G000292375

M25 MAST[illegible]

LONDON STREET ATLAS

CONTENTS

LONDON STREET MAPS

Key to London street maps . . . . . ii-iii
Key to map symbols iii
M25 route planning map 2-3
London street maps 4-191

CENTRAL AREA MAPS

Central London Congestion Charging Zone map 192
Key to central London maps 193
Key to map symbols 193
Central London maps 194-205

INDEX

Index to places, streets, railway stations, hospitals and places of interest 206-350

Published by Collins
An imprint of HarperCollins Publishers
77-85 Fulham Palace Road, Hammersmith, London W6 8JB

www.collins.co.uk

Mapping generated from Collins Bartholomew digital databases

London Underground Map by permission of Transport Trading Limited
Registered User No. 07/4487

The grid on this map is the National Grid taken from the Ordnance Survey map with the permission of the Controller of Her Majesty's Stationery Office.

Printed in China by the South China Printing Company

Hardback	ISBN-13	978 0 00 722749 5	TM12202	Imp 001 NDE
	ISBN-10	0 00 722749 3		
Spiral	ISBN-13	978 0 00 722750 1	TM12203	Imp 001 NDE
	ISBN-10	0 00 722750 7		

e-mail: roadcheck@harpercollins.co.uk

Key to London street maps

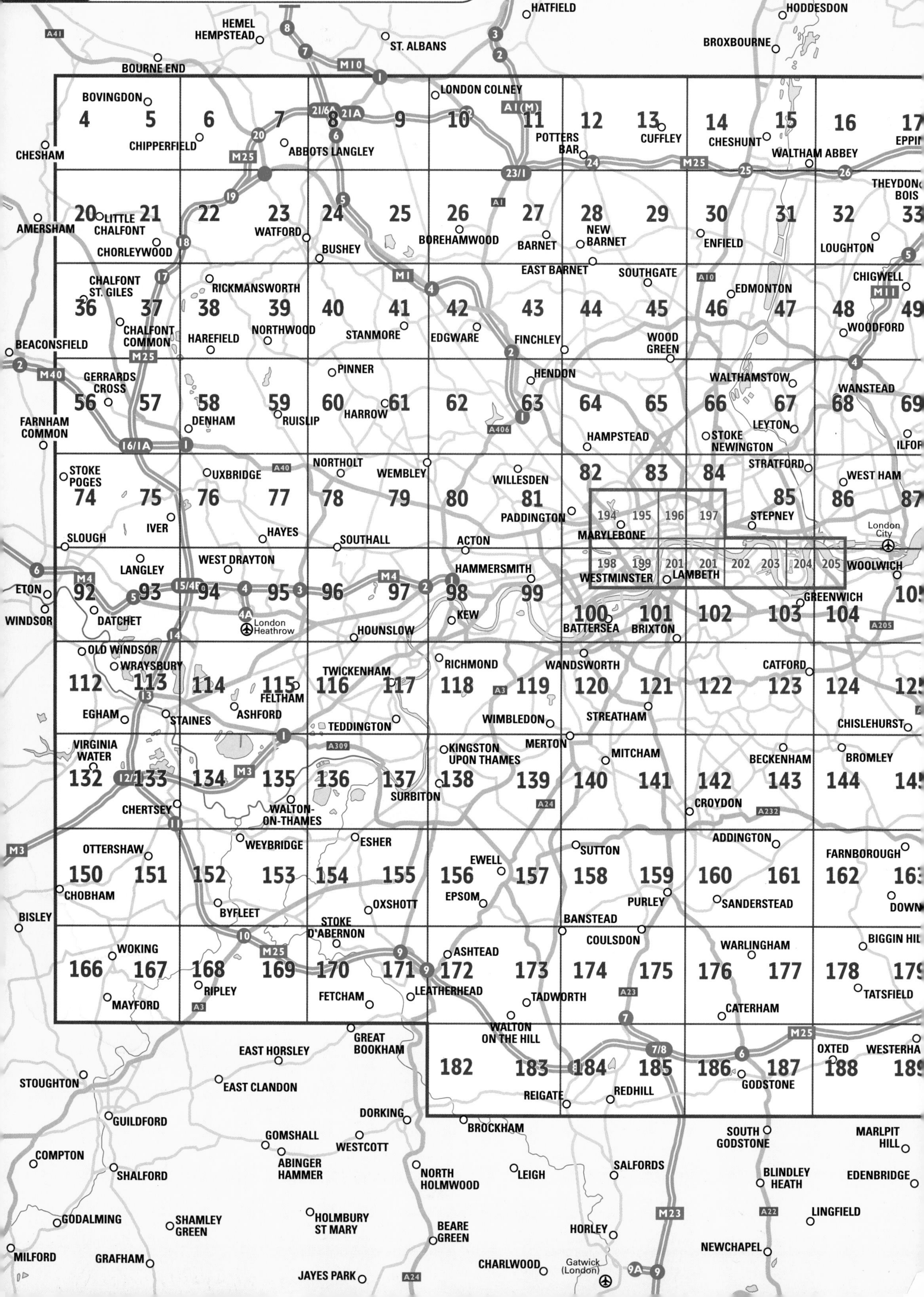

WHEATHAMPSTEAD
WELWYN GARDEN CITY
HERTFORD
HATFIELD
HODDESDON
HEMEL HEMPSTEAD
ST. ALBANS
BROXBOURNE
A41
BOURNE END
M10
BOVINGDON
LONDON COLNEY
A1(M)
21/6A
21A
4 5 6 7 8 9 10 11 12 13 14 15 16 17
CHIPPERFIELD
ABBOTS LANGLEY
POTTERS BAR
CUFFLEY
CHESHUNT
WALTHAM ABBEY
EPPING
CHESHAM
M25
23/1
THEYDON BOIS
20 21 22 23 24 25 26 27 28 29 30 31 32 33
AMERSHAM
LITTLE CHALFONT
WATFORD
BOREHAMWOOD
BARNET
NEW BARNET
ENFIELD
LOUGHTON
CHORLEYWOOD
BUSHEY
A1
EAST BARNET
SOUTHGATE
A10
CHIGWELL
M11
CHALFONT ST. GILES
RICKMANSWORTH
EDMONTON
36 37 38 39 40 41 42 43 44 45 46 47 48 49
CHALFONT COMMON
HAREFIELD
NORTHWOOD
STANMORE
EDGWARE
FINCHLEY
WOOD GREEN
WOODFORD
BEACONSFIELD
M40
M1
PINNER
HENDON
WALTHAMSTOW
WANSTEAD
GERRARDS CROSS
56 57 58 59 60 61 62 63 64 65 66 67 68 69
DENHAM
RUISLIP
HARROW
LEYTON
STOKE NEWINGTON
FARNHAM COMMON
HAMPSTEAD
A406
16/1A
ILFORD
STOKE POGES
UXBRIDGE
A40
NORTHOLT
WEMBLEY
WILLESDEN
82 83 84
STRATFORD
WEST HAM
74 75 76 77 78 79 80 81 85 86 87
194 195 196 197
IVER
PADDINGTON
STEPNEY
HAYES
MARYLEBONE
London City
SLOUGH
SOUTHALL
ACTON
LANGLEY
WEST DRAYTON
HAMMERSMITH
198 199 201 201 202 203 204 205
WOOLWICH
M4
WESTMINSTER
LAMBETH
ETON
92 93 94 95 96 97 98 99
15/4B
4A
WINDSOR
DATCHET
London Heathrow
KEW
GREENWICH
100 101 102 103 104 105
BATTERSEA
BRIXTON
HOUNSLOW
A205
OLD WINDSOR
RICHMOND
WANDSWORTH
CATFORD
WRAYSBURY
TWICKENHAM
112 113 114 115 116 117 118 119 120 121 122 123 124 125
FELTHAM
A3
EGHAM
STAINES
ASHFORD
WIMBLEDON
STREATHAM
CHISLEHURST
TEDDINGTON
VIRGINIA WATER
A309
KINGSTON UPON THAMES
MERTON
MITCHAM
BECKENHAM
BROMLEY
12/1
132 133 134 135 136 137 138 139 140 141 142 143 144 145
M3
SURBITON
CHERTSEY
WALTON-ON-THAMES
A24
CROYDON
A232
ADDINGTON
OTTERSHAW
WEYBRIDGE
ESHER
SUTTON
FARNBOROUGH
EWELL
150 151 152 153 154 155 156 157 158 159 160 161 162 163
CHOBHAM
EPSOM
OXSHOTT
SANDERSTEAD
PURLEY
DOWNE
BISLEY
BYFLEET
STOKE D'ABERNON
BANSTEAD
COULSDON
WOKING
ASHTEAD
WARLINGHAM
BIGGIN HILL
166 167 168 169 170 171 172 173 174 175 176 177 178 179
RIPLEY
FETCHAM
LEATHERHEAD
TADWORTH
A23
TATSFIELD
MAYFORD
CATERHAM
GREAT BOOKHAM
WALTON ON THE HILL
7/8
OXTED
WESTERHAM
EAST HORSLEY
182 183 184 185 186 187 188 189
STOUGHTON
GODSTONE
EAST CLANDON
REIGATE
REDHILL
GUILDFORD
DORKING
BROCKHAM
SOUTH GODSTONE
MARLPIT HILL
GOMSHALL
WESTCOTT
COMPTON
ABINGER HAMMER
NORTH HOLMWOOD
LEIGH
SALFORDS
BLINDLEY HEATH
EDENBRIDGE
SHALFORD
HOLMBURY ST MARY
M23
A22
LINGFIELD
GODALMING
SHAMLEY GREEN
BEARE GREEN
HORLEY
NEWCHAPEL
MILFORD
GRAFHAM
JAYES PARK
A24
CHARLWOOD
Gatwick (London)
9A

Key to map symbols on pages 4-191

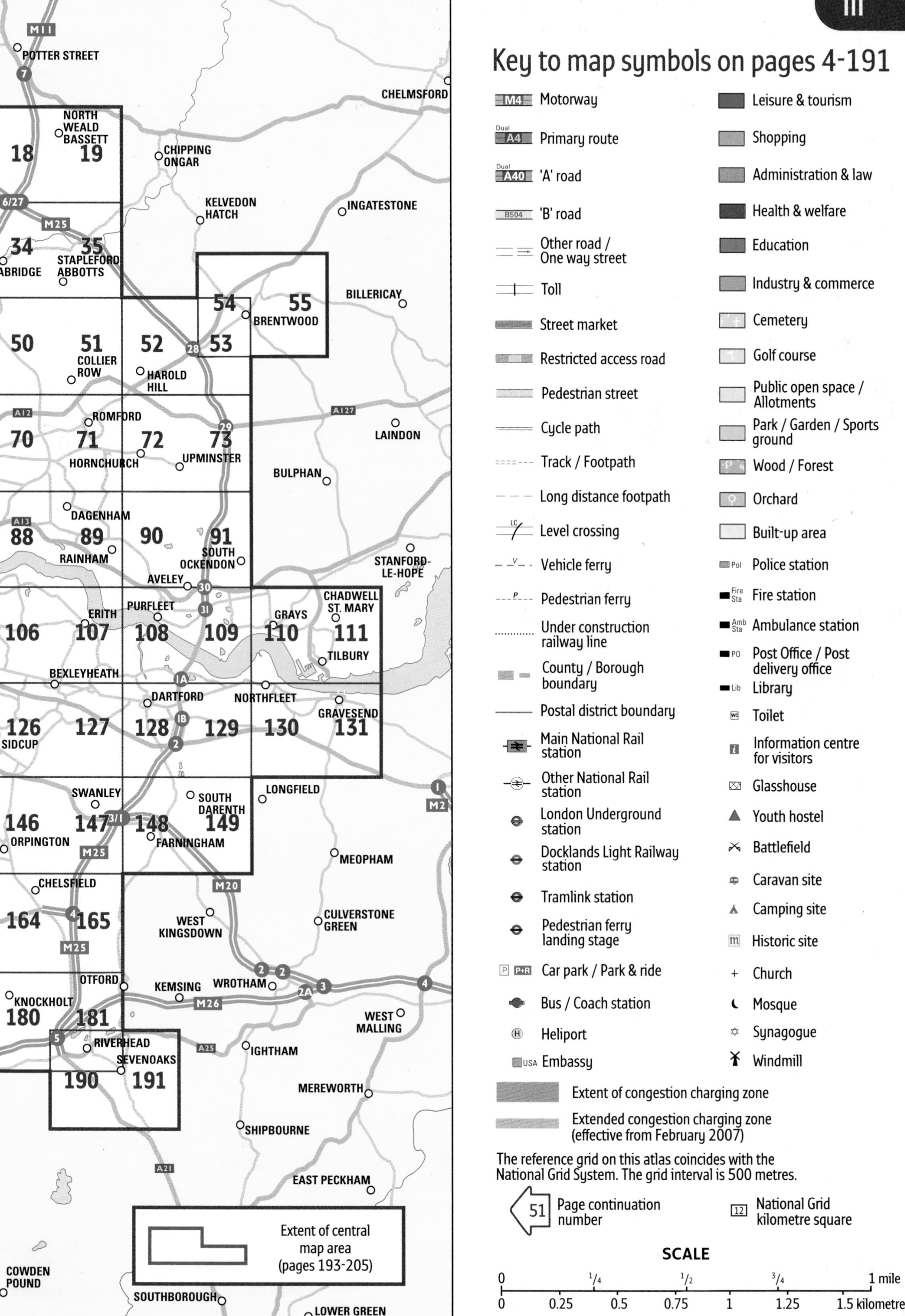
HARLOW
M11
POTTER STREET
7
CHELMSFORD
NORTH WEALD BASSETT
18
19
CHIPPING ONGAR
6/27
M25
KELVEDON HATCH
INGATESTONE
34
35
ABRIDGE
STAPLEFORD ABBOTTS
54
55
BRENTWOOD
BILLERICAY
50
51
COLLIER ROW
52
28
53
HAROLD HILL
A12
A127
ROMFORD
70
71
72
29
73
LAINDON
HORNCHURCH
UPMINSTER
BULPHAN
DAGENHAM
A13
88
89
90
91
RAINHAM
SOUTH OCKENDON
STANFORD-LE-HOPE
AVELEY
30
CHADWELL ST. MARY
31
ERITH
PURFLEET
GRAYS
106
107
108
109
110
111
TILBURY
BEXLEYHEATH
1A
DARTFORD
NORTHFLEET
GRAVESEND
1B
126
127
128
129
130
131
SIDCUP
2
SWANLEY
SOUTH DARENTH
LONGFIELD
M2
146
147
3/1
148
149
ORPINGTON
FARNINGHAM
M25
MEOPHAM
M20
CHELSFIELD
164
4
165
WEST KINGSDOWN
CULVERSTONE GREEN
M25
OTFORD
KEMSING
WROTHAM
2
2
2A
3
4
KNOCKHOLT
M26
180
181
WEST MALLING
5
RIVERHEAD
A25
IGHTHAM
SEVENOAKS
190
191
MEREWORTH
SHIPBOURNE
A21
EAST PECKHAM
Extent of central map area (pages 193-205)
COWDEN POUND
SOUTHBOROUGH
LOWER GREEN
M4 Motorway
Dual A4 Primary route
Dual A40 'A' road
B504 'B' road
Other road / One way street
Toll
Street market
Restricted access road
Pedestrian street
Cycle path
Track / Footpath
Long distance footpath
LC Level crossing
V Vehicle ferry
P Pedestrian ferry
Under construction railway line
County / Borough boundary
Postal district boundary
Main National Rail station
Other National Rail station
London Underground station
Docklands Light Railway station
Tramlink station
Pedestrian ferry landing stage
P P+R Car park / Park & ride
Bus / Coach station
H Heliport
USA Embassy
Leisure & tourism
Shopping
Administration & law
Health & welfare
Education
Industry & commerce
Cemetery
Golf course
Public open space / Allotments
Park / Garden / Sports ground
Wood / Forest
Orchard
Built-up area
Pol Police station
Fire Sta Fire station
Amb Sta Ambulance station
PO Post Office / Post delivery office
Lib Library
WC Toilet
i Information centre for visitors
Glasshouse
Youth hostel
Battlefield
Caravan site
Camping site
Historic site
Church
Mosque
Synagogue
Windmill
Extent of congestion charging zone
Extended congestion charging zone (effective from February 2007)
The reference grid on this atlas coincides with the National Grid System. The grid interval is 500 metres.
51 Page continuation number
12 National Grid kilometre square
SCALE
0
1/4
1/2
3/4
1 mile
0
0.25
0.5
0.75
1
1.25
1.5 kilometres
1:20,000 3.2 inches (8 cm) to 1 mile / 5 cm to 1 km

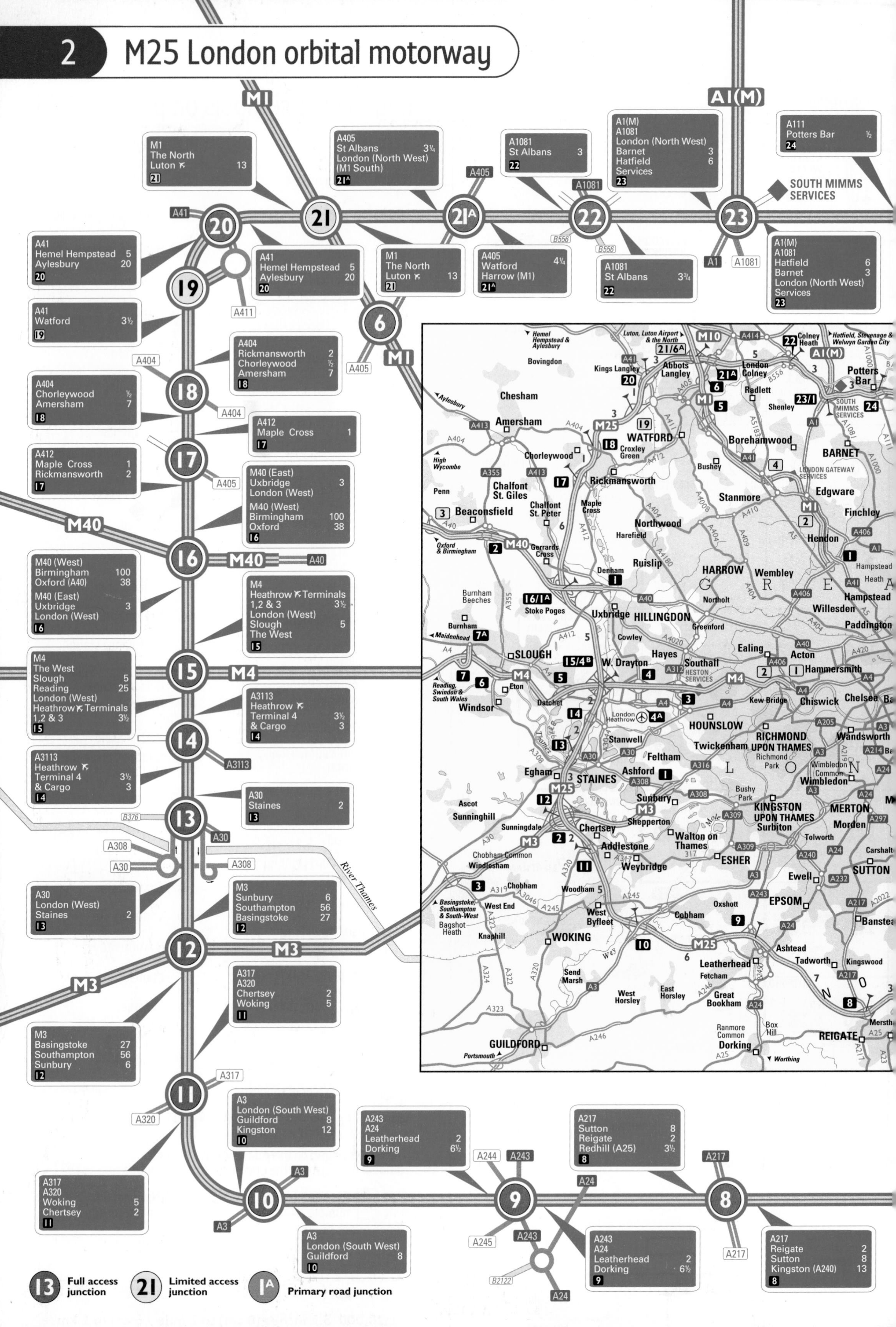

2
M25 London orbital motorway
M1
A1(M)
M1 The North Luton 13 21
A405 St Albans 3¼ London (North West) (M1 South) 21A
A1081 St Albans 3 22
A1(M) A1081 London (North West) 3 Barnet 3 Hatfield 6 Services 23
A111 Potters Bar ½ 24
SOUTH MIMMS SERVICES
A41 Hemel Hempstead 5 Aylesbury 20 20
A41 Hemel Hempstead 5 Aylesbury 20 20
M1 The North Luton 13 21
A405 Watford 4¼ Harrow (M1) 21A
A1081 St Albans 3¾ 22
A1(M) A1081 Hatfield 6 Barnet 3 London (North West) Services 23
A41 Watford 3½ 19
A404 Rickmansworth 2 Chorleywood ½ Amersham 7 18
A404 Chorleywood ½ Amersham 7 18
A412 Maple Cross 1 17
A412 Maple Cross 1 Rickmansworth 2 17
M40 (East) Uxbridge 3 London (West) M40 (West) Birmingham 100 Oxford 38 16
M40 (West) Birmingham 100 Oxford (A40) 38 M40 (East) Uxbridge 3 London (West) 16
M4 Heathrow Terminals 1,2 & 3 3½ London (West) Slough 5 The West 15
M4 The West Slough 5 Reading 25 London (West) Heathrow Terminals 1,2 & 3 3½ 15
A3113 Heathrow Terminal 4 3½ & Cargo 3 14
A3113 Heathrow Terminal 4 3½ & Cargo 3 14
A30 Staines 2 13
A30 London (West) Staines 2 13
M3 Sunbury 6 Southampton 56 Basingstoke 27 12
A317 A320 Chertsey 2 Woking 5 11
M3 Basingstoke 27 Southampton 56 Sunbury 6 12
A3 London (South West) 8 Guildford 12 Kingston 10
A243 A24 Leatherhead 2 Dorking 6½ 9
A217 Sutton 8 Reigate 2 Redhill (A25) 3½ 8
A317 A320 Woking 5 Chertsey 2 11
A3 London (South West) Guildford 8 10
A243 A24 Leatherhead 2 Dorking 6½ 9
A217 Reigate 2 Sutton 8 Kingston (A240) 13 8
M40
M4
M3
River Thames
13 Full access junction
21 Limited access junction
1A Primary road junction
WATFORD
Rickmansworth
Borehamwood
BARNET
Edgware
Stanmore
Northwood
Ruislip
HARROW
Wembley
Hendon
Finchley
Hampstead
Chesham
Amersham
Chalfont St. Giles
Beaconsfield
SLOUGH
Windsor
Uxbridge
HILLINGDON
Hayes
Southall
Ealing
Acton
Hammersmith
Chiswick
HOUNSLOW
Twickenham
RICHMOND UPON THAMES
Wimbledon
Feltham
Ashford
STAINES
Egham
Sunbury
Shepperton
Chertsey
Addlestone
Weybridge
Walton on Thames
ESHER
KINGSTON UPON THAMES
Surbiton
MERTON
Morden
SUTTON
Ewell
EPSOM
Oxshott
Cobham
WOKING
Leatherhead
Ashtead
Great Bookham
Dorking
GUILDFORD
REIGATE
Sunninghill
Ascot
Heathrow

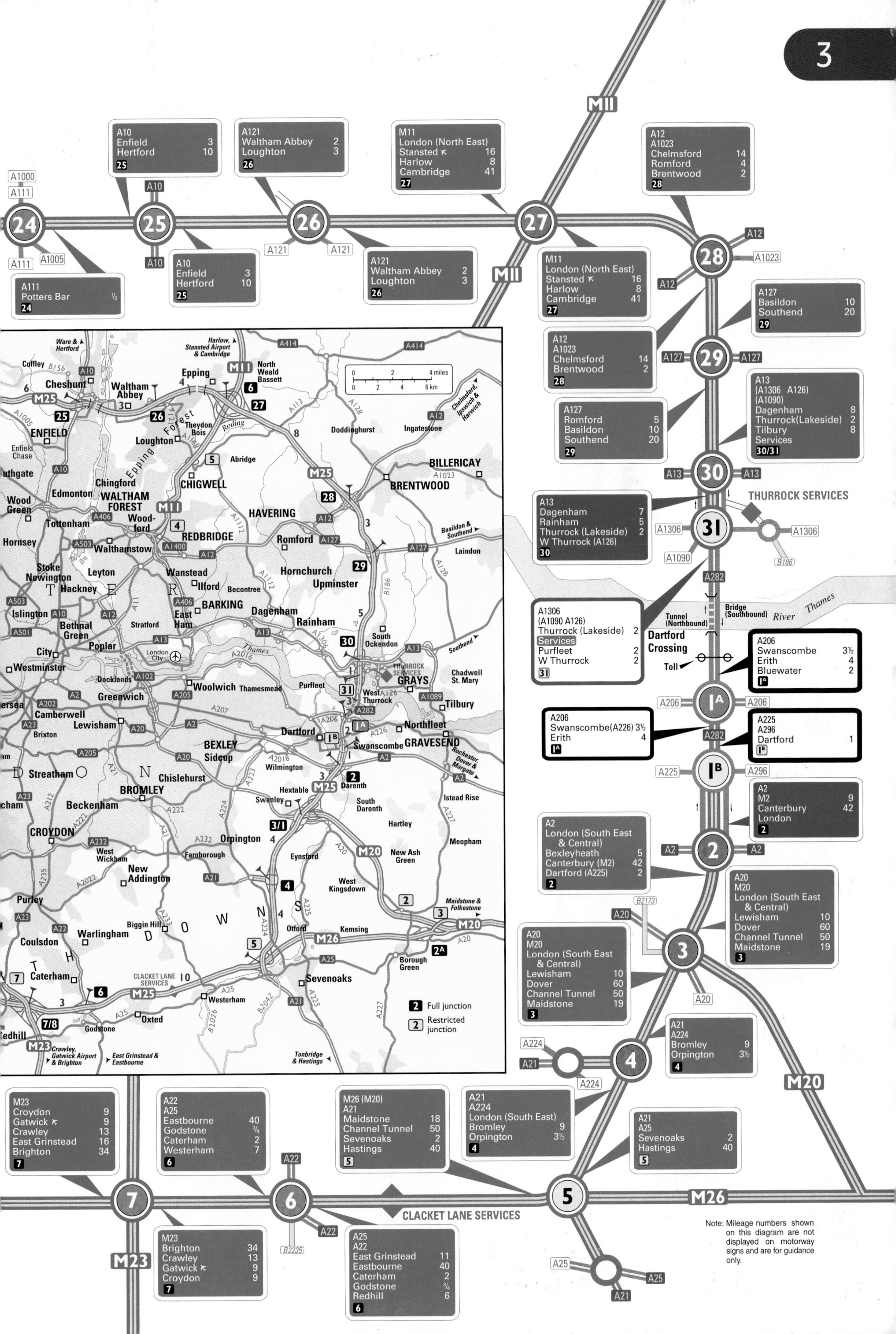
M11
A1000
A111
A10 Enfield 3 Hertford 10 25
A121 Waltham Abbey 2 Loughton 3 26
M11 London (North East) Stansted 16 Harlow 8 Cambridge 41 27
A12 A1023 Chelmsford 14 Romford 4 Brentwood 2 28
24
25
26
27
28
A10
A1005
A111
A121
A12
A1023
A111 Potters Bar ½ 24
A10 Enfield 3 Hertford 10 25
A121 Waltham Abbey 2 Loughton 3 26
M11 London (North East) Stansted 16 Harlow 8 Cambridge 41 27
A12 A1023 Chelmsford 14 Brentwood 2 28
A127 Basildon 10 Southend 20 29
29
A127
A13 (A1306 A126) (A1090) Dagenham 8 Thurrock(Lakeside) 2 Tilbury 8 Services 30/31
A127 Romford 5 Basildon 10 Southend 20 29
30
A13
THURROCK SERVICES
A13 Dagenham 7 Rainham 5 Thurrock (Lakeside) 2 W Thurrock (A126) 30
31
A1306
A1090
B186
A282
Tunnel (Northbound)
Bridge (Southbound)
River Thames
A1306 (A1090 A126) Thurrock (Lakeside) 2 Services Purfleet 2 W Thurrock 2 31
Dartford Crossing
Toll
A206 Swanscombe 3½ Erith 4 Bluewater 2 1A
1A
A206
A206 Swanscombe(A226) 3½ Erith 4 1A
A225 A296 Dartford 1 1B
1B
A225
A296
A2 M2 Canterbury 9 London 42 2
A2 London (South East & Central) Bexleyheath 5 Canterbury (M2) 42 Dartford (A225) 2 2
2
A2
A20 M20 London (South East & Central) Lewisham 10 Dover 60 Channel Tunnel 50 Maidstone 19 3
B2173
A20
3
A20 M20 London (South East & Central) Lewisham 10 Dover 60 Channel Tunnel 50 Maidstone 19 3
A21 A224 Bromley 9 Orpington 3½ 4
A224
A21
4
M20
M23 Croydon 9 Gatwick 9 Crawley 13 East Grinstead 16 Brighton 34 7
A22 A25 Eastbourne 40 Godstone ¾ Caterham 2 Westerham 7 6
M26 (M20) A21 Maidstone 18 Channel Tunnel 50 Sevenoaks 2 Hastings 40 5
A21 A224 London (South East) Bromley 9 Orpington 3½ 4
A21 A25 Sevenoaks 2 Hastings 40 5
A22
7
6
5
M26
CLACKET LANE SERVICES
M23
B2235
M23 Brighton 34 Crawley 13 Gatwick 9 Croydon 9 7
A25 A22 East Grinstead 11 Eastbourne 40 Caterham 2 Godstone ¾ Redhill 6 6
A25
A21
Note: Mileage numbers shown on this diagram are not displayed on motorway signs and are for guidance only.
Ware & Hertford
Harlow, Stansted Airport & Cambridge
Cheshunt
Waltham Abbey
Epping
North Weald Bassett
ENFIELD
Enfield Chase
Theydon Bois
Loughton
Epping Forest
Abridge
Doddinghurst
Ingatestone
Chelmsford, Ipswich & Harwich
BILLERICAY
BRENTWOOD
Chingford
Edmonton
WALTHAM FOREST
CHIGWELL
Woodford
HAVERING
REDBRIDGE
Tottenham
Wood Green
Hornsey
Walthamstow
Romford
Basildon & Southend
Laindon
Stoke Newington
Leyton
Wanstead
Hornchurch
Upminster
Hackney
Ilford
Becontree
Islington
BARKING
Dagenham
East Ham
Rainham
Bethnal Green
Stratford
Poplar
City
London City
Thames
South Ockendon
Southend
Westminster
THURROCK SERVICES
GRAYS
Chadwell St. Mary
Docklands
Woolwich
Thamesmead
Purfleet
West Thurrock
Tilbury
Greenwich
Camberwell
Lewisham
Dartford
Northfleet
Brixton
BEXLEY
Sidcup
Swanscombe
GRAVESEND
Rochester, Dover & Margate
Wilmington
Streatham
Chislehurst
BROMLEY
Darenth
Hextable
Swanley
Istead Rise
Beckenham
South Darenth
Hartley
CROYDON
Orpington
Meopham
West Wickham
Farnborough
Eynsford
New Ash Green
New Addington
West Kingsdown
Purley
Maidstone & Folkestone
Biggin Hill
Warlingham
Kemsing
Otford
Coulsdon
Borough Green
Caterham
CLACKET LANE SERVICES
Sevenoaks
Westerham
Oxted
Godstone
Redhill
Crawley, Gatwick Airport & Brighton
East Grinstead & Eastbourne
Tonbridge & Hastings
0 2 4 miles
0 2 4 6 km
2 Full junction
2 Restricted junction

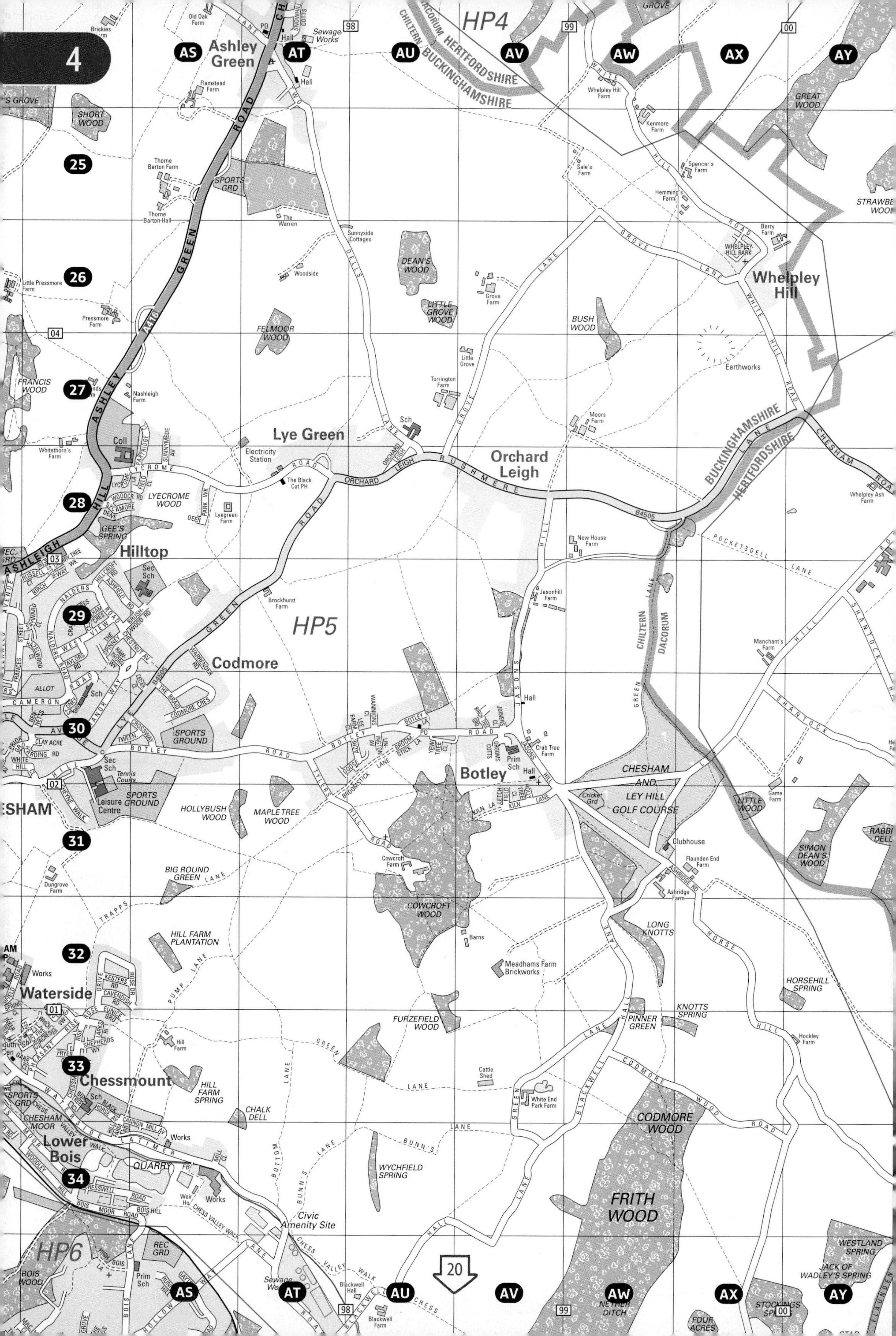

4
Ashley Green
Whelpley Hill
Lye Green
Orchard Leigh
Hilltop
Codmore
Botley
HP4
HP5
HP6
Waterside
Chessmount
Lower Bois
CHILTERN
DACORUM
BUCKINGHAMSHIRE
HERTFORDSHIRE
SHORT WOOD
DEAN'S WOOD
LITTLE GROVE WOOD
FELMOOR WOOD
BUSH WOOD
GREAT WOOD
FRANCIS WOOD
LYECROME WOOD
GEE'S SPRING
HOLLYBUSH WOOD
MAPLE TREE WOOD
BIG ROUND GREEN
COWCROFT WOOD
HILL FARM PLANTATION
LONG KNOTTS
CHESHAM AND LEY HILL GOLF COURSE
LITTLE WOOD
SIMON DEAN'S WOOD
HORSEHILL SPRING
KNOTTS SPRING
PINNER GREEN
FURZEFIELD WOOD
HILL FARM SPRING
CHALK DELL
WYCHFIELD SPRING
CODMORE WOOD
FRITH WOOD
WESTLAND SPRING
JACK OF WADLEY'S SPRING
SPORTS GROUND
Leisure Centre
Civic Amenity Site
Electricity Station
Earthworks
Meadhams Farm Brickworks
20

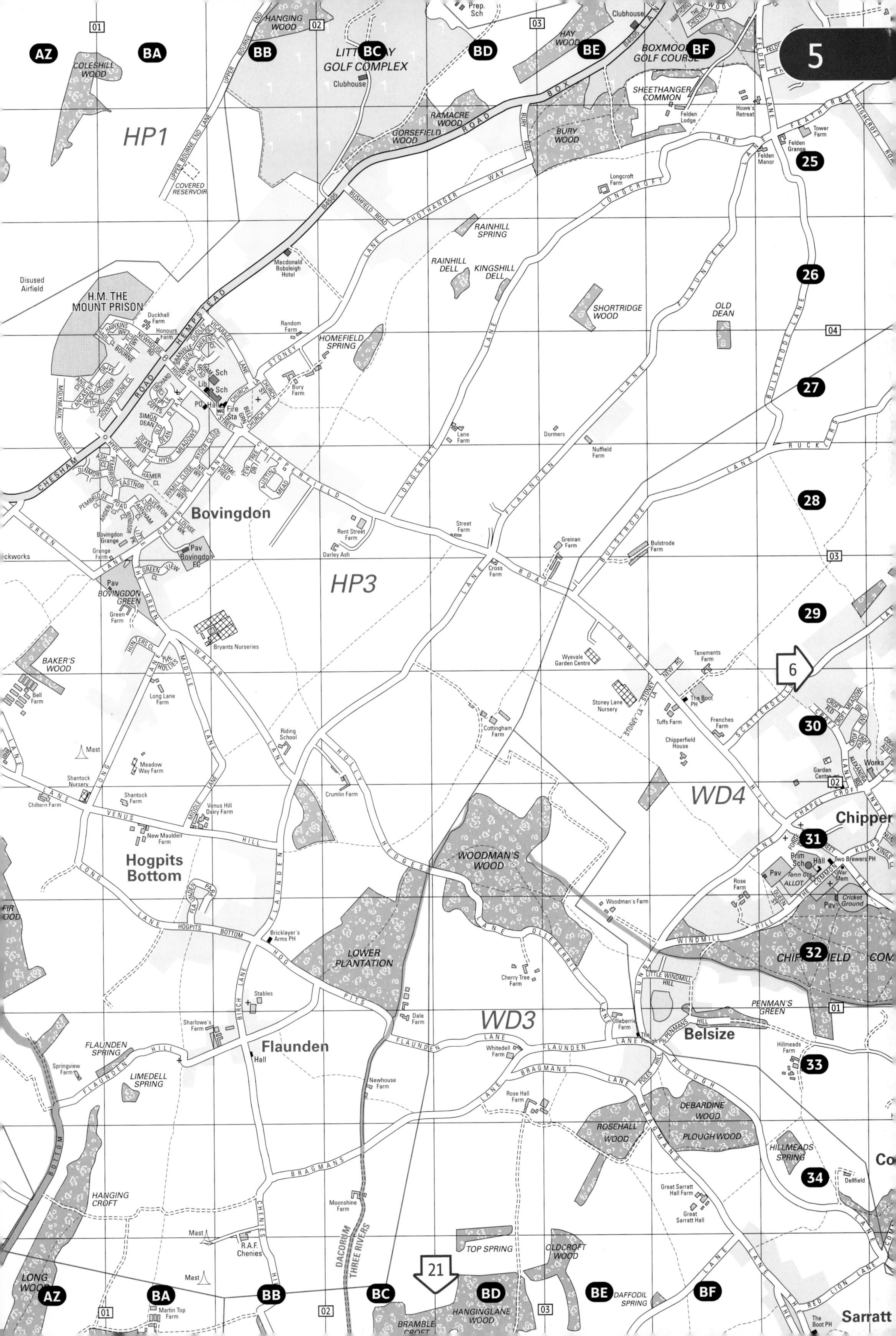
HANGING WOOD
Prep. Sch
Clubhouse
LITTLE HAY GOLF COMPLEX
Clubhouse
HAY WOOD
BOXMOOR GOLF COURSE
SHEETHANGER COMMON
Felden Lodge
Howe's Retreat
FEATHERBED LANE
Tower Farm
Felden Grange
Felden Manor
FELDEN LANE
HIGHCROFT
COLESHILL WOOD
HP1
UPPER BOURNE END LANE
COVERED RESERVOIR
RAMACRE WOOD
GORSEFIELD WOOD
BOX LANE
BURY RISE
BURY WOOD
Longcroft Farm
LONGCROFT LANE
SHOTHANGER WAY
BUSHFIELD ROAD
B4505
RAINHILL SPRING
RAINHILL DELL
KINGSHILL DELL
Macdonald Bobsleigh Hotel
Disused Airfield
H.M. THE MOUNT PRISON
Duckhall Farm
Honours Farm
Random Farm
HOMEFIELD SPRING
SHORTRIDGE WOOD
OLD DEAN
FLAUNDEN LANE
BULSTRODE LANE
HEMPSTEAD ROAD
Sch
Lib
PO
Hall
Fire Sta
CHURCH ST
VICARAGE LANE
STONEY LANE
Bury Farm
MOLYNEAUX AVENUE
CHESHAM ROAD
Lane Farm
Dormers
Nuffield Farm
RUCKLERS LANE
HYDE LANE
HYDE MEADOWS
CHIPPERFIELD ROAD
Bovingdon
Street Farm
Rent Street Farm
Darley Ash
Greinan Farm
Bulstrode Farm
Bovingdon Grange
Grange Farm
Pav
Bovingdon FC
ckworks
GREEN LANE
Cross Farm
HP3
Pav
BOVINGDON GREEN
Green Farm
Bryants Nurseries
TOWER HILL
Wyevale Garden Centre
Tenements Farm
BAKER'S WOOD
Bell Farm
Long Lane Farm
WATER LANE
MIDDLE LANE
Stoney Lane Nursery
The Boot PH
Tuffs Farm
Frenches Farm
Chipperfield House
SCATTERDELLS
Mast
Riding School
Cottingham Farm
Meadow Way Farm
Shantock Nursery
Shantock Farm
Chiltern Farm
VENUS HILL
HOLLY HEDGES LANE
Crumlin Farm
WD4
Garden Centre
Works
CHAPEL CROFT
Chipper
Venus Hill Dairy Farm
New Maulden Farm
Hogpits Bottom
WOODMAN'S WOOD
Prim Sch
Hall
Two Brewers PH
Pav
Tenn Cts
ALLOT
THE COMMON
War Mem
Cricket Ground
Rose Farm
Woodman's Farm
HOGPITS BOTTOM
Bricklayer's Arms PH
FLAUNDEN LANE
LOWER PLANTATION
OLLEBERRIE LANE
WINDMILL HILL
LITTLE WINDMILL HILL
CHIPPERFIELD COM
Cherry Tree Farm
PENMAN'S GREEN
Stables
BIRCH LANE
HOG PITS
Sharlowe's Farm
Dale Farm
WD3
Olleberrie Farm
The Plough PH
Belsize
PENMANS HILL
Hillmeads Farm
FLAUNDEN SPRING
Flaunden
Hall
FLAUNDEN HILL
Whitedell Farm
FLAUNDEN LANE
POLES HILL
PLOUGH LANE
Springview Farm
LIMEDELL SPRING
Newhouse Farm
BRAGMANS LANE
Rose Hall Farm
DEBARDINE WOOD
PLOUGH WOOD
ROSEHALL WOOD
HILLMEADS SPRING
BRAGMANS
HANGING CROFT
Moonshine Farm
Great Sarratt Hall Farm
Great Sarratt Hall
Delfield
DACORUM
THREE RIVERS
Mast
R.A.F. Chenies
CHENIES HILL
TOP SPRING
OLDCROFT WOOD
Mast
LONG WOOD
21
DAFFODIL SPRING
RED LION LANE
HANGINGLANE WOOD
BRAMBLE CROFT
Martin Top Farm
The Boot PH
Sarratt
6
AZ
BA
BB
BC
BD
BE
BF
01
02
03
04
25
26
27
28
29
30
31
32
33
34

Felden
HP3
Apsley
SHENDISH MANOR GOLF COURSE
SHENDISH MANOR CONFERENCE CENTRE
APSLEY MILLS RETAIL PARK
GREAT WOOD
PHASELS WOOD
Phasels Wood Activity Centre
RUCKLERS WOOD
DARK WOOD
MERCEYS WOOD
THE HANGINGS
THE NUCKET
SCATTERDELLS WOOD
THE GROVE
THE WINGS
Kings Langley
KING LANGLEY COMMON
Whippendell Bottom
Whippendell Hill
Chipperfield
WD4
ROOKERY WOOD
CHIPPERFIELD COMMON
PENMAN'S GREEN
Belsize
DACORUM
THREE RIVERS
DEBARDINE WOOD
PLOUGH WOOD
HILLMEADS SPRING
Commonwood
COMMONWOOD COMMON
WD3
Bucks Hill
BERRYBUSHES WOOD
DELLSHOT SPRING
SHEEPCOTE SPRING
HAWK SPRING
BEECHEN BOTTOM
NORTH GROVE WOOD
Sarratt
HIGH SPRING
JUNIPER
OLD DEAN
SHEETHANGER COMMON
A41 KINGS LANGLEY BYPASS
A4251 LONDON ROAD
HEMPSTEAD ROAD
HIGH STREET
WATFORD ROAD
M25

5
22

7
BP
BQ
BR
BS
BT
BU
BV
08
09
10
POTTERS CROUCH PLANTATION
LONG DEANS
HP3
Highwood Hall Farm
High Herts Farm
The Swan PH
Bedmond House
Rose Acre
Radio Station
Sports Hall
Hyde Meadow Farm
HYDE LANE SPRING
Hyde Springs
Hyde Farm
Hyde Lane Farm
Hart Hall Farm
Pimlico House
NEW PLANTATION
Little Abbots
Hart Hall
Green End Farm
White House Farm
Woodlands Poultry Farm
Verulam Farm
NEWLANDS
THREE RIVERS
ST ALBANS
WELLFIELD SPRING
Serge Hill
DEADMAN WOOD
BEDMOND WOOD
White Hart PH
Whitehouse Farm
PIECORNER WOOD
HANGING WOOD
FURZEFIELD WOOD
JOB'S WOOD
Ninnings Farm
Millhouse Farm
Searches Farm
Poultry Farm
Tenements Farm
WD5
Bedmond
Bell Inn PH
BEDMOND PLAYING FIELDS
Prim Sch
MOOR WOOD
LONG SPRING
Hilltop Farm
HIGH VIEW CARAVAN PARK
Leewood Farm
Benmore Farm
Glasshouse
GREAT NOTLEY
M25
M1
Junction 21 M25
Junction 6A M1
25
26
27
28
29
30
31
32
33
34
04
03
02
01
STOWES WOOD
Numbers Farm
LITTLE NOTLEY
Mansion House Farm
COVERED RESERVOIR
LONG WOOD
ROUND WOOD
Depot
Works
Fishing Club
KINGS LANGLEY
8
CEM
Fortunes Farm
BLOOM WOOD
Sports Centre
ABBOTS LANGLEY
MANOR HOUSE GROUNDS
Youth Cen
Manor Lo
Clinic
TANNERS WOOD
LEAVESDEN COUNTRY PARK
WD25
Junction 20
GRAND UNION CANAL
Hunton Bridge
JUNCTION PARK
The Kings Head PH
Langleybury
THE ROOKERY
SPORTS GROUND
Offices
Home Farm
SOUTH WAY PLAYING FLD
Leavesden Studios
Hunton Park
Tennis Courts
Bowl Grn
HILL FARM IND EST
Woodside
Leavesden Green
Kingswood
Garston
Garston Manor Sch
WOODSIDE STADIUM
WOODSIDE PLAYING FIELDS
Leisure Cen
Leisure Centre
Cinema
Cricket Ground
ALBAN WOOD
Comm Cen
Medical Cen
REC
NORTH WATFORD CEMETERY
STANBOROUGH PARK
A405
A41
KINGSWAY (NORTH ORBITAL ROAD)
WATFORD ROAD
NORTH WESTERN AVENUE
23
Airshafts
Hunton Bridge

Potters Crouch
Chiswell Green
How Wood
Bricket Wood
Kingswood
Garston
Meriden
AL2
WD5
WD25
Junction 21A
Junction 21 M25
Junction 6A M1
Junction 6
NORTH ORBITAL ROAD
M25
M1
BRICKET WOOD COMMON
GARSTON PARK
PENFOLD PARK GOLF COURSE
WOODSIDE PLAYING FIELDS
BUILDING RESEARCH ESTABLISHMENT
GRAVEL PIT
Site of Roman Villa
7
24

9
CD
CE
CF
CG
CH
CJ
CK
15
16
17
AL1
AL4
AL2
WD7
NORTH ORBITAL ROAD
A414
A1081
LONDON ROAD
Sopwell House
Sopwell Home Farm
River Ver
CHALKDELL WOOD
Hedges Farm
NORTH ORBITAL COMMERCIAL PARK
Aylett Nursery
COPPICE WOOD
SITE OF SPECIAL SCIENTIFIC INTEREST
25
COLUMBANS SPORTS GRD
VERULAM R.F.C.
Clubho
SPORTS GROUND
SPORTS GRD
Pav
SHENLEY LANE
B5378
Park Street
PARK STREET
A5183
STREET
Radlett Aerodrome (Disused)
GRAVEL PIT
PARK INDUSTRIAL ESTATE
FROGMORE HOME PARK
FROGMORE
Frogmore
SPORTS GROUND
Prim Sch
LONDON COLNEY
26
MORRIS PLAYING FLD
BIG MAYFIELD WOOD
Works
27
BROAD COLNEY LAKES NATURE RESERVE
Fir Tree Farm
Broad Colney Bridge
River Colne
28
Colney Heath Shopping
03
04
29
Arsenal F.C. Training Grounds
ALL SAINTS PASTORAL CENTRE
M25
The Red Cow PH
HAMPDEN PL
VENTURA PARK
QUARRY
COLNEY PARK
10
30
SPORTS GRDS
Premier Travel Inn
Colney Street Farm
The George & Dragon PH
Old Parkbury
Colney Street
Colney Street Bridge
02
HARPERBURY HOSPITAL
HERTSMERE
ST. ALBANS
31
B556
Harper Lane Rail Depot
Pumping Sta
The Black Horse PH
RADLETT GOLF CENTRE
Houndswood Farm
NINE ACRES
HOUND'S WOOD
Harper Lodge Farm and Stables
Netherwylde Farm
RIVERSIDE WAY
32
COW BANKS
01
Wild Farm
Moat
WATLING STREET
WATLING STREET ROMAN ROAD
Hill Farm
33
SHENLEY PARK
PORTERS PARK GOLF COURSE
SAND PLANTATION
Cricket Ground
Clubhouse
34
Oakridge Lane Sewage Treatment Works
Sewage Works
OAKRIDGE LANE
Starveacres
RADLETT
Blackbirds Farm
Auriol Farm
Tykes Water
High Bridge
Fire Sta

LONDON COLNEY
Junction 22
AL4
AL2
WD7
WD6
Ridgehill
Shenley
SHENLEY PARK
Ridge
NORTH A414
A1081 LONDON COLNEY BY-PASS
M25
ST. ALBANS ROAD
COURSERS ROAD
SAND AND GRAVEL PIT
THE WARREN
FREDERICK'S WOOD
WELWYN HATFIELD
HERTSMERE
ST. ALBANS
COPPICE WOOD
(SITE OF SPECIAL SCIENTIFIC INTEREST)
GARDEN WOOD
THE NEW PLANTATION
Tyttenhanger Farm
Tyttenhanger House
Coursers Farm
River Colne
Willows Farm Village
BIG MAYFIELD WOOD
WALSINGHAM WOOD
COBS ASH
ROUND WOOD
REDWELL WOOD
Redwell Wood Farm
BROAD COLNEY LAKES NATURE RESERVE
Colney Fields Shopping Park
RIDGEVIEW LODGE
The Bull PH
BELL LANE
Arsenal F.C. Training Grounds
Gordon Hall Building
UNIVERSITY COLLEGE LONDON SPORTS GROUNDS
Tennis Courts
Salisbury Hall
Salisbury Hall Farm
MOAT
DE HAVILLAND AIRCRAFT HERITAGE CENTRE
SHENLEYBURY
DELL GROVE
Southridge Animal Centre R.S.P.C.A.
PACKHORSE LANE
RECTORY LANE
COMBE WOOD
COW BANKS
Rectory Farm
Shenley Hill Stud Farm
Shenley Hill
Rabley Park Farm
Rabley Park
St. Catherine's Farm
Catherine Bourne
MIMMS LANE
Ravenscroft Farm
LITTLERIDGE WOOD
BIG PURSLEY WOOD
LITTLE PURSLEY WOOD
Ridge Farm
CROSSOAKS LANE
Crossoaks Farm
CROSS OAKS WOOD
The Black Lion PH
BLACK LION HILL
The Garden Nursery
Tokonoma Bonsai
Pursley Farm
LONDON ROAD
SAND PLANTATION
Cricket Ground
WALLED GDN
RADLETT
THE GORSE
Auriol Farm
WOODHALL LANE
GREEN STREET
Wild Farm
Moat
CL CM CN CP CQ CR CS
19 20 21
25 26 27 28 29 30 31 32 33 34
04 03 02 01
9
26

CT
CU
CV
CW
CX
CY
CZ
NORTH MYMMS PARK
North Mymms Park Training Centre
Water End
BROOKMANS PARK
BROOKMANS PARK GOLF COURSE
PELPIN'S WOOD
ROUND WOOD
BRICK KILN WOOD
GOBIONS OPEN SPACE
GOBIONS GARDEN
GOBIONS POND
AL9
CANGSLEY WOOD
Royal Veterinary College (Hawkshead)
HAWKSHEAD WOOD
MYMMSHALL WOOD
SPORTS GROUND
PILVAGE WOOD
Royal Veterinary College (Boltons Park Farm)
WELWYN HATFIELD
HERTSMERE
POTTERS BAR GOLF COURSE
FURZEFIELD WOOD
KING GEORGE V PLAYING FLDS
CRANBORNE INDUSTRIAL ESTATE
Site of Motte & Baileys
Mimms Hall Farm
Warrengate Farm
MUTTON LANE
EN6
South Mimms
POTTERS BAR
Holiday Inn South Mimms
South Mimms Services
Days Inn
Bignell's Corner
Cancer Research UK
Junction 23 (M25) Junction 1 A1(M)
Bentley Heath
A1(M)
M25
12
27
25
26
27
28
29
30
31
32
33
34
22
23
24

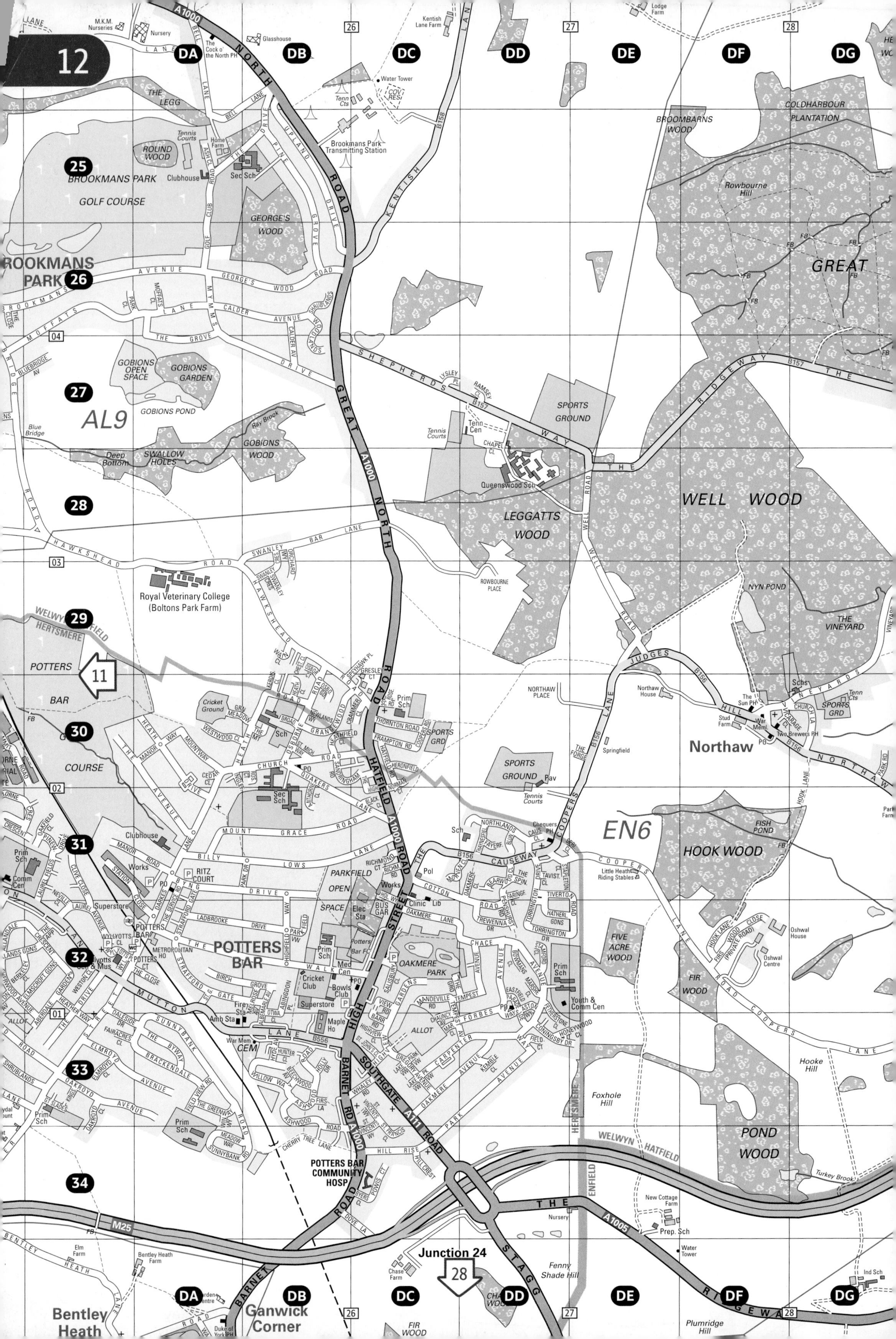

DA
DB
DC
DD
DE
DF
DG
26
27
28
25
26
27
28
29
30
31
32
33
34
04
03
02
01
A1000
NORTH
GREAT NORTH ROAD
M.K.M. Nurseries
Nursery
Glasshouse
The Cock o' the North PH
Kentish Lane Farm
Lodge Farm
Water Tower
COV RESr
Tenn Cts
Brookmans Park Transmitting Station
KENTISH
LANE
B158
THE LEGG
BELL LANE
ROUND WOOD
Tennis Courts
Home Farm
ASHCL
Sec Sch
Clubhouse
BROOKMANS PARK
GOLF COURSE
GEORGE'S WOOD
UPLAND DRIVE
PINE GROVE
GOLF CLUB ROAD
BROOKMANS PARK
GEORGE'S WOOD ROAD
AVENUE
MOFFATS LANE
CALDER AVENUE
CALDER AV
MYMMS DRIVE
WOODLANDS
SHRUBLANDS
THE GROVE
THE CLOSE
BLUEBRIDGE AV
BRIDGE ROAD
GOBIONS OPEN SPACE
GOBIONS GARDEN
GOBIONS POND
AL9
Blue Bridge
Ray Brook
GOBIONS WOOD
Deep Bottom
SWALLOW HOLES
SHEPHERDS WAY
LYSLEY PL
RAMSEY CL
B157
Tennis Courts
Tenn Cen
CHAPEL CL
SPORTS GROUND
Queenswood Sch
LEGGATTS WOOD
ROWBOURNE PLACE
WELL ROAD
BROOMBARNS WOOD
COLDHARBOUR PLANTATION
Rowbourne Hill
FB
GREAT
THE RIDGEWAY
WELL WOOD
NYN POND
THE VINEYARD
HAWKSHEAD ROAD
SWANLEY BAR LANE
SWANLEY CRES
ORCHARD WAY
Royal Veterinary College (Boltons Park Farm)
WELWYN HATFIELD
HERTSMERE
POTTERS BAR
GOLF COURSE
11
SPARROWHAWK PL
GRESLEY CT
Prim Sch
Cricket Ground
WESTWOOD CL
MANOR WAY
MOUNTWAY
Sch
GRANGEWOOD
HEATHFIELD
THORNTON ROAD
FRAMPTON RD
COOPERS RD
SPORTS GRD
HERONFIELD
NORTHAW PLACE
JUDGES HILL
B156
Northaw House
The Sun PH
Stud Farm
War Meml
Schs
Tenn Cts
SPORTS GRD
Two Brewers PH
VINEYARDS
CHURCH LA
Northaw
NORTHAW
HOOK LANE
Springfield
THE FORGE
SPORTS GROUND
Pav
Tennis Courts
CHURCH ROAD
Sec Sch
QUAKERS LANE
HATFIELD ROAD
MOUNT GRACE ROAD
Clubhouse
MANOR ROAD
BILLY LOWS LANE
RICHMOND CT
Works
STATION CLOSE
RITZ COURT
DARKES LA
PARK DR
DRIVE
PARKFIELD OPEN SPACE
Elec Sta
BUS GAR
Clinic
Lib
Pol
COTTON ROAD
OAKMERE LANE
Superstore
THE CAUSEWAY
Chequers PH
COOPERS LANE
EN6
FISH POND
HOOK WOOD
Little Heath Riding Stables
COOPERS
NORTHLANDS
STAPLETON ROAD
TIVERTON ROAD
TORRINGTON DR
HATHERL GDNS
TREWENNA DR
LADBROOKE DRIVE
POTTERS BAR
THE WALK
Prim Sch
Potters Bar FC
Med Cen
OAKMERE PARK
CHACE AVENUE
FIVE ACRE WOOD
Oshwal House
Oshwal Centre
HOOK LANE
PRIVATE ROAD
FIR WOOD
Prim Sch
Youth & Comm Cen
METROPOLITAN HO
STAFFORD GATE
Wyllyotts Cen & Mus
Cricket Club
Bowls Club
Superstore
MANDEVILLE RD
TEMPEST AVENUE
FORBES AVENUE
CONINGSBY DR
HONEYWOOD
COOPERS LANE
Hooke Hill
MUTTON LANE
Amb Sta
Fire Sta
Maple Ho
ALLOT
War Mem
CEM
HIGH STREET
SOUTHGATE ROAD
A111
CARPENTER WAY
KEMBLE CL
PARK AVENUE
OAKMERE AVENUE
SUNNYBANK
THE BYWAY
BRACKENDALE AVENUE
DALESIDE
FAIRACRES CL
ELMROYD AVENUE
OAKROYD CL
Prim Sch
THE GREENWAY
MEADOW WAY
SUNNYBANK RD
Prim Sch
CHERRY TREE LANE
ASHWOOD ROAD
BARNET RD A1000
HILL RISE
HILLCREST
POTTERS BAR COMMUNITY HOSP
Foxhole Hill
HERTSMERE
ENFIELD
WELWYN HATFIELD
POND WOOD
Turkey Brook
New Cottage Farm
Nursery
THE RIDGEWAY
A1005
Prep. Sch
Water Tower
M25
FB
BENTLEY HEATH LANE
Elm Farm
Bentley Heath Farm
Junction 24
28
STAGG
Chase Farm
Fenny Shade Hill
Ind Sch
Bentley Heath
Ganwick Corner
BARNET
Duke of York PH
FIR WOOD
Plumridge Hill

Newgate Street
SG13
WOOD
Justice Hill
Grimes Bottom
Cuffley Camp
Grimes Brook
HOME WOOD
Carbone Bottom
RIDGEWAY
Tolmers Scout Camp
Posten Bridge
WORMLEY WOOD
Cuffley Brook
Newgate Street Bridge
Darnicle Hill Nursery
St. Lawrence Farm
CALVES CROFT
LONG GROVE
DERRYS WOOD
HAZEL GROVE
Tolmers Park Farm
Tolmers Park
Ponsbourne Riding Centre
Boswell's Livery Stables
Clubhouse
GOLF COURSE
Burleigh Farm
Ashfield Nurseries
Nursery
Theobald Nursery
CHESHUNT COMMON
Cuffley
CUFFLEY
Brook Farm
Cuffley Hills Farm
Nyn Manor Farm
Thornton's Farm
Hempshill Brook
Pumping Sta
Coles Hill
Colesdale Farm
Wells Farm
KING GEORGE'S FIELD
NORTHAW BROOK
Soper's Viaduct
Works
WELWYN HATFIELD
BROXBOURNE
NURSERY PLANTATION
CATTLEGATE WOOD
Robin Hill
Northaw Brook
Barvin Hill
Cattlegate Farm
Cattlegate
Woodhurst Farm
Turkey Brook
HERTFORDSHIRE
M25
TILEKILN OSIERS
Owls Hall Farm
The Paddocks
Glasshouse
Oak Hill Farm
Glasgow Stud
South Hill
EN2
Holly Hill Farm
CREWS HILL
Clubhouse
CREWS HILL GOLF COURSE
Woldens Nursery & Garden Centre
Browns of Crews Hill Nurseries
Kings Oak Riding Stables
MUS
Crews Hills
WHITEWEBBS WOOD
Sloeman's Farm
CINDER ASH
CATTLINS
DYSONS OSIERS
Burnt Farm
OLD PARK
EN7
Goffs Oak
Poyndon Farm
SPORTS GRD
The Goff's Oak PH
Springfield Nursery
Weald View Nursery
Rosebury Farm
Elm Farm
Rags Brook
Tanfield Stud Farm
14
29
DH DJ DK DL DM DN DP
25 26 27 28 29 30 31 32 33 34
04 03 02 01

Hammond Street
Flamstead End
Goffs Oak
Bury Green
Bulls Cross
Crews Hill
EN7
EN8
EN2
CHESHUNT PARK
CHESHUNT GOLF COURSE
CATTLINS
HOME WOOD
HOME PLANTATION
HANGING PLANTATION
SOUTH OSIERS
SQUARE PLANTING
BURYGREEN PLANTATION
BROOM HILLS
BULLSCROSS RIDE CEMETERY (JEWISH)
HERTFORDSHIRE
BROXBOURNE
M25
Junction 25
GREAT CAMBRIDGE ROAD
A10
GOFFS LANE
APPLEBY STREET
HAMMOND STREET
NEWGATESTREET ROAD
SILVER STREET
OLD PARK RIDE
WHITEWEBBS ROAD
LIEUTENANT ELLIS WAY
BULLSMOOR
Capel Manor College
Theobalds Park Camping and Caravan Site
Tesco Country Club
ADATH YISROEL CEMETERY
CHESHUNT RESERVOIR (NORTH)
BAISLEY'S WOOD
DERRYS WOOD
SPRING WOOD
CROMWELL WOOD
ROUNDCROFT WOOD
DYSONS OSIERS
CINDER ASH
WHITEWEBBS
25
26
27
28
29
30
31
32
33
34
DQ
DR
DS
DT
DU
DV
DW
13
30
33
34
35
04
03
02
01

Wormley
NAZEING MARSH
Kings Weir
Paynes Farm Nursery
Langridge Nursery
Larksmead Nursery
Clayton Hill
EN10
Turnford Marsh
College
HOLYFIELD LAKE
LEE VALLEY PARK
Sailing Club
Weir
St. Leonards Farm
Netherkidders Farm
Mushroom Farm
COLEMAN'S SHAW
Coach & Horses PH
Denver Lodge Farm
Turnford
ASHLEY
Holyfield Marsh
Holyfield Farm
Marsh Hill
Peartree Farm
GALLEYHILL WOOD
Brookfield Centre
HELL WOOD
THE NIGHTLEYS
Elec Station
Lee Valley Park Tourist Information Centre
Holyfield
NORTH METROPOLITAN PIT
Hayes Hill
North Lodge Farm
Cheshunt Lock
SEVENTY ACRES LAKE
Grubbs Hill
CHESHUNT LAKE
Turnershill Marsh
HOMEFIELD WOOD
Nightingales
Holyfield Fishery
EN9
Monkhams Hall
Young Mariners Base
Police Pit
KENNEL WOOD
CHESHUNT
Thistly Marsh
Hooks Marsh Lake
SPORTS GRD
GRUNDY PARK
Friday Lake
Poultry Farm
Cheshunt Junction
Waltham Common Lock
WALTHAM ABBEY WOODS
LEE VALLEY PARK
Hall Marsh
Hall Marsh Scrape
ALLOT
CHESHUNT
BOWYER'S WATER
Cornmill Meadows
Mile Nursery
Langley Nursery
Lea Valley Nursery
Abbey View Nursery
THEOBALDS GROVE
BROXBOURNE
EPPING FOREST
Marsh Bridge
Crooked Mile Roundabout
Waltham Marsh
WALTHAM CROSS
Cheshunt Marsh
HERTFORDSHIRE
ESSEX
WALTHAM ABBEY (Ruins)
ABBEY GARDENS
Prim Schs.
SPORTS GROUND
LARSENS REC GRD
Britannia Nursery
Hazelmere Marina
TOWN MEAD
Holdbrook
Superstore
Waltham Abbey FC
Swim Pool
SPORTS GROUND
Freezy Water
Works
M25
31
16
RAMMEY MARSH
DEPOT
Cobbin's Brook
Sewardstone Roundabout
Quinton Hill Farm
DX
DY
DZ
EA
EB
EC
ED
25
26
27
28
29
30
31
32
33
34

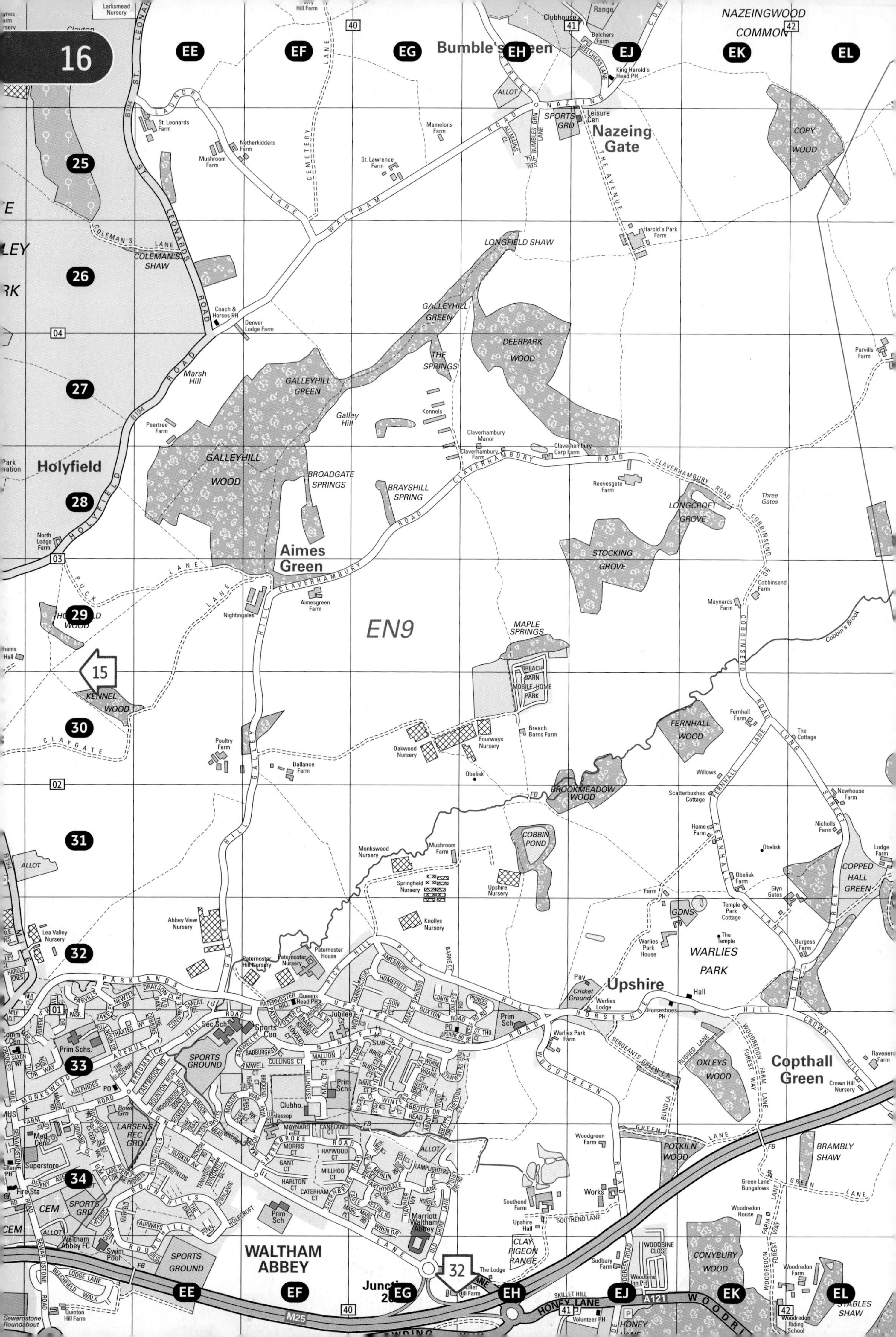

Bumble's Green
Nazeing Gate
NAZEINGWOOD COMMON
COPY WOOD
LONGFIELD SHAW
GALLEYHILL GREEN
DEERPARK WOOD
THE SPRINGS
Marsh Hill
Galley Hill
GALLEYHILL WOOD
Holyfield
BROADGATE SPRINGS
BRAYSHILL SPRING
Aimes Green
LONGCROFT GROVE
STOCKING GROVE
EN9
MAPLE SPRINGS
BREACH BARN MOBILE HOME PARK
KENNEL WOOD
FERNHALL WOOD
BROOKMEADOW WOOD
COBBIN POND
COPPED HALL GREEN
WARLIES PARK
Upshire
OXLEYS WOOD
Copthall Green
POTKILN WOOD
BRAMBLY SHAW
CLAY PIGEON RANGE
CONYBURY WOOD
STABLES SHAW
WALTHAM ABBEY
SPORTS GROUND
LARSENS REC GRD
M25

Epping Green
EPPING LONG GRN
Cobbin's Brook
UPLAND ROAD
EPPING ROAD
Hunters Hall Farm
Hayleys Manor Farm
BARN MEADOW
Pinch Timber Farm
Epping Bury Farm Centre
EPPING BURY FARM CENTRE NATURE TRAIL
NABHILL GROVE
BALLHILL WOOD
ORANGE WOOD
Gills Farm
Cobbin's Bridge
ORANGE FIELD PLANTATION
ORANGE PEEL
GILLS PLANTATION
WINTRY WOOD
LINDSEY STREET
Bury Farm
Shaftesbury Farm
SPRATT'S HEDGEROW WOOD
SPRATT'S HEDGEROW
POND FIELD PLANTATION
JENKINS'S PLANTATION
CM16
BURY LANE
LITTLE ROOKERY WOOD
FITCHES PLANTATION
EPPING CEM
EPPING
The Wood House
The White House
Home Farm
Paris Hall
New Farm
GRIFFIN'S WOOD
Griffin's Wood
COPPED HALL GDNS
Copped Hall (Ruins)
THE SELVAGE
Quality Hotel
Bell Common
Ivy Chimneys
Bower Hill
IVY CHIMNEYS ROAD
M25
BELL COMMON TUNNEL
LORETO CONVENT
THE WARREN
Warren Wood
EPPING THICKS
Great Gregories Farm
Crown Hill Farm
Warren Lodge
Ambresbury Banks
Clubhouse
THEYDON BOIS GOLF COURSE
EPPING FOREST
Little Bronx Livery & Riding Stables
Piercing Hill
Gardners Farm
Junction 6
Junction 27
Long Running
Forest Lodge Stables

18
33

Thornwood
NORTH WEALD AIRFIELD
WINTRY WOOD
THE LOWER FOREST
ST. MARGARET'S HOSPITAL
SPENCER CLOSE HOSPITAL
Coopersale
CM16
GERNON BUSHES
ROUGHTALLEY'S WOOD
BIRCHING COPPICE
Bower Hill
Fiddlers Hamlet
Mount End
Theydon Mount
HOBBS CROSS GOLF CENTRE
BEACHET WOOD
BARBER'S WOOD
Junction 6 (M11)
Junction 27 (M25)
M11
M25
17
34

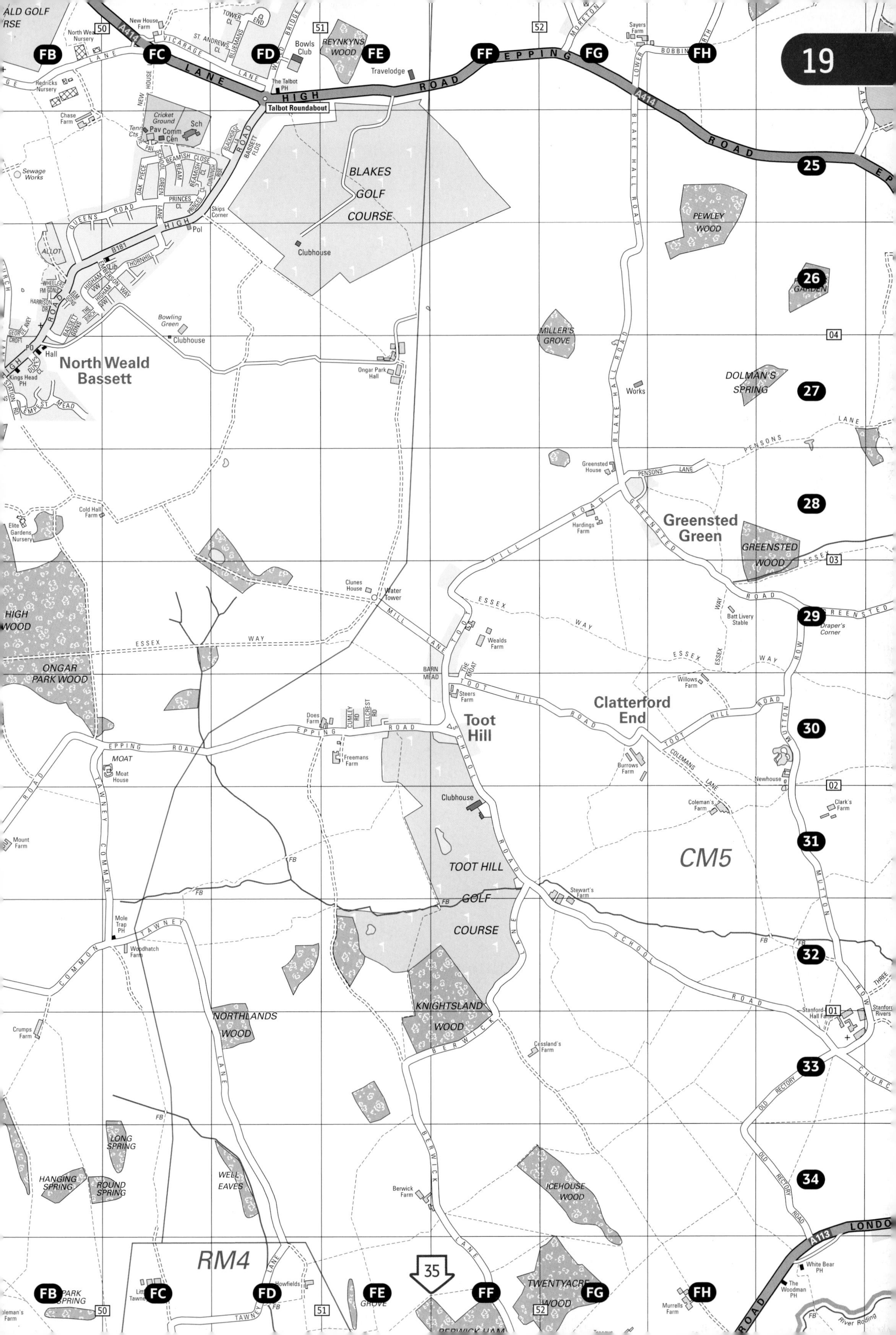

North Weald Bassett
Toot Hill
Greensted Green
Clatterford End
CM5
RM4
BLAKES GOLF COURSE
TOOT HILL GOLF COURSE
Talbot Roundabout
HIGH ROAD
EPPING ROAD
A414
REYNKYNS WOOD
PEWLEY WOOD
MILLER'S GROVE
DOLMAN'S SPRING
GREENSTED WOOD
HIGH WOOD
ONGAR PARK WOOD
NORTHLANDS WOOD
KNIGHTSLAND WOOD
ICEHOUSE WOOD
TWENTYACRE WOOD
LONG SPRING
HANGING SPRING
ROUND SPRING
WELL EAVES
ESSEX WAY
BLAKE HALL ROAD
TOOT HILL ROAD
SCHOOL ROAD
BERWICK LANE
TAWNEY COMMON
MUTTON ROW
OLD RECTORY ROAD
A113
Ongar Park Hall
Clubhouse
Water Tower
Stanford Rivers
Draper's Corner
35

Lower Bois
Chesham Bois
Latimer
Little Chalfont
AMERSHAM
FRITH WOOD
NETHER DITCH
FOUR ACRES
STOCKINGS SPRING
WESTLAND SPRING
JACK OF WADLEY'S SPRING
STAR CLUMP
TOOLEY'S CROFT
SPORTS GROUND
PARKFIELD WOOD
THE GROVE
RECTORY PLANTATION
LATIMER MEWS
LATIMER CONF. CEN
Boer War Mem
DUCK COVER
MARKET READING WOOD
LANE WOOD
ROUND WOOD
BLACKWELL STUBBS
BOIS WOOD
Civic Amenity Site
Sewage Works
Blackwell Hall
Blackwell Farm
Ivy House Farm
Quill Hall Farm
Raans Farm
Corinium Industrial Estate
Boughton Business Park
Latimer Park Farm
WEST WOOD
Tennis Club
Amersham Biosciences
CHALFONT & LATIMER
STATION RD
CHALFONT
Snell's Farm
SNELL'S WOOD
LITTLE CHALFONT GOLF COURSE
STONYDEAN WOOD
LOUDHAM'S WOOD
Burton's Farm
BURTON'S WOOD
Nightingales
Five Diamonds
DOGGETT'S WOOD
NIGHTINGALES WOOD
Rowood Farm
The Gate House
The Sheiling
POLLARDS WOOD
Pollards Park House
Elmswell House
Warren Farm
HAREWOOD DOWNS GOLF COURSE
Harewood Downs House
The Ivy House PH
Clubhouse
Coke's Farm
Little Kimblewick Farm
Bendrose Farm
Amersham & Wycombe Coll
HOBB'S DELL
STANLEY WOOD
WILLOW WOOD
HOVEL WOOD
CEM
Depot
DAY'S WOOD
HIGH WOOD
STRATTON COPSE
BOW WOOD
Lower Bottom House Farm
Upper Bottom House Farm
BAILEY WOOD
BAILEY WOOD BELT
Vache Farm
KILNPOND WOOD
RESERVOIR PLANTATION
Shortenills Environmental Education Centre
Roughwood Farm
Quarrendon Farm
THE LARCHES
BYCROFT PLANTATION
The Chequers PH
A4154 WOODSIDE ROAD
A404 WHITE LION ROAD
A413 LONDON ROAD EAST
A416
B4442
AMERSHAM BYPASS
HP5
HP6
HP7
HP8
AS AT AU AV AW AX AY
35 36 37 38 39 40 41 42 43 44
98 99 00 97 96
4
36

HANGING CROFT
HP3
R.A.F. Chenies
Mast
Moonshine Farm
DACORUM
THREE RIVERS
5
TOP SPRING
OLDCROFT WOOD
PLOUGH WOOD
HILLMEADS SPRING
Great Sarratt Hall Farm
Great Sarratt Hall
LONG WOOD
Martin Top Farm
BRAMBLE CROFT
HANGINGLANE WOOD
DAFFODIL SPRING
Sarratt
The Boot PH
OLDFIELD SPRING
LIMESHILL WOOD
Cricketers Inn PH
DAWES COMMON
SANDFIELD WOOD
FLAUNDEN GROVE
BALDWIN'S WOOD
WALLACE'S WOOD
Valley Farm
Watercress Beds
Moor Cottage
Adams Nurseries
Mill Farm
River Chess
MOUNT WOOD
Green End Business Cen
Chenies Place
PLACEHOUSE COPSE
CONEY WOOD
Greathouse Farm
Manor House
Mountwood Farm
NICHOLAS SPRING
Sarratt Bottom Cottages
Goldingtons
WALK WOOD
Bedford Arms PH
TURVEYLANE WOOD
New Model Farm
Chenies
Football Ground
Cricket Ground
Pav
Chenies Garden Centre
WYBURN WOOD
SCRUBBS WOOD
BLUNTS WOOD
AMERSHAM ROAD
A404
Sarrattmill Bridge
Water Works
MEAD SPRING
Weir
Weirs
22
OLD HANGING WOOD
Great Greenstreet Farm
Little Greenstreet Farm
CHILTON'S WOOD
CHILTERN
THREE RIVERS
WD3
NEW HANGING WOOD
LODGE COPSE
HALSEY'S WOOD
Stubbs Farm
Sec Sch
Field Study Centre
Tennis Club
Chorleywood House
DELL WOOD
MILLFIELD PLANTATION
Lodge Farm
BUCKINGHAMSHIRE
HERTFORDSHIRE
WHITELANDS WOOD
CEM
Highlands Water Gardens
Solesbridge Mill Water Gardens
River Chess
HILLAS WOOD
CARPENTER'S WOOD
Cricket Ground
Prim Sch
LITTLE LADY'S WOOD
White Horse PH
Junction 18
CHORLEYWOOD COMMON
CHORLEYWOOD GOLF COURSE
Arts Centre
Clubhouse
Hall
CHORLEYWOOD
Newhouse Farm
Prim Sch
The Cedars
HOME WOOD
Black Horse PH
Lib
Chorleywood
RICKMANSWORTH ROAD
CROSSLANE WOOD
ROUND WOOD
Fairfield Farm & Livery Stables
Roughwood Park
Berry Farm
THE SCREEN
SOLOMON'S WOOD
The Hall Farm
West Herts Riding School
PHEASANTS WOOD
Penn Farm
Prim Sch
Hill Farm
Chorleywood Bottom
M25
The Swillet
ALLOT
Bullsland Farm
37
Heronsgate
GROVE PING WOOD
HILIPSHILL WOOD
AZ
BA
BB
BC
BD
BE
BF
01
02
03
35
36
37
38
39
40
41
42
43
44
96
97
98
99

Commonwood
Bucks Hill
Sarratt
WD4
WD3
Loudwater
Croxley Green
Junction 18
Junction 19
M25
A404
CHORLEYWOOD ROAD
RICKMANSWORTH ROAD
WATFORD ROAD
SCOTS HILL
GREAT WOOD
HARROCKS WOOD
WELLING GROVE
BEECHENGROVE WOOD
COPTHORNE WOOD
SOLOMON'S WOOD
PHEASANTS WOOD
SCRUBBS WOOD
BLUNTS WOOD
SANDFIELD WOOD
TEMPLEPAN WOOD
JUNIPER HILL
BEECHEN BOTTOM
COMMONWOOD COMMON
HIGH SPRING
SAWPIT SPRING
SHEEPYARD SPRING
BIRCH SPRING
DARTPATH WOOD
MERLIN'S WOOD
MERLIN'S SPRING
WATERDELL SPRING
ROUND SPRING
LONG SPRING
UPPER PLANTATION
MILLFIELD PLANTATION
WILLOW WOOD
MEAD SPRING
HILLMEADS SPRING
SHEEPCOTE SPRING
SPORTS GROUND
Rickmansworth Masonic Sch
York Ho Sch
Prim Sch
River Chess
CHESS VALLEY WALK
BG BH BJ BK BL BM BN
35 36 37 38 39 40 41 42 43 44
05 06 07
99 98 97 96
6
21
38

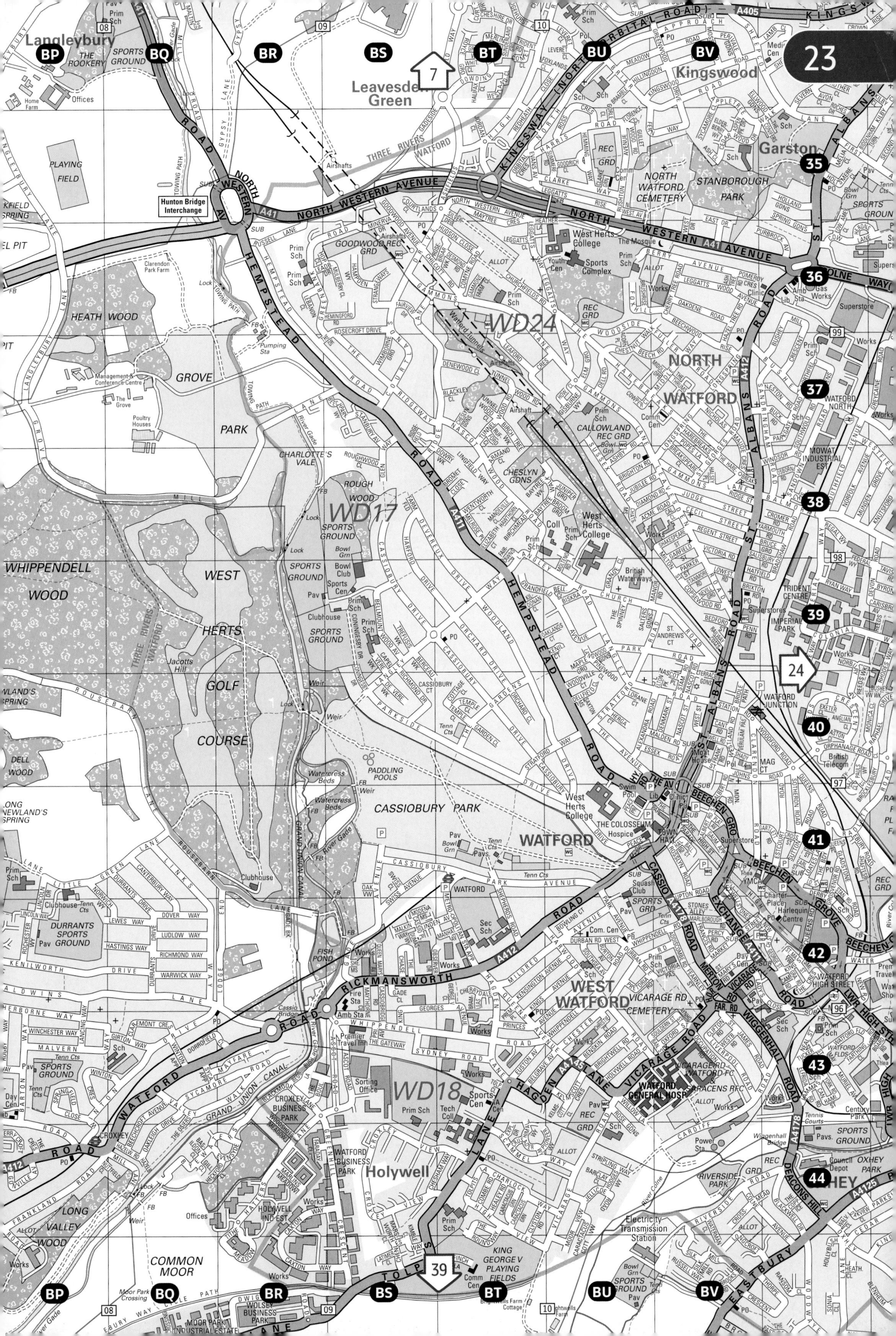
Langleybury
THE ROOKERY
SPORTS GROUND
Leavesden Green
Kingswood
Garston
NORTH ORBITAL ROAD
KINGSWAY (NORTH ORBITAL ROAD)
NORTH WESTERN AVENUE
Hunton Bridge Interchange
PLAYING FIELD
HEATH WOOD
GROVE PARK
The Grove
Management & Conference Centre
Poultry Houses
NORTH WATFORD CEMETERY
STANBOROUGH PARK
GOODWOOD REC GRD
West Herts College
Sports Complex
WD24
Watford Tunnels
NORTH WATFORD
CALLOWLAND REC GRD
CHESLYN GDNS
CHARLOTTE'S VALE
ROUGH WOOD
WD17
HEMPSTEAD ROAD
ST. ALBANS ROAD
WHIPPENDELL WOOD
WEST HERTS GOLF COURSE
Jacotts Hill
THREE RIVERS
WATFORD
DELL WOOD
LONG NEWLAND'S SPRING
CASSIOBURY PARK
PADDLING POOLS
Watercress Beds
GRAND UNION CANAL
THE COLOSSEUM
TOWN HALL
WATFORD
WATFORD JUNCTION
MOWAT INDUSTRIAL EST
TRIDENT CENTRE
IMPERIAL PARK
Harlequin Centre
DURRANTS SPORTS GROUND
RICKMANSWORTH ROAD
WEST WATFORD
VICARAGE RD CEMETERY
WATFORD GENERAL HOSP
FISH POND
WD18
CROXLEY BUSINESS PARK
WATFORD BUSINESS PARK
Holywell
HOLYWELL IND EST
KING GEORGE V PLAYING FIELDS
RIVERSIDE PARK
Electricity Transmission Station
LONG VALLEY WOOD
COMMON MOOR
MOOR PARK INDUSTRIAL ESTATE
WOLSEY BUSINESS PARK
OXHEY PARK
SPORTS GROUND
BP BQ BR BS BT BU BV
7
24
39
35 36 37 38 39 40 41 42 43 44

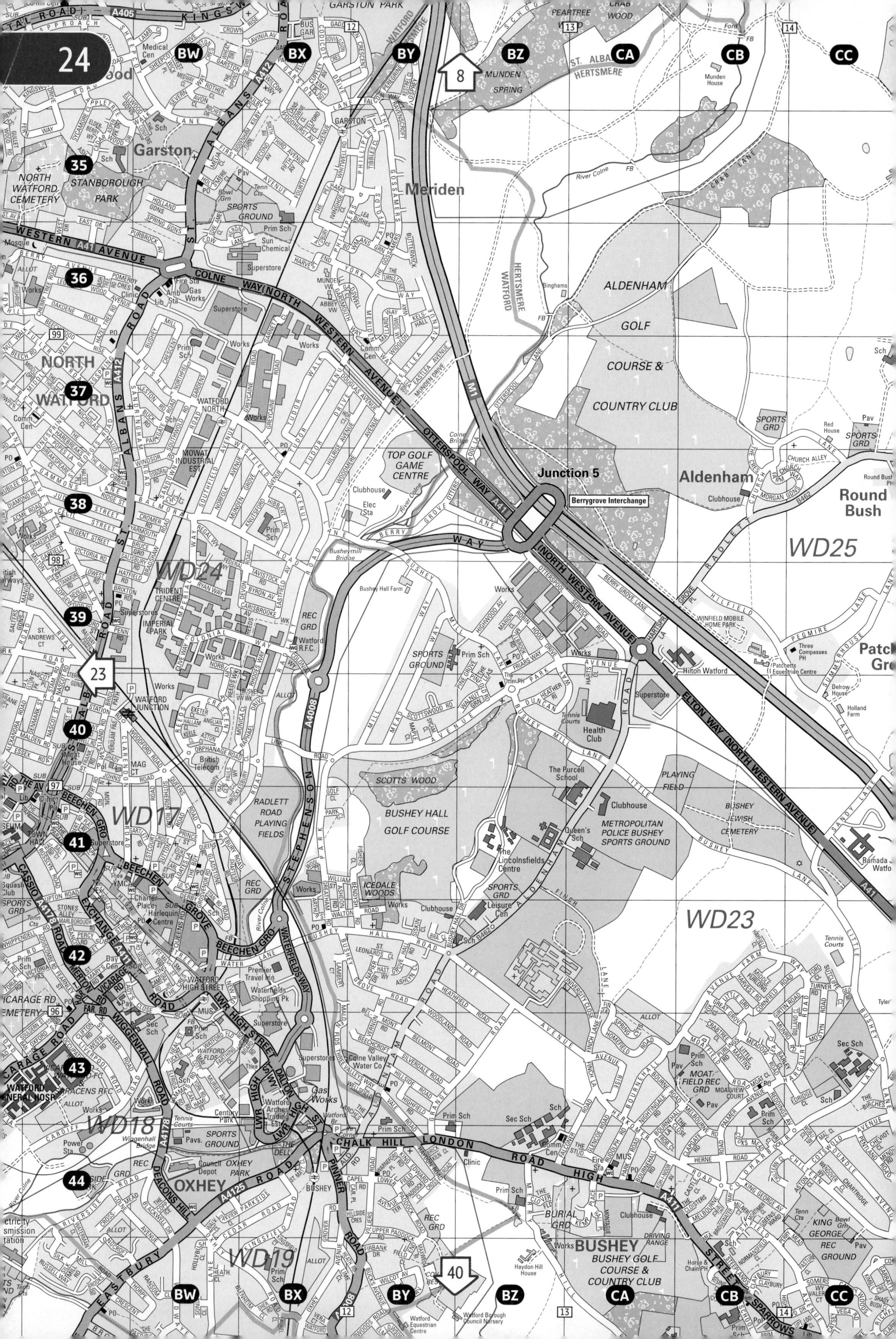
BW
BX
BY
BZ
CA
CB
CC
35
36
37
38
39
40
41
42
43
44
8
23
40
Garston
Meriden
NORTH WATFORD
Aldenham
Round Bush
BUSHEY
OXHEY
WD24
WD25
WD17
WD18
WD19
WD23
Junction 5
Berrygrove Interchange
ALDENHAM GOLF COURSE & COUNTRY CLUB
BUSHEY HALL GOLF COURSE
BUSHEY GOLF COURSE & COUNTRY CLUB
NORTH WATFORD CEMETERY
STANBOROUGH PARK
METROPOLITAN POLICE BUSHEY SPORTS GROUND
BUSHEY JEWISH CEMETERY
RADLETT ROAD PLAYING FIELDS
SCOTTS WOOD
ICEDALE WOODS
TOP GOLF GAME CENTRE
MUNDEN SPRING
WESTERN AVENUE
COLNE WAY (NORTH WESTERN AVENUE)
OTTERSPOOL WAY
ELTON WAY (NORTH WESTERN AVENUE)
ST ALBANS ROAD
STEPHENSON WAY
LONDON ROAD
HIGH STREET
SPARROWS HERNE
Hilton Watford
Watford Junction
Watford North
Bushey
HERTSMERE
WATFORD

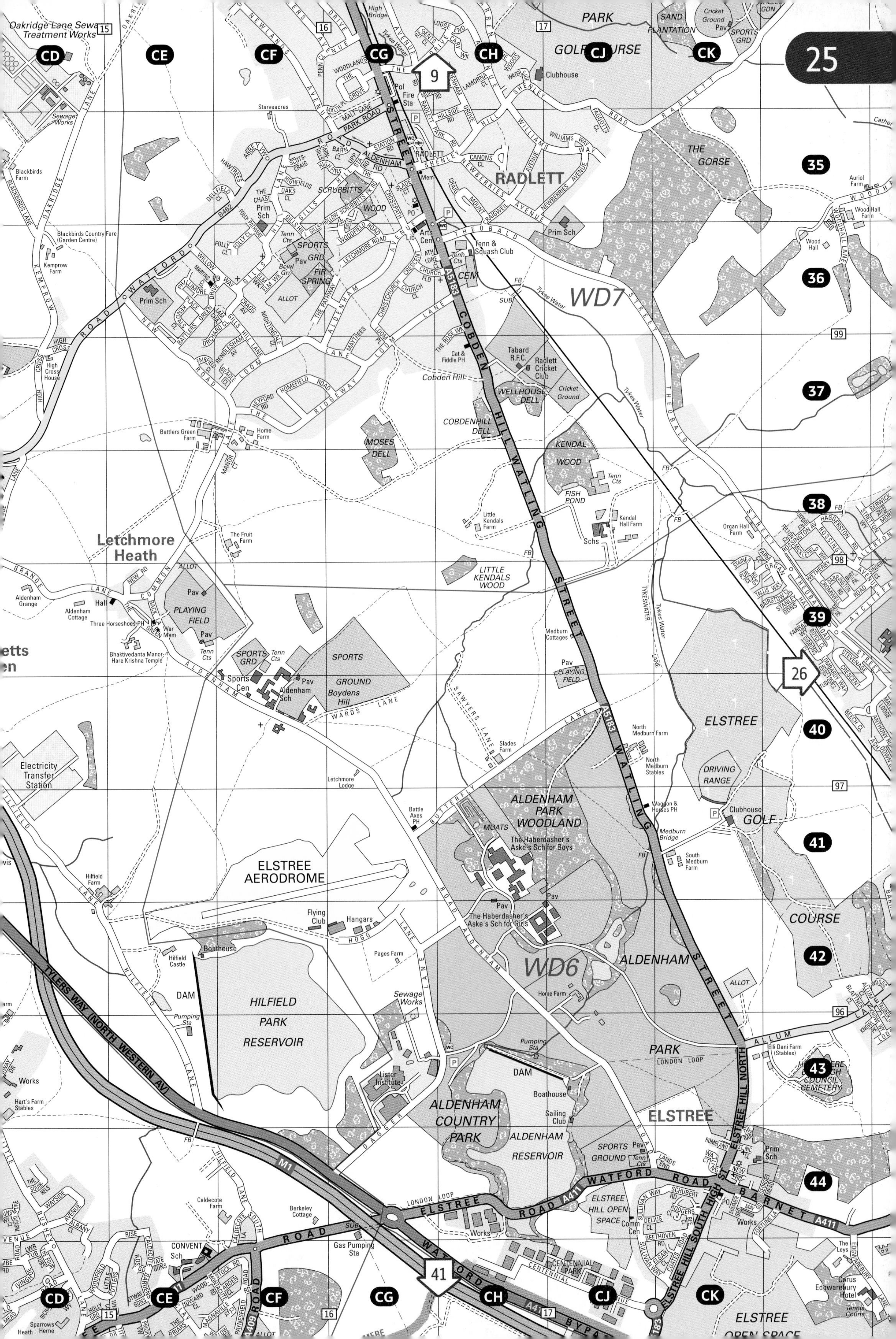

RADLETT
Letchmore Heath
ELSTREE
ELSTREE AERODROME
HILFIELD PARK RESERVOIR
ALDENHAM COUNTRY PARK
ALDENHAM RESERVOIR
ALDENHAM PARK WOODLAND
ALDENHAM PARK
WD7
WD6
THE GORSE
KENDAL WOOD
LITTLE KENDALS WOOD
MOSES DELL
COBDENHILL DELL
WELLHOUSE DELL
SCRUBBITTS WOOD
FIR SPRING
GOLF COURSE
SAND PLANTATION
WATLING STREET
COBDEN HILL
WATFORD ROAD
ELSTREE ROAD
BARNET LANE
ALDENHAM ROAD
THEOBALD STREET
TYLERS WAY (NORTH WESTERN AV)
M1
A5183
A411
Oakridge Lane Sewage Treatment Works
Blackbirds Farm
Blackbirds Country Fare (Garden Centre)
Kemprow Farm
High Cross House
Battlers Green Farm
Home Farm
The Fruit Farm
Aldenham Grange
Aldenham Cottage
Three Horseshoes PH
Bhaktivedanta Manor-Hare Krishna Temple
Electricity Transfer Station
Letchmore Lodge
Battle Axes PH
The Haberdasher's Aske's Sch for Boys
The Haberdasher's Aske's Sch for Girls
Flying Club
Hangars
Pages Farm
Hilfield Farm
Hilfield Castle
Sewage Works
Lister Institute
Organ Hall Farm
Kendal Hall Farm
Little Kendals Farm
Medburn Cottages
Slades Farm
North Medburn Farm
North Medburn Stables
Waggon & Horses PH
Medburn Bridge
South Medburn Farm
Elli Dani Farm (Stables)
Hertsmere Borough Council Cemetery
Edgwarebury Hotel
Corus
Auriol Farm
Wood Hall Farm
Wood Hall
Tabard R.F.C.
Radlett Cricket Club
Tenn & Squash Club
Cat & Fiddle PH
Caldecote Farm
Berkeley Cottage
Gas Pumping Sta
CONVENT Sch
CENTENNIAL PARK
ELSTREE HILL OPEN SPACE
ELSTREE OPEN SPACE
CD CE CF CG CH CJ CK
35 36 37 38 39 40 41 42 43 44
9
26
41

Junction 23 (M25) Junction 1 A1(M)
EN6
EN5
N20
Bentley Heath
Dancers Hill
WROTHAM PARK
DYRHAM PARK GOLF COURSE
DYRHAM PARK
BRIDGEDOWN GOLF COURSE
OLD FOLD MANOR GOLF COURSE
Kitt's End
Monken Hadley
Battle of Barnet 1471
High Barnet
Hadley
BARNET
KING GEORGE'S FIELD
CHIPPING BARNET
BARNET GENERAL HOSP
WHALEBONE PARK
Rowley Green
ARKLEY GOLF COURSE
Arkley
Barnet Gate
Ducks Island
Underhill
WHITINGS HILL OPEN SPACE
WROTHAM PARK OPEN SPACE
ARKLEY LANE OPEN SPACE
ARKLEY OPEN SPACE
HERTFORDSHIRE
HERTSMERE
BARNET
POOR CLARE MONASTERY
OLD ELIZABETHANS (BARNET) MEMORIAL PLAYING FIELDS
GRANGE PLAYING FIELDS
KING GEORGE V PLAYING FIELDS
SOUTH HERTS GOLF
South Mimms Services
Nat Inst for Biological Standards & Control
Research UK
Bignell's Corner
M25
A1(M)
A1081
A1000
A411
ST. ALBANS ROAD
BARNET BY-PASS
GREAT NORTH ROAD
HIGH STREET
WOOD STREET
BARNET ROAD

11
28
43

28
DA
DB
DC
DD
DE
DF
DG
POTTERS BAR COMMUNITY HOSP
M25
12
Junction 24
THE RIDGEWAY
A1005
WELWYN HATFIELD
POND WOOD
New Cottage Farm
Nursery
Prep. Sch
Water Tower
Elm Farm
Bentley Heath Farm
BENTLEY HEATH
35
Bentley Heath
Garden Centre
Ganwick Corner
Duke of York PH
Cricket Ground
Pav
Chase Farm
CHASE WOOD
Fenny Shade Hill
EN6
FIR WOOD
Plumridge Hill
PLUMRIDGE WOOD
Ind Sch
South Barvin Farm
VAULT HILL WOOD
Mausoleum
36
Wrotham Park
Tennis Courts
Pool
WROTHAM
99
PARK
Three Oak Hill
Hornbeam Hills
HERTFORDSHIRE
Cockshot Hill
Deadman's Bottom
Ganwick Farm
SPOILBANK WOOD
Salmon's Brook
Slopers Pond Farm
Plumridge Farm
Roundhedge Hill
HERTSMERE
ENFIELD
37
Wrotham Business Park
WAGGON ROAD
ENFIELD
BARTRAMS QUASH
Tenn Club
Prim Sch
HADLEY WOOD
CLAREMONT ROAD
COURTLEIGH AV
KINGWELL ROAD
Monken Mead Brook
West Lodge Park Hotel
ASH WOOD
38
LANCASTER AVENUE
HADLEY WOOD
Great Broadgates Hill
FERNY HILL
Ferny Hill Farm
BEECH HILL
98
Clubhouse
FERNYHILL WOOD
ROUGH LOT
39
Monken Hadley
Battle of Barnet 1471
Rectory Farm
Prim Sch
Jun Sch
War Memorial
27
CAMLET WAY
BEECH HILL PARK
HADLEY WOOD GOLF COURSE
Green Brook
Bournwell Hill
COVERT WAY OPEN SPACE
Sewit's Hill
FISH PONDS
SEEDFIELD SPINNEY
40
MONKEN HADLEY COMMON
Priddeon's Hill
Newman's Hill
EN4
BEECH HILL LAKE
Water Tower
OAK WOOD
Hadley
97
KING GEORGE'S FIELD
TUDOR GOLF COURSE
TUDOR SPORTS GRD
Clubhouse
Sec Sch
Prim Sch
41
BARNET
EN5
SPORTS GROUND
Gas Works
Ludgrove Hall
SPORTS GROUND
War Memorial
TRENT PARK CEM
BARNET TRADING EST
THE BULL THEATRE
Sports Cen
Barnet Coll
VICTORIA REC GRD
COCKFOSTERS
42
HIGH BARNET
NEW BARNET
COCKFOSTERS
CHIPPING BARNET
96
A110
STATION ROAD
EAST BARNET ROAD
Superstore
NEW BARNET
43
Cinema
BARNET FC
Underhill
Clubhouse
SPORTS GROUND
Health Cen
Lib
ALLOT
Sec Sch
Prim Sch
Middlesex Uni
44
BARNET PLAYING FIELDS
KING GEORGE V PLAYING FIELDS
Prim Sch
B193
EAST BARNET
Oak Hill College
N20
Sec Sch
WYATTS FARM OPEN SPACE
44
OAKLEIGH PARK
OAK HILL PARK
Bandstand
Miniature Golf Course
SOUTH HERTS GOLF
26
27
28

DH
DJ
DK
DL
DM
DN
DP
13
30
45
CREWS HILL GOLF COURSE
Crews Hills
WHITEWEBBS PARK
Botany Bay
CHASE
Clay Hill
HILLY FIELDS PARK
EN2
KING'S OAK PRIVATE HOSPITAL
CHASE FARM HOSPITAL
LAVENDER HILL CEMETERY
Enfield
NUFFIELD HOSP
TRENT PARK GOLF COURSE
Middlesex University
World's End
ENFIELD GOLF COURSE
GRANGE PARK
BUSH HILL PARK GOLF COURSE
OAKWOOD
OAKWOOD PARK
N21
N14
THE RIDGEWAY
A1005
A110
WINDMILL HILL
SLADES HILL
ENFIELD ROAD
HADLEY ROAD
ENFIELD CHASE
TOWN PARK
WILLIAMS WOOD
MOAT WOOD
RIDE WOOD
SHAWS WOOD
FISH POND
Kingswood

DQ
DR
DS
DT
DU
DV
DW
14
Junction 25
BROXBOURNE
BULLSCROSS RIDE
CEMETERY (JEWISH)
COUNTY BROOK PLANTATION
Theobalds Park Camping and Caravan Site
Bulls Cross
Capel Manor College
CAPEL HOUSE
BULLSMOOR
Crews Hill
WHITEWEBBS WOOD
WHITEWEBBS PARK
WHITEWEBBS GOLF COURSE
White Webbs House
WILDWOOD
EN2
Clay Hill
Forty Hill
FORTY HALL COUNTRY PARK
FORTY HALL & MUSEUM
Maiden's Bridge
Bullsmoor
CEMETERY
Crematorium
HILLY FIELDS PARK
Rendlesham Viaduct
LAVENDER HILL CEMETERY
ENFIELD CEMETERY (JEWISH)
QUEEN ELIZABETH STADIUM
EN1
ENFIELD PLAYING FIELDS
ENFIELD
ENFIELD TOWN
ENFIELD CHASE
29
ST. GEORGE'S FIELD
ENFIELD RETAIL PK
Superstores
SOUTHBURY Works
MARTINBRIDGE TRADING ESTATE
Middlesex University
TOWN PARK
BUSH HILL PARK GOLF COURSE
BUSH HILL PARK
GRANGE PARK
N21
N9
JUBILEE PARK
46
GREAT CAMBRIDGE ROAD
SOUTHBURY ROAD
HERTFORD ROAD
WINDMILL HILL
LONDON ROAD
RIDGEWAY
35
36
37
38
39
40
41
42
43
44

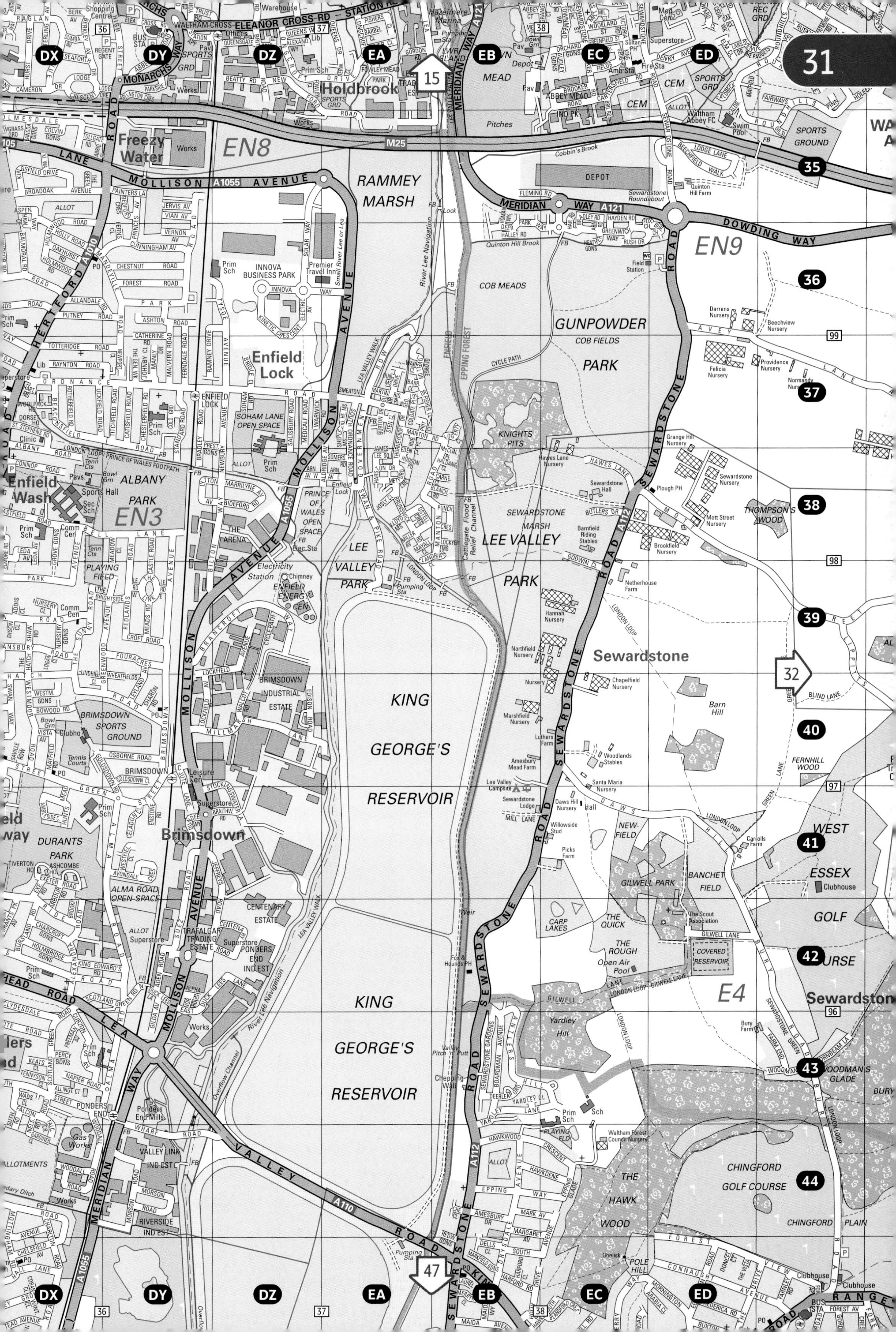

DX
DY
DZ
EA
EB
EC
ED
15
Holdbrook
Waltham Cross
ELEANOR CROSS RD
STATION RD
MONARCHS WAY
Freezy Water
EN8
M25
MOLLISON A1055 AVENUE
RAMMEY MARSH
MERIDIAN WAY A121
DEPOT
Sewardstone Roundabout
DOWDING WAY
EN9
35
36
37
38
39
40
41
42
43
44
INNOVA BUSINESS PARK
Premier Travel Inn
Enfield Lock
COB MEADS
GUNPOWDER PARK
COB FIELDS
HERTFORD A1010 ROAD
ORDNANCE ROAD
SOHAM LANE OPEN SPACE
KNIGHTS PITS
HAWES LANE
SEWARDSTONE ROAD
Enfield Wash
ALBANY PARK
EN3
PRINCE OF WALES OPEN SPACE
SEWARDSTONE MARSH
LEE VALLEY PARK
THOMPSON'S WOOD
THE ARENA
Electricity Station
ENFIELD ENERGY CEN
PLAYING FIELD
Sewardstone
32
BRIMSDOWN INDUSTRIAL ESTATE
KING GEORGE'S RESERVOIR
Barn Hill
BRIMSDOWN SPORTS GROUND
FERNHILL WOOD
Brimsdown
DURANTS PARK
NEW-FIELD
WEST ESSEX GOLF COURSE
ALMA ROAD OPEN SPACE
BANCHET FIELD
GILWELL PARK
The Scout Association
CENTENARY ESTATE
TRAFALGAR TRADING ESTATE
PONDERS END IND EST
CARP LAKES
THE QUICK
THE ROUGH
COVERED RESERVOIR
E4
Sewardstone
Yardley Hill
WOODMAN'S GLADE
Ponders End
VALLEY LINK IND EST
LEA VALLEY A110 ROAD
THE HAWK WOOD
CHINGFORD GOLF COURSE
CHINGFORD PLAIN
POLE HILL
RIVERSIDE IND EST
47
MERIDIAN WAY A1035
36
37
38

EE
EF
EG
EH
EJ
EK
EL
16
41
42
40
WALTHAM ABBEY
Junction 26
M25
A121
DOWDING WAY
HONEY LANE
WOODRIDDEN HILL
SPORTS GROUND
Waltham Abbey FC
Swim Pool
Prim Sch
Marriott Waltham Abbey
Southend Farm
Upshire Hall
Works
CLAY PIGEON RANGE
The Lodge
Skillet Hill Farm
Woodgreen Farm
POTKILN WOOD
BRAMBLY SHAW
Green Lane Bungalows
Woodredon House
CONYBURY WOOD
Woodredon Farm
STABLES SHAW
Woodredon Riding School
Sudbury Farm
WOODBINE CLOSE
Woodbine Inn PH
Volunteer PH
HONEY LANE PLAIN
35
Quinton Hill Farm
Sewardstone Roundabout
EN9
36
Field Station
Inner Lodge
LORD PADGETS WOOD
POPLARS SHAW
WALTHAM ABBEY CEMETERY (JEWISH)
HONEY LANE QUARTERS
SUNSHINE PLAIN
THREE FORESTS WAY
Round Hills
Tile Hill Farm
Beech Hill Park
Darrens Nursery
Beechview Nursery
99
AVEY LANE
Felicia Nursery
Providence Nursery
Normandy Nursery
Hanbury Riding School
BEECH HILL PARK
HIGH BEECH GOLF COURSE
37
SEWARDSTONE ROAD
Avey Lane Farm
Grange Hill Nursery
High Beech Nursery
PYNEST GRN
Pynest Green
High Beech Riding School
Clubho
Duke of Wellington PH
WELLINGTON HILL
Wake Valley
Avey Cottages
Sewardstone Nursery
Plough PH
38
Mott Street Nursery
THOMPSON'S WOOD
Bowl Club
Y.H.A.
Earthworks Tumulus
Court Hill
LITTLE MONK WOOD
Bellringers
Brookfield Nursery
98
King's Oak PH
Epping Forest Field Cen
Netherhouse Farm
Manor House
Prim Sch
Oak Farm
MOTT STREET
MANOR ROAD
Paul's Nursery
Mount Pleasant
BLACKWEIR POND
EPPING
39
Wallsgrove House
ALDERGROVE WOOD
Cricket Ground
Cricket Club
High Beach
Broom Hill
Blackweir Hill
Loughton Camp
Kate's Cellar
BALDWINS POND
Sewardstone
31
Barn Hill
BLIND LANE
Day's Farm
Fairmead, Hackney Scouts Campsite
HILL WOOD
Shelley's Hill
IG10
Robin Hood PH
40
FERNHILL WOOD
Police Training Centre
Pipers Farm
Suntrap Field Study Centre
Elms Caravan & Camping Park
Owl PH
FOREST
Staples Hill
97
LONDON LOOP
Carrolls Farm
WEST
Springfield Farm
Piggeries
WHITEHOUSE PLAIN
Strawberry Hill
41
ESSEX
Clubhouse
ROUND THICKET
FAIRMEAD POND
BANCHET FIELD
GILWELL PARK
The Scout Association
GOLF
GILWELL LANE
42
ALMHOUSE PLAIN
North Long Hills
Fairmead Bottom
STRAWBERRY HILL PONDS
Health Cen
COURSE
E4
Sewardstonebury
Long Hills
Glasshouses
Tenn Cts
96
Bury Farm
Obelisk
Fire Sta
Superstore
Sec Sch
SPORTS GRD
43
WOODMAN'S GLADE
BURY WOOD
HORSE RIDE
Cuckoo Pits
Grimston's Oak
Oaklands Sch
LOUGHTON
CHINGFORD GOLF COURSE
44
Magpie Hill
CONNAUGHT WATER
Warren Hill House
Warren Hill
North Farm House
Tenn Club
CHINGFORD PLAIN
Holmhurst
A104
A1069
QUEEN ELIZABETH'S HUNTING LODGE
48
Clubhouse
Warren Wood PH
Buckhurst Hill
THE WARREN
WARREN POND
Oak Hall
RANGERS ROAD
POLE HILL

EPPING FOREST
THEYDON BOIS GOLF COURSE
Theydon Bois
CM16
Debden Green
Debden
LOUGHTON
RM4
IG7
LOUGHTON GOLF COURSE
WOOLSTON MANOR GOLF COURSE
Junction 6
Junction 27
Junction 5
BIRCH WOOD
RED OAK WOOD
GAUNT'S WOOD
THEYDON PLAIN
THE COPPICE
Long Running
Oak Hill
Jacks Hill
ST.THOMAS'S QUARTERS
BROADSTROOD PLAIN
COPLEY PLAIN
FURZE GROUND
LONG SHAW
BROADFIELD SHAW
THEYDON MEAD
QUEEN MARY & WESTFIELD COLLEGE SPORTS GROUND
THEYDON BOIS CEMETERY
HILLYFIELDS OPEN SPACE
Printing Works
IMPRIMO PARK
PROSPECT BUSINESS PARK
OAKWOOD HILL INDUSTRIAL ESTATE
ABRIDGE PARK
River Roding
M11
A121
A1168
A113
A1112
B172
B1393
17
34
49

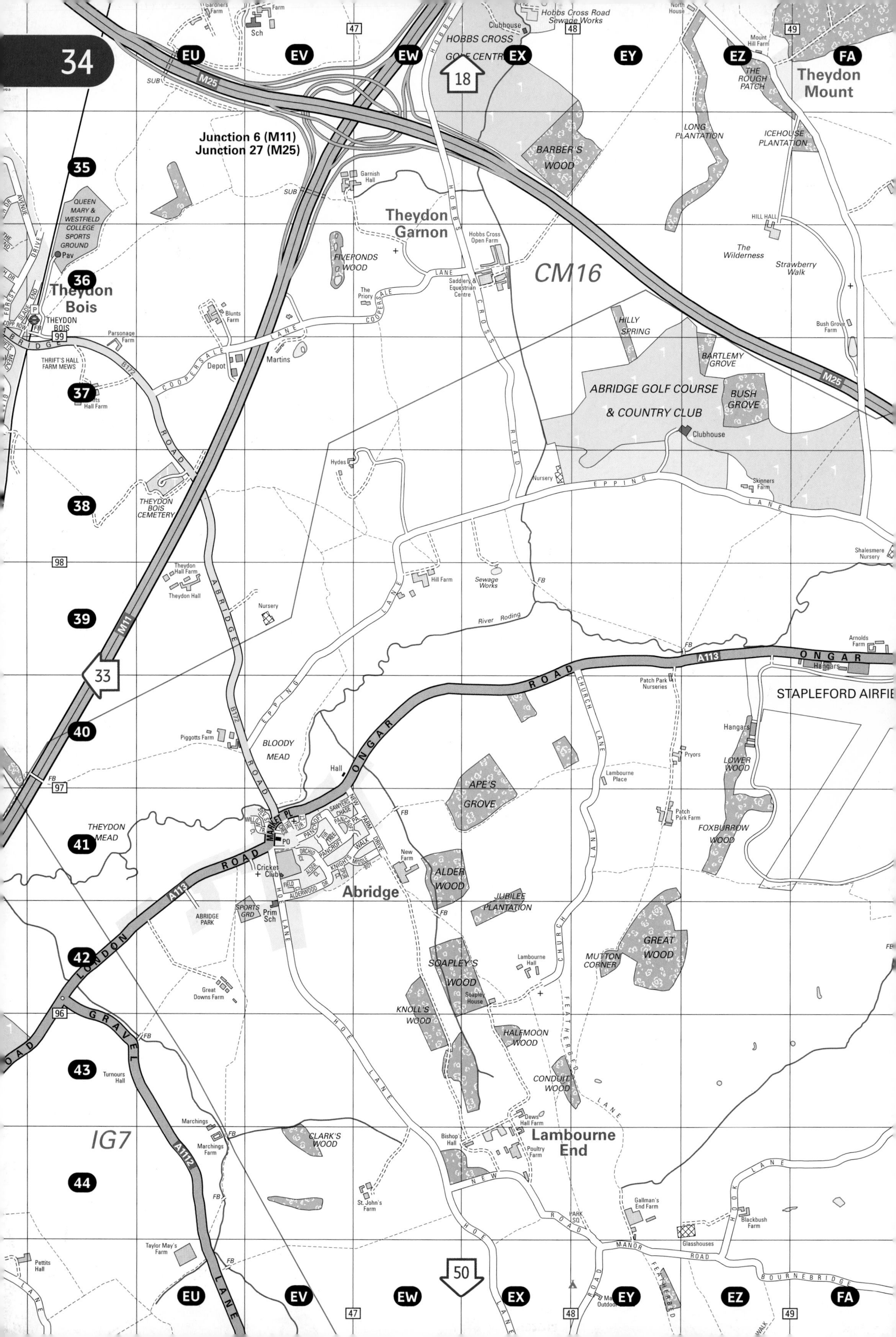
Junction 6 (M11)
Junction 27 (M25)
Theydon Garnon
Theydon Bois
Theydon Mount
CM16
ABRIDGE GOLF COURSE & COUNTRY CLUB
STAPLEFORD AIRFIE
Abridge
Lambourne End
IG7
HOBBS CROSS GOLF CENTRE
BARBER'S WOOD
FIVEPONDS WOOD
QUEEN MARY & WESTFIELD COLLEGE SPORTS GROUND
THEYDON BOIS CEMETERY
BLOODY MEAD
THEYDON MEAD
APE'S GROVE
ALDER WOOD
JUBILEE PLANTATION
SOAPLEY'S WOOD
KNOLL'S WOOD
HALFMOON WOOD
CONDUIT WOOD
CLARK'S WOOD
GREAT WOOD
MUTTON CORNER
LOWER WOOD
FOXBURROW WOOD
HILLY SPRING
BARTLEMY GROVE
BUSH GROVE
LONG PLANTATION
ICEHOUSE PLANTATION
THE ROUGH PATCH
River Roding
ONGAR ROAD
LONDON ROAD
EPPING LANE
HOE LANE
CHURCH LANE
GRAVEL LANE
MANOR ROAD
NEW ROAD
BOURNEBRIDGE LANE
HOOK LANE
COOPERSALE LANE
HOBBS CROSS ROAD
ABRIDGE ROAD
18
33
50
EU EV EW EX EY EZ FA
35 36 37 38 39 40 41 42 43 44
47 48 49 96 97 98 99

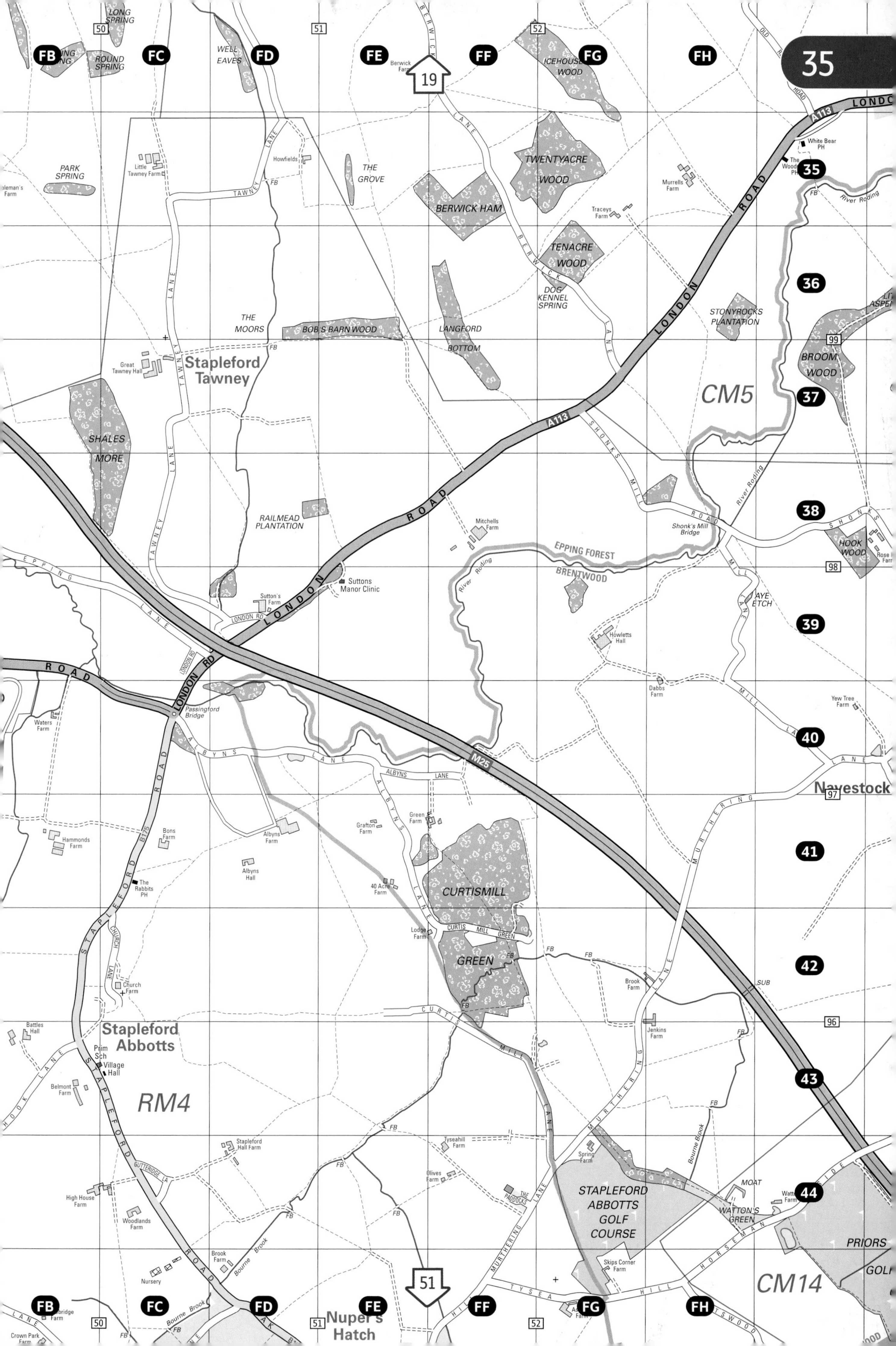
Stapleford Tawney
Stapleford Abbotts
Navestock
Nupers Hatch
RM4
CM5
CM14
LONDON ROAD
A113
M25
STAPLEFORD ROAD
B175
CURTISMILL GREEN
STAPLEFORD ABBOTTS GOLF COURSE
SHALES MORE
BOB'S BARN WOOD
TWENTYACRE WOOD
BERWICK HAM
TENACRE WOOD
ICEHOUSE WOOD
LANGFORD BOTTOM
BROOM WOOD
HOOK WOOD
THE MOORS
THE GROVE
PARK SPRING
ROUND SPRING
LONG SPRING
WELL EAVES
RAILMEAD PLANTATION
STONYROCKS PLANTATION
DOG KENNEL SPRING
EPPING FOREST
BRENTWOOD
River Roding
Bourne Brook
Passingford Bridge
Shonk's Mill Bridge
Suttons Manor Clinic
Albyns Hall
Howletts Hall
Great Tawney Hall
Little Tawney Farm
Hammonds Farm
Mitchells Farm
Tyseahill Farm
Stapleford Hall Farm
Skips Corner Farm
Jenkins Farm
Brook Farm
Lodge Farm
Green Farm
Grafton Farm
40 Acre Farm
Church Farm
Belmont Farm
Battles Hall
Waters Farm
Bons Farm
The Rabbits PH
White Bear PH
Dabbs Farm
Yew Tree Farm
Murrells Farm
Traceys Farm
Howfields
Berwick Farm
Woodlands Farm
High House Farm
Nursery
Olives Farm
Spring Farm
MOAT
WATTON'S GREEN
PRIORS
19
51
FB FC FD FE FF FG FH
35 36 37 38 39 40 41 42 43 44
50 51 52
96 97 98 99

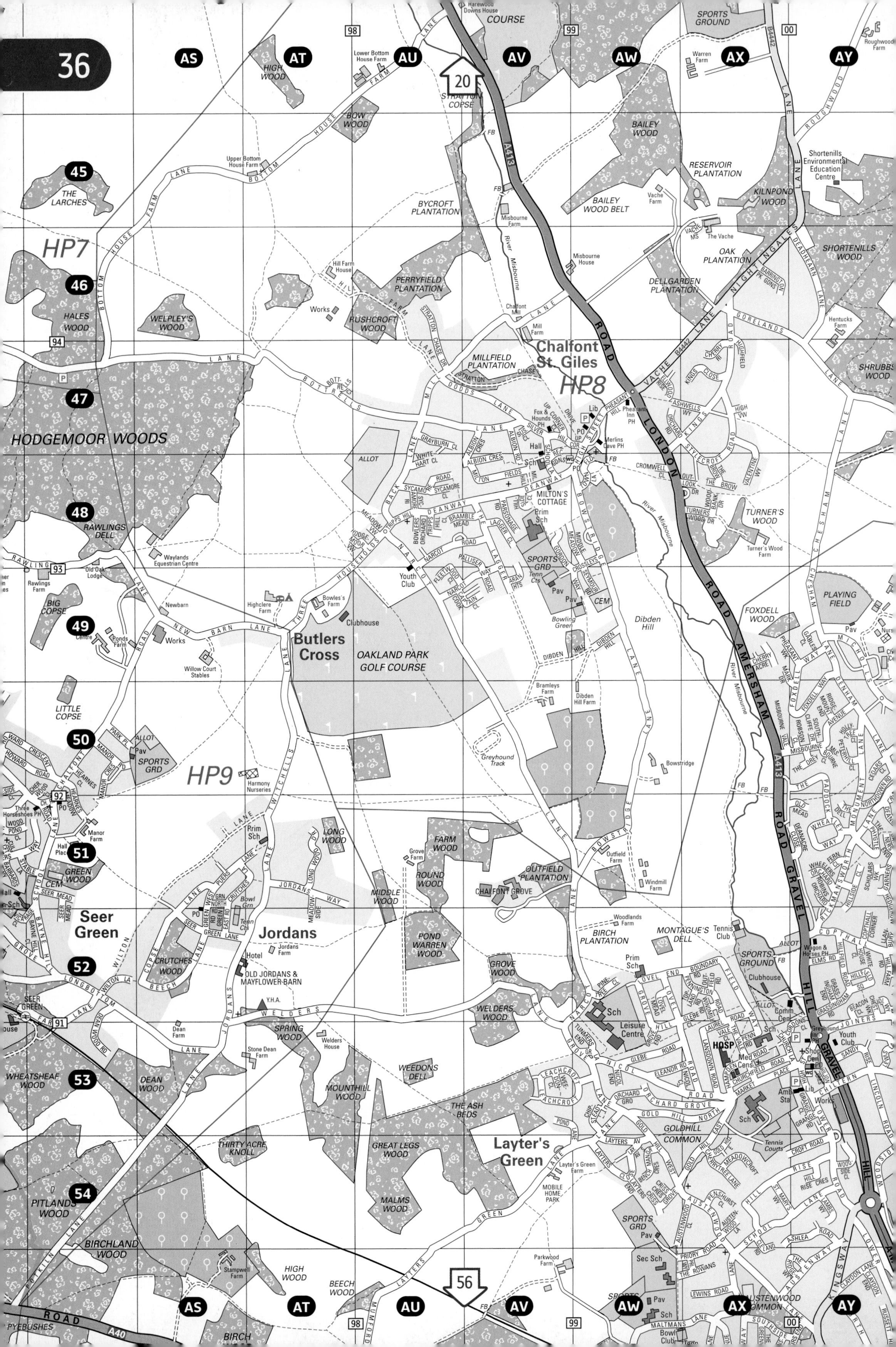
AS
AT
AU
AV
AW
AX
AY
98
99
00
20
56
45
46
47
48
49
50
51
52
53
54
HP7
HP8
HP9
COURSE
Harewood Downs House
SPORTS GROUND
Roughwood Farm
Lower Bottom House Farm
HIGH WOOD
Warren Farm
STRATTON COPSE
BOW WOOD
BAILEY WOOD
A413
RESERVOIR PLANTATION
Shortenills Environmental Education Centre
Upper Bottom House Farm
THE LARCHES
BYCROFT PLANTATION
Misbourne Farm
BAILEY WOOD BELT
Vache Farm
KILNPOND WOOD
The Vache
OAK PLANTATION
SHORTENILLS WOOD
Misbourne House
Hill Farm House
PERRYFIELD PLANTATION
DELLGARDEN PLANTATION
HALES WOOD
WELPLEY'S WOOD
Works
RUSHCROFT WOOD
Chalfont Mill
Mill Farm
Hentucks Farm
Chalfont St. Giles
MILLFIELD PLANTATION
SHRUBBS WOOD
HODGEMOOR WOODS
Pheasant Inn PH
Fox & Hounds PH
Merlins Cave PH
ALLOT
Hall
Sch
MILTON'S COTTAGE
Prim Sch
TURNER'S WOOD
Turner's Wood Farm
RAWLINGS DELL
Waylands Equestrian Centre
Old Oak Lodge
Rawlings Farm
SPORTS GRD
Youth Club
BIG COPSE
Newbarn
Highclere Farm
Bowles's Farm
Clubhouse
CEM
PLAYING FIELD
FOXDELL WOOD
Dibden Hill
Ponds Farm
Works
Butlers Cross
OAKLAND PARK GOLF COURSE
Willow Court Stables
Bowling Green
Bramleys Farm
Dibden Hill Farm
LITTLE COPSE
Greyhound Track
Bowstridge
Harmony Nurseries
Three Horseshoes PH
Manor Farm
LONG WOOD
FARM WOOD
Grove Farm
Outfield Farm
OUTFIELD PLANTATION
Hall Place
GREEN WOOD
ROUND WOOD
MIDDLE WOOD
CHALFONT GROVE
Windmill Farm
Seer Green
Jordans
Woodlands Farm
BIRCH PLANTATION
MONTAGUE'S DELL
Tennis Club
Jordans Farm
POND WARREN WOOD
CRUTCHES WOOD
Hotel
OLD JORDANS & MAYFLOWER BARN
GROVE WOOD
SPORTS GROUND
Clubhouse
Y.H.A.
WELDERS WOOD
Leisure Centre
Youth Club
SEER GREEN
Dean Farm
SPRING WOOD
Welders House
HOSP
Stone Dean Farm
WEEDONS DELL
WHEATSHEAF WOOD
DEAN WOOD
MOUNTHILL WOOD
THE ASH BEDS
GOLDHILL COMMON
THIRTY ACRE KNOLL
GREAT LEGS WOOD
Layter's Green
Layter's Green Farm
Tennis Courts
MOBILE HOME PARK
PITLANDS WOOD
MALMS WOOD
BIRCHLAND WOOD
SPORTS GRD
Parkwood Farm
Sec Sch
Stampwell Farm
HIGH WOOD
BEECH WOOD
AUSTENWOOD COMMON
PYEBUSHES
A40
BIRCH
LONDON ROAD
AMERSHAM ROAD
GRAVEL HILL
CHESHAM LANE
NIGHTINGALES LANE
GORELANDS LANE
BOTTOM HOUSE FARM LANE
NEW BARN LANE
WILTON LANE
LONGBOTTOM LANE
WELDERS LANE
JORDANS LANE
JORDANS WAY
TWITCHELLS LANE
LAYTERS GREEN LANE
MUMFORDS LANE
ASHLEA ROAD
SCHOOL LANE
KINGSWAY

Chorleywood Bottom
The Swillet
Heronsgate
Mill End
Junction 17
NEWLAND PARK
Buckinghamshire Chilterns University College
CHILTERN OPEN AIR MUSEUM
SPORTS GROUND
BOTTOM WOOD
LADYWALK WOOD
WD3
FIVE PLANTATIONS
POLLARDSHILL WOOD
Maple Cross
MAPLE CROSS INDUSTRIAL ESTATE
BEECHEN WOOD
Maple Lodge Sewage Treatment Works
PLAYING FIELDS
FRANKLINS SPRING
Chalfont Common
KILN WOOD
ROBERT'S WOOD
SL9
ROUND ROCKET PLANTATION
QUARRY & LANDFILL SITE
MIDDLE WOOD
BLOOM WOOD
CHALFONT ST. PETER
HOGTROUGH WOOD
GERRARDS CROSS GOLF COURSE
GRAVEL PIT
LYNSTERS LAKE
PYNESFIELD LAKE
SPRINGWELL LAKE
SPRINGWELL CHALK PIT
UB9
Horseshoe Bay
Sailing Club
MOUNT PLEASANT SPORTS GRD
TRAINING CENTRE DURDENT COURT
JUNIPER WOOD
NOCKHILL WOOD
GROVESPRING WOOD
PHILIPSHILL WOOD
NEWLAND GORSE
HERTFORDSHIRE
BUCKINGHAMSHIRE
THREE RIVERS
SOUTH BUCKS
DENHAM WAY
NORTH ORBITAL ROAD
M25
A412
A405

21
38
57

SCREEN
SOLOMON'S WOOD
PHEASANTS WOOD
BG
BH
BJ
BK
BL
BM
BN
22
Batchworth Masonic Sch
HOCKEY PLAYING GRD
FIELD
CRICKET GRD
Clubhouse
SPORTS GROUND
CROXLEY HALL WOOD
Prim Sch
Pav
CEM
SCOTS HILL
WATFORD ROAD
RICKMANSWORTH PARK
FORTUNE COMMON
Scots Br
River Chess
LAYROCK
45
46
47
48
49
50
51
52
53
54
M25
Mill End
Leisure Centre
Swim Pool
Bowl Grn
WILLIAM PENN MULTISPORTS ARENA
Clubho
Moneyhill
Tenn Club
RICKMANSWORTH
Sec Sch
COUN. OFF
MUS
Lib
Watersmeet Cen
Comet House
Croxley Hall Farm
Watercress Beds
River Colne
Lot Mead Lock
Hampton Hall Farm
The Alders
RECTORY RD
RIVERSIDE DRIVE
A404
Batchworth Roundabout
Halfway House PH
Clinics
Boathouse
Weir
Comm Cens
Depot
Prim Sch
ation 17
94
93
92
91
A405
A412
UXBRIDGE ROAD
A412
BATCHWORTH LAKE
WD3
THE AQUADROME
BURY LAKE
Works
Three Valleys Water
Superstore
White Bear PH
MOOR LANE
Green Knoll
Clubhouse
Batchworth
RICKMANSWORTH
MOOR PARK
GOLF
COURSE
MOOR PARK MANSION
GD
LONDON ROAD
Whip & Collar PH
River Colne
Boathouse
GRAND UNION CANAL
Depot
THE GROVE
BATCHWORTH
PARK
Clubhouse
Moor Park Farm
BATCHWORTH HILL
Drayton Ford
STOCKER'S LAKE (NATURE RESERVE)
Stocker's Lock
Stocker's Farm
Pumping Sta
Prim Sch
Froghall Farm
Works
GARRETT WOOD
HIGH WOOD
CHALK PIT
Andrews Ley Farm
Juniper Dell
Greenbroom Spring
GOLF
WOODCOCK HILL CEMETERY
Sandfield Spring
Watercress Beds
SPRINGWELL CHALK PIT
MAPLE CROSS INDUSTRIAL ESTATE
Lock
SPRINGWELL LAKE
HERTFORDSHIRE
HAREFIELD ROAD INDUSTRIAL ESTATE
Pipers Farm
COURSE
Bush Spring
HOME FARM RD
Home Farm House
BATCHWORTH HEATH HILL
Batchworth Heath
Batchworth Heath Farm
Clubhouse
COCKS WOOD
37
Maple Lodge Sewage Treatment Works
Filter Beds
Sludge Beds
LONDON LOOP
THREE RIVERS
Rose & Crown PH
LONG SPRING
PARK WOOD
WOODCOCK HILL
Lynsters Farm
Cripps House Farm
BISHOP'S WOOD
POORFIELD
LOCKWELL WOOD
HILLINGDON
Waybeards Farm
PEARSON'S WOOD
LYNSTERS LAKE
Hill End
White Heath Farm
Harefield Grove
SHRUBS RD
COV RES
WHITE
FRENCH GROVE
ALLOT
WATTS COMMON
COVERED RESERVOIR
Battlers Wells Farm
Works
PARK WOOD
TAYLORS MEADOW
Harefield Grove Farm
BATTLERS WELLS WOOD
JACKETS
PYNESFIELD LAKE
Nature Reserve
Little Bourne Farm (Equestrian Stables)
UB9
Shepherds Hill Farm
MOUNT PLEASANT SPORTS GRD
HAREFIELD HOSPITAL
Pol
Sports Cen
Sec Sch
Shepherds Hill House
NORTHWOOD ROAD
Horseshoe Bay
SPORTS GRD
Health Cen
THE GREEN
FURZEFIELD
DEADMAN'S GROVE
HAREFIELD
Weir
Sailing Club
Colney Farm
Prim Sch
Lib
Comm Cen
The Swan PH
PO
Cricket Ground
ASHAIN SPRING
SCARLET SPRING
Lock
Pavs.
Harefield United FC
KILN POND
RAVENERS SPRING
BREAKSPEAR ROAD
ALLOT
CLAYPITS
DELL
RIVERS
BUCKS
Knightscote Farm
Shooting School
Langley Farm
HIGHBONES
OLD UXBRIDGE ROAD
NORTH WAY
LONDON LOOP TOWING PATH
Grand Union Canal
58
Bourne Farm
05
06
07

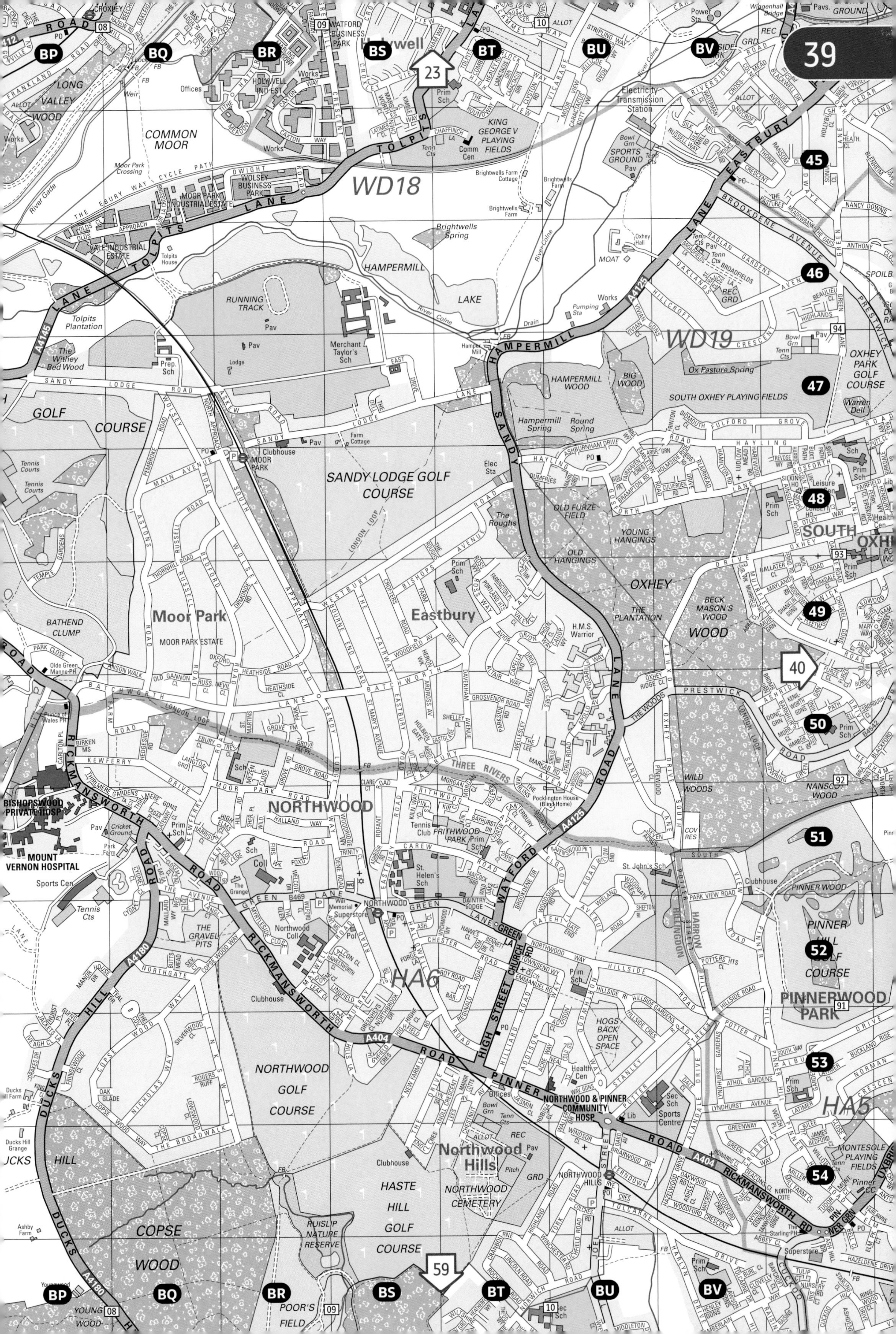
Holywell
WD18
WD19
HA6
HA5
Moor Park
Eastbury
NORTHWOOD
Northwood Hills
OXHEY
SOUTH OXHEY
COMMON MOOR
LONG VALLEY WOOD
KING GEORGE V PLAYING FIELDS
HAMPERMILL LAKE
RUNNING TRACK
Merchant Taylor's Sch
SANDY LODGE GOLF COURSE
GOLF COURSE
OXHEY PARK GOLF COURSE
SOUTH OXHEY PLAYING FIELDS
HAMPERMILL WOOD
BIG WOOD
OXHEY WOODS
BECK MASON'S WOOD
WILD WOODS
NANSCOT WOOD
PINNER WOOD
PINNER HILL GOLF COURSE
PINNERWOOD PARK
MONTESOLE PLAYING FIELDS
NORTHWOOD GOLF COURSE
HASTE HILL GOLF COURSE
NORTHWOOD CEMETERY
RUISLIP NATURE RESERVE
COPSE WOOD
DUCKS HILL
BISHOPSWOOD PRIVATE HOSP
MOUNT VERNON HOSPITAL
NORTHWOOD & PINNER COMMUNITY HOSP
H.M.S. Warrior
THE GRAVEL PITS
HOGS BACK OPEN SPACE
TOLPITS LANE
HAMPERMILL LANE
SANDY LANE
WATFORD ROAD
EASTBURY ROAD
RICKMANSWORTH ROAD
PINNER ROAD
HIGH STREET
GREEN LANE
PRESTWICK ROAD
DUCKS HILL
A4125
A4145
A4180
A404
23
40
59

BW
BX
BY
BZ
CA
CB
CC
24
OXHEY
OXHEY PARK
BUSHEY
CHALK HILL
LONDON ROAD
HIGH STREET
BUSHEY GOLF COURSE & COUNTRY CLUB
KING GEORGE REC GROUND
SPARROWS HERNE
45
46
47
48
49
50
51
52
53
54
EASTBURY LANE
BROOKDENE AVENUE
PINNER ROAD
A4008
A4125
A411
WATFORD HEATH
SHERWOODS WOOD
MARGEHOLES WOOD
WD19
OXHEY PARK GOLF COURSE
SOUTH OXHEY PLAYING FIELDS
Ox Pasture Spring
MERRY HILL
WD23
CARPENDERS PARK
HARTSBOURNE GOLF COURSE & COUNTRY CLUB
HERTSMERE
SOUTH OXHEY
OXHEY LANE
PRESTWICK ROAD
CARPENDERS PARK CEMETERY
WOODWALKS
MUTTON WOOD
LEVELS WOOD
GRIM'S DYKE GOLF COURSE
WEALD WOOD
STONY WOOD
SANDPIT WOOD
39
HERTFORDSHIRE
HARROW
THREE RIVERS
NANSCOT WOOD
SADDLERS MEAD REC GROUND
HATCH END
SHAFTESBURY PLAYING FIELDS
PINNER WOOD
PINNER HILL GOLF COURSE
HA5
PINNERWOOD PARK
UXBRIDGE ROAD
A410
A404
HARROW ARTS CENTRE
HATCH END PLAYING FIELD
RAGHUVANSHI CHARITABLE TRUST SPORTS GROUND
PINNER PARK
HEADSTONE LANE
BANNISTER STADIUM
MONTESOLE PLAYING FIELDS
PINNER GREEN
RICKMANSWORTH ROAD
LITTLE COMMON
ST. THOMAS' DRIVE
60
SPORTS GROUND
HA2
MOAT
RECREATION
HILLINGDON
12
13
14

ELSTREE OPEN SPACE
WD6
Junction 4
ROYAL NATIONAL ORTHOPAEDIC HOSP
BUSHEY HEATH
STANMORE COMMON
PEAR WOOD
CLOISTERS WOOD
BRÖCKLEY HILL
GOLF PARK
HARROW WEALD COMMON
BENTLEY PRIORY OPEN SPACE
BENTLEY PRIORY NATURE RESERVE
DEER PARK
HA7
HA3
STANMORE
HA8
CANONS PARK
STANMORE GOLF COURSE
HARROW WEALD
PRINCE EDWARD PLAYING FIELD
SPORTS GROUND
BELMONT
QUEENSBURY
WEALDSTONE
Canons Corner
HARROW WEALD CEMETERY
Harrow College
Stanmore College
B.U.P.A. HOSPITAL
25
42
61
CD
CE
CF
CG
CH
CJ
CK
45
46
47
48
49
50
51
52
53
54

CL
CM
CN
CP
CQ
CR
CS
26
Stirling Corner
BARNET LANE
BARNET A411
Deacons Hill
DEACONS HILL OPEN SPACE
SCRATCH WOOD
FROGHALL WOOD
BOYS HILL WOOD
THISTLE WOOD
GRAVEL PIT WOOD
CLUMP OF TREES WOOD
TARGET WOOD
LEG OF MUTTON POND
NUT WOOD
MILL HILL GOLF COURSE
HEMMINGS WOOD
STONEY WOOD LAKE
STONEY WOOD
Elstree Manor
Penniwells Farm
Corus Edgwarebury Hotel
ELSTREE OPEN SPACE
ELSTREE HILL SOUTH
WD6
HERTSMERE
BARNET
M1
45
46
Junction 4
Watling Farm Caravan Site
Brockley Grange
Site of Sulloniacae Roman Settlement
47
48
49
50
51
52
53
54
BROCKLEY HILL
BROCKLEY HILL DRIVING RANGE
EDGWAREBURY GOLF COURSE
EDGWARE WAY
A41 (WATFORD BYPASS)
Bury Farm
London Gateway Services
Depot
Days Hotel
EDGWAREBURY CEMETERY
REC GRD
SPORTS GRD
EDGWAREBURY PARK
SPORTS GROUND
SPUR ROAD
Canons Corner
STONEGROVE EST
SPUR RD ESTATE
STANMORE
41
Apex Corner
WATFORD WAY A1
SELVAGE LANE
HALE LANE
A5100
CONVENT
EDGWARE
HA8
STONEGROVE PARK
N London Collegiate Sch
THE LAKE
KING GEORGE V MEML GDNS
CANONS PARK
CANONS PARK SPORTS GROUND
THE SPINNEY
THE BASIN
Broadwalk Shopping Centre
BUS STN
BUS DEPOT
STATION ROAD
HIGH STREET A5
Masons Arms PH
Premier Travel Inn
Edgware Town FC
DEANSBROOK ROAD
EDGWARE COMMUNITY HOSPITAL
BURNT OAK
BURNT OAK BROADWAY A5
LYNDHURST PARK
MILL HILL BROADWAY
WOODCROFT PARK
SPORTS GROUND
WATLING PARK
CHANDOS RECREATION GROUND
PRINCE EDWARD PLAYING FIELD
GOVT BUILDINGS
SPORTS GROUND
HA7
STANMORE MARSH
PLAYING FIELD
HONEYPOT LANE A4140
WHITCHURCH LANE
SILKSTREAM PARK
MONTROSE PLAYING FIELDS
COLINDALE HOSP
BLOOD TRANSFUSION CENTRE
PUBLIC HEALTH LAB.
COLINDALE
COLINDALE BUSINESS PK
CAPITOL IND PK
BRIT. LIB NEWSPAPER COLLECTION
ADASTRAL ESTATE
GRAHAME PARK
AEROVILLE
BRIXTON EST
The Flying Eagle Tavern PH
QUEENSBURY
Superstore
62
EDGWARE ROAD

EAST BARNET
Oak Hill College
OAK HILL PARK
EN4
SOUTH HERTS GOLF COURSE
N20
BROOK FARM OPEN SPACE
WYATTS FARM OPEN SPACE
KING GEORGE V PLAYING FIELDS
OAKLEIGH PARK
DAME ALICE OWEN'S GRD
TOTTERIDGE & WHETSTONE
TOTTERIDGE GREEN
WHETSTONE
SWAN LANE OPEN SPACE
NORTH MIDDLESEX GOLF COURSE
BETHUNE PARK GOLF COURSE
BRUNSWICK PARK
North London Business Park
NEW SOUTHGATE REC GRD
FRIARY PARK
FRIERN BARNET
Consolata Missionary Coll
N12
NORTH FINCHLEY
FINCHLEY
COPPETTS WOOD
GLEBELANDS OPEN SPACE
FINCHLEY MEMORIAL HOSP
VICTORIA PARK
MUSWELL HILL SPORTS GROUND
COPPETTS WOOD HOSP
ST. PANCRAS & ISLINGTON CEMETERY
N3
CHURCH END
FINCHLEY CENTRAL
WEST FINCHLEY
AVENUE HOUSE GRDS
COLDFALL WOOD
N2
N10
DA
DB
DC
DD
DE
DF
DG
28
43
64
45
46
47
48
49
50
51
52
53
54

DH
DJ
DK
DL
DM
DN
DP
29
OAKWOOD
OAKWOOD PARK
WINCHMORE HILL
N14
N21
GROVELANDS PARK
PRIORY HOSPITAL
OSIDGE
SOUTHGATE
SOUTHGATE CEMETERY
PALMERS GREEN
ARNOS PARK
NEW SOUTHGATE
BROOMFIELD PARK
N13
46
N11
BOWES PARK
HAZELWOOD SPORTS GRD
TATEM PARK REC GRD
TOTTENHALL SPORTS GROUND
NEW RIVER SPORTS CENTRE
MUSWELL HILL GOLF COURSE
N22
WOOD GREEN
NOEL PARK
ALEXANDRA PALACE
ALEXANDRA PARK
MUSWELL HILL
HORNSEY
BELMONT REC GRD
65
45
47
48
49
50
51
52
53
54

DQ
DR
DS
DT
DU
DV
DW
30
66
45
N21
N13
N18
N9
N17
N22
LOWER EDMONTON
EDMONTON
UPPER EDMONTON
TOTTENHAM
TOTTENHAM HALE
TOTTENHAM MARSHES
LOCKWOOD RESERVOIR
LEE VALLEY PARK
EDMONTON CEMETERY
FIRS FARM PLAYING FIELDS
CLOWES SPORTS GROUND
THE PAULIN GROUND
CHURCHFIELD REC GRD
CHURCH STREET REC GRD
PYMMES PARK
JUBILEE PARK
TATEM PARK REC GRD
HOLLY-WOOD GDNS
TOTTENHALL SPORTS GROUND
BOUNDARY PLAYING FIELDS
NEW RIVER SPORTS CENTRE
TOTTENHAM CEMETERY
BRUCE CASTLE PARK
LORDSHIP RECREATION GROUND
BELMONT REC GRD
DOWNHILLS PARK
DOWN LANE REC GRD
LEE VALLEY TECHNOPARK
MILMEAD INDUSTRIAL CENTRE
THE ROYAL LONDON ESTATE
MONTAGU RD INDUSTRIAL EST
WINGATE TRADING EST
MOWLEM TRADING ESTATE
NORTH MIDDLESEX HOSPITAL
EDMONTON FEDERATION CEMETERY (JEWISH)
WESTERN SYNAGOGUE CEMETERY
TOTTENHAM PARK CEMETERY
MONTAGU RECREATION GROUND
NORTHUMBERLAND PARK
WHITE HART LANE
TOTTENHAM HOTSPUR FC
BROADWATER FARM EST
TOWER GDNS
PEABODY EST
HAZELWOOD
EDMONTON GREEN
NORTH CIRCULAR ROAD
GREAT CAMBRIDGE ROAD
STERLING WAY
ANGEL ROAD
MERIDIAN WAY
WATERMEAD WAY
LORDSHIP LANE
THE ROUNDWAY
HERTFORD ROAD
FORE STREET
HIGH ROAD
BRUCE GROVE
WESTBURY AVENUE
GREEN LANES
HEDGE LANE
RIDGE AVENUE
A10
A105
A406
A109
A111
A1010
A1055
A1080
B154
B155
B137
Salmon's Brook
Pymme's Brook
The Moselle
Kenninghall

CHINGFORD
CHINGFORD GOLF COURSE
THE HAWK WOOD
POLE HILL
WILLIAM GIRLING RESERVOIR
LEE VALLEY GOLF COURSE
CHINGFORD MOUNT CEMETERY
RIDGEWAY PARK
MANSFIELD PARK
FRIDAY HILL
PIMP HALL PARK
E4
SOUTH CHINGFORD
CHINGFORD HATCH
LARKSWOOD PLAYING FIELDS
LARKS WOOD
HIGHAMS PARK
HALE END
THE HIGHAMS PARK
BOATING LAKE
IG8
EPPING FOREST
WALTHAM FOREST
BANBURY RESERVOIR
DEEPHAMS SEWAGE TREATMENT WORKS
LEE VALLEY PARK
WALTHAMSTOW STADIUM
Crooked Billet Roundabout
Cooks Wharf Roundabout
LEA VALLEY VIADUCT
SOUTHEND RD
E17
LLOYD PARK
Sir George Monoux Coll
WALTHAMSTOW
HIGHAM HILL
CHESTNUTS SHOWGROUND
THORPE COOMBE HOSP
Waterworks Corner
WOODFORD GOLF COURSE
WOODFORD R.F.C.
31
67
48

48
EE
EF
EG
EH
EJ
EK
EL
32
68
47
40
41
42
CHINGFORD GOLF COURSE
CHINGFORD PLAIN
QUEEN ELIZABETH'S HUNTING LODGE
HATCH FOREST
THE WARREN
CHINGFORD GREEN
WHITEHALL PLAIN
Buckhurst Hill
IG10
IG9
IG8
E4
E17
E18
FRIDAY HILL
PIMP HALL PARK
BLUEHOUSE GROVE
SPORTS GROUND
HATCH FOREST
HATCH GROVE
REED'S FOREST
LORD'S BUSHES
Knighton Wood
Woodford Wells
WOODFORD GOLF COURSE
WOODFORD GREEN
THE HIGHAMS PARK
BOATING LAKE
HIGHAMS PARK
HALE END
WOODFORD R.F.C.
EPPING FOREST
WALTHAMSTOW FOREST
Waterworks Corner
SOUTH WOODFORD
WOODFORD
RAY PARK
ASHTON PLAYING FIELD
RODING VALLEY PARK
LUXBOROUGH LANE TREATMENT WORKS
BANCROFT R.F.C.
LOUGHTON RUGBY GROUND
WANSTEAD R.F.C.
OLD MONOVIANS SPORTS GRD
CHILDREN'S BOATING POND
Junction 4
RODING VALLEY
BUCKHURST HILL
HOLLY HOUSE HOSP
NORTH CIRCULAR ROAD
SOUTHEND ROAD
A1069
A110
A104
A121
A1009
A1199
A113
A406
B170
EPPING NEW ROAD
RANGERS ROAD
WHITEHALL ROAD
CHINGFORD LANE
HIGH ROAD
BROADMEAD ROAD
CHIGWELL ROAD
WOODFORD NEW ROAD
PALMERSTON ROAD
QUEENS ROAD

WOOLSTON MANOR GOLF COURSE
SPORTS GROUND
LOUGHTON FC
River Roding
ROLLS PARK
CHIGWELL ROW WATER WORKS
RESERVOIR
Chigwell Row
IG7
METROPOLITAN POLICE SPORTS GRD
Chigwell
CHIGWELL CEMETERY
PLAYING FIELD
CHIGWELL GOLF COURSE
CONVENT OF THE SACRED HEART
Grange Hill
HAINAULT
ILFORD WANDERERS R.F.C.
FAIRLOP OAK PLAYING FIELD
HAINAULT RECREATION GROUND
FOREST ROAD PLAYING FIELD
FOREST INDUSTRIAL PARK
BRACKEN INDUSTRIAL ESTATE
FAIRLOP WATER
Fullwell Cross
IG6
FAIRLOP WATERS GOLF COURSE
DRIVING RANGE
Woodford Bridge
HOSPITAL HILL WOOD
Claybury Woods
COCKED HAT PLANTATION
IG5
CLAYHALL
TIPTREE ESTATE
GARDEN OF REST
BARKINGSIDE CEM
IG2
ALDBOROUGH
EM
EN
EP
EQ
ER
ES
ET
33
69
50

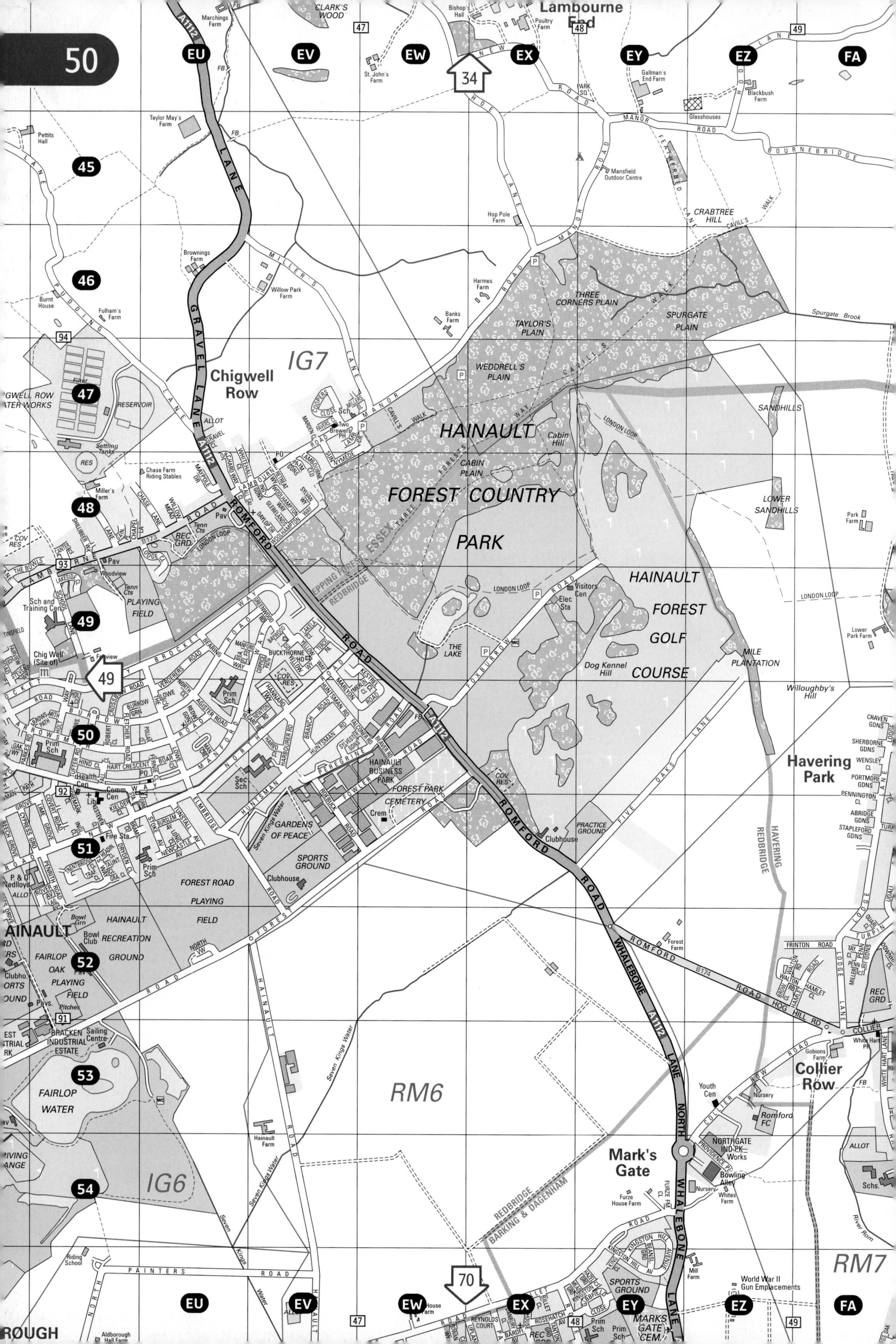
Lambourne End
CLARK'S WOOD
Marchings Farm
Bishop's Hall
Poultry Farm
St. John's Farm
Gallman's End Farm
Blackbush Farm
Glasshouses
MANOR ROAD
BOURNEBRIDGE
34
Taylor May's Farm
Pettits Hall
Mansfield Outdoor Centre
Hop Pole Farm
CRABTREE HILL
CAVILL'S WALK
Brownings Farm
Willow Park Farm
Harmes Farm
Banks Farm
THREE CORNERS PLAIN
TAYLOR'S PLAIN
SPURGATE PLAIN
Spurgate Brook
Burnt House
Fulham's Farm
GRAVEL LANE
Chigwell Row
IG7
WEDDRELL'S PLAIN
RESERVOIR
Filter
Settling Tanks
SANDHILLS
HAINAULT FOREST COUNTRY PARK
CABIN PLAIN
Cabin Hill
LONDON LOOP
Chase Farm Riding Stables
Miller's Farm
LOWER SANDHILLS
Park Farm
ROMFORD ROAD
EPPING FOREST
REDBRIDGE
ESSEX
HAINAULT FOREST GOLF COURSE
Visitors Cen
Elec Sta
THE LAKE
Dog Kennel Hill
MILE PLANTATION
Lower Park Farm
Willoughby's Hill
Chig Well (Site of)
PLAYING FIELD
Sch and Training Cen
49
FOXBURROW ROAD
HAINAULT BUSINESS PARK
FOREST PARK CEMETERY
Crem
Havering Park
Sec Sch
Prim Sch
GARDENS OF PEACE
SPORTS GROUND
Clubhouse
PRACTICE GROUND
FIVE OAKS LANE
HAVERING
REDBRIDGE
FOREST ROAD PLAYING FIELD
HAINAULT RECREATION GROUND
FAIRLOP OAK PLAYING FIELD
HAINAULT
WHALEBONE LANE
Forest Farm
ROMFORD ROAD
HOG HILL RD
COLLIER ROW
Collier Row
BRACKEN INDUSTRIAL ESTATE
Sailing Centre
FAIRLOP WATER
RM6
Seven Kings Water
Youth Cen
Romford FC
NORTHGATE IND PK Works
Bowling Alley
Whites Farm
Mark's Gate
Furze House Farm
IG6
Hainault Farm
REDBRIDGE
BARKING & DAGENHAM
RM7
Riding School
PAINTERS ROAD
70
World War II Gun Emplacements
Mill Farm
SPORTS GROUND
MARKS GATE CEM
Aldborough Hall Farm
EU
EV
EW
EX
EY
EZ
FA
45
46
47
48
49
50
51
52
53
54

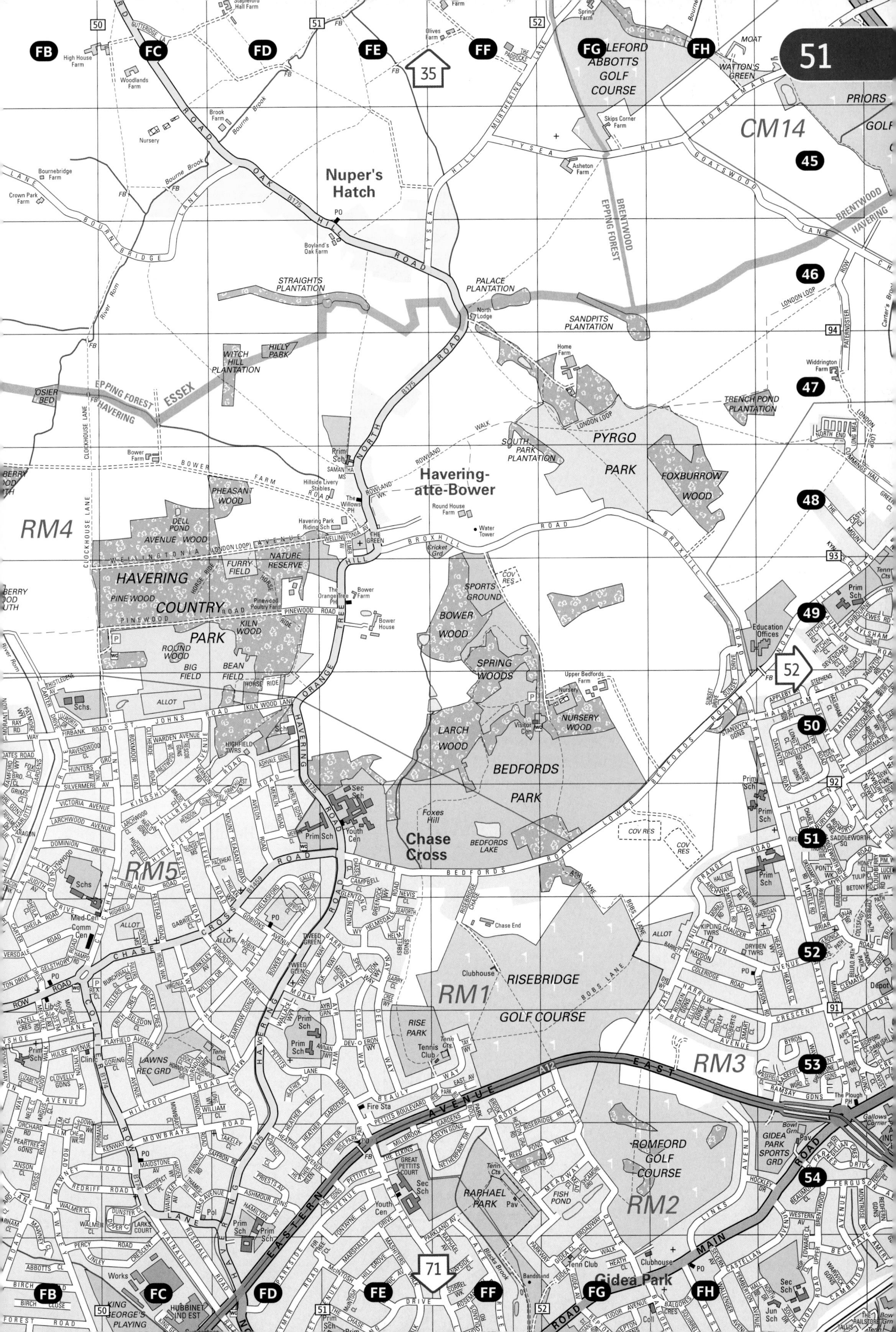

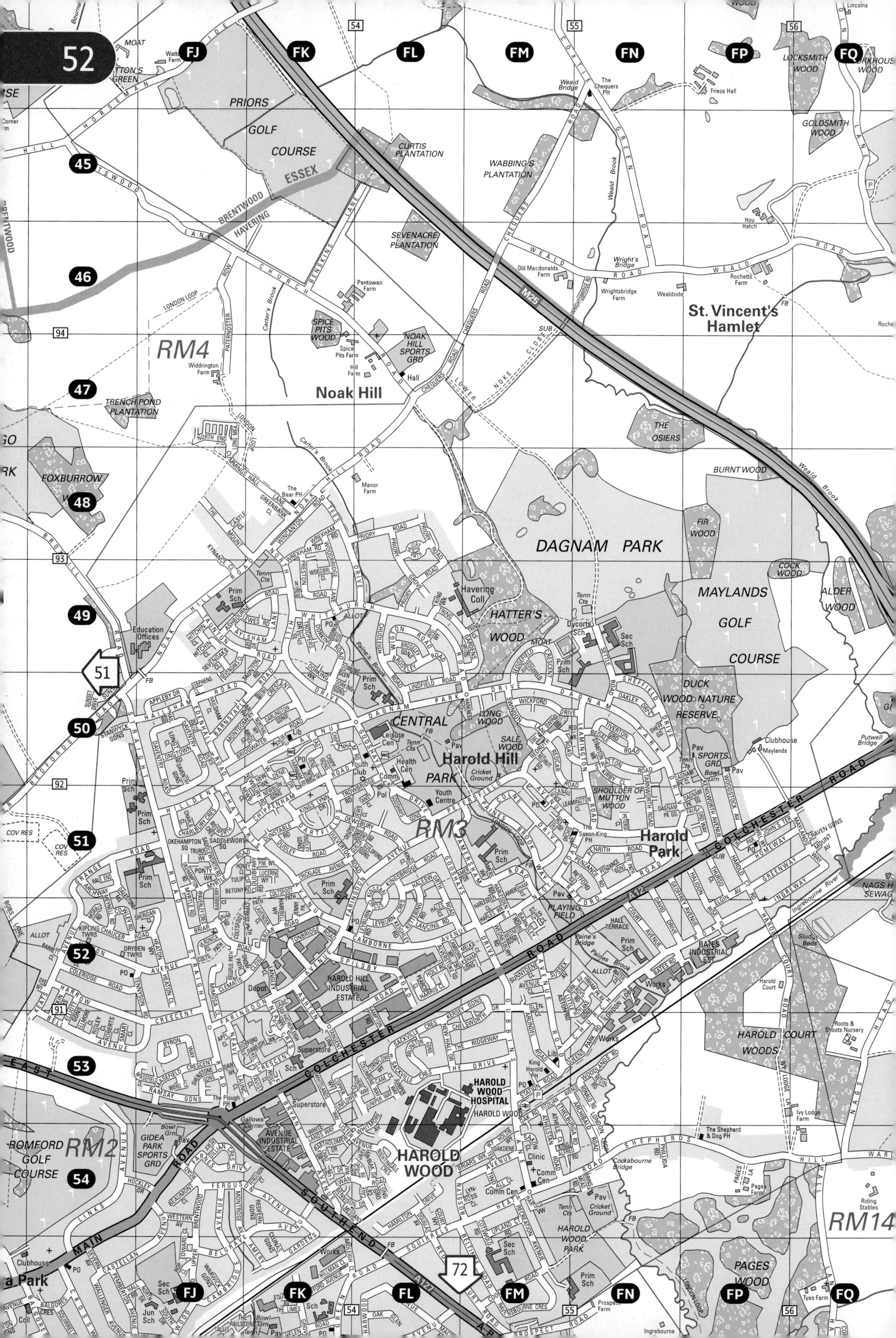
FJ
FK
FL
FM
FN
FP
FQ
45
46
47
48
49
50
51
52
53
54
PRIORS GOLF COURSE
ESSEX
BRENTWOOD
HAVERING
CURTIS PLANTATION
WABBING'S PLANTATION
SEVENACRE PLANTATION
M25
St. Vincent's Hamlet
RM4
Noak Hill
NOAK HILL SPORTS GRD
SPICE PITS WOOD
TRENCH POND PLANTATION
FOXBURROW
THE OSIERS
BURNT WOOD
FIR WOOD
DAGNAM PARK
MAYLANDS GOLF COURSE
COCK WOOD
ALDER WOOD
HATTER'S WOOD
DUCK WOOD NATURE RESERVE
CENTRAL PARK
Harold Hill
RM3
Harold Park
SHOULDER OF MUTTON WOOD
PLAYING FIELD
HAROLD HILL INDUSTRIAL ESTATE
HAROLD COURT WOODS
HAROLD WOOD HOSPITAL
HAROLD WOOD
RM2
ROMFORD GOLF COURSE
GIDEA PARK SPORTS GRD
AVENUE INDUSTRIAL ESTATE
HAROLD WOOD PARK
PAGES WOOD
RM14
COLCHESTER ROAD
SOUTHEND ROAD
A12
A127
51
72

BRENTWOOD
South Weald
Brook Street
Warley
Great Warley
WEALD COUNTRY PARK
WARLEY COUNTRY PARK
CM14
CM15
CM13
Junction 28
BRENTWOOD BYPASS
LONDON ROAD
HIGH STREET
INGRAVE ROAD
SHENFIELD ROAD
ONGAR ROAD
WEALD ROAD
WARLEY ROAD
LITTLE HIGHWOOD HOSP
HIGHWOOD HOSP
ESSEX NUFFIELD HOSP
BRENTWOOD COMM HOSP
MARILLAC HOSPITAL
B.U.P.A. HARTSWOOD HOSP
MASCALLS PARK
HARTSWOOD
KENT'S WOOD
BARRACK WOOD
HOLDEN'S WOOD
ELLEN'S WOOD
LITTLE WARLEY COMMON
GOLF COURSE
BRENTWOOD
HAVERING
ESSEX
TYLERS COMMON
FRONT PARK
THE OAKS

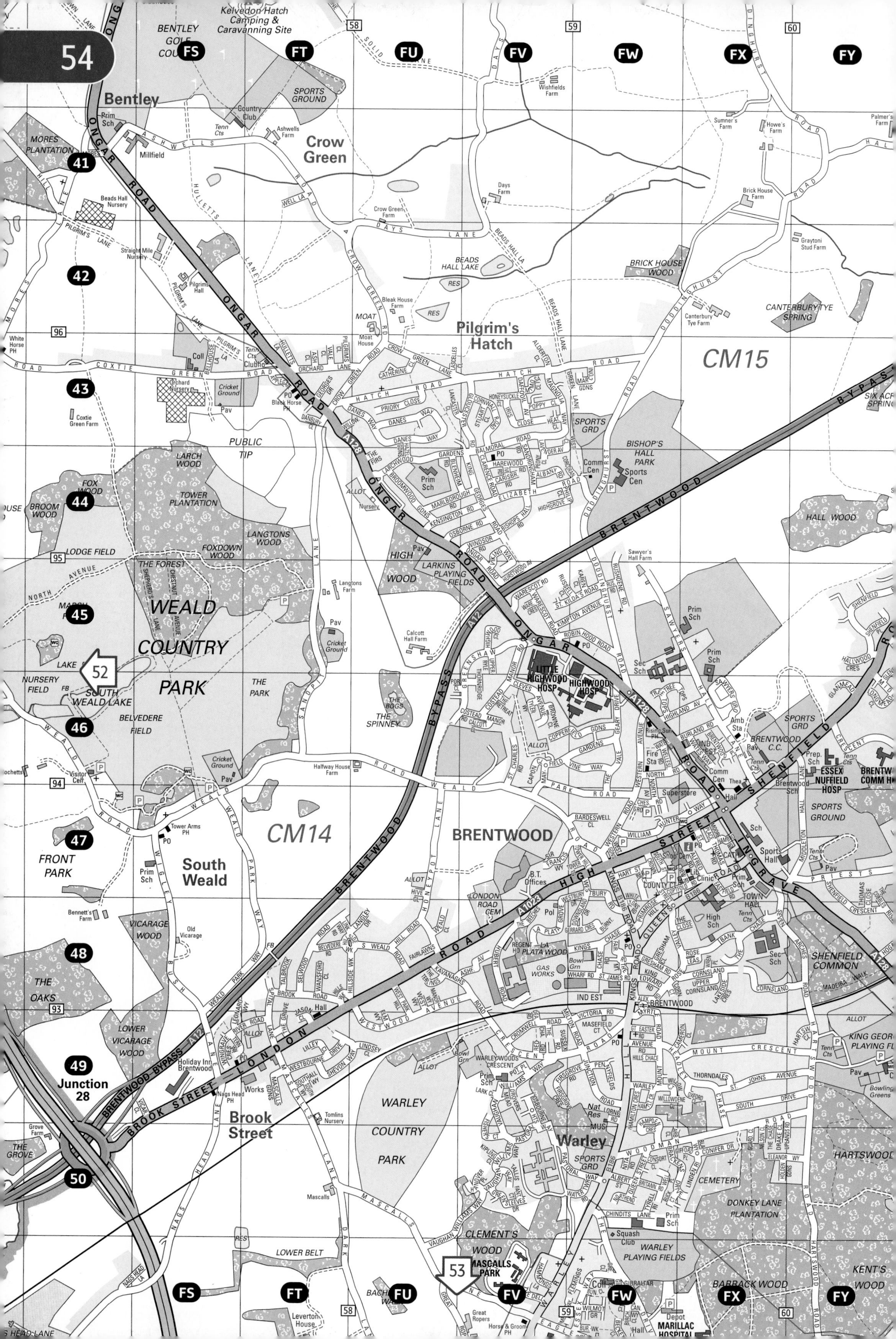

Kelvedon Hatch Camping & Caravanning Site
BENTLEY GOLF COURSE
FS
FT
FU
FV
FW
FX
FY
58
59
60
Bentley
SPORTS GROUND
Country Club
Ashwells Farm
Crow Green
Millfield
MORES PLANTATION
41
Beads Hall Nursery
Wishfields Farm
Sumner's Farm
Howe's Farm
Palmer's Farm
Days Farm
Crow Green Farm
DAYS LANE
BEADS HALL LAKE
RES
Brick House Farm
Graytoni Stud Farm
BRICK HOUSE WOOD
Straight Mile Nursery
42
Pilgrims Hall
Bleak House Farm
MOAT
Moat House
Pilgrim's Hatch
CANTERBURY TYE SPRING
Canterbury Tye Farm
CM15
96
White Horse PH
COXTIE GREEN ROAD
Coll
Tenn Cts
Club
Orchard Nursery
Cricket Ground
43
Coxtie Green Farm
Pav
Black Horse PH
PO
HATCH ROAD
SIX ACRE SPRING
PUBLIC TIP
LARCH WOOD
SPORTS GRD
BISHOP'S HALL PARK
Sports Cen
Comm Cen
Prim Sch
FOX WOOD
44
BROOM WOOD
TOWER PLANTATION
ALLOT
Nursery
HALL WOOD
LANGTONS WOOD
FOXDOWN WOOD
95
LODGE FIELD
NORTH AVENUE
THE FOREST
HIGH WOOD
LARKINS PLAYING FIELDS
Sawyer's Hall Farm
Langtons Farm
45
WEALD COUNTRY PARK
Calcott Hall Farm
Cricket Ground
LAKE
52
NURSERY FIELD
SOUTH WEALD LAKE
THE PARK
THE BOGS
THE SPINNEY
LITTLE HIGHWOOD HOSP
HIGHWOOD HOSP
Sec Sch
46
BELVEDERE FIELD
WEALD ROAD
Halfway House Farm
Fire Sta
Amb Sta
SPORTS GRD
BRENTWOOD C.C.
ESSEX NUFFIELD HOSP
BRENTWOOD COMM H
Visitor Cen
94
Superstore
Brentwood Sch
SPORTS GROUND
Tower Arms PH
47
FRONT PARK
CM14
BRENTWOOD
South Weald
Prim Sch
B.T. Offices
HIGH STREET
Shop Cen
TOWN HALL
Bennett's Farm
VICARAGE WOOD
Old Vicarage
LONDON ROAD CEM
A1023
LA PLATA WOOD
GAS WORKS
High Sch
Sec Sch
SHENFIELD COMMON
48
THE OAKS
93
LOWER VICARAGE WOOD
IND EST
BRENTWOOD
KING GEORGE PLAYING FIELDS
49
Junction 28
Holiday Inn Brentwood
BRENTWOOD BYPASS
A12
LONDON ROAD
BROOK STREET
Nags Head PH
Works
Brook Street
WARLEY COUNTRY PARK
Warley
HARTSWOOD
Grove Farm
THE GROVE
Tomlins Nursery
CEMETERY
50
Mascalls
DONKEY LANE PLANTATION
CLEMENT'S WOOD
MASCALLS PARK
Squash Club
WARLEY PLAYING FIELDS
RES
LOWER BELT
53
BARRACK WOOD
KENT'S WOOD
Leverton House
Great Ropers
Horse & Groom PH
Depot
MARILLAC HOSPITAL
NAGS HEAD LANE

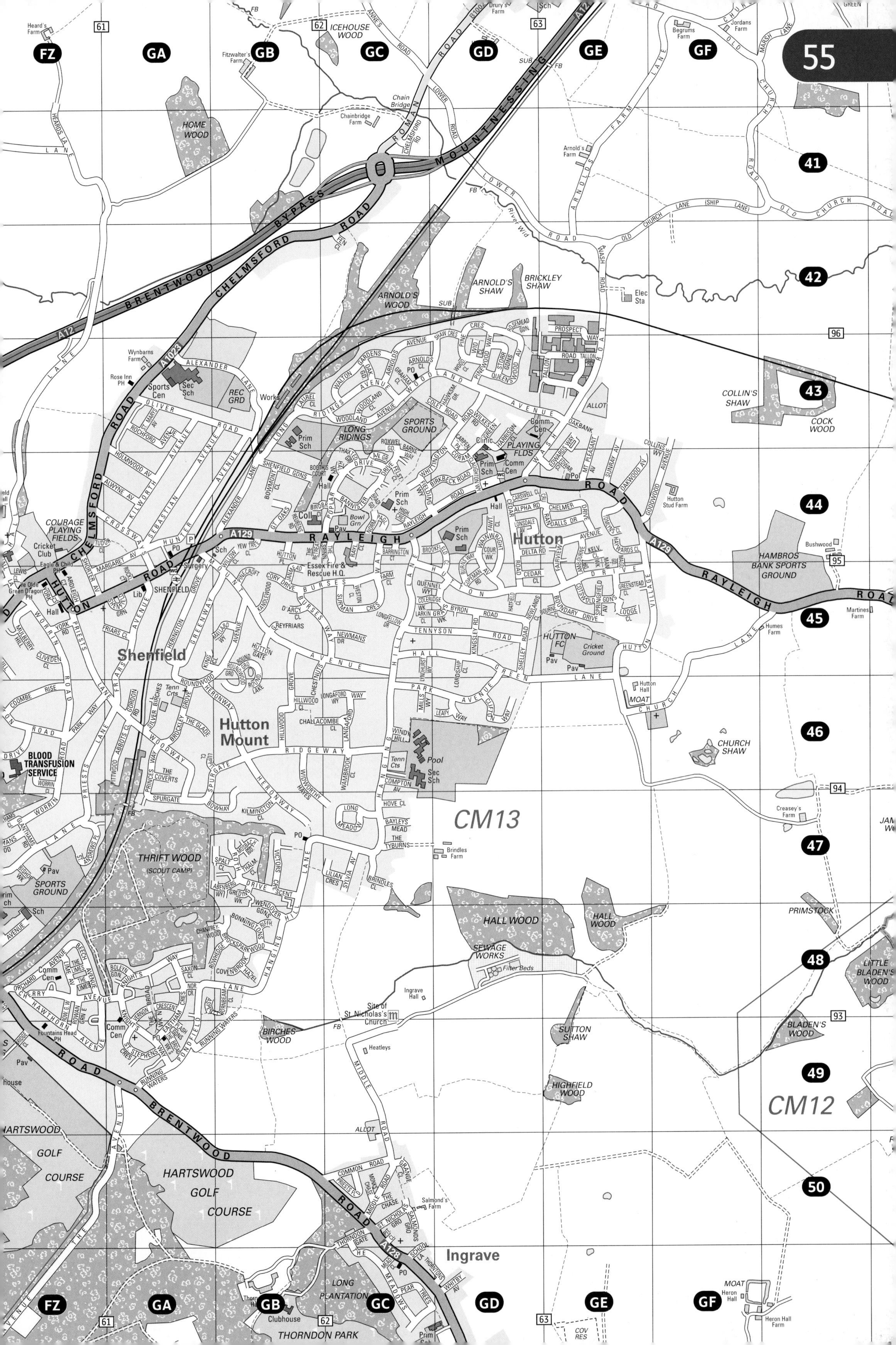
Shenfield
Hutton
Hutton Mount
Ingrave
CM13
CM12
RAYLEIGH ROAD
BRENTWOOD ROAD
CHELMSFORD ROAD
BRENTWOOD BYPASS
MOUNTNESSING
HUTTON ROAD
A12
A129
A128
A1023
HOME WOOD
ICEHOUSE WOOD
ARNOLD'S WOOD
ARNOLD'S SHAW
BRICKLEY SHAW
COLLIN'S SHAW
COCK WOOD
HAMBROS BANK SPORTS GROUND
CHURCH SHAW
THRIFT WOOD
(SCOUT CAMP)
HALL WOOD
SEWAGE WORKS
Filter Beds
SUTTON SHAW
HIGHFIELD WOOD
BIRCHES WOOD
BLADEN'S WOOD
LITTLE BLADEN'S WOOD
PRIMSTOCK
HARTSWOOD GOLF COURSE
LONG PLANTATION
THORNDON PARK
BLOOD TRANSFUSION SERVICE
SPORTS GROUND
LONG RIDINGS
PLAYING FLDS
COURAGE PLAYING FIELDS
REC GRD
Essex Fire & Rescue H.Q.
Cricket Ground
Hutton FC
Site of St Nicholas's Church
Ingrave Hall
Heatleys
Brindles Farm
Salmond's Farm
Heron Hall
Heron Hall Farm
Creasey's Farm
Humes Farm
Martines Farm
Bushwood
Hutton Stud Farm
Hutton Hall
Arnold's Farm
Begrums Farm
Jordans Farm
Chainbridge Farm
Chain Bridge
Fitzwalter's Farm
Heard's Farm
Drury's Farm
Wynbarns Farm
Rose Inn PH
Eagle & Child PH
Ye Olde Green Dragon PH
Fountains Head PH
Clubhouse
FZ GA GB GC GD GE GF
41 42 43 44 45 46 47 48 49 50
61 62 63 93 94 95 96

Layter's Green
GREAT LEGS WOOD
MALMS WOOD
36
AS
AT
AU
AV
AW
AX
AY
MOBILE HOME PARK
SPORTS GRD
Sec Sch
BIRCHLAND WOOD
Stampwell Farm
HIGH WOOD
BEECH WOOD
Parkwood Farm
55
PYEBUSHES
ROAD
A40
BIRCH WOOD
Bellhouse Hotel
OXFORD
SIBLET'S WOOD
CHANTRY WOOD
AUSTENWOOD COMMON
MALTMANS LANE
Bowl Club
Tenn Club
Prim Sch
Mumfords Farm
56
Wapsey's Wood Landfill Site
ROAD
Raylands Farm
CHILTERN
SOUTH BUCKS
89
SAND AND GRAVEL PIT
FURTHER WARREN WOOD
WEST PLANTATION
57
Jarretts Hill
BULSTRODE WAY
GERRARDS CROSS
The Bull Hotel
BULSTRODE
PARK
GERRARDS CROSS
Moat Farm
Bulstrode
GERRARDS CROSS COMMON
58
Slade Farm
HEDGERLEY
MENAGERIE WOOD
88
WAPSEYS
HEDGERLEY GREEN
LANE
GROVE PLANTATION
Bulstrode Camp
Crab Hill
SL9
59
SUTTON'S WOOD
Ponders
HEDGERLEY LANE
LEITH GROVE
French Horn PH
Cricket Ground
Clubhouse
Hedgerley
RSPB NATURE RESERVE
CHURCH WOOD
The White Horse PH
SUB
WINDSOR
60
High Meadows
KILN WOOD
87
HANGING WOOD
MOUNT HILL LANE
MOUNTHILL WOOD
Mount Hill Farm
61
TREETOPS CAMPSITE
FOOTPATH WOOD
HEDGERLEY PARK
BLACK GROVE
Park House
DUKE'S ORCHARD
Riding Stables
M40
FISH POND
ALLOT
COV RES
SL2
PARKSIDE CEMETERY
Tara
PICKERIDGE WOOD
Low Farm
62
Hedgerley Park Farm
TIMBER WOOD
HAY WOOD
86
STOKE WOOD
GRAVEL PIT
FISH POND
Pickeridge Farm
Kestrel Farm
Fulmer
63
Fulmer Hall (Servier Laboratories)
Hall
PO
Prim Sch
Church Farm
Fulmer House Farm
STOKE COMMON ROAD
Alder Bourne
SL3
64
STOKE COMMON
BROCKHURST WOOD
INGRAM'S COPSE
STOKE COMMON
FRAME WOOD
PENN WOOD
Fernacres Farm
Fernacres House
Cricket Grd
Black Firs
Dar Alshams
74
Farnham Common
98
99
00
Framewood Manor
PARSON'S

57
HOGTROUGH WOOD
GERRARDS CROSS GOLF COURSE
NOCKHILL WOOD
JUNIPER WOOD
THREE RIVERS
SOUTH BUCKS
TRAINING CENTRE DURDENT COURT
GREAT HALINGS WOOD
SQUARE COPSE
ROUND COPSE
QUARTERS WOOD
OAKEND WOOD
DENHAM MARSH WOOD
DENHAM AERODROME
NORTHMOOR HILL (NATURE RESERVE)
BATTLESFORD WOOD
RANSTON COVERT
WADLEY COVERT
HOLLY HILL WOOD
NIGHTINGALE WOOD
Rank Film Laboratories
Denham Green
NEWSTEAD WOOD
DENHAM GOLF COURSE
COLLSELS WOOD
DENHAM GOLF CLUB
Higher Denham
UB9
MARTINSFIELD SPORTS GRD
TOM WILLIAM'S WOOD
BRADBURY'S ISLAND
River Misbourne
GALLOWS WOOD
MILL WOOD
LITTLE GALLOWS WOOD
THE RANCHO
CAPS WOOD
MISBOURNE MEADOWS
S BUCKS DISTRICT COUNCIL
BAKER'S WOOD
BUCKINGHAM
Tatling End
OXFORD ROAD
A40
AMERSHAM ROAD
A413
NORTH ORBITAL ROAD
A412
DENHAM AVENUE
M25
M40
NABOTH
GALDWINS WOOD
BROADSPRING WOOD
HAWKS WOOD
FURZENEY WOOD
Junction 16 (M25)
Junction 1a (M40)
Holly Bush
Denham
Denham Roundabout
GOSSAMS WOOD
BROWN'S WOOD
OLDHOUSE WOOD
PARKSPRING WOOD
MOUNT FIDGET WOOD
FULMER RISE ESTATE
BRIDGETTINE CONVENT
LANGLEY COMMON
Langley Corner
SL0
LONG COPPICE
PLAYING FIELD
37
58
75

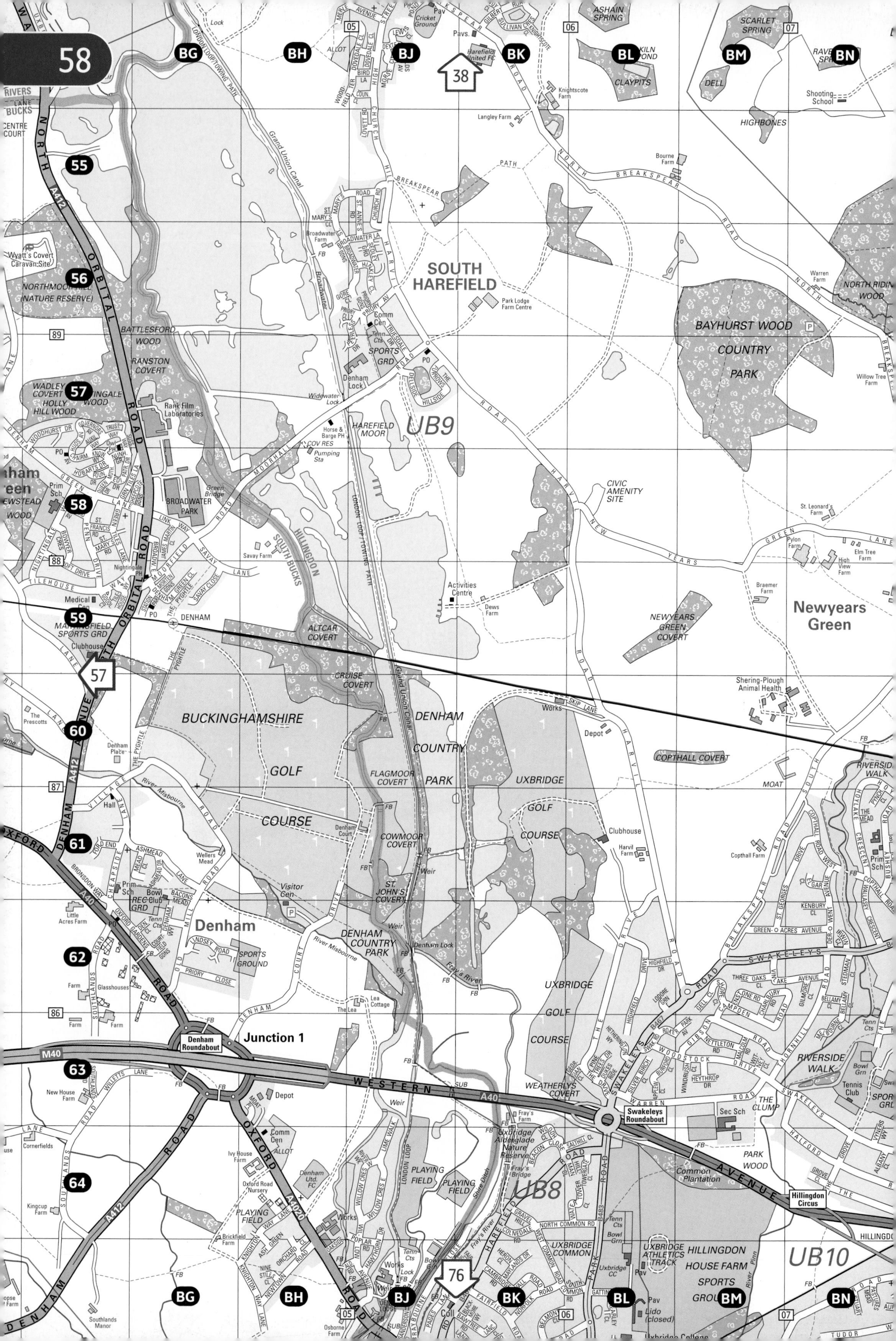
BG
BH
BJ
BK
BL
BM
BN
38
57
76
05
06
07
89
88
87
86
55
56
57
58
59
60
61
62
63
64
SOUTH HAREFIELD
UB9
UB8
UB10
Denham
Newyears Green
ASHAIN SPRING
SCARLET SPRING
KILN POND
CLAYPITS
DELL
HIGHBONES
Shooting School
Knightscote Farm
Langley Farm
Bourne Farm
Warren Farm
NORTH RIDING WOOD
BAYHURST WOOD
COUNTRY
PARK
Willow Tree Farm
Harefield United FC
Cricket Ground
Pavs.
BREAKSPEAR ROAD
NORTH BREAKSPEAR ROAD
HARVIL ROAD
Grand Union Canal
LONDON LOOP TOWING PATH
Park Lodge Farm Centre
Comm Cen
SPORTS GRD
Denham Lock
Widewater Lock
Horse & Barge PH
HAREFIELD MOOR
COV RES
Pumping Sta
Green Bridge
MOORHALL ROAD
Savay Farm
SOUTH BUCKS
HILLINGDON
CIVIC AMENITY SITE
NEW YEARS GREEN LANE
St. Leonard's Farm
Pylon Farm
Elm Tree Farm
High View Farm
Braemer Farm
Activities Centre
Dews Farm
NEWYEARS GREEN COVERT
Wyatt's Covert Caravan Site
NORTHMOOR HILL (NATURE RESERVE)
BATTLESFORD WOOD
RANSTON COVERT
WADLEY COVERT
HOLLY HILL WOOD
Rank Film Laboratories
NORTH ORBITAL ROAD
A412
BROADWATER PARK
DENHAM GREEN LANE
TILEHOUSE
Prim Sch
Medical Cen
MARTINSFIELD SPORTS GRD
Clubhouse
DENHAM
ALTCAR COVERT
CRUISE COVERT
BUCKINGHAMSHIRE
GOLF
COURSE
DENHAM
COUNTRY
PARK
FLAGMOOR COVERT
COWMOOR COVERT
ST. JOHN'S COVERT
Denham Court
Weir
Visitor Cen
DENHAM COUNTRY PARK
Denham Lock
Fray's River
River Misbourne
UXBRIDGE
GOLF
COURSE
Works
SKIP LANE
Depot
Clubhouse
Harvil Farm
Shering-Plough Animal Health
COPTHALL COVERT
MOAT
RIVERSIDE WALK
Copthall Farm
The Prescotts
Denham Place
Hall
Wellers Mead
Prim Sch
Bowl Club
REC GRD
SPORTS GROUND
Little Acres Farm
Glasshouses
Farm
The Lea
Lea Cottage
Denham Roundabout
Junction 1
M40
A40
WESTERN AVENUE
OXFORD ROAD
New House Farm
Cornerfields
Kingcup Farm
Southlands Manor
Depot
Comm Cen
ALLOT
Ivy House Farm
Oxford Road Nursery
Denham Utd. FC
PLAYING FIELD
Brickfield Farm
Works
WEATHERLYS COVERT
Fray's Farm
Uxbridge Alderglade Nature Reserve
Swakeleys Roundabout
SWAKELEYS ROAD
Sec Sch
THE CLUMP
PARK WOOD
Common Plantation
Hillingdon Circus
UXBRIDGE COMMON
Uxbridge CC
UXBRIDGE ATHLETICS TRACK
HILLINGDON HOUSE FARM
SPORTS GROUND
Lido (closed)
Tennis Club
Bowl Grn

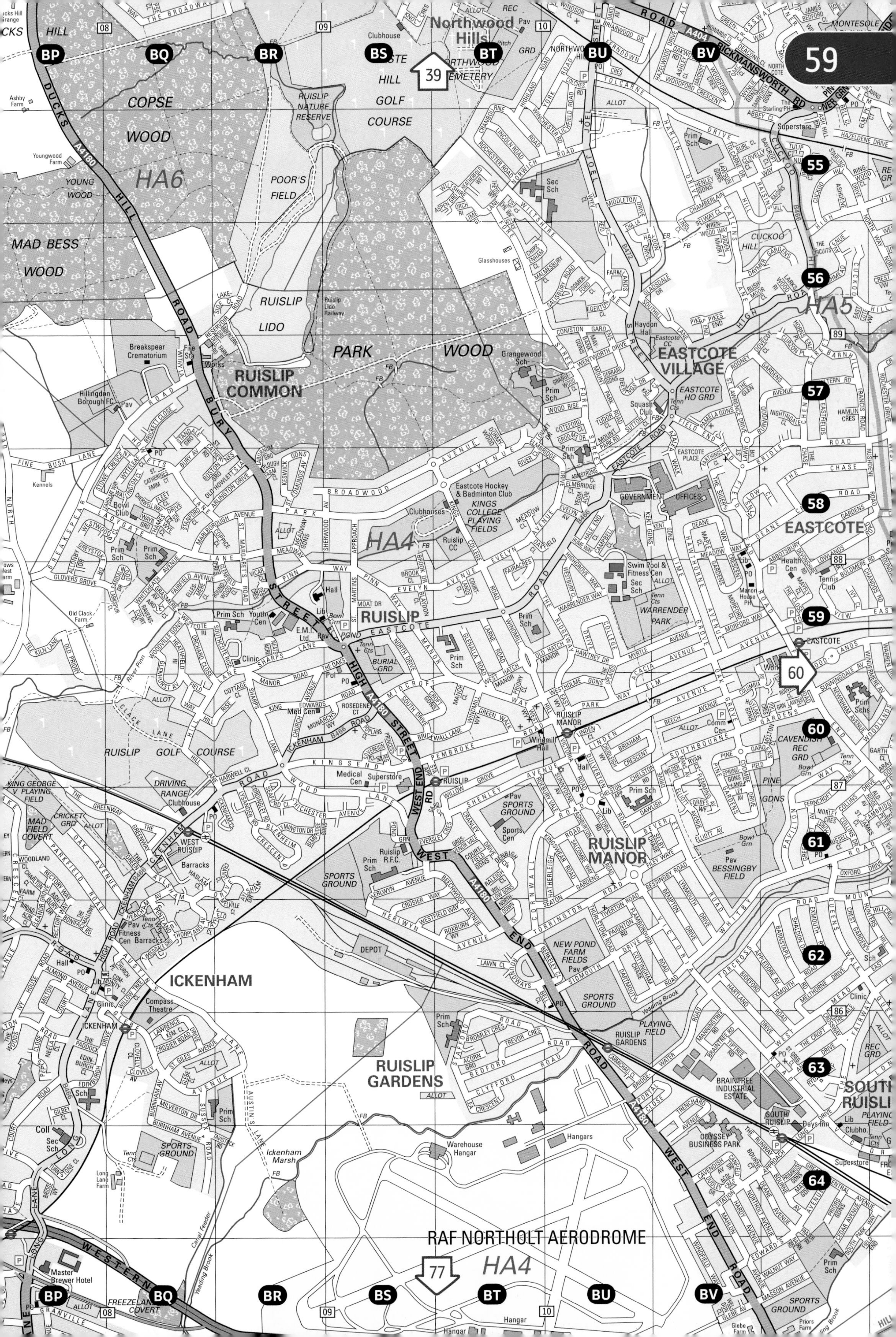
Northwood Hills
HA6
HA4
HA5
COPSE WOOD
YOUNG WOOD
MAD BESS WOOD
RUISLIP NATURE RESERVE
HILL GOLF COURSE
POOR'S FIELD
RUISLIP LIDO
PARK WOOD
RUISLIP COMMON
EASTCOTE VILLAGE
EASTCOTE
RUISLIP
RUISLIP MANOR
RUISLIP GOLF COURSE
ICKENHAM
RUISLIP GARDENS
SOUTH RUISLIP
RAF NORTHOLT AERODROME
KINGS COLLEGE PLAYING FIELDS
WARRENDER PARK
BESSINGBY FIELD
NEW POND FARM FIELDS
CAVENDISH REC GRD
GOVERNMENT OFFICES
BRAINTREE INDUSTRIAL ESTATE
ODYSSEY BUSINESS PARK
Breakspear Crematorium
Hillingdon Borough FC
Master Brewer Hotel
Compass Theatre
Warehouse Hangar
Hangars
DEPOT
Eastcote Hockey & Badminton Club
RICKMANSWORTH RD
DUCKS HILL ROAD
BURY STREET
HIGH STREET
WEST END ROAD
WESTERN AVENUE
39
60
77

BW
BX
BY
BZ
CA
CB
CC
40
78
59
55
56
57
58
59
60
61
62
63
64
PINNER GREEN
PINNER
MONTESOLE PLAYING FIELDS
LITTLE COMMON
CEM
PINNER MEMORIAL PARK
PINNER NEW CEMETERY
REC GRD
CUCKOO HILL
HA5
HA2
HA4
UB5
EASTCOTE VILLAGE
EASTCOTE
PINNER VILLAGE GARDENS
THE CROFT PLAYING FIELD
NORTH HARROW
HEADSTONE
RECREATION GROUND
SPORTS GROUND
WEST HARROW
WEST HARROW REC GRD
RAYNERS LANE
ROXBOURNE PARK
Streamside Reservation
CAVENDISH REC GRD
PINE GDNS
WARRENDER PARK
BESSINGBY FIELD
RECREATION GROUND
NEWTON PARK WEST
NEWTON FM ECOLOGY PK
SOUTH HARROW
ALEXANDRA PARK
ROXETH REC GRD
SOUTH RUISLIP
BRAINTREE INDUSTRIAL ESTATE
ODYSSEY BUSINESS PARK
VICTORIA RETAIL PARK
FROGMORE ESTATE
DEANE PARK
NORTHOLT RECREATION GRD
PLAYING FIELD
EARLSMEAD STADIUM
LORD HALSBURY MEMORIAL GRD
SPORTS GROUND
Civic Amenity Site
Old Lyonian Sports Club
Harrow Mus & Heritage Cen
NORTH HARROW
EASTCOTE
RAYNERS LANE
SOUTH HARROW
SOUTH RUISLIP
NORTHOLT PARK
PINNER ROAD
GEORGE V AVENUE
IMPERIAL DRIVE
ALEXANDRA AVENUE
NORTHOLT RD
WEST END ROAD
HILLINGDON
EALING

CD
CE
CF
CG
CH
CJ
CK
15
16
17
41
BELMONT
HA7
QUEENSBURY
WEALDSTONE
WEALDSTONE CEM
BYRON REC GRD
WAVERLEY INDUSTRIAL ESTATE
HARROW & WEALDSTONE
HA3
KENTON RECREATION GROUND
KENTON
KENTON ROAD
A4006
WOODCOCK PARK
HARROW
HARROW REC GROUND
CEM
HARROW ON THE HILL
HA1
HARROW HILL GOLF COURSE
University of Westminster
NORTHWICK PARK & ST. MARK'S HOSPITALS
NORTHWICK PARK
Northwick Park Pavilion
JOHN BILLAM SPORTS GRD
PRESTON
62
PRESTON PARK
THE GROVE OPEN SPACE
MINIATURE RIFLE RANGE
HARROW SCHOOL PLAYING FIELDS
HARROW SCHOOL GOLF COURSE
PARK LAKE
ST. ANDREW'S AT HARROW HOSP
CLEMENTINE CHURCHILL HOSPITAL
CHASEWOOD PARK
NORTH WEMBLEY
SOUTH KENTON
WEMBLEY COMMERCIAL CENTRE
G.E.C. ESTATE
HA9
FORTY FARM SPORTS GROUND
ROXETH
VALE FARM SPORTS GROUND
WEMBLEY FC
SPORTS GROUND
SPORTS GRD
BUTLER'S GRN
KING EDWARD VII PARK
SUDBURY
BARHAM PARK
HA0
UB6
REC GRD
Sudbury Tower
WEMBLEY CENTRAL
SUDBURY TOWN
SUDBURY HILL
SUDBURY HILL HARROW
GLAXCO WELLCOME
79
A4090
A404
A4005
A312
A409
A4088
A4089
A4140
WATFORD ROAD
HARROW ROAD
EAST LANE
WHITTON AVENUE
GREENFORD ROAD
BRIDGEWATER ROAD
55
56
57
58
59
60
61
62
63
64
86
87
88
89

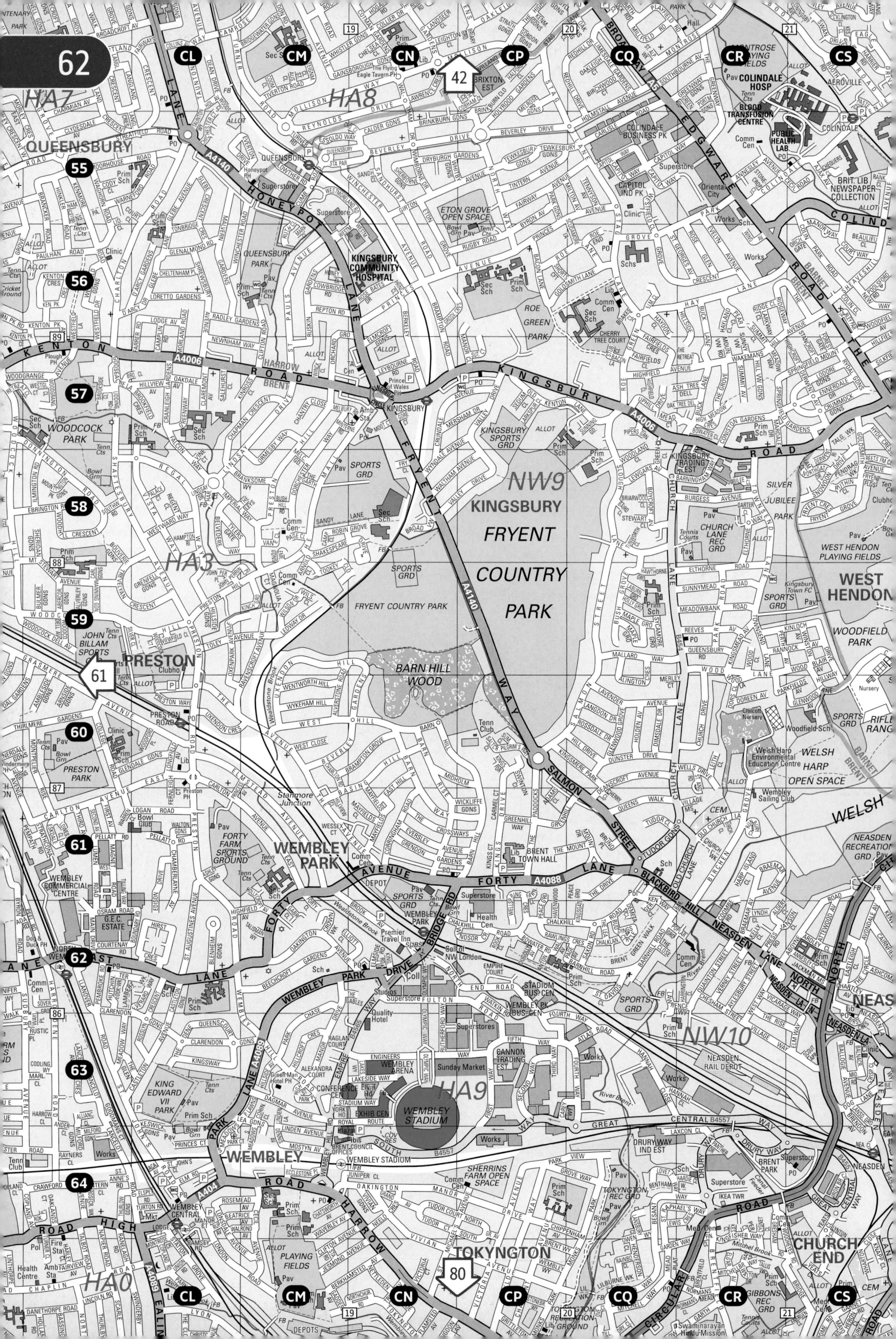
CL
CM
CN
CP
CQ
CR
CS
19
20
21
42
HA7
HA8
QUEENSBURY
55
56
57
58
59
60
61
62
63
64
HONEYPOT LANE
A4140
KENTON ROAD
A4006
KINGSBURY ROAD
KINGSBURY
KINGSBURY COMMUNITY HOSPITAL
QUEENSBURY PARK
ROE GREEN PARK
ETON GROVE OPEN SPACE
COLINDALE HOSP
BLOOD TRANSFUSION CENTRE
PUBLIC HEALTH LAB.
BRIT. LIB NEWSPAPER COLLECTION
COLINDALE
COLINDALE BUSINESS PK
CAPITOL IND PK
Oriental City
MONTROSE PLAYING FIELDS
EDGWARE ROAD
A5
BROADWAY
BARNET
BRENT
HARROW
WOODCOCK PARK
HA3
NW9
KINGSBURY
FRYENT COUNTRY PARK
FRYENT WAY
KINGSBURY TRADING EST
SILVER JUBILEE PARK
CHURCH LANE REC GRD
WEST HENDON PLAYING FIELDS
WEST HENDON
WOODFIELD PARK
JOHN BILLAM SPORTS GRD
PRESTON
61
BARN HILL WOOD
FRYENT COUNTRY PARK
SALMON STREET
PRESTON PARK
PRESTON ROAD
Stanmore Junction
WEMBLEY PARK
FORTY FARM SPORTS GROUND
FORTY AVENUE
FORTY LANE
A4088
BRENT TOWN HALL
BLACKBIRD HILL
NEASDEN LANE
WELSH HARP OPEN SPACE
Welsh Harp Environmental Education Centre
Wembley Sailing Club
NEASDEN RECREATION GRD
WEMBLEY COMMERCIAL CENTRE
G.E.C. ESTATE
EAST LANE
WEMBLEY PARK DRIVE
BRIDGE RD
Coll of NW London
STADIUM BUS CEN
WEMBLEY PK BUS CEN
NW10
NEASDEN RAIL DEPOT
KING EDWARD VII PARK
WEMBLEY ARENA
CONFERENCE CEN
EXHIB CEN
WEMBLEY STADIUM
HA9
CANNON TRADING EST
GREAT CENTRAL WAY
B4557
DRURY WAY IND EST
BRENT PARK
IKEA TWR
WEMBLEY
A404
A4089
HARROW ROAD
HIGH ROAD
WEMBLEY CENTRAL
SHERRINS FARM OPEN SPACE
TOKYNGTON REC GRD
TOKYNGTON
80
PLAYING FIELDS
HA0
NORTH CIRCULAR
CHURCH END
GIBBONS REC GRD
Swaminarayan Hindu Mission
NEASDEN

63
CT
CU
CV
CW
CX
CY
CZ
43
64
81
HOLDERS HILL
SUNNY HILL PARK
RAF MUSEUMS
GARDEN HOSP
CHURCH FARM HOUSE MUS
Middlesex Uni
Thistle Hendon Hall
N3
NORTH CIRCULAR ROAD
REGENTS PARK ROAD
FINCHLEY ROAD
HENDON LANE
CHURCH ROAD
WATFORD WAY
THE BURROUGHS
THE HYDE
HENDON
NW4
HENDON PARK
HENDON CENTRAL
Sch of Jewish Studies
CARMELITE MONASTERY
PRINCES PARK
NW11
HOOP LANE CEMETERY (JEWISH)
GARDEN OF REMEMBRANCE
GOLDERS GREEN
BRENT CROSS
Brent Cross Shopping Centre
Junction 1
Welsh Harp
BRENT RESERVOIR
AQUARIUS BUSINESS PARK
STAPLES CORNER BUSINESS PK
CLITTERHOUSE PLAYING FIELDS
BASING HILL PK
CHILDS HILL PK
CHILDS HILL
EVANS BUSINESS CEN
DOLLIS HILL
GLADSTONE PARK
CRICKLEWOOD
UNIVERSITY COLLEGE SCHOOL SPORTS GRD
HAMPSTEAD CEMETERY
NW8
NW2
WILLESDEN
WEST HAMPSTEAD
Golders Green Hippodrome
European Sch of Management
EDGWARE ROAD
BROADWAY
CRICKLEWOOD BROADWAY
HENDON WAY
GOLDERS GREEN ROAD
SHOOT UP HILL

DA
DB
DC
DD
DE
DF
DG
44
26
27
28
N3
55
56
57
58
59
60
61
62
63
64
89
88
87
86
63
82
NORTH CIRCULAR ROAD
EAST END ROAD
FALLODEN WAY
LYTTELTON ROAD
AYLMER ROAD
GREAT NORTH ROAD
HIGH ROAD
FORTIS GREEN
ARCHWAY ROAD
REGENTS PARK ROAD
FINCHLEY ROAD
NORTH END ROAD
NORTH END WAY
HENDON WAY
HAMPSTEAD LANE
SPANIARDS ROAD
HAVERSTOCK HILL
ROSSLYN HILL
HAMPSTEAD HIGH ST
HEATH STREET
WEST END LANE
COLDFALL WOOD
EAST FINCHLEY CEMETERY
Crematorium
EAST FINCHLEY
N2
NAZARETH HO CONVENT
FORTIS GREEN
ST.LUKE'S WOODSIDE HOSPITAL
HIGHGATE WOOD
SPORTS GRD
CHERRY TREE WOOD
LITTLE WOOD
BIG WOOD
HAMPSTEAD GARDEN SUBURB
LYTTELTON PLAYING FIELDS
NW11
HOOP LANE CEMETERY (JEWISH)
GARDEN OF REMEMBRANCE
GOLDERS GREEN
HAMPSTEAD HEATH EXTENSION
HAMPSTEAD GOLF COURSE
Bunkers Hill
TURNERS WOOD
HIGHGATE GOLF COURSE
Clubhouse
HARINGEY
BARNET
NORTH WOOD
THE IVEAGH BEQUEST - KENWOOD HOUSE
Kenwood House
ATHLONE HOUSE
N6
STOCK POND
CONCERT POND
LILY POND
KENWOOD LADIES POND
KENWOOD
HAMPSTEAD HEATH
SANCTUARY POND
BIRD SANCTUARY POND
BOATING POND
HIGHGATE PONDS
HIGHGATE MEN'S POND
PARLIAMENT HILL
Tumulus
ATHLETICS TRACK
SANDY HEATH
Golders Green Hippodrome
GOLDERS GREEN DEPOT
GOLDERS HILL PARK
SWAN POND
CHILDS HILL
HILL GARDEN
WEST HEATH
LEG OF MUTTON POND
HEATHLANDS
VALE OF HEALTH
VIADUCT POND
NW3
WHITESTONE POND
QUEEN MARY'S HOSP
HAMPSTEAD PONDS
HAMPSTEAD
KEATS HOUSE
ROYAL FREE HOSP
GOSPEL OAK EST
LISMORE CIRCUS
ST. DOMINIC'S PRIORY
MAITLAND PARK ESTATE
ST SILAS ST EST
Univ of London King's Coll
UNIVERSITY COLLEGE SPORTS GRD
HAMPSTEAD CEMETERY
BARNET
CAMDEN
NW8
European Sch of Management
WEST HAMPSTEAD
Camden Arts Centre
FINCHLEY ROAD & FROGNAL
WEST HAMPSTEAD (THAMESLINK)
Shopping Centre
KILBURN
Y.H.A.
Highgate Sch
Tenn & Squash Club
MANOR COURT
AYLMER PARADE

DH
DJ
DK
DL
DM
DN
DP
45
55
56
57
58
59
60
61
62
63
64
66
83
29
30
31
NOEL PARK
ALEXANDRA PALACE
ALEXANDRA PARK
N22
Ice Rink
Pitch 'n' Putt
SPORTS GROUND
RESERVOIR
HORNSEY WATER TREATMENT WORKS
Filter Beds
MUSWELL HILL
THE GROVE
HORNSEY
Shopping City
Gas Works
TURNPIKE LANE
WEST GREEN
DOWNHILLS PARK
BELMONT REC GRD
REC GRD
CHESTNUTS PARK
ST ANN'S HOSPITAL
N8
N10
QUEEN'S WOOD
PRIORY PARK
CROUCH END PLAYING FIELDS
ALLOTMENTS
CROUCH END
HORNSEY TOWN HALL
Clock Tower
STROUD GREEN
STATIONERS PARK
HARRINGAY
TRAIN DEPOT
New River
RAILWAY FLDS
HARRINGAY GREEN LANES
HIGHGATE
SPORTS GRD
Tenn & Squash Club
FINSBURY PARK
N4
AMERICAN GDNS
COV RES
MANOR HOUSE
WEST RESERVOIR
Water Works
Climbing Cen
Bowling Alley
SIX ACRES EST
FINSBURY PARK
Lauderdale Ho
WATERLOW PARK
HIGHGATE CEMETERY
WHITTINGTON HOSPITAL
ARCHWAY
N19
ELTHORNE PARK
Hornsey Rise Health Cen
Sch of Arts
UPPER HOLLOWAY
WHITTINGTON PARK
DARTMOUTH PARK
London Met Uni
TUFNELL PARK
Nags Head Shop Cen
H.M. PRISON HOLLOWAY
City & Islington Coll
HOLLOWAY
LOWER HOLLOWAY
London Metropolitan Uni
N7
EMIRATES STADIUM
ARSENAL FC
ARSENAL
DRAYTON PARK
HIGHBURY
N5
KINGS CRES ESTATE
SPORTS GROUND
HIGHBURY EST
CANONBURY
KENTISH TOWN
NW5
FORUM CLUB
Recycle Cen
PARADISE PARK
Freightliners Farm
MARKET EST
Clock Tower
PENTONVILLE
HIGH ROAD
WESTBURY AVENUE
GREEN LANES
WEST GREEN ROAD
HIGH STREET
PRIORY ROAD
MUSWELL HILL
PARK ROAD
TOTTENHAM LANE
CHURCH LANE
TURNPIKE LANE
WIGHTMAN ROAD
CROUCH HILL
CROUCH END HILL
HORNSEY RISE
HORNSEY ROAD
HORNSEY LANE
ARCHWAY ROAD
HOLLOWAY ROAD
STROUD GREEN ROAD
SEVEN SISTERS ROAD
BLACKSTOCK ROAD
ISLEDON ROAD
TOLLINGTON ROAD
CAMDEN ROAD
CALEDONIAN ROAD
PARKHURST ROAD
JUNCTION ROAD
FORTESS ROAD
BRECKNOCK ROAD
HIGHBURY PARK
HIGHBURY GROVE
ST. PAUL'S ROAD
A1
A103
A105
A201
A400
A503
A504
A1080
A1199
A1201
A5200
A5203
B138
B150
B152

OEL PARK
DQ
DR
DS
DT
DU
DV
DW
46
LORDSHIP RECREATION GROUND
BROADWATER FARM EST
N22
N17
TOTTENHAM MARSHES
LOCKWOOD RESERVOIR
MILMEAD INDUSTRIAL CENTRE
TOTTENHAM HALE
LOCKWOOD INDUSTRIAL PARK
DOWN LANE REC GRD
LEE VALLEY TECHNOPARK
BELMONT REC GRD
55
DOWNHILLS PARK
WEST GREEN
56
57
58
59
60
61
62
63
64
MONUMENT WAY
FERRY LANE
LOW MAYNARD RESERVOIR
Walthamstow Nature Park
Tottenham Hale Retail Park
HIGH CROSS CENTRE
Bowling Alley
RESERVOIR NUMBER FOUR
RESERVOIR NUMBER TWO
RESERVOIR NUMBER ONE
RESERVOIR NUMBER THREE
RESERVOIR NUMBER FIVE
CHESTNUTS PARK
N15
SEVEN SISTERS
ST ANN'S HOSPITAL
SOUTH TOTTENHAM
MARKFIELD REC GRD
Markfield Beam Engine
WARWICK RESERVOIR EAST
WARWICK RESERVOIR WEST
COPPERMILL PLAYING FIELD
Filter Beds
HARRINGAY GREEN LANES
HARRINGAY
RAILWAY FLDS
AMERICAN GDNS
FINSBURY
N4
PARK
65
MANOR HOUSE
AMHURST
STAMFORD HILL
SPRINGHILL SPORTS GRD
SPRINGFIELD PARK
Walthamstow Marsh Nature Reserve
EAST RESERVOIR
WEST RESERVOIR
STAMFORD HILL ESTATE
UPPER CLAPTON
FINSBURY PARK
ABNEY PARK CEMETERY
STOKE NEWINGTON
N16
CLISSOLD PARK
SPORTS GROUND
NORTH MILLFIELDS RECREATION GROUND
E5
SHACKLEWELL
HACKNEY DOWNS
N5
HIGHBURY
E8
DALSTON
84
CANONBURY
KINGSLAND
GRAHAM ROAD
BALLS POND RD
HIGHBURY & ISLINGTON
33
34
35

DX
DY
DZ
EA
EB
EC
ED
HIGHAM HILL
LLOYD PARK
WALTHAMSTOW
47
E17
UPPER WALTHAMSTOW
EPPING FOREST
SNARESBROOK
55
56
57
58
59
60
61
62
63
64
WHIPPS CROSS HOSPITAL
WHIPPS CROSS ROAD
LEA BRIDGE ROAD
A104
A503
FOREST ROAD
HOE STREET
A112
BLACKHORSE ROAD
A1006
MARKHOUSE ROAD
ST. JAMES'S PARK
DOUGLAS EYRE PLAYING FIELDS
LOW HALL SPORTS GROUND
WALTHAMSTOW CEM
LEYTONSTONE
E11
68
E10
LEYTON
HIGH ROAD LEYTON
LEYTON ORIENT FC
ST. PATRICK'S RC CEMETERY
LEA BRIDGE
LEE VALLEY PARK
HACKNEY MARSH
CLAPTON PARK
LOWER CLAPTON
E9
HOMERTON
HACKNEY WICK
EAST CROSS ROUTE
RUCKHOLT ROAD
A106
A12
E15
STRATFORD
STRATFORD INTERNATIONAL (under construction)
Channel Tunnel Rail Link (under construction)
85
36
37
38
NEW SPITALFIELDS MARKET
EASTWAY COMMERCIAL CENTRE
LEE VALLEY CYCLE CIRCUIT
ETON MANOR SPORTS GROUND
WICK COMMUNITY WOODLAND
LEE VALLEY PITCH & PUTT GOLF COURSE
THE WATERWORKS NATURE RESERVE
SEYMOUR ROAD PLAYING FIELD
MARSH LANE PLAYING FIELD
WALTHAM FOREST
NEWHAM
MABLEY GREEN
DRAPERS FIELD REC GRD
SIDMOUTH PARK
RECREATION GROUND
CHOBHAM ROAD
LEYTON ROAD
LEYTONSTONE ROAD
THE GROVE

Waterworks Corner
SOUTH WOODFORD
E18
EPPING FOREST
SPORTS GROUND
Junction 4
RODING HOSP
RECREATION GROUND
IG4
SNARESBROOK
SNARESBROOK CROWN COURT
HOLLOW POND
EAGLE POND
WHIPPS CROSS HOSPITAL
RUGBY FOOTBALL GROUND
WANSTEAD
WANSTEAD GOLF COURSE
LEYTONSTONE
E11
WANSTEAD FLATS
THE BASIN
BUSH WOOD
WANSTEAD PARK
ORNAMENTAL WATERS
SHOULDER OF MUTTON POND
HERONRY POND
PERCH POND
ALDERSBROOK
CITY OF LONDON CEMETERY
JUBILEE POND
MANOR PARK
MANOR PARK CEMETERY
WEST HAM CEMETERY
JEWISH CEMETERY
FOREST GATE
E7
WOODGRANGE PARK CEMETERY
PLASHET JEWISH CEMETERY
E15
STRATFORD
48
67
86
55
56
57
58
59
60
61
62
63
64
EE
EF
EG
EH
EJ
EK
EL

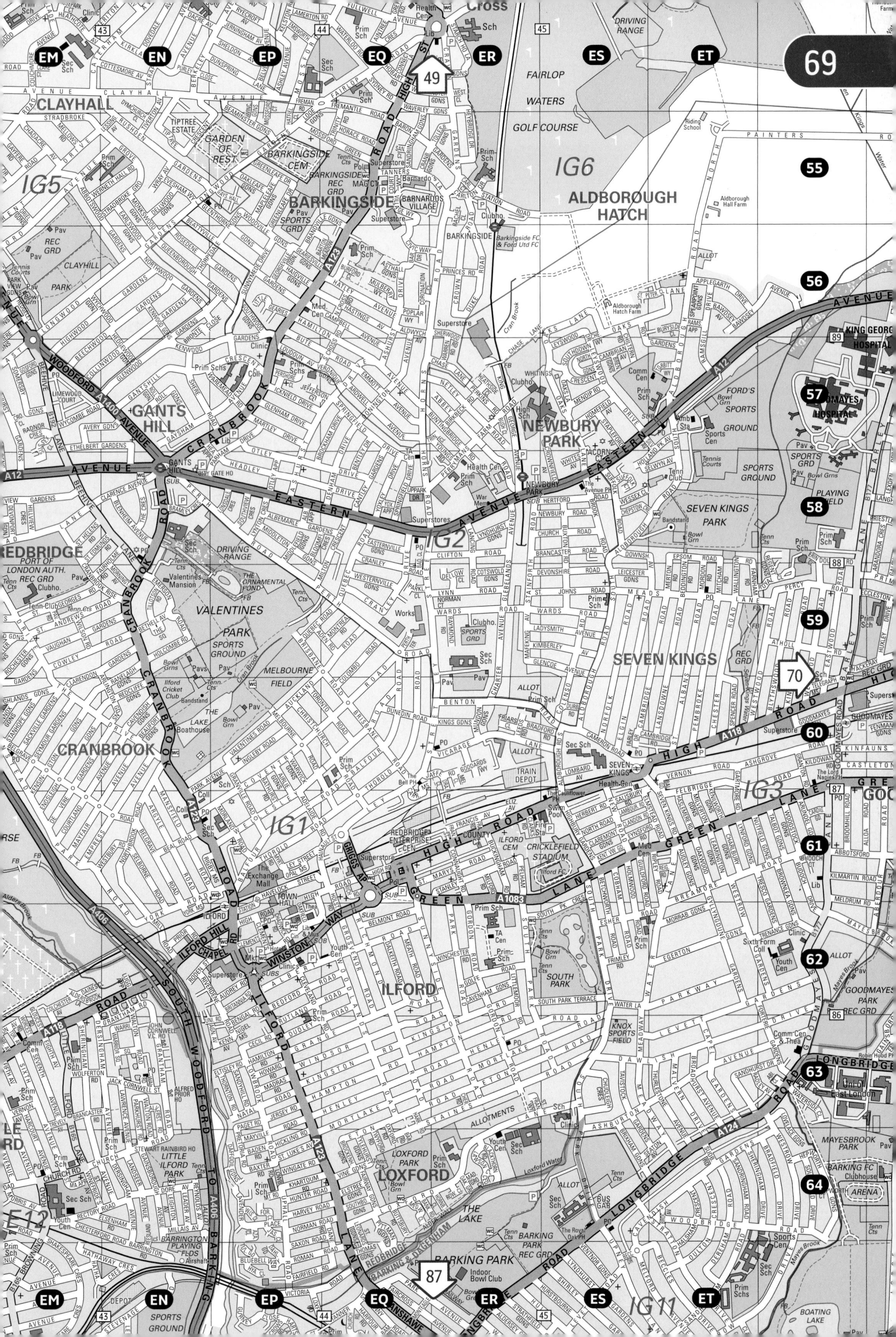
EM
EN
EP
EQ
ER
ES
ET
43
44
45
49
55
56
57
58
59
60
61
62
63
64
70
87
86
88
89
CLAYHALL
IG5
BARKINGSIDE
FAIRLOP WATERS GOLF COURSE
DRIVING RANGE
IG6
ALDBOROUGH HATCH
GARDEN OF REST
BARKINGSIDE CEM
BARKINGSIDE REC GRD
CLAYHALL PARK
GANTS HILL
NEWBURY PARK
IG2
KING GEORGE HOSPITAL
GOODMAYES HOSPITAL
FORD'S SPORTS GROUND
SEVEN KINGS PARK
REDBRIDGE
VALENTINES PARK
MELBOURNE FIELD
SEVEN KINGS
CRANBROOK
IG1
IG3
ILFORD
CRICKLEFIELD STADIUM
SOUTH PARK
KNOX SPORTS FIELD
GOODMAYES PARK
MAYESBROOK PARK
LITTLE ILFORD PARK
LOXFORD PARK
LOXFORD
BARKING PARK
THE LAKE
E12
IG11
EASTERN AVENUE
A12
WOODFORD AVENUE
A1400
CRANBROOK ROAD
A123
HIGH ROAD
A118
GREEN LANE
A1083
LONGBRIDGE ROAD
A124
ILFORD LANE
ILFORD HILL
WINSTON WAY
SOUTH WOODFORD TO BARKING
A406
GOODMAYES ROAD
BARLEY LANE
B177
TRAIN DEPOT
The Exchange Mall
TOWN HALL
Barking FC Clubhouse
Indoor Bowl Club
Uni of East London

70
EU
EV
EW
EX
EY
EZ
FA
50
47
48
49
Mark's Gate
NORTHGATE IND PK
BARKING & DAGENHAM
REDBRIDGE
IG2
RM6
RM8
RM9
IG3
IG11
55
56
57
58
59
60
61
62
63
64
69
88
PAINTERS ROAD
HAINAULT ROAD
BILLET ROAD
EASTERN AVENUE
A12
WHALEBONE LANE NORTH
A1112
WHALEBONE LANE SOUTH
SPORTS GROUND
MARKS GATE CEM
World War II Gun Emplacements
KING GEORGE HOSPITAL
GOODMAYES HOSPITAL
Redbridge College
WARREN PARK GOLF CENTRE
ST. CHADS PARK
CHADWELL HEATH
HIGH ROAD
A118
LONDON ROAD
WESTLANDS PLAYING FIELDS
WEST HAM UNITED FC TRAINING GROUND
SEVEN KINGS
SEVEN KINGS PARK
Grove Farm Retail Park
MIRRAVALE TRADING ESTATE
Becontree Heath
GOODMAYES
GREEN LANE
A1083
GOODMAYES PARK
VALENCE PARK
BECONTREE
VALENCE HO MUS
A124
LONGBRIDGE ROAD
WOOD LANE
Univ of East London
MAYESBROOK PARK
BARKING FC Clubhouse
ARENA
A1153
PORTERS AVENUE
PARSLOES PARK
Leisure Centre
HEATHWAY
A1240
DAGENHAM HEATHWAY
BOATING LAKE

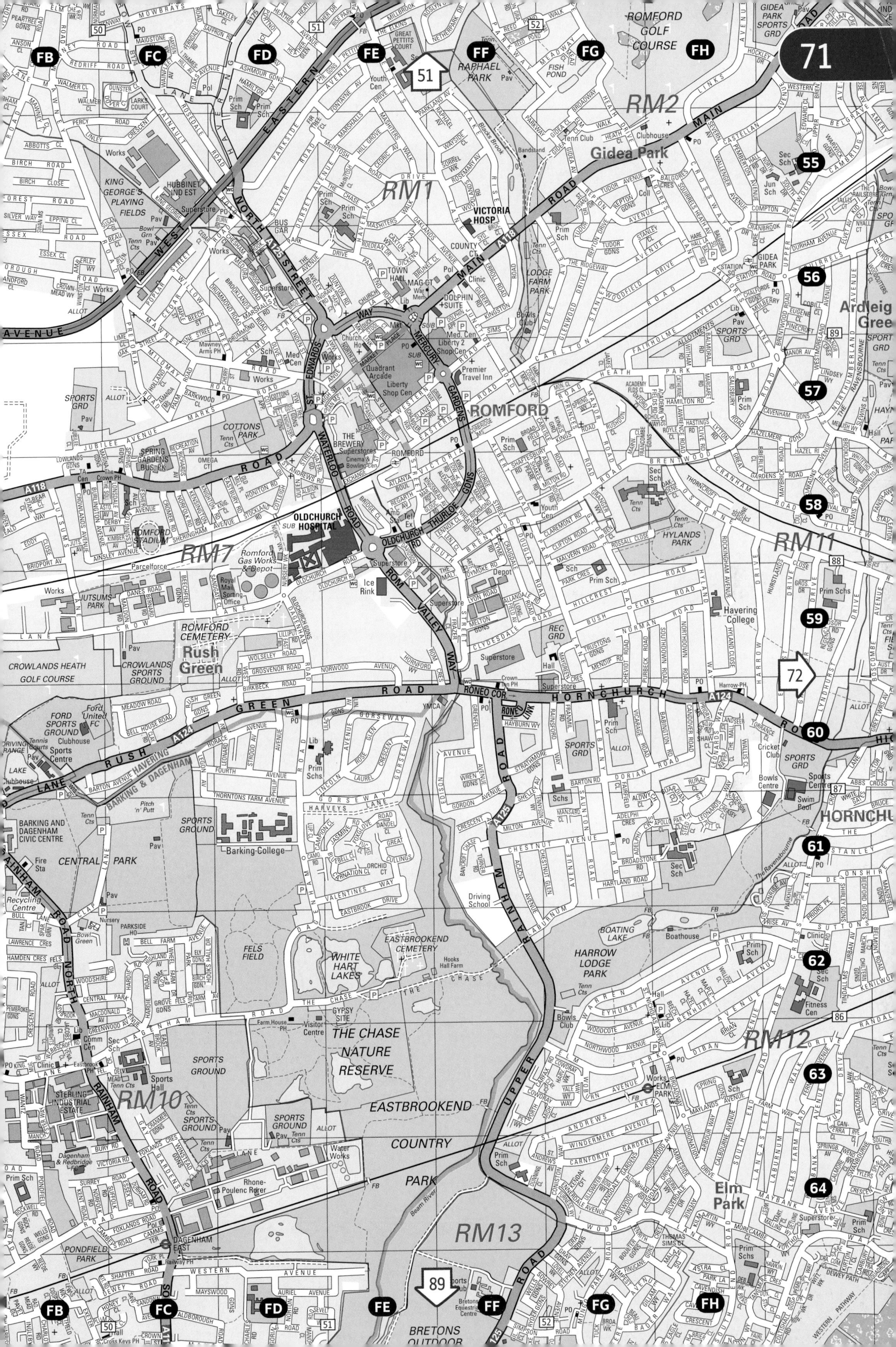
FB
FC
FD
FE
FF
FG
FH
51
ROMFORD GOLF COURSE
RAPHAEL PARK
RM2
Gidea Park
RM1
VICTORIA HOSP
KING GEORGE'S PLAYING FIELDS
NORTH STREET
MAIN ROAD
ROMFORD
COTTONS PARK
OLDCHURCH HOSPITAL
ROMFORD STADIUM
RM7
RM11
HYLANDS PARK
Havering College
ROMFORD CEMETERY
Rush Green
CROWLANDS HEATH GOLF COURSE
RUSH GREEN ROAD
HORNCHURCH ROAD
72
BARKING AND DAGENHAM CIVIC CENTRE
CENTRAL PARK
Barking College
FELS FIELD
WHITE HART LAKES
EASTBROOKEND CEMETERY
THE CHASE NATURE RESERVE
EASTBROOKEND COUNTRY PARK
HARROW LODGE PARK
BOATING LAKE
RM10
RM12
RM13
STERLING INDUSTRIAL ESTATE
Rhone-Poulenc Rorer
DAGENHAM EAST
POUNDFIELD PARK
Elm Park
ELM PARK
UPPER RAINHAM ROAD
HORNCHURCH
89
BRETONS OUTDOOR
50
52
55
56
57
58
59
60
61
62
63
64

FJ
FK
FL
FM
FN
FP
FQ
52
HAROLD WOOD
RM2
RM3
RM11
RM12
55
56
57
58
59
60
61
62
63
64
71
90
PAGES WOOD
HAROLD WOOD PARK
Ardleigh Green
GIDEA PARK
Havering College of Further Educ
Emerson Park
EMERSON PARK
HYLANDS PARK
Havering College
HORNCHURCH
UPMINSTER GOLF COURSE
UPMINSTER
UPMINSTER BRIDGE
UPMINSTER PARK
HORNCHURCH STADIUM
ST. ANDREW'S PARK
ST. GEORGES HOSPITAL
HORNCHURCH CEM
GAYNES PARKWAY
Hacton
Elm Park
Corbets
PARKLANDS OPEN SPACE
ELLIOT PLAYING FIELDS
FIELDERS SPORTS GRD
LANGTON GDNS
HAYNES PARK
Palms Hotel
Ingrebourne Farm
Ingrebourne River
Lillyputts Farm
Chapmans Farm
Tyes Farm
Riding Stables
Prospect Farm
Park Corner Farm
Rainham Lodge Farm
Gardners Cor Hall
Harwood Hall
Lodge Farm
Poultry Farm
White Hart PH
Huntsman & Hounds PH
A127
A124
ARTERIAL ROAD
SOUTHEND ARTERIAL ROAD
HIGH STREET
UPMINSTER ROAD
ST. MARY'S LANE
MAIN ROAD
BRENTWOOD ROAD
LONDON LOOP/INGREBOURNE VALLEY GREENWAY

TYLERS WOOD
Stonyhills House
Cricket Ground
FOXBURROW WOOD
Foxburrows
COOMBE WOOD
53
Tooks Farm
Clap Gate Farm
MAGPIE
PARK
Driving Range
Clubhouse
GOLF COURSE
Suttons Farm
Hole Farm
CM13
PARKER'S SHAW
FOLKES LANE WOODLAND
Howard's Farm
Emery Farm
Upminster Lodge Farm
ESSEX
Preparatory Sch
Warley Garden Centre
LATCHET'S SHAW
SOUTHEND ARTERIAL ROAD
Woodlands Mushroom Farm
Works
CODHAM HALL WOOD
Codham Hall Farm
Codham Hall
Warley Street Flyover
WARLEY HALL WOOD
A127
Tennis Courts
Little Warley Hall Farm
Little Warley Hall
Folkes Farm
ALLOT
BROOKMANS PK
Nursery
POT KILN WOOD
CODHAM HALL WOOD
Great Warley Hall
Junction 29
M25
UPMINSTER TRADING PARK
UPMINSTER HALL PLAYING FIELDS
Health Cen
Comm Cen
Cranham
Sec Sch
BRENTWOOD
HAVERING
CRANHAM BRICKFIELDS
CRANHAM PLAYING FIELDS
FRANKS WOOD
Franks Farm
Monks Farm
Wyncray Farm
The Plough PH
TRAIN DEPOT
Westbury Farm
ST. MARY'S LANE
Elizabeth Lodge Farm
Forest View Nurseries
CLAY TYE WOOD
Cranham Court
Clubhouse
CRANHAM GOLF COURSE
Jobbers Rest PH
Thatched House PH
Sec Sch
Prim Sch
Sewage Works
Bury Farm
Clay Tye Farm
Electricity Station
RM14
Thames Chase Forest Centre
THAMES CHASE FOREST
Cranham Farm
Cranham Hall
Fairplay Farm
Groveland Nurseries
SPRING WOOD
CRANHAM MARSH NATURE RESERVE
MIDDLE WOOD
BONUS WOOD
Whitepost Farm
UPMINSTER CEMETERY
Crem
BRIDGE COTTAGES
North Ockendon
SPORTS GRD
TOP MEADOW GOLF COURSE
Clubhouse
Top Meadow Hotel
Driving Range
The Old White Horse PH
Manor Farm
Hall Farm
91
Nursery
RUSSELLS LAKE
Sullens
B186
B187
B1421
FR FS FT FU FV FW FX
55 56 57 58 59 60 61 62 63 64
86 87 88 89

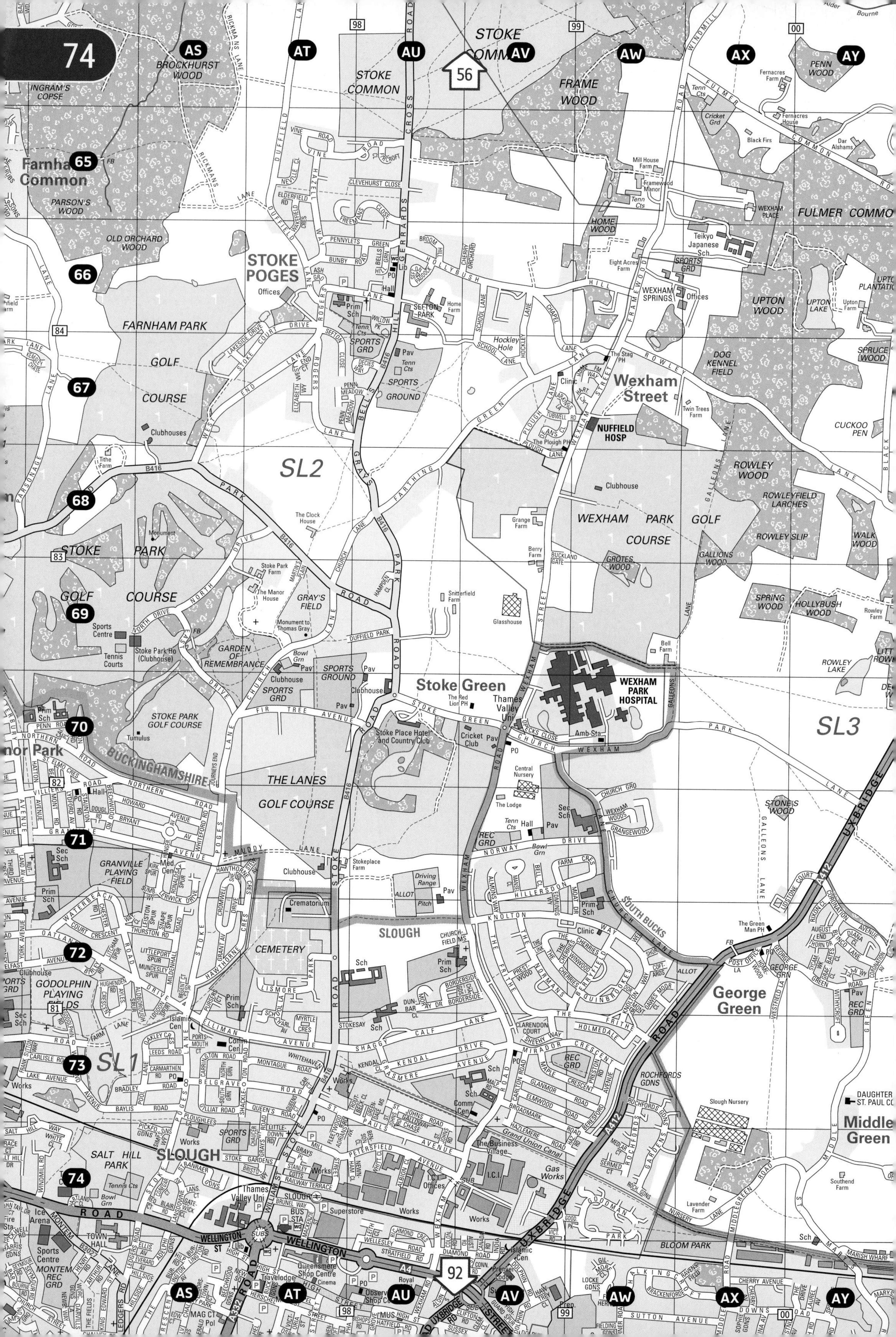

56
AS
AT
AU
AV
AW
AX
AY
BROCKHURST WOOD
INGRAM'S COPSE
Farnham Common
PARSON'S WOOD
OLD ORCHARD WOOD
STOKE COMMON
FRAME WOOD
PENN WOOD
FULMER COMMON
STOKE POGES
Offices
FARNHAM PARK
GOLF
COURSE
Clubhouses
SL2
STOKE
PARK
GOLF
COURSE
Sports Centre
Stoke Park Ho (Clubhouse)
Tennis Courts
GARDEN OF REMEMBRANCE
GRAY'S FIELD
Monument to Thomas Gray
The Manor House
Stoke Park Farm
Tithe Farm
Monument
STOKE PARK GOLF COURSE
Tumulus
SPORTS GRD
SPORTS GROUND
Stoke Green
The Red Lion PH
Thames Valley Uni
Cricket Club
Stoke Place Hotel and Country Club
THE LANES GOLF COURSE
Stokeplace Farm
Clubhouse
Crematorium
CEMETERY
SLOUGH
Driving Range
Wexham Street
NUFFIELD HOSP
Clinic
The Plough PH
The Stag PH
Twin Trees Farm
WEXHAM SPRINGS
Eight Acres Farm
Teikyo Japanese Sch
HOME WOOD
Mill House Farm
Framewood Manor
WEXHAM PLACE
Fernacres Farm
Fernacres House
Black Firs
Dar Alshams
UPTON WOOD
UPTON LAKE
Upton Farm
DOG KENNEL FIELD
SPRUCE WOOD
CUCKOO PEN
ROWLEY WOOD
ROWLEYFIELD LARCHES
ROWLEY SLIP
WALK WOOD
GALLIONS WOOD
SPRING WOOD
HOLLYBUSH WOOD
Rowley Farm
ROWLEY LAKE
WEXHAM PARK GOLF COURSE
GROTES WOOD
Clubhouse
Grange Farm
Berry Farm
Snitterfield Farm
Glasshouse
Bell Farm
WEXHAM PARK HOSPITAL
SL3
Central Nursery
The Lodge
STONE'S WOOD
The Green Man PH
George Green
SL1
GRANVILLE PLAYING FIELD
GODOLPHIN PLAYING FIELDS
SALT HILL PARK
SLOUGH
Ice Arena
Sports Centre
MONTEM REC GRD
TOWN HALL
Thames Valley Uni
BUS STA
Superstore
Queensmere Shop Centre
Travelodge
Cinema
Observ Shop Cen
Royal
I.C.I. Offices
I.C.I.
Gas Works
The Business Village
Grand Union Canal
ROCHFORDS GDNS
Slough Nursery
Lavender Farm
BLOOM PARK
Southend Farm
DAUGHTER ST. PAUL CC
Middle Green
Islamic Cen
Premier Lodge
Works
A412
A4
B416
A332
65
66
67
68
69
70
71
72
73
74
84
83
82
81
98
99
00
92

BROWN'S WOOD
OLDHOUSE WOOD
PARKSPRING WOOD
MOUNT FIDGET WOOD
BRIDGETTINE CONVENT
Langley Corner
LANGLEY COMMON
STRAWBERRY WOOD
HEATHFIELD PLANTATION
NATURE RESERVE
BOWLERS PLANTATION
BLACK PARK COUNTRY PARK
BLACKPARK LAKE
DIAMOND WOOD
CHESTNUT WOOD
FOXES GUTTER
COLUMN LARCHES
LANGLEY PARK WOOD
LANGLEY PARK COUNTRY PARK
ROUGHGROUND WOOD
ARBORETUM
Pinewood Film Studios
Heatherden Hall
THE CLUMP
LONG COPPICE
PLAYING FIELD
BROOM WARREN
Five Points
IVER HEATH
SL0
UB9
CHANDLERS HILL
Ashen Cross
Shreding Green
IVER
IVER GOLF COURSE
BUCKINGHAMSHIRE
SLOUGH
SOUTH BUCKS
Grand Union Canal (Slough Arm)
THE RIDGEWAY ESTATE
FARLOWS LAKE
THORNEY PARK GOLF COURSE
M25
A412
A4007
B470
DENHAM ROAD
SLOUGH ROAD
CHURCH ROAD
PINEWOOD ROAD
BANGORS ROAD NORTH
BANGORS ROAD SOUTH
HIGH STREET
LANGLEY PARK ROAD
THORNEY LANE NORTH
57
76
93

BG
BH
BJ
BK
BL
BM
BN
58
UB9
UB10
UB8
UB7
SL0
65
66
67
68
69
70
71
72
73
74
75
94
UXBRIDGE
UXBRIDGE MOOR
UXBRIDGE COMMON
HILLINGDON
COWLEY
IVER
YIEWSLEY
WEST DRAYTON
HILLINGDON HOUSE FARM SPORTS GROUNDS
UXBRIDGE ATHLETICS TRACK
Uxbridge College (Uxbridge Campus)
HILLINGDON COURT PARK
HILLINGDON GOLF COURSE
HILLINGDON & UXBRIDGE CEMETERY
Brunel University
UNIVERSITY PLAYING FIELDS
HILLINGDON HOSPITAL
COLHAM GREEN REC GRD
HUNTSMOOR PARK
FARLOWS LAKE
LITTLE BRITAIN LAKE
COWLEY LAKE
THORNEY PARK GOLF COURSE
Water Treatment Works
West Drayton Coal Depot
Grand Union Canal (Slough Arm)
Electricity Sub Station
R.A.F. Uxbridge
Hillingdon Circus
Apple Tree Roundabout
Colham Roundabout
ROCKINGHAM REC GRD
CHILTERN BUSINESS VILLAGE
COWLEY BUSINESS PARK
HIGHBRIDGE INDUSTRIAL ESTATE
RAINBOW INDUSTRIAL ESTATE
ZODIAC BUSINESS PARK
THE RIDGEWAY ESTATE
COWLEY HIGH ROAD
COWLEY ROAD
HILLINGDON ROAD
HILLINGDON HILL
FALLING LANE
DENHAM ROAD
OXFORD ROAD
A40
A4007
A4020
A408
A412
A437
B483
M25
BUCKINGHAMSHIRE

RAF NORTHOLT AERODROME
HA4
59
NORTH HILLINGDON
WESTERN AVENUE
A40
Master Brewer Hotel
FREEZELAND COVERT
CUTTHROAT WOOD
GUTTERIDGE WOOD
NATURE RESERVE
MEADOWS NATURE RESERVE
LONDON GOLF CENTRE
Polish War Memorial
WEST END ROAD
Down Barns Moated Site
UB5
WEST LONDON SHOOTING GROUNDS
THE GORSE
HOME COVERT
POLE HILL OPEN SPACE
HARE PLANTATION
Old Abbotsonians R.F.C.
LANE COVERT
YEADING BROOK MEADOWS NATURE RESERVE
GROSVENOR PLAYING FIELD
Hayes R.F.C.
HAYES SHRUB
HAYES PARK
YEADING
78
UB4
BELMORE PLAYING FIELDS
HAYES END
RECREATION GROUND
UXBRIDGE ROAD
A4020
ROSEDALE PARK
GRASSY MEADOW
MEMORIAL GDNS
Hayes Cricket Club
HAYES
BARRA HALL PARK
HAYES STADIUM
BELL HOUSE FLD
Uxbridge College Hayes Community Campus
Lombardy Retail Park
Premier Travel Inn
WARREN PARK
STOCKLEY PARK GOLF COURSE
The Arena
STOCKLEY PARK
UB11
UB3
DAWLEY ROAD
E.M.I. SPORTS GROUND
Grand Union Canal
ADLER IND EST
WARNFORD IND EST
ABERGLEN INDUSTRIAL ESTATE
PROVIDENT INDUSTRIAL ESTATE
95
HAYES BYPASS
A312
MINET COUNTRY PARK
ELYSTAN BUSINESS CENTRE
HAYES METRO CENTRE
HEATHROW INTERCHANGE
HILLINGDON
EALING
BP
BQ
BR
BS
BT
BU
BV
65
66
67
68
69
70
71
72
73
74

BW
BX
BY
BZ
CA
CB
CC
60
65
66
67
68
69
70
71
72
73
74
77
96
HA4
UB5
UB4
UB1
NORTHOLT
GREENFORD
RAVENOR PARK
SOUTHALL
DORMER'S WELLS
BROOKSIDE
HILLINGDON
EALING
LIME TREE PARK GOLF COURSE
LONDON GOLF CENTRE
WEST LONDON SHOOTING GROUNDS
NORTHOLT GOLF COURSE
RECTORY PARK
KENSINGTON & CHELSEA PLAYING FIELDS
MARNHAM FIELDS
JUBILEE PARK
GREENFORD PARK CEMETERY
WEST MIDDLESEX GOLF COURSE
MINET COUNTRY PARK
KING GEORGE'S FIELD
LORD HALSBURY MEMORIAL REC GRD
NORTHOLT RECREATION GRD
ISLIP MANOR PARK
BELVUE PARK
EALING GOLF RANGE
KELVIN INDUSTRIAL ESTATE
THE METROPOLITAN CENTRE
BIRKBECK COLLEGE SPORTS GROUND
SMITHS FARM EST
WARREN PARK
Polish War Memorial
Target Roundabout
Civic Amenity Site
Down Barns Moated Site
Lombardy Retail Park
HEATHROW INTERCHANGE
BROOK INDUSTRIAL ESTATE
HEATHROW PURPLE PARKING
BARRATT INDUSTRIAL PARK
SOUTHALL RAILWAY CENTRE
WESTERN AVENUE
CHURCH ROAD
MANDEVILLE ROAD
RUISLIP ROAD
WEST END ROAD
THE PARKWAY (HAYES BYPASS)
UXBRIDGE ROAD
THE BROADWAY
HIGH STREET
GREENFORD ROAD
WINDMILL LANE
SOUTH ROAD
A312
A40
A4180
A4020
A3005
B455

CD
CE
CF
CG
CH
CJ
CK
61
SUDBURY
HA0
BARHAM PARK
WHITTON AVENUE WEST
A4090
HARROW ROAD
SUDBURY TOWN
SUDBURY & HARROW ROAD
HORSENDEN WOOD
HORSENDEN HILL GOLF COURSE
SUDBURY GOLF COURSE
HORSENDEN HILL
HOME MEAD
SPORTS GROUND
BERKELEY FIELDS
GREAT BRAMSTONES
UB6
GRAND UNION CANAL (PADDINGTON BRANCH)
ALPERTON CEMETERY
ONE TREE HILL REC GRD
GREENFORD
OLDFIELD REC GRD
PERIVALE WOOD (Nature Reserve)
PERIVALE
PERIVALE INDUSTRIAL PARK
PERIVALE NEW BUSINESS CENTRE
WADSWORTH BUSINESS CENTRE
FLEETWAY BUSINESS PARK
SHERATON BUSINESS CEN
METROPOLITAN POLICE TRAFFIC UNIT
ALPERTON SPORTS GROUND
ALPERTON
EALING CENTRAL SPORTS GROUND
Greenford Roundabout
SOUTH GREENFORD
Perivale
WESTERN AVENUE
A40
EALING GOLF COURSE
ATHLETICS TRACK
PERIVALE PARK SPORTS GROUND
PERIVALE PARK GOLF COURSE
PITSHANGER PARK
HANGER LANE
80
HANGER HILL PARK
River Brent
RUISLIP ROAD
BRENT VALLEY PARK
CLEVELAND PARK
CUCKOO PARK
W7
W5
W13
BRENT VALLEY GOLF COURSE
DRAYTON GREEN
EALING
EALING BROADWAY
EALING COMMON
CHURCHFIELDS RECREATION GROUND
KENSINGTON & CHELSEA CEMETERY
UXBRIDGE ROAD
A4020
THE BROADWAY
NEW BROADWAY
WALPOLE PARK
PITSHANGER MANOR & GALL
Thames Valley Uni
HANWELL
HANWELL CEMETERY
EALING HOSPITAL N.H.S. TRUST
LAMMAS PARK
Wharncliffe Viaduct
BARCLAYS BANK SPORTS GROUND
97
65
66
67
68
69
70
71
72
73
74
84
83
82
81
15
16
17

80
62
79
98
CL
CM
CN
CP
CQ
CR
CS
19
20
21
65
66
67
68
69
70
71
72
73
74
HA0
HA9
W3
W5
WEMBLEY
TOKYNGTON
CHURCH END
ALPERTON
STONEBRIDGE
PARK ROYAL
NORTH ACTON
WEST ACTON
EALING
ACTON
EAST ACTON
HARLESDEN
HANGER HILL PARK
EALING COMMON
NORTH CIRCULAR ROAD
WESTERN AVENUE
HANGER LANE
GUNNERSBURY AVENUE
UXBRIDGE ROAD
HIGH STREET
HARROW ROAD
EALING ROAD
HILLSIDE
CRAVEN PARK
CENTRAL MIDDLESEX HOSPITAL
PARK ROYAL CEN.
WEMBLEY STADIUM
WEMBLEY CENTRAL
STONEBRIDGE PARK
HANGER LANE
PARK ROYAL
NORTH EALING
WEST ACTON
ACTON MAIN LINE
EALING BROADWAY
EALING COMMON
ACTON CENTRAL
ACTON TOWN
HARLESDEN
NORTH ACTON

CT
CU
CV
CW
CX
CY
CZ
63
65
66
67
68
69
70
71
72
73
74
82
99
22
23
24
NW2
NW6
NW10
W9
W10
W11
W12
W8
WILLESDEN
WILLESDEN GREEN
BRONDESBURY
BRONDESBURY PARK
KENSAL RISE
KENSAL GREEN
KENSAL TOWN
KILBURN
WEST KILBURN
MAIDA HILL
OLD OAK COMMON
WORMWOOD SCRUBS
NORTH KENSINGTON
NOTTING HILL
SHEPHERD'S BUSH
KENSINGTON
WESTBOURNE GREEN
WILLESDEN NEW CEMETERY
ROUNDWOOD PARK
KING EDWARD VII SPORTS GRD
QUEEN'S PARK
PADDINGTON OLD CEMETERY
ST. MARY'S RC CEMETERY
KENSAL GREEN CEMETERY
GRAND UNION CANAL (Paddington Branch)
LITTLE WORMWOOD SCRUBS REC GRD
LINFORD CHRISTIE STADIUM
QUEEN CHARLOTTE & CHELSEA HOSP
HAMMERSMITH HOSPITAL
H.M. PRISON WORMWOOD SCRUBS
ST CHARLES HOSP
PRINCESS LOUISE HOSP
WORMHOLT PARK
LOFTUS ROAD STADIUM QPR FC
HOLLAND PARK
Holland Park Roundabout
WESTWAY
A40
A404
A4003
A4020
A219
A407
A5
HARROW ROAD
WILLESDEN LANE
SCRUBS LANE
WOOD LANE
UXBRIDGE ROAD
HOLLAND PARK AVENUE
NOTTING HILL GATE
WEST CROSS ROUTE
KILBURN HIGH ROAD
SHOOT UP HILL

DA
DB
DC
DD
DE
DF
DG
64
65
66
67
68
69
70
71
72
73
74
81
194
198
100
WEST HAMPSTEAD
SOUTH HAMPSTEAD
BELSIZE PARK
DESBURY
KILBURN
NW6
NW3
NW8
NW1
W9
W2
W8
W11
SW7
PRIMROSE HILL
ST. JOHN'S WOOD
LISSON GROVE
MAIDA VALE
MAIDA HILL
W KILBURN
THE REGENT'S PARK
WESTBOURNE GREEN
PADDINGTON
BAYSWATER
MARYLEBONE
KENSINGTON GARDENS
HYDE PARK
THE SERPENTINE
KENSINGTON
HOLLAND PARK
ROYAL FREE HOSP
TAVISTOCK CEN
FREUD MUSEUM
LORD'S CRICKET GROUND
LONDON ZOO
QUEEN MARY'S GARDENS
BOATING LAKE
PADDINGTON RECREATION GROUND
PADDINGTON OLD CEMETERY
HOSPITAL OF ST. JOHN & ST. ELIZ
WELLINGTON HOSP
ST. MARY'S HOSP
ROUND POND
KENSINGTON PALACE
SERPENTINE GALLERY
FINCHLEY ROAD
MAIDA VALE
EDGWARE ROAD
BAYSWATER ROAD
KENSINGTON ROAD
KNIGHTSBRIDGE
OXFORD ST
MARYLEBONE ROAD
WESTWAY
A5
A41
A40
A402
A5205
A502
A4202

HOLLOWAY
LOWER HOLLOWAY
HIGHBURY
KENTISH TOWN
CANONBURY
BARNSBURY
N7
KING'S CROSS
CAMDEN TOWN
ISLINGTON
N1
PENTONVILLE PRISON
CALEDONIAN PARK
SOMERS TOWN
PENTONVILLE
FINSBURY
ST. PANCRAS
EUSTON
REGENT'S PARK
WC1
BLOOMSBURY
BRITISH MUSEUM
ST. LUKE'S
EC1
CLERKENWELL
BARBICAN
HOLBORN
LINCOLN'S INN FIELDS
SOHO
WC2
W1
STRAND
AYFAIR
EC4
RIVER THAMES
ST. JAMES'S
SW1
THE GREEN PARK
ST. JAMES'S PARK
SOUTHWARK
SE1
THE BOROUGH
WATERLOO
TATE MODERN
BUCKINGHAM
DH
DJ
DK
DL
DM
DN
DP
65
66
67
68
69
70
71
72
73
74
84
101

HIGHBURY
CANONBURY
KINGSLAND
HACKNEY
DALSTON
DE BEAUVOIR TOWN
SOUTH HACKNEY
HOXTON
HAGGERSTON
BETHNAL GREEN
ST. LUKE'S
CLERKENWELL
SHOREDITCH
BROADGATE
BARBICAN
STEPNEY
WHITECHAPEL
SHADWELL
WAPPING
SOUTHWARK
THE BOROUGH
RIVER THAMES
N1
E8
E2
EC1
EC2
EC4
EC3
E1
SE1
REGENT'S CANAL
LONDON FIELDS
TOWER OF LONDON
TATE MODERN
GUY'S HOSPITAL
ST. PAUL'S CATH
MOORFIELDS EYE HOSP
ROYAL LONDON HOSP
LONDON BRIDGE HOSP
ST. JOSEPH'S HOSPICE
DQ
DR
DS
DT
DU
DV
DW
33
34
35
65
66
67
68
69
70
71
72
73
74
83
102
197
202

85
DX
DY
DZ
EA
EB
EC
ED
67
86
203
204
103
36
37
38
65
66
67
68
69
70
71
72
73
74
HOMERTON
MABLEY GREEN
E9
HACKNEY WICK
STRATFORD INTERNATIONAL (under construction)
Channel Tunnel Rail Link (under construction)
STRATFORD
E15
VICTORIA PARK
OLD FORD
WELL STREET COMMON
HERTFORD UNION CANAL
BOW
MILE END
MILE END PARK
Queen Mary University of London
ROYAL LON. HOSP (ST. CLEMENTS)
TOWER HAMLETS CEMETERY PARK
E3
BROMLEY
DEVONS EST
GROVE HALL PARK
THREE MILLS GREEN
LEE VALLEY PARK
Pumping Station
Gas Works
MEMORIAL GDNS
WEST HAM
MEMORIAL RECREATION GROUND
E16
ELECTRA BUSINESS PARK
BLACKWALL TRADING EST
LIMMO PENINSULA ECOLOGICAL PARK
EAST INDIA DOCK BASIN NATURE RES
CANNING TOWN
STEPNEY GREEN PARK
MILE END STADIUM
LIMEHOUSE
E14
EAST INDIA DOCK RD
BARTLETT PARK
LANSBURY EST
LANGDON PARK
POPLAR
WEST INDIA QUAY
CANARY WHARF
ISLE
WEST INDIA DOCKS
RIVER THAMES
SE16
The Dome Redevelopment (Open 2007)
MERIDIAN GARDENS
NORTH GREENWICH
SE10
BLACKWALL TUNNEL
LIMEHOUSE REACH
TOWER HAMLETS
SOUTHWARK
NEWHAM
WALTHAM FOREST
LEYTON RD
HIGH ST
BOW ROAD
MILE END ROAD
COMMERCIAL ROAD
GROVE RD
BURDETT ROAD
EAST CROSS ROUTE
BLACKWALL TUNNEL NORTHERN APP
ROMFORD ROAD
WEST HAM LANE
CARPENTERS ROAD
WHITE POST LA
ROTHBURY RD
WICK RD
CHAPMAN RD
EASTWAY
CHOBHAM RD
ANGEL LANE
GREAT EASTERN RD
BROADWAY
MANOR ROAD
ASPEN WAY
WESTFERRY RD
PRESTONS ROAD
LOWER LEA CROSSING
SILVERTOWN WAY

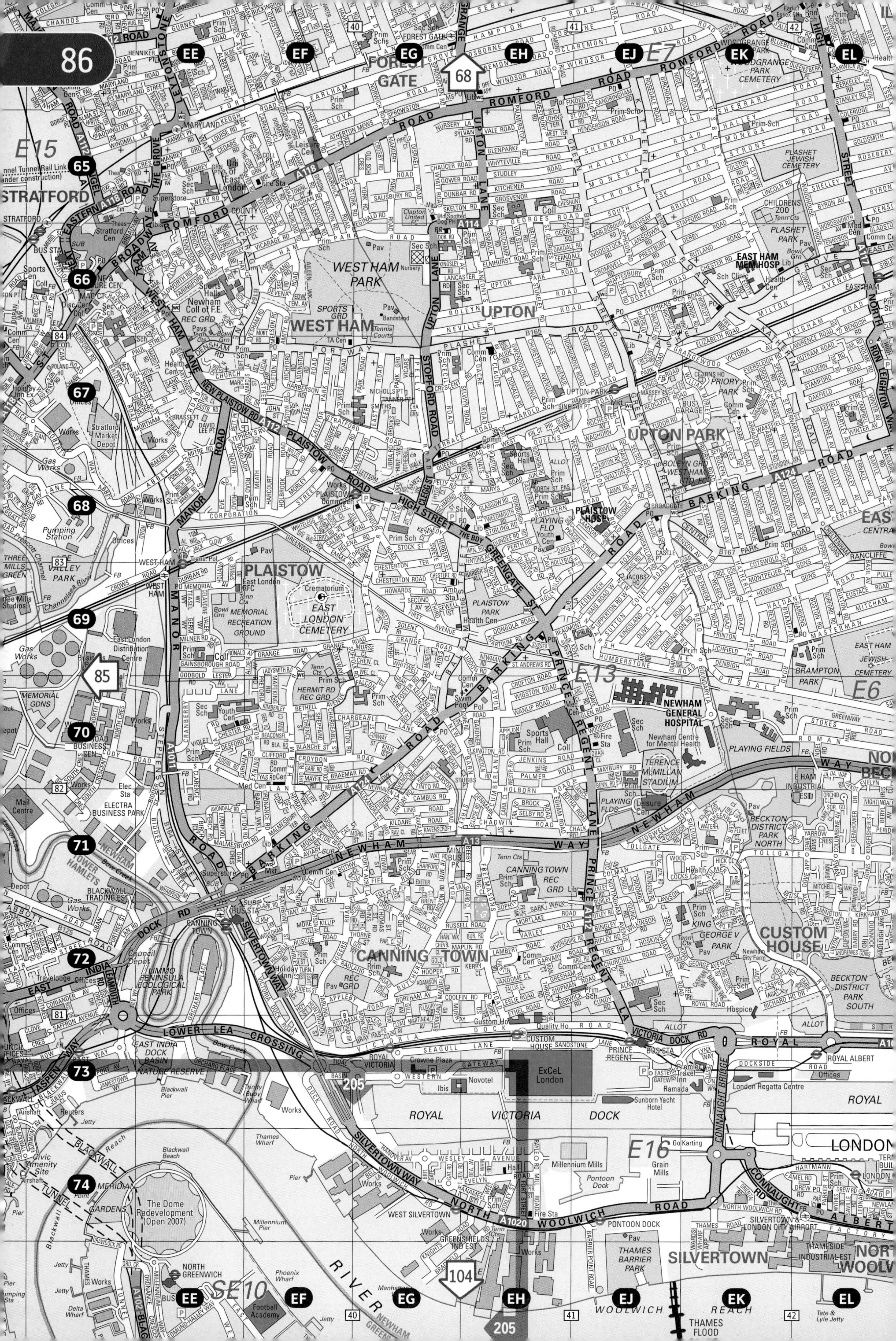
EE
EF
EG
EH
EJ
EK
EL
68
FOREST GATE
E7
E15
STRATFORD
WEST HAM PARK
WEST HAM
UPTON
UPTON PARK
PLAISTOW
EAST LONDON CEMETERY
MEMORIAL RECREATION GROUND
NEWHAM GENERAL HOSPITAL
E13
E6
CANNING TOWN
CUSTOM HOUSE
LIMMO PENINSULA ECOLOGICAL PARK
EAST INDIA DOCK BASIN NATURE RESERVE
ROYAL VICTORIA DOCK
ExCeL London
E16
Millennium Mills
SILVERTOWN
THAMES BARRIER PARK
The Dome Redevelopment (Open 2007)
NORTH GREENWICH
SE10
RIVER
WOOLWICH REACH
THAMES FLOOD
85
104
205
40
41
42
65
66
67
68
69
70
71
72
73
74
ROMFORD ROAD
BARKING ROAD
NEWHAM WAY
PRINCE REGENT LANE
NORTH WOOLWICH ROAD
SILVERTOWN WAY
LOWER LEA CROSSING
UPTON LANE
STOPFORD ROAD
PLAISTOW ROAD
MANOR ROAD
HIGH STREET
GREENGATE ST
WEST HAM LANE
CONNAUGHT BRIDGE
PLASHET PARK
PLASHET JEWISH CEMETERY
EAST HAM JEWISH CEMETERY
BRAMPTON PARK
PRIORY PARK
KING GEORGE V PARK
BECKTON DISTRICT PARK NORTH
BECKTON DISTRICT PARK SOUTH
CANNING TOWN REC GRD
HERMIT RD REC GRD
PLAISTOW PARK
BOLEYN GRD WEST HAM UTD FC
TERENCE McMILLAN STADIUM
WOODGRANGE PARK CEMETERY
EAST HAM MEM HOSP
PLAISTOW HOSP
London Regatta Centre
ROYAL ALBERT
PRINCE REGENT
ROYAL VICTORIA
WEST SILVERTOWN
PONTOON DOCK
LONDON CITY AIRPORT
THAMESIDE INDUSTRIAL EST
Tate & Lyle Jetty

LOXFORD
LITTLE ILFORD PARK
THE LAKE
BARKING PARK
BARKING PARK REC GRD
Indoor Bowl Club
Bowling Greens
LONGBRIDGE ROAD
FANSHAWE AV
BARRINGTON PLAYING FLDS
E12
SPORTS GROUND
Gasholder
NORTHERN RELIEF ROAD
BARKING
BARKING HOSPITAL
UPNEY
BOATING LAKE
TRIPPLESIDE BURIAL GROUND
RIPPLE ROAD
BARKING ROAD REC GRD
ABBEY RETAIL PARK
Mill Pond
IG11
GREAT FIELDS PARK
ALFREDS WAY IND ESTATE
WAYSIDE COMMERCIAL EST
BARKING BYPASS
ALFREDS WAY
FLANDERS RD PLAYING FLDS
Civic Amenity Site
Sewage Works
HAND TROUGH CREEK
CUCKOLD'S HAVEN
LYON BUSINESS PARK
KATELLA TRADING EST
ABBEY WHARF INDUSTRIAL ESTATE
River Roding
ALLOTMENTS
PITCHES
Bowling Alley
Refuse Transfer Station
GOOSELEY'S PLAYING FIELDS
NEWHAM WAY
Filter Beds
BECKTON REACH SEWAGE TREATMENT WORKS
RIVER ROAD BUSINESS PARK
RIVERSIDE INDUSTRIAL ESTATE
Thameside Park City Farm
88
TRAFALGAR BUSINESS CENTRE
CREEKMOUTH
BUZZARD CREEK INDUSTRIAL ESTATE
BECKTON TRIANGLE RETAIL PARK
GATEWAY RETAIL PARK
Nature Reserve
Northern Outfall Sewage Works
ALPINE BUSINESS CEN
Gallions Reach Shopping Park
Gas Works
BARKING FLOOD BARRIER
Gravel Works
BECKTON
DLR DEPOT
NEW BECKTON PARK
GALLIONS REACH
MARGARET NESS OR TRIPCOCK POINT
ALBERT WAY
BECKTON PARK
Uni of East London
ALBERT DOCK
ALBERT BASIN
Norton Healthcare Ltd
CITY AIRPORT
KING GEORGE V DOCK
Newham Coll of Further Ed
SE28
THAMESMEAD
Thamesmere Lake
GALLIONS REACH
ROYAL VICTORIA GDNS
NORTH WOOLWICH
STANDARD INDUSTRIAL ESTATE
105
H.M. PRISON
BIRCHMERE
Birchmere Business Park
Civic Amenity Site
EASTERN WAY
69
EM EN EP EQ ER ES ET
65 66 67 68 69 70 71 72 73 74

88
70
87
106
MAYESBROOK PARK
BARKING FC
ARENA
BOATING LAKE
PARSLOES PARK
RM9
DAGENHAM HEATHWAY
BECONTREE
BARKING HOSPITAL
TRIPPLESIDE BURIAL GROUND
CASTLE GREEN
GORESBROOK SPORTS GROUND
GORESBROOK PARK
BARKING R.F.C.
DAGENHAM LEISURE PK
ALFREDS WAY
RIPPLE ROAD
A13
A123
A1153
A1240
LODGE AVENUE
PORTERS AVENUE
HEATHWAY
ALFREDS WAY IND ESTATE
WAYSIDE COMMERCIAL EST
RENWICK IND ESTATE
RIPPLESIDE COMMERCIAL ESTATE
MAYBELLS COMM EST
TRAIN DEPOT
Freight Depot
FORD MOTOR WORKS
DAGENHAM DOCK
THAMES GATEWAY PARK
RIVERSIDE INDUSTRIAL ESTATE
RIVER ROAD BUSINESS PARK
TRAFALGAR BUSINESS
City Farm & Ecology Park
The Ripple Nature Reserve
IG11
POWER STATION
ALLOTMENTS
CREEKMOUTH
BUZZARD CREEK INDUSTRIAL ESTATE
BARKING FLOOD BARRIER
Barking or False Point
Horse Shoe Corner
Oil Storage Depot
Power Station
BARKING & DAGENHAM
NEWHAM
BEXLEY
GREENWICH
CROSSNESS LIGHTHOUSE
THAMESMEAD NORTH
Ecology Study Area
Crossway Lake
Driving Range
RIVERSIDE GOLF COURSE
SE2
Crossness Pumping Station
COVERED RESERVOIRS
Crossness Sewage Treatment Works
Sludge Incinerator
Thamesmead Lake
THAMESMEAD
MANORWAY GREEN
MOORINGS
CROSSWAY PARK
SPORTS GROUND
Thamesmead Town FC
SOUTHMERE PARK
ERITH MARSHES
LAKESIDE CENTRE
SOUTHMERE
BIRCHMERE PARK
SE28
WOODLAND WAY
DA18
EASTERN WAY
A2016
CENTRAL WAY
HARROW MANORWAY
CARLYLE ROAD
ABBEY WOOD PARK
Bexley Business Academy
H.M. PRISON
EU
EV
EW
EX
EY
EZ
FA
65
66
67
68
69
70
71
72
73
74

BRETONS OUTDOOR CENTRE
BRITTONS PLAYING FIELD
South Hornchurch
RM10
BEAM VALLEY COUNTRY PARK
RAINHAM
RM12
HORNCHURCH COUNTRY PARK
AIRFIELD WOOD
FLIGHTWAY WOOD
FARMFIELD WOOD
LOWFIELD WOOD
HORNCHURCH MARSHES
Riverside Sewage Works
RM13
RAINHAM MARSHES
WENNINGTON MARSHES
DA17
JENNINGTREE POINT LIGHTHOUSE
BELVEDERE INDUSTRIAL ESTATE
ALBRIGHT INDUSTRIAL ESTATE
DENVER INDUSTRIAL ESTATE
FAIRVIEW INDUSTRIAL PARK
Rainham Sunday Market
Old Man's Head
Hornchurch Shoot
Newtons Corner
Dovers Corner
OLD DAGENHAM PARK
PONDFIELD PARK
MANOR ROAD SPORTS GRD
THAMES GATEWAY
NEW ROAD
RAINHAM ROAD
A13
A1306
A125
A1112
71
90
107
FB
FC
FD
FE
FF
FG
FH
65
66
67
68
69
70
71
72
73
74

RM12
HORNCHURCH
COUNTRY
PARK
AIRFIELD WOOD
PINEWOOD
FLIGHTWAY WOOD
FARMFIELD WOOD
LOWFIELD WOOD
ABBEY WOOD
BERWICK WOODS
BERWICK GLADES
BERWICK POND
BONNETTS WOOD
SAND AND GRAVEL PIT
SAND & GRAVEL PIT
Civic Amenity Site
Corbets Tey
PARKLANDS OPEN SPACE
White Post Corner
RAINHAM CEMETERY (JEWISH)
SPRING FARM PARK
WARWICK WOOD
WHITE POST WOOD
RM13
IMPERIAL TRADING EST
KENNINGTON PARK
Wennington
RAINHAM MARSHES
WENNINGTON MARSHES
PURFLEET IND PARK
SPORTS GROUND
A1306 NEW ROAD
A13
GATEWAY
LONDON ROAD
B1335 SANDY LANE
WARWICK LANE
UPMINSTER ROAD NORTH
INGREBOURNE RIVER
Common Watercourse
72
89
108

North Ockendon
SOUTH OCKENDON
North Stifford
Aveley
RM14
RM15
RM16
M25
73
109
Junction 30
HAVERING
THURROCK
UPMINSTER CEMETERY
MIDDLE WOOD
BONUS WOOD
RUSSELL'S LAKE
COYS LAKE
Adventure Centre
SAND AND GRAVEL PIT
FREEMAN'S SHAW
TOP MEADOW GOLF COURSE
THE WILDERNESS
BELHUS WOODS COUNTRY PARK
BELHUS CHASE
BELHUS PARK GOLF COURSE
BELHUS PARK
FORD AVELEY PLANT
The Ockendon Complex
BONNYGATE WOOD
DILKES PARK
Culver Centre
MILLARD'S GARDEN
BRANNETT'S WOOD
HANGMAN'S WOOD
MARDYKE WOODS
DAVY DOWN RIVERSIDE PARK
MARDYKE VALLEY GOLF COURSE
FIELDS OF PEACE
LITTLE PALMER'S SHAW
GREAT PALMER'S SHAW
ARENA ESSEX RACEWAY
KARTING CEN
LAKESIDE COACH PARK
THURROCK ARTERIAL ROAD
SOUTH OCKENDON REC GRD
BRICKBARN WOOD
COMBE WOOD
LOW WELL WOOD
LONG POND
OAK WOOD
ASH PLANTATION
ROOKERY
WHITEHALL WOOD
LITTLE BRICKKILN WOOD
BRICKKILN WOOD
THE SHRUBBERY
South Ockendon Hall
South Ockendon Hall Farm
MOAT
Tumulus
Groves Barns
Kemp's Farm
Manor Farm
Hall Farm
Whitepost Farm
Sullens Farm
FR
FS
FT
FU
FV
FW
FX
65
66
67
68
69
70
71
72
73
74
57
58
59
81
82
83
84

AS
AT
AU
AV
AW
AX
AY
74
SLOUGH
SALT HILL PARK
Thames Valley Uni
Superstore
Works
I.C.I. Offices
Gas Works
The Business Village
Grand Union Canal
BLOOM PARK
Lavender Farm
WELLINGTON ST
WELLINGTON
TOWN HALL
Sports Centre
MONTEM REC GRD
Queensmere Shop Centre
Observatory Shop Centre
Royal Mail
UPTON HOSP
HIGH STREET
ALBERT ST
MERE RD
YEW TREE RD
UXBRIDGE RD
SUSSEX PLACE
LONDON ROAD
SUTTON AVENUE
CHERRY AVENUE
KEDERMISTER PARK
Upton Park
Upton
LASCELLES PLAYING FIELD
HERSCHEL PARK
Amenity Site
75
76
77
78
79
80
81
82
83
84
SL1
SL4
UPTON COURT PARK
MOTOCROSS TRACK
SLOUGH
WINDSOR & MAIDENHEAD
B.M.X. TRACK
Clubhouse
SLOUGH R.F.C.
Cricket Ground
DITTON PARK
Riding Court Farm
Computer Associates
The Manor House
KINGS OAK
DITTON PARK
FISH POND
ETON GOLF COURSE
College Pool
AGARS PLOUGH PLAYING FIELDS
THAMES VALLEY ATHLETICS CENTRE
Fifteen Arch Bri
PLAYING FIELDS
POCOCKS LANE
Eton Coll
Eton College
THE HOME PARK RECREATION GROUND
DATCHET GOLF COURSE
Victoria Bri
KING EDWARD VII AVENUE
WINDSOR ROAD
CUTLERS AIT
WINDSOR & ETON RIVERSIDE
WINDSOR CASTLE
EAST TER LAWN
EAST LAWN
WINDSOR & ETON CENTRAL
ROYAL STATION
Royal Mews Riding Sch
South Slopes
GOLF COURSE
Victoria Barracks
WINDSOR
SUMPTERMEAD AIT
River Thames
DATCHET
Med Cen
DATCHET SPORTS GROUND
DATCHET CEMETERY
The Rising Sun PH
MILL PLACE CARAVAN PARK
Pumping Station
Southlea
Southlea Farm
THE HOME PARK
FROGMORE GARDENS
Royal Mausoleum
Frogmore House
The Aviary
Prince Consort's Home Farm
Adelaide Lodge
PRINCESS MARGARET HOSP
GARRISON SPORTS GROUND
Queen's Cottages
Shaw Farm
Windsor Hall
Glasshouses
ROYAL GARDENS
Albert Bridge
The Lord Nelson PH
Clayhall Farm
Battle Bourne
Manor Farm
NICKCROFT AIT
HAM ISLAND
Sludge Lagoon
Sludge Lagoons
Filter Beds
Sludge Beds
NEW CUT
Ham Bridge
St. George's Farm
Old Windsor Lock
The Manor
Anglo Saxon Palace (site of)
REMENHAM PARK
SUNNYMEADS
Sunnymeads
Sailing Club
GREAT
ALBERT ROAD
KINGS ROAD
112

IVER GOLF COURSE
BUCKINGHAMSHIRE
SLOUGH
SOUTH BUCKS
LANGLEY
Langley
Richings Park
SL0
THORNEY PARK GOLF COURSE
RICHINGS PARK GOLF COURSE AND COUNTRY CLUB
Junction 15 (M25)
Junction 4B (M4)
M4
Junction 5
Brands Hill
Colnbrook
COLNBROOK BYPASS
A4
THE QUEEN MOTHER RESERVOIR
SL3
Poyle
BRITANNIA INDUSTRIAL EST
MCKAY TRADING ESTATE
TRIDENT INDUSTRIAL ESTATE
Horton
Arthur Jacob Nature Reserve
Junction 14
TW19
WRAYSBURY
SURREY
WINDSOR & MAIDENHEAD
M25
Longford Roundabout
STANWELL MOOR
75
94
113

BG
BH
BJ
BK
BL
BM
BN
76
Water Treatment Works
West Drayton Coal Depot
YIEWSLEY
WEST DRAYTON
Horton Ind Park
Horton Bridge
IVER
75
76
77
78
79
80
81
82
83
84
THORNEY PARK GOLF COURSE
Thorney Farm
MILLSIDE COURT
Thorney Weir House
THORNEY
SL0
Tower Arms PH
SPORTS GRD
Clubhouse
Bowl Grn
FAIRWAY AVENUE
HIGH STREET
Health Cen
Works
PROVIDENCE
SPORTS GRD
R.A.F. West Drayton
Prim Sch
Hall
United Biscuits
Youth Cen
Comm Cen
Family Cen
Pol
Lib
Medical Cen
SOUTHLANDS ARTS CEN
THE CLOSES RECREATION GROUND
WEST DRAYTON
CEM.
UB7
Prim Sch
SPORTS GROUND
HEATH GOLF CO
Crowne Plaza Hotel
Novotel Heathrow
HEATHROW COACH CEN
Frays Island Nat Res
MAYFIELD PARK
MAYFIELDS LAKE
Anglers Retreat PH
West Drayton Cricket Club
COLNE PARK CARAVAN SITE
SPORTS GROUND
HARMONDSWORTH MOOR COUNTRY PARK
THE COMMON
Junction 15 (M25)
Junction 4B (M4)
M4
SOUTH BUCKS
Old Slade Farm
Colne Brook
SOUTH BUCKS
HILLINGDON
Bigley Ditch
Sewage Works
Filter Beds
Warehouses
Cement Works
93
Depot
HARMONDSWORTH MOOR COUNTRY PARK
PROSPECT PARK
Homefarm
ALLOT
Scotchlake Farm
British Airways Waterside
Harmondsworth Immigration Detention Cen
Colnbrook Immigration Removal Cen
Sheraton Heathrow Hotel
HARMONDSWORTH CEM
Tithe Barn
The Lodge
Home Farm
Harmondsworth
HOLLOWAY LANE
A3044
Ansell Garden Centre
Holiday Inn Heathrow
Heathrow Garden Centre
Berkeley Nurseries
Sipson
A408
Prim Sch
Works
SIPSON WAR MEML. REC GRD
Holiday Inn
POLAR PARK
Arora International Hotel
COLNBROOK BY-PASS
A4
BATH ROAD
SL3
SLOUGH
M25
HILLINGDON
ACCOMMODATION LANE
STANWELL MOOR RD
Longford Roundabout
Longford
Longford Bridge
Thistle Heathrow
British Airways PLC
NORTHERN PERIMETER ROAD
Fire Sta
COLNBROOK GOLF RANGE
Mad Bridge
Moor Bridge
Kings Bridge
Poyle Channel
Wraysbury River
River Colne
POYLE TECH CEN
M25 under construction
BEDFONT COURT ESTATE
TERMINAL 5 (under construction)
A3044
TW6
Control Tower
Snow Base
TERMINAL 3
Royal Mail
TW19
HILLINGDON
AIRPORT WAY
A3113
Junction 14
SPORTS GROUND
STANWELL MOOR
114
SOUTHERN PERIMETER ROAD
SPELTHORNE
SURREY
CARGO TERMINAL
BRITISH AIRWAYS CARGO CENTRE
05
06
07

BP
BQ
BR
BS
BT
BU
BV
77
UB11
Grand Union Canal
STOCKLEY PARK
E.M.I. SPORTS GROUND
HAYES TOWN
BOTWELL GRN
MINET COUNTRY PARK
PROVIDENT INDUSTRIAL ESTATE
PETER JAMES BUSINESS CENTRE
ADLER IND EST
ABERGLEN INDUSTRIAL ESTATE
WARNFORD IND EST
HAYES & HARLINGTON
Speedmarque Centre
THE SQUIRRELS TRADING ESTATE
INTERNATIONAL TRADING EST
GOVERNMENT BUILDINGS
BOURNE FARM FIELD
ALLOTMENTS
PINKWELL PARK
UB3
NORTH HYDE RD
NORTH HYDE ROAD
STATION ROAD
Cherry Lane Roundabout
CHERRY LANE CEMETERY
SAM PHILIP REC GRD
Premier Travel Inn
Junction 4
Junction 3
M4
THE PARKWAY
BULLS BRIDGE IND EST
Western International Market
NAVIGATOR PARK
LITTLE HARLINGTON FIELD
IMPERIAL COLLEGE SPORTS GROUND
SIPSON MEADOW
SPORTS GROUND
HARLINGTON
HIGH STREET
CRANE MEADOW
CRANFORD
PARK
CRANFORD PARK
AVENUE
TRAVELLERS SITE
BRITISH AIRWAYS SPORTS GROUND
PARKWAY TRADING ESTATE
REDWOOD ESTATE
AIR LINKS INDUSTRIAL ESTATE
96
TW5
Junction 4A
Radisson Edwardian Hotel
Marriott Hotel
Sheraton Skyline
Holiday Inn Ariel
Bowling Alley
Heathrow Airport Visitor Cen
BATH ROAD
A4
Renaissance Hotel
NORTHERN PERIMETER
HEATHROW AIRPORT (LONDON)
TERMINAL 1
TERMINAL 2
Queen's Building
Parking Express
Maintenance Area
Hangar
Perishable Handling Facility
Jurys Inn
TW4
RIVER CRANE
HEATHROW ESTATE
British Airways PLC
HEATHROW INT TRADING ESTATE
RIFLE RANGE
GREEN LANE OPEN SPACE
HATTON
HATTON CROSS
BALANCING RESERVOIR
RADIUS PARK
TW14
GREAT SOUTH WEST ROAD
A30
THE CAUSEWAY
HOUNSLOW HEATH GOLF COURSE
DONKEY WOOD
MERCURY CENTRE
Hounslow Urban Farm
115
75
76
78
79
80
81
82
83
84

SOUTHALL
UB1
UB2
UB3
TW3
TW4
TW5
MINET COUNTRY PARK
HEATHROW PURPLE PARKING
SOUTHALL RAILWAY CENTRE
BARRATT INDUSTRIAL PARK
MIDDLESEX BUSINESS CENTRE
FEATHERSTONE IND EST
SOUTHALL REC GRD
NORWOOD GREEN
TENTELOW LANE SPORTS GROUND
NORTH HYDE
AIRLINKS GOLF COURSE
Junction 3
Heston Services
Travelodge
BRITISH AIRWAYS SPORTS GROUND
PARKWAY TRADING ESTATE
Thorncliffe Hotel (Refugee Centre)
HESTON PARK
HESTON
HESTON INDUSTRIAL MALL
SUTTON PLAYING FIELD
OSTERLEY PARK HOUSE
OSTERLEY
Brentford FC Training Ground
LAMPTON
LAMPTON PARK
HOUNSLOW CIVIC CENTRE
HOUNSLOW WEST
BEAVERSFORD PARK
Cavalry Barracks
HOUNSLOW
INWOOD PARK
GREEN LANE OPEN SPACE
HOUNSLOW HEATH GOLF COURSE
HEATHROW INT TRADING ESTATE
BALANCING RESERVOIR
DONKEY WOOD
MERCURY CENTRE
CENTRAL PARK EST
THE PARKWAY
GREAT WEST ROAD
BATH ROAD
STAINES ROAD
HESTON ROAD
NORWOOD ROAD
UXBRIDGE ROAD
HIGH STREET
BROADWAY
M4
A4
A312
A3005
A3006
A315
A4127
Grand Union Canal
Yeading Brook
BW
BX
BY
BZ
CA
CB
CC
75
76
77
78
79
80
81
82
83
84
12
13
14

78
95
116

HANWELL
HANWELL CEMETERY
EALING HOSPITAL N.H.S. TRUST
W7
BRENT RIVER PARK
ELTHORNE PARK
ELTHORNE PARK EXTENSION
W13
NORTHFIELDS
LAMMAS PARK
WALPOLE PARK
PITSHANGER MANOR & GALL
Thames Valley Uni
EALING COMMON
W5
SOUTH EALING CEMETERY
LITTLE EALING
LONG WOOD (Nature Reserve)
M4
OSTERLEY PARK NT
WYKE GREEN GOLF COURSE
BOSTON MANOR HOUSE
BOSTON MANOR PARK
Junction 2
Grand Union Canal
GlaxoSmithKline
BRENTFORD
BRENTFORD BUSINESS CENTRE
WEST CROSS CENTRE
MACFARLANE SPORT FIELD
GREAT WEST ROAD
A4
A3002
A315
TW7
TW8
TW9
TW1
Brunel University (Osterley Campus)
SPRING GROVE
SYON PARK
SYON HOUSE
Battles of Brentford 1016 & 1642
Syon Reach
RIVER THAMES
KEW
ROYAL BOTANIC GARDEN
QUEEN'S COTTAGE GARDENS
ARBORETUM
PAGODA
ROYAL MID-SURREY GOLF COURSE (OLD DEER PARK)
OBSERVATORY GARDENS
OLD DEER PARK RECREATION GROUND
RICHMOND ATHLETIC GROUND
ROYAL HOSP
RICHMOND GREEN
Richmond Palace Remains
WEST MIDDLESEX UNIVERSITY HOSP
WOODLANDS
ISLEWORTH
ISLEWORTH AIT
MOGDEN SEWAGE TREATMENT WORKS
REDLEES PARK
ST. MARGARETS
TWICKENHAM ROAD
LONDON ROAD
CD
CE
CF
CG
CH
CJ
CK
75
76
77
78
79
80
81
82
83
84
79
98
117

CL
CM
CN
CP
CQ
CR
CS
80
EALING COMMON
ACTON
EAST ACTON
W5
ACTON PARK
THE VALE
SOUTHFIELDS PLAYING FIELDS
75
POPEFIELD PLAYING FIELDS
ACTON TOWN
SOUTH ACTON
BEDFORD PARK
SOUTH EALING
76
GUNNERSBURY PARK MUSEUM
W3
SOUTH EALING CEMETERY
LITTLE EALING
77
CLAYPONDS HOSP
GUNNERSBURY PARK
KENSINGTON CEMETERY
GUNNERSBURY
TURNHAM GREEN
CHISWICK COMMON
Junction 1
Chiswick Rbt
Junction 2
CHISWICK HIGH ROAD
78
TW8
KEW BRIDGE
Kew Bridge
KEW BRIDGE STEAM MUS
BRENTFORD F.C.
W4
BRENTFORD
79
BRENTFORD AIT
CHISWICK
CHISWICK HOUSE GROUNDS
CHISWICK HOUSE
OLIVER'S ISLAND
KEW
Kew Green
97
KEW PALACE
80
ROYAL
GROVE PARK
PUBLIC RECORD OFFICE
RIVER THAMES
BOTANIC GARDENS
81
KEW GARDENS
DUKE'S MEADOW
CIVIL SERVICE SPORTS GROUND
QUEEN'S COTTAGE GARDENS
KEW
DUKE'S MEADOW GOLF COURSE
82
TW9
NORTH SHEEN
NORTH SHEEN CEMETERY
HAMMERSMITH CEMETERY
Chalkers Corner
MORTLAKE
MORTLAKE HIGH ST
83
ROYAL MID-SURREY GOLF COURSE (OLD DEER PARK)
RICHMOND ATHLETIC GROUND
Manor Circus
LOWER MORTLAKE ROAD
UPPER RICHMOND ROAD WEST
Milestone Green
84
RICHMOND
EAST SHEEN
SW14
RICHMOND GREEN
118
EAST SHEEN COMMON (NT)
PALEWELL COMMON
PALEWELL PLAYING FIELDS
CL
CM
CN
CP
CQ
CR
CS

SHEPHERD'S BUSH
81
KENSINGTON
HOLLAND PARK
W11
W14
W12
W6
W8
SW5
SW6
SW13
SW15
HAMMERSMITH
EARLS COURT
CASTELNAU
BARNES
FULHAM
PARSONS GREEN
PUTNEY
WANDSWORTH
ROEHAMPTON
THE WETLANDS CENTRE
BARNES COMMON
RIVER THAMES
OLYMPIA
HOLLAND HOUSE
RAVENSCOURT PARK
BROOK GREEN
WENDELL PARK
THE STAMFORD
CHARING CROSS HOSP
QUEENS CLUB
HAMMERSMITH CEMETERY
FULHAM CEMETERY
BISHOP'S PARK
FULHAM PALACE GARDENS
HURLINGHAM PARK
WANDSWORTH PARK
BARN ELMS PLAYING FIELDS
HARROD'S SPORTS GRD
ROEHAMPTON PRIORY HOSPITAL
UXBRIDGE ROAD
GOLDHAWK ROAD
KING STREET
GREAT WEST ROAD
TALGARTH ROAD
HAMMERSMITH FLYOVER
FULHAM PALACE ROAD
LILLIE ROAD
DAWES ROAD
UPPER RICHMOND ROAD
SOUTH CIRCULAR ROAD
PUTNEY BRIDGE
KENSINGTON HIGH ST
HOLLAND ROAD
NEW KINGS RD
CT
CU
CV
CW
CX
CY
CZ
22
23
24
75
76
77
78
79
80
81
82
83
84
100
119

DA
DB
DC
DD
DE
DF
DG
82
KENSINGTON GARDENS
HYDE PARK
W8
ROUND POND
KENSINGTON PALACE
THE SERPENTINE
198
SW7
KENSINGTON
HOLLAND PARK
75
76
77
78
79
80
81
82
83
84
KENSINGTON ROAD
KENSINGTON GORE
KNIGHTSBRIDGE
ROYAL ALBERT HALL
HARRODS
SOUTH KENSINGTON
SCIENCE MUSEUM
NATURAL HISTORY MUSEUM
VICTORIA & ALBERT MUSEUM
CROMWELL ROAD
BELGRAVIA
BROMPTON
SW5
EARLS COURT
EARLS COURT EXHIBITION CENTRE
SW10
ROYAL MARSDEN HOSP
ROYAL BROMPTON HOSP
ROYAL HOSPITAL CHELSEA
SW3
WEST BROMPTON
BROMPTON CEMETERY
CHELSEA
CHELSEA & WEST. HOSP
STAMFORD BRIDGE CHELSEA FC
99
CHELSEA EMBANKMENT
BATTERSEA PARK
PARSONS GREEN
WALHAM GREEN
SANDS END
EEL BROOK COMMON
HURLINGHAM PARK
SW6
SOUTH PARK
HURLINGHAM CLUB
SW11
CLAPHAM JUNCTION
SW15
SW18
WANDSWORTH
120
26
27
28

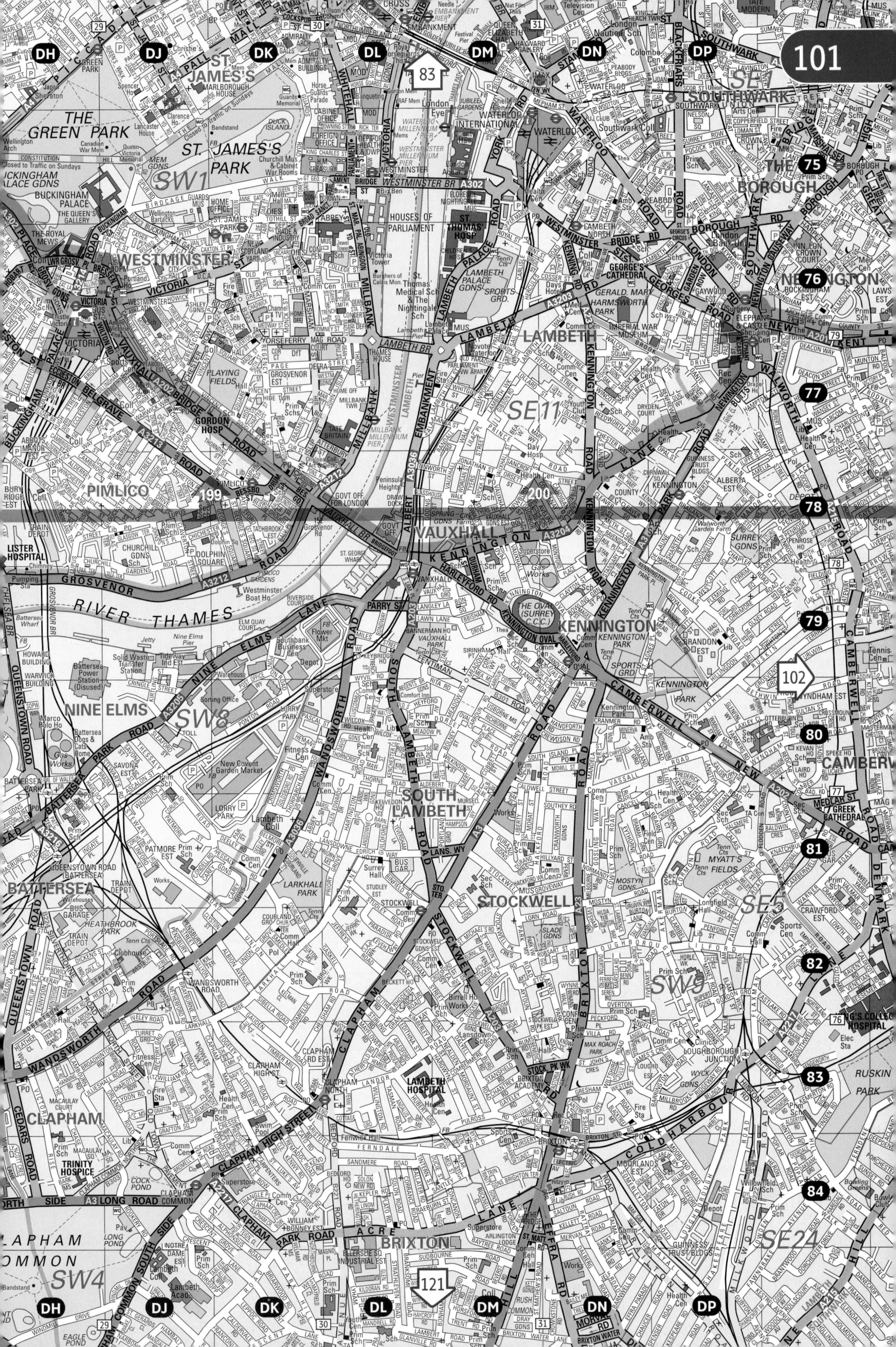

DH
DJ
DK
DL
DM
DN
DP
83
ST. JAMES'S
THE GREEN PARK
ST. JAMES'S PARK
SW1
BUCKINGHAM PALACE
WESTMINSTER
VICTORIA
HOUSES OF PARLIAMENT
ST. THOMAS' HOSP
WATERLOO
SOUTHWARK
SE1
THE BOROUGH
75
76
NEWINGTON
LAMBETH
SE11
77
PIMLICO
199
200
VAUXHALL
78
LISTER HOSPITAL
RIVER THAMES
KENNINGTON
THE OVAL (SURREY C.C.)
79
KENNINGTON PARK
102
80
NINE ELMS
SW8
New Covent Garden Market
CAMBERWELL
SOUTH LAMBETH
81
BATTERSEA
STOCKWELL
LARKHALL PARK
SE5
MYATT'S FIELDS
82
SW9
83
LAMBETH HOSPITAL
LOUGHBOROUGH JUNCTION
RUSKIN PARK
CLAPHAM
TRINITY HOSPICE
BRIXTON
84
SE24
CLAPHAM COMMON
SW4
121
DH
DJ
DK
DL
DM
DN
DP

DQ
DR
DS
DT
DU
DV
DW
84
101
122
75
76
77
78
79
80
81
82
83
84
201
202
SE1
SE11
SE17
SE5
SE15
SE22
SE24
SOUTHWARK
THE BOROUGH
NEWINGTON
WALWORTH
CAMBERWELL
PECKHAM
BERMONDSEY
WAPPING
KENNINGTON
BURGESS PARK
RUSKIN PARK
PECKHAM RYE COMMON
PECKHAM RYE PARK
SOUTHWARK PARK
SURREY GDNS
MYATT'S FIELDS
KENNINGTON PARK
LONDON BRIDGE HOSP
GUY'S HOSPITAL
KING'S COLLEGE HOSPITAL
THE MAUDSLEY HOSPITAL
DULWICH COMMUNITY HOSP
TOWER BRIDGE EXHIBITION
THE POOL
LONDON BRIDGE
TOWER BRIDGE ROAD
TOOLEY ST
JAMAICA ROAD
OLD KENT ROAD
NEW KENT ROAD
WALWORTH ROAD
CAMBERWELL ROAD
CAMBERWELL NEW ROAD
DENMARK HILL
PECKHAM ROAD
PECKHAM HIGH ST
QUEENS ROAD
RYE LANE
EAST DULWICH ROAD
LORDSHIP LANE
GROVE VALE
DOG KENNEL HILL
SOUTHWARK PARK ROAD
ROTHERHITHE NEW ROAD
BOROUGH HIGH STREET
GREAT DOVER STREET
LONG LANE
GRANGE ROAD
ALBANY ROAD
COLDHARBOUR LANE
CHAMPION HILL
NUNHEAD

ROTHERHITHE
SE16
ISLE OF DOGS
WEST INDIA DOCKS
MILLWALL
CUBITT TOWN
E14
SE10
NORTH GREENWICH
DEPTFORD
SE8
SE14
GREENWICH
GREENWICH PARK
NATIONAL MARITIME MUSEUM
SE3
BLACKHEATH
NEW CROSS
NEW CROSS GATE
ST JOHN'S
SE4
LEWISHAM
SE13
BROCKLEY
LADYWELL
HILLY FIELDS
BROCKLEY CEMETERY
LADYWELL CEMETERY
SOUTHWARK
TOWER HAMLETS
LEWISHAM
GREENWICH
85
104
123
DX
DY
DZ
EA
EB
EC
ED
75
76
77
78
79
80
81
82
83
84

LONDON
The Dome Redevelopment (Open 2007)
NORTH GREENWICH
BUS STA
Millennium Pier
Phoenix Wharf
Manhattan Wharf
Football Academy
Gas Works
RIVER THAMES
NEWHAM
GREENWICH
SE10
E16
WEST SILVERTOWN
GREENSHIELDS IND EST
LYLE PARK
PONTOON DOCK
THAMES BARRIER PARK
SILVERTOWN
THAMESIDE INDUSTRIAL EST
SILVERTOWN & LONDON CITY AIRPORT
WOOLWICH REACH
THAMES FLOOD BARRIER
Tate & Lyle Jetty
Barrier Gardens Pier
Barrier Control Building
Greenwich Yacht Club
GREENWICH PENINSULA ECOLOGY PARK
Holiday Inn Express
COUNCIL DEPOT
Cinema
Superstores
BUGSBY'S WAY
A2052
MERIDIAN TRADING ESTATE
ANCHORAGE POINT IND EST
NEW CHARLTON
CABLE TRADE PARK
GREENWICH IND EST
GREENWICH SHOPPING PARK
Stone Lake Retail Pk
MELLISH IND EST
VISITORS CEN
MARYON PARK
THE VALLEY CHARLTON ATHLETIC FC
CHILDRENS ZOO
MARYON WILSON PARK
WOOLWICH ROAD
A206
EAST GREENWICH PLEASAUNCE
WESTCOMBE PARK
Trafalgar Rowing Cen
Power Sta
The Arches Leisure Cen
Uni of Greenwich
QUEEN'S HOUSE
NATIONAL MARITIME MUSEUM
GREENWICH
GREENWICH PARK
FLAMSTEED HOUSE (Old Royal Observatory)
One Tree Hill
The Gardens
Bandstand
THE WILDERNESS (DEER PARK)
RANGER'S HOUSE
Blackheath Gate
CHARLTON
SE7
CHARLTON PARK
Charlton House
RECTORY FIELD Blackheath R.F.C.
HORNFAIR PARK
QUEEN ELIZABETH HOSPITAL
SHOOTERS HILL ROAD
A207
A2
A102
BLACKHEATH
SE3
Christ's Coll for Boys
Morden College
Clarendon Hotel
KIDBROOKE
A2213
ROCHESTER WAY RELIEF RD
SPORTS GROUND
GREENWICH CEMETERY
BLACKHEATH HOSP
BLACKHEATH PARK
SPORTS GROUNDS
FOOTBALL PITCHES
LEE
SE13
SE12
A20
LEE HIGH ROAD
ELTHAM ROAD
MANOR HOUSE GARDENS
MANOR PARK
SUTCLIFFE PARK
Athletics Track
Leisure Cen
KIDBROOKE GREEN (NAT RES)
Referral Unit
UNI OF GREENWICH ATHLETIC GRD
WELL HALL PLEASAUNCE
Lee Green
ELTHAM
A210
EE
EF
EG
EH
EJ
EK
EL
75
76
77
78
79
80
81
82
83
84
86
103
124
205

CITY AIRPORT
KING GEORGE V DOCK
EM
EN
EP
EQ
ER
ES
ET
87
Newham Coll of Further Ed
GALLIONS REACH
NEWHAM
GREENWICH
WOOLWICH FREE FERRY
WOOLWICH FOOT TUNNEL
ROYAL VICTORIA GDNS
STANDARD INDUSTRIAL ESTATE
SE28
H.M. PRISON BELMARSH
WESTERN WAY
EASTERN WAY
West Thamesmead Business Park
THAMESMEAD WEST
BROADWATER GRN
PLUMSTEAD ROAD
PLUMSTEAD HIGH STREET
WOOLWICH ARSENAL
Royal Artillery Barracks
WOOLWICH BARRACK FIELD
SE2
PLUMSTEAD GARDENS
PLUMSTEAD
PLUMSTEAD COMMON
WINN'S COMMON
SE18
WOOLWICH COMMON
Royal Military Academy
GRAND DEPOT RD
SHREWSBURY PARK
SHOOTER'S HILL GOLF COURSE
SHOOTER'S HILL
CLOTHWORKERS WOOD
WOOLWICH CEM
WOOLWICH CEMETERY
106
EAST WICKHAM
EAST WICKHAM OPEN SPACE
HILLVIEW CEMETERY
CASTLEWOOD THERAPY CENTRE
MEMORIAL HOSPITAL
ELTHAM COMMON
CASTLE WOOD
JACK WOOD
OXLEAS WOOD
OXLEAS MEADOW
SHOOTERS HILL
BELLEGROVE ROAD
WELLING
WELLING WAY
DA16
FALCONWOOD FIELD
FALCONWOOD
SHEPHERDLEAS WOOD
ELTHAM PARK NORTH
ELTHAM PARK SOUTH
ELTHAM WARREN GOLF COURSE
ELTHAM CEMETERY
Crematorium
SE9
ROCHESTER WAY
ROCHESTER WAY RELIEF ROAD
EAST ROCHESTER WAY
DA15
125
BLACKFEN
GREENWICH
BEXLEY
75
76
77
78
79
80
81
82
83
84
A205
A206
A207
A209
A2016
A117
A112
A2
A208

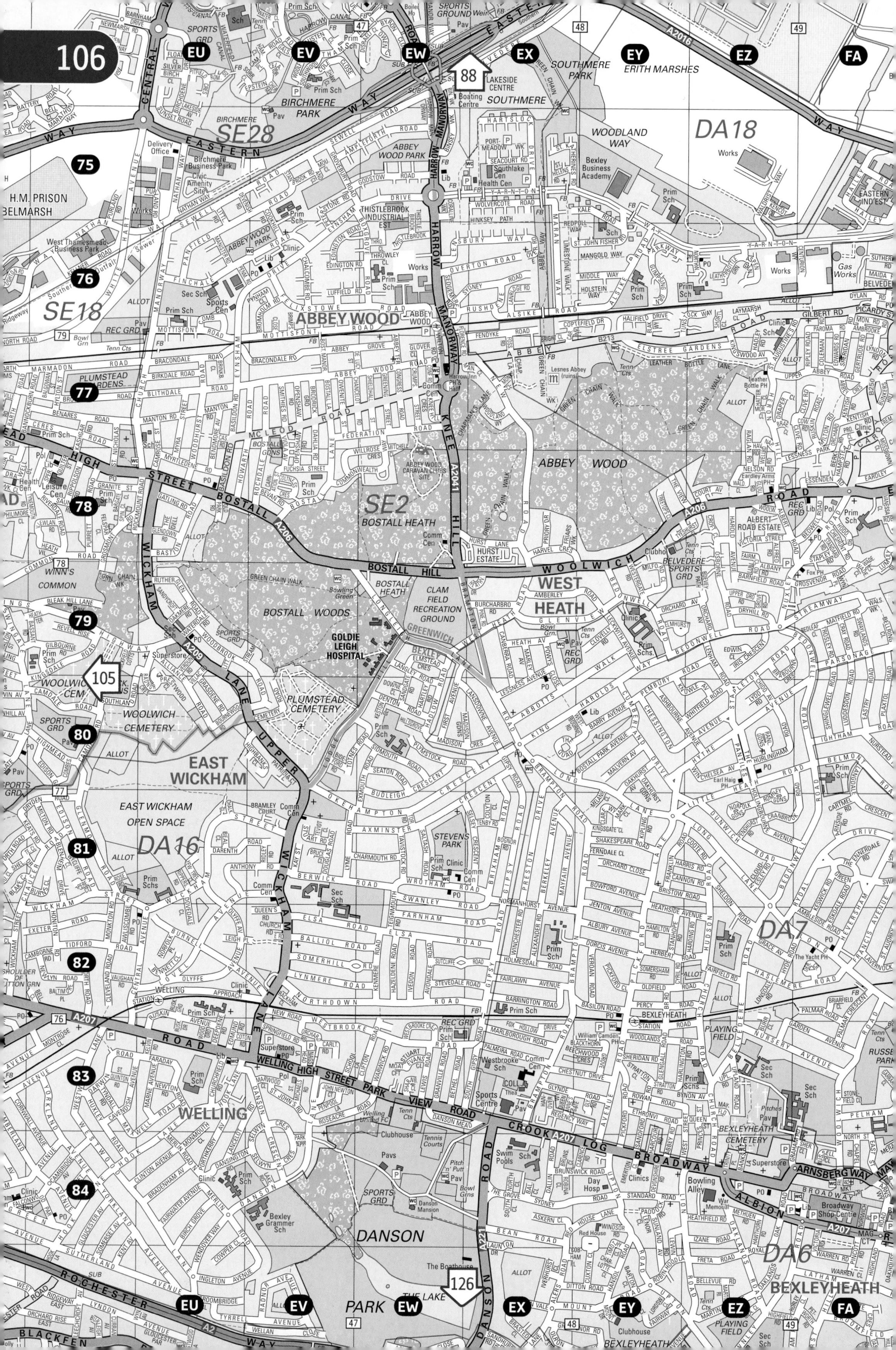
EU
EV
EW
EX
EY
EZ
FA
88
48
49
47
SOUTHMERE PARK
ERITH MARSHES
BIRCHMERE PARK
SOUTHMERE
LAKESIDE CENTRE
SE28
DA18
WOODLAND WAY
Bexley Business Academy
EASTERN WAY
75
H.M. PRISON BELMARSH
West Thamesmead Business Park
ABBEY WOOD PARK
THISTLEBROOK INDUSTRIAL EST
EASTERN IND EST
76
SE18
ABBEY WOOD
77
PLUMSTEAD GARDENS
Lesnes Abbey (ruins)
ABBEY WOOD
78
SE2
BOSTALL HEATH
HIGH STREET
BOSTALL HILL
WOOLWICH ROAD
WINN'S COMMON
WEST HEATH
79
BOSTALL WOODS
GOLDIE LEIGH HOSPITAL
CLAM FIELD RECREATION GROUND
BELVEDERE SPORTS GRD
ALBERT ROAD ESTATE
105
WOOLWICH CEM
WOOLWICH CEMETERY
PLUMSTEAD CEMETERY
80
EAST WICKHAM
EAST WICKHAM OPEN SPACE
DA16
81
STEVENS PARK
82
DA7
WELLING
83
BEXLEYHEATH
BEXLEYHEATH CEMETERY
CROOK LOG
BROADWAY
84
DANSON
DANSON PARK
THE LAKE
126
DA6
BEXLEYHEATH
Bexley Grammer Sch
ROCHESTER WAY
BLACKFEN
A2
A206
A207
A209
A2041
A221
A2016
B213

RAINHAM MARSHES
JENNINGTREE POINT LIGHTHOUSE
FB
FC
FD
FE
FF
FG
FH
50
51
52
89
Depots
Jetty
Works
Wharf
BELVEDERE INDUSTRIAL ESTATE
Pier
ERITH REACH
Depot
RM13
75
WENNINGTON MARSHES
EASTERN WY
ANDERSON WAY
MULBERRY
THAMESMEAD SPINE RD
CHURCH MANORWAY INDUSTRIAL ESTATE
CRABTREE MANORWAY IND EST
BRONZE AGE WAY
Sludge Pipeline
Erith Oil Works
76
RIVER THAMES
FREIGHTMASTER ESTATE
Warehouse
HELIPAD
Coldharbour Point
79
HAVERING
THURROCK
77
DA17
BELVEDERE
FRANK'S PARK
Bexley Coll
Trinity Sch
PLAYING FIELD
HAVERING
BEXLEY
ERITH RANDS
A2016
Landing Stage
Chalk Fm Wharf
Erith Deep Wharf Jetty
78
Crayford
Works
EUROPA TRADING ESTATE
Swim Pool
Lib & Mus
Bexley Coll
LESSNESS HEATH
Atlas Trade Park
A206
ERITH
FRASER ROAD
WHARFSIDE CLOSE
Superstore
Pier
The Saltings
DAYTON
ERITH CEMETERY
Erith Riverside
Health Cen
Works
Concrete Works
Sailing Club
DARENT INDUSTRIAL PARK
QUEEN'S ROAD
CHRISTCHURCH AV
CRESCENT
MANOR ROAD
MANFORD IND EST
ANCHOR BAY IND EST
79
MONASTERY
ERITH & DISTRICT HOSP
Prim Sch
Squash Club
NUMBERLAND HEATH
REC GRD
Sports Centre
ERITH REC GRD
ERITH STADIUM
Erith Town F.C.
BILTON RD
108
Works
LAMB
80
ALLOT
DA8
THE CHURCH TRADING EST
Prim Schs
LESNEY FARM ESTATE
Sec Sch
NORTHUMBERLAND HEATH
Works
NORTHEND TRD EST
SLADE GREEN
POWER IND EST
Lib
Clinic
Comm Cen
The Pheasant PH
COV RES
Prim Sch
NORTH END ROAD
A206
SPORTS GROUND
SPORTS GRD
Tenn Cts
Clubho
MOAT
Howbury Farm
81
CRAYFORD MARSHES
BURSTED WOOD
SLADE GREEN
HOWBURY LANE REC GRDS
RAIL DEPOT
The Grange
82
EVERSLEY AVENUE
BARNEHURST
PARKSIDE AVENUE
OPTIMA PARK
A220
BARNEHURST
Pav
SPORTS GROUND
BARNEHURST GOLF COURSE
Clubhouse
Victoria Scott Court
Chemical Works
76
Chemical Works
BEXLEY
DARTFORD
83
Waste Reception Centre
A2000
THAMES ROAD
Perry Street Farm
Fire Sta
Amb Sta
BUS GAR
MARTENS GROVE PARK
SPORTS GRD
Bowls Club
Adult Ed Cen
Clubhouse
BAKERS FIELD
DA1
Crayside Industrial Est
BOB
Works
SWAN BUSINESS PARK
84
The Woolwich
MARTENS GROVE PARK
SPORTS GRD
BURIAL GRD
Prim Sch
BARNES CRAY
BURNHAM
WATLING STREET
A207
Gas Works
Special Sch
Prim Sch
SHENSTONE PARK
PERRY STREET
CRAYFORD
CRAYFORD MARSHES
River Cray
Stanham Farm
ALLOT
Prim Sch
SPORTS GROUND
Sec Sch
BIGS HILL WOOD
127
ACORN INDUSTRIAL PARK
Stanham River
GRAVEL HILL
LONDON ROAD (WATLING ST)
Bourne Ind Pk
ROMAN WAY
CRAYFORD
REC GRD
Pav

FR
FS
FT
FU
FV
FW
FX
57
58
59
91
HANGMAN'S WOOD
BRANNETT'S WOOD
MARDYKE WOODS
FIELDS OF PEACE
Junction 30
BRICKBARN WOOD
COMBE WOOD
LOW WELL WOOD
A13
ARENA ESSEX RACEWAY
KARTING CEN
SPORTS GRD
LAKESIDE COACH PARK
PILGRIMS LANE CARAVAN PARK
75
CHAFFORD HUNDRED
76
RM16
WARREN GORGE
Thurrock Services
Travelodge
ARTERIAL ROAD
A1306
WEST THURROCK ARTERIAL ROAD NORTH
Premier Travel Inn
Fitness Cen
BUS & COACH STA
Superstore
SHIP LANE CARAVAN SITE
Thurrock FC
Causeway Bri
Mar Dyke Farm
Thurrock Hotel
Junction 31
PURFLEET
Premier Travel Inn
Cinema
Tunnel Estate
ALEXANDRA LAKE
Lakeside
Superstores
Watersport Centre
B186
A126
LION GORGE
77
Oil Depot
Warehouse
Works
West Thurrock
WATERGLADE INDUSTRIAL PK
FROGMORE ESTATE
Distribution Centre
STONEHOUSE LANE
M25
WEST THURROCK WAY
Sec Sch
Sports Hall
South Stifford
MAGNET ESTATE
78
MOTHERWELL WAY
CEM
SPORTS GRD
Formula 1 Hotel
Ibis Hotel
LONDON ROAD
LYNDALE ESTATE
REC GRD
79
110
Ford Distribution Depot
LORRY PARK
WILDLIFE SANCTUARY
OLIVER ROAD
WEST THURROCK MARSHES
RM20
80
Chemical Works
Electricity Sub Station
CANTERBURY WAY
A282
Oil Storage Depot
THURROCK
DARTFORD
QUEEN ELIZABETH II BRIDGE
TUNNEL
81
ST. CLEMENT'S OR FIDDLER'S REACH
DA11
82
STONENESS LIGHTHOUSE
RIVER THAMES
83
SWANSCOMBE MARSHES
DA10
Offices
Warehouse
Campanile Hotel
THAMES EUROPORT
DA2
CROSSWAYS BOULEVARD
NEWTONS COURT
Johnson's Wharf
DA9
84
HIGH STREET
B255
Superstore
Travelodge
STONE CROSSING
Stone
129
LONDON ROAD
A226
Greenhithe
The George & Dragon PH

FY
FZ
GA
GB
GC
GD
GE
75
76
77
78
79
80
81
82
83
84
109
130
61
62
63
77
76
78
79
FIELDS OF PEACE
The Dog & Partridge PH
Stifford Interchange
Pumping Sta
Hogg Lane Roundabout
SPORTS GROUND
THURROCK COMMUNITY HOSPITAL
RM16
THURROCK ARTERIAL ROAD NORTH STIFFORD
A13
A1012
PILGRIMS CARAVAN PK
CHAFFORD HUNDRED
Gas Works
ELIZABETH ROAD
Prim Sch
Amb Sta
Fire Sta
Comm Cen
Health Cen
The Sandmartin PH
WARREN GORGE
DEVONSHIRE ROAD
A126
Badgers Mere
HOGG LANE
LION GORGE
Oil Depot
GRAYS RM17
TA Cen
Works
Kingfisher Height
South Stifford
LONDON ROAD
Superstores
Superstore
Gas Works
MAIDS CROWN RD
ORSETT ROAD
BUS STA
CIVIC OFFICES
CEM
STANLEY RD
CLAREN RD
Thameside Comp
GRAYS PARK
Adult Ed Cen
EAST THURROCK RD
BROADWAY
DOCK ROAD
Sec Sch
Treetops Sch
Med Cen
PALMERS AV
A1013
SOUTHEND ROAD
LODGE LANE
Little Thurrock
Sockett's Heath
STANFORD
THURROCK ATHLETICS STADIUM
KING GEORGE'S FIELD
Blackshots Leisure Centre
Thurrock R.F.C.
HANGMAN'S WOOD
GRAYS NEW CEMETERY
Rookery Hill
GLOBE IND ESTATES
SPORTS GRD
Wharf PH
RM20
Thurrock Yacht Club
Slipway
Grays Beach Riverside Park
The Beach
MANOR WAY IND EST
LITTLE THURROCK MARSHES
Capstan Centre
Superstore
Warehouses
Finnish Terminal
Grain Terminal
A1089
ST ANDREWS RD
DOCK RD
RIVER THAMES
THURROCK
DARTFORD
BROADNESS LIGHTHOUSE
Radar Mast
NORTHFLEET HOPE
BROADNESS SALT MARSHES
Pylon
Pier
Bell Wharf
Jetty
SWANSCOMBE MARSHES
DA11
DA10
BOTANY MARSHES
DARTFORD
GRAVESHAM
KENT
Mole
Lock
PORT OF TILBURY
LOWER ROAD
MANOR WAY
LONDON ROAD
A226
GALLEY HILL ROAD
RIFLE RANGE
The George & Dragon PH
EBBSFLEET INDUSTRIAL ESTATE
ROBINS CREEK
Northfleet Hope
Fire Sta
Tenn Cts
Works

Orsett Heath
CHADWELL ST. MARY
ORSETT GOLF COURSE
GRAVEL PIT
RAINBOW WOOD
ASHEN SHAW
OLD HOUSE WOOD
Linford
SS17
Muckingford
West Tilbury
Low Street
TILBURY MARSHES
Hob Hill
Broom Hill
Hutts Hill
SHROVE HILL WOOD
HALLHILL COMMON
PARSONAGE COMMON
RM18
WEST TILBURY MARSHES
WALTHAM COMMON
EAST TILBURY MARSH
TILBURY
KING GEORGE'S FIELD
Tilbury Energy & Environmental Centre
Tilbury B Power Station
Tilbury Fort
MOAT
Sewage Works
Riverside Business Centre
Fortress Distribution Park
Riverside Rail Terminal
London International Cruise Terminal
Tidal Basin
CUSTOM HOUSE
Thurrock & Basildon College
TERRELS HEATH
Chadwell Place
Tilbury FC
TILBURY STADIUM (KARTING)
RIVER THAMES
THURROCK
GRAVESHAM
GRAVESEND
REACH
131
GF GG GH GJ GK GL GM
75 76 77 78 79 80 81 82 83 84
64 65 66

AS
AT
AU
AV
AW
AX
AY
92
132
85
86
87
88
89
90
91
92
93
94
74
73
72
71
98
99
00
ALBERT ROAD
A308
ROYAL GARDENS
Glasshouses
NEW CUT
Ham Bridge
Manor Farm
Sunnymeads
Sailing Club
Sludge Beds
Filter Beds
HAM ISLAND
Weir
Clayhall Farm
GREAT
PARK
REVIEW GROUND
Battle Bourne
CLAYHALL LANE
MOAT
Tileplace Farm
PETERSHILL COPSE
MILLERS LANE
Peter's Hill
NEWMEADOWS PLANTATION
OLD WINDSOR
STRAIGHT ROAD
CHURCH ROAD
ALLOT
Anglo Saxon Palace (site of)
The Priory
Priory Stables
St. George's Farm
Old Windsor Lock
The Manor
REMENHAM PARK
Old Ferry House
FRIARY ISLAND
MANOR FARM ESTATE
WHARF ROAD
OUSELEY ROAD
WELLEY ROAD
WINDSOR ROAD
B376
Prim Sch
THE GREEN
Sec Sch
The Oxford Blue PH
CRIMP HILL
Mount Place
MOAT
BEAR'S RAILS
RUSH POND
CEM
Windsor Pk Vw Mansion House
Woodside Farm
Med Cen
Prim Sch
Burfield Lodge
RIVER THAMES
The Bells of Ouseley PH
THE EMBANKMENT
B3021
PRINCE OF WALES POND
OLD WINDSOR WOOD
SL4
BEAUMONT HOUSE CONFERENCE CENTRE
War Memorial
Runnymede House
PATS CROFT EYOT
MAGNA CARTA ISLAND
MAGNA CARTA LANE
WITHY BED
DUKE OF YORK PLANTATION
LIDDELL PLANTATION
OLD COVERT
SPORTS GROUND
Priest Hill House
COOPER'S HILL SLOPES NT
RUNNYMEDE
South Lodge Farm
Tennis Courts
MARCHIONESS OF HERTFORD PLANTATION
PRINCESS CHRISTIAN PLANTATION
PRINCE CONSORTS PLANTATION
SULTAN PLANTATION
WILD BOAR ENCLOSURE
WINDSOR & MAIDENHEAD
SURREY
Home Farm
Sch
John F Kennedy Memorial
Magna Carta Monument
Benedictine Nunnery (remains)
A328
Snow Hill
PRINCE OF WALES PLANTATION
QUEEN VICTORIA'S PLANTATION
Spring Hill
GORE PLANTATION
Beech Hill
Ridgemead House
Priest Hill Farm
OAK LANE
PRIEST HILL
Cookes Hill
Park Place
RIDGEMEAD ROAD
Brunel University, Runnymede Campus
Cooper's Hill Slopes
Main Gate Lodges
Bishops Gate
The Dell
BISHOPSGATE ROAD
Fox & Hounds PH
Pumping Sta
COV RES
Chapel Lodge
Royal Lodge
Bishopsgate House
Dell Park Farm
Round Oak
Castle Hill
COOPERS HILL LANE
COOPER'S HILL COPPICE
Air Forces Memorial
CONSERVATORY COVERT
OX POND
GREENBROOM COVERT
KING GEORGE VI CORONATION GROVE
SPORTS GROUND
Royal Holloway Coll (Hall of Residence)
RUNNYMEDE PARK
Chaplain's Lodge
The Vinery
Tennis Courts
COW POND
Savill Court Hotel
ENGLEFIELD GREEN
Castle Hill Farm
CUMBERLAND LODGE
Englefield Green
The Barley Mow PH
TW20
Runnymede Park
Park Close
PROSPECT LANE
MIDDLE HILL
BARLEY MOW ROAD
WILDERNESS
Cumberland Gate
CHAPEL WOOD
The Sun PH
KINGS LANE
WICK LANE
Glasshouse
Parkside House
Meadow Cottage Farm
BOND STREET
MAGNA ROAD
Health Cen
VICTORIA STREET
PO
Hall
Glasshouses
A30
Ripley Springs
THE SAVILL GARDENS
WINDSOR
GREAT
PARK
SL5
Temple Hill
SPORTS GROUND
ST. JUDE'S CEMETERY
ST. JUDE'S ROAD
Prim Sch
Sec Sch
EGHAM HILL
University of London Royal Holloway College
SMITH'S LAWN
ALDER COVERT
FUZZY CLUMP
CORK CLUMP
Cumberland Obelisk
OBELISK POND
Parkwood
Lubbock House
PRUNE HILL
Prince Consort's Statue
SCARLETOAK PLANTATION
Egham Wick
WICK ROAD
LONDON ROAD
FRANK'S PLANTATION
POLO GROUND
Flying Barn
EGHAM WICK PLANTATION
Breakheart Hill
Pav
WEEDEN'S FIELD
JOHNSON'S POND
HEATHER GARDEN
DARKHOLE CLUMP
Eton Bridge
BAKEHAM LANE

93
WRAYSBURY
RESERVOIR
TW19
SL3
Wraysbury
Junction 14
HILLINGDON AIRPORT
M25
STANWELL MOOR
SPORTS GROUND
RUBBISH DUMP
KING GEORGE VI RESERVOIR
GRAVEL PIT
STAINES MOOR
HERON LAKE
Clubhouse
Junction 13
Hythe End
RUNNYMEDE PLEASURE GROUND
RUNNYMEDE NT
WINDSOR ROAD
QUEENSMEAD LAKE
ASHBY REC GRD
114
STAINES
Pooley Green
EGHAM
Egham Hythe
TW18
Thorpe Lea
THORPE LEA REC GRD
BISHOPS WAY REC GRD
Mayflower Nurseries
Proctor & Gamble Laboratories
Milton Park
Great Fosters Hotel
STAINES PARK MINI RAILWAY
Staines Town FC
Sweep's Bridge
Penton Hook Farm
TRUSS'S ISLAND
133
Crabtree Corner

94
113
134
BG
BH
BJ
BK
BL
BM
BN
05
06
07
85
86
87
88
89
90
91
92
93
94
74
73
72
71
HILLINGDON
AIRPORT WAY
A3113
STANWELL MOOR
SPORTS GROUND
Hall
PO
STANWELL MOOR RD
SOUTHERN PERIMETER RD
HILLINGDON
SOUTHERN PERIMETER
SPELTHORNE
SURREY
Vermeulens Garden Centre
Warehouse
HORTON RD
Hithermoor Farm
CHELTENHAM
HAWS LANE
Lower Mill Farm
River Colne
GRAVEL PIT
Bonehead Ditch
KING
GEORGE VI
RESERVOIR
TW19
STAINES
RESERVOIRS
STANWELL MOOR ROAD
A3044
Staines Reservoirs Aqueduct
CARGO TERMINAL
CARGO TERMINAL
BRITISH AIRWAYS CARGO CENTRE
Works
SHORT ROAD
SOUTHAMPTON ROAD W
SOUTHAMPTON ROAD E
SOUTHERN PERIMETER ROAD
BEDFONT ROAD
Virgin Atlantic Cargo
BLACKBURN TRADING ESTATE
CAMGATE CENTRE
Animal Quarantine Station
Mentone Farm
SANCTUARY RD
Cargo Service Centre
Esso West London Oil Terminal
PARK ROAD
B378
HIGH ST
STANWELL
Prim Sch
REC GRD
CEM
ALLOT
Health Cen
Lib
TENN CTS
RECREATION GROUND
SPORTS GRD
Pavs
Pav
HADFIELD ROAD
FALCON DRIVE
CLYDE
HOLYWELL WAY
KINGSWAY
VIOLA AVENUE
Superstore
BURIAL GROUND
ASHFORD HOSPITAL
Fire Sta
SPORTS GROUND
Homers Farm
Warehouse
St George's Nursery
A30
LONDON ROAD
STAINES BYPASS
New Inn Farm
Hengrove Farm
KENILWORTH ROAD
CUMBERLAND ROAD
REC GROUND
STATION CRESCENT
Clinic
Sec Sch
Sch
ASHFORD
Coll
Lib
Pol
Comm Cen
Prim Sch
Tenn Club
STAINES CEM
SHORTWOOD POND
SHORTWOOD COMMON
Shortwood Farm
H.M. Prison Bronzefield
River Ash
Crooked Billet Roundabout
North Thames House
STAINES
Superstores
Elmsleigh Centre
BUS STA
Thames Lodge
Boathouse
CHURCH ROAD
CHESTERFIELD ROAD
WOODTHORPE ROAD
FORDBRIDGE PARK
Ford Bridge
KINGSTON ROAD
ASHFORD MANOR GOLF COURSE
Clubhouse
Electricity Station
GRAVEL PIT
TW17
QUEEN MARY
TW18
ASHFORD ROAD
SPORTS GROUND
COUNCIL OFF.
Leisure Cen
Health Cen
Clinic
Sec Sch
STAINES PARK MINI RAILWAY
COMMERCIAL ROAD
LONDON ROAD
WHEATSHEAF LANE
Clubhouse
Staines Town FC
Sweep's Bridge
Penton Hook Farm
SPORTS GROUND
Clubhouse
Prim Sch
REC GRD
RUNNYMEDE
A320
TRUSS'S ISLAND
THAMES PATH
FISHING TEMPLE
TEMPLE GARDENS
Sweep's Ditch

HATTON
TW6
TERMINAL 4
TW14
BEDFONT RECREATION GROUND
HATTON CEM
EAST BEDFONT
BEDFONT LAKES COUNTRY PARK
H.M. Young Offenders Institution & Remand Centre
LOWER FELTHAM
FELTHAM
FELTHAM ARENAS
GLEBELANDS PLAYING FIELDS
BEDFONT LANE REC GRD
GROSVENOR PARK
FELTHAMHILL
KING GEORGE'S FIELD
LAKESIDE SPORTS GROUND
TW15
TW13
TW16
ASHFORD COMMON WATER TREATMENT WORKS
KEMPTON PARK RACECOURSE
Junction 1
STAINES ROAD
GREAT SOUTH WEST ROAD
HARLINGTON ROAD WEST
CHERTSEY ROAD
HOUNSLOW HEATH GOLF COURSE
95
116
135

BW
BX
BY
BZ
CA
CB
CC
96
HOUNSLOW
TW3
TW4
HOUNSLOW HEATH
HOUNSLOW HEATH GOLF COURSE
DONKEY WOOD
TW14
85
86
87
88
89
90
91
92
93
94
74
73
72
71
115
FELTHAM
WHITTON
BOROUGH CEMETERY
HEATHFIELD REC GRD
TWICKENHAM CEMETERY
CRANE PARK
Crematorium
Sorting Office
SPORTS GROUND
Recreation Centre
HANWORTH PARK
TW13
Hanworth Park House
FELTHAM BUSINESS COMPLEX
HANWORTH TRADING ESTATE
Apex Retail Park
TWICKENHAM PARK GOLF CENTRE
FULWELL PARK
FULWELL GOLF COURSE
HANWORTH
TW12
Hampton Community Coll
PLAYING FIELD
KEMPTON PARK RESERVOIRS
Staines Reservoirs Aqueduct
TWICKENHAM R.F.C. Clubhouse
HALF MOON COVERT
KEMPTON PARK
RACECOURSE
TW16
CARLISLE PARK
HAMPTON
KINGSWAY BUSINESS PARK
ST CLARE BUSINESS PARK
Pantile Bridge
Open Air Pool
136
12
13
14
A315
A314
A316
A312
A313
A305
A311
A244
B358
STAINES ROAD
UXBRIDGE ROAD
HANWORTH ROAD
HAMPTON ROAD WEST
GREAT CHERTSEY ROAD
CHERTSEY RD
TWICKENHAM RD
HARLINGTON ROAD WEST
HARLINGTON ROAD EAST
HOUNSLOW ROAD
HIGH STREET

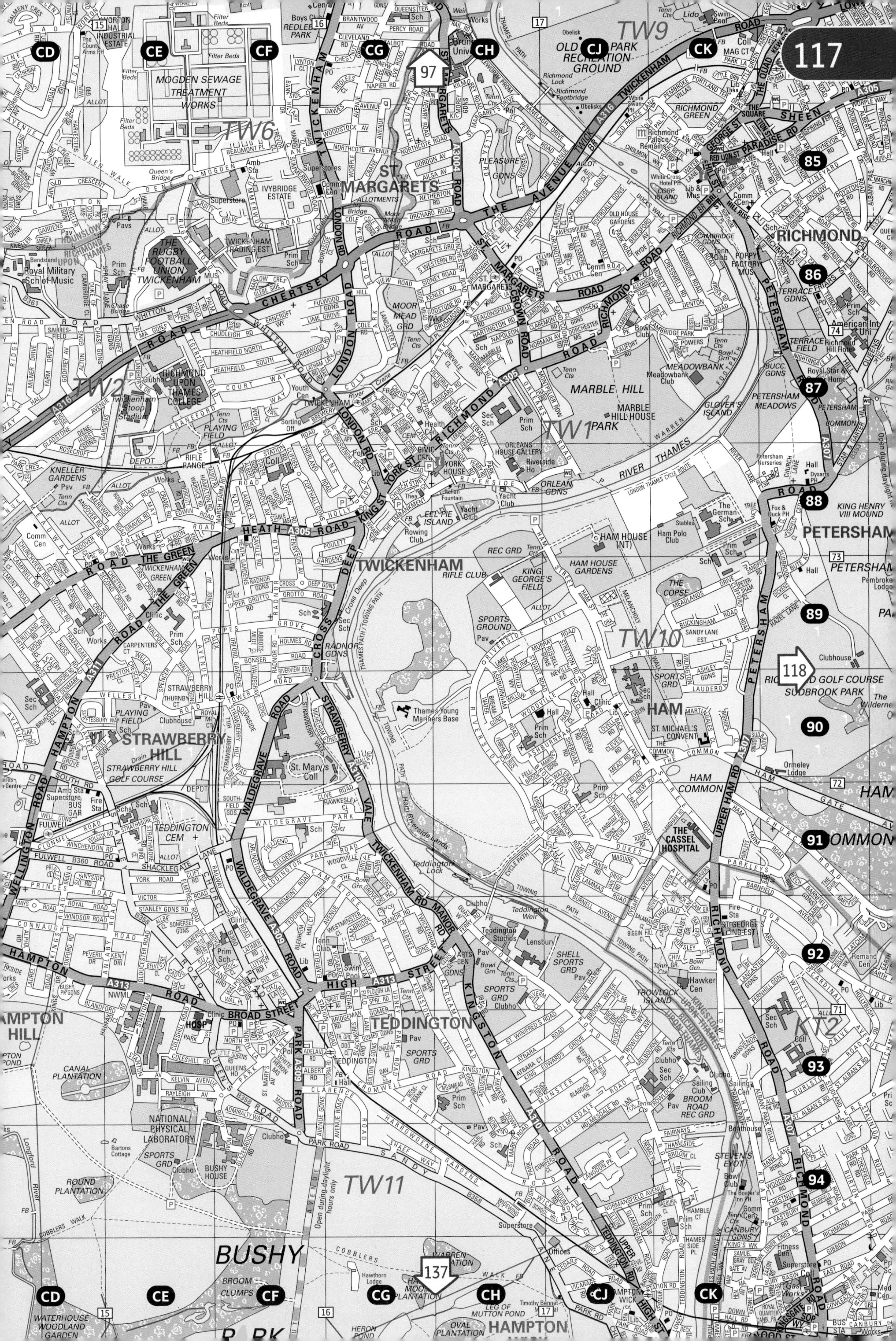
CD
CE
CF
CG
CH
CJ
CK
TW9
OLD DEER PARK RECREATION GROUND
MOGDEN SEWAGE TREATMENT WORKS
TW6
97
ST. MARGARETS
IVYBRIDGE ESTATE
THE RUGBY FOOTBALL UNION TWICKENHAM
TWICKENHAM TRADING EST
Royal Military Sch of Music
HOUNSLOW
RICHMOND UPON THAMES
RICHMOND
RICHMOND GREEN
85
86
87
88
89
90
91
92
93
94
TW2
RICHMOND UPON THAMES COLLEGE
Twickenham Stoop Stadium
MARBLE HILL PARK
MARBLE HILL HOUSE
TW1
ORLEANS HOUSE GALLERY
YORK HOUSE
EEL PIE ISLAND
RIVER THAMES
PETERSHAM MEADOWS
GLOVER'S ISLAND
MEADOWBANK
PETERSHAM
KING HENRY VIII MOUND
HAM HOUSE (NT)
HAM HOUSE GARDENS
KING GEORGE'S FIELD
TWICKENHAM
TWICKENHAM RIFLE CLUB
KNELLER GARDENS
TWICKENHAM GREEN
TW10
HAM
ST. MICHAEL'S CONVENT
HAM COMMON
118
RICHMOND GOLF COURSE
SUDBROOK PARK
Thames Young Mariners Base
STRAWBERRY HILL
STRAWBERRY HILL GOLF COURSE
St. Mary's Coll
TEDDINGTON CEM
Ham Riverside Lands
Teddington Lock
THE CASSEL HOSPITAL
Teddington Weir
SHELL SPORTS GRD
TROWLOCK ISLAND
KT2
TEDDINGTON
HAMPTON HILL
CANAL PLANTATION
NATIONAL PHYSICAL LABORATORY
BUSHY HOUSE
ROUND PLANTATION
TW11
BUSHY
BROOM CLUMPS
WARREN PLANTATION
137
HAMPTON WICK
HAMPTON
LEG OF MUTTON POND
OVAL PLANTATION
HERON POND
WATERHOUSE WOODLAND GARDEN
BROOM ROAD REC GRD
Open during daylight hours only

RICHMOND PARK
RICHMOND
PETERSHAM
HAM
HAM COMMON
EAST SHEEN
SW14
TW10
KT2
COOMBE
East Sheen Common (NT)
East Sheen Cemetery
Richmond Cemetery
Pesthouse Common
Palewell Common
Palewell Playing Fields
Petersham Meadows
Glover's Island
Richmond Golf Course Sudbrook Park
Ham Common
Coombe Hill Golf Course
Coombe Wood Golf Course
Kingston University (Coombe Martin)
Kingston University (Kingston Hill)
Kingston Uni (Dorich House)
The Royal Ballet Sch White Lodge
Pembroke Lodge
Isabella Plantation
Pen Ponds
Sidmouth Wood
Spanker's Hill Wood
Polo Field
98
117
138
CL
CM
CN
CP
CQ
CR
CS
85
86
87
88
89
90
91
92
93
94

119
PUTNEY
WANDSWORTH
ROEHAMPTON
SW15
PUTNEY HEATH
ROEHAMPTON GOLF COURSE
QUEEN MARY'S UNI HOSP
ROEHAMPTON PRIORY HOSPITAL
ROYAL HOSPITAL
Tibbet's Corner
SOUTHFIELDS
SW18
WIMBLEDON PARK
ALL ENGLAND LAWN TENNIS & CROQUET CLUB
SW19
PUTNEY VALE CEMETERY
PUTNEY VALE
WIMBLEDON
COMMON
LONDON SCOTTISH GOLF COURSE
ROYAL WIMBLEDON GOLF COURSE
CANNIZARO PARK
PARKSIDE HOSPITAL
WOLFSON MED. REHAB CENTRE
COPSE HILL
SW20
COTTENHAM PARK
MERTON
RICHMOND PARK GOLF COURSE
99
120
139
CT
CU
CV
CW
CX
CY
CZ
85
86
87
88
89
90
91
92
93
94

120
DA
DB
DC
DD
DE
DF
DG
100
119
140
WANDSWORTH
Wandsworth Town
SOUTHFIELDS
EARLSFIELD
SUMMERSTOWN
WIMBLEDON PARK
SOUTH WIMBLEDON
MERTON
COLLIER'S WOOD
TOOTING GRAVENEY
UPPER TOOTING
BALHAM
SW11
SW17
SW18
SW19
WANDSWORTH COMMON
H.M. PRISON WANDSWORTH
WANDSWORTH CEMETERY
CENTRAL LONDON GOLF CENTRE
SPRINGFIELD HOSPITAL
STREATHAM CEMETERY
LAMBETH CEMETERY
WIMBLEDON CEMETERY
WIMBLEDON STADIUM
ST. GEORGE'S HOSPITAL
LONDON ROAD CEMETERY
FIGGE'S MARSH
BOLINGBROKE HOSP
KING GEORGE'S PARK
SPENCER PARK
GARRATT GREEN
GARRATT PARK
Tooting Bec
Tooting Broadway
CLAPHAM JUNCTION
CLAPHAM COMMON
TRINITY ROAD
GARRATT LANE
MERTON ROAD
DURNSFORD ROAD
HAYDONS ROAD
MERTON HIGH STREET
MITCHAM ROAD
TOOTING HIGH STREET
UPPER TOOTING ROAD
BALHAM HIGH ROAD
WEST HILL
KINGSTON ROAD
BROADWAY
PLOUGH LANE
BURNTWOOD LANE
MERANTUN WAY
WESTERN ROAD

DH
DJ
DK
DL
DM
DN
DP
101
CLAPHAM COMMON
SW4
BRIXTON
CLAPHAM PARK
SW2
SE24
BROCKWELL PARK
HERNE HILL
STREATHAM HILL
SE21
TULSE HILL
PALACE ROAD ESTATE
TOOTING BEC COMMON
TOOTING GRAVENEY COMMON
STREATHAM PARK
STREATHAM
SE27
WEST NORWOOD
WEST NORWOOD CEMETERY
122
STREATHAM COMMON
SW16
NORWOOD GROVE RECREATION GROUND
NORWOOD NEW TOWN
SE19
STREATHAM VALE
BIGGIN WOOD
NORBURY PARK
NORBURY
141
85
86
87
88
89
90
91
92
93
94
H.M. PRISON BRIXTON
BALHAM
CLAPHAM SOUTH
TULSE HILL ESTATE
SACKVILLE ESTATE
WEIR ESTATE
OAKLANDS ESTATE

DQ
DR
DS
DT
DU
DV
DW
102
85
86
87
88
89
90
91
92
93
94
121
142
SE24
SE22
SE21
SE27
SE26
SE19
SE20
HERNE HILL
EAST DULWICH
DULWICH
TULSE HILL
WEST DULWICH
WEST NORWOOD
UPPER SYDENHAM
SYDENHAM
NORWOOD
NORWOOD NEWTOWN
UPPER NORWOOD
PENGE
BROCKWELL PARK
PECKHAM RYE COMMON
PECKHAM RYE PARK
CAMBERWELL OLD CEMETERY
DULWICH PARK
DULWICH & SYDENHAM HILL GOLF COURSE
SYDENHAM HILL WOOD NATURE RESERVE
DULWICH WOOD
WEST NORWOOD CEMETERY
NORWOOD PARK
CRYSTAL PALACE PARK
CRYSTAL PALACE NATIONAL SPORTS CENTRE
HERNE HILL VELODROME
SOUTH BANK UNIVERSITY SPORTS GROUND
DULWICH COMMUNITY HOSP
DULWICH PICTURE GALL
HORNIMAN MUS
BELAIR PARK
BIG WOOD
BEAULIEU HEIGHTS
SYLVAN ESTATE
HALF MOON LANE
DULWICH ROAD
CROXTED ROAD
LORDSHIP LANE
DULWICH COMMON
THURLOW PARK ROAD
NORWOOD ROAD
KNIGHTS HILL
CENTRAL HILL
BEULAH HILL
WESTOW HILL
ANERLEY HILL
ANERLEY ROAD
CRYSTAL PALACE PARADE
CRYSTAL PALACE PARK ROAD
WESTWOOD HILL
KIRKDALE
DARTMOUTH ROAD
LONDON ROAD
COLLEGE ROAD
SYDENHAM HILL
CHURCH ROAD
DULWICH WOOD PK
A205
A214
A215
A216
A2199
A212
A234
A2214
33
34
35
71
72
73
74

LEWISHAM
HILLY FIELDS
103
BROCKLEY
SE4
BROCKLEY CEMETERY
LADYWELL CEMETERY
LADYWELL
UNIVERSITY HOSPITAL LEWISHAM
LEWISHAM PARK
SE13
MANOR PARK
MANOR HOUSE GARDENS
HITHER GREEN
HONOR OAK SPORTS GRD
CAMBERWELL NEW CEMETERY
HONOR OAK PARK
GUY'S U.M.D.S. ATHLETIC GRD
LADYWELL FIELDS
Ladywell Arena
LADYWELL CENTRE
BLYTHE HILL FIELDS
BROCKLEY HILL PARK
MOUNTFIELD PARK PLAYING FIELDS
SE23
BROWNHILL ROAD
S CIRCULAR ROAD
CATFORD
CATFORD BRIDGE
FOREST HILL
STANSTEAD ROAD
SE6
FORSTER MEMORIAL PARK
BELL GREEN
BELLINGHAM
SOUTHEND
MAYOW PARK
LOWER SYDENHAM
HOME PARK
SOUTHEND PARK
BR1
124
BECKENHAM PLACE PARK
GOLF COURSE
SUMMERHOUSE HILL WOOD
LEWISHAM BOROUGH SPORTS GROUND
MIDLAND BANK SPORTS GROUND
WARREN AVE PLAYING FIELDS
NEW BECKENHAM
BR3
KENT C.C.C.
CRYSTAL PALACE FC TRAINING GROUND
ALEXANDRA REC GRD
CATOR PARK
BECKENHAM
BR2
SHORTLANDS GOLF COURSE
BROMLEY PARK
THE SLOANE HOSPITAL
143
DX DY DZ EA EB EC ED
85 86 87 88 89 90 91 92 93 94

HITHER GREEN
SE13
SE12
SE6
GROVE PARK
HITHER GREEN CEMETERY
MOTTINGHAM
ELTHAM
DOWNHAM
PLAISTOW
SUNDRIDGE
SUNDRIDGE PARK GOLF COURSE
ELMSTEAD
ELMSTEAD WOOD
BR1
BR2
BROMLEY PARK
SHORTLANDS GOLF COURSE
THE SLOANE HOSPITAL
Widmore
BROMLEY NORTH
LEWISHAM
GREENWICH
BROMLEY
SUTCLIFFE PARK
MANOR HOUSE GARDENS
MANOR PARK
OLD COLFEIANS SPORTS GROUND
CIVIL SERVICE SPORTS GROUNDS
MIDDLE PARK FIELD
QUEENSCROFT REC GRD
KING JOHN PLAYING FIELDS
UNI OF WESTMINSTER SPORTS GROUND
MOTTINGHAM SPORTS GROUND
CHINBROOK MEADOWS
LOWER MARVELS WOOD
MARVELS WOOD
GROVE PARK CEMETERY
DOWNHAM PLAYING FIELDS
SHAFTESBURY PARK REC GRD
KING'S MEADOW PLAYING FIELDS
LEWISHAM BOROUGH SPORTS GROUND
MIDLAND BANK SPORTS GROUND
WARREN AVE PLAYING FIELDS
ROCKPIT WOOD
LOGSHILL WOOD
ELMSTEAD WOODS
NORTHBROOK PARK
FORSTER MEMORIAL PARK
UNI OF GREENWICH ATHLETIC GRD
A20
A205
A210
A212
A213
A21
B226
S CIRCULAR ROAD
BURNT ASH HILL
BARING ROAD
WESTHORNE AVENUE
SIDCUP ROAD
ELTHAM ROAD
BROMLEY HILL
LONDON ROAD
EE
EF
EG
EH
EJ
EK
EL
104
123
144
85
86
87
88
89
90
91
92
93
94

EM
EN
EP
EQ
ER
ES
ET
105
DA16
ELTHAM PARK SOUTH
ELTHAM WARREN GOLF COURSE
Crematorium
ROCHESTER WAY
RELIEF ROAD
A2
BEXLEY ROAD
BLACKFEN ROAD
A210
ELTHAM HIGH ST
AVERY HILL
AVERY HILL PARK
University of Greenwich Avery Hill Campus
CAMBRIDGE MISSION SPORTS GROUND
CHARLTON ATHLETIC FC TRAINING GRD
FOOTSCRAY PLAYING FIELDS
MILLWALL FC TRAINING GRD
FOOTSCRAY ROAD
A211
ROYAL BLACKHEATH GOLF COURSE
TARN BIRD SANCTUARY
SE9
BLACKFEN
DA15
HOLLY OAK WOOD PK
LAMORBEY
OLD FARM PARK
KING GEORGE'S REC GRD
SIDCUP
126
NEW ELTHAM
FAIRY HILL REC GRD
SIDCUP ROAD
A20
LONGLANDS
JACK NICKLAUS GOLF CENTRE
FLAMINGO PK SPORTS GRD
LONGLANDS REC GRD
MAIN ROAD
SIDCUP BYPASS
STATION ROAD
A222
SIDCUP HIGH STREET
DA14
SIDCUP PLACE
QUEEN MARY'S HOSP
BELMONT LANE OPEN SPACE
Kemnal Manor Stables
CHISLEHURST CEMETERY
Beaver's Wood
Hoblands Wood
OLD ELTHAMIANS SPORTS GRD
UNIVERSITY COLLEGE LONDON SPORTS GRD
BR7
Frognal Corner
SCADBURY PARK NATURE RESERVE
LITTLE WOOD
CHISLEHURST WEST
Ravensbourne Coll
WHYTES WOODLAND
WHITEHORSE HILL
RED HILL
HIGH STREET
CHISLEHURST
CAMDEN PARK
CHISLEHURST GOLF COURSE
CHISLEHURST COMMON
BROMLEY LANE
PERRY STREET
Perry Street Shaw
Bushy Clump
Icehouse Wood
PARK WOOD
Scadbury Moated Manor House Site
Holbrook Wood
The Larches
145
BROMLEY ROAD
WATTS LANE
CHALKPIT
BANSOME
85
86
87
88
89
90
91
92
93
94
43
44
45
71
72
73
74

DA16
DANSON
PARK
THE LAKE
DA6
BEXLEYHEATH
BEXLEYHEATH GOLF COURSE
BEXLEY
BLACKFEN
BEXLEY PARK WOOD
RIVERSIDE WALK
SIDCUP GOLF COURSE
DA15
LAMORBEY PARK
DA5
NORTH CRAY
SIDCUP
DA14
FOOTS CRAY MEADOWS
STABLE MEADOW
GATTONS WOOD
GATTONS PLANTATION
FOOTS CRAY
SCADBURY PARK
NATURE RESERVE
RUXLEY WOOD
BR5
RUXLEY PARK
SIDCUP BYPASS
ROCHESTER WAY
A2
A20
A222
A223
A221
A211
SIDCUP HIGH STREET
SEVENOAKS ROAD
MAIDSTONE ROAD
Crittall's Corner
Ruxley Corner
Queen Mary's Hosp
Rose Bruford College
Sidcup Arts Cen
Goldsmith College Sports Grd
106
125
146

BARNES CRAY
CRAYFORD MARSHES
DA1
CRAYFORD
CRAYFORD GREYHOUND STADIUM
HALL PLACE GARDENS
OLD BEXLEY
DARTFORD HEATH
DARTFORD
DARTFORD GOLF COURSE
North West Kent College
Coldblow
JOYDEN'S WOOD
Joydens Wood
DA2
Hook Green
ROWHILL WOOD
BIRCHWOOD PARK GOLF CENTRE
BR8
Hextable
Swanley Village
SWANLEY
WATLING STREET
LONDON ROAD
DARTFORD ROAD
ROCHESTER WAY
DARTFORD BYPASS
SHEPHERDS LANE
OLD BEXLEY LANE
107
128
147

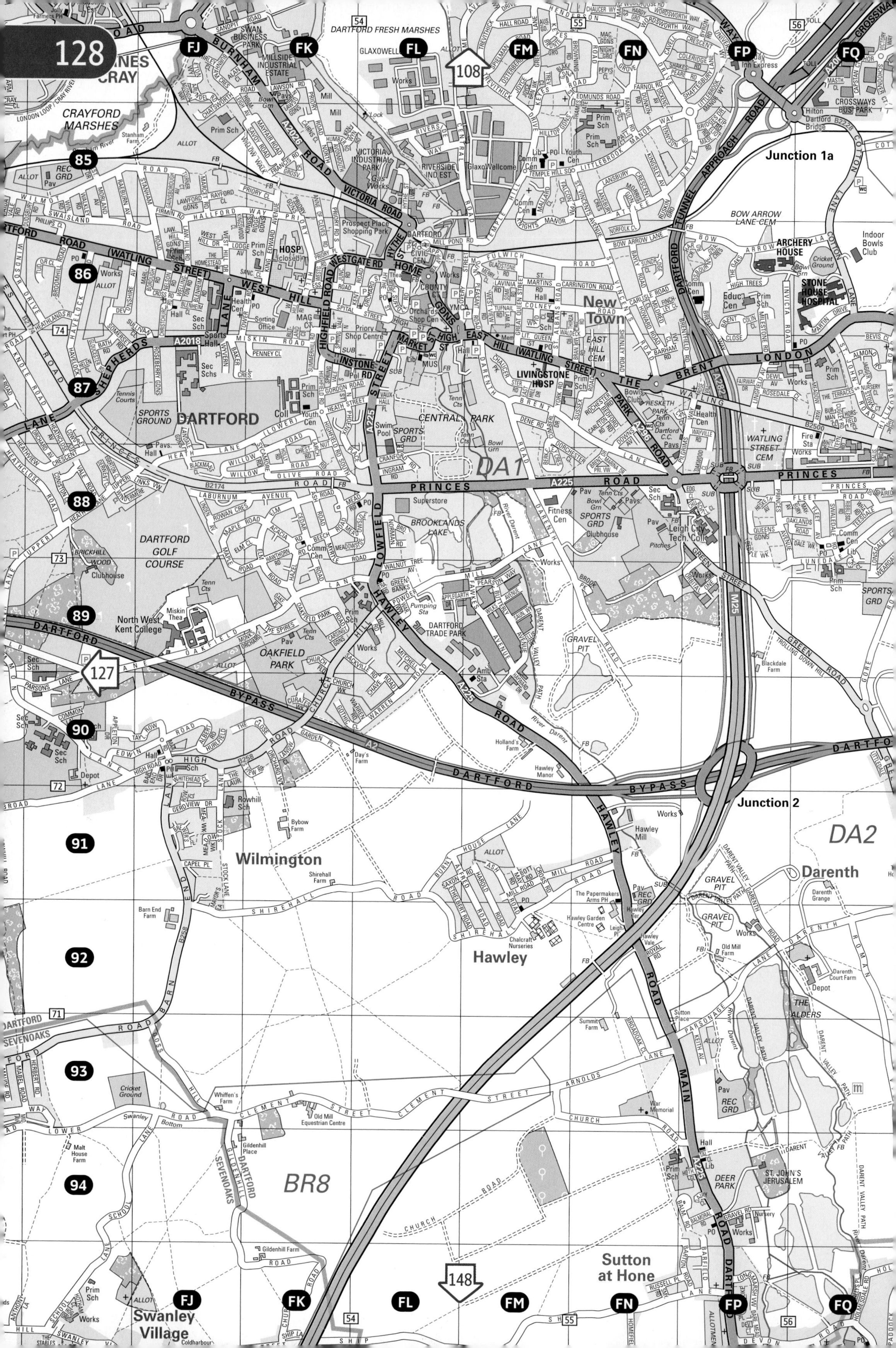
DARTFORD FRESH MARSHES
CRAYFORD MARSHES
108
Junction 1a
GLAXOWELLCOME
VICTORIA INDUSTRIAL PARK
RIVERSIDE IND EST
MILLSIDE INDUSTRIAL ESTATE
SWAN BUSINESS PARK
BURNHAM ROAD
VICTORIA ROAD
TEMPLE HILL
LITTLEBROOK MANOR WAY
BOW ARROW LANE CEM
ARCHERY HOUSE
STONE HOUSE HOSPITAL
CROSSWAYS BUS. PARK
Hilton Dartford Bridge
DARTFORD TUNNEL APPROACH ROAD
DARTFORD
WEST HILL
EAST HILL (WATLING STREET)
HIGH ST
HYTHE ST
HOME GDNS
LIVINGSTONE HOSP
New Town
EAST HILL CEM
WATLING STREET CEM
THE BRENT
LONDON ROAD
PRINCES ROAD
DA1
CENTRAL PARK
SPORTS GROUND
DARTFORD GOLF COURSE
BRICKHILL WOOD
North West Kent College
OAKFIELD PARK
BROOKLANDS LAKE
DARTFORD TRADE PARK
HAWLEY ROAD
LOWFIELD STREET
DARTFORD BYPASS
Junction 2
DA2
Darenth
Wilmington
Hawley
BR8
Sutton at Hone
Swanley Village
127
148
FJ
FK
FL
FM
FN
FP
FQ
85
86
87
88
89
90
91
92
93
94
54
55
56
71
72
73
74
DARTFORD
SEVENOAKS
M25
A2
A225
A226
A282
A2018
B2174
B258
B2500
ST. JOHN'S JERUSALEM
THE ALDERS
DARENT VALLEY PATH

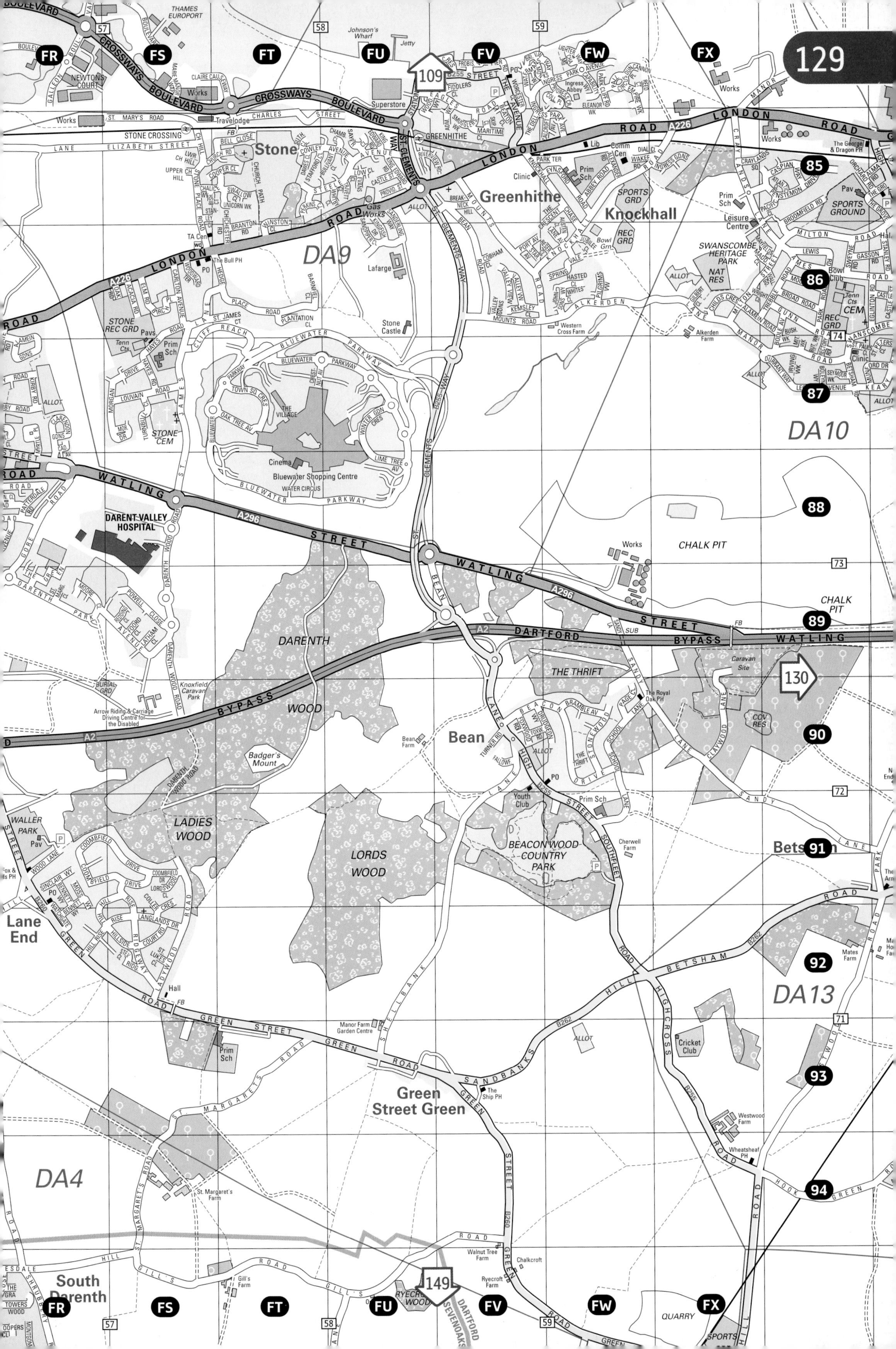
Stone
Greenhithe
Knockhall
DA9
DA10
DA13
DA4
Bluewater Shopping Centre
DARENT VALLEY HOSPITAL
DARENTH WOOD
LADIES WOOD
LORDS WOOD
THE THRIFT
BEACON WOOD COUNTRY PARK
Bean
Lane End
Green Street Green
South Darenth
Betsham
SWANSCOMBE HERITAGE PARK
CHALK PIT
THAMES EUROPORT
CROSSWAYS BOULEVARD
LONDON ROAD
WATLING STREET
DARTFORD BYPASS
A2
A226
A296
B255
B260
B262
ST. CLEMENTS WAY
STONE CROSSING
Stone Castle
Lafarge
Gas Works
Superstore
Travelodge
Johnson's Wharf
Jetty
Knoxfield Caravan Park
Arrow Riding & Carriage Driving Centre for the Disabled
Badger's Mount
Bean Farm
Manor Farm Garden Centre
Cherwell Farm
Mates Farm
Westwood Farm
Wheatsheaf PH
The Ship PH
The Royal Oak PH
The Bull PH
The George & Dragon PH
Alkerden Farm
Western Cross Farm
St. Margaret's Farm
Gill's Farm
Walnut Tree Farm
Ryecroft Farm
Chalkcroft
Cricket Club
QUARRY
WALLER PARK
STONE REC GRD
STONE CEM
Caravan Site
109
130
149
FR
FS
FT
FU
FV
FW
FX
57
58
59
71
72
73
74
85
86
87
88
89
90
91
92
93
94

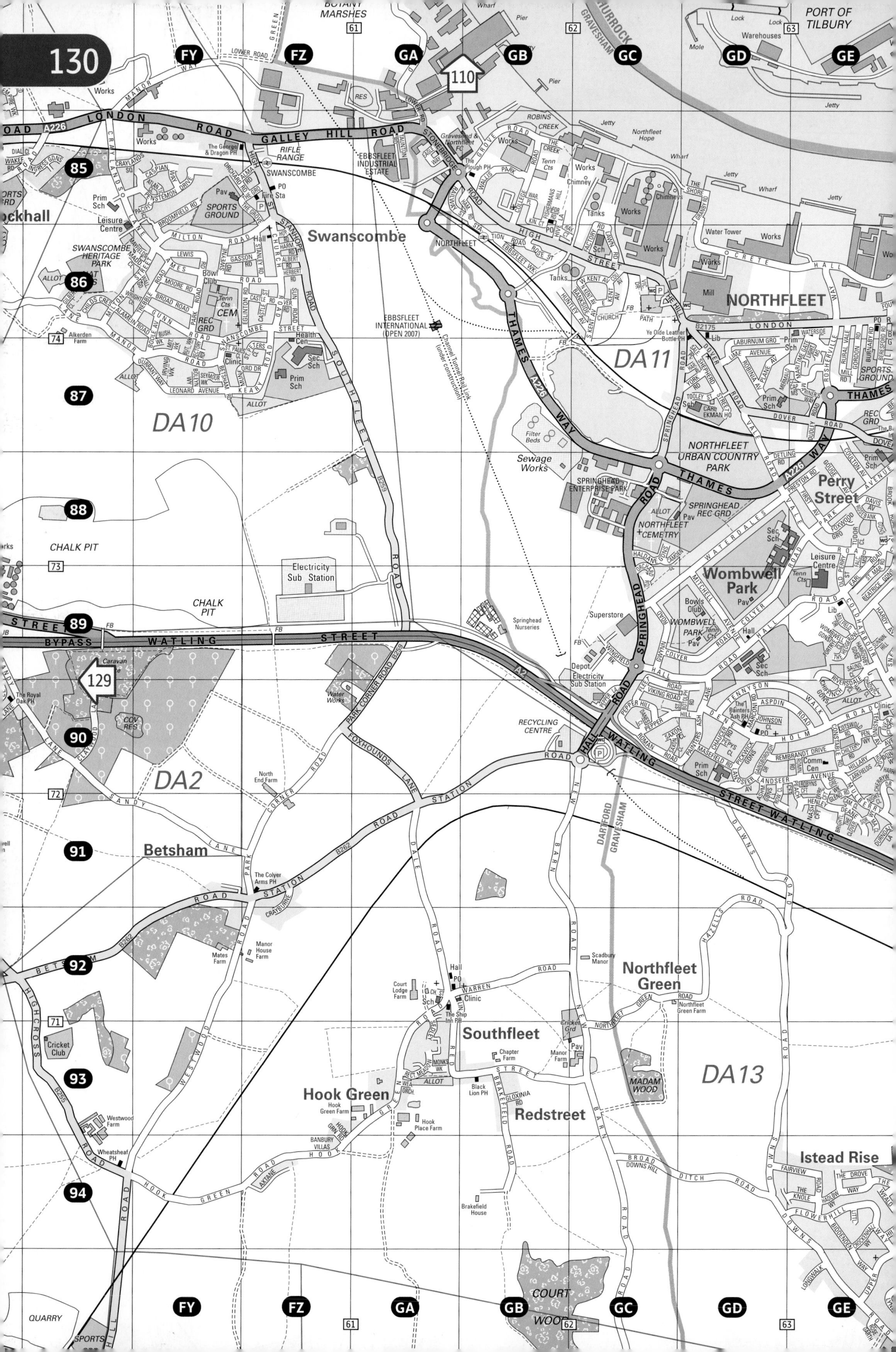
Swanscombe
NORTHFLEET
DA10
DA11
DA2
DA13
Betsham
Southfleet
Hook Green
Redstreet
Northfleet Green
Istead Rise
Perry Street
Wombwell Park
PORT OF TILBURY
EBBSFLEET INTERNATIONAL (OPEN 2007)
NORTHFLEET URBAN COUNTRY PARK
SPRINGHEAD ENTERPRISE PARK
Channel Tunnel Rail Link (under construction)
SWANSCOMBE HERITAGE PARK
EBBSFLEET INDUSTRIAL ESTATE
CHALK PIT
Electricity Sub Station
Sewage Works
MADAM WOOD
COURT WOOD
WATLING STREET
GALLEY HILL ROAD
LONDON ROAD
THAMES WAY
SPRINGHEAD ROAD
STATION ROAD
SOUTHFLEET ROAD
110
129

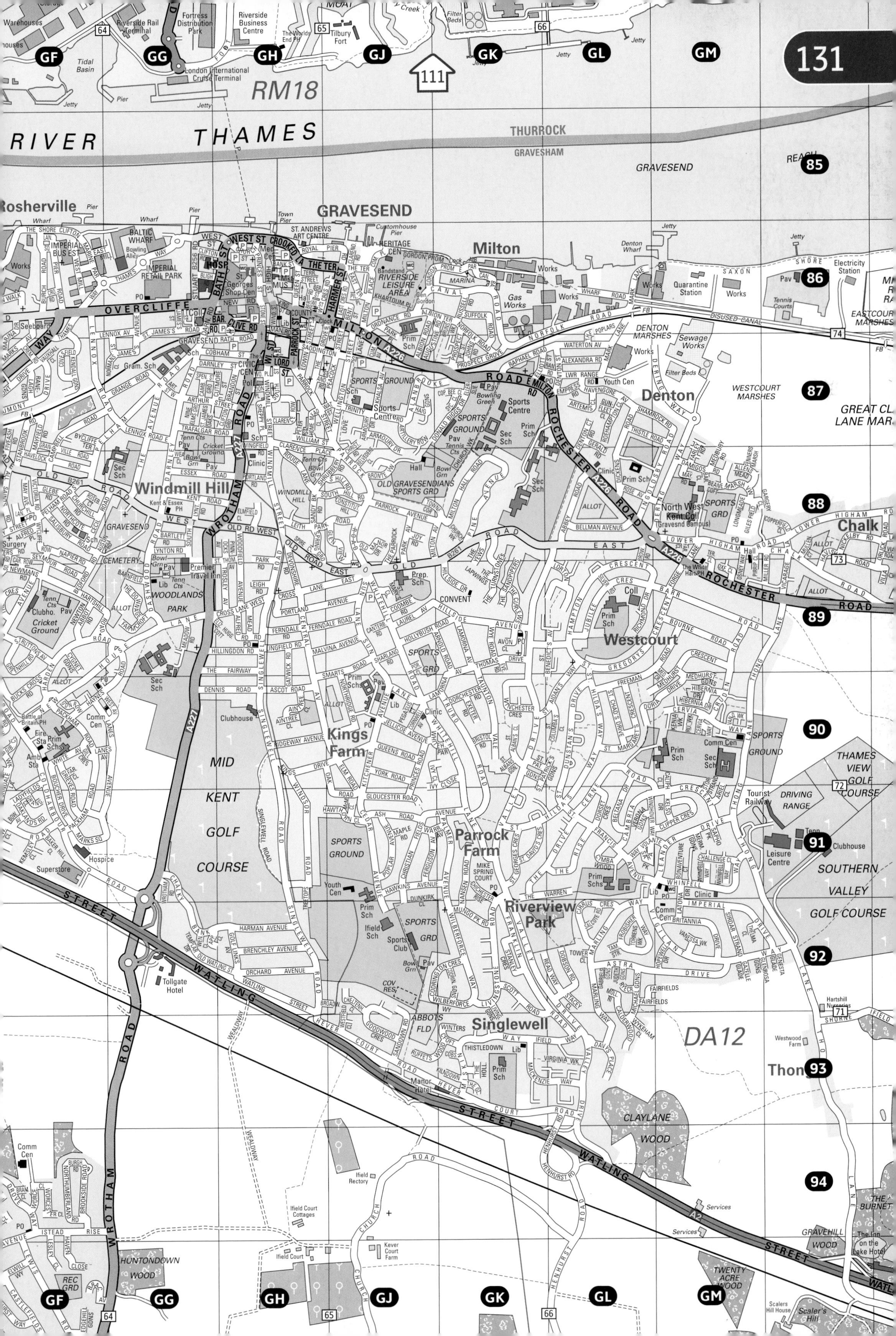
RIVER THAMES
RM18
THURROCK
GRAVESHAM
GRAVESEND
Rosherville
Milton
Denton
Chalk
Windmill Hill
Westcourt
Kings Farm
Parrock Farm
Riverview Park
Singlewell
MID KENT GOLF COURSE
SOUTHERN VALLEY GOLF COURSE
THAMES VIEW GOLF COURSE
DENTON MARSHES
WESTCOURT MARSHES
GREAT CLAYLANE MARSHES
EASTCOURT MARSHES
CLAYLANE WOOD
HUNTONDOWN WOOD
TWENTY ACRE WOOD
GRAVEHILL WOOD
DA12
WATLING STREET
WROTHAM ROAD
ROCHESTER ROAD
OVERCLIFFE
MILTON ROAD
Tilbury Fort
London International Cruise Terminal
Riverside Leisure Area
Old Gravesendians Sports Grd
Woodlands Park
Gravesend Cemetery
Thong
111
GF GG GH GJ GK GL GM
85 86 87 88 89 90 91 92 93 94

VIRGINIA WATER
Wentworth
WENTWORTH
GOLF COURSE
GU25
GU24
SL5
VIRGINIA WATER
Longcross
CHOBHAM COMMON NATIONAL NATURE RESERVE
POLO GROUND
DARKHOLE CLUMP
OXHED CLUMP
The Punch Bowl
THE VALLEY GARDENS
VIRGINIA WATER PLANTATION
EGHAM WICK PLANTATION
WICK POND
BELVEDERE WOOD
FROSTFARM PLANTATION
Royal Holloway College
The American Comm Sch
Callow Hill
GREAT WOOD
KING GEORGE V PLAYING FIELD
Defence Science & Technology Laboratory
BARROW HILLS GOLF COURSE
CHERTSEY COMMON
BLUEBELLE WOOD
KNOWLE GROVE
BEECH WOOD
Broom Hill
Clubhouse
WENTWORTH POND
CHRISTCHURCH ROAD
LONDON ROAD
BLACKNEST ROAD
LONGCROSS ROAD
CHERTSEY ROAD
CHOBHAM LANE

112
150

TW18
TW20
KT16
KT15
Stroude
Thorpe
Thorpe Green
Lyne
CHERTSEY
ADDLESTONE MOOR
LONGSIDE LAKE
MANOR LAKE
THORPE PARK
ST. ANN'S LAKE
Abbey Lake
ST. ANN'S HILL PARK
Junction 2 (M3), Junction 12 (M25)
Lyne Sewage Works
FAN GROVE
THE ROUGH
FOXHILLS GOLF COURSE
Foxhills Country Club
RUNNYMEDE HOSP
ST. PETER'S HOSP
HOSPITAL (CLOSED)
HOMEWOOD PARK
ADDLESTONE CEMETERY
ABBEY MOOR GOLF COURSE
LALEHAM BURWAY
PENTON HOOK ISLAND
PENTON HOOK MARINA
PENTON PARK (Caravan Park)
Great Fosters Hotel
Crabtree Corner
THORPE INDUSTRIAL EST
TASIS England
Mountbatten Pavilion
Junction 11
Kitchenride Corner
Great Cockrow Railway
Silver Birch Caravan Site
ELM FARM CARAVAN PARK
LYNE COPSE
HERSHAM COPSE
RECREATION GROUND
SPORTS GROUND
M25
M3
A320
STAINES ROAD
CHERTSEY LANE
GUILDFORD ROAD
ST. PETER'S WAY
B386
B388
B389
B375
A317
AZ
BA
BB
BC
BD
BE
BF
95
96
97
98
99
100
101
102
103
104
01
02
03
69
68
67
66

113
134
151

QUEEN MARY RESERVOIR
TW18
KT16
KT15
LALEHAM
LALEHAM PARK
LALEHAM GOLF COURSE
LALEHAM BURWAY
LALEHAM PARK SPORTS GROUND
PENTON HOOK
PENTON HOOK ISLAND
PENTON HOOK MARINA
PENTON PARK (Caravan Park)
MANOR LAKE
Abbey Lake
Mountbatten Pavilion
CHERTSEY
CHERTSEY MEADS
RECREATION GROUND
ADDLESTONE MOOR
ADDLESTONE CEMETERY
ABBEY MOOR GOLF COURSE
WOBURN PARK
St. George's College
FORDWATER TRADING EST
WEYBRIDGE TRADING ESTATE
WEYBRIDGE BUSINESS PARK
MEADOWLANDS PARK
HAMHAUGH ISLAND
PHARAOH'S ISLAND
LOCK ISLAND
Shepperton Studios
Laleham Nurseries
Dumsey Eyot
Chertsey Lock
Penton Hook Lock
Shepperton Lock
Weybridge Lock
Black Boy Bridge
Junction 11
THAMES SIDE
STAINES ROAD
CHERTSEY BRIDGE ROAD
CHERTSEY ROAD
LALEHAM ROAD
SHEPPERTON ROAD
WOBURN HILL
WEYBRIDGE ROAD
ST. PETER'S WAY
EASTWORTH ROAD
GUILDFORD STREET
LONDON STREET
BRIDGE ROAD
M3
M25
A317
A318
A320
B375
B376
B377
RIVER THAMES
Abbey River
Burway Ditch
The Bourne
Intake Channel
114
133
152

135
115
136
153
BP
BQ
BR
BS
BT
BU
BV
95
96
97
98
99
100
101
102
103
104
08
09
10
66
67
68
69
A308
A3050
A244
A317
B376
B375
B3366
B385
M3
Junction 1
Staines Reservoirs Aqueduct
ASHFORD COMMON WATER TREATMENT WORKS
WINDMILL ROAD
UPPER HALLIFORD
UPPER HALLIFORD ROAD
UPPER HALLIFORD BYPASS
GASTON BRIDGE ROAD
WALTON BRIDGE RD
LITTLETON
TW17
TW16
SUNBURY
SUNBURY PARK
SUNBURY GOLF COURSE
HAZELWOOD GOLF COURSE
KEMPTON PARK RACECOURSE
LONDON IRISH RUGBY GROUND
GAFLAC SPORTS GROUND
CEDARS REC GRD
SUNBURY CEM
SUNBURY LOCK AIT
Sunbury Locks
WATER TREATMENT WORKS
Gas Works
GRAVEL PIT
KT12
KT13
SHEPPERTON
SHEPPERTON BUSINESS PARK
LONGWOOD BUSINESS PARK
Shepperton Moat House
Shepperton Marina
BISHOP DUPPA'S REC GRD
LAS PALMAS ESTATE
DESBOROUGH ISLAND
D'OYLY CARTE ISLAND
THAMES MEADOW
COWAY SALE
BRIDGE STREET
HEPWORTH WAY
NEW ZEALAND AVENUE
CHURCH ST
TERRACE
HERSHAM ROAD
ELM GROVE REC GRD
GEORGE FROUDE PK
ASHLEY PARK
WALTON-ON-THAMES
WALTON & HERSHAM FC
BROAD WATER
Oatlands Park Hotel
OATLANDS DRIVE
OATLANDS PARK
QUEENS
RYDENS
HOSP
Walton-on-Thames

KEMPTON PARK RACECOURSE
HALF MOON COVERT
PLAYING FIELD
116
HAMPTON
CARLISLE PARK
Open Air Pool
HYDES FIELD
KINGSWAY BUSINESS PARK
UPPER SUNBURY ROAD
A308
EAST
KENTON COURT MEADOW
UPON THAMES
RICHMOND
STAIN HILL RESERVOIRS
GRAND JUNCTION RESERVOIR
TW12
GARRICK'S AIT
HURST PARK
PLATT'S EYOT
SUNBURY COURT
CONFERENCE CENTRE
SUNNYSIDE RESERVOIR
RIVER THAMES
MOLESEY RESERVOIRS
SUNBURY COURT ISLAND
SWAN'S REST ISLAND
RIVERMEAD ISLAND
TW16
SUNBURY
RIVERSIDE ARTS CENTRE
A3050
HURST ROAD
REC GROUND
SPORTS GRD
Sunbury Locks
WATER TREATMENT WORKS
SUNBURY LOCK AIT
LONDON IRISH RUGBY GROUND
SPORTS GROUND
Gas Works
BESSBOROUGH RESERVOIR
KNIGHTS RESERVOIR
WEST MOLESEY
KT8
KT12
GRAVEL PIT
Leisure Cen
WALTON ROAD
B369
APPLE COURT GREEN
135
NEILSON PLAYING FIELD
SPORTS GROUND
Sailing Club
QUEEN ELIZABETH II RESERVOIR
ISLAND BARN RESERVOIR
SAND & GRAVEL PIT
River Mole
River Ember
KT10
Sewage Works
RYDENS ROAD REC GRD
Esher R.F.C.
RYDENS
SANDOWN INDUSTRIAL PARK
Lower Green
Metropolitan Police Dog Training Centre
SANDOWN GOLF COURSE
DRIVING RANGE
SANDOWN PARK RACECOURSE
Karting Centre
Grandstand & Exhibition Centre
HERSHAM VILLAGE GOLF COURSE
CORONATION PLAYING FIELDS
EMBER CENTRE
HERSHAM
Wayneflete's or Wolsey's Tower
GEORGE FROUDE PK
ELM GROVE REC GRD
154
BW
BX
BY
BZ
CA
CB
CC
95
96
97
98
99
100
101
102
103
104

137
BUSHY PARK
TW11
HAMPTON WICK
HAMPTON COURT PARK
(HOME PARK)
HAMPTON COURT PALACE
GOLF COURSE
THE ROYAL PADDOCKS
EAST MOLESEY
THAMES DITTON
WESTON GREEN
HINCHLEY WOOD
LONG DITTON
LITTLEWORTH COMMON
KT7
KT6
KT9
KT1
HOOK
SURBITON
ESHER
THAMES DITTON & ESHER GOLF COURSE
WATERHOUSE WOODLAND GARDEN
WARREN PLANTATION
HALF MOON PLANTATION
OVAL PLANTATION
HAMPTON COURT GREEN
HAMPTON COURT PALACE
THE KINGSFIELD
River Thames
River Mole
River Ember
HAMPTON COURT ROAD
PORTSMOUTH ROAD
KINGSTON BYPASS
SURBITON GENERAL HOSP
Cockcrow Hill
CD
CE
CF
CG
CH
CJ
CK
95
96
97
98
99
100
101
102
103
104
117
138
155

138
CL
CM
CN
CP
CQ
CR
CS
118
137
156
95
96
97
98
99
100
101
102
103
104
COOMBE
COOMBE WOOD GOLF COURSE
KT2
KINGSTON HOSPITAL
NORBITON
KINGSTON UPON THAMES
KINGSTON CEMETERY
KT1
NEW MALDEN
KT8
River Thames
SURBITON CEMETERY
BERRYLANDS
KT3
GREEN LANE REC GRD
HOGSMILL PUBLIC OPEN SPACE
KT5
SURBITON GENERAL HOSP
KT6
SURBITON
FISHPONDS OPEN SPACE
HOGSMILL OPEN SPACE
OLD MALDEN
MAORI SPORTS GROUND
TOLWORTH HOSPITAL
TOLWORTH
KINGSTON UNIVERSITY SPORTS GRD
RIVERHILL SPORTS GRD
WANDGAS ATHLETIC GROUND
KING GEORGES FIELD
KING EDWARD REC GRD
KT9
HOOK
G DITTON
SURREY
KINGSTON BYPASS
A3
A240
A243
A307
A308
A238
A2043
A3210
B3363
B3364
B3370
B284
B283
RICHMOND ROAD
KINGSTON HILL
COOMBE LANE WEST
CAMBRIDGE ROAD
KINGSTON ROAD
LONDON ROAD
PORTSMOUTH ROAD
SURBITON HILL ROAD
EWELL ROAD
BRIGHTON ROAD
MALDEN WAY
HOOK ROAD
PENRHYN ROAD

CT
CU
CV
CW
CX
CY
CZ
119
WOLFSON MED. REHAB CENTRE
COOMBE HILL
OBERON PLAYING FIELD
COTTENHAM PARK
PLAYING FIELDS
SPORTS GROUND
GOLF COURSE
RAYNES PARK SPORTS GRD
KINGSTON BYPASS
BEVERLEY WAY
COOMBE LANE
KINGSTON ROAD
BUSHEY ROAD
NELSON HOSP
WIMBLEDON CHASE
DUNDONALD REC GRD
JOHN INNES REC GRD
MERTON
MERTON PARK
SW19
SW20
PRINCE GEORGE'S PLAYING FIELD
RAYNES PARK
MESSINES PLAYING FLD
JOSEPH HOOD RECREATION GROUND
BUSHEY MEAD
CANNON HILL COMMON
MOSTYN GARDENS
SOUTH MERTON
MORDEN
BEVERLEY PARK
KINGSTON UPON THAMES
MERTON
WEST BARNES
MOTSPUR PARK
RAYNES PARK PLAYING FIELDS
SPORTS GROUND
OLD BLUES R.F.C.
FULHAM F.C. TRAINING GROUND
THE SIR JOSEPH HOOD MEMORIAL PLAYING FIELDS
MORDEN CEMETERY
Crematorium
MORDEN PARK
SM4
MORDEN SPORTS GROUND
Merton Coll
Morden Park Pitch 'n' Putt
140
MORDEN SOUTH
MANOR PARK REC GRD
MERTON & SUTTON JOINT CEMETERY
KING GEORGE'S FIELD
The Woodstock
GARTH ROAD IND CEN
ST. ANTHONY'S HOSP
St. Raphael's Hospice
SM3
SUTTON CEMETERY
KIMPTON TRADE BUSINESS CENTRE
REIGATE AVENUE REC GRD
WORCESTER PARK
CUDDINGTON REC GRD
KT4
NORTH CHEAM
157
SPORTS GRD
SM1
COLLINGWOOD PARK
Oldfields Trading Est
95
96
97
98
99
100
101
102
103
104
22
23
24
66
67
68
69
A3
A24
A217
A238
A298
A2043

DA
DB
DC
DD
DE
DF
DG
120
139
158
SOUTH WIMBLEDON
COLLIER'S WOOD
MERTON
MERTON PARK
SW19
MORDEN
SM4
MORDEN PARK
MITCHAM
ST. HELIER
SM5
ROSEHILL
SM3
SUTTON CEMETERY
BENHILTON
THE WRYTHE
SM1
COLLINGWOOD PARK
LONDON ROAD CEMETERY
FIGGE'S MARSH
MORDEN HALL PARK NT
RAVENSBURY PARK
WATERMEADS NT
MORDEN SPORTS GROUND
MORDEN REC GRD
THOMAS WALL PARK
ST. HELIER OPEN SPACE
SUTTON ARENA
ROSEHILL RECREATION GROUND
ROSEHILL PARK EAST
GREENSHAW WOOD
ST. HELIER HOSP
QUEEN MARY'S HOSP FOR CHILDREN
ROYSTON PARK
THE WRYTHE REC GRD
DALE PARK
POULTER PARK
SPORTS GROUND
MITCHAM GOLF COURS
MITCHAM JUNCTION
MILL GREEN
WILDERNESS ISLAND
BEDD CO
NELSON HOSP
DUNDONALD REC GRD
JOHN INNES REC GRD
MOSTYN GARDENS
ABBEY REC GRD
MERTON INDUSTRIAL PARK
LOMBARD BUSINESS PARK
NELSON TRADING EST
ABBEY IND EST
GRACE BUSINESS CENTRE
EAGLE TRADING EST
KIMPTON TRADE CENTRE
Oldfields Trading Est
REIGATE AVENUE REC GRD
MERANTUN WAY
MORDEN ROAD
LONDON ROAD
EPSOM ROAD
CENTRAL ROAD
BISHOPSFORD ROAD
REIGATE AVENUE
ST. HELIER AVENUE
MORDEN HALL ROAD
WESTERN ROAD
KINGSTON ROAD
MERTON HIGH STREET
CARSHALTON ROAD
STREATHAM ROAD
COMMONSIDE WEST
CRANMER RD
SUTTON COMMON ROAD
OLDFIELDS ROAD
ST. DUNSTAN'S HILL
MIDDLETON ROAD
WRYTHE LANE
Woodstock
95
96
97
98
99
100
101
102
103
104
A24
A217
A236
A237
A238
A239
A297
B286
B278
B2230
26
27
28
66
67
68
69

141
DH
DJ
DK
DL
DM
DN
DP
121
142
159
95
96
97
98
99
100
101
102
103
104
STREATHAM VALE
NORBURY
NORBURY PARK
SE19
SW16
CR7
CR4
CR0
SM6
STREATHAM PARK CEMETERY
POLLARDS HILL
MITCHAM
COMMON
THORNTON HEATH
CROYDON CEMETERY
QUEEN'S ROAD CEMETERY
MAYDAY HOSPITAL
BROAD GREEN
WADDON
WANDLE PARK
HACKBRIDGE
BEDDINGTON
BEDDINGTON PARK
THE GRANGE GARDENS
DUPPAS HILL
CROYDON SUB STATION
Roman Bath House (Site of)
GREEN LANE SPORTS GROUND
LONDON ROAD
MITCHAM ROAD
PURLEY WAY
THORNTON ROAD
CROYDON ROAD
DUPPAS HILL RD

DQ
DR
DS
DT
DU
DV
DW
122
UPPER NORWOOD
WESTOW PARK
SE19
THE LAWNS
BEAULIEU HEIGHTS
SYLVAN ESTATE
SOUTH NORWOOD GROUNDS
SPORTS GROUND
SOUTH NORWOOD LAKE
ORCHARD SCHOOL SPORTS CENTRE
SE20
ANERLEY
BETTS PARK
PENGE
95
96
97
98
99
100
101
102
103
104
GREEN LANE SPORTS GROUND
GRANGEWOOD PARK
CR7
SE25
SELHURST PARK CRYSTAL PALACE FC
SOUTH NORWOOD
BECKENHAM CEMETERY
SOUTH NORWOOD COUNTRY PARK
THORNTON HEATH
NORWOOD JUNCTION
SOUTH NORWOOD REC GRD
CROYDON AND RYLANDS FIELDS
CROYDON SPORTS ARENA
CROYDON DRIVING RANGE
141
MAYDAY HOSPITAL
QUEEN'S ROAD CEMETERY
SELHURST
HEAVERS MEADOW
WOOD SIDE
BROAD GREEN
CR0
ASHBURTON PARK
SHIRLEY OAK HOSPITAL
CROYDON
ADDISCOMBE
WANDLE PARK
EAST CROYDON
WHITGIFT PLAYING FIELDS
SHIRLEY PARK GOLF COURSE
LLOYD PARK
PARK HILL
DUPPAS HILL
SPORTS GROUND
160
LLOYD PARK

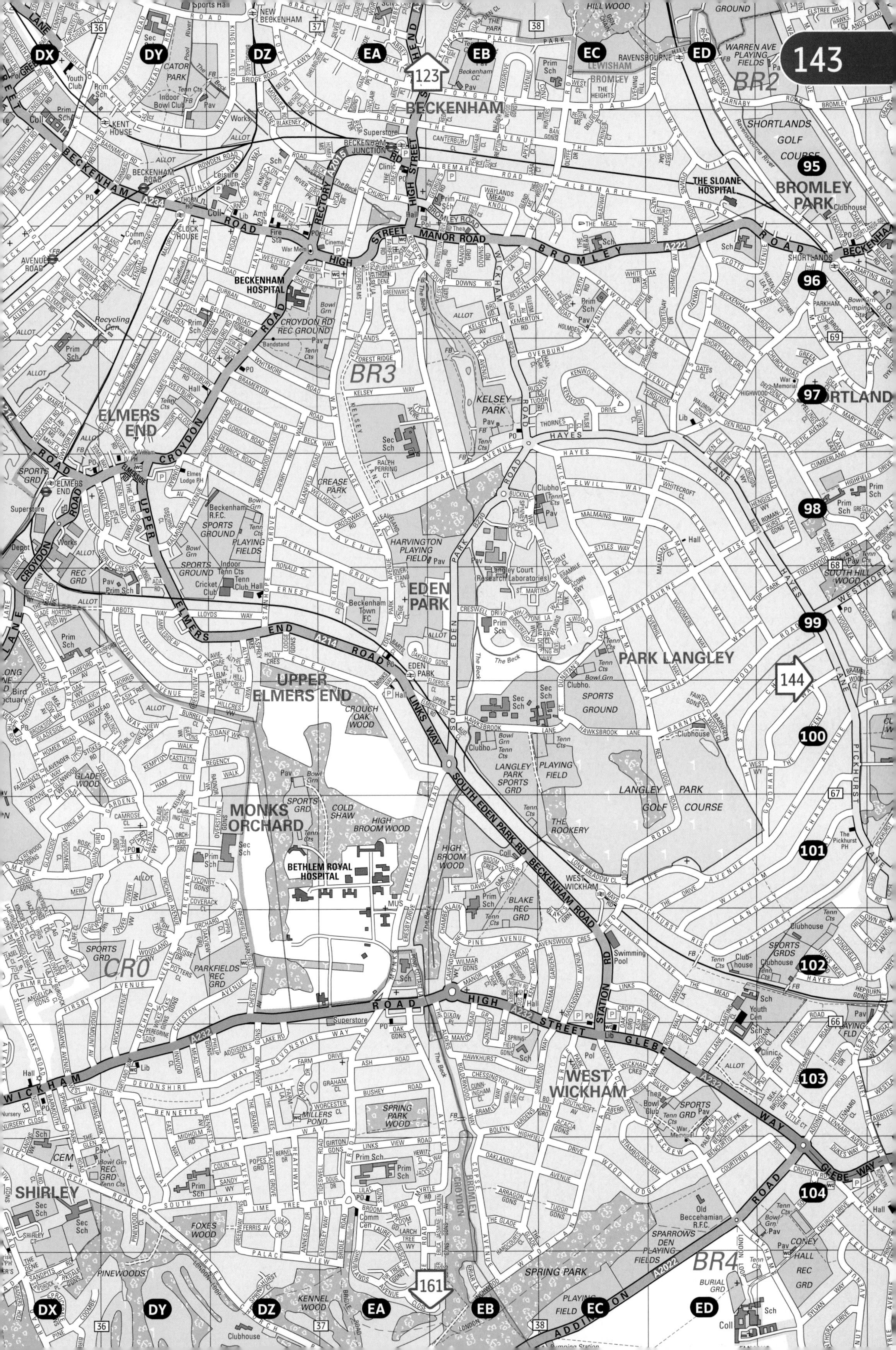
DX
DY
DZ
EA
EB
EC
ED
123
BECKENHAM
BR2
SHORTLANDS GOLF COURSE
BROMLEY PARK
THE SLOANE HOSPITAL
BECKENHAM HOSPITAL
CROYDON RD REC GROUND
BR3
ELMERS END
KELSEY PARK
EDEN PARK
PARK LANGLEY
144
UPPER ELMERS END
MONKS ORCHARD
BETHLEM ROYAL HOSPITAL
LANGLEY PARK GOLF COURSE
WEST WICKHAM
CR0
SHIRLEY
BR4
SPRING PARK
161
BROMLEY ROAD
MANOR ROAD
HIGH STREET
CROYDON ROAD
ELMERS END ROAD
SOUTH EDEN PARK RD
BECKENHAM ROAD
WICKHAM ROAD
GLEBE WAY
ADDINGTON ROAD
HAYES LANE
PICKHURST LANE
95
96
97
98
99
100
101
102
103
104
36
37
38

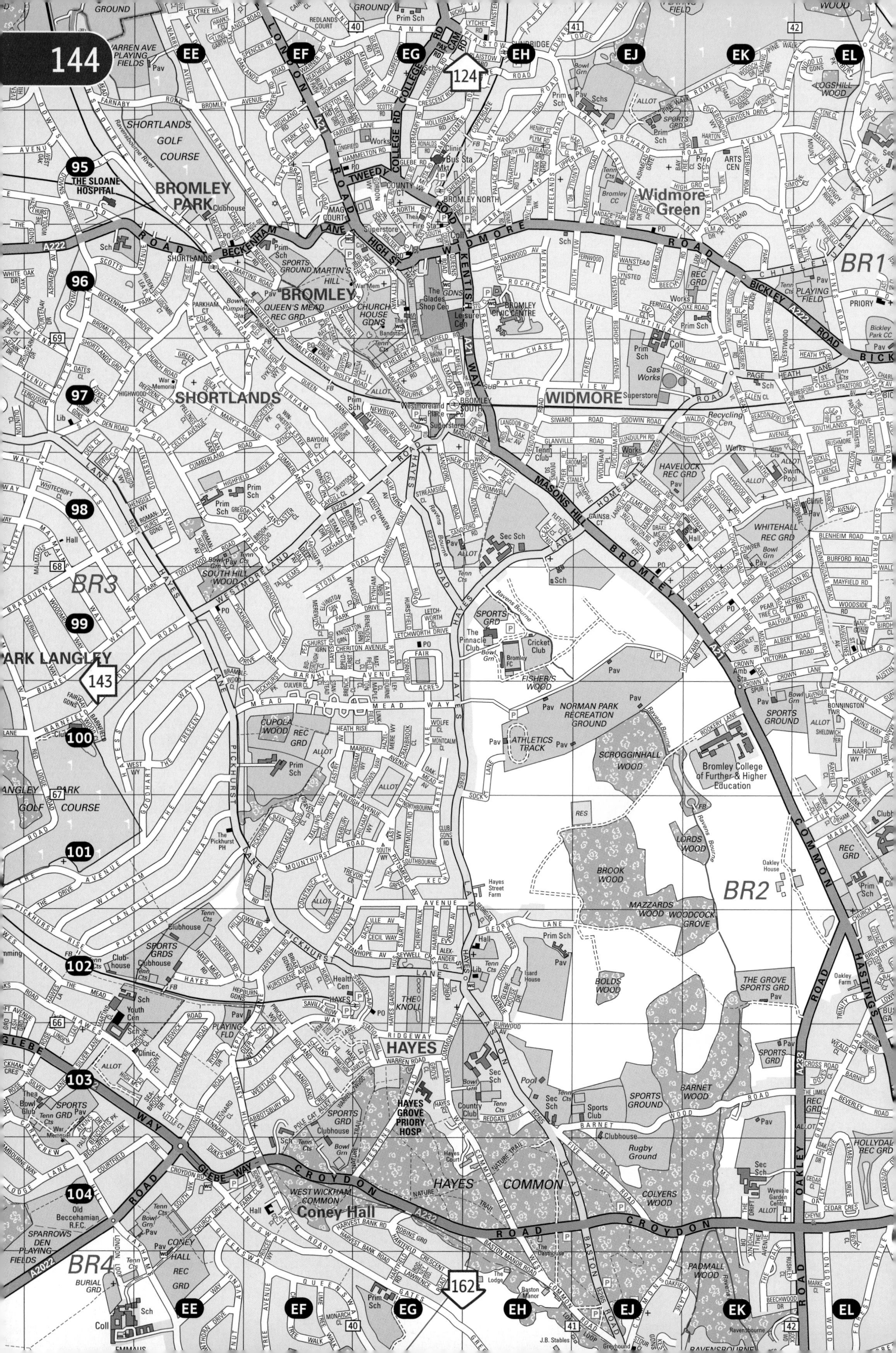
EE
EF
EG
EH
EJ
EK
EL
124
BROMLEY PARK
SHORTLANDS GOLF COURSE
THE SLOANE HOSPITAL
95
96
97
98
99
100
101
102
103
104
BROMLEY
SHORTLANDS
WIDMORE
Widmore Green
BR1
BR2
BR3
BR4
PARK LANGLEY
143
LANGLEY PARK GOLF COURSE
THE GLADES SHOP CEN
BROMLEY CIVIC CENTRE
QUEEN'S MEAD REC GRD
CHURCH HOUSE GDNS
SOUTH HILL WOOD
CUPOLA WOOD
NORMAN PARK RECREATION GROUND
ATHLETICS TRACK
SCROGGINHALL WOOD
Bromley College of Further & Higher Education
LORDS WOOD
BROOK WOOD
MAZZARDS WOOD
WOODCOCK GROVE
BOLDS WOOD
THE GROVE SPORTS GRD
BARNET WOOD
COLYERS WOOD
PADMALL WOOD
HAYES
HAYES COMMON
HAYES GROVE PRIORY HOSP
THE KNOLL
Coney Hall
WEST WICKHAM COMMON
CONEY HALL REC GRD
SPARROWS DEN PLAYING FIELDS
Old Beccehamian R.F.C.
HOLLYDALE REC GRD
WHITEHALL REC GRD
HAVELOCK REC GRD
LOGSHILL WOOD
FISHER'S WOOD
SPORTS GROUND
Rugby Ground
162
A21
A222
A232
A233
A2022
BROMLEY COMMON
HASTINGS ROAD
OAKLEY ROAD
CROYDON ROAD
GLEBE WAY
MASONS HILL
WIDMORE ROAD
BICKLEY ROAD
HAYES LANE
PICKHURST LANE
WESTMORELAND ROAD
BECKENHAM ROAD
LONDON ROAD
HIGH ST
KENTISH WAY
TWEEDY ROAD
COLLEGE RD

CHISLEHURST
CAMDEN PARK
CHISLEHURST COMMON
NATURE RESERVE
EM
EN
EP
EQ
ER
ES
ET
43
44
45
125
CHISLEHURST GOLF COURSE
PARK WOOD
Scadbury Moated Manor House Site
Field-Study Centre
Holbrook Wood
The Larches
CHALKPIT WOOD
BANSOME WOOD
Marjorie McClure Sch
CHISLEHURST
BIRCH WOOD
GOSHILL WOOD
ST. PAUL'S CRAY COMMON
HOBLINGWELL WOOD
HOBLINGWELL WOOD REC GRD
ST. PAUL'S CRAY
BR7
HAWKWOOD ESTATE NT
POND WOOD
WALK WOOD
BICKLEY
Bickley Junction
PETTS WOOD NT
Edlmann Memorial Wood
Willett Memorial Wood
Chislehurst Junction
GREAT THRIFT
95
96
97
98
99
100
101
102
103
104
Bickley Manor Hotel
BLACKBROOK WOOD
Bromley High Sch
THORNET WOOD
JUBILEE COUNTRY PARK
Petts Wood Junction
PETTS WOOD
BR5
POVEREST
146
SOUTHBOROUGH OPEN SPACE
COVET WOOD
POVEREST REC GRD
ST. LUKE'S CEM
PARKFIELD
SOUTHBOROUGH
RECREATION
BROMLEY GOLF COURSE
GROUND
PETTS WOOD REC GRD
SPARROW WOOD
Bromley Common
SPARROW COMMON
ROUNDABOUT WOOD
PLAYING FIELD
Prince's Plain
CROFTON HEATH
ORPINGTON
BR6
GUMPING COMMON
CLAY WOOD
NOBODY'S WOOD
KNOWLEHILL WOOD
POKERIDDEN WOOD
Crofton Roman Villa
ORPINGTON
NEWSTEAD WOOD
DARRICK COMMON
FARNBOROUGH REC GRD
PRINCESS ROYAL UNI HOSP
DARRICK WOOD
163
ORPINGTON HOSPITAL
CROFTON ROAD
SPUR ROAD
A232
A208
A222
A223
B264

NATURE RESERVE
Crittall's Corner
EDGINGTON
SIDCUP
A20 BYPASS
DA14
126
RUXLEY
RUXLEY PARK GOLF COURSE
CRAY VALLEY GOLF COURSE
Scadbury Moated Manor House Site
Field Study Centre
HOBLINGWELL WOOD REC GRD
ST. PAUL'S CRAY
CRAYFIELD IND PARK
MURRAY BUSINESS CEN
SPRINGVALE RETAIL PARK
PAULS CRAY HILL PARK
BR7
BR5
HOCKENDEN WOOD
Simon's Field Shaw
Pilgrim Hill
Barnfield Bank
STAR LANE
CEM
SANDWAY PK
THE WARREN
POVEREST
145
NUGENT IND PARK
ST MARY CRAY
ST. MARY CRAY REC GRD
Shawcroft Sch
CROCKENHILL ROAD
Derry Downs
GRIGG'S CROSS
KYNASTON WOOD
CHILD'S WOOD
Walden Manor
POVEREST REC GRD
PERRY HALL ROAD
A208
PRIORY GARDENS
BROMLEY MUS
GRASSMEADE RECREATION GROUND
COCKMANNINGS ROAD
RAMSDEN
ORPINGTON
A232 SPUR ROAD
COURT ROAD (ORPINGTON BYPASS)
A224
GRIFF'S WOOD
SAGE WENTS
SKIBBS LANE
Byways Nurseries
BR6
Goddington
GODDINGTON PARK
ROUNDS SMALLAMS
LILLY'S WOOD
BLACK BUSH WOOD
ORPINGTON HOSPITAL
164
EU EV EW EX EY EZ FA
47 48 49
95 96 97 98 99 100 101 102 103 104

147
Hextable
Swanley Village
SWANLEY
Crockenhill
Hulberry
BR8
FB
FC
FD
FE
FF
FG
FH
127
148
165
50
51
52
69
68
67
66
95
96
97
98
99
100
101
102
103
104
Junction 3 (M25)
Junction 1 (M20)
KENT
DARTFORD
SEVENOAKS
BROMLEY
SWANLEY PARK
Swanley New Barn Railway
HEXTABLE GDNS
SPORTS GROUND
THE WOODLANDS
White Oak Business Pk
CIVIC CEN
REC GRD
Superstore
Swanley Cen
Leisure Cen
Bowls Cen
Sports Hall
BUS DEPOT
MORETON IND EST
PEDHAM PLACE IND EST
TEARDROP IND EST
Olympic Golf Range
Parkwood Hall Sch
Broom Hill
Tweed Hill
BIRCH WOOD
Windmill Hill Wood
BOURNE WOOD
TILE KILNS WOOD
Hook Spring
ALMA FC
CACKETSHILL WOOD
HEATHFIELD SHAW
HORNCROSS SHAW
THE ROUGHET
ASHEN BANK
PEDHAM PLACE GOLF CENTRE
FOUNTAIN HOY
Fort Farningham (Site Of)
Lullingstone Roman Villa (Remains Of)
Lullingstone Park Farm
Pedham Place Farm
Petham Court
Gosenhill Farm
Westerd Farm
Capricorn Farm
Hulberry Farm
Partridges
Hightrees
Willow Farm
Gables Farm
Skeet Hill Farm
Skeet Hill
Old Park Gate Farm
Park Gate House
Parkgate Farm
Newbarn Farm
EYNSFORD
Pumping Sta
River Darent
Highlands Farm
Highlands Poultry Farm
Harrington's Nursery
Veitchii Nursery
Five Ways Nursery
Lower Daltons Nursery
Coldharbour Farm
Malt House Farm
Gildenhill Place
Stonehill Farm
Timbertops Farm
Burnt House Farm
Upper Hockenden Farm
Birchwood Garden Centre
Glasshouse
Glasshouses
Pembroke House
College Road Nursery
Beechenlea Nursery
Marwood House
Holly Mount
Clubhouse
Depot
SWANLEY BYPASS
A20
M25
M20
B2173
B258
LONDON ROAD
GOLDSEL ROAD
GREEN COURT ROAD
CRAY ROAD
EYNSFORD ROAD
CROCKENHILL LANE
WESTED LANE
DALTONS ROAD
PARKGATE ROAD
HIGHLANDS HILL
SWANLEY VILLAGE ROAD
HIGH STREET
STATION ROAD
LULLINGSTONE AV

Sutton at Hone
Swanley Village
Farningham
Eynsford
FARNINGHAM WOOD NATURE RESERVE
PEDHAM PLACE GOLF CENTRE
BR8
DA4
Junction 3 (M25)
Junction 1 (M20)
128
147
FRANKS
THE FOLLY
RAM'S WOOD
EYNSFORD CASTLE
FIREPOUND SHAW
OLIVERS SHAW
ALCHIN'S WOOD
WESTMINSTER FIELD
BALANCING POND
POLLY SHAW
FOUNTAIN HOY
Eynesford Hill
Fort Farningham (Site Of)
Lullingstone Roman Villa (Remains Of)
SANDHOLE SHAW
ST. JOHN'S JERUSALEM
FARNINGHAM ROAD
Tweed Hill
Broom Hill
Olympic Golf Range
Parkwood Hall Sch
MORETON IND EST
PEDHAM PLACE IND EST
TEARDROP IND EST
GORSE HILL (MAIN ROAD)
DARTFORD ROAD
LONDON ROAD
STATION ROAD
SHIP LANE
CALFSTOCK LANE
EGLANTINE LANE
DONKEY LANE
MAPLESCOMBE LANE
CROCKENHILL LANE
SPAREPENNY LANE
LULLINGSTONE LANE
FJ
FK
FL
FM
FN
FP
FQ
54
55
56
66
67
68
69
95
96
97
98
99
100
101
102
103
104

FR
FS
FT
FU
FV
FW
FX
57
58
59
129
South Darenth
St. Margaret's Farm
Gill's Farm
GILL'S ROAD
RYECROFTS WOOD
Orchard View
DARTFORD SEVENOAKS
Walnut Tree Farm
Chalkcroft
Ryecroft Farm
GREEN STREET
B260
DA2
QUARRY
SPORTS GRD
Wheatsheaf PH
WHITEHILL ROAD
95
Pinden
Works
Mile End Green
Pinden End Farm
Pav
FOOTBALL PITCH
Hall
MAIN ROAD
Lib
96
Longfield
ESSEX ROAD
KENT ROAD
ROWANS CL
STATION ROAD
HARTLEY RD
PO
69
LONGFIELD
CAVENDISH SQ
BRAMBLEFIELD
OAKWOOD RISE
ST MARYS WAY
Sec Sch
97
Dean Bottom Farm
RABBITS ROAD
GORRINGE AV
VICTORIA DR
PRINCE CHARLES AV
ALLOT
SOUTHDOWNS
Tuppence Farm
Rabbits Farm
WILSON LANE
CANADA FARM ROAD
Dean Bottom
CHURCHDOWN WOOD
FAWKHAM ROAD
Horton Kirby
STACK ROAD
Northdown Country Riding Club
STACK LANE
Churchdown Farm
98
Hartley
OLD DOWNS
68
Beeches Farm
Canada Farm
Hill Barn Farm
CASTLE HILL
Hartley Green
99
FAWKHAM VALLEY GOLF COURSE
Country Club
Bowl Grn
SPORTS GRD
CULVEY CL
PENNIS LANE
Sports Ground
Pav
Tenn Cts
Prim Sch
Gay Dawn Farm
Sports Cen
Clubho
SPORTS GRD
Pennis Farm
FAIRBY LANE
100
SCUDDERS HILL
Lone Oak Farm
Kentdown Mushroom Farm
Nursery
SCHOOL LANE
Elec Sta
DA3
VALLEY ROAD
67
101
MUSSENDEN LANE
GATES ROAD
GROVE WOOD
YEWFIELD SHAW
PENNIS WOOD
MANOR ROAD
HORTON WOOD
Grove Farm
Hall
Prim Sch
REDLIBBETS GOLF COURSE
Clubhouse
The Black Lion PH
HOPKINS SPRING WOOD
THREE GATES ROAD
Radio Mast
FAWKHAM MANOR HOSPITAL
Fawkham Manor Farm
HATCHFIELD WOOD
102
FB
The Rookery Pig Farm
M20
Speedgate Farm
White House Farm
SPEEDGATE HILL
66
103
New Ash Green
GABRIEL SPRING WOOD
GABRIEL SPRING ROAD
SCRATCHERS LANE
CHOAKS WOOD
SUN HILL
The Rising Sun PH
War Memorial
PO
Fawkham Green
Westyoke Farm
WEST YOKE
Eaglesfield Equestrian Centre
The Royal Oak PH
FOXBURY
Greyhound Schooling Establishment
104
Bovis Offices
GORSE HILL (MAIN ROAD)
Woodhall Farm
Works
BRANDS HATCH KARTING
HATCH ROAD
Beechcroft Farm Industries
TN15
Sports Cen
SPORTS GROUND
REDHILL
Landway Farm
Leisure Cen
Brands Hatch Place Hotel
SAXTEN'S WOOD
SHETLEY SHAWS
EXPO
Stewart Cen
CHAPMAN
Thistle Brands Hatch
BRANDS HATCH MOTOR RACING
ROGERS WOOD LANE
Ash Place Farm

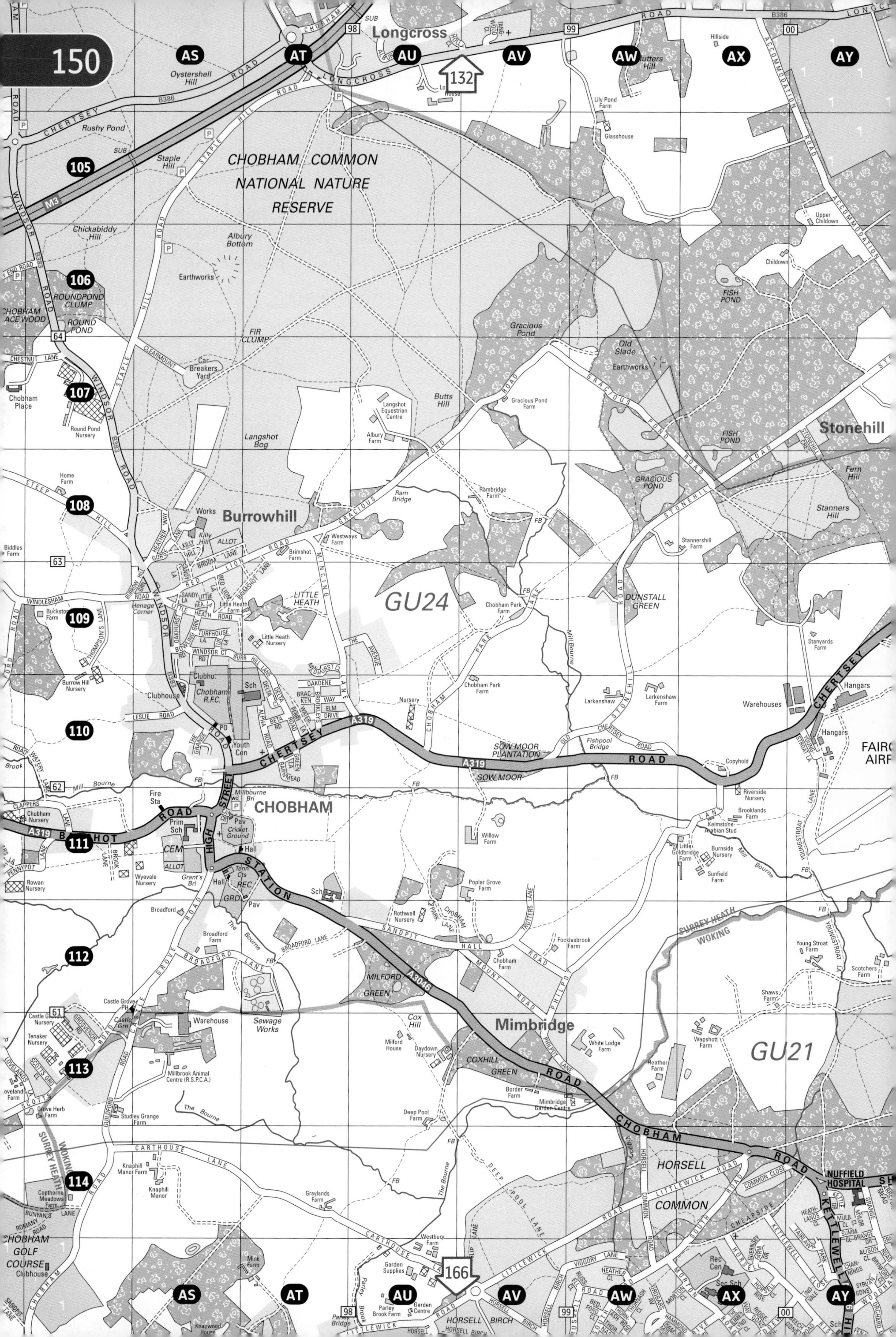

Longcross
CHOBHAM COMMON
NATIONAL NATURE
RESERVE
Oystershell Hill
Rushy Pond
Staple Hill
Chickabiddy Hill
Albury Bottom
Earthworks
ROUNDPOND CLUMP
ROUND POND
FIR CLUMP
Car Breakers Yard
Chobham Place
Round Pond Nursery
Langshot Bog
Langshot Equestrian Centre
Albury Farm
Butts Hill
Gracious Pond
Gracious Pond Farm
Old Slade
Lily Pond Farm
Glasshouse
Hillside
Upper Childown
Childown
FISH POND
Stonehill
Fern Hill
Stanners Hill
GRACIOUS POND
Stannerhill Farm
DUNSTALL GREEN
Stanyards Farm
Hangars
Warehouses
Home Farm
Burrowhill
Works
Biddles Farm
Henage Corner
Buckstone Farm
Burrow Hill Nursery
LITTLE HEATH
Little Heath Farm
Little Heath Nursery
Ram Bridge
Rambridge Farm
Westways Farm
Brimshot Farm
GU24
Chobham Park Farm
Larkenshaw
Larkenshaw Farm
Chobham R.F.C.
Clubhouse
Youth Cen
Nursery
SOW MOOR PLANTATION
SOW MOOR
Fishpool Bridge
Copyhold
CHOBHAM
Millbourne Bri
Fire Sta
Chobham Nursery
Cricket Ground
Willow Farm
Riverside Nursery
Brooklands Farm
Kelmstone Arabian Stud
Little Goldbridge Farm
Burnside Nursery
Sunfield Farm
Wyevale Nursery
Rowan Nursery
Grant's Bri
Poplar Grove Farm
Rothwell Nursery
Broadford
Broadford Farm
Focklesbrook Farm
Chobham Farm
MILFORD GREEN
Castle Grove
Castle Grove Nursery
Tenaker Nursery
Warehouse
Sewage Works
Cox Hill
Milford House
Daydown Nursery
Mimbridge
COXHILL GREEN
White Lodge Farm
Wapshott Farm
Heather Farm
GU21
Young Stroat Farm
Scotchers Farm
Shaws Farm
SURREY HEATH
WOKING
Millbrook Animal Centre (R.S.P.C.A.)
Grove Herb Farm
Studley Grange Farm
Border Farm
Mimbridge Garden Centre
Deep Pool Farm
Knaphill Manor Farm
Knaphill Manor
Graylands Farm
HORSELL COMMON
NUFFIELD HOSPITAL
Copthorne Meadows Farm
CHOBHAM GOLF COURSE
Clubhouse
Mink Farm
Westbury Farm
Garden Supplies
Parley Brook Farm
Garden Centre
Parley Bridge
HORSELL BIRCH
Knapwood House
Sec Sch
Rec Cen
M3
A319
A3046
B386
B383
132
166
AS AT AU AV AW AX AY
105 106 107 108 109 110 111 112 113 114

AZ
BA
BB
BC
BD
BE
BF
133
152
167
GOLF COURSE
Clubhouse
Foxhills Country Club
Foxhills
Tennis Courts
Dower House
Kitchenride Corner
Ten Acre Farm
KT16
Ether Hill
Nursery
HOME WOOD
Botleys Mansion
HOMEWOOD PARK
Hillswood Business Park
Offices
Church Farm
FISH POND
ST. PETER'S HOSP
HOSPITAL (CLOSED)
Silverlands Farm
GUILDFORD ROAD
A320
ST. PETER'S WAY
Junction 11
Woodside Farm
BITTAMS LANE
Simplemarsh Farm
Prim Sch
Sports Cen
Sec Sch
OTTERSHAW
Great Grove Farm
The Otter Nursery
MURRAY ROAD
B3121
SPINNEY HILL
OTTERSHAW MEMORIAL FIELDS
Youth Club
Amb Sta
Queenwood Farm
Coach House
CHOBHAM ROAD
A319
Timber Hill
THE COMMON
Prim Sch
Bousley Farm
Bousley End Stables
ROW TOWN
KT15
Southern Wood Farm
Glasshouses
Rodwell Farm
Hall's Farm
Tusk House
The Mansion
BROX COPSE
BROX LANE
Brox Road Nursery
RUNNYMEDE
SURREY HEATH
Timber Hill
LONG COPSE
OTTERSHAW PARK
SAMSON'S WOOD
LITTLE BLACKMOLE POND
GREAT BLACKMOLE POND
SANDPIT PLANTATION
GREAT WOOD
THE WARREN
WARE COPSE
Anningsley Park Farm
Anningsley Park
BIRCH WOOD
ROSE PARK
Holme Farm
Glasshouse
Fallow Farm
Grange Farm
DECOY PLANTATION
The Bourne
Dunford Bridge
Bonsey's Bridge
McLaren Cars
HOYT WOOD
RUNNYMEDE
WOKING
WOODHAM
Sports Club
NEW ZEALAND GOLF COURSE
Clubhouse
PLAYING FIELD
Sec Sch
BASINGSTOKE CANAL
Electricity Station
WEST BYFLEET
Sheerwater Bridge
ANTHONYS
Danewell Hill
Bleak House PH
HORSELL COMMON
CHERTSEY ROAD
SHEERWATER
SHEERWATER REC GRD
Athletic Club
Prim Sch
Comm Cen
Youth Club
KINGSWEY BUSINESS CENTRE
RIVER COURT
GENESIS BUSINESS PARK
WOKING BUSINESS PARK
Six Cross Roads
WOODHAM ROAD
A245
SPORTS GROUND
Monument Bridge
IND EST
KT14
WEST BYFLEET GOLF COURSE
Pyrford
GU22
OLD WOKING ROAD
Superstore
Health Cen
Clubhouse
Sch
PO
Lib
105
106
107
108
109
110
111
112
113
114
01
02
03
61
62
63
64

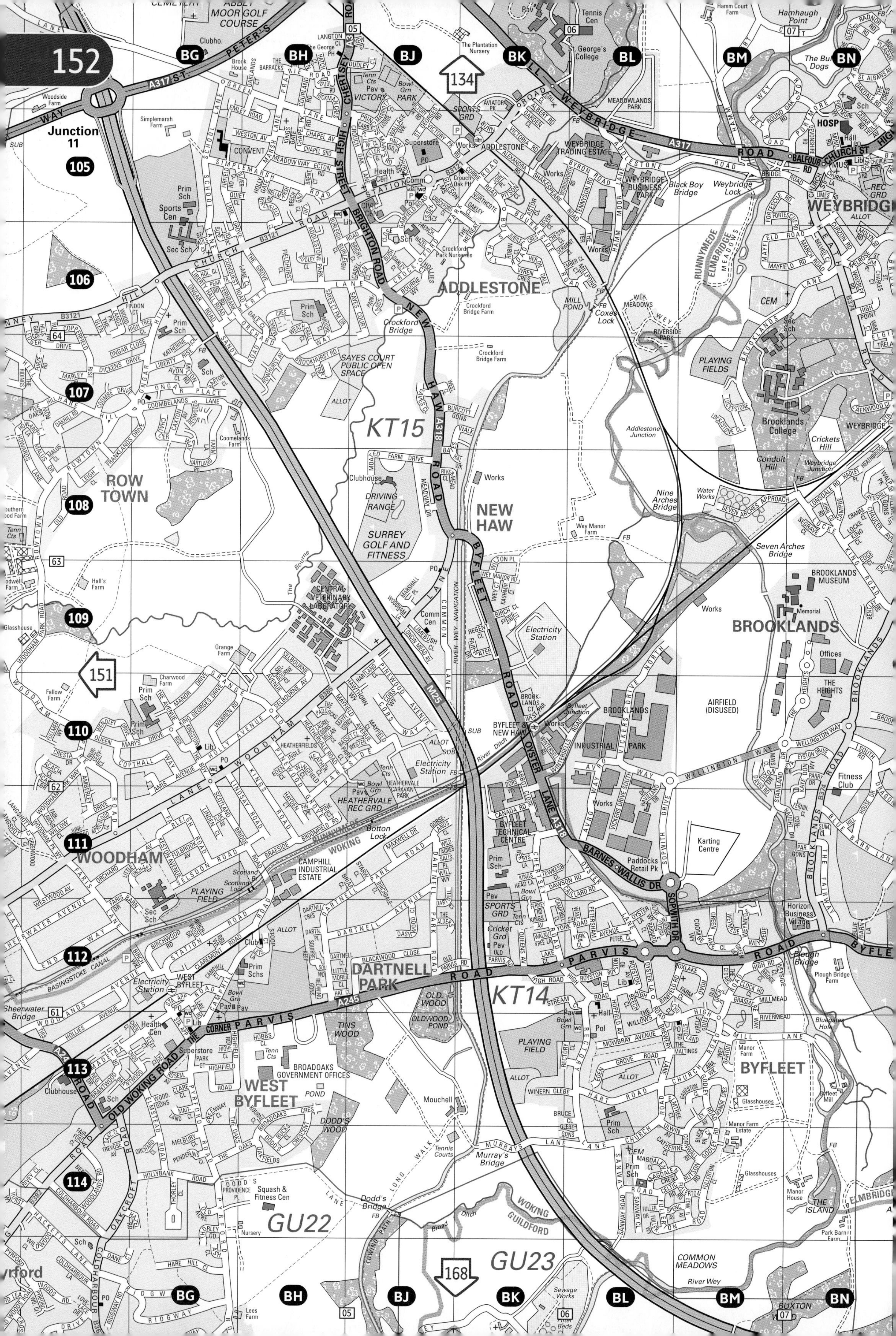
ABBEY MOOR GOLF COURSE
BG
BH
BJ
BK
BL
BM
BN
134
Junction 11
105
106
107
108
109
110
111
112
113
114
151
168
A317 ST. PETER'S WAY
CHERTSEY
HIGH STREET
BRIGHTON ROAD
STATION ROAD
CHURCH ROAD
B3121
ADDLESTONE
VICTORIA PARK
The Plantation Nursery
St. George's College
Tennis Cen
WEYBRIDGE ROAD
A317
WEYBRIDGE TRADING ESTATE
WEYBRIDGE BUSINESS PARK
MEADOWLANDS PARK
Black Boy Bridge
Weybridge Lock
WEYBRIDGE
BALFOUR RD
CHURCH ST
HOSP
The Bull Dogs
Hamhaugh Point
Hamm Court Farm
Simplemarsh Farm
Woodside Farm
CONVENT
Sports Cen
Prim Sch
Sec Sch
Superstore
Health Cen
Crockford Park Nurseries
Crockford Bridge
Crockford Bridge Farm
MILL POND
Coxes Lock
WEY MEADOWS
RIVERSIDE PARK
RUNNYMEDE
ELMBRIDGE
PLAYING FIELDS
CEM
Brooklands College
Crickets Hill
Conduit Hill
Weybridge Junction
Addlestone Junction
Nine Arches Bridge
Water Works
SEVEN ARCHES APPROACH
Seven Arches Bridge
BROOKLANDS MUSEUM
BROOKLANDS
Memorial
Offices
THE HEIGHTS
AIRFIELD (DISUSED)
BROOKLANDS INDUSTRIAL PARK
WELLINGTON WAY
Fitness Club
Karting Centre
Paddocks Retail Pk
BARNES WALLIS DR
SOPWITH DR
SAYES COURT PUBLIC OPEN SPACE
KT15
NEW HAW
A318
NEW HAW ROAD
BYFLEET ROAD
Works
Clubhouse
DRIVING RANGE
SURREY GOLF AND FITNESS
Wey Manor Farm
Electricity Station
ROW TOWN
Coomelands Farm
Hall's Farm
Glasshouse
Grange Farm
Charwood Farm
Fallow Farm
CENTRAL VETERINARY LABORATORY
The Bourne
M25
RIVER WEY NAVIGATION
Byfleet Junction
BYFLEET & NEW HAW
OYSTER LANE
HEATHERVALE REC GRD
HEATHERVALE CARAVAN PARK
Botton Lock
WOODHAM
WOODHAM LANE
SHEERWATER AVENUE
PLAYING FIELD
Scotland Lock
BASINGSTOKE CANAL
CAMPHILL INDUSTRIAL ESTATE
BYFLEET TECHNICAL CENTRE
SPORTS GRD
Cricket Grd
DARTNELL PARK
PARVIS ROAD
A245
OLD WOOD
OLDWOOD POND
TINS WOOD
KT14
WEST BYFLEET
Sheerwater Bridge
BROADOAKS GOVERNMENT OFFICES
DODD'S WOOD
OLD WOKING ROAD
Clubhouse
Mouchell
Tennis Courts
Murray's Bridge
MURRAYS LANE
Dodd's Bridge
Squash & Fitness Cen
GU22
GU23
WOKING
GUILDFORD
Nursery
Lees Farm
BYFLEET
Manor Farm
Glasshouses
Manor Farm Estate
Plough Bridge
Plough Bridge Farm
Bluegates Hole
Byfleet Mill
Horizon Business Village
Manor House
THE ISLAND
Park Barn Farm
ELMBRIDGE
COMMON MEADOWS
River Wey
BUXTON WOOD
Sewage Works
Pyrford

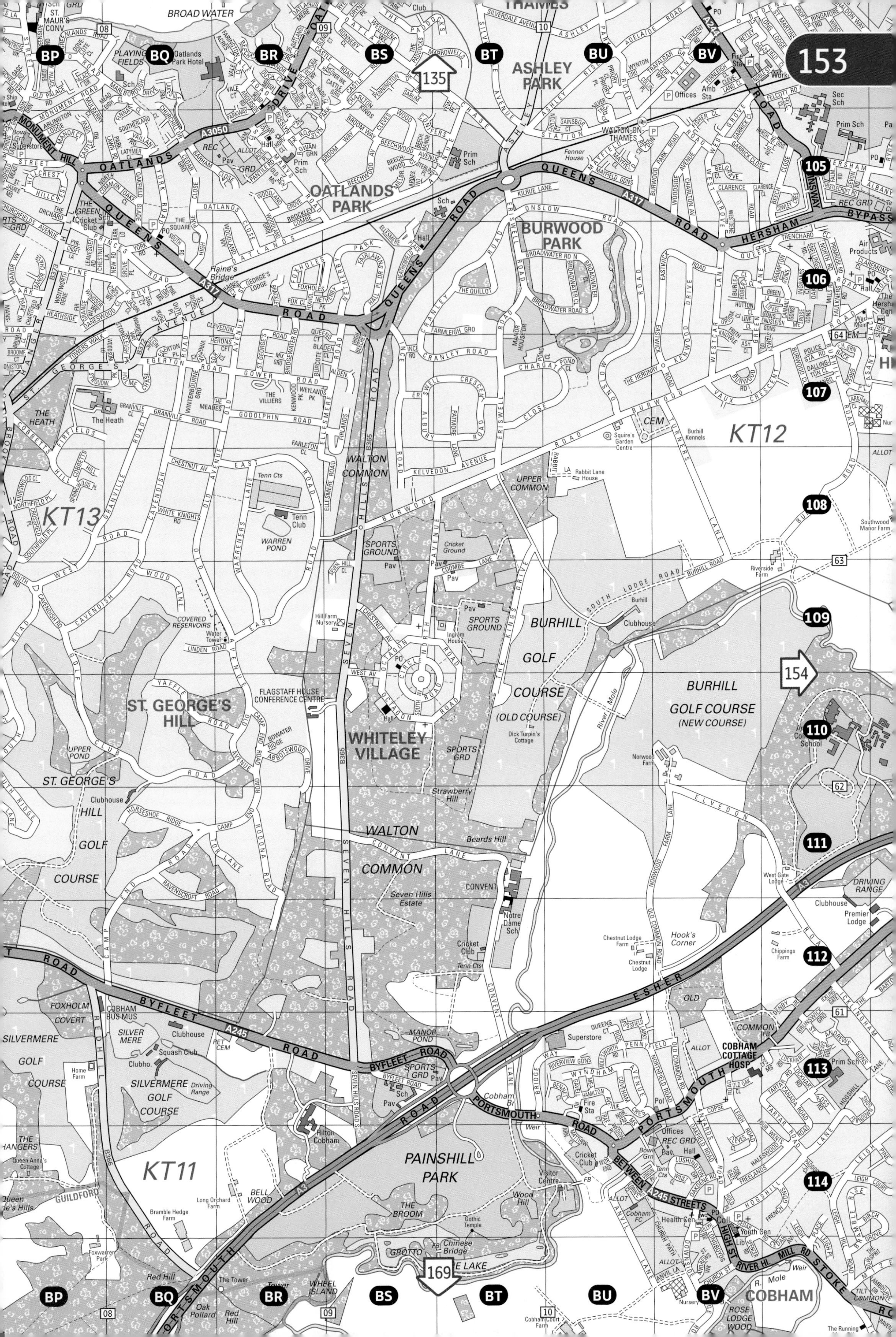
ASHLEY PARK
OATLANDS PARK
BURWOOD PARK
WALTON COMMON
KT13
KT12
KT11
ST. GEORGE'S HILL
WHITELEY VILLAGE
BURHILL GOLF COURSE (OLD COURSE)
BURHILL GOLF COURSE (NEW COURSE)
ST. GEORGE'S HILL GOLF COURSE
SILVERMERE GOLF COURSE
PAINSHILL PARK
COBHAM
QUEENS ROAD
OATLANDS DRIVE
SEVEN HILLS ROAD
PORTSMOUTH ROAD
BYFLEET ROAD
ESHER ROAD
HERSHAM ROAD
BURWOOD ROAD
135
154
169
BP
BQ
BR
BS
BT
BU
BV

BW
BX
BY
BZ
CA
CB
CC
136
153
170
HERSHAM
ESHER
WEST END
KT12
KT11
HERSHAM VILLAGE GOLF COURSE
CORONATION PLAYING FIELDS
SANDOWN PARK RACECOURSE
Grandstand & Exhibition Centre
PRINCESS ALICE HOSPICE
MOORE PLACE GOLF COURSE
HERSHAM RIVERSIDE PARK
WEST END COMMON
CLAREMONT LANDSCAPE GARDEN
Claremont Park
CLAREMONT PARK GOLF COURSE
ARBROOK COMMON
ESHER COMMON
WINTERDOWN WOOD
HORSESHOE CLUMP
BURHILL GOLF COURSE (NEW COURSE)
American Community School
FAIRMILE COMMON
OXSHOTT HEATH
Fairmile
LITTLE HEATH COMMON
WATERCUT COPSE
KNOWLE HILL PARK
COBHAM
COBHAM COTTAGE HOSP
CLAY PLANTATION
PORTSMOUTH ROAD
ESHER BYPASS
HERSHAM BYPASS
HERSHAM ROAD
LAMMAS LANE
COPSEM LANE
WARREN LANE
BURHILL ROAD
BLACKHILLS
SANDY LANE
FAIRMILE LANE
OXSHOTT WAY
STOKE ROAD
A3
A244
A245
A307
105
106
107
108
109
110
111
112
113
114

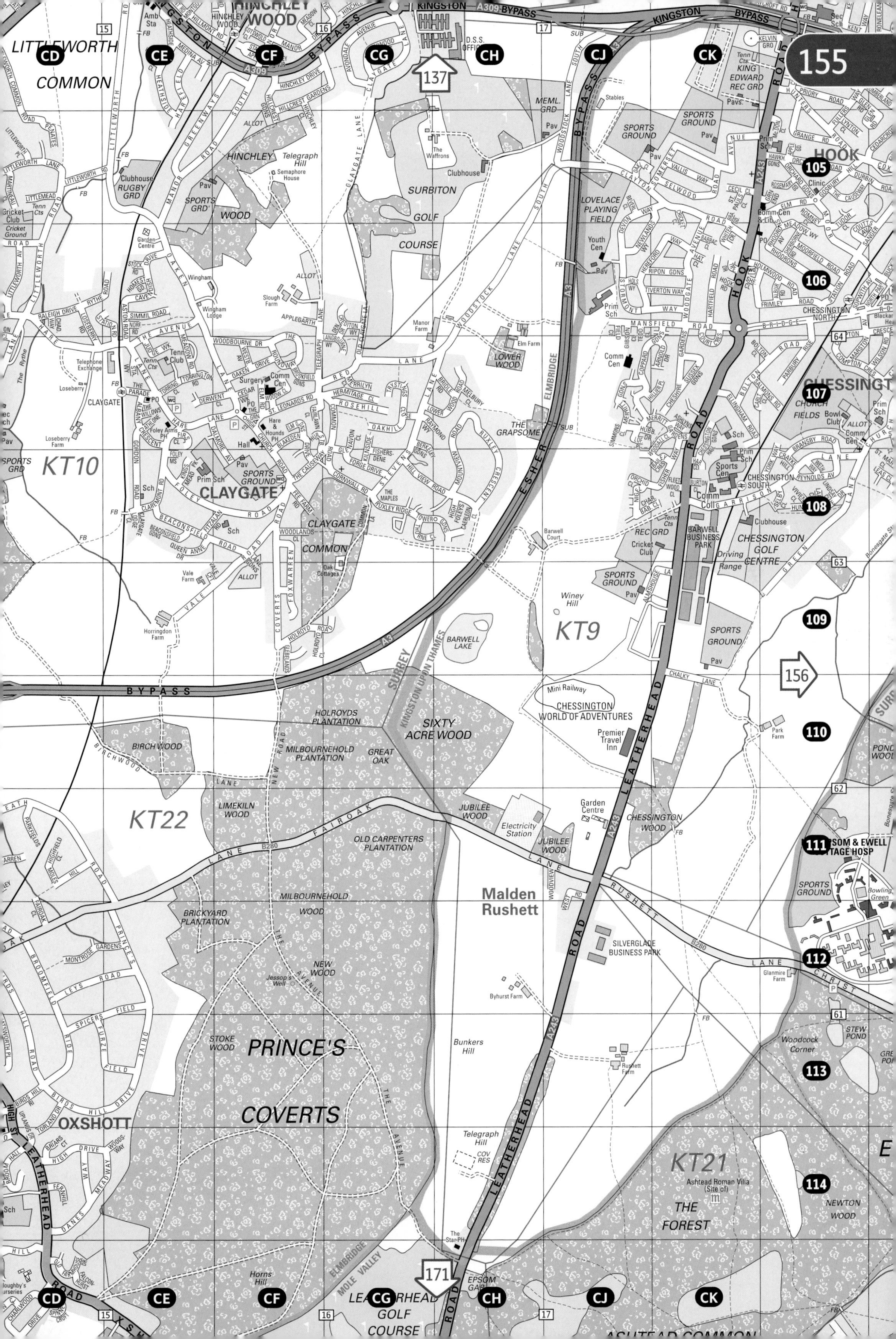
LITTLEWORTH COMMON
HINCHLEY WOOD
KINGSTON BYPASS
137
SURBITON GOLF COURSE
HOOK
CLAYGATE
KT10
CLAYGATE COMMON
CHESSINGTON GOLF CENTRE
KT9
CHESSINGTON WORLD OF ADVENTURES
156
SIXTY ACRE WOOD
BIRCH WOOD
KT22
Malden Rushett
PRINCE'S COVERTS
OXSHOTT
KT21
THE FOREST
LEATHERHEAD GOLF COURSE
171
CD
CE
CF
CG
CH
CJ
CK

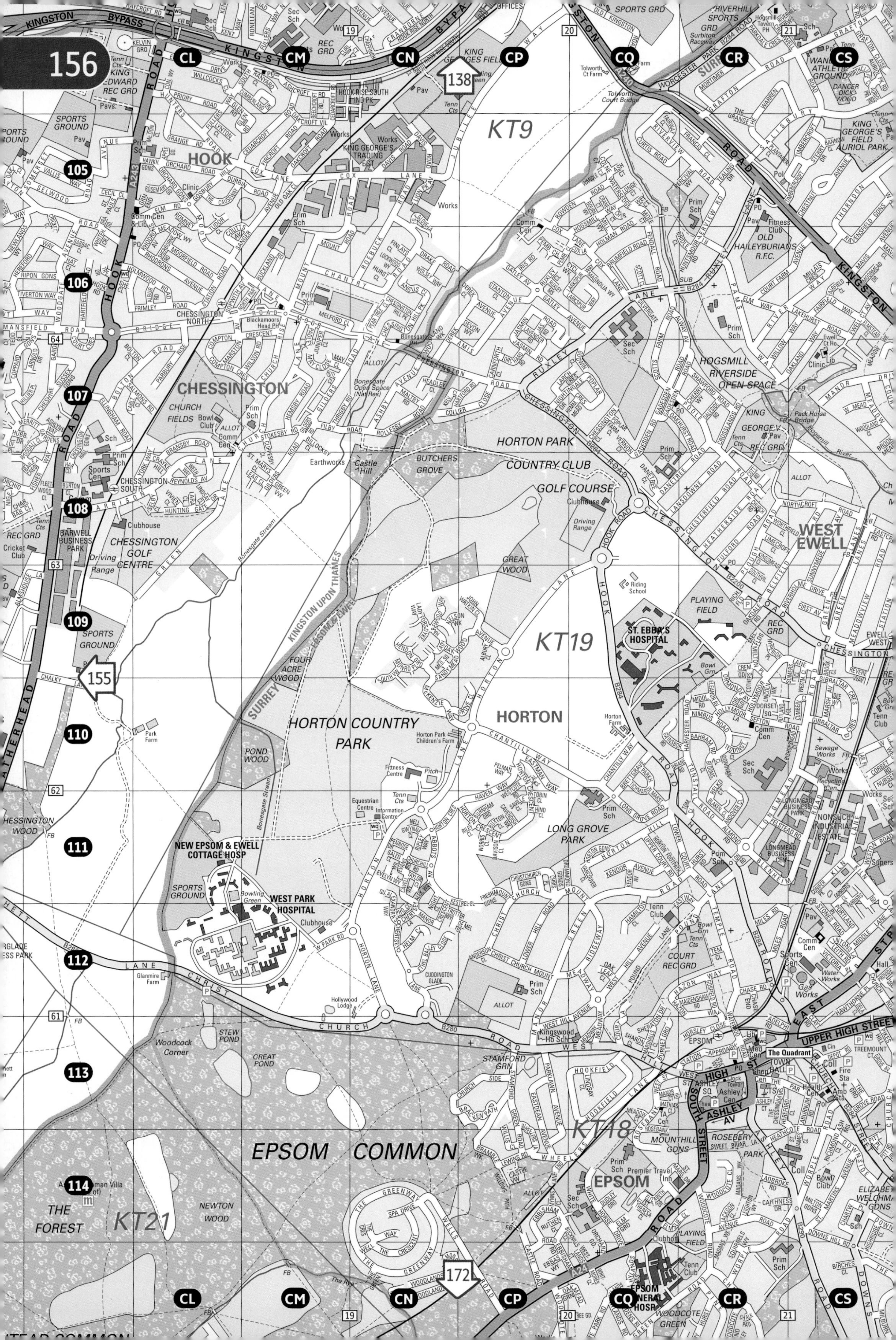
KINGSTON BYPASS
HOOK
KT9
KING GEORGE'S TRADING EST
CHESSINGTON
CHESSINGTON NORTH
CHESSINGTON SOUTH
CHURCH FIELDS
CHESSINGTON GOLF CENTRE
BARWELL BUSINESS PARK
SPORTS GROUND
HORTON PARK COUNTRY CLUB GOLF COURSE
BUTCHERS GROVE
Castle Hill
GREAT WOOD
FOUR ACRE WOOD
KINGSTON UPON THAMES
SURREY
EPSOM & EWELL
HORTON COUNTRY PARK
HORTON
KT19
ST. EBBA'S HOSPITAL
POND WOOD
NEW EPSOM & EWELL COTTAGE HOSP
WEST PARK HOSPITAL
LONG GROVE PARK
HOGSMILL RIVERSIDE OPEN SPACE
KING GEORGE V REC GRD
WEST EWELL
NONSUCH INDUSTRIAL ESTATE
LONGMEAD BUSINESS PARK
COURT REC GRD
UPPER HIGH STREET
The Quadrant
HIGH ST
ASHLEY AV
SOUTH STREET
KT18
EPSOM
EPSOM COMMON
KT21
THE FOREST
NEWTON WOOD
STEW POND
GREAT POND
Woodcock Corner
STAMFORD GRN
ROSEBERY PARK
EPSOM GENERAL HOSP
WOODCOTE GREEN
OLD HAILEYBURIANS R.F.C.
KING GEORGE'S FIELD AURIOL PARK
WANDGAS ATHLETIC GROUND
KING EDWARD REC GRD
CL CM CN CP CQ CR CS
105 106 107 108 109 110 111 112 113 114
138 155 172

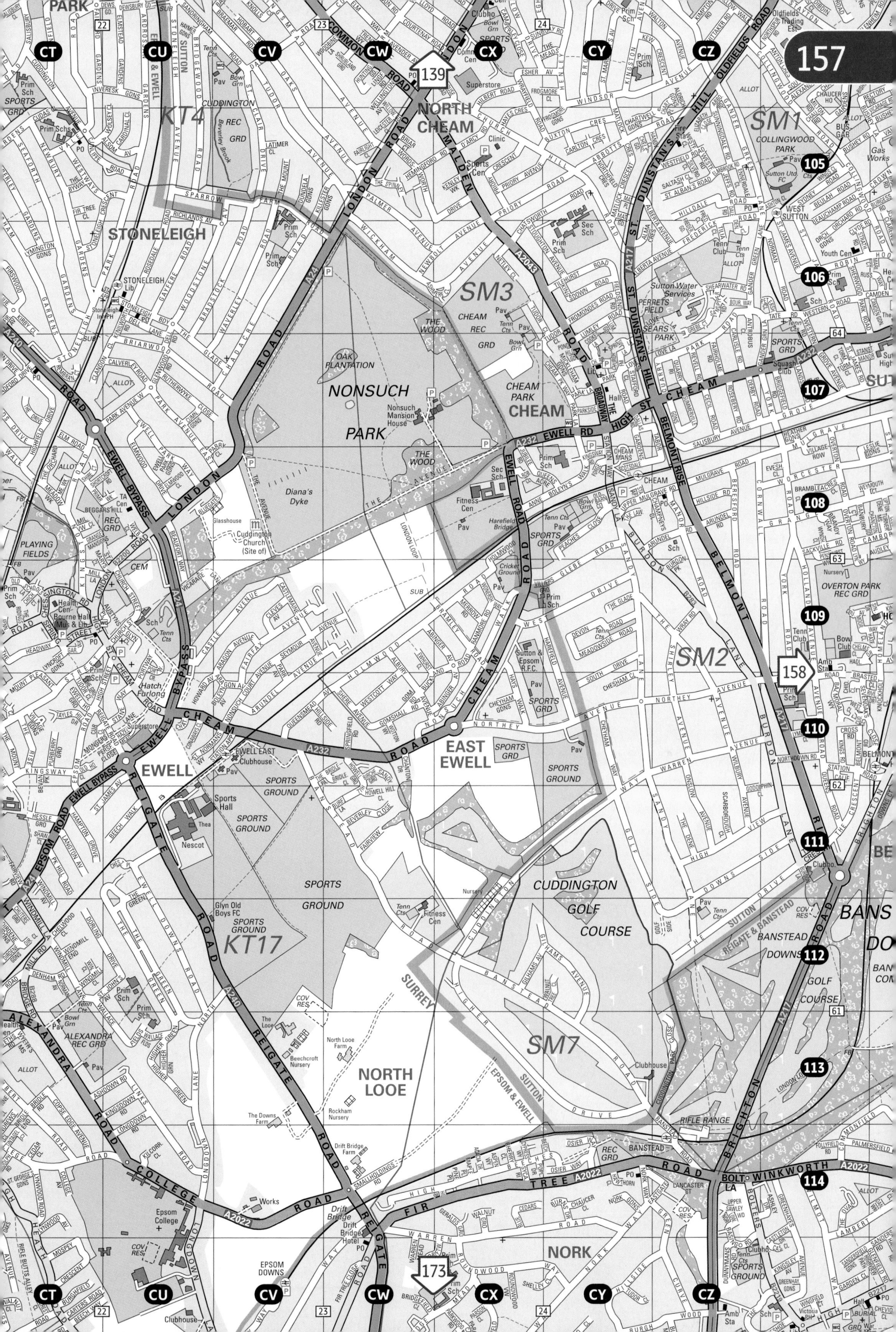
CT
CU
CV
CW
CX
CY
CZ
139
173
158
STONELEIGH
NORTH CHEAM
NONSUCH PARK
CHEAM
EAST EWELL
EWELL
NORTH LOOE
NORK
KT4
KT17
SM1
SM2
SM3
SM7
CUDDINGTON GOLF COURSE
BANSTEAD DOWNS GOLF COURSE
CUDDINGTON REC GRD
CHEAM REC GRD
CHEAM PARK
OAK PLANTATION
THE WOOD
Diana's Dyke
Nonsuch Mansion House
Cuddington Church (Site of)
OVERTON PARK REC GRD
ALEXANDRA REC GRD
COLLINGWOOD PARK
PLAYING FIELDS
SPORTS GROUND
SURREY
EPSOM & EWELL
SUTTON
RIFLE RANGE
Epsom College
EPSOM DOWNS
LONDON ROAD
EWELL BY-PASS
REIGATE ROAD
CHEAM ROAD
EWELL ROAD
BELMONT RISE
ST DUNSTAN'S HILL
BRIGHTON ROAD
COLLEGE ROAD
FIR TREE ROAD
WINKWORTH
A24
A232
A240
A217
A2022
A2043
105
106
107
108
109
110
111
112
113
114

DA
DB
DC
DD
DE
DF
DG
140
157
174
SM1
SM2
SM5
SM7
CARSHALTON
SUTTON
CARSHALTON BEECHES
BELMONT
BANSTEAD DOWNS
LITTLE WOODCOTE
WOODMANSTERNE
ROYSTON PARK
COLLINGWOOD PARK
THE WRYTHE REC GRD
CARSHALTON PARK
THE GROVE
CARSHALTON WAR MEMORIAL HOSP
OVERTON PARK REC GRD
SUTTON HOSPITAL
ROYAL MARSDEN HOSP
WELLFIELD PLANTATION
PLAYING FIELD
OAKS SPORTS CENTRE GOLF COURSE
THE OAKS PARK
H.M. PRISON DOWNVIEW
H.M. PRISON HIGH DOWN
BANSTEAD DOWNS
BANSTEAD COMMON
GOLF COURSE
RIFLE RANGE
SPORTS GROUND
RIFFET WOOD
BIG WOOD
CLOCKHOUSE REC GRD
WOODMANSTERNE PARK RECREATION GROUND
Market Gardens
PROSPECT PLANTATION
CHEAM
BRIGHTON ROAD
BELMONT RISE
CARSHALTON ROAD
WOODMANSTERNE ROAD
WOODMANSTERNE LANE
CROYDON LANE
WINKWORTH ROAD
SUTTON LANE
BANSTEAD ROAD
HIGH ST
A232
A217
A2022
B278
B2218
105
106
107
108
109
110
111
112
113
114

BEDDINGTON
THE GRANGE GARDENS
PARK
WALLINGTON
SM6
SOUTH BEDDINGTON
BANDON HILL CEMETERY
MELLOWS PARK
SOUTH BEDDINGTON SPORTS GROUNDS
ROUNDSHAW PLAYING FIELD
ROUNDSHAW OPEN SPACE
ROUNDSHAW PARK
DUPPAS HILL
CR0
PURLEY WAY PLAYING FIELDS
CR2
HALING PARK
SOUTH CROYDON
WOODCOTE
PURLEY
CR8
PURLEY HOSP
FOXLEY WOOD
RIDDLESDOWN WOOD
HIGHER DRIVE REC GRD
WOODCOTE GROVE REC GRD
WOODCOTE PARK GOLF COURSE
CR5
REEDHAM
KENLEY
SMITHAM
CROYDON ROAD
PURLEY WAY
BRIGHTON ROAD
STAFFORD ROAD
WOODCOTE ROAD
FOXLEY LANE
GODSTONE ROAD
DOWNS COURT ROAD
141
160
175
DH
DJ
DK
DL
DM
DN
DP
29
30
31
61
62
63
64
105
106
107
108
109
110
111
112
113
114

DQ
DR
DS
DT
DU
DV
DW
142
159
176
105
106
107
108
109
110
111
112
113
114
32
33
34
35
61
62
63
64
DUPPAS HILL RD
DUPPAS HILL
BARCLAY RD
FAIRFIELD RD
PARK LANE
HIGH ST
COOMBE ROAD
A212
A2039
PARK HILL
WHITGIFT PLAYING FIELDS
SHIRLEY PARK GOLF COURSE
LLOYD PARK
COOMBE PARK
SPORTS GROUND
PLAYING FIELD
ADDINGTON HILL
COOMBE LODGE PLAYING FIELDS
COOMBE WOOD
COOMBE LANE
BALLARDS PLANTATION
CONDUIT LANE
OAKS ROAD
BRIGHTON ROAD
A235
SOUTH CROYDON
HALING PARK
CR0
PURLEY WAY PLAYING FIELDS
SOUTH END
SOUTHBRIDGE RD
CROHAM RD
CROHAM MANOR ROAD
CROHAM VALLEY ROAD
BALLARDS WAY
CROHAM HURST
CROHAM HURST GOLF COURSE
THRIFT WOOD
UPPER SELSDON ROAD
LITTLEHEATH WOODS
BRAMLEY BANK NATURE RESERVE
THE RUFFETT
HALING GROVE
SOUTH CROYDON REC GRD
SANDERSTEAD ROAD
SANDERSTEAD
PURLEY OAKS
PURLEY BEECHES
SELSDON
SELSDON ROAD
ADDINGTON ROAD
SANDERSTEAD PLANTATION
CR2
SELSDON PARK HOTEL GOLF COURSE
Selsdon Park Hotel
PURLEY
PURLEY HOSP
ROTARY FIELD
PURLEY DOWNS GOLF COURSE
LIMPSFIELD ROAD
RECTORY PARK
A2022
MITCHLEY AVENUE
DOWNS COURT ROAD
GODSTONE ROAD
A22
RIDDLESDOWN
RIDDLESDOWN WOOD
COOMBES WOOD
CR8
MITCHLEY WOOD
RAGGED WOOD
AINSLEY BERRY SHAW
KINGS WOOD
NEWLANDS WOOD
FOXLEY WOOD
HIGHER DRIVE REC GRD
KENLEY
TANDRIDGE
CROYDON
LONDON LOOP

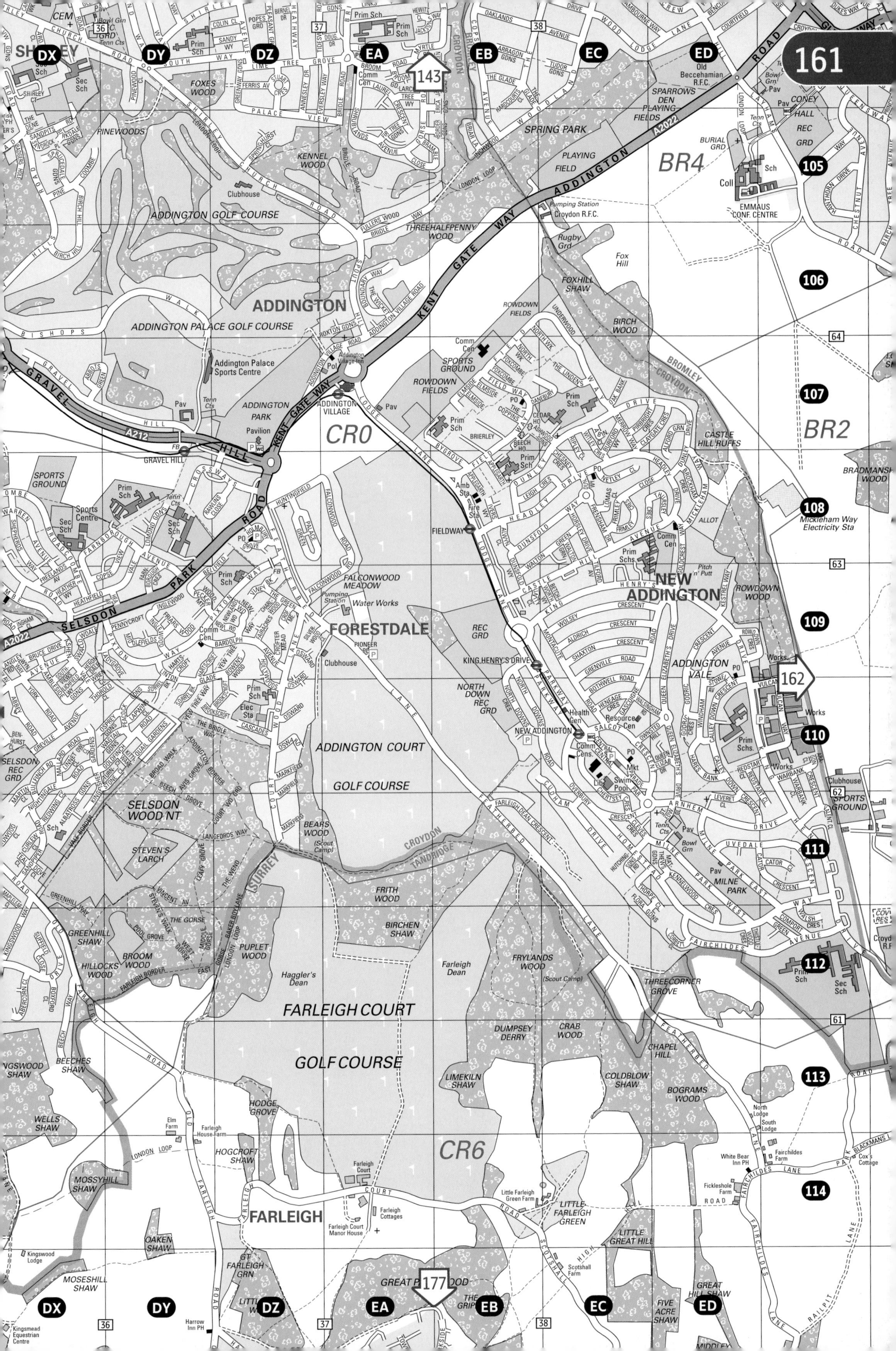
ADDINGTON
ADDINGTON GOLF COURSE
ADDINGTON PALACE GOLF COURSE
FORESTDALE
NEW ADDINGTON
ADDINGTON VALE
ADDINGTON COURT GOLF COURSE
FARLEIGH COURT GOLF COURSE
FARLEIGH
SELSDON WOOD NT
SPRING PARK
CR0
CR6
BR4
BR2
143
162
177

EE
EF
EG
EH
EJ
EK
EL
144
178
161
105
106
107
108
109
110
111
112
113
114
64
63
62
61
40
41
42
GLEBE WAY
CROYDON ROAD
A232
WICKHAM COMMON
Coney Hall
HAYES
COMMON
COLYERS WOOD
Rugby Ground
Hayes Court
NATURE TRAIL
Sec Sch
Wyevale Garden Centre
OAKLEY ROAD
CEDAR CRES
CHEYNE
ALLOT
SPARROWS DEN PLAYING FIELDS
A2022
LAYHAMS ROAD
Tenn Cts
Bowl Grn
Pav
CONEY HALL REC GRD
CHURCH DRIVE
KINGSWAY
QUEENSWAY
PRINCES WAY
HARVEST BANK RD
HARVEST BANK ROAD
ROBINS GRO
HARTFIELD CRESCENT
LAWRENCE RD
GATES GREEN ROAD
Prim Sch
MONARCH CL
CHERRY TREE WALK
LIME TREE WALK
BIRCH TREE AVENUE
CHESTNUT AVE
HAWTHORN DRIVE
SYLVAN WAY
BURIAL GRD
Sch
Coll
EMMAUS CONF. CENTRE
BR4
The Dashhouse
BASTON MANOR ROAD
BASTON ROAD
Hast Hill
The Lodge
Baston Manor
J.B. Stables
LONDON LOOP
COMMONSIDE
OAKFIELD LANE
PADMALL WOOD
Ravensbourne
RAVENSBOURNE OPEN SPACE
Greyhound PH
STOUR CL
WINDMILL DR
KESTON GDNS
LAKES ROAD
The Fox PH
FOX HILL
HEATHFIELD
KESTON AV
Prim Sch
KESTON COMMON
FOREST DRIVE
LONDON WOOD
BEECHWOOD DR
MARKE CL
FOREST RIDGE
HANCOCK
SWIRES SHAW
POULTERS WOOD
Forest Lodge
SOUTH PARK
Earthworks
Rouse Farm
WELL WOOD
NASH LANE
FOX LANE
HERITAGE HILL
Keston
GROVE
FISHPONDS ROAD
GREYS PK CL
REGENTS DR
B265
War Mem
Cricket Ground
Caesar's Camp
Elm Farm Cottage
Graylings Farm
COOPER'S WOOD
LONG SHAW
Fortune Bank Farm
ALLOT
JACKASS LANE
Foxhill Farm
JACKASS SHAW
LEAFY GROVE
Hall
WESTERHAM ROAD
A233
North Pole Farm
NORTH POLE LANE
Nash Farm
Longfield Farm & Cottage
FULLER'S WOOD
JAMES'S WOOD
Stables
Layham's Cattery
The Courtyard
Wilberforce Court
Holwood
BROMLEY CROYDON
CASTLE HILL RUFFS
BRADMANSHILL WOOD
Five Oaks Stables
War Bank
The Temple (Roman Mausoleum)
BR2
Tenn Cts
Mickleham Way Electricity Sta
RUSHFIELD SHAW
BROOMFIELDBANK SHAW
Keston Court Poultry Farm
Roman Villa
RECTORY ROAD
Scout Camp
LONDON LOOP
ALLOT
CR0
Comm Cen
Pitch 'n' Putt
Milchden
CHURCH ROAD
NEW ADDINGTON
ROWDOWN WOOD
Metropolitan Police Dog Training School
ORCHARD PLACE
BLACKNESS LANE
Glebe Farm
DOWNE ROAD
Leaves Green
Layham's Farm
Racing Circuit
Kimberley Farm
ADDINGTON VALE
Works
VULCAN WAY
QUEEN ELIZABETH'S DRIVE
ROWDOWN CRES
Gas Works
GREEN
The Vale Farm
FURZE BOTTOM
Prim Schs.
REDSTART CL
WARBANK CRESCENT
Clubhouse
SPORTS GROUND
Holmshaw Farm
HOPPERSNATCH SHAW
Crown Inn PH
ARNHEM DRIVE
LEVERET CL
Greyhound Training Kennels
Bradmore
Greenacres Riding School
UVEDALE CRESCENT
CATOR CL
MILNE PARK EAST
MILNE PARK WEST
High House Farm
ASHMORE LANE
Colinette Farm
LEAVES GREEN CRES
Milking Lane Farm
MILKING LANE
KENNELWOOD CRES
COMPORT GREEN
The Kings Arms PH
Clubhouse
Higham's Hill
Highams Hill Farm
COV RES
Croydon R.F.C.
FAIRCHILDES AVENUE
Prim Sch
Sec Sch
TERMINAL
THREECORNER GROVE
SHEEPBARN LANE
HELIPAD
MORTIMER ROAD
KEITH PARK
GRICE AV
VINCENT SQ
CHAPEL HILL
FEATHERBED
JEWELS WOOD
JEWELS HILL
SALT BOX HILL
REC GRD
Tenn Cts
HANBURY DR
MAIN ROAD
BOGRAMS WOOD
North Lodge
South Lodge
Hangars
LONDON BIGGIN HILL AIRPORT
SOW WOOD
CHURCH WAY
White Bear Inn PH
Fairchildes Farm
Blackman's Cottages
Cox's Cottage
BLACKMANS LANE
PARK
CR6
TN16
Hangars
CUDHAM LODGE WOODS
FAIRCHILDES LANE
OAKLANDS LANE
CROWN ASH
AIRPORT INDUSTRIAL ESTATE
TANDRIDGE
BROMLEY
SKID HILL LANE
Skid Hill House
SUNNINGVALE
VICTORIA
BIGGIN HILL BUSINESS PARK
Hangar
GREAT HILL SHAW
FIVE ACRE SHAW
CHRISTY ROAD
CROSSLEY
Costains

FARNBOROUGH
BR6
Green Street Green
Downe
Hazelwood
TN14
Single Street
PRINCESS ROYAL UNI HOSP
ORPINGTON HOSPITAL
HIGH ELMS GOLF COURSE
HIGH ELMS COUNTRY PARK
DOWN HO-DARWIN MUSEUM
WEST KENT GOLF COURSE
NEW YEARS WOOD
CUCKOO WOOD
WHITELANDS WOOD
BLACKLANDS
THE ROOKERY
NATURE FIELD
BURNT GORSE
DOWNE BANK (NATURE RESERVE)
LORDFIELD SHAW
HAZEL WOOD
SQUARE SHAW
THOMPSON WOOD
HANG GROVE
TWENTY ACRE SHAW
GREAT MOLLOMS WOOD
LITTLE MOLLOMS WOOD
FOXBERRY WOOD
HOMEFIELD SPRING
BROOM WOOD
HIGH WOOD
KANGLES WOOD
FOXBURROW WOOD
HOOK WOOD
NEWLANDS WOOD
BIRCHES CROFT
JOCKEY'S WOOD
BIRD HOUSE WOOD
LADIES WOOD
SPENCERS GROVE
LEASONS WOOD
BROMLEY CROFT
NINHAMS WOOD
LAKE WOOD
BROOM BANK
DARRICK WOOD
NEWSTEAD WOOD
ROUNDS WOOD
CHURCH END PLANTATION
COCKSETT PLANTATION
RAMUS WOOD
FARNBOROUGH COMMON
SEVENOAKS WAY
SEVENOAKS ROAD
HIGH STREET
SHIRE LANE
CUDHAM LANE NORTH
SNAG LANE
MACE LANE
NORSTED LANE
A21
A223
B2158
145
164
179
EM EN EP EQ ER ES ET
105 106 107 108 109 110 111 112 113 114
43 44 45 61 62 63 64

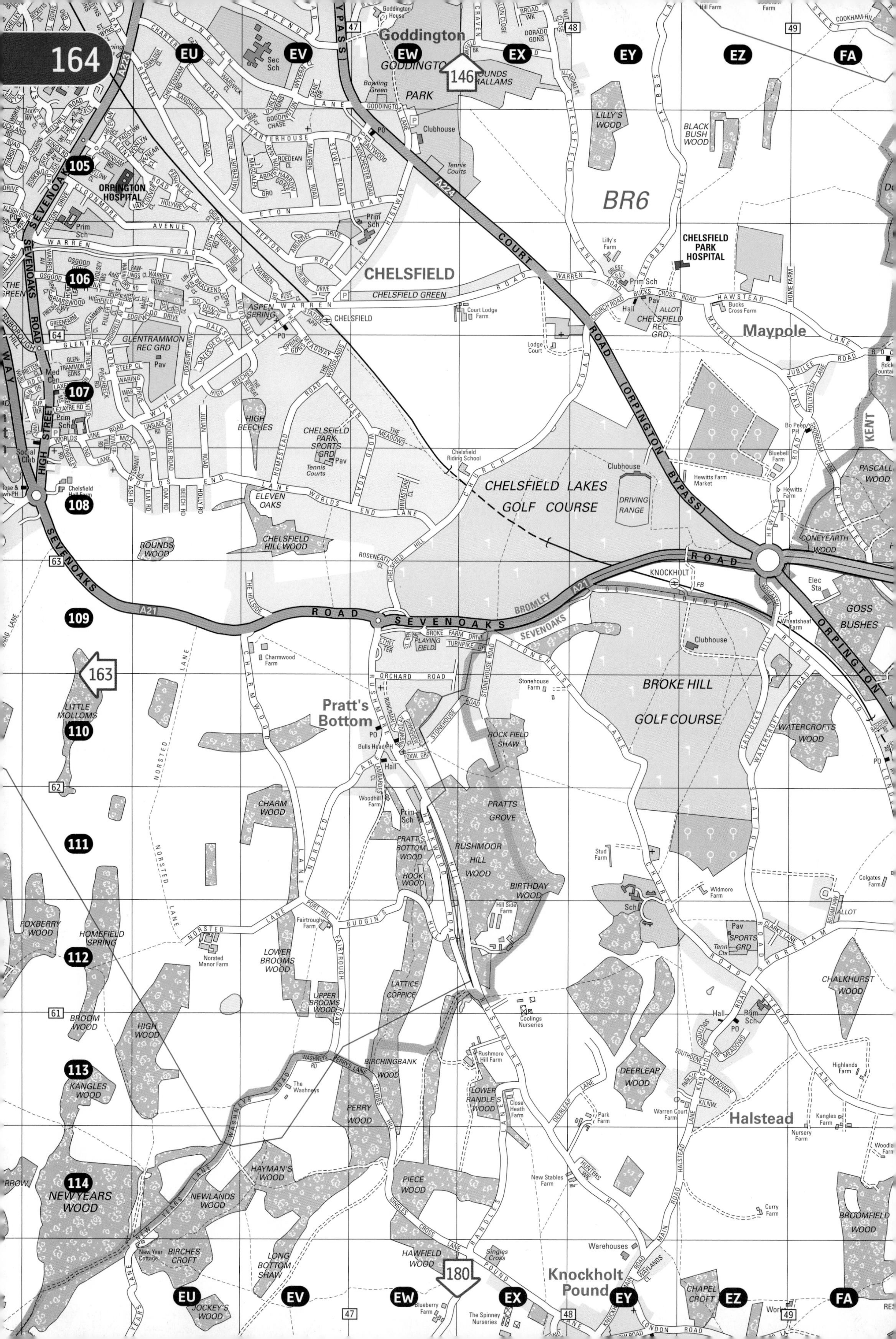
EU
EV
EW
EX
EY
EZ
FA
Goddington
GODDINGTON
PARK
146
Sec Sch
Bowling Green
Clubhouse
Tennis Courts
A224
A223
BR6
LILLY'S WOOD
BLACK BUSH WOOD
105
ORPINGTON HOSPITAL
Prim Sch
CHELSFIELD PARK HOSPITAL
CHELSFIELD
CHELSFIELD GREEN
Lilly's Farm
Prim Sch
Pav
Hall
ALLOT
CHELSFIELD REC GRD
Bucks Cross Farm
Maypole
106
ASPEN SPRING
CHELSFIELD
Court Lodge Farm
Lodge Court
GLENTRAMMON REC GRD
Pav
64
107
HIGH BEECHES
CHELSFIELD PARK SPORTS GRD
Pav
Tennis Courts
Chelsfield Riding School
CHELSFIELD LAKES GOLF COURSE
Clubhouse
DRIVING RANGE
Bo Peep PH
Bluebell Farm
Hewitts Farm Market
Hewitts Farm
PASCALL WOOD
KENT
Social Club
108
Chelsfield Hall Farm
ELEVEN OAKS
CHELSFIELD HILL WOOD
ROUNDS WOOD
CONEYEARTH WOOD
63
A21
KNOCKHOLT
Elec Sta
GOSS BUSHES
109
SEVENOAKS ROAD
BROMLEY
SEVENOAKS
PLAYING FIELD
Wheatsheaf Farm
Clubhouse
163
Charmwood Farm
Stonehouse Farm
BROKE HILL GOLF COURSE
LITTLE MOLLOMS
110
Pratt's Bottom
PO
Bulls Head PH
Hall
ROCK FIELD SHAW
WATERCROFTS WOOD
62
CHARM WOOD
Woodhill Farm
Prim Sch
PRATTS GROVE
111
PRATTS BOTTOM WOOD
HOOK WOOD
RUSHMOOR HILL WOOD
BIRTHDAY WOOD
Stud Farm
Sch
Widmore Farm
Colgates Farm
ALLOT
FOXBERRY WOOD
HOMEFIELD SPRING
112
Norsted Manor Farm
Fairtrough Farm
LOWER BROOMS WOOD
Hill Side Farm
Pav
SPORTS GRD
Tenn Cts
CHALKHURST WOOD
61
BROOM WOOD
HIGH WOOD
UPPER BROOMS WOOD
LATTICE COPPICE
Coolings Nurseries
Hall
Prim Sch
PO
113
KANGLES WOOD
The Washneys
BIRCHINGBANK WOOD
Rushmore Hill Farm
DEERLEAP WOOD
Highlands Farm
PERRY WOOD
LOWER RANDLE'S WOOD
Close Heath Farm
Park Farm
Warren Court Farm
Halstead
Kangles Farm
Nursery Farm
114
NEWYEARS WOOD
HAYMAN'S WOOD
NEWLANDS WOOD
PIECE WOOD
New Stables Farm
Curry Farm
BROOMFIELD WOOD
New Year Cottage
BIRCHES CROFT
LONG BOTTOM SHAW
HAWFIELD WOOD
Singles Cross
180
Warehouses
Knockholt Pound
CHAPEL CROFT
JOCKEY'S WOOD
47
Blueberry Farm
The Spinney Nurseries
48
49

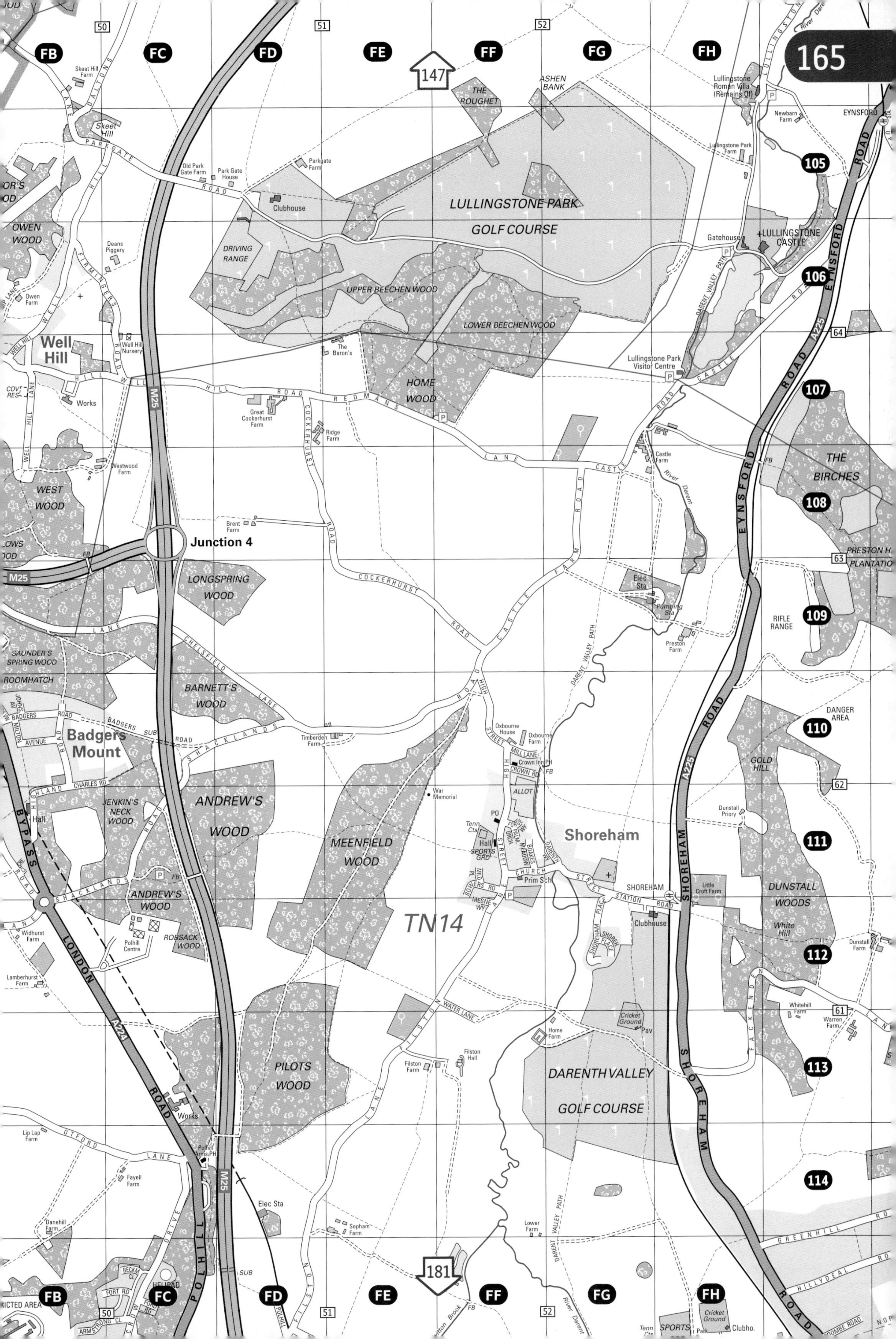
FB
FC
FD
FE
FF
FG
FH
50
51
52
147
181
THE ROUGHET
ASHEN BANK
Skeet Hill Farm
Skeet Hill
DALTONS
PARKGATE ROAD
Old Park Gate Farm
Park Gate House
Parkgate Farm
Clubhouse
LULLINGSTONE PARK GOLF COURSE
DRIVING RANGE
UPPER BEECHEN WOOD
LOWER BEECHEN WOOD
Lullingstone Roman Villa (Remains Of)
Newbarn Farm
EYNSFORD
Lullingstone Park Farm
Gatehouse
LULLINGSTONE CASTLE
DARENT VALLEY PATH
Lullingstone Park Visitor Centre
OWEN WOOD
Deans Piggery
Owen Farm
FIRMINGERS ROAD
Well Hill
Well Hill Nursery
The Baron's
HOME WOOD
WELL HILL
Works
M25
Great Cockerhurst Farm
REDMANS LANE
COCKERHURST ROAD
Ridge Farm
CASTLE ROAD
Castle Farm
River Darent
FB
EYNSFORD ROAD
A225
THE BIRCHES
Westwood Farm
WEST WOOD
Brent Farm
Junction 4
FARM ROAD
PRESTON H PLANTATIO
LONGSPRING WOOD
Elec Sta
Pumping Sta
RIFLE RANGE
Preston Farm
CHELSFIELD LANE
SAUNDER'S SPRING WOOD
ROOMHATCH
BARNETT'S WOOD
HIGH STREET
DANGER AREA
BADGERS ROAD
SHACKLANDS ROAD
Badgers Mount
Timberden Farm
Oxbourne House
Oxbourne Farm
MILL LANE
Crown Inn PH
CROWN RD
GOLD HILL
CHARLES RD
ANDREW'S WOOD
JENKIN'S NECK WOOD
War Memorial
ALLOT
Dunstall Priory
MEENFIELD WOOD
PO
Tenn Cts
Hall
SPORTS GRD
Shoreham
BYPASS
CHURCH STREET
Prim Sch
SHOREHAM
STATION ROAD
Little Croft Farm
DUNSTALL WOODS
White Hill
TN14
Clubhouse
SHOREHAM PLACE
Widhurst Farm
Polhill Centre
ROBSACK WOOD
Dunstall Farm
Lamberhurst Farm
LONDON ROAD
A224
WATER LANE
Cricket Ground
Pav
Whitehill Farm
Warren Farm
FACKENDEN LANE
Home Farm
Filston Hall
Filston Farm
FILSTON LANE
PILOTS WOOD
DARENTH VALLEY GOLF COURSE
SHOREHAM ROAD
Works
Lip Lap Farm
OTFORD LANE
Polhill Arms PH
Fayell Farm
Elec Sta
Danehill Farm
Sepham Farm
Lower Farm
GREENHILL RD
HILLYDEAL ROAD
POLHILL
HELIPAD
BECKM CL
FORT RD
DRIVE
SUB
RICTED AREA
ARMS
Cricket Ground
Clubho.
SPORTS
Tenn Cts
Park
River Darent
Brook
FB
105
106
107
108
109
110
111
112
113
114
61
62
63
64

AS
AT
AU
AV
AW
AX
AY
98
99
00
150
GU21
GU24
GU3
HORSELL COMMON
Horsell
Knaphill
Goldsworth Park
St. John's
Hook Heath
Mount Hermon
Mayford
LITTLEWICK COMMON
GOLDSWORTH PARK REC GRD
GOLDSWORTH PARK TRADING ESTATE
WATERERS PARK
CHOBHAM GOLF COURSE
WOKING GOLF COURSE
WEST HILL GOLF COURSE
WORPLESDON GOLF COURSE
SUTTON GREEN GOLF COURSE
HOE VALLEY LINEAR PARK
WOKING CEMETERY
LOCKFIELD DRIVE
A324
A320
A3046
KETTLEWELL HILL
CHOBHAM ROAD
CARTHOUSE LANE
LITTLEWICK ROAD
BROOKWOOD LYE
SMARTS HEATH
PREY HEATH
BRIDLEY COPSE
Burdenshot Hill
Pye Hill
WORPLESDON
Basingstoke Canal
Crematorium
Superstore
115
116
117
118
119
120
121
122
123
124

WEST BYFLEET GOLF COURSE
Pyrford
WOKING
Maybury
GU22
HOEBRIDGE GOLF CENTRE
PYRFORD COMMON
THE ROUGH
Pyrford Court
Pyrford Village
Newark Priory (Remains)
Old Woking
Westfield
GU4
GU23
Send
Send Marsh
River Wey
River Wey Navigation NT
Broadmead Cut
WOKING PARK
Monument Hill
Fox Hill
Oldhill Copse
Garlick's Arch Copse
Sutton Green
151
168

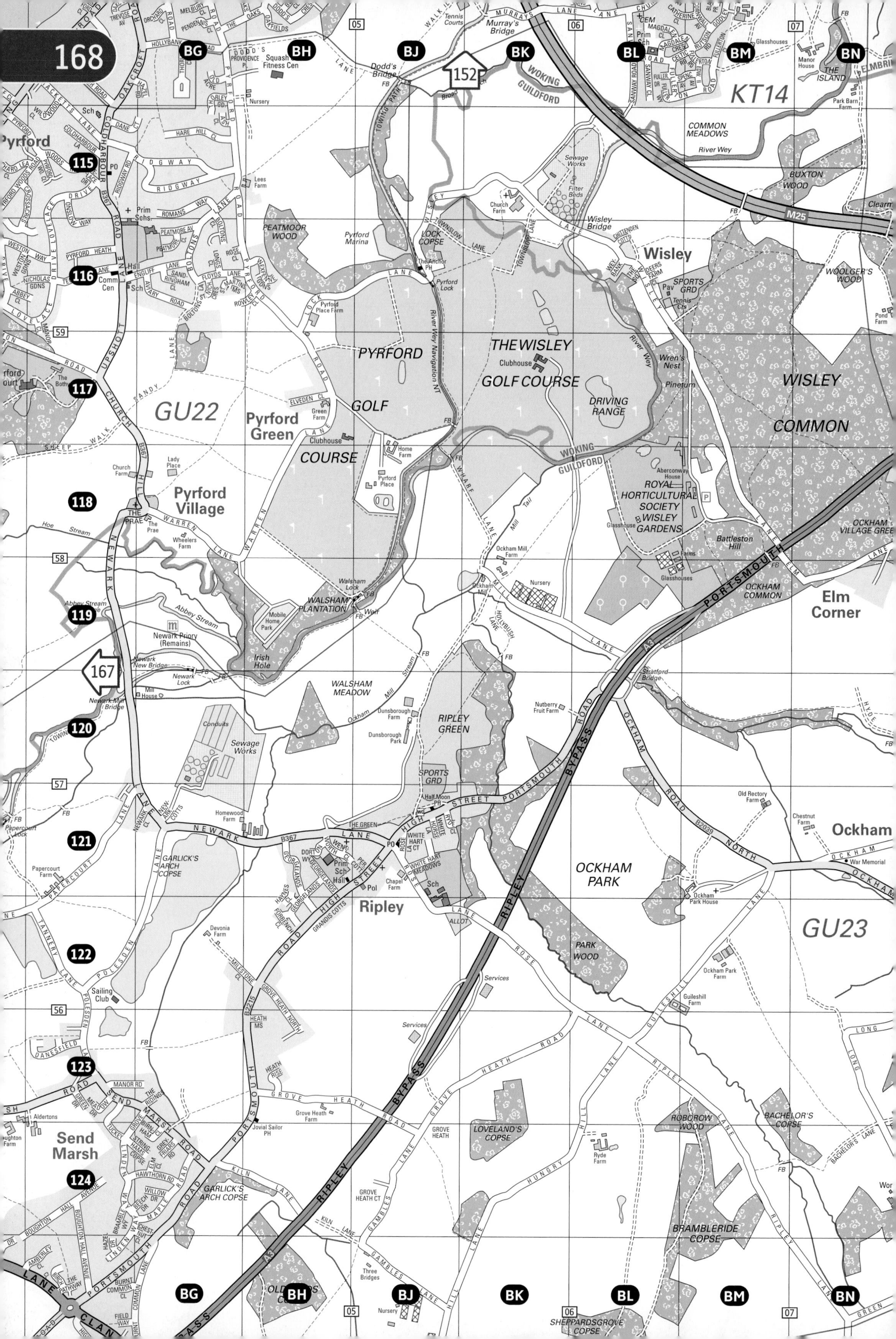
Pyrford
Pyrford Green
Pyrford Village
GU22
PYRFORD GOLF COURSE
THE WISLEY GOLF COURSE
Wisley
WISLEY COMMON
KT14
ROYAL HORTICULTURAL SOCIETY WISLEY GARDENS
Elm Corner
Ockham
OCKHAM PARK
GU23
Ripley
RIPLEY GREEN
Send Marsh
WALSHAM MEADOW
PEATMOOR WOOD
BUXTON WOOD
WOOLGER'S WOOD
PARK WOOD
LOVELAND'S COPSE
ROBOROW WOOD
BRAMBLERIDE COPSE
BACHELOR'S COPSE
GARLICK'S ARCH COPSE
SHEPPARDSGROVE COPSE
M25
A3
PORTSMOUTH ROAD
RIPLEY BYPASS
Newark Priory (Remains)
Wisley Bridge
Dodd's Bridge
Murray's Bridge
River Wey
COMMON MEADOWS
OCKHAM COMMON
Battleston Hill
Wren's Nest
Pinetum
Walsham Lock
Newark Lock
Papercourt Lock
Pyrford Lock
Stratford Bridge
Ockham Park House
Sailing Club
Sewage Works

152
167

PAINSHILL PARK
153
THE BROOM
Gothic Temple
Chinese Bridge
GROTTO
THE LAKE
Hilton Cobham
Long Orchard Farm
BELL WOOD
Bramble Hedge Farm
Foxwarren Park
Red Hill
The Tower
Tower Hill
WHEEL ISLAND
Oak Pollard
Red Hill
PORTSMOUTH ROAD
Junction 10
CHATLEY WOOD
Redhill Bottom
Cockrow Hill
Tumulus
Sandpit Hill
Hut Hill Cottage
Hut Hill
CURRIE'S CLUMP
CHATLEY HEATH
Telegraph Hill
Chatley Semaphore
OCKHAM COMMON
BOLDER MERE
HATCHFORD WOOD
Chatley Farm
THE BOGS
BREACH HILL WOOD
LODGE COPSE
POINTERS ROAD
KT11
River Mole
Cobham Court Farm
Downside Bridge
COBHAM
COBHAM PARK
Cobham Park Nursery
Cobham Stud Farm
Halfpenny Cross
PLOUGH LANE
BRAMBLE WOOD
Poynters Farm
Pointers Green
CHILBROOK ROAD
Cossins House
Cossins Farm
Downside
Pondtail Farm
DOWNSIDE COMMON
BRICKFIELD COPSE
LITTLE BRICKFIELD COPSE
HATCHFORD PARK
M25
NORTON LANE
GOOSE GREEN
Cold Norton Farm
Hazeldene Farm
NORTON WOOD
Highway Farm
Poultry Houses
Wilderness Farm
HUNT'S COPSE
The Black Swan PH
Martyr's Green
Pound Farm
ELMBRIDGE
GUILDFORD
Bull Riding Farm
OLD OAK COMMON
THE NEW PRESERVE
PEAKED ROUGH
ROUNDABOUT
Hurst Hill
May's Green
Bridge End Farm
Upton Farm
TANNERS COPSE
TRULLIBER COPSE
CHAFFERS COPSE
HOOK WOOD
Appstree Farm
SPORTS GROUND
ALMS HEATH
School Farm
SCHOOL LA
STUMPS GROVE
Blackmoor Farm
Barnsthorns
CLAMP ROUGH
Newmarsh Farm
Gun Club
BUSHY THICKET
THICKET COPSE
Banks Way House
LITTLE MORNSHILL WOOD
GALLOWS GROVE
Lord Howard PH
EFFINGHAM JUNCTION
KT24
Slade Farm
THE DRIFT GOLF COURSE
Clubhouse
BARNSTHORNS WOOD
Blue Ride
EFFINGHAM COMMON
Slater's Oak
Norwood Farm
THE DRIFT
DRIFT ROAD
THE FOREST
Cricket Ground
Cricket Club
LOWER FARM ROAD
Lower Farm
PIKES POOL
EVEN WOOD
HORSLEY CAMPING & CARAVAN SITE
Broom House
SPORTS GRD
Hook Farm
Indian Farm
Prim Sch
Manor Farm
BEAUMONT PLANTATION
NEW BARN WOOD
New Barn Farm
PARK WOOD
BIG ROUNDABOUT
ROSE LODGE WOOD
The Running Mare PH
115 116 117 118 119 120 121 122 123 124
170
BP BQ BR BS BT BU BV
08 09 10 56 57 58 59

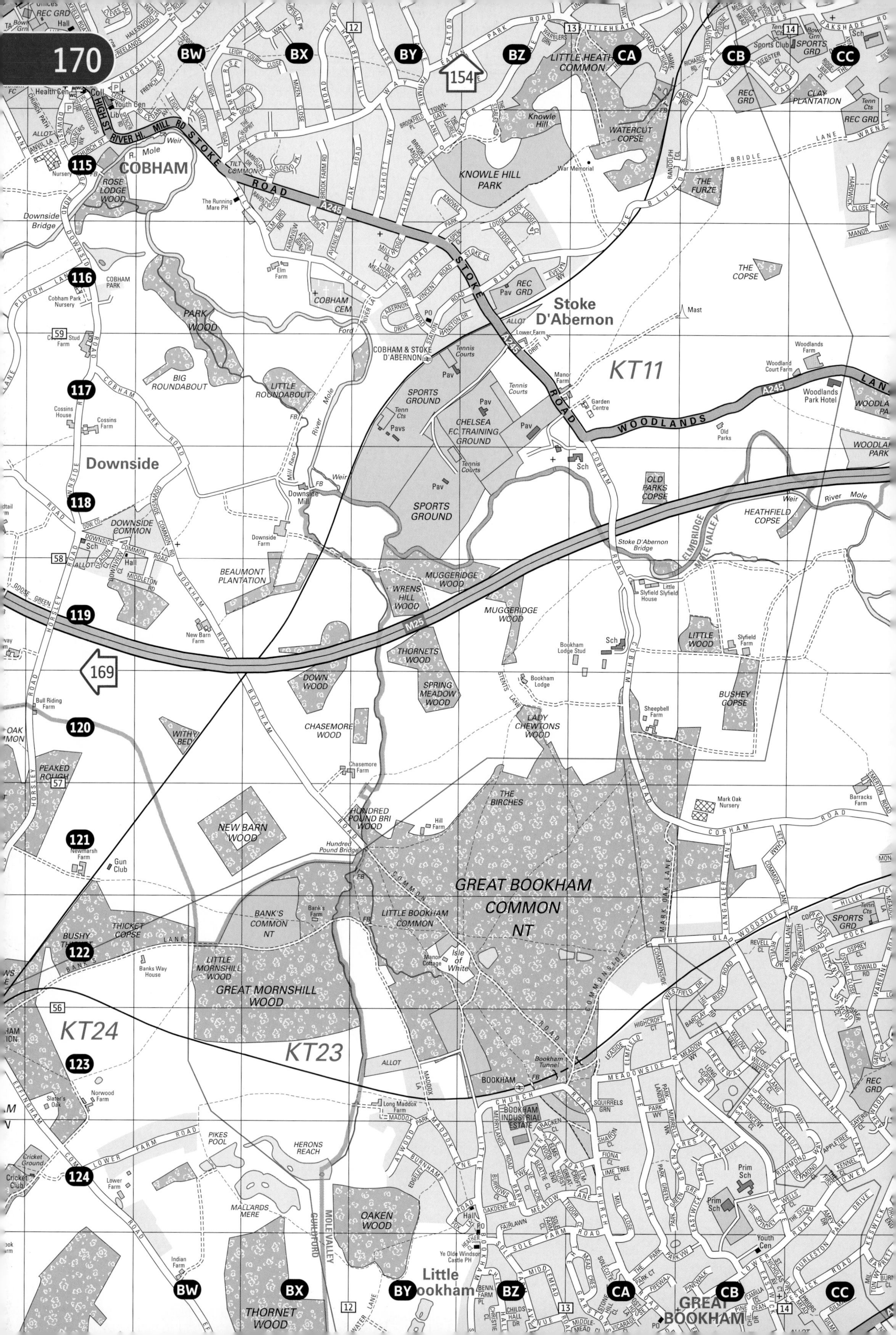
BW
BX
BY
BZ
CA
CB
CC
154
169
12
13
14
56
57
58
59
115
116
117
118
119
120
121
122
123
124
COBHAM
Stoke D'Abernon
Downside
KT11
KT24
KT23
Little Bookham
GREAT BOOKHAM
LITTLE HEATH COMMON
WATERCUT COPSE
Knowle Hill
KNOWLE HILL PARK
War Memorial
THE FURZE
CLAY PLANTATION
REC GRD
SPORTS GRD
Sports Club
R. Mole
ROSE LODGE WOOD
Downside Bridge
The Running Mare PH
STOKE ROAD
A245
Elm Farm
COBHAM CEM
COBHAM PARK
Cobham Park Nursery
PARK WOOD
BIG ROUNDABOUT
LITTLE ROUNDABOUT
River Mole
Cossins House
Cossins Farm
COBHAM & STOKE D'ABERNON
SPORTS GROUND
CHELSEA F.C. TRAINING GROUND
Tennis Courts
Manor Farm
Lower Farm
Garden Centre
Woodlands Farm
Woodland Court Farm
Woodlands Park Hotel
WOODLANDS PARK
WOODLANDS
Old Parks
THE COPSE
Mast
OLD PARKS COPSE
HEATHFIELD COPSE
Weir
Downside Mill
Mill Race
DOWNSIDE COMMON
Downside Farm
BEAUMONT PLANTATION
MUGGERIDGE WOOD
WRENS HILL WOOD
Stoke D'Abernon Bridge
ELMBRIDGE
MOLE VALLEY
Little Slyfield
Slyfield House
LITTLE WOOD
Slyfield Farm
BUSHEY COPSE
New Barn Farm
M25
THORNETS WOOD
DOWN WOOD
SPRING MEADOW WOOD
Bookham Lodge Stud
Bookham Lodge
LADY CHEWTONS WOOD
Sheepbell Farm
CHASEMORE WOOD
Chasemore Farm
WITHY BED
Bull Riding Farm
PEAKED ROUGH
THE BIRCHES
Mark Oak Nursery
Barracks Farm
NEW BARN WOOD
HUNDRED POUND BRI WOOD
Hundred Pound Bridge
Hill Farm
Newmarsh Farm
Gun Club
GREAT BOOKHAM COMMON NT
LITTLE BOOKHAM COMMON
BANK'S COMMON NT
Bank's Farm
THICKET COPSE
BUSHY THICKET
Banks Way House
LITTLE MORNSHILL WOOD
GREAT MORNSHILL WOOD
Manor Cottage
Isle of White
Bookham Tunnel
BOOKHAM
ALLOT
Long Maddox Farm
BOOKHAM INDUSTRIAL ESTATE
Slater's Oak
Norwood Farm
PIKES POOL
HERONS REACH
Cricket Ground
Cricket Club
Lower Farm
MALLARDS MERE
OAKEN WOOD
GUILDFORD
MOLE VALLEY
Indian Farm
THORNET WOOD
Ye Olde Windsor Castle PH
Prim Sch
Youth Cen
REC GRD
COBHAM ROAD
BOOKHAM ROAD
HORSLEY ROAD
DOWNSIDE ROAD
EFFINGHAM COMMON ROAD
LOWER FARM ROAD
CHURCH ROAD
LOWER ROAD
THE GLADE
WOODSIDE
MEADOWSIDE
COMMONSIDE
HIGH ST
RIVER HILL
MILL RD
BLUNDEL LANE
EATON PARK ROAD
LITTLEHEATH

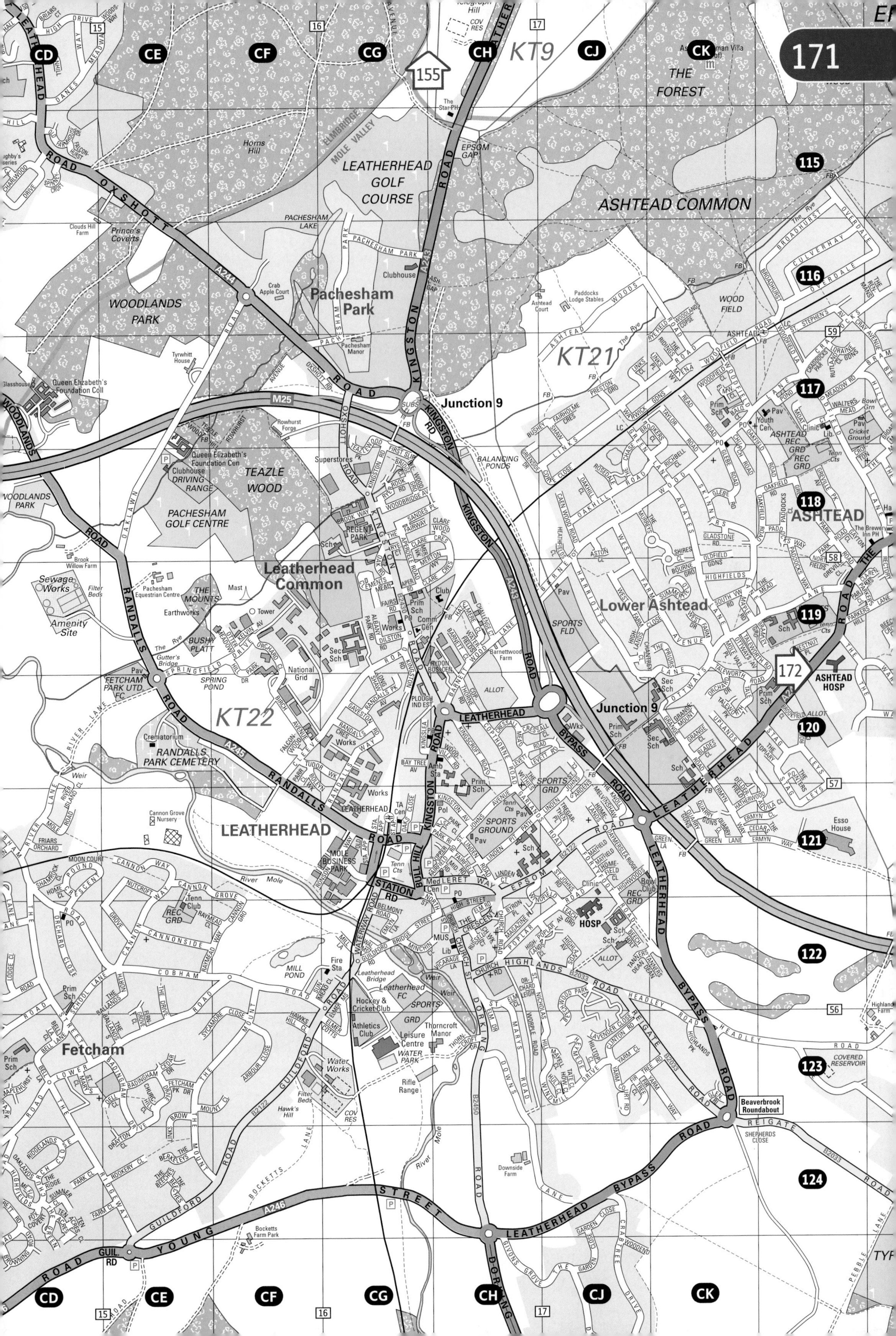
CD
CE
CF
CG
CH
KT9
CJ
CK
155
THE FOREST
LEATHERHEAD GOLF COURSE
Horns Hill
EPSOM GAP
ASHTEAD COMMON
115
116
WOOD FIELD
WOODLANDS PARK
Pachesham Park
KT21
Queen Elizabeth's Foundation Coll
M25
Junction 9
117
TEAZLE WOOD
PACHESHAM GOLF CENTRE
ASHTEAD
118
Leatherhead Common
Lower Ashtead
119
172
ASHTEAD HOSP
KT22
Junction 9
120
RANDALLS PARK CEMETERY
LEATHERHEAD
121
HOSP
122
Fetcham
123
Beaverbrook Roundabout
124
CD
CE
CF
CG
CH
CJ
CK

EPSOM COMMON
ASHTEAD COMMON
NEWTON WOOD
WOOD FIELD
ASHTEAD
Ashtead Park
Woodcote
RAC WOODCOTE PARK COUNTRY CLUB GOLF COURSE
EPSOM GENERAL HOSP
ASHTEAD HOSP
City of London Freemen's School
KT21
KT18
KT22
Langley Vale
LANGLEY BOTTOM WOOD
ADDLESTEAD WOOD
Tyrrell's Wood
TYRRELL'S WOOD
HEADLEY COURT
HAMBLETON WOOD
PIGNUT WOOD
NOWER WOOD
OYSTER HILL NT
TYRRELL'S WOOD GOLF COURSE
HOOK WOOD
GREAT HURST WOOD
LITTLE HURST WOOD
COSTAL WOOD
Beaverbrook Roundabout
LEATHERHEAD BYPASS ROAD
M25
A24
EPSOM & EWELL
MOLE VALLEY
Esso House
THE GROVE
WORLDS END
HALFMOON CLUMP
FISH POND

156
171
182

CT
CU
CV
CW
CX
CY
CZ
157
KT17
NORK
SM7
Epsom College
EPSOM DOWNS
Drift Bridge Hotel
EPSOM GOLF COURSE
BUCKLE'S GAP
NORK PARK
PARK WOOD
SPORTS GROUND
Toyota
TATTENHAM WAY RECREATION GROUND
EPSOM RACE COURSE
EPSOM DOWNS
The Hill
RACE DAY PARKING
Grandstand
Tattenham Corner
TATTENHAM CORNER
Burgh Heath
BURGH HEATH
COVERED RESERVOIR
Superstore
CANONS WOOD
PAGES ACRE
RUFFETT WOOD
Canons Farm
Premier Lodge
174
LANGLEY VALE
WALTON DOWNS
EPSOM & EWELL
REIGATE & BANSTEAD
PIT WOOD
Banstead Athletic FC
Swim Pool
KT20
TADWORTH
THE CHILDRENS TRUST
Legal & General
Garden Farm
KINGSWOOD
Kingswood Warren - BBC Technical Research
WORKHOUSE POND
Cricket Ground
Police Training School
SPORTS GRD
MERE POND
BANSTEAD HEATH
SANDHILL WOOD
Ebbisham Farm
Walton Manor
Walton Manor Farm
Walton on the Hill
Wingfield Stud Farm
The Clock Tower Riding Centre
Clubhouse
BEECHEN
COPSE
183
BANSTEAD
115
116
117
118
119
120
121
122
123
124
56
57
58
59
22
23
24
A217
A240
A2022
B2032
B290
B2220
B2221
B284
B291
B288
BRIGHTON ROAD
REIGATE ROAD
DORKING ROAD
TATTENHAMS WAY
WALTON STREET
CHIPSTEAD LANE

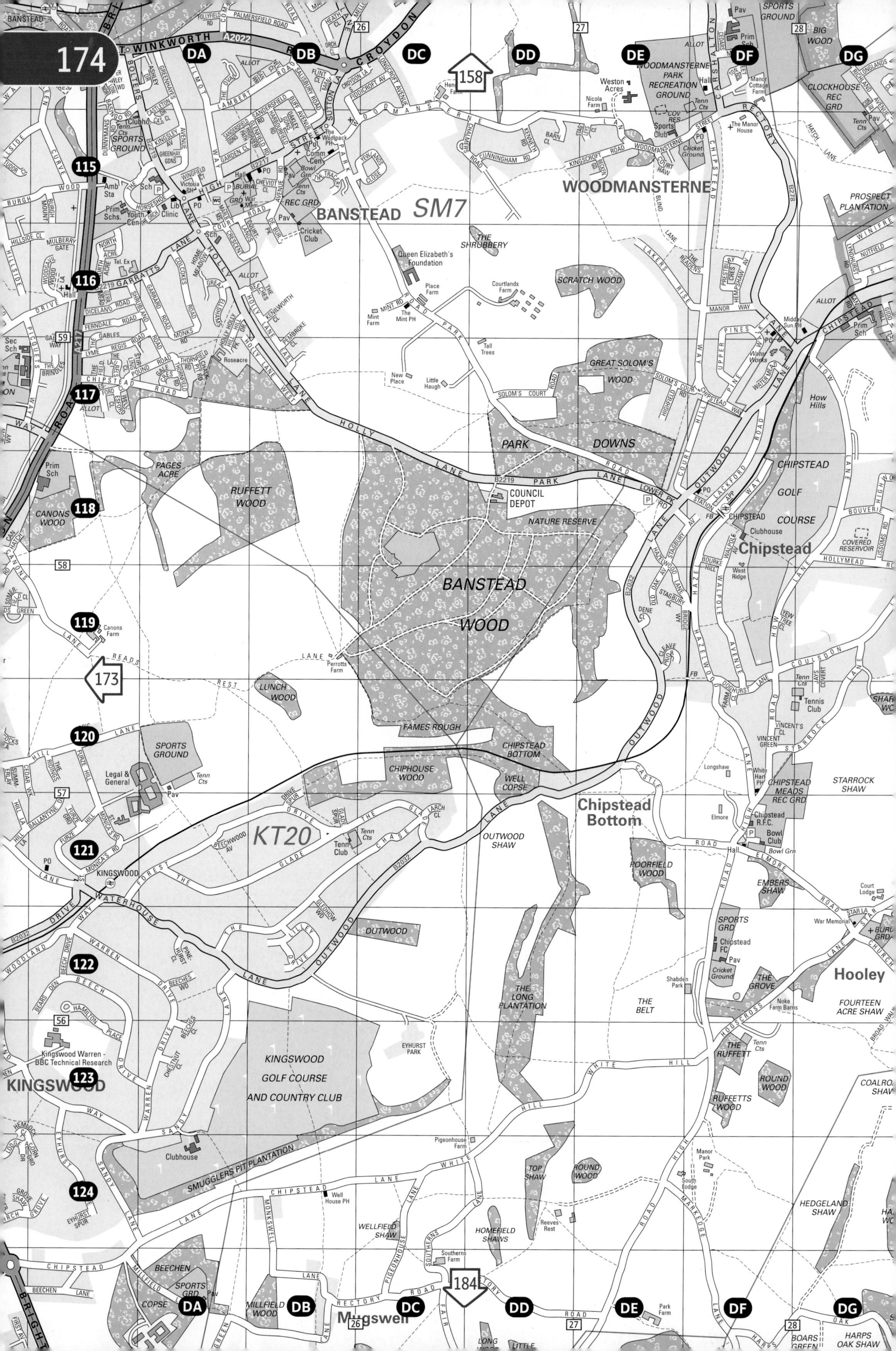
174
DA
DB
DC
DD
DE
DF
DG
158
184
173
BANSTEAD
SM7
WOODMANSTERNE
Chipstead
Chipstead Bottom
Hooley
KINGSWOOD
KT20
Mugswell
BANSTEAD WOOD
PARK DOWNS
GREAT SOLOM'S WOOD
SCRATCH WOOD
THE SHRUBBERY
RUFFETT WOOD
PAGES ACRE
CANONS WOOD
LUNCH WOOD
FAMES ROUGH
CHIPSTEAD BOTTOM
CHIPHOUSE WOOD
WELL COPSE
OUTWOOD SHAW
OUTWOOD
POORFIELD WOOD
THE LONG PLANTATION
THE BELT
CHIPSTEAD GOLF COURSE
How Hills
STARROCK SHAW
CHIPSTEAD MEADS REC GRD
EMBERS SHAW
THE GROVE
FOURTEEN ACRE SHAW
THE RUFFETT
ROUND WOOD
RUFFETTS WOOD
HEDGELAND SHAW
KINGSWOOD GOLF COURSE AND COUNTRY CLUB
SMUGGLERS PIT PLANTATION
TOP SHAW
HOMEFIELD SHAWS
WELLFIELD SHAW
BEECHEN COPSE
MILLFIELD WOOD
BIG WOOD
CLOCKHOUSE REC GRD
PROSPECT PLANTATION
WOODMANSTERNE PARK RECREATION GROUND
COUNCIL DEPOT
NATURE RESERVE
Queen Elizabeth's Foundation
Kingswood Warren - BBC Technical Research
Legal & General
SPORTS GROUND
A2022
A217
B2219
B2217
B2032
B278
115
116
117
118
119
120
121
122
123
124
26
27
28
56
57
58
59

WOODCOTE PARK GOLF COURSE
COULSDON
Old Coulsdon
KENLEY
Chaldon
CR8
CR5
CR3
RH1
HARTLEY BUSHES
COULSDON MANOR GOLF COURSE
COULSDON MANOR HOTEL
STONYFIELD SHAW
ULLSWATER BUSINESS PARK
COULSDON NORTH IND EST
SMITHAM
WOODMANSTERNE
TWINERS WOOD
DUNSTAN'S WOOD
POSTERN WOOD
Cane Hill S.A.S.S. Unit
MARLFIELD SHAW
FARTHING OR FAIRDEAN DOWNS
GRANGE PARK
Coulsdon Coll
BETTS MEAD RECREATION GR
COULSDON COMMON
SPORTS GROUND
DEVILS DEN WOOD
THE DEVILS DEN
SPARKLIE WOOD
HAPPY VALLEY PARK
DITCHES SHAW
BOXERS WOOD
STAR SHAW
THREE CORNERED SHAW
PETERSHOLE SHAW
NETHERNE WOOD
HOSPITAL (closed)
GRASSCUTS SHAW
LORD'S WOOD
ALDERSTEAD HEATH CARAVAN CLUB SITE
ALDERSTEAD HEATH
FURZEFIELD WOOD
FIGGS WOOD
THE GULLET
BROAD WOOD
PILES WOOD
CHURCH GREEN
SURREY NATIONAL GOLF COURSE
RIFLE RANGES
FRYERN BROOM WOOD
WILLEY BROOM WOOD
BROTHERS FIELD
SPARTICLES WOOD
Mersham Tunnel
Junction
CROYDON
TANDRIDGE
REIGATE & BANSTEAD
SURREY
BRIGHTON ROAD
A23
A237
B2030
B2031
B2032
B276
159
176
185
DH
DJ
DK
DL
DM
DN
DP
29
30
31
56
57
58
59
115
116
117
118
119
120
121
122
123
124

160
175
186
DQ
DR
DS
DT
DU
DV
DW
33
34
35
59
58
57
56
115
116
117
118
119
120
121
122
123
124
KENLEY
CR8
CR2
CR5
CR3
Whyteleafe
UPPER WARLINGHAM
Old Coulsdon
Caterham-on-the-Hill
CATERHAM
Hamsey Green
KENLEY AERODROME
KENLEY COMMON
COULSDON COMMON
SURREY NATIONAL GOLF COURSE
RIDDLESDOWN WOOD
KINGS WOOD
RAGGED WOOD
AINSLEY BERRY SHAW
DISPLEY'S WOOD
CROYDON
TANDRIDGE
SURREY
GODSTONE ROAD
CATERHAM BY-PASS
PLAYING FIELDS
SPORTS GROUND
WHYTELEAFE RECREATION GROUND
THE DOBBIN
TITHEPIT SHAW
BETTS MEAD RECREATION GROUND
COXES WOOD
BLIZE WOOD
Joysons Hill
MANOR PARK
Burntwood Hill
WINDMILL SHAW
ROUND SHAW
Stony Hill
PARK SHAW
RYDON'S WOOD
RIFLE RANGES
BROAD WOOD
FRYERN BROOM WOOD
WILLEY BROOM WOOD
Rook Hill
WESTWAY COMMON
QUEEN'S PARK
RUGBY GROUND
CATERHAM DENE HOSP
MARIE CURIE CENTRE
Surrey Hill Gliding Club
Radiocommunications Agency
RAF Mem
Air Training Corps
Gas Works
Warlingham Court Farm
Birchwood House Farm
Tillingdown Farm
Fryern Farm
Wattenden Arms PH
Purley John Fisher R.F.C.
COVERED RESERVOIR
THE NORTH DOWNS

FARLEIGH
CR6
Chelsham
WARLINGHAM
Woldingham Garden Village
Woldingham
GREAT PARK WOOD
HOLT WOOD
WOLDINGHAM GOLF COURSE
161
178
187

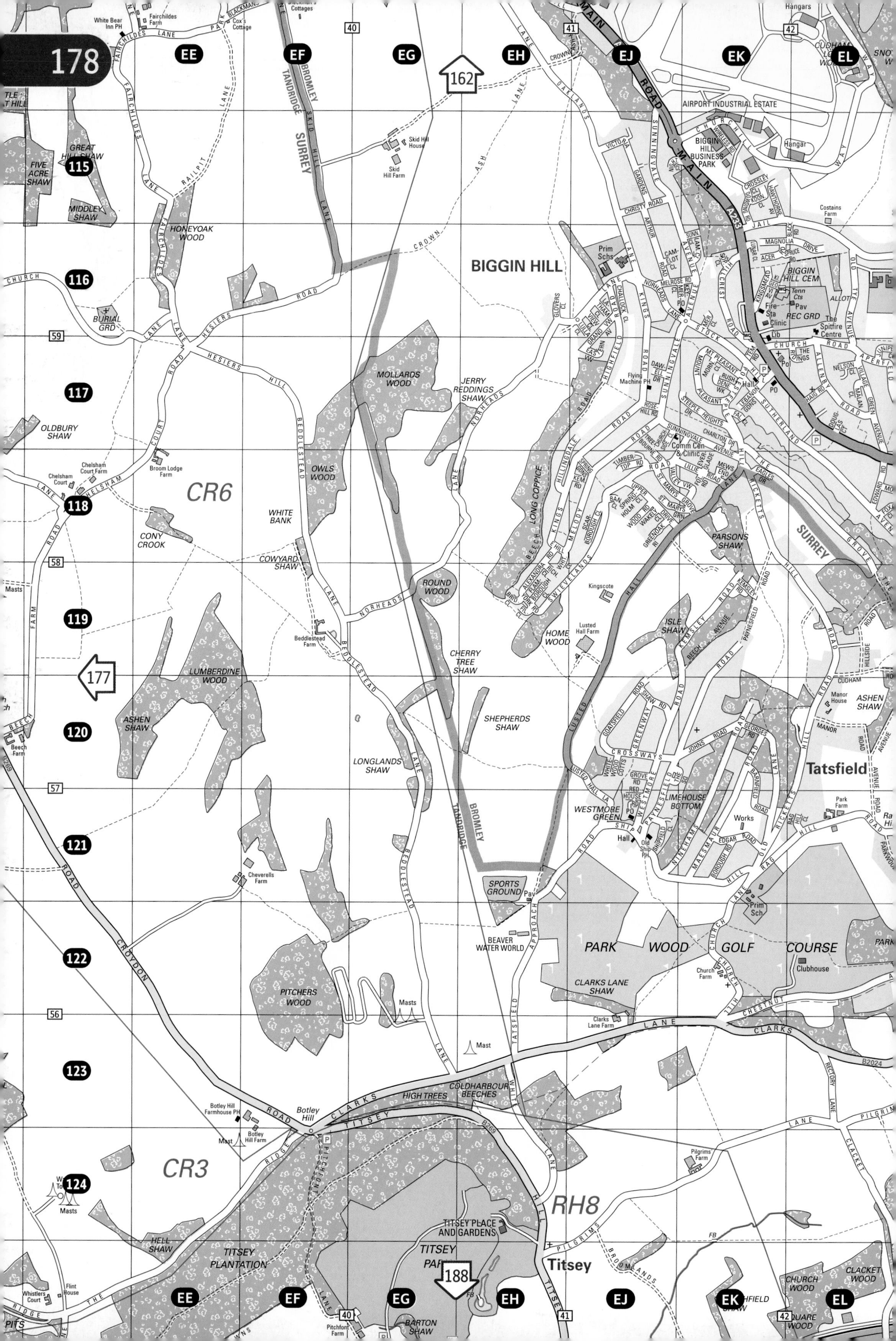

EE
EF
EG
EH
EJ
EK
EL
162
177
188
BIGGIN HILL
Tatsfield
Titsey
CR6
CR3
RH8
SURREY
BROMLEY
TANDRIDGE
AIRPORT INDUSTRIAL ESTATE
BIGGIN HILL BUSINESS PARK
MAIN ROAD
A233
HONEYOAK WOOD
MOLLARDS WOOD
JERRY REDDINGS SHAW
OWLS WOOD
WHITE BANK
CONY CROOK
COWYARD SHAW
ROUND WOOD
LUMBERDINE WOOD
ASHEN SHAW
CHERRY TREE SHAW
SHEPHERDS SHAW
LONGLANDS SHAW
LONG COPPICE
HOME WOOD
PARSONS SHAW
ISLE SHAW
LIMEHOUSE BOTTOM
WESTMORE GREEN
PARK WOOD GOLF COURSE
CLARKS LANE SHAW
PITCHERS WOOD
SPORTS GROUND
BEAVER WATER WORLD
COLDHARBOUR BEECHES
HIGH TREES
Botley Hill
TITSEY PLANTATION
TITSEY PLACE AND GARDENS
HELL SHAW
OLDBURY SHAW
FIVE ACRE SHAW
GREAT HILL SHAW
MIDDLEY SHAW
BURIAL GRD
CHURCH WOOD
CLACKET WOOD
CLARKS LANE
B2024
B269

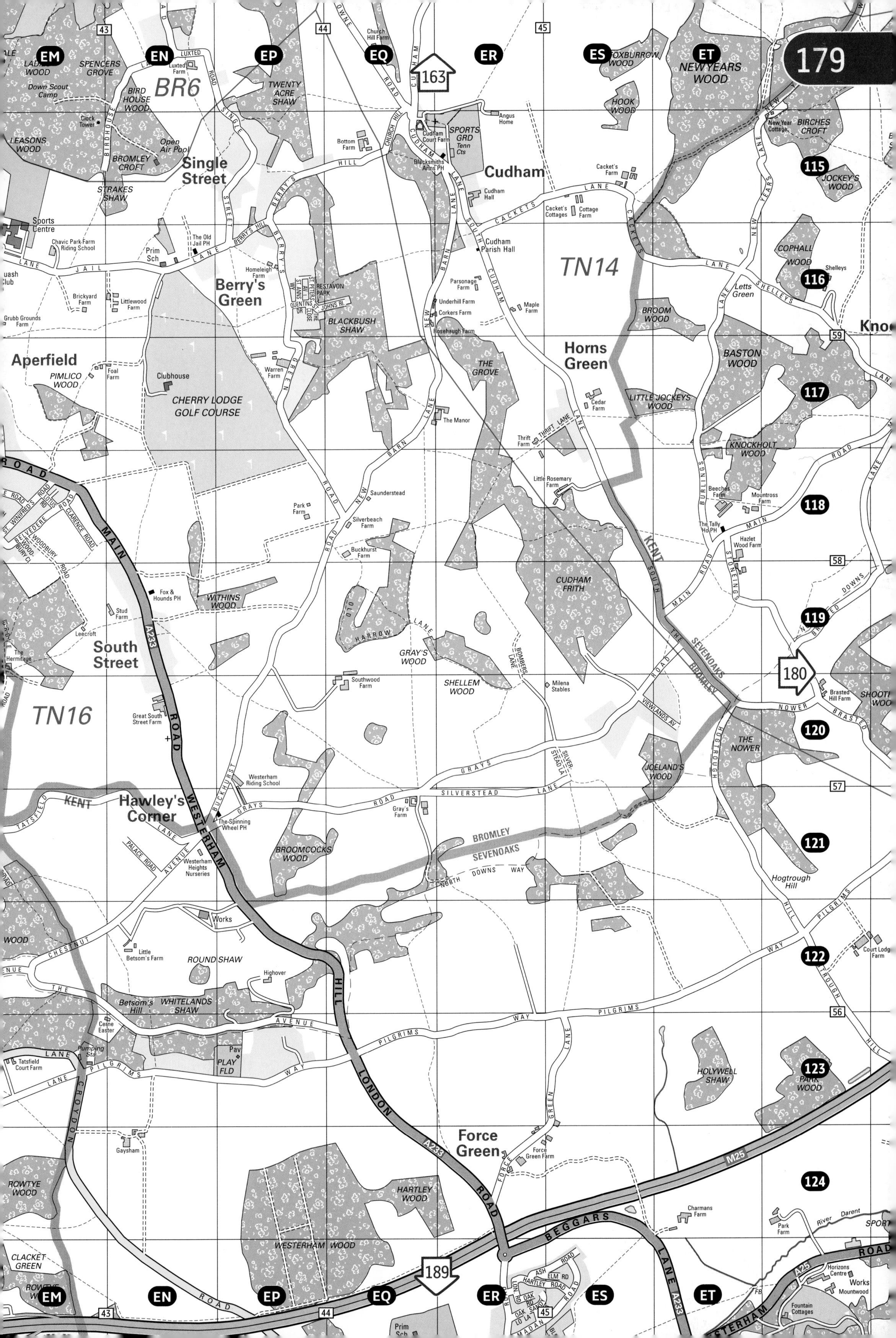

EM
EN
EP
EQ
ER
ES
ET
43
44
45
163
BR6
LADIES WOOD
SPENCERS GROVE
Down Scout Camp
BIRD HOUSE WOOD
Clock Tower
LEASONS WOOD
BROMLEY CROFT
Open Air Pool
Luxted Farm
TWENTY ACRE SHAW
Single Street
STRAKES SHAW
Church Hill Farm
Bottom Farm
Cudham Court Farm
SPORTS GRD
Tenn Cts
Angus Home
Blacksmiths Arms PH
Cudham
Cudham Hall
Cudham Parish Hall
FOXBURROW WOOD
HOOK WOOD
NEWYEARS WOOD
New Year Cottage
BIRCHES CROFT
115
JOCKEY'S WOOD
Cacket's Farm
Cacket's Cottages
Cottage Farm
COPHALL WOOD
Shelleys
116
Letts Green
TN14
Sports Centre
Chavic Park Farm Riding School
The Old Jail PH
Prim Sch
Homeleigh Farm
Berry's Green
RESTAVON PARK
BLACKBUSH SHAW
Brickyard Farm
Littlewood Farm
Grubb Grounds Farm
Parsonage Farm
Underhill Farm
Corkers Farm
Roseheugh Farm
Maple Farm
BROOM WOOD
59
Horns Green
BASTON WOOD
Aperfield
PIMLICO WOOD
Foal Farm
Clubhouse
CHERRY LODGE GOLF COURSE
Warren Farm
THE GROVE
The Manor
Cedar Farm
LITTLE JOCKEYS WOOD
117
Thrift Farm
KNOCKHOLT WOOD
Little Rosemary Farm
Beeches Farm
Mountross Farm
118
The Tally Ho PH
Hazlet Wood Farm
Saunderstead
Park Farm
Silverbeach Farm
Buckhurst Farm
58
CUDHAM FRITH
Fox & Hounds PH
WITHINS WOOD
Stud Farm
Leecroft
The Hermitage
South Street
119
GRAY'S WOOD
SHELLEM WOOD
Milena Stables
180
Brasted Hill Farm
Southwood Farm
TN16
Great South Street Farm
120
THE NOWER
JOELAND'S WOOD
Westerham Riding School
57
Hawley's Corner
The Spinning Wheel PH
Gray's Farm
BROOMCOCKS WOOD
BROMLEY
SEVENOAKS
KENT
Westerham Heights Nurseries
121
Hogtrough Hill
Works
Little Betsom's Farm
ROUND SHAW
Highover
122
Court Lodge Farm
Betsom's Hill
WHITELANDS SHAW
Carne Easter
Pumping Sta
Tatsfield Court Farm
Pav
PLAY FLD
56
HOLYWELL SHAW
123
PARK WOOD
Gaysham
Force Green
Force Green Farm
ROWTYE WOOD
HARTLEY WOOD
M25
124
Charmans Farm
Park Farm
River Darent
WESTERHAM WOOD
CLACKET GREEN
189
Horizons Centre
Works
Mountwood
Fountain Cottages
Prim Sch
A233
A25
MAIN ROAD
WESTERHAM ROAD
LONDON ROAD
HILL
BEGGARS LANE
PILGRIMS WAY
NORTH DOWNS WAY
GRAYS ROAD
SILVERSTEAD LANE
CACKETS LANE
SOUTH CUDHAM
NEW BARN LANE
JAIL LANE
BERRY'S HILL
CHESTNUT AVENUE
CROYDON LANE

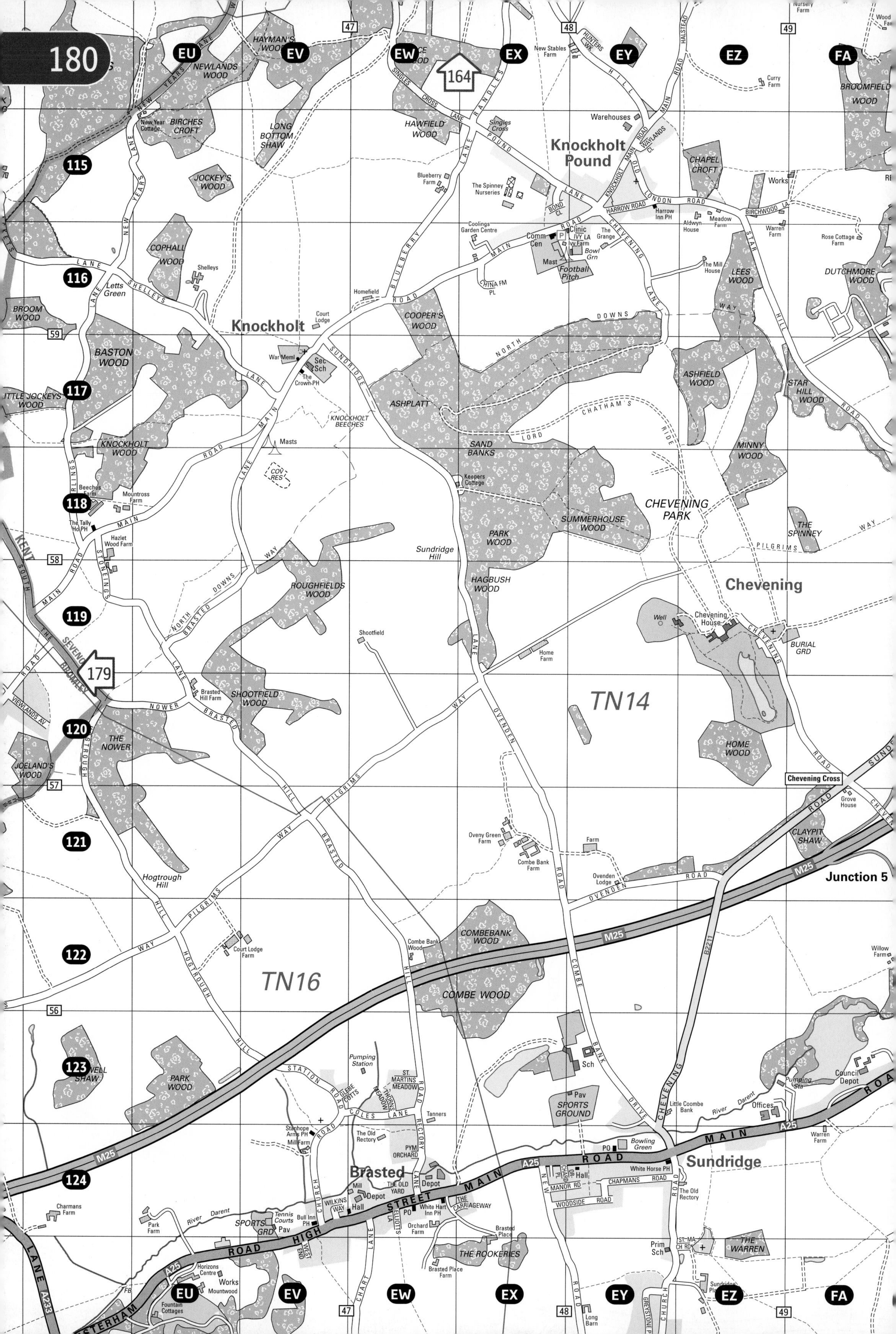
EU
EV
EW
EX
EY
EZ
FA
164
179
HAYMAN'S WOOD
NEWLANDS WOOD
NEW YEARS LANE
New Year Cottage
BIRCHES CROFT
LONG BOTTOM SHAW
JOCKEY'S WOOD
SINGLES CROSS LANE
HAWFIELD WOOD
RANDLES LANE
Singles Cross
POUND LANE
New Stables Farm
HUNTERS WK
HILL
HALSTEAD
MAIN ROAD
Curry Farm
BROOMFIELD WOOD
Warehouses
WAYLANDS CL
Knockholt Pound
CHAPEL CROFT
Works
Blueberry Farm
The Spinney Nurseries
BOND CL
KNOCKHOLT MAIN ROAD
OLD LONDON ROAD
HARROW ROAD
Harrow Inn PH
BIRCHWOOD LA
Aldwyn House
Meadow Farm
Warren Farm
Rose Cottage Farm
Coolings Garden Centre
Comm Cen
Clinic
IVY LA
Ivy Farm
The Grange
Bowl Grn
Mast
Football Pitch
CHEVENING LANE
The Mill House
LEES WOOD
STAR HILL ROAD
DUTCHMORE WOOD
COPHALL WOOD
Shelleys
LANE
SHELLEYS LANE
Letts Green
CHINA FM PL
Homefield
BLUEBERRY LANE
MAIN ROAD
COOPER'S WOOD
NORTH DOWNS WAY
BROOM WOOD
BASTON WOOD
Knockholt
Court Lodge
War Meml
Sec Sch
The Crown PH
SUNDRIDGE
LITTLE JOCKEYS WOOD
ASHPLATT
CHATHAM'S RIDE
ASHFIELD WOOD
STAR HILL WOOD
KNOCKHOLT BEECHES
Masts
KNOCKHOLT WOOD
SAND BANKS
LORD
MINNY WOOD
COV RES
Keepers Cottage
Beeches Farm
Mountross Farm
The Tally Ho PH
Hazlet Wood Farm
STONEINGS
CHEVENING PARK
SUMMERHOUSE WOOD
THE SPINNEY
PARK WOOD
Sundridge Hill
PILGRIMS WAY
KENT
SOUTH MAIN ROAD
HAGBUSH WOOD
Chevening
ROUGHFIELDS WOOD
NORTH DOWNS
BRASTED LANE
Shootfield
Well
Chevening House
BURIAL GRD
THE SEVENOAKS BROMLEY ROAD
VIEWLANDS AV
Home Farm
Brasted Hill Farm
SHOOTFIELD WOOD
NOWER
TN14
OVENDEN
HOGTROUGH
THE NOWER
JOELAND'S WOOD
HOME WOOD
Chevening Cross
Grove House
CLAYPIT SHAW
Oveny Green Farm
Combe Bank Farm
Farm
Ovenden Lodge
OVENDEN ROAD
M25
Junction 5
Hogtrough Hill
PILGRIMS WAY
COMBE ROAD
COMBEBANK WOOD
Combe Bank Wood
Court Lodge Farm
B2211
Willow Farm
TN16
COMBE WOOD
HOGTROUGH HILL
WELL SHAW
PARK WOOD
Pumping Station
STATION ROAD
GLEBE COTTS
THORNS MEADOW
ST. MARTINS MEADOW
Sch
COMBE BANK DRIVE
Pumping Sta
Council Depot
COLES LANE
Tanners
SPORTS GROUND
Pav
CHEVENING ROAD
Little Coombe Bank
River Darent
Offices
Stanhope Arms PH
Mill Farm
The Old Rectory
PYM ORCHARD
RECTORY LANE
PO
Bowling Green
A25
MAIN ROAD
Warren Farm
Brasted
Depot
White Horse PH
Sundridge
NEW CHARD PL
CHARD RD
MANOR RD
Hall
CHAPMANS ROAD
WOODSIDE ROAD
The Old Rectory
Mill
THE OLD YARD
WILKINS WAY
HIGH STREET
White Hart Inn PH
THE CARRIAGEWAY
Charmans Farm
Park Farm
River Darent
SPORTS GRD
Tennis Courts
Bull Inn PH
ELLIOTTS LA
Orchard Farm
Brasted Place
CHART LANE
WEST END
THE ROOKERIES
Prim Sch
ST. MARYS CH RD
THE WARREN
ROAD
Horizons Centre
Works
Mountwood
Brasted Place Farm
LANE
A233
FB
STERHAM
Fountain Cottages
CHURCH
GREYSTONE
Sundridge Place
Long Barn
47
48
49
56
57
58
59
115
116
117
118
119
120
121
122
123
124

FB
FC
FD
FE
FF
FG
FH
165
190
191
Twitton
Otford
TN14
TN13
Dunton Green
Longford
Chipstead
Riverhead
Bessels Green
SEVENOAKS WILDFOWL RESERVE
EAST LAKE
WEST LAKE
CHIPSTEAD LAKE
Morants Court Cross
Bat and Ball Junction
SEVENOAKS HOSP
OTFORD CEMETERY
DEFENCE SCIENCE & TECHNOLOGY LABORATORY FORT HALSTEAD
POLHILL
M25
M26
A224
A225
A25
A21
SEVENOAKS BYPASS
WESTERHAM ROAD
LONDON ROAD
BRADBOURNE VALE ROAD
OTFORD ROAD
DARTFORD ROAD
ST. JOHNS HILL
PILGRIMS WAY
HIGH STREET
STATION ROAD
115
116
117
118
119
120
121
122
123
124
50
51
52
56
57
58
59

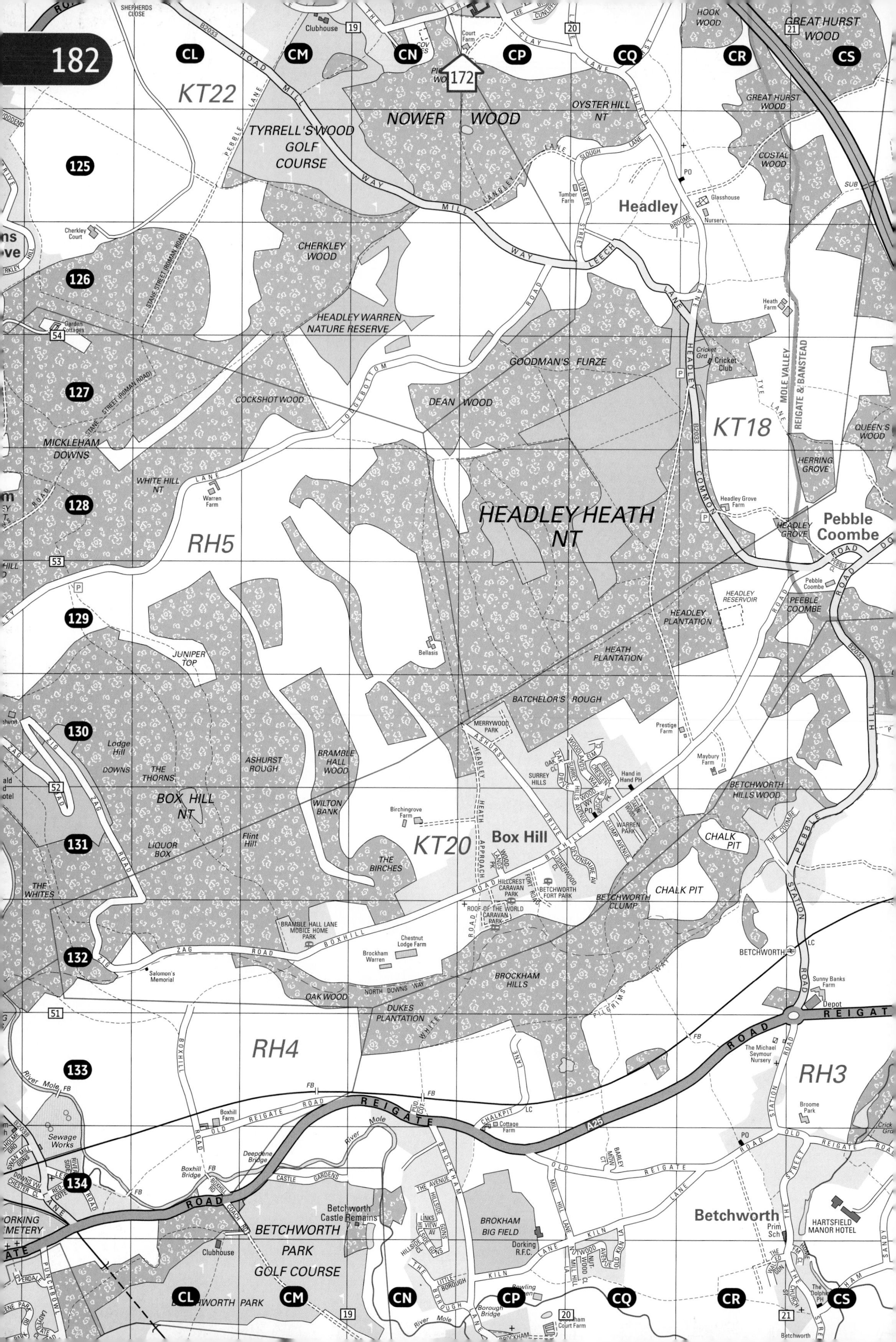

KT22
NOWER WOOD
TYRRELL'S WOOD GOLF COURSE
OYSTER HILL NT
Headley
GREAT HURST WOOD
COSTAL WOOD
CHERKLEY WOOD
HEADLEY WARREN NATURE RESERVE
GOODMAN'S FURZE
DEAN WOOD
COCKSHOT WOOD
MICKLEHAM DOWNS
KT18
QUEEN'S WOOD
HERRING GROVE
WHITE HILL NT
RH5
HEADLEY HEATH NT
Pebble Coombe
HEADLEY RESERVOIR
HEADLEY PLANTATION
PEBBLE COOMBE
JUNIPER TOP
HEATH PLANTATION
BATCHELOR'S ROUGH
Lodge Hill
THE THORNS
ASHURST ROUGH
BRAMBLE HALL WOOD
BOX HILL NT
WILTON BANK
BETCHWORTH HILLS WOOD
KT20
Box Hill
CHALK PIT
LIQUOR BOX
Flint Hill
THE BIRCHES
THE WHITES
BETCHWORTH CLUMP
BROCKHAM HILLS
OAK WOOD
DUKES PLANTATION
RH4
RH3
BETCHWORTH PARK GOLF COURSE
BROKHAM BIG FIELD
Betchworth
HARTSFIELD MANOR HOTEL

173
184
Walton on the Hill
BANSTEAD HEATH
BANSTEAD
KT20
HEATH
WALTON HEATH GOLF COURSE
WALTON HEATH
CHUSSEX PLAIN
Lower Kingswood
Mogador
Marg
Buckland
RH2
REIGATE
REIGATE HEATH GOLF COURSE
REIGATE HEATH
SANDHILL WOOD
WALTON PARK WOOD
LITTLE HEATH
Pfizer
M25
ROUND WOOD
DEWRIDING PLANTATION
Thistle Hill
Lady Hill
Buckland Hills
NORTH DOWNS WAY
PILGRIMS' WAY
Mount Hill
Conybury Hill
Juniper Hill
Colley Hill
THE HORSESHOE
THE SADDLE KNOB
QUEEN'S PARK
NT
MARGERY WOOD NT
FOUR ACRE UPPER WOODS
THE BEECHES
NORTHLAND SHAW
BUSHY SHAW
COLLEYLAND SHAW
BUSHFIELD COPPICE
COLLEY COPSE
COLLEY WOOD
SAND AND GRAVEL PIT
TAP WOOD
ROUND ALDERS
THE ALDERS
MOLE VALLEY
REIGATE & BANSTEAD
BUCKLAND ROAD
A25
ROAD WEST
LONDON ROAD
HIGH STREET
BRIGHTON ROAD
A217
DORKING ROAD
B2032
CHEQUERS LANE
B2220
BEECHEN COPSE
GRUB WOOD
GAS STATION
COVERED RESERVOIR
PRIORY POND
SPORTS GROUND
Kemp's Farm
Underhill Farm
Dowde's Farm
Glebe House
Petty's Farm
Dungate's Farm
Wonham Hill
Sandhills
More Place
Wonham Mill
Dungate Manor
Heathfield Farm
Skimmington Castle PH
Jolly Farmers PH
Black Horse PH
The Mint Arms PH
Yew Tree PH
Site of Reigate Castle
Site of Priory
Old Reigatians R.F.C.
CT
CU
CV
CW
CX
CY
CZ
22
23
24
51
52
53
54
125
126
127
128
129
130
131
132
133
134

DA
DB
DC
DD
DE
DF
DG
174
183
26
27
28
Mugswell
CR5
Lower Kingswood
KT20
Margery
Junction 8
RH2
Gatton
Coles Meads
REIGATE
REDHILL
REIGATE HILL GOLF COURSE
GATTON PARK
THE LAKE
TEMPLE WOOD
NUTWOOD NT
REIGATE HILL NT
MARGERY WOOD NT
Colley Hill
QUEEN'S PARK
THE BEECHES
FOUR ACRE UPPER WOODS
GREAT BUCK WOOD
WINGATE HILL
HALFMOON CLUMP
THE BURPIT
HOP GARDEN POND
ENGINE POND
SERPENTINE WOOD
GREENCLUMP HILL
SPORTS GROUND
UPPER GATTON WOOD
UPPER GATTON PARK
DELL WOOD
COLTS BUSHES
GATWICK WOOD
GRUB WOOD
MILLFIELD WOOD
BEECHEN COPSE
FURZEFIELD COPSE
LONG WOOD
LITTLE WOOD
HOMEFIELD SHAWS
WELLFIELD SHAW
TOP SHAW
HEDGELAND SHAW
BOARS GREEN SHAW
HARPS OAK SHAW
FURZEFIELD SHAW
Ashtead Hill
JUBILEE PLANTATIONS
PARK SHAW
MANSHIPS SHAW
Kingswood Hill
GATTON FIELD SHAW
CATSBRAIN EAST
TOWER WOOD
HIGH BEECHES
GLEBE SHAW
THE CROSSWAYS
MAJORITY PLANTATION
GROVE SHAW
GATLANDS SHAW
CATSBRAIN SHAW
GATTON BOTTOM
TWO ACRE WOOD
BLACKHORSE WOOD
COLLEY WOOD
COLLEY COPSE
WRAY COMMON
REIGATE CEMETERY
PRIORY POND
REDHILL COMMON
BRIGHTON ROAD
A217
A242
A25
A23
M25
GATTON PARK ROAD
REIGATE HILL
CROYDON ROAD
LONDON ROAD
HIGH STREET
STATION RD
125
126
127
128
129
130
131
132
133
134

175
186
Merstham
South Merstham
Holmethorpe
Warwick Wold
Nutfield
Bletchingley
Junction 7
Junction 8 (M23), Junction 7 (M25)
CR3
RH1
M23
M25
A23
A25
B2031
MERCERS PARK COUNTRY PARK
NUTFIELD CEMETERY
PUBLIC TIP
SAND AND GRAVEL PIT
SAND PIT
SEWAGE WORKS
QUARRYSIDE BUSINESS PARK
HOLMETHORPE IND EST
GATTON PARK
THE GROVE
CHURCH HILL
SPARTICLES WOOD
ALDERSTEAD HEATH
FURZEFIELD WOOD
FRYERN BROOM WOOD
WILLEY BROOM WOOD
SIX BROTHERS FIELD
RIDGEBUSHES WOOD
THE SHRUBBERY
COVERED RESERVOIR
Ockley Hill
OCKLEY WOOD
REDLAMS BANK
HERONSWOOD MERE
WITHY SHAW
SPRING BOTTOM
QUARRY WOOD
ROCKY SHAW
PENDELL WOOD
BLACK BUSHES
White Hill
GRUBS WOOD
COCKLEY PLANTATION
PARK WOOD
COOMBES COPPICE
STANLEY'S WOOD
NORTH PARK
SPORTS GRD
FOX HOLE
Furze Hill
Stockers Hill
STENERS HILL
NUTFIELD PRIORY LAKE
Bower Hill
REDSTONE CEMETERY
Castle Hill
Rook Hill
Mersham Tunnel
Airshafts
REIGATE & BANSTEAD
TANDRIDGE

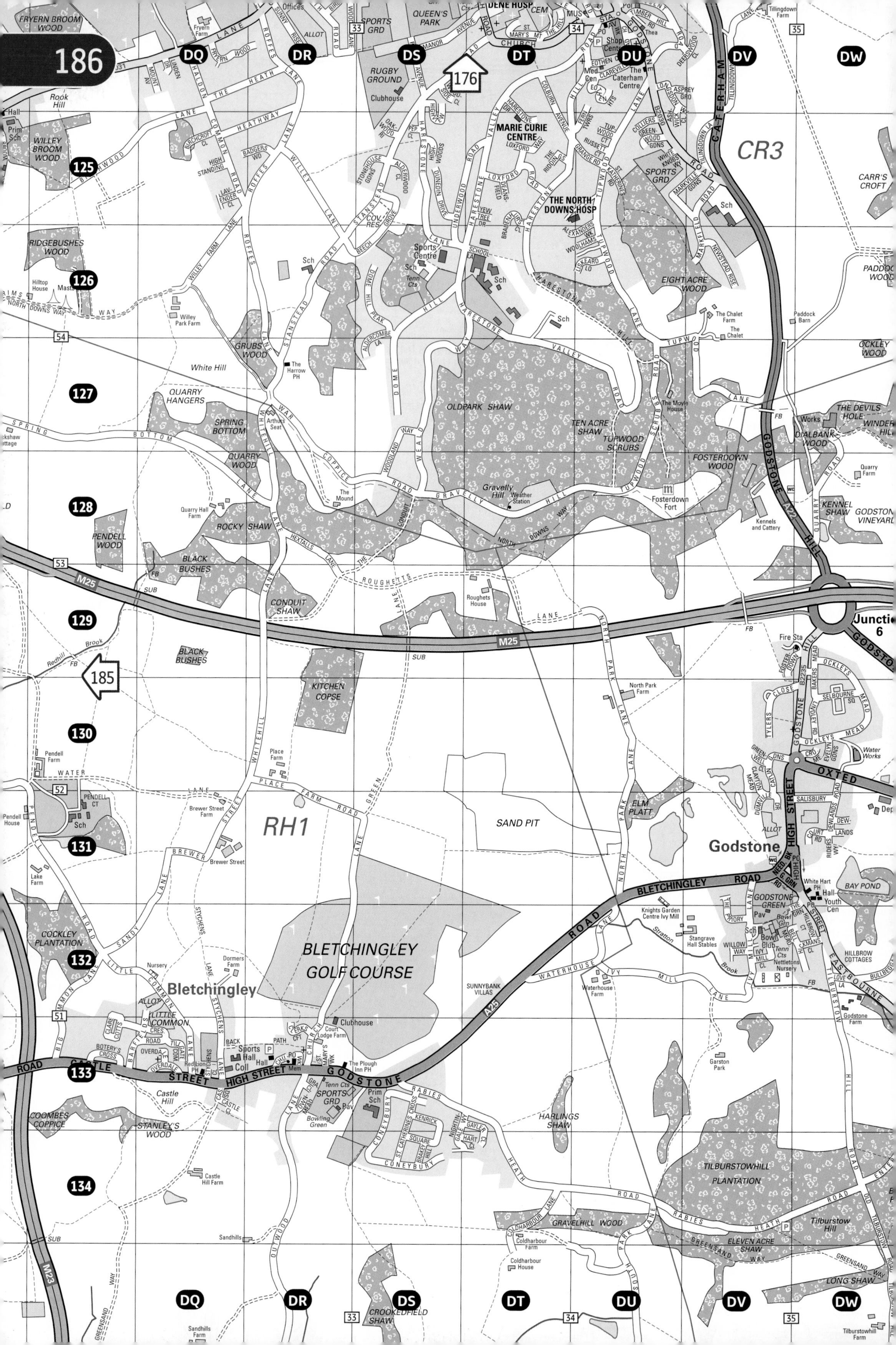
FRYERN BROOM WOOD
DQ
DR
DS
DT
DU
DV
DW
176
QUEEN'S PARK
SPORTS GRD
DENE HOSP
CEM
RUGBY GROUND
Clubhouse
MARIE CURIE CENTRE
THE NORTH DOWNS HOSP
The Caterham Centre
CR3
CATERHAM
CARR'S CROFT
Rook Hill
WILLEY BROOM WOOD
125
RIDGEBUSHES WOOD
126
Hilltop House
Masts
NORTH DOWNS WAY
Willey Park Farm
GRUBS WOOD
The Harrow PH
White Hill
127
QUARRY HANGERS
SPRING BOTTOM
QUARRY WOOD
Arthurs Seat
Sports Centre
Sch
EIGHT ACRE WOOD
The Chalet Farm
The Chalet
Paddock Barn
OCKLEY WOOD
OLDPARK SHAW
TEN ACRE SHAW
TUPWOOD SCRUBS
The Moyle House
FOSTERDOWN WOOD
Fosterdown Fort
THE DEVILS HOLE
Works
DIALBANK WOOD
Quarry Farm
KENNEL SHAW
GODSTONE VINEYARD
Kennels and Cattery
Gravelly Hill
Weather Station
The Mound
128
Quarry Hall Farm
ROCKY SHAW
PENDELL WOOD
BLACK BUSHES
M25
CONDUIT SHAW
Roughets House
129
BLACK BUSHES
185
KITCHEN COPSE
North Park Farm
Junction 6
Fire Sta
130
Pendell Farm
Place Farm
Water Works
52
PENDELL CT
Sch
Pendell House
Brewer Street Farm
RH1
ELM PLATT
SAND PIT
131
Brewer Street
Godstone
OXTED
Lake Farm
BLETCHINGLEY ROAD
White Hart PH
Hall
Youth Cen
BAY POND
COCKLEY PLANTATION
BLETCHINGLEY GOLF COURSE
Knights Garden Centre Ivy Mill
Stangrave Hall Stables
GODSTONE GREEN
Nettletons Nursery
HILLBROW COTTAGES
132
Nursery
Dormers Farm
Bletchingley
SUNNYBANK VILLAS
Waterhouse Farm
A25
51
Clubhouse
Court Lodge Farm
Godstone Farm
Sports Hall
Coll
Red Lion PH
The Plough Inn PH
133
CASTLE STREET
HIGH STREET
GODSTONE ROAD
Prim Sch
SPORTS GRD
Bowling Green
Castle Hill
COOMBES COPPICE
STANLEY'S WOOD
HARLINGS SHAW
Garston Park
134
Castle Hill Farm
TILBURSTOWHILL PLANTATION
GRAVELHILL WOOD
Tilburstow Hill
Sandhills
Coldharbour Farm
Coldharbour House
ELEVEN ACRE SHAW
GREENSAND WAY
LONG SHAW
M23
CROOKEDFIELD SHAW
Sandhills Farm
Tilburstowhill Farm
33
34
35

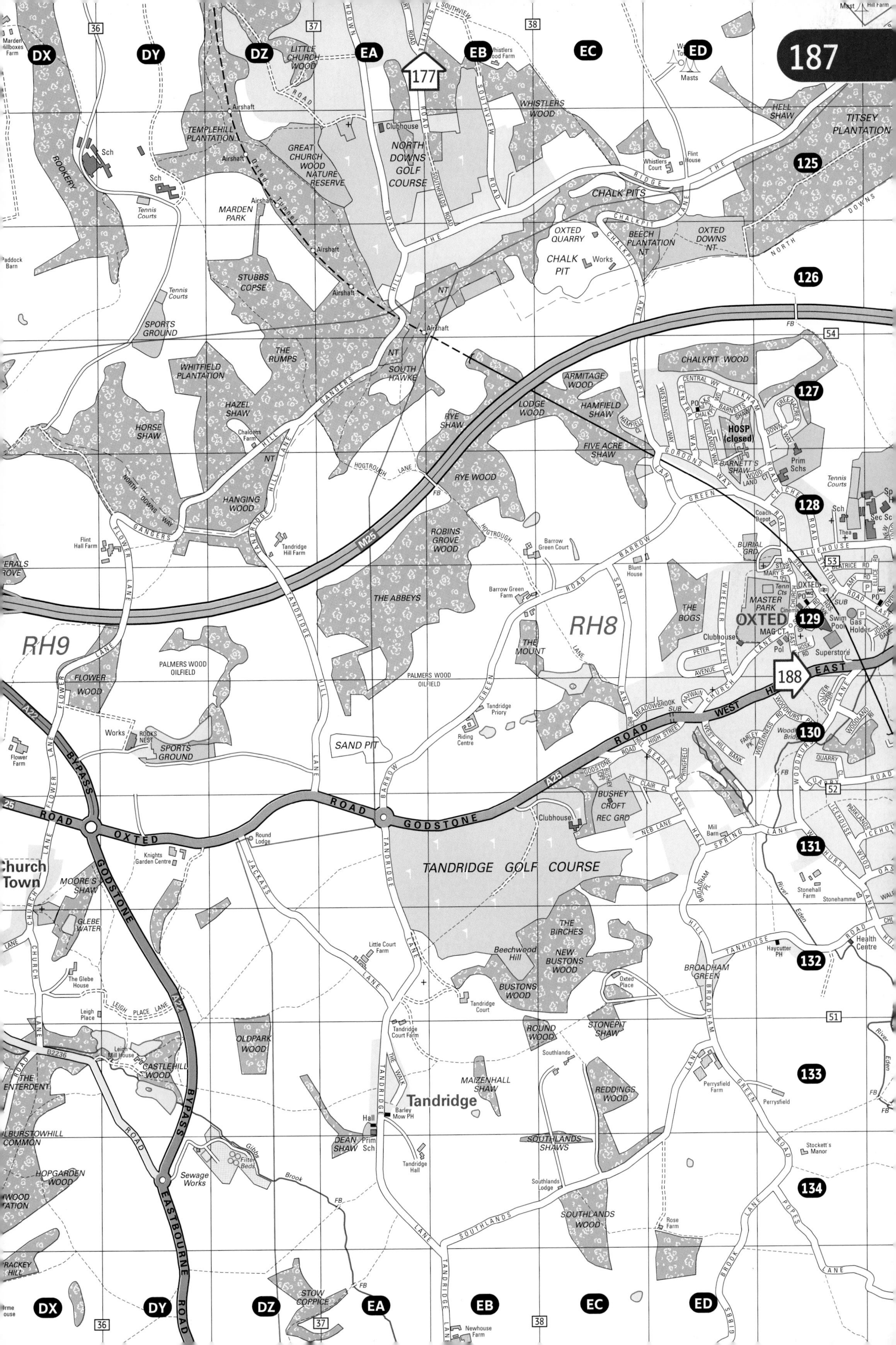
187
177
188
DX
DY
DZ
EA
EB
EC
ED
36
37
38
54
53
52
51
125
126
127
128
129
130
131
132
133
134
RH9
RH8
OXTED
Tandridge
Church Town
LITTLE CHURCH WOOD
TEMPLEHILL PLANTATION
GREAT CHURCH WOOD NATURE RESERVE
NORTH DOWNS GOLF COURSE
WHISTLERS WOOD
Whistlers Wood Farm
HELL SHAW
TITSEY PLANTATION
ROOKERY
Marden Hillboxes Farm
Sch
Tennis Courts
MARDEN PARK
Airshaft
Oxted Tunnel
Clubhouse
Masts
Whistlers Court
Flint House
THE RIDGE
CHALK PITS
OXTED QUARRY
CHALK PIT
Works
BEECH PLANTATION NT
OXTED DOWNS NT
NORTH DOWNS
Paddock Barn
STUBBS COPSE
SPORTS GROUND
THE RUMPS
SOUTH HAWKE
NT
WHITFIELD PLANTATION
HAZEL SHAW
HORSE SHAW
Chaldens Farm
RYE SHAW
LODGE WOOD
ARMITAGE WOOD
HAMFIELD SHAW
FIVE ACRE SHAW
CHALKPIT WOOD
HOSP (closed)
BARNETT'S SHAW
Prim Schs
Tennis Courts
Sec Sch
Coach Depot
BURIAL GRD
HOGTROUGH LANE
RYE WOOD
HANGING WOOD
NORTH DOWNS WAY
GANGERS HILL
Flint Hall Farm
Tandridge Hill Farm
ROBINS GROVE WOOD
Barrow Green Court
Blunt House
Barrow Green Farm
THE ABBEYS
M25
THE BOGS
MASTER PARK
Clubhouse
Superstore
Swim Pool
Gas Holder
THE MOUNT
PALMERS WOOD OILFIELD
FLOWER WOOD
Tandridge Priory
Riding Centre
SAND PIT
Works
ROOKS NEST
SPORTS GROUND
Flower Farm
A22
A25
WEST STREET
EAST HILL
HIGH STREET
GODSTONE ROAD
BUSHEY CROFT REC GRD
Woodhurst Bridge
Round Lodge
Knights Garden Centre
MOORE'S SHAW
GLEBE WATER
TANDRIDGE GOLF COURSE
Mill Barn
Stonehall Farm
Stonehamme
Health Centre
Haycutter PH
River Eden
THE BIRCHES
Beechwood Hill
NEW BUSTONS WOOD
BUSTONS WOOD
BROADHAM GREEN
Oxted Place
Little Court Farm
Tandridge Court
The Glebe House
Leigh Place
LEIGH PLACE LANE
OLDPARK WOOD
ROUND WOOD
STONEPIT SHAW
Tandridge Court Farm
Leigh Mill House
CASTLEHILL WOOD
B2236
THE ENTERDENT
MAIZENHALL SHAW
REDDINGS WOOD
Perrysfield Farm
Perrysfield
Southlands
Barley Mow PH
Hall
Prim Sch
DEAN SHAW
Tandridge Hall
SOUTHLANDS SHAWS
Stockett's Manor
GODSTONE BYPASS
EASTBOURNE ROAD
Sewage Works
Filter Beds
Brook
FB
HOPGARDEN WOOD
Southlands Lodge
SOUTHLANDS WOOD
Rose Farm
POPES LANE
BROOK LANE
B2269
SOUTHLANDS LANE
TANDRIDGE LANE
STOW COPPICE
Newhouse Farm
BRACKEY HILL

EE
EF
EG
EH
EJ
EK
EL
178
TITSEY PLACE AND GARDENS
TITSEY PARK
TITSEY PLANTATION
HELL SHAW
CR3
Titsey
PILGRIMS WAY
BROOMLANDS
CHURCH WOOD
CLACKET WOOD
ROUGHFIELD SHAW
SQUARE WOOD
BARTON SHAW
Pitchfont Farm
Limpsfield Lodge Farm
Park Farm
NORTH DOWNS WAY
OXTED DOWNS NT
BEECH PLANTATION NT
Whistlers Court
125
126
TITSEY ROAD
River Eden
Travel Inn
Clacket Lane Services
TITSEY WOOD
M25
CHALKPIT WOOD
CHALKPIT LANE
127
HOSP (closed)
BARNETT'S SHAW
Prim Schs
ASHEN COPPICE
Broomlands Farm
SAND PIT
GRUBSTREET SHAW
GRUBSTREET COPSE
SPORTS GROUND
128
Tennis Courts
Sports Hall
Sec Sch
Coach Depot
BURIAL GRD
Blunt House
RH8
Limpsfield
LIMPSFIELD
Cricket Club
Cricket Grd
CHART
Peeble Hill
Clubhouse
WESTERHAM ROAD
OXTED
MASTER PARK
129
Swim Pool
Gas Holder
Health Cen
COUNCIL OFF.
Fire Sta
Superstore
187
EAST HILL
WEST HILL
A25
130
ALLOT
GOLF COURSE
LIMPSFIELD COMMON
NT
ANDREWS WOOD
Woodhurst Bridge
Limpsfield Tunnel
WEST HEATH
Wildshaw
Swallowfield
STONESWOOD ROAD
Limpsfield Chart
131
Mill Barn
Stonehall Farm
Stonehamme
THE ALDERS
LITTLE HEATH NT
Chartfield House
Tenchley's Park
TENCHLEY'S WOOD
SPORTS GROUND
HURST GREEN
Health Centre
Haycutter PH
132
Hurst Green
Prim Sch
LOAMPIT WOOD
Boulthurst Farm
Whitegates Farm
Crabbett Wood
Crabbett Wood Farm
CRABBETT WOOD
Tenchleys Manor
133
Perrysfield Farm
Perrysfield
RUNNING TRACK
REC GRD
Pav
Doghurst
ITCHINGWOOD COMMON
Coltsford Mill
FAIRVIEW IND EST
Red Lane Farm
PARISHCROFT WOOD
Parishcroft Wood Farm
Holland
Stockett's Manor
134
Depot
Sewage Works
Filter Beds
POWDERDICK SHAW
The Diamond PH
Conneton Stables
Stockenden Farm
Rose Farm
Clubhouse
Oxted R.F.C.
HONESLAND WOOD
Upper Gincox Farm
COLLESTERS WOOD
MOLLSTONES WOOD
40
41
42
51
52
53
54

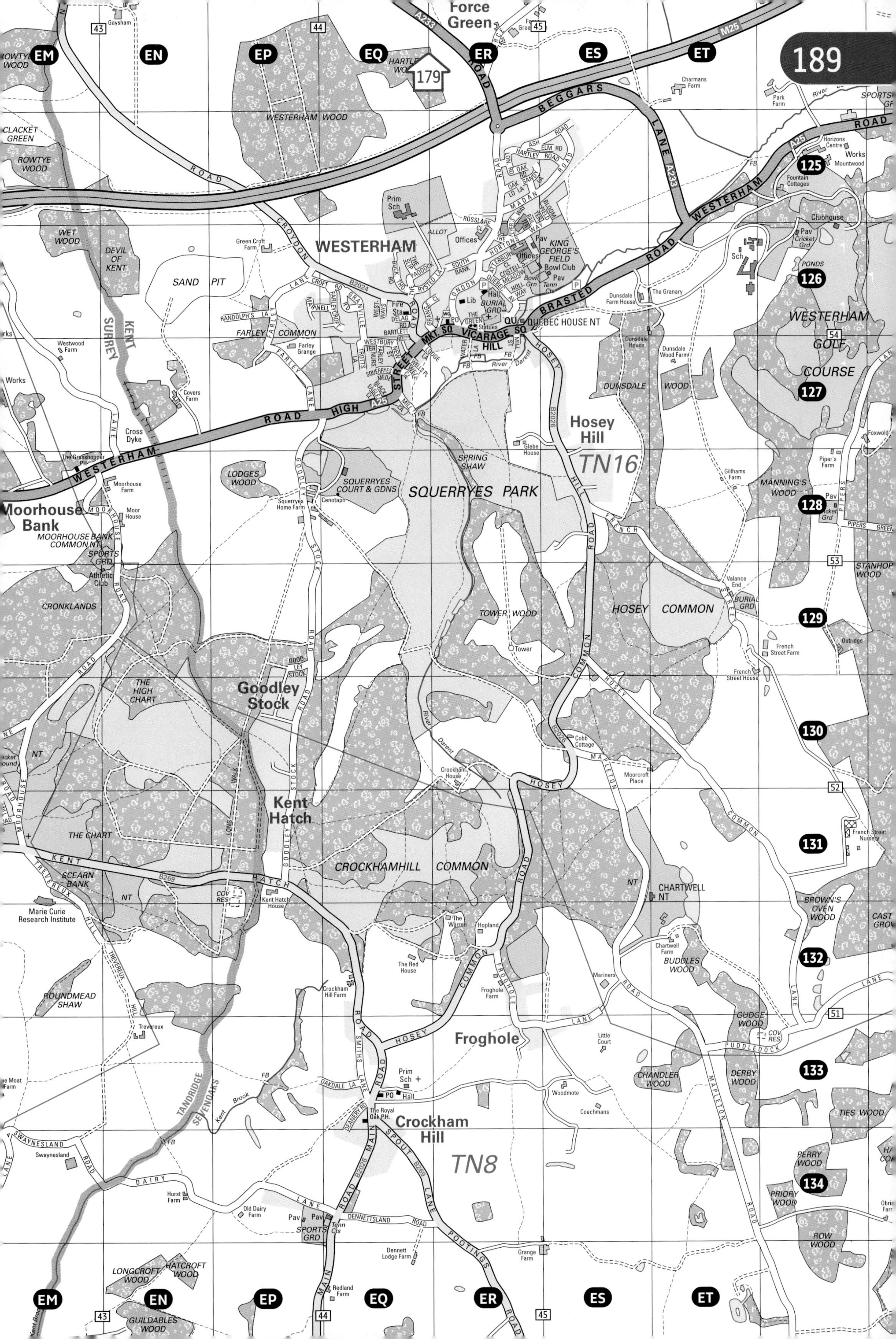

Force Green
179
EM
EN
EP
EQ
ER
ES
ET
M25
A233
BEGGARS LANE
WESTERHAM ROAD
WESTERHAM WOOD
ROWTYE WOOD
CLACKET GREEN
WET WOOD
DEVIL OF KENT
SAND PIT
CROYDON ROAD
WESTERHAM
Prim Sch
Offices
KING GEORGE'S FIELD
Bowl Club
Lib
Hall
Fire Stn
BURIAL GRD
QUEBEC HOUSE NT
MKT. SQ
VICARAGE SQ
BRASTED
HIGH STREET
A25
FARLEY COMMON
Farley Grange
Westwood Farm
Works
Covers Farm
Cross Dyke
SURREY
KENT
The Grasshopper PH
Moorhouse Farm
Moor House
Moorhouse Bank
MOORHOUSE BANK COMMON NT
SPORTS GRD
Athletic Club
CRONKLANDS
LODGES WOOD
SQUERRYES COURT & GDNS
Squerryes Home Farm
Cenotaph
SPRING SHAW
SQUERRYES PARK
Hosey Hill
TN16
B2026
Glebe House
Dunsdale Farm House
The Granary
Dunsdale House
Dunsdale Wood Farm
DUNSDALE
WOOD
Charmans Farm
Park Farm
Horizons Centre
Works
Mountwood
Fountain Cottages
Clubhouse
Pav
Cricket Grd
Sch
PONDS
WESTERHAM GOLF COURSE
125
126
127
128
129
130
131
132
133
134
Foxwold
Piper's Farm
MANNING'S WOOD
Gillhams Farm
FRENCH STREET
Valance End
BURIAL GRD
STANHOPE WOOD
HOSEY COMMON
French Street Farm
French Street House
Outridge
TOWER WOOD
Tower
GOODLEY STOCK
Goodley Stock
THE HIGH CHART
Kent Hatch
THE CHART
LONG WALK
Crockham House
Cobb Cottage
Moorcroft Place
MAPLETON
HOSEY COMMON ROAD
CROCKHAMHILL COMMON
French Street Nursery
KENT HATCH ROAD
B269
SCEARN BANK
NT
COV RES
Kent Hatch House
Marie Curie Research Institute
CHARTWELL NT
BROWN'S OVEN WOOD
The Warren
Hopland
Chartwell Farm
BUDDLES WOOD
The Red House
Crockham Hill Farm
Froghole Farm
Mariners
ROUNDMEAD SHAW
Trevereux
TREVEREUX HILL
Froghole
Little Court
GUDGE WOOD
PUDDLEDOCK
CHANDLER WOOD
DERBY WOOD
Prim Sch
PO
Hall
OAKDALE LA
The Royal Oak PH.
Crockham Hill
Woodmote
Coachmans
TIES WOOD
TANDRIDGE
SEVENOAKS
Kent Brook
SWAYNESLAND
Swaynesland
TN8
PERRY WOOD
PRIORY WOOD
DAIRY LANE
Hurst Farm
Old Dairy Farm
SPORTS GRD
Tenn Cts
DENNETTSLAND ROAD
SPOUT LANE
B2026
MAIN ROAD
POOTINGS ROAD
Dennett Lodge Farm
Grange Farm
ROW WOOD
LONGCROFT WOOD
HATCROFT WOOD
GUILDABLES WOOD
Redland Farm
43
44
45
51
52
53
54

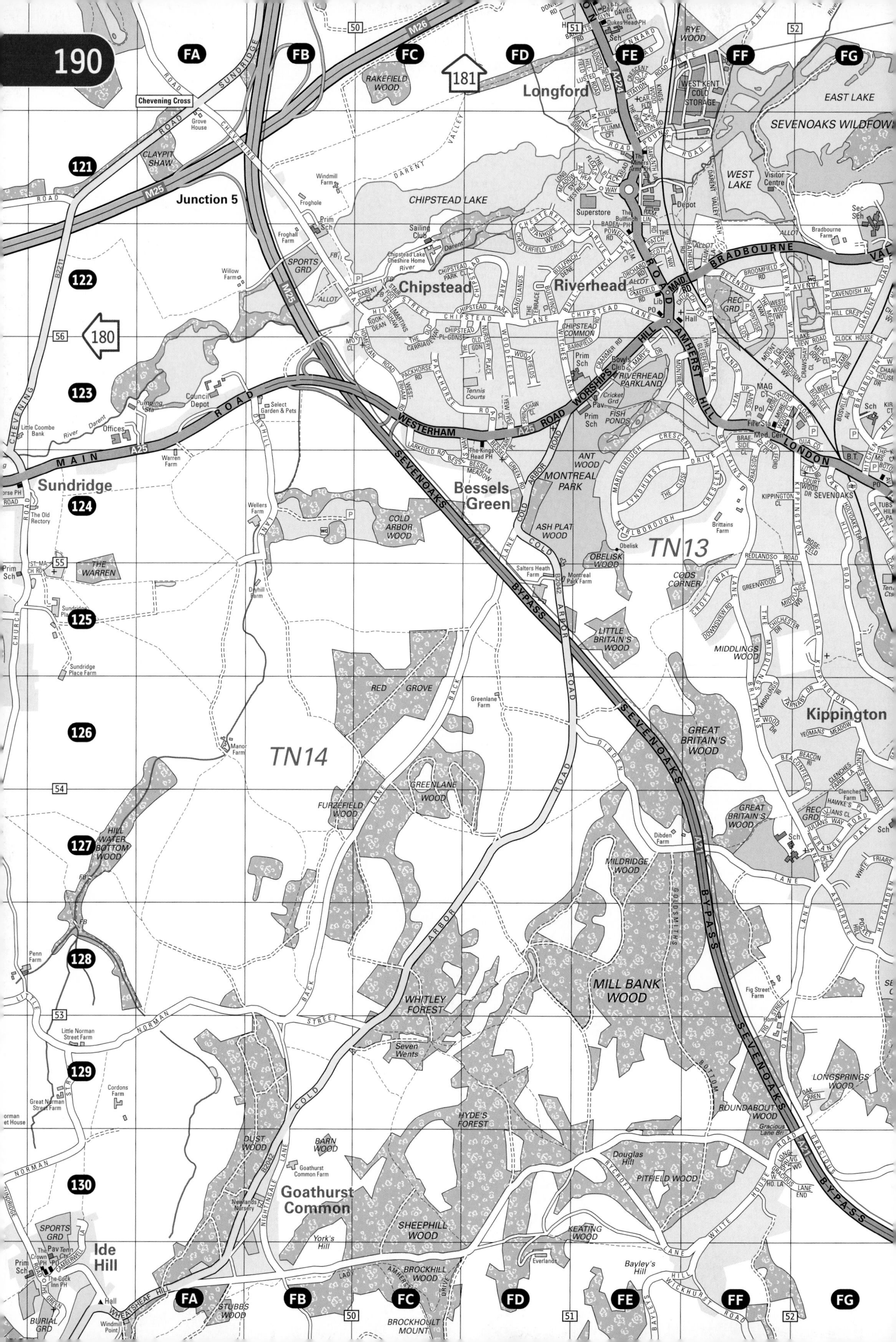

181
180
FA
FB
FC
FD
FE
FF
FG
121
122
123
124
125
126
127
128
129
130
50
51
52
53
54
55
56
Chevening Cross
Junction 5
M25
M26
A21
A25
A224
B2211
B2042
Longford
Chipstead
Riverhead
Bessels Green
Sundridge
Kippington
Goathurst Common
Ide Hill
TN13
TN14
CHIPSTEAD LAKE
EAST LAKE
SEVENOAKS WILDFOW
WEST LAKE
RYE WOOD
RAKEFIELD WOOD
CLAYPIT SHAW
WEST KENT COLD STORAGE
RIVERHEAD PARKLAND
MONTREAL PARK
ANT WOOD
ASH PLAT WOOD
OBELISK WOOD
COLD ARBOR WOOD
THE WARREN
LITTLE BRITAIN'S WOOD
CODS CORNER
MIDDLINGS WOOD
RED GROVE
GREAT BRITAIN'S WOOD
GREENLANE WOOD
FURZEFIELD WOOD
HILL WATER BOTTOM WOOD
MILDRIDGE WOOD
MILL BANK WOOD
WHITLEY FOREST
Seven Wents
HYDE'S FOREST
DUST WOOD
BARN WOOD
PITFIELD WOOD
Douglas Hill
SHEEPHILL WOOD
KEATING WOOD
BROCKHILL WOOD
BROCKHOULT MOUNT
STUBBS WOOD
LONGSPRINGS WOOD
ROUNDABOUT WOOD
Bayley's Hill
York's Hill
Everlands
Goathurst Common Farm
Newlands Nursery
WESTERHAM ROAD
MAIN ROAD
LONDON ROAD
BRADBOURNE VALE
SEVENOAKS BY-PASS
COLD ARBOR ROAD
BACK LANE
DIBDEN LANE
GRACIOUS LANE
WHITE HOUSE ROAD
WICKHURST ROAD
WHEATSHEAF HILL
NORMAN STREET
CHIPSTEAD LANE
AMHERST HILL
KIPPINGTON ROAD
BRITTAINS LANE
Superstore
Sailing Club
Dibden Farm
Salters Heath Farm
Montreal Park Farm
Manor Farm
Dryhill Farm
Wellers Farm
Warren Farm
Penn Farm
Little Norman Street Farm
Great Norman Street Farm
Cordons Farm
Sundridge Place Farm
Greenlane Farm
Fig Street Farm
Froghall Farm
Windmill Farm
Willow Farm
Grove House
Council Depot
Select Garden & Pets
Little Coombe Bank
The Old Rectory
Brittains Farm
Bradbourne Farm
Visitor Centre
Depot
The Kings Head PH
The Cock Inn PH
Windmill Point

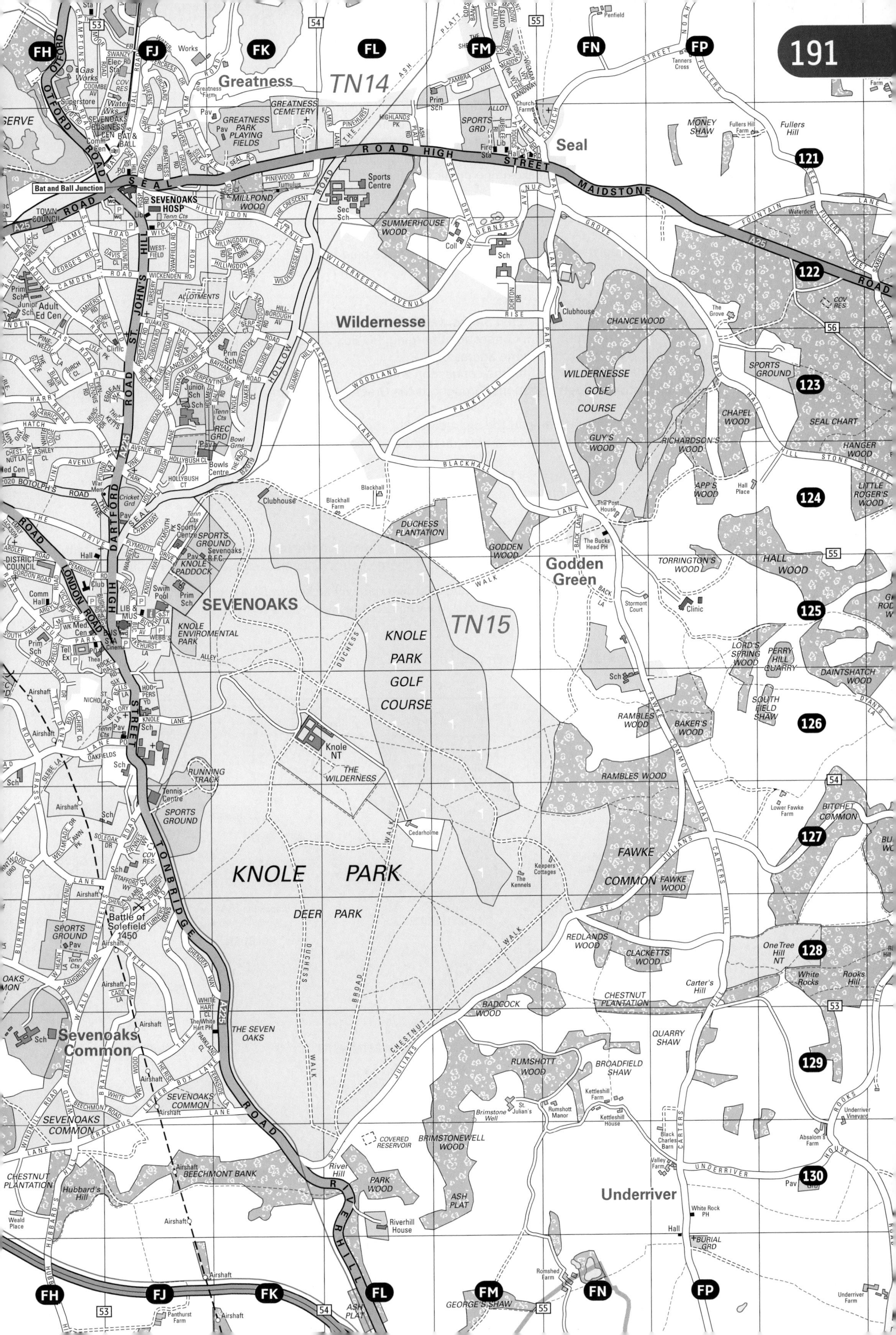
FH
FJ
FK
FL
FM
FN
FP
Greatness
TN14
Works
Penfield
Tanners Cross
FULLERS
Fullers Hill
MONEY SHAW
Seal
HIGH STREET
MAIDSTONE ROAD
A25
SEAL ROAD
OTFORD ROAD
Bat and Ball Junction
GREATNESS PARK PLAYING FIELDS
GREATNESS CEMETERY
SEVENOAKS BUSINESS CEN
SEVENOAKS HOSP
TOWN COUNCIL
MILLPOND WOOD
Sports Centre
Sec Sch
SUMMERHOUSE WOOD
Coll
WILDERNESSE AVENUE
Wildernesse
WILDERNESSE GOLF COURSE
CHANCE WOOD
Clubhouse
GUY'S WOOD
RICHARDSON'S WOOD
CHAPEL WOOD
SPORTS GROUND
SEAL CHART
HANGER WOOD
STONE STREET
LITTLE ROGER'S WOOD
APP'S WOOD
Hall Place
The Grove
BLACKHALL
PARKFIELD
WOODLAND
Blackhall Farm
DUCHESS PLANTATION
GODDEN WOOD
The Post House
The Bucks Head PH
Godden Green
TORRINGTON'S WOOD
HALL WOOD
Clinic
Stormont Court
ST. JOHN'S HILL
DARTFORD ROAD
HIGH STREET
A225
LONDON ROAD
BOTOLPH'S ROAD
SEVENOAKS
SPORTS GROUND
Sevenoaks R.F.C.
KNOLE PADDOCK
KNOLE ENVIROMENTAL PARK
Swim Pool
Prim Sch
KNOLE PARK GOLF COURSE
TN15
DUCHESS
LORD'S SPRING WOOD
PERRY HILL QUARRY
DAINTSHATCH WOOD
SOUTH FIELD SHAW
RAMBLES WOOD
BAKER'S WOOD
FAWKE COMMON ROAD
Knole NT
THE WILDERNESS
RUNNING TRACK
Tennis Centre
SPORTS GROUND
Cedarholme
Lower Fawke Farm
BITCHET COMMON
KNOLE PARK
DEER PARK
Keepers Cottages
The Kennels
FAWKE COMMON
FAWKE WOOD
JULIANS
CARTERS HILL
TONBRIDGE ROAD
Battle of Solefield 1450
REDLANDS WOOD
CLACKETTS WOOD
One Tree Hill NT
White Rocks
Rooks Hill
Carter's Hill
CHESTNUT PLANTATION
BADCOCK WOOD
THE SEVEN OAKS
Sevenoaks Common
CHESTNUT WALK
BROAD WALK
QUARRY SHAW
RUMSHOTT WOOD
BROADFIELD SHAW
St. Julian's
Rumshott Manor
Kettleshill Farm
Kettleshill House
Brimstone Well
BRIMSTONEWELL WOOD
COVERED RESERVOIR
SEVENOAKS COMMON
CHESTNUT PLANTATION
Hubbard's Hill
BEECHMONT BANK
River Hill
PARK WOOD
ASH PLAT
Riverhill House
RIVERHILL
Black Charles Barn
Valley Farm
UNDERRIVER
Underriver
White Rock PH
Hall
BURIAL GRD
Absalom's Farm
Underriver Vineyard
Romshed Farm
GEORGE'S SHAW
Panthurst Farm
Weald Place
Underriver Farm
Airshaft
53
54
55
56
121
122
123
124
125
126
127
128
129
130

London congestion charging zone

- London's congestion charging zone operates inside the 'Inner Ring Road' linking Marylebone Road, Euston Road, Pentonville Road, Tower Bridge, Elephant and Castle, Vauxhall Bridge and Park Lane. The 'Inner Ring Road' provides a route around the charging zone and charges do not apply to vehicles travelling on it. From February 2007 the zone will be extended westwards, with the Park Lane route still being exempt (see map below). The daily operating time is from 7am to 6.30pm (7am to 6pm from 19th February 2007), Monday to Friday, excluding public holidays and the period between Christmas and New Year's Day.

- Payment of the £8 congestion charge, either in advance or on the day of travel, allows the registered vehicle to enter, drive around and leave the congestion zone as many times as required on that one day. Payments can be made in a variety of ways but in all cases the vehicle registration number and the dates to be paid for must be given.
  Charges can be paid:
  - online at www.cclondon.com
  - by phone on 0845 900 1234 (charged at local rate)
  - by text message for drivers who have pre-registered on the website or telephone.
  - by post by requesting an application form from Congestion Charging, PO Box 2982, Coventry, CV7 8WR, or downloading the form from the website and posting to the same address.
  - at self-service machines in major car parks within the congestion zone.
  - at newsagents, convenience stores or petrol stations throughout the Greater London area displaying the PayPoint logo. 

- Regular drivers within the congestion zone can pay the charge weekly, monthly or yearly.
  Residents inside the congestion zone are eligible for a 90% discount upon payment of an annual £10 registration fee.

- On paying the charge the car registration number is held on a database. A series of over 200 cameras in and around the congestion zone record all vehicle number plates and check them against the database.
  - Drivers can pay the £8 charge until 10pm on the day of travel.
  - Drivers who forget to pay by 10pm on the day of travel can pay by midnight on the following charging day but they will then incur a £2 surcharge making the total charge £10. The £10 charge can only be paid by telephone or online.

  Any driver who has not paid before midnight on the following charging day will be sent a £100 penalty charge notice. Payment within 14 days will reduce this to £50. Failure to pay within 28 days will result in the penalty being increased to £150.

- Further information, including vehicles eligible for exemption or a discount, can be found on the website www.cclondon.com or by telephoning 0845 900 1234.

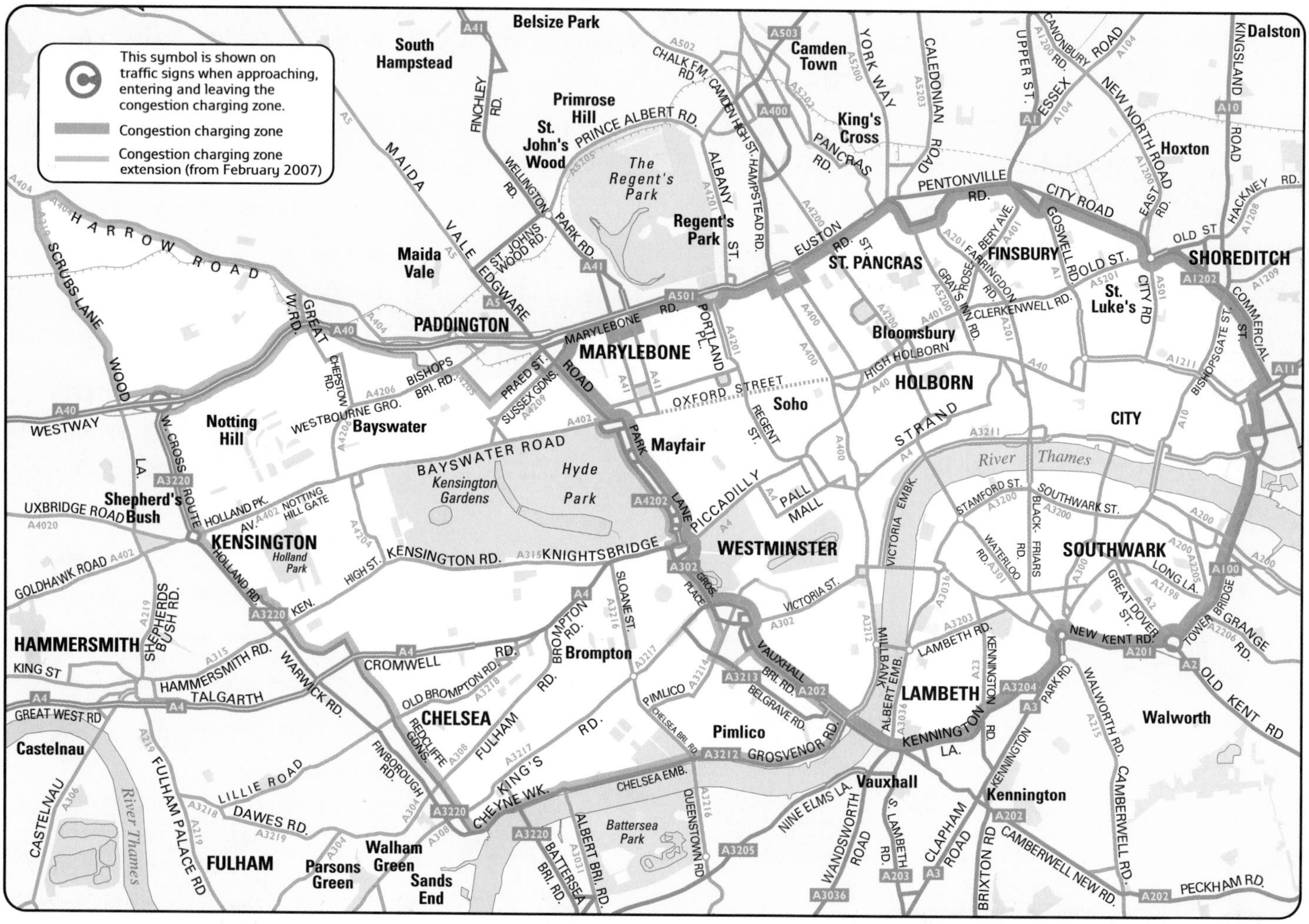

This symbol is shown on traffic signs when approaching, entering and leaving the congestion charging zone.
Congestion charging zone
Congestion charging zone extension (from February 2007)

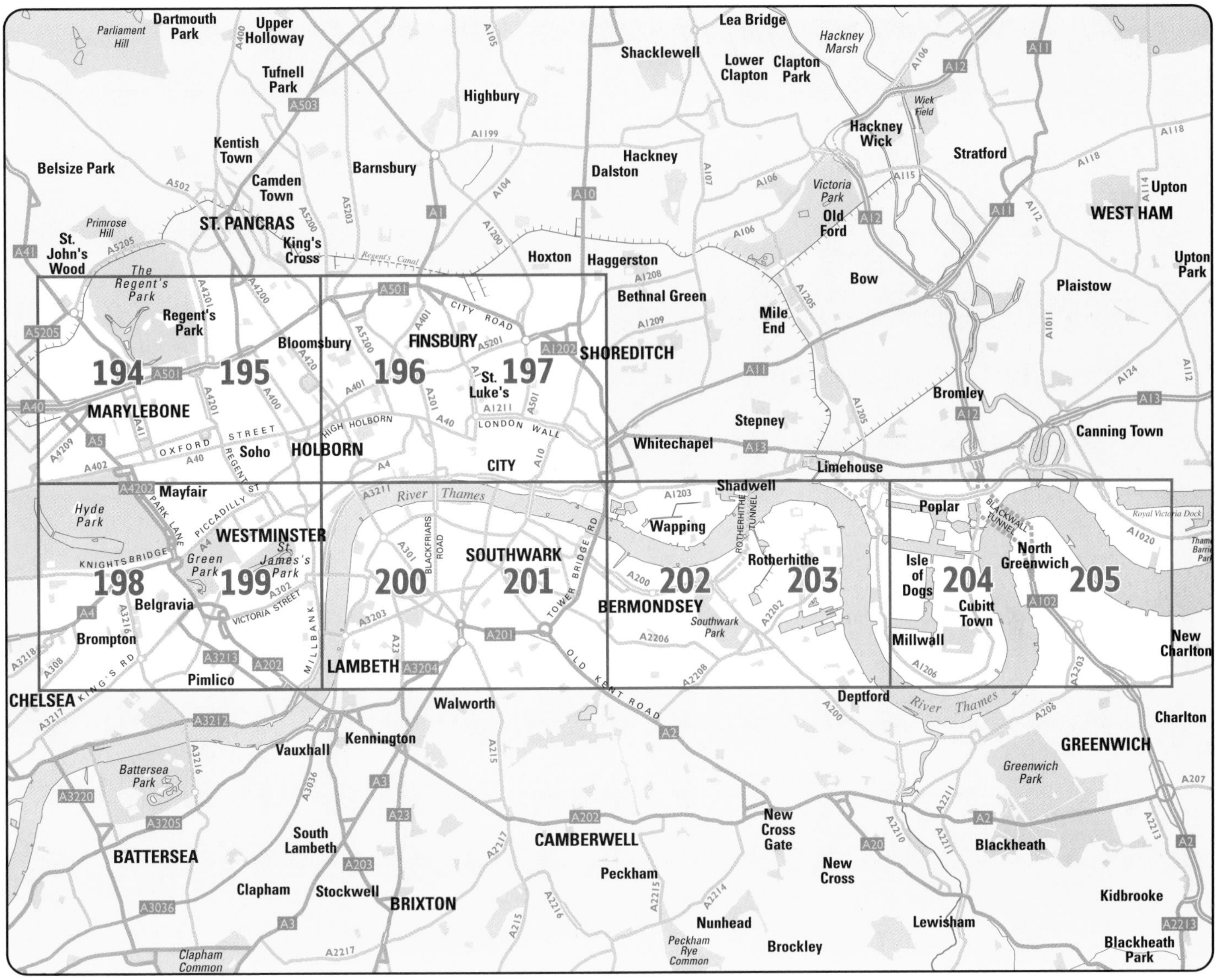

Key to map symbols 194-205

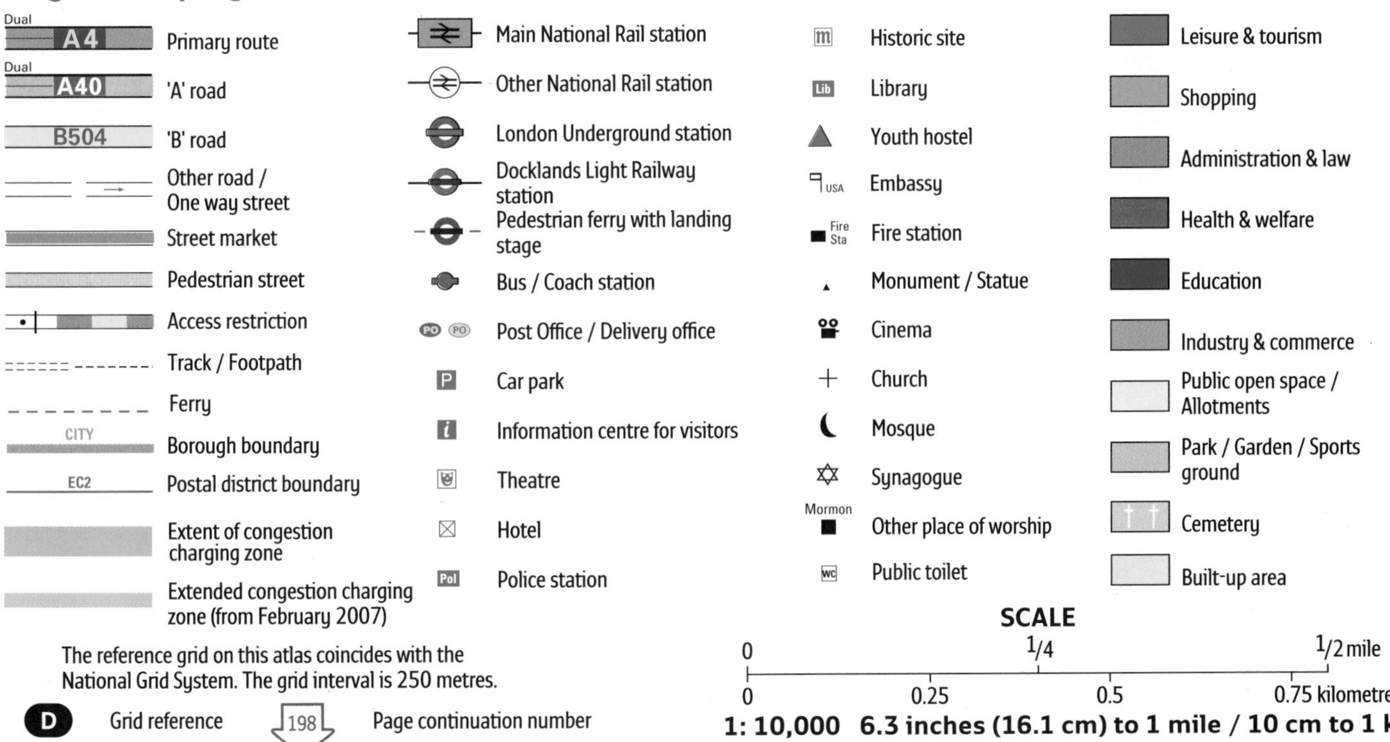
Dual
A4
Primary route
Dual
A40
'A' road
B504
'B' road
Other road / One way street
Street market
Pedestrian street
Access restriction
Track / Footpath
Ferry
CITY
Borough boundary
EC2
Postal district boundary
Extent of congestion charging zone
Extended congestion charging zone (from February 2007)
Main National Rail station
Other National Rail station
London Underground station
Docklands Light Railway station
Pedestrian ferry with landing stage
Bus / Coach station
Post Office / Delivery office
Car park
Information centre for visitors
Theatre
Hotel
Police station
Historic site
Library
Youth hostel
Embassy
Fire Sta
Fire station
Monument / Statue
Cinema
Church
Mosque
Synagogue
Mormon
Other place of worship
Public toilet
Leisure & tourism
Shopping
Administration & law
Health & welfare
Education
Industry & commerce
Public open space / Allotments
Park / Garden / Sports ground
Cemetery
Built-up area
The reference grid on this atlas coincides with the National Grid System. The grid interval is 250 metres.
D
Grid reference
198
Page continuation number
SCALE
0
1/4
1/2 mile
0
0.25
0.5
0.75 kilometre
1: 10,000 6.3 inches (16.1 cm) to 1 mile / 10 cm to 1 km

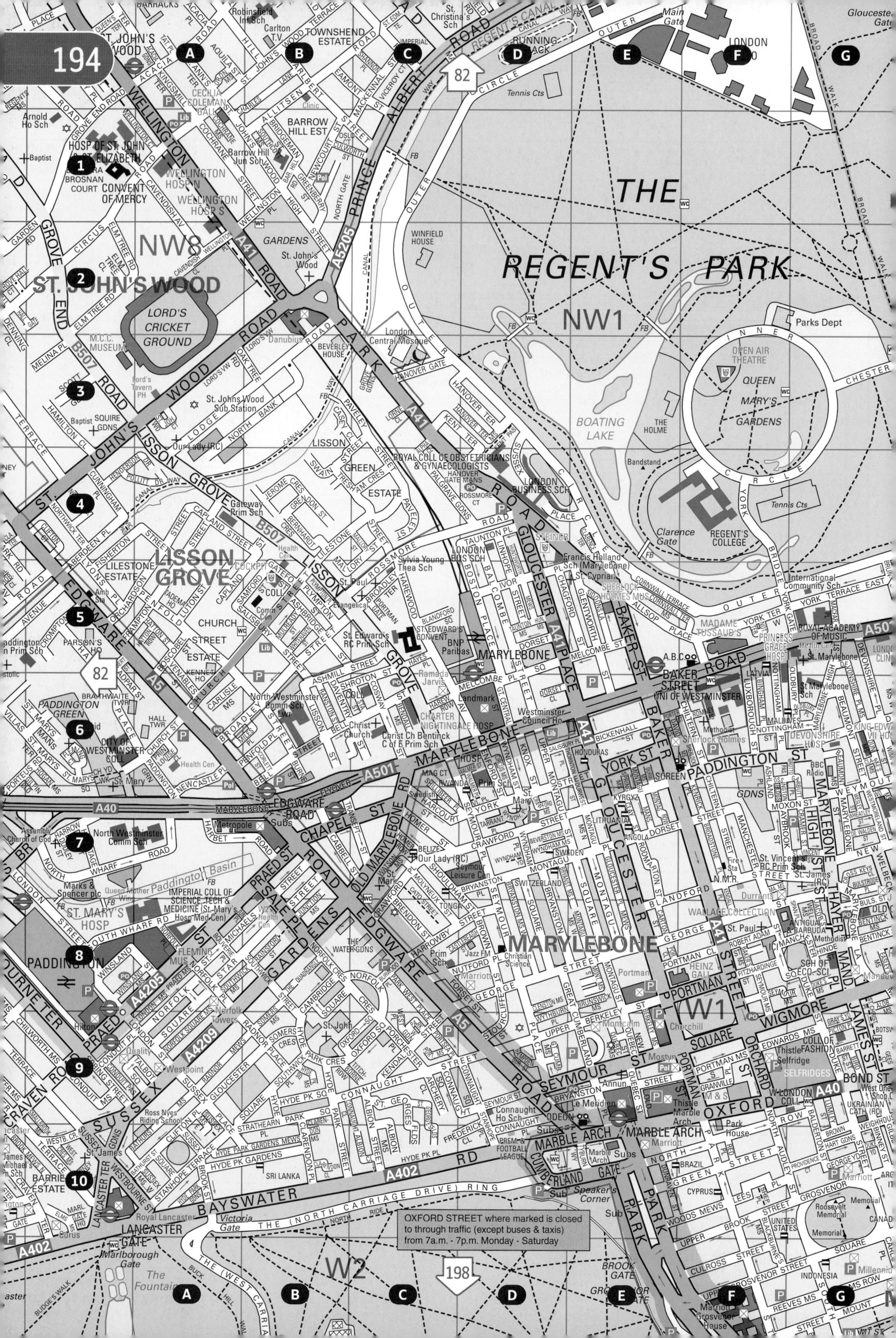
THE REGENT'S PARK
NW1
NW8
W1
W2
ST. JOHN'S WOOD
LISSON GROVE
MARYLEBONE
LORD'S CRICKET GROUND
M.C.C. MUSEUM
WELLINGTON ROAD
ST. JOHN'S WOOD ROAD
PRINCE ALBERT ROAD
PARK ROAD
OUTER CIRCLE
INNER CIRCLE
LONDON ZOO
REGENT'S CANAL
WINFIELD HOUSE
London Central Mosque
HANOVER GATE
BOATING LAKE
OPEN AIR THEATRE
QUEEN MARY'S GARDENS
THE HOLME
Bandstand
Parks Dept
REGENT'S COLLEGE
Clarence Gate
LONDON BUSINESS SCH
YORK BRIDGE
Tennis Cts
MADAME TUSSAUD'S
ROYAL ACADEMY OF MUSIC
BAKER STREET
MARYLEBONE ROAD
BAKER ST
GLOUCESTER PLACE
LISSON GROVE
EDGWARE ROAD
PADDINGTON
PADDINGTON GREEN
Paddington Basin
ST. MARY'S HOSP
PRAED ST
SUSSEX GARDENS
BAYSWATER ROAD
LANCASTER GATE
MARBLE ARCH
OXFORD STREET
PORTMAN SQUARE
WIGMORE ST
SELFRIDGES
WALLACE COLLECTION
PARK LANE
Speaker's Corner
NORTH CARRIAGE DRIVE
THE WEST CARRIAGE DRIVE
The Fountains
A B C D E F G
1 2 3 4 5 6 7 8 9 10
82
198
OXFORD STREET where marked is closed to through traffic (except buses & taxis) from 7a.m. - 7p.m. Monday - Saturday

H
J
K
L
M
N
P
83
REGENT'S PARK
MORNINGTON CRESCENT
CAMDEN
WESTMINSTER
SOMERS TOWN
BRITISH LIBRARY
ST. PANCRAS
KING'S CROSS
KING'S CROSS & ST. PANCRAS
EUSTON
EUSTON ROAD
EUSTON SQUARE
WARREN ST
GT. PORTLAND ST
REGENT'S PARK
PARK CRESCENT
PORTLAND PLACE
ALBANY STREET
HAMPSTEAD ROAD
EVERSHOLT ST
OAKLEY SQ
CROWNDALE RD
PANCRAS ROAD
ST. GEORGE'S CATHEDRAL
CUMBERLAND MARKET EST
CLARENCE GARDENS
ST. PANCRAS CHAMBERS
CAMDEN TOWN HALL
UCL (Main Site)
BLOOMSBURY
GOWER ST
TOTTENHAM CT RD
WOBURN PL
RUSSELL SQ
RUSSELL SQUARE GARDENS
UNIVERSITY OF LONDON SENATE HO
SCH OF ORIENTAL & AFRICAN STUDIES
BIRKBECK COLL
THE BRITISH MUSEUM
BLOOMSBURY
GOODGE ST
GOODGE ST
MORTIMER ST
CAVENDISH SQ
OXFORD CIRCUS
A40 OXFORD ST
TOTTENHAM COURT RD
CENTREPOINT
NEW OXFORD ST
ST. GILES HIGH ST
SHAFTESBURY AV
CHARING CROSS RD
SOHO
LEICESTER SQ
COVENT GARDEN
ROYAL OPERA HO
STRAND
HOLBORN
WC1
WC2
196
1
2
3
4
5
6
7
8
9
10
HOSP FOR CHILDREN
THE NAT HOSP
REGENT ST
NEW BOND ST
CONDUIT ST
HANOVER SQUARE
JOHN LEWIS
DEBENHAMS
PALLADIUM
HAMLEYS
LIBERTY
SOHO SQUARE
MAYFAIR
199
PICCADILLY CIRCUS
Trocadero Cen
NATIONAL GALL
LONG ACRE
BOW ST
JUDD ST
GRAY'S INN RD
SOUTHAMPTON ROW
ST. MARTIN'S LA

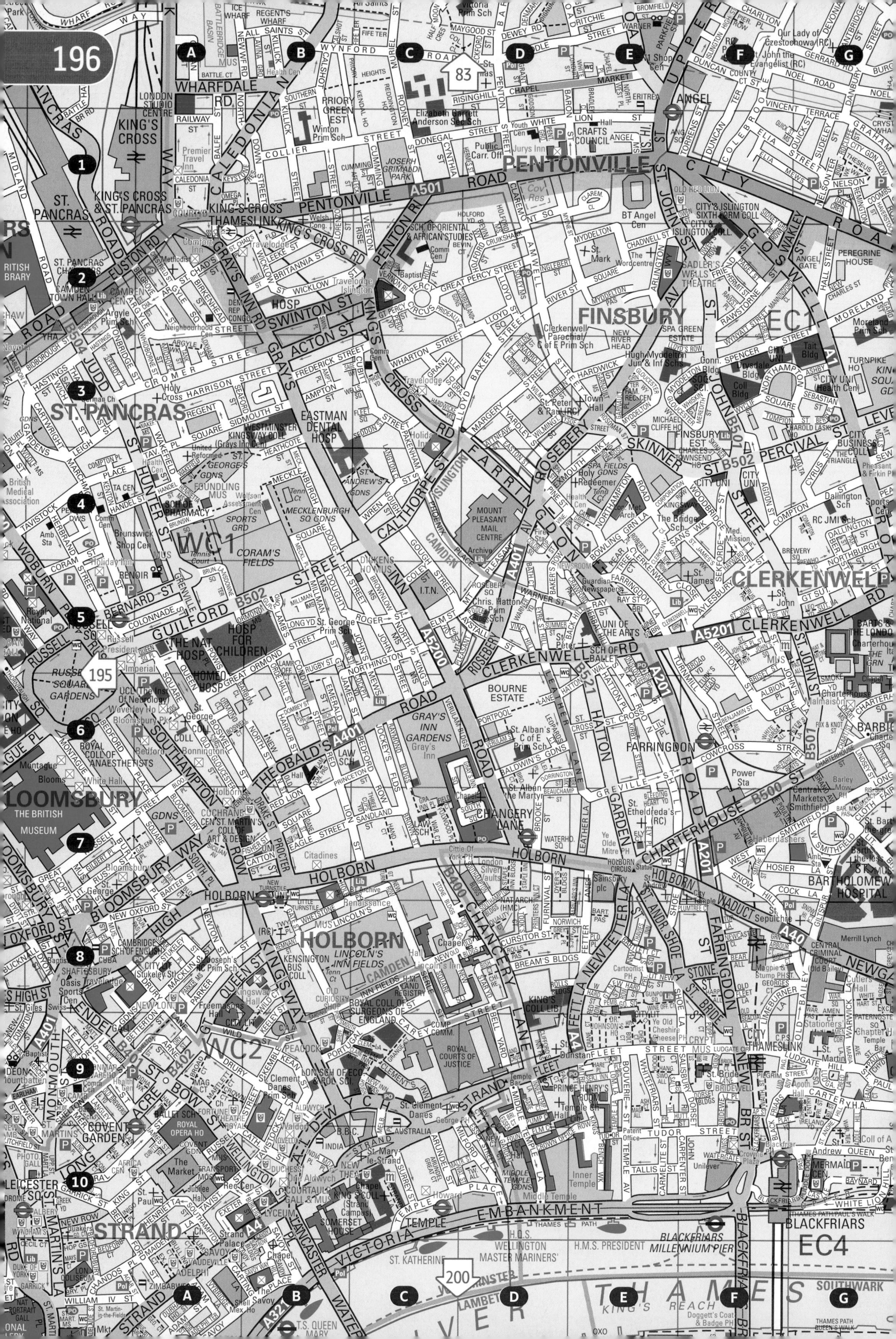
A
B
C
D
E
F
G
1
2
3
4
5
6
7
8
9
10
83
195
200
KING'S CROSS
ST. PANCRAS
KING'S CROSS & ST. PANCRAS
KING'S CROSS THAMESLINK
PENTONVILLE
PENTONVILLE ROAD
A501
ANGEL
CITY ROAD
GOSWELL ROAD
FINSBURY
EC1
ST. PANCRAS
WC1
CORAM'S FIELDS
MECKLENBURGH SQ GDNS
GRAY'S INN ROAD
KING'S CROSS RD
FARRINGDON RD
MOUNT PLEASANT MAIL CENTRE
ROSEBERY AV
CLERKENWELL
CLERKENWELL RD
A5201
FARRINGDON
GUILFORD STREET
B502
HOSP FOR CHILDREN
RUSSELL SQUARE GARDENS
THEOBALD'S ROAD
A401
GRAY'S INN GARDENS
CHANCERY LANE
HOLBORN
HOLBORN VIADUCT
CHARTERHOUSE ST
B500
BLOOMSBURY
THE BRITISH MUSEUM
BLOOMSBURY WAY
HIGH HOLBORN
KINGSWAY
LINCOLN'S INN FIELDS
ROYAL COURTS OF JUSTICE
FLEET STREET
NEW BR ST
FARRINGDON ST
CITY THAMESLINK
WC2
COVENT GARDEN
ROYAL OPERA HO
STRAND
ALDWYCH
SOMERSET HOUSE
TEMPLE
VICTORIA EMBANKMENT
BLACKFRIARS
BLACKFRIARS MILLENNIUM PIER
EC4
H.M.S. PRESIDENT
THAMES
KING'S REACH
SOUTHWARK
BARTHOLOMEW HOSPITAL
CENTRAL CRIMINAL COURT (Old Bailey)
SMITHFIELD
CAMDEN
ISLINGTON

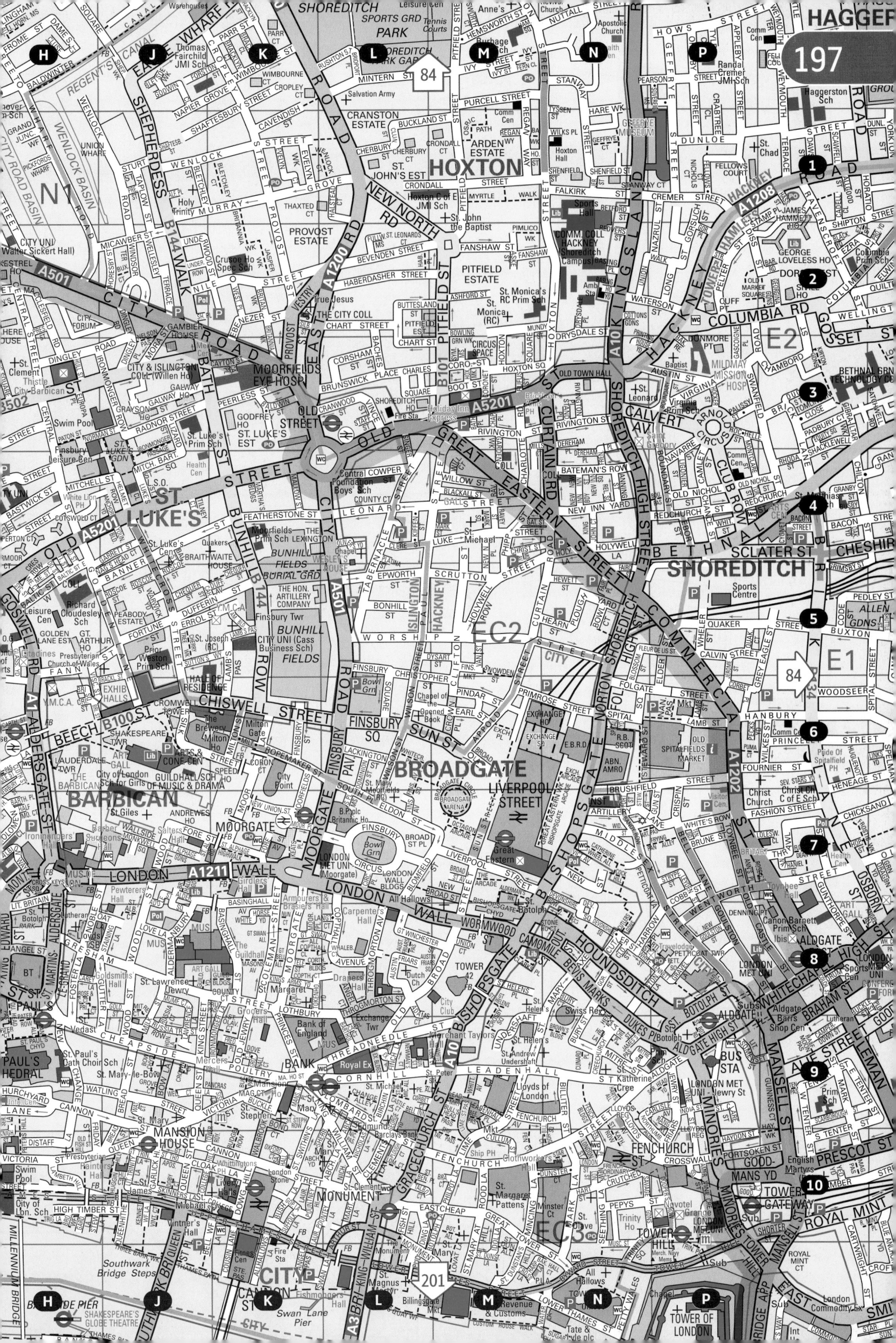

HAGGERSTON
SHOREDITCH
HOXTON
N1
ST. LUKE'S
BARBICAN
BROADGATE
SHOREDITCH
EC2
EC3
E1
E2
CITY
84
201
H J K L M N P
1 2 3 4 5 6 7 8 9 10
CITY ROAD
OLD STREET
GREAT EASTERN STREET
SHOREDITCH HIGH STREET
KINGSLAND ROAD
HACKNEY ROAD
BISHOPSGATE
COMMERCIAL STREET
LONDON WALL
MOORGATE
FINSBURY SQ
LIVERPOOL STREET
ALDERSGATE ST
CHISWELL STREET
HOUNDSDITCH
MINORIES
LEADENHALL
CORNHILL
CHEAPSIDE
FENCHURCH
MONUMENT
MANSION HOUSE
BANK
ALDGATE
TOWER HILL
TOWER OF LONDON
CANNON ST
WHITECHAPEL HIGH ST
COLUMBIA RD
BETHNAL GREEN
SPITALFIELDS MARKET
MOORFIELDS EYE HOSP
BUNHILL FIELDS
ROYAL MINT
Swan Lane Pier
SHAKESPEARE'S GLOBE THEATRE
MILLENNIUM BRIDGE

HYDE PARK
W2
SW7
SW3
BROMPTON
BELGRAVIA
KENSINGTON GARDENS
THE SERPENTINE
THE LONG WATER
BAYSWATER RD
KENSINGTON RD
KNIGHTSBRIDGE
BROMPTON ROAD
CROMWELL ROAD
KING'S ROAD
FULHAM ROAD
SLOANE STREET
PARK LANE
MARBLE ARCH
HYDE PARK CORNER
SOUTH KENSINGTON
SLOANE SQ
VICTORIA & ALBERT MUSEUM
NATURAL HISTORY MUSEUM
SCIENCE MUSEUM
HARRODS
194
82
100

SOHO
MAYFAIR
W1
PICCADILLY CIRCUS
STRAND
NATIONAL GALLERY
TRAFALGAR SQ
CHARING CROSS
LEICESTER SQ
HAYMARKET
REGENT ST
PICCADILLY
GREEN PARK
THE GREEN PARK
ST. JAMES'S
ST. JAMES'S PARK
SW1
PALL MALL
THE MALL
CONSTITUTION HILL
BUCKINGHAM PALACE GARDENS
BUCKINGHAM PALACE
THE QUEEN'S GALLERY
THE ROYAL MEWS
BIRDCAGE WALK
WHITEHALL
HORSE GUARDS
DOWNING ST
PARLIAMENT ST
WESTMINSTER
WESTMINSTER ABBEY
HOUSES OF PARLIAMENT
VICTORIA TOWER GARDENS
VICTORIA EMBANKMENT
VICTORIA ST
VICTORIA
ST. JAMES'S PARK
BUCKINGHAM GATE
MILLBANK
LAMBETH BRI
TATE BRITAIN
MILLBANK TOWER
MILLBANK MILLENNIUM PIER
WESTMINSTER MILLENNIUM PIER
VAUXHALL BRIDGE ROAD
VAUXHALL BRI
PIMLICO
BELGRAVE ROAD
ECCLESTON ST
BUCKINGHAM PALACE ROAD
COACH STA
HORSEFERRY ROAD
PLAYING FIELDS
SE1
ALBERT EMBANKMENT
195
200
101
H
J
K
L
M
N
P
1
2
3
4
5
6
7
8
9
10

STRAND
WC2
EC4
SE1
SE11
SW1
RIVER THAMES
KING'S REACH
VICTORIA EMBANKMENT
ALBERT EMBANKMENT
WATERLOO BRI
WESTMINSTER BRI
LAMBETH BRI
BLACKFRIARS BRI
BLACKFRIARS
WATERLOO
WATERLOO INTERNATIONAL
WATERLOO EAST
CHARING CROSS
EMBANKMENT
WESTMINSTER
LAMBETH NORTH
KENNINGTON
VAUXHALL
HOUSES OF PARLIAMENT
WESTMINSTER ABBEY
TATE BRITAIN
MILLBANK
LAMBETH
ROYAL FESTIVAL HALL
ROYAL NATIONAL
LONDON EYE
COUNTY HALL
ST. THOMAS' HOSP
LAMBETH PALACE GDNS
ARCHBISHOP'S PARK
GERALDINE MARY HARMSWORTH PARK
IMPERIAL WAR MUS
PEABODY ESTATE
STAMFORD STREET
THE CUT
SOUTHWARK
ST. GEORGE'S CIRCUS
ELEPHANT & CASTLE
KENNINGTON LANE
KENNINGTON ROAD
LAMBETH ROAD
WESTMINSTER BRIDGE ROAD
LONDON ROAD
BOROUGH ROAD
KENNINGTON PARK ROAD
NEWINGTON BUTTS
VAUXHALL BRIDGE
A B C D E F G
1 2 3 4 5 6 7 8 9 10
196
199
101

CITY
EC3
TOWER OF LONDON
LONDON BRIDGE HOSPITAL
LONDON BRIDGE CITY PIER
SOUTHWARK CATHEDRAL
H.M.S. BELFAST
TOWER BRIDGE
ST. KATHARINE'S PIER
BANKSIDE PIER
SHAKESPEARE'S GLOBE THEATRE
MILLENNIUM BRIDGE
SOUTHWARK BRIDGE ROAD
CANNON ST
MONUMENT
FENCHURCH ST
TOWER HILL
TOWER HAMLETS
SOUTHWARK
CITY HALL (Greater London Authority)
POTTERS FIELDS PARK
BUTLERS WHARF
DESIGN MUSEUM
GUY'S HOSP
LONDON BRIDGE
THE BOROUGH
BOROUGH HIGH STREET
TOOLEY STREET
BERMONDSEY STREET
ST. THOMAS STREET
LONG LANE
GREAT DOVER STREET
TOWER BRIDGE ROAD
ABBEY STREET
JAMAICA ROAD
BERMONDSEY
GRANGE ROAD
OLD KENT ROAD
BRICKLAYER'S ARMS ROUNDABOUT
NEW KENT ROAD
ELEPHANT & CASTLE
NEWINGTON
WALWORTH
SE17
WALWORTH ROAD
EAST STREET
SURREY SQUARE PARK
FARADAY GARDENS
BERMONDSEY SPA
ROLLS ROAD
SOUTHWARK PARK ROAD
197
202
102
H J K L M N P
1 2 3 4 5 6 7 8 9 10

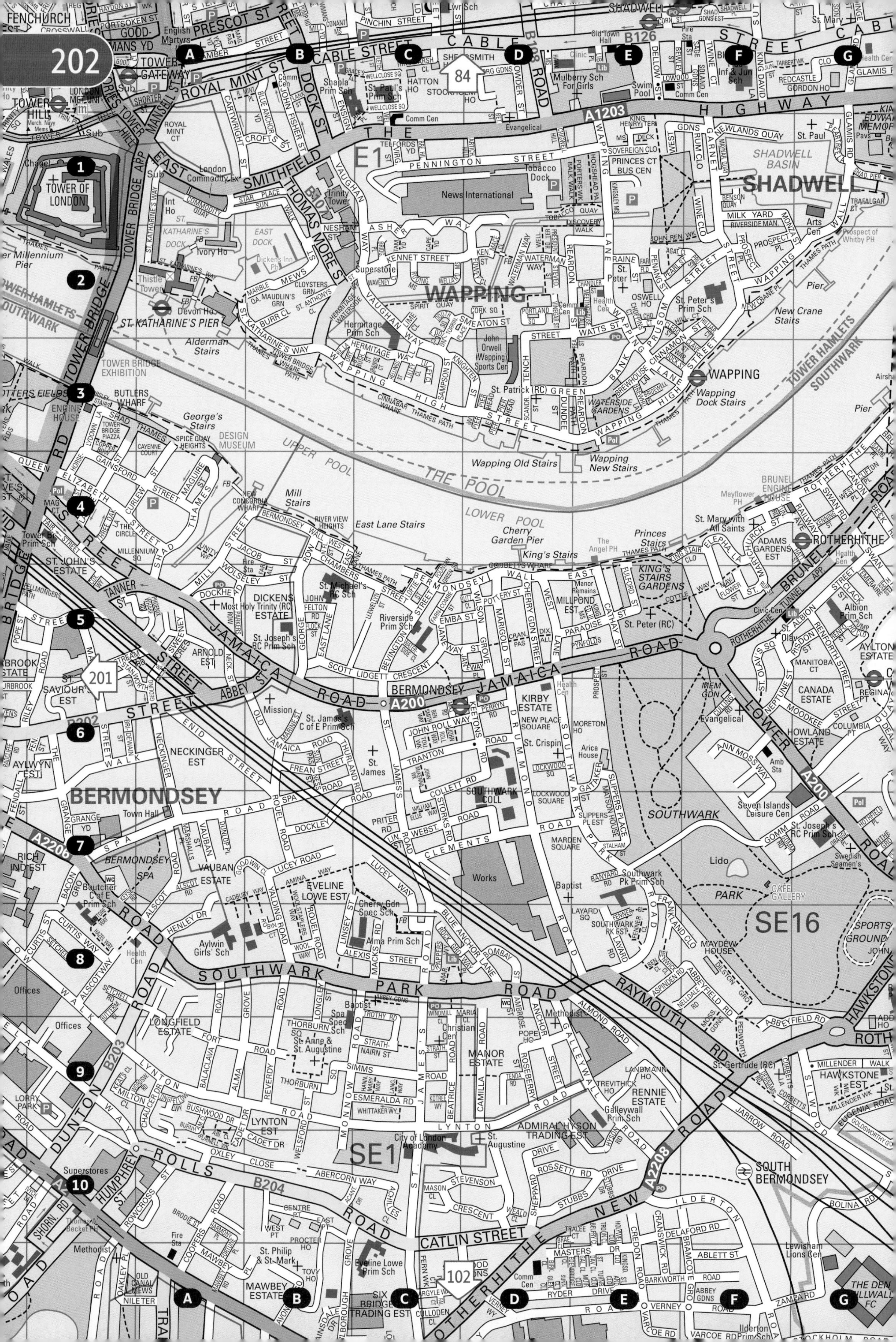

TOWER OF LONDON
TOWER BRIDGE
WAPPING
SHADWELL
SHADWELL BASIN
ROTHERHITHE
BERMONDSEY
SOUTHWARK
SOUTHWARK PARK
SOUTH BERMONDSEY
THE POOL
UPPER POOL
LOWER POOL
E1
SE1
SE16
THE HIGHWAY
CABLE STREET
JAMAICA ROAD
SOUTHWARK PARK ROAD
LOWER ROAD
ROTHERHITHE NEW ROAD
TOWER BRIDGE ROAD
WAPPING HIGH STREET
ST. KATHARINE'S DOCK
News International
DESIGN MUSEUM
TOWER BRIDGE EXHIBITION
THE DEN MILLWALL FC
84
201
102

LIMEHOUSE
RIVER THAMES
ROTHERHITHE
E14
SE8
DEPTFORD
WESTFERRY
CANARY WHARF PIER
HERON QUAYS
WEST INDIA QUAY
MUSEUM IN DOCKLANDS
LIMEHOUSE REACH
GREENLAND DOCK
SOUTH DOCK
GREENLAND PIER
SURREY QUAYS
MASTHOUSE TERRACE
SALTER ROAD
ROTHERHITHE STREET
WESTFERRY ROAD
EVELYN STREET
LOWER ROAD
PLOUGH WAY
GROVE STREET
REDRIFF ROAD
RUSSIA DOCK WOODLAND
ECOLOGICAL PARK
DEPTFORD PARK
PEPYS PARK
SIR JOHN MCDOUGALL GDNS
MILLWALL
TOWER HAMLETS
SOUTHWARK
LEWISHAM
85
103
204

A
B
C
D
E
F
G
1
2
3
4
5
6
7
8
9
10
85
203
103
POPLAR
ISLE OF DOGS
MILLWALL
CUBITT TOWN
E14
SE8
WEST INDIA DOCKS
MILLWALL INNER DOCK
MILLWALL OUTER DOCK
BLACKWALL BASIN
POPLAR DOCK
MUDCHUTE PARK
MILLWALL PARK
ISLAND GARDENS
RIVER THAMES
BLACKWALL REACH
GREENWICH REACH
BLACKWALL TUNNEL
A102
A13
A1206
A1261
ASPEN WAY
WESTFERRY ROAD
WESTFERRY CIRCUS
MANCHESTER ROAD
PRESTONS ROAD
EAST FERRY ROAD
MARSH WALL
WEST INDIA QUAY
CANARY WHARF
HERON QUAYS
SOUTH QUAY
CROSSHARBOUR & LONDON ARENA
MUDCHUTE
ISLAND GARDENS
POPLAR
BLACKWALL
EAST INDIA
ALL SAINTS
MASTHOUSE TERRACE
Billingsgate Mkt
Museum in Docklands
HSBC
Barclays
Citigroup
Canada Square
Cabot Place
Superstore
Independent Newspapers
South Quay Plaza
London Arena (closed)
Telegraph & Express Print Works
Docklands Sailing & Watersport Cen
Great Eastern
Enterprise Centre
41 Millharbour
Harbour Exchange Square
Skylines Village
Britannia International Hotel
Fraser Place
Reuters
Poplar Business Park
Tower Hamlets Coll (Poplar Cen)
Cineworld
Seven Mills Prim Sch
The Barkantine Shopping Par
Arnhem Wf Prim Sch
Harbinger Prim Sch
St. Edmund's RC Prim Sch
St. Luke's Prim Sch
George Green's Sec Sch
Cubitt Town Jun & Inf Sch
Mudchute Farm
Leisure Cen
Greenwich Foot Tunnel
Newcastle Draw Dock
Lovell's Wharf
High Bridge Wharf
Trafalgar Rowing Cen
Palmer's Wharf
Payne's Wharf
Airy's Point
Meridian Gardens
Delta Wharf
New Providence Wharf
TOWER HAMLETS
GREENWICH
LEWISHAM

ExCeL London
ROYAL VICTORIA
E16
SILVERTOWN WAY
NORTH WOOLWICH ROAD
WEST SILVERTOWN
GREENSHIELDS INDUSTRIAL ESTATE
LYLE PARK
The Dome Redevelopment (Open 2007)
NORTH GREENWICH
BUS STA
Football Academy
SE10
GREENWICH PENINSULA ECOLOGY PARK
Millennium Village Sch
SE7
MERIDIAN TRADING ESTATE
GREENWICH INDUSTRIAL ESTATE
GREENWICH SHOPPING PARK
STONE LAKE RETAIL PARK
BUGSBY'S WAY
BLACKWALL TUNNEL APPROACH
WOOLWICH ROAD
A102
A206
A1020
A2203
EAST GREENWICH PLEASAUNCE
WESTCOMBE PARK
NEWHAM
GREENWICH
THAMES
86
104

Notes on how to use the index

The index starting on page 208 combines entries for street names, place names, places of interest, stations and hospitals.

Place names are shown in capital letters,
e.g. **ACTON**, W3 . . . .**80** CN74
These include towns, villages and other localities within the area covered by this atlas.

Places of interest are shown with a star symbol,
e.g. **★British Mus**, WC1 . . . .**195** P7
These include parks, museums, galleries, other important buildings and tourist attractions.

Hospitals and types of station are shown by symbols as listed :-

- H Hospital
- ⇌ Railway station
- ⊖ London Underground station
- DLR Docklands Light Railway station
- Tra Tramlink station
- Riv Pedestrian ferry landing stage

All other entries are for street names. When there is more than one street with exactly the same name then that name is shown only once in the index. It is then followed by a list of entries for each postal district that contains a street with that same name. For example, there are three streets called **Ardley Close** in this atlas and the index entry shows that one of these is in London postal district NW10, one is in London postal district SE6 and one is in Ruislip HA4.
e.g. **Ardley Cl**, NW10 . . . .**62** CS62
SE6 . . . .**123** DY90
Ruislip HA4 . . . .**59** BQ59
All entries are followed by the page number and grid reference on which the name will be found. So, in the example above, **Ardley Close,** NW10 will be found on page **62** in square CS62.
All entries are indexed to the largest scale map on which they are shown.

The index also contains some streets which are not actually named on the maps because there is not enough space. In these cases the adjoining or nearest named thoroughfare to such a street is shown in *italic.* The reference indicates where the unnamed street is located *off* the named thoroughfare.
e.g. **Bacton St**, E2
off Roman Rd **84** DW69
This means that **Bacton Street** is not named on the map, but it is located *off Roman Road* on page **84** in square DW69.

A strict letter-by-letter alphabetical order is followed in this index. All non-alphabetic characters such as spaces, hyphens or apostrophes have not been included in the index order. For example **Belle Vue Road** and **Bellevue Road** will be found listed together.

Standard terms such as **Avenue, Close, Rise** and **Road** are abbreviated in the index but are ordered alphabetically as if given in full. So, for example, **Abbots Ri** comes before **Abbots Rd.**

Names beginning with a definite article (i.e. **The**) are indexed from their second word onwards with the definite article being placed at the end of the name.
e.g. **Avenue, The**, E4 . . . .**47** ED51

The alphabetical order extends to include postal information so that where two or more streets have exactly the same name, London postal district references are given first in alpha-numeric order and are followed by non-London post town references in alphabetical order, e.g. **Ardley Close,** NW10 is followed by **Ardley Close,** SE6 and then **Ardley Close,** Ruislip HA4.

In cases where there are two or more streets of the same name in the same postal area, extra information is given in brackets to aid location. For example, **High St,** Orpington BR6 (Farnborough), and **High St,** Orpington BR6 (Green St Grn), distinguishes between two streets called **High Street** which are both in the post town of Orpington and within the same postal district of BR6.

Extra locational information is also given for some localities within large post towns. This is also to aid location.
e.g. **Acer Rd**, West (Bigg.H.) TN16. . **178** EK116
This street is within the locality of Biggin Hill which is part of the post town of Westerham, and it is within postal district TN16 .

A full list of locality and post town abbreviations used in this atlas is given on the following page.

General abbreviations

Acad	Academy	Conf	Conference	Grd	Ground	Mid	Middle	Sec	Secondary
All	Alley	Cont	Continuing	Grds	Grounds	Mkt	Market	Sen	Senior
App	Approach	Conv	Convent	Grn	Green	Ms	Mews	Shop	Shopping
Arc	Arcade	Cor	Corner	Grns	Greens	Mt	Mount	Spec	Special
Assoc	Association	Cors	Corners	Gro	Grove	Mus	Museum	Sq	Square
Av	Avenue	Cotts	Cottages	Gros	Groves	N	North	St	Street
Ave	Avenue	Cres	Crescent	Gt	Great	NHS	National Health	St.	Saint
BUPA	British United	Ct	Court	HQ	Headquarters		Service	Sta	Station
	Provident	Ctyd	Courtyard	Ho	House	Nat	National	Sts	Streets
	Association	Dep	Depot	Hos	Houses	Nurs	Nursery	Sub	Subway
Bdy	Broadway	Dept	Department	Hosp	Hospital	PO	Post Office	TA	Territorial Army
Bk	Bank	Dev	Development	Hts	Heights	PRU	Pupil Referral Unit	Tech	Technical, Technology
Bldg	Building	Dr	Drive	Ind	Industrial	Par	Parade	Tenn	Tennis
Bldgs	Buildings	Dws	Dwellings	Indep	Independent	Pas	Passage	Ter	Terrace
Boul	Boulevard	E	East	Inf	Infant(s)	Pk	Park	Thea	Theatre
Bowl	Bowling	Ed	Education,	Inst	Institute	Pl	Place	Trd	Trading
Br	Bridge		Educational	Int	International	Pol	Police	Twr	Tower
C of E	Church of England	Embk	Embankment	JM	Junior Mixed	Poly	Polytechnic	Twrs	Towers
Cath	Cathedral	Est	Estate	JMI	Junior Mixed &	Prec	Precinct	Uni	University
Cem	Cemetery	Ex	Exchange		Infant(s)	Prep	Preparatory	Upr	Upper
Cen	Central, Centre	Exhib	Exhibition	Jun	Junior	Prim	Primary	VA	Voluntary Aided
Cft	Croft	FC	Football Club	Junct	Junction	Prom	Promenade	VC	Voluntary Controlled
Cfts	Crofts	Fld	Field	La	Lane	Pt	Point	Vet	Veterinary
Ch	Church	Flds	Fields	Las	Lanes	Quad	Quadrant	Vil	Villas
Chyd	Churchyard	Fm	Farm	Lib	Library	RC	Roman Catholic	Vil	Villa
Circ	Circus	GM	Grant Maintained	Lit	Literary	Rbt	Roundabout	Vw	View
Cl	Close	Gall	Gallery	Lo	Lodge	Rd	Road	W	West
Co	County	Gar	Garage	Lwr	Lower	Rds	Roads	Wd	Wood
CCC	County Cricket Club	Gdn	Garden	Mans	Mansions	Rehab	Rehabilitation	Wds	Woods
Coll	College	Gdns	Gardens	Med	Medical	Ri	Rise	Wf	Wharf
Comb	Combined	Gen	General	Med	Medicine	S	South	Wk	Walk
Comm	Community	Gra	Grange	Mem	Memorial	Sch	School	Wks	Works
Comp	Comprehensive	Gram	Grammar	Met	Metropolitan	Schs	Schools	Yd	Yard

Locality & post town abbreviations

Note: In the following list of abbreviations post towns are in **bold** type.

Abb.L.	**Abbots Langley**
Add.	**Addlestone**
Ald.	Aldenham
Amer.	**Amersham**
Ashf.	**Ashford**
Ashtd.	**Ashtead**
Bad.Dene	Badgers Dene
Bad.Mt	Badgers Mount
Bans.	**Banstead**
Bark.	**Barking**
Barn.	**Barnet**
Barne.	Barnehurst
Beac.	**Beaconsfield**
Beck.	**Beckenham**
Bedd.	Beddington
Bedd.Cor.	Beddington Corner
Belv.	**Belvedere**
Berry's Grn	Berry's Green
Bet.	**Betchworth**
Bex.	**Bexley**
Bexh.	**Bexleyheath**
Bigg.H.	Biggin Hill
Bkhm	Bookham
Bletch.	Bletchingley
Borwd.	**Borehamwood**
Bov.	Bovingdon
Box H.	Box Hill
Brent.	**Brentford**
Brick.Wd	Bricket Wood
Brock.	Brockham
Brom.	**Bromley**
Brook.Pk	Brookmans Park
Brox.	**Broxbourne**
Brwd.	**Brentwood**
Buck.H.	**Buckhurst Hill**
Burgh Hth	Burgh Heath
Bushey Hth	Bushey Heath
Carp.Pk	Carpenders Park
Cars.	**Carshalton**
Cat.	**Caterham**
Ch.End	Church End
Ch.St.G.	**Chalfont St. Giles**
Chad.Hth	Chadwell Heath
Chad.St.M.	Chadwell St. Mary
Chaff.Hun.	Chafford Hundred
Chal.St.P.	Chalfont St. Peter
Chel.	Chelsham
Chels.	Chelsfield
Cher.	**Chertsey**
Chesh.	**Chesham**
Chess.	**Chessington**
Chev.	Chevening
Chig.	**Chigwell**
Chipper.	Chipperfield
Chis.	**Chislehurst**
Chob.Com.	Chobham Common
Chorl.	Chorleywood
Chsht	Cheshunt
Clay.	Claygate
Cob.	**Cobham**
Cockfos.	Cockfosters
Coll.Row	Collier Row
Coln.Hth	Colney Heath
Coln.St	Colney Street
Colnbr.	Colnbrook
Cooper.	Coopersale
Couls.	**Coulsdon**
Cran.	Cranford
Cray.	Crayford
Crock.	Crockenhill
Crock.H.	Crockham Hill
Crox.Grn	Croxley Green
Croy.	**Croydon**
Dag.	**Dagenham**
Dance.H.	Dancers Hill
Dart.	**Dartford**
Denh.	Denham
Dor.	**Dorking**
Down.	Downside
Dunt.Grn	Dunton Green
E.Bed.	East Bedfont
E.Croy.	East Croydon
E.Ewell	East Ewell
E.Hors.	East Horsley
E.Mol.	**East Molesey**
E.Til.	East Tilbury
Ealing Com.	Ealing Common
Eastcote Vill.	Eastcote Village
Eden.	**Edenbridge**
Edg.	**Edgware**
Eff.	Effingham
Eff.Junct.	Effingham Junction
Egh.	**Egham**
Egh.H.	Egham Hythe
Elm Pk	Elm Park
Elm.Wds	Elmstead Woods
Els.	Elstree
Enf.	**Enfield**
Eng.Grn	Englefield Green
Epp.	**Epping**
Epp.Grn	Epping Green
Epsom Com.	Epsom Common
Ewell E.	Ewell East
Ewell W.	Ewell West
Eyns.	Eynsford
Farnboro.	Farnborough
Fawk.	Fawkham
Fawk.Grn	Fawkham Green
Felt.	**Feltham**
Fetch.	Fetcham
Flam.	Flamstead
Flaun.	Flaunden
Fnghm	Farningham
Frog.	Frogmore
Gdse.	**Godstone**
Geo.Grn	George Green
Ger.Cr.	**Gerrards Cross**
Gidea Pk	Gidea Park
Godden Grn	Godden Green
Grav.	**Gravesend**
Green.	**Greenhithe**
Grn St Grn	Green Street Green
Grnf.	**Greenford**
Gt Warley	Great Warley
Guil.	**Guildford**
Hackbr.	Hackbridge
Had.Wd	Hadley Wood
Halst.	Halstead
Han.	Hanworth
Har.	**Harrow**
Har.Hill	Harrow on the Hill
Har.Wld	Harrow Weald
Hare.	Harefield
Harm.	Harmondsworth
Harold Wd	Harold Wood
Hat.	**Hatfield**
Hatt.Cr.	Hatton Cross
Hav.at.Bow.	Havering-atte-Bower
Hedg.	Hedgerley
Hem.H.	**Hemel Hempstead**
Herons.	Heronsgate
Hert.	**Hertford**
Hext.	Hextable
High Barn.	High Barnet
Highams Pk	Highams Park
Hinch.Wd	Hinchley Wood
Hlgdn	Hillingdon
Hmptn H.	Hampton Hill
Hmptn W.	Hampton Wick
Hmptn.	**Hampton**
Hook Grn	Hook Green
Horn.	**Hornchurch**
Hort.Kir.	Horton Kirby
Houns.	**Hounslow**
Houns.W.	Hounslow West
Hthrw Air.	Heathrow Airport
Hthrw Air.N.	Heathrow Airport North
Hutt.	Hutton
Ickhm	Ickenham
Ilf.	**Ilford**
Islw.	**Isleworth**
Ken.	**Kenley**
Kes.	**Keston**
Kgfld	Kingfield
Kgswd	Kingswood
Kings L.	**Kings Langley**
Kings.T.	**Kingston upon Thames**
Knap.	Knaphill
Knock.	Knockholt
Knock.P.	Knockholt Pound
Lamb.End	Lambourne End
Let.Hth	Letchmore Heath
Lmpfld	Limpsfield
Lmpfld Cht.	Limpsfield Chart
Lon.Col.	London Colney
Long Dit.	Long Ditton
Long.	**Longfield**
Longcr.	Longcross
Loud.	Loudwater
Loug.	**Loughton**
Lt.Chal.	Little Chalfont
Lt.Hth	Little Heath
Lt.Warley	Little Warley
Lthd.	**Leatherhead**
Lvsdn	Leavesden
Lwr Kgswd	Lower Kingswood
Lwr Sydenham	Lower Sydenham
Map.Cr.	Maple Cross
Mdgrn	Middlegreen
Merst.	Merstham
Mick.	Mickleham
Mimbr.	Mimbridge
Mitch.	**Mitcham**
Mitch.Com.	Mitcham Common
Mord.	**Morden**
Mots.Pk	Motspur Park
Mtnsg	Mountnessing
N.Finchley	North Finchley
N.Har.	North Harrow
N.Mal.	**New Malden**
N.Mymms	North Mymms
N.Ock.	North Ockendon
N.Stfd	North Stifford
N.Wld Bas.	North Weald Bassett
Nave.	Navestock
Nave.S.	Navestock Side
New Adgtn	New Addington
New Barn.	New Barnet
Northumb.Hth	Northumberland Heath
Norwood Junct.	Norwood Junction
Nthflt	Northfleet
Nthlt.	**Northolt**
Nthwd.	**Northwood**
Nutfld	Nutfield
Ock.	Ockham
Old Wind.	Old Windsor
Old Wok.	Old Woking
Ong.	**Ongar**
Orch.L.	Orchard Leigh
Orp.	**Orpington**
Ott.	Ottershaw
Oxt.	**Oxted**
Petts Wd	Petts Wood
Pilg.Hat.	Pilgrim's Hatch
Pnr.	**Pinner**
Pot.B.	**Potters Bar**
Pr.Bot.	Pratt's Bottom
Pur.	**Purley**
Purf.	**Purfleet**
Rad.	**Radlett**
Rain.	**Rainham**
Red.	**Redhill**
Reig.	**Reigate**
Rich.	**Richmond**
Rick.	**Rickmansworth**
Rod.Val.	Roding Valley
Rom.	**Romford**
Rosh.	Rosherville
Ruis.	**Ruislip**
Runny.	Runnymede
Rush Grn	Rush Green
Russ.Hill	Russell Hill
Rvrhd	Riverhead
S.Croy.	**South Croydon**
S.Darenth	South Darenth
S.Har.	South Harrow
S.Merst.	South Merstham
S.Mimms	South Mimms
S.Norwood	South Norwood
S.Nutfld	South Nutfield
S.Ock.	**South Ockendon**
S.Oxhey	South Oxhey
S.Ruis.	South Ruislip
S.Stfd	South Stifford
S.Wld	South Weald
S.le H.	**Stanford-le-Hope**
Scad.Pk	Scadbury Park
Send M.	Send Marsh
Sev.	**Sevenoaks**
Sheer.	Sheerwater
Shenf.	Shenfield
Shep.	**Shepperton**
Shore.	Shoreham
Short.	Shortlands
Sid.	**Sidcup**
Slade Grn	Slade Green
Slou.	**Slough**
St.Alb.	**St. Albans**
St.Geo.H.	St. George's Hill
St.John's	St. John's
St.M.Cray	St. Mary Cray
St.P.Cray	St. Paul's Cray
Stai.	**Staines**
Stan.	**Stanmore**
Stanw.	Stanwell
Stap.Abb.	Stapleford Abbotts
Stap.Taw.	Stapleford Tawney
Sthflt	Southfleet
Sthl Grn	Southall Green
Sthl.	**Southall**
Stoke D'Ab.	Stoke D'Abernon
Stoke P.	Stoke Poges
Sun.	**Sunbury-on-Thames**
Sund.	Sundridge
Surb.	**Surbiton**
Sutt.	**Sutton**
Sutt.Grn	Sutton Green
Sutt.H.	Sutton at Hone
Swan.	**Swanley**
Swans.	**Swanscombe**
T.Ditt.	**Thames Ditton**
Tad.	**Tadworth**
Tand.	Tandridge
Tats.	Tatsfield
Tedd.	**Teddington**
Th.Hth.	**Thornton Heath**
They.B.	Theydon Bois
They.Gar.	Theydon Garnon
They.Mt	Theydon Mount
Thnwd	Thornwood
Til.	**Tilbury**
Tkgtn	Tokyngton
Turnf.	Turnford
Twick.	**Twickenham**
Tyr.Wd	Tyrrell's Wood
Undrvr	Underriver
Upmin.	**Upminster**
Uxb.	**Uxbridge**
Vir.W.	**Virginia Water**
W.Byf.	**West Byfleet**
W.Croy.	West Croydon
W.Ealing	West Ealing
W.Ewell	West Ewell
W.Hors.	West Horsley
W.Hyde	West Hyde
W.Mol.	**West Molesey**
W.Thur.	West Thurrock
W.Til.	West Tilbury
W.Wick.	**West Wickham**
Wal.Abb.	**Waltham Abbey**
Wal.Cr.	**Waltham Cross**
Wall.	**Wallington**
Walt.	**Walton-on-Thames**
Walt.Hill	Walton on the Hill
Warl.	**Warlingham**
Wat.	**Watford**
Wdf.Grn.	**Woodford Green**
Wdhm	Woodham
Wealds.	Wealdstone
Well.	**Welling**
Wem.	**Wembley**
Wenn.	Wennington
West Dr.	**West Drayton**
West.	**Westerham**
Wey.	**Weybridge**
Whel.Hill	Whelpley Hill
Whiteley Vill.	Whiteley Village
Whyt.	**Whyteleafe**
Wilm.	Wilmington
Wind.	**Windsor**
Wok.	**Woking**
Wold.	Woldingham
Woodside Pk	Woodside Park
Wor.Pk.	**Worcester Park**
Wrays.	Wraysbury
Yiew.	Yiewsley

1 - Adm

1 Canada Sq, E14 204 B2
30 St. Mary Axe, EC3
off St. Mary Axe 84 DS72
99 Bishopsgate, EC2
off Bishopsgate 84 DS72

A

Aaron Hill Rd, E6 87 EN71
Abady Ho, SW1 off Page St 101 DK77
Abberley Ms, SW4
off Cedars Rd 101 DH83
Abberton Wk, Rain. RM13
off Ongar Way 89 FE66
Abbess Cl, E6
off Oliver Gdns 86 EL71
SW2 121 DP88
Abbeville Ms, SW4
off Clapham Pk Rd 101 DK84
Abbeville Rd, N8
off Barrington Rd 65 DK56
SW4 121 DJ86
Abbey Av, Wem. HA0 80 CL68
Abbey Business Cen, SW8
off Ingate Pl 101 DH81
Abbey Cl, E5 66 DU63
SW8 101 DK81
Hayes UB3 77 BV74
Northolt UB5
off Invicta Gro 78 BZ69
Pinner HA5 59 BV55
Romford RM1 71 FG58
Woking GU22 167 BE116
Abbey Ct, Wal.Abb. EN9 15 EB34
Abbey Cres, Belv. DA17 106 FA77
Abbeydale Rd, Wem. HA0 80 CN67
Abbey Dr, SW17
off Church La 120 DG92
Abbots Langley WD5 7 BU32
Dartford DA2 127 FE89
Staines TW18 134 BJ98
Abbeyfield Rd, SE16 202 F8
Abbeyfields Cl, NW10 80 CN68
Abbeyfields Mobile Home Pk,
Cher. KT16 134 BK101
Abbey Gdns, NW8 82 DC68
SE16 202 C8
SW1 off Great Coll St 101 DL76
W6 99 CY79
Chertsey KT16 134 BG100
Chislehurst BR7 145 EN95
Waltham Abbey EN9 15 EC33
Abbey Grn, Cher. KT16 134 BG100
Abbey Gro, SE2 106 EV77
Abbeyhill Rd, Sid. DA15 126 EW89
Abbey Ind Est, Mitch. CR4 140 DF99
Wembley HA0 80 CM67
Abbey La, E15 85 EC68
Beckenham BR3 123 EA94
Abbey Mead Ind Pk, Wal.Abb.
EN9 15 EC34
Abbey Meadows, Cher.
KT16 134 BJ101
Abbey Ms, E17
off Leamington Av 67 EA57
Isleworth TW7 97 CH81
Abbey Orchard St, SW1 199 N6
Abbey Par, SW19
off Merton High St 120 DC94
W5 off Hanger La 80 CM69
Abbey Pk, Beck. BR3 123 EA94
Abbey Pl, Dart. DA1
off Priory Rd N 128 FK85
Abbey Retail Pk, Bark. IG11 87 EP67
Abbey Rd, E15 86 EE68
NW6 82 DB66
NW8 82 DC68
NW10 80 CP68
SE2 106 EX77
SW19 120 DC94
Barking IG11 87 EP66
Belvedere DA17 106 EX77
Bexleyheath DA7 106 EY84
Chertsey KT16 134 BH101
Croydon CR0 141 DP104
Enfield EN1 30 DS43
Gravesend DA12 131 GL88
Greenhithe DA9 129 FW85
Ilford IG2 69 ER57
Shepperton TW17 134 BN102
South Croydon CR2 161 DX110
Virginia Water GU25 132 AX99
Waltham Cross EN8 15 DY34
Woking GU21 166 AW117
Abbey Rd Est, NW8 82 DB67
Abbey St, E13 86 EG70
SE1 201 N6
Abbey Ter, SE2 106 EW77
Abbey Vw, NW7 43 CT48
Radlett WD7 25 CF35
Waltham Abbey EN9 15 EB33
Watford WD25 24 BX36
Abbey Vw Rbt, Wal.Abb. EN9 15 EB33
Abbey Wk, W.Mol. KT8 136 CB97
Abbey Way, SE2 106 EX76
Abbey Wf Ind Est, Bark. IG11 87 ER68
ABBEY WOOD, SE2 106 EV76
⇌ Abbey Wood 106 EW76
Abbey Wd Caravan Club Site,
SE2 106 EW78
Abbey Wd La, Rain. RM13 90 FK68
Abbey Wd Rd, SE2 106 EV77
Abbot Cl, Stai. TW18 114 BK94
West Byfleet (Byfleet)
KT14 152 BK110
Abbot Ct, SW8
off Hartington Rd 101 DL80
Abbots Av, Epsom KT19 156 CN111
Abbotsbury Cl, E15 85 EC68
W14 off Abbotsbury Rd 99 CZ75
Abbotsbury Gdns, Pnr. HA5 60 BW58
Abbotsbury Ms, SE15 102 DW83
Abbotsbury Rd, W14 99 CY75
Bromley BR2 144 EF103
Abbotsbury Rd, Mord. SM4 140 DB99
Abbots Cl, N1 off Alwyne Rd 84 DQ65
Brentwood (Shenf.) CM15 55 GA46
Orpington BR5 145 EQ102
Rainham RM13 90 FJ68
Ruislip HA4 60 BX62
Abbots Dr, Har. HA2 60 CA61
Virginia Water GU25 132 AW98
Abbots Fld, Grav. DA12
off Ruffets Wd 131 GJ93
Abbotsford Av, N15 66 DQ56
Abbotsford Cl, Wok. GU22
off Onslow Cres 167 BA117
Abbotsford Gdns, Wdf.Grn.
IG8 48 EG52
Abbotsford Lo, Nthwd. HA6 39 BS50
Abbotsford Rd, Ilf. IG3 70 EU61
Abbots Gdns, N2 64 DD56
W8 off St. Mary's Pl 100 DB76
Abbots Grn, Croy. CR0 161 DX107
Abbotshade Rd, SE16 203 J2
Abbotshall Av, N14 45 DJ48
Abbotshall Rd, SE6 123 ED88
Abbots La, SE1 201 N3
Kenley CR8 176 DQ116
ABBOTS LANGLEY, WD5 7 BR31
Abbotsleigh Cl, Sutt. SM2 158 DB108
Abbotsleigh Rd, SW16 121 DJ91
Abbots Manor Est, SW1 199 H9
Abbotsmede Cl, Twick. TW1 117 CF89
Abbots Pk, SW2 121 DN88
Abbot's Pl, NW6 82 DB67
Abbots Ri, Kings L. WD4 6 BM26
Redhill RH1 184 DG132
Abbot's Rd, E6 86 EK67
Abbots Rd, Abb.L. WD5 7 BS30
Edgware HA8 42 CQ52
Abbots Ter, N8 65 DL58
Abbotstone Rd, SW15 99 CW83
Abbot St, E8 84 DT65
Abbots Vw, Kings L. WD4 6 BM27
Abbots Wk, W8
off St. Mary's Pl 100 DB76
Caterham CR3
off Tillingdown Hill 176 DV122
Abbots Way, Beck. BR3 143 DY99
Chertsey KT16 133 BF101
Abbotswell Rd, SE4 123 DZ85
Abbotswood Cl, Belv. DA17
off Coptefield Dr 106 EY76
Abbotswood Dr, Wey. KT13 153 BR110
Abbotswood Gdns, Ilf. IG5 69 EM55
Abbotswood Rd, SE22 102 DS84
SW16 121 DK90
Abbotswood Way, Hayes
UB3 77 BV74
Abbott Av, SW20 139 CX96
Abbott Cl, Hmptn. TW12 116 BY93
Northolt UB5 78 BZ65
Abbott Rd, E14 85 EC71
Abbotts Cl, SE28 88 EW73
Romford RM7 71 FB55
Swanley BR8 147 FG98
Uxbridge UB8 76 BK71
Abbotts Cres, E4 47 ED49
Enfield EN2 29 DP40
Abbotts Dr, Wal.Abb. EN9 16 EG34
Wembley HA0 61 CH61
Abbotts Pk Rd, E10 67 EC59
Abbotts Rd, Barn. EN5 28 DB42
Mitcham CR4 141 DJ98
Southall UB1 78 BY74
Sutton SM3 139 CZ104
Abbott's Tilt, Walt. KT12 136 BY104
Abbotts Wk, Bexh. DA7 106 EX80
Abbs Cross Gdns, Horn.
RM12 72 FJ60
Abbs Cross La, Horn. RM12 72 FJ63
Abchurch La, EC4 197 L10
Abchurch Yd, EC4 197 K10
Abdale Rd, W12 81 CV74
Abenberg Way, Brwd. (Hutt.)
CM13 55 GB47
Aberavon Rd, E3 85 DY69
Abercairn Rd, SW16 121 DJ94
Aberconway Rd, Mord.
SM4 140 DB97
Abercorn Cl, NW7 43 CY52
NW8 82 DC69
South Croydon CR2 161 DX112
Abercorn Cres, Har. HA2 60 CB60
Abercorn Gdns, Har. HA3 61 CK59
Romford RM6 70 EV58
Abercorn Gro, Ruis. HA4 59 BR56
Abercorn Ms, Rich. TW10
off Kings Rd 98 CM84
Abercorn Pl, NW8 82 DC69
Abercorn Rd, NW7 43 CY52
Stanmore HA7 41 CJ52
Abercorn Wk, NW8
off Abercorn Pl 82 DC69
Abercorn Way, SE1 202 B10
Woking GU21 166 AU118
Abercrombie Dr, Enf. EN1
off Linwood Cres 30 DU39
Abercrombie St, SW11 100 DE82
Aberdale Ct, SE16
off Poolmans St 103 DX75
Aberdale Gdns, Pot.B. EN6 11 CZ33
Aberdare Cl, W.Wick. BR4 143 EC103
Aberdare Gdns, NW6 82 DB66
NW7 43 CX52
Aberdare Rd, Enf. EN3 30 DW42
Aberdeen La, N5 65 DP64
Aberdeen Par, N18
off Angel Rd 46 DV50
Aberdeen Pk, N5 65 DP64
Aberdeen Pk Ms, N5 66 DQ63
Aberdeen Pl, NW8 82 DD70
Aberdeen Rd, N5 66 DQ63
N18 46 DV50
NW10 63 CT64
Croydon CR0 160 DQ105
Harrow HA3 41 CF54
Aberdeen Sq, E14 203 N2
Aberdeen Ter, SE3 103 ED82
Aberdour Rd, Ilf. IG3 70 EV62
Aberdour St, SE1 201 M8
Aberfeldy St, E14 85 EC72
Aberford Gdns, SE18 104 EL81
Aberford Rd, Borwd. WD6 26 CN40
Aberfoyle Rd, SW16 121 DK93
Abergeldie Rd, SE12 124 EH86
Aberglen Ind Est, Hayes UB3 95 BR75
Abernethy Rd, SE13 104 EE84
Abersham Rd, E8 66 DT64
Abery St, SE18 105 ES77
Abigail Ms, Rom. RM3
off King Alfred Rd 52 FM54
Ability Twrs, EC1
off Macclesfield Rd 84 DQ69
Abingdon Cl, NW1
off Camden Ms 83 DK65
SE1 202 A10
SW19 120 DC93
Uxbridge UB10 76 BM67
Woking GU21 166 AV118
Abingdon Pl, Pot.B. EN6 12 DB32
Abingdon Rd, N3 44 DC54
SW16 141 DL96
W8 100 DA76
Abingdon St, SW1 199 P6
Abingdon Vil, W8 100 DA76
Abingdon Way, Orp. BR6 164 EV105
Abinger Av, Sutt. SM2 157 CW109
Abinger Cl, Bark. IG11 70 EU63
Bromley BR1 144 EL97
Croydon CR0 161 EC107
Wallington SM6 159 DL106
Abinger Gdns, Islw. TW7 97 CE83
Abinger Gro, SE8 103 DZ79
Abinger Ms, W9
off Warlock Rd 82 DA70
Abinger Rd, W4 98 CS76
Ablett St, SE16 102 DW78
Abney Gdns, N16 off Stoke
Newington High St 66 DT61
Aboyne Dr, SW20 139 CU96
Aboyne Est, SW17 120 DD90
Aboyne Rd, NW10 62 CS62
SW17 120 DD90
Abraham Cl, Wat. WD19 39 BV49
ABRIDGE, Rom. RM4 34 EV41
Abridge Cl, Wal.Cr. EN8 31 DX35
Abridge Gdns, Rom. RM5 50 FA51
Abridge Pk, Rom. (Abridge)
RM4 34 EU42
Abridge Rd, Chig. IG7 33 ER44
Epping (They.B.) CM16 33 ES36
Romford (Abridge) RM4 34 EU39
Abridge Way, Bark. IG11 88 EV68
Abyssinia Cl, SW11
off Cairns Rd 100 DE84
Abyssinia Rd, SW11
off Auckland Rd 100 DE84
Acacia Av, N17 46 DR52
Brentford TW8 97 CH80
Hayes UB3 77 BT72
Hornchurch RM12 71 FF61
Mitcham CR4
off Acacia Rd 141 DH96
Ruislip HA4 59 BU60
Shepperton TW17 134 BN99
Staines (Wrays.) TW19 92 AY84
Wembley HA9 62 CL64
West Drayton UB7 76 BM73
Woking GU22 166 AX120
Acacia Cl, SE8 203 K9
SE20 off Selby Rd 142 DU96
Addlestone (Wdhm)
KT15 151 BF110
Orpington BR5 145 ER99
Stanmore HA7 41 CE51
Waltham Cross EN7 14 DS27
Acacia Ct, Wal.Abb. EN9
off Farthingale La 16 EG34
Acacia Dr, Add. (Wdhm)
KT15 151 BF110
Banstead SM7 157 CX114
Sutton SM3 139 CZ102
Upminster RM14 72 FN63
Acacia Gdns, NW8
off Acacia Rd 82 DD68
Upminster RM14 73 FT59
West Wickham BR4 143 EC103
Acacia Gro, SE21 122 DR89
New Malden KT3 138 CR97
Acacia Ms, West Dr. UB7 94 BK79
Acacia Pl, NW8 82 DD68
Acacia Rd, E11 68 EE61
E17 67 DY58
N22 45 DN53
NW8 82 DD68
SW16 141 DL95
W3 80 CQ73
Beckenham BR3 143 DZ97
Dartford DA1 128 FK88
Enfield EN2 30 DR39
Greenhithe DA9 129 FS86
Hampton TW12 116 CA93
Mitcham CR4 141 DH96
Staines TW18 114 BH92
Acacia Wk, Swan. BR8 147 FD96
Acacia Way, Sid. DA15 125 ET88
Academy Flds Cl, Rom. RM2 71 FG57
Academy Flds Rd, Rom.
RM2 71 FH57
Academy Gdns, W8 100 DA75
Croydon CR0 142 DT102
Northolt UB5 78 BX68
Academy Pl, SE18 105 EM81
Academy Rd, SE18 105 EM81
Acanthus Dr, SE1 202 B10
Acanthus Rd, SW11 100 DG83
Accommodation La, West Dr.
UB7 94 BJ79
Accommodation Rd, NW11 63 CZ59
Chertsey (Longcr.) KT16 132 AX104
A.C. Ct, T.Ditt. KT7
off Harvest La 137 CG100
Acer Av, Hayes UB4 78 BY71
Rainham RM13 90 FK69
Acer Rd, West. (Bigg.H.)
TN16 178 EK116
Acers, St.Alb. (Park St) AL2 8 CC28
Acfold Rd, SW6 100 DB81
Achilles Cl, SE1 202 C10
Achilles Pl, Wok. GU21 166 AW117
Achilles Rd, NW6 64 DA64
Achilles St, SE14 103 DY80
Achilles Way, W1 198 G3
Acklam Rd, W10 81 CZ71
Acklington Dr, NW9 42 CS53
Ackmar Rd, SW6 100 DA81
Ackroyd Dr, E3 85 DZ71
Ackroyd Rd, SE23 123 DX87
Acland Cl, SE18
off Clothworkers Rd 105 ER80
Acland Cres, SE5 102 DR84
Acland Rd, NW2 81 CV65
Acle Cl, Ilf. IG6 49 EP52
Acme Rd, Wat. WD24 23 BU38
Acock Gro, Nthlt. UB5 60 CB63
Acol Cres, Ruis. HA4 59 BV64
Acol Rd, NW6 82 DA66
Aconbury Rd, Dag. RM9 88 EV67
Acorn Cl, E4 47 EA50
Chislehurst BR7 125 EQ92
Enfield EN2 29 DP39
Hampton TW12 116 CB93
Slough SL3 off Tamar Way 93 BB78
Stanmore HA7 41 CH52
Acorn Ct, Ilf. IG2 69 ES58
Acorn Gdns, SE19 142 DT95
W3 80 CR71
Acorn Gro, Hayes UB3 95 BT80
Ruislip HA4 59 BT63
Tadworth KT20 173 CY124
Woking GU22
off Old Sch Pl 166 AY121
Acorn Ind Pk, Dart. DA1 127 FG85
Acorn La, Pot.B. (Cuffley)
EN6 13 DL29
Acorn Par, SE15
off Carlton Gro 102 DV80
Acorn Pl, Wat. WD24 23 BU37
Acorn Rd, Dart. DA1 127 FF85
Acorns, The, Chig. IG7 49 ES49
Acorns Way, Esher KT10 154 CC106
Acorn Wk, SE16 203 L2
Acorn Way, SE23 123 DX90
Beckenham BR3 143 EC99
Orpington BR6 163 EP105
Acre Dr, SE22 102 DU84
Acrefield Rd, Ger.Cr. (Chal.St.P.)
SL9 56 AX55
Acre La, SW2 101 DL84
Carshalton SM5 158 DG105
Wallington SM6 158 DG105
Acre Path, Nthlt. UB5
off Arnold Rd 78 BY65
Acre Rd, SW19 120 DD93
Dagenham RM10 89 FB66
Kingston upon Thames
KT2 138 CL95
Acres End, Amer. HP7 20 AS39
Acres Gdns, Tad. KT20 173 CX119
Acre Vw, Horn. RM11 72 FL56
Acre Way, Nthwd. HA6 39 BT53
Acris St, SW18 120 DC85
ACTON, W3 80 CN74
⇌ Acton Central 80 CR74
Acton Cl, N9 46 DU47
Waltham Cross (Chsht)
EN8 15 DY31
Acton Hill Ms, W3
off Uxbridge Rd 80 CP74
Acton La, NW10 80 CS68
W3 98 CQ75
W4 98 CR76
⇌ Acton Main Line 80 CQ72
Acton Ms, E8 84 DT67
Acton Pk Ind Est, W3 98 CR75
Acton St, WC1 196 B3
⊖ Acton Town 98 CN75
Acuba Rd, SW18 120 DB89
Acworth Cl, N9 off Turin Rd 46 DW45
Ada Cl, N11 44 DF48
Ada Ct, W9 off Maida Vale 82 DC69
Ada Gdns, E14 85 ED72
E15 86 EF67
Adair Cl, SE25 142 DV97
Adair Rd, W10 81 CY70
Adair Twr, W10
off Appleford Rd 81 CY70
Adam & Eve Ct, W1 195 L8
Adam & Eve Ms, W8 100 DA76
Adam Cl, SE6 123 DZ91
Adam Ct, SW7
off Gloucester Rd 100 DC77
Adam Rd, E4 47 DZ51
Adams Cl, N3 44 DA52
NW9 62 CP61
Surbiton KT5 138 CM100
Adams Ct, EC2 197 L8
Adamsfield, Wal.Cr. EN7 14 DU27
Adams Gdns Est, SE16 202 F4
Adams Ms, N22 45 DM52
SW17 120 DF89
Adamson Rd, E16 86 EG72
NW3 82 DD66
Adamson Way, Beck. BR3 143 EC99
Adams Pl, N7
off George's Rd 65 DM64
Adams Quarter, Brent. TW8
off Tallow Rd 97 CJ79
Adamsrill Cl, Enf. EN1 30 DR44
Adamsrill Rd, SE26 123 DY91
Adams Rd, N17 46 DR54
Beckenham BR3 143 DY99
Adams Row, W1 198 G1
Adams Sq, Bexh. DA6
off Regency Way 106 EY83
Adam St, WC2 200 A1
Adams Wk, Kings.T. KT1 138 CL96
Adams Way, Croy. CR0 142 DT100
Adam Wk, SW6 99 CW80
Ada Pl, E2 84 DU67
Adare Wk, SW16 121 DM90
Ada Rd, SE5 102 DS80
Wembley HA0 61 CJ62
Adastral Est, NW9 42 CS53
Ada St, E8 84 DV67
Adcock Wk, Orp. BR6
off Borkwood Pk 163 ET105
Adderley Gdns, SE9 125 EN91
Adderley Gro, SW11
off Culmstock Rd 120 DG85
Adderley Rd, Har. HA3 41 CF53
Adderley St, E14 85 EC72
ADDINGTON, Croy. CR0 161 DZ106
Addington Border, Croy.
CR0 161 DY110
Addington Ct, SW14 98 CR83
Addington Dr, N12 44 DC51
Addington Gro, SE26 123 DY91
Addington Rd, E3 85 EA69
E16 86 EE70
N4 65 DN58
Addington Rd, Croy. CR0 141 DN102
South Croydon CR2 160 DU111
West Wickham BR4 144 EE103
Addington Sq, SE5 102 DQ80
Addington St, SE1 200 C5
Tra Addington Village 161 EA107
Addington Village Rd, Croy.
CR0 161 EA106
Addis Cl, Enf. EN3 31 DX39
ADDISCOMBE, Croy. CR0 142 DT102
Tra Addiscombe 142 DU102
Addiscombe Av, Croy. CR0 142 DU101
Addiscombe Cl, Har. HA3 61 CJ57
Addiscombe Ct Rd, Croy.
CR0 142 DS102
Addiscombe Gro, Croy. CR0 142 DR103
Addiscombe Rd, Croy. CR0 142 DS103
Watford WD18 23 BV42
Addison Av, N14 29 DH44
W11 81 CY74
Hounslow TW3 96 CC81
Addison Br Pl, W14 99 CZ77
Addison Cl, Cat. CR3 176 DR122
Northwood HA6 39 BU53
Orpington BR5 145 EQ100
Addison Ct, Epp. CM16 18 EU31
Addison Cres, W14 99 CY76
Addison Dr, SE12
off Eltham Rd 124 EH85
Addison Gdns, W14 99 CX76
Grays RM17
off Palmers Dr 110 GC77
Surbiton KT5 138 CM98
Addison Gro, W4 98 CS76
Addison Pl, W11 81 CY74
Southall UB1
off Longford Av 78 CA73
Addison Rd, E11 68 EG58
E17 67 EB57
SE25 142 DU98
W14 99 CZ76
Bromley BR2 144 EJ99
Caterham CR3 176 DR121
Enfield EN3 30 DW39
Ilford IG6 49 EQ53
Teddington TW11 117 CH93
Woking GU21
off Chertsey Rd 167 AZ117
Addison's Cl, Croy. CR0 143 DZ103
Addison Way, NW11 63 CZ56
Hayes UB3 77 BU72
Northwood HA6 39 BT53
Addle Hill, EC4 196 G10
ADDLESTONE, KT15 152 BJ106
⇌ Addlestone 152 BK105
ADDLESTONE MOOR,
Add. KT15 134 BG103
Addlestone Moor, Add.
KT15 134 BJ103
Addlestone Pk, Add. KT15 152 BH106
Addlestone Rd, Add. KT15 152 BL105
Addle St, EC2 197 J7
Addy Ho, SE16 202 G9
Adecroft Way, W.Mol. KT8 136 CC97
Adela Av, N.Mal. KT3 139 CV99
Adelaide Av, SE4 103 DZ84
Adelaide Cl, SW9
off Broughton Dr 101 DN84
Enfield EN1 30 DT38
Stanmore HA7 41 CG49
Adelaide Cotts, W7 97 CF75
Adelaide Gdns, Rom. RM6 70 EY57
Adelaide Gro, W12 81 CU74
Adelaide Pl, Wey. KT13 153 BR105
Adelaide Rd, E10 67 EB62
NW3 82 DD66
SW18 off Putney Br Rd 120 DA85
W13 79 CG74
Ashford TW15 114 BK92
Chislehurst BR7 125 EP92
Hounslow TW5 96 BY81
Ilford IG1 69 EP61
Richmond TW9 98 CM84
Southall UB2 96 BY77
Surbiton KT6 138 CL99
Teddington TW11 117 CF93
Tilbury RM18 111 GF81
Walton-on-Thames KT12 135 BU104
Adelaide St, WC2 199 P1
Adelaide Ter, Brent. TW8 97 CK78
Adela St, W10
off Kensal Rd 81 CY70
Adelina Gro, E1 84 DW71
Adelina Ms, SW12 121 DK88
Adeline Pl, WC1 195 N7
Adeliza Cl, Bark. IG11
off North St 87 EQ66
Adelphi Ct, SE16
off Poolmans St 103 DX75
Adelphi Cres, Hayes UB4 77 BT69
Hornchurch RM12 71 FG61
Adelphi Gdns, Slou. SL1 92 AS75
Adelphi Rd, Epsom KT17 156 CR113
Adelphi Ter, WC2 200 A1
Adelphi Way, Hayes UB4 77 BT69
Adeney Cl, W6 99 CX79
Aden Gro, N16 66 DR63
Adenmore Rd, SE6 123 EA87
Aden Rd, Enf. EN3 31 DY42
Ilford IG1 69 EP59
Aden Ter, N16 66 DR63
Adhara Rd, Nthwd. HA6
off Vega Cres 39 BT50
Adie Rd, W6 99 CW76
Adine Rd, E13 86 EH70
Adler Ind Est, Hayes UB3 95 BR75
Adler St, E1 84 DU72
Adley St, E5 67 DY64
Adlington Cl, N18 46 DR50
Admaston Rd, SE18 105 EQ80
Admiral Cl, Orp. BR5 146 EX98
Admiral Ct, NW4
off Barton Cl 63 CU57
Admiral Ho, Tedd. TW11
off Twickenham Rd 117 CG91
Admiral Hyson Trd Est,
SE16 202 D9
Admiral Pl, N8 65 DP56
SE16 203 L2
Admirals Cl, E18 68 EH56
Admiral Seymour Rd, SE9 105 EM84
Admirals Gate, SE10 103 EB81
Admiral Sq, SW10 100 DD81

★ Place of interest ⇌ Railway station ⊖ London Underground station DLR Docklands Light Railway station Tra Tramlink station H Hospital Riv Pedestrian ferry landing stage

Admiral Stirling Ct, Wey. KT13 *off Weybridge Rd* 152 BM105
Admiral St, SE8 103 EA82
Admirals Wk, NW3 64 DC62
Coulsdon CR5 175 DM120
Greenhithe DA9 129 FV85
Admirals Way, E14 204 A4
★ **Admiralty Arch**, SW1 199 N2
Admiralty Cl, SE8 *off Reginald Sq* 103 EA80
Admiralty Way, Tedd. TW11 117 CF93
Admiral Wk, W9 82 DA71
Adnams Wk, Rain. RM13 *off Lovell Wk* 89 FF65
Adolf St, SE6 123 EB91
Adolphus Rd, N4 65 DP61
Adolphus St, SE8 103 DZ80
Adomar Rd, Dag. RM8 70 EX62
Adpar St, W2 82 DD70
Adrian Av, NW2 *off North Circular Rd* 63 CV60
Adrian Cl, Barn. EN5 27 CX44
Uxbridge (Hare.) UB9 38 BK53
Adrian Ms, SW10 100 DB79
Adrian Rd, Abb.L. WD5 7 BS31
Adrians Wk, Slou. SL2 74 AT74
Adriatic Bldg, E14 *off Narrow St* 85 DY73
Adrienne Av, Sthl. UB1 78 BZ70
Adstock Ms, Ger.Cr. (Chal.St.P.) SL9 *off Church La* 36 AX53
Adstock Way, Grays (Bad.Dene) RM17 110 FZ77
Advance Rd, SE27 122 DQ91
Advent Ct, Wdf.Grn. IG8 *off Wood La* 48 EF50
Adventurers Ct, E14 *off Newport Av* 85 ED73
Advent Way, N18 47 DX50
Advice Av, Grays RM16 110 GA75
Adys Rd, SE15 102 DT83
Aegean Apts, E16 *off Western Gateway* 86 EG73
Aerodrome Rd, NW4 43 CT54
NW9 43 CT54
Aerodrome Way, Houns. TW5 96 BW79
Aeroville, NW9 42 CS54
Affleck St, N1 196 C1
Afghan Rd, SW11 100 DE82
★ **Africa Cen**, WC2 195 P10
Afton Dr, S.Ock. RM15 91 FV72
Agamemnon Rd, NW6 63 CZ64
Agar Cl, Surb. KT6 138 CM103
Agar Gro, NW1 83 DJ66
Agar Gro Est, NW1 83 DK66
Agar Pl, NW1 83 DJ66
Agars Pl, Slou. (Datchet) SL3 92 AU79
Agar St, WC2 199 P1
Agate Cl, E16 86 EK72
Agate Rd, W6 99 CW76
Agates La, Ashtd. KT21 171 CK118
Agatha Cl, E1 202 E2
Agaton Rd, SE9 125 EQ89
Agave Rd, NW2 63 CW63
Agdon St, EC1 196 F4
Agincourt Rd, NW3 64 DF63
Agister Rd, Chig. IG7 50 EU50
Agnes Av, Ilf. IG1 69 EP63
Agnes Cl, E6 87 EN73
Agnesfield Cl, N12 44 DE51
Agnes Gdns, Dag. RM8 70 EX63
Agnes Rd, W3 81 CT74
Agnes Scott Ct, Wey. KT13 *off Palace Dr* 135 BP104
Agnes St, E14 85 DZ72
Agnew Rd, SE23 123 DX87
Agricola Ct, E3 *off Parnell Rd* 85 DZ67
Agricola Pl, Enf. EN1 30 DT43
Aidan Cl, Dag. RM8 70 EY63
Aileen Wk, E15 86 EF66
Ailsa Av, Twick. TW1 117 CG85
Ailsa Rd, Twick. TW1 117 CH85
Ailsa St, E14 85 EC71
AIMES GREEN, Wal.Abb. EN9 16 EF28
Ainger Ms, NW3 *off Ainger Rd* 82 DF66
Ainger Rd, NW3 82 DF66
Ainsdale Cl, Orp. BR6 145 ER102
Ainsdale Cres, Pnr. HA5 60 CA55
Ainsdale Dr, SE1 102 DU78
Ainsdale Rd, W5 79 CK70
Watford WD19 40 BW48
Ainsdale Way, Wok. GU21 166 AU118
Ainsley Av, Rom. RM7 71 FB58
Ainsley Cl, N9 46 DS46
Ainsley St, E2 84 DV69
Ainslie Wk, SW12 121 DH87
Ainslie Wd Cres, E4 47 EB50
Ainslie Wd Gdns, E4 47 EB49
Ainslie Wd Rd, E4 47 EA50
Ainsty Est, SE16 203 H5
Ainsworth Cl, NW2 63 CU62
SE15 *off Lyndhurst Gro* 102 DS82
Ainsworth Rd, E9 84 DW66
Croydon CR0 141 DP103
Ainsworth Way, NW8 82 DC67
Aintree Av, E6 86 EL67
Aintree Cl, Grav. DA12 131 GH90
Slough (Colnbr.) SL3 93 BE81
Uxbridge UB8 77 BP72
Aintree Cres, Ilf. IG6 49 EQ54
Aintree Est, SW6 *off Dawes Rd* 99 CY80
Aintree Gro, Upmin. RM14 72 FM62
Aintree Rd, Grnf. UB6 79 CH68
Aintree St, SW6 99 CY80
Airco Cl, NW9 *off Capitol Way* 62 CR55
Aird Ct, Hmptn. TW12 *off Oldfield Rd* 136 BZ95
Airdrie Cl, N1 83 DM66
Hayes UB4 *off Glencoe Rd* 78 BY71
Airedale Av, W4 99 CT77
Airedale Av S, W4 *off Netheravon Rd S* 99 CT78
Airedale Cl, Dart. DA2 128 FQ88
Airedale Rd, SW12 120 DF87
W5 97 CJ76
Aire Dr, S.Ock. RM15 91 FV70
Airey Neave Ct, Grays RM17 110 GA75
Airfield Way, Horn. RM12 89 FH65
Airfield Way, Wat. WD25 7 BT34
★ **Air Forces Mem**, Egh. TW20 112 AX91
Airlie Gdns, W8 *off Campden Hill Rd* 82 DA74
Ilford IG1 69 EP60
Air Links Ind Est, Houns. TW5 96 BW78
Air Pk Way, Felt. TW13 115 BV89
Airport Ind Est, West. TN16 162 EK114
Airport Rbt, E16 *off Connaught Br* 86 EK74
Airport Way, Stai. TW19 93 BF84
Air St, W1 199 L1
Airthrie Rd, Ilf. IG3 70 EV61
Aisgill Av, W14 99 CZ78
Aisher Rd, SE28 88 EW73
Aisher Way, Sev. (Rvrhd) TN13 190 FE121
Aislibie Rd, SE12 104 EE84
Aiten Pl, W6 *off Standish Rd* 99 CU77
Aitken Cl, E8 *off Pownall Rd* 84 DU67
Mitcham CR4 140 DF101
Aitken Rd, SE6 123 EB89
Barnet EN5 27 CW43
Ait's Vw, W.Mol. KT8 *off Victoria Av* 136 CB97
Ajax Av, NW9 62 CS55
Ajax Rd, NW6 64 DA64
Akabusi Cl, Croy. CR0 142 DU100
Akehurst La, Sev. TN13 191 FJ125
Akehurst St, SW15 119 CU86
Akenside Rd, NW3 64 DD64
Akerman Rd, SW9 101 DP82
Surbiton KT6 137 CJ100
Akers Way, Rick. (Chorl.) WD3 21 BD44
Alabama St, SE18 105 ER80
Alacross Rd, W5 97 CJ75
Alamaro Lo, SE10 *off Renaissance Wk* 104 EF76
Alamein Gdns, Dart. DA2 129 FR87
Alamein Rd, Swans. DA10 129 FX86
Alanbrooke, Grav. DA12 131 GJ87
Alan Cl, Dart. DA1 108 FJ84
Alandale Dr, Pnr. HA5 39 BV54
Aland Ct, SE16 203 L6
Alander Ms, E17 67 EC56
Alan Dr, Barn. EN5 27 CY44
Alan Gdns, Rom. RM7 70 FA59
Alan Hocken Way, E15 86 EE68
Alan Rd, SW19 119 CY92
Alanthus Cl, SE12 124 EF86
Alan Way, Slou. (Geo.Grn) SL3 74 AY72
Alaska St, SE1 200 D3
Alba Cl, Hayes UB4 *off Ramulis Dr* 78 BX70
Albacore Cres, SE13 123 EB86
Alba Gdns, NW11 63 CY58
Albain Cres, Ashf. TW15 114 BL89
Alba Ms, SW18 120 DA89
Alban Cres, Borwd. WD6 26 CP39
Dartford (Fnghm) DA4 148 FN102
Alban Highwalk, EC2 *off London Wall* 84 DQ71
Albans Vw, Wat. WD25 7 BV33
Albany, W1 199 K1
Albany, The, Wdf.Grn. IG8 48 EF49
Albany Cl, N15 65 DP56
SW14 98 CP84
Bexley DA5 126 EW87
Bushey WD23 25 CD44
Esher KT10 154 CA109
Reigate RH2 184 DA132
Uxbridge UB10 58 BN64
Albany Ct, E4 *off Chelwood Cl* 31 EB44
Epping CM16 17 ET30
Albany Ctyd, W1 199 L1
Albany Cres, Edg. HA8 42 CN52
Esher (Clay.) KT10 155 CE107
Albany Mans, SW11 100 DE80
Albany Ms, N1 *off Barnsbury Pk* 83 DN66
SE5 *off Albany Rd* 102 DQ79
Bromley BR1 124 EG93
Kingston upon Thames KT2 *off Albany Pk Rd* 117 CK93
St. Albans AL2 *off North Orbital Rd* 8 CA27
Sutton SM1 *off Camden Rd* 158 DB106
⇌ **Albany Park** 126 EX89
Albany Pk, Slou. (Colnbr.) SL3 93 BD81
Albany Pk Av, Enf. EN3 30 DW39
Albany Pk Rd, Kings.T. KT2 118 CL93
Leatherhead KT22 171 CG119
Albany Pas, Rich. TW10 118 CM85
Albany Pl, Brent. TW8 *off Albany Rd* 98 CL79
Egham TW20 113 BA91
Albany Rd, E10 67 EA59
E12 68 EK63
E17 67 DY58
N4 65 DM58
N18 46 DV50
SE5 102 DR79
SE17 102 DR79
SW19 120 DB92
W13 79 CH73
Belvedere DA17 106 EZ79
Bexley DA5 126 EW87
Brentford TW8 97 CK79
Brentwood (Pilg.Hat.) CM15 54 FV44
Chislehurst BR7 125 EP92
Enfield EN3 31 DX37
Hornchurch RM12 71 FG60
New Malden KT3 138 CR98
Richmond TW10 *off Albert Rd* 118 CM85
Romford RM6 70 EZ58
Walton-on-Thames KT12 154 BX105
Windsor (Old Wind.) SL4 112 AU85
Albanys, The, Reig. RH2 184 DA131
Albany St, NW1 83 DH68
Albany Ter, NW1 *off Marylebone Rd* 83 DH70
Albany Vw, Buck.H. IG9 48 EG46
Alba Pl, W11 *off Portobello Rd* 81 CZ72
Albatross Cl, E6 87 EM70
Albatross Gdns, S.Croy. CR2 161 DX111
Albatross St, SE18 105 ES80
Albatross Way, SE16 203 H5
Albemarle, SW19 119 CX89
Albemarle App, Ilf. IG2 69 EP58
Albemarle Av, Pot.B. EN6 12 DB33
Twickenham TW2 116 BZ88
Waltham Cross (Chsht) EN8 14 DW28
Albemarle Cl, Grays RM17 110 GA75
Albemarle Gdns, Ilf. IG2 69 EP58
New Malden KT3 138 CR98
Albemarle Pk, Stan. HA7 *off Marsh La* 41 CJ50
Albemarle Rd, Barn. EN4 44 DE45
Beckenham BR3 143 EB95
Albemarle St, W1 199 J1
Albemarle Way, EC1 196 F5
Alberon Gdns, NW11 63 CZ56
Alberta Av, Sutt. SM1 157 CY105
Alberta Est, SE17 200 G10
Alberta Rd, Enf. EN1 30 DT44
Erith DA8 107 FC81
Alberta St, SE17 200 F10
Albert Av, E4 47 EA49
SW8 101 DM80
Chertsey KT16 134 BG97
Albert Barnes Ho, SE1 201 H7
Albert Basin Way, E16 *off Armada Way* 87 EQ73
Albert Bigg Pt, E15 *off Godfrey St* 85 EC68
Albert Br, SW3 100 DE79
SW11 100 DE79
Albert Br Rd, SW11 100 DE80
Albert Carr Gdns, SW16 121 DL92
Albert Cl, E9 *off Northiam St* 84 DV67
N22 45 DK53
Grays RM16 110 GC76
Slough SL1 *off Hencroft St S* 92 AT76
Albert Ct, SW7 *off Prince Consort Rd* 100 DD75
Albert Cres, E4 47 EA49
Albert Dr, SW19 119 CY89
Woking GU21 151 BD114
Albert Embk, SE1 101 DL78
Albert Gdns, E1 85 DX72
Albert Gate, SW1 198 E4
Albert Gro, SW20 139 CX95
Albert Hall Mans, SW7 *off Kensington Gore* 100 DD75
Albertine Cl, Epsom KT17 173 CV116
Albert Mans, SW11 *off Albert Br Rd* 100 DF81
★ **Albert Mem**, SW7 100 DD75
Albert Ms, E14 *off Narrow St* 85 DY73
N4 *off Albert Rd* 65 DM60
SE4 *off Arabin Rd* 103 DY84
W8 *off Victoria Gro* 100 DC76
Albert Murray Cl, Grav. DA12 *off Armoury Dr* 131 GJ87
Albert Pl, N3 44 DA53
N17 *off High Rd* 66 DT55
W8 100 DB75
Albert Rd, E10 67 EC61
E16 86 EL74
E17 67 EA57
E18 68 EH55
N4 65 DM60
N15 66 DS58
N22 45 DJ53
NW4 63 CX56
NW6 81 CZ68
NW7 43 CT50
SE9 124 EL90
SE20 123 DX94
SE25 142 DU98
W5 79 CH70
Addlestone KT15 134 BK104
Ashford TW15 114 BM92
Ashtead KT21 172 CM118
Barnet EN4 28 DC42
Belvedere DA17 106 EZ78
Bexley DA5 126 FA86
Bromley BR2 144 EK99
Buckhurst Hill IG9 48 EK47
Dagenham RM8 70 FA60
Dartford DA2 128 FJ90
Egham (Eng.Grn) TW20 112 AX93
Epsom KT17 157 CT113
Hampton (Hmptn H.) TW12 116 CC92
Harrow HA2 60 CC55
Hayes UB3 95 BS76
Hounslow TW3 96 CA84
Ilford IG1 69 EP62
Kingston upon Thames KT1 138 CM96
Mitcham CR4 140 DF97
New Malden KT3 139 CT98
Orpington (Chels.) BR6 164 EU106
Orpington (St.M.Cray) BR5 146 EV100
Redhill (S.Merst.) RH1 185 DJ129
Richmond TW10 118 CL85
Romford RM1 71 FF57
Southall UB2 96 BX76
Sutton SM1 158 DD106
Swanscombe DA10 130 FZ86
Teddington TW11 117 CF93
Twickenham TW1 117 CF88
Warlingham CR6 177 DZ117
West Drayton UB7 76 BL74
Windsor SL4 92 AS84
Albert Rd Est, Belv. DA17 106 EZ78
Albert Rd N, Reig. RH2 183 CZ133
Watford WD17 23 BV41
Albert Rd S, Wat. WD17 23 BV41
Albert Sq, E15 68 EE64
SW8 101 DM80
Albert St, N12 44 DC50
NW1 83 DH67
Brentwood (Warley) CM14 54 FW50
Slough SL1 92 AT76
Albert Ter, NW1 82 DG67
NW10 80 CR67
W6 *off Beavor La* 99 CU78
Buckhurst Hill IG9 48 EK47
Albert Ter Ms, NW1 *off Regents Pk Rd* 82 DG67
Albert Way, SE15 102 DV80
Albion Av, N10 44 DG53
SW8 101 DK82
Albion Bldgs, EC1 *off Bartholomew Cl* 84 DQ71
Albion Cl, W2 194 C10
Romford RM7 71 FD58
Slough SL2 74 AU74
Albion Cres, Ch.St.G. HP8 36 AV48
Albion Dr, E8 84 DT66
Albion Est, SE16 203 H5
Albion Gro, N16 66 DS63
Albion Hill, Loug. IG10 32 EJ43
Albion Ho, Wok. GU21 167 AZ117
Albion Ms, N1 83 DN67
NW6 *off Kilburn High Rd* 81 CZ66
W2 194 C9
W6 *off Galena Rd* 99 CV77
Albion Par, N16 *off Albion Rd* 66 DR63
Gravesend DA12 131 GK86
Albion Pk, Loug. IG10 32 EK43
Albion Pl, EC1 196 F6
SE25 *off High St* 142 DU97
W6 99 CV77
Albion Riverside Bldg, SW11 100 DE80
Albion Rd, E17 67 EC55
N16 66 DR63
N17 46 DT54
Bexleyheath DA6 106 EZ84
Chalfont St. Giles HP8 36 AV47
Gravesend DA12 131 GJ87
Hayes UB3 77 BS72
Hounslow TW3 96 CA84
Kingston upon Thames KT2 138 CQ95
Sutton SM2 158 DD107
Twickenham TW2 117 CE88
Albion Sq, E8 84 DT66
Albion St, SE16 202 G5
W2 194 C9
Croydon CR0 141 DP102
Albion Ter, E8 84 DT66
Gravesend DA12 131 GJ86
Albion Vil Rd, SE26 122 DW90
Albion Wk, N1 *off Railway St* 83 DL68
Albion Way, EC1 197 H7
SE13 103 EC84
Wembley HA9 *off North End Rd* 62 CP62
Albion Yd, N1 *off Railway St* 83 DL68
Albon Ho, SW18 *off Neville Gill Cl* 120 DB86
Albright Ind Est, Rain. RM13 89 FF71
Albrighton Rd, SE22 102 DS83
Albuhera Cl, Enf. EN2 29 DN39
Albury Av, Bexh. DA7 106 EY82
Isleworth TW7 97 CF80
Sutton SM2 157 CW109
Albury Cl, Cher. (Longcr.) KT16 132 AU104
Epsom KT19 156 CP109
Hampton TW12 116 CA93
Albury Ct, Sutt. SM1 *off Ripley Gdns* 158 DC105
Albury Dr, Pnr. HA5 40 BX52
Albury Gro Rd, Wal.Cr. (Chsht) EN8 15 DX30
Albury Ms, E12 68 EJ60
Albury Ride, Wal.Cr. (Chsht) EN8 15 DX31
Albury Rd, Chess. KT9 156 CL106
Redhill (S.Merst.) RH1 185 DJ129
Walton-on-Thames KT12 153 BS107
Albury St, SE8 103 EA79
Albury Wk, Wal.Cr. (Chsht) EN8 15 DX32
Albyfield, Brom. BR1 145 EM97
Albyn Rd, SE8 103 EA81
Albyns Cl, Rain. RM13 89 FG66
Albyns La, Rom. RM4 35 FC40
Alcester Cres, E5 66 DV61
Alcester Rd, Wall. SM6 159 DH105
Alcock Cl, Wall. SM6 159 DK108
Alcock Rd, Houns. TW5 96 BX80
Alcocks Cl, Tad. KT20 173 CY120
Alcocks La, Tad. (Kgswd) KT20 173 CY120
Alconbury Rd, E5 66 DU61
Alcorn Cl, Sutt. SM3 140 DA103
Alcott Cl, W7 *off Westcott Cres* 79 CF71
Alcuin Ct, Stan. HA7 *off Old Ch La* 41 CJ52
ALDBOROUGH HATCH, Ilf. IG2 69 ES55
Aldborough Rd, Dag. RM10 89 FC65
Upminster RM14 72 FM61
Aldborough Rd N, Ilf. IG2 69 ET57
Aldborough Rd S, Ilf. IG3 69 ES60
Aldborough Spur, Slou. SL1 74 AS72
Aldbourne Rd, W12 81 CT74
Aldbridge St, SE17 201 N10
Aldburgh Ms, W1 194 G8
Aldbury Av, Wem. HA9 80 CP66
Aldbury Cl, Wat. WD25 24 BX36
Aldbury Ms, N9 46 DR45
Aldbury Rd, Rick. (Mill End) WD3 37 BF45
Aldebert Ter, SW8 101 DL80
Aldeburgh Cl, E5 *off Southwold Rd* 66 DV61
Aldeburgh Pl, SE10 205 N9
Woodford Green IG8 48 EG49
Aldeburgh St, SE10 205 M10
Alden Av, E15 86 EF69
ALDENHAM, Wat. WD25 24 CB38
Aldenham Av, Rad. WD7 25 CG36
★ **Aldenham Country Pk**, Borwd. WD6 25 CH43
Aldenham Dr, Uxb. UB8 77 BP70
Aldenham Gro, Rad. WD7 9 CH34
Aldenham Rd, Borwd. (Els.) WD6 25 CH42
Bushey WD23 24 BZ42
Radlett WD7 25 CG35
Watford WD19 24 BX44
Watford (Let.Hth) WD25 25 CE39
Aldenham St, NW1 195 L1
Aldenholme, Wey. KT13 153 BS107
Aldensley Rd, W6 99 CV76
Alder Av, Upmin. RM14 72 FM63
Alderbourne La, Iver SL0 57 BA64
Slough (Fulmer) SL3 56 AX63
Alderbrook Rd, SW12 121 DH86
Alderbury Rd, SW13 99 CU79
Slough SL3 93 AZ75
Alderbury Rd W, Slou. SL3 93 AZ75
Alder Cl, SE15 102 DT79
Egham (Eng.Grn) TW20 112 AY92
St. Albans (Park St) AL2 8 CB28
Aldercombe La, Cat. CR3 186 DS127
Aldercroft, Couls. CR5 175 DM116
Alder Dr, S.Ock. RM15 *off Laburnum Gro* 91 FW70
Alder Gro, NW2 63 CV61
Aldergrove Gdns, Houns. TW3 *off Bath Rd* 96 BY82
Aldergrove Wk, Horn. RM12 *off Airfield Way* 90 FJ65
Alder Ho, NW3 *off Maitland Pk Vil* 82 DF65
Alderman Av, Bark. IG11 88 EU69
Aldermanbury, EC2 197 J8
Aldermanbury Sq, EC2 197 J7
Alderman Cl, Dart. DA1 127 FE87
Alderman Judge Mall, Kings.T. KT1 *off Eden St* 138 CL96
Aldermans Hill, N13 45 DL49
Alderman's Wk, EC2 197 M7
Aldermary Rd, Brom. BR1 144 EG95
Alder Ms, N19 *off Bredgar Rd* 65 DJ61
Aldermoor Rd, SE6 123 DZ90
Alderney Av, Houns. TW5 96 CB80
Alderney Gdns, Nthlt. UB5 78 BZ66
Alderney Ho, N1 *off Clifton Rd* 84 DQ65
Alderney Ms, SE1 201 K6
Alderney Rd, E1 85 DX70
Erith DA8 107 FG80
Alderney St, SW1 199 J10
Alder Rd, SW14 98 CR83
Iver SL0 75 BC68
Sidcup DA14 125 ET90
Uxbridge (Denh.) UB9 76 BJ65
Alders, The, N21 29 DN44
Feltham TW13 116 BY91
Hounslow TW5 96 BZ79
West Byfleet KT14 152 BJ112
West Wickham BR4 143 EB102
Alders Av, Wdf.Grn. IG8 48 EE51
ALDERSBROOK, E12 68 EH61
Aldersbrook Av, Enf. EN1 30 DS40
Aldersbrook Dr, Kings.T. KT2 118 CM93
Aldersbrook La, E12 69 EM62
Aldersbrook Rd, E11 68 EH61
E12 68 EK62
Alders Cl, E11 *off Aldersbrook Rd* 68 EH61
W5 97 CK76
Edgware HA8 42 CQ50
Aldersey Gdns, Bark. IG11 87 ER65
Aldersford Cl, SE4 123 DX85
Aldersgate St, EC1 197 H8
Alders Gro, E.Mol. KT8 *off Esher Rd* 137 CD99
Aldersgrove, Wal.Abb. EN9 *off Roundhills* 16 EE34
Aldersgrove Av, SE9 124 EJ90
Aldershot Rd, NW6 81 CZ67
Alderside Wk, Egh. (Eng.Grn) TW20 112 AY92
Aldersmead Av, Croy. CR0 143 DX100
Aldersmead Rd, Beck. BR3 123 DY94
Alderson Pl, Sthl. UB2 78 CC74
Alderson St, W10 *off Kensal Rd* 81 CY70
Alders Rd, Edg. HA8 42 CQ50
Reigate RH2 184 DB132
Alderstead Heath, Red. RH1 175 DK124
Alderstead La, Red. (Merst.) RH1 185 DK126
Alderton Cl, NW10 62 CR62
Brentwood (Pilg.Hat.) CM15 54 FV43
Loughton IG10 33 EN42
Alderton Cres, NW4 63 CV57
Alderton Hall La, Loug. IG10 33 EN42
Alderton Hill, Loug. IG10 32 EL43
Alderton Ms, Loug. IG10 *off Alderton Hall La* 33 EN42
Alderton Ri, Loug. IG10 33 EN42
Alderton Rd, SE24 102 DQ83
Croydon CR0 142 DT101
Alderton Way, NW4 63 CV57
Loughton IG10 33 EM43
Alderville Rd, SW6 99 CZ82
Alder Wk, Ilf. IG1 69 EQ64
Watford WD25 *off Aspen Pk Dr* 23 BV35
Alder Way, Swan. BR8 147 FD96
Alderwick Dr, Houns. TW3 97 CD83
Alderwood Cl, Cat. CR3 186 DS125
Romford (Abridge) RM4 34 EV41
Alderwood Dr, Rom. (Abridge) RM4 34 EV41
Alderwood Ms, Barn. EN4 28 DC38
Alderwood Rd, SE9 125 ER86
Aldford St, W1 198 F2
⊖ **Aldgate** 197 P8
Aldgate, EC3 197 P9
Aldgate Av, E1 197 P8
Aldgate Barrs Shop Cen, E1 *off Whitechapel High St* 84 DT72
⊖ **Aldgate East** 84 DT72
Aldgate High St, EC3 197 P9
Aldham Dr, S.Ock. RM15 91 FW71
Aldin Av N, Slou. SL1 92 AU75
Aldin Av S, Slou. SL1 92 AU75
Aldine Ct, W12 *off Aldine St* 81 CW74
Aldine Pl, W12 *off Uxbridge Rd* 99 CW75
Aldine St, W12 99 CW75
Aldingham Ct, Horn. RM12 *off Easedale Dr* 71 FG64

Aldingham Gdns, Horn. RM12 71 FG64
Aldington Cl, Dag. RM8 70 EW59
Aldington Rd, SE18 104 EK76
Aldis Ms, SW17 120 DE92
Enfield EN3 *off Martini Dr* 31 EA37
Aldis St, SW17 120 DE92
Aldred Rd, NW6 64 DA64
Aldren Rd, SW17 120 DC90
Aldrich Cres, Croy. (New Adgtn) CR0 161 EC109
Aldriche Way, E4 47 EC51
Aldrich Gdns, Sutt. SM3 139 CZ104
Aldrich Ter, SW18 *off Lidiard Rd* 120 DC89
Aldridge Av, Edg. HA8 42 CP48
Enfield EN3 31 EA38
Ruislip HA4 60 BX61
Stanmore HA7 42 CL53
Aldridge Ri, N.Mal. KT3 138 CS101
Aldridge Rd Vil, W11 81 CZ71
Aldridge Wk, N14 45 DL45
Aldrington Rd, SW16 121 DJ92
Aldsworth Cl, W9 82 DB70
Aldwick Cl, SE9 125 ER90
Aldwick Rd, Croy. CR0 141 DM104
Aldworth Gro, SE13 123 EC86
Aldworth Rd, E15 86 EE66
Aldwych, WC2 196 B10
Aldwych Av, Ilf. IG6 69 EQ56
Aldwych Cl, Horn. RM12 71 FG61
Aldwych Underpass, WC2 *off Kingsway* 83 DM72
Alers Rd, Bexh. DA6 126 EX85
Alesia Cl, N22 *off Nightingale Rd* 45 DL52
Alestan Beck Rd, E16 86 EK71
Alexa Ct, W8 *off Lexham Gdns* 100 DA77
Sutton SM2 *off Mulgrave Rd* 158 DA107
Alexander Av, NW10 81 CV66
Alexander Cl, Barn. EN4 28 DD42
Bromley BR2 144 EG102
Sidcup DA15 125 ES85
Southall UB2 78 CC74
Twickenham TW2 117 CF89
Alexander Ct, Wal.Cr. (Chsht) EN8 15 DX30
Alexander Cres, Cat. CR3 *off Coulsdon Rd* 176 DQ122
Alexander Evans Ms, SE23 *off Sunderland Rd* 123 DX88
★ **Alexander Fleming Laboratory Mus**, W2 194 A8
Alexander Godley Cl, Ashtd. KT21 172 CM119
Alexander Ho, Kings.T. KT2 *off Kingsgate Rd* 138 CL95
Alexander La, Brwd. (Hutt.) CM13, CM15 55 GB44
Alexander Ms, W2 *off Alexander St* 82 DB72
Alexander Pl, SW7 198 B8
Oxted RH8 *off Barrow Grn Rd* 188 EE128
Alexander Rd, N19 65 DL62
Bexleyheath DA7 106 EX82
Chislehurst BR7 125 EP92
Coulsdon CR5 175 DH115
Egham TW20 113 BB92
Greenhithe DA9 129 FW85
St. Albans (Lon.Col.) AL2 9 CJ25
Alexander Sq, SW3 198 B8
Alexander St, W2 82 DA72
Alexanders Wk, Cat. CR3 186 DT126
Alexandra Av, N22 45 DK53
SW11 100 DG81
W4 98 CR80
Harrow HA2 60 BZ60
Southall UB1 78 BZ73
Sutton SM1 140 DA104
Warlingham CR6 177 DZ117
Alexandra Cl, SE8 103 DZ79
Ashford TW15 *off Alexandra Rd* 115 BR94
Grays RM16 111 GH75
Harrow HA2 *off Alexandra Av* 60 CA62
Staines TW18 114 BK93
Swanley BR8 147 FE96
Walton-on-Thames KT12 135 BU103
Alexandra Cotts, SE14 103 DZ81
Alexandra Ct, N14 29 DJ43
N16 *off Belgrade Rd* 66 DT63
W9 *off Maida Vale* 82 DC70
Ashford TW15 *off Alexandra Rd* 115 BR93
Wembley HA9 62 CM63
Alexandra Cres, Brom. BR1 124 EF93
Alexandra Dr, SE19 122 DS92
Surbiton KT5 138 CN101
Alexandra Gdns, N10 65 DH56
W4 98 CS80
Carshalton SM5 158 DG109
Hounslow TW3 96 CB82
Alexandra Gro, N4 65 DP60
N12 44 DB50
Alexandra Ms, N2 *off Fortis Grn* 64 DF55
SW19 *off Alexandra Rd* 120 DA93
★ **Alexandra Palace**, N22 45 DK54
⇌ **Alexandra Palace** 45 DL54
Alexandra Palace Way, N22 65 DJ55
Alexandra Pk Rd, N10 45 DH54
N22 45 DK54
Alexandra Pl, NW8 82 DC67
SE25 142 DR99
Croydon CR0 *off Alexandra Rd* 142 DS102
Alexandra Rd, E6 87 EN69
E10 67 EC62
E17 67 DZ58
E18 68 EH55
N8 65 DN55
N9 46 DV45
N10 45 DH51
N15 66 DR57
Alexandra Rd, NW4 63 CX56
NW8 82 DC66
SE26 123 DX93
SW14 98 CR83
SW19 119 CZ93
W4 98 CR75
Addlestone KT15 152 BK105
Ashford TW15 115 BR94
Borehamwood WD6 26 CR38
Brentford TW8 97 CK79
Brentwood CM14 54 FW48
Croydon CR0 142 DS102
Egham (Eng.Grn) TW20 112 AW93
Enfield EN3 31 DX42
Epsom KT17 157 CT113
Erith DA8 107 FF79
Gravesend DA12 131 GL87
Hounslow TW3 96 CB82
Kings Langley WD4 6 BN29
Kings Langley (Chipper.) WD4 6 BG30
Kingston upon Thames KT2 118 CN94
Mitcham CR4 120 DE94
Rainham RM13 89 FF67
Richmond TW9 98 CM82
Rickmansworth (Sarratt) WD3 22 BG36
Romford RM1 71 FF58
Romford (Chad.Hth) RM6 70 EX58
Thames Ditton KT7 137 CF99
Tilbury RM18 111 GF82
Twickenham TW1 117 CJ86
Uxbridge UB8 76 BK68
Warlingham CR6 177 DY117
Watford WD17 23 BU40
Westerham (Bigg.H.) TN16 178 EH119
Alexandra Sq, Mord. SM4 140 DA99
Alexandra St, E16 86 EG71
SE14 103 DY80
Alexandra Wk, SE19 122 DS92
Dartford (S.Darenth) DA4 *off Gorringe Av* 149 FS96
Alexandra Way, Epsom KT19 156 CN111
Waltham Cross EN8 15 DZ34
Alexandria Rd, W13 79 CG73
Alexis St, SE16 202 B8
Alfan La, Dart. DA2 127 FD92
Alfearn Rd, E5 66 DW63
Alford Grn, Croy. (New Adgtn) CR0 161 ED107
Alford Pl, N1 197 J1
Alford Rd, Erith DA8 107 FD78
Alfoxton Av, N15 65 DP56
Alfreda St, SW11 101 DH81
Alfred Cl, W4 *off Belmont Rd* 98 CR77
Alfred Gdns, Sthl. UB1 78 BY73
Alfred Ms, W1 195 M6
Alfred Pl, WC1 195 M6
Gravesend (Nthflt) DA11 131 GF88
Alfred Prior Ho, E12 69 EN63
Alfred Rd, E15 68 EF64
SE25 142 DU99
W2 82 DA71
W3 80 CQ74
Belvedere DA17 106 EZ78
Brentwood CM14 54 FX47
Buckhurst Hill IG9 48 EK47
Dartford (Hawley) DA2 128 FL91
Feltham TW13 116 BW89
Gravesend DA11 131 GH89
Kingston upon Thames KT1 138 CL97
South Ockendon (Aveley) RM15 90 FQ74
Sutton SM1 158 DC106
Alfred's Gdns, Bark. IG11 87 ES68
Alfred St, E3 85 DZ69
Grays RM17 110 GC79
Alfreds Way, Bark. IG11 87 EQ69
Alfreds Way Ind Est, Bark. IG11 88 EU67
Alfreton Cl, SW19 119 CX90
Alfriston Av, Croy. CR0 141 DL101
Harrow HA2 60 CA58
Alfriston Cl, Dart. DA1 127 FE86
Surbiton KT5 138 CM99
Alfriston Rd, SW11 120 DF85
Algar Cl, Islw. TW7 *off Algar Rd* 97 CG83
Stanmore HA7 41 CF50
Algar Rd, Islw. TW7 97 CG83
Algarve Rd, SW18 120 DB88
Algernon Rd, NW4 63 CU58
NW6 82 DA67
SE13 103 EB84
Algers Cl, Loug. IG10 32 EK43
Algers Mead, Loug. IG10 32 EK43
Algers Rd, Loug. IG10 32 EK43
Algiers Rd, SE13 103 EA84
Alibon Gdns, Dag. RM10 70 FA64
Alibon Rd, Dag. RM9, RM10 70 EZ64
Alice Cl, Barn. EN5 28 DC42
Alice Ct, SW15 *off Deodar Rd* 99 CZ84
Alice Gilliatt Ct, W14 99 CZ79
Alice La, E3 85 DZ67
Alice Ms, Tedd. TW11 *off Luther Rd* 117 CF92
Alice Ruston Pl, Wok. GU22 166 AW119
Alice St, SE1 201 M7
Alice Thompson Cl, SE12 124 EJ89
Alice Walker Cl, SE24 *off Shakespeare Rd* 101 DP84
Alice Way, Houns. TW3 96 CB84
Alicia Av, Har. HA3 61 CH56
Alicia Cl, Har. HA3 61 CJ56
Alicia Gdns, Har. HA3 61 CH56
Alie St, E1 84 DT72
Alington Cres, NW9 62 CQ60
Alington Gro, Wall. SM6 159 DJ109
Alison Cl, E6 87 EN72
Croydon CR0 *off Shirley Oaks Rd* 143 DX102
Woking GU21 166 AY115
Aliwal Rd, SW11 100 DE84
Alkerden La, Green. DA9 129 FW86
Swanscombe DA10 129 FW86
Alkerden Rd, W4 98 CS78
Alkham Rd, N16 66 DT61
Allan Barclay Cl, N15 *off High Rd* 66 DT58
Allan Cl, N.Mal. KT3 138 CR99
Allandale Av, N3 63 CY55
Allandale Cres, Pot.B. EN6 11 CY32
Allandale Pl, Orp. BR6 146 EX104
Allandale Rd, Enf. EN3 31 DX36
Hornchurch RM11 71 FF59
Allan Way, W3 80 CQ71
Allard Cl, Orp. BR5 146 EW101
Waltham Cross (Chsht) EN7 14 DT27
Allard Cres, Bushey (Bushey Hth) WD23 40 CC46
Allard Gdns, SW4 121 DK85
Allardyce St, SW4 101 DM84
Allbrook Cl, Tedd. TW11 117 CE92
Allcot Cl, Felt. TW14 115 BT88
Allcroft Rd, NW5 64 DG64
Allder Way, S.Croy. CR2 159 DP108
Allenby Av, S.Croy. CR2 160 DQ109
Allenby Cl, Grnf. UB6 78 CA69
Allenby Cres, Grays RM17 110 GB78
Allenby Dr, Horn. RM11 72 FL60
Allenby Rd, SE23 123 DY90
SE28 105 EQ76
Southall UB1 78 CA72
Westerham (Bigg.H.) TN16 178 EL117
Allen Cl, Mitch. CR4 141 DH95
Radlett (Shenley) WD7 *off Russet Dr* 10 CL32
Sunbury-on-Thames TW16 135 BV95
Allen Ct, Grnf. UB6 61 CF64
Allendale Av, Sthl. UB1 78 CA72
Allendale Cl, SE5 *off Daneville Rd* 102 DR81
SE26 123 DX92
Dartford DA2 *off Princes Rd* 129 FR88
Allendale Rd, Grnf. UB6 79 CH65
Allen Edwards Dr, SW8 101 DL81
Allenford Ho, SW15 *off Tunworth Cres* 119 CT86
Allen Ho Pk, Wok. GU22 166 AW120
Allen Pl, Twick. TW1 *off Church St* 117 CG88
Allen Rd, E3 85 DZ68
N16 66 DS63
Beckenham BR3 143 DX96
Croydon CR0 141 DM101
Rainham RM13 90 FJ69
Sunbury-on-Thames TW16 135 BV95
Allensbury Pl, NW1 83 DK66
Allens Mead, Grav. DA12 131 GM88
Allens Rd, Enf. EN3 30 DW43
Allen St, W8 100 DA76
Allenswood, SW19 *off Albert Dr* 119 CY88
Allenswood Rd, SE9 104 EL83
Allerford Ct, Har. HA2 60 CB57
Allerford Rd, SE6 123 EB91
Allerton Cl, Borwd. WD6 26 CM38
Allerton Ct, NW4 *off Holders Hill Rd* 43 CX54
Allerton Rd, N16 66 DQ61
Borehamwood WD6 26 CL38
Allerton Wk, N7 *off Durham Rd* 65 DM61
Allestree Rd, SW6 99 CY80
Alleyn Cres, SE21 122 DR89
Alleyndale Rd, Dag. RM8 70 EW61
Alleyn Pk, SE21 122 DR89
Southall UB2 96 BZ77
Alleyn Rd, SE21 122 DR90
Allfarthing La, SW18 120 DB86
Allgood Cl, Mord. SM4 139 CX100
Allgood St, E2 *off Hackney Rd* 84 DT68
Allhallows La, EC4 201 K1
★ **All Hallows-on-the-Wall C of E Ch**, EC2 197 L7
Allhallows Rd, E6 86 EL71
All Hallows Rd, N17 46 DS53
Allhusen Gdns, Slou. (Fulmer) SL3 *off Alderbourne La* 56 AY63
Alliance Cl, Wem. HA0 61 CK63
Alliance Ct, W3 *off Alliance Rd* 80 CP71
Alliance Rd, E13 86 EJ70
SE18 106 EU79
W3 80 CP70
Allied Way, W3 *off Larden Rd* 98 CS75
Allingham Cl, W7 79 CF73
Allingham Ms, N1 *off Allingham St* 84 DQ68
Allingham St, N1 84 DQ68
Allington Av, N17 46 DS51
Allington Cl, SW19 *off High St Wimbledon* 119 CX92
Gravesend DA12 *off Farley Rd* 131 GM88
Greenford UB6 78 CC66
Allington Ct, Enf. EN3 31 DX43
Slough SL2 *off Myrtle Cres* 74 AT73
Allington Rd, NW4 63 CV57
W10 81 CY68
Harrow HA2 60 CC57
Orpington BR6 145 ER103
Allington St, SW1 199 K7
Allison Cl, SE10 *off Dartmouth Hill* 103 EC81
Waltham Abbey EN9 16 EG33
Allison Gro, SE21 122 DS88
Allison Rd, N8 65 DN57
W3 80 CQ72
Allitsen Rd, NW8 194 B1
Allmains Cl, Wal.Abb. EN9 16 EH25
Allnutts Rd, Epp. CM16 18 EU33
Allnutt Way, SW4 121 DK85
Alloa Rd, SE8 203 J10
Ilford IG3 70 EU61
Allonby Dr, Ruis. HA4 59 BP59
Allonby Gdns, Wem. HA9 61 CJ60
Allonby Ho, E14 *off Aston St* 85 DY71
Allotment La, Sev. TN13 191 FJ122
Allotment Way, NW2 *off Midland Ter* 63 CX62
Alloway Cl, Wok. GU21 *off Inglewood* 166 AV118
Alloway Rd, E3 85 DY69
Allports Ms, E1 *off Stepney Grn* 84 DW70
DLR **All Saints** 85 EB73
All Saints Cl, N9 46 DT47
SW8 *off Lansdowne Way* 101 DL81
Chigwell IG7 50 EU48
Swanscombe DA10 *off High St* 130 FZ85
All Saints Cres, Wat. WD25 8 BX33
All Saints Dr, SE3 104 EE82
South Croydon CR2 160 DT112
All Saints La, Rick. (Crox.Grn) WD3 22 BN44
All Saints Ms, Har. HA3 41 CE51
All Saints Pas, SW18 *off Wandsworth High St* 120 DA85
All Saints Rd, SW19 120 DC94
W3 98 CQ76
W11 81 CZ71
Gravesend (Nthflt) DA11 131 GF88
Sutton SM1 140 DB104
All Saints St, N1 83 DM68
All Saints Twr, E10 67 EB59
Allsop Pl, NW1 194 E5
All Souls Av, NW10 81 CV68
All Souls Pl, W1 195 J7
Allum Cl, Borwd. (Els.) WD6 26 CL42
Allum Gro, Tad. KT20 173 CV121
Allum La, Borwd. (Els.) WD6 26 CM42
Allum Way, N20 44 DC46
Allwood Cl, SE26 123 DX91
Allwood Rd, Wal.Cr. EN7 14 DT27
Allyn Cl, Stai. TW18 *off Penton Rd* 113 BF93
Alma Av, E4 47 EC52
Hornchurch RM12 72 FL63
Almack Rd, E5 66 DW63
Alma Cl, Wok. (Knap.) GU21 166 AS118
Alma Cres, Sutt. SM1 157 CY106
Alma Gro, SE1 202 A9
Alma Pl, NW10 *off Harrow Rd* 81 CV69
SE19 122 DT94
Thornton Heath CR7 141 DN99
Alma Rd, N10 44 DG52
SW18 120 DC85
Carshalton SM5 158 DE106
Enfield EN3 31 DY43
Esher KT10 137 CE102
Orpington BR5 146 EX103
Reigate RH2 184 DB133
Sidcup DA14 126 EU90
Southall UB1 78 BY73
Swanscombe DA10 130 FZ85
Alma Row, Har. HA3 41 CD53
Alma Sq, NW8 82 DC69
Alma St, E15 85 ED65
NW5 83 DH65
Alma Ter, SW18 120 DD87
W8 *off Allen St* 100 DA76
Almeida St, N1 83 DP66
Almeric Rd, SW11 100 DF84
Almer Rd, SW20 119 CU94
Almington St, N4 65 DM60
Almners Rd, Cher. (Lyne) KT16 133 BC100
Almond Av, W5 98 CL76
Carshalton SM5 140 DF103
Uxbridge UB10 59 BP62
West Drayton UB7 94 BN76
Woking GU22 166 AX121
Almond Cl, SE15 102 DU82
Bromley BR2 145 EN101
Egham (Eng.Grn) TW20 112 AV93
Feltham TW13 *off Highfield Rd* 115 BU88
Grays RM16 111 GG76
Hayes UB3 77 BS73
Ruislip HA4 *off Roundways* 59 BT62
Shepperton TW17 135 BQ96
Almond Dr, Swan. BR8 147 FD96
Almond Gro, Brent. TW8 97 CH80
Almond Rd, N17 46 DU52
SE16 202 E8
Dartford DA2 128 FQ87
Epsom KT19 156 CR111
Almonds Av, Buck.H. IG9 48 EG47
Almond Way, Borwd. WD6 26 CP42
Bromley BR2 145 EN101
Harrow HA2 40 CB54
Mitcham CR4 141 DK99
Almons Way, Slou. SL2 74 AV71
Almorah Rd, N1 84 DR66
Hounslow TW5 96 BX81
Alms Heath, Wok. (Ock.) GU23 169 BP121
Almshouse La, Chess. KT9 155 CJ109
Enfield EN1 30 DV37
Alnwick Gro, Mord. SM4 *off Bordesley Rd* 140 DB98
Alnwick Rd, E16 86 EJ72
SE12 124 EH87
ALPERTON, Wem. HA0 80 CM67
⊖ **Alperton** 80 CL67
Alperton La, Grnf. UB6 79 CK69
Wembley HA0 79 CK69
Alperton St, W10 81 CY70
Alphabet Gdns, Cars. SM5 140 DD100
Alphabet Sq, E3 *off Hawgood St* 85 EA71
Alpha Cl, NW1 194 C3
Alpha Ct, Whyt. CR3 176 DU118
Alpha Gro, E14 204 A5
Alpha Pl, NW6 82 DA68
SW3 100 DE79
Alpha Rd, E4 47 EB48
N18 46 DU51
SE14 103 DZ81
Brentwood (Hutt.) CM13 55 GD44
Croydon CR0 142 DS102
Enfield EN3 31 DY42
Surbiton KT5 138 CM100
Teddington TW11 117 CD92
Uxbridge UB10 77 BP70
Woking GU22 167 BB116
Woking (Chobham) GU24 150 AT110
Alpha St, SE15 102 DU82
Alpha St N, Slou. SL1 92 AU75
Alpha St S, Slou. SL1 92 AT76
Alpha Way, Egh. TW20 133 BC95
Alphea Cl, SW19 120 DE94
Alpine Av, Surb. KT5 138 CQ103
Alpine Business Cen, E6 87 EN71
Alpine Cl, Croy. CR0 142 DS104
Alpine Copse, Brom. BR1 145 EN96
Alpine Gro, E9 84 DW66
Alpine Rd, E10 67 EB61
SE16 203 H10
Redhill RH1 184 DG131
Walton-on-Thames KT12 135 BU101
Alpine Vw, Cars. SM5 158 DE106
Alpine Wk, Stan. HA7 41 CE47
Alpine Way, E6 87 EN71
Alric Av, NW10 80 CR66
New Malden KT3 138 CS97
Alroy Rd, N4 65 DN59
Alsace Rd, SE17 201 M10
Alscot Rd, SE1 202 A8
Alscot Way, SE1 201 P8
Alsike Rd, SE2 106 EX76
Erith DA18 106 EY76
Alsom Av, Wor.Pk. KT4 157 CU105
Alsop Cl, St.Alb. (Lon.Col.) AL2 10 CL27
Alston Cl, Surb. KT6 137 CH101
Alston Rd, N18 46 DV50
SW17 120 DD91
Barnet EN5 27 CY41
Altair Cl, N17 46 DT51
Altair Way, Nthwd. HA6 39 BT49
Altash Way, SE9 125 EM89
Altenburg Av, W13 97 CH76
Altenburg Gdns, SW11 100 DF84
Alterton Cl, Wok. GU21 166 AU117
Alt Gro, SW19 *off St. George's Rd* 119 CZ94
Altham Gdns, Wat. WD19 40 BX49
Altham Rd, Pnr. HA5 40 BY52
Althea St, SW6 100 DB82
Althorne Gdns, E18 68 EF56
Althorne Way, Dag. RM10 70 FA61
Althorp Cl, Barn. EN5 43 CU45
Althorpe Gro, SW11 *off Westbridge Rd* 100 DD81
Althorpe Ms, SW11 *off Battersea High St* 100 DD81
Althorpe Rd, Har. HA1 60 CC57
Althorp Rd, SW17 120 DF88
Altima Ct, SE22 *off East Dulwich Rd* 102 DU84
Altmore Av, E6 87 EM66
Alton Av, Stan. HA7 41 CF52
Alton Cl, Bex. DA5 126 EY88
Isleworth TW7 97 CF82
Alton Ct, Stai. TW18 133 BE95
Alton Gdns, Beck. BR3 123 EA94
Twickenham TW2 117 CD87
Alton Rd, N17 66 DR55
SW15 119 CU88
Croydon CR0 141 DN104
Richmond TW9 98 CL84
Alton St, E14 85 EB71
Altyre Cl, Beck. BR3 143 DZ99
Altyre Rd, Croy. CR0 142 DR103
Altyre Way, Beck. BR3 143 DZ99
Aluric Cl, Grays RM16 111 GH77
Alvanley Gdns, NW6 64 DB64
Alva Way, Wat. WD19 40 BX47
Alverstoke Rd, Rom. RM3 52 FL52
Alverstone Av, SW19 120 DA89
Barnet EN4 44 DE45
Alverstone Gdns, SE9 125 EQ88
Alverstone Rd, E12 69 EN63
NW2 81 CW66
New Malden KT3 139 CT98
Wembley HA9 62 CM60
Alverston Gdns, SE25 142 DS99
Alverton St, SE8 103 DZ78
Alveston Av, Har. HA3 61 CH55
Alveston Sq, E18 *off Marlborough Rd* 48 EG54
Alvey Est, SE17 201 M9
Alvey St, SE17 201 M10
Alvia Gdns, Sutt. SM1 158 DC105
Alvington Cres, E8 66 DT64
Alway Av, Epsom KT19 156 CQ106
Alwen Gro, S.Ock. RM15 91 FV71
Alwold Cres, SE12 124 EH86
Alwyn Av, W4 98 CR78
Alwyn Cl, Borwd. (Els.) WD6 26 CM44
Croydon (New Adgtn) CR0 161 EB108
Alwyne Av, Brwd. (Shenf.) CM15 55 GA44
Alwyne Ct, Wok. GU21 166 AY116
Alwyne La, N1 *off Alwyne Vil* 83 DP66
Alwyne Pl, N1 84 DQ65
Alwyne Rd, N1 84 DQ66
SW19 119 CZ93
W7 79 CE73
Alwyne Sq, N1 84 DQ65
Alwyne Vil, N1 83 DP66
Alwyn Gdns, NW4 63 CU56
W3 80 CP72
Alwyns Cl, Cher. KT16 *off Alwyns La* 134 BG100
Alwyns La, Cher. KT16 133 BF100
Alyth Gdns, NW11 64 DA58
Alzette Ho, E2 85 DX69
Amalgamated Dr, Brent. TW8 97 CG79
Amanda Cl, Chig. IG7 49 ER51
Amanda Ct, Slou. SL3 92 AX76
Amanda Ms, Rom. RM7 71 FC57
Amazon Apts, N8 *off New River Av* 65 DM55
Amazon St, E1 *off Hessel St* 84 DV72
Ambassador Cl, Houns. TW3 96 BY82
Ambassador Gdns, E6 87 EM71
Ambassador's Ct, SW1 199 L3
Ambassador Sq, E14 204 B9
Amber Av, E17 47 DY53
Amber Ct, SW17 *off Brudenell Rd* 120 DG91
Staines TW18 *off Laleham Rd* 113 BF92
Ambercroft Way, Couls. CR5 175 DP119
Amberden Av, N3 64 DA55
Ambergate St, SE17 200 G10
Amber Gro, NW2 63 CX60
Amber La, Ilf. IG6 49 EP52
Amberley Cl, Orp. BR6 163 ET106
Pinner HA5 60 BZ55
Amberley Ct, Sid. DA14 126 EW92

Amberley Dr, Add. (Wdhm)
KT15 151 BF110
Amberley Gdns, Enf. EN1 46 DS45
Epsom KT19 157 CT105
Amberley Gro, SE26 122 DV91
Croydon CR0 142 DT101
Amberley Rd, E10 67 EA59
N13 45 DM47
SE2 106 EX79
W9 82 DA71
Buckhurst Hill IG9 48 EJ46
Enfield EN1 46 DT45
Amberley Way, Houns. TW4 116 BW85
Morden SM4 139 CZ101
Romford RM7 71 FB56
Uxbridge UB10 76 BL69
Amber Ms, N22
off Brampton Pk Rd 65 DN55
Amberside Cl, Islw. TW7 117 CD86
Amber St, E15
off Great Eastern Rd 85 ED65
Amber Wf, E2 *off Nursery La* 84 DT67
Amberwood Cl, Wall. SM6
off The Chase 159 DL106
Amberwood Ri, N.Mal. KT3 138 CS100
Amblecote, Cob. KT11 154 BY111
Amblecote Cl, SE12 124 EH90
Amblecote Meadows, SE12 124 EH90
Amblecote Rd, SE12 124 EH90
Ambler Rd, N4 65 DP62
Ambleside, SW19
off Albert Dr 119 CY88
Bromley BR1 123 ED93
Epping CM16 18 EU31
Purfleet RM19
off Coniston Av 108 FQ78
Ambleside Av, SW16 121 DK91
Beckenham BR3 143 DY99
Hornchurch RM12 71 FH64
Walton-on-Thames KT12 136 BW102
Ambleside Cl, E9
off Churchill Wk 66 DW64
E10 67 EB59
N17 *off Drapers Rd* 66 DT55
Ambleside Cres, Enf. EN3 31 DX41
Ambleside Dr, Felt. TW14 115 BT88
Ambleside Gdns, SW16 121 DK92
Ilford IG4 68 EL56
South Croydon CR2 161 DX109
Sutton SM2 158 DC107
Wembley HA9 61 CK60
Ambleside Pt, SE15
off Ilderton Rd 102 DW80
Ambleside Rd, NW10 81 CT66
Bexleyheath DA7 106 FA82
Ambleside Wk, Uxb. UB8
off High St 76 BK67
Ambleside Way, Egh. TW20 113 BB94
Ambrey Way, Wall. SM6 159 DK109
Ambrooke Rd, Belv. DA17 106 FA76
Ambrosden Av, SW1 199 L7
Ambrose Av, NW11 63 CY59
Ambrose Cl, E6
off Lovage App 86 EL71
Dartford (Cray.) DA1 107 FF84
Orpington BR6
off Stapleton Rd 145 ET104
Ambrose Ms, SW11 100 DE82
Ambrose St, SE16 202 D8
Ambrose Wk, E3
off Malmesbury Rd 85 EA68
Amelia Cl, W3 80 CP74
Amelia St, SE17 200 G10
Amen Cor, EC4 196 G9
SW17 120 DF93
Amen Ct, EC4 196 G8
Amenity Way, Mord. SM4 139 CW101
America Sq, EC3 197 P10
America St, SE1 201 H3
Amerland Rd, SW18 119 CZ86
Amersham Av, N18 46 DR51
Amersham Cl, Rom. RM3 52 FM51
Amersham Dr, Rom. RM3 52 FL51
Amersham Gro, SE14 103 DZ80
Amersham Pl, Amer. HP7 20 AW39
Amersham Rd, SE14 103 DZ80
Amersham (Lt.Chal.) HP6 20 AX39
Chalfont St. Giles HP8 20 AU43
Croydon CR0 142 DQ100
Gerrards Cross SL9 57 BB59
Gerrards Cross (Chal.St.P.)
SL9 36 AX49
Rickmansworth WD3 21 BB39
Romford RM3 52 FM51
Amersham Vale, SE14 103 DZ80
Amersham Wk, Rom. RM3 52 FM51
Amersham Way, Amer. HP6 20 AX39
Amery Gdns, NW10 81 CV67
Romford RM2 72 FK55
Amery Rd, Har. HA1 61 CG61
Amesbury, Wal.Abb. EN9 16 EG32
Amesbury Av, SW2 121 DL89
Amesbury Cl, Epp. CM16
off Amesbury Rd 17 ET31
Worcester Park KT4 139 CW102
Amesbury Dr, E4 31 EB44
Amesbury Rd, Brom. BR1 144 EK97
Dagenham RM9 88 EX66
Epping CM16 17 ET31
Feltham TW13 116 BX89
Amesbury Twr, SW8
off Westbury St 101 DJ82
Ames Rd, Swans. DA10 130 FY86
Amethyst Cl, N11 45 DK52
Amethyst Rd, E15 67 ED63
Amey Dr, Lthd. (Bkhm)
KT23 170 CC124
Amherst Av, W13 79 CJ72
Amherst Cl, Orp. BR5 146 EU98
Amherst Dr, Orp. BR5 145 ET98
Amherst Hill, Sev. TN13 190 FE122
Amherst Rd, W13 79 CJ72
Sevenoaks TN13 191 FH122
Amhurst Gdns, Islw. TW7 97 CF81
Amhurst Par, N16
off Amhurst Pk 66 DT59
Amhurst Pk, N16 66 DR59
Amhurst Pas, E8 66 DU63
Amhurst Rd, E8 66 DV64
N16 66 DT63
Amhurst Ter, E8 66 DU63
Amhurst Wk, SE28
off Roman Sq 88 EU74
Amidas Gdns, Dag. RM8 70 EV63
Amiel St, E1 84 DW70
Amies St, SW11 100 DF83
Amina Way, SE16 202 B7
Amis Av, Add. (New Haw)
KT15 152 BG111
Epsom KT19 156 CP107
Amis Rd, Wok. GU21 166 AS119
Amity Gro, SW20 139 CW95
Amity Rd, E15 86 EF67
Ammanford Grn, NW9
off Ruthin Cl 62 CS58
Amner Rd, SW11 120 DG86
Amor Rd, W6 99 CW76
Amott Rd, SE15 102 DU83
Amoy Pl, E14 85 EA72
Tra **Ampere Way** 141 DM101
Ampere Way, Croy. CR0 141 DL101
Ampleforth Rd, SE2 106 EV75
Ampthill Sq Est, NW1 195 L1
Ampton Pl, WC1 196 B3
Ampton St, WC1 196 B3
Amroth Cl, SE23 122 DV88
Amroth Grn, NW9
off Fryent Gro 62 CS58
Amstel Way, Wok. GU21 166 AT118
Amsterdam Rd, E14 204 E7
Amundsen Ct, E14
off Napier Av 103 EA78
Amwell Cl, Enf. EN2 30 DR43
Watford WD25
off Phillipers 24 BY35
Amwell Ct, Wal.Abb. EN9 16 EF33
Amwell Ct Est, N4 66 DQ60
Amwell St, EC1 196 D2
Amyand Cotts, Twick. TW1
off Amyand Pk Rd 117 CH86
Amyand La, Twick. TW1
off Marble Hill Gdns 117 CH87
Amyand Pk Gdns, Twick. TW1
off Amyand Pk Rd 117 CH87
Amyand Pk Rd, Twick. TW1 117 CG87
Amy Cl, Wall. SM6
off Mollison Dr 159 DL108
Amy Rd, Oxt. RH8 188 EE129
Amyruth Rd, SE4 123 EA85
Amy Warne Cl, E6
off Evelyn Denington Rd 86 EL70
Anatola Rd, N19
off Dartmouth Pk Hill 65 DH61
Ancaster Cres, N.Mal. KT3 139 CU100
Ancaster Ms, Beck. BR3 143 DX97
Ancaster Rd, Beck. BR3 143 DX97
Ancaster St, SE18 105 ES80
Anchorage Cl, SW19 120 DA92
Anchorage Pt, E14 203 P4
Anchorage Pt Ind Est, SE7 104 EJ76
Anchor & Hope La, SE7 104 EH76
Anchor Bay Ind Est, Erith
DA8 107 FG79
Anchor Boul, Dart. DA2 108 FQ84
Anchor Cl, Bark. IG11 88 EV69
Waltham Cross (Chsht)
EN8 15 DX28
Anchor Ct, Grays RM17 110 GA80
Anchor Dr, Rain. RM13 89 FH69
Anchor Ho, SW18
off Smugglers Way 100 DB84
Anchor Ms, N1
off Balls Pond Rd 84 DS65
SW11 *off Westbridge Rd* 100 DD81
SW12 121 DH86
Anchor Retail Pk, E1 84 DW70
Anchor St, SE16 202 D8
Anchor Ter, E1 *off Cephas Av* 84 DW70
Anchor Wf, E3 *off Watts Gro* 85 EB71
Anchor Yd, EC1 197 J4
Ancill Cl, W6 99 CY79
Ancona Rd, NW10 81 CU68
SE18 105 ER78
Andace Pk Gdns, Brom. BR1 144 EJ95
Andalus Rd, SW9 101 DL83
Ander Cl, Wem. HA0 61 CK63
Anderson Cl, N21 29 DM43
W3 80 CR72
Epsom KT19 156 CP112
Sutton SM3 140 DA102
Uxbridge (Hare.) UB9 38 BG53
Anderson Dr, Ashf. TW15 115 BQ91
Anderson Ho, Bark. IG11
off The Coverdales 87 ER68
Anderson Pl, Houns. TW3 96 CB84
Anderson Rd, E9 85 DX65
Radlett (Shenley) WD7 10 CN33
Weybridge KT13 135 BR104
Woodford Green IG8 68 EK55
Andersons Sq, N1
off Gaskin St 83 DP67
Anderson St, SW3 198 D10
Anderson Way, Belv. DA17 107 FB75
Anderton Cl, SE5 102 DR83
Andmark Ct, Sthl. UB1
off Herbert Rd 78 BZ74
Andover Av, E16
off King George Av 86 EK72
Andover Cl, Epsom KT19 156 CR111
Feltham TW14 115 BT88
Greenford UB6
off Ruislip Rd 78 CB70
Uxbridge UB8 76 BH68
Andover Pl, NW6 82 DB68
Andover Rd, N7 65 DM61
Orpington BR6 145 ER102
Twickenham TW2 117 CD88
Andrea Av, Grays RM16 110 GA75
Andre St, E8 66 DU64
Andrew Borde St, WC2 195 N8
Andrew Cl, Dart. DA1 127 FD85
Ilford IG6 49 ER51
Radlett (Shenley) WD7 10 CM33
Andrewes Gdns, E6 86 EL72
Andrewes Ho, EC2 197 J7
Andrew Pl, SW8
off Cowthorpe Rd 101 DK81
Andrew Reed Ho, SW18
off Linstead Way 119 CY87
Andrews Cl, E6
off Linton Gdns 86 EL72
Buckhurst Hill IG9 48 EJ47
Epsom KT17 157 CT114
Harrow HA1
off Bessborough Rd 61 CD59
Orpington BR5 146 EX96
Andrews Cl, Wor. Pk. KT4 139 CX103
Andrews Crosse, WC2 196 D9
Andrews La, Wal.Cr. (Chsht)
EN7 14 DU28
Andrews Pl, SE9 125 EP86
Dartford DA2 127 FE89
Andrew's Rd, E8 84 DV67
Andrew St, E14 85 EC72
Andrews Wk, SE17
off Dale Rd 101 DP79
Andwell Cl, SE2 106 EV75
ANERLEY, SE20 142 DV95
⇌ **Anerley** 122 DV94
Anerley Gro, SE19 122 DT94
Anerley Hill, SE19 122 DT93
Anerley Pk, SE20 122 DU94
Anerley Pk Rd, SE20 122 DV94
Anerley Rd, SE19 122 DU94
SE20 122 DU94
Anerley Sta Rd, SE20 142 DV95
Anerley St, SW11 100 DF82
Anerley Vale, SE19 122 DT94
Anfield Cl, SW12
off Belthorn Cres 121 DJ87
Angas Ct, Wey. KT13 153 BQ106
⊖ **Angel** 83 DN68
Angel All, E1
off Whitechapel Rd 84 DT72
Angel Cl, N18 46 DT49
Angel Cor Par, N18
off Fore St 46 DU50
Angel Ct, EC2 197 L8
SW1 199 L3
SW17 120 DF91
Angel Edmonton, N18
off Angel Rd 46 DU50
Angelfield, Houns. TW3 96 CB84
Angel Gate, EC1 196 G2
Angel Hill, Sutt. SM1 140 DB104
Angel Hill Dr, Sutt. SM1 140 DB104
Angelica Cl, West Dr. UB7
off Lovibonds Av 76 BL72
Angelica Dr, E6 87 EN71
Angelica Gdns, Croy. CR0 143 DX102
Angelis Apts, N1
off Graham St 83 DP68
Angel La, E15 85 ED65
Hayes UB3 77 BR71
Angell Pk Gdns, SW9 101 DN83
Angell Rd, SW9 101 DN83
Angell Town Est, SW9
off Overton Rd 101 DN82
Angel Ms, E1 *off Cable St* 84 DU73
N1 196 E1
SW15 *off Roehampton*
High St 119 CU87
Angel Pas, EC4 201 K1
Angel Pl, N18 46 DU50
SE1 201 K4
⇌ **Angel Road** 46 DW50
Angel Rd, N18 46 DV50
Harrow HA1 61 CE58
Thames Ditton KT7 137 CG101
Angel Rd Wks, N18 46 DW50
Angel Southside, EC1
off Goswell Rd 83 DN68
Angel Sq, EC1 196 E1
Angel St, EC1 197 H8
Angel Wk, W6 99 CW77
Angel Way, Rom. RM1 71 FE57
Angerstein La, SE3 104 EF80
Angle Cl, Uxb. UB10 76 BN67
Angle Grn, Dag. RM8 70 EW60
Angle Rd, Grays RM20 109 FX79
Anglers Cl, Rich. TW10
off Locksmeade Rd 117 CJ91
Angler's La, NW5 83 DH65
Anglers Reach, Surb. KT6 137 CK99
Anglesea Av, SE18 105 EP77
Anglesea Ms, SE18
off Anglesea Av 105 EP77
Anglesea Pl, Grav. DA11
off Clive Rd 131 GH86
Anglesea Rd, SE18 105 EP77
Kingston upon Thames
KT1 137 CK98
Orpington BR5 146 EW100
Anglesea Ter, W6
off Wellesley Av 99 CV76
Anglesey Cl, Ashf. TW15 114 BN90
Anglesey Ct Rd, Cars. SM5 158 DG107
Anglesey Dr, Rain. RM13 89 FG70
Anglesey Gdns, Cars. SM5 158 DG107
Anglesey Rd, Enf. EN3 30 DV42
Watford WD19 40 BW50
Anglesmede Cres, Pnr. HA5 60 CA55
Anglesmede Way, Pnr. HA5 60 BZ55
Angles Rd, SW16 121 DL91
Anglia Cl, N17 *off Park La* 46 DV52
Anglia Ct, Dag. RM8
off Spring Cl 70 EX60
Anglia Ho, E14 85 DY72
Anglian Cl, Wat. WD24 24 BW40
Anglian Rd, E11 67 ED62
Anglia Wk, E6 87 EM67
Anglo Rd, E3 85 DZ68
Anglo Way, Red. RH1 184 DG132
Angrave Ct, E8 84 DT67
Angrave Pas, E8
off Haggerston Rd 84 DT67
Angus Cl, Chess. KT9 156 CN106
Angus Dr, Ruis. HA4 60 BW63
Angus Gdns, NW9 42 CR53
Angus Home, Sev. (Cudham)
TN14 179 ER115
Angus Rd, E13 86 EJ69
Angus St, SE14 103 DY80
Anhalt Rd, SW11 100 DE80
Ankerdine Cres, SE18 105 EN80
Ankerwycke Priory, Stai. (Wrays.)
TW19 113 AZ89
Anlaby Rd, Tedd. TW11 117 CE92
Anley Rd, W14 99 CX75
Anmersh Gro, Stan. HA7 41 CK53
Annabel Cl, E14 85 EB72
Anna Cl, E8 84 DT67
Annalee Gdns, S.Ock. RM15 91 FV71
Annalee Rd, S.Ock. RM15 91 FV71
Annandale Gro, Uxb. UB10
off Thorpland Av 59 BQ62
Annandale Rd, SE10 104 EF79
W4 98 CS77
Croydon CR0 142 DU103
Annandale Rd, Sid. DA15 125 ES87
Annan Dr, Cars. SM5 158 DG109
Anna Neagle Cl, E7
off Dames Rd 68 EG63
Annan Way, Rom. RM1 51 FD53
Anne Boleyn's Wk, Kings.T.
KT2 118 CL92
Sutton SM3 157 CX108
Anne Case Ms, N.Mal. KT3
off Sycamore Gro 138 CR97
Anne Compton Ms, SE12 124 EF87
Anne Goodman Ho, E1
off Jubilee St 84 DW72
Anne Heart Cl, Grays (Chaff.Hun.)
RM16 109 FX77
Anne of Cleves Rd, Dart.
DA1 128 FK85
Anners Cl, Egh. TW20 133 BC97
Annesley Av, NW9 62 CR55
Annesley Cl, NW10 62 CS62
Annesley Dr, Croy. CR0 143 DZ104
Annesley Rd, SE3 104 EH81
Annesley Wk, N19 65 DJ61
Annesmere Gdns, SE3
off Highbrook Rd 104 EK83
Anne St, E13 86 EG70
Anne's Wk, Cat. CR3 176 DS120
Annett Cl, Shep. TW17 135 BS98
Annette Cl, Har. HA3
off Spencer Rd 41 CE54
Annette Cres, N1
off Essex Rd 84 DQ66
Annette Rd, N7 65 DM63
Annett Rd, Walt. KT12 135 BU101
Anne Way, Ilf. IG6 49 EQ51
West Molesey KT8 136 CB98
Annie Besant Cl, E3 85 DZ67
Annie Brooks Cl, Stai. TW18 113 BD90
Annie Taylor Ho, E12
off Walton Rd 69 EN63
Annifer Way, S.Ock. RM15 91 FV71
Anningsley Pk, Cher. (Ott.)
KT16 151 BD110
Anning St, EC2 197 N4
Annington Rd, N2 64 DF55
Annis Rd, E9 85 DY65
Ann La, SW10 100 DD80
Ann Moss Way, SE16 202 F6
Ann's Cl, SW1 198 E5
Ann's Pl, E1 197 P7
Ann St, SE18 105 ER77
Annsworthy Av, Th.Hth. CR7
off Grange Pk Rd 142 DR97
Annsworthy Cres, SE25
off Grange Rd 142 DR96
Ansdell Rd, SE15 102 DW82
Ansdell St, W8 100 DB76
Ansdell Ter, W8
off Ansdell St 100 DB76
Ansell Gro, Cars. SM5 140 DG102
Ansell Rd, SW17 120 DE90
Anselm Cl, Croy. CR0
off Park Hill Ri 142 DT104
Anselm Rd, SW6 100 DA79
Pinner HA5 40 BZ52
Ansford Rd, Brom. BR1 123 EC92
Ansleigh Pl, W11 81 CX73
Ansley Cl, S.Croy. CR2 160 DV114
Anslow Gdns, Iver SL0 75 BD68
Anson Cl, Hem.H. (Bov.) HP3 5 AZ27
Kenley CR8 176 DR120
Romford RM7 51 FB54
Anson Ho, E1 *off Shandy St* 85 DY70
Anson Pl, SE28 105 ER75
Anson Rd, N7 65 DJ63
NW2 63 CX64
Anson Ter, Nthlt. UB5 78 CB65
Anson Wk, Nthwd. HA6 39 BQ49
Anstead Dr, Rain. RM13 89 FG68
Anstey Rd, SE15 102 DU83
Anstey Wk, N15 65 DP56
Anstice Cl, W4 98 CS80
Anstridge Path, SE9 125 ER86
Anstridge Rd, SE9 125 ER86
Antelope Av, Grays RM16
off Hogg La 110 GA76
Antelope Rd, SE18 105 EM76
Anthony Cl, NW7 42 CS49
Sevenoaks (Dunt.Grn)
TN13 190 FE121
Watford WD19 40 BW46
Anthony La, Swan. BR8 147 FG95
Anthony Rd, SE25 142 DU100
Borehamwood WD6 26 CM40
Greenford UB6 79 CE68
Welling DA16 106 EU81
Anthonys, Wok. GU21 151 BB112
Anthony St, E1
off Commercial Rd 84 DV72
Anthony Way, N18 47 DX51
Anthorne Cl, Pot.B. EN6 12 DB31
Anthus Ms, Nthwd. HA6 39 BS52
Antigua Cl, SE19
off Salters Hill 122 DR92
Antigua Wk, SE19 122 DR92
Antill Rd, E3 85 DY69
N15 66 DT56
Antill Ter, E1 85 DX72
Antlers Hill, E4 31 EB43
Antoinette Ct, Abb.L. WD5
off Dairy Way 7 BT29
Anton Cres, Sutt. SM1 140 DA104
Antoneys Cl, Pnr. HA5 40 BX54
Antonine Hts, SE1
off Long La 102 DS75
Anton Pl, Wem. HA9 62 CP62
Anton Rd, S.Ock. RM15 91 FV70
Anton St, E8 66 DU64
Antrim Gro, NW3 82 DF65
Antrim Mans, NW3 82 DE65
Antrim Rd, NW3 82 DF65
Antrobus Cl, Sutt. SM1 157 CZ106
Antrobus Rd, W4 98 CQ77
Anvil Cl, SW16 121 DJ94
Hemel Hempstead (Bov.) HP3
off Yew Tree Dr 5 BB28
Anvil Ct, Slou. (Langley) SL3
off Blacksmith Row 93 BA77
Anvil La, Cob. KT11 153 BU114
Anvil Pl, St.Alb. AL2 8 CA26
Anvil Rd, Sun. TW16 135 BU97
Anvil Ter, Dart. DA2
off Pinewood Pl 127 FE89
Anworth Cl, Wdf.Grn. IG8 48 EH51
Anyards Rd, Cob. KT11 153 BV113
Apeldoorn Dr, Wall. SM6 159 DL109
Aperdele Rd, Lthd. KT22 171 CG118
APERFIELD, West. TN16 179 EM117
Aperfield Rd, Erith DA8 107 FF79
Westerham (Bigg.H.)
TN16 178 EL117
Apers Av, Wok. GU22 167 AZ121
Apex Cl, Beck. BR3 143 EB95
Apex Cor, NW7 42 CR49
Apex Ind Est, NW10
off Hythe Rd 81 CT70
Apex Retail Pk, Felt. TW13 116 BZ90
Apex Twr, N.Mal. KT3 138 CS97
Aplin Way, Islw. TW7 97 CE81
Apollo, E14 203 P8
Apollo Av, Brom. BR1
off Rodway Rd 144 EH95
Northwood HA6 39 BU50
Apollo Cl, Horn. RM12 71 FH61
★ **Apollo Hammersmith**,
W6 99 CW78
Apollo Pl, E11 68 EE62
SW10 100 DD80
Woking (St.John's) GU21
off Church Rd 166 AU119
★ **Apollo Thea**, W1 195 M10
★ **Apollo Victoria Thea**,
SW1 199 K7
Apollo Way, SE28
off Broadwater Rd 105 ER76
Apostle Way, Th.Hth. CR7 141 DP96
Apothecary St, EC4 196 F9
Appach Rd, SW2 121 DN86
Apple Blossom Ct, SW8
off Pascal St 101 DK80
Appleby Cl, E4 47 EC51
N15 66 DR57
Twickenham TW2 117 CD89
Appleby Ct, W3
off Newport Rd 98 CQ75
Appleby Dr, Rom. RM3 52 FJ50
Appleby Gdns, Felt. TW14 115 BT88
Appleby Grn, Rom. RM3
off Appleby Dr 52 FJ50
Appleby Rd, E8 84 DU66
E16 86 EF72
Appleby St, E2 84 DT68
Waltham Cross (Chsht)
EN7 14 DT26
Apple Cotts, Hem.H. (Bov.)
HP3 5 BA27
Applecroft, St.Alb. (Park St)
AL2 8 CB28
Appledore Av, Bexh. DA7 107 FC81
Ruislip HA4 59 BV62
Appledore Cl, SW17 120 DF89
Bromley BR2 144 EF99
Edgware HA8 42 CN53
Romford RM3 52 FJ53
Appledore Cres, Sid. DA14 125 ES90
Appledore Way, NW7
off Tavistock Av 43 CX52
Appledown Ri, Couls. CR5 175 DJ115
Applefield, Amer. HP7 20 AW39
Appleford Rd, W10 81 CY70
Apple Garth, Brent. TW8 97 CK77
Applegarth, Croy. (New Adgtn)
CR0 161 EB108
Esher (Clay.) KT10 155 CF106
Applegarth Dr, Dart. DA1 128 FL89
Ilford IG2 69 ET56
Applegarth Ho, Erith DA8 107 FF82
Applegarth Rd, SE28 88 EV74
W14 99 CX76
Applegate, Brwd. CM14 54 FT43
Apple Gro, Chess. KT9 156 CL105
Enfield EN1 30 DS41
Apple Mkt, Kings.T. KT1
off Eden St 137 CK96
Apple Orchard, Swan. BR8 147 FD98
Apple Rd, E11 68 EE62
Appleshaw Cl, Grav. DA11 131 GG92
Appleton Cl, Amer. HP7 20 AV40
Bexleyheath DA7 107 FB82
Appleton Dr, Dart. DA2 127 FH90
Appleton Gdns, N.Mal. KT3 139 CU100
Appleton Rd, SE9 104 EL83
Loughton IG10 33 EP41
Appleton Sq, Mitch. CR4
off Silbury Av 140 DE95
Appleton Way, Horn. RM12 72 FK60
Appletree Av, Uxb. UB8 76 BM71
West Drayton UB7 76 BM71
Appletree Cl, SE20
off Jasmine Gro 142 DV95
Leatherhead KT22 170 CC124
Appletree Gdns, Barn. EN4 28 DE42
Appletree La, Slou. SL3 92 AW76
Apple Tree Rbt, West Dr. UB7 76 BM73
Appletree Wk, Wat. WD25 7 BV34
Apple Tree Yd, SW1 199 L2
Applewood Cl, N20 44 DE46
NW2 63 CV62
Uxbridge (Ickhm) UB10 58 BL63
Applewood Dr, E13 86 EH70
Appold St, EC2 197 M6
Erith DA8 107 FF79
Apprentice Way, E5
off Clarence Rd 66 DV63
Approach, The, NW4 63 CX57
W3 80 CR72
Enfield EN1 30 DV40
Orpington BR6 145 ET103
Potters Bar EN6 11 CZ32
Upminster RM14 72 FP62
Approach Cl, N16
off Cowper Rd 66 DS63
Approach Rd, E2 84 DW68
SW20 139 CW96
Ashford TW15 115 BQ93
Barnet EN4 28 DD42
Edgware HA8 42 CP51
Purley CR8 159 DP112
West Molesey KT8 136 CA99
Aprey Gdns, NW4 63 CW56

★ Place of interest ⇌ Railway station ⊖ London Underground station DLR Docklands Light Railway station Tra Tramlink station H Hospital Riv Pedestrian ferry landing stage

April Cl, W7 79 CE73
Ashtead KT21 172 CM117
Feltham TW13 115 BU90
Orpington BR6 163 ET106
April Glen, SE23 123 DX90
April St, E8 66 DT63
Aprilwood Cl, Add. (Wdhm) KT15 151 BF111
Apsledene, Grav. DA12 off Miskin Way 131 GK93
APSLEY, Hem.H. HP3 6 BK25
⇌ Apsley 6 BL25
Apsley Cl, Har. HA2 60 CC57
★ Apsley Ho, Wellington Mus, W1 198 F4
Apsley Rd, SE25 142 DV98
New Malden KT3 138 CQ97
Apsley Way, NW2 63 CU61
W1 198 G4
Aquarius Business Pk, NW2 63 CU60
Aquarius Way, Nthwd. HA6 39 BU50
★ Aquatic Experience, Brent. TW8 97 CH81
Aquila Cl, Lthd. KT22 172 CL121
Aquila St, NW8 82 DD68
Aquinas St, SE1 200 E3
Arabella Dr, SW15 98 CS84
Arabia Cl, E4 47 ED45
Arabin Rd, SE4 103 DY84
Araglen Av, S.Ock. RM15 91 FV71
Aragon Av, Epsom KT17 157 CV109
Thames Ditton KT7 137 CF99
Aragon Cl, Brom. BR2 145 EM102
Croydon (New Adgtn) CR0 162 EE110
Enfield EN2 29 DM38
Loughton IG10 32 EL44
Romford RM5 51 FB51
Sunbury-on-Thames TW16 115 BT94
Aragon Dr, Ilf. IG6 49 EQ52
Ruislip HA4 60 BX60
Aragon Pl, Mord. SM4 139 CX101
Aragon Rd, Kings.T. KT2 118 CL92
Morden SM4 139 CX100
Aragon Twr, SE8 203 M9
Aragon Wk, W.Byf. (Byfleet) KT14 152 BM113
Aran Ct, Wey. KT13 off Mallards Reach 135 BR103
Arandora Cres, Rom. RM6 70 EV59
Aran Dr, Stan. HA7 41 CJ49
Aran Hts, Ch.St.G. HP8 36 AV49
Aran Ms, N7 off Barnsbury Gro 83 DN66
Arbery Rd, E3 85 DY69
Arbor Cl, Beck. BR3 143 EB96
Arbor Ct, N16 off Lordship Rd 66 DR61
Arborfield Cl, SW2 121 DM88
Slough SL1 92 AS76
Arbor Rd, E4 47 ED48
Arbour Cl, Brwd. CM14 54 FW50
Leatherhead (Fetch.) KT22 171 CF123
Arbour Rd, Enf. EN3 31 DX42
Arbour Sq, E1 85 DX72
Arbour Vw, Amer. HP7 20 AV39
Arbour Way, Horn. RM12 71 FH64
Arbroath Grn, Wat. WD19 39 BU48
Arbroath Rd, SE9 104 EL83
Arbrook Chase, Esher KT10 154 CC107
Arbrook Cl, Orp. BR5 146 EU97
Arbrook La, Esher KT10 154 CC107
Arbury Ter, SE26 off Oaksford Av 122 DV90
Arbuthnot La, Bex. DA5 126 EY86
Arbuthnot Rd, SE14 103 DX82
Arbutus St, E8 84 DS67
Arcade, The, EC2 197 M7
Croydon CR0 off High St 142 DQ104
Romford RM3 off Farnham Rd 52 FK50
Arcade Pl, Rom. RM1 71 FE57
Arcadia Av, N3 44 DA53
Arcadia Caravans, Stai. TW18 134 BH95
Arcadia Cl, Cars. SM5 158 DG105
Arcadian Av, Bex. DA5 126 EY86
Arcadian Cl, Bex. DA5 126 EY86
Arcadian Gdns, N22 45 DM52
Arcadian Pl, SW18 119 CY87
Arcadian Rd, Bex. DA5 126 EY86
Arcadia Shop Cen, W5 79 CK73
Arcadia St, E14 85 EA72
Arcany Rd, S.Ock. RM15 91 FV70
Archangel St, SE16 203 J5
Archates Av, Grays RM16 110 GA76
Archbishops Pl, SW2 121 DM86
Archdale Pl, N.Mal. KT3 138 CP97
Archdale Rd, SE22 122 DT85
Archel Rd, W14 99 CZ79
Archer Cl, Kings L. WD4 6 BM29
Kingston upon Thames KT2 118 CL94
Archer Ho, SW11 off Vicarage Cres 100 DD82
Archer Ms, Hmptn. (Hmptn H.) TW12 off Windmill Rd 116 CC93
Archer Rd, SE25 142 DV98
Orpington BR5 146 EU99
Archers Ct, S.Ock. RM15 91 FV71
Archers Dr, Enf. EN3 30 DW40
Archer Sq, SE14 off Knoyle St 103 DY79
Archer St, W1 195 M10
Archer Ter, West Dr. UB7 off Yew Av 76 BL73
Archer Way, Swan. BR8 147 FF96
Archery Cl, W2 194 C9
Harrow HA3 61 CF55
H Archery Ho, Dart. DA2 128 FP86
Archery Rd, SE9 125 EM85
Archery Steps, W2 off St. Georges Flds 82 DE73
Arches, The, SW6 off Munster Rd 99 CZ82
WC2 200 A2
Harrow HA2 60 CB61
Archibald Ms, W1 198 G1
Archibald Rd, N7 65 DK63
Romford RM3 52 FN53
Archibald St, E3 85 EA69
Archie Cl, West Dr. UB7 94 BN75
Archie St, SE1 201 N5
Arch Rd, Walt. KT12 136 BX104
Arch St, SE1 201 H7
⊖ Archway 65 DJ61
Archway, Rom. RM3 51 FH51
Archway Cl, N19 off Archway Rd 65 DJ61
SW19 120 DB91
W10 81 CX71
Wallington SM6 141 DK104
Archway Mall, N19 off Magdala Av 65 DJ61
Archway Ms, SW15 off Putney Br Rd 99 CY84
Archway Rd, N6 64 DF58
N19 65 DJ60
Archway St, SW13 98 CS83
Arcola St, E8 66 DT64
Arcon Dr, Nthlt. UB5 78 BY70
Arctic St, NW5 off Gillies St 64 DG64
Arcus Rd, Brom. BR1 124 EE93
Ardbeg Rd, SE24 122 DR86
Arden Cl, SE28 88 EX72
Bushey (Bushey Hth) WD23 41 CF45
Harrow HA1 61 CD62
Hemel Hempstead (Bov.) HP3 5 BA28
Arden Ct Gdns, N2 64 DD58
Arden Cres, E14 204 A8
Dagenham RM9 88 EW66
Arden Est, N1 197 M1
Arden Gro, Orp. BR6 163 EP105
Arden Ho, SW9 off Grantham Rd 101 DL82
Arden Ms, E17 67 EB57
Arden Mhor, Pnr. HA5 59 BV56
Arden Rd, N3 63 CY55
W13 79 CJ73
Ardent Cl, SE25 142 DS97
Ardesley Wd, Wey. KT13 153 BS105
Ardfern Av, SW16 141 DN97
Ardfillan Rd, SE6 123 ED88
Ardgowan Rd, SE6 124 EE87
Ardilaun Rd, N5 66 DQ63
Ardingly Cl, Croy. CR0 143 DX104
Ardleigh Cl, Horn. RM11 72 FK55
Ardleigh Ct, Brwd. (Shenf.) CM15 55 FZ45
Ardleigh Gdns, Brwd. (Hutt.) CM13 off Fairview Av 55 GE44
Sutton SM3 140 DA101
ARDLEIGH GREEN, Horn. RM11 72 FJ56
Ardleigh Grn Rd, Horn. RM11 72 FK57
Ardleigh Ho, Bark. IG11 off St. Ann's 87 EQ67
Ardleigh Ms, Ilf. IG1 off Bengal Rd 69 EP62
Ardleigh Rd, E17 47 DZ53
N1 84 DR65
Ardleigh Ter, E17 47 DZ53
Ardley Cl, NW10 62 CS62
SE6 123 DY90
Ruislip HA4 59 BQ59
Ardlui Rd, SE27 122 DQ89
Ardmay Gdns, Surb. KT6 138 CL99
Ardmere Rd, SE13 123 ED86
Ardmore La, Buck.H. IG9 48 EH45
Ardmore Pl, Buck.H. IG9 48 EH45
Ardmore Rd, S.Ock. RM15 91 FV70
Ardoch Rd, SE6 123 ED89
Ardra Rd, N9 47 DX48
Ardrossan Gdns, Wor.Pk. KT4 139 CU104
Ardross Av, Nthwd. HA6 39 BS50
Ardshiel Cl, SW15 off Bemish Rd 99 CX83
Ardwell Av, Ilf. IG6 69 EQ57
Ardwell Rd, SW2 121 DL89
Ardwick Rd, NW2 64 DA63
Tramlink Arena 142 DW99
Arena, The, Enf. EN3 31 DZ38
Arena Shop Pk, N4 off Green Las 65 DP58
Arena Sq, Wem. HA9 off Engineers Way 62 CN63
Arewater Grn, Loug. IG10 33 EM39
Argali Ho, Erith DA18 off Kale Rd 106 EY76
Argall Av, E10 67 DX59
Argall Way, E10 67 DX60
Argenta Way, NW10 80 CP66
Argent Cl, Egh. TW20 off Holbrook Meadow 113 BC93
Argent Ct, Grays RM17 110 GA80
Argent St, Grays RM17 110 FY79
Argent Way, Wal.Cr. (Chshst) EN7 14 DR26
Argles Cl, Green. DA9 off Cowley Av 129 FU85
Argon Ms, SW6 100 DA80
Argon Rd, N18 46 DW50
Argosy Gdns, Stai. TW18 113 BF93
Argosy La, Stai. (Stanw.) TW19 114 BK87
Argus Cl, Rom. RM7 51 FB53
Argus Way, Nthlt. UB5 78 BY69
Argyle Av, Houns. TW3 116 CA86
Argyle Cl, W13 79 CG70
Argyle Gdns, Upmin. RM14 73 FR61
Argyle Pas, N17 46 DT53
Argyle Pl, W6 99 CV77
Argyle Rd, E1 85 DX70
E15 68 EE63
E16 86 EJ72
N12 44 DA50
N17 46 DU53
N18 46 DU49
W13 79 CG71
Barnet EN5 27 CW42
Greenford UB6 79 CF69
Harrow HA2 60 CB58
Hounslow TW3 116 CB85
Ilford IG1 69 EN61
Sevenoaks TN13 191 FH125
Teddington TW11 117 CE92
Argyle Sq, WC1 196 A2
Argyle St, WC1 195 P2
Argyle Wk, WC1 196 A3
Argyle Way, SE16 102 DU78
Argyll Av, Sthl. UB1 78 CB74
Argyll Cl, SW9 off Dalyell Rd 101 DM83
Argyll Gdns, Edg. HA8 42 CP54
Argyll Rd, SE18 105 EQ76
W8 100 DA75
Grays RM17 110 GA78
Argyll St, W1 195 K9
Aria Ho, WC2 off Newton St 83 DL72
Arica Ho, SE16 202 E6
Arica Rd, SE4 103 DY84
Ariel Cl, Grav. DA12 131 GM91
Ariel Rd, NW6 82 DA65
Ariel Way, W12 81 CW74
Hounslow TW4 95 BV83
Arisdale Av, S.Ock. RM15 91 FV71
Aristotle Rd, SW4 101 DK83
Ark Av, Grays RM16 110 GA76
Arkell Gro, SE19 121 DP94
Arkindale Rd, SE6 123 EC90
Arklay Cl, Uxb. UB8 76 BM70
ARKLEY, Barn. EN5 27 CU43
Arkley Cres, E17 67 DZ57
Arkley Dr, Barn. EN5 27 CU42
Arkley La, Barn. EN5 27 CU41
Arkley Pk, Barn. EN5 26 CR44
Arkley Rd, E17 67 DZ57
Arkley Vw, Barn. EN5 27 CV42
Arklow Ct, Rick. (Chorl.) WD3 off Station App 21 BD42
Arklow Ho, SE17 off Albany Rd 102 DR79
Arklow Ms, Surb. KT6 off Vale Rd S 138 CL103
Arklow Rd, SE14 103 DZ79
Arkwright Rd, NW3 64 DC64
Slough (Colnbr.) SL3 93 BE82
South Croydon CR2 160 DT110
Tilbury RM18 111 GG82
Arlesey Cl, SW15 119 CY85
Arlesford Rd, SW9 101 DL83
Arlingford Rd, SW2 121 DN85
Arlingham Ms, Wal.Abb. EN9 off Sun St 15 EC33
Arlington, N12 44 DA48
Arlington Av, N1 84 DQ68
Arlington Bldg, E3 off Fairfield Rd 85 EA68
Arlington Cl, SE13 123 ED85
Sidcup DA15 125 ES87
Sutton SM1 140 DA103
Twickenham TW1 117 CJ86
Arlington Ct, W3 off Mill Hill Rd 98 CP75
Hayes UB3 off Shepiston La 95 BR78
Reigate RH2 off Oakfield Dr 184 DB132
Arlington Cres, Wal.Cr. EN8 15 DY34
Arlington Dr, Cars. SM5 140 DF103
Ruislip HA4 59 BR58
Arlington Gdns, W4 98 CQ78
Ilford IG1 69 EN60
Romford RM3 52 FL53
Arlington Grn, NW7 43 CX52
Arlington Lo, SW2 101 DM84
Weybridge KT13 153 BP105
Arlington Ms, Twick. TW1 off Arlington Rd 117 CJ86
Arlington Pl, SE10 off Greenwich S St 103 EC80
Arlington Rd, N14 45 DH47
NW1 83 DH67
W13 79 CH72
Ashford TW15 114 BM92
Richmond TW10 117 CK89
Surbiton KT6 137 CK100
Teddington TW11 117 CF91
Twickenham TW1 117 CJ86
Woodford Green IG8 48 EG53
Arlington Sq, N1 84 DQ67
Arlington St, SW1 199 K2
Arlington Way, EC1 196 E2
Arliss Way, Nthlt. UB5 78 BW67
Arlow Rd, N21 45 DN46
Armada Ct, SE8 off Watergate St 103 EA79
Grays RM16 off Hogg La 110 GA76
Armadale Cl, N17 66 DV56
Armadale Rd, SW6 100 DA80
Feltham TW14 115 BU85
Woking GU21 166 AU117
Armada Way, E6 87 EP71
Armagh Rd, E3 85 DZ67
Armand Cl, Wat. WD17 23 BT38
Armfield Cl, W.Mol. KT8 136 BZ99
Armfield Cres, Mitch. CR4 140 DF96
Armfield Rd, Enf. EN2 30 DR39
Arminger Rd, W12 81 CV74
Armistice Gdns, SE25 off Penge Rd 142 DU97
Armitage Cl, Rick. (Loud.) WD3 22 BK42
Armitage Rd, NW11 63 CZ60
SE10 205 K10
Armor Rd, Purf. RM19 109 FR77
Armour Cl, N7 off Roman Way 83 DM65
Armoury Dr, Grav. DA12 131 GJ87
Armoury Rd, SE8 103 EB82
Armoury Way, SW18 120 DA85
Armstead Wk, Dag. RM10 88 FA66
Armstrong Av, Wdf.Grn. IG8 48 EE51
Armstrong Cl, E6 off Porter Rd 87 EM72
Borehamwood WD6 26 CQ41
Bromley BR1 144 EL97
Dagenham RM8 off Palmer Rd 70 EX60
Pinner HA5 59 BU58
St. Albans (Lon.Col.) AL2 10 CL27
Sevenoaks (Halst.) TN14 181 FB115
Walton-on-Thames KT12 off Sunbury La 135 BU100
Armstrong Cres, Barn. EN4 28 DD41
Armstrong Gdns, Rad. (Shenley) WD7 10 CL32
Armstrong Rd, SE18 105 EQ76
SW7 100 DD76
W3 81 CT74
Egham (Eng.Grn) TW20 112 AW93
Armstrong Rd, Felt. TW13 116 BY92
Armstrong Way, Sthl. UB2 96 CB75
Armytage Rd, Houns. TW5 96 BX80
Arnal Cres, SW18 119 CY87
Arncliffe Cl, N11 44 DG51
Arncroft Ct, Bark. IG11 off Renwick Rd 88 EV69
Arndale Wk, SW18 off Garratt La 120 DB85
Arndale Way, Egh. TW20 off Church Rd 113 BA92
Arne Gro, Orp. BR6 145 ET104
Arne Ho, SE11 200 B10
Arne St, WC2 196 A9
Arnett Cl, Rick. WD3 22 BG44
Arnett Sq, E4 47 DZ51
Arnett Way, Rick. WD3 22 BG44
Arne Wk, SE3 104 EF84
Arneways Av, Rom. RM6 70 EX55
Arneway St, SW1 199 N7
Arnewood Cl, SW15 119 CU88
Leatherhead (Oxshott) KT22 154 CB113
Arney's La, Mitch. CR4 140 DG100
Arngask Rd, SE6 123 ED87
Arnhem Av, S.Ock. (Aveley) RM15 90 FQ74
Arnhem Dr, Croy. (New Adgtn) CR0 161 ED111
Arnhem Pl, E14 203 P7
Arnhem Way, SE22 off East Dulwich Gro 122 DS85
Arnhem Wf, E14 off Arnhem Pl 103 EA76
Arnison Rd, E.Mol. KT8 137 CD98
Arnold Av E, Enf. EN3 31 EA38
Arnold Av W, Enf. EN3 31 DZ38
Arnold Bennett Way, N8 off Burghley Rd 65 DN55
Arnold Circ, E2 197 P3
Arnold Cl, Har. HA3 62 CM59
Arnold Cres, Islw. TW7 117 CD85
Arnold Dr, Chess. KT9 155 CK107
Arnold Est, SE1 202 A5
Arnold Gdns, N13 45 DP50
Arnold Pl, Til. RM18 111 GJ81
Arnold Rd, E3 85 EA69
N15 66 DT55
SW17 120 DF94
Dagenham RM9, RM10 88 EZ66
Gravesend DA12 131 GJ89
Northolt UB5 78 BX65
Staines TW18 114 BJ94
Waltham Abbey EN9 31 EC36
Woking GU21 167 BB116
Arnolds Av, Brwd. (Hutt.) CM13 55 GC43
Arnolds Cl, Brwd. (Hutt.) CM13 55 GC43
Arnolds Fm La, Brwd. (Mtnsg) CM13 55 GE41
Arnolds La, Dart. (Sutt.H.) DA4 128 FM93
⊖ Arnos Grove 45 DJ49
Arnos Gro, N14 45 DK49
Arnos Rd, N11 45 DJ50
Arnott Cl, SE28 off Applegarth Rd 88 EW73
W4 off Fishers La 98 CR77
Arnould Av, SE5 102 DR84
Arnsberg Way, Bexh. DA7 106 FA84
Arnside Gdns, Wem. HA9 61 CK60
Arnside Rd, Bexh. DA7 106 FA81
Arnside St, SE17 102 DQ79
Arnulf St, SE6 123 EB91
Arnulls Rd, SW16 121 DN93
Arodene Rd, SW2 121 DM86
Arosa Rd, Twick. TW1 117 CK86
Arpley Sq, SE20 off High St 122 DW94
Arragon Gdns, SW16 121 DL94
West Wickham BR4 143 EB104
Arragon Rd, E6 86 EK67
SW18 120 DB88
Twickenham TW1 117 CG87
Arran Cl, Erith DA8 107 FD79
Wallington SM6 159 DH105
Arran Dr, E12 68 EK60
Arran Grn, Wat. WD19 off Prestwick Rd 40 BX49
Arran Ms, W5 80 CM74
Arranmore Ct, Bushey WD23 off Bushey Hall Rd 24 BY42
Arran Rd, SE6 123 EB89
Arran Wk, N1 84 DQ66
Arran Way, Esher KT10 136 CB103
Arras Av, Mord. SM4 140 DC99
Arreton Mead, Wok. (Horsell) GU21 150 AY114
Arrol Ho, SE1 201 H7
Arrol Rd, Beck. BR3 142 DW97
Arrow Rd, E3 85 EB69
Arrowscout Wk, Nthlt. UB5 off Argus Way 78 BY69
Arrowsmith Cl, Chig. IG7 49 ET50
Arrowsmith Ho, SE11 200 B10
Arrowsmith Path, Chig. IG7 49 ET50
Arrowsmith Rd, Chig. IG7 49 ES50
Loughton IG10 32 EL41
⊖ Arsenal 65 DN62
★ Arsenal FC, N5 65 DN63
Arsenal Rd, SE9 105 EM82
Arsenal Way, SE18 105 EQ76
Artemis Cl, Grav. DA12 131 GL87
Arterberry Rd, SW20 119 CW94
Arterial Av, Rain. RM13 89 FH70
Arterial Rd N Stifford, Grays RM17 110 FY75
Arterial Rd Purfleet, Purf. RM19 108 FN76
Arterial Rd W Thurrock, Grays RM16, RM20 109 FU76
Artesian Cl, NW10 80 CR66
Hornchurch RM11 71 FF58
Artesian Gro, Barn. EN5 28 DC41
Artesian Rd, W2 82 DA72
Artesian Wk, E11 68 EE62
Arthingworth St, E15 86 EE67
Arthur Ct, SW11 off Charlotte Despard Av 100 DG81
W2 off Queensway 82 DB72
Arthurdon Rd, SE4 123 EA85
Arthur Gro, SE18 105 EQ77
Arthur Henderson Ho, SW6 99 CZ82
Arthur Horsley Wk, E7 off Magpie Cl 68 EF64
★ Arthur Jacob Nature Reserve, Slou. SL3 93 BC83
Arthur Newton Ho, SW11 off Lavender Rd 100 DD83
Arthur Rd, E6 87 EM68
N7 65 DM63
N9 46 DT47
SW19 120 DA90
Kingston upon Thames KT2 118 CN94
New Malden KT3 139 CV99
Romford RM6 70 EW59
Westerham (Bigg.H.) TN16 178 EJ115
Arthur's Br Rd, Wok. GU21 166 AW117
Arthur St, EC4 201 L1
Bushey WD23 24 BX42
Erith DA8 107 FF80
Gravesend DA11 131 GG87
Grays RM17 110 GC79
Arthur St W, Grav. DA11 131 GG87
Arthur Toft Ho, Grays RM17 off New Rd 110 GB79
Arthur Walls Ho, E12 off Grantham Rd 69 EN62
Artichoke Dell, Rick. (Chorl.) WD3 21 BE43
Artichoke Hill, E1 202 D1
Artichoke Pl, SE5 off Camberwell Ch St 102 DR81
Artillery Cl, Ilf. IG2 off Horns Rd 69 EQ58
Artillery La, E1 197 N7
W12 81 CU72
Artillery Mans, SW1 off Victoria St 101 DK76
Artillery Pas, E1 197 N7
Artillery Pl, SE18 105 EM78
SW1 199 M7
Harrow HA3 off Chicheley Rd 40 CC52
Artillery Row, SW1 199 M7
Gravesend DA12 131 GJ87
Artington Cl, Orp. BR6 163 EQ105
Artisan Cl, E6 off Ferndale St 87 EP73
Artizan St, E1 197 N8
Arundel Av, Epsom KT17 157 CV110
Morden SM4 139 CZ98
South Croydon CR2 160 DU110
Arundel Cl, E15 68 EE63
SW11 120 DE85
Bexley DA5 126 EZ86
Croydon CR0 141 DP104
Hampton (Hmptn H.) TW12 116 CB92
Waltham Cross (Chsht) EN8 14 DW29
Arundel Ct, N12 44 DE51
Harrow HA2 60 CA63
Slough SL3 92 AX77
Arundel Dr, Borwd. WD6 26 CQ43
Harrow HA2 60 BZ63
Orpington BR6 164 EV106
Woodford Green IG8 48 EG52
Arundel Gdns, N21 45 DN46
W11 81 CZ73
Edgware HA8 42 CR52
Ilford IG3 70 EU61
Arundel Gt Ct, WC2 196 C10
Arundel Gro, N16 66 DS64
Arundel Pl, N1 83 DN65
Arundel Rd, Abb.L. WD5 7 BU32
Barnet EN4 28 DE41
Croydon CR0 142 DR100
Dartford DA1 108 FJ84
Hounslow TW4 96 BW83
Kingston upon Thames KT1 138 CP96
Romford RM3 52 FM53
Sutton SM2 157 CZ108
Uxbridge UB8 76 BH68
Arundel Sq, N7 83 DN65
Arundel St, WC2 196 C10
Arundel Ter, SW13 99 CV79
Arvon Rd, N5 65 DN64
Asbaston Ter, Ilf. IG1 off Buttsbury Rd 69 EQ64
Ascalon St, SW8 101 DJ80
Ascension Rd, Rom. RM5 51 FC51
Ascham Dr, E4 off Rushcroft Rd 47 EB52
Ascham End, E17 47 DY53
Ascham St, NW5 65 DJ64
Aschurch Rd, Croy. CR0 142 DT101
Ascot Cl, Borwd. (Els.) WD6 26 CN43
Ilford IG6 49 ES51
Northolt UB5 60 CA64
Ascot Gdns, Enf. EN3 30 DW37
Hornchurch RM12 72 FL63
Southall UB1 78 BZ71
Ascot Ms, Wall. SM6 159 DJ109
Ascot Rd, E6 87 EM69
N15 66 DR57
N18 46 DU49
SW17 120 DG93
Feltham TW14 114 BN88
Gravesend DA12 131 GH90
Orpington BR5 145 ET98
Watford WD18 23 BS43
Ascott Av, W5 98 CL75
Ashanti Ms, E8 off Lower Clapton Rd 66 DV64
Ashbeam Cl, Brwd. (Gt Warley) CM13 53 FW51
Ashbourne, St.Alb. AL2 8 BZ31
Ashbourne Av, E18 68 EH56
N20 44 DF47
NW11 63 CZ57
Bexleyheath DA7 106 EY80
Harrow HA2 61 CD61
Ashbourne Cl, N12 44 DB49
W5 80 CN71
Coulsdon CR5 175 DJ118
Ashbourne Ct, E5 off Daubeney Rd 67 DY63
Ashbourne Gro, NW7 42 CR50
SE22 122 DT85
W4 98 CS78
Ashbourne Par, W5 off Ashbourne Rd 80 CM70
Ashbourne Ri, Orp. BR6 163 ER105

★ Place of interest ⇌ Railway station ⊖ London Underground station DLR Docklands Light Railway station Tramlink Tramlink station H Hospital RIV Pedestrian ferry landing stage

Ashbourne Rd, W5 . . . . .80 CM71
Mitcham CR4 . . . . .120 DG93
Romford RM3 . . . . .52 FJ49
Ashbourne Sq, Nthwd. HA6 . .39 BS51
Ashbourne Ter, SW19 . . . . . .120 DA94
Ashbourne Way, NW11
off Ashbourne Av 63 CZ57
Ashbridge Rd, E11 . . . . .68 EE59
Ashbridge St, NW8 . . . . .194 B5
Ashbrook Rd, N19 . . . . .65 DK60
Dagenham RM10 . . . . .71 FB62
Windsor (Old Wind.) SL4 . .112 AV87
Ashburn Gdns, SW7 . . . . . . .100 DC77
Ashburnham Av, Har. HA1 . . .61 CF58
Ashburnham Cl, N2 . . . . .64 DD55
Sevenoaks TN13
off Fiennes Way 191 FJ127
Watford WD19
off Ashburnham Dr 39 BU48
Ashburnham Dr, Wat. WD19 . .39 BU48
Ashburnham Gdns, Har. HA1 .61 CF58
Upminster RM14 . . . . .72 FP60
Ashburnham Gro, SE10 . . . .103 EB80
Ashburnham Pk, Esher KT10 .154 CC105
Ashburnham Pl, SE10 . . . . . .103 EB80
Ashburnham Retreat, SE10 .103 EB80
Ashburnham Rd, NW10 . . . . .81 CW69
SW10 . . . . .100 DC80
Belvedere DA17 . . . . .107 FC77
Richmond TW10 . . . . .117 CH90
Ashburnham Twr, SW10
off World's End Est 100 DD80
Ashburn Pl, SW7 . . . . .100 DC77
Ashburton Av, Croy. CR0 . . .142 DV102
Ilford IG3 . . . . .69 ES63
Ashburton Cl, Croy. CR0 . . . .142 DU102
Ashburton Ct, Pnr. HA5 . . . . .60 BX55
Ashburton Gdns, Croy. CR0 .142 DU103
Ashburton Rd, E16 . . . . .86 EG72
Croydon CR0 . . . . .142 DU102
Ruislip HA4 . . . . .59 BU61
Ashburton Ter, E13
off Grasmere Rd 86 EG68
Ashbury Dr, Uxb. UB10 . . . . .59 BP61
Ashbury Gdns, Rom. RM6 . . .70 EX57
Ashbury Pl, SW19 . . . . .120 DC93
Ashbury Rd, SW11 . . . . .100 DF83
Ashby Av, Chess. KT9 . . . . . .156 CN107
Ashby Cl, Horn. RM11
off Holme Rd 72 FN60
Ashby Gro, N1 . . . . .84 DQ66
Ashby Ms, SE4 . . . . .103 DZ82
SW2 off Prague Pl 121 DL85
Ashby Rd, N15 . . . . .66 DU57
SE4 . . . . .103 DZ82
Watford WD24 . . . . .23 BU38
Ashby St, EC1 . . . . .196 G3
Ashby Wk, Croy. CR0 . . . . .142 DQ100
Ashby Way, West Dr. UB7 . . .94 BN80
Ashchurch Gro, W12 . . . . .99 CU75
Ashchurch Pk Vil, W12 . . . . .99 CU76
Ashchurch Ter, W12 . . . . .99 CU76
Ash Cl, SE20 . . . . .142 DW96
Abbots Langley WD5 . . . . . . .7 BR32
Brentwood (Pilg.Hat.)
CM15 . . . . .54 FT43
Carshalton SM5 . . . . .140 DF103
Edgware HA8 . . . . .42 CQ49
Hatfield AL9 . . . . .12 DA25
New Malden KT3 . . . . .138 CR96
Orpington BR5 . . . . .145 ER99
Redhill (S.Merst.) RH1 . . . . .185 DJ130
Romford RM5 . . . . .51 FB52
Sidcup DA14 . . . . .126 EV90
Slough SL3 . . . . .93 BB76
Stanmore HA7 . . . . .41 CG51
Swanley BR8 . . . . .147 FC96
Uxbridge (Hare.) UB9 . . . . . .38 BK53
Watford WD25 . . . . .23 BV35
Woking GU22 . . . . .166 AY120
Woking (Pyrford) GU22 . . .168 BG115
Ashcombe Av, Surb. KT6 . . .137 CK101
Ashcombe Gdns, Edg. HA8 . .42 CN49
Ashcombe Ho, Enf. EN3 . . . . .31 DX41
Ashcombe Pk, NW2 . . . . .62 CS62
Ashcombe Rd, SW19 . . . . . .120 DA92
Carshalton SM5 . . . . .158 DG107
Redhill (Merst.) RH1 . . . . . .185 DJ127
Ashcombe Sq, N.Mal. KT3 . .138 CQ97
Ashcombe St, SW6 . . . . . . .100 DB82
Ashcombe Ter, Tad. KT20 . . .173 CV120
Ash Copse, St.Alb. (Brick.Wd)
AL2 . . . . .8 BZ31
Ash Ct, Epsom KT19 . . . . . .156 CQ105
Ashcroft, Pnr. HA5 . . . . .40 CA51
Ashcroft Av, Sid. DA15 . . . . .126 EU86
Ashcroft Ct, N20
off Oakleigh Rd N 44 DD47
Ashcroft Cres, Sid. DA15 . . .126 EU86
Ashcroft Dr, Uxb. (Denh.)
UB9 . . . . .57 BF58
Ashcroft Pk, Cob. KT11 . . . .154 BY112
Ashcroft Ri, Couls. CR5 . . . .175 DL116
Ashcroft Rd, E3 . . . . .85 DY69
Chessington KT9 . . . . .138 CM104
Ashcroft Sq, W6 off King St . .99 CW77
Ashdale Cl, Stai. TW19 . . . . .114 BL89
Twickenham TW2 . . . . .116 CC87
Ashdale Gro, Stan. HA7 . . . . .41 CF51
Ashdale Rd, SE12 . . . . .124 EH88
Ashdale Way, Twick. TW2
off Ashdale Cl 116 CC87
Ashdene, SE15 . . . . .102 DV81
Pinner HA5 . . . . .60 BW55
Ashdene Cl, Ashf. TW15 . . . .115 BQ94
Ashdon Cl, Brwd. (Hutt.) CM13
off Poplar Dr 55 GC44
South Ockendon RM15
off Afton Dr 91 FV72
Woodford Green IG8 . . . . . . .48 EH51
Ashdon Rd, NW10 . . . . .80 CS67
Bushey WD23 . . . . .24 BX41
Ashdown Cl, Beck. BR3 . . . .143 EB96
Bexley DA5 . . . . .127 FC87
Ashdown Cres, NW5
off Queen's Cres 64 DG64
Waltham Cross (Chsht)
EN8 . . . . .15 DY28
Ashdown Dr, Borwd. WD6 . . .26 CM40
Ashdown Gdns, S.Croy.
CR2 . . . . .176 DV115
Ashdown Pl, T.Ditt. KT7 . . . .137 CG100
Ashdown Rd, Enf. EN3 . . . . . .30 DW41
Ashdown Rd, Epsom KT17 . .157 CT113
Kingston upon Thames
KT1 . . . . .138 CL96
Uxbridge UB10 . . . . .76 BN68
Ashdown Wk, E14 . . . . .204 A8
Romford RM7 . . . . .51 FB54
Ashdown Way, SW17 . . . . . .120 DG89
Ashen, E6 off Downings 87 EN72
Ashen Cross, Slou. SL3 . . . . .75 BB71
Ashenden Rd, E5 . . . . .67 DX64
Ashen Dr, Dart. DA1 . . . . . . .127 FG86
Ashen Gro, SW19 . . . . .120 DA90
Ashentree Ct, EC4 . . . . .196 E9
Ashen Vale, S.Croy. CR2 . . .161 DX109
Asher Loftus Way, N11 . . . . . .44 DF51
Asher Way, E1 . . . . .202 C2
Ashfield Av, Bushey WD23 . . .24 CB44
Feltham TW13 . . . . .115 BV88
Ashfield Cl, Beck. BR3 . . . . .123 EA94
Richmond TW10 . . . . .118 CL88
Ashfield La, Chis. BR7 . . . . .125 EQ93
Ashfield Par, N14 . . . . .45 DK46
Ashfield Rd, N4 . . . . .66 DQ58
N14 . . . . .45 DJ48
W3 .81 CT74
Ashfields, Loug. IG10 . . . . . . .33 EM40
Reigate RH2 . . . . .184 DB132
Watford WD25 . . . . .23 BT35
Ashfield St, E1 . . . . .84 DV71
Ashfield Yd, E1
off Ashfield St 84 DW71
ASHFORD, TW15 . . . . .114 BM92
⇌ Ashford 114 BL91
Ashford Av, N8 . . . . .65 DL56
Ashford TW15 . . . . .115 BP93
Brentwood CM14 . . . . .54 FV48
Hayes UB4 . . . . .78 BX72
Ashford Cl, E17 . . . . .67 DZ58
Ashford TW15 . . . . .114 BL91
Ashford Cres, Ashf. TW15 . . .114 BL90
Enfield EN3 . . . . .30 DW40
Ashford Gdns, Cob. KT11 . . .170 BX116
Ashford Grn, Wat. WD19 . . . . .40 BX50
H Ashford Hosp, Ashf.
TW15 . . . . .114 BL89
Ashford Ind Est, Ashf. TW15 .115 BQ91
Ashford Ms, N17 . . . . .46 DU53
Ashford Rd, E6 . . . . .87 EN65
E18 . . . . .48 EH54
NW2 . . . . .63 CX63
Ashford TW15 . . . . .115 BQ94
Feltham TW13 . . . . .115 BT90
Iver SL0 . . . . .75 BC66
Staines TW18 . . . . .134 BK95
Ashford St, N1 . . . . .197 M2
Ash Grn, Uxb. (Denh.) UB9 . . .76 BH65
Ash Gro, E8 . . . . .84 DV67
N13 . . . . .46 DQ48
NW2 . . . . .63 CX63
SE20 . . . . .142 DW96
W5 . . . . .98 CL75
Enfield EN1 . . . . .46 DS45
Feltham TW14 . . . . .115 BS88
Hayes UB3 . . . . .77 BR73
Hounslow TW5 . . . . .96 BX81
Slough (Stoke P.) SL2 . . . . . .74 AT66
Southall UB1 . . . . .78 CA71
Staines TW18 . . . . .114 BJ93
Uxbridge (Hare.) UB9 . . . . . .38 BK53
Wembley HA0 . . . . .61 CG63
West Drayton UB7 . . . . .76 BM73
West Wickham BR4 . . . . . .143 EC103
Ashgrove Rd, Ashf. TW15 . . .115 BQ92
Bromley BR1 . . . . .123 ED93
Ilford IG3 . . . . .69 ET60
Sevenoaks TN13 . . . . .190 FG127
Ash Hill Cl, Bushey WD23 . . . .40 CB46
Ash Hill Dr, Pnr. HA5 . . . . . . .60 BW55
Ash Ho, SE1
off Longfield Est 102 DT77
Ashingdon Cl, E4 . . . . .47 EC48
Ashington Ho, E1
off Barnsley St 84 DV70
Ashington Rd, SW6 . . . . .99 CZ82
Ash Island, E.Mol. KT8 . . . . .137 CD97
Ashlake Rd, SW16 . . . . .121 DL91
Ashland Pl, W1 . . . . .194 F6
Ash La, Horn. RM11
off Southend Arterial Rd . .72 FN56
Romford RM1 . . . . .51 FG51
Ashlar Pl, SE18
off Masons Hill 105 EP77
Ashlea Rd, Ger.Cr. (Chal.St.P.)
SL9 . . . . .36 AX54
Ashleigh Av, Egh. TW20 . . . .113 BC94
Ashleigh Cl, Amer. HP7 . . . . .20 AS39
Ashleigh Ct, Wal.Abb. EN9
off Lamplighters Cl 16 EG34
Ashleigh Gdns, Sutt. SM1 . .140 DB103
Upminster RM14 . . . . .73 FR62
Ashleigh Pt, SE23
off Dacres Rd 123 DX90
Ashleigh Rd, SE20 . . . . .142 DV97
SW14 . . . . .98 CS83
Ashley Av, Epsom KT18 . . . .156 CR113
Ilford IG6 . . . . .49 EP54
Morden SM4 . . . . .140 DA99
Ashley Cen, Epsom KT18 . . .156 CR113
Ashley Cl, NW4 . . . . .43 CW54
Pinner HA5 . . . . .39 BV54
Sevenoaks TN13 . . . . .191 FH124
Walton-on-Thames KT12 . .135 BT102
Ashley Ct, Epsom KT18 . . . .156 CR113
Woking GU21 . . . . .166 AT118
Ashley Cres, N22 . . . . .45 DN54
SW11 . . . . .100 DG83
Ashley Dr, Bans. SM7 . . . . . .158 DA114
Borehamwood WD6 . . . . . . .26 CQ43
Isleworth TW7 . . . . .97 CE79
Twickenham TW2 . . . . .116 CB87
Walton-on-Thames KT12 . .135 BU104
Ashley Gdns, N13 . . . . .46 DQ49
SW1 . . . . .199 L7
Orpington BR6 . . . . .163 ES106
Richmond TW10 . . . . .117 CK90
Wembley HA9 . . . . .62 CL61
Ashley Gro, Loug. IG10
off Staples Rd 32 EL41
Ashley La, NW4 . . . . .43 CW54
Croydon CR0 . . . . .159 DP105
ASHLEY PARK, Walt. KT12 . . .135 BT104
Ashley Pk Av, Walt. KT12 . . .135 BT103
Ashley Pk Cres, Walt. KT12 . .135 BT102
Ashley Pk Rd, Walt. KT12 . . .135 BU103
Ashley Pl, SW1 . . . . .199 K7
Ashley Ri, Walt. KT12 . . . . . .153 BU105
Ashley Rd, E4 . . . . .47 EA50
E7 .86 EJ66
N17 . . . . .66 DU55
N19 . . . . .65 DL60
SW19 . . . . .120 DB93
Enfield EN3 . . . . .30 DW40
Epsom KT18 . . . . .156 CR114
Hampton TW12 . . . . .136 CA95
Richmond TW9
off Jocelyn Rd 98 CL83
Sevenoaks TN13 . . . . .191 FH123
Thames Ditton KT7 . . . . . . .137 CF100
Thornton Heath CR7 . . . . . .141 DM98
Uxbridge UB8 . . . . .76 BH68
Walton-on-Thames KT12 . .135 BU102
Woking GU21 . . . . .166 AT118
Ashleys, Rick. WD3 . . . . .37 BF45
Ashley Sq, Epsom KT18 . . . .156 CR113
Ashley Wk, NW7 . . . . .43 CW52
Ashling Rd, Croy. CR0 . . . . .142 DU102
Ashlin Rd, E15 . . . . .67 ED63
Ashlone Rd, SW15 . . . . .99 CW83
Ashlyn Cl, Bushey WD23 . . . .24 BY42
Ashlyn Gro, Horn. RM11 . . . . .72 FK55
Ashlyns Pk, Cob. KT11 . . . . .154 BY113
Ashlyns Rd, Epp. CM16 . . . . .17 ET30
Ashlyns Way, Chess. KT9 . . .155 CK107
Ashmead, N14 . . . . .29 DJ43
Ashmead Dr, Uxb. (Denh.)
UB9 . . . . .58 BG61
Ashmead Gate, Brom. BR1 . .144 EJ95
Ashmead Ho, E9
off Kingsmead Way 67 DY64
Ashmead La, Uxb. (Denh.)
UB9 . . . . .58 BG61
Ashmead Rd, SE8 . . . . .103 EA82
Feltham TW14 . . . . .115 BU88
Ashmeads Ct, Rad. (Shenley)
WD7 . . . . .9 CK33
Ashmere Av, Beck. BR3 . . . .143 ED96
Ashmere Cl, Sutt. SM3 . . . . .157 CW106
Ashmere Gro, SW2 . . . . . . .101 DL84
Ash Ms, Epsom KT18 . . . . . .156 CS113
Ashmill St, NW1 . . . . .194 B6
Ashmole Pl, SW8 . . . . .101 DM79
Ashmole St, SW8 . . . . .101 DM79
Ashmore Cl, SE15 . . . . .102 DT80
Ashmore Ct, Houns. TW5
off Wheatlands 96 CA79
Ashmore Gdns, Grav. (Nthflt)
DA11 . . . . .130 GD91
Ashmore Gro, Well. DA16 . . .105 ER83
Ashmore La, Kes. BR2 . . . . .162 EH111
Ashmore Rd, W9 . . . . .81 CZ70
Ashmount Est, N19
off Ashmount Rd 65 DK59
Ashmount Rd, N15 . . . . .66 DT57
N19 . . . . .65 DJ59
Ashmount Ter, W5
off Murray Rd 97 CK77
Ashmour Gdns, Rom. RM1 . . .51 FD54
Ashneal Gdns, Har. HA1 . . . . .61 CD62
Ashness Gdns, Grnf. UB6 . . .79 CH65
Ashness Rd, SW11 . . . . .120 DF85
Ash Platt, The, Sev. (Seal)
TN14,TN15 . . . . .191 FL121
Ash Platt Rd, Sev. (Seal)
TN15 . . . . .191 FL121
Ash Ride, Enf. EN2 . . . . .29 DN35
Ashridge Cl, Har. HA3 . . . . . .61 CJ58
Hemel Hempstead (Bov.)
HP3 . . . . .5 BA28
Ashridge Cres, SE18 . . . . . . .105 EQ80
Ashridge Dr, St.Alb. (Brick.Wd)
AL2 . . . . .8 BY30
Watford WD19 . . . . .40 BW50
Ashridge Gdns, N13 . . . . . . .45 DK50
Pinner HA5 . . . . .60 BY56
Ashridge Rd, Chesh. HP5 . . . . .4 AW31
Ashridge Way, Mord. SM4 . . .139 CZ97
Sunbury-on-Thames
TW16 . . . . .115 BU93
Ash Rd, E15 . . . . .68 EE64
Croydon CR0 . . . . .143 EA103
Dartford DA1 . . . . .128 FK88
Dartford (Hawley) DA2 . . . .128 FM91
Gravesend DA12 . . . . .131 GJ91
Orpington BR6 . . . . .163 ET108
Shepperton TW17 . . . . .134 BN98
Sutton SM3 . . . . .139 CY101
Westerham TN16 . . . . .189 ER125
Woking GU22 . . . . .166 AX120
Ash Row, Brom. BR2 . . . . . . .145 EN101
ASHTEAD, KT21 . . . . .172 CL118
⇌ Ashtead 171 CK117
Ashtead Gap, Lthd. KT22 . . .171 CH116
H Ashtead Hosp, Ashtd.
KT21 . . . . .172 CL119
ASHTEAD PARK, Ashtd.
KT21 . . . . .172 CN118
Ashtead Rd, E5 . . . . .66 DU59
Ashtead Wds Rd, Ashtd.
KT21 . . . . .171 CJ117
Ashton Cl, Sutt. SM1 . . . . . .158 DA105
Walton-on-Thames KT12 . .153 BV107
Ashton Ct, E4
off Connington Cres 48 EE48
Ashton Gdns, Houns. TW4 . . .96 BZ84
Romford RM6 . . . . .70 EY58
Ashton Rd, E15 . . . . .67 ED64
Enfield EN3 . . . . .31 DY36
Romford RM3 . . . . .52 FK52
Woking GU21 . . . . .166 AT117
Ashton St, E14 . . . . .85 EC73
Ashtree Av, Mitch. CR4 . . . . .140 DD96
Ash Tree Cl, Croy. CR0 . . . . .143 DY100
Ashtree Cl, Orp. BR6 . . . . . .163 EP105
Ash Tree Cl, Surb. KT6 . . . . .138 CL102
Ashtree Ct, Wal.Abb. EN9
off Farthingale La 16 EG34
Ash Tree Dell, NW9 . . . . .62 CQ57
Ash Tree Rd, Wat. WD24 . . . . .23 BV36
Ash Tree Way, Croy. CR0 . . . .143 DY99
Ashurst Cl, SE20 . . . . .142 DV95
Dartford DA1 . . . . .107 FF83
Kenley CR8 . . . . .176 DR115
Northwood HA6 . . . . .39 BS52
Ashurst Dr, Ilf. IG2, IG6 . . . . .69 EP58
Shepperton TW17 . . . . .134 BL99
Tadworth (Box H.) KT20 . . .182 CP130
Ashurst Rd, N12 . . . . .44 DE50
Barnet EN4 . . . . .28 DF43
Tadworth KT20 . . . . .173 CV121
Ashurst Wk, Croy. CR0 . . . . .142 DV103
Ash Vale, Rick. (Map.Cr.) WD3 .37 BD50
Ashvale Dr, Upmin. RM14 . . .73 FS61
Ashvale Gdns, Rom. RM5 . . . .51 FD50
Upminster RM14 . . . . .73 FS61
Ashvale Rd, SW17 . . . . .120 DF92
Ashview Cl, Ashf. TW15 . . . .114 BL93
Ashview Gdns, Ashf. TW15 . .114 BL92
Ashville Rd, E11 . . . . .67 ED61
Ash Wk, SW2 . . . . .121 DM88
South Ockendon RM15 . . . . .91 FX69
Wembley HA0 . . . . .61 CJ63
Ashwater Rd, SE12 . . . . .124 EG88
Ashwell Cl, E6
off Northumberland Rd . . .86 EL72
Ashwells Rd, Brwd. (Pilg.Hat.)
CM15 . . . . .54 FS41
Ashwells Way, Ch.St.G. HP8 . .36 AW47
Ashwick Cl, Cat. CR3 . . . . . .186 DU125
Ashwindham Ct, Wok. GU21
off Raglan Rd 166 AT118
Ashwin St, E8 . . . . .84 DT65
Ashwood, Warl. CR6 . . . . . . .176 DW120
Ashwood Av, Rain. RM13 . . . .89 FH70
Uxbridge UB8 . . . . .76 BN72
Ashwood Gdns, Croy.
(New Adgtn) CR0 . . . . . . .161 EB107
Hayes UB3 off Cranford Dr . .95 BT77
Ashwood Pk, Lthd. (Fetch.)
KT22 . . . . .170 CC124
Woking GU22 . . . . .167 BA118
Ashwood Pl, Dart. (Bean) DA2
off Bean La 129 FV90
Ashwood Rd, E4 . . . . .47 ED48
Egham (Eng.Grn) TW20 . . . .112 AV93
Potters Bar EN6 . . . . .12 DB33
Woking GU22 . . . . .167 AZ118
Ashworth Cl, SE5
off Love Wk 102 DR82
Ashworth Rd, W9 . . . . .82 DB69
Askern Cl, Bexh. DA6 . . . . . .106 EX84
Aske St, N1 . . . . .197 M2
Askew Cres, W12 . . . . .99 CT75
Askew Fm La, Grays RM17 . .110 FY78
Askew Rd, W12 . . . . .81 CT74
Northwood HA6 . . . . .39 BR47
Askham Ct, W12 . . . . .81 CU74
Askham Rd, W12 . . . . .81 CU74
Askill Dr, SW15 . . . . .119 CY85
Askwith Rd, Rain. RM13 . . . . .89 FD69
Asland Rd, E15 . . . . .86 EE67
Aslett St, SW18 . . . . .120 DB87
Asmara Rd, NW2 . . . . .63 CY64
Asmar Cl, Couls. CR5 . . . . . .175 DL115
Asmuns Hill, NW11 . . . . .64 DA57
Asmuns Pl, NW11 . . . . .63 CZ57
Asolando Dr, SE17 . . . . .201 J9
Aspdin Rd, Grav. (Nthflt)
DA11 . . . . .130 GD90
Aspect Ct, SW6
off The Boulevard 100 DC82
Aspen Cl, N19
off Hargrave Pk 65 DJ61
W5 . . . . .98 CM75
Cobham (Stoke D'Ab.)
KT11 . . . . .170 BY116
Orpington BR6 . . . . .164 EU106
St. Albans (Brick.Wd) AL2 . . .8 BY30
Staines TW18 . . . . .113 BF90
Swanley BR8 . . . . .147 FD95
West Drayton UB7 . . . . .76 BM74
Aspen Copse, Brom. BR1 . . .145 EM96
Aspen Ct, Brwd. CM13 . . . . . .55 GA48
Hayes UB3 . . . . .95 BS77
Virginia Water GU25 . . . . .132 AY98
Aspen Dr, Wem. HA0 . . . . . . .61 CG63
Aspen Gdns, W6 . . . . .99 CV78
Ashford TW15 . . . . .115 BQ92
Mitcham CR4 . . . . .140 DG99
Aspen Grn, Erith DA18 . . . . .106 EZ76
Aspen Gro, Pnr. HA5 . . . . . . .59 BT55
Upminster RM14 . . . . .72 FN63
Aspen Ho, NW3
off Maitland Pk Vil 82 DF65
Warlingham CR6
off East Parkside 177 EB115
Aspen La, Nthlt. UB5 . . . . . . .78 BY69
Aspenlea Rd, W6 . . . . .99 CX79
Aspen Pk Dr, Wat. WD25 . . . . .23 BV35
Aspen Sq, Wey. KT13
off Oatlands Dr 135 BR104
Aspen Vale, Whyt. CR3
off Whyteleafe Hill 176 DT118
Aspen Way, E14 . . . . .204 A1
Banstead SM7 . . . . .157 CX114
Enfield EN3 . . . . .31 DX35
Feltham TW13 . . . . .115 BV90
South Ockendon RM15 . . . . .91 FX69
Aspern Gro, NW3 . . . . .64 DE64
Aspinall Rd, SE4 . . . . .103 DX83
Aspinden Rd, SE16 . . . . .202 E8
Aspley Rd, SW18 . . . . .120 DB85
Asplins Rd, N17 . . . . .46 DU53
Asprey Gro, Cat. CR3 . . . . . .176 DU124
Asprey Ms, Beck. BR3 . . . . .143 DZ99
Asprey Pl, Brom. BR1
off Chislehurst Rd 144 EK96
Asquith Cl, Dag. RM8 . . . . . . .70 EW60
Assam St, E1 off White Ch La .84 DU72
Assata Ms, N1
off St. Paul's Rd 83 DP65
Assembly Pas, E1 . . . . .84 DW71
Assembly Wk, Cars. SM5 . . .140 DE101
Assher Rd, Walt. KT12 . . . . .136 BY104
Ass Ho La, Har. HA3 . . . . . . .40 CB49
Assurance Cotts, Belv. DA17
off Heron Hill 106 EZ78
Astall Cl, Har. HA3 . . . . .41 CE53
Astbury Business Pk, SE15
off Station Pas 102 DW81
Astbury Ho, SE11
off Lambeth Wk 101 DN76
Astbury Rd, SE15 . . . . .102 DW81
Astede Pl, Ashtd. KT21 . . . . .172 CM118
Astell St, SW3 . . . . .198 C10
Asters, The, Wal.Cr. EN7 . . . . .14 DR28
Aste St, E14 . . . . .204 D5
Asteys Row, N1 off River Pl . . .83 DP66
Asthall Gdns, Ilf. IG6 . . . . . . .69 EQ56
Astleham Rd, Shep. TW17 . . .134 BL97
Astle St, SW11 . . . . .100 DG82
Astley, Grays RM17 . . . . .110 FZ79
Astley Av, NW2 . . . . .63 CW64
Astley Ho, SE1
off Rowcross St 102 DT77
Aston Av, Har. HA3 . . . . .61 CJ59
Aston Cl, Ashtd. KT21 . . . . . .171 CJ118
Bushey WD23 . . . . .24 CC44
Sidcup DA14 . . . . .126 EU90
Watford WD24 . . . . .24 BW40
Aston Grn, Houns. TW4 . . . . .96 BW82
Aston Ho, SW8
off Wandsworth Rd 101 DK81
Aston Ms, Rom. RM6 . . . . . . .70 EW59
Aston Pl, SW16
off Averil Gro 121 DP93
Aston Rd, SW20 . . . . .139 CW96
W5 .79 CK72
Esher (Clay.) KT10 . . . . . . .155 CE106
Astons Rd, Nthwd. HA6 . . . . .39 BQ48
Aston St, E14 . . . . .85 DY72
Aston Ter, SW12
off Cathles Rd 121 DH86
Astonville St, SW18 . . . . . . .120 DA88
Aston Way, Epsom KT18 . . . .173 CT115
Potters Bar EN6 . . . . .12 DD32
Astor Av, Rom. RM7 . . . . .71 FC58
Astor Cl, Add. KT15 . . . . . . .152 BK105
Kingston upon Thames
KT2 . . . . .118 CP93
Astoria Wk, SW9 . . . . .101 DN83
Astra Cl, Horn. RM12 . . . . . . .89 FH65
Astra Dr, Grav. DA12 . . . . . .131 GL92
Astrop Ms, W6 . . . . .99 CW76
Astrop Ter, W6 . . . . .99 CW76
Astwood Ms, SW7 . . . . .100 DB77
Asylum Rd, SE15 . . . . .102 DV80
Atalanta Cl, Pur. CR8 . . . . . .159 DN110
Atalanta St, SW6 . . . . .99 CX81
Atbara Ct, Tedd. TW11 . . . . .117 CH93
Atbara Rd, Tedd. TW11 . . . . .117 CH93
Atcham Rd, Houns. TW3 . . . . .96 CC84
Atcost Rd, Bark. IG11 . . . . . . .88 EU71
Atheldene Rd, SW18 . . . . . . .120 DB88
Athelney St, SE6 . . . . .123 EA90
Athelstan Cl, Rom. RM3 . . . . .52 FM53
Athelstane Gro, E3 . . . . .85 DZ68
Athelstane Ms, N4
off Stroud Grn Rd 65 DN60
Athelstan Ho, E9
off Kingsmead Way 67 DZ64
Athelstan Rd, Kings.T. KT1 . .138 CM98
Romford RM3 . . . . .52 FM53
Athelstan Way, Orp. BR5 . . .146 EU95
Athelstone Rd, Har. HA3 . . . .41 CD54
Athena Cl, Har. HA2
off Byron Hill Rd 61 CE61
Kingston upon Thames
KT1 . . . . .138 CM97
Athena Ct, SE1 off Long La . .102 DS75
Athenaeum Pl, N10
off Fortis Grn Rd 65 DH55
Athenaeum Rd, N20 . . . . .44 DC46
Athena Pl, Nthwd. HA6
off The Drive 39 BT53
Athenia Cl, Wal.Cr. (Goffs Oak)
EN7 . . . . .13 DN29
Athenlay Rd, SE15 . . . . .123 DX85
Athens Gdns, W9
off Harrow Rd 82 DA70
Atherden Rd, E5 . . . . .66 DW63
Atherfold Rd, SW9 . . . . .101 DL83
Atherley Way, Houns. TW4 . .116 BZ87
Atherstone Ct, W2
off Delamere Ter 82 DB71
Atherstone Ms, SW7 . . . . . . .100 DC77
Atherton Cl, Stai. (Stanw.)
TW19 . . . . .114 BK86
Atherton Dr, SW19 . . . . .119 CX91
Atherton Gdns, Grays RM16 .111 GJ77
Atherton Hts, Wem. HA0 . . . . .79 CJ65
Atherton Ms, E7 . . . . .86 EF65
Atherton Pl, Har. HA2 . . . . . . .61 CD55
Southall UB1 . . . . .78 CA73
Atherton Rd, E7 . . . . .68 EF64
SW13 . . . . .99 CU80
Ilford IG5 . . . . .48 EL54
Atherton St, SW11 . . . . .100 DE82
Athlone, Esher (Clay.) KT10 .155 CE107
Athlone Cl, E5
off Goulton Rd 66 DV64
Radlett WD7 . . . . .25 CH36
H Athlone Ho, N6 . . . . .64 DF60
Athlone Rd, SW2 . . . . .121 DM87
Athlone St, NW5 . . . . .82 DG65
Athlon Rd, Wem. HA0 . . . . . . .79 CK68
Athol Cl, Pnr. HA5 . . . . .39 BV53
Athole Gdns, Enf. EN1 . . . . . .30 DS43
Athol Gdns, Pnr. HA5 . . . . . . .39 BV53
Atholl Ho, W9 off Maida Vale .82 DC69
Atholl Rd, Ilf. IG3 . . . . .70 EU59
Athol Rd, Erith DA8 . . . . . . .107 FC78
Athol Sq, E14 . . . . .85 EC72
Athol Way, Uxb. UB10 . . . . . .76 BN69
Atkin Bldg, WC1
off Gray's Inn 83 DM71
Atkins Cl, Wok. GU21
off Greythorne Rd 166 AU118
Atkins Dr, W.Wick. BR4 . . . .143 ED103
Atkinson Cl, Orp. BR6
off Martindale Av 164 EU106
Atkinson Ho, SW11
off Austin Rd 100 DG81
Atkinson Rd, E16 . . . . .86 EJ71
Atkins Rd, E10 . . . . .67 EB58
SW12 . . . . .121 DK87
Atlanta Boul, Rom. RM1 . . . . .71 FE58
Atlantic Cl, Swans. DA10 . . . .130 FY85
Atlantic Rd, SW9 . . . . .101 DN84
Atlantis Cl, Bark. IG11 . . . . . .88 EV69
Atlas Business Cen, NW2
off Oxgate La 63 CV61
Atlas Gdns, SE7 . . . . .104 EJ77
Atlas Ms, E8 off Dalston La . . .84 DT65
N7 .83 DM65
Atlas Rd, E13 . . . . .86 EG68
N11 . . . . .45 DH51

★ Place of interest ⇌ Railway station ⊖ London Underground station DLR Docklands Light Railway station Tra Tramlink station H Hospital Riv Pedestrian ferry landing stage

Atlas Rd, NW10 ....80 CS69
Dartford DA1
off Cornwall Rd 108 FM83
Wembley HA9 ....62 CQ63
Atlas Trade Pk, Erith DA8 ...107 FD78
Atley Rd, E3 ....85 EA67
Atlip Cen, Wem. HA0
off Atlip Rd 80 CL67
Atlip Rd, Wem. HA0 ....80 CL67
Atney Rd, SW15 ....99 CY84
Atria Rd, Nthwd. HA6 ....39 BU50
Attenborough Cl, Wat. WD19
off Harrow Way 40 BY48
Atterbury Cl, West. TN16 ...189 ER126
Atterbury Rd, N4 ....65 DN58
Atterbury St, SW1 ....199 N9
Attewood Av, NW10 ....62 CS62
Attewood Rd, Nthlt. UB5 ....78 BY65
Attfield Cl, N20 ....44 DD47
Attle Cl, Uxb. UB10 ....76 BN68
Attlee Cl, Hayes UB4 ....77 BV69
Thornton Heath CR7 .....142 DQ100
Attlee Ct, Grays RM17 .....110 GA76
Attlee Dr, Dart. DA1 ....128 FN85
Attlee Rd, SE28 ....88 EV73
Hayes UB4 ....77 BU69
Attlee Ter, E17 ....67 EB56
Attneave St, WC1 ....196 D3
Attwood Cl, S.Croy. CR2 ...160 DV114
Atwater Cl, SW2 ....121 DN88
Atwell Cl, E10
off Belmont Pk Rd 67 EB58
Atwell Pl, T.Ditt. KT7 ....137 CF102
Atwell Rd, SE15 *off Rye La* . .102 DU82
Atwood, Lthd. (Bkhm) KT23 .170 BY124
Atwood Av, Rich. TW9 ....98 CN82
Atwood Rd, W6 ....99 CV77
Atwoods All, Rich. TW9
off Leyborne Pk 98 CN81
Aubert Pk, N5 ....65 DP63
Aubert Rd, N5 ....65 DP63
Aubretia Cl, Rom. RM3 ....52 FL53
Aubrey Av, St.Alb. (Lon.Col.)
AL2 ....9 CJ26
Aubrey Beardsley Ho, SW1
off Vauxhall Br Rd 101 DJ77
Aubrey Moore Pt, E15
off Abbey La 85 EC68
Aubrey Pl, NW8 *off Violet Hill* .82 DC68
Aubrey Rd, E17 ....67 EA55
N8 ....65 DL57
W8 ....81 CZ74
Aubrey Wk, W8 ....81 CZ74
Auburn Cl, SE14 ....103 DY80
Aubyn Hill, SE27 ....122 DQ91
Aubyn Sq, SW15 ....99 CU84
Auckland Av, Rain. RM13 ....89 FF69
Auckland Cl, SE19 ....142 DT95
Enfield EN1 ....30 DV37
Tilbury RM18 ....111 GG82
Auckland Gdns, SE19 ....142 DS95
Auckland Hill, SE27 ....122 DQ91
Auckland Ri, SE19 ....142 DS95
Auckland Rd, E10 ....67 EB62
SE19 ....142 DT95
SW11 ....100 DE84
Caterham CR3 ....176 DS122
Ilford IG1 ....69 EP60
Kingston upon Thames
KT1 ....138 CM98
Potters Bar EN6 ....11 CY32
Auckland St, SE11
off Kennington La 101 DM78
Auden Dr, Borwd. WD6 ....26 CN43
Auden Pl, NW1 ....82 DG67
Sutton SM3
off Wordsworth Dr 157 CW105
Audleigh Pl, Chig. IG7 ....49 EN51
Audley Cl, N10 ....45 DH52
SW11 ....100 DG83
Addlestone KT15 ....152 BH106
Borehamwood WD6 ....26 CN41
Audley Ct, E18 ....68 EF56
Pinner HA5
off Rickmansworth Rd 40 BW54
Audley Dr, E16 ....205 P2
Warlingham CR6 ....176 DW115
Audley Firs, Walt. KT12 .....154 BW105
Audley Gdns, Ilf. IG3 ....69 ET61
Loughton IG10 ....33 EQ40
Waltham Abbey EN9 ....15 EC34
Audley Pl, Sutt. SM2 ....158 DA108
Audley Rd, NW4 ....63 CV58
W5 ....80 CM71
Enfield EN2 ....29 DP40
Richmond TW10 ....118 CM85
Audley Sq, W1 ....198 G2
Audley Wk, Orp. BR5 ....146 EW100
Audrey Cl, Beck. BR3 ....143 EB100
Audrey Gdns, Wem. HA0 ....61 CH61
Audrey Rd, Ilf. IG1 ....69 EP62
Audrey St, E2 ....84 DU68
Audric Cl, Kings.T. KT2 ....138 CN95
Audwick Cl, Wal.Cr. (Chsht)
EN8 ....15 DX28
Augur Cl, Stai. TW18 ....113 BF92
Augurs La, E13 ....86 EH69
Augusta Cl, W.Mol. KT8
off Freeman Dr 136 BZ97
Augusta Rd, Twick. TW2 ....116 CC89
Augusta St, E14 ....85 EB72
August End, Slou. (Geo.Grn)
SL3 ....74 AY72
Augustine Cl, Slou. (Colnbr.)
SL3 ....93 BE83
Augustine Ct, Wal.Abb. EN9
off Beaulieu Dr 15 EB33
Augustine Rd, W14 ....99 CX76
Gravesend DA12 ....131 GJ87
Harrow HA3 ....40 CB53
Orpington BR5 ....146 EX97
Augustus Cl, W12
off Goldhawk Rd 99 CV75
Brentford TW8 ....97 CJ80
Augustus Ct, SE1
off Old Kent Rd 102 DS77
Augustus Ho, NW1
off Augustus St 83 DJ69
Augustus La, Orp. BR6 ....146 EU103
Augustus Rd, SW19 ....119 CY88
Augustus St, NW1 ....195 J1
Aultone Way, Cars. SM5 ....140 DF104
Sutton SM1 ....140 DB103
Aulton Pl, SE11 ....101 DN78
Aurelia Gdns, Croy. CR0 ....141 DM99
Aurelia Rd, Croy. CR0 ....141 DL100
Auriel Av, Dag. RM10 ....89 FD65
Auriga Ms, N1 ....66 DR64
Auriol Cl, Wor.Pk. KT4
off Auriol Pk Rd 138 CS104
Auriol Dr, Grnf. UB6 ....79 CD66
Uxbridge UB10 ....76 BN65
Auriol Pk Rd, Wor.Pk. KT4 ...138 CS104
Auriol Rd, W14 ....99 CY77
Austell Gdns, NW7 ....42 CS48
Austen Cl, SE28 ....88 EV74
Greenhithe DA9 ....129 FW85
Loughton IG10 ....33 ER41
Tilbury RM18
off Coleridge Rd 111 GJ82
Austen Gdns, Dart. DA1 ....108 FM84
Austen Ho, NW6 ....82 DA69
Austen Rd, Erith DA8 ....107 FB80
Harrow HA2 ....60 CB61
Austenway, Ger.Cr. (Chal.St.P.)
SL9 ....56 AX55
Austen Way, Slou. SL3
off Parsons Rd 93 AZ79
Austenwood Cl, Ger.Cr.
(Chal.St.P.) SL9 ....36 AW54
Austenwood La, Ger.Cr.
(Chal.St.P.) SL9 ....36 AX54
Austin Av, Brom. BR2 ....144 EL99
Austin Cl, SE23 ....123 DZ87
Coulsdon CR5 ....175 DP118
Twickenham TW1 ....117 CJ85
Austin Ct, E6 *off Kings Rd* ...86 EJ67
Austin Friars, EC2 ....197 L8
Austin Friars Pas, EC2 ....197 L8
Austin Friars Sq, EC2 ....197 L8
Austin Rd, SW11 ....100 DG81
Gravesend (Nthflt) DA11 ...131 GF88
Hayes UB3 ....95 BT75
Orpington BR5 ....146 EU100
Austin's La, Uxb. UB10 ....59 BR63
Austins Mead, Hem.H. (Bov.)
HP3 ....5 BB28
Austin St, E2 ....197 P3
Austin Waye, Uxb. UB8 ....76 BJ67
Austral Cl, Sid. DA15 ....125 ET90
Austral Dr, Horn. RM11 ....72 FK59
Australia Rd, W12 ....81 CV73
Slough SL1 ....74 AV74
Austral St, SE11 ....200 F8
Austyn Gdns, Surb. KT5 ....138 CP102
Austyns Pl, Epsom KT17 ....157 CU109
Autumn Cl, SW19 ....120 DC93
Enfield EN1 ....30 DU39
Autumn Dr, Sutt. SM2 ....158 DB109
Autumn St, E3 ....85 EA67
Auxiliaries Way, Uxb. UB9 ...57 BF57
Avalon Cl, SW20 ....139 CY96
W13 ....79 CG71
Enfield EN2 ....29 DN40
Orpington BR6 ....146 EX104
Watford WD25 ....8 BY32
Avalon Rd, SW6 ....100 DB81
W13 ....79 CG70
Orpington BR6 ....146 EW103
Avard Gdns, Orp. BR6 ....163 EQ105
Avarn Rd, SW17 ....120 DF93
Avebury Ct, N1 *off Poole St* ...84 DR67
Avebury Pk, Surb. KT6 ....137 CK101
Avebury Rd, E11
off Southwest Rd 67 ED60
SW19 ....139 CZ95
Orpington BR6 ....145 ER104
Avebury St, N1 *off Poole St* ...84 DR67
AVELEY, S.Ock. RM15 ....91 FR73
Aveley Bypass, S.Ock. RM15 .90 FQ73
Aveley Cl, Erith DA8 ....107 FF79
South Ockendon (Aveley)
RM15 ....91 FR74
Aveley Rd, Rom. RM1 ....71 FD56
Upminster RM14 ....90 FP65
Aveline St, SE11 ....200 D10
Aveling Cl, Pur. CR8 ....159 DM113
Aveling Pk Rd, E17 ....47 EA54
Avelon Rd, Rain. RM13 ....89 FG67
Romford RM5 ....51 FD51
Ave Maria La, EC4 ....196 G9
Avenell Rd, N5 ....65 DP62
Avening Rd, SW18
off Brathway Rd 120 DA87
Avening Ter, SW18 ....120 DA86
Avenons Rd, E13 ....86 EG70
Avenue, The, E4 ....47 ED51
E11 (Leytonstone) 68 EF61
E11 (Wanstead) 68 EH58
N3 ....44 DA54
N8 ....65 DN55
N10 ....45 DJ54
N11 ....45 DH49
N17 ....46 DS54
NW6 ....81 CX67
SE10 ....103 ED80
SW4 ....120 DG85
SW11 ....120 DE87
SW18 ....120 DE87
W4 ....98 CS76
W13 ....79 CH73
Addlestone (New Haw)
KT15 ....152 BG110
Barnet EN5 ....27 CY41
Beckenham BR3 ....143 EB95
Betchworth (Brock.) RH3 ..182 CN134
Bexley DA5 ....126 EX87
Brentwood CM13 ....53 FX51
Bromley BR1 ....144 EK97
Bushey WD23 ....24 BZ42
Carshalton SM5 ....158 DG108
Coulsdon CR5 ....175 DK115
Croydon CR0 ....142 DS104
Egham TW20 ....113 BB91
Epsom KT17 ....157 CV108
Esher (Clay.) KT10 ....155 CE107
Gravesend DA11 ....131 GG88
Greenhithe DA9 ....109 FV84
Hampton TW12 ....116 BZ93
Harrow HA3 ....41 CF53
Hornchurch RM12 ....72 FJ61
Avenue, The, Houns. TW3 ...116 CB85
Hounslow (Cran.) TW5 ....95 BU81
Isleworth TW7 ....97 CD79
Keston BR2 ....144 EK104
Leatherhead KT22 ....155 CF112
Loughton IG10 ....32 EK44
Northwood HA6 ....39 BQ51
Orpington BR6 ....145 ET103
Orpington (St.P.Cray) BR5 .126 EV94
Pinner HA5 ....60 BZ58
Pinner (Hatch End) HA5 ...40 CA52
Potters Bar EN6 ....11 CZ30
Radlett WD7 ....9 CG33
Richmond TW9 ....98 CM82
Romford RM1 ....71 FD56
Slough (Datchet) SL3 ....92 AV81
Staines TW18 ....134 BH95
Staines (Wrays.) TW19 ....92 AX83
Sunbury-on-Thames
TW16 ....135 BV95
Surbiton KT5 ....138 CM100
Sutton SM2 ....157 CZ109
Sutton (Cheam) SM3 ....157 CW108
Tadworth KT20 ....173 CV122
Twickenham TW1 ....117 CJ85
Uxbridge (Cowley) UB8 ...76 BK70
Uxbridge (Ickhm) UB10 ....58 BN63
Waltham Abbey (Nazeing)
EN9 ....16 EJ25
Watford WD17 ....23 BU40
Wembley HA9 ....62 CM61
West Drayton UB7 ....94 BL76
West Wickham BR4 ....143 EC101
Westerham TN16 ....179 EM122
Whyteleafe CR3 ....176 DU119
Windsor (Old Wind.) SL4 ...112 AV85
Woking (Chobham) GU24 .150 AT109
Worcester Park KT4 ....139 CT103
Avenue App, Kings L. WD4 ....6 BN30
Avenue Cl, N14 ....29 DJ44
NW8 ....82 DE67
Hounslow TW5
off The Avenue 95 BU81
Romford RM3 ....52 FM52
Tadworth KT20 ....173 CV122
West Drayton UB7 ....94 BK76
Avenue Ct, Tad. KT20
off The Avenue 173 CV123
Avenue Cres, W3 ....98 CP75
Hounslow TW5 ....95 BV80
Avenue Dr, Slou. SL3 ....75 AZ71
Avenue Elmers, Surb. KT6 ...138 CL99
Avenue Gdns, SE25 ....142 DU97
SW14 ....98 CS83
W3 ....98 CP75
Hounslow TW5
off The Avenue 95 BU80
Teddington TW11 ....117 CF94
Avenue Gate, Loug. IG10 ....32 EJ44
Avenue Ind Est, E4 ....47 DZ51
Romford RM3 ....52 FK54
Avenue Ms, N10 ....65 DH55
Avenue Pk Rd, SE27 ....121 DP89
Avenue Ri, Bushey WD23 ....24 CA43
Tra **Avenue Road** 143 DX96
Avenue Rd, E7 ....68 EH64
N6 ....65 DJ59
N12 ....44 DC49
N14 ....45 DH45
N15 ....66 DR57
NW3 ....82 DD66
NW8 ....82 DD66
NW10 ....81 CT68
SE20 ....142 DW95
SE25 ....142 DU96
SW16 ....141 DK96
SW20 ....139 CV96
W3 ....98 CP75
Banstead SM7 ....174 DB115
Beckenham BR3 ....142 DW95
Belvedere DA17 ....107 FC77
Bexleyheath DA7 ....106 EY83
Brentford TW8 ....97 CJ78
Brentwood CM14 ....54 FW49
Caterham CR3 ....176 DR122
Cobham KT11 ....170 BX116
Epping (They.B.) CM16 ....33 ER36
Epsom KT18 ....156 CR114
Erith DA8 ....107 FC80
Feltham TW13 ....115 BT90
Hampton TW12 ....136 CB95
Isleworth TW7 ....97 CF81
Kingston upon Thames
KT1 ....138 CL97
New Malden KT3 ....138 CS98
Pinner HA5 ....60 BY55
Romford (Chad.Hth) RM6 ...70 EV59
Romford (Harold Wd) RM3 .52 FM52
Sevenoaks TN13 ....191 FJ123
Southall UB1 ....96 BZ75
Staines TW18 ....113 BD92
Sutton SM2 ....158 DA110
Teddington TW11 ....117 CG94
Wallington SM6 ....159 DJ108
Westerham (Tats.) TN16 ...178 EL120
Woodford Green IG8 ....48 EJ51
Avenue Rd Est, E11
off High Rd Leytonstone ...67 ED63
Avenue S, Surb. KT5 ....138 CM101
Avenue Ter, N.Mal. KT3
off Kingston Rd 138 CQ97
Watford WD19 ....24 BY44
Averil Gro, SW16 ....121 DP93
Averill St, W6 ....99 CX79
Avern Gdns, W.Mol. KT8 ....136 CB98
Avern Rd, W.Mol. KT8 ....136 CB99
Avery Fm Row, SW1 ....198 G9
Avery Gdns, Ilf. IG2 ....69 EM57
AVERY HILL, SE9 ....125 EQ86
★ **Avery Hill Pk**, SE9 ....125 EQ86
Avery Hill Rd, SE9 ....125 ER86
Avery Row, W1 ....195 H10
Avey La, Loug. IG10 ....32 EH39
Waltham Abbey EN9 ....31 ED36
Aviary Cl, E16 ....86 EF71
Aviary Rd, Wok. GU22 ....168 BG116
Aviator Pk, Add. KT15 ....134 BK104
Aviemore Cl, Beck. BR3 ....143 DZ99
Aviemore Way, Beck. BR3 ...143 DY99
Avignon Rd, SE4 ....103 DX83
Avington Ct, SE1
off Old Kent Rd 102 DS77
Avington Gro, SE20 ....122 DW94
Avion Cres, NW9 ....43 CU53
Avior Dr, Nthwd. HA6 ....39 BT49
Avis Gro, Croy. CR0 ....161 DY110
Avis Sq, E1 ....85 DX72
Avoca Rd, SW17 ....120 DG91
Avocet Cl, SE1 *off Rolls Rd* ..102 DU78
Avocet Ms, SE28 ....105 ER76
Avon Cl, Add. KT15 ....152 BG107
Gravesend DA12 ....131 GK89
Hayes UB4 ....78 BW70
Sutton SM1 ....158 DC105
Watford WD25 ....8 BW34
Worcester Park KT4 ....139 CU103
Avon Ct, Grnf. UB6
off Braund Av 78 CB70
Avondale Av, N12 ....44 DB50
NW2 ....62 CS62
Barnet EN4 ....44 DF46
Esher KT10 ....137 CG104
Staines TW18 ....113 BF94
Worcester Park KT4 ....139 CT102
Avondale Cl, Loug. IG10 ....49 EM45
Walton-on-Thames KT12
off Pleasant Pl 154 BW106
Avondale Ct, E11 ....68 EE60
E16 *off Avondale Rd* 86 EE71
E18 ....48 EH53
Avondale Cres, Enf. EN3 ....31 DY41
Ilford IG4 ....68 EK57
Avondale Dr, Hayes UB3 ....77 BU74
Loughton IG10 ....49 EM45
Avondale Gdns, Houns. TW4 .116 BZ85
Avondale Ho, SE1
off Avondale Sq 102 DU78
Avondale Ms, Brom. BR1
off Avondale Rd 124 EG93
Avondale Pk Gdns, W11 ....81 CY73
Avondale Pk Rd, W11 ....81 CY73
Avondale Pavement, SE1
off Avondale Sq 102 DU78
Avondale Ri, SE15 ....102 DT83
Avondale Rd, E16 ....86 EE71
E17 ....67 EA59
N3 ....44 DC53
N13 ....45 DN47
N15 ....65 DP57
SE9 ....124 EL89
SW14 ....98 CR83
SW19 ....120 DB92
Ashford TW15 ....114 BK90
Bromley BR1 ....124 EE93
Harrow HA3 ....61 CF55
South Croydon CR2 ....160 DQ107
Welling DA16 ....106 EW82
Avondale Sq, SE1 ....102 DU78
Avon Grn, S.Ock. RM15 ....91 FV72
Avonley Rd, SE14 ....102 DW80
Avonmead, Wok. GU21
off Silversmiths Way 166 AW118
Avon Ms, Pnr. HA5 ....40 BZ53
Avonmore Gdns, W14
off Avonmore Rd 99 CZ77
Avonmore Pl, W14
off Avonmore Rd 99 CY77
Avonmore Rd, W14 ....99 CZ77
Avonmouth Rd, Dart. DA1 ...128 FK85
Avonmouth St, SE1 ....201 H6
Avon Path, S.Croy. CR2 ....160 DQ107
Avon Pl, SE1 ....201 J5
Avon Rd, E17 ....67 ED55
SE4 ....103 EA83
Greenford UB6 ....78 CA70
Sunbury-on-Thames
TW16 ....115 BT94
Upminster RM14 ....73 FR58
Avonstowe Cl, Orp. BR6 ....145 EQ104
Avontar Rd, S.Ock. RM15 ....91 FV70
Avon Way, E18 ....68 EG55
Avonwick Rd, Houns. TW3 ....96 CB82
Avril Way, E4 ....47 EC50
Avro Way, Wall. SM6 ....159 DL108
Weybridge KT13 ....152 BL110
Awlfield Av, N17 ....46 DR53
Awliscombe Rd, Well. DA16 .105 ET82
Axe St, Bark. IG11 ....87 EQ67
Axholme Av, Edg. HA8 ....42 CN53
Axis Ct, SE10
off Woodland Cres 104 EE79
SE16 *off East La* 102 DU75
Axis Pk, Slou. (Langley) SL3 .93 BB77
Axminster Cres, Well. DA16 .106 EW81
Axminster Rd, N7 ....65 DL62
Axon Pl, Ilf. IG1 *off High Rd* ..69 EQ61
Axtaine Rd, Orp. BR5 ....146 EX101
Axtane, Grav. (Sthflt) DA13 .130 FZ94
Axtane Cl, Dart. (Sutt.H.)
DA4 ....148 FQ96
Axwood, Epsom KT18 ....172 CQ115
Aybrook St, W1 ....194 F7
Aycliffe Cl, Brom. BR1 ....145 EM98
Aycliffe Rd, W12 ....81 CT74
Borehamwood WD6 ....26 CL39
Ayebridges Av, Egh. TW20 ...113 BC94
Aylands Cl, Wem. HA9
off Preston Rd 62 CL61
Aylands Rd, Enf. EN3 ....30 DW36
Aylesbury Cl, E7
off Atherton Rd 86 EF65
Aylesbury Ct, Sutt. SM1
off Benhill Wd Rd 140 DC104
Aylesbury Est, SE17
off Villa St 102 DR78
Aylesbury Rd, SE17 ....102 DR78
Bromley BR2 ....144 EG97
Aylesbury St, EC1 ....196 F5
NW10 ....62 CR62
Aylesford Av, Beck. BR3 ....143 DY99
Aylesford St, SW1 ....199 M10
Aylesham Cen, The, SE15 ...102 DU81
Aylesham Cl, NW7 ....43 CU52
Aylesham Rd, Orp. BR6 ....145 ET101
Ayles Rd, Hayes UB4 ....77 BV69
Aylestone Av, NW6 ....81 CX67
Aylesworth Spur, Wind.
(Old Wind.) SL4 ....112 AV87
Aylett Rd, SE25 ....142 DV98
Isleworth TW7 ....97 CE82
Upminster RM14 ....72 FQ61
Ayley Cft, Enf. EN1 ....30 DU43
Ayliffe Cl, Kings.T. KT1
off Cambridge Gdns 138 CN96
Aylmer Cl, Stan. HA7 ....41 CG49
Aylmer Dr, Stan. HA7 ....41 CG49
Aylmer Par, N2 ....64 DF57
Aylmer Rd, E11 ....68 EF60
N2 ....64 DE57
W12 ....98 CS75
Dagenham RM8 ....70 EY62
Ayloffe Rd, Dag. RM9 ....88 EZ65
Ayloffs Cl, Horn. RM11 ....72 FL57
Ayloffs Wk, Horn. RM11 ....72 FK57
Aylsham Dr, Uxb. UB10 ....59 BR62
Aylsham La, Rom. RM3 ....52 FJ49
Aylton Est, SE16 ....202 G5
Aylward Rd, SE23 ....123 DX89
SW20 ....139 CZ96
Aylwards Ri, Stan. HA7 ....41 CG49
Aylward St, E1 ....84 DW72
Aylwyn Est, SE1 ....201 P6
Aymer Cl, Stai. TW18 ....133 BE95
Aymer Dr, Stai. TW18 ....133 BE95
Aynhoe Rd, W14 ....99 CX77
Aynho St, Wat. WD18 ....23 BV43
Aynscombe Angle, Orp. BR6 .146 EV101
Aynscombe La, SW14 ....98 CQ83
Aynscombe Path, SW14
off Thames Bk 98 CQ82
Ayot Path, Borwd. WD6 ....26 CN37
Ayr Ct, W3 *off Monks Dr* 80 CN71
Ayres Cl, E13 ....86 EG69
Ayres St, SE1 ....201 J4
Ayr Grn, Rom. RM1 ....51 FE52
Ayron Rd, S.Ock. RM15 ....91 FV70
Ayrsome Rd, N16 ....66 DS62
Ayrton Gould Ho, E2
off Roman Rd 85 DX69
Ayrton Rd, SW7
off Wells Way 100 DD76
Ayr Way, Rom. RM1 ....51 FE52
Aysgarth Ct, Sutt. SM1
off Sutton Common Rd ..140 DB104
Aysgarth Rd, SE21 ....122 DS86
Aytoun Pl, SW9 ....101 DM82
Aytoun Rd, SW9 ....101 DM82
Azalea Cl, W7 ....79 CF74
Ilford IG1 ....69 EP64
St. Albans (Lon.Col.) AL2 ...9 CH27
Azalea Ct, Wok. GU22 ....166 AX119
Woodford Green IG8
off The Bridle Path 48 EE52
Azalea Dr, Swan. BR8 ....147 FD98
Azalea Wk, Pnr. HA5 ....59 BV57
Southall UB2
off Navigator Dr 96 CC75
Azalea Way, Slou. (Geo.Grn) SL3
off Blinco La 74 AY72
Azania Ms, NW5 ....65 DH64
Azenby Rd, SE15 ....102 DT82
Azile Everitt Ho, SE18
off Blendon Ter 105 EQ78
Azof St, SE10 ....205 J9

B

Baalbec Rd, N5 ....65 DP64
Babbacombe Cl, Chess. KT9 .155 CK106
Babbacombe Gdns, Ilf. IG4 ...68 EL56
Babbacombe Rd, Brom. BR1 .144 EG95
Baber Dr, Felt. TW14 ....116 BW86
Babington Ct, WC1
off Orde Hall St 83 DL71
Babington Ri, Wem. HA9 ....80 CN65
Babington Rd, NW4 ....63 CV56
SW16 ....121 DK92
Dagenham RM8 ....70 EW64
Hornchurch RM12 ....71 FH60
Babmaes St, SW1 ....199 L1
Babylon La, Tad. (Lwr Kgswd)
KT20 ....184 DA127
Bacchus Wk, N1 ....197 M1
Bachelor's La, Wok. GU23 ...168 BN124
Baches St, N1 ....197 L3
Back Ch La, E1 ....84 DU73
Back Grn, Walt. KT12 ....154 BW107
Back Hill, EC1 ....196 D5
Backhouse Pl, SE17 ....201 N9
Back La, N8 ....65 DL57
NW3 *off Heath St* 64 DC63
Bexley DA5 ....126 FA87
Brentford TW8 ....97 CK79
Buckhurst Hill IG9 ....48 EK47
Chalfont St. Giles HP8 ...36 AU48
Edgware HA8 ....42 CQ53
Grays (N.Stfd) RM16 ....91 FW74
Purfleet RM19 ....109 FS76
Richmond TW10 ....117 CJ90
Rickmansworth (Chenies)
WD3 ....21 BB38
Romford RM6
off St. Chad's Rd 70 EY59
Sevenoaks (Godden Grn)
TN15 ....191 FN124
Sevenoaks (Ide Hill) TN14 .190 FC126
Watford (Let.Hth) WD25 ...25 CE39
Backley Gdns, SE25 ....142 DU100
Back Path, Red. RH1 ....186 DQ133
Back Rd, Sid. DA14 ....126 EU91
Bacon Gro, SE1 ....201 P7
Bacon La, NW9 ....62 CP56
Edgware HA8 ....42 CN53
Bacon Link, Rom. RM5 ....51 FB51
Bacons Dr, Pot.B. (Cuffley)
EN6 ....13 DL29
Bacons La, N6 ....64 DG60
Bacons Mead, Uxb. (Denh.)
UB9 ....58 BG61
Bacon St, E1 ....84 DT70
E2 ....84 DT70
Bacon Ter, Dag. RM8
off Fitzstephen Rd 70 EV64
Bacton, NW5 ....64 DG64
Bacton St, E2 *off Roman Rd* ..84 DW69
Badburgham Ct, Wal.Abb.
EN9 ....16 EF33
Baddeley Cl, Enf. EN3
off Burton Dr 31 EA37
Baddow Cl, Dag. RM10 ....88 FA67
Woodford Green IG8 ....48 EK51
Baddow Wk, N1 ....84 DQ67
Baden Cl, Stai. TW18 ....114 BG94
Baden Pl, SE1 ....201 K4
Baden Powell Cl, Dag. RM9 ..88 EY67
Surbiton KT6 ....138 CM103

★ Place of interest | Railway station | London Underground station | DLR Docklands Light Railway station | Tra Tramlink station | H Hospital | Riv Pedestrian ferry landing stage

Baden Powell Rd, Sev. TN13 190 FE121
Baden Rd, N8 65 DK56
Ilford IG1 69 EP64
Bader Cl, Ken. CR8 176 DR115
Bader Wk, Grav. (Nthflt) DA11 130 GE90
Bader Way, Rain. RM13 89 FG65
Badger Cl, Felt. TW13
off Sycamore Cl 115 BU90
Hounslow TW4 96 BW83
Ilford IG2 69 EQ59
Badgers Cl, Ashf. TW15
off Fordbridge Rd 114 BM92
Borehamwood WD6
off Kingsley Av 26 CM40
Enfield EN2 29 DP41
Harrow HA1 61 CD58
Hayes UB3 77 BS73
Woking GU21 166 AW118
Badgers Copse, Orp. BR6 145 ET103
Worcester Park KT4 139 CT103
Badgers Cft, N20 43 CY46
SE9 125 EN90
BADGERS DENE, Grays RM17 110 FZ77
Badgers Hill, Vir.W. GU25 132 AW99
Badgers Hole, Croy. CR0 161 DX105
Badgers La, Warl. CR6 176 DW120
BADGERS MOUNT, Sev. TN14 165 FB110
Badgers Mt, Grays (Orsett) RM16 111 GF75
Badgers Ri, Sev. (Bad.Mt) TN14 164 FA110
Badgers Rd, Sev. (Bad.Mt) TN14 165 FB110
Badgers Wk, N.Mal. KT3 138 CS96
Purley CR8 159 DK111
Rickmansworth (Chorl.) WD3 21 BF42
Whyteleafe CR3 176 DT119
Badgers Wd, Cat. (Chaldon) CR3 186 DQ125
Badingham Dr, Lthd. (Fetch.) KT22 171 CE123
Badlis Rd, E17 47 EA54
Badlow Cl, Erith DA8 107 FE80
Badma Cl, N9
off Hudson Way 46 DW48
Badminton Cl, Borwd. WD6 26 CN40
Harrow HA1 61 CE56
Northolt UB5 78 CA65
Badminton Ms, E16 205 N2
Badminton Rd, SW12 120 DG86
Badric Ct, SW11
off Yelverton Rd 100 DD82
Badsworth Rd, SE5 102 DQ80
Baffin Way, E14 204 E1
Bagley Cl, West Dr. UB7 94 BL75
Bagley's La, SW6 100 DB81
Bagleys Spring, Rom. RM6 70 EY56
Bagot Cl, Ashtd. KT21 172 CM116
Bagshot Ct, SE18
off Prince Imperial Rd 105 EN81
Bagshot Rd, Egh. (Eng.Grn) TW20 112 AW94
Enfield EN1 46 DT45
Bagshot St, SE17 102 DS78
Bahram Rd, Epsom KT19 156 CR110
Baildon St, SE8 103 DZ80
Bailey Cl, E4 47 EC49
N11 45 DK52
SE28 off Miles Dr 87 ES74
Purfleet RM19
off Gabion Av 109 FR77
Bailey Cres, Chess. KT9 155 CK108
Bailey Ms, SW2 121 DN85
W4 off Magnolia Rd 98 CP79
Bailey Pl, SE26 123 DX93
Baillie Cl, Rain. RM13 89 FH70
Baillies Wk, W5
off Liverpool Rd 97 CK75
Bainbridge Cl, Rich. (Ham) TW10
off Latchmere Cl 118 CL92
Bainbridge Rd, Dag. RM9 70 EZ63
Bainbridge St, WC1 195 N8
Baines Cl, S.Croy. CR2
off Brighton Rd 160 DQ106
Bainton Mead, Wok. GU21 166 AU117
Baird Av, Sthl. UB1 78 CB73
Baird Cl, E10 off Marconi Rd 67 EA60
NW9 62 CQ58
Bushey WD23
off Ashfield Av 24 CB44
Baird Gdns, SE19 122 DS91
Baird Rd, Enf. EN1 30 DV42
Baird St, EC1 197 J4
Bairny Wd App, Wdf.Grn. IG8
off Broadway Cl 48 EH51
Bairstow Cl, Borwd. WD6 26 CL39
Baizdon Rd, SE3 104 EE82
Bakeham La, Egh. (Eng.Grn) TW20 112 AW94
Baker Boy La, Croy. CR0 161 DZ112
Baker Cres, Dart. DA1 128 FJ87
Baker Hill Cl, Grav. (Nthflt) DA11 131 GF91
Baker La, Mitch. CR4 140 DG96
Baker Pas, NW10
off Baker Rd 80 CS67
Baker Rd, NW10 80 CS67
SE18 104 EL80
Bakers Av, E17 67 EB58
Bakers Cl, Ken. CR8 160 DQ114
Bakers Ct, SE25 142 DS97
Bakers End, SW20 139 CY96
Bakers Fld, N7
off Crayford Rd 65 DK63
Bakers Gdns, Cars. SM5 140 DE103
Bakers Hall Ct, EC3 201 N1
Bakers Hill, E5 66 DW60
Barnet EN5 28 DB40
Bakers La, N6 64 DF57
Epping CM16 17 ET30
Bakers Mead, Gdse. RH9 186 DW130
Baker's Ms, W1 194 F8
Bakers Ms, Orp. BR6 163 ET107
Bakers Pas, NW3
off Heath St 64 DC63
Baker's Rents, E2 197 P3
Bakers Rd, Uxb. UB8 76 BK66
Waltham Cross (Chsht) EN7 14 DV30
Bakers Row, E15 86 EE68
Baker's Row, EC1 196 D5
⊖ Baker Street 194 E6
Baker St, NW1 194 E5
W1 194 E6
Enfield EN1 30 DR41
Potters Bar EN6 27 CY35
Weybridge KT13 152 BN105
Bakers Wd, Uxb. (Denh.) UB9 57 BD60
Baker's Yd, EC1
off Baker's Row 83 DN70
Uxbridge UB8
off Bakers Rd 76 BK66
Bakery Cl, SW9 101 DM81
Bakery Path, Edg. HA8
off Station Rd 42 CP51
Bakery Pl, SW11
off Altenburg Gdns 100 DF84
Bakewell Way, N.Mal. KT3 138 CS96
Balaams La, N14 45 DK47
Balaam St, E13 86 EG69
Balaclava Rd, SE1 202 A9
Surbiton KT6 137 CJ101
Bala Grn, NW9
off Snowdon Dr 62 CS58
Balcaskie Rd, SE9 125 EM85
Balchen Rd, SE3 104 EK82
Balchier Rd, SE22 122 DV86
Balcombe Cl, Bexh. DA6 106 EX84
Balcombe St, NW1 194 D5
Balcon Ct, W5 off Boileau Rd 80 CM72
Balcon Way, Borwd. WD6 26 CQ39
Balcorne St, E9 84 DW66
Balder Ri, SE12 124 EH89
Balderton St, W1 194 G9
Baldocks Rd, Epp. (They.B.) CM16 33 ES35
Baldock St, E3 85 EB68
Baldock Way, Borwd. WD6 26 CM39
Baldry Gdns, SW16 121 DL93
Baldwin Cres, SE5 102 DQ81
Baldwin Gdns, Houns. TW3
off Chamberlain Gdns 96 CC81
Baldwin's Gdns, EC1 196 D6
Baldwins Hill, Loug. IG10 33 EM40
Baldwins La, Rick. (Crox.Grn) WD3 22 BN42
Baldwin St, EC1 197 K3
Baldwin Ter, N1 84 DQ68
Baldwyn Gdns, W3 80 CQ73
Baldwyns Pk, Bex. DA5 127 FD89
Baldwyns Rd, Bex. DA5 127 FD89
Balearic Apts, E16
off Western Gateway 86 EG73
Bale Rd, E1 85 DY71
Balfern Gro, W4 98 CS78
Balfern St, SW11 100 DE81
Balfe St, N1 196 A1
Balfont Cl, S.Croy. CR2 160 DU113
Balfour Av, W7 79 CF74
Woking GU22 166 AY122
Balfour Business Cen, Sthl. UB2 96 BX76
Balfour Gro, N20 44 DF48
Balfour Ho, W10
off St. Charles Sq 81 CX71
Balfour Ms, N9
off The Broadway 46 DU48
W1 198 G2
Balfour Pl, SW15 99 CV84
W1 198 G1
Balfour Rd, N5 66 DQ63
SE25 142 DU98
SW19 120 DB94
W3 80 CQ71
W13 97 CG75
Bromley BR2 144 EK99
Carshalton SM5 158 DF108
Grays RM17 110 GC77
Harrow HA1 61 CD57
Hounslow TW3 96 CB83
Ilford IG1 69 EP61
Southall UB2 96 BX76
Weybridge KT13 152 BN105
Balfour St, SE17 201 K8
Balfron Twr, E14
off St. Leonards Rd 85 EC72
Balgonie Rd, E4 47 ED46
Balgores Cres, Rom. RM2 71 FH55
Balgores La, Rom. RM2 71 FH55
Balgores Sq, Rom. RM2 71 FH56
Balgowan Cl, N.Mal. KT3 138 CS99
Balgowan Rd, Beck. BR3 143 DY97
Balgowan St, SE18 105 ET77
BALHAM, SW12 120 DF88
⇌ Balham 121 DH88
⊖ Balham 121 DH88
Balham Continental Mkt, SW12
off Shipka Rd 121 DH88
Balham Gro, SW12 120 DG87
Balham High Rd, SW12 120 DG88
SW17 120 DG89
Balham Hill, SW12 121 DH87
Balham New Rd, SW12 121 DH87
Balham Pk Rd, SW12 120 DF88
Balham Rd, N9 46 DU47
Balham Sta Rd, SW12 121 DH88
Balkan Wk, E1 202 D1
Balladier Wk, E14 85 EB71
Ballamore Rd, Brom. BR1 124 EG90
Ballance Rd, E9 85 DX65
Ballands N, The, Lthd. (Fetch.) KT22 171 CE122
Ballands S, The, Lthd. (Fetch.) KT22 171 CE123
Ballantine St, SW18 100 DC84
Ballantyne Cl, SE9
off Horning Cl 124 EL91
Ballantyne Dr, Tad. (Kgswd) KT20 173 CZ121
Ballard Cl, Kings.T. KT2 118 CR94
Ballards Cl, Dag. RM10 89 FB67
Ballards Fm Rd, Croy. CR0 160 DU107
South Croydon CR2 160 DU107
Ballards Grn, Tad. KT20 173 CY119
Ballards La, N3 44 DA53
N12 44 DA53
Oxted RH8 188 EJ129
Ballards Ms, Edg. HA8 42 CN51
Ballards Ri, S.Croy. CR2 160 DU107
Ballards Rd, NW2 63 CU61
Dagenham RM10 89 FB67
Ballards Way, Croy. CR0 160 DV107
Ballards Way, S. Croy. CR2 160 DU107
Ballast Quay, SE10 204 G10
Ballater Cl, Wat. WD19 40 BW49
Ballater Rd, SW2 101 DL84
South Croydon CR2 160 DT106
Ball Ct, EC3 off Cornhill 84 DR72
Ballenger Ct, Wat. WD18 23 BV41
Ballina St, SE23 123 DX86
Ballingdon Rd, SW11 120 DG86
Ballinger Pt, E3
off Bromley High St 85 EB69
Ballinger Way, Nthlt. UB5 78 BY70
Balliol Av, E4 47 ED49
Balliol Rd, N17 46 DS53
W10 81 CW72
Welling DA16 106 EV82
Balloch Rd, SE6 123 ED88
Ballogie Av, NW10 62 CS63
Ballow Cl, SE5 off Harris St 102 DS80
Balls Pond Pl, N1
off Balls Pond Rd 84 DR65
Balls Pond Rd, N1 84 DR65
Balmain Cl, W5 79 CK74
Balmer Rd, E3 85 DZ68
Balmes Rd, N1 84 DR67
Balmoral Apts, W2
off Praed St 82 DE71
Balmoral Av, N11 44 DG50
Beckenham BR3 143 DY98
Balmoral Cl, SW15 119 CX86
St. Albans (Park St) AL2 8 CC28
Balmoral Ct, Wor.Pk. KT4 139 CV103
Balmoral Cres, W.Mol. KT8 136 CA97
Balmoral Dr, Borwd. WD6 26 CR43
Hayes UB4 77 BT71
Southall UB1 78 BZ70
Woking GU22 167 BC116
Balmoral Gdns, W13 97 CG76
Bexley DA5 126 EZ87
Ilford IG3 69 ET60
South Croydon CR2 160 DR110
Balmoral Gro, N7 83 DM65
Balmoral Ms, W12 99 CT75
Balmoral Rd, E7 68 EJ63
E10 67 EB61
NW2 81 CV65
Abbots Langley WD5 7 BU32
Brentwood (Pilg.Hat.) CM15 54 FV44
Dartford (Sutt.H.) DA4 128 FP94
Enfield EN3 31 DX36
Harrow HA2 60 CA63
Hornchurch RM12 72 FK62
Kingston upon Thames KT1 138 CM98
Romford RM2 71 FH56
Watford WD24 24 BW38
Worcester Park KT4 139 CV104
Balmoral Way, Sutt. SM2 158 DA110
Balmore Cl, E14 85 EC72
Balmore Cres, Barn. EN4 28 DG43
Balmore St, N19 65 DH61
Balmuir Gdns, SW15 99 CW84
Balnacraig Av, NW10 62 CS63
Balniel Gate, SW1 199 N10
Balquhain Cl, Ashtd. KT21 171 CK117
Baltic Apts, E16
off Western Gateway 86 EG73
Baltic Cl, SW19 120 DD94
Baltic Ct, SE16 203 J4
Baltic Pl, N1
off Kingsland Rd 84 DS67
Baltic Quay, SE16
off Sweden Gate 103 DY77
Baltic St E, EC1 197 H5
Baltic St W, EC1 197 H5
Baltic Wf, Grav. DA11 131 GG86
Baltimore Ho, SW18
off York Rd 100 DC84
Baltimore Pl, Well. DA16 105 ET82
Balvaird Pl, SW1 101 DK78
Balvernie Gro, SW18 119 CZ87
Bamber Ho, Bark. IG11
off St. Margarets 87 EQ67
Bamber Rd, SE15
off Moody Rd 102 DT81
Bamborough Gdns, W12 99 CW75
Bamford Av, Wem. HA0 80 CM67
Bamford Rd, Bark. IG11 87 EQ65
Bromley BR1 123 EC92
Bamford Way, Rom. RM5 51 FB50
Bampfylde Cl, Wall. SM6 141 DJ104
Bampton Dr, NW7 43 CU52
Bampton Rd, SE23 123 DX90
Romford RM3 52 FL53
Bampton Way, Wok. GU21 166 AU118
Banavie Gdns, Beck. BR3 143 EC95
Banbury Cl, Enf. EN2
off Holtwhites Hill 29 DP39
Banbury Ct, WC2 195 P10
Sutton SM2 158 DA108
Banbury Enterprise Cen, Croy. CR0 off Factory La 141 DP103
Banbury Rd, E9 85 DX66
E17 47 DX52
Banbury St, SW11 100 DE82
Watford WD18 23 BU43
Banbury Vil, Grav. DA13 130 FZ94
Banbury Wk, Nthlt. UB5
off Brabazon Rd 78 CA68
Banchory Rd, SE3 104 EH80
Bancroft Av, N2 64 DE57
Buckhurst Hill IG9 48 EG47
Bancroft Chase, Horn. RM12 71 FF61
Bancroft Cl, Ashf. TW15
off Feltham Hill Rd 114 BN92
Bancroft Ct, SW8
off Allen Edwards Dr 101 DL81
Northolt UB5 78 BW67
Reigate RH2 184 DB134
Bancroft Gdns, Har. HA3 40 CC53
Orpington BR6 145 ET102
Bancroft Rd, E1 84 DW69
Harrow HA3 40 CC54
Reigate RH2 184 DA134
Band La, Egh. TW20 113 AZ92
Bandon Cl, Uxb. UB10 76 BM67
Bandon Ri, Wall. SM6 159 DK106
Banfield Rd, SE15 102 DV83
Bangalore St, SW15 99 CW83
Bangor Cl, Nthlt. UB5 60 CB64
Bangors Cl, Iver SL0 75 BE72
Bangors Rd N, Iver SL0 75 BD67
Bangors Rd S, Iver SL0 75 BE71
Banim St, W6 99 CV76
Banister Ms, NW6
off Compayne Gdns 82 DB66
Banister Rd, W10 81 CX69
⊖ Bank 197 K9
DLR Bank 197 K9
Bank, The, N6
off Cholmeley Pk 65 DH60
Bank Av, Mitch. CR4 140 DD96
Bank Ct, Dart. DA1
off High St 128 FL86
Bank End, SE1 201 J2
Bankfoot, Grays (Bad.Dene) RM17 110 FZ77
Bankfoot Rd, Brom. BR1 124 EE91
Bankhurst Rd, SE6 123 DZ87
Bank La, SW15 118 CS85
Kingston upon Thames KT2 118 CL94
Bank Ms, Sutt. SM1
off Sutton Ct Rd 158 DC107
★ Bank of England, EC2 197 K9
★ Bank of England Mus, EC2 197 L9
Bank Pl, Brwd. CM14
off High St 54 FW47
Banksian Wk, Islw. TW7 97 CE81
Banksia Rd, N18 46 DW50
Bankside, SE1 201 H1
Enfield EN2 29 DP39
Gravesend (Nthflt) DA11 130 GC86
Sevenoaks (Dunt.Grn) TN13 190 FE121
South Croydon CR2 160 DT107
Southall UB1 78 BX74
Woking GU21
off Wyndham Rd 166 AV118
Bankside Av, SE13 103 EB83
Northolt UB5
off Townson Av 77 BU68
Bankside Cl, N4 66 DQ58
Bexley DA5 127 FD91
Carshalton SM5 158 DE107
Isleworth TW7 97 CF84
Uxbridge (Hare.) UB9 38 BG51
Westerham (Bigg.H.) TN16 178 EJ118
Bankside Dr, T.Ditt. KT7 137 CH102
★ Bankside Gall, SE1 200 G1
Bankside Lofts, SE1
off Hopton St 83 DP74
Riv Bankside Pier 201 H1
Bankside Rd, Ilf. IG1 69 EQ64
Bankside Way, SE19
off Lunham Rd 122 DS93
Banks La, Bexh. DA6 106 EZ84
Epping CM16 18 EY32
Bank's La, Lthd. (Eff.) KT24 169 BV122
Banks Rd, Borwd. WD6 26 CQ40
Bank St, E14 204 A3
Gravesend DA12 131 GH86
Sevenoaks TN13 191 FH125
Banks Way, E12
off Grantham Rd 69 EN63
Bankton Rd, SW2 101 DN84
Bankwell Rd, SE13 104 EE84
Bann Cl, S.Ock. RM15 91 FV73
Banner Cl, Purf. RM19
off Brimfield Rd 109 FR77
Bannerman Ho, SW8 101 DM79
Banner St, EC1 197 J5
Banning St, SE10 104 EE78
Bannister Cl, SW2
off Ewen Cres 121 DN88
Greenford UB6 61 CD64
Slough SL3 92 AY75
Bannister Dr, Brwd. (Hutt.) CM13 55 GC44
Bannister Gdns, Orp. BR5
off Main Rd 146 EW97
Bannister Ho, E9
off Homerton High St 67 DX64
Bannockburn Rd, SE18 105 ES77
Bannow Cl, Epsom KT19 156 CS105
★ Banqueting Ho, SW1 199 P3
BANSTEAD, SM7 174 DB115
⇌ Banstead 157 CY114
Banstead Gdns, N9 46 DS48
Banstead Rd, Bans. SM7 157 CX112
Carshalton SM5 158 DE107
Caterham CR3 176 DR121
Epsom KT17 157 CV110
Purley CR8 159 DN111
Banstead Rd S, Sutt. SM2 158 DD110
Banstead St, SE15 102 DW83
Banstead Way, Wall. SM6 159 DL106
Banstock Rd, Edg. HA8 42 CP51
Banting Dr, N21 29 DM43
Banton Cl, Enf. EN1
off Central Av 30 DV40
Bantry St, SE5 102 DR80
Banwell Rd, Bex. DA5
off Woodside La 126 EX86
Banyard Rd, SE16 202 E7
Banyards, Horn. RM11 72 FL56
Bapchild Pl, Orp. BR5 146 EW98
Baptist Gdns, NW5
off Queen's Cres 82 DG65
Barandon Wk, W11 81 CX73
Barbara Brosnan Ct, NW8
off Grove End Rd 82 DD68
Barbara Castle Cl, SW6 99 CZ79
Barbara Cl, Shep. TW17 135 BP99
Barbara Hucklesby Cl, N22
off The Sandlings 45 DP54
Barbauld Rd, N16 66 DS62
Barbel Cl, Wal.Cr. EN8 15 EA34
Barber Cl, N21 45 DN45
Barberry Cl, Rom. RM3 52 FJ52
Barber's All, E13 86 EH69
Barbers Rd, E15 85 EB68
BARBICAN, EC2 197 H7
⇌ Barbican 196 G6
⊖ Barbican 196 G6
★ Barbican Arts & Conf Cen, EC2 197 J6
Barbican Rd, Grnf. UB6 78 CB72
Barb Ms, W6 99 CW76
Barbon Cl, WC1 196 A6
Barbot Cl, N9 46 DU48
Barchard St, SW18 120 DB85
Barchester Cl, W7 79 CF74
Barchester Cl, Uxb. UB8 76 BJ70
Barchester Rd, Har. HA3 41 CD54
Slough SL3 93 AZ75
Barchester St, E14 85 EB71
Barclay Cl, SW6 100 DA80
Leatherhead (Fetch.) KT22 170 CB123
Watford WD18 23 BU44
Barclay Oval, Wdf.Grn. IG8 48 EG49
Barclay Path, E17 67 EC57
Barclay Rd, E11 68 EE60
E13 86 EJ70
E17 67 EC57
N18 46 DR51
SW6 100 DA80
Croydon CR0 142 DR104
Barclay Way, Grays (W.Thur.) RM20 109 FT78
Barcombe Av, SW2 121 DL89
Barcombe Cl, Orp. BR5 145 ET97
Barden Cl, Uxb. (Hare.) UB9 38 BJ52
Barden St, SE18 105 ES80
Bardeswell Cl, Brwd. CM14 54 FW47
Bardfield Av, Rom. RM6 70 EX55
Bardney Rd, Mord. SM4 140 DB98
Bardolph Av, Croy. CR0 161 DZ109
Bardolph Rd, N7 65 DL63
Richmond TW9
off St. Georges Rd 98 CM83
Bardon Wk, Wok. GU21
off Bampton Way 166 AV117
Bard Rd, W10 81 CX73
Bardsey Pl, E1
off Mile End Rd 84 DW71
Bardsey Wk, N1
off Clephane Rd 84 DQ65
Bardsley Cl, Croy. CR0 142 DT104
Bardsley La, SE10 103 EC79
Barfett St, W10 81 CZ70
Barfield, Dart. (Sutt.H.) DA4 148 FP95
Barfield Av, N20 44 DE47
Barfield Rd, E11 68 EF60
Bromley BR1 145 EN97
Barfields, Loug. IG10 33 EN42
Redhill (Bletch.) RH1 185 DP133
Barfields Gdns, Loug. IG10
off Barfields 33 EN42
Barfields Path, Loug. IG10 33 EN42
Barfleur La, SE8 203 M9
Barford Cl, NW4 43 CU53
Barford St, N1 83 DN67
Barforth Rd, SE15 102 DV83
Barfreston Way, SE20 142 DV95
Bargate Cl, SE18 105 ET78
New Malden KT3 139 CU101
Barge Ho Rd, E16 87 EP75
Barge Ho St, SE1 200 E2
Barge La, E3
off Birdsfield La 85 DZ67
Bargery Rd, SE6 123 EB88
Barge Wk, E.Mol. KT8 137 CK96
Kingston upon Thames KT1 137 CK95
Walton-on-Thames KT12 136 BX97
Bargrove Cl, SE20 122 DU94
Bargrove Cres, SE6
off Elm La 123 DZ89
Barham Av, Borwd. (Els.) WD6 26 CM41
Barham Cl, Brom. BR2 144 EL102
Chislehurst BR7 125 EP92
Gravesend DA12 131 GM88
Romford RM7 51 FB54
Wembley HA0 79 CH65
Weybridge KT13 153 BQ105
Barham Rd, SW20 119 CU94
Chislehurst BR7 125 EP92
Dartford DA1 128 FN87
South Croydon CR2 160 DQ106
Baring Cl, SE12 124 EG89
Baring Rd, SE12 124 EG87
Barnet EN4 28 DD41
Croydon CR0 142 DU102
Baring St, N1 84 DR67
Barkantine Shop Par, The, E14 203 P5
Bark Burr Rd, Grays RM16 110 FZ75
Barker Cl, Cher. KT16 133 BE101
New Malden KT3 138 CP98
Northwood HA6 39 BT52
Richmond TW9 98 CP82
Barker Dr, NW1 83 DJ66
Barker Ms, SW4 101 DH84
Barker Rd, Cher. KT16 133 BE101
Barker St, SW10 100 DC79
Barker Wk, SW16 121 DK90
Barkham Rd, N17 46 DR52
Barkham Ter, SE1 200 E6
Bark Hart Rd, Orp. BR6 146 EV102
BARKING, IG11 87 EP67
⇌ Barking 87 EQ66
⊖ Barking 87 EQ66
H Barking Hosp, Bark. IG11 87 ET66
Barking Ind Pk, Bark. IG11 87 ET67
Barking Rd, E6 86 EK68
E13 86 EH70
E16 86 EF71
BARKINGSIDE, Ilf. IG6 69 EP55
⊖ Barkingside 69 ER56
Bark Pl, W2 82 DB73
Barkston Gdns, SW5 100 DB77
Barkston Path, Borwd. WD6 26 CN37
Barkway Dr, Orp. BR6 163 EN105
Barkwood Cl, Rom. RM7 71 FC57
Barkworth Rd, SE16 102 DV78
Barlborough St, SE14 102 DW80
Barlby Gdns, W10 81 CX70
Barlby Rd, W10 81 CX71
Barlee Cres, Uxb. UB8 76 BJ71
Barle Gdns, S.Ock. RM15 91 FV72
Barley Brow, Wat. WD25 7 BV31
Barley Cl, Bushey WD23 24 CB43
Wembley HA0
off Harrowdene Rd 61 CK63
Barleycorn Way, E14 85 DZ73
Hornchurch RM11 72 FM58
Barleyfields Cl, Rom. RM6 70 EV59
Barley La, Ilf. IG3 70 EU60

★ Place of interest ⇌ Railway station ⊖ London Underground station DLR Docklands Light Railway station Tra Tramlink station H Hospital Riv Pedestrian ferry landing stage

Barley La, Rom. RM6 70 EV58
Barley Mow Ct, Bet. RH3 182 CQ134
Barley Mow Pas, EC1 196 G7
W4 98 CR78
Barley Mow Rd, Egh. (Eng.Grn)
TW20 112 AW92
Barley Mow Way, Shep.
TW17 134 BN98
Barley Shotts Business Pk, W10
off St. Ervans Rd 81 CZ71
Barlow Cl, Wall. SM6 159 DL108
Barlow Dr, SE18 104 EL81
Barlow Ho, SE16
off Rennie Est 102 DV77
Barlow Pl, W1 199 J1
Barlow Rd, NW6 81 CZ65
W3 80 CP74
Hampton TW12 116 CA94
Barlow St, SE17 201 L9
Barlow Way, Rain. RM13 89 FD71
Barmeston Rd, SE6 123 EB89
Barmor Cl, Har. HA2 40 CB54
Barmouth Av, Grnf. UB6 79 CF68
Barmouth Rd, SW18 120 DC86
Croydon CR0 143 DX103
Barnabas Ct, N21
off Cheyne Wk 29 DN43
Barnabas Rd, E9 67 DX64
Barnaby Cl, Har. HA2 60 CC61
Barnaby Pl, SW7 100 DD77
Barnaby Way, Chig. IG7 49 EP48
Barnacre Cl, Uxb. UB8
off New Peachey La 76 BK72
Barnacres Rd, Hem.H. HP3 6 BM25
Barnard Cl, SE18 105 EN77
Chislehurst BR7 145 ER95
Sunbury-on-Thames TW16
off Oak Gro 115 BV94
Wallington SM6 159 DK108
Barnard Ct, Wok. GU21 166 AS118
Barnard Gdns, Hayes UB4 77 BV70
New Malden KT3 139 CU98
Barnard Gro, E15
off Vicarage La 86 EF66
Barnard Hill, N10 44 DG54
Barnard Ms, SW11 100 DE84
Barnardo Dr, Ilf. IG6 69 EQ56
Barnardo Gdns, E1
off Devonport St 85 DX73
Barnardo St, E1
off Devonport St 85 DX72
Barnardos Village, Ilf. IG6 69 EQ55
Barnard Rd, SW11 100 DE84
Enfield EN1 30 DV40
Mitcham CR4 140 DG97
Warlingham CR6 177 EB119
Barnard's Inn, EC1 196 E8
Barnards Pl, S.Croy. CR2 159 DP109
Barnato Cl, W.Byf. KT14 152 BL112
Barnby Sq, E15 off Barnby St 86 EE67
Barnby St, E15 86 EE67
NW1 195 L1
Barn Cl, Ashf. TW15 115 BP92
Banstead SM7 174 DD115
Epsom KT18
off Woodcote Side 172 CP115
Northolt UB5 78 BW68
Radlett WD7 25 CG35
Barn Cres, Pur. CR8 160 DR113
Stanmore HA7 41 CJ51
Barncroft Cl, Loug. IG10 33 EN43
Uxbridge UB8 77 BP71
Barncroft Grn, Loug. IG10 33 EN43
Barncroft Rd, Loug. IG10 33 EN43
Barneby Cl, Twick. TW2
off Rowntree Rd 117 CE88
BARNEHURST, Bexh. DA7 107 FD83
⇌ Barnehurst 107 FC82
Barnehurst Av, Bexh. DA7 107 FC81
Erith DA8 107 FC81
Barnehurst Cl, Erith DA8 107 FC81
Barnehurst Rd, Bexh. DA7 107 FC82
Barn Elms Pk, SW15 99 CW82
Barn End Dr, Dart. DA2 128 FJ90
Barn End La, Dart. DA2 128 FJ92
BARNES, SW13 99 CU82
⇌ Barnes 99 CU83
Barnes All, Hmptn. TW12
off Hampton Ct Rd 136 CC96
Barnes Av, SW13 99 CU80
Southall UB2 96 BZ77
⇌ Barnes Bridge 98 CS82
Barnes Br, SW13 98 CS82
W4 98 CS82
Barnesbury Ho, SW4 121 DK85
Barnes Cl, E12 68 EK63
★ Barnes Common, SW13 99 CU83
Barnes Ct, E16
off Ridgwell Rd 86 EJ71
Barnet EN5 28 DB42
Woodford Green IG8 48 EK50
BARNES CRAY, Dart. DA1 107 FH84
Barnes Cray Cotts, Dart. DA1
off Maiden La 127 FG85
Barnes Cray Rd, Dart. DA1 107 FG84
Barnesdale Cres, Orp. BR5 146 EU100
Barnes End, N.Mal. KT3 139 CU99
Barnes High St, SW13 99 CT82
H Barnes Hosp, SW14 98 CS83
Barnes Ho, Bark. IG11
off St. Marys 87 ER67
Barnes La, Kings L. WD4 6 BH27
Barnes Pikle, W5 79 CK73
Barnes Ri, Kings L. WD4 6 BM27
Barnes Rd, N18 46 DW49
Ilford IG1 69 EQ64
Barnes St, E14 85 DY72
Barnes Ter, SE8 103 DZ78
Barnes Wallis Dr, Wey. KT13 152 BL111
Barnes Way, Iver SL0 75 BF73
BARNET, EN4 & EN5 27 CZ41
Barnet Bypass, Barn. EN5 26 CS41
Barnet Dr, Brom. BR2 144 EL103
BARNET GATE, Barn. EN5 27 CT44
Barnet Gate La, Barn. EN5 27 CT44
Barnet Gro, E2 84 DU69
Barnet Hill, Barn. EN5 28 DA42
H Barnet Hosp, Barn. EN5 27 CX42
Barnet La, N20 43 CZ46
Barnet EN5 27 CZ44
Borehamwood WD6 25 CK44
★ Barnet Mus, Barn. EN5
off Wood St 27 CY42
Barnet Rd, Barn. EN5 27 CV43
Potters Bar EN6 28 DA35
St. Albans (Lon.Col.) AL2 10 CL27
Barnett Cl, Erith DA8 107 FF82
Leatherhead KT22 171 CH119
Barnet Trd Est, Barn. EN5 27 CZ41
Barnetts Shaw, Oxt. RH8 187 ED127
Barnett St, E1
off Cannon St Rd 84 DV72
Barnett Wd La, Ashtd. KT21 171 CJ119
Leatherhead KT22 171 CH120
Barnet Way, NW7 42 CR45
Barnet Wd Rd, Brom. BR2 144 EJ103
Barney Cl, SE7 104 EJ78
Barnfield, Bans. SM7 158 DB114
Epping CM16 18 EU28
Gravesend DA11 131 GG89
Iver SL0 75 BE72
New Malden KT3 138 CS100
Barnfield Av, Croy. CR0 142 DW103
Kingston upon Thames
KT2 118 CL92
Mitcham CR4 141 DH98
Barnfield Cl, N4
off Crouch Hill 65 DL59
SW17 120 DC90
Coulsdon CR5 176 DQ119
Greenhithe DA9 129 FT86
Swanley BR8 147 FC101
Barnfield Gdns, SE18
off Plumstead
Common Rd 105 EP79
Kingston upon Thames
KT2 118 CL91
Barnfield Pl, E14 204 A9
Barnfield Rd, SE18 105 EP79
W5 79 CJ70
Belvedere DA17 106 EZ79
Edgware HA8 42 CQ53
Orpington BR5 146 EX97
Sevenoaks TN13 190 FD123
South Croydon CR2 160 DS109
Westerham (Tats.) TN16 178 EK120
Barnfield Way, Oxt. RH8 188 EG133
Barnfield Wd Cl, Beck. BR3 143 ED100
Barnfield Wd Rd, Beck. BR3 143 ED100
Barnham Dr, SE28 87 ET74
Barnham Rd, Grnf. UB6 78 CC69
Barnham St, SE1 201 N4
Barnhill, Pnr. HA5 60 BW57
Barn Hill, Wem. HA9 62 CP61
Barnhill Av, Brom. BR2 144 EF99
Barnhill La, Hayes UB4 77 BV69
Barnhill Rd, Hayes UB4 77 BV70
Wembley HA9 62 CQ62
Barnhurst Path, Wat. WD19 40 BW50
Barningham Way, NW9 62 CR58
Barn Lea, Rick. (Mill End)
WD3 38 BG46
Barnlea Cl, Felt. TW13 116 BY89
Barn Mead, Epp. (They.B.)
CM16 33 ES36
Ongar CM5 19 FE29
Barnmead, Wok. (Chobham)
GU24 150 AT110
Barnmead Gdns, Dag. RM9 70 EZ64
Barn Meadow, Epp. CM16
off Upland Rd 17 ET25
Barn Meadow La, Lthd. (Bkhm)
KT23 170 BZ124
Barnmead Rd, Beck. BR3 143 DY95
Dagenham RM9 70 EZ64
Barnock Cl, Dart. DA1 127 FE87
Barn Ri, Wem. HA9 62 CN60
BARNSBURY, N1 83 DM66
Barnsbury Cl, N.Mal. KT3 138 CQ98
Barnsbury Cres, Surb. KT5 138 CQ102
Barnsbury Est, N1
off Barnsbury Rd 83 DN67
Barnsbury Gro, N7 83 DM66
Barnsbury La, Surb. KT5 138 CP103
Barnsbury Pk, N1 83 DN66
Barnsbury Rd, N1 83 DN68
Barnsbury Sq, N1 83 DN66
Barnsbury St, N1 83 DN66
Barnsbury Ter, N1 83 DM66
Barns Ct, Wal.Abb. EN9 16 EG32
Barnscroft, SW20 139 CV97
Barnsdale Av, E14 204 A8
Barnsdale Cl, Borwd. WD6 26 CM39
Barnsdale Rd, W9 81 CZ70
Barnsfield Pl, Uxb. UB8 76 BJ66
Barnsley Rd, Rom. RM3 52 FM52
Barnsley St, E1 84 DV70
Barnstaple Path, Rom. RM3 52 FJ50
Barnstaple Rd, Rom. RM3 52 FJ50
Ruislip HA4 60 BW62
Barnston Wk, N1
off Popham St 84 DQ67
Barnston Way, Brwd. (Hutt.)
CM13 55 GC43
Barn St, N16 off Stoke
Newington Ch St 66 DS62
Barnsway, Kings L. WD4 6 BL28
Barnway, Egh. (Eng.Grn)
TW20 112 AW92
Barn Way, Wem. HA9 62 CN60
Barnwell Rd, SW2 121 DN85
Dartford DA1 108 FM83
Barnwood Cl, N20 43 CZ46
W9 82 DB70
Ruislip HA4
off Lysander Rd 59 BR61
Barnyard, The, Tad. (Walt.Hill)
KT20 173 CU124
Baron Cl, N11 44 DG50
Sutton SM2 158 DB110
Baroness Rd, E2 off Diss St 84 DT69
Baronet Gro, N17
off St. Paul's Rd 46 DU53
Baronet Rd, N17 46 DU53
Baron Gdns, Ilf. IG6 69 EQ55
Baron Gro, Mitch. CR4 140 DE98
Baron Ho, SW19
off Chapter Way 140 DD95
Baron Rd, Dag. RM8 70 EX60
Barons, The, Twick. TW1 117 CH86
⊖ Barons Court 99 CY78
Barons Ct, Wall. SM6
off Whelan Way 141 DK104
Barons Ct Rd, W14 99 CY78
Baronsfield Rd, Twick. TW1 117 CH86
Barons Gate, Barn. EN4 28 DE44
Barons Hurst, Epsom KT18 172 CQ116
Barons Keep, W14 99 CY78
Barons Mead, Har. HA1 61 CE56
Baronsmead Rd, SW13 99 CU81
Baronsmede, W5 98 CM75
Baronsmere Rd, N2 64 DE56
Barons Pl, SE1 200 E5
Baron St, N1 83 DN68
Barons Wk, Croy. CR0 143 DY100
Barons Way, Egh. TW20 113 BD93
Baron Wk, E16 86 EF71
Mitcham CR4 140 DE98
Barque Ms, SE8
off Watergate St 103 EA79
Barrack Path, Wok. GU21 166 AT118
Barrack Rd, Houns. TW4 96 BX84
Barrack Row, Grav. DA11 131 GH86
Barracks, The, Add. KT15 134 BH104
Barracks La, Barn. EN5
off High St 27 CY41
Barra Hall Circ, Hayes UB3 77 BS72
Barra Hall Rd, Hayes UB3 77 BS73
Barrass Cl, Enf. EN3 31 EA37
Barratt Av, N22 45 DM54
Barratt Ind Pk, Sthl. UB1 96 CA75
Barratt Way, Har. HA3
off Tudor Rd 61 CD55
Barrenger Rd, N10 44 DF53
Barrens Brae, Wok. GU22 167 BA118
Barrens Cl, Wok. GU22 167 BA118
Barrens Pk, Wok. GU22 167 BA118
Barrett Cl, Rom. RM3 51 FH52
Barrett Rd, E17 67 EC56
Leatherhead (Fetch.) KT22 170 CC124
Barretts Grn Rd, NW10 80 CQ68
Barretts Gro, N16 66 DS64
Barretts Rd, Sev. (Dunt.Grn)
TN13 181 FD120
Barrett St, W1 194 G9
Barrhill Rd, SW2 121 DL89
Barricane, Wok. GU21 166 AV119
Barrie Cl, Couls. CR5 175 DJ115
Barriedale, SE14 103 DY81
Barrie Est, W2
off Craven Ter 82 DD73
Barrier App, SE7 104 EK76
Barrier Pt Rd, E16 86 EJ74
Barrier Pt Twr, E16
off Barrier Pt Rd 104 EJ75
Barringer Sq, SW17 120 DG91
Barrington Cl, NW5 64 DG64
Ilford IG5 49 EM53
Loughton IG10
off Barrington Rd 33 EQ42
Barrington Ct, W3
off Cheltenham Pl 98 CP75
Brentwood (Hutt.) CM13 55 GC44
Barrington Dr, Uxb. (Hare.)
UB9 38 BG52
Barrington Grn, Loug. IG10 33 EQ42
Barrington Lo, Wey. KT13 153 BQ106
Barrington Pk Gdns, Ch.St.G.
HP8 36 AX46
Barrington Rd, E12 87 EN65
N8 65 DK57
SW9 101 DP83
Bexleyheath DA7 106 EX82
Loughton IG10 33 EQ41
Purley CR8 159 DJ112
Sutton SM3 140 DA102
Barrington Vil, SE18 105 EN81
Barrow Av, Cars. SM5 158 DF108
Barrow Cl, N21 45 DP48
Barrowdene Cl, Pnr. HA5
off Paines La 40 BY54
Barrowell Grn, N21 45 DP47
Barrowfield Cl, N9 46 DV48
Barrowgate Rd, W4 98 CQ78
Barrow Grn Rd, Oxt. RH8 187 EC128
Barrow Hedges Cl, Cars.
SM5 158 DE108
Barrow Hedges Way, Cars.
SM5 158 DE108
Barrow Hill, Wor.Pk. KT4 138 CS103
Barrow Hill Cl, Wor.Pk. KT4
off Barrow Hill 138 CS103
Barrow Hill Est, NW8 194 B1
Barrow Hill Rd, NW8 194 B1
Barrow La, Wal.Cr. (Chsht)
EN7 14 DT30
Barrow Pt Av, Pnr. HA5 40 BY54
Barrow Pt La, Pnr. HA5 40 BY54
Barrow Rd, SW16 121 DK93
Croydon CR0 159 DN106
Barrowsfield, S.Croy. CR2 160 DT112
Barrow Wk, Brent. TW8
off Glenhurst Rd 97 CJ78
Barr Rd, Grav. DA12 131 GM89
Potters Bar EN6 12 DC33
Barrsbrook Fm Rd, Cher.
KT16 133 BE102
Barrs Rd, NW10 80 CR66
Barry Av, N15
off Craven Pk Rd 66 DT58
Bexleyheath DA7 106 EY80
Barry Cl, Grays RM16 111 GG75
Orpington BR6 145 ES104
St. Albans AL2 8 CB25
Barry Ho, SE16
off Rennie Est 102 DV78
Barry Rd, E6 86 EL72
NW10 80 CQ66
SE22 122 DU86
Barset Rd, SE15 102 DW83
Barson Cl, SE20 122 DW94
Barston Rd, SE27 122 DQ90
Barstow Cres, SW2 121 DM88
Barter St, WC1 196 A7
Barters Wk, Pnr. HA5
off High St 60 BY55
Barth Ms, SE18 105 ES77
Bartholomew Cl, EC1 197 H7
SW18 100 DC84
Bartholomew Ct, E14
off Newport Av 85 ED73
Bartholomew Dr, Rom.
(Harold Wd) RM3 52 FK54
Bartholomew La, EC2 197 L9
Bartholomew Pl, EC1 197 H7
Bartholomew Rd, NW5 83 DJ65
Bartholomew Sq, E1
off Coventry Rd 84 DV70
EC1 197 J4
Bartholomew St, SE1 201 K7
Bartholomew Vil, NW5 83 DJ65
Bartholomew Way, Swan.
BR8 147 FE97
Barth Rd, SE18 105 ES77
Bartle Av, E6 86 EL68
Bartle Rd, W11 81 CY72
Bartlett Cl, E14 85 EA72
Bartlett Ct, EC4 196 E8
Bartlett Rd, Grav. DA11 131 GG88
Westerham TN16 189 EQ126
Bartletts Pas, EC4 196 E8
Bartlett St, S.Croy. CR2 160 DR106
Bartlow Gdns, Rom. RM5 51 FD53
Barton, The, Cob. KT11 154 BX112
Barton Av, Rom. RM7 71 FB60
Barton Cl, E6 87 EM72
E9 off Churchill Wk 66 DW64
NW4 63 CU57
SE15 off Kirkwood Rd 102 DV83
Addlestone KT15 152 BG107
Bexleyheath DA6 126 EY85
Chigwell IG7 49 EQ47
Shepperton TW17 135 BP100
Barton Gm, N.Mal. KT3 138 CR96
Barton Ho, SW6
off Wandsworth Br Rd 100 DB83
Barton Meadows, Ilf. IG6 69 EQ56
Barton Rd, W14 99 CY78
Dartford (Sutt.H.) DA4 148 FP95
Hornchurch RM12 71 FG60
Sidcup DA14 126 EY93
Slough SL3 93 AZ75
Bartons, The, Borwd. (Els.)
WD6 25 CK44
Barton St, SW1 199 P6
Bartonway, NW8
off Queen's Ter 82 DD68
Barton Way, Borwd. WD6 26 CN40
Rickmansworth (Crox.Grn)
WD3 23 BP43
Bartram Cl, Uxb. UB8 77 BP70
Bartram Rd, SE4 123 DY85
Bartrams La, Barn. EN4 28 DC38
Bartrop Cl, Wal.Cr. EN7
off Poppy Wk 14 DR28
Barts Cl, Beck. BR3 143 EA99
Barville Cl, SE4
off St. Norbert Rd 103 DY84
Barwell Business Pk, Chess.
KT9 155 CK108
Barwick Dr, Uxb. UB8 77 BP71
Barwick Ho, W3 98 CQ75
Barwick Rd, E7 68 EH63
Barwood Av, W.Wick. BR4 143 EB102
Bascombe Gro, Dart. DA1 127 FE87
Bascombe St, SW2 121 DN86
Basden Gro, Felt. TW13 116 CA89
Basedale Rd, Dag. RM9 88 EV66
Baseing Cl, E6 87 EN73
Basevi Way, SE8 103 EB79
Bashley Rd, NW10 80 CR70
Basil Av, E6 86 EL68
Basildene Rd, Houns. TW4 96 BX82
Basildon Av, Ilf. IG5 49 EN53
Basildon Cl, Sutt. SM2 158 DB109
Watford WD18 23 BQ44
Basildon Rd, SE2 106 EU78
Basil Gdns, SE27 122 DQ92
Croydon CR0
off Primrose La 143 DX102
Basilon Rd, Bexh. DA7 106 EY82
Basil St, SW3 198 D6
Basin App, E14
off Commercial Rd 85 DY72
Basing Cl, T.Ditt. KT7 137 CF101
Basing Ct, SE15 102 DT81
Basingdon Way, SE5 102 DR84
Basing Dr, Bex. DA5 126 EZ86
Basingfield Rd, T.Ditt. KT7 137 CF101
Basinghall Av, EC2 197 K7
Basinghall Gdns, Sutt. SM2 158 DB109
Basinghall St, EC2 197 K8
Basing Hill, NW11 63 CZ60
Wembley HA9 62 CM61
Basing Ho, Bark. IG11
off St. Margarets 87 ER67
Basing Ho Yd, E2 197 N2
Basing Pl, E2 197 N2
Basing Rd, Bans. SM7 157 CZ114
Rickmansworth (Mill End)
WD3 37 BF46
Basing St, W11 81 CZ72
Basing Way, N3 64 DA55
Thames Ditton KT7 137 CF101
Basire St, N1 84 DQ67
Baskerville Rd, SW18 120 DE87
Basket Gdns, SE9 124 EL85
Baslow Cl, Har. HA3 41 CD53
Baslow Wk, E5
off Overbury St 67 DX63
Basnett Rd, SW11 100 DG83
Basque Ct, SE16 203 H5
Bassano St, SE22 122 DT85
Bassant Rd, SE18 105 ET79
Bassein Pk Rd, W12 99 CT75
Basset Cl, Add. (New Haw)
KT15 152 BH110
Bassett Cl, Sutt. SM2 158 DB109
Bassett Dr, Reig. RH2 184 DA133
Bassett Flds, Epp. (N.Wld Bas.)
CM16 19 FD25
Bassett Gdns, Epp. (N.Wld Bas.)
CM16 19 FB26
Isleworth TW7 96 CC80
Bassett Ho, Dag. RM9 88 EV67
Bassett Rd, W10 81 CX72
Uxbridge UB8
off New Windsor St 76 BJ67
Woking GU22 167 BC116
Bassetts Cl, Orp. BR6 163 EP105
H Bassetts Day Cen, Orp.
BR6 163 EP105
Bassett St, NW5 82 DG65
Bassetts Way, Orp. BR6 163 EP105
Bassett Way, Grnf. UB6 78 CB72
Bassingham Rd, SW18 120 DC87
Wembley HA0 79 CK65
Bassishaw Highwalk, EC2
off London Wall 84 DQ71
Bastable Av, Bark. IG11 87 ES68
Bastion Highwalk, EC2
off London Wall 84 DQ71
Bastion Ho, EC2
off London Wall 84 DQ71
Bastion Rd, SE2 106 EU78
Baston Manor Rd, Brom.
BR2 144 EH104
Baston Rd, Brom. BR2 144 EH102
Bastwick St, EC1 197 H4
Basuto Rd, SW6 100 DA81
⇌ Bat & Ball 191 FJ121
Bat & Ball Junct, Sev. TN14 191 FH121
Bat & Ball Rd, Sev. TN14 191 FJ121
Batavia Cl, Sun. TW16 136 BW95
Batavia Ms, SE14
off Goodwood Rd 103 DY80
Batavia Rd, SE14 103 DY80
Sunbury-on-Thames
TW16 135 BV95
Batchelor St, N1 83 DN68
Batchwood Grn, Orp. BR5 146 EU97
BATCHWORTH, Rick. WD3 38 BM47
BATCHWORTH HEATH, Rick.
WD3 38 BN49
Batchworth Heath Hill, Rick.
WD3 38 BN49
Batchworth Hill, Rick. WD3 38 BM48
Batchworth La, Nthwd. HA6 39 BS50
Batchworth Rbt, Rick. WD3 38 BK46
Bateman Cl, Bark. IG11
off Glenny Rd 87 EQ65
Bateman Ho, SE17
off Otto St 101 DP79
Bateman Rd, E4 47 EA51
Rickmansworth (Crox.Grn)
WD3 22 BN44
Bateman's Bldgs, W1 195 M9
Batemans Ms, Brwd. (Warley)
CM14 off Vaughan
Williams Way 54 FV49
Bateman's Row, EC2 197 N4
Bateman St, W1 195 M9
Bates Cl, Slou. (Geo.Grn)
SL3 74 AY72
Bates Cres, SW16 121 DJ94
Croydon CR0 159 DN106
Bates Ind Est, Rom. (Harold Wd)
RM3 52 FP52
Bateson St, SE18 105 ES77
Bateson Way, Wok. GU21 151 BC114
Bates Rd, Rom. RM3 52 FN52
Bate St, E14
off Three Colt St 85 DZ73
Bates Wk, Add. KT15 152 BJ108
B.A.T. Export Ho, Wok. GU21 166 AY117
Bath Cl, SE15 off Asylum Rd 102 DV80
Bath Ct, EC1 196 D5
EC1 (St. Luke's Est)
off Bath St 84 DR69
Bathgate Rd, SW19 119 CX90
Bath Ho Rd, Croy. CR0 141 DL102
Bath Pas, Kings.T. KT1
off St. James Rd 137 CK96
Bath Pl, EC2 197 M3
Barnet EN5 27 CZ41
Bath Rd, E7 86 EK65
N9 46 DV47
W4 98 CS77
Dartford DA1 127 FH87
Hayes UB3 95 BQ81
Hounslow TW3, TW4,
TW5, TW6 96 BX82
Romford RM6 70 EY58
Slough (Colnbr.) SL3 93 BB79
West Drayton UB7 94 BK81
Baths Rd, Brom. BR2 144 EK98
Bath St, EC1 197 J3
Gravesend DA11 131 GH86
Bath Ter, SE1 201 H7
Bathurst Av, SW19
off Brisbane Av 140 DB95
Bathurst Cl, Iver SL0 93 BF75
Bathurst Gdns, NW10 81 CV68
Bathurst Ms, W2
off Sussex Pl 82 DD72
Bathurst Rd, Ilf. IG1 69 EP60
Bathurst St, W2 82 DD73
Bathurst Wk, Iver SL0 93 BE75
Bathway, SE18 105 EN77
Batley Cl, Mitch. CR4 140 DF101
Batley Pl, N16 66 DT62
Batley Rd, N16 off Stoke
Newington High St 66 DT62
Enfield EN2 30 DQ39
Batman Cl, W12 81 CV74
Baton Cl, Purf. RM19 109 FR77
Batoum Gdns, W6 99 CW76
Batson Ho, E1
off Fairclough St 84 DU72
Batson St, W12 99 CU75
Batsworth Rd, Mitch. CR4 140 DD97
Batten Av, Wok. GU21 166 AS119
Battenburg Wk, SE19
off Brabourne Cl 122 DS92
Batten Cl, E6
off Savage Gdns 87 EM72
Batten St, SW11 100 DE83
Battersby Rd, SE6 123 ED89
BATTERSEA, SW11 101 DH81
Battersea Br, SW3 100 DD80
SW11 100 DD80
Battersea Br Rd, SW11 100 DE80
Battersea Ch Rd, SW11 100 DD81
★ Battersea Dogs Home,
SW8 101 DH80
Battersea High St, SW11 100 DD81
★ Battersea Park, SW11 100 DF80
⇌ Battersea Park 101 DH80
Battersea Pk Rd, SW8 101 DH81
SW11 100 DE82
Battersea Ri, SW11 120 DE85
Battersea Sq, SW11
off Battersea High St 100 DD81
Battery Rd, SE28 105 ES75
Battis, The, Rom. RM1
off Waterloo Rd 71 FE58
Battishill Gdns, N1
off Waterloo Ter 83 DP66
Battishill St, N1
off Waterloo Ter 83 DP66

★ Place of interest ⇌ Railway station ⊖ London Underground station DLR Docklands Light Railway station Tra Tramlink station H Hospital Riv Pedestrian ferry landing stage

Battlebridge Ct, N1 *off Wharfdale Rd* 83 DL68
Battle Br La, SE1 201 M3
Battlebridge La, Red. (Merst.) RH1 185 DH130
Battle Br Rd, NW1 195 P1
Battle Cl, SW19 120 DC93
Battledean Rd, N5 65 DP64
Battle Rd, Belv. DA17 107 FC77
Erith DA8 107 FC77
Battlers Grn Dr, Rad. WD7 25 CE37
Batts Hill, Red. RH1 184 DE132
Reigate RH2 184 DD132
Batty St, E1 84 DU72
Baudwin Rd, SE6 124 EE89
Baugh Rd, Sid. DA14 126 EW92
Baulk, The, SW18 120 DA87
Bavant Rd, SW16 141 DL96
Bavaria Rd, N19 65 DL61
Bavdene Ms, NW4 *off The Burroughs* 63 CV56
Bavent Rd, SE5 102 DQ82
Bawdale Rd, SE22 122 DT85
Bawdsey Av, Ilf. IG2 69 ET56
Bawtree Cl, Sutt. SM2 158 DC110
Bawtree Rd, SE14 103 DY80
Uxbridge UB8 76 BK65
Bawtry Rd, N20 44 DF48
Baxendale, N20 44 DC47
Baxendale St, E2 84 DU69
Baxter Av, Red. RH1 184 DE134
Baxter Cl, Slou. SL1 92 AS76
Southall UB2 96 CB75
Uxbridge UB10 77 BP69
Baxter Gdns, Rom. (Noak Hill) RM3 *off Cummings Hall La* 52 FJ48
Baxter Rd, E16 86 EJ72
N1 84 DR65
N18 46 DV49
NW10 80 CS70
Ilford IG1 69 EP64
Bayards, Warl. CR6 176 DW118
Bay Ct, W5 *off Popes La* 98 CL76
Baycroft Cl, Pnr. HA5 60 BW55
Baydon Ct, Brom. BR2 144 EF97
Bayes Cl, SE26 122 DW92
Bayeux, Tad. KT20 173 CX122
Bayfield Rd, SE9 104 EK84
Bayford Ms, E8 *off Bayford St* 84 DV66
Bayford Rd, NW10 81 CX69
Bayford St, E8 84 DV66
Baygrove Ms, Kings.T. (Hmptn W.) KT1 137 CJ95
Bayham Pl, NW1 83 DJ67
Bayham Rd, W4 98 CR76
W13 79 CH73
Morden SM4 140 DB98
Sevenoaks TN13 191 FJ123
Bayham St, NW1 83 DJ67
Bayhurst Dr, Nthwd. HA6 39 BT51
★ **Bayhurst Wood Country Pk**, Uxb. UB9 58 BM56
Bayleys Mead, Brwd. (Hutt.) CM13 55 GC47
Bayley St, WC1 195 M7
Bayley Wk, SE2 *off Woolwich Rd* 106 EY78
Baylin Rd, SW18 *off Garratt La* 120 DB86
Baylis Ms, Twick. TW1 *off Amyand Pk Rd* 117 CG87
Baylis Par, Slou. SL1 *off Stoke Poges La* 74 AS72
Baylis Rd, SE1 200 D5
Bayliss Av, SE28 88 EX73
Bayliss Cl, N21 29 DL43
Southall UB1 78 CB72
Bayly Rd, Dart. DA1 128 FN86
Bay Manor La, Grays RM20 109 FT79
Baymans Wd, Brwd. (Shenf.) CM15 54 FY47
Bayne Cl, E6 *off Savage Gdns* 87 EM72
Baynes Cl, Enf. EN1 30 DU40
Baynes Ms, NW3 *off Belsize La* 82 DD65
Baynes St, NW1 83 DJ66
Baynham Cl, Bex. DA5 126 EZ86
Bayonne Rd, W6 99 CY79
Bays Fm Ct, West Dr. UB7 94 BJ80
Bayshill Ri, Nthlt. UB5 78 CB65
Bayston Rd, N16 66 DT62
BAYSWATER, W2 82 DC72
⊖ **Bayswater** 82 DB73
Bayswater Rd, W2 194 A10
Baythorne St, E3 85 DZ71
Bay Tree Av, Lthd. KT22 171 CG120
Bay Tree Cen, Brwd. CM14 *off High St* 54 FW47
Bay Tree Cl, Brom. BR1 144 EJ95
Ilford IG6 *off Hazel La* 49 EP52
Baytree Cl, St.Alb. (Park St) AL2 8 CB27
Sidcup DA15 125 ET88
Waltham Cross EN7 14 DT27
Baytree Ho, E4 *off Dells Cl* 47 EB45
Baytree Rd, SW2 101 DM84
Baytree Wk, Wat. WD17 23 BT38
Baywood Sq, Chig. IG7 50 EV49
Bazalgette Cl, N.Mal. KT3 138 CR99
Bazalgette Gdns, N.Mal. KT3 138 CR99
Bazely St, E14 85 EC73
Bazile Rd, N21 29 DN44
Beacham Cl, SE7 104 EK78
Beachborough Rd, Brom. BR1 123 EC91
Beachcroft Rd, E11 68 EE62
Beachcroft Way, N19 65 DK60
Beach Gro, Felt. TW13 116 CA89
Beachy Rd, E3 85 EA66
Beacon Cl, Bans. SM7 173 CX116
Gerrards Cross (Chal.St.P.) SL9 36 AY52
Uxbridge UB8 58 BK64
Beacon Dr, Dart. (Bean) DA2 129 FV90
Beaconfield Av, Epp. CM16 17 ET29
Beaconfield Rd, Epp. CM16 17 ET29
Beaconfields, Sev. TN13 190 FF126
Beaconfield Way, Epp. CM16 17 ET29
Beacon Gate, SE14 103 DX83
Beacon Gro, Cars. SM5 158 DG105
Beacon Hill, N7 65 DL64
Purfleet RM19 108 FP78
Beacon Hill, Wok. GU21 166 AW118
Beacon Ri, Sev. TN13 190 FG126
Beacon Rd, SE13 123 ED86
Erith DA8 107 FH80
Hounslow (Hthrw Air.) TW6 114 BN86
Beacon Rd Rbt, Houns. (Hthrw Air.) TW6 115 BP86
Beacons, The, Loug. IG10 33 EN38
Beacons Cl, E6 *off Oliver Gdns* 86 EL71
Beaconsfield Cl, N11 44 DG49
SE3 104 EG79
W4 98 CQ78
Beaconsfield Gdns, Esher (Clay.) KT10 155 CE108
Beaconsfield Par, SE9 *off Beaconsfield Rd* 124 EL91
Beaconsfield Pl, Epsom KT17 156 CS112
Beaconsfield Rd, E10 67 EC61
E16 86 EF70
E17 67 DZ58
N9 46 DU49
N11 44 DG48
N15 66 DS56
NW10 81 CT65
SE3 104 EF80
SE9 124 EL89
SE17 102 DR78
W4 98 CR76
W5 97 CJ75
Bexley DA5 127 FE88
Bromley BR1 144 EK97
Croydon CR0 142 DR100
Enfield EN3 31 DX37
Epsom KT18 172 CR119
Esher (Clay.) KT10 155 CE108
Hayes UB4 78 BW74
New Malden KT3 138 CR96
Southall UB1 78 BZ74
Surbiton KT5 138 CM101
Twickenham TW1 117 CH86
Woking GU22 167 AZ120
Beaconsfield Ter, Rom. RM6 70 EX58
Beaconsfield Ter Rd, W14 99 CY76
Beaconsfield Wk, E6 *off East Ham Manor Way* 87 EN72
SW6 99 CZ81
Beacontree Av, E17 47 ED53
Beacontree Rd, E11 68 EF59
Beacon Way, Bans. SM7 173 CX116
Rickmansworth WD3 38 BG45
★ **Beacon Wd Country Pk**, Dart. DA2 129 FV91
Beadles La, Oxt. RH8 187 ED130
Beadlow Cl, Cars. SM5 *off Olveston Wk* 140 DD100
Beadman Pl, SE27 *off Norwood High St* 121 DP91
Beadman St, SE27 121 DP91
Beadnell Rd, SE23 123 DX88
Beadon Rd, W6 99 CW77
Bromley BR2 144 EG98
Beads Hall La, Brwd. (Pilg.Hat.) CM15 54 FV42
Beaford Gro, SW20 139 CY97
Beagle Cl, Felt. TW13 115 BV91
Radlett WD7 25 CF37
Beagles Cl, Orp. BR5 146 EX103
Beak St, W1 195 L10
Beal Cl, Well. DA16 106 EU81
Beale Cl, N13 45 DP50
Beale Pl, E3 85 DZ68
Beale Rd, E3 85 DZ67
Beales La, Wey. KT13 134 BN104
Beal Rd, Ilf. IG1 69 EN61
Beam Av, Dag. RM10 89 FB67
Beames Rd, NW10 *off Lawrence Av* 80 CR67
Beaminster Gdns, Ilf. IG6 49 EP54
Beaminster Ho, SW8 *off Dorset Rd* 101 DM80
Beamish Cl, Epp. (N.Wld Bas.) CM16 19 FC25
Beamish Dr, Bushey (Bushey Hth) WD23 40 CC46
Beamish Ho, SE16 *off Rennie Est* 102 DW77
Beamish Rd, N9 46 DU46
Orpington BR5 146 EW101
Beam Way, Dag. RM10 89 FD66
BEAN, Dart. DA2 129 FV90
Beanacre Cl, E9 85 DZ65
Beane Cft, Grav. DA12 131 GM88
Bean La, Dart. (Bean) DA2 129 FV89
Bean Rd, Bexh. DA6 106 EX84
Greenhithe DA9 129 FV85
Beanshaw, SE9 125 EN91
Beansland Gro, Rom. RM6 50 EY54
Bear All, EC4 196 F8
Bear Cl, Rom. RM7 71 FB58
Beardell St, SE19 122 DT93
Beardow Gro, N14 29 DJ44
Beard Rd, Kings.T. KT2 118 CM92
Beardsfield, E13 *off Valetta Gro* 86 EG67
Beard's Hill, Hmptn. TW12 136 CA95
Beard's Hill Cl, Hmptn. TW12 *off Beard's Hill* 136 CA95
Beardsley Ter, Dag. RM8 *off Fitzstephen Rd* 70 EV64
Beardsley Way, W3 98 CR75
Beards Rd, Ashf. TW15 115 BS93
Bearfield Rd, Kings.T. KT2 118 CL94
Bear Gdns, SE1 201 H2
Bearing Cl, Chig. IG7 50 EU49
Bearing Way, Chig. IG7 50 EU49
Bear La, SE1 200 G2
Bear Rd, Felt. TW13 116 BX92
Bears Den, Tad. (Kgswd) KT20 173 CZ122
Bears Rails Pk, Wind. (Old Wind.) SL4 112 AT87
Bearstead Ri, SE4 123 DZ85
Bearsted Ter, Beck. BR3 143 EA95
Bear St, WC2 195 N10
Bearwood Cl, Add. KT15 *off Ongar Pl* 152 BG107
Potters Bar EN6 12 DD31
Beasley's Ait La, Sun. TW16 135 BT100
Beasleys Yd, Uxb. UB8 *off Warwick Pl* 76 BJ66
Beaton Cl, SE15 102 DT81
Greenhithe DA9 109 FV84
Beatrice Av, SW16 141 DM97
Wembley HA9 62 CL64
Beatrice Cl, E13 *off Chargeable La* 86 EG70
Pinner HA5 *off Reid Cl* 59 BU56
Beatrice Ct, Buck.H. IG9 48 EK47
Beatrice Gdns, Grav. (Nthflt) DA11 130 GE89
Beatrice Pl, W8 100 DB76
Beatrice Rd, E17 67 EA57
N4 65 DN59
N9 46 DW45
SE1 202 C9
Oxted RH8 188 EE129
Richmond TW10 *off Albert Rd* 118 CM85
Southall UB1 78 BZ74
Beatson Wk, SE16 203 K2
Beattie Cl, Felt. TW14 115 BT88
Leatherhead (Bkhm) KT23 170 BZ124
Beattock Ri, N10 65 DH56
Beatty Rd, N16 66 DS63
Stanmore HA7 41 CJ51
Waltham Cross EN8 15 DZ34
Beatty St, NW1 83 DJ68
Beattyville Gdns, Ilf. IG6 69 EN55
Beauchamp Cl, W4 *off Church Path* 98 CQ76
Beauchamp Ct, Stan. HA7 *off Hardwick Cl* 41 CJ50
Beauchamp Gdns, Rick. (Mill End) WD3 38 BG46
Beauchamp Pl, SW3 198 C6
Beauchamp Rd, E7 86 EH66
SE19 142 DR95
SW11 100 DE84
East Molesey KT8 136 CB99
Sutton SM1 158 DA106
Twickenham TW1 117 CG87
West Molesey KT8 136 CB99
Beauchamp St, EC1 196 D7
Beauchamp Ter, SW15 *off Dryburgh Rd* 99 CV83
Beauclare Cl, Lthd. KT22 *off Delderfield* 171 CK121
Beauclerc Rd, W6 99 CV76
Beauclerk Cl, Felt. TW13 *off Florence Rd* 115 BV88
Beaudesert Ms, West Dr. UB7 94 BL75
Beaufort, E6 *off Newark Knok* 87 EN71
Beaufort Av, Har. HA3 61 CG56
Beaufort Cl, E4 *off Higham Sta Av* 47 EB51
SW15 119 CV87
W5 80 CM71
Epping (N.Wld Bas.) CM16 18 FA27
Grays (Chaff.Hun.) RM16 *off Clifford Rd* 110 FZ76
Reigate RH2 183 CZ133
Romford RM7 71 FC56
Woking GU22 167 BC116
Beaufort Ct, SW6 *off Lillie Rd* 100 DA79
Richmond TW10 *off Beaufort Rd* 117 CJ91
Beaufort Dr, NW11 64 DA56
Beaufort Gdns, NW4 63 CW58
SW3 198 C6
SW16 121 DM94
Hounslow TW5 96 BY81
Ilford IG1 69 EN60
Beaufort Ms, SW6 *off Lillie Rd* 99 CZ79
Beaufort Pk, NW11 64 DA56
Beaufort Rd, W5 80 CM71
Kingston upon Thames KT1 138 CL98
Reigate RH2 183 CZ133
Richmond TW10 117 CJ91
Ruislip HA4 *off Lysander Rd* 59 BR61
Twickenham TW1 117 CJ87
Woking GU22 167 BC116
Beauforts, Egh. (Eng.Grn) TW20 112 AW92
Beaufort St, SW3 100 DD79
Beaufort Way, Epsom KT17 157 CU108
Beaufoy Rd, N17 46 DS52
Beaufoy Wk, SE11 200 C9
Beaulieu Av, E16 205 P2
SE26 122 DV91
Beaulieu Cl, NW9 62 CS56
SE5 102 DR83
Hounslow TW4 116 BZ85
Mitcham CR4 140 DG95
Slough (Datchet) SL3 92 AV81
Twickenham TW1 117 CK87
Watford WD19 40 BW46
Beaulieu Dr, Pnr. HA5 60 BX58
Waltham Abbey EN9 15 EB32
Beaulieu Gdns, N21 46 DQ45
Beaulieu Pl, W4 *off Rothschild Rd* 98 CQ76
Beauly Way, Rom. RM1 51 FE53
Beaumanor Gdns, SE9 125 EN91
Beaumaris Dr, Wdf.Grn. IG8 48 EK52
Beaumaris Grn, NW9 *off Goldsmith Av* 62 CS58
Beaumaris Twr, W3 98 CP75
Beaumont Av, W14 99 CZ78
Harrow HA2 60 CB58
Richmond TW9 98 CM83
Wembley HA0 61 CJ64
Beaumont Cl, Kings.T. KT2 118 CN94
Romford RM2 52 FJ54
Beaumont Cres, W14 99 CZ78
Rainham RM13 89 FG65
Beaumont Dr, Ashf. TW15 115 BR92
Gravesend (Nthflt) DA11 130 GE87
Beaumont Gdns, NW3 64 DA62
Brentwood (Hutt.) CM13 *off Bannister Dr* 55 GC44
Beaumont Gate, Rad. WD7 *off Shenley Hill* 25 CH35
Beaumont Gro, E1 85 DX70
Beaumont Ms, W1 194 G6
Pinner HA5 60 BY55
Beaumont Pl, W1 195 L4
Barnet EN5 27 CZ39
Isleworth TW7 117 CF85
Beaumont Pl, Wat. WD18 *off Brightwell Rd* 23 BU43
Beaumont Ri, N19 65 DK60
Beaumont Rd, E10 67 EB59
E13 86 EH69
SE19 122 DQ93
SW19 119 CY87
W4 98 CQ76
Orpington BR5 145 ER100
Purley CR8 159 DN113
Beaumont Sq, E1 85 DX70
Beaumont St, W1 194 G6
Beaumont Vw, Wal.Cr. (Chsht) EN7 14 DR26
Beaumont Wk, NW3 82 DF66
Beauvais Ter, Nthlt. UB5 78 BX69
Beauval Rd, SE22 122 DT86
Beaverbank Rd, SE9 125 ER88
Beaverbrook Rbt, Lthd. KT22 171 CK123
Beaver Cl, SE20 *off Lullington Rd* 122 DU94
Hampton TW12 136 CB95
Morden SM4 139 CW101
Beaver Gro, Nthlt. UB5 *off Jetstar Way* 78 BY69
Beaver Rd, Ilf. IG6 50 EW50
Beavers Cres, Houns. TW4 96 BW84
Beavers La, Houns. TW4 96 BW83
Beavers La Camp, Houns. TW4 *off Beavers La* 96 BW83
Beaverwood Rd, Chis. BR7 125 ES93
Beavor Gro, W6 *off Beavor La* 99 CU77
Beavor La, W6 99 CU77
Bebbington Rd, SE18 105 ES77
Beblets Cl, Orp. BR6 163 ET106
Beccles Dr, Bark. IG11 87 ES65
Beccles St, E14 85 DZ73
Bec Cl, Ruis. HA4 60 BX62
Beck Cl, SE13 103 EB81
Beck Ct, Beck. BR3 143 DX97
BECKENHAM, BR3 143 EA95
Beckenham Business Cen, Beck. BR3 123 DY92
Beckenham Gdns, N9 46 DS48
Beckenham Gro, Brom. BR2 143 ED96
⇌ **Beckenham Hill** 123 EC92
Beckenham Hill Rd, SE6 123 EB92
Beckenham BR3 123 EB92
H **Beckenham Hosp**, Beck. BR3 143 DZ96
⇌ **Beckenham Junction** 143 EA95
Tra **Beckenham Junction** 143 EA95
Beckenham La, Brom. BR2 144 EE96
Beckenham Pl Pk, Beck. BR3 123 EB94
Tra **Beckenham Road** 143 DY95
Beckenham Rd, Beck. BR3 143 DX95
West Wickham BR4 143 EB101
Beckenshaw Gdns, Bans. SM7 174 DE115
Beckers, The, N16 *off Rectory Rd* 66 DU62
Becket Av, E6 87 EN69
Becket Cl, SE25 142 DU100
Brentwood CM13 53 FW51
Becket Fold, Har. HA1 *off Courtfield Cres* 61 CF57
Becket Rd, N18 46 DW49
Becket St, SE1 201 K6
Beckett Av, Ken. CR8 175 DP115
Beckett Chase, Slou. SL3 *off Ditton Rd* 93 AZ78
Beckett Cl, NW10 80 CR65
SW16 121 DK89
Belvedere DA17 *off Tunstock Way* 106 EY76
Beckett Ho, SW9 101 DL82
Beckett Rd, Couls. CR5 *off Blue Leaves Av* 175 DK122
Becketts Cl, Bex. DA5 127 FC88
Feltham TW14 115 BV86
Orpington BR6 145 ET104
Becketts Pl, Kings.T. (Hmptn W.) KT1 137 CK95
Beckett Wk, Beck. BR3 123 DY93
Beckford Dr, Orp. BR5 145 ER101
Beckford Pl, SE17 *off Walworth Rd* 102 DQ78
Beckford Rd, Croy. CR0 142 DT100
Beck La, Beck. BR3 143 DX97
Becklow Gdns, W12 *off Becklow Rd* 99 CU75
Becklow Ms, W12 *off Becklow Rd* 99 CT75
Becklow Rd, W12 99 CU75
Beckman Cl, Sev. (Halst.) TN14 181 FC115
Beck River Pk, Beck. BR3 143 DZ95
Beck Rd, E8 84 DV67
Becks Rd, Sid. DA14 126 EU90
BECKTON, E6 87 EN71
DLR **Beckton** 87 EN71
DLR **Beckton Park** 87 EM73
Beckton Pk Rbt, E16 *off Royal Albert Way* 87 EM73
Beckton Retail Pk, E6 87 EN71
Beckton Rd, E16 86 EF71
Beckton Triangle Retail Pk, E6 87 EN70
Beck Way, Beck. BR3 143 DZ97
Beckway Rd, SW16 141 DK96
Beckway St, SE17 201 L9
Beckwith Rd, SE24 122 DR86
Beclands Rd, SW17 120 DG93
Becmead Av, SW16 121 DK91
Harrow HA3 61 CH57
Becondale Rd, SE19 122 DS92
BECONTREE, Dag. RM8 70 EY62
⊖ **Becontree** 88 EW66
Becontree Av, Dag. RM8 70 EV63
BECONTREE HEATH, Dag. RM8 70 FA60
Becquerel Ct, SE10 *off West Parkside* 104 EF76
Bective Pl, SW15 *off Bective Rd* 99 CZ84
Bective Rd, E7 68 EG63
SW15 99 CZ84
Becton Pl, Erith DA8 107 FB80
Bedale Rd, Enf. EN2 30 DQ38
Romford RM3 52 FN50
Bedale St, SE1 201 K3
Bedale Wk, Dart. DA2 128 FP88
BEDDINGTON, Croy. CR0 141 DK103
BEDDINGTON CORNER, Mitch. CR4 140 DG101
Beddington Cross, Croy. CR0 141 DK102
Beddington Fm Rd, Croy. CR0 141 DL102
Beddington Gdns, Cars. SM5 158 DG107
Wallington SM6 159 DH107
Beddington Grn, Orp. BR5 145 ET95
Beddington Gro, Wall. SM6 159 DK106
Tra **Beddington Lane** 141 DJ100
Beddington La, Croy. CR0 141 DJ99
Beddington Path, Orp. BR5 145 ET95
Beddington Rd, Ilf. IG3 69 ET59
Orpington BR5 145 ES96
Beddington Trd Pk W, Croy. CR0 141 DL102
Beddlestead La, Warl. CR6 178 EF117
Bede Cl, Pnr. HA5 40 BX53
Bedens Rd, Sid. DA14 126 EY93
Bede Rd, Rom. RM6 70 EW58
Bedevere Rd, N9 46 DU48
Bedfont Cl, Felt. TW14 115 BQ86
Mitcham CR4 140 DG96
Bedfont Ct, Stai. TW19 94 BH84
Bedfont Ct Est, Stai. TW19 94 BG83
Bedfont Grn Cl, Felt. TW14 115 BQ88
Bedfont La, Felt. TW13, TW14 115 BT87
Bedfont Rd, Felt. TW13, TW14 115 BS89
Staines (Stanw.) TW19 114 BL86
Bedford Av, WC1 195 N7
Amersham HP6 20 AW39
Barnet EN5 27 CZ43
Hayes UB4 77 BV72
Bedfordbury, WC2 195 P10
Bedford Cl, N10 44 DG52
W4 98 CS79
Rickmansworth (Chenies) WD3 21 BB38
Woking GU21 166 AW115
Bedford Cor, W4 *off The Avenue* 98 CS77
Bedford Ct, WC2 199 P1
Bedford Cres, Enf. EN3 31 DY35
Bedford Gdns, W8 82 DA74
Hornchurch RM12 72 FJ61
Bedford Hill, SW12 121 DH88
SW16 121 DH88
Bedford Ho, SW4 101 DL84
Bedford Ms, N2 *off Bedford Rd* 64 DE55
SE6 *off Aitken Rd* 123 EB89
BEDFORD PARK, W4 98 CR76
Bedford Pk, Croy. CR0 142 DQ102
Bedford Pk Cor, W4 *off Bath Rd* 98 CS77
Bedford Pas, SW6 *off Dawes Rd* 99 CY80
Bedford Pl, WC1 195 P6
Croydon CR0 142 DR102
Bedford Rd, E6 87 EN67
E17 47 EA54
E18 48 EG54
N2 64 DE55
N8 65 DK58
N9 46 DV45
N15 66 DS56
N22 45 DL53
NW7 42 CS48
SW4 101 DL83
W4 98 CR76
W13 79 CH73
Dartford DA1 128 FN87
Gravesend (Nthflt) DA11 131 GF89
Grays RM17 110 GB78
Harrow HA1 60 CC58
Ilford IG1 69 EP62
Northwood HA6 39 BQ48
Orpington BR6 146 EV103
Ruislip HA4 59 BT63
Sidcup DA15 125 ES90
Twickenham TW2 117 CD90
Worcester Park KT4 139 CW103
Bedford Row, WC1 196 C6
Bedford Sq, WC1 195 N7
Bedford St, WC2 195 P10
Watford WD24 23 BV39
Bedford Ter, SW2 *off Lyham Rd* 121 DL85
Bedford Way, WC1 195 N5
Bedgebury Gdns, SW19 119 CY89
Bedgebury Rd, SE9 104 EK84
Bedivere Rd, Brom. BR1 124 EG90
Bedlam Ms, SE11 200 C8
Bedlow Way, Croy. CR0 159 DM105
BEDMOND, Abb.L. WD5 7 BS27
Bedmond La, Abb.L. WD5 7 BV25
Bedmond Rd, Abb.L. WD5 7 BT29
Bedonwell Rd, SE2 106 EY79
Belvedere DA17 106 FA79
Bexleyheath DA7 106 FA79
Bedser Cl, SE11 *off Harleyford Rd* 101 DM79
Thornton Heath CR7 142 DQ97
Woking GU21 167 BA116
Bedser Dr, Grnf. UB6 61 CD64
Bedster Gdns, W.Mol. KT8 136 CB96
Bedwardine Rd, SE19 122 DS94
Bedwell Gdns, Hayes UB3 95 BS78
Bedwell Rd, N17 46 DS53
Belvedere DA17 106 FA78
Beeby Rd, E16 86 EH71
Beech Av, N20 44 DE46
W3 80 CS74
Brentford TW8 97 CH80
Brentwood CM13 55 FZ48
Buckhurst Hill IG9 48 EH47
Enfield EN2 29 DN35
Radlett WD7 9 CG33
Ruislip HA4 59 BV60
Sidcup DA15 126 EU87
South Croydon CR2 160 DR111

★ Place of interest ⇌ Railway station ⊖ London Underground station DLR Docklands Light Railway station Tra Tramlink station H Hospital Riv Pedestrian ferry landing stage

Beech Av, Swan. BR8 147 FF98
Upminster RM14 72 FP62
Westerham (Tats.) TN16 178 EK119
Beech Cl, N9 30 DU44
SE8 off Clyde St 103 DZ79
SW15 119 CU87
SW19 119 CW93
Ashford TW15 115 BR92
Carshalton SM5 140 DF103
Cobham KT11 154 CA112
Hornchurch RM12 71 FH62
Loughton IG10 33 EP41
Staines (Stanw.) TW19
off St. Mary's Cres 114 BK87
Sunbury-on-Thames TW16
off Harfield Rd 136 BX96
Walton-on-Thames KT12 154 BW105
West Byfleet (Byfleet)
KT14 152 BL112
West Drayton UB7 94 BN76
Beech Cl Ct, Cob. KT11 154 BZ111
Beech Copse, Brom. BR1 145 EM96
South Croydon CR2 160 DS106
Beech Ct, E17 67 ED55
SE9 124 EL86
Ilford IG1
off Riverdene Rd 69 EP62
Beech Cres, Tad. (Box H.)
KT20 182 CQ130
Beechcroft, Ashtd. KT21 172 CM119
Chislehurst BR7 125 EN94
Beechcroft Av, NW11 63 CZ59
Bexleyheath DA7 107 FD81
Harrow HA2 60 CA59
Kenley CR8 176 DR115
New Malden KT3 138 CQ95
Rickmansworth (Crox.Grn)
WD3 23 BQ44
Southall UB1 78 BZ74
Beechcroft Cl, Houns. TW5 96 BY80
Orpington BR6 163 ER105
Beechcroft Gdns, Wem. HA9 62 CM62
Beechcroft Lo, Sutt. SM2
off Devonshire Rd 158 DC108
Beechcroft Manor, Wey.
KT13 135 BR104
Beechcroft Rd, E18 48 EH54
SW14 off Elm Rd 98 CQ83
SW17 120 DE89
Bushey WD23 24 BY43
Chessington KT9 138 CM104
Orpington BR6 163 ER105
Beechdale, N21 45 DM47
Beechdale Rd, SW2 121 DM86
Beech Dell, Kes. BR2 163 EM105
Beechdene, Tad. KT20 173 CV122
Beech Dr, N2 64 DF55
Borehamwood WD6 26 CM40
Reigate RH2 184 DD134
Tadworth (Kgswd) KT20 173 CZ122
Woking (Ripley) GU23 168 BG124
Beechen Cliff Way, Islw. TW7
off Henley Cl 97 CF81
Beechen Gro, Pnr. HA5 60 BZ55
Watford WD17 24 BW42
Beechen La, Tad. (Lwr Kgswd)
KT20 183 CZ125
Beechenlea La, Swan. BR8 147 FH97
Beeches, The, Bans. SM7 174 DB116
Brentwood CM14 54 FV48
Hounslow TW3 96 CB81
Leatherhead (Fetch.) KT22 171 CE124
Rickmansworth (Chorl.)
WD3 21 BF43
St. Albans (Park St) AL2 9 CE27
Swanley BR8 127 FF94
Tilbury RM18 111 GH82
Beeches Av, Cars. SM5 158 DE108
Beeches Cl, SE20
off Genoa Rd 142 DW95
Tadworth (Kgswd) KT20 174 DA123
Beeches Rd, SW17 120 DE90
Sutton SM3 139 CY102
Beeches Wk, Cars. SM5 158 DD109
Beeches Wd, Tad. KT20 174 DA122
Beech Fm Rd, Warl. CR6 177 EC120
Beechfield, Bans. SM7 158 DB113
Kings Langley WD4 6 BM30
Beechfield Cl, Borwd. WD6 26 CL40
Beechfield Cotts, Brom. BR1
off Widmore Rd 144 EJ96
Beechfield Gdns, Rom. RM7 71 FC59
Beechfield Rd, N4 66 DQ58
SE6 123 DZ88
Bromley BR1 144 EJ96
Erith DA8 107 FE80
Beechfield Wk, Wal.Abb. EN9 31 ED35
Beech Gdns, EC2
off Aldersgate St 84 DQ71
W5 98 CL75
Dagenham RM10 89 FB66
Woking GU21 166 AY115
Beech Gro, Add. KT15 152 BH105
Caterham CR3 186 DS126
Croydon CR0 161 DY110
Epsom KT18 173 CV117
Ilford IG6 49 ES51
Mitcham CR4 141 DK98
New Malden KT3 138 CR97
South Ockendon (Aveley)
RM15 90 FQ74
Woking (Mayford) GU22 166 AX123
Beech Hall, Cher. (Ott.) KT16 151 BC108
Beech Hall Cres, E4 47 ED52
Beech Hall Rd, E4 47 EC52
Beech Hill, Barn. EN4 28 DD38
Woking GU22 166 AX123
Beech Hill Av, Barn. EN4 28 DC39
Beech Hill Gdns, Wal.Abb. EN9 32 EH37
Beechhill Rd, SE9 125 EN85
Beech Holt, Lthd. KT22 171 CJ122
Beech Ho, NW3
off Maitland Pk Vil 82 DF65
Croydon CR0 161 EB107
Beech Ho Rd, Croy. CR0 142 DR104
Beech La, Beac. (Jordans)
HP9 36 AS52
Buckhurst Hill IG9 48 EH47
Beech Lawns, N12 44 DD50
Beech Lo, Stai. TW18
off Farm Cl 113 BE92
Beechmeads, Cob. KT11 154 BX113
Beechmont Av, Vir.W. GU25 132 AX99
Beechmont Cl, Brom. BR1 124 EE92
Beechmont Rd, Sev. TN13 191 FH129
Beechmore Gdns, Sutt. SM3 139 CX103
Beechmore Rd, SW11 100 DF81
Beechmount Av, W7 79 CD71
Beecholme, Bans. SM7 157 CY114
Beecholme Av, Mitch. CR4 141 DH95
Beecholme Est, E5
off Prout Rd 66 DV62
Beecholm Ms, Wal.Cr. EN8 15 DX28
Beech Pk, Amer. HP6 20 AV39
Beechpark Way, Wat. WD17 23 BS37
Beech Pl, Epp. CM16 17 ET31
Beech Rd, N11 45 DL51
SW16 141 DL96
Dartford DA1 128 FK88
Epsom KT17 173 CT115
Feltham TW14 115 BS87
Orpington BR6 164 EU108
Redhill (Merst.) RH1 185 DJ126
Reigate RH2 184 DA131
Sevenoaks TN13
off Victoria Rd 191 FH125
Slough SL3 92 AY75
Watford WD24 23 BU37
Westerham (Bigg.H.)
TN16 178 EH118
Weybridge KT13
off St. Marys Rd 153 BR105
Beech Row, Rich. TW10 118 CL91
Beech St, EC2 197 H6
Romford RM7 71 FC56
Beechtree Av, Egh. (Eng.Grn)
TW20 112 AV93
Beech Tree Cl, N1
off Barnsbury Pk 83 DN66
Stanmore HA7 41 CJ50
Beech Tree Glade, E4
off Forest Side 48 EF46
Beech Tree La, Stai. TW18
off Staines Rd 134 BH96
Beech Tree Pl, Sutt. SM1
off St. Nicholas Way 158 DB106
Beech Vale, Wok. GU22
off Hill Vw Rd 167 AZ118
Beechvale Cl, N12 44 DE50
Beech Wk, NW7 42 CS51
Dartford DA1 107 FG84
Epsom KT17 157 CU111
Beech Way, NW10 80 CR66
Beechway, Bex. DA5 126 EX86
Beech Way, Epsom KT17 173 CT115
South Croydon CR2 161 DX113
Twickenham TW2 116 CA90
Beech Waye, Ger.Cr. SL9 57 AZ59
Beechwood Av, N3 63 CZ55
Amersham HP6 20 AW38
Coulsdon CR5 175 DH115
Greenford UB6 78 CB69
Harrow HA2 60 CB62
Hayes UB3 77 BR73
Orpington BR6 163 ES106
Potters Bar EN6 12 DB33
Richmond TW9 98 CN81
Rickmansworth (Chorl.)
WD3 21 BB42
Ruislip HA4 59 BT61
Staines TW18 114 BH93
Sunbury-on-Thames
TW16 115 BU93
Tadworth (Kgswd) KT20 174 DA121
Thornton Heath CR7 141 DP98
Uxbridge UB8 76 BN72
Weybridge KT13 153 BS105
Beechwood Circle, Har. HA2
off Beechwood Gdns 60 CB62
Beechwood Cl, NW7 42 CR50
Amersham HP6 20 AW39
Surbiton KT6 137 CJ101
Waltham Cross (Chsht)
EN7 14 DS26
Weybridge KT13 153 BS105
Woking (Knap.) GU21 166 AS117
Beechwood Ct, Cars. SM5 158 DF105
Sunbury-on-Thames
TW16 115 BU93
Beechwood Cres, Bexh.
DA7 106 EX83
Beechwood Dr, Cob. KT11 154 CA111
Keston BR2 162 EK105
Woodford Green IG8 48 EF50
Beechwood Gdns, NW10
off St. Annes Gdns 80 CM69
Caterham CR3 176 DU122
Harrow HA2 60 CB62
Ilford IG5 69 EM57
Rainham RM13 89 FH71
Slough SL1 92 AS75
Beechwood Gro, W3
off East Acton La 80 CS73
Surbiton KT6 137 CJ101
Beechwood La, Warl. CR6 177 DX119
Beechwood Manor, Wey.
KT13 153 BS105
Beechwood Ms, N9 46 DU47
Beechwood Pk, E18 68 EG55
Leatherhead KT22 171 CJ123
Rickmansworth (Chorl.)
WD3 21 BF42
Beechwood Ri, Chis. BR7 125 EP91
Watford WD24 23 BV36
Beechwood Rd, E8 84 DT65
N8 65 DK56
Caterham CR3 176 DU122
South Croydon CR2 160 DS109
Virginia Water GU25 132 AU101
Woking (Knap.) GU21 166 AS117
Beechwoods Ct, SE19
off Crystal Palace Par 122 DT92
Beechworth Cl, NW3 64 DA61
Beecot La, Walt. KT12 136 BW103
Beecroft La, SE4
off Beecroft Rd 123 DY85
Beecroft Ms, SE4
off Beecroft Rd 123 DY85
Beecroft Rd, SE4 123 DY85
Beehive Cl, E8 84 DT66
Borehamwood (Els.) WD6 25 CK44
Beehive Cl, Uxb. UB10
off Honey Hill 76 BM66
Beehive Ct, Rom. RM3
off Arundel Rd 52 FM52
Beehive La, Ilf. IG1, IG4 69 EM58
Beehive Pas, EC3 197 M9
Beehive Pl, SW9 101 DN83
Beehive Rd, Stai. TW18 113 BF92
Waltham Cross (Chsht)
EN7 13 DP28
Beeken Dene, Orp. BR6
off Isabella Dr 163 EQ105
Beel Cl, Amer. HP7 20 AW39
Beeleigh Rd, Mord. SM4 140 DB98
Beesfield La, Dart. (Fnghm)
DA4 148 FN101
Beeston Cl, E8
off Ferncliff Rd 66 DU64
Watford WD19 40 BX49
Beeston Dr, Wal.Cr. EN8 15 DX27
Beeston Pl, SW1 199 J7
Beeston Rd, Barn. EN4 28 DD44
Beeston Way, Felt. TW14 116 BW86
Beethoven Rd, Borwd. (Els.)
WD6 25 CK44
Beethoven St, W10 81 CY69
Beeton Cl, Pnr. HA5 40 CA52
Begbie Rd, SE3 104 EJ81
Beggars Bush La, Wat. WD18 23 BR43
Beggars Hill, Epsom KT17 157 CT108
Beggars Hollow, Enf. EN2 30 DR37
Beggars La, West. TN16 189 ER125
Beggars Roost La, Sutt. SM1 158 DA107
Begonia Cl, E6 86 EL71
Begonia Pl, Hmptn. TW12
off Gresham Rd 116 CA93
Begonia Wk, W12
off Du Cane Rd 81 CT72
Beira St, SW12 121 DH87
Beken Ct, Wat. WD25
off First Av 24 BW35
Bekesbourne St, E14
off Ratcliffe La 85 DY72
Bekesbourne Twr, Orp. BR5 146 EY102
Belcroft Cl, Brom. BR1
off Hope Pk 124 EF94
Beldam Haw, Sev. (Halst.)
TN14 164 FA112
Beldham Gdns, W.Mol. KT8 136 CB97
Belfairs Dr, Rom. RM6 70 EW59
Belfairs Grn, Wat. WD19
off Heysham Dr 40 BX50
Belfast Rd, N16 66 DT61
SE25 142 DV98
Belfield Rd, Epsom KT19 156 CR109
Belfont Wk, N7 65 DL63
Belford Gro, SE18 105 EN77
Belford Rd, Borwd. WD6 26 CM38
Belfort Rd, SE15 102 DW82
Belfour Ter, N3
off Squires La 44 DB54
Belfry Av, Uxb. (Hare.) UB9 38 BG53
Belfry Cl, SE16 202 E10
Belfry La, Rick. WD3 38 BJ46
Belfry Shop Cen, The, Red.
RH1 184 DF133
Belgrade Rd, N16 66 DS63
Hampton TW12 136 CB95
Belgrave Av, Rom. RM2 72 FJ55
Watford WD18 23 BT43
Belgrave Cl, N14
off Prince George Av 29 DJ43
NW7 42 CR50
W3 off Avenue Rd 98 CP75
Orpington BR5 146 EW98
Walton-on-Thames KT12 153 BV105
Belgrave Ct, E14 203 N1
Belgrave Cres, Sun. TW16 135 BV95
Belgrave Dr, Kings L. WD4 7 BQ28
Belgrave Gdns, N14 29 DK43
NW8 82 DB67
Stanmore HA7
off Copley Rd 41 CJ50
Belgrave Hts, E11 68 EG60
Belgrave Manor, Wok. GU22 166 AY119
Belgrave Ms, Uxb. UB8 76 BK70
Belgrave Ms N, SW1 198 F5
Belgrave Ms S, SW1 198 G6
Belgrave Ms W, SW1 198 F6
Belgrave Pl, SW1 198 G6
Slough SL1 off Clifton Rd 92 AV75
Belgrave Rd, E10 67 EC60
E11 68 EG61
E13 86 EJ70
E17 67 EA57
SE25 142 DT98
SW1 199 K9
SW13 99 CT80
Hounslow TW4 96 BZ83
Ilford IG1 69 EM60
Mitcham CR4 140 DD97
Slough SL1 74 AS73
Sunbury-on-Thames
TW16 135 BV95
Belgrave Sq, SW1 198 F6
Belgrave St, E1 85 DX72
Belgrave Ter, Wdf.Grn. IG8 48 EG48
Tra Belgrave Walk 140 DD97
Belgrave Wk, Mitch. CR4 140 DD97
Belgrave Yd, SW1 199 H7
BELGRAVIA, SW1 198 F7
Belgravia Cl, Barn. EN5 27 CZ41
Belgravia Gdns, Brom. BR1 124 EE93
Belgravia Ho, SW4 121 DK86
Belgravia Ms, Kings.T. KT1 137 CK98
Belgrove St, WC1 195 P2
Belham Rd, Kings L. WD4 6 BM28
Belham Wk, SE5
off D'Eynsford Rd 102 DR81
Belhaven Ct, Borwd. WD6 26 CM39
Belhus Chase, S.Ock. (Aveley)
RM15 91 FR71
Belinda Rd, SW9 101 DP83
Belitha Vil, N1 83 DM66
Bell, The, E17 off Forest Rd 67 EA55
Bellamy Cl, E14 203 P4
W14 off Aisgill Av 99 CZ78
Edgware HA8 42 CQ48
Uxbridge UB10 58 BN62
Watford WD17 23 BU39
Bellamy Dr, Stan. HA7 41 CH53
Bellamy Rd, E4 47 EB51
Enfield EN2 30 DR40
Bellamy Rd, Wal. Cr. (Chsht)
EN8 15 DY29
Bellamy St, SW12 121 DH87
Bellarmine Cl, SE28 105 ET75
Bellasis Av, SW2 121 DL89
Bell Av, Rom. RM3 51 FH53
West Drayton UB7 94 BM77
Bell Br Rd, Cher. KT16 133 BF102
Bell Cl, Abb.L. (Bedmond)
WD5 7 BT27
Greenhithe DA9 129 FT85
Pinner HA5 60 BW55
Ruislip HA4 59 BT62
Slough SL2 74 AV71
Bellclose Rd, West Dr. UB7 94 BL75
BELL COMMON, Epp. CM16 17 ER32
Bell Common, Epp. CM16 17 ES32
Bell Common Tunnel, Epp.
CM16 17 ER33
Bell Ct, Surb. KT5
off Barnsbury La 138 CP103
Bell Cres, Couls. CR5
off Maple Way 175 DH121
Bell Dr, SW18 119 CY87
Bellefield Rd, Orp. BR5 146 EV99
Bellefields Rd, SW9 101 DM83
Bellegrove Cl, Well. DA16 105 ET82
Bellegrove Par, Well. DA16
off Bellegrove Rd 105 ET83
Bellegrove Rd, Well. DA16 105 ER82
Bellenden Rd, SE15 102 DT82
Bellestaines Pleasaunce, E4 47 EA47
Belleville Rd, SW11 120 DF85
Belle Vue, Grnf. UB6 79 CD67
Belle Vue Cl, Stai. TW18 134 BG95
Belle Vue Est, NW4
off Bell La 63 CW56
Belle Vue La, Bushey (Bushey Hth)
WD23 41 CD46
Bellevue Ms, N11 44 DG50
Bellevue Par, SW17
off Bellevue Rd 120 DE88
Belle Vue Pk, Th.Hth. CR7 142 DQ97
Bellevue Pl, E1 84 DW70
Slough SL1 off Albert St 92 AT76
Belle Vue Rd, E17 47 ED54
Bellevue Rd, N11 44 DG49
Belle Vue Rd, NW4
off Bell La 63 CW56
Bellevue Rd, SW13 99 CU82
SW17 120 DE88
W13 79 CH70
Bexleyheath DA6 126 EZ85
Hornchurch RM11 72 FM60
Kingston upon Thames
KT1 138 CL97
Belle Vue Rd, Orp. BR6
off Standard Rd 163 EN110
Bellevue Rd, Rom. RM5 51 FC51
Bellevue Ter, Uxb. (Hare.)
UB9 38 BG52
Bellew St, SW17 120 DC90
Bell Fm Av, Dag. RM10 71 FC62
Bellfield, Croy. CR0 161 DY109
Bellfield Av, Har. HA3 40 CC51
Bellfield Cl, SE3
off Charlton Rd 104 EG80
Bellflower Cl, E6
off Sorrel Gdns 86 EL71
Bellflower Path, Rom. RM3 52 FJ52
Bell Gdns, E17
off Markhouse Rd 67 DZ57
Orpington BR5 146 EW99
Bellgate Ms, NW5 off York Ri 65 DH62
BELL GREEN, SE6 123 DZ90
Bell Grn, SE26 123 DZ90
Hemel Hempstead (Bov.)
HP3 5 BB27
Bell Grn La, SE26 123 DY92
Bell Hill, Croy. CR0
off Surrey St 142 DQ104
Bellhouse La, Brwd. CM14 54 FS43
Bell Ho Rd, Rom. RM7 71 FC60
Bellina Ms, NW5
off Fortess Rd 65 DJ63
BELLINGHAM, SE6 123 EB90
⇌ Bellingham 123 EB90
Bellingham Ct, Bark. IG11
off Renwick Rd 88 EV69
Bellingham Grn, SE6 123 EA90
Bellingham Rd, SE6 123 EB90
Bell Inn Yd, EC3 197 L9
Bell La, E1 197 P7
E16 205 M2
NW4 63 CX56
Abbots Langley (Bedmond)
WD5 7 BT27
Amersham HP6, HP7 20 AV39
Enfield EN3 31 DX38
Hatfield (Brook.Pk) AL9 12 DA25
Leatherhead (Fetch.) KT22 171 CD123
St. Albans (Lon.Col.) AL2 10 CL29
Twickenham TW1
off The Embankment 117 CG88
Wembley HA9
off Magnet Rd 61 CK61
Bell La Cl, Lthd. (Fetch.)
KT22 171 CD123
Bellmaker Ct, E3
off St. Pauls Way 85 EA71
Bellman Av, Grav. DA12 131 GL88
Bellmarsh Rd, Add. KT15 152 BH105
Bell Meadow, SE19
off Dulwich Wd Av 122 DS91
Godstone RH9 186 DV132
Bellmount Wd Av, Wat. WD17 23 BS39
Bello Cl, SE24 121 DP87
Bellot Gdns, SE10 205 J10
Bellot St, SE10 205 J10
Bellring Cl, Belv. DA17 106 FA79
Bell Rd, E.Mol. KT8 137 CD99
Enfield EN1 30 DR39
Hounslow TW3 96 CB84
Bells All, SW6 100 DA82
Bells Gdn Est, SE15
off Buller Cl 102 DU80
Bells Hill, Barn. EN5 27 CX43
Bell's Hill, Slou. (Stoke P.)
SL2 74 AU67
Bells Hill Grn, Slou. (Stoke P.)
SL2 74 AU66
Bells La, Slou. (Horton) SL3 93 BB83
Bell St, NW1 194 B6
Bell St, SE18 104 EL81
Reigate RH2 184 DA134
Bellswood La, Iver SL0 75 BB71
Belltrees Gro, SW16 121 DM92
Bell Water Gate, SE18 105 EN76
Bell Weir Cl, Stai. TW19 113 BB89
Bell Wf La, EC4 197 J10
Bellwood Rd, SE15 103 DX84
Bell Yd, WC2 196 D8
Bell Yd Ms, SE1 201 N5
Belmarsh Rd, SE28
off Western Way 105 ES75
BELMONT, Har. HA3 41 CG54
BELMONT, Sutt. SM2 158 DB111
⇌ Belmont 158 DA110
Belmont Av, N9 46 DU46
N13 45 DL50
N17 66 DQ55
Barnet EN4 28 DF43
New Malden KT3 139 CU99
Southall UB2 96 BY76
Upminster RM14 72 FM61
Welling DA16 105 ES83
Wembley HA0 80 CM67
Belmont Circle, Har. HA3 41 CH53
Belmont Cl, E4 47 ED50
N20 44 DB46
SW4 101 DJ83
Barnet EN4 28 DF42
Uxbridge UB8 76 BK65
Woodford Green IG8 48 EH49
Belmont Cotts, Slou. (Colnbr.)
SL3 off High St 93 BC80
Belmont Ct, NW11 63 CZ57
Belmont Gro, SE13 103 ED83
W4 off Belmont Rd 98 CR77
Belmont Hall Ct, SE13
off Belmont Gro 103 ED83
Belmont Hill, SE13 103 ED83
Belmont La, Chis. BR7 125 EQ92
Stanmore HA7 41 CJ52
Belmont Ms, SW19
off Chapman Sq 119 CX89
Belmont Pk, SE13 103 ED84
Belmont Pk Cl, SE13 103 ED84
Belmont Pk Rd, E10 67 EB58
Belmont Ri, Sutt. SM2 157 CZ107
Belmont Rd, N15 66 DQ56
N17 66 DQ56
SE25 142 DV99
SW4 101 DJ83
W4 98 CR77
Beckenham BR3 143 DZ96
Bushey WD23 24 BY43
Chislehurst BR7 125 EP92
Erith DA8 106 FA80
Grays RM17 110 FZ78
Harrow HA3 61 CF55
Hornchurch RM12 72 FK62
Ilford IG1 69 EQ62
Leatherhead KT22 171 CG122
Sutton SM2 158 DA110
Twickenham TW2 117 CD89
Uxbridge UB8 76 BK66
Wallington SM6 159 DH106
Belmont St, NW1 82 DG66
Belmont Ter, W4
off Belmont Rd 98 CR77
Belmor, Borwd. (Els.) WD6 26 CN43
Belmore Av, Hayes UB4 77 BU72
Woking GU22 167 BD116
Belmore La, N7 65 DK64
Belmore St, SW8 101 DK81
Beloe Cl, SW15 99 CU83
Belper Ct, E5 off Pedro St 67 DX63
Belsham St, E9 84 DW65
BELSIZE, Rick. WD3 5 BF33
Belsize Av, N13 45 DM51
NW3 82 DD65
W13 97 CH76
Belsize Ct, NW3
off Belsize La 64 DE64
Belsize Cres, NW3 64 DD64
Belsize Gdns, Sutt. SM1 158 DB105
Belsize Gro, NW3 82 DE65
Belsize La, NW3 82 DD65
Belsize Ms, NW3
off Belsize La 82 DD65
BELSIZE PARK, NW3 82 DE65
⊖ Belsize Park 64 DE64
Belsize Pk, NW3 82 DD65
Belsize Pk Gdns, NW3 82 DE65
Belsize Pk Ms, NW3
off Belsize La 82 DD65
Belsize Pl, NW3
off Belsize La 82 DD65
Belsize Rd, NW6 82 DB67
Harrow HA3 41 CD52
Belsize Sq, NW3 82 DD65
Belsize Ter, NW3 82 DD65
Belson Rd, SE18 105 EM77
Belswains La, Hem.H. HP3 6 BM25
Beltana Dr, Grav. DA12 131 GL91
Beltane Dr, SW19 119 CX90
Belthorn Cres, SW12 121 DJ87
Beltinge Rd, Rom. RM3 72 FM55
Beltona Gdns, Wal.Cr. (Chsht)
EN8 15 DX27
Belton Rd, E7 86 EH66
E11 68 EE63
N17 66 DS55
NW2 81 CU65
Sidcup DA14 126 EU91
Belton Way, E3 85 EA71
Beltran Rd, SW6 100 DB82
Beltwood Rd, Belv. DA17 107 FC77
BELVEDERE, DA17 107 FB77
⇌ Belvedere 106 FA76
Belvedere Av, SW19 119 CY92
Ilford IG5 49 EP54
Belvedere Bldgs, SE1 200 G5
Belvedere Cl, Esher KT10 154 CB106
Gravesend DA12 131 GJ88
Teddington TW11 117 CE92
Weybridge KT13 152 BN106
Belvedere Ct, N1
off De Beauvoir Cres 84 DS67
N2 64 DD57
Belvedere Dr, SW19 119 CY92
Belvedere Gdns, St.Alb. AL2 8 CA27
West Molesey KT8 136 BZ99
Belvedere Gro, SW19 119 CY92
Belvedere Ho, Felt. TW13 115 BU88

★ Place of interest ⇌ Railway station ⊖ London Underground station DLR Docklands Light Railway station Tra Tramlink station H Hospital Riv Pedestrian ferry landing stage

Belvedere Ind Est, Belv.
DA17 107 FC76
Belvedere Ms, SE3
off Langton Way 104 EH80
SE15 102 DW83
Belvedere Pl, SE1 200 G5
SW2 off Acre La 101 DM84
Belvedere Rd, E10 67 DY60
SE1 200 C4
SE2 88 EX74
SE19 122 DT94
W7 97 CF76
Bexleyheath DA7 106 EZ83
Brentwood CM14 54 FT48
Westerham (Bigg.H.) TN16 179 EM118
Belvedere Sq, SW19 119 CY92
Belvedere Strand, NW9 43 CT54
Belvedere Twr, The, SW10 100 DC81
Belvedere Way, Har. HA3 62 CL58
Belvoir Cl, SE9 124 EL90
Belvoir Rd, SE22 122 DU87
Belvue Cl, Nthlt. UB5 78 CA66
Belvue Rd, Nthlt. UB5 78 CA66
Bembridge Cl, NW6 81 CY66
Bembridge Ct, Slou. SL1
off Park St 92 AT76
Bembridge Gdns, Ruis. HA4 59 BR61
Bemerton Est, N1 83 DM66
Bemerton St, N1 83 DM67
Bemish Rd, SW15 99 CX83
Bempton Dr, Ruis. HA4 59 BV61
Bemsted Rd, E17 67 DZ55
Benares Rd, SE18 105 ET77
Benbow Rd, W6 99 CV76
Benbow St, SE8 103 EA79
Benbow Waye, Uxb. UB8 76 BJ71
Benbury Cl, Brom. BR1 123 EC92
Bence, The, Egh. TW20 133 BB97
Bench Fld, S.Croy. CR2 160 DT107
Bench Manor Cres, Ger.Cr.
(Chal.St.P.) SL9 36 AW54
Bencombe Rd, Pur. CR8 159 DN114
Bencroft, Wal.Cr. (Chsht) EN7 14 DU26
Bencroft Rd, SW16 121 DJ94
Bencurtis Pk, W.Wick. BR4 143 ED104
Bendall Ms, NW1 194 C6
Bendemeer Rd, SW15 99 CX83
Bendish Rd, E6 86 EL66
Bendmore Av, SE2 106 EU78
Bendon Valley, SW18 120 DB87
Bendysh Rd, Bushey WD23 24 BY41
Benedict Cl, Belv. DA17
off Tunstock Way 106 EY76
Orpington BR6 145 ES104
Benedict Dr, Felt. TW14 115 BR87
Benedictine Gate, Wal.Cr.
EN8 15 DY27
Benedict Rd, SW9 101 DM83
Mitcham CR4 140 DD97
Benedict Way, N2 64 DC55
Benenden Grn, Brom. BR2 144 EG99
Benen-Stock Rd, Stai. TW19 113 BF85
Benets Rd, Horn. RM11 72 FN60
Benett Gdns, SW16 141 DL96
Benfleet Cl, Cob. KT11 154 BY112
Sutton SM1 140 DC104
Benfleet Way, N11 44 DG47
Bengal Ct, EC3
off Birchin La 84 DR72
Bengal Rd, Ilf. IG1 69 EP63
Bengarth Dr, Har. HA3 41 CD54
Bengarth Rd, Nthlt. UB5 78 BX67
Bengeo Gdns, Rom. RM6 70 EW58
Bengeworth Rd, SE5 102 DQ83
Harrow HA1 61 CG61
Ben Hale Cl, Stan. HA7 41 CH49
Benham Cl, SW11 100 DD83
Chessington KT9
off Merritt Gdns 155 CJ107
Coulsdon CR5 175 DP118
Benham Gdns, Houns. TW4 116 BZ85
Benham Rd, W7 79 CE71
Benhams Pl, NW3
off Holly Wk 64 DC63
Benhill Av, Sutt. SM1 158 DB105
Benhill Rd, SE5 102 DR80
Sutton SM1 140 DC104
Benhill Wd Rd, Sutt. SM1 140 DC104
BENHILTON, Sutt. SM1 140 DB103
Benhilton Gdns, Sutt. SM1 140 DB104
Benhurst Av, Horn. RM12 71 FH62
Benhurst Cl, S.Croy. CR2 161 DX110
Benhurst Ct, SW16 121 DN92
Benhurst Gdns, S.Croy. CR2 160 DW110
Benhurst La, SW16 121 DN92
Beningfield Dr, St.Alb. (Lon.Col.)
AL2 9 CH27
Benin St, SE13 123 ED87
Benison Ct, Slou. SL1
off Osborne St 92 AT76
Benjafield Cl, N18
off Brettenham Rd 46 DV49
Benjamin Cl, E8 84 DU67
Hornchurch RM11 71 FG58
Benjamin Ms, SW12
off Weir Rd 121 DJ88
Benjamin St, EC1 196 F6
Ben Jonson Rd, E1 85 DY71
Benledi St, E14 85 ED72
Benn Cl, Oxt. RH8 188 EG134
Bennelong Cl, W12 81 CV73
Bennerley Rd, SW11 120 DE85
Bennets Ctyd, SW19
off Watermill Way 140 DC95
Bennetsfield Rd, Uxb. UB11 77 BP74
Bennet's Hill, EC4 196 G10
Bennett Cl, Cob. KT11 153 BU113
Hounslow TW4 116 BY85
Kingston upon Thames
(Hmptn W.) KT1 137 CJ95
Northwood HA6 39 BT52
Welling DA16 106 EU82
Bennett Gro, SE13 103 EB81
Bennett Ho, SW1
off Page St 101 DK77
Bennett Pk, SE3 104 EF83
Bennett Rd, E13 86 EJ70
N16 66 DS63
SW9 101 DN82
Romford RM6 70 EY58
Bennetts Av, Croy. CR0 143 DY103
Greenford UB6 79 CE67
Bennetts Castle La, Dag. RM8 70 EW63
Bennetts Cl, N17 46 DT51
Mitcham CR4 141 DH95
Bennetts Copse, Chis. BR7 124 EL93
Bennett St, SW1 199 K2
W4 98 CS79
Bennetts Way, Croy. CR0 143 DY103
Bennetts Yd, SW1 199 N7
Uxbridge UB8 off High St 76 BJ66
Bennett Way, Dart. (Lane End)
DA2 129 FR91
Benningholme Rd, Edg. HA8 42 CS51
Bennington Rd, N17 46 DS53
Woodford Green IG8 48 EE52
Bennions Cl, Horn. RM12
off Franklin Rd 90 FK65
Bennison Dr, Rom. (Harold Wd)
RM3 52 FK54
Benn St, E9 85 DY65
Benn's Wk, Rich. TW9
off Rosedale Rd 98 CL84
Benrek Cl, Ilf. IG6 49 EQ53
Bensbury Cl, SW15 119 CV87
Bensham Cl, Th.Hth. CR7 142 DQ98
Bensham Gro, Th.Hth. CR7 142 DQ96
Bensham La, Croy. CR0 141 DP101
Thornton Heath CR7 141 DP98
Bensham Manor Rd, Th.Hth.
CR7 142 DQ98
Bensington Ct, Felt. TW14 115 BR86
Benskin Rd, Wat. WD18 23 BU43
Benskins La, Rom. (Noak Hill)
RM4 52 FK46
Bensley Cl, N11 44 DF50
Ben Smith Way, SE16 202 C6
Benson Av, E6 86 EJ68
Benson Cl, Houns. TW3 96 CA84
Slough SL2 74 AU74
Uxbridge UB8 76 BL71
Benson Ct, SW8
off Hartington Rd 101 DL81
Benson Quay, E1 202 F1
Benson Rd, SE23 122 DW88
Croydon CR0 141 DN104
Grays RM17 110 GB79
Bentalls Cen, Kings.T. KT1 137 CK96
Bentfield Gdns, SE9
off Aldersgrove Av 124 EJ90
Benthall Gdns, Ken. CR8 176 DQ116
Benthal Rd, N16 66 DU61
Bentham Av, Wok. GU21 167 BC115
Bentham Ct, N1
off Rotherfield St 84 DQ66
Bentham Ho, SE1
off Falmouth Rd 102 DR76
Bentham Rd, E9 85 DX65
SE28 88 EV73
Bentham Wk, NW10 62 CQ64
Ben Tillet Cl, Bark. IG11 88 EU66
Ben Tillett Cl, E16
off Newland St 87 EM74
Bentinck Cl, NW8
off Prince Albert Rd 82 DE68
Gerrards Cross SL9 56 AX57
Bentinck Ms, W1 194 G8
Bentinck Rd, West Dr. UB7 76 BK74
Bentinck St, W1 194 G8
Bentley Ct, SE13
off Whitburn Rd 103 EC84
Bentley Dr, NW2 63 CZ62
Ilford IG2 69 EQ58
Weybridge KT13 152 BN109
BENTLEY HEATH, Barn. B93 27 CZ35
Bentley Heath La, Barn. EN5 11 CY34
Bentley Ms, Enf. EN1 30 DR44
★ Bentley Priory, Stan. HA7 41 CE48
Bentley Rd, N1
off Tottenham Rd 84 DS65
Bentley St, Grav. DA12 131 GJ86
Bentley Way, Stan. HA7 41 CG50
Woodford Green IG8 48 EG48
Benton Rd, Ilf. IG1 69 ER60
Watford WD19 40 BX50
Bentons La, SE27 122 DQ91
Bentons Ri, SE27 122 DR92
Bentry Cl, Dag. RM8 70 EY61
Bentry Rd, Dag. RM8 70 EY61
Bentworth Rd, W12 81 CV72
Benville Ho, SW8 off Oval Pl 101 DM80
Benwell Ct, Sun. TW16 135 BU95
Benwell Rd, N7 65 DN63
Benwick Cl, SE16 202 E8
Benworth St, E3 85 DZ69
Benyon Path, S.Ock. RM15
off Tyssen Pl 91 FW69
Benyon Rd, N1
off Southgate Rd 84 DR67
Benyon Wf, E8
off Kingsland Rd 84 DS68
Beomonds Row, Cher. KT16
off Heriot Rd 134 BG101
Berberis Wk, West Dr. UB7 94 BL77
Berber Pl, E14
off Birchfield St 85 EA73
Berber Rd, SW11 120 DF85
Berberry Cl, Edg. HA8
off Larkspur Gro 42 CQ49
Berceau Wk, Wat. WD17 23 BS39
Bercta Rd, SE9 125 EQ89
Bere Cl, Green. DA9
off Ingress Pk Av 129 FW85
Beredens La, Brwd. CM13 73 FT55
Berengers Pl, Dag. RM9 88 EV65
Berenger Twr, SW10
off World's End Est 100 DD80
Berenger Wk, SW10
off Blantyre St 100 DD80
Berens Rd, NW10 81 CX69
Orpington BR5 146 EX99
Berens Way, Chis. BR7 145 ET98
Beresford Av, N20 44 DF47
W7 79 CD71
Slough SL2 74 AW74
Surbiton KT5 138 CP102
Twickenham TW1 117 CJ86
Wembley HA0 80 CM67
Beresford Dr, Brom. BR1 144 EK97
Woodford Green IG8 48 EJ49
Beresford Gdns, Enf. EN1 30 DS42
Hounslow TW4 116 BZ85
Romford RM6 70 EY57
Beresford Rd, E4 48 EE46
E17 47 EB53
N2 64 DE55
Beresford Rd, N5 66 DQ64
N8 65 DN57
Gravesend (Nthflt) DA11 130 GE87
Harrow HA1 61 CD57
Kingston upon Thames
KT2 138 CM95
New Malden KT3 138 CQ98
Rickmansworth (Mill End)
WD3 37 BF46
Southall UB1 78 BX74
Sutton SM2 157 CZ108
Beresford Sq, SE18 105 EP77
Beresford St, SE18 105 EP76
Beresford Ter, N5 66 DQ64
Berestede Rd, W6 99 CT78
Bere St, E1 off Cranford St 85 DX73
Bergen Sq, SE16 203 L6
Berger Cl, Orp. BR5 145 ER100
Berger Rd, E9 85 DX65
Berghem Ms, W14
off Blythe Rd 99 CX76
Bergholt Av, Ilf. IG4 68 EL57
Bergholt Cres, N16 66 DS59
Bergholt Ms, NW1
off Rossendale Way 83 DJ66
Berglen Ct, E14
off Branch Rd 85 DY72
Bering Sq, E14 off Napier Av 103 EA78
Bering Wk, E16 86 EK72
Berisford Ms, SW18 120 DC86
Berkeley Av, Bexh. DA7 106 EX81
Greenford UB6 79 CE65
Hounslow TW4 95 BU82
Ilford IG5 49 EN54
Romford RM5 51 FC52
Berkeley Cl, Abb.L. WD5 7 BT32
Borehamwood (Els.) WD6 26 CN43
Hornchurch RM11 72 FP61
Kingston upon Thames
KT2 118 CL94
Orpington BR5 145 ES101
Potters Bar EN6 11 CY32
Ruislip HA4 59 BU62
Staines TW19 113 BD89
Berkeley Ct, N14 29 DJ44
Rickmansworth (Crox.Grn)
WD3 off Mayfare 23 BR43
Wallington SM6 141 DJ104
Weybridge KT13 135 BR103
Berkeley Cres, Barn. EN4 28 DD43
Dartford DA1 128 FM88
Berkeley Dr, Horn. RM11 71 FN60
West Molesey KT8 136 BZ97
Berkeley Gdns, N21 46 DR45
W8 off Brunswick Gdns 82 DA74
Esher (Clay.) KT10 155 CG107
Walton-on-Thames KT12 135 BT101
West Byfleet KT14 151 BF114
Berkeley Ho, E3 85 EA70
Berkeley Ms, W1 194 E8
Berkeley Pl, SW19 119 CX93
Epsom KT18 172 CR115
Berkeley Rd, E12 68 EL64
N8 65 DK57
N15 66 DR58
NW9 62 CN56
SW13 99 CU81
Uxbridge UB10 77 BQ66
Berkeleys, The, Lthd. (Fetch.)
KT22 171 CE124
Berkeley Sq, W1 199 J1
Berkeley St, W1 199 J1
Berkeley Twr, E14 203 N2
Berkeley Wk, N7
off Durham Rd 65 DM61
Berkeley Waye, Houns. TW5 96 BX80
Berkhampstead Rd, Belv.
DA17 106 FA78
Berkhamsted Av, Wem. HA9 80 CM65
Berkley Av, Wal.Cr. EN8 15 DX34
Berkley Cres, Grav. DA12
off Milton Rd 131 GJ86
Berkley Gro, NW1
off Berkley Rd 82 DF66
Berkley Rd, NW1 82 DF66
Gravesend DA12 131 GH86
Berks Hill, Rick. (Chorl.) WD3 21 BC43
Berkshire Cl, Cat. CR3 176 DR122
Berkshire Gdns, N13 45 DN51
N18 46 DV50
Berkshire Rd, E9 85 DZ65
Berkshire Sq, Mitch. CR4
off Berkshire Way 141 DL98
Berkshire Way, Horn. RM11 72 FN57
Mitcham CR4 141 DL98
Bermans Cl, Brwd. (Hutt.) CM13
off Hanging Hill La 55 GB47
Bermans Way, NW10 62 CS63
BERMONDSEY, SE1 201 P7
⊖ Bermondsey 202 C6
Bermondsey Sq, SE1 201 N6
Bermondsey St, SE1 201 M3
Bermondsey Wall E, SE16 202 C5
Bermondsey Wall W, SE16 202 B4
Bermuda Rd, Til. RM18 111 GG82
Bernal Cl, SE28
off Haldane Rd 88 EX73
Bernard Ashley Dr, SE7 104 EH78
Bernard Av, W13 97 CH76
Bernard Cassidy St, E16 86 EF71
Bernard Gdns, SW19 119 CZ92
Bernard Gro, Wal.Abb. EN9
off Beaulieu Dr 15 EB33
Bernard Rd, N15 66 DT57
Romford RM7 71 FC59
Wallington SM6 159 DH105
Bernards Cl, Ilf. IG6 49 EQ51
Bernard Shaw Ho, NW10
off Knatchbull Rd 80 CR67
Bernard St, WC1 195 P5
Gravesend DA12 131 GH86
Bernays Cl, Stan. HA7 41 CJ51
Bernays Gro, SW9 101 DM84
Bernel Dr, Croy. CR0 143 DZ104
Berne Rd, Th.Hth. CR7 142 DQ99
Berners Dr, W13 79 CG72
Berners Ho, Chis. BR7 ... (no)
Bernersmede, SE3
off Blackheath Pk 104 EG83
Berners Ms, W1 195 L7
Berners Pl, W1 195 L8
Berners Rd, N1 83 DN68
N22 45 DN53
Berners St, W1 195 L7
Berney Rd, Croy. CR0 142 DR101
Bernhardt Cres, NW8 194 B4
Bernhart Cl, Edg. HA8 42 CQ52
Bernice Cl, Rain. RM13 90 FJ70
Bernville Way, Har. HA3
off Orchard Gro 62 CM57
Bernwell Rd, E4 48 EE48
Berridge Grn, Edg. HA8 42 CN52
Berridge Ms, NW6
off Hillfield Rd 64 DA64
Berridge Rd, SE19 122 DR92
Berriman Rd, N7 65 DM62
Berrington Dr, Lthd. (E.Hors.)
KT24 169 BT124
Berriton Rd, Har. HA2 60 BZ60
Berry Av, Wat. WD24 23 BU36
Berrybank Cl, E4
off Greenbank Cl 47 EC47
Berry Cl, N21 45 DP46
Dagenham RM10 70 FA64
Hornchurch RM12
off Airfield Way 72 FJ64
Rickmansworth WD3 38 BH45
Berry Ct, Houns. TW4
off Raglan Cl 116 BZ85
Berrydale Rd, Hayes UB4 78 BY70
Berryfield, Slou. SL2 74 AW72
Berryfield Cl, E17 67 EB56
Bromley BR1 144 EL95
Berryfield Rd, SE17 200 G10
Berry Gro La, Wat. WD25 24 CA39
Berryhill, SE9 105 EP84
Berry Hill, Stan. HA7 41 CK49
Berryhill Gdns, SE9 105 EP84
BERRYLANDS, Surb. KT5 138 CM99
⇌ Berrylands 138 CN98
Berrylands, SW20 139 CW97
Orpington BR6 146 EW104
Surbiton KT5 138 CN99
Berrylands Rd, Surb. KT5 138 CM100
Berry La, SE21 122 DR91
Rickmansworth WD3 38 BH46
Walton-on-Thames KT12
off Burwood Rd 154 BX106
Berryman Cl, Dag. RM8
off Bennetts Castle La 70 EW62
Berrymans La, SE26 123 DX91
Berry Meade, Ashtd. KT21 172 CM117
Berry Meade Cl, Ashtd. KT21
off Berry Meade 172 CM117
Berrymead Gdns, W3 80 CQ74
Berrymede Rd, W4 98 CR76
Berry Pl, EC1 196 G3
Berryscroft Ct, Stai. TW18
off Berryscroft Rd 114 BJ94
Berryscroft Rd, Stai. TW18 114 BJ94
BERRY'S GREEN, West.
TN16 179 EP116
Berry's Grn Rd, West. (Berry's Grn)
TN16 179 EP116
Berry's Hill, West. (Berry's Grn)
TN16 179 EP115
Berrys La, W.Byf. (Byfleet)
KT14 152 BK111
Berry St, EC1 196 G4
Berry Wk, Ashtd. KT21 172 CM119
Berry Way, W5 98 CL76
Rickmansworth WD3 38 BH45
Bersham La, Grays (Bad.Dene)
RM17 110 FZ77
Bertal Rd, SW17 120 DD91
Berther Rd, Horn. RM11 72 FK59
Berthold Ms, Wal.Abb. EN9 15 EB33
Berthon St, SE8 103 EA80
Bertie Rd, NW10 81 CU65
SE26 123 DX93
Bertram Cotts, SW19 120 DA94
Bertram Rd, NW4 63 CU58
Enfield EN1 30 DU42
Kingston upon Thames
KT2 118 CN94
Bertram St, N19 65 DH61
Bertram Way, Enf. EN1 30 DT42
Bertrand St, SE13 103 EB83
Bertrand Way, SE28 88 EV73
Bert Rd, Th.Hth. CR7 142 DQ99
Berwick Av, Hayes UB4 78 BX72
Berwick Cl, Stan. HA7
off Gordon Av 41 CF52
Twickenham TW2 116 CA87
Waltham Cross EN8 15 EA34
Berwick Cres, Sid. DA15 125 ES86
Berwick Gdns, Sutt. SM1 140 DC104
Berwick La, Ong. CM5 35 FF36
Berwick Pond Cl, Rain. RM13 90 FK68
Berwick Pond Rd, Rain. RM13 90 FL68
Upminster RM14 90 FM66
Berwick Rd, E16 86 EH72
N22 45 DP53
Borehamwood WD6 26 CM38
Rainham RM13 90 FK68
Welling DA16 106 EV81
Berwick St, W1 195 M9
Berwick Way, Orp. BR6 146 EU102
Sevenoaks TN14 191 FH121
Berwyn Av, Houns. TW3 96 CB81
Berwyn Rd, SE24 121 DP88
Richmond TW10 98 CP84
Beryl Av, E6 86 EL71
Beryl Ho, SE18 off Spinel Cl 105 ET78
Beryl Rd, W6 99 CX78
Berystede, Kings.T. KT2 118 CP94
Besant Ct, N1
off Newington Grn Rd 66 DR64
Besant Pl, SE22
off Hayes Gro 102 DT84
Besant Rd, NW2 63 CY63
Besant Wk, N7
off Newington Barrow Way 65 DM61
Besant Way, NW10 62 CQ64
Besley St, SW16 121 DJ93
Bessant Dr, Rich. TW9 98 CP81
Bessborough Gdns, SW1 199 N10
Bessborough Pl, SW1 199 M10
Bessborough Rd, SW15 119 CU88
Harrow HA1 61 CD60
Bessborough St, SW1 199 M10
BESSELS GREEN, Sev. TN13 190 FC124
Bessels Grn Rd, Sev. TN13 190 FD123
Bessels Meadow, Sev. TN13 190 FD124
Bessels Way, Sev. TN13 190 FC124
Bessemer Cl, Slou. SL3 93 AZ78
Bessemer Rd, SE5 102 DQ82
Bessie Lansbury Cl, E6 87 EN72
Bessingby Rd, Ruis. HA4 59 BU61
Bessingham Wk, SE4
off Frendsbury Rd 103 DX84
Besson St, SE14 102 DW81
Bessy St, E2 off Roman Rd 84 DW69
Bestwood St, SE8 203 J9
Beswick Ms, NW6
off Dresden Cl 82 DB65
Betam Rd, Hayes UB3 95 BR75
Beta Pl, SW4 off Santley St 101 DM84
Beta Rd, Wok. GU22 167 BB116
Woking (Chobham) GU24 150 AT110
Beta Way, Egh. TW20 133 BC95
BETCHWORTH, RH3 182 CR134
⇌ Betchworth 182 CR132
Betchworth Cl, Sutt. SM1
off Turnpike La 158 DD106
Betchworth Fort Pk, Tad. KT20
off Fort Rd 182 CP131
Betchworth Rd, Ilf. IG3 69 ES61
Betchworth Way, Croy. (New Adgtn)
CR0 161 EC109
Betenson Av, Sev. TN13 190 FF122
Betham Rd, Grnf. UB6 79 CD69
Bethany Cl, Horn. RM12 72 FJ61
Bethany Waye, Felt. TW14 115 BS87
Bethecar Rd, Har. HA1 61 CE57
Bethell Av, E16 86 EF70
Ilford IG1 69 EN59
Bethel Rd, Sev. TN13 191 FJ123
Welling DA16 106 EW83
Bethersden Cl, Beck. BR3 123 DZ94
H Bethlem Royal Hosp,
Beck. BR3 143 EA101
BETHNAL GREEN, E2 84 DU68
⇌ Bethnal Green 84 DV70
⊖ Bethnal Green 84 DW69
Bethnal Grn Est, E2 84 DW69
Bethnal Grn Rd, E1 197 P4
E2 197 P4
Bethune Av, N11 44 DF49
Bethune Rd, N16 66 DR59
NW10 80 CR70
Bethwin Rd, SE5 101 DP80
Betjeman Cl, Couls. CR5 175 DM117
Pinner HA5 60 CA56
Waltham Cross EN7
off Rosedale Way 14 DU28
Betley Ct, Walt. KT12 135 BV104
Betony Cl, Croy. CR0
off Primrose La 143 DX102
Betony Rd, Rom. RM3 52 FJ51
Betoyne Av, E4 48 EE49
BETSHAM, Dart. DA13 130 FY91
BETSHAM, Grav. DA13 130 FY91
Betsham Rd, Erith DA8 107 FF80
Gravesend (Sthflt) DA13 129 FX92
Swanscombe DA10 130 FY87
Betstyle Circ, N11 45 DH49
Betstyle Rd, N11 45 DH49
Betterton Dr, Sid. DA14 126 EY89
Betterton Rd, Rain. RM13 89 FE69
Betterton St, WC2 195 P9
Bettles Cl, Uxb. UB8
off Wescott Way 76 BJ68
Bettons Pk, E15 86 EE67
Bettridge Rd, SW6 99 CZ82
Betts Cl, Beck. BR3
off Kendall Rd 143 DY96
Betts Ms, E17 off Queen's Rd 67 DZ58
Betts St, E1 202 D1
Betts Way, SE20 142 DV95
Surbiton KT6 137 CH102
Betula Cl, Ken. CR8 176 DR115
Betula Wk, Rain. RM13 90 FK69
Between Sts, Cob. KT11 153 BU114
Beulah Av, Th.Hth. CR7
off Beulah Rd 142 DQ96
Beulah Cl, Edg. HA8 42 CP48
Beulah Cres, Th.Hth. CR7 142 DQ96
Beulah Gro, Croy. CR0 142 DQ100
Beulah Hill, SE19 121 DP93
Beulah Path, E17
off Addison Rd 67 EB57
Beulah Rd, E17 67 EB57
SW19 119 CZ94
Epping CM16 18 EU29
Hornchurch RM12 72 FJ62
Sutton SM1 158 DA105
Thornton Heath CR7 142 DQ97
Beulah Wk, Cat. (Wold.) CR3 177 DY120
Beult Rd, Dart. DA1 107 FG83
Bevan Av, Bark. IG11 88 EU66
Bevan Ct, Croy. CR0 159 DN106
Bevan Ho, Grays RM16
off Laird Av 110 GD75
Bevan Pk, Epsom KT17 157 CT111
Bevan Pl, Swan. BR8 147 FF98
Bevan Rd, SE2 106 EV78
Barnet EN4 28 DF42
Bevans Cl, Green. DA9
off Johnsons Way 129 FW86
Bevan St, N1 84 DQ67
Bevan Way, Horn. RM12 72 FM63
Bev Callender Cl, SW8
off Daley Thompson Way 101 DH83
Bevenden St, N1 197 L2
Bevercote Wk, Belv. DA17
off Osborne Rd 106 EZ79
Beveridge Rd, NW10 80 CS66
Beverley Av, SW20 139 CT95
Hounslow TW4 96 BZ84
Sidcup DA15 125 ET87
Beverley Cl, N21 46 DQ46
SW11 off Maysoule Rd 100 DD84
SW13 99 CT82
Addlestone KT15 152 BK106
Chessington KT9 155 CJ105
Enfield EN1 30 DS42
Epsom KT17 157 CW111
Hornchurch RM11 72 FM59
Weybridge KT13 135 BS103
Beverley Cotts, SW15
off Kingston Vale 118 CR91
Beverley Ct, N14 45 DJ45
N20 off Farnham Cl 44 DC45

★ Place of interest ⇌ Railway station ⊖ London Underground station DLR Docklands Light Railway station Tra Tramlink station H Hospital Riv Pedestrian ferry landing stage

Beverley Ct, SE4 103 DZ83
Slough SL1 *off Dolphin Rd* 92 AV75
Beverley Cres, Wdf.Grn. IG8 48 EH53
Beverley Dr, Edg. HA8 62 CP55
Beverley Gdns, NW11 63 CY59
SW13 99 CT83
Hornchurch RM11 72 FM59
Stanmore HA7 41 CG53
Waltham Cross (Chsht) EN7 14 DT30
Wembley HA9 62 CM60
Worcester Park KT4 *off Green La* 139 CU102
Beverley Hts, Reig. RH2 184 DB132
Beverley Ho, NW8 194 B3
Beverley La, SW15 119 CT90
Kingston upon Thames KT2 118 CS94
Beverley Ms, E4 *off Beverley Rd* 47 ED51
Beverley Path, SW13 99 CT82
Beverley Rd, E4 47 ED51
E6 86 EK69
SE20 *off Wadhurst Cl* 142 DV96
SW13 99 CT83
W4 99 CT78
Bexleyheath DA7 107 FC82
Bromley BR2 144 EL103
Dagenham RM9 70 EY63
Kingston upon Thames KT1 137 CJ95
Mitcham CR4 141 DK98
New Malden KT3 139 CU98
Ruislip HA4 59 BU61
Southall UB2 96 BY76
Sunbury-on-Thames TW16 135 BT95
Whyteleafe CR3 176 DS116
Worcester Park KT4 139 CW103
Beverley Trd Est, Mord. SM4 *off Garth Rd* 139 CX101
Beverley Way, SW20 139 CT95
New Malden KT3 139 CT95
Beversbrook Rd, N19 65 DK62
Beverstone Rd, SW2 121 DM85
Thornton Heath CR7 141 DN98
Beverston Ms, W1 194 D7
Bevill Allen Cl, SW17 120 DF92
Bevill Cl, SE25 142 DU97
Bevin Cl, SE16 203 K2
Bevin Ct, WC1 196 C2
Bevington Path, SE1 *off Tanner St* 102 DT75
Bevington Rd, W10 81 CY71
Beckenham BR3 143 EB96
Bevington St, SE16 202 C5
Bevin Rd, Hayes UB4 77 BU69
Bevin Sq, SW17 120 DF90
Bevin Way, WC1 196 D2
Bevis Cl, Dart. DA2 128 FQ87
Bevis Marks, EC3 197 N8
Bewcastle Gdns, Enf. EN2 29 DL42
Bew Ct, SE22 *off Lordship La* 122 DU87
Bewdley St, N1 83 DN66
Bewick Ms, SE15 102 DV80
Bewick St, SW8 101 DH82
Bewley Cl, Wal.Cr. (Chsht) EN8 15 DX31
Bewley St, E1 *off Cable St* 84 DV73
SW19 120 DC93
Bewlys Rd, SE27 121 DP92
Bexhill Cl, Felt. TW13 116 BY89
Bexhill Dr, Grays RM17 110 FY79
Bexhill Rd, N11 45 DK50
SE4 123 DZ87
SW14 98 CQ83
Bexhill Wk, E15 *off Mitre Rd* 86 EE67
BEXLEY, DA5 126 FA86
⇌ **Bexley** 126 FA88
Bexley Cl, Dart. DA1 127 FE85
Bexley Gdns, N9 46 DR48
Romford (Chad.Hth) RM6 70 EV57
BEXLEYHEATH, DA6 & DA7 126 EZ85
⇌ **Bexleyheath** 106 EY82
Bexley High St, Bex. DA5 126 FA87
Bexley La, Dart. DA1 127 FE85
Sidcup DA14 126 EW90
Bexley Rd, SE9 125 EP85
Erith DA8 107 FC80
Beynon Rd, Cars. SM5 158 DF106
Bianca Ho, N1 *off Crondall St* 84 DS68
Bianca Rd, SE15 102 DT79
Bibsworth Rd, N3 43 CZ54
Bicester Rd, Rich. TW9 98 CN83
Bickenhall St, W1 194 E6
Bickersteth Rd, SW17 120 DF93
Bickerton Rd, N19 65 DJ61
BICKLEY, Brom. BR1 145 EM97
⇌ **Bickley** 144 EL97
Bickley Cres, Brom. BR1 144 EL98
Bickley Pk Rd, Brom. BR1 144 EL97
Bickley Rd, E10 67 EB59
Bromley BR1 144 EK96
Bickley St, SW17 120 DE92
Bicknell Rd, SE5 102 DQ83
Bickney Way, Lthd. (Fetch.) KT22 170 CC122
Bicknoller Cl, Sutt. SM2 158 DB110
Bicknoller Rd, Enf. EN1 30 DT39
Bicknor Rd, Orp. BR6 145 ES101
Bidborough Cl, Brom. BR2 144 EF99
Bidborough St, WC1 195 P3
Bidbury Cl, SE15 102 DS79
Biddenden Way, SE9 125 EN91
Gravesend (Istead Rise) DA13 130 GE94
Biddenham Turn, Wat. WD25 24 BW35
Bidder St, E16 86 EE71
Biddestone Rd, N7 65 DM63
Biddulph Rd, W9 82 DB69
South Croydon CR2 160 DQ109
Bideford Av, Grnf. UB6 79 CH68
Bideford Cl, Edg. HA8 42 CN53
Feltham TW13 116 BZ90
Romford RM3 52 FJ53
Bideford Gdns, Enf. EN1 46 DS45
Bideford Rd, Brom. BR1 124 EF90
Enfield EN3 31 DZ38
Ruislip HA4 59 BV62
Welling DA16 106 EV80
Bidhams Cres, Tad. KT20 173 CW121
Bidwell Gdns, N11 45 DJ52
Bidwell St, SE15 102 DV81
★ **Big Ben (St. Stephens Tower)**, SW1 200 A5
Bigbury Cl, N17 46 DS52
Big Common La, Red. (Bletch.) RH1 185 DP133
Biggerstaff Rd, E15 85 EC67
Biggerstaff St, N4 65 DN61
Biggin Av, Mitch. CR4 140 DF95
BIGGIN HILL, West. TN16 178 EH116
Biggin Hill, SE19 121 DP94
Biggin Hill Business Pk, West. TN16 178 EK115
Biggin Hill Cl, Kings.T. KT2 117 CJ92
Biggin La, Grays RM16 111 GH79
Biggin Way, SE19 121 DP94
Bigginwood Rd, SW16 121 DP94
Biggs Gro Rd, Wal.Cr. (Chsht) EN7 14 DR27
Biggs Row, SW15 *off Felsham Rd* 99 CX83
Big Hill, E5 66 DV60
Bigland St, E1 84 DV72
Bignell Rd, SE18 105 EP78
Bignell's Cor, Pot.B. (S.Mimms) EN6 11 CU34
Bignold Rd, E7 68 EG63
Bigwood Rd, NW11 64 DB57
Biko Cl, Uxb. UB8 *off Sefton Way* 76 BJ72
Billet Cl, Rom. RM6 70 EX55
Billet La, Horn. RM11 72 FK60
Iver SL0 75 BB69
Slough SL3 75 BB73
Billet Rd, E17 47 DX54
Romford RM6 70 EV55
Staines TW18 114 BG90
Billets Hart Cl, W7 97 CE75
Billet Wks, E17 47 DZ53
Bill Hamling Cl, SE9 125 EM89
Billingford Cl, SE4 103 DX84
Billing Pl, SW10 100 DB80
Billing Rd, SW10 100 DB80
Billings Cl, Dag. RM9 *off Ellerton Rd* 88 EW66
★ **Billingsgate Mkt**, E14 204 C2
Billing St, SW10 100 DB80
Billington Ms, W3 *off High St* 80 CP74
Billington Rd, SE14 103 DX80
Billiter Sq, EC3 197 N10
Billiter St, EC3 197 N9
Bill Nicholson Way, N17 *off High Rd* 46 DT52
Billockby Cl, Chess. KT9 156 CM107
Billson St, E14 204 E9
Billy Lows La, Pot.B. EN6 12 DA31
Bilsby Gro, SE9 124 EK91
Bilton Cl, Slou. (Poyle) SL3 93 BE82
Bilton Rd, Erith DA8 107 FG80
Greenford UB6 79 CH67
Bilton Twrs, W1 *off Great Cumberland Pl* 82 DF72
Bilton Way, Enf. EN3 31 DY39
Hayes UB3 95 BV75
Bina Gdns, SW5 100 DC77
Bincote Rd, Enf. EN2 29 DM41
Binden Rd, W12 99 CT76
Bindon Grn, Mord. SM4 140 DB98
Binfield Rd, SW4 101 DL81
South Croydon CR2 160 DT106
West Byfleet (Byfleet) KT14 152 BL112
Bingfield St, N1 83 DL67
Bingham Cl, S.Ock. RM15 91 FV72
Bingham Ct, N1 *off Halton Rd* 83 DP66
Bingham Dr, Stai. TW18 114 BK94
Woking GU21 166 AT118
Bingham Pl, W1 194 F6
Bingham Pt, SE18 *off Wilmount St* 105 EP77
Bingham Rd, Croy. CR0 142 DU102
Bingham St, N1 84 DR65
Bingley Rd, E16 86 EJ72
Greenford UB6 78 CC71
Sunbury-on-Thames TW16 115 BU94
Binley Ho, SW15 *off Highcliffe Dr* 119 CU86
Binney St, W1 194 G10
Binns Rd, W4 98 CS78
Binns Ter, W4 *off Binns Rd* 98 CS78
Binsey Wk, SE2 88 EW74
Binstead Cl, Hayes UB4 78 BY71
Binyon Cres, Stan. HA7 41 CF50
Birbetts Rd, SE9 125 EM89
Bircham Path, SE4 *off St. Norbert Rd* 103 DX84
Birchanger Rd, SE25 142 DU99
Birch Av, N13 46 DQ48
Caterham CR3 176 DR124
Leatherhead KT22 171 CF120
West Drayton UB7 76 BM72
Birch Cl, E16 86 EE71
N19 *off Hargrave Pk* 65 DJ61
SE15 *off Bournemouth Rd* 102 DU82
Addlestone (New Haw) KT15 152 BK109
Amersham HP6 20 AS37
Brentford TW8 97 CH80
Buckhurst Hill IG9 48 EK48
Dartford (Eyns.) DA4 148 FK104
Hounslow TW3 97 CD83
Iver SL0 75 BD68
Romford RM7 71 FB55
Sevenoaks TN13 191 FH123
South Ockendon RM15 91 FX69
Teddington TW11 117 CG92
Woking GU21 166 AW119
Birch Copse, St.Alb. (Brick.Wd) AL2 8 BY30
Birch Ct, Nthwd. HA6 *off Rickmansworth Rd* 39 BQ51
Birch Cres, Horn. RM11 72 FL56
South Ockendon RM15 91 FX69
Uxbridge UB10 76 BM67
Birchcroft Cl, Cat. (Chaldon) CR3 186 DQ125
Birchdale, Ger.Cr. SL9 56 AX60
Birchdale Cl, W.Byf. KT14 152 BJ111
Birchdale Gdns, Rom. RM6 70 EX59
Birchdale Rd, E7 68 EJ64
Birchdene Dr, SE28 106 EU75
Birchdown Ho, E3 *off Rainhill Way* 85 EB69
Birch Dr, Rick. (Map.Cr.) WD3 37 BD50
Birchen Cl, NW9 62 CR61
Birchend Cl, S.Croy. CR2 160 DR107
Birchen Gro, NW9 62 CR61
Birches, The, N21 29 DM44
SE7 104 EH79
Brentwood CM13 54 FY48
Bushey WD23 24 CC43
Epping (N.Wld Bas.) CM16 19 FB26
Orpington BR6 163 EN105
Swanley BR8 147 FE96
Waltham Abbey EN9 *off Honey La* 16 EF34
Woking GU22 *off Heathside Rd* 167 AZ118
Birches Cl, Epsom KT18 172 CS115
Mitcham CR4 140 DF97
Pinner HA5 60 BY57
Birchfield, Grays (N.Stfd) RM16 91 FX74
Birchfield Cl, Add. KT15 152 BH105
Coulsdon CR5 175 DM116
Birchfield Gro, Epsom KT17 157 CW110
Birchfield Rd, Wal.Cr. (Chsht) EN8 14 DV29
Birchfield St, E14 85 EA73
Birch Gdns, Amer. HP7 20 AS39
Dagenham RM10 71 FC62
Birchgate Ms, Tad. KT20 *off Bidhams Cres* 173 CW121
Birch Grn, NW9 *off Clayton Fld* 42 CS52
Staines TW18 114 BG91
Birch Gro, E11 68 EE62
SE12 124 EF87
W3 80 CN74
Cobham KT11 154 BW114
Potters Bar EN6 12 DA32
Shepperton TW17 135 BS96
Tadworth KT20 173 CY124
Welling DA16 106 EU84
Woking GU22 167 BD115
★ **Birch Hall**, Epp. CM16 33 EQ36
Birch Hill, Croy. CR0 161 DX106
Birchington Cl, Bexh. DA7 107 FB81
Orpington BR5 *off Hart Dyke Rd* 146 EW102
Birchington Rd, N8 65 DK58
NW6 82 DA67
Surbiton KT5 138 CM101
Birchin La, EC3 197 L9
Birchlands Av, SW12 120 DF87
Birch La, Hem.H. (Flaun.) HP3 5 BB33
Purley CR8 159 DL111
Birchmead, Orp. BR6 145 EN103
Watford WD17 23 BT38
Birchmead Av, Pnr. HA5 60 BW56
Birchmere Business Pk, SE28 106 EU75
Birchmere Row, SE3 104 EF82
Birchmore Wk, N5 66 DQ62
Birch Pk, Har. HA3 40 CC52
Birch Pl, Green. DA9 129 FS86
Birch Rd, Felt. TW13 116 BX92
Romford RM7 71 FB55
Birch Row, Brom. BR2 145 EN101
Birch Tree Av, W.Wick. BR4 162 EF106
Birch Tree Gro, Chesh. (Ley Hill) HP5 4 AV30
Birch Tree Wk, Wat. WD17 23 BT37
Birch Tree Way, Croy. CR0 142 DV103
Birch Vale, Cob. KT11 154 CA112
Birch Vw, Epp. CM16 18 EV29
Birchville Ct, Bushey (Bushey Hth) WD23 *off Heathbourne Rd* 41 CE46
Birch Wk, Borwd. WD6 26 CN39
Erith DA8 107 FC79
Mitcham CR4 141 DH95
West Byfleet KT14 152 BG112
Birchway, Hayes UB3 77 BU74
Birch Way, St.Alb. (Lon.Col.) AL2 9 CK27
Warlingham CR6 177 DY118
Birch Wd, Rad. (Shenley) WD7 10 CN34
Birchwood, Wal.Abb. EN9 *off Roundhills* 16 EE34
Birchwood Av, N10 64 DG55
Beckenham BR3 143 DZ98
Sidcup DA14 126 EV89
Wallington SM6 140 DG104
Birchwood Cl, Brwd. (Gt Warley) CM13 53 FW51
Morden SM4 140 DB98
Birchwood Ct, N13 45 DP50
Edgware HA8 42 CQ54
Birchwood Dr, NW3 64 DB62
Dartford DA2 127 FE91
West Byfleet KT14 152 BG112
Birchwood Gro, Hmptn. TW12 116 CA93
Birchwood La, Cat. (Chaldon) CR3 185 DP125
Esher KT10 155 CD110
Leatherhead KT22 155 CD110
Sevenoaks (Knock.) TN14 180 EZ115
Birchwood Pk Av, Swan. BR8 147 FE97
Birchwood Rd, SW17 121 DH92
Dartford DA2 127 FE92
Orpington BR5 145 ER98
Swanley BR8 147 FC95
West Byfleet KT14 152 BG112
Birchwood Ter, Swan. BR8 *off Birchwood Rd* 147 FC95
Birchwood Way, St.Alb. (Park St) AL2 8 CB28
Birdbrook Cl, Brwd. (Hutt.) CM13 55 GB44
Dagenham RM10 89 FC66
Birdbrook Rd, SE3 104 EJ83
Birdcage Wk, SW1 199 L5
Birdham Cl, Brom. BR1 144 EL99
Birdhouse La, Orp. BR6 179 EN115
Birdhurst Av, S.Croy. CR2 160 DR105
Birdhurst Gdns, S.Croy. CR2 160 DR105
Birdhurst Ri, S.Croy. CR2 160 DS106
Birdhurst Rd, SW18 100 DC84
SW19 120 DE93
South Croydon CR2 160 DS106
Bird in Bush Rd, SE15 102 DU80
Bird-in-Hand La, Brom. BR1 144 EK96
Bird-in-Hand Ms, SE23 *off Dartmouth Rd* 122 DW89
Bird-in-Hand Pas, SE23 *off Dartmouth Rd* 122 DW89
Bird La, Brwd. (Gt Warley) CM13 73 FX55
Upminster RM14 73 FR57
Uxbridge (Hare.) UB9 38 BJ54
Birds Fm Av, Rom. RM5 51 FB53
Birdsfield La, E3 85 DZ67
Birds Hill Dr, Lthd. (Oxshott) KT22 155 CD113
Birds Hill Ri, Lthd. (Oxshott) KT22 155 CD113
Birds Hill Rd, Lthd. (Oxshott) KT22 155 CD112
Bird St, W1 194 G9
Birdswood Dr, Wok. GU21 166 AS119
Bird Wk, Twick. TW2 116 BZ88
Birdwood Cl, S.Croy. CR2 161 DX111
Teddington TW11 117 CE91
⇌ **Birkbeck** 142 DW97
Tra **Birkbeck** 142 DW97
Birkbeck Av, W3 80 CQ73
Greenford UB6 78 CC67
Birkbeck Gdns, Wdf.Grn. IG8 48 EF47
Birkbeck Gro, W3 98 CR75
Birkbeck Hill, SE21 121 DP89
Birkbeck Ms, E8 *off Sandringham Rd* 66 DT64
W3 *off Birkbeck Rd* 80 CR74
Birkbeck Pl, SE21 122 DQ88
Birkbeck Rd, E8 66 DT64
N8 65 DL56
N12 44 DC50
N17 46 DT53
NW7 43 CT50
SW19 120 DB92
W3 80 CR74
W5 97 CJ77
Beckenham BR3 142 DW96
Brentwood (Hutt.) CM13 55 GD44
Enfield EN2 30 DR39
Ilford IG2 69 ER57
Romford RM7 71 FD60
Sidcup DA14 126 EU90
Birkbeck St, E2 84 DV69
Birkbeck Way, Grnf. UB6 79 CE67
Birkdale Av, Pnr. HA5 60 CA55
Romford RM3 52 FM52
Birkdale Cl, SE16 *off Masters Dr* 102 DV78
SE28 88 EX72
Orpington BR6 145 ER101
Birkdale Gdns, Croy. CR0 161 DX105
Watford WD19 40 BX48
Birkdale Rd, SE2 106 EU77
W5 80 CL70
Birkenhead Av, Kings.T. KT2 138 CM96
Birkenhead St, WC1 196 A2
Birken Ms, Nthwd. HA6 39 BP50
Birkett Way, Ch.St.G. HP8 20 AX41
Birkhall Rd, SE6 123 ED88
Birkheads Rd, Reig. RH2 184 DA133
Birklands La, St.Alb. AL1 9 CH25
Birkwood Cl, SW12 121 DK87
Birley Rd, N20 44 DC47
Birley St, SW11 100 DG82
Birling Rd, Erith DA8 107 FD80
Birnam Rd, N4 65 DM61
Birnbeck Cl, NW11 63 CZ57
Birnbeck Ct, NW11 *off Finchley Rd* 63 CZ57
Birnham Cl, Wok. (Send M.) GU23 168 BG123
Birrell Ho, SW9 *off Stockwell Rd* 101 DM82
Birse Cres, NW10 62 CS63
Birstall Grn, Wat. WD19 40 BX49
Birstall Rd, N15 66 DS57
Birtley Path, Borwd. WD6 26 CL39
Biscayne Av, E14 *off Fairmont Av* 85 ED74
Biscay Rd, W6 99 CX78
Biscoe Cl, Houns. TW5 96 CA79
Biscoe Way, SE13 103 ED83
Bisenden Rd, Croy. CR0 142 DS103
Bisham Cl, Cars. SM5 140 DF102
Bisham Gdns, N6 64 DG60
Bishop Butt Cl, Orp. BR6 *off Stapleton Rd* 145 ET104
Bishop Cl, W4 98 CQ78
Bishop Duppa's Pk, Shep. TW17 135 BR101
Bishop Fox Way, W.Mol. KT8 136 BZ98
Bishop Ken Rd, Har. HA3 41 CF54
Bishop Kings Rd, W14 99 CY77
Bishop Rd, N14 45 DH45
Bishop's Av, E13 86 EH67
SW6 99 CX82
Bishops Av, Borwd. (Els.) WD6 26 CM43
Bromley BR1 144 EJ96
Northwood HA6 39 BS49
Romford RM6 70 EW58
Bishops Av, The, N2 64 DD59
Bishops Br, W2 82 DC72
Bishops Br Rd, W2 82 DB72
Bishops Cl, E17 67 EB56
N19 *off Wyndham Cres* 65 DJ62
SE9 125 EQ89
Barnet EN5 27 CX44
Bishop's Cl, Couls. CR5 175 DN118
Bishops Cl, Enf. EN1 *off Central Av* 30 DV40
Richmond TW10 117 CK90
Bishop's Cl, Sutt. SM1 140 DA104
Bishops Cl, Uxb. UB10 76 BN68
Bishop's Ct, EC4 196 F8
WC2 196 D8
Bishops Ct, Abb.L. WD5 7 BT31
Greenhithe DA9 129 FS85
Waltham Cross EN8 *off Churchgate* 14 DV30
Bishops Dr, Felt. TW14 115 BR86
Northolt UB5 78 BY67
Bishopsford Rd, Mord. SM4 140 DC101
Bishopsgate, EC2 197 M9
Bishopsgate Arc, EC2 197 N7
Bishopsgate Chyd, EC2 197 M7
Bishopsgate Rd, Egh. (Eng.Grn) TW20 112 AT90
Bishops Gro, N2 64 DD58
Hampton TW12 116 BZ91
Bishop's Hall, Kings.T. KT1 137 CK96
Bishops Hall Rd, Brwd. (Pilg.Hat.) CM15 54 FV44
Bishops Hill, Walt. KT12 135 BU101
Bishopsmead Cl, Epsom KT19 156 CR110
Bishop's Pk, SW6 99 CX82
Bishop's Pk Rd, SW6 99 CX82
Bishops Pk Rd, SW16 141 DL95
Bishops Pl, Sutt. SM1 *off Lind Rd* 158 DC106
Bishops Rd, N6 64 DG58
SW6 99 CZ81
Bishop's Rd, SW11 100 DE80
Bishops Rd, W7 97 CE75
Croydon CR0 141 DP101
Hayes UB3 77 BQ71
Slough SL1 92 AU75
Bishops Sq, E1 *off Brushfield St* 84 DT71
Bishops Ter, SE11 200 E8
Bishopsthorpe Rd, SE26 123 DX91
Bishop St, N1 84 DQ67
Bishops Wk, Chis. BR7 145 EQ95
Croydon CR0 161 DX106
Bishop's Wk, Pnr. HA5 *off High St* 60 BY55
Bishops Way, E2 84 DV68
Egham TW20 113 BD93
Bishops Wd, Wok. GU21 166 AT117
H **Bishopswood Private Hosp**, Nthwd. HA6 39 BP51
Bishopswood Rd, N6 64 DF59
Bishop Wk, Brwd. (Shenf.) CM15 55 FZ47
Bishop Way, NW10 80 CS66
Bishop Wilfred Wd Cl, SE15 *off Moncrieff St* 102 DU82
Biskra, Wat. WD17 23 BU39
Bisley Cl, Wal.Cr. EN8 15 DX33
Worcester Park KT4 139 CW102
Bisley Ho, SW19 119 CX89
Bispham Rd, NW10 80 CM69
Bisson Rd, E15 85 EC68
Bisterne Av, E17 67 ED55
Bittacy Cl, NW7 43 CX51
Bittacy Ct, NW7 *off Bittacy Hill* 43 CY52
Bittacy Hill, NW7 43 CX51
Bittacy Pk Av, NW7 43 CX51
Bittacy Ri, NW7 43 CW51
Bittacy Rd, NW7 43 CX51
Bittams La, Cher. KT16 151 BE105
Bittern Cl, Hayes UB4 78 BX71
Hemel Hempstead HP3 6 BM25
Waltham Cross (Chsht) EN7 14 DQ25
Bitterne Dr, Wok. GU21 166 AT117
Bittern Pl, N22 45 DM54
Bittern St, SE1 201 H5
Bittoms, The, Kings.T. KT1 137 CK97
Bixley Cl, Sthl. UB2 96 BZ77
Black Acre Cl, Amer. HP7 20 AS39
Blackacre Rd, Epp. (They.B.) CM16 33 ES37
Blackall St, EC2 197 M4
Blackberry Cl, Shep. TW17 *off Cherry Way* 135 BS98
Blackberry Fm Cl, Houns. TW5 96 BY80
Blackberry Fld, Orp. BR5 146 EU95
Blackbird Hill, NW9 62 CQ61
Blackbirds La, Wat. (Ald.) WD25 25 CD35
Blackbird Yd, E2 *off Ravenscroft St* 84 DT69
Blackborne Rd, Dag. RM10 88 FA65
Blackborough Cl, Reig. RH2 184 DC134
Black Boy La, N15 66 DQ57
Black Boy Wd, St.Alb. (Brick.Wd) AL2 8 CA30
Blackbridge Rd, Wok. GU22 166 AX119
Blackbrook La, Brom. BR1, BR2 145 EN97
Blackburn, The, Lthd. (Bkhm) KT23 *off Little Bookham St* 170 BZ124
Blackburne's Ms, W1 194 F10
Blackburn Rd, NW6 82 DB65
Blackburn Trd Est, Stai. (Stanw.) TW19 114 BM86
Blackbury Cl, Pot.B. EN6 12 DC31
Blackbush Av, Rom. RM6 70 EX57
Blackbush Cl, Sutt. SM2 158 DB108
Blackdale, Wal.Cr. (Chsht) EN7 14 DU27
Blackdown Av, Wok. GU22 167 BE115
Blackdown Cl, N2 44 DC54
Woking GU22 167 BC116
Blackdown Ter, SE18 *off Prince Imperial Rd* 105 EN80
Black Eagle Cl, West. TN16 189 EQ127
Blackett Cl, Stai. TW18 133 BE96
Blackett St, SW15 99 CX83
Blacketts Wd Dr, Rick. (Chorl.) WD3 21 BB43
Black Fan Cl, Enf. EN2 30 DQ39
BLACKFEN, Sid. DA15 125 ET87
Blackfen Rd, Sid. DA15 125 ES85
Blackford Cl, S.Croy. CR2 159 DP109
Blackford Rd, Wat. WD19 40 BX50
Blackford's Path, SW15 *off Roehampton High St* 119 CU87
⇌ **Blackfriars** 196 G10
⊖ **Blackfriars** 196 G10
Blackfriars Br, EC4 196 F10
SE1 196 F10
Blackfriars Ct, EC4 196 F10
Black Friars La, EC4 196 F10
Riv **Blackfriars Millennium Pier** 196 E10
Blackfriars Pas, EC4 196 F10
Blackfriars Rd, SE1 200 F5
Black Gates, Pnr. HA5 *off Church La* 60 BZ55
Blackhall La, Sev. TN15 191 FK123

★ Place of interest | ⇌ Railway station | ⊖ London Underground station | DLR Docklands Light Railway station | Tra Tramlink station | H Hospital | Riv Pedestrian ferry landing stage

Blackhall Pl, Sev. TN15
off Blackhall La **191** FL124
BLACKHEATH, SE3 . . . .**104** EE81
★ **Blackheath**, SE3 . . . .**103** ED81
⇌ **Blackheath** **104** EE83
Blackheath Av, SE10 . . . . . .**103** ED80
Blackheath Gro, SE3 . . . . . .**104** EF82
Blackheath Hill, SE10 . . . . . .**103** EC81
H **Blackheath Hosp, The**,
SE3 . . . .**104** EE83
BLACKHEATH PARK, SE3 . . .**104** EF84
Blackheath Pk, SE3 . . . .**104** EF83
Blackheath Ri, SE13 . . . .**103** EC82
Blackheath Rd, SE10 . . . . . .**103** EB81
Blackheath Vale, SE3 . . . . . .**104** EE82
Blackheath Village, SE3 . . . .**104** EF82
Blackhills, Esher KT10 . . . . .**154** CA109
Blackhorse Cl, Amer. HP6 . . .**20** AS38
Black Horse Ct, SE1 . . . .**201** L6
Blackhorse Cres, Amer. HP6 . .**20** AS38
Tra **Blackhorse Lane** **142** DU101
Blackhorse La, E17 . . . .**67** DX56
Croydon CR0 . . . .**142** DU101
Epping (N.Wld Bas.) CM16 .**19** FD25
Potters Bar EN6 . . . .**10** CS30
Reigate RH2 . . . .**184** DB129
Blackhorse Ms, E17
off Blackhorse La **67** DX55
Black Horse Pl, Uxb. UB8
off Waterloo Rd **76** BJ67
⇌ **Blackhorse Road** **67** DX56
⊖ **Blackhorse Road** **67** DX56
Blackhorse Rd, E17 . . . .**67** DX56
SE8 . . . .**103** DY78
Sidcup DA14 . . . .**126** EU91
Woking GU22 . . . .**166** AS122
Blackhouse Fm, Egh. TW20
off Coldharbour La **133** BC97
Black Lake Cl, Egh. TW20 . . .**133** BA95
Blacklands Dr, Hayes UB4 . . .**77** BQ70
Blacklands Meadow, Red.
(Nutfld) RH1 . . . .**185** DL133
Blacklands Rd, SE6 . . . .**123** EC91
Blacklands Ter, SW3 . . . .**198** D9
Blackley Cl, Wat. WD17 . . . . .**23** BT37
Black Lion Hill, Rad. (Shenley)
WD7 . . . .**10** CL32
Black Lion La, W6 . . . .**99** CU77
Black Lion Ms, W6
off Black Lion La **99** CU77
Blackmans Cl, Dart. DA1 . . . .**128** FJ88
Blackmans La, Warl. CR6 . . .**162** EE114
Blackmead, Sev. (Rvrhd)
TN13 . . . .**190** FE121
Blackmoor La, Wat. WD18 . . . .**23** BR43
Blackmore Av, Sthl. UB1 . . . . .**79** CD74
Blackmore Cl, Grays RM17 . .**110** GC78
Blackmore Ct, Wal.Abb. EN9 .**16** EG33
Blackmore Cres, Wok. GU21 .**167** BB115
Blackmore Dr, NW10 . . . .**80** CP66
Blackmore Rd, Buck.H. IG9 . . .**48** EL45
Blackmores Gro, Tedd. TW11 .**117** CG93
Blackmore Twr, W3
off Stanley Rd **98** CQ76
Blackmore Way, Uxb. UB8 . . .**76** BK65
Blackness La, Kes. BR2 . . . .**162** EK109
Woking GU22 . . . .**166** AY119
★ **Black Park Country Pk**,
Slou. SL3 . . . .**75** AZ67
Black Pk Rd, Slou. SL3 . . . . . .**75** AZ68
Black Path, E10 . . . .**67** DX59
Blackpool Gdns, Hayes UB4 . .**77** BS70
Blackpool Rd, SE15 . . . .**102** DV82
Black Prince Cl, W.Byf.
(Byfleet) KT14 . . . .**152** BM114
Black Prince Interchange, Bex.
DA5 off East Rochester Way .**127** FB86
Black Prince Rd, SE1 . . . .**200** B9
SE11 . . . .**200** C9
Black Rod Cl, Hayes UB3 . . . .**95** BT76
Blackshaw Pl, N1
off Hertford Rd **84** DS66
Blackshaw Rd, SW17 . . . .**120** DC91
Blackshots La, Grays RM16 . .**110** GD75
Blacksmith Cl, Ashtd. KT21
off Rectory La **172** CM119
Blacksmith Row, Slou. SL3 . . .**93** BA77
Blacksmiths Cl, Rom. RM6 . . . .**70** EW58
Blacksmiths Hill, S.Croy.
CR2 . . . .**160** DU113
Blacksmiths La, Cher. KT16 .**134** BG101
Orpington BR5 . . . .**146** EW99
Rainham RM13 . . . .**89** FF67
Staines TW18 . . . .**134** BH97
Uxbridge (Denh.) UB9 . . . . .**57** BC61
Blacks Rd, W6
off Queen Caroline St **99** CW77
Blackstock Ms, N4
off Blackstock Rd **65** DP61
Blackstock Rd, N4 . . . .**65** DP61
N5 . . . .**65** DP61
Blackstone Est, E8 . . . .**84** DV66
Blackstone Ho, SW1
off Churchill Gdns **101** DJ78
Blackstone Rd, NW2 . . . .**63** CW64
Black Swan Yd, SE1 . . . .**201** M4
Black's Yd, Sev. TN13
off Bank St **191** FJ125
Blackthorn Av, West Dr. UB7 . .**94** BN77
Blackthorn Cl, Wat. WD25 . . . . .**7** BV32
Blackthorn Ct, Houns. TW5 . . .**96** BY80
Blackthorn Dell, Slou. SL3 . . .**92** AW76
Blackthorne Av, Croy. CR0 . .**142** DW101
Blackthorne Cres, Slou.
(Colnbr.) SL3 . . . .**93** BE83
Blackthorne Dr, E4 . . . .**47** ED49
Blackthorne Rd, Slou.
(Colnbr.) SL3 . . . .**93** BE83
Westerham (Bigg.H.) TN16 . .**178** EK116
Blackthorn Gro, Bexh. DA7 . .**106** EX83
Blackthorn Rd, Ilf. IG1 . . . .**69** ER64
Blackthorn St, E3 . . . .**85** EA70
Blackthorn Way, Brwd. CM14 .**54** FX50
Blacktree Ms, SW9 . . . .**101** DN83
DLR **Blackwall** **204** E1
Blackwall La, SE10 . . . .**205** J10
Blackwall Pier, E14 . . . .**205** H1
Blackwall Trd Est, E14 . . . . . .**85** ED71
Blackwall Tunnel, E14 . . . . . .**204** F1
Blackwall Tunnel App, SE10 .**205** H5
Blackwall Tunnel Northern App,
E3 . . . .**85** EA68
E14 . . . .**85** EA68
Blackwall Way, E14 . . . .**204** E1
Blackwater Cl, E7 . . . .**68** EF63
Rainham RM13 . . . .**89** FD71
Blackwater Rd, Sutt. SM1
off High St **158** DB105
Blackwater St, SE22 . . . .**122** DT85
Blackwell Cl, E5 . . . .**67** DX63
Harrow HA3 . . . .**41** CD52
Blackwell Dr, Wat. WD19 . . . . .**24** BW44
Blackwell Gdns, Edg. HA8 . . . .**42** CN48
Blackwell Hall La, Chesh. HP5 .**4** AW33
Blackwell Rd, Kings L. WD4 . . .**6** BN29
Blackwood Av, N18
off Harbet Rd **47** DX50
Blackwood Cl, W.Byf. KT14 . .**152** BJ112
Blackwood Ct, Brox. EN10
off Groom Rd **15** DZ26
Blackwood St, SE17 . . . .**201** K10
Blade Ct, Rom. RM7
off Oldchurch Rd **71** FE58
Blade Ms, SW15
off Deodar Rd **99** CZ84
Bladen Cl, Wey. KT13 . . . . . .**153** BR107
Blades Cl, Lthd. KT22 . . . . . .**171** CK120
Blades Ct, SW15
off Deodar Rd **99** CZ84
Bladindon Dr, Bex. DA5 . . . .**126** EW87
Bladon Gdns, Har. HA2 . . . . . .**60** CB58
Blagdens Cl, N14 . . . .**45** DJ47
Blagdens La, N14 . . . .**45** DK47
Blagdon Rd, SE13 . . . .**123** EB86
New Malden KT3 . . . .**139** CT98
Blagdon Wk, Tedd. TW11 . . . .**117** CJ93
Blagrove Rd, W10 . . . .**81** CY71
Blair Av, NW9 . . . .**62** CS59
Esher KT10 . . . .**136** CC103
Blair Cl, N1 . . . .**84** DQ65
Hayes UB3 . . . .**95** BU77
Sidcup DA15 . . . .**125** ES85
Blairderry Rd, SW2 . . . .**121** DL89
Blair Dr, Sev. TN13 . . . .**191** FH123
Blairhead Dr, Wat. WD19 . . . . .**39** BV48
Blair Rd, Slou. SL1 . . . .**74** AS74
Blair St, E14 . . . .**85** EC72
Blake Apts, N8
off New River Av **65** DM55
Blake Av, Bark. IG11 . . . .**87** ES67
Blakeborough Dr, Rom.
(Harold Wd) RM3 . . . .**52** FL54
Blake Cl, W10 . . . .**81** CW71
Carshalton SM5 . . . .**140** DE101
Rainham RM13 . . . .**89** FF67
Welling DA16 . . . .**105** ES81
Blakeden Dr, Esher (Clay.)
KT10 . . . .**155** CF107
Blake Gdns, SW6 . . . .**100** DB81
Dartford DA1 . . . .**108** FM84
Blake Hall Cres, E11 . . . .**68** EG60
Blake Hall Rd, E11 . . . .**68** EG59
Blakehall Rd, Cars. SM5 . . . .**158** DF107
Blake Hall Rd, Ong. CM5 . . . . .**19** FG25
Blake Ho, Beck. BR3 . . . .**123** EA93
Blake Ms, Rich. TW9
off High Pk Rd **98** CN81
Blakemore Gdns, SW13
off Lonsdale Rd **99** CV79
Blakemore Rd, SW16 . . . .**121** DL90
Thornton Heath CR7 . . . . .**141** DM99
Blakemore Way, Belv. DA17 . .**106** EY76
Blakeney Av, Beck. BR3 . . . . .**143** DZ95
Blakeney Cl, E8
off Ferncliff Rd **66** DU64
N20 . . . .**44** DC46
NW1 off Rossendale Way . . .**83** DK66
Epsom KT19 . . . .**156** CR111
Blakeney Rd, Beck. BR3 . . . .**123** DZ94
Blakenham Rd, SW17 . . . .**120** DF91
Blaker Ct, SE7 off Fairlawn . .**104** EJ80
Blake Rd, E16 . . . .**86** EF70
N11 . . . .**45** DJ52
Croydon CR0 . . . .**142** DS103
Mitcham CR4 . . . .**140** DE97
Blaker Rd, E15 . . . .**85** EC67
Blakes Av, N.Mal. KT3 . . . . . .**139** CT99
Blake's Grn, W.Wick. BR4 . . .**143** EC102
Blakes La, N.Mal. KT3 . . . . . .**139** CT99
Blakesley Av, W5 . . . .**79** CJ72
Blakesley Ho, E12
off Grantham Rd **69** EN62
Blakesley Wk, SW20
off Kingston Rd **139** CZ96
Blakes Rd, SE15 . . . .**102** DS80
Blakes Ter, N.Mal. KT3 . . . . . .**139** CU99
Blake St, SE8
off Watergate St **103** EA79
Blakesware Gdns, N9 . . . .**46** DR45
Blakes Way, Til. RM18
off Coleridge Rd **111** GJ82
Blakewood Cl, Felt. TW13 . . .**116** BW91
Blanchard Cl, SE9 . . . .**124** EL90
Blanchard Dr, Wat. WD18
off Cassio Pl **23** BS42
Blanchard Gro, Enf. EN3 . . . . . .**31** EB38
Blanchard Ms, Rom. (Harold Wd)
RM3 off Avenue Rd **52** FM52
Blanchard Way, E8 . . . .**84** DU65
Blanch Cl, SE15
off Culmore Rd **102** DW80
Blanchedowne, SE5 . . . .**102** DR84
Blanche La, Pot.B. EN6 . . . .**11** CT34
Blanche St, E16 . . . .**86** EF70
Blanchland Rd, Mord. SM4 . .**140** DB99
Blanchmans Rd, Warl. CR6 . .**177** DY118
Blandfield Rd, SW12 . . . .**120** DG86
Blandford Av, Beck. BR3 . . . .**143** DY96
Twickenham TW2 . . . .**116** CB88
Blandford Cl, N2 . . . .**64** DC56
Croydon CR0 . . . .**141** DL104
Romford RM7 . . . .**71** FB56
Slough SL3 . . . .**92** AX76
Woking GU22 . . . .**167** BB117
Blandford Ct, Slou. SL3
off Blandford Rd S **92** AX76
Blandford Cres, E4 . . . .**47** EC45
Blandford Rd, W4 . . . .**98** CS76
W5 . . . .**97** CK75
Beckenham BR3 . . . .**142** DW96
Southall UB2 . . . .**96** CA77
Teddington TW11 . . . .**117** CD92
Blandford Rd N, Slou. SL3 . . . .**92** AX76
Blandford Rd S, Slou. SL3 . . . .**92** AX76
Blandford Sq, NW1 . . . .**194** C5
Blandford St, W1 . . . .**194** E8
Blandford Waye, Hayes UB4 . .**78** BW72
Bland St, SE9 . . . .**104** EK84
Blaney Cres, E6 . . . .**87** EP69
Blanford Ms, Reig. RH2 . . . . .**184** DD134
Blanmerle Rd, SE9 . . . .**125** EP88
Blann Cl, SE9 . . . .**124** EK86
Blantyre St, SW10 . . . .**100** DD80
Blantyre Twr, SW10
off World's End Est **100** DD80
Blantyre Wk, SW10
off Blantyre St **100** DD80
Blashford, NW3 . . . .**82** DF66
Blashford St, SE13 . . . .**123** ED87
Blasker Wk, E14 . . . .**204** A10
Blattner Cl, Borwd. (Els.)
WD6 . . . .**26** CL42
Blawith Rd, Har. HA1 . . . .**61** CE56
Blaxland Ter, Wal.Cr. (Chsht)
EN8 off Davison Dr **15** DX28
Blaydon Cl, N17 . . . .**46** DV52
Ruislip HA4 . . . .**59** BS59
Blaydon Wk, N17 . . . .**46** DV52
Blays Cl, Egh. (Eng.Grn)
TW20 . . . .**112** AW93
Blays La, Egh. (Eng.Grn)
TW20 . . . .**112** AV94
Bleak Hill La, SE18 . . . .**105** ET79
Blean Gro, SE20 . . . .**122** DW94
Bleasdale Av, Grnf. UB6 . . . . .**79** CG68
Blechynden St, W10
off Bramley Rd **81** CX73
Bleddyn Cl, Sid. DA15 . . . . . .**126** EW86
Bledlow Cl, NW8
off Capland St **82** DD70
SE28 . . . .**88** EW73
Bledlow Ri, Grnf. UB6 . . . .**78** CC68
Bleeding Heart Yd, EC1 . . . . .**196** E7
Blegborough Rd, SW16 . . . . .**121** DJ93
Blemundsbury, WC1
off Dombey St **83** DM71
Blencarn Cl, Wok. GU21 . . . .**166** AT116
Blendon Dr, Bex. DA5 . . . . . .**126** EX86
Blendon Path, Brom. BR1 . . . .**124** EF94
Blendon Rd, Bex. DA5 . . . . . .**126** EX86
Blendon Ter, SE18 . . . .**105** EQ78
Blendworth Pt, SW15
off Wanborough Dr **119** CV88
Blenheim Av, Ilf. IG2 . . . .**69** EN58
Blenheim Cl, N21
off Elm Pk Rd **46** DQ46
SE12 . . . .**124** EH88
SW20 . . . .**139** CW97
Dartford DA1 . . . .**128** FJ86
Greenford UB6
off Leaver Gdns **79** CD68
Romford RM7 . . . .**71** FC56
Slough SL3 . . . .**75** AZ74
Upminster RM14 . . . .**73** FS60
Wallington SM6 . . . .**159** DJ108
Watford WD19 . . . .**40** BX45
West Byfleet KT14
off Madeira Rd **151** BF113
Blenheim Ct, N19
off Marlborough Rd **65** DL61
Bromley BR2
off Durham Av **144** EF98
Sidcup DA14 . . . .**125** ER90
Sutton SM2
off Wellesley Rd **158** DC107
Woodford Green IG8
off Navestock Cres **48** EJ52
Blenheim Cres, W11 . . . .**81** CY72
Ruislip HA4 . . . .**59** BR61
South Croydon CR2 . . . .**160** DQ108
Blenheim Dr, Well. DA16 . . . .**105** ET81
Blenheim Gdns, NW2 . . . .**63** CW64
SW2 . . . .**121** DM86
Kingston upon Thames
KT2 . . . .**118** CP94
South Croydon CR2 . . . .**160** DU112
South Ockendon (Aveley)
RM15 . . . .**90** FP74
Wallington SM6 . . . .**159** DJ107
Wembley HA9 . . . .**62** CL62
Woking GU22 . . . .**166** AV119
Blenheim Gro, SE15 . . . .**102** DU82
Blenheim Pk Rd, S.Croy.
CR2 . . . .**160** DQ109
Blenheim Pas, NW8
off Blenheim Ter **82** DC68
Blenheim Pl, Tedd. TW11 . . . .**117** CF92
Blenheim Ri, N15
off Talbot Rd **66** DT56
Blenheim Rd, E6 . . . .**86** EK69
E15 . . . .**68** EE63
E17 . . . .**67** DX55
NW8 . . . .**82** DC68
SE20 off Maple Rd **122** DW94
SW20 . . . .**139** CW97
W4 . . . .**98** CS76
Abbots Langley WD5 . . . .**7** BU33
Barnet EN5 . . . .**27** CX41
Brentwood (Pilg.Hat.)
CM15 . . . .**54** FU44
Bromley BR1 . . . .**144** EL98
Dartford DA1 . . . .**128** FJ86
Epsom KT19 . . . .**156** CR111
Harrow HA2 . . . .**60** CB58
Northolt UB5 . . . .**78** CB65
Orpington BR6 . . . .**146** EW103
Sidcup DA15 . . . .**126** EW88
Slough SL3 . . . .**92** AX77
Sutton SM1 . . . .**140** DA104
Blenheim Shop Cen, SE20 . .**122** DW94
Blenheim St, W1 . . . .**195** H9
Blenheim Ter, NW8 . . . .**82** DC68
Blenheim Way, Epp. (N.Wld Bas.)
CM16 . . . .**18** FA27
Isleworth TW7 . . . .**97** CG81
Blenkarne Rd, SW11 . . . .**120** DF86
Bleriot Rd, Houns. TW5 . . . . . .**96** BW80
Blessbury Rd, Edg. HA8 . . . . . .**42** CQ53
Blessington Cl, SE13 . . . .**103** ED83
Blessington Rd, SE13 . . . .**103** ED83
Blessing Way, Bark. IG11 . . . . .**88** EW69
BLETCHINGLEY, Red. RH1 . . .**186** DQ132
Bletchingley Cl, Red. (Merst.)
RH1 . . . .**185** DJ129
Thornton Heath CR7 . . . . . .**141** DP98
Bletchingley Rd, Gdse. RH9 .**186** DU131
Redhill (Nutfld) RH1 . . . . . .**185** DN133
Redhill (S.Merst.) RH1 . . . . .**185** DJ129
Bletchley Ct, N1 . . . .**197** K1
Bletchley St, N1 . . . .**197** J1
Bletchmore Cl, Hayes UB3 . . . .**95** BR78
Bletsoe Wk, N1
off Cropley St **84** DQ68
Blewbury Ho, SE2
off Yarnton Way **106** EX75
Bligh Rd, Grav. DA11 . . . .**131** GG86
Bligh's Rd, Sev. TN13 . . . .**191** FH125
Blincoe Cl, SW19 . . . .**119** CX89
Blinco La, Slou. (Geo.Grn)
SL3 . . . .**74** AY72
Blind La, Bans. SM7 . . . .**174** DE115
Loughton (High Beach)
IG10 . . . .**32** EE40
Waltham Abbey EN9 . . . .**16** EJ33
Blindman's La, Wal.Cr. (Chsht)
EN8 . . . .**15** DX30
Bliss Cres, SE13 . . . .**103** EB82
Blissett St, SE10 . . . .**103** EC81
Bliss Ms, W10 off Third Av **81** CY69
Blisworth Cl, Hayes UB4
off Braunston Dr **78** BY70
Blithbury Rd, Dag. RM9 . . . . . .**88** EV65
Blithdale Rd, SE2 . . . .**106** EU77
Blithfield St, W8 . . . .**100** DB76
Blockhouse Rd, Grays RM17 .**110** GC79
Blockley Rd, Wem. HA0 . . . . . .**61** CH61
Bloemfontein Av, W12 . . . .**81** CV74
Bloemfontein Rd, W12 . . . .**81** CV73
Bloemfontein Way, W12
off Bloemfontein Rd **81** CV74
Blomfield Ct, SW11
off Westbridge Rd **100** DE81
Blomfield Ms, W2
off Westbourne Ter Rd **82** DC71
Blomfield Rd, W9 . . . .**82** DC71
Blomfield St, EC2 . . . .**197** L7
Blomfield Vil, W2 . . . .**82** DB71
Blomville Rd, Dag. RM8 . . . . . .**70** EY62
Blondell Cl, West Dr. UB7 . . . . .**94** BK79
Blondel St, SW11 . . . .**100** DG82
Blondin Av, W5 . . . .**97** CJ77
Blondin St, E3 . . . .**85** EA68
Bloomburg St, SW1 . . . .**199** L9
Bloomfield Cl, Wok. (Knap.)
GU21 . . . .**166** AS118
Bloomfield Cres, Ilf. IG2 . . . . .**69** EP58
Bloomfield Pl, W1 . . . .**195** J10
Bloomfield Rd, N6 . . . .**64** DG58
SE18 . . . .**105** EP78
Bromley BR2 . . . .**144** EK99
Kingston upon Thames
KT1 . . . .**138** CL98
Waltham Cross (Chsht)
EN7 . . . .**14** DQ25
Bloomfield Ter, SW1 . . . .**198** G10
Westerham TN16 . . . .**189** ES125
Bloom Gro, SE27 . . . .**121** DP90
Bloomhall Rd, SE19 . . . .**122** DR92
Bloom Pk Rd, SW6 . . . .**99** CZ80
BLOOMSBURY, WC1 . . . .**195** N7
Bloomsbury Cl, NW7 . . . .**43** CU52
W5 . . . .**80** CM73
Epsom KT19 . . . .**156** CR110
Bloomsbury Ct, WC1 . . . .**196** A7
Pinner HA5 . . . .**60** BZ55
Bloomsbury Ho, SW4 . . . .**121** DK86
Bloomsbury Pl, SW18
off Fullerton Rd **120** DC85
WC1 . . . .**196** A6
Bloomsbury Sq, WC1 . . . .**196** A7
Bloomsbury St, WC1 . . . .**195** N7
Bloomsbury Way, WC1 . . . . . .**195** P8
Blore Cl, SW8
off Thessaly Rd **101** DK81
Blore Ct, W1 . . . .**195** M9
Blossom Cl, W5 . . . .**98** CL75
Dagenham RM9 . . . .**88** EZ67
South Croydon CR2 . . . .**160** DT106
Blossom La, Enf. EN2 . . . .**30** DQ39
Blossom St, E1 . . . .**197** N6
Blossom Way, Uxb. UB10 . . . . .**76** BM66
West Drayton UB7 . . . .**94** BN77
Blossom Waye, Houns. TW5 . . .**96** BY80
Blount St, E14 . . . .**85** DY72
Bloxam Gdns, SE9 . . . .**124** EL85
Bloxhall Rd, E10 . . . .**67** DZ60
Bloxham Cres, Hmptn. TW12 .**116** BZ94
Bloxworth Cl, Wall. SM6 . . . . .**141** DJ104
Blucher Rd, SE5 . . . .**102** DQ80
Blue Anchor All, Rich. TW9
off Kew Rd **98** CL84
Blue Anchor La, SE16 . . . .**202** C8
Tilbury (W.Til.) RM18 . . . . . .**111** GL77
Blue Anchor Yd, E1 . . . .**84** DU73
Blue Ball La, Egh. TW20 . . . . .**113** AZ92
Blue Ball Yd, SW1 . . . .**199** K3
Blue Barn La, Wey. KT13 . . . . .**152** BN111
Bluebell Av, E12 . . . .**68** EK64
Bluebell Cl, E9
off Moulins Rd **84** DW67
SE26 . . . .**122** DT91
Northolt UB5 . . . .**78** BZ65
Orpington BR6 . . . .**145** EQ103
Romford (Rush Grn) RM7 . . .**71** FE61
Wallington SM6 . . . .**141** DH102
Bluebell Ct, Wok. GU22 . . . . .**166** AX119
Bluebell Dr, Abb.L. (Bedmond)
WD5 . . . .**7** BT27
Waltham Cross EN7 . . . .**14** DR28
Bluebell Way, Ilf. IG1 . . . .**87** EP65
Blueberry Cl, Wdf.Grn. IG8 . . .**48** EG51
Blueberry Gdns, Couls. CR5 .**175** DM116
Blueberry La, Sev. (Knock.)
TN14 . . . .**180** EW116
Bluebird La, Dag. RM10 . . . . . .**88** FA66
Bluebird Way, SE28 . . . .**105** ER75
St. Albans AL2 . . . .**8** BY30
Bluebridge Av, Hat. AL9 . . . . . .**11** CZ27
Bluebridge Rd, Hat. (Brook.Pk)
AL9 . . . .**11** CY26
Blue Cedars, Bans. SM7 . . . .**157** CX114
Blue Cedars Pl, Cob. KT11 . . .**154** BX112
Bluefield Cl, Hmptn. TW12 . . .**116** CA92
Bluegates, Epsom (Ewell)
KT17 . . . .**157** CU108
Bluehouse Gdns, Oxt. RH8 . . .**188** EG128
Bluehouse La, Oxt. RH8 . . . . .**188** EG127
Bluehouse Rd, E4 . . . .**48** EE48
Blue Leaves Av, Couls. CR5 . .**175** DK121
Bluelion Pl, SE1 . . . .**201** M6
Blueprint Apts, SW12
off Balham Gro **121** DH87
Bluett Rd, St.Alb. (Lon.Col.)
AL2 . . . .**9** CK27
Bluewater Ho, SW18
off Smugglers Way **100** DB84
Bluewater Parkway, Green.
(Bluewater) DA9 . . . .**129** FS87
Bluewater Shop Cen, Green.
DA9 . . . .**129** FT88
Blundel La, Cob. (Stoke D'Ab.)
KT11 . . . .**154** CB114
Blundell Cl, E8
off Amhurst Rd **66** DU64
Blundell Rd, Edg. HA8 . . . . . .**42** CR53
Blundell St, N7 . . . .**83** DL66
Blunden Cl, Dag. RM8 . . . .**70** EW60
Blunden Dr, Slou. SL3 . . . .**93** BB77
Blunesfield, Pot.B. EN6 . . . . . .**12** DD31
Blunt Rd, S.Croy. CR2 . . . . . .**160** DR106
Blunts Av, West Dr. UB7 . . . . . .**94** BN80
Blunts La, St.Alb. AL2 . . . .**8** BW27
Blunts Rd, SE9 . . . .**125** EN85
Blurton Rd, E5 . . . .**66** DW63
Blyth Cl, E14 . . . .**204** F8
Borehamwood WD6 . . . .**26** CM39
Twickenham TW1
off Grimwood Rd **117** CF86
Blythe Cl, SE6 . . . .**123** DZ87
Iver SL0 . . . .**75** BF72
Blythe Hill, SE6 . . . .**123** DZ87
Orpington BR5 . . . .**145** ET95
Blythe Hill La, SE6 . . . .**123** DZ87
Blythe Hill Pl, SE23
off Brockley Pk **123** DY87
Blythe Ms, W14 off Blythe Rd .**99** CX76
Blythe Rd, W14 . . . .**99** CX76
Blythe St, E2 . . . .**84** DV69
Blytheswood Pl, SW16
off Curtis Fld Rd **121** DM91
Blythe Vale, SE6 . . . .**123** DZ88
Blyth Rd, E17 . . . .**67** DZ59
SE28 . . . .**88** EW73
Bromley BR1 . . . .**144** EF95
Hayes UB3 . . . .**95** BS75
Blyth's Wf, E14 . . . .**203** L1
Blythswood Rd, Ilf. IG3 . . . .**70** EU60
Blyth Wk, Upmin. RM14 . . . . . .**73** FS58
Blyth Wd Pk, Brom. BR1
off Blyth Rd **144** EF95
Blythwood Rd, N4 . . . .**65** DL59
Pinner HA5 . . . .**40** BX53
Boades Ms, NW3
off New End **64** DD63
Boadicea St, N1
off Copenhagen St **83** DM67
Boakes Cl, NW9 . . . .**62** CQ56
Boakes Meadow, Sev.
(Shore.) TN14 . . . .**165** FF111
Boar Cl, Chig. IG7 . . . .**50** EU50
Boardman Av, E4 . . . .**31** EB43
Boardman Cl, Barn. EN5 . . . . . .**27** CY43
Board Sch Rd, Wok. GU21 . . .**167** AZ116
Boardwalk Pl, E14 . . . .**204** D2
Boar's Head Yd, Brent. TW8
off Brent Way **97** CK80
Boathouse Wk, SE15 . . . .**102** DT80
Richmond TW9 . . . .**98** CL81
Boat Lifter Way, SE16 . . . .**203** L8
Bob Anker Cl, E13
off Chesterton Rd **86** EG69
Bobbin Cl, SW4 . . . .**101** DJ83
Bobby Moore Way, N10 . . . .**44** DF52
Bob Dunn Way, Dart. DA1 . . . .**108** FJ84
Bob Marley Way, SE24
off Mayall Rd **101** DN84
Bobs La, Rom. RM1 . . . .**51** FG52
Bocketts La, Lthd. KT22 . . . . .**171** CF124
Bockhampton Rd, Kings.T.
KT2 . . . .**118** CM94
Bocking St, E8 . . . .**84** DV67
Boddicott Cl, SW19 . . . .**119** CY89
Boddington Gdns, W3 . . . .**98** CN75
Bodell Cl, Grays RM16 . . . . . .**110** GB76
Bodiam Cl, Enf. EN1 . . . .**30** DR40
Bodiam Rd, SW16 . . . .**121** DK94
Bodiam Way, NW10 . . . .**80** CM69
Bodicea Ms, Houns. TW4 . . . .**116** BZ87
Bodle Av, Swans. DA10 . . . . . .**130** FY87
Bodley Cl, Epp. CM16 . . . .**17** ET30
New Malden KT3 . . . .**138** CS99
Bodley Manor Way, SW2
off Hambridge Way **121** DN87
Bodley Rd, N.Mal. KT3 . . . . . .**138** CR100
Bodmin Cl, Har. HA2 . . . .**60** BZ62
Orpington BR5 . . . .**146** EW102
Bodmin Gro, Mord. SM4 . . . . .**140** DB99
Bodmin St, SW18 . . . .**120** DA88
Bodnant Gdns, SW20 . . . .**139** CU97
Bodney Rd, E8 . . . .**66** DV64
Boeing Way, Sthl. UB2 . . . .**95** BV76
Boevey Path, Belv. DA17 . . . .**106** EZ79
Bogey La, Orp. BR6 . . . .**163** EN108
Bognor Gdns, Wat. WD19
off Bowring Grn **40** BW50
Bognor Rd, Well. DA16 . . . . . .**106** EX81
Bohemia Pl, E8 . . . .**84** DV65
Bohn Rd, E1 . . . .**85** DY71
Bohun Gro, Barn. EN4 . . . .**28** DE44
Boileau Par, W5
off Boileau Rd **80** CM72
Boileau Rd, SW13 . . . .**99** CU80
W5 . . . .**80** CM72
Bois Hall Rd, Add. KT15 . . . . .**152** BK105
Bois Hill, Chesh. HP5 . . . .**4** AS34
Bolden St, SE8 . . . .**103** EB82
Bolderwood Way, W.Wick.
BR4 . . . .**143** EB103
Boldmere Rd, Pnr. HA5 . . . .**60** BW59
Boleyn Av, Enf. EN1 . . . .**30** DV39
Epsom KT17 . . . .**157** CV110
Boleyn Cl, E17 . . . .**67** EA56
Grays (Chaff.Hun.) RM16
off Clifford Rd **110** FZ76
Loughton IG10
off Roding Gdns **32** EL44
Staines TW18
off Chertsey La **113** BE92
Boleyn Ct, Buck.H. IG9 . . . . . .**48** EG46

★ Place of interest ⇌ Railway station ⊖ London Underground station DLR Docklands Light Railway station Tra Tramlink station H Hospital Riv Pedestrian ferry landing stage

Boleyn Dr, Ruis. HA4 ... 60 BX61
West Molesey KT8 ... 136 BZ97
Boleyn Gdns, Brwd. CM13 ... 55 GA48
Dagenham RM10 ... 89 FC66
West Wickham BR4 ... 143 EB103
Boleyn Gro, W.Wick. BR4 ... 143 EC103
Boleyn Rd, E6 ... 86 EK68
E7 ... 86 EG66
N16 ... 66 DS64
Boleyn Wk, Lthd. KT22 ... 171 CF120
Boleyn Way, Barn. EN5 ... 28 DC41
Ilford IG6 ... 49 EQ51
Swanscombe DA10 ... 130 FY87
Bolina Rd, SE16 ... 202 G10
Bolingbroke Gro, SW11 ... 100 DE84
H Bolingbroke Hosp, SW11 ... 120 DE85
Bolingbroke Rd, W14 ... 99 CX76
Bolingbroke Wk, SW11 ... 100 DD80
Bolingbroke Way, Hayes UB3 ... 77 BR74
Bolliger Ct, NW10
off Park Royal Rd ... 80 CQ70
Bollo Br Rd, W3 ... 98 CP76
Bollo La, W3 ... 98 CP75
W4 ... 98 CQ77
Bolney Gate, SW7 ... 198 B5
Bolney St, SW8 ... 101 DM80
Bolney Way, Felt. TW13 ... 116 BY90
Bolsover Gro, Red. (Merst.)
RH1 ... 185 DL129
Bolsover St, W1 ... 195 J5
Bolstead Rd, Mitch. CR4 ... 141 DH95
Bolt Cellar La, Epp. CM16 ... 17 ES29
Bolt Ct, EC4 ... 196 E9
Bolters La, Bans. SM7 ... 157 CZ114
Boltmore Cl, NW4 ... 63 CX55
Bolton Cl, SE20 off Selby Rd ... 142 DU96
Chessington KT9 ... 155 CK107
Bolton Cres, SE5 ... 101 DP79
Bolton Dr, Mord. SM4 ... 140 DC101
Bolton Gdns, NW10 ... 81 CX68
SW5 ... 100 DB78
Bromley BR1 ... 124 EF93
Teddington TW11 ... 117 CG93
Bolton Gdns Ms, SW10 ... 100 DB78
Bolton Rd, E15 ... 86 EF65
N18 ... 46 DT50
NW8 ... 82 DB67
NW10 ... 80 CS67
W4 ... 98 CQ80
Chessington KT9 ... 155 CK107
Harrow HA1 ... 60 CC56
Boltons, The, SW10 ... 100 DC78
Wembley HA0 ... 61 CF63
Woodford Green IG8 ... 48 EG49
Boltons Cl, Wok. GU22 ... 168 BG116
Boltons La, Hayes UB3 ... 95 BQ80
Woking GU22 ... 168 BG116
Boltons Pl, SW5 ... 100 DC78
Bolton St, W1 ... 199 J2
Bolton Wk, N7
off Durham Rd ... 65 DM61
Bombay St, SE16 ... 202 D8
Bombers La, West. TN16 ... 179 ER119
Bomer Cl, West Dr. UB7 ... 94 BN80
Bomore Rd, W11 ... 81 CX73
Bonar Pl, Chis. BR7 ... 124 EL94
Bonar Rd, SE15 ... 102 DU80
Bonaventure Ct, Grav. DA12 ... 131 GM91
Bonchester Cl, Chis. BR7 ... 125 EN94
Bonchurch Cl, Sutt. SM2 ... 158 DB108
Bonchurch Rd, W10 ... 81 CY71
W13 ... 79 CH74
Bond Cl, Sev. (Knock.) TN14 ... 180 EX115
West Drayton UB7 ... 76 BM72
Bond Ct, EC4 ... 197 K9
Bondfield Av, Hayes UB4 ... 77 BU69
Bondfield Rd, E6
off Lovage App ... 86 EL71
Bondfield Wk, Dart. DA1 ... 108 FM84
Bond Gdns, Wall. SM6 ... 159 DJ105
Bonding Yd Wk, SE16 ... 203 L5
Bond Rd, Mitch. CR4 ... 140 DE96
Surbiton KT6 ... 138 CM103
Warlingham CR6 ... 177 DX118
⊖ Bond Street ... 194 G9
Bond St, E15 ... 68 EE64
W4 ... 98 CS77
W5 ... 79 CK73
Egham (Eng.Grn) TW20 ... 112 AV92
Grays RM17 ... 110 GC79
Bondway, SW8 ... 101 DL79
Bone Mill La, Gdse. RH9
off Eastbourne Rd ... 187 DY134
Boneta Rd, SE18 ... 105 EM76
Bonfield Rd, SE13 ... 103 EC84
Bonham Gdns, Dag. RM8 ... 70 EX61
Bonham Rd, SW2 ... 121 DM85
Dagenham RM8 ... 70 EX61
Bonheur Rd, W4 ... 98 CR75
Bonhill St, EC2 ... 197 L5
Boniface Gdns, Har. HA3 ... 40 CB52
Boniface Rd, Uxb. UB10 ... 59 BP62
Boniface Wk, Har. HA3 ... 40 CB52
Bonington Ho, Enf. EN1
off Ayley Cft ... 30 DU43
Bonington Rd, Horn. RM12 ... 72 FK64
Bonita Ms, SE4 ... 103 DX83
Bon Marche Ter Ms, SE27
off Gipsy Rd ... 122 DS91
Bonner Hill Rd, Kings.T. KT1 ... 138 CM97
Bonner Rd, E2 ... 84 DW68
Bonners Cl, Wok. GU22 ... 166 AY122
Bonnersfield Cl, Har. HA1 ... 61 CF58
Bonnersfield La, Har. HA1 ... 61 CG58
Bonner St, E2 ... 84 DW68
Bonner Wk, Grays RM16
off Clifford Rd ... 110 FZ76
Bonnett Ms, Horn. RM11 ... 72 FL60
Bonneville Gdns, SW4 ... 121 DJ86
Bonney Gro, Wal.Cr. (Chsht)
EN7 ... 14 DU30
Bonney Way, Swan. BR8 ... 147 FE96
Bonnington Ho, N1
off Killick St ... 83 DM68
Bonningtons, Brwd. CM13 ... 55 GB48
Bonnington Sq, SW8 ... 101 DM79
Bonnington Twr, Brom. BR2 ... 144 EL100
Bonny St, NW1 ... 83 DJ66
Bonser Rd, Twick. TW1 ... 117 CF89
Bonsey Cl, Wok. GU22 ... 166 AY121
Bonsey La, Wok. GU22 ... 166 AY121
Bonseys La, Wok. (Chobham)
GU24 ... 151 AZ110
Bonsor Dr, Tad. KT20 ... 173 CY122
Bonsor St, SE5 ... 102 DS80
Bonville Gdns, NW4
off Handowe Cl ... 63 CU56
Bonville Rd, Brom. BR1 ... 124 EF92
Bookbinders' Cotts, N20
off Manor Dr ... 44 DF48
Booker Cl, E14
off Wallwood St ... 85 DZ71
Booker Rd, N18 ... 46 DU50
⇌ Bookham ... 170 BZ123
Bookham Ct, Lthd. KT23
off Church Rd ... 170 BZ123
Mitcham CR4 ... 140 DD97
Bookham Ind Est, Lthd.
(Bkhm) KT23 ... 170 BZ123
Bookham Rd, Cob. (Down.)
KT11 ... 170 BW119
Book Ms, WC2 ... 195 N9
Boone Ct, N9 ... 46 DW48
Boones Rd, SE13 ... 104 EE84
Boone St, SE13 ... 104 EE84
Boord St, SE10 ... 205 J6
Boothby Rd, N19 ... 65 DK61
Booth Cl, E9
off Victoria Pk Rd ... 84 DV67
SE28 ... 88 EV73
Booth Dr, Stai. TW18 ... 114 BK93
Booth Rd, NW9 ... 42 CS54
Croydon CR0
off Waddon New Rd ... 141 DP103
Booth's Ct, Brwd. (Hutt.)
CM13 ... 55 GB44
Booth's Pl, W1 ... 195 L7
Boot St, N1 ... 197 M3
Bordars Rd, W7 ... 79 CE71
Bordars Wk, W7 ... 79 CE71
Borden Av, Enf. EN1 ... 30 DR44
Border Cres, SE26 ... 122 DV92
Border Gdns, Croy. CR0 ... 161 EB105
Bordergate, Mitch. CR4 ... 140 DE95
Border Rd, SE26 ... 122 DV92
Borderside, Slou. SL2 ... 74 AU72
Borders La, Loug. IG10 ... 33 EN42
Bordesley Rd, Mord. SM4 ... 140 DB98
Bordon Wk, SW15 ... 119 CU87
Boreas Wk, N1 ... 196 G1
Boreham Av, E16 ... 86 EG72
Boreham Cl, E11
off Hainault Rd ... 67 EC60
Boreham Holt, Borwd. (Els.)
WD6 ... 26 CM42
Boreham Rd, N22 ... 46 DQ54
BOREHAMWOOD, WD6 ... 26 CP41
Borehamwood Ind Pk, Borwd.
WD6 ... 26 CR40
Borgard Rd, SE18 ... 105 EM77
Borkwood Pk, Orp. BR6 ... 163 ET105
Borkwood Way, Orp. BR6 ... 163 ES105
Borland Cl, Green. DA9
off Steele Av ... 129 FU85
Borland Rd, SE15 ... 102 DW84
Teddington TW11 ... 117 CH93
Bornedene, Pot.B. EN6 ... 11 CY31
Borneo St, SW15 ... 99 CW83
⊖ Borough ... 201 J5
BOROUGH, THE, SE1 ... 201 H5
Borough High St, SE1 ... 201 H5
Borough Hill, Croy. CR0 ... 141 DP104
★ Borough Mkt, SE1 ... 201 K3
Borough Rd, SE1 ... 200 F6
Isleworth TW7 ... 97 CE81
Kingston upon Thames
KT2 ... 138 CN95
Mitcham CR4 ... 140 DE96
Westerham (Tats.) TN16 ... 178 EK121
Borough Sq, SE1 ... 201 H5
Borough Way, Pot.B. EN6 ... 11 CY32
Borrett Cl, SE17
off Penrose St ... 102 DQ78
Borrodaile Rd, SW18 ... 120 DB86
Borrowdale Av, Har. HA3 ... 41 CG54
Borrowdale Cl, Egh. TW20
off Derwent Rd ... 113 BB94
Ilford IG4 ... 68 EL56
South Croydon CR2 ... 160 DT113
Borrowdale Ct, Enf. EN2 ... 30 DQ39
Borrowdale Dr, S.Croy. CR2 ... 160 DT112
Borthwick Ms, E15
off Borthwick Rd ... 68 EE63
Borthwick Rd, E15 ... 68 EE63
NW9 off West Hendon Bdy ... 63 CT58
Borthwick St, SE8 ... 103 EA78
Borwick Av, E17 ... 67 DZ55
Bosanquet Cl, Uxb. UB8 ... 76 BK70
Bosbury Rd, SE6 ... 123 EC90
Boscastle Rd, NW5 ... 65 DH62
Boscobel Cl, Brom. BR1 ... 145 EM96
Boscobel Pl, SW1 ... 198 G8
Boscobel St, NW8 ... 194 A5
Bosco Cl, Orp. BR6
off Strickland Way ... 163 ET105
Boscombe Av, E10 ... 67 ED59
Grays RM17 ... 110 GD77
Hornchurch RM11 ... 72 FK60
Boscombe Circ, NW9
off Warmwell Av ... 42 CR54
Boscombe Cl, E5 ... 67 DY64
Egham TW20 ... 133 BC95
Boscombe Gdns, SW16 ... 121 DL93
Boscombe Rd, SW17 ... 120 DG93
SW19 ... 140 DB95
W12 ... 81 CU74
Worcester Park KT4 ... 139 CW102
Bose Cl, N3 off Claremont Pk ... 43 CY53
Bosgrove, E4 ... 47 EC46
Boshers Gdns, Egh. TW20 ... 113 AZ93
Boss Ho, SE1 ... 201 P4
Boss St, SE1 ... 201 P4
Bostall Heath, SE2 ... 106 EW78
Bostall Hill, SE2 ... 106 EU78
Bostall La, SE2 ... 106 EV78
Bostall Manorway, SE2 ... 106 EV77
Bostall Pk Av, Bexh. DA7 ... 106 EY80
Bostall Rd, Orp. BR5 ... 126 EV94
Bostal Row, Bexh. DA7
off Harlington Rd ... 106 EZ83
Boston Gdns, W4 ... 98 CS79
Boston Gdns, W7 ... 97 CG77
Brentford TW8 ... 97 CG77
Boston Gro, Ruis. HA4 ... 59 BQ58
★ Boston Manor, Brent.
TW8 ... 97 CH78
⊖ Boston Manor ... 97 CG77
Boston Manor Rd, Brent. TW8 ... 97 CH77
Boston Pk Rd, Brent. TW8 ... 97 CJ78
Boston Pl, NW1 ... 194 D5
Boston Rd, E6 ... 86 EL69
E17 ... 67 EA58
W7 ... 79 CE74
Croydon CR0 ... 141 DM100
Edgware HA8 ... 42 CQ52
Boston St, E2 off Audrey St ... 84 DU68
Bostonthorpe Rd, W7 ... 97 CE75
Boston Vale, W7 ... 97 CG77
Bosun Cl, E14 ... 204 A4
Bosville Av, Sev. TN13 ... 190 FG123
Bosville Dr, Sev. TN13 ... 190 FG123
Bosville Rd, Sev. TN13 ... 190 FG123
Boswell Cl, Orp. BR5
off Killewarren Way ... 146 EW100
Radlett (Shenley) WD7 ... 10 CL32
Boswell Ct, WC1 ... 196 A6
Boswell Path, Hayes UB3
off Croyde Av ... 95 BT77
Boswell Rd, Th.Hth. CR7 ... 142 DQ98
Boswell St, WC1 ... 196 A6
Bosworth Cl, E17 ... 47 DZ53
Bosworth Cres, Rom. RM3 ... 52 FJ51
Bosworth Ho, Erith DA8
off Saltford Cl ... 107 FE78
Bosworth Rd, N11 ... 45 DK51
W10 ... 81 CY70
Barnet EN5 ... 28 DA41
Dagenham RM10 ... 70 FA63
BOTANY BAY, Enf. EN2 ... 29 DK36
Botany Bay La, Chis. BR7 ... 145 EQ97
Botany Cl, Barn. EN4 ... 28 DE42
Botany Rd, Grav. (Nthflt)
DA11 ... 110 GA83
Botany Way, Purf. RM19 ... 108 FP78
Boteley Cl, E4 ... 47 ED47
Botery's Cross, Red. RH1 ... 185 DP133
Botham Cl, Edg. HA8 ... 42 CQ52
Botham Dr, Slou. SL1 ... 92 AS76
Botha Rd, E13 ... 86 EH71
Bothwell Cl, E16 ... 86 EF71
Bothwell Rd, Croy. (New Adgtn)
CR0 ... 161 EC110
Bothwell St, W6
off Delorme St ... 99 CX79
BOTLEY, Chesh. HP5 ... 4 AV30
Botley La, Chesh. HP5 ... 4 AU30
Botley Rd, Chesh. HP5 ... 4 AT30
Botolph All, EC3 ... 197 M10
Botolph La, EC3 ... 197 M10
Botsford Rd, SW20 ... 139 CY96
Bottom Ho Fm La, Ch.St.G.
HP8 ... 36 AT45
Bottom La, Chesh. HP5 ... 4 AT34
Kings Langley WD4 ... 22 BH35
Bottrells Cl, Ch.St.G. HP8 ... 36 AT47
Bottrells La, Ch.St.G. HP8 ... 36 AT47
Bott Rd, Dart. (Hawley) DA2 ... 128 FM91
Botts Ms, W2
off Chepstow Rd ... 82 DA72
Botts Pas, W2
off Chepstow Rd ... 82 DA72
Botwell Common Rd, Hayes
UB3 ... 77 BR73
Botwell Cres, Hayes UB3 ... 77 BS72
Botwell La, Hayes UB3 ... 77 BS74
Boucher Cl, Tedd. TW11 ... 117 CF92
Boucher Dr, Grav. (Nthflt)
DA11 ... 131 GF90
Bouchier Wk, Rain. RM13
off Deere Av ... 89 FG65
Boughton Av, Brom. BR2 ... 144 EF101
Boughton Business Pk, Amer.
HP6 ... 20 AV39
Boughton Hall Av, Wok.
(Send) GU23 ... 167 BF124
Boughton Rd, SE28 ... 105 ES76
Boughton Way, Amer. HP6 ... 20 AW38
Boulcott St, E1 ... 85 DX72
Boulevard, The, SW6 ... 100 DC81
SW17 off Balham High Rd ... 120 DG89
SW18 off Smugglers Way ... 100 DB84
Greenhithe DA9
off Ingress Pk Av ... 109 FW84
Pinner HA5 off Pinner Rd ... 60 CA56
Watford WD18 ... 23 BR43
Woodford Green IG8 ... 49 EN51
Boulevard 25 Retail Pk,
Borwd. WD6 ... 26 CN41
Boulmer Rd, Uxb. UB8 ... 76 BJ69
Boulogne Rd, Croy. CR0 ... 142 DQ100
Boulter Gdns, Rain. RM13 ... 89 FG65
Boulthurst Way, Oxt. RH8 ... 188 EH132
Boulton Ho, Brent. TW8
off Green Dragon La ... 98 CL78
Boulton Rd, Dag. RM8 ... 70 EY62
Boultwood Rd, E6 ... 86 EL72
Bounce Hill, Rom. (Nave.)
RM4 off Mill La ... 35 FH38
Bounces La, N9 ... 46 DV47
Bounces Rd, N9 ... 46 DV46
Boundaries Rd, SW12 ... 120 DF89
Feltham TW13 ... 116 BW88
Boundary Av, E17 ... 67 DZ59
Boundary Cl, SE20
off Haysleigh Gdns ... 142 DU96
Barnet EN5 ... 27 CZ39
Ilford IG3 off Loxford La ... 69 ES63
Kingston upon Thames
KT1 ... 138 CP97
Southall UB2 ... 96 CA78
Boundary Ct, Epp. CM16 ... 17 ER32
Boundary Dr, Brwd. (Hutt.)
CM13 ... 55 GE45
Boundary La, E13 ... 86 EK69
SE17 ... 102 DQ79
Boundary Pk, Wey. KT13 ... 135 BS103
Boundary Pas, E2 ... 197 P4
Boundary Rd, E13 ... 86 EJ68
E17 ... 67 DZ59
N9 ... 30 DW44
N22 ... 65 DP55
NW8 ... 82 DB67
SW19 ... 120 DD93
Ashford TW15 ... 114 BJ92
Boundary Rd, Bark. IG11 ... 87 EQ68
Carshalton SM5 ... 159 DH107
Gerrards Cross (Chal.St.P.)
SL9 ... 36 AX52
Pinner HA5 ... 60 BX58
Romford RM1 ... 71 FG58
Sidcup DA15 ... 125 ES85
Upminster RM14 ... 72 FN62
Wallington SM6 ... 159 DH107
Wembley HA9 ... 62 CL62
Woking GU21 ... 167 BA116
Boundary Row, SE1 ... 200 F4
Boundary St, E2 ... 197 P3
Erith DA8 ... 107 FF80
Boundary Way, Croy. CR0 ... 161 EA106
Watford WD25 ... 7 BV32
Woking GU21 ... 167 BA115
Boundary Yd, Wok. GU21
off Boundary Rd ... 167 BA116
Boundfield Rd, SE6 ... 124 EE90
⊖ Bounds Green ... 45 DK51
Bounds Grn Rd, N11 ... 45 DJ51
N22 ... 45 DJ51
Bourchier Cl, Sev. TN13 ... 191 FH126
Bourchier St, W1 ... 195 M10
Bourdon Pl, W1 ... 195 J10
Bourdon Rd, SE20 ... 142 DW96
Bourdon St, W1 ... 195 J10
Bourke Cl, NW10 ... 80 CS65
SW4 ... 121 DL86
Bourke Hill, Couls. (Chipstead)
CR5 ... 174 DF118
Bourlet Cl, W1 ... 195 K7
Bourn Av, N15 ... 66 DR56
Barnet EN4 ... 28 DD43
Uxbridge UB8 ... 76 BN70
Bournbrook Rd, SE3 ... 104 EK83
Bourne, The, N14 ... 45 DK46
Hemel Hempstead (Bov.)
HP3 ... 5 BA27
Bourne Av, N14 ... 45 DL47
Chertsey KT16 ... 134 BG97
Hayes UB3 ... 95 BQ76
Ruislip HA4 ... 60 BW64
Bournebridge Cl, Brwd. (Hutt.)
CM13 ... 55 GE45
Bournebridge La, Rom.
(Stap.Abb.) RM4 ... 50 EZ45
Bourne Cl, Islw. TW7 ... 97 CE83
Thames Ditton KT7 ... 137 CF103
West Byfleet KT14 ... 152 BH113
Bourne Ct, Ruis. HA4 ... 59 BV64
Bourne Dr, Mitch. CR4 ... 140 DD96
Bourne End, Horn. RM11 ... 72 FN59
Bourne End Rd, Nthwd. HA6 ... 39 BS49
Bourne Est, EC1 ... 196 D6
Bournefield Rd, Whyt. CR3
off Godstone Rd ... 176 DT118
Bourne Gdns, E4 ... 47 EB49
Bourne Gro, Ashtd. KT21 ... 171 CK119
Bournehall Av, Bushey WD23 ... 24 CA43
Bournehall La, Bushey WD23 ... 24 CA44
★ Bourne Hall Mus, Epsom
KT17 ... 157 CT109
Bournehall Rd, Bushey WD23 ... 24 CA44
Bourne Hill, N13 ... 45 DL46
Bourne Hill Cl, N13
off Bourne Hill ... 45 DM47
Bourne Ind Pk, Dart. DA1 ... 127 FE85
Bourne La, Cat. CR3 ... 176 DR121
Bourne Mead, Bex. DA5 ... 127 FD85
Bournemead Av, Nthlt. UB5 ... 77 BU68
Bournemead Cl, Nthlt. UB5 ... 77 BU68
Bourne Meadow, Egh. TW20 ... 133 BB98
Bournemead Way, Nthlt. UB5 ... 77 BV68
Bournemouth Cl, SE15 ... 102 DU82
Bournemouth Rd, SE15 ... 102 DU82
SW19 ... 140 DA95
Bourne Pk Cl, Ken. CR8 ... 176 DS115
Bourne Pl, W4 off Dukes Av ... 98 CR78
Chertsey KT16 ... 134 BH102
Bourne Rd, E7 ... 68 EF62
N8 ... 65 DL58
Bexley DA5 ... 127 FB86
Bromley BR2 ... 144 EK98
Bushey WD23 ... 24 CA43
Dartford DA1 ... 127 FC86
Gravesend DA12 ... 131 GM89
Redhill (S.Merst.) RH1 ... 185 DJ130
Virginia Water GU25 ... 132 AX99
Bourneside, Vir.W. GU25 ... 132 AU101
Bourneside Cres, N14 ... 45 DK46
Bourneside Gdns, SE6 ... 123 EC92
Bourneside Rd, Add. KT15 ... 152 BK105
Bourne St, SW1 ... 198 F9
Croydon CR0
off Waddon New Rd ... 141 DP103
Bourne Ter, W2 ... 82 DB71
Bourne Vale, Brom. BR2 ... 144 EG101
Bournevale Rd, SW16 ... 121 DL91
Bourne Vw, Grnf. UB6 ... 79 CF65
Kenley CR8 ... 176 DR115
Bourne Way, Add. KT15 ... 152 BJ106
Bromley BR2 ... 144 EF103
Epsom KT19 ... 156 CQ105
Sutton SM1 ... 157 CZ106
Swanley BR8 ... 147 FC97
Woking GU22 ... 166 AX122
Bournewood Rd, SE18 ... 106 EU80
Orpington BR5 ... 146 EV101
Bournville Rd, SE6 ... 123 EA87
Bournwell Cl, Barn. EN4 ... 28 DF41
Bourton Cl, Hayes UB3 ... 77 BU74
Bousfield Rd, SE14 ... 103 DX82
Bousley Ri, Cher. (Ott.) KT16 ... 151 BD108
Boutflower Rd, SW11 ... 100 DE84
Boutique Hall, SE13
off Lewisham Cen ... 103 EC84
Bouton Pl, N1
off Waterloo Ter ... 83 DP66
Bouverie Gdns, Har. HA3 ... 61 CK58
Purley CR8 ... 159 DL114
Bouverie Ms, N16
off Bouverie Rd ... 66 DS61
Bouverie Pl, W2 ... 194 A8
Bouverie Rd, N16 ... 66 DS61
Coulsdon (Chipstead) CR5 ... 174 DG118
Harrow HA1 ... 60 CC59
Bouverie St, EC4 ... 196 E9
Bouverie Way, Slou. SL3 ... 92 AY78
Bouvier Rd, Enf. EN3 ... 30 DW38
Boveney Rd, SE23 ... 123 DX87
Bovey Way, S.Ock. RM15 ... 91 FV71
Bovill Rd, SE23 ... 123 DX87
BOVINGDON, Hem.H. HP3 ... 5 BA28
Bovingdon Av, Wem. HA9 ... 80 CN65
Bovingdon Cl, N19
off Brookside Rd ... 65 DJ61
Bovingdon Cres, Wat. WD25 ... 8 BX34
Bovingdon La, NW9 ... 42 CS53
Bovingdon Rd, SW6 ... 100 DB81
Bovingdon Sq, Mitch. CR4
off Leicester Av ... 141 DL98
BOW, E3 ... 85 DZ68
Bow Arrow La, Dart. DA1,
DA2 ... 128 FN86
Bowater Cl, NW9 ... 62 CR57
SW2 ... 121 DL86
Bowater Gdns, Sun. TW16 ... 135 BV96
Bowater Pl, SE3 ... 104 EH80
Bowater Ridge, Wey. KT13 ... 153 BR110
Bowater Rd, SE18 ... 104 EK76
Wembley HA9 ... 62 CP62
Bow Back Rivers Wk, E15 ... 85 EB66
Bow Br Est, E3 ... 85 EB69
DLR Bow Church ... 85 EA69
Bow Chyd, EC4 ... 197 J9
Bow Common La, E3 ... 85 DZ70
Bowden Cl, Felt. TW14 ... 115 BS88
Bowden Dr, Horn. RM11 ... 72 FL60
Bowden St, SE11 ... 101 DN78
Bowditch, SE8 ... 203 M10
Bowdon Rd, E17 ... 67 EA59
Bowen Dr, SE21 ... 122 DS90
Bowen Rd, Har. HA1 ... 60 CC59
Bowen St, E14 ... 85 EB72
Bowens Wd, Croy. CR0 ... 161 DZ109
Bowen Way, Couls. CR5
off Netherne Dr ... 175 DK121
Bower Av, SE10 ... 104 EE81
Bower Cl, Nthlt. UB5 ... 78 BW68
Romford RM5 ... 51 FD52
Bower Ct, Epp. CM16 ... 18 EU32
Woking GU22
off Princess Rd ... 167 BB116
Bowerdean St, SW6 ... 100 DB81
Bower Fm Rd, Rom. (Hav.at.Bow.)
RM4 ... 51 FC48
BOWER HILL, Epp. CM16 ... 18 EU31
Bower Hill, Epp. CM16 ... 18 EU32
Bower Hill Ind Est, Epp. CM16 ... 18 EU32
Bower La, Dart. (Eyns.) DA4 ... 148 FL103
Bowerman Av, SE14 ... 103 DY79
Bowerman Rd, Grays RM16 ... 111 GG77
Bower Rd, Swan. BR8 ... 127 FG94
Bowers Av, Grav. (Nthflt)
DA11 ... 131 GF91
Bowers Rd, Sev. (Shore.)
TN14 ... 165 FF111
Bower St, E1 ... 85 DX72
Bowers Wk, E6 ... 86 EL72
Bower Ter, Epp. CM16
off Bower Hill ... 18 EU32
Bower Vale, Epp. CM16 ... 18 EU32
Bowes Cl, Sid. DA15 ... 126 EV86
BOWES PARK, N22 ... 45 DL51
⇌ Bowes Park ... 45 DL51
Bowes Rd, N11 ... 45 DH50
N13 ... 45 DL50
W3 ... 80 CS73
Dagenham RM8 ... 70 EW63
Staines TW18 ... 113 BE92
Walton-on-Thames KT12 ... 135 BV103
Bowfell Rd, W6 ... 99 CW79
Bowford Av, Bexh. DA7 ... 106 EY81
Bowhay, Brwd. (Hutt.) CM13 ... 55 GA47
Bowhill Cl, SW9 ... 101 DN80
Bowie Cl, SW4 ... 121 DK87
Bow Ind Pk, E15 ... 85 EA66
Bowland Rd, SW4 ... 101 DK84
Woodford Green IG8 ... 48 EJ51
Bowland Yd, SW1 ... 198 E5
Bow La, EC4 ... 197 J9
N12 ... 44 DC53
Morden SM4 ... 139 CY100
Bowl Ct, EC2 ... 197 N5
Bowlers Orchard, Ch.St.G.
HP8 ... 36 AU48
Bowles Grn, Enf. EN1 ... 30 DV36
Bowley Cl, SE19 ... 122 DT93
Bowley La, SE19 ... 122 DT92
Bowling Cl, Uxb. UB10
off Birch Cres ... 76 BM67
Bowling Ct, Wat. WD18 ... 23 BU42
Bowling Grn Cl, SW15 ... 119 CV87
Bowling Grn La, EC1 ... 196 E4
Bowling Grn Pl, SE1 ... 201 K4
Bowling Grn Rd, Wok. (Chobham)
GU24 ... 150 AS109
Bowling Grn Row, SE18
off Samuel St ... 105 EM76
Bowling Grn St, SE11 ... 101 DN79
Bowling Grn Wk, N1 ... 197 M2
Bowls, The, Chig. IG7 ... 49 ES49
Bowls Cl, Stan. HA7 ... 41 CH50
Bowman Av, E16 ... 86 EF73
Bowman Ms, SW18 ... 119 CZ88
Bowmans Cl, W13 ... 79 CH74
Potters Bar EN6 ... 12 DD32
Bowmans Grn, Wat. WD25 ... 24 BX36
Bowmans Lea, SE23 ... 122 DW87
Bowmans Meadow, Wall.
SM6 ... 141 DH104
Bowmans Ms, E1
off Hooper St ... 84 DU72
N7 off Seven Sisters Rd ... 65 DL62
Bowmans Pl, N7
off Holloway Rd ... 65 DL62
Bowmans Rd, Dart. DA1 ... 127 FF87
Bowman's Trd Est, NW9
off Westmoreland Rd ... 62 CM55
Bowmead, SE9 ... 125 EM89
Bowmont Cl, Brwd. (Hutt.)
CM13 ... 55 GB44
Bowmore Wk, NW1
off St. Paul's Cres ... 83 DK66
Bown Cl, Til. RM18 ... 111 GH82
Bowness Cl, E8
off Beechwood Rd ... 84 DT65
Bowness Cres, SW15 ... 118 CS92
Bowness Dr, Houns. TW4 ... 96 BY84
Bowness Rd, SE6 ... 123 EB87
Bexleyheath DA7 ... 107 FB82
Bowness Way, Horn. RM12 ... 71 FG64
Bowood Rd, SW11 ... 100 DG84
Enfield EN3 ... 31 DX40

Bowring Grn, Wat. WD19 40 BW50
⊖ Bow Road 85 DZ69
Bow Rd, E3 85 DZ69
Bowrons Av, Wem. HA0 79 CK66
Bowry Dr, Stai. (Wrays.)
TW19 113 AZ86
Bowsley Ct, Felt. TW13
off Highfield Rd 115 BU89
Bowsprit, The, Cob. KT11 170 BW115
Bowsprit Pt, E14 203 P6
Bow St, E15 68 EE64
WC2 196 A9
Bowstridge La, Ch.St.G. HP8 36 AW51
Bowyer Cl, E6 87 EM71
Bowyer Cres, Uxb. (Denh.)
UB9 57 BF58
Bowyer Pl, SE5 102 DR80
Bowyers Cl, Ashtd. KT21 172 CM118
Bowyer St, SE5 102 DQ80
Boxall Rd, SE21 122 DS86
Boxford Cl, S.Croy. CR2 161 DX112
Boxgrove Rd, SE2 106 EW76
BOX HILL, Tad. KT20 182 CP131
Boxhill Rd, Dor. RH4 182 CL133
Tadworth (Box H.) KT20 182 CP131
Box La, Bark. IG11 88 EV68
Boxley Rd, Mord. SM4 140 DC98
Boxley St, E16 205 P3
Boxmoor Rd, Har. HA3 61 CH56
Romford RM5 51 FC50
Boxoll Rd, Dag. RM9 70 EZ63
Box Ridge Av, Pur. CR8 159 DM112
Boxted Cl, Buck.H. IG9 49 EL46
Boxtree La, Har. HA3 40 CC53
Boxtree Rd, Har. HA3 41 CD52
Boxtree Wk, Orp. BR5 146 EX102
Boxwood Cl, West Dr. UB7
off Hawthorne Cres 94 BM75
Boxwood Way, Warl. CR6 177 DX117
Boxworth Cl, N12 44 DD50
Boxworth Gro, N1
off Richmond Av 83 DM67
Boyard Rd, SE18 105 EP78
Boyce Cl, Borwd. WD6 26 CL39
Boyce St, SE1 200 C3
Boyce Way, E13 86 EG70
Boycroft Av, NW9 62 CQ58
Boyd Av, Sthl. UB1 78 BZ74
Boyd Cl, Kings.T. KT2
off Crescent Rd 118 CN94
Boydell Ct, NW8
off St. John's Wd Pk 82 DD66
Boyd Rd, SW19 120 DD93
Boyd St, E1 84 DU72
Boyes Cres, St.Alb.
(Lon.Col.) AL2 9 CH26
Boyfield St, SE1 200 G5
Boyland Rd, Brom. BR1 124 EF92
Boyle Av, Stan. HA7 41 CG51
Boyle Cl, Uxb. UB10 76 BM68
Boyle Fm Island, T.Ditt. KT7 137 CG100
Boyle Fm Rd, T.Ditt. KT7 137 CG100
Boyle St, W1 195 K10
Boyne Av, NW4 63 CX56
Boyne Rd, SE13 103 EC83
Dagenham RM10 70 FA62
Boyne Ter Ms, W11 81 CZ74
Boyseland Ct, Edg. HA8 42 CQ47
Boyson Rd, SE17 102 DR79
Boyton Cl, E1
off Stayner's Rd 85 DX70
N8 65 DL55
Boyton Rd, N8 65 DL55
Brabant Ct, EC3 197 M10
Brabant Rd, N22 45 DM54
Brabazon Av, Wall. SM6 159 DL108
Brabazon Rd, Houns. TW5 96 BW80
Northolt UB5 78 CA68
Brabazon St, E14 85 EB72
Brabourne Cl, SE19 122 DS92
Brabourne Cres, Bexh. DA7 106 EZ79
Brabourne Hts, NW7 42 CS48
Brabourne Ri, Beck. BR3 143 EC99
Brabourn Gro, SE15 102 DW82
Brace Cl, Wal.Cr. (Chsht) EN7 13 DP25
Bracewell Av, Grnf. UB6 61 CF64
Bracewell Rd, W10 81 CW71
Bracewood Gdns, Croy. CR0 142 DT104
Bracey Ms, N4 *off Bracey St* 65 DL61
Bracey St, N4 65 DL61
Bracken, The, E4
off Hortus Rd 47 EC47
Bracken Av, SW12 120 DG86
Croydon CR0 143 EB104
Brackenbridge Dr, Ruis. HA4 60 BX62
Brackenbury Gdns, W6 99 CV76
Brackenbury Rd, N2 64 DC55
W6 99 CV76
Bracken Cl, E6 87 EM71
Borehamwood WD6 26 CP39
Leatherhead (Bkhm) KT23 170 BZ124
Sunbury-on-Thames TW16
off Cavendish Rd 115 BT93
Twickenham TW2
off Hedley Rd 116 CA87
Woking GU22 167 AZ118
Brackendale, N21 45 DM47
Potters Bar EN6 12 DA33
Brackendale Cl, Houns. TW3 96 CB81
Brackendale Gdns, Upmin.
RM14 72 FQ63
Brackendene, Dart. DA2 127 FE91
St. Albans (Brick.Wd) AL2 8 BZ30
Brackendene Cl, Wok. GU21 167 BA115
Bracken Dr, Chig. IG7 49 EP51
Bracken End, Islw. TW7 117 CD85
Brackenfield Cl, E5 66 DV62
Brackenforde, Slou. SL3 92 AW75
Bracken Gdns, SW13 99 CU82
Brackenhill, Cob. KT11 154 CA111
Bracken Hill Cl, Brom. BR1
off Bracken Hill La 144 EF95
Bracken Hill La, Brom. BR1 144 EF95
Bracken Ind Est, Ilf. IG6 49 ET52
Bracken Ms, E4 *off Hortus Rd* 47 EC47
Romford RM7 70 FA58
Bracken Path, Epsom KT18 156 CP113
Brackens, The, Enf. EN1 46 DS45
Orpington BR6 164 EU106
Brackens Dr, Brwd. CM14 54 FW50
Bracken Way, Wok. (Chobham)
GU24 150 AT110
Brackenwood, Sun. TW16 135 BU95
Brackley, Wey. KT13 153 BR106
Brackley Av, SE15 102 DV83
Brackley Cl, Wall. SM6 159 DL108
Brackley Rd, W4 98 CS78
Beckenham BR3 123 DZ94
Brackley Sq, Wdf.Grn. IG8 48 EK52
Brackley St, EC1 197 H6
Brackley Ter, W4 98 CS78
Bracklyn Cl, N1 *off Parr St* 84 DR68
Bracklyn Ct, N1
off Wimbourne St 84 DR68
Bracklyn St, N1 84 DR68
Bracknell Cl, N22 45 DN53
Bracknell Gdns, NW3 64 DB63
Bracknell Gate, NW3 64 DB64
Bracknell Way, NW3 64 DB63
Bracondale, Esher KT10 154 CC107
Bracondale Rd, SE2 106 EU77
H Bracton Cen, The, Dart.
DA2 127 FF89
Bradbery, Rick. (Map.Cr.)
WD3 37 BD50
Bradbourne Pk Rd, Sev.
TN13 190 FG123
Bradbourne Rd, Bex. DA5 126 FA87
Grays RM17 110 GB79
Sevenoaks TN13 191 FH122
Bradbourne St, SW6 100 DA82
Bradbourne Vale Rd, Sev.
TN13 190 FF122
Bradbury Cl, Borwd. WD6 26 CP39
Southall UB2 96 BZ77
Bradbury Gdns, Slou.
(Fulmer) SL3 56 AX63
Bradbury Ms, N16
off Bradbury St 66 DS64
Bradbury St, N16 66 DS64
Bradd Cl, S.Ock. RM15 91 FW69
Braddock Cl, Islw. TW7 97 CF83
Romford (Coll.Row) RM5 51 FC51
Braddon Rd, Rich. TW9 98 CM83
Braddyll St, SE10 104 EE78
Bradenham Av, Well. DA16 106 EU84
Bradenham Cl, SE17 102 DR79
Bradenham Rd, Har. HA3 61 CH56
Hayes UB4 77 BS69
Bradenhurst Cl, Cat. CR3 186 DT126
Braden St, W9
off Shirland Rd 82 DB70
Bradfield Cl, Wok. GU22 166 AY118
Bradfield Dr, Bark. IG11 70 EU64
Bradfield Ho, SW8
off Wandsworth Rd 101 DK82
Bradfield Rd, E16 205 N4
Ruislip HA4 60 BY64
Bradford Cl, N17
off Commercial Rd 46 DS51
SE26 *off Coombe Rd* 122 DV91
Bromley BR2 145 EM102
Bradford Dr, Epsom KT19 157 CT107
Bradford Rd, W3
off Warple Way 98 CS75
Ilford IG1 69 ER60
Rickmansworth (Herons.)
WD3 37 BC45
Bradgate, Pot.B. (Cuffley) EN6 13 DK27
Bradgate Cl, Pot.B. (Cuffley)
EN6 13 DK28
Bradgate Rd, SE6 123 EA86
Brading Cres, E11 68 EH61
Brading Rd, SW2 121 DM87
Croydon CR0 141 DM100
Brading Ter, W12 99 CV76
Bradiston Rd, W9 81 CZ69
Bradleigh Av, Grays RM17 110 GC77
Bradley Cl, N1
off White Lion St 83 DN68
N7 *off Sutterton St* 83 DM65
Sutton (Belmont) SM2
off Station Rd 158 DA110
Bradley Gdns, W13 79 CH72
Bradley Lynch Ct, E2
off Morpeth St 84 DW69
Bradley Ms, SW17
off Bellevue Rd 120 DF88
Bradley Rd, N22 45 DM54
SE19 122 DQ93
Enfield EN3 31 DY38
Waltham Abbey EN9 31 EC36
Bradley Stone Rd, E6 87 EM71
Bradman Row, Edg. HA8
off Pavilion Way 42 CQ52
Bradmead, SW8 101 DH80
Bradmore Grn, Couls. CR5
off Coulsdon Rd 175 DM118
Hatfield (Brook.Pk) AL9 11 CY26
Bradmore La, Hat. (Brook.Pk)
AL9 11 CW27
Bradmore Pk Rd, W6 99 CV76
Bradmore Way, Couls. CR5 175 DL117
Hatfield (Brook.Pk) AL9 11 CY26
Bradshaw Cl, SW19 120 DA93
Bradshaw Dr, NW7 43 CX52
Bradshawe Waye, Uxb. UB8 76 BL71
Bradshaw Rd, Wat. WD24 24 BW39
Bradshaws Cl, SE25 142 DU97
Bradstock Rd, E9 85 DX65
Epsom KT17 157 CU106
Brad St, SE1 200 E3
Bradwell Av, Dag. RM10 70 FA61
Bradwell Cl, E18 68 EF56
Hornchurch RM12 89 FH65
Bradwell Grn, Brwd. (Hutt.)
CM13 55 GC44
Bradwell Ms, N18
off Lyndhurst Rd 46 DU49
Bradwell Rd, Buck.H. IG9 48 EL46
Bradwell St, E1 85 DX69
Brady Av, Loug. IG10 33 EQ40
Bradymead, E6 87 EN72
Brady St, E1 84 DV70
Braemar Av, N22 45 DL53
NW10 62 CR62
SW19 120 DA89
Bexleyheath DA7 107 FC84
South Croydon CR2 160 DQ109
Thornton Heath CR7 141 DN97
Wembley HA0 79 CK66
Braemar Cl, SE16 202 D10
Braemar Gdns, NW9 42 CR53
Hornchurch RM11 72 FN58
Sidcup DA15 125 ER90
West Wickham BR4 143 EC102
Braemar Rd, E13 86 EF70
N15 66 DS57
Brentford TW8 97 CK79
Worcester Park KT4 139 CV104
Braemer Ho, W9
off Maida Vale 82 DC69
Braeside, Add. (New Haw)
KT15 152 BH111
Beckenham BR3 123 EA92
Braeside Av, SW19 139 CY95
Sevenoaks TN13 190 FF124
Braeside Cl, Pnr. HA5
off The Avenue 40 CA52
Sevenoaks TN13 190 FF123
Braeside Cres, Bexh. DA7 107 FC84
Braeside Rd, SW16 121 DJ94
Braes St, N1 83 DP66
Braesyde Cl, Belv. DA17 106 EZ77
Brafferton Rd, Croy. CR0 160 DQ105
Braganza St, SE17 200 F10
Bragg Cl, Dag. RM8
off Porters Av 88 EV65
Bragmans La, Hem.H. (Flaun.)
HP3 5 BB34
Rickmansworth (Sarratt)
WD3 5 BE33
Braham St, E1 84 DT72
Braid, The, Chesh. HP5 4 AS30
Braid Av, W3 80 CS72
Braid Cl, Felt. TW13 116 BZ89
Braid Ct, W4 *off Lawford Rd* 98 CQ80
Braidwood Pas, EC1
off Aldersgate St 84 DQ71
Braidwood Rd, SE6 123 ED88
Braidwood St, SE1 201 M3
Brailsford Cl, Mitch. CR4 120 DE94
Brailsford Rd, SW2 121 DN85
Brainton Av, Felt. TW14 115 BV87
Braintree Av, Ilf. IG4 68 EL56
Braintree Ind Est, Ruis. HA4 59 BV63
Braintree Rd, Dag. RM10 70 FA62
Ruislip HA4 59 BV63
Braintree St, E2 84 DW69
Braithwaite Av, Rom. RM7 70 FA59
Braithwaite Gdns, Stan. HA7 41 CJ53
Braithwaite Ho, EC1 197 J4
Braithwaite Rd, Enf. EN3 31 DZ41
Braithwaite Twr, W2 82 DD71
Brakefield Rd, Grav. (Sthflt)
DA13 130 GB93
Brakey Hill, Red. (Bletch.)
RH1 186 DS134
Bramah Grn, SW9 101 DN81
★ Bramah Mus, SE1 201 J3
Bramalea Cl, N6 64 DG58
Bramall Cl, E15
off Idmiston Rd 68 EF64
Bramber Ct, Brent. TW8
off Sterling Pl 98 CL77
Bramber Ho, Kings.T. KT2
off Kingsgate Rd 138 CL95
Bramber Rd, N12 44 DE50
W14 99 CZ79
Brambleacres Cl, Sutt. SM2 158 DA108
Bramble Av, Dart. (Bean)
DA2 129 FW90
Bramble Banks, Cars. SM5 158 DG109
Bramblebury Rd, SE18 105 EQ78
Bramble Cl, N15 *off Broad La* 66 DU56
Beckenham BR3 143 EC99
Chigwell IG7 49 EQ46
Croydon CR0 161 EA105
Shepperton TW17
off Halliford Cl 135 BR98
Stanmore HA7 41 CK52
Uxbridge UB8 76 BM71
Watford WD25 7 BU34
Bramble Cft, Erith DA8 107 FC77
Brambledene Cl, Wok. GU21 166 AW118
Brambledown, Stai. TW18 134 BG95
Brambledown Cl, W.Wick.
BR4 144 EE99
Brambledown Rd, Cars.
SM5 158 DG108
South Croydon CR2 160 DS108
Wallington SM6 159 DH108
Bramblefield Cl, Long. DA3 149 FX97
Bramble Gdns, W12
off Wallflower St 81 CT73
Bramble Hall La Mobile Home Pk,
Tad. (Box H.) KT20 182 CM132
Bramble La, Amer. HP7 20 AS41
Hampton TW12 116 BZ93
Sevenoaks TN13 191 FH128
Upminster RM14 90 FQ67
Bramble Mead, Ch.St.G. HP8 36 AU48
Bramble Ri, Cob. KT11 170 BW115
Brambles, The, Chig. IG7
off Clayside 49 EQ50
Waltham Cross EN8 15 DX31
West Drayton UB7 94 BL77
Brambles Cl, Cat. CR3 176 DS122
Isleworth TW7 97 CH80
Brambles Fm Dr, Uxb. UB10 76 BN69
Bramble Wk, Epsom KT18 156 CP114
Bramble Way, Wok. (Ripley)
GU23 167 BF124
Bramblewood, Red. (Merst.)
RH1 185 DH129
Bramblewood Cl, Cars. SM5 140 DE102
Brambling Cl, Bushey WD23 24 BY42
Bramblings, The, E4 47 ED49
Bramcote Av, Mitch. CR4 140 DF98
Bramcote Ct, Mitch. CR4
off Bramcote Av 140 DF98
Bramcote Gro, SE16 202 F10
Bramcote Rd, SW15 99 CV84
Bramdean Cres, SE12 124 EG88
Bramdean Gdns, SE12 124 EG88
Bramerton Rd, Beck. BR3 143 DZ97
Bramerton St, SW3 100 DE79
Bramfield, Wat. WD25
off Garston La 8 BY34
Bramfield Ct, N4
off Queens Dr 66 DQ61
Bramfield Rd, SW11 120 DE86
Bramford Ct, N14 45 DK47
Bramford Rd, SW18 100 DC84
Bramham Gdns, SW5 100 DB78
Chessington KT9 155 CK105
Bramhope La, SE7 104 EH79
Bramlands Cl, SW11 100 DE83
Bramleas, Wat. WD18 23 BT42
Bramley Av, Couls. CR5 175 DJ115
Bramley Cl, E17 47 DY54
N14 29 DH43
Chertsey KT16 134 BH102
Gravesend (Istead Rise)
DA13 131 GF94
Hayes UB3 77 BU73
Orpington BR6 145 EP102
Pinner HA5
off Wiltshire La 59 BT55
South Croydon CR2 159 DP106
Staines TW18 114 BJ93
Swanley BR8 147 FE98
Twickenham TW2 116 CC86
Woodford Green IG8
off Orsett Ter 48 EJ52
Bramley Ct, Wat. WD25
off Orchard Av 7 BV31
Welling DA16 106 EV81
Bramley Cres, SW8
off Pascal St 101 DK80
Ilford IG2 69 EN58
Bramley Gdns, Wat. WD19 40 BW50
Bramley Gro, Ashtd. KT21 172 CL119
Bramley Hill, S.Croy. CR2 159 DP106
Bramley Ho, SW15
off Tunworth Cres 119 CT86
W10 *off Bramley Rd* 81 CX73
Bramley Ho Ct, Enf. EN2 30 DR37
Bramley Pl, Dart. DA1 107 FG84
Bramley Rd, N14 29 DH43
W5 97 CJ76
W10 81 CX73
Sutton SM1 158 DD106
Sutton (Cheam) SM2 157 CX109
Bramley Shaw, Wal.Abb. EN9 16 EF33
Bramley Way, Ashtd. KT21 172 CM117
Hounslow TW4 116 BZ85
West Wickham BR4 143 EB103
Brampton Cl, E5 66 DV61
Waltham Cross (Chsht) EN7 14 DU28
Brampton Gdns, N15
off Brampton Rd 66 DQ57
Walton-on-Thames KT12 154 BW106
Brampton Gro, NW4 63 CV56
Harrow HA3 61 CG56
Wembley HA9 62 CN60
Brampton La, NW4 63 CW56
Brampton Pk Rd, N22 65 DN55
Brampton Rd, E6 86 EK69
N15 66 DQ57
NW9 62 CN56
SE2 106 EW79
Bexleyheath DA7 106 EX80
Croydon CR0 142 DT101
Uxbridge UB10 77 BP68
Watford WD19 39 BU48
Brampton Ter, Borwd. WD6 26 CN38
Bramshaw Gdns, Wat. WD19 40 BX50
Bramshaw Ri, N.Mal. KT3 138 CS100
Bramshaw Rd, E9 85 DX65
Bramshill Cl, Chig. IG7
off Tine Rd 49 ES50
Bramshill Gdns, NW5 65 DH62
Bramshill Rd, NW10 81 CT68
Bramshot Av, SE7 104 EG79
Bramshot Way, Wat. WD19 39 BU47
Bramston Cl, Ilf. IG6 49 ET51
Bramston Rd, NW10 81 CU68
SW17 120 DC90
Bramwell Cl, Sun. TW16 136 BX96
Bramwell Ho, SW1
off Churchill Gdns 101 DJ78
Bramwell Ms, N1 83 DM67
Brancaster Dr, NW7 43 CT52
Brancaster La, Pur. CR8 160 DQ112
Brancaster Pl, Loug. IG10 33 EM41
Brancaster Rd, E12 69 EM63
SW16 121 DL90
Ilford IG2 69 ER58
Brancepeth Gdns, Buck.H. IG9 48 EG47
Branch Hill, NW3 64 DC62
Branch Pl, N1 84 DR67
Branch Rd, E14 85 DY73
Ilford IG6 50 EV50
St. Albans (Park St) AL2 9 CD27
Branch St, SE15 102 DS80
Brancker Cl, Wall. SM6
off Brown Cl 159 DL108
Brancker Rd, Har. HA3 61 CK55
Brancroft Way, Enf. EN3 31 DY39
Brand Cl, N4 65 DP60
Brandesbury Sq, Wdf.Grn.
IG8 49 EN51
Brandlehow Rd, SW15 99 CZ84
Brandon Cl, Grays (Chaff.Hun.)
RM16 110 FZ75
Waltham Cross (Chsht) EN7 14 DS26
Brandon Est, SE17 101 DP79
Brandon Gros Av, S.Ock.
RM15 91 FW69
Brandon Ms, EC2
off The Barbican 84 DR71
Brandon Rd, E17 67 EC55
N7 83 DL66
Dartford DA1 128 FN87
Southall UB2 96 BZ78
Sutton SM1 158 DB105
Brandon St, SE17 201 H9
Gravesend DA11 131 GH87
Brandram Ms, SE13
off Brandram Rd 104 EE83
Brandram Rd, SE13 104 EE83
Brandreth Rd, E6 87 EM72
SW17 121 DH89
Brandries, The, Wall. SM6 141 DK104
BRANDS HILL, Slou. SL3 93 BB79
Brands Rd, Slou. SL3 93 BB79
Brand St, SE10 103 EC80
Brandville Gdns, Ilf. IG6 69 EP56
Brandville Rd, West Dr. UB7 94 BL75
Brandy Way, Sutt. SM2 158 DA108
Branfill Rd, Upmin. RM14 72 FP61
Brangbourne Rd, Brom. BR1 123 EC92
Brangton Rd, SE11 101 DM78
Brangwyn Cres, SW19 140 DD95
Branksea St, SW6 99 CY80
Branksome Av, N18 46 DT50
Branksome Cl, Tedd. TW11 117 CD91
Walton-on-Thames KT12 136 BX103
Branksome Rd, SW2 121 DL85
SW19 140 DA95
Branksome Way, Har. HA3 62 CL58
Branksome Way, N.Mal.
KT3 138 CQ95
Bransby Rd, Chess. KT9 156 CL107
Branscombe Gdns, N21 45 DN45
Branscombe St, SE13 103 EB83
Bransdale Cl, NW6
off West End La 82 DB67
Bransell Cl, Swan. BR8 147 FC100
Bransgrove Rd, Edg. HA8 42 CM53
Branston Cres, Orp. BR5 145 ER102
Branstone Rd, Rich. TW9 98 CM81
Branton Rd, Green. DA9 129 FT86
Brants Wk, W7 79 CE70
Brantwood Av, Erith DA8 107 FC80
Isleworth TW7 97 CG84
Brantwood Cl, E17 67 EB55
West Byfleet KT14
off Brantwood Gdns 152 BG113
Brantwood Ct, W.Byf. KT14
off Brantwood Dr 151 BF113
Brantwood Dr, W.Byf. KT14 151 BF113
Brantwood Gdns, Enf. EN2 29 DL42
Ilford IG4 68 EL56
West Byfleet KT14 151 BF113
Brantwood Rd, N17 46 DT51
SE24 122 DQ85
Bexleyheath DA7 107 FB82
South Croydon CR2 160 DQ109
Brantwood Way, Orp. BR5 146 EW97
Brasenose Dr, SW13 99 CW79
Brasher Cl, Grnf. UB6 61 CD64
Brassett Pt, E15 86 EE67
Brassey Cl, Felt. TW14 115 BU88
Oxted RH8 188 EG129
Brassey Hill, Oxt. RH8 188 EG130
Brassey Rd, NW6 81 CZ65
Oxted RH8 188 EF130
Brassey Sq, SW11 100 DG83
Brassie Av, W3 80 CS72
Brass Tally All, SE16 203 J5
BRASTED, West. TN16 180 EW124
Brasted Cl, SE26 122 DW91
Bexleyheath DA6 126 EX85
Orpington BR6 146 EU103
Sutton SM2 158 DA110
Brasted Hill, Sev. (Knock.)
TN14 180 EU120
Brasted Hill Rd, West. (Brasted)
TN16 180 EV121
Brasted La, Sev. (Knock.)
TN14 180 EU119
Brasted Rd, Erith DA8 107 FE80
Westerham TN16 189 ES126
Brathway Rd, SW18 120 DA87
Bratley St, E1 *off Weaver St* 84 DU70
Brattle Wd, Sev. TN13 191 FH129
Braund Av, Grnf. UB6 78 CB70
Braundton Av, Sid. DA15 125 ET88
Braunston Dr, Hayes UB4 78 BY70
Bravington Cl, Shep. TW17 134 BM99
Bravington Pl, W9
off Bravington Rd 81 CZ70
Bravington Rd, W9 81 CZ68
Bravingtons Wk, N1
off Pentonville Rd 83 DL68
Brawlings La, Ger.Cr.
(Chal.St.P.) SL9 37 BA49
Brawne Ho, SE17
off Hillingdon St 101 DP79
Braxfield Rd, SE4 103 DY84
Braxted Pk, SW16 121 DM93
Bray, NW3 82 DE66
Brayards Rd, SE15 102 DV82
Braybourne Cl, Uxb. UB8 76 BJ65
Braybourne Dr, Islw. TW7 97 CF80
Braybrooke Gdns, SE19
off Fox Hill 122 DT94
Braybrook St, W12 81 CT71
Brayburne Av, SW4 101 DJ82
Bray Cl, Borwd. WD6 26 CQ39
Braycourt Av, Walt. KT12 135 BV101
Bray Cres, SE16 203 H4
Braydon Rd, N16 66 DT60
Bray Dr, E16 86 EF73
Brayfield Ter, N1
off Lofting Rd 83 DN66
Brayford Sq, E1
off Summercourt Rd 84 DW72
Bray Gdns, Wok. GU22 167 BE116
Bray Pas, E16 86 EG73
Bray Pl, SW3 198 D9
Bray Rd, NW7 43 CX51
Cobham (Stoke D'Ab.)
KT11 170 BY116
Bray Springs, Wal.Abb. EN9
off Roundhills 16 EE34
Brayton Gdns, Enf. EN2 29 DK42
Braywood Av, Egh. TW20 113 AZ93
Braywood Rd, SE9 105 ER84
Brazil Cl, Croy. (Bedd.) CR0 141 DL101
Breach Barn Mobile Home Pk,
Wal.Abb. EN9 16 EH29
Breach Barns La, Wal.Abb.
EN9 *off Galley Hill* 16 EF30
Breach La, Dag. RM9 88 FA69
Breach Rd, Grays RM20 109 FT79
Bread & Cheese La, Wal.Cr.
(Chsht) EN7 14 DR25
Bread St, EC4 197 J9
Breakfield, Couls. CR5 175 DL116
Breakneck Hill, Green. DA9 129 FV85
Breakspear Ct, Abb.L. WD5 7 BT30
Breakspeare Cl, Wat. WD24 23 BV38
Breakspeare Rd, Abb.L. WD5 7 BS31
Breakspear Path, Uxb. (Hare.)
UB9 58 BJ55
Breakspear Rd, Ruis. HA4 59 BP59
Breakspear Rd N, Uxb. (Hare.)
UB9 58 BN57
Breakspear Rd S, Uxb. (Ickhm)
UB9, UB10 58 BM62
Breakspears Dr, Orp. BR5 146 EU95
Breakspears Ms, SE4
off Ashby Rd 103 EA82
Breakspears Rd, SE4 103 DZ83
Bream Cl, N17 66 DV56
Bream Gdns, E6 87 EN69

★ Place of interest ⇌ Railway station ⊖ London Underground station DLR Docklands Light Railway station Tra Tramlink station H Hospital Riv Pedestrian ferry landing stage

Breamore Cl, SW15 119 CU88
Breamore Rd, Ilf. IG3 69 ET61
Bream's Bldgs, EC4 196 D8
Bream St, E3 85 EA66
Breamwater Gdns, Rich.
TW10 117 CH90
Brearley Cl, Edg. HA8 42 CQ52
Uxbridge UB8 76 BL65
Breasley Cl, SW15 99 CV84
Brechin Pl, SW7
off Rosary Gdns 100 DC77
Brecknock Rd, N7 65 DJ63
N19 65 DJ63
Brecknock Rd Est, N7 65 DJ63
Breckonmead, Brom. BR1
off Wanstead Rd 144 EJ96
Brecon Cl, Mitch. CR4 141 DL97
Worcester Park KT4 139 CW103
Brecon Grn, NW9
off Goldsmith Av 62 CS58
Brecon Ms, N7
off Brecknock Rd 83 DK65
Brecon Rd, W6 99 CY79
Enfield EN3 30 DW42
Brede Cl, E6 87 EN69
Bredgar, SE13 123 EC85
Bredgar Rd, N19 65 DJ61
Bredhurst Cl, SE20 122 DW93
Bredinghurst, SE22
off Overhill Rd 122 DU87
Bredon Rd, Croy. CR0 142 DT101
Bredune, Ken. CR8 176 DR115
Breech La, Tad. (Walt.Hill)
KT20 173 CU124
Breer St, SW6 100 DB83
Breezers Hill, E1 202 C1
Breeze Ter, Wal.Cr. (Chsht)
EN8 *off Collet Cl* 15 DX28
Brember Rd, Har. HA2 60 CC61
Bremer Ms, E17
off Church La 67 EB56
Bremer Rd, Stai. TW18 114 BG90
Bremner Cl, Swan. BR8 147 FG98
Bremner Rd, SW7 100 DC75
Brenchley Av, Grav. DA11 131 GH92
Brenchley Cl, Brom. BR2 144 EF100
Chislehurst BR7 145 EN95
Brenchley Gdns, SE23 122 DW86
Brenchley Rd, Orp. BR5 145 ET95
Bren Ct, Enf. EN3
off Colgate Pl 31 EA37
Brendans Cl, Horn. RM11 72 FL60
Brenda Rd, SW17 120 DF89
Brenda Ter, Swans. DA10
off Manor Rd 130 FY87
Brende Gdns, W.Mol. KT8 136 CB98
Brendon Av, NW10 62 CS63
Brendon Cl, Erith DA8 107 FE81
Esher KT10 154 CC107
Hayes UB3 95 BQ80
Brendon Ct, Rad. WD7
off The Avenue 9 CH34
Brendon Dr, Esher KT10 154 CC107
Brendon Gdns, Har. HA2 60 CB63
Ilford IG2 69 ES57
Brendon Gro, N2 44 DC54
Brendon Rd, SE9 125 ER89
Dagenham RM8 70 EZ60
Brendon St, W1 194 C8
Brendon Way, Enf. EN1 46 DS45
Brenley Cl, Mitch. CR4 140 DG97
Brenley Gdns, SE9 104 EK84
Brennan Rd, Til. RM18 111 GH82
Brent, The, Dart. DA1, DA2 128 FN87
Brent Cl, Bex. DA5 126 EY88
Dartford DA2 128 FP86
Brentcot Cl, W13 79 CH70
Brent Cres, NW10 80 CM68
⊖ **Brent Cross** 63 CX59
Brent Cross Gdns, NW4
off Haley Rd 63 CX58
Brent Cross Interchange, The,
NW2 *off Hendon Way* 63 CX59
Brent Cross Shop Cen, NW4 63 CW59
Brentfield, NW10 80 CP66
Brentfield Cl, NW10 80 CR65
Brentfield Gdns, NW2
off Hendon Way 63 CX59
Brentfield Ho, NW10
off Stonebridge Pk 80 CR66
Brentfield Rd, NW10 80 CR65
Dartford DA1 128 FN86
BRENTFORD, TW8 97 CK79
⇌ **Brentford** 97 CJ79
Brentford Business Cen, Brent.
TW8 97 CH80
Brentford Cl, Hayes UB4 78 BX70
★ **Brentford FC**, Brent. TW8 97 CK79
Brent Grn, NW4 63 CW57
Brent Grn Wk, Wem. HA9 62 CQ62
Brentham Way, W5 79 CK70
Brenthouse Rd, E9 84 DV66
Brenthurst Rd, NW10 63 CT64
Brentlands Dr, Dart. DA1 128 FN88
Brent La, Dart. DA1 128 FM87
Brent Lea, Brent. TW8 97 CJ80
Brentmead Cl, W7 79 CE73
Brentmead Gdns, NW10 80 CM68
Brentmead Pl, NW11
off North Circular Rd 63 CX58
Brenton St, E14 85 DY72
Brent Pk, NW10 62 CR64
Brent Pk Rd, NW4 63 CV59
NW9 63 CU60
Brent Pl, Barn. EN5 28 DA43
Brent Rd, E16 86 EG71
SE18 105 EP80
Brentford TW8 97 CJ79
South Croydon CR2 160 DV109
Southall UB2 96 BW76
Brent Side, Brent. TW8 97 CJ79
Brentside Cl, W13 79 CG70
Brentside Executive Cen, Brent.
TW8 97 CH79
Brent St, NW4 63 CW56
Brent Ter, NW2 63 CW61
Brentvale Av, Sthl. UB1 79 CD74
Wembley HA0 80 CM67
Brent Vw Rd, NW9 63 CU59
Brent Way, N3 44 DA51
Brentford TW8 97 CK80
Dartford DA2 128 FP86
Wembley HA9 80 CP65
Brentwick Gdns, Brent. TW8 98 CL77
BRENTWOOD, CM13 - CM15 54 FV47
⇌ **Brentwood** 54 FW48
Brentwood Bypass, Brwd.
CM14, CM15 53 FR49
Brentwood Cl, SE9 125 EQ88
H **Brentwood Comm Hosp & Minor Injuries Unit**, Brwd.
CM15 54 FY46
Brentwood Ct, Add. KT15 152 BH105
Brentwood Ho, SE18
off Shooters Hill Rd 104 EK80
★ **Brentwood Mus**, Brwd.
CM14 54 FW49
Brentwood Pl, Brwd. CM15 54 FX46
Brentwood Rd, Brwd. CM13 55 GA49
Grays RM16 111 GH77
Romford RM1, RM2 71 FF58
Brereton Rd, N17 46 DT52
Bressenden Pl, SW1 199 J6
Bressey Av, Enf. EN1 30 DU39
Bressey Gro, E18 48 EF54
Bretlands Rd, Cher. KT16 133 BE103
Brett Cl, N16 *off Yoakley Rd* 66 DS61
Northolt UB5
off Broomcroft Av 78 BX69
Brett Ct, N9 46 DW47
Brett Cres, NW10 80 CR66
Brettell St, SE17
off Merrow St 102 DR78
Brettenham Av, E17 47 EA53
Brettenham Rd, E17 47 EA54
N18 46 DV49
Brett Gdns, Dag. RM9 88 EY66
Brettgrave, Epsom KT19 156 CQ110
Brett Ho Cl, SW15
off Putney Heath La 119 CX86
Brett Pas, E8 *off Kenmure Rd* 66 DV64
Brett Pl, Wat. WD24
off The Harebreaks 23 BU37
Brett Rd, E8 66 DV64
Barnet EN5 27 CW43
Brevet Cl, Purf. RM19 109 FR77
Brewer's Fld, Dart. DA2 128 FJ91
Brewer's Grn, SW1 199 M6
Brewers Hall Gdns, EC2 197 J7
Brewers La, Rich. TW9 117 CK85
Brewer St, W1 195 L10
Redhill (Bletch.) RH1 186 DQ131
★ **Brewery, The**, EC1 197 J6
Brewery, The, Rom. RM1
off Waterloo Rd 71 FE57
Brewery Cl, Wem. HA0 61 CG64
Brewery La, Sev. TN13
off High St 191 FJ125
Twickenham TW1 117 CF87
West Byfleet (Byfleet)
KT14 152 BL113
Brewery Rd, N7 83 DL66
SE18 105 ER78
Bromley BR2 144 EL102
Woking GU21 166 AX117
Brewery Sq, EC1 196 G4
SE1 *off Horselydown La* 84 DT74
Brewery Wk, Rom. RM1 71 FE57
Brewhouse La, E1 202 E3
SW15 99 CY83
Brewhouse Rd, SE18 105 EM77
Brewhouse Wk, SE16 203 K3
Brewhouse Yd, EC1 196 G4
Gravesend DA12
off Queen St 131 GH86
Brewood Rd, Dag. RM8 88 EV65
Brewster Gdns, W10 81 CW71
Brewster Ho, E14 85 DZ73
Brewster Rd, E10 67 EB60
Brian Av, S.Croy. CR2 160 DS112
Brian Cl, Horn. RM12 71 FH63
Briane Rd, Epsom KT19 156 CQ110
Brian Rd, Rom. RM6 70 EW57
Briant Est, SE1
off Cosser St 101 DN76
Briant Ho, SE1
off Hercules Rd 101 DM76
Briants Cl, Pnr. HA5 40 BZ54
Briant St, SE14 103 DX81
Briar Av, SW16 121 DM94
Briarbank Rd, W13 79 CG72
Briar Banks, Cars. SM5 158 DG109
Briar Cl, N2 64 DB55
N13 46 DQ48
Buckhurst Hill IG9 48 EK47
Hampton TW12 116 BZ92
Isleworth TW7 117 CF85
Waltham Cross (Chsht) EN8 14 DW29
Warlingham CR6 177 EA116
West Byfleet KT14 152 BJ111
Briar Ct, Sutt. SM3 157 CW105
Briar Cres, Nthlt. UB5 78 CB65
Briardale Gdns, NW3 64 DA62
Briarfield Av, N3 44 DB54
Briarfield Cl, Bexh. DA7 106 FA82
Briar Gdns, Brom. BR2 144 EF102
Briar Gro, S.Croy. CR2 160 DU113
Briar Hill, Pur. CR8 159 DL111
Briaris Cl, N17 46 DV52
Briar La, Cars. SM5 158 DG109
Croydon CR0 161 EB105
Briarleas Gdns, Upmin. RM14 73 FS59
Briar Pas, SW16 141 DL97
Briar Pl, SW16 141 DM97
Briar Rd, NW2 63 CW63
SW16 141 DL97
Bexley DA5 127 FD90
Harrow HA3 61 CJ57
Romford RM3 52 FJ52
Shepperton TW17 134 BM99
Twickenham TW2 117 CE88
Watford WD25 7 BU34
Woking (Send) GU23 167 BB123
Briars, The, Bushey (Bushey Hth)
WD23 41 CE45
Rickmansworth (Sarratt)
WD3 22 BH36
Slough SL3 93 AZ78
Waltham Cross (Chsht) EN8 15 DY31
Briars Ct, Lthd. KT22 155 CD114
Briars Wk, Rom. RM3 52 FL54
Briarswood, Wal.Cr. EN7 14 DS28
Briarswood Way, Orp. BR6 163 ET106
Briar Wk, SW15 99 CV84
W10 *off Droop St* 81 CY70
Edgware HA8 42 CQ52
West Byfleet KT14 152 BG112
Briar Way, West Dr. UB7 94 BN75
Briarwood, Bans. SM7
off High St 174 DA115
Briarwood Cl, NW9 62 CQ58
Feltham TW13 115 BS90
Briarwood Dr, Nthwd. HA6 39 BU54
Briarwood Rd, SW4 121 DK85
Epsom KT17 157 CU107
Briary Cl, NW3
off Fellows Rd 82 DE66
Briary Ct, E16 *off Turner St* 86 EF72
Sidcup DA14 126 EV92
Briary Gdns, Brom. BR1 124 EH92
Briary Gro, Edg. HA8 42 CP54
Briary La, N9 46 DT48
Brick Ct, EC4 196 D9
Grays RM17
off Columbia Wf Rd 110 GA79
Brickcroft, Brox. EN10 15 DY26
Brickenden Ct, Wal.Abb. EN9 16 EF33
Brickett Cl, Ruis. HA4 59 BQ57
BRICKET WOOD, St.Alb. AL2 8 BZ29
⇌ **Bricket Wood** 8 CA30
Brick Fm Cl, Rich. TW9 98 CP81
Brickfield Cl, Brent. TW8 97 CJ80
Brickfield Cotts, SE18 105 ET79
Brickfield Fm Gdns, Orp.
BR6 163 EQ105
Brickfield La, Barn. EN5 27 CT44
Hayes UB3 95 BR79
Brickfield Rd, SW19 120 DB91
Epping (Cooper.) CM16 18 EX29
Thornton Heath CR7 141 DP95
Brickfields, Har. HA2 61 CD61
Brickfields La, Epp. (Cooper.)
CM16 *off Brickfield Rd* 18 EX29
Brickfields Way, West Dr. UB7 94 BM76
Brick Kiln Cl, Wat. WD19 24 BY44
Brick Kiln La, Oxt. RH8 188 EJ131
Brick La, E1 84 DT71
E2 84 DT69
Enfield EN1, EN3 30 DV40
Stanmore HA7 41 CK52
Bricklayer's Arms Distribution
Cen, SE1 201 N9
Bricklayer's Arms Rbt, SE1 201 K8
Brick St, W1 199 H3
Brickwall La, Ruis. HA4 59 BS60
Brickwood Cl, SE26 122 DV90
Brickwood Rd, Croy. CR0 142 DS103
Brideale Cl, SE15
off Colegrove Rd 102 DT79
Bride Ct, EC4 196 F9
Bride La, EC4 196 F9
Bridel Ms, N1
off Colebrooke Row 83 DP67
Brides Pl, N1
off De Beauvoir Rd 84 DS66
Bride St, N7 83 DM65
Bridewain St, SE1 201 P6
Bridewell Pl, E1 202 E3
EC4 196 F9
Bridford Ms, W1 195 J6
Bridge, The, SW8
off Queenstown Rd 101 DH81
Harrow HA3 61 CE55
Bridge App, NW1 82 DG66
Bridge Av, W6 99 CW78
W7 79 CD71
Upminster RM14 72 FN61
Bridge Barn La, Wok. GU21 166 AW117
Bridge Cl, W10
off Kingsdown Cl 81 CX72
Brentwood CM13 55 FZ49
Dartford DA2 109 FR83
Enfield EN1 30 DV40
Romford RM7 71 FE58
Staines TW18 113 BE91
Teddington TW11
off Shacklegate La 117 CF91
Walton-on-Thames KT12 135 BT101
West Byfleet (Byfleet)
KT14 152 BM112
Woking GU21 166 AW117
Bridge Cotts, Upmin. RM14 73 FU64
Bridge Ct, E14
off Newport Av 85 ED73
Woking GU21 166 AX117
Bridge Dr, N13 45 DM49
Bridge End, E17 47 EC53
Bridge End Cl, Kings.T. KT2
off Clifton Rd 138 CN95
Bridgefield Cl, Bans. SM7 173 CW115
Bridgefield Rd, Sutt. SM1 158 DA107
Bridgefoot, SE1 101 DL78
Bridgefoot La, Pot.B. EN6 11 CX33
Bridge Gdns, N16
off Green Las 66 DR63
Ashford TW15 115 BQ94
East Molesey KT8 137 CD98
Bridge Gate, N21
off Ridge Av 46 DQ45
Bridgeham Cl, Wey. KT13
off Mayfield Rd 152 BN106
Bridge Hill, Epp. CM16 17 ET33
Bridge Ho, NW3
off Adelaide Rd 82 DG66
SW8 *off St. George Wf* 101 DL78
Bridge Ho Quay, E14 204 E3
Bridgeland Rd, E16 86 EG73
Bridgelands Cl, Beck. BR3 123 DZ94
Bridge La, NW11 63 CY57
SW11 100 DE81
Virginia Water GU25 132 AY99
Bridgeman Rd, N1 83 DM66
Teddington TW11 117 CG93
Bridgeman St, NW8 194 B1
Bridge Meadows, SE14 103 DX79
Bridge Ms, Wok. GU21
off Bridge Barn La 166 AX117
Bridgend Rd, SW18 100 DC84
Enfield EN1 30 DW35
Bridgenhall Rd, Enf. EN1 30 DT39
Bridgen Rd, Bex. DA5 126 EY86
Bridge Pk, SW18 120 DA85
Bridge Pl, SW1 199 J8
Amersham HP6 20 AT38
Bridge Pl, Croy. CR0 142 DR101
Bridgepoint Pl, N6
off Hornsey La 65 DJ60
Bridgeport Pl, E1 202 C2
Bridger Cl, Wat. WD25 8 BX33
Bridge Rd, E6 87 EM66
E15 85 ED66
E17 67 DZ59
N9 *off The Broadway* 46 DU48
N22 45 DL53
NW10 80 CS65
Beckenham BR3 123 DZ94
Bexleyheath DA7 106 EY82
Chertsey KT16 134 BH101
Chessington KT9 156 CL106
East Molesey KT8 137 CE98
Epsom KT17 157 CT112
Erith DA8 107 FF81
Grays RM17 110 GB78
Hounslow TW3 97 CD82
Isleworth TW7 97 CD83
Kings Langley WD4 7 BQ33
Orpington BR5 146 EV100
Rainham RM13 89 FF70
Southall UB2 96 BZ75
Sutton SM2 158 DB107
Twickenham TW1 117 CH86
Uxbridge UB8 76 BJ68
Wallington SM6 159 DJ106
Wembley HA9 62 CN62
Weybridge KT13 152 BM105
Bridge Row, Croy. CR0
off Cross Rd 142 DR102
Bridges Ct, SW11 100 DD83
Bridges Dr, Dart. DA1 128 FP85
Bridges La, Croy. CR0 159 DL105
Bridges Pl, SW6 99 CZ81
Bridges Rd, SW19 120 DB93
Stanmore HA7 41 CF50
Bridges Rd Ms, SW19
off Bridges Rd 120 DB93
Bridge St, SW1 199 P5
W4 98 CR77
Leatherhead KT22 171 CG122
Pinner HA5 60 BX55
Richmond TW9 117 CK85
Slough (Colnbr.) SL3 93 BD80
Staines TW18 113 BE91
Walton-on-Thames KT12 135 BT102
Bridge Ter, E15 *off Bridge Rd* 85 ED66
SE13 *off Mercator Rd* 103 ED84
Bridgetown Cl, SE19
off St. Kitts Ter 122 DS92
Bridge Vw, W6 99 CW78
Greenhithe DA9 109 FV84
Bridgeview Ct, Ilf. IG6 49 ER51
Bridgewater Cl, Chis. BR7 145 ES97
Bridgewater Ct, Slou. SL3 93 BA78
Bridgewater Gdns, Edg. HA8 42 CM54
Bridgewater Rd, Ruis. HA4 59 BU63
Wembley HA0 79 CJ66
Weybridge KT13 153 BR107
Bridgewater Sq, EC2 197 H6
Bridgewater St, EC2 197 H6
Bridgewater Way, Bushey
WD23 24 CB44
Bridge Way, N11
off Pymmes Grn Rd 45 DJ48
NW11 63 CZ57
Bridgeway, Bark. IG11 87 ET66
Bridge Way, Cob. KT11 153 BT113
Coulsdon (Chipstead) CR5 174 DE119
Twickenham TW2 116 CC87
Uxbridge UB10 59 BP64
Bridgeway, Wem. HA0 80 CL66
Bridgeway St, NW1 195 L1
Bridge Wf, Cher. KT16 134 BJ102
Bridge Wf Rd, Islw. TW7
off Church St 97 CH83
Bridgewood Cl, SE20 122 DV94
Bridgewood Rd, SW16 121 DK94
Worcester Park KT4 157 CU105
Bridge Wks, Uxb. UB8 76 BJ70
Bridge Yd, SE1 201 L2
Bridgford St, SW18 120 DC90
Bridgman Rd, W4 98 CQ76
Bridgwater Cl, Rom. RM3 52 FK50
Bridgwater Rd, E15 85 EC67
Romford RM3 52 FJ50
Bridgwater Wk, Rom. RM3 52 FK50
Bridle Cl, Enf. EN3 31 DZ37
Epsom KT19 156 CR106
Kingston upon Thames
KT1 137 CK98
Sunbury-on-Thames TW16
off Forge La 135 BU97
Bridle End, Epsom KT17 157 CT114
Bridle La, W1 195 L10
Cobham KT11 170 CB115
Leatherhead KT22 170 CB115
Rickmansworth (Loud.)
WD3 22 BK41
Twickenham TW1 117 CH86
Bridle Ms, Barn. EN5
off High St 27 CZ42
Bridle Path, Croy. CR0 141 DM104
Watford WD17 23 BV40
Bridle Path, The, Epsom KT17 157 CV110
Woodford Green IG8 48 EE52
Bridlepath Way, Felt. TW14 115 BS88
Bridle Rd, Croy. CR0 143 EA104
Epsom KT17 157 CT113
Esher (Clay.) KT10 155 CH107
Pinner HA5 60 BW58
Bridle Rd, The, Pur. CR8 159 DL110
Bridle Way, Croy. CR0 161 EA106
Orpington BR6 163 EQ105
Bridle Way, The, Croy. CR0 161 DY110
Bridleway, The, Wall. SM6 159 DJ105
Bridleway Cl, Epsom KT17 157 CW110
Bridlington Cl, West. (Bigg.H.)
TN16 178 EH119
Bridlington Rd, N9 46 DV45
Watford WD19 40 BX48
Bridport Av, Rom. RM7 71 FB58
Bridport Pl, N1 84 DR68
Bridport Rd, N18 46 DS50
Greenford UB6 78 CB67
Thornton Heath CR7 141 DN97
Bridport Ter, SW8
off Wandsworth Rd 101 DK81
Bridstow Pl, W2
off Talbot Rd 82 DA72
Brief St, SE5 101 DP81
Brier Lea, Tad. (Lwr Kgswd)
KT20 183 CZ126
Brierley, Croy. (New Adgtn)
CR0 161 EB107
Brierley Av, N9 46 DW46
Brierley Cl, SE25 142 DU98
Hornchurch RM11 72 FJ58
Brierley Rd, E11 67 ED63
SW12 121 DJ89
Brierly Gdns, E2
off Royston St 84 DW68
Brier Rd, Tad. KT20 173 CV119
Briery Ct, Rick. (Chorl.) WD3 22 BG42
Briery Fld, Rick. (Chorl.) WD3 22 BG42
Briery Way, Amer. HP6 20 AS37
Brigade Cl, Har. HA2 61 CD61
Brigade Pl, Cat. CR3 176 DQ122
Brigade St, SE3
off Royal Par 104 EF82
Brigadier Av, Enf. EN2 30 DQ39
Brigadier Hill, Enf. EN2 30 DQ38
Briggeford Cl, E5
off Geldeston Rd 66 DU61
Briggs Cl, Mitch. CR4 141 DH95
Bright Cl, Belv. DA17 106 EX77
Brightfield Rd, SE12 124 EF85
Brightlands, Grav. (Nthflt)
DA11 130 GE91
Brightlands Rd, Reig. RH2 184 DC132
Brightling Rd, SE4 123 DZ86
Brightlingsea Pl, E14 85 DZ73
Brightman Rd, SW18 120 DD88
Brighton Av, E17 67 DZ57
Brighton Cl, Add. KT15 152 BJ106
Uxbridge UB10 77 BP66
Brighton Dr, Nthlt. UB5 78 CA65
Brighton Gro, SE14
off Harts La 103 DY81
Brighton Rd, E6 87 EN69
N2 44 DC54
N16 66 DS63
Addlestone KT15 152 BJ105
Banstead SM7 157 CZ114
Coulsdon CR5 175 DJ119
Purley CR8 160 DQ110
South Croydon CR2 160 DQ106
Surbiton KT6 137 CJ100
Sutton SM2 158 DB109
Tadworth KT20 173 CY119
Watford WD24 23 BU38
Brighton Ter, SW9 101 DM84
Brights Av, Rain. RM13 89 FH70
Brightside, The, Enf. EN3 31 DX39
Brightside Av, Stai. TW18 114 BJ94
Brightside Rd, SE13 123 ED86
Bright St, E14 85 EB72
Brightview Cl, St.Alb.
(Brick.Wd) AL2 8 BY29
Brightwell Cl, Croy. CR0
off Sumner Rd 141 DN102
Brightwell Cres, SW17 120 DF92
Brightwell Rd, Wat. WD18 23 BU43
Brig Ms, SE8
off Watergate St 103 EA79
Brigstock Rd, Belv. DA17 107 FB77
Coulsdon CR5 175 DH115
Thornton Heath CR7 141 DN99
Brill Pl, NW1 195 N1
Brimfield Rd, Purf. RM19 109 FR77
Brim Hill, N2 64 DC56
Brimpsfield Cl, SE2 106 EV76
BRIMSDOWN, Enf. EN3 31 DY41
⇌ **Brimsdown** 31 DY41
Brimsdown Av, Enf. EN3 31 DY40
Brimsdown Ind Est, Enf. EN3 31 DZ40
Brimshot La, Wok. (Chobham)
GU24 150 AS109
Brimstone Cl, Orp. BR6 164 EW108
Brimstone Ho, E15
off Victoria St 86 EE66
Brindle Gate, Sid. DA15 125 ES88
Brindles, Horn. RM11 72 FL56
Brindles, The, Bans. SM7 173 CZ117
Brindles Cl, Brwd. (Hutt.)
CM13 55 GC47
Brindley Cl, Bexh. DA7 107 FB83
Wembley HA0 79 CJ67
Brindley Ho, SW2
off New Pk Rd 121 DL87
Brindley St, SE14 103 DZ81
Brindley Way, Brom. BR1 124 EG92
Southall UB1 78 CB73
Brindwood Rd, E4 47 DZ48
Brinkburn Cl, SE2 106 EU77
Edgware HA8 42 CP54
Brinkburn Gdns, Edg. HA8 62 CN55
Brinkley, Kings.T. KT1
off Burritt Rd 138 CN96
Brinkley Rd, Wor.Pk. KT4 139 CV103
Brinklow Cres, SE18 105 EP80
Brinklow Ho, W2 82 DB71
Brinkworth Rd, Ilf. IG5 68 EL55
Brinkworth Way, E9 85 DZ65
Brinley Cl, Wal.Cr. (Chsht)
EN8 14 DW31
Brinsdale Rd, NW4 63 CX56
Brinsley Rd, Har. HA3 41 CD54
Brinsley St, E1
off Watney St 84 DV72
Brinsmead, St.Alb. (Park St)
AL2 9 CD27
Brinsmead Rd, Rom. RM3 52 FN54
Brinsworth Cl, Twick. TW2 117 CD89
Brinton Wk, SE1 200 F3
Brion Pl, E14 85 EC71
Brisbane Av, SW19 140 DB95
Brisbane Ct, N10
off Sydney Rd 45 DH52
Brisbane Ho, Til. RM18 111 GF81
Brisbane Rd, E10 67 EB61
W13 97 CG75
Ilford IG1 69 EP59
Brisbane St, SE5 102 DR80
Briscoe Cl, E11 68 EF61
Briscoe Rd, SW19 120 DD93
Rainham RM13 90 FJ68
Briset Rd, SE9 104 EK83
Briset St, EC1 196 F6
Briset Way, N7 65 DM61
Brisson Cl, Esher KT10 154 BZ107
Bristol Cl, Stai. (Stanw.)
TW19 114 BL86

★ Place of interest ⇌ Railway station ⊖ London Underground station DLR Docklands Light Railway station Tra Tramlink station H Hospital Riv Pedestrian ferry landing stage

Bristol Cl, Wall. SM6 159 DL108
Bristol Gdns, SW15
off Portsmouth Rd 119 CW87
W9 82 DB70
Bristol Ho, SE11
off Lambeth Wk 101 DN76
Bristol Ms, W9
off Bristol Gdns 82 DB70
Bristol Pk Rd, E17 67 DY56
Bristol Rd, E7 86 EJ65
Gravesend DA12 131 GK90
Greenford UB6 78 CB67
Morden SM4 140 DC99
Bristol Way, Slou. SL1 74 AT74
Briston Gro, N8 65 DL58
Briston Ms, NW7 43 CU52
Bristowe Cl, SW2
off Tulse Hill 121 DN86
Bristow Rd, SE19 122 DS92
Bexleyheath DA7 106 EY81
Croydon CR0 159 DL105
Hounslow TW3 96 CC83
★ Britain at War Experience, SE1 201 M3
Britannia Bldg, N1
off Ebenezer St 84 DR69
Britannia Cl, SW4
off Bowland Rd 101 DK84
Erith DA8 107 FF79
Northolt UB5 78 BX69
Britannia Ct, Kings.T. KT2
off Skerne Wk 138 CL95
Britannia Dr, Grav. DA12 131 GM92
Britannia Gate, E16 205 N2
Britannia Ind Est, Slou. (Colnbr.) SL3 93 BD82
Britannia La, Twick. TW2 116 CC87
Britannia Rd, E14 204 A9
N12 44 DC48
SW6 100 DB80
Brentwood (Warley) CM14 54 FW50
Ilford IG1 69 EP62
Surbiton KT5 138 CM101
Waltham Cross EN8 15 DZ34
Britannia Row, N1 83 DP67
Britannia St, WC1 196 B2
Britannia Wk, N1 197 K2
Britannia Way, NW10 80 CP70
SW6 off Britannia Rd 100 DB80
Staines (Stanw.) TW19 114 BK87
★ British Dental Assoc Mus, W1 195 H7
British Gro, W4 99 CT78
British Gro N, W4
off British Gro 99 CT77
British Gro Pas, W4 99 CT78
British Gro S, W4
off British Gro Pas 99 CT78
British Legion Rd, E4 48 EF47
★ British Lib, NW1 195 N2
★ British Lib Newspaper Collection, NW9 62 CS55
★ British Med Assoc, WC1 195 N4
★ British Mus, WC1 195 P7
★ British Red Cross Mus & Archives, SW1 198 F5
British St, E3 85 DZ69
Briton Cl, S.Croy. CR2 160 DS111
Briton Cres, S.Croy. CR2 160 DS111
Briton Hill Rd, S.Croy. CR2 160 DS110
Brittain Rd, Dag. RM8 70 EY62
Walton-on-Thames KT12 154 BX106
Brittains La, Sev. TN13 190 FF123
Brittany Pt, SE11 200 D9
Britten Cl, NW11 64 DB60
Borehamwood (Els.) WD6
off Rodgers Cl 25 CK44
Brittenden Cl, Orp. BR6 163 ES107
Brittenden Par, Orp. BR6
off Glentrammon Rd 163 ET107
Britten Dr, Sthl. UB1 78 CA72
Britten St, SW3 100 DE78
Brittidge Rd, NW10
off Church Rd 80 CS66
Britton Cl, SE6
off Brownhill Rd 123 ED87
Britton St, EC1 196 F5
Brixham Cres, Ruis. HA4 59 BU60
Brixham Gdns, Ilf. IG3 69 ES64
Brixham Rd, Well. DA16 106 EX81
Brixham St, E16 87 EM74
BRIXTON, SW2 101 DL84
⇌ Brixton 101 DN84
⊖ Brixton 101 DN84
★ Brixton Acad, The, SW9 101 DM83
Brixton Est, Edg. HA8 42 CP54
Brixton Hill, SW2 121 DL87
Brixton Hill Pl, SW2
off Brixton Hill 121 DL87
Brixton Oval, SW2 101 DN84
Brixton Rd, SW9 101 DN82
Watford WD24 23 BV39
Brixton Sta Rd, SW9 101 DN84
Brixton Water La, SW2 121 DM85
Broad Acre, St.Alb. (Brick.Wd) AL2 8 BY30
Broadacre, Stai. TW18 114 BG92
Broadacre Cl, Uxb. UB10 59 BP62
Broadbent Cl, N6 65 DH60
Broadbent St, W1 195 H10
Broadberry Ct, N18 46 DV50
Broadbridge Cl, SE3 104 EG80
Broad Cl, Walt. KT12 136 BX104
Broadcoombe, S.Croy. CR2 160 DW108
Broad Ct, WC2 196 A9
Broadcroft Av, Stan. HA7 41 CK54
Broadcroft Rd, Orp. BR5 145 ER101
Broad Ditch Rd, Grav. (Sthflt) DA13 130 GC94
Broadeaves Cl, S.Croy. CR2 160 DS106
Broadfield Cl, NW2 63 CW62
Croydon CR0
off Progress Way 141 DM103
Romford RM1 71 FF57
Tadworth KT20 173 CW120
Broadfield Ct, Bushey (Bushey Hth) WD23 41 CE47
Broadfield La, NW1 83 DL66
Broadfield Rd, SE6 124 EE87
Broadfields, E.Mol. KT8 137 CD100
Harrow HA2 40 CB54
Waltham Cross (Chsht) EN7 13 DP29
Broadfields Av, N21 45 DN45
Broadfields Av, Edg. HA8 42 CP49
Broadfields Hts, Edg. HA8 42 CP49
Broadfields La, Wat. WD19 39 BV46
Broadfield Sq, Enf. EN1 30 DV40
Broadfields Way, NW10 63 CT64
Broadfield Way, Buck.H. IG9 48 EJ48
Broadford La, Wok. (Chobham) GU24 150 AT112
BROADGATE, EC2 197 L6
Broadgate, E13 86 EJ68
EC2 off Liverpool St 84 DS71
Waltham Abbey EN9 16 EF33
Broadgate Circle, EC2 197 M6
Broadgate Rd, E16 86 EK72
Broadgates Av, Barn. EN4 28 DB39
Broadgates Rd, SW18
off Ellerton Rd 120 DD88
BROAD GREEN, Croy. CR0 141 DN100
Broad Grn Av, Croy. CR0 141 DP101
Broadgreen Rd, Wal.Cr. (Chsht) EN7 14 DR26
Broadham Grn Rd, Oxt. RH8 187 ED132
Broadham Pl, Oxt. RH8 187 ED131
Broadhead Strand, NW9 43 CT53
Broadheath Dr, Chis. BR7 125 EM92
Broad Highway, Cob. KT11 154 BX114
Broadhinton Rd, SW4 101 DH83
Broadhurst, Ashtd. KT21 172 CL116
Broadhurst Av, Edg. HA8 42 CP49
Ilford IG3 69 ET63
Broadhurst Cl, NW6
off Broadhurst Gdns 82 DC65
Richmond TW10
off Lower Gro Rd 118 CM85
Broadhurst Gdns, NW6 82 DB65
Chigwell IG7 49 EQ49
Ruislip HA4 60 BW61
Broadhurst Wk, Rain. RM13 89 FG65
Broadlake Cl, St.Alb. (Lon.Col.) AL2 9 CK27
Broadlands, Felt. TW13 116 BZ90
Grays (Bad.Dene) RM17
off Bankfoot 110 FZ78
Broadlands Av, SW16 121 DL89
Enfield EN3 30 DV41
Shepperton TW17 135 BQ100
Broadlands Cl, N6 64 DG59
SW16 121 DL89
Enfield EN3 30 DV41
Waltham Cross EN8 15 DX34
Broadlands Dr, Warl. CR6 176 DW119
Broadlands Rd, N6 64 DF59
Bromley BR1 124 EH91
Broadlands Way, N.Mal. KT3 139 CT100
Broad La, EC2 197 M6
N8 off Tottenham La 65 DM57
N15 66 DT56
Dartford DA2 127 FG91
Hampton TW12 116 CA93
Broad Lawn, SE9 125 EN89
Broadlawns Ct, Har. HA3 41 CF53
Broadley Gdns, Rad. (Shenley) WD7 off Queens Way 10 CL32
Broadley St, NW8 194 A6
Broadley Ter, NW1 194 C5
Broadmark Rd, Slou. SL2 74 AV73
Broadmayne, SE17 201 K10
Broadmead, SE6 123 EA90
Broad Mead, Ashtd. KT21 172 CM117
Broadmead Av, Wor.Pk. KT4 139 CU101
Broadmead Cl, Hmptn. TW12 116 CA93
Pinner HA5 40 BY52
Broadmead Rd, Hayes UB4 78 BY70
Northolt UB5 78 BY70
Woking GU22, GU23 167 BB122
Woodford Green IG8 48 EG51
Broadmeads, Wok. (Send) GU23
off Broadmead Rd 167 BB122
Broad Oak, Sun. TW16 115 BT93
Woodford Green IG8 48 EH50
Broadoak Av, Enf. EN3 31 DX35
Broad Oak Cl, E4 47 EA50
Broadoak Cl, Dart. (Sutt.H.) DA4 128 FN93
Broad Oak Cl, Orp. BR5 146 EU96
Broadoak Rd, Erith DA8 107 FD80
Broadoaks, Epp. CM16 17 ET31
Surbiton KT6 138 CP102
Broadoaks Cres, W.Byf. KT14 152 BH114
Broadoaks Way, Brom. BR2 144 EF99
Broad Platts, Slou. SL3 92 AX76
Broad Ride, Egh. TW20 132 AU96
Virginia Water GU25 132 AU96
Broad Rd, Swans. DA10 130 FY86
Broad Sanctuary, SW1 199 N5
Broadstone Pl, W1 194 F7
Broadstone Rd, Horn. RM12 71 FG61
Broad St, Dag. RM10 88 FA66
Teddington TW11 117 CF93
Broad St Av, EC2 197 M7
Broad St Pl, EC2 197 L7
Broadstrood, Loug. IG10 33 EN38
Broad Vw, NW9 62 CN58
Broadview Av, Grays RM16 110 GD75
Broadview Rd, SW16 121 DK94
Broadwalk, E18 68 EF55
Broad Wk, N21 45 DM47
NW1 195 H3
SE3 104 EJ83
W1 198 F2
Caterham CR3 176 DT122
Coulsdon CR5 174 DG123
Croydon CR0 161 DY110
Epsom KT18
off Chalk La 172 CS117
Epsom (Burgh Hth) KT18 173 CX119
Broadwalk, Har. HA2 60 CA57
Broad Wk, Houns. TW5 96 BX81
Orpington BR6 146 EX104
Richmond TW9 98 CM80
Sevenoaks TN15 191 FL128
Broad Wk, The, W8 82 DB74
East Molesey KT8 137 CF97
Broadwalk, The, Nthwd. HA6 39 BQ54
Broadwalk Ct, W8 82 DA74
Broad Wk La, NW11 63 CZ59
Broad Wk N, The, Brwd. CM13 55 GA49
Broadwalk Shop Cen, Edg. HA8 42 CP51
Broad Wk S, The, Brwd. CM13 55 GA49
Broadwall, SE1 200 E2
Broadwater, Pot.B. EN6 12 DB30
Broadwater Cl, Stai. (Wrays.) TW19 113 AZ87
Walton-on-Thames KT12 153 BU106
Woking GU21 151 BD112
Broad Water Cres, Wey. KT13
off Churchill Dr 135 BQ104
Broadwater Fm Est, N17 46 DR54
Broadwater Gdns, Orp. BR6 163 EP105
Uxbridge (Hare.) UB9 58 BH56
Broadwater La, Uxb. (Hare.) UB9 58 BH56
Broadwater Pk, Uxb. (Denh.) UB9 58 BG58
Broadwater Pl, Wey. KT13
off Oatlands Dr 135 BS103
Broadwater Rd, N17 46 DS53
SE28 105 ER76
SW17 120 DE91
Broadwater Rd N, Walt. KT12 153 BT106
Broadwater Rd S, Walt. KT12 153 BT106
Broadway, E15 85 ED66
SW1 199 M6
Barking IG11 87 EQ67
Bexleyheath DA6 106 EY84
Grays RM17 110 GC79
Rainham RM13 89 FG70
Romford RM2 71 FG55
Staines TW18
off Kingston Rd 114 BH93
Swanley BR8 147 FC100
Tilbury RM18 111 GF82
Broadway, The, E4 47 EC51
E13 86 EH68
N8 65 DL58
N9 46 DU48
N14 off Winchmore Hill Rd 45 DK46
N22 45 DN54
NW7 42 CS50
SW13 off The Terrace 98 CS82
SW19 119 CZ93
W5 79 CK73
W7 off Cherington Rd 79 CE74
W7 (W.Ealing) 79 CG74
W13 79 CG74
Addlestone (New Haw) KT15 152 BG110
Croydon CR0
off Croydon Rd 159 DL105
Dagenham RM8 70 EZ61
Greenford UB6 78 CC70
Harrow HA2 41 CE54
Hornchurch RM12 71 FH63
Loughton IG10 33 EQ42
Pinner HA5 40 BZ52
Southall UB1 78 BX73
Staines (Laleham) TW18 134 BJ97
Stanmore HA7 41 CJ50
Sutton SM1 off Manor La 158 DC106
Sutton (Cheam) SM3 157 CY107
Thames Ditton KT7
off Hampton Ct Way 137 CE102
Watford WD17 24 BW41
Wembley HA9 off East La 62 CL62
Woking GU21 167 AZ117
Woodford Green IG8 48 EH51
Broadway Av, Croy. CR0 142 DR99
Twickenham TW1 117 CH86
Broadway Cl, S.Croy. CR2 160 DV114
Woodford Green IG8 48 EH51
Broadway Ct, SW19 119 CZ93
Broadway E, Uxb. (Denh.) UB9 58 BG58
Broadway Gdns, Mitch. CR4 140 DE98
Broadway Mkt, E8 84 DV67
Broadway Mkt Ms, E8
off Regents Row 84 DU67
Broadway Ms, E5 66 DT59
N13 off Elmdale Rd 45 DM50
N21 off Compton Rd 45 DP46
Broadway Par, N8 65 DL58
Hayes UB3
off Coldharbour La 77 BU74
Hornchurch RM12
off The Broadway 71 FH63
Broadway Pl, SW19
off Hartfield Rd 119 CZ93
Broadway Shop Cen, W6
off Hammersmith Bdy 99 CW77
Bexleyheath DA6 106 FA84
Broadway Wk, E14 204 A6
Broadwick St, W1 195 L10
Broadwood, Grav. DA11 131 GH92
Broadwood Av, Ruis. HA4 59 BS58
Broadwood Rd, Couls. CR5
off Netherne Dr 175 DK121
Broadwood Ter, W8
off Pembroke Rd 99 CZ77
Broad Yd, EC1 196 F5
Brocas Cl, NW3
off Fellows Rd 82 DE66
Brockbridge Ho, SW15
off Tangley Gro 119 CT86
Brockdish Av, Bark. IG11 69 ET64
Brockenhurst, W.Mol. KT8 136 BZ100
Brockenhurst Av, Wor.Pk. KT4 138 CS102
Brockenhurst Cl, Wok. GU21 151 AZ114
Brockenhurst Gdns, NW7 43 CS50
Ilford IG1 69 EQ64
Brockenhurst Ms, N18
off Lyndhurst Rd 46 DU49
Brockenhurst Rd, Croy. CR0 142 DV101
Brockenhurst Way, SW16 141 DK96
Brocket Cl, Chig. IG7
off Burrow Rd 49 ET50
Brocket Rd, Grays RM16 111 GG76
Brocket Way, Chig. IG7 49 ES50
Brock Grn, S.Ock. RM15
off Cam Grn 91 FV72
Brockham Cl, SW19 119 CZ92
Brockham Cres, Croy. (New Adgtn) CR0 161 ED108
Brockham Dr, SW2
off Fairview Pl 121 DM87
Ilford IG2 69 EP58
Brockham Hill Pk, Tad. (Box H.) KT20 182 CQ131
Brockham La, Bet. (Brock.) RH3 182 CN134
Brockham St, SE1 201 J6
Brockhurst Cl, Stan. HA7 41 CF51
Brockill Cres, SE4 103 DY84
Brocklebank Ct, Whyt. CR3 176 DU118
Brocklebank Rd, SE7 205 P9
SW18 120 DC87
Brocklehurst St, SE14 103 DX80
Brocklesbury Cl, Wat. WD24 24 BW41
Brocklesby Rd, SE25 142 DV98
BROCKLEY, SE4 123 DY85
⇌ Brockley 103 DY83
Brockley Av, Stan. HA7 42 CL48
Brockley Cl, Stan. HA7 42 CL49
Brockley Combe, Wey. KT13 153 BR105
Brockley Cres, Rom. RM5 51 FC52
Brockley Cross, SE4
off Endwell Rd 103 DY83
Brockley Footpath, SE15 102 DW84
Brockley Gdns, SE4 103 DZ82
Brockley Gro, SE4 123 DZ85
Brentwood (Hutt.) CM13 55 GA46
Brockley Hall Rd, SE4 123 DY86
Brockley Hill, Stan. HA7 41 CJ46
Brockley Ms, SE4 123 DY85
Brockley Pk, SE23 123 DY87
Brockley Ri, SE23 123 DY86
Brockley Rd, SE4 103 DZ83
Brockleyside, Stan. HA7 41 CK49
Brockley Vw, SE23 123 DY87
Brockley Way, SE4 123 DX85
Brockman Ri, Brom. BR1 123 ED91
Brock Pl, E3 85 EB70
Brock Rd, E13 86 EH71
Brocks Dr, Sutt. SM3 139 CY104
Brockshot Cl, Brent. TW8 97 CK79
Brocksparkwood, Brwd. CM13 55 GB48
Brock St, SE15
off Evelina Rd 102 DW83
Brockton Cl, Rom. RM1 71 FF56
Brock Way, Vir.W. GU25 132 AW99
Brockway Cl, E11 68 EE60
Brockweir, E2 off Cyprus St 84 DW68
Brockwell Av, Beck. BR3 143 EB99
Brockwell Cl, Orp. BR5 145 ET99
★ Brockwell Park, SE24 121 DP86
Brockwell Pk Gdns, SE24 121 DN87
Brockwell Pk Row, SW2 121 DN86
Brodewater Rd, Borwd. WD6 26 CP40
Brodia Rd, N16 66 DS62
Brodick Ho, E3 off Saxon Rd 85 DZ68
Brodie Ho, SE1
off Rowcross St 102 DT77
Brodie Rd, E4 47 EC46
Enfield EN2 30 DQ38
Brodie St, SE1 202 A10
Brodlove La, E1 85 DX73
Brodrick Gro, SE2 106 EV77
Brodrick Rd, SW17 120 DE89
Brograve Gdns, Beck. BR3 143 EB96
Broke Fm Dr, Orp. BR6 164 EW109
Brokengate La, Uxb. (Denh.) UB9 57 BC60
Broken Wf, EC4 197 H10
Brokes Cres, Reig. RH2 184 DA132
Brokesley St, E3 85 DZ70
Brokes Rd, Reig. RH2 184 DA132
Broke Wk, E8 84 DU67
Bromar Rd, SE5 102 DS83
Bromborough Grn, Wat. WD19 40 BW50
Bromefield, Stan. HA7 41 CJ53
Bromefield Ct, Wal.Abb. EN9 16 EG33
Bromehead Rd, E1
off Commercial Rd 84 DW72
Bromehead St, E1
off Commercial Rd 84 DW72
Bromell's Rd, SW4 101 DJ84
Brome Rd, SE9 105 EM83
Bromet Cl, Wat. WD17 23 BT38
Bromfelde Rd, SW4 101 DK82
Bromfelde Wk, SW4 101 DK82
Bromfield St, N1 83 DN68
Bromford Cl, Oxt. RH8 188 EG133
Bromhall Rd, Dag. RM8, RM9 88 EV65
Bromhedge, SE9 125 EM90
Bromholm Rd, SE2 106 EV76
Bromleigh Cl, Wal.Cr. (Chsht) EN8 off Martins Dr 15 DY28
Bromleigh Ct, SE23
off Lapse Wd Wk 122 DV89
BROMLEY, E3 85 EB70
BROMLEY, BR1 & BR2 144 EF96
Bromley, Grays RM17 110 FZ79
Bromley Av, Brom. BR1 124 EE94
⊖ Bromley-by-Bow 85 EB69
BROMLEY COMMON, Brom. BR2 145 EM101
Bromley Common, Brom. BR2 144 EJ98
Bromley Cres, Brom. BR2 144 EF97
Ruislip HA4 59 BT63
Bromley Gdns, Brom. BR2 144 EF97
Bromley Gro, Brom. BR2 143 ED96
Bromley Hall Rd, E14 85 EC71
Bromley High St, E3 85 EB69
Bromley Hill, Brom. BR1 124 EE92
Bromley La, Chis. BR7 125 EQ94
Bromley Mall, The, Brom. BR1 144 EG97
★ Bromley Mus, Orp. BR6 146 EV101
⇌ Bromley North 144 EG95
BROMLEY PARK, Brom. BR1 144 EE95
Bromley Pk, Brom. BR1
off London Rd 144 EF95
Bromley Pl, W1 195 K6
Bromley Rd, E10 67 EB58
E17 47 EA54
N17 46 DT53
N18 46 DR48
SE6 123 EB88
Beckenham BR3 143 EB95
Bromley (Downham) BR1 123 EC91
Bromley (Short.) BR2 143 EC96
Chislehurst BR7 145 EP95
⇌ Bromley South 144 EG97
Bromley St, E1 85 DX71
BROMPTON, SW3 198 B7
Brompton Arc, SW3 198 D5
Brompton Cl, SE20
off Selby Rd 142 DU96
Hounslow TW4 116 BZ85
Brompton Dr, Erith DA8 107 FH80
Brompton Gro, N2 64 DE56
★ Brompton Oratory, SW7 198 B7
Brompton Pk Cres, SW6 100 DB79
Brompton Pl, SW3 198 C6
Brompton Rd, SW1 198 C6
SW3 198 B8
SW7 198 C6
Brompton Sq, SW3 198 B6
Brompton Ter, SE18
off Prince Imperial Rd 105 EN81
Bromwich Av, N6 64 DG61
Bromyard Av, W3 80 CS74
Bromyard Ho, SE15 102 DV80
BRONDESBURY, NW2 81 CY66
⇌ Brondesbury 81 CZ66
Brondesbury Ct, NW2 81 CW65
Brondesbury Ms, NW6
off Willesden La 82 DA66
BRONDESBURY PARK, NW6 81 CW66
⇌ Brondesbury Park 81 CX67
Brondesbury Pk, NW2 81 CV65
NW6 81 CX66
Brondesbury Rd, NW6 81 CZ68
Brondesbury Vil, NW6 81 CZ68
Bronsart Rd, SW6 99 CY80
Bronsdon Way, Uxb. (Denh.) UB9 57 BF61
Bronson Rd, SW20 139 CX96
Bronte Cl, E7
off Bective Rd 68 EG63
Erith DA8 107 FB80
Ilford IG2 69 EN57
Tilbury RM18 111 GJ82
Bronte Gro, Dart. DA1 108 FM84
Bronte Ho, NW6 82 DA69
Bronte Vw, Grav. DA12 131 GJ88
Bronti Cl, SE17 102 DQ78
Bronze Age Way, Belv. DA17 107 FC76
Erith DA8 107 FC76
Bronze St, SE8 103 EA80
Brook Av, Dag. RM10 89 FB66
Edgware HA8 42 CP51
Wembley HA9 62 CN62
Brookbank Av, W7 79 CD71
Brookbank Rd, SE13 103 EA83
Brook Cl, NW7 43 CY52
SW17 120 DG89
SW20 139 CV97
W3 off West Lo Av 80 CN74
Borehamwood WD6 26 CP41
Epsom KT19 156 CS109
Romford RM2 51 FF53
Ruislip HA4 59 BS59
Staines (Stanw.) TW19 114 BM87
Brook Ct, Buck.H. IG9 48 EH46
Brook Cres, E4 47 EA49
N9 46 DV49
Brookdale, N11 45 DJ49
Brookdale Av, Upmin. RM14 72 FN62
Brookdale Cl, Upmin. RM14 72 FP62
Brookdale Rd, E17 67 EA55
SE6 123 EB86
Bexley DA5 126 EY86
Brookdene Av, Wat. WD19 39 BV45
Brookdene Dr, Nthwd. HA6 39 BT52
Brookdene Rd, SE18 105 ET77
Brook Dr, SE11 200 E7
Harrow HA1 60 CC56
Radlett WD7 9 CF33
Ruislip HA4 59 BS58
Sunbury-on-Thames TW16
off Chertsey Rd 115 BS92
Brooke Av, Har. HA2 60 CC62
Brooke Cl, Bushey WD23 40 CC45
Brooke Ct, W10
off Kilburn La 81 CY68
Brookehowse Rd, SE6 123 EB90
Brookend Rd, Sid. DA15 125 ES88
Brooke Rd, E5 66 DU62
E17 67 EC56
N16 66 DT62
Grays RM17 110 GA78
Brooker Rd, Wal.Abb. EN9 15 EC34
Brookers Cl, Ashtd. KT21 171 CJ117
Brooke's Ct, EC1 196 D6
Brookes Mkt, EC1 196 E6
Brooke St, EC1 196 D7
Brooke Way, Bushey WD23
off Richfield Rd 40 CC45
Brook Fm Rd, Cob. KT11 170 BX115
Brookfield, N6 64 DG62
Epping (Thnwd) CM16 18 EW25
Woking GU21 166 AV116
Brookfield Av, E17 67 EC56
NW7 43 CV51
W5 79 CK70
Sutton SM1 158 DD105
Brookfield Cen, Wal.Cr. (Chsht) EN8 15 DX27
Brookfield Cl, NW7 43 CV51
Ashtead KT21 172 CL120
Brentwood (Hutt.) CM13 55 GC44
Chertsey (Ott.) KT16 151 BD107
Brookfield Ct, Grnf. UB6 78 CC69
Harrow HA3 61 CK57
Brookfield Cres, NW7 43 CV51
Harrow HA3 62 CL57
Brookfield Gdns, Esher (Clay.) KT10 155 CF107
Waltham Cross (Chsht) EN8 15 DX27
Brookfield La, Wal.Cr. (Chsht) EN8 15 DX27
Brookfield La W, Wal.Cr. (Chsht) EN8 14 DV28
Brookfield Pk, NW5 65 DH62
Brookfield Path, Wdf.Grn. IG8 48 EE51
Brookfield Pl, Cob. KT11 170 BY115
Brookfield Retail Pk, Wal.Cr. (Chsht) EN8 15 DX26
Brookfield Rd, E9 85 DY65
N9 46 DU48
W4 98 CR75
Brookfields, Enf. EN3 31 DX42
Brookfields Av, Mitch. CR4 140 DE99
Brook Gdns, E4 47 EB49
SW13 99 CT83
Kingston upon Thames KT2 138 CQ95
Brook Gate, W1 198 E1
Brook Grn, W6 99 CX77

★ Place of interest ⇌ Railway station ⊖ London Underground station DLR Docklands Light Railway station Tra Tramlink station H Hospital Riv Pedestrian ferry landing stage

Brook Grn, Wok. (Chobham) GU24
off Brookleys ... 150 AT110
Brook Hill, Oxt. RH8 ... 187 EC130
Brookhill Cl, SE18 ... 105 EP78
Barnet EN4 ... 28 DE43
Brookhill Rd, SE18 ... 105 EP78
Barnet EN4 ... 28 DE43
Brookhouse Gdns, E4 ... 48 EE49
Brookhurst Rd, Add. KT15 ... 152 BH107
Brook Ind Est, Hayes UB4 ... 78 BX74
Brooking Cl, Dag. RM8 ... 70 EW62
Brooking Rd, E7 ... 68 EG64
Brookland Cl, NW11 ... 64 DA56
Brookland Garth, NW11 ... 64 DB56
Brookland Hill, NW11 ... 64 DA56
Brookland Ri, NW11 ... 64 DA56
BROOKLANDS, Wey. KT13 ... 152 BM109
Brooklands, Dart. DA1 ... 128 FL88
Brooklands App, Rom. RM1 ... 71 FD56
Brooklands Av, SW19 ... 120 DB89
Sidcup DA15 ... 125 ER89
Brooklands Cl, Cob. KT11 ... 170 BY115
Romford RM7
off Marshalls Rd ... 71 FD56
Sunbury-on-Thames TW16 ... 135 BS95
Brooklands Ct, Add.
(New Haw) KT15 ... 152 BK110
Weybridge KT13
off Northfield Pl ... 153 BP108
Brooklands Dr, Grnf. UB6 ... 79 CK67
Brooklands Gdns, Horn.
RM11 ... 72 FJ57
Potters Bar EN6 ... 11 CY32
Brooklands Ind Pk, Wey.
KT13 ... 152 BL110
Brooklands La, Rom. RM7 ... 71 FD56
Weybridge KT13 ... 152 BM107
★ **Brooklands Mus**, Wey.
KT13 ... 152 BN109
Brooklands Pk, SE3 ... 104 EG83
Brooklands Pas, SW8
off Belmore St ... 101 DK81
Brooklands Pl, Hmptn. TW12 ... 116 CB92
Brooklands Rd, Rom. RM7 ... 71 FD56
Thames Ditton KT7 ... 137 CF102
Weybridge KT13 ... 153 BP107
Brooklands Way, Red. RH1 ... 184 DE132
Brook La, SE3 ... 104 EH82
Bexley DA5 ... 126 EX86
Bromley BR1 ... 124 EG93
Woking (Send) GU23 ... 167 BE122
Brook La N, Brent. TW8 ... 97 CK78
Brooklea Cl, NW9 ... 42 CS53
Brookleys, Wok. (Chobham)
GU24 ... 150 AT110
Brooklyn Av, SE25 ... 142 DV98
Loughton IG10 ... 32 EL42
Brooklyn Cl, Cars. SM5 ... 140 DE103
Woking GU22 ... 166 AY119
Brooklyn Ct, Wok. GU22
off Brooklyn Rd ... 166 AY119
Brooklyn Gro, SE25 ... 142 DV98
Brooklyn Pas, W12
off Goldhawk Rd ... 99 CV75
Brooklyn Rd, SE25 ... 142 DV98
Bromley BR2 ... 144 EK99
Woking GU22 ... 166 AY118
Brooklyn Way, West Dr. UB7 ... 94 BK76
Brookmans Av, Hat.
(Brook.Pk) AL9 ... 11 CY26
Brookmans Cl, Upmin. RM14 ... 73 FS59
BROOKMANS PARK, Hat. AL9 ... 11 CY26
⇌ **Brookmans Park** ... 11 CX27
Brookmans Pk Dr, Upmin.
RM14 ... 73 FS57
Brookmarsh Ind Est, SE10
off Norman Rd ... 103 EB80
Brook Mead, Epsom KT19 ... 156 CS107
Brookmead Av, Brom. BR1 ... 145 EM99
Brookmead Cl, Orp. BR5 ... 146 EV101
Brook Meadow, N12 ... 44 DB49
Brook Meadow Cl, Wdf.Grn.
IG8 ... 48 EE51
Brookmeadow Way, Wal.Abb. EN9
off Breach Barn Mobile
Home Pk ... 16 EH30
Brookmead Rd, Croy. CR0 ... 141 DJ100
Brookmeads Est, Mitch. CR4 ... 140 DE99
Brookmead Way, Orp. BR5 ... 146 EV100
Brook Ms N, W2
off Craven Ter ... 82 DD73
Brookmill Cl, Wat. WD19
off Brookside Rd ... 39 BV45
Brookmill Rd, SE8 ... 103 EA81
Brook Par, Chig. IG7
off High Rd ... 49 EP48
Brook Pk, Dart. DA1 ... 128 FN89
Brook Pk Cl, N21 ... 29 DP44
Brook Path, Loug. IG10 ... 32 EL42
Brook Pl, Barn. EN5 ... 28 DA43
Brook Ri, Chig. IG7 ... 49 EN48
Brook Rd, N8 ... 65 DL56
N22 ... 65 DM55
NW2 ... 63 CU61
Borehamwood WD6 ... 26 CN40
Brentwood CM14 ... 54 FT48
Buckhurst Hill IG9 ... 48 EG47
Epping CM16 ... 18 EU33
Gravesend (Nthflt) DA11 ... 130 GE88
Ilford IG2 ... 69 ES58
Loughton IG10 ... 32 EL43
Redhill (Merst.) RH1 ... 185 DJ129
Romford RM2 ... 51 FF53
Surbiton KT6 ... 138 CL103
Swanley BR8 ... 147 FD97
Thornton Heath CR7 ... 142 DQ98
Twickenham TW1 ... 117 CG86
Waltham Cross EN8 ... 15 DZ34
Brook Rd S, Brent. TW8 ... 97 CK79
Brooks Av, E6 ... 87 EM70
Brooksbank St, E9 ... 84 DW65
Brooksby Ms, N1
off Brooksby St ... 83 DN66
Brooksby St, N1 ... 83 DN66
Brooksby's Wk, E9 ... 67 DX64
Brooks Cl, SE9 ... 125 EN89
Weybridge KT13 ... 152 BN110
Brookscroft, Croy. CR0 ... 161 DY110
Brookscroft Rd, E17 ... 47 EB53
Brookshill, Har. HA3 ... 41 CD50
Brookshill Av, Har. HA3 ... 41 CD50
Brookshill Dr, Har. HA3 ... 41 CD50
Brookshill Gate, Har.
(Har.Wld) HA3 ... 41 CD50
Brookside, N21 ... 29 DM44
Barnet EN4 ... 28 DE44
Carshalton SM5 ... 158 DG106
Chertsey KT16 ... 133 BE101
Hornchurch RM11 ... 72 FL57
Ilford IG6 ... 49 EQ51
Orpington BR6 ... 145 ET101
Potters Bar EN6 ... 11 CU32
Slough (Colnbr.) SL3 ... 93 BC80
Uxbridge UB10 ... 76 BM66
Waltham Abbey EN9
off Broomstick Hall Rd ... 16 EE33
Brookside Av, Ashf. TW15 ... 114 BJ92
Staines (Wrays.) TW19 ... 92 AY83
Brookside Cl, Barn. EN5 ... 27 CY44
Feltham TW13
off Sycamore Cl ... 115 BU90
Harrow (Kenton) HA3 ... 61 CK57
Harrow (S.Har.) HA2 ... 60 BY63
Brookside Cres, Pot.B. (Cuffley)
EN6 ... 13 DL27
Worcester Park KT4
off Green La ... 139 CU102
Brookside Gdns, Enf. EN1 ... 30 DV37
Brookside Rd, N9 ... 46 DV49
N19 ... 65 DJ61
NW11 ... 63 CY58
Gravesend (Istead Rise)
DA13 ... 131 GF94
Hayes UB4 ... 78 BW73
Watford WD19 ... 39 BV45
Brookside S, Barn. EN4 ... 44 DG45
Brookside Wk, N3 ... 43 CY54
N12 ... 44 DA51
NW4 ... 63 CY56
NW11 ... 63 CY56
Brookside Way, Croy. CR0 ... 143 DX100
Brooks La, W4 ... 98 CN79
Brook's Ms, W1 ... 195 H10
Brook Sq, SE18
off Barlow Dr ... 104 EL81
Brooks Rd, E13 ... 86 EG67
W4 ... 98 CN78
BROOK STREET, Brwd. CM14 ... 54 FS49
Brook St, N17 *off High Rd* ... 46 DT54
W1 ... 194 G10
W2 ... 194 A10
Belvedere DA17 ... 107 FB78
Brentwood CM14 ... 54 FS50
Erith DA8 ... 107 FB79
Kingston upon Thames
KT1 ... 138 CL96
Brooksville Av, NW6 ... 81 CY67
Brooks Way, Orp. BR5 ... 146 EW96
Brook Vale, Erith DA8 ... 107 FB81
Brookview Rd, SW16 ... 121 DJ92
Brookville Rd, SW6 ... 99 CZ80
Brook Wk, N2 ... 44 DD53
Edgware HA8 ... 42 CR51
Brookway, SE3 ... 104 EG83
Brook Way, Chig. IG7 ... 49 EN48
Leatherhead KT22 ... 171 CG118
Rainham RM13 ... 89 FH71
Brookwood Av, SW13 ... 99 CT83
Brookwood Cl, Brom. BR2 ... 144 EF98
Brookwood Rd, SW18 ... 119 CZ88
Hounslow TW3 ... 96 CB81
Broom Av, Orp. BR5 ... 146 EV96
Broom Cl, Brom. BR2 ... 144 EL100
Esher KT10 ... 154 CB106
Teddington TW11 ... 117 CK94
Waltham Cross (Chsht) EN7 ... 14 DU27
Broomcroft Av, Nthlt. UB5 ... 78 BW69
Broomcroft Cl, Wok. GU22 ... 167 BD116
Broomcroft Dr, Wok. GU22 ... 167 BD115
Broome Cl, Epsom (Headley)
KT18 ... 182 CQ126
Broome Pl, S.Ock. (Aveley)
RM15 ... 91 FR74
Broome Rd, Hmptn. TW12 ... 116 BZ94
Broomer Pl, Wal.Cr. EN8 ... 14 DW29
Broome Way, SE5 ... 102 DR80
Broomfield, E17 ... 67 DZ59
St. Albans (Park St) AL2 ... 8 CC27
Staines TW18 ... 114 BG93
Sunbury-on-Thames TW16 ... 135 BU95
Broomfield Av, N13 ... 45 DM50
Broxbourne EN10 ... 15 DY26
Loughton IG10 ... 33 EM44
Broomfield Cl, Rom. RM5 ... 51 FD52
Broomfield Ct, Wey. KT13 ... 153 BP107
Broomfield La, N13 ... 45 DM49
Broomfield Pl, W13
off Broomfield Rd ... 79 CH74
Broomfield Ride, Lthd.
(Oxshott) KT22 ... 155 CD112
Broomfield Ri, Abb.L. WD5 ... 7 BR32
Broomfield Rd, N13 ... 45 DL50
W13 ... 79 CH74
Addlestone (New Haw)
KT15 ... 152 BH111
Beckenham BR3 ... 143 DY97
Bexleyheath DA6 ... 126 FA85
Richmond TW9 ... 98 CM81
Romford RM6 ... 70 EX59
Sevenoaks TN13 ... 190 FF122
Surbiton KT5 ... 138 CM102
Swanscombe DA10 ... 130 FY86
Teddington TW11
off Melbourne Rd ... 117 CJ93
Broomfields, Esher KT10 ... 154 CC106
Broomfield St, E14 ... 85 EA71
Broom Gdns, Croy. CR0 ... 143 EA104
Broom Gro, Wat. WD17 ... 23 BU38
Broomgrove Gdns, Edg. HA8 ... 42 CN53
Broomgrove Rd, SW9 ... 101 DM82
Broom Hall, Lthd. (Oxshott)
KT22 ... 155 CD114
Broomhall End, Wok. GU21
off Broomhall La ... 166 AY116
Broomhall La, Wok. GU21 ... 166 AY116
Broomhall Rd, S.Croy. CR2 ... 160 DR109
Woking GU21 ... 166 AY116
Broom Hill, Slou. (Stoke P.)
SL2 ... 74 AU66
Broomhill Ct, Wdf.Grn. IG8
off Broomhill Rd ... 48 EG51
Broomhill Ri, Bexh. DA6 ... 126 FA85
Broomhill Rd, SW18 ... 120 DA85
Dartford DA1 ... 127 FH86
Ilford IG3 ... 70 EU61
Orpington BR6 ... 146 EU101
Woodford Green IG8 ... 48 EG51
Broomhills, Grav. (Sthflt)
DA13 *off Betsham Rd* ... 130 FY91
Broomhill Wk, Wdf.Grn. IG8 ... 48 EF52
Broomhouse La, SW6 ... 100 DA82
Broomhouse Rd, SW6 ... 100 DA82
Broomlands La, Oxt. RH8 ... 188 EJ125
Broom La, Wok. (Chobham)
GU24 ... 150 AS109
Broomloan La, Sutt. SM1 ... 140 DA103
Broom Lock, Tedd. TW11 ... 117 CJ93
Broom Mead, Bexh. DA6 ... 126 FA85
Broom Pk, Tedd. TW11 ... 117 CK94
Broom Rd, Croy. CR0 ... 143 EA104
Teddington TW11 ... 117 CJ93
Broomsleigh St, NW6 ... 63 CZ64
Broomstick Hall Rd, Wal.Abb.
EN9 ... 16 EE33
Broomstick La, Chesh. HP5 ... 4 AU30
Broom Water, Tedd. TW11 ... 117 CJ93
Broom Water W, Tedd. TW11 ... 117 CJ92
Broom Way, Wey. KT13 ... 153 BS105
Broomwood Cl, Croy. CR0 ... 143 DX99
Broomwood Gdns, Brwd.
(Pilg.Hat.) CM15 ... 54 FU44
Broomwood Rd, SW11 ... 120 DF86
Orpington BR5 ... 146 EV96
Broseley Gdns, Rom. RM3 ... 52 FL49
Broseley Gro, SE26 ... 123 DY92
Broseley Rd, Rom. RM3 ... 52 FL49
Broster Gdns, SE25 ... 142 DT97
Brougham Rd, E8 ... 84 DU67
W3 ... 80 CQ72
Brougham St, SW11 ... 100 DF82
Brough Cl, SW8
off Kenchester Cl ... 101 DL80
Kingston upon Thames
KT2 ... 117 CK92
Broughinge Rd, Borwd. WD6 ... 26 CP40
Broughton Av, N3 ... 63 CY55
Richmond TW10 ... 117 CH90
Broughton Dr, SW9 ... 101 DN84
Broughton Gdns, N6 ... 65 DJ58
Broughton Rd, SW6 ... 100 DB82
W13 ... 79 CH73
Orpington BR6 ... 145 ER103
Sevenoaks (Otford) TN14 ... 181 FG116
Thornton Heath CR7 ... 141 DN100
Broughton Rd App, SW6
off Wandsworth Br Rd ... 100 DB82
Broughton St, SW8 ... 100 DG82
Broughton Way, Rick. WD3 ... 38 BG45
Brouncker Rd, W3 ... 98 CQ75
Brow, The, Ch.St.G. HP8 ... 36 AX48
Watford WD25 ... 7 BV33
Brow Cl, Orp. BR5
off Brow Cres ... 146 EX101
Brow Cres, Orp. BR5 ... 146 EW102
Browells La, Felt. TW13 ... 115 BV89
Brownacres Towpath, Wey.
KT13 ... 135 BP102
Brown Cl, Wall. SM6 ... 159 DL108
Browne Cl, Brwd. CM14 ... 54 FV46
Romford RM5 ... 51 FB50
Brownfield St, E14 ... 85 EB72
Browngraves Rd, Hayes UB3 ... 95 BQ80
Brown Hart Gdns, W1 ... 194 G10
Brownhill Rd, SE6 ... 123 EB87
Browning Av, W7 ... 79 CF72
Sutton SM1 ... 158 DE105
Worcester Park KT4 ... 139 CV102
Browning Cl, E17 ... 67 EC56
W9 *off Randolph Av* ... 82 DC70
Hampton TW12 ... 116 BZ91
Romford (Coll.Row) RM5 ... 50 EZ52
Welling DA16 ... 105 ES81
Browning Ms, W1 ... 195 H7
Browning Rd, E11 ... 68 EF59
E12 ... 87 EM65
Dartford DA1 ... 108 FM84
Enfield EN2 ... 30 DR38
Browning St, SE17 ... 201 J10
Browning Wk, Til. RM18
off Coleridge Rd ... 111 GJ82
Browning Way, Houns. TW5 ... 96 BX81
Brownlea Gdns, Ilf. IG3 ... 70 EU61
Brownlow Cl, Barn. EN4 ... 28 DD43
Brownlow Ms, WC1 ... 196 C5
Brownlow Rd, E7
off Woodford Rd ... 68 EH63
E8 ... 84 DT67
N3 ... 44 DB52
N11 ... 45 DL51
NW10 ... 80 CS66
W13 ... 79 CG74
Borehamwood WD6 ... 26 CN42
Croydon CR0 ... 160 DS105
Redhill RH1 ... 184 DE134
Brownlow St, WC1 ... 196 C7
Brownrigg Rd, Ashf. TW15 ... 114 BN91
Brown Rd, Grav. DA12 ... 131 GL88
Brown's Bldgs, EC3 ... 197 N9
Brownsea Wk, NW7
off Sanders La ... 43 CX51
Browns La, NW5 ... 65 DH64
Brownspring Dr, SE9 ... 125 EP91
Browns Rd, E17 ... 67 EA55
Surbiton KT5 ... 138 CM101
Brown St, W1 ... 194 D8
Brownswell Rd, N2 ... 44 DD54
Brownswood Rd, N4 ... 65 DP62
Broxash Rd, SW11 ... 120 DG86
Broxbourne Av, E18 ... 68 EH56
Broxbourne Rd, E7 ... 68 EG62
Orpington BR6 ... 145 ET101
Broxburn Dr, S.Ock. RM15 ... 91 FV73
Broxburn Par, S.Ock. RM15
off Broxburn Dr ... 91 FV73
Broxhill Rd, Rom. (Hav.at.Bow.)
RM4 ... 51 FH48
Broxholm Rd, SE27 ... 121 DN90
Brox La, Cher. (Ott.) KT16 ... 151 BD109
Brox Rd, Cher. (Ott.) KT16 ... 151 BC107
Broxted Ms, Brwd. (Hutt.) CM13
off Bannister Dr ... 55 GC44
Broxted Rd, SE6 ... 123 DZ89
Broxwood Way, NW8 ... 82 DE67
Bruce Av, Horn. RM12 ... 72 FK61
Bruce Av, Shep. TW17 ... 135 BQ100
★ **Bruce Castle Mus**, N17 ... 46 DS53
Bruce Castle Rd, N17 ... 46 DT53
Bruce Cl, W10
off Ladbroke Gro ... 81 CY71
Welling DA16 ... 106 EV81
West Byfleet (Byfleet)
KT14 ... 152 BK113
Bruce Dr, S.Croy. CR2 ... 161 DX109
Bruce Gdns, N20
off Balfour Gro ... 44 DF48
⇌ **Bruce Grove** ... 46 DT54
Bruce Gro, N17 ... 46 DS53
Orpington BR6 ... 146 EU102
Watford WD24 ... 24 BW38
Bruce Hall Ms, SW17
off Brudenell Rd ... 120 DG91
Bruce Rd, E3 ... 85 EB69
NW10 ... 80 CR66
SE25 ... 142 DR98
Barnet EN5
off St. Albans Rd ... 27 CY41
Harrow HA3 ... 41 CE54
Mitcham CR4 ... 120 DG94
Bruce's Wf Rd, Grays RM17 ... 110 GA79
Bruce Way, Wal.Cr. EN8 ... 15 DX33
Bruckner St, W10 ... 81 CZ69
Brudenell Rd, SW17 ... 120 DF90
Bruffs Meadow, Nthlt. UB5 ... 78 BY65
Bruford Ct, SE8 ... 103 EA79
Bruges Pl, NW1
off Randolph St ... 83 DJ66
Brumana Cl, Wey. KT13 ... 153 BP107
Brumfield Rd, Epsom KT19 ... 156 CQ106
Brummel Cl, Bexh. DA7 ... 107 FC83
★ **Brunei Gall**, WC1 ... 195 N6
Brunel Cl, SE19 ... 122 DT93
Hounslow TW5 ... 95 BV80
Northolt UB5 ... 78 BZ69
Romford RM1 ... 71 FE56
Tilbury RM18 ... 111 GH83
★ **Brunel Engine Ho**, SE16 ... 202 F4
Brunel Est, W2 ... 82 DA71
Brunel Ms, W10
off Kilburn La ... 81 CY69
Brunel Pl, Sthl. UB1 ... 78 CB72
Brunel Rd, E17 ... 67 DY58
SE16 ... 202 F5
W3 ... 80 CS71
Woodford Green IG8 ... 49 EM50
Brunel St, E16
off Victoria Dock Rd ... 86 EF72
Brunel Wk, N15 ... 66 DS56
Twickenham TW2
off Stephenson Rd ... 116 CA87
Brunel Way, Slou. SL1 ... 74 AT74
Brune St, E1 ... 197 P7
Brunner Cl, NW11 ... 64 DB57
Brunner Ct, Cher. (Ott.) KT16 ... 151 BC106
Brunner Rd, E17 ... 67 DZ57
W5 ... 79 CK70
Bruno Pl, NW9 ... 62 CQ61
Brunswick Av, N11 ... 44 DG48
Upminster RM14 ... 73 FS59
Brunswick Cl, Bexh. DA6 ... 106 EX84
Pinner HA5 ... 60 BY58
Thames Ditton KT7 ... 137 CF102
Twickenham TW2 ... 117 CD90
Walton-on-Thames KT12 ... 136 BW103
Brunswick Ct, EC1
off Northampton Sq ... 83 DP69
SE1 ... 201 N5
SW1 *off Regency St* ... 101 DK77
Barnet EN4 ... 28 DD43
Upminster RM14
off Waycross Rd ... 73 FS59
Brunswick Cres, N11 ... 44 DG48
Brunswick Gdns, W5 ... 80 CL69
W8 ... 82 DA74
Ilford IG6 ... 49 EQ52
Brunswick Gro, N11 ... 44 DG48
Cobham KT11 ... 154 BW113
Brunswick Ind Pk, N11 ... 45 DH49
Brunswick Ms, SW16
off Potters La ... 121 DK93
W1 ... 194 E8
BRUNSWICK PARK, N11 ... 44 DF47
Brunswick Pk, SE5 ... 102 DR81
Brunswick Pk Gdns, N11 ... 44 DG47
Brunswick Pk Rd, N11 ... 44 DG47
Brunswick Pl, N1 ... 197 L3
NW1 ... 194 G4
SE19 ... 122 DU94
Brunswick Quay, SE16 ... 203 J7
Brunswick Rd, E10 ... 67 EC60
E14
off Blackwall Tunnel
Northern App ... 85 EC72
N15 ... 66 DS57
W5 ... 79 CK70
Bexleyheath DA6 ... 106 EX84
Enfield EN3 ... 31 EA38
Kingston upon Thames
KT2 ... 138 CN95
Sutton SM1 ... 158 DB105
Brunswick Shop Cen, WC1 ... 195 P4
Brunswick Sq, N17 ... 46 DT51
WC1 ... 196 A5
Brunswick St, E17 ... 67 EC57
Brunswick Vil, SE5 ... 102 DS81
Brunswick Wk, Grav. DA12 ... 131 GK87
Brunswick Way, N11 ... 45 DH49
Brunton Pl, E14 ... 85 DY72
Brushfield St, E1 ... 197 N7
Brushrise, Wat. WD24 ... 23 BU36
Brushwood Cl, E14
off Uamvar St ... 85 EB71
Brushwood Dr, Rick. (Chorl.)
WD3 ... 21 BC42
Brussels Rd, SW11 ... 100 DD84
Bruton Cl, Chis. BR7 ... 125 EM94
Bruton La, W1 ... 199 J1
Bruton Pl, W1 ... 199 J1
Bruton Rd, Mord. SM4 ... 140 DC99
Bruton St, W1 ... 199 J1
Bruton Way, W13 ... 79 CG71
Bryan Av, NW10 ... 81 CV66
Bryan Cl, Sun. TW16 ... 115 BU94
Bryan Rd, SE16 ... 203 M4
Bryan's All, SW6
off Wandsworth Br Rd ... 100 DB82
Bryanston Av, Twick. TW2 ... 116 CB88
Bryanston Cl, Sthl. UB2 ... 96 BZ77
Bryanstone Ct, Sutt. SM1
off Oakhill Rd ... 158 DC105
Bryanstone Rd, N8 ... 65 DK57
Waltham Cross EN8 ... 15 DZ34
Bryanston Ms E, W1 ... 194 D7
Bryanston Ms W, W1 ... 194 D7
Bryanston Pl, W1 ... 194 D7
Bryanston Rd, Til. RM18 ... 111 GJ82
Bryanston Sq, W1 ... 194 D7
Bryanston St, W1 ... 194 D9
Bryant Av, Rom. RM3 ... 52 FK53
Bryant Cl, Barn. EN5 ... 27 CZ43
Bryant Ct, E2 ... 84 DT68
Bryant Rd, Nthlt. UB5 ... 78 BW69
Bryant Row, Rom.
(Noak Hill) RM3
off Cummings Hall La ... 52 FJ48
Bryant St, E15 ... 85 ED66
Bryantwood Rd, N7 ... 65 DN64
Brycedale Cres, N14 ... 45 DK49
Bryce Rd, Dag. RM8 ... 70 EW63
Brydale Ho, SE16 ... 203 H8
Bryden Cl, SE26 ... 123 DY92
Brydges Pl, WC2 ... 199 P1
Brydges Rd, E15 ... 67 ED64
Brydon Wk, N1 *off Outram Pl* ... 83 DL67
Bryer Ct, EC2
off Aldersgate St ... 84 DQ71
Bryett Rd, N7 ... 65 DL62
Brymay Cl, E3 ... 85 EA68
Brynford Cl, Wok. GU21 ... 166 AY115
Brynmaer Rd, SW11 ... 100 DF81
Bryn-y-Mawr Rd, Enf. EN1 ... 30 DT42
Bryony Cl, Loug. IG10 ... 33 EP42
Uxbridge UB8 ... 76 BM71
Bryony Rd, W12 ... 81 CU73
Bryony Way, Sun. TW16 ... 115 BT93
Bubblestone Rd, Sev. (Otford)
TN14 ... 181 FH116
Buccleuch Rd, Slou. (Datchet)
SL3 ... 92 AU80
Buchanan Cl, N21 ... 29 DM43
South Ockendon (Aveley)
RM15 ... 90 FQ74
Buchanan Ct, Borwd. WD6 ... 26 CQ40
Buchanan Gdns, NW10 ... 81 CV68
Buchan Cl, Uxb. UB8 ... 76 BJ69
Buchan Rd, SE15 ... 102 DW83
Bucharest Rd, SW18 ... 120 DC87
Buckbean Path, Rom. RM3
off Clematis Cl ... 52 FJ52
Buckden Cl, N2
off Southern Rd ... 64 DF56
SE12 *off Upwood Rd* ... 124 EF86
Buckettsland La, Borwd. WD6 ... 26 CR38
Buckfast Ct, W13
off Romsey Rd ... 79 CG73
Buckfast Rd, Mord. SM4 ... 140 DB98
Buckfast St, E2 ... 84 DU69
Buckham Thorns Rd, West.
TN16 ... 189 EQ126
Buck Hill Wk, W2 ... 198 A1
Buckhold Rd, SW18 ... 120 DA86
Buckhurst Av, Cars. SM5 ... 140 DE102
Sevenoaks TN13 ... 191 FJ125
Buckhurst Cl, Red. RH1 ... 184 DE132
BUCKHURST HILL, IG9 ... 48 EH45
⊖ **Buckhurst Hill** ... 48 EK47
Buckhurst La, Sev. TN13 ... 191 FJ125
Buckhurst Rd, West. TN16 ... 179 EN121
Buckhurst St, E1 ... 84 DV70
Buckhurst Way, Buck.H. IG9 ... 48 EK49
Buckingham Arc, WC2 ... 200 A1
Buckingham Av, N20 ... 44 DC45
Feltham TW14 ... 115 BV86
Greenford UB6 ... 79 CG67
Thornton Heath CR7 ... 141 DN95
Welling DA16 ... 105 ES84
West Molesey KT8 ... 136 CB97
Buckingham Cl, W5 ... 79 CJ71
Enfield EN1 ... 30 DS40
Hampton TW12 ... 116 BZ92
Hornchurch RM11 ... 72 FK58
Orpington BR5 ... 145 ES101
Buckingham Ct, NW4 ... 63 CU55
Loughton IG10
off Rectory La ... 33 EN40
Buckingham Dr, Chis. BR7 ... 125 EP92
Buckingham Gdns, Edg. HA8 ... 42 CM52
Slough SL1 ... 92 AT75
Thornton Heath CR7 ... 141 DN96
West Molesey KT8
off Buckingham Av ... 136 CB96
Buckingham Gate, SW1 ... 199 K5
Buckingham Gro, Uxb. UB10 ... 76 BN68
Buckingham La, SE23 ... 123 DY87
Buckingham Lo, N10
off Muswell Hill ... 65 DJ56
Buckingham Ms, N1
off Buckingham Rd ... 84 DS65
NW10 *off Buckingham Rd* ... 81 CT68
SW1 ... 199 K6
★ **Buckingham Palace**,
SW1 ... 199 J5
Buckingham Palace Rd,
SW1 ... 199 H9
Buckingham Pl, SW1 ... 199 K6
Buckingham Rd, E10 ... 67 EB62
E11 ... 68 EJ57
E15 ... 68 EF64
E18 ... 48 EF53
N1 ... 84 DS65
N22 ... 45 DL53
NW10 ... 81 CT68
Borehamwood WD6 ... 26 CR42
Edgware HA8 ... 42 CM52
Gravesend DA11
off Dover Rd ... 130 GD87
Hampton TW12 ... 116 BZ91
Harrow HA1 ... 61 CD57
Ilford IG1 ... 69 ER61
Kingston upon Thames
KT1 ... 138 CM98
Mitcham CR4 ... 141 DL99
Richmond TW10 ... 117 CK89
Watford WD24 ... 24 BW37
Buckingham St, WC2 ... 200 A1
Buckingham Way, Wall. SM6 ... 159 DJ109
BUCKLAND, Bet. RH3 ... 183 CU133
Buckland Av, Slou. SL3 ... 92 AV77
Buckland Cl, NW7 ... 43 CU49
Buckland Ct Gdns, Bet. RH3 ... 183 CU133
Buckland Cres, NW3 ... 82 DD66

★ Place of interest ⇌ Railway station ⊖ London Underground station DLR Docklands Light Railway station Tra Tramlink station H Hospital Riv Pedestrian ferry landing stage

Buckland Gate, Slou. (Wexham) SL3 74 AV68
Buckland La, Bet. RH3 183 CT129
Tadworth KT20 183 CT129
Buckland Ri, Pnr. HA5 40 BW53
Buckland Rd, E10 67 EC61
Chessington KT9 156 CM106
Orpington BR6 163 ES105
Reigate RH2 183 CX133
Sutton SM2 157 CW110
Tadworth (Lwr Kgswd) KT20 183 CZ128
Bucklands, The, Rick. WD3 38 BG45
Bucklands Rd, Tedd. TW11 117 CJ93
Buckland St, N1 197 L1
Buckland Wk, W3 98 CQ75
Morden SM4 140 DC98
Buckland Way, Wor.Pk. KT4 139 CW102
Buck La, NW9 62 CR57
Bucklebury, NW1 195 K4
Buckleigh Av, SW20 139 CY97
Buckleigh Rd, SW16 121 DK93
Buckleigh Way, SE19 142 DT95
Buckler Gdns, SE9 off Southold Ri 125 EM90
Bucklers All, SW6 99 CZ79
Bucklersbury, EC4 197 K9
Bucklersbury Pas, EC4 197 K9
Bucklers Ct, Brwd. CM14 54 FW50
Bucklers Way, Cars. SM5 140 DF104
Buckles Ct, Belv. DA17 off Fendyke Rd 106 EX76
Buckles La, S.Ock. RM15 91 FW71
Buckle St, E1 off Leman St 84 DT72
Buckles Way, Bans. SM7 173 CY116
Buckley Cl, SE23 122 DV87
Dartford DA1 107 FF82
Buckley Rd, NW6 81 CZ66
Buckley St, SE1 200 D3
Buckmaster Cl, SW9 off Stockwell Pk Rd 101 DM83
Buckmaster Rd, SW11 100 DE84
Bucknalls Cl, Wat. WD25 8 BY32
Bucknalls Dr, St.Alb. (Brick.Wd) AL2 8 BZ31
Bucknalls La, Wat. WD25 8 BX32
Bucknall St, WC2 195 N8
Bucknall Way, Beck. BR3 143 EB98
Bucknell Cl, SW2 101 DM84
Buckner Rd, SW2 101 DM84
Bucknills Cl, Epsom KT18 156 CP114
Buckrell Rd, E4 47 ED47
Bucks Av, Wat. WD19 40 BY45
Bucks Cl, W.Byf. KT14 152 BH114
Bucks Cross Rd, Grav. (Nthflt) DA11 131 GF90
Orpington BR6 164 EY106
BUCKS HILL, Kings L. WD4 6 BK34
Bucks Hill, Kings L. WD4 6 BK34
Buckstone Cl, SE23 122 DW86
Buckstone Rd, N18 46 DU51
Buck St, NW1 83 DH66
Buckters Rents, SE16 203 K3
Buckthorne Ho, Chig. IG7 50 EV49
Buckthorne Rd, SE4 123 DY86
Buckton Rd, Borwd. WD6 26 CM38
Buck Wk, E17 off Wood St 67 ED56
Budd Cl, N12 44 DB49
Buddings Circle, Wem. HA9 62 CQ62
Budd's All, Twick. TW1 off Arlington Cl 117 CJ85
Budebury Rd, Stai. TW18 114 BG92
Bude Cl, E17 67 DZ57
Budge La, Mitch. CR4 140 DF101
Budgen Dr, Red. RH1 184 DG131
Budge Row, EC4 197 K10
Budge's Wk, W2 82 DC73
Budgin's Hill, Orp. BR6 164 EW112
Budleigh Cres, Well. DA16 106 EW81
Budoch Ct, Ilf. IG3 70 EU61
Budoch Dr, Ilf. IG3 70 EU61
Buer Rd, SW6 99 CY82
Buff Av, Bans. SM7 158 DB114
Buffers La, Lthd. KT22 off Kingston Rd 171 CG119
Bug Hill, Cat. (Wold.) CR3 177 DX120
Bugsby's Way, SE7 205 N9
SE10 205 K8
Buick Ho, Kings.T. KT2 off London Rd 138 CN96
Building 22, SE18 off Carriage St 105 EP76
Building 36, SE18 off Marlborough Rd 105 EQ76
Building 45, SE18 off Hopton Rd 105 EP76
Building 47, SE18 off Marlborough Rd 105 EQ76
Building 48, SE18 off Marlborough Rd 105 EQ76
Building 49, SE18 off Argyll Rd 105 EQ76
Building 50, SE18 off Argyll Rd 105 EQ76
Bulganak Rd, Th.Hth. CR7 142 DQ98
Bulinga St, SW1 199 N9
Bulkeley Cl, Egh. (Eng.Grn) TW20 112 AW91
Bullace La, Dart. DA1 off High St 128 FL86
Bullace Row, SE5 102 DR80
Bull All, Well. DA16 off Welling High St 106 EV83
Bullards Pl, E2 85 DX69
Bullbanks Rd, Belv. DA17 107 FC77
Bullbeggars La, Gdse. RH9 186 DW132
Woking GU21 166 AV116
Bull Cl, Grays RM16 110 FZ75
Bullen Ho, E1 off Collingwood St 84 DV70
Bullen St, SW11 100 DE82
Buller Cl, SE15 102 DU80
Buller Rd, N17 46 DU54
N22 45 DN54
NW10 off Chamberlayne Rd 81 CX69
Barking IG11 87 ES66
Thornton Heath CR7 142 DR96
Bullers Cl, Sid. DA14 126 EY92
Bullers Wd Dr, Chis. BR7 124 EL94
Bullescroft Rd, Edg. HA8 42 CN48
Bullfinch Cl, Sev. TN13 190 FD122
Bullfinch Dene, Sev. TN13 190 FD122
Bullfinch La, Sev. TN13 190 FD122
Bullfinch Rd, S.Croy. CR2 161 DX110
Bullhead Rd, Borwd. WD6 26 CQ41
Bull Hill, Dart. (Hort.Kir.) DA4 148 FQ98
Leatherhead KT22 171 CG121
Bullied Way, SW1 199 J9
Bull Inn Ct, WC2 200 A1
Bullivant Cl, Green. DA9 129 FU85
Bullivant St, E14 85 EC73
Bull La, N18 46 DS50
Chislehurst BR7 125 ER94
Dagenham RM10 71 FB62
Gerrards Cross SL9 56 AX55
Bull Rd, E15 86 EF68
Bullrush Cl, Croy. CR0 142 DS100
Bullrush Gro, Uxb. UB8 76 BJ70
Bull's All, SW14 98 CR82
Bulls Br Ind Est, Sthl. UB2 95 BV77
Bulls Br Rd, Sthl. UB2 95 BV76
Bullsbrook Rd, Hayes UB4 78 BW74
BULLS CROSS, Wal.Cr. EN7 30 DT35
Bulls Cross, Enf. EN2 30 DU37
Bulls Cross Ride, Wal.Cr. EN7 30 DU35
Bulls Gdns, SW3 198 C8
Bull's Head Pas, EC3 197 M9
Bullsland Gdns, Rick. (Chorl.) WD3 21 BB44
Bullsland La, Ger.Cr. SL9 37 BB45
Rickmansworth (Chorl.) WD3 21 BB44
BULLSMOOR, Enf. EN1 30 DV37
Bullsmoor Cl, Wal.Cr. EN8 30 DW35
Bullsmoor Gdns, Wal.Cr. EN8 30 DV35
Bullsmoor La, Enf. EN1, EN3 30 DW35
Waltham Cross EN7 30 DU35
Bullsmoor Ride, Wal.Cr. EN8 30 DW35
Bullsmoor Way, Wal.Cr. EN8 30 DV35
Bullwell Cres, Wal.Cr. (Chsht) EN8 15 DY29
Bull Yd, SE15 off Peckham High St 102 DU81
Gravesend DA12 off High St 131 GH86
Bulmer Gdns, Har. HA3 61 CK59
Bulmer Ms, W11 off Ladbroke Rd 82 DA73
Bulmer Pl, W11 82 DA74
Bulmer Wk, Rain. RM13 90 FJ68
Bulow Est, SW6 off Broughton Rd 100 DB81
Bulrush Cl, Cars. SM5 140 DE103
Bulstrode Av, Houns. TW3 96 BZ82
Bulstrode Ct, Ger.Cr. SL9 56 AX58
Bulstrode Gdns, Houns. TW3 96 BZ83
Bulstrode La, Hem.H. (Felden) HP3 6 BG27
Kings Langley (Chipper.) WD4 5 BE29
Bulstrode Pl, W1 194 G7
Slough SL1 92 AT76
Bulstrode Rd, Houns. TW3 96 CA83
Bulstrode St, W1 194 G8
Bulstrode Way, Ger.Cr. SL9 56 AX57
Bulwer Ct Rd, E11 67 ED60
Bulwer Gdns, Barn. EN5 off Bulwer Rd 28 DC42
Bulwer Rd, E11 67 ED59
N18 46 DS49
Barnet EN5 28 DB42
Bulwer St, W12 81 CW74
Bumbles Grn La, Wal.Abb. EN9 16 EH25
Bunbury Way, Epsom KT17 173 CV116
Bunby Rd, Slou. (Stoke P.) SL2 74 AT66
Bunce Dr, Cat. CR3 176 DR123
Bunces La, Wdf.Grn. IG8 48 EF52
Bundys Way, Stai. TW18 113 BF93
Bungalow Rd, SE25 142 DS98
Woking GU23 169 BQ124
Bungalows, The, SW16 121 DH94
Wallington SM6 159 DH106
Bunhill Row, EC1 197 K4
Bunhouse Pl, SW1 198 F10
Bunkers Hill, NW11 64 DC59
Belvedere DA17 106 FA77
Sidcup DA14 126 EZ90
Bunning Way, N7 83 DL66
Bunns La, NW7 43 CT51
Bunn's La, Chesh. HP5 4 AU34
Bunsen St, E3 off Kenilworth Rd 85 DY68
Buntingbridge Rd, Ilf. IG2 69 ER57
Bunting Cl, N9 off Dunnock Cl 47 DX46
Mitcham CR4 140 DF99
Bunton St, SE18 105 EN76
Bunyan Ct, EC2 off Beech St 84 DQ71
Bunyan Rd, E17 67 DY55
Bunyard Dr, Wok. GU21 151 BC114
Bunyons Cl, Brwd. (Gt Warley) CM13 53 FW51
Buonaparte Ms, SW1 199 M10
H BUPA Bushey Hosp, Bushey WD23 41 CF46
H BUPA Hartswood Hosp, Brwd. CM13 53 FV51
H BUPA Roding Hosp, Ilf. IG4 68 EK55
Burbage Cl, SE1 201 K7
Hayes UB3 77 BR72
Waltham Cross (Chsht) EN8 15 DZ31
Burbage Rd, SE21 122 DR86
SE24 122 DQ86
Burberry Cl, N.Mal. KT3 138 CS96
Burbidge Rd, Shep. TW17 134 BN98
Burbridge Way, N17 46 DT54
Burcham St, E14 85 EB72
Burcharbro Rd, SE2 106 EX79
Burchell Ct, Bushey WD23 off Catsey La 40 CC45
Burchell Rd, E10 67 EB60
SE15 102 DV81
Burchetts Way, Shep. TW17 135 BP100
Burchett Way, Rom. RM6 70 EZ58
Burch Rd, Grav. (Nthflt) DA11 131 GF86
Burchwall Cl, Rom. RM5 51 FC52
Burcote, Wey. KT13 153 BR107
Burcote Rd, SW18 120 DD88
Burcott Gdns, Add. KT15 152 BJ107
Burcott Rd, Pur. CR8 159 DN114
Burden Cl, Brent. TW8 97 CJ78
Burdenshott Av, Rich. TW10 98 CP84
Burden Way, E11 off Brading Cres 68 EH61
Burder Cl, N1 84 DS65
Burder Rd, N1 off Balls Pond Rd 84 DS65
Burdett Av, SW20 139 CU95
Burdett Cl, W7 off Cherington Rd 97 CF75
Sidcup DA14 126 EY92
Burdett Ms, NW3 off Belsize Cres 82 DD65
W2 off Hatherley Gro 82 DB72
Burdett Rd, E3 85 DZ70
E14 85 DZ70
Croydon CR0 142 DR100
Richmond TW9 98 CM83
Burdetts Rd, Dag. RM9 88 EZ67
Burdett St, SE1 200 D6
Burdock Cl, Croy. CR0 143 DX102
Burdock Rd, N17 66 DU55
Burdon La, Sutt. SM2 157 CY108
Burdon Pk, Sutt. SM2 157 CZ109
Burfield Cl, SW17 120 DD91
Burfield Dr, Warl. CR6 176 DW119
Burfield Rd, Rick. (Chorl.) WD3 21 BB43
Windsor (Old Wind.) SL4 112 AU86
Burford Cl, Dag. RM8 70 EW62
Ilford IG6 69 EQ56
Uxbridge UB10 58 BL63
Burford Gdns, N13 45 DM48
Burford La, Epsom KT17 157 CW111
Burford Rd, E6 86 EL69
E15 85 ED66
SE6 123 DZ89
Brentford TW8 98 CL78
Bromley BR1 144 EL98
Sutton SM1 140 DA103
Worcester Park KT4 139 CT101
Burford Wk, SW6 off Cambria St 100 DB80
Burford Way, Croy. (New Adgtn) CR0 161 EC107
Burford Wf Apts, E15 off Cam Rd 85 ED67
Burgate Cl, Dart. DA1 107 FF83
Burges Cl, Horn. RM11 72 FM58
Burges Ct, E6 87 EN66
Burges Gro, SW13 99 CV80
Burges Rd, E6 86 EL66
Burgess Av, NW9 62 CR58
Burgess Business Pk, SE5 102 DR80
Burgess Cl, Felt. TW13 116 BY91
Waltham Cross (Chsht) EN7 14 DQ25
Burgess Ct, Borwd. WD6 off Belford Rd 26 CM38
Burgess Hill, NW2 64 DA63
Burgess Rd, E15 68 EE63
Sutton SM1 158 DB105
Burgess St, E14 85 EA71
Burge St, SE1 201 L7
Burges Way, Stai. TW18 114 BG92
Burghfield, Epsom KT17 173 CT115
Burghfield Rd, Grav. (Istead Rise) DA13 131 GF94
BURGH HEATH, Tad. KT20 173 CX119
Burgh Heath Rd, Epsom KT17 156 CS114
★ Burgh Ho, Hampstead Mus, NW3 off New End Sq 64 DD63
Burghill Rd, SE26 123 DY91
Burghley Av, Borwd. WD6 26 CQ43
New Malden KT3 138 CR95
Burghley Hall Cl, SW19 119 CY87
Burghley Ho, SW19 119 CY90
Burghley Pl, Mitch. CR4 140 DG99
Burghley Rd, E11 68 EE60
N8 65 DN55
NW5 65 DH64
SW19 119 CX91
Grays (Chaff.Hun.) RM16 109 FW76
Burghley Twr, W3 81 CT73
Burgh Mt, Bans. SM7 173 CZ115
Burgh St, N1 83 DP68
Burgh Wd, Bans. SM7 173 CY115
Burgon St, EC4 196 G9
Burgos Cl, Croy. CR0 159 DN107
Burgos Gro, SE10 103 EB81
Burgoyne Rd, N4 65 DP58
SE25 142 DT98
SW9 101 DM83
Sunbury-on-Thames TW16 115 BT93
Burham Cl, SE20 off Maple Rd 122 DW94
Burhill Gro, Pnr. HA5 40 BY54
Burhill Rd, Walt. KT12 154 BW107
Burke Cl, SW15 98 CS84
Burke Ho, SW11 off Maysoule Rd 100 DD84
Burke St, E16 86 EF72
Burket Cl, Sthl. UB2 off Kingsbridge Rd 96 BZ77
Burland Rd, SW11 120 DF85
Brentwood CM15 54 FX46
Romford RM5 51 FC51
Burlea Cl, Walt. KT12 153 BV106
Burleigh Av, Sid. DA15 125 ET85
Wallington SM6 140 DG104
Burleigh Cl, Add. KT15 152 BH106
Romford RM7 71 FB56
Burleigh Gdns, N14 45 DJ46
Ashford TW15 115 BQ92
Burleigh Ho, W10 off St. Charles Sq 81 CX71
Burleigh Pk, Cob. KT11 154 BY112
Burleigh Pl, SW15 119 CX85
Burleigh Rd, Add. KT15 152 BH105
Enfield EN1 30 DS42
Sutton SM3 139 CY102
Uxbridge UB10 77 BP67
Waltham Cross (Chsht) EN8 15 DY32
Burleigh St, WC2 196 B10
Burleigh Wk, SE6 off Muirkirk Rd 123 EC88
Burleigh Way, Enf. EN2 off Church St 30 DR41
Potters Bar (Cuffley) EN6 13 DL30
Burley Cl, E4 47 EA50
SW16 141 DK96
Burley Orchard, Cher. KT16 134 BG100
Burley Rd, E16 86 EJ72
Burlings La, Sev. (Knock.) TN14 179 ET118
Burlington Arc, W1 199 K1
Burlington Av, Rich. TW9 98 CN81
Romford RM7 71 FB58
Slough SL1 92 AS75
Burlington Cl, E6 off Northumberland Rd 86 EL72
W9 81 CZ70
Feltham TW14 115 BR87
Orpington BR6 145 EP103
Pinner HA5 59 BV55
Burlington Gdns, W1 199 K1
W3 80 CQ74
W4 98 CQ78
Romford RM6 70 EY59
Burlington La, W4 98 CS80
Burlington Ms, SW15 119 CZ85
W3 80 CQ74
Burlington Pl, SW6 off Burlington Rd 99 CY82
Reigate RH2 184 DA134
Woodford Green IG8 48 EG48
Burlington Ri, Barn. EN4 44 DE46
Burlington Rd, N10 off Tetherdown 44 DG54
N17 46 DU53
SW6 99 CY82
W4 98 CQ78
Enfield EN2 30 DR39
Isleworth TW7 97 CD81
New Malden KT3 139 CU98
Slough SL1 92 AS75
Thornton Heath CR7 142 DQ96
Burman Cl, Dart. DA2 128 FQ87
Burma Rd, N16 66 DR63
Chertsey (Longcr.) KT16 132 AT104
Burmester Rd, SW17 120 DC90
Burnaby Cres, W4 98 CP79
Burnaby Gdns, W4 98 CQ79
Burnaby Rd, Grav. (Nthflt) DA11 130 GE87
Burnaby St, SW10 100 DC80
Burnbrae Cl, N12 44 DB51
Burnbury Rd, SW12 121 DJ88
Burn Cl, Add. KT15 152 BK105
Leatherhead (Oxshott) KT22 170 CC115
Burncroft Av, Enf. EN3 30 DW40
Burndell Way, Hayes UB4 78 BX71
Burne Jones Ho, W14 99 CZ77
Burnell Av, Rich. TW10 117 CJ92
Welling DA16 106 EU82
Burnell Gdns, Stan. HA7 41 CK53
Burnell Rd, Sutt. SM1 158 DB105
Burnell Wk, SE1 202 A10
Brentwood CM13 53 FW51
Burnels Av, E6 87 EN69
Burness Cl, N7 off Roman Way 83 DM65
Uxbridge UB8 off Whitehall Rd 76 BK68
Burne St, NW1 194 B6
Burnet Gro, Epsom KT19 156 CQ113
Burnett Cl, E9 66 DW64
Burnett Rd, Erith DA8 108 FK79
Burney Av, Surb. KT5 138 CM99
Burney Dr, Loug. IG10 33 EP40
Burney St, SE10 103 EC80
Burnfoot Av, SW6 99 CY81
Burnfoot Ct, SE22 122 DV88
Burnham, NW3 82 DE66
Burnham Av, Uxb. UB10 59 BQ63
Burnham Cl, NW7 43 CU52
SE1 202 A9
Enfield EN1 30 DS38
Harrow (Wealds.) HA3 61 CG56
Burnham Ct, NW4 63 CW56
Burnham Cres, E11 68 EJ56
Dartford DA1 108 FJ84
Burnham Dr, Reig. RH2 184 DA133
Worcester Park KT4 139 CX103
Burnham Gdns, Croy. CR0 142 DT101
Hayes UB3 95 BR76
Hounslow TW4 95 BV81
Burnham Gro, Epsom KT19 156 CP111
Burnham Rd, E4 47 DZ50
Dagenham RM9 88 EV66
Dartford DA1 108 FJ84
Morden SM4 140 DB99
Romford RM7 71 FD55
Sidcup DA14 126 EY89
Burnhams Rd, Lthd. (Bkhm) KT23 170 BY124
Burnham St, E2 84 DW69
Kingston upon Thames KT2 138 CN95
Burnham Way, SE26 123 DZ92
W13 97 CH77
Burnhill Cl, SE15 off Gervase St 102 DV80
Burnhill Rd, Beck. BR3 143 EA96
Burnley Cl, Wat. WD19 40 BW50
Burnley Rd, NW10 63 CU64
SW9 101 DM82
Grays RM20 109 FT81
Burnsall St, SW3 198 C10
Burns Av, Felt. TW14 115 BU86
Romford (Chad.Hth) RM6 70 EW59
Sidcup DA15 126 EV86
Southall UB1 78 CA73
Burns Cl, E17 67 EC56
SW19 120 DD93
Carshalton SM5 158 DG109
Erith DA8 107 FF81
Hayes UB4 77 BT71
Welling DA16 105 ET81
Burns Dr, Bans. SM7 157 CY114
Burnside, Ashtd. KT21 172 CM118
Burnside Av, E4 47 DZ51
Burnside Cl, SE16 203 J2
Barnet EN5 28 DA41
Twickenham TW1 117 CG86
Burnside Cres, Wem. HA0 79 CK67
Burnside Rd, Dag. RM8 70 EW61
Burns Pl, Til. RM18 111 GH81
Burns Rd, NW10 81 CT67
SW11 100 DF82
W13 97 CH75
Wembley HA0 79 CK68
Burns Ter, Esher KT10 off Farm Rd 136 CB103
Burns Way, Brwd. (Hutt.) CM13 55 GD45
Hounslow TW5 96 BX82
Burnt Ash Hill, SE12 124 EF86
Burnt Ash La, Brom. BR1 124 EG93
Burnt Ash Rd, SE12 124 EF85
Burnt Fm Ride, Enf. EN2 13 DP34
Waltham Cross EN7 13 DP31
Burnt Ho La, Dart. (Hawley) DA2 128 FL91
Burnthwaite Rd, SW6 100 DA80
BURNT OAK, Edg. HA8 42 CQ52
⊖ Burnt Oak 42 CQ53
Burnt Oak Bdy, Edg. HA8 42 CP52
Burnt Oak Flds, Edg. HA8 42 CQ53
Burnt Oak La, Sid. DA15 126 EU86
Burntwood, Brwd. CM14 54 FW48
Burntwood Av, Horn. RM11 72 FK58
Burntwood Cl, SW18 120 DD88
Caterham CR3 176 DU121
Burntwood Gra Rd, SW18 120 DD88
Burntwood Gro, Sev. TN13 191 FH127
Burntwood La, SW17 120 DE89
Caterham CR3 176 DU121
Burntwood Rd, Sev. TN13 191 FH128
Burntwood Vw, SE19 off Bowley La 122 DT92
Burnway, Horn. RM11 72 FL59
Buross St, E1 off Commercial Rd 84 DV72
Burpham Cl, Hayes UB4 78 BX71
Burrage Gro, SE18 105 EQ77
Burrage Pl, SE18 105 EP78
Burrage Rd, SE18 105 EQ79
Burrard Rd, E16 86 EH72
NW6 64 DA64
Burr Cl, E1 202 B2
Bexleyheath DA7 106 EZ83
St. Albans (Lon.Col.) AL2 10 CL27
Burrell Cl, Croy. CR0 143 DY100
Edgware HA8 42 CP47
Burrell Row, Beck. BR3 off High St 143 EA96
Burrell St, SE1 200 F2
Burrells Wf Sq, E14 204 B10
Burrell Twr, E10 67 EA59
Burrfield Dr, Orp. BR5 146 EX99
Burr Hill La, Wok. (Chobham) GU24 150 AS109
Burritt Rd, Kings.T. KT1 138 CN96
Burroughs, The, NW4 63 CV57
Burroughs Gdns, NW4 63 CV56
Burroughs Par, NW4 off The Burroughs 63 CV56
Burroway Rd, Slou. SL3 93 BB76
Burrow Cl, Chig. IG7 off Burrow Rd 49 ET50
Burrow Grn, Chig. IG7 49 ET50
BURROWHILL, Wok. GU24 150 AS108
Burrow Rd, SE22 102 DS84
Chigwell IG7 49 ET50
Burrows Chase, Wal.Abb. EN9 31 ED36
Burrows Cl, Lthd. (Bkhm) KT23 170 BZ124
Burrows Ms, SE1 200 F4
Burrows Rd, NW10 81 CW69
Burrow Wk, SE21 off Rosendale Rd 122 DQ87
Burr Rd, SW18 120 DA87
Bursdon Cl, Sid. DA15 125 ET89
Burses Way, Brwd. (Hutt.) CM13 55 GB45
Bursland Rd, Enf. EN3 31 DX42
Burslem Av, Ilf. IG6 50 EU51
Burslem St, E1 84 DU72
Burstead Cl, Cob. KT11 154 BX113
Burstock Rd, SW15 99 CY84
Burston Dr, St.Alb. (Park St) AL2 8 CC28
Burston Rd, SW15 119 CX85
Burston Vil, SW15 off St. John's Av 119 CX85
Burstow Rd, SW20 139 CY95
Burtenshaw Rd, T.Ditt. KT7 137 CG101
Burtley Cl, N4 66 DQ60
Burton Av, Wat. WD18 23 BU42
Burton Cl, Chess. KT9 155 CK108
Thornton Heath CR7 142 DR97
Burton Ct, SW3 off Franklin's Row 100 DF78
Burton Dr, Enf. EN3 31 EA37
Burton Gdns, Houns. TW5 96 BZ81
Burton Gro, SE17 off Portland St 102 DR78
Burtonhole Cl, NW7 43 CX49
Burtonhole La, NW7 43 CY49
Burton La, SW9 101 DN82
Waltham Cross (Chsht) EN7 14 DS29
Burton Ms, SW1 198 G9
Burton Pl, WC1 195 N3
Burton Rd, E18 68 EH55
NW6 81 CZ66
SW9 101 DP82
Kingston upon Thames KT2 118 CL94
Loughton IG10 33 EQ42
Burtons La, Ch.St.G. HP8 21 AZ43
Rickmansworth WD3 21 AZ43
Burtons Rd, Hmptn. (Hmptn H.) TW12 116 CB91
Burton St, WC1 195 N3
Burtons Way, Ch.St.G. HP8 20 AW40
Burtwell La, SE27 122 DR91
Burwash Ct, Orp. BR5 off Rookery Gdns 146 EW99
Burwash Ho, SE1 201 L5
Burwash Rd, SE18 105 ER78
Burway Cres, Cher. KT16 134 BG97
Burwell Av, Grnf. UB6 79 CE65
Burwell Cl, E1 off Bigland St 84 DV72
Burwell Rd, E10 67 DY60
Burwell Wk, E3 85 EA70
Burwood Av, Brom. BR2 144 EH103
Kenley CR8 159 DP114
Pinner HA5 60 BW57
Burwood Cl, Reig. RH2 184 DD134
Surbiton KT6 138 CN102
Walton-on-Thames KT12 154 BW107
Burwood Gdns, Rain. RM13 89 FF69

★ Place of interest | Railway station | ⊖ London Underground station | DLR Docklands Light Railway station | Tramlink station | H Hospital | Pedestrian ferry landing stage

BURWOOD PARK, Walt. KT12 ...153 BT106
Burwood Pk Rd, Walt. KT12 .153 BV105
Burwood Pl, W2 ...194 C8
Burwood Rd, Walt. KT12 ...153 BV107
Bury Av, Hayes UB4 ...77 BS68
Ruislip HA4 ...59 BQ58
Bury Cl, SE16 ...203 J2
Woking GU21 ...166 AX116
Bury Ct, EC3 ...197 N8
Burydell La, St.Alb. (Park St) AL2 ...9 CD27
BURY GREEN, Wal.Cr. EN7 ...14 DV31
Bury Grn Rd, Wal.Cr. (Chsht) EN7 ...14 DU31
Bury Gro, Mord. SM4 ...140 DB99
Bury La, Epp. CM16 ...17 ES31
Rickmansworth WD3 ...38 BK46
Woking GU21 ...166 AW116
Bury Meadows, Rick. WD3 ...38 BK46
Bury Pl, WC1 ...195 P7
Bury Ri, Hem.H. HP3 ...5 BD25
Bury Rd, E4 ...32 EE43
N22 ...65 DN55
Dagenham RM10 ...71 FB64
Epping CM16 ...17 ES31
Buryside Cl, Ilf. IG2 ...69 ET56
Bury St, EC3 ...197 N9
N9 ...46 DU46
SW1 ...199 K2
Ruislip HA4 ...59 BQ57
Bury St W, N9 ...46 DR45
Bury Wk, SW3 ...198 B9
Busbridge Ho, E14 off Brabazon St ...85 EA71
Busby Ms, NW5 off Busby Pl .83 DK65
Busby Pl, NW5 ...83 DK65
Busby St, E2 off Chilton St ...84 DT70
Bushbaby Cl, SE1 ...201 M7
Bushbarns, Wal.Cr. (Chsht) EN7 ...14 DU29
Bushberry Rd, E9 ...85 DY65
Bush Cl, Add. KT15 ...152 BJ106
Ilford IG2 ...69 ER57
Bush Cotts, SW18 off Putney Br Rd ...120 DA85
Bush Ct, W12 off Shepherds Bush Grn ..99 CX75
Bushell Cl, SW2 ...121 DM89
Bushell Grn, Bushey (Bushey Hth) WD23 ...41 CD47
Bushell St, E1 ...202 C3
Bushell Way, Chis. BR7 ...125 EN92
Bush Elms Rd, Horn. RM11 ...71 FG59
Bushetts Gro, Red. (Merst.) RH1 ...185 DH129
BUSHEY, WD23 ...40 CA45
⇌ Bushey ...24 BX44
Bushey Av, E18 ...68 EF55
Orpington BR5 ...145 ER101
Bushey Cl, E4 ...47 EC48
Kenley CR8 ...176 DS116
Uxbridge UB10 ...59 BP61
Bushey Ct, SW20 ...139 CV96
Bushey Cft, Oxt. RH8 ...187 EC130
Bushey Down, SW12 off Bedford Hill ...121 DH89
Bushey Gro Rd, Bushey WD23 ...24 BX42
Bushey Hall Dr, Bushey WD23 ...24 BY42
Bushey Hall Rd, Bushey WD23 ...24 BX42
BUSHEY HEATH, Bushey WD23 ...41 CE46
Bushey Hill Rd, SE5 ...102 DS81
Bushey La, Sutt. SM1 ...158 DA105
Bushey Lees, Sid. DA15 off Fen Gro ...125 ET86
BUSHEY MEAD, SW20 ...139 CX97
Bushey Mill Cres, Wat. WD24 .24 BW37
Bushey Mill La, Bushey WD23 .24 BZ40
Watford WD24 ...24 BW37
Bushey Rd, E13 ...86 EJ68
N15 ...66 DS58
SW20 ...139 CV97
Croydon CR0 ...143 EA103
Hayes UB3 ...95 BS77
Sutton SM1 ...158 DB105
Uxbridge UB10 ...58 BN61
Bushey Shaw, Ashtd. KT21 ...171 CH117
Bushey Vw Wk, Wat. WD24 ...24 BX40
Bushey Way, Beck. BR3 ...143 ED100
Bushfield Cl, Edg. HA8 ...42 CP47
Bushfield Cres, Edg. HA8 ...42 CP47
Bushfield Rd, Hem.H. (Bov.) HP3 ...5 BC25
Bushfields, Loug. IG10 ...33 EN43
Bushfield Wk, Swans. DA10 ...130 FY86
Bush Gro, NW9 ...62 CQ59
Stanmore HA7 ...41 CK53
Bushgrove Rd, Dag. RM8 ...70 EX63
Bush Hill, N21 ...46 DQ45
BUSH HILL PARK, Enf. EN1 ...30 DS43
⇌ Bush Hill Park ...30 DT44
Bush Hill Rd, N21 ...30 DR44
Harrow HA3 ...62 CM58
Bush Ind Est, NW10 ...80 CR70
Bush La, EC4 ...197 K10
Woking (Send) GU23 ...167 BD124
Bushmead Cl, N15 off Copperfield Dr ...66 DT56
Bushmoor Cres, SE18 ...105 EQ80
Bushnell Rd, SW17 ...121 DH89
Bush Rd, E8 ...84 DV67
E11 ...68 EF59
SE8 ...203 J8
Buckhurst Hill IG9 ...48 EK49
Richmond TW9 ...98 CM79
Shepperton TW17 ...134 BM99
Bushway, Dag. RM8 ...70 EX63
Bushwood, E11 ...68 EF60
Bushwood Dr, SE1 ...202 A9
Bushwood Rd, Rich. TW9 ...98 CN79
★ Bushy Park, Tedd. TW11 ...137 CF95
Bushy Pk, Hmptn. (Hmptn H.) TW12 ...137 CF95
Teddington TW11 ...137 CF95
Bushy Pk Gdns, Tedd. TW11 ..117 CD92
Bushy Pk Rd, Tedd. TW11 ...117 CH94
Bushy Rd, Lthd. (Fetch.) KT22 ...170 CB122
Teddington TW11 ...117 CF93
★ Business Design Cen, N1 .83 DN67
Business Village, The, Slou. SL2 ...74 AV74
Butcher Row, E1 ...85 DX73
E14 ...85 DX73
Butchers La, Sev. TN15 ...149 FX103
Butchers Rd, E16 ...86 EG72
Butcher Wk, Swans. DA10 ..130 FY87
Bute Av, Rich. TW10 ...118 CL89
Bute Ct, Wall. SM6 off Bute Rd ...159 DJ106
Bute Gdns, W6 ...99 CX77
Wallington SM6 ...159 DJ106
Bute Gdns W, Wall. SM6 ...159 DJ106
Bute Ms, NW11 off Northway .64 DB57
Bute Rd, Croy. CR0 ...141 DN102
Ilford IG6 ...69 EP57
Wallington SM6 ...159 DJ105
Bute St, SW7 ...100 DD77
Bute Wk, N1 off Marquess Rd .84 DR65
Butler Av, Har. HA1 ...61 CD59
Butler Ct, Wem. HA0 off Harrow Rd ...61 CG63
Butler Ho, Grays RM17 off Argent St ...110 GB79
Butler Pl, SW1 ...199 M6
Butler Rd, NW10 ...81 CT66
Dagenham RM8 ...70 EV63
Harrow HA1 ...60 CC59
Butlers & Colonial Wf, SE1 off Shad Thames ...102 DT75
Butlers Cl, Houns. TW4 ...96 BZ83
Butlers Ct, Wal.Cr. EN8 off Trinity La ...15 DY32
BUTLERS CROSS, Beac. HP9 .36 AT49
Butlers Dene Rd, Cat. (Wold.) CR3 ...177 DZ120
Butlers Dr, E4 ...31 EC38
Butler St, E2 off Knottisford St ...84 DW69
Uxbridge UB10 ...77 BP70
Butlers Wf, SE1 ...202 A3
Butler Wk, Grays RM17 off Palmers Dr ...110 GD77
Buttell Cl, Grays RM17 ...110 GD78
Buttercross La, Epp. CM16 ...18 EU30
Buttercup Cl, Nthlt. UB5 ...78 BY65
Romford RM3 off Copperfields Way ...52 FK53
Buttercup Sq, Stai. (Stanw.) TW19 off Diamedes Av ...114 BK88
Butterfield Cl, N17 off Devonshire Rd ...46 DQ51
SE16 ...202 D5
Twickenham TW1 off Rugby Rd ...117 CF86
Butterfields, E17 ...67 EC57
Butterfield Sq, E6 off Harper Rd ...87 EM72
Butterfly La, SE9 ...125 EP86
Borehamwood (Els.) WD6 ..25 CG41
Butterfly Wk, SE5 off Denmark Hill ...102 DR81
Warlingham CR6 ...176 DW120
Butter Hill, Cars. SM5 ...140 DG104
Wallington SM6 ...140 DG104
Butteridges Cl, Dag. RM9 ...88 EZ67
Butterly Av, Dart. DA1 ...128 FM89
Buttermere Cl, E15 ...67 ED63
SE1 ...201 P8
Feltham TW14 ...115 BT88
Morden SM4 ...139 CX100
Buttermere Dr, SW15 ...119 CY85
Buttermere Gdns, Pur. CR8 ..160 DR113
Buttermere Rd, Orp. BR5 ...146 EX98
Buttermere Wk, E8 ...84 DT65
Buttermere Way, Egh. TW20 off Keswick Rd ...113 BB94
Butterwick, W6 ...99 CW77
Watford WD25 ...24 BY36
Butterworth Gdns, Wdf.Grn. IG8 ...48 EG51
Buttesland St, N1 ...197 L2
Buttfield Cl, Dag. RM10 ...89 FB65
Buttlehide, Rick. (Map.Cr.) WD3 ...37 BD50
Buttmarsh Cl, SE18 ...105 EP78
Button Rd, Grays RM17 ...110 FZ77
Button St, Swan. BR8 ...148 FJ96
Butts, The, Brent. TW8 ...97 CK79
Sevenoaks (Otford) TN14 .181 FH116
Sunbury-on-Thames TW16 off Elizabeth Gdns ...136 BW97
Buttsbury Rd, Ilf. IG1 ...69 EQ64
Butts Cotts, Felt. TW13 ...116 BZ90
Butts Cres, Felt. TW13 ...116 CA90
Butts Grn Rd, Horn. RM11 ...72 FK58
Buttsmead, Nthwd. HA6 ...39 BQ52
Butts Piece, Nthlt. UB5 off Longhook Gdns ...77 BV68
Butts Rd, Brom. BR1 ...124 EE92
Woking GU21 ...166 AY117
Buxhall Cres, E9 ...85 DZ65
Buxted Rd, E8 ...84 DT66
N12 ...44 DE50
SE22 ...102 DS84
Buxton Av, Cat. CR3 ...176 DS121
Buxton Cl, N9 ...46 DW47
Epsom KT19 ...156 CP111
Woodford Green IG8 ...48 EK51
Buxton Ct, N1 ...197 J2
Buxton Cres, Sutt. SM3 ...157 CY105
Buxton Dr, E11 ...68 EE56
New Malden KT3 ...138 CR96
Buxton Gdns, W3 ...80 CP73
Buxton Ho, SW11 off Maysoule Rd ...100 DD84
Buxton La, Cat. CR3 ...176 DR120
Buxton Ms, SW4 ...101 DK82
Buxton Path, Wat. WD19 ...40 BW48
Buxton Rd, E4 ...47 ED45
E6 ...86 EL69
E15 ...68 EE64
E17 ...67 DY56
N19 ...65 DK60
NW2 ...81 CV65
SW14 ...98 CS83
Buxton Rd, Ashf. TW15 ...114 BK92
Epping (They.B.) CM16 ...33 ES36
Erith DA8 ...107 FD80
Grays RM16 ...110 GE75
Ilford IG2 ...69 ES58
Thornton Heath CR7 ...141 DP99
Waltham Abbey EN9 ...16 EG32
Buxton St, E1 ...84 DT70
Buzzard Creek Ind Est, Bark. IG11 ...87 ET71
Byam St, SW6 ...100 DC82
Byards Cft, SW16 ...141 DK95
Byatt Wk, Hmptn. TW12 off Victors Dr ...116 BY93
Bychurch End, Tedd. TW11 off Church Rd ...117 CF92
Bycliffe Ter, Grav. DA11 ...131 GF87
Bycroft Rd, Sthl. UB1 ...78 CA70
Bycroft St, SE20 off Parish La ...123 DX94
Bycullah Av, Enf. EN2 ...29 DP41
Bycullah Rd, Enf. EN2 ...29 DP41
Bye, The, W3 ...80 CS72
Byegrove Ct, SW19 off Byegrove Rd ...120 DD94
Byegrove Rd, SW19 ...120 DD93
Byers Cl, Pot.B. EN6 ...12 DC34
Byewaters, Wat. WD18 ...23 BQ44
Byeway, The, SW14 ...98 CQ83
Bye Way, The, Har. HA3 ...41 CE53
Byeway, The, Rick. WD3 ...38 BL47
Byeways, Twick. TW2 ...116 CB90
Byeways, The, Ashtd. KT21 off Skinners La ...171 CK118
Surbiton KT5 ...138 CN99
Byfeld Gdns, SW13 ...99 CU81
Byfield Cl, SE16 ...203 L4
Byfield Pas, Islw. TW7 ...97 CG83
Byfield Rd, Islw. TW7 ...97 CG83
BYFLEET, W.Byf. KT14 ...152 BM113
⇌ Byfleet & New Haw ...152 BK110
Byfleet Rd, Add. (New Haw) KT15 ...152 BK108
Cobham KT11 ...153 BS113
West Byfleet (Byfleet) KT14 ...152 BN112
Byfleet Tech Cen, W.Byf. (Byfleet) KT14 ...152 BK111
Byford Cl, E15 ...86 EE66
Bygrove, Croy. (New Adgtn) CR0 ...161 EB107
Bygrove St, E14 ...85 EB72
Byland Cl, N21 ...45 DM45
Morden SM4 off Bolton Dr .140 DD101
Bylands, Wok. GU22 ...167 BA119
Bylands Cl, SE2 off Finchale Rd ...106 EV76
SE16 ...203 J2
Byne Rd, SE26 ...122 DW93
Carshalton SM5 ...140 DE103
Bynes Rd, S.Croy. CR2 ...160 DR108
Byng Dr, Pot.B. EN6 ...12 DA31
Byng Pl, WC1 ...195 M5
Byng Rd, Barn. EN5 ...27 CX41
Byng St, E14 ...203 P4
Bynon Av, Bexh. DA7 ...106 EY83
Byre, The, N14 ...29 DH44
Byre Rd, N14 ...28 DG44
Byrne Rd, SW12 ...121 DH88
Byron Av, E12 ...86 EL65
E18 ...68 EF55
NW9 ...62 CP56
Borehamwood WD6 ...26 CN43
Coulsdon CR5 ...175 DL115
Hounslow TW4 ...95 BU82
New Malden KT3 ...139 CU99
Sutton SM1 ...158 DD105
Watford WD24 ...24 BX39
Byron Av E, Sutt. SM1 ...158 DD105
Byron Cl, E8 ...84 DU67
SE26 off Porthcawe Rd ...123 DY91
SE28 ...88 EW74
Hampton TW12 ...116 BZ91
Waltham Cross EN7 off Allard Cl ...14 DT27
Walton-on-Thames KT12 .136 BY102
Woking (Knap.) GU21 ...166 AS117
Byron Ct, W9 off Lanhill Rd ..82 DA70
Enfield EN2 ...29 DP40
Harrow HA1 ...61 CE58
Byron Dr, N2 ...64 DD58
Erith DA8 ...107 FB80
Byron Gdns, Sutt. SM1 ...158 DD105
Tilbury RM18 ...111 GJ81
Byron Hill Rd, Har. HA2 ...61 CD60
Byron Ho, Beck. BR3 ...123 EA93
Slough SL3 ...93 BB78
Byron Ms, NW3 ...64 DE64
W9 off Shirland Rd ...82 DA70
Byron Pl, Lthd. KT22 ...171 CH122
Byron Rd, E10 ...67 EB60
E17 ...67 EA55
NW2 ...63 CV61
NW7 ...43 CU50
W5 ...80 CM74
Addlestone KT15 ...152 BL105
Brentwood (Hutt.) CM13 ...55 GD45
Dartford DA1 ...108 FP84
Harrow HA1 ...61 CE58
Harrow (Wealds.) HA3 ...41 CF54
South Croydon CR2 ...160 DV110
Wembley HA0 ...61 CJ62
Byron St, E14 off St. Leonards Rd ...85 EC72
Byron Ter, N9 ...46 DW45
Byron Way, Hayes UB4 ...77 BT70
Northolt UB5 ...78 BY69
Romford RM3 ...52 FJ53
West Drayton UB7 ...94 BM77
Bysouth Cl, N15 ...66 DR56
Ilford IG5 ...49 EP53
By the Wd, Wat. WD19 ...40 BX47
Bythorn St, SW9 ...101 DM83
Byton Rd, SW17 ...120 DF93
Byward Av, Felt. TW14 ...116 BW86
Byward St, EC3 ...201 N1
Bywater Pl, SE16 ...203 L2
Bywater St, SW3 ...198 D10
Byway, The, Epsom KT19 ...157 CT105
Potters Bar EN6 ...12 DA33
Sutton SM2 ...158 DD109
Bywell Pl, W1 ...195 K7
Bywood Av, Croy. CR0 ...142 DW100
Bywood Cl, Ken. CR8 ...175 DP115
By-Wood End, Ger.Cr. (Chal.St.P.) SL9 ...37 AZ50
Byworth Wk, N19 off Courtauld Rd ...65 DK60

C

Cabbell Pl, Add. KT15 ...152 BJ105
Cabbell St, NW1 ...194 B7
Caberfeigh Pl, Red. RH1 ...184 DD134
Cabinet Way, E4 ...47 DZ51
Cable Pl, SE10 off Diamond Ter ...103 EC81
Cable St, E1 ...84 DU73
Cable Trade Pk, SE7 ...104 EJ77
Cabot Pl, E14 ...204 A2
Cabot Sq, E14 ...204 A2
Cabot Way, E6 off Parr Rd ...86 EK67
Cabrera Av, Vir.W. GU25 ...132 AW100
Cabrera Cl, Vir.W. GU25 ...132 AX100
Cabul Rd, SW11 ...100 DE82
Cacket's Cotts, Sev. (Cudham) TN14 ...179 ES115
Cackets La, Sev. (Cudham) TN14 ...179 ER115
Cactus Cl, SE15 off Lyndhurst Gro ...102 DS82
Cactus Wk, W12 off Du Cane Rd ...81 CT72
Cadbury Cl, Islw. TW7 ...97 CG81
Sunbury-on-Thames TW16 .115 BS94
Cadbury Rd, Sun. TW16 ...115 BS94
Cadbury Way, SE16 ...202 A7
Caddington Cl, Barn. EN4 ...28 DE43
Caddington Rd, NW2 ...63 CY62
Caddis Cl, Stan. HA7 off Daventer Dr ...41 CF52
Caddy Cl, Egh. TW20 ...113 BA92
Cade La, Sev. TN13 ...191 FJ128
Cadell Cl, E2 off Shipton St ..84 DT68
Cade Rd, SE10 ...103 ED81
Cader Rd, SW18 ...120 DC86
Cadet Dr, SE1 ...202 A10
Cadet Pl, SE10 ...205 H10
Cadiz Ct, Dag. RM10 off Rainham Rd S ...89 FD66
Cadiz Rd, Dag. RM10 ...89 FC66
Cadiz St, SE17 ...102 DQ78
Cadley Ter, SE23 ...122 DW89
Cadlocks Hill, Sev. (Halst.) TN14 ...164 EZ110
Cadman Cl, SW9 off Langton Rd ...101 DP80
Cadmer Cl, N.Mal. KT3 ...138 CS98
Cadmore La, Wal.Cr. (Chsht) EN8 ...15 DX28
Cadmus Cl, SW4 off Aristotle Rd ...101 DK83
Cadnam Pt, SW15 off Dilton Gdns ...119 CV88
Cadogan Av, Dart. DA2 ...129 FR87
Cadogan Cl, E9 off Cadogan Ter ...85 DZ66
Beckenham BR3 off Albemarle Rd ...143 ED95
Harrow HA2 ...60 CB63
Teddington TW11 ...117 CE92
Cadogan Ct, Sutt. SM2 ...158 DB107
Cadogan Gdns, E18 ...68 EH55
N3 ...44 DB53
N21 ...29 DN43
SW3 ...198 E8
Cadogan Gate, SW1 ...198 E8
Cadogan La, SW1 ...198 F7
[Riv] Cadogan Pier ...100 DE79
Cadogan Pl, SW1 ...198 E6
Cadogan Rd, SE18 ...105 EQ76
Surbiton KT6 ...137 CK99
Cadogan Sq, SW1 ...198 E7
Cadogan St, SW3 ...198 D9
Cadogan Ter, E9 ...85 DZ65
Cadoxton Av, N15 ...66 DT58
Cadwallon Rd, SE9 ...125 EP89
Caedmon Rd, N7 ...65 DM63
Caenshill Rd, Wey. KT13 ...152 BN108
Caenwood Cl, Wey. KT13 ...152 BN107
Caen Wd Rd, Ashtd. KT21 ...171 CJ118
Caerleon Cl, Esher (Clay.) KT10 ...155 CH108
Sidcup DA14 ...126 EW92
Caerleon Ter, SE2 off Blithdale Rd ...106 EV77
Caernarvon Cl, Horn. RM11 ..72 FN60
Mitcham CR4 ...141 DL97
Caernarvon Dr, Ilf. IG5 ...49 EN53
Caesars Wk, Mitch. CR4 ...140 DF99
Caesars Way, Shep. TW17 ...135 BR100
Cage Pond Rd, Rad. (Shenley) WD7 ...10 CM33
Cage Yd, Reig. RH2 off High St ...184 DA134
Cahill St, EC1 ...197 J5
Cahir St, E14 ...204 B9
Caillard Rd, W.Byf. (Byfleet) KT14 ...152 BL111
Cains La, Felt. TW14 ...115 BS85
Caird St, W10 ...81 CY69
Cairn Av, W5 ...79 CK74
Cairndale Cl, Brom. BR1 ...124 EF94
Cairnfield Av, NW2 ...62 CS62
Cairngorm Cl, Tedd. TW11 off Vicarage Rd ...117 CG92
Cairns Av, Wdf.Grn. IG8 ...48 EL51
Cairns Cl, Dart. DA1 ...128 FK85
Cairns Ms, SE18 off Bell St ..104 EL81
Cairns Rd, SW11 ...120 DE85
Cairn Way, Stan. HA7 ...41 CF51
Cairo New Rd, Croy. CR0 ...141 DP103
Cairo Rd, E17 ...67 EA56
Caishowe Rd, Borwd. WD6 ...26 CP39
Caistor Ms, SW12 off Caistor Rd ...121 DH87
Caistor Pk Rd, E15 ...86 EF67
Caistor Rd, SW12 ...121 DH87
Caithness Dr, Epsom KT18 ..156 CR114
Caithness Gdns, Sid. DA15 ..125 ET86
Caithness Rd, W14 ...99 CX77
Mitcham CR4 ...121 DH94
Calabria Rd, N5 ...83 DP65
Calais Cl, Wal.Cr. EN7 off Argent Way ...14 DR26
Calais Gate, SE5 off Calais St ...101 DP81
Calais St, SE5 ...101 DP81
Calbourne Av, Horn. RM12 ...71 FH64
Calbourne Rd, SW12 ...120 DF87
Calcott Cl, Brwd. CM14 ...54 FV46
Calcott Wk, SE9 ...124 EK91
Calcroft Av, Green. DA9 ...129 FW85
Calcutta Rd, Til. RM18 ...111 GF82
Caldbeck, Wal.Abb. EN9 ...15 ED34
Caldbeck Av, Wor.Pk. KT4 ...139 CU103
Caldecot Av, Wal.Cr. (Chsht) EN7 ...14 DT29
Caldecote Gdns, Bushey WD23 ...25 CE44
Caldecote La, Bushey WD23 ..41 CF45
Caldecot Rd, SE5 ...102 DQ82
Caldecott Way, E5 ...67 DX62
Calder Av, Grnf. UB6 ...79 CF68
Hatfield (Brook.Pk) AL9 ...12 DB26
Calder Cl, Enf. EN1 ...30 DS41
Calder Ct, Slou. SL3 ...93 AZ78
Calder Gdns, Edg. HA8 ...62 CN55
Calderon Pl, W10 off St. Quintin Gdns ...81 CW71
Calderon Rd, E11 ...67 EC63
Calder Rd, Mord. SM4 ...140 DC99
Caldervale Rd, SW4 ...121 DK85
Calder Way, Slou. (Colnbr.) SL3 ...93 BF83
Calderwood, Grav. DA12 ...131 GL92
Calderwood St, SE18 ...105 EN77
Caldicot Grn, NW9 off Snowdon Dr ...62 CS58
Caldwell Rd, Wat. WD19 ...40 BX49
Caldwell St, SW9 ...101 DM80
Caldwell Yd, EC4 off Upper Thames St ...84 DQ73
Caldy Rd, Belv. DA17 ...107 FB76
Caldy Wk, N1 off Clifton Rd ..84 DQ65
Caleb St, SE1 ...201 H4
Caledon Cl, Ilf. IG3 ...70 EV60
⊖ Caledonian Road ...83 DL65
Caledonian Rd, N1 ...196 A1
N7 ...65 DM64
⇌ Caledonian Road & Barnsbury ...83 DM66
Caledonian Sq, NW1 off Canal Boul ...83 DK65
Caledonian Wf, E14 ...204 F9
Caledonia Rd, Stai. TW19 ...114 BL88
Caledonia St, N1 ...196 A1
Caledon Rd, E6 ...86 EL67
St. Albans (Lon.Col.) AL2 ...9 CK26
Wallington SM6 ...158 DG105
Cale St, SW3 ...198 B10
Caletock Way, SE10 ...205 K10
Calfstock La, Dart. (S.Darenth) DA4 ...148 FL98
Calico Row, SW11 off York Pl ...100 DC83
Calidore Cl, SW2 off Endymion Rd ...121 DM86
California Cl, Sutt. SM2 ...158 DA110
California La, Bushey (Bushey Hth) WD23 ...41 CD46
California Rd, N.Mal. KT3 ...138 CQ98
Caliph Cl, Grav. DA12 ...131 GM90
Callaby Ter, N1 off Wakeham St ...84 DR65
Callaghan Cl, SE13 ...104 EE84
Callander Rd, SE6 ...123 EB89
Callan Gro, S.Ock. RM15 ...91 FV73
Callard Av, N13 ...45 DP50
Callcott Rd, NW6 ...81 CZ66
Callcott St, W8 off Hillgate Pl ...82 DA74
Callendar Rd, SW7 ...100 DD76
Calley Down Cres, Croy. (New Adgtn) CR0 ...161 ED110
Callingham Cl, E14 off Wallwood St ...85 DZ71
Callis Fm Cl, Stai. (Stanw.) TW19 off Bedfont Rd ...114 BL86
Callisons Pl, SE10 off Bellot St ...104 EE78
Callis Rd, E17 ...67 DZ58
Callow Fld, Pur. CR8 ...159 DN113
Callow Hill, Vir.W. GU25 ...132 AW97
Callowland Cl, Wat. WD24 ...23 BV38
Callow St, SW3 ...100 DD79
Calluna Ct, Wok. GU22 off Heathside Rd ...167 AZ118
Calmington Rd, SE5 off Albany Rd ...102 DS79
Calmont Rd, Brom. BR1 ...123 ED93
Calmore Cl, Horn. RM12 ...72 FJ64
Calne Av, Ilf. IG5 ...49 EP53
Calonne Rd, SW19 ...119 CX91
Calshot Av, Grays (Chaff.Hun.) RM16 ...110 FZ75
Calshot Rd, Houns. (Hthrw Air.) TW6 ...94 BN82
Calshot St, N1 ...83 DM68
Calshot Way, Enf. EN2 ...29 DP41
Hounslow (Hthrw Air.) TW6 off Calshot Rd ...95 BP82
Calthorpe Gdns, Edg. HA8 off Jesmond Way ...42 CL50
Sutton SM1 ...140 DC104
Calthorpe St, WC1 ...196 C4
Calton Av, SE21 ...122 DS85
Calton Rd, Barn. EN5 ...28 DC44
Calverley Cl, Beck. BR3 ...123 EB93
Calverley Cres, Dag. RM10 ...70 FA61
Calverley Gdns, Har. HA3 ...61 CK59
Calverley Gro, N19 ...65 DK60
Calverley Rd, Epsom KT17 ..157 CU107
Calvert Av, E2 ...197 N3
Calvert Cl, Belv. DA17 ...106 FA77
Epsom KT19 ...156 CP110
Sidcup DA14 ...126 EY93
Calvert Dr, Dart. DA2 ...127 FD89
Calverton, SE5 ...102 DS79
Calverton Rd, E6 ...87 EN67
Calvert Rd, SE10 ...104 EF78
Barnet EN5 ...27 CX40
Calvert's Bldgs, SE1 ...201 K3
Calvert St, NW1 off Chalcot Rd ...82 DG67
Calvin Cl, Orp. BR5 ...146 EX97

★ Place of interest ⇌ Railway station ⊖ London Underground station [DLR] Docklands Light Railway station [Tra] Tramlink station [H] Hospital [Riv] Pedestrian ferry landing stage

Calvin St, E1 197 P5
Calydon Rd, SE7 104 EH78
Calypso Cres, SE15 102 DT80
Calypso Way, SE16 203 M7
Camac Rd, Twick. TW2 117 CD88
Cambalt Rd, SW15 119 CX85
Camberley Av, SW20 139 CV96
Enfield EN1 30 DS42
Camberley Cl, Sutt. SM3 139 CX104
Camberley Rd, Houns. (Hthrw Air.) TW6 94 BN83
Cambert Way, SE3 104 EH84
CAMBERWELL, SE5 102 DQ80
Camberwell Business Cen, SE5 *off Lomond Gro* 102 DR80
Camberwell Ch St, SE5 102 DR81
Camberwell Glebe, SE5 102 DR81
Camberwell Grn, SE5 102 DR81
Camberwell Gro, SE5 102 DR81
Camberwell New Rd, SE5 101 DN80
Camberwell Pas, SE5 *off Camberwell New Rd* 102 DQ81
Camberwell Rd, SE5 102 DQ79
Camberwell Sta Rd, SE5 102 DQ81
Cambeys Rd, Dag. RM10 71 FB64
Camborne Av, W13 97 CH75
Romford RM3 52 FL52
Camborne Cl, Houns. (Hthrw Air.) TW6 *off Camborne Rd* 94 BN83
Camborne Ms, SW18 *off Camborne Rd* 120 DA87
W11 *off St. Marks Rd* 81 CY72
Camborne Rd, SW18 120 DA87
Croydon CR0 142 DU101
Hounslow (Hthrw Air.) TW6 94 BN83
Morden SM4 139 CX99
Sidcup DA14 126 EW90
Sutton SM2 158 DA108
Welling DA16 105 ET82
Camborne Way, Houns. TW5 96 CA81
Hounslow (Hthrw Air.) TW6 *off Camborne Rd* 94 BN83
Romford RM3 52 FL52
Cambourne Av, N9 47 DX45
Cambray Rd, SW12 121 DJ88
Orpington BR6 145 ET101
Cambria Cl, Houns. TW3 96 CA84
Sidcup DA15 125 ER88
Cambria Ct, Felt. TW14 115 BV87
Slough SL3 *off Turner Rd* 92 AW75
Cambria Cres, Grav. DA12 131 GL91
Cambria Gdns, Stai. TW19 114 BL87
Cambria Ho, SE26 *off High Level Dr* 122 DU91
Erith DA8 *off Larner Rd* 107 FE80
Cambrian Av, Ilf. IG2 69 ES57
Cambrian Cl, SE27 121 DP90
Cambrian Grn, NW9 *off Snowdon Dr* 62 CS57
Cambrian Gro, Grav. DA11 131 GG87
Cambrian Rd, E10 67 EA59
Richmond TW10 118 CM86
Cambria Rd, SE5 102 DQ83
Cambria St, SW6 100 DB80
Cambridge Av, NW6 82 DA68
Greenford UB6 61 CF64
New Malden KT3 139 CT96
Romford RM2 72 FJ55
Welling DA16 105 ET84
Cambridge Barracks Rd, SE18 105 EM77
Cambridge Circ, WC2 195 N9
Cambridge Cl, E17 67 DZ58
N22 *off Pellatt Gro* 45 DN53
NW10 *off Lawrence Way* 62 CQ62
SW20 139 CV95
Hounslow TW4 96 BY84
Waltham Cross (Chsht) EN8 14 DW29
West Drayton UB7 94 BK79
Woking GU21 166 AT118
Cambridge Cotts, Rich. TW9 98 CN79
Cambridge Cres, E2 84 DV68
Teddington TW11 117 CG92
Cambridge Dr, SE12 124 EG85
Potters Bar EN6 11 CX31
Ruislip HA4 60 BW61
Cambridge Gdns, N10 44 DG53
N13 45 DN50
N17 *off Great Cambridge Rd* 46 DR52
N21 46 DR45
NW6 82 DA68
W10 81 CY72
Enfield EN1 30 DU40
Grays RM16 111 GG77
Kingston upon Thames KT1 138 CN96
Cambridge Gate, NW1 195 J3
Cambridge Gate Ms, NW1 195 J3
Cambridge Grn, SE9 125 EP88
Cambridge Gro, SE20 142 DV95
W6 99 CV77
Cambridge Gro Rd, Kings.T. KT1 138 CN96
⇌ **Cambridge Heath** 84 DV68
Cambridge Heath Rd, E1 84 DV68
E2 84 DV68
Cambridge Mans, SW11 *off Cambridge Rd* 100 DF81
Cambridge Par, Enf. EN1 *off Great Cambridge Rd* 30 DU39
Cambridge Pk, E11 68 EG59
Twickenham TW1 117 CK87
Cambridge Pk Rd, E11 *off Cambridge Pk* 68 EG59
Cambridge Pl, W8 100 DB75
Cambridge Rd, E4 47 ED46
E11 68 EF58
NW6 82 DA69
SE20 142 DV97
SW11 100 DF81
SW13 99 CT82
SW20 139 CU95
W7 97 CF75
Ashford TW15 115 BQ94
Barking IG11 87 EQ66
Bromley BR1 124 EG94
Carshalton SM5 158 DE107
Hampton TW12 116 BZ94
Harrow HA2 60 CA57
Hounslow TW4 96 BY84
Ilford IG3 69 ES60
Kingston upon Thames KT1 138 CM96
Cambridge Rd, Mitch. CR4 141 DJ97
New Malden KT3 138 CS98
Richmond TW9 98 CN80
Sidcup DA14 125 ES91
Southall UB1 78 BZ74
Teddington TW11 117 CF91
Twickenham TW1 117 CK86
Uxbridge UB8 76 BK65
Walton-on-Thames KT12 135 BV100
Watford WD18 24 BW42
West Molesey KT8 136 BZ98
Cambridge Rd N, W4 98 CP78
Cambridge Rd S, W4 98 CP78
Cambridge Row, SE18 105 EP78
Cambridge Sq, W2 194 B8
Cambridge St, SW1 199 J9
Cambridge Ter, N13 45 DN50
NW1 195 J3
Cambridge Ter Ms, NW1 195 J3
Cambstone Cl, N11 44 DG47
Cambus Cl, Hayes UB4 78 BY71
Cambus Rd, E16 86 EG71
Camdale Rd, SE18 105 ET80
★ **Camden Arts Cen**, NW3 64 DC64
Camden Av, Felt. TW13 116 BW89
Hayes UB4 78 BW73
Camden Cl, Chis. BR7 125 EQ94
Gravesend DA11 130 GC88
Grays RM16 111 GH77
Camden Gdns, NW1 *off Kentish Town Rd* 83 DH66
Sutton SM1 158 DB106
Thornton Heath CR7 141 DP97
Camden Gro, Chis. BR7 125 EP93
Camden High St, NW1 83 DH67
Camden Hill Rd, SE19 122 DS93
Camdenhurst St, E14 85 DY72
Camden La, N7 *off Rowstock Gdns* 83 DK65
★ **Camden Lock Mkt & Waterbuses**, NW1 83 DH66
Camden Lock Pl, NW1 *off Chalk Fm Rd* 83 DH66
Camden Ms, NW1 83 DK65
Camden Pk Rd, NW1 83 DK65
Chislehurst BR7 125 EM94
Camden Pas, N1 83 DP67
⇌ **Camden Road** 83 DJ66
Camden Rd, E11 68 EH58
E17 67 DZ58
N7 65 DK64
NW1 83 DJ67
Bexley DA5 126 EZ88
Carshalton SM5 158 DF105
Grays RM16 110 FY76
Sevenoaks TN13 191 FH122
Sutton SM1 158 DA106
Camden Row, SE3 104 EE82
Camden Sq, NW1 83 DK65
SE15 *off Watts St* 102 DT81
Camden St, NW1 83 DH66
Camden Ter, NW1 *off North Vil* 83 DK65
CAMDEN TOWN, NW1 83 DJ67
⊖ **Camden Town** 83 DH67
Camden Wk, N1 83 DP67
Camden Way, Chis. BR7 125 EM94
Thornton Heath CR7 141 DP97
Camelford Wk, W11 *off St. Marks Rd* 81 CY72
Camel Gro, Kings.T. KT2 117 CK92
Camellia Cl, Rom. RM3 52 FL53
Camellia Ct, Wdf.Grn. IG8 *off The Bridle Path* 48 EE52
Camellia Pl, Twick. TW2 116 CB87
Camellia St, SW8 *off Hartington Rd* 101 DL80
Camelot Cl, SE28 105 ER75
SW19 120 DA91
Westerham (Bigg.H.) TN16 178 EJ116
Camelot Ho, NW1 *off Camden Pk Rd* 83 DK65
Camelot St, SE15 *off Bird in Bush Rd* 102 DV80
Camel Rd, E16 86 EK74
Camera Pl, SW10 100 DD79
Cameron Cl, N18 46 DV49
N20 *off Myddelton Pk* 44 DE47
Bexley DA5 127 FD90
Brentwood CM14 54 FW49
Cameron Dr, Wal.Cr. EN8 15 DX34
Cameron Ho, SE5 *off Comber Gro* 102 DQ80
Cameron Pl, E1 *off Varden St* 84 DV72
SW16 121 DN89
Cameron Rd, SE6 123 DZ89
Bromley BR2 144 EG98
Croydon CR0 141 DP100
Ilford IG3 69 ES60
Cameron Sq, Mitch. CR4 140 DE95
Camerton Cl, E8 *off Buttermere Wk* 84 DT65
Camgate Cen, Stai. (Stanw.) TW19 114 BM86
Cam Grn, S.Ock. RM15 91 FV72
Camilla Cl, Sun. TW16 115 BS93
Camilla Rd, SE16 202 D9
Camille Cl, SE25 142 DU97
Camlan Rd, Brom. BR1 124 EF91
Camlet St, E2 197 P4
Camlet Way, Barn. EN4 28 DA40
Camley St, NW1 83 DK66
★ **Camley St Natural Pk**, NW1 83 DL68
Camm Gdns, Kings.T. KT1 *off Church Rd* 138 CM96
Thames Ditton KT7 137 CE101
Camms Ter, Dag. RM10 71 FC64
Camomile Av, Mitch. CR4 140 DF95
Camomile Rd, Rom. (Rush Grn) RM7 71 FD61
Camomile St, EC3 197 M8
Camomile Way, West Dr. UB7 76 BL72
Campana Rd, SW6 100 DA81
Campbell Av, Ilf. IG6 69 EQ56
Woking GU22 167 AZ121
Campbell Cl, SE18 *off Moordown* 105 EN81
SW16 121 DK91
Romford (Hav.at.Bow.) RM1 51 FE51
Ruislip HA4 59 BU58
Twickenham TW2 117 CD89
Campbell Cl, W. Byf. (Byfleet) KT14 152 BK112
Campbell Ct, N17 46 DT53
SE22 *off Lordship La* 122 DU87
Campbell Cft, Edg. HA8 42 CN50
Campbell Gordon Way, NW2 63 CV63
Campbell Rd, E3 85 EA69
E6 86 EL67
E15 *off Trevelyan Rd* 68 EF63
E17 67 DZ56
N17 46 DU53
W7 79 CE73
Caterham CR3 176 DR121
Croydon CR0 141 DP101
East Molesey KT8 *off Hampton Ct Rd* 137 CF97
Gravesend DA11 131 GF88
Twickenham TW2 117 CD89
Weybridge KT13 152 BN108
Campbell Wk, N1 *off Outram Pl* 83 DL67
Campdale Rd, N7 65 DK62
Campden Cres, Dag. RM8 70 EV63
Wembley HA0 61 CH61
Campden Gro, W8 100 DA75
Campden Hill, W8 100 DA75
Campden Hill Ct, W8 *off Campden Hill Rd* 100 DA75
Campden Hill Gdns, W8 82 DA74
Campden Hill Gate, W8 *off Duchess of Bedford's Wk* 100 DA75
Campden Hill Pl, W11 *off Holland Pk Av* 81 CZ74
Campden Hill Rd, W8 82 DA74
Campden Hill Sq, W8 81 CZ74
Campden Hill Twrs, W11 *off Notting Hill Gate* 82 DA74
Campden Ho Cl, W8 *off Hornton St* 100 DA75
Campden Rd, S.Croy. CR2 160 DS106
Uxbridge UB10 58 BM62
Campden St, W8 82 DA74
Campen Cl, SW19 119 CY89
Camp End Rd, Wey. KT13 153 BR110
Camperdown St, E1 *off Leman St* 84 DT72
Campfield Rd, SE9 124 EK87
Camphill Ct, W.Byf. KT14 152 BG112
Camphill Ind Est, W.Byf. KT14 152 BH111
Camphill Rd, W.Byf. KT14 152 BG112
Campine Cl, Wal.Cr. (Chsht) EN8 *off Welsummer Way* 15 DX28
Campion Cl, E6 87 EM73
Croydon CR0 160 DS105
Gravesend (Nthflt) DA11 130 GE91
Harrow HA3 62 CM58
Romford (Rush Grn) RM7 71 FD61
Uxbridge (Denh.) UB9 *off Lindsey Rd* 58 BG62
Uxbridge (Hlgdn) UB8 76 BM71
Watford WD25 7 BU33
Campion Ct, Grays RM17 110 GD79
Campion Dr, Tad. KT20 173 CV120
Campion Gdns, Wdf.Grn. IG8 48 EG50
Campion Pl, SE28 88 EV74
Campion Rd, SW15 99 CW84
Isleworth TW7 97 CF81
Campions, Epp. CM16 18 EU28
Loughton IG10 33 EN38
Campions, The, Borwd. WD6 26 CN38
Campions Cl, Borwd. WD6 26 CP37
Campion Ter, NW2 63 CX62
Campion Way, Edg. HA8 42 CQ49
Cample La, S.Ock. RM15 91 FU73
Camplin Rd, Har. HA3 62 CL57
Camplin St, SE14 103 DX80
Camp Rd, SW19 119 CW92
Caterham (Wold.) CR3 177 DY120
Gerrards Cross SL9 56 AX59
Campsbourne, The, N8 *off High St* 65 DL56
Campsbourne Rd, N8 65 DL55
Campsey Gdns, Dag. RM9 88 EV66
Campsey Rd, Dag. RM9 88 EV66
Campsfield Rd, N8 *off Campsbourne Rd* 65 DL55
Campshill Pl, SE13 *off Campshill Rd* 123 EC85
Campshill Rd, SE13 123 EC85
Campus Rd, E17 67 DZ58
Campus Way, NW4 *off Greyhound Hill* 63 CV55
Camp Vw, SW19 119 CV92
Cam Rd, E15 85 ED67
Camrose Av, Edg. HA8 42 CM53
Erith DA8 107 FB79
Feltham TW13 115 BV91
Camrose Cl, Croy. CR0 143 DY101
Morden SM4 140 DA98
Camrose St, SE2 106 EU78
Canada Av, N18 46 DQ51
Canada Cres, W3 80 CQ71
Canada Est, SE16 202 G6
Canada Fm Rd, Dart. (S.Darenth) DA4 149 FU98
Longfield DA3 149 FU99
Canada Gdns, SE13 123 EC85
Canada La, Brox. EN10 15 DY25
Canada Rd, W3 80 CQ70
Cobham KT11 154 BW113
Erith DA8 107 FH80
Slough SL1 92 AV75
West Byfleet (Byfleet) KT14 152 BK111
Canadas, The, Brox. EN10 15 DY25
Canada Sq, E14 204 B2
Canada St, SE16 203 H5
⊖ **Canada Water** 202 G5
Canada Way, W12 81 CV73
Canadian Av, SE6 123 EB88
Canadian Mem Av, Egh. TW20 132 AT96
Canal App, SE8 103 DY79
Canal Basin, Grav. DA12 131 GK86
Canal Boul, NW1 83 DK65
Canal Cl, E1 85 DY70
W10 81 CX70
Canal Est, Slou. (Langley) SL3 93 BA75
Canal Gro, SE15 102 DU79
Canal Path, E2 84 DT67
Canal Rd, Grav. DA12 131 GJ86
Canal St, SE5 102 DR79
Canal Wk, N1 84 DR67
NW10 *off West End Cl* 80 CQ66
SE26 122 DW92
Croydon CR0 142 DS100
Canal Way, N1 *off Packington Sq* 84 DQ68
NW1 194 C2
NW8 194 B3
NW10 81 CT70
W2 *off Harrow Rd* 82 DA71
W9 *off Great Western Rd* 81 CZ71
W10 81 CX70
Uxbridge (Hare.) UB9 38 BG51
Canal Way Wk, W10 81 CX70
Canal Wf, Slou. SL3 93 BA75
⊖ **Canary Wharf** 204 B3
DLR **Canary Wharf** 204 A2
RIV **Canary Wharf Pier** 203 N2
Canberra Cl, NW4 63 CU55
Dagenham RM10 89 FD66
Hornchurch RM12 72 FJ63
Canberra Cres, Dag. RM10 89 FD66
Canberra Dr, Hayes UB4 78 BW69
Northolt UB5 78 BW69
Canberra Rd, E6 *off Barking Rd* 87 EM67
SE7 104 EJ79
W13 79 CG74
Bexleyheath DA7 106 EX79
Hounslow (Hthrw Air.) TW6 94 BN83
Canberra Sq, Til. RM18 111 GG82
Canbury Av, Kings.T. KT2 138 CM95
Canbury Ms, SE26 *off Wells Pk Rd* 122 DU90
Canbury Pk Rd, Kings.T. KT2 138 CL95
Canbury Pas, Kings.T. KT2 137 CK95
Canbury Path, Orp. BR5 146 EU98
Cancell Rd, SW9 101 DN81
Candahar Rd, SW11 100 DE82
Cander Way, S.Ock. RM15 91 FV73
Candle Gro, SE15 102 DV83
Candlemakers Apts, SW11 *off York Rd* 100 DD83
Candler St, N15 66 DR58
Candlerush Cl, Wok. GU22 167 BB117
Candlestick La, Wal.Cr. EN7 *off Park La* 14 DV27
Candover Cl, West Dr. UB7 94 BK80
Candover Rd, Horn. RM12 71 FH60
Candover St, W1 195 K7
Candy St, E3 85 DZ67
Cane Hill, Rom. (Harold Wd) RM3 *off Bennison Dr* 52 FK54
Caneland Ct, Wal.Abb. EN9 16 EF34
Canewdon Cl, Wok. GU22 *off Guildford Rd* 166 AY119
Caney Ms, NW2 *off Claremont Rd* 63 CX61
Canfield Dr, Ruis. HA4 59 BV64
Canfield Gdns, NW6 82 DC66
Canfield Pl, NW6 *off Canfield Gdns* 82 DC65
Canfield Rd, Rain. RM13 89 FF67
Woodford Green IG8 48 EL52
Canford Av, Nthlt. UB5 78 BY67
Canford Cl, Enf. EN2 29 DN40
Canford Dr, Add. KT15 134 BH103
Canford Gdns, N.Mal. KT3 138 CR100
Canford Pl, Tedd. TW11 117 CH93
Canford Rd, SW11 120 DG85
Canham Rd, SE25 142 DS97
W3 98 CS75
Can Hatch, Tad. KT20 173 CY118
Canmore Gdns, SW16 121 DJ94
Cann Hall Rd, E11 68 EE63
Canning Cres, N22 45 DM53
Canning Cross, SE5 102 DS82
Canning Pas, W8 100 DC76
Canning Pl, W8 100 DC76
Canning Pl Ms, W8 *off Canning Pl* 100 DC76
Canning Rd, E15 86 EE68
E17 67 DY56
N5 65 DP62
Croydon CR0 142 DT103
Harrow HA3 61 CF55
Cannington Rd, Dag. RM9 88 EW65
CANNING TOWN, E16 86 EG72
⇌ **Canning Town** 86 EE72
⊖ **Canning Town** 86 EE72
DLR **Canning Town** 86 EE72
Canning Town, E16 *off Newham Way* 86 EE71
Cannizaro Rd, SW19 119 CW93
Cannonbury Av, Pnr. HA5 60 BX58
Cannon Cl, SW20 139 CW97
Hampton TW12 *off Hanworth Rd* 116 CB93
Cannon Ct, EC1 *off Northburgh St* 83 DP70
Cannon Cres, Wok. (Chobham) GU24 150 AS111
Cannon Dr, E14 203 P1
Cannon Gate, Slou. SL2 *off Uxbridge Rd* 74 AW73
Cannon Gro, Lthd. (Fetch.) KT22 171 CE121
Cannon Hill, N14 45 DK48
NW6 64 DA64
Cannon Hill La, SW20 139 CY97
Cannon La, NW3 64 DD62
Pinner HA5 60 BY60
Cannon Ms, Wal.Abb. EN9 15 EB33
Cannon Pl, NW3 64 DD62
SE7 104 EL78
Cannon Rd, N14 45 DL48
Bexleyheath DA7 106 EY81
Watford WD18 24 BW43
Cannonside, Lthd. (Fetch.) KT22 171 CE122
⇌ **Cannon Street** 201 K1
⊖ **Cannon Street** 201 K1
Cannon St, EC4 197 H9
Cannon St Rd, E1 84 DV72
Cannon Trd Est, Wem. HA9 62 CP63
Cannon Way, Lthd. (Fetch.) KT22 171 CE121
West Molesey KT8 136 CA98
Cannon Wf Business Cen, SE8 203 K9
Cannon Workshops, E14 203 P1
Canon All, EC4 *off St. Paul's Chyd* 83 DP72
Canon Av, Rom. RM6 70 EW57
Canon Beck Rd, SE16 202 G4
Canonbie Rd, SE23 122 DW87
CANONBURY, N1 84 DQ65
⇌ **Canonbury** 66 DQ64
Canonbury Cres, N1 84 DQ66
Canonbury Gro, N1 84 DQ66
Canonbury La, N1 83 DP66
Canonbury Pk N, N1 84 DQ65
Canonbury Pk S, N1 84 DQ65
Canonbury Pl, N1 83 DP65
Canonbury Rd, N1 83 DP65
Enfield EN1 30 DS39
Canonbury Sq, N1 83 DP66
Canonbury St, N1 84 DQ66
Canonbury Vil, N1 83 DP66
Canonbury Yd, N1 *off New N Rd* 84 DQ67
Canonbury Yd W, N1 *off Compton Rd* 83 DP65
Canon Mohan Cl, N14 *off Farm La* 29 DH44
Canon Rd, Brom. BR1 144 EJ97
Canon Row, SW1 199 P5
Canons Cl, N2 64 DD59
Edgware HA8 42 CM51
Radlett WD7 25 CH35
Reigate RH2 183 CZ133
Canons Cor, Edg. HA8 42 CL49
Canons Dr, Edg. HA8 42 CL51
Canons Gate, Wal.Cr. (Chsht) EN8 15 DZ26
Canon's Hill, Couls. CR5 175 DN117
Canons La, Tad. KT20 173 CY118
Canonsleigh Rd, Dag. RM9 88 EV66
CANONS PARK, Edg. HA8 42 CL52
⊖ **Canons Park** 42 CL52
Canons Pk Cl, Edg. HA8 *off Donnefield Av* 42 CL52
Canon St, N1 84 DQ67
Canons Wk, Croy. CR0 143 DX104
Canopus Way, Nthwd. HA6 39 BU49
Staines TW19 114 BL87
Canrobert St, E2 84 DV69
Cantelowes Rd, NW1 83 DK65
Canterbury Av, Ilf. IG1 68 EL59
Sidcup DA15 126 EW89
Upminster RM14 73 FT60
Canterbury Cl, E6 *off Harper Rd* 87 EM72
Amersham HP7 20 AS39
Beckenham BR3 143 EB95
Chigwell IG7 49 ET48
Dartford DA1 128 FN87
Greenford UB6 78 CB72
Northwood HA6 39 BT51
Worcester Park KT4 139 CX103
Canterbury Cres, SW9 101 DN83
Canterbury Gro, SE27 121 DP90
Canterbury Ho, SE1 *off Royal St* 101 DM76
Borehamwood WD6 26 CN40
Erith DA8 *off Arthur St* 107 FF80
Canterbury Ms, Lthd. (Oxshott) KT22 154 CC113
Canterbury Par, S.Ock. RM15 91 FW69
Canterbury Pl, SE17 200 G9
Canterbury Rd, E10 67 EC59
NW6 82 DA68
Borehamwood WD6 26 CN40
Croydon CR0 141 DM101
Feltham TW13 116 BY90
Gravesend DA12 131 GJ89
Harrow HA1, HA2 60 CB57
Morden SM4 140 DC99
Watford WD17 23 BV40
Canterbury Ter, NW6 82 DA68
Canterbury Way, Brwd. (Gt Warley) CM13 53 FW51
Purfleet RM19 109 FS80
Rickmansworth (Crox.Grn) WD3 23 BQ41
Cantium Retail Pk, SE1 102 DU79
Cantley Gdns, SE19 142 DT95
Ilford IG2 69 EQ58
Cantley Rd, W7 97 CG76
Canton St, E14 85 EA72
Cantrell Rd, E3 85 DZ70
Cantwell Rd, SE18 105 EP80
Canute Gdns, SE16 203 H8
Capability Way, Green. DA9 109 FW84
Cape Cl, Bark. IG11 *off North St* 87 EP65
Capel Av, Wall. SM6 159 DM106
Capel Cl, N20 44 DC48
Bromley BR2 144 EL102
Capel Ct, EC2 197 L9
SE20 *off Melvin Rd* 142 DW95
Capel Gdns, Ilf. IG3 69 ET63
Pinner HA5 60 BZ56
Capella Rd, Nthwd. HA6 39 BT50
Capell Av, Rick. (Chorl.) WD3 21 BC43
Capell Rd, Rick. (Chorl.) WD3 21 BC43
Capell Way, Rick. (Chorl.) WD3 21 BD43
Capel Pl, Dart. DA2 128 FJ91
Capel Pt, E7 68 EH63
Capel Rd, E7 68 EH63
E12 68 EJ63
Barnet EN4 28 DE44
Enfield EN1 30 DV36
Watford WD19 24 BY44
Capel Vere Wk, Wat. WD17 23 BS39
Capener's Cl, SW1 198 F5
Capern Rd, SW18 *off Cargill Rd* 120 DC88
Cape Rd, N17 *off High Cross Rd* 66 DU55
Cape Yd, E1 202 C2
Capital Business Cen, Wem. HA0 79 CK68
Capital E Apts, E16 *off Western Gateway* 86 EG73
Capital Interchange Way, Brent. TW8 98 CN78

★ Place of interest ⇌ Railway station ⊖ London Underground station DLR Docklands Light Railway station Tra Tramlink station H Hospital Riv Pedestrian ferry landing stage

Capital Pk, Wok. (Old Wok.) GU22 167 BB121
Capitol Ind Pk, NW9 62 CQ55
Capitol Way, NW9 62 CQ55
Capland St, NW8 194 A4
Caple Par, NW10
off Harley Rd 80 CS68
Caple Rd, NW10 81 CT68
Capon Cl, Brwd. CM14 54 FV46
Capper St, WC1 195 L5
Caprea Cl, Hayes UB4
off Triandra Way 78 BX71
Capri Rd, Croy. CR0 142 DT102
Capstan Cen, Til. RM18 110 GD80
Capstan Cl, Rom. RM6 70 EV58
Capstan Ct, Dart. DA2 108 FQ84
Capstan Dr, Rain. RM13 89 FG70
Capstan Ms, Grav. DA11 130 GE87
Capstan Ride, Enf. EN2 29 DN40
Capstan Rd, SE8 203 M8
Capstan Sq, E14 204 E5
Capstan's Wf, Wok. GU21 166 AT118
Capstan Way, SE16 203 L3
Capstone Rd, Brom. BR1 124 EF91
Captain Cook Cl, Ch.St.G. HP8 36 AU49
Capthorne Av, Har. HA2 60 BY60
Capuchin Cl, Stan. HA7 41 CH51
Capulet Ms, E16 205 N2
Capulet Sq, E3 *off Talwin St* 85 EB69
Capworth St, E10 67 EA60
Caractacus Cottage Vw, Wat. WD18 39 BU45
Caractacus Grn, Wat. WD18 23 BT44
Caradoc Cl, W2 82 DA72
Caradoc St, SE10 205 H10
Caradon Cl, E11 68 EE60
Woking GU21 166 AV118
Caradon Way, N15 66 DR56
Caravan La, Rick. WD3 38 BL45
Caravel Cl, E14 203 P6
Grays RM16 110 FZ76
Caravelle Gdns, Nthlt. UB5
off Javelin Way 78 BX69
Caravel Ms, SE8
off Watergate St 103 EA79
Caraway Cl, E13 86 EH71
Caraway Pl, Wall. SM6 141 DH104
Carberry Rd, SE19 122 DS93
Carbery Av, W3 98 CM75
Carbis Cl, E4 47 ED46
Carbis Rd, E14 85 DZ72
Carbone Hill, Hert. (Newgate St) SG13 13 DK26
Potters Bar (Cuffley) EN6 13 DJ27
Carbuncle Pas Way, N17 46 DU54
Carburton St, W1 195 J6
Carbury Cl, Horn. RM12 90 FJ65
Cardale St, E14 204 D6
Carden Rd, SE15 102 DV83
Cardiff Rd, W7 97 CG76
Enfield EN3 30 DV42
Watford WD18 23 BV44
Cardiff St, SE18 105 ES80
Cardiff Way, Abb.L. WD5 7 BU32
Cardigan Cl, Wok. GU21 166 AS118
Cardigan Gdns, Ilf. IG3 70 EU61
Cardigan Rd, E3 85 DZ68
SW13 99 CU82
SW19 *off Haydons Rd* 120 DC93
Richmond TW10 118 CL86
Cardigan St, SE11 200 D10
Cardigan Wk, N1
off Ashby Gro 84 DQ66
Cardinal Av, Borwd. WD6 26 CP41
Kingston upon Thames KT2 118 CL92
Morden SM4 139 CY100
Cardinal Bourne St, SE1 201 L7
Cardinal Cap All, SE1
off New Globe Wk 84 DQ73
Cardinal Cl, Chis. BR7 145 ER95
Edgware HA8
off Abbots Rd 42 CR52
Morden SM4 139 CY101
South Croydon CR2 160 DU113
Waltham Cross (Chsht) EN7
off Adamsfield 14 DT26
Worcester Park KT4 157 CU105
Cardinal Ct, Borwd. WD6
off Cardinal Av 26 CP41
Cardinal Cres, N.Mal. KT3 138 CQ96
Cardinal Dr, Ilf. IG6 49 EQ51
Walton-on-Thames KT12 136 BX102
Cardinal Hinsley Cl, NW10 81 CU68
Cardinal Pl, SW15 99 CX84
Cardinal Rd, Felt. TW13 115 BV88
Ruislip HA4 60 BX60
Cardinals Wk, Hmptn. TW12 116 CC94
Sunbury-on-Thames TW16 115 BS93
Cardinals Way, N19 65 DK60
Cardinal Way, Har. HA3
off Wolseley Rd 61 CE55
Rainham RM13 90 FK68
Cardine Ms, SE15 102 DV80
Cardingham, Wok. GU21 166 AU117
Cardington Sq, Houns. TW4 96 BX84
Cardington St, NW1 195 K2
Cardinham Rd, Orp. BR6 163 ET105
Cardozo Rd, N7 65 DL64
Cardrew Av, N12 44 DD50
Cardrew Cl, N12 44 DE50
Cardross St, W6 99 CV76
Cardwell Rd, N7 65 DL63
Carew Cl, N7 65 DM61
Coulsdon CR5 175 DP119
Grays (Chaff.Hun.) RM16 110 FY76
Carew Ct, Sutt. SM2 158 DB109
Carew Rd, N17 46 DU54
W13 97 CJ75
Ashford TW15 115 BQ93
Mitcham CR4 140 DG96
Northwood HA6 39 BS51
Thornton Heath CR7 141 DP97
Wallington SM6 159 DJ107
Carew St, SE5 102 DQ82
Carew Way, Orp. BR5 146 EW102
Watford WD19 40 BZ48
Carey Ct, Bexh. DA6 127 FB85
Carey Gdns, SW8 101 DJ81
Carey La, EC2 197 H8
Carey Pl, SW1 199 M9
Carey Rd, Dag. RM9 70 EY63
Carey's Fld, Sev. (Dunt.Grn) TN13 181 FE120
Carey St, WC2 196 C9
Carey Way, Wem. HA9 62 CP63
Carfax Pl, SW4
off Holwood Pl 101 DK84
Carfax Rd, Hayes UB3 95 BT78
Hornchurch RM12 71 FF63
Carfree Cl, N1
off Bewdley St 83 DN66
Cargill Rd, SW18 120 DB88
Cargreen Pl, SE25
off Cargreen Rd 142 DT98
Cargreen Rd, SE25 142 DT98
Carholme Rd, SE23 123 DZ88
Carisbrooke Av, Bex. DA5 126 EX88
Watford WD24 24 BX39
Carisbrooke Cl, Enf. EN1 30 DT39
Hornchurch RM11 72 FN60
Stanmore HA7 41 CK54
Carisbrooke Ct, Slou. SL1 74 AT73
Carisbrooke Gdns, SE15
off Rosemary Rd 102 DT80
Carisbrooke Ho, Kings.T. KT2
off Kingsgate Rd 138 CL95
Carisbrooke Rd, E17 67 DY56
Bromley BR2 144 EJ98
Mitcham CR4 141 DK98
St. Albans AL2 8 CB26
Carisbrook Rd, Brwd. (Pilg.Hat.) CM15 54 FV44
Carker's La, NW5 65 DH64
Carl Ekman Ho, Grav. DA11 130 GD87
Carleton Av, Wall. SM6 159 DK109
Carleton Cl, Esher KT10 137 CD102
Carleton Pl, Dart. (Hort.Kir.) DA4 148 FQ98
Carleton Rd, N7 65 DK64
Dartford DA1 128 FN87
Waltham Cross (Chsht) EN8 15 DX28
Carleton Vil, NW5
off Leighton Gro 65 DJ64
Carlile Cl, E3 85 DZ68
Carlina Gdns, Wdf.Grn. IG8 48 EH50
Carlingford Gdns, Mitch. CR4 120 DF94
Carlingford Rd, N15 65 DP55
NW3 64 DD63
Morden SM4 139 CX100
Carlisle Av, EC3 197 N9
W3 80 CS72
Carlisle Cl, Kings.T. KT2 138 CN95
Pinner HA5 60 BY59
Carlisle Gdns, Har. HA3 61 CK59
Ilford IG1 68 EL58
Carlisle La, SE1 200 C7
Carlisle Ms, NW8 194 A6
Carlisle Pl, N11 45 DH49
SW1 199 K7
Carlisle Rd, E10 67 EA61
N4 65 DN59
NW6 81 CY67
NW9 62 CQ55
Dartford DA1 128 FN86
Hampton TW12 116 CB94
Romford RM1 71 FG57
Sutton SM1 157 CZ106
Carlisle St, W1 195 M9
Carlisle Wk, E8
off Cumberland Cl 84 DT65
Carlisle Way, SW17 120 DG92
Carlos Pl, W1 198 G1
Carlow St, NW1
off Arlington Rd 83 DJ68
Carlton Av, N14 29 DK43
Feltham TW14 116 BW86
Greenhithe DA9 129 FS86
Harrow HA3 61 CH57
Hayes UB3 95 BS77
South Croydon CR2 160 DS108
Carlton Av E, Wem. HA9 62 CL60
Carlton Av W, Wem. HA0 61 CH61
Carlton Cl, NW3 64 DA61
Borehamwood WD6 26 CR42
Chessington KT9 155 CK107
Edgware HA8 42 CN50
Northolt UB5
off Whitton Av W 60 CC64
Upminster RM14 72 FP61
Woking GU21 151 AZ114
Carlton Ct, SW9 101 DP81
Ilford IG6 69 ER55
Uxbridge UB8 76 BK71
Carlton Cres, Sutt. SM3 157 CY105
Carlton Dr, SW15 119 CY85
Ilford IG6 69 ER55
Carlton Gdns, SW1 199 M3
W5 79 CJ72
Carlton Grn, Red. RH1 184 DE131
Carlton Gro, SE15 102 DV81
Carlton Hill, NW8 82 DB68
Carlton Ho, Felt. TW14 115 BT87
Carlton Ho Ter, SW1 199 M3
Carlton Par, Orp. BR6 146 EV101
Sevenoaks TN13
off St. John's Hill 191 FJ122
Carlton Pk Av, SW20 139 CW96
Carlton Pl, Nthwd. HA6 39 BP50
Weybridge KT13
off Castle Vw Rd 153 BP105
Carlton Rd, E11 68 EF60
E12 68 EK63
E17 47 DY53
N4 65 DN59
N11 44 DG50
SW14 98 CQ83
W4 98 CR75
W5 79 CJ73
Erith DA8 107 FB79
Grays RM16 111 GF75
New Malden KT3 138 CS96
Redhill RH1 184 DF131
Reigate RH2 184 DD132
Romford RM2 71 FG57
Sidcup DA14 125 ET92
Slough SL2 74 AV73
South Croydon CR2 160 DR107
Sunbury-on-Thames TW16 115 BT94
Carlton Rd, Walt. KT12 135 BV101
Welling DA16 106 EV83
Woking GU21 151 BA114
Carlton Sq, E1 *off Argyle Rd* 85 DX70
Carlton St, SW1 199 M1
Carlton Ter, E11 68 EH57
N18 46 DR48
SE26 122 DW90
Carlton Twr Pl, SW1 198 E6
Carlton Vale, NW6 82 DB68
Carlton Vil, SW15
off St. John's Av 119 CX85
Carlwell St, SW17 120 DE92
Carlyle Av, Brom. BR1 144 EK97
Southall UB1 78 BZ73
Carlyle Cl, N2 64 DC58
West Molesey KT8 136 CB96
Carlyle Gdns, Sthl. UB1 78 BZ73
Carlyle Lo, Barn. (New Barn.) EN5 *off Richmond Rd* 28 DC43
Carlyle Ms, E1
off Alderney Rd 85 DX70
Carlyle Pl, SW15 99 CX84
Carlyle Rd, E12 68 EL63
NW10 80 CR67
SE28 88 EV73
W5 97 CJ78
Croydon CR0 142 DU103
Staines TW18 113 BF94
★ **Carlyle's Ho**, SW3 100 DE79
Carlyle Sq, SW3 100 DD78
Carlyon Av, Har. HA2 60 BZ63
Carlyon Cl, Wem. HA0 80 CL67
Carlyon Rd, Hayes UB4 78 BW72
Wembley HA0 80 CL68
Carmalt Gdns, SW15 99 CW84
Walton-on-Thames KT12 154 BW106
Carmarthen Grn, NW9
off Snowdon Dr 62 CS58
Carmarthen Pl, SE1 201 M4
Carmarthen Rd, Slou. SL1 74 AS73
Carmel Cl, Wok. GU22 166 AY118
Carmel Ct, W8
off Holland St 100 DB75
Wembley HA9 62 CP61
Carmelite Cl, Har. HA3 40 CC53
Carmelite Rd, Har. HA3 40 CC53
Carmelite St, EC4 196 E10
Carmelite Wk, Har. HA3 40 CC53
Carmelite Way, Har. HA3 40 CC54
Carmel Way, Rich. TW9
off Taylor Av 98 CP82
Carmen Ct, Borwd. WD6
off Belford Rd 26 CM38
Carmen St, E14 85 EB72
Carmichael Cl, SW11
off Darien Rd 100 DD83
Ruislip HA4 59 BU63
Carmichael Ms, SW18 120 DD87
Carmichael Rd, SE25 142 DU99
Carminia Rd, SW17 121 DH89
Carnaby St, W1 195 K9
Carnach Grn, S.Ock. RM15 91 FV73
Carnac St, SE27 122 DR91
Carnanton Rd, E17 47 ED53
Carnarvon Av, Enf. EN1 30 DT41
Carnarvon Dr, Hayes UB3 95 BQ76
Carnarvon Rd, E10 67 EC58
E15 86 EF65
E18 48 EF53
Barnet EN5 27 CY41
Carnation Cl, Rom. (Rush Grn) RM7 71 FE61
Carnation St, SE2 106 EV78
Carnbrook Rd, SE3 104 EK83
Carnecke Gdns, SE9 124 EL85
Carnegie Cl, Enf. EN3 31 EB38
Surbiton KT6
off Fullers Av 138 CM103
Carnegie Pl, SW19 119 CX90
Carnegie St, N1 83 DM67
Carnet Cl, Dart. DA1 127 FE87
Carnforth Cl, Epsom KT19 156 CP107
Carnforth Gdns, Horn. RM12 71 FG64
Carnforth Rd, SW16 121 DK94
Carnie Lo, SW17
off Manville Rd 121 DH90
Carnoustie Cl, SE28 88 EX72
Carnoustie Dr, N1 83 DM66
Carnwath Rd, SW6 100 DA83
Carol Cl, NW4 63 CX56
Carolina Cl, E15 68 EE64
Carolina Rd, Th.Hth. CR7 141 DP96
Caroline Cl, N10
off Alexandra Pk Rd 45 DH54
SW16 121 DM91
W2 *off Bayswater Rd* 82 DB73
Croydon CR0 160 DS105
Isleworth TW7 97 CD80
West Drayton UB7 94 BK75
Caroline Ct, Ashf. TW15 115 BP93
Stanmore HA7
off The Chase 41 CG51
Caroline Gdns, SE15 102 DV80
Caroline Pl, SW11 100 DG82
W2 82 DB73
Hayes UB3 95 BS80
Watford WD19 24 BY44
Caroline Pl Ms, W2
off Orme La 82 DB73
Caroline Rd, SW19 119 CZ94
Caroline St, E1 85 DX72
Caroline Ter, SW1 198 F9
Caroline Wk, W6 99 CY79
Carol St, NW1 83 DJ67
Carolyn Cl, Wok. GU21 166 AT119
Carolyn Dr, Orp. BR6 146 EU104
Caroon Dr, Rick. (Sarratt) WD3 22 BH36
Carpenders Av, Wat. WD19 40 BY48
CARPENDERS PARK, Wat. WD19 40 BZ47
⇌ **Carpenders Park** 40 BX48
Carpenders Pk, Wat. WD19 40 BY47
Carpenter Cl, Epsom KT17
off West St 157 CT109
Carpenter Gdns, N21 45 DP47
Carpenter Path, Brwd. (Hutt.) CM13 55 GD43
Carpenters Arms La, Epp. (Thnwd) CM16 18 EV25
Carpenters Arms Path, SE9
off Eltham High St 125 EM86
Carpenters Cl, Barn. EN5 28 DB44
Carpenters Ct, Twick. TW2 117 CE89
Carpenters Ms, N7
off North Rd 65 DL64
Carpenters Pl, SW4 101 DK84
Carpenters Rd, E15 85 EB65
Enfield EN1 30 DW36
Carpenter St, W1 199 H1
Carpenters Wd Dr, Rick. (Chorl.) WD3 21 BB42
Carpenter Way, Pot.B. EN6 12 DC33
Carrack Ho, Erith DA8
off Saltford Cl 107 FE78
Carrara Cl, SW9
off Eaton Dr 101 DP84
Carrara Ms, E8 66 DU64
Carrara Wf, SW6 99 CY83
Carr Cl, Stan. HA7 41 CG51
Carr Gro, SE18 104 EL77
Carriage Dr E, SW11 100 DG80
Carriage Dr N, SW11 100 DG79
Carriage Dr S, SW11 100 DF81
Carriage Dr W, SW11 100 DF80
Carriage Ms, Ilf. IG1 69 EQ61
Carriage Pl, N16 66 DR62
SW16 121 DJ92
Carriage St, SE18 105 EP76
Carriageway, The, West. (Brasted) TN16 180 EX124
Carrick Cl, Islw. TW7 97 CG83
Carrick Dr, Ilf. IG6 49 EQ53
Sevenoaks TN13 191 FH123
Carrick Gdns, N17
off Flexmere Rd 46 DS52
Carrick Gate, Esher KT10 136 CC104
Carrick Ms, SE8
off Watergate St 103 EA79
Carrill Way, Belv. DA17 106 EX77
Carrington Av, Borwd. WD6 26 CP43
Hounslow TW3 116 CB85
Carrington Cl, Barn. EN5 27 CU43
Borehamwood WD6 26 CQ43
Croydon CR0 143 DY101
Kingston upon Thames KT2 118 CQ92
Redhill RH1 184 DF133
Carrington Gdns, E7
off Woodford Rd 68 EH63
Carrington Pl, Esher KT10 154 CC105
Carrington Rd, Dart. DA1 128 FM86
Richmond TW10 98 CN84
Slough SL1 74 AS73
Carrington Sq, Har. HA3 40 CC52
Carrington St, W1 199 H3
Carrol Cl, NW5 65 DH63
Carroll Cl, E15 68 EF64
Carroll Hill, Loug. IG10 33 EM41
Carronade Pl, SE28 105 EQ76
Carron Cl, E14 85 EB72
Carroun Rd, SW8 101 DM80
Carroway La, Grnf. UB6
off Cowgate Rd 79 CD69
Carrow Rd, Dag. RM9 88 EV66
Walton-on-Thames KT12
off Kenilworth Dr 136 BX104
Carr Rd, E17 47 DZ54
Northolt UB5 78 CA65
Carrs La, N21 30 DQ43
Carr St, E14 85 DY71
CARSHALTON, SM5 158 DD105
⇌ **Carshalton** 158 DF105
H **Carshalton, Beddington & Wallington War Mem Hosp**, Cars. SM5 158 DF107
CARSHALTON BEECHES, Cars. SM5 158 DD109
⇌ **Carshalton Beeches** 158 DF107
Carshalton Gro, Sutt. SM1 158 DD105
CARSHALTON ON THE HILL, Cars. SM5 158 DG109
Carshalton Pk Rd, Cars. SM5 158 DF106
Carshalton Pl, Cars. SM5 158 DG105
Carshalton Rd, Bans. SM7 158 DF114
Carshalton SM5 158 DC106
Mitcham CR4 140 DG98
Sutton SM1 158 DC106
Carsington Gdns, Dart. DA1 128 FK89
Carslake Rd, SW15 119 CW86
Carson Rd, E16 86 EG70
SE21 122 DR89
Barnet EN4 28 DF42
Carstairs Rd, SE6 123 EC90
Carston Cl, SE12 124 EF85
Carswell Cl, Brwd. (Hutt.) CM13 55 GD44
Ilford IG4
off Roding La S 68 EK56
Carswell Rd, SE6 123 EC87
Cartbridge Cl, Wok. (Send) GU23 *off Send Rd* 167 BB123
Cartel Cl, Purf. RM19 109 FR77
Carter Cl, NW9 62 CR58
Romford RM5 51 FB52
Wallington SM6 159 DK108
Carter Ct, EC4 *off Carter La* 83 DP72
Carter Dr, Rom. RM5 51 FB52
Carteret St, SW1 199 M5
Carteret Way, SE8 203 L9
Carterhatch La, Enf. EN1 30 DU40
Carterhatch Rd, Enf. EN3 30 DW40
Carter La, EC4 196 G9
Carter Pl, SE17 102 DQ78
Carter Rd, E13 86 EH67
SW19 120 DD93
Carters Cl, Wor.Pk. KT4 139 CX103
Cartersfield Rd, Wal.Abb. EN9 15 EC34
Carters Hill, Sev. (Undrvr) TN15 191 FP127
Carters Hill Cl, SE9 124 EJ88
Carters La, SE23 123 DY89
Woking GU22 167 BC120
Carters Rd, Epsom KT17 173 CT115
Carters Row, Grav. (Nthflt) DA11 131 GF88
Carter St, SE17 102 DQ79
Carters Yd, SW18
off Wandsworth High St 120 DA85
Carthew Rd, W6 99 CV76
Carthew Vil, W6 99 CV76
Carthouse La, Wok. GU21 150 AS114
Carthusian St, EC1 197 H6
Cartier Circle, E14 204 C3
Carting La, WC2 200 A1
Cart La, E4 47 ED45
Cartmel, NW1
off Hampstead Rd 83 DJ69
Cartmel Cl, N17
off Heybourne Rd 46 DV52
Reigate RH2 184 DE133
Cartmel Gdns, Mord. SM4 140 DC99
Cartmel Rd, Bexh. DA7 106 FA81
Carton St, W1 194 E8
Cart Path, Wat. WD25 8 BW33
Cartridge Pl, SE18 105 EP76
Cartwright Gdns, WC1 195 P3
Cartwright Rd, Dag. RM9 88 EZ66
Cartwright St, E1 84 DT73
Cartwright Way, SW13 99 CV80
Carver Cl, W4 98 CQ76
Carver Rd, SE24 122 DQ86
Carville Cres, Brent. TW8 98 CL77
Cary Rd, E11 68 EE63
Carysfort Rd, N8 65 DK57
N16 66 DR62
Cary Wk, Rad. WD7 9 CH34
Casby Ho, SE16
off Dickens Est 102 DU76
Cascade Av, N10 65 DJ56
Cascade Cl, Buck.H. IG9
off Cascade Rd 48 EK47
Orpington BR5 146 EW97
Cascade Rd, Buck.H. IG9 48 EK47
Cascades, Croy. CR0 161 DZ110
Cascades Twr, E14
off Westferry Rd 85 EA74
Caselden Cl, Add. KT15 152 BJ106
Casella Rd, SE14 103 DX80
Casewick Rd, SE27 121 DP91
Casey Cl, NW8 194 B3
Casimir Rd, E5 66 DV62
Casino Av, SE24 122 DQ85
Caspian St, SE5 102 DR80
Caspian Wk, E16 86 EK72
Caspian Way, Purf. RM19 108 FN78
Swanscombe DA10 130 FY85
Caspian Wf, E3 *off Violet Rd* 85 EB71
Cassandra Cl, Nthlt. UB5 61 CD63
Cassandra Gate, Wal.Cr. EN8 15 DZ27
Casselden Rd, NW10 80 CR66
H **Cassel Hosp, The**, Rich. TW10 117 CK91
Cassidy Rd, SW6 100 DA80
Cassilda Rd, SE2 106 EU77
Cassilis Rd, E14 204 A5
Twickenham TW1 117 CH85
Cassiobridge, Wat. WD18 23 BR42
Cassiobridge Rd, Wat. WD18 23 BS42
Cassiobury Av, Felt. TW14 115 BT86
Cassiobury Ct, Wat. WD17 23 BT40
Cassiobury Dr, Wat. WD17 23 BT40
★ **Cassiobury Park**, Wat. WD18 23 BS41
Cassiobury Pk, Wat. WD18 23 BS41
Cassiobury Pk Av, Wat. WD18 23 BS41
Cassiobury Rd, E17 67 DX57
Cassio Pl, Wat. WD18 23 BS42
Cassio Rd, Wat. WD18 23 BV41
Cassis Ct, Loug. IG10 33 EQ42
Cassland Rd, E9 84 DW66
Thornton Heath CR7 142 DR98
Casslee Rd, SE6 123 DZ87
Cassocks Sq, Shep. TW17 135 BR100
Casson St, E1 84 DU71
Casstine Cl, Swan. BR8 127 FF94
Castalia Sq, E14 204 D5
Castalia St, E14
off Plevna St 103 EC75
Castano Ct, Abb.L. WD5 7 BS31
Castellain Rd, W9 82 DB70
Castellan Av, Rom. RM2 71 FH55
Castellane Cl, Stan. HA7
off Daventer Dr 41 CF52
Castello Av, SW15 119 CW85
Castell Rd, Loug. IG10 33 EQ39
CASTELNAU, SW13 99 CU79
Castelnau, SW13 99 CV79
Castelnau Gdns, SW13
off Arundel Ter 99 CV79
Castelnau Pl, SW13
off Castelnau 99 CV79
Castelnau Row, SW13
off Lonsdale Rd 99 CV79
Casterbridge, NW6 82 DB67
Casterbridge Rd, SE3 104 EG83
Casterton St, E8
off Wilton Way 84 DV65
Castile Rd, SE18 105 EN77
Castillon Rd, SE6 124 EE89
Castlands Rd, SE6 123 DZ89
Castle Av, E4 47 ED50
Epsom KT17 157 CU109
Rainham RM13 89 FE66
Slough (Datchet) SL3 92 AU79
West Drayton UB7 76 BL73
Castlebar Hill, W5 79 CH71
Castlebar Ms, W5 79 CJ71
⇌ **Castle Bar Park** 79 CF71
Castlebar Pk, W5 79 CH70
Castlebar Rd, W5 79 CJ71
Castle Baynard St, EC4 196 G10
Castlebrook Cl, SE11 200 F8
Castle Cl, E9
off Swinnerton St 67 DY64
SW19 119 CX90
W3 98 CP75
Bromley BR2 144 EE97
Bushey WD23 24 CB44
Redhill (Bletch.) RH1 186 DQ133
Romford RM3 52 FJ48
Sunbury-on-Thames TW16
off Mill Fm Av 115 BS94
Castlecombe Dr, SW19 119 CX87
Castlecombe Rd, SE9 124 EL91
Castle Ct, EC3 197 L9
SE26 *off Champion Rd* 123 DY91
SW15 99 CY83
Castledine Rd, SE20 122 DV94
Castle Dr, Ilf. IG4 68 EL58
Castle Fm Rd, Sev. (Shore.) TN14 165 FF109
Castlefield Rd, Reig. RH2 184 DA133
Castleford Av, SE9 125 EP88
Castleford Cl, N17 46 DT51
Borehamwood WD6 26 CM38
Castle Gdns, Dor. RH4 182 CM134
Castlegate, Rich. TW9 98 CM83
Castle Grn, Wey. KT13 135 BS104

Castle Gro Rd, Wok. (Chobham) GU24 150 AS113
Castlehaven Rd, NW1 83 DH66
Castle Hill, Long. (Fawk.) DA3 149 FX99
Castle Hill Av, Croy. (New Adgtn) CR0 161 EB109
Castle Hill Rd, Egh. TW20 112 AV91
Castle La, SW1 199 L6
Castleleigh Ct, Enf. EN2 30 DR43
Castlemaine Av, Epsom KT17 157 CV109
South Croydon CR2 160 DT106
Castlemaine Twr, SW11 100 DF81
Castlemain St, E1 84 DV71
Castle Ms, N12 off Castle Rd 44 DC50
NW1 off Castle Rd 83 DH65
SW17 120 DE91
Hampton TW12 off Station Rd 136 CB95
Castle Par, Epsom KT17 off Ewell Bypass 157 CU108
Castle Pl, NW1 83 DH65
W4 off Windmill Rd 98 CS77
Castle Pt, E13 86 EJ68
Castlereagh St, W1 194 D8
Castle Rd, N12 44 DC50
NW1 83 DH65
Coulsdon (Chipstead) CR5 174 DE120
Dagenham RM9 88 EV67
Dartford (Eyns.) DA4 165 FH107
Enfield EN3 31 DY39
Epsom KT18 172 CP115
Grays RM17 110 FZ79
Isleworth TW7 97 CF82
Northolt UB5 78 CB65
Sevenoaks (Shore.) TN14 165 FG108
Southall UB2 96 BZ76
Swanscombe DA10 130 FZ86
Weybridge KT13 135 BS104
Woking GU21 151 AZ114
Castle Sq, Red. (Bletch.) RH1 186 DQ133
Castle St, E6 86 EJ68
Greenhithe DA9 129 FU85
Kingston upon Thames KT1 138 CL96
Redhill (Bletch.) RH1 185 DP133
Slough SL1 92 AT76
Swanscombe DA10 130 FZ86
Castleton Av, Bexh. DA7 107 FD81
Wembley HA9 62 CL63
Castleton Cl, Bans. SM7 174 DA115
Croydon CR0 143 DY100
Castleton Dr, Bans. SM7 174 DA115
Castleton Gdns, Wem. HA9 62 CL62
Castleton Rd, E17 47 ED54
SE9 124 EK91
Ilford IG3 70 EU60
Mitcham CR4 141 DK98
Ruislip HA4 60 BX60
Castletown Rd, W14 99 CY78
Castle Vw, Epsom KT18 156 CP114
Castleview Cl, N4 66 DQ60
Castleview Gdns, Ilf. IG1 68 EL58
Castleview Rd, Slou. SL3 92 AW77
Castle Vw Rd, Wey. KT13 153 BP105
Castle Wk, Reig. RH2 off London Rd 184 DA134
Sunbury-on-Thames TW16 off Elizabeth Gdns 136 BW97
Castle Way, SW19 119 CX90
Epsom KT17 off Castle Av 157 CU109
Feltham TW13 116 BW91
Castlewood Dr, SE9 105 EM82
Castlewood Rd, N15 66 DU58
N16 66 DU59
Barnet EN4 28 DD41
H Castlewood Therapy Cen, SE18 105 EN81
Castle Yd, N6 off North Rd 64 DG59
SE1 200 G2
Richmond TW10 off Hill St 117 CK85
Castor La, E14 204 B1
Catalina Av, Grays (Chaff.Hun.) RM16 110 FZ75
Catalina Rd, Houns. (Hthrw Air.) TW6 off Cromer Rd 94 BN82
Catalin Ct, Wal.Abb. EN9 off Howard Cl 15 ED33
Catalpa Ct, SE13 off Hither Grn La 123 ED86
CATERHAM, CR3 176 DU123
⇌ Caterham 176 DU124
Caterham Av, Ilf. IG5 49 EM54
Caterham Bypass, Cat. CR3 176 DV120
Caterham Cl, Cat. CR3 176 DS120
Caterham Ct, Wal.Abb. EN9 16 EF34
H Caterham Dene Hosp, Cat. CR3 176 DT123
Caterham Dr, Couls. CR5 175 DP118
CATERHAM-ON-THE-HILL, Cat. CR3 176 DT122
Caterham Rd, SE13 103 EC83
Catesby St, SE17 201 L9
CATFORD, SE6 123 EB88
⇌ Catford 123 EA87
⇌ Catford Bridge 123 EA87
Catford Bdy, SE6 123 EB87
Catford Gyratory, SE6 off Rushey Grn 123 EB87
Catford Hill, SE6 123 DZ89
Catford Ms, SE6 off Holbeach Rd 123 EB87
Catford Rd, SE6 123 EA88
Cathall Rd, E11 67 ED62
Cathay St, SE16 202 E5
Cathay Wk, Nthlt. UB5 off Brabazon Rd 78 CA68
Cathcart Dr, Orp. BR6 145 ES103
Cathcart Hill, N19 65 DJ62
Cathcart Rd, SW10 100 DC79
Cathcart St, NW5 83 DH65
Cathedral Piazza, SW1 199 K7
Cathedral St, SE1 201 K2
Catherall Rd, N5 66 DQ62
Catherine Cl, Brwd. (Pilg.Hat.) CM15 54 FU43
Grays RM16 110 FZ75
Loughton IG10 off Roding Gdns 33 EM44
West Byfleet (Byfleet) KT14 152 BL114
Catherine Ct, N14 off Conisbee Ct 29 DJ43
Catherine Dr, Rich. TW9 98 CL84
Sunbury-on-Thames TW16 115 BT93
Catherine Gdns, Houns. TW3 97 CD84
Catherine Griffiths Ct, EC1 196 E4
Catherine Gro, SE10 103 EB81
Catherine Howard Ct, Wey. KT13 off Old Palace Rd 135 BP104
Catherine Pl, SW1 199 K6
Harrow HA1 61 CF57
Catherine Rd, Enf. EN3 31 DY36
Romford RM2 71 FH57
Surbiton KT6 137 CK99
Catherine's Cl, West Dr. UB7 off Money La 94 BK76
Catherine St, WC2 196 B10
Catherine Wheel All, E1 197 N7
Catherine Wheel Rd, Brent. TW8 97 CK80
Catherine Wheel Yd, SW1 199 K3
Cat Hill, Barn. EN4 28 DE44
Cathles Rd, SW12 121 DH86
Cathnor Rd, W12 99 CV75
Catisfield Rd, Enf. EN3 31 DY37
Catlin Cres, Shep. TW17 135 BR99
Catlin Gdns, Gdse. RH9 186 DV130
Catling Cl, SE23 122 DW90
Catlins La, Pnr. HA5 59 BV55
Catlin St, SE16 102 DU78
Cator Cl, Croy. (New Adgtn) CR0 162 EE111
Cator Cres, Croy. (New Adgtn) CR0 161 ED111
Cator La, Beck. BR3 143 DZ96
Cato Rd, SW4 101 DK83
Cator Rd, SE26 123 DX93
Carshalton SM5 158 DF106
Cator St, SE15 102 DT79
Cato St, W1 194 C7
Catsey La, Bushey WD23 40 CC45
Catsey Wds, Bushey WD23 40 CC45
Catterick Cl, N11 44 DG51
Catterick Way, Borwd. WD6 26 CM39
Cattistock Rd, SE9 124 EL92
CATTLEGATE, Enf. EN2 13 DL33
Cattlegate Hill, Pot.B. (Northaw) EN6 13 DK31
Cattlegate Rd, Enf. EN2 13 DL34
Potters Bar EN6 13 DK31
Cattley Cl, Barn. EN5 off Wood St 27 CY42
Cattlins Cl, Wal.Cr. (Chsht) EN7 14 DS29
Catton St, WC1 196 B7
Caughley Ho, SE11 off Lambeth Wk 101 DN76
Caulfield Rd, E6 87 EM66
SE15 102 DV82
Causeway, The, N2 64 DE56
SW18 100 DB84
SW19 119 CX92
Carshalton SM5 140 DG104
Chessington KT9 156 CL105
Esher (Clay.) KT10 155 CF108
Feltham TW14 95 BU84
Hounslow TW4 95 BU84
Potters Bar EN6 12 DC31
Staines TW18 113 BC91
Sutton SM2 158 DC109
Teddington TW11 off Broad St 117 CF93
Causeway Cl, Pot.B. EN6 12 DD31
Causeway Ct, Wok. GU21 off Bingham Dr 166 AT118
Causeyware Rd, N9 46 DV45
Causton Rd, N6 65 DH59
Causton Sq, Dag. RM10 88 FA66
Causton St, SW1 199 N9
Cautley Av, SW4 121 DJ85
Cavalier Cl, Rom. RM6 70 EX56
Cavalier Gdns, Hayes UB3 off Hanover Circle 77 BR72
Cavalry Barracks, Houns. TW4 96 BX83
Cavalry Cres, Houns. TW4 96 BX84
Cavalry Gdns, SW15 119 CY85
Cavan Pl, Pnr. HA5 40 BZ53
Cavaye Pl, SW10 off Fulham Rd 100 DC78
Cavell Cres, Dart. DA1 108 FN84
Romford (Harold Wd) RM3 52 FL54
Cavell Dr, Enf. EN2 29 DN40
Cavell Rd, N17 46 DR52
Waltham Cross (Chsht) EN7 14 DT27
Cavell St, E1 84 DV71
Cavell Way, Epsom KT19 156 CN111
Cavendish Av, N3 44 DA54
NW8 194 A1
W13 79 CG71
Erith DA8 107 FC79
Harrow HA1 61 CD63
Hornchurch RM12 89 FH65
New Malden KT3 139 CV99
Ruislip HA4 59 BV64
Sevenoaks TN13 190 FG122
Sidcup DA15 126 EU87
Welling DA16 105 ET83
Woodford Green IG8 48 EH53
Cavendish Cl, N18 46 DV50
NW6 off Cavendish Rd 81 CZ66
NW8 194 A2
Amersham HP6 20 AV39
Hayes UB4 off Westacott 77 BS71
Sunbury-on-Thames TW16 115 BT93
Cavendish Ct, EC3 197 N8
Rickmansworth (Crox.Grn) WD3 off Mayfare 23 BR43
Sunbury-on-Thames TW16 115 BT93
Cavendish Cres, Borwd. (Els.) WD6 26 CN42
Hornchurch RM12 89 FH65
Cavendish Dr, E11 67 ED60
Edgware HA8 42 CM51
Esher (Clay.) KT10 155 CE106
Cavendish Gdns, Bark. IG11 69 ES64
Ilford IG1 69 EN60
Redhill RH1 184 DG133
Romford RM6 70 EY57
South Ockendon RM15 108 FQ75
Cavendish Ms N, W1 195 J6
Cavendish Ms S, W1 195 J7
Cavendish Par, Houns. TW4 off Bath Rd 96 BY82
Cavendish Pl, NW2 81 CX65
W1 195 J8
Bromley BR1 145 EM97
Cavendish Rd, E4 47 EC51
N4 65 DN58
N18 46 DV50
NW6 81 CY66
SW12 121 DH86
SW19 120 DD94
W4 98 CQ81
Barnet EN5 27 CW41
Croydon CR0 141 DP102
New Malden KT3 139 CT99
Redhill RH1 184 DG134
Sunbury-on-Thames TW16 115 BT93
Sutton SM2 158 DC108
Weybridge KT13 153 BQ108
Woking GU22 166 AX119
Cavendish Sq, W1 195 J8
Longfield DA3 149 FX97
Cavendish St, N1 197 K1
Cavendish Ter, Felt. TW13 off High St 115 BU89
Cavendish Wk, Epsom KT19 156 CP111
Cavendish Way, W.Wick. BR4 143 EB102
Cavenham Cl, Wok. GU22 166 AY119
Cavenham Gdns, Horn. RM11 72 FJ57
Ilford IG1 69 ER62
Caverleigh Way, Wor.Pk. KT4 139 CU102
Cave Rd, E13 86 EH68
Richmond TW10 117 CJ91
Caversham Av, N13 45 DN48
Sutton SM3 139 CY103
Caversham Ct, N11 44 DG48
Caversham Flats, SW3 off Caversham St 100 DF79
Caversham Rd, N15 66 DQ56
NW5 83 DJ65
Kingston upon Thames KT1 138 CM96
Caversham St, SW3 100 DF79
Caverswall St, W12 81 CW72
Caveside Cl, Chis. BR7 145 EN95
Cavill's Wk, Chig. IG7 50 EW47
Romford RM4 50 EX47
Cawdor Av, S.Ock. RM15 91 FU73
Cawdor Cres, W7 97 CG77
Cawnpore St, SE19 122 DS92
Cawsey Way, Wok. GU21 166 AY117
Caxton Av, Add. KT15 152 BG107
Caxton Dr, Uxb. UB8 off Chiltern Vw Rd 76 BK68
Caxton Gro, E3 85 EA69
Caxton La, Oxt. RH8 188 EL131
Caxton Ms, Brent. TW8 off The Butts 97 CK79
Caxton Ri, Red. RH1 184 DG133
Caxton Rd, N22 45 DM54
SW19 120 DC92
W12 99 CX75
Southall UB2 96 BX76
Caxton St, SW1 199 L6
Caxton St N, E16 off Victoria Dock Rd 86 EF73
Caxton Way, Rom. RM1 71 FE56
Watford WD18 23 BR44
Cayenne Ct, SE1 202 A3
Cayford Ho, NW3 off Lawn Rd 64 DE64
Caygill Cl, Brom. BR2 144 EF98
Cayley Cl, Wall. SM6 159 DL108
Cayley Rd, Sthl. UB2 off McNair Rd 96 CB76
Cayton Pl, EC1 197 K3
Cayton Rd, Couls. CR5 175 DJ122
Greenford UB6 79 CE68
Cayton St, EC1 197 K3
Cazenove Rd, E17 47 EA53
N16 66 DT61
Cearns Ho, E6 86 EK67
Cearn Way, Couls. CR5 175 DM115
Cecil Av, Bark. IG11 87 ER66
Enfield EN1 30 DT42
Grays RM16 110 FZ75
Hornchurch RM11 72 FL55
Wembley HA9 62 CM64
Cecil Cl, W5 79 CK71
Ashford TW15 115 BQ93
Chessington KT9 155 CK105
Cecil Ct, WC2 199 N1
Barnet EN5 27 CX41
Cecile Pk, N8 65 DL58
Cecilia Cl, N2 64 DC55
★ Cecilia Coleman Gall, NW8 82 DD68
Cecilia Rd, E8 66 DU64
Cecil Pk, Pnr. HA5 60 BY56
Cecil Pl, Mitch. CR4 140 DF99
Cecil Rd, E11 68 EE62
E13 86 EG67
E17 47 EA53
N10 45 DH54
N14 45 DJ46
NW9 62 CS55
NW10 80 CS67
SW19 120 DB94
W3 80 CQ71
Ashford TW15 115 BQ94
Croydon CR0 141 DM100
Enfield EN2 30 DR42
Gravesend DA11 131 GF88
Harrow HA3 61 CE55
Hounslow TW3 96 CC82
Ilford IG1 69 EP63
Iver SL0 75 BE72
Potters Bar EN6 11 CU32
Romford RM6 70 EX59
Sutton SM1 157 CZ107
Waltham Cross (Chsht) EN8 15 DX32
★ Cecil Sharp Ho, NW1 82 DG67
Cecil St, Wat. WD24 23 BV38
Cecil Way, Brom. BR2 144 EG102
Cedar Av, Barn. EN4 44 DE45
Cobham KT11 170 BW115
Enfield EN3 30 DW40
Gravesend DA12 131 GJ91
Hayes UB3 77 BU72
Romford RM6 70 EY57
Ruislip HA4 78 BW65
Sidcup DA15 126 EU87
Twickenham TW2 116 CB86
Upminster RM14 72 FN63
Cedar Av, Wal. Cr. EN8 15 DX33
West Drayton UB7 76 BM74
Cedar Cl, E3 85 DZ67
SE21 122 DQ88
SW15 118 CR91
Borehamwood WD6 26 CP42
Brentwood (Hutt.) CM13 55 GD45
Bromley BR2 144 EL104
Buckhurst Hill IG9 48 EK47
Carshalton SM5 158 DF107
Chesham HP5 4 AS30
East Molesey KT8 off Cedar Rd 137 CE98
Epsom KT17 157 CT114
Esher KT10 154 BZ108
Ilford IG1 69 ER64
Iver SL0 off Thornbridge Rd 75 BC66
Potters Bar EN6 12 DA30
Romford RM7 71 FC56
Staines TW18 134 BJ97
Swanley BR8 147 FC96
Warlingham CR6 177 DY118
Cedar Copse, Brom. BR1 145 EM96
Cedar Ct, E11 off Grosvenor Rd 68 EH57
N1 off Essex Rd 84 DQ66
SE9 124 EL86
SW19 119 CX90
Egham TW20 113 BA91
Epping CM16 18 EU31
Cedar Cres, Brom. BR2 144 EL104
Cedarcroft Rd, Chess. KT9 156 CM105
Cedar Dr, N2 64 DE56
Dartford (Sutt.H.) DA4 148 FP96
Leatherhead (Fetch.) KT22 171 CE123
Loughton IG10 33 EP40
Pinner HA5 40 CA51
Cedar Gdns, Sutt. SM2 158 DC107
Upminster RM14 72 FQ62
Woking GU21 off St. John's Rd 166 AV118
Cedar Gro, W5 98 CL76
Bexley DA5 126 EW86
Southall UB1 78 CA71
Weybridge KT13 153 BQ105
Cedar Hts, Rich. TW10 118 CL88
Cedar Hill, Epsom KT18 172 CQ116
Cedar Ho, Croy. CR0 161 EB107
Sunbury-on-Thames TW16 115 BT94
Cedarhurst, Brom. BR1 off Elstree Hill 124 EE94
Cedarhurst Dr, SE9 124 EJ85
Cedar Lawn Av, Barn. EN5 27 CY43
Cedar Mt, SE9 124 EK88
Cedarne Rd, SW6 100 DB80
Cedar Pk, Cat. CR3 176 DS121
Chigwell IG7 off High Rd 49 EP49
Cedar Pk Gdns, Rom. RM6 70 EX59
Cedar Pk Rd, Enf. EN2 30 DQ38
Cedar Pl, SE7 off Floyd Rd 104 EJ78
Northwood HA6 39 BQ51
Cedar Ri, N14 44 DG45
South Ockendon RM15 off Sycamore Way 91 FX70
Cedar Rd, N17 46 DT53
NW2 63 CW63
Brentwood (Hutt.) CM13 55 GD44
Bromley BR1 144 EJ96
Cobham KT11 153 BV114
Croydon CR0 142 DS103
Dartford DA1 128 FK88
East Molesey KT8 137 CE98
Enfield EN2 29 DP38
Erith DA8 107 FG81
Feltham TW14 115 BR88
Grays RM16 111 GG76
Hornchurch RM12 72 FJ62
Hounslow TW4 96 BW82
Romford RM7 71 FC56
Sutton SM2 158 DC107
Teddington TW11 117 CG92
Watford WD19 24 BW44
Weybridge KT13 152 BN105
Woking GU22 166 AV120
Cedars, Bans. SM7 158 DF114
Cedars, The, E15 off Portway 86 EF67
W13 off Heronsforde 79 CJ72
Buckhurst Hill IG9 48 EG46
Leatherhead KT22 172 CL121
Reigate RH2 184 DD134
Teddington TW11 off Adelaide Rd 117 CF93
West Byfleet (Byfleet) KT14 152 BM112
Cedars Av, E17 67 EA57
Mitcham CR4 140 DG98
Rickmansworth WD3 38 BJ46
Cedars Cl, NW4 63 CX55
SE13 103 ED83
Gerrards Cross (Chal.St.P.) SL9 36 AY50
Cedars Ct, N9 off Church St 46 DS47
Cedars Dr, Uxb. UB10 76 BM68
Cedars Ms, SW4 off Cedars Rd 101 DH84
Cedars Rd, E15 86 EE65
N9 off Church St 46 DU47
N21 45 DP47
SW4 101 DH83
SW13 99 CT82
W4 98 CQ78
Beckenham BR3 143 DY96
Croydon CR0 141 DL104
Kingston upon Thames (Hmptn W.) KT1 137 CJ95
Morden SM4 140 DA98
Cedars Wk, Rick. (Chorl.) WD3 21 BF42
Cedar Ter, Rich. TW9 98 CL84
Cedar Ter Rd, Sev. TN13 191 FJ123
Cedar Tree Gro, SE27 121 DP92
Cedarville Gdns, SW16 121 DM93
Cedar Vista, Rich. TW9 off Kew Rd 98 CL81
Cedar Wk, Esher (Clay.) KT10 155 CF107
Kenley CR8 176 DQ116
Tadworth (Kgswd) KT20 173 CY120
Waltham Abbey EN9 15 ED34
Cedar Way, NW1 83 DK66
Slough SL3 92 AY78
Sunbury-on-Thames TW16 115 BS94
Cedar Wd Dr, Wat. WD25 23 BV35
Cedra Ct, N16 66 DU60
Cedric Av, Rom. RM1 71 FE55
Cedric Rd, SE9 125 EQ90
Celadon Cl, Enf. EN3 31 DY41
Celandine Cl, E14 85 EA71
South Ockendon RM15 91 FW70
Celandine Dr, E8 84 DT66
SE28 88 EV74
Celandine Gro, N14 29 DJ43
Celandine Rd, Walt. KT12 154 BY105
Celandine Way, E15 86 EE69
Celbridge Ms, W2 off Porchester Rd 82 DB72
Celedon Cl, Grays RM16 110 FY75
Celestial Gdns, SE13 103 ED84
Celia Cres, Ashf. TW15 114 BK93
Celia Rd, N19 65 DJ63
Cell Fm Av, Wind. (Old Wind.) SL4 112 AV85
Celtic Av, Brom. BR2 144 EE97
Celtic Rd, W.Byf. (Byfleet) KT14 152 BL114
Celtic St, E14 85 EB71
Cement Block Cotts, Grays RM17 110 GC79
Cemetery La, SE7 104 EL79
Shepperton TW17 135 BP101
Waltham Abbey EN9 16 EF25
Cemetery Rd, E7 68 EF63
N17 46 DS52
SE2 106 EV80
Cenacle Cl, NW3 64 DA62
★ Cenotaph, The, SW1 199 P4
Centaurs Business Cen, Islw. TW7 97 CG79
Centaur St, SE1 200 C6
Centaury Ct, Grays RM17 110 GD79
Centenary Est, Enf. EN3 31 DZ42
Centenary Rd, Enf. EN3 31 DZ42
Centenary Wk, Loug. IG10 32 EH41
Centenary Way, Amer. HP6 20 AT38
Centennial Av, Borwd. (Els.) WD6 41 CH45
Centennial Pk, Borwd. (Els.) WD6 41 CJ45
Central Av, E11 67 ED61
N2 44 DD54
N9 46 DS48
SW11 100 DF80
Enfield EN1 30 DV40
Gravesend DA12 131 GH89
Grays RM20 109 FT77
Hayes UB3 77 BU73
Hounslow TW3 96 CC84
Pinner HA5 60 BZ58
South Ockendon (Aveley) RM15 108 FQ75
Tilbury RM18 111 GG81
Wallington SM6 159 DL106
Waltham Cross EN8 15 DY33
Welling DA16 105 ET82
West Molesey KT8 136 BZ98
Central Circ, NW4 off Hendon Way 63 CV57
★ Central Criminal Ct, Old Bailey, EC4 196 G8
Central Dr, Horn. RM12 72 FL62
Centrale Shop Cen, Croy. CR0 142 DQ103
Central Gdns, Mord. SM4 off Central Rd 140 DB99
Central Hill, SE19 122 DR92
Central Ho, E15 off High St 85 EC68
Barking IG11 off Cambridge Rd 87 EQ66
H Central Middlesex Hosp, NW10 80 CQ69
Central Par, Croy. (New Adgtn) CR0 161 EC110
Feltham TW14 116 BW87
Greenford UB6 79 CG69
Hounslow TW5 off Heston Rd 96 CA80
Surbiton KT6 off St. Mark's Hill 138 CL100
Central Pk Av, Dag. RM10 71 FB62
Central Pk Est, Houns. TW4 116 BX85
Central Pk Rd, E6 86 EK68
Central Pl, SE25 off Portland Rd 142 DV98
Central Rd, Dart. DA1 128 FL85
Morden SM4 140 DA99
Wembley HA0 61 CH64
Worcester Park KT4 139 CU103
Central Sch Footpath, SW14 98 CQ83
Central Sq, NW11 64 DB58
Wembley HA9 off Station Gro 62 CL64
West Molesey KT8 136 BZ98
Central St, EC1 197 H3
Central Wk, Epsom KT19 off Station App 156 CR113
Central Way, NW10 80 CQ69
SE28 88 EU74
Carshalton SM5 158 DE108
Feltham TW14 115 BV85
Oxted RH8 187 ED127
Centre, The, Felt. TW13 115 BU89
Walton-on-Thames KT12 135 BT102
Centre Av, W3 80 CR74
W10 off Harrow Rd 81 CW69
Epping CM16 17 ET32
Centre Cl, Epp. CM16 off Centre Av 17 ET32
Centre Common Rd, Chis. BR7 125 EQ93
Centre Ct Shop Cen, SW19 119 CZ93
Centre Dr, Epp. CM16 17 ET32
Centre Grn, Epp. CM16 off Centre Av 17 ET32
Centre Pt, SE1 202 B10
Centrepoint, WC1 195 N8
Centre Rd, E7 68 EG61
E11 68 EG61
Dagenham RM10 89 FB68
Centre St, E2 84 DV68
Centre Way, E17 47 EC52
N9 46 DW47

★ Place of interest ⇌ Railway station ⊖ London Underground station DLR Docklands Light Railway station Tra Tramlink station H Hospital Riv Pedestrian ferry landing stage

Centreway Apts, Ilf. IG1
off High Rd 69 EQ61
Centric Cl, NW1 off Oval Rd 83 DH67
Centurion Bldg, SW8
off Queenstown Rd 101 DH79
Centurion Cl, N7 83 DM66
Centurion Ct, SE18
off Rush Gro St 105 EN77
Wallington SM6
off Wandle Rd 141 DH104
Centurion La, E3
off Libra Rd 85 DZ68
Centurion Way, Erith DA18 106 FA76
Purfleet RM19 108 FM77
Century Cl, NW4 63 CX57
Century Ct, Wok. GU21 167 AZ116
Century Ms, E5
off Lower Clapton Rd 66 DW63
Century Pk, Wat. WD17 24 BW43
Century Rd, E17 67 DY55
Staines TW18 113 BC92
Century Yd, SE23 122 DW89
Cephas Av, E1 84 DW70
Cephas St, E1 84 DW70
Ceres Rd, SE18 105 ET77
Cerise Rd, SE15 102 DU81
Cerne Cl, Hayes UB4 78 BX73
Cerne Rd, Grav. DA12 131 GL91
Morden SM4 140 DC100
Cerney Ms, W2
off Gloucester Ter 82 DD73
Cerotus Pl, Cher. KT16 133 BF101
Cervantes Ct, W2
off Inverness Ter 82 DB72
Northwood HA6
off Green La 39 BT52
Cervia Way, Grav. DA12 131 GM90
Cester St, E2 off Whiston Rd 84 DU67
Ceylon Rd, W14 99 CX76
Chabot Dr, SE15 102 DV83
Chace Av, Pot.B. EN6 12 DD32
Chadacre Av, Ilf. IG5 69 EM55
Chadacre Rd, Epsom KT17 157 CV107
Chadbourn St, E14 85 EB71
Chad Cres, N9 46 DW48
Chadd Dr, Brom. BR1 144 EL97
Chadd Grn, E13 86 EG67
Chadfields, Til. RM18 111 GG80
Chadview Ct, Rom. (Chad.Hth)
RM6 70 EX59
Chadville Gdns, Rom. RM6 70 EX57
Chadway, Dag. RM8 70 EW60
Chadwell Av, Rom. RM6 70 EV59
Waltham Cross (Chsht) EN8 14 DW28
Chadwell Bypass, Grays
RM16 111 GF78
CHADWELL HEATH, Rom.
RM6 70 EX58
⇌ Chadwell Heath 70 EX59
Chadwell Heath La, Rom.
RM6 70 EV57
Chadwell Hill, Grays RM16 111 GH78
Chadwell La, N8
off New River Av 65 DM56
Chadwell Rd, Grays RM17 110 GC77
CHADWELL ST. MARY, Grays
RM16 111 GJ76
Chadwell St, EC1 196 E2
Chadwick Av, E4 47 ED49
N21 29 DM42
SW19 120 DA93
Chadwick Cl, SW15 119 CT87
W7 off Westcott Cres 79 CF71
Gravesend (Nthflt) DA11 130 GE89
Teddington TW11 117 CG93
Chadwick Dr, Rom. (Harold Wd)
RM3 52 FK54
Chadwick Ms, W4
off Thames Rd 98 CP79
Chadwick Pl, Surb. KT6 137 CJ101
Chadwick Rd, E11 68 EE59
NW10 81 CT67
SE15 102 DT82
Ilford IG1 69 EP62
Chadwick St, SW1 199 N7
Chadwick Way, SE28 88 EX73
Chadwin Rd, E13 86 EH71
Chadworth Way, Esher
(Clay.) KT10 155 CD106
Chaffers Mead, Ashtd. KT21 172 CM116
Chaffinch Av, Croy. CR0 143 DX100
Chaffinch Cl, N9 47 DX46
Croydon CR0 143 DX99
Surbiton KT6 138 CN104
Chaffinch La, Wat. WD18 39 BT45
Chaffinch Rd, Beck. BR3 143 DY95
CHAFFORD HUNDRED, Grays
RM16 110 FY76
⇌ Chafford Hundred 109 FV77
Chafford Wk, Rain. RM13 90 FJ68
Chafford Way, Rom. RM6 70 EW56
Chagford St, NW1 194 D5
Chailey Av, Enf. EN1 30 DT40
Chailey Cl, Houns. TW5
off Springwell Rd 96 BX81
Chailey Pl, Walt. KT12 154 BY105
Chailey St, E5 66 DW62
Chairmans Av, Uxb. (Denh.)
UB9 57 BF58
Chalbury Wk, N1 83 DM68
Chalcombe Rd, SE2 106 EV76
Chalcot Cl, Sutt. SM2 158 DA108
Chalcot Cres, NW1 82 DF67
Chalcot Gdns, NW3 82 DF65
Chalcot Ms, SW16 121 DL90
Chalcot Rd, NW1 82 DG66
Chalcot Sq, NW1 82 DG66
Chalcott Gdns, Surb. KT6 137 CJ102
Chalcroft Rd, SE13 124 EE85
CHALDON, Cat. CR3 175 DN124
Chaldon Common Rd, Cat.
(Chaldon) CR3 176 DQ124
Chaldon Path, Th.Hth. CR7 141 DP98
Chaldon Rd, SW6 99 CY80
Caterham CR3 176 DR124
Chaldon Way, Couls. CR5 175 DL117
Chale Rd, SW2 121 DL86
Chalet Cl, Bex. DA5 127 FD91
Chalet Est, NW7 43 CU49
Chale Wk, Sutt. SM2
off Hulverston Cl 158 DB109
⇌ Chalfont & Latimer 20 AW39
⊖ Chalfont & Latimer 20 AW39
Chalfont Av, Amer. HP6 20 AX39
Wembley HA9 80 CP65
Chalfont Cen for Epilepsy, Ger.Cr.
(Chal.St.P.) SL9 36 AY49
CHALFONT COMMON,
Ger.Cr. SL9 37 AZ49
Chalfont Ct, NW9 63 CT55
Chalfont Grn, N9 46 DS48
Chalfont Gro, Ger.Cr. SL9 36 AV51
Chalfont La, Ger.Cr. SL9 37 BC51
Rickmansworth (Chorl.)
WD3 21 BB43
Rickmansworth (W.Hyde)
WD3 37 BC51
Chalfont Ms, SW19
off Augustus Rd 119 CZ88
Chalfont Pk, Ger.Cr.
(Chal.St.P.) SL9 57 AZ55
Chalfont Rd, N9 46 DS48
SE25 142 DT97
Chalfont St. Giles HP8 37 BB48
Gerrards Cross SL9 37 BB48
Hayes UB3 95 BU75
Rickmansworth (Map.Cr.)
WD3 37 BD49
CHALFONT ST. GILES, HP8 36 AV47
CHALFONT ST. PETER,
Ger.Cr. SL9 37 AZ53
Ⓗ Chalfonts & Gerrards Cross
Hosp, Ger.Cr. SL9 36 AX53
Chalfont Sta Rd, Amer. HP7 20 AW40
Chalfont Wk, Pnr. HA5
off Willows Cl 40 BW54
Chalfont Way, W13 97 CH76
Chalford Cl, W.Mol. KT8 136 CA98
Chalforde Gdns, Rom. RM2 71 FH56
Chalford Rd, SE21 122 DR91
Chalford Wk, Wdf.Grn. IG8 48 EK53
Chalgrove Av, Mord. SM4 140 DA99
Chalgrove Cres, Ilf. IG5 48 EL54
Chalgrove Gdns, N3 63 CY55
Chalgrove Rd, N17 46 DV53
Sutton SM2 158 DD108
Chalice Cl, Wall. SM6
off Lavender Vale 159 DK107
Chalice Way, Green. DA9 129 FS85
Chalkenden Cl, SE20 122 DV94
Chalkers Cor, SW14 98 CP83
⊖ Chalk Farm 82 DG66
Chalk Fm Rd, NW1 82 DG66
Chalk Hill, Wat. WD19 24 BX44
Chalk Hill Rd, W6
off Shortlands 99 CX77
Chalkhill Rd, Wem. HA9 62 CP62
Chalklands, Wem. HA9 62 CQ62
Chalk La, Ashtd. KT21 172 CM119
Barnet EN4 28 DF42
Epsom KT18 172 CR115
Chalkley Cl, Mitch. CR4 140 DF96
Chalkmill Dr, Enf. EN1 30 DV41
Chalk Paddock, Epsom KT18 172 CR115
Chalk Pit Av, Orp. BR5 146 EW97
Chalkpit La, Bet. RH3 182 CP133
Caterham (Wold.) CR3 187 EC125
Oxted RH8 187 EC125
Chalk Pit Rd, Bans. SM7 174 DA117
Epsom KT18 172 CQ119
Chalk Pit Way, Sutt. SM1 158 DC106
Chalkpit Wd, Oxt. RH8 187 ED127
Chalk Rd, E13 86 EH71
Chalkstone Cl, Well. DA16 106 EU81
Chalkwell Pk Av, Enf. EN1 30 DS42
Chalky Bk, Grav. DA11 131 GG91
Chalky La, Chess. KT9 155 CK109
Challacombe Cl, Brwd.
(Hutt.) CM13 55 GB46
Challenge Cl, Grav. DA12 131 GM91
Challenge Ct, Lthd. KT22 171 CH119
Twickenham TW2
off Langhorn Dr 117 CE87
Challenge Rd, Ashf. TW15 115 BQ90
Challice Way, SW2 121 DM88
Challin St, SE20 142 DW95
Challis Rd, Brent. TW8 97 CK78
Challock Cl, West. (Bigg.H.)
TN16 178 EJ116
Challoner Cl, N2 44 DD54
Challoner Cres, W14
off Challoner St 99 CZ78
Challoners Cl, E.Mol. KT8 137 CD98
Challoner St, W14 99 CZ78
Chalmers Ct, Rick. (Crox.Grn)
WD3 22 BM44
Chalmers Ho, SW11
off York Rd 100 DC83
Chalmers Rd, Ashf. TW15 115 BP91
Banstead SM7 174 DD115
Chalmers Rd E, Ashf. TW15 115 BP91
Chalmers Wk, SE17
off Hillingdon St 101 DP79
Chalmers Way, Felt. TW14 115 BU85
Chaloner Ct, SE1 201 K4
Chalsey Rd, SE4 103 DZ84
Chalton Dr, N2 64 DC58
Chalton St, NW1 195 N2
Chalvey Gdns, Slou. SL1 92 AS75
Chalvey Pk, Slou. SL1 92 AS75
Chalvey Rd E, Slou. SL1 92 AS75
Chamberlain Cl, SE28
off Broadwater Rd 105 ER76
Ilford IG1
off Richmond Rd 69 EQ62
Chamberlain Cotts, SE5
off Camberwell Gro 102 DR81
Chamberlain Cres, W.Wick.
BR4 143 EB102
Chamberlain Gdns, Houns.
TW3 96 CC81
Chamberlain La, Pnr. HA5 59 BU56
Chamberlain Pl, E17 67 DY55
Chamberlain Rd, N2 44 DC54
W13 off Midhurst Rd 97 CG75
Chamberlain St, NW1
off Regents Pk Rd 82 DF66
Chamberlain Wk, Felt. TW13
off Burgess Cl 116 BY91
Chamberlain Way, Pnr. HA5 59 BV55
Surbiton KT6 138 CL101
Chamberlayne Av, Wem. HA9 62 CL61
Chamberlayne Rd, NW10 81 CX69
Chambersbury La, Hem.H. HP3 6 BN25
Chambers Cl, Green. DA9 129 FU85
Chambers Gdns, N2 44 DD53
Chambers La, NW10 81 CV66
Chambers Manor Ms, Epp.
CM16 17 EP26
Chambers Pl, S.Croy. CR2
off Rolleston Rd 160 DR108
Chambers Rd, N7 65 DL63
Chambers St, SE16 202 B4
Chamber St, E1 84 DT73
Chambers Wk, Stan. HA7 41 CH50
Chambon Pl, W6
off Beavor La 99 CU77
Chambord St, E2 84 DT69
Champa Cl, N17 46 DT54
Champion Cres, SE26 123 DY91
Champion Gro, SE5 102 DR83
Champion Hill, SE5 102 DR83
Champion Hill Est, SE5 102 DS83
Champion Pk, SE5 102 DR82
Champion Pk Est, SE5
off Denmark Hill 102 DR83
Champion Rd, SE26 123 DY91
Upminster RM14 72 FP61
Champions Way, NW4 43 CV53
NW7 43 CV53
Champness Cl, SE27
off Rommany Rd 122 DR91
Champness Rd, Bark. IG11 87 ET65
Champney Cl, Slou. (Horton)
SL3 93 BA83
Champneys Cl, Sutt. SM2 157 CZ108
Chance Cl, Grays RM16 110 FZ76
Chancellor Gdns, S.Croy.
CR2 159 DP109
Chancellor Gro, SE21 122 DQ89
Chancellor Pas, E14 204 A3
Chancellor Pl, NW9 43 CT54
Chancellors Ct, WC1
off Orde Hall St 83 DM71
Chancellors Rd, W6 99 CW78
Chancellors St, W6 99 CW78
Chancellor Way, Sev. TN13 190 FG122
Chancelot Rd, SE2 106 EV77
Chancel St, SE1 200 F2
Chancery Ct, Dart. DA1
off Downs Av 128 FN87
Chancerygate Cl, Ruis. HA4 60 BY64
Chancerygate Way, Ruis.
HA4 60 BY63
⊖ Chancery Lane 196 D7
Chancery La, WC2 196 D8
Beckenham BR3 143 EB96
Chancery Ms, SW17 120 DE89
Chance St, E1 197 P4
E2 197 P4
Chanctonbury Chase, Red.
RH1 185 DH134
Chanctonbury Cl, SE9 125 EP90
Chanctonbury Gdns, Sutt.
SM2 158 DB108
Chanctonbury Way, N12 43 CZ49
Chandler Av, E16 86 EG71
Chandler Cl, Hmptn. TW12 136 CA95
Chandler Ms, Twick. TW1 117 CG87
Chandler Rd, Loug. IG10 33 EP39
Chandlers Cl, Felt. TW14 115 BT87
Chandlers Dr, Erith DA8 107 FD77
Chandler's La, Rick. WD3 22 BL37
Chandlers Ms, E14 203 P4
Greenhithe DA9 109 FW84
Chandler St, E1 202 E2
Chandlers Way, SW2 121 DN87
Romford RM1 71 FE57
Chandler Way, SE15 102 DT80
Chandon Lo, Sutt. SM2
off Devonshire Rd 158 DC108
Chandos Av, E17 47 EA54
N14 45 DJ48
N20 44 DC46
W5 97 CJ77
Chandos Cl, Amer. HP6 20 AW38
Buckhurst Hill IG9 48 EH47
Chandos Ct, Stan. HA7 41 CH51
Chandos Cres, Edg. HA8 42 CM52
Chandos Mall, Slou. SL1
off High St 92 AT75
Chandos Par, Edg. HA8
off Chandos Cres 42 CM52
Chandos Pl, WC2 199 P1
Chandos Rd, E15 67 ED64
N2 44 DD54
N17 46 DS54
NW2 63 CW64
NW10 80 CS70
Borehamwood WD6 26 CM40
Harrow HA1 60 CC57
Pinner HA5 60 BW59
Staines TW18 113 BD92
Chandos St, W1 195 J7
Chandos Way, NW11 64 DB60
Change All, EC3 197 L9
Chanlock Path, S.Ock. RM15
off Carnach Grn 91 FV73
Channel Cl, Houns. TW5 96 CA81
Channel Gate Rd, NW10
off Old Oak La 81 CT69
Channel Islands Est, N1
off Clifton Rd 84 DQ65
Channelsea Ho Business Cen,
E15 off Canning Rd 85 ED68
Channelsea Rd, E15 85 ED67
Channing Cl, Horn. RM11 72 FM59
Channings, Wok. (Horsell)
GU21 166 AY115
Chantilly Way, Epsom KT19 156 CP110
Chanton Dr, Epsom KT17 157 CW110
Sutton SM2 157 CW110
Chantress Cl, Dag. RM10 89 FC67
Chantrey Cl, Ashtd. KT21 171 CJ119
Chantrey Rd, SW9 101 DM83
Chantreywood, Brwd. CM13 55 GA48
Chantry, The, Uxb. UB8 76 BM69
Chantry Cl, NW7
off Hendon Wd La 27 CT44
SE2 off Felixstowe Rd 106 EW76
W9 off Elgin Av 81 CZ70
Enfield EN2 off Bedale Rd 30 DQ38
Harrow HA3 62 CM57
Kings Langley WD4 6 BN29
Chantry Cl, Sid. DA14
off Ellenborough Rd 126 EY92
Sunbury-on-Thames TW16 115 BU94
West Drayton UB7 76 BK73
Chantry Ct, Cars. SM5 140 DE104
Chantry Cres, NW10
off High Rd 81 CT65
Chantry Ho, Rain. RM13
off Chantry Way 89 FD68
Chantry Hurst, Epsom KT18 172 CR115
Chantry La, Brom. BR2
off Bromley Common 144 EK99
St. Albans (Lon.Col.) AL2 9 CK26
Chantry Pl, Har. HA3 40 CB53
Chantry Rd, Cher. KT16 134 BJ101
Chessington KT9 156 CM106
Harrow HA3 40 CB53
Chantry Sq, W8
off St. Mary's Pl 100 DB76
Chantry St, N1 83 DP67
Chantry Way, Mitch. CR4
off Church Rd 140 DD97
Rainham RM13 89 FD68
Chant Sq, E15 85 ED66
Chant St, E15 85 ED66
Chapel Av, Add. KT15 152 BH105
Chapel Cl, NW10 off High Rd 81 CT65
Dartford DA1 127 FE85
Grays RM20 109 FV79
Hatfield AL9 12 DD27
Watford WD25 7 BT34
Chapel Ct, N2 64 DE55
SE1 201 K4
SE18 off Radnor Cres 106 EU79
Chapel Cft, Kings L. (Chipper.)
WD4 6 BG31
Chapel End, Ger.Cr. (Chal.St.P.)
SL9 off Austenwood La 36 AX54
Chapel Fm Rd, SE9 125 EM90
Chapel Gate Ms, SW4
off Bedford Rd 101 DL83
Chapel Gro, Add. KT15 152 BH105
Epsom KT18 173 CW119
Chapel Hill, Dart. DA1 127 FE85
Chapel Ho St, E14 204 C10
Chapelier Ho, SW18
off Eastfields Av 100 DA84
Chapel La, Chig. IG7 49 ET48
Pinner HA5 60 BX55
Romford RM6 70 EX59
Slough (Stoke P.) SL2 74 AV66
Uxbridge UB8 76 BN72
Chapel Mkt, N1 83 DN68
Chapel Ms, Wdf.Grn. IG8 49 EN51
Chapel Mill Rd, Kings.T. KT1 138 CM97
Chapelmount Rd, Wdf.Grn.
IG8 49 EM51
Chapel Pk Rd, Add. KT15 152 BH105
Chapel Path, E11 68 EG58
Chapel Pl, EC2 197 M3
N1 off Chapel Mkt 83 DN68
N17 off White Hart La 46 DT52
W1 195 H9
Chapel Rd, SE27 121 DP91
W13 79 CH74
Bexleyheath DA7 106 FA84
Epping CM16 17 ET30
Hounslow TW3 96 CB83
Ilford IG1 69 EN62
Oxted RH8 188 EJ130
Redhill RH1 184 DF134
Tadworth KT20 173 CW123
Twickenham TW1 117 CH87
Warlingham CR6 177 DX118
Chapel Row, Uxb. (Hare.)
UB9 38 BJ53
Chapel Side, W2 82 DB73
Chapel Sq, Vir.W. GU25 132 AY98
Chapel Stones, N17 46 DT53
Chapel St, NW1 194 B7
SW1 198 G6
Enfield EN2 30 DQ41
Slough SL1 92 AT75
Uxbridge UB8
off Trumper Way 76 BJ67
Woking GU21 167 AZ117
Chapel Ter, Loug. IG10
off Forest Rd 32 EL42
Chapel Vw, S.Croy. CR2 160 DV107
Chapel Wk, NW4 63 CV56
Coulsdon CR5 175 DK122
Croydon CR0
off Wellesley Rd 142 DQ103
Dartford DA2 127 FE89
Chapel Way, N7
off Sussex Way 65 DM62
Abbots Langley (Bedmond)
WD5 7 BT27
Epsom KT18 173 CW119
Chapel Yd, SW18
off Wandsworth High St 120 DA85
Chaplaincy Gdns, Horn. RM11 72 FL60
Chaplin Cl, SE1 200 E4
Chaplin Cres, Sun. TW16 115 BS93
Chaplin Ms, Slou. SL3
off Ditton Rd 93 AZ78
Chaplin Rd, E15 86 EE68
N17 66 DT55
NW2 81 CU65
Dagenham RM9 88 EY66
Wembley HA0 79 CJ65
Chaplin Sq, N12 44 DD52
Chapman Cl, West Dr. UB7 94 BM76
Chapman Cres, Har. HA3 62 CL57
Chapman Pk Ind Est, NW10 81 CT65
Chapman Pl, N4 65 DP61
Chapman Rd, E9 85 DZ65
Belvedere DA17 106 FA78
Croydon CR0 141 DN102
Chapman's La, SE2 106 EW77
Belvedere DA17 106 EX77
Chapmans La, Orp. BR5 146 EX96
Chapman Sq, SW19 119 CX89
Chapmans Rd, Sev. (Sund.)
TN14 180 EY124
Chapman St, E1 84 DV73
Chapone Pl, W1 195 M9
Chapter Cl, W4
off Beaumont Rd 98 CQ76
Uxbridge UB10 76 BM66
Chapter Ho Ct, EC4 197 H9
Chapter Rd, NW2 63 CU64
SE17 101 DP78
Chapter St, SW1 199 M9
Chapter Way, SW19 140 DC95
Hampton TW12 116 CA91
Chara Pl, W4 98 CR79
Charcot Ho, SW15
off Highcliffe Dr 119 CT86
Charcroft Gdns, Enf. EN3 31 DX42
Chardin Rd, W4
off Elliott Rd 98 CS77
Chardmore Rd, N16 66 DU60
Chard Rd, Houns. (Hthrw Air.) TW6
off Heathrow Tunnel App 95 BP82
Chardwell Cl, E6
off Northumberland Rd 86 EL72
Charecroft Way, W12 99 CX75
W14 99 CX75
Charfield Ct, W9
off Shirland Rd 82 DB70
Charford Rd, E16 86 EG71
Chargate Cl, Walt. KT12 153 BT107
Chargeable La, E13 86 EF70
Chargeable St, E16 86 EF70
Chargrove Cl, SE16 203 J4
Charing Cl, Orp. BR6 163 ET105
⇌ Charing Cross 199 P2
⊖ Charing Cross 199 P2
Charing Cross, SW1 199 P2
Ⓗ Charing Cross Hosp, W6 99 CX79
Charing Cross Rd, WC2 195 N8
Chariot Cl, E3
off Old Ford Rd 85 EA67
Charlbert St, NW8 82 DE68
Charlbury Av, Stan. HA7 41 CK50
Charlbury Cl, Rom. RM3 52 FJ51
Charlbury Cres, Rom. RM3 52 FJ51
Charlbury Gdns, Ilf. IG3 69 ET61
Charlbury Gro, W5 79 CJ72
Charlbury Ho, E12
off Grantham Rd 69 EN62
Charlbury Rd, Uxb. UB10 58 BM62
Charldane Rd, SE9 125 EP90
Charlecote Gro, SE26 122 DV90
Charlecote Rd, Dag. RM8 70 EY62
Charlemont Rd, E6 87 EM69
Charles Babbage Cl, Chess.
KT9 155 CJ108
Charles Barry Cl, SW4 101 DJ83
Charles Burton Ct, E5
off Ashenden Rd 67 DY64
Charles Ch Wk, Ilf. IG1
off Hillview Cres 69 EM58
Charles Cl, Sid. DA14 126 EV91
Charles Cobb Gdns, Croy.
CR0 159 DN106
Charles Coveney Rd, SE15 102 DT81
Charles Cres, Har. HA1 61 CD59
Charles Dickens Ho, E2 84 DV69
Charles Dickens Ter, SE20
off Maple Rd 122 DW94
Charlesfield, SE9 124 EJ90
Charles Flemwell Ms, E16 205 N3
Charles Gdns, Slou. SL2 74 AV72
Charles Gardner Ct, N1
off Haberdasher St 84 DR69
Charles Grinling Wk, SE18 105 EN77
Charles Gro, N14 45 DJ46
Charles Haller St, SW2
off Tulse Hill 121 DN87
Charles Hocking Ho, W3
off Bollo Br Rd 98 CQ75
Charles Ho, N17 off Love La 46 DT52
Chertsey KT16
off Guildford St 133 BF102
Charles La, NW8 194 A1
Charles Mackenzie Ho, SE16
off Linsey St 102 DU77
Charlesmere Gdns, SE28
off Battery Rd 105 ES75
Charles Nex Ms, SE21
off Eastmearn Rd 122 DR89
Charles Pl, NW1 195 L3
Charles Rd, E7 off Lens Rd 86 EJ66
SW19 140 DA95
W13 79 CG72
Dagenham RM10 89 FD65
Romford RM6 70 EX59
Sevenoaks (Bad.Mt) TN14 165 FB110
Staines TW18 114 BK93
Charles II Pl, SW3
off King's Rd 100 DF78
Charles II St, SW1 199 M2
Charles Sevright Dr, NW7 43 CX50
Charles Sq, N1 197 L3
Charles Sq Est, N1
off Pitfield St 84 DR69
Charles St, SW13 98 CS82
W1 199 H2
Chertsey KT16 133 BF102
Croydon CR0 142 DQ104
Enfield EN1 30 DT43
Epping CM16 18 EU32
Grays RM17 110 GB79
Greenhithe DA9 129 FT85
Hounslow TW3 96 BZ82
Uxbridge UB10 77 BP70
Charleston Cl, Felt. TW13
off Vineyard Rd 115 BU90
Charleston St, SE17 201 J9
Charles Townsend Ho, EC1 196 F4
Charles Whincup Rd, E16 205 P2
Charlesworth Pl, SW13
off Eleanor Gro 99 CT83
Charleville Circ, SE26 122 DU92
Charleville Ms, Islw. TW7
off Railshead Rd 97 CH84
Charleville Rd, W14 99 CY78
Charlie Brown's Rbt, E18
off Southend Rd 48 EJ54
Charlie Chaplin Wk, SE1
off Waterloo Rd 83 DN74
Charlieville Rd, Erith DA8
off Northumberland Pk 107 FC80
Charlmont Rd, SW17 120 DF93
Charlock Way, Wat. WD18 23 BT44
Charlotte Av, Slou. SL2 74 AT73
Charlotte Cl, Bexh. DA6 126 EY85
Ilford IG6 off Connor Cl 49 EQ53
Charlotte Ct, W6
off Invermead Cl 99 CU77
Esher KT10 154 CC106
Charlotte Despard Av, SW11 100 DG81
Charlotte Gdns, Rom. RM5 51 FB51
Charlotte Ms, W1 195 L6

Charlotte Ms, W10 **81** CX72
W14 *off Munden St* **99** CY77
Charlotte Pk Av, Brom. BR1 **144** EL97
Charlotte Pl, NW9
off Uphill Dr **62** CQ57
SW1 **199** K9
W1 **195** L7
Grays RM20 **109** FV79
Charlotte Rd, EC2 **197** M4
SW13 **99** CT81
Dagenham RM10 **89** FB65
Wallington SM6 **159** DJ107
Charlotte Row, SW4 **101** DJ83
Charlotte Sq, Rich. TW10
off Greville Rd **118** CM86
Charlotte St, W1 **195** L6
Charlotte Ter, N1 **83** DM67
Charlow Cl, SW6
off Townmead Rd **100** DC82
CHARLTON, SE7 **104** EJ79
⇌ **Charlton** **104** EH78
★ **Charlton Athletic FC**,
SE7 **104** EJ78
Charlton Av, Walt. KT12 **153** BV105
Charlton Ch La, SE7 **104** EJ78
Charlton Cl, Uxb. UB10 **59** BP61
Charlton Cres, Bark. IG11 **87** ET68
Charlton Dene, SE7 **104** EJ80
Charlton Dr, West. (Bigg.H.)
TN16 **178** EK117
Charlton Gdns, Couls. CR5 **175** DJ118
Charlton Kings, Wey. KT13 **135** BS104
Charlton Kings Rd, NW5 **65** DK64
Charlton La, SE7 **104** EK78
Shepperton TW17 **135** BS98
Charlton Pk La, SE7 **104** EK80
Charlton Pk Rd, SE7 **104** EK79
Charlton Pl, N1 **83** DP68
Charlton Rd, N9 **47** DX46
NW10 **80** CS67
SE3 **104** EG80
SE7 **104** EH80
Harrow HA3 **61** CK56
Shepperton TW17 **135** BQ97
Wembley HA9 **62** CM60
Charlton St, Grays RM20 **109** FX79
Charlton Way, SE3 **104** EE81
Charlwood, Croy. CR0 **161** DZ109
Charlwood Cl, Har. HA3
off Kelvin Cres **41** CE52
Charlwood Dr, Lthd. (Oxshott)
KT22 **171** CD115
Charlwood Ho, SW1
off Vauxhall Br Rd **101** DK77
Charlwood Pl, SW1 **199** L9
Charlwood Rd, SW15 **99** CX83
Charlwood St, SW1 **199** L9
Charlwood Ter, SW15
off Cardinal Pl **99** CX84
Charman Rd, Red. RH1 **184** DE134
Charmian Av, Stan. HA7 **61** CK55
Charminster Av, SW19 **140** DB96
Charminster Ct, Surb. KT6 **137** CK101
Charminster Rd, SE9 **124** EK91
Worcester Park KT4 **139** CX102
Charmouth Ho, SW8
off Dorset Rd **101** DM80
Charmouth Rd, Well. DA16 **106** EW81
Charmwood La, Orp. BR6 **164** EV109
Charne, The, Sev. (Otford)
TN14 **181** FG117
Charnock, Swan. BR8 **147** FE98
Charnock Rd, E5 **66** DV62
Charnwood Av, SW19 **140** DA96
Charnwood Cl, N.Mal. KT3 **138** CS98
Charnwood Dr, E18 **68** EH55
Charnwood Gdns, E14 **204** A8
Charnwood Pl, N20 **44** DC48
Charnwood Rd, SE25 **142** DR99
Enfield EN1 **30** DV36
Uxbridge UB10 **76** BN68
Charnwood St, E5 **66** DU61
Charrington Rd, Croy. CR0
off Drayton Rd **141** DP103
Charrington St, NW1 **83** DK68
Charsley Cl, Amer. HP6 **20** AW39
Charsley Rd, SE6 **123** EB89
Charta Rd, Egh. TW20 **113** BC92
Chart Cl, Brom. BR2 **144** EE95
Croydon CR0
off Stockbury Rd **142** DW100
Charter Av, Ilf. IG2 **69** ER60
Charter Cl, Slou. SL1
off Hencroft St S **92** AT76
Charter Ct, N.Mal. KT3 **138** CS97
Charter Cres, Houns. TW4 **96** BY84
Charter Dr, Amer. HP6 **20** AT38
Bexley DA5 **126** EY87
★ **Chartered Insurance Institutes Mus**, EC2
off Aldermanbury **197** J8
★ **Charterhouse**, EC1 **196** G6
Charterhouse Av, Wem. HA0 **61** CJ63
Charterhouse Bldgs, EC1 **196** G5
Charterhouse Dr, Sev. TN13 **190** FG123
Charterhouse Ms, EC1 **196** G6
Charterhouse Rd, E8 **66** DU63
Orpington BR6 **146** EU104
Charterhouse Sq, EC1 **196** G6
Charterhouse St, EC1 **196** E7
Charteris Rd, N4 **65** DN60
NW6 **81** CZ67
Woodford Green IG8 **48** EH52
H **Charter Nightingale Hosp**,
NW1 **194** C6
Charter Pl, Stai. TW18 **114** BG93
Uxbridge UB8 **76** BK66
Watford WD17 **24** BW41
Charter Rd, Kings.T. KT1 **138** CP97
Charter Rd, The, Wdf.Grn. IG8 **48** EE51
Charters Cl, SE19 **122** DS92
Charter Sq, Kings.T. KT1 **138** CP96
Charter Way, N3 **63** CZ56
N14 **29** DJ44
Chartfield Av, SW15 **119** CV85
Chartfield Pl, Wey. KT13 **153** BP106
Chartfield Sq, SW15 **119** CX85
Chartham Gro, SE27
off Royal Circ **121** DN90
Chartham Rd, SE25 **142** DV97
Chart Hills Cl, SE28
off Fairway Dr **88** EY72
Chart La, Reig. RH2 **184** DB134
Chartley Av, NW2 **62** CS62
Stanmore HA7 **41** CF51
Charton Cl, Belv. DA17
off Nuxley Rd **106** EZ79
Chartridge Cl, Barn. EN5 **27** CU43
Bushey WD23 **24** CC44
Chart St, N1 **197** L2
Chartway, Reig. RH2 **184** DB133
Sevenoaks TN13 **191** FJ124
★ **Chartwell**, West. TN16 **189** ET132
Chartwell Cl, SE9 **125** EQ89
Croydon CR0 **142** DR102
Greenford UB6 **78** CB67
Waltham Abbey EN9 **16** EE33
Chartwell Dr, Orp. BR6 **163** ER106
Chartwell Gdns, Sutt. SM3 **157** CY105
Chartwell Pl, Epsom KT18 **156** CS114
Harrow HA2 **61** CD61
Sutton SM3 **157** CZ105
Chartwell Rd, Nthwd. HA6 **39** BT51
Chartwell Way, SE20 **142** DV95
Charville La, Hayes UB4 **77** BS68
Charville La W, Uxb. UB10 **77** BP69
Charwood, SW16 **121** DN91
Charwood Cl, Rad. (Shenley)
WD7 **10** CL33
Chase, The, E12 **68** EK63
SW4 **101** DH83
SW16 **121** DM94
SW20 **139** CY95
Ashtead KT21 **171** CJ118
Bexleyheath DA7 **107** FB83
Brentwood (Cromwell Rd)
CM14 **54** FV49
Brentwood (Ingrave) CM13 **55** GC50
Brentwood (Seven Arches Rd)
CM14 **54** FX48
Brentwood (Woodman Rd)
CM14 **54** FX50
Bromley BR1 **144** EH97
Chigwell IG7 **49** EQ49
Coulsdon CR5 **159** DJ114
Edgware HA8 **42** CP53
Grays RM20 **109** FX79
Hornchurch RM12 **71** FE62
Leatherhead (Oxshott)
KT22 **170** CC115
Loughton IG10 **48** EJ45
Pinner HA5 **60** BZ56
Pinner (Eastcote) HA5 **60** BW58
Radlett WD7 **25** CF35
Romford RM1 **71** FE55
Romford (Chad.Hth) RM6 **70** EY58
Romford (Rush Grn) RM7 **71** FD62
Stanmore HA7 **41** CG50
Sunbury-on-Thames TW16 **135** BV95
Tadworth (Kgswd) KT20 **174** DA122
Upminster RM14 **73** FS62
Uxbridge UB10 **58** BN64
Wallington SM6 **159** DL106
Waltham Cross (Goffs Oak)
EN7 **13** DP28
Watford WD18 **23** BS42
Chase Ct Gdns, Enf. EN2 **30** DQ41
CHASE CROSS, Rom. RM1 **51** FE51
Chase Cross Rd, Rom. RM5 **51** FC52
Chase End, Epsom KT19 **156** CR112
H **Chase Fm Hosp**, Enf. EN2 **29** DN38
Chasefield Rd, SW17 **120** DF91
Chase Gdns, E4 **47** EA49
Twickenham TW2 **117** CD86
Chase Grn, Enf. EN2 **30** DQ41
Chase Grn Av, Enf. EN2 **29** DP40
Chase Hill, Enf. EN2 **30** DQ41
Chase Ho Gdns, Horn. RM11
off Great Nelmes Chase **72** FM57
Chase La, Chig. IG7 **50** EU48
Ilford IG6 **69** ER57
Chaseley Dr, W4 **98** CP78
South Croydon CR2 **160** DR110
Chaseley St, E14 **85** DY72
Chasemore Cl, Mitch. CR4 **140** DF101
Chasemore Gdns, Croy. CR0
off Thorneloe Gdns **159** DP106
Chase Ridings, Enf. EN2 **29** DN40
Chase Rd, N14 **29** DJ44
NW10 **80** CR70
W3 **80** CR70
Brentwood CM14 **54** FW48
Epsom KT19 **156** CR112
Chase Side, N14 **28** DG44
Enfield EN2 **30** DQ41
Chase Side Av, SW20 **139** CY95
Enfield EN2 **30** DQ40
Chaseside Cl, Rom. RM1 **51** FE51
Chase Side Cres, Enf. EN2 **30** DQ39
Chaseside Gdns, Cher. KT16 **134** BH101
Chase Side Pl, Enf. EN2
off Chase Side **30** DQ40
Chase Sq, Grav. DA11
off High St **131** GH86
Chaseville Pk Rd, N21 **29** DL43
Chase Way, N14 **45** DH47
Chasewood Av, Enf. EN2 **29** DP40
Chasewood Pk, Har. HA1 **61** CF62
Chastilian Rd, Dart. DA1 **127** FF87
Chaston Pl, NW5
off Grafton Ter **64** DG64
Chater Ho, E2 *off Roman Rd* **85** DX69
Chatfield Ct, Cat. CR3
off Yorke Gate Rd **176** DR122
Chatfield Rd, SW11 **100** DC83
Croydon CR0 **141** DP102
Chatham Av, Brom. BR2 **144** EF101
Chatham Cl, NW11 **64** DA57
SE18 **105** EP76
Sutton SM3 **139** CZ101
Chatham Hill Rd, Sev. TN14 **191** FJ121
Chatham Pl, E9 **84** DW65
Chatham Rd, E17 **67** DY55
E18 *off Grove Hill* **48** EF54
SW11 **120** DF86
Kingston upon Thames
KT1 **138** CN96
Orpington BR6 **163** EQ106
Chatham St, SE17 **201** K8
Chatsfield, Epsom KT17 **157** CU110
Chatsfield Pl, W5 **80** CL72
Chatsworth Av, NW4 **43** CW54
SW20 **139** CY95
Bromley BR1 **124** EH91
Sidcup DA15 **126** EU88
Wembley HA9 **62** CM64
Chatsworth Cl, NW4 **43** CW54
Borehamwood WD6 **26** CN41
West Wickham BR4 **144** EF103
Chatsworth Ct, W8 **100** DA77
Stanmore HA7
off Marsh La **41** CJ50
Chatsworth Cres, Houns.
TW3 **97** CD84
Chatsworth Dr, Enf. EN1 **46** DU45
Chatsworth Est, E5
off Elderfield Rd **67** DX63
Chatsworth Gdns, W3 **80** CP73
Harrow HA2 **60** CB60
New Malden KT3 **139** CT99
Chatsworth Ms, Wat. WD24 **23** BU38
Chatsworth Par, Orp. BR5
off Queensway **145** EQ99
Chatsworth Pl, Lthd. (Oxshott)
KT22 **155** CD112
Mitcham CR4 **140** DF97
Teddington TW11 **117** CG91
Chatsworth Ri, W5 **80** CM70
Chatsworth Rd, E5 **66** DW62
E15 **68** EF64
NW2 **81** CX65
W4 **98** CQ79
W5 **80** CM70
Croydon CR0 **160** DR105
Dartford DA1 **128** FJ85
Hayes UB4 **77** BV70
Sutton SM3 **157** CX106
Chatsworth Way, SE27 **121** DP90
Chatteris Av, Rom. RM3 **52** FJ51
Chattern Hill, Ashf. TW15 **115** BP91
Chattern Rd, Ashf. TW15 **115** BQ91
Chatterton Ms, N4
off Chatterton Rd **65** DP62
Chatterton Rd, N4 **65** DP62
Bromley BR2 **144** EK98
Chatto Rd, SW11 **120** DF85
Chaucer Av, Hayes UB4 **77** BU71
Hounslow TW4 **95** BV82
Richmond TW9 **98** CN82
Weybridge KT13 **152** BN108
Chaucer Cl, N11 **45** DJ50
Banstead SM7 **157** CY114
Tilbury RM18 **111** GJ82
Chaucer Ct, N16 **66** DS63
Chaucer Dr, SE1 **202** A9
Chaucer Gdns, Sutt. SM1 **140** DA104
Chaucer Grn, Croy. CR0 **142** DV101
Chaucer Ho, SW1
off Churchill Gdns **101** DJ78
Sutton SM1 **140** DA104
Chaucer Pk, Dart. DA1 **128** FM87
Chaucer Rd, E7 **86** EG65
E11 **68** EG58
E17 **47** EC54
SE24 **121** DN85
W3 **80** CQ74
Ashford TW15 **114** BL91
Gravesend (Nthflt) DA11 **130** GD90
Romford RM3 **51** FH52
Sidcup DA15 **126** EW88
Sutton SM1 **158** DA105
Welling DA16 **105** ES81
Chaucer Way, SW19 **120** DD93
Addlestone KT15 **152** BG107
Dartford DA1 **108** FN84
Slough SL1 **74** AT74
Chauncey Cl, N9 **46** DU48
Chauncy Av, Pot.B. EN6 **12** DC33
Chaundrye Cl, SE9 **125** EM86
Chauntler Cl, E16 **86** EH73
Chavecroft Ter, Epsom KT18 **173** CW119
Chave Rd, Dart. DA2 **128** FL90
Chaworth Cl, Cher. (Ott.)
KT16 **151** BC107
Chaworth Rd, Cher. (Ott.)
KT16 **151** BC107
CHEAM, Sutt. SM3 **157** CX107
⇌ **Cheam** **157** CY108
Cheam Cl, Tad. KT20
off Waterfield **173** CW121
Cheam Common Rd, Wor.Pk.
KT4 **139** CV103
Cheam Mans, Sutt. SM3 **157** CY108
Cheam Pk Way, Sutt. SM3 **157** CY107
Cheam Rd, Epsom KT17 **157** CU109
Sutton SM1 **157** CZ107
Sutton (E.Ewell) SM2 **157** CX110
Cheam St, SE15
off Nunhead La **102** DV83
Cheapside, EC2 **197** J9
N13 *off Taplow Rd* **46** DQ49
Woking GU21 **150** AX114
Cheapside La, Uxb. (Denh.)
UB9 **57** BF61
Cheddar Cl, N11 **44** DF51
Cheddar Rd, Houns. (Hthrw Air.)
TW6 *off Cromer Rd* **94** BN82
Cheddar Waye, Hayes UB4 **77** BV72
Cheddington Rd, N18 **46** DS48
Chedworth Cl, E16
off Hallsville Rd **86** EF72
Cheelson Rd, S.Ock. RM15 **91** FW68
Cheeseman Cl, Hmptn. TW12 **116** BY93
Cheesemans Ter, W14 **99** CZ78
Cheldon Av, NW7 **43** CX52
Chelford Rd, Brom. BR1 **123** ED92
Chelmer Cres, Bark. IG11 **88** EV68
Chelmer Dr, Brwd. (Hutt.)
CM13 **55** GE44
South Ockendon RM15 **91** FW73
Chelmer Rd, E9 **67** DX64
Grays RM16 **111** GG78
Upminster RM14 **73** FR58
Chelmsford Av, Rom. RM5 **51** FD52
Chelmsford Cl, E6
off Guildford Rd **87** EM72
W6 **99** CX79
Sutton SM2 **158** DA109
Chelmsford Dr, Upmin. RM14 **72** FM62
Chelmsford Gdns, Ilf. IG1 **68** EL59
Chelmsford Rd, E11 **67** ED60
E17 **67** EA58
E18 **48** EF53
N14 **45** DJ45
Brentwood (Shenf.) CM15 **55** FZ44
Chelmsford Sq, NW10 **81** CW67
CHELSEA, SW3 **100** DD79
H **Chelsea & Westminster Hosp**, SW10 **100** DC79
★ **Chelsea Antique Mkt**,
SW3 **100** DD79
Chelsea Br, SW1 **101** DH79
SW8 **101** DH79
Chelsea Br Rd, SW1 **198** F10
Chelsea Cloisters, SW3
off Lucan Pl **100** DE77
Chelsea Cl, NW10
off Winchelsea Rd **80** CR67
Edgware HA8 **42** CN54
Hampton (Hmptn H.) TW12 **116** CC92
Worcester Park KT4 **139** CU101
Chelsea Cres, SW10
off Harbour Av **100** DC81
Chelsea Embk, SW3 **100** DE79
★ **Chelsea FC**, SW6 **100** DB80
Chelsea Gdns, W13
off Hathaway Gdns **79** CF71
Sutton SM3 **157** CY105
Chelsea Harbour, SW10 **100** DC81
Chelsea Harbour Dr, SW10 **100** DC81
Riv **Chelsea Harbour Pier** **100** DD81
Chelsea Manor Ct, SW3
off Chelsea Manor St **100** DE79
Chelsea Manor Gdns, SW3 **100** DE79
Chelsea Manor St, SW3 **100** DE78
Chelsea Ms, Horn. RM11
off St. Leonards Way **71** FH60
Chelsea Pk Gdns, SW3 **100** DD79
★ **Chelsea Physic Gdn**,
SW3 **100** DF79
Chelsea Reach Twr, SW10
off World's End Est **100** DD80
Chelsea Sq, SW3 **198** A10
Chelsea Vista, SW6
off The Boulevard **100** DC81
Chelsea Wf, SW10 **100** DD80
CHELSFIELD, Orp. BR6 **164** EW106
⇌ **Chelsfield** **164** EV106
Chelsfield Av, N9 **47** DX45
Chelsfield Gdns, SE26 **122** DW90
Chelsfield Grn, N9
off Chelsfield Av **47** DX45
Chelsfield Hill, Orp. BR6 **164** EW109
Chelsfield La, Orp. BR5, BR6 **146** EX101
Orpington (Maypole) BR6 **164** FA108
Sevenoaks TN14 **165** FC109
H **Chelsfield Pk Hosp**, Orp.
BR6 **164** EZ106
Chelsfield Rd, Orp. BR5 **146** EW100
CHELSHAM, Warl. CR6 **177** EA117
Chelsham Cl, Warl. CR6 **177** DY118
Chelsham Common, Warl.
CR6 **177** EA116
Chelsham Common Rd, Warl.
CR6 **177** EA117
Chelsham Ct Rd, Warl. CR6 **177** ED118
Chelsham Rd, SW4 **101** DK83
South Croydon CR2 **160** DR107
Warlingham CR6 **177** EA117
Chelston App, Ruis. HA4 **59** BU61
Chelston Rd, Ruis. HA4 **59** BU60
Chelsworth Cl, Rom. RM3
off Chelsworth Dr **52** FM53
Chelsworth Dr, SE18 **105** ER79
Romford RM3 **52** FL53
Cheltenham Av, Twick. TW1 **117** CG87
Cheltenham Cl, Grav. DA12 **131** GJ92
New Malden KT3
off Northcote Rd **138** CQ97
Northolt UB5 **78** CB65
Cheltenham Gdns, E6 **86** EL68
Loughton IG10 **32** EL44
Cheltenham Pl, W3 **80** CP74
Harrow HA3 **62** CL56
Cheltenham Rd, E10 **67** EC58
SE15 **102** DW84
Orpington BR6 **146** EU104
Cheltenham Ter, SW3 **198** E10
Cheltenham Vil, Stai. TW19 **113** BF86
Chelverton Rd, SW15 **99** CX84
Chelwood, N20
off Oakleigh Rd N **44** DD47
Chelwood Cl, E4 **31** EB44
Coulsdon CR5 **175** DJ119
Epsom KT17 **157** CT112
Northwood HA6 **39** BQ52
Chelwood Gdns, Rich. TW9 **98** CN82
Chelwood Gdns Pas, Rich. TW9
off Chelwood Gdns **98** CN82
Chelwood Wk, SE4 **103** DY84
Chenappa Cl, E13 **86** EG69
Chenduit Way, Stan. HA7 **41** CF50
Cheney Row, E17 **47** DZ53
Cheneys Rd, E11 **68** EE62
Cheney St, Pnr. HA5 **60** BW57
CHENIES, Rick. WD3 **21** BB38
Chenies, The, Dart. DA2 **127** FE91
Orpington BR6 **145** ES100
Chenies Av, Amer. HP6 **20** AW39
Chenies Hill, Hem.H. (Flaun.)
HP3 **5** BB34
★ **Chenies Manor**, Rick. WD3 **21** BA38
Chenies Ms, WC1 **195** M5
Chenies Par, Amer. HP7 **20** AW40
Chenies Pl, NW1 **83** DK68
Chenies Rd, Rick. (Chorl.)
WD3 **21** BD40
Chenies St, WC1 **195** M6
Chenies Way, Wat. WD18 **39** BS45
Cheniston Cl, W.Byf. KT14 **152** BG113
Cheniston Gdns, W8 **100** DB76
Chepstow Av, Horn. RM12 **72** FL62
Chepstow Cl, SW15 **119** CY86
Chepstow Cres, W11 **82** DA73
Ilford IG3 **69** ES58
Chepstow Gdns, Sthl. UB1 **78** BZ72
Chepstow Pl, W2 **82** DA72
Chepstow Ri, Croy. CR0 **142** DS104
Chepstow Rd, W2 **82** DA72
W7 **97** CG76
Croydon CR0 **142** DS104
Chepstow Vil, W11 **81** CZ73
Chequers, Buck.H. IG9
off Hills Rd **48** EH46
Chequers Cl, NW9 **62** CS55
Orpington BR5 **145** ET98
Tadworth (Walt.Hill) KT20 **183** CU125
Chequers Gdns, N13 **45** DP50
Chequers La, Dag. RM9 **88** EZ70
Tadworth (Walt.Hill) KT20 **183** CU125
Watford WD25 **8** BW30
Chequers Orchard, Iver SL0 **75** BF72
Chequers Par, SE9
off Eltham High St **125** EM86
Chequers Rd, Brwd. CM14 **52** FM46
Loughton IG10 **33** EN43
Romford RM3 **52** FL47
Chequers Sq, Uxb. UB8
off The Pavilions **76** BJ66
Chequer St, EC1 **197** J5
Chequers Wk, Wal.Abb. EN9 **16** EF33
Chequers Way, N13 **46** DQ50
Chequer Tree Cl, Wok. (Knap.)
GU21 **166** AS116
Cherbury Cl, SE28 **88** EX72
Cherbury Ct, N1 **197** L1
Cherbury St, N1 **197** L1
Cherchefelle Ms, Stan. HA7 **41** CH50
Cherimoya Gdns, W.Mol. KT8
off Kelvinbrook **136** CB97
Cherington Rd, W7 **79** CF74
Cheriton Av, Brom. BR2 **144** EF99
Ilford IG5 **49** EM54
Cheriton Cl, W5 **79** CJ71
Barnet EN4 **28** DF41
Cheriton Ct, Walt. KT12 **136** BW102
Cheriton Dr, SE18 **105** ER80
Cheriton Sq, SW17 **120** DG89
Cherries, The, Slou. SL2 **74** AV72
Cherry Acre, Ger.Cr. (Chal.St.P.)
SL9 **36** AX49
Cherry Av, Brwd. CM13 **55** FZ48
Slough SL3 **92** AX75
Southall UB1 **78** BX74
Swanley BR8 **147** FD97
Cherry Blossom Cl, N13 **45** DP50
Cherry Cl, E17 *off Eden Rd* **67** EB56
NW9 **42** CS54
SW2 *off Tulse Hill* **121** DN87
W5 **97** CK76
Banstead SM7 **157** CX114
Carshalton SM5 **140** DF103
Morden SM4 **139** CY98
Ruislip HA4
off Roundways **59** BT62
Cherrycot Hill, Orp. BR6 **163** ER105
Cherrycot Ri, Orp. BR6 **163** EQ105
Cherry Cres, Brent. TW8 **97** CH80
Cherry Cft, Rick. (Crox.Grn)
WD3 **22** BN44
Cherrycroft Gdns, Pnr. HA5
off Westfield Pk **40** BZ52
Cherrydale, Wat. WD18 **23** BT42
Cherrydown Av, E4 **47** DZ48
Cherrydown Cl, E4 **47** DZ48
Cherrydown Rd, Sid. DA14 **126** EX89
Cherrydown Wk, Rom. RM7 **51** FB54
Cherry Gdns, Dag. RM9 **70** EZ64
Northolt UB5 **78** CB66
Cherry Gdn St, SE16 **202** D5
Cherry Garth, Brent. TW8 **97** CK77
Cherry Gro, Hayes UB3 **77** BV74
Uxbridge UB8 **77** BP71
Cherry Hill, Barn. EN5 **28** DB44
Harrow HA3 **41** CE51
Rickmansworth (Loud.)
WD3 **22** BH41
St. Albans AL2 **8** CA25
Cherry Hill Gdns, Croy. CR0 **159** DM105
Cherry Hills, Wat. WD19 **40** BY50
Cherry Hollow, Abb.L. WD5 **7** BT31
Cherrylands Cl, NW9 **62** CQ61
Cherry La, West Dr. UB7 **94** BM77
Cherry La Rbt, West Dr. UB7 **95** BP77
Cherry Laurel Wk, SW2
off Beechdale Rd **121** DM86
Cherry Orchard, Amer. HP6 **20** AS37
Ashtead KT21 **172** CP118
Slough (Stoke P.) SL2 **74** AV66
Staines TW18 **114** BG92
West Drayton UB7 **94** BL75
Cherry Orchard Cl, Orp. BR5 **146** EW99
Cherry Orchard Gdns, Croy.
CR0 *off Oval Rd* **142** DR103
West Molesey KT8 **136** BZ97
Cherry Orchard Rd, Brom.
BR2 **144** EL103
Croydon CR0 **142** DR103
West Molesey KT8 **136** CA97
Cherry Ri, Ch.St.G. HP8 **36** AX47
Cherry Rd, Enf. EN3 **30** DW38
Cherry St, Rom. RM7 **71** FD57
Woking GU21 **166** AY118
Cherry Tree Av, St.Alb.
(Lon.Col.) AL2 **9** CK26
Staines TW18 **114** BH93
West Drayton UB7 **76** BM72
Cherry Tree Cl, E9
off Moulins Rd **84** DW67
Grays RM17 **110** GC79
Rainham RM13 **89** FG68
Wembley HA0 **61** CF63
Cherry Tree Ct, NW9 **62** CQ56
Coulsdon CR5 **175** DM118
Cherry Tree Dr, SW16 **121** DL90
South Ockendon RM15 **91** FX70
Cherry Tree Grn, S.Croy. CR2 **160** DV114
Cherry Tree La, Dart. DA2 **127** FF90
Epsom KT19
off Christ Ch Rd **156** CN112
Cherrytree La, Ger.Cr.
(Chal.St.P.) SL9 **36** AX54
Cherry Tree La, Iver SL0 **76** BG67
Potters Bar EN6 **12** DB34
Rainham RM13 **89** FF69
Rickmansworth (Herons.)
WD3 **37** BC46
Slough (Fulmer) SL3 **75** AZ65
Cherry Tree Ri, Buck.H. IG9 **48** EJ49
Cherry Tree Rd, E15
off Wingfield Rd **68** EE64
N2 **64** DF56
Watford WD24 **23** BV36
Cherrytrees, Couls. CR5 **175** DK121
Cherry Tree Wk, EC1 **197** J5
Beckenham BR3 **143** DZ98
West Wickham BR4 **162** EF105
Cherry Tree Way, E13
off Boundary La **86** EJ70

Cherry Tree Way, Stan. HA7 41 CH51
Cherry Wk, Brom. BR2 144 EG102
Grays RM16 111 GG76
Rainham RM13 89 FF68
Rickmansworth (Loud.) WD3 22 BJ40
Cherry Way, Epsom KT19 156 CR107
Shepperton TW17 135 BR98
Slough (Horton) SL3 93 BC83
Cherrywood Av, Egh. (Eng.Grn) TW20 112 AV93
Cherrywood Cl, E3 85 DY69
Kingston upon Thames KT2 118 CN94
Cherrywood Dr, SW15 119 CX85
Gravesend (Nthflt) DA11 130 GE90
Cherrywood La, Mord. SM4 139 CY98
Cherry Wd Way, W5 off Hanger Vale La 80 CN71
Cherston Gdns, Loug. IG10 33 EN42
Cherston Rd, Loug. IG10 33 EN42
CHERTSEY, KT16 134 BG102
⇌ Chertsey 133 BF102
Chertsey Br Rd, Cher. KT16 134 BK101
Chertsey Cl, Ken. CR8 175 DP115
Chertsey Cres, Croy. (New Adgtn) CR0 161 EC110
Chertsey Dr, Sutt. SM3 139 CY103
Chertsey La, Cher. KT16 133 BE95
Epsom KT19 156 CN112
Staines TW18 113 BE92
Chertsey Meads, Cher. KT16 134 BK102
★ Chertsey Mus, Cher. KT16 off Windsor St 134 BG100
Chertsey Rd, E11 67 ED61
Addlestone KT15 134 BH103
Ashford TW15 115 BR94
Feltham TW13 115 BS92
Ilford IG1 69 ER63
Shepperton TW17 134 BN101
Sunbury-on-Thames TW16 115 BR94
Twickenham TW1, TW2 117 CF86
West Byfleet (Byfleet) KT14 152 BK111
Woking GU21 151 BA113
Woking (Chobham) GU24 150 AY110
Chertsey St, SW17 120 DG92
Chervil Cl, Felt. TW13 115 BU90
Chervil Ms, SE28 88 EV74
Cherwell Cl, Rick. (Crox.Grn) WD3 22 BN43
Slough SL3 off Tweed Rd 93 BB79
Cherwell Ct, Epsom KT19 156 CQ105
Cherwell Gro, S.Ock. RM15 91 FV73
Cherwell Ho, NW8 off Church St Est 82 DD70
Cherwell Way, Ruis. HA4 59 BQ58
Cheryls Cl, SW6 100 DB81
Cheseman St, SE26 122 DV90
Chesfield Rd, Kings.T. KT2 118 CL94
Chesham Av, Orp. BR5 145 EP100
Chesham Cl, SW1 198 F7
Romford RM7 71 FD56
Sutton SM2 157 CY110
Chesham Ct, Nthwd. HA6 off Frithwood Av 39 BT51
Chesham Cres, SE20 142 DW96
Chesham La, Ch.St.G. HP8 36 AY48
Gerrards Cross (Chal.St.P.) SL9 36 AY49
Chesham Ms, SW1 198 F6
Chesham Pl, SW1 198 F7
Chesham Rd, SE20 142 DW96
SW19 120 DD92
Hemel Hempstead (Bov.) HP3 4 AY27
Kingston upon Thames KT1 138 CN95
Chesham St, NW10 62 CR62
SW1 198 F7
Chesham Ter, W13 97 CH75
Chesham Way, Wat. WD18 23 BS44
Cheshire Cl, E17 47 EB53
SE4 103 DZ82
Chertsey (Ott.) KT16 151 BC107
Hornchurch RM11 72 FN57
Mitcham CR4 141 DL97
Cheshire Ct, EC4 196 E9
Slough SL1 off Sussex Pl 92 AV75
Cheshire Dr, Wat. (Lvsdn) WD25 7 BT34
Cheshire Gdns, Chess. KT9 155 CK107
Cheshire Ho, N18 46 DV49
Cheshire Rd, N22 45 DM52
Cheshire St, E2 84 DT70
Chesholm Rd, N16 66 DS62
CHESHUNT, Wal.Cr. EN8 15 DX31
⇌ Cheshunt 15 DZ30
H Cheshunt Comm Hosp, Wal.Cr. EN8 15 DY31
Cheshunt Pk, Wal.Cr. (Chsht) EN7 14 DV26
Cheshunt Rd, E7 86 EH65
Belvedere DA17 106 FA78
Cheshunt Wash, Wal.Cr. (Chsht) EN8 15 DY27
Chesil Ct, E2 84 DW68
Chesilton Rd, SW6 99 CZ81
Chesil Way, Hayes UB4 77 BT69
Chesley Gdns, E6 86 EK68
Cheslyn Gdns, Wat. WD17 23 BT37
Chesney Cres, Croy. (New Adgtn) CR0 161 EC108
Chesney St, SW11 100 DG81
Chesnut Est, N17 66 DT55
Chesnut Gro, N17 off Chesnut Rd 66 DU55
Chesnut Rd, N17 66 DT55
Chess Cl, Chesh. (Latimer) HP5 20 AX36
Rickmansworth (Loud.) WD3 22 BK42
Chessell Cl, Th.Hth. CR7 141 DP98
Chessfield Pk, Amer. HP6 20 AY39
Chess Hill, Rick. (Loud.) WD3 22 BK42
Chessholme Ct, Sun. TW16 off Scotts Av 115 BS94
Chessholme Rd, Ashf. TW15 115 BQ93
Chessinghams, The, Epsom KT18 156 CR113
CHESSINGTON, KT9 156 CL107
Chessington Av, N3 63 CY55
Bexleyheath DA7 106 EY80
Chessington Cl, Epsom KT19 156 CQ107
Chessington Ct, Pnr. HA5 60 BZ56
Chessington Hall Gdns, Chess. KT9 155 CK108
Chessington Hill Pk, Chess. KT9 156 CN106
Chessington Lo, N3 63 CZ55
⇌ Chessington North 156 CL106
Chessington Rd, Epsom KT17, KT19 157 CT109
⇌ Chessington South 155 CK108
Chessington Way, W.Wick. BR4 143 EB103
★ Chessington World of Adventures, Chess. KT9 155 CJ110
Chess La, Rick. (Loud.) WD3 22 BK42
Chesson Rd, W14 99 CZ79
Chess Vale Ri, Rick. (Crox.Grn) WD3 22 BM44
Chess Valley Wk, Chesh. HP5 20 AU35
Rickmansworth WD3 22 BL44
Chess Way, Rick. (Chorl.) WD3 22 BG41
Chesswood Way, Pnr. HA5 40 BX54
Chester Av, Rich. TW10 118 CM85
Twickenham TW2 116 BZ88
Upminster RM14 73 FS61
Chester Cl, SW1 198 G5
SW13 99 CV83
Ashford TW15 115 BR92
Loughton IG10 33 EQ39
Potters Bar EN6 12 DB29
Richmond TW10 off Chester Av 118 CM86
Sutton SM1 140 DA103
Uxbridge UB8 77 BP72
Chester Cl N, NW1 195 J2
Chester Cl S, NW1 195 J3
Chester Cotts, SW1 198 F9
Chester Ct, NW1 195 J2
SE5 102 DR80
Chester Cres, E8 off Ridley Rd 66 DT64
Chester Dr, Har. HA2 60 BZ58
Chesterfield Cl, Orp. BR5 146 EX98
Chesterfield Dr, Dart. DA1 127 FH85
Esher KT10 137 CG103
Sevenoaks TN13 190 FD122
Chesterfield Gdns, N4 65 DP57
SE10 off Crooms Hill 103 ED80
W1 199 H2
Chesterfield Gro, SE22 122 DT85
Chesterfield Hill, W1 199 H1
Chesterfield Ms, N4 off Chesterfield Gdns 65 DP57
Ashford TW15 off Chesterfield Rd 114 BL91
Chesterfield Rd, E10 67 EC58
N3 44 DA51
W4 98 CQ79
Ashford TW15 114 BL91
Barnet EN5 27 CX43
Enfield EN3 31 DY37
Epsom KT19 156 CR108
Chesterfield St, W1 199 H2
Chesterfield Wk, SE10 103 ED81
Chesterfield Way, SE15 102 DW80
Hayes UB3 95 BU75
Chesterford Gdns, NW3 64 DB63
Chesterford Ho, SE18 off Shooters Hill Rd 104 EK81
Chesterford Rd, E12 69 EM64
Chester Gdns, W13 79 CG72
Enfield EN3 30 DV44
Morden SM4 140 DC100
Chester Gate, NW1 195 H3
Chester Gibbons Grn, St.Alb. (Lon.Col.) AL2 off High St 9 CK26
Chester Grn, Loug. IG10 33 EQ39
Chester Ms, E17 off Chingford Rd 47 EA54
SW1 199 H6
Chester Path, Loug. IG10 33 EQ39
Chester Pl, NW1 195 H2
Chester Rd, E7 86 EK66
E11 68 EH58
E16 86 EE70
E17 67 DX57
N9 46 DV46
N17 66 DR55
N19 65 DH61
NW1 194 G3
SW19 119 CW93
Borehamwood WD6 26 CQ41
Chigwell IG7 49 EN48
Hounslow TW4 95 BV83
Hounslow (Hthrw Air.) TW6 94 BN83
Ilford IG3 69 ET60
Loughton IG10 33 EP40
Northwood HA6 39 BS52
Sidcup DA15 125 ES85
Watford WD18 23 BU43
Chester Row, SW1 198 F9
Chesters, The, N.Mal. KT3 138 CS95
Chester Sq, SW1 199 H8
Chester Sq Ms, SW1 199 H7
Chester St, E2 84 DU70
SW1 198 G6
Chester Ter, NW1 195 H2
Chesterton Cl, SW18 off Ericcson Cl 120 DA85
Greenford UB6 78 CB68
Chesterton Dr, Red. (Merst.) RH1 185 DL128
Staines TW19 114 BM88
Chesterton Ho, SW11 off Ingrave St 100 DD83
Chesterton Rd, E13 86 EG69
W10 81 CX71
Chesterton Sq, W8 off Pembroke Rd 99 CZ77
Chesterton Ter, E13 86 EG69
Kingston upon Thames KT1 138 CN96
Chesterton Way, Til. RM18 111 GJ82
Chester Way, SE11 200 E9
Chesthunte Rd, N17 46 DQ53
Chestnut All, SW6 off Lillie Rd 99 CZ79
Chestnut Av, E7 68 EH63
N8 65 DL57
SW14 off Thornton Rd 98 CR83
Brentford TW8 97 CK77
Brentwood CM14 54 FS45
Buckhurst Hill IG9 48 EK48
East Molesey KT8 137 CF97
Edgware HA8 42 CL51
Epsom KT19 156 CS105
Esher KT10 137 CD101
Grays RM16 110 GB75
Greenhithe (Bluewater) DA9 129 FT87
Hampton TW12 116 CA94
Hornchurch RM12 71 FF61
Northwood HA6 39 BT54
Rickmansworth WD3 22 BG43
Slough SL3 92 AY75
Teddington TW11 137 CF96
Virginia Water GU25 132 AT98
Walton-on-Thames (Whiteley Vill.) KT12 153 BS109
Wembley HA0 61 CH64
West Drayton UB7 76 BM73
West Wickham BR4 162 EE106
Westerham TN16 178 EK122
Weybridge KT13 153 BQ108
Chestnut Av N, E17 67 EC56
Chestnut Av S, E17 67 EC56
Chestnut Cl, N14 29 DJ43
N16 off Lordship Gro 66 DR61
SE6 123 EC92
SE14 103 DZ81
SW16 121 DN91
Addlestone KT15 152 BK106
Ashford TW15 115 BP91
Buckhurst Hill IG9 48 EK48
Carshalton SM5 140 DF102
Egham (Eng.Grn) TW20 112 AW93
Gerrards Cross (Chal.St.P.) SL9 37 AZ52
Gravesend (Nthflt) DA11 off Burch Rd 131 GF86
Hayes UB3 77 BS73
Hornchurch RM12 off Lancaster Dr 72 FJ63
Orpington BR6 164 EU106
Sidcup DA15 126 EU88
Sunbury-on-Thames TW16 115 BT93
Tadworth KT20 174 DA123
West Drayton UB7 95 BP80
Woking (Ripley) GU23 168 BG124
Chestnut Copse, Oxt. RH8 188 EG132
Chestnut Ct, SW6 off North End Rd 99 CZ79
Amersham HP6 20 AS37
Surbiton KT6 off Penners Gdns 138 CL101
Chestnut Cres, Walt. (Whiteley Vill.) KT12 off Chestnut Av 153 BS109
Chestnut Dr, E11 68 EG58
Bexleyheath DA7 106 EX83
Egham (Eng.Grn) TW20 112 AX93
Harrow HA3 41 CF52
Pinner HA5 60 BX58
Chestnut Glen, Horn. RM12 71 FF61
Chestnut Gro, SE20 122 DV94
SW12 120 DG87
W5 97 CK76
Barnet EN4 28 DF43
Brentwood CM14 54 FW47
Dartford DA2 127 FD91
Ilford IG6 49 ES51
Isleworth TW7 97 CG84
Mitcham CR4 141 DK98
New Malden KT3 138 CR97
South Croydon CR2 160 DV108
Staines TW18 114 BJ93
Wembley HA0 61 CH64
Woking GU22 166 AY120
Chestnut Ho, NW3 off Maitland Pk Vil 82 DF65
Chestnut La, N20 43 CY46
Sevenoaks TN13 191 FH124
Weybridge KT13 153 BP106
Chestnut Manor Cl, Stai. TW18 114 BH92
Chestnut Mead, Red. RH1 off Oxford Rd 184 DE133
Chestnut Pl, SE26 122 DT91
Ashtead KT21 172 CL119
Epsom KT17 157 CU111
Chestnut Ri, SE18 105 ER79
Bushey WD23 40 CB45
Chestnut Rd, SE27 121 DP90
SW20 139 CX96
Ashford TW15 115 BP91
Dartford DA1 128 FK88
Enfield EN3 31 DY36
Kingston upon Thames KT2 118 CL94
Twickenham TW2 117 CE89
Chestnut Row, N3 off Nether St 44 DA52
Chestnuts, Brwd. (Hutt.) CM13 55 GB46
Chestnuts, The, Rom. (Abridge) RM4 34 EV41
Walton-on-Thames KT12 135 BU102
Chestnut Wk, Ger.Cr. (Chal.St.P.) SL9 36 AY52
Sevenoaks TN15 191 FL129
Shepperton TW17 135 BS99
Walton-on-Thames (Whiteley Vill.) KT12 off Octagon Rd 153 BS109
Watford WD24 23 BU37
West Byfleet (Byfleet) KT14 off Royston Rd 152 BL112
Woodford Green IG8 48 EG50
Chestnut Way, Felt. TW13 115 BV90
Cheston Av, Croy. CR0 143 DY103
Chestwood Gro, Uxb. UB10 76 BM66
Cheswick Cl, Dart. DA1 107 FF84
Chesworth Cl, Erith DA8 107 FE81
Chettle Cl, SE1 201 K6
Chettle Ct, N8 65 DN58
Chetwode Dr, Epsom KT18 173 CX118
Chetwode Rd, SW17 120 DF90
Tadworth KT20 173 CW119
Chetwood Wk, E6 86 EL72
Chetwynd Av, Barn. EN4 44 DF46
Chetwynd Dr, Uxb. UB10 76 BM68
Chetwynd Rd, NW5 65 DH63
Chevalier Cl, Stan. HA7 42 CL49
Cheval Pl, SW7 198 C6
Cheval St, E14 203 P6
Cheveley Cl, Rom. RM3 off Chelsworth Dr 52 FM53
Chevely Cl, Epp. (Cooper.) CM16 18 EX29
Cheveney Wk, Brom. BR2 off Marina Cl 144 EG97
CHEVENING, Sev. TN14 180 EZ119
Chevening Cross, Sev. (Chev.) TN14 180 FA120
Chevening La, Sev. (Knock.) TN14 180 EY115
Chevening Rd, NW6 81 CX68
SE10 104 EF78
SE19 122 DR93
Sevenoaks TN13, TN14 180 EZ119
Sevenoaks (Sund.) TN14 180 EY123
Chevenings, The, Sid. DA14 126 EW90
Cheverton Rd, N19 65 DK60
Chevet St, E9 off Kenworthy Rd 67 DY64
Chevington Pl, Horn. RM12 off Chevington Way 72 FK64
Chevington Way, Horn. RM12 72 FK63
Cheviot Cl, Bans. SM7 174 DB115
Bexleyheath DA7 107 FE82
Bushey WD23 24 CC44
Enfield EN1 30 DR40
Hayes UB3 95 BR80
Sutton SM2 158 DD109
Cheviot Gdns, NW2 63 CX61
SE27 121 DP91
Cheviot Gate, NW2 63 CY61
Cheviot Rd, SE27 121 DN92
Hornchurch RM11 71 FG60
Slough SL3 93 BA78
Cheviot Way, Ilf. IG2 69 ES56
Chevron Cl, E16 86 EG72
Chevy Rd, Sthl. UB2 96 CC75
Chewton Rd, E17 67 DY56
Cheyham Gdns, Sutt. SM2 157 CX110
Cheyham Way, Sutt. SM2 157 CY110
Cheyne Av, E18 68 EF55
Twickenham TW2 116 BZ88
Cheyne Cl, NW4 63 CW57
Bromley BR2 144 EL104
Gerrards Cross SL9 56 AY60
Cheyne Ct, SW3 off Flood St 100 DF79
Banstead SM7 off Park Rd 174 DB115
Cheyne Gdns, SW3 100 DE79
Cheyne Hill, Surb. KT5 138 CM98
Cheyne Ms, SW3 100 DE79
Cheyne Path, W7 79 CF71
Cheyne Pl, SW3 100 DF79
Cheyne Rd, Ashf. TW15 115 BR93
Cheyne Row, SW3 100 DE79
Cheyne Wk, N21 29 DP43
NW4 63 CW58
SW3 100 DE79
SW10 100 DD80
Croydon CR0 142 DU103
Longfield DA3 off Cavendish Sq 149 FX97
Cheyneys Av, Edg. HA8 41 CK51
Chichele Gdns, Croy. CR0 160 DS105
Chichele Rd, NW2 63 CX64
Oxted RH8 188 EE128
Chicheley Gdns, Har. HA3 40 CC52
Chicheley Rd, Har. HA3 40 CC52
Chicheley St, SE1 200 C4
Chichester Av, Ruis. HA4 59 BR61
Chichester Cl, E6 86 EL72
SE3 104 EJ81
Grays (Chaff.Hun.) RM16 109 FX77
Hampton TW12 off Maple Cl 116 BZ93
South Ockendon (Aveley) RM15 90 FQ74
Chichester Ct, NW1 off Royal Coll St 83 DJ66
Epsom KT17 157 CT109
Slough SL1 92 AV75
Stanmore HA7 62 CL55
Chichester Dr, Pur. CR8 159 DM112
Sevenoaks TN13 190 FF125
Chichester Gdns, Ilf. IG1 68 EL59
Chichester Ms, SE27 121 DN91
Chichester Rents, WC2 196 D8
Chichester Ri, Grav. DA12 131 GK91
Chichester Rd, E11 68 EE62
N9 46 DU46
NW6 82 DA68
W2 82 DB71
Croydon CR0 142 DS104
Greenhithe DA9 129 FT85
Chichester St, SW1 101 DJ78
Chichester Way, E14 204 F8
Feltham TW14 115 BV87
Watford WD25 8 BY33
Chichester Wf, Erith DA8 107 FE78
Chicksand St, E1 84 DT71
Chiddingfold, N12 44 DA48
Chiddingstone Av, Bexh. DA7 106 EZ80
Chiddingstone Cl, Sutt. SM2 158 DA110
Chiddingstone St, SW6 100 DA82
Chieftan Dr, Purf. RM19 108 FM77
Chieveley Rd, Bexh. DA7 107 FB84
Chiffinch Gdns, Grav. (Nthflt) DA11 130 GE90
Chignell Pl, W13 off The Broadway 79 CG74
CHIGWELL, IG7 49 EP48
⊖ Chigwell 49 EP49
Chigwell Hill, E1 202 D1
Chigwell Hurst Ct, Pnr. HA5 60 BX55
Chigwell La, Loug. IG10 33 EQ43
Chigwell Pk, Chig. IG7 49 EP49
Chigwell Pk Dr, Chig. IG7 49 EN48
Chigwell Ri, Chig. IG7 49 EN47
Chigwell Rd, E18 68 EH55
Woodford Green IG8 48 EJ54
CHIGWELL ROW, Chig. IG7 50 EU47
Chigwell Vw, Rom. RM5 off Lodge La 50 FA51
Chilberton Dr, Red. (S.Merst.) RH1 185 DJ130
Chilbrook Rd, Cob. (Down.) KT11 169 BU118
Chilcombe Ho, SW15 off Fontley Way 119 CU87
Chilcot Cl, E14 off Grundy St 85 EB72
Chilcote La, Amer. (Lt.Chal.) HP7 20 AV39
Chilcott Cl, Wem. HA0 61 CJ63
Chilcott Rd, Wat. WD24 23 BS36
Childebert Rd, SW17 121 DH89
Childeric Rd, SE14 103 DY80
Childerley, Kings.T. KT1 off Burritt Rd 138 CN97
Childerley St, SW6 off Fulham Palace Rd 99 CX81
Childers, The, Wdf.Grn. IG8 49 EM50
Childers St, SE8 103 DY79
Child La, SE10 205 L7
H Children's Trust, The, Tad. KT20 173 CX121
Childs Av, Uxb. (Hare.) UB9 38 BJ54
Childs Cl, Horn. RM11 72 FJ58
Childs Cres, Swans. DA10 129 FX86
CHILDS HILL, NW2 64 DA61
Childs Hill Wk, NW2 63 CZ62
Childs La, SE19 off Westow St 122 DS93
Child's Ms, SW5 off Child's Pl 100 DB77
Child's Pl, SW5 100 DA77
Child's St, SW5 100 DA77
Child's Wk, SW5 off Child's St 100 DA77
Childs Way, NW11 63 CZ57
Chilham Cl, Bex. DA5 126 EZ87
Greenford UB6 79 CG68
Chilham Rd, SE9 124 EL91
Chilham Way, Brom. BR2 144 EG101
Chillerton Rd, SW17 120 DG92
Chillington Dr, SW11 100 DC84
Chillingworth Gdns, Twick. TW1 off Tower Rd 117 CF90
Chillingworth Rd, N7 65 DM64
Chilmark Gdns, N.Mal. KT3 139 CT101
Redhill (Merst.) RH1 185 DL129
Chilmark Rd, SW16 141 DK96
Chilmead La, Red. (Nutfld) RH1 185 DK132
Chilsey Grn Rd, Cher. KT16 133 BE100
Chiltern Av, Bushey WD23 24 CC44
Twickenham TW2 116 CA88
Chiltern Business Village, Uxb. UB8 76 BH68
Chiltern Cl, Bexh. DA7 107 FE81
Borehamwood WD6 26 CM40
Bushey WD23 24 CB44
Croydon CR0 142 DS104
Uxbridge (Ickhm) UB10 59 BP61
Waltham Cross (Chsht) EN7 13 DP27
Watford WD18 off Linden Av 23 BS42
Woking GU22 166 AW122
Worcester Park KT4 off Cotswold Way 139 CW103
Chiltern Dene, Enf. EN2 29 DM42
Chiltern Dr, Rick. (Mill End) WD3 37 BF45
Surbiton KT5 138 CP99
Chiltern Gdns, NW2 63 CX62
Bromley BR2 144 EF98
Hornchurch RM12 72 FJ62
Chiltern Hts, Amer. HP7 20 AU39
Chiltern Hill, Ger.Cr. (Chal.St.P.) SL9 36 AY53
★ Chiltern Open Air Mus, Ch.St.G. HP8 37 AZ47
Chiltern Rd, E3 85 EA70
Gravesend (Nthflt) DA11 130 GE90
Ilford IG2 69 ES56
Pinner HA5 60 BW57
Sutton SM2 158 DB109
Chilterns, The, Sutt. SM2 off Gatton Cl 158 DB109
Chiltern St, W1 194 F6
Chiltern Vw Rd, Uxb. UB8 76 BJ68
Chiltern Way, Wdf.Grn. IG8 48 EG48
Chilthorne Cl, SE6 off Ravensbourne Pk Cres 123 DZ87
Chilton Av, W5 97 CK77
Chilton Ct, Walt. KT12 153 BU105
Chilton Gro, SE8 203 J9
Chiltonian Ind Est, SE12 124 EF86
Chilton Rd, Edg. HA8 42 CN51
Grays RM16 111 GG76
Richmond TW9 98 CN83
Chiltons, The, E18 off Grove Hill 48 EG54
Chiltons Cl, Bans. SM7 off High St 174 DB115
Chilton St, E2 84 DT70
Chilver St, SE10 205 L10
Chilwell Gdns, Wat. WD19 40 BW49
Chilworth Ct, SW19 119 CX88
Chilworth Gdns, Sutt. SM1 140 DC104
Chilworth Ms, W2 82 DC72
Chilworth St, W2 82 DC72
Chimes Av, N13 45 DN50
Chimes Shop Cen, The, Uxb. UB8 76 BK66
China Hall Ms, SE16 202 G7
China Ms, SW2 off Craster Rd 121 DM87
★ Chinatown, W1 off Gerrard St 195 M10
Chinbrook Cres, SE12 124 EH90
Chinbrook Est, SE9 124 EK90
Chinbrook Rd, SE12 124 EH90
Chinchilla Dr, Houns. TW4 96 BW82
Chindits La, Brwd. CM14 54 FW50
Chine, The, N10 65 DJ56
N21 29 DP44
Wembley HA0 61 CH64
Chine Fm Pl, Sev. (Knock.) TN14 180 EX116
Ching Ct, WC2 195 P9
Chingdale Rd, E4 48 EE48
CHINGFORD, E4 47 EB46
⇌ Chingford 48 EE45
Chingford Av, E4 47 EB48
CHINGFORD GREEN, E4 48 EF46
CHINGFORD HATCH, E4 47 EC49
Chingford Ind Cen, E4 47 DY50

★ Place of interest ⇌ Railway station ⊖ London Underground station DLR Docklands Light Railway station Tra Tramlink station H Hospital Riv Pedestrian ferry landing stage

Chingford La, Wdf.Grn. IG8 .. 48 EE49
Chingford Mt Rd, E4 .. 47 EA49
Chingford Rd, E4 .. 47 EA51
E17 .. 47 EB53
Chingley Cl, Brom. BR1 .. 124 EE93
Ching Way, E4 .. 47 DZ51
Chinnery Cl, Enf. EN1 .. 30 DT39
Chinnor Cres, Grnf. UB6 .. 78 CB68
Chipka St, E14 .. 204 D5
Chipley St, SE14 .. 103 DY79
Chipmunk Gro, Nthlt. UB5
off Argus Way .. 78 BY69
Chippendale All, Uxb. UB8
off Chippendale Waye .. 76 BK66
Chippendale Ho, SW1
off Churchill Gdns .. 101 DJ78
Chippendale St, E5 .. 67 DX62
Chippendale Waye, Uxb. UB8 .. 76 BK66
Chippenham Av, Wem. HA9 .. 62 CP64
Chippenham Cl, Pnr. HA5 .. 59 BT56
Romford RM3
off Chippenham Rd .. 52 FK50
Chippenham Gdns, NW6 .. 82 DA69
Romford RM3 .. 52 FK50
Chippenham Ms, W9 .. 82 DA70
Chippenham Rd, W9 .. 82 DA70
Romford RM3 .. 52 FK51
Chippenham Wk, Rom. RM3
off Chippenham Rd .. 52 FK51
CHIPPERFIELD, Kings L. WD4 .. 6 BG31
Chipperfield Cl, Upmin. RM14 .. 73 FS60
Chipperfield Rd, Hem.H.
(Bov.) HP3 .. 5 BB27
Kings Langley WD4 .. 6 BK30
Orpington BR5 .. 146 EU95
CHIPPING BARNET, Barn.
EN5 .. 27 CY42
Chipping Cl, Barn. EN5
off St. Albans Rd .. 27 CY41
CHIPSTEAD, Couls. CR5 .. 174 DF118
CHIPSTEAD, Sev. TN13 .. 190 FC122
⇌ Chipstead .. 174 DF118
Chipstead, Ger.Cr. (Chal.St.P.)
SL9 .. 36 AW53
Chipstead Av, Th.Hth. CR7 .. 141 DP98
CHIPSTEAD BOTTOM, Couls.
CR5 .. 174 DE121
Chipstead Cl, SE19 .. 122 DT94
Coulsdon CR5 .. 174 DG116
Sutton SM2 .. 158 DB109
Chipstead Ct, Wok. (Knap.)
GU21 off Creston Av .. 166 AS117
Chipstead Gdns, NW2 .. 63 CV61
Chipstead Gate, Couls. CR5
off Woodfield Cl .. 175 DJ119
Chipstead La, Couls. CR5 .. 174 DB124
Sevenoaks TN13 .. 190 FC122
Tadworth (Lwr Kgswd)
KT20 .. 183 CZ125
Chipstead Pk, Sev. TN13 .. 190 FD122
Chipstead Pk Cl, Sev. TN13 .. 190 FC122
Chipstead Pl Gdns, Sev.
TN13 .. 190 FC122
Chipstead Rd, Bans. SM7 .. 173 CZ117
Erith DA8 .. 107 FE80
Chipstead Sta Par, Couls.
(Chipstead) CR5
off Station App .. 174 DF118
Chipstead St, SW6 .. 100 DA81
Chipstead Valley Rd, Couls.
CR5 .. 175 DH116
Chipstead Way, Bans. SM7 .. 174 DF115
Chip St, SW4 .. 101 DK83
Chirk Cl, Hayes UB4
off Braunston Dr .. 78 BY70
Chirton Wk, Wok. GU21 .. 166 AU118
Chisenhale Rd, E3 .. 85 DY68
Chisholm Rd, Croy. CR0 .. 142 DS103
Richmond TW10 .. 118 CM86
Chisledon Wk, E9
off Southmoor Way .. 85 DZ65
CHISLEHURST, BR7 .. 125 EN94
⇌ Chislehurst .. 145 EN96
Chislehurst Av, N12 .. 44 DC52
★ Chislehurst Caves, Chis.
BR7 off Caveside Cl .. 145 EN95
Chislehurst Rd, Brom. BR1 .. 144 EK96
Chislehurst BR7 .. 144 EK96
Orpington BR5, BR6 .. 145 ES98
Richmond TW10 .. 118 CL86
Sidcup DA14 .. 126 EU92
CHISLEHURST WEST, Chis.
BR7 .. 125 EM92
Chislet Cl, Beck. BR3 .. 123 EA94
Chisley Rd, N15 .. 66 DS58
Chiswell Ct, Wat. WD24 .. 24 BW38
CHISWELL GREEN, St.Alb. AL2 .. 8 CA26
Chiswell Grn La, St.Alb. AL2 .. 8 BX25
Chiswell Sq, SE3
off Brook La .. 104 EH82
Chiswell St, EC1 .. 197 J6
SE5 off Southampton Way .. 102 DR80
CHISWICK, W4 .. 98 CR79
⇌ Chiswick .. 98 CQ80
Chiswick Br, SW14 .. 98 CQ82
W4 .. 98 CQ82
Chiswick Cl, Croy. CR0 .. 141 DM104
Chiswick Common Rd, W4 .. 98 CR77
Chiswick Ct, Pnr. HA5 .. 60 BZ55
Chiswick Grn Studios, W4
off Evershed Wk .. 98 CQ77
Chiswick High Rd, W4 .. 98 CR77
Brentford TW8 .. 98 CM78
★ Chiswick Ho, W4 .. 98 CS79
Chiswick Ho Grds, W4 .. 98 CR79
Chiswick La, W4 .. 98 CS78
Chiswick La S, W4 .. 99 CT78
H Chiswick Lo, W4 .. 99 CT78
Chiswick Mall, W4 .. 99 CT79
W6 .. 99 CT79
⊖ Chiswick Park .. 98 CQ77
Chiswick Pk, W4 .. 98 CP77
Chiswick Quay, W4 .. 98 CQ81
Chiswick Rd, N9 .. 46 DU47
W4 .. 98 CQ77
Chiswick Rbt, W4 .. 98 CN78
Chiswick Sq, W4
off Hogarth Rbt .. 98 CS79
Chiswick Staithe, W4 .. 98 CQ81
Chiswick Ter, W4
off Acton La .. 98 CQ77
Chiswick Village, W4 .. 98 CP78
Chiswick Wf, W4 .. 99 CT79
Chittenden Cotts, Wok.
(Wisley) GU23 .. 168 BL116
Chitterfield Gate, West Dr.
UB7 .. 94 BN80
Chitty's La, Dag. RM8 .. 70 EX61
Chitty St, W1 .. 195 L6
Chivalry Rd, SW11 .. 120 DE85
Chivenor Gro, Kings.T. KT2 .. 117 CK92
Chivers Rd, E4 .. 47 EB48
Choats Manor Way, Dag.
RM9 .. 88 EZ69
Choats Rd, Bark. IG11 .. 88 EW68
Dagenham RM9 .. 88 EW68
CHOBHAM, Wok. GU24 .. 150 AT111
Chobham Cl, Cher. (Ott.)
KT16 .. 151 BB107
★ Chobham Common
National Nature
Reserve, Wok. GU24 .. 150 AS105
Chobham Gdns, SW19 .. 119 CX89
Chobham La, Cher. (Longcr.)
KT16 .. 132 AV102
Chobham Pk La, Wok. (Chobham)
GU24 .. 150 AU110
Chobham Rd, E15 .. 67 ED64
Chertsey (Ott.) KT16 .. 151 BA108
Woking GU21 .. 166 AY116
Woking (Horsell) GU21 .. 150 AW113
Choice Vw, Ilf. IG1
off High Rd .. 69 EQ61
Choir Grn, Wok. (Knap.)
GU21 .. 166 AS117
Cholmeley Cres, N6 .. 65 DH59
Cholmeley Pk, N6 .. 65 DH60
Cholmley Gdns, NW6
off Fortune Grn Rd .. 64 DA64
Cholmley Rd, T.Ditt. KT7 .. 137 CH100
Cholmondeley Av, NW10 .. 81 CU68
Cholmondeley Wk, Rich.
TW9 .. 117 CJ85
Choppins Ct, E1 .. 202 E2
Chopwell Cl, E15
off Bryant St .. 86 EE66
CHORLEYWOOD, Rick. WD3 .. 21 BE43
⇌ Chorleywood .. 21 BD42
⊖ Chorleywood .. 21 BD42
CHORLEYWOOD BOTTOM,
Rick. WD3 .. 21 BD44
Chorleywood Bottom, Rick.
(Chorl.) WD3 .. 21 BD43
Chorleywood Cl, Rick. WD3 .. 38 BK45
Chorleywood Common, Rick.
(Chorl.) WD3 .. 21 BE42
Chorleywood Cres, Orp. BR5 .. 145 ET96
Chorleywood Ho Dr, Rick.
(Chorl.) WD3 .. 21 BE41
Chorleywood Lo La, Rick.
(Chorl.) WD3
off Rickmansworth Rd .. 21 BF41
Chorleywood Rd, Rick. WD3 .. 22 BG42
Choumert Gro, SE15 .. 102 DU82
Choumert Ms, SE15 .. 102 DU82
Choumert Rd, SE15 .. 102 DT83
Choumert Sq, SE15 .. 102 DU82
Chow Sq, E8 off Arcola St .. 66 DT64
Chrislaine Cl, Stai. (Stanw.)
TW19 .. 114 BK86
Chrisp St, E14 .. 85 EB71
Christabel Cl, Islw. TW7 .. 97 CE83
Christchurch Av, N12 .. 44 DC51
NW6 .. 81 CY66
Erith DA8 .. 107 FD79
Harrow HA3 .. 61 CH56
Rainham RM13 .. 89 FF68
Teddington TW11 .. 117 CG92
Wembley HA0 .. 80 CL65
Christchurch Cl, N12
off Summers La .. 44 DD52
SW19 .. 120 DD94
Enfield EN2 .. 30 DQ40
Christchurch Ct, NW6 .. 81 CY66
Christchurch Cres, Grav. DA12
off Christchurch Rd .. 131 GJ87
Radlett WD7 .. 25 CG36
Christchurch Gdns, Epsom
KT19 .. 156 CP111
Harrow HA3 .. 61 CG56
Christchurch Grn, Wem. HA0 .. 80 CL65
Christchurch Hill, NW3 .. 64 DD62
Christchurch La, Barn. EN5 .. 27 CY40
Christ Ch Mt, Epsom KT19 .. 156 CP112
Christchurch Pk, Sutt. SM2 .. 158 DC108
Christ Ch Pas, EC1 .. 196 G8
Christchurch Pas, NW3 .. 64 DC62
Barnet EN5 .. 27 CY41
Christ Ch Path, Hayes UB3 .. 95 BQ76
Christchurch Pl, Epsom KT19 .. 156 CP111
Christchurch Rd, N8 .. 65 DL58
SW2 .. 121 DM88
SW14 .. 118 CP85
SW19 .. 140 DD95
Christ Ch Rd, Beck. BR3
off Fairfield Rd .. 143 EA96
Christchurch Rd, Dart. DA1 .. 128 FJ87
Christ Ch Rd, Epsom KT19 .. 156 CL112
Christchurch Rd, Grav. DA12 .. 131 GJ88
Ilford IG1 .. 69 EP60
Purley CR8 .. 159 DP110
Sidcup DA15 .. 125 ET91
Christ Ch Rd, Surb. KT5 .. 138 CM100
Christchurch Rd, Til. RM18 .. 111 GG81
Virginia Water GU25 .. 132 AU97
Christchurch Sq, E9
off Victoria Pk Rd .. 84 DW67
Christchurch St, SW3 .. 100 DF79
Christchurch Ter, SW3
off Christchurch St .. 100 DF79
Christchurch Way, SE10 .. 205 J9
Woking GU21
off Church St E .. 167 AZ117
Christian Ct, SE16 .. 203 M3
Christian Flds, SW16 .. 121 DN94
Christian Flds Av, Grav.
DA12 .. 131 GJ91
Christian St, E1 .. 84 DU72
Christie Ct, Wat. WD18 .. 23 BU43
Christie Dr, Croy. CR0 .. 142 DU99
Christie Gdns, Rom. RM6 .. 70 EV58
Christie Rd, E9 .. 85 DY65
Waltham Abbey EN9
off Deer Pk Way .. 31 EB36
Christies Av, Sev. (Bad.Mt)
TN14 .. 164 FA110
Christie Wk, Cat. CR3
off Hambledon Rd .. 176 DR122
Christina Sq, N4
off Adolphus Rd .. 65 DP60
Christina St, EC2 .. 197 M4
Christine Worsley Cl, N21
off Highfield Rd .. 45 DP47
Christopher Av, W7 .. 97 CG76
Christopher Cl, SE16 .. 203 H4
Hornchurch RM12
off Chevington Way .. 72 FK63
Sidcup DA15 .. 125 ET85
Christopher Ct, Tad. KT20
off High St .. 173 CW123
Christopher Gdns, Dag.
RM9 off Wren Rd .. 70 EX64
Christopher Pl, NW1 .. 195 N3
Christopher Rd, Sthl. UB2 .. 95 BV77
Christopher's Ms, W11
off Penzance St .. 81 CY74
Christopher St, EC2 .. 197 L5
Christy Rd, West. (Bigg.H.)
TN16 .. 178 EJ115
Chryssell Rd, SW9 .. 101 DN80
Chubworthy St, SE14 .. 103 DY79
Chucks La, Tad. (Walt.Hill)
KT20 .. 173 CV124
Chudleigh Cres, Ilf. IG3 .. 69 ES63
Chudleigh Gdns, Sutt. SM1 .. 140 DC104
Chudleigh Rd, NW6 .. 81 CX66
SE4 .. 123 DZ85
Romford RM3 .. 52 FL49
Twickenham TW2 .. 117 CF87
Chudleigh St, E1 .. 85 DX72
Chudleigh Way, Ruis. HA4 .. 59 BU60
Chulsa Rd, SE26 .. 122 DV92
Chumleigh St, SE5 .. 102 DS79
Chumleigh Wk, Surb. KT5 .. 138 CM98
Church All, Croy. CR0 .. 141 DN102
Gravesend DA11
off High St .. 131 GH86
Watford (Ald.) WD25 .. 24 CC38
Church App, SE21 .. 122 DR90
Egham TW20 .. 133 BC97
Sevenoaks (Cudham) TN14
off Cudham La S .. 179 EQ115
Staines (Stanw.) TW19 .. 114 BK86
Church Av, E4 .. 47 ED51
NW1 off Kentish Town Rd .. 83 DH65
SW14 .. 98 CR83
Beckenham BR3 .. 143 EA95
Northolt UB5 .. 78 BZ66
Pinner HA5 .. 60 BY58
Ruislip HA4 .. 59 BR60
Sidcup DA14 .. 126 EU92
Southall UB2 .. 96 BY76
Churchbury Cl, Enf. EN1 .. 30 DS40
Churchbury La, Enf. EN1 .. 30 DR41
Churchbury Rd, SE9 .. 124 EK87
Enfield EN1 .. 30 DR40
Church Cl, N20 .. 44 DE48
W8 off Kensington Ch St .. 100 DB75
Addlestone KT15 .. 152 BH105
Edgware HA8 .. 42 CQ50
Hayes UB4 .. 77 BR71
Hounslow TW3 off Bath Rd .. 96 BZ83
Leatherhead (Fetch.) KT22 .. 171 CD124
Loughton IG10 .. 33 EM40
Northwood HA6 .. 39 BT52
Potters Bar (Cuffley) EN6 .. 13 DL29
Radlett WD7 .. 25 CG36
Staines TW18
off The Broadway .. 134 BJ97
Tadworth (Lwr Kgswd) KT20
off Buckland Rd .. 183 CZ127
Uxbridge UB8 .. 76 BH68
West Drayton UB7 .. 94 BL76
Woking (Horsell) GU21 .. 166 AX116
Church Cor, SW17
off Mitcham Rd .. 120 DF92
Church Ct, Reig. RH2 .. 184 DB134
Richmond TW9
off George St .. 117 CK85
Church Cres, E9 .. 85 DX66
N3 .. 43 CZ53
N10 .. 65 DH56
N20 .. 44 DE48
South Ockendon RM15 .. 91 FW69
Churchcroft Cl, SW12
off Endlesham Rd .. 120 DG87
Churchdown, Brom. BR1 .. 124 EE91
Church Dr, NW9 .. 62 CR60
Harrow HA2 .. 60 BZ58
West Wickham BR4 .. 144 EE104
Church Elm La, Dag. RM10 .. 88 FA65
CHURCH END, N3 .. 43 CZ53
CHURCH END, NW10 .. 80 CS65
Church End, E17 .. 67 EB56
NW4 .. 63 CV55
Church Entry, EC4 .. 196 G9
Church Est Almshouses, Rich.
TW9 off St. Mary's Gro .. 98 CM84
Church Fm Cl, Swan. BR8 .. 147 FC100
★ Church Farm Ho Mus,
NW4 .. 63 CV55
Church Fm La, Sutt. SM3 .. 157 CY107
Church Fm Way, Wat. (Ald.)
WD25 .. 24 CB38
Church Fld, Dart. DA2 .. 128 FK89
Epping CM16 .. 18 EU29
Radlett WD7 .. 25 CG36
Sevenoaks TN13 .. 190 FE122
Churchfield Av, N12 .. 44 DC51
Churchfield Cl, Har. HA2 .. 60 CC56
Hayes UB3 off West Av .. 77 BT73
Churchfield Ms, Slou. SL2 .. 74 AU72
Churchfield Path, Wal.Cr.
(Chsht) EN8 .. 14 DW29
Churchfield Pl, Shep. TW17
off Chertsey Rd .. 135 BP101
Weybridge KT13 .. 152 BN105
Churchfield Rd, W3 .. 80 CQ74
W7 .. 97 CE75
W13 .. 79 CH74
Gerrards Cross (Chal.St.P.)
SL9 .. 36 AX53
Reigate RH2 .. 183 CZ133
Walton-on-Thames KT12 .. 135 BU102
Welling DA16 .. 106 EU83
Weybridge KT13 .. 152 BN105
Churchfields, E18 .. 48 EG53
SE10 off Roan St .. 103 EC79
Loughton IG10 .. 32 EL42
Churchfields, W.Mol. KT8 .. 136 CA97
Woking (Horsell) GU21 .. 166 AY116
Churchfields Av, Felt. TW13 .. 116 BZ90
Weybridge KT13 .. 153 BP105
Churchfields Rd, Beck. BR3 .. 143 DX96
Watford WD24 .. 23 BT36
Church Gdns, W5 .. 97 CK75
Wembley HA0 .. 61 CG63
Church Gate, SW6 .. 99 CY83
Churchgate, Wal.Cr. (Chsht)
EN8 .. 14 DV30
Churchgate Rd, Wal.Cr.
(Chsht) EN8 .. 14 DV29
Church Grn, Hayes UB3 .. 77 BT72
Walton-on-Thames KT12 .. 154 BW107
Church Gro, SE13 .. 103 EB84
Amersham HP6 .. 20 AY39
Kingston upon Thames
KT1 .. 137 CJ95
Slough (Wexham) SL3 .. 74 AW71
Church Hill, E17 .. 67 EA56
N21 .. 45 DM45
SE18 .. 105 EM76
SW19 .. 119 CZ92
Abbots Langley (Bedmond)
WD5 .. 7 BT26
Carshalton SM5 .. 158 DF106
Caterham CR3 .. 176 DT124
Dartford DA2 .. 128 FK90
Dartford (Cray.) DA2 .. 107 FE84
Epping CM16 .. 18 EU29
Greenhithe DA9 .. 129 FS85
Harrow HA1 .. 61 CE60
Loughton IG10 .. 32 EL41
Orpington BR6 .. 146 EU101
Purley CR8 .. 159 DL110
Redhill (Merst.) RH1 .. 185 DH126
Redhill (Nutfld) RH1 .. 185 DM133
Sevenoaks (Cudham)
TN14 .. 179 EQ115
Uxbridge (Hare.) UB9 .. 58 BJ55
Westerham (Tats.) TN16 .. 178 EK122
Woking (Horsell) GU21 .. 166 AX116
Woking (Pyrford) GU22 .. 167 BF117
Church Hill Rd, E17 .. 67 EB56
Barnet EN4 .. 44 DF45
Surbiton KT6 .. 138 CL99
Sutton SM3 .. 157 CX105
Church Hill Wd, Orp. BR5 .. 145 ET99
Church Hollow, Purf. RM19 .. 108 FN78
Church Hyde, SE18
off Old Mill Rd .. 105 ES79
Churchill Av, Har. HA3 .. 61 CH58
Uxbridge UB10 .. 77 BP69
Churchill Cl, Dart. DA1 .. 128 FP88
Feltham TW14 .. 115 BT88
Leatherhead (Fetch.) KT22 .. 171 CE123
Uxbridge UB10 .. 77 BP69
Warlingham CR6 .. 176 DW117
Churchill Ct, SE18
off Rush Gro St .. 105 EM77
W5 .. 80 CM70
Northolt UB5 .. 60 CA64
Staines TW18
off Chestnut Gro .. 114 BH93
Churchill Dr, Wey. KT13 .. 135 BQ104
Churchill Gdns, SW1 .. 101 DJ78
W3 .. 80 CN72
Churchill Gdns Rd, SW1 .. 101 DH78
Churchill Ms, Wdf.Grn. IG8
off High Rd Woodford Grn .. 48 EF51
★ Churchill Mus & Cabinet
War Rooms, SW1 .. 199 N4
Churchill Pl, E14 .. 204 C2
Harrow HA1
off Sandridge Cl .. 61 CE56
Churchill Rd, E16 .. 86 EJ72
NW2 .. 81 CV65
NW5 .. 65 DH63
Dartford (Hort.Kir.) DA4 .. 148 FQ98
Edgware HA8 .. 42 CM51
Epsom KT19 .. 156 CN111
Gravesend DA11 .. 131 GF88
Grays RM17 .. 110 GD79
Slough SL3 .. 93 AZ77
South Croydon CR2 .. 160 DQ109
Churchill Ter, E4 .. 47 EA49
Churchill Wk, E9 .. 66 DW64
Churchill Way, Brom. BR1
off Ethelbert Rd .. 144 EG97
Sunbury-on-Thames TW16 .. 115 BU92
Westerham (Bigg.H.) TN16 .. 162 EK113
Church Island, Stai. TW18 .. 113 BD91
Church La, E11 .. 68 EE60
E17 .. 67 EB56
N2 .. 64 DD55
N8 .. 65 DM56
N9 .. 46 DU47
N17 .. 46 DS53
NW9 .. 62 CQ61
SW17 .. 121 DH91
SW19 .. 139 CZ95
W5 .. 97 CJ75
Banstead (Nork) SM7 .. 173 CX117
Brentwood (Gt Warley)
CM13 .. 73 FW58
Brentwood (Hutt.) CM13 .. 55 GE46
Bromley BR2 .. 144 EL102
Caterham (Chaldon) CR3 .. 175 DN123
Chessington KT9 .. 156 CM107
Chislehurst BR7 .. 145 EQ95
Coulsdon CR5 .. 174 DG122
Dagenham RM10 .. 89 FB65
Enfield EN1 .. 30 DR41
Epping (N.Wld Bas.) CM16 .. 19 FB26
Epsom (Headley) KT18 .. 172 CQ124
Gerrards Cross (Chal.St.P.)
SL9 .. 36 AX53
Godstone RH9 .. 187 DX132
Harrow HA3 .. 41 CF53
Hemel Hempstead (Bov.)
HP3 .. 5 BB27
Kings Langley WD4 .. 6 BN29
Loughton IG10 .. 33 EM41
Oxted RH8 .. 188 EE129
Pinner HA5 .. 60 BY55
Potters Bar (Northaw) EN6 .. 12 DG30
Purfleet RM19 .. 108 FN78
Rainham (Wenn.) RM13 .. 90 FK72
Redhill (Bletch.) RH1 .. 186 DR133
Richmond TW10 .. 118 CL88
Rickmansworth (Mill End)
WD3 .. 38 BG46
Church La, Rick. (Sarratt)
WD3 .. 21 BF38
Romford RM1 .. 71 FE56
Romford (Abridge) RM4 .. 34 EY40
Romford (Stap.Abb.) RM4 .. 35 FC42
Slough (Stoke P.) SL2 .. 74 AT69
Slough (Wexham) SL3 .. 74 AW71
Teddington TW11 .. 117 CF92
Thames Ditton KT7 .. 137 CF100
Twickenham TW1 .. 117 CG88
Upminster (N.Ock.) RM14 .. 73 FV64
Uxbridge UB8 .. 76 BH68
Wallington SM6 .. 141 DK104
Waltham Cross (Chsht) EN8 .. 14 DV29
Warlingham CR6 .. 177 DX117
Warlingham (Chel.) CR6 .. 177 EC116
Watford (Ald.) WD25 .. 24 CB38
Westerham TN16 .. 178 EK122
Weybridge KT13 .. 152 BN105
Church La Av, Couls. CR5 .. 175 DH122
Church La Dr, Couls. CR5 .. 175 DH122
Churchley Rd, SE26 .. 122 DV91
Church Manor Est, SW9
off Vassall Rd .. 101 DN80
Church Manorway, SE2 .. 105 ET77
Erith DA8 .. 107 FD76
Church Manorway Ind Est,
Erith DA8 .. 107 FC76
Churchmead Cl, Barn. EN4 .. 28 DE44
Church Meadow, Surb. KT6 .. 137 CJ103
Churchmead Rd, NW10 .. 81 CU65
Church Ms, Add. KT15 .. 152 BJ105
Churchmore Rd, SW16 .. 141 DJ95
Church Mt, N2 .. 64 DD57
Church Paddock Ct, Wall.
SM6 .. 141 DK104
Church Pas, EC2
off Gresham St .. 84 DQ72
Barnet EN5 off Wood St .. 27 CZ42
Surbiton KT6 .. 138 CL99
Church Path, E11 .. 68 EG57
E17 off St. Mary Rd .. 67 EB56
N5 .. 65 DP64
N12 .. 44 DC50
N17 off White Hart La .. 46 DS52
N20 .. 44 DC49
NW10 .. 80 CS66
SW14 .. 98 CR83
SW19 .. 140 DA96
W4 .. 98 CQ76
W7 .. 79 CE74
Cobham KT11 .. 153 BV114
Coulsdon CR5 .. 175 DN118
Gravesend (Nthflt) DA11 .. 130 GC86
Grays RM17 .. 110 GA79
Greenhithe DA9 .. 129 FT85
Mitcham CR4 .. 140 DE97
Southall UB1 .. 78 CA74
Southall (Sthl Grn) UB2 .. 96 BZ76
Woking GU21 off High St .. 167 AZ117
Church Pl, SW1 .. 199 L1
W5 off Church Gdns .. 97 CK75
Mitcham CR4 .. 140 DE97
Twickenham TW1
off Church St .. 117 CG88
Uxbridge (Ickhm) UB10 .. 59 BQ62
Church Ri, SE23 .. 123 DX88
Chessington KT9 .. 156 CM107
Church Rd, E10 .. 67 EB61
E12 .. 68 EL64
E17 .. 47 DY54
N1 .. 84 DQ65
N6 .. 64 DG58
N17 .. 46 DS53
NW4 .. 63 CV56
NW10 .. 80 CS65
SE19 .. 142 DS95
SW13 .. 99 CT82
SW19 (Wimbledon) .. 119 CY91
W3 .. 98 CQ75
W7 .. 79 CF74
Addlestone KT15 .. 152 BG106
Ashford TW15 .. 114 BM90
Ashtead KT21 .. 171 CK117
Barking IG11 .. 87 EQ65
Bexleyheath DA7 .. 106 EZ82
Bromley BR2 .. 144 EG96
Bromley (Short.) BR2 .. 144 EE97
Buckhurst Hill IG9 .. 48 EH46
Caterham CR3 .. 176 DT123
Caterham (Wold.) CR3 .. 177 DX122
Croydon CR0 .. 141 DP104
Dartford (Sutt.H.) DA4 .. 128 FL94
East Molesey KT8 .. 137 CD98
Egham TW20 .. 113 BA92
Enfield EN3 .. 30 DW44
Epsom KT17 .. 156 CS112
Epsom (W.Ewell) KT19 .. 156 CR108
Erith DA8 .. 107 FD78
Esher (Clay.) KT10 .. 155 CF107
Feltham TW13 .. 116 BX92
Gravesend (Cobham) DA12,
DA13 .. 131 GJ94
Greenhithe DA9 .. 129 FS85
Hayes UB3 .. 77 BT72
Hounslow (Cran.) TW5 .. 95 BV78
Hounslow (Heston) TW5 .. 96 CA80
Ilford IG2 .. 69 ER58
Isleworth TW7 .. 97 CD81
Iver SL0 .. 75 BC69
Kenley CR8 .. 176 DR115
Keston BR2 .. 162 EK108
Kingston upon Thames
KT1 .. 138 CM96
Leatherhead KT22 .. 171 CH122
Leatherhead (Bkhm) KT23 .. 170 BZ123
Loughton (High Beach)
IG10 .. 32 EH40
Mitcham CR4 .. 140 DD96
Northolt UB5 .. 78 BZ66
Northwood HA6 .. 39 BT52
Orpington (Chels.) BR6 .. 164 EY106
Orpington (Farnboro.)
BR6 .. 163 EQ106
Potters Bar EN6 .. 12 DB30
Purley CR8 .. 159 DL110
Richmond TW9, TW10 .. 118 CL85

★ Place of interest   ⇌ Railway station   ⊖ London Underground station   DLR Docklands Light Railway station   Tra Tramlink station   H Hospital   Riv Pedestrian ferry landing stage

Church Rd, Rich. (Ham) TW10 118 CM92
Romford (Harold Wd) RM3 52 FN53
Romford (Noak Hill) RM4 52 FK46
Sevenoaks (Halst.) TN14 164 EY111
Sevenoaks (Seal) TN15 191 FM121
Shepperton TW17 135 BP101
Sidcup DA14 126 EU91
Southall UB2 96 BZ76
Stanmore HA7 41 CH50
Surbiton KT6 137 CJ103
Sutton SM3 157 CY107
Swanley BR8 148 FK95
Swanley (Crock.) BR8 147 FD101
Swanscombe DA10 130 FZ86
Teddington TW11 117 CE91
Tilbury RM18 111 GF81
Tilbury (W.Til.) RM18 111 GL79
Uxbridge (Cowley) UB8 76 BK70
Uxbridge (Hare.) UB9 58 BJ55
Wallington SM6 141 DJ104
Warlingham CR6 176 DW117
Watford WD17 23 BU39
Welling DA16 106 EV82
West Byfleet (Byfleet) KT14 152 BM113
West Drayton UB7 94 BK76
Westerham (Bigg.H.) TN16 178 EK117
Westerham (Brasted) TN16 180 EV124
Whyteleafe CR3 176 DT118
Windsor (Old Wind.) SL4 112 AV85
Woking (Horsell) GU21 166 AY116
Woking (St.John's) GU21 166 AU119
Worcester Park KT4 138 CS102
Church Rd Merton, SW19 140 DD95
Church Rd Twr Block, Stan. HA7 *off Church Rd* 41 CJ50
Church Row, NW3 64 DC63
Chislehurst BR7 125 EQ94
Church Side, Epsom KT18 156 CP113
Churchside Cl, West. (Bigg.H.) TN16 178 EJ117
Church Sq, Shep. TW17 135 BP101
Tram **Church Street** 141 DP103
Church St, E15 86 EE67
E16 87 EP74
N9 46 DS47
NW8 194 A6
W2 194 A6
W4 98 CS79
Cobham KT11 169 BV115
Croydon CR0 142 DQ103
Dagenham RM10 89 FB65
Enfield EN2 30 DR41
Epsom KT17 156 CS113
Epsom (Ewell) KT17 157 CU109
Esher KT10 154 CB105
Gravesend DA11 131 GH86
Gravesend (Sthflt) DA13 130 GA92
Grays RM17 110 GC79
Hampton TW12 136 CC95
Hemel Hempstead (Bov.) HP3 5 BB27
Isleworth TW7 97 CH83
Kingston upon Thames KT1 137 CK96
Leatherhead KT22 171 CH122
Reigate RH2 184 DA134
Rickmansworth WD3 38 BL46
Sevenoaks (Seal) TN15 191 FN121
Sevenoaks (Shore.) TN14 165 FF111
Slough SL1 92 AT76
Staines TW18 113 BE91
Sunbury-on-Thames TW16 135 BV97
Sutton SM1 *off High St* 158 DB106
Twickenham TW1 117 CG88
Waltham Abbey EN9 15 EC33
Walton-on-Thames KT12 135 BU102
Watford WD18 24 BW42
Weybridge KT13 152 BN105
Woking (Old Wok.) GU22 167 BC121
Church St E, Wok. GU21 167 AZ117
Church St Est, NW8 194 A5
Church St N, E15 86 EE67
Church St Pas, E15 *off Church St* 86 EE67
Church St W, Wok. GU21 166 AY117
Church Stretton Rd, Houns. TW3 116 CC85
Church Ter, NW4 63 CV55
SE13 104 EE83
SW8 101 DK82
Richmond TW10 117 CK85
CHURCH TOWN, Gdse. RH9 187 DX131
Church Trd Est, The, Erith DA8 107 FG80
Church Vale, N2 64 DF55
SE23 122 DW89
Church Vw, S.Ock. (Aveley) RM15 108 FQ75
Swanley BR8 *off Lime Rd* 147 FD97
Upminster RM14 72 FN61
Churchview Rd, Twick. TW2 117 CD88
Church Vil, Sev. TN13 *off Maidstone Rd* 190 FE122
Church Wk, N6 *off Swains La* 64 DG62
N16 66 DR63
NW2 63 CZ62
NW4 63 CW55
NW9 62 CR61
SW13 99 CU81
SW15 119 CV85
SW16 141 DJ96
SW20 139 CW97
Brentford TW8 97 CJ79
Bushey WD23 *off High St* 24 CA44
Caterham CR3 176 DU124
Chertsey KT16 134 BG101
Dartford DA2 128 FK90
Dartford (Eyns.) DA4 148 FL104
Enfield EN2 *off Church La* 30 DR41
Gravesend DA12 131 GK88
Hayes UB3 77 BT72
Leatherhead KT22 171 CH122
Redhill (Bletch.) RH1 186 DR133
Reigate RH2 *off Reigate Rd* 184 DC134
Richmond TW9 *off Red Lion St* 117 CK85
Church Wk, T. Ditt. KT7 137 CF100
Walton-on-Thames KT12 135 BU102
Weybridge KT13 *off Beales La* 135 BP103
Church Wk Shop Cen, Cat. CR3 *off Church Wk* 176 DU124
Churchward Ho, W14 *off Ivatt Pl* 99 CZ78
Church Way, N20 44 DD48
Churchway, NW1 195 N2
Church Way, Barn. EN4 28 DF42
Edgware HA8 42 CN51
Oxted RH8 188 EF132
South Croydon CR2 160 DT110
Churchwell Path, E9 66 DW64
Churchwood Gdns, Wdf.Grn. IG8 48 EG49
Churchyard Row, SE11 200 G8
Church Yd Wk, W2 *off St. Marys Sq* 82 DD71
Churston Av, E13 86 EH67
Churston Cl, SW2 *off Tulse Hill* 121 DP88
Churston Dr, Mord. SM4 139 CX99
Churston Gdns, N11 45 DJ51
Churton Pl, SW1 199 L9
Churton St, SW1 199 L9
Chusan Pl, E14 *off Commercial Rd* 85 DZ72
Chuters Cl, W.Byf. (Byfleet) KT14 152 BL112
Chuters Gro, Epsom KT17 157 CT112
Chyne, The, Ger.Cr. SL9 57 AZ57
Chyngton Cl, Sid. DA15 125 ET90
Cibber Rd, SE23 123 DX89
Cicada Rd, SW18 120 DC85
Cicely Rd, SE15 102 DU81
Cimba Wd, Grav. DA12 131 GL91
Cinderella Path, NW11 *off North End Rd* 64 DB60
Cinderford Way, Brom. BR1 124 EE91
Cinder Path, Wok. GU22 166 AW119
Cinema Par, W5 *off Ashbourne Rd* 80 CM70
Cinnabar Wf, E1 202 C3
Cinnamon Cl, SE15 *off Pentridge St* 102 DT80
Croydon CR0 141 DL101
Cinnamon Row, SW11 100 DC83
Cinnamon St, E1 202 E3
Cintra Pk, SE19 122 DT94
Circle, The, NW2 62 CS62
NW7 42 CR50
SE1 201 P4
Tilbury RM18 *off Toronto Rd* 111 GG81
Circle Gdns, SW19 140 DA96
West Byfleet (Byfleet) KT14 152 BM113
Circle Rd, Walt. (Whiteley Vill.) KT12 153 BS110
Circuits, The, Pnr. HA5 60 BW56
Circular Rd, N17 66 DT55
Circular Way, SE18 105 EM79
Circus Ms, W1 194 D6
Circus Pl, EC2 197 L7
Circus Rd, NW8 82 DD69
Circus St, SE10 103 EC80
Cirencester St, W2 82 DB71
Cirrus Cl, Wall. SM6 159 DL108
Cirrus Cres, Grav. DA12 131 GL92
Cissbury Ring N, N12 43 CZ50
Cissbury Ring S, N12 43 CZ50
Cissbury Rd, N15 66 DR57
Citadel Pl, SE11 200 B10
Citizen Ho, N7 *off Harvist Est* 65 DN63
Citizen Rd, N7 65 DN63
C.I. Twr, N.Mal. KT3 138 CS97
Citron Ter, SE15 *off Nunhead La* 102 DV83
City Cross Business Pk, SE10 205 J8
City Forum, EC1 197 H2
City Gdn Row, N1 196 G1
City Gate Ho, Ilf. IG2 69 EP58
City Ho, Croy. CR0 141 DP101
City Mill River Towpath, E15 85 EB66
★ **City of Westminster Archives Cen**, SW1 *off St. Ann's St* 199 N6
City Pt, EC2 197 K6
City Rd, EC1 196 F1
⇌ **City Thameslink** 196 F9
★ **City Uni**, EC1 196 F3
City Vw, Ilf. IG1 *off High Rd* 69 EQ61
City Vw Apts, N1 *off Essex Rd* 84 DQ66
Cityview Ct, SE22 122 DU87
City Wk, SE1 *off Long La* 102 DS75
Civic Sq, Til. RM18 111 GG82
Civic Way, Ilf. IG6 69 EQ56
Ruislip HA4 60 BX64
Clabon Ms, SW1 198 D7
Clacket La, West. TN16 178 EL124
Clack La, Ruis. HA4 59 BQ60
Clack St, SE16 202 G5
Clacton Rd, E6 86 EK69
E17 67 DY58
N17 *off Sperling Rd* 46 DT54
Claigmar Gdns, N3 44 DB53
Claire Causeway, Dart. DA2 109 FS84
Claire Ct, N12 44 DC48
Bushey (Bushey Hth) WD23 41 CD46
Pinner HA5 *off Westfield Pk* 40 BZ52
Claire Gdns, Stan. HA7 41 CJ50
Claire Pl, E14 204 A6
Clairvale, Horn. RM11 72 FL59
Clairvale Rd, Houns. TW5 96 BX81
Clairview Rd, SW16 121 DH92
Clairville Ct, Reig. RH2 184 DD134
Clairville Gdns, W7 79 CF74
Clairville Pt, SE23 123 DX90
Clammas Way, Uxb. UB8 76 BJ71
Clamp Hill, Stan. HA7 41 CD49
Clancarty Rd, SW6 100 DA82
Clandon Av, Egh. TW20 113 BC94
Clandon Cl, W3 98 CP75
Epsom KT17 157 CT107
Clandon Gdns, N3 64 DA55
Clandon Rd, Ilf. IG3 69 ES61
Clandon St, SE8 103 EA82
Clanricarde Gdns, W2 82 DA73
Clapgate Rd, Bushey WD23 24 CB44
CLAPHAM, SW4 101 DH83
★ **Clapham Common**, SW4 100 DG84
⊖ **Clapham Common** 101 DJ84
Clapham Common, SW4 *off Clapham Common S Side* 101 DJ84
Clapham Common N Side, SW4 101 DH84
Clapham Common S Side, SW4 121 DH86
Clapham Common W Side, SW4 100 DG84
Clapham Cres, SW4 101 DK84
Clapham Est, SW11 100 DE84
⇌ **Clapham High Street** 101 DK83
Clapham High St, SW4 101 DK84
⇌ **Clapham Junction** 100 DD84
Clapham Manor St, SW4 101 DJ83
⊖ **Clapham North** 101 DL83
CLAPHAM PARK, SW4 121 DK86
Clapham Pk Est, SW4 121 DK86
Clapham Pk Rd, SW4 101 DK84
Clapham Rd, SW9 101 DL83
Clapham Rd Est, SW4 101 DK83
⊖ **Clapham South** 121 DH86
Clap La, Dag. RM10 71 FB62
Claps Gate La, E6 87 EN70
⇌ **Clapton** 66 DV61
Clapton Common, E5 66 DT59
CLAPTON PARK, E5 67 DY63
Clapton Pk Est, E5 *off Blackwell Cl* 67 DX63
Clapton Pas, E5 66 DW64
Clapton Sq, E5 66 DW64
Clapton Ter, N16 *off Oldhill St* 66 DU60
Clapton Way, E5 66 DU63
Clara Pl, SE18 105 EN77
Clare Cl, N2 *off Thomas More Way* 64 DC55
Borehamwood (Els.) WD6 26 CM44
West Byfleet KT14 152 BG113
Clare Cor, SE9 125 EP87
Clare Cotts, Red. (Bletch.) RH1 185 DP133
Clare Ct, Cat. (Wold.) CR3 177 EA123
Northwood HA6 39 BS50
South Ockendon (Aveley) RM15 108 FQ75
Clare Cres, Lthd. KT22 171 CG118
Claredale, Wok. GU22 166 AY119
Claredale St, E2 84 DU68
Clare Gdns, E7 68 EG63
W11 *off Westbourne Pk Rd* 81 CY72
Barking IG11 87 ET65
Egham TW20 *off Mowbray Cres* 113 BA92
Clare Hill, Esher KT10 154 CB107
Clare Ho, E3 85 DZ67
Clare La, N1 84 DQ66
Clare Lawn Av, SW14 118 CR85
Clare Mkt, WC2 196 B9
Clare Ms, SW6 *off Waterford Rd* 100 DB80
Claremont, St.Alb. (Brick.Wd) AL2 8 CA31
Waltham Cross (Chsht) EN7 14 DT29
Claremont Av, Esher KT10 154 BZ107
Harrow HA3 62 CL57
New Malden KT3 139 CU99
Sunbury-on-Thames TW16 135 BV95
Walton-on-Thames KT12 154 BX105
Woking GU22 166 AY119
Claremont Cl, E16 87 EN74
N1 196 E1
SW2 *off Christchurch Rd* 121 DM88
Grays RM16 *off Premier Av* 110 GC76
Orpington BR6 163 EN105
South Croydon CR2 176 DV115
Walton-on-Thames KT12 154 BW106
Claremont Ct, Surb. KT6 *off St. James Rd* 137 CK100
Claremont Cres, Dart. DA1 107 FE84
Rickmansworth (Crox.Grn) WD3 23 BQ43
Claremont Dr, Esher KT10 154 CB108
Shepperton TW17 135 BP100
Woking GU22 166 AY119
Claremont End, Esher KT10 154 CB107
Claremont Gdns, Ilf. IG3 69 ES61
Surbiton KT6 138 CL99
Upminster RM14 73 FR60
Claremont Gro, W4 *off Edensor Gdns* 98 CS80
Woodford Green IG8 48 EJ51
★ **Claremont Landscape Gdns**, Esher KT10 154 BZ108
Claremont La, Esher KT10 154 CB105
CLAREMONT PARK, Esher KT10 154 CB108
Claremont Pk, N3 43 CY53
Claremont Pk Rd, Esher KT10 154 CB107
Claremont Pl, Grav. DA11 *off Cutmore St* 131 GH87
Claremont Rd, E7 68 EH64
E17 47 DY54
N6 65 DJ59
NW2 63 CX62
W9 81 CY68
W13 79 CG71
Barnet EN4 28 DD37
Bromley BR1 144 EL98
Croydon CR0 142 DU102
Esher (Clay.) KT10 155 CE108
Harrow HA3 41 CE54
Hornchurch RM11 71 FG58
Redhill RH1 184 DG131
Staines TW18 113 BD92
Surbiton KT6 138 CL100
Swanley BR8 127 FE94
Teddington TW11 117 CF92
Twickenham TW1 117 CH86
West Byfleet KT14 152 BG112
Claremont Sq, N1 196 D1
Claremont St, E16 87 EN74
N18 46 DU51
SE10 103 EB79
Claremont Way, NW2 63 CW60
Claremount Cl, Epsom KT18 173 CW117
Claremount Gdns, Epsom KT18 173 CW117
Clarence Av, SW4 121 DK86
Bromley BR1 144 EL98
Ilford IG2 69 EN58
New Malden KT3 138 CQ96
Upminster RM14 72 FN61
Clarence Cl, Barn. EN4 28 DD43
Bushey (Bushey Hth) WD23 41 CF45
Walton-on-Thames KT12 154 BW105
Clarence Ct, Egh. TW20 *off Clarence St* 113 AZ93
Clarence Cres, SW4 121 DK86
Sidcup DA14 126 EV90
Clarence Dr, Egh. (Eng.Grn) TW20 112 AW91
Clarence Gdns, NW1 195 J3
Clarence Gate, Wdf.Grn. IG8 49 EN51
Clarence Gate Gdns, NW1 *off Glentworth St* 82 DF70
★ **Clarence Ho**, SW1 199 L4
Clarence La, SW15 118 CS86
Clarence Ms, E5 66 DV64
SE16 203 H3
SW12 121 DH87
Clarence Pl, E5 66 DV64
Gravesend DA12 131 GH87
Clarence Rd, E5 66 DV63
E12 68 EK64
E16 86 EE70
E17 47 DX54
N15 66 DQ57
N22 45 DL52
NW6 81 CZ66
SE8 103 EB79
SE9 124 EL89
SW19 120 DB93
W4 98 CN78
Bexleyheath DA6 106 EY84
Brentwood (Pilg.Hat.) CM15 54 FV44
Bromley BR1 144 EK97
Croydon CR0 142 DR101
Enfield EN3 30 DV43
Grays RM17 110 GA79
Richmond TW9 98 CM81
Sidcup DA14 126 EV90
Sutton SM1 158 DB105
Teddington TW11 117 CF93
Wallington SM6 159 DH106
Walton-on-Thames KT12 153 BV105
Westerham (Bigg.H.) TN16 179 EM118
Clarence Row, Grav. DA12 131 GH87
Clarence St, Egh. TW20 113 AZ93
Kingston upon Thames KT1 138 CL96
Richmond TW9 98 CL84
Southall UB2 96 BX76
Staines TW18 113 BE91
Clarence Ter, NW1 194 E4
Hounslow TW3 96 CB84
Clarence Wk, SW4 101 DL82
Clarence Way, NW1 83 DH66
Clarence Way Est, NW1 83 DH66
Clarenden Pl, Dart. DA2 127 FD92
Clarendon Cl, E9 84 DW66
W2 194 B10
Orpington BR5 146 EU97
Clarendon Ct, Slou. SL2 74 AV73
Clarendon Cres, Twick. TW2 117 CD90
Clarendon Cross, W11 *off Portland Rd* 81 CY73
Clarendon Dr, SW15 99 CW84
Clarendon Flds, Rick. WD3 22 BM38
Clarendon Gdns, NW4 63 CV55
W9 82 DC70
Dartford DA2 129 FR87
Ilford IG1 69 EM60
Wembley HA9 62 CL63
Clarendon Gate, Cher. (Ott.) KT16 151 BD107
Clarendon Grn, Orp. BR5 146 EU98
Clarendon Gro, NW1 195 M2
Mitcham CR4 140 DF97
Orpington BR5 146 EU97
Clarendon Ms, W2 194 B9
Ashtead KT21 172 CL119
Bexley DA5 127 FB88
Borehamwood WD6 *off Clarendon Rd* 26 CN41
Clarendon Path, Orp. BR5 146 EU97
Clarendon Pl, W2 194 B10
Sevenoaks TN13 *off Clarendon Rd* 190 FG125
Clarendon Ri, SE13 103 EC83
Clarendon Rd, E11 67 ED60
E17 67 EB58
E18 68 EG55
N8 65 DM55
N15 65 DP56
N18 46 DU51
N22 45 DM54
SW19 120 DE94
W5 80 CL70
W11 81 CY73
Ashford TW15 114 BM91
Borehamwood WD6 26 CN41
Croydon CR0 141 DP103
Gravesend DA12 131 GJ86
Harrow HA1 61 CE58
Hayes UB3 95 BT75
Redhill RH1 184 DF133
Sevenoaks TN13 190 FG124
Wallington SM6 159 DJ107
Waltham Cross (Chsht) EN8 15 DX29
Watford WD17 23 BV40
Clarendon St, SW1 101 DH78
Clarendon Ter, W9 *off Lanark Pl* 82 DC70
Clarendon Wk, W11 81 CY72
Clarendon Way, N21 30 DQ44
Chislehurst BR7 145 ET97
Orpington BR5 145 ET97
Clarens St, SE6 123 DZ89
Clare Pk, Amer. HP7 20 AS40
Clare Pl, SW15 *off Minstead Gdns* 119 CT87
Clare Pt, NW2 *off Claremont Rd* 63 CX60
Clare Rd, E11 67 ED58
NW10 81 CU66
SE14 103 DZ81
Greenford UB6 79 CD65
Clare Rd, Houns. TW4 96 BZ83
Staines (Stanw.) TW19 114 BL87
Clare St, E2 84 DV68
Claret Gdns, SE25 142 DS98
Clareville Gro, SW7 100 DC77
Clareville Rd, Cat. CR3 176 DU124
Orpington BR5 145 EQ103
Clareville St, SW7 100 DC77
Clare Way, Bexh. DA7 106 EY81
Sevenoaks TN13 191 FJ127
Clare Wd, Lthd. KT22 171 CH118
Clarewood Wk, SW9 101 DP84
Clarges Ms, W1 199 H2
Clarges St, W1 199 J2
Claribel Rd, SW9 101 DP82
Clarice Way, Wall. SM6 159 DL109
Claridge Rd, Dag. RM8 70 EX60
Clarina Rd, SE20 *off Evelina Rd* 123 DX94
Clarissa Rd, Rom. RM6 70 EX59
Clarissa St, E8 84 DT67
Clark Cl, Erith DA8 107 FG81
Clarkebourne Dr, Grays RM17 110 GD79
Clarke Grn, Wat. WD25 23 BU35
Clarke Ms, N9 *off Plevna Rd* 46 DV48
Clarke Path, N16 66 DU60
Clarkes Av, Wor.Pk. KT4 139 CX102
Clarkes Dr, Uxb. UB8 76 BL71
Clarke's Ms, W1 194 G6
Clarke Way, Wat. WD25 23 BU35
Clarkfield, Rick. (Mill End) WD3 38 BH46
Clark Lawrence Ct, SW11 *off Winstanley Rd* 100 DD83
Clarks La, Epp. CM16 17 ET31
Sevenoaks (Halst.) TN14 164 EZ112
Warlingham CR6 178 EF123
Westerham TN16 178 EK123
Clarks Mead, Bushey WD23 40 CC45
Clarkson Rd, E16 86 EF72
Clarkson Row, NW1 195 K1
Clarksons, The, Bark. IG11 87 EQ68
Clarkson St, E2 84 DV69
Clarks Pl, EC2 197 M8
Clarks Rd, Ilf. IG1 69 ER61
Clark St, E1 84 DV71
Clark Way, Houns. TW5 96 BX80
Classon Cl, West Dr. UB7 94 BL75
Claston Cl, Dart. DA1 *off Iron Mill La* 107 FE84
CLATTERFORD END, Ong. CM5 19 FG30
Claude Rd, E10 67 EC61
E13 86 EH67
SE15 102 DV82
Claude St, E14 203 P8
Claudia Jones Way, SW2 121 DL86
Claudian Way, Grays RM16 111 GH76
Claudia Pl, SW19 119 CY88
Claudius Cl, Stan. HA7 41 CK48
Claughton Rd, E13 86 EJ68
Claughton Way, Brwd. (Hutt.) CM13 55 GD44
Clauson Av, Nthlt. UB5 60 CB64
Clavell St, SE10 103 EC79
Claverdale Rd, SW2 121 DM87
Claverhambury Rd, Wal.Abb. EN9 16 EF29
Clavering Av, SW13 99 CV79
Clavering Cl, Twick. TW1 117 CG91
Clavering Rd, E12 68 EK60
Claverings Ind Est, N9 47 DX47
Clavering Way, Brwd. (Hutt.) CM13 *off Poplar Dr* 55 GC44
Claverley Gro, N3 44 DA52
Claverley Vil, N3 44 DB52
Claverton Cl, Hem.H. (Bov.) HP3 5 BA28
Claverton St, SW1 101 DJ78
Clave St, E1 202 F3
Claxton Gro, W6 99 CX78
Claxton Path, SE4 *off Billingford Cl* 103 DX84
Clay Av, Mitch. CR4 141 DH96
Claybank Gro, SE13 *off Algernon Rd* 103 EB83
Claybourne Ms, SE19 *off Church Rd* 122 DS94
Claybridge Rd, SE12 124 EJ91
Claybrook Cl, N2 64 DD55
Claybrook Rd, W6 99 CX79
Clayburn Gdns, S.Ock. RM15 91 FV73
Claybury, Bushey WD23 40 CB45
Claybury Bdy, Ilf. IG5 68 EL55
Claybury Hall, Wdf.Grn. IG8 49 EM52
Claybury Rd, Wdf.Grn. IG8 48 EL52
Claydon Dr, Croy. CR0 159 DL105
Claydon End, Ger.Cr. (Chal.St.P.) SL9 56 AY55
Claydon La, Ger.Cr. (Chal.St.P.) SL9 56 AY55
Claydon Rd, Wok. GU21 166 AU116
Claydown Ms, SE18 *off Woolwich New Rd* 105 EN78
Clayfarm Rd, SE9 125 EQ89
CLAYGATE, Esher KT10 155 CE108
⇌ **Claygate** 155 CD107
Claygate Cl, Horn. RM12 71 FG63
Claygate Cres, Croy. (New Adgtn) CR0 161 EC107
Claygate La, Esher KT10 137 CG103
Thames Ditton KT7 137 CG102
Waltham Abbey EN9 15 ED30
Claygate Lo Cl, Esher (Clay.) KT10 155 CE108
Claygate Rd, W13 97 CH76
CLAYHALL, Ilf. IG5 49 EM54
Clayhall Av, Ilf. IG5 68 EL55
Clayhall La, Wind. (Old Wind.) SL4 112 AT85
CLAY HILL, Enf. EN2 30 DQ37
Clay Hill, Enf. EN2 30 DQ37
Clayhill, Surb. KT5 138 CN99
Clayhill Cres, SE9 124 EK91
Claylands Pl, SW8 101 DN80
Claylands Rd, SW8 101 DM79
Clay La, Bushey (Bushey Hth) WD23 41 CE45
Edgware HA8 42 CN46
Epsom (Headley) KT18 172 CP124
Staines (Stanw.) TW19 114 BM87
Claymill Ho, SE18 105 EQ78

★ Place of interest ⇌ Railway station ⊖ London Underground station DLR Docklands Light Railway station Tram Tramlink station H Hospital Riv Pedestrian ferry landing stage

Claymore Cl, Mord. SM4 ...140 DA101
Claymore Ct, E17
off Billet Rd ...47 DY53
Claypit Hill, Wal.Abb. EN9 ...32 EJ36
Claypole Dr, Houns. TW5 ...96 BY81
Claypole Rd, E15 ...85 EC68
Clayponds Av, Brent. TW8 ...98 CL77
Clayponds Gdns, W5 ...97 CK77
H Clayponds Hosp, W5 ...98 CL77
Clayponds La, Brent. TW8 ...98 CL78
Clay Rd, The, Loug. IG10 ...32 EL39
Clayside, Chig. IG7 ...49 EQ51
Clays La, E15 ...67 EB64
Clay's La, Loug. IG10 ...33 EN39
Clays La Cl, E15 ...67 EB64
Clay St, W1 ...194 E7
Clayton Av, Upmin. RM14 ...72 FP64
Wembley HA0 ...80 CL66
Clayton Cl, E6
off Brandreth Rd ...87 EM72
Clayton Cres, N1 ...83 DL67
Brentford TW8 ...97 CK78
Clayton Cft Rd, Dart. DA2 ...127 FG89
Clayton Dr, SE8 ...203 K10
Clayton Fld, NW9 ...42 CS52
Clayton Mead, Gdse. RH9 ...186 DV130
Clayton Ms, SE10 ...103 ED81
Clayton Rd, SE15 ...102 DU81
Chessington KT9 ...155 CJ105
Epsom KT17 ...156 CS113
Hayes UB3 ...95 BS75
Isleworth TW7 ...97 CE83
Romford RM7 ...71 FC60
Clayton St, SE11 ...101 DN79
Clayton Ter, Hayes UB4
off Jollys La ...78 BX71
Clayton Wk, Amer. HP7 ...20 AW39
Clayton Way, Uxb. UB8 ...76 BK70
Clay Tye Rd, Upmin. RM14 ...73 FW63
Claywood Cl, Orp. BR6 ...145 ES101
Claywood La, Dart. (Bean)
DA2 ...129 FX90
Clayworth Cl, Sid. DA15 ...126 EV86
Cleall Av, Wal.Abb. EN9
off Quaker La ...15 EC34
Cleanthus Cl, SE18
off Cleanthus Rd ...105 EP81
Cleanthus Rd, SE18 ...105 EP81
Clearbrook Way, E1
off West Arbour St ...84 DW72
Cleardown, Wok. GU22 ...167 BB118
Clearmount, Wok. (Chobham)
GU24 ...150 AS107
Clears, The, Reig. RH2 ...183 CY132
Clearwater Ter, W11
off Lorne Gdns ...99 CX75
Clearwell Dr, W9 ...82 DB70
Cleave Av, Hayes UB3 ...95 BS77
Orpington BR6 ...163 ES107
Cleaveland Rd, Surb. KT6 ...137 CK99
Cleave Prior, Couls. (Chipstead)
CR5 ...174 DE119
Cleaverholme Cl, SE25 ...142 DV100
Cleaver Sq, SE11 ...200 E10
Cleaver St, SE11 ...200 E10
Cleeve Ct, Felt. TW14
off Kilross Rd ...115 BS88
Cleeve Hill, SE23 ...122 DV88
Cleeve Pk Gdns, Sid. DA14 ...126 EV89
Cleeve Rd, Lthd. KT22 ...171 CF120
Cleeve Way, SW15
off Danebury Av ...119 CT87
Sutton SM1 ...140 DB102
Clegg Ho, SE3 off Pinto Way .104 EH84
Clegg St, E1 ...202 E2
E13 ...86 EG68
Cleland Path, Loug. IG10 ...33 EP39
Cleland Rd, Ger.Cr. (Chal.St.P.)
SL9 ...36 AX54
Clematis Cl, Rom. RM3 ...52 FJ52
Clematis Gdns, Wdf.Grn. IG8 .48 EG50
Clematis St, W12 ...81 CT73
Clem Attlee Ct, SW6 ...99 CZ79
Clem Attlee Par, SW6
off North End Rd ...99 CZ79
Clemence Rd, Dag. RM10 ...89 FC67
Clemence St, E14 ...85 DZ71
Clement Av, SW4 ...101 DK84
Clement Cl, NW6 ...81 CW66
W4 off Acton La ...98 CR77
Purley CR8
off Croftleigh Av ...175 DP116
Clement Gdns, Hayes UB3 ...95 BS77
Clementhorpe Rd, Dag. RM9 .88 EW65
Clementina Rd, E10 ...67 DZ60
H Clementine Churchill Hosp,
Har. HA1 ...61 CF62
Clementine Cl, W13
off Balfour Rd ...97 CH75
Clementine Wk, Wdf.Grn. IG8
off Salway Cl ...48 EG52
Clement Rd, SW19 ...119 CY92
Beckenham BR3 ...143 DX96
Waltham Cross (Chsht) EN8 .15 DY27
Clements Av, E16 ...86 EG73
Clements Cl, Slou. SL1 ...92 AV75
Clements Ct, Houns. TW4 ...96 BX84
Ilford IG1
off Clements La ...69 EP62
Clement's Inn, WC2 ...196 C9
Clement's Inn Pas, WC2 ...196 C9
Clements La, EC4 ...197 L10
Ilford IG1 ...69 EP62
Clements Mead, Lthd. KT22 .171 CG119
Clements Pl, Brent. TW8 ...97 CK78
Clements Rd, E6 ...87 EM66
SE16 ...202 C7
Ilford IG1 ...69 EP62
Rickmansworth (Chorl.)
WD3 ...21 BD43
Walton-on-Thames KT12 .135 BV103
Clement St, Swan. BR8 ...128 FK93
Clement Way, Upmin. RM14 ..72 FM62
Clenches Fm La, Sev. TN13 ..190 FG126
Clenches Fm Rd, Sev. TN13 .190 FG126
Clendon Way, SE18
off Polthorne Gro ...105 ER77
Clennam St, SE1 ...201 J4
Clensham Ct, Sutt. SM1
off Sutton Common Rd ..140 DA103
Clensham La, Sutt. SM1 ...140 DA103
Clenston Ms, W1 ...194 D8
★ Cleopatra's Needle, WC2 .200 B2
Clephane Rd, N1 ...84 DQ65
Clere St, EC2 ...197 L4
Clerics Wk, Shep. TW17
off Gordon Rd ...135 BR100
CLERKENWELL, EC1 ...196 F5
Clerkenwell Cl, EC1 ...196 E4
Clerkenwell Grn, EC1 ...196 E5
Clerkenwell Rd, EC1 ...196 D5
Clerks Cft, Red. (Bletch.) RH1 .186 DR133
Clerks Piece, Loug. IG10 ...33 EM41
Clermont Rd, E9 ...84 DW67
Clevedon, Wey. KT13 ...153 BQ106
Clevedon Cl, N16
off Smalley Cl ...66 DT62
Clevedon Gdns, Hayes UB3 ..95 BR76
Hounslow TW5 ...95 BV81
Clevedon Rd, SE20 ...143 DX95
Kingston upon Thames
KT1 ...138 CN96
Twickenham TW1 ...117 CK86
Clevehurst Cl, Slou. (Stoke P.)
SL2 ...74 AT65
Cleveland Av, SW20 ...139 CZ96
W4 ...99 CT77
Hampton TW12 ...116 BZ94
Cleveland Cl, Walt. KT12 ...135 BV104
Cleveland Cres, Borwd. WD6 .26 CQ43
Cleveland Dr, Stai. TW18 ...134 BH96
Cleveland Gdns, N4 ...66 DQ57
NW2 ...63 CX61
SW13 ...99 CT82
W2 ...82 DC72
Worcester Park KT4 ...138 CS103
Cleveland Gro, E1
off Cleveland Way ...84 DW70
Cleveland Ms, W1 ...195 K6
Cleveland Pk, Stai. TW19 ...114 BL86
Cleveland Pk Av, E17 ...67 EA56
Cleveland Pk Cres, E17 ...67 EA56
Cleveland Pl, SW1 ...199 L2
Cleveland Ri, Mord. SM4 ...139 CX101
Cleveland Rd, E18 ...68 EG55
N1 ...84 DR66
N9 ...46 DV45
SW13 ...99 CT82
W4 off Antrobus Rd ...98 CQ76
W13 ...79 CH71
Ilford IG1 ...69 EP62
Isleworth TW7 ...97 CG84
New Malden KT3 ...138 CS98
Uxbridge UB8 ...76 BK68
Welling DA16 ...105 ET82
Worcester Park KT4 ...138 CS103
Cleveland Row, SW1 ...199 K3
Cleveland Sq, W2 ...82 DC72
Cleveland St, W1 ...195 K5
Cleveland Ter, W2 ...82 DC72
Cleveland Way, E1 ...84 DW70
Cleveley Cl, SE7 ...104 EK77
Cleveley Cres, W5 ...80 CL68
Cleveleys Rd, E5 ...66 DV62
Cleverly Est, W12 ...81 CU74
Cleve Rd, NW6 ...82 DA66
Sidcup DA14 ...126 EX90
Cleves Av, Brwd. CM14 ...54 FV46
Epsom KT17 ...157 CV109
Cleves Cl, Cob. KT11 ...153 BV114
Loughton IG10 ...32 EL44
Cleves Cres, Croy. (New Adgtn)
CR0 ...161 EC111
Cleves Rd, E6 ...86 EK67
Richmond TW10 ...117 CJ90
Cleves Wk, Ilf. IG6 ...49 EQ52
Cleves Way, Hmptn. TW12 ...116 BZ94
Ruislip HA4 ...60 BX60
Sunbury-on-Thames TW16 .115 BT93
Cleves Wd, Wey. KT13 ...153 BS105
Clewer Cres, Har. HA3 ...41 CD53
Clewer Ho, SE2
off Wolvercote Rd ...106 EX75
Clichy Est, E1 ...84 DW71
Clifden Ms, E5
off Clifden Rd ...67 DX63
Clifden Rd, E5 ...66 DW64
Brentford TW8 ...97 CK79
Twickenham TW1 ...117 CF88
Cliff End, Pur. CR8 ...159 DP112
Cliffe Rd, S.Croy. CR2 ...160 DR106
Cliffe Wk, Sutt. SM1
off Turnpike La ...158 DC106
Clifford Av, SW14 ...98 CP83
Chislehurst BR7 ...125 EM93
Ilford IG5 ...49 EP53
Wallington SM6 ...159 DJ105
Clifford Cl, Nthlt. UB5 ...78 BY67
Clifford Dr, SW9 ...101 DP84
Clifford Gdns, NW10 ...81 CW68
Hayes UB3 ...95 BR77
Clifford Gro, Ashf. TW15 ...114 BN91
Clifford Haigh Ho, SW6
off Fulham Palace Rd ...99 CX80
Clifford Rd, E16 ...86 EF70
E17 ...47 EC54
N9 ...30 DW44
SE25 ...142 DU98
Barnet EN5 ...28 DB41
Grays (Chaff.Hun.) RM16 ..110 FZ75
Hounslow TW4 ...96 BX83
Richmond TW10 ...117 CK89
Wembley HA0 ...79 CK67
Clifford's Inn Pas, EC4 ...196 D9
Clifford St, W1 ...199 K1
Clifford Way, NW10 ...63 CT63
Cliff Pl, S.Ock. RM15 ...91 FX69
Cliff Reach, Green. (Bluewater)
DA9 ...129 FS87
Cliff Rd, NW1 ...83 DK65
Cliff Ter, SE8 ...103 EA82
Cliffview Rd, SE13 ...103 EA83
Cliff Vil, NW1 ...83 DK65
Cliff Wk, E16 ...86 EF71
Clifton Av, E17 ...67 DX55
N3 ...43 CZ53
W12 ...81 CT74
Feltham TW13 ...116 BW90
Stanmore HA7 ...41 CH54
Sutton SM2 ...158 DB111
Wembley HA9 ...80 CM65
Clifton Cl, Add. KT15 ...134 BH103
Caterham CR3 ...176 DR123
Orpington BR6 ...163 EQ106
Waltham Cross (Chsht)
EN8 ...15 DY29
Clifton Ct, N4
off Biggerstaff St ...65 DN61
NW8 off Edgware Rd ...82 DD70
Woodford Green IG8
off Snakes La W ...48 EG51
Clifton Cres, SE15 ...102 DV80
Clifton Est, SE15
off Consort Rd ...102 DV81
Clifton Gdns, N15 ...66 DT58
NW11 ...63 CZ58
W4 off Dolman Rd ...98 CR77
W9 ...82 DC70
Enfield EN2 ...29 DL42
Uxbridge UB10 ...77 BP68
Clifton Gro, E8 ...84 DU65
Gravesend DA11 ...131 GH87
Clifton Hill, NW8 ...82 DB68
Clifton Marine Par, Grav.
DA11 ...131 GF86
Clifton Pk Av, SW20 ...139 CW96
Clifton Pl, SE16 ...202 G4
W2 ...194 A10
Banstead SM7
off Court Rd ...174 DA116
Clifton Ri, SE14 ...103 DY80
Clifton Rd, E7 ...86 EK65
E16 ...86 EE71
N1 ...84 DQ65
N3 ...44 DC53
N8 ...65 DK58
N22 ...45 DJ53
NW10 ...81 CU68
SE25 ...142 DS98
SW19 ...119 CX93
W9 ...82 DC70
Coulsdon CR5 ...175 DH115
Gravesend DA11 ...131 GG86
Greenford UB6 ...78 CC70
Harrow HA3 ...62 CM57
Hornchurch RM11 ...71 FG58
Hounslow (Hthrw Air.) TW6
off Inner Ring E ...95 BP83
Ilford IG2 ...69 ER58
Isleworth TW7 ...97 CD82
Kingston upon Thames
KT2 ...118 CM94
Loughton IG10 ...32 EL42
Sidcup DA14 ...125 ES91
Slough SL1 ...92 AV75
Southall UB2 ...96 BY77
Teddington TW11 ...117 CE91
Wallington SM6 ...159 DH106
Watford WD18 ...23 BV43
Welling DA16 ...106 EW83
Cliftons La, Reig. RH2 ...183 CX131
Clifton's Rbt, SE12
off Westhorne Av ...124 EJ86
Clifton St, EC2 ...197 M6
Clifton Ter, N4 ...65 DN61
Clifton Vil, W9 ...82 DB71
Clifton Wk, E6 ...86 EL72
W6 off Galena Rd ...99 CV77
Dartford DA2
off Osbourne Rd ...128 FP86
Clifton Way, SE15 ...102 DV80
Borehamwood WD6 ...26 CN39
Brentwood (Hutt.) CM13 ...55 GD46
Wembley HA0 ...80 CL67
Woking GU21 ...166 AT117
Climb, The, Rick. WD3 ...22 BH44
Clinch Ct, E16 ...86 EG71
Cline Rd, N11 ...45 DJ51
Clinger Ct, N1
off Pitfield St ...84 DS67
★ Clink Prison Mus, SE1 ...201 K2
Clink St, SE1 ...201 J2
Clinton Av, E.Mol. KT8 ...136 CC98
Welling DA16 ...105 ET84
Clinton Cl, Wey. KT13 ...135 BP104
Clinton Cres, Ilf. IG6 ...49 ES51
Clinton Rd, E3 ...85 DY69
E7 ...68 EG63
N15 ...66 DR56
Leatherhead KT22 ...171 CJ123
Clinton Ter, Sutt. SM1
off Manor La ...158 DC105
Clipper Boul, Dart. DA2 ...109 FS83
Clipper Boul W, Dart. DA2 ...109 FR83
Clipper Cl, SE16 ...203 H4
Clipper Cres, Grav. DA12 ...131 GM91
Clipper Way, SE13 ...103 EC84
Clippesby Cl, Chess. KT9 ...156 CM108
Clipstone Ms, W1 ...195 K5
Clipstone Rd, Houns. TW3 ...96 CA83
Clipstone St, W1 ...195 J6
Clissold Cl, N2 ...64 DF55
Clissold Ct, N4 ...66 DQ61
Clissold Cres, N16 ...66 DR62
Clissold Rd, N16 ...66 DR62
Clitheroe Av, Har. HA2 ...60 CA60
Clitheroe Gdns, Wat. WD19 ...40 BX48
Clitheroe Rd, SW9 ...101 DL82
Romford RM5 ...51 FC50
Clitherow Av, W7 ...97 CG76
Clitherow Pas, Brent. TW8 ...97 CJ78
Clitherow Rd, Brent. TW8 ...97 CJ78
Clitterhouse Cres, NW2 ...63 CW60
Clitterhouse Rd, NW2 ...63 CW60
Clive Av, N18
off Claremont St ...46 DU51
Dartford DA1 ...127 FF86
Clive Cl, Pot.B. EN6 ...11 CZ31
Clive Ct, W9 off Maida Vale ..82 DC70
Cliveden Cl, N12
off Woodside Av ...44 DC49
Brentwood (Shenf.) CM15 .55 FZ45
Cliveden Pl, SW1 ...198 F8
Shepperton TW17 ...135 BP100
Cliveden Rd, SW19 ...139 CZ95
Clivedon Ct, W13 ...79 CH71
Clivedon Rd, E4 ...48 EE50
Clive Par, Nthwd. HA6
off Maxwell Rd ...39 BS52
Clive Pas, SE21 off Clive Rd ..122 DR90
Clive Rd, SE21 ...122 DR90
SW19 ...120 DE93
Belvedere DA17 ...106 FA77
Brentwood CM13 ...53 FW52
Enfield EN1 ...30 DU42
Esher KT10 ...154 CB105
Feltham TW14 ...115 BU86
Gravesend DA11 ...131 GH86
Romford RM2 ...71 FH57
Clive Rd, Twick. TW1 ...117 CF91
Clivesdale Dr, Hayes UB3 ...77 BV74
Clive Way, Enf. EN1 ...30 DU42
Watford WD24 ...24 BW39
Cloak La, EC4 ...197 J10
⇌ Clock House ...143 DY96
Clockhouse Av, Bark. IG11 ...87 EQ67
Clockhouse Cl, SW19 ...119 CW90
Clock Ho Cl, W.Byf. (Byfleet)
KT14 ...152 BM112
Clockhouse La, Ashf. TW15 ..114 BN91
Feltham TW14 ...115 BP89
Grays RM16 ...91 FX74
Romford RM5 ...51 FB52
Clock Ho La, Sev. TN13 ...190 FG123
Clockhouse La E, Egh. TW20 .113 BB94
Clockhouse La W, Egh. TW20 .113 BA94
Clock Ho Mead, Lthd.
(Oxshott) KT22 ...154 CB114
Clockhouse Ms, Rick. (Chorl.) WD3
off Chorleywood Ho Dr ...21 BE41
Clockhouse Pl, SW15 ...119 CY85
Feltham TW14 ...115 BQ88
Clock Ho Rd, Beck. BR3 ...143 DY97
Clockhouse Rbt, Felt. TW14 ..115 BP88
★ Clockmakers Company Collection,
The, Guildhall Lib, EC2 ..197 J8
Clock Twr Ms, N1
off Arlington Av ...84 DQ67
SE28 ...88 EV73
Clock Twr Pl, N7 ...83 DL65
Clock Twr Rd, Islw. TW7 ...97 CF83
Cloister Cl, Rain. RM13 ...89 FH70
Teddington TW11 ...117 CH92
Cloister Gdns, SE25 ...142 DV100
Edgware HA8 ...42 CQ50
Cloister Rd, NW2 ...63 CZ62
W3 ...80 CQ71
Cloisters, The, Bushey WD23 .24 CB44
Rickmansworth WD3 ...38 BL45
Woking GU22 ...167 BB121
Cloisters Av, Brom. BR2 ...145 EM99
Cloisters Business Cen, SW8
off Battersea Pk Rd ...101 DH80
Cloisters Mall, Kings.T. KT1
off Union St ...137 CK96
Clonard Way, Pnr. HA5 ...40 CA51
Clonbrock Rd, N16 ...66 DS63
Cloncurry St, SW6 ...99 CX82
Clonmel Cl, Har. HA2 ...61 CD61
Clonmell Rd, N17 ...66 DR55
Clonmel Rd, SW6 ...99 CZ80
Teddington TW11 ...117 CD91
Clonmore St, SW18 ...119 CZ88
Cloonmore Av, Orp. BR6 ...163 ET105
Clorane Gdns, NW3 ...64 DA62
Close, The, E4
off Beech Hall Rd ...47 EC52
N14 ...45 DK47
N20 ...43 CZ47
SE3 off Heath La ...103 ED82
Barnet EN4 ...28 DF44
Beckenham BR3 ...143 DY98
Bexley DA5 ...126 FA86
Brentwood CM14 ...54 FW48
Bushey WD23 ...24 CB43
Carshalton SM5 ...158 DE109
Dartford DA2 ...128 FJ90
Grays RM16 ...110 GC75
Harrow HA2 ...40 CC54
Hatfield AL9 ...11 CY26
Isleworth TW7 ...97 CD82
Iver SL0 ...75 BC69
Mitcham CR4 ...140 DF98
New Malden KT3 ...138 CQ96
Orpington BR5 ...145 ES100
Pinner (Eastcote) HA5 ...60 BW59
Pinner (Rayners La) HA5 ...60 BZ59
Potters Bar EN6 ...12 DA32
Purley (Pampisford Rd)
CR8 ...159 DP110
Purley (Russ.Hill) CR8 ...159 DM110
Radlett WD7 ...9 CF33
Richmond TW9 ...98 CP83
Rickmansworth WD3 ...38 BJ46
Romford RM6 ...70 EY58
Sevenoaks TN13 ...190 FE124
Sidcup DA14 ...126 EV92
Sutton SM3 ...139 CZ101
Uxbridge UB10 ...76 BL66
Uxbridge (Hlgdn) UB10 ...76 BN67
Virginia Water GU25 ...132 AW99
Wembley (Barnhill Rd) HA9 .62 CQ62
Wembley (Lyon Pk Av) HA0 .80 CL65
West Byfleet KT14 ...152 BG113
Westerham (Berry's Grn)
TN16 ...179 EP116
Closemead Cl, Nthwd. HA6 ..39 BQ51
Cloth Ct, EC1 ...196 G7
Cloth Fair, EC1 ...196 G7
Clothier St, E1 ...197 N8
Cloth St, EC1 ...197 H6
Clothworkers Rd, SE18 ...105 ER80
Cloudberry Rd, Rom. RM3 ...52 FK51
Cloudesdale Rd, SW17 ...121 DH89
Cloudesley Pl, N1 ...83 DN67
Cloudesley Rd, N1 ...83 DN67
Bexleyheath DA7 ...106 EZ81
Erith DA8 ...107 FF81
Cloudesley Sq, N1 ...83 DN67
Cloudesley St, N1 ...83 DN67
Clouston Cl, Wall. SM6 ...159 DL106
Clova Rd, E7 ...86 EF65
Clove Cres, E14 ...85 ED73
Clove Hitch Quay, SW11 ...100 DC83
Clovelly Av, NW9 ...63 CT56
Uxbridge UB10 ...59 BQ63
Warlingham CR6 ...176 DV118
Clovelly Cl, Pnr. HA5 ...59 BV55
Uxbridge UB10 ...59 BQ63
Clovelly Ct, Horn. RM11 ...72 FN61
Clovelly Gdns, SE19 ...142 DT95
Enfield EN1 ...46 DS45
Romford RM7 ...51 FB53
Clovelly Rd, N8 ...65 DK56
W4 ...98 CQ75
W5 ...97 CJ75
Bexleyheath DA7 ...106 EY79
Hounslow TW3 ...96 CA82
Clovelly Way, E1
off Jamaica St ...84 DW72
Harrow HA2 ...60 BZ61
Orpington BR6 ...145 ET100
Clover Cl, E11 off Norman Rd .67 ED61
Clover Ct, Grays RM17
off Churchill Rd ...110 GD79
Woking GU22 ...166 AX118
Cloverdale Gdns, Sid. DA15 .125 ET86
Clover Fld, The, Bushey WD23 .24 BZ44
Clover Hill, Couls. CR5 ...175 DH121
Clover Leas, Epp. CM16 ...17 ET30
Cloverleys, Loug. IG10 ...32 EK43
Clover Ms, SW3 off Dilke St .100 DF79
Clovers, The, Grav. (Nthflt)
DA11 ...130 GE91
Clover Way, Wall. SM6 ...140 DG102
Clove St, E13 off Barking Rd .86 EG70
Clowders Rd, SE6 ...123 DZ90
Clowser Cl, Sutt. SM1
off Turnpike La ...158 DC106
Cloysters Grn, E1 ...202 B2
Cloyster Wd, Edg. HA8 ...41 CK52
Club Gdns Rd, Brom. BR2 ...144 EG101
Club Row, E1 ...197 P4
E2 ...197 P4
Clump, The, Rick. WD3 ...22 BG43
Clump Av, Tad. (Box H.) KT20 .182 CQ131
Clumps, The, Ashf. TW15 ...115 BR91
Clunas Gdns, Rom. RM2 ...52 FK54
Clunbury Av, Sthl. UB2 ...96 BZ78
Clunbury St, N1 ...197 L1
Cluny Est, SE1 ...201 M6
Cluny Ms, SW5 ...100 DA77
Cluny Pl, SE1 ...201 M6
Cluse Ct, N1 off Dame St ...84 DQ68
Clutterbucks, Rick. (Sarratt)
WD3 ...22 BG36
Clutton St, E14 ...85 EB71
Clydach Rd, Enf. EN1 ...30 DT42
Clyde Av, S.Croy. CR2 ...176 DV115
Clyde Circ, N15 ...66 DS56
Clyde Cl, Red. RH1 ...184 DG133
Clyde Ct, Red. RH1
off Clyde Cl ...184 DG133
Clyde Cres, Upmin. RM14 ...73 FS58
Clyde Pl, E10 ...67 EB59
Clyde Rd, N15 ...66 DS56
N22 ...45 DK53
Croydon CR0 ...142 DT102
Staines (Stanw.) TW19 ...114 BK88
Sutton SM1 ...158 DA106
Wallington SM6 ...159 DJ106
Clydesdale, Enf. EN3 ...31 DX42
Clydesdale Av, Stan. HA7 ...61 CK55
Clydesdale Cl, Borwd. WD6 ...26 CR43
Isleworth TW7 ...97 CF83
Clydesdale Gdns, Rich. TW10 .98 CP84
Clydesdale Ho, Erith DA18
off Kale Rd ...106 EY75
Clydesdale Rd, W11 ...81 CZ72
Hornchurch RM11 ...71 FF59
Clydesdale Wk, Brox. EN10
off Tarpan Way ...15 DZ25
Clyde St, SE8 ...103 DZ79
Clyde Ter, SE23 ...122 DW89
Clyde Vale, SE23 ...122 DW89
Clyde Way, Rom. RM1 ...51 FE53
Clydon Cl, Erith DA8 ...107 FE79
Clyfford Rd, Ruis. HA4 ...59 BT63
Clymping Dene, Felt. TW14 ..115 BV87
Clyston Rd, Wat. WD18 ...23 BT44
Clyston St, SW8 ...101 DJ82
Clyve Way, Stai. TW18 ...133 BE95
Coach & Horses Yd, W1 ...195 J10
Coach Ho La, N5
off Highbury Hill ...65 DP63
SW19 ...119 CX91
Coach Ho Ms, SE14
off Waller Rd ...103 DX82
Coachhouse Ms, SE20 ...122 DV94
Coach Ho Ms, SE23 ...123 DX86
Coach Ho Yd, SW18
off Ebner St ...100 DB84
Coachmaker Ms, SW4
off Fenwick Pl ...101 DL83
W4 off Berrymede Rd ...98 CR76
Coach Rd, Bet. (Brock.) RH3 .182 CL134
Chertsey (Ott.) KT16 ...151 BC107
Coach Yd Ms, N19
off Trinder Rd ...65 DL60
Coal Ct, Grays RM17
off Columbia Wf Rd ...110 GA79
Coaldale Wk, SE21
off Lairdale Cl ...122 DQ87
Coalecroft Rd, SW15 ...99 CW84
Coalport Ho, SE11
off Walnut Tree Wk ...101 DN77
Coal Rd, Til. RM18 ...111 GL77
Coal Wf Rd, W12
off Sterne St ...81 CX74
Coates Av, SW18 ...120 DE86
Coates Cl, Th.Hth. CR7 ...142 DQ97
Coates Dell, Wat. WD25 ...8 BY33
Coates Hill Rd, Brom. BR1 ..145 EN96
Coates Rd, Borwd. (Els.) WD6 .41 CK45
Coate St, E2 ...84 DU68
Coates Wk, Brent. TW8 ...98 CL78
Coates Way, Wat. WD25 ...8 BX33
Cobb Cl, Borwd. WD6 ...26 CQ43
Slough (Datchet) SL3 ...92 AX81
Cobbett Cl, Enf. EN3 ...30 DW36
Cobbett Rd, SE9 ...104 EL83
Twickenham TW2 ...116 CA88
Cobbetts Av, Ilf. IG4 ...68 EK57
Cobbetts Cl, Wok. GU21 ...166 AV117
Cobbetts Hill, Wey. KT13 ...153 BP107
Cobbett St, SW8 ...101 DM80
Cobb Grn, Wat. WD25 ...7 BV32
Cobbins, The, Wal.Abb. EN9 .16 EE33
Cobbinsend Rd, Wal.Abb. EN9 .16 EK29
Cobble La, N1
off Edwards Ms ...83 DP66
Cobble Ms, N5 ...66 DQ62
Cobblers Wk, E.Mol. KT8 ...137 CG95
Hampton TW12 ...116 CC94
Kingston upon Thames
KT2 ...137 CG95
Teddington TW11 ...137 CG95
Cobbles, The, Brwd. CM15 ...54 FY47
Upminster RM14 ...73 FT59

Cobblestone Pl, Croy. CR0
off Oakfield Rd 142 DQ102
Cobbold Est, NW10 . . . . .81 CT65
Cobbold Ms, W12
off Cobbold Rd 99 CT75
Cobbold Rd, E11 . . . . .68 EF62
NW10 . . . . .81 CT65
W12 . . . . .98 CS75
Cobb's Ct, EC4
off Carter La 83 DP72
Cobb's Rd, Houns.TW4 . . . . .96 BZ84
Cobb St, E1 . . . . .197 P7
Cobden Cl, Uxb. UB8 . . . . . . .76 BJ67
Cobden Hill, Rad. WD7 . . . . . .25 CH36
Cobden Rd, E11 . . . . .68 EE62
SE25 . . . . .142 DU99
Orpington BR6 . . . . .163 ER105
Sevenoaks TN13 . . . . .191 FJ123
COBHAM, KT11 . . . . .169 BV115
Cobham, Grays RM16 . . . . . .110 GB75
⇌ Cobham & Stoke
D'Abernon 170 BY117
Cobham Av, N.Mal. KT3 . . . .139 CU99
★ Cobham Bus Mus, Cob.
KT11 . . . . .153 BQ112
Cobham Cl, SW11 . . . . .120 DE86
Bromley BR2 . . . . .144 EL101
Edgware HA8 . . . . .42 CP54
Enfield EN1 . . . . .30 DU41
Greenhithe DA9 . . . . .129 FV86
Sidcup DA15
off Park Mead 126 EV86
Wallington SM6 . . . . .159 DL107
H Cobham Cottage Hosp,
Cob. KT11 . . . . .153 BV113
Cobham Gate, Cob. KT11 . . .153 BV114
Cobham Ho, Bark. IG11
off St. Margarets 87 EQ67
Erith DA8 off Boundary St . .107 FF80
Cobham Ms, NW1
off Agar Gro 83 DK66
Cobham Pk, Cob. KT11 . . . . .169 BV116
Cobham Pk Rd, Cob. KT11 . . .169 BV117
Cobham Pl, Bexh. DA6 . . . . .126 EX85
Cobham Rd, E17 . . . . .47 EC53
N22 . . . . .65 DP55
Cobham (Stoke D'Ab.) KT11 170 CA118
Hounslow TW5 . . . . .96 BW80
Ilford IG3 . . . . .69 ES61
Kingston upon Thames
KT1 . . . . .138 CN95
Leatherhead (Fetch.) KT22 . .171 CE122
Cobham St, Grav. DA11 . . . .131 GG87
Cobham Ter, Green. DA9
off Bean Rd 129 FV85
Cobill Cl, Horn. RM11 . . . . . . .72 FJ56
Cobland Rd, SE12 . . . . .124 EJ91
Coborn Rd, E3 . . . . .85 DZ69
Coborn St, E3 . . . . .85 DZ69
Cobourg Rd, SE5 . . . . .102 DT79
Cobourg St, NW1 . . . . .195 L3
Cobsdene, Grav. DA12 . . . . .131 GK93
Cobs Way, Add. (New Haw)
KT15 . . . . .152 BJ110
Coburg Cl, SW1 . . . . .199 L8
Coburg Cres, SW2 . . . . .121 DM88
Coburg Gdns, Ilf. IG5 . . . . . .48 EK54
Coburg Rd, N22 . . . . .65 DM55
Cochrane Ms, NW8 . . . . .194 A1
Cochrane Rd, SW19 . . . . . . .119 CZ94
Cochrane St, NW8 . . . . .194 A1
Cockayne Way, SE8 . . . . . . .203 L10
Cockerell Rd, E17 . . . . .67 DY59
Cockerhurst Rd, Sev.
(Shore.) TN14 . . . . .165 FD107
Cocker Rd, Enf. EN1 . . . . . . .30 DV36
Cockett Rd, Slou. SL3 . . . . . .92 AY76
COCKFOSTERS, Barn. EN4 . . .28 DE42
⊖ Cockfosters 28 DG42
Cockfosters Par, Barn. EN4
off Cockfosters Rd 28 DG42
Cockfosters Rd, Barn. EN4 . . .28 DF40
Cock Hill, E1 . . . . .197 N7
Cock La, EC1 . . . . .196 F7
Leatherhead (Fetch.) KT22 . .170 CC122
Cockle Way, Rad. (Shenley)
WD7 . . . . .10 CL33
Cockmannings La, Orp. BR5 .146 EX102
Cockmannings Rd, Orp. BR5 .146 EX101
Cockpit Steps, SW1 . . . . . . .199 N5
Cockpit Yd, WC1 . . . . .196 C6
Cocks Cres, N.Mal. KT3 . . . .139 CT98
Cocksett Av, Orp. BR6 . . . . .163 ES107
Cockspur Ct, SW1 . . . . .199 N2
Cockspur St, SW1 . . . . .199 N2
Cocksure La, Sid. DA14 . . . .126 FA90
Cock's Yd, Uxb. UB8
off Bakers Rd 76 BK66
Coda Cen, The, SW6 . . . . .99 CY81
Code St, E1 . . . . .84 DT70
Codham Hall La, Brwd.
(Gt Warley) CM13 . . . . . . .73 FV56
Codicote Dr, Wat. WD25 . . . . . .8 BX34
Codicote Ter, N4
off Green Las 66 DQ61
Codling Cl, E1 . . . . .202 C2
Codling Way, Wem. HA0 . . . . .61 CK63
CODMORE, Chesh. HP5 . . . . . .4 AS29
Codmore Cres, Chesh. HP5 . . .4 AS30
Codmore Wd Rd, Chesh. HP5 . .4 AW33
Codrington Ct, Wok. GU21
off Raglan Rd 166 AS118
Codrington Cres, Grav.
DA12 . . . . .131 GJ92
Codrington Gdns, Grav.
DA12 . . . . .131 GK92
Codrington Hill, SE23 . . . . .123 DY87
Codrington Ms, W11
off Blenheim Cres 81 CY72
Cody Cl, Har. HA3 . . . . .61 CK55
Wallington SM6
off Alcock Cl 159 DK108
Cody Rd, E16 . . . . .85 ED70
Cody Rd Business Cen, E16 . .85 ED70
Coe Av, SE25 . . . . .142 DU100
Coe's All, Barn. EN5
off Wood St 27 CY42
Coftards, Slou. SL2 . . . . .74 AW72
Cogan Av, E17 . . . . .47 DY53
Cohen Cl, Wal.Cr. EN8 . . . . . . .15 DY31
Coin St, SE1 . . . . .200 D2
Coity Rd, NW5 . . . . .82 DG65
Cokers La, SE21
off Perifield 122 DR88
Coke's Fm La, Ch.St.G. HP8 . .20 AV41
Coke's La, Amer. HP7 . . . . . . .20 AW41
Chalfont St. Giles HP8 . . . .20 AU42
Coke St, E1 . . . . .84 DU72
Colas Ms, NW6
off Birchington Rd 82 DA67
Colbeck Ms, SW7 . . . . .100 DB77
Colbeck Rd, Har. HA1 . . . . . . .60 CC59
Colberg Pl, N16 . . . . .66 DS59
Colborne Way, Wor.Pk. KT4 . .139 CW104
Colbrook Av, Hayes UB3 . . . . .95 BR76
Colbrook Cl, Hayes UB3 . . . . .95 BR76
Colburn Av, Cat. CR3 . . . . . .176 DT124
Pinner HA5 . . . . .40 BY51
Colburn Way, Sutt. SM1 . . . .140 DD104
Colby Ms, SE19
off Gipsy Hill 122 DS92
Colby Rd, SE19 . . . . .122 DS92
Walton-on-Thames KT12
off Winchester Rd 135 BU102
Colchester Av, E12 . . . . .69 EM62
Colchester Dr, Pnr. HA5 . . . . .60 BX57
Colchester Rd, E10 . . . . .67 EC59
E17 . . . . .67 EA58
Edgware HA8 . . . . .42 CQ52
Northwood HA6 . . . . .39 BU54
Romford RM3 . . . . .52 FK53
Colchester St, E1
off Braham St 84 DT72
Colcokes Rd, Bans. SM7 . . . .174 DA116
Cold Arbor Rd, Sev.TN13 . . .190 FD124
Coldbath Sq, EC1 . . . . .196 D4
Coldbath St, SE13 . . . . .103 EB81
COLDBLOW, Bex. DA5 . . . . . .127 FC89
Cold Blow Cres, Bex. DA5 . . .127 FD88
Cold Blow La, SE14 . . . . . . .103 DX80
Cold Blows, Mitch. CR4 . . . .140 DG97
Coldershaw Rd, W13 . . . . .79 CG74
Coldfall Av, N10 . . . . .44 DF54
Coldham Gro, Enf. EN3 . . . . . .31 DY37
Cold Harbour, E14 . . . . .204 E3
Coldharbour Cl, Egh.TW20 . .133 BC97
Coldharbour Crest, SE9
off Great Harry Dr 125 EN90
Coldharbour La, SE5 . . . . . .101 DN84
SW9 . . . . .101 DN84
Bushey WD23 . . . . .24 CB44
Egham TW20 . . . . .133 BC97
Hayes UB3 . . . . .77 BU73
Purley CR8 . . . . .159 DN110
Rainham RM13 . . . . .89 FE72
Redhill (Bletch.) RH1 . . . . .186 DT134
Woking GU22 . . . . .167 BF115
Coldharbour La Ind Est, SE5
off Coldharbour La 102 DQ82
Coldharbour Pl, SE5
off Denmark Hill 102 DR82
Coldharbour Rd, Croy. CR0 . .159 DN106
Gravesend (Nthflt) DA11 . .130 GE89
West Byfleet KT14 . . . . . . .151 BF114
Woking GU22 . . . . .151 BF115
Coldharbour Way, Croy. CR0 .159 DN106
Coldshott, Oxt. RH8 . . . . . . .188 EG133
Coldstream Gdns, SW18 . . . .119 CZ86
Coldstream Rd, Cat. CR3 . . .176 DQ121
Cole Av, Grays RM16 . . . . . . .111 GJ77
Colebeck Ms, N1 . . . . .83 DP65
Colebert Av, E1 . . . . .84 DW70
Colebrook, Cher. (Ott.) KT16 .151 BD107
Colebrook Cl, NW7 . . . . .43 CX52
SW15 off West Hill 119 CX87
Colebrooke Av, W13 . . . . .79 CH72
Colebrooke Dr, E11 . . . . .68 EH59
Colebrooke Pl, N1
off St. Peters St 83 DP67
Colebrooke Ri, Brom. BR2 . . .144 EE96
Colebrooke Rd, Red. RH1 . . .184 DE132
Colebrooke Row, N1 . . . . . . .196 F1
Colebrook Gdns, Loug. IG10 . .33 EP40
Colebrook Ho, E14
off Brabazon St 85 EB72
Colebrook La, Loug. IG10 . . . .33 EP40
Colebrook Path, Loug. IG10 . . .33 EP40
Colebrook Pl, Cher. (Ott.)
KT16 . . . . .151 BB108
Colebrook Rd, SW16 . . . . . . .141 DL95
Colebrook St, Erith DA8 . . . .107 FF78
Colebrook Way, N11 . . . . .45 DH50
Coleby Path, SE5
off Harris St 102 DR80
Colechurch Ho, SE1
off Avondale Sq 102 DU78
Cole Cl, SE28 . . . . .88 EV74
Coledale Dr, Stan. HA7 . . . . . .41 CJ53
Coleford Rd, SW18 . . . . .120 DC85
Cole Gdns, Houns.TW5 . . . . . .95 BU80
Colegrave Rd, E15 . . . . .67 ED64
Colegrove Rd, SE15 . . . . . . .102 DT80
Coleherne Ct, SW5 . . . . .100 DB78
Coleherne Ms, SW10 . . . . . . .100 DB78
Coleherne Rd, SW10 . . . . . . .100 DB78
Colehill Gdns, SW6
off Fulham Palace Rd 99 CY82
Colehill La, SW6 . . . . .99 CY81
Coleman Cl, SE25 . . . . .142 DU96
Coleman Flds, N1 . . . . .84 DQ67
Coleman Rd, SE5 . . . . .102 DS80
Belvedere DA17 . . . . .106 FA77
Dagenham RM9 . . . . .88 EY65
Colemans Heath, SE9 . . . . . .125 EP90
Colemans La, Ong. CM5 . . . . .19 FH30
Coleman's La, Wal.Abb. EN9 . .15 ED26
Coleman St, EC2 . . . . .197 K8
Colenso Dr, NW7 . . . . .43 CU52
Colenso Rd, E5 . . . . .66 DW63
Ilford IG2 . . . . .69 ES60
Cole Pk Gdns, Twick. TW1 . . .117 CG86
Cole Pk Rd, Twick. TW1 . . . . .117 CG86
Cole Pk Vw, Twick. TW1
off Hill Vw Rd 117 CG86
Colepits Wd Rd, SE9 . . . . . . .125 EQ85
Coleraine Rd, N8 . . . . .65 DN55
SE3 . . . . .104 EF79
Coleridge Av, E12 . . . . .86 EL65
Sutton SM1 . . . . .158 DE105
Coleridge Cl, SW8 . . . . .101 DH82
Waltham Cross (Chsht) EN7 .14 DT27
Coleridge Cres, Slou. (Colnbr.)
SL3 . . . . .93 BE81
Coleridge Gdns, NW6
off Fairhazel Gdns 82 DC66
SW10 . . . . .100 DB80
Coleridge Ho, SW1
off Churchill Gdns 101 DJ78
Coleridge La, N8
off Coleridge Rd 65 DL58
Coleridge Rd, E17 . . . . .67 DZ56
N4 .65 DN61
N8 .65 DK58
N12 . . . . .44 DC50
Ashford TW15 . . . . .114 BL91
Croydon CR0 . . . . .142 DW101
Dartford DA1 . . . . .108 FN84
Romford RM3 . . . . .51 FH52
Tilbury RM18 . . . . .111 GJ82
Coleridge Sq, SW10 . . . . . . .100 DC80
W13 off Berners Dr 79 CG72
Coleridge Wk, NW11 . . . . .64 DA56
Brentwood (Hutt.) CM13 . . .55 GC45
Coleridge Way, Borwd. WD6 . .26 CN42
Hayes UB4 . . . . .77 BU72
Orpington BR6 . . . . .146 EU100
West Drayton UB7 . . . . .94 BM77
Cole Rd, Twick. TW1 . . . . . . .117 CG86
Watford WD17
off Stamford Rd 23 BV39
Colesburg Rd, Beck. BR3 . . .143 DZ97
Coles Cres, Har. HA2 . . . . .60 CB61
Colescroft Hill, Pur. CR8 . . . .175 DN115
Colesdale, Pot.B. (Cuffley)
EN6 . . . . .13 DL30
Coles Grn, Bushey (Bushey Hth)
WD23 . . . . .40 CC46
Loughton IG10 . . . . .33 EN39
Coles Grn Ct, NW2 . . . . .63 CU61
Coles Grn Rd, NW2 . . . . .63 CU60
Coleshill Rd, Tedd. TW11 . . . .117 CE93
Coles La, West. (Brasted)
TN16 . . . . .180 EW123
Colesmead Rd, Red. RH1 . . .184 DF131
COLES MEADS, Red. RH1 . . .184 DF131
Colestown St, SW11 . . . . . . .100 DE82
Cole St, SE1 . . . . .201 J5
Colet Cl, N13 . . . . .45 DP51
Colet Gdns, W14 . . . . .99 CX77
Colet Rd, Brwd. (Hutt.) CM13 .55 GC43
Colets Orchard, Sev.
(Otford) TN14 . . . . .181 FH116
Coley Av, Wok. GU22 . . . . . .167 BA118
Coley St, WC1 . . . . .196 C5
Colfe Rd, SE23 . . . . .123 DY88
Colgate Pl, Enf. EN3 . . . . .31 EA37
Colham Av, West Dr. UB7 . . . .76 BL74
Colham Grn Rd, Uxb. UB8 . . . .76 BN71
Colham Mill Rd, West Dr. UB7 .94 BK75
Colham Rd, Uxb. UB8 . . . . . . .76 BM70
Colham Rbt, Uxb. UB8 . . . . . .76 BN72
Colina Ms, N15
off Harringay Rd 65 DP57
Colina Rd, N15 . . . . .65 DP57
Colin Cl, NW9 . . . . .62 CS56
Croydon CR0 . . . . .143 DZ104
Dartford DA2 . . . . .128 FP86
West Wickham BR4 . . . . . . .144 EF104
Colin Cres, NW9 . . . . .63 CT56
⊖ Colindale 62 CS55
Colindale Av, NW9 . . . . .62 CR55
Colindale Business Pk, NW9 .62 CQ55
H Colindale Hosp, NW9 . . . . .42 CS54
Colindeep Gdns, NW4 . . . . . . .63 CU57
Colindeep La, NW4 . . . . .62 CS55
NW9 . . . . .62 CS55
Colin Dr, NW9 . . . . .63 CT57
Colinette Rd, SW15 . . . . .99 CW84
Colin Gdns, NW9 . . . . .63 CT57
Colin Par, NW9
off Edgware Rd 62 CS56
Colin Pk Rd, NW9 . . . . .62 CS56
Colin Rd, NW10 . . . . .81 CU65
Caterham CR3 . . . . .176 DU123
Colinton Rd, Ilf. IG3 . . . . .70 EV61
★ Coliseum, The, WC2 . . . . .199 P1
Coliston Pas, SW18
off Coliston Rd 120 DA87
Coliston Rd, SW18 . . . . .120 DA87
Collamore Av, SW18 . . . . . . .120 DE88
Collapit Cl, Har. HA1 . . . . . . .60 CB57
Collard Av, Loug. IG10 . . . . . .33 EQ40
Collard Grn, Loug. IG10 . . . . .33 EQ40
Collard Pl, NW1
off Harmood St 83 DH66
College App, SE10 . . . . .103 EC79
College Av, Egh. TW20 . . . . .113 BB93
Epsom KT17 . . . . .157 CT114
Grays RM17 . . . . .110 GB77
Harrow HA3 . . . . .41 CE53
Slough SL1 . . . . .92 AS76
College Cl, E9 off Median Rd .66 DW64
N18 . . . . .46 DT50
Addlestone KT15 . . . . .134 BK104
Grays RM17 . . . . .110 GC77
Harrow HA3 . . . . .41 CE52
Hatfield (N.Mymms) AL9 . . .11 CX28
Twickenham TW2
off Meadway 117 CD88
College Ct, Wal.Cr. (Chsht)
EN8 . . . . .14 DW30
College Cres, NW3 . . . . .82 DD65
Redhill RH1 . . . . .184 DG131
College Cross, N1 . . . . .83 DN66
College Dr, Ruis. HA4 . . . . . . .59 BU59
Thames Ditton KT7 . . . . . . .137 CE101
College Gdns, E4 . . . . .47 EB45
N18 . . . . .46 DT50
SE21 . . . . .122 DS88
SW17 . . . . .120 DE89
Enfield EN2 . . . . .30 DR39
Ilford IG4 . . . . .68 EL57
New Malden KT3 . . . . .139 CT99
College Grn, SE19 . . . . .122 DS94
College Gro, NW1
off St. Pancras Way 83 DK67
College Hill, EC4 . . . . .197 J10
College Hill Rd, Har. HA3 . . . .41 CF53
College La, NW5 . . . . .65 DH63
Woking GU22 . . . . .166 AW119
College Ms, SW1 . . . . .199 P6
SW18 off St. Ann's Hill 120 DB85
★ College of Arms, EC4 . . . .196 G10
College Pk Cl, SE13 . . . . . . .103 ED84
College Pk Rd, N17
off College Rd 46 DT51
College Pl, E17 . . . . .68 EE56
NW1 . . . . .83 DJ67
SW10 off Hortensia Rd . . .100 DC80
Greenhithe DA9 . . . . .109 FW84
College Pt, E15 . . . . .86 EF65
College Rd, E17 . . . . .67 EC57
N17 . . . . .46 DT51
N21 . . . . .45 DN47
NW10 . . . . .81 CW68
SE19 . . . . .122 DT92
SE21 . . . . .122 DS87
SW19 . . . . .120 DD93
W13 . . . . .79 CH72
Abbots Langley WD5 . . . . . . .7 BT31
Bromley BR1 . . . . .124 EG94
Croydon CR0 . . . . .142 DR103
Enfield EN2 . . . . .30 DR40
Epsom KT17 . . . . .157 CU114
Gravesend (Nthflt) DA11 . . .130 GB85
Grays RM17 . . . . .110 GC77
Harrow (Har.Hill) HA1 . . . . . .61 CE58
Harrow (Har.Wld) HA3 . . . . .41 CE53
Isleworth TW7 . . . . .97 CF81
Swanley BR8 . . . . .147 FE95
Waltham Cross (Chsht) EN8 .14 DV30
Wembley HA9 . . . . .61 CK60
Woking GU22 . . . . .167 BB116
College Row, E9 . . . . .67 DX64
College Slip, Brom. BR1 . . . .144 EG95
College St, EC4 . . . . .197 J10
College Ter, E3 . . . . .85 DZ69
N3 off Hendon La 43 CZ54
College Vw, SE9 . . . . .124 EK88
College Wk, Kings.T. KT1
off Grange Rd 138 CL97
College Way, Ashf. TW15 . . . .114 BM91
Hayes UB3 . . . . .77 BU73
Northwood HA6 . . . . .39 BR51
College Yd, NW5
off College La 65 DH63
Watford WD24
off Gammons La 23 BV38
Collent St, E9 . . . . .84 DW65
Coller Cres, Dart. (Lane End)
DA2 . . . . .129 FS91
Colless Rd, N15 . . . . .66 DT57
Collet Cl, Wal.Cr. (Chsht) EN8 .15 DX28
Collet Gdns, Wal.Cr. (Chsht)
EN8 off Collet Cl 15 DX28
Collett Rd, SE16 . . . . .202 C7
Collett Way, Sthl. UB2 . . . . . .78 CB74
Colley Hill La, Slou. (Hedg.)
SL2 . . . . .56 AT62
Colleyland, Rick. (Chorl.) WD3 .21 BD42
Colley La, Reig. RH2 . . . . . . .183 CY132
Colley Manor Dr, Reig. RH2 .183 CX133
Colley Way, Reig. RH2 . . . . .183 CY131
Collier Cl, E6 off Trader Rd . . .87 EP73
Epsom KT19 . . . . .156 CN107
Collier Dr, Edg. HA8 . . . . .42 CN54
COLLIER ROW, Rom. RM5 . . . .50 FA53
Collier Row La, Rom. RM5 . . .51 FB52
Collier Row Rd, Rom. RM5 . . .50 EZ53
Colliers, Cat. CR3 . . . . .186 DU125
Colliers Cl, Wok. GU21 . . . . .166 AV117
Colliers Shaw, Kes. BR2 . . . .162 EK105
Collier St, N1 . . . . .196 B1
Colliers Water La, Th.Hth.
CR7 . . . . .141 DN99
COLLIER'S WOOD, SW19 . . . .120 DD94
⊖ Colliers Wood 120 DD94
Collindale Av, Erith DA8 . . . .107 FB79
Sidcup DA15 . . . . .126 EU88
Collingbourne Rd, W12 . . . . . .81 CV74
Collingham Gdns, SW5 . . . . .100 DB77
H Collingham Gdns Hosp,
SW5 . . . . .100 DB77
Collingham Pl, SW5 . . . . . . .100 DB77
Collingham Rd, SW5 . . . . . . .100 DB77
Collings Cl, N22
off Whittington Rd 45 DM51
Collington Cl, Grav. (Nthflt)
DA11 off Beresford Rd . . .130 GE87
Collington St, SE10
off Hoskins St 103 ED78
Collingtree Rd, SE26 . . . . . . .122 DW91
Collingwood Av, N10 . . . . . . .64 DG55
Surbiton KT5 . . . . .138 CQ102
Collingwood Cl, SE20 . . . . . .142 DV95
Twickenham TW2 . . . . .116 CA86
Collingwood Dr, St.Alb.
(Lon.Col.) AL2 . . . . .9 CK25
Collingwood Pl, Walt. KT12 .135 BU104
Collingwood Rd, E17 . . . . . . .67 EA58
N15 . . . . .66 DS56
Mitcham CR4 . . . . .140 DE96
Rainham RM13 . . . . .89 FF68
Sutton SM1 . . . . .140 DA104
Uxbridge UB8 . . . . .77 BP70
Collingwood St, E1 . . . . .84 DV70
Collins Av, Stan. HA7 . . . . . . .42 CL54
Collins Dr, Ruis. HA4 . . . . . . .60 BW61
Collinson St, SE1 . . . . .201 H5
Collinson Wk, SE1 . . . . .201 H5
Collins Rd, N5 . . . . .66 DQ63
Collins Sq, SE3
off Tranquil Vale 104 EF82
Collins St, SE3 . . . . .104 EE82
Collins Way, Brwd. (Hutt.)
CM13 . . . . .55 GE43
Collin's Yd, N1
off Islington Grn 83 DP67
Collinwood Av, Enf. EN3 . . . . .30 DW41
Collinwood Gdns, Ilf. IG5 . . . .69 EM57
Collis All, Twick. TW2
off The Green 117 CE88
Collison Pl, N16 . . . . .66 DS61
Colls Rd, SE15 . . . . .102 DW81
Collyer Av, Croy. CR0 . . . . . .159 DL105
Collyer Pl, SE15
off Peckham High St 102 DU81
Collyer Rd, Croy. CR0 . . . . . .159 DL105
St. Albans (Lon.Col.) AL2 . . .9 CJ27
Colman Cl, Epsom KT18 . . . .173 CW117
Colman Rd, E16 . . . . .86 EJ71
Colman Way, Red. RH1 . . . . .184 DE132
Colmar Cl, E1
off Alderney Rd 85 DX70
Colmer Pl, Har. HA3 . . . . .41 CD52
Colmer Rd, SW16 . . . . .141 DL95
Colmore Ms, SE15 . . . . .102 DV81
Colmore Rd, Enf. EN3 . . . . . . .30 DW42
COLNBROOK, Slou. SL3 . . . . .93 BD80
Colnbrook Bypass, Slou. SL3 .93 BF80
West Drayton UB7 . . . . .93 BF80
Colnbrook Cl, St.Alb.
(Lon.Col.) AL2 . . . . .10 CL27
Colnbrook Ct, Slou. SL3 . . . . .93 BF81
Colnbrook St, SE1 . . . . .200 F7
Colndale Rd, Slou. (Colnbr.)
SL3 . . . . .93 BE82
Colne Av, Rick. (Mill End) WD3 .38 BG47
Watford WD19 . . . . .23 BV44
West Drayton UB7 . . . . .94 BJ75
Colne Bk, Slou. (Horton) SL3 .93 BC83
Colnebridge Cl, Stai. TW18
off Clarence St 113 BE91
Colne Br Retail Pk, Wat. WD17
off Lower High St 24 BX43
Colne Cl, S.Ock. RM15 . . . . . .91 FW73
Colne Ct, Epsom KT19 . . . . .156 CQ105
Colnedale Rd, Uxb. UB8 . . . . .58 BK64
Colne Dr, Rom. RM3 . . . . .52 FM51
Walton-on-Thames KT12 . .136 BX104
Colne Gdns, St.Alb. (Lon.Col.)
AL2 . . . . .10 CL27
Colne Ho, Bark. IG11 . . . . . . .87 EP65
Colne Mead, Rick. (Mill End)
WD3 off Uxbridge Rd 38 BG47
Colne Orchard, Iver SL0 . . . . .75 BF72
Colne Pk Caravan Site,
West Dr. UB7 . . . . .94 BJ77
Colne Reach, Stai. TW19 . . . .113 BF85
Colne Rd, E5 . . . . .67 DY63
N21 . . . . .46 DR45
Twickenham TW1, TW2 . . . .117 CE88
Colne St, E13 off Grange Rd .86 EG69
Colne Valley, Upmin. RM14 . . .73 FS58
Colne Way, Stai. TW19 . . . . .113 BB90
Watford WD24, WD25 . . . . . .24 BY37
Colney Flds Shop Pk, St.Alb.
(Lon.Col.) AL2 . . . . .10 CM28
Colney Hatch La, N10 . . . . . . .44 DG52
N11 . . . . .44 DF51
Colney Rd, Dart. DA1 . . . . . .128 FM86
COLNEY STREET, St.Alb. AL2 .9 CE31
Cologne Rd, SW11 . . . . .100 DD84
Colombo Rd, Ilf. IG1 . . . . .69 EQ60
Colombo St, SE1 . . . . .200 F3
Colomb St, SE10 . . . . .104 EE78
Colonels La, Cher. KT16 . . . .134 BG100
Colonels Wk, Enf. EN2 . . . . . .29 DP41
Colonial Av, Twick. TW2 . . . .116 CC85
Colonial Dr, W4 . . . . .98 CQ77
Colonial Rd, Felt. TW14 . . . .115 BS87
Slough SL1 . . . . .92 AU75
Colonial Way, Wat. WD24 . . . .24 BX39
Colonnade, WC1 . . . . .195 P5
Colonnades, The, W2 . . . . . . .82 DB72
Colonnade Wk, SW1 . . . . . . .199 H9
Colony Ms, N1
off Mildmay Gro N 66 DR64
Colorado Apts, N8
off New River Av 65 DM56
Colosseum Ter, NW1
off Albany St 83 DH70
Colson Gdns, Loug. IG10 . . . .33 EN42
Colson Path, Loug. IG10 . . . . .33 EN42
Colson Rd, Croy. CR0 . . . . . .142 DS103
Loughton IG10 . . . . .33 EP42
Colson Way, SW16 . . . . .121 DJ91
Colsterworth Rd, N15 . . . . . . .66 DT56
Colston Av, Cars. SM5 . . . . .158 DE105
Colston Cl, Cars. SM5
off West St 158 DF105
Colston Cres, Wal.Cr.
(Chsht) EN7 . . . . .13 DP27
Colston Rd, E7 . . . . .86 EK65
SW14 . . . . .98 CQ84
Colthurst Cres, N4 . . . . .66 DQ61
Colthurst Dr, N9 . . . . .46 DV48
Coltishall Rd, Horn. RM12 . . . .90 FJ65
Coltman St, E14
off Halley St 85 DY71
Colt Ms, Enf. EN3
off Martini Dr 31 EA37
Coltness Cres, SE2 . . . . .106 EV78
Colton Gdns, N17 . . . . .66 DQ55
Colton Rd, Har. HA1 . . . . .61 CE57
Coltsfoot Ct, Grays RM17 . . .110 GD79
Coltsfoot Dr, West Dr. UB7 . . .76 BL72
Coltsfoot La, Oxt. RH8 . . . . .188 EF133
Coltsfoot Path, Rom. RM3 . . . .52 FJ52
Columbia Av, Edg. HA8 . . . . . .42 CP53
Ruislip HA4 . . . . .59 BV60
Worcester Park KT4 . . . . . .139 CT101
Columbia Pt, SE16 . . . . .202 G6
Columbia Rd, E2 . . . . .197 P2
E13 . . . . .86 EF70
Broxbourne EN10 . . . . .15 DY26
Columbia Sq, SW14
off Upper Richmond Rd W .98 CQ84
Columbia Wf Rd, Grays
RM17 . . . . .110 GA79
Columbine Av, E6 . . . . .86 EL71
South Croydon CR2 . . . . . .159 DP108
Columbine Way, SE13 . . . . . .103 EC82
Romford RM3 . . . . .52 FL53
Columbus Ct, SE16
off Rotherhithe St 84 DW74
Columbus Ctyd, E14 . . . . . . .204 P2
Columbus Gdns, Nthwd. HA6 .39 BU53
Columbus Sq, Erith DA8 . . . .107 FF79
Colva Wk, N19 off Chester Rd .65 DH61
Colvestone Cres, E8 . . . . .66 DT64
Colview Ct, SE9
off Mottingham La 124 EK88
Colville Est, N1 . . . . .84 DR67
Colville Gdns, W11 . . . . .81 CZ72
Colville Hos, W11 . . . . .81 CZ72
Colville Ms, W11
off Lonsdale Rd 81 CZ72
Colville Pl, W1 . . . . .195 L7
Colville Rd, E11 . . . . .67 EC62
E17 . . . . .47 DY54
N9 .46 DV46
W3 .98 CP76
W11 . . . . .81 CZ72
Colville Sq, W11 . . . . .81 CZ72
Colville Ter, W11 . . . . .81 CZ72
Colvin Cl, SE26 . . . . .122 DW92
Colvin Gdns, E4 . . . . .47 EC48
E11 . . . . .68 EH56
Ilford IG6 . . . . .49 EQ53

Colvin Gdns, Wal. Cr. EN8 . . . 31 DX35
Colvin Rd, E6 . . . 86 EL66
Thornton Heath CR7 . . . 141 DN99
Colwall Gdns, Wdf.Grn. IG8 . . 48 EG50
Colwell Rd, SE22 . . . 122 DT85
Colwick Cl, N6 . . . 65 DK59
Colwith Rd, W6 . . . 99 CW79
Colwood Gdns, SW19 . . . 120 DD94
Colworth Gro, SE17 . . . 201 J9
Colworth Rd, E11 . . . 68 EE58
Croydon CR0 . . . 142 DU102
Colwyn Av, Grnf. UB6 . . . 79 CF68
Colwyn Cl, SW16 . . . 121 DJ92
Colwyn Cres, Houns. TW3 . . . 96 CC81
Colwyn Grn, NW9
off Snowdon Dr . . . 62 CS58
Colwyn Ho, SE1
off Hercules Rd . . . 101 DN76
Colwyn Rd, NW2 . . . 63 CV62
Colyer Cl, N1 . . . 83 DM68
SE9 . . . 125 EP89
Colyer Rd, Grav. (Nthflt)
DA11 . . . 130 GC89
Colyers Cl, Erith DA8 . . . 107 FD81
Colyers La, Erith DA8 . . . 107 FC81
Colyers Wk, Erith DA8
off Colyers La . . . 107 FE81
Colyton Cl, Well. DA16 . . . 106 EX81
Wembley HA0
off Bridgewater Rd . . . 79 CJ65
Woking GU21 . . . 166 AW118
Colyton La, SW16 . . . 121 DN92
Colyton Rd, SE22 . . . 122 DV85
Colyton Way, N18 . . . 46 DU50
Combe, The, NW1 . . . 195 J3
Combe Av, SE3 . . . 104 EF80
Combe Bk Dr, Sev. (Sund.)
TN14 . . . 180 EY122
Combedale Rd, SE10 . . . 205 M10
Combe Lo, SE7
off Elliscombe Rd . . . 104 EJ79
Combemartin Rd, SW18 . . . 119 CY87
Combe Ms, SE3 . . . 104 EF80
Comber Cl, NW2 . . . 63 CV62
Comber Gro, SE5 . . . 102 DQ81
Comber Ho, SE5
off Comber Gro . . . 102 DQ80
Combermere Rd, SW9 . . . 101 DM83
Morden SM4 . . . 140 DB100
Combe Rd, Wat. WD18 . . . 23 BT44
Comberton Rd, E5 . . . 66 DV61
Combeside, SE18 . . . 105 ET80
Combwell Cres, SE2 . . . 106 EU76
Comely Bk Rd, E17 . . . 67 EC57
Comeragh Cl, Wok. GU22 . . . 166 AU119
Comeragh Ms, W14 . . . 99 CY78
Comeragh Rd, W14 . . . 99 CY78
Comer Cres, Sthl. UB2
off Windmill Av . . . 96 CC75
Comerford Rd, SE4 . . . 103 DY84
Comer Ho, Barn. EN5
off Station Rd . . . 28 DC42
Comet Cl, E12 . . . 68 EK63
Purfleet RM19 . . . 108 FN77
Watford WD25 . . . 7 BT34
Comet Pl, SE8 . . . 103 EA80
Comet Rd, Stai. (Stanw.)
TW19 . . . 114 BK87
Comet St, SE8 . . . 103 EA80
Comforts Fm Av, Oxt. RH8 . . . 188 EF133
Comfort St, SE15 . . . 102 DS79
Comfrey Ct, Grays RM17 . . . 110 GD79
Commerce Rd, N22 . . . 45 DM53
Brentford TW8 . . . 97 CJ80
Commerce Way, Croy. CR0 . . . 141 DM103
Commercial Pl, Grav. DA12 . . . 131 GJ86
Commercial Rd, E1 . . . 84 DU72
E14 . . . 84 DW72
N17 . . . 46 DS51
N18 . . . 46 DS50
Staines TW18 . . . 114 BG93
Commercial St, E1 . . . 197 P5
Commercial Way, NW10 . . . 80 CP68
SE15 . . . 102 DT80
Woking GU21 . . . 167 AZ117
Commerell St, SE10 . . . 205 J10
Commodity Quay, E1 . . . 202 A1
Commodore Ho, SW18
off York Rd . . . 100 DC84
Commodore St, E1 . . . 85 DY70
Common, The, E15 . . . 86 EE65
W5 . . . 80 CL73
Kings Langley (Chipper.)
WD4 . . . 6 BG32
Richmond TW10 . . . 117 CK90
Southall UB2 . . . 96 BW77
Stanmore HA7 . . . 41 CE47
West Drayton UB7 . . . 94 BJ77
Common Cl, Wok. GU21 . . . 150 AX114
Commondale, SW15 . . . 99 CW83
Commonfield Rd, Bans.
SM7 . . . 158 DA114
Common Gate Rd, Rick.
(Chorl.) WD3 . . . 21 BD43
Common La, Add. (New Haw)
KT15 . . . 152 BJ109
Dartford DA2 . . . 127 FG89
Esher (Clay.) KT10 . . . 155 CG108
Kings Langley WD4 . . . 6 BM28
Radlett WD7 . . . 25 CE39
Watford (Let.Hth) WD25 . . . 25 CE39
Commonmeadow La, Wat.
(Ald.) WD25 . . . 8 CB33
Common Mile Cl, SW4 . . . 121 DK85
Common Rd, SW13 . . . 99 CU83
Brentwood (Ingrave) CM13 . . . 55 GC50
Esher (Clay.) KT10 . . . 155 CG107
Leatherhead KT23 . . . 170 BY121
Rickmansworth (Chorl.)
WD3 . . . 21 BD42
Slough (Langley) SL3 . . . 93 BA77
Stanmore HA7 . . . 41 CD49
Commonside, Epsom KT18 . . . 172 CN115
Keston BR2 . . . 162 EJ105
Leatherhead (Bkhm) KT23 . . . 170 CA122
Commonside Cl, Couls. CR5
off Coulsdon Rd . . . 175 DP120
Sutton SM2 . . . 158 DB111
Commonside E, Mitch. CR4 . . . 140 DF97
Commonside W, Mitch. CR4 . . . 140 DF97
Commonwealth Av, W12 . . . 81 CV73
Hayes UB3 . . . 77 BR72
Commonwealth Rd, N17 . . . 46 DU52
Commonwealth Rd, Cat.
CR3 . . . 176 DU123
Commonwealth Way, SE2 . . . 106 EV78
COMMONWOOD, Kings L.
WD4 . . . 6 BH34
Commonwood La, Kings L.
WD4 . . . 22 BH35
Community Cl, Houns. TW5 . . . 95 BV81
Uxbridge UB10 . . . 59 BQ62
Community La, N7 . . . 65 DK64
Community Rd, E15 . . . 67 ED64
Greenford UB6 . . . 78 CC67
Community Wk, Esher KT10
off High St . . . 154 CC105
Community Way, Rick. (Crox.Grn)
WD3 *off Barton Way* . . . 23 BP43
Como Rd, SE23 . . . 123 DY89
Como St, Rom. RM7 . . . 71 FD57
Compass Cl, Ashf. TW15 . . . 115 BQ94
Edgware HA8
off Glendale Av . . . 42 CM49
Compass Hill, Rich. TW10 . . . 117 CK86
Compass Ho, SW18
off Smugglers Way . . . 100 DB84
Compass La, Brom. BR1
off North St . . . 144 EG95
Compayne Gdns, NW6 . . . 82 DB66
Comport Grn, Croy. (New Adgtn)
CR0 . . . 162 EE112
Compton Av, E6 . . . 86 EK68
N1 . . . 83 DP65
N6 . . . 64 DE59
Brentwood (Hutt.) CM13 . . . 55 GC46
Romford RM2 . . . 71 FH55
Wembley HA0 . . . 61 CJ63
Compton Cl, E3 . . . 85 EA71
NW1 . . . 195 J3
NW11 *off The Vale* . . . 63 CX62
SE15 *off Commercial Way* . . . 102 DU80
W13 . . . 79 CG72
Edgware HA8 . . . 42 CQ52
Esher KT10 . . . 154 CC106
Compton Ct, SE19
off Victoria Cres . . . 122 DS92
Compton Cres, N17 . . . 46 DQ52
W4 . . . 98 CQ79
Chessington KT9 . . . 156 CL107
Northolt UB5 . . . 78 BX67
Compton Gdns, Add. KT15
off Monks Cres . . . 152 BH106
St. Albans AL2 . . . 8 CB26
Compton Ho, SW11
off Parkham St . . . 100 DE81
Compton Pas, EC1 . . . 196 G4
Compton Pl, WC1 . . . 195 P4
Erith DA8 . . . 107 FF79
Watford WD19 . . . 40 BY48
Compton Ri, Pnr. HA5 . . . 60 BY57
Compton Rd, N1 . . . 83 DP65
N21 . . . 45 DN46
NW10 . . . 81 CX69
SW19 . . . 119 CZ93
Croydon CR0 . . . 142 DV102
Hayes UB3 . . . 77 BS73
Compton St, EC1 . . . 196 F4
Compton Ter, N1 . . . 83 DP65
Computer Ho, Brent. TW8 . . . 97 CJ79
Comreddy Cl, Enf. EN2 . . . 29 DP39
Comus Pl, SE17 . . . 201 M9
Comyne Rd, Wat. WD24 . . . 23 BT36
Comyn Rd, SW11 . . . 100 DE84
Comyns, The, Bushey (Bushey Hth)
WD23 . . . 40 CC46
Comyns Cl, E16 . . . 86 EF71
Comyns Rd, Dag. RM9 . . . 88 FA66
Conant Ms, E1 *off Back Ch La* . . . 84 DU73
Conaways Cl, Epsom KT17 . . . 157 CU110
Concanon Rd, SW2 . . . 101 DM84
Concert Hall App, SE1 . . . 200 C3
Concord Cl, Nthlt. UB5 . . . 78 BY69
Concorde Cl, Houns. TW3 . . . 96 CB82
Uxbridge UB10 . . . 76 BL68
Concorde Dr, E6 . . . 87 EM71
Concorde Way, SE16 . . . 203 H9
Concord Rd, W3 . . . 80 CP70
Enfield EN3 . . . 30 DW43
Concord Ter, Har. HA2
off Coles Cres . . . 60 CB61
Concourse, The, N9
off New Rd . . . 46 DU47
NW9 . . . 43 CT53
Concrete Cotts, Wok. (Wisley)
GU23 *off Wisley La* . . . 168 BL116
Condell Rd, SW8 . . . 101 DJ81
Conder St, E14 *off Salmon La* . . . 85 DY72
Condor Path, Nthlt. UB5
off Brabazon Rd . . . 78 CA68
Condor Rd, Stai. TW18 . . . 134 BH97
Condor Wk, Horn. RM12
off Heron Flight Av . . . 89 FH66
Condover Cres, SE18 . . . 105 EP80
Condray Pl, SW11 . . . 100 DE80
Conduit, The, Red. (Bletch.)
RH1 . . . 186 DS129
Conduit Av, SE10
off Crooms Hill . . . 103 ED80
Conduit Ct, WC2 . . . 195 P10
Conduit La, N18 . . . 46 DW50
Croydon CR0 . . . 160 DU106
Enfield EN3 *off Morson Rd* . . . 31 DY44
South Croydon CR2 . . . 160 DU106
Conduit Ms, SE18 . . . 105 EP78
W2 . . . 82 DD72
Conduit Pas, W2
off Conduit Pl . . . 82 DD72
Conduit Pl, W2 . . . 82 DD72
Conduit Rd, SE18 . . . 105 EP78
Slough SL3 . . . 92 AY78
Conduit St, W1 . . . 195 J10
Conduit Way, NW10 . . . 80 CQ66
Conegar Ct, Slou. SL1 . . . 74 AS74
Conewood St, N5 . . . 65 DP62
Coney Acre, SE21 . . . 122 DQ88
Coney Burrows, E4
off Wyemead Cres . . . 48 EE47
Coneybury, Red. (Bletch.)
RH1 . . . 186 DS134
Coneybury Cl, Warl. CR6 . . . 176 DV119
Coney Gro, Uxb. UB8 . . . 76 BN69
Coneygrove Path, Nthlt. UB5
off Arnold Rd . . . 78 BY65
CONEY HALL, W.Wick. BR4 . . . 144 EF104
Coney Hill Rd, W.Wick. BR4 . . . 144 EE103
Coney Way, SW8 . . . 101 DM79
Conference Cl, E4
off Greenbank Cl . . . 47 EC47
★ **Conference Forum, The**,
E1 . . . 84 DU72
Conference Rd, SE2 . . . 106 EW77
Congleton Gro, SE18 . . . 105 EQ78
Congo Dr, N9 . . . 46 DW48
Congo Rd, SE18 . . . 105 ER78
Congress Rd, SE2 . . . 106 EW77
Congreve Rd, SE9 . . . 105 EM83
Waltham Abbey EN9 . . . 16 EE33
Congreve St, SE17 . . . 201 M8
Congreve Wk, E16 . . . 86 EK71
Conical Cor, Enf. EN2 . . . 30 DQ40
Conifer Av, Rom. RM5 . . . 51 FB50
Conifer Cl, Orp. BR6 . . . 163 ER105
Reigate RH2 . . . 184 DA132
Waltham Cross EN7 . . . 14 DT29
Conifer Dr, Brwd. CM14 . . . 54 FX50
Conifer Gdns, SW16 . . . 121 DL90
Enfield EN1 . . . 30 DS44
Sutton SM1 . . . 140 DB103
Conifer La, Egh. TW20 . . . 113 BC92
Conifer Pk, Epsom KT17 . . . 156 CS111
Conifers, Wey. KT13 . . . 153 BS105
Conifers, The, Wat. WD25 . . . 24 BW35
Conifers Cl, Tedd. TW11 . . . 117 CH94
Conifer Way, Hayes UB3
off Longmead Rd . . . 77 BU73
Swanley BR8 . . . 147 FC95
Wembley HA0 . . . 61 CJ62
Coniger Rd, SW6 . . . 100 DA82
Coningesby Dr, Wat. WD17 . . . 23 BS39
Coningham Ms, W12
off Percy Rd . . . 81 CU74
Coningham Rd, W12 . . . 99 CV75
Coningsby Av, NW9 . . . 42 CS54
Coningsby Cotts, W5
off Coningsby Rd . . . 97 CK75
Coningsby Dr, Pot.B. EN6 . . . 12 DD33
Coningsby Gdns, E4 . . . 47 EB51
Coningsby Rd, N4 . . . 65 DP59
W5 . . . 97 CJ75
South Croydon CR2 . . . 160 DQ109
Conington Rd, SE13 . . . 103 EB82
Conisbee Ct, N14 . . . 29 DJ43
Conisborough Cres, SE6 . . . 123 EC90
Coniscliffe Cl, Chis. BR7 . . . 145 EN95
Coniscliffe Rd, N13 . . . 46 DQ48
Conista Ct, Wok. GU21
off Roundthorn Way . . . 166 AT116
Coniston Av, Bark. IG11 . . . 87 ES66
Greenford UB6 . . . 79 CH69
Purfleet RM19 . . . 108 FQ79
Upminster RM14 . . . 72 FQ63
Welling DA16 . . . 105 ES83
Coniston Cl, N20 . . . 44 DC48
SW13 *off Lonsdale Rd* . . . 99 CT80
SW20 . . . 139 CX100
W4 . . . 98 CQ81
Barking IG11
off Coniston Av . . . 87 ES66
Bexleyheath DA7 . . . 107 FC81
Dartford DA1 . . . 127 FH88
Erith DA8 . . . 107 FE80
Coniston Ct, Wey. KT13 . . . 153 BP107
Conistone Way, N7 . . . 83 DL66
Coniston Gdns, N9 . . . 46 DW46
NW9 . . . 62 CR57
Ilford IG4 . . . 68 EL56
Pinner HA5 . . . 59 BU56
Sutton SM2 . . . 158 DD107
Wembley HA9 . . . 61 CJ60
Coniston Ho, SE5 . . . 102 DQ80
Coniston Rd, N10 . . . 45 DH54
N17 . . . 46 DU51
Bexleyheath DA7 . . . 107 FC81
Bromley BR1 . . . 124 EE93
Coulsdon CR5 . . . 175 DJ116
Croydon CR0 . . . 142 DU101
Kings Langley WD4 . . . 6 BM28
Twickenham TW2 . . . 116 CB86
Woking GU22 . . . 167 BB120
Coniston Wk, E9
off Clifden Rd . . . 66 DW64
Coniston Way, Chess. KT9 . . . 138 CL104
Egham TW20 . . . 113 BB94
Hornchurch RM12 . . . 71 FG64
Reigate RH2 . . . 184 DE133
Conlan St, W10 . . . 81 CY70
Conley Rd, NW10 . . . 80 CS65
Conley St, SE10 . . . 205 J10
Connaught Av, E4 . . . 47 ED45
SW14 . . . 98 CQ83
Ashford TW15 . . . 114 BL91
Barnet EN4 . . . 44 DF46
Enfield EN1 . . . 30 DS40
Grays RM16 . . . 110 GB75
Hounslow TW4 . . . 116 BY85
Loughton IG10 . . . 32 EK42
Connaught Br, E16 . . . 86 EK74
Connaught Cl, E10 . . . 67 DY61
W2 . . . 194 B9
Enfield EN1 . . . 30 DS40
Sutton SM1 . . . 140 DD103
Uxbridge UB8 *off New Rd* . . . 77 BQ70
Connaught Ct, E17
off Orford Rd . . . 67 EB56
Buckhurst Hill IG9 . . . 48 EH46
Connaught Dr, NW11 . . . 64 DA56
Weybridge KT13 . . . 152 BN111
Connaught Gdns, N10 . . . 65 DH57
N13 . . . 45 DP49
Morden SM4 . . . 140 DC98
Connaught Hts, Uxb. UB10
off Uxbridge Rd . . . 77 BQ70
Connaught Hill, Loug. IG10 . . . 32 EK42
Connaught La, Ilf. IG1
off Connaught Rd . . . 69 ER61
Connaught Ms, SE18 . . . 105 EN78
Ilford IG1
off Connaught Rd . . . 69 ER61
Connaught Pl, W2 . . . 194 D10
Connaught Rd, E4 . . . 48 EE45
E11 . . . 67 ED60
E16 . . . 86 EK74
E17 . . . 67 EA57
N4 . . . 65 DN59
NW10 . . . 80 CS67
SE18 . . . 105 EN78
W13 . . . 79 CH73
Barnet EN5 . . . 27 CX44
Connaught Rd, Har. HA3 . . . 41 CF53
Hornchurch RM12 . . . 72 FK62
Ilford IG1 . . . 69 ER61
New Malden KT3 . . . 138 CS98
Richmond TW10
off Albert Rd . . . 118 CM85
Slough SL1 . . . 92 AV75
Sutton SM1 . . . 140 DD103
Teddington TW11 . . . 117 CD92
Connaught Rbt, E16
off Connaught Br . . . 86 EK73
Connaught Sq, W2 . . . 194 D9
Connaught St, W2 . . . 194 B9
Connaught Way, N13 . . . 45 DP49
Connect La, Ilf. (Barkingside)
IG6 . . . 49 EQ54
Connell Cres, W5 . . . 80 CM70
Connemara Cl, Borwd. WD6 . . . 26 CQ44
Connington Cres, E4 . . . 47 ED48
Connop Rd, Enf. EN3 . . . 31 DX38
Connor Cl, E11 . . . 68 EE60
Ilford IG6 . . . 49 EP53
Connor Ct, SW11
off Alfreda St . . . 101 DH81
Connor Rd, Dag. RM9 . . . 70 EZ63
Connor St, E9
off Lauriston Rd . . . 85 DX67
Conolly Rd, W7 . . . 79 CE74
Conquest Rd, Add. KT15 . . . 152 BG106
Conrad Cl, Grays RM16 . . . 110 GB75
Conrad Dr, Wor.Pk. KT4 . . . 139 CW102
Conrad Gdns, Grays RM16 . . . 110 GA75
Conrad Ho, N16 . . . 66 DS64
Consfield Av, N.Mal. KT3 . . . 139 CU98
Consort Cl, Brwd. CM14 . . . 54 FW50
Consort Ms, Islw. TW7 . . . 117 CD85
Consort Rd, SE15 . . . 102 DV81
Consort Way, Uxb. (Denh.) UB9
off Knowland Way . . . 57 BF58
Cons St, SE1 . . . 200 E4
Constable Av, E16 . . . 205 P2
Constable Cl, N11
off Friern Barnet La . . . 44 DF50
NW11 . . . 64 DB58
Hayes UB4
off Charville La . . . 77 BQ69
Constable Cres, N15 . . . 66 DU57
Constable Gdns, Edg. HA8 . . . 42 CN53
Isleworth TW7 . . . 117 CD85
Constable Ho, E14
off Cassilis Rd . . . 103 EA75
NW3 *off Adelaide Rd* . . . 82 DD66
Constable Ms, Dag. RM8
off Stonard Rd . . . 70 EV63
Constable Rd, Grav. (Nthflt)
DA11 . . . 130 GE90
Constable Wk, SE21 . . . 122 DT90
Constance Cres, Brom. BR2 . . . 144 EF101
Constance Rd, Croy. CR0 . . . 141 DP101
Enfield EN1 . . . 30 DS44
Sutton SM1 . . . 158 DC105
Twickenham TW2 . . . 116 CB87
Constance St, E16
off Albert Rd . . . 86 EL74
Constantine Pl, Uxb. (Hlgdn)
UB10 . . . 76 BM67
Constantine Rd, NW3 . . . 64 DE63
Constitution Hill, SW1 . . . 199 H4
Gravesend DA12 . . . 131 GJ88
Woking GU22 . . . 166 AY119
Constitution Ri, SE18 . . . 105 EN81
Consul Av, Dag. RM9 . . . 89 FC69
Consul Gdns, Swan. BR8 . . . 127 FG94
Content St, SE17 . . . 201 J9
Contessa Cl, Orp. BR6 . . . 163 ES106
Control Twr Rd, Houns.
(Hthrw Air.) TW6 . . . 94 BN83
Convair Wk, Nthlt. UB5
off Kittiwake Rd . . . 78 BX69
Convent Cl, Beck. BR3 . . . 123 EC94
Convent Gdns, W5 . . . 97 CJ77
W11 *off Kensington Pk Rd* . . . 81 CZ72
Convent Hill, SE19 . . . 122 DQ93
Convent La, Cob. KT11 . . . 153 BS111
Convent Rd, Ashf. TW15 . . . 114 BN92
Convent Way, Sthl. UB2 . . . 96 BW77
Conway Cl, Rain. RM13 . . . 89 FG66
Stanmore HA7 . . . 41 CG51
Conway Cres, Grnf. UB6 . . . 79 CE68
Romford RM6 . . . 70 EW59
Conway Dr, Ashf. TW15 . . . 115 BQ93
Hayes UB3 . . . 95 BQ76
Sutton SM2 . . . 158 DB107
Conway Gdns, Enf. EN2 . . . 30 DS38
Grays RM17 . . . 110 GB80
Mitcham CR4 . . . 141 DK98
Wembley HA9 . . . 61 CJ59
Conway Gro, W3 . . . 80 CR71
Conway Ms, W1 . . . 195 K5
Conway Rd, N14 . . . 45 DL48
N15 . . . 65 DP57
NW2 . . . 63 CW61
SE18 . . . 105 ER77
SW20 . . . 139 CW95
Feltham TW13 . . . 116 BX92
Hounslow TW4 . . . 116 BZ87
Hounslow (Hthrw Air.) TW6
off Inner Ring E . . . 95 BP83
Conway St, E13 . . . 86 EG70
W1 . . . 195 K5
Conway Wk, Hmptn. TW12
off Fearnley Cres . . . 116 BZ93
Conybeare, NW3
off King Henry's Rd . . . 82 DE66
Conybury Cl, Wal.Abb. EN9 . . . 16 EG32
Cony Cl, Wal.Cr. (Chsht) EN7 . . . 14 DS26
Conyers Cl, Walt. KT12 . . . 154 BX106
Woodford Green IG8 . . . 48 EE51
Conyers Rd, SW16 . . . 121 DK92
Conyer St, E3 . . . 85 DY68
Conyers Way, Loug. IG10 . . . 33 EP41
Cooden Cl, Brom. BR1
off Plaistow La . . . 124 EH94
Cook Ct, SE16
off Rotherhithe St . . . 84 DW74
Cookes Cl, E11 . . . 68 EF61
Cookes La, Sutt. SM3 . . . 157 CY107
Cooke St, Bark. IG11
off St. Ann's . . . 87 EQ67
Cookham Cl, Sthl. UB2 . . . 96 CB75
Cookham Cres, SE16 . . . 203 H4
Cookham Dene Cl, Chis. BR7 . . . 145 ER95
Cookham Hill, Orp. BR6 . . . 146 FA104
Cookham Rd, Sid. DA14 . . . 126 FA94
Swanley BR8 . . . 146 FA95
Cookhill Rd, SE2 . . . 106 EV75
Cook Rd, Dag. RM9 . . . 88 EY67
Cooks Cl, E14 *off Cabot Sq* . . . 85 EA74
Romford RM5 . . . 51 FC53
Cook's Hole Rd, Enf. EN2 . . . 29 DP38
Cooks Mead, Bushey WD23 . . . 24 CB44
Cookson Gro, Erith DA8 . . . 107 FB80
Cook Sq, Erith DA8 . . . 107 FF80
Cook's Rd, E15 . . . 85 EB68
Cooks Rd, SE17 . . . 101 DP79
Cooks Wf Rbt, N18 . . . 47 DY50
Coolfin Rd, E16 . . . 86 EG72
Coolgardie Av, E4 . . . 47 EC50
Chigwell IG7 . . . 49 EN48
Coolgardie Rd, Ashf. TW15 . . . 115 BQ92
Coolhurst Rd, N8 . . . 65 DK58
Cool Oak La, NW9 . . . 62 CS59
Coomassie Rd, W9
off Bravington Rd . . . 81 CZ70
COOMBE, Kings.T. KT2 . . . 118 CQ94
Coombe, The, Bet. RH3 . . . 182 CR131
Coombe Av, Croy. CR0 . . . 160 DS105
Sevenoaks TN14 . . . 181 FH120
Coombe Bk, Kings.T. KT2 . . . 138 CS95
Coombe Cl, Edg. HA8 . . . 42 CM54
Hounslow TW3 . . . 96 CA84
Coombe Cor, N21 . . . 45 DP46
Coombe Cres, Hmptn. TW12 . . . 116 BY94
Coombe Dr, Add. KT15 . . . 151 BF107
Kingston upon Thames
KT2 . . . 118 CR94
Ruislip HA4 . . . 59 BV60
Coombe End, Kings.T. KT2 . . . 118 CR94
Coombefield Cl, N.Mal. KT3 . . . 138 CS99
Coombe Gdns, SW20 . . . 139 CU96
New Malden KT3 . . . 139 CT98
Coombe Hts, Kings.T. KT2 . . . 118 CS94
Coombe Hill Glade, Kings.T.
KT2 . . . 118 CS94
Coombe Hill Rd, Kings.T. KT2 . . . 118 CS94
Rickmansworth (Mill End)
WD3 . . . 38 BG45
Coombe Ho Chase, N.Mal.
KT3 . . . 138 CR95
Coombehurst Cl, Barn. EN4 . . . 28 DF40
Coombelands La, Add. KT15 . . . 152 BG107
Tram **Coombe Lane** . . . 160 DW106
Coombe La, SW20 . . . 139 CU95
Croydon CR0 . . . 160 DV106
Walton-on-Thames
(Whiteley Vill.) KT12 . . . 153 BT109
Coombe La W, Kings.T. KT2 . . . 118 CS94
Coombe Lea, Brom. BR1 . . . 144 EL97
Coombe Neville, Kings.T.
KT2 . . . 118 CR94
Coombe Pk, Kings.T. KT2 . . . 118 CR92
Coombe Ridings, Kings.T.
KT2 . . . 118 CQ92
Coombe Ri, Brwd. (Shenf.)
CM15 . . . 55 FZ46
Kingston upon Thames
KT2 . . . 138 CQ95
Coombe Rd, N22 . . . 45 DN53
NW10 . . . 62 CR62
SE26 . . . 122 DV91
W4 . . . 98 CS78
W13 *off Northcroft Rd* . . . 97 CH76
Bushey WD23 . . . 40 CC45
Croydon CR0 . . . 160 DR105
Gravesend DA12 . . . 131 GJ89
Hampton TW12 . . . 116 BZ93
Kingston upon Thames
KT2 . . . 138 CN95
New Malden KT3 . . . 138 CS96
Romford RM3 . . . 72 FM55
Coomber Way, Croy. CR0 . . . 141 DK101
Coombes Rd, Dag. RM9 . . . 88 EZ67
St. Albans (Lon.Col.) AL2 . . . 9 CH26
Coombe Vale, Ger.Cr. SL9 . . . 56 AY60
Coombe Wk, Sutt. SM1 . . . 140 DB104
Coombe Way, W.Byf. (Byfleet)
KT14 . . . 152 BM112
Coombewood Dr, Rom. RM6 . . . 70 EZ58
Coombe Wd Hill, Pur. CR8 . . . 160 DQ112
Coombe Wd Rd, Kings.T. KT2 . . . 118 CQ92
Coombfield Dr, Dart.
(Lane End) DA2 . . . 129 FR91
Coombs St, N1 . . . 196 G1
Coomer Ms, SW6
off Coomer Pl . . . 99 CZ79
Coomer Pl, SW6 . . . 99 CZ79
Coomer Rd, SW6
off Coomer Pl . . . 99 CZ79
Cooms Wk, Edg. HA8
off East Rd . . . 42 CQ53
Cooperage Cl, N17
off Brantwood Rd . . . 46 DT51
Cooper Av, E17 . . . 47 DX53
Cooper Cl, SE1 . . . 200 E5
Greenhithe DA9 . . . 129 FT85
Cooper Cres, Cars. SM5 . . . 140 DF104
Cooper Rd, NW4 . . . 63 CX58
NW10 . . . 63 CT64
Croydon CR0 . . . 159 DN105
COOPERSALE, Epp. CM16 . . . 18 EX29
Coopersale Cl, Wdf.Grn. IG8
off Navestock Cres . . . 48 EJ52
Coopersale Common, Epp.
(Cooper.) CM16 . . . 18 EX28
Coopersale La, Epp. CM16 . . . 34 EU37
Coopersale Rd, E9 . . . 67 DX64
Coopersale St, Epp. CM16 . . . 18 EW32
Coopers Cl, E1 . . . 84 DW70
Chigwell IG7 . . . 50 EV47
Dagenham RM10 . . . 89 FB65
Dartford (S.Darenth) DA4 . . . 148 FQ95
Staines TW18 . . . 113 BE92
Coopers Ct, Rom. (Gidea Pk)
RM2 *off Kidman Cl* . . . 72 FJ55
Coopers Cres, Borwd. WD6 . . . 26 CQ39
Coopers Dr, Dart. DA2 . . . 127 FE89
Coopers Hill La, Egh. TW20 . . . 112 AY91
Coopers Hill Rd, Red. RH1 . . . 185 DM133
Coopers La, E10 . . . 67 EB60
NW1 . . . 83 DK68

Cooper's La, SE12 124 EH89
Coopers La, Pot.B. EN6 12 DD31
Staines TW18
off Kingston Rd 114 BG91
Coopers La Rd, Pot.B. EN6 12 DE31
Coopers Ms, Beck. BR3 143 EA96
Watford WD25
off High Elms La 8 BW31
Coopers Rd, SE1 102 DT78
Gravesend (Nthflt) DA11 130 GE88
Potters Bar EN6 12 DC30
Cooper's Row, EC3 197 P10
Coopers Row, Iver SL0 75 BC70
Coopers Shaw Rd, Til. RM18 111 GK80
Cooper St, E16
off Lawrence St 86 EF71
Coopers Wk, E15
off Maryland St 68 EE64
Waltham Cross (Chsht) EN8 15 DX28
Coopers Yd, N1 off Upper St 83 DP66
Cooper's Yd, SE19
off Westow Hill 122 DS93
Coote Gdns, Dag. RM8 70 EZ62
Coote Rd, Bexh. DA7 106 EZ81
Dagenham RM8 70 EZ62
Copeland Dr, E14 204 A8
Copeland Ho, SE11
off Lambeth Rd 101 DM76
Copeland Rd, E17 67 EB57
SE15 102 DU82
Copeman Cl, SE26 122 DW92
Copeman Rd, Brwd. (Hutt.)
CM13 55 GD45
Copenhagen Gdns, W4 98 CQ75
Copenhagen Pl, E14 85 DZ72
Copenhagen St, N1 83 DL67
Copenhagen Way, Walt.
KT12 135 BV104
Cope Pl, W8 100 DA76
Copers Cope Rd, Beck. BR3 123 DZ93
Cope St, SE16 203 H8
Copford Cl, Wdf.Grn. IG8 48 EL51
Copford Wk, N1
off Popham St 84 DQ67
Copgate Path, SW16 121 DM93
Copinger Wk, Edg. HA8
off North Rd 42 CP53
Copland Av, Wem. HA0 61 CK64
Copland Cl, Wem. HA0 61 CJ64
Copland Ms, Wem. HA0
off Copland Rd 80 CL65
Copland Rd, Wem. HA0 80 CL65
Copleigh Dr, Tad. KT20 173 CY120
Copleston Ms, SE15
off Copleston Rd 102 DT82
Copleston Pas, SE15 102 DT83
Copleston Rd, SE15 102 DT83
Copley Cl, SE17
off Hillingdon St 101 DP79
W7 79 CF71
Redhill RH1 184 DE132
Woking GU21 166 AS119
Copley Dene, Brom. BR1 144 EK95
Copley Pk, SW16 121 DM93
Copley Rd, Stan. HA7 41 CJ50
Copley St, E1 85 DX71
Copley Way, Tad. KT20 173 CX120
Copmans Wick, Rick. (Chorl.)
WD3 21 BD43
Coppard Gdns, Chess. KT9 155 CJ107
Copped Hall, SE21
off Glazebrook Cl 122 DR89
Coppelia Rd, SE3 104 EF84
Coppen Rd, Dag. RM8 70 EZ59
Copperas St, SE8 103 EB79
Copper Beech Cl, Grav.
DA12 131 GK87
Ilford IG5 49 EN53
Orpington BR5 146 EW99
Woking GU22 166 AV121
Copper Beech Ct, Loug. IG10 33 EN39
Copper Beech Ct, Islw. TW7
off Eversley Cres 97 CD81
Copper Beech Rd, S.Ock.
RM15 91 FW69
Copper Cl, N17 46 DV52
SE19 off Auckland Rd 122 DT94
Copperdale Rd, Hayes UB3 95 BU75
Copperfield, Chig. IG7 49 ER51
Copperfield App, Chig. IG7 49 ER51
Copperfield Av, Uxb. UB8 76 BN71
Copperfield Cl, S.Croy. CR2 160 DQ111
Copperfield Ct, Lthd. KT22
off Kingston Rd 171 CG121
Pinner HA5
off Copperfield Way 60 BZ56
Copperfield Dr, N15 66 DT56
Copperfield Gdns, Brwd.
CM14 54 FV46
Copperfield Ms, N18 46 DS50
Copperfield Ri, Add. KT15 151 BF106
Copperfield Rd, E3 85 DY70
SE28 88 EW72
Copperfields, Dart. DA1
off Spital St 128 FL86
Leatherhead (Fetch.) KT22 170 CC122
Copperfield St, SE1 200 G4
Copperfields Way, Rom. RM3 52 FK53
Copperfield Ter, Slou. SL2
off Mirador Cres 74 AV73
Copperfield Way, Chis. BR7 125 EQ93
Pinner HA5 60 BZ56
Coppergate Cl, Brom. BR1 144 EH95
Coppergate Ct, Wal.Abb. EN9
off Farthingale La 16 EG34
Copper Mead Cl, NW2 63 CW62
Copper Ms, W4
off Reynolds Rd 98 CQ76
Copper Mill Dr, Islw. TW7 97 CF82
Coppermill La, E17 66 DW58
Copper Mill La, SW17 120 DC91
Coppermill La, Rick. WD3 37 BE52
Uxbridge (Hare.) UB9 37 BE52
Coppermill Rd, Stai. (Wrays.)
TW19 93 BC84
Copper Ridge, Ger.Cr.
(Chal.St.P.) SL9 37 AZ50
Copper Row, SE1 201 P3
Coppetts Cl, N12 44 DE52
Coppetts Rd, N10 44 DG54
H Coppetts Wd Hosp, N10 44 DF53
Coppice, The, Ashf. TW15
off School Rd 115 BP93
Enfield EN2 29 DP42
Watford WD19 24 BW44
West Drayton UB7 76 BL72
Coppice Cl, SW20 139 CW97
Beckenham BR3 143 EB98
Ruislip HA4 59 BR58
Stanmore HA7 41 CF51
Coppice Dr, SW15 119 CV86
Staines (Wrays.) TW19 112 AX87
Coppice End, Wok. GU22 167 BE116
Coppice La, Reig. RH2 183 CZ132
Coppice Path, Chig. IG7 50 EV49
Coppice Row, Epp. CM16 33 EM36
Coppice Wk, N20 44 DA48
Coppice Way, E18 68 EF56
Coppies Gro, N11 44 DG49
Copping Cl, Croy. CR0 160 DS105
Coppins, The, Croy. (New Adgtn)
CR0 161 EB107
Harrow HA3 41 CE51
Coppins La, Iver SL0 75 BF71
Coppock Cl, SW11 100 DE82
Coppsfield, W.Mol. KT8
off Hurst Rd 136 CA97
Copse, The, E4 48 EF46
Caterham CR3
off Tupwood La 186 DU126
Leatherhead (Fetch.) KT22 170 CB123
Copse Av, W.Wick. BR4 143 EB104
Copse Cl, SE7 104 EH79
Northwood HA6 39 BQ54
West Drayton UB7 94 BK76
Copse Edge Av, Epsom KT17 157 CT113
Copse Glade, Surb. KT6 137 CK102
COPSE HILL, SW20 119 CU94
Copse Hill, SW20 119 CV94
Purley CR8 159 DL113
Sutton SM2 158 DB108
Copse La, Beac. (Jordans)
HP9 36 AS52
Copsem Dr, Esher KT10 154 CB107
Copsem La, Esher KT10 154 CB107
Leatherhead (Oxshott)
KT22 154 CC111
Copsem Way, Esher KT10 154 CC107
Copsen Wd, Lthd. KT22 154 CC111
Copse Rd, Cob. KT11 153 BV113
Woking GU21 166 AT118
Copse Vw, S.Croy. CR2 161 DX109
Copse Wd, Iver SL0 75 BD67
Copsewood Cl, Sid. DA15 125 ES86
Copse Wd Ct, Reig. RH2
off Green La 184 DE132
Copsewood Rd, Wat. WD24 23 BV39
Copse Wd Way, Nthwd. HA6 39 BQ52
Coptain Ho, SW18
off Eastfields Av 100 DA84
Coptefield Dr, Belv. DA17 106 EX76
Coptfold Rd, Brwd. CM14 54 FW47
Copthall Av, EC2 197 L8
Copthall Bldgs, EC2 197 K8
Copthall Cl, EC2 197 K8
Gerrards Cross (Chal.St.P.)
SL9 37 AZ52
Copthall Cor, Ger.Cr. (Chal.St.P.)
SL9 36 AY52
Copthall Ct, EC2 197 K8
Copthall Dr, NW7 43 CU52
Copthall Gdns, NW7 43 CU52
Twickenham TW1 117 CF88
COPTHALL GREEN, Wal.Abb.
EN9 16 EK33
Copthall La, Ger.Cr. (Chal.St.P.)
SL9 36 AY52
Copthall Rd E, Uxb. UB10 58 BN61
Copthall Rd W, Uxb. UB10 58 BN61
Copthall Way, Add. (New Haw)
KT15 151 BF110
Copt Hill La, Tad. KT20 173 CY120
Copthorne Av, SW12 121 DK87
Bromley BR2 145 EM103
Ilford IG6 49 EP51
Copthorne Chase, Ashf.
TW15 off Ford Rd 114 BM91
Copthorne Cl, Rick. (Crox.Grn)
WD3 22 BM43
Shepperton TW17 135 BQ100
Copthorne Gdns, Horn. RM11 72 FN57
Copthorne Ms, Hayes UB3 95 BS77
Copthorne Ri, S.Croy. CR2 160 DR113
Copthorne Rd, Lthd. KT22 171 CH120
Rickmansworth (Crox.Grn)
WD3 22 BM44
Coptic St, WC1 195 P7
Copwood Cl, N12 44 DD49
Coral Apts, E16
off Western Gateway 86 EG73
Coral Cl, Rom. RM6 70 EW56
Coraline Cl, Sthl. UB1 78 BZ69
Coralline Wk, SE2 106 EW75
Coral Row, SW11
off Gartons Way 100 DC83
Coral St, SE1 200 E5
Coram Grn, Brwd. (Hutt.)
CM13 55 GD44
Coram St, WC1 195 P5
Coran Cl, N9 47 DX45
Corban Rd, Houns. TW3 96 CA83
Corbar Cl, Barn. EN4 28 DD38
Corbden Cl, SE15 102 DT81
Corbet Cl, Wall. SM6 140 DG102
Corbet Ct, EC3 197 L9
Corbet Pl, E1 197 P6
Corbet Rd, Epsom KT17 156 CS110
Corbets Av, Upmin. RM14 72 FP64
CORBETS TEY, Upmin. RM14 90 FQ65
Corbets Tey Rd, Upmin.
RM14 72 FP63
Corbett Cl, Croy. CR0 161 ED112
Corbett Gro, N22 45 DL52
Corbett Ho, Wat. WD19 40 BW48
Corbett Rd, E11 68 EJ58
E17 67 EC55
Corbetts La, SE16 202 F9
Corbetts Pas, SE16 202 F9
Corbicum, E11 68 EE59
Corbidge Ct, SE8
off Glaisher St 103 EB79
Corbiere Ct, SW19
off Thornton Rd 119 CX93
Corbiere Ho, N1 84 DS67
Corbin Ho, E3
off Bromley High St 85 EB69
Corbins La, Har. HA2 60 CB62
Corbridge Cres, E2 84 DV68
Corbridge Ms, Rom. RM1 71 FF57
Corby Cl, Egh. (Eng.Grn)
TW20 112 AW93
St. Albans AL2 8 CA25
Corby Cres, Enf. EN2 29 DL42
Corby Dr, Egh. (Eng.Grn)
TW20 112 AV93
Corbylands Rd, Sid. DA15 125 ES87
Corbyn St, N4 65 DL60
Corby Rd, NW10 80 CR68
Corby Way, E3 off Knapp Rd 85 EA70
Corcorans, Brwd. (Pilg.Hat.)
CM15 54 FV44
Cordelia Cl, SE24 101 DP84
Cordelia Gdns, Stai. TW19 114 BL87
Cordelia Rd, Stai. TW19 114 BL87
Cordelia St, E14 85 EB72
Cordell Cl, Wal.Cr. (Chsht)
EN8 15 DY28
Cordell Ho, N15
off Newton Rd 66 DT57
Corderoy Pl, Cher. KT16 133 BE100
Cordingley Rd, Ruis. HA4 59 BR61
Cording St, E14
off Chrisp St 85 EB71
Cordons Cl, Ger.Cr. (Chal.St.P.)
SL9 36 AX53
Cordrey Gdns, Couls. CR5 175 DL115
Cordwainers Wk, E13
off Richmond St 86 EG68
Cord Way, E14 204 A6
Cordwell Rd, SE13 124 EE85
Corefield Cl, N11
off Benfleet Way 44 DG47
Corelli Rd, SE3 104 EL82
Corfe Av, Har. HA2 60 CA63
Corfe Cl, Ashtd. KT21 171 CJ118
Borehamwood WD6 26 CR41
Hayes UB4 78 BW72
Corfe Ho, SW8 off Dorset Rd 101 DM80
Corfe Twr, W3 98 CP75
Corfield Rd, N21 29 DM43
Corfield St, E2 84 DV69
Corfton Rd, W5 80 CL72
Coriander Av, E14 85 ED72
Cories Cl, Dag. RM8 70 EX61
Corinium Cl, Wem. HA9 62 CM63
Corinium Ind Est, Amer. HP6 20 AT38
Corinne Rd, N19 65 DJ63
Corinthian Manorway, Erith
DA8 107 FD77
Corinthian Rd, Erith DA8 107 FD77
Corinthian Way, Stai. (Stanw.)
TW19 off Clare Rd 114 BK87
Corker Wk, N7 65 DM61
Corkran Rd, Surb. KT6 137 CK101
Corkscrew Hill, W.Wick. BR4 143 ED103
Cork Sq, E1 202 D2
Cork St, W1 199 K1
Cork St Ms, W1 199 K1
Cork Tree Way, E4 47 DY50
Corlett St, NW1 194 B6
Cormongers La, Red. (Nutfld)
RH1 185 DK131
Cormont Rd, SE5 101 DP81
Cormorant Cl, E17 47 DX53
Cormorant Ho, Enf. EN3
off Alma Rd 31 DX43
Cormorant Pl, Sutt. SM1
off Sandpiper Rd 157 CZ106
Cormorant Rd, E7 68 EF63
Cormorant Wk, Horn. RM12
off Heron Flight Av 89 FH65
Cornbury Rd, Edg. HA8 41 CK52
Cornelia Dr, Hayes UB4 78 BW70
Cornelia Pl, Erith DA8
off Queen St 107 FE79
Cornelia St, N7 83 DM65
Cornell Cl, Sid. DA14 126 EY93
Cornell Way, Rom. RM5 50 FA50
Corner, The, W.Byf. KT14 152 BG113
Corner Fm Cl, Tad. KT20 173 CW122
Corner Grn, SE3 104 EG83
Corner Ho St, WC2 199 P2
Corner Mead, NW9 43 CT52
Cornerside, Ashf. TW15 115 BQ94
Corney Reach Way, W4 98 CS80
Corney Rd, W4 98 CS79
Cornfield Cl, Uxb. UB8
off The Greenway 76 BK68
Cornfield Rd, Bushey WD23 24 CB42
Cornflower La, Croy. CR0 143 DX102
Cornflower Ter, SE22 122 DV86
Cornflower Way, Rom. RM3 52 FL53
Cornford Cl, Brom. BR2 144 EG99
Cornford Gro, SW12 121 DH89
Cornhill, EC3 197 L9
Cornhill Cl, Add. KT15 134 BH103
Cornhill Dr, Enf. EN3
off Ordnance Rd 31 DY37
Cornish Ct, N9 46 DV45
Cornish Gro, SE20 122 DV94
Cornish Ho, SE17 off Otto St 101 DP79
Brentford TW8
off Green Dragon La 98 CM78
Cornmill, Wal.Abb. EN9 15 EB33
Corn Mill Dr, Orp. BR6 145 ET101
Cornmill La, SE13 103 EB83
Cornmill Ms, Wal.Abb. EN9
off Highbridge St 15 EB33
Cornmow Dr, NW10 63 CT64
Cornshaw Rd, Dag. RM8 70 EX60
Cornsland, Brwd. CM14 54 FX48
Cornsland Cl, Upmin. RM14 72 FQ55
Cornsland Ct, Brwd. CM14 54 FW48
Cornthwaite Rd, E5 66 DW62
Cornwall Av, E2 84 DW69
N3 44 DA52
N22 45 DL53
Esher (Clay.) KT10
off The Causeway 155 CF108
Southall UB1 78 BZ71
Welling DA16 105 ES83
West Byfleet (Byfleet)
KT14 152 BM114
Cornwall Cl, Bark. IG11 87 ET65
Cornwall Cl, Horn. RM11 72 FN56
Waltham Cross EN8 15 DY33
Cornwall Cres, W11 81 CY73
Cornwall Dr, Orp. BR5 126 EW94
Cornwall Gdns, NW10 81 CV65
SW7 100 DB76
Cornwall Gdns Wk, SW7
off Cornwall Gdns 100 DB76
Cornwall Gate, Purf. RM19
off Fanns Ri 108 FN77
Cornwall Gro, W4 98 CS78
Cornwallis Av, N9 46 DV47
SE9 125 ER89
Cornwallis Cl, Cat. CR3 176 DQ122
Erith DA8 107 FF79
Cornwallis Ct, SW8
off Hartington Rd 101 DL81
Cornwallis Gro, N9 46 DV47
Cornwallis Rd, E17 67 DX56
N9 46 DV47
N19 65 DL61
SE18 105 EQ76
Dagenham RM9 70 EX63
Cornwallis Sq, N19 65 DL61
Cornwallis Wk, SE9 105 EM83
Cornwall Ms S, SW7 100 DC76
Cornwall Ms W, SW7
off Cornwall Gdns 100 DB76
Cornwall Rd, N4 65 DN59
N15 66 DR57
N18 off Fairfield Rd 46 DU50
SE1 200 D2
Brentwood (Pilg.Hat.)
CM15 54 FV43
Croydon CR0 141 DP103
Dartford DA1 108 FM83
Esher (Clay.) KT10 155 CG108
Harrow HA1 60 CC58
Pinner HA5 40 BZ52
Ruislip HA4 59 BT62
Sutton SM2 157 CZ108
Twickenham TW1 117 CG88
Uxbridge UB8 76 BK65
Windsor SL4 112 AU86
Cornwall Sq, SE11 200 F10
Cornwall St, E1
off Watney St 84 DV73
Cornwall Ter, NW1 194 E5
Cornwall Ter Ms, NW1 194 E5
Cornwall Way, Stai. TW18 113 BE93
Corn Way, E11 67 ED62
Cornwell Av, Grav. DA12 131 GJ90
Cornwood Cl, N2 64 DD57
Cornwood Dr, E1 84 DW72
Cornworthy Rd, Dag. RM8 70 EW64
Corona Rd, SE12 124 EG87
Coronation Av, N16
off Victorian Rd 66 DT62
Slough (Geo.Grn) SL3 74 AY72
Windsor SL4 92 AT81
Coronation Cl, Bex. DA5 126 EX86
Ilford IG6 69 EQ56
Coronation Dr, Horn. RM12 71 FH63
Coronation Hill, Epp. CM16 17 ET30
Coronation Rd, E13 86 EJ69
NW10 80 CN70
Hayes UB3 95 BT77
Coronation Wk, Twick. TW2 116 BZ88
Coronet St, N1 197 M3
Corporation Av, Houns. TW4 96 BY84
Corporation Row, EC1 196 E4
Corporation St, E15 86 EE68
N7 65 DL64
Corrance Rd, SW2 101 DL84
Corran Way, S.Ock. RM15 91 FV73
Corri Av, N14 45 DK49
Corrib Dr, Sutt. SM1 158 DE106
Corrie Gdns, Vir.W. GU25 132 AW101
Corrie Rd, Add. KT15 152 BK105
Woking GU22 167 BC120
Corrigan Av, Couls. CR5 158 DG114
Corrigan Cl, NW4 63 CW55
Corringham Ct, NW11
off Corringham Rd 64 DA59
Corringham Rd, NW11 64 DA59
Wembley HA9 62 CN61
Corringway, NW11 64 DB59
W5 80 CN70
Corris Grn, NW9
off Snowdon Dr 62 CS58
Corry Dr, SW9 101 DP84
Corsair Cl, Stai. TW19 114 BK87
Corsair Rd, Stai. TW19 114 BL87
Corscombe Cl, Kings.T. KT2 118 CQ92
Corsehill St, SW16 121 DJ93
Corsham St, N1 197 L3
Corsica St, N5 83 DP65
Cortayne Rd, SW6 99 CZ82
Cortina Dr, Dag. RM9 89 FC69
Cortis Rd, SW15 119 CV86
Cortis Ter, SW15 119 CV86
Cortland Cl, Dart. DA1 127 FE86
Corunna Rd, SW8 101 DJ81
Corunna Ter, SW8 101 DJ81
Corve La, S.Ock. RM15 91 FV73
Corvette Sq, SE10
off Feathers Pl 103 ED79
Corwell Gdns, Uxb. UB8 77 BQ72
Corwell La, Uxb. UB8 77 BQ72
Cory Dr, Brwd. (Hutt.) CM13 55 GB45
Coryton Path, W9
off Ashmore Rd 81 CZ70
Cosbycote Av, SE24 122 DQ85
Cosdach Av, Wall. SM6 159 DK108
Cosedge Cres, Croy. CR0 159 DN106
Cosgrove Cl, N21 46 DQ47
Hayes UB4
off Kingsash Dr 78 BY70
Cosmo Pl, WC1 196 A6
Cosmur Cl, W12 99 CT76
Cossall Wk, SE15 102 DV81
Cossar Ms, SW2
off Tulse Hill 121 DN86
Cosser St, SE1 200 D6
Costa St, SE15 102 DU82
Costead Manor Rd, Brwd.
CM14 54 FV46
Costell's Meadow, West.
TN16 189 ER126
Costons Av, Grnf. UB6 79 CD69
Costons La, Grnf. UB6 79 CD69
Coston Wk, SE4
off Hainford Cl 103 DX84
Cosway St, NW1 194 C6
Cotall St, E14 85 EA72
Coteford Cl, Loug. IG10 33 EP40
Pinner HA5 59 BU57
Coteford St, SW17 120 DF91
Cotelands, Croy. CR0 142 DS104
Cotesbach Rd, E5 66 DW62
Cotesmore Gdns, Dag. RM8 70 EW63
Cotford Rd, Th.Hth. CR7 142 DQ98
Cotham St, SE17 201 J9
Cotherstone, Epsom KT19 156 CR110
Cotherstone Rd, SW2 121 DM88
Cotlandswick, St.Alb.
(Lon.Col.) AL2 9 CJ26
Cotleigh Av, Bex. DA5 126 EX89
Cotleigh Rd, NW6 82 DA66
Romford RM7 71 FD58
Cotman Cl, NW11 64 DC58
SW15 119 CX86
Cotmandene Cres, Orp. BR5 146 EU96
Cotman Gdns, Edg. HA8 42 CN54
Cotman Ms, Dag. RM8
off Highgrove Rd 70 EW64
Cotmans Cl, Hayes UB3 77 BU74
Coton Rd, Well. DA16 106 EU83
Cotsford Av, N.Mal. KT3 138 CQ99
Cotswold Av, Bushey WD23 24 CC44
Cotswold Cl, Bexh. DA7 107 FE82
Esher KT10 137 CF104
Kingston upon Thames
KT2 118 CP93
Staines TW18 114 BG92
Uxbridge UB8 76 BJ67
Cotswold Ct, EC1 197 H4
N11 44 DG49
Cotswold Gdns, E6 86 EK69
NW2 63 CX61
Brentwood (Hutt.) CM13 55 GE45
Ilford IG2 69 ER59
Cotswold Gate, NW2
off Cotswold Gdns 63 CY60
Cotswold Grn, Enf. EN2
off Cotswold Way 29 DM42
Cotswold Ms, SW11
off Battersea High St 100 DD81
Cotswold Ri, Orp. BR6 145 ET100
Cotswold Rd, Grav. (Nthflt)
DA11 130 GE90
Hampton TW12 116 CA93
Romford RM3 52 FM54
Sutton SM2 158 DB110
Cotswold St, SE27
off Norwood High St 121 DP91
Cotswold Way, Enf. EN2 29 DM42
Worcester Park KT4 139 CW103
Cottage Av, Brom. BR2 144 EL102
Cottage Cl, Cher. (Ott.) KT16 151 BC107
Harrow HA2 61 CE61
Rickmansworth (Crox.Grn)
WD3 22 BM44
Ruislip HA4 59 BR60
Watford WD17 23 BT40
Cottage Fm Way, Egh. TW20
off Green Rd 133 BC97
Cottage Fld Cl, Sid. DA14 126 EW88
Cottage Gdns, Wal.Cr. EN8 14 DW29
Cottage Grn, SE5 102 DR80
Cottage Gro, SW9 101 DL83
Surbiton KT6 137 CK100
Cottage Pl, SW3 198 B6
Cottage Rd, N7
off Caledonian Rd 83 DM65
Epsom KT19 156 CR108
Cottage St, E14 85 EB73
Cottage Wk, N16
off Smalley Cl 66 DT62
Cottenham Dr, NW9 63 CT55
SW20 119 CV94
Cottenham Par, SW20
off Durham Rd 139 CV96
COTTENHAM PARK, SW20 139 CV95
Cottenham Pk Rd, SW20 119 CV94
Cottenham Pl, SW20 119 CV94
Cottenham Rd, E17 67 DZ56
Cotterill Rd, Surb. KT6 138 CL103
Cottesbrooke Cl, Slou.
(Colnbr.) SL3 93 BD81
Cottesbrook St, SE14
off Nynehead St 103 DY80
Cottesloe Ms, SE1 200 E6
Cottesmore Av, Ilf. IG5 49 EN54
Cottesmore Gdns, W8 100 DB76
Cottimore Av, Walt. KT12 135 BV102
Cottimore Cres, Walt. KT12 135 BV101
Cottimore La, Walt. KT12 136 BW102
Cottimore Ter, Walt. KT12 135 BV101
Cottingham Chase, Ruis. HA4 59 BU62
Cottingham Rd, SE20 123 DX94
SW8 101 DM80
Cottington Rd, Felt. TW13 116 BX91
Cottington St, SE11 200 E10
Cottle Way, SE16 202 E5
Cotton Av, W3 80 CR72
Cotton Cl, E11 68 EE61
Dagenham RM9
off Flamstead Rd 88 EW66
Cottongrass Cl, Croy. CR0
off Cornflower La 143 DX102
Cotton Hill, Brom. BR1 123 ED91
Cotton La, Dart. DA2 128 FQ86
Greenhithe DA9 128 FQ85
Cotton Rd, Pot.B. EN6 12 DC31
Cotton Row, SW11 100 DC83
Cottons App, Rom. RM7 71 FD57
Cottons Ct, Rom. RM7 71 FD57
Cottons Gdns, E2 197 N2
Cottons La, SE1 201 L2
Cotton St, E14 85 EC73
Cottrell Ct, SE10
off Greenroof Way 104 EF77
Cottrill Gdns, E8
off Marcon Pl 84 DV65
Cotts Cl, W7
off Westcott Cres 79 CF71
Couchmore Av, Esher KT10 137 CE103
Ilford IG5 49 EM54
Coulgate St, SE4 103 DY83
COULSDON, CR5 175 DJ116
Coulsdon Common, Cat.
CR3 176 DQ121
Coulsdon Ct Rd, Couls. CR5 175 DM116
Coulsdon La, Couls. (Chipstead)
CR5 174 DF119

★ Place of interest ⇌ Railway station ⊖ London Underground station DLR Docklands Light Railway station Tra Tramlink station H Hospital Riv Pedestrian ferry landing stage

Coulsdon N Ind Est, Couls. CR5 175 DK116
Coulsdon Pl, Cat. CR3 176 DR122
Coulsdon Ri, Couls. CR5 175 DL117
Coulsdon Rd, Cat. CR3 176 DQ122
Coulsdon CR5 175 DM115
⇌ Coulsdon South 175 DK116
Coulson Cl, Dag. RM8 70 EW59
Coulson St, SW3 198 D10
Coulter Cl, Hayes UB4
off Berrydale Rd 78 BY70
Potters Bar (Cuffley) EN6 13 DK27
Coulter Rd, W6 99 CV76
Coulton Av, Grav. (Nthflt) DA11 130 GE87
Council Av, Grav. (Nthflt) DA11 130 GC86
Council Cotts, Wok. (Wisley) GU23 off Wisley La 168 BK115
Councillor St, SE5 102 DQ80
Counter Ct, SE1
off Borough High St 84 DR74
Counter St, SE1 201 M3
Countess Cl, Uxb. (Hare.) UB9 38 BJ54
Countess Rd, NW5 65 DJ64
Countisbury Av, Enf. EN1 46 DT45
Countisbury Gdns, Add. KT15
off Addlestone Pk 152 BH106
Country Way, Felt. TW13 115 BV94
Sunbury-on-Thames TW16 115 BV94
County Gate, SE9 125 EQ90
Barnet EN5 28 DB44
County Gro, SE5 102 DQ81
★ County Hall, SE1 200 B4
County Rd, E6 87 EP71
Thornton Heath CR7 141 DP96
County St, SE1 201 J7
Coupland Pl, SE18 105 EQ78
Courage Cl, Horn. RM11 72 FJ58
Courage Wk, Brwd. (Hutt.) CM13 55 GD44
Courcy Rd, N8 65 DN55
Courier Rd, Dag. RM9 89 FC70
Courland Gro, SW8 101 DK81
Courland Gro Hall, SW8 101 DK82
Courland Rd, Add. KT15 134 BH104
Courland St, SW8 101 DK81
Course, The, SE9 125 EN90
Coursers Rd, St.Alb. (Coln.Hth) AL4 10 CN27
Court, The, Ruis. HA4 60 BY63
Warlingham CR6 177 DY118
Courtauld Cl, SE28 88 EU74
★ Courtauld Inst of Art, WC2 196 B10
Courtauld Rd, N19 65 DK60
Courtaulds, Kings L. (Chipper.) WD4 6 BH30
Court Av, Belv. DA17 106 EZ78
Coulsdon CR5 175 DN118
Romford RM3 52 FN52
Court Bushes Rd, Whyt. CR3 176 DU120
Court Cl, Har. HA3 62 CL55
Twickenham TW2 116 CB90
Wallington SM6 159 DK108
Court Cl Av, Twick. TW2 116 CB90
Court Cres, Chess. KT9 155 CK106
Swanley BR8 147 FE98
Court Downs Rd, Beck. BR3 143 EB96
★ Court Dress Collection, Kensington Palace, W8 100 DB75
Court Dr, Croy. CR0 159 DM105
Stanmore HA7 42 CL49
Sutton SM1 158 DE105
Uxbridge UB10 76 BM67
Courtenay Av, N6 64 DE58
Harrow HA3 40 CC53
Sutton SM2 158 DA109
Courtenay Dr, Beck. BR3 143 ED96
Grays (Chaff.Hun.) RM16
off Clifford Rd 110 FZ76
Courtenay Gdns, Har. HA3 40 CC54
Upminster RM14 72 FQ60
Courtenay Ms, E17
off Cranbrook Ms 67 DY57
Courtenay Pl, E17 67 DY57
Courtenay Rd, E11 68 EF62
E17 67 DX56
SE20 123 DX94
Wembley HA9 61 CK62
Woking GU21 167 BA116
Worcester Park KT4 139 CW104
Courtenay Sq, SE11
off Courtenay St 101 DN78
Courtenay St, SE11 200 D10
Courtens Ms, Stan. HA7 41 CJ52
Court Fm Av, Epsom KT19 156 CR106
Court Fm Rd, SE9 124 EK89
Northolt UB5 78 CA66
Warlingham CR6 176 DU118
Courtfield, W5
off Castlebar Hill 79 CJ71
Courtfield Av, Har. HA1 61 CF57
Courtfield Cres, Har. HA1 61 CF57
Courtfield Gdns, SW5 100 DB77
W13 79 CG72
Ruislip HA4 59 BT61
Uxbridge (Denh.) UB9 58 BG62
Courtfield Ms, SW5
off Courtfield Gdns 100 DC77
Courtfield Ri, W.Wick. BR4 143 ED104
Courtfield Rd, SW7 100 DB77
Ashford TW15 115 BP93
Court Gdns, N7 83 DN65
Courtgate Cl, NW7 43 CT51
Court Grn Hts, Wok. GU22 166 AW120
Court Haw, Bans. SM7 174 DE115
Court Hill, Couls. (Chipstead) CR5 174 DE118
South Croydon CR2 160 DS112
Courthill Rd, SE13 103 EC84
Courthope Rd, NW3 64 DF63
SW19 119 CY92
Greenford UB6 79 CD68
Courthope Vil, SW19 119 CY94
Court Ho Gdns, N3 44 DA51
Courthouse Rd, N12 44 DB51
Courtland Av, E4 48 EF47
NW7 42 CR48
SW16 121 DM94
Ilford IG1 69 EM61
Courtland Cl, Wdf.Grn. IG8 48 EJ53
Courtland Dr, Chig. IG7 49 EP48
Courtland Gro, SE28 88 EX73
Courtland Rd, E6
off Harrow Rd 86 EL67
Courtlands, Rich. TW10 98 CN84
Courtlands Av, SE12 124 EH85
Bromley BR2 144 EF102
Esher KT10 154 BZ107
Hampton TW12 116 BZ93
Richmond TW9 98 CP82
Slough SL3 92 AX77
Courtlands Cl, Ruis. HA4 59 BT59
South Croydon CR2 160 DT110
Watford WD24 23 BS35
Courtlands Cres, Bans. SM7 174 DA116
Courtlands Dr, Epsom KT19 156 CS107
Watford WD17, WD24 23 BS37
Courtlands Rd, Surb. KT5 138 CN101
Court La, SE21 122 DS86
Epsom KT19 156 CQ113
Iver SL0 76 BG74
Court La Gdns, SE21 122 DS87
Courtleas, Cob. KT11 154 CA113
Courtleet Dr, Erith DA8 107 FB81
Courtleigh Av, Barn. EN4 28 DD38
Courtleigh Gdns, NW11 63 CY56
Courtman Rd, N17 46 DQ52
Court Mead, Nthlt. UB5 78 BZ69
Courtmead Cl, SE24 122 DQ86
Courtnell St, W2 82 DA72
Courtney Cl, SE19 122 DS93
Courtney Cres, Cars. SM5 158 DF108
Courtney Pl, Cob. KT11 154 BZ112
Croydon CR0 141 DN104
Courtney Rd, N7
off Bryantwood Rd 65 DN64
SW19 120 DE94
Croydon CR0 141 DN104
Grays RM16 111 GJ75
Hounslow (Hthrw Air.) TW6 94 BN83
Courtney Way, Houns. (Hthrw Air.) TW6 94 BN83
Court Par, Wem. HA0 61 CH62
Courtrai Rd, SE23 123 DY86
Court Rd, SE9 124 EL89
SE25 142 DT96
Banstead SM7 174 DA116
Caterham CR3 176 DR123
Dartford (Lane End) DA2 129 FS92
Godstone RH9 186 DW131
Orpington BR6 146 EV101
Southall UB2 96 BZ77
Uxbridge UB10 59 BP64
Courtside, N8 65 DK58
Court St, E1
off Whitechapel Rd 84 DV71
Bromley BR1 144 EG96
Court Way, NW9 62 CS56
W3 80 CQ71
Ilford IG6 69 EQ55
Romford RM3 52 FL54
Twickenham TW2 117 CF87
Courtway, Wdf.Grn. IG8 48 EJ50
Courtway, The, Wat. WD19 40 BY47
Court Wd Dr, Sev. TN13 190 FG124
Court Wd Gro, Croy. CR0 161 DZ111
Court Wd La, Croy. CR0 161 DZ111
Court Yd, SE9 124 EL86
Courtyard, The, N1 83 DM66
Keston BR2 162 EL107
Courtyards, The, Slou. SL3
off Waterside Dr 93 BA75
Cousin La, EC4 201 K1
Cousins Cl, West Dr. UB7 76 BL73
Couthurst Rd, SE3 104 EH79
Coutts Av, Chess. KT9 156 CL106
Coutts Cres, NW5 64 DG62
Coval Gdns, SW14 98 CP84
Coval La, SW14 98 CP84
Coval Pas, SW14 off Coval Rd 98 CQ84
Coval Rd, SW14 98 CP84
Coveham Cres, Cob. KT11 153 BU113
Covelees Wall, E6 87 EN72
Covell Ct, SE8
off Reginald Sq 103 EA80
Covenbrook, Brwd. CM13 55 GB48
★ Covent Garden, WC2 196 A10
⊖ Covent Garden 195 P10
Coventry Cl, E6
off Harper Rd 87 EM72
NW6 off Kilburn High Rd 82 DA67
Coventry Rd, E1 84 DV70
E2 84 DV70
SE25 142 DU98
Ilford IG1 69 EP60
Coventry St, W1 199 M1
Coverack Cl, N14 29 DJ44
Croydon CR0 143 DY101
Coverdale Cl, Stan. HA7 41 CH50
Coverdale Ct, Enf. EN3
off Raynton Rd 31 DY37
Coverdale Gdns, Croy. CR0
off Park Hill Ri 142 DT104
Coverdale Rd, N11 44 DG51
NW2 81 CX66
W12 81 CV74
Coverdales, The, Bark. IG11 87 EQ68
Coverley Cl, E1 84 DU71
Brentwood (Gt Warley) CM13
off Wilmot Grn 53 FW51
Covert, The, Nthwd. HA6 39 BQ53
Orpington BR6 145 ES100
Coverton Rd, SW17 120 DE92
Covert Rd, Ilf. IG6 49 ET51
Coverts, The, Brwd. (Hutt.) CM13 55 GA46
Coverts Rd, Esher (Clay.) KT10 155 CF109
Covert Way, Barn. EN4 28 DC40
Covesfield, Grav. DA11 131 GF87
Covet Wd Cl, Orp. BR5 145 ET100
Covey Cl, SW19 140 DB96
Covington Gdns, SW16 121 DP94
Covington Way, SW16 121 DM93
Cowan Cl, E6 off Oliver Gdns 86 EL71
Cowbridge La, Bark. IG11 87 EP66
Cowbridge Rd, Har. HA3 62 CM56
Cowcross St, EC1 196 F6
Cowdenbeath Path, N1 83 DM67
Cowden Rd, Orp. BR6 145 ET101
Cowden St, SE6 123 EA91
Cowdray Rd, Uxb. UB10 77 BQ67
Cowdray Way, Horn. RM12 71 FF63
Cowdrey Cl, Enf. EN1 30 DS40
Cowdrey Ct, Dart. DA1 127 FH87
Cowdrey Rd, SW19 120 DB92
Cowdry Rd, E9
off East Cross Route 85 DZ65
Cowen Av, Har. HA2 60 CC61
Cowgate Rd, Grnf. UB6 79 CD68
Cowick Rd, SW17 120 DF91
Cowings Mead, Nthlt. UB5 78 BY66
Cowland Av, Enf. EN3 30 DW42
Cow La, Grnf. UB6 79 CD68
Watford WD25 24 BW36
Cow Leaze, E6 87 EN72
Cowleaze Rd, Kings.T. KT2 138 CL95
Cowles, Wal.Cr. (Chsht) EN7 14 DT27
COWLEY, Uxb. UB8 76 BJ70
Cowley Av, Cher. KT16 133 BF101
Greenhithe DA9 129 FT85
Cowley Business Pk, Uxb. UB8 76 BJ69
Cowley Cl, S.Croy. CR2 160 DW109
Cowley Cres, Uxb. UB8 76 BJ71
Walton-on-Thames KT12 154 BW105
Cowley Hill, Borwd. WD6 26 CP37
Cowley La, E11 off West St 68 EE62
Chertsey KT16 133 BF101
Cowley Mill Rd, Uxb. UB8 76 BH68
Cowley Pl, NW4 63 CW57
Cowley Rd, E11 68 EH57
SW9 101 DN81
SW14 98 CS83
W3 81 CT74
Ilford IG1 69 EM59
Romford RM3 51 FH52
Uxbridge UB8 76 BJ68
Cowley St, SW1 199 P6
Cowling Cl, W11
off Wilsham St 81 CY74
Cowper Av, E6 86 EL66
Sutton SM1 158 DD105
Tilbury RM18 111 GH81
Cowper Cl, Brom. BR2 144 EK98
Chertsey KT16 133 BF100
Welling DA16 126 EU85
Cowper Ct, Wat. WD24 23 BU37
Cowper Gdns, N14 29 DJ44
Wallington SM6 159 DJ107
Cowper Rd, N14 45 DH46
N16 66 DS64
N18 46 DU50
SW19 120 DC93
W3 80 CR74
W7 79 CF73
Belvedere DA17 106 FA77
Bromley BR2 144 EK98
Kingston upon Thames KT2 118 CM92
Rainham RM13 89 FG70
Cowpers Ct, EC3
off Birchin La 84 DR72
Cowper St, EC2 197 L4
Cowper Ter, W10
off St. Marks Rd 81 CX71
Cowslip Cl, Uxb. UB10 76 BL66
Cowslip La, Wok. GU21 166 AV115
Cowslip Rd, E18 48 EH54
Cowthorpe Rd, SW8 101 DK81
Cox Cl, Rad. (Shenley) WD7 10 CM32
Coxdean, Epsom KT18 173 CW119
Coxe Pl, Har. (Wealds.) HA3 61 CG56
Cox La, Chess. KT9 156 CM105
Epsom KT19 156 CP106
Coxley Ri, Pur. CR8 160 DQ113
Coxmount Rd, SE7 104 EK78
Coxson Way, SE1 201 P5
Cox's Wk, SE21 122 DU88
Coxwell Rd, SE18 105 ER78
SE19 122 DS94
Coxwold Path, Chess. KT9
off Garrison La 156 CL108
Crabbs Cft Cl, Orp. BR6
off Ladycroft Way 163 EQ106
Crab Hill, Beck. BR3 123 ED94
Crab La, Wat. (Ald.) WD25 24 CB35
Crabtree Av, Rom. RM6 70 EX56
Wembley HA0 80 CL68
Crabtree Cl, E2 84 DT68
Bushey WD23 24 CB43
Crabtree Cor, Egh. TW20 133 BB95
Crabtree Dr, Lthd. KT22 171 CJ124
Crabtree Hill, Rom. (Abridge) RM4 50 EZ45
Crabtree La, SW6 99 CX80
Crabtree Manorway Ind Est, Belv. DA17 107 FB76
Crabtree Manorway N, Belv. DA17 107 FC75
Crabtree Manorway S, Belv. DA17 107 FC76
Crabtree Rd, Egh. TW20 133 BC96
Cracknell Cl, Enf. EN1 30 DV37
Craddock Rd, Enf. EN1 30 DT41
Craddocks Av, Ashtd. KT21 172 CL117
Craddocks Par, Ashtd. KT21 172 CL117
Craddock St, NW5
off Prince of Wales Rd 82 DG65
Cradley Rd, SE9 125 ER88
Cragg Av, Rad. WD7 25 CF36
Craigdale Rd, Horn. RM11 71 FF58
Craig Dr, Uxb. UB8 77 BP72
Craigen Av, Croy. CR0 142 DV102
Craigerne Rd, SE3 104 EH80
Craig Gdns, E18 48 EF54
Craigholm, SE18 105 EN82
Craigmore Twr, Wok. GU22
off Guildford Rd 166 AY119
Craig Mt, Rad. WD7 25 CH35
Craigmuir Pk, Wem. HA0 80 CM67
Craignair Rd, SW2 121 DN87
Craignish Av, SW16 141 DM96
Craig Pk Rd, N18 46 DV50
Craig Rd, Rich. TW10 117 CJ91
Craigs Ct, SW1 199 P2
Craigs Wk, Wal.Cr. (Chsht) EN8 off Davison Dr 15 DX28
Craigton Rd, SE9 105 EM84
Craigweil Av, Rad. WD7 25 CH35
Craigweil Cl, Stan. HA7 41 CK50
Craigweil Dr, Stan. HA7 41 CK50
Craigwell Av, Felt. TW13 115 BU90
Craigwell Cl, Stai. TW18 133 BE95
Craik Ct, NW6
off Carlton Vale 81 CZ68
Crail Row, SE17 201 L9
Cramer Ct, N.Mal. KT3
off Warwick Rd 138 CQ97
Cramer St, W1 194 G7
Crammerville Wk, Rain. RM13 89 FH70
Cramond Cl, W6 99 CY79
Cramond Ct, Felt. TW14 115 BS88
Crampshaw La, Ashtd. KT21 172 CM119
Crampton Rd, SE20 122 DW93
Cramptons Rd, Sev. TN14 181 FH120
Crampton St, SE17 201 H9
Cranberry Cl, Nthlt. UB5
off Parkfield Av 78 BX68
Cranberry La, E16 86 EE70
Cranborne Av, Sthl. UB2 96 CA77
Surbiton KT6 138 CN104
Cranborne Cl, Pot.B. EN6 11 CY31
Cranborne Cres, Pot.B. EN6 11 CY31
Cranborne Gdns, Upmin. RM14 72 FP61
Cranborne Ind Est, Pot.B. EN6 11 CY30
Cranborne Rd, Bark. IG11 87 ER67
Potters Bar EN6 11 CY30
Waltham Cross (Chsht) EN8 15 DX32
Cranborne Waye, Hayes UB4 78 BW73
Cranbourn All, WC2
off Cranbourn St 83 DK73
Cranbourne Av, E11 68 EH56
Cranbourne Cl, SW16 141 DL97
Walton-on-Thames KT12 154 BW107
Cranbourne Dr, Pnr. HA5 60 BX57
Cranbourne Gdns, NW11 63 CY57
Ilford IG6 69 EQ55
Cranbourne Pas, SE16 202 D5
Cranbourne Rd, E12
off High St N 68 EL64
E15 67 EC63
N10 45 DH54
Northwood HA6 59 BT55
Cranbourn St, WC2 195 N10
CRANBROOK, Ilf. IG1 69 EM60
Cranbrook Cl, Brom. BR2 144 EG100
Cranbrook Dr, Esher KT10 136 CC102
Romford RM2 71 FH56
Twickenham TW2 116 CB88
Cranbrook Ho, Erith DA8
off Boundary St 107 FF80
Cranbrook Ms, E17 67 DY57
Cranbrook Pk, N22 45 DM53
Cranbrook Ri, Ilf. IG1 69 EM59
Cranbrook Rd, SE8 103 EA81
SW19 119 CY94
W4 98 CS78
Barnet EN4 28 DD44
Bexleyheath DA7 106 EZ81
Hounslow TW4 96 BZ84
Ilford IG1, IG2, IG6 69 EN59
Thornton Heath CR7 142 DQ96
Cranbrook St, E2 off Mace St 85 DX68
Cranbury Rd, SW6 100 DB82
Crandon Wk, Dart. (S.Darenth) DA4 off Gorringe Av 149 FS96
Crane Av, W3 80 CQ73
Isleworth TW7 117 CG85
Cranebank Ms, Twick. TW1 97 CG84
Cranebrook, Twick. TW2
off Manor Rd 116 CC89
Crane Cl, Dag. RM10 88 FA65
Harrow HA2 60 CC62
Crane Ct, EC4 196 E9
Epsom KT19 156 CQ105
Cranefield Dr, Wat. WD25 8 BY32
Craneford Cl, Twick. TW2 117 CF87
Craneford Way, Twick. TW2 117 CE87
Crane Gdns, Hayes UB3 95 BT77
Crane Gro, N7 83 DN65
Crane Ho, SE15
off Talfourd Pl 102 DT81
Cranell Grn, S.Ock. RM15 91 FV74
Crane Lo Rd, Houns. TW5 95 BV79
Crane Pk Rd, Twick. TW2 116 CB89
Crane Rd, Twick. TW2 117 CE88
Cranesbill Cl, NW9
off Annesley Av 62 CR55
Cranes Dr, Surb. KT5 138 CL98
Cranes Pk, Surb. KT5 138 CL98
Cranes Pk Av, Surb. KT5 138 CL98
Cranes Pk Cres, Surb. KT5 138 CM98
Crane St, SE10 103 ED78
SE15 102 DT81
Craneswater, Hayes UB3 95 BT80
Craneswater Pk, Sthl. UB2 96 BZ78
Cranes Way, Borwd. WD6 26 CQ43
Crane Way, Twick. TW2 116 CC87
Cranfield Cl, SE27
off Dunelm Gro 122 DQ90
Cranfield Ct, Wok. GU21
off Martindale Rd 166 AU118
Cranfield Cres, Pot.B. (Cuffley) EN6 13 DL29
Cranfield Dr, NW9 42 CS52
Cranfield Rd, SE4 103 DZ83
Cranfield Rd E, Cars. SM5 158 DG109
Cranfield Rd W, Cars. SM5 158 DF109
Cranfield Row, SE1 200 E6
CRANFORD, Houns. TW5 95 BU80
Cranford Av, N13 45 DL50
Staines TW19 114 BL87
Cranford Cl, SW20 139 CV95
Purley CR8 160 DQ113
Staines TW19 114 BL87
Cranford Cotts, E1
off Cranford St 85 DX73
Cranford Dr, Hayes UB3 95 BT77
Cranford La, Hayes UB3 95 BR79
Hounslow (Hthrw Air.) TW6 95 BT83
Hounslow (Hthrw Air.N.) TW6 95 BT81
Hounslow (Heston) TW5 96 BX80
Cranford Pk Rd, Hayes UB3 95 BT77
Cranford Ri, Esher KT10 154 CC106
Cranford Rd, Dart. DA1 128 FL88
Cranford St, E1 85 DX73
Cranford Way, N8 65 DM57
CRANHAM, Upmin. RM14 73 FS59
Cranham Gdns, Upmin. RM14 73 FS60
Cranham Rd, Horn. RM11 71 FH58
Cranhurst Rd, NW2 63 CW64
Cranleigh Cl, SE20 142 DV96
Bexley DA5 127 FB86
Orpington BR6 146 EU104
South Croydon CR2 160 DU112
Waltham Cross (Chsht) EN7 14 DU28
Cranleigh Ct, Mitch. CR4
off Phipps Br Rd 140 DD97
Cranleigh Dr, Swan. BR8 147 FE98
Cranleigh Gdns, N21 29 DN43
SE25 142 DS97
Barking IG11 87 ER66
Harrow HA3 62 CL57
Kingston upon Thames KT2 118 CM93
Loughton IG10 33 EM44
South Croydon CR2 160 DU112
Southall UB1 78 BZ72
Sutton SM1 140 DB103
Cranleigh Gdns Ind Est, Sthl. UB1 off Cranleigh Gdns 78 BZ71
Cranleigh Ms, SW11 100 DE82
Cranleigh Rd, N15 66 DQ57
SW19 140 DA97
Esher KT10 136 CC102
Feltham TW13 115 BT91
Cranleigh St, NW1 195 L1
Cranley Dene Ct, N10 65 DH56
Cranley Dr, Ilf. IG2 69 EQ59
Ruislip HA4 59 BT61
Cranley Gdns, N10 65 DJ56
N13 45 DM48
SW7 100 DC78
Wallington SM6 159 DJ108
Cranley Ms, SW7 100 DC78
Cranley Par, SE9
off Beaconsfield Rd 124 EL91
Cranley Pl, SW7 100 DD77
Cranley Rd, E13 86 EH71
Ilford IG2 69 EQ58
Walton-on-Thames KT12 153 BS106
Cranmer Av, W13 97 CH76
Cranmer Cl, Mord. SM4 139 CX100
Potters Bar EN6 12 DB30
Ruislip HA4 60 BX60
Stanmore HA7 41 CJ52
Warlingham CR6 177 DY117
Weybridge KT13 152 BN108
Cranmer Ct, SW3 198 C9
SW4 101 DK83
Hampton (Hmptn H.) TW12
off Cranmer Rd 116 CB92
Cranmer Fm Cl, Mitch. CR4 140 DF98
Cranmer Gdns, Dag. RM10 71 FC63
Warlingham CR6 177 DY117
Cranmer Ho, SW11
off Surrey La 100 DE81
Cranmer Rd, E7 68 EH63
SW9 101 DN80
Croydon CR0 141 DP104
Edgware HA8 42 CP48
Hampton (Hmptn H.) TW12 116 CB92
Hayes UB3 77 BR72
Kingston upon Thames KT2 118 CL92
Mitcham CR4 140 DF98
Sevenoaks TN13 190 FE123
Cranmer Ter, SW17 120 DD92
Cranmore Av, Islw. TW7 96 CC80
Cranmore Rd, Brom. BR1 124 EE90
Chislehurst BR7 125 EM92
Cranmore Way, N10 65 DJ56
Cranston Cl, Houns. TW3 96 BY82
Uxbridge UB10 59 BR61
Cranston Est, N1 197 L1
Cranston Gdns, E4 47 EB50
Cranston Pk Av, Upmin. RM14 72 FP63
Cranston Rd, SE23 123 DY88
Cranswick Rd, SE16 202 E10
Crantock Rd, SE6 123 EB89
Cranwell Cl, E3 85 EB70
Cranwell Gro, Shep. TW17 134 BM98
Cranwich Av, N21 46 DR45
Cranwich Rd, N16 66 DR59
Cranwood St, EC1 197 K3
Cranworth Cres, E4 47 ED46
Cranworth Gdns, SW9 101 DN81
Craster Rd, SW2 121 DM87
Crathie Rd, SE12 124 EH86
Cravan Av, Felt. TW13 115 BU89
Craven Av, W5 79 CJ73
Southall UB1 78 BZ71
Craven Cl, Hayes UB4 78 BU72
Craven Gdns, SW19 120 DA92
Barking IG11 87 ES68
Ilford IG6 49 ER54
Romford (Coll.Row) RM5 50 FA50
Romford (Harold Wd) RM3 52 FQ51
Craven Hill, W2 82 DC73
Craven Hill Gdns, W2 82 DC73
Craven Hill Ms, W2 82 DC73
Craven Ms, SW11
off Taybridge Rd 100 DG83
Craven Pk, NW10 80 CS67
Craven Pk Ms, NW10 80 CS66
Craven Pk Rd, N15 66 DT58
NW10 80 CS67
Craven Pas, WC2 199 P2
Craven Rd, NW10 80 CR67
W2 82 DC73
W5 79 CJ73
Croydon CR0 142 DV102
Kingston upon Thames KT2 138 CM95
Orpington BR6 146 EX104
Craven St, WC2 199 P2
Craven Ter, W2 82 DC73
Craven Wk, N16 66 DU59
Crawford Av, Wem. HA0 61 CK64
Crawford Cl, Islw. TW7 97 CE82
Crawford Compton Cl, Horn. RM12 90 FJ65
Crawford Est, SE5 102 DQ82
Crawford Gdns, N13 45 DP48
Northolt UB5 78 BZ69
Crawford Ms, W1 194 D7
Crawford Pas, EC1 196 D5
Crawford Pl, W1 194 C8
Crawford Rd, SE5 102 DQ81
Crawfords, Swan. BR8 127 FE94
Crawford St, NW10
off Fawood Av 80 CR66

★ Place of interest ⇌ Railway station ⊖ London Underground station DLR Docklands Light Railway station Tra Tramlink station H Hospital Riv Pedestrian ferry landing stage

Crawford St, W1 194 D7
Crawley Rd, E10 67 EB60
N22 46 DQ54
Enfield EN1 46 DS45
Crawshaw Rd, Cher. (Ott.)
KT16 151 BD107
Crawshay Cl, Sev. TN13 190 FG123
Crawshay Ct, SW9
off Eythorne Rd 101 DN81
Crawthew Gro, SE22 102 DT84
Cray Av, Ashtd. KT21 172 CL116
Orpington BR5 146 EV99
Craybrooke Rd, Sid. DA14 126 EV91
Crayburne, Grav. (Sthflt)
DA13 130 FZ92
Craybury End, SE9 125 EQ89
Cray Cl, Dart. DA1 107 FG84
Craydene Rd, Erith DA8 107 FF81
Crayfield Ind Pk, Orp. BR5 146 EW96
CRAYFORD, Dart. DA1 127 FD85
⇌ **Crayford** 127 FE86
Crayford Cl, E6
off Neatscourt Rd 86 EL71
Crayford High St, Dart. DA1 107 FE84
Crayford Rd, N7 65 DK63
Dartford DA1 127 FF85
Crayford Way, Dart. DA1 127 FF85
Crayke Hill, Chess. KT9 156 CL108
Craylands, Orp. BR5 146 EW97
Craylands La, Swans. DA10 129 FX85
Craylands Sq, Swans. DA10 129 FX85
Craymill Sq, Dart. DA1 107 FF82
Crayonne Cl, Sun. TW16 135 BS95
Cray Riverway, Dart. DA1 127 FG85
Cray Rd, Belv. DA17 106 FA79
Sidcup DA14 126 EW94
Swanley BR8 147 FB100
Crayside Ind Est, Dart. DA1 107 FH84
Cray Valley Rd, Orp. BR5 146 EU99
Crealock Gro, Wdf.Grn. IG8 48 EF50
Crealock St, SW18 120 DB86
Creasey Cl, Horn. RM11 71 FH61
Creasy Cl, Abb.L. WD5 7 BT31
Creasy Est, SE1 201 M7
Crebor St, SE22 122 DU86
Credenhall Dr, Brom. BR2 145 EM102
Credenhill St, SW16 121 DJ93
Crediton Hill, NW6 64 DB64
Crediton Rd, E16
off Pacific Rd 86 EG72
NW10 81 CX67
Crediton Way, Esher (Clay.)
KT10 155 CG106
Credon Rd, E13 86 EJ68
SE16 202 E10
Credo Way, Grays RM20 109 FV79
Creechurch La, EC3 197 N9
Creechurch Pl, EC3 197 N9
Creed Ct, EC4
off Ludgate Hill 83 DP72
Creed La, EC4 196 G9
Creed's Fm Yd, Epp. CM16 17 ES32
Creek, The, Grav. DA11 130 GB85
Sunbury-on-Thames TW16 135 BU99
CREEKMOUTH, Bark. IG11 88 EU70
Creek Rd, SE8 103 EA79
SE10 103 EA79
Barking IG11 87 ET69
East Molesey KT8 137 CE98
Creekside, SE8 103 EB80
Rainham RM13 89 FE70
Creek Way, Rain. RM13 89 FE71
Creeland Gro, SE6
off Catford Hill 123 DZ88
Cree Way, Rom. RM1 51 FE52
Crefeld Cl, W6 99 CX79
Creffield Rd, W3 80 CM73
W5 80 CM73
Creighton Av, E6 86 EK68
N2 64 DE55
N10 44 DG54
Creighton Cl, W12 81 CU73
Creighton Rd, N17 46 DS52
NW6 81 CX68
W5 97 CK76
Cremer St, E2 197 P1
Cremorne Est, SW10
off Milman's St 100 DD80
Cremorne Gdns, Epsom
KT19 156 CR109
Cremorne Rd, SW10 100 DC80
Gravesend (Nthflt) DA11 131 GF87
Crescent, EC3 197 P10
Crescent, The, E17 67 DY57
N11 44 DF49
NW2 63 CV62
SW13 99 CT82
SW19 120 DA90
W3 80 CS72
Abbots Langley WD5 7 BT30
Ashford TW15 114 BM92
Barnet EN5 28 DB41
Beckenham BR3 143 EA95
Bexley DA5 126 EW87
Caterham CR3 177 EA123
Chertsey KT16
off Western Av 134 BG97
Croydon CR0 142 DR99
Egham TW20 112 AY93
Epping CM16 17 ET32
Epsom KT18 156 CN114
Gravesend (Nthflt) DA11 131 GF89
Greenhithe DA9 129 FW85
Harrow HA2 61 CD60
Hayes UB3 95 BQ80
Ilford IG2 69 EN58
Leatherhead KT22 171 CH122
Loughton IG10 32 EK43
New Malden KT3 138 CQ96
Reigate RH2 *off Chartway* 184 DB134
Rickmansworth (Crox.Grn)
WD3 23 BP44
St. Albans (Brick.Wd) AL2 8 CA30
Sevenoaks TN13 191 FK121
Shepperton TW17 135 BT101
Sidcup DA14 125 ET91
Slough SL1 92 AS75
Southall UB1 96 BZ75
Crescent, The, Surb. KT6 138 CL99
Sutton SM1 158 DD105
Sutton (Belmont) SM2 158 DA111
Upminster RM14 73 FS59
Watford WD18 24 BW42
Watford (Ald.) WD25 24 CB37
Wembley HA0 61 CH61
West Molesey KT8 136 CA98
West Wickham BR4 144 EE100
Weybridge KT13 134 BN104
Crescent Arc, SE10
off Creek Rd 103 EC79
Crescent Av, Grays RM17 110 GD78
Hornchurch RM12 71 FF61
Crescent Cotts, Sev. TN13 181 FE120
Crescent Ct, Surb. KT6 137 CK99
Crescent Dr, Brwd. (Shenf.)
CM15 54 FY46
Orpington BR5 145 EP100
Crescent E, Barn. EN4 28 DC38
Crescent Gdns, SW19 120 DA90
Ruislip HA4 59 BV58
Swanley BR8 147 FC96
Crescent Gro, SW4 101 DJ84
Mitcham CR4 140 DE98
Crescent Ho, SE13
off Ravensbourne Pl 103 EB82
Crescent La, SW4 121 DK85
Crescent Ms, N22
off Palace Gates Rd 45 DL53
Crescent Pl, SW3 198 B8
Crescent Ri, N22 45 DK53
Barnet EN4 28 DE43
Crescent Rd, E4 48 EE45
E6 86 EJ67
E10 67 EB61
E13 86 EG67
E18 48 EJ54
N3 43 CZ53
N8 65 DK59
N9 46 DU46
N11 44 DF49
N15 *off Carlingford Rd* 65 DP55
N22 45 DK53
SE18 105 EP78
SW20 139 CX95
Barnet EN4 28 DE43
Beckenham BR3 143 EB96
Brentwood CM14 54 FV49
Bromley BR1 124 EG94
Caterham CR3 176 DU124
Dagenham RM10 71 FB63
Enfield EN2 29 DP41
Erith DA8 107 FF79
Kingston upon Thames
KT2 118 CN94
Redhill (Bletch.) RH1 186 DQ133
Shepperton TW17 135 BQ99
Sidcup DA15 125 ET90
South Ockendon (Aveley)
RM15 108 FQ75
Crescent Row, EC1 197 H5
Crescent Stables, SW15
off Upper Richmond Rd 99 CY84
Crescent St, N1 83 DM66
Crescent Vw, Loug. IG10 32 EK44
Crescent Wk, S.Ock. (Aveley)
RM15 108 FQ75
Crescent Way, N12 44 DE51
SE4 103 EA83
SW16 121 DM94
Orpington BR6 163 ES106
South Ockendon (Aveley)
RM15 91 FR74
Crescent W, Barn. EN4 28 DC38
Crescent Wd Rd, SE26 122 DU90
Cresford Rd, SW6 100 DB81
Crespigny Rd, NW4 63 CV58
Cressage Cl, Sthl. UB1 78 CA70
Cressall Cl, Lthd. KT22 171 CH120
Cressall Mead, Lthd. KT22 171 CH120
Cress End, Rick. WD3
off Springwell Av 38 BG46
Cresset Rd, E9 84 DW65
Cresset St, SW4 101 DK83
Cressfield Cl, NW5 64 DG64
Cressida Rd, N19 65 DJ60
Cressingham Gro, Sutt. SM1 158 DC105
Cressingham Rd, SE13 103 EC83
Edgware HA8 42 CR51
Cressington Cl, N16
off Wordsworth Rd 66 DS64
Cress Ms, Brom. BR1 123 ED92
Cresswell Gdns, SW5 100 DC78
Cresswell Pk, SE3 104 EF83
Cresswell Pl, SW10 100 DC78
Cresswell Rd, SE25 142 DU98
Feltham TW13 116 BY91
Twickenham TW1 117 CK86
Cresswell Way, N21 45 DN45
Cressy Ct, E1 *off Cressy Pl* 84 DW71
W6 99 CV76
Cressy Pl, E1 84 DW71
Cressy Rd, NW3 64 DF64
Crest, The, N13 45 DN49
NW4 63 CW57
Surbiton KT5 138 CN99
Waltham Cross (Chsht) EN7
off Orchard Way 13 DP27
Cresta Dr, Add. (Wdhm)
KT15 151 BF110
Crest Av, Grays RM17 110 GB80
Crestbrook Av, N13 45 DP48
Crestbrook Pl, N13 45 DP48
Crest Cl, Sev. (Bad.Mt) TN14 165 FB111
Crest Dr, Enf. EN3 30 DW38
Crestfield St, WC1 196 A2
Crest Gdns, Ruis. HA4 60 BW62
Cresthill Av, Grays RM17 110 GC77
Creston Av, Wok. (Knap.)
GU21 166 AS116
Creston Way, Wor.Pk. KT4 139 CX102
Crest Rd, NW2 63 CT62
Bromley BR2 144 EF101
South Croydon CR2 160 DV108
Crest Vw, Green. DA9
off Woodland Way 109 FU84
Pinner HA5 60 BX56
Crest Vw Dr, Orp. BR5 145 EP99
Crestway, SW15 119 CV86
Crestwood Way, Houns. TW4 116 BZ85
Creswell Dr, Beck. BR3 143 EB99
Creswick Rd, W3 80 CP73
Creswick Wk, E3
off Addington Rd 85 EA69
NW11 63 CZ56
Crete Hall Rd, Grav. DA11 130 GD86
Creton St, SE18 105 EN76
Creukhorne Rd, NW10
off Church Rd 80 CS66
Crewdson Rd, SW9 101 DN80
Crewe Pl, NW10 81 CT69
Crewe's Av, Warl. CR6 176 DW116
Crewe's Cl, Warl. CR6 176 DW116
Crewe's Fm La, Warl. CR6 177 DX116
Crewe's La, Warl. CR6 177 DX116
CREWS HILL, Enf. EN2 29 DP35
⇌ **Crews Hill** 13 DM34
Crews St, E14 203 P8
Crewys Rd, NW2 63 CZ61
SE15 102 DV82
Crichton Av, Wall. SM6 159 DK106
Crichton Rd, Cars. SM5 158 DF107
Crichton St, SW8
off Westbury St 101 DJ82
Cricketers Arms Rd, Enf. EN2 30 DQ40
Cricketers Cl, N14 45 DJ45
Chessington KT9 155 CK105
Erith DA8 107 FE78
Cricketers Ct, SE11 200 F9
Cricketers Ms, SW18
off East Hill 120 DB85
Cricketers Ter, Cars. SM5
off Wrythe La 140 DE104
Cricketfield Rd, E5 66 DV63
Cricket Fld Rd, Uxb. UB8 76 BK67
Cricketfield Rd, West Dr. UB7 94 BJ77
Cricket Grn, Mitch. CR4 140 DF97
Cricket Grd Rd, Chis. BR7 145 EP95
Cricket La, Beck. BR3 123 DY93
Cricket Way, Wey. KT13 135 BS103
Cricklade Av, SW2 121 DL89
Romford RM3 52 FK51
CRICKLEWOOD, NW2 63 CX62
⇌ **Cricklewood** 63 CX63
Cricklewood Bdy, NW2 63 CW62
Cricklewood La, NW2 63 CX63
Cridland St, E15
off Church St 86 EF67
Crieff Ct, Tedd. TW11 117 CJ94
Crieff Rd, SW18 120 DC86
Criffel Av, SW2 121 DK89
Crimp Hill, Egh. (Eng.Grn)
TW20 112 AU90
Crimp Hill Rd, Wind. (Old Wind.)
SL4 112 AU88
Crimscott St, SE1 201 N7
Crimsworth Rd, SW8 101 DK81
Crinan St, N1 83 DL68
Cringle St, SW8 101 DJ80
Cripplegate St, EC2 197 H6
Cripps Grn, Hayes UB4
off Stratford Rd 77 BV70
Crispe Ho, Bark. IG11
off Dovehouse Mead 87 ER68
Crispen Rd, Felt. TW13 116 BY91
Crispian Cl, NW10 62 CS63
Crispin Cl, Ashtd. KT21 172 CM118
Croydon CR0
off Harrington Cl 141 DL103
Crispin Cres, Croy. CR0 141 DK104
Crispin Pl, E1 *off Lamb St* 84 DT71
Crispin Rd, Edg. HA8 42 CQ51
Crispin St, E1 197 P7
Crispin Way, Uxb. UB8 76 BM70
Crisp Rd, W6 99 CW78
Criss Cres, Ger.Cr. (Chal.St.P.)
SL9 36 AW54
Criss Gro, Ger.Cr. (Chal.St.P.)
SL9 36 AW54
Cristowe Rd, SW6 99 CZ82
Criterion Ms, N19 65 DK61
Crittall's Cor, Sid. DA14 126 EW94
Crockenhall Way, Grav.
(Istead Rise) DA13 130 GE94
CROCKENHILL, Swan. BR8 147 FD101
Crockenhill La, Dart. (Eyns.)
DA4 148 FJ102
Swanley BR8 147 FG101
Crockenhill Rd, Orp. BR5 146 EX99
Swanley BR8 146 EZ100
Crockerton Rd, SW17 120 DF89
Crockford Cl, Add. KT15 152 BJ105
Crockford Pk Rd, Add. KT15 152 BJ106
CROCKHAM HILL, Eden. TN8 189 EQ133
Crockham Way, SE9 125 EN91
Crocus Cl, Croy. CR0
off Cornflower La 143 DX102
Crocus Fld, Barn. EN5 27 CZ44
Croffets, Tad. KT20 173 CX121
Croft, The, E4 48 EE47
NW10 81 CT68
W5 80 CL71
Barnet EN5 27 CX42
Hounslow TW5 96 BY79
Loughton IG10 33 EN40
Pinner HA5 *off Rayners La* 60 BZ59
Ruislip HA4 60 BW63
St. Albans AL2 8 CA25
Swanley BR8 147 FC97
Wembley HA0 61 CJ64
Croft Av, W.Wick. BR4 143 EC102
Croft Cl, NW7 42 CS48
Belvedere DA17 106 EZ78
Chislehurst BR7 125 EM91
Hayes UB3 95 BQ80
Kings Langley (Chipper.)
WD4 6 BG30
Uxbridge UB10 76 BN66
Croft Ct, Borwd. WD6 26 CR41
Croftdown Rd, NW5 64 DG62
Croft End Cl, Chess. KT9
off Ashcroft Rd 138 CM104
Croft End Rd, Kings L.
(Chipper.) WD4 6 BG30
Crofters, The, Wind. SL4 112 AU86
Crofters Cl, Islw. TW7
off Ploughmans End 117 CD85
Crofters Ct, SE8
off Croft St 103 DY77
Crofters Mead, Croy. CR0 161 DZ109
Crofters Rd, Nthwd. HA6 39 BS49
Crofters Way, NW1 83 DK67
Croft Fld, Kings L. (Chipper.)
WD4 6 BG30
Croft Gdns, W7 97 CG75
Croft Gdns, Ruis. HA4 59 BT60
Croft La, Kings L. (Chipper.)
WD4 6 BG30
Croftleigh Av, Pur. CR8 175 DN116
Croft Lo Cl, Wdf.Grn. IG8 48 EH51
Croft Meadow, Kings L.
(Chipper.) WD4 6 BG30
Croft Ms, N12 44 DC48
Crofton, Ashtd. KT21 172 CL118
Crofton Av, W4 98 CR80
Bexley DA5 126 EX87
Orpington BR6 145 EQ103
Walton-on-Thames KT12 136 BW104
Crofton Cl, Cher. (Ott.) KT16 151 BC108
Croftongate Way, SE4 123 DY85
Crofton Gro, E4 47 ED49
Crofton La, Orp. BR5, BR6 145 ER101
⇌ **Crofton Park** 123 DZ85
Crofton Pk Rd, SE4 123 DZ86
Crofton Rd, E13 86 EH70
SE5 102 DS81
Grays RM16 110 GE76
Orpington BR6 145 EN104
Crofton Ter, E5
off Studley Cl 67 DY64
Richmond TW9 98 CM84
Crofton Way, Barn. EN5
off Wycherley Cres 28 DB44
Enfield EN2 29 DN40
Croft Rd, SW16 141 DN95
SW19 120 DC94
Bromley BR1 124 EG93
Caterham (Wold.) CR3 177 DZ122
Enfield EN3 31 DY39
Gerrards Cross (Chal.St.P.)
SL9 36 AY54
Sutton SM1 158 DE106
Westerham TN16 189 EP126
Crofts, The, Shep. TW17 135 BS98
Croftside, SE25 *off Sunny Bk* 142 DU97
Crofts La, N22 45 DN52
Crofts Rd, Har. HA1 61 CG58
Crofts St, E1 202 B1
Croft St, SE8 203 K9
Croftway, NW3 64 DA63
Richmond TW10 117 CH90
Croft Way, Sev. TN13 190 FF125
Sidcup DA15 125 ES90
Crogsland Rd, NW1 82 DG66
Croham Cl, S.Croy. CR2 160 DS107
Croham Manor Rd, S.Croy.
CR2 160 DS106
Croham Mt, S.Croy. CR2 160 DS108
Croham Pk Av, S.Croy. CR2 160 DT106
Croham Rd, S.Croy. CR2 160 DR106
Croham Valley Rd, S.Croy.
CR2 160 DT107
Croindene Rd, SW16 141 DL95
Cromartie Rd, N19 65 DK59
Cromarty Rd, Edg. HA8 42 CP47
Crombie Cl, Ilf. IG4 69 EM57
Crombie Rd, Sid. DA15 125 ER88
Cromer Cl, Uxb. UB8 77 BQ72
Crome Rd, NW10 80 CS65
Cromer Pl, Orp. BR6
off Andover Rd 145 ER102
Cromer Rd, E10 *off James La* 67 ED58
N17 46 DU54
SE25 142 DV97
SW17 120 DG93
Barnet EN5 28 DC42
Hornchurch RM11 72 FK59
Hounslow (Hthrw Air.) TW6 94 BN83
Romford RM7 71 FC58
Romford (Chad.Hth) RM6 70 EY58
Watford WD24 24 BW38
Woodford Green IG8 48 EG49
Cromer St, WC1 196 A3
Cromer Ter, E8 *off Ferncliff Rd* 66 DU64
Cromer Vil Rd, SW18 119 CZ86
Cromford Cl, Orp. BR6 145 ES104
Cromford Path, E5
off Overbury St 67 DX63
Cromford Rd, SW18 120 DA85
Cromford Way, N.Mal. KT3 138 CR95
Cromlix Cl, Chis. BR7 145 EP96
Crompton Pl, Enf. EN3
off Brunswick Rd 31 EA38
Crompton St, W2 82 DD70
Cromwell Av, N6 65 DH60
W6 99 CV78
Bromley BR2 144 EH98
New Malden KT3 139 CT99
Waltham Cross (Chsht) EN7 14 DU30
Cromwell Cl, N2 64 DD56
W3 *off High St* 80 CQ74
Bromley BR2 144 EH98
Chalfont St. Giles HP8 36 AW48
Walton-on-Thames KT12 135 BV102
Cromwell Cres, SW5 100 DA77
Cromwell Dr, Slou. SL1 74 AS72
Cromwell Gdns, SW7 198 A7
Cromwell Gro, W6 99 CW76
Caterham CR3 176 DQ121
Cromwell Highwalk, EC2
off Beech St 84 DQ71
H **Cromwell Hosp, The**,
SW5 100 DB77
Cromwell Ind Est, E10 67 DY60
Cromwell Ms, SW7 198 A8
Cromwell Pl, N6 65 DH60
SW7 198 A8
SW14 98 CQ83
W3 *off Grove Pl* 80 CQ74
Cromwell Rd, E7 86 EJ66
E17 67 EC57
N3 44 DC54
N10 44 DG52
SW5 100 DB77
SW7 100 DB77
SW9 101 DP81
SW19 120 DA92
Beckenham BR3 143 DY96
Borehamwood WD6 26 CL39
Brentwood (Warley) CM14 54 FV49
Caterham CR3 176 DQ121
Croydon CR0 142 DR101
Feltham TW13 115 BV88
Grays RM17 110 GA77
Hayes UB3 77 BR72
Hounslow TW3 96 CA84
Kingston upon Thames
KT2 138 CL95
Cromwell Rd, Red. RH1 184 DF133
Teddington TW11 117 CG93
Waltham Cross (Chsht) EN7 14 DV28
Walton-on-Thames KT12 135 BV102
Wembley HA0 80 CL68
Worcester Park KT4 138 CR104
Cromwells Mere, Rom. RM1
off Havering Rd 51 FD51
Cromwell St, Houns. TW3 96 CA84
Cromwell Twr, EC2 197 J6
Cromwell Wk, Red. RH1 184 DF134
Crondace Rd, SW6 100 DA81
Crondall Ct, N1 197 M1
Crondall Ho, SW15
off Fontley Way 119 CU88
Crondall St, N1 197 L1
Cronin St, SE15 102 DT80
Crooked Billet, SW19
off Woodhayes Rd 119 CW93
Crooked Billet Rbt, E17 47 EA52
Staines TW18 114 BG91
Crooked Billet Yd, E2
off Kingsland Rd 84 DS69
Crooked La, Grav. DA12 131 GH86
Crooked Mile, Wal.Abb. EN9 15 EC33
Crooked Mile Rbt, Wal.Abb.
EN9 15 EC33
Crooked Usage, N3 63 CY55
Crooke Rd, SE8 203 K10
Crookham Rd, SW6 99 CZ81
Crook Log, Bexh. DA6 106 EX83
Crookston Rd, SE9 105 EN83
Croombs Rd, E16 86 EJ71
Crooms Hill, SE10 103 ED80
Crooms Hill Gro, SE10 103 EC80
Cropley Ct, N1
off Cropley St 84 DR68
Cropley St, N1 84 DR68
Croppath Rd, Dag. RM10 70 FA63
Cropthorne Ct, W9 82 DC69
Crosby Cl, Felt. TW13 116 BY91
Crosby Ct, SE1 201 K4
Crosby Rd, E7 86 EG65
Dagenham RM10 89 FB68
Crosby Row, SE1 201 K5
Crosby Sq, EC3 197 M9
Crosby Wk, E8
off Beechwood Rd 84 DT65
SW2 121 DN87
Crosier Cl, SE3 104 EL81
Crosier Rd, Uxb. (Ickhm)
UB10 59 BQ63
Crosier Way, Ruis. HA4 59 BS62
Crosland Pl, SW11
off Taybridge Rd 100 DG83
Crossacres, Wok. GU22 167 BE115
Cross Av, SE10 103 ED79
Crossbow Rd, Chig. IG7 49 ET50
Crossbrook Rd, SE3 104 EL82
Crossbrook St, Wal.Cr.
(Chsht) EN8 15 DX31
Cross Cl, SE15
off Gordon Rd 102 DV82
Cross Deep, Twick. TW1 117 CF89
Cross Deep Gdns, Twick. TW1 117 CF89
Crossfield Pl, Wey. KT13 153 BP108
Crossfield Rd, N17 66 DQ55
NW3 82 DD66
Crossfields, Loug. IG10 33 EP43
Crossfield St, SE8 103 EA80
Crossford St, SW9 101 DM82
Crossgate, Edg. HA8 42 CN48
Greenford UB6 79 CH65
DLR **Crossharbour & London Arena** 204 C6
Crossing Rd, Epp. CM16 18 EU32
Cross Keys Cl, N9
off Balham Rd 46 DU47
W1 194 G7
Sevenoaks TN13 190 FG127
Cross Keys Sq, EC1 197 H7
Cross Lances Rd, Houns.
TW3 96 CB84
Crossland Rd, Red. RH1 184 DG134
Thornton Heath CR7 141 DP100
Crosslands, Cher. KT16 133 BE104
Crosslands Av, W5 80 CM74
Southall UB2 96 BZ78
Crosslands Rd, Epsom KT19 156 CR107
Cross La, EC3 201 M1
N8 65 DM55
Bexley DA5 126 EZ87
Chertsey (Ott.) KT16 151 BB107
Cross La E, Grav. DA12 131 GH89
Cross Las, Ger.Cr. (Chal.St.P.)
SL9 36 AY50
Cross Las Cl, Ger.Cr. (Chal.St.P.)
SL9 *off Cross Las* 37 AZ50
Cross La W, Grav. DA11 131 GH89
Crosslet St, SE17 201 L8
Crosslet Vale, SE10 103 EB81
Crossley Cl, West. (Bigg.H.)
TN16 178 EK115
Crossleys, Ch.St.G. HP8 36 AW49
Crossley St, N7 83 DN65
Crossmead, SE9 125 EM88
Watford WD19 23 BV44
Crossmead Av, Grnf. UB6 78 CA69
Crossmount Ho, SE5 102 DQ80
Crossness La, SE28 88 EX73
★ **Crossness Pumping Sta**,
SE2 88 EY72
Crossness Rd, Bark. IG11 87 ET69
Crossoaks La, Borwd. WD6 26 CR35
Potters Bar (S.Mimms) EN6 10 CS34
Crosspath, The, Rad. WD7 25 CG35
Cross Rd, E4 48 EE46
N11 45 DH50
N22 45 DN52
SE5 102 DS82
SW19 120 DA94
Bromley BR2 144 EL103
Croydon CR0 142 DR102
Dartford DA1 128 FJ86
Dartford (Hawley) DA2 128 FM91
Enfield EN1 30 DS42
Feltham TW13 116 BY91
Gravesend (Nthflt) DA11 131 GF86
Harrow HA1 61 CD56
Harrow (S.Har.) HA2 60 CB62
Harrow (Wealds.) HA3 41 CG54
Kingston upon Thames
KT2 118 CM94

★ Place of interest ⇌ Railway station ⊖ London Underground station DLR Docklands Light Railway station Tra Tramlink station H Hospital Riv Pedestrian ferry landing stage

Cross Rd, Orp. BR5 .146 EV99
Purley CR8 .159 DP113
Romford RM7 .70 FA55
Romford (Chad.Hth) RM6 .70 EW59
Sidcup DA14
off Sidcup Hill .126 EV91
Sutton SM2 .158 DD106
Sutton (Belmont) SM2 .158 DA110
Tadworth KT20 .173 CW122
Uxbridge UB8
off New Windsor St .76 BJ67
Waltham Cross EN8 .15 DY33
Watford WD19 .24 BY44
Weybridge KT13 .135 BR104
Woodford Green IG8 .49 EM51
Cross Rds, Loug. (High Beach)
IG10 .32 EH40
Cross St, N1 .83 DP67
SW13 .98 CS82
Erith DA8 off Bexley Rd .107 FE78
Hampton (Hmptn H.) TW12 .116 CC92
Uxbridge UB8 .76 BJ66
Watford WD17 .24 BW41
Cross Ter, Wal.Abb. EN9
off Stonyshotts .16 EE34
Crossthwaite Av, SE5 .102 DR84
Crosstrees Ho, E14
off Cassilis Rd .103 EA76
Crosswall, EC3 .197 P10
Crossway, N12 .44 DD51
N16 .66 DS64
NW9 .63 CT56
SE28 .88 EW72
SW20 .139 CW98
W13 .79 CG70
Chesham HP5 .4 AS30
Dagenham RM8 .70 EW62
Enfield EN1 .46 DS45
Hayes UB3 .77 BU74
Orpington BR5 .145 ER98
Pinner HA5 .39 BV54
Ruislip HA4 .60 BW63
Walton-on-Thames KT12 .135 BV103
Woodford Green IG8 .48 EJ49
Crossway, The, N22 .45 DP52
SE9 .124 EK89
Cross Way, The, Har. HA3 .41 CE54
Crossway, The, Uxb. UB10 .76 BM68
Crossways, N21 .30 DQ44
Brentwood (Shenf.) CM15 .55 GA44
Egham TW20 .113 BD93
Romford RM2 .71 FH55
South Croydon CR2 .161 DY108
Sunbury-on-Thames TW16 .115 BT94
Sutton SM2 .158 DD109
Westerham (Tats.) TN16 .178 EJ120
Crossways, The, Couls. CR5 .175 DM119
Hounslow TW5 .96 BZ80
Redhill (S.Merst.) RH1 .185 DJ130
Wembley HA9 .62 CN61
Crossways Boul, Dart. DA2 .108 FQ84
Greenhithe DA9 .109 FT84
Crossways Business Pk, Dart.
DA2 .108 FQ84
Crossways La, Reig. RH2 .184 DC128
Crossways Rd, Beck. BR3 .143 EA98
Mitcham CR4 .141 DH97
Crosswell Cl, Shep. TW17 .135 BQ96
Croston St, E8 .84 DU67
Crothall Cl, N13 .45 DM48
Crouch Av, Bark. IG11 .88 EV68
Crouch Cl, Beck. BR3 .123 EA93
Crouch Cft, SE9 .125 EN90
CROUCH END, N8 .65 DJ58
Crouch End Hill, N8 .65 DK59
Crouch Hall Rd, N8 .65 DK58
⇌ Crouch Hill .65 DM59
Crouch Hill, N4 .65 DL58
N8 .65 DL58
Crouch La, Wal.Cr. (Chsht)
EN7 .14 DQ28
Crouchman's Cl, SE26 .122 DT90
Crouch Oak La, Add. KT15 .152 BJ105
Crouch Rd, NW10 .80 CR66
Grays RM16 .111 GG78
Crouch Valley, Upmin. RM14 .73 FS59
Crowborough Cl, Warl. CR6 .177 DY117
Crowborough Dr, Warl. CR6 .177 DY118
Crowborough Path, Wat. WD19
off Prestwick Rd .40 BX49
Crowborough Rd, SW17 .120 DG93
Crowden Way, SE28 .88 EW73
Crowder Cl, N12 .44 DC53
Crowder St, E1 .84 DV73
Crow Dr, Sev. (Halst.) TN14 .181 FC115
Crowfoot Cl, E9
off Lee Conservancy Rd .67 DZ64
SE28 .87 ES74
CROW GREEN, Brwd. CM15 .54 FT41
Crow Grn La, Brwd. (Pilg.Hat.)
CM15 .54 FU43
Crow Grn Rd, Brwd. (Pilg.Hat.)
CM15 .54 FT43
Crowhurst Cl, SW9 .101 DN82
Crowhurst Mead, Gdse. RH9 .186 DW130
Crowhurst Way, Orp. BR5 .146 EW99
Crowland Av, Hayes UB3 .95 BS77
Crowland Gdns, N14 .45 DL45
Crowland Rd, N15 .66 DT57
Thornton Heath CR7 .142 DR98
Crowlands Av, Rom. RM7 .71 FB58
Crowland Ter, N1 .84 DR66
Crowland Wk, Mord. SM4 .140 DB100
Crow La, Rom. RM7 .70 EZ59
Crowley Cres, Croy. CR0 .159 DN106
Crowline Wk, N1
off St. Paul's Rd .84 DR65
Crowmarsh Gdns, SE23
off Tyson Rd .122 DW87
Crown Arc, Kings.T. KT1
off Union St .137 CK96
Crown Ash Hill, West. TN16 .162 EH114
Crown Ash La, Warl. CR6 .178 EG116
Westerham TN16 .178 EG116
Crown Cl, E3 .85 EA67
N22 off Winkfield Rd .45 DN53
NW6 .82 DB65
NW7 .43 CT47
Hayes UB3 .95 BT75
Orpington BR6 .164 EU105
Slough (Colnbr.) SL3 .93 BC80
Walton-on-Thames KT12 .136 BW101
Crown Ct, EC2 .197 J9
Crown Ct, SE12 .124 EH86
WC2 .196 A9
Bromley BR2
off Victoria Rd .144 EK99
Crown Dale, SE19 .121 DP93
Crowndale Rd, NW1 .83 DJ68
Crownfield Av, Ilf. IG2 .69 ES57
Crownfield Rd, E15 .67 ED64
Crownfields, Sev. TN13 .191 FH125
Crown Hill, Croy. CR0
off Church St .142 DQ103
Epping CM16 .17 EM33
Waltham Abbey EN9 .17 EM33
Crownhill Rd, NW10 .81 CT67
Woodford Green IG8 .48 EL52
Crown Ho, Bark. IG11
off Linton Rd .87 EQ66
Crown La, N14 .45 DJ46
SW16 .121 DN92
Bromley BR2 .144 EK99
Chislehurst BR7 .145 EQ95
Morden SM4 .140 DB97
Virginia Water GU25 .132 AX100
Crown La Gdns, SW16 .121 DN92
Crown La Spur, Brom. BR2 .144 EK100
Crown Meadow, Slou.
(Colnbr.) SL3 .93 BB80
Crownmead Way, Rom. RM7 .71 FB56
Crown Ms, E13
off Waghorn Rd .86 EJ67
W6 .99 CU77
Crown Office Row, EC4 .196 D10
Crown Pas, SW1 .199 L3
Kingston upon Thames
KT1 off Church St .137 CK96
Watford WD18
off The Crescent .24 BW42
Crown Pl, EC2 .197 M6
NW5 off Kentish Town Rd .83 DH65
SE16 off Varcoe Rd .102 DV78
Crown Pt Par, SE19
off Beulah Hill .121 DP93
Crown Reach, SW1
off Grosvenor Rd .101 DK78
Crown Ri, Cher. KT16 .133 BF102
Watford WD25 .8 BW34
Crown Rd, N10 .44 DG52
Borehamwood WD6 .26 CN39
Enfield EN1 .30 DV42
Grays RM17 .110 GA79
Ilford IG6 .69 ES56
Morden SM4 .140 DB98
New Malden KT3 .138 CQ95
Orpington BR6 .164 EU106
Ruislip HA4 .60 BX64
Sevenoaks (Shore.) TN14 .165 FF110
Sutton SM1 .158 DB105
Twickenham TW1 .117 CH86
Virginia Water GU25 .132 AW100
Crown Sq, Wok. GU21
off Commercial Way .167 AZ117
Crownstone Rd, SW2 .121 DN85
Crown St, SE5 .102 DQ80
W3 .80 CP74
Brentwood CM14 .54 FW47
Dagenham RM10 .89 FC65
Egham TW20 .113 BA92
Harrow HA2 .61 CD60
Crown Ter, Rich. TW9 .98 CM84
Crowntree Cl, Islw. TW7 .97 CF79
Crown Wk, Uxb. UB8
off The Pavilions .76 BJ66
Wembley HA9 .62 CM62
Crown Way, West Dr. UB7 .76 BM74
Crown Wds La, SE9 .105 EP82
SE18 .105 EP82
Crown Wds Way, SE9 .125 ER85
Crown Wks, E2 off Temple St .84 DV68
Crown Yd, Houns. TW3
off High St .96 CC83
Crowshott Av, Stan. HA7 .41 CJ53
Crows Rd, E15 .85 ED69
Barking IG11 .87 EP65
Epping CM16 .17 ET30
Crowstone Rd, Grays RM16 .110 GC75
Crowther Av, Brent. TW8 .98 CL77
Crowther Cl, SW6
off Coomer Pl .99 CZ79
Crowther Rd, SE25 .142 DU98
Crowthorne Cl, SW18 .119 CZ88
Crowthorne Rd, W10 .81 CX72
Croxdale Rd, Borwd. WD6 .26 CM40
Croxden Cl, Edg. HA8 .62 CM55
Croxden Wk, Mord. SM4 .140 DC100
Croxford Gdns, N22 .45 DP52
Croxford Way, Rom. RM7
off Horace Av .71 FD60
⊖ Croxley .23 BP44
Croxley Business Pk, Wat.
WD18 .23 BR43
Croxley Cl, Orp. BR5 .146 EV96
CROXLEY GREEN, Rick. WD3 .22 BN43
Croxley Grn, Orp. BR5 .146 EV95
Croxley Rd, W9 .81 CZ69
Croxley Vw, Wat. WD18 .23 BS44
Croxted Cl, SE21 .122 DQ87
Croxted Ms, SE24
off Croxted Rd .122 DQ86
Croxted Rd, SE21 .122 DQ87
SE24 .122 DQ87
Croxteth Ho, SW8
off Wandsworth Rd .101 DK82
Croyde Av, Grnf. UB6 .78 CC69
Hayes UB3 .95 BS77
Croyde Cl, Sid. DA15 .125 ER87
CROYDON, CR0 .142 DR103
Croydon Flyover, Croy. CR0 .159 DP105
Croydon Gro, Croy. CR0 .141 DP102
Croydon La, Bans. SM7 .158 DB114
Croydon La S, Bans. SM7 .158 DB114
★ Croydon Mus, Croy. CR0 .142 DQ104
Croydon Rd, E13 .86 EF70
SE20 .142 DV96
Beckenham BR3 .143 DY98
Bromley BR2 .144 EF104
Caterham CR3 .176 DU122
Croydon (Bedd.) CR0 .159 DL105
Croydon (Mitch.Com.) CR0 .140 DG98
Hounslow (Hthrw Air.) TW6 .95 BP82
Keston BR2 .144 EJ104
Mitcham CR4 .140 DG98
Reigate RH2 .184 DB134
Wallington SM6 .159 DH105
Croydon Rd, Warl. CR6 .177 ED122
West Wickham BR4 .144 EE104
Westerham TN16 .179 EM123
Croydon Valley Trade Pk, Croy. CR0
off Beddington Fm Rd .141 DL101
Croyland Rd, N9 .46 DU46
Croylands Dr, Surb. KT6 .138 CL101
Croysdale Av, Sun. TW16 .135 BU97
Crozier Dr, S.Croy. CR2 .160 DV110
Crozier Ho, SE3
off Ebdon Way .104 EH83
Crozier Ter, E9 .67 DX64
Crucible Cl, Rom. RM6 .70 EV58
Crucifix La, SE1 .201 M4
Cruden Ho, SE17
off Hillingdon St .101 DP79
Cruden Rd, Grav. DA12 .131 GM90
Cruden St, N1 .83 DP67
Cruick Av, S.Ock. RM15 .91 FW73
Cruikshank Rd, E15 .68 EE63
Cruikshank St, WC1 .196 D2
Crummock Gdns, NW9 .62 CS57
Crumpsall St, SE2 .106 EW77
Crundale Av, NW9 .62 CN57
Crundal Twr, Orp. BR5 .146 EW102
Crunden Rd, S.Croy. CR2 .160 DR108
Crusader Cl, Purf. RM19
off Centurion Way .108 FN77
Crusader Gdns, Croy. CR0
off Cotelands .142 DS104
Crusader Industrial Est, N4
off Hermitage Rd .66 DQ58
Crusader Way, Wat. WD18 .23 BT44
Crushes Cl, Brwd. (Hutt.)
CM13 .55 GE44
Crusoe Ms, N16 .66 DR61
Crusoe Rd, Erith DA8 .107 FD78
Mitcham CR4 .120 DF94
Crutched Friars, EC3 .197 N10
Crutches La, Beac. (Jordans)
HP9 .36 AS51
Crutchfield La, Walt. KT12 .135 BV103
Crutchley Rd, SE6 .124 EE89
Crystal Av, Horn. RM12 .72 FL63
Crystal Ct, SE19
off College Rd .122 DT92
Crystal Ho, SE18
off Spinel Cl .105 ET78
⇌ Crystal Palace .122 DU93
Crystal Palace Caravan Club,
SE19 .122 DT92
★ Crystal Palace FC, SE25 .142 DS98
★ Crystal Palace Nat
Sport Cen, SE19 .122 DU93
Crystal Palace Par, SE19 .122 DT93
★ Crystal Palace Pk, SE19 .122 DT92
Crystal Palace Pk Rd, SE26 .122 DU92
Crystal Palace Rd, SE22 .102 DU84
Crystal Palace Sta Rd, SE19 .122 DU93
Crystal Ter, SE19 .122 DR93
Crystal Vw Ct, Brom. BR1
off Winlaton Rd .123 ED91
Crystal Way, Dag. RM8 .70 EW60
Harrow HA1 .61 CF57
Crystal Wf, N1 .196 G1
Cuba Dr, Enf. EN3 .30 DW40
Cuba St, E14 .203 P4
Cubitt Sq, Sthl. UB2
off Windmill Av .78 CC74
Cubitt Steps, E14 .204 A2
Cubitt St, WC1 .196 C3
Croydon CR0 .159 DM106
Cubitts Yd, WC2 .196 A10
Cubitt Ter, SW4 .101 DJ83
CUBITT TOWN, E14 .204 E6
Cuckmans Dr, St.Alb. AL2 .8 CA25
Cuckoo Av, W7 .79 CE70
Cuckoo Dene, W7 .79 CD71
Cuckoo Hall La, N9 .46 DW45
Cuckoo Hill, Pnr. HA5 .60 BW55
Cuckoo Hill Dr, Pnr. HA5 .60 BW55
Cuckoo Hill Rd, Pnr. HA5 .60 BW56
Cuckoo La, W7 .79 CE73
Cuckoo Pound, Shep. TW17 .135 BS99
Cudas Cl, Epsom KT19 .157 CT105
Cuddington Av, Wor.Pk. KT4 .139 CT104
Cuddington Cl, Tad. KT20 .173 CW120
Cuddington Glade, Epsom
KT19 .156 CN112
Cuddington Pk Cl, Bans.
SM7 .157 CZ113
Cuddington Way, Sutt. SM2 .157 CX112
CUDHAM, Sev. TN14 .179 ER115
Cudham Cl, Sutt. (Belmont)
SM2 .158 DA110
Cudham Dr, Croy. (New Adgtn)
CR0 .161 EC110
Cudham La N, Orp. BR6 .163 ES110
Sevenoaks (Cudham) TN14 .163 ER112
Cudham La S, Sev. TN14 .179 EQ115
Cudham Pk Rd, Sev.
(Cudham) TN14 .163 ES110
Cudham Rd, Orp. BR6 .163 EN111
Westerham (Tats.) TN16 .178 EL120
Cudham St, SE6 .123 EC87
Cudworth St, E1 .84 DV70
Cuff Cres, SE9 .124 EK86
CUFFLEY, Pot.B. EN6 .13 DM29
⇌ Cuffley .13 DM29
Cuffley Av, Wat. WD25 .8 BX34
Cuffley Hill, Wal.Cr. (Chsht)
EN7 .13 DN29
Cuff Pt, E2 .197 P2
Cugley Rd, Dart. DA2 .128 FQ87
Culford Gdns, SW3 .198 E9
Culford Gro, N1 .84 DS65
Culford Ms, N1
off Culford Rd .84 DS65
Culford Rd, N1 .84 DS66
Grays RM16 .110 GC75
Culgaith Gdns, Enf. EN2 .29 DL42
Cullen Sq, S.Ock. RM15 .91 FW73
Cullen Way, NW10 .80 CQ70
Cullera Cl, Nthwd. HA6 .39 BT51
Cullerne Cl, Epsom (Ewell)
KT17 .157 CT110
Cullesden Rd, Ken. CR8 .175 DP115
Culling Rd, SE16 .202 F6
Cullings Ct, Wal.Abb. EN9 .16 EF33
Cullington Cl, Har. HA3 .61 CG56
Cullingworth Rd, NW10 .63 CU64
Culloden Cl, SE16 .102 DU78
Culloden Rd, Enf. EN2 .29 DP40
Culloden St, E14 .85 EC72
Cullum St, EC3 .197 M10
Culmington Rd, W13 .97 CJ75
South Croydon CR2 .160 DQ109
Culmore Rd, SE15 .102 DV80
Culmstock Rd, SW11 .120 DG85
Culpeper Cl, Ilf. IG6 .49 EP51
Culpepper Cl, N18 .46 DV50
Culross Cl, N15 .66 DQ56
Culross St, W1 .198 F1
Culsac Rd, Surb. KT6 .138 CL103
Culverden Rd, SW12 .121 DJ89
Watford WD19 .39 BV48
Culver Dr, Oxt. RH8 .188 EE130
Culver Gro, Stan. HA7 .41 CJ54
Culverhay, Ashtd. KT21 .172 CL116
Culverhouse Gdns, SW16 .121 DM90
Culverlands Cl, Stan. HA7 .41 CH49
Culverley Rd, SE6 .123 EB88
Culvers Av, Cars. SM5 .140 DF103
Culvers Retreat, Cars. SM5 .140 DF102
Culverstone Cl, Brom. BR2 .144 EF100
Culvers Way, Cars. SM5 .140 DF103
Culvert La, Uxb. UB8 .76 BH68
Culvert Pl, SW11 .100 DG82
Culvert Rd, N15 .66 DS57
SW11 .100 DF82
Culworth St, NW8 .194 B1
Cumberland Av, NW10 .80 CP69
Gravesend DA12 .131 GJ87
Hornchurch RM12 .72 FL62
Welling DA16 .105 ES83
Cumberland Cl, E8 .84 DT65
SW20 off Lansdowne Rd .119 CX94
Amersham HP7 .20 AV39
Epsom KT19 .156 CS110
Hornchurch RM12 .72 FL62
Ilford IG6 .49 EQ53
Twickenham TW1
off Westmorland Cl .117 CH86
Cumberland Ct, Well. DA16
off Bellegrove Rd .105 ES82
Cumberland Cres, W14 .99 CY77
Cumberland Dr, Bexh. DA7 .106 EY80
Chessington KT9 .138 CM104
Dartford DA1 .128 FM87
Esher KT10 .137 CG103
Cumberland Gdns, NW4 .43 CY54
WC1 .196 C2
Cumberland Gate, W1 .194 D10
Cumberland Mkt, NW1 .195 J2
Cumberland Mkt Est, NW1 .195 J2
Cumberland Mills Sq, E14 .204 F10
Cumberland Pk, NW10 .81 CU69
W3 .80 CQ73
Cumberland Pl, NW1 .195 H2
SE6 .124 EF88
Sunbury-on-Thames TW16 .135 BU98
Cumberland Rd, E12 .68 EK63
E13 .86 EH71
E17 .47 DY54
N9 .46 DW46
N22 .45 DM54
SE25 .142 DV100
SW13 .99 CT81
W3 .80 CQ73
W7 .97 CF75
Ashford TW15 .114 BK90
Bromley BR2 .144 EE98
Grays (Chaff.Hun.) RM16 .110 FY75
Harrow HA1 .60 CB57
Richmond TW9 .98 CN80
Stanmore HA7 .62 CM55
Cumberlands, Ken. CR8 .176 DR115
Cumberland St, SW1 .199 J10
Staines TW18 .113 BD92
Cumberland Ter, NW1 .195 H1
Cumberland Ter Ms, NW1 .195 H1
Cumberland Vil, W3
off Cumberland Rd .80 CQ73
Cumberlow Av, SE25 .142 DT97
Cumbernauld Gdns, Sun.
TW16 .115 BT92
Cumberton Rd, N17 .46 DR53
Cumbrae Cl, Slou. SL2
off St. Pauls Av .74 AU74
Cumbrae Gdns, Surb. KT6 .137 CK103
Cumbrian Av, Bexh. DA7 .107 FE81
Cumbrian Gdns, NW2 .63 CX61
Cumbrian Way, Uxb. UB8
off Chippendale Waye .76 BK66
★ Cuming Mus, SE17 .201 H9
Cumley Rd, Ong. CM5 .19 FE30
Cummings Hall La, Rom.
(Noak Hill) RM3 .52 FJ48
Cumming St, N1 .196 B1
Cumnor Gdns, Epsom KT17 .157 CU107
Cumnor Ri, Ken. CR8 .176 DQ117
Cumnor Rd, Sutt. SM2 .158 DC107
Cunard Cres, N21 .30 DR44
Cunard Pl, EC3 .197 N9
Cunard Rd, NW10 .80 CR69
Cunard St, SE5
off Albany Rd .102 DS79
Cunard Wk, SE16 .203 J8
Cundy Rd, E16 .86 EJ72
Cundy St, SW1 .198 G9
Cundy St Est, SW1 .198 G9
Cunliffe Cl, Epsom (Headley)
KT18 .172 CP124
Cunliffe Rd, Epsom KT19 .157 CT105
Cunliffe St, SW16 .121 DJ93
Cunningham Av, Enf. EN3 .31 DY36
Cunningham Cl, Rom. RM6 .70 EW57
West Wickham BR4 .143 EB103
Cunningham Pk, Har. HA1 .60 CC57
Cunningham Pl, NW8 .82 DD70
Cunningham Ri, Epp.
(N.Wld Bas.) CM16 .19 FC25
Cunningham Rd, N15 .66 DU56
Banstead SM7 .174 DD115
Waltham Cross (Chsht) EN8 .15 DY27
Cunnington St, W4 .98 CQ76
Cupar Rd, SW11 .100 DG81
Cupola Cl, Brom. BR1 .124 EH92
Curates Wk, Dart. DA1 .128 FK90
Cureton St, SW1 .199 N9
Curfew Bell Rd, Cher. KT16 .133 BF101
Curfew Ho, Bark. IG11
off St. Ann's .87 EQ67
Curie Gdns, NW9
off Pasteur Cl .42 CS54
Curlew Cl, SE28 .88 EX73
Curlew Cl, S. Croy. CR2 .161 DX111
Curlew Ct, Surb. KT6 .138 CM104
Curlew Ho, Enf. EN3
off Allington Ct .31 DX43
Curlews, The, Grav. DA12 .131 GK89
Curlew St, SE1 .201 P4
Curlew Ter, Ilf. IG5
off Tiptree Cres .69 EN55
Curlew Way, Hayes UB4 .78 BX71
Curling Cl, Couls. CR5 .175 DM120
Curling La, Grays (Bad.Dene)
RM17 .110 FZ78
Curness St, SE13 .103 EC84
Curnick's La, SE27
off Chapel Rd .122 DQ91
Curnock Est, NW1
off Plender St .83 DJ67
Curran Av, Sid. DA15 .125 ET85
Wallington SM6 .140 DG104
Curran Cl, Uxb. UB8 .76 BJ70
Currey Rd, Grnf. UB6 .79 CD65
Curricle St, W3 .80 CS74
Currie Hill Cl, SW19 .119 CZ91
Curry Ri, NW7 .43 CX51
Cursitor St, EC4 .196 D8
Curtain Pl, EC2
off Curtain Rd .84 DS69
Curtain Rd, EC2 .197 M5
Curthwaite Gdns, Enf. EN2 .29 DK42
Curtis Cl, Rick. (Mill End)
WD3 .38 BG46
Curtis Dr, W3 .80 CR72
Curtis Fld Rd, SW16 .121 DM91
Curtis Ho, N11 .45 DH50
Curtis La, Wem. HA0
off Montrose Cres .80 CL65
Curtismill Cl, Orp. BR5 .146 EV97
Curtis Mill Grn, Rom. (Nave.)
RM4 .35 FF42
Curtis Mill La, Rom. (Nave.)
RM4 .35 FF42
Curtismill Way, Orp. BR5 .146 EV97
Curtis Rd, Epsom KT19 .156 CQ105
Hornchurch RM11 .72 FM60
Hounslow TW4 .116 BZ87
Curtiss Dr, Wat. (Lvsdn) WD25 .7 BT34
Curtis St, SE1 .201 P8
Curtis Way, SE1 .201 P8
SE28 off Tawney Rd .88 EV73
Curvan Cl, Epsom KT17 .157 CT110
Curve, The, W12 .81 CU73
Curwen Av, E7
off Woodford Rd .68 EH63
Curwen Rd, W12 .99 CU75
Curzon Av, Enf. EN3 .31 DX43
Stanmore HA7 .41 CG53
Curzon Cl, Orp. BR6 .163 ER105
Weybridge KT13
off Curzon Rd .152 BN105
Curzon Cres, NW10 .81 CT66
Barking IG11 .87 ET68
Curzon Dr, Grays RM17 .110 GC80
Curzon Gate, W1 .198 G3
Curzon Mall, Slou. SL1
off High St .92 AT75
Curzon Pl, Pnr. HA5 .60 BW57
Curzon Rd, N10 .45 DH54
W5 .79 CH70
Thornton Heath CR7 .141 DN100
Weybridge KT13 .152 BN105
Curzon Sq, W1 .198 G3
Curzon St, W1 .198 G3
Cusack Cl, Twick. TW1
off Waldegrave Rd .117 CF91
Cussons Cl, Wal.Cr. (Chsht)
EN7 .14 DU29
CUSTOM HOUSE, E16 .86 EK72
⇌ Custom House .86 EH73
DLR Custom House for ExCeL .86 EH73
Custom Ho Reach, SE16 .203 M5
Custom Ho Wk, EC3 .201 M1
Cut, The, SE1 .200 E4
Cutcombe Rd, SE5 .102 DQ82
Cuthberga Cl, Bark. IG11
off George St .87 EQ66
Cuthbert Gdns, SE25 .142 DS97
Cuthbert Rd, E17 .67 EC55
N18 off Fairfield Rd .46 DU50
Croydon CR0 .141 DP103
Cuthberts Cl, Wal.Cr. (Chsht)
EN7 .14 DT29
Cuthbert St, W2 .82 DD70
Cut Hills, Egh. TW20 .132 AV95
Virginia Water GU25 .132 AU96
Cuthill Wk, SE5 .102 DR81
Cutlers Gdns, E1 .197 N8
Cutlers Gdns Arc, EC2
off Cutler St .84 DS72
Cutlers Sq, E14 .204 A9
Cutlers Ter, N1
off Balls Pond Rd .84 DR65
Cutler St, E1 .197 N8
Cutmore St, Grav. DA11 .131 GH87
Cutthroat All, Rich. TW10
off Ham St .117 CJ89
★ Cutty Sark, SE10 .103 EC79
Cutty Sark Ct, Green. DA9
off Low Cl .129 FU85
DLR Cutty Sark for Maritime
Greenwich .103 EC79
Cutty Sark Gdns, SE10
off King William Wk .103 EC79
Cuxton Cl, Bexh. DA6 .126 EY85
Cyclamen Cl, Hmptn. TW12
off Gresham Rd .116 CA93
Cyclamen Rd, Swan. BR8 .147 FD98
Cyclamen Way, Epsom
KT19 .156 CP106
Cyclops Ms, E14 .203 P8
Cygnet Av, Felt. TW14 .116 BW87
Cygnet Cl, NW10 .62 CR64
Borehamwood WD6 .26 CQ39
Northwood HA6 .39 BQ52
Woking GU21 .166 AV116
Cygnet Gdns, Grav. (Nthflt)
DA11 .131 GF89
Cygnets, The, Felt. TW13 .116 BY91

A B C D E F G H I J K L M N O P Q R S T U V W X Y Z

★ Place of interest ⇌ Railway station ⊖ London Underground station DLR Docklands Light Railway station Tra Tramlink station H Hospital Riv Pedestrian ferry landing stage

Cygnets, The, Stai. TW18
off Edgell Rd .113 BF92
Cygnets Cl, Red. RH1 .184 DG132
Cygnet St, E1 off Sclater St .84 DT70
Cygnet Vw, Grays RM20 .109 FT77
Cygnet Way, Hayes UB4 .78 BX71
Cygnus Business Cen, NW10 .81 CT65
Cymbeline Ct, Har. HA1 .61 CF58
Cynthia St, N1 .196 C1
Cyntra Pl, E8 .84 DV66
Cypress Av, Enf. EN2 .29 DN35
Twickenham TW2 .116 CC87
Cypress Cl, E5
off Rossington St .66 DU61
Waltham Abbey EN9 .15 ED34
Cypress Ct, Vir.W. GU25 .132 AY98
Cypress Gdns, SE4 .123 DY85
Cypress Gro, Ilf. IG6 .49 ES51
Cypress Path, Rom. RM3 .52 FK52
Cypress Pl, W1 .195 L5
Cypress Rd, SE25 .142 DS96
Harrow HA3 .41 CD54
Cypress Tree Cl, Sid. DA15
off White Oak Gdns .125 ET87
Cypress Wk, Egh. (Eng.Grn)
TW20 .112 AV93
Watford WD25
off Cedar Wd Dr .23 BV35
Cypress Way, Bans. SM7 .157 CX114
DLR Cyprus .87 EN73
Cyprus Av, N3 .43 CY54
Cyprus Cl, N4
off Atterbury Rd .65 DP58
Cyprus Gdns, N3 .43 CY54
Cyprus Pl, E2 .84 DW68
E6 .87 EN73
Cyprus Rd, N3 .43 CZ54
N9 .46 DT47
Cyprus Rbt, E16
off Royal Albert Way .87 EN73
Cyprus St, E2 .84 DW68
Cyrena Rd, SE22 .122 DT86
Cyril Mans, SW11 .100 DF81
Cyril Rd, Bexh. DA7 .106 EY82
Orpington BR6 .146 EU101
Cyrus St, EC1 .196 G4
Czar St, SE8 .103 EA79

D

Dabbling Cl, Erith DA8 .107 FH80
Dabbs Hill La, Nthlt. UB5 .60 CB64
D'Abernon Cl, Esher KT10 .154 CA105
D'Abernon Dr, Cob. (Stoke D'Ab.)
KT11 .170 BY116
Dabin Cres, SE10 .103 EC81
Dacca St, SE8 .103 DZ79
Dace Rd, E3 .85 EA66
Dacre Av, Ilf. IG5 .49 EN54
South Ockendon (Aveley)
RM15 .91 FR74
Dacre Cl, Chig. IG7 .49 EQ49
Greenford UB6 .78 CB68
Dacre Cres, S.Ock. (Aveley)
RM15 .91 FR74
Dacre Gdns, SE13 .104 EE84
Borehamwood WD6 .26 CR43
Chigwell IG7 .49 EQ49
Dacre Pk, SE13 .104 EE83
Dacre Pl, SE13 .104 EE83
Dacre Rd, E11 .68 EF60
E13 .86 EH67
Croydon CR0 .141 DL101
Dacres Rd, SE23 .123 DX90
Dacre St, SW1 .199 M6
Dade Way, Sthl. UB2 .96 BZ78
Daerwood Cl, Brom. BR2 .145 EM102
Daffodil Av, Brwd. (Pilg.Hat.)
CM15 .54 FV43
Daffodil Cl, Croy. CR0 .143 DX102
Daffodil Gdns, Ilf. IG1 .69 EP64
Daffodil Pl, Hmptn. TW12
off Gresham Rd .116 CA93
Daffodil St, W12 .81 CT73
Daffone Rd, SW17 .120 DG90
DAGENHAM, RM8 - RM10 .88 FA65
Dagenham Av, Dag. RM9 .88 EY67
⇌ Dagenham Dock .88 EZ68
⊖ Dagenham East .71 FC64
⊖ Dagenham Heathway .88 EZ65
Dagenham Rd, E10 .67 DZ60
Dagenham RM10 .71 FC63
Rainham RM13 .89 FD66
Romford RM7 .71 FD62
Dagger La, Borwd. (Els.) WD6 .25 CG44
Dagmar Av, Wem. HA9 .62 CM63
Dagmar Gdns, NW10 .81 CX68
Dagmar Ms, Sthl. UB2
off Dagmar Rd .96 BY76
Dagmar Pas, N1 off Cross St .83 DP67
Dagmar Rd, N4 .65 DN59
N15 off Cornwall Rd .66 DR56
N22 .45 DK53
SE5 .102 DS81
SE25 .142 DS99
Dagenham RM10 .89 FC66
Kingston upon Thames
KT2 .138 CM95
Southall UB2 .96 BY76
Dagmar Ter, N1 .83 DP67
Dagnall Cres, Uxb. UB8 .76 BJ71
Dagnall Pk, SE25 .142 DS100
Dagnall Rd, SE25 .142 DS99
Dagnall St, SW11 .100 DF82
Dagnam Pk Cl, Rom. RM3 .52 FN50
Dagnam Pk Dr, Rom. RM3 .52 FL50
Dagnam Pk Gdns, Rom. RM3 .52 FN51
Dagnam Pk Sq, Rom. RM3 .52 FP51
Dagnan Rd, SW12 .121 DH87
Dagonet Gdns, Brom. BR1 .124 EG90
Dagonet Rd, Brom. BR1 .124 EG90
Dahlia Cl, Wal.Cr. (Chsht) EN7 .14 DQ25
Dahlia Dr, Swan. BR8 .147 FF96
Dahlia Gdns, Ilf. IG1 .87 EP65
Dahlia Gdns, Mitch. CR4 .141 DK98
Dahlia Rd, SE2 .106 EV77
Dahomey Rd, SW16 .121 DJ93
Daiglen Dr, S.Ock. RM15 .91 FU73
Daimler Way, Wall. SM6 .159 DL108
Daines Cl, E12 .69 EM62
South Ockendon RM15 .91 FU70
Dainford Cl, Brom. BR1 .123 ED92
Dainton Cl, Brom. BR1 .144 EH95
Daintry Cl, Har. HA3 .61 CG56
Daintry Lo, Nthwd. HA6 .39 BT52
Daintry Way, E9
off Osborne Rd .85 DZ65
Dairsie Rd, SE9 .105 EN83
Dairy Cl, NW10 .81 CU67
Dartford (Sutt.H.) DA4 .128 FP94
Thornton Heath CR7 .142 DQ96
Dairy Fm Pl, SE15
off Queens Rd .102 DW81
Dairyglen Av, Wal.Cr. EN8 .15 DY31
Dairy La, SE18 .105 EM77
Edenbridge (Crock.H.) TN8 .189 EN134
Dairyman Cl, NW2
off Claremont Rd .63 CY62
Dairy Ms, SW9 .101 DL83
Dairy Wk, SW19 .119 CY91
Dairy Way, Abb.L. WD5 .7 BT29
Daisy Cl, Croy. CR0 .143 DX102
Daisy Dobbins Wk, N19
off Hillrise Rd .65 DL59
Daisy La, SW6 .100 DA83
Daisy Rd, E16
off Cranberry La .86 EE70
E18 .48 EH54
Dakin Pl, E1
off White Horse Rd .85 DY71
Dakota Cl, Wall. SM6 .159 DM108
Dakota Gdns, E6 .86 EL70
Northolt UB5
off Argus Way .78 BY69
Dalberg Rd, SW2 .101 DN84
Dalberg Way, SE2
off Lanridge Rd .106 EX76
Dalby Rd, SW18 .100 DC84
Dalby St, NW5 .83 DH65
Dalcross Rd, Houns. TW4 .96 BY82
Dale, The, Kes. BR2 .162 EK105
Waltham Abbey EN9 .16 EE34
Dale Av, Edg. HA8 .42 CM53
Hounslow TW4 .96 BY83
Dalebury Rd, SW17 .120 DE89
Dale Cl, SE3 .104 EG83
Addlestone KT15 .152 BH106
Barnet EN5 .28 DB44
Dartford DA1 .127 FF86
Pinner HA5 .39 BV53
South Ockendon RM15 .91 FU72
Dale Dr, Hayes UB4 .77 BT70
Dale End, Dart. DA1
off Dale Rd .127 FF86
Dale Gdns, Wdf.Grn. IG8 .48 EH49
Dalegarth Gdns, Pur. CR8 .160 DR113
Dale Grn Rd, N11 .45 DH48
Dale Gro, N12 .44 DC50
Daleham Av, Egh. TW20 .113 BA93
Daleham Dr, Uxb. UB8 .77 BP72
Daleham Gdns, NW3 .64 DD64
Daleham Ms, NW3 .82 DD65
Dalehead, NW1 .195 K1
Dalemain Ms, E16 .205 N2
Dale Pk Av, Cars. SM5 .140 DF103
Dale Pk Rd, SE19 .142 DQ95
Dale Rd, NW5 off Grafton Rd .64 DG64
SE17 .101 DP79
Dartford DA1 .127 FF86
Gravesend (Sthflt) DA13 .130 GA91
Greenford UB6 .78 CB71
Purley CR8 .159 DN112
Sunbury-on-Thames TW16 .115 BT94
Sutton SM1 .157 CZ105
Swanley BR8 .147 FC96
Walton-on-Thames KT12 .135 BT101
Dale Row, W11
off St. Marks Rd .81 CY72
Daleside, Ger.Cr. SL9 .56 AY60
Orpington BR6 .164 EU106
Daleside Cl, Orp. BR6 .164 EU107
Daleside Dr, Pot.B. EN6 .11 CZ32
Daleside Gdns, Chig. IG7 .49 EQ48
Daleside Rd, SW16 .121 DH92
Epsom KT19 .156 CR107
Dales Path, Borwd. WD6
off Farriers Way .26 CR43
Dales Rd, Borwd. WD6 .26 CR43
Dalestone Ms, Rom. RM3 .51 FH51
Dale St, W4 .98 CS78
Dale Vw, Epsom (Headley)
KT18 .172 CP123
Erith DA8 .107 FF82
Woking GU21 .166 AU118
Dale Vw Av, E4 .47 EC47
Dale Vw Cres, E4 .47 EC47
Dale Vw Gdns, E4 .47 ED48
Daleview Rd, N15 .66 DS58
Dale Wk, Dart. DA2 .128 FQ88
Dalewood Cl, Horn. RM11 .72 FM59
Dalewood Gdns, Wor.Pk.
KT4 .139 CV103
Dale Wd Rd, Orp. BR6 .145 ES101
Daley St, E9 .85 DX65
Daley Thompson Way, SW8 .101 DH82
Dalgarno Gdns, W10 .81 CW71
Dalgarno Way, W10 .81 CW70
Dalgleish St, E14 .85 DY72
Daling Way, E3 .85 DY67
Dalkeith Gro, Stan. HA7 .41 CK50
Dalkeith Rd, SE21 .122 DQ88
Ilford IG1 .69 EQ62
Dallas Rd, NW4 .63 CU59
SE26 .122 DV91
W5 .80 CM71
Sutton SM3 .157 CY107
Dallas Ter, Hayes UB3 .95 BT76
Dallega Cl, Hayes UB3
off Dawley Rd .77 BR73
Dallinger Rd, SE12 .124 EF86
Dalling Rd, W6 .99 CV76
Dallington Cl, Walt. KT12 .154 BW107
Dallington Sq, EC1
off Dallington St .83 DP70
Dallington St, EC1 .196 G4
Dallin Rd, SE18 .105 EP80
Bexleyheath DA6 .106 EX84
Dalmain Rd, SE23 .123 DX88
Dalmally Rd, Croy. CR0 .142 DT101
Dalmeny Av, N7 .65 DK63
SW16 .141 DN96
Dalmeny Cl, Wem. HA0 .79 CJ65
Dalmeny Cres, Houns. TW3 .97 CD84
Dalmeny Rd, N7 .65 DK62
Barnet EN5 .28 DC44
Carshalton SM5 .158 DG108
Erith DA8 .107 FB81
Worcester Park KT4 .139 CV104
Dalmeyer Rd, NW10 .81 CT65
Dalmore Av, Esher (Clay.)
KT10 .155 CF107
Dalmore Rd, SE21 .122 DQ89
Dalroy Cl, S.Ock. RM15 .91 FU72
Dalrymple Cl, N14 .45 DK45
Dalrymple Rd, SE4 .103 DY84
DALSTON, E8 .84 DU66
Dalston Gdns, Stan. HA7 .42 CL53
⇌ Dalston Kingsland .84 DS65
Dalston La, E8 .84 DT65
Dalton Av, Mitch. CR4 .140 DE96
Dalton Cl, Hayes UB4 .77 BR70
Orpington BR6 .145 ES104
Purley CR8 .160 DQ112
Dalton Grn, Slou. SL3
off Ditton Rd .93 AZ78
Dalton Rd, Har. (Har.Wld)
HA3 .41 CD54
Daltons Rd, Orp. BR6 .147 FB104
Swanley BR8 .147 FC102
Dalton St, SE27 .121 DP89
Dalton Way, Wat. WD17 .24 BX43
Dalwood St, SE5 .102 DS81
Dalyell Rd, SW9 .101 DM83
Damascene Wk, SE21
off Lovelace Rd .122 DQ88
Damask Cres, E16
off Cranberry La .86 EE70
Damer Ter, SW10
off Tadema Rd .100 DC80
Dames Rd, E7 .68 EG62
Dame St, N1 .84 DQ68
Dameswick Vw, St.Alb. AL2 .8 CA27
Damien St, E1 .84 DV72
Damigos Rd, Grav. DA12 .131 GM88
Damon Cl, Sid. DA14 .126 EV90
Damson Ct, Swan. BR8 .147 FD98
Damson Dr, Hayes UB3 .77 BU73
Damson Way, Cars. SM5 .158 DF110
Damsonwood Rd, Sthl. UB2 .96 CA76
Danbrook Rd, SW16 .141 DL95
Danbury Cl, Brwd. (Pilg.Hat.)
CM15 .54 FT43
Romford RM6 .70 EX55
Danbury Cres, S.Ock. RM15 .91 FV72
Danbury Ms, Wall. SM6 .159 DH105
Danbury Rd, Loug. IG10 .48 EL45
Rainham RM13 .89 FF67
Danbury St, N1 .83 DP68
Danbury Way, Wdf.Grn. IG8 .48 EJ51
Danby St, SE15 .102 DT83
Dancer Rd, SW6 .99 CZ81
Richmond TW9 .98 CN83
DANCERS HILL, Barn. EN5 .27 CW35
Dancers Hill Rd, Barn. EN5 .27 CY36
Dancers La, Barn. EN5 .27 CW35
Dandelion Cl, Rom. (Rush Grn)
RM7 .71 FE61
Dando Cres, SE3 .104 EH83
Dandridge Cl, SE10 .205 L10
Slough SL3 .92 AX77
Danebury, Croy. (New Adgtn)
CR0 .161 EB107
Danebury Av, SW15 .118 CS86
Daneby Rd, SE6 .123 EB90
Dane Cl, Amer. HP7 .20 AT41
Bexley DA5 .126 FA87
Orpington BR6 .163 ER106
Dane Ct, Wok. GU22 .167 BF115
Danecourt Gdns, Croy. CR0 .142 DT104
Danecroft Rd, SE24 .122 DQ85
Danehill Wk, Sid. DA14
off Hatherley Rd .126 EU90
Danehurst Cl, Egh. TW20 .112 AY93
Danehurst Gdns, Ilf. IG4 .68 EL57
Danehurst St, SW6 .99 CY81
Daneland, Barn. EN4 .28 DF44
Danemead Gro, Nthlt. UB5 .60 CB64
Danemere St, SW15 .99 CW83
Dane Pl, E3 off Roman Rd .85 DZ68
Dane Rd, N18 .46 DW48
SW19 .140 DC95
W13 .79 CJ74
Ashford TW15 .115 BQ93
Ilford IG1 .69 EQ64
Sevenoaks (Otford) TN14 .181 FE117
Southall UB1 .78 BY73
Warlingham CR6 .177 DX117
Danes, The, St.Alb. (Park St)
AL2 .8 CC28
Danesbury Rd, Felt. TW13 .115 BV88
Danes Cl, Grav. (Nthflt) DA11 .130 GC90
Leatherhead (Oxshott)
KT22 .154 CC114
Danescombe, SE12
off Winn Rd .124 EG88
Danes Ct, Wem. HA9
off North End Rd .62 CP62
Danescourt Cres, Sutt. SM1 .140 DC103
Danescroft, NW4 .63 CX57
Danescroft Av, NW4 .63 CX57
Danescroft Gdns, NW4 .63 CX57
Danesdale Rd, E9 .85 DY65
Danesfield, SE5 .102 DS79
Woking (Ripley) GU23 .167 BF123
Danesfield Cl, Walt. KT12 .135 BV104
Danes Gate, Har. HA1 .61 CE55
Daneshill, Red. RH1 .184 DE133
Danes Hill, Wok. GU22 .167 BA118
Daneshill Cl, Red. RH1 .184 DE133
Danes Rd, Rom. RM7 .71 FC59
Dane St, WC1 .196 B7
Danes Way, Brwd. (Pilg.Hat.)
CM15 .54 FU43
Leatherhead (Oxshott)
KT22 .155 CD114
Daneswood Av, SE6 .123 EC90
Danewood Cl, Wey. KT13 .153 BP106
Danethorpe Rd, Wem. HA0 .79 CK65
Danetree Cl, Epsom KT19 .156 CQ108
Danetree Rd, Epsom KT19 .156 CQ108
Danette Gdns, Dag. RM10 .70 EZ61
Daneville Rd, SE5 .102 DR81
Dangan Rd, E11 .68 EG58
Daniel Bolt Cl, E14
off Uamvar St .85 EB71
Daniel Cl, N18 .46 DW49
SW17 .120 DE93
Grays RM16 .111 GH76
Grays (Chaff.Hun.) RM16 .110 FY75
Hounslow TW4
off Harvey Rd .116 BZ87
Daniel Gdns, SE15 .102 DT80
Daniell Way, Croy. CR0 .141 DL102
Daniel Pl, NW4 .63 CV58
Daniel Rd, W5 .80 CM73
Daniels La, Warl. CR6 .177 DZ116
Daniels Rd, SE15 .102 DW83
Daniel Way, Bans. SM7 .158 DB114
Dan Leno Wk, SW6
off Britannia Rd .100 DB80
Dan Mason Dr, W4 .98 CR82
Dansey Pl, W1 .195 M10
Dansington Rd, Well. DA16 .106 EU84
Danson Cres, Well. DA16 .106 EV83
Danson Interchange, Sid. DA15
off East Rochester Way .126 EW86
Danson La, Well. DA16 .106 EU84
Danson Mead, Well. DA16 .106 EW83
★ Danson Park, Well. DA16 .106 EW84
Danson Pk, Bexh. DA6 .106 EW84
Danson Rd, Bex. DA5 .126 EX85
Bexleyheath DA6 .126 EX85
Danson Underpass, Sid. DA15
off Danson Rd .126 EW85
Dante Pl, SE11 .200 G8
Dante Rd, SE11 .200 F8
Danube Apts, N8
off New River Av .65 DM56
Danube St, SW3 .198 C10
Danvers Rd, N8 .65 DK56
Danvers St, SW3 .100 DD79
Danvers Way, Cat. CR3 .176 DQ123
Danyon Cl, Rain. RM13 .90 FJ68
Danziger Way, Borwd. WD6 .26 CQ39
Daphne Gdns, E4
off Gunners Gro .47 EC48
Daphne St, SW18 .120 DC86
Daplyn St, E1 off Hanbury St .84 DU71
D'Arblay St, W1 .195 L9
Darby Cl, Cat. CR3 .176 DQ122
Darby Cres, Sun. TW16 .136 BW96
Darby Dr, Wal.Abb. EN9 .15 EC33
Darby Gdns, Sun. TW16 .136 BW96
Darcy Av, Wall. SM6 .159 DJ105
Darcy Cl, N20 .44 DD47
D'Arcy Cl, Brwd. (Hutt.) CM13 .55 GB45
Darcy Cl, Couls. CR5 .175 DP119
Waltham Cross (Chsht)
EN8 .15 DY31
D'Arcy Dr, Har. HA3 .61 CK56
Darcy Gdns, Dag. RM9 .88 EZ67
D'Arcy Gdns, Har. HA3 .62 CL56
D'Arcy Pl, Ashtd. KT21 .172 CM117
Bromley BR2 .144 EG98
Darcy Rd, SW16 .141 DL96
D'Arcy Rd, Ashtd. KT21 .172 CM117
Darcy Rd, Islw. TW7
off London Rd .97 CG81
D'Arcy Rd, Sutt. SM3 .157 CX105
Dare Gdns, Dag. RM8 .70 EY62
Darell Rd, Rich. TW9 .98 CN83
Darent Cl, Sev. (Chipstead)
TN13 .190 FC122
DARENTH, Dart. DA2 .128 FQ91
Darenth Gdns, West. TN16
off Quebec Av .189 ER126
Darenth Hill, Dart. (Darenth)
DA2 .128 FQ92
Darenth Interchange, Dart. DA2
off Dartford Bypass .128 FP90
Darenth La, Sev. (Dunt.Grn)
TN13 .190 FE121
South Ockendon RM15 .91 FU72
Darenth Pk Av, Dart. DA2 .129 FR89
Darenth Rd, N16 .66 DT59
Dartford DA1 .128 FM87
Dartford (Darenth) DA2 .128 FP91
Welling DA16 .106 EU81
Darenth Way, Sev. (Shore.)
TN14 .165 FG111
Darenth Wd Rd, Dart. DA2 .129 FS89
Darent Ind Pk, Erith DA8 .108 FJ79
Darent Mead, Dart. (Sutt.H.)
DA4 .148 FP95
H Darent Valley Hosp, Dart.
DA2 .129 FS88
Darent Valley Path, Dart. DA1,
DA2, DA4 .128 FM89
Sevenoaks TN13, TN14 .181 FG115
Darfield Rd, SE4 .123 DZ85
Darfield Way, W10 .81 CX72
Darfur St, SW15 .99 CX83
Dargate Cl, SE19
off Chipstead Cl .122 DT94
Darien Rd, SW11 .100 DD83
Darkes La, Pot.B. EN6 .12 DA32
Dark Ho Wk, EC3
off King William St .84 DR73
Dark La, Brwd. (Gt Warley)
CM14 .53 FU52
Waltham Cross (Chsht) EN7 .14 DU31
Darlands Dr, Barn. EN5 .27 CX43
Darlan Rd, SW6 .99 CZ80
Darlaston Rd, SW19 .119 CX94
Darley Cl, Add. KT15 .152 BJ106
Croydon CR0 .143 DY100
Darley Cft, St.Alb. AL2 .8 CB28
Darley Dr, N.Mal. KT3 .138 CR96
Darley Gdns, Mord. SM4 .140 DB100
Darley Rd, N9 .46 DT46
SW11 .120 DF86
Darling Rd, SE4 .103 EA83
Darling Row, E1 .84 DV70
Darlington Gdns, Rom. RM3 .52 FK50
Darlington Path, Rom. RM3
off Darlington Gdns .52 FK50
Darlington Rd, SE27 .121 DP92
Darlton Cl, Dart. DA1 .107 FF83
Darmaine Cl, S.Croy. CR2
off Churchill Rd .160 DQ108
Darnaway Pl, E14
off Abbott Rd .85 EC72
Darndale Cl, E17 .47 DZ54
Darnets Fld, Sev. (Otford)
TN14 .181 FF117
Darnhills, Rad. WD7 .25 CG35
Darnicle Hill, Wal.Cr. (Chsht)
EN7 .13 DM25
Darnley Ho, E14 .85 DY72
Darnley Pk, Wey. KT13 .135 BP104
Darnley Rd, E9 .84 DV65
Gravesend DA11 .131 GG88
Grays RM17
off Stanley Rd .110 GB79
Woodford Green IG8 .48 EG53
Darnley St, Grav. DA11 .131 GG87
Darnley Ter, W11
off St. James's Gdns .81 CY74
Darns Hill, Swan. BR8 .147 FC101
Darrell Cl, Slou. SL3 .93 AZ77
Darrell Rd, SE22 .122 DU85
Darren Cl, N4 .65 DM59
Darrick Wd Rd, Orp. BR6 .145 ER103
Darrington Rd, Borwd. WD6 .26 CL39
Darris Cl, Hayes UB4 .78 BY70
Darsley Dr, SW8 .101 DK81
Dart Cl, Slou. SL3 .93 BB79
Upminster RM14 .73 FR58
Dartfields, Rom. RM3 .52 FK51
DARTFORD, DA1 & DA2;
DA4 .128 FJ87
⇌ Dartford .128 FL86
Dartford Av, N9 .30 DW44
Dartford Bypass, Bex. DA5 .127 FE88
Dartford DA2 .127 FH89
Dartford Gdns, Rom. (Chad.Hth)
RM6 off Heathfield Pk Dr .70 EV58
★ Dartford Heath, Dart.
DA1 .127 FG88
Dartford Heath, Bex. DA5
off Dartford Bypass .127 FF88
Dartford Ho, SE1
off Longfield Est .102 DT77
★ Dartford Mus, Dart. DA1 .128 FL87
Dartford Rd, Bex. DA5 .127 FC88
Dartford DA1 .127 FG86
Dartford (Fnghm) DA4 .148 FP95
Sevenoaks TN13 .191 FJ124
Dartford St, SE17 .102 DQ79
Dartford Trade Pk, Dart. DA1 .128 FL89
Dartford Tunnel, Dart. DA1 .109 FR83
Purfleet RM19 .109 FR83
Dartford Tunnel App Rd, Dart.
DA1 .128 FN86
Dart Grn, S.Ock. RM15 .91 FV72
Dartmoor Wk, E14 .204 A8
Dartmouth Av, Wok. GU21 .151 BC114
Dartmouth Cl, W11 .81 CZ72
Dartmouth Grn, Wok. GU21 .151 BD114
Dartmouth Gro, SE10 .103 EC81
Dartmouth Hill, SE10 .103 EC81
Dartmouth Ho, Kings.T. KT2
off Kingsgate Rd .138 CL95
DARTMOUTH PARK, NW5 .65 DH62
Dartmouth Pk Av, NW5 .65 DH62
Dartmouth Pk Hill, N19 .65 DH60
NW5 .65 DH60
Dartmouth Pk Rd, NW5 .65 DH63
Dartmouth Path, Wok. GU21 .151 BD114
Dartmouth Pl, SE23
off Dartmouth Rd .122 DW89
W4 .98 CS79
Dartmouth Rd, E16
off Fords Pk Rd .86 EG72
NW2 .81 CX65
NW4 .63 CU58
SE23 .122 DW90
SE26 .122 DW90
Bromley BR2 .144 EG101
Ruislip HA4 .59 BU62
Dartmouth Row, SE10 .103 EC82
Dartmouth St, SW1 .199 M5
Dartmouth Ter, SE10 .103 ED81
Dartnell Av, W.Byf. KT14 .152 BH112
Dartnell Cl, W.Byf. KT14 .152 BH112
Dartnell Ct, W.Byf. KT14 .152 BJ112
Dartnell Cres, W.Byf. KT14 .152 BH112
DARTNELL PARK, W.Byf.
KT14 .152 BJ112
Dartnell Pk Rd, W.Byf. KT14 .152 BJ111
Dartnell Pl, W.Byf. KT14 .152 BH112
Dartnell Rd, Croy. CR0 .142 DT101
Dartrey Twr, SW10
off World's End Est .100 DD80
Dartrey Wk, SW10
off World's End Est .100 DD80
Dart St, W10 .81 CY69
Dartview Cl, Grays RM17 .110 GE77
Darvel Cl, Wok. GU21 .166 AU116
Darvells Yd, Rick. WD3
off Common Rd .21 BD42
Darville Rd, N16 .66 DT62
Darwell Cl, E6 .87 EN68
Darwen Pl, E2 off Wharf Pl .84 DV67
Darwin Cl, N11 .45 DH48
Orpington BR6 .163 ER106
Darwin Ct, SE17
off Catesby St .102 DR77
Darwin Dr, Sthl. UB1 .78 CB72
Darwin Gdns, Wat. WD19
off Barnhurst Path .40 BW50
Darwin Rd, N22 .45 DP53
W5 .97 CJ78
Slough SL3 .93 AZ75
Tilbury RM18 .111 GF81
Welling DA16 .105 ET83
Darwin St, SE17 .201 L8
Daryngton Dr, Grnf. UB6 .79 CD68
Dashwood Cl, Bexh. DA6 .126 FA85
Slough SL3 .92 AW77
West Byfleet KT14 .152 BJ112
Dashwood Rd, N8 .65 DM58
Gravesend DA11 .131 GG89
Dassett Rd, SE27 .121 DP92
Datchelor Pl, SE5 .102 DR81
DATCHET, Slou. SL3 .92 AW81
⇌ Datchet .92 AV81
Datchet Pl, Slou. (Datchet)
SL3 .92 AV81
Datchet Rd, SE6 .123 DZ90
Slough SL3 .92 AT77
Slough (Horton) SL3 .93 AZ83
Windsor (Old Wind.) SL4 .92 AU84
Datchworth Ct, N4
off Queens Dr .66 DQ62
Date St, SE17 .102 DQ78

★ Place of interest ⇌ Railway station ⊖ London Underground station DLR Docklands Light Railway station Tra Tramlink station H Hospital Riv Pedestrian ferry landing stage

Daubeney Gdns, N17 46 DQ52
Daubeney Rd, E5 67 DY63
N17 46 DQ52
Daubeney Twr, SE8 203 M9
Dault Rd, SW18 120 DC86
Davall Ho, Grays RM17
off Argent St 110 GB79
Davema Cl, Chis. BR7
off Brenchley Cl 145 EN95
Davenant Rd, N19 65 DK61
Croydon CR0
off Duppas Hill Rd 159 DP105
Davenant St, E1 84 DU71
Davenham Av, Nthwd. HA6 39 BT49
Davenport Cl, Tedd. TW11 117 CG93
Davenport Ho, SE11
off Walnut Tree Wk 101 DN77
Davenport Rd, SE6 123 EB86
Sidcup DA14 126 EX89
Daventer Dr, Stan. HA7 41 CF52
Daventry Av, E17 67 EA57
Daventry Cl, Slou. (Colnbr.)
SL3 93 BF81
Daventry Gdns, Rom. RM3 52 FJ50
Daventry Grn, Rom. RM3
off Hailsham Rd 52 FJ50
Daventry Rd, Rom. RM3 52 FJ50
Daventry St, NW1 194 B6
Davern Cl, SE10 205 K9
Davey Cl, N7 83 DM65
N13 45 DM50
Davey Rd, E9 85 EA66
Davey St, SE15 102 DT79
David Av, Grnf. UB6 79 CE69
David Cl, Hayes UB3 95 BR80
David Dr, Rom. RM3 52 FN51
Davidge St, SE1 200 F5
David Lee Pt, E15 86 EE67
David Ms, W1 194 E6
David Rd, Dag. RM8 70 EY61
Slough (Colnbr.) SL3 93 BF82
Davidson Gdns, SW8 101 DL80
Davidson La, Har. HA1
off Grove Hill 61 CF59
Davidson Rd, Croy. CR0 142 DT100
Davidson Way, Rom. RM7 71 FE58
Davids Rd, SE23 122 DW88
David St, E15 85 ED65
David's Way, Ilf. IG6 49 ES52
David Twigg Cl, Kings.T. KT2 138 CL95
Davies Cl, Croy. CR0 142 DU100
Rainham RM13 90 FJ69
Davies La, E11 68 EE61
Davies Ms, W1 195 H10
Davies St, W1 195 H10
Davington Gdns, Dag. RM8 70 EV64
Davington Rd, Dag. RM8 88 EV65
Davinia Cl, Wdf.Grn. IG8
off Deacon Way 49 EM51
Davis Av, Grav. (Nthflt) DA11 130 GE88
Davis Cl, Sev. TN13 191 FJ122
Davison Cl, Epsom KT19 156 CP111
Waltham Cross EN8 15 DX28
Davison Dr, Wal.Cr. (Chsht)
EN8 15 DX28
Davison Rd, Slou. SL3 93 AZ78
Davis Rd, W3 81 CT74
Chessington KT9 156 CN105
Grays (Chaff.Hun.) RM16 110 FZ76
South Ockendon (Aveley)
RM15 91 FR74
Weybridge KT13 152 BM110
Davis St, E13 86 EH68
Davisville Rd, W12 99 CU75
Davos Cl, Wok. GU22 166 AY119
Davys Pl, Grav. DA12 131 GL93
Dawell Dr, West. (Bigg.H.)
TN16 178 EJ117
Dawes Av, Horn. RM12 72 FK62
Isleworth TW7 117 CG85
Dawes Cl, Green. DA9 129 FT85
Dawes Ct, Esher KT10 154 CB105
Dawes Ho, SE17 201 L9
Dawes La, Rick. (Sarratt) WD3 21 BE37
Dawes Moor Cl, Slou. SL2 74 AW72
Dawes Rd, SW6 99 CY80
Uxbridge UB10 76 BL68
Dawes St, SE17 201 L10
Dawley Av, Uxb. UB8 77 BQ71
Dawley Grn, S.Ock. RM15 91 FU72
Dawley Par, Hayes UB3
off Dawley Rd 77 BQ73
Dawley Ride, Slou. (Colnbr.)
SL3 93 BE81
Dawley Rd, Hayes UB3 77 BR73
Uxbridge UB8 77 BQ73
Dawlish Av, N13 45 DL49
SW18 120 DB89
Greenford UB6 79 CG68
Dawlish Dr, Ilf. IG3 69 ES63
Pinner HA5 60 BY57
Ruislip HA4 59 BU61
Dawlish Rd, E10 67 EC61
N17 66 DU55
NW2 81 CX65
Dawlish Wk, Rom. RM3 52 FJ53
Dawnay Gdns, SW18 120 DD89
Dawnay Rd, SW18 120 DC89
Dawn Cl, Houns. TW4 96 BY83
Dawn Cres, E15 *off Bridge Rd* 85 ED67
Dawn Redwood Cl, Slou.
(Horton) SL3 93 BA83
Dawpool Rd, NW2 63 CT61
Daws Hill, E4 31 EC41
Daws La, NW7 43 CT50
Dawson Av, Bark. IG11 87 ES66
Orpington BR5 146 EV96
Dawson Cl, SE18 105 EQ77
Hayes UB3 77 BR71
Dawson Dr, Rain. RM13 89 FH66
Swanley BR8 127 FE94
Dawson Gdns, Bark. IG11
off Dawson Av 87 ET66
Dawson Hts Est, SE22 122 DU87
Dawson Pl, W2 82 DA73
Dawson Rd, NW2 63 CW64
Kingston upon Thames
KT1 138 CM97
West Byfleet (Byfleet)
KT14 152 BK111
Dawson St, E2 84 DT68
Dax Ct, Sun. TW16
off Thames St 136 BW97
Daybrook Rd, SW19 140 DB96
Daylesford Av, SW15 99 CU84
Daylop Dr, Chig. IG7 50 EV48
Daymer Gdns, Pnr. HA5 59 BV56
Daymerslea Ridge, Lthd.
KT22 171 CJ121
Days Acre, S.Croy. CR2 160 DT110
Daysbrook Rd, SW2 121 DM89
Days La, Brwd. (Pilg.Hat.)
CM15 54 FU42
Sidcup DA15 125 ES87
Dayton Dr, Erith DA8 108 FK78
Dayton Gro, SE15 102 DW81
Deacon Cl, Cob. (Down.)
KT11 169 BV119
Purley CR8 159 DL109
Deacon Ms, N1 84 DR66
Deacon Pl, Cat. CR3 176 DQ123
Deacon Rd, NW2 63 CU64
Kingston upon Thames
KT2 138 CM95
Deacons Cl, Borwd. (Els.)
WD6 26 CN42
Pinner HA5 39 BV54
Deacons Hill, Wat. WD19 24 BW44
Deacon's Hill Rd, Borwd. (Els.)
WD6 26 CM42
Deacons Leas, Orp. BR6 163 ER105
Deacons Ri, N2 64 DD57
Deacons Wk, Hmptn. TW12
off Bishops Gro 116 BZ91
Deacon Way, SE17 201 H8
Woodford Green IG8 49 EM52
Deadhearn La, Ch.St.G. HP8 36 AY46
Deadman's Ash La, Rick.
(Sarratt) WD3 22 BH36
Deakin Cl, Wat. WD18
off Chenies Way 39 BS45
Deal Ms, W5 *off Darwin Rd* 97 CK77
Deal Porters Way, SE16 202 G6
Deal Rd, SW17 120 DG93
Deals Gateway, SE13 103 EA81
Deal St, E1 84 DU71
Dealtry Rd, SW15 99 CW84
Deal Wk, SW9
off Mandela St 101 DN80
Deanacre Cl, Ger.Cr.
(Chal.St.P.) SL9 36 AY51
DEAN BOTTOM, Dart. DA4 149 FV97
Dean Bradley St, SW1 199 P7
Dean Cl, E9
off Churchill Wk 66 DW64
SE16 203 J3
Uxbridge UB10 76 BM66
Woking GU22 167 BE115
Dean Ct, SW8
off Thorncroft St 101 DL80
Wembley HA0 61 CH62
Deancroft Rd, Ger.Cr.
(Chal.St.P.) SL9 36 AY51
Deancross St, E1 84 DW72
Dean Dr, Stan. HA7 42 CL54
Deane Av, Ruis. HA4 60 BW64
Deane Cft Rd, Pnr. HA5 59 BV58
Deanery Cl, N2 64 DE56
Deanery Ms, W1 198 G2
Deanery Rd, E15 86 EE65
Edenbridge (Crock.H.) TN8 189 EQ134
Deanery St, W1 198 G2
Deane Way, Ruis. HA4 59 BV58
Dean Farrar St, SW1 199 M6
Dean Fld, Hem.H. (Bov.) HP3 5 BA27
Dean Gdns, E17 67 ED56
W13 *off Northfield Av* 79 CH74
Deanhill Rd, SW14 98 CP84
Dean La, Red. RH1 175 DH123
Dean Rd, NW2 81 CW65
SE28 88 EU73
Croydon CR0 160 DR105
Hampton TW12 116 CA92
Hounslow TW3 116 CB85
Dean Ryle St, SW1 199 P8
Deansbrook Cl, Edg. HA8 42 CQ51
Deansbrook Rd, Edg. HA8 42 CQ51
Deans Bldgs, SE17 201 K9
Deans Cl, W4 98 CP79
Abbots Langley WD5 7 BR32
Amersham HP6 20 AT37
Dean's Cl, Croy. CR0 142 DT104
Deans Cl, Edg. HA8 42 CQ51
Slough (Stoke P.) SL2 74 AV67
Tadworth (Walt.Hill) KT20 173 CV124
Deans Ct, EC4 196 G9
Deanscroft Av, NW9 62 CQ61
Deans Dr, N13 45 DP51
Edgware HA8 42 CR50
Deans Factory Est, Rain. RM13
off Lambs La N 90 FK70
Deansfield, Cat. CR3 186 DT125
Dean's Gate Cl, SE23 123 DX90
Deans La, W4 98 CP79
Edgware HA8 42 CQ51
Redhill (Nutfld) RH1 185 DN133
Tadworth (Walt.Hill) KT20 173 CV124
Deans Ms, W1 195 J8
Deans Rd, W7 79 CF74
Brentwood CM14 54 FV49
Redhill (S.Merst.) RH1 185 DJ130
Sutton SM1 140 DB104
Dean Stanley St, SW1 199 P7
Dean St, E7 68 EG64
W1 195 M8
Deans Wk, Couls. CR5 175 DN118
Deansway, N2 64 DD56
N9 46 DS48
Deans Way, Edg. HA8 42 CQ50
Dean's Yd, SW1 199 N6
Dean Trench St, SW1 199 P7
Dean Wk, Edg. HA8
off Deansbrook Rd 42 CQ51
Deanway, Ch.St.G. HP8 36 AU48
Dean Way, Sthl. UB2 96 CB75
Dearne Cl, Stan. HA7 41 CG50
De'Arn Gdns, Mitch. CR4 140 DE97
Dearsley Ho, Rain. RM13 89 FD68
Dearsley Rd, Enf. EN1 30 DU41
Deason St, E15 *off High St* 85 EC67
De Barowe Ms, N5
off Leigh Rd 65 DP63
DEBDEN, Loug. IG10 33 ER41
⊖ **Debden** 33 EQ42
Debden Cl, NW9
off Kenley Av 42 CS54
Debden Cl, Kings.T. KT2 117 CK92
Woodford Green IG8 48 EJ52
DEBDEN GREEN, Loug. IG10 33 EQ38
Debden Grn, Loug. IG10 33 EP38
Debden La, Loug. IG10 33 EP38
Debden Rd, Loug. IG10 33 EP38
Debden Wk, Horn. RM12 89 FH65
De Beauvoir Cres, N1 84 DS67
De Beauvoir Est, N1 84 DR67
De Beauvoir Rd, N1 84 DS67
De Beauvoir Sq, N1 84 DS66
DE BEAUVOIR TOWN, N1 84 DR67
Debenham Rd, Wal.Cr.
(Chsht) EN7 14 DV27
Debnams Rd, SE16 202 F9
De Bohun Av, N14 29 DH44
Deborah Cl, Islw. TW7 97 CE81
Deborah Cres, Ruis. HA4 59 BR59
Debrabant Cl, Erith DA8 107 FD79
De Brome Rd, Felt. TW13 116 BW88
De Burgh Gdns, Tad. KT20 173 CX119
De Burgh Pk, Bans. SM7 174 DB115
Deburgh Rd, SW19 120 DC94
Decies Way, Slou. (Stoke P.)
SL2 74 AU67
Decima St, SE1 201 M6
Deck Cl, SE16 203 J4
Decoy Av, NW11 63 CY57
De Crespigny Pk, SE5 102 DR82
Dee Cl, Upmin. RM14 73 FS58
Deeley Rd, SW8 101 DK81
Deena Cl, W3 80 CM72
Deepdale, SW19 119 CX91
Deepdale Av, Brom. BR2 144 EF98
Deepdale Cl, N11 44 DG51
Deepdene, W5 80 CM70
Potters Bar EN6 11 CX31
Deepdene Av, Croy. CR0 142 DT104
Deepdene Cl, E11 68 EG56
Deepdene Ct, N21 29 DP44
Bromley BR2 144 EE97
Deepdene Gdns, SW2 121 DM87
Deepdene Path, Loug. IG10 33 EN42
Deepdene Pt, SE23
off Dacres Rd 123 DX90
Deepdene Rd, SE5 102 DR84
Loughton IG10 33 EN42
Welling DA16 106 EU83
Deep Fld, Slou. (Datchet) SL3 92 AV80
Deepfield Way, Couls. CR5 175 DL116
Deep Pool La, Wok. (Chobham)
GU24 150 AV114
Deepwell Cl, Islw. TW7 97 CG81
Deepwood La, Grnf. UB6
off Cowgate Rd 79 CD69
Deerbrook Rd, SE24 121 DP88
Deercote Ct, Wal.Cr. EN8
off Turners Hill 15 DX30
Deerdale Rd, SE24 102 DQ84
Deere Av, Rain. RM13 89 FG65
Deerfield Cl, NW9
off Rookery Cl 63 CT57
Deerhurst Cl, Felt. TW13 115 BU91
Deerhurst Cres, Hmptn.
(Hmptn H.) TW12 116 CC92
Deerhurst Rd, NW2 81 CX65
SW16 121 DM92
Deerings Dr, Pnr. HA5 59 BU57
Deerings Rd, Reig. RH2 184 DB134
Deerleap Gro, E4 31 EB43
Deerleap La, Sev. TN14 164 EX113
Dee Rd, Rich. TW9 98 CM84
Deer Pk Cl, Kings.T. KT2 118 CP94
Deer Pk Gdns, Mitch. CR4 140 DD97
Deer Pk Rd, SW19 140 DB96
Deer Pk Wk, Chesh. HP5 4 AS28
Deer Pk Way, Wal.Abb. EN9 31 EB36
West Wickham BR4 144 EF103
Deers Fm Cl, Wok. (Wisley)
GU23 168 BL116
Deerswood Cl, Cat. CR3 176 DU124
Deeside Rd, SW17 120 DD90
Dee St, E14 85 EC72
Deeves Hall La, Pot.B. EN6 10 CS33
Dee Way, Epsom KT19 156 CS110
Romford RM1 51 FE53
Defence Cl, SE28
off Miles Dr 87 ES74
Defiance Wk, SE18 105 EM76
Defiant Way, Wall. SM6 159 DL108
Defoe Av, Rich. TW9 98 CN80
Defoe Cl, SE16 203 M5
SW17 120 DE93
Erith DA8 *off Selkirk Dr* 107 FE81
Defoe Ho, EC2 197 J6
Defoe Par, Grays RM16 111 GH76
Defoe Pl, EC2 *off Beech St* 84 DQ71
SW17 *off Lessingham Av* 120 DF91
Defoe Rd, N16 66 DS61
Defoe Way, Rom. RM5 51 FB51
De Frene Rd, SE26 123 DX91
De Gama Pl, E14
off Maritime Quay 103 EA78
Degema Rd, Chis. BR7 125 EP92
Dehar Cres, NW9 63 CT59
Dehavilland Cl, Nthlt. UB5 78 BX69
De Havilland Ct, Ilf. IG1
off Vicarage La 69 ER60
Radlett (Shenley) WD7
off Armstrong Gdns 10 CL32
De Havilland Dr, SE18 105 EP79
Weybridge KT13 152 BL111
★ **De Havilland Mosquito Aircraft Mus**, St.Alb. AL2 10 CP29
De Havilland Rd, Edg. HA8 42 CP54
Hounslow TW5 96 BW80
De Havilland Way, Abb.L.
WD5 7 BT32
Staines (Stanw.) TW19 114 BK86
Dekker Rd, SE21 122 DS86
Delabole Rd, Red. (Merst.)
RH1 185 DL129
Delacourt Rd, SE3
off Old Dover Rd 104 EH80
Delafield Ho, E1
off Christian St 84 DU72
Delafield Rd, SE7 104 EH78
Grays RM17 110 GD78
Delaford Cl, Iver SL0 75 BF72
Delaford Rd, SE16 202 E10
Delaford St, SW6 99 CY80
Delagarde Rd, West. TN16 189 EQ126
Delamare Cres, Croy. CR0 142 DW100
Delamare Rd, Wal.Cr. (Chsht)
EN8 15 DZ30
Delamere Gdns, NW7 42 CR51
Delamere Rd, SW20 139 CX95
W5 80 CL74
Borehamwood WD6 26 CP39
Hayes UB4 78 BX73
Delamere St, W2
off Westbourne Ter Ms 82 DC71
Delamere Ter, W2 82 DB71
Delancey Pas, NW1
off Delancey St 83 DH67
Delancey St, NW1 83 DH67
Delaporte Cl, Epsom KT17 156 CS112
De Lapre Cl, Orp. BR5 146 EX101
De Lara Way, Wok. GU21 166 AX118
Delargy Cl, Grays RM16 111 GH76
De Laune St, SE17 101 DP78
Delaware Rd, W9 82 DB70
Delawyk Cres, SE24 122 DQ86
Delcombe Av, Wor.Pk. KT4 139 CW102
Delderfield, Lthd. KT22 171 CK120
Delft Way, SE22
off East Dulwich Gro 122 DS85
Delhi Rd, Enf. EN1 46 DT45
Delhi St, N1 83 DL67
Delia St, SW18 120 DB87
Delisle Rd, SE28 87 ES74
Delius Cl, Borwd. (Els.) WD6 25 CJ44
Delius Gro, E15 85 ED68
Dell, The, SE2 106 EU78
SE19 142 DT95
Bexley DA5 127 FE88
Brentford TW8 97 CJ79
Brentwood (Gt Warley)
CM13 53 FV51
Feltham TW14 115 BV87
Gerrards Cross (Chal.St.P.)
SL9 36 AY51
Greenhithe DA9 129 FV85
Northwood HA6 39 BS47
Pinner HA5 40 BX54
Radlett WD7 25 CG36
Reigate RH2 184 DA133
Tadworth KT20 173 CW121
Waltham Abbey EN9
off Greenwich Way 31 EC36
Wembley HA0 61 CH64
Woking GU21 166 AW118
Woodford Green IG8 48 EH48
Della Path, E5 66 DU62
Dellbow Rd, Felt. TW14
off Central Way 115 BV85
Dell Cl, E15 85 ED67
Leatherhead (Fetch.) KT22 171 CE123
Wallington SM6 159 DK105
Woodford Green IG8 48 EH48
Dell Fm Rd, Ruis. HA4 59 BR57
Dellfield Cl, Beck. BR3 143 EC95
Radlett WD7 25 CE35
Watford WD17 23 BU40
Dellfield Cres, Uxb. UB8 76 BJ70
Dellfield Par, Uxb. (Cowley)
UB8 *off High St* 76 BJ70
Dell La, Epsom KT17 157 CU106
Dellmeadow, Abb.L. WD5 7 BS30
Dellors Cl, Barn. EN5 27 CX43
Dellow Cl, Ilf. IG2 69 ER59
Dellow St, E1 84 DV73
Dell Ri, St.Alb. (Park St) AL2 8 CB26
Dell Rd, Enf. EN3 30 DW38
Epsom KT17 157 CU107
Grays RM17 110 GB77
Watford WD24 23 BU37
West Drayton UB7 94 BM76
Dells Cl, E4 47 EB45
Teddington TW11
off Middle La 117 CF93
Dellside, Uxb. (Hare.) UB9 58 BJ57
Dell Side, Wat. WD24
off The Harebreaks 23 BU37
Dell's Ms, SW1 199 L9
Dell Wk, N.Mal. KT3 138 CS96
Dell Way, W13 79 CJ72
Dellwood, Rick. WD3 38 BH46
Dellwood Gdns, Ilf. IG5 69 EN55
Delmare Cl, SW9
off Brighton Ter 101 DM84
Delme Cres, SE3 104 EH82
Delmey Cl, Croy. CR0
off Radcliffe Rd 142 DT104
Deloraine St, SE8 103 EA81
Delorme St, W6 99 CX79
Delta Cl, Wok. (Chobham)
GU24 150 AT110
Worcester Park KT4 138 CS104
Delta Ct, NW2 63 CU61
Delta Gain, Wat. WD19 40 BX47
Delta Gro, Nthlt. UB5 78 BX69
Delta Rd, Brwd. (Hutt.) CM13 55 GD44
Woking GU21 167 BA116
Woking (Chobham) GU24 150 AT110
Worcester Park KT4 138 CS104
Delta St, E2
off Wellington Row 84 DU69
Delta Way, Egh. TW20 133 BC95
De Luci Rd, Erith DA8 107 FC78
De Lucy St, SE2 106 EV77
Delvan Cl, SE18
off Ordnance Rd 105 EN80
Delvers Mead, Dag. RM10 71 FC63
Delverton Rd, SE17 101 DP78
Delves, Tad. KT20 173 CX121
Delvino Rd, SW6 100 DA81
De Mandeville Gate, Enf. EN1
off Southbury Rd 30 DU42
De Mel Cl, Epsom KT19 156 CP112
Demesne Rd, Wall. SM6 159 DK106
Demeta Cl, Wem. HA9 62 CQ62
De Montfort Par, SW16
off Streatham High Rd 121 DL90
De Montfort Rd, SW16 121 DL90
De Morgan Rd, SW6 100 DB83
Dempster Cl, Surb. KT6 137 CJ102
Dempster Rd, SW18 120 DC85
Denbar Par, Rom. RM7
off Mawney Rd 71 FC56
Denberry Dr, Sid. DA14 126 EV90
Denbigh Cl, NW10 80 CS66
W11 81 CZ73
Chislehurst BR7 125 EM93
Hornchurch RM11 72 FN56
Ruislip HA4 59 BT61
Denbigh Cl, Sthl. UB1 78 BZ72
Sutton SM1 157 CZ106
Denbigh Dr, Hayes UB3 95 BQ75
Denbigh Gdns, Rich. TW10 118 CM85
Denbigh Ms, SW1 199 K9
Denbigh Pl, SW1 199 K10
Denbigh Rd, E6 86 EK69
W11 81 CZ73
W13 79 CH73
Hounslow TW3 96 CB82
Southall UB1 78 BZ72
Denbigh St, SW1 199 K9
Denbigh Ter, W11 81 CZ73
Denbridge Rd, Brom. BR1 145 EM96
Denby Rd, Cob. KT11 154 BW113
Den Cl, Beck. BR3 143 ED97
Dendridge Cl, Enf. EN1 30 DV37
Dene, The, W13 79 CH71
Croydon CR0 161 DX105
Sevenoaks TN13 191 FH126
Sutton SM2 157 CZ111
Wembley HA9 62 CL63
West Molesey KT8 136 BZ99
Dene Av, Houns. TW3 96 BZ83
Sidcup DA15 126 EV87
Dene Cl, SE4 103 DY83
Bromley BR2 144 EF102
Coulsdon CR5 174 DE119
Dartford DA2 127 FE91
Worcester Park KT4 139 CT103
Dene Ct, Stan. HA7 41 CJ50
Denecroft Cres, Uxb. UB10 77 BP67
Denecroft Gdns, Grays RM17 110 GD76
Dene Dr, Orp. BR6 146 EV104
Denefield Dr, Ken. CR8 176 DR115
Dene Gdns, Stan. HA7 41 CJ50
Thames Ditton KT7 137 CG103
Dene Holm Rd, Grav.
(Nthflt) DA11 130 GD90
Denehurst Gdns, NW4 63 CW58
W3 80 CP74
Richmond TW10 98 CN84
Twickenham TW2 117 CD87
Woodford Green IG8 48 EH49
Dene Path, S.Ock. RM15 91 FU72
Dene Pl, Wok. GU21 166 AV118
Dene Rd, N11 44 DF46
Ashtead KT21 172 CM119
Buckhurst Hill IG9 48 EK46
Dartford DA1 128 FM87
Northwood HA6 39 BS51
Denewood, Barn. EN5 28 DC43
Denewood Cl, Wat. WD17 23 BT37
Denewood Rd, N6 64 DF58
Denford St, SE10 205 K10
Dengie Wk, N1 *off Basire St* 84 DQ67
DENHAM, Uxb. UB9 58 BG62
⇌ **Denham** 58 BG59
★ **Denham Aerodrome**, Uxb.
UB9 57 BD57
Denham Av, Uxb. (Denh.)
UB9 57 BF61
Denham Cl, Uxb. (Denh.)
UB9 58 BG62
Welling DA16
off Park Vw Rd 106 EW83
Denham Ct Dr, Uxb. (Denh.)
UB9 58 BH63
Denham Cres, Mitch. CR4 140 DF98
Denham Dr, Ilf. IG2 69 EQ58
Denham Gdn Village, Uxb. UB9
off Denham Grn La 57 BF58
⇌ **Denham Golf Club** 57 BD59
DENHAM GREEN, Uxb. UB9 57 BE58
Denham Grn Cl, Uxb. (Denh.)
UB9 58 BG59
Denham Grn La, Uxb. (Denh.)
UB9 57 BE57
Denham La, Ger.Cr. (Chal.St.P.)
SL9 37 BA53
Denham Lo, Uxb. UB9 76 BJ65
Denham Rd, N20 44 DF48
Egham TW20 113 BA91
Epsom KT17 157 CT112
Feltham TW14 116 BW86
Iver SL0 75 BD67
Uxbridge (Denh.) UB9 75 BE65
Denham Rbt, Uxb. UB9 58 BG63
Denham St, SE10 205 M10
Denham Wk, Ger.Cr. (Chal.St.P.)
SL9 37 AZ51
Denham Way, Bark. IG11 87 ES67
Borehamwood WD6 26 CR39
Rickmansworth (Map.Cr.)
WD3 37 BE50
Uxbridge (Denh.) UB9 58 BG62
Denholme Rd, W9 81 CZ69
Denholme Wk, Rain. RM13
off Ryder Gdns 89 FF65
Denison Cl, N2 64 DC55
Denison Rd, SW19 120 DD93
W5 79 CJ70
Feltham TW13 115 BT91
Deniston Av, Bex. DA5 126 EY88
Denis Way, SW4
off Gauden Rd 101 DK83
Denleigh Gdns, N21 45 DN46
Thames Ditton KT7 137 CE100
Denman Dr, NW11 64 DA57
Ashford TW15 115 BP93
Esher (Clay.) KT10 155 CG106
Denman Dr N, NW11 64 DA57
Denman Dr S, NW11 64 DA57
Denman Pl, W1
off Great Windmill St 83 DK73
Denman Rd, SE15 102 DT81
Denman St, W1 199 M1
Denmark Av, SW19 119 CY94
Denmark Ct, Mord. SM4 140 DA99
Denmark Gdns, Cars. SM5 140 DF104
Denmark Gro, N1 83 DN68
⇌ **Denmark Hill** 102 DR82
Denmark Hill, SE5 102 DR81
Denmark Hill Dr, NW9 63 CT56
Denmark Hill Est, SE5 102 DR84
Denmark Pl, E3
off Kitcat Ter 85 EA69

★ Place of interest ⇌ Railway station ⊖ London Underground station DLR Docklands Light Railway station Tram Tramlink station H Hospital Riv Pedestrian ferry landing stage

Denmark Pl, WC2 195 N8
Denmark Rd, N8 65 DN56
NW6 81 CZ68
SE5 102 DQ81
SE25 142 DU99
SW19 119 CX93
W13 79 CH73
Bromley BR1 144 EH95
Carshalton SM5 140 DF104
Kingston upon Thames KT1 138 CL97
Twickenham TW2 117 CD90
Denmark St, E11
off High Rd Leytonstone 68 EE62
E13 86 EH71
N17 46 DV53
WC2 195 N9
Watford WD17 23 BV40
Denmark Wk, SE27 122 DQ91
Denmead Cl, Ger.Cr. SL9 56 AY59
Denmead Ho, SW15
off Highcliffe Dr 119 CT86
Denmead Rd, Croy. CR0 141 DP102
Dennan Rd, Surb. KT6 138 CM102
Dennard Way, Orp. BR6 163 EP105
Denner Rd, E4 47 EA47
Denne Ter, E8 84 DT67
Dennett Rd, Croy. CR0 141 DN102
Dennetts Gro, SE14
off Dennetts Rd 103 DX82
Dennettsland Rd, Eden. (Crock.H.) TN8 189 EQ134
Dennetts Rd, SE14 102 DW81
Denning Av, Croy. CR0 159 DN105
Denning Cl, NW8 82 DC69
Hampton TW12 116 BZ93
Denning Pt, E1 197 P8
Denning Rd, NW3 64 DD63
Dennington Cl, E5
off Detmold Rd 66 DV61
Dennington Pk Rd, NW6 82 DA65
Denningtons, The, Wor.Pk. KT4 138 CS103
Dennis Av, Wem. HA9 62 CM64
Dennis Cl, Ashf. TW15 115 BR93
Redhill RH1 184 DE132
Dennises La, Upmin. RM14 91 FS67
Dennis Gdns, Stan. HA7 41 CJ50
Dennis La, Stan. HA7 41 CH48
Dennison Pt, E15 85 EC66
Dennis Pk Cres, SW20 139 CY95
Dennis Reeve Cl, Mitch. CR4 140 DF95
Dennis Rd, E.Mol. KT8 136 CC98
Gravesend DA11 131 GG90
South Ockendon RM15 91 FU66
Denny Av, Wal.Abb. EN9 15 ED34
Denny Cl, E6 off Linton Gdns 86 EL71
Denny Cres, SE11 200 E9
Denny Gdns, Dag. RM9
off Canonsleigh Rd 88 EV66
Denny Gate, Wal.Cr. EN8 15 DZ27
Denny Rd, N9 46 DV46
Slough SL3 93 AZ77
Denny St, SE11 200 E10
Den Rd, Brom. BR2 143 ED97
Densham Dr, Pur. CR8 159 DN114
Densham Rd, E15 86 EE67
Densole Cl, Beck. BR3
off Kings Hall Rd 143 DY95
Densworth Gro, N9 46 DW47
Dent Cl, S.Ock. RM15 91 FU72
DENTON, Grav. DA12 131 GL87
Denton, NW1
off Malden Cres 82 DG65
Denton Cl, Barn. EN5 27 CW43
Denton Ct Rd, Grav. DA12 131 GL87
Denton Gro, Walt. KT12 136 BX103
Denton Rd, N8 65 DM57
N18 46 DS49
Bexley DA5 127 FE89
Dartford DA1 127 FE88
Twickenham TW1 117 CK86
Welling DA16 106 EW80
Denton St, SW18 120 DB86
Gravesend DA12 131 GL87
Denton Ter, Bex. DA5
off Denton Rd 127 FE89
Denton Way, E5 67 DX62
Woking GU21 166 AT118
Dents Gro, Tad. (Lwr Kgswd) KT20 183 CZ128
Dents Rd, SW11 120 DF86
Denvale Wk, Wok. GU21 166 AU118
Denver Cl, Orp. BR6 145 ES100
Denver Ind Est, Rain. RM13 89 FF71
Denver Rd, N16 66 DS59
Dartford DA1 127 FG87
Denyer St, SW3 198 C9
Denziloe Av, Uxb. UB10 77 BP69
Denzil Rd, NW10 63 CT64
Deodara Cl, N20 44 DE48
Deodar Rd, SW15 99 CY84
★ Department for Environment, Food & Rural Affairs (D.E.F.R.A.), SW1 199 P2
★ Department for Transport (D.f.T.), SW1 199 N8
★ Department of Health & Dept for Work & Pensions (D.W.P.), SW1 199 P4
Depot App, NW2 63 CX63
Depot Rd, W12 81 CW73
Epsom KT17 156 CS113
Hounslow TW3 97 CD83
DEPTFORD, SE8 103 DZ78
⇌ Deptford 103 DZ80
DLR Deptford Bridge 103 EA81
Deptford Br, SE8 103 EA81
Deptford Bdy, SE8 103 EA81
Deptford Ch St, SE8 103 EA79
Deptford Ferry Rd, E14 204 A9
Deptford Grn, SE8 103 EA79
Deptford High St, SE8 103 EA79
Deptford Strand, SE8 203 N9
Deptford Wf, SE8 203 M8
De Quincey Ho, SW1
off Lupus St 101 DJ78
De Quincey Ms, E16 205 N2
De Quincey Rd, N17 46 DR53
Derby Arms Rd, Epsom KT18 173 CT117
Derby Av, N12 44 DC50
Harrow HA3 41 CD53
Romford RM7 71 FC58
Upminster RM14 72 FM62
Derby Cl, Epsom KT18 173 CV119
Derby Ct, E5 off Overbury St 67 DX63
Derby Gate, SW1 199 P4
Derby Hill, SE23 122 DW89
Derby Hill Cres, SE23 122 DW89
Derby Ho, SE11
off Walnut Tree Wk 101 DN77
Derby Rd, E7 86 EJ66
E9 85 DX67
E18 48 EF53
N18 46 DW50
SW14 98 CP84
SW19 off Russell Rd 120 DA94
Croydon CR0 141 DP103
Enfield EN3 30 DV43
Grays RM17 110 GB78
Greenford UB6 78 CB67
Hounslow TW3 96 CB84
Surbiton KT5 138 CN102
Sutton SM1 157 CZ107
Uxbridge UB8 76 BJ68
Watford WD17 24 BW41
Derby Rd Br, Grays RM17 110 GB79
Derby Rd Ind Est, Houns. TW3
off Derby Rd 96 CB84
Derbyshire St, E2 84 DU69
Derby Sq, The, Epsom KT19
off High St 156 CR113
Derby Stables Rd, Epsom KT18 172 CS117
Derby St, W1 198 G3
Dereham Pl, EC2 197 N3
Romford RM5 51 FB51
Dereham Rd, Bark. IG11 87 ET65
Derek Av, Epsom KT19 156 CN106
Wallington SM6 159 DH105
Wembley HA9 80 CP66
Derek Cl, Epsom (Ewell) KT19 156 CP106
Derek Walcott Cl, SE24
off Shakespeare Rd 121 DP85
Derham Gdns, Upmin. RM14 72 FQ62
Deri Av, Rain. RM13 89 FH70
Dericote St, E8 84 DU67
Deridene Cl, Stai. (Stanw.) TW19 off Bedfont Rd 114 BL86
Derifall Cl, E6 87 EM71
Dering Pl, Croy. CR0 160 DQ105
Dering Rd, Croy. CR0 160 DQ105
Dering St, W1 195 H9
Dering Way, Grav. DA12 131 GM87
Derinton Rd, SW17 120 DF91
Derley Rd, Sthl. UB2 96 BW76
Dermody Gdns, SE13 123 ED85
Dermody Rd, SE13 123 ED85
Deronda Rd, SE24 121 DP88
De Ros Pl, Egh. TW20 113 BA93
Deroy Cl, Cars. SM5 158 DF107
Derrick Av, S.Croy. CR2 160 DQ110
Derrick Gdns, SE7
off Anchor & Hope La 104 EJ77
Derrick Rd, Beck. BR3 143 DZ97
Derry Av, S.Ock. RM15 91 FU72
Derrydown, Wok. GU22 166 AW121
DERRY DOWNS, Orp. BR5 146 EX100
Derry Downs, Orp. BR5 146 EW100
Derry Rd, Croy. CR0 141 DL104
Derry St, W8 100 DB75
Dersingham Av, E12 69 EN64
Dersingham Rd, NW2 63 CY62
Derwent Av, N18 46 DR50
NW7 42 CR50
NW9 62 CS57
SW15 118 CS91
Barnet EN4 44 DF46
Pinner HA5 40 BY51
Uxbridge UB10 58 BN62
Derwent Cl, Add. KT15 152 BK106
Amersham HP7 20 AV39
Dartford DA1 127 FH88
Esher (Clay.) KT10 155 CE107
Feltham TW14 115 BT88
Watford WD25 8 BW34
Derwent Cres, N20 44 DC48
Bexleyheath DA7 106 FA82
Stanmore HA7 41 CJ54
Derwent Dr, Hayes UB4 77 BS71
Orpington BR5 145 ER101
Purley CR8 160 DR113
Derwent Gdns, Ilf. IG4 68 EL56
Wembley HA9 61 CJ59
Derwent Gro, SE22 102 DT84
Derwent Par, S.Ock. RM15 91 FU72
Derwent Ri, NW9 62 CS58
Derwent Rd, N13 45 DM49
SE20 142 DU96
SW20 139 CX100
W5 97 CJ76
Egham TW20 113 BB94
Southall UB1 78 CA72
Twickenham TW2 116 CB86
Derwent St, SE10 205 H10
Derwent Wk, Wall. SM6 159 DH108
Derwentwater Rd, W3 80 CQ74
Derwent Way, Horn. RM12 71 FH64
Derwent Yd, W5
off Northfield Av 97 CJ76
De Salis Rd, Uxb. UB10 77 BQ70
Desborough Cl, W2 82 DB71
Shepperton TW17 134 BN101
Desborough Ho, W14
off North End Rd 99 CZ79
Desborough St, W2
off Cirencester St 82 DB71
Desenfans Rd, SE21 122 DS86
Desford Ct, Ashf. TW15
off Desford Way 114 BM89
Desford Ms, E16
off Desford Rd 86 EE70
Desford Rd, E16 86 EE70
Desford Way, Ashf. TW15 114 BM89
★ Design Mus, SE1 202 A3
Desmond Rd, Wat. WD24 23 BT36
Desmond St, SE14 103 DY79
Desmond Tutu Dr, SE23
off St. Germans Rd 123 DY88
Despard Rd, N19 65 DJ60
Desvignes Dr, SE13
off Hither Grn La 123 ED86
Detillens La, Oxt. RH8 188 EG129
Detling Cl, Horn. RM12 72 FJ64
Detling Rd, Brom. BR1 124 EG92
Erith DA8 107 FD80
Gravesend (Nthflt) DA11 130 GD88
Detmold Rd, E5 66 DW61
Devalls Cl, E6 87 EN73
Devana End, Cars. SM5 140 DF104
Devas Rd, SW20 139 CW95
Devas St, E3 85 EB70
Devenay Rd, E15 86 EF66
Devenish Rd, SE2 106 EU75
Deventer Cres, SE22 122 DS85
Deveraux Cl, Beck. BR3 143 EC99
De Vere Gdns, W8 100 DC75
Ilford IG1 69 EM61
Deverell St, SE1 201 K7
De Vere Ms, W8
off Canning Pl 100 DC76
Devereux Ct, WC2 196 D9
Devereux Dr, Wat. WD17 23 BS38
Devereux La, SW13 99 CV80
Devereux Rd, SW11 120 DF86
Grays RM16 110 FZ76
De Vere Wk, Wat. WD17 23 BS40
Deverill Ct, SE20 142 DW95
Deverills Way, Slou. SL3 93 BC77
Deveron Gdns, S.Ock. RM15 91 FU71
Deveron Way, Rom. RM1 51 FE53
Devey Cl, Kings.T. KT2 118 CS94
Devils La, Egh. TW20 113 BD94
Devitt Cl, Ashtd. KT21 172 CN116
Devizes St, N1 off Poole St 84 DR67
Devoke Way, Walt. KT12 136 BX103
Devon Av, Twick. TW2 116 CC88
Devon Cl, N17 66 DT55
Buckhurst Hill IG9 48 EH47
Greenford UB6 79 CJ67
Kenley CR8 176 DT116
Devon Ct, Buck.H. IG9 48 EH46
Dartford (Sutt.H.) DA4 148 FP95
Devon Cres, Red. RH1 184 DD134
Devoncroft Gdns, Twick. TW1 117 CG87
Devon Gdns, N4 65 DP58
Devonhurst Pl, W4
off Heathfield Ter 98 CR78
Devonia Gdns, N18 46 DQ51
Devonia Rd, N1 83 DP68
Devon Mans, SE1
off Tooley St 102 DT75
Devonport Gdns, Ilf. IG1 69 EM58
Devonport Ms, W12
off Devonport Rd 81 CV74
Devonport Rd, W12 99 CV75
Devonport St, E1 84 DW72
Devon Ri, N2 64 DD56
Devon Rd, Bark. IG11 87 ES67
Dartford (Sutt.H.) DA4 148 FP95
Redhill (S.Merst.) RH1 185 DJ130
Sutton SM2 157 CY109
Walton-on-Thames KT12 154 BW105
Watford WD24 24 BX39
Devons Est, E3 85 EB69
Devonshire Av, Dart. DA1 127 FH86
Sutton SM2 158 DC108
Tadworth (Box H.) KT20 182 CQ131
Woking GU21 151 BC114
Devonshire Cl, E15 68 EE63
N13 45 DN49
W1 195 H6
Devonshire Cres, NW7 43 CX52
Devonshire Dr, SE10 103 EB80
Surbiton KT6 137 CK102
Devonshire Gdns, N17 46 DQ51
N21 46 DQ45
W4 98 CQ80
Devonshire Gro, SE15 102 DV79
Devonshire Hill La, N17 46 DQ51
H Devonshire Hosp, W1 194 G6
Devonshire Ho, Sutt. SM2
off Devonshire Av 158 DC108
Devonshire Ms, SW10
off Park Wk 100 DD79
W4 off Glebe St 98 CS78
Devonshire Ms N, W1 195 H6
Devonshire Ms S, W1 195 H6
Devonshire Ms W, W1 195 H5
Devonshire Pas, W4 98 CS78
Devonshire Pl, NW2 64 DA62
W1 194 G5
W8 off St. Mary's Pl 100 DB76
Devonshire Pl Ms, W1 194 G5
Devonshire Rd, E16 86 EH72
E17 67 EA58
N9 46 DW46
N13 45 DM49
N17 46 DQ51
NW7 43 CX52
SE9 124 EL89
SE23 122 DW88
SW19 120 DE94
W4 98 CS78
W5 97 CJ76
Bexleyheath DA6 106 EY84
Carshalton SM5 158 DG105
Croydon CR0 142 DR101
Feltham TW13 116 BY90
Gravesend DA12 131 GH88
Grays RM16 110 FY77
Harrow HA1 61 CD58
Hornchurch RM12 72 FJ61
Ilford IG2 69 ER59
Orpington BR6 146 EU101
Pinner (Eastcote) HA5 60 BW58
Pinner (Hatch End) HA5 40 BZ53
Southall UB1 78 CA71
Sutton SM2 158 DC108
Weybridge KT13 152 BN105
Devonshire Row, EC2 197 N7
Devonshire Row Ms, W1 195 J5
Devonshire Sq, EC2 197 N8
Bromley BR2 144 EH98
Devonshire St, W1 194 G6
W4 98 CS78
Devonshire Ter, W2 82 DC72
Devonshire Way, Croy. CR0 143 DY103
Hayes UB4 77 BV72
DLR Devons Road 85 EB70
Devons Rd, E3 85 EA71
Devon St, SE15 102 DV79
Devon Way, Chess. KT9 155 CJ106
Devon Way, Epsom KT19 156 CP106
Uxbridge UB10 76 BM68
Devon Waye, Houns. TW5 96 BZ80
De Walden St, W1 194 G7
Dewar Spur, Slou. SL3
off Ditton Rd 93 AZ78
Dewar St, SE15 102 DU83
Dewberry Gdns, E6 86 EL71
Dewberry St, E14 85 EC71
Dewey Path, Horn. RM12 90 FJ65
Dewey Rd, N1 83 DN68
Dagenham RM10 89 FB65
Dewey St, SW17 120 DF92
Dewgrass Gro, Wal.Cr. EN8 31 DX35
Dewhurst Rd, W14 99 CX76
Waltham Cross (Chsht) EN8 14 DW29
Dewlands, Gdse. RH9 186 DW131
Dewlands Av, Dart. DA2 128 FP87
Dewlands Ct, NW4
off Holders Hill Rd 43 CX54
Dewsbury Cl, Pnr. HA5 60 BZ58
Romford RM3 52 FL51
Dewsbury Ct, W4
off Chiswick Rd 98 CQ77
Dewsbury Gdns, Rom. RM3 52 FK51
Worcester Park KT4 139 CU104
Dewsbury Rd, NW10 63 CU64
Romford RM3 52 FK51
Dewsbury Ter, NW1
off Camden High St 83 DH67
Dexter Cl, Grays RM17 110 GA76
Dexter Ho, Erith DA18
off Kale Rd 106 EY76
Dexter Rd, Barn. EN5 27 CX44
Uxbridge (Hare.) UB9 38 BJ54
Deyncourt Gdns, Upmin. RM14 72 FQ61
Deyncourt Rd, N17 46 DQ53
Deynecourt Gdns, E11 68 EJ56
D'Eynsford Rd, SE5 102 DR81
Dhonan Ho, SE1
off Longfield Est 102 DT77
Diadem Ct, W1 195 M9
Dial Cl, Green. DA9 129 FW85
Dialmead, Pot.B. EN6
off Crossoaks La 11 CT34
Dial Wk, The, W8 100 DB75
Diamedes Av, Stai. (Stanw.) TW19 114 BK87
Diameter Rd, Orp. BR5 145 EP101
Diamond Cl, Dag. RM8 70 EW60
Grays RM16 110 FZ76
Diamond Rd, Ruis. HA4 60 BX63
Slough SL1 92 AU75
Watford WD24 23 BU38
Diamond St, NW10 80 CR66
SE15 102 DS80
Diamond Ter, SE10 103 EC81
Diamond Way, SE8
off Crossfield St 103 EA80
Diana Cl, E18 48 EH53
SE8 off Staunton St 103 DZ79
Grays (Chaff.Hun.) RM16 110 FZ76
Sidcup DA14 126 EY89
Slough (Geo.Grn) SL3 74 AY72
Diana Gdns, Surb. KT6 138 CM103
Diana Ho, SW13 99 CT81
★ Diana Princess of Wales Mem, W2 198 A3
Diana Rd, E17 67 DZ55
Dianne Way, Barn. EN4 28 DE43
Dianthus Cl, SE2
off Carnation St 106 EV78
Chertsey KT16 133 BE101
Dianthus Ct, Wok. GU22 166 AX118
Diban Av, Horn. RM12 71 FH63
Dibden Hill, Ch.St.G. HP8 36 AW49
Dibden La, Sev. (Ide Hill) TN14 190 FE126
Dibden Row, SE1
off Gerridge St 101 DN76
Dibden St, N1 83 DP67
Dibdin Cl, Sutt. SM1 140 DA104
Dibdin Ho, W9 off Maida Vale 82 DB68
Dibdin Rd, Sutt. SM1 140 DA104
Diceland Rd, Bans. SM7 173 CZ116
Dicey Av, NW2 63 CW64
Dickens Av, N3 44 DC53
Dartford DA1 108 FN84
Tilbury RM18 111 GH81
Uxbridge UB8 77 BP72
Dickens Cl, Erith DA8 107 FB80
Hayes UB3 off Croyde Av 95 BS77
Richmond TW10 118 CL89
Waltham Cross EN7 14 DU26
Dickens Dr, Add. KT15 151 BF107
Chislehurst BR7 125 EQ93
Dickens Est, SE1 202 B5
SE16 202 B5
Dickens Ho, NW6 82 DA69
★ Dickens Ho Mus, WC1 196 C5
Dickens La, N18 46 DS50
Dickens Ms, EC1
off Turnmill St 83 DP70
Dickenson Cl, N9
off Croyland Rd 46 DU46
Dickenson Rd, N8 65 DL59
Feltham TW13 116 BW92
Dickensons La, SE25 142 DU99
Dickensons Pl, SE25 142 DU100
Dickens Pl, Slou. (Colnbr.) SL3 93 BE81
Dickens Ri, Chig. IG7 49 EN48
Dickens Rd, E6 86 EK68
Gravesend DA12 131 GL88
Dickens Sq, SE1 201 J6
Dickens St, SW8 101 DH82
Dickens Way, Rom. RM1 71 FE56
Dickenswood Cl, SE19 121 DP94
Dickerage La, N.Mal. KT3 138 CQ97
Dickerage Rd, Kings.T. KT1 138 CQ95
New Malden KT3 138 CQ95
Dickinson Av, Rick. (Crox.Grn) WD3 22 BN44
Dickinson Ct, EC1
off Northburgh St 83 DP70
Dickinson Quay, Hem.H. HP3 6 BL25
Dickinson Sq, Rick. (Crox.Grn) WD3 22 BN44
Dickson, Wal.Cr. (Chsht) EN7 14 DT27
Dickson Fold, Pnr. HA5 60 BX56
Dickson Rd, SE9 104 EL83
Dick Turpin Way, Felt. TW14 95 BT84
Didsbury Cl, E6
off Barking Rd 87 EM67
Dieppe Cl, W14 99 CZ78
Digby Cres, N4 66 DQ61
Digby Gdns, Dag. RM10 88 FA67
Digby Pl, Croy. CR0 142 DT104
Digby Rd, E9 85 DX65
Barking IG11 87 ET66
Digby St, E2 84 DW69
Digby Wk, Horn. RM12
off Pembrey Way 90 FJ65
Digby Way, W.Byf. (Byfleet) KT14 off High Rd 152 BM112
Dig Dag Hill, Wal.Cr. (Chsht) EN7 14 DT27
Digdens Ri, Epsom KT18 172 CQ115
Diggon St, E1
off Stepney Way 85 DX71
Dighton Ct, SE5 102 DQ79
Dighton Rd, SW18 120 DC85
Dignum St, N1
off Cloudesley Rd 83 DN68
Digswell Cl, Borwd. WD6 26 CN38
Digswell St, N7
off Holloway Rd 83 DN65
Dilhorne Cl, SE12 124 EH90
Dilke St, SW3 100 DF79
Dilloway Yd, Sthl. UB2
off The Green 96 BY75
Dillwyn Cl, SE26 123 DY91
Dilston Cl, Nthlt. UB5
off Yeading La 78 BW69
Dilston Gro, SE16 202 F8
Dilston Rd, Lthd. KT22 171 CG119
Dilton Gdns, SW15 119 CU88
Dilwyn Ct, E17
off Hillyfield 47 DY54
Dimes Pl, W6 off King St 99 CV77
Dimmock Dr, Grnf. UB6 61 CD64
Dimmocks La, Rick. (Sarratt) WD3 22 BH36
Dimond Cl, E7 68 EG63
Dimsdale Dr, NW9 62 CQ60
Enfield EN1 30 DU44
Dimsdale Wk, E13
off Stratford Rd 86 EG67
Dimson Cres, E3 85 EA70
Dingle, The, Uxb. UB10 77 BP68
Dingle Cl, Barn. EN5 27 CT44
Dingle Gdns, E14 204 A1
Dingle Rd, Ashf. TW15 115 BP92
Dingley La, SW16 121 DK89
Dingley Pl, EC1 197 J3
Dingley Rd, EC1 197 H3
Dingwall Av, Croy. CR0 142 DQ103
Dingwall Gdns, NW11 64 DA58
Dingwall Rd, SW18 120 DC87
Carshalton SM5 158 DF109
Croydon CR0 142 DR103
Dinmont St, E2 off Coate St 84 DV68
Dinmore, Hem.H. (Bov.) HP3 5 AZ28
Dinsdale Cl, Wok. GU22 167 AZ118
Dinsdale Gdns, SE25 142 DS99
Barnet EN5 28 DB43
Dinsdale Rd, SE3 104 EF79
Dinsmore Rd, SW12 121 DH87
Dinton Rd, SW19 120 DD93
Kingston upon Thames KT2 118 CM94
Diploma Av, N2 64 DE56
Diploma Ct, N2
off Diploma Av 64 DE56
Dirdene Cl, Epsom KT17 157 CT112
Dirdene Gdns, Epsom KT17 157 CT112
Dirdene Gro, Epsom KT17 156 CS112
Dirleton Rd, E15 86 EF67
Disbrowe Rd, W6 99 CY79
Discovery Business Pk, SE16
off St. James's Rd 102 DU76
Discovery Wk, E1 202 D1
Dishforth La, NW9 42 CS53
Disney Ms, N4
off Chesterfield Gdns 65 DP57
Disney Pl, SE1 201 J4
Disney St, SE1 201 J4
Dison Cl, Enf. EN3 31 DX39
Disraeli Cl, SE28 88 EW74
W4 off Acton La 98 CR77
Disraeli Ct, Slou. SL3
off Sutton Pl 93 BB79
Disraeli Gdns, SW15
off Fawe Pk Rd 99 CZ84
Disraeli Rd, E7 86 EG65
NW10 80 CQ68
SW15 99 CY84
W5 79 CK74
Diss St, E2 197 P2
Distaff La, EC4 197 H10
Distillery La, W6
off Fulham Palace Rd 99 CW78
Distillery Rd, W6 99 CW78
Distillery Wk, Brent. TW8 98 CL79
Distin St, SE11 200 D9
District Rd, Wem. HA0 61 CH64
Ditch All, SE10 103 EB81
Ditchburn St, E14 204 E1
Ditches La, Cat. CR3 175 DM122
Coulsdon CR5 175 DL120
Ditches Ride, The, Loug. IG10 33 EN37
Ditchfield Rd, Hayes UB4 78 BY70
Dittisham Rd, SE9 124 EL91
Ditton Cl, T.Ditt. KT7 137 CG101
Dittoncroft Cl, Croy. CR0 160 DS105
Ditton Gra Cl, Surb. KT6 137 CK102
Ditton Gra Dr, Surb. KT6 137 CK102
Ditton Hill, Surb. KT6 137 CJ102
Ditton Hill Rd, Surb. KT6 137 CJ102
Ditton Lawn, T.Ditt. KT7 137 CG102
Ditton Pk, Slou. SL3 92 AX78
Ditton Pk Rd, Slou. SL3 92 AY79
Ditton Pl, SE20 142 DV95
Ditton Reach, T.Ditt. KT7 137 CH100
Ditton Rd, Bexh. DA6 126 EX85
Slough SL3 93 AZ79
Slough (Datchet) SL3 92 AX81
Southall UB2 96 BZ77
Surbiton KT6 138 CL102
Divis Way, SW15 119 CV86
Dixon Clark Ct, N1
off Canonbury Rd 83 DP65
Dixon Cl, E6
off Brandreth Rd 87 EM72
Dixon Dr, Wey. KT13 152 BM110

★ Place of interest ⇌ Railway station ⊖ London Underground station DLR Docklands Light Railway station Tra Tramlink station H Hospital Riv Pedestrian ferry landing stage

Dixon Ho, W10 81 CX72
Dixon Pl, W.Wick. BR4 143 EB102
Dixon Rd, SE14 103 DY81
SE25 142 DS97
Dixon's All, SE16 202 D5
Dixons Hill Cl, Hat. (N.Mymms)
AL9 11 CV25
Dixons Hill Rd, Hat. (N.Mymms)
AL9 11 CU25
Dobbin Cl, Har. HA3 41 CG54
Dobell Path, SE9
off Dobell Rd 125 EM85
Dobell Rd, SE9 125 EM85
Dobree Av, NW10 81 CV66
Dobson Cl, NW6 82 DD66
Dobson Rd, Grav. DA12 131 GL92
Doby Ct, EC4 197 J10
Dockers Tanner Rd, E14 203 P7
Dockett Eddy La, Shep.
TW17 134 BM102
Dockhead, SE1 202 A5
Dock Hill Av, SE16 203 J4
Dockland St, E16 87 EN74
Dockley Rd, SE16 202 B7
Dock Rd, E16 205 L1
Brentford TW8 97 CK80
Grays RM17 110 GD79
Tilbury RM18 111 GF82
Dockside Rd, E16 86 EK73
Dock St, E1 84 DU73
Dockwell Cl, Felt. TW14 95 BU84
Dockyard Ind Est, SE18
off Woolwich Ch St 104 EL76
Doctor Johnson Av, SW17 121 DH90
★ Doctor Johnson's Ho,
EC4 196 E9
Doctors Cl, SE26 122 DW92
Doctors La, Cat. (Chaldon)
CR3 175 DN123
Docwra's Bldgs, N1 84 DS65
Dodbrooke Rd, SE27 121 DN90
Dodd Ho, SE16
off Rennie Est 102 DV77
Doddinghurst Rd, Brwd.
CM15 54 FW44
Doddington Gro, SE17 101 DP79
Doddington Pl, SE17 101 DP79
Dodd's Cres, W.Byf. KT14 152 BH114
Dodds La, Ch.St.G. HP8 36 AU47
Dodd's La, Wok. GU22 152 BG114
Dodsley Pl, N9 46 DV48
Dodson St, SE1 200 E5
Dod St, E14 85 DZ72
Doebury Wk, SE18
off Prestwood Cl 106 EU79
Doel Cl, SW19 120 DC94
Doggets Ct, Barn. EN4 28 DE43
Doggett Rd, SE6 123 EA87
Doggetts Fm Rd, Uxb. (Denh.)
UB9 57 BC59
Doggetts Wd Cl, Ch.St.G. HP8 20 AV42
Doggetts Wd La, Ch.St.G. HP8 20 AV41
Doghurst Av, Hayes UB3 95 BP80
Doghurst Dr, West Dr. UB7 95 BP80
Doghurst La, Couls. (Chipstead)
CR5 174 DF120
Dog Kennel Hill, SE22 102 DS83
Dog Kennel Hill Est, SE22 102 DS83
Dog Kennel La, Rick. (Chorl.)
WD3 21 BF42
Dog La, NW10 62 CS63
Dogwood Cl, Grav. (Nthflt)
DA11 130 GE91
Doherty Rd, E13 86 EG70
Dokal Ind Est, Sthl. UB2
off Hartington Rd 96 BY76
Dolben St, SE1 200 F3
Dolby Rd, SW6 99 CZ82
Dolland St, SE11 101 DM78
Dollis Av, N3 43 CZ53
Dollis Brook Wk, Barn. EN5 27 CY44
Dollis Cres, Ruis. HA4 60 BW60
DOLLIS HILL, NW2 63 CV62
⊖ Dollis Hill 63 CU64
Dollis Hill Av, NW2 63 CV62
Dollis Hill La, NW2 63 CV62
Dollis Ms, N3 off Dollis Pk 43 CZ53
Dollis Pk, N3 43 CZ53
Dollis Rd, N3 43 CY52
NW7 43 CY52
Dollis Valley Dr, Barn. EN5 27 CZ44
Dollis Valley Grn Wk, N20
off Totteridge La 44 DC47
Barnet EN5 27 CY44
Dollis Valley Way, Barn. EN5 27 CZ44
Dolman Cl, N3
off Avondale Rd 44 DC54
Dolman Rd, W4 98 CR77
Dolman St, SW4 101 DM84
Dolphin App, Rom. RM1 71 FF56
Dolphin Cl, SE16 203 H4
SE28 88 EX72
Surbiton KT6 137 CK100
Dolphin Ct, NW11 63 CY58
Slough SL1 92 AV75
Staines TW18 114 BG90
Dolphin Ct N, Stai. TW18 114 BG90
Dolphin Est, Sun. TW16 135 BS95
Dolphin Ho, SW18
off Smugglers Way 100 DB84
Dolphin La, E14 204 B1
Dolphin Pt, Purf. RM19 109 FS78
Dolphin Rd, Nthlt. UB5 78 BZ68
Slough SL1 92 AV75
Sunbury-on-Thames TW16 135 BS95
Dolphin Rd N, Sun. TW16 135 BS95
Dolphin Rd S, Sun. TW16 135 BR95
Dolphin Rd W, Sun. TW16 135 BR95
Dolphin Sq, SW1 101 DJ78
W4 98 CS80
Dolphin St, Kings.T. KT1 138 CL95
Dolphin Twr, SE8
off Abinger Gro 103 DZ79
Dolphin Way, Purf. RM19 109 FS78
Dombey St, WC1 196 B6
★ Dome, The, SE10 205 H3
Dome Hill, Cat. CR3 186 DS127
Dome Hill Pk, SE26 122 DT91
Dome Hill Peak, Cat. CR3 186 DS126
Domett Cl, SE5 102 DR84
Dome Way, Red. RH1 184 DF133
Domfe Pl, E5
off Rushmore Rd 66 DW63
Domingo St, EC1 197 H4
Dominica Cl, E13 86 EJ68
Dominic Ct, Wal.Abb. EN9 15 EB33
Dominion Cl, Houns. TW3 97 CD82
Dominion Dr, Rom. RM5 51 FB51
Dominion Rd, Croy. CR0 142 DT101
Southall UB2 96 BY76
Dominion St, EC2 197 L6
★ Dominion Thea, W1 195 N8
Dominion Way, Rain. RM13 89 FG69
Domonic Dr, SE9 125 EP91
Domville Cl, N20 44 DD47
Donald Biggs Dr, Grav. DA12 131 GK87
Donald Dr, Rom. RM6 70 EW57
Donald Rd, E13 86 EJ67
Croydon CR0 141 DM100
Donaldson Rd, NW6 81 CZ67
SE18 105 EN81
Donald Wds Gdns, Surb.
KT5 138 CP103
Donato Dr, SE15
off Tower Mill Rd 102 DS80
Doncaster Dr, Nthlt. UB5 60 BZ64
Doncaster Gdns, N4
off Stanhope Gdns 66 DQ58
Northolt UB5 60 BZ64
Doncaster Grn, Wat. WD19 40 BW50
Doncaster Rd, N9 46 DV45
Doncaster Way, Upmin. RM14 72 FM62
Doncel Ct, E4 47 ED45
Doncella Cl, Grays (Chaff.Hun.)
RM16 109 FX76
Donegal St, N1 196 C1
Doneraile St, SW6 99 CX82
Dongola Rd, E1 85 DY71
E13 86 EH69
N17 66 DS55
Dongola Rd W, E13
off Balaam St 86 EH69
Donington Av, Ilf. IG6 69 EQ57
Donkey All, SE22 122 DU87
Donkey La, Dart. (Fnghm)
DA4 148 FP103
Enfield EN1 30 DU40
West Drayton UB7 94 BJ77
Donkin Ho, SE16
off Rennie Est 102 DV77
Donnay Cl, Ger.Cr. SL9 56 AX58
Donne Ct, SE24 122 DQ86
Donnefield Av, Edg. HA8 42 CL52
Donne Gdns, Wok. GU22 167 BE115
Donne Pl, SW3 198 C8
Mitcham CR4 141 DH98
Donne Rd, Dag. RM8 70 EW61
Donnington Ct, NW10
off Donnington Rd 81 CV66
Donnington Rd, NW10 81 CV66
Harrow HA3 61 CK57
Sevenoaks (Dunt.Grn)
TN13 181 FD120
Worcester Park KT4 139 CU103
Donnybrook Rd, SW16 121 DJ94
Donovan Av, N10 45 DH54
Donovan Cl, Epsom KT19 156 CR110
Don Phelan Cl, SE5 102 DR81
Don Way, Rom. RM1 51 FE52
Doods Pk Rd, Reig. RH2 184 DC133
Doods Rd, Reig. RH2 184 DC133
Doods Way, Reig. RH2 184 DD133
Doone Cl, Tedd. TW11 117 CG93
Doon St, SE1 200 D3
Dorado Gdns, Orp. BR6 146 EX104
Doral Way, Cars. SM5 158 DF106
Dorando Cl, W12 81 CV73
Doran Dr, Red. RH1 184 DD134
Doran Gdns, Red. RH1 184 DD134
Doran Gro, SE18 105 ES80
Doran Wk, E15 85 EC66
Dora Rd, SW19 120 DA92
Dora St, E14 85 DZ72
Dora Way, SW9 101 DN82
Dorchester Av, N13 46 DQ49
Bexley DA5 126 EX88
Harrow HA2 60 CC58
Dorchester Cl, Dart. DA1 128 FM87
Northolt UB5 60 CB64
Orpington BR5
off Grovelands Rd 126 EU94
Dorchester Ct, N14 45 DH45
SE24 122 DQ85
Rickmansworth (Crox.Grn)
WD3 off Mayfare 23 BQ43
Woking GU22 167 BA116
Dorchester Dr, SE24 122 DQ85
Feltham TW14 115 BS86
Dorchester Gdns, E4 47 EA49
NW11 64 DA56
Dorchester Gro, W4 98 CS78
Dorchester Ms, N.Mal. KT3
off Elm Rd 138 CR98
Twickenham TW1 117 CJ87
Dorchester Rd, Grav. DA12 131 GK90
Morden SM4 140 DB101
Northolt UB5 60 CB64
Weybridge KT13 135 BP104
Worcester Park KT4 139 CW102
Dorchester Way, Har. HA3 62 CM58
Dorchester Waye, Hayes UB4 78 BW72
Dorcis Av, Bexh. DA7 106 EY82
Dordrecht Rd, W3 80 CS74
Dore Av, E12 69 EN64
Doreen Av, NW9 62 CR60
Dore Gdns, Mord. SM4 140 DB101
Dorell Cl, Sthl. UB1 78 BZ71
Doria Dr, Grav. DA12 131 GL90
Dorian Rd, Horn. RM12 71 FG60
Doria Rd, SW6 99 CZ82
Doric Dr, Tad. KT20 173 CZ120
Doric Way, NW1 195 M2
Dorie Ms, N12 44 DB49
Dorien Rd, SW20 139 CX96
Dorin Ct, Warl. CR6 176 DV119
Dorincourt, Wok. GU22 167 BE115
Doris Av, Erith DA8 107 FC81
Doris Rd, E7 86 EG66
Ashford TW15 115 BR93
Dorking Cl, SE8 103 DZ79
Worcester Park KT4 139 CX103
Dorking Gdns, Rom. RM3 52 FK50
Dorking Glen, Rom. RM3 52 FK49
Dorking Ri, Rom. RM3 52 FK49
Dorking Rd, Epsom KT18 172 CN116
Leatherhead KT22 171 CH122
Dorking Rd, Rom. RM3 52 FK49
Tadworth KT20 173 CX123
Dorking Wk, Rom. RM3 52 FK49
Dorkins Way, Upmin. RM14 73 FS59
Dorlcote Rd, SW18 120 DD87
Dorling Dr, Epsom KT17 157 CT112
Dorly Cl, Shep. TW17 135 BS99
Dorman Pl, N9
off Balham Rd 46 DU47
Dormans Cl, Nthwd. HA6 39 BR52
Dorman Wk, NW10
off Garden Way 62 CR64
Dorman Way, NW8 82 DD67
Dorma Trd Pk, E10 67 DX60
Dormay St, SW18 120 DB85
Dormer Cl, E15 86 EF65
Barnet EN5 27 CX43
Dormers Av, Sthl. UB1 78 CA72
Dormers Ri, Sthl. UB1 78 CB72
DORMER'S WELLS, Sthl. UB1 78 CB73
Dormers Wells La, Sthl. UB1 78 CA72
Dormywood, Ruis. HA4 59 BT57
Dornberg Cl, SE3 104 EG80
Dornberg Rd, SE3
off Banchory Rd 104 EH80
Dorncliffe Rd, SW6 99 CY82
Dornels, Slou. SL2 74 AW72
Dorney, NW3 82 DE66
Dorney Gro, Wey. KT13 135 BP103
Dorney Ri, Orp. BR5 145 ET98
Dorney Way, Houns. TW4 116 BY85
Dornfell St, NW6 63 CZ64
Dornford Gdns, Couls. CR5 176 DQ119
Dornton Rd, SW12 121 DH89
South Croydon CR2 160 DR106
Dorothy Av, Wem. HA0 80 CL66
Dorothy Evans Cl, Bexh. DA7 107 FB84
Dorothy Gdns, Dag. RM8 70 EV63
Dorothy Rd, SW11 100 DF83
Dorrell Pl, SW9
off Brixton Rd 101 DN84
Dorrien Wk, SW16 121 DK89
Dorrington Ct, SE25 142 DS96
Dorrington Gdns, Horn. RM12 72 FK60
Dorrington Pt, E3
off Bromley High St 85 EB69
Dorrington St, EC1 196 D6
Dorrington Way, Beck. BR3 143 EC99
Dorrit Ms, N18 46 DS49
Dorrit St, SE1 201 J4
Dorrit Way, Chis. BR7 125 EQ93
Dorrofield Cl, Rick. (Crox.Grn)
WD3 23 BQ43
Dors Cl, NW9 62 CR60
Dorset Av, Hayes UB4 77 BS69
Romford RM1 71 FD55
Southall UB2 96 CA77
Welling DA16 105 ET84
Dorset Bldgs, EC4 196 F9
Dorset Cl, NW1 194 D6
Hayes UB4 77 BS69
Dorset Cres, Grav. DA12 131 GL91
Dorset Dr, Edg. HA8 42 CM51
Woking GU22 167 BB117
Dorset Est, E2 84 DT69
Dorset Gdns, Mitch. CR4 141 DM98
Dorset Ho, Enf. EN3 31 DX37
Dorset Ms, N3 44 DA53
SW1 199 H6
Dorset Pl, E15 85 ED65
Dorset Ri, EC4 196 F9
Dorset Rd, E7 86 EJ66
N15 66 DR56
N22 45 DL53
SE9 124 EL89
SW8 101 DM80
SW19 140 DA95
W5 97 CJ76
Ashford TW15 114 BK90
Beckenham BR3 143 DX97
Harrow HA1 60 CC58
Mitcham CR4 140 DE96
Sutton SM2 158 DA110
Dorset Sq, NW1 194 D5
Epsom KT19 156 CR110
Dorset St, W1 194 E7
Sevenoaks TN13
off High St 191 FJ125
Dorset Way, Twick. TW2 117 CD88
Uxbridge UB10 76 BM68
West Byfleet (Byfleet)
KT14 152 BK110
Dorset Waye, Houns. TW5 96 BZ80
Dorton Cl, SE15
off Chandler Way 102 DS80
Dorton Dr, Sev. TN15 191 FM122
Dorton Way, Wok. (Ripley)
GU23 168 BH121
Dorville Cres, W6 99 CV76
Dorville Rd, SE12 124 EF85
Dothill Rd, SE18 105 ER80
Douai Gro, Hmptn. TW12 136 CC95
Doubleday Rd, Loug. IG10 33 EQ41
Doughty Ms, WC1 196 B5
Doughty St, WC1 196 B4
Douglas Av, E17 47 EA53
New Malden KT3 139 CV98
Romford RM3 52 FL54
Watford WD24 24 BX37
Wembley HA0 80 CL66
Douglas Cl, Grays (Chaff.Hun.)
RM16 110 FY76
Stanmore HA7 41 CG50
Wallington SM6 159 DL108
Douglas Ct, Cat. CR3 176 DQ122
Westerham TN16 178 EL117
Douglas Cres, Hayes UB4 78 BW70
Douglas Dr, Croy. CR0 143 EA104
Douglas La, Stai. (Wrays.)
TW19 113 AZ85
Douglas Ms, NW2 63 CY62
Banstead SM7
off North Acre 173 CZ116
Douglas Path, E14 204 E10
Douglas Rd, E4 48 EE45
E16 86 EG71
N1 84 DQ66
N22 45 DN53
NW6 81 CZ67
Addlestone KT15 134 BH104
Esher KT10 136 CB103
Hornchurch RM11 71 FF58
Hounslow TW3 96 CB83
Douglas Rd, Ilf. IG3 70 EU58
Kingston upon Thames
KT1 138 CP96
Reigate RH2 184 DA133
Staines (Stanw.) TW19 114 BK86
Surbiton KT6 138 CM103
Welling DA16 106 EV81
Douglas Sq, Mord. SM4 140 DA100
Douglas St, SW1 199 M9
Douglas Ter, E17
off Douglas Av 47 EA53
Douglas Way, SE8 103 DZ80
Doug Siddons Ct, Grays
RM17 off Elm Rd 110 GC79
Doulton Ho, SE11
off Lambeth Wk 101 DM76
Doulton Ms, NW6
off Dresden Cl 82 DB65
Doultons, The, Stai. TW18 114 BG94
Dounesforth Gdns, SW18 120 DB88
Dounsell Ct, Brwd. (Pilg.Hat.)
CM15 off Ongar Rd 54 FU44
Douro Pl, W8 100 DB76
Douro St, E3 85 EA68
Douthwaite Sq, E1 202 C2
Dove App, E6 86 EL71
Dove Cl, NW7 43 CT52
Northolt UB5
off Wayfarer Rd 78 BX70
South Croydon CR2 161 DX111
Wallington SM6 159 DM108
Dovecot Cl, Pnr. HA5 59 BV57
Dovecote Av, N22 65 DN55
Dovecote Cl, Wey. KT13 135 BP104
Dovecote Gdns, SW14
off Avondale Rd 98 CR83
Dove Ct, EC2 197 K9
Dovedale Av, Har. HA3 61 CJ58
Ilford IG5 49 EN54
Dovedale Cl, Uxb. (Hare.)
UB9 38 BJ54
Welling DA16 106 EU82
Dovedale Ri, Mitch. CR4 120 DF94
Dovedale Rd, SE22 122 DV85
Dartford DA2 128 FQ88
Dovedon Cl, N14 45 DL47
Dove Ho Gdns, E4 47 EA47
Dovehouse Grn, Wey. KT13
off Rosslyn Pk 153 BR105
Dovehouse Mead, Bark. IG11 87 ER68
Dovehouse St, SW3 198 B10
Dove La, Pot.B. EN6 12 DB34
Dove Ms, SW5 100 DC77
Doveney Cl, Orp. BR5 146 EW97
Dove Pk, Pnr. HA5 40 CA52
Rickmansworth (Chorl.)
WD3 21 BB44
Dover Cl, NW2 off Brent Ter 63 CX61
Romford RM5 51 FC54
Dovercourt Av, Th.Hth. CR7 141 DN98
Dovercourt Est, N1 84 DR65
Dovercourt Gdns, Stan. HA7 42 CL50
Dovercourt La, Sutt. SM1 140 DC104
Dovercourt Rd, SE22 122 DS86
Doverfield, Wal.Cr. EN7 14 DQ29
Doverfield Rd, SW2 121 DL86
Dover Flats, SE1
off Old Kent Rd 102 DS77
Dover Gdns, Cars. SM5 140 DF104
Dover Ho Rd, SW15 99 CU84
Doveridge Gdns, N13 45 DP49
Dove Rd, N1 84 DR65
Dove Row, E2 84 DU67
Dover Pk Dr, SW15 119 CV86
Dover Patrol, SE3
off Kidbrooke Way 104 EH82
Dover Rd, E12 68 EJ61
N9 46 DW47
SE19 122 DR93
Gravesend (Nthflt) DA11 130 GD87
Romford RM6 70 EY58
Dover Rd E, Grav. DA11 130 GE87
Dovers Cor, Rain. RM13 89 FG69
Doversmead, Wok. (Knap.)
GU21 166 AS116
Dover St, W1 199 J1
Dover Way, Rick. (Crox.Grn)
WD3 23 BQ42
Dover Yd, W1 199 K2
Doves Cl, Brom. BR2 144 EL103
Doves Yd, N1 83 DN67
Dovet Ct, SW8
off Mursell Est 101 DM81
Doveton Rd, S.Croy. CR2 160 DR106
Doveton St, E1
off Malcolm Rd 84 DW70
Dove Wk, SW1 198 F10
Hornchurch RM12
off Heron Flight Av 89 FH65
Dowanhill Rd, SE6 123 ED88
Dowdeswell Cl, SW15 98 CS84
Dowding Pl, Stan. HA7 41 CG51
Dowding Rd, Uxb. UB10 76 BM66
Westerham (Bigg.H.) TN16 178 EK115
Dowding Wk, Grav. (Nthflt)
DA11 130 GE90
Dowding Way, Horn. RM12 89 FH66
Waltham Abbey EN9 31 ED36
Watford (Lvsdn) WD25 7 BT34
Dowdney Cl, NW5 65 DJ64
Dower Av, Wall. SM6 159 DH109
Dowgate Hill, EC4 197 K10
Dowland St, W10 81 CY68
Dowlas Est, SE5
off Dowlas St 102 DS80
Dowlas St, SE5 102 DS80
Dowlerville Rd, Orp. BR6 163 ET107
Dowman Cl, SW19
off Nelson Gro Rd 140 DB95
Downage, NW4 63 CW55
Downage, The, Grav. DA11 131 GG89
Downalong, Bushey (Bushey Hth)
WD23 41 CD46
Downbank Av, Bexh. DA7 107 FD81
Downbarns Rd, Ruis. HA4 60 BX62
Downbury Ms, SW18
off Merton Rd 120 DA86
Down Cl, Nthlt. UB5 77 BV68
Downderry Rd, Brom. BR1 123 ED90
DOWNE, Orp. BR6 163 EM111
Downe Av, Sev. (Cudham)
TN14 163 EQ112
Downe Cl, Well. DA16 106 EW80
Downend, SE18
off Moordown 105 EP80
Downer Dr, Rick. (Sarratt)
WD3 22 BG36
Downe Rd, Kes. BR2 162 EK109
Mitcham CR4 140 DF96
Sevenoaks (Cudham) TN14 163 EQ114
Downers Cotts, SW4
off The Pavement 101 DJ84
Downes Cl, Twick. TW1
off St. Margarets Rd 117 CH86
Downes Ct, N21 45 DN46
Downfield, Wor.Pk. KT4 139 CT102
Downfield Cl, W9 82 DB70
Downfield Rd, Wal.Cr.
(Chsht) EN8 15 DY31
Down Hall Rd, Kings.T. KT2 137 CK95
DOWNHAM, Brom. BR1 124 EF92
Downham Cl, Rom. RM5 50 FA52
Downham La, Brom. BR1
off Downham Way 123 ED92
Downham Rd, N1 84 DR66
Downham Way, Brom. BR1 123 ED92
Downhills Av, N17 66 DR55
Downhills Pk Rd, N17 66 DQ55
Downhills Way, N17 66 DQ55
★ Down Ho - Darwin Mus,
Orp. BR6 163 EN112
Downhurst Av, NW7 42 CR50
Downing Cl, Har. HA2 60 CC55
Downing Dr, Grnf. UB6 79 CD67
Downing Rd, Dag. RM9 88 EZ67
Downings, E6 87 EN72
Downing St, SW1 199 P4
Downings Wd, Rick. (Map.Cr.)
WD3 37 BD50
Downland Cl, N20 44 DC46
Coulsdon CR5 159 DH114
Epsom KT18 173 CV118
Downland Gdns, Epsom
KT18 173 CV118
Downlands, Wal.Abb. EN9 16 EE34
Downlands Rd, Pur. CR8 159 DL113
Downland Way, Epsom KT18 173 CV118
Downleys Cl, SE9 124 EL89
Downman Rd, SE9 104 EL83
Down Pl, W6 99 CV77
Down Rd, Tedd. TW11 117 CH93
Downs, The, SW20 119 CX94
Downs Av, Chis. BR7 125 EM92
Dartford DA1 128 FN87
Epsom KT18 156 CS114
Pinner HA5 60 BZ58
Downs Br Rd, Beck. BR3 143 ED95
Downsbury Ms, SW18
off Merton Rd 120 DA85
Downs Ct, Sutt. SM2 158 DB111
Downs Ct Rd, Pur. CR8 159 DP112
Downsell Rd, E15 67 EC63
Downsfield Rd, E17 67 DY58
Downshall Av, Ilf. IG3 69 ES58
Downs Hill, Beck. BR3 123 ED94
Gravesend (Sthflt) DA13 130 GC94
Downs Hill Rd, Epsom KT18 156 CS114
Downshire Hill, NW3 64 DD63
Downs Ho Rd, Epsom KT18 173 CT118
DOWNSIDE, Cob. KT11 169 BV118
Downside, Cher. KT16 133 BF102
Epsom KT18 156 CS114
Sunbury-on-Thames TW16 135 BU95
Twickenham TW1 117 CF90
Downside Br Rd, Cob. KT11 169 BV115
Downside Cl, SW19 120 DC93
Downside Common, Cob.
(Down.) KT11 169 BV118
Downside Common Rd, Cob.
(Down.) KT11 169 BV118
Downside Cres, NW3 64 DE64
W13 79 CG70
Downside Orchard, Wok.
GU22 off Park Rd 167 BA117
Downside Rd, Cob. (Down.)
KT11 169 BV116
Sutton SM2 158 DD107
Downside Wk, Nthlt. UB5 78 BZ69
Downsland Dr, Brwd. CM14 54 FW48
Downs La, E5 off Downs Rd 66 DV63
Leatherhead KT22 171 CH123
Downs Pk Rd, E5 66 DU64
E8 66 DT64
Downs Rd, E5 66 DU63
Beckenham BR3 143 EB96
Coulsdon CR5 175 DK118
Enfield EN1 30 DS42
Epsom KT18 172 CS115
Gravesend (Istead Rise)
DA13 130 GD91
Purley CR8 159 DP111
Slough SL3 92 AX75
Sutton SM2 158 DB110
Thornton Heath CR7 142 DQ95
Downs Side, Sutt. SM2 157 CZ111
Down St, W1 199 H3
West Molesey KT8 136 CA99
Down St Ms, W1 199 H3
Downs Vw, Islw. TW7 97 CF80
Tadworth KT20 173 CV121
Downsview Av, Wok. GU22 167 AZ121
Downsview Cl, Orp. BR6 164 EW110
Swanley BR8 147 FF97
Downsview Gdns, SE19 121 DP94
Downsview Rd, SE19 122 DQ94
Sevenoaks TN13 190 FF125
Downs Way, Epsom KT18 173 CT116
Downsway, Orp. BR6 163 ES106
Downs Way, Oxt. RH8 188 EE127
Downsway, S.Croy. CR2 160 DS111
Downs Way, Tad. KT20 173 CV121
Downsway, Whyt. CR3 176 DT116
Downsway, The, Sutt. SM2 158 DC109
Downs Way Cl, Tad. KT20 173 CU121
Downs Wd, Epsom KT18 173 CV117
Downswood, Reig. RH2 184 DE131
Downton Av, SW2 121 DL89
Downtown Rd, SE16 203 L4
Downview Cl, Cob. (Down.)
KT11 169 BV119

★ Place of interest ⇌ Railway station ⊖ London Underground station DLR Docklands Light Railway station Tra Tramlink station H Hospital Riv Pedestrian ferry landing stage

Down Way, Nthlt. UB5 77 BV69
Dowrey St, N1
off Richmond Av 83 DN67
Dowry Wk, Wat. WD17 23 BT38
Dowsett Rd, N17 46 DT54
Dowson Cl, SE5 102 DR84
Doyce St, SE1 201 H4
Doyle Cl, Erith DA8 107 FE81
Doyle Gdns, NW10 81 CU67
Doyle Rd, SE25 142 DU98
Doyle Way, Til. RM18
off Coleridge Rd 111 GJ82
D'Oyley St, SW1 198 F8
D'Oyly Carte Island, Wey.
KT13 135 BP102
Doynton St, N19 65 DH61
Draco St, SE17 102 DQ79
Dragonfly Cl, E13
off Hollybush St 86 EH69
Dragon La, Wey. KT13 152 BN110
Dragon Rd, SE15 102 DS79
Dragoon Rd, SE8 103 DZ78
Dragor Rd, NW10 80 CQ70
Drake Av, Cat. CR3 176 DQ122
Slough SL3 92 AX77
Staines TW18 113 BF92
Drake Cl, SE16 203 J4
Brentwood CM14 54 FX50
Drake Ct, SE19 122 DT92
W12 99 CW75
Harrow HA2 60 BZ60
Drake Cres, SE28 88 EW72
Drakefell Rd, SE4 103 DX82
SE14 103 DX82
Drakefield Rd, SW17 120 DG90
Drake Ho, SW8
off St. George Wf 101 DL78
Drakeley Ct, N5
off Highbury Hill 65 DP63
Drake Ms, Brom. BR2 144 EJ98
Hornchurch RM12
off Fulmar Rd 89 FG66
Drake Rd, SE4 103 EA83
Chessington KT9 156 CN106
Croydon CR0 141 DM101
Grays (Chaff.Hun.) RM16 110 FY76
Harrow HA2 60 BZ61
Mitcham CR4 140 DG100
Drakes Cl, Esher KT10 154 CA106
Waltham Cross (Chsht) EN8 15 DX28
Drakes Ctyd, NW6 81 CZ66
Drakes Dr, Nthwd. HA6 39 BP53
Drake St, WC1 196 B7
Enfield EN2 30 DR39
Drakes Wk, E6 87 EM67
Drakes Way, Wok. GU22 166 AX122
Drakewood Rd, SW16 121 DK94
Draper Cl, Belv. DA17 106 EZ77
Isleworth TW7 97 CD82
Draper Ct, Horn. RM12 72 FL61
Draper Ho, SE1 200 G8
Draper Pl, N1 off Dagmar Ter 83 DP67
Drapers' Cres, Walt. KT12
off Octagon Rd 153 BT110
Draper's Gdns, EC2
off Copthall Av 84 DR72
Drapers Rd, E15 67 ED63
N17 66 DT55
Enfield EN2 29 DP40
Drappers Way, SE16 202 C8
Draven Cl, Brom. BR2 144 EF101
Drawdock Rd, SE10 204 G3
Drawell Cl, SE18 105 ES78
Drax Av, SW20 119 CV94
Draxmont, SW19 119 CY93
Draycot Rd, E11 68 EH58
Surbiton KT6 138 CN102
Draycott Av, SW3 198 C8
Harrow HA3 61 CH58
Draycott Cl, NW2 63 CX62
SE5 off Caspian St 102 DR80
Harrow HA3 61 CH58
Draycott Ms, SW6
off New Kings Rd 99 CZ82
Draycott Pl, SW3 198 D9
Draycott Ter, SW3 198 E8
Drayford Cl, W9 81 CZ70
Dray Gdns, SW2 121 DM85
Draymans Ms, SE15
off Chadwick Rd 102 DT82
Draymans Way, Islw. TW7 97 CF83
Drayside Ms, Sthl. UB2
off Kingston Rd 96 BZ75
Drayson Cl, Wal.Abb. EN9 16 EE32
Drayson Ms, W8 100 DA75
Drayton Av, W13 79 CG73
Loughton IG10 33 EM44
Orpington BR6 145 EP102
Potters Bar EN6 11 CY32
Drayton Br Rd, W7 79 CF73
W13 79 CF73
Drayton Cl, Houns. TW4 116 BZ85
Ilford IG1 69 ER60
Leatherhead (Fetch.) KT22 171 CE124
Drayton Ford, Rick. WD3 38 BG48
Drayton Gdns, N21 45 DP45
SW10 100 DC78
W13 79 CG73
West Drayton UB7 94 BL75
⇌ Drayton Green 79 CF72
Drayton Grn, W13 79 CG73
Drayton Grn Rd, W13 79 CH73
Drayton Gro, W13 79 CG73
⇌ Drayton Park 65 DN63
Drayton Pk, N5 65 DN64
Drayton Pk Ms, N5
off Drayton Pk 65 DN64
Drayton Rd, E11 67 ED60
N17 46 DS54
NW10 81 CT67
W13 79 CG73
Borehamwood WD6 26 CN42
Croydon CR0 141 DP103
Drayton Waye, Har. HA3 61 CH58
Drenon Sq, Hayes UB3 77 BT73
Dresden Cl, NW6 82 DB65
Dresden Ho, SE11
off Lambeth Wk 101 DM77
Dresden Rd, N19 65 DK60
Dresden Way, Wey. KT13 153 BQ106
Dressington Av, SE4 123 EA86
Drew Av, NW7 43 CY51
Drew Gdns, Grnf. UB6 79 CF65
Drew Pl, Cat. CR3 176 DR123
Drew Rd, E16 86 EL74
Drewstead Rd, SW16 121 DK89
Drey, The, Ger.Cr. (Chal.St.P.)
SL9 36 AY50
Driffield Rd, E3 85 DY68
Drift, The, Brom. BR2 144 EK104
Drift La, Cob. KT11 170 BZ117
Drift Rd, Lthd. KT24 169 BT124
Drift Way, Rich. TW10 118 CM88
Slough (Colnbr.) SL3 93 BC81
Driftway, The, Bans. SM7 173 CW115
Leatherhead KT22
off Downs La 171 CH123
Mitcham CR4 140 DG95
Driftwood Av, St.Alb. AL2 8 CA26
Driftwood Dr, Ken. CR8 175 DP117
Drill Hall Rd, Cher. KT16 134 BG101
Drinkwater Rd, Har. HA2 60 CB61
Drive, The, E4 47 ED45
E17 67 EB56
E18 68 EG56
N3 44 DA52
N6 64 DF57
N11 45 DJ51
NW10 off Longstone Av 81 CT67
NW11 63 CY59
SW6 off Fulham Rd 99 CY82
SW16 141 DM97
SW20 119 CW94
W3 80 CQ72
Ashford TW15 115 BR94
Banstead SM7 173 CY117
Barking IG11 87 ET66
Barnet (High Barn.) EN5 27 CY41
Barnet (New Barn.) EN5 28 DC44
Beckenham BR3 143 EA96
Bexley DA5 126 EW86
Brentwood CM13 54 FW50
Buckhurst Hill IG9 48 EJ45
Chislehurst BR7 145 ET97
Chislehurst (Scad.Pk) BR7 145 ES95
Cobham KT11 154 BY114
Coulsdon CR5 159 DL114
Edgware HA8 42 CN50
Enfield EN2 30 DR39
Epsom KT19 157 CT107
Epsom (Headley) KT18 172 CN124
Erith DA8 107 FB80
Esher KT10 136 CC102
Feltham TW14 116 BW87
Gerrards Cross (Chal.St.P.)
SL9 36 AY52
Gravesend DA12 131 GK91
Harrow HA2 60 CA59
Hatfield (Brook.Pk) AL9 12 DA25
Hounslow TW3 97 CD82
Ilford IG1 69 EM60
Isleworth TW7 97 CD82
Kingston upon Thames
KT2 118 CQ94
Leatherhead (Fetch.) KT22 171 CE122
Leatherhead (Tyr.Wd)
KT22 172 CN124
Loughton IG10 32 EL41
Morden SM4 140 DD99
Northwood HA6 39 BS54
Orpington BR6 145 ET103
Potters Bar EN6 11 CZ33
Radlett WD7 9 CG34
Rickmansworth WD3 22 BJ44
Romford (Coll.Row) RM5 51 FC53
Romford (Harold Wd) RM3 52 FL53
Sevenoaks TN13 191 FH124
Sidcup DA14 126 EV90
Slough SL3 92 AY75
Slough (Datchet) SL3 92 AV81
Staines (Wrays.) TW19 112 AX85
Surbiton KT6 138 CL101
Sutton SM2 157 CZ112
Thornton Heath CR7 142 DR98
Uxbridge UB10 58 BL63
Virginia Water GU25 133 AZ99
Wallington SM6 159 DJ110
Waltham Cross (Chsht) EN7 13 DP28
Watford WD17 23 BR37
Wembley HA9 62 CQ61
West Wickham BR4 143 ED101
Woking GU22 166 AV120
Drive Mead, Couls. CR5 159 DL114
Drive Rd, Couls. CR5 175 DM119
Drive Spur, Tad. KT20 174 DB121
Driveway, The, E17
off Hoe St 67 EB58
Potters Bar (Cuffley) EN6 13 DL28
Droitwich Cl, SE26 122 DU90
Dromey Gdns, Har. HA3 41 CF52
Dromore Rd, SW15 119 CY86
Dronfield Gdns, Dag. RM8 70 EW64
Droop St, W10 81 CY70
Drop La, St.Alb. (Brick.Wd) AL2 8 CB30
Drovers Mead, Brwd. (Warley)
CM14 54 FV49
Drovers Pl, SE15 102 DV80
Drovers Rd, S.Croy. CR2 160 DR106
Droveway, Loug. IG10 33 EP40
Drove Way, The, Grav.
(Istead Rise) DA13 130 GE94
Druce Rd, SE21 122 DS86
Drudgeon Way, Dart. (Bean)
DA2 129 FV90
Druids Cl, Ashtd. KT21 172 CM120
Druid St, SE1 201 N4
Druids Way, Brom. BR2 143 ED98
Drumaline Ridge, Wor.Pk.
KT4 138 CS103
Drummond Av, Rom. RM7 71 FD56
Drummond Cl, Erith DA8 107 FE81
Drummond Cres, NW1 195 M2
Drummond Dr, Stan. HA7 41 CF52
Drummond Gdns, Epsom
KT19 156 CP111
Drummond Gate, SW1 199 N10
Drummond Pl, Twick. TW1 117 CH86
Drummond Rd, E11 68 EH58
SE16 202 D6
Croydon CR0 142 DQ103
Romford RM7 71 FD56
Drummonds, The, Buck.H. IG9 48 EH47
Epping CM16 18 EU30
Drummonds Pl, Rich. TW9 98 CL84
Drummond St, NW1 195 K4
Drum St, E1
off Whitechapel High St 84 DT72
Drury Cres, Croy. CR0 141 DN103
Drury La, WC2 196 A9
Drury Rd, Har. HA1 60 CC59
Drury Way, NW10 62 CR64
Drury Way Ind Est, NW10 62 CQ64
Dryad St, SW15 99 CX83
Dryburgh Gdns, NW9 62 CN55
Dryburgh Rd, SW15 99 CV83
Dryden Av, W7 79 CF72
Dryden Cl, Ilf. IG6 49 ET51
Dryden Ct, SE11 200 E9
Dryden Pl, Til. RM18
off Fielding Av 111 GH81
Dryden Rd, SW19 120 DC93
Enfield EN1 30 DS44
Harrow HA3 41 CF53
Welling DA16 105 ES81
Dryden St, WC2 196 A9
Dryden Twrs, Rom. RM3 51 FH52
Dryden Way, Orp. BR6 146 EU102
Dryfield Cl, NW10 80 CQ65
Dryfield Rd, Edg. HA8 42 CQ51
Dryfield Wk, SE8
off New King St 103 EA79
Dryhill La, Sev. (Sund.) TN14 190 FB123
Dryhill Rd, Belv. DA17 106 EZ79
Dryland Av, Orp. BR6 163 ET105
Drylands Rd, N8 65 DL58
Drynham Pk, Wey. KT13 135 BS104
Drysdale Av, E4 47 EB45
Drysdale Cl, Nthwd. HA6
off Northbrook Dr 39 BS52
Drysdale Pl, N1 197 N2
Drysdale St, N1 197 N3
Duarte Pl, Grays RM16 110 FZ76
Dublin Av, E8 84 DU67
Du Burstow Ter, W7 97 CE75
Ducal St, E2 off Brick La 84 DT69
Du Cane Cl, W12 81 CW72
Du Cane Ct, SW17 120 DG88
Du Cane Rd, W12 81 CT72
Duchess Cl, N11 45 DH50
Sutton SM1 158 DC105
Duchess Ct, Wey. KT13 135 BR104
Duchess Gro, Buck.H. IG9 48 EH47
Duchess Ms, W1 195 J7
Duchess of Bedford's Wk,
W8 100 DA75
Duchess St, W1 195 J7
Duchess Wk, Sev. TN15 191 FL125
Duchy Rd, Barn. EN4 28 DD38
Duchy St, SE1 200 E2
Ducie St, SW4 101 DM84
Duckett Ms, N4
off Duckett Rd 65 DP58
Duckett Rd, N4 65 DP58
Ducketts Rd, Dart. DA1 127 FF85
Duckett St, E1 85 DX70
Ducking Stool Ct, Rom. RM1 71 FE56
Duck La, W1 195 M9
Epping (Thnwd) CM16 18 EW26
Duck Lees La, Enf. EN3 31 DY42
Ducks Hill, Nthwd. HA6 39 BP54
Ducks Hill Rd, Nthwd. HA6 39 BP54
Ruislip HA4 39 BP54
DUCKS ISLAND, Barn. EN5 27 CX44
Ducks Wk, Twick. TW1 117 CJ85
Du Cros Dr, Stan. HA7 41 CK51
Du Cros Rd, W3
off The Vale 80 CS74
Dudden Hill La, NW10 63 CT63
Duddington Cl, SE9 124 EK91
Dudley Av, Har. HA3 61 CJ55
Waltham Cross EN8 15 DX32
Dudley Cl, Add. KT15 134 BJ104
Grays (Chaff.Hun.) RM16 110 FY75
Hemel Hempstead (Bov.)
HP3 5 BA27
Dudley Ct, NW11 63 CZ56
Slough SL1 off Upton Rd 92 AU76
Dudley Dr, Mord. SM4 139 CY101
Ruislip HA4 59 BV64
Dudley Gdns, W13 97 CH75
Harrow HA2 61 CD60
Romford RM3 52 FK51
Dudley Gro, Epsom KT18 156 CQ114
Dudley Ho, W2
off North Wf Rd 82 DD71
Dudley Ms, SW2
off Bascombe St 121 DN86
Dudley Pl, Hayes UB3 95 BR77
Dudley Rd, E17 47 EA54
N3 44 DB54
NW6 81 CY68
SW19 120 DA93
Ashford TW15 114 BM92
Feltham TW14 115 BQ88
Gravesend (Nthflt) DA11 130 GE87
Harrow HA2 60 CC61
Ilford IG1 69 EP63
Kingston upon Thames
KT1 138 CM97
Richmond TW9 98 CM82
Romford RM3 52 FK51
Southall UB2 96 BX75
Walton-on-Thames KT12 135 BU100
Dudley St, W2 82 DD71
Dudlington Rd, E5 66 DW61
Dudmaston Ms, SW3 198 A10
Dudrich Ms, SE22
off Melbourne Gro 122 DT85
Dudsbury Rd, Dart. DA1 127 FG86
Sidcup DA14 126 EV93
Dudset La, Houns. TW5 95 BU81
Duffell Ho, SE11 200 C10
Dufferin Av, EC1 197 K5
Dufferin St, EC1 197 J5
Duffield Cl, Grays (Daniel Cl)
RM16 110 FY75
Grays (Davis Rd) RM16 110 FZ76
Harrow HA1 61 CF57
Duffield Dr, N15
off Copperfield Dr 66 DT56
Duffield La, Slou. (Stoke P.)
SL2 74 AT65
Duffield Pk, Slou. (Stoke P.)
SL2 74 AU69
Duffield Rd, Tad. (Walt.Hill)
KT20 173 CV124
Duffins Orchard, Cher. (Ott.)
KT16 151 BC108
Duff St, E14 85 EB72
Dufour's Pl, W1 195 L9
Dugard Way, SE11 200 F8
Dugdale Hill La, Pot.B. EN6 11 CY33
Dugdales, Rick. (Crox.Grn)
WD3 22 BN42
Duggan Dr, Chis. BR7 124 EL92
Dugolly Av, Wem. HA9 62 CP62
Duke Gdns, Ilf. IG6
off Duke Rd 69 ER56
Duke Humphrey Rd, SE3 104 EE81
Duke of Cambridge Cl, Twick.
TW2 117 CD86
Duke of Edinburgh Rd, Sutt.
SM1 140 DD103
Duke of Wellington Av, SE18 105 EP76
Duke of Wellington Pl, SW1 198 G4
Duke of York Sq, SW3 198 E9
Duke of York St, SW1 199 L2
Duke Rd, W4 98 CR78
Ilford IG6 69 ER56
Dukes Av, N3 44 DB53
N10 65 DJ55
W4 98 CR78
Edgware HA8 42 CM51
Epping (They.B.) CM16 33 ES35
Grays RM17 110 GA75
Harrow HA1 61 CE56
Harrow (N.Har.) HA2 60 BZ58
Hounslow TW4 96 BY84
Kingston upon Thames
KT2 117 CJ91
New Malden KT3 139 CT97
Northolt UB5 78 BY66
Richmond TW10 117 CJ91
Dukes Cl, Ashf. TW15 115 BQ91
Epping (N.Wld Bas.) CM16 19 FB27
Gerrards Cross SL9 56 AX60
Hampton TW12 116 BZ92
Dukes Ct, E6 87 EN67
Woking GU21 167 AZ117
Dukes Gate, W4
off Acton La 98 CQ77
Dukes Grn Av, Felt. TW14 115 BU85
Dukes Head Yd, N6
off Highgate High St 65 DH60
Dukes Hill, Cat. (Wold.) CR3 177 DY120
Duke Shore Pl, E14 203 M1
Duke Shore Wf, E14 203 M1
Dukes Kiln Dr, Ger.Cr. SL9 56 AW60
Dukes La, W8 100 DA75
Gerrards Cross SL9 56 AY59
Dukes Lo, Nthwd. HA6
off Eastbury Av 39 BS50
Duke's Meadows, W4 98 CR81
Dukes Ms, N10 off Dukes Av 65 DH55
Duke's Ms, W1 194 G8
Dukes Orchard, Bex. DA5 127 FC88
Duke's Pas, E17 67 EC56
Dukes Pl, EC3 197 N9
Dukes Ride, Ger.Cr. SL9 56 AY60
Uxbridge UB10 58 BL63
Dukes Rd, E6 87 EN67
W3 80 CN71
Duke's Rd, WC1 195 N3
Dukes Rd, Walt. KT12 154 BX106
Dukesthorpe Rd, SE26 123 DX91
Duke St, SW1 199 L2
W1 194 G8
Richmond TW9 97 CK84
Sutton SM1 158 DD105
Watford WD17 24 BW41
Woking GU21 167 AZ117
Duke St Hill, SE1 201 L2
Dukes Valley, Ger.Cr. SL9 56 AV61
Dukes Way, Uxb. UB8
off Waterloo Rd 76 BJ67
West Wickham BR4 144 EE104
Dukes Wd Av, Ger.Cr. SL9 56 AY60
Dukes Wd Dr, Ger.Cr. SL9 56 AW60
Duke's Yd, W1 194 G10
Dulas St, N4
off Everleigh St 65 DM60
Dulford St, W11 81 CY73
Dulka Rd, SW11 120 DF85
Dulverton Rd, SE9 125 EQ89
Romford RM3 52 FK51
Ruislip HA4 59 BU60
South Croydon CR2 160 DW110
DULWICH, SE21 122 DS87
★ Dulwich Coll Picture Gall,
SE21 122 DS87
Dulwich Common, SE21 122 DS88
SE22 122 DS88
H Dulwich Comm Hosp,
SE22 102 DS84
Dulwich Lawn Cl, SE22
off Colwell Rd 122 DT85
Dulwich Oaks, The, SE21 122 DS90
Dulwich Rd, SE24 121 DN85
Dulwich Village, SE21 122 DS86
Dulwich Way, Rick. (Crox.Grn)
WD3 22 BN43
Dulwich Wd Av, SE19 122 DS91
Dulwich Wd Pk, SE19 122 DS91
Dumas Way, Wat. WD18 23 BS42
Dumbarton Av, Wal.Cr. EN8 15 DX34
Dumbarton Rd, SW2 121 DL86
Dumbleton Cl, Kings.T. KT1
off Gloucester Rd 138 CP95
Dumbletons, The, Rick.
(Map.Cr.) WD3 37 BE49
Dumbreck Rd, SE9 105 EM84
Dumfries Cl, Wat. WD19 39 BT48
Dumont Rd, N16 66 DS62
Dumpton Pl, NW1
off Gloucester Av 82 DG66
Dumville Dr, Gdse. RH9 186 DV131
Dunally Pk, Shep. TW17 135 BR101
Dunbar Av, SW16 141 DN96
Beckenham BR3 143 DY98
Dagenham RM10 70 FA62
Dunbar Cl, Hayes UB4 77 BU71
Slough SL2 74 AU72
Dunbar Ct, Sutt. SM1 158 DD106
Walton-on-Thames KT12 136 BW103
Dunbar Gdns, Dag. RM10 70 FA64
Dunbar Rd, E7 86 EG65
N22 45 DN53
Dunbar Rd, N. Mald. KT3 138 CQ98
Dunbar St, SE27 122 DQ90
Dunblane Cl, Edg. HA8
off Tayside Dr 42 CP47
Dunblane Rd, SE9 104 EL83
Dunboe Pl, Shep. TW17 135 BQ101
Dunboyne Rd, NW3 64 DF64
Dunbridge Ho, SW15
off Highcliffe Dr 119 CT86
Dunbridge St, E2 84 DU70
Duncan Cl, Barn. EN5 28 DC42
Duncan Gdns, Stai. TW18 114 BG93
Duncan Gro, W3 80 CS72
Duncannon Pl, Green. DA9 109 FW84
Duncannon St, WC2 199 P1
Duncan Rd, E8 84 DV67
Richmond TW9 98 CL84
Tadworth KT20 173 CY119
Duncan St, N1 83 DP68
Duncan Ter, N1 196 F1
Duncan Way, Bushey WD23 24 BZ40
Dunch St, E1 off Watney St 84 DV72
Duncombe Cl, Amer. HP6 20 AS38
Duncombe Ct, Stai. TW18 113 BF94
Duncombe Hill, SE23 123 DY87
Duncombe Rd, N19 65 DK60
Duncrievie Rd, SE13 123 ED86
Duncroft, SE18 105 ES80
Duncroft Cl, Reig. RH2 183 CZ133
Dundalk Rd, SE4 103 DY83
Dundas Gdns, W.Mol. KT8 136 CB97
Dundas Ms, Enf. EN3 31 EA37
Dundas Rd, SE15 102 DW82
Dundee Ho, W9
off Maida Vale 82 DC69
Dundee Rd, E13 86 EH68
SE25 142 DV99
Dundee St, E1 202 D3
Dundee Way, Enf. EN3 31 DY41
Dundela Gdns, Wor.Pk. KT4 157 CV105
Dundonald Cl, E6
off Northumberland Rd 86 EL72
Tra Dundonald Road 119 CZ94
Dundonald Rd, NW10 81 CX67
SW19 119 CY94
Dundrey Cres, Red. (Merst.)
RH1 185 DL129
Dunedin Dr, Cat. CR3 186 DS125
Dunedin Ho, E16
off Manwood St 87 EM74
Dunedin Rd, E10 67 EB62
Ilford IG1 69 EQ60
Rainham RM13 89 FF69
Dunedin Way, Hayes UB4 78 BW70
Dunelm Gro, SE27 122 DQ91
Dunelm St, E1 85 DX72
Dunfee Way, W.Byf. KT14 152 BL112
Dunfield Gdns, SE6 123 EB91
Dunfield Rd, SE6 123 EB92
Dunford Rd, N7 65 DM63
Dungarvan Av, SW15 99 CU84
Dungates La, Bet. (Buckland)
RH3 183 CU133
Dunheved Cl, Th.Hth. CR7 141 DN100
Dunheved Rd N, Th.Hth. CR7 141 DN100
Dunheved Rd S, Th.Hth. CR7 141 DN100
Dunheved Rd W, Th.Hth. CR7 141 DN100
Dunhill Pt, SW15
off Dilton Gdns 119 CV88
Dunholme Grn, N9 46 DT48
Dunholme La, N9
off Dunholme Rd 46 DT48
Dunholme Rd, N9 46 DT48
Dunkeld Rd, SE25 142 DR98
Dagenham RM8 70 EV61
Dunkellin Gro, S.Ock. RM15 91 FU71
Dunkellin Way, S.Ock. RM15 91 FU72
Dunkery Rd, SE9 124 EK91
Dunkin Rd, Dart. DA1 108 FN84
Dunkirk Cl, Grav. DA12 131 GJ92
Dunkirk St, SE27
off Waring St 122 DQ91
Dunlace Rd, E5 66 DW63
Dunleary Cl, Houns. TW4 116 BZ87
Dunley Dr, Croy. (New Adgtn)
CR0 161 EB108
Dunlin Ho, W13 79 CF70
Dunloe Av, N17 66 DR55
Dunloe St, E2 197 P1
Dunlop Cl, Dart. DA1 108 FL83
Dunlop Pl, SE16 202 A7
Dunlop Rd, Til. RM18 111 GF81
Dunmail Dr, Pur. CR8 160 DS114
Dunmore Pt, E2 197 P3
Dunmore Rd, NW6 81 CY67
SW20 139 CW95
Dunmow Cl, Felt. TW13 116 BY91
Loughton IG10 32 EL44
Romford RM6 70 EW57
Dunmow Dr, Rain. RM13 89 FF67
Dunmow Ho, Dag. RM9 88 EV67
Dunmow Rd, E15 67 ED63
Dunmow Wk, N1
off Popham St 84 DQ67
Dunnage Cres, SE16 203 L8
Dunnets, Wok. (Knap.) GU21 166 AS117
Dunning Cl, S.Ock. RM15 91 FU72
Dunningford Cl, Horn. RM12 71 FF64
Dunn Mead, NW9
off Field Mead 43 CT52
Dunnock Cl, N9 47 DX46
Borehamwood WD6 26 CN42
Dunnock Rd, E6 86 EL72
Dunns Pas, WC1 196 A8
Dunn St, E8 66 DT64
Dunny La, Kings L. (Chipper.)
WD4 5 BE32
Dunnymans Rd, Bans. SM7 173 CZ115
Dunollie Pl, NW5
off Dunollie Rd 65 DJ64
Dunollie Rd, NW5 65 DJ64
Dunoon Rd, SE23 122 DW87
Dunraven Dr, Enf. EN2 29 DN40
Dunraven Rd, W12 81 CU74
Dunraven St, W1 194 E10
Dunsany Rd, W14 99 CX76
Dunsborough Pk, Wok.
(Ripley) GU23 168 BJ120
Dunsbury Cl, Sutt. SM2
off Nettlecombe Cl 158 DB109
Dunsfold Ri, Couls. CR5 159 DK113
Dunsfold Way, Croy. (New Adgtn)
CR0 161 EB108

★ Place of interest ⇌ Railway station ⊖ London Underground station DLR Docklands Light Railway station Tra Tramlink station H Hospital Riv Pedestrian ferry landing stage

Dunsford Way, SW15
off Dover Pk Dr ...119 CV86
Dunsmore Cl, Bushey WD23 ..25 CD44
Hayes UB4 ...78 BX70
Dunsmore Rd, Walt. KT12 ...135 BV100
Dunsmore Way, Bushey
WD23 ...25 CD44
Dunsmure Rd, N16 ...66 DS60
Dunspring La, Ilf. IG5 ...49 EP54
Dunstable Cl, Rom. RM3
off Dunstable Rd ...52 FK51
Dunstable Ms, W1 ...194 G6
Dunstable Rd, Rich. TW9 ...98 CL84
Romford RM3 ...52 FK51
West Molesey KT8 ...136 BZ98
Dunstall Grn, Wok. (Chobham)
GU24 ...150 AW109
Dunstall Rd, SW20 ...119 CV93
Dunstall Way, W.Mol. KT8 ...136 CB97
Dunstan Cl, N2
off Thomas More Way ...64 DC55
Dunstan Rd, NW11 ...63 CZ60
Coulsdon CR5 ...175 DK117
Dunstans Gro, SE22 ...122 DV86
Dunstans Rd, SE22 ...122 DU87
Dunster Av, Mord. SM4 ...139 CX102
Dunster Cl, Barn. EN5 ...27 CX42
Romford RM5 ...51 FC54
Uxbridge (Hare.) UB9 ...38 BH53
Dunster Ct, EC3 ...197 M10
Borehamwood WD6
off Kensington Way ...26 CR41
Dunster Cres, Horn. RM11 ...72 FN61
Dunster Dr, NW9 ...62 CQ60
Dunster Gdns, NW6 ...81 CZ66
Dunsterville Way, SE1 ...201 L5
Dunster Way, Har. HA2 ...60 BY62
Wallington SM6
off Helios Rd ...140 DG102
Dunston Rd, E8 ...84 DT67
SW11 ...100 DG82
Dunston St, E8 ...84 DT67
Dunton Cl, Surb. KT6 ...138 CL102
DUNTON GREEN,
Sev. TN13 ...181 FC119
⇌ **Dunton Green** ...181 FF119
Dunton Rd, E10 ...67 EB59
SE1 ...201 P10
Romford RM1 ...71 FE56
Duntshill Rd, SW18 ...120 DB88
Dunvegan Cl, W.Mol. KT8 ...136 CB98
Dunvegan Rd, SE9 ...105 EM84
Dunwich Rd, Bexh. DA7 ...106 EZ81
Dunworth Ms, W11
off Portobello Rd ...81 CZ72
Duplex Ride, SW1 ...198 E5
Dupont Rd, SW20 ...139 CX96
Duppas Av, Croy. CR0
off Violet La ...159 DP105
Duppas Cl, Shep. TW17 ...135 BR99
Duppas Hill La, Croy. CR0
off Duppas Hill Rd ...159 DP105
Duppas Hill Rd, Croy. CR0 ...159 DP105
Duppas Hill Ter, Croy. CR0 ...141 DP104
Duppas Rd, Croy. CR0 ...141 DN104
Dupre Cl, Grays (Chaff.Hun.)
RM16 ...110 FY76
Dupree Rd, SE7 ...205 P10
Dura Den Cl, Beck. BR3 ...123 EB94
Durand Cl, Cars. SM5 ...140 DF102
Durand Gdns, SW9 ...101 DM81
Durands Wk, SE16 ...203 L4
Durand Way, NW10 ...80 CQ66
Durant Rd, Swan. BR8 ...127 FG93
Durants Pk Av, Enf. EN3 ...31 DX42
Durants Rd, Enf. EN3 ...30 DW42
Durant St, E2 ...84 DU68
Durban Gdns, Dag. RM10 ...89 FC66
Durban Rd, E15 ...86 EE69
E17 ...47 DZ53
N17 ...46 DS51
SE27 ...122 DQ91
Beckenham BR3 ...143 DZ96
Ilford IG2 ...69 ES60
Durban Rd E, Wat. WD18 ...23 BU42
Durban Rd W, Wat. WD18 ...23 BU42
Durbin Rd, Chess. KT9 ...156 CL105
Durdans Rd, Sthl. UB1 ...78 BZ72
Durell Gdns, Dag. RM9 ...70 EX64
Durell Rd, Dag. RM9 ...70 EX64
Durfey Pl, SE5
off Edmund St ...102 DR80
Durfold Dr, Reig. RH2 ...184 DC134
Durford Cres, SW15 ...119 CU88
Durham Av, Brom. BR2 ...144 EF98
Hounslow TW5 ...96 BZ78
Romford RM2 ...72 FJ56
Woodford Green IG8 ...48 EK50
Durham Cl, SW20
off Durham Rd ...139 CV96
Durham Hill, Brom. BR1 ...124 EF91
Durham Ho St, WC2 ...200 A1
Durham Pl, SW3
off Smith St ...100 DF78
Ilford IG1 *off Eton Rd* ...69 EQ63
Durham Ri, SE18 ...105 EQ78
Durham Rd, E12 ...68 EK63
E16 ...86 EE70
N2 ...64 DE55
N7 ...65 DM61
N9 ...46 DU47
SW20 ...139 CV95
W5 ...97 CK76
Borehamwood WD6 ...26 CQ41
Bromley BR2 ...144 EF97
Dagenham RM10 ...71 FC64
Feltham TW14 ...116 BW87
Harrow HA1 ...60 CB57
Sidcup DA14 ...126 EV92
Durham Row, E1 ...85 DY71
Durham St, SE11 ...101 DM78
Durham Ter, W2 ...82 DB72
Durham Wf, Brent. TW8
off London Rd ...97 CJ80
Durham Yd, E2
off Teesdale St ...84 DV69
Durian Way, Erith DA8 ...107 FH80
Durley Av, Pnr. HA5 ...60 BY59
Durley Gdns, Orp. BR6 ...164 EV105
Durley Rd, N16 ...66 DS59
Durlston Rd, E5 ...66 DU61
Kingston upon Thames
KT2 ...118 CL93
Durndale La, Grav. (Nthflt)
DA11 ...131 GF91
Durnell Way, Loug. IG10 ...33 EN41
Durnford St, N15 ...66 DS57
SE10 *off Greenwich Ch St* ...103 EC79
Durning Rd, SE19 ...122 DR92
Durnsford Av, SW19 ...120 DA89
Durnsford Rd, N11 ...45 DK53
SW19 ...120 DA89
Durrants Cl, Rain. RM13 ...90 FJ68
Durrants Dr, Rick. (Crox.Grn)
WD3 ...23 BQ42
Durrant Way, Orp. BR6 ...163 ER106
Swanscombe DA10 ...130 FY87
Durrell Rd, SW6 ...99 CZ81
Durrell Way, Shep. TW17 ...135 BR100
Durrington Av, SW20 ...139 CW95
Durrington Pk Rd, SW20 ...119 CW94
Durrington Rd, E5 ...67 DY63
Durrington Twr, SW8
off Westbury St ...101 DJ82
Dursley Cl, SE3 ...104 EJ82
Dursley Gdns, SE3 ...104 EK81
Dursley Rd, SE3 ...104 EJ82
Durward St, E1 ...84 DV71
Durweston Ms, W1 ...194 E6
Durweston St, W1 ...194 E6
Dury Falls Cl, Horn. RM11 ...72 FM60
Dury Rd, Barn. EN5 ...27 CZ39
Dutch Barn Cl, Stai. (Stanw.)
TW19 ...114 BK86
Dutch Elm Av, Wind. SL4 ...92 AT80
Dutch Gdns, Kings.T. KT2
off Windmill Ri ...118 CP94
Dutch Yd, SW18
off Wandsworth High St ...120 DA85
Dutton St, SE10 ...103 EC81
Dutton Way, Iver SL0 ...75 BE72
Duxberry Cl, Brom. BR2
off Southborough La ...144 EL99
Duxford Cl, Horn. RM12 ...89 FH65
Duxford Ho, SE2
off Wolvercote Rd ...106 EX75
Dwight Ct, SW6
off Burlington Rd ...99 CY82
Dwight Rd, Wat. WD18 ...39 BR45
Dye Ho La, E3 ...85 EA67
Dyer's Bldgs, EC1 ...196 D7
Dyers Hall Rd, E11 ...68 EE60
Dyers La, SW15 ...99 CV84
Dyers Way, Rom. RM3 ...51 FH52
Dyke Dr, Orp. BR5 ...146 EW102
Dykes Path, Wok. GU21
off Bentham Av ...167 BC115
Dykes Way, Brom. BR2 ...144 EF97
Dykewood Cl, Bex. DA5 ...127 FE90
Dylan Cl, Borwd. (Els.) WD6
off Coates Rd ...41 CK45
Dylan Rd, SE24 ...101 DP84
Belvedere DA17 ...106 FA76
Dylways, SE5 ...102 DR84
Dymchurch Cl, Ilf. IG5 ...49 EN54
Orpington BR6 ...163 ES105
Dymes Path, SW19
off Queensmere Rd ...119 CX89
Dymock St, SW6 ...100 DB83
Dymoke Rd, Horn. RM11 ...71 FF59
Dymond Est, SW17
off Glenburnie Rd ...120 DE90
Dyneley Rd, SE12 ...124 EJ91
Dyne Rd, NW6 ...81 CZ66
Dynevor Rd, N16 ...66 DS62
Richmond TW10 ...118 CL85
Dynham Rd, NW6 ...82 DA66
Dyott St, WC1 ...195 P8
Dyrham La, Barn. EN5 ...27 CU36
Dysart Av, Kings.T. KT2 ...117 CJ92
Dysart St, EC2 ...197 M5
Dyson Rd, E11 ...68 EE58
E15 ...86 EF65
Dysons Cl, Wal.Cr. EN8 ...15 DX33
Dysons Rd, N18 ...46 DV50

E

Eade Rd, N4 ...66 DQ59
Eagans Cl, N2 *off Market Pl* ...64 DE55
Eagle Av, Rom. RM6 ...70 EY58
Eagle Cl, SE16 *off Varcoe Rd* ...102 DW78
Amersham HP6 ...20 AT37
Enfield EN3 ...30 DW42
Hornchurch RM12 ...89 FH65
Wallington SM6 ...159 DL107
Waltham Abbey EN9 ...16 EG34
Eagle Ct, EC1 ...196 F6
Eagle Dr, NW9 ...42 CS54
Eagle Hts, SW11
off Bramlands Cl ...100 DE83
Eagle Hill, SE19 ...122 DR93
Eagle Ho Ms, SW4
off Narbonne Av ...121 DJ85
Eagle La, E11 ...68 EG56
Eagle Lo, NW11
off Golders Grn Rd ...63 CY58
Eagle Ms, N1
off Tottenham Rd ...84 DS65
Eagle Pl, SW1 ...199 L1
SW7 *off Old Brompton Rd* ...100 DC78
Eagle Rd, Wem. HA0 ...79 CK66
Eagles Dr, West. (Tats.) TN16 ...178 EK118
Eaglesfield Rd, SE18 ...105 EP80
Eagles Rd, Green. DA9 ...109 FV84
Eagle St, WC1 ...196 B7
Eagle Ter, Wdf.Grn. IG8 ...48 EH52
Eagle Trd Est, Mitch. CR4 ...140 DF100
Eagle Way, Brwd. CM13 ...53 FV51
Gravesend (Nthflt) DA11 ...130 GA85
Eagle Wf Rd, N1 ...84 DQ68
Eagling Cl, E3
off Rounton Rd ...85 EA69
Ealdham Sq, SE9 ...104 EJ84
EALING, W5 ...79 CJ73
⇌ **Ealing Broadway** ...79 CK73
⊖ **Ealing Broadway** ...79 CK73
Ealing Bdy Shop Cen, W5 ...79 CK73
Ealing Cl, Borwd. WD6 ...26 CR39
★ **Ealing Common**, W5 ...80 CL74
⊖ **Ealing Common** ...80 CM74
Ealing Common, W5
off Gunnersbury Av ...80 CM73
Ealing Downs Ct, Grnf. UB6
off Perivale La ...79 CG69
Ealing Grn, W5 ...79 CK74
H **Ealing Hosp**, Sthl. UB1 ...79 CD75
Ealing Pk Gdns, W5 ...97 CJ77
Ealing Rd, Brent. TW8 ...97 CK78
Northolt UB5 ...78 CA66
Wembley HA0 ...79 CK67
Ealing Village, W5 ...80 CL72
Eamont Cl, Ruis. HA4
off Allonby Dr ...59 BP59
Eamont St, NW8 ...82 DE68
Eardemont Cl, Dart. DA1 ...107 FF84
Eardley Cres, SW5 ...100 DA78
Eardley Pt, SE18
off Wilmount St ...105 EP77
Eardley Rd, SW16 ...121 DJ92
Belvedere DA17 ...106 FA78
Sevenoaks TN13 ...191 FH124
Earhart Way, Houns. TW4 ...95 BU83
Earl Cl, N11 ...45 DH50
Earldom Rd, SW15 ...99 CW84
Earle Gdns, Kings.T. KT2 ...118 CL93
Earleswood, Cob. KT11 ...154 BX112
Earlham Gro, E7 ...68 EF64
N22 ...45 DM52
Earlham St, WC2 ...195 N9
Earl Ri, SE18 ...105 ER77
Earl Rd, SW14 *off Elm Rd* ...98 CQ84
Gravesend (Nthflt) DA11 ...130 GE89
EARLS COURT, SW5 ...99 CZ78
⊖ **Earls Court** ...100 DA78
★ **Earls Court Exhib Cen**,
SW5 ...100 DA78
Earls Ct Gdns, SW5 ...100 DB77
Earls Ct Rd, SW5 ...100 DA77
W8 ...100 DA77
Earls Ct Sq, SW5 ...100 DB78
Earls Cres, Har. HA1 ...61 CE56
Earlsdown Ho, Bark. IG11
off Wheelers Cross ...87 ER68
Earlsferry Way, N1 ...83 DM66
EARLSFIELD, SW18 ...120 DC88
⇌ **Earlsfield** ...120 DC88
Earlsfield Ho, Kings.T. KT2
off Kingsgate Rd ...137 CK95
Earlsfield Rd, SW18 ...120 DC88
Earlshall Rd, SE9 ...105 EM84
Earls La, Pot.B. EN6 ...10 CS32
Earlsmead, Har. HA2 ...60 BZ63
Earlsmead Rd, N15 ...66 DT57
NW10 ...81 CW68
Earl's Path, Loug. IG10 ...32 EJ40
Earls Ter, W8 ...99 CZ76
Earlsthorpe Ms, SW12 ...120 DG86
Earlsthorpe Rd, SE26 ...123 DX91
Earlstoke St, EC1 ...196 F2
Earlston Gro, E9 ...84 DV67
Earl St, EC2 ...197 M6
Watford WD17 ...24 BW41
Earls Wk, W8 ...100 DA76
Dagenham RM8 ...70 EV63
Earls Way, Orp. BR6
off Station Rd ...145 ET103
Earlswood Av, Th.Hth. CR7 ...141 DN99
Earlswood Gdns, Ilf. IG5 ...69 EN55
Earlswood St, SE10 ...104 EE78
Early Ms, NW1
off Arlington Rd ...83 DH67
Earnshaw St, WC2 ...195 N8
Earsby St, W14 ...99 CY77
Easby Cres, Mord. SM4 ...140 DB100
Easebourne Rd, Dag. RM8 ...70 EW64
Easedale Dr, Horn. RM12 ...71 FG64
Easedale Ho, Islw. TW7
off Summerwood Rd ...117 CF85
Eashing Pt, SW15
off Wanborough Dr ...119 CV88
Easington Way, S.Ock. RM15 ...91 FU71
Easley's Ms, W1 ...194 G8
East 10 Enterprise Pk, E10
off Argall Way ...67 DY60
EAST ACTON, W3 ...80 CR74
⊖ **East Acton** ...81 CT72
East Acton La, W3 ...80 CS73
East Arbour St, E1 ...85 DX72
East Av, E12 ...86 EL66
E17 ...67 EB56
Hayes UB3 ...95 BT75
Southall UB1 ...78 BZ73
Wallington SM6 ...159 DM106
Walton-on-Thames (Whiteley Vill.)
KT12 *off Octagon Rd* ...153 BT110
East Bk, N16 ...66 DS59
Eastbank Rd, Hmptn.
(Hmptn H.) TW12 ...116 CC92
EAST BARNET, Barn. EN4 ...28 DE44
East Barnet Rd, Barn. EN4 ...28 DE44
EAST BEDFONT, Felt. TW14 ...115 BS88
Eastbourne Av, W3 ...80 CR72
Eastbourne Gdns, SW14 ...98 CQ83
Eastbourne Ms, W2 ...82 DC72
Eastbourne Rd, E6 ...87 EN69
E15 ...86 EE67
N15 ...66 DS58
SW17 ...120 DG93
W4 ...98 CQ79
Brentford TW8 ...97 CJ78
Feltham TW13 ...116 BX89
Godstone RH9 ...186 DW132
Eastbourne Ter, W2 ...82 DC72
Eastbournia Av, N9 ...46 DV48
Eastbridge, Slou. SL2
off Victoria Rd ...74 AV74
Eastbrook Av, N9 ...46 DW45
Dagenham RM10 ...71 FC63
Eastbrook Cl, Wok. GU21 ...167 BA116
Eastbrook Dr, Rom. RM7 ...71 FE62
Eastbrook Rd, SE3 ...104 EH80
Waltham Abbey EN9 ...16 EE33
EASTBURY, Nthwd. HA6 ...39 BS49
Eastbury Av, Bark. IG11 ...87 ES67
Enfield EN1 ...30 DS39
Northwood HA6 ...39 BS50
Eastbury Ct, Bark. IG11 ...87 ES67
Eastbury Gro, W4 ...98 CS78
★ **Eastbury Ho**, Bark. IG11 ...87 ET67
Eastbury Pl, Nthwd. HA6
off Eastbury Av ...39 BT50
Eastbury Rd, E6 ...87 EN70
Kingston upon Thames
KT2 ...118 CL94
Northwood HA6 ...39 BS51
Eastbury Rd, Orp. BR5 ...145 ER100
Romford RM7 ...71 FD58
Watford WD19 ...39 BV45
Eastbury Sq, Bark. IG11 ...87 ET67
Eastbury Ter, E1 ...85 DX70
Eastcastle St, W1 ...195 K8
Eastcheap, EC3 ...197 L10
East Churchfield Rd, W3 ...80 CR74
Eastchurch Rd, Houns.
(Hthrw Air.) TW6 ...95 BS82
East Cl, W5 ...80 CN70
Barnet EN4 ...28 DG42
Greenford UB6 ...78 CC68
Rainham RM13 ...89 FH70
St. Albans AL2 ...8 CB25
Eastcombe Av, SE7 ...104 EH79
East Common, Ger.Cr. SL9 ...56 AY58
EASTCOTE, Pnr. HA5 ...60 BW58
⊖ **Eastcote** ...60 BW59
Eastcote, Orp. BR6 ...145 ET102
Eastcote Av, Grnf. UB6 ...61 CG64
Harrow HA2 ...60 CB61
West Molesey KT8 ...136 BZ99
Eastcote La, Har. HA2 ...60 CA62
Northolt UB5 ...78 CA66
Eastcote La N, Nthlt. UB5 ...78 BZ65
Eastcote Pl, Pnr. HA5 ...59 BV58
Eastcote Rd, Har. HA2 ...60 CC62
Pinner HA5 ...60 BX57
Pinner (Eastcote Vill.) HA5 ...59 BU58
Ruislip HA4 ...59 BS59
Welling DA16 ...105 ER82
Eastcote St, SW9 ...101 DM82
Eastcote Vw, Pnr. HA5 ...60 BW56
EASTCOTE VILLAGE, Pnr.
HA5 ...59 BV57
Eastcourt, Sun. TW16 ...136 BW96
East Ct, Wem. HA0 ...61 CJ61
East Cres, N11 ...44 DF49
Enfield EN1 ...30 DT43
East Cres Rd, Grav. DA12 ...131 GJ86
Eastcroft Rd, Epsom KT19 ...156 CS108
East Cross Cen, E15 ...85 EA65
East Cross Route, E3 ...85 DZ66
E9 ...85 DZ66
⇌ **East Croydon** ...142 DR103
Tram **East Croydon** ...142 DR103
Eastdean Av, Epsom KT18 ...156 CP113
East Dene Dr, Rom. (Harold Hill)
RM3 ...52 FK50
Eastdown Pk, SE13 ...103 ED84
East Dr, Cars. SM5 ...158 DE109
Northwood HA6 ...39 BS47
Orpington BR5 ...146 EV100
Slough (Stoke P.) SL2 ...74 AS69
Virginia Water GU25 ...132 AU101
Watford WD25 ...23 BV35
East Duck Lees La, Enf. EN3 ...31 DY42
EAST DULWICH, SE22 ...122 DU86
⇌ **East Dulwich** ...102 DS84
East Dulwich Gro, SE22 ...122 DS86
East Dulwich Rd, SE15 ...102 DT84
SE22 ...102 DT84
East End Rd, N2 ...64 DC55
N3 ...44 DA54
East End Way, Pnr. HA5 ...60 BY55
East Entrance, Dag. RM10 ...89 FB68
Eastern Av, E11 ...68 EJ58
Chertsey KT16 ...134 BG97
Grays (W.Thur.) RM20 ...109 FT78
Ilford IG2, IG4 ...68 EL58
Pinner HA5 ...60 BX59
Romford RM6 ...70 EW56
South Ockendon (Aveley)
RM15 ...90 FQ74
Waltham Cross EN8 ...15 DY33
Eastern Av E, Rom. RM1,
RM2, RM3 ...71 FD55
Eastern Av W, Rom. RM1,
RM5, RM6, RM7 ...70 EY56
Eastern Gateway, E16 ...86 EJ73
Eastern Ind Est, Erith DA18 ...106 FA75
Eastern Pathway, Horn. RM12 ...90 FJ67
Eastern Perimeter Rd, Houns.
(Hthrw Air.) TW6 ...95 BT83
Eastern Quay Apts, E16
off Rayleigh Rd ...86 EH74
Eastern Rd, E13 ...86 EH68
E17 ...67 EC57
N2 ...64 DF55
N22 ...45 DL53
SE4 ...103 EA84
Grays RM17 ...110 GD77
Romford RM1 ...71 FE57
Eastern Rbt, Ilf. IG1
off Winston Way ...69 EQ61
Eastern Vw, West. (Bigg.H.)
TN16 ...178 EJ117
Easternville Gdns, Ilf. IG2 ...69 EQ58
Eastern Way, SE2 ...88 EX74
SE28 ...106 EU75
Belvedere DA17 ...107 FB75
Erith DA18 ...88 EX74
Grays RM17 ...110 GA79
EAST EWELL, Sutt. SM2 ...157 CX110
East Ferry Rd, E14 ...204 C8
Eastfield Av, Wat. WD24 ...24 BX39
Eastfield Cl, Slou. SL1
off St. Laurence Way ...92 AU76
Eastfield Cotts, Hayes UB3 ...95 BS78
Eastfield Gdns, Dag. RM10 ...70 FA63
Eastfield Par, Pot.B. EN6 ...12 DD32
Eastfield Rd, E17 ...67 EA56
N8 ...65 DL55
Brentwood CM14 ...54 FX47
Dagenham RM9, RM10 ...70 FA63
Enfield EN3 ...31 DX38
Waltham Cross EN8 ...15 DY32
Eastfields, Pnr. HA5 ...60 BW57
Eastfields Av, SW18 ...100 DA84
Eastfields Rd, W3 ...80 CQ71
Mitcham CR4 ...140 DG96
Eastfield St, E14 ...85 DY71
EAST FINCHLEY, N2 ...64 DE56
⊖ **East Finchley** ...64 DE56
East Gdns, SW17 ...120 DE93
Woking GU22 ...167 BC117
Eastgate, Bans. SM7 ...157 CY114
Eastgate Business Pk, E10 ...67 DY60
Eastgate Cl, SE28 ...88 EX72
Eastglade, Nthwd. HA6 ...39 BS50
Pinner HA5 ...60 BY55
East Gorse, Croy. CR0 ...161 DY112
East Grn, Hem.H. HP3 ...6 BM25
East Hall La, Rain. (Wenn.)
RM13 ...90 FK72
East Hall Rd, Orp. BR5 ...146 EY101
EAST HAM, E6 ...86 EL68
⊖ **East Ham** ...86 EL66
Eastham Cl, Barn. EN5 ...27 CY43
Eastham Cres, Brwd. CM13 ...55 GA49
East Ham Ind Est, E6 ...86 EL70
East Ham Manor Way, E6 ...87 EN72
East Ham Shop Hall, E6
off Myrtle Rd ...86 EL67
East Harding St, EC4 ...196 E8
East Heath Rd, NW3 ...64 DD62
East Hill, SW18 ...120 DB85
Dartford DA1 ...128 FM87
Dartford (S.Darenth) DA4 ...148 FQ95
Oxted RH8 ...188 EE129
South Croydon CR2 ...160 DS110
Wembley HA9 ...62 CN61
Westerham (Bigg.H.) TN16 ...178 EH118
Woking GU22 ...167 BC116
East Hill Dr, Dart. DA1 ...128 FM87
East Hill Rd, Oxt. RH8 ...188 EE129
Eastholm, NW11 ...64 DB56
East Holme, Erith DA8 ...107 FD81
Eastholme, Hayes UB3 ...77 BU74
DLR **East India** ...85 ED73
East India Dock Rd, E14 ...85 EA72
East India Way, Croy. CR0 ...142 DT102
East Kent Av, Grav. (Nthflt)
DA11 ...130 GC86
Eastlake Ho, NW8
off Frampton St ...82 DD70
Eastlake Rd, SE5 ...101 DP82
Eastlands Cl, Oxt. RH8
off Eastlands Way ...187 ED127
Eastlands Cres, SE21 ...122 DT86
Eastlands Way, Oxt. RH8 ...187 ED127
East La, SE16 ...202 B5
Abbots Langley WD5 ...7 BU29
Dartford (S.Darenth) DA4 ...149 FR96
Kingston upon Thames
KT1 *off High St* ...137 CK97
Wembley HA0, HA9 ...61 CK62
Eastlea Av, Wat. WD25 ...24 BY37
Eastlea Ms, E16
off Desford Rd ...86 EE70
Eastleigh Av, Har. HA2 ...60 CB61
Eastleigh Cl, NW2 ...62 CS62
Sutton SM2 ...158 DB108
Eastleigh Rd, E17 ...47 DZ54
Bexleyheath DA7 ...107 FC82
Hounslow (Hthrw Air.) TW6
off Cranford La ...95 BT83
Eastleigh Wk, SW15 ...119 CU87
Eastleigh Way, Felt. TW14 ...115 BU88
East Lo La, Enf. EN2 ...29 DK36
H **Eastman Dental Hosp**,
WC1 ...196 B3
Eastman Rd, W3 ...80 CR74
Eastman Way, Epsom KT19 ...156 CP110
East Mascalls, SE7
off Mascalls Rd ...104 EJ79
East Mead, Ruis. HA4 ...60 BX62
Eastmead, Wok. GU21 ...166 AV117
Eastmead Av, Grnf. UB6 ...78 CB69
Eastmead Cl, Brom. BR1 ...144 EL96
Eastmearn Rd, SE21 ...122 DQ89
East Mill, Grav. DA11 ...131 GF86
East Milton Rd, Grav. DA12 ...131 GK87
EAST MOLESEY, KT8 ...137 CD98
Eastmont Rd, Esher KT10 ...137 CE103
Eastmoor Pl, SE7
off Eastmoor St ...104 EK76
Eastmoor St, SE7 ...104 EK76
East Mt St, E1 ...84 DV71
Eastney Rd, Croy. CR0 ...141 DP102
Eastney St, SE10 ...103 ED78
Eastnor, Hem.H. (Bov.) HP3 ...5 BA28
Eastnor Rd, SE9 ...125 EQ88
Easton Gdns, Borwd. WD6 ...26 CR42
Easton St, WC1 ...196 D3
East Pk Cl, Rom. RM6 ...70 EX57
East Parkside, SE10 ...205 K5
Warlingham CR6 ...177 EA116
East Pas, EC1 ...196 G6
East Pier, E1 ...202 D3
East Pl, SE27
off Pilgrim Hill ...122 DQ91
East Pt, SE1 ...202 B10
East Poultry Av, EC1 ...196 F7
⊖ **East Putney** ...119 CY85
East Ramp, Houns. (Hthrw Air.)
TW6 ...95 BP81
East Ridgeway, Pot.B. (Cuffley)
EN6 ...13 DK29
East Rd, E15 ...86 EG67
N1 ...197 K3
SW3 *off Royal Hosp Rd* ...100 DG78
SW19 ...120 DC93
Barnet EN4 ...44 DG46
Edgware HA8 ...42 CP53
Enfield EN3 ...30 DW38
Feltham TW14 ...115 BR87
Kingston upon Thames
KT2 ...138 CL95
Reigate RH2 ...183 CZ133
Romford (Chad.Hth) RM6 ...70 EY57
Romford (Rush Grn) RM7 ...71 FD59
Welling DA16 ...106 EV82
West Drayton UB7 ...94 BM77
Weybridge KT13 ...153 BR108
East Rochester Way, SE9 ...105 ES84
Bexley DA5 ...126 EX86
Sidcup DA15 ...105 ES84
East Row, E11 ...68 EG58
W10 ...81 CY70
Eastry Av, Brom. BR2 ...144 EF100
Eastry Rd, Erith DA8 ...106 FA80
EAST SHEEN, SW14 ...98 CR84
East Sheen Av, SW14 ...98 CR84
Eastside Rd, NW11 ...63 CZ56
East Smithfield, E1 ...202 A1
East St, SE17 ...201 J10
Barking IG11 ...87 EQ66
Bexleyheath DA7 ...106 FA84

East St, Brent. TW8 ...97 CJ80
Bromley BR1 ...144 EG96
Chertsey KT16 ...134 BG101
Epsom KT17 ...156 CS113
Grays RM17 ...110 GC79
Grays (S.Stfd) RM20 ...110 FY79
East Surrey Gro, SE15 ...102 DT80
★ **East Surrey Mus**, Cat. CR3 ...176 DU124
East Tenter St, E1 ...84 DT72
East Ter, Grav. DA12 ...131 GJ86
East Thurrock Rd, Grays RM17 ...110 GB79
East Twrs, Pnr. HA5 ...60 BX57
East Vw, E4 ...47 EC50
Barnet EN5 ...27 CZ41
Eastview Av, SE18 ...105 ES80
Eastville Av, NW11 ...63 CZ58
East Wk, Barn. EN4 ...44 DG45
Hayes UB3 ...77 BU74
Reigate RH2 ...184 DB134
Eastway, E9 ...85 DZ65
East Way, E11 ...68 EH57
Bromley BR2 ...144 EG101
Croydon CR0 ...143 DY103
Eastway, Epsom KT19 ...156 CQ112
East Way, Hayes UB3 ...77 BU74
Eastway, Mord. SM4 ...139 CX99
East Way, Ruis. HA4 ...59 BU60
Eastway, Wall. SM6 ...159 DJ105
Eastway Commercial Cen, E9 ...67 EA64
Eastway Cres, Har. HA2
off Eliot Dr ...60 CB61
Eastwell Cl, Beck. BR3 ...143 DY95
Eastwick Ct, SW19
off Victoria Dr ...119 CX88
Eastwick Cres, Rick. (Mill End) WD3 ...37 BF47
Eastwick Dr, Lthd. (Bkhm) KT23 ...170 CA123
EAST WICKHAM, Well. DA16 ...106 EU80
Eastwick Pk Av, Lthd. (Bkhm) KT23 ...170 CB124
Eastwick Rd, Walt. KT12 ...153 BV106
Eastwood Cl, E18
off George La ...48 EG54
N7 *off Eden Gro* ...65 DN64
N17
off Northumberland Gro ...46 DV52
Eastwood Dr, Rain. RM13 ...89 FH72
Eastwood Rd, E18 ...48 EG54
N10 ...44 DG54
Ilford IG3 ...70 EU59
West Drayton UB7 ...94 BN75
East Woodside, Bex. DA5 ...126 EY88
Eastwood St, SW16 ...121 DJ93
Eastworth Rd, Cher. KT16 ...134 BG102
Eatington Rd, E10 ...67 ED57
Eaton Cl, SW1 ...198 F9
Stanmore HA7 ...41 CH49
Eaton Dr, SW9 ...101 DP84
Kingston upon Thames KT2 ...118 CN94
Romford RM5 ...51 FB52
Eaton Gdns, Dag. RM9 ...88 EY66
Eaton Gate, SW1 ...198 F8
Northwood HA6 ...39 BQ51
Eaton Ho, E14
off Westferry Circ ...85 DZ73
Eaton La, SW1 ...199 J7
Eaton Ms N, SW1 ...198 F8
Eaton Ms S, SW1 ...198 G8
Eaton Ms W, SW1 ...198 G8
Eaton Pk, Cob. KT11 ...154 BY114
Eaton Pk Rd, N13 ...45 DN47
Cobham KT11 ...154 BY114
Eaton Pl, SW1 ...198 F7
Eaton Ri, E11 ...68 EJ57
W5 ...79 CK72
Eaton Rd, NW4 ...63 CW57
Enfield EN1 ...30 DS41
Hounslow TW3 ...97 CD84
Sidcup DA14 ...126 EX89
Sutton SM2 ...158 DD107
Upminster RM14 ...73 FS61
Eaton Row, SW1 ...199 H7
Eatons Mead, E4 ...47 EA47
Eaton Sq, SW1 ...199 H6
Longfield DA3
off Bramblefield Cl ...149 FX97
Eaton Ter, SW1 ...198 F8
Eaton Ter Ms, SW1 ...198 F8
Eatonville Rd, SW17 ...120 DF89
Eatonville Vil, SW17
off Eatonville Rd ...120 DF89
Eaves Cl, Add. KT15 ...152 BJ107
Ebbas Way, Epsom KT18 ...172 CP115
Ebb Ct, E16 *off Armada Way* ...87 EQ73
Ebbisham Cen, The, Epsom KT19 *off High St* ...156 CR113
Ebbisham Dr, SW8 ...101 DM79
Ebbisham La, Tad. (Walt.Hill) KT20 ...173 CT121
Ebbisham Rd, Epsom KT18 ...156 CP114
Worcester Park KT4 ...139 CW103
Ebbsfleet Ind Est, Grav. (Nthflt) DA11 ...130 GA85
⇌ **Ebbsfleet International** ...130 GA86
Ebbsfleet Rd, NW2 ...63 CY64
Ebbsfleet Wk, Grav. (Nthflt) DA11 ...130 GB86
Ebdon Way, SE3 ...104 EH83
Ebenezer Ho, SE11 ...200 E9
Ebenezer St, N1 ...197 K2
Ebenezer Wk, SW16 ...141 DJ95
Ebley Cl, SE15 ...102 DT79
Ebner St, SW18 ...120 DB85
Ebor St, E1 ...197 P4
Ebrington Rd, Har. HA3 ...61 CK58
Ebsworth St, SE23 ...123 DX87
Eburne Rd, N7 ...65 DL62
Ebury App, Rick. WD3
off Ebury Rd ...38 BK46
Ebury Br, SW1 ...199 H10
Ebury Br Est, SW1 ...199 H10
Ebury Br Rd, SW1 ...100 DG78
Ebury Cl, Kes. BR2 ...144 EL104
Northwood HA6 ...39 BQ50
Ebury Ms, SE27 ...121 DP90
SW1 ...198 G8
Ebury Ms E, SW1 ...199 H8
Ebury Rd, Rick. WD3 ...38 BK46
Watford WD17 ...24 BW41
Ebury Sq, SW1 ...198 G9
Ebury St, SW1 ...199 H8
Ebury Way Cycle Path, The, Rick. WD3 ...39 BP45
Watford WD18 ...39 BP45
Ecclesbourne Cl, N13 ...45 DN50
Ecclesbourne Gdns, N13 ...45 DN50
Ecclesbourne Rd, N1 ...84 DQ66
Thornton Heath CR7 ...142 DQ99
Eccles Rd, SW11 ...100 DF84
Eccleston Br, SW1 ...199 J8
Eccleston Cl, Barn. EN4 ...28 DF42
Orpington BR6 ...145 ER102
Eccleston Cres, Rom. RM6 ...70 EU59
Ecclestone Ct, Wem. HA9
off St. John's Rd ...62 CL64
Ecclestone Pl, Wem. HA9 ...62 CM64
Eccleston Ms, SW1 ...198 G7
Eccleston Pl, SW1 ...199 H8
Eccleston Rd, W13 ...79 CG73
Eccleston Sq, SW1 ...199 J9
Eccleston Sq Ms, SW1 ...199 K9
Eccleston St, SW1 ...199 H7
Echelforde Dr, Ashf. TW15 ...114 BN91
Echo Hts, E4
off Mount Echo Dr ...47 EB46
Echo Sq, Grav. DA12
off Old Rd E ...131 GJ89
Eckersley St, E1
off Buxton St ...84 DU70
Eckford St, N1 ...83 DN68
Eckington Ho, N15
off Fladbury Rd ...66 DR58
Eckstein Rd, SW11 ...100 DE84
Eclipse Ho, N22
off Station Rd ...45 DM54
Eclipse Rd, E13 ...86 EH71
Ecton Rd, Add. KT15 ...152 BH105
Ector Rd, SE6 ...124 EE89
Edbrooke Rd, W9 ...82 DA70
Eddiscombe Rd, SW6 ...99 CZ82
Eddy Cl, Rom. RM7 ...71 FB58
Eddystone Rd, SE4 ...123 DY85
Eddystone Twr, SE8 ...203 L9
Eddystone Wk, Stai. TW19 ...114 BL87
Ede Cl, Houns. TW3 ...96 BZ83
Edenbridge Cl, SE16
off Masters Dr ...102 DV78
Orpington BR5 ...146 EX98
Edenbridge Rd, E9 ...85 DX66
Enfield EN1 ...30 DS44
Eden Cl, NW3 ...64 DA61
W8 *off Adam & Eve Ms* ...100 DA76
Addlestone (New Haw) KT15 ...152 BH110
Bexley DA5 ...127 FD91
Enfield EN3 ...31 EA38
Slough SL3 ...93 BA78
Wembley HA0 ...79 CK67
Edencourt Rd, SW16 ...121 DH93
Edendale Rd, Bexh. DA7 ...107 FD81
Edenfield Gdns, Wor.Pk. KT4 ...139 CT104
Eden Grn, S.Ock. RM15 ...91 FV71
Eden Gro, E17 ...67 EB57
N7 ...65 DM64
Eden Gro Rd, W.Byf. (Byfleet) KT14 ...152 BL113
Edenhall Cl, Rom. RM3 ...52 FJ50
Edenhall Glen, Rom. RM3 ...52 FJ50
Edenhall Rd, Rom. RM3 ...52 FJ50
Edenham Way, W10
off Elkstone Rd ...81 CZ71
Edenhurst Av, SW6 ...99 CZ83
Eden Ms, SW17
off Huntspill St ...120 DC90
EDEN PARK, Beck. BR3 ...143 EA99
⇌ **Eden Park** ...143 EA99
Eden Pk Av, Beck. BR3 ...143 DY98
Eden Pl, Grav. DA12
off Lord St ...131 GH87
Eden Rd, E17 ...67 EB57
SE27 ...121 DP92
Beckenham BR3 ...143 DY98
Bexley DA5 ...127 FC91
Croydon CR0 ...160 DR105
Edenside Rd, Lthd. (Bkhm) KT23 ...170 BZ124
Edensor Gdns, W4 ...98 CS80
Edensor Rd, W4 ...98 CS80
Eden St, Kings.T. KT1 ...137 CK96
Edenvale, Wal.Cr. EN7
off Goffs La ...14 DV29
Edenvale Cl, Mitch. CR4
off Edenvale Rd ...120 DG94
Edenvale Rd, Mitch. CR4 ...120 DG94
Edenvale St, SW6 ...100 DB82
Eden Wk, Kings.T. KT1
off Eden St ...138 CL96
Eden Wk Shop Cen, Kings.T. KT1 ...138 CL96
Eden Way, Beck. BR3 ...143 DZ99
Warlingham CR6 ...177 DY118
Ederline Av, SW16 ...141 DM97
Edgar Cl, Swan. BR8 ...147 FF97
Edgar Kail Way, SE22 ...102 DS84
Edgarley Ter, SW6 ...99 CY81
Edgar Rd, E3 ...85 EB69
Hounslow TW4 ...116 BZ87
Romford RM6 ...70 EX59
South Croydon CR2 ...160 DR109
West Drayton UB7 ...76 BL73
Westerham (Tats.) TN16 ...178 EK121
Edgbaston Dr, Rad. (Shenley) WD7 ...10 CL32
Edgbaston Rd, Wat. WD19 ...39 BV48
Edgeborough Way, Brom. BR1 ...124 EK94
Edgebury, Chis. BR7 ...125 EP91
Edgebury Wk, Chis. BR7 ...125 EQ91
Edge Cl, Wey. KT13 ...152 BN108
Edgecombe Ho, SW19 ...119 CY88
Edgecoombe, S.Croy. CR2 ...160 DW108
Edgecoombe Cl, Kings.T. KT2 ...118 CR94
Edgecote Cl, W3
off Cheltenham Pl ...80 CQ74
Edgecot Gro, N15
off Oulton Rd ...66 DS57
Edgefield Av, Bark. IG11 ...87 ET66
Edgefield Cl, Dart. DA1 ...128 FP88
Edge Hill, SE18 ...105 EP79
SW19 ...119 CX94
Edge Hill Av, N3 ...64 DA55
Edge Hill Ct, SW19 ...119 CX94
Edgehill Ct, Walt. KT12
off St. Johns Dr ...136 BW102
Edgehill Gdns, Dag. RM10 ...70 FA63
Edgehill Rd, W13 ...79 CJ71
Chislehurst BR7 ...125 EQ90
Mitcham CR4 ...141 DH95
Purley CR8 ...159 DN110
Edgeley, Lthd. (Bkhm) KT23 ...170 BY124
Edgeley La, SW4
off Edgeley Rd ...101 DK83
Edgeley Rd, SW4 ...101 DK83
Edgell Cl, Vir.W. GU25 ...133 AZ97
Edgell Rd, Stai. TW18 ...113 BF92
Edgel St, SW18
off Ferrier St ...100 DB84
Edgepoint Cl, SE27
off Knights Hill ...121 DP92
Edge St, W8
off Kensington Ch St ...82 DA74
Edgewood Dr, Orp. BR6 ...163 ET106
Edgewood Grn, Croy. CR0 ...143 DX102
Edgeworth Av, NW4 ...63 CU57
Edgeworth Cl, NW4 ...63 CU57
Whyteleafe CR3 ...176 DU118
Edgeworth Cres, NW4 ...63 CU57
Edgeworth Rd, SE9 ...104 EJ84
Barnet EN4 ...28 DE42
Edgington Rd, SW16 ...121 DK93
Edgington Way, Sid. DA14 ...126 EW94
Edgson Ho, SW1
off Ebury Br Rd ...101 DH78
EDGWARE, HA8 ...42 CP50
⊖ **Edgware** ...42 CP51
Edgwarebury Gdns, Edg. HA8 ...42 CN50
Edgwarebury La, Borwd. (Els.) WD6 ...42 CL45
Edgware HA8 ...42 CN49
H **Edgware Comm Hosp**, Edg. HA8 ...42 CP52
Edgware Ct, Edg. HA8
off Cavendish Dr ...42 CN51
⊖ **Edgware Road** ...194 B7
Edgware Rd, NW2 ...63 CV60
NW9 ...62 CR55
W2 ...194 C8
Edgware Rd Sub, W2
off Edgware Rd ...82 DE71
Edgware Way, Edg. HA8 ...42 CM49
Edinburgh Av, Rick. (Mill End) WD3 ...22 BG44
Edinburgh Cl, E2
off Russia La ...84 DW68
Pinner HA5 ...60 BX59
Uxbridge UB10 ...59 BP63
Edinburgh Ct, SW20 ...139 CX99
Edinburgh Cres, Wal.Cr. EN8 ...15 DY33
Edinburgh Dr, Abb.L. WD5 ...7 BU32
Romford RM7
off Eastern Av W ...71 FC56
Staines TW18 ...114 BK93
Uxbridge (Denh.) UB9 ...57 BF58
Uxbridge (Ickhm) UB10 ...59 BP63
Edinburgh Gate, SW1 ...198 D4
Edinburgh Ho, W9 ...82 DC69
Edinburgh Ms, Til. RM18 ...111 GH82
Edinburgh Rd, E13 ...86 EH68
E17 ...67 EA57
N18 ...46 DU50
W7 ...97 CF75
Sutton SM1 ...140 DC103
Edington Rd, SE2 ...106 EV76
Enfield EN3 ...30 DW40
Edison Av, Horn. RM12 ...71 FF61
Edison Cl, E17 *off Exeter Rd* ...67 EA57
Hornchurch RM12
off Edison Av ...71 FF60
West Drayton UB7 ...94 BM75
Edison Ct, SE10 ...205 L8
Edison Dr, Sthl. UB1 ...78 CB72
Wembley HA9 ...62 CL62
Edison Gro, SE18 ...105 ET80
Edison Rd, N8 ...65 DK58
Bromley BR2 ...144 EG96
Enfield EN3 ...31 DZ40
Welling DA16 ...105 ET81
Edis St, NW1 ...82 DG67
Edith Cavell Cl, N19
off Hornsey Ri Gdns ...65 DK59
Edith Cavell Way, SE18 ...104 EL81
Edith Gdns, Surb. KT5 ...138 CP101
Edith Gro, SW10 ...100 DC79
Edithna St, SW9 ...101 DL83
Edith Nesbit Wk, SE9 ...124 EL85
Edith Rd, E6 ...86 EK66
E15 *off Chandos Rd* ...67 ED64
N11 ...45 DK52
SE25 ...142 DR99
SW19 ...120 DB93
W14 ...99 CY77
Orpington BR6 ...164 EU106
Romford RM6 ...70 EX58
Edith Row, SW6 ...100 DB81
Edith St, E2 ...84 DU68
Edith Summerskill Ho, SW6
off Clem Attlee Ct ...99 CZ80
Edith Ter, SW10 ...100 DC80
Edith Vil, SW15
off Bective Rd ...99 CY84
W14 ...99 CZ77
Edith Yd, SW10
off World's End Est ...100 DC80
Edmansons Cl, N17
off Bruce Gro ...46 DS53
Edmeston Cl, E9 ...85 DY65
Edmonds Ct, W.Mol. KT8
off Avern Rd ...136 CB98
EDMONTON, N9 ...46 DU49
⇌ **Edmonton Green** ...46 DU47
Edmonton Grn, N9
off Hertford Rd ...46 DV47
Edmonton Grn Shop Cen, N9 ...46 DV47
Edmund Gro, Felt. TW13 ...116 BZ89
Edmund Halley Way, SE10 ...205 H5
Edmund Hurst Dr, E6 ...87 EP71
Edmund Rd, Grays (Chaff.Hun.) RM16 ...109 FX75
Mitcham CR4 ...140 DE97
Edmund Rd, Orp. BR5 ...146 EW100
Rainham RM13 ...89 FE68
Welling DA16 ...106 EU83
Edmunds Av, Orp. BR5 ...146 EX97
Edmunds Cl, Hayes UB4 ...78 BW71
Edmund St, SE5 ...102 DR80
Edmunds Wk, N2 ...64 DE56
Edmunds Way, Slou. SL2 ...74 AV71
Edna Rd, SW20 ...139 CX96
Edna St, SW11 ...100 DE81
Edrich Ho, SW4 ...101 DL81
Edric Ho, SW1 *off Page St* ...101 DK77
Edrick Rd, Edg. HA8 ...42 CQ51
Edrick Wk, Edg. HA8 ...42 CQ51
Edric Rd, SE14 ...103 DX80
Edridge Cl, Bushey WD23 ...24 CC43
Hornchurch RM12 ...72 FK64
Edridge Rd, Croy. CR0 ...142 DQ104
Edulf Rd, Borwd. WD6 ...26 CP39
Edward Amey Cl, Wat. WD25 ...24 BW36
Edward Av, E4 ...47 EB51
Morden SM4 ...140 DD99
Edward Cl, N9 ...46 DT45
NW2 ...63 CX63
Abbots Langley WD5 ...7 BT32
Grays (Chaff.Hun.) RM16 ...109 FX76
Hampton (Hmptn H.) TW12
off Edward Rd ...116 CC92
Northolt UB5 ...78 BW68
Romford RM2 ...72 FJ55
Edward Ct, E16
off Alexandra St ...86 EG71
Staines TW18 ...114 BJ93
Waltham Abbey EN9 ...16 EF33
Edwardes Pl, W8
off Edwardes Sq ...99 CZ76
Edwardes Sq, W8 ...100 DA76
Edward Gro, Barn. EN4 ...28 DD43
Edward Ms, NW1 ...195 J1
Edward Pauling Ho, Felt. TW14
off Westmacott Dr ...115 BT87
Edward Pl, SE8 ...103 DZ79
Edward Rd, E17 ...67 DX56
SE20 ...123 DX94
Barnet EN4 ...28 DD43
Bromley BR1 ...124 EH94
Chislehurst BR7 ...125 EP92
Coulsdon CR5 ...175 DK115
Croydon CR0 ...142 DS101
Feltham TW14 ...115 BR85
Hampton (Hmptn H.) TW12 ...116 CC92
Harrow HA2 ...60 CC55
Northolt UB5 ...78 BW68
Romford RM6 ...70 EY58
Westerham (Bigg.H.) TN16 ...178 EL118
Edward's Av, Ruis. HA4 ...77 BV65
Edwards Cl, Brwd. (Hutt.) CM13 ...55 GE44
Worcester Park KT4 ...139 CX103
Edwards Cotts, N1
off Compton Av ...83 DP65
Edwards Ct, Slou. SL1 ...92 AS75
Waltham Cross EN8
off Turners Hill ...15 DX31
Edwards Dr, N11
off Gordon Rd ...45 DK52
Edward II Av, W.Byf. (Byfleet) KT14 ...152 BM114
Edwards Gdns, Swan. BR8
off Ladds Way ...147 FD98
Edwards La, N16 ...66 DR61
Edwards Ms, N1 ...83 DN66
W1 ...194 F9
Edward Sq, N1
off Caledonian Rd ...83 DM67
SE16 ...203 L2
Edwards Rd, Belv. DA17 ...106 FA77
Edward St, E16 ...86 EG70
SE8 ...103 DZ79
SE14 ...103 DY80
Edward's Way, SE4
off Adelaide Av ...123 EA85
Edwards Way, Brwd. (Hutt.) CM13 ...55 GE44
Edwards Yd, Wem. HA0
off Mount Pleasant ...80 CL67
Edward Temme Av, E15 ...86 EF66
Edward Tyler Rd, SE12 ...124 EH89
Edward Way, Ashf. TW15 ...114 BM89
Edwina Gdns, Ilf. IG4 ...68 EL57
Edwin Av, E6 ...87 EN68
Edwin Cl, Bexh. DA7 ...106 EZ79
Rainham RM13 ...89 FF69
Edwin Hall Pl, SE13
off Hither Grn La ...123 ED86
Edwin Pl, Croy. CR0
off Cross Rd ...142 DR102
Edwin Rd, Dart. DA2 ...127 FH90
Edgware HA8 ...42 CR51
Twickenham TW1, TW2 ...117 CF88
Edwin's Mead, E9
off Lindisfarne Way ...67 DY63
Edwin St, E1 ...84 DW70
E16 ...86 EG71
Gravesend DA12 ...131 GH87
Edwyn Cl, Barn. EN5 ...27 CW44
Edwyn Ho, SW18
off Neville Gill Cl ...120 DB86
Eel Brook Cl, SW6
off King's Rd ...100 DB81
Eel Brook Studios, SW6
off Moore Pk Rd ...100 DA80
Eel Pie Island, Twick. TW1 ...117 CG88
Effie Pl, SW6 ...100 DA80
Effie Rd, SW6 ...100 DA80
Effingham Cl, Sutt. SM2 ...158 DB108
Effingham Common, Lthd. (Eff.) KT24 ...169 BU123
Effingham Common Rd, Lthd. (Eff.) KT24 ...169 BU123
Effingham Ct, Wok. GU22
off Constitution Hill ...166 AY118
⇌ **Effingham Junction** ...169 BU123
Effingham Rd, N8 ...65 DN57
SE12 ...124 EE85
Croydon CR0 ...141 DM101
Surbiton KT6 ...137 CH101
Effort St, SW17 ...120 DE92
Effra Par, SW2 ...121 DN85
Effra Rd, SW2 ...101 DN84
SW19 ...120 DB93
Egan Way, Hayes UB3 ...77 BS73
Egbert St, NW1 ...82 DG67
Egbury Ho, SW15
off Tangley Gro ...119 CT86
Egdean Wk, Sev. TN13 ...191 FJ123
Egeremont Rd, SE13 ...103 EB82
Egerton Av, Swan. BR8 ...127 FF94
Egerton Cl, Dart. DA1 ...127 FH88
Pinner HA5 ...59 BU56
Egerton Cres, SW3 ...198 C8
Egerton Dr, SE10 ...103 EB81
Egerton Gdns, NW4 ...63 CV56
NW10 ...81 CW67
SW3 ...198 B7
W13 ...79 CH72
Ilford IG3 ...69 ET62
Egerton Gdns Ms, SW3 ...198 C7
Egerton Pl, SW3 ...198 C7
Weybridge KT13 ...153 BQ107
Egerton Rd, N16 ...66 DT59
SE25 ...142 DS97
New Malden KT3 ...139 CT98
Twickenham TW2 ...117 CE87
Wembley HA0 ...80 CM66
Weybridge KT13 ...153 BQ107
Egerton Ter, SW3 ...198 C7
Egerton Way, Hayes UB3 ...95 BP80
Eggardon Ct, Nthlt. UB5
off Lancaster Rd ...78 CC65
Egg Fm La, Kings L. WD4 ...7 BP30
Egg Hall, Epp. CM16 ...18 EU29
EGHAM, TW20 ...113 BA93
⇌ **Egham** ...113 BA92
Egham Bypass, Egh. TW20 ...113 AZ92
Egham Cl, SW19 ...119 CY89
Sutton SM3 ...139 CY103
Egham Cres, Sutt. SM3 ...139 CX104
Egham Hill, Egh. TW20 ...112 AX93
EGHAM HYTHE, Stai. TW18 ...113 BE93
★ **Egham Mus**, Egh. TW20 ...113 BA92
Egham Rd, E13 ...86 EH71
EGHAM WICK, Egh. TW20 ...112 AU94
Eglantine La, Dart. (Hort.Kir.) DA4 ...148 FN101
Eglantine Rd, SW18 ...120 DC85
Egleston Rd, Mord. SM4 ...140 DB100
Egley Dr, Wok. GU22 ...166 AX122
Egley Rd, Wok. GU22 ...166 AX122
Eglington Ct, SE17
off Carter St ...102 DQ79
Eglington Rd, E4 ...47 ED45
Eglinton Hill, SE18 ...105 EP79
Eglinton Rd, SE18 ...105 EN79
Swanscombe DA10 ...130 FZ86
Eglise Rd, Warl. CR6 ...177 DY117
Egliston Ms, SW15 ...99 CW83
Egliston Rd, SW15 ...99 CW83
Eglon Ms, NW1
off Berkley Rd ...82 DF66
Egmont Av, Surb. KT6 ...138 CM102
Egmont Pk Rd, Tad. (Walt.Hill) KT20 ...183 CU125
Egmont Rd, N.Mal. KT3 ...139 CT98
Surbiton KT6 ...138 CM102
Sutton SM2 ...158 DC108
Walton-on-Thames KT12 ...135 BV101
Egmont St, SE14 ...103 DX80
Egmont Way, Tad. KT20
off Oatlands Rd ...173 CY119
Egremont Ho, SE13
off Conington Rd ...103 EB82
Egremont Rd, SE27 ...121 DN90
Egret Way, Hayes UB4 ...78 BX71
Eider Cl, E7 ...68 EF64
Hayes UB4 *off Cygnet Way* ...78 BX71
Eighteenth Rd, Mitch. CR4 ...141 DL98
Eighth Av, E12 ...69 EM63
Hayes UB3 ...77 BU74
Eileen Rd, SE25 ...142 DR99
Eindhoven Cl, Cars. SM5 ...140 DG102
Eisenhower Dr, E6 ...86 EL71
Elaine Gro, NW5 ...64 DG64
Elam Cl, SE5 ...101 DP82
Elam St, SE5 ...101 DP82
Eland Pl, Croy. CR0
off Eland Rd ...141 DP104
Eland Rd, SW11 ...100 DF83
Croydon CR0 ...141 DP104
Elan Rd, S.Ock. RM15 ...91 FU71
Elba Pl, SE17 ...201 J8
Elberon Av, Croy. CR0 ...141 DJ100
Elbe St, SW6 ...100 DC82
Elborough Rd, SE25 ...142 DU99
Elborough St, SW18 ...120 DA88
Elbow Meadow, Slou. (Colnbr.) SL3 ...93 BF81
Elbury Dr, E16 ...86 EG72
Elcho St, SW11 ...100 DE80
Elcot Av, SE15 ...102 DV80
Elder Av, N8 ...65 DL57
Elderbek Cl, Wal.Cr. EN7 ...14 DU28
Elderberry Cl, Ilf. IG6
off Hazel La ...49 EP52
Elderberry Gro, SE27
off Linton Gro ...122 DQ92
Elderberry Rd, W5 ...98 CL75
Elderberry Way, E6 ...87 EM69
Watford WD25 ...23 BV35
Elder Cl, N20 ...44 DB47
Sidcup DA15 ...125 ET88
West Drayton UB7
off Yew Av ...76 BL73
Elder Ct, Bushey (Bushey Hth) WD23 ...41 CE47
Elderfield Pl, SW17 ...121 DH91
Elderfield Rd, E5 ...66 DW63
Slough (Stoke P.) SL2 ...74 AT65
Elderfield Wk, E11 ...68 EH57
Elderflower Way, E15 ...86 EE66
Elder Gdns, SE27 ...122 DQ91
Elder Oak Cl, SE20 ...142 DV95
Elder Rd, SE27 ...122 DQ92
Eldersley Cl, Red. RH1 ...184 DF132
Elderslie Cl, Beck. BR3 ...143 EB99
Elderslie Rd, SE9 ...125 EN85
Elder St, E1 ...197 P6
Elderton Rd, SE26 ...123 DY91
Eldertree Pl, Mitch. CR4
off Eldertree Way ...141 DJ95
Eldertree Way, Mitch. CR4 ...141 DH95
Elder Wk, N1 *off Essex Rd* ...83 DP67
SE13 *off Bankside Av* ...103 EC83
Elder Way, Rain. RM13 ...90 FK69
Slough (Langley) SL3 ...93 AZ75

★ Place of interest ⇌ Railway station ⊖ London Underground station DLR Docklands Light Railway station Tra Tramlink station H Hospital Riv Pedestrian ferry landing stage

Elderwood Pl, SE27
off Elder Rd 122 DQ92
Eldon Av, Borwd. WD6 26 CN40
Croydon CR0 142 DW103
Hounslow TW5 96 CA80
Eldon Gro, NW3 64 DD64
Eldon Pk, SE25 142 DV98
Eldon Rd, E17 67 DZ56
N9 46 DW47
N22 45 DP53
W8 100 DB76
Caterham CR3 176 DR121
Eldon St, EC2 197 L7
Eldon Way, NW10 80 CP68
Eldred Dr, Orp. BR5 146 EW103
Eldred Gdns, Upmin. RM14 73 FS59
Eldred Rd, Bark. IG11 87 ES67
Eldrick Ct, Felt. TW14 115 BR88
Eldridge Cl, Felt. TW14 115 BU88
Eleanor Av, Epsom KT19 156 CR110
Eleanor Cl, N15
off Arnold Rd 66 DT55
SE16 203 H4
Eleanor Cres, NW7 43 CX49
Eleanor Cross Rd, Wal.Cr.
EN8 15 DY34
Eleanor Gdns, Barn. EN5 27 CX43
Dagenham RM8 70 EZ62
Eleanor Gro, SW13 98 CS83
Uxbridge (Ickhm) UB10 59 BP62
Eleanor Rd, E8 84 DV66
E15 86 EF65
N11 45 DL51
Gerrards Cross (Chal.St.P.)
SL9 36 AW53
Waltham Cross EN8 15 DY33
Eleanor St, E3 85 EA69
Eleanor Wk, SE18
off Samuel St 105 EM77
Greenhithe DA9 109 FW84
Eleanor Way, Brwd. CM14 54 FX50
Waltham Cross EN8 15 DZ34
Electra Business Pk, E16 85 ED71
Electric Av, SW9 101 DN84
Enfield EN3 31 DZ36
Electric La, SW9 101 DN84
Electric Par, E18
off George La 48 EG54
Surbiton KT6 137 CK100
Elektron Ho, E14
off Blackwall Way 85 ED73
⇌ **Elephant & Castle** 201 H8
⊖ **Elephant & Castle** 201 H8
Elephant & Castle, SE1 200 G7
Elephant & Castle Shop Cen, SE1
off Elephant & Castle 102 DQ77
Elephant La, SE16 202 F4
Elephant Rd, SE17 201 H8
Elers Rd, W13 97 CJ75
Hayes UB3 95 BR77
Eleven Acre Ri, Loug. IG10 33 EM41
Eley Est, N18 46 DW50
Eley Rd, N18 47 DX50
Elfindale Rd, SE24 122 DQ85
Elfin Gro, Tedd. TW11
off Broad St 117 CF92
Elford Cl, SE3 104 EH84
Elfort Rd, N5 65 DN63
Elfrida Cres, SE6 123 EA91
Elfrida Rd, Wat. WD18 24 BW43
Elf Row, E1 84 DW73
Elfwine Rd, W7 79 CE71
Elgal Cl, Orp. BR6 163 EP106
Elgar Av, NW10 80 CR65
SW16 141 DL97
W5 98 CL75
Surbiton KT5 138 CP101
Elgar Cl, E13 *off Bushey Rd* 86 EJ68
SE8 *off Comet St* 103 EA80
Borehamwood (Els.) WD6 41 CK45
Buckhurst Hill IG9 48 EK47
Uxbridge UB10 58 BN61
Elgar Gdns, Til. RM18 111 GH81
Elgar St, SE16 203 L6
Elgin Av, W9 82 DB69
W12 99 CU75
Ashford TW15 115 BQ93
Harrow HA3 41 CH54
Romford RM3 52 FP52
Elgin Cl, W12 99 CV75
Elgin Cres, W11 81 CZ72
Caterham CR3 176 DU122
Hounslow (Hthrw Air.) TW6
off Eastern Perimeter Rd 95 BS82
Elgin Dr, Nthwd. HA6 39 BS52
Elgin Ms, W11
off Ladbroke Gro 81 CY72
Elgin Ms N, W9
off Randolph Av 82 DB69
Elgin Ms S, W9
off Randolph Av 82 DB69
Elgin Pl, Wey. KT13 153 BQ107
Elgin Rd, N22 45 DJ54
Croydon CR0 142 DT102
Ilford IG3 69 ES60
Sutton SM1 140 DC104
Wallington SM6 159 DJ107
Waltham Cross (Chsht) EN8 14 DW30
Weybridge KT13 152 BN106
Elgood Av, Nthwd. HA6 39 BU51
Elgood Cl, W11
off Avondale Pk Rd 81 CY73
Elham Cl, Brom. BR1 124 EK94
Elia Ms, N1 196 F1
Elias Pl, SW8 101 DN79
Elia St, N1 196 F1
Elibank Rd, SE9 105 EN84
Elim Est, SE1 201 M6
Elim Way, E13 86 EF69
Eliot Bk, SE23 122 DV89
Eliot Cotts, SE3
off Eliot Pl 104 EE82
Eliot Ct, N15
off Tynemouth Rd 66 DT56
Eliot Dr, Har. HA2 60 CB61
Eliot Gdns, SW15 99 CU84
Eliot Hill, SE13 103 EC82
Eliot Ms, NW8 82 DC68
Eliot Pk, SE13 103 EC83
Eliot Pl, SE3 104 EE82
Eliot Rd, Dag. RM9 70 EX63
Dartford DA1 128 FP85
Eliot Vale, SE3 103 ED82
Elizabethan Cl, Stai.
(Stanw.) TW19
off Elizabethan Way 114 BK87
Elizabethan Way, Stai.
(Stanw.) TW19 114 BK87
Elizabeth Av, N1 84 DQ67
Amersham HP6 20 AV39
Enfield EN2 29 DP41
Ilford IG1 69 ER61
Staines TW18 114 BJ93
Elizabeth Blackwell Ho, N22
off Progress Way 45 DN53
Elizabeth Br, SW1 199 H9
Elizabeth Cl, E14
off Grundy St 85 EB72
W9 *off Randolph Av* 82 DC70
Barnet EN5 27 CX41
Romford RM7 51 FB53
Sutton SM1 157 CZ105
Tilbury RM18 111 GH82
Elizabeth Clyde Cl, N15 66 DS56
Elizabeth Cotts, Rich. (Kew)
TW9 98 CM81
Elizabeth Ct, SW1 199 N7
Gravesend DA11
off St. James's Rd 131 GG86
Kingston upon Thames KT2
off Lower Kings Rd 138 CL95
Watford WD17 23 BT38
Woodford Green IG8
off Navestock Cres 48 EJ52
Elizabeth Dr, Epp. (They.B.)
CM16 33 ES36
Elizabeth Est, SE17 102 DR79
Elizabeth Fry Pl, SE18 104 EL81
Elizabeth Fry Rd, E8
off Lamb La 84 DV66
Elizabeth Gdns, W3 81 CT74
Isleworth TW7 97 CG84
Stanmore HA7 41 CJ51
Sunbury-on-Thames TW16 136 BW97
Elizabeth Huggins Cotts,
Grav. DA11 131 GG89
Elizabeth Ms, NW3 82 DE65
Elizabeth Pl, N15 66 DR56
Elizabeth Ride, N9 46 DV45
Elizabeth Rd, E6 86 EK67
N15 66 DS57
Brentwood (Pilg.Hat.) CM15 54 FV44
Grays RM16 110 FZ76
Rainham RM13 89 FH71
Elizabeth Sq, SE16 203 K1
Elizabeth St, SW1 198 G8
Greenhithe DA9 129 FS85
Elizabeth Ter, SE9 125 EM86
Elizabeth Way, SE19 122 DR94
Feltham TW13 116 BW91
Orpington BR5 146 EW99
Slough (Stoke P.) SL2 74 AT67
Eliza Cook Cl, Green. DA9
off Watermans Way 109 FV84
Elkanette Ms, N20
off Ridgeview Rd 44 DC47
Elkington Pt, SE11 200 D9
Elkington Rd, E13 86 EH70
Elkins, The, Rom. RM1 51 FE54
Elkins Rd, Slou. (Hedg.) SL2 56 AS61
Elkstone Rd, W10 81 CZ71
Ella Cl, Beck. BR3 143 EA96
Ellaline Rd, W6 99 CX79
Ella Ms, NW3 *off Cressy Rd* 64 DF64
Ellanby Cres, N18 46 DV49
Elland Rd, SE15 102 DW84
Walton-on-Thames KT12 136 BX103
Ella Rd, N8 65 DL59
Ellement Cl, Pnr. HA5 60 BX57
Ellenborough Pl, SW15 99 CU84
Ellenborough Rd, N22 46 DQ53
Sidcup DA14 126 EX92
Ellenbridge Way, S.Croy. CR2 160 DS109
Ellenbrook Cl, Wat. WD24
off Hatfield Rd 23 BV39
Ellen Cl, Brom. BR1 144 EK97
Ellen Ct, N9
off Densworth Gro 46 DW47
Ellen St, E1 84 DU72
Ellen Webb Dr, Har. (Wealds.)
HA3 61 CE55
Elleray Rd, Tedd. TW11 117 CF93
Ellerby St, SW6 99 CX81
Ellerdale Cl, NW3
off Ellerdale Rd 64 DC63
Ellerdale Rd, NW3 64 DC64
Ellerdale St, SE13 103 EB84
Ellerdine Rd, Houns. TW3 96 CC84
Ellerker Gdns, Rich. TW10 118 CL86
Ellerman Av, Twick. TW2 116 BZ88
Ellerman Rd, Til. RM18 111 GF82
Ellerslie, Grav. DA12 131 GK87
Ellerslie Gdns, NW10 81 CU67
Ellerslie Rd, W12 81 CV74
Ellerslie Sq Ind Est, SW2 121 DL85
Ellerton, NW6 *off Mill La* 63 CZ64
Ellerton Gdns, Dag. RM9 88 EW66
Ellerton Rd, SW13 99 CU81
SW18 120 DD88
SW20 119 CU94
Dagenham RM9 88 EW66
Surbiton KT6 138 CM103
Ellery Rd, SE19 122 DR94
Ellery St, SE15 102 DV82
Ellesborough Cl, Wat. WD19 40 BW50
Ellesmere Av, NW7 42 CR48
Beckenham BR3 143 EB96
Ellesmere Cl, E11 68 EF57
Ruislip HA4 59 BQ59
Ellesmere Dr, S.Croy. CR2 160 DV114
Ellesmere Gdns, Ilf. IG4 68 EL57
Ellesmere Gro, Barn. EN5 27 CZ43
Ellesmere Pl, Walt. KT12 153 BS106
Ellesmere Rd, E3 85 DY68
NW10 63 CU64
W4 98 CR79
Greenford UB6 78 CC70
Twickenham TW1 117 CJ86
Weybridge KT13 153 BR107
Ellesmere St, E14 85 EB72
Ellice Rd, Oxt. RH8 188 EF129
Elliman Av, Slou. SL2 74 AS73
Ellingfort Rd, E8 84 DV66
Ellingham Rd, E15 67 ED63
W12 99 CU75
Chessington KT9 155 CK107
Ellington Rd, N10 65 DH56
Feltham TW13 115 BT91
Hounslow TW3 96 CB82
Ellington St, N7 83 DN65
Ellington Way, Epsom KT18 173 CV117
Elliot Cl, E15 86 EE66
Elliot Rd, NW4 63 CV58
Stanmore HA7 41 CG51
Elliott Av, Ruis. HA4 59 BV61
Elliott Cl, Wem. HA9 62 CM62
Elliott Gdns, Rom. RM3 51 FH53
Shepperton TW17 134 BN98
Elliott Rd, SW9 101 DP80
W4 98 CS77
Bromley BR2 144 EK98
Thornton Heath CR7 141 DP98
Elliotts Cl, Uxb. (Cowley)
UB8 76 BJ71
Elliotts La, West. (Brasted)
TN16 180 EW124
Elliott's Pl, N1
off St. Peters St 83 DP67
Elliott Sq, NW3 82 DE66
Elliotts Row, SE11 200 F8
Elliott St, Grav. DA12 131 GK87
Ellis Av, Ger.Cr. (Chal.St.P.)
SL9 37 AZ53
Rainham RM13 89 FG71
Slough SL1 92 AS75
Ellis Cl, NW10 *off High Rd* 81 CV65
SE9 125 EQ89
Coulsdon CR5 175 DM120
Swanley BR8 147 FD98
Elliscombe Rd, SE7 104 EJ78
Ellis Ct, W7 79 CF71
Ellis Fm Cl, Wok. GU22 166 AX122
Ellisfield Dr, SW15 119 CT87
Ellison Gdns, Sthl. UB2 96 BZ77
Ellison Ho, SE13
off Lewisham Rd 103 EC82
Ellison Rd, SW13 99 CT82
SW16 121 DK94
Sidcup DA15 125 ER88
Ellis Rd, Couls. CR5 175 DM120
Mitcham CR4 140 DF100
Southall UB2 78 CC74
Ellis St, SW1 198 E8
Elliston Ho, SE18 105 EN77
Ellis Way, Dart. DA1 128 FM89
Ellmore Cl, Rom. RM3 51 FH53
Ellora Rd, SW16 121 DK92
Ellsworth St, E2 84 DV69
Ellwood Ct, W9
off Clearwell Dr 82 DB70
Ellwood Gdns, Wat. WD25 7 BV34
Ellwood Ri, Ch.St.G. HP8 36 AW47
Elmar Rd, N15 66 DR56
Elm Av, W5 80 CL74
Carshalton SM5 158 DF110
Ruislip HA4 59 BU60
Upminster RM14 72 FP62
Watford WD19 40 BY45
Elmbank, N14 45 DL45
Elmbank Av, Barn. EN5 27 CW42
Egham (Eng.Grn) TW20 112 AV93
Elm Bk Dr, Brom. BR1 144 EK96
Elm Bk Gdns, SW13 98 CS82
Elmbank Way, W7 79 CD71
Elmbourne Dr, Belv. DA17 107 FB77
Elmbourne Rd, SW17 120 DG90
Elmbridge Av, Surb. KT5 138 CP99
Elmbridge Cl, Ruis. HA4 59 BU58
Elmbridge Dr, Ruis. HA4 59 BT57
Elmbridge La, Wok. GU22 167 AZ119
★ **Elmbridge Mus**, Wey.
KT13 152 BN105
Elmbridge Rd, Ilf. IG6 50 EU51
Elmbridge Wk, E8
off Wilman Gro 84 DU66
Elmbrook Cl, Sun. TW16 135 BV95
Elmbrook Gdns, SE9 104 EL84
Elmbrook Rd, Sutt. SM1 157 CZ105
Elm Cl, E11 68 EH58
N19 *off Hargrave Pk* 65 DJ61
NW4 63 CX57
SW20 *off Grand Dr* 139 CW98
Buckhurst Hill IG9 48 EK47
Carshalton SM5 140 DF102
Dartford DA1 128 FJ88
Harrow HA2 60 CB58
Hayes UB3 77 BU72
Leatherhead KT22 171 CH122
Romford RM7 51 FB54
South Croydon CR2 160 DS107
Staines (Stanw.) TW19 114 BK88
Surbiton KT5 138 CQ101
Tadworth (Box H.) KT20 182 CQ130
Twickenham TW2 116 CB89
Waltham Abbey EN9 15 ED34
Warlingham CR6 177 DX117
Woking GU21 166 AX115
Woking (Ripley) GU23 168 BG124
ELM CORNER, Wok. GU23 168 BN119
Elmcote Way, Rick. (Crox.Grn)
WD3 22 BM44
Elm Ct, EC4 196 D10
Mitcham CR4
off Armfield Cres 140 DF96
Sunbury-on-Thames TW16 115 BT94
Elmcourt Rd, SE27 121 DP89
Elm Cres, W5 80 CL74
Kingston upon Thames
KT2 138 CL95
Elmcroft, N8 65 DM57
Leatherhead KT23 170 CA124
Elm Cft, Slou. (Datchet) SL3 92 AW81
Elmcroft Av, E11 68 EH57
N9 30 DV44
NW11 63 CZ59
Sidcup DA15 125 ET86
Elmcroft Cl, E11 68 EH56
W5 79 CK72
Chessington KT9 138 CL104
Feltham TW14 115 BT86
Elmcroft Cres, NW11 63 CY59
Harrow HA2 60 CA55
Elmcroft Dr, Ashf. TW15 114 BN92
Chessington KT9 138 CL104
Elmcroft Gdns, NW9 62 CN57
Elmcroft Rd, Orp. BR6 146 EU101
Elmcroft St, E5 66 DW63
Elmdale Rd, N13 45 DM50
Elmdene, Surb. KT5 138 CQ102
Elmdene Av, Horn. RM11 72 FM57
Elmdene Cl, Beck. BR3 143 DZ99
Elmdene Ct, Wok. GU22
off Constitution Hill 166 AY118
Elmdene Rd, SE18 105 EP78
Elmdon Rd, Houns. TW4 96 BX82
Hounslow (Hatt.Cr.) TW6 95 BT83
South Ockendon RM15 91 FU71
Elm Dr, Har. HA2 60 CB58
Leatherhead KT22 171 CH122
Sunbury-on-Thames TW16 136 BW96
Swanley BR8 147 FD96
Waltham Cross (Chsht) EN8 15 DY28
Woking (Chobham) GU24 150 AT110
Elmer Av, Rom. (Hav.at.Bow.)
RM4 51 FE48
Elmer Cl, Enf. EN2 29 DM41
Rainham RM13 89 FG66
Elmer Cotts, Lthd. KT22 171 CG123
Elmer Gdns, Edg. HA8 42 CP52
Isleworth TW7 97 CD83
Rainham RM13 89 FG66
Elmer Ms, Lthd. (Fetch.)
KT22 171 CG123
Elmer Rd, SE6 123 EC87
Elmers Dr, Tedd. TW11
off Kingston Rd 117 CH93
ELMERS END, Beck. BR3 143 DY97
⇌ **Elmers End** 143 DX98
Tramlink **Elmers End** 143 DX98
Elmers End Rd, SE20 142 DW96
Beckenham BR3 142 DW96
Elmerside Rd, Beck. BR3 143 DY98
Elmers Rd, SE25 142 DU101
Elm Fm Caravan Pk, Cher.
(Lyne) KT16 133 BC101
Elmfield, Lthd. (Bkhm) KT23 170 CA123
Elmfield Av, N8 65 DL57
Mitcham CR4 140 DG95
Teddington TW11 117 CF92
Elmfield Cl, Grav. DA11 131 GH88
Harrow HA1 61 CE61
Potters Bar EN6 11 CY33
Elmfield Pk, Brom. BR1 144 EG97
Elmfield Rd, E4 47 EC47
E17 67 DX58
N2 64 DD55
SW17 120 DG89
Bromley BR1 144 EG97
Potters Bar EN6 11 CY33
Southall UB2 96 BY76
Elmfield Way, W9 82 DA71
South Croydon CR2 160 DT109
Elm Friars Wk, NW1 83 DK66
Elm Gdns, N2 64 DC55
Enfield EN2 30 DR38
Epping (N.Wld Bas.) CM16 19 FB26
Epsom KT18 173 CW119
Esher (Clay.) KT10 155 CF107
Mitcham CR4 141 DK98
Elmgate Av, Felt. TW13 115 BV90
Elmgate Gdns, Edg. HA8 42 CR50
Elm Grn, W3 80 CS72
Elmgreen Cl, E15
off Church St N 86 EE67
Elm Gro, N8 65 DL58
NW2 63 CX63
SE15 102 DT82
SW19 119 CY94
Caterham CR3 176 DS122
Epsom KT18 156 CQ114
Erith DA8 107 FD80
Harrow HA2 60 CA59
Hornchurch RM11 72 FL58
Kingston upon Thames
KT2 138 CL95
Orpington BR6 145 ET102
Sutton SM1 158 DB105
Watford WD24 23 BU37
West Drayton UB7
off Willow Av 76 BM73
Woodford Green IG8 48 EF50
Elmgrove Cres, Har. HA1 61 CF57
Elmgrove Gdns, Har. HA1 61 CG57
Elm Gro Par, Wall. SM6
off Butter Hill 140 DG104
Elm Gro Rd, SW13 99 CU82
W5 98 CL75
Cobham KT11 170 BX116
Elmgrove Rd, Croy. CR0 142 DV101
Harrow HA1 61 CF57
Weybridge KT13 152 BN105
Elm Hall Gdns, E11 68 EH58
Elmhurst, Belv. DA17 106 EY79
Elmhurst Av, N2 64 DD55
Mitcham CR4 121 DH94
Elmhurst Dr, E18 48 EG54
Hornchurch RM11 72 FJ60
Elmhurst Mans, SW4
off Edgeley Rd 101 DK83
Elmhurst Rd, E7 86 EH66
N17 46 DS54
SE9 124 EL89
Enfield EN3 30 DW37
Slough SL3 93 BA76
Elmhurst St, SW4 101 DK83
Elmhurst Vil, SE15
off Cheltenham Rd 102 DW84
Elmhurst Way, Loug. IG10 49 EM45
Elmington Cl, Bex. DA5 127 FB86
Elmington Est, SE5 102 DR80
Elmington Rd, SE5 102 DR81
Elmira St, SE13 103 EB83
Elm La, SE6 123 DZ89
Woking GU23 169 BP118
Elm Lawn Cl, Uxb. UB8
off Park Rd 76 BL66
Elmlea Dr, Hayes UB3
off Grange Rd 77 BS71
Elmlee Cl, Chis. BR7 125 EM93
Elmley Cl, E6
off Lovage App 86 EL71
Elmley St, SE18 105 ER77
Elm Ms, Rich. TW10
off Grove Rd 118 CM86
Elmore Cl, Wem. HA0 80 CL68
Elmore Rd, E11 67 EC62
Coulsdon (Chipstead) CR5 174 DF121
Enfield EN3 31 DX39
Elmores, Loug. IG10 33 EN41
Elmore St, N1 84 DQ66
Elm Par, Horn. RM12
off St. Nicholas Av 71 FH63
ELM PARK, Horn. RM12 71 FH64
⊖ **Elm Park** 71 FH63
Elm Pk, SW2 121 DM86
Stanmore HA7 41 CH50
Elm Pk Av, N15 66 DT57
Hornchurch RM12 71 FG63
Elm Pk Ct, Pnr. HA5 60 BW55
Elm Pk Gdns, NW4 63 CX57
SW10 100 DD78
Elmpark Gdns, S.Croy. CR2 160 DW110
Elm Pk La, SW3 100 DD78
Elm Pk Mans, SW10
off Park Wk 100 DC79
Elm Pk Rd, E10 67 DY60
N3 43 CZ52
N21 46 DQ45
SE25 142 DT97
SW3 100 DD79
Pinner HA5 40 BW54
Elm Pl, SW7 100 DD78
Elm Quay Ct, SW8 101 DK79
Elm Rd, E7 86 EF65
E11 67 ED61
E17 67 EC57
N22 *off Granville Rd* 45 DP53
SW14 98 CQ83
Barnet EN5 27 CZ42
Beckenham BR3 143 DZ96
Chessington KT9 156 CL105
Dartford DA1 128 FK88
Epsom KT17 157 CT107
Erith DA8 107 FG81
Esher (Clay.) KT10 155 CF107
Feltham TW14 115 BR88
Gravesend DA12 131 GJ90
Grays RM17 110 GC79
Greenhithe DA9 129 FS86
Kingston upon Thames
KT2 138 CM95
Leatherhead KT22 171 CH122
New Malden KT3 138 CR98
Orpington BR6 164 EU108
Purley CR8 159 DP113
Redhill RH1 184 DE134
Romford RM7 51 FB54
Sidcup DA14 126 EU91
South Ockendon (Aveley)
RM15 90 FQ74
Thornton Heath CR7 142 DR98
Wallington SM6 140 DG102
Warlingham CR6 177 DX117
Wembley HA9 62 CL64
Westerham TN16 189 ES125
Woking GU21 166 AX118
Woking (Horsell) GU21 167 AZ115
Elm Rd W, Sutt. SM3 139 CZ101
Elm Row, NW3 64 DC62
Elmroyd Av, Pot.B. EN6 11 CZ33
Elmroyd Cl, Pot.B. EN6 11 CZ33
Elms, The, SW13 99 CT83
Elms Av, N10 65 DH55
NW4 63 CX57
Elmscott Gdns, N21 30 DQ44
Elmscott Rd, Brom. BR1 124 EF92
Elms Ct, Wem. HA0 61 CF63
Elms Cres, SW4 121 DJ86
Elmscroft Gdns, Pot.B. EN6 11 CY32
Elmsdale Rd, E17 67 DZ56
Elms Fm Rd, Horn. RM12 72 FJ64
Elms Gdns, Dag. RM9 70 EZ63
Wembley HA0 61 CG63
Elmshaw Rd, SW15 119 CU85
Elmshorn, Epsom KT17 173 CW116
Elmshurst Cres, N2 64 DD56
Elmside, Croy. (New Adgtn)
CR0 161 EB107
Elmside Rd, Wem. HA9 62 CN62
Elms La, Wem. HA0 61 CG63
Elmsleigh Av, Har. HA3 61 CH56
Elmsleigh Cen, The, Stai.
TW18 113 BF91
Elmsleigh Ct, Sutt. SM1 140 DB104
Elmsleigh Rd, Stai. TW18 113 BF92
Twickenham TW2 117 CD89
Elmslie Cl, Epsom KT18 156 CQ114
Woodford Green IG8 49 EM51
Elmslie Pt, E3 85 DZ71
Elms Ms, W2 82 DD73
Elms Pk Av, Wem. HA0 61 CG63
Elms Rd, SW4 121 DJ85
Gerrards Cross (Chal.St.P.)
SL9 36 AY52
Harrow HA3 41 CE52
ELMSTEAD, Chis. BR7 124 EK92
Elmstead Av, Chis. BR7 125 EM92
Wembley HA9 62 CL60
Elmstead Cl, N20 44 DA47
Epsom KT19 156 CS106
Sevenoaks TN13 190 FE122
Elmstead Cres, Well. DA16 106 EW79
Elmstead Gdns, Wor.Pk. KT4 139 CU104
Elmstead Glade, Chis. BR7 125 EM93
Elmstead La, Chis. BR7 125 EM92
Elmstead Rd, Erith DA8 107 FE81
Ilford IG3 69 ES61
West Byfleet KT14 152 BG113
⇌ **Elmstead Woods** 124 EL93
Elmstone Rd, SW6 100 DA81
Elm St, WC1 196 C5
Elmsway, Ashf. TW15 114 BM92
Elmswood, Lthd. (Bkhm)
KT23 170 BZ124
Elmsworth Av, Houns. TW3 96 CB82
Elm Ter, NW2 64 DA62
SE9 125 EN86
Grays RM20 109 FV79
Harrow HA3 41 CD52
Elm Tree Av, Esher KT10 137 CD101
Elm Tree Cl, NW8 82 DD69
Ashford TW15
off Convent Rd 115 BP92
Chertsey KT16 133 BE103
Northolt UB5 78 BZ68
Elmtree Cl, W.Byf. (Byfleet)
KT14 152 BL113
Elm Tree Rd, NW8 82 DD69
Elmtree Rd, Tedd. TW11 117 CE91

★ Place of interest ⇌ Railway station ⊖ London Underground station DLR Docklands Light Railway station Tram Tramlink station H Hospital Riv Pedestrian ferry landing stage

Elm Tree Wk, Rick. (Chorl.)
WD3 21 BF42
Elm Wk, NW3 64 DA61
SW20 139 CW98
Orpington BR6 145 EM104
Radlett WD7 25 CF36
Romford RM2 71 FG55
Elm Way, N11 44 DG51
NW10 62 CS63
Brentwood CM14 54 FU48
Epsom KT19 156 CR106
Rickmansworth WD3 38 BH46
Worcester Park KT4 139 CW104
Elmwood Av, N13 45 DL50
Borehamwood WD6 26 CP42
Feltham TW13 115 BU89
Harrow HA3 61 CG57
Elmwood Cl, Ashtd. KT21 171 CK117
Epsom KT17 157 CU108
Wallington SM6 140 DG103
Elmwood Ct, SW11 101 DH81
Ashtead KT21
off Elmwood Cl 171 CK117
Wembley HA0 61 CG62
Elmwood Cres, NW9 62 CQ56
Elmwood Dr, Bex. DA5 126 EY87
Epsom KT17 157 CU107
Elmwood Gdns, W7 79 CE72
Elmwood Pk, Ger.Cr. SL9 56 AY60
Elmwood Rd, SE24 122 DR85
W4 98 CQ79
Croydon CR0 141 DP101
Mitcham CR4 140 DF97
Redhill RH1 184 DG130
Slough SL2 74 AV73
Elmworth Gro, SE21 122 DR89
Elnathan Ms, W9
off Shirland Rd 82 DB70
Elphinstone Rd, E17 47 DZ54
Elphinstone St, N5
off Avenell Rd 65 DP63
Elrick Cl, Erith DA8
off Queen St 107 FE79
Elrington Rd, E8 84 DU65
Woodford Green IG8 48 EG50
Elruge Cl, West Dr. UB7 94 BK76
Elsa Rd, Well. DA16 106 EV82
Elsa St, E1 85 DY71
Elsdale St, E9 84 DW65
Elsden Ms, E2
off Old Ford Rd 84 DW68
Elsden Rd, N17 46 DT53
Elsdon Rd, Wok. GU21 166 AU117
Elsenham Rd, E12 69 EN64
Elsenham St, SW18 119 CZ88
Elsham Rd, E11 68 EE62
W14 99 CY75
Elsham Ter, W14 99 CY75
Elsiedene Rd, N21 46 DQ45
Elsiemaud Rd, SE4 123 DZ85
Elsie Rd, SE22 102 DT84
Elsinge Rd, Enf. EN1 30 DV36
Elsinore Av, Stai. TW19 114 BL87
Elsinore Gdns, NW2 63 CY62
Elsinore Rd, SE23 123 DY88
Elsinore Way, Rich. TW9
off Lower Richmond Rd 98 CP83
Elsley Rd, SW11 100 DF83
Elspeth Rd, SW11 100 DF84
Wembley HA0 62 CL64
Elsrick Av, Mord. SM4 140 DA99
Elstan Way, Croy. CR0 143 DY101
Elstead Ct, Sutt. SM3
off Stonecot Hill 139 CY102
Elsted St, SE17 201 L9
Elstow Cl, SE9 125 EN85
Ruislip HA4 60 BX59
Elstow Gdns, Dag. RM9 88 EY67
Elstow Rd, Dag. RM9 88 EY66
ELSTREE, Borwd. WD6 25 CK43
★ Elstree Aerodrome,
Borwd. WD6 25 CF41
⇌ Elstree & Borehamwood 26 CM42
Elstree Cl, Horn. RM12 89 FH66
Elstree Gdns, N9 46 DV46
Belvedere DA17 106 EY77
Ilford IG1 69 EQ64
Elstree Hill, Brom. BR1 124 EE94
Elstree Hill N, Borwd. (Els.)
WD6 25 CK44
Elstree Hill S, Borwd. (Els.)
WD6 41 CJ45
Elstree Pk, Borwd. WD6 26 CR44
Elstree Rd, Borwd. (Els.) WD6 25 CG44
Bushey (Bushey Hth) WD23 41 CD45
Elstree Way, Borwd. WD6 26 CP41
Elswick Rd, SE13 103 EB82
Elswick St, SW6 100 DC82
Elsworth Cl, Felt. TW14 115 BS88
Elsworthy, T.Ditt. KT7 137 CE100
Elsworthy Ri, NW3 82 DE66
Elsworthy Rd, NW3 82 DE67
Elsworthy Ter, NW3 82 DE66
Elsynge Rd, SW18 120 DD85
ELTHAM, SE9 124 EK86
⇌ Eltham 125 EM85
Eltham Grn, SE9 124 EJ85
Eltham Grn Rd, SE9 104 EJ84
Eltham High St, SE9 125 EM86
Eltham Hill, SE9 124 EK85
★ Eltham Palace, SE9 124 EL87
Eltham Palace Rd, SE9 124 EJ86
Eltham Pk Gdns, SE9 105 EN84
Eltham Rd, SE9 124 EJ85
SE12 124 EF85
Elthiron Rd, SW6 100 DA81
Elthorne Av, W7 97 CF75
Elthorne Ct, Felt. TW13 116 BW88
Elthorne Pk Rd, W7 97 CF75
Elthorne Rd, N19 65 DK61
NW9 62 CR59
Uxbridge UB8 76 BK68
Elthorne Way, NW9 62 CR58
Elthruda Rd, SE13 123 ED86
Eltisley Rd, Ilf. IG1 69 EP63
Elton Av, Barn. EN5 27 CZ43
Greenford UB6 79 CF65
Wembley HA0 61 CH64
Elton Cl, Kings.T. KT1 117 CJ94
Elton Ho, E3 85 DZ67
Elton Pk, Wat. WD17 23 BV40
Elton Pl, N16 66 DS64
Elton Rd, Kings.T. KT2 138 CM95
Purley CR8 159 DJ112
Elton Way, Wat. WD25 24 CB40
Eltringham St, SW18 100 DC84
Elvaston Ms, SW7 100 DC76
Elvaston Pl, SW7 100 DC76
Elveden Cl, Wok. GU22 168 BH117
Elveden Pl, NW10 80 CN68
Elveden Rd, NW10 80 CN68
Elvedon Rd, Cob. KT11 153 BV111
Feltham TW13 115 BT90
Elvendon Rd, N13 45 DL51
Elver Gdns, E2
off St. Peter's Cl 84 DU68
Elverson Ms, SE8 103 EB82
DLR Elverson Road 103 EB82
Elverson Rd, SE8 103 EB82
Elverton St, SW1 199 M8
Elvet Av, Rom. RM2 72 FJ56
Elvin Dr, Grays (N.Stfd)
RM16 91 FX74
Elvington Grn, Brom. BR2 144 EF99
Elvington La, NW9 42 CS53
Elvino Rd, SE26 123 DY92
Elvis Rd, NW2 81 CW65
Elwell Cl, Egh. TW20
off Mowbray Cres 113 BA92
Elwick Rd, S.Ock. RM15 91 FW72
Elwill Way, Beck. BR3 143 EC98
Elwin St, E2 84 DU69
Elwood St, N5 65 DP62
Elwyn Gdns, SE12 124 EG87
Ely Cl, Amer. HP7 20 AS39
Erith DA8 107 FF82
New Malden KT3 139 CT96
Ely Ct, EC1 196 E7
Ely Gdns, Borwd. WD6 26 CR43
Dagenham RM10 71 FC62
Ilford IG1
off Canterbury Av 68 EL59
Elyne Rd, N4 65 DN58
Ely Pl, EC1 196 E7
Woodford Green IG8 49 EN51
Ely Rd, E10 67 EC58
Croydon CR0 142 DR99
Hounslow (Hthrw Air.) TW6
off Eastern Perimeter Rd 95 BT82
Hounslow (Houns.W.) TW4 96 BW83
Elysian Av, Orp. BR5 145 ES100
Elysium Bldg, The, SE8
off Trundleys Rd 103 DX78
Elysium Pl, SW6
off Fulham Pk Gdns 99 CZ82
Elysium St, SW6
off Fulham Pk Gdns 99 CZ82
Elystan Business Cen, Hayes
UB4 78 BW73
Elystan Cl, Wall. SM6 159 DH109
Elystan Pl, SW3 198 C10
Elystan St, SW3 198 B9
Elystan Wk, N1
off Cloudesley Rd 83 DN67
Emanuel Av, W3 80 CQ72
Emanuel Dr, Hmptn. TW12 116 BZ92
⊖ Embankment 200 A2
Embankment, SW15 99 CX82
Embankment, The, Stai.
(Wrays.) TW19 112 AW87
Twickenham TW1 117 CG88
Embankment Gdns, SW3 100 DF79
RIV Embankment Pier 200 B2
Embankment Pl, WC2 200 A2
Embassy Ct, Sid. DA14 126 EV90
Welling DA16
off Welling High St 106 EV83
Embassy Gdns, Beck. BR3
off Blakeney Rd 143 DZ95
Emba St, SE16 202 C5
Ember Cen, Walt. KT12 136 BY103
Ember Cl, Add. KT15 152 BK106
Orpington BR5 145 EQ101
Embercourt Rd, T.Ditt. KT7 137 CE100
Ember Fm Av, E.Mol. KT8 137 CD100
Ember Fm Way, E.Mol. KT8 137 CD100
Ember Gdns, T.Ditt. KT7 137 CE101
Ember La, E.Mol. KT8 137 CD101
Esher KT10 137 CD101
Ember Rd, Slou. SL3 93 BB76
Emberson Way, Epp. (N.Wld Bas.)
CM16 19 FC26
Emberton, SE5 102 DS79
Emberton Ct, EC1
off Northampton Sq 83 DP69
Embleton Rd, SE13 103 EB83
Watford WD19 39 BU48
Embleton Wk, Hmptn. TW12
off Fearnley Cres 116 BZ93
Embry Cl, Stan. HA7 41 CG49
Embry Dr, Stan. HA7 41 CG51
Embry Way, Stan. HA7 41 CG50
Emden Cl, West Dr. UB7 94 BN75
Emden St, SW6 100 DB81
Emerald Cl, E16 86 EL72
Emerald Ct, Slou. SL1 92 AS75
Emerald Gdns, Dag. RM8 70 FA60
Emerald Rd, NW10
off Lawrence Av 80 CR67
Emerald Sq, Sthl. UB2 96 BX76
Emerald St, WC1 196 B6
Emerson Apts, N8
off New River Av 65 DM56
Emerson Dr, Horn. RM11 72 FK59
Emerson Gdns, Har. HA3 62 CM58
EMERSON PARK, Horn. RM11 72 FL58
⇌ Emerson Park 72 FL59
Emerson Rd, Ilf. IG1 69 EN59
Emersons Av, Swan. BR8 127 FF94
Emerson St, SE1 201 H2
Emerton Cl, Bexh. DA6 106 EY84
Emerton Rd, Lthd. KT22 170 CC120
Emery Hill St, SW1 199 L7
Emery St, SE1 200 E6
Emes Rd, Erith DA8 107 FC80
Emilia Cl, Enf. EN3 30 DV43
Emily Davidson Dr, Epsom
KT18 173 CV118
Emily Jackson Cl, Sev. TN13 191 FH124
Emley Rd, Add. KT15 134 BG104
Emlyn Gdns, W12 98 CS75
Emlyn La, Lthd. KT22 171 CG122
Emlyn Rd, W12 98 CS75
Emmanuel Lo, Wal.Cr. (Chsht)
EN8 off College Rd 14 DW30
Emmanuel Rd, SW12 121 DJ88
Northwood HA6 39 BT52
Emma Rd, E13 86 EF68
Emma St, E2 84 DV68
Emmaus Way, Chig. IG7 49 EN50
Emmett Cl, Rad. (Shenley)
WD7 10 CL33
Emmetts Cl, Wok. GU21 166 AW117
Emmott Av, Ilf. IG6 69 EQ57
Emmott Cl, E1 85 DY70
NW11 64 DC58
Emms Pas, Kings.T. KT1 137 CK96
Emperor's Gate, SW7 100 DB76
Empire Av, N18 46 DQ50
Empire Ct, Wem. HA9 62 CP62
Empire Rd, Grnf. UB6 79 CJ67
Empire Sq, N7 65 DL62
SE1 off Long La 102 DR75
SE20 off High St 123 DX94
Empire Wk, Green. DA9 109 FW84
Empire Way, Wem. HA9 62 CM63
Empire Wf Rd, E14 204 F9
Empress App, SW6
off Lillie Rd 100 DA79
Empress Av, E4 47 EA52
E12 68 EJ61
Ilford IG1 69 EM61
Woodford Green IG8 48 EF52
Empress Dr, Chis. BR7 125 EP93
Empress Ms, SE5 102 DQ82
Empress Pl, SW6 100 DA78
Empress Rd, Grav. DA12 131 GL87
Empress St, SE17 102 DQ79
Empson St, E3 85 EB70
Emsworth Cl, N9 46 DW46
Emsworth Rd, Ilf. IG6 49 EP54
Emsworth St, SW2 121 DM89
Emu Rd, SW8 101 DH82
Ena Rd, SW16 141 DL97
Enborne Grn, S.Ock. RM15 91 FU71
Enbrook St, W10 81 CY69
Endale Cl, Cars. SM5 140 DF103
Endeavour Ho, Barn. EN5 28 DC42
Endeavour Rd, Wal.Cr.
(Chsht) EN8 15 DY27
Endeavour Way, SW19 120 DB91
Barking IG11 88 EU68
Croydon CR0 141 DK101
Endell St, WC2 195 P8
Enderby St, SE10 104 EE78
Enderley Cl, Har. HA3
off Enderley Rd 41 CE53
Enderley Rd, Har. HA3 41 CE53
Endersby Rd, Barn. EN5 27 CW43
Endersleigh Gdns, NW4 63 CU56
Endlebury Rd, E4 47 EB47
Endlesham Rd, SW12 120 DG87
Endsleigh Cl, S.Croy. CR2 160 DW110
Endsleigh Gdns, WC1 195 M4
Ilford IG1 69 EM61
Surbiton KT6 137 CJ100
Walton-on-Thames KT12 154 BW106
Endsleigh Ind Est, Sthl. UB2 96 BZ77
Endsleigh Pl, WC1 195 N4
Endsleigh Rd, W13 79 CG73
Redhill (S.Merst.) RH1 185 DJ129
Southall UB2 96 BY77
Endsleigh St, WC1 195 M4
Endway, Surb. KT5 138 CN101
Endwell Rd, SE4 103 DY82
Endymion Rd, N4 65 DN59
SW2 121 DM86
Energen Cl, NW10 80 CS65
ENFIELD, EN1 - EN3 30 DT41
⇌ Enfield Chase 30 DQ41
Enfield Cl, Uxb. UB8
off Villier St 76 BK68
ENFIELD HIGHWAY, Enf. EN3 30 DW41
ENFIELD LOCK, Enf. EN3 31 DZ37
⇌ Enfield Lock 31 DY37
Enfield Retail Pk, Enf. EN1 30 DV41
Enfield Rd, N1 84 DS66
W3 98 CP75
Brentford TW8 97 CK78
Enfield EN2 29 DK42
Hounslow (Hthrw Air.) TW6
off Eastern Perimeter Rd 95 BS82
ENFIELD TOWN, Enf. EN2 30 DR40
⇌ Enfield Town 30 DS42
Enfield Wk, Brent. TW8 97 CK78
ENFIELD WASH, Enf. EN3 31 DX38
Enford St, W1 194 D6
Engadine Cl, Croy. CR0 142 DT104
Engadine St, SW18 119 CZ88
Engate St, SE13 103 EC84
Engayne Gdns, Upmin. RM14 72 FP60
Engel Pk, NW7 43 CW51
Engineer Cl, SE18 105 EN79
Engineers Way, Wem. HA9 62 CN63
Englands La, NW3 82 DF65
Loughton IG10 33 EN40
England Way, N.Mal. KT3 138 CP98
Englefield Cl, Croy. CR0
off Queen's Rd 142 DQ100
Egham (Eng.Grn) TW20
off Alexandra Rd 112 AW93
Enfield EN2 29 DN40
Orpington BR5 145 ET98
Englefield Cres, Orp. BR5 145 ET98
ENGLEFIELD GREEN, Egh.
TW20 112 AV92
Englefield Grn, Egh. (Eng.Grn)
TW20 112 AW91
Englefield Path, Orp. BR5 145 ET98
Englefield Rd, N1 84 DR65
Orpington BR5 146 EU98
Engleheart Dr, Felt. TW14 115 BT86
Engleheart Rd, SE6 123 EB87
Englehurst, Egh. (Eng.Grn)
TW20 112 AW93
Englemere Pk, Lthd. (Oxshott)
KT22 154 CB114
Englewood Rd, SW12 121 DH86
Engliff La, Wok. GU22 167 BF116
English Gdns, Stai. (Wrays.)
TW19 92 AX84
English Grds, SE1 201 M3
English St, E3 85 DZ70
Enid Cl, St.Alb. (Brick.Wd) AL2 8 BZ31
Enid St, SE16 202 A6
Enmore Av, SE25 142 DU99
Enmore Gdns, SW14 118 CR85
Enmore Rd, SE25 142 DU99
SW15 99 CW84
Southall UB1 78 CA70
Ennerdale Av, Horn. RM12 71 FG64
Stanmore HA7 61 CJ55
Ennerdale Cl, Felt. TW14 115 BT88
Sutton SM1 157 CZ105
Ennerdale Dr, NW9 62 CS57
Watford WD25 8 BW33
Ennerdale Gdns, Wem. HA9 61 CJ60
Ennerdale Ho, E3 85 DZ70
Ennerdale Rd, Bexh. DA7 106 FA81
Richmond TW9 98 CM82
Ennersdale Rd, SE13 123 ED85
Ennismore Av, W4 99 CT77
Greenford UB6 79 CE65
Ennismore Gdns, SW7 198 B5
Thames Ditton KT7 137 CE100
Ennismore Gdns Ms, SW7 198 B6
Ennismore Ms, SW7 198 B6
Ennismore St, SW7 198 B6
Ennis Rd, N4 65 DN60
SE18 105 EQ79
Ensign Cl, Pur. CR8 159 DN110
Staines (Stanw.) TW19 114 BK88
Ensign Dr, N13 46 DQ48
Ensign Ho, SW8
off St. George Wf 101 DL79
Ensign St, E1 84 DU73
Ensign Way, Stai. (Stanw.)
TW19 114 BK88
Wallington SM6 159 DL108
Enslin Rd, SE9 125 EN86
Ensor Ms, SW7
off Cranley Gdns 100 DD78
Enstone Rd, Enf. EN3 31 DY41
Uxbridge UB10 58 BM62
Enterdent, The, Gdse. RH9 187 DX133
Enterdent Rd, Gdse. RH9 186 DW134
Enterprise Cl, Croy. CR0 141 DN102
Enterprise Way, NW10 81 CU69
SW18 100 DA84
Teddington TW11 117 CF92
Enterprize Way, SE8 203 M8
Eothen Cl, Cat. CR3 176 DU124
Eothen Hts, Cat. CR3 176 DU124
Epirus Ms, SW6 100 DA80
Epirus Rd, SW6 99 CZ80
EPPING, CM16 17 ES31
⊖ Epping 18 EU31
Epping Cl, E14 204 A8
Romford RM7 71 FB55
★ Epping Forest,
Epp. & Loug. 32 EJ39
★ Epping Forest District Mus,
Wal.Abb. EN9 off Sun St 15 EC33
Epping Glade, E4 31 EC44
Epping La, Rom. (Stap.Taw.)
RM4 34 EV40
Epping New Rd, Buck.H. IG9 48 EH47
Loughton IG10 32 EH43
Epping Pl, N1
off Liverpool Rd 83 DN65
Epping Rd, Epp. CM16 33 EM36
Epping (Epp.Grn) CM16 18 ER27
Epping (N.Wld Bas.) CM16 18 EW28
Ongar (Toot Hill) CM5 19 FC30
Epping Way, E4 31 EB44
Epple Rd, SW6 99 CZ81
EPSOM, KT17 - KT19 156 CQ114
⇌ Epsom 156 CR113
Epsom Cl, Bexh. DA7 107 FB83
Northolt UB5 60 BZ64
⇌ Epsom Downs 173 CV115
Epsom Downs, Epsom KT18 173 CU118
Epsom Downs Metro Cen, Tad.
KT20 off Waterfield 173 CV120
Epsom Gap, Lthd. KT22 171 CH115
H Epsom Gen Hosp,
Epsom KT18 172 CQ115
Epsom La N, Epsom KT18 173 CV118
Tadworth KT20 173 CV118
Epsom La S, Tad. KT20 173 CW121
★ Epsom Racecourse, Epsom
KT18 173 CT118
Epsom Rd, E10 67 EC58
Ashtead KT21 172 CM118
Croydon CR0 159 DN105
Epsom KT17 157 CT110
Ilford IG3 69 ET58
Leatherhead KT22 171 CH121
Morden SM4 139 CZ101
Sutton SM3 139 CZ101
Epsom Sq, Houns. (Hthrw Air.) TW6
off Eastern Perimeter Rd 95 BT82
Epsom Way, Horn. RM12 72 FM63
Epstein Rd, SE28 88 EU74
Epworth Rd, Islw. TW7 97 CH80
Epworth St, EC2 197 L5
Equity Sq, E2
off Shacklewell St 84 DT69
Erasmus St, SW1 199 N9
Erconwald St, W12 81 CT72
Erebus Dr, SE28 105 EQ76
Eresby Dr, Beck. BR3 143 EA102
Eresby Pl, NW6 82 DA66
Erica Ct, Swan. BR8
off Azalea Dr 147 FE98
Woking GU22 166 AX118
Erica Gdns, Croy. CR0 161 EB105
Erica St, W12 81 CU73
Eric Clarke La, Bark. IG11 87 EP70
Eric Cl, E7 68 EG63
Ericcson Cl, SW18 120 DA85
Eric Rd, E7 68 EG63
NW10 off Church Rd 81 CT65
Romford RM6 70 EX59
Eric Steele Ho, St.Alb. AL2 8 CB27
Eric St, E3 85 DZ70
Eridge Grn Cl, Orp. BR5
off Petten Gro 146 EW102
Eridge Rd, W4 98 CR76
Erin Cl, Brom. BR1 124 EE94
Ilford IG3 70 EU58
Erindale, SE18 105 ER79
Erindale Ter, SE18 105 ER79
Eriswell Cres, Walt. KT12 153 BS107
Eriswell Rd, Walt. KT12 153 BT105
ERITH, DA8; DA18 107 FD79
⇌ Erith 107 FE78
H Erith & District Hosp,
Erith DA8 107 FD79
Erith Ct, Purf. RM19 108 FN77
Erith Cres, Rom. RM5 51 FC53
Erith High St, Erith DA8 107 FE78
★ Erith Lib & Mus, Erith DA8
off Walnut Tree Rd 107 FE78
Erith Riverside, Erith DA8 107 FE79
Erith Rd, Belv. DA17 106 FA78
Bexleyheath DA7 107 FB84
Erith DA8 107 FB84
Erkenwald Cl, Cher. KT16 133 BE101
Erlanger Rd, SE14 103 DX81
Erlesmere Gdns, W13 97 CG76
Ermine Cl, Houns. TW4 96 BW82
Waltham Cross (Chsht) EN7 14 DV31
Ermine Ho, N17
off Moselle St 46 DT52
Ermine Rd, N15 66 DT58
SE13 103 EB83
Ermine Side, Enf. EN1 30 DU43
Ermington Rd, SE9 125 EQ89
Ermyn Cl, Lthd. KT22 171 CK121
Ermyn Way, Lthd. KT22 171 CK121
Ernald Av, E6 86 EL68
Ernan Cl, S.Ock. RM15 91 FU71
Ernan Rd, S.Ock. RM15 91 FU71
Erncroft Way, Twick. TW1 117 CF86
Ernest Av, SE27 121 DP91
Ernest Cl, Beck. BR3 143 EA99
Ernest Gdns, W4 98 CP79
Ernest Gro, Beck. BR3 143 DZ99
Ernest Rd, Horn. RM11 72 FL58
Kingston upon Thames
KT1 138 CP96
Ernest Sq, Kings.T. KT1 138 CP96
Ernest St, E1 85 DX70
Ernle Rd, SW20 119 CV94
Ernshaw Pl, SW15
off Carlton Dr 119 CY85
★ Eros, W1 199 M1
Erpingham Rd, SW15 99 CW83
Erridge Rd, SW19 140 DA96
Erriff Dr, S.Ock. RM15 91 FT71
Errington Cl, Grays RM16
off Cedar Rd 111 GH76
Errington Rd, W9 81 CZ70
Errol Gdns, Hayes UB4 77 BV70
New Malden KT3 139 CU98
Erroll Rd, Rom. RM1 71 FF56
Errol St, EC1 197 J5
Erskine Cl, Sutt. SM1 140 DE104
Erskine Cres, N17 66 DV56
Erskine Hill, NW11 64 DA57
Erskine Ms, NW3
off Erskine Rd 82 DF66
Erskine Rd, E17 67 DZ56
NW3 82 DF66
Sutton SM1 158 DD105
Watford WD19 40 BW48
Erwood Rd, SE7 104 EL78
Esam Way, SW16 121 DN92
Escott Gdns, SE9 124 EL91
Escott Pl, Cher. (Ott.) KT16 151 BC107
Escot Way, Barn. EN5 27 CW43
Escreet Gro, SE18 105 EN77
Esdaile Gdns, Upmin. RM14 73 FR59
ESHER, KT10 154 CB105
⇌ Esher 137 CD103
Esher Av, Rom. RM7 71 FC58
Sutton SM3 139 CX104
Walton-on-Thames KT12 135 BU101
Esher Bypass, Chess. KT9 155 CH108
Cobham KT11 153 BU112
Esher KT10 155 CH108
Esher Cl, Bex. DA5 126 EY88
Esher KT10 154 CB106
Esher Common, Esher KT10
off Esher Bypass 154 CC110
Esher Cres, Houns. (Hthrw Air.) TW6
off Eastern Perimeter Rd 95 BS82
Esher Gdns, SW19 119 CX89
Esher Grn, Esher KT10 154 CB105
Esher Ms, Mitch. CR4 140 DF97
Esher Pk Av, Esher KT10 154 CC105
Esher Pl Av, Esher KT10 154 CB105
Esher Rd, E.Mol. KT8 137 CD100
Ilford IG3 69 ES62
Walton-on-Thames KT12 154 BX106
Eskdale, NW1 195 K1
St. Albans (Lon.Col.) AL2 10 CM27
Eskdale Av, Nthlt. UB5 78 BZ67
Eskdale Cl, Dart. DA2 128 FQ89
Wembley HA9 61 CK61
Eskdale Gdns, Pur. CR8 160 DR114
Eskdale Rd, Bexh. DA7 106 FA82
Uxbridge UB8 76 BH68
Eskley Gdns, S.Ock. RM15 91 FV70
Eskmont Ridge, SE19 122 DS94
Esk Rd, E13 86 EG70
Esk Way, Rom. RM1 51 FD52
Esmar Cres, NW9 63 CU59
Esme Ho, SW15 99 CT84
Esmeralda Rd, SE1 202 C9
Esmond Cl, Rain. RM13
off Dawson Dr 89 FH66
Esmond Rd, NW6 81 CZ67
W4 98 CR77
Esmond St, SW15 99 CY84
Esparto St, SW18 120 DB87
Essendene Cl, Cat. CR3 176 DS123
Essendene Rd, Cat. CR3 176 DS123
Essenden Rd, Belv. DA17 106 FA78
South Croydon CR2 160 DS108
Essendine Rd, W9 82 DA70
Essex Av, Islw. TW7 97 CE83
Essex Cl, E17 67 DY56
Addlestone KT15 152 BJ105
Morden SM4 139 CX101
Romford RM7 71 FB56
Ruislip HA4 60 BX60
Essex Ct, EC4 196 D9
SW13 99 CT82
Essex Gdns, N4 65 DP58
Hornchurch RM11 72 FM57
Essex Gro, SE19 122 DR93
Essex Ho, E14 off Giraud St 85 EB72
Essex La, Kings L. WD4 7 BS33
H Essex Nuffield Hosp, Brwd.
CM15 54 FY46
Essex Pk, N3 44 DB51
Essex Pk Ms, W3 80 CS74
Essex Pl, W4 98 CQ77

Essex Pl Sq, W4
off Chiswick High Rd 98 CR77
≠ **Essex Road** 84 DQ66
Essex Rd, E4 48 EE46
E10 67 EC58
E12 68 EL64
E17 67 DY58
E18 48 EH54
N1 83 DP67
NW10 80 CS66
W3 80 CQ73
W4 off Belmont Rd 98 CR77
Barking IG11 87 ER66
Borehamwood WD6 26 CN41
Dagenham RM10 71 FC64
Dartford DA1 128 FK86
Enfield EN2 30 DR42
Gravesend DA11 131 GG88
Grays RM20 109 FU79
Longfield DA3 149 FX96
Romford RM7 71 FB56
Romford (Chad.Hth) RM6 70 EW59
Watford WD17 23 BU40
Essex Rd S, E11 67 ED59
Essex St, E7 68 EG64
WC2 196 D10
Essex Twr, SE20 142 DV95
Essex Vil, W8 100 DA75
Essex Way, Brwd. CM13 53 FW51
Epping CM16 18 EV32
Ongar CM5 19 FF29
Essex Wf, E5 66 DW61
Essian St, E1 85 DY71
Essoldo Way, Edg. HA8 62 CM55
Estate Way, E10 67 DZ60
Estcourt Rd, SE25 142 DV100
SW6 99 CZ80
Watford WD17 24 BW41
Estella Av, N.Mal. KT3 139 CV98
Estelle Rd, NW3 64 DF63
Esterbrooke St, SW1 199 M9
Este Rd, SW11 100 DE83
Esther Cl, N21 45 DN45
Esther Rd, E11 68 EE59
Estoria Cl, SW2 121 DN87
★ **Estorick Collection of Modern Italian Art**, N1 83 DP65
Estreham Rd, SW16 121 DK93
Estridge Cl, Houns. TW3 96 CA84
Estuary Cl, Bark. IG11 88 EV69
Eswyn Rd, SW17 120 DF91
Etchingham Pk Rd, N3 44 DB52
Etchingham Rd, E15 67 EC63
Eternit Wk, SW6 99 CW81
Etfield Gro, Sid. DA14 126 EV92
Ethel Bailey Cl, Epsom KT19 156 CN112
Ethelbert Cl, Brom. BR1 144 EG97
Ethelbert Gdns, Ilf. IG2 69 EM57
Ethelbert Rd, SW20 139 CX95
Bromley BR1 144 EG97
Dartford (Hawley) DA2 128 FL91
Erith DA8 107 FC80
Orpington BR5 146 EX97
Ethelbert St, SW12 121 DH88
Ethelburga Rd, Rom. RM3 52 FM53
Ethelburga St, SW11 100 DE81
Ethelburga Twr, SW11
off Rosenau Rd 100 DE81
Etheldene Av, N10 65 DJ56
Ethelden Rd, W12 81 CV74
Ethel Rd, E16 86 EH72
Ashford TW15 114 BL92
Ethel St, SE17 201 H9
Ethel Ter, Orp. BR6 164 EW109
Ethelwine Pl, Abb.L. WD5
off The Crescent 7 BT30
Etheridge Grn, Loug. IG10 33 EQ41
Etheridge Rd, NW2 63 CW59
Loughton IG10 33 EP40
Etherley Rd, N15 66 DQ57
Etherow St, SE22 122 DU86
Etherstone Grn, SW16 121 DN91
Etherstone Rd, SW16 121 DN91
Ethnard Rd, SE15 102 DV79
Ethorpe Cl, Ger.Cr. SL9 56 AY57
Ethorpe Cres, Ger.Cr. SL9 56 AY57
Ethronvi Rd, Bexh. DA7 106 EY83
Etloe Rd, E10 67 EA61
Eton Av, N12 44 DC52
NW3 82 DD66
Barnet EN4 28 DE44
Hounslow TW5 96 BZ79
New Malden KT3 138 CR99
Wembley HA0 61 CH63
Eton Cl, SW18 120 DB87
Slough (Datchet) SL3 92 AU79
Eton Coll Rd, NW3 82 DF65
Eton Ct, NW3 off Eton Av 82 DD66
Staines TW18
off Richmond Rd 113 BF92
Wembley HA0 off Eton Av 61 CJ63
Eton Garages, NW3
off Lambolle Pl 82 DE65
Eton Gro, NW9 62 CN55
SE13 104 EE83
Eton Hall, NW3
off Eton Coll Rd 82 DF65
Eton Pl, NW3
off Haverstock Hill 82 DG66
Eton Ri, NW3
off Eton Coll Rd 82 DF65
Eton Rd, NW3 82 DF66
Hayes UB3 95 BT80
Ilford IG1 69 EQ64
Orpington BR6 164 EV105
Slough (Datchet) SL3 92 AT78
Eton St, Rich. TW9 118 CL85
Eton Vil, NW3 82 DF65
Eton Way, Dart. DA1 108 FJ84
Etta St, SE8 103 DY79
Etton Cl, Horn. RM12 72 FL61
Ettrick St, E14 85 EC72
Etwell Pl, Surb. KT5 138 CM100
Euclid Way, Grays RM20 109 FT78
Euesden Cl, N9 46 DV48
Eugene Cl, Rom. RM2 72 FJ56
Eugenia Rd, SE16 202 G9
Eureka Rd, Kings.T. KT1
off Washington Rd 138 CN96
Euro Cl, NW10 off Strode Rd 81 CU65
Europa Pl, EC1 197 H3
Europa Trd Est, Erith DA8 107 FD78
Europe Rd, SE18 105 EM76
Eustace Bldg, SW8
off Queenstown Rd 101 DH79
Eustace Pl, SE18
off Borgard Rd 105 EM77
Eustace Rd, E6 86 EL69
SW6 100 DA80
Romford RM6 70 EX59
≠ **Euston** 195 L2
⊖ **Euston** 195 L2
Euston Av, Wat. WD18 23 BT43
Euston Cen, NW1
off Triton Sq 83 DJ70
Euston Gro, NW1 195 M3
Euston Rd, N1 195 P2
NW1 195 J5
Croydon CR0 141 DN102
⊖ **Euston Square** 195 L4
Euston Sq, NW1 195 M3
Euston Sta Colonnade, NW1 195 M3
Euston St, NW1 195 L4
Euston Twr, NW1 195 K4
Evandale Rd, SW9 101 DN82
Evangelist Rd, NW5 65 DH63
Evans Av, Wat. WD25 23 BT35
Evans Business Cen, NW2 63 CU62
Evans Cl, E8
off Buttermere Wk 84 DT65
Greenhithe DA9 129 FU85
Rickmansworth (Crox.Grn)
WD3 off New Rd 22 BN43
Evansdale, Rain. RM13
off New Zealand Way 89 FF69
Evans Gro, Felt. TW13 116 CA89
Evans Rd, SE6 124 EE89
Evanston Av, E4 47 EC52
Evanston Gdns, Ilf. IG4 68 EL58
Eva Rd, Rom. RM6 70 EW59
H **Evelina Children's Hosp**,
SE1 200 B6
Evelina Rd, SE15 102 DW83
SE20 123 DX94
Eveline Lowe Est, SE16 202 B7
Eveline Rd, Mitch. CR4 140 DF95
Evelyn Av, NW9 62 CR56
Ruislip HA4 59 BT58
Evelyn Cl, Twick. TW2 116 CB87
Woking GU22 166 AX120
Evelyn Ct, N1 197 K1
Evelyn Cres, Sun. TW16 135 BT95
Evelyn Denington Rd, E6 86 EL70
Evelyn Dr, Pnr. HA5 40 BX52
Evelyn Fox Ct, W10 81 CW71
Evelyn Gdns, SW7 100 DD78
Godstone RH9 186 DW130
Richmond TW9 off Kew Rd 98 CL84
Evelyn Gro, W5 80 CM74
Southall UB1 78 BZ72
Evelyn Rd, E16 205 P2
E17 67 EC56
SW19 120 DB92
W4 98 CR76
Barnet EN4 28 DF42
Richmond TW9 98 CL83
Richmond (Ham) TW10 117 CJ90
Evelyns Cl, Uxb. UB8 76 BN72
Evelyn Sharp Cl, Rom. RM2
off Amery Gdns 72 FK55
Evelyn St, SE8 203 K9
Evelyn Ter, Rich. TW9 98 CL83
Evelyn Wk, N1 197 K1
Brentwood CM13
off Essex Way 53 FW51
Evelyn Way, Cob. (Stoke D'Ab.)
KT11 170 BZ116
Epsom KT19 156 CN111
Sunbury-on-Thames TW16 135 BT95
Wallington SM6 159 DK105
Evelyn Yd, W1 195 M8
Evening Hill, Beck. BR3 123 EC94
Evensyde, Wat. WD18 23 BR44
Evenwood Cl, SW15 119 CY85
Everard Av, Brom. BR2 144 EG102
Slough SL1 92 AS75
Everard La, Cat. CR3
off Tillingdown Hill 176 DU122
Everard Way, Wem. HA9 62 CL62
Everatt Cl, SW18
off Amerland Rd 119 CZ86
Everdon Rd, SW13 99 CU79
Everest Cl, Grav. (Nthflt)
DA11 130 GE90
Everest Ct, Wok. GU21
off Langmans Way 166 AS116
Everest Pl, E14 85 EC71
Swanley BR8 147 FD98
Everest Rd, SE9 125 EM85
Staines (Stanw.) TW19 114 BK87
Everett Cl, Bushey (Bushey Hth)
WD23 41 CE46
Pinner HA5 59 BT55
Waltham Cross (Chsht) EN7 14 DQ25
Everett Wk, Belv. DA17
off Osborne Rd 106 EZ78
Everglade, West. (Bigg.H.)
TN16 178 EK118
Everglade Strand, NW9 43 CT53
Evergreen Ct, Stai. (Stanw.) TW19
off Evergreen Way 114 BK87
Evergreen Oak Av, Wind. SL4 92 AU83
Evergreen Sq, E8 84 DT66
Evergreen Way, Hayes UB3 77 BT73
Staines (Stanw.) TW19 114 BK87
Everilda St, N1 83 DM67
Evering Rd, E5 66 DT62
N16 66 DT62
Everington Rd, N10 44 DF54
Everington St, W6 99 CX79
Everitt Rd, NW10 80 CR69
Everlands Cl, Wok. GU22 166 AY118
Everleigh St, N4 65 DM60
Eve Rd, E11 68 EE63
E15 86 EE68
N17 66 DS55
Isleworth TW7 97 CG84
Woking GU21 167 BB115
Eversfield Gdns, NW7 42 CS52
Eversfield Rd, Reig. RH2 184 DB134
Richmond TW9 98 CM82
Evershed Wk, W4 98 CR77
Eversholt St, NW1 83 DJ68
Evershot Rd, N4 65 DM60
Eversleigh Gdns, Upmin.
RM14 73 FR60
Eversleigh Rd, E6 86 EK67
N3 43 CZ52
SW11 100 DF83
Barnet EN5 28 DC43
Eversley Av, Bexh. DA7 107 FD82
Wembley HA9 62 CN61
Eversley Cl, N21 29 DM44
Loughton IG10 33 EQ41
Eversley Cres, N21 29 DM44
Isleworth TW7 97 CD81
Ruislip HA4 59 BS61
Eversley Cross, Bexh. DA7 107 FE82
Eversley Mt, N21 29 DM44
Eversley Pk, SW19 119 CV92
Eversley Pk Rd, N21 29 DM44
Eversley Rd, SE7 104 EH79
SE19 122 DR94
Surbiton KT5 138 CM98
Eversley Way, Croy. CR0 161 EA105
Egham TW20 133 BC96
Everthorpe Rd, SE15 102 DT83
Everton Bldgs, NW1 195 K3
Everton Dr, Stan. HA7 62 CM55
Everton Rd, Croy. CR0 142 DU102
Evesham Av, E17 47 EA54
Evesham Cl, Grnf. UB6 78 CB68
Reigate RH2 183 CZ133
Sutton SM2 158 DA108
Evesham Ct, W13
off Tewkesbury Rd 79 CG74
Evesham Grn, Mord. SM4 140 DB100
Evesham Rd, E15 86 EF67
N11 45 DJ50
Gravesend DA12 131 GK89
Morden SM4 140 DB100
Reigate RH2 183 CZ134
Evesham Rd N, Reig. RH2 183 CZ133
Evesham St, W11 81 CX73
Evesham Wk, SE5
off Love Wk 102 DR82
SW9 101 DN82
Evesham Way, SW11 100 DG83
Ilford IG5 69 EN55
Evreham Rd, Iver SL0 75 BE72
Evry Rd, Sid. DA14 126 EW93
Ewald Rd, SW6 99 CZ82
Ewanrigg Ter, Wdf.Grn. IG8 48 EJ50
Ewan Rd, Rom. (Harold Wd)
RM3 52 FK54
Ewart Gro, N22 45 DN53
Ewart Pl, E3 off Roman Rd 85 DZ68
Ewart Rd, SE23 123 DX87
Ewe Cl, N7 83 DL65
EWELL, Epsom KT17 157 CU110
Ewell Bypass, Epsom KT17 157 CU108
Ewell Ct Av, Epsom KT19 156 CS106
Ewell Downs Rd, Epsom
KT17 157 CU111
≠ **Ewell East** 157 CV110
Ewell Ho Gro, Epsom KT17 157 CT110
Ewellhurst Rd, Ilf. IG5 48 EL54
Ewell Pk Gdns, Epsom KT17 157 CU108
Ewell Pk Way, Epsom (Ewell)
KT17 157 CU107
Ewell Rd, Surb. KT6 138 CL100
Surbiton (Long Dit.) KT6 137 CH101
Sutton SM3 157 CY107
≠ **Ewell West** 156 CS109
Ewelme Rd, SE23 122 DW88
Ewen Cres, SW2 121 DN87
Ewer St, SE1 201 H3
Ewhurst Av, S.Croy. CR2 160 DT109
Ewhurst Cl, E1 84 DW71
Sutton SM2 157 CW109
Ewhurst Ct, Mitch. CR4
off Phipps Br Rd 140 DD97
Ewhurst Rd, SE4 123 DZ86
Exbury Rd, SE6 123 EA89
Excel Ct, WC2 199 N1
★ **ExCeL London**, E16 86 EH73
ExCeL Marina, E16 205 P1
Excelsior Cl, Kings.T. KT1
off Washington Rd 138 CN96
Excelsior Gdns, SE13 103 EC82
ExCeL Waterfront, E16
off Western Gateway 86 EH73
Exchange Arc, EC2 197 N6
Exchange Bldgs, E1
off Cutler St 84 DS72
Exchange Cl, N11
off Benfleet Way 44 DG47
Exchange Ct, WC2 200 A1
Exchange Ho, N8 65 DL58
Exchange Mall, The, Ilf. IG1 69 EP61
Exchange Pl, EC2 197 M6
Exchange Rd, Wat. WD18 23 BV42
Exchange Sq, EC2 197 M6
Exchange St, Rom. RM1 71 FE57
Exchange Wk, Pnr. HA5 60 BY59
Exeforde Av, Ashf. TW15 114 BN91
Exeter Cl, E6 off Harper Rd 87 EM72
Watford WD24 24 BW40
Exeter Gdns, Ilf. IG1 68 EL60
Exeter Ho, SW15
off Putney Heath 119 CW86
Exeter Ms, NW6
off West Hampstead Ms 82 DB65
SW6 off Farm La 100 DA80
Exeter Rd, E16 86 EG71
E17 67 EA57
N9 46 DW47
N14 45 DH46
NW2 63 CY64
Croydon CR0 142 DS101
Dagenham RM10 89 FB65
Enfield EN3 31 DX41
Feltham TW13 116 BZ90
Gravesend DA12 131 GK90
Harrow HA2 60 BY61
Hounslow (Hthrw Air.) TW6 95 BS82
Welling DA16 105 ET82
Exeter St, WC2 196 A10
Exeter Way, SE14 103 DZ80
Hounslow (Hthrw Air.) TW6 95 BS83
Exford Gdns, SE12 124 EH88
Exford Rd, SE12 124 EH89
Exhibition Cl, W12 81 CW73
Exhibition Rd, SW7 198 A5
Exmoor Cl, Ilf. IG6 49 EQ53
Exmoor St, W10 81 CX70
Exmouth Mkt, EC1 196 D4
Exmouth Ms, NW1 195 L3
Exmouth Pl, E8 84 DV66
Exmouth Rd, E17 67 DZ57
Bromley BR2 144 EH97
Grays RM17 110 GB79
Hayes UB4 77 BS69
Ruislip HA4 60 BW62
Welling DA16 106 EW81
Exmouth St, E1
off Commercial Rd 84 DW72
Exning Rd, E16 86 EF70
Exon St, SE17 201 M10
Explorer Av, Stai. TW19 114 BL88
Explorer Dr, Wat. WD18 23 BT44
Express Dr, Ilf. IG3 70 EV60
Exton Cres, NW10
off Marshall St 80 CR66
Exton Gdns, Dag. RM8 70 EW64
Exton Rd, NW10 80 CQ66
Exton St, SE1 200 D3
Eyebright Cl, Croy. CR0
off Primrose La 143 DX102
Eyhurst Av, Horn. RM12 71 FG62
Eyhurst Cl, NW2 63 CU61
Tadworth (Kgswd) KT20 173 CZ123
Eyhurst Pk, Tad. KT20 174 DC123
Eyhurst Spur, Tad. KT20 173 CZ124
Eylewood Rd, SE27 122 DQ92
Eynella Rd, SE22 122 DT87
Eynham Rd, W12 81 CW72
EYNSFORD, Dart. DA4 148 FL103
★ **Eynsford Castle**,
Dart. DA4 148 FK103
Eynsford Cl, Orp. BR5 145 EQ101
Eynsford Cres, Bex. DA5 126 EW88
Eynsford Rd, Dart. (Fnghm)
DA4 148 FM102
Greenhithe DA9 129 FW85
Ilford IG3 69 ES61
Sevenoaks TN14 165 FH108
Swanley BR8 147 FD100
Eynsham Dr, SE2 106 EU77
Eynswood Dr, Sid. DA14 126 EV92
Eyot Gdns, W6 99 CT78
Eyot Grn, W4
off Chiswick Mall 99 CT79
Eyre Cl, Rom. RM2 71 FH56
Eyre Ct, NW8 off Finchley Rd 82 DD68
Eyre St Hill, EC1 196 D5
Eyston Dr, Wey. KT13 152 BN110
Eythorne Rd, SW9 101 DN81
Ezra St, E2 84 DT69

F

Faber Gdns, NW4 63 CU57
Fabian Rd, SW6 99 CZ80
Fabian St, E6 87 EM70
Fackenden La, Sev. (Shore.)
TN14 165 FH113
Factory La, N17 46 DT54
Croydon CR0 141 DN102
Factory Rd, E16 86 EL74
Gravesend (Nthflt) DA11 130 GC86
Factory Sq, SW16 121 DL93
Factory Yd, W7
off Uxbridge Rd 79 CE74
Faesten Way, Bex. DA5 127 FE90
Faggotts Cl, Rad. WD7 25 CJ35
Faggs Rd, Felt. TW14 115 BU85
Fagus Av, Rain. RM13 90 FK69
Faints Cl, Wal.Cr. (Chsht) EN7 14 DS29
Fairacre, N.Mal. KT3 138 CS97
Fairacres, SW15 99 CU84
Fair Acres, Brom. BR2 144 EG99
Fairacres, Cob. KT11 154 BX112
Croydon CR0 161 DZ109
Ruislip HA4 59 BT59
Tadworth KT20 173 CW121
Fairacres Cl, Pot.B. EN6 11 CZ33
Fairbairn Cl, Pur. CR8 159 DN113
Fairbairn Grn, SW9 101 DN81
Fairbank Av, Orp. BR6 145 EP103
Fairbank Est, N1 off East Rd 84 DR68
Fairbanks Rd, N17 66 DT55
Fairbourne, Cob. KT11 154 BX113
Fairbourne Cl, Wok. GU21 166 AU118
Fairbourne La, Cat. CR3 176 DQ122
Fairbourne Rd, N17 66 DS55
Fairbridge Rd, N19 65 DK61
Fairbrook Cl, N13 45 DN50
Fairbrook Rd, N13 45 DN51
Fairburn Cl, Borwd. WD6 26 CN39
Fairburn Ct, SW15
off Mercier Rd 119 CY85
Fairburn Ho, W14
off Ivatt Pl 99 CZ78
Fairby Ho, SE1
off Longfield Est 102 DT77
Fairby Rd, SE12 124 EH85
Faircharm Trd Est, SE8 103 EB80
Fairchild Cl, SW11
off Wye St 100 DD82
Fairchildes Av, Croy. (New Adgtn)
CR0 161 ED112
Fairchildes La, Warl. CR6 161 ED114
Fairchild Pl, EC2 197 N5
Fairchild St, EC2 197 N5
Fair Cl, Bushey WD23
off Claybury 40 CB45
Fairclough St, E1 84 DU72
Faircross Av, Bark. IG11 87 EQ65
Romford RM5 51 FD52
Fairdale Gdns, SW15 99 CV84
Hayes UB3 77 BU74
Fairdene Rd, Couls. CR5 175 DK117
Fairey Av, Hayes UB3 95 BT77
Fairfax Av, Epsom KT17 157 CV109
Redhill RH1 184 DE133
Fairfax Cl, Walt. KT12 135 BV102
Fairfax Gdns, SE3 104 EK81
Fairfax Ms, E16 205 P2
SW15 99 CW84
Fairfax Pl, NW6 82 DC66
W14 99 CY76
Fairfax Rd, N8 65 DN56
NW6 82 DC66
W4 98 CS76
Grays RM17 110 GB78
Teddington TW11 117 CG93
Tilbury RM18 111 GF81
Woking GU22 167 BB120
Fairfax Way, N10 44 DG52
Fairfield App, Stai. (Wrays.)
TW19 112 AX86
Fairfield Av, NW4 63 CV58
Edgware HA8 42 CP51
Ruislip HA4 59 BQ59
Slough (Datchet) SL3 92 AW80
Staines TW18 113 BF91
Twickenham TW2 116 CB88
Upminster RM14 72 FQ62
Watford WD19 40 BW48
Fairfield Cl, N12 44 DC49
Enfield EN3
off Scotland Grn Rd N 31 DY42
Epsom (Ewell) KT19 156 CS106
Hornchurch RM12 71 FG60
Mitcham CR4 120 DE94
Northwood HA6
off Thirlmere Gdns 39 BP50
Radlett WD7 25 CE37
Sidcup DA15 125 ET86
Slough (Datchet) SL3 92 AX80
Fairfield Ct, NW10 81 CU67
Northwood HA6
off Windsor Cl 39 BU54
Fairfield Cres, Edg. HA8 42 CP51
Fairfield Dr, SW18 120 DB85
Greenford UB6 79 CJ67
Harrow HA2 60 CC55
Fairfield E, Kings.T. KT1 138 CL96
Fairfield Gdns, N8
off Elder Av 65 DL57
Fairfield Gro, SE7 104 EK78
★ **Fairfield Halls**, Croy. CR0 142 DR104
Fairfield N, Kings.T. KT1 138 CL96
Fairfield Pk, Cob. KT11 154 BX114
Fairfield Path, Croy. CR0 142 DR104
Fairfield Pathway, Horn.
RM12 90 FJ66
Fairfield Pl, Kings.T. KT1 138 CL97
Fairfield Rd, E3 85 EA68
E17 47 DY54
N8 65 DL57
N18 46 DU49
W7 97 CG76
Beckenham BR3 143 EA96
Bexleyheath DA7 106 EZ82
Brentwood CM14 54 FW48
Bromley BR1 124 EG94
Croydon CR0 142 DS104
Epping CM16 18 EV29
Ilford IG1 87 EP65
Kingston upon Thames
KT1 138 CL96
Leatherhead KT22 171 CH121
Orpington BR5 145 ER100
Southall UB1 78 BZ72
Staines (Wrays.) TW19 112 AX86
Uxbridge UB8 76 BK65
West Drayton UB7 76 BL74
Woodford Green IG8 48 EG51
Fairfields, Cher. KT16 134 BG102
Gravesend DA12 131 GL92
Fairfields Cl, NW9 62 CQ57
Fairfields Cres, NW9 62 CQ56
Fairfield S, Kings.T. KT1 138 CL97
Fairfields Rd, Houns. TW3 96 CC83
Fairfield St, SW18 120 DB85
Fairfield Trade Pk, Kings.T.
KT1 138 CM97
Fairfield Wk, Lthd. KT22
off Fairfield Rd 171 CH121
Waltham Cross (Chsht) EN8 15 DY28
Fairfield Way, Barn. EN5 28 DA43
Coulsdon CR5 159 DK114
Epsom KT19 156 CS106
Fairfield W, Kings.T. KT1 138 CL96
Fairfolds, Wat. WD25 24 BY36
Fairfoot Rd, E3 85 EA70
Fairford Av, Bexh. DA7 107 FD81
Croydon CR0 143 DX99
Fairford Cl, Croy. CR0 143 DY99
Reigate RH2 184 DC132
Romford RM3
off Fairford Way 52 FP51
West Byfleet KT14 151 BF114
Fairford Ct, Sutt. SM2
off Grange Rd 158 DB108
Fairford Gdns, Wor.Pk. KT4 139 CT104
Fairford Ho, SE11 200 E9
Fairford Way, Rom. RM3 52 FP51
Fairgreen, Barn. EN4 28 DF41
Fairgreen E, Barn. EN4 28 DF41
Fairgreen Par, Mitch. CR4
off London Rd 140 DF97
Fairgreen Rd, Th.Hth. CR7 141 DP99
Fairham Av, S.Ock. RM15 91 FU73
Fairhaven, Egh. TW20 113 AZ92
Fairhaven Av, Croy. CR0 143 DX100
Fairhaven Cres, Wat. WD19 39 BU48
Fairhaven Rd, Red. RH1 184 DG130
Fairhazel Gdns, NW6 82 DB65
Fairholme, Felt. TW14 115 BR87
Fairholme Av, Rom. RM2 71 FG57
Fairholme Cl, N3 63 CY56
Fairholme Cres, Ashtd. KT21 171 CJ117
Hayes UB4 77 BT70
Fairholme Gdns, N3 63 CY55
Upminster RM14 73 FT59
Fairholme Rd, W14 99 CY78
Ashford TW15 114 BL92
Croydon CR0 141 DN101
Harrow HA1 61 CF57
Ilford IG1 69 EM59
Sutton SM1 157 CZ107
Fairholt Cl, N16 66 DS60
Fairholt Rd, N16 66 DR60
Fairholt St, SW7 198 C6
Fairkytes Av, Horn. RM11 72 FK60
Fairland Rd, E15 86 EF65
Fairlands Av, Buck.H. IG9 48 EG47
Sutton SM1 140 DA103
Thornton Heath CR7 141 DM98
Fairlands Ct, SE9
off North Pk 125 EN86
Fair La, Couls. CR5 184 DC125
Fairlawn, SE7 104 EJ79

★ Place of interest ≠ Railway station ⊖ London Underground station DLR Docklands Light Railway station Tra Tramlink station H Hospital Riv Pedestrian ferry landing stage

Fairlawn, Lthd. (Bkhm) KT23 ... 170 BZ124
Fairlawn Av, N2 ... 46 DE56
W4 ... 98 CQ77
Bexleyheath DA7 ... 106 EX82
Fairlawn Cl, N14 ... 29 DJ44
Esher (Clay.) KT10 ... 155 CF107
Feltham TW13 ... 116 BZ91
Kingston upon Thames KT2 ... 118 CQ93
Fairlawn Dr, Wdf.Grn. IG8 ... 48 EG52
Fairlawnes, Wall. SM6 off Maldon Rd ... 159 DH106
Fairlawn Gdns, Sthl. UB1 ... 78 BZ73
Fairlawn Gro, W4 ... 98 CQ77
Banstead SM7 ... 158 DD113
Fairlawn Pk, SE26 ... 123 DY92
Woking GU21 ... 150 AY114
Fairlawn Rd, SW19 ... 119 CZ94
Banstead SM7 ... 158 DD112
Carshalton SM5 ... 158 DC111
Fairlawns, Add. (Wdhm) KT15 ... 151 BF111
Brentwood CM14 ... 54 FU48
Pinner HA5 ... 40 BW54
Sunbury-on-Thames TW16 ... 135 BU97
Twickenham TW1 ... 117 CJ86
Watford WD17 ... 23 BT38
Weybridge KT13 ... 153 BS106
Fairlawns Cl, Horn. RM11 ... 72 FM59
Staines TW18 ... 114 BH93
Fairlead Ho, E14 off Cassilis Rd ... 103 EA76
Fairlea Pl, W5 ... 79 CK70
Fairley Way, Wal.Cr. (Chsht) EN7 ... 14 DV28
Fairlie Gdns, SE23 ... 122 DW87
Fairlight Av, E4 ... 47 ED47
NW10 ... 80 CS68
Woodford Green IG8 ... 48 EG51
Fairlight Cl, E4 ... 47 ED47
Worcester Park KT4 ... 157 CW105
Fairlight Dr, Uxb. UB8 ... 76 BK65
Fairlight Rd, SW17 ... 120 DD91
⊖ Fairlop ... 49 ER53
Fairlop Cl, Horn. RM12 ... 89 FH65
Fairlop Gdns, Ilf. IG6 ... 49 EQ52
Fairlop Rd, E11 ... 67 ED59
Ilford IG6 ... 49 EQ54
Fairmark Dr, Uxb. UB10 ... 76 BN65
Fairmead, Brom. BR1 ... 145 EM98
Surbiton KT5 ... 138 CP102
Woking GU21 ... 166 AW118
Fairmead Cl, Brom. BR1 ... 145 EM98
Hounslow TW5 ... 96 BX80
New Malden KT3 ... 138 CR97
Fairmead Cres, Edg. HA8 ... 42 CQ48
Fairmead Gdns, Ilf. IG4 ... 68 EL57
Fairmead Ho, E9 off Kingsmead Way ... 67 DY63
Fairmead Rd, N19 ... 65 DK62
Croydon CR0 ... 141 DM102
Loughton IG10 ... 32 EH42
Fairmeads, Cob. KT11 ... 154 BZ113
Loughton IG10 ... 33 EP40
Fairmead Side, Loug. IG10 ... 32 EJ43
FAIRMILE, Cob. KT11 ... 154 BZ112
Fairmile Av, SW16 ... 121 DK92
Cobham KT11 ... 154 BY114
Fairmile Ct, Cob. KT11 ... 154 BY112
Fairmile Ho, Tedd. TW11 off Twickenham Rd ... 117 CG91
Fairmile La, Cob. KT11 ... 154 BX112
Fairmile Pk Copse, Cob. KT11 ... 154 BZ112
Fairmile Pk Rd, Cob. KT11 ... 154 BZ113
Fairmont Av, E14 ... 204 F2
Fairmont Cl, Belv. DA17 ... 106 EZ78
Fairmount Rd, SW2 ... 121 DM86
Fairoak Cl, Ken. CR8 ... 175 DP115
Leatherhead (Oxshott) KT22 ... 155 CD112
Orpington BR5 ... 145 EP101
Fairoak Dr, SE9 ... 125 ER85
Fairoak Gdns, Rom. RM1 ... 51 FE54
Fairoak La, Chess. KT9 ... 155 CF111
Leatherhead (Oxshott) KT22 ... 155 CF111
Fairseat Cl, Bushey (Bushey Hth) WD23 off Hive Rd ... 41 CE47
Fairs Rd, Lthd. KT22 ... 171 CG119
Fairstead Wk, N1 off Popham Rd ... 84 DQ67
Fair St, SE1 ... 201 N4
Hounslow TW3 off High St ... 96 CC83
Fairthorn Rd, SE7 ... 205 N10
Fairtrough Rd, Orp. BR6 ... 164 EV112
Fairview, Epsom KT17 ... 157 CW111
Erith DA8 off Guild Rd ... 107 FF80
Potters Bar EN6 off Hawkshead Rd ... 12 DB29
Fairview Av, Brwd. (Hutt.) CM13 ... 55 GE45
Rainham RM13 ... 90 FK68
Wembley HA0 ... 79 CK65
Woking GU22 ... 166 AY118
Fairview Cl, E17 ... 47 DY53
Chigwell IG7 ... 49 ES49
Woking GU22 off Fairview Av ... 167 AZ118
Fairview Ct, Ashf. TW15 ... 114 BN92
Fairview Cres, Har. HA2 ... 60 CA60
Fairview Dr, Chig. IG7 ... 49 ES49
Orpington BR6 ... 163 ER105
Shepperton TW17 ... 134 BM99
Watford WD17 ... 23 BS36
Fairview Gdns, Wdf.Grn. IG8 ... 48 EH53
Fairview Ind Est, Oxt. RH8 ... 188 EG133
Fairview Ind Pk, Rain. RM13 ... 89 FD71
Fairview Pl, SW2 ... 121 DM87
Fairview Rd, N15 ... 66 DT57
SW16 ... 141 DM95
Chigwell IG7 ... 49 ES49
Enfield EN2 ... 29 DN39
Epsom KT17 ... 157 CT111
Gravesend (Istead Rise) DA13 ... 130 GD94
Sutton SM1 ... 158 DD106
Fairview Way, Edg. HA8 ... 42 CN49
Fairwater Av, Well. DA16 ... 106 EU84
Fairwater Dr, Add. (New Haw) KT15 ... 152 BK109
Fairway, SW20 ... 139 CW97
Bexleyheath DA6 ... 126 EY85
Carshalton SM5 ... 158 DC111
Chertsey KT16 ... 134 BH102
Orpington BR5 ... 145 ER99
Virginia Water GU25 ... 132 AV100
Woodford Green IG8 ... 48 EJ50
Fairway, The, N13 ... 46 DQ48
N14 ... 29 DH44
NW7 ... 42 CR48
W3 ... 80 CS72
Abbots Langley WD5 ... 7 BR32
Barnet EN5 ... 28 DB44
Bromley BR1 ... 145 EM99
Gravesend DA11 ... 131 GG89
Leatherhead KT22 ... 171 CG118
New Malden KT3 ... 138 CR95
Northolt UB5 ... 78 CC65
Northwood HA6 ... 39 BS49
Ruislip HA4 ... 60 BX62
Upminster RM14 ... 72 FQ59
Uxbridge UB10 ... 76 BM68
Wembley HA0 ... 61 CH62
West Molesey KT8 ... 136 CB97
Weybridge KT13 ... 152 BN111
Fairway Av, NW9 ... 62 CP55
Borehamwood WD6 ... 26 CP40
West Drayton UB7 ... 76 BJ74
Fairway Cl, NW11 ... 64 DC59
Croydon CR0 ... 143 DY99
Epsom KT19 ... 156 CQ105
Hounslow TW4 ... 116 BW85
St. Albans (Park St) AL2 ... 8 CC27
West Drayton UB7 off Fairway Av ... 76 BK74
Woking GU22 ... 166 AU119
Fairway Ct, NW7 off The Fairway ... 42 CR48
Fairway Dr, SE28 ... 88 EX72
Dartford DA2 ... 128 FP87
Greenford UB6 ... 78 CB66
Fairway Gdns, Beck. BR3 ... 143 ED100
Ilford IG1 ... 69 EQ64
Fairways, Ashf. TW15 ... 115 BP93
Kenley CR8 ... 176 DQ117
Stanmore HA7 ... 42 CL54
Teddington TW11 ... 117 CK94
Waltham Abbey EN9 ... 16 EE34
Fairways, The, Wal.Cr. (Chsht) EN8 ... 15 DX26
Fairweather Cl, N15 ... 66 DS56
Fairweather Rd, N16 ... 66 DU58
Fairwyn Rd, SE26 ... 123 DY91
Fakenham Cl, NW7 ... 43 CU52
Northolt UB5 off Goodwood Dr ... 78 CA65
Fakruddin St, E1 ... 84 DU70
Falaise, Egh. TW20 ... 112 AY92
Falcon Av, Brom. BR1 ... 144 EL98
Grays RM17 ... 110 GB79
Falconberg Ct, W1 ... 195 N8
Falconberg Ms, W1 ... 195 M8
Falcon Cl, W4 off Sutton La S ... 98 CQ79
Dartford DA1 ... 128 FM85
Northwood HA6 ... 39 BS52
Waltham Abbey EN9 off Kestrel Rd ... 16 EG34
Falcon Ct, EC4 ... 196 D9
Woking GU21 ... 151 BC113
Falcon Cres, Enf. EN3 ... 31 DX43
Falcon Dr, Stai. (Stanw.) TW19 ... 114 BK86
Falconer Rd, Bushey WD23 ... 24 BZ44
Ilford IG6 ... 50 EV50
Falconer Wk, N7 off Newington Barrow Way ... 65 DM61
Falcon Gro, SW11 ... 100 DE83
Falcon Ho, W13 ... 79 CF70
Falconhurst, Lthd. (Oxshott) KT22 ... 171 CD115
Falcon La, SW11 ... 100 DE83
Falcon Ms, Grav. DA11 ... 130 GE88
Falcon Pk Ind Est, NW10 ... 63 CT64
Falcon Rd, SW11 ... 100 DE82
Enfield EN3 ... 31 DX43
Hampton TW12 ... 116 BZ94
Falcons Cl, West. (Bigg.H.) TN16 ... 178 EK117
Falcon St, E13 ... 86 EG70
Falcon Ter, SW11 ... 100 DE83
Falcon Way, E11 ... 68 EG56
E14 ... 204 C8
NW9 ... 42 CS54
Feltham TW14 ... 115 BV85
Harrow HA3 ... 62 CL57
Hornchurch RM12 ... 89 FG66
Sunbury-on-Thames TW16 ... 135 BS96
Watford WD25 ... 8 BY34
FALCONWOOD, Well. DA16 ... 105 ER83
⇌ Falconwood ... 105 EQ84
Falconwood, SE9 off Rochester Way Relief Rd ... 105 ER84
Egham TW20 ... 112 AY92
Leatherhead KT24 ... 171 CF120
Falconwood Av, Well. DA16 ... 105 ER82
Falconwood Par, Well. DA16 ... 105 ES84
Falconwood Rd, Croy. CR0 ... 161 EA108
Falcourt Cl, Sutt. SM1 ... 158 DB106
Falkirk Cl, Horn. RM11 ... 72 FN60
Falkirk Gdns, Wat. WD19 off Blackford Rd ... 40 BX50
Falkirk Ho, W9 ... 82 DB69
Falkirk St, N1 ... 197 N1
Falkland Av, N3 ... 44 DA52
N11 ... 44 DG49
Falkland Pk Av, SE25 ... 142 DS97
Falkland Pl, NW5 off Falkland Rd ... 65 DJ64
Falkland Rd, N8 ... 65 DN56
NW5 ... 65 DJ64
Barnet EN5 ... 27 CY40
Fallaize Av, Ilf. IG1 off Riverdene Rd ... 69 EP63
Falling La, West Dr. UB7 ... 76 BL73
Falloden Way, NW11 ... 64 DA56
Fallow Cl, Chig. IG7 ... 49 ET50
Fallow Ct, SE16 off Argyle Way ... 102 DU78
Fallow Ct Av, N12 ... 44 DC52
Fallowfield, Dart. (Bean) DA2 ... 129 FV90
Stanmore HA7 ... 41 CG48
Fallowfield Cl, Uxb. (Hare.) UB9 ... 38 BJ53
Fallowfield Ct, Stan. HA7 ... 41 CG48
Fallow Flds, Loug. IG10 ... 48 EJ45
Fallowfields Dr, N12 ... 44 DE51
Fallows Cl, N2 ... 44 DC54
Fallsbrook Rd, SW16 ... 121 DJ94
Falman Cl, N9 off Croyland Rd ... 46 DU46
Falmer Rd, E17 ... 67 EB55
N15 ... 66 DQ57
Enfield EN1 ... 30 DS42
Falmouth Av, E4 ... 47 ED50
Falmouth Cl, N22 ... 45 DM52
SE12 ... 124 EF85
Falmouth Gdns, Ilf. IG4 ... 68 EL57
Falmouth Ho, Kings.T. KT2 off Kingsgate Rd ... 137 CK95
Falmouth Rd, SE1 ... 201 J6
Walton-on-Thames KT12 ... 154 BW105
Falmouth St, E15 ... 67 ED64
Falmouth Way, E17 off Gosport Rd ... 67 DZ57
Falstaff Cl, Dart. DA1 ... 127 FE87
Falstaff Ms, Hmptn. (Hmptn H.) TW12 off Hampton Rd ... 117 CD92
Falstone, Wok. GU21 ... 166 AV118
Fambridge Cl, SE26 ... 123 DZ91
Fambridge Rd, Dag. RM8 ... 70 FA60
Famet Av, Pur. CR8 ... 160 DQ113
Famet Cl, Pur. CR8 ... 160 DQ113
Famet Wk, Pur. CR8 ... 160 DQ113
★ Family Records Cen, Public Record Office, EC1 ... 196 E3
Fane St, W14 off North End Rd ... 99 CZ79
Fangrove Pk, Cher. (Lyne) KT16 ... 133 BB102
★ Fan Mus, SE10 ... 103 EC80
Fanns Ri, Purf. RM19 ... 108 FN77
Fann St, EC1 ... 197 H5
EC2 ... 197 H5
Fanshawe Av, Bark. IG11 ... 87 EQ65
Fanshawe Cres, Dag. RM9 ... 70 EY64
Hornchurch RM11 ... 72 FK58
Fanshawe Rd, Grays RM16 ... 111 GG76
Richmond TW10 ... 117 CJ91
Fanshaw St, N1 ... 197 M2
Fantasia Ct, Brwd. (Warley) CM14 ... 54 FV50
Fanthorpe St, SW15 ... 99 CW83
Faraday Av, Sid. DA14 ... 126 EU89
Faraday Cl, N7 off Bride St ... 83 DM65
Watford WD18 ... 23 BR44
Faraday Lo, SE10 off Renaissance Wk ... 104 EF76
★ Faraday Mus, W1 ... 199 K1
Faraday Pl, W.Mol. KT8 ... 136 CA98
Faraday Rd, E15 ... 86 EF65
SW19 ... 120 DA93
W3 ... 80 CQ73
W10 ... 81 CY71
Southall UB1 ... 78 CB73
Welling DA16 ... 106 EU83
West Molesey KT8 ... 136 CA98
Faraday Way, SE18 ... 104 EK76
Croydon CR0 off Ampere Way ... 141 DM102
Orpington BR5 ... 146 EV98
Fareham Rd, Felt. TW14 ... 116 BW87
Fareham St, W1 ... 195 M8
Farewell Pl, Mitch. CR4 ... 140 DE95
Faringdon Av, Brom. BR2 ... 145 EP100
Romford RM3 ... 52 FJ53
Faringford Cl, Pot.B. EN6 ... 12 DD31
Faringford Rd, E15 ... 86 EE66
Farington Acres, Wey. KT13 ... 135 BR104
Faris Barn Dr, Add. (Wdhm) KT15 ... 151 BF112
Faris La, Add. (Wdhm) KT15 ... 151 BF111
Farjeon Rd, SE3 ... 104 EK81
FARLEIGH, Warl. CR6 ... 161 DZ114
Farleigh Av, Brom. BR2 ... 144 EF100
Farleigh Border, Croy. CR0 ... 161 DY112
Farleigh Ct Rd, Warl. CR6 ... 161 DZ114
Farleigh Dean Cres, Croy. CR0 ... 161 EB111
Farleigh Pl, N16 off Farleigh Rd ... 66 DT63
Farleigh Rd, N16 ... 66 DT63
Addlestone (New Haw) KT15 ... 152 BG111
Warlingham CR6 ... 177 DX118
Farleton Cl, Wey. KT13 ... 153 BR107
Farley Common, West. TN16 ... 189 EP126
Farleycroft, West. TN16 ... 189 EQ126
Farley Dr, Ilf. IG3 ... 69 ES60
Farley La, West. TN16 ... 189 EP127
Farley Ms, SE6 ... 123 EC87
Farley Nurs, West. TN16 ... 189 EQ127
Farley Pk, Oxt. RH8 ... 187 ED130
Farley Pl, SE25 ... 142 DU98
Farley Rd, SE6 ... 123 EB87
Gravesend DA12 ... 131 GM88
South Croydon CR2 ... 160 DV108
Farlington Pl, SW15 off Roehampton La ... 119 CV87
Farlow Cl, Grav. (Nthflt) DA11 ... 131 GF90
Farlow Rd, SW15 ... 99 CX83
Farlton Rd, SW18 ... 120 DB87
Farman Gro, Nthlt. UB5 off Wayfarer Rd ... 78 BX69
Farm Av, NW2 ... 63 CY62
SW16 ... 121 DL91
Harrow HA2 ... 60 BZ59
Swanley BR8 ... 147 FC97
Wembley HA0 ... 79 CJ65
Farmborough Cl, Har. HA1 off Pool Rd ... 61 CD59
Farm Cl, SW6 off Farm La ... 100 DA80
Amersham HP6 ... 20 AX39
Barnet EN5 ... 27 CW43
Borehamwood WD6 ... 25 CK38
Brentwood (Hutt.) CM13 ... 55 GC45
Buckhurst Hill IG9 ... 48 EJ48
Chertsey (Lyne) KT16 ... 133 BA100
Coulsdon (Chipstead) CR5 ... 174 DF120
Dagenham RM10 ... 89 FC66
Leatherhead (Fetch.) KT22 ... 171 CD124
Potters Bar (Cuffley) EN6 ... 13 DK27
Radlett WD7 ... 10 CL30
Farm Cl, Shep. TW17 ... 134 BN101
Southall UB1 ... 78 CB73
Staines TW18 ... 113 BE92
Sutton SM2 ... 158 DD108
Uxbridge UB10 ... 59 BP61
Wallington SM6 ... 159 DJ110
Waltham Cross (Chsht) EN8 ... 14 DW30
West Byfleet (Byfleet) KT14 ... 152 BM112
West Wickham BR4 ... 144 EE104
Farmcote Rd, SE12 ... 124 EG88
Farm Ct, NW4 ... 63 CU55
Farm Cres, St.Alb. (Lon.Col.) AL2 ... 9 CG26
Slough SL2 ... 74 AV71
Farmcroft, Grav. DA11 ... 131 GG89
Farmdale Rd, SE10 ... 205 N10
Carshalton SM5 ... 158 DE108
Farm Dr, Croy. CR0 ... 143 DZ103
Purley CR8 ... 159 DK112
Farm End, E4 ... 32 EE43
Northwood HA6 off Drakes Dr ... 39 BP53
Farmer Rd, E10 ... 67 EB60
Farmers Cl, Wat. WD25 ... 7 BV33
Farmers Ct, Wal.Abb. EN9 off Winters Way ... 16 EG33
Farmers Rd, SE5 ... 101 DP80
Staines TW18 ... 113 BE92
Farmer St, W8 off Uxbridge St ... 82 DA74
Farm Fld, Wat. WD17 ... 23 BS38
Farmfield Rd, Brom. BR1 ... 124 EE92
Farm Flds, S.Croy. CR2 ... 160 DS111
Farm Hill Rd, Wal.Abb. EN9 ... 15 EC34
Farm Ho Cl, Brox. EN10 ... 15 DZ25
Farmhouse Cl, Wok. GU22 ... 167 BD115
Farmhouse Rd, SW16 ... 121 DJ94
Farmilo Rd, E17 ... 67 DZ59
Farmington Av, Sutt. SM1 ... 140 DD104
Farmlands, Enf. EN2 ... 29 DN39
Pinner HA5 ... 59 BU56
Farmlands, The, Nthlt. UB5 ... 78 BZ65
Farmland Wk, Chis. BR7 ... 125 EP92
Farm La, N14 ... 28 DG44
SW6 ... 100 DA79
Addlestone KT15 ... 152 BG107
Ashtead KT21 ... 172 CN116
Carshalton SM5 ... 158 DF110
Croydon CR0 ... 143 DZ103
Epsom KT18 ... 172 CP119
Purley CR8 ... 159 DJ110
Rickmansworth (Loud.) WD3 ... 22 BH41
Woking (Send) GU23 ... 167 BC124
Farm La Trd Cen, SW6 off Farm La ... 100 DA79
Farmleigh, N14 ... 45 DJ45
Farmleigh Gro, Walt. KT12 ... 153 BT106
Farm Pl, W8 off Uxbridge St ... 82 DA74
Dartford DA1 ... 107 FG84
Farm Rd, N21 ... 45 DP46
NW10 ... 80 CR67
Edgware HA8 ... 42 CP51
Esher KT10 ... 136 CB102
Grays (Orsett) RM16 ... 111 GF75
Hounslow TW4 ... 116 BY88
Morden SM4 ... 140 DB99
Northwood HA6 ... 39 BQ50
Rainham RM13 ... 90 FJ69
Rickmansworth (Chorl.) WD3 ... 21 BA42
Sevenoaks TN14 ... 191 FJ121
Staines TW18 ... 114 BH93
Sutton SM2 ... 158 DD108
Warlingham CR6 ... 177 DY119
Woking GU22 ... 167 BB120
Farmstead Rd, SE6 ... 123 EB91
Harrow HA3 ... 41 CD53
Farm St, W1 ... 199 H1
Farm Vale, Bex. DA5 ... 127 FB86
Farmview, Cob. KT11 ... 170 BX116
Farm Vw, Tad. (Lwr Kgswd) KT20 ... 183 CZ127
Farm Wk, NW11 ... 63 CZ57
Farm Way, Buck.H. IG9 ... 48 EJ49
Bushey WD23 ... 24 CB42
Farmway, Dag. RM8 ... 70 EW63
Farm Way, Horn. RM12 ... 71 FH63
Northwood HA6 ... 39 BS49
Staines TW19 ... 113 BF86
Worcester Park KT4 ... 139 CW104
Farnaby Dr, Sev. TN13 ... 190 FF126
Farnaby Rd, SE9 ... 104 EJ84
Bromley BR1, BR2 ... 123 ED94
Farnan Av, E17 ... 47 EA54
Farnan Rd, SW16 ... 121 DL92
FARNBOROUGH, Orp. BR6 ... 163 EP106
Farnborough Av, E17 ... 67 DY55
South Croydon CR2 ... 161 DX108
Farnborough Cl, Wem. HA9 ... 62 CP61
Farnborough Common, Orp. BR6 ... 145 EM104
Farnborough Cres, Brom. BR2 off Saville Row ... 144 EF102
South Croydon CR2 ... 161 DY109
Farnborough Hill, Orp. BR6 ... 163 ER106
Farnborough Ho, SW15 off Fontley Way ... 119 CU88
Farnborough Way, Orp. BR6 ... 163 EQ105
Farncombe St, SE16 ... 202 C5
Farndale Av, N13 ... 45 DP48
Farndale Cres, Grnf. UB6 ... 78 CC69
Farnell Ms, SW5 off Earls Ct Sq ... 100 DB78
Farnell Pl, W3 ... 80 CP73
Farnell Rd, Islw. TW7 ... 97 CD83
Staines TW18 ... 114 BG90
Farnes Dr, Rom. RM2 ... 52 FJ54
Farnham Cl, N20 ... 44 DC45
Hemel Hempstead (Bov.) HP3 ... 5 BA28
Farnham Gdns, SW20 ... 139 CV96
Farnham Pl, SE1 ... 200 G3
Farnham Rd, Ilf. IG3 ... 69 ET59
Romford RM3 ... 52 FK50
Welling DA16 ... 106 EW82
Farnham Royal, SE11 off Kennington La ... 101 DM78
FARNINGHAM, Dart. DA4 ... 148 FN100
Farningham Cres, Cat. CR3 off Commonwealth Rd ... 176 DU123
Farningham Hill Rd, Dart. (Fnghm) DA4 ... 148 FJ99
⇌ Farningham Road ... 148 FP96
Farningham Rd, N17 ... 46 DU52
Caterham CR3 ... 176 DU123
Farnley, Wok. GU21 ... 166 AT117
Farnley Rd, E4 ... 48 EE45
SE25 ... 142 DR98
Farnol Rd, Dart. DA1 ... 108 FN84
Farnsworth Ct, SE10 off West Parkside ... 104 EF76
Faro Cl, Brom. BR1 ... 145 EN96
Faroe Rd, W14 ... 99 CX76
Faroma Wk, Enf. EN2 ... 29 DN39
Farquhar Rd, SE19 ... 122 DT92
SW19 ... 120 DA90
Farquharson Rd, Croy. CR0 ... 142 DQ102
Farraline Rd, Wat. WD18 ... 23 BV42
Farrance Rd, Rom. RM6 ... 70 EY58
Farrance St, E14 ... 85 DZ72
Farrans Ct, Har. HA3 ... 61 CH59
Farrant Av, N22 ... 45 DN54
Farrant Cl, Orp. BR6 ... 164 EU108
Farrant Way, Borwd. WD6 ... 26 CL39
Farr Av, Bark. IG11 ... 88 EU68
Farrell Ho, E1 ... 84 DW72
Farren Rd, SE23 ... 123 DY89
Farrer Ms, N8 off Farrer Rd ... 65 DJ56
Farrer Rd, N8 ... 65 DJ56
Harrow HA3 ... 62 CL57
Farrer's Pl, Croy. CR0 ... 161 DX105
Farrier Cl, Sun. TW16 ... 135 BU98
Uxbridge UB8 off Horseshoe Dr ... 76 BN72
Farrier Pl, Sutt. SM1 ... 140 DA104
Farrier Rd, Nthlt. UB5 ... 78 CA68
Farriers Cl, Epsom KT17 ... 156 CS111
Gravesend DA12 ... 131 GM88
Hemel Hempstead (Bov.) HP3 off Chipperfield Rd ... 5 BB28
Farriers Ct, Sutt. SM3 off Forge La ... 157 CY108
Watford WD25 ... 7 BV32
Farriers End, Brox. EN10 ... 15 DZ26
Farriers Ms, SE15 off Machell Rd ... 102 DW83
Farriers Rd, Epsom KT17 ... 156 CS112
Farrier St, NW1 ... 83 DH66
Farriers Way, Borwd. WD6 ... 26 CQ44
Farrier Wk, SW10 ... 100 DC79
⇌ Farringdon ... 196 E6
⊖ Farringdon ... 196 E6
Farringdon La, EC1 ... 196 E5
Farringdon Rd, EC1 ... 196 D4
Farringdon St, EC4 ... 196 F8
Farringford Cl, St.Alb. AL2 ... 8 CA26
Farrington Av, Orp. BR5 ... 146 EV97
Farrington Pl, Chis. BR7 ... 125 ER94
Northwood HA6 ... 39 BT49
Farrins Rents, SE16 ... 203 K3
Farrow La, SE14 ... 102 DW80
Farrow Pl, SE16 ... 203 K6
Farr Rd, Enf. EN2 ... 30 DR39
Farthingale Ct, Wal.Abb. EN9 ... 16 EG34
Farthingale La, Wal.Abb. EN9 ... 16 EG34
Farthingale Wk, E15 ... 85 ED66
Farthing All, SE1 ... 202 B5
Farthing Cl, Dart. DA1 ... 108 FM84
Watford WD18 ... 24 BW43
Farthing Ct, NW7 ... 43 CY52
Farthing Flds, E1 ... 202 E2
Farthing Grn La, Slou. (Stoke P.) SL2 ... 74 AU68
Farthings, Wok. (Knap.) GU21 ... 166 AS116
Farthings, The, Kings.T. KT2 off Brunswick Rd ... 138 CN95
Farthings Cl, E4 ... 48 EE48
Pinner HA5 ... 59 BV58
Farthing St, Orp. BR6 ... 163 EM108
Farwell Rd, Sid. DA14 ... 126 EV90
Farwig La, Brom. BR1 ... 144 EF95
Fashion St, E1 ... 197 P7
Fashoda Rd, Brom. BR2 ... 144 EK98
Fassett Rd, E8 ... 84 DU65
Kingston upon Thames KT1 ... 138 CL98
Fassett Sq, E8 ... 84 DU65
Fassnidge Way, Uxb. UB8 off Oxford Rd ... 76 BJ66
Fauconberg Rd, W4 ... 98 CQ79
Faulkner Cl, Dag. RM8 ... 70 EX59
Faulkner's All, EC1 ... 196 F6
Faulkners Rd, Walt. KT12 ... 154 BW106
Faulkner St, SE14 ... 102 DW81
Fauna Cl, Rom. RM6 ... 70 EW59
Faunce St, SE17 off Harmsworth St ... 101 DP78
Favart Rd, SW6 ... 100 DA81
Faverolle Grn, Wal.Cr. EN8 ... 15 DX28
Faversham Av, E4 ... 48 EE46
Enfield EN1 ... 30 DR44
Faversham Cl, Chig. IG7 ... 50 EV47
Faversham Rd, SE6 ... 123 DZ87
Beckenham BR3 ... 143 DZ96
Morden SM4 ... 140 DB100
Fawcett Cl, SW11 ... 100 DD82
SW16 ... 121 DN91
Fawcett Est, E5 ... 66 DU60
Fawcett Rd, NW10 ... 81 CT67
Croydon CR0 ... 142 DQ104
Fawcett St, SW10 ... 100 DC79
Fawcus Cl, Esher (Clay.) KT10 off Dalmore Av ... 155 CF107
Fawe Pk Rd, SW15 ... 99 CZ84
Fawe St, E14 ... 85 EB71
Fawke Common, Sev. (Undrvr) TN15 ... 191 FP127
Fawke Common Rd, Sev. TN15 ... 191 FP126
Fawkes Av, Dart. DA1 ... 128 FM89
FAWKHAM GREEN, Long. DA3 ... 149 FV104
Fawkham Grn Rd, Long. (Fawk.Grn) DA3 ... 149 FV104
Fawkham Ho, SE1 off Longfield Est ... 102 DT77
H Fawkham Manor Hosp, Long. DA3 ... 149 FW102
Fawkham Rd, Long. DA3 ... 149 FX97
Fawley Rd, NW6 ... 64 DB64
Fawnbrake Av, SE24 ... 121 DP85
Fawn Rd, E13 ... 86 EJ68
Chigwell IG7 ... 49 ET50
Fawns Manor Cl, Felt. TW14 ... 115 BQ88

★ Place of interest ⇌ Railway station ⊖ London Underground station DLR Docklands Light Railway station Tra Tramlink station H Hospital Riv Pedestrian ferry landing stage

Fawns Manor Rd, Felt. TW14 115 BR88
Fawood Av, NW10 80 CR66
Fawsley Cl, Slou. (Colnbr.)
SL3 93 BE80
Fawters Cl, Brwd. (Hutt.)
CM13 55 GD44
Fayerfield, Pot.B. EN6 12 DD31
Faygate Cres, Bexh. DA6 126 FA85
Faygate Rd, SW2 121 DM89
Fay Grn, Abb.L. WD5 7 BR33
Fayland Av, SW16 121 DJ92
Faymore Gdns, S.Ock. RM15 91 FU72
Fearney Mead, Rick. (Mill End)
WD3 38 BG46
Fearnley Cres, Hmptn. TW12 116 BY92
Fearnley St, Wat. WD18 23 BV42
Fearns Mead, Brwd. CM14
off Bucklers Ct 54 FW50
Fearon St, SE10 205 M10
Featherbed La, Abb.L. (Bedmond)
WD5 off Sergehill La 7 BV26
Croydon CR0 161 DZ108
Romford RM4 50 EY45
Warlingham CR6 161 ED113
Feathers La, Stai. (Wrays.)
TW19 113 BA89
Feathers Pl, SE10 103 ED79
Featherstone Av, SE23 122 DV89
Featherstone Gdns, Borwd.
WD6 26 CQ42
Featherstone Ind Est, Sthl.
UB2 96 BY75
Featherstone Rd, NW7 43 CV51
Southall UB2 96 BY76
Featherstone St, EC1 197 K4
Featherstone Ter, Sthl. UB2 96 BY76
Featley Rd, SW9 101 DP83
Federal Rd, Grnf. UB6 79 CJ68
Federal Way, Wat. WD24 24 BW38
Federation Rd, SE2 106 EV77
Fee Fm Rd, Esher (Clay.)
KT10 155 CF108
Feenan Highway, Til. RM18 111 GH80
Feeny Cl, NW10
off Sonia Gdns 63 CT63
Felbridge Av, Stan. HA7 41 CG53
Felbridge Cl, SW16 121 DN91
Sutton SM2 158 DC109
Felbrigge Rd, Ilf. IG3 69 ET61
Felcott Cl, Walt. KT12 136 BW104
Felcott Rd, Walt. KT12 136 BW104
Felday Rd, SE13 123 EB86
Felden Cl, Pnr. HA5 40 BY52
Watford WD25 8 BX34
Felden St, SW6 99 CZ81
Feldman Cl, N16 66 DU60
Felgate Ms, W6 99 CV77
Felhampton Rd, SE9 125 EP89
Felhurst Cres, Dag. RM10 71 FB63
Felicia Way, Grays RM16 111 GH77
Felipe Rd, Grays (Chaff.Hun.)
RM16 109 FW76
Felix Av, N8 65 DL58
Felix La, Shep. TW17 135 BS100
Felix Pl, SW2 off Talma Rd 121 DN85
Felix Rd, W13 79 CG73
Walton-on-Thames KT12 135 BU100
Felixstowe Ct, E16
off Fishguard Way 87 EP74
Felixstowe Rd, N9 46 DU49
N17 66 DT55
NW10 81 CV69
SE2 106 EV76
Fellbrigg Rd, SE22 122 DT85
Fellbrigg St, E1
off Headlam St 84 DV70
Fellbrook, Rich. TW10 117 CH90
Fellmongers Path, SE1 201 N5
Fellmongers Yd, Croy. CR0
off Surrey St 142 DQ103
Fellowes Cl, Hayes UB4
off Paddington Cl 78 BX70
Fellowes Rd, Cars. SM5 140 DE104
Fellows Ct, E2 197 P1
Fellows Rd, NW3 82 DD66
Fell Rd, Croy. CR0 142 DQ104
Felltram Ms, SE7
off Woolwich Rd 104 EG78
Felltram Way, SE7 205 N10
Fell Wk, Edg. HA8
off East Rd 42 CP53
Felmersham Cl, SW4
off Haselrigge Rd 101 DK84
Felmingham Rd, SE20 142 DW96
Felnex Trd Est, Wall. SM6 140 DG103
Felsberg Rd, SW2 121 DL86
Fels Cl, Dag. RM10 71 FB62
Fels Fm Av, Dag. RM10 71 FC62
Felsham Rd, SW15 99 CX83
Felspar Cl, SE18 105 ET78
Felstead Av, Ilf. IG5 49 EN53
Felstead Cl, Brwd. (Hutt.)
CM13 55 GC44
Felstead Gdns, E14
off Ferry St 103 EC78
Felstead Rd, E11 68 EG59
Epsom KT19 156 CR111
Loughton IG10 48 EL45
Orpington BR6 146 EU103
Romford RM5 51 FC51
Waltham Cross EN8 15 DY32
Felstead St, E9 85 DZ65
Felsted Rd, E16 86 EK72
FELTHAM, TW13 & TW14 115 BU89
⇌ Feltham 115 BV88
Feltham Av, E.Mol. KT8 137 CE98
Felthambrook Way, Felt.
TW13 115 BV90
Feltham Business Complex,
Felt. TW13 115 BV89
FELTHAMHILL, Felt. TW13 115 BT92
Feltham Hill Rd, Ashf. TW15 115 BP92
Feltham Rd, Ashf. TW15 115 BP91
Mitcham CR4 140 DF96
Felton Cl, Borwd. WD6 26 CL38
Broxbourne EN10 15 DZ25
Orpington BR5 145 EP100
Felton Gdns, Bark. IG11
off Sutton Rd 87 ES67
Felton Ho, SE3 off Ryan Cl 104 EH84
Felton Lea, Sid. DA14 125 ET92
Felton Rd, W13
off Camborne Av 97 CJ75
Felton Rd, Bark. IG11
off Sutton Rd 87 ES68
Felton St, N1 84 DR67
Fencepiece Rd, Chig. IG7 49 EQ50
Ilford IG6 49 EQ50
Fenchurch Av, EC3 197 M9
Fenchurch Bldgs, EC3 197 N9
Fenchurch Pl, EC3 197 N10
⇌ Fenchurch Street 197 N10
Fenchurch St, EC3 197 M10
Fen Cl, Brwd. (Shenf.) CM15 55 GC42
Fen Ct, EC3 197 M10
Fendall Rd, Epsom KT19 156 CQ106
Fendall St, SE1 201 N7
Fendt Cl, E16 off Bowman Av 86 EF73
Fendyke Rd, Belv. DA17 106 EX76
Fenelon Pl, W14 99 CZ77
Fengates Rd, Red. RH1 184 DE134
Fen Gro, Sid. DA15 125 ET86
Fenham Rd, SE15 102 DU80
Fen La, SW13
off Queen Elizabeth Wk 99 CV81
Upminster (N.Ock.) RM14 73 FW64
Fenman Ct, N17
off Shelbourne Rd 46 DV53
Fenman Gdns, Ilf. IG3 70 EV60
Fenn Cl, Brom. BR1 124 EG93
Fennel Cl, E16
off Cranberry La 86 EE70
Croydon CR0
off Primrose La 143 DX102
Fennells Mead, Epsom KT17 157 CT109
Fennel St, SE18 105 EN79
Fenner Cl, SE16 202 E8
Fenner Ho, Walt. KT12 153 BU105
Fenner Rd, Grays RM16 109 FW77
Fenners Marsh, Grav. DA12 131 GM88
Fenner Sq, SW11
off Thomas Baines Rd 100 DD83
Fenning St, SE1 201 M4
Fenn St, E9 66 DW64
Fenns Way, Wok. GU21 166 AY115
Fenstanton Av, N12 44 DD50
Fen St, E16
off Huntingdon St 86 EF73
Fens Way, Swan. BR8 127 FG93
Fenswood Cl, Bex. DA5 126 FA85
Fentiman Rd, SW8 101 DL79
Fentiman Way, Har. HA2 60 CB61
Hornchurch RM11 72 FL60
Fenton Av, Stai. TW18 114 BJ93
Fenton Cl, E8 off Laurel St 84 DT65
SW9 101 DM82
Chislehurst BR7 125 EM92
Redhill RH1 184 DG134
★ Fenton Ho, NW3 64 DC62
Fenton Rd, N17 46 DQ52
Grays (Chaff.Hun.) RM16 110 FY75
Redhill RH1 184 DG134
Fentons Av, E13 86 EH68
Fenwick Cl, SE18
off Ritter St 105 EN79
Woking GU21 166 AV118
Fenwick Gro, SE15 102 DU83
Fenwick Path, Borwd. WD6 26 CM38
Fenwick Pl, SW9 101 DL83
South Croydon CR2
off Columbine Av 159 DP108
Fenwick Rd, SE15 102 DU83
Ferdinand Pl, NW1
off Ferdinand St 82 DG66
Ferdinand St, NW1 82 DG65
Ferguson Av, Grav. DA12 131 GJ91
Romford RM2 52 FJ54
Surbiton KT5 138 CM99
Ferguson Cl, E14 203 P9
Bromley BR2 143 EC97
Ferguson Ct, Rom. RM2 52 FK54
Ferguson Dr, W3 80 CR72
Fergus Rd, N5
off Calabria Rd 65 DP64
Ferme Pk Rd, N4 65 DL57
N8 65 DL57
Fermor Rd, SE23 123 DY88
Fermoy Rd, W9 81 CZ70
Greenford UB6 78 CB70
Fern Av, Mitch. CR4 141 DK98
Fernbank, Buck.H. IG9 48 EH46
Fernbank Av, Horn. RM12 72 FJ63
Walton-on-Thames KT12 136 BY101
Wembley HA0 61 CF63
Fernbank Ms, SW12 121 DJ86
Fernbank Rd, Add. KT15 152 BG106
Fernbrook Av, Sid. DA15
off Blackfen Rd 125 ES85
Fernbrook Cres, SE13 124 EE86
Fernbrook Dr, Har. HA2 60 CB59
Fernbrook Rd, SE13 124 EE86
Ferncliff Rd, E8 66 DU64
Fern Cl, N1 off Ivy St 84 DS68
Erith DA8
off Hollywood Way 107 FH81
Warlingham CR6 177 DY118
Ferncroft Av, N12 44 DE51
NW3 64 DA62
Ruislip HA4 60 BW61
Ferndale, Brom. BR1 144 EJ96
Ferndale Av, E17 67 ED57
Chertsey KT16 133 BE104
Hounslow TW4 96 BY83
Ferndale Cl, Bexh. DA7 106 EY81
Ferndale Ct, SE3 104 EF80
Ferndale Cres, Uxb. UB8 76 BJ69
Ferndale Rd, E7 86 EH66
E11 68 EE61
N15 66 DT58
SE25 142 DV99
SW4 101 DL84
SW9 101 DM83
Ashford TW15 114 BK92
Banstead SM7 173 CZ116
Enfield EN3 31 DY37
Gravesend DA12 131 GH89
Romford RM5 51 FC54
Woking GU21 167 AZ116
Ferndale St, E6 87 EP73
Ferndale Ter, Har. HA1 61 CF56
Ferndale Way, Orp. BR6 163 ER106
Ferndell Av, Bex. DA5 127 FD90
Fern Dene, W13
off Templewood 79 CH71
Ferndene, St.Alb. (Brick.Wd)
AL2 8 BZ31
Ferndene Rd, SE24 102 DQ84
Fernden Way, Rom. RM7 71 FB58
Ferndown, Horn. RM11 72 FM58
Northwood HA6 39 BU54
Ferndown Av, Orp. BR6 145 ER102
Ferndown Cl, Pnr. HA5 40 BY52
Sutton SM2 158 DD107
Ferndown Gdns, Cob. KT11 154 BW113
Ferndown Rd, SE9 124 EK87
Watford WD19 40 BW48
Fernery, The, Stai. TW18 113 BE92
Fernes Cl, Uxb. UB8 76 BJ72
Ferney Ct, W.Byf. (Byfleet)
KT14 off Ferney Rd 152 BK112
Ferney Meade Way, Islw. TW7 97 CG82
Ferney Rd, Barn. EN4 44 DG45
Waltham Cross (Chsht) EN7 14 DR26
West Byfleet (Byfleet) KT14 152 BK112
Fern Gro, Felt. TW14 115 BV87
Ferngrove Cl, Lthd. (Fetch.)
KT22 171 CE123
Fernhall Dr, Ilf. IG4 68 EK57
Fernhall La, Wal.Abb. EN9 16 EK31
Fernham Rd, Th.Hth. CR7 142 DQ97
Fernhead Rd, W9 81 CZ70
Fernheath Way, Dart. DA2 127 FD92
Fernhill, Lthd. (Oxshott) KT22 155 CD114
Fernhill Cl, Wok. GU22 166 AW120
Fernhill Ct, E17 47 ED54
Fernhill Gdns, Kings.T. KT2 117 CK92
Fernhill La, Wok. GU22 166 AW120
Fernhill Pk, Wok. GU22 166 AW120
Fernhills, Kings L. WD4 7 BR33
Fernhill St, E16 87 EM74
Fernholme Rd, SE15 123 DX85
Fernhurst Gdns, Edg. HA8 42 CN51
Fernhurst Rd, SW6 99 CY81
Ashford TW15 115 BQ91
Croydon CR0 142 DU101
Fernie Cl, Chig. IG7 50 EU50
Fernihough Cl, Wey. KT13 152 BN111
Fernlands Cl, Cher. KT16 133 BE104
Fern La, Houns. TW5 96 BZ78
Fernlea, Lthd. (Bkhm) KT23 170 CB124
Fernlea Rd, SW12 121 DH88
Mitcham CR4 140 DG96
Fernleigh Cl, W9 81 CZ69
Croydon CR0
off Stafford Rd 159 DN105
Walton-on-Thames KT12 135 BV104
Fernleigh Ct, Har. HA2 40 CB54
Wembley HA9 62 CL61
Fernleigh Rd, N21 45 DN47
Fernsbury St, WC1 196 D3
Ferns Cl, Enf. EN3 31 DY36
South Croydon CR2 160 DV110
Fernshaw Rd, SW10 100 DC79
Fernside, NW11
off Finchley Rd 64 DA61
Buckhurst Hill IG9 48 EH46
Fernside Av, NW7 42 CR48
Feltham TW13 115 BV91
Fernside La, Sev. TN13 191 FJ129
Fernside Rd, SW12 120 DF88
Fernsleigh Cl, Ger.Cr. (Chal.St.P.)
SL9 36 AY51
Ferns Rd, E15 86 EF65
Fern St, E3 85 EA70
Fernthorpe Rd, SW16 121 DJ93
Ferntower Rd, N5 66 DR64
Fern Twrs, Cat. CR3 186 DU125
Fern Wk, SE16
off Argyle Way 102 DU78
Ashford TW15
off Ferndale Rd 114 BK92
Fern Way, Wat. WD25 23 BU35
Fernways, Ilf. IG1
off Cecil Rd 69 EP63
Fernwood, SW19
off Albert Dr 119 CZ88
Fernwood Av, SW16 121 DK91
Wembley HA0
off Bridgewater Rd 61 CJ64
Fernwood Cl, Brom. BR1 144 EJ96
Fernwood Cres, N20 44 DF48
Ferny Hill, Barn. EN4 28 DF38
Ferranti Cl, SE18 104 EK76
Ferraro Cl, Houns. TW5 96 CA79
Ferrers Av, Wall. SM6 159 DK105
West Drayton UB7 94 BK75
Ferrers Rd, SW16 121 DK92
Ferrestone Rd, N8 65 DM56
Ferrey Ms, SW9 101 DN82
Ferriby Cl, N1
off Bewdley St 83 DN66
Ferrier Pt, E16
off Forty Acre La 86 EG71
Ferrier St, SW18 100 DB84
Ferriers Way, Epsom KT18 173 CW119
Ferring Cl, Har. HA2 60 CC60
Ferrings, SE21 122 DS89
Ferris Av, Croy. CR0 143 DZ104
Ferris Rd, SE22 102 DU84
Ferron Rd, E5 66 DV62
Ferro Rd, Rain. RM13 89 FG70
Ferrour Ct, N2 64 DD55
Ferry Av, Stai. TW18 113 BE94
Ferrybridge Ho, SE11
off Lambeth Rd 101 DM76
Ferryhills Cl, Wat. WD19 40 BW48
Ferry La, N17 66 DU56
SW13 99 CT79
Brentford TW8 98 CL79
Chertsey KT16 134 BH98
Rainham RM13 89 FE72
Richmond TW9 98 CM79
Shepperton TW17 134 BN102
Staines (Laleham) TW18 134 BJ97
Staines (Wrays.) TW19 113 BB89
Ferryman's Quay, SW6 100 DC82
Ferrymead Av, Grnf. UB6 78 CA69
Ferrymead Dr, Grnf. UB6 78 CA68
Ferrymead Gdns, Grnf. UB6 78 CC68
Ferrymoor, Rich. TW10 117 CH90
Ferry Pl, SE18
off Woolwich High St 105 EN76
Ferry Rd, SW13 99 CU80
Teddington TW11 117 CH92
Thames Ditton KT7 137 CH100
Tilbury RM18 111 GG83
Twickenham TW1 117 CH88
West Molesey KT8 136 CA97
Ferry Sq, Brent. TW8 98 CL79
Ferry Sq, Shep. TW17 135 BP101
Ferry St, E14 204 D10
Feryby Rd, Grays RM16 111 GH76
Festing Rd, SW15 99 CX83
Festival Cl, Bex. DA5 126 EX88
Erith DA8 off Betsham Rd 107 FF80
Uxbridge UB10 77 BP67
Festival Path, Wok. GU21 166 AT119
Festival Wk, Cars. SM5 158 DF106
Festoon Way, E16 86 EK73
FETCHAM, Lthd. KT22 171 CD123
Fetcham Common La, Lthd.
(Fetch.) KT22 170 CB121
Fetcham Pk Dr, Lthd.
(Fetch.) KT22 171 CE123
Fetherstone Cl, Pot.B. EN6 12 DD32
Fetter La, EC4 196 E9
Ffinch St, SE8 103 EA80
Fiddicroft Av, Bans. SM7 158 DB114
Fiddlers Cl, Green. DA9 109 FV84
FIDDLERS HAMLET, Epp.
CM16 18 EW32
Fidler Pl, Bushey WD23
off Ashfield Av 24 CB44
Field Cl, E4 47 EB51
NW2 63 CU61
Bromley BR1 144 EJ96
Buckhurst Hill IG9 48 EJ48
Chesham HP5 4 AS28
Chessington KT9 155 CJ106
Hayes UB3 95 BQ80
Hounslow TW4 95 BV81
Romford (Abridge) RM4 34 EV41
Ruislip HA4
off Field Way 59 BQ60
South Croydon CR2 160 DV114
West Molesey KT8 136 CB99
Fieldcommon La, Walt. KT12 136 BZ101
Field Ct, WC1 196 C7
Oxted RH8
off Silkham Rd 188 EE127
Field End, Barn. EN5 27 CV42
Coulsdon CR5 159 DK114
Northolt UB5 78 BX65
Ruislip HA4 78 BW65
Fieldend, Twick. TW1 117 CF91
Field End Cl, Wat. WD19 40 BY45
Field End Ms, Wat. WD19
off Field End Cl 40 BY45
Fieldend Rd, SW16 141 DJ95
Field End Rd, Pnr. HA5 59 BV58
Ruislip HA4 60 BY63
Fielders Cl, Enf. EN1
off Woodfield Cl 30 DS42
Harrow HA2 60 CC60
Fielders Way, Rad. (Shenley)
WD7 10 CL33
Fieldfare Rd, SE28 88 EW73
Fieldgate La, Mitch. CR4 140 DE97
Fieldgate St, E1 84 DU71
Fieldhouse Cl, E18 48 EG53
Fieldhouse Rd, SW12 121 DJ88
Fieldhurst, Slou. SL3 93 AZ78
Fieldhurst Cl, Add. KT15 152 BH106
Fielding Av, Til. RM18 111 GH81
Twickenham TW2 116 CC90
Fielding Gdns, Slou. SL3 92 AW75
Fielding Ho, NW6 82 DA69
Fielding Ms, SW13
off Castelnau 99 CV79
Fielding Rd, W4 98 CR76
W14 99 CX76
Fieldings, The, SE23 122 DW88
Banstead SM7 173 CZ117
Woking GU21 166 AT116
Fieldings Rd, Wal.Cr. (Chsht)
EN8 15 DZ29
Fielding St, SE17 102 DQ79
Fielding Wk, W13 97 CH76
Fielding Way, Brwd.
(Hutt.) CM13 55 GC44
Field La, Brent. TW8 97 CJ80
Teddington TW11 117 CG92
Field Mead, NW7 42 CS52
NW9 42 CS52
Field Pl, N.Mal. KT3 139 CT100
Field Rd, E7 68 EF63
N17 66 DR55
W6 99 CY78
Feltham TW14 115 BV86
South Ockendon (Aveley)
RM15 90 FQ74
Uxbridge (Denh.) UB9 57 BE63
Watford WD19 24 BY44
Fields Ct, Pot.B. EN6 12 DD33
Fieldsend Rd, Sutt. SM3 157 CY106
Fields Est, E8 84 DU66
Fieldside Cl, Orp. BR6
off State Fm Av 163 EQ105
Fieldside Rd, Brom. BR1 123 ED92
Fields Pk Cres, Rom. RM6 70 EX57
Field St, WC1 196 B2
Fieldview, SW18 120 DD88
Field Vw, Egh. TW20 113 BC92
Feltham TW13 115 BR91
Field Vw Cl, Rom. RM7 70 FA55
Fieldview Ct, Stai. TW18
off Burges Way 114 BG93
Field Vw Ri, St.Alb. (Brick.Wd)
AL2 8 BY29
Field Vw Rd, Pot.B. EN6 12 DA33
Trm Fieldway 161 EB108
Field Way, NW10
off Twybridge Way 80 CQ66
Croydon CR0 161 EB107
Fieldway, Dag. RM8 70 EV63
Field Way, Ger.Cr. (Chal.St.P.)
SL9 36 AX52
Greenford UB6 78 CB67
Hemel Hempstead (Bov.)
HP3 5 BA27
Fieldway, Orp. BR5 145 ER100
Field Way, Rick. WD3 38 BH46
Ruislip HA4 59 BQ60
Uxbridge UB8 76 BK70
Fieldway Cres, N5 65 DN64
Fiennes Cl, Dag. RM8 70 EW60
Fiennes Way, Sev. TN13 191 FJ127
Fiesta Dr, Dag. RM9 89 FC70
Fifehead Cl, Ashf. TW15 114 BL93
Fife Rd, E16 86 EG71
N22 45 DP52
SW14 118 CQ85
Fife Rd, Kings.T. KT1 138 CL96
Fife Ter, N1 83 DM68
Fifield Path, SE23
off Bampton Rd 123 DX90
Fifth Av, E12 69 EM63
W10 81 CY69
Grays RM20 109 FU79
Hayes UB3 77 BT74
Watford WD25 24 BX35
Fifth Cross Rd, Twick. TW2 117 CD89
Fifth Way, Wem. HA9 62 CP63
Figges Rd, Mitch. CR4 120 DG94
Figgs Wd, Couls. CR5 175 DJ122
Fig St, Sev. TN14 190 FF129
Fig Tree Cl, NW10
off Craven Pk 80 CS67
Filby Rd, Chess. KT9 156 CM107
Filey Av, N16 66 DU60
Filey Cl, Sutt. SM2 158 DC108
Westerham (Bigg.H.) TN16 178 EH119
Filey Waye, Ruis. HA4 59 BU61
Filigree Ct, SE16 203 L3
Fillebrook Av, Enf. EN1 30 DS40
Fillebrook Rd, E11 67 ED60
Filmer La, Sev. TN14 191 FL121
Filmer Rd, SW6 99 CY81
Filston La, Sev. TN14 165 FE113
Filston Rd, Erith DA8
off Riverdale Rd 107 FB78
Filton Cl, NW9 off Kenley Av 42 CS54
Finborough Rd, SW10 100 DB78
SW17 120 DF93
Finchale Rd, SE2 106 EU76
Fincham Cl, Uxb. UB10
off Aylsham Dr 59 BQ61
Finch Av, SE27 122 DR91
Finch Cl, NW10 62 CR64
Barnet EN5 28 DA43
Finchdean Ho, SW15
off Tangley Gro 119 CT87
Finch Dr, Felt. TW14 116 BX87
Finches Av, Rick. (Crox.Grn)
WD3 22 BM41
Finch Gdns, E4 47 EA50
Finch Grn, Rick. (Chorl.) WD3 21 BF42
Finchingfield Av, Wdf.Grn.
IG8 48 EJ52
Finch La, EC3 197 L9
Amersham HP7 20 AV40
Bushey WD23 24 CA43
FINCHLEY, N3 44 DB53
⊖ Finchley Central 44 DA53
Finchley Cl, Dart. DA1 128 FN86
Finchley Ct, N3 44 DB51
Finchley La, NW4 63 CW56
H Finchley Mem Hosp, N12 44 DC52
Finchley Pk, N12 44 DC49
Finchley Pl, NW8 82 DD68
⊖ Finchley Road 82 DC65
Finchley Rd, NW2 64 DA62
NW3 82 DC65
NW8 82 DD67
NW11 63 CZ58
Grays RM17 110 GB79
⇌ Finchley Road & Frognal 64 DC64
Finchley Way, N3 44 DA52
Finch Ms, SE15 102 DT80
Finden Rd, E7 68 EH64
Findhorn Av, Hayes UB4 77 BV71
Findhorn St, E14 85 EC72
Findon Cl, SW18
off Wimbledon Pk Rd 120 DA86
Harrow HA2 60 CB62
Findon Ct, Add. KT15 151 BF106
Findon Gdns, Rain. RM13 89 FG71
Findon Rd, N9 46 DV46
W12 99 CU75
Fine Bush La, Uxb. (Hare.)
UB9 59 BP58
Fingal St, SE10 205 L10
Finglesham Cl, Orp. BR5
off Westwell Cl 146 EX102
Finians Cl, Uxb. UB10 76 BM66
Finland Quay, SE16 203 L7
Finland Rd, SE4 103 DY83
Finland St, SE16 203 L6
Finlay Gdns, Add. KT15 152 BJ105
Finlays Cl, Chess. KT9 156 CN106
Finlay St, SW6 99 CX81
Finnart Cl, Wey. KT13 153 BQ105
Finnart Ho Dr, Wey. KT13
off Vaillant Rd 153 BQ105
Finney La, Islw. TW7 97 CG81
Finnis St, E2 84 DV69
Finnymore Rd, Dag. RM9 88 EY66
FINSBURY, EC1 196 E2
Finsbury Av, EC2 197 L7
Finsbury Av Sq, EC2 197 L7
Finsbury Circ, EC2 197 L7
Finsbury Cotts, N22 45 DL52
Finsbury Ct, Wal.Cr. EN8
off Parkside 15 DY34
Finsbury Est, EC1 196 E3
Finsbury Ho, N22 45 DL53
Finsbury Mkt, EC2 197 M5
FINSBURY PARK, N4 65 DN60
★ Finsbury Park, N4 65 DP59
⇌ Finsbury Park 65 DN61
⊖ Finsbury Park 65 DN61
Finsbury Pk Av, N4 66 DQ58
Finsbury Pk Rd, N4 65 DP61
Finsbury Pavement, EC2 197 L6
Finsbury Rd, N22 45 DM53
Finsbury Sq, EC2 197 L6
Finsbury St, EC2 197 K6
Finsbury Twr, EC1 197 K5
Finsbury Way, Bex. DA5 126 EZ86
Finsen Rd, SE5 102 DQ83
Finstock Rd, W10 81 CX72
Finucane Dr, Orp. BR5 146 EW101
Finucane Gdns, Rain. RM13 89 FG65
Finucane Ri, Bushey (Bushey Hth)
WD23 40 CC47
Finway Ct, Wat. WD18
off Whippendell Rd 23 BT43
Fiona Cl, Lthd. (Bkhm) KT23 170 CA124
Firbank Cl, E16 86 EK71

Firbank Cl, Enf. EN2
off Gladbeck Way 30 DQ42
Firbank Dr, Wat. WD19 ......40 BY45
Woking GU21 ....166 AV119
Firbank La, Wok. GU21 .....166 AV119
Firbank Pl, Egh. (Eng.Grn)
TW20 ....112 AV93
Firbank Rd, SE15 ....102 DV82
Romford RM5 ....51 FB50
Fir Cl, Walt. KT12 ....135 BU101
Fircroft Cl, Slou. (Stoke P.)
SL2 ....74 AU65
Woking GU22 ....167 AZ118
Fircroft Ct, Wok. GU22
off Fircroft Cl 167 AZ118
Fircroft Gdns, Har. HA1 ......61 CE62
Fircroft Rd, SW17 ....120 DF89
Chessington KT9 ....156 CM105
Egham TW20
off Bagshot Rd 112 AW94
Fir Dene, Orp. BR6 ....145 EM104
Firdene, Surb. KT5 ....138 CQ102
Fire Bell All, Surb. KT6 .....138 CL100
Firecrest Dr, NW3 ....64 DB62
Firefly Cl, Wall. SM6 ....159 DL108
Firefly Gdns, E6
off Jack Dash Way 86 EL70
★ **Firepower**, SE18 ....105 EP76
Fire Sta All, Barn. EN5
off Christchurch La 27 CZ40
Firethorn Cl, Edg. HA8
off Larkspur Gro 42 CQ49
Firfield Rd, Add. KT15 ......152 BG105
Firfields, Wey. KT13 ....153 BP107
Fir Gra Av, Wey. KT13 ......153 BP106
Fir Gro, N.Mal. KT3 ....139 CT100
Woking (St.John's) GU21 .166 AU119
Fir Gro Rd, SW9
off Marcella Rd 101 DN82
Firham Pk Av, Rom. RM3 ....52 FN52
Firhill Rd, SE6 ....123 EA91
Firlands, Wey. KT13 ....153 BS107
Firmingers Rd, Orp. BR6 ....165 FB106
Firmin Rd, Dart. DA1 ....128 FJ85
Fir Rd, Felt. TW13 ....116 BX92
Sutton SM3 ....139 CZ102
Firs, The, E17 *off Leucha Rd* ..67 DY57
N20 ....44 DD46
W5 ....79 CK71
Bexley DA5
off Dartford Rd 127 FD88
Brentwood (Pilg.Hat.) CM15 .54 FU44
Caterham CR3
off Yorke Gate Rd 176 DR122
Leatherhead (Bkhm) KT23 ..170 CC124
Tadworth KT20
off Brighton Rd 183 CZ126
Waltham Cross (Chsht) EN7 .14 DS27
Firs Av, N10 ....64 DG55
N11 ....44 DG51
SW14 ....98 CQ84
Firsby Av, Croy. CR0 ....143 DX102
Firsby Rd, N16 ....66 DT60
Firs Cl, N10 *off Firs Av* 64 DG55
SE23 ....123 DX87
Esher (Clay.) KT10 ......155 CE107
Iver SL0
off Thornbridge Rd 75 BC67
Mitcham CR4 ....141 DH96
Firscroft, N13 ....46 DQ48
Firsdene Cl, Cher. (Ott.) KT16
off Slade Rd 151 BD107
Firs Dr, Houns. TW5 ....95 BV80
Loughton IG10 ....33 EN39
Slough SL3 ....75 AZ74
Firs End, Ger.Cr. (Chal.St.P.)
SL9 ....56 AY55
Firsgrove Cres, Brwd. CM14 ..54 FV49
Firsgrove Rd, Brwd. CM14 ...54 FV49
Firside Gro, Sid. DA15 ......125 ET88
Firs La, N13 ....46 DQ48
N21 ....46 DQ47
Potters Bar EN6 ....12 DB33
Firs Pk Av, N21 ....46 DR46
Firs Pk Gdns, N21 ....46 DQ46
Firs Rd, Ken. CR8 ....175 DP115
First Av, E12 ....68 EL63
E13 ....86 EG69
E17 ....67 EA57
N18 ....46 DW49
NW4 ....63 CW56
SW14 ....98 CS83
W3 ....81 CT74
W10 ....81 CZ70
Bexleyheath DA7 ....106 EW80
Dagenham RM10 ....89 FB68
Enfield EN1 ....30 DT44
Epsom KT19 ....156 CS109
Gravesend (Nthflt) DA11 ..130 GE88
Grays RM20 ....109 FU79
Greenford UB6 ....79 CD66
Hayes UB3 ....77 BT74
Romford RM6 ....70 EW57
Tadworth (Lwr Kgswd)
KT20 ....183 CY125
Waltham Abbey EN9
off Breach Barn Mobile Home Pk 16 EH30
Walton-on-Thames KT12 .135 BV100
Watford WD25 ....24 BW35
Wembley HA9 ....61 CK61
West Molesey KT8 ....136 BZ98
First Cl, W.Mol. KT8 ....136 CC97
First Cross Rd, Twick. TW2 ...117 CE89
First Dr, NW10 ....80 CQ66
First Slip, Lthd. KT22 ......171 CG118
First St, SW3 ....198 C8
Firstway, SW20 ....139 CW96
First Way, Wem. HA9 ....62 CP63
Firs Wk, Nthwd. HA6 ....39 BR51
Woodford Green IG8 ......48 EG50
Firswood Av, Epsom KT19 ..157 CT106
Firs Wd Cl, Pot.B. EN6 ....12 DF32
Firth Gdns, SW6 ....99 CY81
Fir Tree Av, Mitch. CR4 .....140 DG96
Slough (Stoke P.) SL2 .....74 AT70
West Drayton UB7 ....94 BN76
Fir Tree Cl, SW16 ....121 DJ92
Fir Tree Cl, W5 ....80 CL72
Epsom KT17 ....173 CW115
Epsom (Ewell) KT19 .....157 CT105
Esher KT10 ....154 CC106
Grays RM17 ....110 GD79
Leatherhead KT22 ....171 CJ123
Orpington BR6 ....163 ET106
Romford RM1 ....71 FD55
Firtree Ct, Borwd. (Els.) WD6 .26 CM42
Fir Tree Gdns, Croy. CR0 ....161 EA105
Fir Tree Gro, Cars. SM5 .....158 DF108
Fir Tree Hill, Rick. WD3 ......22 BM38
Fir Tree Pl, Ashf. TW15
off Percy Av 114 BN92
Fir Tree Rd, Bans. SM7 .....157 CW114
Epsom KT17 ....173 CV116
Hounslow TW4 ....96 BY84
Leatherhead KT22 ....171 CJ123
Fir Trees, Rom. (Abridge)
RM4 ....34 EV41
Fir Trees Cl, SE16 ....203 L3
Fir Tree Wk, Dag. RM10
off Wheel Fm Dr 71 FC62
Enfield EN1 ....30 DR41
Reigate RH2 ....184 DD134
Firwood Cl, Wok. GU21 .....166 AS119
Firwood Rd, Vir.W. GU25 ....132 AS100
Fisher Cl, E9
off Brooksby's Wk 67 DX64
Croydon CR0 *off Grant Rd* ..142 DT102
Enfield EN3 ....31 EA37
Greenford UB6 ....78 CA69
Kings Langley WD4 ....6 BN29
Walton-on-Thames KT12 .153 BV105
Fisherman Cl, Rich. TW10
off Locksmeade Rd 117 CJ91
Fishermans Dr, SE16 ....203 J4
Fishermans Hill, Grav. DA11 .130 GB85
Fisherman's Wk, E14 ....203 P2
Fishermans Wk, SE28
off Tugboat St 105 ES75
Fisher Rd, Har. HA3 ....41 CF54
Fishers Cl, SW16
off Garrad's Rd 121 DK90
Bushey WD23 ....24 BY41
Waltham Cross EN8 ......15 EA34
Fishers Ct, SE14
off Besson St 103 DX81
Brentwood (Warley) CM14 .54 FV49
Fishersdene, Esher (Clay.)
KT10 ....155 CG108
Fishers Grn La, Wal.Abb. EN9 .15 EB29
Fishers La, W4 ....98 CR77
Epping CM16 ....17 ES32
Fisher St, E16 ....86 EG71
WC1 ....196 A7
Fishers Way, Belv. DA17 .....89 FC74
Fisherton St, NW8 ....82 DD70
Fishguard Spur, Slou. SL1 ...92 AV75
Fishguard Way, E16 ....105 EP75
Fishing Temple, Stai. TW18 ..133 BF95
Fishponds Rd, SW17 ....120 DE91
Keston BR2 ....162 EK106
Fish St Hill, EC3 ....197 L10
Fitzalan Rd, N3 ....63 CY55
Esher (Clay.) KT10 ......155 CE108
Fitzalan St, SE11 ....200 D8
Fitzgeorge Av, W14 ....99 CY77
New Malden KT3 ....138 CR95
Fitzgerald Av, SW14 ....98 CS83
Fitzgerald Cl, E11
off Fitzgerald Rd 68 EG57
Fitzgerald Ho, E14 ....85 EB72
Hayes UB3 ....77 BV74
Fitzgerald Rd, E11 ....68 EG57
SW14 ....98 CR83
Thames Ditton KT7 ......137 CG100
Fitzhardinge St, W1 ....194 F8
Fitzherbert Ho, Rich. TW10
off Kingsmead 118 CM86
Fitzhugh Gro, SW18 ....120 DD86
Fitzilian Av, Rom. RM3 ....52 FM53
Fitzjames Av, W14 ....99 CY77
Croydon CR0 ....142 DU103
Fitzjohn Av, Barn. EN5 ....27 CY43
Fitzjohn's Av, NW3 ....64 DD64
Fitzmaurice Ho, SE16
off Rennie Est 102 DV77
Fitzmaurice Pl, W1 ....199 J2
Fitzneal St, W12 ....81 CT72
Fitzrobert Pl, Egh. TW20 ....113 BA93
Fitzroy Cl, N6 ....64 DF60
Fitzroy Ct, W1 ....195 L5
Fitzroy Cres, W4 ....98 CR80
Fitzroy Gdns, SE19 ....122 DS94
Fitzroy Ms, W1 ....195 K5
Fitzroy Pk, N6 ....64 DF60
Fitzroy Rd, NW1 ....82 DG67
Fitzroy Sq, W1 ....195 K5
Fitzroy St, W1 ....195 K5
Fitzroy Yd, NW1
off Fitzroy Rd 82 DG67
Fitzsimmons Ct, NW10
off Knatchbull Rd 80 CR67
Fitzstephen Rd, Dag. RM8 ...70 EV64
Fitzwarren Gdns, N19 ....65 DJ60
Fitzwilliam Av, Rich. TW9 ....98 CM82
Fitzwilliam Ms, E16 ....205 M2
Fitzwilliam Rd, SW4 ....101 DJ83
Fitzwygram Cl, Hmptn.
(Hmptn H.) TW12 ....116 CC92
Five Acre, NW9 ....43 CT53
Fiveacre Cl, Th.Hth. CR7 ....141 DN100
Five Acres, Kings L. WD4 .....6 BM29
St. Albans (Lon.Col.) AL2 ...9 CK25
Five Acres Av, St.Alb.
(Brick.Wd) AL2 ....8 BZ29
Fiveash Rd, Grav. DA11 .....131 GF87
Five Bell All, E14
off Three Colt St 85 DZ73
Five Elms Rd, Brom. BR2 ....144 EH104
Dagenham RM9 ....70 EZ62
Five Flds Cl, Wat. WD19 ......40 BZ48
Five Oaks, Add. KT15 ....151 BF107
Five Oaks La, Chig. IG7 ....50 EY51
Five Oaks Ms, Brom. BR1 ....124 EG90
Five Points, Iver SL0 ....75 BC69
Fives Ct, SE11 ....200 F8
Five Ways Cor, NW4 ....43 CV53
Fiveways Rd, SW9 ....101 DN82
Five Wents, Swan. BR8 ......147 FG96
Fladbury Rd, N15 ....66 DR58
Fladgate Rd, E11 ....68 EE58
Flag Cl, Croy. CR0 ....143 DX102
Flagstaff Cl, Wal.Abb. EN9 ...15 EB33
Flagstaff Ho, SW8
off St. George Wf 101 DL79
Flagstaff Rd, Wal.Abb. EN9 ...15 EB33
Flag Wk, Pnr. HA5
off Eastcote Rd 59 BU58
Flambard Rd, Har. HA1 ....61 CG58
Flamborough Cl, West.
(Bigg.H.) TN16 ....178 EH119
Flamborough Rd, Ruis. HA4 ..59 BU62
Flamborough St, E14 ....85 DY72
Flamborough Wk, E14
off Flamborough St 85 DY72
Flamingo Gdns, Nthlt. UB5
off Jetstar Way 78 BY69
Flamingo Wk, Horn. RM12 ...89 FG65
FLAMSTEAD END, Wal.Cr.
EN7 ....14 DU28
Flamstead End Rd, Wal.Cr.
(Chsht) EN8 ....14 DV28
Flamstead Gdns, Dag. RM9
off Flamstead Rd 88 EW66
Flamstead Rd, Dag. RM9 ....88 EW66
Flamsted Av, Wem. HA9 .....80 CN65
★ **Flamsteed Ho Mus**,
SE10 ....103 ED80
Flamsteed Rd, SE7 ....104 EL78
Flanchford Rd, W12 ....99 CT76
Reigate RH2 ....183 CX134
Flanders Ct, Egh. TW20 .....113 BC92
Flanders Cres, SW17 ....120 DF94
Flanders Rd, E6 ....87 EM68
W4 ....98 CS77
Flanders Way, E9 ....85 DX65
Flandrian Cl, Enf. EN3 ....31 EA38
Flank St, E1 *off Dock St* 84 DU73
Flash La, Enf. EN2 ....29 DP37
Flask Cotts, NW3
off New End Sq 64 DD63
Flask Wk, NW3 ....64 DD63
Flat Iron Sq, SE1
off Union St 84 DQ74
FLAUNDEN, Hem.H. HP3 .....5 BB33
Flaunden Bottom, Chesh.
HP5 ....20 AY36
Hemel Hempstead (Flaun.)
HP3 ....20 AY35
Flaunden Hill, Hem.H. (Flaun.)
HP3 ....5 AZ33
Flaunden La, Hem.H. (Bov.)
HP3 ....5 BB32
Rickmansworth WD3 ....5 BD33
Flaunden Pk, Hem.H. (Flaun.)
HP3 ....5 BA32
Flavell Ms, SE10 ....205 J10
Flaxen Cl, E4 *off Flaxen Rd* ..47 EB48
Flaxen Rd, E4 ....47 EB48
Flaxley Rd, Mord. SM4 .....140 DB100
Flaxman Ct, W1 ....195 M9
Flaxman Rd, SE5 ....101 DP82
Flaxman Ter, WC1 ....195 N3
Flaxton Rd, SE18 ....105 ER81
Flecker Cl, Stan. HA7 ....41 CF50
Fleece Dr, N9 ....46 DU49
Fleece Rd, Surb. KT6 ....137 CJ102
Fleece Wk, N7 *off Manger Rd* .83 DL65
Fleeming Cl, E17
off Pennant Ter 47 DZ54
Fleeming Rd, E17 ....47 DZ54
Fleet Av, Dart. DA2 ....128 FQ88
Upminster RM14 ....73 FR58
Fleet Cl, Ruis. HA4 ....59 BQ58
Upminster RM14 ....73 FR58
West Molesey KT8 ....136 BZ99
Fleetdale Par, Dart. DA2
off Fleet Av 128 FQ88
Fleet La, W.Mol. KT8 ....136 BZ100
Fleet Pl, EC4
off Farringdon St 83 DN72
Fleet Rd, NW3 ....64 DE64
Dartford DA2 ....128 FQ88
Gravesend (Nthflt) DA11 ..130 GC90
Fleetside, W.Mol. KT8 ......136 BZ100
Fleet Sq, WC1 ....196 C3
Fleet St, EC4 ....196 D9
Fleet St Hill, E1
off Weaver St 84 DU70
Fleetway, Egh. TW20 ....133 BC97
Fleetway Business Pk, Grnf.
UB6 ....79 CH68
Fleetwood Cl, E16 ....86 EK71
Chalfont St. Giles HP8 .....36 AU49
Chessington KT9 ....155 CK108
Croydon CR0 ....142 DT104
Tadworth KT20 ....173 CW120
Fleetwood Ct, E6
off Evelyn Denington Rd ..87 EM71
West Byfleet KT14 ....152 BG113
Fleetwood Gro, W3
off East Acton La 80 CS73
Fleetwood Rd, NW10 ....63 CU64
Kingston upon Thames
KT1 ....138 CP97
Slough SL2 ....74 AT74
Fleetwood Sq, Kings.T. KT1 .138 CP97
Fleetwood St, N16
off Stoke Newington Ch St .66 DS61
Fleetwood Way, Wat. WD19 ..40 BW49
Fleming Cl, W9
off Chippenham Rd 82 DA70
Waltham Cross (Chsht) EN7 .14 DU26
Fleming Ct, W2
off St. Marys Ter 82 DD71
Croydon CR0 ....159 DN106
Fleming Dr, N21 ....29 DM43
Fleming Gdns, Rom. (Harold Wd)
RM3 *off Bartholomew Dr* .52 FK54
Tilbury RM18
off Fielding Av 111 GJ81
Fleming Mead, Mitch. CR4 ..120 DE94
Fleming Rd, SE17 ....101 DP79
Grays (Chaff.Hun.) RM16 .109 FW77
Southall UB1 ....78 CB72
Waltham Abbey EN9 ....31 EB35
Flemings, Brwd. CM13 ....53 FW51
Fleming Wk, NW9
off Pasteur Cl 42 CS54
Fleming Way, SE28 ....88 EX73
Isleworth TW7 ....97 CF83
Flemish Flds, Cher. KT16 ...134 BG101
Flemming Av, Ruis. HA4 ......59 BV60
Flempton Rd, E10 ....67 DY59
Fletcher Cl, E6
off Trader Rd 87 EP72
Chertsey (Ott.) KT16 .....151 BE107
Fletcher La, E10 ....67 EC59
Fletcher Path, SE8
off New Butt La 103 EA80
Fletcher Rd, W4 ....98 CQ76
Chertsey (Ott.) KT16 .....151 BD107
Chigwell IG7 ....49 ET50
Fletchers Cl, Brom. BR2 ....144 EH98
Fletcher St, E1 *off Cable St* ...84 DU73
Fletching Rd, E5 ....66 DW62
SE7 ....104 EJ79
Fletton Rd, N11 ....45 DL52
Fleur de Lis St, E1 ....197 N5
Fleur Gates, SW19
off Princes Way 119 CX87
Flexmere Gdns, N17
off Flexmere Rd 46 DR53
Flexmere Rd, N17 ....46 DR53
Flight App, NW9 ....43 CT54
Flimwell Cl, Brom. BR1 .....124 EE92
Flint Cl, E15 ....86 EF66
Banstead SM7 ....158 DB114
Redhill RH1 ....184 DF133
Flint Down Cl, Orp. BR5 ....146 EU95
Flintlock Cl, Stai. TW19 ......94 BG84
Flintmill Cres, SE3 ....104 EL82
Flinton St, SE17 ....201 N10
Flint St, SE17 ....201 L9
Grays RM20 ....109 FV79
Flitcroft St, WC2 ....195 N8
Floathaven Cl, SE28 ....88 EU74
Floats, The, Sev. (Rvrhd)
TN13 ....190 FE121
Flock Mill Pl, SW18 ....120 DB88
Flockton St, SE16 ....202 B5
Flodden Rd, SE5 ....102 DQ81
Flood La, Twick. TW1
off Church La 117 CG88
Flood Pas, SE18
off Samuel St 105 EM77
Flood St, SW3 ....100 DE78
Flood Wk, SW3 ....100 DE79
Flora Cl, E14 ....85 EB72
Stanmore HA7 ....42 CL48
Flora Gdns, W6 ....99 CV77
Croydon CR0 ....161 EC111
Romford RM6 ....70 EW58
Floral Ct, Ashtd. KT21
off Rosedale 171 CJ118
Floral Dr, St.Alb. (Lon.Col.)
AL2 ....9 CK26
Floral Pl, N1
off Northampton Gro 66 DR64
Floral St, WC2 ....195 P10
Flora St, Belv. DA17
off Victoria St 106 EZ78
Florence Av, Add. (New Haw)
KT15 ....152 BG111
Enfield EN2 ....30 DQ41
Morden SM4 ....140 DC99
Florence Cantwell Wk, N19
off Hillrise Rd 65 DL59
Florence Cl, Grays RM20 .....110 FY79
Hornchurch RM12 ....72 FL61
Walton-on-Thames KT12
off Florence Rd 135 BV101
Watford WD25 ....23 BU35
Florence Ct, W9
off Maida Vale 82 DC69
Florence Dr, Enf. EN2 ....30 DQ41
Florence Elson Cl, E12
off Grantham Rd 69 EN63
Florence Gdns, W4 ....98 CQ79
Romford RM6
off Roxy Av 70 EW59
Staines TW18 ....114 BH94
Florence Nightingale Ho, N1
off Nightingale Rd 84 DQ65
★ **Florence Nightingale Mus**,
SE1 ....200 B5
Florence Rd, E6 ....86 EJ67
E13 ....86 EF68
N4 ....65 DN60
SE2 ....106 EW76
SE14 ....103 DZ81
SW19 ....120 DB93
W4 ....98 CR76
W5 ....80 CL73
Beckenham BR3 ....143 DX96
Bromley BR1 ....144 EG95
Feltham TW13 ....115 BV88
Kingston upon Thames
KT2 ....118 CM94
South Croydon CR2 .....160 DR109
Southall UB2 ....96 BX77
Walton-on-Thames KT12 .135 BV101
Florence St, E16 ....86 EF70
N1 ....83 DP66
NW4 ....63 CW56
Florence Ter, SE14 ....103 DZ81
Florence Way, SW12 ....120 DF88
Uxbridge UB8
off Wyvern Way 76 BJ67
Florey Sq, N21
off Highlands Av 29 DM43
Florfield Pas, E8
off Reading La 84 DV65
Florfield Rd, E8
off Reading La 84 DV65
Florian Av, Sutt. SM1 ......158 DD105
Florian Rd, SW15 ....99 CY84
Florida Cl, Bushey (Bushey Hth)
WD23 ....41 CD47
Florida Ct, Brom. BR2
off Westmoreland Rd 144 EF98
Florida Rd, Th.Hth. CR7 .....141 DP95
Florida St, E2 ....84 DU69
Florin Ct, SE1 *off Tanner St* ..102 DT75
Floris Pl, SW4
off Fitzwilliam Rd 101 DJ83
Floriston Av, Uxb. UB10 .....77 BQ66
Floriston Cl, Stan. HA7 ....41 CH53
Floriston Ct, Nthlt. UB5 ......60 CB64
Floriston Gdns, Stan. HA7 ....41 CH53
Floss St, SW15 ....99 CW82
Flower & Dean Wk, E1
off Thrawl St 84 DT71
Flower Cres, Cher. (Ott.)
KT16 ....151 BB107
Flowerfield, Sev. (Otford)
TN14 ....181 FF117
Flowerhill Way, Grav. (Istead Rise)
DA13 ....130 GE94
Flower La, NW7 ....43 CT50
Godstone RH9 ....187 DY128
Flower Ms, NW11 ....63 CY58
Flower Pot Cl, N15
off St. Ann's Rd 66 DT58
Flowers Cl, NW2 ....63 CU62
Flowersmead, SW17 ....120 DG89
Flowers Ms, N19
off Archway Rd 65 DJ61
Flower Wk, The, SW7 ....100 DC75
Floyd Rd, SE7 ....104 EJ78
Floyds La, Wok. GU22 ......168 BG116
Floyer Cl, Rich. TW10 ....118 CM85
Fludyer St, SE13 ....104 EE84
Flux's La, Epp. CM16 ....18 EU33
Flyer's Way, The, West. TN16 .189 ER126
Fogerty Cl, Enf. EN3 ....31 EB37
Foley Ms, Esher (Clay.) KT10 .155 CE108
Foley Rd, Esher (Clay.) KT10 .155 CE108
Westerham (Bigg.H.) TN16 .178 EK118
Foley St, W1 ....195 K7
Folgate St, E1 ....197 N6
Foliot Ho, N1
off Priory Grn Est 83 DM68
Foliot St, W12 ....81 CT72
Folkes La, Upmin. RM14 ......73 FT57
Folkestone Ct, Slou. SL3 .....93 BA78
Folkestone Rd, E6 ....87 EN68
E17 ....67 EB56
N18 ....46 DU49
Folkingham La, NW9 ....42 CR53
Folkington Cor, N12 ....43 CZ50
Follet Dr, Abb.L. WD5 ....7 BT31
Follett Cl, Wind. (Old Wind.)
SL4 ....112 AV86
Follett St, E14 ....85 EC72
Folly Cl, Rad. WD7 ....25 CF36
Follyfield Rd, Bans. SM7 ....158 DA114
Folly La, E4 ....47 DZ52
E17 ....47 DY53
Folly Ms, W11
off Portobello Rd 81 CZ72
Folly Pathway, Rad. WD7 ....25 CF35
Folly Wall, E14 ....204 E5
Fontaine Rd, SW16 ....121 DM94
Fontarabia Rd, SW11 ....100 DG84
Fontayne Av, Chig. IG7 ....49 EQ49
Rainham RM13 ....89 FE66
Romford RM1 ....51 FE54
Fontenoy Rd, SW12 ....121 DH89
Fonteyne Gdns, Wdf.Grn.
IG8 *off Lechmere Av* 48 EK54
Fonthill Cl, SE20
off Selby Rd 142 DU96
Fonthill Ms, N4
off Lennox Rd 65 DN61
Fonthill Rd, N4 ....65 DM60
Font Hills, N2 ....44 DC54
Fontley Way, SW15 ....119 CU87
Fontmell Cl, Ashf. TW15 .....114 BN92
Fontmell Pk, Ashf. TW15 ....114 BM92
Fontwell Cl, Har. HA3 ....41 CE52
Northolt UB5 ....78 CA65
Fontwell Dr, Brom. BR2 .....145 EN99
Fontwell Pk Gdns, Horn.
RM12 ....72 FL63
Foord Cl, Dart. DA2 ....129 FS89
Football La, Har. HA1 ....61 CE60
Footbury Hill Rd, Orp. BR6 ..146 EU101
Footpath, The, SW15 ....119 CU85
FOOTS CRAY, Sid. DA14 ....126 EV93
Foots Cray High St, Sid.
DA14 ....126 EW93
Foots Cray La, Sid. DA14 ...126 EW88
Footscray Rd, SE9 ....125 EN86
Forbench Cl, Wok. (Ripley)
GU23 ....168 BH122
Forbes Av, Pot.B. EN6 ....12 DD33
Forbes Cl, NW2 ....63 CU62
Hornchurch RM11
off St. Leonards Way 71 FH60
Forbes Ct, SE19 ....122 DS92
Forbes St, E1 *off Ellen St* 84 DU72
Forbes Way, Ruis. HA4 ....59 BV61
Forburg Rd, N16 ....66 DU60
FORCE GREEN, West. TN16 ..179 ER124
Force Grn La, West. TN16 ...179 ER124
Fordbridge Cl, Cher. KT16 ...134 BH102
Fordbridge Rd, Ashf. TW15 ..114 BL93
Shepperton TW17 ....135 BS100
Sunbury-on-Thames TW16 .135 BS100
Ford Cl, E3 *off Roman Rd* 85 DY68
Ashford TW15 ....114 BL93
Bushey WD23 ....24 CC42
Harrow HA1 ....61 CD59
Rainham RM13 ....89 FF66
Shepperton TW17 ....134 BN98
Thornton Heath CR7 .....141 DP100
Fordcroft Rd, Orp. BR5 .....146 EV99
Forde Av, Brom. BR1 ....144 EJ97
Fordel Rd, SE6 ....123 ED88
Ford End, Uxb. (Denh.) UB9 ..57 BF61
Woodford Green IG8 ......48 EH51
Fordham Cl, Barn. EN4 ......28 DE41
Hornchurch RM11 ....72 FN59
Fordham Rd, Barn. EN4 ......28 DD41
Fordham St, E1 ....84 DU72
Fordhook Av, W5 ....80 CM73
Fordingley Rd, W9 ....81 CZ69
Fordington Ho, SE26
off Sydenham Hill Est ..122 DV90
Fordington Rd, N6 ....64 DF57
Ford La, Iver SL0 ....76 BG72
Rainham RM13 ....89 FF66
Fordmill Rd, SE6 ....123 EA89
Ford Rd, E3 ....85 DY67
Ashford TW15 ....114 BM91
Chertsey KT16 ....134 BH102
Dagenham RM9, RM10 ....88 EZ66
Gravesend (Nthflt) DA11 .130 GB85
Woking (Old Wok.) GU22 .167 BB120
Fords Gro, N21 ....46 DQ46
Fords Pk Rd, E16 ....86 EG72
Ford Sq, E1 ....84 DV71
Ford St, E3 ....85 DY67
E16 ....86 EF72
Fordwater Rd, Cher. KT16 ...134 BH102
Fordwater Trd Est, Cher.
KT16 ....134 BJ102
Fordwich Cl, Orp. BR6 ......145 ET101
Fordwych Rd, NW2 ....63 CY63

Fordyce Cl, Horn. RM11 72 FM59
Fordyce Ho, SW16
off Colson Way 121 DJ91
Fordyce Rd, SE13 123 EC86
Fordyke Rd, Dag. RM8 70 EZ61
Forefield, St.Alb. AL2 8 CA27
★ **Foreign & Commonwealth Office**, SW1 199 P4
Foreign St, SE5 101 DP82
Foreland Ct, NW4 43 CY53
Foreland St, SE18
off Plumstead Rd 105 ER77
Foremark Cl, Ilf. IG6 49 ET50
Foreshore, SE8 203 N9
Forest, The, E11 68 EE56
Forest App, E4 48 EE45
Woodford Green IG8 48 EF52
Forest Av, E4 48 EE45
Chigwell IG7 49 EN50
Forest Business Pk, E17 67 DX59
Forest Cl, E11 68 EF57
NW6 81 CY66
Chislehurst BR7 145 EN95
Waltham Abbey EN9 32 EH37
Woking GU22 167 BD115
Woodford Green IG8 48 EH48
Forest Ct, E4 48 EF46
E11 48 EE56
Forest Cres, Ashtd. KT21 172 CN116
Forest Cft, SE23 122 DV89
FORESTDALE, Croy. CR0 161 EA109
Forestdale, N14 45 DK49
Forest Dr, E12 68 EK62
Epping (They.B.) CM16 33 ES36
Keston BR2 162 EL105
Sunbury-on-Thames TW16 115 BT94
Tadworth (Kgswd) KT20 173 CZ121
Woodford Green IG8 47 ED52
Forest Dr E, E11 67 ED59
Forest Dr W, E11 67 EC59
Forest Edge, Buck.H. IG9 48 EJ49
Forester Rd, SE15 102 DV84
Foresters Cl, Wall. SM6 159 DK108
Waltham Cross EN7 14 DS27
Woking GU21 166 AT118
Foresters Cres, Bexh. DA7 107 FB84
Foresters Dr, E17 67 ED56
Wallington SM6 159 DK108
Forest Gdns, N17 46 DT54
FOREST GATE, E7 68 EG64
⇌ **Forest Gate** 68 EG64
Forest Gate, NW9 62 CS56
Forest Glade, E4 48 EE49
E11 68 EE58
Epping (N.Wld Bas.) CM16 18 EY27
Forest Gro, E8 84 DT65
Forest Hts, Buck.H. IG9 48 EG47
FOREST HILL, SE23 123 DX88
⇌ **Forest Hill** 122 DW89
Forest Hill, SE23
off Waldram Cres 122 DW89
Forest Hill Business Cen, SE23 122 DW89
Forest Hill Ind Est, SE23
off Perry Vale 122 DW89
Forest Hill Rd, SE22 122 DV85
SE23 122 DV85
Forestholme Cl, SE23 122 DW89
Forest Ind Pk, Ilf. IG6 49 ES53
Forest La, E7 68 EE64
E15 68 EE64
Chigwell IG7 49 EN50
Leatherhead KT24 169 BT124
Forest Mt Rd, Wdf.Grn. IG8 47 ED52
Fore St, EC2 197 J7
N9 46 DU50
N18 46 DT51
Pinner HA5 59 BU57
Fore St Av, EC2 197 K7
Forest Ridge, Beck. BR3 143 EA97
Keston BR2 162 EL105
Forest Ri, E17 67 ED57
Forest Rd, E7 68 EG63
E8 84 DT65
E11 67 ED59
E17 66 DW56
N9 46 DV46
N17 66 DW56
Enfield EN3 31 DY36
Erith DA8 107 FG81
Feltham TW13 116 BW89
Ilford IG6 49 ES53
Leatherhead KT24 169 BU123
Loughton IG10 32 EK41
Richmond TW9 98 CN80
Romford RM7 71 FB55
Sutton SM3 140 DA102
Waltham Cross (Chsht) EN8 15 DX29
Watford WD25 7 BV33
Woking GU22 167 BD115
Woodford Green IG8 48 EG48
Forest Side, E4 48 EF45
E7 *off Capel Rd* 68 EH63
Buckhurst Hill IG9 48 EJ46
Epping CM16 17 ER33
Waltham Abbey EN9 32 EJ36
Worcester Park KT4 139 CT102
Forest St, E7 68 EG64
Forest Vw, E4 47 ED45
E11
off High Rd Leytonstone 68 EF59
Forest Vw Av, E10 67 ED57
Forest Vw Rd, E12 68 EL63
E17 47 EC53
Loughton IG10 32 EK42
Forest Wk, N10 45 DH53
Bushey WD23
off Millbrook Rd 24 BZ39
Forest Way, N19
off Hargrave Pk 65 DJ61
Ashtead KT21 172 CM117
Loughton IG10 32 EL41
Orpington BR5 145 ET99
Sidcup DA15 125 ER87
Waltham Abbey EN9 32 EK35
Woodford Green IG8 48 EH49
Forfar Rd, N22 45 DP53
SW11 100 DG81
Forge, The, Pot.B. (Northaw)
EN6 12 DE30
Forge Av, Couls. CR5 175 DN120
Forge Br La, Couls. CR5 175 DH121
Forge Cl, Brom. BR2 144 EG102
Forge Cl, Hayes UB3
off High St 95 BR79
Kings Langley (Chipper.)
WD4 6 BG31
Forge Cotts, W5
off Ealing Grn 79 CK74
Forge Dr, Esher (Clay.) KT10 155 CG108
Forge End, St.Alb. AL2 8 CA26
Woking GU21 166 AY117
Forgefield, West. (Bigg.H.)
TN16 *off Main Rd* 178 EK116
Forge La, Dart. (Hort.Kir.)
DA4 148 FQ98
Feltham TW13 116 BY92
Gravesend DA12 131 GM89
Northwood HA6 39 BS52
Richmond TW10
off Petersham Rd 118 CL88
Sunbury-on-Thames TW16 135 BU97
Sutton SM3 157 CY108
Forge Ms, Croy. CR0
off Addington Village Rd 161 EA106
Forge Pl, NW1
off Malden Cres 82 DG65
Forge Way, Sev. (Shore.)
TN14 165 FF111
Forlong Path, Nthlt. UB5
off Arnold Rd 78 BY65
Forman Pl, N16
off Farleigh Rd 66 DT63
Formation, The, E16
off Woolwich Manor Way 105 EP75
Formby Av, Stan. HA7 61 CJ55
Formby Cl, Slou. SL3 93 BC77
Formosa St, W9 82 DB71
Formunt Cl, E16
off Vincent St 86 EF71
Forres Gdns, NW11 64 DA58
Forrester Path, SE26 123 DX91
Forrest Gdns, SW16 141 DM97
Forris Av, Hayes UB3 77 BT74
Forset St, W1 194 C8
Forstal Cl, Brom. BR2
off Ridley Rd 144 EG97
Forster Cl, E17 47 ED52
Forster Rd, E17 67 DY58
N17 66 DT55
SW2 121 DL87
Beckenham BR3 143 DY97
Croydon CR0
off Windmill Rd 142 DQ101
Forsters Cl, Rom. RM6 70 EZ58
Forster's Way, SW18 120 DB88
Forsters Way, Hayes UB4 77 BV72
Forston St, N1
off Cropley St 84 DR68
Forsyte Cres, SE19 142 DS95
Forsyth Gdns, SE17 101 DP79
Forsyth Ho, SW1
off Tachbrook St 101 DJ78
Forsythia Cl, Ilf. IG1 69 EP64
Forsythia Gdns, Slou. SL3 92 AY76
Forsyth Path, Wok. GU21 151 BD113
Forsyth Pl, Enf. EN1 30 DS43
Forsyth Rd, Wok. GU21 151 BC114
Forterie Gdns, Ilf. IG3 70 EU62
Fortescue Av, E8
off Mentmore Ter 84 DV66
Twickenham TW2 116 CC90
Fortescue Rd, SW19 120 DD94
Edgware HA8 42 CR53
Weybridge KT13 152 BM105
Fortess Gro, NW5
off Fortess Rd 65 DH64
Fortess Rd, NW5 65 DH64
Fortess Wk, NW5
off Fortess Rd 65 DH64
Fortess Yd, NW5
off Fortess Rd 65 DJ63
Forthbridge Rd, SW11 100 DG84
Forth Rd, Upmin. RM14 73 FR58
Fortin Cl, S.Ock. RM15 91 FU73
Fortin Path, S.Ock. RM15 91 FU73
Fortin Way, S.Ock. RM15 91 FU73
Fortis Cl, E16 86 EJ72
FORTIS GREEN, N2 64 DF56
Fortis Grn, N2 64 DE56
N10 64 DE56
Fortis Grn Av, N2 64 DF55
Fortis Grn Rd, N10 64 DG55
Fortismere Av, N10 64 DG55
Fort La, Reig. RH2 184 DB130
Fortnam Rd, N19 65 DK61
★ **Fortnum & Mason**, W1 199 K2
Fortnums Acre, Stan. HA7 41 CF51
Fortress Distribution Pk, Til.
RM18 111 GG84
Fort Rd, SE1 202 A9
Northolt UB5 78 CA66
Sevenoaks (Halst.) TN14 181 FC115
Tadworth (Box H.) KT20 182 CP131
Tilbury RM18 111 GH84
Fortrose Cl, E14 *off Oban St* 85 ED72
Fortrose Gdns, SW2 121 DL88
Fortrye Cl, Grav. (Nthflt)
DA11 130 GE89
Fort St, E1 197 N7
E16 86 EH74
Fortuna Cl, N7
off Jupiter Way 83 DM65
Fortune Gate Rd, NW10 80 CS67
Fortune Grn Rd, NW6 64 DA63
Fortune La, Borwd. (Els.) WD6 25 CK44
Fortune Pl, SE1
off Mawbey Pl 102 DT78
Fortunes Mead, Nthlt. UB5 78 BY65
Fortune St, EC1 197 J5
Fortune Wk, SE28
off Broadwater Rd 105 ER76
Fortune Way, NW10 81 CU69
Forty Acre La, E16 86 EG71
Forty Av, Wem. HA9 62 CM62
Forty Cl, Wem. HA9 62 CM61
Forty Footpath, SW14 98 CQ83
Fortyfoot Rd, Lthd. KT22 171 CJ121
★ **Forty Hall & Mus**, Enf.
EN2 30 DT38
FORTY HILL, Enf. EN2 30 DS37
Forty Hill, Enf. EN2 30 DT38
Forty La, Wem. HA9 62 CP61
Forum, The, W.Mol. KT8 136 CB98
Forum Cl, E3 *off Old Ford Rd* 85 EA67
★ **Forum Club**, NW5 65 DH64
Forum Magnum Sq, SE1 200 B4
Forumside, Edg. HA8
off Station Rd 42 CN51
Forum Way, Edg. HA8
off High St 42 CN51
Forval Cl, Mitch. CR4 140 DF99
Forward Dr, Har. HA3 61 CF56
Fosbury Ms, W2
off Inverness Ter 82 DB73
Foscote Ms, W9
off Amberley Rd 82 DA71
Foscote Rd, NW4 63 CV58
Foskett Rd, SW6 99 CZ82
Foss Av, Croy. CR0 159 DN106
Fossdene Rd, SE7 104 EH78
Fossdyke Cl, Hayes UB4 78 BY71
Fosse Way, W13 79 CG71
West Byfleet KT14
off Brantwood Dr 151 BF113
Fossil Rd, SE13 103 EA83
Fossington Rd, Belv. DA17 106 EX77
Foss Rd, SW17 120 DD91
Fossway, Dag. RM8 70 EW61
Foster Cl, Wal.Cr. (Chsht) EN8 15 DX30
Fosterdown, Gdse. RH9 186 DV129
Foster La, EC2 197 H8
Foster Rd, E13 86 EG70
W3 80 CS73
W4 98 CR78
Fosters Cl, E18 48 EH53
Chislehurst BR7 125 EM92
Foster St, NW4 63 CW56
Foster Wk, NW4 *off Foster St* 63 CW56
Fothergill Cl, E13 86 EG68
Fothergill Dr, N21 29 DL43
Fotheringham Rd, Enf. EN1 30 DT42
Fotherley Rd, Rick. (Mill End)
WD3 37 BF47
Foubert's Pl, W1 195 K9
Foulden Rd, N16 66 DT63
Foulden Ter, N16
off Foulden Rd 66 DT63
Foulis Ter, SW7 198 A10
Foulser Rd, SW17 120 DF90
Foulsham Rd, Th.Hth. CR7 142 DQ97
Founder Cl, E6 *off Trader Rd* 87 EP72
Founders Ct, EC2 197 K8
Founders Dr, Uxb. (Denh.)
UB9 57 BF58
Founders Gdns, SE19 122 DQ94
★ **Foundling Mus**, WC1 196 A4
Foundry Cl, SE16 203 K2
Foundry Gate, Wal.Cr. EN8
off York Rd 15 DY34
Foundry La, Slou. (Horton)
SL3 93 BB83
Foundry Ms, NW1 195 L4
Hounslow TW3
off Station Rd 96 CB84
Foundry Pl, E1
off Redman's Rd 84 DW71
Fountain Cl, E5
off Lower Clapton Rd 66 DV62
Uxbridge UB8 *off New Rd* 77 BQ71
Fountain Ct, EC4 196 D10
SW6 *off The Boulevard* 100 DC82
Dartford (Eyns.) DA4
off Pollyhaugh 148 FL103
Fountain Dr, SE19 122 DT91
Carshalton SM5 158 DF109
Fountain Grn Sq, SE16 202 C4
Fountain Ho, SW8
off St. George Wf 101 DL78
Fountain La, Sev. TN15 191 FP122
Fountain Ms, N5
off Highbury Gra 66 DQ63
NW3 82 DF65
Fountain Pl, SW9 101 DN81
Waltham Abbey EN9 15 EC34
Fountain Rd, SW17 120 DD92
Thornton Heath CR7 142 DQ96
Fountains, The, Loug. IG10
off Fallow Flds 48 EK45
Fountains Av, Felt. TW13 116 BZ90
Fountains Cl, Felt. TW13 116 BZ89
Fountains Cres, N14 45 DL45
Fountain Sq, SW1 199 H8
Fountain St, E2
off Columbia Rd 84 DT69
Fountain Wk, Grav. (Nthflt)
DA11 130 GE86
Fountayne Rd, N15 66 DU56
N16 66 DU61
Fount St, SW8 101 DK80
Fouracres, SW12
off Little Dimocks 121 DH89
Four Acres, Cob. KT11 154 BY113
Fouracres, Enf. EN3 31 DY39
Fourland Wk, Edg. HA8 42 CQ51
Fournier St, E1 197 P6
Four Seasons Cl, E3 85 EA68
Four Seasons Cres, Sutt. SM3
off Kimpton Rd 139 CZ103
Fourth Av, E12 69 EM63
W10 81 CY70
Grays RM20 109 FU79
Hayes UB3 77 BT74
Romford RM7 71 FD60
Watford WD25 24 BX35
Fourth Cross Rd, Twick. TW2 117 CD89
Fourth Dr, Couls. CR5 175 DK116
Fourth Way, Wem. HA9 62 CQ63
Four Tubs, The, Bushey WD23 41 CD45
Four Wents, Cob. KT11 153 BV113
Four Wents, The, E4
off Kings Rd 47 ED47
Fowey Av, Ilf. IG4 68 EK57
Fowey Cl, E1 202 D2
Fowler Cl, SW11 100 DD83
Fowler Rd, E7 68 EG63
N1 *off Halton Rd* 83 DP66
Ilford IG6 50 EV51
Mitcham CR4 140 DG96
Fowlers Cl, Sid. DA14
off Thursland Rd 126 EY92
Fowlers Mead, Wok. (Chobham)
GU24 *off Windsor Rd* 150 AS110
Fowlers Wk, W5 79 CK70
Fowley Cl, Wal.Cr. EN8 15 DZ34
Fowley Mead Pk, Wal.Cr. EN8 15 EA34
Fownes St, SW11 100 DE83
Foxacre, Cat. CR3
off Town End Cl 176 DS122
Fox & Knot St, EC1 196 G6
Foxberry Rd, SE4 103 DY83
Foxberry Wk, Grav. (Nthflt)
DA11 *off Rowmarsh Cl* 130 GD91
Foxborough Cl, Slou. SL3 93 BA78
Foxborough Gdns, SE4 123 EA86
Foxbourne Rd, SW17 120 DG89
Foxburrow Rd, Chig. IG7 50 EX50
Foxbury Av, Chis. BR7 125 ER93
Foxbury Cl, Brom. BR1 124 EH93
Orpington BR6 164 EU106
Foxbury Dr, Orp. BR6 164 EU107
Foxbury Rd, Brom. BR1 124 EG93
Fox Cl, E1 84 DW70
E16 86 EG71
Borehamwood (Els.) WD6
off Rodgers Cl 25 CK44
Bushey WD23 24 CB42
Orpington BR6 164 EU106
Romford RM5 51 FB50
Weybridge KT13 153 BR106
Woking GU22 167 BD115
Foxcombe, Croy. (New Adgtn)
CR0 161 EB107
Foxcombe Cl, E6
off Boleyn Rd 86 EK68
Foxcombe Rd, SW15
off Alton Rd 119 CU88
Foxcote, SE5 102 DS78
Fox Covert, Lthd. (Fetch.)
KT22 171 CD124
Foxcroft Rd, SE18 105 EP81
Foxdell, Nthwd. HA6 39 BR51
Foxdell Way, Ger.Cr.
(Chal.St.P.) SL9 36 AY50
Foxearth Cl, West. (Bigg.H.)
TN16 178 EL118
Foxearth Rd, S.Croy. CR2 160 DW110
Foxearth Spur, S.Croy. CR2 160 DW109
Foxes Dale, SE3 104 EG83
Bromley BR2 143 ED97
Foxes Dr, Wal.Cr. EN7 14 DU29
Foxes Grn, Grays (Orsett)
RM16 111 GG75
Foxes La, Pot.B. (Cuffley) EN6 13 DL28
Foxfield Cl, Nthwd. HA6 39 BT51
Foxfield Rd, Orp. BR6 145 ER103
Foxglove Cl, N9 46 DW46
Sidcup DA15 126 EU86
Southall UB1 78 BY73
Staines (Stanw.) TW19 114 BK88
Foxglove Gdns, E11 68 EJ56
Purley CR8 159 DL111
Foxglove La, Chess. KT9 156 CN105
Foxglove Path, SE28
off Crowfoot Cl 87 ES74
Foxglove Rd, Rom. (Rush Grn)
RM7 71 FE61
South Ockendon RM15 91 FW71
Foxglove St, W12 81 CT73
Foxglove Way, Wall. SM6 141 DH102
Foxgrove, N14 45 DL48
Fox Gro, Walt. KT12 135 BV101
Foxgrove Av, Beck. BR3 123 EB94
Foxgrove Dr, Wok. GU21 167 BA115
Foxgrove Path, Wat. WD19 40 BX50
Foxgrove Rd, Beck. BR3 123 EB94
Foxhall Rd, Upmin. RM14 72 FQ64
Foxham Rd, N19 65 DK62
Foxhanger Gdns, Wok. GU22
off Oriental Rd 167 BA116
Foxherne, Slou. SL3 92 AW75
Fox Hill, SE19 122 DT94
Keston BR2 162 EJ106
Foxhill, Wat. WD24 23 BU36
Fox Hill Gdns, SE19 122 DT94
Foxhills, Wok. GU21 166 AW117
Foxhills Cl, Cher. (Ott.) KT16 151 BB107
Foxhills Ms, Cher. KT16 133 BB104
Foxhills Rd, Cher. (Ott.) KT16 151 BA105
Foxhole Rd, SE9 124 EL85
Foxholes, Wey. KT13 153 BR106
Fox Hollow Cl, SE18 105 ES78
Fox Hollow Dr, Bexh. DA7 106 EX83
Foxholt Gdns, NW10 80 CQ66
Foxhome Cl, Chis. BR7 125 EN93
Foxhounds La, Grav. DA13 130 GA90
Fox Ho, SW11
off Maysoule Rd 100 DD84
Chertsey KT16
off Fox La N 133 BF102
Fox Ho Rd, Belv. DA17 107 FB77
Foxlake Rd, W.Byf. (Byfleet)
KT14 152 BM112
Foxlands Cl, Wat. WD25 7 BU34
Foxlands Cres, Dag. RM10 71 FC64
Foxlands La, Dag. RM10 71 FC64
Foxlands Rd, Dag. RM10 71 FC64
Fox La, N13 45 DM48
W5 80 CL70
Caterham CR3 175 DP121
Keston BR2 162 EH106
Leatherhead (Bkhm) KT23 170 BY124
Reigate RH2 184 DB131
Fox La N, Cher. KT16 133 BF102
Fox La S, Cher. KT16
off Guildford St 133 BF102
Foxlees, Wem. HA0 61 CG63
Foxley Cl, E8
off Ferncliff Rd 66 DU64
Loughton IG10 33 EP40
Foxley Ct, Sutt. SM2 158 DC108
Foxley Gdns, Pur. CR8 159 DP113
Foxley Hill Rd, Pur. CR8 159 DN112
Foxley La, Pur. CR8 159 DK111
Foxley Rd, SW9 101 DN80
Kenley CR8 159 DP114
Thornton Heath CR7 141 DP98
Foxleys, Wat. WD19 40 BY48
Foxley Sq, SW9
off Cancell Rd 101 DP80
Fox Manor Way, Grays RM20 109 FV79
Foxmead Cl, Enf. EN2 29 DM41
Foxmoor Ct, Uxb. (Denh.) UB9
off North Orbital Rd 58 BG58
Foxmore St, SW11 100 DF81
Foxon Cl, Cat. CR3 176 DS121
Foxon La, Cat. CR3 176 DR121
Foxon La Gdns, Cat. CR3 176 DS121
Fox Rd, E16 86 EF71
Slough SL3 92 AX77
Fox's Path, Mitch. CR4 140 DE96
Foxton Gro, Mitch. CR4 140 DD96
Foxton Rd, Grays RM20 109 FX79
Foxwarren, Esher (Clay.)
KT10 155 CF109
Foxwell Ms, SE4
off Foxwell St 103 DY83
Foxwell St, SE4 103 DY83
Foxwood Chase, Wal.Abb.
EN9 31 EC35
Foxwood Cl, NW7 42 CS49
Feltham TW13 115 BV90
Foxwood Grn Cl, Enf. EN1 30 DS44
Foxwood Gro, Grav. (Nthflt)
DA11 130 GE88
Orpington BR6 164 EW110
Foxwood Rd, SE3 104 EF84
Dartford (Bean) DA2 129 FV90
Foyle Dr, S.Ock. RM15 91 FU71
Foyle Rd, N17 46 DU53
SE3 104 EF79
Frailey Cl, Wok. GU22 167 BB116
Frailey Hill, Wok. GU22 167 BB116
Framewood Rd, Slou. SL2,
SL3 74 AW66
Framfield Cl, N12 44 DA48
Framfield Ct, Enf. EN1 30 DS44
Framfield Rd, N5 65 DP64
W7 79 CE72
Mitcham CR4 120 DG94
Framlingham Cl, E5
off Detmold Rd 66 DW61
Framlingham Cres, SE9 124 EL91
Frampton Cl, Sutt. SM2 158 DA108
Frampton Pk Rd, E9 84 DW65
Frampton Rd, Epp. CM16 18 EU28
Hounslow TW4 116 BY85
Potters Bar EN6 12 DC30
Frampton St, NW8 82 DD70
Francemary Rd, SE4 123 EA85
Frances Av, Grays (Chaff.Hun.)
RM16 109 FW77
Frances Gdns, S.Ock. RM15 91 FT72
Frances Rd, E4 47 EA51
Frances St, SE18 105 EM77
Franche Ct Rd, SW17 120 DC90
Francis Av, Bexh. DA7 106 FA82
Feltham TW13 115 BU90
Ilford IG1 69 ER61
Francis Barber Cl, SW16
off Well Cl 121 DM91
Franciscan Rd, SW17 120 DF92
Francis Chichester Way,
SW11 100 DG81
Francis Cl, E14 204 F8
Epsom KT19 156 CR105
Shepperton TW17 134 BN98
Francisco Cl, Grays (Chaff.Hun.)
RM16 109 FW76
Francis Gro, SW19 119 CZ93
Francis Rd, E10 67 EC60
N2 *off Lynmouth Rd* 64 DF56
Caterham CR3 176 DR122
Croydon CR0 141 DP101
Dartford DA1 128 FK85
Greenford UB6 79 CJ67
Harrow HA1 61 CG57
Hounslow TW4 96 BX82
Ilford IG1 69 ER61
Orpington BR5 146 EX97
Pinner HA5 60 BW57
Wallington SM6 159 DJ107
Watford WD18 23 BV42
Francis St, E15 68 EE64
SW1 199 K8
Ilford IG1 69 ER61
Francis Ter, N19
off Junction Rd 65 DJ62
Francis Ter Ms, N19
off Junction Rd 65 DJ62
Francis Wk, N1
off Bingfield St 83 DM67
Francklyn Gdns, Edg. HA8 42 CN48
Francombe Gdns, Rom. RM1 71 FG58
Franconia Rd, SW4 121 DJ85
Frank Bailey Wk, E12
off Gainsborough Av 69 EN64
Frank Burton Cl, SE7
off Victoria Way 104 EH78
Frank Dixon Cl, SE21 122 DS88
Frank Dixon Way, SE21 122 DS88
Frankfurt Rd, SE24 122 DQ85
Frankham St, SE8 103 EA80
Frankland Cl, SE16 202 E7
Rickmansworth (Crox.Grn)
WD3 38 BN45
Woodford Green IG8 48 EJ50
Frankland Rd, E4 47 EA50
SW7 *off Armstrong Rd* 100 DD76
Rickmansworth (Crox.Grn)
WD3 23 BP44
Franklands Dr, Add. KT15 151 BF108
Franklin Av, Wal.Cr. (Chsht)
EN7 14 DV30
Franklin Cl, N20 44 DC45
SE13 103 EB81
SE27 121 DP90
Kingston upon Thames
KT1 138 CN97
Franklin Cres, Mitch. CR4 141 DJ98
Franklin Ho, NW9 63 CT59
Franklin Pas, SE9 104 EL83
Franklin Pl, SE13 103 EB81
Franklin Rd, SE20 122 DW94
Bexleyheath DA7 106 EY81
Dartford DA2 127 FE89
Gravesend DA12 131 GK92
Hornchurch RM12 90 FJ65
Watford WD17 23 BV40
Franklins Ms, Har. HA2 60 CC61
Franklin Sq, W14
off Marchbank Rd 99 CZ78
Franklin's Row, SW3 198 E10
Franklin St, E3 85 EB69
N15 66 DS58
Franklin Way, Croy. CR0 141 DL101
Franklyn Gdns, Ilf. IG6 49 ER51
Franklyn Rd, NW10 81 CT66
Walton-on-Thames KT12 135 BU100

★ Place of interest ⇌ Railway station ⊖ London Underground station DLR Docklands Light Railway station Tra Tramlink station H Hospital Riv Pedestrian ferry landing stage

Frank Martin Ct, Wal.Cr. EN7 .14 DU30
Franks Av, N.Mal. KT3 .138 CQ98
Franks La, Dart. (Hort.Kir.) DA4 .148 FN98
Frank St, E13 .86 EG70
Frankswood Av, Orp. BR5 .145 EP99
West Drayton UB7 .76 BM72
Frank Towell Ct, Felt. TW14
off Glebelands Rd .115 BU88
Franlaw Cres, N13 .46 DQ49
Franmil Rd, Horn. RM12 .71 FG60
Fransfield Gro, SE26 .122 DV90
Frant Cl, SE20 .122 DW94
Franthorne Way, SE6 .123 EB89
Frant Rd, Th.Hth. CR7 .141 DP99
Fraser Cl, E6
off Linton Gdns .86 EL72
Bexley DA5
off Dartford Rd .127 FC88
Fraser Ho, Brent. TW8
off Green Dragon La .98 CM78
Fraser Rd, E17 .67 EB57
N9 .46 DV48
Erith DA8 .107 FC78
Greenford UB6 .79 CH67
Waltham Cross (Chsht) EN8 .15 DY28
Fraser St, W4 .98 CS78
Frating Cres, Wdf.Grn. IG8 .48 EG51
Frays Av, West Dr. UB7 .94 BK75
Frays Cl, West Dr. UB7 .94 BK76
Frays Lea, Uxb. UB8 .76 BJ68
Frays Waye, Uxb. UB8 .76 BJ67
Frazer Av, Ruis. HA4 .60 BW64
Frazer Cl, Rom. RM1 .71 FF59
Frazier St, SE1 .200 D5
Frean St, SE16 .202 B6
Freda Corbett Cl, SE15
off Bird in Bush Rd .102 DU80
Frederica Rd, E4 .47 ED45
Frederica St, N7
off Caledonian Rd .83 DM66
Frederick Andrews Ct, Grays RM17 .110 GD79
Frederick Cl, W2 .194 C10
Sutton SM1 .157 CZ105
Frederick Ct, NW2
off Douglas Ms .63 CY62
Frederick Cres, SW9 .101 DP80
Enfield EN3 .30 DW40
Frederick Gdns, Croy. CR0 .141 DP100
Sutton SM1 .157 CZ106
Frederick Pl, SE18 .105 EP78
Frederick Rd, SE17
off Chapter Rd .101 DP78
Rainham RM13 .89 FD68
Sutton SM1 .157 CZ106
Frederick's Pl, EC2 .197 K9
Fredericks Pl, N12 .44 DC49
Frederick Sq, SE16 .203 K1
Frederick's Row, EC1 .196 F2
Frederick St, WC1 .196 B3
Frederick Ter, E8
off Haggerston Rd .84 DT67
Frederick Vil, W7
off Lower Boston Rd .79 CE74
Frederic Ms, SW1 .198 E5
Frederic St, E17 .67 DY57
Fredora Av, Hayes UB4 .77 BT70
Fred White Wk, N7
off Market Rd .83 DL65
Fred Wigg Twr, E11 .68 EF61
Freeborne Gdns, Rain. RM13
off Mungo Pk Rd .89 FG65
Freedom Cl, E17 .67 DY56
Freedom Rd, N17 .46 DR54
Freedom St, SW11 .100 DF82
Freedown La, Sutt. SM2 .158 DC113
Freegrove Rd, N7 .65 DL64
Freeland Pk, NW4 .43 CY54
Freeland Rd, W5 .80 CM73
Freelands Av, S.Croy. CR2 .161 DX109
Freelands Gro, Brom. BR1 .144 EH95
Freelands Rd, Brom. BR1 .144 EH95
Cobham KT11 .153 BV114
Freeland Way, Erith DA8
off Slade Grn Rd .107 FG81
Freeling St, N1
off Caledonian Rd .83 DM66
Freeman Cl, Nthlt. UB5 .78 BY66
Shepperton TW17 .135 BS98
Freeman Ct, N7
off Tollington Way .65 DL62
Freeman Dr, W.Mol. KT8 .136 BZ97
Freeman Rd, Grav. DA12 .131 GL90
Morden SM4 .140 DD99
Freemans Cl, Slou. (Stoke P.) SL2 .74 AT65
Freemans La, Hayes UB3 .77 BS73
Freemantle Av, Enf. EN3 .31 DX43
Freemantle St, SE17 .201 M10
Freeman Way, Horn. RM11 .72 FL58
★ Freemason's Hall, United Grand Lo of England, WC2 .196 A8
Freemasons Rd, E16 .86 EH71
Croydon CR0 .142 DS102
Free Prae Rd, Cher. KT16 .134 BG102
Freesia Cl, Orp. BR6 .163 ET106
Freethorpe Cl, SE19 .142 DR95
Free Trade Wf, E1
off The Highway .85 DX73
Freezeland Way, Uxb. UB10
off Long La .77 BP65
FREEZY WATER, Wal.Cr. EN8 .31 DY35
★ Freightliners City Fm, N7 .83 DM65
Freightmaster Est, Rain. RM13 .107 FG76
Freke Rd, SW11 .100 DG83
Fremantle Ho, Til. RM18 .111 GF81
Fremantle Rd, Belv. DA17 .106 FA77
Ilford IG6 .49 EQ54
Fremont St, E9 .84 DW67
French Apts, The, Pur. CR8
off Lansdowne Rd .159 DN112
Frenchaye, Add. KT15 .152 BJ106
Frenches, The, Red. RH1 .184 DG132
Frenches Cl, Red. RH1
off Frenches Rd .184 DG132
Frenches Dr, Red. RH1
off The Frenches .184 DG132
Frenches Rd, Red. RH1 .184 DG132
French Gdns, Cob. KT11 .154 BW114
French Ordinary Ct, EC3 .197 N10
French Pl, E1 .197 N4
French St, Sun. TW16 .136 BW96
Westerham TN16 .189 ES128
French's Wells, Wok. GU21 .166 AV117
Frendsbury Rd, SE4 .103 DY84
Frensham, Wal.Cr. (Chsht) EN7 .14 DT27
Frensham Cl, Sthl. UB1 .78 BZ70
Frensham Ct, Mitch. CR4 .140 DD97
Frensham Dr, SW15 .119 CU89
Croydon (New Adgtn) CR0 .161 EC108
Frensham Rd, SE9 .125 ER89
Kenley CR8 .159 DP114
Frensham St, SE15 .102 DU79
Frensham Way, Epsom KT17 .173 CW116
Frere St, SW11 .100 DE82
Freshfield Av, E8 .84 DT66
Freshfield Cl, SE13
off Mercator Rd .103 ED84
Freshfield Dr, N14 .45 DH45
Freshfields, Croy. CR0 .143 DZ101
Freshfields Av, Upmin. RM14 .72 FP64
Freshford St, SW18 .120 DC90
Freshmount Gdns, Epsom KT19 .156 CP111
Freshwater Cl, SW17 .120 DG93
Freshwater Rd, SW17 .120 DG93
Dagenham RM8 .70 EX60
Freshwell Av, Rom. RM6 .70 EW56
Fresh Wf Est, Bark. IG11
off Fresh Wf Rd .87 EP67
Fresh Wf Rd, Bark. IG11 .87 EP67
Freshwood Cl, Beck. BR3 .143 EB95
Freshwood Way, Wall. SM6 .159 DH109
Freston Gdns, Barn. EN4 .28 DG43
Freston Pk, N3 .43 CZ54
Freston Rd, W10 .81 CX73
W11 .81 CX73
Freta Rd, Bexh. DA6 .126 EZ85
★ Freud Mus, NW3 .82 DC65
Frewin Rd, SW18 .120 DD88
Friar Ms, SE27 .121 DP90
Friar Rd, Hayes UB4 .78 BX70
Orpington BR5 .146 EU99
Friars, The, Chig. IG7 .49 ES49
Friars Av, N20 .44 DE48
SW15 .119 CT90
Brentwood (Shenf.) CM15 .55 GA46
Friars Cl, E4 .47 EC48
N2 .64 DD56
SE1 .200 F3
Brentwood (Shenf.) CM15 .55 FZ45
Ilford IG1 .69 ER60
Northolt UB5
off Broomcroft Av .78 BX69
Friars Gdns, W3
off St. Dunstans Av .80 CR72
Friars Gate Cl, Wdf.Grn. IG8 .48 EG49
Friars La, Rich. TW9 .117 CK85
Friars Mead, E14 .204 D7
Friars Ms, SE9 .125 EN85
Friars Orchard, Lthd. (Fetch.) KT22 .171 CD121
Friars Pl La, W3 .80 CR73
Friars Ri, Wok. GU22 .167 BA118
Friars Rd, E6 .86 EK67
Virginia Water GU25 .132 AX98
Friars Stile Pl, Rich. TW10
off Friars Stile Rd .118 CL86
Friars Stile Rd, Rich. TW10 .118 CL86
Friar St, EC4 .196 G9
Friars Wk, N14 .45 DH46
SE2 .106 EX78
Friars Way, W3 .80 CR72
Bushey WD23 .24 BZ39
Chertsey KT16 .134 BG100
Kings Langley WD4 .6 BN30
Friars Wd, Croy. CR0 .161 DY109
Friary, The, Wind. (Old Wind.) SL4 .112 AW86
Friary Cl, N12 .44 DE50
Friary Ct, SW1 .199 L3
Woking GU21 .166 AT118
Friary Est, SE15 .102 DU79
Friary Island, Stai. (Wrays.) TW19 .112 AW86
Friary La, Wdf.Grn. IG8 .48 EG49
Friary Pk Est, W3
off Friary Rd .80 CR72
Friary Rd, N12 .44 DD49
SE15 .102 DU80
W3 .80 CR72
Staines (Wrays.) TW19 .112 AW86
Friary Way, N12 .44 DE49
FRIDAY HILL, E4 .47 ED47
Friday Hill, E4 .48 EE47
Friday Hill E, E4 .48 EE48
Friday Hill W, E4 .48 EE47
Friday Rd, Erith DA8 .107 FD78
Mitcham CR4 .120 DF94
Friday St, EC4 .197 H9
Frideswide Pl, NW5
off Islip St .65 DJ64
Friendly Pl, SE13
off Lewisham Rd .103 EB81
Friendly St, SE8 .103 EA81
Friendly St Ms, SE8
off Friendly St .103 EA82
Friends Av, Wal.Cr. EN8 .15 DX31
Friendship Wk, Nthlt. UB5
off Wayfarer Rd .78 BX69
Friendship Way, E15
off Carpenters Rd .85 EC67
Friends Rd, Croy. CR0 .142 DR104
Purley CR8 .159 DP112
Friend St, EC1 .196 F2
Friends Wk, Stai. TW18 .113 BF92
Uxbridge UB8
off Bakers Rd .76 BK66
FRIERN BARNET, N11 .44 DE49
Friern Barnet La, N11 .44 DE49
N20 .44 DE49
Friern Barnet Rd, N11 .44 DF50
Friern Br Retail Pk, N11 .45 DH51
Friern Cl, Wal.Cr. EN7 .14 DS26
Friern Ct, N20 .44 DD48
Friern Mt Dr, N20 .44 DC45
Friern Pk, N12 .44 DC50
Friern Rd, SE22 .122 DU86
Friern Watch Av, N12 .44 DC49
Frigate Ms, SE8
off Watergate St .103 EA79
Frimley Av, Horn. RM11 .72 FN60
Wallington SM6 .159 DL106
Frimley Cl, SW19 .119 CY89
Croydon (New Adgtn) CR0 .161 EC108
Frimley Ct, Sid. DA14 .126 EV92
Frimley Cres, Croy. (New Adgtn) CR0 .161 EC108
Frimley Gdns, Mitch. CR4 .140 DE97
Frimley Rd, Chess. KT9 .156 CL106
Ilford IG3 .69 ES62
Frimley Way, E1 .85 DX70
Fringewood Cl, Nthwd. HA6 .39 BP53
Frinstead Gro, Orp. BR5 .146 EX98
Frinstead Ho, W10 .81 CX73
Frinsted Rd, Erith DA8 .107 FD80
Frinton Cl, Wat. WD19 .39 BV47
Frinton Dr, Wdf.Grn. IG8 .47 ED52
Frinton Ms, Ilf. IG2
off Bramley Cres .69 EN58
Frinton Rd, E6 .86 EK69
N15 .66 DS58
SW17 .120 DG93
Romford RM5 .50 EZ52
Sidcup DA14 .126 EY89
Friston Path, Chig. IG7 .49 ES50
Friston St, SW6 .100 DB82
Friswell Pl, Bexh. DA6 .106 FA84
Fritham Cl, N.Mal. KT3 .138 CS100
Frith Ct, NW7 .43 CY52
Frithe, The, Slou. SL2 .74 AV72
Frith Knowle, Walt. KT12 .153 BV106
Frith La, NW7 .43 CY52
Frith Rd, E11 .67 EC63
Croydon CR0 .142 DQ103
Friths Dr, Reig. RH2 .184 DB131
Frith St, W1 .195 M9
Frithville Gdns, W12 .81 CW74
Frithwald Rd, Cher. KT16 .133 BF101
Frithwood Av, Nthwd. HA6 .39 BS51
Frizlands La, Dag. RM10 .71 FB63
Frobisher Cl, Bushey WD23 .24 CA44
Kenley CR8 *off Hayes La* .176 DQ117
Pinner HA5 .60 BX59
Frobisher Cres, EC2
off Beech St .84 DQ71
Staines TW19 .114 BL87
Frobisher Gdns, Stai. TW19 .114 BL87
Frobisher Pas, E14 .204 A2
Frobisher Pl, SE15
off St. Mary's Rd .102 DW81
Frobisher Rd, E6 .87 EM72
N8 .65 DN56
Erith DA8 .107 FF80
Frobisher St, SE10 .104 EE79
Frobisher Way, Grav. DA12 .131 GL92
Greenhithe DA9 .109 FV84
Froggy La, Uxb. (Denh.) UB9 .57 BD62
Froghall La, Chig. IG7 .49 ER49
FROGHOLE, Eden. TN8 .189 ER133
Froghole La, Eden. TN8 .189 ER132
Frogley Rd, SE22 .102 DT84
Frogmoor La, Rick. WD3 .38 BK47
FROGMORE, St.Alb. AL2 .9 CE28
Frogmore, SW18 .120 DA85
St. Albans AL2 .9 CD27
Frogmore Av, Hayes UB4 .77 BS69
Frogmore Cl, Sutt. SM3 .139 CX104
Frogmore Dr, Wind. SL4 .92 AS81
Frogmore Est, Ruis. HA4 .60 BX64
Frogmore Gdns, Hayes UB4 .77 BS70
Sutton SM3 .157 CY105
Frogmore Home Pk, St.Alb. AL2 .9 CD28
Frogmore Ind Est, NW10 .80 CQ69
Frognal, NW3 .64 DC64
Frognal Av, Har. HA1 .61 CF56
Sidcup DA14 .126 EU92
Frognal Cl, NW3 .64 DC64
Frognal Cor, Sid. DA14
off Chislehurst Rd .125 ET93
Frognal Ct, NW3 .82 DC65
Frognal Gdns, NW3 .64 DC63
Frognal La, NW3 .64 DB64
Frognal Par, NW3
off Frognal Ct .82 DC65
Frognal Pl, Sid. DA14 .126 EU93
Frognal Ri, NW3 .64 DC63
Frognal Way, NW3 .64 DC63
Froissart Rd, SE9 .124 EK85
Frome Rd, N22
off Westbury Av .65 DP55
Frome St, N1 .84 DQ68
Fromondes Rd, Sutt. SM3 .157 CY106
Front La, Upmin. RM14 .73 FS59
Frostic Wk, E1 .84 DT71
Froude St, SW8 .101 DH82
Frowyke Cres, Pot.B. EN6 .11 CU32
Fruen Rd, Felt. TW14 .115 BT87
Fruiterers Pas, EC4
off Southwark Br .84 DQ73
Fryatt Rd, N17 .46 DR52
Fry Cl, Rom. RM5 .50 FA50
Fryday Gro Ms, SW12
off Weir Rd .121 DJ87
Fryent Cl, NW9 .62 CN58
Fryent Cres, NW9 .62 CS58
Fryent Flds, NW9 .62 CS58
Fryent Gro, NW9 .62 CS58
Fryent Way, NW9 .62 CN57
Fryern Wd, Cat. (Chaldon) CR3 .176 DQ124
Frying Pan All, E1 .197 P7
Fry Rd, E6 .86 EK66
NW10 .81 CT67
Fryston Av, Couls. CR5 .159 DH114
Croydon CR0 .142 DU103
Fuchsia Cl, Rom. (Rush Grn) RM7 .71 FE61
Fuchsia St, SE2 .106 EV78
Fulbeck Dr, NW9 .42 CS53
Fulbeck Wk, Edg. HA8
off Knightswood Cl .42 CP47
Fulbeck Way, Har. HA2 .40 CC54
Fulbourne Cl, Red. RH1
off Dennis Cl .184 DE132
Fulbourne Rd, E17 .47 EC53
Fulbourne St, E1
off Durward St .84 DV71
Fulbrook Av, Add. (New Haw) KT15 .152 BG111
Fulbrook La, S.Ock. RM15 .91 FT73
Fulbrook Rd, N19
off Junction Rd .65 DJ63
Fulford Gro, Wat. WD19 .39 BV47
Fulford Rd, Cat. CR3 .176 DR121
Epsom KT19 .156 CR108
Fulford St, SE16 .202 E5
FULHAM, SW6 .99 CY82
⊖ Fulham Broadway .100 DA80
Fulham Bdy, SW6 .100 DA80
Fulham Bdy Retail Cen, SW6
off Fulham Bdy .100 DA80
Fulham Cl, Uxb. UB10
off Uxbridge Rd .77 BQ70
Fulham Ct, SW6
off Shottendane Rd .100 DA81
★ Fulham FC, SW6 .99 CX81
Fulham High St, SW6 .99 CY82
★ Fulham Palace Mus, SW6 .99 CX82
Fulham Palace Rd, SW6 .99 CX80
W6 .99 CW78
Fulham Pk Gdns, SW6 .99 CZ82
Fulham Pk Rd, SW6 .99 CZ82
Fulham Rd, SW3 .100 DC79
SW6 .99 CY82
SW10 .100 DB80
Fullarton Cres, S.Ock. RM15 .91 FT72
Fullbrooks Av, Wor.Pk. KT4 .139 CT102
Fuller Cl, E2
off St. Matthew's Row .84 DU70
Orpington BR6 .163 ET106
Fuller Gdns, Wat. WD24
off Fuller Rd .23 BV37
Fuller Rd, Dag. RM8 .70 EV62
Watford WD24 .23 BV37
Fullers Av, Surb. KT6 .138 CM103
Woodford Green IG8 .48 EF52
Fullers Cl, Rom. RM5 .51 FC52
Waltham Abbey EN9 .16 EG33
★ Fuller's Griffin Brewery, W4 .99 CT79
Fullers Hill, West. TN16
off Market Sq .189 ER126
Fullers La, Rom. RM5 .51 FC52
Fullers Rd, E18 .48 EF53
Fuller St, NW4 .63 CW56
Fullers Way N, Surb. KT6 .138 CM104
Fullers Way S, Chess. KT9 .156 CL105
Fullers Wd, Croy. CR0 .161 EA106
Fullers Wd La, Red. (S.Nutfld) RH1 .185 DJ134
Fuller Ter, Ilf. IG1
off Oaktree Gro .69 EQ64
Fullerton Cl, W.Byf. (Byfleet) KT14 .152 BM114
Fullerton Dr, W.Byf. (Byfleet) KT14 .152 BL114
Fullerton Rd, SW18 .120 DC85
Carshalton SM5 .158 DE109
Croydon CR0 .142 DT101
West Byfleet (Byfleet) KT14 .152 BM114
Fullerton Way, W.Byf. (Byfleet) KT14 .152 BL114
Fuller Way, Hayes UB3 .95 BT78
Rickmansworth (Crox.Grn) WD3 .22 BN43
Fullmer Way, Add. (Wdhm) KT15 .151 BF110
Fullwell Av, Ilf. IG5, IG6 .49 EM53
FULLWELL CROSS, Ilf. IG6 .49 ER53
Fullwell Cross Rbt, Ilf. IG6
off High St .49 ER54
Fullwoods Ms, N1 .197 L2
Fulmar Cl, Surb. KT5 .138 CM100
Fulmar Rd, Horn. RM12 .89 FG66
Fulmead St, SW6 .100 DB81
FULMER, Slou. SL3 .56 AX63
Fulmer Cl, Hmptn. TW12 .116 BY92
Fulmer Common Rd, Iver SL0 .75 AZ65
Slough (Fulmer) SL3 .75 AZ65
Fulmer Dr, Ger.Cr. SL9 .56 AY61
Fulmer La, Ger.Cr. SL9 .57 BB60
Slough (Fulmer) SL3 .56 AY62
Fulmer Ri Est, Slou. (Fulmer) SL3 .75 AZ65
Fulmer Rd, E16 .86 EK71
Gerrards Cross SL9 .56 AY59
Slough (Fulmer) SL3 .56 AY63
Fulmer Way, W13 .97 CH76
Gerrards Cross SL9 .56 AY58
Fulready Rd, E10 .67 ED57
Fulstone Cl, Houns. TW4 .96 BZ84
Fulthorp Rd, SE3 .104 EF82
Fulton Ms, W2
off Porchester Ter .82 DC73
Fulton Rd, Wem. HA9 .62 CN62
⇌ Fulwell .117 CD91
Fulwell Pk Av, Twick. TW2 .116 CB89
Fulwell Rd, Tedd. TW11 .117 CD91
Fulwich Rd, Dart. DA1 .128 FM86
Fulwood Av, Wem. HA0 .80 CM67
Fulwood Cl, Hayes UB3 .77 BT72
Fulwood Gdns, Twick. TW1 .117 CF86
Fulwood Pl, WC1 .196 C7
Fulwood Wk, SW19 .119 CY88
Furber St, W6 .99 CV76
Furham Feild, Pnr. HA5 .40 CA52
Furley Rd, SE15 .102 DU80
Furlong Cl, Wall. SM6 .141 DH102
Furlong Rd, N7 .83 DN65
Furlough, The, Wok. GU22
off Pembroke Rd .167 BA117
Furmage St, SW18 .120 DB87
Furneaux Av, SE27 .121 DP92
Furner Cl, Dart. DA1 .107 FF83
Furness Cl, Grays RM16 .111 GH78
Furness Rd, NW10 .81 CU68
SW6 .100 DB82
Harrow HA2 .60 CB59
Morden SM4 .140 DB101
Furness Way, Horn. RM12 .71 FG64
Furnival Cl, Vir.W. GU25 .132 AX100
Furnival St, EC4 .196 D8
Furrow La, E9 .66 DW64
Furrows, The, Uxb. (Hare.) UB9 .58 BJ57
Walton-on-Thames KT12 .136 BW103
Furrows Pl, Cat. CR3 .176 DT123
Fursby Av, N3 .44 DA51
Further Acre, NW9 .43 CT54
Furtherfield, Abb.L. WD5 .7 BS32
Furtherfield Cl, Croy. CR0 .141 DN100
Further Grn Rd, SE6 .124 EE87
Furzebushes La, St.Alb. AL2 .8 BY25
Furze Cl, Red. RH1 .184 DF133
Watford WD19 .40 BW50
FURZEDOWN, SW17 .120 DG92
Furzedown Cl, Egh. TW20 .112 AY93
Furzedown Dr, SW17 .121 DH92
Furzedown Hall, SW17
off Spalding Rd .121 DH92
Furzedown Rd, SW17 .121 DH92
Sutton SM2 .158 DC111
Furze Fm Cl, Rom. RM6 .50 EY54
Furze Fld, Lthd. (Oxshott) KT22 .155 CD113
Furzefield, Wal.Cr. (Chsht) EN8 .14 DV28
Furzefield Cl, Chis. BR7 .125 EP93
Furzefield Rd, SE3 .104 EH79
Furzeground Way, Uxb. UB11 .77 BQ74
Furze Gro, Tad. KT20 .173 CZ121
Furzeham Rd, West Dr. UB7 .94 BL75
Furze Hill, Pur. CR8 .159 DL111
Redhill RH1
off Linkfield La .184 DE133
Tadworth (Kgswd) KT20 .173 CZ120
Furzehill Par, Borwd. WD6
off Shenley Rd .26 CN41
Furzehill Rd, Borwd. WD6 .26 CN42
Furzehill Sq, Orp. (St.M.Cray) BR5 .146 EV98
Furze La, Pur. CR8 .159 DL111
Furze Rd, Add. KT15 .151 BF107
Thornton Heath CR7 .142 DQ97
Furze St, E3 .85 EA71
Furze Vw, Rick. (Chorl.) WD3 .21 BC44
Furzewood, Sun. TW16 .135 BU95
Fuschia Ct, Wdf.Grn. IG8
off The Bridle Path .48 EE52
Fusedale Way, S.Ock. RM15 .91 FT73
Fyfe Way, Brom. BR1
off Widmore Rd .144 EG96
Fyfield Cl, Brom. BR2 .143 ED98
Fyfield Ct, E7 .86 EG65
Fyfield Rd, E17 .67 ED55
SW9 .101 DN83
Enfield EN1 .30 DS41
Rainham RM13 .89 FF67
Woodford Green IG8 .48 EJ52
Fynes St, SW1 .199 M8

G

Gabion Av, Purf. RM19 .109 FR77
Gable Cl, Abb.L. WD5 .7 BS32
Dartford DA1 .127 FG85
Pinner HA5 .40 CA52
Gable Ct, SE26
off Lawrie Pk Av .122 DV91
Gables, The, Bans. SM7 .173 CZ117
Leatherhead (Oxshott) KT22 .154 CC112
Wembley HA9 .62 CM62
Gables Av, Ashf. TW15 .114 BM92
Borehamwood WD6 .26 CM41
Gables Cl, SE5 .102 DS81
SE12 .124 EG88
Gerrards Cross (Chal.St.P.) SL9 .36 AY49
Slough (Datchet) SL3 .92 AU79
Woking (Kgfld) GU22
off Kingfield Rd .167 AZ120
Gables Ct, Wok. (Kgfld) GU22
off Kingfield Rd .167 AZ120
Gables Way, Bans. SM7 .173 CZ117
Gabriel Cl, Felt. TW13 .116 BX91
Grays (Chaff.Hun.) RM16 .109 FW76
Romford RM5 .51 FC52
Gabrielle Cl, Wem. HA9 .62 CM62
Gabrielle Ct, NW3 .82 DD65
Gabriel Ms, NW2
off Crewys Rd .63 CZ61
Gabriels Gdns, Grav. DA12 .131 GL92
Gabriel Spring Rd, Long. (Fawk.Grn) DA3 .149 FR103
Gabriel Spring Rd (East), Long. (Fawk.Grn) DA3 .149 FS103
Gabriel St, SE23 .123 DX87
Gabriel's Wf, SE1 .200 D2
Gad Cl, E13 .86 EH69
Gaddesden Av, Wem. HA9 .80 CM65
Gaddesden Cres, Wat. WD25 .8 BX34
Gade Av, Wat. WD18 .23 BS42
Gade Bk, Rick. (Crox.Grn) WD3 .23 BR42
Gade Cl, Hayes UB3 .77 BV74
Watford WD18 .23 BS42
Gadesden Rd, Epsom KT19 .156 CQ107
Gadeside, Wat. WD25 .23 BS35
Gade Twr, Hem.H. HP3 .6 BN25
Gade Valley Cl, Kings L. WD4 .6 BN28
Gade Vw Gdns, Kings L. WD4 .7 BQ32
Gadsbury Cl, NW9 .63 CT58
Gadsden Cl, Upmin. RM14 .73 FS58
Gadswell Cl, Wat. WD25 .24 BX36
Gadwall Cl, E16
off Freemasons Rd .86 EH72
Gadwall Way, SE28 .105 ER75
Gage Rd, E16
off Malmesbury Rd .86 EE71
Gage St, WC1 .196 A6
Gainford St, N1
off Richmond Av .83 DN67
Gainsboro Gdns, Grnf. UB6 .61 CE64
Gainsborough Av, E12 .69 EN64
Dartford DA1 .128 FJ85
Tilbury RM18 .111 GG81
Gainsborough Cl, Beck. BR3 .123 EA94
Esher KT10
off Lime Tree Av .137 CE102
Gainsborough Ct, N12 .44 DB50
W12 *off Lime Gro* .99 CW75
Bromley BR2 .144 EJ98
Walton-on-Thames KT12 .153 BU105
Gainsborough Dr, Grav. (Nthflt) DA11 .130 GD90
South Croydon CR2 .160 DU113
Gainsborough Gdns, NW3 .64 DD62
NW11 .63 CZ59
Edgware HA8 .42 CM54
Isleworth TW7 .117 CD85
Gainsborough Ho, E14 .204 A5

★ Place of interest ⇌ Railway station ⊖ London Underground station DLR Docklands Light Railway station Tra Tramlink station H Hospital Riv Pedestrian ferry landing stage

Gainsborough Ho, Enf. EN1
off Ayley Cft 30 DU43
Gainsborough Ms, SE26
off Panmure Rd 122 DV90
Gainsborough Pl, Chig. IG7 49 ET48
Gainsborough Rd, E11 68 EE59
E15 86 EE69
N12 44 DB50
W4 99 CT77
Dagenham RM8 70 EV63
Epsom KT19 156 CQ110
Hayes UB4 77 BQ68
New Malden KT3 138 CR101
Rainham RM13 89 FG67
Richmond TW9 98 CM83
Woodford Green IG8 48 EL51
Gainsborough Sq, Bexh. DA6
off Regency Way 106 EX83
Gainsborough St, E9
off Trowbridge Rd 85 DZ65
Gainsborough Studios, N1
off Poole St 84 DR67
Gainsford Rd, E17 67 DZ56
Gainsford St, SE1 201 P4
Gairloch Rd, SE5 102 DS82
Gaisford St, NW5 83 DJ65
Gaist Av, Cat. CR3 176 DU122
Gaitskell Ct, SW11 100 DE82
Gaitskell Rd, SE9 125 EQ88
Gaitskell Way, SE1
off Lant St 102 DQ75
Galahad Rd, N9 46 DU48
Bromley BR1 124 EG90
Galata Rd, SW13 99 CU80
Galatea Sq, SE15
off Scylla Rd 102 DV83
Galaxy, E14 *off Crews St* 103 EA77
Galba Ct, Brent. TW8
off Augustus Cl 97 CK80
Galbraith St, E14 204 D6
Galdana Av, Barn. EN5 28 DC41
Galeborough Av, Wdf.Grn.
IG8 47 ED52
Gale Cl, Hmptn. TW12
off Stewart Cl 116 BY93
Mitcham CR4 140 DD97
Gale Cres, Bans. SM7 174 DA117
Galena Ho, SE18
off Grosmont Rd 105 ET78
Galena Rd, W6 99 CV77
Galen Cl, Epsom KT19 156 CN111
Galen Pl, WC1 196 A7
Galesbury Rd, SW18 120 DC86
Gales Gdns, E2 84 DV69
Gale St, E3 85 EA71
Dagenham RM9 88 EX67
Gales Way, Wdf.Grn. IG8 48 EL52
Galey Grn, S.Ock. RM15
off Bovey Way 91 FV71
Galgate Cl, SW19 119 CY88
Gallants Fm Rd, Barn. EN4 44 DE45
Galleon Boul, Dart. DA2 109 FR84
Galleon Cl, SE16 202 G4
Erith DA8 107 FD77
Galleon Ho, SW8
off St. George Wf 101 DL79
Galleon Ms, Grav. DA11
off Maritime Gate 130 GE87
Galleon Rd, Grays (Chaff.Hun.)
RM16 109 FW77
Galleons Dr, Bark. IG11 88 EU69
Galleons La, Slou. (Geo.Grn)
SL3 74 AX71
Gallery Gdns, Nthlt. UB5 78 BX68
Gallery Rd, SE21 122 DR88
Galley Hill, Wal.Abb. EN9 16 EF30
Galley Hill Rd, Grav. (Nthflt)
DA11 130 FZ85
Swanscombe DA10 130 FZ85
Galley La, Barn. EN5 27 CV41
Galleymead Rd, Slou.
(Colnbr.) SL3 93 BF81
Galleywall Rd, SE16 202 D9
Galleywood Cres, Rom. RM5 51 FD51
Galliard Cl, N9 30 DW44
Galliard Rd, N9 46 DU46
Gallia Rd, N5 65 DP64
Gallions Cl, Bark. IG11 88 EU69
DLR **Gallions Reach** 87 EP72
Gallions Reach Shop Pk, E6 87 EQ71
Gallions Rd, E16
off Armada Way 87 EQ73
SE7 104 EH77
Gallions Rbt, E16 87 EP73
Gallions Vw Rd, SE28
off Goldfinch Rd 105 ES75
Gallon Cl, SE7 104 EJ77
Gallop, The, S.Croy. CR2 160 DV108
Sutton SM2 158 DC108
Gallops, The, Tad. KT20 183 CV126
Gallosson Rd, SE18 105 ES77
Galloway Chase, Slou. SL2 74 AU73
Galloway Cl, Brox. EN10 15 DZ26
Galloway Dr, Dart. DA1 127 FE87
Galloway Path, Croy. CR0 160 DR105
Galloway Rd, W12 81 CU74
Gallows Cor, Rom. (Harold Wd)
RM3 52 FK53
Gallows Hill, Kings L. WD4 7 BQ31
Gallows Hill La, Abb.L. WD5 7 BQ32
Gallus Cl, N21 29 DM44
Gallus Sq, SE3 104 EH83
Galpins Rd, Th.Hth. CR7 141 DM98
Galsworthy Av, E14 85 DY71
Romford RM6 70 EV59
Galsworthy Cl, SE28 88 EV74
Galsworthy Cres, SE3
off Merriman Rd 104 EJ81
Galsworthy Rd, NW2 63 CY63
Chertsey KT16 134 BG101
Kingston upon Thames
KT2 118 CP94
Tilbury RM18 111 GJ81
Galsworthy Ter, N16
off Hawksley Rd 66 DS62
Galton St, W10 81 CY70
Galva Cl, Barn. EN4 28 DG42
Galvani Way, Croy. CR0
off Ampere Way 141 DM102
Galveston Rd, SW15 119 CZ85
Galway Cl, SE16
off Masters Dr 102 DV78
Galway Ho, EC1 197 J3
Galway St, EC1 197 J3
Gambetta St, SW8 101 DH82
Gambia St, SE1 200 G3
Gambier Ho, EC1 197 J2
Gambles La, Wok. (Ripley)
GU23 168 BJ124
Gambole Rd, SW17 120 DE91
Games Rd, Barn. EN4 28 DF41
Gamlen Rd, SW15 99 CX84
Gammons Fm Cl, Wat. WD24 23 BT36
Gammons La, Brox. EN10 14 DT25
Watford WD24 23 BV38
Gamuel Cl, E17 67 EA58
Gander Grn Cres, Hmptn.
TW12 136 CA95
Gander Grn La, Sutt.
SM1, SM3 139 CY103
Ganders Ash, Wat. WD25 7 BU33
Gandhi Cl, E17 67 EA58
Gandolfi St, SE15
off Dragon Rd 102 DS79
Gangers Hill, Cat. (Wold.)
CR3 187 EA127
Godstone RH9 187 EA127
Gant Ct, Wal.Abb. EN9 16 EF34
Ganton St, W1 195 K10
Ganton Wk, Wat. WD19
off Woodhall La 40 BY49
GANTS HILL, Ilf. IG2 69 EN57
⊖ **Gants Hill** 69 EN58
Gants Hill, Ilf. IG2
off Eastern Av 69 EN58
Gantshill Cres, Ilf. IG2 69 EN57
GANWICK CORNER, Barn.
EN5 28 DB35
Gap Rd, SW19 120 DA92
Garage Rd, W3 80 CN72
Garbrand Wk, Epsom KT17 157 CT109
Garbutt Pl, W1 194 G6
Garbutt Rd, Upmin. RM14 72 FQ61
Garden Av, Bexh. DA7 106 FA83
Mitcham CR4 121 DH94
Garden City, Edg. HA8 42 CN51
Garden Cl, E4 47 EA50
SE12 124 EH90
SW15 119 CV87
Addlestone KT15 152 BK105
Ashford TW15 115 BQ93
Banstead SM7 174 DA115
Barnet EN5 27 CW42
Hampton TW12 116 BZ92
Leatherhead KT22 171 CJ124
Northolt UB5 78 BY67
Ruislip HA4 59 BS61
Wallington SM6 159 DL106
Watford WD17 23 BT40
Garden Cotts, Orp. BR5
off Main Rd 146 EW96
Garden Ct, EC4 196 D10
N12 *off Holden Rd* 44 DB50
Richmond TW9 98 CM81
Stanmore HA7 41 CJ50
West Molesey KT8
off Avern Rd 136 CB98
Garden End, Amer. HP6 20 AS37
Gardeners Cl, N11 44 DG47
SE9 124 EL90
Gardeners Rd, Croy. CR0 141 DP102
H **Garden Hosp, The**, NW4 63 CW55
Gardenia Rd, Enf. EN1 30 DS44
Gardenia Way, Wdf.Grn. IG8 48 EG50
Garden La, SW2
off Christchurch Rd 121 DM88
Bromley BR1 124 EH93
Garden Ms, W2
off Linden Gdns 82 DA73
Slough SL1
off Littledown Rd 74 AT74
Garden Pl, E8
off Haggerston Rd 84 DT67
Dartford DA2 128 FK90
Garden Reach, Ch.St.G. HP8 20 AX41
Garden Rd, NW8 82 DC69
SE20 142 DW95
Abbots Langley WD5 7 BS31
Bromley BR1 124 EH94
Richmond TW9 98 CN83
Sevenoaks TN13 191 FK122
Walton-on-Thames KT12 135 BV100
Garden Row, SE1 200 F7
Gravesend (Nthflt) DA11 131 GF90
Gardens, The, SE22 102 DU84
Beckenham BR3 143 EC96
Esher KT10 154 CA105
Feltham TW14 115 BR85
Harrow HA1 60 CC58
Hatfield (Brook.Pk) AL9 11 CY27
Pinner HA5 60 BZ58
Watford WD17 23 BT40
★ **Gardens of the Rose**,
St.Alb. AL2 8 BY26
Garden St, E1 85 DX71
Garden Ter, SW1 199 M10
Garden Wk, EC2 197 M3
Beckenham BR3
off Hayne Rd 143 DZ95
Coulsdon CR5 175 DH123
Garden Way, NW10 80 CQ65
Loughton IG10 33 EN38
Gardiner Av, NW2 63 CW64
Gardiner Cl, Dag. RM8 70 EX63
Enfield EN3 31 DX44
Orpington BR5 146 EW96
H **Gardiner Hill Unit**, SW17 120 DE89
Gardner Cl, E11 68 EH58
Gardner Ct, EC1
off St. John St 83 DP70
Gardner Gro, Felt. TW13 116 BZ89
Gardner Pl, Felt. TW14 115 BV86
Gardner Rd, E13 86 EH70
Gardners La, EC4 197 H10
Gardnor Rd, NW3
off Flask Wk 64 DD63
Gard St, EC1 196 G2
Garendon Gdns, Mord. SM4 140 DB101
Garendon Rd, Mord. SM4 140 DB101
Gareth Cl, Wor.Pk. KT4
off Burnham Dr 139 CX103
Gareth Gro, Brom. BR1 124 EG91
Garfield Ms, SW11
off Garfield Rd 100 DG83
Garfield Rd, E4 47 ED46
E13 86 EF70
Garfield Rd, SW11 100 DG83
SW19 120 DC92
Addlestone KT15 152 BJ106
Enfield EN3 30 DW42
Twickenham TW1 117 CG88
Garfield St, Wat. WD24 23 BV38
Garford St, E14 203 P1
Garganey Wk, SE28 88 EX73
Garibaldi St, SE18 105 ES77
Garland Cl, Wal.Cr. EN8 15 DY31
Garland Dr, Houns. TW3 96 CC82
Garland Ho, Kings.T. KT2
off Kingsgate Rd 138 CL95
Garland Rd, SE18 105 ER80
Stanmore HA7 42 CL53
Garlands Ct, Croy. CR0
off Chatsworth Rd 160 DR105
Garlands Rd, Lthd. KT22 171 CH121
Garland Way, Cat. CR3 176 DR122
Hornchurch RM11 72 FL56
Garlichill Rd, Epsom KT18 173 CV117
Garlick Hill, EC4 197 J10
Garlies Rd, SE23 123 DY90
Garlinge Rd, NW2 81 CZ65
Garman Cl, N18 46 DR50
Garman Rd, N17 46 DW52
Garnault Ms, EC1 196 E3
Garnault Pl, EC1 196 E3
Garnault Rd, Enf. EN1 30 DT38
Garner Cl, Dag. RM8 70 EX60
Garner Dr, Brox. EN10 15 DY26
Garner Rd, E17 47 EC53
Garners Cl, Ger.Cr.
(Chal.St.P.) SL9 36 AY51
Garners End, Ger.Cr.
(Chal.St.P.) SL9 36 AY51
Garners Rd, Ger.Cr.
(Chal.St.P.) SL9 36 AY51
Garner St, E2 *off Coate St* 84 DU68
Garnet Rd, NW10 80 CS65
Thornton Heath CR7 142 DR98
Garnet St, E1 202 F1
Garnett Cl, SE9 105 EM83
Watford WD24 24 BX37
Garnett Dr, St.Alb. (Brick.Wd)
AL2 8 BZ29
Garnett Rd, NW3 64 DF64
Garnett Way, E17
off McEntee Av 47 DY53
Garnet Wk, E6
off Kingfisher St 86 EL71
Garnham Cl, N16
off Garnham St 66 DT61
Garnham St, N16 66 DT61
Garnies Cl, SE15 102 DT80
Garnon Mead, Epp. (Cooper.)
CM16 18 EX28
Garrad's Rd, SW16 121 DK90
Garrard Cl, Bexh. DA7 106 FA83
Chislehurst BR7 125 EP92
Garrard Rd, Bans. SM7 174 DA116
Garrard Wk, NW10
off Garnet Rd 80 CS65
Garratt Cl, Croy. CR0 159 DL105
Garratt La, SW17 120 DD91
SW18 120 DB85
Garratt Rd, Edg. HA8 42 CN52
Garratts La, Bans. SM7 173 CZ116
Garratts Rd, Bushey WD23 40 CC45
Garratt Ter, SW17 120 DE91
Garrett Cl, W3 *off Jenner Av* 80 CR71
Garrett St, EC1 197 J4
Garrick Av, NW11 63 CY58
Garrick Cl, SW18 100 DC84
W5 80 CL70
Richmond TW9
off Old Palace La 117 CK85
Staines TW18 114 BG94
Walton-on-Thames KT12 153 BV105
Garrick Cres, Croy. CR0 142 DS103
Garrick Dr, NW4 43 CW54
SE28 *off Broadwater Rd* 105 ER76
Garrick Gdns, W.Mol. KT8 136 CA97
Garrick Pk, NW4 43 CX54
Garrick Rd, NW9 63 CT58
Greenford UB6 78 CB70
Richmond TW9 98 CN82
Garricks Ho, Kings.T. KT1 137 CK96
Garrick St, WC2 195 P10
Gravesend DA11
off Barrack Row 131 GH86
Garrick Way, NW4 63 CX56
Garrison Cl, SE18
off Red Lion La 105 EN80
Hounslow TW4 116 BZ85
Garrison La, Chess. KT9 155 CK108
Garrison Par, Purf. RM19
off Comet Cl 108 FN77
Garrison Rd, E3
off Old Ford Rd 85 EA67
Garrolds Cl, Swan. BR8 147 FD96
Garron La, S.Ock. RM15 91 FT72
Garry Cl, Rom. RM1 51 FE52
Garry Way, Rom. RM1 51 FE52
Garsdale Cl, N11 44 DG51
Garside Cl, SE28
off Goosander Way 105 ER76
Hampton TW12 116 CB93
Garsington Ms, SE4 103 DZ83
Garsmouth Way, Wat. WD25 24 BX36
Garson Cl, Esher KT10
off Garson Rd 154 BZ107
Garson La, Stai. (Wrays.)
TW19 112 AX87
Garson Mead, Esher KT10 154 BZ106
Garson Rd, Esher KT10 154 BZ107
GARSTON, Wat. WD25 24 BW35
⇌ **Garston** 24 BX35
Garston Cres, Wat. WD25 8 BW34
Garston Dr, Wat. WD25 8 BW34
Garston Gdns, Ken. CR8
off Godstone Rd 176 DR115
Garston La, Ken. CR8 160 DR114
Watford WD25 8 BX34
Garston Pk Par, Wat. WD25 8 BX34
Garter Way, SE16 203 H5
Garth, The, N12
off Holden Rd 44 DB50
Abbots Langley WD5 7 BR33
Cobham KT11 154 BY113
Hampton (Hmptn H.) TW12
off Uxbridge Rd 116 CB93
Harrow HA3 62 CM58
Garth Cl, W4 98 CR78
Kingston upon Thames
KT2 118 CM92
Morden SM4 139 CX101
Ruislip HA4 60 BX60
Garth Ct, W4 *off Garth Rd* 98 CR78
Garth Ho, NW2
off Granville Rd 63 CZ61
Garthland Dr, Barn. EN5 27 CV43
Garth Ms, W5
off Greystoke Gdns 80 CL70
Garthorne Rd, SE23 123 DX87
Garth Rd, NW2 63 CZ61
W4 98 CR79
Kingston upon Thames
KT2 118 CM92
Morden SM4 139 CW100
Sevenoaks TN13 191 FJ128
South Ockendon RM15 91 FW70
Garth Rd Ind Cen, Mord.
SM4 139 CX101
Garthside, Rich. TW10 118 CL92
Garthway, N12 44 DE51
Gartlett Rd, Wat. WD17 24 BW41
Gartmoor Gdns, SW19 119 CZ88
Gartmore Rd, Ilf. IG3 69 ET60
Garton Pl, SW18 120 DC86
Gartons Cl, Enf. EN3 30 DW43
Gartons Way, SW11 100 DC83
Garvary Rd, E16 86 EH72
Garvock Dr, Sev. TN13 190 FG126
Garway Rd, W2 82 DB72
Garwood Cl, N17 46 DV53
Gascoigne Gdns, Wdf.Grn.
IG8 48 EE52
Gascoigne Pl, E2 197 P3
Gascoigne Rd, Bark. IG11 87 EQ67
Croydon (New Adgtn) CR0 161 EC110
Weybridge KT13 135 BP104
Gascony Av, NW6 82 DA66
Gascoyne Cl, Pot.B. EN6 11 CU32
Romford RM3 52 FK52
Gascoyne Dr, Dart. DA1 107 FF82
Gascoyne Rd, E9 85 DX66
Gaselee St, E14 204 E1
Gaskarth Rd, SW12 121 DH86
Edgware HA8 42 CQ53
Gaskell Rd, N6 64 DF58
Gaskell St, SW4 101 DL82
Gaskin St, N1 83 DP67
Gaspar Cl, SW5
off Courtfield Gdns 100 DB77
Gaspar Ms, SW5
off Courtfield Gdns 100 DB77
Gassiot Rd, SW17 120 DF91
Gassiot Way, Sutt. SM1 140 DD104
Gasson Rd, Swans. DA10 130 FY86
Gastein Rd, W6 99 CX79
Gaston Bell Cl, Rich. TW9 98 CM83
Gaston Br Rd, Shep. TW17 135 BS99
Gaston Rd, Mitch. CR4 140 DG97
Gaston Way, Shep. TW17 135 BR99
Gataker St, SE16 202 E6
Gatcombe Ms, W5 80 CM73
Gatcombe Rd, E16 205 N2
N19 65 DK62
Gatcombe Way, Barn. EN4 28 DF41
Gate Cl, Borwd. WD6 26 CQ39
Gate End, Nthwd. HA6 39 BU52
Gateforth St, NW8 194 B5
Gatehill Rd, Nthwd. HA6 39 BT52
Gatehope Dr, S.Ock. RM15 91 FT72
Gatehouse Cl, Kings.T. KT2 118 CQ94
Gatehouse Sq, SE1
off Southwark Br Rd 84 DQ74
Gateley Rd, SW9 101 DM83
Gate Ms, SW7 198 C5
Gater Dr, Enf. EN2 30 DR39
Gatesborough St, EC2 197 M4
Gatesden Cl, Lthd. (Fetch.)
KT22 170 CC123
Gatesden Rd, Lthd. (Fetch.)
KT22 170 CC123
Gates Grn Rd, Kes. BR2 162 EG105
West Wickham BR4 144 EF104
Gateshead Rd, Borwd. WD6 26 CM39
Gateside Rd, SW17 120 DF90
Gatestone Rd, SE19 122 DS93
Gate St, WC2 196 B8
Gateway, SE17 102 DQ79
Weybridge KT13
off Palace Dr 135 BP104
Gateway, The, Wat. WD18 23 BS43
Woking GU21 151 BB114
Gateway Arc, N1
off Islington High St 83 DP68
Gateway Business Cen,
SE26 123 DY93
Gateway Cl, Nthwd. HA6 39 BQ51
Gateway Ho, Bark. IG11
off St. Ann's 87 EQ67
Gateway Ind Est, NW10 81 CT69
Gateway Ms, E8
off Shacklewell La 66 DT64
Gateway Retail Pk, E6 87 EP70
Gateway Rd, E10 67 EB62
Gateways, The, SW3 198 C9
Waltham Cross EN7 14 DR28
Gatewick Cl, Slou. SL1 74 AS74
Gatfield Gro, Felt. TW13 116 CA89
Gathorne Rd, N22 45 DN54
Gathorne St, E2 *off Mace St* 85 DX68
Gatley Av, Epsom KT19 156 CP106
Gatliff Cl, SW1
off Ebury Br Rd 101 DH78
Gatliff Rd, SW1 100 DG78
Gatling Rd, SE2 106 EU78
Gatonby St, SE15 102 DT81
Gatting Cl, Edg. HA8 42 CQ52
Gatting Way, Uxb. UB8 76 BL65
GATTON, Reig. RH2 184 DF128
Gatton Bottom, Red.
(Merst.) RH1 185 DH127
Reigate RH2 184 DE128
Gatton Cl, Reig. RH2 184 DC131
Sutton SM2 158 DB109
Gatton Pk, Reig. RH2 184 DF129
Gatton Pk Rd, Red. RH1 184 DD132
Reigate RH2 184 DD132
Gatton Rd, SW17 120 DE91
Reigate RH2 184 DC131
Gattons Way, Sid. DA14 126 EZ91
Gatward Cl, N21 29 DP44
Gatward Grn, N9 46 DS47
Gatwick Rd, SW18 119 CZ87
Gravesend DA12 131 GH90
Gatwick Way, Horn. RM12
off Haydock Cl 72 FM63
Gauden Cl, SW4 101 DK83
Gauden Rd, SW4 101 DK82
Gaumont App, Wat. WD17 23 BV41
Gaumont Ter, W12
off Lime Gro 99 CW75
Gauntlet Cl, Nthlt. UB5 78 BY66
Gauntlet Cres, Ken. CR8 176 DR120
Gauntlett Ct, Wem. HA0 61 CH64
Gauntlett Rd, Sutt. SM1 158 DD106
Gaunt St, SE1 200 G6
Gautrey Rd, SE15 102 DW82
Gautrey Sq, E6 87 EM72
Gavell Rd, Cob. KT11 153 BU113
Gavel St, SE17 201 L8
Gavenny Path, S.Ock. RM15 91 FT72
Gaverick Ms, E14 203 P8
Gaveston Cl, W.Byf. (Byfleet)
KT14 152 BM113
Gavestone Cres, SE12 124 EH87
Gavestone Rd, SE12 124 EH87
Gaveston Rd, Lthd. KT22 171 CG120
Gaviller Pl, E5
off Clarence Rd 66 DV63
Gavina Cl, Mord. SM4 140 DE99
Gavin St, SE18 105 ES77
Gaviots Cl, Ger.Cr. SL9 57 AZ60
Gaviots Grn, Ger.Cr. SL9 56 AY60
Gaviots Way, Ger.Cr. SL9 56 AY59
Gawain Wk, N9
off Galahad Rd 46 DU48
Gawber St, E2 84 DW69
Gawsworth Cl, E15
off Ash Rd 68 EE64
Gawthorne Av, NW7
off Lane App 43 CY50
Gawthorne Ct, E3
off Mostyn Gro 85 EA68
Gay Cl, NW2 63 CV64
Gaydon Ho, W2 82 DB71
Gaydon La, NW9 42 CS53
Gayfere Rd, Epsom KT17 157 CU106
Ilford IG5 69 EM55
Gayfere St, SW1 199 P7
Gayford Rd, W12 99 CT75
Gay Gdns, Dag. RM10 71 FC63
Gayhurst, SE17
off Hopwood Rd 102 DR79
Gayhurst Rd, E8 84 DU66
Gayler Cl, Red. (Bletch.) RH1 186 DT133
Gaylor Rd, Nthlt. UB5 60 BZ64
Tilbury RM18 110 GE81
Gaynes Ct, Upmin. RM14 72 FP63
Gaynesford Rd, SE23 123 DX89
Carshalton SM5 158 DF108
Gaynes Hill Rd, Wdf.Grn. IG8 48 EL51
Gaynes Pk, Epp. (Cooper.)
CM16 18 EY31
Gaynes Pk Rd, Upmin. RM14 72 FN63
Gaynes Rd, Upmin. RM14 72 FP61
Gay Rd, E15 85 ED68
Gaysham Av, Ilf. IG2 69 EN57
Gaysham Hall, Ilf. IG5 69 EP55
Gay St, SW15 99 CX83
Gayton Cl, Amer. HP6 20 AS35
Ashtead KT21 172 CL118
Gayton Ct, Har. HA1 61 CF58
Gayton Cres, NW3 64 DD63
Gayton Ho, E3 85 EA70
Gayton Rd, NW3 64 DD63
SE2 *off Florence Rd* 106 EW76
Harrow HA1 61 CF58
Gayville Rd, SW11 120 DF86
Gaywood Av, Wal.Cr. (Chsht)
EN8 15 DX30
Gaywood Cl, SW2 121 DM88
Gaywood Est, SE1 200 G7
Gaywood Rd, E17 67 EA55
Ashtead KT21 172 CM118
Gaywood St, SE1 200 G7
Gaza St, SE17
off Braganza St 101 DP78
Gazelle Glade, Grav. DA12 131 GM92
Gazelle Ho, E15
off Manbey Pk Rd 86 EE65
Geariesville Gdns, Ilf. IG6 69 EP56
Gearing Cl, SW17 120 DG91
Geary Dr, Brwd. CM14, CM15 54 FW46
Geary Rd, NW10 63 CU64
Geary St, N7 65 DM64
G.E.C. Est, Wem. HA9 61 CK62
Geddes Pl, Bexh. DA6
off Market Pl 106 FA84
Geddes Rd, Bushey WD23 24 CC42
Gedeney Rd, N17 46 DQ53
Gedling Pl, SE1 202 A6
Geere Rd, E15 86 EF67
Gees Ct, W1 194 G9
Gee St, EC1 197 H4
Geffrye Ct, N1 197 N1
Geffrye Est, N1
off Stanway St 84 DS68
★ **Geffrye Mus**, E2 197 N1
Geffrye St, E2 84 DT68
Geisthorp Ct, Wal.Abb. EN9 16 EG33
Geldart Rd, SE15 102 DV80
Geldeston Rd, E5 66 DU61
Gellatly Rd, SE14 102 DW82
Gell Cl, Uxb. UB10 58 BM62
Gelsthorpe Rd, Rom. RM5 51 FB52
Gemini Gro, Nthlt. UB5
off Javelin Way 78 BY69
Gemmell Cl, Pur. CR8 159 DM114
General Gordon Pl, SE18 105 EP77
Generals Wk, The, Enf. EN3 31 DY37
General Wolfe Rd, SE10 103 ED81
Genesis Business Pk, Wok.
GU21 167 BC115
Genesis Cl, Stai. (Stanw.)
TW19 114 BM88
Genesta Rd, SE18 105 EP79
Geneva Cl, Shep. TW17 135 BS96
Geneva Dr, SW9 101 DN84

Geneva Gdns, Rom. RM6 ....70 EY57
Geneva Rd, Kings.T. KT1 ....138 CL98
Thornton Heath CR7 ....142 DQ99
Genever Cl, E4 ....47 EA50
Genista Rd, N18 ....46 DV50
Genoa Av, SW15 ....119 CW85
Genoa Rd, SE20 ....142 DW95
Genotin Ms, Horn. RM12 ....72 FJ64
Genotin Rd, Enf. EN1 ....30 DR41
Genotin Ter, Enf. EN1
off Genotin Rd 30 DR41
Gentian Row, SE13
off Sparta St 103 EC81
Gentlemans Row, Enf. EN2 ....30 DQ41
Gentry Gdns, E13
off Whitwell Rd 86 EG70
Geoffrey Av, Rom. RM3 ....52 FN51
Geoffrey Cl, SE5 ....102 DQ82
Geoffrey Gdns, E6 ....86 EL68
Geoffrey Rd, SE4 ....103 DZ83
George Avey Cft, Epp. (N.Wld Bas.)
CM16 ....19 FB26
George Beard Rd, SE8 ....203 M9
George Belt Ho, E2
off Smart St 85 DX69
George Comberton Wk, E12
off Gainsborough Av 69 EN64
George Ct, WC2 ....200 A1
George Cres, N10 ....44 DG52
George Crook's Ho, Grays
RM17 *off New Rd* 110 GB79
George Downing Est, N16
off Cazenove Rd 66 DT61
George Eliot Ho, SW1
off Vauxhall Br Rd 101 DJ77
George Elliston Ho, SE1
off Old Kent Rd 102 DU78
George V Av, Pnr. HA5 ....60 CA55
George V Cl, Pnr. HA5
off George V Av 60 CA55
Watford WD18 ....23 BT42
George V Way, Grnf. UB6 ....79 CH67
Rickmansworth (Sarratt)
WD3 ....22 BG36
George Gange Way, Har.
(Wealds.) HA3 ....61 CE55
GEORGE GREEN, Slou. SL3 ....74 AX72
George Grn Dr, Slou.
(Geo.Grn) SL3 ....75 AZ71
George Grn Rd, Slou.
(Geo.Grn) SL3 ....74 AX72
George Gro Rd, SE20 ....142 DU95
★ **George Inn**, SE1 ....201 K3
George Inn Yd, SE1 ....201 K3
Georgelands, Wok. (Ripley)
GU23 ....168 BH121
George La, E18 ....48 EG54
SE13 ....123 EC86
Bromley BR2 ....144 EH102
George La Rbt, E18
off George La 48 EG54
George Lansbury Ho, N22
off Progress Way 45 DN53
George Loveless Ho, E2
off Diss St 84 DT69
George Lovell Dr, Enf. EN3 ....31 EA37
George Lowe Ct, W2
off Bourne Ter 82 DB71
George Mathers Rd, SE11 ....200 F8
George Ms, NW1 ....195 K3
Enfield EN2 *off Sydney Rd* 30 DR41
George Pl, N17
off Dongola Rd 66 DS55
George Rd, E4 ....47 EA51
Kingston upon Thames
KT2 ....118 CP94
New Malden KT3 ....139 CT98
George Row, SE16 ....202 B5
Georges Cl, Orp. BR5 ....146 EW97
Georges Dr, Brwd. (Pilg.Hat.)
CM15 ....54 FT43
Georges Mead, Borwd.
(Els.) WD6 ....25 CK44
George Sq, SW19
off Mostyn Rd 139 CZ97
George's Rd, N7 ....65 DM64
Georges Rd, West. (Tats.)
TN16 ....178 EK120
Georges Sq, SW6
off North End Rd 99 CZ79
Georges Ter, Cat. CR3
off Coulsdon Rd 176 DR122
Tra **George Street** 142 DQ103
George St, E16 ....86 EF72
W1 ....194 E8
W7 *off The Broadway* 79 CE74
Barking IG11 ....87 EQ66
Croydon CR0 ....142 DR103
Grays RM17 ....110 GA79
Hounslow TW3 ....96 BZ82
Richmond TW9 ....117 CK85
Romford RM1 ....71 FF58
Southall UB2 ....96 BY77
Staines TW18 ....113 BF91
Uxbridge UB8 ....76 BK66
Watford WD18 ....24 BW42
George's Wd Rd, Hat.
(Brook.Pk) AL9 ....12 DA26
George Tilbury Ho, Grays
RM16 ....111 GH75
Georgetown Cl, SE19
off St. Kitts Ter 122 DR92
Georgette Pl, SE10
off King George St 103 EC80
Georgeville Gdns, Ilf. IG6 ....69 EP56
Georgewood Rd, Hem.H. HP3 ....6 BM25
George Wyver Cl, SW19
off Beaumont Rd 119 CY87
George Yd, EC3 ....197 L9
W1 ....194 G10
Georgiana St, NW1 ....83 DJ67
Georgian Cl, Brom. BR2 ....144 EH101
Staines TW18 ....114 BH91
Stanmore HA7 ....41 CG52
Uxbridge UB10 ....58 BL63
Georgian Ct, SW16
off Gleneldon Rd 121 DL91
Wembley HA9 ....80 CN65
Georgian Way, Har. HA1 ....61 CD61
Georgia Rd, N.Mal. KT3 ....138 CQ98
Thornton Heath CR7 ....141 DP95
Georgina Gdns, E2
off Columbia Rd 84 DT69
Geraint Rd, Brom. BR1 ....124 EG91
Geraldine Rd, SW18 ....120 DC85
W4 ....98 CN79
Geraldine St, SE11 ....200 F7
Gerald Ms, SW1 ....198 G8
Gerald Rd, E16 ....86 EF70
SW1 ....198 G8
Dagenham RM8 ....70 EZ61
Gravesend DA12 ....131 GL87
Geralds Gro, Bans. SM7 ....157 CX114
Gerard Av, Houns. TW4 ....116 CA87
Gerard Gdns, Rain. RM13 ....89 FE68
Gerard Pl, E9
off Groombridge Rd 85 DX66
Gerard Rd, SW13 ....99 CT81
Harrow HA1 ....61 CG58
Gerards Cl, SE16 ....102 DW78
Gerda Rd, SE9 ....125 EQ89
Gerdview Dr, Dart. DA2 ....128 FJ91
Germander Way, E15 ....86 EE69
Gernigan Ho, SW18
off Fitzhugh Gro 120 DD86
Gernon Cl, Rain. RM13
off Jordans Way 90 FK68
Gernon Rd, E3 ....85 DY68
Geron Way, NW2 ....63 CV60
Gerpins La, Upmin. RM14 ....90 FM68
Gerrard Cres, Brwd. CM14 ....54 FV48
Gerrard Gdns, Pnr. HA5 ....59 BU57
Gerrard Pl, W1 ....195 N10
Gerrard Rd, N1 ....83 DP68
Gerrards Cl, N14 ....29 DJ43
GERRARDS CROSS, SL9 ....56 AX58
⇌ **Gerrards Cross** 56 AY57
Gerrards Cross Rd, Slou.
(Stoke P.) SL2 ....74 AU66
Gerrards Mead, Bans. SM7 ....173 CZ116
Gerrard St, W1 ....195 M10
Gerridge St, SE1 ....200 E5
Gerry Raffles Sq, E15
off Great Eastern Rd 85 ED65
Gertrude Rd, Belv. DA17 ....106 FA77
Gertrude St, SW10 ....100 DC79
Gervase Cl, Wem. HA9 ....62 CQ62
Gervase Rd, Edg. HA8 ....42 CQ53
Gervase St, SE15 ....102 DV80
Gews Cor, Wal.Cr. (Chsht)
EN8 ....15 DX29
Ghent St, SE6 ....123 EA89
Ghent Way, E8 *off Tyssen St* 84 DT65
Giant Arches Rd, SE24 ....122 DQ87
Giant Tree Hill, Bushey
(Bushey Hth) WD23 ....41 CD46
Gibbard Ms, SW19 ....119 CX92
Gibbfield Cl, Rom. RM6 ....70 EY55
Gibbins Rd, E15 ....85 EC66
Gibbon Rd, SE15 ....102 DW82
W3 ....80 CS73
Kingston upon Thames
KT2 ....138 CL95
Gibbons Cl, Borwd. WD6 ....26 CL39
Gibbons Ms, NW11
off Hayes Cres 63 CZ57
Gibbons Rents, SE1
off Magdalen St 84 DS74
Gibbons Rd, NW10 ....80 CR65
Gibbon Wk, SW15 ....99 CU84
Gibbs Av, SE19 ....122 DR92
Gibbs Cl, SE19 ....122 DR92
Waltham Cross (Chsht) EN8 ....15 DX29
Gibbs Couch, Wat. WD19 ....40 BX48
Gibbs Grn, W14 ....99 CZ78
Edgware HA8 ....42 CQ50
Gibbs Rd, N18 ....46 DW49
Gibbs Sq, SE19 ....122 DR92
Gibraltar Cl, Brwd. (Gt Warley)
CM13 ....53 FW51
Gibraltar Cres, Epsom KT19 ....156 CS110
Gibraltar Ho, Brwd. CM13 ....53 FW51
Gibraltar Wk, E2 ....84 DT69
Gibson Cl, E1
off Colebert Av 84 DW70
N21 ....29 DN44
Chessington KT9 ....155 CJ107
Epping (N.Wld Bas.) CM16
off Beamish Cl 19 FC25
Gravesend (Nthflt) DA11 ....131 GF90
Isleworth TW7 ....97 CD83
Gibson Ct, Rom. RM1
off Regarth Av 71 FE58
Slough SL3 ....93 AZ78
Gibson Gdns, N16
off Northwold Rd 66 DT61
Gibson Ms, Twick. TW1
off Richmond Rd 117 CJ87
Gibson Pl, Stai. (Stanw.)
TW19 ....114 BJ86
Gibson Rd, SE11 ....200 C9
Dagenham RM8 ....70 EW60
Sutton SM1 ....158 DB106
Uxbridge UB10 ....58 BM63
Gibson's Hill, SW16 ....121 DN93
Gibson Sq, N1 ....83 DN67
Gibson St, SE10 ....104 EE78
Gidd Hill, Couls. CR5 ....174 DG116
Gidea Av, Rom. RM2 ....71 FG55
Gidea Cl, Rom. RM2 ....71 FG55
South Ockendon RM15
off Tyssen Pl 91 FW69
GIDEA PARK, Rom. RM2 ....71 FG55
⇌ **Gidea Park** 72 FJ56
Gideon Cl, Belv. DA17 ....107 FB77
Gideon Ms, W5 ....97 CK75
Gideon Rd, SW11 ....100 DG83
Gidian Ct, St.Alb. AL2 ....9 CD27
Giesbach Rd, N19 ....65 DJ61
Giffard Rd, N18 ....46 DS50
Giffin St, SE8 ....103 EA80
Gifford Gdns, W7 ....79 CD71
Gifford Pl, Brwd. (Warley)
CM14 ....54 FX50
Giffordside, Grays RM16 ....111 GH78
Gifford St, N1 ....83 DL66
Gift La, E15 ....86 EE67
Giggs Hill, Orp. BR5 ....146 EU96
Giggs Hill Gdns, T.Ditt. KT7 ....137 CG102
Giggs Hill Rd, T.Ditt. KT7 ....137 CG101
Gilbert Cl, SE18 ....105 EM81
Gilbert Cl, Swans. DA10 ....129 FX86
Gilbert Gro, Edg. HA8 ....42 CR53
Gilbert Ho, EC2
off The Barbican 84 DQ71
SE8 *off McMillan St* 103 EA79
SW1 *off Churchill Gdns* 101 DJ78
Gilbert Pl, WC1 ....195 P7
Gilbert Rd, SE11 ....200 E9
SW19 ....120 DC94
Belvedere DA17 ....106 FA76
Bromley BR1 ....124 EG94
Grays (Chaff.Hun.) RM16 ....109 FW76
Pinner HA5 ....60 BX56
Romford RM1 ....71 FF56
Uxbridge (Hare.) UB9 ....38 BK54
Gilbert St, E15 ....68 EE63
W1 ....194 G9
Enfield EN3 ....30 DW37
Hounslow TW3 *off High St* 96 CC83
Gilbert Way, Croy. CR0
off Beddington Fm Rd 141 DL102
Slough SL3 ....93 AZ78
Gilbey Cl, Uxb. UB10 ....59 BP63
Gilbey Rd, SW17 ....120 DE91
Gilbeys Yd, NW1 ....82 DG66
Gilbourne Rd, SE18 ....105 ET79
Gilda Av, Enf. EN3 ....31 DY43
Gilda Cres, N16 ....66 DU60
Gildea Cl, Pnr. HA5 ....40 CA52
Gildea St, W1 ....195 J7
Gilden Cres, NW5 ....64 DG64
Gildenhill Rd, Swan. BR8 ....128 FJ94
Gildersome St, SE18
off Nightingale Vale 105 EN79
Gilders Rd, Chess. KT9 ....156 CM107
Giles Cl, Rain. RM13 ....90 FK68
Giles Coppice, SE19 ....122 DT91
Giles Fld, Grav. DA12 ....131 GM88
Giles Travers Cl, Egh. TW20 ....133 BC97
Gilfrid Cl, Uxb. UB8 ....77 BP72
Gilhams Av, Bans. SM7 ....157 CX112
Gilkes Cres, SE21 ....122 DS86
Gilkes Pl, SE21 ....122 DS86
Gillam Way, Rain. RM13 ....89 FG65
Gillan Grn, Bushey (Bushey Hth)
WD23 ....40 CC47
Gillards Ms, E17
off Gillards Way 67 EA56
Gillards Way, E17 ....67 EA56
Gill Av, E16 ....86 EG72
Gill Cl, Wat. WD18 ....23 BQ44
Gill Cres, Grav. (Nthflt) DA11 ....131 GF90
Gillender St, E3 ....85 EC70
E14 ....85 EC70
Gillespie Rd, N5 ....65 DN62
Gillett Av, E6 ....86 EL68
Gillette Cor, Islw. TW7 ....97 CG80
Gillett Rd, Th.Hth. CR7 ....142 DR98
Gillett St, N16 ....66 DS64
Gillfoot, NW1 ....195 K1
Gillham Ter, N17 ....46 DU51
Gilliam Gro, Pur. CR8 ....159 DN110
Gillian Cres, Rom. RM2 ....52 FJ54
Gillian Pk Rd, Sutt. SM3 ....139 CZ102
Gillian St, SE13 ....123 EB85
Gilliat Cl, Iver SL0
off Grange Way 75 BF72
Gilliat Rd, Slou. SL1 ....74 AS73
Gilliat's Grn, Rick. (Chorl.)
WD3 ....21 BD42
Gillies St, NW5 ....64 DG64
Gilling Ct, NW3 ....82 DE65
Gillingham Ms, SW1 ....199 K8
Gillingham Rd, NW2 ....63 CY62
Gillingham Row, SW1 ....199 K8
Gillingham St, SW1 ....199 J8
Gillison Wk, SE16 ....202 C6
Gillman Dr, E15 ....86 EF67
Gillmans Rd, Orp. BR5 ....146 EV102
Gills Hill, Rad. WD7 ....25 CF35
Gills Hill La, Rad. WD7 ....25 CF36
Gills Hollow, Rad. WD7 ....25 CF36
Gill's Rd, Dart. (S.Darenth)
DA2, DA4 ....149 FS95
Gill St, E14 ....85 DZ72
Gillum Cl, Barn. EN4 ....44 DF46
Gilmore Cl, Slou. SL3 ....92 AW75
Uxbridge UB10 ....58 BN62
Gilmore Cres, Ashf. TW15 ....114 BN92
Gilmore Rd, SE13 ....103 ED84
Gilmour Cl, Wal.Cr. EN7 ....30 DU35
Gilpin Av, SW14 ....98 CR84
Gilpin Cl, W2 *off Porteus Rd* 82 DC71
Mitcham CR4 ....140 DE96
Gilpin Cres, N18 ....46 DT50
Twickenham TW2 ....116 CB87
Gilpin Rd, E5 ....67 DY63
Gilpin Way, Hayes UB3 ....95 BR80
Gilroy Cl, Rain. RM13 ....89 FF65
Gilroy Way, Orp. BR5 ....146 EV101
Gilsland, Wal.Abb. EN9 ....32 EE35
Gilsland Rd, Th.Hth. CR7 ....142 DR98
Gilstead Ho, Bark. IG11 ....88 EV68
Gilstead Rd, SW6 ....100 DB82
Gilston Rd, SW10 ....100 DC78
Gilton Rd, SE6 ....124 EE90
Giltspur St, EC1 ....196 G8
Gilwell Cl, E4
off Antlers Hill 31 EB42
Gilwell La, E4 ....31 EC42
Gilwell Pk, E4 ....31 EC41
Gimcrack Hill, Lthd. KT22
off Dorking Rd 171 CH123
Gippeswyck Cl, Pnr. HA5
off Uxbridge Rd 40 BX53
⇌ **Gipsy Hill** 122 DS92
Gipsy Hill, SE19 ....122 DS92
Gipsy La, SW15 ....99 CU83
Grays RM17 ....110 GC79
Gipsy Rd, SE27 ....122 DQ91
Welling DA16 ....106 EX81
Gipsy Rd Gdns, SE27 ....122 DQ91
Giralda Cl, E16
off Fulmer Rd 86 EK71
Giraud St, E14 ....85 EB72
Girdlers Rd, W14 ....99 CX77
Girdlestone Wk, N19 ....65 DJ61
Girdwood Rd, SW18 ....119 CY87
Girling Way, Felt. TW14 ....95 BU83
Girona Cl, Grays (Chaff.Hun.)
RM16 ....109 FW76
Gironde Rd, SW6 ....99 CZ80
Girtin Rd, Bushey WD23 ....24 CB43
Girton Av, NW9 ....62 CN55
Girton Cl, Nthlt. UB5 ....78 CC65
Girton Ct, Wal.Cr. EN8 ....15 DY30
Girton Gdns, Croy. CR0 ....143 EA104
Girton Rd, SE26 ....123 DX92
Northolt UB5 ....78 CC65
Girton Vil, W10 ....81 CX72
Girton Way, Rick. (Crox.Grn)
WD3 ....23 BQ43
Gisborne Gdns, Rain. RM13 ....89 FF69
Gisbourne Cl, Wall. SM6 ....141 DK104
Gisburne Way, Wat. WD24 ....23 BU37
Gisburn Rd, N8 ....65 DM56
Gissing Wk, N1
off Lofting Rd 83 DN66
Gittens Cl, Brom. BR1 ....124 EF91
Given Wilson Wk, E13 ....86 EF68
Glacier Way, Wem. HA0 ....79 CK68
Gladbeck Way, Enf. EN2 ....29 DP42
Gladding Rd, E12 ....68 EK63
Waltham Cross (Chsht) EN7 ....13 DP25
Glade, The, N21 ....29 DM44
SE7 ....104 EJ80
Brentwood (Hutt.) CM13 ....55 GA46
Bromley BR1 ....144 EK96
Coulsdon CR5 ....175 DN119
Croydon CR0 ....143 DX99
Enfield EN2 ....29 DN41
Epsom KT17 ....157 CU106
Gerrards Cross SL9 ....56 AX60
Ilford IG5 ....49 EM53
Leatherhead (Fetch.) KT22 ....170 CA122
Sevenoaks TN13 ....191 FH123
Staines TW18 ....114 BH94
Sutton SM2 ....157 CY109
Tadworth KT20 ....174 DA121
Upminster RM14 ....72 FQ64
West Byfleet KT14 ....151 BE113
West Wickham BR4 ....143 EB104
Woodford Green IG8 ....48 EH48
Glade Cl, Surb. KT6 ....137 CK103
Glade Ct, Ilf. IG5
off The Glade 49 EM53
Glade Gdns, Croy. CR0 ....143 DY101
Glade La, Sthl. UB2 ....96 CB75
Glades, The, Grav. DA12 ....131 GK93
Gladeside, N21 ....29 DM44
Croydon CR0 ....143 DX100
Gladeside Cl, Chess. KT9
off Leatherhead Rd 155 CK108
Gladeside Ct, Warl. CR6 ....176 DV120
Gladesmore Rd, N15 ....66 DT58
Glade Spur, Tad. KT20 ....174 DB121
Glades Shop Cen, The, Brom.
BR1 ....144 EG96
Gladeswood Rd, Belv. DA17 ....107 FB77
Gladeway, The, Wal.Abb. EN9 ....15 ED33
Gladiator St, SE23 ....123 DY86
Glading Ter, N16 ....66 DT62
Gladioli Cl, Hmptn. TW12
off Gresham Rd 116 CA93
Gladsdale Dr, Pnr. HA5 ....59 BU56
Gladsmuir Cl, Walt. KT12 ....136 BW103
Gladsmuir Rd, N19 ....65 DJ60
Barnet EN5 ....27 CY40
Gladstone Av, E12 ....86 EL66
N22 ....45 DN54
Feltham TW14 ....115 BU86
Twickenham TW2 ....117 CD87
Gladstone Ct, SW1
off Regency St 101 DK77
SW19 *off Gladstone Rd* 120 DA94
Gladstone Gdns, Houns. TW3
off Palmerston Rd 96 CC81
Gladstone Ms, N22
off Pelham Rd 45 DN54
NW6 *off Cavendish Rd* 81 CZ66
SE20 ....122 DW94
Gladstone Par, NW2
off Edgware Rd 63 CV60
Gladstone Pk Gdns, NW2 ....63 CV62
Gladstone Pl, E3
off Roman Rd 85 DZ68
Barnet EN5 ....27 CX42
Gladstone Rd, SW19 ....120 DA94
W4 *off Acton La* 98 CR76
Ashtead KT21 ....171 CK118
Buckhurst Hill IG9 ....48 EH46
Croydon CR0 ....142 DR101
Dartford DA1 ....128 FM86
Kingston upon Thames
KT1 ....138 CN97
Orpington BR6 ....163 EQ106
Southall UB2 ....96 BY76
Surbiton KT6 ....137 CK103
Watford WD17 ....24 BW41
Gladstone St, SE1 ....200 F6
Gladstone Ter, SE27
off Bentons La 122 DQ91
Gladstone Way, Har.
(Wealds.) HA3 ....61 CE55
Gladwell Rd, N8 ....65 DM58
Bromley BR1 ....124 EG93
Gladwyn Rd, SW15 ....99 CX83
Gladys Rd, NW6 ....82 DA66
Glaisher St, SE8 ....103 EA79
Glaisyer Way, Iver SL0 ....75 BC68
Glamis Cl, Wal.Cr. (Chsht)
EN7 ....14 DU29
Glamis Cres, Hayes UB3 ....95 BQ76
Glamis Dr, Horn. RM11 ....72 FL60
Glamis Pl, E1 ....84 DW73
Glamis Rd, E1 ....84 DW73
Glamis Way, Nthlt. UB5 ....78 CC65
Glamorgan Cl, Mitch. CR4 ....141 DL97
Glamorgan Rd, Kings.T. KT1 ....117 CJ94
Glanfield Rd, Beck. BR3 ....143 DZ98
Glanleam Rd, Stan. HA7 ....41 CK49
Glanmead, Brwd. (Shenf.)
CM15 ....54 FY46
Glanmor Rd, Slou. SL2 ....74 AV73
Glanthams Cl, Brwd.
(Shenf.) CM15 ....54 FY47
Glanthams Rd, Brwd.
(Shenf.) CM15 ....55 FZ47
Glanty, The, Egh. TW20 ....113 BB91
Glanville Dr, Horn. RM11 ....72 FM60
Glanville Ms, Stan. HA7 ....41 CG50
Glanville Rd, SW2 ....121 DL85
Bromley BR2 ....144 EH97
Glasbrook Av, Twick. TW2 ....116 BZ88
Glasbrook Rd, SE9 ....124 EK87
Glaserton Rd, N16 ....66 DS59
Glasford St, SW17 ....120 DF93
Glasgow Ho, W9 ....82 DB68
Glasgow Rd, E13 ....86 EH68
N18 *off Aberdeen Rd* 46 DV50
Glasgow Ter, SW1 ....101 DJ78
Glasier Ct, E15
off Glenavon Rd 86 EE66
Glaskin Ms, E9
off Danesdale Rd 85 DY65
Glasse Cl, W13 ....79 CG73
Glasshill St, SE1 ....200 G4
Glasshouse Cl, Uxb. UB8 ....77 BP71
Glasshouse Flds, E1 ....85 DX73
Glasshouse St, W1 ....199 L1
Glasshouse Wk, SE11 ....200 A10
Glasshouse Yd, EC1 ....197 H5
Glasslyn Rd, N8 ....65 DK57
Glassmill La, Brom. BR2 ....144 EF96
Glass St, E2 *off Coventry Rd* 84 DV70
Glass Yd, SE18
off Woolwich High St 105 EN76
Glastonbury Av, Wdf.Grn. IG8 ....48 EK52
Glastonbury Cl, Orp. BR5 ....146 EW102
Glastonbury Ho, SW1 ....199 H10
Glastonbury Pl, E1
off Sutton St 84 DW72
Glastonbury Rd, N9 ....46 DU46
Morden SM4 ....140 DA101
Glastonbury St, NW6 ....63 CZ64
Glaucus St, E3 ....85 EB71
Glazbury Rd, W14 ....99 CY77
Glazebrook Cl, SE21 ....122 DR89
Glazebrook Rd, Tedd. TW11 ....117 CF94
Glebe, The, SE3 ....104 EE83
SW16 ....121 DK91
Chislehurst BR7 ....145 EQ95
Kings Langley WD4 ....6 BN29
Watford WD25 ....8 BW33
West Drayton UB7 ....94 BM77
Worcester Park KT4 ....139 CT102
Glebe Av, Enf. EN2 ....29 DP41
Harrow HA3 ....62 CL55
Mitcham CR4 ....140 DE96
Ruislip HA4 ....77 BV65
Uxbridge UB10 ....59 BQ63
Woodford Green IG8 ....48 EG51
Glebe Cl, W4
off Prince of Wales Ter 98 CS78
Gerrards Cross (Chal.St.P.)
SL9 ....36 AX52
South Croydon CR2 ....160 DT111
Uxbridge UB10 ....59 BQ63
Glebe Cotts, Sutt. SM1
off Vale Rd 158 DB105
Westerham (Brasted) TN16 ....180 EV123
Glebe Ct, W7 ....79 CD73
Coulsdon CR5 ....175 DH115
Mitcham CR4 ....140 DF97
Sevenoaks TN13
off Oak La 191 FH126
Stanmore HA7 ....41 CJ50
Glebe Cres, NW4 ....63 CW56
Harrow HA3 ....62 CL55
Glebefield, The, Sev. TN13 ....190 FF123
Glebe Gdns, N.Mal. KT3 ....138 CS101
West Byfleet (Byfleet)
KT14 ....152 BK114
Glebe Ho Dr, Brom. BR2 ....144 EH102
Glebe Hyrst, SE19
off Giles Coppice 122 DT91
South Croydon CR2 ....160 DT112
Glebeland Gdns, Shep.
TW17 ....135 BQ100
Glebelands, Chig. IG7 ....50 EV48
Dartford DA1 ....107 FF84
Esher (Clay.) KT10 ....155 CF109
West Molesey KT8 ....136 CB99
Glebelands Av, E18 ....48 EG54
Ilford IG2 ....69 ER59
Glebelands Cl, N12 ....44 DD53
Glebelands Rd, Felt. TW14 ....115 BU87
Glebe La, Barn. EN5 ....27 CU43
Harrow HA3 ....62 CL56
Sevenoaks TN13 ....191 FH126
Glebe Ms, Sid. DA15
off Christopher Cl 125 ET85
Glebe Path, Mitch. CR4 ....140 DE97
Glebe Pl, SW3 ....100 DE79
Dartford (Hort.Kir.) DA4 ....148 FQ98
Glebe Rd, E8
off Middleton Rd 84 DT66
N3 ....44 DC53
N8 ....65 DM56
NW10 ....81 CT65
SW13 ....99 CU82
Ashtead KT21 ....171 CK118
Bromley BR1 ....144 EG95
Carshalton SM5 ....158 DF107
Dagenham RM10 ....89 FB65
Egham TW20 ....113 BC93
Gerrards Cross (Chal.St.P.)
SL9 ....36 AW53
Gravesend DA11 ....131 GF88
Hayes UB3 ....77 BT74
Rainham RM13 ....90 FJ69
Redhill (Merst.) RH1 ....175 DH124
Staines TW18 ....114 BH93
Stanmore HA7 ....41 CJ50
Sutton SM2 ....157 CY109
Uxbridge UB8 ....76 BJ68
Warlingham CR6 ....177 DX117
Windsor (Old Wind.) SL4 ....112 AV85
Glebe Side, Twick. TW1 ....117 CF86
Glebe St, W4 ....98 CS78
Glebe Ter, W4 *off Glebe St* 98 CS78
Glebe Way, Erith DA8 ....107 FE79
Feltham TW13 ....116 CA90
Hornchurch RM11 ....72 FL59
South Croydon CR2 ....160 DT111
West Wickham BR4 ....143 EC103
Glebeway, Wdf.Grn. IG8 ....48 EJ50
Gledhow Gdns, SW5 ....100 DC77
Gledhow Wd, Tad. KT20 ....174 DB121
Gledstanes Rd, W14 ....99 CY78
Gledwood Av, Hayes UB4 ....77 BT71
Gledwood Cres, Hayes UB4 ....77 BT71
Gledwood Dr, Hayes UB4 ....77 BT71
Gledwood Gdns, Hayes UB4 ....77 BT71
Gleed Av, Bushey (Bushey Hth)
WD23 ....41 CD47
Gleeson Dr, Orp. BR6 ....163 ET106
Gleeson Ms, Add. KT15 ....152 BJ105
Glegg Pl, SW15 ....99 CX84

★ Place of interest   ⇌ Railway station   ⊖ London Underground station   DLR Docklands Light Railway station   Tra Tramlink station   H Hospital   Riv Pedestrian ferry landing stage

Glen, The, Add. KT15 151 BF106
Bromley BR2 144 EE96
Croydon CR0 143 DX103
Enfield EN2 29 DP42
Northwood HA6 39 BR52
Orpington BR6 145 EM104
Pinner HA5 60 BY59
Pinner (Eastcote) HA5 59 BV57
Rainham RM13 90 FJ70
Slough SL3 92 AW77
Southall UB2 96 BZ78
Wembley HA9 61 CK63
Glenaffric Av, E14 204 F9
Glen Albyn Rd, SW19 119 CX89
Glenalla Rd, Ruis. HA4 59 BT59
Glenalmond Rd, Har. HA3 62 CL56
Glenalvon Way, SE18 104 EL77
Glena Mt, Sutt. SM1 158 DC105
Glenarm Rd, E5 66 DW64
Glen Av, Ashf. TW15 114 BN91
Glenavon Cl, Esher (Clay.) KT10 155 CG108
Glenavon Gdns, Slou. SL3 92 AW77
Glenavon Rd, E15 86 EE66
Glenbarr Cl, SE9
off Dumbreck Rd 105 EP83
Glenbow Rd, Brom. BR1 124 EE93
Glenbrook N, Enf. EN2 29 DM42
Glenbrook Rd, NW6 64 DA64
Glenbrook S, Enf. EN2 29 DM42
Glenbuck Ct, Surb. KT6
off Glenbuck Rd 137 CK100
Glenbuck Rd, Surb. KT6 137 CK100
Glenburnie Rd, SW17 120 DF90
Glencairn Dr, W5 79 CH70
Glencairne Cl, E16 86 EK71
Glencairn Rd, SW16 141 DL95
Glen Cl, Shep. TW17 134 BN98
Tadworth (Kgswd) KT20 173 CY123
Glencoe Av, Ilf. IG2 69 ER59
Glencoe Dr, Dag. RM10 70 FA63
Glencoe Rd, Bushey WD23 24 CA44
Hayes UB4 78 BY71
Weybridge KT13 134 BN104
Glencorse Grn, Wat. WD19
off Caldwell Rd 40 BX49
Glen Ct, Stai. TW18 113 BF94
Glen Cres, Wdf.Grn. IG8 48 EH51
Glendale, Swan. BR8 147 FF99
Glendale Av, N22 45 DN52
Edgware HA8 42 CM49
Romford RM6 70 EW59
Glendale Cl, SE9
off Dumbreck Rd 105 EN83
Brentwood (Shenf.) CM15 54 FY45
Woking GU21 166 AW118
Glendale Dr, SW19 119 CZ92
Glendale Gdns, Wem. HA9 61 CK60
Glendale Ms, Beck. BR3 143 EB95
Glendale Ri, Ken. CR8 175 DP115
Glendale Rd, Erith DA8 107 FC77
Gravesend (Nthflt) DA11 130 GE91
Glendale Wk, Wal.Cr. (Chsht) EN8 15 DY30
Glendale Way, SE28 88 EW73
Glendall St, SW9 101 DM84
Glendarvon St, SW15 99 CX83
Glendevon Cl, Edg. HA8
off Tayside Dr 42 CP48
Glendish Rd, N17 46 DU53
Glendor Gdns, NW7 42 CR49
Glendower Cres, Orp. BR6 146 EU100
Glendower Gdns, SW14
off Glendower Rd 98 CR83
Glendower Pl, SW7 100 DD77
Glendower Rd, E4 47 ED46
SW14 98 CR83
Glendown Rd, SE2 106 EU78
Glendun Rd, W3 80 CS73
Gleneagle Ms, SW16
off Ambleside Av 121 DK92
Gleneagle Rd, SW16 121 DK92
Gleneagles, Stan. HA7 41 CH51
Gleneagles Cl, SE16
off Ryder Dr 102 DV78
Orpington BR6 145 ER102
Romford RM3 52 FM52
Staines (Stanw.) TW19 114 BK86
Watford WD19 40 BX49
Gleneagles Grn, Orp. BR6
off Tandridge Dr 145 ER102
Gleneagles Twr, Sthl. UB1 78 CC72
Gleneldon Ms, SW16 121 DL91
Gleneldon Rd, SW16 121 DL91
Glenelg Rd, SW2 121 DL85
Glenesk Rd, SE9 105 EN83
Glenfarg Rd, SE6 123 ED88
Glenfield Cres, Ruis. HA4 59 BR59
Glenfield Rd, SW12 121 DJ88
W13 97 CH75
Ashford TW15 115 BP93
Banstead SM7 174 DB115
Glenfield Ter, W13 97 CH75
Glenfinlas Way, SE5 101 DP80
Glenforth St, SE10 205 L10
Glengall Causeway, E14 203 P6
Glengall Gro, E14 204 D6
Glengall Rd, NW6 81 CZ67
SE15 102 DT79
Bexleyheath DA7 106 EY83
Edgware HA8 42 CP48
Woodford Green IG8 48 EG51
Glengall Ter, SE15 102 DT79
Glen Gdns, Croy. CR0 141 DN104
Glengarnock Av, E14 204 E9
Glengarry Rd, SE22 122 DS85
Glenham Dr, Ilf. IG2 69 EP57
Glenhaven Av, Borwd. WD6 26 CN41
Glenhead Cl, SE9
off Dumbreck Rd 105 EP83
Glenheadon Cl, Lthd. KT22
off Glenheadon Ri 171 CK123
Glenheadon Ri, Lthd. KT22 171 CK123
Glenhill Cl, N3 44 DA54
Glenhouse Rd, SE9 125 EN85
Glenhurst Av, NW5 64 DG63
Bexley DA5 126 EZ88
Ruislip HA4 59 BQ59
Glenhurst Ct, SE19 122 DT92
Glenhurst Ri, SE19 122 DQ94
Glenhurst Rd, N12 44 DD50
Brentford TW8 97 CJ79
Glenilla Rd, NW3 82 DE65
Glenister Ho, Hayes UB3 77 BV74
Glenister Pk Rd, SW16 121 DK94
Glenister Rd, SE10 205 K10
Glenister St, E16 87 EN74
Glenkerry Ho, E14
off Burcham St 85 EC72
Glenlea Path, SE9
off Well Hall Rd 125 EM85
Glenlea Rd, SE9 125 EM85
Glenlion Ct, Wey. KT13 135 BS104
Glenloch Rd, NW3 82 DE65
Enfield EN3 30 DW40
Glen Luce, Wal.Cr. EN8 15 DX31
Glenluce Rd, SE3 104 EG80
Glenlyon Rd, SE9 125 EN85
Glenmere Av, NW7 43 CU52
Glenmere Row, SE12
off Burnt Ash Rd 124 EF86
Glen Ms, E17 off Glen Rd 67 DZ57
Glenmill, Hmptn. TW12 116 BZ92
Glenmore Cl, Add. KT15 134 BH104
Glenmore Gdns, Abb.L. WD5
off Stewart Cl 7 BU32
Glenmore Rd, NW3 82 DE65
Welling DA16 105 ET81
Glenmore Way, Bark. IG11 88 EU69
Glenmount Path, SE18
off Raglan Rd 105 EQ78
Glenn Av, Pur. CR8 159 DP111
Glennie Rd, SE27 121 DN90
Glenny Rd, Bark. IG11 87 EQ65
Glenorchy Cl, Hayes UB4 78 BY71
Glenparke Rd, E7 86 EH65
Glen Ri, Wdf.Grn. IG8 48 EH51
Glen Rd, E13 86 EJ70
E17 67 DZ57
Chessington KT9 138 CL104
Glen Rd End, Wall. SM6 159 DH109
Glenrosa Gdns, Grav. DA12 131 GM92
Glenrosa St, SW6 100 DC82
Glenrose Ct, Sid. DA14 126 EV92
Glenroy St, W12 81 CW72
Glensdale Rd, SE4 103 DZ83
Glenshee Cl, Nthwd. HA6
off Rickmansworth Rd 39 BQ51
Glenshiel Rd, SE9 125 EN85
Glenside, Chig. IG7 49 EP51
Glenside Cl, Ken. CR8 176 DR115
Glenside Cotts, Slou. SL1 92 AT76
Glentanner Way, SW17 120 DD90
Glen Ter, E14 204 E4
Glentham Gdns, SW13
off Glentham Rd 99 CV79
Glentham Rd, SW13 99 CU79
Glenthorne Av, Croy. CR0 142 DV102
Glenthorne Cl, Sutt. SM3 140 DA102
Uxbridge UB10
off Uxbridge Rd 76 BN69
Glenthorne Gdns, Ilf. IG6 69 EN55
Sutton SM3 140 DA102
Glenthorne Ms, W6
off Glenthorne Rd 99 CV77
Glenthorne Rd, E17 67 DY57
N11 44 DF50
W6 99 CW77
Kingston upon Thames KT1 138 CM98
Glenthorpe Rd, Mord. SM4 139 CX99
Glenton Cl, Rom. RM1 51 FE51
Glenton Rd, SE13 104 EE84
Glenton Way, Rom. RM1 51 FE52
Glentrammon Av, Orp. BR6 163 ET107
Glentrammon Cl, Orp. BR6 163 ET107
Glentrammon Gdns, Orp. BR6 163 ET107
Glentrammon Rd, Orp. BR6 163 ET107
Glentworth St, NW1 194 E5
Glenure Rd, SE9 125 EN85
Glenview, SE2 106 EX79
Glen Vw, Grav. DA12 131 GJ88
Glenview Rd, Brom. BR1 144 EK96
Glenville Av, Enf. EN2 30 DQ38
Glenville Gro, SE8 103 DZ80
Glenville Ms, SW18 120 DB87
Glenville Rd, Kings.T. KT2 138 CN95
Glen Wk, Islw. TW7 117 CD85
Glen Way, Wat. WD17 23 BS38
Glenwood Av, NW9 62 CS60
Rainham RM13 89 FH70
Glenwood Cl, Har. HA1 61 CF57
Glenwood Ct, E18
off Clarendon Rd 68 EG55
Glenwood Dr, Rom. RM2 71 FG56
Glenwood Gdns, Ilf. IG2 69 EN57
Glenwood Gro, NW9 62 CQ60
Glenwood Rd, N15 65 DP57
NW7 42 CS48
SE6 123 DZ88
Epsom KT17 157 CU107
Hounslow TW3 97 CD83
Glenwood Way, Croy. CR0 143 DX100
Glenworth Av, E14 204 F9
Gliddon Dr, E5 66 DV63
Gliddon Rd, W14 99 CY77
Glimpsing Grn, Erith DA18 106 EY76
Glisson Rd, Uxb. UB10 76 BN68
Gload Cres, Orp. BR5 146 EX103
Global App, E3
off Hancock Rd 85 EB68
Globe Ind Estates, Grays RM17 110 GC78
Globe Pond Rd, SE16 203 K3
Globe Rd, E1 84 DW69
E2 84 DW69
E15 68 EF64
Hornchurch RM11 71 FG58
Woodford Green IG8 48 EJ51
Globe Rope Wk, E14 204 D9
Globe St, SE1 201 J6
Globe Ter, E2 off Globe Rd 84 DW69
Globe Town, E2 off Mace St 85 DX68
Globe Wf, SE16 203 J1
Globe Yd, W1 195 H9
Glossop Rd, S.Croy. CR2 160 DR109
Gloster Rd, N.Mal. KT3 138 CS98
Woking GU22 167 BA120
Gloucester Arc, SW7
off Gloucester Rd 100 DC77
Gloucester Av, NW1 82 DG66
Grays RM16 110 GC75
Hornchurch RM11 72 FN56
Sidcup DA15 125 ES89
Waltham Cross EN8 15 DY33
Gloucester Av, Well. DA16 105 ET84
Gloucester Circ, SE10 103 EC80
Gloucester Cl, NW10 80 CR66
Thames Ditton KT7 137 CG102
Gloucester Ct, Rich. TW9 98 CN80
Tilbury RM18 off Dock Rd 111 GF82
Uxbridge (Denh.) UB9
off Moorfield Rd 58 BG58
Gloucester Cres, NW1 83 DH67
Staines TW18 114 BK93
Gloucester Dr, N4 65 DP61
NW11 64 DA56
Staines TW18 113 BC90
Gloucester Gdns, NW11 63 CZ59
W2 off Bishops Br Rd 82 DC72
Barnet EN4 28 DG42
Ilford IG1 68 EL59
Sutton SM1 140 DB103
Gloucester Gate, NW1 83 DH68
Gloucester Gate Ms, NW1
off Gloucester Gate 83 DH68
Gloucester Gro, Edg. HA8 42 CR53
Gloucester Ho, NW6 82 DA68
Gloucester Ms, E10
off Gloucester Rd 67 EA59
W2 82 DC72
Gloucester Ms W, W2
off Cleveland Ter 82 DC72
Gloucester Par, Sid. DA15 126 EU85
Gloucester Pk, SW7
off Courtfield Rd 100 DC77
Gloucester Pl, NW1 194 D4
W1 194 E6
Gloucester Pl Ms, W1 194 E7
⊖ Gloucester Road 100 DC77
Gloucester Rd, E10 67 EA59
E11 68 EH57
E12 69 EM62
E17 47 DX54
N17 46 DR54
N18 46 DT50
SW7 100 DC76
W3 98 CQ75
W5 97 CJ75
Barnet EN5 28 DC43
Belvedere DA17 106 EZ78
Brentwood (Pilg.Hat.) CM15 54 FV43
Croydon CR0 142 DR100
Dartford DA1 127 FH87
Enfield EN2 30 DQ38
Feltham TW13 116 BW88
Gravesend DA12 131 GJ91
Hampton TW12 116 CB94
Harrow HA1 60 CB57
Hounslow TW4 96 BY84
Kingston upon Thames KT1 138 CP96
Redhill RH1 184 DF133
Richmond TW9 98 CN80
Romford RM1 71 FE58
Teddington TW11 117 CE92
Twickenham TW2 116 CC88
Gloucester Sq, E2
off Whiston Rd 84 DU67
W2 194 A9
Woking GU21, GU22
off Church St E 167 AZ117
Gloucester St, SW1 101 DJ78
Gloucester Ter, W2 82 DD73
Gloucester Wk, W8 100 DA75
Woking GU21 167 AZ117
Gloucester Way, EC1 196 E3
Glover Cl, SE2 106 EW77
Waltham Cross EN7
off Allwood Rd 14 DT27
Glover Dr, N18 46 DW51
Glover Rd, Pnr. HA5 60 BX58
Glovers Cl, West. (Bigg.H.) TN16 178 EH116
Glovers Gro, Ruis. HA4 59 BP59
Gloxinia Rd, Grav. (Sthflt) DA13 130 GB93
Gloxinia Wk, Hmptn. TW12 116 CA93
Glycena Rd, SW11 100 DF83
Glyn Av, Barn. EN4 28 DD42
Glyn Cl, SE25 142 DS96
Epsom KT17 157 CU109
Glyn Ct, SW16 121 DN90
Stanmore HA7 41 CH51
Glyn Davies Cl, Sev. (Dunt.Grn) TN13 181 FE120
Glyndebourne Pk, Orp. BR6 145 EP103
Glynde Ms, SW3 198 C7
Glynde Rd, Bexh. DA7 106 EX83
Glynde St, SE4 123 DZ86
Glyndon Rd, SE18 105 EQ77
Glyn Dr, Sid. DA14 126 EV91
Glynfield Rd, NW10 80 CS66
Glynne Rd, N22 45 DN54
Glyn Rd, E5 67 DX62
Enfield EN3 30 DW42
Worcester Park KT4 139 CX103
Glyn St, SE11
off Kennington La 101 DM78
Glynswood, Ger.Cr. (Chal.St.P.) SL9 37 AZ52
Glynswood Pl, Nthwd. HA6 39 BP52
Glynwood Ct, SE23 122 DW89
Goaters All, SW6 99 CZ80
GOATHURST COMMON, Sev. TN14 190 FB130
Goat La, Enf. EN1 30 DT38
Surbiton KT6 137 CJ103
Goat Rd, Mitch. CR4 140 DG101
Goatsfield Rd, West. (Tats.) TN16 178 EJ120
Goatswood La, Rom. (Nave.) RM4 51 FH45
Goat Wf, Brent. TW8 98 CL79
Gobions Av, Rom. RM5 51 FD52
Gobions Way, Pot.B. EN6
off Swanley Bar La 12 DB28
Godalming Av, Wall. SM6 159 DL106
Godalming Rd, E14 85 EB71
Godbold Rd, E15 86 EE69
Goddard Cl, Shep. TW17
off Magdalene Rd 134 BM97
Goddard Pl, N19 65 DJ62
Goddard Rd, Beck. BR3 143 DX98
Goddards Way, Ilf. IG1 69 ER60
GODDEN GREEN, Sev. TN15 191 FN125
H Godden Grn Clinic, Sev. TN15 191 FP125
GODDINGTON, Orp. BR6 146 EW104
Goddington Chase, Orp. BR6 164 EV105
Goddington La, Orp. BR6 146 EU104
Godfrey Av, Nthlt. UB5 78 BY67
Twickenham TW2 117 CD87
Godfrey Hill, SE18 104 EL77
Godfrey Ho, EC1 197 K3
Godfrey Rd, SE18 105 EM77
Godfrey St, E15 85 EC68
SW3 198 C10
Godfrey Way, Houns. TW4 116 BY87
Goding St, SE11 101 DL78
Godley Cl, SE14
off Kender St 102 DW81
Godley Rd, SW18 120 DD88
West Byfleet (Byfleet) KT14 152 BM113
Godliman St, EC4 197 H9
Godman Rd, SE15 102 DV82
Grays RM16 111 GG76
Godolphin Cl, N13 45 DP51
Sutton SM2 157 CZ111
Godolphin Pl, W3 80 CR73
Godolphin Rd, W12 99 CV75
Weybridge KT13 153 BR107
Godric Cres, Croy. (New Adgtn) CR0 161 ED110
Godson Rd, Croy. CR0 141 DN104
Godson St, N1 83 DN68
GODSTONE, RH9 186 DV131
Godstone Bypass, Gdse. RH9 186 DW129
Godstone Grn, Gdse. RH9 186 DV131
Godstone Grn Rd, Gdse. RH9 186 DV131
Godstone Hill, Gdse. RH9 186 DV127
Godstone Rd, Cat. CR3 176 DU124
Kenley CR8 176 DR115
Oxted RH8 187 EA131
Purley CR8 159 DN112
Redhill (Bletch.) RH1 186 DR133
Sutton SM1 158 DC105
Twickenham TW1 117 CG86
Whyteleafe CR3 176 DT116
Godstow Rd, SE2 106 EW75
Godwin Cl, E4 31 EC38
N1 off Napier Gro 84 DQ68
Epsom KT19 156 CQ107
Godwin Ct, NW1
off Crowndale Rd 83 DJ68
Godwin Ho, NW6
off Tollgate Gdns 82 DB68
Godwin Rd, E7 68 EH63
Bromley BR2 144 EJ97
Goffers Rd, SE3 103 ED81
Goffs Cres, Wal.Cr. (Chsht) EN7 13 DP29
Goffs La, Wal.Cr. (Chsht) EN7 14 DU29
GOFFS OAK, Wal.Cr. EN7 14 DQ29
Goffs Oak Av, Wal.Cr. (Chsht) EN7 13 DP28
Goffs Rd, Ashf. TW15 115 BR93
Gogmore Fm Cl, Cher. KT16 133 BF101
Gogmore La, Cher. KT16 134 BG101
Goidel Cl, Wall. SM6 159 DK105
Golborne Gdns, W10
off Golborne Rd 81 CZ70
Golborne Ms, W10
off Portobello Rd 81 CY71
Golborne Rd, W10 81 CY71
Goldace, Grays RM17 110 FZ79
Golda Cl, Barn. EN5 27 CX44
Goldbeaters Gro, Edg. HA8 42 CS51
Goldcliff Cl, Mord. SM4 140 DA100
Goldcrest Cl, E16
off Sheerwater Rd 86 EK71
SE28 88 EW73
Goldcrest Ms, W5 79 CK71
Goldcrest Way, Bushey WD23 40 CC46
Croydon (New Adgtn) CR0 161 ED109
Purley CR8 159 DK110
Golden Ct, Rich. TW9
off George St 117 CK85
Golden Cres, Hayes UB3 77 BT74
Golden Cross Ms, W11
off Basing St 81 CZ72
★ Golden Hinde, SE1 201 K2
Golden Jubilee Br, SE1 200 B3
WC2 200 B2
Golden La, EC1 197 H5
Golden La Est, EC1 197 H5
Golden Manor, W7 79 CE73
Golden Plover Cl, E16
off Maplin Rd 86 EH72
Golden Sq, W1 195 L10
Golden Yd, NW3 off Heath St 64 DC63
Golders Cl, Edg. HA8 42 CP50
Golders Gdns, NW11 63 CY59
GOLDERS GREEN, NW11 64 DA59
⊖ Golders Green 64 DA59
Golders Grn Cres, NW11 63 CZ59
Golders Grn Rd, NW11 63 CY58
Golders Manor Dr, NW11 63 CX58
Golders Pk Cl, NW11 64 DA60
Golders Ri, NW4 63 CX57
Golders Way, NW11 63 CZ59
Goldfinch Cl, Orp. BR6 164 EU106
Goldfinch Rd, SE28 105 ER76
South Croydon CR2 161 DY110
Goldfinch Way, Borwd. WD6 26 CN42
Goldfort Wk, Wok. GU21
off Langmans Way 166 AS116
Goldhawk Ms, W12
off Devonport Rd 99 CV75
⊖ Goldhawk Road 99 CW75
Goldhawk Rd, W6 99 CT77
W12 99 CU76
Goldhaze Cl, Wdf.Grn. IG8 48 EK52
Gold Hill, Edg. HA8 42 CR51
Gold Hill E, Ger.Cr. (Chal.St.P.) SL9 36 AX54
Gold Hill N, Ger.Cr. (Chal.St.P.) SL9 36 AW53
Gold Hill W, Ger.Cr. (Chal.St.P.) SL9 36 AW53
Goldhurst Ter, NW6 82 DB66
H Goldie Leigh Hosp, SE2 106 EW79
Golding Cl, Chess. KT9
off Coppard Gdns 155 CJ107
Goldingham Av, Loug. IG10 33 EQ40
Golding Rd, Sev. TN13 191 FJ122
Goldings, The, Wok. GU21 166 AT116
Goldings Hill, Loug. IG10 33 EN39
Goldings Ri, Loug. IG10 33 EN39
Goldings Rd, Loug. IG10 33 EN39
Golding St, E1 84 DU72
Golding Ter, SW11
off Longhedge St 100 DG82
Goldington Cres, NW1 83 DK68
Goldington St, NW1 83 DK68
Gold La, Edg. HA8 42 CR51
Goldman Cl, E2 84 DU70
Goldmark Ho, SE3
off Lebrun Sq 104 EH83
Goldney Rd, W9 82 DA70
Goldrill Dr, N11 44 DG47
Goldrings Rd, Lthd. (Oxshott) KT22 154 CC113
Goldring Way, St.Alb. (Lon.Col.) AL2 9 CH27
Goldsboro Rd, SW8 101 DK81
Goldsborough Cres, E4 47 EC47
Goldsdown Cl, Enf. EN3 31 DY40
Goldsdown Rd, Enf. EN3 31 DX40
Goldsel Rd, Swan. BR8 147 FD99
Goldsmid St, SE18
off Sladedale Rd 105 ES78
Goldsmith, Grays RM17 110 FZ79
Goldsmith Av, E12 86 EL65
NW9 63 CT58
W3 80 CR73
Romford RM7 70 FA59
Goldsmith Cl, W3 80 CR74
Harrow HA2 60 CB60
Goldsmith La, NW9 62 CP56
Goldsmith Rd, E10 67 EA60
E17 47 DX54
N11 44 DF50
SE15 102 DU81
W3 80 CR74
Goldsmiths Bottom, Sev. TN14 190 FE127
Goldsmiths Cl, Wok. GU21 166 AW118
★ Goldsmiths' Hall, EC2 197 J8
Goldsmith's Row, E2 84 DU68
Goldsmith's Sq, E2 84 DU68
Goldsmith St, EC2 197 J8
Goldsworth Orchard, Wok. GU21
off St. John's Rd 166 AU118
GOLDSWORTH PARK, Wok. GU21 166 AU117
Goldsworth Pk Trd Est, Wok. GU21 166 AU116
Goldsworth Rd, Wok. GU21 166 AW118
Goldsworthy Gdns, SE16 202 G9
Goldwell Rd, Th.Hth. CR7 141 DM98
Goldwin Cl, SE14 102 DW81
Goldwing Cl, E16 86 EG72
Golf Cl, Bushey WD23 24 BX41
Stanmore HA7 41 CJ52
Thornton Heath CR7
off Kensington Av 141 DN95
Woking GU22 151 BE114
Golf Club Dr, Kings.T. KT2 118 CR94
Golf Club Rd, Hat. AL9 12 DA26
Weybridge KT13 153 BP109
Woking GU22 166 AU120
Golfe Rd, Ilf. IG1 69 ER62
Golf Ho Rd, Oxt. RH8 188 EJ129
Golf Links Av, Grav. DA11 131 GH92
Golf Ride, Enf. EN2 29 DN35
Golf Rd, W5 off Boileau Rd 80 CM72
Bromley BR1 145 EN97
Kenley CR8 176 DR118
Golf Side, Sutt. SM2 157 CY111
Twickenham TW2 117 CD90
Golfside Cl, N20 44 DE48
New Malden KT3 138 CS96
Goliath Cl, Wall. SM6 159 DL108
Gollogly Ter, SE7 104 EJ78
Gomer Gdns, Tedd. TW11 117 CG93
Gomer Pl, Tedd. TW11 117 CG93
Gomm Rd, SE16 202 F7
Gomshall Av, Wall. SM6 159 DL106
Gomshall Gdns, Ken. CR8 176 DS115
Gomshall Rd, Sutt. SM2 157 CW110
Gondar Gdns, NW6 63 CZ64
Gonson St, SE8 103 EB79
Gonston Cl, SW19 119 CY89
Gonville Av, Rick. (Crox.Grn) WD3 23 BP44
Gonville Cres, Nthlt. UB5 78 CB65
Gonville Rd, Th.Hth. CR7 141 DM99
Gonville St, SW6
off Putney Br App 99 CY83
Gooch Ho, E5 66 DV62
Goodall Rd, E11 67 EC62
Gooden Ct, Har. HA1 61 CE62
Goodenough Cl, Couls. CR5 175 DN120
Goodenough Rd, SW19 119 CZ94
Goodenough Way, Couls. CR5 175 DM120
Gooderham Ho, Grays RM16 111 GH75
Goodey Rd, Bark. IG11 87 ET66
Goodge Pl, W1 195 L7
⊖ Goodge Street 195 L6
Goodge St, W1 195 L7
Goodhall Cl, Stan. HA7 41 CG51
Goodhall St, NW10 80 CS69
Goodhart Pl, E14 85 DY73
Goodhart Way, W.Wick. BR4 144 EE101
Goodhew Rd, Croy. CR0 142 DU100
Gooding Cl, N.Mal. KT3 138 CQ98
Goodinge Cl, N7 83 DL65
Goodlake Ct, Uxb. (Denh.) UB9 57 BF59
GOODLEY STOCK, West. TN16 189 EP130
Goodley Stock, West. TN16 189 EP129
Goodley Stock Rd, Eden. (Crock.H.) TN8 189 EP131
Westerham TN16 189 EP128
Goodman Cres, SW2 121 DK89
Goodman Pk, Slou. SL2 74 AW74
Goodman Pl, Stai. TW18 113 BF91
Goodman Rd, E10 67 EC59
Goodmans Ct, E1 197 P10
Wembley HA0 61 CK63

Goodman's Stile, E1 84 DU72
Goodmans Yd, E1 197 P10
GOODMAYES, Ilf. IG3 70 EV61
≠ Goodmayes 70 EU60
Goodmayes Av, Ilf. IG3 70 EU60
H Goodmayes Hosp, Ilf. IG3 70 EU57
Goodmayes La, Ilf. IG3 70 EU63
Goodmayes Rd, Ilf. IG3 70 EU60
Goodmead Rd, Orp. BR6 146 EU101
Goodrich Cl, Wat. WD25 23 BU35
Goodrich Rd, SE22 122 DT86
Goodson Rd, NW10 80 CS66
Goods Way, NW1 83 DL68
Goodway Gdns, E14 85 ED72
Goodwill Dr, Har. HA2 60 CA60
Goodwin Cl, SE16 202 A7
Mitcham CR4 140 DD97
Goodwin Ct, Barn. EN4 28 DE44
Waltham Cross EN8 15 DY28
Goodwin Dr, Sid. DA14 126 EX90
Goodwin Gdns, Croy. CR0 159 DP107
Goodwin Rd, N9 46 DW46
W12 99 CU75
Croydon CR0 159 DP106
Goodwins Ct, WC2 195 P10
Goodwin St, N4
off Fonthill Rd 65 DN61
Goodwood Av, Brwd. (Hutt.)
CM13 55 GE44
Enfield EN3 30 DW37
Hornchurch RM12 72 FL63
Watford WD24 23 BS35
Goodwood Cl, Mord. SM4 140 DA98
Stanmore HA7 41 CJ50
Goodwood Cres, Grav. DA12 131 GJ93
Goodwood Dr, Nthlt. UB5 78 CA65
Goodwood Path, Borwd. WD6
off Stratfield Rd 26 CN41
Goodwood Rd, SE14 103 DY80
Redhill RH1 184 DF132
Goodwyn Av, NW7 42 CS50
Goodwyns Vale, N10 44 DG53
Goodyers Av, Rad. WD7 9 CF33
Goodyers Gdns, NW4 63 CX57
Goosander Way, SE28 105 ER76
Goose Acre, Chesh. HP5 4 AT30
Gooseacre La, Har. HA3 61 CK57
Goosefields, Rick. WD3 22 BJ44
Goose Grn, Cob. KT11 169 BU119
Goose Grn Cl, Orp. BR5 146 EU96
Goose La, Wok. GU22 166 AV122
Gooseley La, E6 87 EN69
Goosens Cl, Sutt. SM1
off Turnpike La 158 DC106
Goose Sq, E6 off Harper Rd 87 EM72
Gooshays Dr, Rom. RM3 52 FL50
Gooshays Gdns, Rom. RM3 52 FL51
Gophir La, EC4 197 K10
Gopsall St, N1 84 DR67
Goral Mead, Rick. WD3 38 BK46
Gordon Av, E4 48 EE51
SW14 98 CS84
Hornchurch RM12 71 FF61
South Croydon CR2 160 DQ110
Stanmore HA7 41 CH51
Twickenham TW1 117 CG85
Gordonbrock Rd, SE4 123 EA85
Gordon Cl, E17 67 EA58
N19 off Highgate Hill 65 DJ60
Chertsey KT16 133 BE104
Staines TW18 114 BH93
Gordon Ct, W12 81 CW72
Gordon Cres, Croy. CR0 142 DS102
Hayes UB3 95 BU76
Gordondale Rd, SW19 120 DA89
Gordon Dr, Cher. KT16 133 BE104
Shepperton TW17 135 BR100
Gordon Gdns, Edg. HA8 42 CP54
Gordon Gro, SE5 101 DP82
≠ Gordon Hill 29 DP39
Gordon Hill, Enf. EN2 30 DQ39
H Gordon Hosp, SW1 199 M9
Gordon Ho, E1 off Glamis Rd 84 DW73
Gordon Ho Rd, NW5 64 DG63
Gordon Pl, W8 100 DA75
Gravesend DA12
off East Ter 131 GJ86
Gordon Prom, Grav. DA12 131 GJ86
Gordon Prom E, Grav. DA12 131 GJ86
Gordon Rd, E4 48 EE45
E11 68 EG58
E15 67 EC63
E18 48 EH53
N3 43 CZ52
N9 46 DV47
N11 45 DK52
SE15 102 DV82
W4 98 CP79
W5 79 CJ73
W13 79 CH73
Ashford TW15 114 BL90
Barking IG11 87 ES67
Beckenham BR3 143 DZ97
Belvedere DA17 107 FC77
Brentwood (Shenf.) CM15 55 GA46
Carshalton SM5 158 DF107
Caterham CR3 176 DR121
Dartford DA1 128 FK87
Enfield EN2 30 DQ39
Esher (Clay.) KT10 155 CE107
Gravesend (Nthflt) DA11 130 GE87
Grays RM16 111 GF75
Harrow HA3 61 CE55
Hounslow TW3 96 CC84
Ilford IG1 69 ER62
Kingston upon Thames
KT2 138 CM95
Redhill RH1 184 DG131
Richmond TW9 98 CM82
Romford RM6 70 EZ58
Sevenoaks TN13 191 FH125
Shepperton TW17 135 BR100
Sidcup DA15 125 ES85
Southall UB2 96 BY77
Staines TW18 113 BC91
Surbiton KT5 138 CM101
Waltham Abbey EN9 15 EA34
West Drayton UB7 76 BL73
Gordon Sq, WC1 195 N5
Gordon St, E13
off Grange Rd 86 EG69
WC1 195 M4
Gordons Way, Oxt. RH8 187 ED128
Gordon Way, Barn. EN5 27 CZ42
Bromley BR1 144 EG95
Chalfont St. Giles HP8 36 AV48
Gore Cl, Uxb. (Hare.) UB9 58 BH56
Gore Ct, NW9 62 CN57
Gorefield Pl, NW6 82 DA68
Gorelands La, Ch.St.G. HP8 37 AZ47
Gore Rd, E9 84 DW67
SW20 139 CW96
Dartford DA2 128 FQ90
Goresbrook Rd, Dag. RM9 88 EV67
Goresbrook Village, Dag. RM9
off Goresbrook Rd 88 EV67
Gore St, SW7 100 DC76
Gorham Pl, W11 off Mary Pl 81 CY73
Goring Cl, Rom. RM5 51 FC53
Goring Gdns, Dag. RM8 70 EW63
Goring Rd, N11 45 DL51
Dagenham RM10 89 FD65
Staines TW18 113 BD92
Gorings Sq, Stai. TW18 113 BE91
Goring St, EC3 197 N8
Goring Way, Grnf. UB6 78 CC68
Gorle Cl, Wat. WD25 7 BU34
Gorleston Rd, N15 66 DR57
Gorleston St, W14 99 CY77
Gorman Rd, SE18 105 EM77
Gorringe Av, Dart. (S.Darenth)
DA4 149 FR96
Gorringe Pk Av, Mitch. CR4 120 DF94
Gorse Cl, E16 86 EG72
Tadworth KT20 173 CV120
Gorse Hill, Dart. (Fnghm)
DA4 148 FL100
Gorse Hill La, Vir.W. GU25 132 AX98
Gorse Hill Rd, Vir.W. GU25 132 AX98
Gorselands Cl, W.Byf. KT14 152 BJ111
Gorse La, Wok. (Chobham)
GU24 150 AS108
Gorse Ri, SW17 120 DG92
Gorse Rd, Croy. CR0 161 EA105
Orpington BR5 146 FA103
Gorse Wk, West Dr. UB7 76 BL72
Gorseway, Rom. RM7 71 FD61
Gorst Rd, NW10 80 CQ70
SW11 120 DF86
Gorsuch Pl, E2 197 P2
Gorsuch St, E2 197 P2
Gosberton Rd, SW12 120 DG88
Gosbury Hill, Chess. KT9 156 CL105
Gosfield Rd, Dag. RM8 70 FA61
Epsom KT19 156 CR112
Gosfield St, W1 195 K6
Gosford Gdns, Ilf. IG4 69 EM57
Gosforth La, Wat. WD19 40 BW48
Gosforth Path, Wat. WD19 39 BU48
Goshawk Gdns, Hayes UB4 77 BS69
Goslett Ct, Bushey WD23
off Bournehall Av 24 CA43
Goslett Yd, WC2 195 N9
Gosling Cl, Grnf. UB6 78 CA69
Gosling Grn, Slou. SL3 92 AY76
Gosling Rd, Slou. SL3 92 AY76
Gosling Way, SW9 101 DN81
Gospatrick Rd, N17 46 DQ52
GOSPEL OAK, NW5 64 DG63
≠ Gospel Oak 64 DG63
Gospel Oak Est, NW5 64 DF64
Gosport Dr, Horn. RM12 90 FJ65
Gosport Rd, E17 67 DZ57
Gosport Wk, N17
off Yarmouth Cres 66 DV57
Gossage Rd, SE18 105 ER78
Uxbridge UB10 76 BM66
Gossamers, The, Wat. WD25 24 BY36
Gosset St, E2 84 DT69
Goss Hill, Dart. DA2 128 FJ93
Swanley BR8 128 FJ93
Gosshill Rd, Chis. BR7 145 EN96
Gossington Cl, Chis. BR7
off Beechwood Ri 125 EP91
Gosterwood St, SE8 103 DY79
Gostling Rd, Twick. TW2 116 CA88
Goston Gdns, Th.Hth. CR7 141 DN97
Goswell Rd, EC1 197 H5
Gothic Cl, Dart. DA1 128 FK90
Gothic Ct, Hayes UB3
off Sipson La 95 BR79
Gothic Rd, Twick. TW2 117 CD89
Gottfried Ms, NW5
off Fortess Rd 65 DJ63
Goudhurst Rd, Brom. BR1 124 EE92
Gouge Av, Grav. (Nthflt)
DA11 130 GE88
Gough Rd, E15 68 EF63
Enfield EN1 30 DV40
Gough Sq, EC4 196 E8
Gough St, WC1 196 C4
Gough Wk, E14
off Saracen St 85 EA72
Gould Ct, SE19 122 DT92
Goulden Ho App, SW11 100 DE82
Goulding Gdns, Th.Hth. CR7 141 DP96
Gould Rd, Felt. TW14 115 BS87
Twickenham TW2 117 CE88
Goulds Grn, Uxb. UB8 77 BP72
Gould Ter, E8
off Kenmure Rd 66 DV64
Goulston St, E1 197 P8
Goulton Rd, E5 66 DV63
Gourley Pl, N15
off Gourley St 66 DS57
Gourley St, N15 66 DS57
Gourock Rd, SE9 125 EN85
Govan St, E2 off Whiston Rd 84 DU67
Government Row, Enf. EN3 31 EA38
Governors Av, Uxb. (Denh.)
UB9 57 BF57
Governors Cl, Amer. HP6 20 AT37
Govett Av, Shep. TW17 135 BQ99
Govier Cl, E15 86 EE66
Gowan Av, SW6 99 CY81
Gowan Rd, NW10 81 CV65
Gowar Fld, Pot.B. EN6 11 CU32
Gower, The, Egh. TW20 133 BB97
Gower Cl, SW4 121 DJ86
Gower Ct, WC1 195 M4
Gower Ms, WC1 195 M7
Gower Pl, WC1 195 L4
Gower Rd, E7 86 EG65
Isleworth TW7 97 CF79
Weybridge KT13 153 BR107
Gowers, The, Amer. HP6 20 AS36
Gowers La, Grays (Orsett)
RM16 111 GF75
Gower St, WC1 195 L4
Gower's Wk, E1 84 DU72
Gowland Pl, Beck. BR3 143 DZ96
Gowlett Rd, SE15 102 DU83
Gowlland Cl, Croy. CR0 142 DU101
Gowrie Pl, Cat. CR3 176 DQ122
Gowrie Rd, SW11 100 DG83
Graburn Way, E.Mol. KT8 137 CD97
Grace Av, Bexh. DA7 106 EZ82
Radlett (Shenley) WD7 9 CK33
Grace Business Cen, Mitch.
CR4 140 DF99
Gracechurch St, EC3 197 L10
Grace Cl, SE9 124 EK90
Borehamwood WD6 26 CR39
Edgware HA8
off Pavilion Way 42 CQ52
Ilford IG6 49 ET51
Gracedale Rd, SW16 121 DH92
Gracefield Gdns, SW16 121 DL90
Grace Jones Cl, E8
off Parkholme Rd 84 DU65
Grace Path, SE26 122 DW91
Grace Pl, E3
off St. Leonards St 85 EB69
Grace Rd, Croy. CR0 142 DQ100
Grace's All, E1 84 DU73
Graces Ms, SE5 102 DS82
Graces Rd, SE5 102 DS82
Grace St, E3 85 EB69
Gracious La, Sev. TN13 190 FG130
Gracious La End, Sev. TN14 190 FF130
Gracious Pond Rd, Wok.
(Chobham) GU24 150 AT108
Gradient, The, SE26 122 DU91
Graduate Pl, SE1 off Long La 102 DS76
Graeme Rd, Enf. EN1 30 DR40
Graemesdyke Av, SW14 98 CP83
Grafton Cl, W13 79 CG72
Hounslow TW4 116 BY88
Slough (Geo.Grn) SL3 74 AY72
West Byfleet KT14
off Madeira Rd 151 BF113
Worcester Park KT4 138 CS104
Grafton Ct, Felt. TW14 115 BR88
Grafton Cres, NW1 83 DH65
Grafton Gdns, N4 66 DQ58
Dagenham RM8 70 EY61
Grafton Ho, E3 85 EA69
Grafton Ms, W1 195 K5
Grafton Pk Rd, Wor.Pk. KT4 138 CS103
Grafton Pl, NW1 195 M3
Grafton Rd, NW5 64 DG64
W3 80 CQ73
Croydon CR0 141 DN102
Dagenham RM8 70 EY61
Enfield EN2 29 DM41
Harrow HA1 60 CC57
New Malden KT3 138 CS97
Worcester Park KT4 138 CR104
Graftons, The, NW2
off Hermitage La 64 DA62
Grafton Sq, SW4 101 DJ83
Grafton St, W1 199 J1
Grafton Ter, NW5 64 DF64
Grafton Way, W1 195 K5
WC1 195 K5
West Molesey KT8 136 BZ98
Grafton Yd, NW5
off Prince of Wales Rd 83 DH65
Graham Av, W13 97 CH75
Mitcham CR4 140 DG95
Graham Cl, Brwd. (Hutt.)
CM13 55 GC43
Croydon CR0 143 EA103
Grahame Pk Est, NW9 42 CS53
Grahame Pk Way, NW7 43 CT52
NW9 43 CT54
Graham Gdns, Surb. KT6 138 CL102
Graham Rd, E8 84 DT65
E13 86 EG70
N15 65 DP55
NW4 63 CV58
SW19 119 CZ94
W4 98 CR76
Bexleyheath DA6 106 FA84
Hampton TW12 116 CA91
Harrow HA3 61 CE55
Mitcham CR4 140 DG95
Purley CR8 159 DN113
Graham St, N1 196 G1
Graham Ter, SW1 198 F9
Grainger Cl, Nthlt. UB5
off Lancaster Rd 60 CC64
Grainger Rd, N22 46 DQ53
Isleworth TW7 97 CF82
Grainge's Yd, Uxb. UB8
off Cross St 76 BJ66
Gramer Cl, E11
off Norman Rd 67 ED61
Grampian Cl, Hayes UB3 95 BR80
Orpington BR6
off Clovelly Way 145 ET100
Sutton SM2 158 DC108
Grampian Gdns, NW2 63 CY60
Grampian Ho, N9
off Plevna Rd 46 DV47
Grampian Way, Slou. SL3 93 BA78
Gramsci Way, SE6 123 EB90
Granard Av, SW15 119 CV85
Granard Rd, SW12 120 DF87
Granaries, The, Wal.Abb. EN9 16 EE34
Granary Cl, N9 off Turin Rd 46 DW45
Granary Rd, E1 84 DV70
Granary Sq, N1
off Liverpool Rd 83 DN65
Granary St, NW1 83 DK67
Granby Pk Rd, Wal.Cr.
(Chsht) EN7 14 DT28
Granby Pl, SE1 200 D5
Granby Rd, SE9 105 EM82
Gravesend DA11 130 GD85
Granby St, E2 84 DT70
Granby Ter, NW1 195 K1
Grand Arc, N12
off Ballards La 44 DC50
Grand Av, EC1 196 G6
N10 64 DG56
Surbiton KT5 138 CP99
Wembley HA9 62 CN64
Grand Av E, Wem. HA9 62 CP64
Grand Dep Rd, SE18 105 EN78
Grand Dr, SW20 139 CW96
Southall UB2 96 CC75
Granden Rd, SW16 141 DL96
Grandfield Av, Wat. WD17 23 BT39
Grandis Cotts, Wok.
(Ripley) GU23 168 BH122
Grandison Rd, SW11 120 DF85
Worcester Park KT4 139 CW103
Grand Junct Wf, N1 197 H1
Grand Par Ms, SW15
off Upper Richmond Rd 119 CY85
Grand Stand Rd, Epsom
KT18 173 CT117
Grand Union Canal Wk, W7 97 CE76
Grand Union Cl, W9
off Woodfield Rd 81 CZ71
Grand Union Cres, E8 84 DU66
Grand Union Ind Est, NW10 80 CP68
Grand Union Wk, NW1 83 DH66
Grand Vw Av, West.
(Bigg.H.) TN16 178 EJ117
Grand Wk, E1 off Solebay St 85 DY70
Granfield St, SW11 100 DD81
Grange, The, N2
off Central Av 44 DD54
N20 44 DC46
SE1 201 P6
SW19 119 CX93
Croydon CR0 143 DZ103
Dartford (S.Darenth) DA4 149 FR95
Walton-on-Thames KT12 135 BV103
Wembley HA0 80 CN66
Windsor (Old Wind.) SL4 112 AV85
Woking (Chobham) GU24 150 AS110
Worcester Park KT4 138 CR104
Grange Av, N12 44 DC50
N20 43 CY45
SE25 142 DS96
Barnet EN4 44 DE46
Stanmore HA7 41 CH54
Twickenham TW2 117 CE89
Woodford Green IG8 48 EG51
Grangecliffe Gdns, SE25 142 DS96
Grange Cl, Brwd. (Ingrave)
CM13 55 GC50
Edgware HA8 42 CQ50
Gerrards Cross (Chal.St.P.)
SL9 36 AY53
Hayes UB3 77 BS71
Hounslow TW5 96 BZ79
Leatherhead KT22 171 CK120
Redhill (Bletch.) RH1 186 DR133
Redhill (Merst.) RH1 185 DH128
Sidcup DA15 126 EU90
Staines (Wrays.) TW19 112 AY86
Watford WD17 23 BU39
West Molesey KT8 136 CB98
Westerham TN16 189 EQ126
Woodford Green IG8 48 EG52
Grange Ct, WC2 196 C9
Chigwell IG7 49 EQ47
Loughton IG10 32 EK43
Northolt UB5 78 BW68
Staines TW18 114 BG92
Waltham Abbey EN9 15 EC34
Walton-on-Thames KT12 135 BU103
Grangecourt Rd, N16 66 DS60
Grange Cres, SE28 88 EW72
Chigwell IG7 49 ER50
Dartford DA2 128 FP86
Grangedale Cl, Nthwd. HA6 39 BS53
Grange Dr, Chis. BR7 124 EL93
Orpington BR6
off Rushmore Hill 164 EW109
Redhill (Merst.) RH1
off London Rd S 185 DH128
Woking GU21 150 AY114
Grange Fm Cl, Har. HA2 60 CC61
Grange Flds, Ger.Cr. (Chal.St.P.)
SL9 off Lower Rd 36 AY53
Grange Gdns, N14 45 DK46
NW3 64 DB62
SE25 142 DS96
Banstead SM7 158 DB113
Pinner HA5 60 BZ56
Grange Gro, N1 84 DP65
GRANGE HILL, Chig. IG7 49 ER51
⊖ Grange Hill 49 ER49
Grange Hill, SE25 142 DS96
Edgware HA8 42 CQ50
Grangehill Pl, SE9
off Westmount Rd 105 EM83
Grangehill Rd, SE9 105 EM84
Grange Ho, Bark. IG11
off St. Margarets 87 ER67
Erith DA8 107 FG82
Grange La, SE21 122 DT89
Watford (Let.Hth) WD25 25 CD39
Grange Mans, Epsom KT17 157 CT108
Grange Meadow, Bans. SM7 158 DB113
Grangemill Rd, SE6 123 EA90
Grangemill Way, SE6 123 EA89
Grangemount, Lthd. KT22 171 CK120
GRANGE PARK, N21 29 DP43
≠ Grange Park 29 DP43
Grange Pk, W5 80 CL74
Woking GU21 166 AY115
Grange Pk Av, N21 29 DP44
Grange Pk Pl, SW20 119 CV94
Grange Pk Rd, E10 67 EB60
Thornton Heath CR7 142 DR98
Grange Pl, NW6 82 DA66
Staines TW18 134 BJ96
Walton-on-Thames KT12 135 BU103
Grange Rd, E10 67 EA60
E13 86 EF69
E17 67 DY57
N6 64 DG58
N17 46 DU51
N18 46 DU51
NW10 81 CV65
SE1 201 N6
SE19 142 DR98
SE25 142 DR98
SW13 99 CU81
W4 98 CP78
W5 79 CK74
Grange Rd, Add. (New Haw)
KT15 152 BG110
Borehamwood (Els.) WD6 26 CM43
Bushey WD23 24 BY43
Caterham CR3 186 DU125
Chessington KT9 156 CL105
Edgware HA8 42 CR51
Egham TW20 113 AZ92
Gerrards Cross (Chal.St.P.)
SL9 36 AY53
Gravesend DA11 131 GG87
Grays RM17 110 GB79
Harrow HA1 61 CG58
Harrow (S.Har.) HA2 61 CD61
Hayes UB3 77 BS72
Ilford IG1 69 EP63
Kingston upon Thames
KT1 138 CL97
Leatherhead KT22 171 CK120
Orpington BR6 145 EQ103
Romford RM3 51 FH51
Sevenoaks TN13 190 FG127
South Croydon CR2 160 DQ110
South Ockendon (Aveley)
RM15 90 FQ74
Southall UB1 96 BY75
Sutton SM2 158 DA108
Thornton Heath CR7 142 DR98
Walton-on-Thames KT12 154 BY105
West Molesey KT8 136 CB98
Woking GU21 150 AY114
Granger Way, Rom. RM1 71 FG58
Grange St, N1 84 DR67
Grange Vale, Sutt. SM2 158 DB108
Grange Vw Rd, N20 44 DC46
Grange Wk, SE1 201 N6
Grange Wk Ms, SE1
off Grange Wk 102 DS76
Grangeway, N12 44 DB49
NW6 off Messina Av 82 DA66
Grange Way, Erith DA8 107 FH80
Iver SL0 75 BF72
Grangeway, Wdf.Grn. IG8 48 EJ49
Grangeway, The, N21 29 DP44
Grangeway Gdns, Ilf. IG4 68 EL57
Grangeways Cl, Grav.
(Nthflt) DA11 131 GF91
Grangewood, Bex. DA5
off Hurst Rd 126 EZ88
Potters Bar EN6 12 DB30
Slough (Wexham) SL3 74 AW71
Grangewood Av, Grays
RM16 110 GE76
Rainham RM13 90 FJ70
Grangewood Cl, Brwd. CM13
off Knight's Way 55 GA48
Pinner HA5 59 BU57
Grangewood Dr, Sun. TW16
off Forest Dr 115 BT94
Grangewood La, Beck. BR3 123 DZ93
Grangewood St, E6 86 EJ67
Grangewood Ter, SE25
off Grange Rd 142 DR96
Grange Yd, SE1 201 P7
Granham Gdns, N9 46 DT47
Granite Apts, E15
off Windmill La 85 ED65
Granite St, SE18 105 ET78
Granleigh Rd, E11 68 EE61
Gransden Av, E8 84 DV66
Gransden Rd, W12
off Wendell Rd 99 CT75
Grant Av, Slou. SL1 74 AS72
Grantbridge St, N1 83 DP68
Grantchester Cl, Har. HA1 61 CF62
Grant Cl, N14 45 DJ45
Shepperton TW17 135 BP100
Grantham Cl, Edg. HA8 42 CL48
Grantham Gdns, Rom. RM6 70 EZ58
Grantham Grn, Borwd. WD6 26 CQ43
Grantham Pl, W1 199 H3
Grantham Rd, E12 69 EN63
SW9 101 DL82
W4 98 CS80
Grantley Pl, Esher KT10 154 CB106
Grantley Rd, Houns. TW4 96 BW82
Grantley St, E1 85 DX69
Grantock Rd, E17 47 ED53
Granton Av, Upmin. RM14 72 FM61
Granton Rd, SW16 141 DJ95
Ilford IG3 70 EU60
Sidcup DA14 126 EW93
Grant Pl, Croy. CR0 142 DT102
Grant Rd, SW11 100 DD84
Croydon CR0 142 DT102
Harrow HA3 61 CE55
Grants Cl, N17 46 DS54
NW7 43 CW52
Grants La, Oxt. RH8 188 EJ132
Grant's Quay Wf, EC3 201 L1
Grant St, E13 86 EG69
N1 off Chapel Mkt 83 DN68
Grantully Rd, W9 82 DB69
Grant Way, Islw. TW7 97 CG79
Granville Av, N9 46 DW48
Feltham TW13 115 BU89
Hounslow TW3 116 CA85
Granville Cl, Croy. CR0 142 DS103
West Byfleet (Byfleet) KT14
off Church Rd 152 BM113
Weybridge KT13 153 BQ107
Granville Ct, N1 84 DR67
Granville Dene, Hem.H.
(Bov.) HP3 5 BA27
Granville Gdns, SW16 141 DM95
W5 80 CM74
Granville Gro, SE13 103 EC83
Granville Ind Est, NW2
off Granville Rd 63 CZ61
Granville Ms, Sid. DA14 126 EU91
Granville Pk, SE13 103 EC83
Granville Pl, N12 (N.Finchley)
off High Rd 44 DC52
SW6 off Maxwell Rd 100 DB80
W1 194 F9
Pinner HA5 60 BX55
Granville Pl, NW2
off Granville Rd 63 CZ61
Granville Rd, E17 67 EB58
E18 48 EH54
N4 65 DM58
N12 44 DB52
N13 off Russell Rd 45 DM51

★ Place of interest ≠ Railway station ⊖ London Underground station DLR Docklands Light Railway station Tra Tramlink station H Hospital Riv Pedestrian ferry landing stage

Granville Rd, N22 . . . . .45 DP53
NW2 . . . . .63 CZ61
NW6 . . . . .82 DA68
SW18 . . . . .120 DA87
SW19 off Russell Rd 120 DA94
Barnet EN5 . . . . .27 CW42
Epping CM16 . . . . .18 EV29
Gravesend DA11 . . . . .131 GF87
Hayes UB3 . . . . .95 BT77
Ilford IG1 . . . . .69 EP60
Oxted RH8 . . . . .188 EF129
Sevenoaks TN13 . . . . .190 FG124
Sidcup DA14 . . . . .126 EU91
Uxbridge UB10 . . . . .77 BP65
Watford WD18 . . . . .24 BW42
Welling DA16 . . . . .106 EW83
Westerham TN16 . . . . .189 EQ126
Weybridge KT13 . . . . .153 BQ107
Woking GU22 . . . . .167 AZ120
Granville Sq, SE15 . . . . .102 DS80
WC1 . . . . .196 C3
Granville St, WC1 . . . . .196 C3
Grape St, WC2 . . . . .195 P8
Graphite Sq, SE11 . . . . .200 B10
Grapsome Cl, Chess. KT9
off Nigel Fisher Way 155 CJ108
Grasdene Rd, SE18 . . . . .106 EU80
Grasgarth Cl, W3
off Creswick Rd 80 CQ73
Grasholm Way, Slou. SL3 . . . .93 BC77
Grasmere Av, SW15 . . . . . . .118 CR91
SW19 . . . . .140 DA97
W3 . . . . .80 CQ73
Hounslow TW3 . . . . .116 CB86
Orpington BR6 . . . . .145 EP104
Ruislip HA4 . . . . .59 BQ59
Slough SL2 . . . . .74 AU73
Wembley HA9 . . . . .61 CK59
Grasmere Cl, Egh. TW20
off Keswick Rd 113 BB94
Feltham TW14 . . . . .115 BT88
Loughton IG10 . . . . .33 EM40
Watford WD25 . . . . .7 BV32
Grasmere Ct, N22
off Palmerston Rd 45 DM51
Grasmere Gdns, Har. HA3 . . .41 CG54
Ilford IG4 . . . . .69 EM57
Orpington BR6 . . . . .145 EP104
Grasmere Pt, SE15
off Ilderton Rd 102 DW80
Grasmere Rd, E13 . . . . .86 EG68
N10 . . . . .45 DH53
N17 . . . . .46 DU51
SE25 . . . . .142 DV100
SW16 . . . . .121 DM92
Bexleyheath DA7 . . . . .107 FC81
Bromley BR1 . . . . .144 EF95
Orpington BR6 . . . . .145 EP104
Purley CR8 . . . . .159 DP111
Grasmere Way, W.Byf.
(Byfleet) KT14 . . . . .152 BM112
Grassfield Cl, Couls. CR5 . . .175 DH119
Grasshaven Way, SE28 . . . . . .87 ET74
Grassingham End, Ger.Cr.
(Chal.St.P.) SL9 . . . . .36 AY52
Grassingham Rd, Ger.Cr.
(Chal.St.P.) SL9 . . . . .36 AY52
Grassington Cl, N11 . . . . .44 DG50
St. Albans (Brick.Wd) AL2 . . .8 CA30
Grassington Rd, Sid. DA14 . .126 EU91
Grassmere Rd, Horn. RM11 . .72 FM56
Grassmount, SE23 . . . . .122 DV89
Purley CR8 . . . . .159 DJ110
Grass Pk, N3 . . . . .43 CZ53
Grassway, Wall. SM6 . . . . . .159 DJ105
Grassy La, Sev. TN13 . . . . . .191 FH126
Grasvenor Av, Barn. EN5 . . . .28 DA44
Gratton Rd, W14 . . . . .99 CY76
Gratton Ter, NW2 . . . . .63 CX62
Gravel Cl, Chig. IG7 . . . . .50 EU47
Graveley, Kings.T. KT1
off Willingham Way 138 CN96
Graveley Av, Borwd. WD6 . . . .26 CQ42
Tra Gravel Hill 161 DY108
Gravel Hill, N3 . . . . .43 CZ54
Bexleyheath DA6 . . . . .127 FB85
Croydon CR0 . . . . .161 DX107
Gerrards Cross (Chal.St.P.)
SL9 . . . . .36 AY53
Leatherhead KT22
off North St 171 CH121
Loughton (High Beach)
IG10 . . . . .32 EG38
Uxbridge UB8 . . . . .58 BK64
Gravel Hill Cl, Bexh. DA6 . . .127 FB85
Gravel La, E1 . . . . .197 P8
Chigwell IG7 . . . . .50 EU46
Gravelly Hill, Cat. CR3 . . . . .186 DS128
Gravelly Ride, SW19 . . . . . . .119 CV91
Gravel Pit La, SE9 . . . . .125 EQ85
Gravel Pit Way, Orp. BR6 . . .146 EU103
Gravel Rd, Brom. BR2 . . . . . .144 EL103
Dartford (Sutt.H.) DA4 . . . .128 FP94
Twickenham TW2 . . . . .117 CE88
Gravelwood Cl, Chis. BR7 . . .125 EQ90
Graveney Gro, SE20 . . . . . . .122 DW94
Graveney Rd, SW17 . . . . . . .120 DE91
GRAVESEND, DA11 - DA13 . .131 GJ85
⇌ Gravesend 131 GG87
H Gravesend & N Kent Hosp,
Grav. DA11 . . . . .131 GG86
Gravesend Rd, W12 . . . . .81 CU73
Gravesham Ct, Grav. DA12
off Clarence Row 131 GH87
★ Gravesham Mus, Grav.
DA11 . . . . .131 GH86
Gray Av, Dag. RM8 . . . . .70 EZ60
Grayburn Cl, Ch.St.G. HP8 . . .36 AU47
Gray Gdns, Rain. RM13 . . . . .89 FG65
Grayham Cres, N.Mal. KT3 . .138 CR98
Grayham Rd, N.Mal. KT3 . . .138 CR98
Grayland Cl, Brom. BR1 . . . .144 EK95
Graylands, Epp. (They.B.)
CM16 . . . . .33 ER37
Woking GU21 . . . . .166 AY116
Graylands Cl, Wok. GU21 . . .166 AY116
Grayling Cl, E16
off Cranberry La 86 EE70
Grayling Rd, N16 . . . . .66 DR61
Graylings, The, Abb.L. WD5 . . .7 BR33
Grayling Sq, E2 . . . . .84 DU69
Gray Pl, Cher. (Ott.) KT16
off Clarendon Gate 151 BD107

GRAYS, RM16 & RM17;
RM20 . . . . .110 GA78
⇌ Grays 110 GA79
Grayscroft Rd, SW16 . . . . . . .121 DK94
Grays End Cl, Grays RM17 . .110 GA76
Grays Fm Rd, Orp. BR5 . . . .146 EV95
Grayshott Rd, SW11 . . . . . . .100 DG82
★ Gray's Inn, WC1 . . . . .196 C6
Gray's Inn Pl, WC1 . . . . .196 C7
Gray's Inn Rd, WC1 . . . . .196 B3
Gray's Inn Sq, WC1 . . . . .196 D6
Grays La, Ashf. TW15 . . . . . .115 BP91
Gray's La, Ashtd. KT21 . . . . .172 CM119
Epsom KT18 . . . . .172 CN120
Grayson Ho, EC1 . . . . .197 J3
Grays Pk Rd, Slou.
(Stoke P.) SL2 . . . . .74 AU68
Grays Pl, Slou. SL2 . . . . .74 AT74
Grays Rd, Slou. SL1 . . . . .74 AT74
Uxbridge UB10 . . . . .76 BL67
Westerham TN16 . . . . .179 EP121
Grays Town Shop Cen, Grays
RM17 off High St 110 GA79
Gray St, SE1 . . . . .200 E5
Grays Wk, Brwd. (Hutt.)
CM13 . . . . .55 GD45
Grayswood Gdns, SW20
off Farnham Gdns 139 CV96
Grayswood Pt, SW15
off Norley Vale 119 CU88
Gray's Yd, W1 . . . . .194 G9
Graywood Ct, N12 . . . . .44 DC52
Grazebrook Rd, N16 . . . . .66 DR61
Grazeley Cl, Bexh. DA6 . . . . .127 FC85
Grazeley Ct, SE19
off Gipsy Hill 122 DS91
Great Acre Ct, SW4
off St. Alphonsus Rd 101 DK84
Great Amwell La, N8
off New River Av 65 DM56
Great Arthur Ho, EC1 . . . . . .197 H5
Great Bell All, EC2 . . . . .197 K8
Great Benty, West Dr. UB7 . . .94 BL77
★ Great Bookham Common,
Lthd. KT23 . . . . .170 BZ121
Great Brownings, SE21 . . . . .122 DT91
Great Bushey Dr, N20 . . . . . . .44 DB46
Great Cambridge Junct, N18
off North Circular Rd 46 DR49
Great Cambridge Rd, N9 . . . .46 DS46
N17 . . . . .46 DR50
N18 . . . . .46 DR50
Broxbourne (Turnf.) EN10 . .15 DY26
Enfield EN1 . . . . .30 DU42
Waltham Cross (Chsht) EN8 .14 DW34
Great Castle St, W1 . . . . . . .195 J8
Great Cen Av, Ruis. HA4 . . . . .60 BW64
Great Cen St, NW1 . . . . .194 D6
Great Cen Way, NW10 . . . . . . .62 CS64
Wembley HA9 . . . . .62 CQ63
Great Chapel St, W1 . . . . . . .195 M8
Great Chart St, SW11 . . . . . .100 DD84
Great Chertsey Rd, W4 . . . . . .98 CQ82
Feltham TW13 . . . . .116 CA90
Great Ch La, W6 . . . . .99 CX78
Great Coll St, SW1 . . . . .199 P6
Great Cross Av, SE10 . . . . . .104 EE80
Great Cullings, Rom. RM7 . . . .71 FE61
Great Cumberland Ms, W1 . .194 D9
Great Cumberland Pl, W1 . . .194 D8
Great Dover St, SE1 . . . . . . .201 J5
Greatdown Rd, W7 . . . . .79 CF70
Great Eastern Enterprise
Cen, E14 . . . . .204 B5
Great Eastern Rd, E15 . . . . . . .85 ED66
Brentwood CM14 . . . . .54 FW49
Great Eastern St, EC2 . . . . . .197 M3
Great Eastern Wk, EC2 . . . . .197 N7
Great Ellshams, Bans. SM7 . .174 DA116
Great Elms Rd, Brom. BR2 . .144 EJ98
Great Fld, NW9 . . . . .42 CS53
Greatfield Av, E6 . . . . .87 EM70
Greatfield Cl, N19
off Warrender Rd 65 DJ63
SE4 . . . . .103 EA84
Greatfields Dr, Uxb. UB8 . . . .76 BN71
Greatfields Rd, Bark. IG11 . . .87 ER67
Great Fleete Way, Bark. IG11
off Choats Rd 88 EW68
Great Galley Cl, Bark. IG11 . . .88 EV69
Great Gdns Rd, Horn. RM11 . .71 FH58
Great Gatton Cl, Croy. CR0 . .143 DY101
Great George St, SW1 . . . . . .199 N5
Great Gregories La, Epp.
CM16 . . . . .17 ES33
Great Gro, Bushey WD23 . . . .24 CB42
Great Gros, Wal.Cr. EN7 . . . . .14 DS28
Great Guildford St, SE1 . . . . .201 H2
Greatham Rd, Bushey WD23 .24 BX41
Greatham Wk, SW15 . . . . . . .119 CU88
Great Harry Dr, SE9 . . . . . . .125 EN90
Greathurst End, Lthd.
(Bkhm) KT23 . . . . .170 BZ124
Great James St, WC1 . . . . . .196 B5
Great Julians, Rick. WD3
off Grove Cres 22 BN42
Great Marlborough St, W1 . .195 K9
Great Maze Pond, SE1 . . . . .201 L4
Great Nelmes Chase, Horn.
RM11 . . . . .72 FM57
Greatness La, Sev. TN14 . . . .191 FJ121
Greatness Rd, Sev. TN14 . . . .191 FJ121
Great Newport St, WC2
off Charing Cross Rd 83 DK73
Great New St, EC4 . . . . .196 E8
Great N Leisure Pk, N12 . . . . .44 DD52
Great N Rd, N2 . . . . .64 DE56
N6 .64 DE56
Barnet EN5 . . . . .27 CZ38
Barnet (New Barn.) EN5 . . . .28 DA43
Potters Bar EN6 . . . . .12 DB27
Great N Way, NW4 . . . . .43 CW54
Great Oaks, Brwd. (Hutt.)
CM13 . . . . .55 GB44
Chigwell IG7 . . . . .49 EQ49
Greatorex St, E1 . . . . .84 DU71
Great Ormond St, WC1 . . . . .196 A6
H Great Ormond St Hosp
for Children, The, WC1 . . .196 A5
Great Owl Rd, Chig. IG7 . . . . .49 EN48
Great Pk, Kings L. WD4 . . . . . .6 BM30
Great Percy St, WC1 . . . . . . .196 C2
Great Peter St, SW1 . . . . . . .199 M7

Great Pettits Ct, Rom. RM1 . . .51 FE54
⊖ Great Portland Street . . .195 J5
Great Portland St, W1 . . . . . .195 J6
Great Pulteney St, W1 . . . . . .195 L10
Great Queen St, WC2 . . . . . .196 A9
Dartford DA1 . . . . .128 FM87
Great Ropers La, Brwd. CM13 .53 FU51
Great Russell St, WC1 . . . . . .195 N8
Great St. Helens, EC3 . . . . . .197 M8
Great St. Thomas Apostle,
EC4 . . . . .197 J10
Great Scotland Yd, SW1 . . . .199 P3
Great Slades, Pot.B. EN6 . . . . .11 CZ33
Great Smith St, SW1 . . . . . . .199 N6
Great South-West Rd, Felt.
TW14 . . . . .115 BQ87
Hounslow TW4 . . . . .95 BT84
Great Spilmans, SE22 . . . . . .122 DS85
Great Stockwood Rd, Wal.Cr.
(Chsht) EN7 . . . . .14 DR26
Great Strand, NW9 . . . . .43 CT53
Great Suffolk St, SE1 . . . . . .200 G3
Great Sutton St, EC1 . . . . . . .196 G5
Great Swan All, EC2 . . . . . . .197 K8
Great Tattenhams, Epsom
KT18 . . . . .173 CV118
Great Thrift, Orp. BR5 . . . . . .145 EQ98
Great Till Cl, Sev. (Otford)
TN14 . . . . .181 FE116
Great Titchfield St, W1 . . . . .195 K8
Great Twr St, EC3 . . . . .197 M10
Great Trinity La, EC4 . . . . . .197 J10
Great Turnstile, WC1 . . . . . . .196 C7
GREAT WARLEY, Brwd. CM14 .53 FV53
Great Warley St, Brwd.
(Gt Warley) CM13 . . . . .53 FU53
Great Western Rd, W2 . . . . . . .81 CZ71
W9 .81 CZ71
W11 . . . . .81 CZ71
Great W Rd, W4 . . . . .98 CP78
W6 .99 CT78
Brentford TW8 . . . . .98 CP78
Hounslow TW5 . . . . .96 BX82
Isleworth TW7 . . . . .97 CE80
Great Winchester St, EC2 . . .197 L8
Great Windmill St, W1 . . . . . .195 M10
Greatwood, Chis. BR7 . . . . . .125 EN94
Greatwood Cl, Cher.
(Ott.) KT16 . . . . .151 BC109
Great Woodcote Dr, Pur.
CR8 . . . . .159 DK110
Great Woodcote Pk, Pur.
CR8 . . . . .159 DK110
Great Yd, SE1 . . . . .201 N4
Greaves Cl, Bark. IG11
off Norfolk Rd 87 ES66
Greaves Pl, SW17 . . . . .120 DE91
Greaves Twr, SW10
off World's End Est 100 DC80
Grebe Av, Hayes UB4
off Cygnet Way 78 BX72
Grebe Cl, E7
off Cormorant Rd 68 EF64
E17 . . . . .47 DY52
Barking IG11 . . . . .88 EU70
Grebe Ct, Sutt. SM1 . . . . . . .157 CZ106
Grebe Crest, Grays RM20 . . .109 FU77
Grecian Cres, SE19 . . . . . . .121 DP93
Greding Wk, Brwd. (Hutt.)
CM13 . . . . .55 GB47
Gredo Ho, Bark. IG11 . . . . . . .88 EV69
Greek Ct, W1 . . . . .195 N9
★ Greek Orthodox Cath
of the Divine Wisdom
(St. Sophia), W2 . . . . .82 DB73
Greek St, W1 . . . . .195 N9
Greek Yd, WC2 . . . . .195 P10
Green, The, E4 . . . . .47 EC46
E11 . . . . .68 EH58
E15 . . . . .86 EE65
N9 .46 DU47
N14 . . . . .45 DK48
N21 . . . . .45 DN45
SW14 . . . . .98 CQ83
SW19 . . . . .119 CX92
W3 .80 CS72
W5 off High St 79 CK73
Bexleyheath DA7 . . . . .106 FA81
Bromley BR1
off Downham Way 124 EG90
Bromley (Hayes) BR2 . . . . .144 EG101
Carshalton SM5 . . . . .158 DG105
Caterham (Wold.) CR3 . . . .177 EA123
Chalfont St. Giles HP8
off High St 36 AW47
Croydon CR0 . . . . .161 DZ109
Dartford DA2 . . . . .129 FR89
Epping (They.B.) CM16 . . . . .33 ES37
Epsom KT17 . . . . .157 CU111
Esher (Clay.) KT10 . . . . . . .155 CF107
Feltham TW13 . . . . .115 BV89
Hayes UB3 off Wood End . .77 BS72
Hemel Hempstead (Bov.)
HP3 . . . . .5 BA29
Hounslow TW5
off Heston Rd 96 CA79
Leatherhead (Fetch.) KT22 . .171 CD124
Morden SM4 . . . . .139 CY98
New Malden KT3 . . . . .138 CQ97
Orpington (Pr.Bot.) BR6
off Rushmore Hill 164 EW110
Orpington (St.P.Cray) BR5
off The Avenue 126 EV94
Rainham (Wenn.) RM13 . . . .90 FL73
Richmond TW9 . . . . .117 CK85
Rickmansworth (Crox.Grn)
WD3 . . . . .22 BN44
Rickmansworth (Sarratt)
WD3 . . . . .22 BG35
Romford (Havat.Bow.)
RM4 . . . . .51 FE48
Sevenoaks TN13 . . . . .191 FK122
Shepperton TW17 . . . . .135 BS98
Sidcup DA14 . . . . .126 EU91
Slough (Datchet) SL3 . . . . .92 AV80
South Ockendon RM15 . . . . .91 FW69
Southall UB2 . . . . .96 BY76
Staines (Wrays.) TW19 . . . .112 AY86
Sutton SM1 . . . . .140 DB104
Tadworth (Burgh Hth)
KT20 . . . . .173 CY119
Tilbury (W.Til.) RM18 . . . . .111 GL79
Twickenham TW2 . . . . .117 CE88

Green, The, Uxb. (Hare.) UB9 .38 BJ53
Uxbridge (Ickhm) UB10 . . . .59 BQ61
Waltham Abbey EN9
off Sewardstone Rd 15 EC34
Waltham Cross (Chsht) EN8 .14 DW28
Walton-on-Thames (Whiteley Vill.)
KT12 off Octagon Rd 153 BS110
Warlingham CR6 . . . . .177 DX117
Watford (Let.Hth) WD25 . . .25 CE39
Welling DA16 . . . . .105 ES84
Wembley HA0 . . . . .61 CG61
West Drayton UB7 . . . . .94 BK76
Westerham TN16 . . . . .189 ER126
Woking (Ripley) GU23 . . . .168 BH121
Woodford Green IG8 . . . . . .48 EG50
Greenacre, Dart. DA1
off Oakfield La 128 FL89
Woking (Knap.) GU21
off Mead Ct 166 AS116
Greenacre Cl, Barn. EN5 . . . . .27 CZ38
Northolt UB5 . . . . .60 BZ64
Swanley BR8 . . . . .147 FE98
Greenacre Ct, Egh. (Eng.Grn)
TW20 . . . . .112 AW93
Greenacre Gdns, E17 . . . . . . .67 EC56
Greenacre Pl, Wall. (Hackbr.)
SM6 off Park Rd 141 DH103
Greenacres, N3 . . . . .43 CY54
SE9 . . . . .125 EN86
Bushey (Bushey Hth) WD23 .41 CD47
Green Acres, Croy. CR0 . . . .142 DT104
Greenacres, Epp. CM16 . . . . .17 ET29
Leatherhead (Bkhm) KT23 . .170 CB124
Oxted RH8 . . . . .188 EE127
Greenacres Av, Uxb. UB10 . . .58 BM62
Greenacres Cl, Orp. BR6 . . .163 EQ105
Rainham RM13 . . . . .90 FL69
Greenacres Dr, Stan. HA7 . . . .41 CH52
Greenacre Sq, SE16 . . . . . . .203 J4
Greenacre Wk, N14 . . . . .45 DL48
Greenall Cl, Wal.Cr. (Chsht)
EN8 . . . . .15 DY30
Green Arbour Ct, EC1 . . . . . .196 F8
Green Av, NW7 . . . . .42 CR49
W13 . . . . .97 CH76
Greenaway Av, N18 . . . . .47 DX51
Greenaway Gdns, NW3 . . . . . .64 DB63
Green Bk, E1 . . . . .202 D3
N12 . . . . .44 DB49
Greenbank, Wal.Cr. (Chsht)
EN8 . . . . .14 DV28
Greenbank Av, Wem. HA0 . . . .61 CG64
Greenbank Cl, E4 . . . . .47 EC47
Romford RM3 . . . . .52 FK48
Greenbank Cres, NW4 . . . . . .63 CY56
Greenbank Rd, Wat. WD17 . . .23 BR36
Greenbanks, Dart. DA1 . . . . .128 FL89
Upminster RM14 . . . . .73 FS60
Greenbay Rd, SE7 . . . . .104 EK80
Greenberry St, NW8 . . . . . . .194 B1
Greenbrook Av, Barn. EN4 . . .28 DC39
Greenbury Cl, Rick. (Chorl.)
WD3 . . . . .21 BC41
Green Cl, NW9 . . . . .62 CQ58
NW11 . . . . .64 DC59
Bromley BR2 . . . . .144 EE97
Carshalton SM5 . . . . .140 DF103
Feltham TW13 . . . . .116 BY92
Hatfield AL9
off Station Rd 11 CY26
Waltham Cross (Chsht) EN8 .15 DY32
Greencoat Pl, SW1 . . . . .199 L8
Greencoat Row, SW1 . . . . . . .199 L7
Greencourt Av, Croy. CR0 . . .142 DV103
Edgware HA8 . . . . .42 CP53
Greencourt Gdns, Croy. CR0 .142 DV102
Greencourt Rd, Orp. BR5 . . .145 ER99
Green Ct Rd, Swan. BR8 . . . .147 FD99
Greencrest Pl, NW2
off Dollis Hill La 63 CU62
Green Cft, Edg. HA8
off Deans La 42 CQ50
Greencroft Av, Ruis. HA4 . . . .60 BW61
Greencroft Cl, E6
off Neatscourt Rd 86 EL71
Greencroft Gdns, NW6 . . . . . .82 DB66
Enfield EN1 . . . . .30 DS41
Greencroft Rd, Houns. TW5 . .96 BZ81
Green Curve, Bans. SM7 . . . .157 CZ114
Green Dale, SE5 . . . . .102 DR84
SE22 . . . . .122 DS85
Green Dale Cl, SE22
off Green Dale 122 DS85
Greendale Ms, Slou. SL2 . . . .74 AU73
Greendale Wk, Grav. (Nthflt)
DA11 . . . . .130 GE90
Green Dragon Ct, SE1 . . . . . .201 K2
Green Dragon La, N21 . . . . . .29 DP44
Brentford TW8 . . . . .98 CL78
Green Dragon Yd, E1
off Old Montague St 84 DU71
Green Dr, Slou. SL3 . . . . .92 AY77
Southall UB1 . . . . .78 CA74
Woking (Ripley) GU23 . . . .167 BF123
Green E Rd, Beac.
(Jordans) HP9 . . . . .36 AS52
Green Edge, Wat. WD25
off Clarke Grn 23 BU35
Greene Fielde End, Stai. TW18 .114 BK94
Green End, N21 . . . . .45 DP47
Chessington KT9 . . . . .156 CL105
Green End Business Cen,
Rick. (Sarratt) WD3 . . . . . .22 BG37
Greenend Rd, W4 . . . . .98 CS75
Greenfarm Cl, Orp. BR6 . . . .163 ET106
Greenfell Mans, SE8
off Glaisher St 103 EB79
Greenfield Av, Surb. KT5 . . .138 CP101
Watford WD19 . . . . .40 BX47
Greenfield Dr, N2 . . . . .64 DF56
Greenfield End, Ger.Cr.
(Chal.St.P.) SL9 . . . . .36 AY51
Greenfield Gdns, NW2 . . . . . .63 CY61
Dagenham RM9 . . . . .88 EX67
Orpington BR5 . . . . .145 ER101
Greenfield Link, Couls. CR5 .175 DL115
Greenfield Rd, E1 . . . . .84 DU71
N15 . . . . .66 DS57
Dagenham RM9 . . . . .88 EW67
Dartford DA2 . . . . .127 FD92
Greenfields, Loug. IG10 . . . . .33 EN42
Potters Bar (Cuffley) EN6
off South Dr 13 DL30

Greenfields Cl, Brwd.
(Gt Warley) CM13 . . . . .53 FW51
Loughton IG10 . . . . .33 EN42
Greenfield St, Wal.Abb. EN9 . .15 EC34
Greenfield Way, Har. HA2 . . . .60 CB55
GREENFORD, UB6 . . . . .78 CB69
⇌ Greenford 79 CD67
⊖ Greenford 79 CD67
Greenford Av, W7 . . . . .79 CE70
Southall UB1 . . . . .78 BZ73
Greenford Gdns, Grnf. UB6 . .78 CB69
Greenford Rd, Grnf. UB6 . . . .78 CC71
Harrow HA1 . . . . .61 CE64
Southall UB1 . . . . .78 CC74
Sutton SM1 . . . . .158 DB105
Greenford Rbt, Grnf. UB6 . . . .79 CD68
Green Gdns, Orp. BR6 . . . . .163 EQ106
Greengate, Grnf. UB6 . . . . . . .79 CH65
Greengate St, E13 . . . . .86 EH68
Green Glade, Epp. (They.B.)
CM16 . . . . .33 ES37
Green Glades, Horn. RM11 . . .72 FM58
Greenhalgh Wk, N2 . . . . .64 DC56
Greenham Cl, SE1 . . . . .200 D5
Greenham Cres, E4 . . . . .47 DZ51
Greenham Rd, N10 . . . . .44 DG54
Greenham Wk, Wok. GU21 . . .166 AW118
Greenhaven Dr, SE28 . . . . . . .88 EV72
Greenhayes Av, Bans. SM7 . .158 DA114
Greenhayes Cl, Reig. RH2 . . .184 DC134
Greenhayes Gdns, Bans.
SM7 . . . . .174 DA115
Greenheys Cl, Nthwd. HA6 . . .39 BS53
Greenheys Dr, E18 . . . . .68 EF55
Greenheys Pl, Wok. GU22
off White Rose La 167 AZ118
Greenhill, NW3
off Prince Arthur Rd 64 DD63
SE18 . . . . .105 EM78
Green Hill, Buck.H. IG9 . . . . .48 EJ46
Orpington BR6 . . . . .162 EL112
Greenhill, Sutt. SM1 . . . . . . .140 DC103
Wembley HA9 . . . . .62 CP61
Greenhill Av, Cat. CR3 . . . . .176 DV121
Greenhill Cres, Wat. WD18 . . .23 BS44
Greenhill Gdns, Nthlt. UB5 . . .78 BZ68
Greenhill Gro, E12 . . . . .68 EL63
Green Hill La, Warl. CR6 . . . .177 DY117
Greenhill Pk, NW10 . . . . .80 CS67
Barnet EN5 . . . . .28 DB43
Greenhill Rd, NW10 . . . . .80 CS67
Gravesend (Nthflt) DA11 . .131 GF89
Harrow HA1 . . . . .61 CE58
Greenhills Cl, Rick. WD3 . . . . .22 BH43
Greenhill's Rents, EC1 . . . . .196 G6
Greenhills Ter, N1
off Baxter Rd 84 DR65
Greenhill Ter, SE18 . . . . .105 EM78
Northolt UB5 . . . . .78 BZ68
Greenhill Way, Croy. CR0 . . .161 DX111
Harrow HA1 . . . . .61 CE58
Wembley HA9 . . . . .62 CP61
GREENHITHE, DA9 . . . . .129 FV85
⇌ Greenhithe 129 FU85
Greenhithe Cl, Sid. DA15 . . .125 ES87
Greenholm Rd, SE9 . . . . . . .125 EP85
Green Hundred Rd, SE15 . . .102 DU79
Greenhurst La, Oxt. RH8 . . . .188 EG132
Greenhurst Rd, SE27 . . . . . .121 DN92
Greening St, SE2 . . . . .106 EW77
Greenlake Ter, Stai. TW18 . . .113 BF94
Greenland Cres, Sthl. UB2 . . .96 BW76
Greenland Ms, SE8
off Trundleys Rd 103 DX78
Riv Greenland Pier 203 M7
Greenland Pl, NW1
off Greenland Rd 83 DH67
Greenland Quay, SE16 . . . . .203 J8
Greenland Rd, NW1 . . . . .83 DJ67
Barnet EN5 . . . . .27 CW44
Greenlands, Cher. KT16 . . . .133 BC104
Greenlands La, NW4 . . . . .43 CV53
Greenlands Rd, Stai. TW18 . .114 BG91
Weybridge KT13 . . . . .135 BP104
Greenland St, NW1
off Camden High St 83 DH67
Greenland Way, Croy. CR0 . .141 DK101
Green La, E4 . . . . .32 EE41
NW4 . . . . .63 CX57
SE9 . . . . .125 EN89
SE20 . . . . .123 DX94
SW16 . . . . .121 DM94
W7 .97 CE75
Addlestone KT15 . . . . .134 BG104
Amersham HP6 . . . . .20 AS38
Ashtead KT21 . . . . .171 CJ117
Brentwood (Pilg.Hat.) CM15 .54 FV43
Brentwood (Warley) CM14 . .53 FU52
Caterham CR3 . . . . .176 DQ122
Chertsey KT16 . . . . .133 BE103
Chesham HP5 . . . . .4 AV33
Chessington KT9 . . . . .156 CL109
Chigwell IG7 . . . . .49 ER47
Chislehurst BR7 . . . . .125 EP91
Cobham KT11 . . . . .154 BY112
Coulsdon CR5 . . . . .184 DA125
Dagenham RM8 . . . . .70 EU60
Edgware HA8 . . . . .42 CN50
Egham TW20 . . . . .113 BB91
Egham (Thorpe) TW20 . . . .133 BD95
Feltham TW13 . . . . .116 BY92
Harrow HA1 . . . . .61 CE62
Hemel Hempstead (Bov.)
HP3 . . . . .5 AZ28
Hounslow TW4 . . . . .95 BV83
Ilford IG1, IG3 . . . . .69 EQ61
Leatherhead KT22 . . . . . . .171 CK121
Morden SM4 . . . . .140 DB100
New Malden KT3 . . . . .138 CQ99
Northwood HA6 . . . . .39 BT52
Purley CR8 . . . . .159 DJ111
Redhill RH1 . . . . .184 DE132
Redhill (Bletch.) RH1 . . . . .186 DS131
Reigate RH2 . . . . .183 CZ134
Rickmansworth (Crox.Grn)
WD3 . . . . .22 BM43
Shepperton TW17 . . . . .135 BQ100

Green La, Slough (Datchet) SL3 92 AV81
South Ockendon RM15 91 FR69
Staines TW18 133 BE95
Stanmore HA7 41 CH49
Sunbury-on-Thames TW16 115 BT94
Tadworth (Lwr Kgswd) KT20 183 CZ126
Thornton Heath CR7 141 DN95
Upminster RM14 91 FR68
Uxbridge UB8 77 BQ71
Waltham Abbey EN9 16 EJ34
Walton-on-Thames KT12 153 BV107
Warlingham CR6 177 DY116
Watford WD19 40 BW46
West Byfleet (Byfleet) KT14 152 BM112
West Molesey KT8 136 CB99
Woking (Chobham) GU24 150 AT110
Woking (Mayford) GU24 *off Copper Beech Cl* 166 AV121
Woking (Ock.) GU23 169 BP124
Worcester Park KT4 139 CU102
Green La Av, Walt. KT12 154 BW106
Green La Cl, Cher. KT16 133 BE103
West Byfleet (Byfleet) KT14 152 BM112
Green La Gdns, Th.Hth. CR7 142 DQ96
Green Las, N4 66 DQ60
N8 65 DP55
N13 45 DM51
N15 65 DP55
N16 66 DQ62
N21 45 DP46
Epsom KT19 156 CS109
Greenlaw Gdns, N.Mal. KT3 139 CT101
Greenlawn La, Brent. TW8 97 CK77
Green Lawns, Ruis. HA4 60 BW60
Greenlaw St, SE18 105 EN76
Green Leaf Av, Wall. SM6 159 DK105
Greenleaf Cl, SW2 *off Tulse Hill* 121 DN87
Greenleafe Dr, Ilf. IG6 69 EP56
Greenleaf Rd, E6 *off Redclyffe Rd* 86 EJ67
E17 67 DZ55
Greenlea Pk, SW19 140 DE95
Green Leas, Sun. TW16 115 BT93
Waltham Abbey EN9 *off Roundhills* 15 ED34
Green Leas Cl, Sun. TW16 *off Green Leas* 115 BT93
Greenleaves Ct, Ashf. TW15 *off Redleaves Av* 115 BP93
Greenleigh Av, Orp. BR5 146 EV98
Greenlink Wk, Rich. TW9 *off Melliss Av* 98 CP81
Green Man Gdns, W13 79 CG73
Green Man La, W13 79 CG74
Feltham TW14 95 BU84
Green Manor Way, Grav. DA11 110 FZ84
Green Man Pas, W13 79 CG73
Green Man Rbt, E11 68 EF59
Greenman St, N1 84 DQ66
Green Mead, Esher KT10 *off Winterdown Gdns* 154 BZ107
Greenmead Cl, SE25 142 DU99
Green Meadow, Pot.B. EN6 12 DA30
Greenmeads, Wok. GU22 166 AY122
Green Moor Link, N21 45 DP45
Greenmoor Rd, Enf. EN3 30 DW40
Green N Rd, Beac. (Jordans) HP9 36 AS51
Greenoak Pl, Barn. EN4 28 DF40
Greenoak Ri, West. (Bigg.H.) TN16 178 EJ118
Greenoak Way, SW19 119 CX91
Greenock Rd, SW16 141 DK95
W3 98 CP76
Greenock Way, Rom. RM1 51 FE51
Greeno Cres, Shep. TW17 134 BN99
⊖ **Green Park** 199 K3
Green Pk, Stai. TW18 113 BE90
★ **Green Park, The**, SW1 199 J4
Greenpark Ct, Wem. HA0 79 CJ66
Green Pk Way, Grnf. UB6 79 CE67
Green Pl, SE10 205 H4
Dartford DA1 127 FE85
Green Pt, E15 86 EE65
Green Pond Cl, E17 67 DZ55
Green Pond Rd, E17 67 DY55
Green Ride, Epp. CM16 33 EP35
Loughton IG10 32 EG43
Green Rd, N14 29 DH44
N20 44 DC48
Egham (Thorpe) TW20 133 BB98
Greenroof Way, SE10 205 L7
Greensand Cl, Red. (S.Merst.) RH1 185 DK128
Green Sand Rd, Red. RH1 184 DG133
Greensand Way, Gdse. RH9 186 DV134
Greens Cl, The, Loug. IG10 33 EN40
Green's Ct, W1 195 M10
Green's End, SE18 105 EP77
Greenshank Cl, E17 *off Banbury Rd* 47 DY52
Greenshaw, Brwd. CM14 54 FV46
Greenshields Ind Est, E16 205 P3
Greenside, Bex. DA5 126 EY88
Borehamwood WD6 26 CN38
Dagenham RM8 70 EW60
Swanley BR8 147 FD96
Greenside Cl, N20 44 DD47
SE6 123 ED89
Greenside Dr, Ashtd. KT21 171 CH118
Greenside Rd, W12 99 CU76
Croydon CR0 141 DN101
Weybridge KT13 135 BP104
Greenside Wk, West. (Bigg.H.) TN16 *off Kings Rd* 178 EH118
Greenslade Av, Ashtd. KT21 172 CP119
Greenslade Rd, Bark. IG11 87 ER66
Greensleeves Dr, Brwd. (Warley) CM14 54 FV50
Greenstead Av, Wdf.Grn. IG8 48 EJ52
Greenstead Cl, Brwd. (Hutt.) CM13 55 GE45
Greenstead Cl, Wdf. Grn. IG8 *off Greenstead Gdns* 48 EJ51
Greenstead Gdns, SW15 119 CU85
Woodford Green IG8 48 EJ51
GREENSTED GREEN, Ong. CM5 19 FH28
Greensted Rd, Loug. IG10 48 EL45
Ongar CM5 19 FG28
Greenstone Ms, E11 68 EG58
GREEN STREET, Borwd. WD6 26 CP37
Green St, E7 86 EH65
E13 86 EJ67
W1 194 E10
Borehamwood WD6 26 CN36
Enfield EN3 30 DW40
Radlett (Shenley) WD7 26 CN36
Rickmansworth (Chorl.) WD3 21 BC40
Sunbury-on-Thames TW16 135 BU95
GREEN STREET GREEN, Dart. DA2 129 FU93
GREEN STREET GREEN, Orp. BR6 163 ES107
Green St Grn Rd, Dart. DA1, DA2 128 FP88
Greensward, Bushey WD23 24 CB44
Green Ter, EC1 196 E3
Green Tiles La, Uxb. (Denh.) UB9 57 BF58
Greentrees, Epp. CM16 18 EU31
Green Vale, W5 80 CM72
Bexleyheath DA6 126 EX85
Greenvale Rd, SE9 105 EM84
Green Verges, Stan. HA7 41 CK52
Green Vw, Chess. KT9 156 CM108
Greenview Av, Beck. BR3 143 DY100
Croydon CR0 143 DY100
Greenview Cl, W3 80 CS74
Green Vw Cl, Hem.H. (Bov.) HP3 5 BA29
Greenview Ct, Ashf. TW15 *off Village Way* 114 BM91
Green Wk, NW4 63 CX57
SE1 201 M7
Buckhurst Hill IG9 48 EL45
Dartford DA1 107 FF84
Hampton TW12 *off Orpwood Cl* 116 BZ93
Ruislip HA4 59 BT60
Southall UB2 96 CA78
Woodford Green IG8 48 EL51
Green Wk, The, E4 47 EC46
Greenway, N14 45 DL47
N20 44 DA47
Green Way, SE9 124 EK85
Greenway, SW20 139 CW98
Brentwood (Hutt.) CM13 55 GA45
Green Way, Brom. BR2 144 EL100
Greenway, Chis. BR7 125 EN92
Dagenham RM8 70 EW61
Harrow HA3 62 CL57
Hayes UB4 77 BV70
Leatherhead (Bkhm) KT23 170 CB123
Pinner HA5 39 BV54
Green Way, Red. RH1 184 DE132
Greenway, Rom. RM3 52 FP51
Green Way, Sun. TW16 135 BU98
Greenway, Wall. SM6 159 DJ105
Westerham (Tats.) TN16 178 EJ120
Woodford Green IG8 48 EJ50
Greenway, The, NW9 42 CR54
Enfield EN3 31 DX35
Epsom KT18 172 CN115
Gerrards Cross (Chal.St.P.) SL9 56 AX55
Harrow HA3 41 CE53
Hounslow TW4 96 BZ84
Orpington BR5 146 EV100
Oxted RH8 188 EH133
Pinner HA5 60 BZ58
Potters Bar EN6 12 DA33
Rickmansworth (Mill End) WD3 38 BG45
Uxbridge UB8 76 BJ68
Uxbridge (Ickhm) UB10 59 BQ61
Greenway Av, E17 67 ED56
Greenway Cl, N4 66 DQ61
N11 44 DG51
N15 *off Copperfield Dr* 66 DT56
N20 44 DA47
NW9 42 CR54
West Byfleet KT14 152 BG113
Greenway Dr, Stai. TW18 134 BK95
Greenway Gdns, NW9 42 CR54
Croydon CR0 143 DZ104
Greenford UB6 78 CA69
Harrow HA3 41 CE54
Greenways, Abb.L. WD5 7 BS32
Beckenham BR3 143 EA96
Egham TW20 112 AY92
Esher KT10 155 CE105
Tadworth (Walt.Hill) KT20 183 CV125
Waltham Cross (Chsht) EN7 13 DP29
Woking GU22 *off Pembroke Rd* 167 BA117
Greenways, The, Twick. TW1 *off South Western Rd* 117 CG86
Greenwell Cl, Gdse. RH9 186 DV130
Greenwell St, W1 195 J5
Green W Rd, Beac. (Jordans) HP9 36 AS52
GREENWICH, SE10 103 ED79
⇌ **Greenwich** 103 EB80
DLR **Greenwich** 103 EB80
Greenwich Ch St, SE10 103 EC79
Greenwich Ct, Wal.Cr. EN8 *off Parkside* 15 DY34
Greenwich Cres, E6 *off Swan App* 86 EL71
Greenwich Foot Tunnel, E14 103 EC78
SE10 103 EC78
Greenwich Hts, SE18 *off Master Gunner Pl* 104 EL80
Greenwich High Rd, SE10 103 EB81
Greenwich Ho, SE13 *off Hither Grn La* 123 ED86
Greenwich Ind Est, SE7 205 P9
Greenwich Mkt, SE10 *off King William Wk* 103 EC79
★ **Greenwich Pk**, SE10 103 ED80
Greenwich Pk St, SE10 103 ED78
★ **Greenwich Pier**, SE10 103 EC79
Greenwich Quay, SE8 103 EB79
Greenwich Shop Pk, SE7 205 N9
Greenwich S St, SE10 103 EB81
Greenwich Vw Pl, E14 204 B7
Greenwich Way, Wal.Abb. EN9 31 EC36
Greenwood Av, Dag. RM10 71 FB63
Enfield EN3 31 DY40
Waltham Cross (Chsht) EN7 14 DV31
Greenwood Cl, Add. (Wdhm) KT15 151 BF111
Amersham HP6 20 AS37
Bushey (Bushey Hth) WD23 *off Langmead Dr* 41 CE45
Morden SM4 139 CY98
Orpington BR5 145 ES100
Sidcup DA15 *off Hurst Rd* 126 EU89
Thames Ditton KT7 137 CG102
Waltham Cross (Chsht) EN7 14 DV31
Greenwood Ct, SW1 199 K10
Greenwood Dr, E4 *off Avril Way* 47 EC50
Watford WD25 7 BV34
Greenwood Gdns, N13 45 DP48
Caterham CR3 186 DU125
Ilford IG6 49 EQ52
Oxted RH8 188 EG134
Radlett (Shenley) WD7 10 CL33
Greenwood Ho, Grays RM17 *off Argent St* 110 GB79
Greenwood La, Hmptn. (Hmptn H.) TW12 116 CB92
Greenwood Pk, Kings.T. KT2 118 CS94
Greenwood Pl, NW5 *off Highgate Rd* 65 DH64
Greenwood Rd, E8 84 DU65
E13 *off Valetta Gro* 86 EF68
Bexley DA5 127 FD91
Chigwell IG7 50 EV49
Croydon CR0 141 DP101
Isleworth TW7 97 CE83
Mitcham CR4 141 DK97
Thames Ditton KT7 137 CG102
Woking GU21 166 AS120
Greenwoods, The, Har. (S.Har.) HA2 60 CC61
Greenwood Ter, NW10 80 CR67
Greenwood Way, Sev. TN13 190 FF125
Green Wrythe Cres, Cars. SM5 140 DE102
Green Wrythe La, Cars. SM5 140 DD100
Greenyard, Wal.Abb. EN9 15 EC33
Greer Rd, Har. HA3 40 CC53
Greet St, SE1 200 E3
Greg Cl, E10 67 EC58
Gregor Ms, SE3 104 EG80
Gregory Av, Pot.B. EN6 12 DC33
Gregory Cl, Brom. BR2 144 EE98
Woking GU21 166 AW117
Gregory Cres, SE9 124 EK87
Gregory Dr, Wind. (Old Wind.) SL4 112 AV86
Gregory Ms, Wal.Abb. EN9 *off Beaulieu Dr* 15 EB33
Gregory Pl, W8 100 DB75
Gregory Rd, Rom. RM6 70 EX56
Southall UB2 96 CA76
Gregson Cl, Borwd. WD6 26 CQ39
Gregson's Ride, Loug. IG10 33 EN38
Greig Cl, N8 65 DL57
Greig Ter, SE17 *off Lorrimore Sq* 101 DP79
Grenaby Av, Croy. CR0 142 DR101
Grenaby Rd, Croy. CR0 142 DR101
Grenada Rd, SE7 104 EJ80
Grenade St, E14 85 DZ73
Grenadier Pl, Cat. CR3 176 DQ122
Grenadier St, E16 87 EN74
Grenadine Cl, Wal.Cr. EN7 14 DT27
Grena Gdns, Rich. TW9 98 CM84
Grenard Cl, SE15 102 DU80
Grena Rd, Rich. TW9 98 CM84
Grendon Gdns, Wem. HA9 62 CN61
Grendon Ho, N1 *off Priory Grn Est* 83 DM68
Grendon St, NW8 194 B4
Grenfell Av, Horn. RM12 71 FF60
Grenfell Cl, Borwd. WD6 26 CQ39
Grenfell Gdns, Har. HA3 62 CL59
Grenfell Ho, SE5 *off Comber Gro* 102 DQ80
Grenfell Rd, W11 81 CX73
Mitcham CR4 120 DF93
Grenfell Twr, W11 81 CX73
Grenfell Wk, W11 81 CX73
Grennell Cl, Sutt. SM1 140 DD103
Grennell Rd, Sutt. SM1 140 DC103
Grenoble Gdns, N13 45 DN51
Grenville Cl, N3 43 CZ53
Cobham KT11 154 BX113
Surbiton KT5 138 CQ102
Waltham Cross EN8 15 DX32
Grenville Ct, SE19 *off Lymer Av* 122 DT92
Grenville Gdns, Wdf.Grn. IG8 48 EJ53
Grenville Ms, N19 *off Grenville Rd* 65 DL60
SW7 100 DC77
Hampton TW12 116 CB92
Grenville Pl, NW7 42 CR50
SW7 100 DC76
Grenville Rd, N19 65 DL60
Croydon (New Adgtn) CR0 161 EC109
Grays (Chaff.Hun.) RM16 109 FW78
Grenville St, WC1 196 A5
Gresham Av, N20 44 DF49
Warlingham CR6 177 DY118
Gresham Cl, Bex. DA5 126 EY86
Brentwood CM14 54 FW48
Enfield EN2 30 DQ41
Oxted RH8 188 EF128
Gresham Dr, Rom. RM6 70 EV57
Gresham Gdns, NW11 63 CY60
Gresham Pl, N19 65 DK61
Gresham Rd, E6 87 EM68
E16 86 EH72
NW10 62 CR64
SE25 142 DU98
SW9 101 DN83
Beckenham BR3 143 DY96
Brentwood CM14 54 FW48
Edgware HA8 42 CM51
Hampton TW12 116 CA93
Hounslow TW3 96 CC81
Gresham Rd, Oxted RH8 188 EF128
Staines TW18 113 BF92
Uxbridge UB10 76 BN68
Gresham St, EC2 197 H8
Gresham Way, SW19 120 DA90
Gresley Cl, E17 67 DY58
N15 *off Clinton Rd* 66 DR56
Gresley Ct, Pot.B. EN6 12 DC29
Gresley Rd, N19 65 DJ60
Gressenhall Rd, SW18 119 CZ86
Gresse St, W1 195 M7
Gresswell Cl, Sid. DA14 126 EU90
Greswell St, SW6 99 CX81
Gretton Rd, N17 46 DS52
Greville Av, S.Croy. CR2 161 DX110
Greville Cl, Ashtd. KT21 172 CL119
Twickenham TW1 117 CH87
Greville Ct, E5 *off Napoleon Rd* 66 DV63
Greville Hall, NW6 *off Greville Pl* 82 DB68
Greville Ms, NW6 *off Greville Rd* 82 DB68
Greville Pk Av, Ashtd. KT21 172 CL118
Greville Pk Rd, Ashtd. KT21 172 CL118
Greville Pl, NW6 82 DB68
Greville Rd, E17 67 EC56
NW6 82 DB67
Richmond TW10 118 CM86
Greville St, EC1 196 E7
Grey Alders, Bans. SM7 *off High Beeches* 157 CW114
Greycaine Rd, Wat. WD24 24 BX37
Grey Cl, NW11 64 DC58
Greycoat Pl, SW1 199 M7
Greycoat St, SW1 199 M7
Greycot Rd, Beck. BR3 123 EA92
Grey Eagle St, E1 197 P6
Greyfell Cl, Stan. HA7 *off Coverdale Cl* 41 CH50
Greyfields Cl, Pur. CR8 159 DP113
Greyfriars, Brwd. (Hutt.) CM13 55 GB45
Greyfriars Pas, EC1 196 G8
Greyfriars Rd, Wok. (Ripley) GU23 168 BG124
Greyhound Hill, NW4 63 CU55
Greyhound La, SW16 121 DK93
Grays (Orsett) RM16 111 GG75
Potters Bar EN6 11 CU33
Greyhound Rd, N17 66 DS55
NW10 81 CV69
W6 99 CX79
W14 99 CY79
Sutton SM1 158 DC106
Greyhound Ter, SW16 141 DJ95
Greyhound Way, Dart. DA1 127 FE86
Greys Pk Cl, Kes. BR2 162 EJ106
Greystead Rd, SE23 122 DW87
Greystoke Av, Pnr. HA5 60 CA55
Greystoke Dr, Ruis. HA4 59 BP58
Greystoke Gdns, W5 80 CL70
Enfield EN2 29 DK42
Greystoke Pk Ter, W5 79 CK69
Greystoke Pl, EC4 196 D8
Greystone Cl, S.Croy. CR2 160 DW111
Greystone Gdns, Har. HA3 61 CJ58
Ilford IG6 49 EQ54
Greystone Path, E11 *off Grove Rd* 68 EF59
Greystones Dr, Reig. RH2 184 DC132
Greyswood Av, N18 47 DX51
Greyswood St, SW16 121 DH93
Greythorne Rd, Wok. GU21 166 AU118
Grey Twrs Av, Horn. RM11 72 FK60
Grey Twrs Gdns, Horn. RM11 *off Grey Twrs Av* 72 FK60
Grice Av, West. (Bigg.H.) TN16 162 EH113
Gridiron Pl, Upmin. RM14 72 FP62
Grierson Rd, SE23 123 DX87
Grieves Rd, Grav. (Nthflt) DA11 131 GF90
Griffin Av, Upmin. RM14 73 FS58
Griffin Cen, The, Felt. TW14 115 BV85
Griffin Cl, NW10 63 CV64
Griffin Manor Way, SE28 105 ER76
Griffin Rd, N17 46 DS54
SE18 105 ER78
Griffins, The, Grays RM16 110 GB75
Griffins Cl, N21 46 DR45
Griffin Wk, Green. DA9 *off Church Rd* 129 FT85
Griffin Way, Sun. TW16 135 BU96
Griffith Cl, Dag. RM8 *off Gibson Rd* 70 EW60
Griffiths Cl, Wor.Pk. KT4 139 CV103
Griffiths Rd, SW19 120 DA94
Griffon Way, Wat. (Lvsdn) WD25 7 BT34
Grifon Rd, Grays (Chaff.Hun.) RM16 109 FW76
Griggs App, Ilf. IG1 69 EQ61
Griggs Gdns, Horn. RM12 *off Tylers Cres* 72 FJ64
Griggs Pl, SE1 201 N7
Griggs Rd, E10 67 EC58
Grilse Cl, N9 46 DV49
Grimsby Gro, E16 87 EP74
Grimsby St, E2 *off Cheshire St* 84 DU70
Grimsdyke Cres, Barn. EN5 27 CW41
Grimsdyke Rd, Pnr. HA5 40 BY52
Grimsel Path, SE5 *off Laxley Cl* 101 DP80
Grimshaw Cl, N6 64 DG59
Grimshaw Way, Rom. RM1 71 FF57
Grimstone Cl, Rom. RM5 51 FB51
Grimston Rd, SW6 99 CZ82
Grimthorpe Ho, EC1 *off Percival St* 83 DP69
Grimwade Av, Croy. CR0 142 DU104
Grimwade Cl, SE15 102 DW83
Grimwood Rd, Twick. TW1 117 CF87
Grindall Cl, Croy. CR0 *off Hillside Rd* 159 DP105
Grindal St, SE1 200 D5
Grindleford Av, N11 44 DG47
Grindley Gdns, Croy. CR0 142 DT100
Grinling Pl, SE8 103 EA79
Grinstead Rd, SE8 103 DY78
Grisedale Cl, Pur. CR8 160 DS114
Grisedale Gdns, Pur. CR8 160 DS114
Grittleton Av, Wem. HA9 80 CP65
Grittleton Rd, W9 82 DA70
Grizedale Ter, SE23 122 DV89
Grobars Av, Wok. GU21 166 AW115
Grocer's Hall Ct, EC2 197 K9
Grogan Cl, Hmptn. TW12 116 BZ93
Groombridge Cl, Walt. KT12 153 BV106
Welling DA16 126 EU85
Groombridge Rd, E9 85 DX66
Groom Cl, Brom. BR2 144 EH98
Groom Cres, SW18 120 DD87
Groomfield Cl, SW17 120 DG91
Groom Pl, SW1 198 G6
Groom Rd, Brox. EN10 15 DZ26
Grooms Cotts, Chesh. HP5 4 AV30
Grooms Dr, Pnr. HA5 59 BU57
Grosmont Rd, SE18 105 ET78
Grosse Way, SW15 119 CV86
Grosvenor Av, N5 66 DQ64
SW14 98 CS83
Carshalton SM5 158 DF107
Harrow HA2 60 CB58
Hayes UB4 77 BS68
Kings Langley WD4 7 BQ28
Richmond TW10 *off Grosvenor Rd* 118 CL85
Grosvenor Cl, Iver SL0 75 BD69
Loughton IG10 33 EP39
Grosvenor Cotts, SW1 198 F8
Grosvenor Ct, N14 45 DJ45
NW6 81 CX67
Rickmansworth (Crox.Grn) WD3 *off Mayfare* 23 BR43
Slough SL1 74 AS72
Grosvenor Cres, NW9 62 CN56
SW1 198 G5
Dartford DA1 128 FK85
Uxbridge UB10 77 BP66
Grosvenor Cres Ms, SW1 198 F5
Grosvenor Dr, Horn. RM11 72 FJ60
Loughton IG10 33 EP39
Grosvenor Est, SW1 199 N8
Grosvenor Gdns, E6 86 EK69
N10 65 DJ55
N14 29 DK43
NW2 63 CW64
NW11 63 CZ58
SW1 199 H6
SW14 98 CS83
Kingston upon Thames KT2 117 CK93
Upminster RM14 73 FR60
Wallington SM6 159 DJ108
Woodford Green IG8 48 EG51
Grosvenor Gdns Ms E, SW1 199 J6
Grosvenor Gdns Ms N, SW1 199 H7
Grosvenor Gdns Ms S, SW1 199 J7
Grosvenor Gate, W1 198 E1
Grosvenor Hill, SW19 119 CY93
W1 195 H10
Grosvenor Pk, SE5 102 DQ79
Grosvenor Pk Rd, E17 67 EA57
Grosvenor Path, Loug. IG10 33 EP39
Grosvenor Pl, SW1 198 G5
Weybridge KT13 *off Vale Rd* 135 BR104
Grosvenor Ri E, E17 67 EB57
Grosvenor Rd, E6 86 EK67
E7 86 EH65
E10 67 EC60
E11 68 EG57
N3 43 CZ52
N9 46 DV46
N10 45 DH53
SE25 142 DU98
SW1 101 DH79
W4 98 CP78
W7 79 CG74
Belvedere DA17 106 FA79
Bexleyheath DA6 126 EX85
Borehamwood WD6 26 CN41
Brentford TW8 97 CK79
Dagenham RM8 70 EZ60
Epsom KT18 172 CR119
Hounslow TW3 96 BZ83
Ilford IG1 69 EQ62
Northwood HA6 39 BT50
Orpington BR5 145 ES100
Richmond TW10 118 CL85
Romford RM7 71 FD59
Southall UB2 96 BZ76
Staines TW18 114 BG94
Twickenham TW1 117 CG87
Wallington SM6 159 DH107
Watford WD17 24 BW42
West Wickham BR4 143 EB102
Grosvenor Sq, W1 194 G10
Kings Langley WD4 *off Grosvenor Av* 7 BQ28
Grosvenor St, W1 195 H10
Grosvenor Ter, SE5 101 DP80
Grosvenor Vale, Ruis. HA4 59 BT61
Grosvenor Way, E5 66 DW61
Grosvenor Wf Rd, E14 204 F9
Grote's Bldgs, SE3 104 EE82
Grote's Pl, SE3 104 EE82
Groton Rd, SW18 120 DB89
Grotto Pas, W1 194 G6
Grotto Rd, Twick. TW1 117 CF89
Weybridge KT13 135 BP104
Grove, The, E15 86 EE65
N3 44 DA53
N4 65 DM59
N6 64 DG60
N8 65 DK57
N13 45 DN50
N14 29 DJ43
NW9 62 CR57
NW11 63 CY59
SE22 *off Dulwich Common* 122 DU88
W5 79 CK74
Addlestone KT15 152 BH106
Bexleyheath DA6 106 EX84
Brentwood CM14 54 FT49
Caterham CR3 175 DP121
Chesham (Latimer) HP5 20 AX36
Coulsdon CR5 175 DK115
Edgware HA8 42 CP49
Egham TW20 113 BA92
Enfield EN2 29 DN40
Epsom KT17 156 CS113
Epsom (Ewell) KT17 157 CT110
Esher KT10 136 CB102
Gravesend DA12 131 GH87

★ Place of interest | ⇌ Railway station | ⊖ London Underground station | DLR Docklands Light Railway station | Tra Tramlink station | H Hospital | Riv Pedestrian ferry landing stage

Grove,The, Grnf. UB6 ....78 CC72
Hatfield (Brook.Pk) AL9 ....12 DA27
Isleworth TW7 ....97 CE81
Potters Bar EN6 ....12 DC32
Radlett WD7 ....9 CG34
Sidcup DA14 ....126 EY91
Slough SL1 ....92 AU75
Stanmore HA7 ....41 CG47
Swanley BR8 ....147 FF97
Swanscombe DA10 ......130 FZ85
Teddington TW11 ....117 CG91
Twickenham TW1
off Bridge Rd 117 CH86
Upminster RM14 ....72 FP63
Uxbridge UB10 ....58 BN64
Walton-on-Thames KT12 .135 BV101
Watford WD17 ....23 BQ37
West Wickham BR4 ......143 EB104
Westerham (Bigg.H.) TN16 .178 EK118
Woking GU21 ....167 AZ116
Grove Av, N3 ....44 DA52
N10 ....45 DJ54
W7 ....79 CE72
Epsom KT17 ....156 CS113
Pinner HA5 ....60 BY56
Sutton SM1 ....158 DA107
Twickenham TW1 ....117 CF88
Grove Bk, Wat. WD19 ....40 BX46
Grovebarns, Stai. TW18 .....114 BG93
Grovebury Cl, Erith DA8 ....107 FD79
Grovebury Gdns, St.Alb.
(Park St) AL2 ....8 CC27
Grovebury Rd, SE2 ....106 EV75
Grove Cl, N14 off Avenue Rd .45 DH45
SE23 ....123 DX88
Bromley BR2 ....144 EG103
Epsom KT19 ....156 CP110
Feltham TW13 ....116 BY91
Gerrards Cross (Chal.St.P.)
SL9 off Grove La 36 AW53
Kingston upon Thames
KT1 ....138 CM98
Slough SL1 off Alpha St S .92 AU76
Uxbridge UB10 ....59 BN64
Windsor (Old Wind.) SL4 ..112 AV87
Grove Cotts, SW3 ....100 DE79
Grove Ct, SE3 ....104 EG81
Barnet EN5 off High St 27 CZ41
East Molesey KT8
off Walton Rd 137 CD99
Waltham Abbey EN9
off Highbridge St 15 EB33
Grove Cres, E18 ....48 EF54
NW9 ....62 CQ56
Feltham TW13 ....116 BY91
Kingston upon Thames
KT1 ....138 CL97
Rickmansworth (Crox.Grn)
WD3 ....22 BN42
Walton-on-Thames KT12 .135 BV101
Grove Cres Rd, E15 ....85 ED65
Grovedale Cl, Wal.Cr.
(Chsht) EN7 ....14 DT30
Grovedale Rd, N19 ....65 DK61
Grove End, E18
off Grove Hill 48 EF54
NW5 off Chetwynd Rd 65 DH63
Gerrards Cross (Chal.St.P.)
SL9 ....36 AW53
Grove End Gdns, NW8
off Grove End Rd 82 DD68
Grove End La, Esher KT10 ..137 CD102
Grove End Rd, NW8 ....82 DD69
Grove Fm Ct, Mitch. CR4
off Brookfields Av 140 DF98
Grove Fm Pk, Nthwd. HA6 ...39 BR50
Grove Fm Retail Pk, Rom.
(Chad.Hth) RM6 ....70 EW59
Grove Footpath, Surb. KT5 ..138 CL98
Grove Gdns, NW4 ....63 CU56
NW8 ....194 C3
Dagenham RM10 ....71 FC62
Enfield EN3 ....31 DX39
Teddington TW11 ....117 CG91
Grove Grn Rd, E11 ....67 EC62
Grove Hall Ct, NW8
off Hall Rd 82 DC69
Grove Hall Rd, Bushey WD23 .24 BY42
Grove Heath, Wok. (Ripley)
GU23 ....168 BJ124
Grove Heath Ct, Wok. (Ripley)
GU23 ....168 BJ124
Grove Heath N, Wok. (Ripley)
GU23 ....168 BH122
Grove Heath Rd, Wok. (Ripley)
GU23 ....168 BJ123
Groveherst Rd, Dart. DA1 ...108 FM83
Grove Hill, E18 ....48 EF54
Gerrards Cross (Chal.St.P.)
SL9 ....36 AW52
Harrow HA1 ....61 CE59
Grove Hill Rd, SE5 ....102 DS83
Harrow HA1 ....61 CE59
Grovehill Rd, Red. RH1 ....184 DE134
Grove Ho Rd, N8 ....65 DL56
Groveland Av, SW16 ....121 DM94
Groveland Ct, EC4 ....197 J9
Groveland Rd, Beck. BR3 ...143 DZ97
Grovelands, St.Alb.
(Park St) AL2 ....8 CB27
West Molesey KT8 ......136 CA98
Grovelands Cl, SE5 ....102 DS82
Harrow HA2 ....60 CB62
Grovelands Ct, N14 ....45 DK45
Grovelands Rd, N13 ....45 DM49
N15 ....66 DU58
Orpington BR5 ....126 EU94
Purley CR8 ....159 DL112
Grovelands Way, Grays
RM17 ....110 FZ78
Groveland Way, N.Mal. KT3 .138 CQ99
Grove La, SE5 ....102 DR81
Chesham HP5 ....4 AV27
Chigwell IG7 ....49 ET48
Coulsdon CR5 ....158 DG113
Epping CM16 off High St ..18 EU30
Gerrards Cross (Chal.St.P.)
SL9 ....36 AW53
Kingston upon Thames
KT1 ....138 CL98
Uxbridge UB8 ....76 BM70
Grove La Ter, SE5
off Grove La 102 DS83
Groveley Rd, Sun. TW16 ....115 BT92
Grove Mkt Pl, SE9 ....125 EM86
Grove Ms, W6 ....99 CW76
W11 off Portobello Rd 81 CZ72
Grove Mill La, Wat. WD17 ....23 BP37
Grove Mill Pl, Cars. SM5 ....140 DG104
GROVE PARK, SE12 ....124 EG89
GROVE PARK, W4 ....98 CP80
⇌ Grove Park 124 EG90
Grove Pk, E11 ....68 EH58
NW9 ....62 CQ56
SE5 ....102 DS82
Grove Pk Av, E4 ....47 EB52
Grove Pk Br, W4 ....98 CQ80
Grove Pk Gdns, W4 ....98 CP79
Grove Pk Ms, W4 ....98 CQ80
Grove Pk Rd, N15 ....66 DS56
SE9 ....124 EJ90
W4 ....98 CP80
Rainham RM13 ....89 FG67
Grove Pk Ter, W4 ....98 CP79
Grove Pas, E2 ....84 DV68
Teddington TW11 ....117 CG92
Grove Path, Wal.Cr. (Chsht)
EN7 ....14 DU31
Grove Pl, NW3
off Christchurch Hill 64 DD62
SW12 ....121 DH86
W3 ....80 CQ74
W5 off The Grove 79 CK74
Banstead SM7 ....158 DF112
Barking IG11
off Clockhouse Av 87 EQ67
Watford WD25 ....24 CB39
Weybridge KT13 ....153 BQ106
Grove Rd, E3 ....85 DX67
E4 ....47 EB49
E11 ....68 EF59
E17 ....67 EB58
E18 ....48 EF54
N11 ....45 DH50
N12 ....44 DD50
N15 ....66 DS57
NW2 ....81 CW65
SW13 ....99 CT82
SW19 ....120 DC94
W3 ....80 CQ74
W5 ....79 CK73
Amersham HP6 ....20 AT37
Ashtead KT21 ....172 CM118
Barnet EN4 ....28 DE41
Belvedere DA17 ....106 EZ79
Bexleyheath DA7 ....107 FC84
Borehamwood WD6 ....26 CN39
Brentford TW8 ....97 CJ78
Chertsey KT16 ....133 BF100
East Molesey KT8 ....137 CD98
Edgware HA8 ....42 CN51
Epsom KT17 ....156 CS113
Gravesend (Nthflt) DA11 ..130 GB85
Grays RM17 ....110 GC79
Hounslow TW3 ....96 CB84
Isleworth TW7 ....97 CE81
Mitcham CR4 ....141 DH96
Northwood HA6 ....39 BR50
Oxted RH8
off Southlands La 187 EC134
Pinner HA5 ....60 BZ57
Richmond TW10 ....118 CM86
Rickmansworth (Mill End)
WD3 ....38 BG47
Romford RM6 ....70 EV59
Sevenoaks TN14 ....191 FJ121
Sevenoaks (Seal) TN15 ...191 FN122
Shepperton TW17 ....135 BQ100
Surbiton KT6 ....137 CK99
Sutton SM1 ....158 DB107
Thornton Heath CR7 .....141 DN98
Twickenham TW2 ....117 CD90
Uxbridge UB8 ....76 BK66
Westerham (Tats.) TN16 ..178 EJ120
Woking GU21 ....167 AZ116
Grove Rd W, Enf. EN3 ......30 DW37
Grover Rd, Wat. WD19 ....40 BX45
Grove Shaw, Tad. (Kgswd)
KT20 ....173 CY124
Groveside Cl, W3 ....80 CN72
Carshalton SM5 ....140 DE103
Groveside Rd, E4 ....48 EE47
Grovestile Waye, Felt. TW14 .115 BR87
Grove St, N18 ....46 DT51
SE8 ....203 M8
Grove Ter, NW5 ....65 DH62
Teddington TW11 ....117 CG91
Grove Ter Ms, NW5
off Grove Ter 65 DH62
Grove Vale, SE22 ....102 DS84
Chislehurst BR7 ....125 EN93
Grove Vil, E14 ....85 EB73
Groveway, SW9 ....101 DM81
Dagenham RM8 ....70 EX63
Grove Way, Esher KT10 ....136 CC101
Rickmansworth (Chorl.)
WD3 ....21 BB42
Uxbridge UB8 ....76 BK66
Wembley HA9 ....62 CP64
Grovewood, Rich. TW9
off Sandycombe Rd 98 CN81
Grovewood Cl, Rick.
(Chorl.) WD3 ....21 BB43
Grove Wd Hill, Couls. CR5 ..159 DK114
Grovewood Pl, Wdf.Grn. IG8 .49 EM51
Grubb St, Oxt. RH8 ....188 EJ128
Grummant Rd, SE15 ....102 DT81
Grundy St, E14 ....85 EB72
Gruneisen Rd, N3 ....44 DB52
Guardian Av, Grays (N.Stfd)
RM16 ....109 FX75
Guardian Cl, Horn. RM11 ....71 FH60
Guards Av, Cat. CR3 ....176 DQ122
Guardsman Cl, Brwd. CM14 ..54 FX50
★ Guards Mus, SW1 ....199 L5
Gubbins La, Rom. RM3 .....52 FM52
Gubyon Av, SE24 ....121 DP85
Guerin Sq, E3 ....85 DZ69
Guernsey Cl, Houns. TW5 ....96 CA81
Guernsey Fm Dr, Wok. GU21 .166 AX115
Guernsey Gro, SE24 ....122 DQ87
Guernsey Ho, N1
off Clifton Rd 84 DQ65
Enfield EN3
off Eastfield Rd 31 DX38
Guernsey Rd, E11 ....67 ED60
Guibal Rd, SE12 ....124 EH87
Guildersfield Rd, SW16 .....121 DL94
Guildford Av, Felt. TW13 ....115 BT89
Guildford Gdns, Rom. RM3 ..52 FL51
Guildford Gro, SE10 ....103 EB81
Guildford La, Wok. GU22 ...166 AX120
Guildford Rd, E6 ....86 EL72
E17 ....47 EC53
SW8 ....101 DL81
Chertsey KT16 ....133 BE102
Croydon CR0 ....142 DR100
Ilford IG3 ....69 ES61
Leatherhead (Fetch.) KT22 ..171 CG122
Romford RM3 ....52 FL51
Woking GU22 ....166 AY119
Woking (Mayford) GU22 ..166 AX122
Guildford St, Cher. KT16 ....134 BG101
Staines TW18 ....114 BG93
Guildford Way, Wall. SM6 ...159 DL106
★ Guildhall, The, EC2 .....197 K8
★ Guildhall Art Gall,
Guildhall Lib, EC2 ......197 J8
Guildhall Bldgs, EC2 ......197 K8
Guildhall Yd, EC2 ....197 J8
Guildhouse St, SW1 ....199 K8
Guildown Av, N12 ....44 DB49
Guild Rd, SE7 ....104 EK78
Erith DA8 ....107 FF80
Guildsway, E17 ....47 DZ53
Guileshill La, Wok. (Ock.)
GU23 ....168 BL123
Guilford Av, Surb. KT5 .....138 CM99
Guilford Pl, WC1 ....196 B5
Guilford St, WC1 ....196 A5
Guilford Vil, Surb. KT5
off Alpha Rd 138 CM100
Guilsborough Cl, NW10 .....80 CS66
Guinevere Gdns, Wal.Cr. EN8 .15 DY31
Guinness Cl, E9 ....85 DY66
Hayes UB3 ....95 BR76
Guinness Ct, E1
off Mansell St 84 DT72
Woking GU21
off Iveagh Rd 166 AT118
Guinness Sq, SE1 ....201 M8
Guinness Trust Bldgs, SE1
off Snowsfields 102 DS75
SE11 ....200 G10
SW3 ....198 D9
SW9 ....101 DP84
W6 off Fulham Palace Rd ..99 CW78
Guinness Trust Est, N16
off Holmleigh Rd 66 DS60
Guion Rd, SW6 ....99 CZ82
Gulland Cl, Bushey WD23 ....24 CC43
Gulland Wk, N1
off Nightingale Rd 84 DQ65
Gull Cl, Wall. SM6 ....159 DL108
Gullet Wd Rd, Wat. WD25 ....23 BU35
Gulliver Cl, Nthlt. UB5 ......78 BZ67
Gulliver Rd, Sid. DA15 .....125 ES89
Gulliver St, SE16 ....203 M6
Gull Wk, Horn. RM12
off Heron Flight Av 89 FH66
Gulston Wk, SW3 ....198 E9
Gumleigh Rd, W5 ....97 CJ77
Gumley Gdns, Islw. TW7 .....97 CG83
Gumley Rd, Grays RM20 ....109 FX79
Gumping Rd, Orp. BR5 .....145 EQ103
Gundulph Rd, Brom. BR2 ...144 EJ97
Gunfleet Cl, Grav. DA12 ....131 GL87
Gun Hill, Til. (W.Til.) RM18 ..111 GK79
Gunmakers La, E3 ....85 DY67
Gunnell Cl, SE26 ....122 DU92
Croydon CR0 ....142 DU100
Gunner Dr, Enf. EN3 ....31 EA37
Gunner La, SE18 ....105 EN78
GUNNERSBURY, W4 ....98 CP77
⇌ Gunnersbury 98 CP78
⊖ Gunnersbury 98 CP78
Gunnersbury Av, W3 ....98 CN76
W4 ....98 CN76
W5 ....80 CM74
Gunnersbury Cl, W4
off Grange Rd 98 CP78
Gunnersbury Ct, W3
off Bollo La 98 CP75
Gunnersbury Cres, W3 ......98 CN75
Gunnersbury Dr, W5 ....98 CM75
Gunnersbury Gdns, W3 ......98 CN75
Gunnersbury La, W3 ....98 CN76
Gunnersbury Ms, W4
off Chiswick High Rd 98 CP78
★ Gunnersbury Park, W3 ...98 CM77
Gunnersbury Pk, W3 ....98 CM77
W5 ....98 CM77
★ Gunnersbury Park Mus &
Art Cen, W3 ....98 CN76
Gunners Gro, E4 ....47 EC48
Gunners Rd, SW18 ....120 DD89
Gunnery Ter, SE18 ....105 EQ77
Gunning Rd, Grays RM17 ...110 GD78
Gunning St, SE18 ....105 ES77
Gunn Rd, Swans. DA10 .....130 FY86
Gunpowder Sq, EC4 ....196 E8
Gunstor Rd, N16 ....66 DS63
Gun St, E1 ....197 P7
Gunter Gro, SW10 ....100 DC79
Edgware HA8 ....42 CR53
Gunters Mead, Esher KT10 ..154 CC110
Gunterstone Rd, W14 ....99 CY77
Gunthorpe St, E1 ....84 DT71
Gunton Rd, E5 ....66 DV62
SW17 ....120 DG93
Gunwhale Cl, SE16 ....203 J3
Gurdon Rd, SE7 ....104 EG78
Gurnard Cl, West Dr. UB7
off Trout Rd 76 BK73
Gurnell Gro, W13 ....79 CF70
Gurney Cl, E15
off Gurney Rd 68 EE64
E17 ....47 DX53
Barking IG11 ....87 EP65
Gurney Cres, Croy. CR0 ....141 DM102
Gurney Dr, N2 ....64 DC57
Gurney Rd, E15 ....68 EE64
SW6 ....100 DC83
Carshalton SM5 ....158 DG105
Northolt UB5 ....77 BV69
Guthrie St, SW3 ....198 B10
Gutteridge La, Rom.
(Stap.Abb.) RM4 ....35 FC44
Gutter La, EC2 ....197 J8
Guyatt Gdns, Mitch. CR4
off Ormerod Gdns 140 DG96
Guy Barnett Gro, SE3
off Casterbridge Rd 104 EG83
Guy Rd, Wall. SM6 ....141 DK104
Guyscliff Rd, SE13 ....123 EC85
Guysfield Cl, Rain. RM13 ....89 FG67
Guysfield Dr, Rain. RM13 ....89 FG67
H Guy's Hosp, SE1 ....201 L4
Guy St, SE1 ....201 L4
Gwalior Rd, SW15
off Felsham Rd 99 CX83
Gwendolen Av, SW15 ......119 CX85
Gwendolen Cl, SW15 ......119 CX85
Gwendolen Ho, Stai. TW19
off Yeoman Dr 114 BL88
Gwendoline Av, E13 ....86 EH67
Gwendwr Rd, W14 ....99 CY78
Gwent Cl, Wat. WD25 ....8 BX34
Gwillim Cl, Sid. DA15 ......126 EU85
Gwydor Rd, Beck. BR3 .....143 DX98
Gwydyr Rd, Brom. BR2 .....144 EF97
Gwyn Cl, SW6 ....100 DC80
Gwynne Av, Croy. CR0 .....143 DX101
Gwynne Cl, W4
off Pumping Sta Rd 99 CT79
Gwynne Pk Av, Wdf.Grn. IG8 .49 EM51
Gwynne Pl, WC1 ....196 C3
Gwynne Rd, SW11 ....100 DD82
Caterham CR3 ....176 DR123
Gwynn Rd, Grav. (Nthflt)
DA11 ....130 GC89
Gyfford Wk, Wal.Cr. EN7 .....14 DV31
Gylcote Cl, SE5 ....102 DR84
Gyles Pk, Stan. HA7 ....41 CJ53
Gyllyngdune Gdns, Ilf. IG3 ...69 ET61
Gypsy Cor, W3 ....80 CR71
Gypsy La, Kings L. WD4 .....23 BR35
Slough (Stoke P.) SL2 .....56 AS63

H

Haarlem Rd, W14 ....99 CX76
Haberdasher Est, N1
off Haberdasher St 84 DR69
Haberdasher Pl, N1 ....197 L2
Haberdasher St, N1 ....197 L2
Habgood Rd, Loug. IG10 .....32 EL41
Habitat Cl, SE15
off Gordon Rd 102 DV82
Haccombe Rd, SW19
off Haydons Rd 120 DC93
HACKBRIDGE, Wall. SM6 ...141 DH103
⇌ Hackbridge 141 DH103
Hackbridge Grn, Wall. SM6 ..140 DG103
Hackbridge Pk Gdns,
Cars. SM5 ....140 DG103
Hackbridge Rd, Wall. SM6 ..140 DG103
Hacketts La, Wok. GU22 ....151 BF114
Hackford Rd, SW9 ....101 DM81
Hackford Wk, SW9 ....101 DM81
Hackforth Cl, Barn. EN5 .....27 CV43
Hackington Cres, Beck. BR3 .123 EA93
HACKNEY, E8 ....84 DV65
⇌ Hackney Central 84 DV65
★ Hackney City Fm, E2 .....84 DU68
Hackney Cl, Borwd. WD6 ....26 CR43
⇌ Hackney Downs 66 DV64
Hackney Gro, E8
off Reading La 84 DV65
★ Hackney Marsh, E9 ....67 DY62
★ Hackney Mus, E8 ....84 DV65
Hackney Rd, E2 ....197 P3
HACKNEY WICK, E9 ....67 EA64
⇌ Hackney Wick 85 EA65
Hackworth Pt, E3
off Rainhill Way 85 EB69
Hacon Sq, E8
off Richmond Rd 84 DV66
HACTON, Rain. RM13 ....72 FM64
Hacton Dr, Horn. RM12 ......72 FK63
Hacton La, Horn. RM12 ......72 FM62
Upminster RM14 ....72 FM64
Hadar Cl, N20 ....44 DA46
Hadden Rd, SE28 ....105 ES76
Hadden Way, Grnf. UB6 .....79 CD65
Haddestoke Gate, Wal.Cr.
(Chsht) EN8 ....15 DZ26
Haddington Rd, Brom. BR1 .123 ED90
Haddon Cl, Borwd. WD6 .....26 CN41
Enfield EN1 ....30 DU44
New Malden KT3 ....139 CT99
Weybridge KT13 ....135 BR104
Haddonfield, SE8 ....203 J9
Haddon Gro, Sid. DA15 .....126 EU87
Haddon Rd, Orp. BR5 ......146 EW99
Rickmansworth (Chorl.)
WD3 ....21 BC43
Sutton SM1 ....158 DB105
Haddo St, SE10 ....103 EB79
Hadfield Cl, Sthl. UB1
off Adrienne Av 78 BZ69
Hadfield Rd, Stai. (Stanw.)
TW19 ....114 BK86
Hadlands Cl, Hem.H.
(Bov.) HP3 ....5 AZ26
Hadleigh Cl, E1
off Mantus Rd 84 DW70
SW20 ....139 CZ96
Hadleigh Dr, Sutt. SM2 ....158 DA109
Hadleigh Rd, N9 ....46 DV45
Hadleigh St, E2 ....84 DW70
Hadleigh Wk, E6 ....86 EL72
HADLEY, Barn. EN5 ....27 CZ40
Hadley Cl, N21 ....29 DN44
Borehamwood (Els.) WD6 ..26 CM44
Hadley Common, Barn. EN5 ..28 DA40
Hadley Gdns, W4 ....98 CR78
Southall UB2 ....96 BZ78
Hadley Grn, Barn. EN5 ......27 CZ40
Hadley Grn Rd, Barn. EN5 ...27 CZ40
Hadley Grn W, Barn. EN5 ....27 CZ40
Hadley Gro, Barn. EN5 ......27 CY40
Hadley Hts, Barn. EN5
off Hadley Rd 28 DB40
Hadley Highstone, Barn. EN5 .27 CZ39
Hadley Pl, Wey. KT13 .....152 BN108
Hadley Ridge, Barn. EN5 ....27 CZ41
Hadley Rd, Barn. (Had.Wd)
EN4 ....29 DH38
Hadley Rd, Barn. (New Barn.)
EN5 ....28 DB42
Belvedere DA17 ....106 EZ77
Enfield EN2 ....29 DL38
Mitcham CR4 ....141 DK98
Hadley St, NW1 ....83 DH65
Hadley Way, N21 ....29 DN44
HADLEY WOOD, Barn. EN4 ..28 DD38
⇌ Hadley Wood 28 DC38
Hadley Wd Ri, Ken. CR8 ....175 DP115
Hadlow Pl, SE19 ....122 DU94
Hadlow Rd, Sid. DA14 .....126 EU91
Welling DA16 ....106 EW80
Hadlow Way, Grav. (Istead Rise)
DA13 ....130 GE94
Hadrian Cl, E3
off Old Ford Rd 85 EA67
Staines TW19 ....114 BL87
Hadrian Ct, Sutt. SM2
off Stanley Rd 158 DB108
Hadrian Est, E2 ....84 DU68
Hadrian Ms, N7
off Roman Way 83 DM66
Hadrians Ride, Enf. EN1 .....30 DT43
Hadrian St, SE10 ....104 EE78
Hadrian Way, Stai. (Stanw.)
TW19 ....114 BL87
Hadyn Pk Rd, W12 ....99 CU75
Hafer Rd, SW11 ....100 DF84
Hafton Rd, SE6 ....124 EE88
Hagden La, Wat. WD18 ......23 BT43
Haggard Rd, Twick. TW1 ....117 CH87
HAGGERSTON, E2 ....84 DT68
Haggerston Rd, E8 ....84 DT66
Borehamwood WD6 ....26 CL38
Haggerston Studios, E8
off Kingsland Rd 84 DS67
Hague St, E2
off Derbyshire St 84 DU69
Ha-Ha Rd, SE18 ....105 EM79
Haig Gdns, Grav. DA12 .....131 GJ87
Haig Pl, Mord. SM4
off Green La 140 DA100
Haig Rd, Grays RM16 ......111 GG76
Stanmore HA7 ....41 CJ50
Uxbridge UB8 ....77 BP71
Westerham (Bigg.H.) TN16 ..178 EL117
Haig Rd E, E13 ....86 EJ69
Haig Rd W, E13 ....86 EJ69
Haigville Gdns, Ilf. IG6 ......69 EP56
Hailes Cl, SW19 ....120 DC93
Haileybury Av, Enf. EN1 .....30 DT44
Haileybury Rd, Orp. BR6 ....164 EU105
Hailey Rd, Erith DA18 ......106 FA75
Hailsham Av, SW2 ....121 DM89
Hailsham Cl, Rom. RM3 .....52 FJ50
Surbiton KT6 ....137 CK101
Hailsham Dr, Har. HA1 ......61 CD55
Hailsham Gdns, Rom. RM3 ..52 FJ50
Hailsham Rd, SW17 ....120 DG93
Romford RM3 ....52 FJ50
Hailsham Ter, N18 ....46 DQ50
Haimo Rd, SE9 ....124 EK85
HAINAULT, Ilf. IG6 ....49 ES52
⊖ Hainault 49 ES52
Hainault Business Pk, Ilf. IG6 .50 EW50
Hainault Ct, E17 ....67 ED56
★ Hainault Forest Country Pk,
Chig. IG7 ....50 EW47
Hainault Gore, Rom. RM6 ...70 EY57
Hainault Gro, Chig. IG7 .....49 EQ49
Hainault Rd, E11 ....67 EC60
Chigwell IG7 ....49 EP48
Romford RM5 ....51 FC54
Romford (Chad.Hth) RM6 ...70 EZ58
Romford (Lt.Hth) RM6 .....70 EV55
Hainault St, SE9 ....125 EP88
Ilford IG1 ....69 EP61
Haines Ct, Wey. KT13 ......153 BR106
Haines Wk, Mord. SM4
off Dorchester Rd 140 DB101
Haines Way, Wat. WD25 .....7 BU34
Hainford Cl, SE4 ....103 DX84
Haining Cl, W4
off Wellesley Rd 98 CN78
Hainthorpe Rd, SE27 ......121 DP90
Hainton Cl, E1 ....84 DV72
Halberd Ms, E5
off Knightland Rd 66 DV61
Halbutt Gdns, Dag. RM9 .....70 EZ62
Halbutt St, Dag. RM9 ....70 EZ63
Halcomb St, N1 ....84 DS67
Halcot Av, Bexh. DA6 ......127 FB85
Halcrow St, E1 off Newark St .84 DV71
Halcyon Way, Horn. RM11 ...72 FM60
Haldane Cl, N10 ....45 DH52
Enfield EN3 ....31 EB38
Haldane Gdns, Grav. DA11 ..130 GC88
Haldane Pl, SW18 ....120 DB88
Haldane Rd, E6 ....86 EK69
SE28 ....88 EX73
SW6 ....99 CZ80
Southall UB1 ....78 CC72
Haldan Rd, E4 ....47 EC51
Haldon Cl, Chig. IG7
off Arrowsmith Rd 49 ES50
Haldon Rd, SW18 ....119 CZ85
Hale, The, E4 ....47 ED52
N17 ....66 DU55
Hale Cl, E4 ....47 EC48
Edgware HA8 ....42 CQ50
Orpington BR6 ....163 EQ105
Hale Dr, NW7 ....42 CQ51
HALE END, E4 ....47 ED51
Hale End, Rom. RM3 ....51 FH51
Woking GU22 ....166 AV121
Hale End Cl, Ruis. HA4 ......59 BU58
Hale End Rd, E4 ....47 ED51
E17 ....47 ED53
Woodford Green IG8 ......47 ED52
Halefield Rd, N17 ....46 DU53
Hale Gdns, N17 ....66 DU55
W3 ....80 CN74
Hale Gro Gdns, NW7 ....42 CR50
Hale La, NW7 ....42 CR50
Edgware HA8 ....42 CP50
Sevenoaks (Otford) TN14 ..181 FE117

★ Place of interest ⇌ Railway station ⊖ London Underground station DLR Docklands Light Railway station Tra Tramlink station H Hospital Riv Pedestrian ferry landing stage

Hal - Han

Hale Path, SE27 121 DP91
Hale Rd, E6 86 EL70
N17 60 DU55
Halesowen Rd, Mord. SM4 140 DB101
Hales Prior, N1
off Calshot St 83 DM68
Hales St, SE8
off Deptford High St 103 EA80
Hale St, E14 85 EB73
Staines TW18 113 BE91
Haleswood, Cob. KT11 153 BV114
Halesworth Cl, E5
off Theydon Rd 66 DW61
Romford RM3 52 FL52
Halesworth Rd, SE13 103 EB83
Romford RM3 52 FL51
Hale Wk, W7 79 CE71
Haley Rd, NW4 63 CW58
Half Acre, Brent. TW8 97 CK79
Halfacre Hill, Ger.Cr. (Chal.St.P.) SL9 36 AY53
Half Acre Rd, W7 79 CE74
Halfhide La, Brox. (Turnf.) EN10 15 DY26
Waltham Cross (Chsht) EN8 15 DX27
Halfhides, Wal.Abb. EN9 15 ED33
Half Moon Ct, EC1 197 H7
Half Moon Cres, N1 83 DM68
Half Moon La, SE24 122 DQ86
Epping CM16 17 ET31
Half Moon Pas, E1
off Braham St 84 DT72
Half Moon St, W1 199 J2
Halford Cl, Edg. HA8 42 CP54
Halford Rd, E10 67 ED57
SW6 100 DA79
Richmond TW10 118 CL85
Uxbridge UB10 58 BN64
Halfway Ct, Purf. RM19 108 FN77
Halfway Grn, Walt. KT12 135 BV104
Halfway St, Sid. DA15 125 ER87
Haliburton Rd, Twick. TW1 117 CG85
Haliday Wk, N1
off Balls Pond Rd 84 DR65
Halidon Cl, E9 *off Urswick Rd* 66 DW64
Halidon Ri, Rom. RM3 52 FP51
Halifax Cl, St.Alb. AL2 8 BZ30
Teddington TW11 117 CD93
Watford (Lvsdn) WD25 7 BT34
Halifax Rd, Enf. EN2 30 DQ40
Greenford UB6 78 CB67
Rickmansworth (Herons.) WD3 37 BC45
Halifax St, SE26 122 DV91
Halifield Dr, Belv. DA17 106 EY76
Haling Down Pas, S.Croy. CR2 160 DQ109
Haling Gro, S.Croy. CR2 160 DQ108
Haling Pk, S.Croy. CR2 160 DQ107
Haling Pk Gdns, S.Croy. CR2 159 DP107
Haling Pk Rd, S.Croy. CR2 159 DP106
Haling Rd, S.Croy. CR2 160 DR107
Halings La, Uxb. (Denh.) UB9 57 BE56
Halkin Arc, SW1 198 F6
Halkingcroft, Slou. SL3 92 AW75
Halkin Ms, SW1 198 F6
Halkin Pl, SW1 198 F6
Halkin St, SW1 198 G5
Hall, The, SE3 104 EG83
Hallam Cl, Chis. BR7 125 EM92
Watford WD24 24 BW40
Hallam Gdns, Pnr. HA5 40 BY52
Hallam Ms, W1 195 J6
Hallam Rd, N15 65 DP56
SW13 99 CV83
Hallam St, W1 195 J5
Halland Way, Nthwd. HA6 39 BR51
Hall Av, N18
off Weir Hall Av 46 DR51
South Ockendon (Aveley) RM15 90 FQ74
Hall Cl, W5 80 CL71
Rickmansworth (Mill End) WD3 38 BG46
Hall Ct, Slou. (Datchet) SL3 92 AV80
Teddington TW11 117 CF92
Hall Cres, S.Ock. (Aveley) RM15 108 FQ75
Hall Dr, SE26 122 DW92
W7 79 CE72
Uxbridge (Hare.) UB9 38 BJ53
Halley Gdns, SE13 103 ED84
Halley Rd, E7 86 EJ65
E12 86 EK65
Waltham Abbey EN9 31 EB36
Halleys App, Wok. GU21 166 AU118
Halleys Ct, Wok. GU21
off Halleys App 166 AU118
Halley St, E14 85 DY71
Halleys Wk, Add. KT15 152 BJ108
Hall Fm Cl, Stan. HA7 41 CH49
Hall Fm Dr, Twick. TW2 117 CD87
Hallfield Est, W2 82 DC72
Hallford Way, Dart. DA1 128 FJ85
Hall Gdns, E4 47 DZ49
Hall Gate, NW8 *off Hall Rd* 82 DC69
Hall Grn La, Brwd. (Hutt.) CM13 55 GC45
Hall Hill, Oxt. RH8 187 ED131
Sevenoaks (Seal) TN15 191 FP123
Halliards, The, Walt. KT12
off Felix Rd 135 BU100
Halliday Cl, Rad. (Shenley) WD7 10 CL32
Halliday Ho, E1
off Christian St 84 DU72
Halliday Sq, Sthl. UB2 79 CD74
Halliford Cl, Shep. TW17 135 BR98
Halliford Rd, Shep. TW17 135 BS99
Sunbury-on-Thames TW16 135 BS99
Halliford St, N1 84 DQ66
Halliloo Valley Rd, Cat. (Wold.) CR3 177 DZ119
Hallingbury Ct, E17 67 EB55
Hallings Wf Studios, E15
off Channelsea Rd 85 ED67
Hallington Cl, Wok. GU21 166 AV117
Halliwell Rd, SW2 121 DM86
Halliwick Rd, N10 44 DG53
Hall La, E4 47 DY50
Hall La, NW4 43 CU53
Brentwood (Shenf.) CM15 55 FZ44
Hayes UB3 95 BR80
South Ockendon RM15 91 FX68
Upminster RM14 72 FQ60
Hallmark Trd Est, NW10
off Great Cen Way 62 CQ63
Hallmead Rd, Sutt. SM1 140 DB104
Hall Oak Wk, NW6
off Barlow Rd 81 CZ65
Hallowell Av, Croy. CR0 159 DL105
Hallowell Cl, Mitch. CR4 140 DG97
Hallowell Rd, Nthwd. HA6 39 BS52
Hallowes Cres, Wat. WD19
off Hayling Rd 39 BU48
Hallowfield Way, Mitch. CR4 140 DD98
Hallows Gro, Sun. TW16 115 BT92
Hall Pk Rd, Upmin. RM14 72 FQ64
★ Hall Pl, Bex. DA5 127 FC86
Hall Pl, W2 82 DD70
Woking GU21 167 BA116
Hall Pl Cres, Bex. DA5 127 FC85
Hall Pl Dr, Wey. KT13 153 BS106
Hall Rd, E6 87 EM67
E15 67 ED63
NW8 82 DC69
Dartford DA1 108 FM84
Gravesend (Nthflt) DA11 130 GC90
Isleworth TW7 117 CD85
Romford (Chad.Hth) RM6 70 EW58
Romford (Gidea Pk) RM2 71 FH55
South Ockendon (Aveley) RM15 108 FQ75
Wallington SM6 159 DH109
Hallside Rd, Enf. EN1 30 DT38
Hallsland Way, Oxt. RH8 188 EF133
Hall St, EC1 196 G2
N12 44 DC50
Hallsville Rd, E16 86 EF72
Hallswelle Rd, NW11 63 CZ57
Hall Ter, Rom. RM3 52 FN52
South Ockendon (Aveley) RM15 109 FR75
Hall Twr, W2 194 A6
Hall Vw, SE9 124 EK89
Hall Way, Pur. CR8 159 DP113
Hallwood Cres, Brwd. (Shenf.) CM15 54 FY45
Hallywell Cres, E6 87 EM71
Halons Rd, SE9 125 EN87
Halpin Pl, SE17 201 L9
Halsbrook Rd, SE3 104 EK83
Halsbury Cl, Stan. HA7 41 CH49
Halsbury Rd, W12 81 CV74
Halsbury Rd E, Nthlt. UB5 60 CC63
Halsbury Rd W, Nthlt. UB5 60 CB64
Halsend, Hayes UB3 77 BV74
Halsey Ms, SW3 198 D8
Halsey Pk, St.Alb. (Lon.Col.) AL2 10 CM27
Halsey Pl, Wat. WD24 23 BV38
Halsey Rd, Wat. WD18 23 BV41
Halsey St, SW3 198 D8
Halsham Cres, Bark. IG11 87 ET65
Halsmere Rd, SE5 101 DP81
HALSTEAD, Sev. TN14 164 EZ113
Halstead Cl, Croy. CR0
off Charles St 142 DQ104
Halstead Ct, N1 197 L1
Halstead Gdns, N21 46 DR46
Halstead Hill, Wal.Cr. (Chsht) EN7 14 DS29
Halstead La, Sev. (Knock.) TN14 164 EZ114
Halstead Rd, E11 68 EG57
N21 46 DQ46
Enfield EN1 30 DS42
Erith DA8 107 FE81
Halstead Way, Brwd. (Hutt.) CM13 55 GC44
Halston Cl, SW11 120 DF86
Halstow Rd, NW10 81 CX69
SE10 205 M10
Halsway, Hayes UB3 77 BU74
Halter Cl, Borwd. WD6 26 CR43
Halton Cl, N11 44 DF51
Halton Cross St, N1 83 DP67
Halton Pl, N1 *off Dibden St* 84 DQ67
Halton Rd, N1 83 DP66
Grays RM16 111 GJ76
Halt Robin La, Belv. DA17
off Halt Robin Rd 107 FB77
Halt Robin Rd, Belv. DA17 106 FA77
HAM, Rich. TW10 117 CK90
Ham, The, Brent. TW8 97 CJ80
Hambalt Rd, SW4 121 DJ85
Hamble Cl, Ruis. HA4
off Chichester Av 59 BS61
Woking GU21 166 AU117
Hamble Ct, Tedd. TW11 117 CK94
Hambledon Cl, Uxb. UB8
off Aldenham Dr 77 BP70
Hambledon Gdns, SE25 142 DT97
Hambledon Hill, Epsom KT18 172 CQ116
Hambledon Pl, SE21 122 DS88
Hambledon Rd, SW18 119 CZ87
Caterham CR3 176 DR123
Hambledon Vale, Epsom KT18 172 CQ116
Hambledown Rd, Sid. DA15 125 ER87
Hamble La, S.Ock. RM15 91 FT71
Hamble St, SW6 100 DB83
Hambleton Cl, Wor.Pk. KT4 139 CW103
Hamble Wk, Nthlt. UB5
off Brabazon Rd 78 CA68
Woking GU21 166 AU118
Hambley Ho, SE16
off Manor Est 102 DV77
Hamblings Cl, Rad. (Shenley) WD7 9 CK33
Hambridge Way, SW2 121 DN87
Hambro Av, Brom. BR2 144 EG102
Hambrook Rd, SE25 142 DV97
Hambro Rd, SW16 121 DK93
Brentwood CM14 54 FX47
Hambrough Rd, Sthl. UB1 78 BY74
Hamburgh Ct, Wal.Cr. EN8 15 DX28
Ham Cl, Rich. TW10 117 CJ90
Ham Common, Rich. TW10 118 CM91
Ham Cft Cl, Felt. TW13 115 BU90
Hamden Cres, Dag. RM10 71 FB62
Hamel Cl, Har. HA3 61 CK55
Hamelin St, E14
off St. Leonards Rd 85 EC72
Hamer Cl, Hem.H. (Bov.) HP3 5 BA28
Hamerton Rd, Grav. (Nthflt) DA11 130 GB85
Hameway, E6 87 EN70
Ham Fm Rd, Rich. TW10 117 CK91
Hamfield Cl, Oxt. RH8 187 EC127
Hamfrith Rd, E15 86 EF65
Ham Gate Av, Rich. TW10 117 CK90
Hamhaugh Island, Shep. TW17 134 BN103
★ Ham Ho, Rich. TW10 117 CJ88
Hamilton Av, N9 46 DU45
Cobham KT11 153 BU113
Ilford IG6 69 EP56
Romford RM1 51 FD54
Surbiton KT6 138 CP102
Sutton SM3 139 CY103
Woking GU22 167 BE115
Hamilton Cl, N17 66 DT55
NW8 82 DD69
SE16 203 L5
Barnet EN4 28 DE42
Chertsey KT16 133 BF102
Epsom KT19 156 CQ112
Feltham TW13 115 BT92
Potters Bar EN6 11 CU33
Purley CR8 159 DP112
St. Albans (Brick.Wd) AL2 8 CA30
Hamilton Ct, W5 80 CM73
W9 *off Maida Vale* 82 DC69
Hamilton Cres, N13 45 DN49
Brentwood CM14 54 FW49
Harrow HA2 60 BZ62
Hounslow TW3 116 CB85
Hamilton Dr, Rom. RM3 52 FL54
Hamilton Gdns, NW8 82 DC69
Hamilton Ho, SW8
off St. George Wf 101 DL79
Hamilton La, N5
off Hamilton Pk 65 DP63
Hamilton Mead, Hem.H. (Bov.) HP3 5 BA27
Hamilton Ms, SW18
off Merton Rd 120 DA88
W1 199 H4
Hamilton Pk, N5 65 DP63
Hamilton Pk W, N5 65 DP63
Hamilton Pl, N19
off Wedmore St 65 DK62
W1 198 G3
Sunbury-on-Thames TW16 115 BV94
Tadworth (Kgswd) KT20 173 CZ122
Hamilton Rd, E15 86 EE69
E17 47 DY54
N2 64 DC55
N9 46 DU45
NW10 63 CU64
NW11 63 CX59
SE27 122 DR91
SW19 120 DB94
W4 98 CS75
W5 80 CL73
Barnet EN4 28 DE42
Bexleyheath DA7 106 EY82
Brentford TW8 97 CK79
Feltham TW13 115 BT91
Harrow HA1 61 CE57
Hayes UB3 77 BV73
Ilford IG1 69 EP63
Kings Langley WD4 7 BQ33
Romford RM2 71 FH57
Sidcup DA15 126 EU91
Southall UB1 78 BZ74
Thornton Heath CR7 142 DR97
Twickenham TW2 117 CE88
Uxbridge UB8 76 BK71
Watford WD19 39 BV48
Hamilton Rd Ind Est, SE27 122 DR91
Hamilton Sq, N12
off Sandringham Gdns 44 DD51
SE1 201 L4
Hamilton St, SE8
off Deptford High St 103 EA79
Watford WD18 24 BW43
Hamilton Ter, NW8 82 DB68
Hamilton Wk, Erith DA8 107 FF80
Hamilton Way, N3 44 DA51
N13 45 DP49
Wallington SM6 159 DK109
Ham Island, Wind. (Old Wind.) SL4 92 AX84
Ham La, Egh. (Eng.Grn) TW20 112 AV91
Windsor (Old Wind.) SL4 92 AX84
Hamlea Cl, SE12 124 EF85
Hamlet, The, SE5 102 DR83
Hamlet Cl, SE13 104 EE84
Romford RM5 50 FA52
St. Albans AL2 8 BZ30
Hamlet Gdns, W6 99 CU77
Hamlet Ho, Erith DA8
off Waterhead Cl 107 FE80
Hamlet Ms, SE21
off Thurlow Pk Rd 122 DR88
Hamleton Ter, Dag. RM9
off Flamstead Rd 88 EW66
Hamlet Rd, SE19 122 DT94
Romford RM5 50 FA52
Hamlet Sq, NW2 63 CY62
Hamlets Way, E3 85 DZ70
Hamlet Way, SE1 201 L4
★ Hamleys, W1 195 K10
Hamlin Cres, Pnr. HA5 60 BW57
Hamlin Rd, Sev. TN13 190 FE121
Hamlyn Cl, Edg. HA8 42 CL48
Hamlyn Gdns, SE19 122 DS94
Hamm Ct, Wey. KT13 134 BL103
Hammelton Grn, SW9
off Cromwell Rd 101 DP81
Hammelton Rd, Brom. BR1 144 EF95
Hammer Par, Wat. WD25 7 BU33
Hammers Gate, St.Alb. AL2 8 CA25
Hammers La, NW7 43 CU50
HAMMERSMITH, W6 99 CW78
⊖ Hammersmith 99 CW77
Hammersmith Br, SW13 99 CV79
W6 99 CV79
Hammersmith Br Rd, W6 99 CW78
Hammersmith Bdy, W6 99 CW77
Hammersmith Flyover, W6 99 CW78
Hammersmith Gro, W6 99 CW76
[H] Hammersmith Hosp, W12 81 CT72
Hammersmith Rd, W6 99 CX77
W14 99 CX77
Hammersmith Ter, W6 99 CU78
Hammet Cl, Hayes UB4 78 BX71
Hammett St, EC3 197 P10
Hamm Moor La, Add. KT15 152 BL106
Hammond Av, Mitch. CR4 141 DH96
Hammond Cl, Barn. EN5 27 CY43
Greenford UB6
off Lilian Board Way 61 CD64
Hampton TW12 136 CA95
Waltham Cross (Chsht) EN7 14 DS26
Woking GU21 166 AW115
Hammond Rd, Enf. EN1 30 DV40
Southall UB2 96 BY76
Woking GU21 166 AW115
Hammonds Cl, Dag. RM8 70 EW62
Hammonds La, Brwd. CM13 53 FV51
HAMMOND STREET, Wal.Cr. EN7 14 DR26
Hammond St, NW5 83 DJ65
Hammondstreet Rd, Wal.Cr. (Chsht) EN7 14 DR26
Hammond Way, SE28
off Oriole Way 88 EV73
Hamond Cl, S.Croy. CR2 159 DP109
Hamonde Cl, Edg. HA8 42 CP47
Hamond Sq, N1
off Hoxton St 84 DS68
Ham Pk Rd, E7 86 EF66
E15 86 EF66
Hampden Av, Beck. BR3 143 DY96
Hampden Cl, NW1 195 N1
Epping (N.Wld Bas.) CM16 18 FA27
Slough (Stoke P.) SL2 74 AU69
Hampden Cres, Brwd. CM14 54 FW49
Waltham Cross (Chsht) EN7 14 DV31
Hampden Gurney St, W1 194 D9
Hampden La, N17 46 DT53
Hampden Pl, St.Alb. (Frog.) AL2 9 CE29
Hampden Rd, N8 65 DN56
N10 44 DG52
N17 46 DU53
N19 *off Holloway Rd* 65 DK61
Beckenham BR3 143 DY96
Gerrards Cross (Chal.St.P.) SL9 36 AX53
Grays RM17 110 GB78
Harrow HA3 40 CC53
Kingston upon Thames KT1 138 CN97
Romford RM5 51 FB52
Slough SL3 93 AZ76
Hampden Sq, N14
off Osidge La 45 DH46
Hampden Way, N14 45 DH47
Watford WD17 23 BS36
Hampermill La, Wat. WD19 39 BT47
Hampshire Cl, N18
off Berkshire Gdns 46 DV50
Hampshire Hog La, W6
off King St 99 CV77
Hampshire Rd, N22 45 DM52
Hornchurch RM11 72 FN56
Hampshire St, NW5
off Torriano Av 83 DK65
Hampson Way, SW8 101 DM81
HAMPSTEAD, NW3 64 DD63
⊖ Hampstead 64 DC63
Hampstead Av, Wdf.Grn. IG8 49 EN52
Hampstead Cl, SE28 88 EV74
St. Albans (Brick.Wd) AL2 8 BZ31
Hampstead Gdns, NW11 64 DA58
Romford (Chad.Hth) RM6 70 EV57
HAMPSTEAD GARDEN SUBURB, N2 64 DC57
Hampstead Grn, NW3 64 DE64
Hampstead Gro, NW3 64 DC62
★ Hampstead Heath, NW3 64 DD61
⇌ Hampstead Heath 64 DE63
Hampstead Hts, N2 44 DC56
Hampstead High St, NW3 64 DC63
Hampstead Hill Gdns, NW3 64 DD63
Hampstead La, N6 64 DD59
NW3 64 DD59
Hampstead Rd, NW1 83 DJ68
Hampstead Sq, NW3 64 DC62
Hampstead Wk, E3
off Waterside Cl 85 DZ67
Hampstead Way, NW11 64 DC60
HAMPTON, TW12 136 CB95
⇌ Hampton 136 CA95
Hampton Cl, N11 45 DH50
NW6 82 DA69
SW20 119 CW94
⇌ Hampton Court 137 CE98
Hampton Ct, N1 *off Upper St* 83 DP65
Hampton Ct Av, E.Mol. KT8 137 CD99
Hampton Ct Cres, E.Mol. KT8 137 CD97
★ Hampton Court Palace & Pk, E.Mol. KT8 137 CE97
Hampton Ct Par, E.Mol. KT8
off Creek Rd 137 CE98
Hampton Ct Rd, E.Mol. KT8 137 CF97
Hampton TW12 136 CC96
Kingston upon Thames KT1 137 CF97
Hampton Ct Way, E.Mol. KT8 137 CE100
Thames Ditton KT7 137 CE103
Hampton Cres, Grav. DA12 131 GL89
Hampton Fm Ind Est, Felt. TW13 116 BZ90
Hampton Gro, Epsom KT17 157 CT111
HAMPTON HILL, Hmptn. TW12 116 CC93
Hampton Hill Business Pk, Hmptn. TW12 *off Wellington Rd* 116 CC92
Hampton La, Felt. TW13 116 BY91
Hampton Mead, Loug. IG10 33 EP41
Hampton Ms, NW10
off Minerva Rd 80 CR69
Hampton Ri, Har. HA3 62 CL58
Hampton Rd, E4 47 DZ50
E7 68 EH64
E11 67 ED60
Croydon CR0 142 DQ100
Hampton (Hmptn H.) TW12 117 CD92
Ilford IG1 69 EP63
Teddington TW11 117 CD92
Twickenham TW2 117 CD90
Worcester Park KT4 139 CU103
Hampton Rd E, Felt. TW13 116 BZ90
Hampton Rd W, Felt. TW13 116 BY89
Hampton St, SE1 200 G9
SE17 200 G9
HAMPTON WICK, Kings.T. KT1 137 CH95
⇌ Hampton Wick 137 CJ95
Ham Ridings, Rich. TW10 118 CM92
HAMSEY GREEN, Warl. CR6 176 DW116
Hamsey Grn Gdns, Warl. CR6 176 DV116
Hamsey Way, S.Croy. CR2 176 DV115
Hamshades Cl, Sid. DA15 125 ET90
Ham St, Rich. TW10 117 CJ89
Ham Vw, Croy. CR0 143 DY100
Ham Yd, W1 195 M10
Hanah Ct, SW19 119 CX94
Hanameel St, E16 205 N2
Hana Ms, E5 *off Goulton Rd* 66 DW63
Hanbury Cl, NW4 63 CW55
Waltham Cross (Chsht) EN8 15 DX29
Hanbury Dr, E11
off High Rd Leytonstone 68 EF59
N21 29 DM43
Westerham (Bigg.H.) TN16 162 EH113
Hanbury Ms, N1 *off Mary St* 84 DQ67
Hanbury Path, Wok. GU21 151 BD114
Hanbury Rd, N17 46 DV54
W3 98 CP75
Hanbury St, E1 197 P6
Hanbury Wk, Bex. DA5 127 FE90
Hancock Ct, Borwd. WD6 26 CQ39
Hancock Rd, E3 85 EC69
SE19 122 DR93
Handa Wk, N1
off Clephane Rd 84 DR65
Hand Ct, WC1 196 C7
Handcroft Rd, Croy. CR0 141 DP101
Handel Cl, Edg. HA8 42 CM51
Handel Cres, Til. RM18 111 GG80
Handel Pl, NW10 80 CR65
Handel St, WC1 195 P4
Handel Way, Edg. HA8 42 CN52
Handen Rd, SE12 124 EE85
Handforth Rd, SW9 101 DN80
Ilford IG1
off Winston Way 69 EP62
Handley Gro, NW2 63 CX62
Handley Page Rd, Wall. SM6 159 DM108
Handley Rd, E9 84 DW66
Handowe Cl, NW4 63 CU56
Handpost Hill, Pot.B. (Northaw) EN6 13 DH28
Handside Cl, Wor.Pk. KT4 139 CX102
Hands Wk, E16 86 EG72
Handsworth Av, E4 47 ED51
Handsworth Rd, N17 66 DR55
Handsworth Way, Wat. WD19
off Hayling Rd 39 BU48
Handtrough Way, Bark. IG11
off Fresh Wf Rd 87 EP68
Hanford Cl, SW18 120 DA88
Hanford Rd, S.Ock. (Aveley) RM15 90 FQ74
Hanford Row, SW19 119 CW93
Hangar Ruding, Wat. WD19 40 BZ48
Hanger Grn, W5 80 CN70
Hanger Hill, Wey. KT13 153 BP107
⊖ Hanger Lane 80 CM69
Hanger La, W5 80 CM70
Hanger Vale La, W5 80 CM72
Hanger Vw Way, W3 80 CN72
Hanging Hill La, Brwd. CM13 55 GB48
Hanging Sword All, EC4 196 E9
Hangrove Hill, Orp. BR6 163 EP113
Hankey Pl, SE1 201 L5
Hankins La, NW7 42 CS48
Hanley Gdns, N4 65 DM60
Hanley Pl, Beck. BR3 123 EA94
Hanley Rd, N4 65 DL60
Hanmer Wk, N7
off Newington Barrow Way 65 DM62
Hannah Cl, NW10 62 CQ63
Beckenham BR3 143 EC97
Hannah Ct, N13 45 DM47
Hannah Mary Way, SE1 202 C9
Hannah Ms, Wall. SM6 159 DJ108
Hannards Way, Ilf. IG6 50 EV50
Hannay La, N8 65 DK59
Hannay Wk, SW16 121 DK89
Hannell Rd, SW6 99 CY80
Hannen Rd, SE27
off Norwood High St 121 DP90
Hannibal Rd, E1 84 DW71
Staines (Stanw.) TW19 114 BK87
Hannibal Way, Croy. CR0 159 DM106
Hannington Rd, SW4 101 DH83
Hanover Av, E16 205 M2
Feltham TW13 115 BU88
Hanover Circle, Hayes UB3 77 BQ72
Hanover Cl, Egh. (Eng.Grn) TW20 112 AV93
Redhill (Merst.) RH1 185 DJ128
Richmond TW9 98 CN80
Slough SL1 92 AU76
Sutton SM3 157 CZ105
Hanover Ct, SE19
off Anerley Rd 122 DT94
W12 *off Uxbridge Rd* 81 CU74
Woking GU22
off Midhope Rd 166 AY119
Hanover Dr, Chis. BR7 125 EQ91
Hanover Gdns, SE11 101 DN79
Abbots Langley WD5 7 BT30
Ilford IG6 49 EQ52
Hanover Gate, NW1 194 C3
Hanover Gate Mans, NW1 194 C4
Hanover Ho, Surb. KT6
off Lenelby Rd 138 CN102
Hanover Pk, SE15 102 DU81
Hanover Pl, E3
off Brokesley St 85 DZ69
WC2 196 A9
Brentwood (Warley) CM14 54 FV50
Hanover Rd, N15 66 DT56
NW10 81 CW66
SW19 120 DC94
Hanover Sq, W1 195 J9
Hanover Steps, W2
off St. George's Flds 82 DE72
Hanover St, W1 195 J9
Croydon CR0
off Abbey Rd 141 DP104
Hanover Ter, NW1 194 C3

★ Place of interest ⇌ Railway station ⊖ London Underground station DLR Docklands Light Railway station Tra Tramlink station H Hospital Riv Pedestrian ferry landing stage

Hanover Ter Ms, NW1 194 C3
Hanover Wk, Wey. KT13 135 BS104
Hanover Way, Bexh. DA6 106 EX83
Hanover W Ind Est, NW10 80 CR68
Hanover Yd, N1 *off Noel Rd* 83 DP68
Hansard Ms, W14
off Holland Rd 99 CX75
Hansart Way, Enf. EN2
off The Ridgeway 29 DN39
Hanscomb Ms, SW4
off Bromell's Rd 101 DJ84
Hans Cres, SW1 198 D6
Hanselin Cl, Stan. HA7 41 CF50
Hansen Dr, N21 29 DM43
Hanshaw Dr, Edg. HA8 42 CR53
Hansler Gro, E.Mol. KT8 137 CD98
Hansler Rd, SE22 122 DT85
Hansol Rd, Bexh. DA6 126 EY85
Hanson Cl, SW12 121 DH87
SW14 98 CQ83
Beckenham BR3 123 EB93
Loughton IG10 33 EQ40
West Drayton UB7 94 BM76
Hanson Dr, Loug. IG10 33 EQ40
Hanson Gdns, Sthl. UB1 96 BY75
Hanson Grn, Loug. IG10 33 EQ40
Hanson St, W1 195 K6
Hans Pl, SW1 198 E6
Hans Rd, SW3 198 D6
Hans St, SW1 198 E7
Hanway Pl, W1 195 M8
Hanway Rd, W7 79 CD72
Hanway St, W1 195 M8
HANWELL, W7 79 CF74
⇌ **Hanwell** 79 CE73
HANWORTH, Felt. TW13 116 BX91
Hanworth La, Cher. KT16 133 BF102
Hanworth Rd, Felt. TW13 115 BV88
Hampton TW12 116 CB93
Hounslow TW3, TW4 96 CB83
Sunbury-on-Thames TW16 115 BU94
Hanworth Ter, Houns. TW3 96 CB84
Hanworth Trd Est, Felt. TW13 116 BY90
Hanyards End, Pot.B.
(Cuffley) EN6 13 DL28
Hanyards La, Pot.B.
(Cuffley) EN6 13 DK28
Hapgood Cl, Grnf. UB6 61 CD64
Harads Pl, E1 202 C1
Harben Rd, NW6 82 DC66
Harberson Rd, E15 86 EF67
SW12 121 DH88
Harberton Rd, N19 65 DJ60
Harbet Rd, E4 47 DX50
N18 47 DX50
W2 194 A7
Harbex Cl, Bex. DA5 127 FB87
Harbinger Rd, E14 204 B9
Harbledown Pl, Orp. BR5 146 EW98
Harbledown Rd, SW6 100 DA81
South Croydon CR2 160 DU111
Harbord Cl, SE5
off De Crespigny Pk 102 DR82
Harbord St, SW6 99 CX81
Harborne Cl, Wat. WD19 40 BW50
Harborough Av, Sid. DA15 125 ES87
Harborough Rd, SW16 121 DM91
Harbour Av, SW10 100 DC81
Harbourer Cl, Ilf. IG6 50 EV50
Harbourer Rd, Ilf. IG6 50 EV50
Harbour Ex Sq, E14 204 C5
Harbourfield Rd, Bans. SM7 174 DB115
Harbour Reach, SW6
off The Boulevard 100 DC81
Harbour Rd, SE5 102 DQ83
Harbour Yd, SW10
off Harbour Av 100 DC81
Harbridge Av, SW15 119 CT87
Harbury Rd, Cars. SM5 158 DE109
Harbut Rd, SW11 100 DD84
Harcombe Rd, N16 66 DS62
Harcourt, Stai. (Wrays.) TW19 112 AY86
Harcourt Av, E12 69 EM63
Edgware HA8 42 CQ48
Sidcup DA15 126 EW86
Wallington SM6 159 DH105
Harcourt Cl, Egh. TW20 113 BC93
Isleworth TW7 97 CG83
Harcourt Fld, Wall. SM6 159 DH105
Harcourt Lo, Wall. SM6
off Croydon Rd 159 DH105
Harcourt Ms, Rom. RM2 71 FF57
Harcourt Rd, E15 86 EF68
N22 45 DK53
SE4 103 DY84
SW19 *off Russell Rd* 120 DA94
Bexleyheath DA6 106 EY84
Bushey WD23 24 CC43
Thornton Heath CR7 141 DM100
Wallington SM6 159 DH105
Harcourt St, W1 194 C7
Harcourt Ter, SW10 100 DB78
Hardcastle Cl, Croy. CR0 142 DU100
Hardcourts Cl, W.Wick. BR4 143 EB104
Hardell Cl, Egh. TW20 113 BA92
Hardel Ri, SW2 121 DP89
Hardel Wk, SW2
off Papworth Way 121 DN87
Harden Fm Cl, Couls. CR5 175 DJ121
Harden Rd, Grav. (Nthflt)
DA11 131 GF90
Hardens Manorway, SE7 104 EK76
Harders Rd, SE15 102 DV82
Hardess St, SE24
off Herne Hill Rd 102 DQ83
Hardie Cl, NW10 62 CR64
Hardie Rd, Dag. RM10 71 FC62
Harding Cl, SE17
off Hillingdon St 102 DQ79
Croydon CR0 142 DT104
Watford WD25 8 BW33
Hardinge Cl, Uxb. UB8 77 BP72
Hardinge Cres, SE18 105 EQ76
Hardinge Rd, N18 46 DS50
NW10 81 CV67
Hardinge St, E1 84 DW72
Harding Ho, Hayes UB3 77 BV72
Harding Rd, Bexh. DA7 106 EZ82
Epsom KT18 172 CS119
Grays RM16 111 GG76
Hardings Cl, Iver SL0 75 BD69
Harding's Cl, Kings.T. KT2 138 CM95
Hardings La, SE20 123 DX93
Harding Spur, Slou. SL3
off Parsons Rd 93 AZ78
Hardings Row, Iver SL0 75 BC69
Hardley Cres, Horn. RM11 72 FK56
Hardman Rd, SE7 205 P10
Kingston upon Thames
KT2 138 CL96
Hardwick Cl, Lthd. (Oxshott)
KT22 170 CC115
Stanmore HA7 41 CJ50
Hardwick Cres, Dart. DA2 128 FP86
Hardwicke Av, Houns. TW5 96 CA81
Hardwicke Gdns, Amer. HP6 20 AS38
Hardwicke Ho, E3
off Bromley High St 85 EB69
Hardwicke Ms, WC1 196 C3
Hardwicke Pl, St.Alb.
(Lon.Col.) AL2 9 CK27
Hardwicke Rd, N13 45 DL51
W4 98 CR77
Reigate RH2 184 DA133
Richmond TW10 117 CJ91
Hardwicke St, Bark. IG11 87 EQ67
Hardwick Grn, W13 79 CH71
Hardwick La, Cher. (Lyne)
KT16 133 BC101
Hardwick St, EC1 196 E3
Hardwicks Way, SW18
off Buckhold Rd 120 DA85
Hardwidge St, SE1 201 M4
Hardy Av, E16 205 N2
Gravesend (Nthflt) DA11 130 GE89
Ruislip HA4 59 BV64
Hardy Cl, SE16 203 J5
Barnet EN5 27 CY44
Pinner HA5 60 BX59
Hardy Gro, Dart. DA1 108 FN84
Hardy Pas, N22
off Cranbrook Pk 45 DM53
Hardy Rd, E4 47 DZ51
SE3 104 EF80
SW19 120 DB94
Hardy's Ms, E.Mol. KT8 137 CE98
Hardy Way, Enf. EN2 29 DN39
Hare & Billet Rd, SE3 103 ED81
Harebell Dr, E6 87 EN71
Harebell Hill, Cob. KT11 154 BX114
Harebell Way, Rom. RM3 52 FK52
Harebreaks, The, Wat. WD24 23 BV38
Harecastle Cl, Hayes UB4 78 BY70
Hare Ct, EC4 196 D9
Harecourt Rd, N1 84 DQ65
Hare Cres, Wat. WD25 7 BU32
Harecroft, Lthd. (Fetch.)
KT22 170 CB123
Haredale Rd, SE24 102 DQ84
Haredon Cl, SE23 122 DW87
HAREFIELD, Uxb. UB9 38 BL53
Harefield, Esher KT10 155 CE105
Harefield Av, Sutt. SM2 157 CY109
Harefield Cl, Enf. EN2 29 DN39
[H] **Harefield Hosp**, Uxb. UB9 38 BJ53
Harefield Ms, SE4 103 DZ83
Harefield Rd, N8 65 DK57
SE4 103 DZ83
SW16 121 DM94
Rickmansworth WD3 38 BK50
Sidcup DA14 126 EX89
Uxbridge UB8 76 BK65
Harefield Rd Ind Est, Rick.
WD3 38 BL49
Hare Hall La, Rom. RM2 71 FH56
Hare Hill, Add. KT15 151 BF107
Hare Hill Cl, Wok. (Pyrford)
GU22 168 BG115
Harelands Cl, Wok. GU21 166 AW117
Harelands La, Wok. GU21 166 AW117
Hare La, Esher (Clay.) KT10 155 CE107
Hare Marsh, E2
off Cheshire St 84 DU70
Harendon, Tad. KT20 173 CW121
Hare Pl, EC4 196 E9
Hare Row, E2 84 DV68
Hares Bk, Croy. (New Adgtn)
CR0 161 ED110
Haresfield Rd, Dag. RM10 88 FA65
Harestone Dr, Cat. CR3 176 DT124
Harestone Hill, Cat. CR3 186 DT126
Harestone La, Cat. CR3 186 DS125
[H] **Harestone Marie Curie Cen**,
Cat. CR3 186 DT125
Harestone Valley Rd,
Cat. CR3 186 DT126
Hare St, SE18 105 EN76
Hare Ter, Grays RM20
off Mill La 109 FX78
Hare Wk, N1 197 N1
Harewood, Rick. WD3 22 BH43
Harewood Av, NW1 194 C5
Northolt UB5 78 BY66
Harewood Cl, Nthlt. UB5 78 BZ66
Reigate RH2 184 DC132
Harewood Dr, Ilf. IG5 49 EM54
Harewood Gdns, S.Croy.
CR2 176 DV115
Harewood Hill, Epp.
(They.B.) CM16 33 ES35
Harewood Pl, W1 195 J9
Slough SL1 92 AU76
Harewood Rd, SW19 120 DE93
Brentwood (Pilg.Hat.) CM15 54 FV44
Chalfont St. Giles HP8 20 AW41
Isleworth TW7 97 CF80
South Croydon CR2 160 DS107
Watford WD19 39 BV48
Harewood Row, NW1 194 C6
Harewood Ter, Sthl. UB2 96 BZ77
Harfield Gdns, SE5 102 DS83
Harfield Rd, Sun. TW16 136 BX96
Harford Cl, E4 47 EB45
Harford Dr, Wat. WD17 23 BS38
Harford Ms, N19
off Wedmore St 65 DK62
Harford Rd, E4 47 EB45
Harford St, E1 85 DY70
Harford Wk, N2 64 DD57
Harfst Way, Swan. BR8 147 FC95
Hargood Cl, Har. HA3 62 CL58
Hargood Rd, SE3 104 EJ81
Hargrave Pk, N19 65 DJ61
Hargrave Pl, N7
off Brecknock Rd 65 DK64
Hargrave Rd, N19 65 DJ61
Hargreaves Av, Wal.Cr.
(Chsht) EN7 14 DV30
Hargreaves Cl, Wal.Cr.
(Chsht) EN7 14 DV31
Hargwyne St, SW9 101 DM83
Haringey Pk, N8 65 DL58
Haringey Pas, N4 65 DP58
N8 65 DN56
Haringey Rd, N8 65 DL56
Harington Ter, N9 46 DR48
N18 46 DR48
Harkett Cl, Har. HA3
off Byron Rd 41 CF54
Harkett Ct, Har. HA3 41 CF54
Harkness, Wal.Cr. (Chsht) EN7 14 DU29
Harkness Cl, Epsom KT17 173 CW116
Romford RM3 52 FM50
Harkness Ho, E1
off Christian St 84 DU72
Harland Av, Croy. CR0 142 DT104
Sidcup DA15 125 ER90
Harland Cl, SW19 140 DB97
Harland Rd, SE12 124 EG88
Harlands Gro, Orp. BR6 163 EP105
Harlech Gdns, Houns. TW5 96 BW79
Pinner HA5 60 BX59
Harlech Rd, N14 45 DL48
Abbots Langley WD5 7 BU31
Harlech Twr, W3 98 CP75
Harlequin Av, Brent. TW8 97 CG79
Harlequin Cen, Wat. WD17 24 BW42
Harlequin Cl, Hayes UB4
off Cygnet Way 78 BX71
Isleworth TW7 117 CE85
Harlequin Ho, Erith DA18
off Kale Rd 106 EY76
Harlequin Rd, Tedd. TW11 117 CH94
★ **Harlequins R.L.**, Twick.
TW2 117 CE87
Harlescott Rd, SE15 103 DX84
HARLESDEN, NW10 80 CS68
⇌ **Harlesden** 80 CR68
⊖ **Harlesden** 80 CR68
Harlesden Cl, Rom. RM3 52 FM52
Harlesden Gdns, NW10 81 CT67
Harlesden La, NW10 81 CU67
Harlesden Rd, NW10 81 CU67
Romford RM3 52 FM51
Harlesden Wk, Rom. RM3 52 FM52
Harleston Cl, E5
off Theydon Rd 66 DW61
Harley Cl, Wem. HA0 79 CK65
Harley Ct, E11
off Blake Hall Rd 68 EG59
Harley Cres, Har. HA1 61 CD56
Harleyford, Brom. BR1 144 EH95
Harleyford Rd, SE11 101 DM79
Harleyford St, SE11 101 DN79
Harley Gdns, SW10 100 DC78
Orpington BR6 163 ES105
Harley Gro, E3 85 DZ69
Harley Pl, W1 195 H7
Harley Rd, NW3 82 DD66
NW10 80 CS68
Harrow HA1 61 CD56
Harley St, W1 195 H7
[H] **Harley St Clinic, The**, W1 195 H6
Harling Ct, SW11
off Latchmere Rd 100 DF82
Harlinger St, SE18 104 EL76
HARLINGTON, Hayes UB3 95 BQ79
Harlington Cl, Hayes UB3
off New Rd 95 BQ80
Harlington Rd, Bexh. DA7 106 EY83
Hounslow (Hthrw Air.) TW6 95 BT84
Uxbridge UB8 77 BP71
Harlington Rd E, Felt. TW13,
TW14 115 BV87
Harlington Rd W, Felt. TW14 115 BV86
Harlow Gdns, Rom. RM5 51 FC51
Harlow Rd, N13 46 DR48
Rainham RM13 89 FF67
Harlton Ct, Wal.Abb. EN9 16 EF34
Harlyn Dr, Pnr. HA5 59 BV55
Harman Av, Grav. DA11 131 GH92
Woodford Green IG8 48 EF52
Harman Cl, E4 47 ED49
NW2 63 CY62
SE1 *off Avondale Sq* 102 DU78
Harman Dr, NW2 63 CY62
Sidcup DA15 125 ET86
Harman Pl, Pur. CR8 159 DP111
Harman Rd, Enf. EN1 30 DT43
Harmer Rd, Swans. DA10 130 FZ86
Harmer St, Grav. DA12 131 GJ86
HARMONDSWORTH, West Dr.
UB7 94 BK79
Harmondsworth La, West Dr.
UB7 94 BL79
Harmondsworth Rd, West Dr.
UB7 94 BL78
Harmony Cl, NW11 63 CY57
Wallington SM6 159 DL109
Harmony Pl, SE1 202 A10
Harmony Ter, Har. HA2
off Goldsmith Cl 60 CB60
Harmony Way, NW4
off Victoria Rd 63 CW56
Harmood Gro, NW1
off Clarence Way 83 DH66
Harmood Pl, NW1
off Harmood St 83 DH66
Harmood St, NW1 83 DH66
Harmsworth Ms, SE11 200 F7
Harmsworth St, SE17 101 DP78
Harmsworth Way, N20 43 CZ46
Harnetts Cl, Swan. BR8 147 FD100
Harold Av, Belv. DA17 106 EZ78
Hayes UB3 95 BT76
Harold Ct Rd, Rom. RM3 52 FP51
Harold Cres, Wal.Abb. EN9 15 EC32
Harold Est, SE1 201 N7
Harold Gibbons Ct, SE7 104 EJ79
HAROLD HILL, Rom. RM3 52 FL50
Harold Hill Ind Est, Rom.
RM3 52 FK52
Harold Laski Ho, EC1 196 F3
HAROLD PARK, Rom. RM3 52 FN51
Harold Pl, SE11 101 DN78
Harold Rd, E4 47 EC49
E11 68 EE60
E13 86 EH67
N8 65 DM57
Harold Rd, N15 66 DT57
NW10 80 CR69
SE19 122 DS93
Dartford (Hawley) DA2 128 FM91
Sutton SM1 158 DD105
Woodford Green IG8 48 EG53
Haroldstone Rd, E17 67 DX57
Harold Vw, Rom. RM3 52 FM54
HAROLD WOOD, Rom. RM3 52 FL54
⇌ **Harold Wood** 52 FM53
[H] **Harold Wd Hosp**, Rom.
RM3 52 FL54
Harp All, EC4 196 F8
Harpenden Rd, E12 68 EJ61
SE27 121 DP90
Harpenmead Pt, NW2
off Granville Rd 63 CZ61
[H] **Harperbury Hosp**,
Rad. WD7 9 CJ31
Harper Cl, N14
off Alexandra Ct 29 DJ43
Grays (Chaff.Hun.) RM16 109 FW78
Harper La, Rad. WD7 9 CG32
Harper Ms, SW17 120 DC90
Harper Rd, E6 87 EM72
SE1 201 H6
Harpers Yd, N17
off Ruskin Rd 46 DT53
Harpesford Av, Vir.W. GU25 132 AV99
Harp Island Cl, NW10 62 CR61
Harp La, EC3 201 M1
Harpley Sq, E1 84 DW69
Harpour Rd, Bark. IG11 87 EQ65
Harp Rd, W7 79 CF70
Harpsden St, SW11 100 DG81
Harps Oak La, Red.
(Merst.) RH1 184 DF125
Harpswood Cl, Couls. CR5 175 DJ122
Harpur Ms, WC1 196 B6
Harpurs, Tad. KT20 173 CX122
Harpur St, WC1 196 B6
Harraden Rd, SE3 104 EJ81
Harrap Chase, Grays (Bad.Dene)
RM17 110 FZ78
Harrap St, E14 85 EC73
Harrier Av, E11
off Eastern Av 68 EH58
Harrier Cl, Horn. RM12 89 FH65
Harrier Ms, SE28 105 ER76
Harrier Rd, NW9 42 CS54
Harriers Cl, W5 80 CL73
Harrier Way, E6 87 EM70
Waltham Abbey EN9 16 EG34
Harriescourt, Wal.Abb. EN9 16 EG32
Harries Rd, Hayes UB4 78 BW70
Harriet Cl, E8 84 DU67
Harriet Gdns, Croy. CR0 142 DU103
Harriet St, SW1 198 E5
Harriet Tubman Cl, SW2 121 DN87
Harriet Wk, SW1 198 E5
Harriet Walker Way, Rick.
WD3 37 BF45
Harriet Way, Bushey WD23 41 CD45
HARRINGAY, N8 65 DN57
⇌ **Harringay** 65 DN58
Harringay Gdns, N8 65 DP56
⇌ **Harringay Green Lanes** 65 DP58
Harringay Rd, N15 65 DP57
Harrington Cl, NW10 62 CR62
Croydon CR0 141 DL103
Harrington Ct, W10
off Dart St 81 CZ69
Croydon CR0
off Altyre Rd 142 DS103
Harrington Cres, Grays
(N.Stfd) RM16 91 FX74
Harrington Gdns, SW7 100 DB77
Harrington Hill, E5 66 DV60
Harrington Ho, NW1 195 K2
[Tra] **Harrington Road** 142 DW97
Harrington Rd, E11 68 EE60
SE25 142 DU98
SW7 100 DD77
Harrington Sq, NW1 195 K1
Harrington St, NW1 195 K2
Harrington Way, SE18 104 EK76
Harriott Cl, SE10 205 K9
Harriotts Cl, Ashtd. KT21
off Harriotts La 171 CJ120
Harriotts La, Ashtd. KT21 171 CJ119
Harris Cl, Enf. EN2 29 DP39
Gravesend (Nthflt) DA11 130 GE90
Hounslow TW3 96 CA81
Romford RM3 52 FL52
Harris La, Rad. (Shenley) WD7 10 CN34
Harrison Cl, N20 44 DE46
Brentwood (Hutt.) CM13 55 GD43
Northwood HA6 39 BQ51
Harrison Ct, Shep. TW17
off Greeno Cres 135 BP99
Harrison Dr, Epp. (N.Wld Bas.)
CM16 19 FB26
Harrison Rd, Dag. RM10 89 FB65
Harrisons Ri, Croy. CR0 141 DP104
Harrison St, WC1 196 A3
Harrisons Wf, Purf. RM19 108 FN78
Harrison Wk, Wal.Cr.
(Chsht) EN8 15 DX30
Harrison Way, Sev. TN13 190 FG122
Waltham Abbey EN9 31 EC36
Harris Rd, Bexh. DA7 106 EY81
Dagenham RM9 70 EZ64
Watford WD25 23 BU35
Harris St, E17 67 DZ59
SE5 102 DR80
Harris Way, Sun. TW16 135 BS95
★ **Harrods**, SW1 198 D6
Harrogate Ct, Slou. SL3 93 BA78
Harrogate Rd, Wat. WD19 40 BW48
Harrold Rd, Dag. RM8 70 EV64
HARROW, HA1 - HA3 61 CD59
⇌ **Harrow & Wealdstone** 61 CE56
⊖ **Harrow & Wealdstone** 61 CE56
★ **Harrow Arts Cen**,
Pnr. HA5 40 CB52
Harrow Av, Enf. EN1 30 DT44
Harroway Rd, SW11 100 DD82
Harrow Bottom Rd, Vir.W.
GU25 133 AZ100
Harrowby Gdns, Grav.
(Nthflt) DA11 130 GE89
Harrowby St, W1 194 C8
Harrow Cl, Add. KT15 134 BH103
Harrow Cl, Chess. KT9 155 CK108
Hornchurch RM11 71 FH60
Harrow Cres, Rom. RM3 51 FH52
Harrowdene Cl, Wem. HA0 61 CK63
Harrowdene Gdns, Tedd.
TW11 117 CG93
Harrowdene Rd, Wem. HA0 61 CK62
Harrow Dr, N9 46 DT46
Hornchurch RM11 71 FH60
Harrowes Meade, Edg. HA8 42 CN48
Harrow Flds Gdns, Har. HA1 61 CE62
Harrow Gdns, Orp. BR6 164 EV105
Warlingham CR6 177 DZ115
Harrowgate Rd, E9 85 DY65
Harrow Grn, E11
off Harrow Rd 68 EE62
Harrow La, E14 204 D1
Harrow Manorway, SE2 88 EW74
Harrow Mkt, Slou. SL3 93 BA76
★ **Harrow Mus & Heritage Cen**,
Har. HA2 60 CC55
HARROW ON THE HILL,
Har. HA1 61 CE61
⇌ **Harrow on the Hill** 61 CE58
⊖ **Harrow on the Hill** 61 CE58
Harrow Pk, Har. HA1 61 CE61
Harrow Pas, Kings.T. KT1
off Market Pl 137 CK96
Harrow Pl, E1 197 N8
Harrow Rd, E6 86 EL67
E11 68 EE62
NW10 81 CV69
W2 81 CZ70
W9 81 CZ70
W10 81 CX70
Barking IG11 87 ES67
Carshalton SM5 158 DE106
Feltham TW14 114 BN88
Ilford IG1 69 EQ63
Sevenoaks (Knock.) TN14 180 EY115
Slough SL3 93 AZ76
Warlingham CR6 177 DZ115
Wembley HA0 61 CJ64
Wembley (Tkgtn) HA9 62 CM64
★ **Harrow Sch**, Har. HA1 61 CE60
Harrow Vw, Har. HA1, HA2 61 CD56
Hayes UB3 77 BU72
Uxbridge UB10 77 BQ69
Harrow Vw Rd, W5 79 CH70
Harrow Way, Shep. TW17 135 BQ96
Watford WD19 40 BY48
HARROW WEALD, Har. HA3 41 CD53
Harrow Weald Pk, Har. HA3 41 CD51
Harston Dr, Enf. EN3 31 EA38
Hart Cl, Red. (Bletch.) RH1 186 DT134
Hart Cor, Grays RM20 109 FX78
Hart Cres, Chig. IG7 49 ET50
Hart Dyke Cres, Swan. BR8
off Hart Dyke Rd 147 FD97
Hart Dyke Rd, Orp. BR5 146 EW102
Swanley BR8 147 FD97
Harte Rd, Houns. TW3 96 BZ82
Hartfield Av, Borwd. (Els.)
WD6 26 CN43
Northolt UB5 77 BV68
Hartfield Cl, Borwd. (Els.)
WD6 26 CN43
Hartfield Cres, SW19 119 CZ94
West Wickham BR4 144 EG104
Hartfield Gro, SE20 142 DV95
Hartfield Pl, Grav. (Nthflt)
DA11 130 GD87
Hartfield Rd, SW19 119 CZ94
Chessington KT9 155 CK106
West Wickham BR4 162 EG105
Hartfield Ter, E3 85 EA68
Hartford Av, Har. HA3 61 CG55
Hartforde Rd, Borwd. WD6 26 CN40
Hartford Rd, Bex. DA5 126 FA86
Epsom KT19 156 CN107
Hart Gro, W5 80 CN74
Southall UB1 78 CA71
Harthall La, Hem.H. HP3 7 BS26
Kings Langley WD4 7 BP28
Hartham Cl, N7 65 DL64
Isleworth TW7 97 CG81
Hartham Rd, N7 65 DL64
N17 46 DT54
Isleworth TW7 97 CF81
Harting Rd, SE9 124 EL91
Hartington Cl, Har. HA1 61 CE63
Hartington Ct, W4 98 CP80
Hartington Pl, Reig. RH2 184 DA132
Hartington Rd, E16 86 EH72
E17 67 DY58
SW8 101 DL81
W4 98 CP80
W13 79 CH73
Southall UB2 96 BY76
Twickenham TW1 117 CH87
Hartismere Rd, SW6 99 CZ80
Hartlake Rd, E9 85 DX65
Hartland Cl, N21
off Elmscott Gdns 30 DQ44
Addlestone (New Haw)
KT15 152 BJ110
Edgware HA8 42 CN47
Hartland Dr, Edg. HA8 42 CN47
Ruislip HA4 59 BV62
Hartland Rd, E15 86 EF66
N11 44 DF50
NW1 83 DH66
NW6 81 CZ68
Addlestone KT15 152 BG108
Epping CM16 18 EU31
Hampton (Hmptn H.) TW12 116 CB91
Hornchurch RM12 71 FG61
Isleworth TW7 97 CG83
Morden SM4 140 DA101
Waltham Cross (Chsht) EN8 15 DX30
Hartlands Cl, Bex. DA5 126 EZ86
Hartland Way, Croy. CR0 143 DY103
Morden SM4 139 CZ101
Hartlepool Ct, E16
off Fishguard Way 87 EP74
Hartley Av, E6 86 EL67
NW7 43 CT50

★ Place of interest ⇌ Railway station ⊖ London Underground station DLR Docklands Light Railway station Tra Tramlink station H Hospital Riv Pedestrian ferry landing stage

Hartley Cl, NW7 ... 43 CT50
Bromley BR1 ... 145 EM96
Slough (Stoke P.) SL3 ... 74 AW67
Hartley Copse, Wind. (Old Wind.) SL4 ... 112 AU86
Hartley Down, Pur. CR8 ... 159 DM114
Hartley Fm Est, Pur. CR8 ... 175 DM115
HARTLEY GREEN, Long. DA3 ... 149 FX99
Hartley Hill, Pur. CR8 ... 175 DM115
Hartley Ho, SE1 off Longfield Est ... 102 DT77
Hartley Old Rd, Pur. CR8 ... 159 DM114
Hartley Rd, E11 ... 68 EF60
Croydon CR0 ... 141 DP101
Welling DA16 ... 106 EW80
Westerham TN16 ... 189 ER125
Hartley St, E2 ... 84 DW69
Hartley Way, Pur. CR8 ... 175 DM115
Hartmann Rd, E16 ... 86 EL74
Hartmoor Ms, Enf. EN3 ... 31 DX37
Hartnoll St, N7 off Eden Gro ... 65 DM64
Harton Cl, Brom. BR1 ... 144 EK95
Harton Rd, N9 ... 46 DV47
Harton St, SE8 ... 103 EA81
Hartopp Pt, SW6 off Pellant Rd ... 99 CY80
Hart Rd, W.Byf. (Byfleet) KT14 ... 152 BL113
Hartsbourne Av, Bushey (Bushey Hth) WD23 ... 40 CC47
Hartsbourne Cl, Bushey (Bushey Hth) WD23 ... 41 CD47
Hartsbourne Rd, Bushey (Bushey Hth) WD23 ... 41 CD47
Harts Cl, Bushey WD23 ... 24 CA40
Hartscroft, Croy. CR0 ... 161 DY109
Harts Gro, Wdf.Grn. IG8 ... 48 EG50
Hartshill Cl, Uxb. UB10 ... 76 BN65
Hartshill Rd, Grav. (Nthflt) DA11 ... 131 GF89
Hartshill Wk, Wok. GU21 ... 166 AV116
Hartshorn All, EC3 ... 197 N9
Hartshorn Gdns, E6 ... 87 EN70
Hartslands Rd, Sev. TN13 ... 191 FJ123
Harts La, SE14 ... 103 DY80
Barking IG11 ... 87 EP65
Hartslock Dr, SE2 ... 106 EX75
Hartsmead Rd, SE9 ... 125 EM89
Hartspring La, Bushey WD23 ... 24 CA39
Watford WD25 ... 24 CA39
Hart St, EC3 ... 197 N10
Brentwood CM14 ... 54 FW47
Hartsway, Enf. EN3 ... 30 DW42
Hartswood Cl, Brwd. CM14 ... 54 FY49
Hartswood Gdns, W12 ... 99 CT76
Hartswood Grn, Bushey (Bushey Hth) WD23 ... 41 CD47
Hartswood Rd, W12 ... 99 CT75
Brentwood CM14 ... 54 FY49
Hartsworth Cl, E13 ... 86 EF68
Hartville Rd, SE18 ... 105 ES77
Hartwell Cl, SW2 off Challice Way ... 121 DM88
Hartwell Dr, E4 ... 47 EC51
Hartwell St, E8 off Dalston La ... 84 DT65
Harvard Hill, W4 ... 98 CP79
Harvard La, W4 ... 98 CP78
Harvard Rd, SE13 ... 123 EC85
W4 ... 98 CP78
Isleworth TW7 ... 97 CE81
Harvard Wk, Horn. RM12 ... 71 FG63
Harvel Cl, Orp. BR5 ... 146 EU97
Harvel Cres, SE2 ... 106 EX78
Harvest Bk Rd, W.Wick. BR4 ... 144 EF104
Harvest Ct, Shep. TW17 ... 134 BN98
Harvest End, Wat. WD25 ... 24 BX36
Harvester Rd, Epsom KT19 ... 156 CR110
Harvesters Cl, Islw. TW7 ... 117 CD85
Harvest La, Loug. IG10 ... 48 EK45
Thames Ditton KT7 ... 137 CG100
Harvest Rd, Bushey WD23 ... 24 CB42
Egham (Eng.Grn) TW20 ... 112 AX92
Feltham TW13 ... 115 BU91
Harvest Way, Swan. BR8 ... 147 FD101
Harvey, Grays RM16 ... 110 GB75
Harvey Dr, Hmptn. TW12 ... 136 CB95
Harveyfields, Wal.Abb. EN9 ... 15 EC34
Harvey Gdns, E11 off Harvey Rd ... 68 EF60
SE7 ... 104 EJ78
Loughton IG10 ... 33 EP41
Harvey Ho, Brent. TW8 off Green Dragon La ... 98 CL78
Harvey Pt, E16 off Fife Rd ... 86 EG71
Harvey Rd, E11 ... 68 EE60
N8 ... 65 DM57
SE5 ... 102 DR81
Hounslow TW4 ... 116 BZ87
Ilford IG1 ... 69 EP64
Northolt UB5 ... 78 BW66
Rickmansworth (Crox.Grn) WD3 ... 22 BN44
St. Albans (Lon.Col.) AL2 ... 9 CJ26
Slough SL3 ... 93 BB76
Uxbridge UB10 ... 76 BN68
Walton-on-Thames KT12 ... 135 BU101
Harveys La, Rom. RM7 ... 71 FD61
Harvey St, N1 ... 84 DR67
Harvill Rd, Sid. DA14 ... 126 EX92
Harvil Rd, Uxb. (Hare.) UB9 ... 58 BK58
Uxbridge (Ickhm) UB10 ... 58 BL60
Harvington Wk, E8 off Wilman Gro ... 84 DU66
Harvist Est, N7 ... 65 DN63
Harvist Rd, NW6 ... 81 CX69
Harwater Dr, Loug. IG10 ... 33 EM40
Harwell Cl, Ruis. HA4 ... 59 BR60
Harwell Pas, N2 ... 64 DF56
Harwood Av, Brom. BR1 ... 144 EH96
Hornchurch RM11 ... 72 FL55
Mitcham CR4 ... 140 DE97
Harwood Cl, N12 ... 44 DE51
Wembley HA0 off Harrowdene Rd ... 61 CK63
Harwood Dr, Uxb. UB10 ... 76 BM67
Harwood Gdns, Wind. (Old Wind.) SL4 ... 112 AV87
Harwood Hall La, Upmin. RM14 ... 90 FP65
Harwood Rd, SW6 ... 100 DA80
Harwoods Rd, Wat. WD18 ... 23 BU42
Harwoods Yd, N21 off Wades Hill ... 45 DN45
Harwood Ter, SW6 ... 100 DB81
Hascombe Ter, SE5 off Love Wk ... 102 DR82
Haselbury Rd, N9 ... 46 DS49
N18 ... 46 DS49
Haseldine Rd, St.Alb. (Lon.Col.) AL2 ... 9 CK26
Haseley End, SE23 off Tyson Rd ... 122 DW87
Haselrigge Rd, SW4 ... 101 DK84
Haseltine Rd, SE26 ... 123 DZ91
Haselwood Dr, Enf. EN2 ... 29 DP42
Haskard Rd, Dag. RM9 ... 70 EX63
Hasker St, SW3 ... 198 C8
Haslam Av, Sutt. SM3 ... 139 CY102
Haslam Cl, N1 ... 83 DN66
Uxbridge UB10 ... 59 BQ61
Haslam St, SE15 ... 102 DT80
Haslemere Av, NW4 ... 63 CX58
SW18 ... 120 DB89
W7 ... 97 CG76
W13 ... 97 CG76
Barnet EN4 ... 44 DF46
Hounslow TW5 ... 96 BW82
Mitcham CR4 ... 140 DD96
Haslemere Cl, Hmptn. TW12 ... 116 BZ92
Wallington SM6 off Stafford Rd ... 159 DL106
Haslemere Gdns, N3 ... 63 CZ55
Haslemere Heathrow Est, Houns. TW4 ... 95 BV82
Haslemere Rd, N8 ... 65 DK59
N21 ... 45 DP47
Bexleyheath DA7 ... 106 EZ82
Ilford IG3 ... 69 ET61
Thornton Heath CR7 ... 141 DP99
Hasler Cl, SE28 ... 88 EV73
Haslett Rd, Shep. TW17 ... 135 BS96
Hasluck Gdns, Barn. EN5 ... 28 DC44
Hassard St, E2 off Hackney Rd ... 84 DT68
Hassendean Rd, SE3 ... 104 EH79
Hassett Rd, E9 ... 85 DX65
Hassocks Cl, SE26 ... 122 DV90
Hassocks Rd, SW16 ... 141 DK95
Hassock Wd, Kes. BR2 ... 162 EK105
Hassop Rd, NW2 ... 63 CX63
Hassop Wk, SE9 ... 124 EL91
Hasted Cl, Green. DA9 ... 129 FW86
Hasted Rd, SE7 ... 104 EK78
Hastings Av, Ilf. IG6 ... 69 EQ56
Hastings Cl, SE15 ... 102 DU80
Barnet EN5 off Leicester Rd ... 28 DC42
Grays RM17 ... 110 FY79
Wembley HA0 ... 61 CJ63
Hastings Dr, Surb. KT6 ... 137 CJ100
Hastings Ho, SE18 ... 105 EM77
Hastings Rd, N11 ... 45 DJ50
N17 ... 66 DR55
W13 ... 79 CH73
Bromley BR2 ... 144 EL102
Croydon CR0 ... 142 DT102
Romford RM2 ... 71 FH57
Hastings St, SE18 ... 105 EQ76
WC1 ... 195 P3
Hastings Way, Bushey WD23 ... 24 BY42
Rickmansworth (Crox.Grn) WD3 ... 23 BP42
Hastingwood Trd Est, N18 ... 47 DX51
Hastoe Cl, Hayes UB4 ... 78 BY70
Hat & Mitre Ct, EC1 ... 196 G5
Hatch, The, Enf. EN3 ... 31 DX39
Hatcham Ms Business Cen, SE14 off Hatcham Pk Rd ... 103 DX81
Hatcham Pk Ms, SE14 off Hatcham Pk Rd ... 103 DX81
Hatcham Pk Rd, SE14 ... 103 DX81
Hatcham Rd, SE15 ... 102 DW79
Hatchard Rd, N19 ... 65 DK61
Hatch Cl, Add. KT15 ... 134 BH104
Hatchcroft, NW4 ... 63 CV55
HATCH END, Pnr. HA5 ... 40 BY51
⇌ Hatch End ... 40 BZ52
Hatchers Ms, SE1 ... 201 N5
Hatchett Rd, Felt. TW14 ... 115 BQ88
Hatch Gdns, Tad. KT20 ... 173 CX120
Hatch Gro, Rom. RM6 ... 70 EY56
Hatchlands Rd, Red. RH1 ... 184 DE134
Hatch La, E4 ... 47 ED49
Cobham KT11 ... 169 BP119
Coulsdon CR5 ... 174 DG115
West Drayton UB7 ... 94 BK80
Woking (Ock.) GU23 ... 169 BP120
Hatch Pl, Kings.T. KT2 ... 118 CM92
Hatch Rd, SW16 ... 141 DL96
Brentwood (Pilg.Hat.) CM15 ... 54 FU43
Hatch Side, Chig. IG7 ... 49 EN50
Hatchwood Cl, Wdf.Grn. IG8 off Sunset Av ... 48 EF49
Hatcliffe Cl, SE3 ... 104 EF83
Hatcliffe St, SE10 ... 205 K10
Hatfield Cl, SE14 off Reaston St ... 103 DX80
Brentwood (Hutt.) CM13 ... 55 GD45
Hornchurch RM12 ... 72 FK64
Ilford IG6 ... 69 EP55
Mitcham CR4 ... 140 DD98
Sutton SM2 ... 158 DA109
West Byfleet KT14 ... 152 BH112
Hatfield Mead, Mord. SM4 off Central Rd ... 140 DA99
Hatfield Ms, Dag. RM9 ... 88 EY66
Hatfield Rd, E15 ... 68 EE64
W4 ... 98 CR75
W13 ... 79 CG74
Ashtead KT21 ... 172 CM119
Dagenham RM9 ... 88 EY65
Grays (Chaff.Hun.) RM16 ... 109 FX77
Potters Bar EN6 ... 12 DC30
Slough SL1 ... 92 AU75
Watford WD24 ... 23 BV39
Hatfields, SE1 ... 200 E2
Loughton IG10 ... 33 EP41
Hathaway Cl, Brom. BR2 ... 145 EM102
Hathaway Cl, Ilf. IG6 ... 49 EP51
Ruislip HA4 off Stafford Rd ... 59 BT63
Stanmore HA7 ... 41 CG50
Hathaway Cres, E12 ... 87 EM65
Hathaway Gdns, W13 ... 79 CF71
Grays RM17 off Hathaway Rd ... 110 GB76
Romford RM6 ... 70 EX57
Hathaway Rd, Croy. CR0 ... 141 DP101
Grays RM17 ... 110 GB77
Hatherleigh Cl, NW7 ... 43 CX52
Chessington KT9 ... 155 CK106
Morden SM4 ... 140 DA98
Hatherleigh Gdns, Pot.B. EN6 ... 12 DD32
Hatherleigh Rd, Ruis. HA4 ... 59 BU61
Hatherleigh Way, Rom. RM3 ... 52 FK53
Hatherley Cres, Sid. DA14 ... 126 EU89
Hatherley Gdns, E6 ... 86 EK68
N8 ... 65 DL58
Hatherley Gro, W2 ... 82 DB72
Hatherley Ms, E17 ... 67 EA56
Hatherley Rd, E17 ... 67 DZ56
Richmond TW9 ... 98 CM82
Sidcup DA14 ... 126 EU91
Hatherley St, SW1 ... 199 L8
Hathern Gdns, SE9 ... 125 EN91
Hatherop Rd, Hmptn. TW12 ... 116 BZ94
Hathersage Ct, N1 off Newington Grn ... 66 DR64
Hatherwood, Lthd. KT22 ... 171 CK121
Hathorne Cl, SE15 ... 102 DV82
Hathway St, SE15 off Gibbon Rd ... 102 DW82
Hathway Ter, SE14 off Kitto Rd ... 103 DX82
Hatley Av, Ilf. IG6 ... 69 EQ56
Hatley Cl, N11 ... 44 DF50
Hatley Rd, N4 ... 65 DM61
Hatteraick St, SE16 ... 202 G4
Hattersfield Cl, Belv. DA17 ... 106 EZ77
Hatters La, Wat. WD18 ... 23 BR44
HATTON, Felt. TW14 ... 95 BT84
Hatton Cl, SE18 ... 105 ER80
Gravesend (Nthflt) DA11 ... 130 GE90
Grays (Chaff.Hun.) RM16 ... 109 FX76
⊖ Hatton Cross ... 95 BT84
Hatton Gdn, EC1 ... 196 E6
Hatton Gdns, Mitch. CR4 ... 140 DF99
Hatton Grn, Felt. TW14 ... 95 BU84
Hatton Gro, West Dr. UB7 ... 94 BK75
Hatton Ho, E1 off Cable St ... 84 DU73
Hatton Ms, Green. DA9 ... 109 FW84
Hatton Pl, EC1 ... 196 E5
Hatton Rd, Croy. CR0 ... 141 DN102
Feltham TW14 ... 115 BS85
Waltham Cross (Chsht) EN8 ... 15 DX29
Hatton Row, NW8 ... 194 A5
Hatton St, NW8 ... 194 A5
Hatton Wall, EC1 ... 196 D6
Haul Rd, NW1 ... 83 DL68
Haunch of Venison Yd, W1 ... 195 H9
Hauteville Ct Gdns, W6 off Stamford Brook Av ... 99 CT76
Havana Cl, Rom. RM1 off Exchange St ... 71 FE57
Havana Rd, SW19 ... 120 DA89
Havannah St, E14 ... 204 A5
Havant Rd, E17 ... 67 EC55
Havelock Pl, Har. HA1 ... 61 CE58
Havelock Rd, N17 ... 46 DU54
SW19 ... 120 DC92
Belvedere DA17 ... 106 EZ77
Bromley BR2 ... 144 EJ98
Croydon CR0 ... 142 DT102
Dartford DA1 ... 127 FH87
Gravesend DA11 ... 131 GF88
Harrow HA3 ... 61 CE55
Kings Langley WD4 ... 6 BN28
Southall UB2 ... 96 BZ76
Havelock St, N1 ... 83 DL67
Ilford IG1 ... 69 EP61
Havelock Ter, SW8 ... 101 DH80
Havelock Wk, SE23 ... 122 DW88
Haven, The, SE26 off Springfield Rd ... 122 DV92
Grays RM16 ... 111 GF78
Richmond TW9 ... 98 CN83
Sunbury-on-Thames TW16 ... 115 BU94
Haven Cl, SE9 ... 125 EM90
SW19 ... 119 CX90
Esher KT10 ... 137 CE103
Gravesend (Istead Rise) DA13 ... 131 GF94
Hayes UB4 ... 77 BS71
Sidcup DA14 ... 126 EW93
Swanley BR8 ... 147 FF96
Haven Ct, Esher KT10 off Portsmouth Rd ... 137 CE103
Havengore Av, Grav. DA12 ... 131 GL87
Haven Grn, W5 ... 79 CK72
Haven Grn Ct, W5 off Haven Grn ... 79 CK72
Havenhurst Ri, Enf. EN2 ... 29 DN40
Haven La, W5 ... 80 CL72
Haven Ms, E3 off St. Pauls Way ... 85 DZ71
N1 off Liverpool Rd ... 83 DN66
Haven Pl, W5 off The Broadway ... 79 CK73
Esher KT10 ... 137 CE103
Grays RM16 ... 110 GC75
Haven Rd, Ashf. TW15 ... 115 BP91
Havensfield, Kings L. (Chipper.) WD4 ... 6 BH31
Haven St, NW1 off Castlehaven Rd ... 83 DH66
Haven Ter, W5 off The Broadway ... 79 CK73
Haven Way, Epsom KT19 ... 156 CP111
Havenwood, Wem. HA9 ... 62 CP62
Havenwood Cl, Brwd. (Gt Warley) CM13 off Wilmot Grn ... 53 FW51
Haverfield Gdns, Rich. TW9 ... 98 CN80
Haverfield Rd, E3 ... 85 DY69
Haverford Way, Edg. HA8 ... 42 CM53
Haverhill Rd, E4 ... 47 EC46
SW12 ... 121 DJ88
HAVERING-ATTE-BOWER, Rom. RM4 ... 51 FE48
Havering Dr, Rom. RM1 ... 71 FE56
Havering Gdns, Rom. RM6 ... 70 EW57
HAVERING PARK, Rom. RM5 ... 50 FA50
Havering Rd, Rom. RM1 ... 71 FD55
Havering St, E1 off Devonport St ... 85 DX72
Havering Way, Bark. IG11 ... 88 EV69
Havers Av, Walt. KT12 ... 154 BX106
Haversfield Est, Brent. TW8 ... 98 CL78
Haversham Cl, Twick. TW1 ... 117 CK86
Haversham Pl, N6 ... 64 DF61
Haverstock Ct, Orp. BR5 ... 146 EU96
Haverstock Hill, NW3 ... 64 DE64
Haverstock Pl, N1 off Haverstock St ... 83 DP69
Haverstock Rd, NW5 ... 64 DG64
Haverstock St, N1 ... 196 G1
Haverthwaite Rd, Orp. BR6 ... 145 ER103
Havil St, SE5 ... 102 DS80
Havisham Pl, SE19 ... 121 DP93
Hawarden Gro, SE24 ... 122 DQ87
Hawarden Hill, NW2 ... 63 CU62
Hawarden Rd, E17 ... 67 DX56
Caterham CR3 ... 176 DQ121
Hawbridge Rd, E11 ... 67 ED60
Hawes Cl, Nthwd. HA6 ... 39 BT52
Hawes La, E4 ... 31 EC38
West Wickham BR4 ... 143 ED102
Hawes Rd, N18 ... 46 DV51
Bromley BR1 ... 144 EH95
Tadworth KT20 off Hatch Gdns ... 173 CX120
Hawes St, N1 ... 83 DP66
Haweswater Dr, Wat. WD25 ... 8 BW33
Haweswater Ho, Islw. TW7 off Summerwood Rd ... 117 CF85
Hawfield Bk, Orp. BR6 ... 146 EX104
Hawfield Gdns, St.Alb. (Park St) AL2 ... 9 CD26
Hawgood St, E3 ... 85 EA71
Hawk Cl, Wal.Abb. EN9 ... 16 EG34
Hawkdene, E4 ... 31 EB44
Hawke Pk Rd, N22 ... 65 DP55
Hawke Pl, SE16 ... 203 J4
Hawke Rd, SE19 ... 122 DS93
Hawkesbury Rd, SW15 ... 119 CV85
Hawkes Cl, Grays RM17 off New Rd ... 110 GB79
Hawkesfield Rd, SE23 ... 123 DY89
Hawkesley Cl, Twick. TW1 ... 117 CG91
Hawke's Pl, Sev. TN13 ... 190 FG127
Hawkes Rd, Felt. TW14 ... 115 BU87
Mitcham CR4 ... 140 DE95
Hawkesworth Cl, Nthwd. HA6 ... 39 BS52
Hawke Twr, SE14 off Nynehead St ... 103 DY79
Hawkewood Rd, Sun. TW16 ... 135 BU97
Hawkhirst Rd, Ken. CR8 ... 176 DR115
Hawkhurst, Cob. KT11 ... 154 CA114
Hawkhurst Gdns, Chess. KT9 ... 156 CL105
Romford RM5 ... 51 FD51
Hawkhurst Rd, SW16 ... 141 DK95
Hawkhurst Way, N.Mal. KT3 ... 138 CR99
West Wickham BR4 ... 143 EB103
Hawkinge Wk, Orp. BR5 ... 146 EV97
Hawkinge Way, Horn. RM12 ... 90 FJ65
Hawkins Av, Grav. DA12 ... 131 GJ91
Hawkins Cl, NW7 off Hale La ... 42 CR50
Borehamwood WD6 off Banks Rd ... 26 CQ40
Harrow HA1 ... 61 CD59
Hawkins Dr, Grays (Chaff.Hun.) RM16 ... 109 FX75
Hawkins Rd, NW10 ... 80 CS66
Teddington TW11 ... 117 CH93
Hawkins Ter, SE7 ... 104 EL78
Hawkins Way, SE6 ... 123 EA92
Hemel Hempstead (Bov.) HP3 ... 5 BA26
Hawkley Gdns, SE27 ... 121 DP89
Hawkridge, NW5 off Warden Rd ... 82 DG65
Hawkridge Cl, Rom. RM6 ... 70 EW59
Hawkridge Dr, Grays RM17 ... 110 GD78
Hawksbrook La, Beck. BR3 ... 143 EB100
Hawkshaw Cl, SW2 off Tierney Rd ... 121 DL87
Hawkshead, NW1 ... 195 K2
Hawkshead Cl, Brom. BR1 ... 124 EE94
Hawkshead La, Hat. (N.Mymms) AL9 ... 11 CW28
Hawkshead Rd, NW10 ... 81 CT66
W4 ... 98 CS75
Potters Bar EN6 ... 12 DB29
Hawks Hill, Epp. (N.Wld Bas.) CM16 ... 18 FA27
Hawk's Hill, Lthd. KT22 ... 171 CF123
Hawkshill Cl, Esher KT10 ... 154 CA107
Hawks Hill Cl, Lthd. (Fetch.) KT22 ... 171 CF122
Hawkshill Way, Esher KT10 ... 154 BZ107
Hawkslade Rd, SE15 ... 123 DX85
Hawksley Rd, N16 ... 66 DS62
Hawksmead Cl, Enf. EN3 ... 31 DX35
Hawks Ms, SE10 off Luton Pl ... 103 EC80
Hawksmoor, Rad. (Shenley) WD7 ... 10 CN33
Hawksmoor Cl, E6 off Allhallows Rd ... 86 EL72
SE18 ... 105 ES78
Hawksmoor Grn, Brwd. (Hutt.) CM13 ... 55 GD43
Hawksmoor Ms, E1 off Cable St ... 84 DV73
Hawksmoor St, W6 ... 99 CX79
Hawksmouth, E4 ... 47 EB45
Hawks Rd, Kings.T. KT1 ... 138 CM96
Hawkstone Est, SE16 ... 202 G9
Hawkstone Rd, SE16 ... 202 G9
Hawksview, Cob. KT11 ... 154 BZ113
Hawksway, Stai. TW18 ... 113 BF90
Hawkswell Cl, Wok. GU21 ... 166 AT117
Hawkswell Wk, Wok. GU21 off Lockfield Dr ... 166 AS117
Hawkswood Gro, Slou. (Fulmer) SL3 ... 75 AZ65
Hawkswood La, Ger.Cr. SL9 ... 57 AZ64
Hawk Ter, Ilf. IG5 off Tiptree Cres ... 69 EN55
Hawkwell Ct, E4 off Colvin Gdns ... 47 EC48
Hawkwell Ho, Dag. RM8 ... 70 FA60
Hawkwell Wk, N1 off Basire St ... 84 DQ67
Hawkwood Cres, E4 ... 31 EB44
Hawkwood La, Chis. BR7 ... 145 EQ95
Hawkwood Mt, E5 ... 66 DV60
Hawlands Dr, Pnr. HA5 ... 60 BY59
HAWLEY, Dart. DA2 ... 128 FM92
Hawley Cl, Hmptn. TW12 ... 116 BZ93
Hawley Cres, NW1 ... 83 DH66
Hawley Ms, NW1 off Hawley St ... 83 DH66
Hawley Mill, Dart. DA2 ... 128 FN91
Hawley Rd, N18 ... 47 DX50
NW1 ... 83 DH66
Dartford DA1, DA2 ... 128 FL89
HAWLEY'S CORNER, West. TN16 ... 179 EN121
Hawley St, NW1 ... 83 DH66
Hawley Ter, Dart. DA2 off Hawley Rd ... 128 FN92
Hawley Vale, Dart. DA2 ... 128 FN92
Hawley Way, Ashf. TW15 ... 114 BN92
Haws La, Stai. TW19 ... 114 BG86
Hawstead La, Orp. BR6 ... 164 EZ106
Hawstead Rd, SE6 ... 123 EB86
Hawsted, Buck.H. IG9 ... 48 EH45
Hawthorn Av, E3 ... 85 DZ67
N13 ... 45 DL50
Brentwood CM13 ... 55 FZ48
Carshalton SM5 ... 158 DG108
Rainham RM13 ... 89 FH70
Richmond TW9 off Kew Rd ... 98 CL82
Thornton Heath CR7 ... 141 DP95
Hawthorn Cen, Har. HA1 ... 61 CF56
Hawthorn Cl, Abb.L. WD5 ... 7 BU32
Banstead SM7 ... 157 CY114
Gravesend DA12 ... 131 GH91
Hampton TW12 ... 116 CA92
Hounslow TW5 ... 95 BV80
Iver SL0 ... 75 BD68
Orpington BR5 ... 145 ER100
Watford WD17 ... 23 BT38
Woking GU22 ... 166 AY120
Hawthorn Cotts, Well. DA16 off Hook La ... 106 EU83
Hawthorn Cres, SW17 ... 120 DG92
South Croydon CR2 ... 160 DW111
Hawthornden Cl, N12 off Fallowfields Dr ... 44 DE51
Hawthorndene Cl, Brom. BR2 ... 144 EF103
Hawthorndene Rd, Brom. BR2 ... 144 EF103
Hawthorn Dr, Har. HA2 ... 60 BZ58
Uxbridge (Denh.) UB9 ... 76 BJ65
West Wickham BR4 ... 162 EE105
Hawthorne Av, Har. HA3 ... 61 CG58
Mitcham CR4 ... 140 DD96
Ruislip HA4 ... 59 BV58
Waltham Cross (Chsht) EN7 ... 14 DV31
Westerham (Bigg.H.) TN16 ... 178 EK115
Hawthorne Cl, N1 ... 84 DS65
Bromley BR1 ... 145 EM97
Sutton SM1 off Aultone Way ... 140 DC103
Waltham Cross (Chsht) EN7 ... 14 DV31
Hawthorne Ct, Nthwd. HA6 off Ryefield Cres ... 39 BU54
Walton-on-Thames KT12 off Ambleside Av ... 136 BX103
Hawthorne Cres, Slou. SL1 ... 74 AS71
West Drayton UB7 ... 94 BM75
Hawthorne Fm Av, Nthlt. UB5 ... 78 BY67
Hawthorne Gro, NW9 ... 62 CQ59
Hawthorne Ms, Grnf. UB6 off Greenford Rd ... 78 CC72
Hawthorne Pl, Epsom KT17 ... 156 CS112
Hayes UB3 ... 77 BT73
Hawthorne Rd, E17 ... 67 EA55
Bromley BR1 ... 144 EL97
Radlett WD7 ... 9 CG34
Staines TW18 ... 113 BC92
Hawthorne Way, N9 ... 46 DS47
Staines (Stanw.) TW19 ... 114 BK87
Hawthorn Gdns, W5 ... 97 CK76
Hawthorn Gro, SE20 ... 122 DV94
Barnet EN5 ... 27 CT44
Enfield EN2 ... 30 DR38
Hawthorn Hatch, Brent. TW8 ... 97 CH80
Hawthorn La, Sev. TN13 ... 190 FF122
Hawthorn Ms, NW7 off Holders Hill Rd ... 43 CY53
Hawthorn Pl, Erith DA8 ... 107 FC78
Hawthorn Rd, N8 ... 65 DK55
N18 ... 46 DT50
NW10 ... 81 CU66
Bexleyheath DA6 ... 106 EZ84
Brentford TW8 ... 97 CH80
Buckhurst Hill IG9 ... 48 EK49
Dartford DA1 ... 128 FK88
Feltham TW13 ... 115 BU88
Sutton SM1 ... 158 DE107
Wallington SM6 ... 159 DH108
Woking GU22 ... 166 AX120
Woking (Ripley) GU23 ... 168 BG124
Hawthorns, Wdf.Grn. IG8 ... 48 EG48
Hawthorns, The, Ch.St.G. HP8 ... 20 AW40
Epsom KT17 off Ewell Bypass ... 157 CT107
Loughton IG10 ... 33 EN42
Oxted RH8 ... 188 EG133
Rickmansworth (Map.Cr.) WD3 ... 37 BD50
Slough (Colnbr.) SL3 ... 93 BF81
Hawthorn Wk, W10 off Droop St ... 81 CY70
Hawthorn Way, Add. (New Haw) KT15 ... 152 BJ110
Shepperton TW17 ... 135 BR98
Hawtrees, Rad. WD7 ... 25 CF35
Hawtrey Av, Nthlt. UB5 ... 78 BX68
Hawtrey Cl, Slou. SL1 ... 92 AV75
Hawtrey Dr, Ruis. HA4 ... 59 BU59
Hawtrey Rd, NW3 ... 82 DE66
Haxted Rd, Brom. BR1 off North Rd ... 144 EH95
Hayburn Way, Horn. RM12 ... 71 FF60
Hay Cl, E15 ... 86 EE66
Borehamwood WD6 ... 26 CQ40
Haycroft Cl, Couls. CR5 off Caterham Dr ... 175 DP118
Haycroft Gdns, NW10 ... 81 CU67
Haycroft Rd, SW2 ... 121 DL85

Haycroft Rd, Surb. KT6 . . . . .138 CL104
Hay Currie St, E14 . . . . .85 EB72
Hayday Rd, E16 . . . . .86 EG71
Hayden Ct, Add. (New Haw)
KT15 . . . . .152 BH111
Hayden Rd, Wal.Abb. EN9 . . .31 EE35
Haydens Cl, Orp. BR5 . . . . . .146 EV100
Haydens Pl, W11
off Portobello Rd 81 CZ72
Hayden Way, Rom. RM5 . . . . .51 FC54
Haydn Av, Pur. CR8 . . . . .159 DN114
Haydns Ms, W3
off Emanuel Av 80 CQ72
Haydock Av, Nthlt. UB5 . . . . .78 CA65
Haydock Cl, Horn. RM12 . . . . .72 FM63
Haydock Grn, Nthlt. UB5
off Haydock Av 78 CA65
Haydon Cl, NW9 . . . . .62 CQ56
Enfield EN1
off Mortimer Dr 30 DS44
Romford RM3 . . . . .51 FH52
Haydon Dr, Pnr. HA5 . . . . .59 BU56
Haydon Pk Rd, SW19 . . . . . . .120 DB92
Haydon Rd, Dag. RM8 . . . . . .70 EW61
Watford WD19 . . . . .24 BY44
⇌ Haydons Road 120 DC92
Haydons Rd, SW19 . . . . .120 DB92
Haydon St, EC3 . . . . .197 P10
Haydon Wk, E1
off Mansell St 84 DT73
Haydon Way, SW11 . . . . .100 DD84
HAYES, Brom. BR2 . . . . .144 EG103
HAYES, UB3 & UB4 . . . . .77 BS72
⇌ Hayes 144 EF102
Hayes, The, Epsom KT18 . . . .172 CR119
⇌ Hayes & Harlington 95 BT76
Hayes Barton, Wok. GU22 . . .167 BD116
Hayes Bypass, Hayes UB3,
UB4 . . . . .78 BX70
Hayes Chase, W.Wick. BR4 . .144 EE99
Hayes Cl, Brom. BR2 . . . . . . .144 EG103
Grays RM20 . . . . .109 FW79
Hayes Ct, SW2 . . . . .121 DL88
Hayes Cres, NW11 . . . . .63 CZ57
Sutton SM3 . . . . .157 CX105
Hayes Dr, Rain. RM13 . . . . . . .89 FH66
HAYES END, Hayes UB3 . . . . .77 BQ71
Hayes End Cl, Hayes UB4 . . . .77 BR70
Hayes End Dr, Hayes UB4 . . .77 BR70
Hayes End Rd, Hayes UB4 . . .77 BR70
Hayesford Pk Dr, Brom. BR2 .144 EF99
Hayes Gdn, Brom. BR2 . . . . .144 EG103
Hayes Gro, SE22 . . . . .102 DT84
Hayes Hill, Brom. BR2 . . . . . .144 EE102
Hayes Hill Rd, Brom. BR2 . . .144 EF102
Hayes La, Beck. BR3 . . . . . . .143 EC97
Bromley BR2 . . . . .144 EG99
Kenley CR8 . . . . .160 DQ114
Hayes Mead Rd, Brom. BR2 .144 EE102
Hayes Metro Cen, Hayes
UB4 . . . . .78 BW73
Hayes Pk, Hayes UB4 . . . . . . .77 BS70
Hayes Pl, NW1 . . . . .194 C5
Hayes Rd, Brom. BR2 . . . . . .144 EG98
Greenhithe DA9 . . . . .129 FS87
Southall UB2 . . . . .95 BV77
Hayes St, Brom. BR2 . . . . . .144 EH102
HAYES TOWN, Hayes UB3 . . .95 BS75
Hayes Wk, Brox. EN10
off Landau Way 15 DZ25
Potters Bar EN6
off Hyde Av 12 DB33
Hayes Way, Beck. BR3 . . . . . .143 EC98
Hayes Wd Av, Brom. BR2 . . .144 EH102
Hayfield Cl, Bushey WD23 . . .24 CB42
Hayfield Pas, E1
off Stepney Grn 84 DW70
Hayfield Rd, Orp. BR5 . . . . . .146 EU99
Hayfield Yd, E1
off Mile End Rd 84 DW70
Haygarth Pl, SW19 . . . . .119 CX92
Hay Grn, Horn. RM11 . . . . . . .72 FN58
Haygreen Cl, Kings.T. KT2 . . .118 CP93
Hay Hill, W1 . . . . .199 J1
Hayland Cl, NW9 . . . . .62 CR56
Hay La, NW9 . . . . .62 CR56
Slough (Fulmer) SL3 . . . . . . .56 AX63
Hayles St, SE11 . . . . .200 F8
Haylett Gdns, Kings.T. KT1
off Anglesea Rd 137 CK98
Hayling Av, Felt. TW13 . . . . . .115 BU90
Hayling Cl, N16
off Boleyn Rd 66 DS64
Hayling Rd, Wat. WD19 . . . . . .39 BV47
Haymaker Cl, Uxb. UB10
off Honey Hill 76 BM66
Hayman Cres, Hayes UB4 . . . .77 BR68
Hayman St, N1 off Cross St . .83 DP66
Haymarket, SW1 . . . . .199 M1
Haymarket Arc, SW1 . . . . . . .199 M1
Haymeads Dr, Esher KT10 . . .154 CC107
Haymer Gdns, Wor.Pk. KT4 . .139 CU104
Haymerle Rd, SE15 . . . . .102 DU79
Haymill Cl, Grnf. UB6 . . . . . . .79 CF69
Hayne Rd, Beck. BR3 . . . . . . .143 DZ96
Haynes Cl, N11 . . . . .44 DG48
N17 . . . . .46 DV52
SE3 . . . . .104 EE83
Slough SL3 . . . . .93 AZ78
Woking (Ripley) GU23 . . . . .168 BH122
Haynes Dr, N9 . . . . .46 DV48
Haynes La, SE19 . . . . .122 DS93
Haynes Pk Ct, Horn. RM11
off Slewins Cl 72 FJ57
Haynes Rd, Grav. (Nthflt)
DA11 . . . . .131 GF90
Hornchurch RM11 . . . . .72 FK57
Wembley HA0 . . . . .80 CL66
Hayne St, EC1 . . . . .196 G6
Haynt Wk, SW20 . . . . .139 CY97
★ Hay's Galleria, SE1 . . . . .201 M2
Hay's La, SE1 . . . . .201 M3
Haysleigh Gdns, SE20 . . . . .142 DU96
Hay's Ms, W1 . . . . .199 H1
Haysoms Cl, Rom. RM1 . . . . .71 FE56
Haystall Cl, Hayes UB4 . . . . .77 BS68
Hay St, E2 . . . . .84 DU67
Hays Wk, Sutt. SM2 . . . . .157 CX110
Hayter Ct, E11 . . . . .68 EH61
Hayter Rd, SW2 . . . . .121 DL85
Hayton Cl, E8
off Buttermere Wk 84 DT65
Haywain, Oxt. RH8 . . . . .187 ED130
Hayward Cl, SW19 . . . . .140 DB95
Dartford DA1 . . . . .127 FD85
Hayward Dr, Dart. DA1 . . . . .128 FM89
★ Hayward Gall, SE1 . . . . . .200 C2
Hayward Gdns, SW15 . . . . . .119 CW86
Hayward Rd, N20 . . . . .44 DC47
Thames Ditton KT7 . . . . . . .137 CG102
Haywards Cl, Brwd. (Hutt.)
CM13 . . . . .55 GE44
Romford (Chad.Hth) RM6 . .70 EV57
Hayward's Pl, EC1 . . . . .196 F5
Haywood Cl, Pnr. HA5 . . . . . .40 BX54
Haywood Ct, Wal.Abb. EN9 . .16 EF34
Haywood Dr, Rick. (Chorl.)
WD3 . . . . .21 BF43
Haywood Pk, Rick. (Chorl.)
WD3 . . . . .21 BF43
Haywood Ri, Orp. BR6 . . . . .163 ES105
Haywood Rd, Brom. BR2 . . .144 EK98
Hayworth Cl, Enf. EN3
off Green St 31 DY40
Hazel Av, West Dr. UB7 . . . . . .94 BN76
Hazelbank, Rick. (Crox.Grn)
WD3 . . . . .23 BQ44
Surbiton KT5 . . . . .138 CQ102
Hazelbank Ct, Cher. KT16 . . .134 BJ102
Hazelbank Rd, SE6 . . . . .123 ED89
Chertsey KT16 . . . . .134 BJ102
Hazelbourne Rd, SW12 . . . . .121 DH86
Hazelbrouck Gdns, Ilf. IG6 . . .49 ER52
Hazelbury Av, Abb.L. WD5 . . . .7 BQ32
Hazelbury Cl, SW19 . . . . . . .140 DA96
Hazelbury Grn, N9 . . . . .46 DS48
Hazelbury La, N9 . . . . .46 DS48
Hazel Cl, N13 . . . . .46 DR48
N19 off Hargrave Pk 65 DJ61
NW9 . . . . .42 CS54
SE15 . . . . .102 DU82
Brentford TW8 . . . . .97 CH80
Croydon CR0 . . . . .143 DX101
Egham (Eng.Grn) TW20 . . .112 AV93
Hornchurch RM12 . . . . .71 FH62
Mitcham CR4 . . . . .141 DK98
Twickenham TW2 . . . . .116 CC87
Waltham Cross EN7 . . . . . . .14 DS26
Hazel Ct, Rad. (Shenley) WD7 .10 CM33
Hazelcroft, Pnr. HA5 . . . . .40 CA51
Hazelcroft Cl, Uxb. UB10 . . . .76 BM66
Hazeldean Rd, NW10 . . . . . . .80 CR66
Hazeldene, Add. KT15 . . . . .152 BJ106
Waltham Cross EN8 . . . . . . .15 DY32
Hazeldene Ct, Ken. CR8 . . . .176 DR115
Hazeldene Dr, Pnr. HA5 . . . . .60 BW55
Hazeldene Gdns, Uxb. UB10 . .77 BQ67
Hazeldene Rd, Ilf. IG3 . . . . . .70 EV61
Welling DA16 . . . . .106 EW82
Hazeldon Rd, SE4 . . . . .123 DY85
Hazel Dr, Erith DA8 . . . . .107 FH81
South Ockendon RM15 . . . .91 FW69
Hazeleigh, Brwd. CM13 . . . . . .55 GB48
Hazeleigh Gdns, Wdf.Grn. IG8 .48 EL50
Hazel End, Swan. BR8 . . . . . .147 FE99
Hazel Gdns, Edg. HA8 . . . . . . .42 CP49
Grays RM16 . . . . .110 GE76
Hazelgreen Cl, N21 . . . . .45 DP46
Hazel Gro, SE26 . . . . .123 DX91
Enfield EN1
off Dimsdale Dr 30 DU44
Feltham TW13 . . . . .115 BU88
Orpington BR6 . . . . .145 EP103
Romford RM6 . . . . .70 EY55
Staines TW18 . . . . .114 BH93
Watford WD25
off Cedar Wd Dr 23 BV35
Wembley HA0
off Carlyon Rd 80 CL67
Hazel Gro Est, SE26 . . . . . . .123 DX91
Hazel Ho, NW3
off Maitland Pk Rd 82 DF65
Hazelhurst, Beck. BR3 . . . . . .143 ED95
Hazelhurst Rd, SW17 . . . . . .120 DC91
Hazel La, Ilf. IG6 . . . . .49 EP52
Richmond TW10 . . . . .118 CL89
Hazell Cres, Rom. RM5 . . . . . .51 FB53
Hazells Rd, Grav. DA13 . . . . .130 GD92
Hazellville Rd, N19 . . . . .65 DK59
Hazell Way, Slou. (Stoke P.)
SL2 . . . . .74 AT65
Hazel Mead, Barn. EN5 . . . . . .27 CV43
Epsom KT17 . . . . .157 CU110
Hazelmere Cl, Felt. TW14 . . . .115 BR86
Leatherhead KT22 . . . . . . .171 CH119
Northolt UB5 . . . . .78 BZ68
Hazelmere Dr, Nthlt. UB5 . . . .78 BZ68
Hazelmere Gdns, Horn. RM11 .71 FH57
Hazelmere Rd, NW6 . . . . .82 DA67
Northolt UB5 . . . . .78 BZ68
Orpington BR5 . . . . .145 EQ98
Hazelmere Wk, Nthlt. UB5 . . .78 BZ68
Hazelmere Way, Brom. BR2 .144 EG100
Hazel Ms, N8
off Alexandra Rd 65 DN55
Hazel Ri, Horn. RM11 . . . . . . .72 FJ58
Hazel Rd, E15 off Burgess Rd .68 EE64
NW10 . . . . .81 CW69
Dartford DA1 . . . . .128 FK89
Erith DA8 . . . . .107 FG81
St. Albans (Park St) AL2 . . . .8 CB28
West Byfleet KT14 . . . . . . .152 BG114
Hazeltree La, Nthlt. UB5 . . . . .78 BY69
Hazel Tree Rd, Wat. WD24 . . . .23 BV37
Hazel Wk, Brom. BR2 . . . . . .145 EN100
Hazel Way, E4 . . . . .47 DZ51
SE1 . . . . .201 P8
Coulsdon (Chipstead) CR5 . .174 DF119
Leatherhead (Fetch.) KT22 . .170 CC122
HAZELWOOD, Sev. TN14 . . . .163 ER111
Hazelwood, Loug. IG10 . . . . . .32 EK43
Hazelwood Av, Mord. SM4 . .140 DB98
Hazelwood Cl, W5 . . . . .98 CL75
Harrow HA2 . . . . .60 CB56
Hazelwood Ct, NW10
off Neasden La N 62 CS62
Hazelwood Cres, N13 . . . . . . .45 DN49
Hazelwood Cft, Surb. KT6 . . .138 CL100
Hazelwood Dr, Pnr. HA5 . . . . .39 BV54
Hazelwood Gdns, Brwd.
(Pilg.Hat.) CM15 . . . . .54 FU44
Hazelwood Gro, S.Croy. CR2 .160 DV113
Hazelwood Hts, Oxt. RH8 . . .188 EG131
Hazelwood La, N13 . . . . .45 DN49
Abbots Langley WD5 . . . . . .7 BQ32
Coulsdon (Chipstead) CR5 . .174 DF119
Hazelwood Pk Cl, Chig. IG7 . .49 ES50
Hazelwood Rd, E17 . . . . .67 DY57
Enfield EN1 . . . . .30 DT44
Oxted RH8 . . . . .188 EH132
Rickmansworth (Crox.Grn)
WD3 . . . . .23 BQ44
Sevenoaks (Cudham) TN14 .163 ER112
Woking (Knap.) GU21 . . . . .166 AS118
Hazlebury Rd, SW6 . . . . .100 DB82
Hazledean Rd, Croy. CR0 . . .142 DR103
Hazledene Rd, W4 . . . . .98 CQ79
Hazlemere Gdns, Wor.Pk.
KT4 . . . . .139 CV102
Hazlemere Rd, Slou. SL2 . . . .74 AW74
Hazlewell Rd, SW15 . . . . . . .119 CV85
Hazlewood Cl, E5
off Mandeville St 67 DY62
Hazlewood Cres, W10 . . . . . . .81 CY70
Hazlewood Twr, W10
off Golborne Rd 81 CZ70
Hazlitt Cl, Felt. TW13 . . . . . . .116 BY91
Hazlitt Ms, W14
off Hazlitt Rd 99 CY76
Hazlitt Rd, W14 . . . . .99 CY76
Hazon Way, Epsom KT19 . . . .156 CR112
Heacham Av, Uxb. UB10 . . . . .59 BQ62
Headcorn Pl, Th.Hth. CR7
off Headcorn Rd 141 DM98
Headcorn Rd, N17 . . . . .46 DT52
Bromley BR1 . . . . .124 EF92
Thornton Heath CR7 . . . . .141 DM98
Headfort Pl, SW1 . . . . .198 G5
Headingley Cl, Ilf. IG6 . . . . . .49 ET51
Radlett (Shenley) WD7 . . . .10 CL32
Waltham Cross (Chsht)
EN7 . . . . .14 DT26
Headington Rd, SW18 . . . . . .120 DC88
Headlam Rd, SW4 . . . . .121 DK86
Headlam St, E1 . . . . .84 DV70
HEADLEY, Epsom KT18 . . . .182 CQ125
Headley App, Ilf. IG2 . . . . . . .69 EN57
Headley Av, Wall. SM6 . . . . .159 DM106
Headley Chase, Brwd. CM14 .54 FW49
Headley Cl, Epsom KT19 . . . .156 CN107
Headley Common, Brwd. CM13
off Warley Gap 53 FV52
Headley Common Rd, Epsom
(Headley) KT18 . . . . .182 CR127
Tadworth KT20 . . . . .182 CR127
Headley Ct, SE26 . . . . .122 DV92
Headley Dr, Croy. (New Adgtn)
CR0 . . . . .161 EB108
Epsom KT18 . . . . .173 CV119
Ilford IG2 . . . . .69 EP58
Headley Gro, Tad. KT20 . . . . .173 CV120
★ Headley Heath, Epsom
KT18 . . . . .182 CP128
Headley Heath App, Dor.
(Mick.) RH5 . . . . .182 CP130
Tadworth (Box H.) KT20 . .182 CP130
Headley Rd, Epsom (Tyr.Wd)
KT18 . . . . .172 CN123
Epsom (Woodcote) KT18 .172 CP118
Leatherhead KT22 . . . . . . .171 CK123
Head's Ms, W11
off Westbourne Gro 82 DA72
HEADSTONE, Har. HA2 . . . . . .60 CC56
Headstone Dr, Har. HA1, HA3 .61 CE55
Headstone Gdns, Har. HA2 . . .60 CC56
⇌ Headstone Lane 40 CB53
Headstone La, Har. HA2, HA3 .60 CB56
Headstone Rd, Har. HA1 . . . . .61 CE57
Head St, E1 . . . . .85 DX72
Headway, The, Epsom KT17 .157 CT109
Headway Cl, Rich. TW10
off Locksmeade Rd 117 CJ91
Heald St, SE14 . . . . .103 DZ81
Healey Dr, Orp. BR6 . . . . . . .163 ET105
Healey Rd, Wat. WD18 . . . . . .23 BT44
Healey St, NW1 . . . . .83 DH65
Heanor Ct, E5 off Pedro St . . .67 DX62
Heards La, Brwd. (Shenf.)
CM15 . . . . .55 FZ41
Hearne Ct, Ch.St.G. HP8
off Gordon Way 36 AV48
Hearne Rd, W4 . . . . .98 CN79
Hearn Ri, Nthlt. UB5 . . . . . . .78 BX67
Hearn Rd, Rom. RM1 . . . . . . .71 FF58
Hearn's Bldgs, SE17 . . . . . . .201 L9
Hearnshaw St, E14
off Maroon St 85 DY72
Hearn's Rd, Orp. BR5 . . . . . .146 EW98
Hearn St, EC2 . . . . .197 N5
Hearnville Rd, SW12 . . . . . . .120 DG88
H Heart Hosp, The, W1 . . . . .194 G7
Heath, The, W7
off Lower Boston Rd 79 CE74
Caterham (Chaldon) CR3 .176 DQ124
Radlett WD7 . . . . .9 CG33
Heathacre, Slou. (Colnbr.) SL3
off Park St 93 BE81
Heatham Pk, Twick. TW2 . . . .117 CF87
Heath Av, Bexh. DA7 . . . . . . .106 EX79
Heathbourne Rd, Bushey
(Bushey Hth) WD23 . . . . . .41 CE47
Stanmore HA7 . . . . .41 CE47
Heathbridge, Wey. KT13 . . . .152 BN108
Heath Brow, NW3
off North End Way 64 DC62
Heath Cl, NW11 . . . . .64 DB59
W5 . . . . .80 CM70
Banstead SM7 . . . . .158 DB114
Hayes UB3 . . . . .95 BR80
Orpington BR5
off Sussex Rd 146 EW100
Potters Bar EN6 . . . . .12 DB30
Romford RM2 . . . . .71 FG55
Staines (Stanw.) TW19 . . . .114 BJ86
Heathclose, Swan. BR8
off Bonney Way 147 FE96
Heath Cl, Vir.W. GU25 . . . . . .132 AX98
Heathclose Av, Dart. DA1 . . .127 FH87
Heathclose Rd, Dart. DA1 . . .127 FG88
Heathcock Ct, WC2
off Strand 83 DL73
Heathcote, Tad. KT20 . . . . . .173 CX121
Heathcote Av, Ilf. IG5 . . . . . . .49 EM54
Heathcote Ct, Ilf. IG5
off Heathcote Av 49 EM54
Heathcote Gro, E4 . . . . .47 EC48
Heathcote Pt, E9 off Wick Rd .85 DX65
Heathcote Rd, Epsom KT18 .156 CR114
Twickenham TW1 . . . . .117 CH86
Heathcote St, WC1 . . . . .196 B4
Heathcote Way, West Dr. UB7
off Tavistock Rd 76 BK74
Heath Cotts, Pot.B. EN6
off Heath Rd 12 DB30
Heath Ct, SE9 . . . . .125 EQ88
Hounslow TW4 . . . . .96 BZ84
Uxbridge UB8 . . . . .76 BL66
Heathcroft, NW11 . . . . .64 DB60
W5 . . . . .80 CM70
Heathcroft Av, Sun. TW16 . . .115 BT94
Heathcroft Gdns, E17 . . . . . . .47 ED53
Heathdale Av, Houns. TW4 . . .96 BY83
Heathdene, Tad. KT20
off Brighton Rd 173 CY119
Heathdene Dr, Belv. DA17 . . .107 FB77
Heathdene Rd, SW16 . . . . . .121 DM94
Wallington SM6 . . . . .159 DH108
Heathdown Rd, Wok. GU22 .167 BD115
Heath Dr, NW3 . . . . .64 DB63
SW20 . . . . .139 CW98
Epping (They.B.) CM16 . . . .33 ES35
Potters Bar EN6 . . . . .12 DA30
Romford RM2 . . . . .51 FG53
Sutton SM2 . . . . .158 DC109
Tadworth (Walt.Hill) KT20 .183 CU125
Woking (Send) GU23 . . . .167 BB123
Heathedge, SE26 . . . . .122 DV89
Heath End Rd, Bex. DA5 . . . .127 FE88
Heather Av, Rom. RM1 . . . . . .51 FD54
Heatherbank, SE9 . . . . .105 EM82
Chislehurst BR7 . . . . .145 EN96
Heatherbank Cl, Cob. KT11 . .154 BX111
Dartford DA1 . . . . .127 FE86
Heather Cl, E6 . . . . .87 EP72
N7
off Newington Barrow Way .65 DM62
SE13 . . . . .123 ED86
SW8 . . . . .101 DH83
Abbots Langley WD5 . . . . . .7 BU32
Addlestone (New Haw)
KT15 . . . . .152 BH110
Brentwood (Pilg.Hat.) CM15 .54 FV43
Hampton TW12 . . . . .136 BZ95
Isleworth TW7
off Harvesters Cl 117 CD85
Redhill RH1 . . . . .185 DH130
Romford RM1 . . . . .51 FD53
Tadworth KT20 . . . . .173 CY122
Uxbridge UB8
off Violet Av 76 BM71
Woking GU21 . . . . .166 AW115
Heatherdale Cl, Kings.T. KT2 .118 CN93
Heatherdene Cl, N12
off Bow La 44 DC53
Mitcham CR4 . . . . .140 DE98
Heatherden Grn, Iver SL0 . . . .75 BC67
Heather Dr, Dart. DA1 . . . . . .127 FG87
Enfield EN2 . . . . .29 DP40
Romford RM1 . . . . .51 FD54
Heather End, Swan. BR8 . . . .147 FD98
Heatherfield La, Walt. KT12 .153 BS106
Heatherfields, Add. (New Haw)
KT15 . . . . .152 BH110
Heatherfold Way, Pnr. HA5 . . .59 BT55
Heather Gdns, NW11 . . . . . . .63 CY58
Romford RM1 . . . . .51 FD54
Sutton SM2 . . . . .158 DA107
Waltham Abbey EN9 . . . . . .31 EC36
Heather Glen, Rom. RM1 . . . .51 FD54
Heatherlands, Sun. TW16 . . .115 BU93
Heather La, Wat. WD24 . . . . . .23 BT35
West Drayton UB7 . . . . . . .76 BL72
Heatherley Dr, Ilf. IG5 . . . . . .68 EL55
Heather Pk Dr, Wem. HA0 . . . .80 CN66
Heather Pl, Esher KT10
off Park Rd 154 CB105
Heather Ri, Bushey WD23 . . . .24 BZ40
Heather Rd, E4 . . . . .47 DZ51
NW2 . . . . .63 CT61
SE12 . . . . .124 EG89
Heathers, The, Stai. TW19 . . .114 BM87
Heatherset Cl, Esher KT10 . .154 CC106
Heatherset Gdns, SW16 . . . .121 DM94
Heatherside Dr, Vir.W. GU25 .132 AU100
Heatherside Rd, Epsom
KT19 . . . . .156 CR108
Sidcup DA14 off Wren Rd .126 EX90
Heatherton Ter, N3 . . . . .44 DB54
Heathervale Caravan Pk, Add.
(New Haw) KT15 . . . . . . .152 BJ110
Heathervale Rd, Add.
(New Haw) KT15 . . . . . . .152 BH110
Heather Wk, W10
off Droop St 81 CY70
Edgware HA8 . . . . .42 CP50
Twickenham TW2
off Stephenson Rd 116 CA87
Walton-on-Thames (Whiteley Vill.)
KT12 off Octagon Rd 153 BT110
Heather Way, Pot.B. EN6 . . . .11 CZ32
Romford RM1 . . . . .51 FD54
South Croydon CR2 . . . . . .161 DX109
Stanmore HA7 . . . . .41 CF51
Woking (Chobham) GU24 .150 AS108
Heatherwood Cl, E12 . . . . . . .68 EJ61
Heatherwood Dr, Hayes UB4
off Charville La 77 BR68
Heath Fm Ct, Wat. WD17
off Grove Mill La 23 BR37
Heathfield, E4 . . . . .47 EC48
Chislehurst BR7 . . . . .125 EQ93
Cobham KT11 . . . . .154 CA114
Heathfield Av, SW18
off Heathfield Rd 120 DD87
South Croydon CR2 . . . . .161 DY109
Heathfield Cl, E16 . . . . .86 EK71
Keston BR2 . . . . .162 EJ106
Potters Bar EN6 . . . . .12 DB30
Watford WD19 . . . . .40 BW45
Woking GU22 . . . . .167 BA118
Heathfield Dr, Mitch. CR4 . . .140 DE95
Heathfield Gdns, NW11 . . . . .63 CX58
SE3 . . . . .104 EE82
SW18 . . . . .120 DD86
W4 . . . . .98 CQ78
Croydon CR0
off Coombe Rd 160 DR105
Heathfield La, Chis. BR7 . . . .125 EP93
Heathfield N, Twick. TW2 . . . .117 CF87
Heathfield Pk, NW2 . . . . .81 CW65
Heathfield Pk Dr, Rom.
(Chad.Hth) RM6 . . . . .70 EV57
Heathfield Ri, Ruis. HA4 . . . . .59 BQ59
Heathfield Rd, SW18 . . . . . . .120 DC86
W3 . . . . .98 CP75
Bexleyheath DA6 . . . . .106 EZ84
Bromley BR1 . . . . .124 EF94
Bushey WD23 . . . . .24 BY42
Croydon CR0 . . . . .160 DR105
Keston BR2 . . . . .162 EJ106
Sevenoaks TN13 . . . . .190 FF122
Walton-on-Thames KT12 .154 BY105
Woking GU22 . . . . .167 BA118
Heathfields Cl, Ashtd. KT21 .171 CJ118
Heathfields Ct, Houns. TW4
off Heathlands Way 116 BY85
Heathfield S, Twick. TW2 . . . .117 CF87
Heathfield Sq, SW18 . . . . . . .120 DD87
Heathfield St, W11
off Portland Rd 81 CY73
Heathfield Ter, SE18 . . . . . . .105 ET79
W4 . . . . .98 CQ78
Heathfield Vale, S.Croy. CR2 .161 DX109
Heath Gdns, Twick. TW1 . . . .117 CF88
Heathgate, NW11 . . . . .64 DB58
Heathgate Pl, NW3
off Agincourt Rd 64 DF64
Heath Gro, SE20
off Maple Rd 122 DW94
Sunbury-on-Thames TW16 .115 BT94
Heath Hurst Rd, NW3 . . . . . . .64 DE63
Heathhurst Rd, S.Croy. CR2 .160 DS109
Heathland Rd, N16 . . . . .66 DS60
Heathlands, Tad. KT20 . . . . . .173 CX122
Heathlands Cl, Sun. TW16 . . .135 BU96
Twickenham TW1 . . . . .117 CF89
Woking GU21 . . . . .150 AY114
Heathlands Ri, Dart. DA1 . . . .127 FH86
Heathlands Way, Houns.
TW4 . . . . .116 BY85
Heath La, SE3 . . . . .103 ED82
Dartford (Lower) DA1 . . . .128 FJ88
Dartford (Upper) DA1 . . . .127 FG89
Heathlee Rd, SE3 . . . . .104 EF84
Dartford DA1 . . . . .127 FE86
Heathley End, Chis. BR7 . . . .125 EQ93
Heathmans Rd, SW6 . . . . .99 CZ81
Heath Mead, SW19 . . . . .119 CX90
Heath Ms, Wok. (Ripley)
GU23 . . . . .168 BH123
Heath Pk Ct, Rom. RM2
off Heath Pk Rd 71 FG57
Heath Pk Dr, Brom. BR1 . . . .144 EL97
Heath Pk Rd, Rom. RM2 . . . . .71 FG57
Heath Pas, NW3 . . . . .64 DB61
Heath Ridge Grn, Cob. KT11 .154 CA113
Heath Ri, SW15 . . . . .119 CX86
Bromley BR2 . . . . .144 EF100
Virginia Water GU25 . . . . .132 AX98
Woking (Ripley) GU23 . . . .168 BH123
Heath Rd, SW8 . . . . .101 DH82
Bexley DA5 . . . . .127 FC88
Caterham CR3 . . . . .176 DR123
Dartford DA1 . . . . .127 FF86
Grays RM16 . . . . .111 GG75
Harrow HA1 . . . . .60 CC59
Hounslow TW3 . . . . .96 CB84
Leatherhead (Oxshott)
KT22 . . . . .154 CC112
Potters Bar EN6 . . . . .12 DA30
Romford RM6 . . . . .70 EX59
Thornton Heath CR7 . . . . .142 DQ97
Twickenham TW1, TW2 . . .117 CF88
Uxbridge UB10 . . . . .77 BQ70
Watford WD19 . . . . .40 BX45
Weybridge KT13 . . . . .152 BN106
Woking GU21 . . . . .167 AZ115
★ Heathrow Airport (London),
Houns. TW6 . . . . .95 BP81
Heathrow Cl, West Dr. UB7 . . .94 BH81
Heathrow Ho, Houns. TW5
off Bath Rd 95 BU81
Heathrow Interchange,
Hayes UB4 . . . . .78 BW74
Heathrow Int Trd Est,
Houns. TW4 . . . . .95 BV83
⇌ Heathrow Terminal 4 . . . .115 BP85
⊖ Heathrow Terminal 4 . . . .115 BP85
⇌ Heathrow Terminals 1,2,3 .95 BP83
⊖ Heathrow Terminals 1,2,3 .95 BP83
Heathrow Tunnel App, Houns.
(Hthrw Air.) TW6 . . . . .95 BP83
Heathrow Vehicle Tunnel, Houns.
(Hthrw Air.) TW6 . . . . .95 BP81
Heaths Cl, Enf. EN1 . . . . .30 DS40
Heath Side, NW3 . . . . .64 DD63
Heathside, Esher KT10 . . . . .137 CE104
Hounslow TW4 . . . . .116 BZ87
Heath Side, Orp. BR5 . . . . . .145 EQ102
Heathside, Wey. KT13 . . . . . .153 BP106
Heathside Av, Bexh. DA7 . . .106 EY81
Heathside Cl, Esher KT10 . . .137 CE104
Ilford IG2 . . . . .69 ER57
Northwood HA6 . . . . .39 BR50
Heathside Ct, Tad. KT20 . . . .173 CV123
Heathside Cres, Wok. GU22 .167 AZ117
Heathside Gdns, Wok. GU22 .167 BA117
Heathside Pk Rd, Wok. GU22 .167 AZ118
Heathside Pl, Epsom KT18 . .173 CX118
Heathside Rd, Nthwd. HA6 . . .39 BR49
Woking GU22 . . . . .167 AZ118
Heathstan Rd, W12 . . . . .81 CU72
Heath St, NW3 . . . . .64 DC62
Dartford DA1 . . . . .128 FK87
Heath Vw, N2 . . . . .64 DC56
Heathview Av, Dart. DA1 . . .127 FE86
Heath Vw Cl, N2 . . . . .64 DC56
Heathview Ct, SW19 . . . . . . .119 CX89
Heathview Cres, Dart. DA1 . .127 FG88
Heathview Dr, SE2 . . . . .106 EX79
Heathview Gdns, SW15 . . . .119 CW87
Heath Vw Gdns, Grays RM16 .110 GC75
Heath Vw Rd, Grays RM16 . .110 GC75
Heathview Rd, Th.Hth. CR7 . .141 DN98
Heath Vil, SE18 . . . . .105 ET78
SW18 off Cargill Rd 120 DC88
Heathville Rd, N19 . . . . .65 DL59
Heathwall St, SW11 . . . . . . .100 DF83
Heathway, SE3 . . . . .104 EF80

★ Place of interest ⇌ Railway station ⊖ London Underground station DLR Docklands Light Railway station Tra Tramlink station H Hospital Riv Pedestrian ferry landing stage

Heathway, Cat. (Chaldon) CR3 186 DQ125
Croydon CR0 143 DZ104
Dagenham RM9, RM10 88 FA66
Heath Way, Erith DA8 107 FC81
Heathway, Iver SL0 75 BD68
Leatherhead (E.Hors.) KT24 169 BT124
Woodford Green IG8 48 EJ49
Heathway Ind Est, Dag. RM10 off Manchester Way 71 FB63
Heathwood Gdns, SE7 104 EL77
Swanley BR8 147 FC96
Heathwood Pt, SE23 off Dacres Rd 123 DX90
Heathwood Wk, Bex. DA5 127 FE88
Heaton Av, Rom. RM3 51 FH52
Heaton Cl, E4 47 EC48
Romford RM3 52 FJ52
Heaton Ct, Wal.Cr. (Chsht) EN8 15 DX29
Heaton Gra Rd, Rom. RM2 51 FF54
Heaton Rd, SE15 102 DU83
Mitcham CR4 120 DG94
Heaton Way, Rom. RM3 52 FJ52
Heaven Tree Cl, N1 66 DQ64
Heaver Rd, SW11 off Wye St 100 DD83
Heavitree Cl, SE18 105 ER78
Heavitree Rd, SE18 105 ER78
Hebden Ct, E2 off Laburnum St 84 DT67
Hebden Ter, N17 off Commercial Rd 46 DS51
Hebdon Rd, SW17 120 DE90
Heber Rd, NW2 63 CX64
SE22 122 DT86
Hebron Rd, W6 99 CV76
Hecham Cl, E17 47 DY54
Heckets Ct, Esher KT10 154 CC111
Heckfield Pl, SW6 off Fulham Rd 100 DA80
Heckford Cl, Wat. WD18 23 BQ44
Heckford St, E1 off The Highway 85 DX73
Hector St, SE18 105 ES77
Heddington Gro, N7 65 DM64
Heddon Cl, Islw. TW7 97 CG84
Heddon Ct Av, Barn. EN4 28 DF43
Heddon Ct Par, Barn. EN4 off Cockfosters Rd 28 DG43
Heddon Rd, Barn. EN4 28 DF43
Heddon St, W1 195 K10
Hedge Hill, Enf. EN2 29 DP39
Hedge La, N13 45 DP48
Hedgeley, Ilf. IG4 69 EM56
Hedgemans Rd, Dag. RM9 88 EX66
Hedgemans Way, Dag. RM9 88 EY65
Hedge Pl Rd, Green. DA9 129 FT86
Hedgerley Ct, Wok. GU21 166 AW117
Hedgerley Gdns, Grnf. UB6 78 CC68
Hedgerley Grn, Slou. (Hedg.) SL2 56 AT58
Hedgerley La, Ger.Cr. SL9 56 AV59
Slough SL2 56 AS58
Hedgerow, Ger.Cr. (Chal.St.P.) SL9 36 AY51
Hedgerow La, Barn. EN5 27 CV43
Hedgerows, The, Grav. (Nthflt) DA11 130 GE89
Hedgerow Wk, Wal.Cr. EN8 15 DX30
Hedgers Cl, Loug. IG10 off Newmans La 33 EN42
Hedgers Gro, E9 85 DY65
Hedger St, SE11 200 F8
Hedgeside Rd, Nthwd. HA6 39 BQ50
Hedge Wk, SE6 123 EB91
Hedgewood Gdns, Ilf. IG5 69 EN57
Hedgley Ms, SE12 off Hedgley St 124 EF85
Hedgley St, SE12 124 EF85
Hedingham Cl, N1 off Popham Rd 84 DQ66
Hedingham Ho, Kings.T. KT2 off Kingsgate Rd 138 CL95
Hedingham Rd, Dag. RM8 70 EV64
Grays (Chaff.Hun.) RM16 109 FW78
Hornchurch RM11 72 FN60
Hedley Av, Grays RM20 109 FW80
Hedley Cl, Rom. RM1 off High St 71 FE57
Hedley Rd, Twick. TW2 116 CA87
Hedley Row, N5 off Poets Rd 66 DR64
Hedworth Av, Wal.Cr. EN8 15 DX33
Heenan Cl, Bark. IG11 off Glenny Rd 87 EQ65
Heene Rd, Enf. EN2 30 DR39
Heideck Gdns, Brwd. (Hutt.) CM13 off Victors Cres 55 GB47
Heidegger Cres, SW13 off Wyatt Dr 99 CV80
Heigham Rd, E6 86 EK66
Heighton Gdns, Croy. CR0 159 DP106
Heights, The, SE7 104 EJ78
Beckenham BR3 123 EC94
Loughton IG10 33 EM40
Northolt UB5 60 BZ64
Waltham Abbey (Nazeing) EN9 16 EH25
Weybridge KT13 152 BN110
Heights Cl, SW20 119 CV94
Banstead SM7 173 CY116
★ Heinz Gall, R.I.B.A., W1 194 F8
Heiron St, SE17 101 DP79
Helby Rd, SW4 121 DK86
Helder Gro, SE12 124 EF87
Helder St, S.Croy. CR2 160 DR107
Heldmann Cl, Houns. TW3 97 CD84
Helegan Cl, Orp. BR6 163 ET105
Helena Cl, Barn. EN4 28 DD38
Helena Pl, E9 off Fremont St 84 DW67
Helena Rd, E13 86 EF68
E17 67 EA57
NW10 63 CV64
W5 79 CK71
Helena Sq, SE16 203 K1
Helen Av, Felt. TW14 115 BV87
Helen Cl, N2 off Thomas More Way 64 DC55
Helen Cl, Dart. DA1 127 FH87
West Molesey KT8 136 CB98
Helen Rd, Horn. RM11 72 FK55
Helens Gate, Wal.Cr. EN8 15 DZ26
Helenslea Av, NW11 63 CZ60
Helen's Pl, E2 off Roman Rd 84 DW69
Helen St, SE18 off Wilmount St 105 EP77
Helford Cl, Ruis. HA4 off Chichester Av 59 BS61
Helford Wk, Wok. GU21 166 AU118
Helford Way, Upmin. RM14 73 FR58
Helgiford Gdns, Sun. TW16 115 BS94
Helios Rd, Wall. SM6 140 DG102
Helix Gdns, SW2 off Helix Rd 121 DM86
Helix Rd, SW2 121 DM86
Helleborine, Grays (Bad.Dene) RM17 110 FZ78
Hellen Way, Wat. WD19 40 BW49
Hellings St, E1 202 C3
Helm Cl, Epsom KT19 156 CN112
Helme Cl, SW19 119 CZ92
Helmet Row, EC1 197 J4
Helmore Rd, Bark. IG11 87 ET66
Helmsdale, Wok. GU21 off Winnington Way 166 AV118
Helmsdale Cl, Hayes UB4 78 BY70
Romford RM1 51 FE52
Helmsdale Rd, SW16 141 DJ95
Romford RM1 51 FE52
Helmsley Pl, E8 84 DV66
Helperby Rd, NW10 80 CS66
Helsinki Sq, SE16 203 L6
Helston Cl, Pnr. HA5 40 BZ52
Helston Pl, Abb.L. WD5 off Shirley Rd 7 BT32
Helvellyn Cl, Egh. TW20 113 BB94
Helvetia St, SE6 123 DZ89
Hemans St, SW8 101 DK80
Hemberton Rd, SW9 101 DL83
Hemery Rd, Grnf. UB6 61 CD64
Hemingford Cl, N12 44 DD50
Hemingford Rd, N1 83 DM67
Sutton SM3 157 CW105
Watford WD17 23 BS36
Heming Rd, Edg. HA8 42 CP52
Hemington Av, N11 44 DF50
Hemingway Cl, NW5 off Oak Village 64 DG63
Hemlock Cl, Tad. (Kgswd) KT20 173 CY123
Hemlock Rd, W12 81 CT73
Hemmen La, Hayes UB3 77 BT72
Hemming Cl, Hmptn. TW12 off Chandler Cl 136 CA95
Hemmings Cl, Sid. DA14 126 EV89
Hemmings Mead, Epsom KT19 156 CP107
Hemming St, E1 84 DU70
Hemming Way, Wat. WD25 23 BU35
Hemnall St, Epp. CM16 17 ET31
Hempshaw Av, Bans. SM7 174 DF116
Hempson Av, Slou. SL3 92 AW76
Hempstead Cl, Buck.H. IG9 48 EG47
Hempstead Rd, E17 47 ED54
Hemel Hempstead (Bov.) HP3 5 BA27
Kings Langley WD4 6 BM26
Watford WD17 23 BT39
Hemp Wk, SE17 201 L8
Hemsby Rd, Chess. KT9 156 CM107
Hemstal Rd, NW6 82 DA66
Hemsted Rd, Erith DA8 107 FE80
Hemswell Dr, NW9 42 CS53
Hemsworth Ct, N1 off Hemsworth St 84 DS68
Hemsworth St, N1 84 DS68
Hemus Pl, SW3 off Chelsea Manor St 100 DE78
Hen & Chicken Ct, EC4 off Fleet St 83 DN72
Henbane Path, Rom. RM3 off Clematis Cl 52 FK52
Henbit Cl, Tad. KT20 173 CV119
Henbury Way, Wat. WD19 40 BX48
Henchman St, W12 81 CT72
Hencroft St N, Slou. SL1 92 AT75
Hencroft St S, Slou. SL1 92 AT76
Hendale Av, NW4 63 CU55
Henderson Cl, NW10 80 CQ65
Hornchurch RM11 71 FH61
Henderson Dr, NW8 off Cunningham Pl 82 DD70
Dartford DA1 108 FM84
H Henderson Hosp, Sutt. SM2 158 DB109
Henderson Pl, Abb.L. (Bedmond) WD5 7 BT27
Henderson Rd, E7 86 EJ65
N9 46 DV46
SW18 120 DE87
Croydon CR0 142 DR100
Hayes UB4 77 BU69
Westerham (Bigg.H.) TN16 162 EJ112
Hendham Rd, SW17 120 DE89
HENDON, NW4 63 CV56
⇌ Hendon 63 CU58
Hendon Av, N3 43 CY53
⊖ Hendon Central 63 CW57
Hendon Gdns, Rom. RM5 51 FC51
Hendon Gro, Epsom KT19 156 CN109
Hendon Hall Ct, NW4 off Parson St 63 CX55
Hendon La, N3 63 CY55
Hendon Pk Row, NW11 63 CZ58
Hendon Rd, N9 46 DU47
Hendon Way, NW2 63 CZ62
NW4 63 CV58
Staines (Stanw.) TW19 114 BK86
Hendon Wd La, NW7 27 CT44
Hendren Cl, Grnf. UB6 off Dimmock Dr 61 CD64
Hendre Rd, SE1 201 N9
Hendrick Av, SW12 120 DF86
Heneage Cres, Croy. (New Adgtn) CR0 161 EC110
Heneage La, EC3 197 N9
Heneage St, E1 84 DT71
Henfield Cl, N19 65 DJ60
Bexley DA5 126 FA86
Henfield Rd, SW19 139 CZ95
Hengelo Gdns, Mitch. CR4 140 DD98
Hengist Rd, SE12 124 EH87
Erith DA8 107 FB80
Hengist Way, Brom. BR2 144 EE98
Hengrave Rd, SE23 123 DX87
Hengrove Ct, Bex. DA5 off Hurst Rd 126 EY88
Hengrove Cres, Ashf. TW15 114 BK90
Henhurst Rd, Grav. (Cobham) DA12 131 GK94
Henley Av, Sutt. SM3 139 CY104
Henley Cl, SE16 off St. Marychurch St 102 DW75
Greenford UB6 78 CC68
Isleworth TW7 97 CF81
Henley Ct, N14 45 DJ45
Woking GU22 167 BB120
Henley Cross, SE3 104 EH83
Henley Deane, Grav. (Nthflt) DA11 130 GE91
Henley Dr, SE1 202 A8
Kingston upon Thames KT2 119 CT94
Henley Gdns, Pnr. HA5 59 BV55
Romford RM6 70 EY57
Henley Prior, N1 off Collier St 83 DM68
Henley Rd, E16 105 EM75
N18 46 DS49
NW10 81 CW67
Ilford IG1 69 EQ63
Henley St, SW11 100 DG82
Henley Way, Felt. TW13 116 BX92
Henlow Pl, Rich. TW10 off Sandpits Rd 117 CK89
Hennel Cl, SE23 122 DW90
Hennessy Ct, Wok. GU21 151 BC113
Hennessy Rd, N9 46 DW47
Henniker Gdns, E6 86 EK69
Henniker Ms, SW3 off Callow St 100 DD79
Henniker Pt, E15 67 ED64
Henniker Rd, E15 67 ED64
Henningham Rd, N17 46 DR53
Henning St, SW11 100 DE81
Henrietta Cl, SE8 103 EA79
Henrietta Ms, WC1 196 A4
Henrietta Pl, W1 195 H9
Henrietta St, E15 67 EC64
WC2 196 A10
Henriques St, E1 84 DU72
Henry Addlington Cl, E6 87 EP71
Henry Cl, Enf. EN2 30 DS38
Henry Cooper Way, SE9 124 EK90
Henry Darlot Dr, NW7 43 CX50
Henry De Gray Cl, Grays RM17 110 FZ77
Henry Dent Cl, SE5 102 DR83
Henry Dickens Ct, W11 81 CX74
Henry Doulton Dr, SW17 121 DH91
Henry Jackson Rd, SW15 99 CX83
Henry Macaulay Av, Kings.T. KT2 137 CK95
Henry Rd, E6 86 EL68
N4 66 DQ60
Barnet EN4 28 DD43
Henry's Av, Wdf.Grn. IG8 48 EF50
Henryson Rd, SE4 123 EA85
Henry St, Brom. BR1 144 EH95
Grays RM17 off East Thurrock Rd 110 GC79
Henry's Wk, Ilf. IG6 49 ER52
Henry Tate Ms, SW16 121 DN92
Henry Wise Ho, SW1 off Vauxhall Br Rd 101 DJ77
Hensford Gdns, SE26 off Wells Pk Rd 122 DV91
Henshall Pt, E3 off Bromley High St 85 EB69
Henshall St, N1 84 DR65
Henshawe Rd, Dag. RM8 70 EX62
Henshaw St, SE17 201 K8
Hensley Pt, E9 off Wick Rd 85 DX65
Henslowe Rd, SE22 122 DU85
Henslow Way, Wok. GU21 151 BD114
Henson Av, NW2 63 CW64
Henson Cl, Orp. BR6 145 EP103
Henson Path, Har. HA3 61 CK55
Henson Pl, Nthlt. UB5 78 BW67
Henstridge Pl, NW8 82 DE68
Hensworth Rd, Ashf. TW15 114 BK93
Henty Cl, SW11 100 DE80
Henty Wk, SW15 119 CV85
Henville Rd, Brom. BR1 144 EH95
Henwick Rd, SE9 104 EK83
Henwood Side, Wdf.Grn. IG8 off Love La 49 EM51
Hepburn Cl, Grays (Chaff.Hun.) RM16 109 FX77
Hepburn Gdns, Brom. BR2 144 EE102
Hepburn Ms, SW11 off Webbs Rd 120 DF85
Hepple Cl, Islw. TW7 97 CH82
Hepplestone Cl, SW15 119 CV86
Hepscott Rd, E9 85 EA66
Hepworth Ct, SW1 off Gatliff Rd 101 DH78
Barking IG11 70 EU64
Hepworth Gdns, Bark. IG11 70 EU64
Hepworth Rd, SW16 121 DL94
Hepworth Wk, NW3 off Haverstock Hill 64 DE64
Hepworth Way, Walt. KT12 135 BT102
Heracles Cl, Wall. SM6 159 DL108
Herald Gdns, Wall. SM6 141 DH104
Herald's Pl, SE11 200 F8
Herald St, E2 off Three Colts La 84 DV70
Herald Wk, Dart. DA1 off Temple Hill Sq 128 FM85
Herbal Hill, EC1 196 E5
Herbert Cres, SW1 198 E6
Woking (Knap.) GU21 166 AS118
Herbert Gdns, NW10 81 CV68
W4 off Magnolia Rd 98 CP79
Romford RM6 70 EX59
St. Albans AL2 8 CB29
Herbert Ms, SW2 off Bascombe St 121 DN86
Herbert Morrison Ho, SW6 off Clem Attlee Ct 99 CZ79
Herbert Pl, SE18 off Plumstead Common Rd 105 EP79
Herbert Rd, E12 68 EL63
Herbert Rd, E17 67 DZ59
N11 45 DL52
N15 66 DT57
NW9 63 CU58
SE18 105 EN80
SW19 119 CZ94
Bexleyheath DA7 106 EY82
Bromley BR2 144 EK99
Hornchurch RM11 72 FL59
Ilford IG3 69 ES61
Kingston upon Thames KT1 138 CM97
Southall UB1 78 BZ74
Swanley BR8 127 FH93
Swanscombe DA10 130 FZ86
Herbert St, E13 86 EG68
NW5 82 DG65
Herbert Ter, SE18 off Herbert Rd 105 EP79
Herbrand St, WC1 195 P4
Hercies Rd, Uxb. UB10 76 BM66
Hercules Pl, N7 off Hercules St 65 DL62
Hercules Rd, SE1 200 C7
Hercules St, N7 65 DL62
Hercules Way, Wat. (Lvsdn) WD25 7 BT34
Hereford Av, Barn. EN4 44 DF46
Hereford Cl, Epsom KT18 156 CR113
Staines TW18 134 BH95
Hereford Copse, Wok. GU22 166 AV119
Hereford Ct, Sutt. SM2 off Worcester Rd 158 DA108
Hereford Gdns, SE13 off Longhurst Rd 124 EE85
Ilford IG1 68 EL59
Pinner HA5 60 BY57
Twickenham TW2 116 CC88
Hereford Ho, NW6 82 DA68
Hereford Ms, W2 off Hereford Rd 82 DA72
Hereford Pl, SE14 off Royal Naval Pl 103 DZ80
Hereford Retreat, SE15 off Bird in Bush Rd 102 DU80
Hereford Rd, E3 off Ordell Rd 85 DZ68
E11 68 EH57
W2 82 DA72
W3 80 CP73
W5 97 CJ76
Feltham TW13 116 BW88
Hereford Sq, SW7 100 DC77
Hereford St, E2 84 DU70
Hereford Way, Chess. KT9 155 CJ106
Herent Dr, Ilf. IG5 68 EL56
Hereward Av, Pur. CR8 159 DN111
Hereward Cl, Wal.Abb. EN9 15 ED32
Hereward Gdns, N13 45 DN50
Hereward Grn, Loug. IG10 33 EQ39
Hereward Rd, SW17 120 DF91
Herga Ct, Har. HA1 61 CE62
Watford WD17 23 BU40
Herga Rd, Har. HA3 61 CF56
Herington Gro, Brwd. (Hutt.) CM13 55 GA45
Heriot Av, E4 47 EA47
Heriot Rd, NW4 63 CW57
Chertsey KT16 134 BG101
Heriots Cl, Stan. HA7 41 CG49
Heritage Cl, SW9 101 DP83
Uxbridge UB8 76 BJ70
Heritage Hill, Kes. BR2 162 EJ106
Heritage Pl, SW18 off Earlsfield Rd 120 DC88
Heritage Vw, Har. HA1 61 CF62
Heritage Wk, Rick. (Chorl.) WD3 off Chenies Rd 21 BE41
Herkomer Cl, Bushey WD23 24 CB44
Herkomer Rd, Bushey WD23 24 CA43
Herlwyn Av, Ruis. HA4 59 BS62
Herlwyn Gdns, SW17 120 DF91
Hermes Cl, W9 off Chippenham Rd 82 DA70
Hermes St, N1 196 D1
Hermes Wk, Nthlt. UB5 off Hotspur Rd 78 CA68
Hermes Way, Wall. SM6 159 DK108
Herm Ho, Enf. EN3 off Eastfield Rd 31 DX38
Hermiston Av, N8 65 DL57
Hermitage, The, SE23 122 DW88
SW13 99 CT81
Feltham TW13 115 BT90
Richmond TW10 117 CK85
Uxbridge UB8 76 BL65
Hermitage Cl, E18 68 EF56
SE2 off Felixstowe Rd 106 EW76
Enfield EN2 29 DP40
Esher (Clay.) KT10 155 CG107
Shepperton TW17 134 BN98
Slough SL3 92 AW76
Hermitage Ct, E18 68 EG56
NW2 off Hermitage La 64 DA62
Potters Bar EN6 off Southgate Rd 12 DC33
Hermitage Gdns, NW2 64 DA62
SE19 122 DQ93
Hermitage La, N18 46 DR50
NW2 64 DA62
SE25 142 DU100
SW16 121 DM94
Croydon CR0 142 DU100
Hermitage Path, SW16 141 DL95
Hermitage Rd, N4 65 DP59
N15 65 DP59
SE19 122 DQ94
Kenley CR8 176 DQ116
Woking GU21 166 AT119
Hermitage Row, E8 66 DU64
Hermitage St, W2 82 DD71
Hermitage Wk, E18 68 EF56
Hermitage Wall, E1 202 C3
Hermitage Waterside, E1 202 B2
Hermitage Way, Stan. HA7 41 CG53
Hermitage Wds Cres, Wok. GU21 166 AS119
Hermit Pl, NW6 off Belsize Rd 82 DB67
Hermit Rd, E16 86 EF71
Hermit St, EC1 196 F2
Hermon Gro, Hayes UB3 77 BU74
Hermon Hill, E11 68 EG57
Hermon Hill, E18 68 EG57
Herndon Cl, Egh. TW20 113 BA91
Herndon Rd, SW18 120 DC85
Herne Cl, NW10 off North Circular Rd 62 CR64
Hayes UB3 77 BT72
HERNE HILL, SE24 122 DQ85
⇌ Herne Hill 121 DP86
Herne Hill, SE24 122 DQ86
Herne Hill Ho, SE24 off Railton Rd 121 DP86
Herne Hill Rd, SE24 102 DQ83
Herne Ms, N18 off Lyndhurst Rd 46 DU49
Herne Pl, SE24 121 DP85
Herne Rd, Bushey WD23 24 CB44
Surbiton KT6 137 CK103
Hernes Cl, Stai. TW18 off Staines Rd 134 BH95
Heron Cl, E17 47 DZ54
NW10 80 CS65
Buckhurst Hill IG9 48 EG46
Hemel Hempstead HP3 6 BM25
Rickmansworth WD3 38 BK47
Sutton SM1 off Sandpiper Rd 157 CZ106
Uxbridge UB8 76 BK65
Heron Ct, Brom. BR2 144 EJ98
Heron Cres, Sid. DA14 125 ES90
Heron Dale, Add. KT15 152 BK106
Herondale, S.Croy. CR2 161 DX109
Herondale Av, SW18 120 DD88
Heron Dr, N4 66 DQ61
Slough SL3 93 BB77
Heronfield, Egh. (Eng.Grn) TW20 112 AV93
Potters Bar EN6 12 DC30
Heron Flight Av, Horn. RM12 89 FG66
Herongate Rd, E12 68 EJ61
Swanley BR8 127 FE93
Waltham Cross (Chsht) EN8 15 DY27
Heron Hill, Belv. DA17 106 EZ77
Heron Ms, Ilf. IG1 off Balfour Rd 69 EP61
Heron Pl, SE16 203 L2
Uxbridge (Hare.) UB9 38 BG51
Heron Quay, E14 203 P3
DLR Heron Quays 204 A3
Heron Rd, SE24 102 DQ84
Croydon CR0 off Tunstall Rd 142 DS103
Twickenham TW1 97 CG84
Heronry, The, Walt. KT12 153 BU107
Herons, The, E11 68 EF58
Herons Cft, Wey. KT13 153 BR107
Heronsforde, W13 79 CJ72
HERONSGATE, Rick. WD3 37 BD45
Heronsgate, Edg. HA8 42 CN50
Heronsgate Rd, Rick. (Chorl.) WD3 21 BB44
Heronslea, Wat. WD25 24 BW36
Heronslea Dr, Stan. HA7 42 CL50
Heron's Pl, Islw. TW7 97 CH83
Heron Sq, Rich. TW9 off Bridge St 117 CK85
Herons Ri, Barn. EN4 28 DE42
Heronswood, Wal.Abb. EN9 off Roundhills 16 EE34
Heron Trd Est, W3 off Alliance Rd 80 CP70
Heron Wk, Nthwd. HA6 39 BS49
Woking GU21 off Blackmore Cres 151 BC114
Heronway, Brwd. (Hutt.) CM13 55 GA46
Heron Way, Felt. TW14 95 BU84
Grays RM20 109 FV78
Upminster RM14 73 FS60
Heronway, Wdf.Grn. IG8 48 EJ49
Herrick Rd, N5 66 DQ62
Herrick St, SW1 199 N8
Herries St, W10 81 CY68
Herringham Rd, SE7 104 EJ76
Herrings La, Cher. KT16 134 BG100
Herrongate Cl, Enf. EN1 30 DT40
Hersant Cl, NW10 81 CU67
Herschell Ms, SE5 off Bicknell Rd 102 DQ83
Herschell Rd, SE23 123 DY87
Herschel Pk Dr, Slou. SL1 92 AT75
Herschel St, Slou. SL1 92 AT75
HERSHAM, Walt. KT12 154 BX107
⇌ Hersham 136 BY104
Hersham Bypass, Walt. KT12 153 BV106
Hersham Cen, The, Walt. KT12 154 BX106
Hersham Cl, SW15 119 CU87
Hersham Gdns, Walt. KT12 154 BW105
Hersham Rd, Walt. KT12 154 BW105
Hertford Av, SW14 118 CR85
Hertford Cl, Barn. EN4 28 DD41
Hertford Ct, N13 off Green Las 45 DN48
Hertford Pl, W1 195 K5
Hertford Rd, N1 84 DS67
N2 64 DE55
N9 46 DV47
Barking IG11 87 EP66
Barnet EN4 28 DC41
Enfield EN3 30 DW41
Ilford IG2 69 ES58
Waltham Cross EN8 31 DX37
Hertford Sq, Mitch. CR4 off Hertford Way 141 DL98
Hertford St, W1 199 H2
Hertford Wk, Belv. DA17 off Hoddesdon Rd 106 FA78
Hertford Way, Mitch. CR4 141 DL98
Hertslet Rd, N7 65 DM62
Hertsmere Ind Pk, Borwd. WD6 26 CR41
Hertsmere Rd, E14 203 P1
Hervey Cl, N3 44 DA53
Hervey Pk Rd, E17 67 DY56
Hervey Rd, SE3 104 EH81
Hesa Rd, Hayes UB3 77 BU72
Hesewall Cl, SW4 off Brayburne Av 101 DJ82
Hesiers Hill, Warl. CR6 178 EE117
Hesiers Rd, Warl. CR6 178 EE117
Hesketh Av, Dart. DA2 128 FP88
Hesketh Pl, W11 81 CY73
Hesketh Rd, E7 68 EG62

★ Place of interest · ⇌ Railway station · ⊖ London Underground station · DLR Docklands Light Railway station · Tra Tramlink station · H Hospital · Riv Pedestrian ferry landing stage

Heslop Rd, SW12 .120 DF88
Hesper Ms, SW5 .100 DB78
Hesperus Cres, E14 .204 B9
Hessel Rd, W13 .97 CG75
Hessel St, E1 .84 DV72
Hesselyn Dr, Rain. RM13 .89 FH66
Hessle Gro, Epsom KT17 .157 CT111
Hestercombe Av, SW6 .99 CY82
Hesterman Way, Croy. CR0 .141 DL102
Hester Rd, N18 .46 DU50
SW11 .100 DE80
Hester Ter, Rich. TW9
off Chilton Rd .98 CN83
Hestia Ho, SE1 *off Long La* .102 DS75
HESTON, Houns. TW5 .96 BZ80
Heston Av, Houns. TW5 .96 BY80
Heston Gra La, Houns. TW5 .96 BZ79
Heston Ind Mall, Houns. TW5 .96 BZ80
Heston Rd, Houns. TW5 .96 CA80
Heston St, SE14 .103 DZ81
Heswell Grn, Wat. WD19
off Fairhaven Cres .39 BU48
Hetherington Rd, SW4 .101 DL84
Shepperton TW17 .135 BQ96
Hetherington Way, Uxb. UB10 .58 BL63
Hethersett Cl, Reig. RH2 .184 DC131
Hetley Gdns, SE19 .122 DT94
Hetley Rd, W12 .81 CV74
Heton Gdns, NW4 .63 CU56
Heusden Way, Ger.Cr. SL9 .57 AZ60
Hevelius Cl, SE10 .205 K10
Hever Ct Rd, Grav. DA12 .131 GH93
Hever Cft, SE9 .125 EN91
Hever Gdns, Brom. BR1 .145 EN97
Heverham Rd, SE18 .105 ES77
Heversham Rd, Bexh. DA7 .106 FA82
Hevingham Dr, Rom. RM3 .70 EW57
Hewens Rd, Hayes UB4 .77 BQ70
Uxbridge UB10 .77 BQ70
Hewer St, W10 .81 CX71
Hewers Way, Tad. KT20 .173 CV120
Hewett Cl, Stan. HA7 .41 CH49
Hewett Pl, Swan. BR8 .147 FD98
Hewett Rd, Dag. RM8 .70 EX64
Hewetts Quay, Bark. IG11 .87 EP67
Hewett St, EC2 .197 N5
Hewins Cl, Wal.Abb. EN9
off Broomstick Hall Rd .16 EE33
Hewish Rd, N18 .46 DS49
Hewison St, E3 .85 DZ68
Hewitt Av, N22 .45 DP54
Hewitt Cl, Croy. CR0 .143 EA104
Hewitt Rd, N8 .65 DN57
Hewitts Rd, Orp. BR6 .164 EZ108
Hewlett Rd, E3 .85 DY68
Hexagon, The, N6 .64 DF60
Hexal Rd, SE6 .124 EE90
Hexham Gdns, Islw. TW7 .97 CG80
Hexham Rd, SE27 .122 DQ89
Barnet EN5 .28 DB42
Morden SM4 .140 DB102
HEXTABLE, Swan. BR8 .127 FG94
Hextalls La, Red. (Bletch.)
RH1 .186 DR128
Heybourne Rd, N17 .46 DV52
Heybridge Av, SW16 .121 DL94
Heybridge Dr, Ilf. IG6 .49 ER54
Heybridge Way, E10 .67 DY59
Heyford Av, SW8 .101 DL80
SW20 .139 CZ97
Heyford Rd, Mitch. CR4 .140 DE96
Radlett WD7 .25 CF37
Heyford Ter, SW8
off Heyford Av .101 DL80
Heygate St, SE17 .201 H9
Heylyn Sq, E3
off Malmesbury Rd .85 DZ69
Heymede, Lthd. KT22 .171 CJ123
Heynes Rd, Dag. RM8 .70 EW63
Heysham Dr, Wat. WD19 .40 BW50
Heysham La, NW3 .64 DB62
Heysham Rd, N15 .66 DR58
Heythorp Cl, Wok. GU21 .166 AT117
Heythorp St, SW18 .119 CZ88
Heythrop Dr, Uxb. (Ickhm)
UB10 .58 BM63
Heywood Av, NW9 .42 CS53
Heyworth Rd, E5 .66 DV63
E15 .68 EF64
Hibbert Av, Wat. WD24 .24 BX38
Hibbert Lo, Ger.Cr. (Chal.St.P.)
SL9 *off Gold Hill E* .36 AX54
Hibbert Rd, E17 .67 DZ59
Harrow HA3 .41 CF54
Hibbert St, SW11 .100 DC83
Hibberts Way, Ger.Cr. SL9
off North Pk .56 AY56
Hibbs Cl, Swan. BR8 .147 FD96
Hibernia Dr, Grav. DA12 .131 GM90
Hibernia Gdns, Houns. TW3 .96 CA84
Hibernia Pt, SE2
off Wolvercote Rd .106 EX75
Hibernia Rd, Houns. TW3 .96 CA84
Hibiscus Cl, Edg. HA8
off Campion Way .42 CQ49
Hichisson Rd, SE15 .122 DW85
Hickin Cl, SE7 .104 EK77
Hickin St, E14 .204 D6
Hickling Rd, Ilf. IG1 .69 EP64
Hickman Av, E4 .47 EC51
Hickman Cl, E16 .86 EK71
Hickman Rd, Rom. RM6 .70 EW59
Hickmans Cl, Gdse. RH9 .186 DW132
Hickmore Wk, SW4 .101 DJ83
Hickory Cl, N9 .46 DU45
Hicks Av, Grnf. UB6 .79 CD68
Hicks Cl, SW11 .100 DE83
Hicks St, SE8 .203 K10
Hidcote Cl, Wok. GU22 .167 BB116
Hidcote Gdns, SW20 .139 CV97
Hide, E6 *off Downings* .87 EN72
Hideaway, The, Abb.L. WD5 .7 BU31
Hide Pl, SW1 .199 M9
Hide Rd, Har. HA1 .61 CD56
Hides St, N7
off Sheringham Rd .83 DM65
Hide Twr, SW1 .199 M9
Higgins Rd, Wal.Cr. (Chsht)
EN7 .14 DR27
Higgins Wk, Hmptn. TW12
off Abbott Cl .116 BY93
High Acres, Abb.L. WD5 .7 BR32
Enfield EN2 *off Old Pk Vw* .29 DN41
HIGHAM HILL, E17 .47 DY54
Higham Hill Rd, E17 .47 DY54
Higham Pl, E17 .67 DY55
Higham Rd, N17 .66 DR55
Woodford Green IG8 .48 EG51
Highams Ct, E4 *off Friars Cl* .47 ED48
Highams Lo Business Cen,
E17 .67 DY55
HIGHAMS PARK, E4 .47 ED50
⇌ **Highams Park** .47 ED51
Highams Pk Ind Est, E4 .47 EC51
Higham Sta Av, E4 .47 EB51
Higham St, E17 .67 DY55
Higham Vw, Epp. (N.Wld Bas.)
CM16 .19 FB26
Highbanks Cl, Well. DA16 .106 EV80
Highbanks Rd, Pnr. HA5 .40 CB50
Highbank Way, N8 .65 DN58
HIGH BARNET, Barn. EN5 .27 CX40
⊖ **High Barnet** .28 DA42
Highbarns, Hem.H. HP3 .6 BN25
Highbarrow Cl, Pur. CR8 .159 DM110
Highbarrow Rd, Croy. CR0 .142 DU101
HIGH BEECH, Loug. IG10 .32 EG39
High Beech, S.Croy. CR2 .160 DS108
High Beeches, Bans. SM7 .157 CX114
Gerrards Cross SL9 .56 AX60
Orpington BR6 .164 EU107
Sidcup DA14 .126 EY92
Weybridge KT13 .153 BS107
High Beeches Cl, Pur. CR8 .159 DK110
High Beech Rd, Loug. IG10 .32 EK42
High Br, SE10 .103 ED78
Highbridge Ind Est, Uxb. UB8 .76 BJ66
Highbridge Rd, Bark. IG11 .87 EP67
Highbridge St, Wal.Abb. EN9 .15 EA33
High Br Wf, SE10 .103 ED78
Highbrook Rd, SE3 .104 EK83
High Broom Cres, W.Wick.
BR4 .143 EB101
HIGHBURY, N5 .65 DP64
⇌ **Highbury & Islington** .83 DP65
⊖ **Highbury & Islington** .83 DP65
Highbury Av, Th.Hth. CR7 .141 DN96
Highbury Cl, N.Mal. KT3 .138 CQ98
West Wickham BR4 .143 EB103
Highbury Cor, N5 .83 DN65
Highbury Cres, N5 .65 DN64
Highbury Est, N5 .66 DQ64
Highbury Gdns, Ilf. IG3 .69 ES61
Highbury Gra, N5 .65 DP63
Highbury Gro, N5 .83 DP65
Highbury Hill, N5 .65 DN62
Highbury Ms, N7
off Holloway Rd .83 DN65
Highbury New Pk, N5 .66 DQ64
Highbury Pk, N5 .65 DP62
Highbury Pl, N5 .83 DP65
Highbury Quad, N5 .66 DQ62
Highbury Rd, SW19 .119 CY92
Highbury Sq, N14
off Burleigh Gdns .45 DJ46
Highbury Sta Rd, N1 .83 DN65
Highbury Ter, N5 .65 DP64
Highbury Ter Ms, N5 .65 DP64
High Canons, Borwd. WD6 .26 CQ37
High Cedar Dr, SW20 .119 CV94
Highclere Cl, Ken. CR8 .176 DQ115
Highclere Rd, N.Mal. KT3 .138 CR97
Highclere St, SE26 .123 DY91
Highcliffe Dr, SW15 .119 CT86
Highcliffe Gdns, Ilf. IG4 .68 EL57
High Cl, Rick. WD3 .22 BJ43
Highcombe, SE7 .104 EH79
Highcombe Cl, SE9 .124 EK88
High Coombe Pl, Kings.T.
KT2 .118 CR94
Highcroft, NW9 .62 CR57
Highcroft Av, Wem. HA0 .80 CN67
Highcroft Ct, Lthd. (Bkhm)
KT23 .170 CA123
Highcroft Gdns, NW11 .63 CZ58
Highcroft Rd, N19 .65 DL59
Hemel Hempstead
(Felden) HP3 .6 BG25
High Cross, Wat. (Ald.) WD25 .25 CD37
High Cross Cen, N15 .66 DU56
High Cross Rd, N17 .66 DU55
Highcross Rd, Grav.
(Sthflt) DA13 .129 FX92
Highcross Way, SW15 .119 CU88
Highdaun Dr, SW16 .141 DM98
Highdown, Wor.Pk. KT4 .138 CS103
Highdown La, Sutt. SM2 .158 DB111
Highdown Rd, SW15 .119 CV86
High Dr, Cat. (Wold.) CR3 .177 DZ122
Leatherhead (Oxshott)
KT22 .155 CD114
New Malden KT3 .138 CQ95
High Elms, Chig. IG7 .49 ES49
Upminster RM14 .73 FS60
Woodford Green IG8 .48 EG50
High Elms Cl, Nthwd. HA6 .39 BR51
High Elms La, Wat. WD25 .7 BV31
High Elms Rd, Orp. BR6 .163 EP110
HIGHER DENHAM, Uxb. UB9 .57 BB59
Higher Dr, Bans. SM7 .157 CX112
Purley CR8 .159 DN113
Higher Grn, Epsom KT17 .157 CU113
Highfield, Bans. SM7 .174 DE117
Bushey (Bushey Hth) WD23 .41 CE47
Chalfont St. Giles HP8 .36 AX47
Kings Langley WD4 .6 BL28
Watford WD19 .40 BZ48
Highfield Av, NW9 .62 CQ57
NW11 .63 CX59
Erith DA8 .107 FB79
Greenford UB6 .61 CE64
Orpington BR6 .163 ET106
Pinner HA5 .60 BZ57
Wembley HA9 .62 CL62
Highfield Cl, N22 .45 DN53
NW9 .62 CQ57
SE13 .123 ED86
Egham (Eng.Grn) TW20 .112 AW93
Leatherhead (Oxshott)
KT22 .155 CD111
Northwood HA6 .39 BS53
Romford RM5 .51 FC51
Surbiton KT6 .137 CJ102
West Byfleet KT14 .152 BG113
Highfield Ct, N14 .29 DJ44
Highfield Cres, Horn. RM12 .72 FM61
Highfield Cres, Nthwd. HA6 .39 BS53
Highfield Dr, Brom. BR2 .144 EE98
Caterham CR3 .176 DU122
Epsom KT19 .157 CT108
Uxbridge (Ickhm) UB10 .58 BL63
West Wickham BR4 .143 EB103
Highfield Gdns, NW11 .63 CY58
Grays RM16 .110 GD75
Highfield Grn, Epp. CM16 .17 ES31
Highfield Hill, SE19 .122 DR94
Highfield Link, Rom. RM5 .51 FC51
Highfield Ms, NW6
off Compayne Gdns .82 DB66
Highfield Pl, Epp. CM16 .17 ES31
Highfield Rd, N21 .45 DP47
NW11 .63 CY58
W3 .80 CP71
Bexleyheath DA6 .126 EZ85
Bromley BR1 .145 EM98
Bushey WD23 .24 BY43
Caterham CR3 .176 DU122
Chertsey KT16 .134 BG102
Chislehurst BR7 .145 ET97
Dartford DA1 .128 FK87
Feltham TW13 .115 BU89
Hornchurch RM12 .72 FM61
Isleworth TW7 .97 CF81
Northwood HA6 .39 BS53
Purley CR8 .159 DM110
Romford RM5 .51 FC52
Sunbury-on-Thames TW16 .135 BT98
Surbiton KT5 .138 CQ101
Sutton SM1 .158 DE106
Waltham Cross (Chsht) EN7 .14 DS26
Walton-on-Thames KT12 .135 BU102
West Byfleet KT14 .152 BG113
Westerham (Bigg.H.) TN16 .178 EJ117
Woodford Green IG8 .48 EL52
Highfield Rd S, Dart. DA1 .128 FK87
Highfields, Ashtd. KT21 .171 CK119
Leatherhead (Fetch.) KT22 .171 CD124
Potters Bar (Cuffley) EN6 .13 DL28
Radlett WD7 .25 CF35
Highfields Gro, N6 .64 DF60
Highfield Twr, Rom. RM5 .51 FD50
Highfield Way, Horn. RM12 .72 FM61
Potters Bar EN6 .12 DB32
Rickmansworth WD3 .22 BH44
High Firs, Rad. WD7 .25 CF35
Swanley BR8 .147 FE98
High Foleys, Esher (Clay.)
KT10 .155 CH108
High Gables, Loug. IG10 .32 EK43
High Garth, Esher KT10 .154 CC107
HIGHGATE, N6 .64 DG61
⊖ **Highgate** .65 DH58
Highgate Av, N6 .65 DH58
★ **Highgate Cem**, N6 .64 DG60
Highgate Cl, N6 .64 DG59
Highgate High St, N6 .64 DG60
Highgate Hill, N6 .65 DH60
N19 .65 DH60
Highgate Ho, SE26
off Sydenham Hill Est .122 DU90
H **Highgate Mental Health Cen**,
N19 .65 DH61
Highgate Rd, NW5 .65 DH63
Highgate Wk, SE23 .122 DW89
Highgate W Hill, N6 .64 DG61
High Gro, SE18 .105 ER80
Highgrove, Brwd. (Pilg.Hat.)
CM15 .54 FV44
High Gro, Brom. BR1 .144 EJ95
Highgrove Cl, N11
off Balmoral Av .44 DG50
Chislehurst BR7 .144 EL95
Highgrove Ms, Cars. SM5 .140 DF104
Grays RM17 .110 GC78
Highgrove Rd, Dag. RM8 .70 EW64
Highgrove Way, Ruis. HA4 .59 BU58
High Hill Est, E5
off Mount Pleasant La .66 DV60
High Hill Ferry, E5 .66 DV60
High Hill Rd, Warl. CR6 .177 EC115
High Holborn, WC1 .196 A8
High Ho La, Grays (Orsett)
RM16 .111 GJ75
Tilbury (W.Til.) RM18 .111 GK77
Highland Av, W7 .79 CE72
Brentwood CM15 .54 FW46
Dagenham RM10 .71 FC62
Loughton IG10 .32 EL44
Highland Cotts, Wall. SM6 .159 DH105
Highland Ct, E18 .48 EH53
Highland Cft, Beck. BR3 .123 EB92
Highland Dr, Bushey WD23 .40 CC45
Highland Pk, Felt. TW13 .115 BT91
Highland Rd, SE19 .122 DS93
Bexleyheath DA6 .126 FA85
Bromley BR1, BR2 .144 EF95
Northwood HA6 .39 BT54
Purley CR8 .159 DN114
Sevenoaks (Bad.Mt) TN14 .165 FB111
Highlands, Ashtd. KT21 .171 CJ119
Watford WD19 .40 BW46
Highlands, The, Edg. HA8 .42 CP54
Potters Bar EN6 .28 DB43
Rickmansworth WD3 .38 BH45
Highlands Av, N21 .29 DM43
W3 .80 CQ73
Leatherhead KT22 .171 CJ122
Highlands Cl, N4
off Mount Vw Rd .65 DL59
Gerrards Cross (Chal.St.P.)
SL9 .37 AZ52
Hounslow TW3 .96 CB81
Leatherhead KT22 .171 CH122
Highlands End, Ger.Cr.
(Chal.St.P.) SL9 .36 AY52
Highlands Gdns, Ilf. IG1 .69 EM60
Highlands Heath, SW15 .119 CW87
Highlands Hill, Swan. BR8 .147 FG96
Highlands La, Ger.Cr.
(Chal.St.P.) SL9 .37 AZ51
Woking GU22 .166 AY122
Highlands Pk, Lthd. KT22 .171 CK123
Sevenoaks (Seal) TN15 .191 FL121
Highlands Rd, Barn. EN5 .28 DA43
Leatherhead KT22 .171 CH122
Orpington BR5 .146 EV101
Reigate RH2 .184 DD133
High La, W7 .79 CD72
Caterham CR3 .177 DZ119
High La, Warl. CR6 .177 DZ118
High Lawns, Har. HA1 .61 CE62
Highlea Cl, NW9 .42 CS53
High Level Dr, SE26 .122 DU91
Highlever Rd, W10 .81 CW71
Highmead, SE18 .105 ET80
High Mead, Chig. IG7 .49 EQ47
Harrow HA1 .61 CE57
West Wickham BR4 .143 ED103
Highmead Cres, Wem. HA0 .80 CM66
High Meadow Cl, Pnr. HA5
off Daymer Gdns .59 BV56
High Meadow Cres, NW9 .62 CR57
High Meadow Pl, Cher. KT16 .133 BF100
High Meadows, Chig. IG7 .49 ER50
High Meads Rd, E16 .86 EK72
Highmore Rd, SE3 .104 EE80
High Mt, NW4 .63 CU58
High Oaks, Enf. EN2 .29 DM38
High Pk Av, Rich. TW9 .98 CN81
High Pk Rd, Rich. TW9 .98 CN81
High Path, SW19 .140 DB95
High Pine Cl, Wey. KT13 .153 BQ106
High Pines, Warl. CR6 .176 DW119
High Pt, N6 .64 DG59
SE9 .125 EP90
Weybridge KT13 .152 BN106
High Ridge, Pot.B. (Cuffley)
EN6 .13 DL27
Highridge Cl, Epsom KT18 .172 CS115
High Ridge Cl, Hem.H. HP3 .6 BK25
High Ridge Rd, Hem.H. HP3 .6 BK25
High Rd, N2 .64 DE56
N11 .45 DH50
N12 .44 DC51
N15 .66 DT58
N17 .46 DT53
N20 .44 DC45
N22 .65 DN55
NW10 (Willesden) .81 CV65
Buckhurst Hill IG9 .48 EH47
Bushey (Bushey Hth) WD23 .41 CD46
Chigwell IG7 .49 EM50
Coulsdon (Chipstead) CR5 .174 DF121
Dartford (Wilm.) DA2 .128 FJ90
Epping CM16 .17 ER32
Epping (N.Wld Bas.) CM16 .19 FB27
Epping (Thnwd) CM16 .18 EV28
Harrow (Har.Wld) HA3 .41 CE52
Ilford IG1 .69 EP62
Ilford (Seven Kings) IG3 .69 ET60
Loughton IG10 .48 EJ45
Pinner HA5 .59 BV56
Reigate RH2 .184 DD126
Romford (Chad.Hth) RM6 .70 EV60
Uxbridge UB8 .76 BJ71
Watford (Lvsdn) WD25 .23 BT35
Wembley HA0, HA9 .61 CK64
West Byfleet (Byfleet)
KT14 .152 BM112
High Rd Ickenham, Uxb.
UB10 .59 BP62
High Rd Leyton, E10 .67 EB60
E15 .67 EC62
High Rd Leytonstone, E11 .68 EE63
E15 .68 EE63
High Rd Turnford, Brox. EN10 .15 DY25
High Rd Woodford Grn, E18 .48 EF52
Woodford Green IG8 .48 EF52
Highshore Rd, SE15 .102 DT82
High Silver, Loug. IG10 .32 EK42
High Standing, Cat. (Chaldon)
CR3 .186 DQ125
Highstead Cres, Erith DA8 .107 FE81
Highstone Av, E11 .68 EG58
High St, E11 .68 EG57
E13 .86 EG68
E15 .85 EC68
E17 .67 DZ57
N8 .65 DL56
N14 .45 DK46
NW7 .43 CV49
NW10 (Harlesden) .81 CT68
SE20 .122 DV93
SE25 (S.Norwood) .142 DT98
W3 .80 CP74
W5 .79 CK73
Abbots Langley WD5 .7 BS31
Abbots Langley (Bedmond)
WD5 .7 BT27
Addlestone KT15 .152 BH105
Banstead SM7 .174 DA115
Barnet EN5 .27 CY41
Beckenham BR3 .143 EA96
Borehamwood (Els.) WD6 .25 CK44
Brentford TW8 .97 CK79
Brentwood CM14 .54 FV47
Bromley BR1 .144 EG96
Bushey WD23 .24 CA44
Carshalton SM5 .158 DG105
Caterham CR3 .176 DS123
Chalfont St. Giles HP8 .36 AW48
Chislehurst BR7 .125 EP93
Cobham KT11 .153 BV114
Croydon CR0 .142 DQ103
Dartford DA1 .128 FL86
Dartford (Bean) DA2 .129 FV90
Dartford (Eyns.) DA4 .148 FL103
Dartford (Fnghm) DA4 .148 FM100
Edgware HA8 .42 CN51
Egham TW20 .113 BA92
Epping CM16 .17 ET31
Epsom KT19 .156 CR113
Epsom (Ewell) KT17 .157 CT109
Esher KT10 .154 CB105
Esher (Clay.) KT10 .155 CF107
Feltham TW13 .115 BT90
Gerrards Cross (Chal.St.P.)
SL9 .36 AY53
Godstone RH9 .186 DV131
Gravesend DA11 .131 GH86
Gravesend (Nthflt) DA11 .130 GB86
Grays RM17 .110 GA79
Greenhithe DA9 .109 FV84
Hampton TW12 .116 CC93
Harrow HA1, HA2 .61 CE60
Harrow (Wealds.) HA3 .61 CE55
Hayes UB3 .95 BS78
Hemel Hempstead (Bov.)
HP3 .5 BA27
Hornchurch RM11, RM12 .72 FK60
Hounslow TW3 .96 CC83
Hounslow (Cran.) TW5 .95 BV80
High St, Ilf. (Barkingside) IG6 .49 EQ54
Iver SL0 .75 BE72
Kings Langley WD4 .6 BN29
Kingston upon Thames
KT1 .137 CK96
Kingston upon Thames
(Hmptn W.) KT1 .137 CJ95
Leatherhead KT22 .171 CH122
Leatherhead (Oxshott)
KT22 .155 CD113
New Malden KT3 .138 CS97
Northwood HA6 .39 BT53
Orpington BR6 .146 EU102
Orpington (Downe) BR6 .163 EN111
Orpington (Farnboro.) BR6 .163 EP106
Orpington (Grn St Grn)
BR6 .163 ET108
Orpington (St.M.Cray) BR5 .146 EW98
Oxted RH8 .187 ED130
Oxted (Lmpfld) RH8 .188 EG128
Pinner HA5 .60 BY55
Potters Bar EN6 .12 DC33
Purfleet RM19 .108 FN78
Purley CR8 .159 DN111
Redhill RH1 .184 DF134
Redhill (Bletch.) RH1 .186 DQ133
Redhill (Merst.) RH1 .185 DH128
Redhill (Nutfld) RH1 .185 DM133
Reigate RH2 .184 DA134
Rickmansworth WD3 .38 BK46
Romford RM1 .71 FE57
Ruislip HA4 .59 BS59
St. Albans (Lon.Col.) AL2 .9 CJ25
Sevenoaks TN13 .191 FJ125
Sevenoaks (Chipstead)
TN13 .190 FC122
Sevenoaks (Otford) TN14 .181 FF116
Sevenoaks (Seal) TN15 .191 FL121
Sevenoaks (Shore.) TN14 .165 FF110
Shepperton TW17 .135 BP100
Slough SL1 .92 AU75
Slough (Colnbr.) SL3 .93 BC80
Slough (Datchet) SL3 .92 AV81
Slough (Langley) SL3 .93 AZ78
South Ockendon (Aveley)
RM15 .91 FR74
Southall UB1 .78 BZ74
Staines TW18 .113 BF91
Staines (Stanw.) TW19 .114 BK86
Staines (Wrays.) TW19 .112 AY86
Sutton SM1 .158 DB105
Sutton (Cheam) SM3 .157 CY107
Swanley BR8 .147 FF98
Swanscombe DA10 .130 FZ85
Tadworth KT20 .173 CW123
Teddington TW11 .117 CG92
Thames Ditton KT7 .137 CG101
Thornton Heath CR7 .142 DQ98
Twickenham (Whitton)
TW2 .116 CC87
Uxbridge UB8 .76 BK67
Uxbridge (Cowley) UB8 .76 BJ70
Uxbridge (Hare.) UB9 .38 BJ54
Waltham Cross EN8 .15 DY34
Waltham Cross (Chsht) EN8 .15 DX29
Walton-on-Thames KT12 .135 BU102
Watford WD17 .23 BV41
Wembley HA9 .62 CM63
West Drayton (Harm.) UB7 .94 BK79
West Drayton (Yiew.) UB7 .76 BK74
West Molesey KT8 .136 CA98
West Wickham BR4 .143 EB102
Westerham TN16 .189 EQ127
Westerham (Brasted) TN16 .180 EV124
Weybridge KT13 .152 BN105
Woking GU21 .166 AY117
Woking (Chobham) GU24 .150 AS111
Woking (Horsell) GU21 .166 AV115
Woking (Old Wok.) GU22 .167 BB121
Woking (Ripley) GU23 .168 BJ121
High St Colliers Wd, SW19 .120 DD94
⊖ **High Street Kensington** .100 DB75
High St Ms, SW19 .119 CY92
High St N, E6 .86 EL67
E12 .68 EL64
High St Ponders End, Enf.
EN3 .30 DW42
High St S, E6 .87 EM68
High St Wimbledon, SW19 .119 CX92
High Timber St, EC4 .197 H10
High Tor Cl, Brom. BR1
off Babbacombe Rd .124 EH94
High Tor Vw, SE28 .87 ES74
High Tree Cl, Add. KT15 .151 BF106
High Tree Ct, W7 .79 CE73
High Trees, SW2 .121 DN88
Barnet EN4 .28 DE43
Croydon CR0 .143 DY102
Dartford DA2 .128 FP86
High Trees Cl, Cat. CR3 .176 DT123
High Trees Ct, Brwd. CM14
off Warley Mt .54 FW49
Highview, Cat. CR3 .176 DS124
High Vw, Ch.St.G. HP8 .36 AX47
Highview, Nthlt. UB5 .78 BY69
High Vw, Pnr. HA5 .60 BW56
Rickmansworth (Chorl.)
WD3 .22 BG42
Sutton SM2 .157 CZ111
Watford WD18 .23 BT44
Highview, Wok. (Knap.) GU21
off Mulgrave Way .166 AS117
Highview Av, Edg. HA8 .42 CQ49
High Vw Av, Grays RM17 .110 GC78
Highview Av, Wall. SM6 .159 DM106
High Vw Caravan Pk, Kings L.
WD4 .7 BR28
High Vw Cl, SE19 .142 DT96
Loughton IG10 .32 EJ43
Highview Cl, Pot.B. EN6 .12 DC33
Highview Cres, Brwd. (Hutt.)
CM13 .55 GC44
Highview Gdns, N3 .63 CY55
N11 .45 DJ50
Edgware HA8 .42 CQ49
High Vw Gdns, Grays RM17 .110 GC78
Highview Gdns, Pot.B. EN6 .12 DC33

Highview Gdns, Upmin.
RM14 . . . . .72 FP61
Highview Ho, Rom. RM6 . . . .70 EY56
Highview Path, Bans. SM7 . .174 DA115
High Vw Rd, E18 . . . . .68 EF55
SE19 . . . . .122 DR93
Highview Rd, W13 . . . . .79 CG71
Sidcup DA14 . . . . .126 EV91
Highway, The, E1 . . . . .202 C1
E14 . . . . .202 C1
Orpington BR6 . . . . .164 EW106
Stanmore HA7 . . . . .41 CF53
Sutton SM2 . . . . .158 DC109
Highwold, Couls. (Chipstead)
CR5 . . . . .174 DG118
Highwood, Brom. BR2 . . . . . .144 EE97
Highwood Av, N12 . . . . .44 DC49
Bushey WD23 . . . . .24 BZ39
Highwood Cl, SE22 . . . . .122 DU88
Brentwood CM14 . . . . .54 FV45
Kenley CR8 . . . . .176 DQ117
Orpington BR6 . . . . .145 EQ103
Highwood Dr, Orp. BR6 . . . .145 EQ103
Highwood Gdns, Ilf. IG5 . . . . .69 EM57
Highwood Gro, NW7 . . . . .42 CR50
Highwood Hall La, Hem.H.
HP3 . . . . .7 BQ25
HIGHWOOD HILL, NW7 . . . . . .43 CU47
Highwood Hill, NW7 . . . . .43 CT47
H **Highwood Hosp**, Brwd.
CM15 . . . . .54 FW45
Highwood La, Loug. IG10 . . . .33 EN43
Highwood Rd, N19 . . . . .65 DL62
Highwoods, Cat. CR3 . . . . . .186 DS125
Leatherhead KT22 . . . . . . .171 CJ121
High Worple, Har. HA2 . . . . . .60 BZ59
Highworth Rd, N11 . . . . .45 DK51
Hilary Av, Mitch. CR4 . . . . . .140 DG97
Hilary Cl, SW6 . . . . .100 DB80
Erith DA8 . . . . .107 FC81
Hornchurch RM12 . . . . .72 FK64
Hilary Rd, W12 . . . . .81 CT72
Slough SL3 . . . . .92 AY75
Hilbert Rd, Sutt. SM3 . . . . . .139 CX104
Hilborough Way, Orp. BR6 . .163 ER106
Hilda Lockert Wk, SW9
off Fiveways Rd 101 DP82
Hilda May Av, Swan. BR8 . . .147 FE97
Hilda Rd, E6 . . . . .86 EK66
E16 . . . . .86 EE70
Hilda Ter, SW9 . . . . .101 DN82
Hilda Vale Cl, Orp. BR6 . . . . .163 EP105
Hilda Vale Rd, Orp. BR6 . . . .163 EN105
Hildenborough Gdns, Brom.
BR1 . . . . .124 EE93
Hilden Dr, Erith DA8 . . . . . .107 FH80
Hildenlea Pl, Brom. BR2 . . . .144 EE96
Hildenley Cl, Red. (Merst.) RH1
off Malmstone Av 185 DK128
Hilders, The, Ashtd. KT21 . . .172 CP117
Hildreth St, SW12 . . . . .121 DH88
Hildreth St Ms, SW12
off Hildreth St 121 DH88
Hildyard Rd, SW6 . . . . .100 DA79
Hiley Rd, NW10 . . . . .81 CW69
Hilfield La, Wat. (Ald.) WD25 . .25 CD41
Hilfield La S, Bushey WD23 . .25 CF44
Hilgrove Rd, NW6 . . . . .82 DC66
Hiliary Gdns, Stan. HA7 . . . . .41 CJ54
Hiljon Cres, Ger.Cr. (Chal.St.P.)
SL9 . . . . .36 AY53
Hill, The, Cat. CR3 . . . . .176 DT124
Gravesend (Nthflt) DA11 . .130 GC86
Hillars Heath Rd, Couls. CR5 .175 DL115
Hillary Av, Grav. (Nthflt)
DA11 . . . . .130 GE90
Hillary Cres, Walt. KT12 . . . . .136 BW102
Hillary Dr, Islw. TW7 . . . . . . .97 CF84
Hillary Ri, Barn. EN5 . . . . . . .28 DA42
Hillary Rd, Sthl. UB2 . . . . . . .96 CA76
Hill Barn, S.Croy. CR2 . . . . . .160 DS111
Hillbeck Cl, SE15 . . . . .102 DW80
Hillbeck Way, Grnf. UB6 . . . . .79 CD67
Hillborne Cl, Hayes UB3 . . . . .95 BU78
Hillborough Av, Sev. TN13 . . .191 FK122
Hillborough Cl, SW19 . . . . . .120 DC94
Hillbrook Gdns, Wey. KT13 . .152 BN108
Hillbrook Rd, SW17 . . . . . . .120 DF90
Hill Brow, Brom. BR1 . . . . . .144 EK95
Dartford DA1 . . . . .127 FF86
Hillbrow, N.Mal. KT3 . . . . . .139 CT97
Hillbrow Cl, Bex. DA5 . . . . . .127 FD91
Hillbrow Cotts, Gdse. RH9 . .186 DW132
Hillbrow Ct, Gdse. RH9 . . . .186 DW132
Hillbrow Rd, Brom. BR1 . . . .124 EE94
Esher KT10 . . . . .154 CC105
Hillbury Av, Har. HA3 . . . . . . .61 CH57
Hillbury Cl, Warl. CR6 . . . . .176 DV118
Hillbury Gdns, Warl. CR6 . . .176 DW118
Hillbury Rd, SW17 . . . . .121 DH90
Warlingham CR6 . . . . .176 DU117
Whyteleafe CR3 . . . . .176 DU117
Hill Cl, NW2 . . . . .63 CV62
NW11 . . . . .64 DA58
Barnet EN5 . . . . .27 CW43
Chislehurst BR7 . . . . .125 EP92
Cobham KT11 . . . . .154 CA112
Gravesend (Istead Rise)
DA13 . . . . .130 GE94
Harrow HA1 . . . . .61 CE62
Purley CR8 . . . . .160 DQ113
Stanmore HA7 . . . . .41 CH49
Woking GU21 . . . . .166 AX115
Hillcote Av, SW16 . . . . .121 DN94
Hill Ct, Nthlt. UB5 . . . . .60 CA64
Hillcourt Av, N12 . . . . .44 DB51
Hillcourt Est, N16 . . . . .66 DR60
Hillcourt Rd, SE22 . . . . .122 DV86
Hill Cres, N20 . . . . .44 DB47
Bexley DA5 . . . . .127 FC88
Harrow HA1 . . . . .61 CG57
Hornchurch RM11 . . . . .72 FJ58
Surbiton KT5 . . . . .138 CM99
Worcester Park KT4 . . . . . .139 CW103
Hillcrest, N6 . . . . .64 DG59
N21 . . . . .45 DP45
Hill Crest, Pot.B. EN6 . . . . . . .12 DC34
Sevenoaks TN13 . . . . .190 FG122
Hill Crest, Sid. DA15 . . . . . . .126 EU87
Hillcrest, Wey. KT13 . . . . . . .153 BP105
Hillcrest Av, NW11 . . . . .63 CY57
Chertsey KT16 . . . . .151 BE105
Edgware HA8 . . . . .42 CP49
Grays RM20 . . . . .109 FU79
Pinner HA5 . . . . .60 BX56
Hillcrest Caravan Pk, Tad.
(Box H.) KT20 . . . . .182 CP131
Hillcrest Cl, SE26 . . . . .122 DU91
Beckenham BR3 . . . . .143 DZ99
Epsom KT18 . . . . .173 CT115
Waltham Cross (Goffs Oak)
EN7 . . . . .14 DQ29
Hillcrest Ct, Sutt. SM2
off Eaton Rd 158 DD107
Hillcrest Dr, Green. DA9
off Riverview Rd 129 FV85
Hillcrest Gdns, N3 . . . . .63 CY56
NW2 . . . . .63 CU62
Esher KT10 . . . . .137 CF104
Hillcrest Par, Couls. CR5 . . . .159 DH114
Hillcrest Rd, E17 . . . . .47 ED54
E18 . . . . .48 EF54
W3 .80 CN74
W5 .80 CL71
Bromley BR1 . . . . .124 EG92
Dartford DA1 . . . . .127 FF87
Hornchurch RM11 . . . . .71 FG59
Loughton IG10 . . . . .32 EK44
Ongar CM5 . . . . .19 FE30
Orpington BR6 . . . . .146 EU103
Purley CR8 . . . . .159 DM110
Radlett (Shenley) WD7 . . . .10 CN33
Westerham (Bigg.H.) TN16 . .178 EK116
Whyteleafe CR3 . . . . .176 DT117
Hillcrest Vw, Beck. BR3 . . . . .143 DZ100
Hillcrest Way, Epp. CM16 . . . .18 EU31
Hillcrest Waye, Ger.Cr. SL9 . . .57 AZ59
Hillcroft, Loug. IG10 . . . . .33 EN40
Hillcroft Av, Pnr. HA5 . . . . . . .60 BZ58
Purley CR8 . . . . .159 DJ113
Hillcroft Cres, W5 . . . . .80 CL72
Ruislip HA4 . . . . .60 BX62
Watford WD19 . . . . .39 BV46
Wembley HA9 . . . . .62 CM63
Hillcroft Rd, E6 . . . . .87 EP71
Hillcroome Rd, Sutt. SM2 . . .158 DD107
Hillcross Av, Mord. SM4 . . . .139 CZ99
Hilldale Rd, Sutt. SM1 . . . . . .157 CZ105
Hilldeane Rd, Pur. CR8 . . . . .159 DN109
Hilldene Av, Rom. RM3 . . . . . .52 FJ51
Hilldene Cl, Rom. RM3 . . . . . .52 FK50
Hilldown Rd, SW16 . . . . .121 DL94
Bromley BR2 . . . . .144 EE102
Hill Dr, NW9 . . . . .62 CQ60
SW16 . . . . .141 DM97
Hilldrop Cres, N7 . . . . .65 DK64
Hilldrop Est, N7 . . . . .65 DK64
Hilldrop La, N7 . . . . .65 DK64
Hilldrop Rd, N7 . . . . .65 DK64
Bromley BR1 . . . . .124 EG93
HILL END, Uxb. UB9 . . . . .38 BH51
Hillend, SE18 . . . . .105 EN81
Hill End, Orp. BR6
off The Approach 145 ET103
Hill End Rd, Uxb. (Hare.) UB9 .38 BH51
Hillersdon, Slou. SL2 . . . . . . .74 AV71
Hillersdon Av, SW13 . . . . .99 CU82
Edgware HA8 . . . . .42 CM50
Hillery Cl, SE17 . . . . .201 L9
Hilley Fld La, Lthd. (Fetch.)
KT22 . . . . .170 CC122
Hill Fm Av, Wat. WD25 . . . . . . .7 BU33
Hill Fm Cl, Wat. WD25 . . . . . . .7 BU33
Hill Fm Ind Est, Wat. WD25 . . . .7 BT33
Hill Fm La, Ch.St.G. HP8 . . . . .36 AT46
Hill Fm Rd, W10 . . . . .81 CW71
Gerrards Cross (Chal.St.P.)
SL9 . . . . .36 AY52
Uxbridge UB10
off Austin's La 59 BR63
Hillfield Av, N8 . . . . .65 DL57
NW9 . . . . .62 CS57
Wembley HA0 . . . . .80 CL66
Hillfield Cl, Har. HA2 . . . . . . .60 CC56
Redhill RH1 . . . . .184 DG134
Hillfield Ct, NW3 . . . . .64 DE64
Hillfield Ms, N8 . . . . .65 DM56
Hillfield Par, Mord. SM4 . . . .140 DE100
Hillfield Pk, N10 . . . . .65 DH56
N21 . . . . .45 DN47
Hillfield Pk Ms, N10 . . . . .65 DH56
Hillfield Rd, NW6 . . . . .63 CZ64
Gerrards Cross (Chal.St.P.)
SL9 . . . . .36 AY52
Hampton TW12 . . . . .116 BZ94
Redhill RH1 . . . . .184 DG134
Sevenoaks (Dunt.Grn)
TN13 . . . . .181 FE120
Hillfield Sq, Ger.Cr. (Chal.St.P.)
SL9 . . . . .36 AY52
Hillfoot Av, Rom. RM5 . . . . . . .51 FC53
Hillfoot Rd, Rom. RM5 . . . . . . .51 FC53
Hillgate Pl, SW12 . . . . .121 DH87
W8 .82 DA74
Hillgate St, W8 . . . . .82 DA74
Hill Gate Wk, N6 . . . . .65 DJ58
Hill Gro, Felt. TW13
off Watermill Way 116 BZ89
Hillgrove, Ger.Cr. (Chal.St.P.)
SL9 . . . . .37 AZ53
Hill Gro, Rom. RM1 . . . . .71 FE55
Hill Hall, Epp. (They.Mt) CM16 .34 EZ35
Hillhouse, Wal.Abb. EN9 . . . . .16 EF33
Hill Ho Av, Stan. HA7 . . . . . . .41 CF52
Hill Ho Cl, N21 . . . . .45 DN45
Gerrards Cross (Chal.St.P.) SL9
off Rickmansworth La 36 AY52
Hill Ho Dr, Hmptn. TW12 . . . .136 CA95
Weybridge KT13 . . . . .152 BN111
Hill Ho Rd, SW16 . . . . .121 DM92
Hillhouse Rd, Dart. DA2 . . . . .128 FQ87
Hillhurst Gdns, Cat. CR3 . . . .176 DS120
Hilliard Rd, Nthwd. HA6 . . . . .39 BT53
Hilliards Ct, E1 . . . . .202 E2
Hilliards Rd, Uxb. UB8 . . . . . .76 BK72
Hillier Cl, Barn. EN5 . . . . .28 DB44
Hillier Gdns, Croy. CR0 . . . . .159 DN106
Hillier Pl, Chess. KT9 . . . . . .155 CK107
Hillier Rd, SW11 . . . . .120 DF86
Hilliers Av, Uxb. UB8
off Harlington Rd 76 BN69
Hilliers La, Croy. CR0 . . . . . .141 DL104
Hillingdale, West. (Bigg.H.)
TN16 . . . . .178 EH118
HILLINGDON, Uxb. UB 76 BN69
⊖ **Hillingdon** 58 BN64
Hillingdon Av, Sev. TN13 . . . .191 FJ121
Staines TW19 . . . . .114 BL88
Hillingdon Circ, Uxb. UB10 . . .58 BN64
Hillingdon Hill, Uxb. UB10 . . .76 BL69
H **Hillingdon Hosp**, Uxb.
UB8 . . . . .76 BM71
Hillingdon Ri, Sev. TN13 . . . .191 FK122
Hillingdon Rd, Bexh. DA7 . . .107 FC82
Gravesend DA11 . . . . .131 GG89
Uxbridge UB10 . . . . .76 BL67
Watford WD25 . . . . .7 BU34
Hillingdon St, SE17 . . . . .101 DP80
Hillington Gdns, Wdf.Grn. IG8 .48 EK54
Hill La, Ruis. HA4 . . . . .59 BQ60
Tadworth (Kgswd) KT20 . . .173 CY121
Hill Leys, Pot.B. (Cuffley) EN6 .13 DL28
Hillman Cl, Horn. RM11 . . . . . .72 FK55
Uxbridge UB8 . . . . .58 BL64
Hillman Dr, W10 . . . . .81 CW70
Hillman St, E8 . . . . .84 DV65
Hillmarton Rd, N7 . . . . .65 DL64
Hillmead Dr, SW9 . . . . .101 DP84
Hillmont Rd, Esher KT10 . . . .137 CE104
Hillmore Gro, SE26 . . . . .123 DX92
Hillmount, Wok. GU22
off Constitution Hill 166 AY119
Hill Pk Dr, Lthd. KT22 . . . . . .171 CF119
Hill Path, SW16
off Valley Rd 121 DM92
Hillpoint, Rick. (Loud.) WD3 . .22 BJ43
Hillreach, SE18 . . . . .105 EM78
Hill Ri, N9 . . . . .30 DV44
NW11 . . . . .64 DB56
SE23 *off London Rd* 122 DV88
Dartford (Lane End) DA2 . .129 FR92
Esher KT10 . . . . .137 CH103
Gerrards Cross (Chal.St.P.)
SL9 . . . . .36 AX54
Greenford UB6 . . . . .78 CC66
Potters Bar EN6 . . . . .12 DC34
Potters Bar (Cuffley) EN6 . .13 DK27
Richmond TW10 . . . . .117 CK85
Rickmansworth WD3 . . . . . .22 BH44
Ruislip HA4 . . . . .59 BQ60
Slough SL3 . . . . .93 BA79
Upminster RM14 . . . . .72 FN61
Hillrise, Walt. KT12 . . . . .135 BT101
Hillrise Av, Wat. WD24 . . . . . .24 BX38
Hill Ri Cres, Ger.Cr. (Chal.St.P.)
SL9 . . . . .36 AY54
Hillrise Rd, N19 . . . . .65 DL59
Romford RM5 . . . . .51 FC51
Hill Rd, N10 . . . . .44 DF53
NW8 . . . . .82 DC68
Brentwood CM14 . . . . .54 FU48
Carshalton SM5 . . . . .158 DE107
Dartford DA2 . . . . .128 FL89
Epping (They.B.) CM16 . . . .33 ES37
Harrow HA1 . . . . .61 CG57
Leatherhead (Fetch.) KT22 . .170 CB122
Mitcham CR4 . . . . .141 DH95
Northwood HA6 . . . . .39 BR51
Pinner HA5 . . . . .60 BY57
Purley CR8 . . . . .159 DM112
Sutton SM1 . . . . .158 DB106
Wembley HA0 . . . . .61 CH62
Hillsborough Grn, Wat. WD19
off Ashburnham Dr 39 BU48
Hillsborough Rd, SE22 . . . . .122 DS85
Hills Chace, Brwd. CM14 . . . .54 FW49
Hillsgrove, Well. DA16 . . . . . .106 EW80
Hillside, NW9 . . . . .62 CR56
NW10 . . . . .80 CQ67
SW19 . . . . .119 CX93
Banstead SM7 . . . . .173 CY115
Barnet EN5 . . . . .28 DC43
Dartford (Fnghm) DA4 . . . .148 FM101
Dartford (Lane End) DA2 . .129 FS92
Erith DA8 . . . . .107 FD77
Grays RM17 . . . . .110 GD77
Slough SL1 . . . . .92 AS75
Uxbridge (Hare.) UB9 . . . . .58 BJ57
Virginia Water GU25 . . . . .132 AW100
Woking GU22 . . . . .166 AX120
Hillside, The, Orp. BR6 . . . . .164 EV109
Hillside Av, N11 . . . . .44 DF51
Borehamwood WD6 . . . . . . .26 CP42
Gravesend DA12 . . . . .131 GK89
Purley CR8 . . . . .159 DP113
Waltham Cross (Chsht)
EN8 . . . . .15 DX31
Wembley HA9 . . . . .62 CM63
Woodford Green IG8 . . . . . .48 EJ50
Hillside Cl, NW8 . . . . .82 DB68
Abbots Langley WD5 . . . . . . .7 BS32
Banstead SM7 . . . . .173 CY116
Chalfont St. Giles HP8 . . . .36 AV48
Gerrards Cross (Chal.St.P.)
SL9 . . . . .36 AY51
Morden SM4 . . . . .139 CY98
Woodford Green IG8 . . . . . .48 EJ50
Hillside Ct, Swan. BR8 . . . . .147 FG98
Hillside Cres, Enf. EN2 . . . . . .30 DR38
Harrow HA2 . . . . .60 CC60
Northwood HA6 . . . . .39 BU53
Waltham Cross (Chsht) EN8 .15 DX31
Watford WD19 . . . . .24 BY44
Hillside Dr, Edg. HA8 . . . . . . .42 CN51
Gravesend DA12 . . . . .131 GK89
Hillside Est, N15 . . . . .66 DT58
Hillside Gdns, E17 . . . . .67 ED55
N6 .64 DG58
SW2 . . . . .121 DN89
Addlestone KT15 . . . . .151 BF107
Barnet EN5 . . . . .27 CY42
Betchworth (Brock.) RH3 . .182 CN134
Edgware HA8 . . . . .42 CM49
Harrow HA3 . . . . .62 CL59
Northwood HA6 . . . . .39 BU52
Wallington SM6 . . . . .159 DJ108
Hillside Gro, N14 . . . . .45 DK45
NW7 . . . . .43 CU52
Hillside La, Brom. BR2 . . . . .144 EG103
Hillside Pas, SW2 . . . . .121 DM89
Hillside Ri, Nthwd. HA6 . . . . . .39 BU52
Hillside Rd, N15 . . . . .66 DS59
SW2 . . . . .121 DN89
W5 .80 CL71
Hillside Rd, Ashtd. KT21 . . . .172 CM117
Bromley BR2 . . . . .144 EF97
Bushey WD23 . . . . .24 BY43
Coulsdon CR5 . . . . .175 DM118
Croydon CR0 . . . . .159 DP106
Dartford DA1 . . . . .127 FG86
Epsom KT17 . . . . .157 CV110
Northwood HA6 . . . . .39 BU52
Pinner HA5 . . . . .39 BV52
Radlett WD7 . . . . .25 CH35
Rickmansworth (Chorl.)
WD3 . . . . .21 BC43
Sevenoaks TN13 . . . . .191 FK123
Southall UB1 . . . . .78 CA70
Surbiton KT5 . . . . .138 CM99
Sutton SM2 . . . . .157 CZ108
Westerham (Tats.) TN16 . .178 EL119
Whyteleafe CR3 . . . . .176 DU118
Hillside Wk, Brwd. CM14 . . . .54 FU48
Hills La, Nthwd. HA6 . . . . .39 BS53
Hillsleigh Rd, W8 . . . . .81 CZ74
Hillsmead Way, S.Croy. CR2 .160 DU113
Hills Ms, W5 . . . . .80 CL73
Hills Pl, W1 . . . . .195 K9
Hills Rd, Buck.H. IG9 . . . . . . .48 EH46
Hillstowe St, E5 . . . . .66 DW61
Hill St, W1 . . . . .198 G2
Richmond TW9 . . . . .117 CK85
Hillswood Business Pk,
Cher. KT16 . . . . .151 BC105
Hillswood Dr, Cher. KT16 . . . .151 BC105
Hill Top, NW11 . . . . .64 DB56
Loughton IG10 . . . . .33 EN40
Morden SM4 . . . . .140 DA100
Sutton SM3 . . . . .139 CZ101
Hilltop Av, NW10 . . . . .80 CQ66
Hilltop Cl, Lthd. KT22 . . . . . .171 CJ123
Hill Top Cl, Loug. IG10 . . . . . .33 EN41
Hilltop Cl, Wal.Cr. (Chsht)
EN7 . . . . .14 DT26
Hilltop Gdns, NW4 . . . . .43 CV54
Dartford DA1 . . . . .128 FM85
Orpington BR6 . . . . .145 ES103
Hilltop La, Cat. (Chaldon)
CR3 . . . . .185 DN126
Redhill RH1 . . . . .185 DN126
Hill Top Pl, Loug. IG10 . . . . . .33 EN41
Hilltop Rd, NW6 . . . . .82 DA66
Grays RM20 . . . . .109 FV79
Kings Langley WD4 . . . . .7 BR27
Whyteleafe CR3 . . . . .176 DS117
Hill Top Vw, Wdf.Grn. IG8 . . . .49 EM51
Hilltop Wk, Cat. (Wold.) CR3 .177 DY120
Hilltop Way, Stan. HA7 . . . . . .41 CG48
Hillview, SW20 . . . . .119 CV94
Mitcham CR4 . . . . .141 DL98
Whyteleafe CR3 . . . . .176 DT117
Hillview Av, Har. HA3 . . . . . . .62 CL57
Hornchurch RM11 . . . . .72 FJ58
Hillview Cl, Pnr. HA5 . . . . . . .40 BZ51
Purley CR8 . . . . .159 DP111
Hill Vw Cl, Tad. KT20 . . . . . . .173 CW121
Hillview Cl, Wem. HA9 . . . . . .62 CM61
Hillview Ct, Wok. GU22 . . . . .167 AZ118
Hillview Cres, Ilf. IG1 . . . . . . .69 EM58
Hill Vw Cres, Orp. BR6 . . . . .145 ET102
Hill Vw Dr, SE28 . . . . .87 ES74
Welling DA16 . . . . .105 ES82
Hillview Gdns, NW4 . . . . .63 CX56
Hill Vw Gdns, NW9 . . . . .62 CR57
Hillview Gdns, Har. HA2 . . . . .60 CA55
Waltham Cross (Chsht) EN8 .15 DX27
Hillview Rd, NW7 . . . . .43 CX49
Chislehurst BR7 . . . . .125 EN92
Hill Vw Rd, Esher (Clay.)
KT10 . . . . .155 CG108
Orpington BR6 . . . . .145 ET102
Hillview Rd, Pnr. HA5 . . . . . . .40 BZ52
Hill Vw Rd, Stai. (Wrays.)
TW19 . . . . .112 AX86
Hillview Rd, Sutt. SM1 . . . . .140 DC104
Hill Vw Rd, Twick. TW1 . . . . .117 CG86
Woking GU22 . . . . .167 AZ118
Hillway, N6 . . . . .64 DG61
NW9 . . . . .62 CS60
Hill Waye, Ger.Cr. SL9 . . . . . .57 AZ58
Hillwood Cl, Brwd. (Hutt.)
CM13 . . . . .55 GB46
Hillwood Gro, Brwd. (Hutt.)
CM13 . . . . .55 GB46
Hillworth Rd, SW2 . . . . .121 DN87
Hillyard Rd, W7 . . . . .79 CE71
Hillyard St, SW9 . . . . .101 DN81
Hillyfield, E17 . . . . .47 DY54
Hillyfield Cl, E9
off Mabley St 67 DY64
Hillyfields, Loug. IG10 . . . . . . .33 EN40
Hilly Flds Cres, SE4 . . . . .103 EA83
Hilperton Rd, Slou. SL1 . . . . . .92 AS75
Hilsea Pt, SW15
off Wanborough Dr 119 CV88
Hilsea St, E5 . . . . .66 DW63
Hilton Av, N12 . . . . .44 DD50
Hilton Cl, Uxb. UB8 . . . . .76 BH68
DLR **Hilton Docklands Nelson
Dock Pier** 203 M2
Hilton Way, S.Croy. CR2 . . . .176 DV115
Hilversum Cres, SE22
off East Dulwich Gro 122 DS85
Himalayan Way, Wat. WD18 . . .23 BT44
Himley Rd, SW17 . . . . .120 DE92
Hinchley Cl, Esher KT10 . . . .137 CF104
Hinchley Dr, Esher KT10 . . . .137 CF104
Hinchley Manor, Esher KT10
off Manor Rd N 137 CF104
Hinchley Way, Esher KT10 . .137 CG104
HINCHLEY WOOD, Esher
KT10 . . . . .137 CF104
⇌ **Hinchley Wood** 137 CF104
Hinckley Rd, SE15 . . . . .102 DU84
Hind Cl, Chig. IG7 . . . . .49 ET50
Hind Ct, EC4 . . . . .196 E9
Hind Cres, Erith DA8 . . . . . . .107 FD79
Hinde Ms, W1
off Marylebone La 82 DG72
Hindes Rd, Har. HA1 . . . . .61 CD57
Hinde St, W1 . . . . .194 G8
Hind Gro, E14 . . . . .85 EA72
Hindhead Cl, N16 . . . . .66 DS60
Uxbridge UB8
off Aldenham Dr 77 BP71
Hindhead Gdns, Nthlt. UB5 . . .78 BY67
Hindhead Grn, Wat. WD19 . . . .40 BW50
Hindhead Pt, SW15
off Wanborough Dr 119 CV88
Hindhead Way, Wall. SM6 . . .159 DL106
Hind Ho, N7 *off Harvist Est* . . .65 DN63
Hindmans Rd, SE22 . . . . .122 DU85
Hindmans Way, Dag. RM9 . . . .88 EZ70
Hindmarsh Cl, E1
off Cable St 84 DU73
Hindon Ct, SW1 . . . . .199 K8
Hindrey Rd, E5 . . . . .66 DV64
Hindsley's Pl, SE23 . . . . .122 DW89
Hind Ter, Grays RM20
off Mill La 109 FX78
Hine Cl, Couls. CR5 . . . . .175 DJ122
Epsom KT19 . . . . .156 CP111
Hinkler Rd, Har. HA3 . . . . .61 CK55
Hinkley Cl, Uxb. (Hare.) UB9 . .58 BJ56
Hinksey Cl, Slou. SL3 . . . . . . .93 BB76
Hinksey Path, SE2 . . . . .106 EX76
Hinstock Rd, SE18 . . . . .105 EQ79
Hinton Av, Houns. TW4 . . . . . .96 BX84
Hinton Cl, SE9 . . . . .124 EL88
Hinton Rd, N18 . . . . .46 DS49
SE24 . . . . .101 DP83
Uxbridge UB8 . . . . .76 BJ67
Wallington SM6 . . . . .159 DJ107
Hipley St, Wok. GU22 . . . . . .167 BB121
Hippodrome Ms, W11
off Portland Rd 81 CY73
Hippodrome Pl, W11 . . . . .81 CY73
Hirst Ct, SW1 *off Gatliff Rd* . .101 DH78
Hirst Cres, Wem. HA9 . . . . . . .62 CL62
Hitcham Rd, E17 . . . . .67 DZ59
Hitchcock Cl, Shep. TW17 . . .134 BM97
Hitchen Hatch La, Sev. TN13 .190 FG124
Hitchin Cl, Rom. RM3 . . . . . . .52 FJ49
Hitchin Sq, E3 . . . . .85 DY68
Hithe Gro, SE16 . . . . .202 G7
Hitherbroom Rd, Hayes UB3 . .77 BU74
Hither Fm Rd, SE3 . . . . .104 EJ83
Hitherfield Rd, SW16 . . . . . . .121 DM89
Dagenham RM8 . . . . .70 EY61
HITHER GREEN, SE13 . . . . . .124 EE86
⇌ **Hither Green** 124 EE86
Hither Grn La, SE13 . . . . . . .123 EC85
Hitherlands, SW12 . . . . .121 DH89
Hither Meadow, Ger.Cr. (Chal.St.P.)
SL9 *off Lower Rd* 36 AY54
Hithermoor Rd, Stai. TW19 . .114 BG85
Hitherwell Dr, Har. HA3 . . . . . .41 CD53
Hitherwood Cl, Horn. RM12
off Swanbourne Dr 72 FK63
Reigate RH2 . . . . .184 DD132
Hitherwood Dr, SE19 . . . . . .122 DT91
Hive, The, Grav. (Nthflt) DA11
off Fishermans Hill 130 GB85
Hive Cl, Brwd. CM14 . . . . .54 FU47
Bushey (Bushey Hth) WD23 .41 CD47
Hive La, Grav. (Nthflt) DA11 .130 GB86
Hive Rd, Bushey (Bushey Hth)
WD23 . . . . .41 CD47
★ **H.M.S. Belfast**, SE1 . . . . . .201 N2
★ **H.M.S. President**, EC4 . . .200 E1
★ **H.M. Treasury**, SW1 . . . . . .199 P4
Hoadly Rd, SW16 . . . . .121 DK90
Hobart Cl, N20
off Oakleigh Rd N 44 DE47
Hayes UB4 . . . . .78 BX70
Hobart Dr, Hayes UB4 . . . . . . .78 BX70
Hobart Gdns, Th.Hth. CR7 . . .142 DR97
Hobart La, Hayes UB4 . . . . . . .78 BX70
Hobart Pl, SW1 . . . . .199 H6
Richmond TW10
off Chisholm Rd 118 CM86
Hobart Rd, Dag. RM9 . . . . . . .70 EX63
Hayes UB4 . . . . .78 BX70
Ilford IG6 . . . . .49 EQ54
Tilbury RM18 . . . . .111 GG81
Worcester Park KT4 . . . . . .139 CV104
Hobarts Dr, Uxb. (Denh.) UB9 .57 BF58
Hobbayne Rd, W7 . . . . .79 CD72
Hobbes Wk, SW15 . . . . .119 CV85
Hobbs Cl, Wal.Cr. (Chsht) EN8 .15 DX29
West Byfleet KT14 . . . . . . .152 BH113
Hobbs Cross Rd, Epp.
(They.Gar.) CM16 . . . . .34 EW35
Hobbs Grn, N2 . . . . .64 DC55
Hobbs Ms, Ilf. IG3
off Ripley Rd 69 ET61
Hobbs Pl Est, N1
off Pitfield St 84 DS67
Hobbs Rd, SE27 . . . . .122 DQ91
Hobby Horse Cl, Wal.Cr. (Chsht) EN7
off Great Stockwood Rd . .14 DR26
Hobby St, Enf. EN3
off Falcon Rd 31 DX43
Hobday St, E14 . . . . .85 EB71
Hobill Wk, Surb. KT5 . . . . . . .138 CM100
Hoblands End, Chis. BR7 . . .125 ES93
Hobsons Pl, E1
off Hanbury St 84 DU71
Hobury St, SW10 . . . . .100 DC79
Hockenden La, Swan. BR8 . .147 FB96
Hockering Gdns, Wok. GU22 .167 BA117
Hockering Rd, Wok. GU22 . . .167 BA118
Hocker St, E2 . . . . .197 P3
Hockett Cl, SE8 . . . . .203 L8
Hockley Av, E6 . . . . .86 EL68
Hockley Ct, E18
off Churchfields 48 EG53
Hockley Dr, Rom. RM2 . . . . . .51 FH54
Hockley La, Slou. (Stoke P.)
SL2 . . . . .74 AV67
Hockley Ms, Bark. IG11 . . . . . .87 ES68
Hocroft Av, NW2 . . . . .63 CZ62
Hocroft Rd, NW2 . . . . .63 CZ63
Hocroft Wk, NW2 . . . . .63 CZ62
Hodder Dr, Grnf. UB6 . . . . . . .79 CF68
Hoddesdon Rd, Belv. DA17 . . .106 FA78
Broxbourne EN10 . . . . .15 DX27
Hodes Row, NW3 . . . . .64 DG63
off Estelle Rd 64 DG63
Hodford Rd, NW11 . . . . .63 CZ61
Hodgemoor Vw, Ch.St.G.
HP8 . . . . .36 AT48
Hodges Cl, Grays (Chaff.Hun.)
RM16 . . . . .109 FX78
Hodges Way, Wat. WD18 . . . . .23 BU44
Hodgkin Cl, SE28
off Fleming Way 88 EX73
Hodgkins Ms, Stan. HA7 . . . . .41 CH50
Hodister Cl, SE5
off Badsworth Rd 102 DQ80

★ Place of interest ⇌ Railway station ⊖ London Underground station DLR Docklands Light Railway station Tra Tramlink station H Hospital Riv Pedestrian ferry landing stage

Hodnet Gro, SE16 203 H8
Hodsoll Ct, Orp. BR5 146 EX100
Hodson Cl, Har. HA2 60 BZ62
Hodson Cres, Orp. BR5 146 EX100
Hodson Pl, Enf. EN3 31 EA38
Hoe, The, Wat. WD19 40 BX47
Hoebrook Cl, Wok. GU22 166 AX121
Hoechst, Houns. TW4 96 BW83
Hoe La, Enf. EN1, EN3 30 DU38
Romford (Abridge) RM4 34 EV43
Hoe St, E17 67 EA56
Hoffmann Gdns, S.Croy. CR2 160 DU108
Hofland Rd, W14 99 CX76
Hogan Ms, W2 off Porteus Rd 82 DD71
Hogan Way, E5
off Geldeston Rd 66 DU61
Hogarth Av, Ashf. TW15 115 BQ93
Brentwood CM15 54 FY48
Hogarth Business Pk, W4 98 CS79
Hogarth Cl, E16 86 EK71
W5 80 CL71
Uxbridge UB8 76 BJ69
Hogarth Ct, EC3 197 N10
SE19 off Fountain Dr 122 DT91
Bushey WD23
off Steeplands 40 CB45
Hogarth Cres, SW19 140 DD95
Croydon CR0 142 DQ101
Hogarth Gdns, Houns. TW5 96 CA80
Hogarth Hill, NW11 63 CZ56
Hogarth La, W4 98 CS79
Hogarth Pl, SW5
off Hogarth Rd 100 DB77
Hogarth Reach, Loug. IG10 33 EM43
Hogarth Rd, SW5 100 DB77
Dagenham RM8 70 EV64
Edgware HA8 42 CN54
Hogarth Rbt, W4 99 CT79
Hogarth Rbt Flyover, W4
off Burlington La 98 CS79
★ Hogarth's Ho, W4
off Hogarth La 98 CS79
Hogarth Way, Hmptn. TW12 136 CC95
Hogg La, Borwd. (Els.) WD6 25 CG42
Grays RM16, RM17 110 GA76
Hogg La Rbt, Grays RM16 110 FZ75
Hog Hill Rd, Rom. RM5 50 EZ52
Hog Pits, Hem.H. (Flaun.) HP3 5 BB32
HOGPITS BOTTOM, Hem.H.
HP3 5 BA31
Hogpits Bottom, Hem.H.
(Flaun.) HP3 5 BA32
Hogscross La, Couls.
(Chipstead) CR5 174 DF123
Hogshead Pas, E1 202 E1
Hogshill La, Cob. KT11 154 BX112
Hogs La, Grav. DA11 130 GD90
Hogsmill Way, Epsom KT19 156 CQ106
Hogs Orchard, Swan. BR8 147 FH95
Hogtrough Hill, West.
(Brasted) TN16 179 ET120
Hogtrough La, Gdse. RH9 187 EA128
Oxted RH8 187 EB128
Holbeach Cl, NW9 42 CS53
Holbeach Gdns, Sid. DA15 125 ES86
Holbeach Ms, SW12
off Harberson Rd 121 DH88
Holbeach Rd, SE6 123 EA87
Holbeck La, Wal.Cr. (Chsht)
EN7 14 DT26
Holbeck Row, SE15 102 DU80
Holbein Gate, Nthwd. HA6 39 BS50
Holbein Ms, SW1 198 F10
Holbein Pl, SW1 198 F9
Holbein Ter, Dag. RM8
off Marlborough Rd 70 EV63
Holberton Gdns, NW10 81 CV69
HOLBORN, WC2 196 B8
⊖ Holborn 196 A7
Holborn, EC1 196 D7
Holborn Circ, EC1 196 E7
Holborn Pl, WC1 196 B7
Holborn Rd, E13 86 EH70
Holborn Viaduct, EC1 196 E7
Holborn Way, Mitch. CR4 140 DF96
Holbreck Pl, Wok. GU22
off Heathside Rd 167 AZ118
Holbrook Cl, N19
off Dartmouth Pk Hill 65 DH60
Enfield EN1 30 DT39
Holbrooke Ct, N7 65 DL63
Holbrooke Pl, Rich. TW10
off Hill Ri 117 CK85
Holbrook La, Chis. BR7 125 ER94
Holbrook Meadow, Egh.
TW20 113 BC93
Holbrook Rd, E15 86 EF68
Holbrook Way, Brom. BR2 145 EM100
Holburne Cl, SE3 104 EJ81
Holburne Gdns, SE3 104 EK81
Holburne Rd, SE3 104 EJ81
Holcombe Hill, NW7 43 CU48
Holcombe Rd, N17 66 DT55
Ilford IG1 69 EN59
Holcombe St, W6 99 CV78
Holcon Ct, Red. RH1 184 DG131
Holcote Cl, Belv. DA17
off Blakemore Way 106 EY76
Holcroft Rd, E9 84 DW66
HOLDBROOK, Wal.Cr. EN8 15 EA34
Holdbrook N, Wal.Cr. EN8
off Eleanor Way 15 DZ34
Holdbrook S, Wal.Cr. EN8
off Queens Way 15 DZ34
Holdbrook Way, Rom. RM3 52 FM54
Holden Av, N12 44 DB50
NW9 62 CQ60
Holdenby Rd, SE4 123 DY85
Holden Cl, Dag. RM8 70 EV62
Holden Gdns, Brwd. CM14 54 FX50
Holdenhurst Av, N12 44 DB52
Holden Pl, Cob. KT11 153 BV114
Holden Pt, E15
off Waddington Rd 85 ED65
Holden Rd, N12 44 DB50
Holden St, SW11 100 DG82
Holden Way, Upmin. RM14 73 FR59
Holder Cl, N3 44 DB52
Holdernesse Cl, Islw. TW7 97 CG81
Holdernesse Rd, SW17 120 DF90
Holderness Way, SE27 121 DP92
HOLDERS HILL, NW4 43 CX54
Holders Hill Av, NW4 43 CX54
Holders Hill Circ, NW7
off Dollis Rd 43 CY52
Holders Hill Cres, NW4 43 CX54
Holders Hill Dr, NW4 63 CX55
Holders Hill Gdns, NW4 43 CY54
Holders Hill Rd, NW4 43 CX54
NW7 43 CX54
Holecroft, Wal.Abb. EN9 16 EE34
Hole Fm La, Brwd. CM13 73 FV55
Holegate St, SE7
off Westmoor St 104 EK76
Holford Ho, SE16
off Manor Est 102 DV77
Holford Ms, WC1 196 D1
Holford Pl, WC1 196 C2
Holford Rd, NW3 64 DC62
Grays RM16 111 GK76
Stanford-le-Hope (Linford)
SS17 111 GL75
Tilbury RM18 111 GK76
Holford St, WC1 196 D2
Holford Yd, WC1 196 C1
Holgate Av, SW11 100 DD83
Holgate Gdns, Dag. RM10 70 FA64
Holgate Rd, Dag. RM10 70 FA64
HOLLAND, Oxt. RH8 188 EG134
Holland Av, SW20 139 CT95
Sutton SM2 158 DA109
Holland Cl, Barn. EN5 44 DD45
Bromley BR2 144 EF103
Redhill RH1 184 DF134
Romford RM7 71 FC57
Stanmore HA7 41 CH50
Holland Ct, E17
off Evelyn Rd 67 EC56
NW7 43 CU51
Holland Cres, Oxt. RH8 188 EG133
Holland Dr, SE23 123 DY90
Holland Gdns, W14 99 CY76
Brentford TW8 98 CL79
Egham TW20 133 BF96
Watford WD25 24 BW35
Holland Gro, SW9 101 DN80
★ Holland Ho & Pk, W8 99 CZ75
Holland La, Oxt. RH8 188 EG133
⊖ Holland Park 81 CY74
Holland Pk, W8 99 CZ75
W11 99 CY75
Holland Pk Av, W11 99 CY75
Ilford IG3 69 ES58
Holland Pk Gdns, W14 81 CY74
Holland Pk Ms, W11 81 CY74
Holland Pk Rd, W14 99 CZ76
Holland Pk Rbt, W11 99 CX75
Holland Pas, N1
off Basire St 84 DQ67
Holland Pl, W8
off Kensington Ch St 100 DB75
Holland Ri Ho, SW9
off Clapham Rd 101 DM80
Holland Rd, E6 87 EM67
E15 86 EE69
NW10 81 CU67
SE25 142 DU99
W14 99 CX75
Oxted RH8 188 EG133
Wembley HA0 79 CK65
Hollands, The, Felt. TW13 116 BX91
Woking GU22
off Montgomery Rd 166 AY118
Worcester Park KT4 139 CT102
Holland St, SE1 200 G2
W8 100 DA75
Holland Vil Rd, W14 99 CY75
Holland Wk, N19
off Duncombe Rd 65 DK60
W8 99 CZ75
Stanmore HA7 41 CG50
Holland Way, Brom. BR2 144 EF103
Hollar Rd, N16
off Stoke Newington High St 66 DT62
Hollen St, W1 195 M8
Holles Cl, Hmptn. TW12 116 CA93
Holles St, W1 195 J8
Holley Rd, W3 98 CS75
Hollickwood Av, N12 44 DF51
Holliday Sq, SW11
off Fowler Cl 100 DD83
Hollidge Way, Dag. RM10 89 FB65
Hollies, The, E11 68 EG57
N20 off Oakleigh Pk N 44 DD46
Gravesend DA12 131 GK93
Harrow HA3 61 CG56
Hemel Hempstead (Bov.)
HP3 5 BA29
Hollies Av, Sid. DA15 125 ET89
West Byfleet KT14 151 BF113
Hollies Cl, SW16 121 DN93
Twickenham TW1 117 CF89
Hollies Ct, Add. KT15 152 BJ106
Hollies End, NW7 43 CV50
Hollies Rd, W5 97 CJ77
Hollies Way, SW12
off Bracken Av 120 DG87
Potters Bar EN6 12 DC31
Holligrave Rd, Brom. BR1 144 EG95
Hollingbourne Av, Bexh. DA7 106 EZ80
Hollingbourne Gdns, W13 79 CH71
Hollingbourne Rd, SE24 122 DQ85
Hollingbourne Twr, Orp. BR5 146 EX102
Hollingsworth Rd, Croy. CR0 160 DV107
Hollington Cres, N.Mal. KT3 139 CT100
Hollington Rd, E6 87 EM69
N17 46 DU54
Hollingworth Cl, W.Mol. KT8 136 BZ98
Hollingworth Rd, Orp. BR5 145 EP100
Hollingworth Way, West.
TN16 189 ER126
Hollis Pl, Grays RM17
off Ward Av 110 GA77
Hollman Gdns, SW16 121 DP93
Hollow, The, Wdf.Grn. IG8 48 EF49
HOLLOWAY, N7 65 DK64
Holloway Cl, West Dr. UB7 94 BL78
Holloway Dr, Vir.W. GU25 132 AY98
Holloway Hill, Cher. KT16 133 BC104
Holloway La, Rick. (Chenies)
WD3 21 BD36
West Drayton UB7 94 BL79
⊖ Holloway Road 65 DM64
Holloway Rd, E6 87 EM69
E11 68 EE62
N7 65 DM63
Holloway Rd, N19 65 DK61
Holloway St, Houns. TW3 96 CB83
Hollow Cotts, Purf. RM19 108 FN78
Hollowfield Av, Grays RM17 110 GD77
Hollowfield Wk, Nthlt. UB5 78 BY65
Hollow Hill La, Iver SL0 75 BB73
Hollow La, Vir.W. GU25 132 AY97
Hollows, The, Brent. TW8
off Kew Br Rd 98 CM79
Hollow Wk, Rich. TW9
off Kew Rd 98 CL80
Hollow Way La, Amer. HP6 20 AS35
Chesham HP5 20 AS35
Holly Av, Add. (New Haw)
KT15 152 BG110
Stanmore HA7 42 CL54
Walton-on-Thames KT12 136 BX102
Hollybank Cl, Hmptn. TW12 116 CA92
Hollybank Rd, W.Byf. KT14 152 BG114
Holly Bk Rd, Wok. GU22 166 AV121
Hollyberry La, NW3
off Holly Wk 64 DC63
Hollybrake Cl, Chis. BR7 125 ER94
Hollybush Cl, E11 68 EG57
Harrow HA3 41 CE53
Sevenoaks TN13 191 FJ124
Watford WD19 40 BW45
Hollybush Ct, Sev. TN13 191 FJ124
Hollybush Gdns, E2 84 DV69
Hollybush Hill, E11 68 EF58
Holly Bush Hill, NW3 64 DC63
Hollybush Hill, Slou.
(Stoke P.) SL2 74 AU66
Holly Bush La, Hmptn. TW12 116 BZ94
Hollybush La, Iver SL0 75 BB72
Orpington BR6 164 FA107
Holly Bush La, Sev. TN13 191 FJ123
Hollybush La, Uxb. (Denh.)
UB9 57 BE63
Woking (Ripley) GU23 168 BK119
Hollybush Pl, E2
off Bethnal Grn Rd 84 DV69
Hollybush Rd, Grav. DA12 131 GJ89
Kingston upon Thames
KT2 118 CL92
Holly Bush Steps, NW3
off Heath St 64 DC63
Hollybush St, E13 86 EH69
Holly Bush Vale, NW3
off Heath St 64 DC63
Hollybush Way, Wal.Cr. EN7 14 DU28
Holly Cl, NW10
off Hawkins Rd 80 CS66
Beckenham BR3 143 EC98
Buckhurst Hill IG9 48 EK48
Chertsey (Longcr.) KT16 132 AU104
Egham (Eng.Grn) TW20 112 AV93
Feltham TW13 116 BY92
Wallington SM6 159 DH108
Woking GU21 166 AV119
Hollycombe, Egh. (Eng.Grn)
TW20 112 AW91
Holly Cottage Ms, Uxb. UB8
off Pield Heath Rd 76 BN71
Holly Ct, SE10
off West Parkside 104 EF76
Sutton SM2
off Worcester Rd 158 DA108
Holly Cres, Beck. BR3 143 DZ99
Woodford Green IG8 47 ED52
Hollycroft Av, NW3 64 DA62
Wembley HA9 62 CM61
Hollycroft Cl, S.Croy. CR2 160 DS106
West Drayton UB7 94 BN79
Hollycroft Gdns, West Dr. UB7 94 BN79
Hollydale Cl, Nthlt. UB5
off Dorchester Rd 60 CB63
Hollydale Dr, Brom. BR2 145 EM104
Hollydale Rd, SE15 102 DW81
Hollydene, SE15 102 DV81
Hollydown Way, E11 67 ED62
Holly Dr, E4 47 EB45
Brentford TW8 97 CG79
Potters Bar EN6 12 DB33
South Ockendon RM15 91 FX70
Windsor SL4 112 AS85
Holly Fm Rd, Sthl. UB2 96 BY78
Hollyfield Av, N11 44 DF50
Hollyfield Rd, Surb. KT5 138 CM101
Hollyfields, Brox. EN10 15 DY26
Holly Gdns, Bexh. DA7 107 FC84
West Drayton UB7 94 BM75
Holly Gate, Add. KT15 152 BH105
Holly Grn, Wey. KT13 135 BR104
Holly Gro, NW9 62 CQ59
SE15 102 DT82
Bushey WD23 41 CD45
Pinner HA5 40 BY53
Hollyhedge Rd, Cob. KT11 153 BV114
Holly Hedges La, Hem.H.
(Bov.) HP3 5 BC30
Rickmansworth WD3 5 BC30
Holly Hedge Ter, SE13 123 ED85
Holly Hill, N21 29 DM44
NW3 64 DC63
Holly Hill Dr, Bans. SM7 174 DA116
Holly Hill Pk, Bans. SM7 174 DA117
Holly Hill Rd, Belv. DA17 107 FB78
Erith DA8 107 FB78
Holly Ho, Brwd. CM15
off Sawyers Hall La 54 FX46
H Holly Ho Hosp, Buck.H.
IG9 48 EH47
Holly La, Bans. SM7 174 DA116
Holly La E, Bans. SM7 174 DA116
Holly La W, Bans. SM7 174 DA117
Holly Lo Gdns, N6 64 DG61
Holly Lo Mobile Home Pk, Tad.
(Lwr Kgswd) KT20 183 CY126
Hollymead, Cars. SM5 140 DF104
Hollymead Rd, Couls.
(Chipstead) CR5 174 DG118
Hollymeoak Rd, Couls. CR5 175 DH119
Holly Ms, SW10
off Drayton Gdns 100 DC78
Hollymoor La, Epsom KT19 156 CR110
Holly Mt, NW3
off Holly Bush Hill 64 DC63
Hollymount Cl, SE10 103 EC81
Holly Pk, N3 63 CZ55
N4 65 DM59
Holly Pk Est, N4
off Blythwood Rd 65 DL59
Holly Pk Gdns, N3 64 DA55
Holly Pk Rd, N11 44 DG50
W7 79 CF74
Holly Pl, NW3 off Holly Wk 64 DC63
Holly Rd, E11 68 EF59
W4 off Dolman Rd 98 CR77
Dartford DA1 128 FK88
Enfield EN3 31 DX36
Hampton (Hmptn H.) TW12 116 CC93
Hounslow TW3 96 CB84
Orpington BR6 164 EU108
Twickenham TW1 117 CG88
Holly St, E8 84 DT65
Holly Ter, N6
off Highgate W Hill 64 DG60
N20 off Swan La 44 DC47
Holly Tree Av, Swan. BR8 147 FE96
Hollytree Cl, SW19 119 CX88
Holly Tree Cl, Chesh.
(Ley Hill) HP5 4 AV31
Hollytree Cl, Ger.Cr.
(Chal.St.P.) SL9 36 AY50
Holly Tree Rd, Cat. CR3
off Elm Gro 176 DS122
Holly Vw Cl, NW4 63 CU58
Holly Village, N6
off Swains La 65 DH61
Holly Wk, NW3 64 DC63
Enfield EN2 30 DQ41
Richmond TW9 98 CL82
Holly Way, Mitch. CR4 141 DK98
Hollywood Ct, Borwd. (Els.)
WD6 off Deacon's Hill Rd 26 CM42
Hollywood Gdns, Hayes UB4 77 BV72
Hollywood Ms, SW10
off Hollywood Rd 100 DC79
Hollywood Rd, E4 47 DY50
SW10 100 DC79
Hollywoods, Croy. CR0 161 DZ109
Hollywood Way, Erith DA8 107 FH81
Woodford Green IG8 47 ED52
Holman Ho, E2
off Roman Rd 85 DX68
Holman Rd, SW11 100 DD82
Epsom KT19 156 CQ106
Holmbank Dr, Shep. TW17 135 BS98
Holmbridge Gdns, Enf. EN3 31 DX42
Holmbrook Dr, NW4 63 CX57
Holmbury Ct, SW17 120 DF90
SW19 off Cavendish Rd 120 DE94
Holmbury Gdns, Hayes UB3
off Church Rd 77 BT74
Holmbury Gro, Croy. CR0 161 DZ108
Holmbury Pk, Brom. BR1 124 EL94
Holmbury Vw, E5 66 DV60
Holmbush Rd, SW15 119 CY86
Holm Cl, Add. (Wdhm) KT15 151 BE112
Holmcote Gdns, N5 66 DQ64
Holmcroft, Tad. (Walt.Hill)
KT20 183 CV125
Holmcroft Way, Brom. BR2 145 EM99
Holmdale Cl, Borwd. WD6 26 CM40
Holmdale Gdns, NW4 63 CX57
Holmdale Rd, NW6 64 DA64
Chislehurst BR7 125 EQ92
Holmdale Ter, N15 66 DS59
Holmdene Av, NW7 43 CU51
SE24 122 DQ85
Harrow HA2 60 CB55
Holmdene Cl, Beck. BR3 143 EC96
Holmead Rd, SW6 100 DB80
Holmebury Cl, Bushey
(Bushey Hth) WD23 41 CE47
Holme Chase, Wey. KT13 153 BQ107
Holme Cl, Wal.Cr. (Chsht)
EN8 15 DY31
Holme Ct, Islw. TW7
off Twickenham Rd 97 CG83
Holmedale, Slou. SL2 74 AW73
Holmefield Ct, NW3 82 DE65
Holme Lacey Rd, SE12 124 EF86
Holme Lea, Wat. WD25
off Kingsway 8 BW34
Holme Pk, Borwd. WD6 26 CM40
Holme Rd, E6 86 EL67
Hornchurch RM11 72 FN60
Holmes Av, E17 67 DZ55
NW7 43 CY50
Holmes Cl, SE22 102 DU84
Purley CR8 159 DM113
Woking GU22 167 AZ121
Holmesdale, Wal.Cr. EN8 31 DX35
Holmesdale Av, SW14 98 CP83
Holmesdale Cl, SE25 142 DT97
Holmesdale Hill, Dart.
(S.Darenth) DA4 148 FQ95
Holmesdale Rd, N6 65 DH59
SE25 142 DR99
Bexleyheath DA7 106 EX82
Croydon CR0 142 DR99
Dartford (S.Darenth) DA4 148 FQ95
Reigate RH2 184 DA133
Richmond TW9 98 CM81
Sevenoaks TN13 191 FJ123
Teddington TW11 117 CJ93
Holmesley Rd, SE23 123 DY86
Holmes Pl, SW10
off Fulham Rd 100 DC79
Holmes Rd, NW5 65 DH64
SW19 120 DC94
Twickenham TW1 117 CF89
Holmes Ter, SE1 200 D4
HOLMETHORPE, Red. RH1 185 DH132
Holmethorpe Av, Red. RH1 185 DH131
Holmethorpe Ind Est,
Red. RH1 185 DH131
Holme Way, Stan. HA7 41 CF51
Holmewood Gdns, SW2 121 DM87
Holmewood Rd, SE25 142 DS97
SW2 121 DL87
Holmfield Av, NW4 63 CX57
Holm Gro, Uxb. UB10 76 BN66
Holmhurst Rd, Belv. DA17 107 FB78
Holmlea Rd, Slou. (Datchet)
SL3 92 AX81
Holmlea Wk, Slou. (Datchet)
SL3 92 AW81
Holmleigh Av, Dart. DA1 108 FJ84
Holmleigh Rd, N16 66 DS60
Holmleigh Rd Est, N16
off Holmleigh Rd 66 DT60
Holm Oak Cl, SW15
off West Hill 119 CZ86
Holm Oak Ms, SW4
off King's Av 121 DL85
Holmsdale Cl, Iver SL0 75 BF72
Holmsdale Gro, Bexh. DA7 107 FE82
Holmshaw Cl, SE26 123 DY91
Holmshill La, Borwd. WD6 26 CS36
Holmside Ri, Wat. WD19 39 BV48
Holmside Rd, SW12 120 DG86
Holmsley Cl, N.Mal. KT3 139 CT100
Holmsley Ho, SW15
off Tangley Gro 119 CT87
Holms St, E2 84 DU68
Holmstall Av, Edg. HA8 62 CQ55
Holm Wk, SE3
off Blackheath Pk 104 EG82
Holmwood Av, Brwd.
(Shenf.) CM15 55 GA44
South Croydon CR2 160 DT113
Holmwood Cl, Add. KT15 152 BG106
Harrow HA2 60 CC55
Northolt UB5 78 CB65
Sutton SM2 157 CX109
Holmwood Gdns, N3 44 DA54
Wallington SM6 159 DH107
Holmwood Gro, NW7 42 CR50
Holmwood Rd, Chess. KT9 155 CK106
Enfield EN3 31 DX36
Ilford IG3 69 ES61
Sutton SM2 157 CW110
Holmwood Vil, SE7 205 N10
Holne Chase, N2 64 DC58
Morden SM4 139 CZ100
Holness Rd, E15 86 EF65
Holroyd Cl, Esher (Clay.)
KT10 155 CF109
Holroyd Rd, SW15 99 CW84
Esher (Clay.) KT10 155 CF109
Holsart Cl, Tad. KT20 173 CV122
Holstein Av, Wey. KT13 152 BN105
Holstein Way, Erith DA18 106 EY76
Holstock Rd, Ilf. IG1 69 EQ62
Holsworth Cl, Har. HA2 60 CC57
Holsworthy Sq, WC1 196 C5
Holsworthy Way, Chess. KT9 155 CJ106
Holt, The, Ilf. IG6 49 EQ51
Wallington SM6 159 DJ105
Holt Cl, N10 64 DG56
SE28 88 EV73
Borehamwood (Els.) WD6 26 CM42
Chigwell IG7 49 ET50
Holt Ct, E15 off Clays La 67 EC64
Holton St, E1 85 DX70
Holt Rd, E16 86 EL74
Romford RM3 52 FL52
Wembley HA0 61 CH62
Holtsmere Cl, Wat. WD25 24 BW35
Holt Way, Chig. IG7 49 ET50
Holtwhite Av, Enf. EN2 30 DQ40
Holtwhites Hill, Enf. EN2 29 DP39
Holtwood Rd, Lthd. (Oxshott)
KT22 154 CC113
Holwell Pl, Pnr. HA5 60 BY56
Holwood Cl, Walt. KT12 136 BW103
Holwood Pk Av, Orp. BR6 163 EM105
Holwood Pl, SW4 101 DK84
Holybourne Av, SW15 119 CU87
HOLYFIELD, Wal.Abb. EN9 15 ED28
Holyfield Rd, Wal.Abb. EN9 15 EC29
Holyhead Cl, E3 85 EA69
E6 off Valiant Way 87 EM71
Holyoake Av, Wok. GU21 166 AW117
Holyoake Ct, SE16 203 L4
Holyoake Cres, Wok. GU21 166 AW117
Holyoake Ter, Sev. TN13 190 FG124
Holyoake Wk, N2 64 DC55
W5 79 CJ70
Holyoak Rd, SE11 200 F8
Holyport Rd, SW6 99 CW80
Holyrood Av, Har. HA2 60 BY63
Holyrood Gdns, Edg. HA8 62 CP55
Grays RM16 111 GJ77
Holyrood Ms, E16 205 N2
Holyrood Rd, Barn. EN5 28 DC44
Holyrood St, SE1 201 M3
HOLYWELL, Wat. WD18 23 BS44
Holywell Cl, SE3 104 EG79
SE16 202 E10
Orpington BR6 164 EU105
Staines TW19 114 BL88
Holywell Ind Est, Wat. WD18 23 BR44
Holywell La, EC2 197 N4
Holywell Rd, Wat. WD18 23 BU43
Holywell Row, EC2 197 M5
Holywell Way, Stai. TW19 114 BL88
Homan Ct, N12 44 DC49
Home Cl, Cars. SM5 140 DF103
Leatherhead (Fetch.) KT22 171 CD121
Northolt UB5 78 BZ69
Virginia Water GU25 132 AX100
Homecroft Gdns, Loug. IG10 33 EP42
Homecroft Rd, N22 46 DQ53
SE26 122 DW92
Homedean Rd, Sev. (Chipstead)
TN13 190 FC122
Home Fm, Orp. BR6 164 FA106
Home Fm Cl, Cher. (Ott.)
KT16 151 BA108
Esher KT10 154 CB107
Shepperton TW17 135 BS98
Tadworth KT20 173 CX117
Thames Ditton KT7 137 CF101
Home Fm Gdns, Walt. KT12 136 BW103
Homefarm Rd, W7 79 CE72
Home Fm Rd, Rick. WD3 38 BN49
Home Fm Way, Slou.
(Stoke P.) SL3 74 AW67
Homefield, Hem.H. (Bov.) HP3 5 BB28
Waltham Abbey EN9 16 EG32
Walton-on-Thames KT12 154 BX105
Homefield Av, Ilf. IG2 69 ES57
Homefield Cl, NW10 80 CQ65
Addlestone (Wdhm) KT15 151 BE112
Epping CM16 18 EU30
Hayes UB4 78 BW70
Leatherhead KT22 171 CJ121
Orpington BR5 146 EV98
Swanley BR8 147 FF97

★ Place of interest | ⇌ Railway station | ⊖ London Underground station | DLR Docklands Light Railway station | Tra Tramlink station | H Hospital | Riv Pedestrian ferry landing stage

Homefield Fm Rd, Dart. (Sutt.H.) DA4 148 FM96
Homefield Gdns, N2 64 DD55
Mitcham CR4 140 DC96
Tadworth KT20 173 CW120
Homefield Ms, Beck. BR3 143 EA95
Homefield Pk, Sutt. SM1 158 DB107
Homefield Ri, Orp. BR6 146 EU102
Homefield Rd, SW19 119 CX93
W4 99 CT77
Bromley BR1 144 EJ95
Bushey WD23 24 CA43
Coulsdon CR5 175 DP119
Edgware HA8 42 CR51
Radlett WD7 25 CF37
Rickmansworth (Chorl.) WD3 21 BC42
Sevenoaks TN13 190 FE122
Walton-on-Thames KT12 136 BY101
Warlingham CR6 176 DW119
Wembley HA0 61 CG63
Homefield St, N1 197 M1
Homefirs Ho, Wem. HA9 off Wembley Pk Dr 62 CM62
Home Gdns, Dag. RM10 71 FC62
Dartford DA1 128 FL86
Home Hill, Swan. BR8 127 FF94
Homeland Dr, Sutt. SM2 158 DB109
Homelands, Lthd. KT22 171 CJ121
Homelands Dr, SE19 122 DS94
Home Lea, Orp. BR6 163 ET106
Homeleigh Ct, Wal.Cr. EN8 14 DV29
Homeleigh Rd, SE15 123 DX85
Homemead, SW12 121 DH89
Gravesend DA12 off Home Mead Cl 131 GH87
Home Mead, Stan. HA7 41 CJ53
Home Mead Cl, Grav. DA12 131 GH87
Home Meadow, Bans. SM7 174 DA116
Homemead Rd, Brom. BR2 145 EM99
Croydon CR0 141 DJ100
★ Home Office, SW1 199 M5
Home Orchard, Dart. DA1 128 FL86
Home Pk, Oxt. RH8 188 EG131
Home Pk Mill Link Rd, Kings L. WD4 7 BP31
Home Pk Rd, SW19 120 DA90
Home Pk Wk, Kings.T. KT1 137 CK98
Homer Cl, Bexh. DA7 107 FC81
Homer Dr, E14 203 P9
Home Rd, SW11 100 DE82
Homer Rd, E9 85 DY65
Croydon CR0 143 DX100
Homer Row, W1 194 C7
Homersham Rd, Kings.T. KT1 138 CN96
Homer St, W1 194 C7
HOMERTON, E9 67 DY64
⇌ Homerton 85 DX65
Homerton Gro, E9 67 DX64
Homerton High St, E9 66 DW64
Homerton Rd, E9 67 DY64
Homerton Row, E9 66 DW64
Homerton Ter, E9 off Morning La 84 DW65
H Homerton Uni Hosp, E9 67 DX64
Homesdale Cl, E11 68 EG57
Homesdale Rd, Brom. BR1, BR2 144 EJ98
Caterham CR3 176 DR123
Orpington BR5 145 ES101
Homesfield, NW11 64 DA57
Homestall Rd, SE22 122 DW85
Homestead, The, N11 45 DH49
Dartford DA1 128 FJ86
Homestead Cl, St.Alb. (Park St) AL2 8 CC27
Homestead Gdns, Esher (Clay.) KT10 155 CE106
Homestead Paddock, N14 29 DH43
Homestead Pk, NW2 63 CT62
Homestead Rd, SW6 99 CZ80
Caterham CR3 176 DR123
Dagenham RM8 70 EZ61
Orpington BR6 164 EV108
Rickmansworth WD3 off Park Rd 38 BK45
Staines TW18 114 BH93
Homestead Way, Croy. (New Adgtn) CR0 161 EC111
Homewaters Av, Sun. TW16 135 BT95
Home Way, Rick. (Mill End) WD3 37 BF46
Homeway, Rom. RM3 52 FP51
Homewillow Cl, N21 29 DP44
Homewood, Slou. (Geo.Grn) SL3 74 AX72
Homewood Av, Pot.B. (Cuffley) EN6 13 DL27
Homewood Cl, Hmptn. TW12 off Fearnley Cres 116 BZ93
Homewood Cres, Chis. BR7 125 ES93
Homewood La, Pot.B. EN6 13 DJ27
Homildon Ho, SE26 off Sydenham Hill Est 122 DU90
Honduras St, EC1 197 H4
Honeybourne Rd, NW6 64 DB64
Honeybourne Way, Orp. BR5 145 ER102
Honey Brook, Wal.Abb. EN9 16 EE33
Honeybrook Rd, SW12 121 DJ87
Honey Cl, Dag. RM10 89 FB65
Honeycroft, Loug. IG10 33 EN42
Honeycroft Hill, Uxb. UB10 76 BL66
Honeyden Rd, Sid. DA14 126 EY93
Honey Hill, Uxb. UB10 76 BM66
Honey La, EC2 197 J9
Waltham Abbey EN9 32 EG35
Honeyman Cl, NW6 81 CX66
Honeypot Cl, NW9 62 CM56
Honeypot La, NW9 62 CM55
Brentwood CM14 54 FU48
Stanmore HA7 62 CM55
Honeypots Rd, Wok. GU22 166 AX122
Honeysett Rd, N17 off Reform Row 46 DT54
Honeysuckle Cl, Brwd. (Pilg.Hat.) CM15 54 FV43
Iver SL0 75 BC72
Honeysuckle Cl, Rom. RM3 52 FJ51
Southall UB1 78 BY73
Honeysuckle Gdns, Croy. CR0 143 DX101
Honeywell Rd, SW11 120 DF86
Honeywood Cl, Pot.B. EN6 12 DE33
Honeywood Rd, NW10 81 CT68
Isleworth TW7 97 CG84
Honeywood Wk, Cars. SM5 158 DF105
Honister Cl, Stan. HA7 41 CH53
Honister Gdns, Stan. HA7 41 CH52
Honister Hts, Pur. CR8 160 DR114
Honister Pl, Stan. HA7 41 CH53
Honiton Gdns, NW7 43 CX52
Honiton Ho, Enf. EN3 off Exeter Rd 31 DX41
Honiton Rd, NW6 81 CZ68
Romford RM7 71 FD58
Welling DA16 105 ET82
Honley Rd, SE6 123 EB87
Honnor Gdns, Islw. TW7 97 CD82
Honnor Rd, Stai. TW18 114 BK94
HONOR OAK, SE23 122 DW86
HONOR OAK PARK, SE4 123 DY86
⇌ Honor Oak Park 123 DX86
Honor Oak Pk, SE23 122 DW86
Honor Oak Ri, SE23 122 DW86
Honor Oak Rd, SE23 122 DW88
Hood Av, N14 29 DH44
SW14 118 CQ85
Orpington BR5 146 EV99
Hood Cl, Croy. CR0 off Parson's Mead 141 DP102
Hoodcote Gdns, N21 45 DP45
Hood Ct, EC4 196 E9
Hood Rd, SW20 119 CT94
Rainham RM13 89 FE67
Hood Wk, Rom. RM7 51 FB53
HOOK, Chess. KT9 156 CL105
Hook, The, Barn. EN5 28 DD44
Hookers Rd, E17 67 DX55
Hook Fm Rd, Brom. BR2 144 EK99
Hookfield, Epsom KT19 156 CQ113
Hookfields, Grav. (Nthflt) DA11 130 GE90
Hook Gate, Enf. EN1 30 DV36
HOOK GREEN, Dart. DA2 127 FG91
HOOK GREEN, Grav. DA13 130 FZ93
Hook Grn La, Dart. DA2 127 FF90
Hook Grn Rd, Grav. (Sthflt) DA13 130 FY94
HOOK HEATH, Wok. GU22 166 AV120
Hook Heath Av, Wok. GU22 166 AV119
Hook Heath Gdns, Wok. GU22 166 AT121
Hook Heath Rd, Wok. GU22 166 AW121
Hook Hill, S.Croy. CR2 160 DS110
Hook Hill La, Wok. GU22 166 AV121
Hook Hill Pk, Wok. GU22 166 AV121
Hooking Grn, Har. HA2 60 CB57
Hook Junct, Surb. KT6 off Kingston Bypass 138 CL104
Hook La, Pot.B. EN6 12 DF32
Romford RM4 34 EZ44
Welling DA16 125 ET85
Hook Ri N, Surb. KT6 138 CN104
Hook Ri S, Surb. KT6 138 CN104
Hook Ri S Ind Pk, Surb. KT6 138 CN104
Hook Rd, Chess. KT9 155 CK106
Epsom KT19 156 CR111
Surbiton KT6 138 CL104
Hooks Cl, SE15 off Woods Rd 102 DV81
Hooks Hall Dr, Dag. RM10 71 FC62
Hookstone Way, Wdf.Grn. IG8 48 EK52
Hook Wk, Edg. HA8 42 CQ51
Hookwood Cor, Oxt. RH8 off Hookwood La 188 EH128
Hookwood La, Oxt. RH8 188 EH128
Hookwood Rd, Orp. BR6 164 EW111
Hool Cl, NW9 off Kingsbury Rd 62 CQ57
HOOLEY, Couls. CR5 174 DG122
Hooper Dr, Uxb. UB8 77 BP71
Hooper Rd, E16 86 EG72
Hooper's Ct, SW3 198 D5
Hoopers Ms, W3 off Churchfield Rd 80 CQ74
Hooper's Ms, Bushey WD23 40 CB46
Hooper St, E1 84 DU72
Hoopers Yd, Sev. TN13 191 FJ126
Hoop La, NW11 63 CZ59
Hope Cl, N1 off Wallace Rd 84 DQ65
SE12 124 EH90
Brentford TW8 off Burford Rd 98 CL78
Romford (Chad.Hth) RM6 70 EW56
Sutton SM1 158 DC106
Woodford Green IG8 off West Gro 48 EJ51
Hopedale Rd, SE7 104 EH79
Hopefield Av, NW6 81 CY68
Hope Gdns, W3 off Park Rd N 98 CP75
Hope Grn, Wat. WD25 7 BU33
Hope La, SE9 125 EP89
Hope Pk, Brom. BR1 124 EF94
Hope Rd, Swans. DA10 130 FZ86
Hopes Cl, Houns. TW5 off Old Cote Dr 96 CA79
Hope St, SW11 100 DD83
Hope Ter, Grays RM20 109 FX78
Hopetown St, E1 off Brick La 84 DT71
Hopewell Cl, Grays (Chaff.Hun.) RM16 109 FX78
Hopewell Dr, Grav. DA12 131 GM92
Hopewell St, SE5 102 DR80
Hopewell Yd, SE5 off Hopewell St 102 DR80
Hope Wf, SE16 off St. Marychurch St 102 DW75
Hopfield, Wok. (Horsell) GU21 166 AY116
Hopfield Av, W.Byf. (Byfleet) KT14 152 BL112
Hopgarden La, Sev. TN13 190 FG128
Hop Gdns, WC2 199 P1
Hop Gdn Way, Wat. WD25 8 BW31
Hopgood St, W12 off Macfarlane Rd 81 CW74
Hopkins Cl, N10 44 DG52
Romford RM2 72 FJ55
Hopkins Ms, E15 off West Rd 86 EF67
Hopkinsons Pl, NW1 off Fitzroy Rd 82 DG67
Hopkins St, W1 195 L9
Hoppers Rd, N13 45 DN47
N21 45 DN47
Hoppett Rd, E4 48 EE48
Hoppety, The, Tad. KT20 173 CX122
Hopping La, N1 off St. Mary's Gro 83 DP65
Hoppingwood Av, N.Mal. KT3 138 CS97
Hoppit Rd, Wal.Abb. EN9 15 EB32
Hoppner Rd, Hayes UB4 77 BQ68
Hop St, SE10 205 L8
Hopton Gdns, SE1 200 G2
New Malden KT3 139 CU100
Hopton Rd, SE18 105 EP76
SW16 121 DL92
Hopton St, SE1 200 G2
Hoptree Cl, N12 off Woodside Pk Rd 44 DB49
Hopwood Cl, SW17 120 DC90
Watford WD17 23 BR36
Hopwood Rd, SE17 102 DR79
Hopwood Wk, E8 off Wilman Gro 84 DU66
Horace Av, Rom. RM7 71 FC60
Horace Bldg, SW8 off Queenstown Rd 101 DH80
Horace Rd, E7 68 EH63
Ilford IG6 69 EQ55
Kingston upon Thames KT1 138 CM97
Horatio Ct, SE16 off Rotherhithe St 84 DW74
Horatio Pl, E14 204 E4
SW19 off Kingston Rd 140 DA95
Horatio St, E2 84 DT68
Horatius Way, Croy. CR0 159 DM106
Horbury Cres, W11 82 DA73
Horbury Ms, W11 off Ladbroke Rd 81 CZ73
Horder Rd, SW6 99 CY81
Hordle Prom E, SE15 off Garnies Cl 102 DT80
Hordle Prom N, SE15 off Daniel Gdns 102 DT80
Hordle Prom S, SE15 off Garnies Cl 102 DT80
Horizon Business Village, Wey. KT13 152 BN112
Horizon Way, SE7 104 EH77
Horksley Gdns, Brwd. (Hutt.) CM13 off Bannister Dr 55 GC44
Horle Wk, SE5 101 DP82
Horley Cl, Bexh. DA6 126 FA85
Horley Rd, SE9 124 EL91
Hormead Rd, W9 81 CZ70
Hornbeam Av, Upmin. RM14 72 FN63
Hornbeam Chase, S.Ock. RM15 91 FX69
Hornbeam Cl, NW7 43 CT48
SE11 200 D8
Barking IG11 off Marine Dr 88 EU69
Borehamwood WD6 26 CN39
Brentwood CM13 55 GB48
Buckhurst Hill IG9 off Hornbeam Rd 48 EK48
Epping (They.B.) CM16 33 ES37
Ilford IG1 69 ER64
Northolt UB5 60 BZ64
Hornbeam Cres, Brent. TW8 97 CH80
Hornbeam Gdns, Slough SL1 off Upton Rd 92 AU76
New Malden KT3 139 CU100
Hornbeam Gro, E4 48 EE48
Hornbeam Ho, NW3 off Maitland Pk Vil 82 DF65
Hornbeam La, E4 32 EE43
Bexleyheath DA7 107 FC82
Hornbeam Rd, Buck.H. IG9 48 EK48
Epping (They.B.) CM16 33 ER37
Hayes UB4 78 BW71
Hornbeams, St.Alb. (Brick.Wd) AL2 8 BZ30
Hornbeams Av, Enf. EN1 30 DW35
Hornbeam Sq, E3 off Hawthorn Av 85 DZ67
Hornbeams Ri, N11 44 DG51
Hornbeam Ter, Cars. SM5 140 DE102
Hornbeam Wk, Rich. TW10 118 CM90
Walton-on-Thames (Whiteley Vill.) KT12 off Octagon Rd 153 BT109
Hornbeam Way, Brom. BR2 145 EN100
Waltham Cross EN7 14 DT29
Hornbill Cl, Uxb. UB8 76 BK72
Hornblower Cl, SE16 203 K8
Hornbuckle Cl, Har. HA2 61 CD61
Hornby Cl, NW3 82 DD66
Horncastle Cl, SE12 124 EG87
Horncastle Rd, SE12 124 EG87
HORNCHURCH, RM11 & RM12 72 FJ61
⊖ Hornchurch 72 FK62
Hornchurch Cl, Kings.T. KT2 117 CK91
Hornchurch Hill, Whyt. CR3 176 DT117
Hornchurch Rd, Horn. RM11, RM12 71 FG60
Horndean Cl, SW15 off Bessborough Rd 119 CU88
Horndon Cl, Rom. RM5 51 FC53
Horndon Grn, Rom. RM5 51 FC53
Horndon Rd, Rom. RM5 51 FC53
Horner La, Mitch. CR4 140 DD96
Horne Rd, Shep. TW17 134 BN98
Hornets, The, Wat. WD18 23 BV42
Horne Way, SW15 99 CW82
Hornfair Rd, SE7 104 EJ79
Hornford Way, Rom. RM7 71 FE59
Hornhill Rd, Ger.Cr. SL9 37 BB50
Rickmansworth (Map.Cr.) WD3 37 BD50
Horniman Dr, SE23 122 DV88
★ Horniman Mus, SE23 122 DV88
Horning Cl, SE9 124 EL91
Horn La, SE10 205 M9
W3 80 CQ73
Woodford Green IG8 48 EG51
Horn Link Way, SE10 205 M8
Hornminster Glen, Horn. RM11 72 FN61
Horn Pk Cl, SE12 124 EH85
Horn Pk La, SE12 124 EH85
Hornsby La, Grays (Orsett) RM16 111 GG75
Horns Cft Cl, Bark. IG11 off Thornhill Gdns 87 ES66
Horns End Pl, Pnr. HA5 60 BW56
HORNSEY, N8 65 DM55
⇌ Hornsey 65 DM56
Hornsey La, N6 65 DH60
N19 65 DJ60
Hornsey La Est, N19 off Hornsey La 65 DK59
Hornsey La Gdns, N6 65 DJ59
Hornsey Pk Rd, N8 65 DM55
Hornsey Ri, N19 65 DK59
Hornsey Ri Gdns, N19 65 DK59
Hornsey Rd, N7 65 DM61
N19 65 DL60
Hornsey St, N7 65 DM64
HORNS GREEN, Sev. TN14 179 ES117
Hornshay St, SE15 102 DW79
Horns Rd, Ilf. IG2, IG6 69 EQ57
Hornton Pl, W8 100 DA75
Hornton St, W8 82 DA74
Horsa Rd, SE12 124 EJ87
Erith DA8 107 FC80
Horse & Dolphin Yd, W1 195 N10
Horsebridge Cl, Dag. RM9 88 EY67
Horsecroft, Bans. SM7 off Lyme Regis Rd 173 CZ117
Horsecroft Cl, Orp. BR6 146 EV102
Horsecroft Rd, Edg. HA8 42 CR52
Horse Fair, Kings.T. KT1 137 CK96
Horseferry Pl, SE10 103 EC79
Horseferry Rd, E14 85 DY73
SW1 199 M7
Horse Guards Av, SW1 199 P3
★ Horse Guards Par, SW1 199 N3
Horse Guards Rd, SW1 199 N3
Horse Hill, Chesh. HP5 4 AX32
Horse Leaze, E6 87 EN72
HORSELL, Wok. GU21 166 AY116
Horsell Birch, Wok. GU21 166 AV115
Horsell Common, Wok. GU21 150 AX114
Horsell Common Rd, Wok. GU21 150 AW114
Horsell Ct, Cher. KT16 off Stepgates 134 BH101
Horsell Moor, Wok. GU21 166 AX117
Horsell Pk, Wok. GU21 166 AX116
Horsell Pk Cl, Wok. GU21 166 AX116
Horsell Ri, Wok. GU21 166 AX115
Horsell Ri Cl, Wok. GU21 166 AX115
Horsell Rd, N5 65 DN64
Orpington BR5 146 EV95
Horsell Vale, Wok. GU21 166 AY115
Horsell Way, Wok. GU21 166 AW116
Horselydown La, SE1 201 P4
Horseman Side, Brwd. (Nave.S.) CM14 51 FH45
Horsemans Ride, St.Alb. AL2 8 CA26
Horsemongers Ms, SE1 201 J5
Horsemoor Cl, Slou. SL3 93 BA77
Horsenden Av, Grnf. UB6 61 CE64
Horsenden Cres, Grnf. UB6 61 CF64
Horsenden La N, Grnf. UB6 79 CF65
Horsenden La S, Grnf. UB6 79 CG67
Horse Ride, SW1 199 L3
Tadworth KT20 183 CY125
Horse Rd, E7 off Centre Rd 68 EH62
Horseshoe, The, Bans. SM7 173 CZ115
Coulsdon CR5 159 DK113
Horseshoe Business Pk, St.Alb. (Brick.Wd) AL2 8 CA30
Horseshoe Cl, E14 204 D10
NW2 63 CV61
Waltham Abbey EN9 16 EG34
Horse Shoe Ct, EC1 off Northburgh St 83 DP70
Horse Shoe Cres, Nthlt. UB5 78 CA68
Horseshoe Dr, Uxb. UB8 76 BN72
Horse Shoe Grn, Sutt. SM1 off Aultone Way 140 DB103
Horseshoe Hill, Wal.Abb. EN9 16 EJ33
Horseshoe La, N20 43 CX46
Enfield EN2 off Chase Side 30 DQ41
Watford WD25 7 BV32
Horseshoe Ms, SW2 off Acre La 101 DL84
Horseshoe Ridge, Wey. KT13 153 BQ111
Horse Yd, N1 off Essex Rd 83 DP67
Horsfeld Gdns, SE9 124 EL85
Horsfeld Rd, SE9 124 EK85
Horsfield Cl, Dart. DA2 128 FQ87
Horsford Rd, SW2 121 DM85
Horsham Av, N12 44 DE50
Horsham Rd, Bexh. DA6 126 FA85
Feltham TW14 115 BQ86
Horsley Cl, Epsom KT19 156 CR113
Horsleydown Old Stairs, SE1 201 P3
Horsley Dr, Croy. (New Adgtn) CR0 161 EC108
Kingston upon Thames KT2 117 CK92
Horsley Rd, E4 47 EC47
Bromley BR1 off Palace Rd 144 EH95
Cobham KT11 169 BV119
Horsleys, Rick. (Map.Cr.) WD3 37 BD50
Horsley St, SE17 102 DR79
Horsmonden Cl, Orp. BR6 145 ES101
Horsmonden Rd, SE4 123 DZ85
Hortensia Rd, SW10 100 DC80
Horticultural Pl, W4 off Heathfield Ter 98 CR78
HORTON, Epsom KT19 156 CP110
HORTON, Slou. SL3 93 BA83
Horton Av, NW2 63 CY63
Horton Br Rd, West Dr. UB7 76 BM74
Horton Cl, West Dr. UB7 76 BM74
★ Horton Country Pk, Epsom KT19 156 CM110
Horton Cres, Epsom KT19 156 CP110
Horton Footpath, Epsom KT19 156 CQ111
Horton Gdns, Epsom KT19 156 CQ111
Horton Hill, Epsom KT19 156 CQ111
Horton Ind Pk, West Dr. UB7 76 BM74
HORTON KIRBY, Dart. DA4 149 FR98
Horton La, Epsom KT19 156 CP110
★ Horton Park Children's Fm, Epsom KT19 156 CN110
Horton Rd, E8 84 DV65
Dartford (Hort.Kir.) DA4 148 FQ97
Slough (Colnbr.) SL3 93 BA81
Slough (Datchet) SL3 92 AV80
Slough (Poyle) SL3 93 BE83
Staines TW19 114 BG85
West Drayton UB7 76 BN74
Horton St, SE13 103 EB83
Hortons Way, West. TN16 189 ER126
Horton Way, Croy. CR0 143 DX99
Dartford (Fnghm) DA4 148 FM101
Hortus Rd, E4 47 EC47
Southall UB2 96 BZ75
Horvath Cl, Wey. KT13 153 BR105
Horwood Cl, Rick. WD3 off Thellusson Way 38 BG45
Horwood Ct, Wat. WD24 24 BX37
Hosack Rd, SW17 120 DF89
Hoser Av, SE12 124 EG89
Hosey Common La, West. TN16 189 ES130
Hosey Common Rd, Eden. TN8 189 EQ133
Westerham TN16 189 ER130
HOSEY HILL, West. TN16 189 ES127
Hosey Hill, West. TN16 189 ER127
Hosier La, EC1 196 F7
Hoskins Cl, E16 86 EJ72
Hayes UB3 off Cranford Dr 95 BT78
Hoskins Rd, Oxt. RH8 188 EE129
Hoskins St, SE10 103 ED78
Hoskins Wk, Oxt. RH8 188 EE129
Hospital Br Rd, Twick. TW2 116 CB87
H Hospital of St. John & St. Elizabeth, NW8 82 DD68
Hospital Rd, E9 off Homerton Row 67 DX64
Hounslow TW3 96 CA83
Sevenoaks TN13 191 FJ121
Hospital Way, SE13 123 ED86
Hotham Cl, Dart. (Sutt.H.) DA4 128 FP94
Swanley BR8 147 FH95
West Molesey KT8 off Garrick Gdns 136 CA97
Hotham Rd, SW15 99 CW83
SW19 120 DC94
Hotham Rd Ms, SW19 off Haydons Rd 120 DC94
Hotham St, E15 86 EE67
Hothfield Pl, SE16 202 G7
Hotspur Rd, Nthlt. UB5 78 CA68
Hotspur St, SE11 200 D10
Houblon Rd, Rich. TW10 118 CL85
Houblons Hill, Epp. (Cooper.) CM16 18 EW31
Houghton Cl, E8 off Buttermere Wk 84 DT65
Hampton TW12 116 BY93
Houghton Rd, N15 off West Grn Rd 66 DT57
Houghton St, WC2 196 C9
Houlder Cres, Croy. CR0 159 DP107
Houndsden Rd, N21 29 DM44
Houndsditch, EC3 197 N8
Houndsfield Rd, N9 46 DV45
HOUNSLOW, TW3 -TW6 96 BZ84
⇌ Hounslow 116 CB85
Hounslow Av, Houns. TW3 116 CB85
Hounslow Business Pk, Houns. TW3 off Alice Way 96 CB84
⊖ Hounslow Central 96 CA83
⊖ Hounslow East 96 CC82
Hounslow Gdns, Houns. TW3 116 CB85
★ Hounslow Heath, Houns. TW4 116 BY86
Hounslow Rd, Felt. TW14 115 BV88
Feltham (Han.) TW13 116 BX91
Twickenham TW2 116 CC86
HOUNSLOW WEST, Houns. TW4 96 BX83
⊖ Hounslow West 96 BY82
Houseman Way, SE5 off Hopewell St 102 DR80
★ Houses of Parliament, SW1 200 A5
Houston Pl, Esher KT10 off Lime Tree Av 137 CE102
Houston Rd, SE23 123 DY89
Surbiton KT6 137 CH100
Hove Av, E17 67 DZ57
Hove Cl, Brwd. (Hutt.) CM13 55 GC47
Grays RM17 110 GA79
Hoveden Rd, NW2 63 CY64
Hove Gdns, Sutt. SM1 140 DB102
Hoveton Rd, SE28 88 EW72
Hoveton Way, Ilf. IG6 49 EP52
Howard Agne Cl, Hem.H. (Bov.) HP3 5 BA27
Howard Av, Bex. DA5 126 EW88
Epsom KT17 157 CU110
Howard Bldg, SW8 101 DH79
Howard Business Pk, Wal.Abb. EN9 off Farm Hill Rd 15 ED33
Howard Cl, N11 44 DG47
NW2 63 CY63
W3 80 CP72
Ashtead KT21 172 CM118
Bushey (Bushey Hth) WD23 41 CE45
Hampton TW12 116 CC93
Leatherhead KT22 171 CJ123
Loughton IG10 32 EL44
Sunbury-on-Thames TW16 off Catherine Dr 115 BT93
Tadworth (Walt.Hill) KT20 183 CT125
Waltham Abbey EN9 15 ED34
Watford WD24 23 BU37
Howard Ct, Reig. RH2 184 DC133
Howard Dr, Borwd. WD6 26 CR42
Howard Ms, N5 off Hamilton Pk 65 DP63
Slough SL3 off Laburnum Gro 93 BB79
Howard Pl, Reig. RH2 184 DA132
Howard Rd, E6 87 EM68
E11 68 EE62
E17 67 EA55
N15 66 DS58
N16 66 DR63
NW2 63 CX63

A B C D E F G H I J K L M N O P Q R S T U V W X Y Z

Howard Rd, SE20 142 DW95
SE25 142 DU99
Barking IG11 87 ER67
Bromley BR1 124 EG94
Coulsdon CR5 175 DJ115
Dartford DA1 128 FN86
Grays (Chaff.Hun.) RM16 109 FW76
Ilford IG1 69 EP63
Isleworth TW7 97 CF83
Leatherhead (Eff.Junct.)
KT24 169 BU122
New Malden KT3 138 CS97
Southall UB1 78 CB72
Surbiton KT5 138 CM100
Upminster RM14 72 FQ61
Howards Cl, Pnr. HA5 39 BV54
Woking GU22 167 BA120
Howards Crest Cl, Beck. BR3 143 EC96
Howards La, SW15 119 CV85
Addlestone KT15 151 BE107
Howards Rd, E13 86 EG69
Woking GU22 167 AZ120
Howards Thicket, Ger.Cr. SL9 56 AW61
Howard St, T.Ditt. KT7 137 CH101
Howards Wd Dr, Ger.Cr. SL9 56 AX61
Howard Wk, N2 64 DC56
Howard Way, Barn. EN5 27 CX43
Howarth Ct, E15
off Smithies Ct 67 EC64
Howarth Rd, SE2 106 EU78
Howberry Cl, Edg. HA8 41 CK51
Howberry Rd, Edg. HA8 41 CK51
Stanmore HA7 41 CK51
Thornton Heath CR7 142 DR95
Howbury La, Erith DA8 107 FG82
Howbury Rd, SE15 102 DW83
Howcroft Cres, N3 44 DA52
Howcroft La, Grnf. UB6
off Cowgate Rd 79 CD69
Howden Cl, SE28 88 EX73
Howden Rd, SE25 142 DT96
Howden St, SE15 102 DU83
Howe Cl, Rad. (Shenley) WD7 10 CL32
Romford RM7 50 FA53
Howe Dr, Cat. CR3 176 DR122
Howell Cl, Rom. RM6 70 EX57
Howell Hill Cl, Epsom KT17 157 CW111
Howell Hill Gro, Epsom
KT17 157 CW110
Howell Wk, SE1 200 G9
Howerd Way, SE18
off Barlow Dr 104 EL81
Howes Cl, N3 64 DA55
Howfield Pl, N17 66 DT55
Howgate Rd, SW14 98 CR83
Howick Pl, SW1 199 L7
Howie St, SW11 100 DE80
Howitt Cl, N16 off Allen Rd 66 DS63
NW3 off Howitt Rd 82 DE65
Howitt Rd, NW3 82 DE65
Howitts Cl, Esher KT10 154 CA107
Howland Est, SE16 202 G6
Howland Ms E, W1 195 L6
Howland St, W1 195 K6
Howland Way, SE16 203 L5
How La, Couls. (Chipstead)
CR5 174 DG117
Howletts La, Ruis. HA4 59 BQ57
Howletts Rd, SE24 122 DQ86
Howley Pl, W2 82 DC71
Howley Rd, Croy. CR0 141 DP104
Hows Cl, Uxb. UB8
off Hows Rd 76 BJ67
Howse Rd, Wal.Abb. EN9
off Deer Pk Way 31 EB35
Howsman Rd, SW13 99 CU79
Howson Rd, SE4 103 DY84
Howson Ter, Rich. TW10 118 CL86
Hows Rd, Uxb. UB8 76 BJ67
Hows St, E2 84 DT68
Howton Pl, Bushey (Bushey Hth)
WD23 41 CD46
HOW WOOD, St.Alb. AL2 8 CC27
⇌ How Wood 8 CC28
How Wd, St.Alb. (Park St) AL2 8 CB28
HOXTON, N1 197 M1
Hoxton Mkt, N1 197 M3
Hoxton Sq, N1 197 M3
Hoxton St, N1 197 N3
Hoylake Cres, Uxb. (Ickhm)
UB10 58 BN60
Hoylake Gdns, Mitch. CR4 141 DJ97
Romford RM3 52 FN53
Ruislip HA4 59 BV60
Watford WD19 40 BX49
Hoylake Rd, W3 80 CS72
Hoyland Cl, SE15
off Commercial Way 102 DV80
Hoyle Rd, SW17 120 DE92
Hoy St, E16 86 EF72
Hoy Ter, Grays RM20 109 FX78
★ H.Q.S. Wellington, Master
Mariners' Hall, WC2 196 D10
Hubbard Dr, Chess. KT9 155 CJ107
Hubbard Rd, SE27 122 DQ91
Hubbards Chase, Horn. RM11 72 FN57
Hubbards Cl, Horn. RM11 72 FN57
Uxbridge UB8 77 BP72
Hubbards Rd, Rick. (Chorl.)
WD3 21 BD43
Hubbard St, E15 86 EE67
Hubbinet Ind Est, Rom. RM7 71 FC55
Hubert Gro, SW9 101 DL83
Hubert Rd, E6 86 EK69
Brentwood CM14 54 FV48
Rainham RM13 89 FF69
Slough SL3 92 AX76
Hucknall Cl, Rom. RM3 52 FM51
Huddart St, E3 85 DZ71
Huddleston Cl, E2 84 DW68
Huddlestone Cres, Red.
(Merst.) RH1 185 DK128
Huddlestone Rd, E7 68 EF63
NW2 81 CV65
Huddleston Rd, N7 65 DK63
Hudson Apts, N8
off New River Av 65 DM56
Hudson Av, Uxb. (Denh.) UB9 57 BF58
Hudson Cl, E15 off Park Gro 86 EG67
Watford WD24 23 BT36
Hudson Ct, E14
off Maritime Quay 103 EA78
SW19 120 DB94
Hudson Gdns, Orp. BR6
off Superior Dr 163 ET107
Hudson Pl, SE18 105 EQ78
Slough SL3 off Ditton Rd 93 AZ78
Hudson Rd, Bexh. DA7 106 EZ82
Hayes UB3 95 BR79
Hudsons, Tad. KT20 173 CX121
Hudson's Pl, SW1 199 J8
Hudson Way, N9 46 DW48
NW2 off Gratton Ter 63 CX62
Huggin Ct, EC4 197 J10
Huggin Hill, EC4 197 J10
Huggins Pl, SW2
off Roupell Rd 121 DM88
Hughan Rd, E15 67 ED64
Hugh Dalton Av, SW6 99 CZ79
Hughenden Av, Har. HA3 61 CH57
Hughenden Gdns, Nthlt. UB5 78 BW69
Hughenden Rd, Wor.Pk. KT4 139 CU101
Hughendon Ter, E15
off Westdown Rd 67 EC63
Hughes Cl, N12
off Coleridge Rd 44 DC50
Hughes Rd, Ashf. TW15 115 BQ94
Grays RM16 111 GG76
Hayes UB3 77 BV73
Hughes Ter, SW9
off Styles Gdns 101 DP83
Hughes Wk, Croy. CR0
off St. Saviours Rd 142 DQ101
Hugh Gaitskell Cl, SW6 99 CZ79
Hugh Ms, SW1 199 J9
Hugh St, SW1 199 J9
Hugo Cl, Wat. WD18
off Malkin Way 23 BS42
Hugo Gdns, Rain. RM13 89 FF65
Hugo Gryn Way, Rad. (Shenley)
WD7 10 CL31
Hugon Rd, SW6 100 DB83
Hugo Rd, N19 65 DJ63
Huguenot Pl, E1 84 DT71
SW18 120 DC85
Huguenot Sq, SE15
off Scylla Rd 102 DV83
HULBERRY, Swan. BR8 147 FG103
Hullbridge Ms, N1
off Sherborne St 84 DR67
Hull Cl, SE16 203 J4
Sutton SM2
off Yarbridge Cl 158 DB110
Waltham Cross (Chsht) EN7 14 DR26
Hulletts La, Brwd. (Pilg.Hat.)
CM15 54 FT43
Hull Pl, E16
off Fishguard Way 87 EQ74
Hull St, EC1 197 H3
Hulme Pl, SE1 201 J5
Hulse Av, Bark. IG11 87 ER65
Romford RM7 51 FB53
Hulse Ter, Ilf. IG1
off Buttsbury Rd 69 EQ64
Hulsewood Cl, Dart. DA2 127 FH90
Hulton Cl, Lthd. KT22 171 CJ123
Hulverston Cl, Sutt. SM2 158 DB110
Humber Av, S.Ock. RM15 91 FT72
Humber Cl, West Dr. UB7 76 BK74
Humber Dr, W10 81 CX70
Upminster RM14 73 FR58
Humber Rd, NW2 63 CV61
SE3 104 EF79
Dartford DA1 128 FK85
Humberstone Rd, E13 86 EJ69
Humberton Cl, E9
off Marsh Hill 67 DY64
Humber Way, Slou. SL3 93 BA77
Humbolt Rd, W6 99 CY79
Hume Av, Til. RM18 111 GG83
Hume Cl, Til. RM18 111 GG83
Humes Av, W7 97 CE76
Hume Ter, E16
off Prince Regent La 86 EJ72
Hume Way, Ruis. HA4 59 BU58
Hummer Rd, Egh. TW20 113 BA91
Humphrey Cl, Ilf. IG5 49 EM53
Leatherhead (Fetch.) KT22 170 CC122
Humphrey St, SE1 201 P10
Humphries Cl, Dag. RM9 70 EZ63
Hundred Acre, NW9 43 CT54
Hungerdown, E4 47 EC46
Hungerford Av, Slou. SL2 74 AS71
Hungerford Br, SE1 200 A2
WC2 200 A2
Hungerford La, WC2 199 P2
Hungerford Rd, N7 65 DK64
Hungerford Sq, Wey. KT13
off Rosslyn Pk 153 BR105
Hungerford St, E1
off Commercial Rd 84 DV72
Hungry Hill, Wok. (Ripley) GU23
off Hungry Hill La 168 BK124
Hungry Hill La, Wok. (Send)
GU23 168 BK124
Hunsdon Cl, Dag. RM9 88 EY65
Hunsdon Dr, Sev. TN13 191 FH123
Hunsdon Rd, SE14 103 DX79
Hunslett St, E2
off Royston St 84 DW68
Hunstanton Cl, Slou. (Colnbr.)
SL3 93 BC80
Hunston Rd, Mord. SM4 140 DB102
Hunt Cl, W11 81 CX74
Hunter Av, Brwd. (Shenf.)
CM15 55 GA44
Hunter Cl, SE1 201 L7
SW12 off Balham Pk Rd 120 DG88
Borehamwood WD6 26 CQ43
Potters Bar EN6 12 DB33
Wallington SM6 159 DL108
Huntercrombe Gdns, Wat.
WD19 40 BW50
Hunter Dr, Horn. RM12 72 FJ63
Hunter Ho, Felt. TW13 115 BU88
Hunter Rd, SW20 139 CW95
Ilford IG1 69 EP64
Thornton Heath CR7 142 DR97
Hunters, The, Beck. BR3 143 EC95
Hunters Cl, Bex. DA5 127 FE90
Epsom KT19
off Marshalls Cl 156 CQ113
Hemel Hempstead (Bov.)
HP3 5 BA29
Hunters Ct, Rich. TW9
off Friars La 117 CK85
Huntersfield Cl, Reig. RH2 184 DB131
Hunters Gate, Red. (Nutfld)
RH1 185 DM133
Watford WD25
off Hunters La 7 BU33
Hunters Gro, Har. HA3 61 CJ56
Hayes UB3 77 BU74
Orpington BR6 163 EP105
Romford RM5 51 FB50
Hunters Hall Rd, Dag. RM10 70 FA63
Hunters Hill, Ruis. HA4 60 BW62
Hunters La, Wat. WD25 7 BT33
Hunters Meadow, SE19
off Dulwich Wd Av 122 DS91
Hunters Reach, Wal.Cr. EN7 14 DT29
Hunters Ride, St.Alb. (Brick.Wd)
AL2 8 CA31
Hunters Rd, Chess. KT9 138 CL104
Hunters Sq, Dag. RM10 70 FA63
Hunter St, WC1 196 A4
Hunters Wk, Sev. (Knock.)
TN14 164 EY114
Hunters Way, Croy. CR0 160 DS105
Enfield EN2 29 DN39
Hunter Wk, E13 86 EG68
Borehamwood WD6
off Hunter Cl 26 CQ43
Hunting Cl, Esher KT10 154 CA105
Huntingdon Cl, Mitch. CR4 141 DL97
Huntingdon Gdns, W4 98 CQ80
Worcester Park KT4 139 CW104
Huntingdon Pl, Slou. SL3
off Meadfield Rd 93 BB76
Huntingdon Rd, N2 64 DE55
N9 46 DW46
Redhill RH1 184 DF134
Woking GU21 166 AT117
Huntingdon St, E16 86 EF72
N1 83 DM66
Huntingfield, Croy. CR0 161 DZ108
Huntingfield Rd, SW15 99 CU84
Huntingfield Way, Egh.
TW20 113 BD94
Hunting Gate Cl, Enf. EN2 29 DN41
Hunting Gate Dr, Chess.
KT9 156 CL108
Hunting Gate Ms, Sutt. SM1 140 DB104
Twickenham TW2
off Colne Rd 117 CE88
Huntings Rd, Dag. RM10 88 FA65
Huntland Cl, Rain. RM13 89 FH71
Huntley Av, Grav. (Nthflt)
DA11 130 GB86
Huntley Cl, Stai. (Stanw.) TW19
off Cambria Gdns 114 BL87
Huntley Dr, N3 44 DA51
Huntley Ho, Walt. KT12
off Octagon Rd 153 BT109
Huntley St, WC1 195 L5
Huntley Way, SW20 139 CU96
Huntly Rd, SE25 142 DS98
HUNTON BRIDGE, Kings L.
WD4 7 BP33
Hunton Br Hill, Kings L. WD4 7 BQ33
Hunton St, E1 84 DU70
Hunt Rd, Grav. (Nthflt) DA11 130 GE90
Southall UB2 96 CA76
Hunt's Cl, SE3 104 EG82
Hunt's Ct, WC2 199 N1
Hunts La, E15 85 EC68
Huntsman Cl, Warl. CR6 176 DW119
Huntsman Rd, Ilf. IG6 50 EU51
Huntsmans Cl, Felt. TW13 115 BV91
Leatherhead (Fetch.) KT22
off The Green 171 CD124
Huntsmans Dr, Upmin. RM14 72 FQ64
Huntsman St, SE17 201 L9
Hunts Mead, Enf. EN3 31 DX41
Hunts Mead Cl, Chis. BR7 125 EM94
Huntsmoor Rd, Epsom KT19 156 CR106
Huntspill St, SW17 120 DC90
Hunts Slip Rd, SE21 122 DS90
Huntsworth Ms, NW1 194 D5
Hurdwick Pl, NW1
off Harrington Sq 83 DJ68
Hurley Cl, Walt. KT12 135 BV103
Hurley Cres, SE16 203 J4
Hurley Ho, SE11 200 E9
Hurley Rd, Grnf. UB6 78 CB72
Hurlfield, Dart. DA2 128 FJ90
Hurlford, Wok. GU21 166 AU117
Hurlingham Business Pk,
SW6 100 DA83
Hurlingham Ct, SW6 99 CZ83
Hurlingham Gdns, SW6 99 CZ83
★ Hurlingham Ho, SW6 100 DA83
★ Hurlingham Park, SW6 99 CZ82
Hurlingham Retail Pk, SW6
off Carnwath Rd 100 DB83
Hurlingham Rd, SW6 99 CZ82
Bexleyheath DA7 106 EZ80
Hurlingham Sq, SW6 100 DA83
Hurlock St, N5 65 DP62
Hurlstone Rd, SE25 142 DR99
Hurn Ct Rd, Houns. TW4
off Renfrew Rd 96 BX82
Hurnford Cl, S.Croy. CR2 160 DS110
Huron Cl, Orp. BR6
off Winnipeg Dr 163 ET107
Huron Rd, SW17 120 DG89
Broxbourne EN10 15 DY26
Hurren Cl, SE3 104 EE83
Hurricane Rd, Wall. SM6 159 DL108
Hurricane Way, Abb.L. WD5
off Abbey Dr 7 BU32
Epping (N.Wld Bas.) CM16 18 EZ27
Slough SL3 93 BB78
Hurry Cl, E15 86 EE66
Hursley Rd, Chig. IG7
off Tufter Rd 49 ET50
Hurst Av, E4 47 EA49
N6 65 DJ58
Hurstbourne, Esher (Clay.)
KT10 155 CF107
Hurstbourne Gdns, Bark. IG11 87 ES65
Hurstbourne Ho, SW15
off Tangley Gro 119 CT86
Hurstbourne Rd, SE23 123 DY88
Hurst Cl, E4 47 EA48
NW11 64 DB58
Bromley BR2 144 EF102
Chessington KT9 156 CN106
Northolt UB5 78 BZ65
Hurst Cl, Wok. GU22 166 AW120
Hurstcourt Rd, Sutt. SM1 140 DB103
Hurstdene Av, Brom. BR2 144 EF102
Staines TW18 114 BH93
Hurstdene Gdns, N15 66 DS59
Hurst Dr, Tad. (Walt.Hill)
KT20 183 CU126
Waltham Cross EN8 15 DX34
Hurst Est, SE2 106 EX78
Hurstfield, Brom. BR2 144 EG99
Hurstfield Cres, Hayes UB4 77 BS70
Hurstfield Rd, W.Mol. KT8 136 CA97
HURST GREEN, Oxt. RH8 188 EG132
⇌ Hurst Green 188 EF132
Hurst Grn Cl, Oxt. RH8 188 EG132
Hurst Grn Rd, Oxt. RH8 188 EF132
Hurst Gro, Walt. KT12 135 BT102
Hurstlands, Oxt. RH8 188 EG132
Hurstlands Cl, Horn. RM11 72 FJ59
Hurst La, SE2 106 EX78
East Molesey KT8 136 CC98
Egham TW20 133 BA96
Epsom (Headley) KT18 172 CQ124
Hurstleigh Cl, Red. RH1 184 DF132
Hurstleigh Dr, Red. RH1 184 DF132
Hurstleigh Gdns, Ilf. IG5 49 EM53
Hurstmead Ct, Edg. HA8 42 CP49
Hurst Pk Av, Horn. RM12
off Newmarket Way 72 FL63
Hurst Pl, Nthwd. HA6 39 BP53
Hurst Ri, Barn. EN5 28 DA41
Hurst Rd, E17 67 EB55
N21 45 DN46
Bexley DA5 126 EX88
Buckhurst Hill IG9 48 EK46
Croydon CR0 160 DR106
East Molesey KT8 136 CA97
Epsom KT19 156 CR111
Epsom (Headley) KT18 172 CR123
Erith DA8 107 FC80
Sidcup DA15 126 EU89
Tadworth (Walt.Hill) KT20 172 CR123
Walton-on-Thames KT12 136 BW99
West Molesey KT8 136 BY97
Hurst Springs, Bex. DA5 126 EY88
Hurst St, SE24 121 DP86
Hurst Vw Rd, S.Croy. CR2 160 DS108
Hurst Way, Sev. TN13 191 FJ127
South Croydon CR2 160 DS107
Woking (Pyrford) GU22 151 BE114
Hurstway Wk, W11 81 CX73
Hurstwood Av, E18 68 EH56
Bexley DA5 126 EY88
Bexleyheath DA7 107 FE81
Brentwood (Pilg.Hat.)
CM15 54 FV45
Erith DA8 107 FE81
Hurstwood Ct, Upmin. RM14 72 FQ60
Hurstwood Dr, Brom. BR1 145 EM97
Hurstwood Rd, NW11 63 CY56
Hurtwood Rd, Walt. KT12 136 BZ101
Hurworth Av, Slou. SL3 92 AW76
Huson Cl, NW3 82 DE66
Hussain Cl, Har. HA1 61 CF63
Hussars Cl, Houns. TW4 96 BY83
Husseywell Cres, Brom. BR2 144 EG102
Hutchingsons Rd, Croy.
(New Adgtn) CR0 161 EC111
Hutchings St, E14 203 P5
Hutchings Wk, NW11 64 DB56
Hutchins Cl, E15
off Gibbins Rd 85 EC66
Hornchurch RM12 72 FL62
Hutchinson Ter, Wem. HA9 61 CK62
Hutchins Rd, SE28 88 EU73
Hutson Ter, Purf. RM19
off London Rd Purfleet 109 FR79
HUTTON, Brwd. CM13 55 GD44
Hutton Cl, Grnf. UB6
off Mary Peters Dr 61 CD64
Walton-on-Thames KT12 153 BV106
Woodford Green IG8 48 EH51
Hutton Dr, Brwd. (Hutt.)
CM13 55 GD45
Hutton Gdns, Har. HA3 40 CC52
Hutton Gate, Brwd. (Hutt.)
CM13 55 GB45
Hutton Gro, N12 44 DB50
Hutton La, Har. HA3 40 CC52
HUTTON MOUNT, Brwd.
CM13 55 GB46
Hutton Pl, Brwd. (Hutt.)
CM13 55 GB44
Hutton Rd, Brwd. (Shenf.)
CM15 55 FZ45
Hutton Row, Edg. HA8 42 CQ52
Hutton St, EC4 196 E9
Hutton Village, Brwd. (Hutt.)
CM13 55 GE45
Hutton Wk, Har. HA3 40 CC52
Huxbear St, SE4 123 DZ85
Huxley Cl, Nthlt. UB5 78 BY67
Uxbridge UB8 76 BK70
Huxley Dr, Rom. RM6 70 EV59
Huxley Gdns, NW10 80 CM69
Huxley Par, N18 46 DR50
Huxley Pl, N13 45 DP49
Huxley Rd, E10 67 EC61
N18 46 DR49
Welling DA16 105 ET83
Huxley Sayze, N18 46 DR50
Huxley St, W10 81 CY69
Hyacinth Cl, Hmptn. TW12
off Gresham Rd 116 CA93
Ilford IG1 87 EP65
Hyacinth Ct, Pnr. HA5
off Tulip Ct 60 BW55
Hyacinth Dr, Uxb. UB10 76 BL66
Hyacinth Rd, SW15 119 CU88
Hyburn Cl, St.Alb. (Brick.Wd)
AL2 8 BZ30
Hycliffe Gdns, Chig. IG7 49 EQ49
HYDE, THE, NW9 63 CT56
Hyde, The, NW9 62 CS57
Hyde Av, Pot.B. EN6 12 DB33
Hyde Cl, E13 86 EG68
Ashford TW15 off Hyde Ter 115 BS93
Barnet EN5 27 CZ41
Grays (Chaff.Hun.) RM16 109 FX76
Hyde Ct, N20 44 DD48
Waltham Cross EN8
off Parkside 15 DY34
Hyde Cres, NW9 62 CS57
Hyde Dr, Orp. BR5 146 EV98
Hyde Est Rd, NW9 63 CT57
Hyde Fm Ms, SW12
off Telferscot Rd 121 DK88
Hydefield Cl, N21 46 DR46
Hydefield Ct, N9 46 DS47
Hyde Ho, NW9 62 CS57
Hyde La, SW11
off Battersea Br Rd 100 DE81
Hemel Hempstead HP3 7 BR26
Hemel Hempstead (Bov.)
HP3 5 BA27
St. Albans (Frog.) AL2 9 CE28
Woking (Ock.) GU23 168 BN120
Hyde Meadows, Hem.H.
(Bov.) HP3 5 BA28
★ Hyde Park, W2 198 B2
Hyde Pk, SW7 198 B2
W1 198 B2
Hyde Pk Av, N21 46 DQ47
⊖ Hyde Park Corner 198 F4
Hyde Pk Cor, W1 198 G4
Hyde Pk Cres, W2 194 B9
Hyde Pk Gdns, N21 46 DQ46
W2 194 A10
Hyde Pk Gdns Ms, W2 194 A10
Hyde Pk Gate, SW7 100 DC75
Hyde Pk Gate Ms, SW7
off Hyde Pk Gate 100 DC75
Hyde Pk Pl, W2 194 C10
Hyde Pk Sq, W2 194 B9
Hyde Pk Sq Ms, W2 194 B9
Hyde Pk St, W2 194 B9
Hyderabad Way, E15 86 EE66
Hyde Rd, N1 84 DR67
Bexleyheath DA7 106 EZ82
Richmond TW10
off Albert Rd 118 CM85
South Croydon CR2 160 DS113
Watford WD17 23 BU40
Hyder Rd, Grays RM16 111 GJ76
Hydeside Gdns, N9 46 DT47
Hydes Pl, N1 off Compton Av 83 DP66
Hyde St, SE8
off Deptford High St 103 EA79
Hyde Ter, Ashf. TW15 115 BS93
Hydethorpe Av, N9 46 DT47
Hydethorpe Rd, SW12 121 DJ88
Hyde Vale, SE10 103 EC80
Hyde Wk, Mord. SM4 140 DA101
Hyde Way, N9 46 DT47
Hayes UB3 95 BT77
Hyland Cl, Horn. RM11 71 FH59
Hylands Cl, Epsom KT18 172 CQ115
Hylands Ms, Epsom KT18 172 CQ115
Hylands Rd, E17 47 ED54
Epsom KT18 172 CQ115
Hyland Way, Horn. RM11 71 FH59
Hylton St, SE18 105 ET77
Hyndewood, SE23 123 DX90
Hyndford Cres, Green. DA9
off Ingress Pk Av 129 FW85
Hyndman St, SE15 102 DV79
Hynton Rd, Dag. RM8 70 EW61
Hyperion Pl, Epsom KT19 156 CR109
Hyrons Cl, Amer. HP6 20 AS38
Hyrstdene, S.Croy. CR2 159 DP105
Hyson Rd, SE16 202 E10
Hythe, The, Stai. TW18 113 BE92
Hythe Av, Bexh. DA7 106 EZ80
Hythe Cl, N18 46 DU49
Orpington BR5
off Sandway Rd 146 EW98
HYTHE END, Stai. TW19 113 BB90
Hythe End Rd, Stai. (Wrays.)
TW19 113 BA89
Hythe Fld Av, Egh. TW20 113 BD93
Hythe Pk Rd, Egh. TW20 113 BC92
Hythe Path, Th.Hth. CR7 142 DR97
Hythe Rd, NW10 81 CU70
Staines TW18 113 BD92
Thornton Heath CR7 142 DR96
Hythe Rd Ind Est, NW10 81 CU69
Hythe St, Dart. DA1 128 FL86
Hythe St Lwr, Dart. DA1 128 FL85
Hyver Hill, NW7 26 CR44

I

Ian Sq, Enf. EN3
off Lansbury Rd 31 DX39
Ibbetson Path, Loug. IG10 33 EP41
Ibbotson Av, E16 86 EF72
Ibbott St, E1 off Mantus Rd 84 DW70
Iberian Av, Wall. SM6 159 DK105
Ibex Ho, E15 off Forest La 86 EE65
Ibis La, W4 98 CQ81
Ibis Way, Hayes UB4
off Cygnet Way 78 BX72
Ibscott Cl, Dag. RM10 89 FC65
Ibsley Gdns, SW15 119 CU88
Ibsley Way, Barn. EN4 28 DE43
★ Ice Ho, Holland Pk, W8 99 CZ75
Icehouse Wd, Oxt. RH8 188 EE131
Iceland Rd, E3 85 EA67
Iceland Wf, SE16
off Plough Way 103 DY77
Iceni Ct, E3 off Roman Rd 85 DZ67
Ice Wf, N1 off New Wf Rd 83 DL68
Ice Wf Marina, N1
off New Wf Rd 83 DL68
Ickburgh Est, E5
off Ickburgh Rd 66 DV62
Ickburgh Rd, E5 66 DV62
ICKENHAM, Uxb. UB10 59 BQ62
⊖ Ickenham 59 BQ63
Ickenham Cl, Ruis. HA4 59 BR61
Ickenham Rd, Ruis. HA4 59 BR60
Uxbridge (Ickhm) UB10 59 BQ61
Ickleton Rd, SE9 124 EL91
Icklingham Gate, Cob. KT11 154 BW112
Icklingham Rd, Cob. KT11 154 BW112
Icknield Dr, Ilf. IG2 69 EP57
Ickworth Pk Rd, E17 67 DY56

★ Place of interest ⇌ Railway station ⊖ London Underground station DLR Docklands Light Railway station Tra Tramlink station H Hospital Riv Pedestrian ferry landing stage

Ida Rd, N15 66 DR57
Ida St, E14 85 EC72
Iden Cl, Brom. BR2 144 EE97
Idlecombe Rd, SW17 120 DG93
Idmiston Rd, E15 68 EF64
SE27 122 DQ90
Worcester Park KT4 139 CT101
Idmiston Sq, Wor.Pk. KT4 139 CT101
Idol La, EC3 201 M1
Idonia St, SE8 103 DZ80
Iffley Cl, Uxb. UB8 76 BK66
Iffley Rd, W6 99 CV76
Ifield Rd, SW10 100 DB79
Ifield Way, Grav. DA12 131 GK93
Ifor Evans Pl, E1
off Mile End Rd 85 DX70
Ightham Rd, Erith DA8 106 FA80
Ikea Twr, NW10 62 CR64
Ikona Ct, Wey. KT13 153 BQ106
Ilbert St, W10 81 CX69
Ilchester Gdns, W2 82 DB73
Ilchester Pl, W14 99 CZ76
Ilchester Rd, Dag. RM8 70 EV64
Ildersly Gro, SE21 122 DR89
Ilderton Rd, SE15 102 DW80
SE16 202 E10
Ilex Cl, Egh. (Eng.Grn) TW20 112 AV94
Sunbury-on-Thames TW16
off Oakington Dr 136 BW96
Ilex Ho, N4 65 DM59
Ilex Rd, NW10 81 CT65
Ilex Way, SW16 121 DN92
ILFORD, IG1 - IG6 69 EQ62
⇌ Ilford 69 EN62
Ilford Hill, Ilf. IG1 69 EN62
Ilford La, Ilf. IG1 69 EP62
Ilfracombe Cres, Horn. RM12 72 FJ63
Ilfracombe Gdns, Rom. RM6 70 EV59
Ilfracombe Rd, Brom. BR1 124 EF90
Iliffe St, SE17 200 G10
Iliffe Yd, SE17 200 G10
Ilkeston Ct, E5
off Overbury St 67 DX63
Ilkley Cl, SE19 122 DR93
Ilkley Rd, E16 86 EJ71
Watford WD19 40 BX50
Illingworth Cl, Mitch. CR4 144 DD97
Illingworth Way, Enf. EN1 30 DS42
Ilmington Rd, Har. HA3 61 CK58
Ilminster Gdns, SW11 100 DE84
Imber Cl, N14 45 DJ45
Esher KT10 off Ember La 137 CD102
Imber Ct Trd Est, E.Mol. KT8 137 CD100
Imber Gro, Esher KT10 137 CD101
Imber Pk Rd, Esher KT10 137 CD102
Imber St, N1 84 DR67
Imer Pl, T.Ditt. KT7 137 CF101
Imperial Av, N16
off Victorian Rd 66 DT62
Imperial Business Est, Grav.
DA11 131 GF86
Imperial Cl, Har. HA2 60 CA58
★ Imperial Coll of Science,
Tech & Med, SW7 100 DD76
Imperial Coll Rd, SW7 100 DD76
Imperial Ct, NW8
off Prince Albert Rd 82 DE68
Imperial Cres, SW6 100 DC82
Weybridge KT13
off Churchill Dr 135 BQ104
Imperial Dr, Grav. DA12 131 GM92
Harrow HA2 60 CA59
Imperial Gdns, Mitch. CR4 141 DH97
Imperial Ms, E6
off Central Pk Rd 86 EJ68
Imperial Pk, Wat. WD24 24 BW39
Imperial Retail Pk, Grav.
DA11 131 GG86
Imperial Rd, N22 45 DL53
SW6 100 DB81
Feltham TW14 115 BS87
Imperial Sq, SW6 100 DB81
Imperial St, E3 85 EC69
Imperial Trd Est, Rain. RM13 90 FJ70
★ Imperial War Mus, SE1 200 E7
Imperial Way, Chis. BR7 125 EQ90
Croydon CR0 159 DM107
Harrow HA3 62 CL58
Watford WD24 24 BW39
Imperial Wf, SW6 100 DC82
Imprimo Pk, Loug. IG10 33 ER42
Imre Cl, W12
off Ellerslie Rd 81 CV74
Inca Dr, SE9 125 EP87
Inca Ter, N15 off Milton Rd 65 DP55
Ince Rd, Walt. KT12 153 BS107
Inchmery Rd, SE6 123 EB89
Inchwood, Croy. CR0 161 EB105
Independent Pl, E8
off Downs Pk Rd 66 DT64
Independents Rd, SE3
off Blackheath Village 104 EF83
Inderwick Rd, N8 65 DM57
Indescon Ct, E14 204 A5
India Pl, WC2 196 B10
India Rd, Slou. SL1 92 AV75
India St, EC3 197 P9
India Way, W12 81 CV73
Indigo Ms, E14 off Ashton St 85 EC73
N16 66 DR62
Indus Rd, SE7 104 EJ80
Industry Ter, SW9
off Canterbury Cres 101 DN83
Ingal Rd, E13 86 EG70
Ingate Pl, SW8 101 DH81
Ingatestone Rd, E12 68 EJ60
SE25 142 DV98
Woodford Green IG8 48 EG52
Ingelow Rd, SW8 101 DH82
Ingels Mead, Epp. CM16 17 ET29
Ingersoll Rd, W12 81 CV74
Enfield EN3 30 DW38
Ingestre Ct, W1
off Broadwick St 83 DJ73
Ingestre Pl, W1 195 L9
Ingestre Rd, E7 68 EG63
NW5 65 DH63
Ingham Cl, S.Croy. CR2 161 DX109
Ingham Rd, NW6 64 DA63
South Croydon CR2 160 DW109
Inglebert St, EC1 196 D2
Ingleboro Dr, Pur. CR8 160 DR113
Ingleborough St, SW9 101 DN82
Ingleby Dr, Har. HA1 61 CD62
Ingleby Gdns, Chig. IG7 50 EV48
Ingleby Rd, N7 off Bryett Rd 65 DL62
Dagenham RM10 89 FB65
Grays RM16 111 GH76
Ilford IG1 69 EP60
Ingleby Way, Chis. BR7 125 EN92
Wallington SM6 159 DK109
Ingle Cl, Pnr. HA5 60 BY55
Ingledew Rd, SE18 105 ER78
Inglefield, Pot.B. EN6 12 DA30
Ingleglen, Horn. RM11 72 FN59
Inglehurst, Add. (New Haw)
KT15 152 BH110
Inglehurst Gdns, Ilf. IG4 69 EM57
Inglemere Rd, SE23 123 DX90
Mitcham CR4 120 DF94
Inglesham Wk, E9 85 DZ65
Ingleside, Slou. (Colnbr.) SL3 93 BE81
Ingleside Cl, Beck. BR3 123 EA94
Ingleside Gro, SE3 104 EF79
Inglethorpe St, SW6 99 CX81
Ingleton Av, Well. DA16 126 EU85
Ingleton Rd, N18 46 DU51
Carshalton SM5 158 DE109
Ingleton St, SW9 101 DN82
Ingleway, N12 44 DD51
Inglewood, Cher. KT16 133 BF104
Croydon CR0 161 DY109
Woking GU21 166 AV118
Inglewood Cl, E14 204 A8
Hornchurch RM12 72 FK63
Ilford IG6 49 ET51
Inglewood Copse, Brom.
BR1 144 EL96
Inglewood Gdns, St.Alb. AL2
off North Orbital Rd 9 CE25
Inglewood Ms, Surb. KT6 138 CN102
Inglewood Rd, NW6 64 DA64
Bexleyheath DA7 107 FD84
Inglis Barracks, NW7 43 CX50
Inglis Rd, W5 80 CM73
Croydon CR0 142 DT102
Inglis St, SE5 101 DP81
Ingoldsby Rd, Grav. DA12 131 GL88
Ingram Av, NW11 64 DC59
Ingram Cl, SE11 200 C8
Stanmore HA7 41 CJ50
Ingram Ho, E3 off Daling Way 85 DY68
Ingram Rd, N2 64 DE56
Dartford DA1 128 FL88
Grays RM17 110 GD77
Thornton Heath CR7 142 DQ95
Ingrams Cl, Walt. KT12 154 BW106
Ingram Way, Grnf. UB6 79 CD67
Ingrave Ho, Dag. RM9 88 EV67
Ingrave Rd, Brwd. CM13,
CM15 54 FX47
Romford RM1 71 FD56
Ingrave St, SW11 100 DD83
Ingrebourne Gdns, Upmin.
RM14 72 FQ60
Ingrebourne Rd, Rain. RM13 89 FH70
Ingrebourne Valley Grn Way,
Horn. RM12 72 FK64
Ingress Gdns, Green. DA9 129 FX85
Ingress Pk Av, Green. DA9 109 FV84
Ingress St, W4
off Devonshire Rd 98 CS78
Ingreway, Rom. RM3 52 FP52
Inigo Jones Rd, SE7 104 EL80
Inigo Pl, WC2 195 P10
Inkerman Rd, NW5 83 DH65
Woking (Knap.) GU21 166 AS118
Inkerman Ter, W8
off Allen St 100 DA76
Inkerman Way, Wok. GU21 166 AS118
Inks Grn, E4 47 EC50
Inkster Ho, SW11
off Ingrave St 100 DE83
Inman Rd, NW10 80 CS67
SW18 120 DC87
Inmans Row, Wdf.Grn. IG8 48 EG49
Inner Circ, NW1 194 F3
Inner Pk Rd, SW19 119 CX88
Inner Ring E, Houns. (Hthrw Air.)
TW6 95 BP83
Inner Ring W, Houns. (Hthrw Air.)
TW6 94 BN83
Inner Temple La, EC4 196 D9
Innes Cl, SW20 139 CY96
Innes Gdns, SW15 119 CV86
Innes St, SE15 102 DS80
Innes Yd, Croy. CR0
off Whitgift St 142 DQ104
Inniskilling Rd, E13 86 EJ68
Innova Business Pk, Enf. EN3 31 DZ36
Innovation Cl, Wem. HA0 80 CL67
Innova Way, Enf. EN3 31 DZ36
Inskip Cl, E10 67 EB61
Inskip Dr, Horn. RM11 72 FL60
Inskip Rd, Dag. RM8 70 EX60
★ Institute of Contemporary
Arts (I.C.A.), SW1 199 N2
Institute Pl, E8 66 DV64
Institute Rd, Epp. (Cooper.)
CM16 18 EX29
Instone Rd, Dart. DA1 128 FK87
Integer Gdns, E11 67 ED59
Interchange E Ind Est, E5
off Grosvenor Way 66 DW61
International Av, Houns. TW5 96 BW78
International Trd Est, Sthl.
UB2 95 BV76
International Way, Sun.
TW16 135 BS95
Inveraray Pl, SE18
off Old Mill Rd 105 ER79
Inver Cl, E5 off Theydon Rd 66 DW61
Inverclyde Gdns, Rom. RM6 70 EX56
Inver Ct, W2
off Inverness Ter 82 DB72
W6 off Invermead Cl 99 CU76
Inveresk Gdns, Wor.Pk. KT4 139 CT104
Inverforth Cl, NW3
off North End Way 64 DC61
Inverforth Rd, N11 45 DH50
Inverine Rd, SE7 104 EH78
Invermead Cl, W6 99 CU77
Invermore Pl, SE18 105 EQ77
Inverness Av, Enf. EN1 30 DS39
Inverness Dr, Ilf. IG6 49 ES51
Inverness Gdns, W8
off Vicarage Gate 82 DB74
Inverness Ms, E16 87 EQ74
W2 off Inverness Ter 82 DB73
Inverness Pl, W2 82 DB73
Inverness Rd, N18
off Aberdeen Rd 46 DV50
Hounslow TW3 96 BZ84
Southall UB2 96 BY77
Worcester Park KT4 139 CX102
Inverness St, NW1 83 DH67
Inverness Ter, W2 82 DB73
Inverton Rd, SE15 103 DX84
Invicta Cl, E3
off Hawgood St 85 EA71
Chislehurst BR7 125 EN92
Feltham TW14 115 BT88
Invicta Gro, Nthlt. UB5 78 BZ69
Invicta Plaza, SE1 200 F2
Invicta Rd, SE3 104 EG80
Dartford DA2 128 FP86
Inville Rd, SE17 102 DR78
Inwen Ct, SE8 103 DY78
Inwood Av, Couls. CR5 175 DN120
Hounslow TW3 96 CC83
Inwood Cl, Croy. CR0 143 DY103
Inwood Ct, Walt. KT12 136 BW103
Inwood Rd, Houns. TW3 96 CB84
Inworth St, SW11 100 DE82
Inworth Wk, N1
off Popham St 84 DQ67
Iona Cl, SE6 123 EA87
Morden SM4 140 DB101
Ionian Bldg, E14
off Narrow St 85 DY73
Ionia Wk, Grav. DA12
off Cervia Way 131 GM90
Ion Sq, E2 off Hackney Rd 84 DU68
Ipswich Rd, SW17 120 DG93
Ireland Cl, E6
off Bradley Stone Rd 87 EM71
Ireland Pl, N22 45 DL52
Ireland Yd, EC4 196 G9
Irene Rd, SW6 100 DA81
Cobham (Stoke D'Ab.)
KT11 154 CA114
Orpington BR6 145 ET101
Ireton Av, Walt. KT12 135 BS103
Ireton Cl, N10 44 DG52
Ireton Pl, Grays RM17
off Russell Rd 110 GA77
Ireton St, E3
off Tidworth Rd 85 EA70
Iris Av, Bex. DA5 126 EY85
Iris Cl, E6 86 EL71
Brentwood (Pilg.Hat.) CM15 54 FV43
Croydon CR0 143 DX102
Surbiton KT6 138 CM101
Iris Ct, Pnr. HA5 60 BW55
Iris Cres, Bexh. DA7 106 EZ79
Iris Path, Rom. RM3
off Clematis Cl 52 FJ52
Iris Rd, Epsom (W.Ewell)
KT19 156 CP106
Iris Wk, Edg. HA8 off Ash Cl 42 CQ49
Irkdale Av, Enf. EN1 30 DT39
Iron Br Cl, NW10 62 CS64
Southall UB2 78 CC74
Iron Br Rd, Uxb. UB11 94 BN75
West Drayton UB7 94 BN75
Iron Mill La, Dart. DA1 107 FE84
Iron Mill Pl, SW18
off Garratt La 120 DB86
Dartford DA1 107 FF84
Iron Mill Rd, SW18 120 DB86
Ironmonger La, EC2 197 K9
Ironmonger Pas, EC1 197 J4
Ironmonger Row, EC1 197 J3
Ironmongers Pl, E14 204 A9
Ironside Cl, SE16 203 H4
Ironside Rd, Brent. TW8 97 CJ80
Irons Way, Rom. RM5 51 FC52
Irvine Av, Har. HA3 61 CG55
Irvine Cl, E14 off Uamvar St 85 EB71
N20 44 DE47
Irvine Gdns, S.Ock. RM15 91 FT72
Irvine Pl, Vir.W. GU25 132 AY99
Irvine Way, Orp. BR6 145 ET101
Irving Av, Nthlt. UB5 78 BX67
Irving Gro, SW9 101 DM82
Irving Ms, N1 off Alwyne Rd 84 DQ65
Irving Rd, W14 99 CX76
Irving St, WC2 199 N1
Irving Wk, Swans. DA10 130 FY87
Irving Way, NW9 63 CT57
Swanley BR8 147 FD96
Irwin Av, SE18 105 ES80
Irwin Cl, Uxb. UB10 58 BN62
Irwin Gdns, NW10 81 CV67
Isaac Way, SE1 201 J4
Isabel Gate, Wal.Cr. (Chsht)
EN8 15 DZ26
Isabel Hill Cl, Hmptn. TW12
off Upper Sunbury Rd 136 CB95
Isabella Cl, N14 45 DJ45
Isabella Ct, Rich. TW10
off Grove Rd 118 CM86
Isabella Dr, Orp. BR6 163 EQ105
Isabella Ms, N1
off Balls Pond Rd 84 DS65
Isabella Pl, Kings.T. KT2 118 CM92
Isabella Rd, E9 66 DW64
Isabella St, SE1 200 F3
Isabelle Cl, Wal.Cr. (Goffs Oak)
EN7 14 DQ29
Isabel St, SW9 101 DM81
Isambard Cl, Uxb. UB8 76 BK69
Isambard Ms, E14 204 E7
Isambard Pl, SE16 202 G3
Isbell Gdns, Rom. RM1 51 FE52
Isel Way, SE22
off East Dulwich Gro 122 DS85
Isham Rd, SW16 141 DL96
Isis Cl, SW15 99 CW84
Ruislip HA4 59 BQ58
Isis Dr, Upmin. RM14 73 FS58
Isis St, SW18 120 DC89
Island, The, Stai. (Wrays.)
TW19 113 BA90
Island, The, West Dr. UB7 94 BH81
Island Cl, Stai. TW18 113 BE91
Island Fm Av, W.Mol. KT8 136 BZ99
Island Fm Rd, W.Mol. KT8 136 BZ99
DLR Island Gardens 204 D9
Island Rd, SE16 203 H9
Mitcham CR4 120 DF94
Island Row, E14 85 DZ72
Isla Rd, SE18 105 EQ79
Islay Gdns, Houns. TW4 116 BX85
Islay Wk, N1 off Douglas Rd 84 DQ65
Isledon Rd, N7 65 DN62
Islehurst Cl, Chis. BR7 145 EN95
ISLEWORTH, TW7 97 CF83
⇌ Isleworth 97 CF82
Isleworth Business Complex, Islw.
TW7 off St. John's Rd 97 CF82
Isleworth Prom, Twick. TW1 97 CH84
ISLINGTON, N1 83 DM67
Islington Grn, N1 83 DP67
Islington High St, N1 196 E1
Islington Pk Ms, N1
off Islington Pk St 83 DP66
Islington Pk St, N1 83 DN66
Islip Gdns, Edg. HA8 42 CR52
Northolt UB5 78 BY66
Islip Manor Rd, Nthlt. UB5 78 BY66
Islip St, NW5 65 DJ64
Ismailia Rd, E7 86 EH66
★ Ismaili Cen & Zamana Gall,
SW7 198 A8
Ismay Ct, Slou. SL2
off Elliman Av 74 AS73
Isom Cl, E13 off Belgrave Rd 86 EH69
ISTEAD RISE, Grav. DA13 130 GE94
Istead Ri, Grav. DA13 131 GF94
Itchingwood Common Rd,
Oxt. RH8 188 EJ133
Ivanhoe Cl, Uxb. UB8 76 BK71
Ivanhoe Dr, Har. HA3 61 CG55
Ivanhoe Rd, SE5 102 DT83
Hounslow TW4 96 BX83
Ivatt Pl, W14 99 CZ78
Ivatt Way, N17 65 DP55
Iveagh Av, NW10 80 CN68
Iveagh Cl, E9 85 DX67
NW10 80 CN68
Northwood HA6 39 BP53
Iveagh Rd, Wok. GU21 166 AT118
Iveagh Ter, NW10
off Iveagh Av 80 CN68
Ivedon Rd, Well. DA16 106 EW82
Ive Fm Cl, E10 67 EA61
Ive Fm La, E10 67 EA61
Iveley Rd, SW4 101 DJ82
IVER, SL0 75 BF72
⇌ Iver 93 BF75
Iverdale Cl, Iver SL0 75 BC73
Ivere Dr, Barn. EN5 28 DB44
IVER HEATH, Iver SL0 75 BD69
Iverhurst Cl, Bexh. DA6 126 EX85
Iver La, Iver SL0 76 BH71
Uxbridge UB8 76 BH71
Iverna Ct, W8 100 DA76
Iverna Gdns, W8 100 DA76
Feltham TW14 115 BR85
Iver Rd, Brwd. (Pilg.Hat.)
CM15 54 FV44
Iver SL0 76 BG72
Iverson Rd, NW6 81 CZ65
Ivers Way, Croy. (New Adgtn)
CR0 161 EB108
Ives Gdns, Rom. RM1
off Sims Cl 71 FF56
Ives Rd, E16 86 EE71
Slough SL3 93 AZ76
Ives St, SW3 198 C8
Ivestor Ter, SE23 122 DW87
Ivimey St, E2 84 DU69
Ivinghoe Cl, Enf. EN1 30 DS40
Watford WD25 24 BX35
Ivinghoe Rd, Bushey WD23 41 CD45
Dagenham RM8 70 EV64
Rickmansworth (Mill End)
WD3 38 BG45
Ivor Gro, SE9 125 EP88
Ivor Pl, NW1 194 D5
Ivor St, NW1 83 DJ66
Ivory Ct, Felt. TW13 115 BU88
Ivorydown, Brom. BR1 124 EG91
Ivory Sq, SW11
off Gartons Way 100 DC83
Ivy Bower Cl, Green. DA9
off Riverview Rd 129 FV85
Ivybridge Cl, Twick. TW1 117 CG86
Uxbridge UB8 76 BL69
Ivybridge Est, Islw. TW7 117 CF85
Ivybridge La, WC2 200 A1
IVY CHIMNEYS, Epp. CM16 17 ES32
Ivy Chimneys Rd, Epp. CM16 17 ES32
Ivychurch Cl, SE20 122 DW94
Ivychurch La, SE17 201 P10
Ivy Cl, Dart. DA1 128 FN87
Gravesend DA12 131 GJ90
Harrow HA2 60 BZ63
Pinner HA5 60 BW59
Sunbury-on-Thames TW16 136 BW96
Ivy Cotts, E14 off Grove Vil 85 EB73
Ivy Ct, SE16 off Argyle Way 102 DU78
Ivy Cres, W4 98 CQ77
Ivydale Rd, SE15 103 DX83
Carshalton SM5 140 DF103
Ivyday Gro, SW16 121 DM90
Ivydene, W.Mol. KT8 136 BZ99
Ivydene Cl, Sutt. SM1 158 DC105
Ivy Gdns, N8 65 DL58
Mitcham CR4 141 DK97
Ivy Ho La, Sev. TN14 181 FD118
Ivyhouse Rd, Dag. RM9 88 EX65
Ivy Ho Rd, Uxb. UB10 59 BP62
Ivy La, Houns. TW4 96 BZ84
Sevenoaks (Knock.) TN14 180 EY116
Woking GU22 167 BB118
Ivy Lea, Rick. WD3
off Springwell Av 38 BG46
Ivy Lo La, Rom. RM3 52 FP53
Ivy Mill Cl, Gdse. RH9 186 DV132
Ivy Mill La, Gdse. RH9 186 DU132
Ivymount Rd, SE27 121 DN90
Ivy Pl, Surb. KT5
off Alpha Rd 138 CM100
Ivy Rd, E16 off Pacific Rd 86 EG72
E17 67 EA58
Ivy Rd, N14 45 DJ45
NW2 63 CW63
SE4 103 DZ84
SW17 off Tooting High St 120 DE92
Hounslow TW3 96 CB84
Surbiton KT6 138 CN102
Ivy St, N1 84 DS68
Ivy Wk, Dag. RM9 88 EY65
Ixworth Pl, SW3 198 B10
Izane Rd, Bexh. DA6 106 EZ84

J

Jacaranda Cl, N.Mal. KT3 138 CS97
Jacaranda Gro, E8 84 DT66
Jackass La, Kes. BR2 162 EH107
Oxted (Tand.) RH8 187 DZ131
Jack Barnett Way, N22 45 DM54
Jack Clow Rd, E15 86 EE68
Jack Cornwell St, E12 69 EN63
Jack Dash Way, E6 86 EL70
Jackets La, Nthwd. HA6 39 BP53
Uxbridge (Hare.) UB9 38 BN52
Jacketts Fld, Abb.L. WD5 7 BT31
Jack Goodchild Way, Kings.T.
KT1 off Kingston Rd 138 CP97
Jacklin Grn, Wdf.Grn. IG8 48 EG49
Jackman Ms, NW10 62 CS62
Jackmans La, Wok. GU21 166 AU119
Jackman St, E8 84 DV67
Jacks La, Uxb. (Hare.) UB9 38 BG53
Jackson Cl, E9 84 DW66
Epsom KT18 156 CR114
Greenhithe DA9
off Cowley Av 129 FU85
Hornchurch RM11 72 FM56
Uxbridge UB10
off Jackson Rd 76 BL66
Jackson Ct, E11
off Brading Cres 68 EH60
Jackson Rd, N7 65 DM63
Barking IG11 87 ER67
Barnet EN4 28 DE44
Bromley BR2 144 EL103
Uxbridge UB10 76 BL66
Jacksons Dr, Wal.Cr. EN7 14 DU28
Jacksons La, N6 64 DG59
Jacksons Pl, Croy. CR0
off Cross Rd 142 DR102
Jackson St, SE18 105 EN79
Jacksons Way, Croy. CR0 143 EA104
Jackson Way, Epsom KT19
off Lady Harewood Way 156 CN109
Southall UB2 96 CB75
Jack Walker Ct, N5 65 DP63
Jacob Ho, Erith DA18
off Kale Rd 106 EX75
Jacobs Av, Rom. (Harold Wd)
RM3 52 FL54
Jacobs Cl, Dag. RM10 71 FB63
Jacobs Ho, E13 86 EJ69
Jacobs La, Dart. (Hort.Kir.)
DA4 148 FQ97
Jacob St, SE1 202 A4
Jacob's Well Ms, W1 194 G8
Jacqueline Cl, Nthlt. UB5
off Canford Av 78 BZ67
Jade Cl, E16 86 EK72
NW2 63 CX59
Dagenham RM8 70 EW60
Jaffe Rd, Ilf. IG1 69 EQ60
Jaffray Pl, SE27
off Chapel Rd 121 DP91
Jaffray Rd, Brom. BR2 144 EK98
Jaggard Way, SW12 120 DF87
Jagger Cl, Dart. DA2 128 FQ87
Jago Cl, SE18 105 EQ79
Jago Wk, SE5 102 DR80
Jail La, West. (Bigg.H.) TN16 178 EK116
Jamaica Rd, SE1 202 A5
SE16 202 D6
Thornton Heath CR7 141 DP100
Jamaica St, E1 84 DW72
James Av, NW2 63 CW64
Dagenham RM8 70 EZ60
James Bedford Cl, Pnr. HA5 40 BW54
James Boswell Cl, SW16
off Curtis Fld Rd 121 DN91
James Clavell Sq, SE18
off Duke of Wellington Av 105 EP76
James Cl, E13
off Richmond St 86 EG68
NW11 off Woodlands 63 CY58
Bushey WD23
off Aldenham Rd 24 BY43
Romford RM2 71 FG57
James Collins Cl, W9
off Fermoy Rd 81 CZ70
James Ct, N1 off Morton Rd 84 DQ66
James Dudson Ct, NW10 80 CQ66
James Gdns, N22 45 DP52
James Hammett Ho, E2
off Ravenscroft St 84 DT69
James Joyce Wk, SE24
off Shakespeare Rd 101 DP84
James La, E10 67 ED59
E11 67 ED58
James Lee Sq, Enf. EN3 31 EA38
James Martin Cl, Uxb. (Denh.)
UB9 58 BG58
James Meadow, Slou. SL3 93 AZ79
James Newman Ct, SE9
off Great Harry Dr 125 EN90
Jameson Cl, W3 off Acton La 98 CQ75
Jameson Ct, E2 84 DW68
Jameson Ho, SE11
off Glasshouse Wk 101 DM78
Jameson St, W8 82 DA74
James Pl, N17 46 DT53
James Riley Pt, E15
off Carpenters Rd 85 EC67
James Rd, Dart. DA1 127 FG87
James's Cotts, Rich. TW9
off Kew Rd 98 CN80
James Sinclair Pt, E13 86 EJ67
James St, W1 194 G8
WC2 196 A10
Barking IG11 87 EQ66
Enfield EN1 30 DT43
Epping CM16 17 ET28

James St, Houns. TW3 97 CD83
James Ter, SW14
off Mullins Path 98 CR83
Jamestown Rd, NW1 83 DH67
Jamestown Way, E14 204 G1
James Watt Way, Erith DA8 107 FF79
James Way, Wat. WD19 40 BX49
James Yd, E4 47 ED51
Jamieson Ho, Houns. TW4 116 BZ87
Jamnagar Cl, Stai. TW18 113 BF93
Jamuna Cl, E14 85 DY71
Jane St, E1
off Commercial Rd 84 DV72
Janet St, E14 204 A6
Janeway Pl, SE16 202 D5
Janeway St, SE16 202 C5
Janice Ms, Ilf. IG1
off Oakfield Rd 69 EP62
Janmead, Brwd. (Hutt.) CM13 55 GB45
Janoway Hill La, Wok. GU21 166 AW119
Jansen Wk, SW11
off Hope St 100 DD84
Janson Cl, E15 *off Janson Rd* 68 EE64
NW10 62 CR62
Janson Rd, E15 68 EE64
Jansons Rd, N15 66 DS55
Japan Cres, N4 65 DM60
Japan Rd, Rom. RM6 70 EX58
Japonica Cl, Wok. GU21 166 AW118
Jardine Rd, E1 85 DX73
Jarman Ho, E1 *off Jubilee St* 84 DW71
Jarrah Cotts, Purf. RM19
off London Rd Purfleet 109 FR79
Jarrett Cl, SW2 121 DP88
Jarrow Cl, Mord. SM4 140 DB99
Jarrow Rd, N17 66 DV56
SE16 202 F9
Romford RM6 70 EW58
Jarrow Way, E9 67 DY63
Jarvis Cleys, Wal.Cr. (Chsht)
EN7 14 DT26
Jarvis Cl, Bark. IG11
off Westbury Rd 87 ER67
Barnet EN5 27 CX43
Jarvis Rd, SE22
off Melbourne Gro 102 DS84
South Croydon CR2 160 DR107
Jarvis Way, Rom. (Harold Wd)
RM3 52 FL54
Jasmin Cl, Nthwd. HA6 39 BT53
Jasmine Cl, Ilf. IG1 69 EP64
Orpington BR6 145 EP103
Southall UB1 78 BY73
Woking GU21 166 AT116
Jasmine Gdns, Croy. CR0 143 EB104
Harrow HA2 60 CA61
Jasmine Gro, SE20 142 DV95
Jasmine Rd, Rom. (Rush Grn)
RM7 71 FE61
Jasmine Sq, E3
off Birdsfield La 85 DZ67
Jasmine Ter, West Dr. UB7 94 BN75
Jasmine Way, E.Mol. KT8
off Hampton Ct Way 137 CE98
Jasmin Rd, Epsom KT19 156 CP106
Jason Cl, Brwd. CM14 54 FT49
Weybridge KT13 153 BQ106
Jason Ct, W1
off Marylebone La 82 DG72
Jasons Hill, Chesh. HP5 4 AV30
Jason Wk, SE9 125 EN91
Jasper Cl, Enf. EN3 30 DW38
Jasper Pas, SE19 122 DT93
Jasper Rd, E16 86 EK72
SE19 122 DT92
Jasper Wk, N1 197 K2
Javelin Way, Nthlt. UB5 78 BX69
Jaycroft, Enf. EN2
off The Ridgeway 29 DN39
Jay Gdns, Chis. BR7 125 EM91
Jay Ms, SW7 100 DC75
Jays Covert, Couls. CR5 174 DG119
Jazzfern Ter, Wem. HA0
off Maybank Av 61 CG64
Jean Batten Cl, Wall. SM6 159 DM108
Jebb Av, SW2 121 DL86
Jebb St, E3 85 EA68
Jedburgh Rd, E13 86 EJ69
Jedburgh St, SW11 100 DG84
Jeddo Rd, W12 99 CT75
Jefferson Cl, W13 97 CH76
Ilford IG2 69 EP57
Slough SL3 93 BA77
Jefferson Wk, SE18
off Kempt St 105 EN79
Jeffreys Pl, NW1
off Jeffreys St 83 DJ66
Jeffreys Rd, SW4 101 DL82
Enfield EN3 31 DZ41
Jeffreys St, NW1 83 DH66
Jeffreys Wk, SW4 101 DL82
Jeffries Ho, NW10 80 CQ67
Jeffs Cl, Hmptn. TW12
off Uxbridge Rd 116 CB93
Jeffs Rd, Sutt. SM1 157 CZ105
Jeger Av, E2 84 DT67
Jeken Rd, SE9 104 EJ84
Jelf Rd, SW2 121 DN85
Jellicoe Av, Grav. DA12 131 GJ90
Jellicoe Av W, Grav. DA12
off Kitchener Av 131 GJ90
Jellicoe Gdns, Stan. HA7 41 CF51
Jellicoe Ho, SW8
off St. George Wf 101 DL79
Jellicoe Rd, E13
off Jutland Rd 86 EG70
N17 46 DR52
Watford WD18 23 BU44
Jemma Knowles Cl, SW2
off Neil Wates Cres 121 DN88
Jemmett Cl, Kings.T. KT2 138 CP95
Jengar Cl, Sutt. SM1 158 DB105
Jenkins Av, St.Alb. (Brick.Wd)
AL2 8 BY30
Jenkins La, E6 87 EN68
Barking IG11 87 EP68
Jenkinson Ho, E2 *off Usk St* 85 DX69
Jenkins Rd, E13 86 EH70
Jenner Av, W3 80 CR71
Jenner Cl, Sid. DA14 126 EU91
Jenner Ho, SE3 104 EE79
Jenner Pl, SW13 99 CV79
Jenner Rd, N16 66 DT61
Jenner Way, Epsom KT19
off Monro Pl 156 CN109
Jennett Rd, Croy. CR0 141 DN104
Jennifer Rd, Brom. BR1 124 EF90
Jennings Cl, Add. (New Haw)
KT15 *off Woodham La* 152 BJ109
Surbiton KT6 137 CJ101
Jennings Rd, SE22 122 DT86
Jennings Way, Barn. EN5 27 CW41
Jenningtree Rd, Erith DA8 107 FH80
Jenningtree Way, Belv. DA17 107 FC75
Jenny Hammond Cl, E11
off Newcomen Rd 68 EF62
Jenny Path, Rom. RM3 52 FK52
Jennys Way, Couls. CR5 175 DJ122
Jenson Way, SE19 122 DT94
Jenton Av, Bexh. DA7 106 EY81
Jephson Rd, E7 86 EJ66
Jephson St, SE5
off Grove La 102 DR81
Jephtha Rd, SW18 120 DA86
Jeppos La, Mitch. CR4 140 DF98
Jepps Cl, Wal.Cr. EN7
off Little Gro Av 14 DS27
Jepson Ho, SW6
off Pearscroft Rd 100 DB81
Jerdan Pl, SW6 100 DA80
Jeremiah St, E14 85 EB72
Jeremys Grn, N18 46 DV49
Jermyn St, SW1 199 K2
Jerningham Av, Ilf. IG5 49 EP54
Jerningham Rd, SE14 103 DY82
Jerome Cres, NW8 194 B4
Jerome Pl, Kings.T. KT1
off Wadbrook St 137 CK96
Jerome St, E1 197 P6
Jerome Twr, W3 98 CP75
Jerrard St, N1 197 N1
SE13 103 EB83
Jersey Av, Stan. HA7 41 CH54
Jersey Cl, Cher. KT16 133 BF104
Jersey Dr, Orp. BR5 145 ER100
Jersey Ho, N1 *off Clifton Rd* 84 DQ65
Enfield EN3
off Eastfield Rd 31 DX38
Jersey Par, Houns. TW5 96 CB81
Jersey Rd, E11 67 ED60
E16 *off Prince Regent La* 86 EJ72
SW17 121 DH93
W7 97 CG75
Hounslow TW3, TW5 96 CB81
Ilford IG1 69 EP63
Isleworth TW7 97 CE79
Rainham RM13 89 FG66
Jersey St, E2
off Bethnal Grn Rd 84 DV69
Jerusalem Pas, EC1 196 F5
Jervis Av, Enf. EN3 31 DY35
Jervis Ct, W1 195 J9
Jervis Rd, SW6 *off Lillie Rd* 99 CZ79
Jerviston Gdns, SW16 121 DN93
Jesmond Av, Wem. HA9 80 CM65
Jesmond Cl, Mitch. CR4 141 DH97
Jesmond Rd, Croy. CR0 142 DT101
Jesmond Way, Stan. HA7 42 CL50
Jessam Av, E5 66 DV60
Jessamine Pl, Dart. DA2 128 FQ87
Jessamine Rd, W7 79 CE74
Jessamine Ter, Swan. BR8
off Birchwood Rd 147 FC95
Jessamy Rd, Wey. KT13 135 BP103
Jessel Dr, Loug. IG10 33 EQ39
Jessel Ho, SW1 *off Page St* 101 DK77
Jesse Rd, E10 67 EC60
Jessett Cl, Erith DA8
off West St 107 FD77
Jessica Rd, SW18 120 DC86
Jessie Blythe La, N19 65 DL59
Jessiman Ter, Shep. TW17 134 BN99
Jessop Av, Sthl. UB2 96 BZ77
Jessop Rd, SE24
off Milkwood Rd 101 DP84
Jessop Sq, E14 203 P3
Jessops Way, Croy. CR0 141 DJ100
Jessup Cl, SE18 105 EQ77
Jethou Ho, N1
off Nightingale Rd 84 DQ65
Jetstar Way, Nthlt. UB5 78 BY69
Jetty Wk, Grays RM17 110 GA79
Jevington Way, SE12 124 EH89
Jewel Rd, E17 67 EA55
Jewels Hill, West. (Bigg.H.)
TN16 162 EG112
★ Jewel Twr, Houses of Parliament,
SW1 199 P6
★ Jewish Mus, NW1 83 DH67
Jewry St, EC3 197 P9
Jew's Row, SW18 100 DB84
Jews Wk, SE26 122 DV91
Jeymer Av, NW2 63 CV64
Jeymer Dr, Grnf. UB6 78 CC67
Jeypore Pas, SW18
off Jeypore Rd 120 DC86
Jeypore Rd, SW18 120 DC87
Jigger Mast Ho, SE18
off Woolwich Ch St 105 EN76
Jillian Cl, Hmptn. TW12 116 CA94
Jim Bradley Cl, SE18
off John Wilson St 105 EN77
Jim Griffiths Ho, SW6
off Clem Attlee Ct 99 CZ79
Joan Cres, SE9 124 EK87
Joan Gdns, Dag. RM8 70 EY61
Joan Rd, Dag. RM8 70 EY61
Joan St, SE1 200 F3
Jocelyn Rd, Rich. TW9 98 CL83
Jocelyn St, SE15 102 DU81
Jockey's Flds, WC1 196 C6
Jodane St, SE8 203 M9
Jodrell Cl, Islw. TW7 97 CG81
Jodrell Rd, E3 85 DZ67
Jodrell Way, Grays (W.Thur.)
RM20 109 FT78
Joel St, Nthwd. HA6 59 BU55
Pinner HA5 59 BU55
Johanna St, SE1 200 D5
John Adam St, WC2 200 A1
John Aird Ct, W2 82 DC71
John Archer Way, SW18 120 DD86
John Ashby Cl, SW2 121 DL86
John Austin Cl, Kings.T. KT2
off Queen Elizabeth Rd 138 CM95
John Barnes Wk, E15 86 EF65
John Bradshaw Rd, N14
off High St 45 DK46
John Burns Dr, Bark. IG11 87 ES66
Johnby Cl, Enf. EN3 31 DY37
John Campbell Rd, N16 66 DS64
John Carpenter St, EC4 196 F10
John Cobb Rd, Wey. KT13 152 BN108
John Cornwell VC Ho, E12 69 EN63
John Drinkwater Cl, E11
off Browning Rd 68 EF59
John Fearon Wk, W10
off Parry Rd 81 CZ69
John Felton Rd, SE16 202 B5
John Fisher St, E1 84 DU73
John Gooch Dr, Enf. EN2 29 DP39
John Harrison Ho, E1
off Philpot St 84 DV72
John Harrison Way, SE10 205 K7
John Horner Ms, N1
off Frome St 84 DQ68
H John Howard Cen, E9 85 DY65
John Islip St, SW1 199 P9
John Keats Ho, N22 45 DM52
John Kennedy Ho, SE16 202 G8
John Maurice Cl, SE17 201 K8
John McKenna Wk, SE16 202 C6
John Newton Ct, Well.
DA16 106 EV83
John Parker Cl, Dag. RM10 89 FB66
John Parker Sq, SW11
off Thomas Baines Rd 100 DD83
John Penn St, SE13 103 EB81
John Perrin Pl, Har. HA3 62 CL59
John Princes St, W1 195 J8
John Rennie Wk, E1 202 E2
John Roll Way, SE16 202 C6
John Ruskin St, SE5 101 DP80
Johns Av, NW4 63 CW56
Johns Cl, Ashf. TW15 115 BQ91
Johnsdale, Oxt. RH8 188 EF129
John Silkin La, SE8 203 J9
Johns La, Mord. SM4 140 DC99
John's Ms, WC1 196 C5
John Smith Av, SW6 99 CZ80
John Smith Ms, E14
off Newport Av 85 ED73
Johnson Cl, E8 84 DU67
Gravesend (Nthflt) DA11 130 GD90
Johnson Ho, E2
off Roberta St 84 DU69
Johnson Rd, NW10 80 CR67
Bromley BR2 144 EK99
Croydon CR0 142 DR101
Hounslow TW5 96 BW80
Johnsons Av, Sev. (Bad.Mt)
TN14 165 FB110
Johnsons Cl, Cars. SM5 140 DF104
Johnson's Ct, EC4
off Fleet St 83 DN72
Johnsons Ct, Sev. (Seal)
TN15 *off School La* 191 FM121
Johnsons Dr, Hmptn. TW12 136 CC95
Johnson's Pl, SW1 101 DJ78
Johnson St, E1 *off Cable St* 84 DW73
Southall UB2 96 BW76
Johnsons Way, NW10 80 CP70
Greenhithe DA9 129 FW86
Johnsons Yd, Uxb. UB8
off Redford Way 76 BJ66
John Spencer Sq, N1 83 DP65
John's Pl, E1 *off Damien St* 84 DV72
Johns Rd, West. (Tats.) TN16 178 EK120
John's Ter, Croy. CR0 142 DR102
Romford RM3 52 FP51
Johnston Cl, SW9
off Hackford Rd 101 DM81
Johnstone Rd, E6 87 EM69
Johnston Rd, Wdf.Grn. IG8 48 EG50
Johnston Ter, NW2
off Kara Way 63 CX62
John St, E15 86 EF67
SE25 142 DU98
WC1 196 C5
Enfield EN1 30 DT43
Grays RM17 110 GC79
Hounslow TW3 96 BY82
Johns Wk, Whyt. CR3 176 DU119
John Trundle Ct, EC2
off The Barbican 84 DQ71
John Walsh Twr, E11 68 EF61
John Watkin Cl, Epsom
KT19 156 CP109
John William Cl, Grays
(Chaff.Hun.) RM16 109 FX78
John Williams Cl, SE14 103 DX79
Kingston upon Thames KT2
off Henry Macaulay Av 137 CK95
John Wilson St, SE18 105 EN76
John Woolley Cl, SE13 104 EE84
Joiner's Arms Yd, SE5
off Denmark Hill 102 DR81
Joiners Cl, Chesh. (Ley Hill)
HP5 4 AV30
Gerrards Cross (Chal.St.P.)
SL9 37 AZ52
Joiners La, Ger.Cr. (Chal.St.P.)
SL9 36 AY53
Joiners Pl, N5
off Leconfield Rd 66 DR63
Joiner St, SE1 201 L3
Joiners Way, Ger.Cr. (Chal.St.P.)
SL9 36 AY52
Joiners Yd, N1
off Caledonia St 83 DL68
Joinville Pl, Add. KT15 152 BK105
Jolliffe Rd, Red. RH1 185 DJ126
Jollys La, Har. HA2 61 CD60
Hayes UB4 78 BX71
Jonathan Ct, W4
off Windmill Rd 98 CS77
Jonathan St, SE11 200 B10
Jones Rd, E13
off Holborn Rd 86 EH70
Waltham Cross (Chsht) EN7 13 DP30
Jones St, W1 199 H1
Jones Wk, Rich. TW10
off Pyrland Rd 118 CM86
Jonquil Gdns, Hmptn. TW12
off Partridge Rd 116 BZ93
Jonson Cl, Hayes UB4 77 BU71
Mitcham CR4 141 DH98
Jordan Cl, Dag. RM10
off Muggeridge Rd 71 FB63
Jordan Cl, Har. HA2
off Hamilton Cres 60 BZ62
South Croydon CR2 160 DT111
Watford WD25 23 BT35
Jordan Ct, SW15
off Charlwood Rd 99 CX84
Jordan Rd, Grnf. UB6 79 CH67
JORDANS, Beac. HP9 36 AT52
Jordans Cl, Islw. TW7 97 CE81
Staines (Stanw.) TW19 114 BJ87
Jordans La, Beac. (Jordans)
HP9 36 AS53
Jordans Rd, Rick. WD3 38 BG45
Jordans Way, Beac. (Jordans)
HP9 36 AT51
Rainham RM13 90 FK68
St. Albans (Brick.Wd) AL2 8 BZ30
Joseph Av, W3 80 CR72
Joseph Conrad Ho, SW1
off Tachbrook St 101 DJ77
Joseph Hardcastle Cl, SE14 103 DX80
Josephine Av, SW2 121 DM85
Tadworth (Lwr Kgswd)
KT20 183 CZ126
Josephine Cl, Tad. (Lwr Kgswd)
KT20 183 CZ127
Joseph Locke Way, Esher
KT10 136 CA103
Joseph Powell Cl, SW12
off Hazelbourne Rd 121 DJ86
Joseph Ray Rd, E11 68 EE61
Joseph St, E3 85 DZ70
Joseph Trotter Cl, EC1
off Myddelton St 83 DN69
Joshua Cl, N10 45 DH52
South Croydon CR2 159 DP108
Joshua St, E14
off St. Leonards Rd 85 EC72
Joshua Wk, Wal.Cr. EN8
off Longcroft Dr 15 EA34
Josling Cl, Grays RM17 110 FZ79
Joslings Cl, W12
off Bloemfontein Rd 81 CV73
Joslin Rd, Purf. RM19 108 FQ78
Joslyn Cl, Enf. EN3 31 EA38
Joubert St, SW11 100 DF82
Journeys End, Slou. (Stoke P.)
SL2 74 AS71
Jowett St, SE15 102 DT80
Joyce Av, N18 46 DT50
Joyce Ct, Wal.Abb. EN9 15 ED34
Joyce Dawson Way, SE28
off Thamesmere Dr 88 EU73
Joyce Dawson Way Shop Arc, SE28
off Thamesmere Dr 88 EU73
Joyce Grn La, Dart. DA1 108 FL81
Joyce Grn Wk, Dart. DA1 108 FM84
Joyce Page Cl, SE7
off Lansdowne La 104 EK79
Joyce Wk, SW2 121 DN86
JOYDENS WOOD, Bex. DA5 127 FC92
Joydens Wd Rd, Bex. DA5 127 FD91
Joydon Dr, Rom. RM6 70 EV58
Joyes Cl, Rom. RM3 52 FK49
Joyners Cl, Dag. RM9 70 EZ63
Joy Rd, Grav. DA12 131 GJ88
Jubb Powell Ho, N15 66 DS58
Jubilee Av, E4 47 EC51
Romford RM7 71 FB57
St. Albans (Lon.Col.) AL2 9 CK26
Twickenham TW2 116 CC88
Jubilee Cl, NW9 62 CR58
NW10 *off Nicoll Rd* 81 CT68
Greenhithe DA9 129 FW86
Pinner HA5 40 BW54
Romford RM7 71 FB57
Staines (Stanw.) TW19 114 BJ87
Jubilee Ct, Stai. TW18
off Leacroft 114 BG92
Waltham Abbey EN9 16 EF33
Jubilee Cres, E14 204 E7
N9 46 DU46
Addlestone KT15 152 BK106
Gravesend DA12 131 GL89
Jubilee Dr, Ruis. HA4 60 BX63
★ Jubilee Gdns, SE1 200 B3
Jubilee Gdns, Sthl. UB1 78 CA72
Jubilee La, W5 *off Haven La* 80 CL72
Jubilee Pl, SW3 198 C10
Jubilee Ri, Sev. (Seal) TN15 191 FM121
Jubilee Rd, Grays RM20 109 FV79
Greenford UB6 79 CH67
Orpington BR6 164 FA107
Sutton SM3 157 CX108
Watford WD24 23 BU38
Jubilee St, E1 84 DW72
Jubilee Wk, Wat. WD19 39 BV49
Jubilee Way, SW19 140 DB95
Chessington KT9 156 CN105
Feltham TW14 115 BT88
Sidcup DA14 126 EU89
Slough (Datchet) SL3 92 AW80
Judd St, WC1 195 P3
Jude St, E16 86 EF72
Judeth Gdns, Grav. DA12 131 GL92
Judge Heath La, Hayes UB3 77 BQ72
Uxbridge UB8 77 BQ72
Judges Hill, Pot.B. EN6 12 DE29
Judge St, Wat. WD24 23 BV38
Judge Wk, Esher (Clay.) KT10 155 CE107
Judith Av, Rom. RM5 51 FB51
Juer St, SW11 100 DE80
Jug Hill, West. (Bigg.H.) TN16
off Hillcrest Rd 178 EK116
Juglans Rd, Orp. BR6 146 EU102
Jules Thorn Av, Enf. EN1 30 DT41
Julia Gdns, Bark. IG11 88 EX68
Julia Garfield Ms, E16
off Evelyn Rd 86 EH74
Juliana Cl, N2 64 DC55
Julian Av, W3 80 CP73
Julian Cl, Barn. EN5 28 DB41
Woking GU21 166 AW118
Julian Hill, Har. HA1 61 CE61
Weybridge KT13 152 BN108
Julian Pl, E14 204 C10
Julian Rd, Orp. BR6 164 EU107
Julians Cl, Sev. TN13 190 FG127
Julians Way, Sev. TN13 190 FG127
Julian Tayler Path, SE23 122 DV89
Julia St, NW5
off Oak Village 64 DG63
Julien Rd, W5 97 CJ76
Julien Rd, Couls. CR5 175 DK115
Juliette Rd, E13 86 EF68
Juliette Way, S.Ock. RM15 108 FM75
Julius Caesar Way, Stan. HA7 41 CK49
Julius Nyerere Cl, N1
off Copenhagen St 83 DM67
Junction App, SE13 103 EC83
SW11 100 DE83
Junction Av, W10
off Harrow Rd 81 CW69
Junction Ms, W2 194 B8
Junction Pk, Kings L. WD4 7 BQ33
Junction Pl, W2 194 B8
Junction Rd, E13 86 EH68
N9 46 DU46
N17 66 DU55
N19 65 DJ63
W5 97 CK77
Ashford TW15 115 BQ92
Brentford TW8 97 CK77
Brentwood CM14 54 FW49
Dartford DA1 128 FK86
Harrow HA1 61 CE58
Romford RM1 71 FF56
South Croydon CR2 160 DR106
Junction Rd E, Rom. RM6
off Kenneth Rd 70 EY59
Junction Rd W, Rom. RM6 70 EY59
Junction Shop Cen, The, SW11
off St. John's Hill 100 DE84
June Cl, Couls. CR5 159 DH114
Junewood Cl, Add. (Wdhm)
KT15 151 BF111
Juniper Av, St.Alb. (Brick.Wd)
AL2 8 CA31
Juniper Cl, Barn. EN5 27 CX43
Broxbourne EN10 15 DZ25
Chessington KT9 156 CM107
Rickmansworth WD3 38 BK48
Wembley HA9 62 CM64
Westerham (Bigg.H.) TN16 178 EL117
Juniper Ct, Slou. SL1
off Nixey Cl 92 AU75
Juniper Cres, NW1 82 DG66
Juniper Dr, SW18
off York Rd 100 DC84
Juniper Gdns, SW16
off Leonard Rd 141 DJ95
Radlett (Shenley) WD7 10 CL33
Sunbury-on-Thames TW16 115 BT93
Juniper Gate, Rick. WD3 38 BK47
Juniper Gro, Wat. WD17 23 BU38
Juniper La, E6 86 EL71
Juniper Rd, Ilf. IG1 69 EN63
Juniper St, E1 84 DW73
Juniper Wk, Swan. BR8 147 FD96
Juniper Way, Hayes UB3 77 BR73
Romford RM3 52 FL53
Juno Way, SE14 103 DX79
Jupiter Way, N7 83 DM65
Jupp Rd, E15 85 ED66
Jupp Rd W, E15 85 EC67
Jurgens Rd, Purf. RM19
off London Rd Purfleet 109 FR79
Jury St, Grav. DA11
off Princes St 131 GH86
Justice Wk, SW3
off Lawrence St 100 DE79
Justin Cl, Brent. TW8 97 CK80
Justines Pl, E2
off Palmers Rd 85 DX69
Justin Rd, E4 47 DZ51
Jute La, Enf. EN3 31 DY40
Jutland Cl, N19
off Sussex Way 65 DL60
Jutland Gdns, Couls. CR5 175 DM120
Jutland Pl, Egh. TW20
off Mullens Rd 113 BC92
Jutland Rd, E13 86 EG70
SE6 123 EC87
Jutsums Av, Rom. RM7 71 FB58
Jutsums La, Rom. RM7 71 FB58
Juxon Cl, Har. HA3
off Augustine Rd 40 CB53
Juxon St, SE11 200 C8

K

Kaduna Cl, Pnr. HA5 59 BU57
Kale Rd, Erith DA18 106 EY75
Kambala Rd, SW11 100 DD82
Kandlewood, Brwd. (Hutt.)
CM13 55 GB45
Kangley Br Rd, SE26 123 DZ92
Kaplan Dr, N21 29 DL43
Karanjia Ct, NW2 81 CW65
Kara Way, NW2 63 CX63
Karen Cl, Brwd. CM15 54 FW45
Rainham RM13 89 FE68
Karen Ct, SE4
off Wickham Rd 103 DZ83
Bromley BR1 *off Blyth Rd* 144 EF95
Karen Ter, E11
off Montague Rd 68 EF61
Karenza Ct, Wem. HA9
off Lulworth Av 61 CJ59
Kariba Cl, N9 46 DW48
Karina Cl, Chig. IG7 49 ES50
Karma Way, Har. HA2 60 CA60
Karoline Gdns, Grnf. UB6
off Oldfield La N 79 CD68
Kashgar Rd, SE18 105 ET78
Kashmir Cl, Add. (New Haw)
KT15 152 BK109
Kashmir Rd, SE7 104 EK80
Kassala Rd, SW11 100 DF81
Katella Trd Est, Bark. IG11 87 ES69
Kates Cl, Barn. EN5 27 CU43
Katharine St, Croy. CR0 142 DQ104
Katherine Cl, SE16 203 H3
Addlestone KT15 152 BG107
Katherine Gdns, SE9 104 EK84
Ilford IG6 49 EQ52
Katherine Ms, Whyt. CR3 176 DT117

★ Place of interest | Railway station | London Underground station | DLR Docklands Light Railway station | Tra Tramlink station | H Hospital | Riv Pedestrian ferry landing stage

Katherine Pl, Abb.L. WD5 7 BU32
Katherine Rd, E6 86 EK66
E7 86 EJ64
Twickenham TW1
off London Rd 117 CG88
Katherine Sq, W11
off Wilsham St 81 CY74
Kathleen Av, W3 80 CQ71
Wembley HA0 80 CL66
Kathleen Rd, SW11 100 DF83
Kavanaghs Rd, Brwd. CM14 54 FU48
Kavanaghs Ter, Brwd. CM14
off Kavanaghs Rd 54 FV48
Kaye Don Way, Wey. KT13 152 BN111
Kayemoor Rd, Sutt. SM2 158 DE108
Kay Rd, SW9 101 DL82
Kays Ter, E18 *off Walpole Rd* 48 EF53
Kay St, E2 84 DU68
Welling DA16 106 EV81
Kay Way, SE10
off Greenwich High Rd 103 EB80
Kaywood Cl, Slou. SL3 92 AW76
Kean St, WC2 196 B9
Kearton Cl, Ken. CR8 176 DQ117
Keary Rd, Swans. DA10 130 FY87
Keatley Grn, E4 47 DZ51
Keats Av, E16 205 P2
Redhill RH1 184 DG132
Romford RM3 51 FH52
Keats Cl, E11
off Nightingale La 68 EH57
NW3 *off Keats Gro* 64 DE63
SE1 201 P9
SW19 120 DD93
Chigwell IG7 49 EQ51
Enfield EN3 31 DX43
Hayes UB4 77 BU71
Keats Gdns, Til. RM18 111 GH82
Keats Gro, NW3 64 DD63
★ Keats Ho, NW3 64 DE63
Keats Ho, SW1
off Churchill Gdns 101 DJ78
Beckenham BR3 123 EA93
Keats Pl, EC2 197 K7
Keats Rd, Belv. DA17 107 FC76
Welling DA16 105 ES81
Keats Wk, Brwd. (Hutt.) CM13
off Byron Rd 55 GD45
Keats Way, Croy. CR0 142 DW100
Greenford UB6 78 CB71
West Drayton UB7 94 BM77
Keble Cl, Nthlt. UB5 60 CC64
Worcester Park KT4 139 CT102
Keble Pl, SW13
off Somerville Av 99 CV79
Keble St, SW17 120 DC91
Keble Ter, Abb.L. WD5 7 BT32
Kechill Gdns, Brom. BR2 144 EG101
Kedelston Ct, E5
off Redwald Rd 67 DY63
Kedeston Ct, Sutt. SM1
off Hurstcourt Rd 140 DB102
Kedleston Dr, Orp. BR5 145 ET100
Kedleston Wk, E2
off Middleton St 84 DV69
Keedonwood Rd, Brom. BR1 124 EE92
Keel Cl, SE16 203 J3
Barking IG11 88 EW68
Keel Ct, E14 *off Newport Av* 85 ED73
Keele Cl, Wat. WD24 24 BW40
Keeley Rd, Croy. CR0 142 DQ103
Keeley St, WC2 196 B9
Keeling Ho, E2
off Claredale St 84 DV68
Keeling Rd, SE9 124 EK85
Keely Cl, Barn. EN4 28 DE43
Keemor Cl, SE18
off Llanover Rd 105 EN80
Keensacre, Iver SL0 75 BD68
Keens Cl, SW16 121 DK92
Keens Rd, Croy. CR0 160 DQ105
Keens Yd, N1
off St. Paul's Rd 83 DP65
Keep, The, SE3 104 EG82
Kingston upon Thames
KT2 118 CM93
Keepers Ms, Tedd. TW11 117 CJ93
Keepers Wk, Vir.W. GU25 132 AX99
Keep La, N11
off Gardeners Cl 44 DG47
Keetons Rd, SE16 202 D6
Keevil Dr, SW19 119 CX87
Keighley Cl, N7 65 DL63
Keighley Rd, Rom. RM3 52 FL52
Keightley Dr, SE9 125 EQ88
Keilder Cl, Uxb. UB10
off Charnwood Rd 76 BN68
Keildon Rd, SW11 100 DF84
Keir, The, SW19
off West Side Common 119 CW92
Keir Hardie Est, E5
off Springfield 66 DV60
Keir Hardie Ho, W6
off Lochaline St 99 CW79
Keir Hardie Way, Bark. IG11 88 EU66
Hayes UB4 77 BU69
Keith Av, Dart. (Sutt.H.) DA4 128 FP93
Keith Connor Cl, SW8
off Daley Thompson Way 101 DH83
Keith Gro, W12 99 CU75
Keith Pk Cres, West. (Bigg.H.)
TN16 162 EH112
Keith Pk Rd, Uxb. UB10 76 BM66
Keith Rd, E17 47 DZ53
Barking IG11 87 ER68
Hayes UB3 95 BS76
Keith Way, Horn. RM11 72 FL59
Kelbrook Rd, SE3 104 EL83
Kelburn Way, Rain. RM13
off Dominion Way 89 FG69
Kelby Path, SE9 125 EP90
Kelceda Cl, NW2 63 CU61
Kelf Gro, Hayes UB3 77 BT72
Kelfield Gdns, W10 81 CW72
Kelfield Ms, W10
off Kelfield Gdns 81 CX72
Kelland Cl, N8 *off Palace Rd* 65 DK57
Kelland Rd, E13 86 EG70
Kellaway Rd, SE3 104 EJ82
Keller Cres, E12 68 EK63
Kellerton Rd, SE13 124 EE85
Kellett Rd, SW2 101 DN84
Kelling Gdns, Croy. CR0 141 DP101
Kellino St, SW17 120 DF91
Kellner Rd, SE28 105 ET76
Kell St, SE1 200 G6
Kelly Av, SE15 102 DT80
Kelly Cl, NW10 62 CR62
Shepperton TW17 135 BS96
Kelly Ct, Borwd. WD6 26 CQ40
Kelly Ms, W9
off Woodfield Rd 81 CZ71
Kelly Rd, NW7 43 CY51
Kelly St, NW1 83 DH65
Kelly Way, Rom. RM6 70 EY57
Kelman Cl, SW4 101 DK82
Waltham Cross EN8 15 DX31
Kelmore Gro, SE22 102 DU84
Kelmscott Cl, E17 47 DZ54
Watford WD18 23 BU43
Kelmscott Cres, Wat. WD18 23 BU43
Kelmscott Gdns, W12 99 CU76
Kelmscott Rd, SW11 120 DE85
Kelross Pas, N5
off Kelross Rd 66 DQ63
Kelross Rd, N5 65 DP63
Kelsall Cl, SE3 104 EH82
Kelsall Ms, Rich. TW9 98 CP81
Kelsey Gate, Beck. BR3 143 EB96
Kelsey La, Beck. BR3 143 EA96
Kelsey Pk Av, Beck. BR3 143 EB96
Kelsey Pk Rd, Beck. BR3 143 EA96
Kelsey Rd, Orp. BR5 146 EV96
Kelsey Sq, Beck. BR3 143 EA96
Kelsey St, E2 84 DV70
Kelsey Way, Beck. BR3 143 EA97
Kelshall, Wat. WD25 24 BY36
Kelshall Ct, N4
off Brownswood Rd 66 DQ61
Kelsie Way, Ilf. IG6 49 ES52
Kelso Dr, Grav. DA12 131 GM91
Kelson Ho, E14 204 E6
Kelso Pl, W8 100 DB76
Kelso Rd, Cars. SM5 140 DC101
Kelston Rd, Ilf. IG6 49 EP54
Kelvedon Av, Walt. KT12 153 BS108
Kelvedon Cl, Brwd. (Hutt.)
CM13 55 GE44
Kingston upon Thames
KT2 118 CM93
Kelvedon Ho, SW8 101 DL81
Kelvedon Rd, SW6 99 CZ80
Kelvedon Wk, Rain. RM13
off Ongar Way 89 FE66
Kelvedon Way, Wdf.Grn. IG8 49 EM51
Kelvin Av, N13 45 DM51
Leatherhead KT22 171 CF119
Teddington TW11 117 CE93
Kelvinbrook, W.Mol. KT8 136 CB97
Kelvin Cl, Epsom KT19 156 CN107
Kelvin Cres, Har. HA3 41 CE52
Kelvin Dr, Twick. TW1 117 CH86
Kelvin Gdns, Croy. CR0 141 DL101
Southall UB1 78 CA72
Kelvin Gro, SE26 122 DV90
Chessington KT9 138 CL104
Kelvington Cl, Croy. CR0 143 DY101
Kelvington Rd, SE15 123 DX85
Kelvin Ind Est, Grnf. UB6 78 CB66
Kelvin Par, Orp. BR6 145 ES102
Kelvin Rd, N5 65 DP63
Tilbury RM18 111 GG82
Welling DA16 106 EU83
Kember St, N1
off Carnoustie Dr 83 DM66
Kemble Cl, Pot.B. EN6 12 DD33
Weybridge KT13 153 BR105
Kemble Cotts, Add. KT15
off Emley Rd 134 BG104
Kemble Dr, Brom. BR2 144 EL104
Kemble Par, Pot.B. EN6
off High St 12 DC32
Kemble Rd, N17 46 DU53
SE23 123 DX88
Croydon CR0 141 DN104
Kembleside Rd, West.
(Bigg.H.) TN16 178 EJ118
Kemble St, WC2 196 B9
Kemerton Rd, SE5 102 DQ83
Beckenham BR3 143 EB96
Croydon CR0 142 DT101
Kemeys St, E9 67 DY64
Kemishford, Wok. GU22 166 AU123
Kemnal Rd, Chis. BR7 125 ER91
Kemp Ct, SW8
off Hartington Rd 101 DL80
Kempe Cl, Slou. SL3 93 BC77
Kempe Rd, NW6 81 CX68
Enfield EN1 30 DV36
Kemp Gdns, Croy. CR0
off St. Saviours Rd 142 DQ100
Kempis Way, SE22
off East Dulwich Gro 122 DS85
Kemplay Rd, NW3 64 DD63
Kemp Pl, Bushey WD23 24 CA44
Kemp Rd, Dag. RM8 70 EX60
Kemprow, Wat. (Ald.) WD25 25 CD36
Kemp's Ct, W1 195 L9
Kemps Dr, E14 *off Morant St* 85 EA73
Northwood HA6 39 BT52
Kempsford Gdns, SW5 100 DA78
Kempsford Rd, SE11 200 E9
Kemps Gdns, SE13
off Thornford Rd 123 EC85
Kempshott Rd, SW16 121 DK94
Kempson Rd, SW6 100 DA81
Kempthorne Rd, SE8 203 L8
Kempton Av, Horn. RM12 72 FM63
Northolt UB5 78 CA65
Sunbury-on-Thames TW16 135 BV95
Kempton Cl, Erith DA8 107 FC79
Uxbridge UB10 59 BQ63
Kempton Ct, E1
off Durward St 84 DV71
Sunbury-on-Thames TW16 135 BV95
≠ Kempton Park
(Race days only) 115 BV94
★ Kempton Park Racecourse,
Sun. TW16 116 BW94
Kempton Rd, E6 87 EM67
Hampton TW12 136 BZ96
Kempton Wk, Croy. CR0 143 DY100
Kempt St, SE18 105 EN79
Kemsing Cl, Bex. DA5 126 EY87
Bromley BR2 144 EF103
Thornton Heath CR7 142 DQ98
Kemsing Rd, SE10 205 M10
Kemsley, SE13 123 EC85
Kemsley Cl, Grav. (Nthflt)
DA11 131 GF91
Greenhithe DA9 129 FV86
Kemsley Rd, West. (Tats.)
TN16 178 EK119
Kenbury Cl, Uxb. UB10 58 BN62
Kenbury Gdns, SE5
off Kenbury St 102 DQ82
Kenbury St, SE5 102 DQ82
Kenchester Cl, SW8 101 DL80
Kencot Cl, Erith DA18 106 EZ75
Kendal, Purf. RM19 108 FQ78
Kendal Av, N18 46 DR49
W3 80 CN70
Barking IG11 87 ES66
Epping CM16 18 EU31
Kendal Cl, SW9 101 DP80
Feltham TW14
off Ambleside Dr 115 BT88
Hayes UB4 77 BS68
Reigate RH2 184 DD133
Slough SL2 74 AU73
Woodford Green IG8 48 EF47
Kendal Cft, Horn. RM12 71 FG64
Kendal Dr, Slou. SL2 74 AU73
Kendale, Grays RM16 111 GH76
Kendale Rd, Brom. BR1 124 EE92
Kendal Gdns, N18 46 DR49
Sutton SM1 140 DC103
Kendal Ho, N1 *off Collier St* 83 DM68
Kendall Av, Beck. BR3 143 DY96
South Croydon CR2 160 DR109
Kendall Av S, S.Croy. CR2 160 DQ110
Kendall Ct, SW19 120 DD93
Borehamwood WD6
off Gregson Cl 26 CQ39
Kendall Gdns, Grav. DA11 131 GF87
Kendall Pl, W1 194 F7
Kendall Rd, SE18 104 EL81
Beckenham BR3 143 DY96
Isleworth TW7 97 CG82
Kendalmere Cl, N10 45 DH53
Kendal Par, N18
off Great Cambridge Rd 46 DR49
Kendal Pl, SW15 119 CZ85
Kendal Rd, NW10 63 CU63
Waltham Abbey EN9
off Deer Pk Way 31 EC36
Kendals Cl, Rad. WD7 25 CE36
Kendal Steps, W2
off St. Georges Flds 82 DE72
Kendal St, W2 194 C9
Kender St, SE14 102 DW80
Kendoa Rd, SW4 101 DK84
Kendon Cl, E11 68 EH57
Kendor Av, Epsom KT19 156 CQ111
Kendra Hall Rd, S.Croy. CR2 159 DP108
Kendrey Gdns, Twick. TW2 117 CE86
Kendrick Ms, SW7
off Reece Ms 100 DD77
Kendrick Pl, SW7 100 DD77
Kendrick Rd, Slou. SL3 92 AV76
Kenelm Cl, Har. HA1 61 CG62
Kenerne Dr, Barn. EN5 27 CY43
Kenford Cl, Wat. WD25 7 BV32
Kenia Wk, Grav. DA12 131 GM90
Kenilford Rd, SW12 121 DH87
Kenilworth Av, E17 47 EA54
SW19 120 DA92
Cobham (Stoke D'Ab.)
KT11 154 CB114
Harrow HA2 60 BZ63
Romford RM3 52 FP50
Kenilworth Cl, Bans. SM7 174 DB116
Borehamwood WD6 26 CQ41
Slough SL1 92 AT76
Kenilworth Ct, SW15
off Lower Richmond Rd 99 CX83
Watford WD17 23 BU39
Kenilworth Cres, Enf. EN1 30 DS39
Kenilworth Dr, Borwd. WD6 26 CQ41
Rickmansworth (Crox.Grn)
WD3 23 BP42
Walton-on-Thames KT12 136 BX104
Kenilworth Gdns, SE18 105 EP82
Hayes UB4 77 BT71
Hornchurch RM12 72 FJ62
Ilford IG3 69 ET61
Loughton IG10 33 EM44
Southall UB1 78 BZ69
Staines TW18 114 BJ92
Watford WD19 40 BW50
Kenilworth Rd, E3 85 DY68
NW6 81 CZ67
SE20 143 DX95
W5 80 CL74
Ashford TW15 114 BK90
Edgware HA8 42 CQ48
Epsom KT17 157 CU107
Orpington BR5 145 EQ100
KENLEY, CR8 176 DQ116
≠ Kenley 160 DQ114
Kenley, N17
off Gloucester Rd 46 DR54
Kenley Av, NW9 42 CS53
Kenley Cl, Barn. EN4 28 DE42
Bexley DA5 126 FA87
Caterham CR3 176 DR120
Chislehurst BR7 145 ES97
Kenley Gdns, Horn. RM12 72 FM61
Thornton Heath CR7 141 DP98
Kenley La, Ken. CR8 160 DQ114
Kenley Rd, SW19 139 CZ96
Kingston upon Thames
KT1 138 CP96
Twickenham TW1 117 CG86
Kenley Wk, W11 81 CY73
Sutton SM3 157 CX105
Kenlor Rd, SW17 120 DD92
Kenmare Dr, N17 46 DT54
Mitcham CR4 120 DF94
Kenmare Gdns, N13 45 DP49
Kenmare Rd, Th.Hth. CR7 141 DN100
Kenmere Gdns, Wem. HA0 80 CN67
Kenmere Rd, Well. DA16 106 EW82
Kenmont Gdns, NW10 81 CV69
Kenmore Av, Har. HA3 61 CG56
Kenmore Cl, Rich. TW9
off Kent Rd 98 CN80
Kenmore Cres, Hayes UB4 77 BT69
Kenmore Gdns, Edg. HA8 42 CP54
Kenmore Rd, Har. HA3 61 CK55
Kenley CR8 159 DP114
Kenmure Rd, E8 66 DV64
Kenmure Yd, E8
off Kenmure Rd 66 DV64
Kennacraig Cl, E16 205 N3
Kennard Rd, E15 85 ED66
N11 44 DF50
Kennard St, E16 87 EM74
SW11 100 DG82
Kennedy Av, Enf. EN3 30 DW44
Kennedy Cl, E13 86 EG68
Mitcham CR4 140 DG96
Orpington BR5 145 ER102
Pinner HA5 40 BZ51
Waltham Cross (Chsht) EN8 15 DX28
Kennedy Gdns, Sev. TN13 191 FJ123
Kennedy Ho, SE11
off Vauxhall Wk 101 DM78
Kennedy Path, W7
off Harp Rd 79 CF70
Kennedy Rd, W7 79 CE71
Barking IG11 87 ES67
Kennedy Wk, SE17
off Flint St 102 DR77
Kennel Cl, Lthd. (Fetch.)
KT22 170 CC124
Kennel La, Lthd. (Fetch.)
KT22 170 CC122
Kennelwood Cres, Croy.
(New Adgtn) CR0 161 ED111
Kennet Cl, SW11
off Maysoule Rd 100 DD84
Upminster RM14 73 FS58
Kennet Grn, S.Ock. RM15 91 FV73
Kenneth Av, Ilf. IG1 69 EP63
Kenneth Cres, NW2 63 CV64
Kenneth Gdns, Stan. HA7 41 CG51
Kenneth More Rd, Ilf. IG1
off Oakfield Rd 69 EP62
Kennet Ho, NW8 194 A6
Kenneth Rd, Bans. SM7 174 DD115
Romford RM6 70 EX59
Kenneth Robbins Ho, N17 46 DV52
Kennet Rd, W9 81 CZ70
Dartford DA1 107 FG83
Isleworth TW7 97 CF83
Kennet Sq, Mitch. CR4 140 DE95
Kennet St, E1 202 C2
Kennett Ct, Swan. BR8 147 FE97
Kennett Dr, Hayes UB4 78 BY71
Kennett Rd, Slou. SL3 93 BB76
Kennet Wf La, EC4 197 J10
Kenninghall, N18 46 DV50
Kenninghall Rd, E5 66 DU62
N18 46 DW50
Kenning St, SE16 202 G4
Kennings Way, SE11 200 F10
Kenning Ter, N1 84 DS67
KENNINGTON, SE11 101 DN79
⊖ Kennington 200 F10
Kennington Grn, SE11
off Montford Pl 101 DN78
Kennington La, SE11 200 E10
Kennington Oval, SE11 101 DM79
Kennington Pk, SW9 101 DN80
Kennington Pk Est, SE11
off Harleyford St 101 DN79
Kennington Pk Gdns, SE11 101 DP79
Kennington Pk Pl, SE11 101 DN79
Kennington Pk Rd, SE11 101 DN79
Kennington Rd, SE1 200 D6
SE11 200 D7
Kenny Dr, Cars. SM5 158 DF109
Kenny Rd, NW7 43 CY50
Kenrick Pl, W1 194 F6
Kenrick Sq, Red. (Bletch.)
RH1 186 DS133
KENSAL GREEN, NW10 81 CW69
≠ Kensal Green 81 CW69
⊖ Kensal Green 81 CW69
★ Kensal Green Cem, W10 81 CW69
KENSAL RISE, NW6 81 CX68
≠ Kensal Rise 81 CW68
Kensal Rd, W10 81 CY70
KENSAL TOWN, W10 81 CX70
Kensal Wf, W10
off Ladbroke Gro 81 CX70
KENSINGTON, W8 99 CZ75
Kensington Av, E12 86 EL65
Thornton Heath CR7 141 DN95
Watford WD18 23 BT42
Kensington Ch Ct, W8 100 DB75
Kensington Ch St, W8 82 DA74
Kensington Ch Wk, W8 100 DB75
Kensington Cl, N11 44 DG50
Kensington Ct, NW7
off Grenville Pl 42 CR50
W8 100 DB75
Kensington Ct Gdns, W8
off Kensington Ct Pl 100 DB76
Kensington Ct Ms, W8
off Kensington Ct Pl 100 DB75
Kensington Ct Pl, W8 100 DB76
Kensington Dr, Wdf.Grn. IG8 48 EK53
★ Kensington Gdns, W2 82 DC74
Kensington Gdns, Ilf. IG1 69 EM61
Kingston upon Thames KT1
off Portsmouth Rd 137 CK97
Kensington Gdns Sq, W2 82 DB72
Kensington Gate, W8 100 DC76
Kensington Gore, SW7 100 DD75
Kensington Grn, W8
off St. Mary's Pl 100 DB76
Kensington Hall Gdns, W14
off Beaumont Av 99 CZ78
Kensington High St, W8 100 DA76
W14 99 CY77
Kensington Mall, W8 82 DA74
≠ Kensington (Olympia) 99 CY76
⊖ Kensington (Olympia) 99 CY76
★ Kensington Palace, W8 100 DB75
Kensington Palace Gdns, W8 82 DB74
Kensington Pk Gdns, W11 81 CZ73
Kensington Pk Ms, W11
off Kensington Pk Rd 81 CZ72
Kensington Pk Rd, W11 81 CZ73
Kensington Pl, W8 82 DA74
Kensington Rd, SW7 198 A5
W8 100 DB75
Brentwood (Pilg.Hat.)
CM15 54 FU44
Northolt UB5 78 CA69
Romford RM7 71 FC58
Kensington Sq, W8 100 DB75
Kensington Ter, S.Croy. CR2
off Sanderstead Rd 160 DR108
Kensington Village, W14
off Avonmore Rd 99 CZ77
Kensington Way, Borwd. WD6 26 CR41
Kent Av, W13 79 CH71
Dagenham RM9 88 FA70
Welling DA16 125 ET85
Kent Cl, Borwd. WD6 26 CR38
Mitcham CR4 141 DL98
Orpington BR6 163 ES107
Staines TW18 114 BK93
Uxbridge UB8 76 BJ65
Kent Dr, Barn. EN4 28 DG42
Hornchurch RM12 72 FK63
Teddington TW11 117 CE92
Kentford Way, Nthlt. UB5 78 BY67
Kent Gdns, W13 79 CH71
Ruislip HA4 59 BV58
Kent Gate Way, Croy. CR0 161 EA106
KENT HATCH, Eden. TN8 189 EP131
Kent Hatch Rd, Eden.
(Crock.H.) TN8 189 EM131
Oxted RH8 188 EJ129
≠ Kent House 143 DY95
Kent Ho La, Beck. BR3 123 DY92
Kent Ho Rd, SE26 143 DX95
Beckenham BR3 123 DY92
Kentish Bldgs, SE1 201 K3
Kentish La, Hat. AL9 12 DC25
Kentish Rd, Belv. DA17 106 FA77
KENTISH TOWN, NW5 83 DJ65
≠ Kentish Town 65 DJ64
⊖ Kentish Town 65 DJ64
Kentish Town Rd, NW1 83 DH66
NW5 83 DH66
≠ Kentish Town West 82 DG65
Kentish Way, Brom. BR1 144 EG96
Kentlea Rd, SE28 105 ES75
Kentmere Rd, SE18 105 ES77
KENTON, Har. HA3 61 CH57
≠ Kenton 61 CH58
⊖ Kenton 61 CH58
Kenton Av, Har. HA1 61 CF59
Southall UB1 78 CA73
Sunbury-on-Thames TW16 136 BY96
Kenton Ct, W14
off Kensington High St 99 CZ76
Kenton Gdns, Har. HA3 61 CJ57
Kenton La, Har. HA3 61 CJ55
Kenton Pk Av, Har. HA3 61 CK56
Kenton Pk Cl, Har. HA3 61 CJ56
Kenton Pk Cres, Har. HA3 61 CK56
Kenton Pk Rd, Har. HA3 61 CJ56
Kenton Rd, E9 85 DX65
Harrow HA1, HA3 61 CK57
Kenton St, WC1 195 P4
Kenton Way, Hayes UB4
off Exmouth Rd 77 BS69
Woking GU21 166 AT117
Kent Pas, NW1 194 D4
Kent Rd, N21 46 DR46
W4 98 CQ76
Dagenham RM10 71 FB64
Dartford DA1 128 FK86
East Molesey KT8 136 CC98
Gravesend DA11 131 GG88
Grays RM17 110 GC79
Kingston upon Thames
KT1 *off The Bittoms* 137 CK97
Longfield DA3 149 FX96
Orpington BR5 146 EV100
Richmond TW9 98 CN80
West Wickham BR4 143 EB102
Woking GU22 167 BB116
Kents Pas, Hmptn. TW12 136 BZ95
Kent St, E2 84 DT68
E13 86 EJ69
Kent Ter, NW1 194 C3
Kent Vw, S.Ock. (Aveley)
RM15 108 FQ75
Kent Vw Gdns, Ilf. IG3 69 ES61
Kent Way, Surb. KT6 138 CL104
Kentwell Cl, SE4 103 DY84
Kentwode Grn, SW13 99 CU80
Kent Yd, SW7 198 C5
Kenver Av, N12 44 DD51
Kenward Rd, SE9 124 EJ85
Kenway, Rain. RM13 90 FJ69
Romford RM5 51 FC54
Ken Way, Wem. HA9 62 CQ61
Kenway Cl, Rain. RM13 90 FJ69
Kenway Dr, Amer. HP7 20 AV39
Kenway Rd, SW5 100 DB77
Kenway Wk, Rain. RM13 90 FK69
Kenwood Av, N14 29 DK43
SE14 *off Besson St* 103 DX81
Kenwood Cl, NW3 64 DD60
West Drayton UB7 94 BN79
Kenwood Dr, Beck. BR3 143 EC97
Rickmansworth (Mill End)
WD3 37 BF47
Walton-on-Thames KT12 153 BV107
Kenwood Gdns, E18 68 EH55
Ilford IG2 69 EN56
★ Kenwood Ho, The Iveagh
Bequest, NW3 64 DE60
Kenwood Pk, Wey. KT13 153 BR107
Kenwood Ridge, Ken. CR8 175 DP117
Kenwood Rd, N6 64 DF58
N9 46 DU46
Kenworth Cl, Wal.Cr. EN8 15 DX33
Kenworthy Rd, E9 67 DY64
Kenwyn Dr, NW2 62 CS62
Kenwyn Rd, SW4 101 DK84
SW20 139 CW95
Dartford DA1 128 FK85
Kenya Rd, SE7 104 EK80
Kenyngton Dr, Sun. TW16 115 BU92
Kenyngton Pl, Har. HA3 61 CJ57
Kenyon St, SW6 99 CX81
Keogh Rd, E15 86 EE65
Kepler Rd, SW4 101 DL84
Keppel Rd, E6 87 EM66
Dagenham RM9 70 EY63
Keppel Row, SE1 201 H3

★ Place of interest ≠ Railway station ⊖ London Underground station DLR Docklands Light Railway station Tra Tramlink station H Hospital Riv Pedestrian ferry landing stage

Keppel Spur, Wind. (Old Wind.) SL4 112 AV87
Keppel St, WC1 195 N6
Kerbela St, E2 *off Cheshire St* 84 DU70
Kerbey St, E14 85 EB72
Kerdistone Cl, Pot.B. EN6 12 DB30
Kerfield Cres, SE5 102 DR81
Kerfield Pl, SE5 102 DR81
Kernow Cl, Horn. RM12 72 FL61
Kerri Cl, Barn. EN5 27 CW42
Kerridge Ct, N1 84 DS65
Kerrill Av, Couls. CR5 175 DN119
Kerrison Pl, W5 79 CK74
Kerrison Rd, E15 85 ED67
SW11 100 DE83
W5 79 CK74
Kerrison Vil, W5 *off Kerrison Pl* 79 CK74
Kerry Av, S.Ock. (Aveley) RM15 108 FM75
Stanmore HA7 41 CK49
Kerry Cl, E16 86 EH72
N13 45 DM47
Upminster RM14 73 FT59
Kerry Ct, Stan. HA7 41 CK49
Kerry Dr, Upmin. RM14 73 FT59
Kerry Ho, E1 *off Sidney St* 84 DW72
Kerry Path, SE14 103 DZ79
Kerry Rd, SE14 103 DZ79
Kerry Ter, Wok. GU21 167 BB116
Kersey Dr, S.Croy. CR2 160 DW112
Kersey Gdns, SE9 124 EL91
Romford RM3 52 FL53
Kersfield Rd, SW15 119 CX86
Kershaw Cl, SW18 120 DC86
Grays (Chaff.Hun.) RM16 109 FW77
Hornchurch RM11 72 FK59
Kershaw Rd, Dag. RM10 70 FA62
Kersley Ms, SW11 100 DF82
Kersley Rd, N16 66 DS62
Kersley St, SW11 100 DF82
Kerstin Cl, Hayes UB3 *off St. Mary's Rd* 77 BT73
Kerswell Cl, N15 66 DS57
Kerwick Cl, N7 *off Sutterton St* 83 DM66
Keslake Rd, NW6 81 CX68
Kessock Cl, N17 66 DV57
Kesteven Cl, Ilf. IG6 49 ET51
Kestlake Rd, Bex. DA5 *off East Rochester Way* 126 EW86
KESTON, BR2 162 EJ106
Keston Av, Add. (New Haw) KT15 152 BG111
Coulsdon CR5 175 DN119
Keston BR2 162 EJ106
Keston Cl, N18 46 DR48
Welling DA16 106 EW80
Keston Gdns, Kes. BR2 162 EJ105
Keston Ms, Wat. WD17 *off Nascot Rd* 23 BV40
Keston Pk Cl, Kes. BR2 145 EM104
Keston Rd, N17 66 DR55
SE15 102 DU83
Thornton Heath CR7 141 DN100
Kestral Ct, Wall. SM6 *off Carew Rd* 159 DJ106
Kestrel Av, E6 *off Swan App* 86 EL71
SE24 121 DP85
Staines TW18 113 BF90
Kestrel Cl, NW9 42 CS54
NW10 62 CR64
Epsom KT19 156 CN111
Hornchurch RM12 89 FH66
Ilford IG6 50 EW49
Kingston upon Thames KT2 117 CK91
Watford WD25 8 BY34
Kestrel Ho, EC1 197 H2
SW8 *off St. George Wf* 101 DL79
W13 79 CF70
Enfield EN3 *off Alma Rd* 31 DY43
Kestrel Pl, SE14 *off Milton Ct Rd* 103 DY79
Kestrel Rd, Wal.Abb. EN9 16 EG34
Kestrels, The, St.Alb. (Brick.Wd) AL2 8 BZ31
Kestrel Way, Croy. (New Adgtn) CR0 161 ED109
Hayes UB3 95 BR75
Keswick Av, SW15 118 CS92
SW19 140 DA96
Hornchurch RM11 72 FK60
Keswick Bdy, SW15 *off Upper Richmond Rd* 119 CY85
Keswick Cl, Sutt. SM1 158 DC105
Keswick Ct, Slou. SL2 *off Stoke Rd* 74 AT73
Keswick Dr, Enf. EN3 30 DW36
Keswick Gdns, Ilf. IG4 68 EL57
Purfleet RM19 108 FQ79
Ruislip HA4 59 BR58
Wembley HA9 62 CL63
Keswick Ms, W5 80 CL74
Keswick Rd, SW15 119 CY85
Bexleyheath DA7 106 FA82
Egham TW20 113 BB94
Orpington BR6 145 ET102
Twickenham TW2 116 CC86
West Wickham BR4 144 EE103
Kettering Rd, Enf. EN3 *off Beaconsfield Rd* 31 DX37
Romford RM3 52 FL52
Kettering St, SW16 121 DJ93
Kett Gdns, SW2 121 DM85
Kettlebaston Rd, E10 67 DZ60
Kettlewell Cl, N11 44 DG51
Woking GU21 150 AX114
Kettlewell Ct, Swan. BR8 147 FF96
Kettlewell Dr, Wok. GU21 150 AY114
Kettlewell Hill, Wok. GU21 150 AY114
Ketton Grn, Red. (Merst.) RH1 *off Malmstone Av* 185 DK128
Kevan Dr, Wok. (Send) GU23 167 BE124
Kevan Ho, SE5 102 DQ80
Kevelioc Rd, N17 46 DQ53
Kevin Cl, Houns. TW4 96 BX82
Kevington Cl, Orp. BR5 145 ET98
Kevington Dr, Chis. BR7 145 ET98
Orpington BR5 145 ET98
KEW, Rich. TW9 98 CN79
≠ **Kew Bridge** 98 CM78
Kew Br, Brent. TW8 98 CM79
Richmond TW9 98 CM79
Kew Br Arches, Rich. TW9 *off Kew Br* 98 CM79
Kew Br Ct, W4 98 CN78
Kew Br Rd, Brent. TW8 98 CM79
★ **Kew Bridge Steam Mus**, Brent. TW8 98 CM78
Kew Cres, Sutt. SM3 139 CY104
Kewferry Dr, Nthwd. HA6 39 BP50
Kewferry Rd, Nthwd. HA6 39 BQ51
Kew Foot Rd, Rich. TW9 98 CL84
≠ **Kew Gardens** 98 CM81
⊖ **Kew Gardens** 98 CM81
Kew Gdns Rd, Rich. TW9 98 CM80
Kew Grn, Rich. TW9 98 CN80
Kew Meadows Path, Rich. TW9 98 CP82
★ **Kew Observatory**, Rich. TW9 97 CH83
★ **Kew Palace**, Royal Botanic Gdns, Rich. TW9 98 CL80
Kew Retail Pk, Rich. TW9 98 CP81
Kew Rd, Rich. TW9 98 CN79
Keybridge Ho, SW8 101 DL79
Key Cl, E1 84 DV70
Keyes Rd, NW2 63 CX64
Dartford DA1 108 FM84
Keyham Ho, W2 *off Westbourne Pk Rd* 82 DA71
Keymer Cl, West. (Bigg.H.) TN16 178 EK116
Keymer Rd, SW2 121 DM89
Keynes Cl, N2 64 DF55
Keynsham Av, Wdf.Grn. IG8 48 EE49
Keynsham Gdns, SE9 124 EL85
Keynsham Rd, SE9 124 EK85
Morden SM4 140 DB102
Keynsham Wk, Mord. SM4 140 DB102
Keys, The, Brwd. (Gt Warley) CM13 *off Eagle Way* 53 FW51
Keyse Rd, SE1 201 P7
Keysham Av, Houns. TW5 *off The Avenue* 95 BU81
Keys Ho, Enf. EN3 *off Beaconsfield Rd* 31 DX37
Keystone Cres, N1 196 A1
Keywood Dr, Sun. TW16 115 BU93
Keyworth Cl, E5 67 DY63
Keyworth Pl, SE1 *off Keyworth St* 101 DP76
Keyworth St, SE1 200 G6
Kezia Ms, SE8 *off Trundleys Rd* 103 DY78
Kezia St, SE8 *off Trundleys Rd* 103 DY78
Khalsa Av, Grav. DA12 131 GJ87
Khalsa Ct, N22 *off Acacia Rd* 45 DP53
Khama Rd, SW17 120 DE91
Khartoum Pl, Grav. DA12 131 GJ86
Khartoum Rd, E13 86 EH69
SW17 120 DD91
Ilford IG1 69 EP64
Khyber Rd, SW11 100 DE82
Kibworth St, SW8 101 DM80
KIDBROOKE, SE3 104 EH83
≠ **Kidbrooke** 104 EH83
Kidbrooke Gdns, SE3 104 EG82
Kidbrooke Gro, SE3 104 EG81
Kidbrooke Interchange, SE3 *off Rochester Way Relief Rd* 104 EJ83
Kidbrooke La, SE9 104 EL84
Kidbrooke Pk Cl, SE3 104 EH81
Kidbrooke Pk Rd, SE3 104 EH81
Kidbrooke Way, SE3 104 EH82
Kidderminster Pl, Croy. CR0 *off Kidderminster Rd* 141 DP102
Kidderminster Rd, Croy. CR0 141 DP102
Kidderpore Av, NW3 64 DA63
Kidderpore Gdns, NW3 64 DA63
Kidd Pl, SE7 104 EL78
Kidman Cl, Rom. (Gidea Pk) RM2 72 FJ55
Kielder Cl, Ilf. IG6 49 ET51
Kiffen St, EC2 197 L4
Kilberry Cl, Islw. TW7 97 CD81
KILBURN, NW6 82 DA68
⊖ **Kilburn** 81 CZ65
Kilburn Br, NW6 *off Kilburn High Rd* 82 DA67
Kilburn Gate, NW6 *off Kilburn Priory* 82 DB68
≠ **Kilburn High Road** 82 DA67
Kilburn High Rd, NW6 81 CZ66
Kilburn La, W9 81 CX69
W10 81 CX69
⊖ **Kilburn Park** 82 DA68
Kilburn Pk Rd, NW6 82 DA69
Kilburn Pl, NW6 82 DA67
Kilburn Priory, NW6 82 DB67
Kilburn Sq, NW6 82 DA67
Kilburn Vale, NW6 *off Belsize Rd* 82 DB67
Kilby Cl, Wat. WD25 24 BX35
Kilby Ct, SE10 *off Child La* 104 EF76
Kilcorral Cl, Epsom KT17 157 CU114
Kildare Cl, Ruis. HA4 60 BW60
Kildare Gdns, W2 82 DA72
Kildare Rd, E16 86 EG71
Kildare Ter, W2 82 DA72
Kildare Wk, E14 *off Farrance St* 85 EA72
Kildonan Cl, Wat. WD17 23 BT39
Kildoran Rd, SW2 121 DL85
Kildowan Rd, Ilf. IG3 70 EU60
Kilgour Rd, SE23 123 DY86
Kilkie St, SW6 100 DC82
Killarney Rd, SW18 120 DC86
Killasser Ct, Tad. KT20 173 CW123
Killburns Mill Cl, Wall. SM6 *off London Rd* 159 DH105
Killearn Rd, SE6 123 ED88
Killester Gdns, Wor.Pk. KT4 157 CV105
Killewarren Way, Orp. BR5 146 EW100
Killick Cl, Sev. (Dunt.Grn) TN13 190 FE121
Killick St, N1 83 DM68
Killieser Av, SW2 121 DL89
Killip Cl, E16 86 EF72
Killowen Av, Nthlt. UB5 60 CC64
Killowen Rd, E9 85 DX65
Killy Hill, Wok. (Chobham) GU24 150 AS108
Killyon Rd, SW8 101 DJ82
Killyon Ter, SW8 101 DJ82
Kilmaine Rd, SW6 99 CY80
Kilmarnock Gdns, Dag. RM8 *off Lindsey Rd* 70 EW62
Kilmarnock Pk, Reig. RH2 184 DB133
Kilmarnock Rd, Wat. WD19 40 BX49
Kilmarsh Rd, W6 99 CW77
Kilmartin Av, SW16 141 DM97
Kilmartin Rd, Ilf. IG3 70 EU61
Kilmartin Way, Horn. RM12 71 FH64
Kilmington Cl, Brwd. (Hutt.) CM13 55 GB47
Kilmington Rd, SW13 99 CU79
Kilmiston Av, Shep. TW17 135 BQ100
Kilmorey Gdns, Twick. TW1 117 CH85
Kilmorey Rd, Twick. TW1 97 CH84
Kilmorie Rd, SE23 123 DY88
Kiln Av, Amer. HP6 20 AW38
Kiln Cl, Hayes UB3 *off Brickfield La* 95 BR79
Kilndown, Grav. DA12 131 GK93
Kilner St, E14 85 EA71
Kiln La, Chesh. (Ley Hill) HP5 4 AV31
Epsom KT17 156 CS111
Woking (Ripley) GU23 168 BH124
Kiln Ms, SW17 120 DD92
Kiln Pl, NW5 64 DG64
Kiln Rd, Epp. (N.Wld Bas.) CM16 18 FA27
Kilnside, Esher (Clay.) KT10 155 CG108
Kiln Way, Grays (Bad.Dene) RM17 110 FZ78
Northwood HA6 39 BS51
Kilnwood, Sev. (Halst.) TN14 164 EZ113
Kiln Wd La, Rom. (Hav.at.Bow.) RM4 51 FD50
Kilpatrick Way, Hayes UB4 78 BY71
Kilravock St, W10 81 CY69
Kilross Rd, Felt. TW14 115 BR88
Kilrue La, Walt. KT12 153 BT105
Kilrush Ter, Wok. GU21 167 BA116
Kilsby Wk, Dag. RM9 *off Rugby Rd* 88 EV65
Kilsha Rd, Walt. KT12 135 BV100
Kilsmore La, Wal.Cr. (Chsht) EN8 15 DX28
Kilvinton Dr, Enf. EN2 30 DR38
Kilworth Av, Brwd. (Shenf.) CM15 55 GA44
Kimbell Gdns, SW6 99 CY81
Kimbell Pl, SE3 *off Tudway Rd* 104 EJ84
Kimberley Av, E6 86 EL68
SE15 102 DV82
Ilford IG2 69 ER59
Romford RM7 71 FC58
Kimberley Cl, Slou. SL3 93 AZ77
Kimberley Dr, Sid. DA14 126 EX89
Kimberley Gdns, N4 65 DP57
Enfield EN1 30 DT41
Kimberley Gate, Brom. BR1 *off Oaklands Rd* 124 EF94
Kimberley Ind Est, E17 47 DZ53
Kimberley Pl, Pur. CR8 *off Brighton Rd* 159 DN111
Kimberley Ride, Cob. KT11 154 CB113
Kimberley Rd, E4 48 EE46
E11 67 ED61
E16 86 EF70
E17 47 DZ53
N17 46 DU54
N18 46 DV51
NW6 81 CY67
SW9 101 DL82
Beckenham BR3 143 DX96
Croydon CR0 141 DP100
Kimberley Way, E4 48 EE46
Kimber Rd, SW18 120 DA87
Kimble Cl, Wat. WD18 23 BS44
Kimble Cres, Bushey WD23 40 CC45
Kimble Rd, SW19 120 DD93
Kimbolton Cl, SE12 124 EF86
Kimbolton Grn, Borwd. WD6 26 CQ42
Kimbolton Row, SW3 198 B9
Kimmeridge Gdns, SE9 124 EL91
Kimmeridge Rd, SE9 124 EL91
Kimpton Av, Brwd. CM15 54 FV45
Kimpton Ho, SW15 *off Fontley Way* 119 CU87
Kimpton Link Business Cen, Sutt. SM3 *off Kimpton Rd* 139 CZ103
Kimpton Pl, Wat. WD25 8 BX34
Kimpton Rd, SE5 102 DR81
Sutton SM3 139 CZ103
Kimptons Cl, Pot.B. EN6 11 CX33
Kimptons Mead, Pot.B. EN6 11 CX32
Kimpton Trade & Business Cen, Sutt. SM3 139 CZ103
Kinburn Dr, Egh. TW20 112 AY92
Kinburn St, SE16 203 H4
Kincaid Rd, SE15 102 DV80
Kincardine Gdns, W9 *off Harrow Rd* 81 CZ70
Kinch Gro, Wem. HA9 62 CM59
Kincraig Dr, Sev. TN13 190 FG124
Kinder Cl, SE28 88 EX73
Kindersley Way, Abb.L. WD5 7 BQ31
Kinder St, E1 *off Cannon St Rd* 84 DV72
Kinderton Cl, N14 45 DJ46
Kinefold Ho, N7 *off York Way* 83 DL65
Kinetic Cres, Enf. EN3 31 DZ36
Kinfauns Av, Horn. RM11 72 FJ58
Kinfauns Rd, SW2 121 DN89
Ilford IG3 70 EU60
Kingaby Gdns, Rain. RM13 89 FG66
King Acre Ct, Stai. TW18 *off Moor La* 113 BE90
King Alfred Av, SE6 123 EA90
King Alfred Rd, Rom. RM3 52 FM54
King & Queen Cl, SE9 *off St. Keverne Rd* 124 EL91
King & Queen St, SE17 201 J9
King & Queen Wf, SE16 203 H2
King Arthur Cl, SE15 102 DW80
King Arthur Ct, Wal.Cr. EN8 15 DX31
King Charles Cres, Surb. KT5 138 CM101
King Charles Rd, Rad. (Shenley) WD7 10 CL32
Surbiton KT5 138 CM99
King Charles St, SW1 199 N4
King Charles Ter, E1 *off Sovereign Cl* 84 DV73
King Charles Wk, SW19 *off Princes Way* 119 CY88
Kingcup Cl, Croy. CR0 143 DX101
King David La, E1 84 DW73
Kingdon Rd, NW6 82 DA65
King Edward Av, Dart. DA1 128 FK86
Rainham RM13 90 FK68
King Edward Dr, Chess. KT9 *off Kelvin Gro* 138 CL104
Grays RM16 110 GE75
King Edward Ms, SW13 99 CU81
King Edward Rd, E10 67 EC60
E17 67 DY55
Barnet EN5 28 DA42
Brentwood CM14 54 FW48
Greenhithe DA9 129 FU85
Radlett (Shenley) WD7 10 CM33
Romford RM1 71 FF58
Waltham Cross EN8 15 DY33
Watford WD19 24 BY44
King Edward VII Av, Wind. SL4 92 AS80
H **King Edward VII's Hosp for Officers**, W1 194 G6
King Edward's Gdns, W3 80 CN74
King Edwards Gro, Tedd. TW11 117 CH93
King Edward's Pl, W3 *off King Edward's Gdns* 80 CN74
King Edwards Rd, E9 84 DV67
N9 46 DV45
Barking IG11 87 ER67
King Edward's Rd, Enf. EN3 31 DX42
King Edwards Rd, Ruis. HA4 59 BR60
King Edward St, EC1 197 H8
King Edward III Ms, SE16 202 E5
King Edward Wk, SE1 200 E6
Kingfield Cl, Wok. GU22 167 AZ120
Kingfield Dr, Wok. GU22 167 AZ120
Kingfield Gdns, Wok. GU22 167 AZ120
Kingfield Grn, Wok. GU22 167 AZ120
Kingfield Rd, W5 79 CK70
Woking GU22 166 AY120
Kingfield St, E14 204 E9
Kingfisher Av, E11 *off Eastern Av* 68 EH58
Kingfisher Cl, SE28 88 EW73
Brentwood (Hutt.) CM13 55 GA45
Harrow (Har.Wld) HA3 41 CF52
Northwood HA6 39 BP53
Orpington BR5 146 EX98
Walton-on-Thames KT12 154 BY106
Kingfisher Ct, SW19 *off Queensmere Rd* 119 CY89
Enfield EN2 *off Mount Vw* 29 DM38
Surbiton KT6 *off Ewell Rd* 138 CM101
Sutton SM1 *off Sandpiper Rd* 157 CZ106
Woking GU21 *off Vale Fm Rd* 166 AX117
Woking (Sheer.) GU21 *off Blackmore Cres* 151 BC114
Kingfisher Dr, Green. DA9 129 FU85
Hemel Hempstead HP3 6 BM25
Redhill RH1 184 DG131
Richmond TW10 117 CH91
Staines TW18 113 BF91
Kingfisher Gdns, S.Croy. CR2 161 DX111
Kingfisher Height, Grays RM17 110 GA78
Kingfisher Ho, SW18 *off York Rd* 100 DC84
Kingfisher Lure, Kings L. WD4 7 BP29
Rickmansworth (Loud.) WD3 22 BH42
Kingfisher Ms, SE13 103 EB84
Kingfisher Pl, N22 *off Clarendon Rd* 45 DM54
Kingfisher Rd, Upmin. RM14 73 FT60
Kingfisher Sq, SE8 103 DZ79
Kingfisher St, E6 86 EL71
Kingfisher Wk, NW9 *off Eagle Dr* 42 CS54
Kingfisher Way, NW10 62 CR64
Beckenham BR3 143 DX99
King Frederik IX Twr, SE16 203 M6
King Gdns, Croy. CR0 159 DP106
King George Av, E16 86 EK72
Bushey WD23 24 CB44
Ilford IG2 69 ER57
Walton-on-Thames KT12 136 BX102
King George Cl, Rom. RM7 71 FC55
Sunbury-on-Thames TW16 115 BS92
DLR **King George V** 87 EN74
H **King George Hosp**, Ilf. IG3 70 EV57
King George Rd, Wal.Abb. EN9 15 EC34
King Georges Av, Wat. WD18 23 BS43
King Georges Dr, Add. (New Haw) KT15 152 BG110
Southall UB1 78 BZ71
King George VI Av, Mitch. CR4 140 DF98
Westerham TN16 178 EK116
King George Sq, Rich. TW10 118 CM86
King Georges Rd, Brwd. (Pilg.Hat.) CM15 54 FV44
King George's Trd Est, Chess. KT9 156 CN105
King George St, SE10 103 EC80
Kingham Cl, SW18 120 DC87
W11 99 CY75
King Harolds Way, Bexh. DA7 106 EX80
King Henry Ms, Har. HA2 61 CE60
Orpington BR6 *off Osgood Av* 163 ET106
King Henry's Ct, Wal.Abb. EN9 *off Deer Pk Way* 31 EC36
Tra **King Henry's Drive** 161 EB109
King Henry's Dr, Croy. (New Adgtn) CR0 161 EC109
King Henry's Ms, Enf. EN3 31 EA37
King Henry's Reach, W6 99 CW79
King Henry's Rd, NW3 82 DE66
Kingston upon Thames KT1 138 CP97
King Henry St, N16 66 DS64
King Henry's Wk, N1 84 DS65
King Henry Ter, E1 202 E1
Kinghorn St, EC1 197 H7
King James Av, Pot.B. (Cuffley) EN6 13 DL29
King James Ct, SE1 200 G5
King James St, SE1 200 G5
King John Ct, EC2 197 N4
King John's Cl, Stai. (Wrays.) TW19 112 AW86
King John St, E1 85 DX71
King Johns Wk, SE9 124 EK88
Kinglake Ct, Wok. GU21 *off Raglan Rd* 166 AS118
Kinglake Est, SE17 201 N10
Kinglake St, SE17 102 DS78
Kinglet Cl, E7 *off Romford Rd* 86 EG65
Kingly Ct, W1 195 K10
Kingly St, W1 195 K9
Kingsand Rd, SE12 124 EG89
Kings Arbour, Sthl. UB2 96 BY78
Kings Arms Ct, E1 *off Old Montague St* 84 DU71
Kings Arms Yd, EC2 197 K8
Kingsash Dr, Hayes UB4 78 BY70
Kings Av, N10 64 DG55
N21 45 DP46
King's Av, SW4 121 DK87
SW12 121 DK88
Kings Av, W5 79 CK72
Bromley BR1 124 EF93
Buckhurst Hill IG9 48 EK47
Carshalton SM5 158 DE108
Greenford UB6 78 CB72
Hounslow TW3 96 CB81
New Malden KT3 138 CS98
Romford RM6 70 EZ58
Sunbury-on-Thames TW16 115 BT92
Watford WD18 23 BT42
West Byfleet (Byfleet) KT14 152 BK112
Woodford Green IG8 48 EH51
Kings Bench St, SE1 200 G4
Kings Bench Wk, EC4 196 E9
Kingsbridge Av, W3 98 CM75
Kingsbridge Circ, Rom. RM3 52 FL51
Kingsbridge Cl, Rom. RM3 52 FL51
Kingsbridge Ct, E14 *off Dockers Tanner Rd* 103 EA76
Kingsbridge Cres, Sthl. UB1 78 BZ71
Kingsbridge Dr, NW7 43 CX52
Kingsbridge Rd, W10 81 CW72
Barking IG11 87 ER68
Morden SM4 139 CX101
Romford RM3 52 FL51
Southall UB2 96 BZ77
Walton-on-Thames KT12 135 BV101
Kingsbridge Way, Hayes UB4 77 BS69
Kingsbrook, Lthd. KT22 *off Ryebrook Rd* 171 CG118
KINGSBURY, NW9 62 CP58
⊖ **Kingsbury** 62 CN57
Kingsbury Circle, NW9 62 CN57
H **Kingsbury Comm Hosp**, NW9 62 CN56
Kingsbury Cres, Stai. TW18 113 BD91
Kingsbury Dr, Wind. (Old Wind.) SL4 112 AV86
Kingsbury Rd, N1 84 DS65
NW9 62 CP57
Kingsbury Ter, N1 84 DS65
Kingsbury Trd Est, NW9 62 CQ58
Kings Butts, SE9 *off Strongbow Cres* 125 EM85
Kings Chace Vw, Enf. EN2 *off Crofton Way* 29 DN40
Kings Chase, Brwd. CM14 54 FW48
East Molesey KT8 136 CC97
Kingsclere Cl, SW15 119 CU87
Kingsclere Ct, Barn. EN5 *off Gloucester Rd* 28 DC43
Kingsclere Pl, Enf. EN2 *off Chase Side* 30 DQ40
Kingscliffe Gdns, SW19 119 CZ88
Kings Cl, E10 67 EB59
NW4 63 CX56
Chalfont St. Giles HP8 36 AX47
Dartford DA1 107 FE84
Kings Langley (Chipper.) WD4 6 BH31
Northwood HA6 39 BT51
Staines TW18 114 BK94
Thames Ditton KT7 137 CG100
Walton-on-Thames KT12 135 BV102
King's Cl, Wat. WD18 *off Lady's Cl* 23 BV42
H **King's Coll Hosp**, SE5 102 DR82
Kings Coll Rd, NW3 82 DE66
Ruislip HA4 59 BT58
Kingscote Rd, W4 98 CR76
Croydon CR0 142 DV101
New Malden KT3 138 CR97
Kingscote St, EC4 196 F10
Kings Ct, E13 86 EH67
W6 *off King St* 99 CU77
Tadworth KT20 173 CW122
Wembley HA9 62 CP61
Kingscourt Rd, SW16 121 DK90
Kings Ct S, SW3 *off Chelsea Manor Gdns* 100 DE78
Kings Cres, N4 66 DQ62
Kings Cres Est, N4 66 DQ61
Kingscroft Rd, NW2 81 CZ65
Banstead SM7 174 DD115
Leatherhead KT22 171 CH120
KING'S CROSS, N1 83 DK67
≠ **King's Cross** 195 P1
King's Cross Br, N1 196 A2
King's Cross Rd, WC1 196 C2
⊖ **King's Cross St. Pancras** 195 P1
≠ **King's Cross Thameslink** 196 A1
Kingsdale Ct, Wal.Abb. EN9 *off Lamplighters Cl* 16 EG34
Kingsdale Gdns, W11 81 CX74
Kingsdale Rd, SE18 105 ET80
SE20 123 DX94
Kingsdene, Tad. KT20 173 CV121
Kingsdown Av, W3 80 CS73
W13 97 CH75

★ Place of interest ≠ Railway station ⊖ London Underground station DLR Docklands Light Railway station Tra Tramlink station H Hospital Riv Pedestrian ferry landing stage

Kingsdown Av, S.Croy. CR2 .159 DP109
Kingsdown Cl, SE16
off Masters Dr .102 DV78
W10 .81 CX72
Gravesend DA12
off Farley Rd .131 GM88
Kingsdowne Rd, Surb. KT6 .138 CL101
Kingsdown Rd, E11 .68 EE62
N19 .65 DL61
Epsom KT17 .157 CU113
Sutton SM3 .157 CY106
Kingsdown Way, Brom. BR2 .144 EG101
Kings Dr, Edg. HA8 .42 CM49
Gravesend DA12 .131 GH90
Surbiton KT5 .138 CN101
Teddington TW11 .117 CD92
Thames Ditton KT7 .137 CH100
Wembley HA9 .62 CP61
Kings Dr, The, Walt. KT12 .153 BT110
Kingsend, Ruis. HA4 .59 BR60
KINGS FARM, Grav. DA12 .131 GJ90
Kings Fm Av, Rich. TW10 .98 CN84
Kings Fm Rd, Rick. (Chorl.)
WD3 .21 BD44
Kingsfield Av, Har. HA2 .60 CB56
Kingsfield Ct, Wat. WD19 .40 BX45
Kingsfield Dr, Enf. EN3 .31 DX35
Kingsfield Ho, SE9 .124 EK90
Kingsfield Rd, Har. HA1 .61 CD59
Watford WD19 .40 BX45
Kingsfield Ter, Dart. DA1
off Priory Rd S .128 FK86
Kingsfield Way, Enf. EN3 .31 DX35
Kingsford St, NW5 .64 DF64
Kingsford Way, E6 .87 EM71
Kings Gdns, NW6
off West End La .82 DA66
Ilford IG1 .69 ER60
Upminster RM14 .73 FS59
King's Garth Ms, SE23
off London Rd .122 DW89
Kings Gate, Add. KT15 .152 BH105
Kingsgate, Wem. HA9 .62 CQ62
Kingsgate Av, N3 .64 DA55
Kingsgate Cl, Bexh. DA7 .106 EY81
Orpington BR5
off Main Rd .146 EW97
Kingsgate Pl, NW6 .82 DA66
Kingsgate Rd, NW6 .82 DA66
Kingston upon Thames
KT2 .138 CL95
Kings Grn, Loug. IG10 .32 EL41
Kingsground, SE9 .124 EL87
Kings Gro, SE15 .102 DV80
Romford RM1 .71 FG57
Kingshall Ms, SE13
off Lewisham Rd .103 EC83
Kings Hall Rd, Beck. BR3 .123 DY94
Kings Head Hill, E4 .47 EB45
Kings Head La, W.Byf.
(Byfleet) KT14 .152 BK111
Kings Head Yd, SE1 .201 K3
Kings Highway, SE18 .105 ES79
Kings Hill, Loug. IG10 .32 EL40
Kingshill Av, Har. HA3 .61 CH56
Hayes UB4 .77 BS69
Northolt UB5 .77 BU69
Romford RM5 .51 FC51
Worcester Park KT4 .139 CU101
Kingshill Cl, Hayes UB4 .77 BU69
Kingshill Dr, Har. HA3 .61 CH55
Kingshold Est, E9
off Victoria Pk Rd .84 DW67
Kingshold Rd, E9 .84 DW66
Kingsholm Gdns, SE9 .104 EK84
Kingshurst Rd, SE12 .124 EG87
Kingside Business Pk, SE18
off Woolwich Ch St .104 EL76
King's Keep, SW15
off Westleigh Av .119 CX86
Kings Keep, Kings.T. KT1
off Beaufort Rd .138 CL98
KINGSLAND, N1 .84 DS65
Kingsland, NW8
off Broxwood Way .82 DE67
Potters Bar EN6 .11 CZ33
Kingsland Basin, N1
off Kingsland Rd .84 DS67
Kingsland Grn, E8 .84 DS65
Kingsland High St, E8 .66 DT64
Kingsland Pas, E8
off Kingsland Grn .84 DS65
Kingsland Rd, E2 .197 N2
E8 .84 DS68
E13 .86 EJ69
Kingsland Shop Cen, E8 .84 DT65
Kings La, Egh. (Eng.Grn)
TW20 .112 AU92
Kings Langley (Chipper.)
WD4 .6 BG31
Sutton SM1 .158 DD107
KINGS LANGLEY, WD4 .6 BM30
⇌ Kings Langley .7 BQ30
Kings Langley Bypass, Kings L.
WD4 .6 BK28
Kingslawn Cl, SW15
off Howards La .119 CV85
Kingslea, Lthd. KT22 .171 CG120
Kingsleigh Cl, Brent. TW8 .97 CK79
Kingsleigh Pl, Mitch. CR4 .140 DF97
Kingsleigh Wk, Brom. BR2
off Stamford Dr .144 EF98
Kingsley Av, W13 .79 CG72
Banstead SM7 .174 DA115
Borehamwood WD6 .26 CM40
Dartford DA1 .128 FN85
Egham (Eng.Grn) TW20 .112 AV93
Hounslow TW3 .96 CC82
Southall UB1 .78 CA73
Sutton SM1 .158 DD105
Waltham Cross (Chsht) EN8 .14 DV29
Kingsley Cl, N2 .64 DC57
Dagenham RM10 .71 FB63
Kingsley Ct, Edg. HA8 .42 CP47
Kingsley Dr, Wor.Pk. KT4
off Badgers Copse .139 CT103
Kingsley Flats, SE1
off Old Kent Rd .102 DS77
Kingsley Gdns, E4 .47 EA50
Hornchurch RM11 .72 FK56
Kingsley Ms, E1 .202 E1
W8 off Stanford Rd .100 DB76
Chislehurst BR7 .125 EP93
Kingsley Pl, N6 .64 DG59
Kingsley Rd, E7 .86 EG66
E17 .47 EC54
N13 .45 DN49
NW6 .81 CZ67
SW19 .120 DB92
Brentwood (Hutt.) CM13 .55 GD45
Croydon CR0 .141 DN102
Harrow HA2 .60 CC63
Hounslow TW3 .96 CC82
Ilford IG6 .49 EQ53
Loughton IG10 .33 ER41
Orpington BR6 .163 ET107
Pinner HA5 .60 BZ56
Kingsley St, SW11 .100 DF83
Kingsley Wk, Grays RM16 .111 GG77
Kingsley Way, N2 .64 DC58
Kingsley Wd Dr, SE9 .125 EM90
Kingslyn Cres, SE19 .142 DS95
Kings Lynn Cl, Rom. RM3
off Kings Lynn Dr .52 FK51
Kings Lynn Dr, Rom. RM3 .52 FK51
Kings Lynn Path, Rom. RM3
off Kings Lynn Dr .52 FK51
Kings Mall, W6 .99 CW77
Kingsman Par, SE18
off Woolwich Ch St .105 EM76
Kingsman St, SE18 .105 EM76
Kingsmead, Barn. EN5 .28 DA42
Potters Bar (Cuffley) EN6 .13 DL28
Richmond TW10 .118 CM86
Waltham Cross EN8 .15 DX28
Westerham (Bigg.H.) TN16 .178 EK116
Kingsmead Av, N9 .46 DV46
NW9 .62 CR59
Mitcham CR4 .141 DJ97
Romford RM1 .71 FE58
Sunbury-on-Thames TW16 .136 BW97
Surbiton KT6 .138 CN103
Worcester Park KT4 .139 CV104
Kingsmead Cl, Epsom KT19 .156 CR108
Sidcup DA15 .126 EU89
Teddington TW11 .117 CH93
Kingsmead Dr, Nthlt. UB5 .78 BZ66
Kingsmead Est, E9 .67 DY64
Kingsmead Ho, E9
off Kingsmead Way .67 DY63
Kings Meadow, Kings L. WD4 .6 BN28
Kings Mead Pk, Esher (Clay.)
KT10 .155 CE108
Kingsmead Rd, SW2 .121 DN89
Kingsmead Way, E9 .67 DY63
Kingsmere Cl, SW15
off Felsham Rd .99 CY83
Kingsmere Pk, NW9 .62 CP60
Kingsmere Pl, N16 .66 DR60
Kingsmere Rd, SW19 .119 CX89
Kings Ms, SW4 off King's Av .121 DL85
King's Ms, WC1 .196 C5
Kings Ms, Chig. IG7 .49 EQ47
Kingsmill Business Pk,
Kings.T. KT1 .138 CM97
Kingsmill Gdns, Dag. RM9 .70 EZ64
Kingsmill Rd, Dag. RM9 .70 EZ64
Kingsmill Ter, NW8 .82 DD68
Kingsnympton Pk, Kings.T.
KT2 .118 CP93
Kings Oak, Rom. RM7 .70 FA55
H King's Oak Private Hosp,
Enf. EN2 .29 DN38
King's Orchard, SE9 .124 EL86
Kings Paddock, Hmptn.
TW12 .136 CC95
Kings Par, Cars. SM5
off Wrythe La .140 DE104
Kingspark Ct, E18 .68 EG55
King's Pas, E11 .68 EE59
Kings Pas, Kings.T. KT1 .137 CK96
Kings Pl, SE1 .201 H5
W4 .98 CQ78
Buckhurst Hill IG9 .48 EJ47
Loughton IG10 .48 EK45
King Sq, EC1 .197 H3
King's Reach Twr, SE1 .200 E2
Kings Ride Gate, Rich. TW10 .98 CN84
Kingsridge, SW19 .119 CY89
Kingsridge Gdns, Dart. DA1 .128 FK86
Kings Rd, E4 .47 ED46
E6 .86 EJ67
E11 .68 EE59
King's Rd, N17 .46 DT53
Kings Rd, N18 .46 DU50
N22 .45 DM53
NW10 .81 CV66
SE25 .142 DU97
King's Rd, SW1 .198 C10
SW3 .198 C10
SW6 .100 DB81
SW10 .100 DB81
Kings Rd, SW14 .98 CR83
SW19 .120 DA93
W5 .79 CK71
Addlestone (New Haw)
KT15 .152 BH110
Barking IG11 off North St .87 EQ66
Barnet EN5 .27 CW41
Brentwood CM14 .54 FW48
Chalfont St. Giles HP8 .36 AX47
Egham TW20 .113 BA91
Feltham TW13 .116 BW88
Harrow HA2 .60 BZ61
Kingston upon Thames
KT2 .118 CL94
Mitcham CR4 .140 DG97
Orpington BR6 .163 ET105
Richmond TW10 .118 CM85
Romford RM1 .71 FG57
St. Albans (Lon.Col.) AL2 .9 CJ26
Slough SL1 .92 AS76
Surbiton KT6 .137 CJ102
Sutton SM2 .158 DA110
Teddington TW11 .117 CD92
Twickenham TW1 .117 CH86
King's Rd, Uxb. UB8 .76 BK68
Kings Rd, Wal.Cr. EN8 .15 DY34
Walton-on-Thames KT12 .135 BV103
West Drayton UB7 .94 BM75
Westerham (Bigg.H.) TN16 .178 EJ116
Kings Rd, Wok. GU21 .167 BA116
Kings Rd Bungalows, Har.
HA2 off Kings Rd .60 BZ62
King's Scholars' Pas, SW1 .199 K7
King Stairs Cl, SE16 .202 E4
King's Ter, NW1
off Plender St .83 DJ67
Kings Ter, Islw. TW7
off Worple Rd .97 CG83
Kingsthorpe Rd, SE26 .123 DX91
⇌ Kingston .138 CL95
Kingston Av, Felt. TW14 .115 BS86
Leatherhead KT22 .171 CH121
Sutton SM3 .139 CY104
West Drayton UB7 .76 BM73
Kingston Br, Kings.T. KT1 .137 CK96
Kingston Bypass, SW15 .118 CS91
SW20 .118 CS91
Esher KT10 .137 CG104
New Malden KT3 .139 CT95
Surbiton KT5, KT6 .138 CL104
Kingston Cl, Nthlt. UB5 .78 BZ67
Romford RM6 .70 EY55
Teddington TW11 .117 CH93
Kingston Ct, Grav. (Nthflt)
DA11 .130 GB85
Kingston Cres, Ashf. TW15 .114 BJ92
Beckenham BR3 .143 DZ95
Kingston Gdns, Croy. CR0 .141 DL104
Kingston Hall Rd, Kings.T.
KT1 .137 CK97
Kingston Hill, Kings.T. KT2 .118 CQ93
Kingston Hill Av, Rom. RM6 .70 EY55
Kingston Hill Pl, Kings.T. KT2 .118 CQ91
H Kingston Hosp, Kings.T.
KT2 .138 CP95
Kingston Ho Gdns, Lthd. KT22
off Upper Fairfield Rd .171 CH121
Kingston La, Tedd. TW11 .117 CG92
Uxbridge UB8 .76 BL69
West Drayton UB7 .94 BM75
Kingston Lo, N.Mal. KT3
off Kingston Rd .138 CS98
★ Kingston Mus & Heritage
Cen, Kings.T. KT1 .138 CL96
Kingston Pk Est, Kings.T.
KT2 .118 CP93
Kingston Pl, Har. HA3
off Richmond Gdns .41 CF52
Kingston Ri, Add. (New Haw)
KT15 .152 BG110
Kingston Rd, N9 .46 DU47
SW15 .119 CU88
SW19 .139 CZ95
SW20 .139 CW96
Ashford TW15 .114 BL93
Barnet EN4 .28 DD43
Epsom KT17, KT19 .156 CS106
Ilford IG1 .69 EP63
Kingston upon Thames
KT1 .138 CP97
Leatherhead KT22 .171 CG117
New Malden KT3 .138 CR98
Romford RM1 .71 FF56
Southall UB2 .96 BZ75
Staines TW18 .114 BH93
Surbiton KT5 .138 CP103
Teddington TW11 .117 CH92
Worcester Park KT4 .138 CP103
Kingston Sq, SE19 .122 DR92
KINGSTON UPON THAMES,
KT1 & KT2 .138 CL96
KINGSTON VALE, SW15 .118 CS91
Kingston Vale, SW15 .118 CR91
Kingstown St, NW1 .82 DG67
King St, E13 .86 EG70
EC2 .197 J9
N2 .64 DD55
N17 .46 DT53
SW1 .199 L3
W3 .80 CP74
W6 .99 CU77
WC2 .195 P10
Chertsey KT16 .134 BG102
Gravesend DA12 .131 GH86
Richmond TW9 .117 CK85
Southall UB2 .96 BY76
Twickenham TW1 .117 CG88
Watford WD18 .24 BW42
Kings Wk, Grays RM17 .110 GA79
King's Wk, Kings.T. KT2 .137 CK95
Kings Wk, S.Croy. CR2 .160 DV114
Kings Wk Shop Mall, SW3
off King's Rd .100 DF78
Kings Warren, Lthd. (Oxshott)
KT22 .154 CC111
Kingswater Pl, SW11
off Battersea Ch Rd .100 DE80
Kingsway, N12 .44 DC51
SW14 .98 CP83
WC2 .196 B8
Croydon CR0 .159 DM106
Enfield EN3 .30 DV43
Gerrards Cross (Chal.St.P.)
SL9 .56 AY55
Kings Way, Har. HA1 .61 CE56
Kingsway, Hayes UB3 .77 BQ71
Iver SL0 off High St .75 BE72
New Malden KT3 .139 CW98
Orpington BR5 .145 ES99
Potters Bar (Cuffley) EN6 .13 DL30
Staines TW19 .114 BK88
Watford WD25 .8 BW34
Wembley HA9 .62 CL63
West Wickham BR4 .144 EE104
Woking GU21 .166 AX118
Woodford Green IG8 .48 EJ50
Kingsway, The, Epsom KT17 .157 CT111
Kingsway Av, S.Croy. CR2 .160 DW109
Woking GU21 .166 AX118
Kingsway Business Pk,
Hmptn. TW12 .136 BZ95
Kingsway Cres, Har. HA2 .60 CC56
Kingsway Pl, EC1 .196 E4
Kingsway Rd, Sutt. SM3 .157 CY108
Kingsway Shop Cen, NW3
off Hampstead High St .64 DC63
Kingswear Rd, NW5 .65 DH62
Ruislip HA4 .59 BU61
Kingswell Ride, Pot.B.
(Cuffley) EN6 .13 DL30
Kingswey Business Pk, Wok.
GU21 .151 BC114
Kings Wf, E8
off Kingsland Rd .84 DS67
KINGSWOOD, Tad. KT20 .173 CY123
KINGSWOOD, Wat. WD25 .7 BV34
⇌ Kingswood .173 CZ121
Kingswood Av, NW6 .81 CY67
Belvedere DA17 .106 EZ77
Bromley BR2 .144 EE97
Hampton TW12 .116 CB93
Hounslow TW3 .96 BZ81
South Croydon CR2 .176 DV115
Swanley BR8 .147 FF98
Thornton Heath CR7 .141 DN99
Kingswood Cl, N20 .28 DC44
SW8 .101 DL80
Ashford TW15 .115 BQ91
Dartford DA1 .128 FJ86
Egham (Eng.Grn) TW20 .112 AX91
Enfield EN1 .30 DS43
New Malden KT3 .139 CT100
Orpington BR6 .145 ER101
Surbiton KT6 .138 CL101
Weybridge KT13 .153 BP108
Kingswood Ct, SE13
off Hither Grn La .123 ED86
Kingswood Creek, Stai.
(Wrays.) TW19 .112 AX85
Kingswood Dr, SE19 .122 DS91
Carshalton SM5 .140 DF102
Sutton SM2 .158 DB109
Kingswood Est, SE21
off Bowen Dr .122 DS91
Kingswood Gra, Tad. KT20
off Babylon La .184 DA127
Kingswood La, S.Croy. CR2 .160 DW113
Warlingham CR6 .176 DW115
Kingswood Ms, N15
off Harringay Rd .65 DP57
Kingswood Pk, N3 .43 CZ54
Kingswood Pl, SE13 .104 EE84
Kingswood Ri, Egh. (Eng.Grn)
TW20 .112 AX92
Kingswood Rd, E11 .68 EE59
SE20 .122 DW93
SW2 .121 DL86
SW19 .119 CZ94
W4 .98 CQ76
Bromley BR2 .143 ED98
Ilford IG3 .70 EU60
Sevenoaks (Dunt.Grn)
TN13 .181 FE120
Tadworth KT20 .173 CV121
Watford WD25 .7 BV34
Wembley HA9 .62 CN62
Kingswood Ter, W4
off Kingswood Rd .98 CQ76
Kingswood Way, S.Croy.
CR2 .160 DW113
Wallington SM6 .159 DL106
Kingsworth Cl, Beck. BR3 .143 DY99
Kingsworthy Cl, Kings.T. KT1 .138 CM97
King's Yd, SW15
off Stanbridge Rd .99 CW83
Kingthorpe Rd, NW10 .80 CR66
Kingthorpe Ter, NW10 .80 CR65
Kingwell Rd, Barn. EN4 .28 DD38
Kingweston Cl, NW2
off Windmill Dr .63 CY62
King William IV Gdns, SE20
off St. John's Rd .122 DW93
King William La, SE10
off Trafalgar Rd .104 EE78
King William St, EC4 .201 L1
King William Wk, SE10 .103 EC79
Kingwood Rd, SW6 .99 CX81
Kinlet Rd, SE18 .105 EQ81
Kinloch Dr, NW9 .62 CS59
Kinloch St, N7
off Hornsey Rd .65 DM62
Kinloss Ct, N3
off Haslemere Gdns .63 CZ56
Kinloss Gdns, N3 .63 CZ56
Kinloss Rd, Cars. SM5 .140 DC101
Kinnaird Av, W4 .98 CQ80
Bromley BR1 .124 EF93
Kinnaird Cl, Brom. BR1 .124 EF93
Kinnaird Ho, N6
off Hornsey La .65 DK59
Kinnaird Way, Wdf.Grn. IG8 .49 EM51
Kinnear Rd, W12 .99 CT75
Kinnerton Pl N, SW1 .198 E5
Kinnerton Pl S, SW1 .198 E5
Kinnerton St, SW1 .198 F5
Kinnerton Yd, SW1 .198 E5
Kinnoul Rd, W6 .99 CY79
Kinross Av, Wor.Pk. KT4 .139 CU103
Kinross Cl, Edg. HA8
off Tayside Dr .42 CP47
Harrow HA3 .62 CM57
Sunbury-on-Thames TW16 .115 BT92
Kinross Dr, Sun. TW16 .115 BT92
Kinross Ter, E17 .47 DZ54
Kinsale Rd, SE15 .102 DU83
Kintore Way, SE1 .201 P8
Kintyre Cl, SW16 .141 DM97
Kinveachy Gdns, SE7 .104 EL78
Kinver Rd, SE26 .122 DW91
Kipings, Tad. KT20 .173 CX122
Kipling Av, Til. RM18 .111 GH81
Kipling Cl, Brwd. (Warley)
CM14 .54 FV50
Kipling Dr, SW19 .120 DD93
Kipling Est, SE1 .201 L5
Kipling Pl, Stan. HA7
off Uxbridge Rd .41 CF51
Kipling Rd, Bexh. DA7 .106 EY81
Dartford DA1 .128 FP85
Kipling St, SE1 .201 L5
Kipling Ter, N9 .46 DR48
Kipling Twr, W3 .98 CQ76
Kipling Twrs, Rom. RM3 .51 FH52
KIPPINGTON, Sev. TN13 .190 FG126
Kippington Cl, Sev. TN13 .190 FF124
Kippington Dr, SE9 .124 EK88
Kippington Ho, Sev. TN13
off Kippington Rd .190 FG126
Kippington Rd, Sev. TN13 .190 FG124
Kirby Cl, Epsom KT19 .157 CT106
Ilford IG6 .49 ES51
Loughton IG10 .48 EL45
Northwood HA6 .39 BT51
Romford RM3 .52 FN50
Kirby Est, SE16 .202 D6
Kirby Gro, SE1 .201 M4
Kirby Rd, Dart. DA2 .128 FQ87
Woking GU21 .166 AW117
Kirby St, EC1 .196 E6
Kirby Way, Uxb. UB8 .76 BM70
Walton-on-Thames KT12 .136 BW100
Kirchen Rd, W13 .79 CH73
Kirkby Cl, N11
off Coverdale Rd .44 DG51
Kirkcaldy Grn, Wat. WD19
off Trevose Way .40 BW48
Kirk Ct, Sev. TN13 .190 FG123
Kirkdale, SE26 .122 DV89
Kirkdale Rd, E11 .68 EE60
Kirkfield Cl, W13
off Broomfield Rd .79 CH74
Kirkham Rd, E6 .86 EL72
Kirkham St, SE18 .105 ES79
Kirkland Av, Ilf. IG5 .49 EN54
Woking GU21 .166 AS116
Kirkland Cl, Sid. DA15 .125 ES86
Kirkland Dr, Enf. EN2 .29 DP39
Kirkland Wk, E8 .84 DT65
Kirk La, SE18 .105 EQ79
Kirkleas Rd, Surb. KT6 .138 CL102
Kirklees Rd, Dag. RM8 .70 EW64
Thornton Heath CR7 .141 DN99
Kirkley Rd, SW19 .140 DA95
Kirkly Cl, S.Croy. CR2 .160 DS109
Kirkman Pl, W1 .195 M7
Kirkmichael Rd, E14
off Dee St .85 EC72
Kirk Ri, Sutt. SM1 .140 DB104
Kirk Rd, E17 .67 DZ58
Kirkside Rd, SE3 .104 EG79
Kirkstall Av, N17 .66 DR56
Kirkstall Gdns, SW2 .121 DK88
Kirkstall Rd, SW2 .121 DK88
Kirkstead Ct, E5
off Mandeville St .67 DY62
Kirksted Rd, Mord. SM4 .140 DB102
Kirkstone Way, Brom. BR1 .124 EE94
Kirk St, WC1 .196 B5
Kirkton Rd, N15 .66 DS56
Kirkwall Pl, E2 .84 DW69
Kirkwall Spur, Slou. SL1 .74 AS71
Kirkwood Rd, SE15 .102 DV82
Kirn Rd, W13 off Kirchen Rd .79 CH73
Kirrane Cl, N.Mal. KT3 .139 CT99
Kirtley Rd, SE26 .123 DY91
Kirtling St, SW8 .101 DJ80
Kirton Cl, W4 off Dolman Rd .98 CR77
Hornchurch RM12 .90 FJ65
Kirton Gdns, E2
off Chambord St .84 DT69
Kirton Rd, E13 .86 EJ68
Kirton Wk, Edg. HA8 .42 CQ52
Kirwyn Way, SE5 .101 DP80
Kitcat Ter, E3 .85 EA69
Kitchener Av, Grav. DA12 .131 GJ90
Kitchener Rd, E7 .86 EH65
E17 .47 EB53
N2 .64 DE55
N17 .66 DR55
Dagenham RM10 .89 FB65
Thornton Heath CR7 .142 DR97
Kitchenride Cor, Cher. KT16 .151 BA105
Kite Pl, E2 off Nelson Gdns .84 DU69
Kite Yd, SW11
off Cambridge Rd .100 DF81
Kitley Gdns, SE19 .142 DT95
Kitsmead La, Cher. (Longcr.)
KT16 .132 AX103
Kitson Rd, SE5 .102 DQ80
SW13 .99 CU81
Kitswell Way, Rad. WD7 .9 CF33
Kitters Grn, Abb.L. WD5
off High St .7 BS31
Kittiwake Cl, S.Croy. CR2 .161 DY110
Kittiwake Pl, Sutt. SM1
off Sandpiper Rd .157 CZ106
Kittiwake Rd, Nthlt. UB5 .78 BX69
Kittiwake Way, Hayes UB4 .78 BX71
Kitto Rd, SE14 .103 DX82
KITT'S END, Barn. EN5 .27 CY37
Kitt's End Rd, Barn. EN5 .27 CX36
Kiver Rd, N19 .65 DK61
Klea Av, SW4 .121 DJ86
Knapdale Cl, SE23 .122 DV89
Knapmill Rd, SE6 .123 EA89
Knapmill Way, SE6 .123 EB89
Knapp Cl, NW10 .80 CS65
Knapp Rd, E3 .85 EA70
Ashford TW15 .114 BM91
Knapton Ms, SW17
off Seely Rd .120 DG93
Knaresborough Dr, SW18 .120 DB88
Knaresborough Pl, SW5 .100 DB77
Knatchbull Rd, NW10 .80 CR67
SE5 .102 DQ81
Knebworth Av, E17 .47 EA53
Knebworth Cl, Barn. EN5 .28 DB42
Knebworth Path, Borwd.
WD6 .26 CR42
Knebworth Rd, N16
off Nevill Rd .66 DS63
Knee Hill, SE2 .106 EW77
Knee Hill Cres, SE2 .106 EW77
Kneller Gdns, Islw. TW7 .117 CD85
Kneller Rd, SE4 .103 DY84
New Malden KT3 .138 CS101
Twickenham TW2 .116 CC86
Knevett Ter, Houns. TW3 .96 CA84
Knight Cl, Dag. RM8 .70 EW61
Knighten St, E1 .202 C3
Knighthead Pt, E14 .203 P6
Knightland Rd, E5 .66 DV61
Knighton Cl, Rom. RM7 .71 FD58
South Croydon CR2 .159 DP108
Woodford Green IG8 .48 EH49
Knighton Dr, Wdf.Grn. IG8 .48 EG49
Knighton Grn, Buck.H. IG9
off High Rd .48 EH47
Knighton La, Buck.H. IG9 .48 EH47
Knighton Pk Rd, SE26 .123 DX92
Knighton Rd, E7 .68 EG62
Romford RM7 .71 FC58
Sevenoaks (Otford) TN14 .181 FF116
Knighton Way La, Uxb.
(Denh.) UB9 .76 BH65
Knightrider Ct, EC4
off Godliman St .84 DQ73
Knightrider St, EC4 .197 H10

Knights Arc, SW1 . . . 198 D5
Knights Av, W5 . . . 98 CL75
⊖ Knightsbridge . . . 198 D5
Knightsbridge, SW1 . . . 198 E5
SW7 . . . 198 C5
Knightsbridge Cl, Slou. (Langley) SL3 off High St . . . 93 BA77
Knightsbridge Cres, Stai. TW18 . . . 114 BH93
Knightsbridge Gdns, Rom. RM7 . . . 71 FD57
Knightsbridge Grn, SW1 . . . 198 D5
Knights Cl, E9 off Churchill Wk . . . 66 DW64
Egham TW20 . . . 113 BD93
West Molesey KT8 . . . 136 BZ99
Knightscote Cl, Uxb. UB9 . . . 38 BK54
Knights Ct, Kings.T. KT1 . . . 138 CL97
Romford RM6 . . . 70 EY58
Knights Fld, Dart. (Eyns.) DA4 . . . 148 FL104
Knights Hill, SE27 . . . 121 DP92
Knights Hill Sq, SE27 . . . 121 DP91
Knights La, N9 . . . 46 DU48
Knights Manor Way, Dart. DA1 . . . 128 FM86
Knights Ms, Sutt. SM2 off York Rd . . . 158 DA108
Knights Pk, Kings.T. KT1 . . . 138 CL97
Knights Pl, Red. RH1 off Noke Dr . . . 184 DG133
Knight's Pl, Twick. TW2 off May Rd . . . 117 CE88
Knights Ridge, Orp. BR6 off Stirling Dr . . . 164 EV106
Knights Rd, E16 . . . 205 N4
Stanmore HA7 . . . 41 CJ49
Knights Wk, SE11 . . . 200 F9
Romford (Abridge) RM4 . . . 34 EV41
Knight's Way, Brwd. CM13 . . . 55 GA48
Knights Way, Ilf. IG6 . . . 49 EQ51
Knightswood, Wok. GU21 . . . 166 AT118
Knightswood Cl, Edg. HA8 . . . 42 CQ47
Knightswood Rd, Rain. RM13 . 89 FG68
Knightwood Cres, N.Mal. KT3 . . . 138 CS100
Knipp Hill, Cob. KT11 . . . 154 BZ113
Knivet Rd, SW6 . . . 100 DA79
Knobs Hill Rd, E15 . . . 85 EB67
KNOCKHALL, Green. DA9 . . . 129 FW85
Knockhall Chase, Green. DA9 . . . 129 FV85
Knockhall Rd, Green. DA9 . . 129 FW86
KNOCKHOLT, Sev. TN14 . . . 180 EU116
⇌ Knockholt . . . 164 EY109
Knockholt Cl, Sutt. SM2 . . . 158 DB110
Knockholt Main Rd, Sev. (Knock.) TN14 . . . 180 EY115
KNOCKHOLT POUND, Sev. TN14 . . . 180 EX115
Knockholt Rd, SE9 . . . 124 EK85
Sevenoaks (Halst.) TN14 . 164 EZ113
Knole, The, SE9 . . . 125 EN91
Gravesend (Istead Rise) DA13 . . . 130 GE94
Knole Cl, Croy. CR0 off Stockbury Rd . . . 142 DW100
Knole Gate, Sid. DA15 off Woodside Cres . . . 125 ES90
★ Knole Ho & Pk, Sev. TN15 . . . 191 FL126
Knole La, Sev. TN13 . . . 191 FJ126
Knole Rd, Dart. DA1 . . . 127 FG87
Sevenoaks TN13 . . . 191 FK123
Knole Way, Sev. TN13 . . . 191 FJ125
Knoll, The, W13 . . . 79 CJ71
Beckenham BR3 . . . 143 EB95
Bromley BR2 . . . 144 EG103
Chertsey KT16 . . . 133 BF102
Cobham KT11 . . . 154 CA113
Leatherhead KT22 . . . 171 CJ120
Knoll Ct, SE19 . . . 122 DT92
Knoll Cres, Nthwd. HA6 . . . 39 BS53
Knoll Dr, N14 . . . 44 DG45
Knollmead, Surb. KT5 . . . 138 CQ102
Knoll Pk Rd, Cher. KT16 . . . 133 BF102
Knoll Ri, Orp. BR6 . . . 145 ET102
Knoll Rd, SW18 . . . 120 DC85
Bexley DA5 . . . 126 FA87
Sidcup DA14 . . . 126 EV92
Knolls, The, Epsom KT17 . . 173 CW116
Knolls Cl, Wor.Pk. KT4 . . . 139 CV104
Knollys Cl, SW16 . . . 121 DN90
Knollys Rd, SW16 . . . 121 DN90
Knolton Way, Slou. SL2 . . . 74 AW72
Knottisford St, E2 . . . 84 DW69
Knotts Grn Ms, E10 . . . 67 EB58
Knotts Grn Rd, E10 . . . 67 EB58
Knotts Pl, Sev. TN13 . . . 190 FG124
Knowland Way, Uxb. (Denh.) UB9 . . . 57 BF58
Knowle, The, Tad. KT20 . . . 173 CW121
Knowle Av, Bexh. DA7 . . . 106 EY80
Knowle Cl, SW9 . . . 101 DN83
Knowle Gdns, W.Byf. KT14 off Madeira Rd . . . 151 BF113
Knowle Grn, Stai. TW18 . . . 114 BG92
Knowle Gro, Vir.W. GU25 . . . 132 AW101
Knowle Gro Cl, Vir.W. GU25 . 132 AW101
Knowle Hill, Vir.W. GU25 . . . 132 AV101
Knowle Pk, Cob. KT11 . . . 170 BY115
Knowle Pk Av, Stai. TW18 . . . 114 BH93
Knowle Rd, Brom. BR2 . . . 144 EL103
Twickenham TW2 . . . 117 CE88
Knowles Cl, West Dr. UB7 . . . 76 BL74
Knowles Hill Cres, SE13 . . . 123 ED85
Knowles Ho, SW18 off Neville Gill Cl . . . 120 DB86
Knowles Wk, SW4 . . . 101 DJ83
Knowl Hill, Wok. GU22 . . . 167 BB119
Knowl Pk, Borwd. (Els.) WD6 . 26 CL43
Knowlton Grn, Brom. BR2 . . . 144 EF99
Knowl Way, Borwd. (Els.) WD6 . 26 CL42
Knowsley Av, Sthl. UB1 . . . 78 CA74
Knowsley Rd, SW11 . . . 100 DF82
Knoxfield Caravan Pk, Dart. DA2 . . . 129 FS90
Knox Rd, E7 . . . 86 EF65
Knox St, W1 . . . 194 D6
Knoyle St, SE14 . . . 103 DY79
Knutsford Av, Wat. WD24 . . . 24 BX38
Kohat Rd, SW19 . . . 120 DB92
Koh-i-noor Av, Bushey WD23 . 24 CA44
Koonowla Cl, West. (Bigg.H.) TN16 . . . 178 EK115
Kooringa, Warl. CR6 . . . 176 DV119
Korda Cl, Shep. TW17 . . . 134 BM97
Kossuth St, SE10 . . . 205 H10
Kotree Way, SE1 . . . 202 C9
Kramer Ms, SW5 off Kempsford Gdns . . . 100 DA78
Kreedman Wk, E8 . . . 66 DU64
Kreisel Wk, Rich. TW9 . . . 98 CM79
Kuala Gdns, SW16 . . . 141 DM95
Kuhn Way, E7 off Forest La . . . 68 EG64
Kydbrook Cl, Orp. BR5 . . . 145 EQ101
Kylemore Cl, E6 off Parr Rd . . 86 EK68
Kylemore Rd, NW6 . . . 82 DA66
Kymberley Rd, Har. HA1 . . . 61 CE58
Kyme Rd, Horn. RM11 . . . 71 FF58
Kynance Cl, Rom. RM3 . . . 52 FJ48
Kynance Gdns, Stan. HA7 . . . 41 CJ53
Kynance Ms, SW7 . . . 100 DB76
Kynance Pl, SW7 . . . 100 DC76
Kynaston Av, N16 off Dynevor Rd . . . 66 DT62
Thornton Heath CR7 . . . 142 DQ99
Kynaston Cl, Har. HA3 . . . 41 CD52
Kynaston Cres, Th.Hth. CR7 . 142 DQ99
Kynaston Rd, N16 . . . 66 DS62
Bromley BR1 . . . 124 EG92
Enfield EN2 . . . 30 DR39
Orpington BR5 . . . 146 EV101
Thornton Heath CR7 . . . 142 DQ99
Kynaston Wd, Har. HA3 . . . 41 CD52
Kynersley Cl, Cars. SM5 off William St . . . 140 DF104
Kynoch Rd, N18 . . . 46 DW49
Kyrle Rd, SW11 . . . 120 DG85
Kytes Dr, Wat. WD25 . . . 8 BX33
Kytes Est, Wat. WD25 . . . 8 BX33
Kyverdale Rd, N16 . . . 66 DT61

L

Laburnham Cl, Upmin. RM14 . 73 FU59
Wembley HA0 off Highcroft Av . . . 80 CN67
Laburnham Gdns, Upmin. RM14 . . . 73 FT59
Laburnum Av, N9 . . . 46 DS47
N17 . . . 46 DR52
Dartford DA1 . . . 128 FJ88
Hornchurch RM12 . . . 71 FF62
Sutton SM1 . . . 140 DE104
Swanley BR8 . . . 147 FC97
West Drayton UB7 . . . 76 BM73
Laburnum Cl, E4 . . . 47 DZ51
N11 . . . 44 DG51
SE15 off Clifton Way . . . 102 DW80
Waltham Cross (Chsht) EN8 . 15 DX31
Laburnum Ct, E2 off Laburnum St . . . 84 DT67
Stanmore HA7 . . . 41 CJ49
Laburnum Cres, Sun. TW16 off Batavia Rd . . . 135 BV95
Laburnum Gdns, N21 . . . 46 DQ47
Croydon CR0 . . . 143 DX101
Laburnum Gro, N21 . . . 46 DQ47
NW9 . . . 62 CQ59
Gravesend (Nthflt) DA11 . . 130 GD87
Hounslow TW3 . . . 96 BZ84
New Malden KT3 . . . 138 CR96
Ruislip HA4 . . . 59 BR58
St. Albans AL2 . . . 8 CB25
Slough SL3 . . . 93 BB79
South Ockendon RM15 . . . 91 FW69
Southall UB1 . . . 78 BZ70
Laburnum Ho, Dag. RM10 off Bradwell Av . . . 70 FA61
Laburnum Pl, Egh. (Eng.Grn) TW20 . . . 112 AV93
Laburnum Rd, SW19 . . . 120 DC94
Chertsey KT16 . . . 134 BG102
Epping (Cooper.) CM16 . . . 18 EW29
Epsom KT18 . . . 156 CS113
Hayes UB3 . . . 95 BT77
Mitcham CR4 . . . 140 DG96
Woking GU22 . . . 166 AX120
Laburnum St, E2 . . . 84 DT67
Laburnum Wk, Horn. RM12 . . 72 FJ64
Laburnum Way, Brom. BR2 . . 145 EN101
Staines TW19 . . . 114 BM88
Waltham Cross (Chsht) EN7 off Millcrest Rd . . . 13 DP28
Lacebark Cl, Sid. DA15 . . . 125 ET87
Lacewing Cl, E13 off Sewell St . . . 86 EG69
Lacey Av, Couls. CR5 . . . 175 DN120
Lacey Cl, N9 . . . 46 DU47
Egham TW20 . . . 113 BD94
Lacey Dr, Couls. CR5 . . . 175 DN120
Dagenham RM8 . . . 70 EV63
Edgware HA8 . . . 42 CL49
Hampton TW12 . . . 136 BZ95
Lacey Grn, Couls. CR5 . . . 175 DN120
Lacey Wk, E3 . . . 85 EA68
Lackford Rd, Couls. (Chipstead) CR5 . . . 174 DF118
Lackington St, EC2 . . . 197 L6
Lackmore Rd, Enf. EN1 . . . 30 DW35
Lacock Cl, SW19 . . . 120 DC93
Lacock Ct, W13 off Singapore Rd . . . 79 CG74
Lacon Rd, SE22 . . . 102 DU84
Lacrosse Way, SW16 . . . 141 DK95
Lacy Rd, SW15 . . . 99 CX84
Ladas Rd, SE27 . . . 122 DQ91
Ladbroke Ct, Red. RH1 . . . 184 DG132
Ladbroke Cres, W11 off Ladbroke Gro . . . 81 CY72
Ladbroke Gdns, W11 . . . 81 CZ73
⊖ Ladbroke Grove . . . 81 CY72
Ladbroke Gro, W10 . . . 81 CX70
W11 . . . 81 CY72
Redhill RH1 . . . 184 DG133
Ladbroke Ms, W11 off Ladbroke Rd . . . 81 CY74
Ladbroke Rd, W11 . . . 81 CZ74
Enfield EN1 . . . 30 DT44
Epsom KT18 . . . 156 CR114
Redhill RH1 . . . 184 DG133
Ladbroke Sq, W11 . . . 81 CZ73
Ladbroke Ter, W11 . . . 81 CZ73
Ladbroke Wk, W11 . . . 81 CZ74
Ladbrook Cl, Pnr. HA5 . . . 60 BZ57
Ladbrooke Cl, Pot.B. EN6 off Strafford Gate . . . 12 DA32
Ladbrooke Cres, Sid. DA14 . . 126 EX90
Ladbrooke Dr, Pot.B. EN6 . . . 12 DA32
Ladbrook Rd, SE25 . . . 142 DR97
Ladderstile Ride, Kings.T. KT2 . . . 118 CP92
Ladderswood Way, N11 . . . 45 DJ50
Ladds Way, Swan. BR8 . . . 147 FD98
Ladlands, SE22 off Overhill Rd . . . 122 DU87
Lady Aylesford Av, Stan. HA7 . 41 CH50
Lady Booth Rd, Kings.T. KT1 . 138 CL96
Ladycroft Gdns, Orp. BR6 . . . 163 EQ106
Ladycroft Rd, SE13 . . . 103 EB83
Ladycroft Wk, Stan. HA7 . . . 41 CK53
Ladycroft Way, Orp. BR6 . . . 163 EQ106
Lady Dock Path, SE16 . . . 203 K5
Ladyfield Cl, Loug. IG10 . . . 33 EP42
Ladyfields, Grav. (Nthflt) DA11 . . . 131 GF91
Loughton IG10 . . . 33 EP42
Lady Forsdyke Way, Epsom KT19 . . . 156 CN109
Ladygate La, Ruis. HA4 . . . 59 BP58
Ladygrove, Croy. CR0 . . . 161 DY109
Lady Harewood Way, Epsom KT19 . . . 156 CN109
Lady Hay, Wor.Pk. KT4 . . . 139 CT103
Lady Margaret Rd, N19 . . . 65 DJ63
NW5 . . . 65 DJ64
Southall UB1 . . . 78 BZ71
Ladymeadow, Kings L. WD4 . . 6 BK27
Lady's Cl, Wat. WD18 . . . 23 BV42
Ladysmith Av, E6 . . . 86 EL68
Ilford IG2 . . . 69 ER59
Ladysmith Cl, NW7 . . . 43 CU52
Ladysmith Rd, E16 . . . 86 EF69
N17 . . . 46 DU54
N18 . . . 46 DV50
SE9 . . . 125 EN86
Enfield EN1 . . . 30 DS41
Harrow HA3 . . . 41 CE54
Lady Somerset Rd, NW5 . . . 65 DH63
Ladythorpe Cl, Add. KT15 off Church Rd . . . 152 BH105
Ladywalk, Rick. (Map.Cr.) WD3 . . . 37 BE50
LADYWELL, SE13 . . . 123 EA85
⇌ Ladywell . . . 123 EB85
Ladywell Cl, SE4 off Adelaide Av . . . 103 DZ84
Ladywell Hts, SE4 . . . 123 DZ86
Ladywell Rd, SE13 . . . 123 EA85
Ladywell St, E15 off Plaistow Gro . . . 86 EF67
Ladywood Av, Orp. BR5 . . . 145 ES99
Ladywood Cl, Rick. WD3 . . . 22 BH41
Ladywood Rd, Dart. (Lane End) DA2 . . . 129 FS92
Surbiton KT6 . . . 138 CN103
Lady Yorke Pk, Iver SL0 . . . 75 BD65
Lafone Av, Felt. TW13 off Alfred Rd . . . 116 BW88
Lafone St, SE1 . . . 201 P4
Lagado Ms, SE16 . . . 203 J3
Lagger, The, Ch.St.G. HP8 . . . 36 AV48
Lagger Cl, Ch.St.G. HP8 . . . 36 AV48
Laglands Cl, Reig. RH2 . . . 184 DC132
Lagonda Av, Ilf. IG6 . . . 49 ET51
Lagonda Way, Dart. DA1 . . . 108 FJ84
Lagoon Rd, Orp. BR5 . . . 146 EV99
Laidlaw Dr, N21 . . . 29 DM42
Laing Cl, Ilf. IG6 . . . 49 ER51
Laing Dean, Nthlt. UB5 . . . 78 BW67
Laing Ho, SE5 off Comber Gro . . . 102 DQ80
Laings Av, Mitch. CR4 . . . 140 DF96
Lainlock Pl, Houns. TW3 off Spring Gro Rd . . . 96 CB81
Lainson St, SW18 . . . 120 DA87
Lairdale Cl, SE21 . . . 122 DQ88
Laird Av, Grays RM16 . . . 110 GD75
Laird Ho, SE5 . . . 102 DQ80
Lairs Cl, N7 off Manger Rd . . 83 DL65
Laitwood Rd, SW12 . . . 121 DH88
Lakanal, SE5 off Dalwood St 102 DS81
Lake, The, Bushey (Bushey Hth) WD23 . . . 40 CC46
Lake Av, Brom. BR1 . . . 124 EG93
Rainham RM13 . . . 90 FK68
Lake Cl, SW19 off Lake Rd . . 119 CZ92
Dagenham RM8 . . . 70 EW62
West Byfleet (Byfleet) KT14 . 152 BK112
Lakedale Rd, SE18 . . . 105 ES79
Lake Dr, Bushey (Bushey Hth) WD23 . . . 40 CC47
Lakefield Cl, SE20 off Limes Av . . . 122 DV94
Lakefield Rd, N22 . . . 45 DP54
Lakefields Cl, Rain. RM13 . . . 90 FK68
Lake Gdns, Dag. RM10 . . . 70 FA64
Richmond TW10 . . . 117 CH89
Wallington SM6 . . . 141 DH104
Lakehall Gdns, Th.Hth. CR7 . 141 DP99
Lakehall Rd, Th.Hth. CR7 . . . 141 DP99
Lake Ho Rd, E11 . . . 68 EG62
Lakehurst Rd, Epsom KT19 . 156 CS106
Lakeland Cl, Chig. IG7 . . . 50 EV49
Harrow HA3 . . . 41 CD51
Lakenheath, N14 . . . 29 DK44
Lake Ri, Grays RM20 . . . 109 FU77
Romford RM1 . . . 71 FF55
Lake Rd, SW19 . . . 119 CZ92
Croydon CR0 . . . 143 DZ103
Romford RM6 . . . 70 EX56
Virginia Water GU25 . . . 132 AV98
Laker Pl, SW15 . . . 119 CZ86
Lakers Ri, Bans. SM7 . . . 174 DE116
Lakeside, W13 off Edgehill Rd . . . 79 CJ72
Beckenham BR3 . . . 143 EB97
Enfield EN2 . . . 29 DK42
Grays RM20 . . . 109 FV77
Rainham RM13 . . . 90 FL68
Redhill RH1 . . . 184 DG132
Wallington SM6 off Derek Av . . . 141 DH104
Weybridge KT13 . . . 135 BS103
Woking GU21 . . . 166 AS119
Lakeside Av, SE28 . . . 88 EU74
Ilford IG4 . . . 68 EK56
Lakeside Cl, SE25 . . . 142 DU96
Chigwell IG7 . . . 49 ET49
Ruislip HA4 . . . 59 BR56
Sidcup DA15 . . . 126 EW85
Woking GU21 . . . 166 AS119
Lakeside Ct, N4 . . . 65 DP61
Borehamwood (Els.) WD6 off Cavendish Cres . . . 26 CN43
Lakeside Cres, Barn. EN4 . . . 28 DF43
Brentwood CM14 . . . 54 FX48
Weybridge KT13 off Churchill Dr . . . 135 BQ104
Lakeside Dr, NW10 . . . 80 CM69
Bromley BR2 . . . 144 EL104
Esher KT10 . . . 154 CC107
Slough (Stoke P.) SL2 . . . 74 AS67
Lakeside Gra, Wey. KT13 . . . 135 BQ104
Lakeside Pl, St.Alb. (Lon.Col.) AL2 . . . 9 CK27
Lakeside Rd, N13 . . . 45 DM49
W14 . . . 99 CX76
Slough SL3 . . . 93 BF80
Waltham Cross (Chsht) EN8 . 14 DW28
Lakeside Way, Wem. HA9 . . . 62 CN63
Lakes Rd, Kes. BR2 . . . 162 EJ106
Lakeswood Rd, Orp. BR5 . . . 145 EP100
Lake Vw, Edg. HA8 . . . 42 CM50
Potters Bar EN6 . . . 12 DC33
Lakeview Ct, SW19 off Victoria Dr . . . 119 CY89
Lakeview Rd, SE27 . . . 121 DN92
Lake Vw Rd, Sev. TN13 . . . 190 FG122
Lakeview Rd, Well. DA16 . . . 106 EV84
Lakis Cl, NW3 off Flask Wk . . 64 DC63
LALEHAM, Stai. TW18 . . . 134 BJ97
Laleham Av, NW7 . . . 42 CR48
Laleham Cl, Stai. TW18 off Worple Rd . . . 134 BH95
Laleham Ct, Wok. GU21 . . . 166 AY116
★ Laleham Heritage Cen, Stai. TW18 . . . 134 BJ97
Laleham Pk, Stai. TW18 . . . 134 BJ98
Laleham Reach, Cher. KT16 . 134 BH96
Laleham Rd, SE6 . . . 123 EC86
Shepperton TW17 . . . 134 BM98
Staines TW18 . . . 113 BF92
Lalor St, SW6 . . . 99 CY82
Lambarde Av, SE9 . . . 125 EN91
Lambarde Dr, Sev. TN13 . . . 190 FG123
Lambarde Rd, Sev. TN13 . . . 190 FG122
Lambardes Cl, Orp. BR6 . . . 164 EW110
Lamb Cl, Nthlt. UB5 . . . 78 BY69
Tilbury RM18 off Coleridge Rd . . . 111 GJ82
Watford WD25 . . . 8 BW34
Lamberhurst Cl, Orp. BR5 . . 146 EX102
Lamberhurst Rd, SE27 . . . 121 DN91
Dagenham RM8 . . . 70 EZ60
Lambert Av, Rich. TW9 . . . 98 CP83
Slough SL3 . . . 92 AY75
Lambert Cl, West. (Bigg.H.) TN16 . . . 178 EK116
Lambert Ct, Bushey WD23 . . . 24 BX42
Lambert Jones Ms, EC2 off The Barbican . . . 84 DQ71
Lambert Rd, E16 . . . 86 EH72
N12 . . . 44 DD50
SW2 . . . 121 DL85
Banstead SM7 . . . 158 DA114
Lamberts Pl, Croy. CR0 . . . 142 DR102
Lamberts Rd, Surb. KT5 . . . 138 CL99
Lambert St, N1 . . . 83 DN66
Lambert Wk, Wem. HA9 . . . 61 CK62
Lambert Way, N12 off Woodhouse Rd . . . 44 DC50
LAMBETH, SE1 . . . 200 B6
Lambeth Br, SE1 . . . 200 A8
SW1 . . . 200 A8
Lambeth High St, SE1 . . . 200 B9
Lambeth Hill, EC4 . . . 197 H10
H Lambeth Hosp, SW9 . . . 101 DL83
⊖ Lambeth North . . . 200 D5
★ Lambeth Palace, SE1 . . . 200 B7
Lambeth Palace Rd, SE1 . . . 200 B7
Lambeth Rd, SE1 . . . 200 C7
SE11 . . . 200 C7
Croydon CR0 . . . 141 DN101
Lambeth Twrs, SE11 off Kennington Rd . . . 101 DN76
Lambeth Wk, SE1 . . . 200 C8
SE11 . . . 200 C8
Lambfold Ho, N7 off York Way . 83 DL65
Lambkins Ms, E17 off Barrett Rd . . . 67 EC56
Lamb La, E8 . . . 84 DV66
Lamble St, NW5 . . . 64 DG64
Lambley Rd, Dag. RM9 . . . 88 EV65
Lambly Hill, Vir.W. GU25 . . . 132 AY97
Lambolle Pl, NW3 . . . 82 DE65
Lambolle Rd, NW3 . . . 82 DE65
Lambourn Chase, Rad. WD7 . . 25 CF36
Lambourn Cl, W7 . . . 97 CF75
South Croydon CR2 . . . 159 DP109
Lambourne Av, SW19 . . . 119 CZ91
Lambourne Cl, Chig. IG7 . . . 50 EV48
Lambourne Ct, Wdf.Grn. IG8 off Navestock Cres . . . 48 EJ52
Lambourne Cres, Chig. IG7 . . 50 EV47
Woking GU21 . . . 151 BD113
Lambourne Dr, Brwd. (Hutt.) CM13 . . . 55 GE45
Cobham KT11 . . . 170 BX115
LAMBOURNE END, Rom. RM4 . . . 34 EX44
Lambourne Gdns, E4 . . . 47 EA47
Barking IG11 off Lambourne Rd . . . 87 ET66
Enfield EN1 . . . 30 DT40
Hornchurch RM12 . . . 72 FK61
Lambourne Gro, SE16 . . . 203 H9
Kingston upon Thames KT1 off Kenley Rd . . . 138 CP96
Lambourne Pl, SE3 off Shooters Hill Rd . . . 104 EH81
Lambourne Rd, E11 . . . 67 EC59
Barking IG11 . . . 87 ES66
Chigwell IG7 . . . 49 ES49
Ilford IG3 . . . 69 ES61
Lambourn Rd, SW4 . . . 101 DH83
Lambrook Ter, SW6 . . . 99 CY81
Lamb's Bldgs, EC1 . . . 197 K5
Lambs Cl, N9 off Winchester Rd . . . 46 DU47
Potters Bar (Cuffley) EN6 . . 13 DM29
Lambs Conduit Pas, WC1 . . . 196 B6
Lamb's Conduit St, WC1 . . . 196 B5
Lambscroft Av, SE9 . . . 124 EJ90
Lambscroft Way, Ger.Cr. (Chal.St.P.) SL9 . . . 36 AY54
Lambs La N, Rain. RM13 . . . 90 FJ70
Lambs La S, Rain. RM13 . . . 89 FH71
Lambs Meadow, Wdf.Grn. IG8 . . . 48 EK54
Lambs Ms, N1 off Colebrooke Row . . . 83 DP67
Lamb's Pas, EC1 . . . 197 K6
Lambs Ter, N9 . . . 46 DR47
Lamb St, E1 . . . 197 P6
Lambs Wk, Enf. EN2 . . . 30 DQ40
Lambton Av, Wal.Cr. EN8 . . . 15 DX32
Lambton Ms, N19 off Lambton Rd . . . 65 DL60
Lambton Pl, W11 off Westbourne Gro . . . 81 CZ72
Lambton Rd, N19 . . . 65 DL60
SW20 . . . 139 CW95
Lamb Wk, SE1 . . . 201 M5
Lamerock Rd, Brom. BR1 . . . 124 EF91
Lamerton Rd, Ilf. IG6 . . . 49 EP54
Lamerton St, SE8 . . . 103 EA79
Lamford Cl, N17 . . . 46 DR52
Lamington St, W6 . . . 99 CV77
Lamlash St, SE11 . . . 200 F8
Lammas Av, Mitch. CR4 . . . 140 DG96
Lammas Cl, Stai. TW18 . . . 113 BE90
Lammas Ct, Stai. TW19 . . . 113 BD89
Lammas Dr, Stai. TW18 . . . 113 BD90
Lammas Grn, SE26 . . . 122 DV90
Lammas La, Esher KT10 . . . 154 CA106
Lammas Pk, W5 . . . 97 CJ75
Lammas Pk Gdns, W5 . . . 97 CJ75
Lammas Pk Rd, W5 . . . 79 CJ74
Lammas Rd, E9 . . . 85 DX66
E10 . . . 67 DY61
Richmond TW10 . . . 117 CJ91
Watford WD18 . . . 24 BW43
Lammermoor Rd, SW12 . . . 121 DH87
Lamont Rd, SW10 . . . 100 DC79
Lamont Rd Pas, SW10 off Lamont Rd . . . 100 DD79
LAMORBEY, Sid. DA15 . . . 125 ET88
Lamorbey Cl, Sid. DA15 . . . 125 ET88
Lamorna Av, Grav. DA12 . . . 131 GJ90
Lamorna Cl, E17 . . . 47 EC53
Orpington BR6 . . . 146 EU101
Radlett WD7 . . . 9 CH34
Lamorna Gro, Stan. HA7 . . . 41 CK53
Lampard Gro, N16 . . . 66 DT60
Lampern Sq, E2 off Nelson Gdns . . . 84 DU69
Lampeter Cl, NW9 . . . 62 CS58
Woking GU22 . . . 166 AY118
Lampeter Sq, W6 off Humbolt Rd . . . 99 CY79
Lamplighter Cl, E1 off Cleveland Way . . . 84 DW70
Lamplighters Cl, Dart. DA1 . . 128 FM86
Waltham Abbey EN9 . . . 16 EG34
Lampmead Rd, SE12 . . . 124 EE85
Lamp Office Ct, WC1 . . . 196 B5
Lamport Cl, SE18 . . . 105 EM77
LAMPTON, Houns. TW3 . . . 96 CB81
Lampton Av, Houns. TW3 . . . 96 CB81
Lampton Ho Cl, SW19 . . . 119 CX91
Lampton Pk Rd, Houns. TW3 . 96 CB82
Lampton Rd, Houns. TW3 . . . 96 CB82
Lamson Rd, Rain. RM13 . . . 89 FF70
Lanacre Av, NW9 . . . 43 CT53
Lanark Cl, W5 . . . 79 CJ71
Lanark Ms, W9 off Lanark Rd . 82 DC69
Lanark Pl, W9 . . . 82 DC70
Lanark Rd, W9 . . . 82 DB68
Lanark Sq, E14 . . . 204 C6
Lanata Wk, Hayes UB4 off Ramulis Dr . . . 78 BX70
Lanbury Rd, SE15 . . . 103 DX84
Lancashire Ct, W1 . . . 195 J10
Lancaster Av, E18 . . . 68 EH56
SE27 . . . 121 DP89
SW19 . . . 119 CX92
Barking IG11 . . . 87 ES66
Barnet EN4 . . . 28 DD38
Mitcham CR4 . . . 141 DL99
Lancaster Cl, N1 off Hertford Rd . . . 84 DS66
N17 off Park La . . . 46 DU52
NW9 . . . 43 CT52
Ashford TW15 . . . 114 BL91
Brentwood (Pilg.Hat.) CM15 . . . 54 FU43
Bromley BR2 . . . 144 EF98
Egham TW20 . . . 112 AX92
Kingston upon Thames KT2 . . . 117 CK92
Staines (Stanw.) TW19 . . . 114 BL86
Woking GU21 . . . 167 BA116
Lancaster Cotts, Rich. TW10 off Lancaster Pk . . . 118 CL86
Lancaster Ct, SE27 . . . 121 DP89
SW6 . . . 99 CZ80
W2 off Lancaster Gate . . . 82 DC73
Banstead SM7 . . . 157 CZ114
Walton-on-Thames KT12 . 135 BU101
Lancaster Dr, E14 . . . 204 E3
NW3 . . . 82 DE65
Hemel Hempstead (Bov.) HP3 . . . 5 AZ27
Hornchurch RM12 . . . 71 FH64
Loughton IG10 . . . 32 EL44
Lancaster Gdns, SW19 . . . 119 CY92
W13 . . . 97 CH75
Bromley BR1 . . . 144 EL99
Kingston upon Thames KT2 . . . 117 CK92
⊖ Lancaster Gate . . . 82 DD73
Lancaster Gate, W2 . . . 82 DC73
Lancaster Gro, NW3 . . . 82 DD65
★ Lancaster Ho, SW1 . . . 199 K4

★ Place of interest ⇌ Railway station ⊖ London Underground station DLR Docklands Light Railway station Tra Tramlink station H Hospital Riv Pedestrian ferry landing stage

Lancaster Ms, SW18
off East Hill 120 DB85
W2 .... 82 DC73
Richmond TW10
off Richmond Hill 118 CL86
Lancaster Pk, Rich. TW10 .... 118 CL85
Lancaster Pl, SW19 .... 119 CX92
WC2 .... 196 B10
Hounslow TW4 .... 96 BW82
Ilford IG1 off Staines Rd 69 EQ63
Twickenham TW1 .... 117 CG86
Lancaster Rd, E7 .... 86 EG66
E11 .... 68 EE61
E17 .... 47 DX54
N4 .... 65 DN59
N11 .... 45 DK51
N18 .... 46 DT50
NW10 .... 63 CT64
SE25 .... 142 DT96
SW19 .... 119 CX92
W11 .... 81 CY72
Barnet EN4 .... 28 DD43
Enfield EN2 .... 30 DR39
Epping (N.Wld Bas.) CM16 .... 18 FA26
Grays (Chaff.Hun.) RM16 .... 109 FX78
Harrow HA2 .... 60 CA57
Northolt UB5 .... 78 CC65
Southall UB1 .... 78 BY73
Uxbridge UB8 .... 76 BK65
Lancaster St, SE1 .... 200 G5
Lancaster Ter, W2 .... 82 DD73
Lancaster Wk, W2 .... 82 DC74
Hayes UB3 .... 77 BQ72
Lancaster Way, Abb.L. WD5 .... 7 BT31
Worcester Park KT4 .... 139 CV101
Lancaster W, W11
off Grenfell Rd 81 CX73
Lancastrian Rd, Wall. SM6 .... 159 DL108
Lancefield St, W10 .... 81 CZ69
Lancell St, N16
off Stoke Newington Ch St 66 DS61
Lancelot Av, Wem. HA0 .... 61 CK63
Lancelot Cres, Wem. HA0 .... 61 CK63
Lancelot Gdns, Barn. EN4 .... 44 DG45
Lancelot Pl, SW7 .... 198 D5
Lancelot Rd, Ilf. IG6 .... 49 ES51
Welling DA16 .... 106 EU84
Wembley HA0 .... 61 CK64
Lance Rd, Har. HA1 .... 60 CC59
Lancer Sq, W8 off Old Ct Pl 100 DB75
Lancey Cl, SE7
off Cleveley Cl 104 EK77
Lanchester Rd, N6 .... 64 DF57
Lanchester Way, SE14 .... 102 DW81
Lancing Gdns, N9 .... 46 DT46
Lancing Rd, W13
off Drayton Grn Rd 79 CH73
Croydon CR0 .... 141 DM100
Feltham TW13 .... 115 BT89
Ilford IG2 .... 69 ER58
Orpington BR6 .... 146 EU103
Romford RM3 .... 52 FL52
Lancing St, NW1 .... 195 M3
Lancing Way, Rick. (Crox.Grn)
WD3 .... 23 BP43
Lancresse Cl, Uxb. UB8 .... 76 BK65
Lancresse Ct, N1 .... 84 DS67
Landale Gdns, Dart. DA1 .... 128 FJ87
Landau Way, Brox. EN10 .... 15 DZ26
Erith DA8 .... 108 FK78
Landcroft Rd, SE22 .... 122 DT86
Landells Rd, SE22 .... 122 DT86
Lander Rd, Grays RM17 .... 110 GD78
Landford Cl, Rick. WD3 .... 38 BL47
Landford Rd, SW15 .... 99 CW83
Landgrove Rd, SW19 .... 120 DA92
Landmann Ho, SE16 .... 202 E9
Landmann Way, SE14 .... 103 DX79
Landmark Hts, E5 .... 67 DY63
Landmead Rd, Wal.Cr.
(Chsht) EN8 .... 15 DY29
Landon Pl, SW1 .... 198 D6
Landons Cl, E14 .... 204 E2
Landon Wk, E14
off Cottage St 85 EB73
Landon Way, Ashf. TW15
off Courtfield Rd 115 BP93
Landor Rd, SW9 .... 101 DL83
Landor Wk, W12 .... 99 CU75
Landra Gdns, N21 .... 29 DP44
Landridge Dr, Enf. EN1 .... 30 DV38
Landridge Rd, SW6 .... 99 CZ82
Landrock Rd, N8 .... 65 DL58
Landscape Rd, Warl. CR6 .... 176 DV119
Woodford Green IG8 .... 48 EH52
Landsdown Cl, Barn. EN5 .... 28 DC42
Landseer Av, E12 .... 69 EN64
Gravesend (Nthflt) DA11 .... 130 GD90
Landseer Cl, SW19
off Thorburn Way 140 DD95
Edgware HA8 .... 42 CN54
Hornchurch RM11 .... 71 FH60
Landseer Rd, N19 .... 65 DL62
Enfield EN1 .... 30 DU43
New Malden KT3 .... 138 CR101
Sutton SM1 .... 158 DA107
Lands End, Borwd. (Els.) WD6 .... 25 CK44
Landstead Rd, SE18 .... 105 ER80
Landway, The, Orp. BR5 .... 146 EW97
Lane, The, NW8
off Marlborough Pl 82 DC68
SE3 .... 104 EG83
Chertsey KT16 .... 134 BG97
Virginia Water GU25 .... 132 AY97
Lane App, NW7 .... 43 CY50
Lane Av, Green. DA9 .... 129 FW86
Lane Cl, NW2 .... 63 CV62
Addlestone KT15 .... 152 BG106
LANE END, Dart. DA2 .... 129 FR92
Lane End, Bexh. DA7 .... 107 FB83
Epsom KT18 .... 156 CP114
Lane Gdns, Bushey (Bushey Hth)
WD23 .... 41 CE45
Esher (Clay.) KT10 .... 155 CF108
Lane Ms, E12
off Colchester Av 69 EM62
Lanercost Cl, SW2 .... 121 DN89
Lanercost Gdns, N14 .... 45 DL45
Lanercost Rd, SW2 .... 121 DN89
Lanes Av, Grav. (Nthflt) DA11 .... 131 GG90
Lanesborough Pl, SW1 .... 198 G4
Laneside, Chis. BR7 .... 125 EP92
Edgware HA8 .... 42 CQ50
Laneside Av, Dag. RM8 .... 70 EZ59
Laneway, SW15 .... 119 CV85
Lane Wd Cl, Amer. HP7 .... 20 AT39
Lanfranc Rd, E3 .... 85 DY68
Lanfrey Pl, W14
off North End Rd 99 CZ78
Langaller La, Lthd. KT22 .... 170 CB122
Langbourne Av, N6 .... 64 DG61
Langbourne Pl, E14 .... 204 B10
Langbourne Way, Esher
(Clay.) KT10 .... 155 CG107
Langbrook Rd, SE3 .... 104 EK83
Lang Cl, Lthd. (Fetch.) KT22 .... 170 CB123
Langcroft Cl, Cars. SM5 .... 140 DF104
Langdale, NW1 .... 195 K2
Langdale Av, Mitch. CR4 .... 140 DF97
Langdale Cl, SE17 .... 102 DQ79
SW14 .... 98 CP84
Dagenham RM8 .... 70 EW60
Orpington BR6
off Grasmere Rd 145 EP104
Woking GU21 .... 166 AW116
Langdale Cres, Bexh. DA7 .... 106 FA80
Langdale Dr, Hayes UB4 .... 77 BS68
Langdale Gdns, Grnf. UB6 .... 79 CH69
Hornchurch RM12 .... 71 FG64
Waltham Cross EN8 .... 31 DX35
Langdale Rd, SE10 .... 103 EC80
Thornton Heath CR7 .... 141 DN98
Langdale St, E1
off Burslem St 84 DV72
Langdale Wk, Grav. (Nthflt)
DA11 off Landseer Av 130 GE90
Langdon Ct, NW10 .... 80 CS67
Langdon Cres, E6 .... 87 EN68
Langdon Dr, NW9 .... 62 CQ60
Langdon Pk, Tedd. TW11 .... 117 CJ94
Langdon Pk Rd, N6 .... 65 DJ59
Langdon Pl, SW14
off Rosemary La 98 CQ83
Langdon Rd, E6 .... 87 EN67
Bromley BR2 .... 144 EH97
Morden SM4 .... 140 DC99
Langdons Ct, Sthl. UB2 .... 96 CA76
Langdon Shaw, Sid. DA14 .... 125 ET92
Langdon Wk, Mord. SM4 .... 140 DC99
Langdon Way, SE1 .... 202 C9
Langford Cl, E8 .... 66 DU64
N15 .... 66 DS58
NW8 off Langford Pl 82 DC68
W3 .... 98 CP75
Langford Ct, NW8 .... 82 DC68
Langford Cres, Barn. EN4 .... 28 DF42
Langford Grn, SE5 .... 102 DS83
Brentwood (Hutt.) CM13 .... 55 GC44
Langford Ms, N1
off Liverpool Rd 83 DN66
Langford Pl, NW8 .... 82 DC68
Sidcup DA14 .... 126 EU90
Langford Rd, SW6 .... 100 DB82
Barnet EN4 .... 28 DE42
Woodford Green IG8 .... 48 EJ51
Langfords, Buck.H. IG9 .... 48 EK47
Langfords Way, Croy. CR0 .... 161 DY111
Langham Cl, N15
off Langham Rd 65 DP55
Langham Ct, Horn. RM11 .... 72 FK59
Langham Dene, Ken. CR8 .... 175 DP115
Langham Dr, Rom. RM6 .... 70 EV58
Langham Gdns, N21 .... 29 DN43
W13 .... 79 CH73
Edgware HA8 .... 42 CQ52
Richmond TW10 .... 117 CJ91
Wembley HA0 .... 61 CJ61
Langham Ho Cl, Rich. TW10 .... 117 CK91
Langham Pk Pl, Brom. BR2 .... 144 EF98
Langham Pl, N15 .... 65 DP55
W1 .... 195 J7
W4 off Hogarth Rbt 98 CS79
Egham TW20 .... 113 AZ92
Langham Rd, N15 .... 65 DP55
SW20 .... 139 CW95
Edgware HA8 .... 42 CQ51
Teddington TW11 .... 117 CH92
Langham St, W1 .... 195 J7
Langhedge Cl, N18
off Langhedge La 46 DT51
Langhedge La, N18 .... 46 DT50
Langhedge La Ind Est, N18 .... 46 DT51
Langholm Cl, SW12
off King's Av 121 DK87
Langholme, Bushey WD23 .... 40 CC46
Langhorn Dr, Twick. TW2 .... 117 CE87
Langhorne Rd, Dag. RM10 .... 88 FA66
Langland Ct, Nthwd. HA6 .... 39 BQ52
Langland Cres, Stan. HA7 .... 62 CL55
Langland Dr, Pnr. HA5 .... 40 BY52
Langland Gdns, NW3 .... 64 DB64
Croydon CR0 .... 143 DZ103
Langlands Dr, Dart. (Lane End)
DA2 .... 129 FS92
Langlands Ri, Epsom KT19
off Burnet Gro 156 CQ113
Langler Rd, NW10 .... 81 CW68
LANGLEY, Slou. SL3 .... 93 BA76
≠ Langley 93 BA75
Langley Av, Ruis. HA4 .... 59 BV60
Surbiton KT6 .... 137 CK102
Worcester Park KT4 .... 139 CX103
Langley Broom, Slou. SL3 .... 93 AZ78
LANGLEYBURY, Kings L. WD4 .... 7 BP34
Langleybury La, Kings L.
WD4 .... 23 BP37
Langley Business Cen,
Slou. (Langley) SL3 .... 93 BA75
Langley Cl, Epsom KT18 .... 172 CR119
Romford RM3 .... 52 FK52
Langley Cor, Slou. (Fulmer)
SL3 .... 75 AZ65
Langley Ct, WC2 .... 195 P10
Beckenham BR3 .... 143 EB99
Langley Cres, E11 .... 68 EJ59
Dagenham RM9 .... 88 EW66
Edgware HA8 .... 42 CQ48
Hayes UB3 .... 95 BT80
Kings Langley WD4 .... 6 BN30
Langley Dr, E11 .... 68 EH59
W3 .... 80 CP74
Langley Dr, Brent. CM14 .... 54 FU48
Langley Gdns, Brom. BR2 .... 144 EJ98
Dagenham RM9 .... 88 EW66
Orpington BR5 .... 145 EP100
Langley Gro, N.Mal. KT3 .... 138 CS96
Langley Hill, Kings L. WD4 .... 6 BM29
Langley Hill Cl, Kings L. WD4 .... 6 BN29
Langley La, SW8 .... 101 DM79
Abbots Langley WD5 .... 7 BT31
Epsom (Headley) KT18 .... 182 CP125
Langley Lo La, Kings L. WD4 .... 6 BN31
Langley Meadow, Loug. IG10 .... 33 ER40
Langley Oaks Av, S.Croy.
CR2 .... 160 DU110
Langley Pk, NW7 .... 42 CS51
★ Langley Park Country Pk,
Slou. SL3 .... 75 BA70
Langley Pk Rd, Iver SL0 .... 75 BC72
Slough SL3 .... 93 BA75
Sutton SM1, SM2 .... 158 DC106
Langley Quay, Slou.
(Langley) SL3 .... 93 BA75
Langley Rd, SW19 .... 139 CZ95
Abbots Langley WD5 .... 7 BS31
Beckenham BR3 .... 143 DY98
Isleworth TW7 .... 97 CF82
Kings Langley (Chipper.)
WD4 .... 6 BH30
Slough SL3 .... 92 AW75
South Croydon CR2 .... 161 DX109
Staines TW18 .... 113 BF93
Surbiton KT6 .... 138 CL101
Watford WD17 .... 23 BU39
Welling DA16 .... 106 EW79
Langley Row, Barn. EN5 .... 27 CZ39
Langley St, WC2 .... 195 P9
LANGLEY VALE, Epsom
KT18 .... 172 CR120
Langley Vale Rd, Epsom
KT18 .... 172 CR118
Langley Wk, Wok. GU22
off Midhope Rd 166 AY119
Langley Way, Wat. WD17 .... 23 BS40
West Wickham BR4 .... 143 ED102
Langmans La, Wok. GU21 .... 166 AV118
Langmans Way, Wok. GU21 .... 166 AS116
Langmead Dr, Bushey (Bushey Hth)
WD23 .... 41 CD46
Langmead St, SE27
off Beadman St 121 DP91
Langmore Ct, Bexh. DA6
off Regency Way 106 EX83
Langport Ct, Walt. KT12 .... 136 BW102
Langridge Ms, Hmptn. TW12
off Oak Av 116 BZ93
Langroyd Rd, SW17 .... 120 DF89
Langshott Cl, Add. (Wdhm)
KT15 .... 151 BE111
Langside Av, SW15 .... 99 CU84
Langside Cres, N14 .... 45 DK48
Langstone Way, NW7 .... 43 CX52
Langston Hughes Cl, SE24
off Shakespeare Rd 101 DP84
Langston Rd, Loug. IG10 .... 33 EQ43
Lang St, E1 .... 84 DW70
Langthorn Ct, EC2 .... 197 K8
Langthorne Cres, Grays
RM17 .... 110 GC77
Langthorne Rd, E11 .... 67 ED62
Langthorne St, SW6 .... 99 CX80
Langton Av, E6 .... 87 EN69
N20 .... 44 DC45
Epsom KT17 .... 157 CT111
Langton Cl, WC1 .... 196 C3
Addlestone KT15 .... 134 BH104
Woking GU21 .... 166 AT117
Langton Gro, Nthwd. HA6 .... 39 BQ50
Langton Ho, SW16
off Colson Way 121 DJ91
Langton Pl, SW18
off Merton Rd 120 DA88
Langton Ri, SE23 .... 122 DV87
Langton Rd, NW2 .... 63 CW62
SW9 .... 101 DP80
Harrow HA3 .... 40 CC52
West Molesey KT8 .... 136 CC98
Langton St, SW10 .... 100 DC79
Langton Way, SE3 .... 104 EF81
Croydon CR0 .... 160 DS105
Egham TW20 .... 113 BC93
Grays RM16 .... 111 GJ77
Langtry Pl, SW6
off Seagrave Rd 100 DA79
Langtry Rd, NW8 .... 82 DB67
Northolt UB5 .... 78 BX68
Langtry Wk, NW8
off Alexandra Pl 82 DC66
Langwood Chase, Tedd.
TW11 .... 117 CJ93
Langwood Cl, Ashtd. KT21 .... 172 CN117
Langwood Gdns, Wat. WD17 .... 23 BU39
Langworth Cl, Dart. DA2 .... 128 FK90
Langworth Dr, Hayes UB4 .... 77 BU72
Lanhill Rd, W9 .... 82 DA70
Lanier Rd, SE13 .... 123 EC86
Lanigan Dr, Houns. TW3 .... 116 CB85
Lankaster Gdns, N2 .... 44 DD53
Lankers Dr, Har. HA2 .... 60 BZ58
Lankester Sq, Oxt. RH8
off Eastlands Way 187 ED128
Lankton Cl, Beck. BR3 .... 143 EC95
Lannock Rd, Hayes UB3 .... 77 BS74
Lannoy Pt, SW6
off Pellant Rd 99 CY80
Lannoy Rd, SE9 .... 125 EQ88
Lanrick Rd, E14 .... 85 ED72
Lanridge Rd, SE2 .... 106 EX76
Lansbury Av, N18 .... 46 DR50
Barking IG11 .... 88 EU66
Feltham TW14 .... 115 BV86
Romford RM6 .... 70 EY57
Lansbury Cl, NW10 .... 62 CQ64
Lansbury Cres, Dart. DA1 .... 128 FN85
Lansbury Dr, Hayes UB4 .... 77 BT71
Lansbury Est, E14 .... 85 EB72
Lansbury Gdns, E14 .... 85 ED72
Tilbury RM18 .... 111 GG81
Lansbury Rd, Enf. EN3 .... 31 DX39
Lansbury Way, N18 .... 46 DS50
Lanscombe Wk, SW8 .... 101 DL81
Lansdell Rd, Mitch. CR4 .... 140 DG96
Lansdown Cl, Walt. KT12
off St. Johns Dr 136 BW102
Lansdown Cl, Wok. GU21 .... 166 AT119
Lansdowne Av, Bexh. DA7 .... 106 EX80
Orpington BR6 .... 145 EP102
Slough SL1 .... 74 AS74
Lansdowne Cl, SW20 .... 119 CX94
Surbiton KT5
off Kingston Rd 138 CP103
Twickenham TW1
off Lion Rd 117 CF88
Watford WD25 .... 8 BX34
Lansdowne Copse, Wor.Pk.
KT4 off The Avenue 139 CU103
Lansdowne Ct, Pur. CR8 .... 159 DP110
Slough SL1 .... 74 AS74
Worcester Park KT4
off The Avenue 139 CU103
Lansdowne Cres, W11 .... 81 CY73
Lansdowne Dr, E8 .... 84 DU65
Lansdowne Gdns, SW8 .... 101 DL81
Lansdowne Grn, SW8
off Hartington Rd 101 DL81
Lansdowne Gro, NW10 .... 62 CS63
Lansdowne Hill, SE27 .... 121 DP90
Lansdowne La, SE7 .... 104 EK79
Lansdowne Ms, SE7 .... 104 EK78
W11 off Lansdowne Rd 81 CZ74
Lansdowne Pl, SE1 .... 201 L7
SE19 .... 122 DT94
Lansdowne Ri, W11 .... 81 CY73
Lansdowne Rd, E4 .... 47 EA47
E11 .... 68 EF61
E17 .... 67 EA57
E18 .... 68 EG55
N3 .... 43 CZ52
N10 .... 45 DJ54
N17 .... 46 DT53
SW20 .... 119 CW94
W11 .... 81 CY73
Bromley BR1 .... 124 EG94
Croydon CR0 .... 142 DR103
Epsom KT19 .... 156 CQ108
Harrow HA1 .... 61 CE59
Hounslow TW3 .... 96 CB83
Ilford IG3 .... 69 ET60
Purley CR8 .... 159 DN112
Sevenoaks TN13 .... 191 FK122
Staines TW18 .... 114 BH94
Stanmore HA7 .... 41 CJ51
Tilbury RM18 .... 111 GF82
Uxbridge UB8 .... 77 BP72
Lansdowne Row, W1 .... 199 J2
Lansdowne Sq, Grav.
(Nthflt) DA11 .... 131 GF86
Lansdowne Ter, WC1 .... 196 A5
Lansdowne Wk, W11 .... 81 CY74
Lansdowne Way, SW8 .... 101 DK81
Lansdowne Wd Cl, SE27 .... 121 DP90
Lansdown Pl, Grav.
(Nthflt) DA11 .... 131 GF88
Lansdown Rd, E7 .... 86 EJ66
Gerrards Cross (Chal.St.P.)
SL9 .... 36 AX53
Sidcup DA14 .... 126 EV90
Lansfield Av, N18 .... 46 DU49
Lantern Cl, SW15 .... 99 CU84
Orpington BR6 .... 163 EP105
Wembley HA0 .... 61 CK64
Lanterns Ct, E14 .... 204 A5
Lantern Way, West Dr. UB7 .... 94 BL75
Lant St, SE1 .... 201 H4
Lanvanor Rd, SE15 .... 102 DW82
Lapford Cl, W9 .... 81 CZ70
La Plata Gro, Brwd. CM14 .... 54 FV48
Lapponum Wk, Hayes UB4
off Lochan Cl 78 BX71
Lapse Wd Wk, SE23 .... 122 DV88
Lapstone Gdns, Har. HA3 .... 61 CJ58
Lapwing Cl, Erith DA8 .... 107 FH80
South Croydon CR2 .... 161 DY110
Lapwing Ct, Surb. KT6
off Chaffinch Cl 138 CN104
Lapwings, The, Grav. DA12 .... 131 GK89
Lapwing Ter, E7
off Hampton Rd 68 EK64
Lapwing Twr, SE8
off Abinger Gro 103 DZ79
Lapwing Way, Abb.L. WD5 .... 7 BU31
Hayes UB4 .... 78 BX72
Lapworth Cl, Orp. BR6 .... 146 EW103
Lara Cl, SE13 .... 123 EC86
Chessington KT9 .... 156 CL108
Larbert Rd, SW16 .... 141 DJ95
Larby Pl, Epsom KT17 .... 156 CS110
Larch Av, W3 .... 80 CS74
St. Albans (Brick.Wd) AL2 .... 8 BY30
Larch Cl, E13 .... 86 EH70
N11 .... 44 DG52
N19 off Bredgar Rd 65 DJ61
SE8 off Clyde St 103 DZ79
SW12 .... 121 DH89
Tadworth KT20 .... 174 DC121
Waltham Cross EN7
off The Firs 14 DS27
Warlingham CR6 .... 177 DY119
Larch Cres, Epsom KT19 .... 156 CP107
Hayes UB4 .... 78 BW70
Larchdene, Orp. BR6 .... 145 EN103
Larch Dr, W4
off Gunnersbury Av 98 CN78
Larches, The, N13 .... 46 DQ48
Amersham HP6 .... 20 AV38
Bushey WD23 .... 24 BY43
Northwood HA6
off Rickmansworth Rd 39 BQ51
Uxbridge UB10 .... 77 BP69
Woking GU21 .... 166 AY116
Larches Av, SW14 .... 98 CR84
Enfield EN1 .... 30 DW35
Larch Grn, NW9
off Clayton Fld 42 CS53
Larch Gro, Sid. DA15 .... 125 ET88
Larch Rd, E10
off Walnut Rd 67 EA61
NW2 .... 63 CW63
Dartford DA1 .... 128 FK87
Larch Tree Way, Croy. CR0 .... 143 EA104
Larch Wk, Swan. BR8 .... 147 FD96
Larch Way, Brom. BR2 .... 145 EN101
Larchwood Av, Rom. RM5 .... 51 FB51
Larchwood Cl, Bans. SM7 .... 173 CY116
Romford RM5 .... 51 FC51
Larchwood Dr, Egh. (Eng.Grn)
TW20 .... 112 AV93
Larchwood Gdns, Brwd.
(Pilg.Hat.) CM15 .... 54 FU44
Larchwood Rd, SE9 .... 125 EP89
Larcombe Cl, Croy. CR0 .... 160 DT105
Larcom St, SE17 .... 201 J9
Larden Rd, W3 .... 80 CS74
Largewood Av, Surb. KT6 .... 138 CN103
Largo Wk, Erith DA8
off Selkirk Dr 107 FE81
Larissa St, SE17 .... 201 L10
Lark Av, Stai. TW18
off Kestrel Av 113 BF90
Larkbere Rd, SE26 .... 123 DY91
Lark Cl, Brwd. (Warley) CM14 .... 54 FV49
Larken Cl, Bushey WD23
off Larken Dr 40 CC46
Larken Dr, Bushey WD23 .... 40 CC46
Larkfield, Cob. KT11 .... 153 BU113
Larkfield Av, Har. HA3 .... 61 CH55
Larkfield Cl, Brom. BR2 .... 144 EF103
Larkfield Rd, Rich. TW9 .... 98 CL84
Sevenoaks TN13 .... 190 FC123
Sidcup DA14 .... 125 ET90
Larkfields, Grav. (Nthflt)
DA11 .... 130 GE90
Larkhall Cl, Walt. KT12 .... 154 BW107
Larkhall La, SW4 .... 101 DK82
Larkhall Ri, SW4 .... 101 DJ83
Larkham Cl, Felt. TW13 .... 115 BS90
Larkhill Ter, SE18
off Prince Imperial Rd 105 EN80
Larkin Cl, Brwd. (Hutt.) CM13 .... 55 GC45
Coulsdon CR5 .... 175 DM117
Larkings La, Slou. (Stoke P.)
SL2 .... 74 AV67
Lark Row, E2 .... 84 DW67
Larksfield, Egh. (Eng.Grn)
TW20 .... 112 AW94
Larksfield Gro, Enf. EN1 .... 30 DV39
Larks Gro, Bark. IG11
off Thornhill Gdns 87 ES66
Larkshall Ct, Rom. RM7 .... 51 FC54
Larkshall Cres, E4 .... 47 EC49
Larkshall Rd, E4 .... 47 EC50
Larkspur Cl, E6 .... 86 EL71
N17 off Fryatt Rd 46 DR52
NW9 .... 62 CQ57
Orpington BR6 .... 146 EW103
Ruislip HA4 .... 59 BQ59
South Ockendon RM15 .... 91 FW69
Larkspur Gro, Edg. HA8 .... 42 CQ49
Larkspur Way, Epsom KT19 .... 156 CQ106
Larkswood Cl, Erith DA8 .... 107 FG81
Larkswood Ct, E4 .... 47 ED50
Larkswood Leisure Pk, E4
off New Rd 47 EC49
Larkswood Ri, Pnr. HA5 .... 60 BW56
Larkswood Rd, E4 .... 47 EA49
Lark Way, Cars. SM5 .... 140 DE101
Larkway Cl, NW9 .... 62 CR56
Larmans Rd, Enf. EN3 .... 30 DW36
Larnach Rd, W6 .... 99 CX79
Larne Rd, Ruis. HA4 .... 59 BT59
Larner Rd, Erith DA8 .... 107 FE80
La Roche Cl, Slou. SL3 .... 92 AW76
Larpent Av, SW15 .... 119 CW85
Larsen Dr, Wal.Abb. EN9 .... 15 ED34
Larwood Cl, Grnf. UB6 .... 61 CD64
Lascelles Av, Har. HA1 .... 61 CD59
Lascelles Cl, E11 .... 67 ED61
Brentwood (Pilg.Hat.) CM15 .... 54 FU43
Lascelles Rd, Slou. SL3 .... 92 AV76
Lascotts Rd, N22 .... 45 DM51
Las Palmas Est, Shep. TW17 .... 135 BQ101
Lassa Rd, SE9 .... 124 EL85
Lassell St, SE10 .... 103 ED78
Lasseter Pl, SE3
off Vanbrugh Hill 104 EF79
Lasswade Rd, Cher. KT16 .... 133 BF101
Latchett Rd, E18 .... 48 EH53
Latchford Pl, Chig. IG7
off Manford Way 50 EV49
Latching Cl, Rom. RM3
off Troopers Dr 52 FK49
Latchingdon Ct, E17 .... 67 DX56
Latchingdon Gdns, Wdf.Grn.
IG8 .... 48 EL51
Latchmere Cl, Rich. TW10 .... 118 CL92
Latchmere La, Kings.T. KT2 .... 118 CM93
Latchmere Pas, SW11
off Cabul Rd 100 DE82
Latchmere Rd, SW11 .... 100 DF82
Kingston upon Thames
KT2 .... 118 CL94
Latchmere St, SW11 .... 100 DF82
Latchmoor Av, Ger.Cr.
(Chal.St.P.) SL9 .... 56 AX56
Latchmoor Gro, Ger.Cr.
(Chal.St.P.) SL9 .... 56 AX56
Latchmoor Way, Ger.Cr.
(Chal.St.P.) SL9 .... 56 AX56
Lateward Rd, Brent. TW8 .... 97 CK79
Latham Cl, E6
off Oliver Gdns 86 EL72
Dartford DA2 .... 129 FS89
Twickenham TW1 .... 117 CG87
Westerham (Bigg.H.)
TN16 .... 178 EJ116
Latham Ho, E1 .... 85 DX72
Latham Rd, Bexh. DA6 .... 126 FA85
Twickenham TW1 .... 117 CF87
Lathams Way, Croy. CR0 .... 141 DM102
Lathkill Cl, Enf. EN1 .... 46 DU45
Lathom Rd, E6 .... 87 EM66
LATIMER, Chesh. HP5 .... 20 AY36
Latimer, SE17
off Beaconsfield Rd 102 DS78
Latimer Av, E6 .... 87 EM67
Latimer Cl, Amer. HP6 .... 20 AW39
Pinner HA5 .... 40 BW53
Watford WD18 .... 39 BS45
Woking GU22 .... 167 BB116
Worcester Park KT4 .... 157 CV105
Latimer Dr, Horn. RM12 .... 72 FK62
Latimer Gdns, Pnr. HA5 .... 40 BW53
Latimer Pl, W10 .... 81 CW72
⊖ Latimer Road 81 CX73
Latimer Rd, E7 .... 68 EH63
N15 .... 66 DS58
SW19 .... 120 DB93
W10 .... 81 CW72
Barnet EN5 .... 28 DB41
Chesham HP5 .... 20 AU36

★ Place of interest · ≠ Railway station · ⊖ London Underground station · DLR Docklands Light Railway station · Tra Tramlink station · H Hospital · Riv Pedestrian ferry landing stage

Latimer Rd, Croy. CR0
off Abbey Rd 141 DP104
Rickmansworth (Chenies) WD3 21 BB38
Teddington TW11 117 CF92
Latitude Ct, E16
off Armada Way 87 EQ73
Latona Dr, Grav. DA12 131 GM92
Latona Rd, SE15 102 DU79
La Tourne Gdns, Orp. BR6 145 EQ104
Lattimer Pl, W4 98 CS79
Latton Cl, Esher KT10 154 CB105
Walton-on-Thames KT12 136 BY101
Latymer Cl, Wey. KT13 153 BQ105
Latymer Ct, W6 99 CX77
Latymer Rd, N9 46 DT46
Latymer Way, N9 46 DR47
Lauder Cl, Nthlt. UB5 78 BX68
Lauderdale Dr, Rich. TW10 117 CK90
Lauderdale Pl, EC2
off Beech St 84 DQ71
Lauderdale Rd, W9 82 DB69
Kings Langley WD4 7 BQ33
Lauderdale Twr, EC2 197 H6
Laud St, SE11 200 B10
Croydon CR0 142 DQ104
Laughton Ct, Borwd. WD6
off Banks Rd 26 CR40
Laughton Rd, Nthlt. UB5 78 BX67
Launcelot Rd, Brom. BR1 124 EG91
Launcelot St, SE1 200 D5
Launceston Cl, Rom. RM3 52 FJ53
Launceston Gdns, Grnf. UB6 79 CJ67
Launceston Pl, W8 100 DC76
Launceston Rd, Grnf. UB6 79 CJ67
Launch St, E14 204 D6
Launders Gate, W3 98 CP75
Launders La, Rain. RM13 90 FM69
Laundress La, N16 66 DU62
Laundry La, N1
off Greenman St 84 DQ67
Waltham Abbey EN9 16 EE25
Laundry Ms, SE23 123 DY87
Laundry Rd, W6 99 CY79
Launton Dr, Bexh. DA6 106 EX84
Laura Cl, E11 68 EJ57
Enfield EN1 30 DS43
Lauradale Rd, N2 64 DF56
Laura Dr, Swan. BR8 127 FG94
Laura Pl, E5 66 DW63
Laurel Apts, SE17
off Townsend St 102 DS77
Laurel Av, Egh. (Eng.Grn) TW20 112 AV92
Gravesend DA12 131 GJ89
Potters Bar EN6 11 CZ32
Slough SL3 92 AY75
Twickenham TW1 117 CF88
Laurel Bk Gdns, SW6
off New Kings Rd 99 CZ82
Laurel Bk Rd, Enf. EN2 30 DQ39
Laurel Bk Vil, W7
off Lower Boston Rd 79 CE74
Laurel Cl, N19
off Hargrave Pk 65 DJ61
SW17 120 DE92
Brentwood (Hutt.) CM13 55 GB43
Dartford DA1
off Willow Rd 128 FJ88
Ilford IG6 49 EQ51
Sidcup DA14 126 EU90
Slough (Colnbr.) SL3 93 BE80
Watford WD19 40 BX45
Woking GU21 151 BD113
Laurel Ct, Pot.B. (Cuffley) EN6
off Station Rd 13 DM29
Laurel Cres, Croy. CR0 143 EA104
Romford RM7 71 FE60
Woking GU21 151 BC113
Laurel Dr, N21 45 DN45
Oxted RH8 188 EF131
South Ockendon RM15 91 FX70
Laurel Flds, Pot.B. EN6 11 CZ31
Laurel Gdns, E4 47 EB45
NW7 42 CR48
W7 79 CE74
Addlestone (New Haw) KT15 152 BH110
Bromley BR1 144 EL98
Hounslow TW4 96 BY84
Laurel Gro, SE20 122 DV94
SE26 123 DX91
Laurel La, Horn. RM12
off Station La 72 FL61
West Drayton UB7 94 BL77
Laurel Lo La, Barn. EN5 27 CW36
Laurel Manor, Sutt. SM2 158 DC108
Laurel Pk, Har. HA3 41 CF52
Laurel Rd, SW13 99 CU82
SW20 139 CV95
Gerrards Cross (Chal.St.P.) SL9 36 AX53
Hampton (Hmptn H.) TW12 117 CD92
Laurels, The, Bans. SM7 173 CZ117
Cobham KT11 170 BY115
Dartford DA2 128 FJ90
Waltham Cross EN7 14 DS27
Weybridge KT13 135 BR104
Laurels Rd, Iver SL0 75 BD68
Laurel St, E8 84 DT65
Laurel Vw, N12 44 DB48
Laurel Way, E18 68 EF56
N20 44 DA48
Laurence Ms, W12
off Askew Rd 99 CU75
Laurence Pountney Hill, EC4 197 K10
Laurence Pountney La, EC4 197 K10
Laurie Gro, SE14 103 DY81
Laurie Rd, W7 79 CE71
Laurier Rd, NW5 65 DH62
Croydon CR0 142 DT101
Laurimel Cl, Stan. HA7
off September Way 41 CH51
Laurino Pl, Bushey (Bushey Hth) WD23 40 CC47
Lauriston Rd, E9 85 DX67
SW19 119 CX93
Lausanne Rd, N8 65 DN56
SE15 102 DW81
Lauser Rd, Stai. (Stanw.) TW19 114 BJ87
Lavell St, N16 66 DR63
Lavender Av, NW9 62 CQ60
Brentwood (Pilg.Hat.) CM15 54 FV43
Mitcham CR4 140 DE95
Worcester Park KT4 139 CW104
Lavender Cl, SW3
off Danvers St 100 DD79
Bromley BR2 144 EL100
Carshalton SM5 158 DG105
Caterham (Chaldon) CR3 186 DQ125
Coulsdon CR5 175 DJ119
Leatherhead KT22 171 CJ123
Romford RM3 52 FK52
Waltham Cross (Chsht) EN7 14 DT27
Lavender Ct, W.Mol. KT8
off Molesham Way 136 CB97
Lavender Dr, Uxb. UB8 76 BM71
Lavender Gdns, SW11 100 DF84
Enfield EN2 29 DP39
Harrow HA3
off Uxbridge Rd 41 CE51
Lavender Gate, Lthd. KT22 154 CB113
Lavender Gro, E8 84 DT66
Mitcham CR4 140 DE95
Lavender Hill, SW11 100 DE84
Enfield EN2 29 DN39
Swanley BR8 147 FD97
Lavender Pk Rd, W.Byf. KT14 152 BG112
Lavender Pl, Ilf. IG1 69 EP64
Lavender Ri, West Dr. UB7 94 BN75
Lavender Rd, SE16 203 K2
SW11 100 DD83
Carshalton SM5 158 DG105
Croydon CR0 141 DM100
Enfield EN2 30 DR39
Epsom KT19 156 CP106
Sutton SM1 158 DD105
Uxbridge UB8 76 BM71
Woking GU22 167 BB116
Lavender St, E15
off Manbey Gro 86 EE65
Lavender Sweep, SW11 100 DF84
Lavender Ter, SW11
off Falcon Rd 100 DE83
Lavender Vale, Wall. SM6 159 DK107
Lavender Wk, SW11 100 DF84
Mitcham CR4 140 DG97
Lavender Way, Croy. CR0 143 DX100
Lavengro Rd, SE27 122 DQ89
Lavenham Rd, SW18 119 CZ89
Lavernock Rd, Bexh. DA7 106 FA82
Lavers Rd, N16 66 DS62
Laverstoke Gdns, SW15 119 CU87
Laverton Ms, SW5
off Laverton Pl 100 DB77
Laverton Pl, SW5 100 DB77
Lavidge Rd, SE9 124 EL89
Lavina Gro, N1
off Wharfdale Rd 83 DM68
Lavington Cl, E9
off Beanacre Cl 85 DZ65
Lavington Rd, W13 79 CH74
Croydon CR0 141 DM104
Lavington St, SE1 200 G3
Lavinia Av, Wat. WD25 8 BX34
Lavinia Rd, Dart. DA1 128 FM86
Lavrock La, Rick. WD3 38 BM45
Lawdons Gdns, Croy. CR0 159 DP105
Lawford Av, Rick. (Chorl.) WD3 21 BC44
Lawford Cl, Horn. RM12 72 FJ63
Rickmansworth (Chorl.) WD3 21 BC44
Wallington SM6 159 DL109
Lawford Gdns, Dart. DA1 128 FJ85
Kenley CR8 176 DQ116
Lawford Rd, N1 84 DS66
NW5 83 DJ65
W4 98 CQ80
Law Ho, Bark. IG11 88 EU68
Lawless St, E14 85 EB73
Lawley Rd, N14 45 DH45
Lawley St, E5 66 DW63
Lawn, The, Sthl. UB2 96 CA78
Lawn Av, West Dr. UB7 94 BJ75
Lawn Cl, N9 46 DT45
Bromley BR1 124 EH93
New Malden KT3 138 CS96
Ruislip HA4 59 BT62
Slough (Datchet) SL3 92 AW80
Swanley BR8 147 FC96
Lawn Cres, Rich. TW9 98 CN82
Lawn Fm Gro, Rom. RM6 70 EY56
Lawn Gdns, W7 79 CE74
Lawn Ho Cl, E14 204 D4
Lawn La, SW8 101 DL79
Lawn Pk, Sev. TN13 191 FH127
Lawn Rd, NW3 64 DF64
Beckenham BR3 123 DZ94
Gravesend DA11 130 GC86
Uxbridge UB8
off New Windsor St 76 BJ67
Lawns, The, E4 47 EA50
SE3 off Lee Ter 104 EF83
SE19 142 DR95
Pinner HA5 40 CB52
Radlett (Shenley) WD7 10 CL33
Sidcup DA14 126 EV91
Sutton SM2 157 CY108
Lawns Ct, Wem. HA9
off The Avenue 62 CM61
Lawns Cres, Grays RM17 110 GD79
Lawnside, SE3 104 EF84
Lawns Way, Rom. RM5 51 FC52
Lawn Ter, SE3 104 EE83
Lawn Vale, Pnr. HA5 40 BX54
Lawrance Gdns, Wal.Cr. (Chsht) EN8 15 DX28
Lawrance Sq, Grav. DA11
off Haynes Rd 131 GF90
Lawrence Av, E12 69 EN63
E17 47 DX53
N13 45 DP49
NW7 42 CS49
NW10 80 CR67
New Malden KT3 138 CR100
Lawrence Bldgs, N16 66 DT62
Lawrence Campe Cl, N20
off Friern Barnet La 44 DD48
Lawrence Cl, E3 85 EA68
N15 off Lawrence Rd 66 DS55
Lawrence Ct, NW7 42 CS50
Lawrence Cres, Dag. RM10 71 FB62
Lawrence Cres, Edg. HA8 42 CN54
Lawrence Dr, Uxb. UB10 59 BQ63
Lawrence Gdns, NW7 43 CT48
Tilbury RM18 111 GH80
Lawrence Hill, E4 47 EA47
Lawrence Hill Gdns, Dart. DA1 128 FJ86
Lawrence Hill Rd, Dart. DA1 128 FJ86
Lawrence La, EC2 197 J9
Betchworth (Buckland) RH3 183 CV131
Lawrence Orchard, Rick. (Chorl.) WD3 21 BD43
Lawrence Pl, N1
off Outram Pl 83 DL67
Lawrence Rd, E6 86 EK67
E13 86 EH67
N15 66 DS56
N18 46 DV49
SE25 142 DT98
W5 97 CK77
Erith DA8 107 FB80
Hampton TW12 116 BZ94
Hayes UB4 77 BQ68
Hounslow TW4 96 BW84
Pinner HA5 60 BX57
Richmond TW10 117 CJ91
Romford RM2 71 FH57
West Wickham BR4 162 EG105
Lawrence St, E16 86 EF71
NW7 43 CT49
SW3 100 DE79
Lawrence Way, NW10 62 CQ62
Lawrence Weaver Cl, Mord. SM4 off Green La 140 DA100
Lawrie Pk Av, SE26 122 DV92
Lawrie Pk Cres, SE26 122 DV92
Lawrie Pk Gdns, SE26 122 DV91
Lawrie Pk Rd, SE26 122 DV93
Laws Cl, SE25 142 DR98
Lawson Cl, E16 86 EJ71
SW19 119 CX90
Ilford IG1 69 ER64
Lawson Est, SE1 201 K7
Lawson Gdns, Dart. DA1 128 FK85
Pinner HA5 59 BV55
Lawson Rd, Dart. DA1 108 FK84
Enfield EN3 30 DW39
Southall UB1 78 BZ70
Lawson Wk, Cars. SM5 158 DF110
Law St, SE1 201 L6
Lawton Rd, E3 85 DY69
E10 67 EC60
Barnet EN4 28 DD41
Loughton IG10 33 EP41
Laxcon Cl, NW10 62 CQ64
Laxey Rd, Orp. BR6 163 ET107
Laxley Cl, SE5 101 DP80
Laxton Gdns, Rad. (Shenley) WD7 10 CL32
Redhill (Merst.) RH1 185 DK128
Laxton Pl, NW1 195 J4
Layard Rd, SE16 202 E8
Enfield EN1 30 DT39
Thornton Heath CR7 142 DR96
Layard Sq, SE16 202 E8
Layborne Av, Rom. RM3
off Cummings Hall La 52 FJ48
Layburn Cres, Slou. SL3 93 BB79
Laycock St, N1 83 DN65
Layer Gdns, W3 80 CN73
Layfield Cl, NW4 63 CV59
Layfield Cres, NW4 63 CV59
Layfield Rd, NW4 63 CV59
Layhams Rd, Kes. BR2 162 EF106
West Wickham BR4 143 ED104
Laymarsh Cl, Belv. DA17 106 EZ76
Laymead Cl, Nthlt. UB5 78 BY65
Laystall St, EC1 196 D5
Layters Av, Ger.Cr. (Chal.St.P.) SL9 36 AW54
Layters Av S, Ger.Cr. (Chal.St.P.) SL9 36 AW54
Layters Cl, Ger.Cr. (Chal.St.P.) SL9 36 AW54
Layters End, Ger.Cr. (Chal.St.P.) SL9 36 AW54
LAYTER'S GREEN, Ger.Cr. SL9 36 AV54
Layters Grn La, Ger.Cr. (Chal.St.P.) SL9 56 AU55
Layter's Grn Mobile Home Pk, Ger.Cr. (Chal.St.P.) SL9
off Layters Grn La 36 AV54
Layters Way, Ger.Cr. SL9 56 AX56
Layton Ct, Wey. KT13
off Castle Vw Rd 153 BP105
Layton Cres, Croy. CR0 159 DN106
Layton Pl, Rich. (Kew) TW9
off Station Av 98 CN81
Layton Rd, Brent. TW8 97 CK78
Hounslow TW3 96 CB84
Laytons Bldgs, SE1 201 J4
Laytons La, Sun. TW16 135 BT96
Layzell Wk, SE9
off Mottingham La 124 EK88
Lazar Wk, N7
off Briset Way 65 DM61
Lea, The, Egh. TW20 133 BB95
Leabank Cl, Har. HA1 61 CE62
Leabank Sq, E9 85 EA65
Leabank Vw, N15 66 DU58
Leabourne Rd, N16 66 DU58
LEA BRIDGE, E5 67 DX62
Lea Br Rd, E5 66 DW62
E10 67 DY60
E17 67 ED56
Lea Bushes, Wat. WD25 24 BY35
Leachcroft, Ger.Cr. (Chal.St.P.) SL9 36 AV53
Leach Gro, Lthd. KT22 171 CJ122
Lea Cl, Bushey WD23 24 CB43
Twickenham TW2 116 BZ87
Lea Cres, Ruis. HA4 59 BT63
Leacroft, Stai. TW18 114 BH91
Leacroft Av, SW12 120 DF87
Leacroft Cl, Ken. CR8 176 DQ116
Staines TW18 114 BH91
West Drayton UB7 76 BL72
Leacroft Rd, Iver SL0 75 BD72
Leadale Av, E4 47 EA47
Leadale Rd, N15 66 DU58
N16 66 DU58
Leadbeaters Cl, N11
off Goldsmith Rd 44 DF50
Leadbetter Dr, Wat. WD25 23 BR36
★ **Leadenhall Mkt**, EC3 197 M9
Leadenhall Pl, EC3 197 M9
Leadenhall St, EC3 197 M9
Leadenham Ct, E3
off Spanby Rd 85 EA70
Leader Av, E12 69 EN64
Leadings, The, Wem. HA9 62 CQ62
Leaf Cl, Nthwd. HA6 39 BR52
Thames Ditton KT7 137 CE99
Leaf Gro, SE27 121 DN92
Leafield Cl, SW16 121 DP93
Woking GU21
off Winnington Way 166 AV118
Leafield La, Sid. DA14 126 EZ91
Leafield Rd, SW20 139 CZ97
Sutton SM1 140 DA103
Leaford Cres, Wat. WD24 23 BT37
Leaforis Rd, Wal.Cr. EN7 14 DU28
Leafy Gro, Croy. CR0 161 DY111
Keston BR2 162 EJ106
Leafy Oak Rd, SE12 124 EJ90
Leafy Way, Brwd. (Hutt.) CM13 55 GD46
Croydon CR0 142 DT103
Lea Gdns, Wem. HA9 62 CL63
Leagrave St, E5 66 DW62
Lea Hall Rd, E10 67 EA60
Leaholme Way, Ruis. HA4 59 BP58
Leahurst Rd, SE13 123 ED85
Lea Interchange, E9
off East Cross Route 67 EA64
Leake St, SE1 200 C4
Lealand Rd, N15 66 DT58
Leamington Av, E17 67 EA57
Bromley BR1 124 EJ92
Morden SM4 139 CZ98
Orpington BR6 163 ES105
Leamington Cl, E12 68 EL64
Bromley BR1 124 EJ92
Hounslow TW3 116 CC85
Romford RM3 52 FM51
Leamington Cres, Har. HA2 60 BY62
Leamington Gdns, Ilf. IG3 69 ET61
Leamington Pk, W3 80 CR71
Leamington Pl, Hayes UB4 77 BT70
Leamington Rd, Rom. RM3 52 FN50
Southall UB2 96 BX77
Leamington Rd Vil, W11 81 CZ71
Leamore St, W6 99 CV77
Lea Mt, Wal.Cr. EN7 14 DS28
Leamouth Rd, E6
off Remington Rd 86 EL72
E14 85 ED72
Leander Ct, SE8 103 EA81
Leander Dr, Grav. DA12 131 GM91
Leander Gdns, Wat. WD25 24 BY37
Leander Rd, SW2 121 DM86
Northolt UB5 78 CA68
Thornton Heath CR7 141 DM98
Learner Dr, Har. HA2 60 CA61
Lea Rd, Beck. BR3
off Fairfield Rd 143 EA96
Enfield EN2 30 DR39
Grays RM16 111 GG78
Sevenoaks TN13 191 FJ127
Southall UB2 96 BY77
Waltham Abbey EN9 15 EA34
Learoyd Gdns, E6 87 EN73
Leas, The, Bushey WD23 24 BZ39
Staines TW18
off Raleigh Ct 114 BG91
Upminster RM14 73 FR59
Leas Cl, Chess. KT9 156 CM108
Leas Dale, SE9 125 EN90
Leas Dr, Iver SL0 75 BE72
Leas Grn, Chis. BR7 125 ET93
Leaside, Lthd. (Bkhm) KT23 170 CA123
Leaside Av, N10 64 DG55
Leaside Ct, Uxb. UB10
off The Larches 77 BP69
Leaside Rd, E5 66 DW60
Leas La, Warl. CR6 177 DX118
Leasowes Rd, E10 67 EA60
Lea Sq, E3 off Lefevre Wk 85 DZ67
Leas Rd, Warl. CR6 177 DX118
Leasway, Brwd. CM14 54 FX48
Upminster RM14 72 FQ62
Leathart Cl, Horn. RM12
off Dowding Way 89 FH66
Leatherbottle Grn, Erith DA18 106 EZ76
Leather Bottle La, Belv. DA17 106 EY77
Leather Cl, Mitch. CR4 140 DG96
Leatherdale St, E1
off Portelet Rd 85 DX70
Leather Gdns, E15
off Abbey Rd 86 EE67
LEATHERHEAD, KT22 - KT24 171 CF121
⇌ **Leatherhead** 171 CG121
Leatherhead Bypass Rd, Lthd. KT22 171 CH120
Leatherhead Cl, N16 66 DT60
LEATHERHEAD COMMON, Lthd. KT22 171 CF119
H **Leatherhead Hosp**, Lthd. KT22 171 CJ122
★ **Leatherhead Mus of Local History**, Lthd. KT22 171 CH122
Leatherhead Rd, Ashtd. KT21 171 CK121
Chessington KT9 155 CJ111
Leatherhead KT22 171 CK121
Leatherhead (Oxshott) KT22 155 CD114
Leather La, EC1 196 E7
Hornchurch RM11
off North St 72 FK60
★ **Leather Mkt Bermondsey**, SE1 201 M5
Leathermarket Ct, SE1 201 M5
Leathermarket St, SE1 201 M5
Leather Rd, SE16 203 H9
Leathersellers Cl, Barn. EN5
off The Avenue 27 CY42
Leathsail Rd, Har. HA2 60 CB62
Leathwaite Rd, SW11 100 DF84
Leathwell Rd, SE8 103 EB82
Lea Vale, Dart. DA1 107 FD84
Lea Valley Rd, E4 31 DX43
Lea Valley Rd, Enf. EN3 31 DX43
Lea Valley Trd Est, N18 47 DX50
Lea Valley Viaduct, E4 47 DX50
N18 47 DX50
Lea Valley Wk, E3 85 EC70
E5 67 DY62
E9 67 DY62
E10 67 DY62
E14 85 EB71
E15 85 EC69
E17 46 DW53
N9 47 DY46
N15 66 DU58
N16 66 DU58
N17 46 DW53
N18 46 DW53
Enfield EN3 31 DZ41
Waltham Abbey EN9 15 DZ30
Waltham Cross EN8 15 DZ30
Leaveland Cl, Beck. BR3 143 EA98
Leaver Gdns, Grnf. UB6 79 CD68
Leavesden Ct, Abb.L. WD5 7 BU31
LEAVESDEN GREEN, Wat. WD25 7 BT34
Leavesden Rd, Stan. HA7 41 CG51
Watford WD24 23 BV38
Weybridge KT13 153 BP106
LEAVES GREEN, Kes. BR2 162 EK109
Leaves Grn Cres, Kes. BR2 162 EJ111
Leaves Grn Rd, Kes. BR2 162 EK111
Leaview, Wal.Abb. EN9 15 EB33
Lea Vw Hos, E5
off Springfield 66 DV60
Leaway, E10 67 DX60
Leazes Av, Cat. (Chaldon) CR3 175 DN123
Leazes La, Cat. CR3 175 DN123
Lebanon Av, Felt. TW13 116 BX92
Lebanon Cl, Wat. WD17 23 BR36
Lebanon Ct, Twick. TW1 117 CH87
Lebanon Dr, Cob. KT11 154 CA113
Lebanon Gdns, SW18 120 DA86
Westerham (Bigg.H.) TN16 178 EK117
Lebanon Pk, Twick. TW1 117 CH87
Tra **Lebanon Road** 142 DS103
Lebanon Rd, SW18 120 DA85
Croydon CR0 142 DS102
Lebrun Sq, SE3 104 EH83
Lechmere App, Wdf.Grn. IG8 48 EJ54
Lechmere Av, Chig. IG7 49 EQ49
Woodford Green IG8 48 EK54
Lechmere Rd, NW2 81 CV65
Leckford Rd, SW18 120 DC89
Leckhampton Pl, SW2
off Scotia Rd 121 DN87
Leckwith Av, Bexh. DA7 106 EY79
Lecky St, SW7 100 DD78
Leclair Ho, SE3
off Gallus Sq 104 EH83
Leconfield Av, SW13 99 CT83
Leconfield Rd, N5 66 DR63
Leconfield Wk, Horn. RM12
off Airfield Way 90 FJ65
Le Corte Cl, Kings L. WD4 6 BM29
Leda Av, Enf. EN3 31 DX39
Leda Rd, SE18 105 EM76
Ledbury Est, SE15 102 DV80
Ledbury Ms N, W11
off Ledbury Rd 82 DA73
Ledbury Ms W, W11
off Ledbury Rd 82 DA73
Ledbury Pl, Croy. CR0 160 DR105
Ledbury Rd, W11 81 CZ72
Croydon CR0 160 DQ105
Reigate RH2 183 CZ133
Ledbury St, SE15 102 DU80
Ledger Dr, Add. KT15 151 BF106
Ledgers Rd, Warl. CR6 177 EA116
Ledrington Rd, SE19 122 DU93
Ledway Dr, Wem. HA9 62 CM59
LEE, SE12 104 EE84
⇌ **Lee** 124 EG86
Lee, The, Nthwd. HA6 39 BT50
Lee Av, Rom. RM6 70 EY58
Lee Br, SE13 103 EC83
Leechcroft Av, Sid. DA15 125 ET85
Swanley BR8 147 FF97
Leechcroft Rd, Wall. SM6 140 DG104
Leech La, Epsom (Headley) KT18 182 CQ126
Leatherhead KT22 182 CQ126
Lee Ch St, SE13 104 EE84
Lee Cl, E17 47 DX53
Barnet EN5 28 DC42
Lee Conservancy Rd, E9 67 DZ64
Leecroft Rd, Barn. EN5 27 CY43
Leeds Cl, Orp. BR6 146 EX103
Leeds Pl, N4
off Tollington Pk 65 DM61
Leeds Rd, Ilf. IG1 69 ER60
Slough SL1 74 AS73
Leeds St, N18 46 DU50
Lee Fm Cl, Chesh. HP5 4 AU30
Leefern Rd, W12 99 CU75
Leefe Way, Pot.B. EN6 13 DK28
Lee Gdns Av, Horn. RM11 72 FN60
Leegate, SE12 124 EF85
Leegate Cl, Wok. GU21
off Sythwood 166 AV116
Lee Grn, SE12
off Lee High Rd 124 EF85
Orpington BR5 146 EU99
Lee Grn La, Epsom KT18 172 CP124
Lee Gro, Chig. IG7 49 EN47
Lee High Rd, SE12 103 ED83
SE13 103 ED83
Leeke St, WC1 196 B2
Leeland Rd, W13 79 CG74
Leeland Ter, W13 79 CG74
Leeland Way, NW10 63 CT63
Leeming Rd, Borwd. WD6 26 CM39
Lee Pk, SE3 104 EF84
Lee Pk Way, N9 47 DX49
N18 47 DX49
Leerdam Dr, E14 204 E7
Lee Rd, NW7 43 CX52
SE3 104 EF83

★ Place of interest ⇌ Railway station ⊖ London Underground station DLR Docklands Light Railway station Tra Tramlink station H Hospital Riv Pedestrian ferry landing stage

Lee Rd, SW19 140 DB95
Enfield EN1 30 DU44
Greenford UB6 79 CJ67
Lees, The, Croy. CR0 143 DZ103
Lees Av, Nthwd. HA6 59 BT53
Leeside, Barn. EN5 27 CY43
Potters Bar EN6
off Wayside 12 DD31
Leeside Ct, SE16 203 H2
Leeside Cres, NW11 63 CZ58
Leeside Rd, N17 46 DV51
Leeson Rd, SE24 101 DN84
Leesons Hill, Chis. BR7 145 ES97
Orpington BR5 146 EU97
Leesons Way, Orp. BR5 145 ET96
Lees Pl, W1 194 F10
Lees Rd, Uxb. UB8 77 BP70
Lee St, E8 84 DT67
Lee Ter, SE3 104 EE83
SE13 104 EE83
★ **Lee Valley Pk**, E10 15 DZ31
Lee Valley Pathway, E9 67 DZ62
E10 66 DW59
E17 66 DW59
Waltham Abbey EN9 15 EA31
Lee Valley Technopark, N17 66 DU55
Lee Vw, Enf. EN2 29 DP39
Leeward Gdns, SW19 119 CZ93
Leeway, SE8 203 M10
Leeway Cl, Pnr. HA5 40 BZ52
Leewood Cl, SE12
off Upwood Rd 124 EF86
Leewood Pl, Swan. BR8 147 FD98
Lefevre Wk, E3 85 DZ67
Lefroy Rd, W12 99 CT75
Legard Rd, N5 65 DP63
Legatt Rd, SE9 124 EK85
Leggatt Rd, E15 85 EC68
Leggatts Cl, Wat. WD24 23 BT36
Leggatts Pk, Pot.B. EN6 12 DD29
Leggatts Ri, Wat. WD25 23 BU35
Leggatts Way, Wat. WD24 23 BT36
Leggatts Wd Av, Wat. WD24 23 BV36
Legge St, SE13 123 EC85
Leghorn Rd, NW10 81 CT68
SE18 105 ER78
Legion Cl, N1 83 DN65
Legion Ct, Mord. SM4 140 DA100
Legion Rd, Grnf. UB6 78 CC67
Legion Ter, E3
off Lefevre Wk 85 DZ67
Legion Way, N12 44 DE52
Legon Av, Rom. RM7 71 FC60
Legrace Av, Houns. TW4 96 BX82
Leicester Av, Mitch. CR4 141 DL98
Leicester Cl, Wor.Pk. KT4 157 CW105
Leicester Ct, WC2 195 N10
Leicester Gdns, Ilf. IG3 69 ES59
Leicester Ms, N2
off Leicester Rd 64 DE55
Leicester Pl, WC2 195 N10
Leicester Rd, E11 68 EH57
N2 64 DE55
Barnet EN5 28 DB43
Croydon CR0 142 DS101
Tilbury RM18 111 GF81
⊖ **Leicester Square** 195 N10
Leicester Sq, WC2 199 N1
Leicester St, WC2 195 N10
Leigh, The, Kings.T. KT2 118 CS93
Leigham Av, SW16 121 DL90
Leigham Cl, Wall. SM6
off Stafford Rd 159 DJ107
Leigham Ct Rd, SW16 121 DL89
Leigham Dr, Islw. TW7 97 CE80
Leigham Vale, SW2 121 DM90
SW16 121 DM90
Leigh Av, Ilf. IG4 68 EK56
Leigh Cl, Add. KT15 151 BF108
New Malden KT3 138 CR98
Leigh Cor, Cob. KT11
off Leigh Hill Rd 154 BW114
Leigh Ct, SE4
off Lewisham Way 103 EA82
Borehamwood WD6
off Banks Rd 26 CR40
Harrow HA2 61 CE60
Leigh Ct Cl, Cob. KT11 154 BW114
Leigh Cres, Croy. (New Adgtn)
CR0 161 EB108
Leigh Dr, Rom. RM3 52 FK49
Leigh Gdns, NW10 81 CW68
Leigh Hill Rd, Cob. KT11 154 BW114
Leigh Hunt Dr, N14 45 DK46
Leigh Hunt St, SE1 201 H4
Leigh Orchard Cl, SW16 121 DM90
Leigh Pk, Slou. (Datchet) SL3 92 AV80
Leigh Pl, EC1 196 D6
Cobham KT11 170 BW115
Dartford DA2
off Hawley Rd 128 FN92
Feltham TW13 116 BW88
Welling DA16 106 EU82
Leigh Pl La, Gdse. RH9 187 DY132
Leigh Rd, E6 87 EN65
E10 67 EC59
N5 65 DP63
Cobham KT11 153 BV113
Gravesend DA11 131 GH89
Hounslow TW3 97 CD84
Leigh Rodd, Wat. WD19 40 BZ48
Leigh St, WC1 195 P4
Leigh Ter, Orp. BR5
off Saxville Rd 146 EV97
Leighton Av, E12 69 EN64
Pinner HA5 60 BY55
Leighton Cl, Edg. HA8 42 CN54
Leighton Cres, NW5 65 DJ64
Leighton Gdns, NW10 81 CV68
South Croydon CR2 160 DV113
Tilbury RM18 111 GG80
Leighton Gro, NW5 65 DJ64
★ **Leighton Ho Mus**, W14 99 CZ76
Leighton Pl, NW5 65 DJ64
Leighton Rd, NW5 65 DK64
W13 97 CG75
Enfield EN1 30 DT43
Harrow (Har.Wld) HA3 41 CD54
Leighton St, Croy. CR0 141 DP102
Leighton Way, Epsom KT18 156 CR114
Leila Parnell Pl, SE7 104 EJ79
Leinster Av, SW14 98 CQ83
Leinster Gdns, W2 82 DC72
Leinster Ms, W2 82 DC73
Barnet EN5 *off Union St* 27 CY41
Leinster Pl, W2 82 DC72
Leinster Rd, N10 65 DH56
Leinster Sq, W2 82 DA72
Leinster Ter, W2 82 DC73
Leiston Spur, Slou. SL1 74 AS72
Leisure La, W.Byf. KT14 152 BH112
Leisure Way, N12 44 DD52
Leith Cl, NW9 62 CR60
Slough SL1 74 AU74
Leithcote Gdns, SW16 121 DM91
Leithcote Path, SW16 121 DM90
Leith Hill, Orp. BR5 146 EU95
Leith Hill Grn, Orp. BR5
off Leith Hill 146 EU95
Leith Pk Rd, Grav. DA12 131 GH88
Leith Rd, N22 45 DP53
Epsom KT17 156 CS112
Leith Yd, NW6 *off Quex Rd* 82 DA67
Lela Av, Houns. TW4 96 BW82
Lelitia Cl, E8
off Pownall Rd 84 DU67
Leman St, E1 84 DT72
Lemark Cl, Stan. HA7 41 CJ50
Le May Av, SE12 124 EH90
Lemmon Rd, SE10 104 EE79
Lemna Rd, E11 68 EE59
Lemonfield Dr, Wat. WD25 8 BY32
Lemon Gro, Felt. TW13 115 BU88
Lemonwell Ct, SE9
off Lemonwell Dr 125 EQ85
Lemonwell Dr, SE9 125 EQ85
Lemsford Cl, N15 66 DU57
Lemsford Ct, N4
off Brownswood Rd 66 DQ61
Borehamwood WD6 26 CQ42
Lemuel St, SW18 120 DB86
Lena Cres, N9 46 DW47
Lena Gdns, W6 99 CW76
Lena Kennedy Cl, E4 47 EB51
Lenanton Steps, E14 204 A4
Lendal Ter, SW4 101 DK83
Lenelby Rd, Surb. KT6 138 CN102
Len Freeman Pl, SW6
off John Smith Av 99 CZ80
Lenham Rd, SE12 104 EF84
Bexleyheath DA7 106 EZ79
Sutton SM1 158 DB105
Thornton Heath CR7 142 DR96
Lenmore Av, Grays RM17 110 GC76
Lennard Av, W.Wick. BR4 144 EE103
Lennard Cl, W.Wick. BR4 144 EE103
Lennard Rd, SE20 122 DW93
Beckenham BR3 123 DX93
Bromley BR2 145 EM102
Croydon CR0 142 DQ102
Sevenoaks (Dunt.Grn)
TN13 181 FE120
Lennard Row, S.Ock.
(Aveley) RM15 91 FR74
Lennon Rd, NW2 63 CW64
Lennox Av, Grav. DA11 131 GF86
Lennox Cl, Grays (Chaff.Hun.)
RM16 109 FW77
Romford RM1 71 FF58
Lennox Gdns, NW10 63 CT63
SW1 198 D7
Croydon CR0 159 DP105
Ilford IG1 69 EM60
Lennox Gdns Ms, SW1 198 D7
Lennox Rd, E17 67 DZ58
N4 65 DM61
Gravesend DA11 131 GF86
Lennox Rd E, Grav. DA11 131 GG87
Lenor Cl, Bexh. DA6 106 EY84
Lensbury Av, SW6
off The Boulevard 100 DC82
Lensbury Cl, Wal.Cr. (Chsht)
EN8 *off Ashdown Cres* 15 DY28
Lensbury Way, SE2 106 EW76
Lens Rd, E7 86 EJ66
Len Taylor Cl, Hayes UB4
off Derwent Dr 77 BS70
Lenthall Av, Grays RM17 110 GA75
Lenthall Ho, SW1
off Churchill Gdns 101 DJ78
Lenthall Rd, E8 84 DU66
Loughton IG10 33 ER42
Lenthorp Rd, SE10 205 K10
Lentmead Rd, Brom. BR1 124 EF90
Lenton Path, SE18 105 ER79
Lenton Ri, Rich. TW9
off Evelyn Ter 98 CL83
Lenton St, SE18 105 ER77
Leof Cres, SE6 123 EB92
Leominster Rd, Mord. SM4 140 DC100
Leominster Wk, Mord. SM4 140 DC100
Leonard Av, Mord. SM4 140 DC99
Romford RM7 71 FD60
Sevenoaks (Otford) TN14 181 FH116
Swanscombe DA10 130 FY87
Leonard Pl, N16 *off Allen Rd* 66 DS63
Leonard Rd, E4 47 EA51
E7 68 EG63
N9 46 DT48
SW16 141 DJ95
Southall UB2 96 BX76
Leonard Robbins Path, SE28
off Tawney Rd 88 EV73
Leonard St, E16 86 EL74
EC2 197 L4
Leonard Way, Brwd. CM14 54 FS49
Leontine Cl, SE15 102 DU80
Leopards Ct, EC1 196 D6
Leopold Av, SW19 119 CZ92
Leopold Ms, E9
off Fremont St 84 DW67
Leopold Rd, E17 67 EA57
N2 64 DD55
N18 46 DV50
NW10 80 CS66
SW19 119 CZ91
W5 80 CM74
Leopold St, E3 85 DZ71
Leopold Ter, SW19
off Dora Rd 120 DA92
Leo St, SE15 102 DV80
Leo Yd, EC1 196 G5
Le Personne Rd, Cat. CR3 176 DR122
Leppoc Rd, SW4 121 DK85
Leret Way, Lthd. KT22 171 CH121
Leroy St, SE1 201 M8
Lerry Cl, W14 *off Thaxton Rd* 99 CZ79
Lerwick Dr, Slou. SL1 74 AS71
Lescombe Cl, SE23 123 DY90
Lescombe Rd, SE23 123 DY90
Lesley Cl, Bex. DA5 127 FB87
Gravesend (Istead Rise)
DA13 131 GF94
Swanley BR8 147 FD97
Leslie Gdns, Sutt. SM2 158 DA108
Leslie Gro, Croy. CR0 142 DS102
Leslie Gro Pl, Croy. CR0
off Leslie Gro 142 DS102
Leslie Pk Rd, Croy. CR0 142 DS102
Leslie Rd, E11 67 EC63
E16 86 EH72
N2 64 DD55
Woking (Chobham) GU24 150 AS110
Leslie Smith Sq, SE18
off Nightingale Vale 105 EN79
★ **Lesnes Abbey (ruins)**,
Erith DA18 106 EX77
Lesney Fm Est, Erith DA8 107 FD80
Lesney Pk, Erith DA8 107 FD79
Lesney Pk Rd, Erith DA8 107 FD79
Lessar Av, SW4 121 DJ85
Lessingham Av, SW17 120 DF91
Ilford IG5 69 EN55
Lessing St, SE23 123 DY87
Lessington Av, Rom. RM7 71 FC58
Lessness Av, Bexh. DA7 106 EX80
LESSNESS HEATH, Belv. 107 FB78
Lessness Pk, Belv. DA17 106 EZ78
Lessness Rd, Belv. DA17
off Stapley Rd 106 FA78
Morden SM4 140 DC100
Lester Av, E15 86 EE69
Lestock Cl, SE25 142 DU97
Leston Cl, Rain. RM13 89 FG69
Leswin Pl, N16 *off Leswin Rd* 66 DT62
Leswin Rd, N16 66 DT62
Letchfield, Chesh. (Ley Hill)
HP5 4 AV31
Letchford Gdns, NW10 81 CU69
Letchford Ms, NW10
off Letchford Gdns 81 CU69
Letchford Ter, Har. HA3 40 CB53
LETCHMORE HEATH, Wat.
WD25 25 CD38
Letchmore Rd, Rad. WD7 25 CG36
Letchworth Av, Felt. TW14 115 BT87
Letchworth Cl, Brom. BR2 144 EG99
Watford WD19 40 BX50
Letchworth Dr, Brom. BR2 144 EG99
Letchworth St, SW17 120 DF91
Lethbridge Cl, SE13 103 EC81
Letter Box La, Sev. TN13 191 FJ129
Letterstone Rd, SW6
off Varna Rd 99 CZ80
Lettice St, SW6 99 CZ81
Lett Rd, E15 85 ED66
Lettsom St, SE5 102 DS82
Lettsom Wk, E13 86 EG68
Leucha Rd, E17 67 DY57
Levana Cl, SW19 119 CY88
Levehurst Way, SW4 101 DL82
Leven Cl, Wal.Cr. EN8 15 DX33
Watford WD19 40 BX50
Levendale Rd, SE23 123 DY89
Leven Dr, Wal.Cr. EN8 15 DX33
Leven Rd, E14 85 EC71
Leven Way, Hayes UB3 77 BS72
Leveret Cl, Croy. (New Adgtn)
CR0 161 ED111
Watford WD25 7 BU34
Leverett St, SW3 198 C8
Leverholme Gdns, SE9 125 EN90
Leverson St, SW16 121 DJ93
Lever Sq, Grays RM16 111 GG77
Lever St, EC1 196 G3
Leverton Pl, NW5
off Leverton St 65 DJ64
Leverton St, NW5 65 DJ64
Leverton Way, Wal.Abb. EN9 15 EC33
Leveson Rd, Grays RM16 111 GH76
Levett Gdns, Ilf. IG3 69 ET63
Levett Rd, Bark. IG11 87 ES65
Leatherhead KT22 171 CH120
Levine Gdns, Bark. IG11 88 EX68
Levison Way, N19
off Grovedale Rd 65 DK61
Lewes Cl, Grays RM17 110 GA79
Northolt UB5 78 CA65
Lewesdon Cl, SW19 119 CX88
Lewes Rd, N12 44 DE50
Bromley BR1 144 EK96
Romford RM3 52 FJ49
Leweston Pl, N16 66 DT59
Lewes Way, Rick. (Crox.Grn)
WD3 23 BQ42
Lewey Ho, E3 85 DZ70
Lewgars Av, NW9 62 CQ58
Lewin Rd, SW14 98 CR83
SW16 121 DK93
Bexleyheath DA6 106 EY84
Lewins Rd, Epsom KT18 156 CP114
Gerrards Cross (Chal.St.P.)
SL9 56 AX55
Lewis Av, E17 47 EA53
Lewis Cl, N14
off Orchid Rd 45 DJ45
Addlestone KT15 152 BJ105
Brentwood (Shenf.) CM15 55 FZ45
Uxbridge (Hare.) UB9 38 BJ54
Lewis Cres, NW10 62 CQ64
Lewis Gdns, N2 44 DD54
Lewis Gro, SE13 103 EC83
LEWISHAM, SE13 103 EB84
⇌ **Lewisham** 103 EC83
DLR **Lewisham** 103 EC83
Lewisham Cen, SE13 103 EC83
Lewisham High St, SE13 103 EC83
Lewisham Hill, SE13 103 EC82
Lewisham Pk, SE13 123 EB86
Lewisham Rd, SE13 103 EB81
Lewisham St, SW1 199 N5
Lewisham Way, SE4 103 DZ81
SE14 103 DZ81
Lewis La, Ger.Cr. (Chal.St.P.)
SL9 36 AY53
Lewis Pl, E8 66 DU64
Lewis Rd, Horn. RM11 72 FJ58
Mitcham CR4 140 DD96
Richmond TW10
off Red Lion St 117 CK85
Sidcup DA14 126 EW90
Southall UB1 96 BY75
Sutton SM1 158 DB105
Swanscombe DA10 130 FY86
Welling DA16 106 EW83
Lewis St, NW1 83 DH65
Lewiston Cl, Wor.Pk. KT4 139 CV101
Lewis Way, Dag. RM10 89 FB65
Lexden Dr, Rom. RM6 70 EV58
Lexden Rd, W3 80 CP73
Mitcham CR4 141 DK98
Lexham Ct, Grnf. UB6 79 CD67
Lexham Gdns, W8 100 DB76
Lexham Gdns Ms, W8 100 DB76
Lexham Ho, Bark. IG11
off St. Margarets 87 ER67
Lexham Ms, W8 100 DA77
Lexham Wk, W8
off Lexham Gdns 100 DB76
Lexington, The, EC1 197 K4
Lexington Bldg, E3
off Fairfield Rd 85 EA68
Lexington Cl, Borwd. WD6 26 CM41
Lexington Ct, Pur. CR8 160 DQ110
Lexington Pl, Kings.T. KT1 117 CK94
Lexington St, W1 195 L9
Lexington Way, Barn. EN5 27 CX42
Upminster RM14 73 FT58
Lexton Gdns, SW12 121 DK88
Leyborne Av, W13 97 CH75
Leyborne Pk, Rich. TW9 98 CN81
Leybourne Av, W.Byf.
(Byfleet) KT14 152 BM113
Leybourne Cl, Brom. BR2 144 EG100
West Byfleet (Byfleet) KT14
off Leybourne Av 152 BM113
Leybourne Rd, E11 68 EF60
NW1 83 DH66
NW9 62 CN57
Uxbridge UB10 77 BQ67
Leybourne St, NW1
off Hawley St 83 DH66
Leybridge Ct, SE12 124 EG85
Leyburn Cl, E17
off Church La 67 EB56
Leyburn Cres, Rom. RM3 52 FL52
Leyburn Gdns, Croy. CR0 142 DS103
Leyburn Gro, N18 46 DU51
Leyburn Rd, N18 46 DU51
Romford RM3 52 FL52
Leycroft Cl, Loug. IG10 33 EN43
Leycroft Gdns, Erith DA8 107 FH81
Leydenhatch La, Swan. BR8 147 FC95
Leyden St, E1 197 P7
Leydon Cl, SE16 203 J3
Leyfield, Wor.Pk. KT4 138 CS102
Leyhill Cl, Swan. BR8 147 FE99
Ley Hill Rd, Hem.H. (Bov.) HP3 4 AX30
Leyland Av, Enf. EN3 31 DY40
Leyland Cl, Wal.Cr. (Chsht)
EN8 14 DW28
Leyland Gdns, Wdf.Grn. IG8 48 EJ50
Leyland Rd, SE12 124 EG85
Leylands La, Stai. TW19 113 BF85
Leylang Rd, SE14 103 DX80
Leys, The, N2 64 DC56
Harrow HA3 62 CM58
Leys Av, Dag. RM10 89 FC66
Leys Cl, Dag. RM10 89 FC66
Harrow HA1 61 CD57
Uxbridge (Hare.) UB9 38 BK53
Leysdown Av, Bexh. DA7 107 FC84
Leysdown Rd, SE9 124 EL89
Leysfield Rd, W12 99 CU75
Leys Gdns, Barn. EN4 28 DG43
Leyspring Rd, E11 68 EF60
Leys Rd, Lthd. (Oxshott)
KT22 155 CD112
Leys Rd E, Enf. EN3 31 DY39
Leys Rd W, Enf. EN3 31 DY39
Ley St, Ilf. IG1, IG2 69 EP61
Leyswood Dr, Ilf. IG2 69 ES57
Leythe Rd, W3 98 CQ75
LEYTON, E11 67 EB60
⊖ **Leyton** 67 EC62
Leyton Business Cen, E10 67 EA61
Leyton Cross Rd, Dart. DA2 127 FF90
Leyton Gra, E10
off Goldsmith Rd 67 EB60
Leyton Gra Est, E10 67 EA60
Leyton Grn Rd, E10 67 EC58
Leyton Ind Village, E10 67 DX59
⇌ **Leyton Midland Road** 67 EC60
★ **Leyton Orient FC**, E10 67 EB62
Leyton Pk Rd, E10 67 EC62
Leyton Rd, E15 67 ED64
SW19 120 DC94
LEYTONSTONE, E11 67 ED59
⊖ **Leytonstone** 68 EE60
⇌ **Leytonstone High Road** 68 EE61
Leytonstone Rd, E15 68 EE64
Leywick St, E15 86 EE68
Lezayre Rd, Orp. BR6 163 ET107
Liardet St, SE14 103 DY79
Liberia Rd, N5 83 DP65
★ **Liberty**, W1 195 K9
Liberty 2 Shop Cen,
Rom. RM1 71 FF57
Liberty Av, SW19 140 DD95
Liberty Cl, N18 46 DT49
Liberty Hall Rd, Add. KT15 152 BG106
Liberty Ho, Cher. KT16
off Guildford St 133 BF102
Liberty La, Add. KT15 152 BG106
Liberty Ms, SW12 121 DH86
Liberty Ri, Add. KT15 152 BG107
Liberty Shop Cen, Rom. RM1 71 FE57
Liberty St, SW9 101 DM81
Libra Rd, E3 85 DZ67
E13 86 EG68
Library Hill, Brwd. CM14
off Coptfold Rd 54 FX47
Library Pl, E1 *off Cable St* 84 DV73
Library St, SE1 200 F5
Library Way, Twick. TW2
off Nelson Rd 116 CC87
Licenced Victuallers Nat Homes,
Uxb. (Denh.) UB9
off Denham Grn La 57 BF58
Lichfield Cl, Barn. EN4 28 DF41
Lichfield Ct, Rich. TW9
off Sheen Rd 98 CL84
Lichfield Gdns, Rich. TW9 98 CL84
Lichfield Gro, N3 44 DA53
Lichfield Rd, E3 85 DY69
E6 86 EK69
N9 *off Winchester Rd* 46 DU47
NW2 63 CY63
Dagenham RM8 70 EV63
Hounslow TW4 96 BW83
Northwood HA6 59 BU55
Richmond TW9 98 CM81
Woodford Green IG8 48 EE49
Lichfield Ter, Upmin. RM14 73 FS61
Lichfield Way, S.Croy. CR2 161 DX110
Lichlade Cl, Orp. BR6 163 ET105
Lickey Ho, W14
off North End Rd 99 CZ79
Lidbury Rd, NW7 43 CY51
Lidcote Gdns, SW9 101 DN82
Liddall Way, West Dr. UB7 76 BM74
Liddell Cl, Har. HA3 61 CK55
Liddell Gdns, NW10 81 CW68
Liddell Rd, NW6 82 DA65
Lidding Rd, Har. HA3 61 CK57
Liddington Rd, E15 86 EF67
Liddon Rd, E13 86 EH69
Bromley BR1 144 EJ97
Liden Cl, E17 *off Hitcham Rd* 67 DZ60
Lidfield Rd, N16 66 DR63
Lidgate Rd, SE15
off Chandler Way 102 DT80
Lidiard Rd, SW18 120 DC89
Lidlington Pl, NW1 195 K1
Lido Sq, N17 46 DR54
Lidstone Cl, Wok. GU21 166 AV117
Lidstone Ct, Slou. (Geo.Grn)
SL3 74 AX72
Lidyard Rd, N19 65 DJ60
Lieutenant Ellis Way, Wal.Cr.
EN7, EN8 14 DT31
★ **Lifetimes Mus**, Croy. CR0 142 DQ104
Liffler Rd, SE18 105 ES78
Liffords Pl, SW13 99 CT82
Lifford St, SW15 99 CX84
Lightcliffe Rd, N13 45 DN49
Lighter Cl, SE16 203 L8
Lighterman Ms, E1 85 DX72
Lighterman's Ms, Grav.
DA11 130 GE87
Lightermans Rd, E14 204 A5
Lightermans Way, Green.
DA9 109 FW84
Lightfoot Rd, N8 65 DL57
Lightley Cl, Wem. HA0
off Stanley Av 80 CM66
Lightswood Cl, Wal.Cr.
(Chsht) EN7 14 DR27
Ligonier St, E2 197 P4
Lilac Av, Enf. EN1 30 DW36
Woking GU22 166 AX120
Lilac Cl, E4 47 DZ51
Brentwood (Pilg.Hat.) CM15
off Magnolia Way 54 FV43
Waltham Cross (Chsht) EN7 14 DV31
Lilac Gdns, W5 97 CK76
Croydon CR0 143 EA104
Hayes UB3 77 BS72
Romford RM7 71 FE60
Swanley BR8 147 FD97
Lilac Ms, N8 *off Courcy Rd* 65 DN55
Lilac Pl, SE11 200 B9
West Drayton UB7
off Cedar Av 76 BM73
Lilac St, W12 81 CU73
Lilah Ms, Brom. BR2
off Beckenham La 144 EE96
Lila Pl, Swan. BR8 147 FE98
Lilburne Gdns, SE9 124 EL85
Lilburne Rd, SE9 124 EL85
Lilburne Wk, NW10 80 CQ65
Lile Cres, W7 79 CE71
Lilestone Est, NW8
off Fisherton St 82 DD70
Lilestone St, NW8 194 B4
Lilford Rd, SE5 101 DP82
Lilian Barker Cl, SE12 124 EG85
Lilian Board Way, Grnf. UB6 61 CD64
Lilian Cl, N16
off Barbauld Rd 66 DS62
Lilian Cres, Brwd. (Hutt.)
CM13 55 GC47
Lilian Gdns, Wdf.Grn. IG8 48 EH53
Lilian Rd, SW16 141 DJ95
Lillechurch Rd, Dag. RM8 88 EV65
Lilleshall Rd, Mord. SM4 140 DD100
Lilley Cl, E1 202 C3
Brentwood CM14 54 FT49
Lilley Dr, Tad. (Kgswd) KT20 174 DB122
Lilley La, NW7 42 CR50
Lillian Av, W3 98 CN75
Lillian Rd, SW13 99 CU79
Lillie Rd, SW6 99 CY80
Westerham (Bigg.H.) TN16 178 EK118
Lillieshall Rd, SW4 101 DH83
Lillie Yd, SW6 100 DA79
Lillington Ho, N7
off Harvist Est 65 DN63
Lillington Gdns Est, SW1 199 L9
Lilliots La, Lthd. KT22
off Kingston Rd 171 CG119
Lilliput Av, Nthlt. UB5 78 BZ67
Lilliput Rd, Rom. RM7 71 FD59
Lily Cl, W14 99 CY77
Lily Dr, West Dr. UB7 94 BK77
Lily Gdns, Wem. HA0 79 CJ68
Lily Pl, EC1 196 E6
Lily Rd, E17 67 EA58
Lilyville Rd, SW6 99 CZ81
Limbourne Av, Dag. RM8 70 EZ59
Limburg Rd, SW11 100 DF84
Lime Av, Brwd. CM13 55 FZ48
Gravesend (Nthflt) DA11 130 GD87
Upminster RM14 72 FN63
West Drayton UB7 76 BM73
Windsor SL4 92 AT80
Limeburner La, EC4 196 F9
Limebush Cl, Add. (New Haw)
KT15 152 BJ109

★ Place of interest ⇌ Railway station ⊖ London Underground station DLR Docklands Light Railway station Tra Tramlink station H Hospital Riv Pedestrian ferry landing stage

Lime Cl, E1 202 C2
Bromley BR1 144 EL98
Buckhurst Hill IG9 48 EK48
Carshalton SM5 140 DF103
Harrow HA3 41 CF54
Pinner HA5 59 BT55
Romford RM7 71 FC56
South Ockendon RM15 91 FW69
Watford WD19 40 BX45
Lime Ct, Mitch. CR4
off Lewis Rd 140 DD96
Lime Cres, Sun.TW16 136 BW96
Limecroft Cl, Epsom KT19 156 CR108
Limedene Cl, Pnr. HA5 40 BX53
Lime Gro, E4 47 DZ51
N20 43 CZ46
W12 99 CW75
Addlestone KT15 152 BG105
Hayes UB3 77 BR73
Ilford IG6 49 ET51
New Malden KT3 138 CR97
Orpington BR6 145 EP103
Ruislip HA4 59 BV59
Sidcup DA15 125 ET86
Twickenham TW1 117 CF86
Warlingham CR6 177 DY118
Woking GU22 166 AY121
Limeharbour, E14 204 C5
LIMEHOUSE, E14 85 DY73
⇌ Limehouse 85 DY72
DLR Limehouse 85 DY72
Limehouse Causeway, E14 85 DZ73
Limehouse Flds Est, E14 85 DY71
Limehouse Link, E14 203 N1
Limekiln Dr, SE7 104 EH79
Limekiln Pl, SE19 122 DT94
Lime Meadow Av, S.Croy.
CR2 160 DU113
Lime Pit La, Sev. (Dunt.Grn)
TN13 181 FC117
Limerick Cl, SW12 121 DJ87
Limerick Gdns, Upmin. RM14 73 FT59
Limerick Ms, N2
off Bedford Rd 64 DE55
Lime Rd, Epp. CM16 17 ET31
Richmond TW9
off St. Mary's Gro 98 CM84
Swanley BR8 147 FD97
Lime Row, Erith DA18
off Northwood Pl 106 EZ76
Limerston St, SW10 100 DC79
Limes, The, W2
off Linden Gdns 82 DA73
Brentwood CM13 55 FZ48
Bromley BR2 144 EL103
Hornchurch RM11 72 FK55
Purfleet RM19
off Tank Hill Rd 108 FN78
Woking (Horsell) GU21 166 AX115
Limes Av, E11 68 EH56
N12 44 DC49
NW7 42 CS51
NW11 63 CY59
SE20 122 DV94
SW13 99 CT82
Carshalton SM5 140 DF102
Chigwell IG7 49 ER51
Croydon CR0 141 DN104
Limes Av, The, N11 45 DH50
Limes Cl, Ashf. TW15 114 BN92
Limes Ct, Brwd. CM15
off Sawyers Hall La 54 FX46
Limesdale Gdns, Edg. HA8 42 CQ54
Limes Fld Rd, SW14
off White Hart La 98 CS83
Limesford Rd, SE15 103 DX84
Limes Gdns, SW18 120 DA86
Limes Gro, SE13 103 EC84
Limes Pl, Croy. CR0 142 DR101
Limes Rd, Beck. BR3 143 EB96
Croydon CR0 142 DR100
Egham TW20 113 AZ92
Waltham Cross (Chsht) EN8 15 DX32
Weybridge KT13 152 BN105
Limes Row, Orp. BR6 163 EP106
Limestone Wk, Erith DA18 106 EX76
Lime St, E17 67 DY56
EC3 197 M10
Lime St Pas, EC3 197 M9
Limes Wk, SE15 102 DV84
W5 off Chestnut Gro 97 CK75
Lime Ter, W7 off Manor Ct Rd 79 CE73
Lime Tree Av, Esher KT10 137 CD102
Greenhithe (Bluewater)
DA9 129 FU88
Thames Ditton KT7 137 CD102
Lime Tree Cl, E18
off Ashbourne Av 68 EJ56
Limetree Cl, SW2 121 DM88
Lime Tree Cl, Lthd. (Bkhm)
KT23 170 CA124
Lime Tree Ct, St.Alb. (Lon.Col.)
AL2 9 CH26
Leatherhead KT22 171 CJ121
Lime Tree Gro, Croy. CR0 143 DZ104
Lime Tree Pl, Mitch. CR4 141 DH95
Lime Tree Rd, Houns. TW5 96 CB81
Limetree Ter, Well. DA16
off Hook La 106 EU83
Limetree Wk, SW17
off Church La 120 DG92
Lime Tree Wk, Amer. HP7 20 AT39
Bushey (Bushey Hth) WD23 41 CE46
Enfield EN2 30 DQ38
Rickmansworth WD3 22 BH43
Sevenoaks TN13 191 FH125
Virginia Water GU25 132 AY98
West Wickham BR4 162 EF105
Lime Wk, E15 off Church St N 86 EE67
Uxbridge (Denh.) UB9 58 BJ64
Limewood Cl, E17 67 DZ56
W13 off St. Stephens Rd 79 CH72
Beckenham BR3 143 EC99
Limewood Ct, Ilf. IG4 69 EM57
Limewood Rd, Erith DA8 107 FC80
Lime Wks Rd, Red. (Merst.)
RH1 185 DJ126
LIMPSFIELD, Oxt. RH8 188 EG128
Limpsfield Av, SW19 119 CX89
Thornton Heath CR7 141 DM99
LIMPSFIELD CHART, Oxt.
RH8 188 EL130
Limpsfield Rd, S.Croy. CR2 160 DU112
Warlingham CR6 176 DW116
Linacre Cl, SE15 102 DV83
Linacre Ct, W6 99 CX78
Linacre Rd, NW2 81 CV65
Linberry Wk, SE8 203 M9
Linchfield Rd, Slou.
(Datchet) SL3 92 AW81
Linchmere Rd, SE12 124 EF87
Lincoln Av, N14 45 DJ48
SW19 119 CX90
Romford RM7 71 FD60
Twickenham TW2 116 CB89
Lincoln Cl, SE25
off Woodside Grn 142 DV100
Erith DA8 107 FF82
Greenford UB6 78 CC67
Harrow HA2 60 BZ57
Hornchurch RM11 72 FN57
Lincoln Ct, N16 66 DR59
Borehamwood WD6 26 CR43
Lincoln Cres, Enf. EN1 30 DS43
Lincoln Dr, Rick. (Crox.Grn)
WD3 23 BP42
Watford WD19 40 BW48
Woking GU22 167 BE115
Lincoln Gdns, Ilf. IG1 68 EL59
Lincoln Grn Rd, Orp. BR5 145 ET99
Lincoln Ms, NW6
off Willesden La 81 CZ67
SE21 122 DR88
Lincoln Pk, Amer. HP7 20 AS39
Lincoln Rd, E7 86 EK65
E13 86 EH70
E18 off Grove Rd 48 EG53
N2 64 DE55
SE25 142 DV97
Enfield EN1, EN3 30 DU43
Erith DA8 107 FF82
Feltham TW13 116 BZ90
Gerrards Cross (Chal.St.P.)
SL9 36 AY53
Harrow HA2 60 BZ57
Mitcham CR4 141 DL99
New Malden KT3 138 CQ97
Northwood HA6 59 BT55
Sidcup DA14 126 EV92
Wembley HA0 79 CK65
Worcester Park KT4 139 CV102
Lincolns, The, NW7 43 CT48
Lincolns Flds, Epp. CM16 17 ET29
Lincolnshott, Grav. (Sthflt)
DA13 130 GB92
★ Lincoln's Inn, WC2 196 C8
Lincoln's Inn Flds, WC2 196 B8
Lincoln St, E11 68 EE61
SW3 198 D9
Lincoln Wk, Epsom KT19 156 CR110
Lincoln Way, Enf. EN1 30 DV43
Rickmansworth (Crox.Grn)
WD3 23 BP42
Sunbury-on-Thames TW16 135 BS95
Lincombe Rd, Brom. BR1 124 EF90
Lindal Cres, Enf. EN2 29 DL42
Lindale Cl, Vir.W. GU25 132 AT98
Lindales, The, N17
off Brantwood Rd 46 DT51
Lindal Rd, SE4 123 DZ85
Lindbergh Rd, Wall. SM6 159 DL109
Linden Av, NW10 81 CX68
Coulsdon CR5 175 DH116
Dartford DA1 128 FJ88
Enfield EN1 30 DU39
Hounslow TW3 116 CB85
Ruislip HA4 59 BU60
Thornton Heath CR7 141 DP98
Watford WD18 23 BS42
Wembley HA9 62 CM64
Linden Chase Rd, Sev. TN13 191 FH122
Linden Cl, N14 29 DJ44
Addlestone (New Haw)
KT15 152 BG111
Orpington BR6 164 EU106
Purfleet RM19 108 FQ79
Ruislip HA4 59 BU60
Stanmore HA7 41 CH50
Tadworth KT20 173 CX120
Thames Ditton KT7 137 CF101
Waltham Cross EN7 14 DV30
Linden Ct, W12 81 CW74
Egham (Eng.Grn) TW20 112 AV93
Leatherhead KT22 171 CH121
Linden Cres, Grnf. UB6 79 CF65
Kingston upon Thames
KT1 138 CM96
Woodford Green IG8 48 EH51
Linden Dr, Cat. (Chaldon)
CR3 176 DQ124
Gerrards Cross (Chal.St.P.)
SL9 off Woodside Hill 36 AY54
Lindenfield, Chis. BR7 145 EP96
Linden Gdns, W2 82 DA73
W4 98 CR78
Enfield EN1 30 DU39
Leatherhead KT22 171 CJ121
Linden Gro, SE15 102 DV83
SE26 122 DW93
New Malden KT3 138 CS97
Teddington TW11
off Waldegrave Rd 117 CF92
Walton-on-Thames KT12 135 BT103
Warlingham CR6 177 DY118
Linden Ho, Slou. SL3 93 BB78
Linden Lawns, Wem. HA9 62 CM63
Linden Lea, N2 64 DC57
Watford WD25 7 BU33
Linden Leas, W.Wick. BR4 143 ED103
Linden Ms, N1 66 DR64
W2 off Linden Gdns 82 DA73
Linden Pas, W4
off Linden Gdns 98 CR78
Linden Pit Path, Lthd. KT22 171 CH121
Linden Pl, Epsom KT17
off East St 156 CS112
Mitcham CR4 140 DE98
Linden Ri, Brwd. CM14 54 FX50
Linden Rd, E17 off High St 67 DZ57
N10 65 DH56
N11 44 DF47
N15 66 DQ56
Hampton TW12 116 CA94
Leatherhead KT22 171 CH121
Weybridge KT13 153 BQ109
Lindens, The, N12 44 DD50
W4 98 CQ81
Lindens, The, Croy. (New Adgtn)
CR0 161 EC107
Loughton IG10 33 EM43
Linden Sq, Sev. TN13
off London Rd 190 FE122
Uxbridge (Hare.) UB9 38 BG51
Linden St, Rom. RM7 71 FD56
Linden Wk, N19
off Hargrave Pk 65 DJ61
Linden Way, N14 29 DJ44
Purley CR8 159 DJ110
Shepperton TW17 135 BQ99
Woking GU22 167 AZ121
Woking (Ripley) GU23 167 BF124
Lindeth Cl, Stan. HA7 41 CH51
Lindfield Gdns, NW3 64 DB64
Lindfield Rd, W5 79 CJ70
Croydon CR0 142 DT100
Romford RM3 52 FL50
Lindfield St, E14 85 EA72
Lindhill Cl, Enf. EN3 31 DX39
Lindisfarne Cl, Grav. DA12
off St. Benedict's Av 131 GL89
Lindisfarne Rd, SW20 119 CU94
Dagenham RM8 70 EW62
Lindisfarne Way, E9 67 DY63
Lindley Est, SE15
off Bird in Bush Rd 102 DU80
Lindley Pl, Rich. (Kew) TW9 98 CN81
Lindley Rd, E10 67 EB61
Godstone RH9 186 DW130
Walton-on-Thames KT12 136 BX104
Lindley St, E1 84 DW71
Lindore Rd, SW11 100 DF84
Lindores Rd, Cars. SM5 140 DC101
Lindo St, SE15 off Selden Rd 102 DW82
Lind Rd, Sutt. SM1 158 DC106
Lindrop St, SW6 100 DC82
Lindsay Cl, Chess. KT9 156 CL108
Epsom KT19 156 CQ113
Staines (Stanw.) TW19 114 BK85
Lindsay Ct, SW11
off Battersea High St 100 DD81
Lindsay Dr, Har. HA3 62 CL58
Shepperton TW17 135 BR100
Lindsay Pl, Wal.Cr. EN7 14 DV30
Lindsay Rd, Add. (New Haw)
KT15 152 BG110
Hampton (Hmptn H.) TW12 116 CB91
Worcester Park KT4 139 CV103
Lindsay Sq, SW1 199 N10
Lindsell St, SE10 103 EC81
Lindsey Cl, Brwd. CM14 54 FU49
Bromley BR1 144 EK97
Mitcham CR4 141 DL98
Lindsey Gdns, Felt. TW14 115 BR87
Lindsey Ms, N1 84 DQ66
Lindsey Rd, Dag. RM8 70 EW63
Uxbridge (Denh.) UB9 58 BG62
Lindsey St, EC1 196 G6
Epping CM16 17 ER28
Lindsey Way, Horn. RM11 72 FJ57
Lind St, SE8 103 EB82
Lindum Rd, Tedd. TW11 117 CJ94
Lindvale, Wok. GU21 166 AY115
Lindway, SE27 121 DP92
Lindwood Cl, E6
off Northumberland Rd 86 EL71
Linfield Cl, NW4 63 CW55
Walton-on-Thames KT12 153 BV106
Linfields, Amer. HP7 20 AW40
LINFORD, S.le H. SS17 111 GM75
Linford Rd, E17 67 EC55
Grays RM16 111 GH78
Tilbury (W.Til.) RM18 111 GJ77
Linford St, SW8 101 DJ81
Lingards Rd, SE13 103 EC84
Lingey Cl, Sid. DA15 125 ET89
Lingfield Av, Dart. DA2 128 FP87
Kingston upon Thames
KT1 138 CL98
Upminster RM14 72 FM62
Lingfield Cl, Enf. EN1 30 DS44
Northwood HA6 39 BS52
Lingfield Cres, SE9 105 ER84
Lingfield Gdns, N9 46 DV45
Coulsdon CR5 175 DP119
Lingfield Rd, SW19 119 CX92
Gravesend DA12 131 GH89
Worcester Park KT4 139 CW104
Lingfield Way, Wat. WD17 23 BT38
Lingham St, SW9 101 DL82
Lingholm Way, Barn. EN5 27 CX43
Lingmere Cl, Chig. IG7 49 EQ47
Lingmoor Dr, Wat. WD25 8 BW33
Ling Rd, E16 86 EG71
Erith DA8 107 FC79
Lingrove Gdns, Buck.H. IG9
off Beech La 48 EH47
Lings Coppice, SE21 122 DR89
Lingwell Rd, SW17 120 DE90
Lingwood Gdns, Islw. TW7 97 CE80
Lingwood Rd, E5 66 DU59
Linhope St, NW1 194 D4
Linington Av, Chesh. HP5 4 AU30
Link, The, SE9 125 EN90
W3 80 CP72
Enfield EN3 31 DY39
Northolt UB5
off Eastcote La 60 BZ64
Pinner HA5 60 BW59
Slough SL2 74 AV72
Wembley HA0
off Nathans Rd 61 CJ60
Link Av, Wok. GU22 167 BD115
Link Cen, The, Dag. RM10
off Heathway 88 FA65
Linkfield, Brom. BR2 144 EG100
West Molesey KT8 136 CA97
Linkfield Cor, Red. RH1
off Hatchlands Rd 184 DE133
Linkfield Gdns, Red. RH1
off Hatchlands Rd 184 DE134
Linkfield La, Red. RH1 184 DE133
Linkfield Rd, Islw. TW7 97 CF82
Linkfield St, Red. RH1 184 DE134
Link La, Wall. SM6 159 DK107
Linklea Cl, NW9 42 CS52
Link Rd, N11 44 DG49
Addlestone KT15
off Weybridge Rd 152 BL105
Dagenham RM9 89 FB68
Feltham TW14 115 BT87
Link Rd, Rick. (Chenies) WD3 21 BA37
Slough (Datchet) SL3 92 AW80
Wallington SM6 140 DG102
Watford WD24 24 BX40
Links, The, E17 67 DY56
Waltham Cross (Chsht) EN8 15 DX26
Walton-on-Thames KT12 135 BU103
Links Av, Mord. SM4 140 DA98
Romford RM2 51 FH54
Links Brow, Lthd. (Fetch.)
KT22 171 CE124
Links Cl, Ashtd. KT21 171 CJ117
Linkscroft Av, Ashf. TW15 115 BP93
Links Dr, N20 44 DA46
Borehamwood (Els.) WD6 26 CM41
Radlett WD7 9 CF33
Links Gdns, SW16 121 DN94
Links Grn Way, Cob. KT11 154 CA114
Linkside, N12 43 CZ51
Chigwell IG7 49 EQ50
New Malden KT3 138 CS96
Linkside Cl, Enf. EN2 29 DM41
Linkside Gdns, Enf. EN2 29 DM41
Links Pl, Ashtd. KT21 171 CK117
Links Rd, NW2 63 CT61
SW17 120 DF93
W3 80 CN72
Ashford TW15 114 BL92
Ashtead KT21 171 CJ118
Epsom KT17 157 CU113
West Wickham BR4 143 EC102
Woodford Green IG8 48 EG50
Links Side, Enf. EN2 29 DN41
Link St, E9 84 DW65
Links Vw, N3 43 CZ52
Dartford DA1 128 FJ88
Links Vw Av, Bet. (Brock.)
RH3 182 CN134
Links Vw Cl, Stan. HA7 41 CG51
Links Vw Rd, Croy. CR0 143 EA104
Hampton (Hmptn H.) TW12 116 CC92
Linksway, NW4 43 CX54
Links Way, Beck. BR3 143 EA100
Linksway, Nthwd. HA6 39 BQ53
Links Way, Rick. (Crox.Grn)
WD3 23 BQ41
Links Yd, E1 off Spelman St 84 DU71
Linkway, N4 66 DQ59
SW20 139 CV97
Link Way, Brom. BR2 144 EL101
Linkway, Dag. RM8 70 EW63
Link Way, Horn. RM11 72 FL60
Pinner HA5 40 BX53
Linkway, Rich. TW10 117 CH89
Link Way, Stai. TW18 114 BH93
Uxbridge (Denh.) UB9 58 BG58
Linkway, Wok. GU22 167 BC117
Linkway, The, Barn. EN5 28 DB44
Sutton SM2 158 DC109
Link Way Rd, Brwd. CM14 54 FT48
Linkwood Wk, NW1
off Maiden La 83 DK66
Linley Cres, Rom. RM7 71 FB55
Linley Rd, N17 46 DS54
★ Linley Sambourne Ho,
W8 100 DA75
Linnell Cl, NW11 64 DB58
Linnell Dr, NW11 64 DB58
Linnell Rd, N18
off Fairfield Rd 46 DU50
SE5 102 DS82
Linnet Cl, N9 47 DX46
SE28 88 EW73
Bushey WD23 40 CC45
South Croydon CR2 161 DX110
Linnet Ms, SW12 120 DG87
Linnet Rd, Abb.L. WD5 7 BU31
Linnett Cl, E4 47 EC49
Linnet Ter, Ilf. IG5
off Tiptree Cres 69 EN55
Linnet Way, Purf. RM19 108 FP78
Linom Rd, SW4 101 DL84
Linscott Rd, E5 66 DW63
Linsdell Rd, Bark. IG11 87 EQ67
Linsey St, SE16 202 B8
Linslade Cl, Houns. TW4
off Heathlands Way 116 BY85
Pinner HA5 59 BV55
Linslade Rd, Orp. BR6 164 EU107
Linstead St, NW6 82 DA66
Linstead Way, SW18 119 CY87
Linsted Ct, SE9 125 ES86
Linster Gro, Borwd. WD6 26 CQ43
Lintaine Cl, W6
off Moylan Rd 99 CY79
Linthorpe Av, Wem. HA0 79 CJ65
Linthorpe Rd, N16 66 DS59
Barnet EN4 28 DE41
Linton Av, Borwd. WD6 26 CM39
Linton Cl, Mitch. CR4 140 DF101
Welling DA16
off Anthony Rd 106 EV81
Linton Gdns, E6 86 EL72
Linton Glade, Croy. CR0 161 DY109
Linton Gro, SE27 121 DP92
Linton Rd, Bark. IG11 87 EQ66
Lintons, The, Bark. IG11 87 EQ66
Lintons La, Epsom KT17 156 CS112
Linton St, N1 84 DQ67
Lintott Ct, Stai. (Stanw.)
TW19 114 BK86
Linver Rd, SW6 100 DA82
Linwood Cl, SE5 102 DT82
Linwood Cres, Enf. EN1 30 DU39
Linzee Rd, N8 65 DL56
Lion Av, Twick. TW1
off Lion Rd 117 CF88
Lion Cl, SE4 123 EA86
Shepperton TW17 134 BL97
Lion Ct, Borwd. WD6 26 CQ39
Lionel Gdns, SE9 124 EK85
Lionel Ms, W10
off Telford Rd 81 CY71
Lionel Oxley Ho, Grays
RM17 off New Rd 110 GB79
Lionel Rd, SE9 124 EK85
Lionel Rd N, Brent. TW8 98 CL77
Lionel Rd S, Brent. TW8 98 CM78
Lion Gate Gdns, Rich. TW9 98 CM83
Lion Gate Ms, SW18
off Merton Rd 120 DA87
Lion Grn Rd, Couls. CR5 175 DK115
Lion La, Red. RH1 184 DF133
Lion Pk Av, Chess. KT9 156 CN105
Lion Plaza, EC2
off Threadneedle St 84 DR72
Lion Rd, E6 87 EM71
N9 46 DU47
Bexleyheath DA6 106 EZ84
Croydon CR0 142 DQ99
Twickenham TW1 117 CF88
Lions Cl, SE9 124 EJ90
Lion Way, Brent. TW8 97 CK80
Lion Wf Rd, Islw. TW7 97 CH83
Lion Yd, SW4
off Tremadoc Rd 101 DK84
Liphook Cl, Horn. RM12
off Petworth Way 71 FF63
Liphook Cres, SE23 122 DW87
Liphook Rd, Wat. WD19 40 BX49
Lippitts Hill, Loug. (High Beach)
IG10 32 EE39
Lipsham Cl, Bans. SM7 158 DD113
Lipton Cl, SE28
off Aisher Rd 88 EW73
Lipton Rd, E1 off Bower St 85 DX72
Lisbon Av, Twick. TW2 116 CC89
Lisbon Cl, E17 47 DZ54
Lisburne Rd, NW3 64 DF63
Lisford St, SE15 102 DT81
Lisgar Ter, W14 99 CZ77
Liskeard Cl, Chis. BR7 125 EQ93
Liskeard Gdns, SE3 104 EG81
Liskeard Lo, Cat. CR3 186 DU126
Lisle Cl, SW17 121 DH91
Lisle Pl, Grays RM17 110 GA76
Lisle St, WC2 195 N10
Lismore Circ, NW5 64 DG64
Lismore Cl, Islw. TW7 97 CG82
Lismore Pk, Slou. SL2 74 AT72
Lismore Rd, N17 66 DR55
South Croydon CR2 160 DS107
Lismore Wk, N1
off Clephane Rd 84 DQ65
Lissant Cl, Surb. KT6 137 CK101
Lissenden Gdns, NW5 64 DG63
Lissoms Rd, Couls. (Chipstead)
CR5 174 DG118
Lisson Grn Est, NW8 194 B3
LISSON GROVE, NW8 194 A5
Lisson Gro, NW1 194 B4
NW8 194 A3
Lisson St, NW1 194 B6
Lister Av, Rom. RM3 52 FK54
Lister Cl, W3 80 CR71
Mitcham CR4 140 DE95
Lister Ct, NW9
off Pasteur Cl 42 CS54
Lister Gdns, N18 46 DQ50
H Lister Hosp, The, SW1 101 DH78
Lister Ho, SE3 104 EE79
Lister Rd, E11 68 EE60
Tilbury RM18 111 GG82
Lister Wk, SE28
off Haldane Rd 88 EX73
Liston Rd, N17 46 DU53
SW4 101 DJ83
Liston Way, Wdf.Grn. IG8
off Navestock Cres 48 EJ52
Listowel Cl, SW9
off Mandela St 101 DN80
Listowel Rd, Dag. RM10 70 FA62
Listria Pk, N16 66 DS61
Litchfield Av, E15 86 EE65
Morden SM4 139 CZ101
Litchfield Gdns, NW10 81 CU65
Cobham KT11
off Between Sts 153 BU114
Litchfield Rd, Sutt. SM1 158 DC105
Litchfield St, WC2 195 N10
Litchfield Way, NW11 64 DB57
Lithos Rd, NW3 82 DB65
Little Acre, Beck. BR3 143 EA97
Little Albany St, NW1 195 J4
Little Argyll St, W1 195 K9
Little Aston Rd, Rom. RM3 52 FM52
Little Belhus Cl, S.Ock. RM15 91 FU70
Little Benty, West Dr. UB7 94 BK78
Little Birch Cl, Add. (New Haw)
KT15 152 BK109
Little Birches, Sid. DA15 125 ES89
Little Boltons, The, SW5 100 DB78
SW10 100 DB78
Little Bookham Common,
Lthd. (Bkhm) KT23 170 BY122
Little Bookham St, Lthd.
(Bkhm) KT23 170 BZ124
Little Bornes, SE21 122 DS91
Little Britain, EC1 197 H8
Littlebrook Cl, Croy. CR0 143 DX100
Littlebrook Gdns, Wal.Cr.
(Chsht) EN8 14 DW30
Littlebrook Manor Way, Dart.
DA1 128 FN85
Little Brownings, SE23 122 DV89
Littlebury Rd, SW4 101 DK83
Little Bury St, N9 46 DR46
Little Bushey La, Bushey
WD23 25 CD44
Little Bushey La Footpath,
Bushey WD23
off Little Bushey La 41 CD45
Little Cedars, N12
off Woodside Av 44 DC49
LITTLE CHALFONT, Amer.
HP7 20 AW40
LITTLE CHALFONT, Ch.St.G.
HP8 20 AW40
Little Chester St, SW1 198 G6
Little Cloisters, SW1
off Tufton St 101 DK76
Little Coll La, EC4
off Upper Thames St 84 DR73
Little Coll St, SW1 199 P6
Littlecombe, SE7 104 EH79
Littlecombe Cl, SW15 119 CX86
Little Common, Stan. HA7 41 CG48
Little Common La, Red.
(Bletch.) RH1 185 DP132
Littlecote Cl, SW19 119 CX87

★ Place of interest ⇌ Railway station ⊖ London Underground station DLR Docklands Light Railway station Tra Tramlink station H Hospital Riv Pedestrian ferry landing stage

Littlecote Pl, Pnr. HA5 40 BY53
Little Ct, W.Wick. BR4 144 EE103
Littlecourt Rd, Sev. TN13 190 FG124
Littlecroft, SE9 105 EN83
Gravesend (Istead Rise) DA13 130 GE94
Littlecroft Rd, Egh. TW20 113 AZ92
Littledale, SE2 106 EU79
Dartford DA2 128 FQ90
Little Dean's Yd, SW1 199 P6
Little Dimocks, SW12 121 DH89
Little Dormers, Ger.Cr. SL9 57 AZ56
Little Dorrit Ct, SE1 201 J4
Littledown Rd, Slou. SL1 74 AT74
Little Dragons, Loug. IG10 32 EK42
LITTLE EALING, W5 97 CJ77
Little Ealing La, W5 97 CJ77
Little E Fld, Couls. CR5 off Blue Leaves Av 175 DK121
Little Edward St, NW1 195 J2
Little Elms, Hayes UB3 95 BR80
Little Essex St, WC2 196 D10
Little Ferry Rd, Twick. TW1 off Ferry Rd 117 CH88
Littlefield Cl, N19 off Tufnell Pk Rd 65 DJ63
Kingston upon Thames KT1 off Fairfield W 138 CL96
Littlefield Rd, Edg. HA8 42 CQ52
Little Friday Rd, E4 48 EE47
Little Gaynes Gdns, Upmin. RM14 72 FP63
Little Gaynes La, Upmin. RM14 72 FM63
Little Geaires, Ilf. IG6 69 EP56
Little George St, SW1 199 P5
Little Gerpins La, Upmin. RM14 90 FM67
Little Gra, Grnf. UB6 off Perivale La 79 CG69
Little Graylings, Abb.L. WD5 7 BS33
Little Grn, Rich. TW9 97 CK84
Little Grn La, Cher. KT16 133 BE104
Rickmansworth (Crox.Grn) WD3 23 BP41
Little Grn St, NW5 off College La 65 DH63
Little Gregories La, Epp. (They.B.) CM16 33 ER35
Littlegrove, Barn. EN4 28 DE44
Little Gro, Bushey WD23 24 CB42
Little Gro Av, Wal.Cr. (Chsht) EN7 14 DS27
Little Halliards, Walt. KT12 off Felix Rd 135 BU100
Little Hayes, Kings L. WD4 6 BN29
Little Heath, SE7 104 EL79
Romford (Chad.Hth) RM6 70 EV56
Littleheath La, Cob. KT11 154 CA114
Little Heath La, Wok. (Chobham) GU24 150 AS109
Little Heath Rd, Bexh. DA7 106 EZ81
Littleheath Rd, S.Croy. CR2 160 DV108
Little Heath Rd, Wok. (Chobham) GU24 150 AS109
H Little Highwood Hosp, Brwd. CM15 54 FV45
Little Hill, Rick. (Herons.) WD3 21 BC44
★ Little Holland Ho, Cars. SM5 158 DE108
Little How Cft, Abb.L. WD5 7 BQ31
LITTLE ILFORD, E12 68 EL64
Little Ilford La, E12 69 EM63
Littlejohn Rd, W7 79 CF72
Orpington BR5 146 EU100
Little Julians Hill, Sev. TN13 190 FG128
Little London Cl, Uxb. UB8 77 BP71
Little Marlborough St, W1 195 K9
Little Martins, Bushey WD23 24 CB43
Littlemead, Esher KT10 155 CD105
Little Mead, Wok. GU21 166 AT116
Littlemede, SE9 125 EM90
Littlemoor Rd, Ilf. IG1 69 ER62
Littlemore Rd, SE2 106 EU75
Little Moreton Cl, W.Byf. KT14 152 BH112
Little Moss La, Pnr. HA5 40 BY54
Little Newport St, WC2 195 N10
Little New St, EC4 196 E8
Little Oaks Cl, Shep. TW17 134 BM98
Little Orchard, Add. (Wdhm) KT15 151 BF111
Woking GU21 151 BA114
Little Orchard Cl, Abb.L. WD5 7 BR32
Pinner HA5 off Barrow Pt La 40 BY54
Little Oxhey La, Wat. WD19 40 BX50
Little Pk, Hem.H. (Bov.) HP3 5 BA28
Little Pk Dr, Felt. TW13 116 BX89
Little Pk Gdns, Enf. EN2 30 DQ41
Little Pipers Cl, Wal.Cr. (Chsht) EN7 13 DP29
Little Plucketts Way, Buck.H. IG9 48 EJ46
Little Portland St, W1 195 K8
Littleport Spur, Slou. SL1 74 AS72
Little Potters, Bushey WD23 41 CD45
Little Queens Rd, Tedd. TW11 117 CF93
Little Queen St, Dart. DA1 128 FM87
Little Redlands, Brom. BR1 144 EL96
Little Reeves Av, Amer. HP7 20 AT39
Little Riding, Wok. GU22 167 BB116
Little Rd, Croy. CR0 off Lower Addiscombe Rd 142 DS102
Hayes UB3 95 BT75
Little Roke Av, Ken. CR8 159 DP114
Little Roke Rd, Ken. CR8 160 DQ114
Littlers Cl, SW19 off Runnymede 140 DD95
Little Russell St, WC1 195 P7
Little Russets, Brwd. (Hutt.) CM13 off Hutton Village 55 GE45
Little St. James's St, SW1 199 K3
Little St. Leonards, SW14 98 CQ83
Little Sanctuary, SW1 199 N5
Little Smith St, SW1 199 N6
Little Somerset St, E1 197 P9
Littlestock Rd, Wal.Cr. (Chsht) EN7 14 DR26
Littlestone Cl, Beck. BR3 off Abbey La 123 EA93
Little Strand, NW9 43 CT54
Little Stream Cl, Nthwd. HA6 39 BS50
Little St, Wal.Abb. EN9 off Greenwich Way 31 EC36
Little Sutton La, Slou. SL3 93 BC78
Little Thrift, Orp. BR5 145 EQ98
LITTLE THURROCK, Grays RM17 110 GD76
Little Titchfield St, W1 195 K7
LITTLETON, Shep. TW17 135 BP97
Littleton Av, E4 48 EF46
Littleton Cres, Har. HA1 61 CF61
Littleton Ho, SW1 off Lupus St 101 DJ78
Littleton La, Shep. TW17 134 BK101
Littleton Rd, Ashf. TW15 115 BQ94
Harrow HA1 61 CF61
Littleton St, SW18 120 DC89
Little Trinity La, EC4 197 J10
Little Turnstile, WC1 196 B8
★ Little Venice (Waterbuses), W2 82 DC71
Littlewick Common, Wok. (Knap.) GU21 166 AS115
Littlewick Rd, Wok. GU21 150 AW114
Little Windmill Hill, Kings L. (Chipper.) WD4 5 BE32
Littlewood, SE13 123 EC85
Sevenoaks TN13 191 FJ122
Littlewood Cl, W13 97 CH76
Little Wd Cl, Orp. BR5 146 EU95
LITTLE WOODCOTE, Cars. SM5 158 DG111
Little Woodcote Est, Cars. SM5 off Woodmansterne La 158 DG111
Wallington SM6 off Woodmansterne La 158 DG111
Little Woodcote La, Cars. SM5 159 DH112
Purley CR8 159 DH112
Wallington SM6 159 DH112
Littleworth Av, Esher KT10 155 CD106
Littleworth Common Rd, Esher KT10 137 CD104
Littleworth La, Esher KT10 155 CD105
Littleworth Pl, Esher KT10 155 CD105
Littleworth Rd, Esher KT10 155 CE105
Livermere Rd, E8 84 DT67
Liverpool Gro, SE17 102 DR78
Liverpool Rd, E10 67 EC58
E16 86 EE71
N1 83 DN68
N7 65 DN64
W5 97 CK75
Kingston upon Thames KT2 118 CN94
Thornton Heath CR7 142 DQ97
Watford WD18 23 BV43
⇌ Liverpool Street 197 M7
⊖ Liverpool Street 197 M7
Liverpool St, EC2 197 M7
Livesey Cl, Kings.T. KT1 138 CM97
★ Livesey Mus for Children, SE15 102 DV79
Livesey Pl, SE15 off Peckham Pk Rd 102 DU79
Livingstone Ct, E10 off Matlock Rd 67 EC58
Barnet EN5 off Christchurch La 27 CY40
Livingstone Gdns, Grav. DA12 131 GK92
H Livingstone Hosp, Dart. DA1 128 FM87
Livingstone Pl, E14 off Ferry St 103 EC78
Livingstone Rd, E15 85 EC67
E17 67 EB58
N13 45 DL51
SW11 off Winstanley Rd 100 DD83
Caterham CR3 176 DR122
Gravesend DA12 131 GK92
Hounslow TW3 96 CC84
Southall UB1 78 BX73
Thornton Heath CR7 142 DQ96
Livingstone Ter, Rain. RM13 89 FE67
Livingstone Wk, SW11 100 DD83
Livonia St, W1 195 L9
Livsey Cl, SE28 105 EQ76
Lizard St, EC1 197 J3
Lizban St, SE3 104 EH80
Llanbury Cl, Ger.Cr. (Chal.St.P.) SL9 36 AY52
Llanelly Rd, NW2 63 CZ61
Llanover Rd, SE18 105 EN79
Wembley HA9 61 CK62
Llanthony Rd, Mord. SM4 140 DD100
Llanvanor Rd, NW2 63 CZ61
Llewellyn St, SE16 202 C5
Lloyd Av, SW16 141 DL95
Coulsdon CR5 158 DG114
Lloyd Baker St, WC1 196 C3
Lloyd Ct, Pnr. HA5 60 BX57
Lloyd Ms, Enf. EN3 31 EA38
Tram Lloyd Park 160 DT105
Lloyd Pk, E17 47 EA54
Lloyd Pk Av, Croy. CR0 160 DT105
Lloyd Rd, E6 87 EM67
E17 67 DX56
Dagenham RM9 88 EZ65
Worcester Park KT4 139 CW104
Lloyd's Av, EC3 197 N9
★ Lloyds of London, EC3 197 M9
Lloyds Pl, SE3 104 EE82
Lloyd Sq, WC1 196 D2
Lloyd's Row, EC1 196 E3
Lloyd St, WC1 196 D2
Lloyds Way, Beck. BR3 143 DY99
Loampit Hill, SE13 103 EA82
Loampit Vale, SE13 103 EB83
Loanda Cl, E8 off Clarissa St 84 DT67
Loates La, Wat. WD17 24 BW41
Loats Rd, SW2 121 DL86
Lobelia Cl, E6 off Sorrel Gdns 86 EL71
Local Board Rd, Wat. WD17 24 BX43
Locarno Rd, W3 80 CQ74
Greenford UB6 78 CC70
Lochaber Rd, SE13 104 EE84
Lochaline St, W6 99 CW79
Lochan Cl, Hayes UB4 78 BY70
Lochinvar St, SW12 121 DH87
Lochmere Cl, Erith DA8 107 FB79
Lochnagar St, E14 85 EC71
Lock Bldg, The, E15 off High St 85 EC68
Lock Chase, SE3 104 EE83
Lock Cl, Add. (Wdhm) KT15 151 BE113
Southall UB2 off Navigator Dr 96 CC75
Locke Cl, Rain. RM13 69 FF65
Locke Gdns, Slou. SL3 92 AW75
Locke King Cl, Wey. KT13 152 BN108
Locke King Rd, Wey. KT13 152 BN108
Lockesfield Pl, E14 204 C10
Lockesley Dr, Orp. BR5 145 ET100
Lockesley Sq, Surb. KT6 137 CK100
Lockestone, Wey. KT13 152 BM107
Lockestone Cl, Wey. KT13 152 BM107
Locket Rd, Har. HA3 61 CE55
Locke Way, Wok. GU21 off The Broadway 167 AZ117
Lockfield Av, Enf. EN3 31 DY40
Lockfield Dr, Wok. GU21 166 AT118
Lockgate Cl, E9 off Lee Conservancy Rd 67 DZ64
Lockhart Cl, N7 83 DM65
Enfield EN3 30 DV43
Lockhart Rd, Cob. KT11 154 BW113
Lockhart St, E3 85 DZ70
Lockhurst St, E5 67 DX63
Lockie Pl, SE25 142 DU97
Lockier Wk, Wem. HA9 61 CK62
Lockington Rd, SW8 101 DH81
Lock Island, Shep. TW17 134 BN103
Lock La, Wok. GU22 168 BH116
Lockmead Rd, N15 66 DU58
SE13 103 EC83
Lock Ms, NW1 off Northpoint Sq 83 DK65
Lock Rd, Rich. TW10 117 CJ91
Locks La, Mitch. CR4 140 DF95
Locksley Dr, Wok. GU21 off Robin Hood Rd 166 AT118
Locksley Est, E14 85 DZ72
Locksley St, E14 85 DZ71
Locksmeade Rd, Rich. TW10 117 CJ91
Locksons Cl, E14 off Broomfield St 85 EB71
Lockswood Cl, Barn. EN4 28 DF42
Lockton St, W10 81 CX73
Lockwood Cl, SE26 123 DX91
Lockwood Ind Pk, N17 66 DV55
Lockwood Path, Wok. GU21 151 BD113
Lockwood Pl, E4 47 EA51
Lockwood Sq, SE16 202 D6
Lockwood Wk, Rom. RM1 off Western Rd 71 FE57
Lockwood Way, E17 47 DX54
Chessington KT9 156 CN106
Lockyer Est, SE1 201 L4
Lockyer Ms, Enf. EN3 31 EB38
Lockyer Rd, Purf. RM19 108 FQ79
Lockyer St, SE1 201 L5
Locomotive Dr, Felt. TW14 115 BU88
Loddiges Rd, E9 84 DW66
Loddon Spur, Slou. SL1 74 AS73
Loder Cl, Wok. GU21 151 BD113
Loder St, SE15 102 DW81
Lodge Av, SW14 98 CS83
Borehamwood (Els.) WD6 26 CM43
Croydon CR0 141 DN104
Dagenham RM8, RM9 88 EU67
Dartford DA1 128 FJ86
Harrow HA3 62 CL56
Romford RM2 71 FG56
Lodgebottom Rd, Lthd. KT22 182 CM127
Lodge Cl, N18 46 DQ50
Brentwood (Hutt.) CM13 55 GE45
Chigwell IG7 50 EU48
Cobham (Stoke D'Ab.) KT11 170 BZ115
Edgware HA8 42 CM51
Egham (Eng.Grn) TW20 112 AX92
Epsom KT17 off Howell Hill Gro 157 CW110
Isleworth TW7 97 CH81
Leatherhead (Fetch.) KT22 171 CD122
Orpington BR6 146 EV102
Uxbridge UB8 76 BJ70
Wallington SM6 140 DG102
Lodge Ct, Horn. RM12 72 FL61
Wembley HA0 62 CL64
Lodge Cres, Orp. BR6 146 EW103
Waltham Cross EN8 15 DX34
Lodge Dr, N13 45 DN49
Rickmansworth (Loud.) WD3 22 BJ42
Lodge End, Rad. WD7 9 CH34
Rickmansworth (Crox.Grn) WD3 23 BR42
Lodge Gdns, Beck. BR3 143 DZ99
Lodge Hill, SE2 106 EV80
Ilford IG4 68 EL56
Purley CR8 175 DN115
Welling DA16 106 EV80
Lodgehill Pk Cl, Har. HA2 60 CB61
Lodge La, N12 44 DC50
Bexley DA5 126 EX86
Chalfont St. Giles HP8 21 AZ41
Croydon (New Adgtn) CR0 161 EA107
Grays RM16, RM17 110 GA75
Romford RM5 50 FA52
Waltham Abbey EN9 31 ED35
Westerham TN16 189 EQ127
Lodge Pl, Sutt. SM1 158 DB106
Lodge Rd, NW4 63 CW56
NW8 194 A3
Bromley BR1 124 EH94
Croydon CR0 141 DP100
Leatherhead (Fetch.) KT22 170 CC122
Sutton SM1 off Throwley Way 158 DB106
Wallington SM6 159 DH106
Lodge Vil, Wdf.Grn. IG8 48 EF52
Lodge Wk, Warl. CR6 177 EA116
Lodge Way, Ashf. TW15 114 BL89
Shepperton TW17 135 BQ96
Lodore Gdns, NW9 62 CS57
Lodore Grn, Uxb. UB10 58 BL62
Lodore St, E14 85 EC72
Loewen Rd, Grays RM16 111 GG76
Lofthouse Pl, Chess. KT9 155 CJ107
Loftie St, SE16 202 C5
Lofting Rd, N1 83 DM66
Loftus Rd, W12 81 CV74
Barking IG11 off Tanner St 87 EQ65
Logan Cl, Enf. EN3 31 DX39
Hounslow TW4 96 BZ83
Logan Ct, Rom. RM1 off Logan Ms 71 FE57
Logan Ms, W8 100 DA77
Romford RM1 71 FE57
Logan Pl, W8 100 DA77
Logan Rd, N9 46 DV47
Wembley HA9 62 CL61
Loggetts, The, SE21 122 DS89
Logs Hill, Brom. BR1 124 EL94
Chislehurst BR7 124 EL94
Logs Hill Cl, Chis. BR7 144 EL95
Lois Dr, Shep. TW17 135 BP99
Lolesworth Cl, E1 off Commercial St 84 DT71
Lollard St, SE11 200 C8
Loman Path, S.Ock. RM15 91 FT72
Loman St, SE1 200 G4
Lomas Cl, Croy. CR0 161 EC108
Lomas Dr, E8 84 DT66
Lomas St, E1 84 DU71
Lombard Av, Enf. EN3 30 DW39
Ilford IG3 69 ES60
Lombard Business Pk, SW19 140 DC96
Lombard Ct, EC3 197 L10
W3 off Crown St 80 CP74
Lombard La, EC4 196 E9
Lombard Rd, N11 45 DH50
SW11 100 DD82
SW19 140 DB96
Lombards, The, Horn. RM11 72 FM59
Lombard St, EC3 197 L9
Dartford (Hort.Kir.) DA4 148 FQ99
Lombard Wall, SE7 205 P7
Lombardy Cl, Ilf. IG6 off Hazel La 49 EP52
Woking GU21 off Nethercote Av 166 AT117
Lombardy Pl, W2 off Bark Pl 82 DB73
Lombardy Retail Pk, Hayes UB3 77 BV73
Lombardy Way, Borwd. WD6 26 CL39
Lomond Cl, N15 66 DS56
Wembley HA0 80 CM66
Lomond Gdns, S.Croy. CR2 161 DY108
Lomond Gro, SE5 102 DR80
Loncin Mead Av, Add. (New Haw) KT15 152 BJ109
Loncroft Rd, SE5 102 DS79
Londesborough Rd, N16 66 DS63
Londinium Twr, E1 off Mansell St 84 DT73
★ London Aquarium, SE1 200 B4
★ London Biggin Hill Airport, West. TN16 162 EK113
★ London Brass Rubbing Cen, St. Martin-in-the-Fields Ch, WC2 199 P1
⇌ London Bridge 201 M3
⊖ London Bridge 201 M3
London Br, EC4 201 L2
SE1 201 L2
RIV London Bridge City Pier 201 M2
H London Br Hosp, SE1 201 L2
London Br St, SE1 201 K3
London Br Wk, SE1 201 L2
★ London Butterfly Ho, Syon Pk, Brent. TW8 97 CH81
★ London Canal Mus, The, N1 off New Wf Rd 83 DL68
★ London Cen Mosque, NW8 194 C3
H London Chest Hosp, E2 84 DW68
★ London City Airport, E16 87 EM74
DLR London City Airport 86 EL74
H London Clinic, The, W1 194 G5
LONDON COLNEY, St.Alb. AL2 10 CL26
London Colney Bypass, St.Alb. AL2 9 CK25
★ London Commodity Exchange, E1 202 A1
★ London Dungeon, SE1 201 L3
★ London Eye, SE1 200 B4
⇌ London Fields 84 DV66
London Flds, E8 84 DV66
London Flds E Side, E8 84 DV66
London Flds W Side, E8 84 DU66
★ London Fire Brigade Mus, SE1 201 H4
H London Foot Hosp & Sch of Podiatric Med, The, W1 195 K5
★ London Heathrow Airport, Houns. TW6 95 BP81
H London Indep Hosp, E1 85 DX71
London La, E8 84 DV66
Bromley BR1 124 EF94
★ London Met Archives, EC1 196 E4
London Ms, W2 194 A9
★ London Palladium, W1 195 K9
London Pav, The, W1 199 M1
★ London Peace Pagoda, SW11 100 DF79
★ London Regatta Cen, E16 86 EK73
London Rd, E13 86 EG68
SE1 200 F6
SE23 122 DV88
SW16 141 DM95
SW17 140 DF96
Ashford TW15 114 BH90
Barking IG11 87 EP66
Borehamwood WD6 10 CN34
Brentford TW8 97 CJ80
Brentwood CM14 54 FS49
Bromley BR1 124 EF94
Bushey WD23 24 BY44
Caterham CR3 176 DR123
Chalfont St. Giles HP8 36 AW47
Croydon CR0 141 DP101
Dartford (Cray.) DA1 127 FD85
Dartford (Fnghm) DA4 148 FL100
Dartford (Stone) DA2 128 FP87
Egham (Eng.Grn) TW20 132 AV95
London Rd, Enf. EN2 30 DR41
Epsom KT17 157 CT109
Feltham TW14 114 BH90
Gravesend (Nthflt) DA11 130 GD86
Grays RM17, RM20 109 FW79
Greenhithe DA9 129 FS86
Harrow HA1 61 CE61
Hounslow TW3 96 CC83
Isleworth TW7 97 CF82
Kingston upon Thames KT2 138 CM96
Mitcham CR4 140 DF96
Mitcham (Bedd.Cor.) CR4 140 DG101
Morden SM4 140 DA99
Ongar CM5 35 FH36
Radlett (Shenley) WD7 10 CM33
Redhill RH1 184 DG132
Reigate RH2 184 DA134
Rickmansworth WD3 38 BM47
Romford (Abridge) RM4 33 ET42
Romford (Chad.Hth) RM6, RM7 70 FA58
Romford (Stap.Taw.) RM4 35 FC40
Sevenoaks TN13 190 FF123
Sevenoaks (Dunt.Grn) TN13 181 FD118
Sevenoaks (Halst.) TN14 165 FB112
Slough SL3 93 AZ78
Slough (Datchet) SL3 92 AV80
South Ockendon (Aveley) RM15 90 FM74
Staines TW18 113 BF91
Stanmore HA7 41 CJ50
Sutton SM3 139 CX104
Swanley BR8 147 FC95
Swanscombe DA10 129 FV85
Thornton Heath CR7 141 DN99
Tilbury RM18 111 GH82
Twickenham TW1 117 CG85
Virginia Water GU25 132 AV95
Wallington SM6 159 DH105
Wembley HA9 80 CL65
Westerham TN16 179 EQ123
London Rd E, Amer. HP7 20 AT42
London Rd N, Red. (Merst.) RH1 185 DH125
London Rd Purfleet, Purf. RM19 108 FN78
London Rd S, Red. (Merst.) RH1 184 DG130
London Rd W Thurrock, Grays RM20 109 FS79
Londons Cl, Upmin. RM14 72 FQ64
★ London Silver Vaults, WC2 196 D7
London Stile, W4 off Wellesley Rd 98 CN78
★ London Stone, EC4 197 K10
London St, EC3 197 N10
W2 82 DD72
Chertsey KT16 134 BG101
★ London Transport Mus, WC2 196 A10
★ London Trocadero, The, W1 199 M1
London Wall, EC2 197 J7
London Wall Bldgs, EC2 197 L7
★ London Wildlife Trust, NW1 83 DK67
★ London Zoo, NW1 82 DG68
Lonesome Way, SW16 141 DH95
Long Acre, WC2 195 P10
Orpington BR6 146 EX103
Longacre Pl, Cars. SM5 off Beddington Gdns 158 DG107
Longacre Rd, E17 47 ED53
Longaford Way, Brwd. (Hutt.) CM13 55 GB46
Long Barn Cl, Wat. WD25 7 BV32
Longbeach Rd, SW11 100 DF83
Longberrys, NW2 63 CZ62
Longboat Row, Sthl. UB1 78 BZ72
Longbourne Way, Cher. KT16 133 BF100
Longboyds, Cob. KT11 153 BV114
Longbridge Rd, Bark. IG11 87 EQ66
Dagenham RM8 70 EU63
Longbridge Way, SE13 123 EC85
Uxbridge UB8 76 BH68
Longbury Cl, Orp. BR5 146 EV97
Longbury Dr, Orp. BR5 146 EV97
Longcliffe Path, Wat. WD19 off Gosforth La 39 BU48
Long Copse Cl, Lthd. (Bkhm) KT23 170 CB123
Long Ct, Purf. RM19 108 FN77
Longcroft, SE9 125 EM90
Watford WD19 39 BV45
Longcroft Av, Bans. SM7 158 DC114
Longcroft Dr, Wal.Cr. EN8 15 DZ34
Longcrofte Rd, Edg. HA8 41 CK52
Longcroft La, Hem.H. (Bov.) HP3 5 BC28
Longcroft Ri, Loug. IG10 33 EN43
Longcroft Rd, Rick. (Map.Cr.) WD3 37 BD50
Longcrofts, Wal.Abb. EN9 off Roundhills 16 EE34
LONGCROSS, Cher. KT16 132 AU104
⇌ Longcross 132 AT102
Longcross Rd, Cher. (Longcr.) KT16 132 AY104
Long Deacon Rd, E4 48 EE46
LONG DITTON, Surb. KT10 137 CJ102
Longdon Wd, Kes. BR2 162 EL105
Longdown La N, Epsom KT17 157 CU114
Longdown La S, Epsom KT17 157 CU114
Longdown Rd, SE6 123 EA91
Epsom KT17 157 CU114
Long Dr, W3 80 CS72
Greenford UB6 78 CB67
Ruislip HA4 60 BX63
Long Elmes, Har. HA3 40 CB53
Long Elms, Abb.L. WD5 7 BR33
Long Elms Cl, Abb.L. WD5 off Long Elms 7 BR33
Long Fallow, St.Alb. AL2 8 CA27
Longfellow Dr, Brwd. (Hutt.) CM13 55 GC45
Longfellow Rd, E17 67 DZ58
Worcester Park KT4 139 CU103

★ Place of interest · ⇌ Railway station · ⊖ London Underground station · DLR Docklands Light Railway station · Tram Tramlink station · H Hospital · RIV Pedestrian ferry landing stage

Longfellow Way, SE1 ......**202** A9
Long Fld, NW9 ....**42** CS52
Longfield, Brom. BR1 ......**144** EF95
Loughton IG10 ....**32** EJ43
Longfield Av, E17 ....**67** DY56
NW7 ....**43** CU52
W5 ....**79** CJ73
Enfield EN3 ....**30** DW37
Hornchurch RM11 ....**71** FF59
Wallington SM6 ....**140** DG102
Wembley HA9 ....**62** CL60
Longfield Cres, SE26 ....**122** DW90
Tadworth KT20 ....**173** CW120
Longfield Dr, SW14 ....**118** CP85
Mitcham CR4 ....**120** DE94
Longfield Est, SE1 ....**202** A9
Longfield La, Wal.Cr.
(Chsht) EN7 ....**14** DU27
Longfield Rd, W5 ....**79** CJ73
Longfield St, SW18 ....**120** DA87
Longfield Wk, W5 ....**79** CJ72
LONGFORD, Sev. TN13 .....**181** FD120
LONGFORD, West Dr. UB7 ..**94** BH81
Longford Av, Felt. TW14 ....**115** BS86
Southall UB1 ....**78** CA73
Staines TW19 ....**114** BL88
Longford Cl, Hmptn. (Hmptn H.)
TW12 ....**116** CA91
Hayes UB4
off Longford Gdns **78** BX73
Longford Ct, E5 *off Pedro St* **.67** DX63
NW4 ....**63** CX56
Epsom KT19 ....**156** CQ105
Longford Gdns, Hayes UB4 ..**78** BX73
Sutton SM1 ....**140** DC104
Longford Ho, E1
off Jubilee St **84** DW72
Longford Rd, Twick. TW2 ....**116** CA88
Longford Rbt, West Dr. UB7 ..**94** BH81
Longford St, NW1 ....**195** J4
Longford Wk, SW2
off Papworth Way **121** DN87
Longford Way, Stai. TW19 ...**114** BL88
Long Grn, Chig. IG7 ....**49** ES49
Long Gro, Rom. (Harold Wd)
RM3 ....**52** FL54
Long Gro Rd, Epsom KT19 ..**156** CQ111
Longhayes Av, Rom. RM6 ....**70** EX56
Longhayes Ct, Rom. RM6
off Longhayes Av **70** EX56
Longheath Gdns, Croy. CR0 ..**142** DW99
Longhedge Ho, SE26 ....**122** DT91
Long Hedges, Houns. TW3 ...**96** CA81
Longhedge St, SW11 ......**100** DG82
Long Hill, Cat. (Wold.) CR3 ..**177** DX121
Longhill Rd, SE6 ....**123** ED89
Longhook Gdns, Nthlt. UB5 ..**77** BU68
Longhope Cl, SE15 ....**102** DS79
Longhouse Rd, Grays RM16 .**111** GH76
Longhurst Rd, SE13 ....**123** ED85
Croydon CR0 ....**142** DV100
Longland Ct, SE1
off Rolls Rd **102** DU78
Longland Dr, N20 ....**44** DB48
LONGLANDS, Chis. BR7 .....**125** EQ90
Longlands Av, Couls. CR5 ...**158** DG114
Longlands Cl, Wal.Cr.
(Chsht) EN8 ....**15** DX32
Longlands Ct, W11
off Portobello Rd **81** CZ73
Mitcham CR4
off Summerhill Way **140** DG95
Longlands Pk Cres, Sid.
DA15 ....**125** ES90
Longlands Rd, Sid. DA15 ...**125** ES90
Long La, EC1 ....**196** G6
N2 ....**44** DC54
N3 ....**44** DB52
SE1 ....**201** K5
Bexleyheath DA7 ....**106** EX80
Croydon CR0 ....**142** DW99
Grays RM16 ....**110** GA75
Hemel Hempstead (Bov.)
HP3 ....**5** AZ31
Rickmansworth (Herons.)
WD3 ....**21** BC44
Rickmansworth (Mill End)
WD3 ....**37** BF47
Staines (Stanw.) TW19 ....**114** BM87
Uxbridge UB10 ....**76** BN69
Longleat Ho, SW1
off Rampayne St **101** DK78
Longleat Ms, Orp. BR5
off High St **146** EW98
Longleat Rd, Enf. EN1 ....**30** DS43
Longleat Way, Felt. TW14 ....**115** BR87
Longlees, Rick. (Map.Cr.) WD3 **.37** BC50
Longleigh La, SE2 ....**106** EW79
Bexleyheath DA7 ....**106** EW79
Longlents Ho, NW10 ....**80** CR67
Longley Av, Wem. HA0 ....**80** CM67
Longley Ct, SW8
off Lansdowne Way **101** DL81
Longley Rd, SW17 ....**120** DE93
Croydon CR0 ....**141** DP101
Harrow HA1 ....**60** CC57
Long Leys, E4 ....**47** EB51
Longley St, SE1 ....**202** B9
Longley Way, NW2 ....**63** CW62
Long Lo Dr, Walt. KT12 .....**136** BW104
Longmans Cl, Wat. WD18
off Byewaters **23** BQ44
Long Mark Rd, E16
off Fulmer Rd **86** EK71
Longmarsh La, SE28 ....**87** ES74
Longmarsh Vw, Dart.
(Sutt.H.) DA4 ....**148** FP95
Long Mead, NW9 ....**43** CT53
Longmead, Chis. BR7 ....**145** EN96
Longmead Business Cen,
Epsom KT19 ....**156** CR111
Longmead Business Pk,
Epsom KT19 ....**156** CS111
Longmead Cl, Brwd.
(Shenf.) CM15 ....**54** FY46
Caterham CR3 ....**176** DS122
Longmead Dr, Sid. DA14 ....**126** EX89
Longmeade, Grav. DA12 ....**131** GM88
Long Meadow, NW5
off Torriano Av **65** DK64
Brentwood (Hutt.) CM13 ....**55** GC47
Romford (Noak Hill) RM3 ..**52** FJ48
Sevenoaks (Rvrhd) TN13 ..**190** FD121
Long Meadow Cl, W.Wick.
BR4 ....**143** EC101
Longmeadow Rd, Sid. DA15 .**125** ES88
Longmead Rd, SW17 ......**120** DF92
Epsom KT19 ....**156** CR111
Hayes UB3 ....**77** BT73
Thames Ditton KT7 ......**137** CE101
Longmere Gdns, Tad. KT20 ..**173** CW119
Longmoor, Wal.Cr. (Chsht)
EN8 ....**15** DY29
Longmoore St, SW1 ....**199** K9
Longmoor Pt, SW15
off Norley Vale **119** CV88
Longmore Av, Barn. EN4,
EN5 ....**28** DC44
Longmore Cl, Rick. (Map.Cr.)
WD3 ....**37** BF49
Longmore Rd, Walt. KT12 ....**154** BY105
Longnor Rd, E1 ....**85** DX69
Long Pond Rd, SE3 ....**104** EE81
Longport Cl, Ilf. IG6 ....**50** EU51
Long Reach, Wok. (Ock.)
GU23 ....**168** BN123
Long Reach Ct, Bark. IG11 ...**87** ER68
Longreach Rd, Bark. IG11 ...**87** ET70
Erith DA8 ....**107** FH80
Longridge Gro, Wok. GU22
off Old Woking Rd **151** BE114
Longridge La, Sthl. UB1 .....**78** CB73
Longridge Rd, SW5 ....**100** DA77
Long Ridings Av, Brwd.
(Hutt.) CM13 ....**55** GB43
Long Rd, SW4 ....**101** DH84
Longs Cl, Wok. GU22 ......**168** BG116
Long's Ct, WC2 ....**195** M10
Longs Ct, Rich. TW9
off Crown Ter **98** CM84
Longsdon Way, Cat. CR3 ....**176** DU124
Long Shaw, Lthd. KT22 .....**171** CG119
Longshaw Rd, E4 ....**47** ED48
Longshore, SE8 ....**203** M9
Longside Cl, Egh. TW20 ....**133** BC95
Longspring, Wat. WD24 .....**23** BV38
Longspring Wd, Sev. TN14 ..**190** FF130
Longstaff Cres, SW18 ......**120** DA86
Longstaff Rd, SW18 ....**120** DA86
Longstone Av, NW10 ....**81** CT66
Longstone Ct, SE1 ....**201** J5
Longstone Rd, SW17 ......**121** DH92
Iver SL0 ....**75** BC68
Long St, E2 ....**197** P2
Waltham Abbey EN9 ....**16** EL32
Longthornton Rd, SW16 ....**141** DJ96
Longthorpe Ct, W6
off Invermead Cl **99** CU76
Longton Av, SE26 ....**122** DU91
Longton Gro, SE26 ....**122** DV91
Longton Ho, SE11
off Lambeth Wk **101** DM77
Longtown Cl, Rom. RM3 ....**52** FJ50
Longtown Rd, Rom. RM3 ....**52** FJ50
Longview Way, Rom. RM5 ...**51** FD53
Longville Rd, SE11 ....**200** F8
Long Wk, SE1 ....**201** N6
SE18 ....**105** EP79
SW13 ....**98** CS82
Chalfont St. Giles HP8 ....**20** AX41
Epsom KT18 ....**173** CX119
New Malden KT3 ....**138** CQ97
Waltham Abbey EN9 ......**15** EA30
West Byfleet KT14 ....**152** BJ114
Longwalk Rd, Uxb. UB11 ....**77** BP74
Longwood Av, Slou. SL3 ....**93** BB78
Longwood Business Pk, Sun.
TW16 ....**135** BT99
Longwood Cl, Upmin. RM14 **.72** FQ64
Longwood Dr, SW15 ....**119** CU86
Long Wd Dr, Beac. (Jordans)
HP9 ....**36** AT51
Longwood Gdns, Ilf. IG5, IG6 **.69** EM56
Longwood Rd, Ken. CR8 ....**176** DR116
Longworth Cl, SE28 ....**88** EX72
Long Yd, WC1 ....**196** B5
Loning, The, NW9 ....**62** CS56
Enfield EN3 ....**30** DW38
Lonsdale Av, E6 ....**86** EK69
Brentwood (Hutt.) CM13 ...**55** GD44
Romford RM7 ....**71** FC58
Wembley HA9 ....**62** CL64
Lonsdale Cl, E6
off Lonsdale Av **86** EL70
SE9 ....**124** EK90
Edgware HA8
off Orchard Dr **42** CM50
Pinner HA5 ....**40** BY52
Uxbridge UB8 ....**77** BQ71
Lonsdale Cres, Dart. DA2 ...**128** FQ88
Ilford IG2 ....**69** EP58
Lonsdale Dr, Enf. EN2 ......**29** DL43
Lonsdale Gdns, Th.Hth. CR7 **.141** DM98
Lonsdale Ms, W11
off Lonsdale Rd **81** CZ72
Richmond TW9
off Elizabeth Cotts **98** CN81
Lonsdale Pl, N1
off Barnsbury St **83** DN66
Lonsdale Rd, E11 ....**68** EF59
NW6 ....**81** CZ68
SE25 ....**142** DV98
SW13 ....**99** CU79
W4 ....**99** CT77
W11 ....**81** CZ72
Bexleyheath DA7 ....**106** EZ82
Southall UB2 ....**96** BX76
Weybridge KT13 ....**152** BN108
Lonsdale Sq, N1 ....**83** DN66
Loobert Rd, N15 ....**66** DS55
Looe Gdns, Ilf. IG6 ....**69** EP55
Loom La, Rad. WD7 ....**25** CG37
Loom Pl, Rad. WD7 ....**25** CG36
Loop Rd, Chis. BR7 ....**125** EQ93
Epsom KT18
off Woodcote Side **172** CQ116
Waltham Abbey EN9 ......**15** EB32
Woking GU22 ....**167** AZ121
Lopen Rd, N18 ....**46** DS49
Loraine Cl, Enf. EN3 ....**30** DW43
Loraine Gdns, Ashtd. KT21 ..**172** CL117
Loraine Rd, N7 ....**65** DM63
W4 ....**98** CP79
Lorane Ct, Wat. WD17 ....**23** BU40
Lord Amory Way, E14 ....**204** D4
Lord Av, Ilf. IG5 ....**69** EM56
Lord Chancellor Wk, Kings.T.
KT2 ....**138** CQ95
Lord Chatham's Ride, Sev.
TN14 ....**180** EX117
Lordell Pl, SW19 ....**119** CW93
Lorden Wk, E2 ....**84** DU69
Lord Gdns, Ilf. IG5 ....**68** EL56
Lord Hills Br, W2
off Porchester Rd **82** DB71
Lord Hills Rd, W2 ....**82** DB71
Lord Holland La, SW9
off St. Lawrence Way **101** DN81
Lord Knyvett Cl, Stai.
(Stanw.) TW19 ....**114** BK86
Lord Knyvetts Ct, Stai.
(Stanw.) TW19
off De Havilland Way **114** BL86
Lord Napier Pl, W6
off Upper Mall **99** CU78
Lord N St, SW1 ....**199** P7
Lord Roberts Ms, SW6
off Waterford Rd **100** DB80
Lord Roberts Ter, SE18 .....**105** EN78
★ **Lord's**, Middlesex CCC &
Mus, NW8 ....**194** A2
Lordsbury Fld, Wall. SM6 ...**159** DJ110
Lord's Cl, SE21 ....**122** DQ89
Lords Cl, Felt. TW13 ....**116** BY89
Radlett (Shenley) WD7 ....**10** CL32
Lordsgrove Cl, Tad. KT20
off Whitegate Way **173** CV120
Lordship Cl, Brwd. (Hutt.)
CM13 ....**55** GD46
Lordship Gro, N16 ....**66** DR61
Lordship La, N17 ....**46** DQ53
N22 ....**45** DN54
SE22 ....**122** DT86
Lordship La Est, SE22 ......**122** DU88
Lordship Pk, N16 ....**66** DQ61
Lordship Pk Ms, N16
off Allerton Rd **66** DQ61
Lordship Pl, SW3
off Cheyne Row **100** DE79
Lordship Rd, N16 ....**66** DR61
Northolt UB5 ....**78** BY66
Waltham Cross (Chsht) EN7 .**14** DV30
Lordship Ter, N16 ....**66** DR61
Lordsmead Rd, N17 ....**46** DS53
Lord St, E16 ....**86** EL74
Gravesend DA12 ....**131** GH87
Watford WD17 ....**24** BW41
Lord's Vw, NW8 ....**194** A3
Lordswood Cl, Bexh. DA6 ...**126** EY85
Dartford (Lane End) DA2 ..**129** FS91
Lords Wd Ho, Couls. CR5 ...**175** DK122
Lord Warwick St, SE18 .....**105** EM76
Lorenzo St, WC1 ....**196** B2
Loretto Gdns, Har. HA3 .....**62** CL56
Lorian Cl, N12 ....**44** DB49
Lorian Dr, Reig. RH2 ....**184** DC133
Loriners Cl, Cob. KT11 ......**153** BU114
Loring Rd, N20 ....**44** DE47
SE14 ....**103** DY81
Isleworth TW7 ....**97** CF82
Loris Rd, W6 ....**99** CW76
Lorn Ct, SW9 ....**101** DN82
Lorne Av, Croy. CR0 ....**143** DX101
Lorne Cl, NW8 ....**194** C3
Lorne Gdns, E11 ....**68** EJ56
W11 ....**99** CX75
Croydon CR0 ....**143** DX101
Lorne Rd, E7 ....**68** EH63
E17 ....**67** EA57
N4 ....**65** DM60
Brentwood CM14 ....**54** FW49
Harrow HA3 ....**41** CF54
Richmond TW10
off Albert Rd **118** CM85
Lorn Rd, SW9 ....**101** DM82
Lorraine Chase, S.Ock. RM15 **.108** FM75
Lorraine Pk, Har. HA3 ....**41** CE52
Lorrimore Rd, SE17 ....**101** DP79
Lorrimore Sq, SE17 ....**101** DP79
Lorton Cl, Grav. DA12 ......**131** GL89
Loseberry Rd, Esher (Clay.)
KT10 ....**155** CD106
Lossie Dr, Iver SL0 ....**75** BB73
Lothair Rd, W5 ....**97** CK75
Lothair Rd N, N4 ....**65** DP58
Lothair Rd S, N4 ....**65** DN59
Lothbury, EC2 ....**197** K8
Lothian Av, Hayes UB4 ......**77** BV71
Lothian Cl, Wem. HA0 ....**61** CG63
Lothian Rd, SW9 ....**101** DP81
Lothian Wd, Tad. KT20 ......**173** CV122
Lothrop St, W10 ....**81** CY69
Lots Rd, SW10 ....**100** DC80
Lotus Cl, SE21 ....**122** DQ90
Lotus Rd, West. (Bigg.H.)
TN16 ....**179** EM118
Loubet St, SW17 ....**120** DF93
Loudhams Rd, Amer. HP7 ....**20** AW39
Loudhams Wd La, Ch.St.G.
HP8 ....**20** AX40
Loudoun Av, Ilf. IG6 ....**69** EP57
Loudoun Rd, NW8 ....**82** DC67
LOUDWATER, Rick. WD3 .....**22** BK41
Loudwater Cl, Sun. TW16 ...**135** BU98
Loudwater Dr, Rick. (Loud.)
WD3 ....**22** BJ42
Loudwater Hts, Rick. (Loud.)
WD3 ....**22** BH41
Loudwater La, Rick. WD3 ....**22** BK42
Loudwater Ridge, Rick.
(Loud.) WD3 ....**22** BJ42
Loudwater Rd, Sun. TW16 ...**135** BU98
Loughborough Est, SW9
off Loughborough Rd ...**101** DP82
⇌ **Loughborough Junction** .**101** DP83
Loughborough Pk, SW9 .....**101** DP84
Loughborough Rd, SW9 ....**101** DN82
Loughborough St, SE11 .....**200** C10
Lough Rd, N7 ....**83** DM65
LOUGHTON, IG10 ....**33** EM43
⊖ **Loughton** **32** EL43
Loughton Ct, Wal.Abb. EN9 ..**16** EH33
Loughton La, Epp. (They.B.)
CM16 ....**33** ER38
Loughton Way, Buck.H. IG9 ..**48** EK46
Louisa Cl, E9
off Wetherell Rd **85** DX67
Louisa Gdns, E1
off Louisa St **85** DX70
Louisa Ho, SW15 ....**98** CS84
Louisa St, E1 ....**85** DX70
Louise Aumonier Wk, N19
off Hillrise Rd **65** DL59
Louise Bennett Cl, SE24
off Shakespeare Rd **101** DP84
Louise Ct, E11
off Grosvenor Rd **68** EH57
Louise Gdns, Rain. RM13 ....**89** FE69
Louise Rd, E15 ....**86** EE65
Louise Wk, Hem.H. (Bov.) HP3 **.5** BA28
Louis Gdns, Chis. BR7 ......**125** EM91
Louis Ms, N10 ....**45** DH53
Louisville Rd, SW17 ....**120** DG90
Louvaine Rd, SW11 ....**100** DD84
Louvain Rd, Green. DA9 ....**129** FS87
Louvain Way, Wat. WD25 .....**7** BV32
Lovage App, E6 ....**86** EL71
Lovat Cl, NW2 ....**63** CT62
Lovat La, EC3 ....**201** M1
Lovatt Cl, Edg. HA8 ....**42** CP51
Lovatt Dr, Ruis. HA4 ....**59** BU57
Lovatts, Rick. (Crox.Grn) WD3 **.22** BN42
Lovat Wk, Houns. TW5
off Cranford La **96** BY80
Loveday Rd, W13 ....**79** CH74
Love Grn La, Iver SL0 ....**75** BD71
Lovegrove St, SE1 ....**102** DU78
Lovegrove Wk, E14 ....**204** D3
Love Hill La, Slou. SL3 ......**75** BA73
Lovekyn Cl, Kings.T. KT2
off Queen Elizabeth Rd ..**138** CM96
Lovelace Av, Brom. BR2 ....**145** EN100
Lovelace Cl, Lthd. (Eff.Junct.)
KT24 ....**169** BU123
Lovelace Dr, Wok. GU22 ....**167** BF115
Lovelace Gdns, Bark. IG11 ...**70** EU63
Surbiton KT6 ....**137** CK101
Walton-on-Thames KT12 .**154** BW106
Lovelace Grn, SE9 ....**105** EM83
Lovelace Rd, SE21 ....**122** DQ89
Barnet EN4 ....**44** DE45
Surbiton KT6 ....**137** CJ101
Lovelands La, Tad. (Lwr Kgswd)
KT20 ....**184** DB127
Love La, EC2 ....**197** J8
N17 ....**46** DT52
SE18 ....**105** EP77
SE25 ....**142** DV97
Abbots Langley WD5 ......**7** BT30
Bexley DA5 ....**126** EZ86
Godstone RH9 ....**186** DW132
Gravesend DA12 ....**131** GJ87
Iver SL0 ....**75** BD72
Kings Langley WD4 ....**6** BL29
Mitcham CR4 ....**140** DE97
Morden SM4 ....**140** DA101
Pinner HA5 ....**60** BY55
South Ockendon (Aveley)
RM15 ....**108** FQ75
Surbiton KT6 ....**137** CK103
Sutton SM3 ....**157** CY106
Tadworth (Walt.Hill) KT20 .**183** CT126
Woodford Green IG8 ....**49** EM51
Lovel Av, Well. DA16 ....**106** EU82
Lovel End, Ger.Cr. (Chal.St.P.)
SL9 ....**36** AW52
Lovelinch Cl, SE15 ....**102** DW79
Lovell Ho, E8 ....**84** DU67
Lovell Pl, SE16 ....**203** L6
Lovell Rd, Enf. EN1 ....**30** DV35
Richmond TW10 ....**117** CJ90
Southall UB1 ....**78** CB72
Lovell Wk, Rain. RM13 ......**89** FG65
Lovel Mead, Ger.Cr. (Chal.St.P.)
SL9 ....**36** AW52
Lovelock Cl, Ken. CR8 ......**176** DQ117
Lovel Rd, Ger.Cr. (Chal.St.P.)
SL9 ....**36** AW52
Loveridge Ms, NW6
off Loveridge Rd **81** CZ65
Loveridge Rd, NW6 ....**81** CZ65
Lovering Rd, Wal.Cr. (Chsht)
EN7 ....**14** DQ26
Lovers La, Green. DA9 ......**109** FX84
Lovers Wk, N3 ....**44** DA52
NW7 ....**43** CZ51
SE10 ....**104** EE79
Lover's Wk, W1 ....**198** F2
Lovett Dr, Cars. SM5 ......**140** DC101
Lovett Rd, St.Alb. (Lon.Col.)
AL2 ....**9** CG26
Staines TW18 ....**113** BB91
Uxbridge (Hare.) UB9 ......**58** BJ55
Lovett's Pl, SW18
off Old York Rd **100** DB84
Lovett Way, NW10 ....**62** CQ64
Love Wk, SE5 ....**102** DR82
Lovibonds Av, Orp. BR6 .....**163** EP105
West Drayton UB7 ....**76** BM72
Lowbell La, St.Alb. (Lon.Col.)
AL2 ....**10** CL27
Lowbrook Rd, Ilf. IG1 ....**69** EP64
Low Cl, Green. DA9 ....**129** FU85
Low Cross Wd La, SE21 .....**122** DT90
Lowdell Cl, West Dr. UB7 ....**76** BL72
Lowden Rd, N9 ....**46** DV46
SE24 ....**101** DP84
Southall UB1 ....**78** BY73
Lowe, The, Chig. IG7 ....**50** EU50
Lowe Av, E16 ....**86** EG71
Lowe Cl, Chig. IG7 ....**50** EU50
Lowell St, E14 ....**85** DY72
Lowen Rd, Rain. RM13 ....**89** FD68
Lower Addiscombe Rd,
Croy. CR0 ....**142** DS102
Lower Addison Gdns, W14 ...**99** CY75
Lower Alderton Hall La,
Loug. IG10 ....**33** EN43
LOWER ASHTEAD, Ashtd.
KT21 ....**171** CJ119
Lower Barn Rd, Pur. CR8 ...**160** DR112
Lower Bedfords Rd, Rom.
RM1 ....**51** FE51
Lower Belgrave St, SW1 ....**199** H7
Lower Boston Rd, W7 ....**79** CE74
Lower Br Rd, Red. RH1 .....**184** DF134
Lower Broad St, Dag. RM10 ..**88** FA67
Lower Bury La, Epp. CM16 ...**17** ES31
Lower Camden, Chis. BR7 ...**125** EM94
Lower Ch Hill, Green. DA9 ..**129** FS85
Lower Ch St, Croy. CR0
off Waddon New Rd **141** DP103
LOWER CLAPTON, E5 ....**67** DX63
Lower Clapton Rd, E5 ....**66** DV64
Lower Clarendon Wk, W11
off Lancaster Rd **81** CY72
Lower Common S, SW15 ....**99** CV83
Lower Coombe St, Croy.
CR0 ....**160** DQ105
Lower Ct Rd, Epsom KT19 ..**156** CQ111
Lower Cft, Swan. BR8 ......**147** FF98
Lower Downs Rd, SW20 ....**139** CX95
Lower Drayton Pl, Croy. CR0
off Drayton Rd **141** DP103
Lower Dunnymans, Bans.
SM7 *off Basing Rd* **157** CZ114
LOWER EDMONTON, N9 ....**46** DT46
Lower Fm Rd, Lthd. (Eff.)
KT24 ....**169** BV124
LOWER FELTHAM, Felt.
TW13 ....**115** BS90
Lower George St, Rich. TW9
off George St **117** CK85
Lower Gravel Rd, Brom. BR2 **.144** EL102
LOWER GREEN, Esher KT10 **.136** CA103
Lower Grn Gdns, Wor.Pk.
KT4 ....**139** CU102
Lower Grn Rd, Esher KT10 ..**136** CB103
Lower Grn W, Mitch. CR4 ...**140** DE97
Lower Grosvenor Pl, SW1 ...**199** H6
Lower Gro Rd, Rich. TW10 ...**118** CM86
Lower Guild Hall, Green.
(Bluewater) DA9
off Bluewater Parkway ..**129** FU88
Lower Hall La, E4 ....**47** DY50
Lower Hampton Rd, Sun.
TW16 ....**136** BW97
Lower Ham Rd, Kings.T. KT2 **.117** CK93
Lower Higham Rd, Grav.
DA12 ....**131** GM88
Lower High St, Wat. WD17 ...**24** BX44
Lower Hill Rd, Epsom KT19 **.156** CP112
LOWER HOLLOWAY, N7 .....**65** DM64
Lower James St, W1 ....**195** L10
Lower John St, W1 ....**195** L10
Lower Kenwood Av, Enf. EN2 **.29** DK43
Lower Kings Rd, Kings.T.
KT2 ....**138** CL95
LOWER KINGSWOOD, Tad.
KT20 ....**184** DA127
Lower Lea Crossing, E14 ....**86** EE73
E16 ....**86** EE73
Lower Maidstone Rd, N11
off Telford Rd **45** DJ51
Lower Mall, W6 ....**99** CV78
Lower Mardyke Av, Rain.
RM13 ....**89** FC68
Lower Marsh, SE1 ....**200** D5
Lower Marsh La, Kings.T.
KT1 ....**138** CM98
Lower Mast Ho, SE18
off Woolwich Ch St **105** EN76
Lower Mead, Iver SL0 ....**75** BD69
Lower Meadow, Wal.Cr. EN8 **.15** DX27
Lower Merton Ri, NW3 ......**82** DE66
Lower Morden La, Mord.
SM4 ....**139** CW100
Lower Mortlake Rd, Rich.
TW9 ....**98** CL84
Lower Noke Cl, Brwd. CM14 **.52** FL47
Lower Northfield, Bans.
SM7 ....**157** CZ114
Lower Paddock Rd, Wat.
WD19 ....**24** BY44
Lower Pk Rd, N11 ....**45** DJ50
Belvedere DA17 ....**106** FA76
Coulsdon (Chipstead) CR5 **.174** DE118
Loughton IG10 ....**32** EK43
Lower Pillory Down, Cars.
SM5 ....**158** DG113
Lower Plantation, Rick.
(Loud.) WD3 ....**22** BJ41
Lower Queens Rd, Buck.H.
IG9 ....**48** EK47
Lower Range Rd, Grav.
DA12 ....**131** GL87
Lower Richmond Rd, SW14 ..**98** CP83
SW15 ....**99** CW83
Richmond TW9 ....**98** CN83
Lower Rd, SE1
off Station App **101** DN75
SE8 ....**202** F6
SE16 ....**203** H8
Belvedere DA17 ....**106** FA76
Brentwood (Mtnsg) CM13,
CM15 ....**55** GD41
Erith DA8 ....**107** FD77
Gerrards Cross SL9 ....**36** AY53
Gravesend (Nthflt) DA11 ..**110** FY84
Harrow HA2 ....**61** CD61
Hemel Hempstead HP3 .....**6** BN25
Kenley CR8 ....**159** DP113
Leatherhead KT22, KT23 ..**171** CD123
Loughton IG10 ....**33** EN40
Orpington BR5 ....**146** EV101
Rickmansworth (Chorl.)
WD3 ....**21** BC42
Sutton SM1 ....**158** DC105
Swanley BR8 ....**127** FF94
Uxbridge (Denh.) UB9 .....**57** BC59
Lower Robert St, WC2
off John Adam St **83** DL73
Lower Rose Gall, Green.
(Bluewater) DA9
off Bluewater Parkway ..**129** FU88
Lower Sandfields, Wok.
(Send) GU23 ....**167** BD124
Lower Sand Hills, T.Ditt. KT7 **.137** CJ101
Lower Sawley Wd, Bans. SM7
off Upper Sawley Wd ...**157** CZ114
Lower Shott, Wal.Cr. (Chsht)
EN7 ....**14** DT26
Lower Sloane St, SW1 .....**198** F9
Lower Sq, Islw. TW7 ....**97** CH83
Lower Sta Rd, Dart. (Cray.)
DA1 ....**127** FE86
Lower Strand, NW9 ....**43** CT54
Lower Sunbury Rd, Hmptn.
TW12 ....**136** BZ96

★ Place of interest ⇌ Railway station ⊖ London Underground station DLR Docklands Light Railway station Tra Tramlink station H Hospital Riv Pedestrian ferry landing stage

Lower Swaines, Epp. CM16 ..17 ES30
LOWER SYDENHAM, SE26 ..123 DX91
⇌ Lower Sydenham ..123 DZ92
Lower Sydenham Ind Est,
SE26 ..123 DZ92
Lower Tail, Wat. WD19 ..40 BY48
Lower Talbot Wk, W11
off Talbot Wk ..81 CY72
Lower Teddington Rd,
Kings.T. KT1 ..137 CK95
Lower Ter, NW3 ..64 DC62
Lower Thames St, EC3 ..201 L1
Lower Thames Wk, Green.
(Bluewater) DA9
off Bluewater Parkway ..129 FU88
Lower Tub, Bushey WD23 ..41 CD45
Lower Wd Rd, Esher (Clay.)
KT10 ..155 CG107
Lowestoft Cl, E5
off Theydon Rd ..66 DW61
Lowestoft Ms, E16 ..105 EP75
Lowestoft Rd, Wat. WD24 ..23 BV39
Loweswater Cl, Wat. WD25 ..8 BW33
Wembley HA9 ..61 CK61
Lowfield Rd, NW6 ..82 DA66
W3 ..80 CQ72
Lowfield St, Dart. DA1 ..128 FL89
Low Hall Cl, E4 ..47 EA45
Low Hall La, E17 ..67 DY58
Lowick Rd, Har. HA1 ..61 CE56
Lowlands Dr, Stai. (Stanw.)
TW19 ..114 BK85
Lowlands Gdns, Rom. RM7 ..71 FB58
Lowlands Rd, Har. HA1 ..61 CE59
Pinner HA5 ..60 BW59
South Ockendon (Aveley)
RM15 ..90 FP74
Lowman Rd, N7 ..65 DM63
Lowndes Cl, SW1 ..198 G7
Lowndes Ct, W1 ..195 K9
Bromley BR1
off Queens Rd ..144 EG96
Lowndes Pl, SW1 ..198 F7
Lowndes Sq, SW1 ..198 E5
Lowndes St, SW1 ..198 E6
Lowood Ct, SE19 ..122 DT92
Lowood St, E1 off Dellow St ..84 DV73
Lowry Cl, Erith DA8 ..107 FD77
Lowry Cres, Mitch. CR4 ..140 DE96
Lowry Ho, E14
off Cassilis Rd ..103 EA75
Lowry Rd, Dag. RM8 ..70 EV63
Lowshoe La, Rom. RM5 ..51 FB53
Lowson Gro, Wat. WD19 ..40 BY45
LOW STREET, Til. RM18 ..111 GM79
Low St La, Til. (E.Til.) RM18 ..111 GM78
Lowswood Cl, Nthwd. HA6 ..39 BQ53
Lowther Cl, Borwd. (Els.) WD6 ..26 CM43
Lowther Dr, Enf. EN2 ..29 DL42
Lowther Gdns, SW7 ..198 A5
Lowther Hill, SE23 ..123 DY87
Lowther Rd, E17 ..47 DY54
N7 off Mackenzie Rd ..65 DN64
SW13 ..99 CT81
Kingston upon Thames
KT2 ..138 CM95
Stanmore HA7 ..62 CM55
Lowthorpe, Wok. GU21
off Shilburn Way ..166 AU118
Lowth Rd, SE5 ..102 DQ82
LOXFORD, Ilf. IG1 ..69 EQ64
Loxford Av, E6 ..86 EK68
Loxford La, Ilf. IG1, IG3 ..69 EQ64
Loxford Rd, Bark. IG11 ..87 EP65
Caterham CR3 ..186 DT125
Loxford Ter, Bark. IG11
off Fanshawe Av ..87 EQ65
Loxford Way, Cat. CR3 ..186 DT125
Loxham Rd, E4 ..47 EA52
Loxham St, WC1 ..196 A3
Loxley Cl, SE26 ..123 DX92
Loxley Rd, SW18 ..120 DD88
Hampton TW12 ..116 BZ91
Loxton Rd, SE23 ..123 DX88
Loxwood Cl, Felt. TW14 ..115 BR88
Orpington BR5 ..146 EX103
Loxwood Rd, N17 ..66 DS55
Lubbock Rd, Chis. BR7 ..125 EM94
Lubbock St, SE14 ..102 DW80
Lucan Dr, Stai. TW18 ..114 BK94
Lucan Pl, SW3 ..198 B9
Lucan Rd, Barn. EN5 ..27 CY41
Lucas Av, E13 ..86 EH67
Harrow HA2 ..60 CA61
Lucas Cl, NW10 off Pound La ..81 CU66
Lucas Ct, SW11
off Strasburg Rd ..100 DG81
Harrow HA2 ..60 CA60
Waltham Abbey EN9 ..16 EF33
Lucas Cres, Green. DA9
off Ingress Pk Av ..129 FW85
Lucas Gdns, N2 ..44 DC54
Lucas Rd, SE20 ..122 DW93
Grays RM17 ..110 GA76
Lucas Sq, NW11
off Hampstead Way ..64 DA58
Lucas St, SE8 ..103 EA81
Lucern Cl, Wal.Cr. (Chsht) EN7 ..14 DS27
Lucerne Cl, N13 ..45 DL49
Woking GU22
off Claremont Av ..166 AY119
Lucerne Ct, Erith DA18
off Middle Way ..106 EY76
Lucerne Gro, E17 ..67 ED56
Lucerne Ms, W8
off Kensington Mall ..82 DA74
Lucerne Rd, N5 ..65 DP63
Orpington BR6 ..145 ET102
Thornton Heath CR7 ..141 DP99
Lucerne Way, Rom. RM3 ..52 FK51
Lucey Rd, SE16 ..202 B7
Lucey Way, SE16 ..202 C7
Lucida Ct, Wat. WD18
off Whippendell Rd ..23 BS43
Lucie Av, Ashf. TW15 ..115 BP93
Lucien Rd, SW17 ..120 DG91
SW19 ..120 DB89
Lucknow St, SE18 ..105 ES80
Lucorn Cl, SE12 ..124 EF86
Lucton Ms, Loug. IG10 ..33 EP42
Luctons Av, Buck.H. IG9 ..48 EJ46
Lucy Cres, W3 ..80 CQ71
Lucy Gdns, Dag. RM8 ..70 EY62
Luddesdon Rd, Erith DA8 ..106 FA80
Luddington Av, Vir.W. GU25 ..133 AZ96
Ludford Cl, Croy. CR0
off Warrington Rd ..159 DP105
Ludgate Bdy, EC4 ..196 F9
Ludgate Circ, EC4 ..196 F9
Ludgate Hill, EC4 ..196 F9
Ludgate Sq, EC4 ..196 G9
Ludham Cl, SE28
off Rollesby Way ..88 EW72
Ilford IG6 ..49 EQ53
Ludlow Cl, Brom. BR2
off Aylesbury Rd ..144 EG97
Harrow HA2 ..60 BZ63
Ludlow Mead, Wat. WD19 ..39 BV48
Ludlow Pl, Grays RM17 ..110 GB76
Ludlow Rd, W5 ..79 CJ70
Feltham TW13 ..115 BU91
Ludlow St, EC1 ..197 H4
Ludlow Way, N2 ..64 DC56
Rickmansworth (Crox.Grn)
WD3 ..23 BQ42
Ludovick Wk, SW15 ..98 CS84
Ludwick Ms, SE14 ..103 DY80
Luffield Rd, SE2 ..106 EV76
Luffman Rd, SE12 ..124 EH90
Lugard Rd, SE15 ..102 DV82
Lugg App, E12 ..69 EN62
Luke Ho, E1 ..84 DV72
Luke St, EC2 ..197 M4
Lukin Cres, E4 ..47 ED48
Lukin St, E1 ..84 DW72
Lukintone Cl, Loug. IG10 ..32 EL44
Lullarook Cl, West. (Bigg.H.)
TN16 ..178 EJ116
Lullingstone Av, Swan. BR8 ..147 FF97
Lullingstone Cl, Orp. BR5
off Lullingstone Cres ..126 EV94
Lullingstone Cres, Orp. BR5 ..126 EU94
Lullingstone La, SE13 ..123 ED86
Dartford (Eyns.) DA4 ..148 FJ104
★ Lullingstone Park Visitor Cen,
Dart. DA4 ..165 FG107
Lullingstone Rd, Belv. DA17 ..106 EZ79
★ Lullingstone Roman Vil,
Dart. DA4 ..147 FH104
Lullington Garth, N12 ..43 CZ50
Borehamwood WD6 ..26 CP43
Bromley BR1 ..124 EE94
Lullington Rd, SE20 ..122 DU94
Dagenham RM9 ..88 EY66
Lulot Gdns, N19 ..65 DH61
Lulworth, NW1 off Agar Pl ..83 DJ66
SE17 ..201 K10
Lulworth Av, Houns. TW5 ..96 CB80
Waltham Cross (Chsht) EN7 ..13 DP29
Wembley HA9 ..61 CJ59
Lulworth Cl, Har. HA2 ..60 BZ62
Lulworth Cres, Mitch. CR4 ..140 DE96
Lulworth Dr, Pnr. HA5 ..60 BX59
Romford RM5 ..51 FB50
Lulworth Gdns, Har. HA2 ..60 BY61
Lulworth Ho, SW8
off Dorset Rd ..101 DM80
Lulworth Rd, SE9 ..124 EL89
SE15 ..102 DV82
Welling DA16 ..105 ET82
Lulworth Waye, Hayes UB4 ..78 BW72
Lumen Rd, Wem. HA9 ..61 CK61
Lumiere Ct, SW17 ..120 DG89
Lumley Cl, Belv. DA17 ..106 FA79
Lumley Ct, WC2 ..200 A1
Lumley Gdns, Sutt. SM3 ..157 CY106
Lumley Rd, Sutt. SM3 ..157 CY107
Lumley St, W1 ..194 G9
Lunar Cl, West. (Bigg.H.)
TN16 ..178 EK116
Luna Rd, Th.Hth. CR7 ..142 DQ97
Lundin Wk, Wat. WD19
off Woodhall La ..40 BX49
Lund Pt, E15
off Carpenters Rd ..85 EC67
Lundy Dr, Hayes UB3 ..95 BS77
Lundy Wk, N1 off Clifton Rd ..84 DQ65
Lunedale Rd, Dart. DA2 ..128 FQ88
Lunedale Wk, Dart. DA2
off Lunedale Rd ..128 FP88
Lunghurst Rd, Cat. (Wold.)
CR3 ..177 DZ120
Lunham Rd, SE19 ..122 DS93
Lupin Cl, SW2 off Palace Rd ..121 DP89
Croydon CR0
off Primrose La ..143 DX102
Romford (Rush Grn) RM7 ..71 FD61
West Drayton UB7
off Magnolia St ..94 BK78
Lupin Cres, Ilf. IG1
off Bluebell Way ..87 EP65
Lupino Ct, SE11 ..200 C9
Lupin Pt, SE1 off Abbey St ..102 DT75
Luppit Cl, Brwd. (Hutt.) CM13 ..55 GA46
Lupton Cl, SE12 ..124 EH90
Lupton St, NW5 ..65 DJ63
Lupus St, SW1 ..101 DH79
Luralda Gdns, E14 ..204 E10
Lurgan Av, W6 ..99 CX79
Lurline Gdns, SW11 ..100 DG81
Luscombe Ct, Brom. BR2 ..144 EE96
Luscombe Way, SW8 ..101 DL80
Lushes Ct, Loug. IG10
off Lushes Rd ..33 EP43
Lushes Rd, Loug. IG10 ..33 EP43
Lushington Dr, Cob. KT11 ..153 BV114
Lushington Rd, NW10 ..81 CV68
SE6 ..123 EB92
Lushington Ter, E8
off Wayland Av ..66 DU64
Lusted Hall La, West. (Tats.)
TN16 ..178 EJ120
Lusted Rd, Sev. TN13 ..181 FE120
Luther Cl, Edg. HA8 ..42 CQ47
Luther King Cl, E17 ..67 DY58
Luther Ms, Tedd. TW11
off Luther Rd ..117 CF92
Luther Rd, Tedd. TW11 ..117 CF92
Luton Pl, SE10 ..103 EC80
Luton Rd, E13
off Croydon Rd ..86 EG70
Luton Rd, E17 ..67 DZ55
Sidcup DA14 ..126 EW90
Luton St, NW8 ..194 A5
Lutton Ter, NW3
off Flask Wk ..64 DD63
Luttrell Av, SW15 ..119 CV85
Lutwyche Rd, SE6 ..123 DZ89
Lutyens Ho, SW1
off Churchill Gdns ..101 DJ78
Luxborough La, Chig. IG7 ..48 EL48
Luxborough St, W1 ..194 F6
Luxborough Twr, W1
off Luxborough St ..82 DG71
Luxembourg Ms, E15
off Leytonstone Rd ..68 EE64
Luxemburg Gdns, W6 ..99 CX77
Luxfield Rd, SE9 ..124 EL88
Luxford St, SE16 ..203 H9
Luxmore St, SE4 ..103 DZ81
Luxor St, SE5 ..101 DP82
Luxted Rd, Orp. BR6 ..163 EN112
Lyall Av, SE21 ..122 DS90
Lyall Ms, SW1 ..198 F7
Lyall Ms W, SW1 ..198 F7
Lyall St, SW1 ..198 F7
Lyal Rd, E3 ..85 DY68
Lycée, The, SE11
off Stannary St ..101 DN78
Lycett Pl, W12
off Becklow Rd ..99 CU75
Lych Gate, Wat. WD25 ..8 BX33
Lych Gate Rd, Orp. BR6 ..146 EU102
Lych Gate Wk, Hayes UB3 ..77 BT73
Lych Way, Wok. GU21 ..166 AX116
Lyconby Gdns, Croy. CR0 ..143 DY101
Lycrome Rd, Chesh. HP5 ..4 AS28
Lydd Cl, Sid. DA14 ..125 ES90
Lydden Ct, SE9 ..125 ES86
Lydden Gro, SW18 ..120 DB87
Lydden Rd, SW18 ..120 DB87
Lydd Rd, Bexh. DA7 ..106 EZ80
Lydeard Rd, E6 ..87 EM66
Lydele Cl, Wok. GU21 ..167 AZ115
Lydford Cl, N16
off Pellerin Rd ..66 DS64
Lydford Rd, N15 ..66 DR57
NW2 ..81 CX65
W9 ..81 CZ70
Lydhurst Av, SW2 ..121 DM89
Lydia Rd, Erith DA8 ..107 FF79
Lydney Cl, SW19
off Princes Way ..119 CY89
Lydon Rd, SW4 ..101 DJ83
Lydstep Rd, Chis. BR7 ..125 EN91
Lye, The, Tad. KT20 ..173 CW122
LYE GREEN, Chesh. HP5 ..4 AT27
Lye La, St.Alb. (Brick.Wd) AL2 ..8 CA30
Lyfield, Lthd. (Oxshott) KT22 ..154 CB114
Lyford Rd, SW18 ..120 DD87
Lyford St, SE18 off Woodhill ..104 EL77
Lygon Ho, SW6
off Fulham Palace Rd ..99 CX80
Lygon Pl, SW1 ..199 H7
Lyham Cl, SW2 ..121 DL86
Lyham Rd, SW2 ..121 DL85
Lyle Cl, Mitch. CR4 ..140 DG101
Lyle Pk, Sev. TN13 ..191 FH123
Lymbourne Cl, Sutt. SM2 ..158 DA110
Lyme Fm Rd, SE12 ..104 EG84
Lyme Gro, E9
off St. Thomas's Sq ..84 DW66
Lymer Av, SE19 ..122 DT92
Lyme Regis Rd, Bans. SM7 ..173 CZ117
Lyme Rd, Well. DA16 ..106 EV81
Lymescote Gdns, Sutt. SM1 ..140 DA103
Lyme St, NW1 ..83 DJ66
Lyme Ter, NW1
off Royal Coll St ..83 DJ66
Lyminge Cl, Sid. DA14 ..125 ET91
Lyminge Gdns, SW18 ..120 DE88
Lymington Av, N22 ..45 DN54
Lymington Cl, E6
off Valiant Way ..87 EM71
SW16 ..141 DK96
Lymington Dr, Ruis. HA4 ..59 BR61
Lymington Gdns, Epsom
KT19 ..157 CT106
Lymington Rd, NW6 ..82 DB65
Dagenham RM8 ..70 EX60
Lyminster Cl, Hayes UB4
off West Quay Dr ..78 BY71
Lympstone Gdns, SE15 ..102 DU80
Lynbridge Gdns, N13 ..45 DP49
Lynbrook Cl, Rain. RM13 ..89 FD68
Lynbrook Gro, SE15 ..102 DS80
Lynceley Gra, Epp. CM16 ..18 EU29
Lynch, The, Uxb. UB8
off New Windsor St ..76 BJ67
Lynch Cl, SE3 off Paragon Pl ..104 EF82
Uxbridge UB8
off New Windsor St ..76 BJ67
Lynchen Cl, Houns. TW5
off The Avenue ..95 BU81
Lynch Wk, SE8 off Prince St ..103 DZ79
Lyncott Cres, SW4 ..101 DH84
Lyncroft Av, Pnr. HA5 ..60 BY57
Lyncroft Gdns, NW6 ..64 DA64
W13 ..97 CJ75
Epsom KT17 ..157 CT109
Hounslow TW3 ..96 CC84
Lyndale, NW2 ..63 CZ63
Lyndale Av, NW2 ..63 CZ62
Lyndale Cl, SE3 ..104 EF79
Lyndale Ct, W.Byf. KT14
off Parvis Rd ..152 BG113
Lyndale Est, Grays RM20 ..109 FV79
Lyndale Rd, Red. RH1 ..184 DF131
Lynden Way, Swan. BR8 ..147 FC97
Lyndhurst Av, N12 ..44 DF51
NW7 ..42 CS51
SW16 ..141 DK96
Pinner HA5 ..39 BV53
Southall UB1 ..78 CB74
Sunbury-on-Thames TW16 ..135 BU97
Surbiton KT5 ..138 CP102
Twickenham TW2 ..116 BZ88
Lyndhurst Cl, NW10 ..62 CR62
Bexleyheath DA7 ..107 FB83
Croydon CR0 ..142 DT104
Orpington BR6 ..163 EP105
Woking GU21 ..166 AX115
Lyndhurst Ct, E18
off Churchfields ..48 EG53
Lyndhurst Ct, Sutt. SM2
off Overton Rd ..158 DA108
Lyndhurst Dr, E10 ..67 EC59
Hornchurch RM11 ..72 FJ60
New Malden KT3 ..138 CS100
Sevenoaks TN13 ..190 FE124
Lyndhurst Gdns, N3 ..43 CY53
NW3 ..64 DD64
Barking IG11 ..87 ES65
Enfield EN1 ..30 DS42
Ilford IG2 ..69 ER58
Pinner HA5 ..39 BV53
Lyndhurst Gro, SE15 ..102 DS82
Lyndhurst Ho, SW15
off Ellisfield Dr ..119 CU87
Lyndhurst Ri, Chig. IG7 ..49 EN49
Lyndhurst Rd, E4 ..47 EC52
N18 ..46 DU49
N22 ..45 DM51
NW3 ..64 DD64
Bexleyheath DA7 ..107 FB83
Coulsdon CR5 ..174 DG116
Greenford UB6 ..78 CB70
Thornton Heath CR7 ..141 DN98
Lyndhurst Sq, SE15 ..102 DT81
Lyndhurst Ter, NW3 ..64 DD64
Lyndhurst Way, SE15 ..102 DT81
Brentwood (Hutt.) CM13 ..55 GC45
Chertsey KT16 ..133 BE104
Sutton SM2 ..158 DA108
Lyndon Av, Pnr. HA5 ..40 BY51
Sidcup DA15 ..125 ET85
Wallington SM6 ..140 DG104
Lyndon Rd, Belv. DA17 ..106 FA77
Lyndon Yd, SW17 ..120 DB91
Lyndwood Dr, Wind.
(Old Wind.) SL4 ..112 AU86
LYNE, Cher. KT16 ..133 BA102
Lyne Cl, Vir.W. GU25 ..133 AZ100
Lyne Cres, E17 ..47 DZ53
Lyne Crossing Rd, Cher.
(Lyne) KT16 ..133 BA100
Lynegrove Av, Ashf. TW15 ..115 BQ92
Lyneham Dr, NW9
off Kenley Av ..42 CS54
Lyneham Wk, E5
off Boscombe Cl ..67 DY64
Pinner HA5 ..59 BT55
Lyne La, Cher. (Lyne) KT16 ..133 BA100
Egham TW20 ..133 BA99
Virginia Water GU25 ..133 BA100
Lyne Rd, Vir.W. GU25 ..132 AX100
Lynette Av, SW4 ..121 DH86
Lynett Rd, Dag. RM8 ..70 EX61
Lynford Cl, Barn. EN5
off Rowley La ..27 CT43
Edgware HA8 ..42 CQ52
Lynford Gdns, Edg. HA8 ..42 CP48
Ilford IG3 ..69 ET61
Lynhurst Cres, Uxb. UB10 ..77 BQ66
Lynhurst Rd, Uxb. UB10 ..77 BQ66
Lynmere Rd, Well. DA16 ..106 EV82
Lyn Ms, E3 off Tredegar Sq ..85 DZ69
N16 ..66 DS63
Lynmouth Av, Enf. EN1 ..30 DT44
Morden SM4 ..139 CX101
Lynmouth Dr, Ruis. HA4 ..59 BV61
Lynmouth Gdns, Grnf. UB6 ..79 CH67
Hounslow TW5 ..96 BX81
Lynmouth Ri, Orp. BR5 ..146 EV98
Lynmouth Rd, E17 ..67 DY58
N2 ..64 DF55
N16 ..66 DT60
Greenford UB6 ..79 CH67
Lynn Cl, Ashf. TW15
off Goffs Rd ..115 BR92
Harrow HA3 ..41 CD54
Lynne Cl, Orp. BR6 ..163 ET107
South Croydon CR2 ..160 DW111
Lynne Wk, Esher KT10 ..154 CC106
Lynne Way, Nthlt. UB5 ..78 BX68
Lynn Ms, E11 off Lynn Rd ..68 EE61
Lynn Rd, E11 ..68 EE61
SW12 ..121 DH87
Ilford IG2 ..69 ER59
Lynn St, Enf. EN2 ..30 DR39
Lynross Cl, Rom. RM3 ..52 FM54
Lynscott Way, S.Croy. CR2 ..159 DP109
Lynsted Cl, Bexh. DA6 ..127 FB85
Bromley BR1 ..144 EJ96
Lynsted Ct, Beck. BR3
off Churchfields Rd ..143 DY96
Lynsted Gdns, SE9 ..104 EK83
Lynton Av, N12 ..44 DD49
NW9 ..63 CT56
W13 ..79 CG72
Orpington BR5 ..146 EV98
Romford RM7 ..50 FA53
Lynton Cl, NW10 ..62 CS64
Chessington KT9 ..156 CL105
Isleworth TW7 ..97 CF84
Lynton Cres, Ilf. IG2 ..69 EP58
Lynton Crest, Pot.B. EN6
off Strafford Gate ..12 DA32
Lynton Est, SE1 ..202 B9
Lynton Gdns, N11 ..45 DK51
Enfield EN1 ..46 DS45
Lynton Mead, N20 ..44 DA48
Lynton Par, Wal.Cr. EN8
off Turners Hill ..15 DX30
Lynton Rd, E4 ..47 EB50
N8 ..65 DK57
NW6 ..81 CZ67
SE1 ..202 A9
W3 ..80 CN73
Croydon CR0 ..141 DN100
Gravesend DA11 ..131 GG88
Harrow HA2 ..60 BY61
New Malden KT3 ..138 CR99
Lynton Rd S, Grav. DA11 ..131 GG88
Lynton Ter, W3 off Lynton Rd ..80 CQ72
Lynton Wk, Hayes UB4 ..77 BS69
Lynwood Av, Couls. CR5 ..175 DH115
Egham TW20 ..112 AY93
Epsom KT17 ..157 CT114
Slough SL3 ..92 AX76
Lynwood Cl, E18 ..48 EJ53
Harrow HA2 ..60 BY62
Romford RM5 ..51 FB51
Woking GU21 ..151 BD113
Lynwood Dr, Nthwd. HA6 ..39 BT53
Romford RM5 ..51 FB51
Worcester Park KT4 ..139 CU103
Lynwood Gdns, Croy. CR0 ..159 DM105
Southall UB1 ..78 BZ72
Lynwood Gro, N21 ..45 DN46
Orpington BR6 ..145 ES101
Lynwood Hts, Rick. WD3 ..22 BH43
Lynwood Rd, SW17 ..120 DF90
W5 ..80 CL70
Epsom KT17 ..157 CT114
Redhill RH1 ..184 DG132
Thames Ditton KT7 ..137 CF103
Lynx Way, E16 ..86 EK73
Lyon Business Pk, Bark. IG11 ..87 ES68
Lyon Meade, Stan. HA7 ..41 CJ53
Lyon Pk Av, Wem. HA0 ..80 CL65
Lyon Rd, SW19 ..140 DC95
Harrow HA1 ..61 CF58
Romford RM1 ..71 FF59
Walton-on-Thames KT12 ..136 BY103
Lyonsdene, Tad. (Lwr Kgswd)
KT20 ..183 CZ127
Lyonsdown Av, Barn. EN5 ..28 DC44
Lyonsdown Rd, Barn. EN5 ..28 DC44
Lyons Pl, NW8 ..82 DD70
Lyon St, N1
off Caledonian Rd ..83 DM66
Lyons Wk, W14 ..99 CY77
Lyon Way, Grnf. UB6 ..79 CE67
Lyoth Rd, Orp. BR5 ..145 EQ103
Lyric Dr, Grnf. UB6 ..78 CB70
Lyric Ms, SE26 ..122 DW91
Lyric Rd, SW13 ..99 CT81
Lyric Sq, W6 off King St ..99 CW77
★ Lyric Thea, W6 ..99 CW77
Lysander Cl, Hem.H. (Bov.)
HP3 ..5 AZ27
Lysander Gdns, Surb. KT6
off Ewell Rd ..138 CM100
Lysander Gro, N19 ..65 DK60
Lysander Ho, E2
off Temple St ..84 DV68
Lysander Ms, N19
off Lysander Gro ..65 DK60
Lysander Rd, Croy. CR0 ..159 DM107
Ruislip HA4 ..59 BR61
Lysander Way, Abb.L. WD5 ..7 BU32
Orpington BR6 ..145 EQ104
Lysias Rd, SW12 ..120 DG86
Lysia St, SW6 ..99 CX80
Lysley Pl, Hat. (Brook.Pk) AL9 ..12 DC27
Lysons Wk, SW15 ..119 CU85
Lyster Ms, Cob. KT11 ..153 BV113
Lytchet Rd, Brom. BR1 ..124 EH94
Lytchet Way, Enf. EN3 ..30 DW39
Lytchgate Cl, S.Croy. CR2 ..160 DS108
Lytcott Dr, W.Mol. KT8
off Freeman Dr ..136 BZ98
Lytcott Gro, SE22 ..122 DT85
Lyte St, E2
off Bishops Way ..84 DW68
Lytham Av, Wat. WD19 ..40 BX50
Lytham Cl, SE28 ..88 EY72
Lytham Gro, W5 ..80 CM69
Lytham St, SE17 ..102 DR78
Lyttelton Cl, NW3 ..82 DE66
Lyttelton Rd, E10 ..67 EB62
N2 ..64 DC57
Lyttleton Rd, N8 ..65 DN55
Lytton Av, N13 ..45 DN47
Enfield EN3 ..31 DY38
Lytton Cl, N2 ..64 DD57
Loughton IG10 ..33 ER41
Northolt UB5 ..78 BZ66
Lytton Gdns, Wall. SM6 ..159 DK105
Lytton Gro, SW15 ..119 CX85
Lytton Pk, Cob. KT11 ..154 BZ112
Lytton Rd, E11 ..68 EE59
Barnet EN5 ..28 DC42
Grays RM16 ..111 GG77
Pinner HA5 ..40 BY52
Romford RM2 ..71 FH57
Woking GU22 ..167 BB116
Lytton Strachey Path, SE28
off Titmuss Av ..88 EV73
Lyveden Rd, SE3 ..104 EH80
SW17 ..120 DE93
Lywood Cl, Tad. KT20 ..173 CW122

M

Mabbotts, Tad. KT20 ..173 CX121
Mabbutt Cl, St.Alb. (Brick.Wd)
AL2 ..8 BY30
Mabel Rd, Swan. BR8 ..127 FG93
Mabel St, Wok. GU21 ..166 AX117
Maberley Cres, SE19 ..122 DU94
Maberley Rd, SE19 ..142 DT95
Beckenham BR3 ..143 DX97
Mabledon Pl, WC1 ..195 N3
Mablethorpe Rd, SW6 ..99 CY80
Mabley St, E9 ..85 DY65
McAdam Dr, Enf. EN2 ..29 DP40
Macaret Cl, N20 ..44 DB45
MacArthur Cl, E7 ..86 EG65
Erith DA8 ..107 FE78
MacArthur Ter, SE7 ..104 EL79
Macaulay Av, Esher KT10 ..137 CE103
Macaulay Ct, SW4 ..101 DH83
Macaulay Rd, E6 ..86 EK68
SW4 ..101 DH83
Caterham CR3 ..176 DS122
Macaulay Sq, SW4 ..101 DH84
Macaulay Way, SE28
off Booth Cl ..88 EV73
McAuley Cl, SE1 ..200 D6
SE9 ..125 EP85
Macauley Ms, SE13 ..103 EC82
Macbean St, SE18 ..105 EN76
Macbeth St, W6 ..99 CV78
McCall Cl, SW4
off Jeffreys Rd ..101 DL82
McCall Cres, SE7 ..104 EL78
McCarthy Rd, Felt. TW13 ..116 BX92
Macclesfield Br, NW1 ..82 DE68
Macclesfield Rd, EC1 ..197 H2
SE25 ..142 DV99
Macclesfield St, W1 ..195 N10
McClintock Pl, Enf. EN3 ..31 EB38
McCoid Way, SE1 ..201 H5
McCrone Ms, NW3
off Belsize La ..82 DD65

★ Place of interest ⇌ Railway station ⊖ London Underground station DLR Docklands Light Railway station Tra Tramlink station H Hospital Riv Pedestrian ferry landing stage

McCudden Rd, Dart. DA1
off Cornwall Rd 108 FM83
McCullum Rd, E3 85 DZ67
McDermott Cl, SW11 100 DE83
McDermott Rd, SE15 102 DU83
Macdonald Av, Dag. RM10 71 FB62
Hornchurch RM11 72 FL56
Macdonald Rd, E7 68 EG63
E17 47 EC54
N11 44 DF50
N19 65 DJ61
Macdonald Way, Horn. RM11 72 FL56
Macdonnell Gdns, Wat. WD25
off High Rd 23 BT35
McDonough Cl, Chess. KT9 156 CL105
McDowall Cl, E16 86 EF71
McDowall Rd, SE5 102 DQ81
Macduff Rd, SW11 100 DG81
Mace Cl, E1 202 D2
Mace Ct, Grays RM17 110 GE79
Mace La, Sev. (Cudham)
TN14 163 ER113
McEntee Av, E17 47 DY53
Mace St, E2 85 DX68
McEwen Way, E15 85 ED67
Macey Ho, SW11
off Surrey La 100 DE81
Macfarland Gro, SE15 102 DS80
MacFarlane La, Islw. TW7 97 CF79
Macfarlane Rd, W12 81 CW74
Macfarren Pl, NW1 194 G5
McGrath Rd, E15 68 EF64
McGredy, Wal.Cr. (Chsht) EN7 14 DV29
Macgregor Rd, E16 86 EJ71
McGregor Rd, W11 81 CZ72
Machell Rd, SE15 102 DW83
McIntosh Cl, Rom. RM1 71 FE55
Wallington SM6 159 DL108
Macintosh Cl, Wal.Cr. EN7 14 DR26
McIntosh Rd, Rom. RM1 71 FE55
Mackay Rd, SW4 101 DH83
McKay Rd, SW20 119 CV94
McKay Trd Est, Slou.
(Colnbr.) SL3 93 BE82
McKellar Cl, Bushey (Bushey Hth)
WD23 40 CC47
Mackennal St, NW8 194 C1
Mackenzie Mall, Slou. SL1
off High St 92 AT75
Mackenzie Rd, N7 83 DM65
Beckenham BR3 142 DW96
Mackenzie St, Slou. SL1 74 AT74
Mackenzie Wk, E14 204 A3
McKenzie Way, Epsom KT19 156 CN110
Mackenzie Way, Grav. DA12 131 GK93
McKerrell Rd, SE15 102 DU81
Mackeson Rd, NW3 64 DF63
Mackie Rd, SW2 121 DN87
Mackintosh La, E9
off Homerton High St 67 DX64
Macklin St, WC2 196 A8
Mackrow Wk, E14
off Robin Hood La 85 EC73
Macks Rd, SE16 202 C8
Mackworth St, NW1 195 K2
Maclaren Ms, SW15
off Clarendon Dr 99 CW84
Maclean Rd, SE23 123 DY86
Maclennan Av, Rain. RM13 90 FK69
Macleod Cl, Grays RM17 110 GD77
Macleod Rd, N21 29 DL43
McLeod Rd, SE2 106 EV77
McLeod's Ms, SW7
off Emperor's Gate 100 DC77
Macleod St, SE17 102 DQ78
Maclise Rd, W14 99 CY76
McMillan Cl, Grav. DA12 131 GJ91
Macmillan Gdns, Dart. DA1 108 FN84
McMillan St, SE8 103 EA79
McMillan Student Village,
SE8 off Creek Rd 103 EA79
Macmillan Way, SW17 121 DH91
McNair Rd, Sthl. UB2 96 CB75
McNeil Rd, SE5 102 DS82
McNicol Dr, NW10 80 CQ68
Macoma Rd, SE18 105 ER79
Macoma Ter, SE18 105 ER79
Maconochies Rd, E14 204 B10
Macon Way, Upmin. RM14 73 FT59
Macquarie Way, E14 204 C9
McRae La, Mitch. CR4 140 DF101
Macroom Rd, W9 81 CZ69
Mac's Pl, EC4 196 D8
★ Madame Tussaud's, NW1 194 F5
Madan Rd, West. TN16 189 ER125
Madans Wk, Epsom KT18 156 CR114
Mada Rd, Orp. BR6 145 EP104
Maddams St, E3 85 EB70
Madden Cl, Swans. DA10 129 FX86
Maddison Cl, N2 off Long La 44 DC54
Teddington TW11 117 CF93
Maddocks Cl, Sid. DA14 126 EY92
Maddock Way, SE17 101 DP79
Maddox La, Lthd. (Bkhm)
KT23 170 BY123
Maddox Pk, Lthd. (Bkhm)
KT23 170 BY123
Maddox St, W1 195 J10
Madeira Av, Brom. BR1 124 EE94
Madeira Cl, W.Byf. KT14
off Brantwood Gdns 152 BG113
Madeira Cres, W.Byf. KT14
off Brantwood Gdns 152 BG113
Madeira Gro, Wdf.Grn. IG8 48 EJ51
Madeira Rd, E11 67 ED60
N13 45 DP49
SW16 121 DL92
Mitcham CR4 140 DF98
West Byfleet KT14 151 BF113
Madeira Wk, Brwd. CM15 54 FY48
Reigate RH2 184 DD133
Madeleine Cl, Rom. RM3 70 EW58
Madeley Rd, W5 80 CL72
Madeline Gro, Ilf. IG1 69 ER64
Madeline Rd, SE20 142 DU95
Madells, Epp. CM16 17 ET31
Madge Gill Way, E6
off Ron Leighton Way 86 EL67
Madinah Rd, E8 84 DU65
Madingley, Kings.T. KT1
off St. Peters Rd 138 CN96
Madison Cres, Bexh. DA7 106 EW80
Madison Gdns, Bexh. DA7 106 EW80
Madison Gdns, Brom. BR2 144 EF97
Madison Way, Sev. TN13 190 FF123
Madras Pl, N7 83 DN65
Madras Rd, Ilf. IG1 69 EP63
Madresfield Ct, Rad. (Shenley)
WD7 off Russet Dr 10 CL32
Madrid Rd, SW13 99 CU81
Madrigal La, SE5 101 DP80
Madron St, SE17 201 N10
Maesmaur Rd, West. (Tats.)
TN16 178 EK121
Mafeking Av, E6 86 EK68
Brentford TW8 98 CL79
Ilford IG2 69 ER59
Mafeking Rd, E16 86 EF70
N17 46 DU54
Enfield EN1 30 DT41
Staines (Wrays.) TW19 113 BB89
Magazine Pl, Lthd. KT22 171 CH122
Magazine Rd, Cat. CR3 175 DP122
Magdala Av, N19 65 DH61
Magdala Rd, Islw. TW7 97 CG83
South Croydon CR2
off Napier Rd 160 DR108
Magdalen Cl, W.Byf.
(Byfleet) KT14 152 BL114
Magdalen Cres, W.Byf.
(Byfleet) KT14 152 BL114
Magdalene Cl, SE15
off Pilkington Rd 102 DV82
Magdalene Gdns, E6 87 EN70
Magdalene Rd, Shep. TW17 134 BM98
Magdalen Gdns, Brwd.
(Hutt.) CM13 55 GE44
Magdalen Gro, Orp. BR6 164 EV105
Magdalen Ms, NW3
off Frognal 82 DC65
Magdalen Pas, E1
off Prescot St 84 DT73
Magdalen Rd, SW18 120 DC88
Magdalen St, SE1 201 M3
Magee St, SE11 101 DN79
Magellan Pl, E14
off Maritime Quay 103 EA77
Maggie Blakes Causeway,
SE1 off Shad Thames 84 DT74
Magna Carta La, Stai.
(Wrays.) TW19 112 AX88
★ Magna Carta Monument,
Egh. TW20 112 AX89
Magna Rd, Egh. (Eng.Grn)
TW20 112 AV93
Magnaville Rd, Bushey
(Bushey Hth) WD23 41 CE45
Magnet Est, Grays RM20 109 FW78
Magnet Rd, Grays RM20 109 FW79
Wembley HA9 61 CK61
Magnin Cl, E8 off Wilde Cl 84 DU67
Magnolia Av, Abb.L. WD5 7 BU32
Magnolia Cl, E10 67 EA61
Kingston upon Thames
KT2 118 CP93
St. Albans (Park St) AL2 9 CD27
Magnolia Ct, Felt. TW13
off Highfield Rd 115 BU88
Harrow HA3 62 CM59
Wallington SM6
off Parkgate Rd 159 DH106
Magnolia Dr, West. (Bigg.H.)
TN16 178 EK116
Magnolia Gdns, Edg. HA8 42 CQ49
Slough SL3 92 AW76
Magnolia Pl, SW4 121 DK85
W5 79 CK71
Magnolia Rd, W4 98 CP79
Magnolia St, West Dr. UB7 94 BK77
Magnolia Way, Brwd.
(Pilg.Hat.) CM15 54 FV43
Epsom KT19 156 CQ106
Magnum Cl, Rain. RM13 90 FJ70
Magnum Ho, Kings.T. KT2
off London Rd 138 CN95
Magpie All, EC4 196 E9
Magpie Cl, E7 68 EF64
NW9 off Eagle Dr 42 CS54
Coulsdon CR5
off Ashbourne Cl 175 DJ118
Enfield EN1 30 DU39
Magpie Hall Cl, Brom. BR2 144 EL100
Magpie Hall La, Brom. BR2 145 EM99
Magpie Hall Rd, Bushey
(Bushey Hth) WD23 41 CE47
Magpie La, Brwd. CM13 53 FW54
Magpie Pl, SE14
off Milton Ct Rd 103 DY79
Magri Wk, E1 off Ashfield St 84 DW71
Maguire Dr, Rich. TW10 117 CJ91
Maguire St, SE1 202 A4
Mahlon Av, Ruis. HA4 59 BV64
Mahogany Cl, SE16 203 L3
Mahon Cl, Enf. EN1 30 DT39
Maida Av, E4 47 EB45
W2 82 DC71
MAIDA HILL, W9 81 CZ70
Maida Rd, Belv. DA17 106 FA76
MAIDA VALE, W9 82 DB70
⊖ Maida Vale 82 DC69
Maida Vale, W9 82 DB68
Maida Vale Rd, Dart. DA1 127 FG85
Maida Way, E4 47 EB45
Maiden Erlegh Av, Bex. DA5 126 EY88
Maiden La, NW1 83 DK66
SE1 201 J2
WC2 200 A1
Dartford DA1 107 FG83
Maiden Pl, NW5
off Dartmouth Pk Hill 65 DH62
Maiden Rd, E15 86 EE66
Maidenshaw Rd, Epsom
KT19 156 CR112
Maidenstone Hill, SE10 103 EC81
Maids of Honour Row, Rich.
TW9 off The Green 117 CK85
Maidstone Av, Rom. RM5 51 FC54
Maidstone Bldgs Ms, SE1 201 J3
Maidstone Ho, E14
off Carmen St 85 EB72
Maidstone Rd, N11 45 DJ51
Grays RM17 110 GA79
Sevenoaks TN13 190 FE122
Sevenoaks (Seal) TN15 191 FN121
Sidcup DA14 126 EX93
Swanley BR8 147 FB95
Maidstone St, E2
off Audrey St 84 DU68
Main Av, Enf. EN1 30 DT43
Northwood HA6 39 BQ48
Main Dr, Ger.Cr. SL9 56 AW57
Iver SL0 93 BE77
Wembley HA9 61 CK62
Main Par, Rick. (Chorl.) WD3
off Whitelands Av 21 BC42
Main Par Flats, Rick. (Chorl.)
WD3 off Whitelands Av 21 BC42
Main Ride, Egh. TW20 112 AS93
Mainridge Rd, Chis. BR7 125 EN91
Main Rd, Dart. (Fnghm) DA4 148 FL100
Dartford (Sutt.H.) DA4 128 FP93
Edenbridge (Crock.H.) TN8 189 EQ134
Longfield DA3 149 FX96
Orpington BR5 146 EW95
Romford RM1, RM2 71 FF56
Sevenoaks (Knock.) TN14 180 EV117
Sevenoaks (Sund.) TN14 180 EX124
Sidcup DA14 125 ES90
Swanley (Crock.) BR8 147 FD100
Swanley (Hext.) BR8 127 FF94
Westerham TN16 162 EJ113
Main St, Felt. TW13 116 BX92
Maisemore St, SE15
off Peckham Pk Rd 102 DU80
Maisie Webster Cl, Stai. (Stanw.)
TW19 off Lauser Rd 114 BK87
Maitland Cl, Houns. TW4 96 BZ83
Walton-on-Thames KT12 136 BY103
West Byfleet KT14 152 BG113
Maitland Cl Est, SE10
off Greenwich High Rd 103 EB80
Maitland Pk Est, NW3 82 DF65
Maitland Pk Rd, NW3 82 DF65
Maitland Pk Vil, NW3 82 DF65
Maitland Pl, E5
off Lower Clapton Rd 66 DW63
Maitland Rd, E15 86 EF65
SE26 123 DX93
Maizey Ct, Brwd. (Pilg.Hat.)
CM15 off Danes Way 54 FU43
Majendie Rd, SE18 105 ER78
Majestic Way, Mitch. CR4 140 DF96
Major Cl, SW9 101 DP83
Major Rd, E15 67 EC64
SE16 202 C6
Majors Fm Rd, Slou. SL3 92 AX80
Makepeace Av, N6 64 DG61
Makepeace Rd, E11 68 EG56
Northolt UB5 78 BY68
Makins St, SW3 198 C9
Malabar St, E14 203 P5
Malam Gdns, E14
off Wades Pl 85 EB73
Malan Cl, West. (Bigg.H.)
TN16 178 EL117
Malan Sq, Rain. RM13 89 FH65
Malbrook Rd, SW15 99 CV84
Malcolm Ct, Stan. HA7 41 CJ50
Malcolm Cres, NW4 63 CU58
Malcolm Dr, Surb. KT6 138 CL102
Malcolm Pl, E2 84 DW70
Malcolm Rd, E1 84 DW70
SE20 122 DW94
SE25 142 DU100
SW19 119 CY93
Coulsdon CR5 175 DK115
Uxbridge UB10 58 BM63
Malcolms Way, N14 29 DJ43
Malcolm Way, E11 68 EG57
Malden Av, SE25 142 DV98
Greenford UB6 61 CE64
Malden Cl, Amer. HP6 20 AT38
Malden Ct, N.Mal. KT3 139 CV97
Malden Cres, NW1 82 DG65
Malden Flds, Bushey WD23 24 BX42
Malden Grn Av, Wor.Pk.
KT4 139 CT102
Malden Hill, N.Mal. KT3 139 CT97
Malden Hill Gdns, N.Mal.
KT3 139 CT97
Malden Junct, N.Mal. KT3
off Malden Way 139 CT99
⇌ Malden Manor 138 CS101
Malden Pk, N.Mal. KT3 139 CT100
Malden Pl, NW5
off Grafton Ter 64 DG64
Malden Rd, NW5 64 DG64
Borehamwood WD6 26 CN41
New Malden KT3 138 CS99
Sutton SM3 157 CX105
Watford WD17 23 BU40
Worcester Park KT4 139 CT101
MALDEN RUSHETT,
Chess. KT9 155 CH111
Malden Way, N.Mal. KT3 139 CT99
Maldon Cl, E15
off Maryland St 67 ED64
N1 off Popham Rd 84 DQ67
SE5 102 DS83
Maldon Ct, Wall. SM6
off Maldon Rd 159 DJ106
Maldon Rd, N9 46 DT48
W3 80 CQ73
Romford RM7 71 FC59
Wallington SM6 159 DH106
Maldon Wk, Wdf.Grn. IG8 48 EJ51
Malet Cl, Egh. TW20 113 BD93
Malet Pl, WC1 195 M5
Malet St, WC1 195 M5
Maley Av, SE27 121 DP89
Malford Ct, E18 48 EG54
Malford Gro, E18 68 EF56
Malfort Rd, SE5 102 DS83
Malham Cl, N11
off Catterick Cl 44 DG51
Malham Rd, SE23 123 DX88
Malins Cl, Barn. EN5 27 CV43
Malkin Way, Wat. WD18 23 BS42
Mall, The, N14 45 DL48
SW1 199 L4
SW14 118 CQ85
W5 80 CL73
Croydon CR0 142 DQ103
Harrow HA3 62 CM58
Hornchurch RM11 71 FH60
St. Albans (Park St) AL2 8 CC27
Surbiton KT6 137 CK99
Mallams Ms, SW9
off St. James's Cres 101 DP83
Mallard Cl, E9
off Berkshire Rd 85 DZ65
NW6 82 DA68
W7 97 CE75
Barnet EN5 off The Hook 28 DD44
Dartford DA1 128 FM85
Redhill RH1 184 DG131
Twickenham TW2
off Stephenson Rd 116 CA87
Upminster RM14 73 FT59
Mallard Path, SE28 105 ER76
Mallard Pl, Twick. TW1 117 CG90
Mallard Pt, E3
off Rainhill Way 85 EB69
Mallard Rd, Abb.L. WD5 7 BU31
South Croydon CR2 161 DX110
Mallards, The, Hem.H. HP3
off Kingfisher Dr 6 BM25
Staines TW18 134 BH96
Mallards Reach, Wey. KT13 135 BR103
Mallards Rd, Bark. IG11 88 EU70
Woodford Green IG8 48 EH52
Mallard Wk, Beck. BR3 143 DX99
Sidcup DA14 126 EW92
Mallard Way, NW9 62 CQ59
Brentwood (Hutt.) CM13 55 GB45
Northwood HA6 39 BQ52
Wallington SM6 159 DJ109
Watford WD25 24 BY37
Mallet Dr, Nthlt. UB5 60 BZ64
Mallet Rd, SE13 123 ED86
★ Mall Galleries, SW1 199 N2
Malling, SE13 123 EC85
Malling Cl, Croy. CR0 142 DW100
Malling Gdns, Mord. SM4 140 DC100
Malling Way, Brom. BR2 144 EF101
Mallinson Cl, Horn. RM12 72 FJ64
Mallinson Rd, SW11 120 DE85
Croydon CR0 141 DK104
Mallion Ct, Wal.Abb. EN9 16 EF33
Mallord St, SW3 100 DD79
Mallory Cl, E14
off Uamvar St 85 EB71
SE4 103 DY84
Mallory Gdns, Barn. EN4 44 DG45
Mallory St, NW8 194 C4
Mallow Cl, Croy. CR0
off Marigold Way 143 DX102
Gravesend (Nthflt) DA11 130 GE91
Tadworth KT20 173 CV119
Mallow Ct, Grays RM17 110 GD79
Mallow Mead, NW7 43 CY52
Mallows, The, Uxb. UB10 59 BP62
Mallow St, EC1 197 K4
Mallow Wk, Wal.Cr. (Goffs Oak)
EN7 14 DR28
Mall Rd, W6 99 CV78
Mall Shop Cen, The, Dag.
RM10 off Heathway 88 FA65
Mallys Pl, Dart. (S.Darenth)
DA4 148 FQ95
Malmains Cl, Beck. BR3 143 ED99
Malmains Way, Beck. BR3 143 EC98
Malm Cl, Rick. WD3 38 BK47
Malmesbury, E2
off Cyprus St 84 DW68
Malmesbury Cl, Pnr. HA5 59 BT56
Malmesbury Rd, E3 85 DZ69
E16 86 EE71
E18 48 EF53
Morden SM4 140 DC101
Malmesbury Ter, E16 86 EF71
Malmsmead Ho, E9
off Kingsmead Way 67 DY64
Malmstone Av, Red. (Merst.)
RH1 185 DJ128
Malory Cl, Beck. BR3 143 DY96
Malpas Dr, Pnr. HA5 60 BX57
Malpas Rd, E8 84 DV65
SE4 103 DZ82
Dagenham RM9 88 EX65
Grays RM16 111 GJ76
Slough SL2 74 AV73
Malta Rd, E10 67 EA60
Tilbury RM18 111 GF82
Malta St, EC1 196 G4
Maltby Cl, Orp. BR6 146 EU102
Maltby Dr, Enf. EN1 30 DV38
Maltby Rd, Chess. KT9 156 CN107
Maltby St, SE1 201 P5
Malt Hill, Egh. TW20 112 AY92
Malt Ho Cl, Wind. (Old Wind.)
SL4 112 AV87
Malthouse Dr, W4 98 CS79
Feltham TW13 116 BX92
Malthouse Pas, SW13
off The Terrace 98 CS82
Malthouse Pl, Rad. WD7 9 CG34
Malthus Path, SE28
off Owen Cl 88 EW74
Malting Ho, E14 85 DZ73
Maltings, The, Kings L. WD4 7 BQ33
Orpington BR6 145 ET102
Oxted RH8 188 EF131
Romford RM1 71 FF59
Staines TW18
off Church St 113 BE91
West Byfleet (Byfleet) KT14 152 BM113
Maltings Cl, E3
off Twelvetrees Cres 85 EC70
SW13 off Cleveland Gdns 98 CS82
Maltings Dr, Epp. CM16
off Palmers Hill 18 EU29
Maltings La, Epp. CM16 18 EU29
Maltings Ms, Sid. DA15
off Station Rd 126 EU90
Maltings Pl, SE1
off Tower Br Rd 102 DS75
SW6 100 DB81
Malting Way, Islw. TW7 97 CF83
Malt La, Rad. WD7 25 CG35
Maltmans La, Ger.Cr.
(Chal.St.P.) SL9 56 AW55
Malton Ms, SE18
off Malton St 105 ES79
W10 off Cambridge Gdns 81 CY72
Malton Rd, W10
off St. Marks Rd 81 CY72
Malton St, SE18 105 ES79
Maltravers St, WC2 196 C10
Malt St, SE1 102 DU79
Malus Cl, Add. KT15 151 BF108
Malus Dr, Add. KT15 151 BF107
Malva Cl, SW18
off St. Ann's Hill 120 DB85
Malvern Av, E4 47 ED52
Bexleyheath DA7 106 EY80
Harrow HA2 60 BY62
Malvern Cl, SE20
off Derwent Rd 142 DU96
W10 81 CZ71
Bushey WD23 24 CC44
Chertsey (Ott.) KT16 151 BC107
Mitcham CR4 141 DJ97
Surbiton KT6 138 CL102
Uxbridge UB10 59 BP61
Malvern Ct, SE14
off Avonley Rd 102 DW80
SW7 198 A9
Slough SL3 off Hill Ri 93 BA79
Sutton SM2
off Overton Rd 158 DA108
Malvern Dr, Felt. TW13 116 BX92
Ilford IG3 69 ET63
Woodford Green IG8 48 EJ50
Malvern Gdns, NW2 63 CY61
NW6 off Carlton Vale 81 CZ68
Harrow HA3 62 CL55
Loughton IG10 33 EM44
Malvern Ms, NW6
off Malvern Rd 82 DA69
Malvern Pl, NW6 81 CZ69
Malvern Rd, E6 86 EL67
E8 84 DU66
E11 68 EE61
N8 65 DM55
N17 66 DU55
NW6 82 DA69
Enfield EN3 31 DY37
Grays RM17 110 GD77
Hampton TW12 116 CA94
Hayes UB3 95 BS80
Hornchurch RM11 71 FG58
Orpington BR6 164 EV105
Surbiton KT6 138 CL103
Thornton Heath CR7 141 DN98
Malvern Ter, N1 83 DN67
N9 off Latymer Rd 46 DT46
Malvern Way, W13
off Templewood 79 CH71
Rickmansworth (Crox.Grn)
WD3 23 BP43
Malvina Av, Grav. DA12 131 GH89
Malwood Rd, SW12 121 DH86
Malyons, The, Shep. TW17
off Gordon Rd 135 BR100
Malyons Rd, SE13 123 EB85
Swanley BR8 127 FF94
Malyons Ter, SE13 123 EB85
Managers St, E14 204 E3
Manatee Pl, Wall. SM6
off Croydon Rd 141 DK104
Manaton Cl, SE15 102 DV83
Manaton Cres, Sthl. UB1 78 CA72
Manbey Gro, E15 86 EE65
Manbey Pk Rd, E15 86 EE65
Manbey Rd, E15 86 EE65
Manbey St, E15 86 EE65
Manbre Rd, W6 99 CW79
Manbrough Av, E6 87 EM69
Manchester Ct, E16 86 EH72
Manchester Dr, W10 81 CY70
Manchester Gro, E14 204 D10
Manchester Ms, W1 194 F7
Manchester Rd, E14 204 D10
N15 66 DR58
Thornton Heath CR7 142 DQ97
Manchester Sq, W1 194 F8
Manchester St, W1 194 F7
Manchester Way, Dag. RM10 71 FB63
Manchuria Rd, SW11 120 DG86
Manciple St, SE1 201 K5
Mandalay Rd, SW4 121 DJ85
Mandarin St, E14
off Salter St 85 EA73
Mandarin Way, Hayes UB4 78 BX72
Mandela Cl, NW10 80 CQ66
Mandela Rd, E16 86 EG72
Mandela St, NW1 83 DJ67
SW9 101 DN80
Mandela Way, SE1 201 N8
Mandel Ho, SW18
off Eastfields Av 100 DA84
Mandeville Cl, SE3
off Vanbrugh Pk 104 EF80
SW20 139 CY95
Watford WD17 23 BT38
Mandeville Ct, E4 47 DY49
Egham TW20 113 BA91
Mandeville Dr, Surb. KT6 137 CK102
Mandeville Ho, SE1
off Rolls Rd 102 DT77
Mandeville Ms, SW4
off Clapham Pk Rd 101 DL84
Mandeville Pl, W1 194 G8
Mandeville Rd, N14 45 DH47
Enfield EN3 31 DX36
Isleworth TW7 97 CG82
Northolt UB5 78 CA66
Potters Bar EN6 12 DC32
Shepperton TW17 134 BN99
Mandeville St, E5 67 DY62
Mandeville Wk, Brwd. (Hutt.)
CM13 55 GE44
Mandrake Rd, SW17 120 DF90
Mandrake Way, E15 86 EE66
Mandrell Rd, SW2 121 DL85
Manette St, W1 195 N9
Manford Cl, Chig. IG7 50 EU49
Manford Cross, Chig. IG7 50 EU50
Manford Ind Est, Erith DA8 107 FG79
Manford Way, Chig. IG7 49 ES49
Manfred Rd, SW15 119 CZ85
Manger Rd, N7 83 DL65
Mangold Way, Erith DA18 106 EY76
Manhattan Av, Wat. WD18 23 BT42
Manhattan Bldg, E3
off Fairfield Rd 85 EA68
Manhattan Wf, E16 205 M4
Manilla St, E14 203 P4

★ Place of interest ⇌ Railway station ⊖ London Underground station DLR Docklands Light Railway station Tra Tramlink station H Hospital Riv Pedestrian ferry landing stage

Manister Rd, SE2 106 EU76
Manitoba Ct, SE16 202 G5
Manitoba Gdns, Orp. BR6
off Superior Dr 163 ET107
Manley Ct, N16
off Stoke Newington High St 66 DT62
Manley St, NW1 82 DG67
Manly Dixon Dr, Enf. EN3 31 DY37
Mannamead, Epsom KT18 172 CS119
Mannamead Cl, Epsom KT18
off Mannamead 172 CS119
Mann Cl, Croy. CR0
off Salem Pl 142 DQ104
Manneby Prior, N1
off Cumming St 83 DM68
Manningford Cl, EC1 196 F2
Manning Gdns, Har. HA3 61 CK59
Manning Pl, Rich. TW10
off Grove Rd 118 CM86
Manning Rd, E17
off Southcote Rd 67 DY57
Dagenham RM10 88 FA65
Orpington BR5 146 EX99
Manning St, S.Ock. (Aveley)
RM15 90 FQ74
Manningtree Cl, SW19 119 CY88
Manningtree Rd, Ruis. HA4 59 BV63
Manningtree St, E1
off White Ch La 84 DU72
Mannin Rd, Rom. RM6 70 EV59
Mannock Dr, Loug. IG10 33 EQ40
Mannock Ms, E18 48 EH53
Mannock Rd, N22 65 DP55
Dartford DA1
off Barnwell Rd 108 FM83
Manns Cl, Islw. TW7 117 CF85
Manns Rd, Edg. HA8 42 CN51
Manoel Rd, Twick. TW2 116 CC89
Manor Av, SE4 103 DZ82
Caterham CR3 176 DS124
Hornchurch RM11 72 FJ57
Hounslow TW4 96 BX83
Northolt UB5 78 BZ66
Manorbrook, SE3 104 EG84
Manor Chase, Wey. KT13 153 BP106
Manor Circ, Rich. TW9 98 CN83
Manor Cl, E17 *off Manor Rd* 47 DY54
NW7 *off Manor Dr* 42 CR50
NW9 62 CP57
SE28 88 EW72
Barnet EN5 27 CY42
Dagenham RM10 89 FD65
Dartford (Cray.) DA1 107 FD84
Dartford (Wilm.) DA2 127 FG90
Romford RM1 *off Manor Rd* 71 FG57
Ruislip HA4 59 BT60
South Ockendon (Aveley)
RM15 90 FQ74
Warlingham CR6 177 DY117
Woking GU22 167 BF116
Worcester Park KT4 138 CS102
Manor Cl S, S.Ock. (Aveley)
RM15 *off Manor Cl* 90 FQ74
Manor Cotts, Nthwd. HA6 39 BT53
Manor Cotts App, N2 44 DC54
Manor Ct, E10
off Grange Pk Rd 67 EB60
N2 64 DF57
SW6 *off Bagley's La* 100 DB81
Enfield EN1 30 DV36
Radlett WD7 25 CF38
Twickenham TW2 116 CC89
Wembley HA9 62 CL64
Weybridge KT13 153 BP105
Manor Ct Rd, W7 79 CE73
Manor Cres, Epsom KT19 156 CN112
Hornchurch RM11 72 FJ57
Surbiton KT5 138 CN100
West Byfleet (Byfleet)
KT14 152 BM113
Manorcrofts Rd, Egh. TW20 113 BA93
Manordene Cl, T.Ditt. KT7 137 CG102
Manordene Rd, SE28 88 EW72
Manor Dr, N14 45 DH45
N20 44 DE48
NW7 42 CR50
Addlestone (New Haw)
KT15 152 BG110
Epsom KT19 156 CS107
Esher KT10 137 CF103
Feltham TW13
off Lebanon Av 116 BX92
St. Albans AL2 8 CA27
Sunbury-on-Thames TW16 135 BU96
Surbiton KT5 138 CM100
Wembley HA9 62 CM63
Manor Dr, The, Wor.Pk. KT4 138 CS102
Manor Dr N, N.Mal. KT3 138 CR101
Worcester Park KT4 138 CS102
Manor Est, SE16 202 D9
Manor Fm, Dart. (Fnghm)
DA4 148 FM101
Manor Fm Av, Shep. TW17 135 BP100
Manor Fm Cl, Wor.Pk. KT4 138 CS102
Manor Fm Dr, E4 48 EE48
Manor Fm Est, Stai. (Wrays.)
TW19 112 AW86
Manor Fm La, Egh. TW20 113 BA92
Manor Fm Rd, Enf. EN1 30 DV35
Thornton Heath CR7 141 DN96
Wembley HA0 79 CK68
Manorfield Cl, N19
off Junction Rd 65 DJ63
Manor Flds, SW15 119 CX86
Manorfields Cl, Chis. BR7 145 ET97
Manor Gdns, N7 65 DL62
SW20 139 CZ96
W3 98 CN77
W4 *off Devonshire Rd* 98 CS78
Hampton TW12 116 CB94
Richmond TW9 98 CM84
Ruislip HA4 60 BW64
South Croydon CR2 160 DT107
Sunbury-on-Thames TW16 135 BU96
Manor Gate, Nthlt. UB5 78 BY66
Manorgate Rd, Kings.T. KT2 138 CN95
Manor Grn Rd, Epsom KT19 156 CP113
Manor Gro, SE15 102 DW79
Manor Gro, Beck. BR3 143 EB96
Richmond TW9 98 CN84
Manor Hall Av, NW4 43 CW54
Manor Hall Dr, NW4 43 CX54
Manorhall Gdns, E10 67 EA60
⊖ **Manor House** 65 DP59
Manor Ho Ct, Epsom KT18 156 CQ113
Shepperton TW17 135 BP101
Manor Ho Dr, NW6 81 CX66
Northwood HA6 39 BP52
Walton-on-Thames KT12 153 BT107
Manor Ho Est, Stan. HA7
off Old Ch La 41 CH51
Manor Ho Gdns, Abb.L. WD5 7 BR31
Manor Ho La, Slou. (Datchet)
SL3 92 AV80
Manor Ho Way, Islw. TW7 97 CH83
Manor La, SE12 124 EE86
SE13 104 EE84
Feltham TW13 115 BU89
Gerrards Cross SL9 56 AX59
Hayes UB3 95 BR79
Longfield (Fawk.Grn) DA3 149 FW101
Sevenoaks TN15 149 FW103
Sunbury-on-Thames TW16 135 BU96
Sutton SM1 158 DC106
Tadworth (Lwr Kgswd)
KT20 184 DA129
Manor La Ter, SE13 104 EE84
Manor Leaze, Egh. TW20 113 BB92
Manor Ms, NW6
off Cambridge Av 82 DA68
SE4 103 DZ82
Manor Mt, SE23 122 DW88
Manor Par, NW10
off Station Rd 81 CT68
MANOR PARK, E12 68 EL63
⇌ **Manor Park** 68 EK63
Manor Pk, SE13 103 ED84
Chislehurst BR7 145 ER96
Richmond TW9 98 CM84
Staines TW18 113 BD90
Manor Pk Cl, W.Wick. BR4 143 EB102
Manor Pk Cres, Edg. HA8 42 CN51
Manor Pk Dr, Har. HA2 60 CB55
Manor Pk Gdns, Edg. HA8 42 CN50
Manor Pk Par, SE13
off Lee High Rd 103 ED84
Manor Pk Rd, E12 68 EK63
N2 64 DD55
NW10 81 CT67
Chislehurst BR7 145 EQ95
Sutton SM1 158 DC106
West Wickham BR4 143 EB102
Manor Pl, SE17 101 DP78
Chislehurst BR7 145 ER95
Dartford DA1
off Highfield Rd S 128 FL88
Feltham TW14 115 BU88
Mitcham CR4 141 DJ97
Staines TW18 114 BH92
Sutton SM1 158 DB105
Walton-on-Thames KT12
off Manor Rd 135 BT101
Manor Rd, E10 67 EA59
E15 86 EE69
E16 86 EE69
E17 47 DY54
N16 66 DR61
N17 46 DU53
N22 45 DL51
SE25 142 DU98
SW20 139 CZ96
W13 79 CG73
Ashford TW15 114 BM92
Barking IG11 87 ET65
Barnet EN5 27 CY43
Beckenham BR3 143 EB96
Bexley DA5 127 FB88
Chigwell IG7 49 EP50
Dagenham RM10 89 FC65
Dartford DA1 107 FE84
East Molesey KT8 137 CD98
Enfield EN2 30 DR40
Erith DA8 107 FF79
Gravesend DA12 131 GH86
Grays RM17 110 GC79
Grays (W.Thur.) RM20 109 FW79
Harrow HA1 61 CG58
Hayes UB3 77 BU72
Loughton IG10 32 EH44
Loughton (High Beach) IG10 32 EH38
Mitcham CR4 141 DJ98
Potters Bar EN6 11 CZ31
Redhill (S.Merst.) RH1 185 DJ129
Reigate RH2 183 CZ132
Richmond TW9 98 CM83
Romford RM1 71 FG57
Romford (Chad.Hth) RM6 70 EX58
Romford (Lamb.End) RM4 50 EW47
Ruislip HA4 59 BR60
St. Albans (Lon.Col.) AL2 9 CJ26
Sevenoaks (Sund.) TN14 180 EX124
Sidcup DA15 125 ET90
Sutton SM2 157 CZ108
Swanscombe DA10 129 FX86
Teddington TW11 117 CH92
Tilbury RM18 111 GG82
Twickenham TW2 116 CC89
Wallington SM6 159 DH105
Waltham Abbey EN9 15 ED33
Walton-on-Thames KT12 135 BT101
Watford WD17 23 BV39
West Wickham BR4 143 EB103
Westerham (Tats.) TN16 178 EL120
Woking GU21 166 AW116
Woking (Ripley) GU23 167 BF123
Woodford Green IG8 49 EM51
Manor Rd N, Esher KT10 137 CF104
Thames Ditton KT7 137 CG103
Wallington SM6 159 DH105
Manor Rd S, Esher KT10 155 CE105
Manorside, Barn. EN5 27 CY42
Manorside Cl, SE2 106 EW77
Manor Sq, Dag. RM8 70 EX61
Manor Vale, Brent. TW8 97 CJ78
Manor Vw, N3 44 DB54
Manor Wk, Wey. KT13 153 BP106
Manor Way, E4 47 ED49
NW9 62 CS55
SE3 104 EF84
SE23 122 DW87
SE28 88 EW74
Manor Way, Bans. SM7 174 DF116
Beckenham BR3 143 EA96
Bexley DA5 126 FA88
Bexleyheath DA7 107 FD83
Borehamwood WD6 26 CQ42
Brentwood CM14 54 FU48
Bromley BR2 144 EL100
Egham TW20 113 AZ93
Manorway, Enf. EN1 46 DS45
Manor Way, Grays RM17 110 GB80
Harrow HA2 60 CB56
Leatherhead (Oxshott)
KT22 170 CC115
Mitcham CR4 141 DJ97
Orpington BR5 145 EQ98
Potters Bar EN6 12 DA30
Purley CR8 159 DL112
Rainham RM13 89 FE70
Rickmansworth (Crox.Grn)
WD3 22 BN42
Ruislip HA4 59 BS59
South Croydon CR2 160 DS107
Southall UB2 96 BX77
Swanscombe DA10 109 FX84
Waltham Cross (Chsht) EN8
off Russells Ride 15 DY31
Woking GU22 167 BB121
Manorway, Wdf.Grn. IG8 48 EJ50
Manor Way, Wor.Pk. KT4 138 CS102
Manor Way, The, Wall. SM6 159 DH105
Manor Waye, Uxb. UB8 76 BK67
Manor Way Ind Est, Grays
RM17 110 GC80
Manor Wd Rd, Pur. CR8 159 DL113
Manpreet Ct, E12
off Morris Av 69 EM64
Manresa Rd, SW3 100 DE78
Mansard Beeches, SW17 120 DG92
Mansard Cl, Horn. RM12 71 FG61
Pinner HA5 60 BX55
Manse Cl, Hayes UB3 95 BR79
Mansel Cl, Slou. SL2 74 AV71
Mansel Gro, E17 47 EA53
Mansell Rd, W3 98 CR75
Greenford UB6 78 CB71
Mansell St, E1 202 A1
Mansell Way, Cat. CR3 176 DR122
Mansel Rd, SW19 119 CY93
Mansergh Cl, SE18 104 EL80
Manse Rd, N16 66 DT62
Manser Rd, Rain. RM13 89 FE69
Manse Way, Swan. BR8 147 FG98
Mansfield Av, N15 66 DR56
Barnet EN4 28 DF44
Ruislip HA4 59 BV60
Mansfield Cl, N9 30 DU44
Orpington BR5 146 EX101
Weybridge KT13 153 BP106
Mansfield Dr, Hayes UB4 77 BS70
Redhill (Merst.) RH1 185 DK128
Mansfield Gdns, Horn. RM12 72 FK61
Mansfield Hill, E4 47 EB46
Mansfield Ms, W1 195 H7
Mansfield Pl, NW3
off New End 64 DC63
Mansfield Rd, E11 68 EH58
E17 67 DZ56
NW3 64 DF64
W3 80 CP70
Chessington KT9 155 CJ106
Ilford IG1 69 EN61
South Croydon CR2 160 DR107
Swanley BR8 127 FE93
Mansfield St, W1 195 H7
Mansford St, E2 84 DU68
Manship Rd, Mitch. CR4 120 DG94
Mansion Cl, SW9
off Cowley Rd 101 DN81
Mansion Gdns, NW3 64 DB62
★ **Mansion Ho**, EC4 197 K9
⊖ **Mansion House** 197 J10
Mansion Ho Pl, EC4 197 K9
Mansion Ho St, EC4 197 K9
Mansion La, Iver SL0 75 BC74
Manson Ms, SW7 100 DC77
Manson Pl, SW7 100 DD77
Manstead Gdns, Rain. RM13 89 FH72
Mansted Gdns, Rom. RM6 70 EW59
Manston Av, Sthl. UB2 96 CA77
Manston Cl, SE20
off Garden Rd 142 DW95
Waltham Cross (Chsht) EN8 14 DW30
Manstone Rd, NW2 63 CY64
Manston Gro, Kings.T. KT2 117 CK92
Manston Way, Horn. RM12 89 FH65
Manthorp Rd, SE18 105 EQ78
Mantilla Rd, SW17 120 DG91
Mantle Rd, SE4 103 DY83
Mantlet Cl, SW16 121 DJ94
Mantle Way, E15
off Romford Rd 86 EE66
Manton Av, W7 97 CF75
Manton Cl, Hayes UB3 77 BS73
Manton Rd, SE2 106 EU77
Enfield EN3 31 EA37
Mantua St, SW11 100 DD83
Mantus Cl, E1 *off Mantus Rd* 84 DW70
Mantus Rd, E1 84 DW70
Manus Way, N20
off Blakeney Cl 44 DC47
Manville Gdns, SW17 121 DH89
Manville Rd, SW17 120 DG89
Manwood Rd, SE4 123 DZ85
Manwood St, E16 87 EM74
Manygate La, Shep. TW17 135 BQ101
Manygates, SW12 121 DH89
Mapesbury Ms, NW4
off Station Rd 63 CU58
Mapesbury Rd, NW2 81 CY66
Mapeshill Pl, NW2 81 CW65
Mape St, E2 84 DV70
Maple Av, E4 47 DZ50
W3 80 CS74
Harrow HA2 60 CB61
Upminster RM14 72 FP62
West Drayton UB7 76 BL73
Maple Cl, N3 44 DA51
N16 66 DU58
SW4 121 DK86
Brentwood CM13
off Cherry Av 55 FZ48
Buckhurst Hill IG9 48 EK48
Bushey WD23 24 BY40
Maple Cl, Epp. (They.B.) CM16
off Loughton La 33 ER36
Hampton TW12 116 BZ93
Hayes UB4 78 BX69
Hornchurch RM12 71 FH62
Ilford IG6 49 ES50
Mitcham CR4 141 DH95
Orpington BR5 145 ER99
Ruislip HA4 59 BV58
Swanley BR8 147 FE96
Whyteleafe CR3 176 DT117
Maple Ct, Egh. (Eng.Grn) TW20
off Ashwood Rd 112 AV93
Erith DA8 107 FF80
New Malden KT3 138 CS97
Maple Cres, Sid. DA15 126 EU86
Slough SL2 74 AV73
Maplecroft Cl, E6
off Allhallows Rd 86 EL72
MAPLE CROSS, Rick. WD3 37 BD49
Maple Cross Ind Est, Rick.
(Map.Cr.) WD3 37 BF49
Mapledale Av, Croy. CR0 142 DU103
Mapledene, Chis. BR7
off Kemnal Rd 125 EQ92
Mapledene Rd, E8 84 DT66
Maple Dr, S.Ock. RM15 91 FX70
Maplefield, St.Alb. (Park St)
AL2 8 CB29
Maplefield La, Ch.St.G. HP8 20 AV41
Maple Gdns, Edg. HA8 42 CS52
Staines TW19 114 BL89
Maple Gate, Loug. IG10 33 EN40
Maple Gro, NW9 62 CQ59
W5 97 CK76
Brentford TW8 97 CH80
Southall UB1 78 BZ71
Watford WD17 23 BU39
Woking GU22 166 AY121
Maple Hill, Hem.H. (Bov.) HP3
off Ley Hill Rd 4 AX30
Maple Ho, NW3
off Maitland Pk Vil 82 DF65
Maplehurst, Lthd. KT22 171 CD123
Maplehurst Cl, Dart. DA2
off Sandringham Dr 127 FE89
Kingston upon Thames
KT1 138 CL98
Maple Ind Est, Felt. TW13
off Maple Way 115 BV90
Maple Leaf Cl, Abb.L. WD5 7 BU32
Mapleleaf Cl, S.Croy. CR2 161 DX111
Maple Leaf Cl, West. (Bigg.H.)
TN16 *off Main Rd* 178 EK116
Maple Leaf Dr, Sid. DA15 125 ET88
Mapleleafe Gdns, Ilf. IG6 69 EP55
Maple Leaf Sq, SE16 203 J4
Maple Lo Cl, Rick. (Map.Cr.)
WD3 37 BE49
Maple Ms, NW6
off Kilburn Pk Rd 82 DB68
SW16 121 DM92
Maple Pl, N17 *off Park La* 46 DU52
W1 195 L5
Banstead SM7 157 CX114
West Drayton UB7
off Maple Av 76 BM73
Maple Rd, E11 68 EE58
SE20 142 DV95
Ashtead KT21 171 CK119
Dartford DA1 128 FJ88
Gravesend DA12 131 GJ91
Grays RM17 110 GC79
Hayes UB4 78 BW69
Surbiton KT6 138 CL99
Whyteleafe CR3 176 DT117
Woking (Ripley) GU23 168 BG124
Maples, The, Bans. SM7 158 DB114
Chertsey (Ott.) KT16 151 BB107
Esher (Clay.) KT10 155 CG108
Waltham Cross (Goffs Oak)
EN7 14 DS28
Maplescombe La, Dart.
(Fnghm) DA4 148 FN104
Maples Pl, E1 *off Raven Row* 84 DV71
Maple Springs, Wal.Abb. EN9 16 EG33
Maplestead Rd, SW2 121 DM87
Dagenham RM9 88 EV67
Maple St, E2 84 DU68
W1 195 K6
Romford RM7 71 FC56
Maplethorpe Rd, Th.Hth. CR7 141 DP98
Mapleton Cl, Brom. BR2 144 EG100
Mapleton Cres, SW18 120 DB86
Enfield EN3 30 DW38
Mapleton Rd, E4 47 EC48
SW18 120 DB86
Edenbridge TN8 189 ET133
Enfield EN1 30 DV40
Westerham TN16 189 ES130
Maple Wk, W10 *off Droop St* 81 CX70
Sutton SM2 158 DB110
Maple Way, Couls. CR5 175 DH121
Feltham TW13 115 BU90
Waltham Abbey EN9
off Breach Barn Mobile
Home Pk 16 EH30
Maplin Cl, N21 29 DM44
Maplin Ho, SE2
off Wolvercote Rd 106 EX75
Maplin Pk, Slou. SL3 93 BC75
Maplin Rd, E16 86 EG72
Maplin St, E3 85 DZ69
Mapperley Dr, Wdf.Grn. IG8
off Forest Dr 48 EE52
Marabou Cl, E12 68 EL64
Maran Way, Erith DA18 106 EX75
Marathon Ho, NW1
off Marylebone Rd 82 DF71
Marathon Way, SE28 105 ET75
Marban Rd, W9 81 CZ69
★ **Marble Arch**, W1 194 E10
⊖ **Marble Arch** 194 E10
Marble Arch Apts, W1
off Harrowby St 82 DE72
Marble Cl, W3 80 CP74
Marble Dr, NW2 63 CX60
Marble Hill Cl, Twick. TW1 117 CH87
Marble Hill Gdns, Twick. TW1 117 CH87
★ **Marble Hill Ho**, Twick.
TW1 117 CJ87
Marble Ho, SE18
off Felspar Cl 105 ET78
Marble Quay, E1 202 B2
Marbles Way, Tad. KT20 173 CX119
Marbrook Ct, SE12 124 EJ90
Marcella Rd, SW9 101 DN82
Marcellina Way, Orp. BR6 145 ES104
Marcet Rd, Dart. DA1 128 FJ85
Marchant Rd, E11 67 ED61
Marchant St, SE14 103 DY79
Marchbank Rd, W14 99 CZ79
Marchmant Cl, Horn. RM12 72 FJ62
Marchmont Gdns, Rich. TW10
off Marchmont Rd 118 CM85
Marchmont Rd, Rich. TW10 118 CM85
Wallington SM6 159 DJ108
Marchmont St, WC1 195 P4
March Rd, Twick. TW1 117 CG87
Weybridge KT13 152 BN106
Marchside Cl, Houns. TW5 96 BX81
Marchwood Cl, SE5 102 DS80
Marchwood Cres, W5 79 CJ72
Marcia Rd, SE1 201 N9
Marcilly Rd, SW18 120 DD85
Marconi Gdns, Brwd.
(Pilg.Hat.) CM15 54 FW43
Marconi Rd, E10 67 EA60
Gravesend (Nthflt) DA11 130 GD90
Marconi Way, Sthl. UB1 78 CB72
Marcon Pl, E8 84 DV65
Marco Rd, W6 99 CW76
Marcourt Lawns, W5 80 CL70
Marcus Ct, E15 86 EE67
Marcuse Rd, Cat. CR3 176 DR123
Marcus Garvey Ms, SE22
off St. Aidan's Rd 122 DV85
Marcus Garvey Way, SE24 101 DN84
Marcus Rd, Dart. DA1 127 FG87
Marcus St, E15 86 EF67
SW18 120 DB86
Marcus Ter, SW18 120 DB86
Mardale Dr, NW9 62 CR57
Mardell Rd, Croy. CR0 143 DX99
Marden Av, Brom. BR2 144 EG100
Marden Cl, Chig. IG7 50 EV47
Marden Cres, Bex. DA5 127 FC85
Croydon CR0 141 DM100
Marden Pk, Cat. (Wold.) CR3 187 DZ125
Marden Rd, N17 66 DS55
Croydon CR0 141 DM100
Romford RM1 71 FE58
Marden Sq, SE16 202 D7
Marder Rd, W13 97 CG75
Mardyke Cl, Rain. RM13 89 FC68
Mardyke Ho, SE17
off Townsend St 102 DS77
Rainham RM13
off Lower Mardyke Av 89 FD68
Marechal Niel Av, Sid. DA15 125 ER90
Maresfield, Croy. CR0 142 DS104
Maresfield Gdns, NW3 64 DC64
Mare St, E8 84 DV67
Marfleet Cl, Cars. SM5 140 DE103
Margaret Av, E4 31 EB44
Brentwood (Shenf.) CM15 55 FZ45
Margaret Bondfield Av, Bark.
IG11 88 EU66
Margaret Bldgs, N16
off Margaret Rd 66 DT60
Margaret Cl, Abb.L. WD5 7 BT32
Epping CM16
off Margaret Rd 18 EU29
Potters Bar EN6 12 DC33
Romford RM2
off Margaret Rd 71 FH57
Staines TW18
off Charles Rd 114 BK93
Waltham Abbey EN9 15 ED33
Margaret Ct, W1 195 K8
Margaret Dr, Horn. RM11 72 FM60
Margaret Gardner Dr, SE9 125 EM89
Margaret Ingram Cl, SW6
off John Smith Av 99 CZ80
Margaret Lockwood Cl,
Kings.T. KT1 138 CM98
Margaret Rd, N16 66 DT60
Barnet EN4 28 DD42
Bexley DA5 126 EX86
Epping CM16 18 EU29
Romford RM2 71 FH57
Margaret Sq, Uxb. UB8 76 BJ67
Margaret St, W1 195 J8
Margaretta Ter, SW3 100 DE79
Margaretting Rd, E12 68 EJ61
Margaret Way, Couls. CR5 175 DP118
Ilford IG4 68 EL58
Margate Rd, SW2 121 DL85
Margeholes, Wat. WD19 40 BY47
MARGERY, Tad. KT20 184 DA129
Margery Gro, Tad. (Lwr Kgswd)
KT20 183 CY129
Margery La, Tad. (Lwr Kgswd)
KT20 183 CZ129
Margery Pk Rd, E7 86 EG65
Margery Rd, Dag. RM8 70 EX62
Margery St, WC1 196 D3
Margery Wd La, Tad. (Lwr Kgswd)
KT20 183 CZ129
Margherita Pl, Wal.Abb. EN9 16 EF34
Margherita Rd, Wal.Abb. EN9 16 EG34
Margin Dr, SW19 119 CX92
Margravine Gdns, W6 99 CX78
Margravine Rd, W6 99 CX78
Marham Dr, NW9
off Kenley Av 42 CS54
Marham Gdns, SW18 120 DE88
Morden SM4 140 DC100
Maria Cl, SE1 202 D8
Mariam Gdns, Horn. RM12 72 FM61
Marian Cl, Hayes UB4 78 BX70
Marian Ct, Sutt. SM1 158 DB106
Marian Pl, E2 84 DV68
Marian Rd, SW16 141 DJ95
Marian Sq, E2
off Pritchard's Rd 84 DU68
Marian St, E2
off Hackney Rd 84 DV68
Marian Way, NW10 81 CT66
Maria Ter, E1 85 DX71
Maria Theresa Cl, N.Mal. KT3 138 CR99
Maricas Av, Har. HA3 41 CD53
Marie Curie, SE5
off Dalwood St 102 DS81
Marie Lloyd Gdns, N19
off Hornsey Ri Gdns 65 DL59

★ Place of interest | ⇌ Railway station | ⊖ London Underground station | DLR Docklands Light Railway station | Tra Tramlink station | H Hospital | Riv Pedestrian ferry landing stage

Marie Lloyd Wk, E8
off Forest Rd 84 DU65
Marie Manor Way, Dart. DA2 109 FS84
Mariette Way, Wall. SM6 159 DL109
Marigold All, SE1 200 F1
Marigold Cl, Sthl. UB1
off Lancaster Rd 78 BY73
Marigold Rd, N17 46 DW52
Marigold St, SE16 202 D5
Marigold Way, E4
off Silver Birch Av 47 DZ51
Croydon CR0 143 DX102
H Marillac Hosp, Brwd.
CM13 53 FX51
Marina App, Hayes UB4 78 BY71
Marina Av, N.Mal. KT3 139 CV99
Marina Cl, Brom. BR2 144 EG97
Chertsey KT16 134 BH102
Marina Dr, Dart. DA1 128 FN88
Gravesend (Nthflt) DA11 131 GF87
Welling DA16 105 ES82
Marina Gdns, Rom. RM7 71 FC58
Waltham Cross (Chsht) EN8 14 DW30
Marina Pl, Kings.T. KT1 137 CK95
Marina Way, Iver SL0 75 BF73
Teddington TW11
off Fairways 117 CK94
Marine Dr, SE18 105 EM77
Barking IG11 88 EV70
Marinefield Rd, SW6 100 DB82
Mariner Gdns, Rich. TW10 117 CJ90
Mariner Rd, E12
off Dersingham Av 69 EN63
Mariners Cl, Barn. EN4
off Lancaster Rd 28 DD43
Mariners Ct, Green. DA9
off High St 109 FV84
Mariners Ms, E14 204 F8
Mariners Wk, Erith DA8
off Frobisher Rd 107 FF79
Mariner's Way, Grav. DA11 130 GE87
Marine St, SE16 202 B6
Marine Twr, SE8
off Abinger Gro 103 DZ79
Marion Av, Shep. TW17 135 BP99
Marion Cl, Bushey WD23 24 BZ39
Ilford IG6 49 ER52
Marion Cres, Orp. BR5 146 EU99
Marion Gro, Wdf.Grn. IG8 48 EE50
Marion Rd, NW7 43 CU50
Thornton Heath CR7 142 DQ99
Marischal Rd, SE13 103 ED83
Marisco Cl, Grays RM16 111 GH77
Marish La, Uxb. (Denh.) UB9 57 BC56
Marish Wf, Slou. (Mdgrn) SL3 92 AY75
Maritime Cl, Green. DA9 129 FV85
Maritime Gate, Grav. DA11 130 GE87
Maritime Ho, SE18
off Green's End 105 EP77
Barking IG11
off Linton Rd 87 EQ66
Maritime Quay, E14 204 A10
Maritime St, E3 85 DZ70
Marius Pas, SW17
off Marius Rd 120 DG89
Marius Rd, SW17 120 DG89
Marjorams Av, Loug. IG10 33 EM40
Marjorie Gro, SW11 100 DF84
Marjorie Ms, E1
off Arbour Sq 85 DX72
Markab Rd, Nthwd. HA6 39 BT50
Mark Av, E4 31 EB44
Mark Cl, Bexh. DA7 106 EY81
Southall UB1
off Longford Av 78 CB74
Mark Dr, Ger.Cr. (Chal.St.P.)
SL9 36 AX49
Marke Cl, Kes. BR2 162 EL105
Markedge La, Couls. CR5 174 DE124
Redhill (Merst.) RH1 184 DF126
Markeston Grn, Wat. WD19 40 BX49
Market, The, Cars. SM5
off Wrythe La 140 DC102
Sutton SM1 off Rose Hill 140 DC102
Market App, W12
off Lime Gro 99 CW75
Market Ct, W1 195 K8
Market Dr, W4 98 CS80
Market Est, N7 83 DL65
Marketfield Rd, Red. RH1 184 DF134
Marketfield Way, Red. RH1 184 DF134
Market Hill, SE18 105 EN76
Market La, W12
off Goldhawk Rd 99 CW75
Edgware HA8 42 CQ53
Iver SL0 93 BC75
Slough SL3 93 BC76
Market Link, Rom. RM1 71 FE56
Market Meadow, Orp. BR5 146 EW98
Market Ms, W1 199 H3
Market Pl, N2 64 DE55
NW11 64 DC56
SE16 202 C8
W1 195 K8
W3 80 CQ74
Bexleyheath DA6 106 FA84
Brentford TW8 97 CJ80
Dartford DA1
off Market St 128 FL87
Enfield EN2 off The Town 30 DR41
Gerrards Cross (Chal.St.P.)
SL9 36 AX53
Kingston upon Thames
KT1 137 CK96
Romford RM1 71 FE57
Romford (Abridge) RM4 34 EV41
Tilbury RM18 111 GF82
Market Rd, N7 83 DL65
Richmond TW9 98 CN83
Market Row, SW9
off Atlantic Rd 101 DN84
Market Service Rd, The, Sutt.
SM1 off Rosehill Av 140 DC102
Market Sq, E14 off Chrisp St 85 EB72
N9 off New Rd 46 DU47
Bromley BR1 144 EG96
Staines TW18
off Clarence St 113 BE91
Uxbridge UB8
off The Pavilions 76 BJ66
Waltham Abbey EN9
off Leverton Way 15 EC33
Westerham TN16 189 EQ127
Market Sq, Wok. GU21
off Cawsey Way 166 AY117
Market St, E1 off Steward St 84 DT71
E6 87 EM68
SE18 105 EN77
Dartford DA1 128 FL87
Watford WD18 23 BV42
Market Way, E14
off Kerbey St 85 EB72
Wembley HA0 off Turton Rd 62 CL64
Westerham TN16
off Costell's Meadow 189 ER126
Market Yd Ms, SE1 201 N6
Markfield, Croy. CR0 161 DZ110
Markfield Gdns, E4 47 EB45
Markfield Rd, N15 66 DU56
Caterham CR3 186 DV126
Markham Pl, SW3 198 D10
Markham Rd, Wal.Cr. (Chsht)
EN7 14 DQ26
Markham Sq, SW3 198 D10
Markham St, SW3 198 C10
Markhole Cl, Hmptn. TW12
off Priory Rd 116 BZ94
Markhouse Av, E17 67 DY58
Markhouse Rd, E17 67 DZ57
Markland Ho, W10 81 CX73
Mark La, EC3 201 N1
Gravesend DA12 131 GL86
Markmanor Av, E17 67 DY59
Mark Oak La, Lthd. KT22 170 CA122
Mark Rd, N22 45 DP54
Marksbury Av, Rich. TW9 98 CN83
MARK'S GATE, Rom. RM6 50 EY54
Mark Sq, EC2 197 M4
Marks Rd, Rom. RM7 71 FC57
Warlingham CR6 177 DY118
Marks Sq, Grav. (Nthflt) DA11 131 GF91
Mark St, E15 86 EE66
EC2 197 M4
Reigate RH2 184 DB133
Markville Gdns, Cat. CR3 186 DU125
Mark Wade Cl, E12
off Westmorland Cl 68 EK61
Markway, Sun. TW16 136 BW96
Mark Way, Swan. BR8 147 FG99
Markwell Cl, SE26
off Longton Gro 122 DV91
Markyate Rd, Dag. RM8 70 EV64
Marlands Rd, Ilf. IG5 68 EL55
Marlborough, SW3 198 C8
Marlborough Av, E8 84 DU67
N14 45 DJ48
Edgware HA8 42 CP48
Ruislip HA4 59 BQ58
Marlborough Cl, N20
off Marlborough Gdns 44 DF48
SE17 200 G9
SW19 120 DE93
Grays RM16 110 GC75
Orpington BR6
off Aylesham Rd 145 ET101
Upminster RM14 73 FS60
Walton-on-Thames KT12
off Arch Rd 136 BX104
Marlborough Ct, W1 195 K9
W8 100 DA77
Wallington SM6
off Cranley Gdns 159 DJ108
Marlborough Cres, W4 98 CR76
Hayes UB3 95 BR80
Sevenoaks TN13 190 FE124
Marlborough Dr, Ilf. IG5 68 EL55
Weybridge KT13 135 BQ104
Marlborough Gdns, N20 44 DF48
Upminster RM14 73 FR60
Marlborough Gate Ho, W2
off Elms Ms 82 DD73
Marlborough Gro, SE1 102 DU78
Marlborough Hill, NW8 82 DC67
Harrow HA1 61 CF56
★ Marlborough Ho, SW1 199 L3
Marlborough La, SE7 104 EJ79
Marlborough Ms, Bans. SM7 174 DA115
Marlborough Pk Av, Sid.
DA15 126 EU87
Marlborough Pl, NW8 82 DC68
Marlborough Rd, E4 47 EA51
E7 86 EJ66
E15 off Borthwick Rd 68 EE63
E18 68 EG55
N9 46 DT46
N19 65 DK61
N22 45 DL52
SE18 105 EP76
SW1 199 L3
SW19 120 DE93
W4 98 CQ78
W5 97 CK75
Ashford TW15 114 BK92
Bexleyheath DA7 106 EX83
Brentwood (Pilg.Hat.)
CM15 54 FU44
Bromley BR2 144 EJ98
Dagenham RM8 70 EV63
Dartford DA1 128 FJ86
Feltham TW13 116 BX89
Hampton TW12 116 CA93
Isleworth TW7 97 CH81
Richmond TW10 118 CL86
Romford RM7 70 FA56
Slough SL3 92 AX77
South Croydon CR2 160 DQ108
Southall UB2 96 BW76
Sutton SM1 140 DA104
Uxbridge UB10 77 BP70
Watford WD18 23 BV42
Woking GU21 167 BA116
Marlborough St, SW3 198 B9
Marlborough Yd, N19 65 DK61
Marld, The, Ashtd. KT21 172 CM118
Marle Gdns, Wal.Abb. EN9 15 EC32
Marler Rd, SE23 123 DY88
Marlescroft Way, Loug. IG10 33 EP43
Marley Av, Bexh. DA7 106 EX79
Marley Cl, N15
off Stanmore Rd 65 DP56
Addlestone KT15 151 BF107
Greenford UB6 78 CA69
Marley Wk, NW2
off Lennon Rd 63 CW64
Marl Fld Cl, Wor.Pk. KT4 139 CU102
Marlin Cl, Sun. TW16 115 BT93
Marlingdene Cl, Hmptn.
TW12 116 CA93
Marlings Cl, Chis. BR7 145 ES98
Whyteleafe CR3 176 DS117
Marlings Pk Av, Chis. BR7 145 ES98
Marling Way, Grav. DA12 131 GL92
Marlins, The, Nthwd. HA6 39 BT51
Marlins Cl, Rick. (Chorl.) WD3 21 BE40
Sutton SM1
off Turnpike La 158 DC106
Marlins Meadow, Wat. WD18 23 BR44
Marlin Sq, Abb.L. WD5 7 BT31
Marloes Cl, Wem. HA0 61 CK63
Marloes Rd, W8 100 DB76
Marlow Av, Purf. RM19 108 FN77
Marlow Cl, SE20 142 DV97
Marlow Ct, NW6 81 CX66
NW9 63 CT55
Marlow Cres, Twick. TW1 117 CF86
Marlow Dr, Sutt. SM3 139 CX103
Marlowe Cl, Chis. BR7 125 ER93
Ilford IG6 49 EQ53
Marlowe Ct, SE19
off Lymer Av 122 DT92
Marlowe Gdns, SE9 125 EN86
Romford RM3
off Shenstone Gdns 52 FJ53
Marlowe Path, SE8
off Glaisher St 103 EB79
Marlowe Rd, E17 67 EC56
Marlowes, The, NW8 82 DD67
Dartford DA1 107 FD84
Marlowe Sq, Mitch. CR4 141 DJ98
Marlowe Way, Croy. CR0 141 DL103
Marlow Gdns, Hayes UB3 95 BR76
Marlow Rd, E6 87 EM69
SE20 142 DV97
Southall UB2 96 BZ76
Marlow Way, SE16 203 H4
Marlpit Av, Couls. CR5 175 DL117
Marlpit La, Couls. CR5 175 DK116
Marl Rd, SW18 100 DB84
Marl St, SW18 off Marl Rd 100 DC84
Marlton St, SE10 205 L10
Marlwood Cl, Sid. DA15 125 ES89
Marlyon Rd, Ilf. IG6 50 EV50
Marmadon Rd, SE18 105 ET77
Marmara Apts, E16
off Western Gateway 86 EG73
Marmion App, E4 47 EA49
Marmion Av, E4 47 DZ49
Marmion Cl, E4 47 DZ49
Marmion Ms, SW11
off Taybridge Rd 100 DG83
Marmion Rd, SW11 100 DG84
Marmont Rd, SE15 102 DU81
Marmora Rd, SE22 122 DW86
Marmot Rd, Houns. TW4 96 BX83
Marne Av, N11 45 DH49
Welling DA16 106 EU83
Marnell Way, Houns. TW4 96 BX83
Marne St, W10 81 CY69
Marney Rd, SW11 100 DG84
Marneys Cl, Epsom KT18 172 CN115
Marnfield Cres, SW2 121 DM88
Marnham Av, NW2 63 CY63
Marnham Cres, Grnf. UB6 78 CB69
Marnock Rd, SE4 123 DY85
Maroon St, E14 85 DY71
Maroons Way, SE6 123 EA92
Marquess Est, N1
off Nightingale Rd 84 DQ65
Marquess Rd, N1 84 DR65
Marquis Cl, Wem. HA0 80 CM66
Marquis Rd, N4 65 DM60
N22 45 DM51
NW1 83 DK65
Marrabon Cl, Sid. DA15 126 EU88
Marram Ct, Grays RM17
off Medlar Rd 110 GE79
Marrick Cl, SW15 99 CU84
Marrilyne Av, Enf. EN3 31 DZ38
Marriott Cl, Felt. TW14 115 BR86
Marriott Ter, Rick. (Chorl.) WD3 21 BF42
Marriott Lo Cl, Add. KT15 152 BJ105
Marriott Rd, E15 86 EE67
N4 65 DM60
N10 44 DF53
Barnet EN5 27 CX41
Dartford DA1 128 FN87
Marriotts Cl, NW9 63 CT58
Mar Rd, S.Ock. RM15 91 FW70
Marrowells, Wey. KT13 135 BS104
Marryat Cl, Houns. TW4 96 BZ84
Marryat Pl, SW19 119 CY91
Marryat Rd, SW19 119 CX92
Enfield EN1 30 DV35
Marryat Sq, SW6 99 CY81
Marsala Rd, SE13 103 EB84
Marsden Rd, N9 46 DV47
SE15 102 DT83
Marsden St, NW5 82 DG65
Marsden Way, Orp. BR6 163 ET105
Marshall Cl, SW18
off Allfarthing La 120 DC86
Harrow HA1 off Bowen Rd 61 CD59
Hounslow TW4 116 BZ85
South Croydon CR2 160 DU113
Marshall Dr, Hayes UB4 77 BT71
Marshall Est, NW7 43 CU49
Marshall Path, SE28
off Attlee Rd 88 EV73
Marshall Pl, Add. (New Haw)
KT15 152 BJ109
Marshall Rd, E10 67 EB62
N17 46 DR53
Marshalls Cl, N11 45 DH49
Epsom KT19 156 CQ113
Marshalls Dr, Rom. RM1 71 FE55
Marshall's Gro, SE18 104 EL77
Marshalls Pl, SE16 202 A7
Marshalls Rd, Rom. RM7 71 FD56
Marshall's Rd, Sutt. SM1 158 DB105
Marshall St, NW10 80 CR66
W1 195 L9
Marshalsea Rd, SE1 201 J4
Marsham Cl, Chis. BR7 125 EP92
Marsham La, Ger.Cr. SL9 56 AY58
Marsham Lo, Ger.Cr. SL9 56 AY58
Marsham St, SW1 199 N7
Marsham Way, Ger.Cr. SL9 56 AY57
Marsh Av, Epsom KT19 156 CS110
Mitcham CR4 140 DF96
Marshbrook Cl, SE3 104 EK83
Marsh Cl, NW7 43 CT48
Waltham Cross EN8 15 DZ33
Marsh Ct, SW19 140 DC95
Marshcroft Dr, Wal.Cr.
(Chsht) EN8 15 DY30
Marsh Dr, NW9 63 CT58
Marshe Cl, Pot.B. EN6 12 DD32
Marsh Fm Rd, Twick. TW2 117 CF88
Marshfield, Slou. (Datchet)
SL3 92 AW81
Marshfield St, E14 204 D6
Marshfoot Rd, Grays RM16,
RM17 110 GE78
Marshgate La, E15 85 EB67
Marshgate Path, SE28
off Tom Cribb Rd 105 EQ76
Marshgate Sidings, E15 85 EB67
Marsh Grn Rd, Dag. RM10 88 FA67
Marsh Hill, E9 67 DY64
Marsh La, E10 67 EA61
N17 46 DV52
NW7 42 CS49
Addlestone KT15 152 BH105
Stanmore HA7 41 CJ50
Marsh Rd, Pnr. HA5 60 BY56
Wembley HA0 79 CK68
Marshside Cl, N9 46 DW46
Marsh St, E14 204 B9
Dartford DA1 108 FN82
Marsh Ter, Orp. BR5
off Buttermere Rd 146 EX98
Marsh Vw, Grav. DA12 131 GM88
Marsh Wall, E14 203 P3
Marsh Way, Rain. RM13 89 FD70
Marsland Cl, SE17 101 DP78
Marston, Epsom KT19 156 CQ111
Marston Av, Chess. KT9 156 CL107
Dagenham RM10 70 FA61
Marston Cl, NW6 82 DC66
Dagenham RM10 70 FA62
Marston Ct, Walt. KT12
off St. Johns Dr 136 BW102
Marston Dr, Warl. CR6 177 DY118
Marston Ho, Grays RM17 110 GA79
Marston Rd, Ilf. IG5 48 EL53
Teddington TW11 117 CH92
Woking GU21 166 AV117
Marston Way, SE19 121 DP94
Marsworth Av, Pnr. HA5 40 BX53
Marsworth Cl, Hayes UB4 78 BY71
Watford WD18 23 BS44
Marsworth Ho, E2
off Whiston Rd 84 DU67
Martaban Rd, N16 66 DS61
Martara Ms, SE17
off Penrose St 102 DQ78
Martello St, E8 84 DV66
Martello Ter, E8 84 DV66
Martell Rd, SE21 122 DR90
Martel Pl, E8 off Dalston La 84 DT65
Marten Rd, E17 47 EA54
Martens Av, Bexh. DA7 107 FC84
Martens Cl, Bexh. DA7 107 FC84
Martha Ct, E2 84 DV68
Martham Cl, SE28 88 EX73
Ilford IG6 49 EP53
Martha Rd, E15 86 EE65
Martha's Bldgs, EC1 197 K4
Martha St, E1 84 DV72
Marthorne Cres, Har. HA3 41 CD54
Martina Ter, Chig. IG7
off Manford Way 49 ES50
Martin Bowes Rd, SE9 105 EM83
Martinbridge Trd Est, Enf. EN1 30 DU43
Martin Cl, N9 47 DX46
South Croydon CR2 161 DX111
Uxbridge UB10
off Valley Rd 76 BL68
Warlingham CR6 176 DV116
Martin Cres, Croy. CR0 141 DN102
Martindale, SW14 118 CQ85
Iver SL0 75 BD70
Martindale Av, E16 86 EG73
Orpington BR6 164 EU106
Martindale Rd, SW12 121 DH87
Hounslow TW4 96 BY83
Woking GU21 166 AT118
Martin Dene, Bexh. DA6 126 EZ85
Martin Dr, Dart. (Stone) DA2 128 FQ86
Northolt UB5 60 BZ64
Rainham RM13 89 FH70
Martineau Cl, Esher KT10 155 CD105
Martineau Ms, N5
off Martineau Rd 65 DP63
Martineau Rd, N5 65 DP63
Martineau St, E1 84 DW73
Martingale Cl, Sun. TW16 135 BU98
Martingales Cl, Rich. TW10 117 CK90
Martin Gdns, Dag. RM8 70 EW63
Martin Gro, Mord. SM4 140 DA97
Martini Dr, Enf. EN3 31 EA37
Martin La, EC4 197 L10
Martin Ri, Bexh. DA6 126 EZ85
Martin Rd, Dag. RM8 70 EW63
Dartford DA2 128 FJ90
Slough SL1 92 AS76
South Ockendon (Aveley)
RM15 91 FR73
Martins Cl, Orp. BR5 146 EX97
Radlett WD7 25 CE36
West Wickham BR4 143 ED102
Martins Dr, Wal.Cr. (Chsht)
EN8 15 DY28
Martinsfield Cl, Chig. IG7 49 ES49
Martins Mt, Barn. EN5 28 DA42
Martins Pl, SE28
off Martin St 87 ES74
Martin's Plain, Slou.
(Stoke P.) SL2 74 AT69
Martins Rd, Brom. BR2 144 EE96
Martins Shaw, Sev. (Chipstead)
TN13 190 FC122
Martinstown Cl, Horn. RM11 72 FN58
Martin St, SE28 87 ES74
Martins Wk, N8
off Alexandra Rd 65 DN55
N10 44 DG53
SE28 87 ES74
Borehamwood WD6
off Siskin Cl 26 CN42
Martinsyde, Wok. GU22 167 BC117
Martin Way, SW20 139 CY97
Martin Way, Mord. SM4 139 CY97
Woking GU21 166 AU118
Martlands Ind Est, Wok.
GU22 166 AU123
Martlesham Cl, Horn. RM12 72 FJ64
Martlesham Wk, NW9
off Kenley Av 42 CS53
Martlet Gro, Nthlt. UB5 78 BX69
Martlett Ct, WC2 196 A9
Martley Dr, Ilf. IG2 69 EP57
Martock Cl, Har. HA3 61 CG56
Martock Gdns, N11 44 DF50
Marton Cl, SE6 123 EA90
Marton Rd, N16 66 DS61
MARTYR'S GREEN, Wok.
KT11 169 BR120
Martyrs La, Wok. GU21 151 BB112
Martys Yd, NW3
off Hampstead High St 64 DD63
Marvell Av, Hayes UB4 77 BU71
Marvels Cl, SE12 124 EH89
Marvels La, SE12 124 EH89
Marville Rd, SW6 99 CZ80
Marvin St, E8
off Sylvester Rd 84 DV65
Marwell, West. TN16 189 EP126
Marwell Cl, Rom. RM1 71 FG57
West Wickham BR4
off Deer Pk Way 144 EF103
Marwood Cl, Kings L. WD4 6 BN29
Welling DA16 106 EV83
Marwood Dr, NW7 43 CX52
Mary Adelaide Cl, SW15 118 CS91
Mary Ann Gdns, SE8 103 EA79
Maryatt Av, Har. HA2 60 CB61
Marybank, SE18 105 EM77
Mary Cl, Stan. HA7 62 CM56
Mary Datchelor Cl, SE5 102 DR81
Maryfield Cl, Bex. DA5 127 FE90
Marygold Wk, Amer. HP6 20 AV39
Mary Grn, NW8 82 DB67
Maryhill Cl, Ken. CR8 176 DQ117
⇌ Maryland 86 EE65
Maryland Ind Est, E15
off Maryland Rd 67 ED64
Maryland Pk, E15 68 EE64
Maryland Pt, E15
off The Grove 86 EE65
Maryland Rd, E15 67 ED64
N22 45 DM51
Thornton Heath CR7 141 DP95
Maryland Sq, E15 68 EE64
Marylands Rd, W9 82 DA70
Maryland St, E15 67 ED64
Maryland Wk, N1
off Popham St 84 DQ67
Maryland Way, Sun. TW16 135 BU96
Mary Lawrenson Pl, SE3 104 EF80
MARYLEBONE, NW1 194 D8
⇌ Marylebone 194 D5
⊖ Marylebone 194 D5
Marylebone Flyover, NW1 194 A7
W2 194 A7
Marylebone Gdns, Rich. TW9
off Manor Rd 98 CM84
Marylebone High St, W1 194 G6
Marylebone La, W1 195 H9
Marylebone Ms, W1 195 H7
Marylebone Pas, W1 195 L8
Marylebone Rd, NW1 194 C6
Marylebone St, W1 194 G7
Marylee Way, SE11 200 C10
Mary Macarthur Ho, E2
off Warley St 85 DX69
W6 off Field Rd 99 CY79
Maryon Gro, SE7 104 EL77
Maryon Ms, NW3
off South End Rd 64 DE63
Maryon Rd, SE7 104 EL77
SE18 104 EL77
Mary Peters Dr, Grnf. UB6 61 CD64
Mary Pl, W11 81 CY73
Mary Rose Cl, Grays (Chaff.Hun.)
RM16 109 FW77
Hampton TW12
off Ashley Rd 136 CA95
Mary Rose Mall, E6
off Frobisher Rd 87 EN71
Maryrose Way, N20 44 DD46
Mary Seacole Cl, E8
off Clarissa St 84 DT67
Maryside, Slou. SL3 92 AY75
Mary's Ter, Twick. TW1 117 CG87
Mary St, E16 off Barking Rd 86 EF71
N1 84 DQ67
Mary Ter, NW1 83 DH67
Mary Way, Wat. WD19 40 BW49
Masbro Rd, W14 99 CX76
Mascalls Ct, SE7
off Victoria Way 104 EJ79
Mascalls Gdns, Brwd. CM14 54 FT49
Mascalls La, Brwd. CM14 54 FT49
H Mascalls Pk, Brwd. CM14 53 FV51
Mascalls Rd, SE7 104 EJ79
Mascotte Rd, SW15 99 CX84
Mascotts Cl, NW2 63 CV62
Masefield Av, Borwd. WD6 26 CP43
Southall UB1 78 CA73
Stanmore HA7 41 CF50
Masefield Cl, Erith DA8 107 FF81
Romford RM3 52 FJ53
Masefield Ct, Brwd. CM14 54 FW49
Masefield Cres, N14 29 DJ44
Romford RM3 52 FJ53
Masefield Dr, Upmin. RM14 72 FQ59
Masefield Gdns, E6 87 EN70
Masefield La, Hayes UB4 77 BV70
Masefield Rd, Dart. DA1 128 FP85
Gravesend (Nthflt) DA11 130 GD90
Grays RM16 110 GE75
Hampton TW12
off Wordsworth Rd 116 BZ91
Masefield Vw, Orp. BR6 145 EQ104
Masefield Way, Stai. TW19 114 BM88
Masham Ho, Erith DA18
off Kale Rd 106 EX75
Mashie Rd, W3 80 CS72

Mashiters Hill, Rom. RM1 51 FD53
Mashiters Wk, Rom. RM1 71 FE55
Maskall Cl, SW2 121 DN88
Maskani Wk, SW16
off Bates Cres 121 DJ94
Maskell Rd, SW17 120 DC90
Maskelyne Cl, SW11 100 DE81
Mason Bradbear Ct, N1
off St. Paul's Rd 84 DR65
Mason Cl, E16 86 EG73
SE16 202 C10
SW20 139 CX95
Bexleyheath DA7 107 FB83
Borehamwood WD6 26 CQ40
Hampton TW12 136 BZ95
Mason Dr, Rom. (Harold Wd)
RM3 off Whitmore Av 52 FL54
Masonic Hall Rd, Cher. KT16 133 BF100
Mason Rd, Sutt. SM1
off Manor Pl 158 DB106
Woodford Green IG8 48 EE49
Masons Arms Ms, W1 195 J9
Masons Av, EC2 197 K8
Croydon CR0 142 DQ104
Harrow HA3 61 CF56
Masons Ct, Wem. HA9
off Mayfields 62 CN61
Masons Grn La, W3 80 CN71
Masons Hill, SE18 105 EP77
Bromley BR1, BR2 144 EG97
Masons Pl, EC1
off Moreland St 83 DP69
Mason's Pl, EC1 196 G2
Masons Pl, Mitch. CR4 140 DF95
Masons Rd, Enf. EN1 30 DW36
Mason St, SE17 201 L9
Masons Yd, EC1
off Moreland St 83 DP69
Mason's Yd, SW1 199 L2
SW19
off High St Wimbledon 119 CX92
Mason Way, Wal.Abb. EN9 16 EF34
Massey Cl, N11 off Grove Rd 45 DH50
Massey Ct, E6 86 EJ67
Massie Rd, E8 off Graham Rd 84 DU65
Massingberd Way, SW17 121 DH91
Massinger St, SE17 201 M9
Massingham St, E1 85 DX70
Masson Av, Ruis. HA4 78 BW65
Master Cl, Oxt. RH8
off Church La 188 EE129
Master Gunner Pl, SE18 104 EL80
Masterman Ho, SE5 102 DQ80
Masterman Rd, E6 86 EL69
Masters Cl, SW16 121 DJ93
Masters Dr, SE16 102 DV78
Masters St, E1 85 DX71
Masthead Cl, Dart. DA2 108 FQ84
DLR Masthouse Terrace 204 A10
Masthouse Ter, E14 204 A9
Mast Leisure Pk, SE16 203 J7
Mastmaker Rd, E14 204 A5
Mast Quay, SE18
off Woolwich Ch St 105 EN76
Maswell Pk Cres, Houns.
TW3 116 CC85
Maswell Pk Rd, Houns. TW3 116 CB85
Matcham Rd, E11 68 EE62
Matchless Dr, SE18 105 EN80
Matfield Cl, Brom. BR2 144 EG99
Matfield Rd, Belv. DA17 106 FA79
Matham Gro, SE22 102 DT84
Matham Rd, E.Mol. KT8 137 CD99
Matheson Rd, W14 99 CZ77
Mathews Av, E6 87 EN68
Mathews Pk Av, E15 86 EF65
Mathias Cl, Epsom KT18 156 CQ113
Mathisen Way, Slou.
(Colnbr.) SL3 93 BE81
Matilda Cl, SE19
off Elizabeth Way 122 DR94
Matilda St, N1 83 DM67
Matlock Cl, SE24 102 DQ84
Barnet EN5 27 CX43
Matlock Ct, SE5
off Denmark Hill Est 102 DR84
Matlock Cres, Sutt. SM3 157 CY105
Watford WD19 40 BW48
Matlock Gdns, Horn. RM12 72 FL62
Sutton SM3 157 CY105
Matlock Pl, Sutt. SM3 157 CY105
Matlock Rd, E10 67 EC58
Caterham CR3 176 DS121
Matlock St, E14 85 DY72
Matlock Way, N.Mal. KT3 138 CR95
Matrimony Pl, SW8 101 DJ82
Matson Ct, Wdf.Grn. IG8
off The Bridle Path 48 EE52
Matson Ho, SE16 202 E6
Matthew Arnold Cl, Cob.
KT11 153 BU114
Staines TW18
off Elizabeth Av 114 BJ93
Matthew Cl, W10 81 CX70
Matthew Ct, Mitch. CR4 141 DK99
Matthew Parker St, SW1 199 N5
Matthews Cl, Rom. (Hav.at.Bow.)
RM3 off Oak Rd 52 FM53
Matthews Gdns, Croy.
(New Adgtn) CR0 161 ED111
Matthews La, Stai. TW18
off Kingston Rd 114 BG91
Matthews Rd, Grnf. UB6 61 CD64
Matthews St, SW11 100 DF82
Matthews Yd, WC2 195 P9
Matthias Rd, N16 66 DR64
Mattingley Way, SE15
off Daniel Gdns 102 DT80
Mattison Rd, N4 65 DN58
Mattock La, W5 79 CH74
W13 79 CH74
Maud Cashmore Way, SE18 105 EM76
Maud Chadburn Pl, SW4
off Balham Hill 121 DH86
Maude Cres, Wat. WD24 23 BV37
Maude Rd, E17 67 DY57
SE5 102 DS81
Swanley BR8 127 FG93
Maudesville Cotts, W7
off The Broadway 79 CE74
Maude Ter, E17 67 DY56
Maud Gdns, E13 86 EF67
Barking IG11 87 ET68
Maudlin's Grn, E1 202 B2
Maud Rd, E10 67 EC62
E13 86 EF68
Maudslay Rd, SE9 105 EM83
H Maudsley Hosp, SE5 102 DR82
Maudsley Ho, Brent. TW8
off Green Dragon La 98 CL78
Maud St, E16 86 EF71
Maud Wilkes Cl, NW5 65 DJ64
Mauleverer Rd, SW2 121 DL85
Maundeby Wk, NW10
off Neasden La 80 CS65
Maunder Cl, Grays (Chaff.Hun.)
RM16 109 FX77
Maunder Rd, W7 79 CF74
Maunsel St, SW1 199 M8
Maurer Ct, SE10
off Renaissance Wk 104 EF76
Maurice Av, N22 45 DP54
Caterham CR3 176 DR122
Maurice Brown Cl, NW7 43 CX50
Maurice St, W12 81 CV72
Maurice Wk, NW11 64 DC56
Maurier Cl, Nthlt. UB5 78 BW67
Mauritius Rd, SE10 205 J9
Maury Rd, N16 66 DU61
Mauveine Gdns, Houns. TW3 96 CA84
Mavelstone Cl, Brom. BR1 144 EL95
Mavelstone Rd, Brom. BR1 144 EL95
Maverton Rd, E3 85 EA67
Mavis Av, Epsom KT19 156 CS106
Mavis Cl, Epsom KT19 156 CS106
Mavis Gro, Horn. RM12 72 FL61
Mavis Wk, E6 86 EL71
Mawbey Est, SE1 102 DT78
Mawbey Ho, SE1
off Old Kent Rd 102 DU78
Mawbey Pl, SE1 102 DT78
Mawbey Rd, SE1
off Old Kent Rd 102 DT78
Chertsey (Ott.) KT16 151 BD107
Mawbey St, SW8 101 DL80
Mawney Cl, Rom. RM7 51 FB54
Mawney Rd, Rom. RM7 71 FC56
Mawson Cl, SW20 139 CY96
Mawson La, W4
off Great W Rd 99 CT79
Maxey Gdns, Dag. RM9 70 EY63
Maxey Rd, SE18 105 EQ77
Dagenham RM9 70 EY63
Maxfield Cl, N20 44 DC45
Maxilla Gdns, W10
off Cambridge Gdns 81 CX72
Maxilla Wk, W10
off Kingsdown Cl 81 CX72
Maximfeldt Rd, Erith DA8 107 FE78
Maxim Rd, N21 29 DN44
Dartford DA1 127 FE85
Erith DA8 107 FE77
Maxted Pk, Har. HA1 61 CE59
Maxted Rd, SE15 102 DT83
Maxwell Cl, Croy. CR0 141 DL102
Hayes UB3 77 BU73
Rickmansworth (Mill End)
WD3 38 BG47
Maxwell Dr, W.Byf. KT14 152 BJ111
Maxwell Gdns, Orp. BR6 145 ET104
Maxwell Ri, Wat. WD19 40 BY45
Maxwell Rd, SW6 100 DB80
Ashford TW15 115 BQ93
Borehamwood WD6 26 CP41
Northwood HA6 39 BR52
Welling DA16 106 EU84
West Drayton UB7 94 BM77
Maxwelton Av, NW7 42 CR50
Maxwelton Cl, NW7 42 CR50
Maya Angelou Ct, E4
off Bailey Cl 47 EC49
Maya Cl, SE15 102 DV82
Mayall Cl, Enf. EN3 31 EA38
Mayall Rd, SE24 121 DP85
Maya Pl, N11 45 DK52
Maya Rd, N2 64 DC56
May Av, Grav. (Nthflt) DA11 131 GF88
Orpington BR5 146 EV99
May Av Ind Est, Grav. (Nthflt)
DA11 off May Av 131 GF88
Maybank Av, E18 48 EH54
Hornchurch RM12 71 FH64
Wembley HA0 61 CF64
Maybank Gdns, Pnr. HA5 59 BU57
Maybank Lo, Horn. RM12
off Maybank Av 72 FJ64
Maybank Rd, E18 48 EH53
May Bate Av, Kings.T. KT2 137 CK95
Maybells Commercial Est,
Bark. IG11 88 EX68
Mayberry Pl, Surb. KT5 138 CM101
Maybourne Cl, SE26 122 DV92
Maybourne Ri, Wok. GU22 166 AX124
Maybrick Rd, Horn. RM11 72 FJ58
Maybrook Meadow Est,
Bark. IG11 88 EU66
MAYBURY, Wok. GU22 167 BB117
Maybury Av, Dart. DA2 128 FQ88
Waltham Cross (Chsht) EN8 14 DV28
Maybury Cl, Enf. EN1 30 DV38
Loughton IG10 33 EP42
Orpington BR5 145 EP99
Tadworth KT20
off Ballards Grn 173 CY119
Maybury Gdns, NW10 81 CV65
Maybury Hill, Wok. GU22 167 BB116
Maybury Ms, N6 65 DJ59
Maybury Rd, E13 86 EJ70
Barking IG11 87 ET68
Woking GU21 167 AZ117
Maybury St, SW17 120 DE92
Maybush Rd, Horn. RM11 72 FL59
Maychurch Cl, Stan. HA7 41 CK52
May Cl, Chess. KT9 156 CM107
Maycock Gro, Nthwd. HA6 39 BT51
May Cotts, Wat. WD18 24 BW43
May Ct, SW19 140 DB95
Grays RM17 off Medlar Rd 110 GE79
Maycroft, Pnr. HA5 39 BV54
Maycroft Av, Grays RM17 110 GD78
Maycroft Gdns, Grays RM17 110 GD78
Maycroft Rd, Wal.Cr. (Chsht)
EN7 14 DS26
Maycross Av, Mord. SM4 139 CZ97
Mayday Gdns, SE3 104 EL82
Mayday Rd, Th.Hth. CR7 141 DP100
H Mayday Uni Hosp,
Th.Hth. CR7 141 DP100
Maydew Ho, SE16 202 F8
Maydwell Lo, Borwd. WD6 26 CM40
Mayell Cl, Lthd. KT22 171 CJ123
Mayerne Rd, SE9 124 EK85
Mayer Rd, Wal.Abb. EN9
off Deer Pk Way 31 EB36
Mayesbrook Rd, Bark. IG11 87 ET67
Dagenham RM8 70 EU62
Ilford IG3 70 EU62
Mayes Cl, Swan. BR8 147 FG98
Warlingham CR6 177 DX118
Mayesford Rd, Rom. RM6 70 EW59
Mayes Rd, N22 45 DN54
Mayeswood Rd, SE12 124 EJ90
MAYFAIR, W1 199 H1
Mayfair Av, Bexh. DA7 106 EX81
Ilford IG1 69 EM61
Romford RM6 70 EX58
Twickenham TW2 116 CC87
Worcester Park KT4 139 CU102
Mayfair Cl, Beck. BR3 143 EB95
Surbiton KT6 138 CL102
Mayfair Gdns, N17 46 DR51
Woodford Green IG8 48 EG52
Mayfair Ms, NW1
off Regents Pk Rd 82 DF66
Mayfair Pl, W1 199 J2
Mayfair Rd, Dart. DA1 128 FK85
Mayfair Ter, N14 45 DK45
Mayfare, Rick. (Crox.Grn)
WD3 23 BR43
Mayfield, Bexh. DA7 106 EZ83
Leatherhead KT22 171 CJ121
Waltham Abbey EN9 15 ED34
Mayfield Av, N12 44 DC49
N14 45 DK47
W4 98 CS77
W13 97 CH76
Addlestone (New Haw)
KT15 152 BH110
Gerrards Cross SL9 56 AX56
Harrow HA3 61 CH57
Orpington BR6 145 ET102
Woodford Green IG8 48 EG52
Mayfield Cl, E8
off Forest Rd 84 DT65
SW4 121 DK85
Addlestone (New Haw)
KT15 152 BJ110
Ashford TW15 115 BP93
Thames Ditton KT7 137 CH102
Uxbridge UB10 77 BP69
Walton-on-Thames KT12 153 BU105
Mayfield Cres, N9 30 DV44
Thornton Heath CR7 141 DM98
Mayfield Dr, Pnr. HA5 60 BZ56
Mayfield Gdns, NW4 63 CX58
W7 79 CD72
Addlestone (New Haw)
KT15 152 BH110
Brentwood CM14 54 FV46
Staines TW18 113 BF93
Walton-on-Thames KT12 153 BU105
Mayfield Mans, SW15
off West Hill 119 CX87
Mayfield Pk, West Dr. UB7 94 BJ76
Mayfield Rd, E4 47 EC47
E8 84 DT66
E13 86 EF70
E17 47 DY54
N8 65 DM58
SW19 139 CZ95
W3 80 CP73
W12 98 CS75
Belvedere DA17 107 FC77
Bromley BR1 144 EL99
Dagenham RM8 70 EW60
Enfield EN3 31 DX40
Gravesend DA11 131 GF87
South Croydon CR2 160 DR109
Sutton SM2 158 DD107
Thornton Heath CR7 141 DM98
Walton-on-Thames KT12 153 BU105
Weybridge KT13 152 BM106
Mayfields, Grays RM16 110 GC75
Swanscombe DA10 129 FX86
Wembley HA9 62 CN61
Mayfields Cl, Wem. HA9 62 CN61
Mayflower Cl, SE16 203 J8
Ruislip HA4
off Leaholme Way 59 BQ58
South Ockendon RM15 91 FW70
Mayflower Ct, SE16
off St. Marychurch St 102 DW75
Mayflower Rd, SW9 101 DL83
Grays (Chaff.Hun.) RM16 109 FW78
St. Albans (Park St) AL2 8 CB27
Mayflower St, SE16 202 F5
Mayfly Cl, Orp. BR5 146 EX98
Pinner HA5 60 BW59
Mayfly Gdns, Nthlt. UB5
off Ruislip Rd 78 BX69
MAYFORD, Wok. GU22 166 AW122
Mayford Cl, SW12 120 DF87
Beckenham BR3 143 DX97
Woking GU22 166 AX122
Mayford Grn, Wok. GU22
off Smarts Heath Rd 166 AX122
Mayford Rd, SW12 120 DF87
May Gdns, Borwd. (Els.) WD6 25 CK44
Wembley HA0 79 CJ68
Maygoods Cl, Uxb. UB8 76 BK71
Maygoods Grn, Uxb. UB8
off Worcester Rd 76 BK71
Maygoods La, Uxb. UB8 76 BK71
Maygood St, N1 83 DM68
Maygoods Vw, Uxb. UB8
off Benbow Waye 76 BJ71
Maygreen Cres, Horn. RM11 71 FG59
Maygrove Rd, NW6 81 CZ65
Mayhew Cl, E4 47 EA48
Mayhill Rd, SE7 104 EH79
Barnet EN5 27 CY44
Mayhurst Av, Wok. GU22 167 BC116
Mayhurst Cl, Wok. GU22 167 BC116
Mayhurst Cres, Wok. GU22 167 BC116
Maylands Av, Horn. RM12 71 FH63
Maylands Dr, Sid. DA14 126 EX90
Uxbridge UB8 76 BK65
Maylands Rd, Wat. WD19 40 BW49
Maylands Way, Rom. RM3 52 FQ51
Maynard Cl, N15
off Brunswick Rd 66 DS56
SW6 off Cambria St 100 DB80
Erith DA8 107 FF80
Maynard Ct, Enf. EN3
off Harston Dr 31 EA38
Waltham Abbey EN9 16 EF34
Maynard Path, E17 67 EC57
Maynard Pl, Pot.B. EN6 13 DL29
Maynard Rd, E17 67 EC57
Maynards, Horn. RM11 72 FL59
Maynards Quay, E1 202 F1
Maynooth Gdns, Cars. SM5 140 DF101
Mayo Cl, Wal.Cr. (Chsht) EN8 14 DW28
Mayola Rd, E5 66 DW63
Mayo Rd, NW10 80 CS65
Croydon CR0 142 DR99
Walton-on-Thames KT12 135 BT101
Mayor's La, Dart. DA2 128 FJ92
Mayow Rd, SE23 123 DX90
SE26 123 DX91
Mayplace Av, Dart. DA1 107 FG84
Mayplace Cl, Bexh. DA7 107 FB83
Mayplace La, SE18 105 EP80
Mayplace Rd E, Bexh. DA7 107 FB83
Dartford DA1 107 FC83
Mayplace Rd W, Bexh. DA7 106 FA84
MAYPOLE, Orp. BR6 164 EZ106
Maypole Cres, Erith DA8 108 FK79
Ilford IG6 49 ER52
Maypole Dr, Chig. IG7 50 EU48
Maypole Rd, Grav. DA12 131 GM88
Orpington BR6 164 EZ106
May Rd, E4 47 EA51
E13 86 EG68
Dartford (Hawley) DA2 128 FM91
Twickenham TW2 117 CE88
Mayroyd Av, Surb. KT6 138 CN103
May's Bldgs Ms, SE10
off Crooms Hill 103 EC80
Mays Cl, Wey. KT13 152 BM110
Mays Ct, WC2 199 P1
Maysfield Rd, Wok. (Send)
GU23 167 BD123
MAY'S GREEN, Cob. KT11 169 BT121
Mays Gro, Wok. (Send) GU23 167 BD123
Mays Hill Rd, Brom. BR2 144 EE96
Mays La, E4 47 ED47
Barnet EN5 27 CY43
Maysoule Rd, SW11 100 DD84
Mays Rd, Tedd. TW11 117 CD92
Mayston Ms, SE10
off Westcombe Hill 104 EG78
May St, W14
off North End Rd 99 CZ78
Mayswood Gdns, Dag. RM10 89 FC65
Maythorne Cl, Wat. WD18 23 BS42
Mayton St, N7 65 DM62
Maytree Cl, Edg. HA8 42 CQ48
Rainham RM13 89 FE68
Maytree Cres, Wat. WD24 23 BT35
Maytree Gdns, W5
off South Ealing Rd 97 CK75
May Tree La, Stan. HA7 41 CF52
Maytrees, Rad. WD7 25 CG37
Maytree Wk, SW2 121 DN89
Mayville Est, N16
off King Henry St 66 DS64
Mayville Rd, E11 68 EE61
Ilford IG1 69 EP64
May Wk, E13 86 EH68
Maywater Cl, S.Croy. CR2 160 DR111
Maywin Dr, Horn. RM11 72 FM60
Maywood Cl, Beck. BR3 123 EB94
⇌ Maze Hill 104 EE79
Maze Hill, SE3 104 EE79
SE10 104 EE79
Mazenod Av, NW6 82 DA66
Maze Rd, Rich. TW9 98 CN80
Mead, The, N2 44 DC54
W13 79 CH71
Ashtead KT21 172 CL119
Beckenham BR3 143 EC95
Uxbridge UB10 58 BN61
Wallington SM6 159 DK107
Waltham Cross (Chsht) EN8 14 DW29
Watford WD19 40 BY48
West Wickham BR4 143 ED102
Mead Av, Slou. SL3 93 BB75
Mead Cl, Egh. TW20 113 BB93
Grays RM16 110 GB75
Harrow HA3 41 CD53
Loughton IG10 33 EP40
Redhill RH1 184 DG131
Romford RM2 51 FG54
Slough SL3 93 BB75
Swanley BR8 147 FG99
Uxbridge (Denh.) UB9 58 BG61
Mead Ct, NW9 62 CQ57
Egham TW20
off Holbrook Meadow 113 BC93
Waltham Abbey EN9 15 EB34
Woking (Knap.) GU21 166 AS116
Mead Cres, E4 47 EC49
Dartford DA1 off Beech Rd 128 FK88
Sutton SM1 158 DE105
Meadcroft Rd, SE11 101 DP79
Meade Cl, W4 98 CN79
Meade Ct, Tad. (Walt.Hill)
KT20 173 CU124
Mead End, Ashtd. KT21 172 CM116
Meades, The, Wey. KT13 153 BQ107
Meadfield, Edg. HA8 42 CP47
Mead Fld, Har. HA2
off Kings Rd 60 BZ62
Meadfield Av, Slou. SL3 93 BA76
Meadfield Grn, Edg. HA8 42 CP47
Meadfield Rd, Slou. SL3 93 BA76
Meadfoot Rd, SW16 121 DJ94
Meadgate Av, Wdf.Grn. IG8 48 EL50
Mead Gro, Rom. RM6 70 EY55
Mead Ho La, Hayes UB4 77 BR70
Meadhurst Rd, Cher. KT16 134 BH102
Meadlands Dr, Rich. TW10 117 CK89
Mead La, Cher. KT16 134 BH102
Meadow, The, Chis. BR7 125 EQ93
Meadow Av, Croy. CR0 143 DX100
Meadow Bk, N21 29 DM44
Meadowbank, NW3 82 DF66
SE3 104 EF83
Kings Langley WD4 6 BN30
Surbiton KT5 138 CM100
Watford WD19 40 BW45
Meadowbank Cl, SW6 99 CW80
Meadowbank Gdns, Houns.
TW5 95 BU82
Meadowbank Rd, NW9 62 CR59
Meadowbanks, Barn. EN5 27 CT43
Meadowbrook, Oxt. RH8 187 EC130
Meadowbrook Cl, Slou.
(Colnbr.) SL3 93 BF82
Meadow Cl, E4
off Mount Echo Av 47 EB46
E9 67 DZ64
SE6 123 EA92
SW20 139 CW98
Barking IG11 87 ET67
Barnet EN5 27 CZ44
Bexleyheath DA6 126 EZ85
Chislehurst BR7 125 EP92
Enfield EN3 31 DY38
Esher KT10 137 CF104
Hounslow TW4 116 CA86
Northolt UB5 78 CA68
Purley CR8 159 DK113
Richmond TW10 118 CL88
Ruislip HA4 59 BT58
St. Albans (Brick.Wd) AL2 8 CA29
St. Albans (Lon.Col.) AL2 9 CK27
Sevenoaks TN13 190 FG123
Sutton SM1
off Aultone Way 140 DC103
Walton-on-Thames KT12 154 BZ105
Windsor (Old Wind.) SL4 112 AV86
Meadow Ct, Epsom KT18 156 CQ113
Redhill RH1 185 DJ130
Staines TW18 113 BE90
Meadowcourt Rd, SE3 104 EF84
Meadowcroft, Brom. BR1 145 EM97
Bushey WD23 24 CB44
Gerrards Cross (Chal.St.P.)
SL9 36 AX54
Meadowcroft Rd, N13 45 DN47
Meadowcross, Wal.Abb. EN9 16 EE34
Meadow Dr, N10 65 DH55
NW4 43 CW54
Amersham HP6 20 AS37
Woking (Ripley) GU23 167 BF123
Meadowford Cl, SE28 88 EU73
Meadow Gdns, Edg. HA8 42 CP51
Staines TW18 113 BD92
Meadow Garth, NW10 80 CQ65
Meadowgate Cl, NW7 43 CT50
Meadow Hill, Couls. CR5 159 DJ113
New Malden KT3 138 CS100
Purley CR8 159 DJ113
Meadowlands, Cob. KT11 153 BU113
Hornchurch RM11 72 FL59
Oxted RH8 188 EG134
Meadowlands Pk, Add. KT15 134 BL104
Meadow La, SE12 124 EH90
Leatherhead (Fetch.) KT22 170 CC121
Meadowlea Cl, West Dr. UB7 94 BK79
Meadow Ms, SW8 101 DM79
Meadow Pl, SW8 101 DL80
W4 off Edensor Rd 98 CS80
Meadow Ri, Couls. CR5 159 DK113
Meadow Rd, SW8 101 DM79
SW19 120 DC94
Ashford TW15 115 BR92
Ashtead KT21 172 CL117
Barking IG11 87 ET66
Borehamwood WD6 26 CP40
Bromley BR2 144 EE95
Bushey WD23 24 CB43
Dagenham RM9 88 EZ65
Epping CM16 17 ET29
Esher (Clay.) KT10 155 CE107
Feltham TW13 116 BY89
Gravesend DA11 131 GG89
Loughton IG10 32 EL43
Pinner HA5 60 BX57
Romford RM7 71 FC60
Slough SL3 92 AY76
Southall UB1 78 BZ73
Sutton SM1 158 DE106
Virginia Water GU25 132 AS99
Watford WD25 7 BU34
Meadow Row, SE1 201 H7
Meadows, The, Amer. HP7 20 AS39
Orpington BR6 164 EW107
Sevenoaks (Halst.) TN14 164 EZ113
Warlingham CR6 177 DX117
Meadows Cl, E10 67 EA61
Meadows End, Sun. TW16 135 BU95
Meadowside, SE9 104 EJ84
Beaconsfield (Jordans)
HP9 36 AT52
Dartford DA1 128 FK88
Leatherhead (Bkhm) KT23 170 CA123
Walton-on-Thames KT12 136 BW103
Meadow Side, Wat. WD25 7 BV31
Meadowside Rd, Sutt. SM2 157 CY109
Upminster RM14 72 FQ64
Meadows Leigh Cl, Wey.
KT13 135 BQ104
Meadow Stile, Croy. CR0
off High St 142 DQ104
Meadowsweet Cl, E16
off Monarch Dr 86 EK71
SW20 139 CW98
Meadow Vw, Ch.St.G. HP8 36 AU48
Chertsey KT16 134 BJ102
Harrow HA1 61 CE60
Meadowview, Orp. BR5 146 EW97
Meadow Vw, Sid. DA15 126 EV87
Staines TW19 113 BF85
Meadowview Rd, SE6 123 DZ92
Bexley DA5 126 EY86
Epsom KT19 156 CS109
Meadow Vw Rd, Hayes UB4 77 BQ70
Thornton Heath CR7 141 DP99
Meadow Wk, E18 68 EG56
Dagenham RM9 88 EZ65
Dartford DA2 128 FJ91
Epsom KT17, KT19 156 CS107
Tadworth (Walt.Hill) KT20 173 CV124
Wallington SM6 141 DH104
Meadow Way, NW9 62 CR57
Abbots Langley (Bedmond)
WD5 7 BT27

★ Place of interest ⇌ Railway station ⊖ London Underground station DLR Docklands Light Railway station Tra Tramlink station H Hospital Riv Pedestrian ferry landing stage

Meadow Way, Add. KT15 ... 152 BH105
Chessington KT9 ... 156 CL106
Chigwell IG7 ... 49 EQ48
Dartford DA2 ... 128 FQ87
Kings Langley WD4 ... 6 BN30
Leatherhead (Bkhm) KT23 ... 170 CB123
Orpington BR6 ... 145 EN104
Potters Bar EN6 ... 12 DA34
Rickmansworth WD3 ... 38 BJ45
Ruislip HA4 ... 59 BV58
Tadworth KT20 ... 173 CY118
Upminster RM14 ... 72 FQ62
Wembley HA9 ... 61 CK63
Windsor (Old Wind.) SL4 ... 112 AV86
Meadow Way, The, Har. HA3 ... 41 CE53
Meadow Waye, Houns. TW5 ... 96 BY79
Mead Path, SW17 ... 120 DC92
Mead Pl, E9 ... 84 DW65
Croydon CR0 ... 141 DP102
Rickmansworth WD3 ... 38 BH46
Mead Plat, NW10 ... 80 CQ65
Mead Rd, Cat. CR3 ... 176 DT123
Chislehurst BR7 ... 125 EQ93
Dartford DA1 ... 128 FK88
Edgware HA8 ... 42 CN51
Gravesend DA11 ... 131 GH89
Radlett (Shenley) WD7 ... 10 CM33
Richmond TW10 ... 117 CJ90
Uxbridge UB8 ... 76 BK66
Walton-on-Thames KT12 ... 154 BY105
Mead Row, SE1 ... 200 D6
Meads, The, Edg. HA8 ... 42 CR51
St. Albans (Brick.Wd) AL2 ... 8 BZ29
Sutton SM3 ... 139 CY104
Upminster RM14 ... 73 FS61
Uxbridge UB8 ... 76 BL70
Meads La, Ilf. IG3 ... 69 ES59
Meads Rd, N22 ... 45 DP54
Enfield EN3 ... 31 DY39
Meadsway, Brwd. CM13 ... 53 FV51
Mead Ter, Wem. HA9
off Meadow Way ... 61 CK63
Meadvale Rd, W5 ... 79 CH70
Croydon CR0 ... 142 DT101
Mead Wk, Slou. SL3 ... 93 BB75
Meadway, N14 ... 45 DK47
NW11 ... 64 DB58
SW20 ... 139 CW98
Ashford TW15 ... 114 BN91
Barnet EN5 ... 28 DA42
Beckenham BR3 ... 143 EC95
Mead Way, Brom. BR2 ... 144 EF100
Bushey WD23 ... 24 BY40
Coulsdon CR5 ... 175 DL118
Croydon CR0 ... 143 DY103
Meadway, Enf. EN3 ... 30 DW36
Epsom KT19 ... 156 CQ112
Esher KT10 ... 154 CB109
Grays RM17 ... 110 GD77
Ilford IG3 ... 69 ES63
Leatherhead (Oxshott)
KT22 ... 155 CD114
Romford RM2 ... 51 FG54
Ruislip HA4 ... 59 BR58
Sevenoaks (Halst.) TN14 ... 164 EZ113
Staines TW18 ... 114 BG94
Surbiton KT5 ... 138 CQ102
Twickenham TW2 ... 117 CD88
Warlingham CR6 ... 176 DW115
Woodford Green IG8 ... 48 EJ50
Meadway, The, SE3
off Heath La ... 103 ED82
Buckhurst Hill IG9 ... 48 EK46
Loughton IG10 ... 33 EM44
Orpington BR6 ... 164 EV106
Potters Bar (Cuffley) EN6 ... 13 DM28
Sevenoaks TN13 ... 190 FF122
Meadway Cl, NW11 ... 64 DB58
Barnet EN5 ... 28 DA42
Pinner HA5
off Highbanks Rd ... 40 CB51
Staines TW18 ... 113 BF94
Meadway Ct, NW11 ... 64 DB58
Meadway Dr, Add. KT15 ... 152 BJ108
Woking GU21 ... 166 AW116
Meadway Gdns, Ruis. HA4 ... 59 BR58
Meadway Gate, NW11 ... 64 DA58
Meadway Pk, Ger.Cr. SL9 ... 56 AX60
Meaford Way, SE20 ... 122 DV94
Meakin Est, SE1 ... 201 M6
Meanley Rd, E12 ... 68 EL63
Meard St, W1 ... 195 M9
Meare Cl, Tad. KT20 ... 173 CW123
Meath Cl, Orp. BR5 ... 146 EV99
Meath Rd, E15 ... 86 EF68
Ilford IG1 ... 69 EQ62
Meath St, SW11 ... 101 DH81
Mecklenburgh Pl, WC1 ... 196 B4
Mecklenburgh Sq, WC1 ... 196 B4
Mecklenburgh St, WC1 ... 196 B4
Medburn St, NW1 ... 83 DK68
Medbury Rd, Grav. DA12 ... 131 GM88
Medcalf Rd, Enf. EN3 ... 31 DZ37
Medcroft Gdns, SW14 ... 98 CQ84
Medebourne Cl, SE3 ... 104 EG83
Mede Cl, Stai. (Wrays.) TW19 ... 112 AX88
Mede Fld, Lthd. (Fetch.) KT22 ... 171 CD124
Medesenge Way, N13 ... 45 DP51
Medfield St, SW15 ... 119 CV87
Medhurst Cl, E3
off Arbery Rd ... 85 DY68
Woking (Chobham) GU24 ... 150 AT109
Medhurst Cres, Grav. DA12 ... 131 GM90
Medhurst Gdns, Grav. DA12 ... 131 GM90
Median Rd, E5 ... 66 DW64
★ Medici Galleries, W1 ... 199 J1
Medick Ct, Grays RM17 ... 110 GE79
Medina Av, Esher KT10 ... 137 CE104
Medina Gro, N7
off Medina Rd ... 65 DN62
Medina Ho, Erith DA8
off Waterhead Cl ... 107 FE80
Medina Rd, N7 ... 65 DN62
Grays RM17 ... 110 GD77
Medina Sq, Epsom KT19 ... 156 CN109
Medlake Rd, Egh. TW20 ... 113 BC93
Medland Cl, Wall. SM6 ... 140 DG102
Medland Ho, E14
off Branch Rd ... 85 DY73
Medlar Cl, Nthlt. UB5
off Parkfield Av ... 78 BY68
Medlar Ct, Slou. SL2 ... 74 AW74
Medlar Rd, Grays RM17 ... 110 GD79
Medlar St, SE5 ... 102 DQ81
Medley Rd, NW6 ... 82 DA65
Medman Cl, Uxb. UB8
off Chiltern Vw Rd ... 76 BJ68
Medora Rd, SW2 ... 121 DM87
Romford RM7 ... 71 FD56
Medow Mead, Rad. WD7 ... 9 CF33
Medusa Rd, SE6 ... 123 EB86
Medway Bldgs, E3
off Medway Rd ... 85 DY68
Medway Cl, Croy. CR0 ... 142 DW100
Ilford IG1 ... 69 EQ64
Watford WD25 ... 8 BW34
Medway Dr, Grnf. UB6 ... 79 CF68
Medway Gdns, Wem. HA0 ... 61 CG63
Medway Ms, E3
off Medway Rd ... 85 DY68
Medway Par, Grnf. UB6 ... 79 CF68
Medway Rd, E3 ... 85 DY68
Dartford DA1 ... 107 FG83
Medway St, SW1 ... 199 N7
Medwin St, SW4 ... 101 DM84
Meecham Ct, SW11
off Shuttleworth Rd ... 100 DD82
Meerbrook Rd, SE3 ... 104 EJ83
Meeson Rd, E15 ... 86 EF67
Meesons La, Grays RM17 ... 110 FZ77
Meeson St, E5 ... 67 DY63
Meeting Fld Path, E9
off Chatham Pl ... 84 DW65
Meeting Ho All, E1 ... 202 E2
Meeting Ho La, SE15 ... 102 DV81
Megg La, Kings L. (Chipper.)
WD4 ... 6 BH29
Mehetabel Rd, E9 ... 84 DW65
Meister Cl, Ilf. IG1 ... 69 ER60
Melancholy Wk, Rich. TW10 ... 117 CJ89
Melanda Cl, Chis. BR7 ... 125 EM92
Melanie Cl, Bexh. DA7 ... 106 EY81
Melba Gdns, Til. RM18 ... 111 GG80
Melba Way, SE13 ... 103 EB81
Melbourne Av, N13 ... 45 DM51
W13 ... 79 CG74
Pinner HA5 ... 60 CB55
Melbourne Cl, Orp. BR6 ... 145 ES101
Uxbridge UB10 ... 58 BN63
Wallington SM6
off Melbourne Rd ... 159 DJ106
Melbourne Ct, E5
off Daubeney Rd ... 67 DY63
N10 off Sydney Rd ... 45 DH52
SE20 ... 122 DU94
Melbourne Gdns, Rom. RM6 ... 70 EY57
Melbourne Gro, SE22 ... 102 DS84
Melbourne Ho, Hayes UB4 ... 78 BW70
Melbourne Ms, SE6 ... 123 EC87
SW9 ... 101 DN81
Melbourne Pl, WC2 ... 196 C10
Melbourne Rd, E6 ... 87 EM67
E10 ... 67 EB59
E17 ... 67 DY56
SW19 ... 140 DA95
Bushey WD23 ... 24 CB44
Ilford IG1 ... 69 EP60
Teddington TW11 ... 117 CJ93
Tilbury RM18 ... 110 GE81
Wallington SM6 ... 159 DH106
Melbourne Sq, SW9
off Melbourne Ms ... 101 DN81
Melbourne Ter, SW6
off Waterford Rd ... 100 DB80
Melbourne Way, Enf. EN1 ... 30 DT44
Melbray Ms, SW6
off Hurlingham Rd ... 99 CZ82
Melbury Av, Sthl. UB2 ... 96 CB76
Melbury Cl, Cher. KT16 ... 134 BG101
Chislehurst BR7 ... 124 EL93
Esher (Clay.) KT10 ... 155 CH107
West Byfleet KT14 ... 152 BG114
Melbury Ct, W8 ... 99 CZ76
Melbury Dr, SE5
off Sedgmoor Pl ... 102 DS80
Melbury Gdns, SW20 ... 139 CV95
Melbury Rd, W14 ... 99 CZ76
Harrow HA3 ... 62 CM57
Melcombe Gdns, Har. HA3 ... 62 CM58
Melcombe Ho, SW8
off Dorset Rd ... 101 DM80
Melcombe Pl, NW1 ... 194 D6
Melcombe St, NW1 ... 194 E5
Meldex Cl, NW7 ... 43 CW51
Meldon Cl, SW6
off Bagley's La ... 100 DB81
Meldone Cl, Surb. KT5 ... 138 CP100
Meldrum Cl, Orp. BR5
off Killewarren Way ... 146 EW100
Oxted RH8 ... 188 EF132
Meldrum Rd, Ilf. IG3 ... 70 EU61
Melfield Gdns, SE6 ... 123 EB91
Melford Av, Bark. IG11 ... 87 ES65
Melford Cl, Chess. KT9 ... 156 CM106
Melford Rd, E6 ... 87 EM70
E11 ... 68 EE61
E17 ... 67 DY56
SE22 ... 122 DU87
Ilford IG1 ... 69 ER61
Melfort Av, Th.Hth. CR7 ... 141 DP97
Melfort Rd, Th.Hth. CR7 ... 141 DP97
Melgund Rd, N5 ... 65 DN64
Melia Cl, Wat. WD19 ... 24 BW35
Melina Cl, Hayes UB3
off Middleton Rd ... 77 BR71
Melina Pl, NW8 ... 82 DD69
Melina Rd, W12 ... 99 CV75
Melior Pl, SE1 ... 201 M4
Melior St, SE1 ... 201 L4
Meliot Rd, SE6 ... 123 ED89
Melksham Cl, Rom. RM3 ... 52 FL52
Melksham Dr, Rom. RM3
off Melksham Gdns ... 52 FM52
Melksham Gdns, Rom. RM3 ... 52 FL52
Melksham Grn, Rom. RM3
off Melksham Gdns ... 52 FM52
Meller Cl, Croy. CR0 ... 141 DL104
Melling Dr, Enf. EN1 ... 30 DU39
Melling St, SE18 ... 105 ES79
Mellish Cl, Bark. IG11 ... 87 ET67
Mellish Gdns, Wdf.Grn. IG8 ... 48 EG50
Mellish Ind Est, SE18 ... 104 EL76
Mellish St, E14 ... 203 P6
Mellish Way, Horn. RM11 ... 72 FJ57
Mellison Rd, SW17 ... 120 DE92
Melliss Av, Rich. TW9 ... 98 CP81
Mellitus St, W12 ... 81 CT72
Mellor Cl, Walt. KT12 ... 136 BZ101
Mellow Cl, Bans. SM7 ... 158 DB114
Mellow La E, Hayes UB4 ... 77 BQ69
Mellow La W, Uxb. UB10 ... 77 BQ69
Mellows Rd, Ilf. IG5 ... 69 EM55
Wallington SM6 ... 159 DK106
Mells Cres, SE9 ... 125 EM91
Mell St, SE10
off Trafalgar Rd ... 104 EE78
Melody La, N5 ... 65 DP64
Melody Rd, SW18 ... 120 DC85
Westerham (Bigg.H.) TN16 ... 178 EJ118
Melon Pl, W8
off Kensington Ch St ... 100 DA75
Melon Rd, E11 ... 68 EE62
SE15 ... 102 DU81
Melrose Av, N22 ... 45 DP53
NW2 ... 63 CV64
SW16 ... 141 DM97
SW19 ... 120 DA89
Borehamwood WD6 ... 26 CP43
Dartford DA1 ... 127 FE87
Greenford UB6 ... 78 CB68
Mitcham CR4 ... 121 DH94
Potters Bar EN6 ... 12 DB32
Twickenham TW2 ... 116 CB87
Melrose Cl, SE12 ... 124 EG88
Greenford UB6 ... 78 CB68
Hayes UB4 ... 77 BU71
Melrose Ct, W13
off Williams Rd ... 79 CG74
Melrose Cres, Orp. BR6 ... 163 ER105
Melrose Dr, Sthl. UB1 ... 78 CA74
Melrose Gdns, W6 ... 99 CW76
Edgware HA8 ... 42 CP54
New Malden KT3 ... 138 CR97
Walton-on-Thames KT12 ... 154 BW106
Melrose Pl, Wat. WD17 ... 23 BT38
Melrose Rd, SW13 ... 99 CT82
SW18 ... 119 CZ86
SW19 ... 140 DA96
W3 off Stanley Rd ... 98 CQ76
Coulsdon CR5 ... 175 DH115
Pinner HA5 ... 60 BZ56
Westerham (Bigg.H.) TN16 ... 178 EJ116
Weybridge KT13 ... 152 BN106
Melrose Ter, W6 ... 99 CW75
Melsa Rd, Mord. SM4 ... 140 DC100
Melstock Av, Upmin. RM14 ... 72 FQ63
Melthorne Dr, Ruis. HA4 ... 60 BW62
Melthorpe Gdns, SE3 ... 104 EL81
Melton Cl, Ruis. HA4 ... 60 BW60
Melton Ct, SW7 ... 198 A9
Sutton SM2 ... 158 DC108
Melton Flds, Epsom KT19 ... 156 CR109
Melton Gdns, Rom. RM1 ... 71 FF59
Melton Pl, Epsom KT19 ... 156 CR109
Melton Rd, Red. (S.Merst.)
RH1 ... 185 DJ130
Melton St, NW1 ... 195 L3
Melville Av, SW20 ... 119 CU94
Greenford UB6 ... 61 CF64
South Croydon CR2 ... 160 DT106
Melville Cl, Uxb. UB10 ... 59 BR62
Melville Gdns, N13 ... 45 DP50
Melville Pl, N1 off Essex Rd ... 84 DQ66
Melville Rd, E17 ... 67 DZ55
NW10 ... 80 CR66
SW13 ... 99 CU81
Rainham RM13 ... 89 FG70
Romford RM5 ... 51 FB52
Sidcup DA14 ... 126 EW89
Melville Vil Rd, W3
off High St ... 80 CR74
Melvin Rd, SE20 ... 142 DW95
Melvinshaw, Lthd. KT22 ... 171 CJ121
Melvyn Cl, Wal.Cr. (Chsht)
EN7 ... 13 DP28
Melyn Cl, N7 off Anson Rd ... 65 DJ63
Memel Ct, EC1 ... 197 H5
Memel St, EC1 ... 197 H5
Memess Path, SE18 ... 105 EN79
Memorial Av, E15 ... 86 EE69
Memorial Cl, Houns. TW5 ... 96 BZ79
Memorial Hts, Ilf. IG2
off Eastern Av ... 69 ER58
H Memorial Hosp, SE18 ... 105 EN82
Menai Pl, E3 off Blondin St ... 85 EA68
Mendip Cl, SE26 ... 122 DW91
Hayes UB3 ... 95 BR80
Slough SL3 ... 93 BA78
Worcester Park KT4 ... 139 CW102
Mendip Dr, NW2 ... 63 CX61
Mendip Ho, N9 off New Rd ... 46 DU48
Mendip Rd, SW11 ... 100 DC83
Bexleyheath DA7 ... 107 FE81
Bushey WD23 ... 24 CC44
Hornchurch RM11 ... 71 FG59
Ilford IG2 ... 69 ES57
Mendora Rd, SW6 ... 99 CY80
Mendoza Cl, Horn. RM11 ... 72 FL57
Menelik Rd, NW2 ... 63 CY63
Menlo Gdns, SE19 ... 122 DR94
Menon Dr, N9 ... 46 DV48
Menotti St, E2
off Dunbridge St ... 84 DU70
Menthone Pl, Horn. RM11 ... 72 FK59
Mentmore Cl, Har. HA3 ... 61 CJ58
Mentmore Ter, E8 ... 84 DV66
Meon Cl, Tad. KT20 ... 173 CV122
Meon Ct, Islw. TW7 ... 97 CE82
Meon Rd, W3 ... 98 CQ75
Meopham Rd, Mitch. CR4 ... 141 DJ95
Mepham Cres, Har. HA3 ... 40 CC52
Mepham Gdns, Har. HA3 ... 40 CC52
Mepham St, SE1 ... 200 C3
Mera Dr, Bexh. DA7 ... 106 FA84
Merantun Way, SW19 ... 140 DC95
Merbury Cl, SE13 ... 123 EC85
SE28 ... 87 ER74
Merbury Rd, SE28 ... 105 ES75
Mercator Pl, E14 ... 204 A10
Mercator Rd, SE13 ... 103 ED84
Mercer Cl, T.Ditt. KT7 ... 137 CF101
Merceron St, E1 ... 84 DV70
Mercer Pl, Pnr. HA5
off Crossway ... 40 BW54
Mercers Cl, SE10 ... 205 K9
Mercers Ms, N19
off Mercers Rd ... 65 DK62
Mercers Pl, W6 ... 99 CW77
Mercers Rd, N19 ... 65 DK62
Mercer St, WC2 ... 195 P9
Mercer Wk, Uxb. UB8
off The Pavilions ... 76 BJ66
Merchants Cl, SE25
off Clifford Rd ... 142 DU98
Merchants Ho, SE10
off Hoskins St ... 103 ED78
Merchants Row, SE10
off Hoskins St ... 103 ED78
Merchant St, E3 ... 85 DZ69
Merchiston Rd, SE6 ... 123 ED89
Merchland Rd, SE9 ... 125 EQ88
Mercia Gro, SE13 ... 103 EC84
Mercia Wk, Wok. GU21
off Commercial Way ... 167 AZ117
Mercier Rd, SW15 ... 119 CY85
Mercury Cen, Felt. TW14 ... 115 BV85
Mercury Gdns, Rom. RM1 ... 71 FE56
Mercury Way, SE14 ... 103 DX79
Mercy Ter, SE13 ... 103 EB84
Merebank La, Croy. CR0 ... 159 DM106
Mere Cl, SW15 ... 119 CX87
Orpington BR6 ... 145 EP103
Meredith Av, NW2 ... 63 CW64
Meredith Cl, Pnr. HA5 ... 40 BX52
Meredith Ms, SE4 ... 103 DZ84
Meredith Rd, Grays RM16 ... 111 GG77
Meredith St, E13 ... 86 EG69
EC1 ... 196 F3
Meredyth Rd, SW13 ... 99 CU82
Mere End, Croy. CR0 ... 143 DX101
Merefield Gdns, Tad. KT20 ... 173 CX119
Mere Rd, Shep. TW17 ... 135 BP100
Slough SL1 ... 92 AT76
Tadworth KT20 ... 173 CV124
Weybridge KT13 ... 135 BR104
Mere Side, Orp. BR6 ... 145 EN103
Mereside Pl, Vir.W. GU25 ... 132 AX100
Meretone Cl, SE4 ... 103 DY84
Merevale Cres, Mord. SM4 ... 140 DC100
Mereway Rd, Twick. TW2 ... 117 CD88
Merewood Cl, Brom. BR1 ... 145 EN96
Merewood Gdns, Croy. CR0 ... 143 DX101
Merewood Rd, Bexh. DA7 ... 107 FC82
Mereworth Cl, Brom. BR2 ... 144 EF99
Mereworth Dr, SE18 ... 105 EP80
Merganser Gdns, SE28
off Avocet Ms ... 105 ER76
MERIDEN, Wat. WD25 ... 24 BY35
Meriden Cl, Brom. BR1 ... 124 EK94
Ilford IG6 ... 49 EQ53
Meriden Way, Wat. WD25 ... 24 BY36
Meridian Ct, SE16
off East La ... 102 DU75
Meridian Gate, E14 ... 204 D4
Meridian Pl, E14 ... 204 D4
Meridian Rd, SE7 ... 104 EK80
Meridian Sq, E15 ... 85 ED66
Meridian Trd Est, SE7 ... 104 EH77
Meridian Wk, N17
off Commercial Rd ... 46 DS51
Meridian Way, N9 ... 46 DW50
N18 ... 46 DW51
Enfield EN3 ... 31 DX44
Waltham Abbey EN9 ... 31 EB35
Meriel Wk, Green. DA9
off The Avenue ... 109 FV84
Merifield Rd, SE9 ... 104 EJ84
Merino Cl, E11 ... 68 EJ56
Merino Pl, Sid. DA15
off Blackfen Rd ... 126 EU86
Merivale Rd, SW15 ... 99 CY84
Harrow HA1 ... 60 CC59
Merland Cl, Tad. KT20 ... 173 CW120
Merland Grn, Tad. KT20 ... 173 CW120
Merland Ri, Epsom KT18 ... 173 CW119
Tadworth KT20 ... 173 CW119
Merle Av, Uxb. (Hare.) UB9 ... 38 BH54
Merlewood, Sev. TN13 ... 191 FH123
Merlewood Cl, Cat. CR3 ... 176 DR120
Merlewood Dr, Chis. BR7 ... 145 EM95
Merley Ct, NW9 ... 62 CQ60
Merlin Cl, Croy. CR0 ... 160 DS105
Grays (Chaff.Hun.) RM16 ... 110 FY76
Ilford IG6 ... 50 EW50
Mitcham CR4 ... 140 DE97
Northolt UB5 ... 78 BW69
Romford RM5 ... 51 FD51
Slough SL3 ... 93 BB79
Wallington SM6 ... 159 DM107
Waltham Abbey EN9 ... 16 EG34
Merlin Ct, Brom. BR2
off Durham Av ... 144 EF98
Woking GU21
off Blackmore Cres ... 151 BC114
Merlin Cres, Edg. HA8 ... 42 CM53
Merlin Gdns, Brom. BR1 ... 124 EG90
Romford RM5 ... 51 FD51
Merling Cl, Chess. KT9
off Coppard Gdns ... 155 CK106
Merlin Gro, Beck. BR3 ... 143 DZ98
Ilford IG6 ... 49 EP52
Merlin Ho, Enf. EN3
off Allington Ct ... 31 DX43
Merlin Rd, E12 ... 68 EJ61
Romford RM5 ... 51 FD51
Welling DA16 ... 106 EU84
Merlin Rd N, Well. DA16 ... 106 EU84
Merlins Av, Har. HA2 ... 60 BZ62
Merlin St, WC1 ... 196 D3
Merlin Way, Epp. (N.Wld Bas.)
CM16 ... 18 FA27
Watford (Lvsdn) WD25 ... 7 BT34
Mermagen Dr, Rain. RM13 ... 89 FH66
Mermaid Cl, Grav. DA11 ... 130 GD87
Mermaid Ct, SE1 ... 201 K4
SE16 ... 203 M3
Mermaid Twr, SE8
off Abinger Gro ... 103 DZ79
Mermerus Gdns, Grav. DA12 ... 131 GM91
Merredene St, SW2 ... 121 DM86
Merriam Av, E9 ... 85 DZ65
Merriam Cl, E4 ... 47 EC50
Merrick Rd, Sthl. UB2 ... 96 BZ75
Merrick Sq, SE1 ... 201 J6
Merridale, SE12 ... 124 EG85
Merridene, N21 ... 29 DP44
Merrielands Cres, Dag. RM9 ... 88 EZ67
Merrilands Rd, Wor.Pk. KT4 ... 139 CW102
Merrilees Rd, Sid. DA15 ... 125 ES88
Merrilyn Cl, Esher (Clay.)
KT10 ... 155 CG107
Merriman Rd, SE3 ... 104 EJ81
Merrington Rd, SW6 ... 100 DA79
Merrin Hill, S.Croy. CR2 ... 160 DS111
Merrion Av, Stan. HA7 ... 41 CK50
Merrion Wk, SE17
off Dawes St ... 102 DR78
Merritt Gdns, Chess. KT9 ... 155 CJ107
Merritt Rd, SE4 ... 123 DZ85
Merrivale, N14 ... 29 DK44
Merrivale Av, Ilf. IG4 ... 68 EK56
Merrivale Gdns, Wok. GU21 ... 166 AW117
Merrow Rd, Sutt. SM2 ... 157 CX109
Merrows Cl, Nthwd. HA6
off Rickmansworth Rd ... 39 BQ51
Merrow St, SE17 ... 102 DQ79
Merrow Wk, SE17 ... 201 L10
Merrow Way, Croy. (New Adgtn)
CR0 ... 161 EC107
Merrydown Way, Chis. BR7 ... 144 EL95
Merryfield, SE3 ... 104 EF82
Merryfield Gdns, Stan. HA7 ... 41 CJ50
Merryfield Ho, SE9
off Grove Pk Rd ... 124 EJ90
Merryfields, Uxb. UB8
off Valley Rd ... 76 BL68
Merryfields Way, SE6 ... 123 EB87
MERRY HILL, Bushey WD23 ... 40 CA46
Merryhill Cl, E4 ... 47 EB45
Merry Hill Mt, Bushey WD23 ... 40 CB46
Merry Hill Rd, Bushey WD23 ... 40 CB46
Merryhills Cl, West. (Bigg.H.)
TN16 ... 178 EK116
Merryhills Ct, N14 ... 29 DJ43
Merryhills Dr, Enf. EN2 ... 29 DK42
Merrylands, Cher. KT16 ... 133 BE104
Merrylands Rd, Lthd.
(Bkhm) KT23 ... 170 BZ123
Merrymeet, Bans. SM7 ... 158 DF114
Merryweather Cl, Dart. DA1 ... 128 FM86
Merrywood Gro, Tad. (Lwr Kgswd)
KT20 ... 183 CX130
Merrywood Pk, Reig. RH2 ... 184 DB132
Tadworth (Box H.) KT20 ... 182 CP130
Mersea Ho, Bark. IG11 ... 87 EP65
Mersey Av, Upmin. RM14 ... 73 FR58
Mersey Rd, E17 ... 67 DZ55
Mersey Wk, Nthlt. UB5
off Brabazon Rd ... 78 CA68
Mersham Dr, NW9 ... 62 CN57
Mersham Pl, SE20 ... 142 DV95
Mersham Rd, Th.Hth. CR7 ... 142 DR97
MERSTHAM, Red. RH1 ... 185 DJ128
⇌ Merstham ... 185 DJ128
Merstham Rd, Red. RH1 ... 185 DN129
Merten Rd, Rom. RM6 ... 70 EY59
Merthyr Ter, SW13 ... 99 CV79
MERTON, SW19 ... 140 DA95
Merton Av, W4 ... 99 CT77
Northolt UB5 ... 60 CC64
Uxbridge UB10 ... 77 BP66
Merton Ct, Ilf. IG1
off Castleview Gdns ... 69 EM58
Merton Gdns, Orp. BR5 ... 145 EP99
Tadworth KT20 ... 173 CX119
Merton Hall Gdns, SW20 ... 139 CY95
Merton Hall Rd, SW19 ... 139 CY95
Merton High St, SW19 ... 120 DB94
Merton Ind Pk, SW19 ... 140 DC95
Merton La, N6 ... 64 DF61
Merton Mans, SW20 ... 139 CX96
MERTON PARK, SW19 ... 140 DA96
Tram Merton Park ... 140 DA95
Merton Pk Par, SW19
off Kingston Rd ... 139 CZ95
Merton Pl, Grays RM16 ... 111 GG77
Merton Ri, NW3 ... 82 DE66
Merton Rd, E17 ... 67 EC57
SE25 ... 142 DU99
SW18 ... 120 DA85
SW19 ... 120 DB94
Barking IG11 ... 87 ET66
Enfield EN2 ... 30 DR38
Harrow HA2 ... 60 CC60
Ilford IG3 ... 69 ET59
Slough SL1 ... 92 AU76
Watford WD18 ... 23 BV42
Merton Wk, Lthd. KT22 ... 171 CG118
Merton Way, Lthd. KT22 ... 171 CG119
Uxbridge UB10 ... 77 BP66
West Molesey KT8 ... 136 CB98
Merttins Rd, SE15 ... 123 DX85
Meru Cl, NW5 ... 64 DG63
Mervan Rd, SW2 ... 101 DN84
Mervyn Av, SE9 ... 125 EQ90
Mervyn Rd, W13 ... 97 CG76
Shepperton TW17 ... 135 BQ101
Meryfield Cl, Borwd. WD6 ... 26 CM40
Mesne Way, Sev. (Shore.)
TN14 ... 165 FF112
Messaline Av, W3 ... 80 CQ72
Messant Cl, Rom. (Harold Wd)
RM3 ... 52 FK54
Messent Rd, SE9 ... 124 EJ85
Messeter Pl, SE9 ... 125 EN86
Messina Av, NW6 ... 82 DA66
Metcalf Rd, Ashf. TW15 ... 115 BP92
Metcalf Wk, Felt. TW13
off Cresswell Rd ... 116 BY91
Meteor St, SW11 ... 100 DG84
Meteor Way, Wall. SM6 ... 159 DL108
Metford Cres, Enf. EN3 ... 31 EA38
Methley St, SE11 ... 101 DN78
★ Methodist Cen Hall,
SW1 ... 199 N5
Methuen Cl, Edg. HA8 ... 42 CN52
Methuen Pk, N10 ... 45 DH54
Methuen Rd, Belv. DA17 ... 107 FB77
Bexleyheath DA6 ... 106 EZ84
Edgware HA8 ... 42 CN52
Methwold Rd, W10 ... 81 CX71
Metro Cen Hts, SE1 ... 201 H7
Metro Ind Cen, Islw. TW7 ... 97 CE82
Metropolis Cen, Borwd. WD6 ... 26 CN41
Metropolitan Cen, The, Grnf.
UB6 ... 78 CB67
Metropolitan Cl, E14
off Broomfield St ... 85 EA71
Metropolitan Ho, Pot.B. EN6 ... 12 DA32

★ Place of interest ⇌ Railway station ⊖ London Underground station DLR Docklands Light Railway station Tram Tramlink station H Hospital Riv Pedestrian ferry landing stage

Metropolitan Ms, Wat. WD18
off Linden Av 23 BS42
Metropolitan Sta App, Wat.
WD18 23 BT41
Meux Cl, Wal.Cr. (Chsht) EN7 14 DU31
Mews, The, N1
off St. Paul St 84 DQ67
N8 *off Turnpike La* 65 DN55
Grays RM17 110 GC77
Ilford IG4 68 EK57
Romford RM1
off Market Link 71 FE56
Sevenoaks TN13 190 FG123
Twickenham TW1
off Bridge Rd 117 CH86
Mews Deck, E1 202 E1
Mews End, West. (Bigg.H.)
TN16 178 EK118
Mews Pl, Wdf.Grn. IG8 48 EG49
Mews St, E1 202 B2
Mexfield Rd, SW15 119 CZ85
Meyer Grn, Enf. EN1 30 DU38
Meyer Rd, Erith DA8 107 FC79
Meymott St, SE1 200 F3
Meynell Cres, E9 85 DX66
Meynell Gdns, E9 85 DX66
Meynell Rd, E9 85 DX66
Romford RM3 51 FH52
Meyrick Cl, Wok. (Knap.)
GU21 166 AS116
Meyrick Rd, NW10 81 CU65
SW11 100 DD83
Mezen Cl, Nthwd. HA6 39 BR50
Miah Ter, E1
off Wapping High St 84 DU74
Miall Wk, SE26 123 DY91
Micawber Av, Uxb. UB8 76 BN70
Micawber St, N1 197 J2
Michael Cliffe Ho, EC1 196 E3
Michael Faraday Ho, SE17
off Beaconsfield Rd 102 DS78
Michael Gdns, Grav. DA12 131 GL92
Hornchurch RM11 72 FK56
Michael Gaynor Cl, W7 79 CF74
Michaelmas Cl, SW20 139 CW97
Michael Rd, E11 68 EE60
SE25 142 DS97
SW6 100 DB81
Michaels Cl, SE13 104 EE84
Michaels La, Long. (Fawk.Grn)
DA3 149 FV103
Sevenoaks TN15 149 FV103
Michael Stewart Ho, SW6
off Clem Attlee Ct 99 CZ79
Micheldever Rd, SE12 124 EE86
Michelham Gdns, Tad. KT20
off Waterfield 173 CW120
Twickenham TW1 117 CF90
Michels Row, Rich. TW9
off Kew Foot Rd 98 CL84
Michel Wk, SE18 105 EP78
Michigan Av, E12 68 EL63
Michigan Bldg, E14 204 E1
Michigan Cl, Brox. EN10 15 DY26
Michleham Down, N12 43 CZ49
Micholls Av, Ger.Cr. SL9 36 AY49
Micklefield Way, Borwd. WD6 26 CL38
Mickleham Cl, Orp. BR5 145 ET96
Mickleham Gdns, Sutt. SM3 157 CY107
Mickleham Rd, Orp. BR5 145 ET95
Mickleham Way, Croy.
(New Adgtn) CR0 161 ED108
Micklethwaite Rd, SW6 100 DA79
Midas Ind Est, Uxb. UB8 76 BH68
Midas Met Ind Est, The, Mord.
SM4 *off Garth Rd* 139 CX102
Midcroft, Ruis. HA4 59 BS60
Mid Cross La, Ger.Cr.
(Chal.St.P.) SL9 36 AY50
Middle Boy, Rom. (Abridge)
RM4 34 EW41
Middle Cl, Amer. HP6 20 AT37
Coulsdon CR5 175 DN120
Epsom KT17 *off Middle La* 156 CS112
Middle Cres, Uxb. (Denh.)
UB9 57 BD59
Middle Dartrey Wk, SW10
off World's End Est 100 DD80
Middle Dene, NW7 42 CR48
Middle Fld, NW8 82 DD67
Middlefielde, W13 79 CH71
Middlefield Gdns, Ilf. IG2 69 EP58
Middlefields, Croy. CR0 161 DY109
Middle Furlong, Bushey
WD23 24 CB42
Middle Gorse, Croy. CR0 161 DY112
MIDDLE GREEN, Slou. SL3 74 AY73
Middle Grn, Slou. SL3 74 AY74
Staines TW18 114 BK94
Middle Grn Cl, Surb. KT5
off Alpha Rd 138 CM100
Middlegreen Rd, Slou. SL3 74 AX74
Middleham Gdns, N18 46 DU51
Middleham Rd, N18 46 DU51
Middle Hill, Egh. TW20 112 AW91
Middle La, N8 65 DL57
Epsom KT17 156 CS112
Hemel Hempstead (Bov.)
HP3 5 BA29
Sevenoaks (Seal) TN15
off Church Rd 191 FM121
Teddington TW11 117 CF93
Middle La Ms, N8
off Middle La 65 DL57
Middle Meadow, Ch.St.G.
HP8 36 AW48
Middle Ope, Wat. WD24 23 BV37
Middle Pk Av, SE9 124 EK86
Middle Path, Har. HA2
off Middle Rd 61 CD60
Middle Rd, E13
off London Rd 86 EG68
SW16 141 DK96
Barnet EN4 28 DE44
Brentwood (Ingrave) CM13 55 GC50
Harrow HA2 61 CD61
Leatherhead KT22 171 CH121
Uxbridge (Denh.) UB9 57 BC59
Middle Rd, Wal. Abb. EN9 15 EB32
Middle Row, W10 81 CY70
Middlesborough Rd, N18 46 DU51
Middlesex Business Cen,
Sthl. UB2 96 CA75
Middlesex Cl, Sthl. UB1 78 CB70
Middlesex Ct, W4
off British Gro 99 CT77
★ **Middlesex Guildhall**,
SW1 199 P5
Middlesex Ho, Wem. HA0 79 CK67
Middlesex Pas, EC1 196 G7
Middlesex Rd, Mitch. CR4 141 DL99
Middlesex St, E1 197 N7
Middlesex Wf, E5 66 DW61
Middle St, EC1 197 H6
Croydon CR0 *off Surrey St* 142 DQ104
Middle Temple, EC4 196 D10
Middle Temple La, EC4 196 D9
Middleton Av, E4 47 DZ49
Greenford UB6 79 CD68
Sidcup DA14 126 EW93
Middleton Cl, E4 47 DZ48
Middleton Dr, SE16 203 J5
Pinner HA5 59 BU55
Middleton Gdns, Ilf. IG2 69 EP58
Middleton Gro, N7 65 DL64
Middleton Hall La, Brwd.
CM15 54 FY47
Middleton Ms, N7
off Middleton Gro 65 DL64
Middleton Pl, W1 195 K7
Middleton Rd, E8 84 DT66
NW11 64 DA59
Brentwood (Shenf.) CM15 54 FY46
Carshalton SM5 140 DE101
Cobham (Down.) KT11 169 BV119
Epsom KT19 156 CR110
Hayes UB3 77 BR71
Morden SM4 140 DC100
Rickmansworth (Mill End)
WD3 38 BG46
Middleton St, E2 84 DV69
Middleton Way, SE13 103 ED84
Middle Wk, Wok. GU21
off Commercial Way 166 AY117
Middleway, NW11 64 DB57
Middle Way, SW16 141 DK96
Erith DA18 106 EY76
Hayes UB4 78 BW70
Watford WD24 23 BV37
Middle Way, The, Har. HA3 41 CF54
Middle Yd, SE1 201 L2
Middlings, The, Sev. TN13 190 FF125
Middlings Ri, Sev. TN13 190 FF126
Middlings Wd, Sev. TN13 190 FF125
Midfield Av, Bexh. DA7 107 FC83
Swanley BR8 127 FH93
Midfield Par, Bexh. DA7 107 FC83
Midfield Way, Orp. BR5 146 EV95
Midford Pl, W1 195 L5
Midgarth Cl, Lthd. (Oxshott)
KT22 154 CC114
Midholm, NW11 64 DB56
Wembley HA9 62 CN60
Midholm Cl, NW11 64 DB56
Midholm Rd, Croy. CR0 143 DY103
Midhope Cl, Wok. GU22 166 AY119
Midhope Gdns, Wok. GU22
off Midhope Rd 166 AY119
Midhope Rd, Wok. GU22 166 AY119
Midhope St, WC1 196 A3
Midhurst Av, N10 64 DG55
Croydon CR0 141 DN101
Midhurst Cl, Horn. RM12 71 FG63
Midhurst Gdns, Uxb. UB10 77 BQ66
Midhurst Hill, Bexh. DA6 126 FA86
Midhurst Rd, W13 97 CG75
Midhurst Way, E5 66 DU63
Midland Cres, NW3
off Finchley Rd 82 DC65
Midland Pl, E14 204 D10
Midland Rd, E10 67 EC59
NW1 195 N1
Midland Ter, NW2 63 CX62
NW10 80 CS70
Midleton Rd, N.Mal. KT3 138 CQ97
Midlothian Rd, E3
off Burdett Rd 85 DZ70
Midmoor Rd, SW12 121 DJ88
SW19 139 CX95
Midship Cl, SE16 203 J3
Midship Pt, E14 203 P5
Midstrath Rd, NW10 62 CS63
Mid St, Red. (S.Nutfld) RH1 185 DM134
Midsummer Av, Houns. TW4 96 BZ84
Midway, Sutt. SM3 139 CZ101
Walton-on-Thames KT12 135 BV103
Midway Av, Cher. KT16 134 BG97
Egham TW20 133 BB97
Midway Cl, Stai. TW18 114 BH90
Midwinter Cl, Well. DA16
off Hook La 106 EU83
Midwood Cl, NW2 63 CV62
Miena Way, Ashtd. KT21 171 CK117
Miers Cl, E6 87 EN67
Mighell Av, Ilf. IG4 68 EK57
Mike Spring Ct, Grav. DA12 131 GK91
Milan Rd, Sthl. UB1 96 BZ75
Milborne Gro, SW10 100 DC78
Milborne St, E9 84 DW65
Milborough Cres, SE12 124 EE86
Milbourne La, Esher KT10 154 CC107
Milbrook, Esher KT10 154 CC107
Milburn Dr, West Dr. UB7 76 BL73
Milburn Wk, Epsom KT18 172 CS115
Milcombe Cl, Wok. GU21
off Inglewood 166 AV118
Milcote St, SE1 200 F5
Mildenhall Rd, E5 66 DW63
Slough SL1 74 AS72
Mildmay Av, N1 84 DR65
Mildmay Gro N, N1 66 DR64
Mildmay Gro S, N1 66 DR64
Mildmay Pk, N1 66 DR64
Mildmay Pl, N16
off Boleyn Rd 66 DS64
Sevenoaks (Shore.) TN14 165 FF111
Mildmay Rd, N1 66 DS64
Ilford IG1 *off Albert Rd* 69 EP62
Romford RM7 71 FC57
Mildmay St, N1 84 DR65
Mildred Av, Borwd. WD6 26 CN42
Mildred Av, Hayes UB3 95 BR77
Northolt UB5 60 CB64
Watford WD18 23 BT42
Mildred Cl, Dart. DA1 128 FN86
Mildred Rd, Erith DA8 107 FE78
Mile Cl, Wal.Abb. EN9 15 EC33
MILE END, E1 85 DX69
⊖ **Mile End** 85 DY69
Mile End, The, E17 47 DX53
MILE END GREEN, Dart.
DA2 149 FW96
H **Mile End Hosp**, E1 85 DX70
Mile End Pl, E1 85 DX70
Mile End Rd, E1 84 DW71
E3 84 DW71
Mile Path, Wok. GU22 166 AV120
Mile Rd, Wall. SM6 141 DJ102
Miles Cl, SE28 *off Miles Dr* 87 ES74
Miles Dr, SE28 87 ER74
Miles La, Cob. KT11 154 BY113
Milespit Hill, NW7 43 CV50
Miles Pl, NW1 194 A6
Surbiton KT5
off Villiers Av 138 CM98
Miles Rd, N8 65 DL55
Epsom KT19 156 CR112
Mitcham CR4 140 DE97
Miles St, SW8 101 DL79
Milestone Cl, N9
off Chichester Rd 46 DU47
Sutton SM2 158 DD107
Woking (Ripley) GU23 168 BG122
Milestone Dr, Pur. CR8 159 DM114
Milestone Grn, SW14 98 CQ84
Milestone Rd, SE19 122 DT93
Dartford DA2 128 FP86
Miles Way, N20 44 DE47
Milfoil St, W12 81 CU73
Milford Cl, SE2 106 EY79
Milford Gdns, Croy. CR0
off Tannery Cl 143 DX99
Edgware HA8 42 CN52
Wembley HA0 61 CK64
Milford Gro, Sutt. SM1 158 DC105
Milford La, WC2 196 C10
Milford Ms, SW16 121 DM90
Milford Rd, W13 79 CH74
Southall UB1 78 CA73
Milford Twrs, SE6
off Thomas La 123 EB87
Milking La, Kes. BR2 162 EK111
Orpington BR6 162 EL112
Milk St, E16 87 EP74
EC2 197 J9
Bromley BR1 124 EH93
Milkwell Gdns, Wdf.Grn. IG8 48 EH52
Milkwell Yd, SE5 102 DQ81
Milkwood Rd, SE24 121 DP85
Milk Yd, E1 202 F1
Millais Av, E12 69 EN64
Millais Cres, Epsom KT19 156 CS106
Millais Gdns, Edg. HA8 42 CN54
Millais Pl, Til. RM18 111 GG80
Millais Rd, E11 67 EC63
Enfield EN1 30 DT43
New Malden KT3 138 CS100
Millais Way, Epsom KT19 156 CQ105
Millan Cl, Add. (New Haw)
KT15 152 BH110
Milland Ct, Borwd. WD6 26 CR39
Millard Cl, N16
off Boleyn Rd 66 DS64
Millard Ter, Dag. RM10
off Church Elm La 88 FA65
Mill Av, Uxb. UB8 76 BJ68
Millbank, SW1 199 P7
Staines TW18 114 BH92
Millbank Ct, SW1
off John Islip St 101 DK78
RIV **Millbank Millennium Pier** 200 A9
Millbank Twr, SW1 199 P9
Millbank Way, SE12 124 EG85
Millbourne Rd, Felt. TW13 116 BY91
Mill Br Pl, Uxb. UB8 76 BH68
Millbro, Swan. BR8 127 FG94
Millbrook, Wey. KT13 153 BS105
Millbrook Av, Well. DA16 105 ER84
Millbrook Gdns, Rom.
(Chad.Hth) RM6 70 EZ58
Romford (Gidea Pk) RM2 51 FE54
Millbrook Pl, NW1
off Hampstead Rd 83 DJ68
Millbrook Rd, N9 46 DV46
SW9 101 DP83
Bushey WD23 24 BZ39
Mill Brook Rd, Orp. BR5 146 EW98
Millbrook Way, Slou.
(Colnbr.) SL3 93 BE82
Mill Cl, Cars. SM5 140 DG103
Chesham HP5 4 AS34
Hemel Hempstead HP3 6 BN25
Leatherhead (Bkhm) KT23 170 CA124
West Drayton UB7 94 BK76
Mill Cor, Barn. EN5 27 CZ39
Mill Ct, E10 67 EC62
Millcrest Rd, Wal.Cr. (Chsht)
EN7 13 DP28
Millcroft Ho, SE6 123 EC91
Millen Ct, Dart. (Hort.Kir.)
DA4 148 FP98
MILL END, Rick. WD3 37 BF46
Millender Wk, SE16 202 G9
Millennium Br, EC4 197 H10
SE1 197 H10
Millennium Cl, E16
off Russell Rd 86 EH72
Uxbridge UB8 76 BH68
Millennium Dr, E14 204 F8
Millennium Harbour, E14 203 N4
Millennium Pl, E2 84 DV68
Millennium Sq, SE1 201 P4
Millennium Way, SE10 205 H4
Millennium Wf, Rick. WD3
off Wharf La 38 BL45
Miller Av, Enf. EN3 31 EA38
Miller Cl, Brom. BR1 124 EG92
Mitcham CR4 140 DF101
Pinner HA5 40 BW54
Romford RM5 50 FA52
Miller Pl, Ger.Cr. SL9 56 AX57
Miller Rd, SW19 120 DD93
Croydon CR0 141 DM102
Miller's Av, E8 66 DT64
Millers Cl, NW7 43 CU49
Chigwell IG7 50 EV47
Rickmansworth (Chorl.)
WD3 21 BE41
Staines TW18 114 BH92
Millers Copse, Epsom KT18 172 CR119
Millers Ct, W4
off Chiswick Mall 99 CT78
Millers Grn Cl, Enf. EN2 29 DP41
Miller's La, Chig. IG7 50 EV46
Millers La, Wind. SL4 112 AT86
Millers Meadow Cl, SE3
off Meadowcourt Rd 124 EF85
Miller's Ter, E8 66 DT64
Miller St, NW1 83 DJ68
Millers Way, W6 99 CW75
Miller Wk, SE1 200 E3
Millet Rd, Grnf. UB6 78 CB69
Mill Fm Av, Sun. TW16 115 BS94
Mill Fm Cl, Pnr. HA5 40 BW54
Mill Fm Cres, Houns. TW4 116 BY88
Millfield, Sun. TW16 135 BR95
Millfield Av, E17 47 DY53
Millfield Dr, Grav. (Nthflt)
DA11 130 GE89
Millfield La, N6 64 DF61
Tadworth (Lwr Kgswd)
KT20 183 CZ125
Millfield Pl, N6 64 DG61
Millfield Rd, Edg. HA8 42 CQ54
Hounslow TW4 116 BY88
Millfields Cl, Orp. BR5 146 EV97
Millfields Cotts, Orp. BR5
off Millfields Cl 146 EV98
Millfields Est, E5
off Denton Way 67 DX62
Millfields Rd, E5 66 DW63
Millford, Wok. GU21 166 AV117
Mill Gdns, SE26 122 DV91
Mill Grn, Mitch. CR4
off London Rd 140 DG101
Mill Grn Business Pk, Mitch.
CR4 *off Mill Grn Rd* 140 DG101
Mill Grn Rd, Mitch. CR4 140 DF101
Millgrove St, SW11 100 DG82
Millharbour, E14 204 B6
Millhaven Cl, Rom. RM6 70 EV58
Millhedge Cl, Cob. KT11 170 BY116
MILL HILL, NW7 43 CU50
Mill Hill, SW13
off Mill Hill Rd 99 CU82
Brentwood (Shenf.) CM15 54 FY45
⇌ **Mill Hill Broadway** 42 CS51
Mill Hill Circ, NW7
off Watford Way 43 CT50
⊖ **Mill Hill East** 43 CX52
Mill Hill Gro, W3
off Mill Hill Rd 80 CP74
Mill Hill Ind Est, NW7 43 CT51
Mill Hill La, Bet. (Brock.) RH3 182 CP134
Mill Hill Rd, SW13 99 CU82
W3 98 CP75
Mill Hill Ter, W3
off Mill Hill Rd 80 CQ74
Millhoo Ct, Wal.Abb. EN9 16 EF34
Mill Ho Cl, Dart. (Eyns.) DA4
off Mill La 148 FL102
Millhouse La, Abb.L. (Bedmond)
WD5 7 BT27
Mill Ho La, Cher. KT16 133 BB98
Egham TW20 133 BB98
Millhouse Pl, SE27 121 DP91
Millicent Rd, E10 67 DZ60
Milligan St, E14 203 N1
Milliners Ct, Loug. IG10
off The Croft 33 EN40
Milliners Ho, SW18
off Eastfields Av 100 DA84
Milling Rd, Edg. HA8 42 CR52
Millington Rd, Hayes UB3 95 BS76
Mill La, E4 31 EB41
NW6 63 CZ64
SE18 105 EN78
Carshalton SM5 158 DF105
Chalfont St. Giles HP8 36 AU47
Croydon CR0 141 DM104
Dartford (Eyns.) DA4 148 FL102
Egham TW20 133 BC98
Epsom KT17 157 CT109
Gerrards Cross SL9 57 AZ58
Grays RM20 109 FX78
Grays (Chaff.Hun.) RM16 109 FX77
Kings Langley WD4 6 BN29
Leatherhead (Fetch.) KT22 171 CG122
Ongar (Toot Hill) CM5 19 FE29
Orpington (Downe) BR6 163 EN110
Oxted RH8 188 EF132
Oxted (Lmpfld Cht.) RH8 189 EM131
Redhill (S.Merst.) RH1 185 DJ131
Rickmansworth (Crox.Grn)
WD3 23 BQ44
Romford (Chad.Hth) RM6 70 EY58
Romford (Nave.) RM4 35 FH40
Sevenoaks TN14 191 FJ121
Sevenoaks (Shore.) TN14 165 FF110
Slough (Horton) SL3 93 BB83
Waltham Cross EN8 15 DY28
West Byfleet (Byfleet) KT14 152 BM113
Westerham TN16 189 EQ127
Woking (Ripley) GU23 168 BK119
Woodford Green IG8 48 EF50
Mill La Trd Est, Croy. CR0 141 DM104
Millman Ms, WC1 196 B5
Millman Pl, WC1
off Millman St 83 DM70
Millman St, WC1 196 B5
Millmark Gro, SE14 103 DY82
Millmarsh La, Enf. EN3 31 DY40
Mill Mead, Stai. TW18 113 BF91
Millmead, W.Byf. (Byfleet)
KT14 152 BM112
Mill Mead Rd, N17 66 DV56
Mill Pk Av, Horn. RM12 72 FL61
Mill Pl, E14
off Commercial Rd 85 DY72
Chislehurst BR7 145 EP95
Dartford DA1 107 FG84
Kingston upon Thames
KT1 138 CM97
Slough (Datchet) SL3 92 AX82
Mill Pl Caravan Pk, Slou.
(Datchet) SL3 92 AW82
Mill Plat, Islw. TW7 97 CG82
Mill Plat Av, Islw. TW7 97 CG82
Mill Pond Cl, SW8
off Thorparch Rd 101 DK80
Sevenoaks TN14 191 FJ121
Millpond Ct, Add. KT15 152 BL106
Millpond Est, SE16 202 D5
Millpond Pl, Cars. SM5 140 DG104
Mill Pond Rd, Dart. DA1 128 FL86
Mill Ridge, Edg. HA8 42 CM50
Mill Rd, E16 86 EH74
SW19 120 DC94
Cobham KT11 170 BW115
Dartford (Hawley) DA2 128 FM91
Epsom KT17 157 CT112
Erith DA8 107 FC80
Esher KT10 136 CA103
Gravesend (Nthflt) DA11 130 GE87
Ilford IG1 69 EN62
Purfleet RM19 108 FP79
Sevenoaks (Dunt.Grn)
TN13 190 FE121
South Ockendon (Aveley)
RM15 90 FQ73
Tadworth KT20 173 CX123
Twickenham TW2 116 CC89
West Drayton UB7 94 BJ76
Mill Row, N1 84 DS67
Mills Cl, Uxb. UB10 76 BN68
Mills Ct, EC2 197 N3
Mills Gro, E14
off Dewberry St 85 EC71
NW4 63 CX55
Mill Shaw, Oxt. RH8 188 EF132
Mill Shot Cl, SW6 99 CW80
Millside, Cars. SM5 140 DF103
Millside Ct, Iver SL0 94 BH75
Millside Ind Est, Dart. DA1 108 FK84
Millside Pl, Islw. TW7 97 CH82
Millsmead Way, Loug. IG10 33 EM40
Millson Cl, N20 44 DD47
Mills Rd, Walt. KT12 154 BW106
Mills Row, W4 98 CR77
Mills Spur, Wind. (Old Wind.)
SL4 112 AV87
Millstead Cl, Tad. KT20 173 CV122
Millstone Cl, Dart. (S.Darenth)
DA4 148 FQ96
Millstone Ms, Dart. (S.Darenth)
DA4 148 FQ95
Millstream Cl, N13 45 DN50
Millstream Rd, SE1 201 P5
Mill St, SE1 202 A5
W1 195 J10
Kingston upon Thames
KT1 138 CL97
Slough SL2 74 AT74
Slough (Colnbr.) SL3 93 BD80
Westerham TN16 189 ER127
Mills Way, Brwd. (Hutt.) CM13 55 GC46
Millthorne Cl, Rick. (Crox.Grn)
WD3 22 BM43
Mill Vale, Brom. BR2 144 EF96
Mill Vw, St.Alb. (Park St)
AL2 *off Park St* 9 CD27
Mill Vw Cl, Epsom (Ewell)
KT17 157 CT108
Millview Cl, Reig. RH2 184 DD132
Mill Vw Gdns, Croy. CR0 143 DX104
MILLWALL, E14 204 B8
Millwall Dock Rd, E14 203 P6
★ **Millwall FC**, SE16 102 DW78
Millway, NW7 42 CS50
Mill Way, Bushey WD23 24 BY40
Feltham TW14 115 BV85
Leatherhead KT22 172 CM124
Millway, Reig. RH2 184 DD134
Mill Way, Rick. (Mill End)
WD3 37 BF46
Millway Gdns, Nthlt. UB5 78 BZ65
Millwell Cres, Chig. IG7 49 ER50
Millwood Rd, Houns. TW3 116 CC85
Orpington BR5 146 EW97
Millwood St, W10
off St. Charles Sq 81 CY71
Millwrights Wk, Hem.H. HP3
off Stephenson Wf 6 BM25
Mill Yd, E1 *off Cable St* 84 DU73
Milman Cl, Pnr. HA5 60 BX55
Milman Rd, NW6 81 CY68
Milman's St, SW10 100 DD79
Milmead Ind Cen, N17 46 DV54
Milne Ct, E18
off Churchfields 48 EG53
Milne Feild, Pnr. HA5 40 CA52
Milne Gdns, SE9 124 EL85
Milne Pk E, Croy. (New Adgtn)
CR0 161 ED111
Milne Pk W, Croy. (New Adgtn)
CR0 161 ED111
Milner App, Cat. CR3 176 DU121
Milner Cl, Cat. CR3 176 DT121
Watford WD25 7 BV34
Milner Ct, Bushey WD23 24 CB44
Milner Dr, Cob. KT11 154 BZ112
Twickenham TW2 117 CD87
Milner Pl, N1 83 DN67
Carshalton SM5
off High St 158 DG105
Milner Rd, E15 86 EE69
SW19 140 DB95
Caterham CR3 176 DU122
Dagenham RM8 70 EW61
Kingston upon Thames
KT1 137 CK97
Morden SM4 140 DD99
Thornton Heath CR7 142 DR97
Milner Sq, N1 83 DP66
Milner St, SW3 198 D8
Milner Wk, SE9 125 ER89
Milne Way, Uxb. (Hare.) UB9 38 BH53
Milnthorpe Rd, W4 98 CR79
Milo Gdns, SE22 *off Milo Rd* 122 DT86
Milo Rd, SE22 122 DT86
Milroy Av, Grav. (Nthflt) DA11 130 GE89
Milroy Wk, SE1 200 F2
Milson Rd, W14 99 CY76
MILTON, Grav. DA12 131 GK86
Milton Av, E6 86 EK66
N6 65 DJ59
NW9 62 CQ55
NW10 80 CQ67
Barnet EN5 27 CZ43
Croydon CR0 142 DR101

★ Place of interest ⇌ Railway station ⊖ London Underground station DLR Docklands Light Railway station Tra Tramlink station H Hospital RIV Pedestrian ferry landing stage

Milton Av, Ger.Cr. (Chal.St.P.) SL9 56 AX56
Gravesend DA12 131 GJ88
Hornchurch RM12 71 FF61
Sevenoaks (Bad.Mt) TN14 165 FB110
Sutton SM1 140 DD104
Milton Cl, N2 64 DC57
SE1 201 P9
Hayes UB4 77 BU72
Slough (Horton) SL3 93 BA83
Sutton SM1 140 DD104
Milton Ct, EC2 197 K6
Romford (Chad.Hth) RM6
off Cross Rd 70 EW59
Uxbridge UB10 59 BP62
Waltham Abbey EN9 15 EC34
Milton Ct Rd, SE14 103 DY79
Milton Cres, Ilf. IG2 69 EQ59
Milton Dr, Borwd. WD6 26 CP43
Shepperton TW17 134 BL98
Milton Flds, Ch.St.G. HP8 36 AV48
Milton Gdn Est, N16
off Milton Gro 66 DS63
Milton Gdns, Epsom KT18 156 CS114
Staines TW19
off Chesterton Dr 114 BM88
Tilbury RM18 111 GH81
Milton Gro, N11 45 DJ50
N16 66 DR63
Milton Hall Rd, Grav. DA12 131 GK88
Milton Hill, Ch.St.G. HP8 36 AV48
Milton Pk, N6 65 DJ59
Milton Pl, N7 *off George's Rd* 65 DN64
Gravesend DA12 131 GJ86
Milton Rd, E17 67 EA56
N6 65 DJ59
N15 65 DP56
NW7 43 CU50
NW9 *off West Hendon Bdy* 63 CU59
SE24 121 DP86
SW14 98 CR83
SW19 120 DC93
W3 80 CR74
W7 79 CF73
Addlestone KT15 152 BG107
Belvedere DA17 106 FA77
Brentwood CM14 54 FV49
Caterham CR3 176 DR121
Croydon CR0 142 DR102
Egham TW20 113 AZ92
Gravesend DA12 131 GJ86
Grays RM17 110 GB78
Hampton TW12 116 CA94
Harrow HA1 61 CE56
Mitcham CR4 120 DG94
Romford RM1 71 FG58
Sevenoaks (Dunt.Grn) TN13 190 FE121
Sutton SM1 140 DA104
Swanscombe DA10 130 FY86
Uxbridge UB10 58 BN63
Wallington SM6 159 DJ107
Walton-on-Thames KT12 136 BX104
Welling DA16 105 ET81
★ **Milton's Cottage**, Ch.St.G. HP8 36 AV48
Milton St, EC2 197 K6
Swanscombe DA10 129 FX86
Waltham Abbey EN9 15 EC34
Watford WD24 23 BV38
Milton Way, West Dr. UB7 94 BM77
Milverton Dr, Uxb. UB10 59 BQ63
Milverton Gdns, Ilf. IG3 69 ET61
Milverton Ho, SE23 123 DY90
Milverton Rd, NW6 81 CW66
Milverton St, SE11 101 DN78
Milverton Way, SE9 125 EN91
Milward St, E1
off Stepney Way 84 DV71
Milward Wk, SE18
off Spearman St 105 EN79
MIMBRIDGE, Wok. GU24 150 AV113
Mimms Hall Rd, Pot.B. EN6 11 CX31
Mimms La, Pot.B. (S.Mimms) EN6 10 CQ33
Radlett (Shenley) WD7 10 CN33
Mimosa Cl, Brwd. (Pilg.Hat.) CM15 54 FV43
Orpington BR6
off Berrylands 146 EW104
Romford RM3 52 FJ52
Mimosa Rd, Hayes UB4 78 BW71
Mimosa St, SW6 99 CZ81
Mina Av, Slou. SL3 92 AX75
Minard Rd, SE6 124 EE87
Mina Rd, SE17 102 DS78
SW19 140 DA95
Minchenden Cres, N14 45 DJ48
Minchin Cl, Lthd. KT22 171 CG122
Mincing La, EC3 197 M10
Woking (Chobham) GU24 150 AT108
Minden Rd, SE20 142 DV95
Sutton SM3 139 CZ103
Minehead Rd, SW16 121 DM92
Harrow HA2 60 CA62
Mineral Cl, Barn. EN5 27 CW44
Mineral St, SE18 105 ES77
Minera Ms, SW1 198 G8
Minerva Cl, SW9 101 DN80
Sidcup DA14 125 ES90
Staines TW19 114 BG85
Minerva Dr, Wat. WD24 23 BS36
Minerva Rd, E4 47 EB52
NW10 80 CQ70
Kingston upon Thames KT1 138 CM96
Minerva St, E2 84 DV68
Minet Av, NW10 80 CS68
Minet Dr, Hayes UB3 77 BU74
Minet Gdns, NW10 80 CS68
Hayes UB3 77 BU74
Minet Rd, SW9 101 DP82
Minford Gdns, W14 99 CX75
Mingard Wk, N7
off Hornsey Rd 65 DM62
Ming St, E14 85 EA73
Ministers Gdns, St.Alb. AL2
off Frogmore 9 CE28
★ **Ministry of Defence**, SW1 199 P3
Ministry Way, SE9 125 EM89
Miniver Pl, EC4
off Garlick Hill 84 DQ73
Mink Ct, Houns. TW4 96 BW83
Minniedale, Surb. KT5 138 CM99
Minnow St, SE17 *off East St* 102 DS77
Minnow Wk, SE17 201 N9
Minorca Rd, Wey. KT13 152 BN105
Minories, EC3 197 P10
Minshull Pl, Beck. BR3 123 EA94
Minshull St, SW8
off Wandsworth Rd 101 DK81
Minson Rd, E9 85 DX67
Minstead Gdns, SW15 119 CT87
Minstead Way, N.Mal. KT3 138 CS100
Minster Av, Sutt. SM1
off Leafield Rd 140 DA103
Minster Ct, EC3
off Mincing La 84 DS73
Hornchurch RM11 72 FN61
St. Albans (Frog.) AL2 9 CE28
Minster Dr, Croy. CR0 160 DS105
Minster Gdns, W.Mol. KT8 136 BZ98
Minsterley Av, Shep. TW17 135 BS98
Minster Pavement, EC3
off Mincing La 84 DS73
Minster Rd, NW2 63 CY64
Bromley BR1 124 EH94
Minster Wk, N8
off Lightfoot Rd 65 DL56
Minster Way, Horn. RM11 72 FM60
Slough SL3 93 AZ75
Minstrel Gdns, Surb. KT5 138 CM98
Mint Business Pk, E16 86 EG71
Mint Cl, Uxb. (Hlgdn) UB10 77 BP69
Mintern Cl, N13 45 DP48
Minterne Av, Sthl. UB2 96 CA77
Minterne Rd, Har. HA3 62 CM57
Minterne Waye, Hayes UB4 78 BW72
Mintern St, N1 84 DR68
Mint La, Tad. (Lwr Kgswd) KT20 184 DA129
Minton Ho, SE11
off Walnut Tree Wk 101 DN77
Minton Ms, NW6
off Dresden Cl 82 DB65
Mint Rd, Bans. SM7 174 DC116
Wallington SM6 159 DH105
Mint St, SE1 201 H4
Mint Wk, Croy. CR0
off High St 142 DQ104
Warlingham CR6 177 DX118
Woking (Knap.) GU21 166 AS117
Mirabel Rd, SW6 99 CZ80
Mirador Cres, Slou. SL2 74 AV73
Miramar Way, Horn. RM12 72 FK64
Miranda Cl, E1 *off Sidney St* 84 DW71
Miranda Ct, W3 *off Queens Dr* 80 CM72
Miranda Rd, N19 65 DJ60
Mirfield St, SE7 104 EK77
Miriam Rd, SE18 105 ES78
Mirravale Trd Est, Dag. RM8 70 EZ59
Mirren Cl, Har. HA2 60 BZ63
Mirrie La, Uxb. (Denh.) UB9 57 BC57
Mirror Path, SE9
off Lambscroft Av 124 EJ90
Misbourne Av, Ger.Cr. (Chal.St.P.) SL9 36 AY50
Misbourne Cl, Ger.Cr. (Chal.St.P.) SL9 36 AY50
Misbourne Ct, Slou. SL3
off High St 93 BA77
Misbourne Meadows, Uxb. (Denh.) UB9 57 BC60
Misbourne Rd, Uxb. UB10 76 BN67
Misbourne Vale, Ger.Cr. (Chal.St.P.) SL9 36 AX50
Miskin Rd, Dart. DA1 128 FJ87
Miskin Way, Grav. DA12 131 GK93
Missenden Cl, Felt. TW14 115 BT88
Missenden Gdns, Mord. SM4 140 DC100
Mission Gro, E17 67 DY57
Mission Pl, SE15 102 DU81
Mission Sq, Brent. TW8 98 CL79
Mistletoe Cl, Croy. CR0
off Marigold Way 143 DX102
Misty's Fld, Walt. KT12 136 BW102
Mitali Pas, E1
off Back Ch La 84 DU72
MITCHAM, CR4 140 DG97
Tramlink **Mitcham** 140 DE98
Mitcham Gdn Village, Mitch. CR4 140 DG99
Mitcham Ind Est, Mitch. CR4 140 DG95
⇌ **Mitcham Junction** 140 DG99
Tramlink **Mitcham Junction** 140 DG99
Mitcham La, SW16 121 DJ93
Mitcham Pk, Mitch. CR4 140 DF98
Mitcham Rd, E6 86 EL69
SW17 120 DF92
Croydon CR0 141 DL100
Ilford IG3 69 ET59
Mitchell Av, Grav. (Nthflt) DA11 130 GD89
Mitchellbrook Way, NW10 80 CR65
Mitchell Cl, SE2 106 EW77
Abbots Langley WD5 7 BU32
Belvedere DA17 107 FC76
Dartford DA1 128 FL89
Hemel Hempstead (Bov.) HP3 5 AZ27
Rainham RM13 90 FJ68
Mitchell Rd, N13 45 DP50
Orpington BR6 163 ET105
Mitchell's Pl, SE21
off Dulwich Village 122 DS87
Mitchell St, EC1 197 H4
Mitchell Wk, E6 86 EL71
Amersham HP6 20 AS38
Swanscombe DA10 130 FY87
Mitchell Way, NW10 80 CQ65
Bromley BR1 144 EG95
Mitchison Rd, N1 84 DR65
Mitchley Av, Pur. CR8 160 DQ113
South Croydon CR2 160 DQ113
Mitchley Gro, S.Croy. CR2 160 DU113
Mitchley Hill, S.Croy. CR2 160 DT113
Mitchley Rd, N17 66 DU55
Mitchley Vw, S.Croy. CR2 160 DU113
Mitford Cl, Chess. KT9
off Merritt Gdns 155 CJ107
Mitford Rd, N19 65 DL61
Mitre, The, E14
off Three Colt St 85 DZ73
Mitre Av, E17
off Greenleaf Rd 67 DZ55
Mitre Cl, Brom. BR2
off Beckenham La 144 EF96
Shepperton TW17 135 BR100
Sutton SM2 158 DC108
Mitre Ct, EC2 197 J8
EC4 196 E9
Mitre Rd, E15 86 EE68
SE1 200 E4
Mitre Sq, EC3 197 N9
Mitre St, EC3 197 N9
Mitre Way, W10 81 CV70
Mixbury Gro, Wey. KT13 153 BR107
Mixnams La, Cher. KT16 134 BG97
Mizen Cl, Cob. KT11 154 BX114
Mizen Way, Cob. KT11 170 BW115
Mizzen Mast Ho, SE18
off Woolwich Ch St 105 EN76
Moat, The, N.Mal. KT3 138 CS95
Ongar CM5 19 FF29
Moat Cl, Bushey WD23 24 CB43
Orpington BR6 163 ET107
Sevenoaks (Chipstead) TN13 190 FB123
Moat Ct, Ashtd. KT21 172 CL117
Moat Cres, N3 64 DB55
Moat Cft, Well. DA16 106 EW83
Moat Dr, E13 *off Boundary Rd* 86 EJ68
Harrow HA1 60 CC56
Ruislip HA4 59 BS59
Slough SL2 74 AW71
Moated Fm Dr, Add. KT15 152 BJ108
Moat Fm Rd, Nthlt. UB5 78 BZ65
Moatfield Rd, Bushey WD23 24 CB43
Moat La, Erith DA8 107 FG81
Moat Pl, SW9 101 DM83
W3 80 CP72
Uxbridge (Denh.) UB9 58 BH63
Moatside, Enf. EN3 31 DX42
Feltham TW13 116 BW91
Moatview Ct, Bushey WD23 24 CB43
Moberley Rd, SW4 121 DK87
Modbury Gdns, NW5
off Queen's Cres 82 DG65
Modder Pl, SW15 99 CX84
Model Cotts, SW14
off Upper Richmond Rd W 98 CQ84
Model Fm Cl, SE9 124 EL90
Modena Ms, Wat. WD18 23 BS42
Modling Ho, E2 84 DW68
Moelwyn Hughes Ct, N7
off Hilldrop Cres 65 DK64
Moelyn Ms, Har. HA1 61 CG57
Moffat Ho, SE5
off Comber Gro 102 DQ80
Moffat Rd, N13 45 DL51
SW17 120 DE91
Thornton Heath CR7 142 DQ96
Moffats Cl, Hat. AL9 12 DA26
Moffats La, Hat. AL9 11 CZ26
MOGADOR, Tad. KT20 183 CY129
Mogador Cotts, Tad. KT20
off Mogador Rd 183 CX128
Mogador Rd, Tad. (Lwr Kgswd) KT20 183 CX128
Mogden La, Islw. TW7 117 CE85
Mohmmad Khan Rd, E11
off Harvey Rd 68 EF60
Moira Cl, N17 46 DS54
Moira Rd, SE9 105 EM84
Moir Cl, S.Croy. CR2 160 DU109
Molash Rd, Orp. BR5 146 EX98
Molasses Row, SW11
off Cinnamon Row 100 DC83
Mole Abbey Gdns, W.Mol. KT8 *off New Rd* 136 CA97
Mole Business Pk, Lthd. KT22 171 CG121
Mole Ct, Epsom KT19 156 CQ105
Molember Ct, E.Mol. KT8 137 CE99
Molember Rd, E.Mol. KT8 137 CE99
Mole Rd, Lthd. (Fetch.) KT22 171 CD121
Walton-on-Thames KT12 154 BX106
Molescroft, SE9 125 EQ90
Molesey Av, W.Mol. KT8 136 BZ98
Molesey Cl, Walt. KT12 154 BY105
Molesey Dr, Sutt. SM3 139 CY103
Hospital **Molesey Hosp**, W.Mol. KT8 136 CA99
Molesey Pk Av, W.Mol. KT8 136 CB99
Molesey Pk Cl, E.Mol. KT8 136 CC99
Molesey Pk Rd, E.Mol. KT8 137 CD99
West Molesey KT8 136 CB99
Molesey Rd, Walt. KT12 154 BX106
West Molesey KT8 136 BY99
Molesford Rd, SW6 100 DA81
Molesham Cl, W.Mol. KT8 136 CB97
Molesham Way, W.Mol. KT8 136 CB97
Moles Hill, Lthd. (Oxshott) KT22 155 CD111
Molesworth Rd, Cob. KT11 153 BU113
Molesworth St, SE13 103 EC83
Mole Valley Pl, Ashtd. KT21 171 CK119
Mollands La, S.Ock. RM15 91 FW70
Mollison Av, Enf. EN3 31 DY43
Mollison Dr, Wall. SM6 159 DL107
Mollison Ri, Grav. DA12 131 GL92
Mollison Sq, Wall. SM6
off Mollison Dr 159 DL108
Mollison Way, Edg. HA8 42 CN54
Molloy Ct, Wok. GU21
off Courtenay Rd 167 BA116
Molly Huggins Cl, SW12 121 DJ87
Molteno Rd, Wat. WD17 23 BU39
Molyneaux Av, Hem.H. (Bov.) HP3 5 AZ27
Molyneux Dr, SW17 121 DH91
Molyneux Rd, Wey. KT13 152 BN106
Molyneux St, W1 194 C7
Monahan Av, Pur. CR8 159 DM112
Monarch Cl, Felt. TW14 115 BS87
Rainham RM13
off Whymark Cl 89 FG68
Tilbury RM18 111 GH82
West Wickham BR4 162 EF105
Monarch Dr, E16 86 EK71
Monarch Ms, E17 67 EB57
SW16 121 DN92
Monarch Par, Mitch. CR4
off London Rd 140 DF96
Monarch Pl, Buck.H. IG9 48 EJ47
Monarch Rd, Belv. DA17 106 FA76
Monarchs Ct, NW7
off Grenville Pl 42 CR50
Monarchs Way, Ruis. HA4 59 BR60
Waltham Cross EN8 15 DY34
Monarch Way, Ilf. IG2
off Eastern Av 69 ER58
Mona Rd, SE15 102 DW82
Monastery Gdns, Enf. EN2 30 DR40
Mona St, E16 86 EF71
Monaveen Gdns, W.Mol. KT8 136 CA97
Monck St, SW1 199 N7
Monclar Rd, SE5 102 DR84
Moncorvo Cl, SW7 198 B5
Moncrieff Cl, E6
off Linton Gdns 86 EL72
Moncrieff Pl, SE15
off Rye La 102 DU82
Moncrieff St, SE15 102 DU82
Mondial Way, Hayes UB3 95 BQ80
Monega Rd, E7 86 EJ65
E12 86 EK65
Money Av, Cat. CR3 176 DR122
MONEYHILL, Rick. WD3 38 BH46
Moneyhill Par, Rick. WD3
off Uxbridge Rd 38 BH46
Money Hill Rd, Rick. WD3 38 BJ46
Money La, West Dr. UB7 94 BK76
Money Rd, Cat. CR3 176 DR122
Mongers La, Epsom KT17 157 CT110
Monica Cl, Wat. WD24 24 BW40
Monier Rd, E3 85 EA66
Monivea Rd, Beck. BR3 123 DZ94
Monkchester Cl, Loug. IG10 33 EN39
Monk Dr, E16 86 EG72
MONKEN HADLEY, Barn. EN5 27 CZ39
Monkfrith Av, N14 29 DH44
Monkfrith Cl, N14 45 DH45
Monkfrith Way, N14 44 DG45
Monkhams Av, Wdf.Grn. IG8 48 EG50
Monkhams Dr, Wdf.Grn. IG8 48 EH49
Monkhams La, Buck.H. IG9 48 EH48
Woodford Green IG8 48 EG50
Monkleigh Rd, Mord. SM4 139 CY97
Monk Pas, E16 *off Monk Dr* 86 EG73
Monks Av, Barn. EN5 28 DC44
West Molesey KT8 136 BZ99
Monks Chase, Brwd. (Ingrave) CM13 55 GC50
Monks Cl, SE2 106 EX77
Enfield EN2 30 DQ40
Harrow HA2 60 CB61
Ruislip HA4 60 BX63
Monks Cres, Add. KT15 152 BH106
Walton-on-Thames KT12 135 BV102
Monksdene Gdns, Sutt. SM1 140 DB104
Monks Dr, W3 80 CN71
Monks Grn, Lthd. (Fetch.) KT22 170 CC121
Monksgrove, Loug. IG10 33 EN43
Monksmead, Borwd. WD6 26 CQ42
MONKS ORCHARD, Croy. CR0 143 DZ101
Monks Orchard, Dart. DA1 128 FJ89
Monks Orchard Rd, Beck. BR3 143 EA102
Monks Pk, Wem. HA9 80 CQ65
Monks Pk Gdns, Wem. HA9 80 CP65
Monks Pl, Cat. CR3
off Tillingdown Hill 176 DV122
Monk's Ridge, N20 43 CV46
Monks Rd, Bans. SM7 174 DA116
Enfield EN2 30 DQ40
Virginia Water GU25 132 AX98
Monk St, SE18 105 EN77
Monks Wk, Cher. KT16 133 BE98
Gravesend (Sthflt) DA13 130 GA93
Monk's Wk, Reig. RH2 184 DB134
Monks Way, NW11
off Hurstwood Rd 63 CZ56
Beckenham BR3 143 EA99
Orpington BR5 145 EQ102
Staines TW18 114 BK94
West Drayton UB7 94 BL79
Monks Well, Green. DA9 109 FV84
Monkswell Ct, N10 44 DG53
Monkswell La, Couls. CR5 174 DB124
Monkswood Av, Wal.Abb. EN9 15 ED33
Monkswood Gdns, Borwd. WD6 26 CR42
Ilford IG5 69 EN55
Monkton Rd, Well. DA16 105 ET82
Monkton St, SE11 200 E8
Monkville Av, NW11 63 CZ56
Monkwell Sq, EC2 197 J7
Monkwood Cl, Rom. RM1 71 FG57
Monmouth Av, E18 68 EH56
Kingston upon Thames KT1 117 CJ94
Monmouth Cl, W4
off Beaumont Rd 98 CR76
Mitcham CR4
off Recreation Way 141 DL98
Welling DA16 106 EU84
Monmouth Gro, Brent. TW8
off Sterling Pl 98 CL77
Monmouth Ho, NW5
off Raglan St 83 DH65
Monmouth Pl, W2
off Monmouth Rd 82 DA72
Monmouth Rd, E6 87 EM69
N9 46 DV47
W2 82 DB72
Dagenham RM9 70 EZ64
Hayes UB3 95 BS77
Watford WD17 23 BV41
Monmouth St, WC2 195 P9
Monnery Rd, N19 65 DJ62
Monnow Grn, S.Ock. (Aveley) RM15 *off Monnow Rd* 90 FQ73
Monnow Rd, SE1 202 B10
South Ockendon (Aveley) RM15 90 FQ73
Mono La, Felt. TW13 115 BV89
Monoux Gro, E17 47 EA53
Monroe Cres, Enf. EN1 30 DV39
Monroe Dr, SW14 118 CP85
Monro Gdns, Har. HA3 41 CE52
Monro Pl, Epsom KT19 156 CN109
Monro Way, E5 66 DV63
Monsal Ct, E5 *off Redwald Rd* 67 DY63
Monsell Ct, N4
off Monsell Rd 65 DP62
Monsell Gdns, Stai. TW18 113 BE92
Monsell Rd, N4 65 DP62
Monson Rd, NW10 81 CU68
SE14 103 DX80
Redhill RH1 184 DF130
Mons Wk, Egh. TW20 113 BC92
Mons Way, Brom. BR2 144 EL100
Montacute Rd, SE6 123 DZ87
Bushey (Bushey Hth) WD23 41 CE45
Croydon (New Adgtn) CR0 161 EC109
Morden SM4 140 DD100
Montagu Cres, N18 46 DV49
Montague Av, SE4 103 DZ84
W7 79 CF74
South Croydon CR2 160 DS112
Montague Cl, SE1 201 K2
Walton-on-Thames KT12 135 BU101
Montague Dr, Cat. CR3
off Drake Av 176 DQ122
Montague Gdns, W3 80 CN73
Montague Hall Pl, Bushey WD23 24 CA44
Montague Pl, WC1 195 N6
Montague Rd, E8 66 DU64
E11 68 EF61
N8 65 DM57
N15 66 DU56
SW19 120 DB94
W7 79 CF74
W13 79 CH72
Croydon CR0 141 DP102
Hounslow TW3 96 CB83
Richmond TW10 118 CL86
Slough SL1 74 AT73
Slough (Datchet) SL3 92 AV81
Uxbridge UB8 76 BK66
Montague Sq, SE15
off Clifton Way 102 DW80
Montague St, EC1 197 H7
WC1 195 P6
Montague Waye, Sthl. UB2 96 BY76
Montagu Gdns, N18 46 DV49
Wallington SM6 159 DJ105
Montagu Mans, W1 194 E6
Montagu Ms N, W1 194 E7
Montagu Ms S, W1 194 E8
Montagu Ms W, W1 194 E8
Montagu Pl, W1 194 D7
Montagu Rd, N9 46 DW49
N18 46 DV50
NW4 63 CU58
Montagu Rd Ind Est, N18 46 DW49
Montagu Row, W1 194 E7
Montagu Sq, W1 194 E7
Montagu St, W1 194 E8
Montaigne Cl, SW1 199 N9
Montalt Rd, Wdf.Grn. IG8 48 EF50
Montana Cl, S.Croy. CR2 160 DR110
Montana Gdns, SE26 123 DZ92
Sutton SM1 *off Lind Rd* 158 DC106
Montana Rd, SW17 120 DG91
SW20 139 CW95
Montayne Rd, Wal.Cr. (Chsht) EN8 15 DX32
Montbelle Rd, SE9 125 EP90
Montbretia Cl, Orp. BR5 146 EW98
Montcalm Cl, Brom. BR2 144 EG100
Hayes UB4 *off Ayles Rd* 77 BV69
Montcalm Rd, SE7 104 EK80
Montclare St, E2 197 P3
Monteagle Av, Bark. IG11 87 EQ65
Monteagle Way, SE15 102 DV83
Montefiore St, SW8 101 DH82
Montego Cl, SE24
off Railton Rd 101 DN84
Montem Rd, SE23 123 DZ87
New Malden KT3 138 CS98
Montem St, N4
off Thorpedale Rd 65 DM60
Montenotte Rd, N8 65 DJ57
Monterey Cl, NW7
off The Broadway 42 CS50
Bexley DA5 127 FC89
Montesole Ct, Pnr. HA5 40 BW54
Montevetro, SW11 100 DD81
Montford Pl, SE11 101 DN78
Montford Rd, Sun. TW16 135 BU98
Montfort Gdns, Ilf. IG6 49 EQ51
Montfort Pl, SW19 119 CX88
Montgolfier Wk, Nthlt. UB5
off Jetstar Way 78 BY69
Montgomerie Ms, SE23 122 DW87
Montgomery Av, Esher KT10 137 CE104
Montgomery Cl, Grays RM16 110 GC75
Mitcham CR4 141 DL98
Sidcup DA15 125 ET86
Montgomery Ct, W4
off St. Thomas' Rd 98 CQ79
Montgomery Cres, Rom. RM3 52 FJ50
Montgomery Dr, Wal.Cr. (Chsht) EN8 15 DY28
Montgomery Gdns, Sutt. SM2 158 DD108
Montgomery Pl, Slou. SL2 74 AW72
Montgomery Rd, W4 98 CQ77
Dartford (S.Darenth) DA4 149 FR95
Edgware HA8 42 CM51
Woking GU22 166 AY118
Montgomery St, E14 204 C3
Montholme Rd, SW11 120 DF86
Monthope Rd, E1
off Casson St 84 DU71
Montolieu Gdns, SW15 119 CV85
Montpelier Av, W5 79 CJ71
Bexley DA5 126 EX87
Montpelier Cl, Uxb. UB10 76 BN67
Montpelier Gdns, E6 86 EK69
Romford RM6 70 EW59
Montpelier Gro, NW5 65 DJ64
Montpelier Ms, SW7 198 C6
Montpelier Pl, E1 84 DW72
SW7 198 C6
Montpelier Ri, NW11 63 CY59
Wembley HA9 61 CK60
Montpelier Rd, N3 44 DC53
SE15 102 DV81

Montpelier Rd, W5 79 CK71
Purley CR8 159 DP110
Sutton SM1 158 DC105
Montpelier Row, SE3 104 EF82
Twickenham TW1 117 CH87
Montpelier Sq, SW7 198 C5
Montpelier St, SW7 198 C5
Montpelier Ter, SW7 198 C5
Montpelier Vale, SE3 104 EF82
Montpelier Wk, SW7 198 C6
Montpelier Way, NW11 63 CY59
Montrave Rd, SE20 122 DW93
Montreal Pl, WC2 196 B10
Montreal Rd, Ilf. IG1 69 EQ59
Sevenoaks TN13 190 FE123
Tilbury RM18 111 GG82
Montrell Rd, SW2 121 DL88
Montrose Av, NW6 81 CY68
Edgware HA8 42 CQ54
Romford RM2 52 FJ54
Sidcup DA15 126 EU87
Slough (Datchet) SL3 92 AW80
Twickenham TW2 116 CB87
Welling DA16 105 ER83
Montrose Cl, Ashf. TW15 115 BQ93
Welling DA16 105 ET83
Woodford Green IG8 48 EG49
Montrose Ct, SW7 198 A5
Montrose Cres, N12 44 DC51
Wembley HA0 80 CL65
Montrose Gdns, Lthd. (Oxshott) KT22 155 CD112
Mitcham CR4 140 DF97
Sutton SM1 140 DB103
Montrose Pl, SW1 198 G5
Montrose Rd, Felt. TW14 115 BR86
Harrow HA3 41 CE54
Montrose Wk, Wey. KT13 135 BP104
Montrose Way, SE23 123 DX88
Slough (Datchet) SL3 92 AX81
Montrouge Cres, Epsom KT17 173 CW116
Montserrat Av, Wdf.Grn. IG8 47 ED52
Montserrat Cl, SE19 122 DR92
Montserrat Rd, SW15 99 CY84
⊖ Monument 197 L10
★ Monument, The, EC3 201 L1
Monument Gdns, SE13 123 EC85
Monument Grn, Wey. KT13 135 BP104
Monument Hill, Wey. KT13 153 BP105
Monument La, Ger.Cr. (Chal.St.P.) SL9 36 AY51
Monument Rd, Wey. KT13 153 BP105
Woking GU21 151 BA114
Monument St, EC3 197 L10
Monument Way, N17 66 DT55
Monument Way E, Wok. GU21 167 BB115
Monument Way W, Wok. GU21 167 BA115
Monza St, E1 202 F1
Moodkee St, SE16 202 F6
Moody Rd, SE15 102 DT80
Moody St, E1 85 DX69
Moon Ct, Lthd. KT22 171 CD121
Moon La, Barn. EN5 27 CZ41
Moon St, N1 83 DP67
Moorcroft Gdns, Brom. BR2 off Southborough Rd 144 EL99
Moorcroft La, Uxb. UB8 76 BN71
Moorcroft Rd, SW16 121 DL90
Moorcroft Way, Pnr. HA5 60 BY57
Moordown, SE18 105 EN81
Moore Av, Grays RM20 110 FY78
Tilbury RM18 111 GH82
Moore Cl, SW14 off Little St. Leonards 98 CQ83
Addlestone KT15 152 BH106
Dartford DA2 129 FR89
Mitcham CR4 141 DH96
Wallington SM6 off Brabazon Av 159 DL109
Moore Cres, Dag. RM9 88 EV67
Moorefield Rd, N17 46 DT54
Moore Gro Cres, Egh. TW20 112 AY94
Moorehead Way, SE3 104 EH83
Moore Ho, E14 204 A5
Mooreland Rd, Brom. BR1 124 EF94
Moore Pk Rd, SW6 100 DB80
Moore Rd, SE19 122 DQ93
Swanscombe DA10 130 FY86
Moores Pl, Brwd. CM14 54 FX47
Moore St, SW3 198 D8
Moore Wk, E7 off Stracey Rd 68 EG63
Moore Way, Sutt. SM2 158 DA109
Moorey Cl, E15 off Stephen's Rd 86 EF67
Moorfield Av, W5 79 CK70
Moorfield Rd, Chess. KT9 156 CL106
Enfield EN3 30 DW39
Orpington BR6 146 EU101
Uxbridge UB8 76 BK72
Uxbridge (Hare.) UB9 58 BG59
Moorfields, EC2 197 K7
Moorfields Cl, Stai. TW18 133 BE95
H Moorfields Eye Hosp, EC1 197 K3
Moorfields Highwalk, EC2 off Fore St 84 DR71
⇌ Moorgate 197 K7
⊖ Moorgate 197 K7
Moorgate, EC2 197 K8
Moorgate Pl, EC2 197 K8
Moorhall Rd, Uxb. (Hare.) UB9 58 BH58
Moorhayes Dr, Stai. TW18 134 BJ97
Moorhen Cl, Erith DA8 107 FH80
Moorholme, Wok. GU22 off Oakbank 166 AY119
MOORHOUSE BANK, West. TN16 189 EM128
Moorhouse Rd, W2 82 DA72
Harrow HA3 61 CK55
Oxted RH8 189 EM131
Westerham TN16 189 EM128
Moorhurst Av, Wal.Cr. (Chsht) EN7 13 DN29
Moorings, SE28 88 EV73
Moorings, The, Wind. SL4 off Straight Rd 112 AW87
Moorings Ho, Brent. TW8 off Tallow Rd 97 CJ80
Moorland Cl, Rom. RM5 51 FB52
Twickenham TW2 off Telford Rd 116 CA87
Moorland Rd, SW9 101 DP84
West Drayton UB7 94 BJ79
Moorlands, St.Alb. (Frog.) AL2 off Frogmore 9 CE28
Moorlands, The, Wok. GU22 167 AZ121
Moorlands Av, NW7 43 CV51
Moorlands Est, SW9 101 DN84
Moor La, EC2 197 K7
Chessington KT9 156 CL105
Rickmansworth WD3 38 BM47
Rickmansworth (Sarratt) WD3 21 BE36
Staines TW18, TW19 113 BE90
Upminster RM14 73 FS60
West Drayton UB7 94 BJ79
Woking GU22 166 AY122
Moor La Crossing, Wat. WD18 39 BQ46
Moormead Dr, Epsom KT19 156 CS106
Moor Mead Rd, Twick. TW1 117 CG86
Moormede Cres, Stai. TW18 113 BF91
Moor Mill La, St.Alb. (Coln.St) AL2 9 CE29
MOOR PARK, Nthwd. HA6 39 BQ49
⊖ Moor Park 39 BR48
Moor Pk Est, Nthwd. HA6 39 BQ49
Moor Pk Gdns, Kings.T. KT2 118 CS94
Moor Pk Ind Est, Wat. WD18 39 BQ45
★ Moor Park Mansion, Rick. WD3 38 BN48
Moor Pk Rd, Nthwd. HA6 39 BR50
Moor Pl, EC2 197 K7
Moor Rd, The, Sev. TN14 181 FH120
Moorside Rd, Brom. BR1 124 EE90
Moorsom Way, Couls. CR5 175 DK117
Moorstown Ct, Slou. SL1 92 AS75
Moor St, W1 195 N9
Moortown Rd, Wat. WD19 40 BW49
Moor Vw, Wat. WD18 39 BU45
Moot Ct, NW9 62 CN57
Moran Cl, St.Alb. (Brick.Wd) AL2 8 BZ31
Morant Gdns, Rom. RM5 51 FB50
Morant Pl, N22 off Commerce Rd 45 DM53
Morant Rd, Grays RM16 111 GH76
Morants Ct Cross, Sev. (Dunt.Grn) TN14 181 FB118
Morants Ct Rd, Sev. (Dunt.Grn) TN13 181 FC118
Morant St, E14 85 EA73
Mora Rd, NW2 63 CW63
Mora St, EC1 197 J3
Morat St, SW9 101 DM81
Moravian Pl, SW10 off Milman's St 100 DD79
Moravian St, E2 84 DW69
Moray Av, Hayes UB3 77 BT74
Moray Cl, Edg. HA8 off Pentland Av 42 CP47
Romford RM1 51 FE52
Moray Dr, Slou. SL2 74 AU72
Moray Ms, N7 off Durham Rd 65 DM61
Moray Rd, N4 65 DM61
Moray Way, Rom. RM1 51 FD52
Mordaunt Gdns, Dag. RM9 88 EY66
Mordaunt Ho, NW10 80 CR67
Mordaunt Rd, NW10 80 CR67
Mordaunt St, SW9 101 DM83
MORDEN, SM4 140 DA97
⊖ Morden 140 DB97
Morden Cl, Tad. KT20 173 CX120
Morden Ct, Mord. SM4 140 DB98
Morden Gdns, Grnf. UB6 61 CF64
Mitcham CR4 140 DD98
★ Morden Hall Pk N.T., Mord. SM4 140 DB97
Morden Hall Rd, Mord. SM4 140 DB97
Morden Hill, SE13 103 EC82
Morden La, SE13 103 EC81
MORDEN PARK, Mord. SM4 139 CY99
Tra Morden Road 140 DB96
Morden Rd, SE3 104 EG82
SW19 120 DB94
Mitcham CR4 140 DC98
Romford RM6 70 EY59
Morden Rd Ms, SE3 104 EG82
⇌ Morden South 140 DA99
Morden St, SE13 103 EB81
Morden Way, Sutt. SM3 140 DA101
Morden Wf Rd, SE10 205 H7
Mordon Rd, Ilf. IG3 69 ET59
Mordred Rd, SE6 124 EE89
Moreau Wk, Slou. (Geo.Grn) SL3 off Alan Way 74 AY72
Morecambe Cl, E1 85 DX71
Hornchurch RM12 71 FH64
Morecambe Gdns, Stan. HA7 41 CK49
Morecambe St, SE17 201 J9
Morecambe Ter, N18 46 DR49
More Cl, E16 86 EF72
W14 99 CY77
Purley CR8 159 DN111
Morecoombe Cl, Kings.T. KT2 118 CP94
Moree Way, N18 46 DU49
Moreland Av, Grays RM16 110 GC75
Slough (Colnbr.) SL3 93 BC80
Moreland Cl, Slou. (Colnbr.) SL3 off Moreland Av 93 BC80
Moreland Dr, Ger.Cr. SL9 57 AZ59
Moreland St, EC1 196 G2
Moreland Way, E4 47 EB48
More La, Esher KT10 136 CB103
Morel Ct, Sev. TN13 191 FH122
Morella Cl, Vir.W. GU25 132 AW98
Morella Rd, SW12 120 DF87
Morell Cl, Barn. EN5 off Galdana Av 28 DC41
Morello Av, Uxb. UB8 77 BP71
Morello Cl, Swan. BR8 147 FD98
Morello Dr, Slou. SL3 75 AZ74
More London Pl, SE1 201 M3
More London Riverside, SE1 201 N3
Moremead, Wal.Abb. EN9 15 ED33
Moremead Rd, SE6 123 DZ91
Morena St, SE6 123 EB87
Moresby Av, Surb. KT5 138 CP101
Moresby Rd, E5 66 DV60
Moresby Wk, SW8 101 DH82
Moretaine Rd, Ashf. TW15 off Hengrove Cres 114 BK90
Moreton Av, Islw. TW7 97 CE81
Moreton Cl, E5 66 DW61
N15 66 DR58
NW7 43 CW51
SW1 199 L10
Swanley BR8 off Bonney Way 147 FE96
Waltham Cross (Chsht) EN7 14 DV27
Moreton Gdns, Wdf.Grn. IG8 48 EL50
Moreton Ho, SE16 202 E6
Moreton Ind Est, Swan. BR8 147 FH98
Moreton Pl, SW1 199 L10
Moreton Rd, N15 66 DR58
South Croydon CR2 160 DR106
Worcester Park KT4 139 CU103
Moreton St, SW1 199 L10
Moreton Ter, SW1 199 L10
Moreton Ter Ms N, SW1 199 L10
Moreton Ter Ms S, SW1 199 L10
Moreton Twr, W3 80 CP74
Morewood Cl, Sev. TN13 190 FF123
Morewood Cl Ind Pk, Sev. TN13 off Morewood Cl 190 FF123
Morford Cl, Ruis. HA4 59 BV59
Morford Way, Ruis. HA4 59 BV59
Morgan Av, E17 67 ED56
Morgan Cl, Dag. RM10 88 FA66
Northwood HA6 39 BT51
Morgan Ct, SW11 off Battersea High St 100 DD81
Morgan Cres, Epp. (They.B.) CM16 33 ER36
Morgan Dr, Green. DA9 129 FS87
Morgan Gdns, Wat. (Ald.) WD25 24 CB38
Morgan Ho, SW1 off Vauxhall Br Rd 101 DJ77
Morgan Rd, N7 65 DN64
W10 81 CZ71
Bromley BR1 124 EG94
Morgans La, SE1 201 M3
Hayes UB3 77 BR71
Morgan St, E3 85 DY69
E16 86 EF71
Morgan Way, Rain. RM13 90 FJ69
Woodford Green IG8 48 EL51
Moriatry Cl, N7 65 DL63
Morie St, SW18 120 DB85
Morieux Rd, E10 67 DZ60
Moring Rd, SW17 120 DG91
Morkyns Wk, SE21 122 DS90
Morland Av, Croy. CR0 142 DS102
Dartford DA1 127 FH85
Morland Cl, NW11 64 DB60
Hampton TW12 116 BZ92
Mitcham CR4 140 DE97
Morland Est, E8 off Richmond Rd 84 DU66
Morland Gdns, NW10 80 CR66
Southall UB1 78 CB74
Morland Ms, N1 off Lofting Rd 83 DN66
Morland Rd, E17 67 DX57
SE20 123 DX93
Croydon CR0 142 DS102
Dagenham RM10 88 FA66
Harrow HA3 62 CL57
Ilford IG1 69 EP61
Sutton SM1 158 DC106
Morland Way, Wal.Cr. (Chsht) EN8 15 DY28
Morley Av, E4 47 ED52
N18 46 DU49
N22 45 DN54
Morley Cl, Orp. BR6 145 EP103
Slough SL3 93 AZ75
Morley Cres, Edg. HA8 42 CQ47
Ruislip HA4 60 BW61
Morley Cres E, Stan. HA7 41 CJ54
Morley Cres W, Stan. HA7 41 CJ54
Morley Hill, Enf. EN2 30 DR38
Morley Rd, E10 67 EC60
E15 86 EF68
SE13 103 EC84
Barking IG11 87 ER67
Chislehurst BR7 145 EQ95
Romford RM6 70 EY57
South Croydon CR2 160 DT110
Sutton SM3 139 CZ102
Twickenham TW1 117 CK86
Morley Sq, Grays RM16 111 GG77
Morley St, SE1 200 E6
Morna Rd, SE5 102 DQ82
Morning La, E9 84 DW65
Morning Ri, Rick. (Loud.) WD3 22 BK41
Morningside Rd, Wor.Pk. KT4 139 CV103
Mornington Av, W14 99 CZ77
Bromley BR1 144 EJ97
Ilford IG1 69 EN59
Mornington Cl, West. (Bigg.H.) TN16 178 EK117
Woodford Green IG8 48 EG49
Mornington Ct, Bex. DA5 127 FC88
⊖ Mornington Crescent 83 DH68
Mornington Cres, NW1 83 DJ68
Hounslow TW5 95 BV81
Mornington Gro, E3 85 EA69
Mornington Ms, SE5 102 DQ81
Mornington Pl, NW1 off Mornington Ter 83 DH68
Mornington Rd, E4 47 ED45
E11 68 EF60
SE8 103 DZ80
Ashford TW15 115 BQ92
Greenford UB6 78 CB71
Loughton IG10 33 EQ41
Radlett WD7 9 CG34
Woodford Green IG8 48 EF49
Mornington St, NW1 83 DH68
Mornington Ter, NW1 83 DH67
Mornington Wk, Rich. TW10 117 CJ91
Morocco St, SE1 201 M5
Morpeth Av, Borwd. WD6 26 CM38
Morpeth Gro, E9 85 DX67
Morpeth Rd, E9 84 DW67
Morpeth St, E2 85 DX69
Morpeth Ter, SW1 199 K7
Morpeth Wk, N17 off West Rd 46 DV52
Morrab Gdns, Ilf. IG3 69 ET62
Morrells Yd, SE11 off Cleaver St 101 DN78
Morrice Cl, Slou. SL3 93 AZ77
Morris Av, E12 69 EM64
Morris Cl, Croy. CR0 143 DY100
Gerrards Cross (Chal.St.P.) SL9 37 AZ53
Orpington BR6 145 ES104
Morris Ct, E4 47 EB48
Enfield EN3 off Martini Dr 31 EA37
Waltham Abbey EN9 16 EF34
Morris Gdns, SW18 120 DA87
Dartford DA1 128 FN85
Morrish Rd, SW2 121 DL87
Morrison Av, E4 47 EA51
N17 66 DS55
Morrison Rd, SW9 off Marcella Rd 101 DN82
Barking IG11 88 EY68
Hayes UB4 77 BV69
Morrison St, SW11 100 DG83
Morris Pl, N4 65 DN61
Morris Rd, E14 85 EB71
E15 68 EE63
Dagenham RM8 70 EZ61
Isleworth TW7 97 CF83
Romford RM3 51 FH52
Morris St, E1 84 DV72
Morriston Cl, Wat. WD19 40 BW50
Morris Way, St.Alb. (Lon.Col.) AL2 10 CL26
Morse Cl, E13 86 EG69
Uxbridge (Hare.) UB9 38 BJ54
Morshead Rd, W9 82 DA69
Morson Rd, Enf. EN3 31 DY44
Morston Cl, Tad. KT20 off Waterfield 173 CV120
Morston Gdns, SE9 125 EM91
Morten Cl, SW4 121 DK86
Morten Gdns, Uxb. (Denh.) UB9 58 BG59
Morteyne Rd, N17 46 DR53
Mortham St, E15 85 ED67
Mortimer Cl, NW2 63 CZ62
SW16 121 DK89
Bushey WD23 24 CB44
Mortimer Cres, NW6 82 DB67
Worcester Park KT4 138 CR104
Mortimer Dr, Enf. EN1 30 DR43
Mortimer Est, NW6 82 DB67
Mortimer Gate, Wal.Cr. EN8 15 DZ27
Mortimer Ho, W11 off St. Anns Rd 81 CX74
Mortimer Mkt, WC1 195 L5
Mortimer Pl, NW6 82 DB67
Mortimer Rd, E6 87 EM69
N1 84 DS66
NW10 81 CW69
W13 79 CJ72
Erith DA8 107 FD79
Mitcham CR4 140 DF95
Orpington BR6 146 EU103
Slough SL3 92 AX76
Westerham (Bigg.H.) TN16 162 EJ112
Mortimer Sq, W11 off St. Anns Rd 81 CX73
Mortimer St, W1 195 K8
Mortimer Ter, NW5 off Gordon Ho Rd 65 DH63
MORTLAKE, SW14 98 CQ83
⇌ Mortlake 98 CQ83
Mortlake Cl, Croy. CR0 off Richmond Rd 141 DL104
Mortlake Dr, Mitch. CR4 140 DE95
Mortlake High St, SW14 98 CR83
Mortlake Rd, E16 86 EH72
Ilford IG1 69 EQ63
Richmond TW9 98 CN80
Mortlake Sta Pas, SW14 off Sheen La 98 CQ83
Mortlake Ter, Rich. TW9 off Kew Rd 98 CN80
Mortlock Cl, SE15 off Cossall Wk 102 DV82
Morton, Tad. KT20 173 CX121
Morton Cl, E1 off Deancross St 84 DW72
Uxbridge UB8 76 BM70
Wallington SM6 159 DM108
Woking GU21 166 AW115
Morton Ct, Nthlt. UB5 60 CC64
Morton Cres, N14 45 DK49
Morton Gdns, Wall. SM6 159 DJ106
Morton Ms, SW5 off Earls Ct Gdns 100 DB77
Morton Pl, SE1 200 D7
Morton Rd, E15 86 EF66
N1 84 DQ66
Morden SM4 140 DD99
Woking GU21 166 AW115
Morton Way, N14 45 DJ48
Morvale Cl, Belv. DA17 106 EZ77
Morval Rd, SW2 121 DN85
Morven Cl, Pot.B. EN6 12 DC31
Morven Rd, SW17 120 DF90
Morville Ho, SW18 off Fitzhugh Gro 120 DD86
Morville St, E3 85 EA68
Morwell St, WC1 195 N7
Mosbach Gdns, Brwd. (Hutt.) CM13 55 GB47
Moscow Pl, W2 off Moscow Rd 82 DB73
Moscow Rd, W2 82 DA73
Moseley Row, SE10 205 L8
Moselle Av, N22 45 DN54
Moselle Cl, N8 off Miles Rd 65 DM55
Moselle Ho, N17 off William St 46 DT52
Moselle Pl, N17 off High Rd 46 DT52
Moselle Rd, West. (Bigg.H.) TN16 178 EL118
Moselle St, N17 46 DT52
Mospey Cres, Epsom KT17 173 CT115
Moss Bk, Grays RM17 110 FZ78
Mossborough Cl, N12 44 DB51
Mossbury Rd, SW11 100 DE83
Moss Cl, E1 off Old Montague St 84 DU71
N9 46 DU46
Pinner HA5 40 BZ54
Moss Cl, Rick. WD3 38 BK47
Mossdown Cl, Belv. DA17 106 FA77
Mossendew Cl, Uxb. (Hare.) UB9 38 BK53
Mossfield, Cob. KT11 153 BU113
Mossford Ct, Ilf. IG6 69 EP55
Mossford Grn, Ilf. IG6 69 EP55
Mossford La, Ilf. IG6 49 EP54
Mossford St, E3 85 DZ70
Moss Gdns, Felt. TW13 115 BU89
South Croydon CR2 off Warren Av 161 DX108
Moss Hall Ct, N12 44 DB51
Moss Hall Cres, N12 44 DB51
Moss Hall Gro, N12 44 DB51
Mossington Gdns, SE16 202 F9
Moss La, Pnr. HA5 60 BZ55
Romford RM1 off Wheatsheaf Rd 71 FF58
Mosslea Rd, SE20 122 DW93
Bromley BR2 144 EK99
Orpington BR6 145 EQ104
Whyteleafe CR3 176 DT116
Mossop St, SW3 198 C8
Moss Rd, Dag. RM10 88 FA66
South Ockendon RM15 91 FW71
Watford WD25 7 BV34
Moss Side, St.Alb. (Brick.Wd) AL2 8 BZ30
Mossville Gdns, Mord. SM4 139 CZ97
Moss Way, Dart. (Lane End) DA2 129 FR91
Moston Cl, Hayes UB3 off Fuller Way 95 BT78
Mostyn Av, Wem. HA9 62 CM64
Mostyn Gdns, NW10 81 CX68
Mostyn Gro, E3 85 DZ68
Mostyn Rd, SW9 101 DN81
SW19 139 CZ95
Bushey WD23 24 CC43
Edgware HA8 42 CR52
Mosul Way, Brom. BR2 144 EL100
Mosyer Dr, Orp. BR5 146 EX103
Motcomb St, SW1 198 E6
Moth Cl, Wall. SM6 159 DL108
Mothers' Sq, E5 66 DV63
Motherwell Way, Grays RM20 109 FU78
Motley Av, EC2 197 M4
Motley St, SW8 off St. Rule St 101 DJ82
MOTSPUR PARK, N.Mal. KT3 139 CU100
⇌ Motspur Park 139 CV99
Motspur Pk, N.Mal. KT3 139 CT100
MOTTINGHAM, SE9 124 EJ89
⇌ Mottingham 124 EL88
Mottingham Gdns, SE9 124 EK88
Mottingham La, SE9 124 EJ88
SE12 124 EJ88
Mottingham Rd, N9 31 DX44
SE9 124 EL89
Mottisfont Rd, SE2 106 EU76
Motts Hill La, Tad. KT20 173 CU123
Mott St, E4 31 ED38
Loughton (High Beach) IG10 32 EF39
Mouchotte Cl, West. (Bigg.H.) TN16 162 EH112
Moulins Rd, E9 84 DW67
Moulsford Ho, N7 65 DK64
Moultain Hill, Swan. BR8 147 FG98
Moulton Av, Houns. TW3 96 BY82
Moultrie Way, Upmin. RM14 73 FS59
Mound, The, SE9 125 EN90
Moundfield Rd, N16 66 DU58
Mount, The, N20 44 DC47
NW3 off Heath St 64 DC63
W3 80 CP74
Brentwood CM14 54 FW48
Coulsdon CR5 174 DG115
Epsom (Ewell) KT17 157 CT110
Esher KT10 154 CA107
Leatherhead (Fetch.) KT22 171 CE123
New Malden KT3 139 CT97
Potters Bar EN6 12 DB30
Rickmansworth WD3 22 BJ44
Romford RM3 52 FJ48
Tadworth (Lwr Kgswd) KT20 183 CZ126
Virginia Water GU25 132 AX100
Waltham Cross (Chsht) EN7 14 DR26
Warlingham CR6 176 DU119
Wembley HA9 62 CP61
Weybridge KT13 135 BS103
Woking GU21 166 AX118
Woking (St.John's) GU21 166 AU119
Worcester Park KT4 157 CV105
Mountacre Cl, SE26 122 DT91
Mount Adon Pk, SE22 122 DU87
Mountague Pl, E14 85 EC73
Mountain Ho, SE11 200 B10
Mount Angelus Rd, SW15 119 CT87
Mount Ararat Rd, Rich. TW10 118 CL85
Mount Ash Rd, SE26 122 DV90
Mount Av, E4 47 EA48
W5 79 CK71
Brentwood CM13 55 GA44
Caterham (Chaldon) CR3 176 DQ124
Romford RM3 52 FQ51
Southall UB1 78 CA72
Mountbatten Cl, SE18 105 ES79
SE19 122 DS92
Slough SL1 92 AU76
Mountbatten Ct, SE16 off Rotherhithe St 84 DW74
Buckhurst Hill IG9 48 EK47
Mountbatten Gdns, Beck. BR3 off Balmoral Av 143 DY98
Mountbatten Ms, SW18 off Inman Rd 120 DC88
Mountbel Rd, Stan. HA7 41 CG53
Mount Cl, W5 79 CJ71
Barnet EN4 28 DG42
Bromley BR1 144 EL95
Carshalton SM5 158 DG109
Kenley CR8 176 DQ116
Leatherhead (Fetch.) KT22 171 CE123
Sevenoaks TN13 190 FF123
Woking GU22 166 AV121
Mount Cl, The, Vir.W. GU25 132 AX100
Mountcombe Cl, Surb. KT6 138 CL101
Mount Cor, Felt. TW13 116 BX89

★ Place of interest ⇌ Railway station ⊖ London Underground station DLR Docklands Light Railway station Tra Tramlink station H Hospital Riv Pedestrian ferry landing stage

Mount Ct, SW15
off Weimar St 99 CY83
West Wickham BR4 144 EE103
Mount Cres, Brwd. CM14 54 FX49
Mount Culver Av, Sid. DA14 126 EX93
Mount Dr, Bexh. DA6 126 EY85
Harrow HA2 60 BZ57
St. Albans (Park St) AL2 9 CD25
Wembley HA9 62 CQ61
Mount Dr, The, Reig. RH2 184 DC132
Mountearl Gdns, SW16 121 DM90
Mount Echo Av, E4 47 EB47
Mount Echo Dr, E4 47 EB46
MOUNT END, Epp. CM16 18 EZ32
Mount Ephraim La, SW16 121 DK90
Mount Ephraim Rd, SW16 121 DK90
Mount Est, The, E5
off Mount Pleasant La 66 DV61
Mount Felix, Walt. KT12 135 BT102
Mountfield Cl, SE6 123 ED87
Mountfield Rd, E6 87 EN68
N3 64 DA55
W5 79 CK72
Mountfield Ter, SE6
off Mountfield Cl 123 ED87
Mountfield Way, Orp. BR5 146 EW98
Mountfort Cres, N1
off Barnsbury Sq 83 DN66
Mountfort Ter, N1
off Barnsbury Sq 83 DN66
Mount Gdns, SE26 122 DV90
Mount Grace Rd, Pot.B. EN6 12 DA31
Mount Gro, Edg. HA8 42 CQ48
Mountgrove Rd, N5 65 DP62
Mount Harry Rd, Sev. TN13 190 FG123
MOUNT HERMON, Wok.
GU22 166 AX118
Mount Hermon Cl, Wok.
GU22 166 AX118
Mount Hermon Rd, Wok.
GU22 166 AX119
Mount Hill La, Ger.Cr. SL9 56 AV60
Mounthurst Rd, Brom. BR2 144 EF101
Mountington Pk Cl, Har. HA3 61 CK58
Mountjoy Cl, SE2 106 EV75
Mountjoy Ho, EC2
off The Barbican 84 DQ71
Mount La, Uxb. (Denh.) UB9 57 BD61
Mount Lee, Egh. TW20 112 AY92
Mount Ms, Hmptn. TW12 136 CB95
Mount Mills, EC1 196 G3
Mountnessing Bypass,
Brwd. CM15 55 GD41
Mount Nod Rd, SW16 121 DM90
Mount Pk, Cars. SM5 158 DG109
Mount Pk Av, Har. HA1 61 CD61
South Croydon CR2 159 DP109
Mount Pk Cres, W5 79 CK72
Mount Pk Rd, W5 79 CK71
Harrow HA1 61 CD62
Pinner HA5 59 BU57
Mount Pl, W3 off High St 80 CP74
Mount Pleasant, SE27 122 DQ91
WC1 196 C5
Barnet EN4 28 DE42
Epsom KT17 157 CT110
Ruislip HA4 60 BW61
Uxbridge (Hare.) UB9 38 BG53
Wembley HA0 80 CL67
Westerham (Bigg.H.) TN16 178 EK117
Weybridge KT13 134 BN104
Mount Pleasant Av, Brwd.
(Hutt.) CM13 55 GE44
Mount Pleasant Cres, N4 65 DM59
Mount Pleasant Hill, E5 66 DV61
Mount Pleasant La, E5 66 DV61
St. Albans (Brick.Wd) AL2 8 BY30
Mount Pleasant Pl, SE18 105 ER77
Mount Pleasant Rd, E17 47 DY54
N17 46 DS54
NW10 81 CW66
SE13 123 EB86
W5 79 CJ70
Caterham CR3 176 DU123
Chigwell IG7 49 ER49
Dartford DA1 128 FM86
New Malden KT3 138 CQ97
Romford RM5 51 FD51
Mount Pleasant Vil, N4 65 DM59
Mount Pleasant Wk, Bex.
DA5 127 FC85
Mount Rd, NW2 63 CV62
NW4 63 CU58
SE19 122 DR93
SW19 120 DA89
Barnet EN4 28 DE43
Bexleyheath DA6 126 EX85
Chessington KT9 156 CM106
Dagenham RM8 70 EZ60
Dartford DA1 127 FF86
Epping CM16 18 EW32
Feltham TW13 116 BY90
Hayes UB3 95 BT75
Ilford IG1 69 EP64
Mitcham CR4 140 DE96
New Malden KT3 138 CR97
Woking GU22 166 AV121
Woking (Chobham) GU24 150 AV112
Mount Row, W1 199 H1
Mountsfield Cl, Stai. TW19 114 BG86
Mountsfield Ct, SE13 123 ED86
Mountside, Felt. TW13 116 BY90
Stanmore HA7 41 CF53
Mounts Pond Rd, SE3 103 ED82
Mount Sq, The, NW3
off Heath St 64 DC62
Mounts Rd, Green. DA9 129 FV85
Mount Stewart Av, Har. HA3 61 CK58
Mount St, W1 198 G1
Mount St Ms, W1
off Mount St 83 DH73
Mount Ter, E1
off New Rd 84 DV71
Mount Vernon, NW3 64 DC63
H Mount Vernon Hosp,
Nthwd. HA6 39 BP51
Mount Vw, NW7 42 CR48
W5 79 CK70
Enfield EN2 29 DM38
Mountview, Nthwd. HA6 39 BT51
Mount Vw, Rick. WD3 38 BH46
St. Albans (Lon.Col.) AL2 10 CL27
Mountview Cl, NW11 64 DB60
Mountview Ct, N8
off Green Las 65 DP56
Mount Vw Rd, E4 47 EC45
N4 65 DL59
NW9 62 CR56
Mountview Rd, Esher
(Clay.) KT10 155 CH108
Orpington BR6 146 EU101
Waltham Cross (Chsht) EN7 14 DS26
Mount Vil, SE27 121 DP90
Mount Way, Cars. SM5 158 DG109
Mountway, Pot.B. EN6 12 DA30
Mountwood, W.Mol. KT8 136 CA97
Mountwood Cl, S.Croy. CR2 160 DV110
Movers La, Bark. IG11 87 ER67
Mowat Ind Est, Wat. WD24 24 BW38
Mowatt Cl, N19 65 DK60
Mowbray Av, W.Byf. (Byfleet)
KT14 152 BL113
Mowbray Cres, Egh. TW20 113 BA92
Mowbray Rd, NW6 81 CY66
SE19 142 DT95
Barnet EN5 28 DC42
Edgware HA8 42 CN49
Richmond TW10 117 CJ90
Mowbrays Cl, Rom. RM5 51 FC53
Mowbrays Rd, Rom. RM5 51 FC54
Mowbrey Gdns, Loug. IG10 33 EQ40
Mowlem St, E2 84 DV68
Mowlem Trd Est, N17 46 DW52
Mowll St, SW9 101 DN80
Moxom Av, Wal.Cr. (Chsht)
EN8 15 DY30
Moxon Cl, E13
off Whitelegg Rd 86 EF68
Moxon St, W1 194 F7
Barnet EN5 27 CZ41
Moye Cl, E2 off Dove Row 84 DU67
Moyers Rd, E10 67 EC59
Moylan Rd, W6 99 CY79
Moyne Ct, Wok. GU21
off Iveagh Rd 166 AT118
Moyne Pl, NW10 80 CN68
Moynihan Dr, N21 29 DL43
Moys Cl, Croy. CR0 141 DL100
Moyser Rd, SW16 121 DH92
Mozart St, W10 81 CZ69
Mozart Ter, SW1 198 G9
Muchelney Rd, Mord. SM4 140 DC100
Muckhatch La, Egh. TW20 133 BB97
MUCKINGFORD, S.le H.
SS17 111 GM76
Muckingford Rd, S.le H.
(Linford) SS17 111 GM77
Tilbury (W.Til.) RM18 111 GL77
DLR Mudchute 204 C8
Muddy La, Slou. SL2 74 AS71
Mudlands Ind Est, Rain.
RM13 89 FE69
Mud La, W5 79 CK71
Mudlarks Boul, SE10
off John Harrison Way 104 EF76
Muggeridge Cl, S.Croy. CR2 160 DR106
Muggeridge Rd, Dag. RM10 71 FB63
MUGSWELL, Couls. CR5 184 DB125
Muirdown Av, SW14 98 CQ84
Muir Dr, SW18 120 DD86
Muirfield, W3 80 CS72
Muirfield Cl, SE16
off Ryder Dr 102 DV78
Watford WD19 40 BW49
Muirfield Cres, E14 204 B6
Muirfield Grn, Wat. WD19 40 BW49
Muirfield Rd, Wat. WD19 40 BX49
Woking GU21 166 AU118
Muirkirk Rd, SE6 123 EC88
Muir Rd, E5 66 DU62
Muir St, E16 off Newland St 87 EM74
Mulberry Av, Stai. TW19 114 BL88
Windsor SL4 92 AT82
Mulberry Business Cen,
SE16 203 J5
Mulberry Cl, E4 47 EA47
N8 65 DL57
NW3 off Hampstead High St 64 DD63
NW4 63 CW55
SE7 off Charlton Pk Rd 104 EK79
SE22 122 DU85
SW3 off Beaufort St 100 DD79
SW16 121 DJ91
Amersham HP7 20 AT39
Barnet EN4 28 DD42
Northolt UB5
off Parkfield Av 78 BY68
Romford RM2 71 FH56
St. Albans (Park St) AL2 8 CB28
Watford WD25 23 BS36
Weybridge KT13 135 BP104
Woking GU21 150 AY114
Mulberry Ct, EC1
off Northampton Sq 83 DP69
Barking IG11
off Westrow Dr 87 ET65
Mulberry Cres, Brent. TW8 97 CH80
West Drayton UB7 94 BN75
Mulberry Dr, Purf. RM19 108 FM77
Slough SL3 92 AY78
Mulberry Gdns, Rad.
(Shenley) WD7 10 CL33
Mulberry Gate, Bans. SM7 173 CZ116
Mulberry Hill, Brwd.
(Shenf.) CM15 55 FZ45
Mulberry La, Croy. CR0 142 DT102
Mulberry Ms, SE14
off Lewisham Way 103 DZ81
Wallington SM6
off Ross Rd 159 DJ107
Mulberry Par, West Dr. UB7 94 BN76
Mulberry Pl, SE9 104 EK84
W6 off Chiswick Mall 99 CU78
Mulberry Rd, E8 84 DT66
Gravesend (Nthflt) DA11 130 GE90
Mulberry St, E1 off Adler St 84 DU72
Mulberry Tree Ms, W4
off Clovelly Rd 98 CQ75
Mulberry Trees, Shep. TW17 135 BQ101
Mulberry Wk, SW3 100 DD79
Mulberry Way, E18 48 EH54
Belvedere DA17 107 FC75
Ilford IG6 69 EQ56
Mulgrave Rd, NW10 63 CT63
SE18 105 EM77
SW6 99 CZ79
Mulgrave Rd, W5 79 CK69
Croydon CR0 142 DR104
Harrow HA1 61 CG61
Sutton SM2 158 DA107
Mulgrave Way, Wok. (Knap.)
GU21 166 AS118
Mulholland Cl, Mitch. CR4 141 DH96
Mulkern Rd, N19 65 DK60
Mullards Cl, Mitch. CR4 140 DF102
Mullein Ct, Grays RM17 110 GD79
Mullens Rd, Egh. TW20 113 BB92
Muller Rd, SW4 121 DK86
Mullet Gdns, E2
off St. Peter's Cl 84 DU68
Mullins Path, SW14 98 CR83
Mullion Cl, Har. HA3 40 CB53
Mullion Wk, Wat. WD19
off Ormskirk Rd 40 BX49
Mull Wk, N1 off Clephane Rd 84 DQ65
Mulready St, NW8 194 B5
Multi-way, W3 off Valetta Rd 98 CS75
Multon Rd, SW18 120 DD87
Mulvaney Way, SE1 201 L5
Mumford Ct, EC2 197 J8
Mumford Mills, SE10
off Greenwich High Rd 103 EB81
Mumford Rd, SE24
off Railton Rd 121 DP85
Mumfords La, Ger.Cr.
(Chal.St.P.) SL9 56 AU55
Muncaster Cl, Ashf. TW15 114 BN91
Muncaster Rd, SW11 120 DF85
Ashford TW15 115 BP92
Muncies Ms, SE6 123 EC89
Mundania Rd, SE22 122 DV86
Munday Rd, E16 86 EG72
Mundells, Wal.Cr. EN7 14 DU27
Munden Dr, Wat. WD25 24 BY37
Munden Gro, Wat. WD24 24 BW38
Munden St, W14 99 CY77
Munden Vw, Wat. WD25 24 BX36
Mundesley Cl, Wat. WD19 40 BW49
Mundesley Spur, Slou. SL1 74 AS72
Mundford Rd, E5 66 DW61
Mundon Gdns, Ilf. IG1 69 ER60
Mund St, W14 99 CZ78
Mundy St, N1 197 M2
Munford Dr, Swans. DA10 130 FY87
Mungo Pk Cl, Bushey (Bushey Hth)
WD23 40 CC47
Mungo Pk Rd, Grav. DA12 131 GK92
Rainham RM13 89 FG65
Mungo Pk Way, Orp. BR5 146 EW101
Munnery Way, Orp. BR6 145 EN104
Munnings Gdns, Islw. TW7 117 CD85
Munro Dr, N11 45 DJ51
Munro Ms, W10 81 CY71
Munro Rd, Bushey WD23 24 CB43
Munro Ter, SW10 100 DD80
Munslow Gdns, Sutt. SM1 158 DD105
Munster Av, Houns. TW4 96 BZ84
Munster Ct, Tedd. TW11 117 CJ93
Munster Gdns, N13 45 DP49
Munster Ms, SW6
off Lillie Rd 99 CY80
Munster Rd, SW6 99 CZ81
Teddington TW11 117 CH93
Munster Sq, NW1 195 J3
Munton Rd, SE17 201 J8
Murchison Av, Bex. DA5 126 EX88
Murchison Rd, E10 67 EC61
Murdoch Cl, Stai. TW18 114 BG92
Murdock Cl, E16
off Rogers Rd 86 EF72
Murdock St, SE15 102 DV79
Murfett Cl, SW19 119 CY89
Murfitt Way, Upmin. RM14 72 FN63
Muriel Av, Wat. WD18 24 BW43
Muriel St, N1 83 DM68
Murillo Rd, SE13 103 ED84
Murphy St, SE1 200 D5
Murray Av, Brom. BR1 144 EH96
Hounslow TW3 116 CB85
Murray Business Cen, Orp.
BR5 146 EV97
Murray Cres, Pnr. HA5 40 BX53
Murray Grn, Wok. GU21
off Bunyard Dr 151 BC114
Murray Gro, N1 197 J1
Murray Ms, NW1 83 DK66
Murray Rd, SW19 119 CX93
W5 97 CJ77
Chertsey (Ott.) KT16 151 BC107
Northwood HA6 39 BS53
Orpington BR5 146 EV97
Richmond TW10 117 CH89
Murrays La, W.Byf. (Byfleet)
KT14 152 BK114
Murray Sq, E16 86 EG72
Murray St, NW1 83 DK66
Murrays Yd, SE18 105 EP77
Murray Ter, NW3
off Flask Wk 64 DD63
W5 off Murray Rd 97 CK77
Murrells Wk, Lthd. (Bkhm)
KT23 170 CA123
Murreys, The, Ashtd. KT21 171 CK118
Murry Cl, SE28 87 ES74
Mursell Est, SW8 101 DM81
Murthering La, Rom. RM4 35 FG43
Murtwell Dr, Chig. IG7 49 EQ51
Musard Rd, W6 99 CY79
W14 99 CY79
Musbury St, E1 84 DW72
Muscal, W6 99 CY79
Muscatel Pl, SE5
off Dalwood St 102 DS81
Muschamp Rd, SE15 102 DT83
Carshalton SM5 140 DE103
Muscovy Ho, Erith DA18
off Kale Rd 106 EY75
Muscovy St, EC3 201 N1
★ Museum in Docklands,
E14 204 A1
★ Museum Interpretative Cen
& Nature Reserve, E6
off Norman Rd 87 EM70
Museum La, SW7
off Exhibition Rd 100 DD76
★ Museum of Childhood at
Bethnal Grn, E2 84 DV69
★ Museum of Gdn History,
SE1 200 B7
★ Museum of Instruments,
Royal Coll of Music, SW7 100 DD76
★ Museum of London, EC2 197 H7
★ Museum of Richmond, Rich.
TW9 117 CK85
Museum Pas, E2
off Victoria Pk Sq 84 DW69
Museum St, WC1 195 P7
Musgrave Cl, Barn. EN4 28 DC39
Waltham Cross EN7
off Allwood Rd 14 DT27
Musgrave Cres, SW6 100 DA81
Musgrave Rd, Islw. TW7 97 CF81
Musgrove Rd, SE14 103 DX81
Musjid Rd, SW11
off Kambala Rd 100 DD82
Muskalls Cl, Wal.Cr. (Chsht)
EN7 14 DU27
Musket Cl, Barn. EN4
off East Barnet Rd 28 DD43
Musquash Way, Houns. TW4 96 BW82
Mussenden La, Dart.
(Hort.Kir.) DA4 148 FQ99
Longfield (Fawk.Grn) DA3 149 FS101
Mustard Mill Rd, Stai. TW18 113 BF91
Muston Rd, E5 66 DV61
Mustow Pl, SW6
off Munster Rd 99 CZ82
Muswell Av, N10 45 DH54
MUSWELL HILL, N10 65 DH55
Muswell Hill, N10 65 DH55
Muswell Hill Bdy, N10 65 DH55
Muswell Hill Pl, N10 65 DH56
Muswell Hill Rd, N6 64 DG58
N10 64 DG56
Muswell Ms, N10
off Muswell Rd 65 DH55
Muswell Rd, N10 65 DH55
Mutchetts Cl, Wat. WD25 8 BY33
Mutrix Rd, NW6 82 DA67
Mutton La, Pot.B. EN6 11 CY31
Mutton Pl, NW1
off Harmood St 83 DH65
Muybridge Rd, N.Mal. KT3 138 CQ96
Myatt Rd, SW9 101 DP81
Mycenae Rd, SE3 104 EG80
Myddelton Av, Enf. EN1 30 DS38
Myddelton Cl, Enf. EN1 30 DT39
Myddelton Gdns, N21 45 DP45
Myddelton Pk, N20 44 DD48
Myddelton Pas, EC1 196 E2
Myddelton Rd, N8 65 DL56
Myddelton Sq, EC1 196 E2
Myddelton St, EC1 196 E3
Myddleton Av, N4 66 DQ61
Myddleton Ms, N22 45 DL52
Myddleton Path, Wal.Cr.
(Chsht) EN7 14 DV31
Myddleton Rd, N22 45 DL52
Uxbridge UB8 76 BJ67
Myers La, SE14 103 DX79
Mygrove Cl, Rain. RM13 90 FK68
Mygrove Gdns, Rain. RM13 90 FK68
Mygrove Rd, Rain. RM13 90 FK68
Myles Ct, Wal.Cr. EN7 14 DQ29
Mylis Cl, SE26 122 DV91
Mylius Cl, SE14
off Kender St 102 DW81
Mylne Cl, Wal.Cr. EN8 14 DW27
Mylne St, EC1 196 D1
Mylor Cl, Wok. GU21 150 AY114
Mymms Dr, Hat. AL9 12 DA26
Mynns Cl, Epsom KT18 156 CP114
Mynterne Ct, SW19
off Swanton Gdns 119 CX88
Myra St, SE2 106 EU78
Myrdle St, E1 84 DU71
Myrke, The, Slou. (Datchet)
SL3 92 AT77
Myrna Cl, SW19 120 DE94
Myron Pl, SE13 103 EC83
Myrtle Av, Felt. TW14 95 BS84
Ruislip HA4 59 BU59
Myrtleberry Cl, E8
off Beechwood Rd 84 DT65
Myrtle Cl, Barn. EN4 44 DF46
Erith DA8 107 FE81
Slough (Colnbr.) SL3 93 BE81
Uxbridge UB8
off Violet Av 76 BM71
West Drayton UB7 94 BM76
Myrtle Cres, Slou. SL2 74 AT73
Myrtledene Rd, SE2 106 EU78
Myrtle Gdns, W7 79 CE74
Myrtle Gro, Enf. EN2 30 DR38
New Malden KT3 138 CQ96
South Ockendon (Aveley)
RM15 108 FQ75
Myrtle Pl, Dart. DA2 129 FR87
Myrtle Rd, E6 86 EL67
E17 67 DY58
N13 46 DQ48
W3 80 CQ74
Brentwood CM14 54 FW49
Croydon CR0 143 EA104
Dartford DA1 128 FK88
Hampton (Hmptn H.) TW12 116 CC93
Hounslow TW3 96 CC82
Ilford IG1 69 EP61
Romford RM3 52 FJ51
Sutton SM1 158 DC106
Myrtleside Cl, Nthwd. HA6 39 BR52
Myrtle Wk, N1 197 M1
Mysore Rd, SW11 100 DF83
Myton Rd, SE21 122 DR90

N

N1 Shop Cen, N1 83 DN68
Nadine Ct, Wall. SM6
off Woodcote Rd 159 DJ109
Nadine St, SE7 104 EJ78
Nafferton Ri, Loug. IG10 32 EK43
Nagle Cl, E17 47 ED54
Nags Head, N7
off Holloway Rd 65 DL63
Nag's Head Ct, EC1 197 H5
Nags Head La, Brwd. CM14 53 FR51
Upminster RM14 52 FQ53
Welling DA16 106 EV83
Nags Head Rd, Enf. EN3 30 DW42
Nags Head Shop Cen, N7 65 DM63
Nailsworth Cres, Red.
(Merst.) RH1 185 DK129
Nailzee Cl, Ger.Cr. SL9 56 AY59
Nairn Ct, Til. RM18
off Dock Rd 111 GF82
Nairne Gro, SE24 122 DR85
Nairn Grn, Wat. WD19 39 BU48
Nairn Rd, Ruis. HA4 78 BW65
Nairn St, E14 85 EC71
Nallhead Rd, Felt. TW13 116 BW92
Namba Roy Cl, SW16 121 DM91
Namton Dr, Th.Hth. CR7 141 DM98
Nan Clark's La, NW7 43 CT47
Nancy Downs, Wat. WD19 40 BW45
Nankin St, E14 85 EA72
Nansen Rd, SW11 100 DG84
Gravesend DA12 131 GK91
Nansen Village, N12 44 DB49
Nant Ct, NW2
off Granville Rd 63 CZ61
Nantes Cl, SW18 100 DC84
Nantes Pas, E1 197 P6
Nant Rd, NW2 63 CZ61
Nant St, E2
off Cambridge Heath Rd 84 DV69
Naoroji St, WC1 196 D3
Nap, The, Kings L. WD4 6 BN29
Napier Av, E14 204 A10
SW6 99 CZ83
Napier Cl, SE8
off Amersham Vale 103 DZ80
W14 off Napier Rd 99 CZ76
Hornchurch RM11 71 FH60
St. Albans (Lon.Col.) AL2 9 CK25
West Drayton UB7 94 BM76
Napier Ct, SW6
off Ranelagh Gdns 99 CZ83
Waltham Cross (Chsht) EN8
off Flamstead End Rd 14 DV28
Napier Dr, Bushey WD23 24 BY42
Napier Gro, N1 197 J1
Napier Ho, Rain. RM13 89 FF69
Napier Pl, W14 99 CZ76
Napier Rd, E6 87 EN67
E11 68 EE63
E15 86 EE68
N17 66 DS55
NW10 81 CV69
SE25 142 DV98
W14 99 CZ76
Ashford TW15 115 BR94
Belvedere DA17 106 EZ77
Bromley BR2 144 EH98
Enfield EN3 31 DX43
Gravesend (Nthflt) DA11 131 GF88
Hounslow (Hthrw Air.) TW6 94 BK81
Isleworth TW7 97 CG84
South Croydon CR2 160 DR108
Wembley HA0 61 CK64
Napier Ter, N1 83 DP66
Napier Wk, Ashf. TW15 115 BR94
Napoleon Rd, E5 66 DV62
Twickenham TW1 117 CH87
Napsbury Av, St.Alb.
(Lon.Col.) AL2 9 CJ26
Napton Cl, Hayes UB4 78 BY70
Narbonne Av, SW4 121 DJ85
Narboro Ct, Rom. RM1
off Manor Rd 71 FG57
Narborough Cl, Uxb. UB10
off Aylsham Dr 59 BQ61
Narborough St, SW6 100 DB82
Narcissus Rd, NW6 64 DA64
Narcot La, Ch.St.G. HP8 36 AU48
Gerrards Cross (Chal.St.P.)
SL9 36 AV52
Narcot Rd, Ch.St.G. HP8 36 AU48
Narcot Way, Ch.St.G. HP8 36 AU49
Nare Rd, S.Ock. (Aveley)
RM15 90 FQ73
Naresby Fold, Stan. HA7 41 CJ51
Narford Rd, E5 66 DU62
Narrow Boat Cl, SE28
off Ridge Cl 105 ER75
Narrow La, Warl. CR6 176 DV119
Narrow St, E14 85 DY73
Narrow Way, Brom. BR2 144 EL100
Nascot Pl, Wat. WD17 23 BV39
Nascot Rd, Wat. WD17 23 BV40
Nascot St, W12 81 CW72
Watford WD17 23 BV40
Nascot Wd Rd, Wat. WD17 23 BT37
Naseberry Ct, E4
off Merriam Cl 47 EC50
Naseby Cl, NW6 82 DC66
Isleworth TW7 97 CE81
Naseby Ct, Walt. KT12
off Clements Rd 136 BW103
Naseby Rd, SE19 122 DR93
Dagenham RM10 70 FA62
Ilford IG5 49 EM53
Nash Cl, Borwd. (Els.) WD6 26 CM42
Sutton SM1 140 DD104
Nash Ct, E14 204 B3
Nash Cft, Grav. (Nthflt) DA11 130 GE91
Nash Dr, Red. RH1 184 DF132
Nash Gdns, Red. RH1 184 DF132
Nash Grn, Brom. BR1 124 EG93
Hemel Hempstead HP3 6 BM25
Nash Ho, SW1 off Lupus St 101 DH78
Nash La, Kes. BR2 162 EG106
Nash Mills La, Hem.H. HP3 6 BM26
Nash Rd, N9 46 DW47
SE4 103 DX84
Romford RM6 70 EX56
Slough SL3 93 AZ77
Nash St, NW1 195 J3
Nash's Yd, Uxb. UB8
off Bakers Rd 76 BK66
Nash Way, Har. HA3 61 CH58
Nasmyth St, W6 99 CV76
Nassau Path, SE28
off Disraeli Cl 88 EW74
Nassau Rd, SW13 99 CT81
Nassau St, W1 195 K7

M
N

★ Place of interest ⇌ Railway station ⊖ London Underground station DLR Docklands Light Railway station Tra Tramlink station H Hospital Riv Pedestrian ferry landing stage

Nassington Rd, NW3 ... 64 DE63
Natalie Cl, Felt. TW14 ... 115 BR87
Natalie Ms, Twick. TW2 *off Sixth Cross Rd* ... 117 CD90
Natal Rd, N11 ... 45 DL51
SW16 ... 121 DK93
Ilford IG1 ... 69 EP63
Thornton Heath CR7 ... 142 DR97
Nathan Cl, Upmin. RM14 ... 73 FS60
Nathaniel Cl, E1 *off Thrawl St* ... 84 DT71
Nathans Rd, Wem. HA0 ... 61 CJ60
Nathan Way, SE28 ... 105 ES77
★ **National Army Mus**, SW3 ... 100 DF79
H **National Blood Service**, SW17 ... 120 DD92
H **National Blood Service/ Brentwood Transfusion Cen**, Brwd. CM15 ... 55 FZ46
★ **National Gall**, WC2 ... 199 N1
H **National Hosp for Neurology & Neurosurgery, The**, WC1 ... 196 A5
★ **National Maritime Mus**, SE10 ... 103 ED79
★ **National Portrait Gall**, WC2 ... 199 N1
National Ter, SE16 *off Bermondsey Wall E* ... 102 DV75
Nation Way, E4 ... 47 EC46
★ **Natural History Mus**, SW7 ... 100 DD76
Naunton Way, Horn. RM12 ... 72 FK62
Naval Row, E14 ... 85 EC73
Naval Wk, Brom. BR1 *off High St* ... 144 EG97
Navarino Gro, E8 ... 84 DU65
Navarino Rd, E8 ... 84 DU65
Navarre Gdns, Rom. RM5 ... 51 FB51
Navarre Rd, E6 ... 86 EL68
Navarre St, E2 ... 197 P4
Navenby Wk, E3 *off Burwell Wk* ... 85 EA70
Navestock Cl, E4 *off Mapleton Rd* ... 47 EC48
Navestock Cres, Wdf.Grn. IG8 ... 48 EJ53
Navestock Ho, Bark. IG11 ... 88 EV68
Navigation Ct, E16 *off Armada Way* ... 87 EQ73
Navigator Dr, Sthl. UB2 ... 96 CC75
Navigator Pk, Sthl. UB2 ... 96 BW77
Navy St, SW4 ... 101 DK83
Naxos Bldg, E14 ... 203 P5
Nayim Pl, E8 *off Amhurst Rd* ... 66 DV64
Naylor Gro, Enf. EN3 *off South St* ... 31 DX43
Naylor Rd, N20 ... 44 DC47
SE15 ... 102 DV80
Naylor Ter, Slou. (Colnbr.) SL3 *off Vicarage Way* ... 93 BC80
Nazareth Gdns, SE15 ... 102 DV82
NAZEING GATE, Wal.Abb. EN9 ... 16 EJ25
Nazeing Wk, Rain. RM13 *off Ongar Way* ... 89 FF67
Nazrul St, E2 ... 197 P2
Neagle Cl, Borwd. WD6 *off Balcon Way* ... 26 CQ39
Neal Av, Sthl. UB1 ... 78 BZ70
Neal Cl, Ger.Cr. SL9 ... 57 BB60
Northwood HA6 ... 39 BU53
Neal Ct, Wal.Abb. EN9 ... 16 EF33
Nealden St, SW9 ... 101 DM83
Neale Cl, N2 ... 64 DC55
Neal St, WC2 ... 195 P9
Watford WD18 ... 24 BW43
Neal's Yd, WC2 ... 195 P9
Near Acre, NW9 ... 43 CT53
NEASDEN, NW2 ... 62 CS62
⊖ **Neasden** ... 62 CS64
Neasden Cl, NW10 ... 62 CS64
Neasden La, NW10 ... 62 CS63
Neasden La N, NW10 ... 62 CR62
Neasham Rd, Dag. RM8 ... 70 EV64
Neate St, SE5 ... 102 DT79
Neath Gdns, Mord. SM4 ... 140 DC100
Neathouse Pl, SW1 ... 199 K8
Neats Acre, Ruis. HA4 ... 59 BR59
Neatscourt Rd, E6 ... 86 EK71
Neave Cres, Rom. RM3 ... 52 FJ53
Neb La, Oxt. RH8 ... 187 EC131
Nebraska St, SE1 ... 201 K5
★ **NEC Harlequins R.F.C.**, Twick. TW2 ... 117 CE87
Neckinger, SE16 ... 202 A6
Neckinger Est, SE16 ... 202 A6
Neckinger St, SE1 ... 202 A5
Nectarine Way, SE13 ... 103 EB82
Needham Rd, W11 *off Westbourne Gro* ... 82 DA72
Needham Ter, NW2 *off Kara Way* ... 63 CX62
Needleman St, SE16 ... 203 H5
Needles Bk, Gdse. RH9 ... 186 DV131
Neela Cl, Uxb. UB10 ... 59 BP63
Neeld Cres, NW4 ... 63 CV57
Wembley HA9 ... 62 CN64
Neeld Par, Wem. HA9 *off Harrow Rd* ... 62 CN64
Neil Cl, Ashf. TW15 ... 115 BQ92
Neil Wates Cres, SW2 ... 121 DN88
Nelgarde Rd, SE6 ... 123 EA87
Nella Rd, W6 ... 99 CX79
Nelldale Rd, SE16 ... 202 F8
Nellgrove Rd, Uxb. UB10 ... 77 BP70
Nell Gwynn Cl, Rad. (Shenley) WD7 ... 10 CL32
Nell Gwynne Av, Shep. TW17 ... 135 BR100
Nell Gwynne Cl, Epsom KT19 ... 156 CN111
Nello James Gdns, SE27 ... 122 DR91
Nelmes Cl, Horn. RM11 ... 72 FM57
Nelmes Cres, Horn. RM11 ... 72 FL57
Nelmes Rd, Horn. RM11 ... 72 FL59
Nelmes Way, Horn. RM11 ... 72 FL56
Nelson Cl, NW6 ... 82 DA69
Brentwood (Warley) CM14 ... 54 FX50
Nelson Cl, Croy. CR0 ... 141 DP102
Feltham TW14 ... 115 BT88
Romford RM7 ... 51 FB53
Slough SL3 ... 92 AX77
Uxbridge UB10 ... 77 BP69
Walton-on-Thames KT12 ... 135 BV102
Westerham (Bigg.H.) TN16 ... 178 EL117
Nelson Ct, SE16 *off Brunel Rd* ... 84 DW74
Nelson Gdns, E2 ... 84 DU69
Hounslow TW3 ... 116 CA86
Nelson Gro Rd, SW19 ... 140 DB95
H **Nelson Hosp**, SW20 ... 139 CZ96
Nelson La, Uxb. UB10 *off Nelson Rd* ... 77 BP69
Nelson Mandela Cl, N10 ... 44 DG54
Nelson Mandela Rd, SE3 ... 104 EJ83
Nelson Pas, EC1 ... 197 J3
Nelson Pl, N1 ... 196 G1
Sidcup DA14 *off Sidcup High St* ... 126 EU91
Nelson Rd, E4 ... 47 EB51
E11 ... 68 EG56
N8 ... 65 DM57
N9 ... 46 DV47
N15 ... 66 DS56
SE10 ... 103 EC79
SW19 ... 120 DB94
Ashford TW15 ... 114 BL92
Belvedere DA17 ... 106 EZ78
Bromley BR2 ... 144 EJ98
Caterham CR3 ... 176 DR123
Dartford DA1 ... 128 FJ86
Enfield EN3 ... 31 DX44
Gravesend (Nthflt) DA11 ... 131 GF89
Harrow HA1 ... 61 CD60
Hounslow TW3, TW4 ... 116 CA86
Hounslow (Hthrw Air.) TW6 ... 94 BM81
New Malden KT3 ... 138 CR99
Rainham RM13 ... 89 FF68
Sidcup DA14 *off Sidcup High St* ... 126 EU91
South Ockendon RM15 ... 91 FW68
Stanmore HA7 ... 41 CJ51
Twickenham TW2 ... 116 CC86
Uxbridge UB10 ... 77 BP69
★ **Nelson's Column**, WC2 ... 199 P2
Nelson Sq, SE1 ... 200 F4
Nelson's Row, SW4 ... 101 DK84
Nelson St, E1 ... 84 DV72
E6 ... 87 EM68
E16 *off Huntingdon St* ... 86 EF72
Nelsons Yd, NW1 *off Mornington Cres* ... 83 DJ68
Nelson Ter, N1 ... 196 G1
Nelson Trd Est, SW19 ... 140 DB95
Nelson Wk, SE16 ... 203 L3
Epsom KT19 ... 156 CN109
Nelwyn Av, Horn. RM11 ... 72 FM57
Nemoure Rd, W3 ... 80 CQ73
Nene Gdns, Felt. TW13 ... 116 BZ89
Nene Rd, Houns. (Hthrw Air.) TW6 ... 95 BP81
Nepaul Rd, SW11 ... 100 DE82
Nepean St, SW15 ... 119 CU86
Neptune Cl, Rain. RM13 ... 89 FF68
Neptune Ct, Borwd. WD6 *off Clarendon Rd* ... 26 CN41
Neptune Rd, Har. HA1 ... 61 CD58
Hounslow (Hthrw Air.) TW6 ... 95 BR81
Neptune St, SE16 ... 202 F6
Neptune Wk, Erith DA8 ... 107 FD77
Nero Ct, Brent. TW8 *off Justin Cl* ... 97 CK80
Nesbit Rd, SE9 ... 104 EK84
Nesbitt Cl, SE3 *off Hurren Cl* ... 104 EE83
Nesbitts All, Barn. EN5 *off Bath Pl* ... 27 CZ41
Nesbitt Sq, SE19 *off Coxwell Rd* ... 122 DS94
Nesham St, E1 ... 202 B2
Ness Rd, Erith DA8 ... 108 FK79
Ness St, SE16 ... 202 B6
Nesta Rd, Wdf.Grn. IG8 ... 48 EE51
Nestles Av, Hayes UB3 ... 95 BT76
Neston Rd, Wat. WD24 ... 24 BW37
Nestor Av, N21 ... 29 DP44
Nethan Dr, S.Ock. (Aveley) RM15 ... 90 FQ73
Netheravon Rd, W4 ... 99 CT77
W7 ... 79 CF74
Netheravon Rd S, W4 ... 99 CT78
Netherbury Rd, W5 ... 97 CK76
Netherby Gdns, Enf. EN2 ... 29 DL42
Netherby Pk, Wey. KT13 ... 153 BS106
Netherby Rd, SE23 ... 122 DW87
Nether Cl, N3 ... 44 DA52
Nethercote Av, Wok. GU21 ... 166 AT117
Nethercourt Av, N3 ... 44 DA51
Netherfield Gdns, Bark. IG11 ... 87 ER65
Netherfield Rd, N12 ... 44 DB50
SW17 ... 120 DG90
Netherford Rd, SW4 ... 101 DJ82
Netherhall Gdns, NW3 ... 82 DC65
Netherhall Way, NW3 *off Netherhall Gdns* ... 64 DC64
Netherlands, The, Couls. CR5 ... 175 DJ119
Netherlands Rd, Barn. EN5 ... 28 DD44
Netherleigh Cl, N6 ... 65 DH60
Nethern Ct Rd, Cat. (Wold.) CR3 ... 177 EA123
Netherne Dr, Couls. CR5 ... 175 DH121
Netherne La, Couls. CR5 ... 175 DK121
Redhill RH1 ... 175 DJ123
Netherpark Dr, Rom. RM2 ... 51 FF54
Nether St, N3 ... 44 DA53
N12 ... 44 DA52
Netherton Gro, SW10 ... 100 DC79
Netherton Rd, N15 ... 66 DR58
Twickenham TW1 ... 117 CH85
Netherwood, N2 ... 44 DD54
Netherwood Pl, W14 *off Netherwood Rd* ... 99 CX76
Netherwood Rd, W14 ... 99 CX76
Netherwood St, NW6 ... 81 CZ66
Netley Cl, Croy. (New Adgtn) CR0 ... 161 EC108
Sutton SM3 ... 157 CX106
Netley Dr, Walt. KT12 ... 136 BZ101
Netley Gdns, Mord. SM4 ... 140 DC101
Netley Rd, E17 ... 67 DZ57
Netley Rd, Brent. TW8 ... 98 CL79
Hounslow (Hthrw Air.) TW6 ... 95 BR81
Ilford IG2 ... 69 ER57
Morden SM4 ... 140 DC101
Netley St, NW1 ... 195 K3
Nettlecombe Cl, Sutt. SM2 ... 158 DB109
Nettleden Av, Wem. HA9 ... 80 CN65
Nettlefold Pl, SE27 ... 121 DP90
Nettlestead Cl, Beck. BR3 ... 143 DZ95
Nettleton Rd, SE14 ... 103 DX81
Hounslow (Hthrw Air.) TW6 ... 95 BP81
Uxbridge UB10 ... 58 BM63
Nettlewood Rd, SW16 ... 121 DK94
Neuchatel Rd, SE6 ... 123 DZ89
Nevada Cl, N.Mal. KT3 *off Georgia Rd* ... 138 CQ98
Nevada St, SE10 ... 103 EC79
Nevell Rd, Grays RM16 ... 111 GH76
Nevern Pl, SW5 ... 100 DA77
Nevern Rd, SW5 ... 100 DA77
Nevern Sq, SW5 ... 100 DA77
Nevil Cl, Nthwd. HA6 ... 39 BQ50
Neville Av, N.Mal. KT3 ... 138 CR95
Neville Cl, E11 ... 68 EF62
NW1 ... 195 N1
NW6 ... 81 CZ68
SE15 ... 102 DU80
W3 *off Acton La* ... 98 CQ75
Banstead SM7 ... 158 DB114
Esher KT10 ... 154 BZ107
Hounslow TW3 ... 96 CB82
Potters Bar EN6 ... 11 CZ31
Sidcup DA15 ... 125 ET91
Slough (Stoke P.) SL2 ... 74 AT65
Neville Dr, N2 ... 64 DC58
Neville Gdns, Dag. RM8 ... 70 EX62
Neville Gill Cl, SW18 ... 120 DA86
Neville Pl, N22 ... 45 DM53
Neville Rd, E7 ... 86 EG66
NW6 ... 81 CZ68
W5 ... 79 CK70
Croydon CR0 ... 142 DR101
Dagenham RM8 ... 70 EX61
Ilford IG6 ... 49 EQ53
Kingston upon Thames KT1 ... 138 CN96
Richmond TW10 ... 117 CJ90
Nevilles Ct, NW2 ... 63 CU62
Neville St, SW7 ... 100 DD78
Neville Ter, SW7 ... 100 DD78
Neville Wk, Cars. SM5 *off Green Wrythe La* ... 140 DE101
Nevill Gro, Wat. WD24 ... 23 BV39
Nevill Rd, N16 ... 66 DS63
Nevill Way, Loug. IG10 *off Valley Hill* ... 48 EL45
Nevin Dr, E4 ... 47 EB46
Nevinson Cl, SW18 ... 120 DD86
Nevis Cl, Rom. RM1 ... 51 FE51
Nevis Rd, SW17 ... 120 DG89
New Acres Rd, SE28 ... 105 ES75
NEW ADDINGTON, Croy. CR0 ... 161 ED109
Tra **New Addington** ... 161 EC110
Newall Rd, Houns. (Hthrw Air.) TW6 ... 95 BQ81
New Arc, Uxb. UB8 *off High St* ... 76 BK67
Newark Cl, Wok. (Ripley) GU23 ... 168 BG121
Newark Cotts, Wok. (Ripley) GU23 ... 168 BG121
Newark Ct, Walt. KT12 ... 136 BW102
Newark Cres, NW10 ... 80 CR69
Newark Grn, Borwd. WD6 ... 26 CR41
Newark Knok, E6 ... 87 EN72
Newark La, Wok. (Ripley) GU23 ... 167 BF118
Newark Par, NW4 *off Greyhound Hill* ... 63 CU55
Newark Rd, S.Croy. CR2 ... 160 DR107
Newark St, E1 ... 84 DV71
Newark Way, NW4 ... 63 CU56
New Ash Cl, N2 *off Oakridge Dr* ... 64 DD55
NEW ASH GREEN, Long. DA3 ... 149 FX103
New Atlas Wf, E14 ... 203 N7
New Barn Cl, Wall. SM6 ... 159 DM107
NEW BARNET, Barn. EN5 ... 28 DB42
⇌ **New Barnet** ... 28 DD43
New Barn La, Beac. HP9 ... 36 AS49
Sevenoaks (Cudham) TN14 ... 179 EQ116
Westerham TN16 ... 179 EQ118
Whyteleafe CR3 ... 176 DS117
New Barn Rd, Grav. (Sthflt) DA13 ... 130 GC90
Swanley BR8 ... 147 FE95
New Barns Av, Mitch. CR4 ... 141 DK98
New Barn St, E13 ... 86 EG70
New Barns Way, Chig. IG7 ... 49 EP48
New Battlebridge La, Red. RH1 ... 185 DH130
NEW BECKENHAM, Beck. BR3 ... 123 DZ93
⇌ **New Beckenham** ... 123 DZ94
Newberries Av, Rad. WD7 ... 25 CJ35
New Berry La, Walt. KT12 ... 154 BX106
Newbery Rd, Erith DA8 ... 107 FF81
Newbiggin Path, Wat. WD19 ... 40 BW49
Newbolt Av, Sutt. SM3 ... 157 CW106
Newbolt Rd, Stan. HA7 ... 41 CF51
New Bond St, W1 ... 195 H9
Newborough Grn, N.Mal. KT3 ... 138 CR98
New Brent St, NW4 ... 63 CW57
Newbridge Pt, SE23 *off Windrush La* ... 123 DX90
New Br St, EC4 ... 196 F9
New Broad St, EC2 ... 197 M7
New Bdy, W5 ... 79 CJ73
Hampton (Hmptn H.) TW12 *off Hampton Rd* ... 117 CD92
New Bdy Bldgs, W5 *off New Bdy* ... 79 CK73
Newburgh Rd, W3 ... 80 CQ74
Grays RM17 ... 110 GD78
Newburgh St, W1 ... 195 K9
New Burlington Ms, W1 ... 195 K10
New Burlington Pl, W1 ... 195 K10
New Burlington St, W1 ... 195 K10
Newburn St, SE11 ... 101 DM78
Newbury Av, Enf. EN3 ... 31 DZ38
Newbury Cl, Dart. DA2 *off Lingfield Av* ... 128 FP87
Northolt UB5 ... 78 BZ65
Romford RM3 ... 52 FK51
Newbury Gdns, Epsom KT19 ... 157 CT105
Romford RM3 ... 52 FK51
Upminster RM14 ... 72 FM62
Newbury Ho, N22 ... 45 DL53
Newbury Ms, NW5 *off Malden Rd* ... 82 DG65
NEWBURY PARK, Ilf. IG2 ... 69 ER57
⊖ **Newbury Park** ... 69 ER58
Newbury Rd, E4 ... 47 EC51
Bromley BR2 ... 144 EG97
Hounslow (Hthrw Air.) TW6 ... 94 BM81
Ilford IG2 ... 69 ER58
Romford RM3 ... 52 FK50
Newbury St, EC1 ... 197 H7
Newbury Wk, Rom. RM3 ... 52 FK50
Newbury Way, Nthlt. UB5 ... 78 BY65
New Butt La, SE8 ... 103 EA80
New Butt La N, SE8 *off Reginald Rd* ... 103 EA80
Newby Cl, Enf. EN1 ... 30 DS40
Newby Pl, E14 ... 85 EC73
Newby St, SW8 ... 101 DH83
New Caledonian Wf, SE16 ... 203 M6
Newcastle Av, Ilf. IG6 ... 50 EU51
Newcastle Cl, EC4 ... 196 F8
Newcastle Pl, W2 ... 194 A7
Newcastle Row, EC1 ... 196 E4
New Cavendish St, W1 ... 195 J6
New Change, EC4 ... 197 H9
New Chapel Sq, Felt. TW13 ... 115 BV88
New Charles St, EC1 ... 196 G2
NEW CHARLTON, SE7 ... 104 EJ77
New Ch Ct, SE19 *off Waldegrave Rd* ... 122 DU94
New Ch Rd, SE5 ... 102 DQ80
New City Rd, E13 ... 86 EJ69
New Cl, SW19 ... 140 DC97
Feltham TW13 ... 116 BY92
New Coll Ct, NW3 *off Finchley Rd* ... 82 DC65
New Coll Ms, N1 *off Islington Pk St* ... 83 DN66
New Coll Par, NW3 *off Finchley Rd* ... 82 DD65
Newcombe Gdns, SW16 ... 121 DL91
Hounslow TW4 ... 96 BZ84
Newcombe Pk, NW7 ... 42 CS50
Wembley HA0 ... 80 CM67
Newcombe Ri, West Dr. UB7 ... 76 BL72
Newcombe St, W8 *off Kensington Pl* ... 82 DA74
Newcomen Rd, E11 ... 68 EF62
SW11 ... 100 DD83
Newcomen St, SE1 ... 201 K4
Newcome Path, Rad. (Shenley) WD7 *off Newcome Rd* ... 10 CN34
Newcome Rd, Rad. (Shenley) WD7 ... 10 CN34
New Compton St, WC2 ... 195 N9
New Concordia Wf, SE1 ... 202 B4
New Coppice, Wok. GU21 ... 166 AT119
New Cotts, Rain. (Wenn.) RM13 ... 90 FJ72
New Ct, EC4 ... 196 D10
Addlestone KT15 ... 134 BJ104
Newcourt, Uxb. UB8 ... 76 BJ71
Newcourt St, NW8 ... 194 B1
★ **New Covent Garden Flower Mkt**, SW8 ... 101 DK79
★ **New Covent Garden Mkt**, SW8 ... 101 DK80
New Crane Pl, E1 ... 202 F2
Newcroft Cl, Uxb. UB8 ... 76 BM71
NEW CROSS, SE14 ... 103 DY81
⇌ **New Cross** ... 103 DZ80
⊖ **New Cross** ... 103 DZ80
NEW CROSS GATE, SE14 ... 103 DX81
⇌ **New Cross Gate** ... 103 DY81
⊖ **New Cross Gate** ... 103 DY81
New Cross Rd, SE14 ... 102 DW80
Newdales Cl, N9 *off Balham Rd* ... 46 DU47
Newdene Av, Nthlt. UB5 ... 78 BX68
Newdigate Grn, Uxb. (Hare.) UB9 ... 38 BK53
Newdigate Rd, Uxb. (Hare.) UB9 ... 38 BJ53
Newdigate Rd E, Uxb. (Hare.) UB9 ... 38 BK53
Newell St, E14 ... 85 DZ72
NEW ELTHAM, SE9 ... 125 EN89
⇌ **New Eltham** ... 125 EP88
New End, NW3 ... 64 DC63
New End Sq, NW3 ... 64 DD63
Newent Cl, SE15 ... 102 DS80
Carshalton SM5 ... 140 DF102
H **New Epsom & Ewell Cottage Hosp**, Epsom KT19 ... 156 CL111
New Fm Av, Brom. BR2 ... 144 EG98
New Fm Cl, Stai. TW18 ... 134 BJ95
New Fm Dr, Rom. (Abridge) RM4 ... 34 EV41
New Fm La, Nthwd. HA6 ... 39 BS53
New Ferry App, SE18 ... 105 EN76
New Fetter La, EC4 ... 196 E8
Newfield Cl, Hmptn. TW12 *off Percy Rd* ... 136 CA95
Newfield Ri, NW2 ... 63 CV62
New Ford Rd, Wal.Cr. EN8 ... 15 DZ34
New Forest La, Chig. IG7 ... 49 EN51
Newgale Gdns, Edg. HA8 ... 42 CM53
New Gdn Dr, West Dr. UB7 *off Drayton Gdns* ... 94 BL75
Newgate, Croy. CR0 ... 142 DQ102
Newgate Cl, Felt. TW13 ... 116 BY89
Newgate St, E4 ... 48 EF48
EC1 ... 196 G8
Newgatestreet Rd, Wal.Cr. (Chsht) EN7 ... 13 DP27
Newgate St Village, Hert. SG13 ... 13 DL25
New Globe Wk, SE1 ... 201 H2
New Goulston St, E1 ... 197 P8
New Grn Pl, SE19 *off Hawke Rd* ... 122 DS93
New Hall Cl, Hem.H. (Bov.) HP3 ... 5 BA27
Newhall Ct, Wal.Abb. EN9 ... 16 EF33
New Hall Dr, Rom. RM3 ... 52 FL53
Newhall Gdns, Walt. KT12 ... 136 BW103
H **Newham Cen for Mental Health**, E13 ... 86 EK70
Newhams Row, SE1 ... 201 N5
H **Newham Uni Hosp**, E13 ... 86 EJ70
Gateway Surgical Cen, E13 ... 86 EK70
Newham Way, E6 ... 86 EJ71
E16 ... 86 EF71
Newhaven Cl, Hayes UB3 ... 95 BT77
Newhaven Cres, Ashf. TW15 ... 115 BR92
Newhaven Gdns, SE9 ... 104 EK84
Newhaven La, E16 ... 86 EF70
Newhaven Rd, SE25 ... 142 DR99
NEW HAW, Add. KT15 ... 152 BK108
New Haw Rd, Add. KT15 ... 152 BJ106
New Heston Rd, Houns. TW5 ... 96 BZ80
New Horizons Ct, Brent. TW8 *off Shield Dr* ... 97 CG79
Newhouse Av, Rom. RM6 ... 70 EX55
Newhouse Cl, N.Mal. KT3 ... 138 CS101
Newhouse Cres, Wat. WD25 ... 7 BV32
New Ho La, Grav. DA11 ... 131 GF90
Newhouse Rd, Hem.H. (Bov.) HP3 ... 5 BA26
Newhouse Wk, Mord. SM4 ... 140 DC101
Newick Cl, Bex. DA5 ... 127 FB86
Newick Rd, E5 ... 66 DV62
Newing Grn, Brom. BR1 ... 124 EK94
NEWINGTON, SE1 ... 201 H8
Newington Barrow Way, N7 ... 65 DM62
Newington Butts, SE1 ... 200 G9
SE11 ... 200 G9
Newington Causeway, SE1 ... 200 G7
Newington Grn, N1 ... 66 DR64
N16 ... 66 DR64
Newington Grn Rd, N1 ... 84 DR65
New Inn Bdy, EC2 ... 197 N4
New Inn Pas, WC2 ... 196 C9
New Inn Sq, EC2 ... 197 N4
New Inn St, EC2 ... 197 N4
New Inn Yd, EC2 ... 197 N4
New James Ct, SE15 *off Nunhead La* ... 102 DV83
New Jersey Ter, SE15 *off Nunhead La* ... 102 DV83
New Jubilee Ct, Wdf.Grn. IG8 *off Grange Av* ... 48 EG52
New Kent Rd, SE1 ... 201 H7
New Kings Rd, SW6 ... 99 CZ82
New King St, SE8 ... 103 EA79
Newland Cl, Pnr. HA5 ... 40 BY51
Newland Ct, EC1 *off Bath St* ... 84 DR70
Wembley HA9 *off Forty Av* ... 62 CN61
Newland Dr, Enf. EN1 ... 30 DV39
Newland Gdns, W13 ... 97 CG75
Newland Rd, N8 ... 65 DL55
Newlands, Abb.L. (Bedmond) WD5 ... 7 BT26
Newlands, The, Wall. SM6 ... 159 DJ108
Newlands Av, Rad. WD7 ... 9 CF34
Thames Ditton KT7 ... 137 CE102
Woking GU22 ... 167 AZ121
Newlands Cl, Brwd. (Hutt.) CM13 ... 55 GD45
Edgware HA8 ... 42 CL48
Southall UB2 ... 96 BY78
Walton-on-Thames KT12 ... 154 BY105
Wembley HA0 ... 79 CJ65
Newlands Ct, SE9 ... 125 EN86
Newlands Dr, Slou. (Colnbr.) SL3 ... 93 BE83
Newlands Pk, SE26 ... 123 DX92
Newlands Pl, Barn. EN5 ... 27 CX43
Newlands Quay, E1 ... 202 F1
Newlands Rd, SW16 ... 141 DL96
Woodford Green IG8 ... 48 EF47
Newlands Ter, SW8 *off Queenstown Rd* ... 101 DH82
Newland St, E16 ... 86 EL74
Newlands Wk, Wat. WD25 *off Trevellance Way* ... 8 BX33
Newlands Way, Chess. KT9 ... 155 CJ106
Potters Bar EN6 ... 12 DB30
Newlands Wd, Croy. CR0 ... 161 DZ109
New La, Guil. (Sutt.Grn) GU4 ... 166 AY122
Newling Cl, E6 *off Porter Rd* ... 87 EM72
New Lo Dr, Oxt. RH8 ... 188 EF128
New London St, EC3 ... 197 N10
New Lydenburg St, SE7 ... 104 EJ76
Newlyn Cl, Orp. BR6 ... 163 ET105
St. Albans (Brick.Wd) AL2 ... 8 BY30
Uxbridge UB8 ... 76 BN71
Newlyn Gdns, Har. HA2 ... 60 BZ59
Newlyn Rd, N17 ... 46 DT53
NW2 *off Tilling Rd* ... 63 CW60
Barnet EN5 ... 27 CZ42
Welling DA16 ... 105 ET82
NEW MALDEN, KT3 ... 138 CR97
⇌ **New Malden** ... 138 CS97
Newman Cl, Horn. RM11 ... 72 FL57
Newman Pas, W1 ... 195 L7
Newman Rd, E13 ... 86 EH69
E17 *off Southcote Rd* ... 67 DX57
Bromley BR1 ... 144 EG95
Croydon CR0 ... 141 DM102
Hayes UB3 ... 77 BV73
Newmans Cl, Loug. IG10 ... 33 EP41
Newman's Ct, EC3 ... 197 L9
Newmans Dr, Brwd. (Hutt.) CM13 ... 55 GC45
Newmans La, Loug. IG10 ... 33 EN41
Surbiton KT6 ... 137 CK100
Newmans Rd, Grav. (Nthflt) DA11 ... 131 GF89
Newman's Row, WC2 ... 196 C7
Newman St, W1 ... 195 L7
Newmans Way, Barn. EN4 ... 28 DC39
Newman Yd, W1 ... 195 L8
Newmarket Av, Nthlt. UB5 ... 60 CA64
Newmarket Grn, SE9 *off Middle Pk Av* ... 124 EK87
Newmarket Way, Horn. RM12 ... 72 FL63
Newmarsh Rd, SE28 ... 87 ET74
New Mill Rd, Orp. BR5 ... 146 EW95
Newminster Rd, Mord. SM4 ... 140 DC100
New Mt St, E15 ... 85 ED66
Newnes Path, SW15 *off Putney Pk La* ... 99 CV84
Newnham Av, Ruis. HA4 ... 60 BW60
Newnham Cl, Loug. IG10 ... 32 EK44
Northolt UB5 ... 60 CC64
Slough SL2 ... 74 AU74

★ Place of interest ⇌ Railway station ⊖ London Underground station DLR Docklands Light Railway station Tra Tramlink station H Hospital Riv Pedestrian ferry landing stage

Newnham Cl, Th. Hth. CR7 ... 142 DQ96
Newnham Gdns, Nthlt. UB5 ... 60 CC64
Newnham Ms, N22
off Newnham Rd ... 45 DM53
Newnham Pl, Grays RM16 ... 111 GG77
Newnham Rd, N22 ... 45 DM53
Newnhams Cl, Brom. BR1 ... 145 EM97
Newnham Ter, SE1 ... 200 D6
Newnham Way, Har. HA3 ... 62 CL57
New N Pl, EC2 ... 197 M5
New N Rd, N1 ... 197 L1
Ilford IG6 ... 49 ER52
New N St, WC1 ... 196 B6
Newnton Cl, N4 ... 66 DR59
New Oak Rd, N2 ... 44 DC54
New Orleans Wk, N19 ... 65 DK59
New Oxford St, WC1 ... 195 N8
New Par, Ashf. TW15
off Church Rd ... 114 BM91
Rickmansworth (Chorl.) WD3
off Whitelands Av ... 21 BC42
Rickmansworth (Crox.Grn)
WD3 off The Green ... 22 BM44
New Par Flats, Rick. (Chorl.)
WD3 off Whitelands Av ... 21 BC42
New Pk Av, N13 ... 46 DQ48
New Pk Cl, Nthlt. UB5 ... 78 BY65
New Pk Ct, SW2 ... 121 DL87
New Pk Par, SW2
off Doverfield Rd ... 121 DL86
New Pk Rd, SW2 ... 121 DK88
Ashford TW15 ... 115 BQ92
Uxbridge (Hare.) UB9 ... 39 BJ53
New Peachey La, Uxb. UB8 ... 76 BK72
Newpiece, Loug. IG10 ... 33 EP41
New Pl Gdns, Upmin. RM14 ... 73 FR61
New Pl Sq, SE16 ... 202 D6
New Plaistow Rd, E15 ... 86 EE67
New Plymouth Ho, Rain.
RM13 ... 89 FF69
Newport Av, E13 ... 86 EH70
E14 ... 204 G1
Newport Cl, Enf. EN3 ... 31 DY37
Newport Ct, WC2 ... 195 N10
Newport Mead, Wat. WD19
off Kilmarnock Rd ... 40 BX49
Newport Pl, WC2 ... 195 N10
Newport Rd, E10 ... 67 EC61
E17 ... 67 DY56
SW13 ... 99 CU81
W3 ... 98 CQ75
Hayes UB4 ... 77 BR71
Hounslow (Hthrw Air.) TW6 ... 94 BN81
Newports, Swan. BR8 ... 147 FD101
Newport St, SE11 ... 200 B9
New Printing Ho Sq, WC1
off Gray's Inn Rd ... 83 DM70
New Priory Ct, NW6
off Mazenod Av ... 82 DA66
New Providence Wf, E14 ... 204 F2
Newquay Cres, Har. HA2 ... 60 BY61
Newquay Gdns, Wat. WD19
off Fulford Gro ... 39 BV47
Newquay Rd, SE6 ... 123 EB89
New Quebec St, W1 ... 194 E9
New Ride, SW7 ... 198 D4
New River Av, N8 ... 65 DM55
New River Ct, N5 ... 66 DR63
Waltham Cross (Chsht)
EN7 off Pengelly Cl ... 14 DV30
New River Cres, N13 ... 45 DP49
New River Head, EC1 ... 196 E2
New River Trd Est, Wal.Cr.
(Chsht) EN8 ... 15 DX26
New River Wk, N1 ... 84 DQ65
New River Way, N4 ... 66 DR59
New Rd, E1 ... 84 DV71
E4 ... 47 EB49
N8 ... 65 DL57
N9 ... 46 DU48
N17 ... 46 DT53
N22 ... 46 DQ53
NW7 ... 43 CY52
NW7 (Barnet Gate) ... 43 CT45
SE2 ... 106 EX77
Amersham HP6 ... 20 AS37
Borehamwood (Els.) WD6 ... 25 CK44
Brentford TW8 ... 97 CK79
Brentwood CM14 ... 54 FX47
Chalfont St. Giles HP8 ... 20 AY41
Chertsey KT16 ... 133 BF101
Dagenham RM9, RM10 ... 88 FA67
Dartford (S.Darenth) DA4 ... 148 FQ96
Epping CM16 ... 18 FA32
Esher KT10 ... 136 CC104
Esher (Clay.) KT10 ... 155 CF110
Feltham TW14 ... 115 BV88
Feltham (E.Bed.) TW14 ... 115 BR86
Feltham (Han.) TW13 ... 116 BY92
Gravesend DA11 ... 131 GH86
Grays RM17 ... 110 GA79
Grays (Manor Way) RM17 ... 110 GB79
Harrow HA1 ... 61 CF63
Hayes UB3 ... 95 BQ80
Hounslow TW3 ... 96 CB84
Ilford IG3 ... 69 ES61
Kings Langley (Chipper.)
WD4 ... 5 BF30
Kingston upon Thames
KT2 ... 118 CN94
Leatherhead KT22 ... 155 CF110
Mitcham CR4 ... 140 DF102
Orpington BR6 ... 146 EU101
Oxted (Lmpfld) RH8 ... 188 EH130
Potters Bar (S.Mimms) EN6 ... 11 CU33
Radlett WD7 ... 25 CE36
Radlett (Shenley) WD7 ... 10 CN34
Rainham RM13 ... 89 FG69
Richmond TW10 ... 117 CJ91
Rickmansworth (Ch.End)
WD3 ... 21 BF39
Rickmansworth (Crox.Grn)
WD3 ... 22 BN43
Romford (Abridge) RM4 ... 34 EX44
Sevenoaks (Sund.) TN14 ... 180 EX124
Shepperton TW17 ... 135 BP97
Slough (Datchet) SL3 ... 92 AX81
Slough (Langley) SL3 ... 93 BA76
Staines TW18 ... 113 BC92
Swanley BR8 ... 147 FF97
Swanley (Hext.) BR8 ... 127 FF94
Tadworth KT20 ... 173 CW123
Uxbridge UB8 ... 77 BQ70
New Rd, Wat. WD17 ... 24 BW42
Watford (Let.Hth) WD25 ... 25 CE39
Welling DA16 ... 106 EV82
West Molesey KT8 ... 136 CA97
Weybridge KT13 ... 153 BQ106
New Rd Hill, Kes. BR2 ... 162 EL109
Orpington BR6 ... 162 EL109
New Row, WC2 ... 195 P10
Newry Rd, Twick. TW1 ... 97 CG84
Newsam Av, N15 ... 66 DR57
★ New Scotland Yd, SW1 ... 199 M6
Newsham Rd, Wok. GU21 ... 166 AT117
Newsholme Dr, N21 ... 29 DM43
NEW SOUTHGATE, N11 ... 45 DK49
⇌ New Southgate ... 45 DH50
New Spring Gdns Wk, SE11
off Goding St ... 101 DL78
New Sq, WC2 ... 196 C8
Feltham TW14 ... 115 BQ88
Slough SL1 ... 92 AT75
New Sq Pas, WC2
off New Sq ... 83 DM72
Newstead Av, Orp. BR6 ... 145 ER104
Newstead Ri, Cat. CR3 ... 186 DV126
Newstead Rd, SE12 ... 124 EE87
Newstead Wk, Cars. SM5 ... 140 DC101
Newstead Way, SW19 ... 119 CX91
New St, EC2 ... 197 N7
Staines TW18 ... 114 BG91
Watford WD18 ... 24 BW42
Westerham TN16 ... 189 EQ127
New St Hill, Brom. BR1 ... 124 EH92
New St Sq, EC4 ... 196 E8
New Swan Yd, Grav. DA12
off Bank St ... 131 GH86
New Tank Hill Rd, Purf.
RM19 ... 108 FN76
Newteswell Dr, Wal.Abb. EN9 ... 15 ED32
Newton Abbot Rd, Grav.
(Nthflt) DA11 ... 131 GF89
Newton Av, N10 ... 44 DG53
W3 ... 98 CQ75
Newton Cl, E17 ... 67 DY58
Harrow HA2 ... 60 CA61
Slough SL3 ... 93 AZ75
Newton Ct, Wind. (Old Wind.)
SL4 ... 112 AU86
Newton Cres, Borwd. WD6 ... 26 CQ42
Newton Gro, W4 ... 98 CS77
Newton Ho, Enf. EN3
off Exeter Rd ... 31 DX41
Newton La, Wind. (Old Wind.)
SL4 ... 112 AV86
Newton Pl, E14 ... 203 P8
Newton Rd, E15 ... 67 ED64
N15 ... 66 DT57
NW2 ... 63 CW62
SW19 ... 119 CY94
W2 ... 82 DA72
Chigwell IG7 ... 50 EV50
Harrow HA3 ... 41 CE54
Isleworth TW7 ... 97 CF82
Purley CR8 ... 159 DJ112
Tilbury RM18 ... 111 GG82
Welling DA16 ... 106 EU83
Wembley HA0 ... 80 CM66
Newtons Cl, Rain. RM13 ... 89 FF66
Newtons Ct, Dart. DA2 ... 109 FR84
Newtonside Orchard,
Wind. SL4 ... 112 AU86
Newton St, WC2 ... 196 A8
Newtons Yd, SW18
off Wandsworth High St ... 120 DA85
Newton Wk, Edg. HA8
off North Rd ... 42 CP53
Newton Way, N18 ... 46 DQ50
Newton Wd, Ashtd. KT21 ... 156 CL114
Newton Wd Rd, Ashtd. KT21 ... 172 CM116
NEW TOWN, Dart. DA1 ... 128 FN86
Newtown Rd, Uxb. (Denh.)
UB9 ... 76 BH65
Newtown St, SW11
off Strasburg Rd ... 101 DH81
New Trinity Rd, N2 ... 64 DD55
New Turnstile, WC1 ... 196 B7
New Union Cl, E14 ... 204 E6
New Union St, EC2 ... 197 K7
H New Victoria Hosp,
Kings.T. KT2 ... 138 CS95
New Wanstead, E11 ... 68 EF58
New Way Rd, NW9 ... 62 CS56
New Wf Rd, N1 ... 83 DL68
New Wickham La, Egh.
TW20 ... 113 BA94
New Windsor St, Uxb. UB8 ... 76 BJ67
NEWYEARS GREEN, Uxb.
UB9 ... 58 BN59
New Years Grn La, Uxb.
(Hare.) UB9 ... 58 BL58
New Years La, Orp. BR6 ... 164 EU114
Sevenoaks (Knock.) TN14 ... 179 ET116
New Zealand Av, Walt. KT12 ... 135 BT102
New Zealand Way, W12 ... 81 CV73
Rainham RM13 ... 89 FF69
Niagara Av, W5 ... 97 CJ77
Niagara Cl, N1
off Cropley St ... 84 DR68
Waltham Cross (Chsht) EN8 ... 15 DX29
Nibthwaite Rd, Har. HA1 ... 61 CE57
Nicholas Cl, Grnf. UB6 ... 78 CB68
South Ockendon RM15 ... 91 FW69
Watford WD24 ... 23 BV37
Nicholas Ct, E13
off Tunmarsh La ... 86 EH69
Nicholas Gdns, W5 ... 97 CK75
Woking GU22 ... 167 BE116
Nicholas La, EC4 ... 197 L10
Nicholas Ms, W4
off Short Rd ... 98 CS79
Nicholas Pas, EC4 ... 197 L10
Nicholas Rd, E1 ... 84 DW70
Borehamwood (Els.) WD6 ... 26 CM44
Croydon CR0 ... 159 DL105
Dagenham RM8 ... 70 EZ61
Nicholas Wk, Grays RM16
off Godman Rd ... 111 GH75
Nicholas Way, Nthwd. HA6 ... 39 BQ53
Nicholay Rd, N19 ... 65 DK60
Nichol Cl, N14 ... 45 DK46
Nicholes Rd, Houns. TW3 ... 96 CA84
Nichol La, Brom. BR1 ... 124 EG94
Nicholl Rd, Epp. CM16 ... 17 ET31
Nicholls Av, Uxb. UB8 ... 76 BN70
Nichollsfield Wk, N7
off Hillmarton Rd ... 65 DM64
Nicholls Pt, E15
off Park Gro ... 86 EG67
Nicholl St, E2 ... 84 DU67
Nichols Cl, N4
off Osborne Rd ... 65 DN60
Chessington KT9
off Merritt Gdns ... 155 CJ107
Nichols Ct, E2 ... 197 P1
Nichols Grn, W5 ... 80 CL71
Nicholson Ms, Egh. TW20
off Nicholson Wk ... 113 BA92
Nicholson Rd, Croy. CR0 ... 142 DT102
Nicholson St, SE1 ... 200 F3
Nicholson Wk, Egh. TW20 ... 113 BA92
Nicholson Way, Sev. TN13 ... 191 FK122
Nickelby Cl, SE28 ... 88 EW72
Uxbridge UB8 ... 77 BP72
Nickols Wk, SW18
off Jew's Row ... 100 DB84
Nicola Cl, Har. HA3 ... 41 CD54
South Croydon CR2 ... 160 DQ107
Nicola Ms, Ilf. IG6 ... 49 EP52
Nicol Cl, Ger.Cr. (Chal.St.P.)
SL9 ... 36 AX53
Twickenham TW1
off Cassilis Rd ... 117 CH86
Nicol End, Ger.Cr. (Chal.St.P.)
SL9 ... 36 AW53
Nicoll Pl, NW4 ... 63 CV58
Nicoll Rd, NW10 ... 80 CS67
Nicoll Way, Borwd. WD6 ... 26 CR43
Nicol Rd, Ger.Cr. (Chal.St.P.)
SL9 ... 36 AW53
Nicolson Dr, Bushey (Bushey Hth)
WD23 ... 40 CC46
Nicolson Rd, Orp. BR5 ... 146 EX101
Nicosia Rd, SW18 ... 120 DE87
Niederwald Rd, SE26 ... 123 DY91
Nield Rd, Hayes UB3 ... 95 BT75
Nield Way, Rick. WD3 ... 37 BF45
Nigel Cl, Nthlt. UB5
off Church Rd ... 78 BY67
Nigel Fisher Way, Chess.
KT9 ... 155 CJ108
Nigel Ms, Ilf. IG1 ... 69 EP63
Nigel Playfair Av, W6
off King St ... 99 CV77
Nigel Rd, E7 ... 68 EJ64
SE15 ... 102 DU83
Nigeria Rd, SE7 ... 104 EJ80
Nightingale Av, E4 ... 48 EE50
Harrow HA1 ... 61 CH59
Leatherhead (W.Hors.)
KT24 ... 169 BR124
Upminster RM14 ... 73 FT60
Nightingale Cl, E4 ... 48 EE49
W4 off Grove Pk Ter ... 98 CQ79
Abbots Langley WD5 ... 7 BU31
Carshalton SM5 ... 140 DG103
Cobham KT11 ... 154 BX111
Epsom KT19 ... 156 CN112
Gravesend (Nthflt) DA11 ... 130 GE91
Pinner HA5 ... 60 BW57
Radlett WD7 ... 25 CF36
Westerham (Bigg.H.) TN16 ... 178 EJ115
Nightingale Ct, E11
off Nightingale La ... 68 EH57
Slough SL1
off St. Laurence Way ... 92 AU76
Nightingale Cres, Lthd.
(W.Hors.) KT24 ... 169 BQ124
Romford RM3 ... 52 FL54
Nightingale Dr, Epsom
KT19 ... 156 CP107
Nightingale Est, E5 ... 66 DU62
Nightingale Gro, SE13 ... 123 ED85
Dartford DA1 ... 108 FN84
Nightingale Hts, SE18
off Nightingale Vale ... 105 EP79
Nightingale Ho, E1
off Thomas More St ... 84 DU74
Nightingale La, E11 ... 68 EG57
N6 ... 64 DE60
N8 ... 65 DL56
SW4 ... 120 DF87
SW12 ... 120 DF87
Bromley BR1 ... 144 EJ96
Richmond TW10 ... 118 CL87
Sevenoaks (Ide Hill) TN14 ... 190 FB130
Nightingale Ms, E3
off Chisenhale Rd ... 85 DY68
E11 ... 68 EG57
SE11 ... 200 E8
Kingston upon Thames
KT1 off South La ... 137 CK97
Nightingale Pl, SE18 ... 105 EN79
SW10 off Fulham Rd ... 100 DC79
Rickmansworth WD3
off Nightingale Rd ... 38 BK45
Nightingale Rd, E5 ... 66 DV62
N1 ... 84 DQ65
N9 ... 30 DW44
N22 ... 45 DL53
NW10 ... 81 CT68
W7 ... 79 CF74
Bushey WD23 ... 24 CA43
Carshalton SM5 ... 140 DF104
Esher KT10 ... 154 BZ106
Hampton TW12 ... 116 CA92
Orpington BR5 ... 145 EQ100
Rickmansworth WD3 ... 38 BJ46
South Croydon CR2 ... 161 DX111
Waltham Cross (Chsht) EN7 ... 14 DQ25
Walton-on-Thames KT12 ... 135 BV101
West Molesey KT8 ... 136 CB99
Nightingales, Wal.Abb. EN9
off Roundhills ... 16 EE34
Nightingales, The, Stai.
TW19 ... 114 BM87
Nightingales Cor, Amer. HP7
off Chalfont Sta Rd ... 20 AW40
Nightingale Shott, Egh.
TW20 ... 113 AZ93
Nightingales La, Ch.St.G. HP8 ... 36 AX46
Nightingale Sq, SW12 ... 120 DG87
Nightingale Vale, SE18 ... 105 EN79
Nightingale Wk, SW4 ... 121 DH86
Nightingale Way, E6 ... 86 EL71
Redhill (Bletch.) RH1 ... 186 DS134
Swanley BR8 ... 147 FE97
Uxbridge (Denh.) UB9 ... 57 BF59
Nile Cl, N16 off Evering Rd ... 66 DT62
Nile Dr, N9 ... 46 DW47
Nile Path, SE18
off Jackson St ... 105 EN79
Nile Rd, E13 ... 86 EJ68
Nile St, N1 ... 197 J2
Nile Ter, SE15 ... 102 DT78
Nimbus Rd, Epsom KT19 ... 156 CR110
Nimegen Way, SE22 ... 122 DS85
Nimmo Dr, Bushey (Bushey Hth)
WD23 ... 41 CD45
Nimrod Cl, Nthlt. UB5 ... 78 BX69
Nimrod Pas, N1
off Tottenham Rd ... 84 DS65
Nimrod Rd, SW16 ... 121 DH93
Nina Mackay Cl, E15
off Arthingworth St ... 86 EE67
Nine Acres Cl, E12 ... 68 EL64
Nineacres Way, Couls. CR5 ... 175 DL116
NINE ELMS, SW8 ... 101 DH80
Nine Elms Av, Uxb. UB8 ... 76 BK71
Nine Elms Cl, Felt. TW14 ... 115 BT88
Uxbridge UB8 ... 76 BK72
Nine Elms Gro, Grav. DA11 ... 131 GG87
Nine Elms La, SW8 ... 101 DJ80
Ninefields, Wal.Abb. EN9 ... 16 EF33
Ninehams Cl, Cat. CR3 ... 176 DR120
Ninehams Gdns, Cat. CR3 ... 176 DR120
Ninehams Rd, Cat. CR3 ... 176 DR121
Westerham (Tats.) TN16 ... 178 EJ121
Nine Stiles Cl, Uxb. (Denh.)
UB9 ... 76 BH65
Nineteenth Rd, Mitch. CR4 ... 141 DL98
Ninhams Wd, Orp. BR6 ... 163 EN105
Ninnings Rd, Ger.Cr.
(Chal.St.P.) SL9 ... 37 AZ52
Ninnings Way, Ger.Cr.
(Chal.St.P.) SL9 ... 37 AZ52
Ninth Av, Hayes UB3 ... 77 BU73
Nisbet Ho, E9
off Homerton High St ... 67 DX64
Nisbett Wk, Sid. DA14
off Sidcup High St ... 126 EU91
Nita Rd, Brwd. CM14 ... 54 FW50
Nithdale Rd, SE18 ... 105 EP80
Nithsdale Gro, Uxb. UB10
off Tweeddale Gro ... 59 BQ62
Niton Cl, Barn. EN5 ... 27 CX44
Niton Rd, Rich. TW9 ... 98 CN83
Niton St, SW6 ... 99 CX80
Niven Cl, Borwd. WD6 ... 26 CQ39
Nixey Cl, Slou. SL1 ... 92 AU75
N.L.A. Twr, Croy. CR0 ... 142 DR103
No. 1 St, SE18
off Duke of Wellington Av ... 105 EP76
NOAK HILL, Rom. RM4 ... 52 FK47
Noak Hill Rd, Rom. RM3 ... 52 FJ49
Nobel Dr, Hayes UB3 ... 95 BR80
Nobel Rd, N18 ... 46 DW50
Noble St, EC2 ... 197 H8
Walton-on-Thames KT12 ... 135 BV104
Nobles Way, Egh. TW20 ... 112 AY93
Noel Coward Ho, SW1
off Vauxhall Br Rd ... 101 DJ77
NOEL PARK, N22 ... 45 DN54
Noel Pk Rd, N22 ... 45 DN54
Noel Rd, E6 ... 86 EL70
N1 ... 83 DP68
W3 ... 80 CP72
Noel Sq, Dag. RM8 ... 70 EW63
Noel St, W1 ... 195 L9
Noel Ter, SE23
off Dartmouth Rd ... 122 DW89
Noke Dr, Red. RH1 ... 184 DG133
Noke Fm Barns, Couls. CR5 ... 174 DF122
Noke La, St.Alb. AL2 ... 8 BY26
Noke Side, St.Alb. AL2 ... 8 CA27
Nolan Way, E5 ... 66 DU63
Nolton Pl, Edg. HA8 ... 42 CM53
Nonsuch Cl, Ilf. IG6 ... 49 EP51
Nonsuch Ct Av, Epsom KT17 ... 157 CV110
Nonsuch Ho, SW19
off Chapter Way ... 140 DD95
Nonsuch Ind Est, Epsom
KT17 ... 156 CS111
★ Nonsuch Mansion Ho,
Sutt. SM3 ... 157 CW107
Nonsuch Wk, Sutt. SM2 ... 157 CW110
Nora Gdns, NW4 ... 63 CX56
NORBITON, Kings.T. KT2 ... 138 CP96
⇌ Norbiton ... 138 CN95
Norbiton Av, Kings.T. KT1 ... 138 CN96
Norbiton Common Rd,
Kings.T. KT1 ... 138 CP97
Norbiton Rd, E14 ... 85 DZ72
Norbreck Gdns, NW10
off Lytham Gro ... 80 CM69
Norbreck Par, NW10
off Lytham Gro ... 80 CM69
Norbroke St, W12 ... 81 CT73
Norburn St, W10
off Chesterton Rd ... 81 CY71
NORBURY, SW16 ... 141 DN95
⇌ Norbury ... 141 DM95
Norbury Av, SW16 ... 141 DM95
Hounslow TW3 ... 117 CD85
Thornton Heath CR7 ... 141 DN96
Watford WD24 ... 24 BW39
Norbury Cl, SW16 ... 141 DN95
Norbury Ct Rd, SW16 ... 141 DL97
Norbury Cres, SW16 ... 141 DM95
Norbury Cross, SW16 ... 141 DL97
Norbury Gdns, Rom. RM6 ... 70 EX57
Norbury Gro, NW7 ... 42 CS48
Norbury Hill, SW16 ... 121 DN94
Norbury Ri, SW16 ... 141 DL97
Norbury Rd, E4 ... 47 EA50
Feltham TW13 ... 115 BT90
Reigate RH2 ... 183 CZ134
Thornton Heath CR7 ... 142 DQ96
Norcombe Gdns, Har. HA3 ... 61 CJ58
Norcott Cl, Hayes UB4 ... 78 BW70
Norcott Rd, N16 ... 66 DU61
Norcroft Gdns, SE22 ... 122 DU87
Norcutt Rd, Twick. TW2 ... 117 CE88
Nordenfeldt Rd, Erith DA8 ... 107 FD78
Nordmann Pl, S.Ock. RM15 ... 91 FX70
Norfield Rd, Dart. DA2 ... 127 FC91
Norfolk Av, N13 ... 45 DP51
N15 ... 66 DT58
South Croydon CR2 ... 160 DU110
Watford WD24 ... 24 BW38
Norfolk Cl, N2 off Park Rd ... 64 DE55
Norfolk Cl, N13 ... 45 DP51
Barnet EN4 ... 28 DG42
Dartford DA1 ... 128 FN86
Twickenham TW1
off Cassilis Rd ... 117 CH86
Norfolk Cres, W2 ... 194 C8
Sidcup DA15 ... 125 ES87
Norfolk Fm Cl, Wok. GU22 ... 167 BD116
Norfolk Fm Rd, Wok. GU22 ... 167 BD115
Norfolk Gdns, Bexh. DA7 ... 106 EZ81
Borehamwood WD6 ... 26 CR42
Norfolk Ho, SE3 ... 104 EE79
SW1 off Regency St ... 101 DK77
Norfolk Ho Rd, SW16 ... 121 DK90
Norfolk Ms, W10
off Blagrove Rd ... 81 CZ71
Norfolk Pl, W2 ... 194 A8
Grays (Chaff.Hun.) RM16 ... 109 FW78
Welling DA16 ... 106 EU82
Norfolk Rd, E6 ... 87 EM67
E17 ... 47 DX54
NW8 ... 82 DD67
NW10 ... 80 CS66
SW19 ... 120 DE94
Barking IG11 ... 87 ES66
Barnet EN5 ... 28 DA41
Dagenham RM10 ... 71 FB64
Enfield EN3 ... 30 DV44
Esher (Clay.) KT10 ... 155 CE106
Feltham TW13 ... 116 BW88
Gravesend DA12 ... 131 GK86
Harrow HA1 ... 60 CB57
Ilford IG3 ... 69 ES60
Rickmansworth WD3 ... 38 BL46
Romford RM7 ... 71 FC58
Thornton Heath CR7 ... 142 DQ97
Upminster RM14 ... 72 FN62
Uxbridge UB8 ... 76 BK65
Norfolk Row, SE1 ... 200 B8
Norfolk Sq, W2 ... 194 A9
Norfolk Sq Ms, W2 ... 194 A9
Norfolk St, E7 ... 68 EG63
Norfolk Ter, W6 off Field Rd ... 99 CY78
Norgrove Pk, Ger.Cr. SL9 ... 56 AY56
Norgrove St, SW12 ... 120 DG87
Norheads La, Warl. CR6 ... 178 EG119
Westerham (Bigg.H.) TN16 ... 178 EJ116
Norhyrst Av, SE25 ... 142 DT97
NORK, Bans. SM7 ... 173 CY115
Nork Gdns, Bans. SM7 ... 157 CY114
Nork Ri, Bans. SM7 ... 173 CX116
Nork Way, Bans. SM7 ... 173 CY115
Norland Ho, W11 ... 81 CX74
Norland Pl, W11 ... 81 CY74
Norland Rd, W11 ... 81 CX74
Norlands Cres, Chis. BR7 ... 145 EP95
Norlands Gate, Chis. BR7 ... 145 EP95
Norlands La, Egh. TW20 ... 133 BE97
Norland Sq, W11 ... 81 CY74
Norley Vale, SW15 ... 119 CU88
Norlington Rd, E10 ... 67 EC60
E11 ... 67 EC60
Norman Av, N22 ... 45 DP53
Epsom KT17 ... 157 CT112
Feltham TW13 ... 116 BY89
South Croydon CR2 ... 160 DQ110
Southall UB1 ... 78 BY73
Twickenham TW1 ... 117 CH87
Normanby Cl, SW15 ... 119 CZ85
Normanby Rd, NW10 ... 63 CT63
Norman Cl, Epsom KT18 ... 173 CV119
Orpington BR6 ... 145 EQ104
Romford RM5 ... 51 FB54
Waltham Abbey EN9 ... 15 ED33
Norman Colyer Ct, Epsom
KT19 off Hollymoor La ... 156 CR110
Norman Ct, Ilf. IG2 ... 69 ER59
Potters Bar EN6 ... 12 DC30
Woodford Green IG8
off Monkhams Av ... 48 EH50
Norman Cres, Brwd. CM13 ... 55 GA48
Hounslow TW5 ... 96 BX81
Pinner HA5 ... 40 BW53
Normand Gdns, W14
off Greyhound Rd ... 99 CY79
Normand Ms, W14
off Normand Rd ... 99 CZ79
Normand Rd, W14 ... 99 CZ79
Normandy Av, Barn. EN5 ... 27 CZ43
Normandy Cl, SE26 ... 123 DY90
Normandy Dr, Hayes UB3 ... 77 BQ72
Normandy Rd, SW9 ... 101 DN81
Normandy Ter, E16 ... 86 EH72
Normandy Wk, Egh. TW20
off Mullens Rd ... 113 BC92
Normandy Way, Erith DA8 ... 107 FE81
Norman Gro, E3 ... 85 DY68
Normanhurst, Ashf. TW15 ... 114 BN92
Brentwood (Hutt.) CM13 ... 55 GC44
Normanhurst Av, Bexh. DA7 ... 106 EX81
Normanhurst Dr, Twick. TW1
off St. Margarets Rd ... 117 CH85
Normanhurst Rd, SW2 ... 121 DM89
Orpington BR5 ... 146 EV96
Walton-on-Thames KT12 ... 136 BX103
Norman Rd, E6 ... 87 EM70
E11 ... 67 ED61
N15 ... 66 DT57
SE10 ... 103 EB80
SW19 ... 120 DC94
Ashford TW15 ... 115 BR93
Belvedere DA17 ... 107 FB76
Dartford DA1 ... 128 FL88
Hornchurch RM11 ... 71 FG59
Ilford IG1 ... 69 EP64
Sutton SM1 ... 158 DA106
Thornton Heath CR7 ... 141 DP99
Normans, The, Slou. SL2 ... 74 AV72
Norman's Bldgs, EC1
off Ironmonger Row ... 84 DQ69
Normans Cl, NW10 ... 80 CR65
Gravesend DA11 ... 131 GG87
Uxbridge UB8 ... 76 BL71
Normansfield Av, Tedd. TW11 ... 117 CJ94
Normansfield Cl, Bushey
WD23 ... 40 CB45
Normanshire Av, E4 ... 47 EC49

Normanshire Dr, E4 ...47 EA49
Normans Mead, NW10 ...80 CR65
Norman St, EC1 ...197 H3
Normanton Av, SW19 ...120 DA89
Normanton Pk, E4 ...48 EE48
Normanton Rd, S.Croy. CR2 .160 DS107
Normanton St, SE23 ...123 DX89
Norman Way, N14 ...45 DL47
W3 ...80 CP71
Normington Cl, SW16 ...121 DN92
Norrice Lea, N2 ...64 DD57
Norris Cl, Epsom KT19 ...156 CP111
St. Albans (Lon.Col.) AL2 ...9 CH26
Norris Rd, Stai. TW18 ...113 BF91
Norris St, SW1 ...199 M1
Norris Way, Dart. DA1 ...107 FF83
Norroy Rd, SW15 ...99 CX84
Norrys Cl, Barn. EN4 ...28 DF43
Norrys Rd, Barn. EN4 ...28 DF42
Norseman Cl, Ilf. IG3 ...70 EV60
Norseman Way, Grnf. UB6
off Olympic Way ...78 CB67
Norstead Pl, SW15 ...119 CU89
Norsted La, Orp. BR6 ...164 EU110
North Access Rd, E17 ...67 DX58
North Acre, NW9 ...42 CS53
Banstead SM7 ...173 CZ116
NORTH ACTON, W3 ...80 CR70
⊖ **North Acton** ...80 CR70
North Acton Rd, NW10 ...80 CR69
Northallerton Way, Rom.
RM3 ...52 FK50
Northall Rd, Bexh. DA7 ...107 FC82
Northampton Gro, N1 ...66 DR64
Northampton Pk, N1 ...84 DQ65
Northampton Rd, EC1 ...196 E4
Croydon CR0 ...142 DU103
Enfield EN3 ...31 DY42
Northampton Row, EC1 ...196 E3
Northampton Sq, EC1 ...196 F3
Northampton St, N1 ...84 DQ66
Northanger Rd, SW16 ...121 DL93
North App, Nthwd. HA6 ...39 BQ47
Watford WD25 ...23 BT35
North Arc, Croy. CR0
off North End ...142 DQ103
North Audley St, W1 ...194 F9
North Av, N18 ...46 DU49
W13 ...79 CH72
Brentwood CM14 ...53 FR45
Carshalton SM5 ...158 DF108
Harrow HA2 ...60 CB58
Hayes UB3 ...77 BU73
Radlett (Shenley) WD7 ...10 CL32
Richmond TW9
off Sandycombe Rd ...98 CN81
Southall UB1 ...78 BZ73
Walton-on-Thames (Whiteley Vill.)
KT12 ...153 BS109
NORTHAW, Pot.B. EN6 ...12 DF30
Northaw Pl, Pot.B. EN6 ...12 DD30
Northaw Rd E, Pot.B. (Cuffley)
EN6 ...13 DK31
Northaw Rd W, Pot.B. EN6 ...12 DG30
North Bk, NW8 ...194 A3
Northbank Rd, E17 ...47 EC54
NORTH BECKTON, E6 ...86 EL70
North Birkbeck Rd, E11 ...67 ED62
Northborough Rd, SW16 ...141 DK97
Northbourne, Brom. BR2 ...144 EG101
Northbourne Rd, SW4 ...101 DK84
North Branch Av, W10
off Harrow Rd ...81 CW69
Northbrook Dr, Nthwd. HA6 ...39 BS53
Northbrook Rd, N22 ...45 DL52
SE13 ...123 ED85
Barnet EN5 ...27 CY44
Croydon CR0 ...142 DR99
Ilford IG1 ...69 EN61
Northburgh St, EC1 ...196 G4
North Carriage Dr, W2 ...194 B10
NORTH CHEAM, Sutt. SM3 .139 CW104
Northchurch, SE17 ...201 L10
Northchurch Rd, N1 ...84 DR66
Wembley HA9 ...80 CM65
Northchurch Ter, N1 ...84 DS66
North Circular Rd, E4 (A406) .47 DZ52
E6 (A406) ...87 EP68
E11 (A406) ...48 EJ54
E12 (A406) ...69 EN64
E17 (A406) ...47 DZ52
E18 (A406) ...48 EJ54
N3 (A406) ...64 DB55
N11 (A406) ...44 DD53
N12 (A406) ...44 DD53
N13 (A406) ...45 DN50
N18 (A406) ...46 DS50
NW2 (A406) ...62 CS62
NW10 (A406) ...80 CP66
NW11 (A406) ...63 CY56
W3 (A406) ...98 CM75
W4 (A406) ...98 CM75
W5 (A406) ...98 CM75
Barking (A406) IG11 ...87 EP68
Ilford (A406) IG1, IG4 ...68 EL60
Northcliffe Cl, Wor.Pk. KT4 ..138 CS104
Northcliffe Dr, N20 ...43 CZ46
North Cl, Barn. EN5 ...27 CW43
Bexleyheath DA6 ...106 EX84
Chigwell IG7 ...50 EU50
Dagenham RM10 ...88 FA67
Feltham TW14 *off North Rd* .115 BR86
Morden SM4 ...139 CY98
St. Albans AL2 ...8 CB25
North Colonnade, E14 ...204 A2
North Common, Wey. KT13 .153 BP105
North Common Rd, W5 ...80 CL73
Uxbridge UB8 ...58 BK64
Northcote, Add. KT15 ...152 BK105
Leatherhead (Oxshott)
KT22 ...154 CC114
Pinner HA5 ...40 BW54
Northcote Av, W5 ...80 CL73
Isleworth TW7 ...117 CG85
Southall UB1 ...78 BY73
Surbiton KT5 ...138 CN101
Northcote Ms, SW11
off Northcote Rd ...100 DE84
Northcote Rd, E17 ...67 DY56
NW10 ...80 CS66
SW11 ...100 DE84
Croydon CR0 ...142 DR100
Gravesend DA11 ...131 GF88
New Malden KT3 ...138 CQ97
Sidcup DA14 ...125 ES91
Twickenham TW1 ...117 CG85
North Cotts, St.Alb.
(Lon.Col.) AL2 ...9 CG25
Northcott Av, N22 ...45 DL53
Northcotts, Abb.L. WD5
off Long Elms ...7 BR33
North Countess Rd, E17 ...47 DZ54
Northcourt, Rick. (Mill End)
WD3 *off Springwell Av* ...38 BG46
NORTH CRAY, Sid. DA14 ...126 FA90
North Cray Rd, Bex. DA5 ...126 EZ90
Sidcup DA14 ...126 EY93
North Cres, E16 ...85 ED70
N3 ...43 CZ54
WC1 ...195 M6
Northcroft Cl, Egh. (Eng.Grn)
TW20 ...112 AV92
Northcroft Gdns, Egh.
(Eng.Grn) TW20 ...112 AV92
Northcroft Rd, W13 ...97 CH75
Egham (Eng.Grn) TW20 ...112 AV92
Epsom KT19 ...156 CR108
Northcroft Ter, W13
off Northcroft Rd ...97 CH75
Northcroft Vil, Egh. (Eng.Grn)
TW20 ...112 AV92
North Cross Rd, SE22 ...122 DT85
Ilford IG6 ...69 EQ56
North Dene, NW7 ...42 CR48
Northdene, Chig. IG7 ...49 ER50
North Dene, Houns. TW3 ...96 CB81
Northdene Gdns, N15 ...66 DT58
North Down, S.Croy. CR2 ...160 DS111
Northdown Cl, Ruis. HA4 ...59 BT62
Northdown Gdns, Ilf. IG2 ...69 ES57
Northdown Rd, Cat. (Wold.)
CR3 ...177 EA123
Gerrards Cross (Chal.St.P.)
SL9 ...36 AY51
Hornchurch RM11 ...71 FH59
Longfield DA3 ...149 FX96
Sutton SM2 ...158 DA110
Welling DA16 ...106 EV82
North Downs Cres, Croy.
(New Adgtn) CR0 ...161 EB110
🅷 **North Downs Private Hosp, The**, Cat. CR3 ...186 DT125
North Downs Rd, Croy.
(New Adgtn) CR0 ...161 EB110
Northdown St, N1 ...83 DM68
North Downs Way, Bet. RH3 .183 CU130
Caterham CR3 ...185 DN126
Godstone RH9 ...187 DY128
Oxted RH8 ...188 EE126
Redhill RH1 ...184 DG128
Reigate RH2 ...184 DD130
Sevenoaks TN13, TN14 ...181 FD118
Tadworth KT20 ...183 CX130
Westerham TN16 ...179 ER121
North Dr, SW16 ...121 DJ91
Hounslow TW3 ...96 CC82
Orpington BR6 ...163 ES105
Romford RM2 ...72 FJ55
Ruislip HA4 ...59 BS59
Slough SL2 ...74 AS69
Virginia Water GU25 ...132 AS100
⇌ **North Dulwich** ...122 DR85
⊖ **North Ealing** ...80 CM72
North End, NW3 ...64 DC61
Northend, Brwd. CM14 ...54 FW50
North End, Buck.H. IG9 ...48 EJ45
Croydon CR0 ...142 DQ103
Romford (Noak Hill) RM3 ...52 FJ47
North End Av, NW3 ...64 DC61
North End Cres, W14 ...99 CZ77
North End Ho, W14 ...99 CY77
North End La, Orp. BR6 ...163 EN110
North End Par, W14
off North End Rd ...99 CY77
North End Rd, NW11 ...64 DA60
SW6 ...99 CZ79
W14 ...99 CY77
Northend Rd, Dart. DA1 ...107 FF80
Erith DA8 ...107 FF80
North End Rd, Wem. HA9 ...62 CN62
Northend Trd Est, Erith DA8 .107 FE81
North End Way, NW3 ...64 DC61
Northern Av, N9 ...46 DT47
Northernhay Wk, Mord. SM4 .139 CY98
Northern Perimeter Rd, Houns.
(Hthrw Air.) TW6 ...95 BQ81
Northern Perimeter Rd W, Houns.
(Hthrw Air.) TW6 ...94 BK81
Northern Relief Rd, Bark. IG11 .87 EP66
Northern Rd, E13 ...86 EH67
Northern Service Rd, Barn.
EN5 ...27 CY41
Northey Av, Sutt. SM2 ...157 CZ110
North Eyot Gdns, W6 ...99 CU78
Northey St, E14 ...85 DY73
Northfield, Loug. IG10 ...32 EK42
Northfield Av, W5 ...97 CH75
W13 ...97 CH75
Orpington BR5 ...146 EW100
Pinner HA5 ...60 BX56
Northfield Cl, Brom. BR1 ...144 EL95
Hayes UB3 ...95 BT76
Northfield Ct, Stai. TW18 ...134 BH95
Northfield Cres, Sutt. SM3 ..157 CY105
Northfield Fm Ms, Cob.
KT11 ...153 BU113
Northfield Gdns, Dag. RM9
off Northfield Rd ...70 EZ63
Watford WD24 ...24 BW37
Northfield Ind Est, NW10 ...80 CN69
Northfield Pk, Hayes UB3 ...95 BT76
Northfield Path, Dag. RM9 ...70 EZ62
Northfield Pl, Wey. KT13 ...153 BP108
Northfield Rd, E6 ...87 EM66
N16 ...66 DS59
W13 ...97 CH75
Barnet EN4 ...28 DE41
Borehamwood WD6 ...26 CP39
Cobham KT11 ...153 BU113
Dagenham RM9 ...70 EZ63
Enfield EN3 ...30 DV43
Northfield Rd, Houns. TW5 ...96 BX79
Staines TW18 ...134 BH95
Waltham Cross EN8 ...15 DY32
⊖ **Northfields** ...97 CH76
Northfields, SW18 ...100 DA84
Ashtead KT21 ...172 CL119
Grays RM17 ...110 GC77
Northfields Ind Est, Wem.
HA0 ...80 CN67
Northfields Rd, W3 ...80 CP71
NORTH FINCHLEY, N12 ...44 DD50
NORTHFLEET, Grav. DA10 ...130 GD86
⇌ **Northfleet** ...130 GA86
NORTHFLEET GREEN,
Grav. DA13 ...130 GC92
Northfleet Grn Rd, Grav.
DA13 ...130 GC93
North Flockton St, SE16 ...202 B4
North Gdn, E14
off Westferry Circ ...85 DZ74
North Gdns, SW19 ...120 DD94
North Gate, NW8 ...194 B1
Northgate, Nthwd. HA6 ...39 BQ52
Northgate Dr, NW9 ...62 CS58
Northgate Ind Pk, Rom. RM5 .50 EZ54
Northgate Path, Borwd. WD6 .26 CM39
North Glade, The, Bex. DA5 .126 EZ87
North Gower St, NW1 ...195 L3
North Grn, NW9
off Clayton Fld ...42 CS52
Slough SL1 ...74 AS73
⊖ **North Greenwich** ...205 H4
North Gro, N6 ...64 DG59
N15 ...66 DR57
Chertsey KT16 ...133 BF100
NORTH HARROW, Har. HA2 ...60 CA58
⊖ **North Harrow** ...60 CA57
North Hatton Rd, Houns.
(Hthrw Air.) TW6 ...95 BR81
North Hill, N6 ...64 DF58
Rickmansworth WD3 ...21 BE40
North Hill Av, N6 ...64 DG58
North Hill Dr, Rom. RM3 ...52 FK48
North Hill Grn, Rom. RM3 ...52 FK49
NORTH HILLINGDON, Uxb.
UB10 ...77 BQ66
NORTH HYDE, Sthl. UB2 ...96 BY77
North Hyde Gdns, Hayes UB3 .95 BU77
North Hyde La, Houns. TW5 ...96 BY78
Southall UB2 ...96 BY78
North Hyde Rd, Hayes UB3 ...95 BT76
Northiam, N12 ...44 DA48
Northiam St, E9 ...84 DV67
Northington St, WC1 ...196 B5
NORTH KENSINGTON, W10 ...81 CW72
North Kent Av, Grav.
(Nthflt) DA11 ...130 GC86
Northlands, Pot.B. EN6 ...12 DD31
Northlands Av, Orp. BR6 ...163 ES105
Northlands St, SE5 ...102 DQ82
North La, Tedd. TW11 ...117 CF93
North Lo Cl, SW15 ...119 CX85
🅷 **North London Blood Transfusion Cen**, NW9 ...42 CR54
North London Business Pk,
N11 ...44 DF47
🅷 **North London Nuffield Hosp**,
Enf. EN2 ...29 DN40
NORTH LOOE, Epsom KT17 .157 CW113
North Mall, N9
off Edmonton Grn Shop Cen ...46 DV47
North Mead, Red. RH1 ...184 DF131
North Ms, WC1 ...196 C5
🅷 **North Middlesex Uni Hosp**,
N18 ...46 DS50
North Mymms Pk, Hat. AL9 ...11 CT25
NORTH OCKENDON, Upmin.
RM14 ...73 FV64
Northolm, Edg. HA8 ...42 CR49
Northolme Cl, Grays RM16
off Premier Av ...110 GC76
Northolme Gdns, Edg. HA8 ...42 CN53
Northolme Ri, Orp. BR6 ...145 ES103
Northolme Rd, N5 ...66 DQ63
NORTHOLT, UB5 ...78 BZ66
⊖ **Northolt** ...78 CA66
Northolt, N17 *off Griffin Rd* ...46 DS54
★ **Northolt Aerodrome**,
Ruis. HA4 ...77 BT65
Northolt Av, Ruis. HA4 ...59 BV64
Northolt Gdns, Grnf. UB6 ...61 CF64
⇌ **Northolt Park** ...60 CB63
Northolt Rd, Har. HA2 ...60 CB63
Hounslow (Hthrw Air.) TW6 ...94 BK81
Northolt Way, Horn. RM12 ...90 FJ65
North Orbital Rd, Rick. WD3 ...37 BE52
St. Albans AL1, AL2, AL4 ...9 CK25
Uxbridge (Denh.) UB9 ...57 BF60
Watford WD25 ...7 BU34
Northover, Brom. BR1 ...124 EF90
North Par, Chess. KT9 ...156 CL106
North Pk, SE9 ...125 EM86
Gerrards Cross (Chal.St.P.)
SL9 ...56 AY56
Iver SL0 ...93 BC76
North Pk La, Gdse. RH9 ...186 DU129
North Pas, SW18 ...100 DA84
North Perimeter Rd, Uxb.
UB8 *off Kingston La* ...76 BL69
North Pl, Mitch. CR4 ...120 DF94
Teddington TW11 ...117 CF93
Waltham Abbey EN9
off Highbridge St ...15 EB33
Northpoint, Brom. BR1
off Sherman Rd ...144 EG95
Northpoint Cl, Sutt. SM1 ...140 DC104
Northpoint Sq, NW1 ...83 DK65
North Pole La, Kes. BR2 ...162 EF107
North Pole Rd, W10 ...81 CW71
Northport St, N1 ...84 DR67
North Ride, W2 ...198 B1
Northridge Rd, Grav. DA12 ...131 GJ90
North Riding, St.Alb.
(Brick.Wd) AL2 ...8 CA30
North Rd, N6 ...64 DG59
N7 ...83 DL65
N9 ...46 DV46
SE18 ...105 ES77
SW19 ...120 DC93
W5 ...97 CK76
Belvedere DA17 ...107 FB76
Brentford TW8 ...98 CL79
North Rd, Brent. CM14 ...54 FW46
Bromley BR1 ...144 EH95
Dartford DA1 ...127 FF86
Edgware HA8 ...42 CP53
Feltham TW14 ...115 BR86
Hayes UB3 ...77 BR71
Ilford IG3 ...69 ES61
Purfleet RM19 ...109 FR77
Richmond TW9 ...98 CN83
Rickmansworth (Chorl.)
WD3 ...21 BD43
Romford (Chad.Hth) RM6 ...70 EY57
Romford (Hav.at.Bow.) RM4 .51 FE48
South Ockendon RM15 ...91 FW68
Southall UB1 ...78 CA73
Surbiton KT6 ...137 CK100
Waltham Cross EN8 ...15 DY33
Walton-on-Thames KT12 .154 BW106
West Drayton UB7 ...94 BM76
West Wickham BR4 ...143 EB102
Woking GU21 ...167 BA116
North Rd Av, Brwd. CM14 ...54 FW46
Northrop Rd, Houns.
(Hthrw Air.) TW6 ...95 BS81
North Row, W1 ...194 E10
North Several, SE3
off Orchard Rd ...103 ED82
NORTH SHEEN, Rich. TW9 ...98 CN82
⇌ **North Sheen** ...98 CN84
Northside Rd, Brom. BR1
off Mitchell Way ...144 EG95
North Side Wandsworth Common, SW18 ...120 DC85
Northspur Rd, Sutt. SM1 ...140 DA104
North Sq, N9
off St. Martins Rd ...46 DV47
NW11 ...64 DA57
Northstead Rd, SW2 ...121 DN89
North St, E13 ...86 EG68
NW4 ...63 CW57
SW4 ...101 DJ83
Barking IG11 ...87 EP65
Bexleyheath DA7 ...106 FA84
Bromley BR1 ...144 EG95
Carshalton SM5 ...140 DF104
Dartford DA1 ...128 FK87
Egham TW20 ...113 AZ92
Gravesend DA12
off South St ...131 GH87
Hornchurch RM11 ...72 FK59
Isleworth TW7 ...97 CG83
Leatherhead KT22 ...171 CG121
Redhill RH1 ...184 DF133
Romford RM1, RM5 ...71 FD55
North St Pas, E13 ...86 EH68
North Tenter St, E1 ...84 DT72
North Ter, SW3 ...198 B7
Windsor SL4
off Windsor Castle ...92 AS80
Northumberland All, EC3 ...197 N9
Northumberland Av, E12 ...68 EJ60
WC2 ...199 P2
Enfield EN1 ...30 DV39
Hornchurch RM11 ...72 FJ57
Isleworth TW7 ...97 CF81
Welling DA16 ...105 ER84
Northumberland Cl, Erith
DA8 ...107 FC80
Staines (Stanw.) TW19 ...114 BL86
Northumberland Cres, Felt.
TW14 ...115 BS86
Northumberland Gdns, N9 ...46 DT48
Bromley BR1 ...145 EN98
Isleworth TW7 ...97 CG80
Mitcham CR4 ...141 DK99
Northumberland Gro, N17 ...46 DV52
NORTHUMBERLAND HEATH,
Erith DA8 ...107 FC80
⇌ **Northumberland Park** ...46 DV53
Northumberland Pk, N17 ...46 DT52
Erith DA8 ...107 FC80
Northumberland Pl, W2 ...82 DA72
Richmond TW10 ...117 CK85
Northumberland Rd, E6 ...86 EL72
E17 ...67 EA59
Barnet EN5 ...28 DC44
Gravesend (Istead Rise)
DA13 ...131 GF94
Harrow HA2 ...60 BZ57
Northumberland Row, Twick.
TW2 *off Colne Rd* ...117 CE88
Northumberland St, WC2 ...199 P2
Northumberland Way, Erith
DA8 ...107 FC81
Northumbria St, E14 ...85 EA72
North Verbena Gdns, W6
off St. Peter's Sq ...99 CU78
Northview, N7 ...65 DL62
North Vw, SW19 ...119 CV92
W5 ...79 CJ70
Ilford IG6 ...50 EU52
Pinner HA5 ...60 BW59
Northview, Swan. BR8 ...147 FE96
North Vw Av, Til. RM18 ...111 GG81
Northview Cres, NW10 ...63 CT63
North Vw Cres, Epsom KT18 .173 CV117
North Vw Dr, Wdf.Grn. IG8 ...48 EK54
North Vw Rd, N8 ...65 DK55
Sevenoaks TN14
off Seal Rd ...191 FJ121
North Vil, NW1 ...83 DK65
North Wk, W2
off Bayswater Rd ...82 DC73
Croydon (New Adgtn)
CR0 ...161 EB106
NORTH WATFORD, Wat.
WD24 ...23 BV37
North Way, N9 ...46 DW47
N11 ...45 DJ51
NW9 ...62 CP55
Northway, NW11 ...64 DB57
Morden SM4 ...139 CY97
North Way, Pnr. HA5 ...60 BW55
Northway, Rick. WD3 ...38 BK45
North Way, Uxb. UB10 ...76 BL66
Northway, Wall. SM6 ...159 DJ105
Northway Circ, NW7 ...42 CR49
Northway Cres, NW7 ...42 CR49
Northway Ho, N20 ...44 DC46
Northway Rd, SE5 ...102 DQ83
Croydon CR0 ...142 DT100
Northways Par, NW3
off Finchley Rd ...82 DD66
North Weald Airfield, Epp.
(N.Wld Bas.) CM16 ...18 EZ26
NORTH WEALD BASSETT,
Epp. CM16 ...19 FB27
North Weald Cl, Horn. RM12 .89 FH66
Northweald La, Kings.T. KT2 .117 CK92
NORTH WEMBLEY, Wem.
HA0 ...61 CH61
⇌ **North Wembley** ...61 CK62
⊖ **North Wembley** ...61 CK62
North Western Av, Wat.
WD24, WD25 ...24 BW36
Northwest Pl, N1
off Chapel Mkt ...83 DN68
North Wf Rd, W2 ...82 DD71
Northwick Av, Har. HA3 ...61 CG58
Northwick Circle, Har. HA3 ...61 CJ58
Northwick Cl, NW8
off Northwick Ter ...82 DD70
Harrow HA1 ...61 CH60
⊖ **Northwick Park** ...61 CG59
🅷 **Northwick Pk Hosp**,
Har. HA1 ...61 CH59
Northwick Pk Rd, Har. HA1 ...61 CF58
Northwick Rd, Wat. WD19 ...40 BW49
Wembley HA0
off Glacier Way ...79 CK67
Northwick Ter, NW8 ...82 DD70
Northwick Wk, Har. HA1 ...61 CF59
Northwold Dr, Pnr. HA5
off Cuckoo Hill ...60 BW55
Northwold Est, E5 ...66 DU61
Northwold Rd, E5 ...66 DT61
N16 ...66 DT61
NORTHWOOD, HA6 ...39 BR51
⊖ **Northwood** ...39 BS52
Northwood, Grays RM16 ...111 GH75
🅷 **Northwood & Pinner Comm Hosp**, Nthwd. HA6 ...39 BU53
Northwood Av, Horn. RM12 ...71 FG63
Purley CR8 ...159 DN113
Northwood Cl, Wal.Cr. EN7 ...14 DT27
North Wd Ct, SE25
off Regina Rd ...142 DU97
Northwood Gdns, N12 ...44 DD50
Greenford UB6 ...61 CF64
Ilford IG5 ...69 EN56
Northwood Hall, N6 ...65 DJ59
NORTHWOOD HILLS,
Nthwd. HA6 ...39 BT54
⊖ **Northwood Hills** ...39 BU54
Northwood Ho, SE27 ...122 DR91
Northwood Pl, Erith DA18 ...106 EZ76
Northwood Rd, N6 ...65 DH59
SE23 ...123 DZ88
Carshalton SM5 ...158 DG107
Hounslow (Hthrw Air.) TW6 ...94 BK81
Thornton Heath CR7 ...141 DP96
Uxbridge (Hare.) UB9 ...38 BJ53
Northwood Twr, E17 ...67 EC56
Northwood Way, SE19
off Roman Ri ...122 DR93
Northwood HA6 ...39 BU52
Uxbridge (Hare.) UB9 ...38 BK53
NORTH WOOLWICH, E16 ...104 EL75
⇌ **North Woolwich** ...105 EN75
★ **North Woolwich Old Sta Mus**, E16 ...105 EN75
North Woolwich Rd, E16 ...205 L2
North Woolwich Rbt, E16
off North Woolwich Rd ...86 EK74
North Worple Way, SW14 ...98 CR83
Nortoft Rd, Ger.Cr. (Chal.St.P.)
SL9 ...37 AZ51
Norton Av, Surb. KT5 ...138 CP101
Norton Cl, E4 ...47 EA50
Borehamwood WD6 ...26 CN39
Enfield EN1 *off Brick La* ...30 DV40
Norton Folgate, E1 ...197 N6
Norton Gdns, SW16 ...141 DL96
Norton La, Cob. KT11 ...169 BT119
Norton Rd, E10 ...67 DZ60
Dagenham RM10 ...89 FD65
Uxbridge UB8 ...76 BK69
Wembley HA0 ...79 CK65
Norval Rd, Wem. HA0 ...61 CH61
Norvic Ho, Erith DA8
off Waterhead Cl ...107 FF80
Norway Dr, Slou. SL2 ...74 AV71
Norway Gate, SE16 ...203 L6
Norway Pl, E14
off Commercial Rd ...85 DZ72
Norway St, SE10 ...103 EB79
Norway Wk, Rain. RM13
off The Glen ...90 FJ70
Norwich Ho, E14
off Cordelia St ...85 EB72
Norwich Ms, Ilf. IG3
off Ashgrove Rd ...70 EU60
Norwich Pl, Bexh. DA6 ...106 FA84
Norwich Rd, E7 ...68 EG64
Dagenham RM9 ...88 FA68
Greenford UB6 ...78 CB67
Northwood HA6 ...59 BT55
Thornton Heath CR7 ...142 DQ97
Norwich St, EC4 ...196 D8
Norwich Wk, Edg. HA8 ...42 CQ52
Norwich Way, Rick. (Crox.Grn)
WD3 ...23 BP41
NORWOOD, SE19 ...122 DS93
Norwood Av, Rom. RM7 ...71 FE59
Wembley HA0 ...80 CM67
Norwood Cl, NW2 ...63 CY62
Southall UB2 ...96 CA77
Twickenham TW2
off Fourth Cross Rd ...117 CD89
Norwood Cres, Houns.
(Hthrw Air.) TW6 ...95 BQ81
Norwood Dr, Har. HA2 ...60 BZ58
Norwood Fm La, Cob. KT11 .153 BU111
Norwood Gdns, Hayes UB4 ...78 BW70
Southall UB2 ...96 BZ77
NORWOOD GREEN, Sthl.
UB2 ...96 CA77
Norwood Grn Rd, Sthl. UB2 ...96 CA77
Norwood High St, SE27 ...121 DP90
⇌ **Norwood Junction** ...142 DT98
Norwood La, Iver SL0 ...75 BD70
NORWOOD NEW TOWN,
SE19 ...122 DQ93
Norwood Pk Rd, SE27 ...122 DQ92
Norwood Rd, SE24 ...121 DP88
SE27 ...121 DP89

Norwood Rd, Sthl. UB2 .....96 BZ77
Waltham Cross (Chsht) EN8 .15 DY30
Norwood Ter, Sthl. UB2
off Tentelow La 96 CB77
Notley End, Egh. (Eng.Grn)
TW20 .....112 AW93
Notley St, SE5 .....102 DR80
Notre Dame Est, SW4 .....101 DJ84
Notson Rd, SE25 .....142 DV98
Notting Barn Rd, W10 .....81 CX70
Nottingdale Sq, W11
off Wilsham St 81 CY74
Nottingham Av, E16 .....86 EJ71
Nottingham Cl, Wat. WD25 .....7 BU33
Woking GU21 .....166 AT118
Nottingham Ct, WC2 .....195 P9
Woking GU21
off Nottingham Cl 166 AT118
Nottingham Pl, W1 .....194 F5
Nottingham Rd, E10 .....67 EC58
SW17 .....120 DF88
Isleworth TW7 .....97 CF82
Rickmansworth (Herons.)
WD3 .....37 BC45
South Croydon CR2 .....160 DQ105
Nottingham St, W1 .....194 F6
Nottingham Ter, NW1 .....194 F5
NOTTING HILL, W11 .....81 CY73
⊖ Notting Hill Gate 82 DA73
Notting Hill Gate, W11 .....82 DA74
Nova, E14 .....203 P8
Nova Ms, Sutt. SM3 .....139 CY102
Novar Cl, Orp. BR6 .....145 ET101
Nova Rd, Croy. CR0 .....141 DP101
Novar Rd, SE9 .....125 EQ88
Novello St, SW6 .....100 DA81
Novello Way, Borwd. WD6 .....26 CR39
Nowell Rd, SW13 .....99 CU79
Nower, The, Sev. TN14 .....179 ET119
Nower Hill, Pnr. HA5 .....60 BZ56
Noyna Rd, SW17 .....120 DF90
Nuding Cl, SE13 .....103 EA83
Nuffield Rd, Swan. BR8 .....127 FG93
H Nuffield Speech & Language
Unit, W5 .....79 CJ71
Nugent Ind Pk, Orp. BR5 .....146 EW99
Nugent Rd, N19 .....65 DL60
SE25 .....142 DT97
Nugents Ct, Pnr. HA5
off St. Thomas' Dr 40 BY53
Nugents Pk, Pnr. HA5 .....40 BY53
Nugent Ter, NW8 .....82 DC68
Numa Ct, Brent. TW8
off Justin Cl 97 CK80
★ No. 2 Willow Rd, NW3 .....64 DE63
Nunappleton Way, Oxt. RH8 .188 EG132
Nun Ct, EC2 .....197 K8
Nuneaton Rd, Dag. RM9 .....88 EX66
Nunfield, Kings L. (Chipper.)
WD4 .....6 BH31
NUNHEAD, SE15 .....102 DW83
⇌ Nunhead 102 DW82
Nunhead Cres, SE15 .....102 DV83
Nunhead Est, SE15 .....102 DV84
Nunhead Grn, SE15 .....102 DV83
Uxbridge (Denh.) UB9 .....57 BF58
Nunhead Gro, SE15 .....102 DV83
Nunhead La, SE15 .....102 DV83
Nunhead Pas, SE15
off Peckham Rye 102 DU83
Nunnington Cl, SE9 .....124 EL90
Nunns Rd, Enf. EN2 .....30 DQ40
Nunns Way, Grays RM17 .....110 GD77
Nunsbury Dr, Brox. EN10 .....15 DY25
Nuns Wk, Vir.W. GU25 .....132 AX99
NUPER'S HATCH, Rom. RM4 .51 FE45
Nupton Dr, Barn. EN5 .....27 CW44
Nurse Cl, Edg. HA8
off Gervase Rd 42 CQ53
Nursery, The, Erith DA8 .....107 FF80
Nursery Av, N3 .....44 DC54
Bexleyheath DA7 .....106 EZ83
Croydon CR0 .....143 DX103
Nursery Cl, SE4 .....103 DZ82
SW15 .....99 CX84
Addlestone (Wdhm) KT15 .151 BF110
Amersham HP7 .....20 AS39
Croydon CR0 .....143 DX103
Dartford DA2 .....128 FQ87
Enfield EN3 .....31 DX39
Epsom KT17 .....156 CS110
Feltham TW14 .....115 BV87
Orpington BR6 .....146 EU101
Romford RM6 .....70 EX58
Sevenoaks TN13 .....191 FJ122
South Ockendon RM15 .....91 FW70
Swanley BR8 .....147 FC96
Tadworth (Walt.Hill) KT20 .183 CU125
Woking GU21 .....166 AW116
Woodford Green IG8 .....48 EH50
Nursery Ct, N17
off Nursery St 46 DT52
Nursery Gdns, Chis. BR7 .....125 EP93
Enfield EN3 .....31 DX39
Hounslow TW4 .....116 BZ85
Staines TW18 .....114 BH94
Sunbury-on-Thames TW16 .135 BT96
Waltham Cross EN7 .....14 DR28
Nursery La, E2 .....84 DT67
E7 .....86 EG65
W10 .....81 CW71
Slough SL3 .....74 AW74
Uxbridge UB8 .....76 BK70
Nurserymans Rd, N11 .....44 DG47
Nursery Pl, Sev. TN13 .....190 FD122
Windsor (Old Wind.) SL4
off Gregory Dr 112 AV86
Nursery Rd, E9
off Morning La 84 DW65
N2 .....44 DD53
N14 .....45 DJ45
SW9 .....101 DM84
Broxbourne EN10 .....15 DY25
Loughton IG10 .....32 EJ43
Loughton (High Beach) IG10 .32 EH39
Pinner HA5 .....60 BW55
Sunbury-on-Thames TW16 .135 BS96
Sutton SM1 .....158 DC105
Tadworth (Walt.Hill) KT20 .183 CU125
Thornton Heath CR7 .....142 DR98
Nursery Rd Merton, SW19 .....140 DB96
Nursery Rd Mitcham,
Mitch. CR4 .....140 DE97
Nursery Rd Wimbledon,
SW19 off Worple Rd 119 CY94
Nursery Row, SE17 .....201 K9
Barnet EN5
off St. Albans Rd 27 CY41
Nursery St, N17 .....46 DT52
Nursery Wk, NW4 .....63 CV55
Romford RM7 .....71 FD59
Nursery Way, Stai. (Wrays.)
TW19 .....112 AX86
Nursery Waye, Uxb. UB8 .....76 BK67
Nurstead Rd, Erith DA8 .....106 FA80
Nutberry Av, Grays RM16 .....110 GA75
Nutberry Cl, Grays RM16
off Long La 110 GA75
Nutbourne St, W10 .....81 CY69
Nutbrook St, SE15 .....102 DU83
Nutbrowne Rd, Dag. RM9 .....88 EZ67
Nutcroft Gro, Lthd. (Fetch.)
KT22 .....171 CE121
Nutcroft Rd, SE15 .....102 DV80
NUTFIELD, Red. RH1 .....185 DM133
Nutfield Cl, N18 .....46 DU51
Carshalton SM5 .....140 DE104
Nutfield Gdns, Ilf. IG3 .....69 ET61
Northolt UB5 .....78 BW68
Nutfield Marsh Rd, Red.
(Nutfld) RH1 .....185 DJ130
Nutfield Rd, E15 .....67 EC63
NW2 .....63 CU61
SE22 .....122 DT85
Coulsdon CR5 .....174 DG116
Redhill RH1 .....184 DG134
Redhill (S.Merst.) RH1 .....185 DJ129
Thornton Heath CR7 .....141 DP98
Nutfield Way, Orp. BR6 .....145 EN103
Nutford Pl, W1 .....194 C8
Nuthatch Cl, Stai. TW19 .....114 BM88
Nuthatch Gdns, SE28 .....105 ER75
Nuthurst Av, SW2 .....121 DM89
Nutkin Wk, Uxb. UB8
off Park Rd 76 BL66
Nutley Cl, Swan. BR8 .....147 FF95
Nutley Ct, Reig. RH2
off Nutley La 183 CZ134
Nutley La, Reig. RH2 .....183 CZ133
Nutley Ter, NW3 .....82 DC65
Nutmead Cl, Bex. DA5 .....127 FC88
Nutmeg Cl, E16
off Cranberry La 86 EE70
Nutmeg La, E14 .....85 ED72
Nuttall St, N1 .....84 DS68
Nutter La, E11 .....68 EJ58
Nuttfield Cl, Rick. (Crox.Grn)
WD3 .....23 BP44
Nutt Gro, Edg. HA8 .....41 CK47
Nut Tree Cl, Orp. BR6 .....146 EX104
Nutt St, SE15 .....102 DT80
Nutty La, Shep. TW17 .....135 BQ98
Nutwell St, SW17 .....120 DE92
Nutwood Gdns, Wal.Cr. (Chsht)
EN7 off Great Stockwood Rd .14 DS26
Nuxley Rd, Belv. DA17 .....106 EZ79
Nyall Ct, Rom. (Gidea Pk)
RM2 .....72 FJ56
Nyanza St, SE18 .....105 ER79
Nye Bevan Est, E5 .....67 DX62
Nyefield Pk, Tad. (Walt.Hill)
KT20 .....183 CU126
Nye Way, Hem.H. (Bov.) HP3 ..5 BA28
Nylands Av, Rich. TW9 .....98 CN81
Nymans Gdns, SW20
off Hidcote Gdns 139 CV97
Nynehead St, SE14 .....103 DY80
Nyon Gro, SE6 .....123 DZ89
Nyssa Cl, Wdf.Grn. IG8
off Gwynne Pk Av 49 EM51
Nyth Cl, Upmin. RM14 .....73 FR58
Nyton Cl, N19
off Courtauld Rd 65 DL60

O

O2 Shop Cen, NW3
off Finchley Rd 82 DC65
Oakapple Cl, S.Croy. CR2 .....160 DV114
Oak Apple Ct, SE12 .....124 EG89
Oak Av, N8 .....65 DL56
N10 .....45 DH52
N17 .....46 DR52
Croydon CR0 .....143 EA103
Egham TW20 .....113 BC94
Enfield EN2 .....29 DM38
Hampton TW12 .....116 BY92
Hounslow TW5 .....96 BX80
St. Albans (Brick.Wd) AL2 ..8 CA30
Sevenoaks TN13 .....191 FH128
Upminster RM14 .....72 FP62
Uxbridge UB10 .....59 BP61
West Drayton UB7 .....94 BN76
Oakbank, Brwd. (Hutt.) CM13 .55 GE43
Oak Bk, Croy. (New Adgtn)
CR0 .....161 EC107
Oakbank, Lthd. (Fetch.) KT22 .170 CC123
Woking GU22 .....166 AY119
Oakbank Av, Walt. KT12 .....136 BZ101
Oakbank Gro, SE24 .....102 DQ84
Oakbark Ho, Brent. TW8
off High St 97 CJ80
Oakbrook Cl, Brom. BR1 .....124 EH91
Oakbury Rd, SW6 .....100 DB82
Oak Cl, N14 .....45 DH45
Dartford DA1 .....107 FE84
Sutton SM1 .....140 DC103
Tadworth (Box H.) KT20 .....182 CP130
Waltham Abbey EN9 .....15 ED34
Oakcombe Cl, N.Mal. KT3
off Traps La 138 CS95
Oak Cottage Cl, SE6 .....124 EF88
Oak Cres, E16 .....86 EE71
Oakcroft Cl, Pnr. HA5 .....39 BV54
West Byfleet KT14 .....151 BF114
Oakcroft Rd, SE13 .....103 ED82
Chessington KT9 .....156 CM105
West Byfleet KT14 .....151 BF114
Oakcroft Vil, Chess. KT9 .....156 CM105
Oakdale, N14 .....45 DH46
Oakdale Av, Har. HA3 .....62 CL57
Northwood HA6 .....39 BU54
Oakdale Cl, Wat. WD19 .....40 BW49
Oakdale Gdns, E4 .....47 EC50
Oakdale La, Eden. (Crock.H.)
TN8 .....189 EP133
Oakdale Rd, E7 .....86 EH66
E11 .....67 ED61
E18 .....48 EH54
N4 .....66 DQ58
SE15 .....102 DW83
SW16 .....121 DL92
Epsom KT19 .....156 CR109
Watford WD19 .....40 BW48
Weybridge KT13 .....134 BN104
Oakdale Way, Mitch. CR4
off Wolseley Rd 140 DG101
Oakdene, SE15
off Carlton Gro 102 DV81
Oak Dene, W13 off The Dene .79 CH71
Oakdene, Rom. RM3 .....52 FM54
Tadworth KT20 .....173 CY120
Waltham Cross (Chsht) EN8 .15 DY30
Woking (Chobham) GU24 .150 AT110
Oakdene Av, Chis. BR7 .....125 EN92
Erith DA8 .....107 FC79
Thames Ditton KT7 .....137 CG102
Oakdene Cl, Horn. RM11 .....71 FH58
Pinner HA5 .....40 BZ52
Oakdene Dr, Surb. KT5 .....138 CQ101
Oakdene Ms, Sutt. SM3 .....139 CZ102
Oakdene Par, Cob. KT11
off Anyards Rd 153 BV114
Oakdene Pk, N3 .....43 CZ52
Oakdene Rd, Cob. KT11 .....153 BV114
Leatherhead (Bkhm) KT23 .170 BZ124
Orpington BR5 .....145 ET99
Redhill RH1 .....184 DE134
Sevenoaks TN13 .....190 FG122
Uxbridge UB10 .....77 BP68
Watford WD24 .....23 BV36
Oakden St, SE11 .....200 E8
Oak Dr, Tad. (Box H.) KT20 .182 CP130
Oake Ct, SW15
off Portinscale Rd 119 CY85
Oaken Coppice, Ashtd. KT21 .172 CN119
Oak End Dr, Iver SL0 .....75 BC68
Oaken Dr, Esher (Clay.) KT10 .155 CF107
Oak End Way, Add. (Wdhm)
KT15 .....151 BE112
Gerrards Cross SL9 .....57 AZ57
Oakengate Wd, Tad. KT20 .....182 CQ131
Oakenholt Ho, SE2
off Hartslock Dr 106 EX75
Oaken La, Esher (Clay.) KT10 .155 CE106
Oakenshaw Cl, Surb. KT6 .....138 CL101
Oakes Cl, E6
off Savage Gdns 87 EM72
Oakeshott Av, N6 .....64 DG61
Oakey La, SE1 .....200 D6
Oak Fm, Borwd. WD6 .....26 CQ43
Oakfield, E4 .....47 EB50
Rickmansworth (Mill End)
WD3 .....37 BF45
Woking GU21 .....166 AS116
Oakfield Av, Har. HA3 .....61 CH55
Oakfield Cl, N.Mal. KT3
off Blakes La 139 CT99
Potters Bar EN6 .....11 CZ31
Ruislip HA4 .....59 BT58
Weybridge KT13 .....153 BQ105
Oakfield Ct, N8 .....65 DL59
NW2 off Hendon Way 63 CX59
Borehamwood WD6 .....26 CP41
Oakfield Dr, Reig. RH2 .....184 DA132
Oakfield Gdns, N18 .....46 DS49
SE19 .....122 DS92
Beckenham BR3 .....143 EA99
Carshalton SM5 .....140 DE102
Greenford UB6 .....79 CD70
Oakfield Glade, Wey. KT13 .....153 BQ105
Oakfield La, Bex. DA5 .....127 FE89
Dartford DA1, DA2 .....127 FG89
Keston BR2 .....162 EJ105
Oakfield Pk Rd, Dart. DA1 .....128 FK89
Oakfield Pl, Dart. DA1 .....128 FK89
Oakfield Rd, E6 .....86 EL67
E17 .....47 DY54
N3 .....44 DB53
N4 .....65 DN58
N14 .....45 DL48
SE20 .....122 DV94
SW19 .....119 CX90
Ashford TW15 .....115 BP92
Ashtead KT21 .....171 CK117
Cobham KT11 .....153 BV113
Croydon CR0 .....142 DQ102
Ilford IG1 .....69 EP61
Orpington BR6
off Goodmead Rd 146 EU101
Oakfields, Sev. TN13 .....191 FH126
Walton-on-Thames KT12 .135 BU102
West Byfleet KT14 .....152 BH114
Oakfields Rd, NW11 .....63 CY58
Oakfield St, SW10 .....100 DC79
Oakford Rd, NW5 .....65 DJ63
Oak Gdns, Croy. CR0 .....143 EA103
Edgware HA8 .....42 CQ54
Oak Glade, Epp. (Cooper.) CM16
off Coopersale Common .18 EX29
Epsom KT19
off Christ Ch Rd 156 CN112
Northwood HA6 .....39 BP53
Oak Glen, Horn. RM11 .....72 FL55
Oak Grn, Abb.L. WD5 .....7 BS32
Oak Grn Way, Abb.L. WD5 .....7 BS32
Oak Gro, NW2 .....63 CY63
Ruislip HA4 .....59 BV59
Sunbury-on-Thames TW16 .115 BV94
West Wickham BR4 .....143 EC103
Oak Gro Rd, SE20 .....142 DW95
Oakhall Ct, E11 .....68 EH58
Oakhall Dr, Sun. TW16 .....115 BT92
Oak Hall Rd, E11 .....68 EH58
Oakham Cl, SE6
off Rutland Wk 123 DZ89
Barnet EN4 .....28 DF41
Oakham Dr, Brom. BR2 .....144 EF98
Oakhampton Rd, NW7 .....43 CX52
Oak Hill, Epsom KT18 .....172 CR116
Oakhill, Esher (Clay.) KT10 .155 CG107
Oak Hill, Surb. KT6 .....138 CL101
Woodford Green IG8 .....47 ED52
Oakhill Av, NW3 .....64 DB63
Pinner HA5 .....40 BY54
Oakhill Cl, Ashtd. KT21 .....171 CJ118
Oakhill Cl, Rick. (Map.Cr.)
WD3 .....37 BE49
Oak Hill Cl, Wdf.Grn. IG8 .....47 ED52
Oakhill Ct, SW19 .....119 CX94
Oak Hill Cres, Surb. KT6 .....138 CL101
Woodford Green IG8 .....47 ED52
Oakhill Dr, Surb. KT6 .....138 CL101
Oakhill Gdns, Wey. KT13 .....135 BS103
Oak Hill Gdns, Wdf.Grn. IG8 ..48 EE53
Oak Hill Gro, Surb. KT6 .....138 CL100
Oak Hill Pk, NW3 .....64 DB63
Oak Hill Pk Ms, NW3 .....64 DC63
Oakhill Path, Surb. KT6 .....138 CL100
Oakhill Pl, SW15
off Oakhill Rd 120 DA85
Oakhill Rd, SW15 .....119 CZ85
SW16 .....141 DL95
Addlestone KT15 .....151 BF107
Ashtead KT21 .....171 CJ118
Beckenham BR3 .....143 EC96
Orpington BR6 .....145 ET102
Purfleet RM19 .....108 FP78
Rickmansworth (Map.Cr.)
WD3 .....37 BD49
Oak Hill Rd, Rom. (Stap.Abb.)
RM4 .....51 FD45
Sevenoaks TN13 .....190 FG124
Surbiton KT6 .....138 CL100
Oakhill Rd, Sutt. SM1 .....140 DB104
Oak Hill Way, NW3 .....64 DC63
Oak Ho, NW3
off Maitland Pk Vil 82 DF65
Oakhouse Rd, Bexh. DA6 .....126 FA85
Oakhurst, Wok. (Chobham)
GU24 .....150 AS109
Oakhurst Av, Barn. EN4 .....44 DE45
Bexleyheath DA7 .....106 EY80
Oakhurst Cl, E17 .....68 EE56
Chislehurst BR7 .....145 EM95
Ilford IG6 .....49 EQ53
Teddington TW11 .....117 CE92
Oakhurst Gdns, E4 .....48 EF46
E17 .....68 EE56
Bexleyheath DA7 .....106 EY80
Oakhurst Gro, SE22 .....102 DU84
Oakhurst Pl, Wat. WD18
off Cherrydale 23 BT42
Oakhurst Ri, Cars. SM5 .....158 DE110
Oakhurst Rd, Enf. EN3 .....31 DX36
Epsom KT19 .....156 CQ107
Oakington Av, Amer. HP6 .....20 AY39
Harrow HA2 .....60 CA59
Hayes UB3 .....95 BR77
Wembley HA9 .....62 CM62
Oakington Cl, Sun. TW16 .....136 BW96
Oakington Dr, Sun. TW16 .....136 BW96
Oakington Manor Dr, Wem.
HA9 .....62 CN64
Oakington Rd, W9 .....82 DA70
Oakington Way, N8 .....65 DL58
Oakland Gdns, Brwd. (Hutt.)
CM13 .....55 GC43
Oakland Pl, Buck.H. IG9 .....48 EG47
Oakland Rd, E15 .....67 ED63
Oaklands, N21 .....45 DM47
Kenley CR8 .....160 DQ114
Leatherhead (Fetch.) KT22 .171 CD124
Twickenham TW2 .....116 CC87
Oaklands Av, N9 .....30 DV44
Esher KT10 .....137 CD102
Hatfield AL9 .....11 CY27
Isleworth TW7 .....97 CF79
Romford RM1 .....71 FE55
Sidcup DA15 .....125 ET87
Thornton Heath CR7 .....141 DN98
Watford WD19 .....39 BV46
West Wickham BR4 .....143 EB104
Oaklands Cl, Bexh. DA6 .....126 EZ85
Chessington KT9 .....155 CJ105
Orpington BR5 .....145 ES100
Oaklands Ct, W12
off Uxbridge Rd 81 CV74
Addlestone KT15 .....134 BH104
Watford WD17 .....23 BU39
Wembley HA0 .....61 CK64
Oaklands Dr, S.Ock. RM15 .....91 FW71
Oaklands Est, SW4 .....121 DJ86
Oaklands Gdns, Ken. CR8 .....160 DQ114
Oaklands Gate, Nthwd. HA6
off Green La 39 BS51
Oaklands Gro, W12 .....81 CU74
Oaklands La, Barn. EN5 .....27 CV42
Westerham (Bigg.H.) TN16 .162 EH113
Oaklands Ms, NW2
off Oaklands Rd 63 CX63
Oaklands Pk Av, Ilf. IG1
off High Rd 69 ER61
Oaklands Pl, SW4
off St. Alphonsus Rd 101 DJ84
Oaklands Rd, N20 .....43 CZ45
NW2 .....63 CX63
SW14 .....98 CR83
W7 .....97 CF75
Bexleyheath DA6 .....106 EZ84
Bromley BR1 .....124 EE94
Dartford DA2 .....128 FP88
Gravesend (Nthflt) DA11 .....131 GF91
Waltham Cross (Chsht) EN7 .14 DS26
Oaklands Way, Tad. KT20 .....173 CW122
Wallington SM6 .....159 DK108
Oakland Way, Epsom KT19 .....156 CR107
Oak La, E14 .....85 DZ73
N2 .....44 DD54
N11 .....45 DK51
Egham (Eng.Grn) TW20 .....112 AW90
Isleworth TW7 .....97 CE84
Potters Bar (Cuffley) EN6 .....13 DM28
Sevenoaks TN13 .....190 FG127
Twickenham TW1 .....117 CG87
Woking GU22
off Beaufort Rd 167 BC116
Woodford Green IG8 .....48 EF49
Oaklawn Rd, Lthd. KT22 .....171 CE118
Oak Leaf Cl, Epsom KT19 .....156 CQ112
Oakleafe Gdns, Ilf. IG6 .....69 EP55
Oaklea Pas, Kings.T. KT1 .....137 CK97
Oakleigh Av, N20 .....44 DD47
Edgware HA8 .....42 CP54
Surbiton KT6 .....138 CN102
Oakleigh Cl, N20 .....44 DF48
Swanley BR8 .....147 FE97
Oakleigh Ct, Barn. EN4
off Church Hill Rd 28 DE44
Oakleigh Ct, Edg. HA8 .....42 CQ54
Oakleigh Cres, N20 .....44 DE47
Oakleigh Dr, Rick. (Crox.Grn)
WD3 .....23 BQ44
Oakleigh Gdns, N20 .....44 DC46
Edgware HA8 .....42 CM50
Orpington BR6 .....163 ES105
Oakleigh Ms, N20
off Oakleigh Rd N 44 DC47
OAKLEIGH PARK, N20 .....44 DD46
⇌ Oakleigh Park 44 DD45
Oakleigh Pk Av, Chis. BR7 .....145 EN95
Oakleigh Pk N, N20 .....44 DD46
Oakleigh Pk S, N20 .....44 DE47
Oakleigh Ri, Epp. CM16
off Bower Hill 18 EU32
Oakleigh Rd, Pnr. HA5 .....40 BZ51
Uxbridge UB10 .....77 BQ66
Oakleigh Rd N, N20 .....44 DD47
Oakleigh Rd S, N11 .....44 DG48
Oakleigh Way, Mitch. CR4 .....141 DH95
Surbiton KT6 .....138 CN102
Oakley Av, W5 .....80 CN73
Barking IG11 .....87 ET66
Croydon CR0 .....159 DL105
Oakley Cl, E4 .....47 EC48
E6 off Northumberland Rd .86 EL72
W7 .....79 CE73
Addlestone KT15 .....152 BK105
Grays RM20 .....109 FW79
Isleworth TW7 .....97 CD81
Oakley Ct, Loug. IG10
off Hillyfields 33 EN40
Mitcham CR4
off London Rd 140 DG102
Oakley Cres, EC1 .....196 G1
Slough SL1 .....74 AS73
Oakley Dr, SE9 .....125 ER88
SE13 .....123 ED86
Bromley BR2 .....144 EL104
Romford RM3 .....52 FN50
Oakley Gdns, N8 .....65 DM57
SW3 .....100 DE79
Banstead SM7 .....174 DB115
Oakley Pk, Bex. DA5 .....126 EW87
Oakley Pl, SE1 .....102 DT78
Oakley Rd, N1 .....84 DR66
SE25 .....142 DV99
Bromley BR2 .....144 EL104
Harrow HA1 .....61 CE58
Warlingham CR6 .....176 DU118
Oakley Sq, NW1 .....195 L1
Oakley St, SW3 .....100 DE79
Oakley Wk, W6 .....99 CX79
Oakley Yd, E2 off Bacon St 84 DT70
Oak Lo Av, Chig. IG7 .....49 ER50
Oak Lo Cl, Stan. HA7
off Dennis La 41 CJ50
Walton-on-Thames KT12 .154 BW106
Oak Lo Dr, W.Wick. BR4 .....143 EB101
Oak Lo La, West. TN16 .....189 ER125
Oaklodge Way, NW7 .....43 CT50
Oak Manor Dr, Wem. HA9
off Oakington Manor Dr 62 CM64
Oakmead Av, Brom. BR2 .....144 EG100
Oakmeade, Pnr. HA5 .....40 CA51
Oakmead Gdns, Edg. HA8 .....42 CR49
Oakmead Grn, Epsom KT18 .172 CP115
Oakmead Pl, Mitch. CR4 .....140 DE95
Oakmead Rd, SW12 .....120 DG88
Croydon CR0 .....141 DK100
Oakmere Av, Pot.B. EN6 .....12 DC33
Oakmere Cl, Pot.B. EN6 .....12 DD31
Oakmere La, Pot.B. EN6 .....12 DC32
Oakmere Rd, SE2 .....106 EU79
Oakmoor Way, Chig. IG7 .....49 ES50
Oakmount Pl, Orp. BR6 .....145 ER102
Oak Pk, W.Byf. KT14 .....151 BE113
Oak Pk Gdns, SW19 .....119 CX87
Oak Pk Ms, N16
off Brooke Rd 66 DT62
Oak Path, Bushey WD23
off Ashfield Av 24 CB44
Oak Piece, Epp. (N.Wld Bas.)
CM16 .....19 FC25
Oak Pl, SW18 off East Hill 120 DB85
Oakridge, St.Alb. (Brick.Wd)
AL2 .....8 BZ29
Oakridge Av, Rad. WD7 .....9 CF34
Oakridge Dr, N2 .....64 DD55
Oakridge La, Brom. BR1
off Downham Way 123 ED92
Radlett WD7 .....9 CF33
Watford (Ald.) WD25 .....25 CD35
Oakridge Rd, Brom. BR1 .....123 ED91
Oak Ri, Buck.H. IG9 .....48 EK48
Oak Rd, W5 off The Broadway .79 CK73
Caterham CR3 .....176 DS122
Cobham KT11 .....170 BX115
Epping CM16 .....17 ET30
Erith (Northumb.Hth) DA8 .....107 FC80
Erith (Slade Grn) DA8 .....107 FG81
Gravesend DA12 .....131 GJ90
Grays RM17 .....110 GC79
Greenhithe DA9 .....129 FS86
Leatherhead KT22 .....171 CG118
New Malden KT3 .....138 CR96
Orpington BR6 .....164 EU108
Reigate RH2 .....184 DB133
Romford RM3 .....52 FM53
Westerham TN16 .....189 ER125
Oak Row, SW16 .....141 DJ96
Oakroyd Av, Pot.B. EN6 .....11 CZ33
Oakroyd Cl, Pot.B. EN6 .....11 CZ34
Oaks, The, N12 .....44 DB49
SE18 .....105 EQ78
Dartford DA2 .....128 FP86
Epsom KT18 .....157 CT114
Hayes UB4
off Charville La 77 BQ68
Ruislip HA4 .....59 BS59
Staines TW18
off Moormede Cres 113 BF91
Swanley BR8 .....147 FE96
Tadworth KT20 .....173 CW123
Watford WD19 .....40 BW46
West Byfleet KT14 .....152 BG113

★ Place of interest ⇌ Railway station ⊖ London Underground station DLR Docklands Light Railway station Tra Tramlink station H Hospital Riv Pedestrian ferry landing stage

Oaks, The, Wdf. Grn. IG8 48 EE51
Oaks Av, SE19 122 DS92
Feltham TW13 51 BY89
Romford RM5 51 FC54
Worcester Park KT4 139 CV104
Oaks Cl, Lthd. KT22 171 CG121
Radlett WD7 25 CF35
Oaksford Av, SE26 122 DV90
Oaks Gro, E4 48 EE47
Oakshade Rd, Brom. BR1 123 ED91
Leatherhead (Oxshott) KT22 154 CC114
Oakshaw, Oxt. RH8 187 ED127
Oakshaw Rd, SW18 120 DB87
Oakside, Uxb. (Denh.) UB9 76 BH65
Oakside Ct, Ilf. IG6 off Fencepiece Rd 49 ER54
Oaks La, Croy. CR0 142 DW104
Ilford IG2 69 ES57
Oak Sq, Sev. TN13 off High St 191 FJ126
Oaks Rd, Croy. CR0 160 DV106
Kenley CR8 159 DP114
Reigate RH2 184 DC133
Staines (Stanw.) TW19 114 BK86
Woking GU21 166 AY117
Oaks Sq, The, Epsom KT19 off Waterloo Rd 156 CR113
Oaks Track, Cars. SM5 158 DF111
Wallington SM6 159 DH110
Oak St, Rom. RM7 71 FC57
Oaks Way, Cars. SM5 158 DF108
Epsom KT18 off Epsom La N 173 CV119
Kenley CR8 160 DQ114
Surbiton KT6 137 CK103
Oakthorpe Rd, N13 45 DN50
Oaktree Av, N13 45 DP48
Oak Tree Av, Green. (Bluewater) DA9 129 FT87
Oak Tree Cl, W5 off Pinewood Gro 79 CJ72
Abbots Langley WD5 7 BR32
Oaktree Cl, Brwd. CM13 off Hawthorn Av 55 FZ49
Oak Tree Cl, Loug. IG10 33 EQ39
Stanmore HA7 41 CJ52
Virginia Water GU25 132 AX101
Oaktree Cl, Wal.Cr. EN7 13 DP28
Oak Tree Ct, Borwd. (Els.) WD6 off Barnet La 25 CK44
Oak Tree Dell, NW9 62 CQ57
Oak Tree Dr, N20 44 DB46
Egham (Eng.Grn) TW20 112 AW92
Slough SL3 93 BB78
Oak Tree Gdns, Brom. BR1 124 EH92
Oaktree Gro, Ilf. IG1 69 ER64
Oak Tree Rd, NW8 194 A3
Oaktree Wk, Cat. CR3 176 DS122
Oak Vw, Wat. WD18 23 BS41
Oakview Cl, Wal.Cr. EN7 14 DV28
Watford WD19 24 BW44
Oakview Gdns, N2 64 DD56
Oakview Gro, Croy. CR0 143 DY102
Oakview Rd, SE6 123 EB92
Oak Village, NW5 64 DG63
Oak Wk, Wall. SM6 off Helios Rd 140 DG102
Oak Warren, Sev. TN13 190 FG129
Oak Way, N14 45 DH45
Oakway, SW20 139 CW98
Oak Way, W3 80 CS74
Ashtead KT21 172 CN116
Oakway, Brom. BR2 143 ED96
Oak Way, Croy. CR0 143 DX100
Feltham TW14 115 BS88
Oakway, Wok. GU21 166 AS119
Oakway Cl, Bex. DA5 126 EY86
Oakway Pl, Rad. WD7 off Watling St 9 CG34
Oakways, SE9 125 EP86
Oakwell Dr, Pot.B. EN6 13 DH32
OAKWOOD, N14 29 DK44
⊖ Oakwood 29 DJ43
Oakwood, Wall. SM6 159 DH109
Waltham Abbey EN9 off Roundhills 31 ED35
Oakwood Av, N14 45 DK45
Beckenham BR3 143 EC96
Borehamwood WD6 26 CP42
Brentwood (Hutt.) CM13 55 GE44
Bromley BR2 144 EH97
Epsom KT19 156 CN109
Mitcham CR4 140 DD96
Purley CR8 159 DP112
Southall UB1 78 CA73
Oakwood Chase, Horn. RM11 72 FM58
Oakwood Cl, N14 29 DJ44
SE13 off Hither Grn La 123 ED86
Chislehurst BR7 125 EM93
Dartford DA1 128 FP88
Redhill RH1 184 DG134
Woodford Green IG8 off Green Wk 48 EL51
Oakwood Ct, W14 99 CZ76
Oakwood Cres, N21 29 DL44
Greenford UB6 79 CG65
Oakwood Dr, SE19 122 DR93
Bexleyheath DA7 107 FD84
Edgware HA8 42 CQ51
Sevenoaks TN13 191 FH123
Oakwood Gdns, Ilf. IG3 69 ET61
Orpington BR6 145 EQ103
Sutton SM1 140 DA103
Oakwood Hill, Loug. IG10 33 EM44
Oakwood Hill Ind Est, Loug. IG10 33 EQ43
Oakwood La, W14 99 CZ76
Oakwood Pk Rd, N14 45 DK45
Oakwood Pl, Croy. CR0 141 DN100
Oakwood Ri, Cat. CR3 186 DS125
Oakwood Rd, NW11 64 DB57
SW20 139 CU95
Croydon CR0 141 DN100
Orpington BR6 145 EQ103
Pinner HA5 39 BV54
Redhill (Merst.) RH1 185 DN129
St. Albans (Brick.Wd) AL2 8 BY29
Oakwood Rd, Vir. W. GU25 132 AW99
Woking GU21 166 AS119
Oakwood Vw, N14 29 DK44
Oakworth Rd, W10 81 CW71
Oarsman Pl, E.Mol. KT8 137 CE98
Oast Ho Cl, Stai. (Wrays.) TW19 112 AY87
Oasthouse Way, Orp. BR5 146 EV98
Oast Rd, Oxt. RH8 188 EF131
Oates Cl, Brom. BR2 143 ED97
Oates Rd, Rom. RM5 51 FB50
Oatfield Ho, N15 off Bushey Rd 66 DS58
Oatfield Rd, Orp. BR6 145 ET102
Tadworth KT20 173 CV120
Oatland Ri, E17 47 DY54
Oatlands Av, Wey. KT13 153 BR106
Oatlands Chase, Wey. KT13 135 BS104
Oatlands Cl, Wey. KT13 153 BQ105
Oatlands Dr, Wey. KT13 135 BR104
Oatlands Grn, Wey. KT13 135 BR104
Oatlands Mere, Wey. KT13 135 BR104
OATLANDS PARK, Wey. KT13 153 BR105
Oatlands Rd, Enf. EN3 30 DW39
Tadworth KT20 173 CY119
Oat La, EC2 197 H8
Oban Cl, E13 86 EJ70
Oban Ho, E14 off Oban St 85 ED72
Barking IG11 off Wheelers Cross 87 ER68
Oban Rd, E13 86 EJ69
SE25 142 DR98
Oban St, E14 85 ED72
Obelisk Ride, Egh. TW20 112 AS93
Oberon Cl, Borwd. WD6 26 CQ39
Oberon Way, Shep. TW17 134 BL97
Oberstein Rd, SW11 100 DD84
Oborne Cl, SE24 121 DP85
O'Brien Ho, E2 off Roman Rd 85 DX69
Observatory Gdns, W8 100 DA75
Observatory Ms, E14 204 F8
Observatory Rd, SW14 98 CQ84
Observatory Shop Cen, Slou. SL1 92 AU75
Observatory Wk, Red. RH1 off Lower Br Rd 184 DF134
Observer Dr, Wat. WD18 23 BS42
Occupation La, SE18 105 EP81
W5 97 CK77
Occupation Rd, SE17 201 H10
W13 97 CH75
Watford WD18 23 BV43
Ocean Est, E1 85 DX70
Ocean St, E1 85 DX71
Ocean Wf, E14 203 P5
Ockenden Cl, Wok. GU22 off Ockenden Rd 167 AZ118
Ockenden Gdns, Wok. GU22 off Ockenden Rd 167 AZ118
Ockenden Rd, Wok. GU22 167 AZ118
⇌ Ockendon 91 FX69
Ockendon Ms, N1 off Ockendon Rd 84 DR65
Ockendon Rd, N1 84 DR65
Upminster RM14 72 FQ64
OCKHAM, Wok. GU23 168 BN121
Ockham Dr, Lthd. (W.Hors.) KT24 169 BR124
Orpington BR5 126 EU94
Ockham La, Cob. KT11 169 BT118
Woking (Ock.) GU23 169 BP120
Ockham Pk, Wok. GU23 off Ripley Bypass 168 BL120
Ockham Rd N, Lthd. KT24 169 BQ124
Woking (Ock.) GU23 168 BN121
Ockley Ct, Sutt. SM1 off Oakhill Rd 158 DC105
Ockley Rd, SW16 121 DL90
Croydon CR0 141 DM101
Ockleys Mead, Gdse. RH9 186 DW129
Octagon Arc, EC2 197 M7
Octagon Rd, Walt. (Whiteley Vill.) KT12 153 BS109
Octavia Cl, Mitch. CR4 140 DE99
Octavia Ms, W9 off Bravington Rd 81 CZ70
Octavia Rd, Islw. TW7 97 CF82
Octavia St, SW11 100 DE81
Octavia Way, SE28 off Booth Cl 88 EV73
Staines TW18 114 BG93
Octavius St, SE8 103 EA80
Odard Rd, W.Mol. KT8 off Down St 136 CA98
Oddesey Rd, Borwd. WD6 26 CP39
Odell Cl, Bark. IG11 87 ET66
Odell Wk, SE13 off Bankside Av 103 EC83
Odeon, The, Bark. IG11 off Longbridge Rd 87 ER66
Odessa Rd, E7 68 EF62
NW10 81 CU68
Odessa St, SE16 203 M5
Odger St, SW11 100 DF82
Odhams Wk, WC2 196 A9
Odyssey Business Pk, Ruis. HA4 59 BV64
Offa's Mead, E9 off Lindisfarne Way 67 DY63
Offenbach Ho, E2 85 DX68
Offenham Rd, SE9 125 EM91
Offers Ct, Kings.T. KT1 off Winery La 138 CM97
Offerton Rd, SW4 101 DJ83
Offham Slope, N12 43 CZ50
Offley Pl, Islw. TW7 97 CD82
Offley Rd, SW9 101 DN80
Offord Cl, N17 46 DU52
Offord Rd, N1 83 DM66
Offord St, N1 83 DM66
Ogilby St, SE18 105 EM77
Oglander Rd, SE15 102 DT84
Ogle St, W1 195 K6
Oglethorpe Rd, Dag. RM10 70 EZ62
Ohio Rd, E13 86 EF70
Oil Mill La, W6 99 CU78
Okeburn Rd, SW17 120 DG92
Okehampton Cl, N12 44 DD50
Okehampton Cres, Well. DA16 106 EV81
Okehampton Rd, NW10 81 CW67
Romford RM3 52 FJ51
Okehampton Sq, Rom. RM3 52 FJ51
Okemore Gdns, Orp. BR5 146 EW98
Olaf St, W11 81 CX73
Old Acre, Wok. GU22 152 BG114
Oldacre Ms, SW12 off Balham Gro 121 DH87
★ Old Admiralty Bldgs (M.o.D.), SW1 199 N3
Old Amersham Rd, Ger.Cr. SL9 57 BB60
Old Av, W.Byf. KT14 151 BE113
Weybridge KT13 153 BR107
Old Av Cl, W.Byf. KT14 151 BE113
Old Bailey, EC4 196 G9
Old Barge Ho All, SE1 off Upper Grd 83 DN74
Old Barn Cl, Sutt. SM2 157 CY108
Old Barn La, Ken. CR8 176 DT116
Rickmansworth (Crox.Grn) WD3 22 BM43
Old Barn Ms, Rick. (Crox.Grn) WD3 off Old Barn La 22 BM43
Old Barn Rd, Epsom KT18 172 CQ117
Old Barn Way, Bexh. DA7 107 FD83
Old Barrack Yd, SW1 198 F4
Old Barrowfield, E15 off Stephen's Rd 86 EF67
Old Bath Rd, Slou. (Colnbr.) SL3 93 BE81
Old Bellgate Pl, E14 203 P7
Oldberry Rd, Edg. HA8 42 CR51
Old Bethnal Grn Rd, E2 84 DU69
OLD BEXLEY, Bex. DA5 127 FB87
Old Bexley La, Bex. DA5 127 FD89
Dartford DA1 127 FF88
Old Billingsgate Wk, EC3 off Lower Thames St 84 DS73
Old Bond St, W1 199 K1
Oldborough Rd, Wem. HA0 61 CJ61
Old Brewers Yd, WC2 195 P9
Old Brewery Ms, NW3 off Hampstead High St 64 DD63
Old Br Cl, Nthlt. UB5 78 CA68
Old Br St, Kings.T. (Hmptn W.) KT1 137 CK96
Old Broad St, EC2 197 L9
Old Bromley Rd, Brom. BR1 123 ED92
Old Brompton Rd, SW5 100 DA78
SW7 100 DA78
Old Bldgs, WC2 196 D8
Old Burlington St, W1 195 K10
Oldbury Cl, Cher. KT16 off Oldbury Rd 133 BE101
Orpington BR5 146 EX98
Oldbury Pl, W1 194 G6
Oldbury Rd, Cher. KT16 133 BE101
Enfield EN1 30 DU40
Old Canal Ms, SE15 off Nile Ter 102 DT78
Old Carriageway, The, Sev. TN13 190 FC123
Old Castle St, E1 197 P7
Old Cavendish St, W1 195 H8
Old Change Ct, EC4 off Carter La 84 DQ72
Old Chapel Rd, Swan. BR8 147 FC101
Old Charlton Rd, Shep. TW17 135 BQ99
Old Chelsea Ms, SW3 off Danvers St 100 DD79
Old Chertsey Rd, Wok. (Chobham) GU24 150 AV110
Old Chestnut Av, Esher KT10 154 CA107
Old Chorleywood Rd, Rick. WD3 off Chorleywood Rd 22 BK44
Oldchurch Gdns, Rom. RM7 71 FD59
H Oldchurch Hosp, Rom. RM7 71 FE58
Old Ch La, NW9 62 CQ61
Brentwood (Mtnsg) CM13 55 GE42
Greenford UB6 off Perivale La 79 CG69
Stanmore HA7 41 CJ52
Old Ch Path, Esher KT10 off High St 154 CB105
Oldchurch Ri, Rom. RM7 71 FD59
Old Ch Rd, E1 85 DX72
E4 47 EA49
Oldchurch Rd, Rom. RM7 71 FD59
Old Ch St, SW3 100 DD78
Old Claygate La, Esher (Clay.) KT10 155 CG107
Old Clem Sq, SE18 off Kempt St 105 EN79
Old Coach Rd, Cher. KT16 133 BD99
Old Coal Yd, SE28 off Pettman Cres 105 ER77
Old Common Rd, Cob. KT11 153 BU112
Rickmansworth (Chorl.) WD3 off Common Rd 21 BD42
Old Compton St, W1 195 M10
Old Cote Dr, Houns. TW5 96 CA79
OLD COULSDON, Couls. CR5 175 DN119
Old Ct, Ashtd. KT21 172 CL119
Old Ct Pl, W8 100 DB75
★ Old Curiosity Shop, WC2 196 B8
Old Dairy Ms, SW12 120 DG88
Old Dairy Sq, N21 off Wades Hill 45 DN45
Old Dartford Rd, Dart. (Fnghm) DA4 148 FM100
Old Dean, Hem.H. (Bov.) HP3 5 BA27
Old Deer Pk Gdns, Rich. TW9 98 CL83
Old Devonshire Rd, SW12 121 DH87
Old Dock App Rd, Grays RM17 110 GE77
Old Dock Cl, Rich. TW9 off Watcombe Cotts 98 CN79
Old Dover Rd, SE3 104 EG80
Olden La, Pur. CR8 159 DN112
Old Esher Cl, Walt. KT12 154 BX106
Old Esher Rd, Walt. KT12 154 BX106
Old Farleigh Rd, S.Croy. CR2 160 DW110
Warlingham CR6 161 DY113
Old Fm Av, N14 45 DJ45
Sidcup DA15 125 ER88
Old Fm Cl, Houns. TW4 96 BZ84
Old Fm Gdns, Swan. BR8 147 FF97
Old Farmhouse Dr, Lthd. (Oxshott) KT22 171 CD115
Old Fm Pas, Hmptn. TW12 136 CC95
Old Fm Rd, N2 44 DD53
Hampton TW12 116 BZ93
West Drayton UB7 94 BK75
Old Fm Rd E, Sid. DA15 126 EU89
Old Fm Rd W, Sid. DA15 125 ET89
Old Ferry Dr, Stai. (Wrays.) TW19 112 AW86
Old Fld Cl, Amer. HP6 20 AY39
Oldfield Cl, Brom. BR1 145 EM98
Greenford UB6 61 CE64
Stanmore HA7 41 CG50
Waltham Cross (Chsht) EN8 15 DY28
Oldfield Dr, Wal.Cr. (Chsht) EN8 15 DY28
Oldfield Fm Gdns, Grnf. UB6 79 CD67
Oldfield Gdns, Ashtd. KT21 171 CK119
Oldfield Gro, SE16 203 H9
Oldfield La N, Grnf. UB6 79 CE65
Oldfield La S, Grnf. UB6 78 CC70
Oldfield Ms, N6 65 DJ59
Oldfield Rd, N16 66 DS62
NW10 81 CT66
SW19 119 CY93
W3 off Valetta Rd 99 CT75
Bexleyheath DA7 106 EY82
Bromley BR1 145 EM98
Hampton TW12 136 BZ95
St. Albans (Lon.Col.) AL2 9 CK25
Oldfields Circ, Nthlt. UB5 78 CC65
Oldfields Rd, Sutt. SM1 139 CZ104
Oldfields Trd Est, Sutt. SM1 140 DA104
Oldfield Wd, Wok. GU22 off Maybury Hill 167 BB117
Old Fish St Hill, EC4 197 H10
Old Fleet La, EC4 196 F8
Old Fold Cl, Barn. EN5 off Old Fold La 27 CZ39
Old Fold La, Barn. EN5 27 CZ39
Old Fold Vw, Barn. EN5 27 CW41
OLD FORD, E3 85 DZ66
Old Ford Rd, E2 84 DW68
E3 85 DY68
Old Forge Cl, Stan. HA7 41 CG49
Watford WD25 7 BU33
Old Forge Cres, Shep. TW17 135 BP100
Old Forge Ms, W12 off Goodwin Rd 99 CV75
Old Forge Rd, N19 off Elthorne Rd 65 DK61
Enfield EN1 30 DT38
Old Forge Way, Sid. DA14 126 EV91
Old Fox Cl, Cat. CR3 175 DP121
Old Fox Footpath, S.Croy. CR2 off Essenden Rd 160 DS108
Old Gannon Cl, Nthwd. HA6 39 BQ50
Old Gdn, The, Sev. TN13 190 FD123
Old Gloucester St, WC1 196 A6
Old Gro Cl, Wal.Cr. (Chsht) EN7 14 DR26
Old Hall Cl, Pnr. HA5 40 BY53
Old Hall Dr, Pnr. HA5 40 BY53
Oldham Ter, W3 80 CQ74
Old Harrow La, West. TN16 179 EQ119
Old Hatch Manor, Ruis. HA4 59 BT59
Old Hill, Chis. BR7 145 EN95
Orpington BR6 163 ER107
Woking GU22 166 AX120
Oldhill St, N16 66 DU60
Old Homesdale Rd, Brom. BR2 144 EJ98
Old Hosp Cl, SW12 120 DF88
Old Ho Cl, SW19 119 CY92
Epsom KT17 157 CT110
Old Ho Gdns, Twick. TW1 117 CJ85
Old Ho La, Kings L. WD4 22 BL35
Old Howlett's La, Ruis. HA4 59 BQ58
Old Jamaica Rd, SE16 202 B6
Old James St, SE15 102 DV83
Old Jewry, EC2 197 K9
Old Kenton La, NW9 62 CP57
Old Kent Rd, SE1 201 L7
SE15 102 DS77
Old Kingston Rd, Wor.Pk. KT4 138 CQ104
Old La, Cob. KT11 169 BP117
Westerham (Tats.) TN16 178 EK121
Old La Gdns, Cob. KT11 169 BT122
Old Lo La, Ken. CR8 175 DN115
Purley CR8 159 DM113
Old Lo Pl, Twick. TW1 off St. Margarets Rd 117 CH86
Old Lo Way, Stan. HA7 41 CG50
Old London Rd, Epsom KT18 173 CU118
Kingston upon Thames KT2 138 CL96
Sevenoaks (Bad.Mt) TN14 164 FA110
Sevenoaks (Knock.P.) TN14 180 EY115
Old Maidstone Rd, Sid. DA14 126 EZ94
OLD MALDEN, Wor.Pk. KT4 138 CR102
Old Malden La, Wor.Pk. KT4 138 CR103
Old Malt Way, Wok. GU21 166 AX117
Old Manor Dr, Grav. DA12 131 GJ88
Isleworth TW7 116 CC86
Old Manor Ho Ms, Shep. TW17 off Squires Br Rd 134 BN97
Old Manor Rd, Sthl. UB2 96 BX77
Old Manor Way, Bexh. DA7 107 FD82
Chislehurst BR7 125 EM92
Old Manor Yd, SW5 off Earls Ct Rd 100 DB77
Old Mkt Sq, E2 197 P2
Old Marylebone Rd, NW1 194 C7
Old Mead, Ger.Cr. (Chal.St.P.) SL9 36 AY51
Old Ms, Har. HA1 off Hindes Rd 61 CE57
Old Mill Cl, Dart. (Eyns.) DA4 148 FL102
Old Mill Ct, E18 68 EJ55
Old Mill La, Red. (Merst.) RH1 185 DH128
Uxbridge UB8 76 BH72
Old Mill Pl, Rom. RM7 71 FD58
Old Mill Rd, SE18 105 ER79
Kings Langley WD4 7 BQ33
Uxbridge (Denh.) UB9 58 BG62
Old Mitre Ct, EC4 off Fleet St 83 DN72
Old Montague St, E1 84 DU71
Old Nichol St, E2 197 P4
Old N St, WC1 196 B6
Old Nurs Pl, Ashf. TW15 off Park Rd 115 BP92
Old Oak Av, Couls. (Chipstead) CR5 174 DE119
Old Oak Cl, Chess. KT9 156 CM105
Cobham KT11 153 BV113
OLD OAK COMMON, NW10 81 CT71
Old Oak Common La, NW10 80 CS71
W3 80 CS71
Old Oak La, NW10 80 CS69
Old Oak Rd, W3 81 CT73
Old Oaks, Wal.Abb. EN9 16 EE32
★ Old Operating Thea Mus & Herb Garret, SE1 201 L3
Old Orchard, St.Alb. (Park St) AL2 8 CC26
Sunbury-on-Thames TW16 136 BW96
West Byfleet (Byfleet) KT14 152 BM112
Old Orchard, The, NW3 off Nassington Rd 64 DF63
Old Orchard Cl, Barn. EN4 28 DD38
Uxbridge UB8 76 BN72
Old Otford Rd, Sev. TN14 181 FH117
Old Palace La, Rich. TW9 117 CJ85
Old Palace Rd, Croy. CR0 141 DP104
Weybridge KT13 135 BP104
Old Palace Ter, Rich. TW9 off King St 117 CK85
Old Palace Yd, SW1 199 P6
Richmond TW9 117 CJ85
Old Paradise St, SE11 200 B8
Old Pk Av, SW12 120 DG86
Enfield EN2 30 DQ42
Old Parkbury La, St.Alb. (Coln.St) AL2 9 CF30
Old Pk Gro, Enf. EN2 30 DQ42
Old Pk La, W1 198 G3
Old Pk Ms, Houns. TW5 96 BZ80
Old Pk Ride, Wal.Cr. EN7 14 DT33
Old Pk Ridings, N21 29 DP44
Old Pk Rd, N13 45 DM49
SE2 106 EU78
Enfield EN2 29 DP41
Old Pk Rd S, Enf. EN2 29 DP42
Old Pk Vw, Enf. EN2 29 DN41
Old Parvis Rd, W.Byf. KT14 152 BK112
Old Perry St, Chis. BR7 125 ES94
Gravesend (Nthflt) DA11 130 GE89
Old Polhill, Sev. TN14 181 FD115
Old PO La, SE3 104 EH83
Old Pound Cl, Islw. TW7 97 CG81
Old Priory, Uxb. (Hare.) UB9 59 BP59
Old Pye St, SW1 199 M6
Old Quebec St, W1 194 E9
Old Queen St, SW1 199 N5
Old Rectory Cl, Tad. (Walt.Hill) KT20 173 CU124
Old Rectory Gdns, Edg. HA8 42 CN51
Old Rectory La, Uxb. (Denh.) UB9 57 BE59
Old Redding, Har. HA3 40 CC49
Old Reigate Rd, Bet. RH3 182 CP134
Dorking RH4 182 CL134
Oldridge Rd, SW12 120 DG87
Old River Lea Towpath, E15 off City Mill River Towpath 85 EB66
Old Rd, SE13 104 EE84
Addlestone KT15 151 BF108
Betchworth (Buckland) RH3 182 CR134
Dartford DA1 107 FD84
Enfield EN3 30 DW39
Old Rd E, Grav. DA12 131 GH88
Old Rd W, Grav. DA11 131 GF88
Old Rope Wk, Sun. TW16 off The Avenue 135 BV97
Old Royal Free Pl, N1 off Liverpool Rd 83 DN67
Old Royal Free Sq, N1 83 DN67
Old Ruislip Rd, Nthlt. UB5 78 BX68
Olds App, Wat. WD18 39 BP46
Old Savill's Cotts, Chig. IG7 off The Chase 49 EQ49
Old Sch Cl, SE10 205 J7
SW19 140 DA96
Beckenham BR3 143 DX96
Old Sch Ct, Stai. (Wrays.) TW19 112 AY87
Old Sch Cres, E7 86 EG65
Old Sch Ms, Stai. TW18 113 BD92
Weybridge KT13 153 BR105
Old Sch Pl, Croy. CR0 159 DN105
Woking GU22 166 AY121
Old Sch Rd, Uxb. UB8 76 BM70
Old Schs La, Epsom KT17 157 CT109
Old Sch Sq, E14 off Pelling St 85 EA72
Thames Ditton KT7 137 CF100
Olds Cl, Wat. WD18 39 BP46
Old Seacoal La, EC4 196 F8
Old Shire La, Ger.Cr. SL9 37 BA46
Rickmansworth (Chorl.) WD3 21 BB44
Waltham Abbey EN9 32 EG35
Old Slade La, Iver SL0 93 BE76
Old Solesbridge La, Rick. (Chorl.) WD3 22 BG41
Old S Cl, Pnr. HA5 40 BX53
Old S Lambeth Rd, SW8 101 DL80
★ Old Spitalfields Mkt, E1 197 P6
Old Sq, WC2 196 C8
Old Sta App, Lthd. KT22 171 CG121
Old Sta Rd, Hayes UB3 95 BT76
Loughton IG10 32 EL43
Old Sta Yd, Brom. BR2 off Bourne Way 144 EF102
Oldstead Rd, Brom. BR1 123 ED91
Old Stockley Rd, West Dr. UB7 95 BP75
⇌ Old Street 197 K3
⊖ Old Street 197 K3
Old St, E13 86 EH68
EC1 197 H4
Old Studio Cl, Croy. CR0 142 DR101
Old Swan Yd, Cars. SM5 158 DF105
Old Thea Ct, SE1 off Park St 84 DQ74
Old Tilburstow Rd, Gdse. RH9 186 DW134
Old Town, SW4 101 DJ83
Croydon CR0 141 DP104
Old Tram Yd, SE18 off Lakedale Rd 105 ES77
Old Tye Av, West. (Bigg.H.) TN16 178 EL116

★ Place of interest ⇌ Railway station ⊖ London Underground station DLR Docklands Light Railway station Tra Tramlink station H Hospital Riv Pedestrian ferry landing stage

Old Uxbridge Rd, Rick. (W.Hyde) WD3 37 BE53
Old Wk, The, Sev. (Otford) TN14 181 FH117
Old Watford Rd, St.Alb. (Brick.Wd) AL2 8 BY30
Old Watling St, Grav. DA11 131 GG92
Old Westhall Cl, Warl. CR6 176 DW119
Old Wf Way, Wey. KT13
off Weybridge Rd 152 BM105
OLD WINDSOR, Wind. SL4 112 AU86
Old Windsor Lock, Wind. (Old Wind.) SL4 112 AW85
OLD WOKING, Wok. GU22 167 BA121
Old Woking Rd, W.Byf. KT14 151 BF113
Woking GU22 167 BE116
Old Woolwich Rd, SE10 103 ED79
Old Yd, The, West. TN16 180 EW124
Old York Rd, SW18 120 DB85
Oleander Cl, Orp. BR6 163 ER106
O'Leary Sq, E1 84 DW71
Olga St, E3 85 DY68
Olinda Rd, N16 66 DT58
Oliphant St, W10 81 CX69
Olive Gro, N15 66 DQ56
Oliver Av, SE25 142 DT97
Oliver Cl, W4 98 CP79
Addlestone KT15 152 BG105
Grays RM20 109 FT80
St. Albans (Park St) AL2 9 CD27
Oliver Cres, Dart. (Fnghm) DA4 148 FM101
Oliver Gdns, E6 86 EL72
Oliver-Goldsmith Est, SE15 102 DU81
Oliver Gro, SE25 142 DT98
Oliver Ms, SE15 102 DU82
Olive Rd, E13 86 EJ69
NW2 63 CW63
SW19 *off Norman Rd* 120 DC94
W5 97 CK76
Dartford DA1 128 FK88
Oliver Rd, E10 67 EB61
E17 67 EC57
NW10 80 CQ68
Brentwood (Shenf.) CM15 55 GA43
Grays RM20 109 FT81
New Malden KT3 138 CQ96
Rainham RM13 89 FF67
Sutton SM1 158 DD105
Swanley BR8 147 FD97
Olivers Yd, EC1 197 L4
Olive St, Rom. RM7 71 FD57
Olivette St, SW15 99 CX83
Olivia Dr, Slou. SL3 93 AZ78
Olivia Gdns, Uxb. (Hare.) UB9 38 BJ53
Ollards Gro, Loug. IG10 32 EK42
Olleberrie La, Rick. (Sarratt) WD3 5 BD32
Ollerton Grn, E3 85 DZ67
Ollerton Rd, N11 45 DK50
Olley Cl, Wall. SM6 159 DL108
Ollgar Cl, W12 81 CT74
Olliffe St, E14 204 E7
Olmar St, SE1 102 DU79
Olney Rd, SE17 101 DP79
Olron Cres, Bexh. DA6 126 EX85
Olven Rd, SE18 105 EQ80
Olveston Wk, Cars. SM5 140 DD100
Olwen Ms, Pnr. HA5 40 BX54
Olyffe Av, Well. DA16 106 EU82
Olyffe Dr, Beck. BR3 143 EC95
★ **Olympia**, W14 99 CY76
Olympia Ms, W2
off Queensway 82 DB73
Olympia Way, W14 99 CY76
Olympic Way, Grnf. UB6 78 CB67
Wembley HA9 62 CN63
Olympus Gro, N22 45 DN53
Olympus Sq, E5
off Nolan Way 66 DU62
Oman Av, NW2 63 CW63
O'Meara St, SE1 201 J3
Omega Bldg, SW18
off Smugglers Way 100 DB84
Omega Cl, E14 204 B6
Omega Ct, Rom. RM7 71 FC58
Omega Pl, N1 196 A1
Omega Rd, Wok. GU21 167 BA115
Omega St, SE14 103 EA81
Ommaney Rd, SE14 103 DX81
Omnibus Way, E17 47 EA54
Ondine Rd, SE15 102 DT84
Onega Gate, SE16 203 K6
O'Neill Path, SE18
off Kempt St 105 EN79
One Tree Cl, SE23 122 DW86
Ongar Cl, Add. KT15 151 BF107
Romford RM6 70 EW57
Ongar Hill, Add. KT15 152 BG107
Ongar Par, Add. KT15
off Ongar Hill 152 BG107
Ongar Pl, Add. KT15 152 BG107
Ongar Rd, SW6 100 DA79
Addlestone KT15 152 BG106
Brentwood CM15 54 FV45
Romford RM4 34 EW40
Ongar Way, Rain. RM13 89 FE67
Onra Rd, E17 67 EA59
Onslow Av, Rich. TW10 118 CL85
Sutton SM2 157 CZ110
Onslow Cl, E4 47 EC47
W10 *off Dowland St* 81 CZ69
Thames Ditton KT7 137 CE102
Woking GU22 167 BA117
Onslow Cres, SW7 198 A9
Chislehurst BR7 145 EP95
Woking GU22 167 BA117
Onslow Dr, Sid. DA14 126 EX89
Onslow Gdns, E18 68 EH55
N10 65 DH57
N21 29 DN43
SW7 100 DD78
South Croydon CR2 160 DU112
Thames Ditton KT7 137 CE102
Wallington SM6 159 DJ107
Onslow Ms, Cher. KT16 134 BG100
Onslow Ms E, SW7
off Cranley Pl 100 DD77
Onslow Ms W, SW7
off Cranley Pl 100 DD77
Onslow Rd, Croy. CR0 141 DM101
New Malden KT3 139 CU98
Richmond TW10 118 CL85
Onslow Rd, Walt. KT12 153 BT105
Onslow Sq, SW7 198 A8
Onslow St, EC1 196 E5
Onslow Way, T.Ditt. KT7 137 CE102
Woking GU22 167 BF115
Ontario Cl, Brox. EN10 15 DY25
Ontario St, SE1 200 G7
Ontario Way, E14 203 P1
On The Hill, Wat. WD19 40 BY47
Onyx Ms, E15
off Vicarage La 86 EE65
Opal Cl, E16 86 EK72
Opal Ct, Slou. (Wexham) SL3 *off Wexham St* 74 AV70
Opal Ms, NW6
off Priory Pk Rd 81 CZ67
Ilford IG1 69 EP61
Opal St, SE11 200 F9
Opecks Cl, Slou. (Wexham) SL2 74 AV70
Openshaw Rd, SE2 106 EV77
Openview, SW18 120 DC88
Ophelia Gdns, NW2
off Hamlet Sq 63 CY62
Ophir Ter, SE15 102 DU81
Opossum Way, Houns. TW4 96 BW82
Oppenheim Rd, SE13 103 EC82
Oppidans Ms, NW3
off Meadowbank 82 DF66
Oppidans Rd, NW3 82 DF66
Optima Pk, Dart. DA1 107 FG83
Orange Ct, E1 202 C3
Orange Ct La, Orp. BR6 163 EN109
Orange Gro, E11 67 ED62
Chigwell IG7 49 EQ51
Orange Hill Rd, Edg. HA8 42 CQ52
Orange Pl, SE16 202 G7
Orangery, The, Rich. TW10 117 CJ89
Orangery La, SE9 125 EM85
Orange Sq, SW1 198 G9
Orange St, WC2 199 M1
Orange Tree Hill, Rom. (Hav.at.Bow.) RM4 51 FD50
Orange Yd, W1 195 N9
Oransay Rd, N1 84 DQ65
Oransay Wk, N1
off Oransay Rd 84 DQ65
Oratory La, SW3 198 A10
Orbain Rd, SW6 99 CY80
Orbel St, SW11 100 DE81
Orbital Cres, Wat. WD25 23 BT35
Orbital One, Dart. DA1 128 FP89
Orb St, SE17 201 K9
Orchard, The, N14 29 DH43
N21 30 DR44
NW11 64 DA57
SE3 103 ED82
W4 98 CR77
W5 *off Montpelier Rd* 79 CK71
Banstead SM7 174 DA115
Epsom KT17 157 CT108
Epsom (Ewell) KT17
off Tayles Hill Dr 157 CT110
Hounslow TW3 96 CC82
Kings Langley WD4 6 BN29
Rickmansworth (Crox.Grn) WD3 *off Green La* 22 BM43
Sevenoaks (Dunt.Grn) TN13 181 FE120
Swanley BR8 147 FD96
Virginia Water GU25 132 AY99
Weybridge KT13 153 BP105
Woking GU22 166 AY122
Orchard Av, N3 64 DA55
N14 29 DJ44
N20 44 DD47
Addlestone (Wdhm) KT15 151 BF111
Ashford TW15 115 BQ93
Belvedere DA17 106 EY79
Brentwood CM13 55 FZ48
Croydon CR0 143 DY101
Dartford DA1 127 FH87
Feltham TW14 115 BR85
Gravesend DA11 131 GH92
Hounslow TW5 96 BY80
Mitcham CR4 140 DG102
New Malden KT3 138 CS96
Rainham RM13 90 FJ70
Southall UB1 78 BY74
Thames Ditton KT7 137 CG102
Watford WD25 7 BV32
Orchard Cl, E4
off Chingford Mt Rd 47 EA49
E11 68 EH56
N1 84 DQ66
NW2 63 CU62
SE23 *off Brenchley Gdns* 122 DW86
SW20 *off Grand Dr* 139 CW98
W10 81 CY71
Ashford TW15 115 BQ93
Banstead SM7 158 DB114
Bexleyheath DA7 106 EY81
Borehamwood (Els.) WD6 26 CM42
Bushey (Bushey Hth) WD23 41 CD46
Edgware HA8 42 CL51
Egham TW20 113 BB92
Epsom (W.Ewell) KT19 156 CP107
Leatherhead KT22 171 CF119
Leatherhead (E.Hors.) KT24 169 BT124
Leatherhead (Fetch.) KT22 171 CD122
Northolt UB5 60 CC64
Potters Bar (Cuffley) EN6 13 DL28
Radlett WD7 25 CE37
Rickmansworth (Chorl.) WD3 21 BD42
Ruislip HA4 59 BQ59
South Ockendon RM15 91 FW70
Surbiton KT6 137 CH101
Uxbridge (Denh.) UB9 76 BH65
Walton-on-Thames KT12 135 BV101
Watford WD17 23 BT40
Wembley HA0 80 CL67
Woking GU22 167 BB116
Orchard Ct, Hem.H. (Bov.) HP3 5 BA27
Isleworth TW7
off Thornbury Av 97 CD80
Twickenham TW2 117 CD89
Wallington SM6
off Parkgate Rd 159 DH106
Worcester Park KT4 139 CU102
Orchard Cres, Edg. HA8 42 CQ50
Enfield EN1 30 DT39
Orchard Dr, SE3
off Orchard Rd 104 EE82
Ashtead KT21 171 CK120
Edgware HA8 42 CM50
Epping (They.B.) CM16 33 ES36
Grays RM17 110 GA75
Rickmansworth (Chorl.) WD3 21 BC41
St. Albans (Park St) AL2 8 CB27
Uxbridge UB8 76 BK70
Watford WD17 23 BT39
Woking GU21 167 AZ115
Orchard End, Cat. CR3 176 DS122
Leatherhead (Fetch.) KT22 170 CC124
Weybridge KT13 135 BS103
Orchard End Av, Amer. HP7 20 AT39
Orchard Est, Wdf.Grn. IG8 48 EJ52
Orchard Gdns, Chess. KT9 156 CL105
Epsom KT18 156 CQ114
Sutton SM1 158 DA106
Waltham Abbey EN9 15 EC34
Orchard Gate, NW9 62 CS56
Esher KT10 137 CD102
Greenford UB6 79 CH65
Orchard Grn, Orp. BR6 145 ES103
Orchard Gro, SE20 122 DU94
Croydon CR0 143 DY101
Edgware HA8 42 CN53
Gerrards Cross (Chal.St.P.) SL9 36 AW53
Harrow HA3 62 CM57
Orpington BR6 145 ET103
Orchard Hill, SE13
off Coldbath St 103 EB82
Carshalton SM5 158 DF106
Dartford DA1 127 FE85
Orchard Ho, Erith DA8
off Northend Rd 107 FF81
Orchard La, SW20 139 CV95
Brentwood (Pilg.Hat.) CM15 54 FT43
East Molesey KT8 137 CD100
Woodford Green IG8 48 EJ49
Orchard Lea Cl, Wok. GU22 167 BE115
ORCHARD LEIGH, Chesh. HP5 4 AV28
Orchard Leigh, Chesh. HP5 4 AU28
Orchardleigh, Lthd. KT22 171 CH122
Orchardleigh Av, Enf. EN3 30 DW40
Orchard Mains, Wok. GU22 166 AW119
Orchardmede, N21 30 DR44
Orchard Ms, N1
off Southgate Gro 84 DR66
N6 *off Orchard Rd* 65 DH59
Orchard Path, Slou. SL3 75 BA72
Orchard Pl, E5 66 DV64
E14 86 EE73
N17 46 DT52
Keston BR2 162 EJ109
Sevenoaks (Sund.) TN14 180 EY124
Waltham Cross (Chsht) EN8 *off Turners Hill* 15 DX30
Orchard Ri, Croy. CR0 143 DY102
Kingston upon Thames KT2 138 CQ95
Pinner HA5 59 BT55
Richmond TW10 98 CP84
Orchard Ri E, Sid. DA15 125 ET85
Orchard Ri W, Sid. DA15 125 ES85
Orchard Rd, N6 65 DH59
SE3 104 EE82
SE18 105 ER77
Barnet EN5 27 CZ42
Belvedere DA17 106 FA77
Brentford TW8 97 CJ79
Bromley BR1 144 EJ95
Chalfont St. Giles HP8 36 AW47
Chessington KT9 156 CL105
Dagenham RM10 88 FA67
Enfield EN3 30 DW43
Feltham TW13 115 BU88
Gravesend (Nthflt) DA11 130 GC89
Hampton TW12 116 BZ94
Hayes UB3 77 BT73
Hounslow TW4 116 BZ85
Kingston upon Thames KT1 138 CL96
Mitcham CR4 140 DG102
Orpington (Farnboro.) BR6 163 EP106
Orpington (Pr.Bot.) BR6 164 EW110
Reigate RH2 184 DB134
Richmond TW9 98 CN83
Romford RM7 51 FB53
Sevenoaks (Otford) TN14 181 FF116
Sevenoaks (Rvrhd) TN13 190 FE122
Sidcup DA14 125 ES91
South Croydon CR2 160 DV114
South Ockendon RM15 91 FW70
Sunbury-on-Thames TW16
off Hanworth Rd 115 BV94
Sutton SM1 158 DA106
Swanscombe DA10 130 FY85
Twickenham TW1 117 CG85
Welling DA16 106 EV83
Windsor (Old Wind.) SL4 112 AV86
Orchards, The, Epp. CM16 18 EU32
Orchards Cl, W.Byf. KT14 152 BG114
Orchardson Ho, NW8
off Orchardson St 82 DD70
Orchardson St, NW8 82 DD70
Orchard Sq, W14 *off Sun Rd* 99 CZ78
Orchards Residential Pk, The, Slou. SL3 75 AZ74
Orchards Shop Cen, Dart. DA1 128 FL86
Orchard St, E17 67 DY56
W1 194 F9
Dartford DA1 128 FL86
Orchard Ter, Enf. EN1
off Great Cambridge Rd 30 DU44
Orchard Vw, Cher. KT16 134 BG100
Uxbridge UB8 76 BK70
Orchard Vil, Sid. DA14 126 EV93
Orchard Wk, Kings.T. KT2
off Clifton Rd 138 CN95
Orchard Way, Add. KT15 152 BH106
Ashford TW15 114 BM89
Beckenham BR3 143 DY99
Chigwell IG7 50 EU48
Croydon CR0 143 DY102
Dartford DA2 128 FK90
Enfield EN1 30 DS41
Esher KT10 154 CC107
Hemel Hempstead (Bov.) HP3 5 BA28
Orchard Way, Oxt. RH8 188 EG133
Potters Bar EN6 12 DB28
Rickmansworth (Mill End) WD3 38 BG45
Slough SL3 74 AY74
Sutton SM1 158 DD105
Tadworth (Lwr Kgswd) KT20 183 CZ126
Waltham Cross (Chsht) EN7 13 DP27
Orchard Waye, Uxb. UB8 76 BK68
Orchehill Av, Ger.Cr. SL9 56 AX56
Orchehill Ct, Ger.Cr. SL9 56 AY57
Orchehill Ri, Ger.Cr. SL9 56 AY57
Orchestra Cl, Edg. HA8
off Symphony Cl 42 CP52
Orchid Cl, E6 86 EL71
Chessington KT9 155 CJ108
Romford (Abridge) RM4 34 EV41
Southall UB1 78 BY72
Waltham Cross (Goffs Oak) EN7 14 DQ30
Orchid Ct, Egh. TW20 113 BB91
Romford RM7 71 FE61
Orchid Rd, N14 45 DJ45
Orchid St, W12 81 CU73
Orchis Gro, Grays (Bad.Dene) RM17 110 FZ78
Orchis Way, Rom. RM3 52 FM51
Orde Hall St, WC1 196 B5
Ordell Rd, E3 85 DZ68
Ordnance Cl, Felt. TW13 115 BU90
Ordnance Cres, SE10 204 G4
Ordnance Hill, NW8 82 DD67
Ordnance Ms, NW8
off St. Ann's Ter 82 DD68
Ordnance Rd, E16 86 EF71
SE18 105 EN79
Enfield EN3 31 DX37
Gravesend DA12 131 GJ86
Oregano Cl, West Dr. UB7
off Camomile Way 76 BM72
Oregano Dr, E14 85 ED72
Oregon Av, E12 69 EM63
Oregon Cl, N.Mal. KT3
off Georgia Rd 138 CQ98
Oregon Sq, Orp. BR6 145 ER102
Orestes Ms, NW6
off Aldred Rd 64 DA64
Oreston Rd, Rain. RM13 90 FK69
Orford Ct, SE27 121 DP89
Orford Gdns, Twick. TW1 117 CF89
Orford Rd, E17 67 EA57
E18 68 EH55
SE6 123 EB90
Organ Hall Rd, Borwd. WD6 26 CL39
Organ La, E4 47 EC47
Oriel Cl, Mitch. CR4 141 DK98
Oriel Ct, NW3 *off Heath St* 64 DC63
Oriel Dr, SW13 99 CV79
Oriel Gdns, Ilf. IG5 69 EM55
Oriel Pl, NW3 *off Heath St* 64 DC63
Oriel Rd, E9 85 DX65
Oriel Way, Nthlt. UB5 78 CB66
Oriental City, NW9 62 CR55
Oriental Cl, Wok. GU22
off Oriental Rd 167 BA117
Oriental Rd, E16 86 EK74
Woking GU22 167 BA117
Oriental St, E14
off Morant St 85 EA73
Orient Ind Pk, E10 67 EA61
Orient St, SE11 200 F8
Orient Way, E5 67 DX62
E10 67 DY61
Oriole Cl, Abb.L. WD5 7 BU31
Oriole Way, SE28 88 EV73
Orion Ho, E1 *off Coventry Rd* 84 DV70
Orion Pt, E14 203 P8
Orion Rd, N11 45 DH51
Orion Way, Nthwd. HA6 39 BT49
Orissa Rd, SE18 105 ES78
Orkney St, SW11 100 DG82
Orlando Gdns, Epsom KT19 156 CR110
Orlando Rd, SW4 101 DJ83
Orleans Cl, Esher KT10 137 CD103
★ **Orleans Ho Gall**, Twick. TW1 117 CH88
Orleans Rd, SE19 122 DR93
Twickenham TW1 117 CH87
Orlestone Gdns, Orp. BR6 164 EY106
Orleston Ms, N7 83 DN65
Orleston Rd, N7 83 DN65
Orley Fm Rd, Har. HA1 61 CE62
Orlop St, SE10 104 EE78
Ormanton Rd, SE26 122 DU91
Orme Ct, W2 82 DB73
Orme Ct Ms, W2 *off Orme La* 82 DB73
Orme La, W2 82 DB73
Ormeley Rd, SW12 121 DH88
Orme Rd, Kings.T. KT1 138 CP96
Sutton SM1 *off Grove Rd* 158 DB107
Ormerod Gdns, Mitch. CR4 140 DG96
Ormesby Cl, SE28
off Wroxham Rd 88 EX73
Ormesby Dr, Pot.B. EN6 11 CX32
Ormesby Way, Har. HA3 62 CM58
Orme Sq, W2
off Bayswater Rd 82 DB73
Ormiston Gro, W12 81 CV74
Ormiston Rd, SE10 104 EG78
Ormond Av, Hmptn. TW12 136 CB95
Richmond TW10
off Ormond Rd 117 CK85
Ormond Cl, WC1 196 A6
Romford (Harold Wd) RM3
off Chadwick Dr 52 FK54
Ormond Cres, Hmptn. TW12 136 CB95
Ormond Dr, Hmptn. TW12 116 CB94
Ormonde Av, Epsom KT19 156 CR109
Orpington BR6 145 EQ103
Ormonde Gate, SW3 100 DF78
Ormonde Pl, SW1 198 F9
Ormonde Ri, Buck.H. IG9 48 EJ46
Ormonde Rd, SW14 98 CP83
Northwood HA6 39 BR49
Woking GU21 166 AW116
Ormonde Ter, NW8 82 DF67
Ormond Ms, WC1 196 A5
Ormond Rd, N19 65 DL60
Richmond TW10 117 CK85
Ormond Yd, SW1 199 L2
Ormsby, Sutt. SM2
off Grange Rd 158 DB108
Ormsby Gdns, Grnf. UB6 78 CC68
Ormsby Pl, N16
off Victorian Gro 66 DT62
Ormsby Pt, SE18
off Vincent Rd 105 EP77
Ormsby St, E2 84 DT68
Ormside St, SE15 102 DW79
Ormside Way, Red. RH1 185 DH130
Ormskirk Rd, Wat. WD19 40 BX49
Ornan Rd, NW3 64 DE64
Orpen Wk, N16 66 DS62
Orphanage Rd, Wat. WD17, WD24 24 BW40
Orpheus St, SE5 102 DR81
ORPINGTON, BR5 & BR6 145 ES102
⇌ **Orpington** 145 ET103
Orpington Bypass, Orp. BR6 146 EV103
Sevenoaks TN14 164 FA109
Orpington Gdns, N18 46 DS48
Ⓗ **Orpington Hosp**, Orp. BR6 163 ET105
Orpington Rd, N21 45 DP46
Chislehurst BR7 145 ES97
Orpin Rd, Red. (S.Merst.) RH1 185 DH130
Orpwood Cl, Hmptn. TW12 116 BZ92
ORSETT HEATH, Grays RM16 111 GG75
Orsett Heath Cres, Grays RM16 111 GG76
Orsett Rd, Grays RM17 110 GA78
Orsett St, SE11 200 C10
Orsett Ter, W2 82 DC72
Woodford Green IG8 48 EJ53
Orsman Rd, N1 84 DS67
Orton St, E1 202 B3
Orville Rd, SW11 100 DD82
Orwell Cl, Hayes UB3 77 BS73
Rainham RM13 89 FD71
Orwell Ct, N5 66 DQ63
Orwell Rd, E13 86 EJ68
Osbaldeston Rd, N16 66 DU61
Osberton Rd, SE12 124 EG85
Osbert St, SW1 199 M9
Osborn Cl, E8 84 DU67
Osborne Av, Stai. TW19 114 BL88
Osborne Cl, Barn. EN4 28 DF41
Beckenham BR3 143 DY98
Feltham TW13 116 BX92
Hornchurch RM11 71 FH58
Osborne Ct, Pot.B. EN6 12 DB29
Osborne Gdns, Pot.B. EN6 12 DB30
Thornton Heath CR7 142 DQ96
Osborne Gro, E17 67 DZ56
N4 65 DN60
Osborne Ms, E17
off Osborne Gro 67 DZ56
Osborne Pl, Sutt. SM1 158 DD106
Osborne Rd, E7 68 EH64
E9 85 DZ65
E10 67 EB62
N4 65 DM60
N13 45 DN48
NW2 81 CV65
W3 98 CP76
Belvedere DA17 106 EZ78
Brentwood (Pilg.Hat.) CM15 54 FU44
Buckhurst Hill IG9 48 EH46
Dagenham RM9 70 EZ64
Egham TW20 113 AZ93
Enfield EN3 31 DY40
Hornchurch RM11 71 FH58
Hounslow TW3 96 BZ83
Kingston upon Thames KT2 118 CL94
Potters Bar EN6 12 DB30
Redhill RH1 184 DG131
Southall UB1 78 CC72
Thornton Heath CR7 142 DQ96
Uxbridge UB8
off Oxford Rd 76 BJ66
Waltham Cross (Chsht) EN8 15 DY27
Walton-on-Thames KT12 135 BU102
Watford WD24 24 BW38
Osborne Sq, Dag. RM9 70 EZ63
Osborne St, Slou. SL1 92 AT75
Osborne Ter, SW17
off Church La 120 DG92
Osborne Way, Chess. KT9
off Bridge Rd 156 CM106
Osborn Gdns, NW7 43 CX52
Osborn La, SE23 123 DY87
Osborn St, E1 84 DT71
Osborn Ter, SE3 *off Lee Rd* 104 EF84
Osbourne Av, Kings L. WD4 6 BM28
Osbourne Hts, Brwd. (Warley) CM14 54 FV49
Osbourne Rd, Dart. DA2 128 FP86
Oscar Faber Pl, N1
off St. Peter's Way 84 DS66
Oscar St, SE8 103 EA81
Oseney Cres, NW5 83 DJ65
Osgood Av, Orp. BR6 163 ET106
Osgood Gdns, Orp. BR6 163 ET106
OSIDGE, N14 45 DH46
Osidge La, N14 44 DG46
Osier Cres, N10 44 DF53
Osier La, SE10 205 L7
Osier Ms, W4 99 CT79
Osier Pl, Egh. TW20 113 BC93
Osiers, The, Rick. (Crox.Grn) WD3 23 BQ44
Osiers Rd, SW18 100 DA84
Osier St, E1 84 DW70
Osier Way, E10 67 EB62
Banstead SM7 157 CY114
Mitcham CR4 140 DE99
Oslac Rd, SE6 123 EB92
Oslo Ct, NW8 194 B1
Oslo Sq, SE16 203 L6
Osman Cl, N15
off Tewkesbury Rd 66 DR58
Osman Rd, N9 46 DU48
W6 *off Batoum Gdns* 99 CW76
Osmington Ho, SW8
off Dorset Rd 101 DM80
Osmond Cl, Har. HA2 60 CC61

★ Place of interest ⇌ Railway station ⊖ London Underground station DLR Docklands Light Railway station Tra Tramlink station H Hospital Riv Pedestrian ferry landing stage

Osmond Gdns, Wall. SM6 159 DJ106
Osmund St, W12
off Braybrook St 81 CT72
Osnaburgh St, NW1 195 J5
NW1 (north section) 195 J3
Osnaburgh Ter, NW1 195 J4
Osney Ho, SE2
off Hartslock Dr 106 EX75
Osney Wk, Cars. SM5 140 DD100
Osney Way, Grav. DA12 131 GM89
Osprey Cl, E6 off Dove App 86 EL71
E11 68 EG56
E17 47 DY52
Bromley BR2 144 EL102
Leatherhead (Fetch.) KT22 170 CC122
Sutton SM1
off Sandpiper Rd 157 CZ106
Watford WD25 8 BY34
West Drayton UB7 94 BK75
Osprey Ct, Wal.Abb. EN9 16 EG34
Osprey Gdns, S.Croy. CR2 161 DX110
Osprey Hts, SW11
off Bramlands Cl 100 DE83
Osprey Ms, Enf. EN3 30 DX43
Osprey Rd, Wal.Abb. EN9 16 EG34
Ospringe Cl, SE20 122 DW94
Ospringe Ct, SE9
off Alderwood Rd 125 ER86
Ospringe Rd, NW5 65 DJ63
Osram Ct, W6 off Lena Gdns 99 CW76
Osram Rd, Wem. HA9 61 CK62
Osric Path, N1 197 M1
Ossian Ms, N4 65 DM59
Ossian Rd, N4 65 DM59
Ossington Bldgs, W1 194 F6
Ossington Cl, W2
off Ossington St 82 DA73
Ossington St, W2 82 DA73
Ossory Rd, SE1 102 DU78
Ossulston St, NW1 195 M1
Ossulton Pl, N2
off East End Rd 64 DC55
Ossulton Way, N2 64 DC56
Ostade Rd, SW2 121 DM87
Ostell Cres, Enf. EN3 31 EA38
Osten Ms, SW7
off Emperor's Gate 100 DC77
Osterberg Rd, Dart. DA1 108 FM84
OSTERLEY, Islw. TW7 96 CC80
⊖ Osterley 97 CD80
Osterley Av, Islw. TW7 97 CD80
Osterley Cl, Orp. BR5
off Leith Hill 146 EU95
Osterley Ct, Islw. TW7 97 CD81
Osterley Cres, Islw. TW7 97 CE81
Osterley Gdns, Th.Hth. CR7 142 DQ96
Osterley Ho, E14
off Giraud St 85 EB72
Osterley La, Islw. TW7 97 CE78
Southall UB2 96 CA78
Osterley Pk, Islw. TW7 97 CD78
★ Osterley Park Ho, Islw.
TW7 96 CC78
Osterley Pk Rd, Sthl. UB2 96 BZ76
Osterley Pk Vw Rd, W7 97 CE75
Osterley Rd, N16 66 DS63
Isleworth TW7 97 CE80
Osterley Views, Sthl. UB2
off West Pk Rd 79 CD74
Oster Ter, E17
off Southcote Rd 67 DX57
Ostlers Dr, Ashf. TW15 115 BQ92
Ostliffe Rd, N13 46 DQ50
Oswald Bldg, SW8
off Queenstown Rd 101 DH79
Oswald Cl, Lthd. (Fetch.)
KT22 170 CC122
Oswald Rd, Lthd. (Fetch.)
KT22 170 CC122
Southall UB1 78 BY74
Oswald's Mead, E9
off Lindisfarne Way 67 DY63
Oswald St, E5 67 DX62
Oswald Ter, NW2
off Temple Rd 63 CW62
Osward, Croy. CR0 161 DZ109
Osward Pl, N9 46 DV47
Osward Rd, SW17 120 DF89
Oswell Ho, E1 202 E2
Oswin St, SE11 200 G8
Oswyth Rd, SE5 102 DS82
OTFORD, Sev. TN14 181 FG116
Otford Cl, SE20 142 DW95
Bexley DA5
off Southwold Rd 127 FB86
Bromley BR1 145 EN97
Otford Cres, SE4 123 DZ86
Otford La, Sev. (Halst.) TN14 164 EZ112
Otford Rd, Sev. TN14 181 FH118
Othello Cl, SE11 200 F10
Otho Ct, Brent. TW8 97 CK80
Otis St, E3 85 EC69
Otley App, Ilf. IG2 69 EP58
Otley Dr, Ilf. IG2 69 EP57
Otley Rd, E16 86 EJ72
Otley Ter, E5 67 DX61
Otley Way, Wat. WD19 40 BW48
Otlinge Rd, Orp. BR5 146 EX98
Ottawa Ct, Brox. EN10 15 DY25
Ottawa Gdns, Dag. RM10 89 FD66
Ottawa Rd, Til. RM18 111 GG82
Ottaway St, E5
off Stellman Cl 66 DU62
Ottenden Cl, Orp. BR6
off Southfleet Rd 163 ES105
Otterbourne Rd, E4 47 ED48
Croydon CR0 142 DQ103
Otterburn Gdns, Islw. TW7 97 CG80
Otterburn Ho, SE5 102 DQ80
Otterburn St, SW17 120 DF93
Otter Cl, E15 85 EC67
Chertsey (Ott.) KT16 151 BB107
Otterden St, SE6 123 EA91
Otterfield Rd, West Dr. UB7 76 BL73
Ottermead La, Cher. (Ott.)
KT16 151 BC107
Otter Meadow, Lthd. KT22 171 CF119
Otter Rd, Grnf. UB6 78 CC70
Otters Cl, Orp. BR5 146 EX98
OTTERSHAW, Cher. KT16 151 BC106
Ottershaw Pk, Cher. (Ott.)
KT16 151 BA109
Otterspool La, Wat. WD25 24 BY38
Otterspool Service Rd, Wat.
WD25 24 BZ39
Otterspool Way, Wat. WD25 24 BY37
Otto Cl, SE26 122 DV90
Ottoman Ter, Wat. WD17
off Ebury Rd 24 BW41
Otto St, SE17 101 DP79
Ottways Av, Ashtd. KT21 171 CK119
Ottways La, Ashtd. KT21 171 CK120
Otway Gdns, Bushey WD23 41 CE45
Otways Cl, Pot.B. EN6 12 DB32
Oulton Cl, E5
off Mundford Rd 66 DW61
SE28 off Rollesby Way 88 EW72
Oulton Cres, Bark. IG11 87 ET65
Potters Bar EN6 11 CX32
Oulton Rd, N15 66 DR57
Oulton Way, Wat. WD19 40 BY49
Oundle Av, Bushey WD23 24 CC44
Ousden Cl, Wal.Cr. (Chsht)
EN8 15 DY30
Ousden Dr, Wal.Cr. (Chsht)
EN8 15 DY30
Ouseley Rd, SW12 120 DF88
Staines (Wrays.) TW19 112 AW87
Windsor (Old Wind.) SL4 112 AW87
Outer Circle, NW1 194 F5
Outfield Rd, Ger.Cr. (Chal.St.P.)
SL9 36 AX52
Outgate Rd, NW10 81 CT66
Outlook Dr, Ch.St.G. HP8 36 AX48
Outram Pl, N1 83 DL67
Weybridge KT13 153 BQ106
Outram Rd, E6 86 EL67
N22 45 DK53
Croydon CR0 142 DT102
Outwich St, EC3 197 N8
Outwood La, Couls. CR5 174 DF118
Tadworth (Kgswd) KT20 174 DB122
⊖ Oval 101 DN79
★ Oval, The, Surrey CCC,
SE11 101 DM79
Oval, The, E2 84 DV68
Banstead SM7 158 DA114
Broxbourne EN10 15 DY25
Sidcup DA15 126 EU87
Oval Gdns, Grays RM17 110 GC76
Oval Pl, SW8 101 DM80
Oval Rd, NW1 83 DH67
Croydon CR0 142 DS102
Oval Rd N, Dag. RM10 89 FB67
Oval Rd S, Dag. RM10 89 FB68
Oval Way, SE11 101 DM78
Gerrards Cross SL9 56 AY56
Ovenden Rd, Sev. (Sund.)
TN14 180 EX120
Overbrae, Beck. BR3 123 EA93
Overbrook Wk, Edg. HA8 42 CN52
Overbury Av, Beck. BR3 143 EB97
Overbury Cres, Croy.
(New Adgtn) CR0 161 EC110
Overbury Rd, N15 66 DR58
Overbury St, E5 67 DX63
Overcliffe, Grav. DA11 131 GG86
Overcliff Rd, SE13 103 EA83
Grays RM17 110 GD78
Overcourt Cl, Sid. DA15 126 EV86
Overdale, Ashtd. KT21 172 CL115
Redhill (Bletch.) RH1 186 DQ133
Overdale Av, N.Mal. KT3 138 CQ96
Overdale Rd, W5 97 CJ76
Overdown Rd, SE6 123 EA91
Overhill, Warl. CR6 176 DW119
Overhill Rd, SE22 122 DU87
Purley CR8 159 DN109
Overhill Way, Beck. BR3 143 ED99
Overlea Rd, E5 66 DU59
Overmead, Sid. DA15 125 ER87
Swanley BR8 147 FE99
Oversley Ho, W2 82 DA71
Overstand Cl, Beck. BR3 143 EA99
Overstone Gdns, Croy. CR0 143 DZ101
Overstone Rd, W6 99 CW76
Overstrand Ho, Horn. RM12
off Sunrise Av 71 FH61
Overstream, Rick. (Loud.)
WD3 22 BH42
Over The Misbourne,
Ger.Cr. SL9 57 BA58
Uxbridge (Denh.) UB9 57 BC58
Overthorpe Cl, Wok. (Knap.)
GU21 166 AS117
Overton Cl, NW10 80 CQ65
Isleworth TW7
off Avenue Rd 97 CF81
Overton Ct, E11 68 EG59
Overton Dr, E11 68 EH59
Romford RM6 70 EW59
Overton Ho, SW15
off Tangley Gro 119 CT87
Overton Rd, E10 67 DY60
N14 29 DL43
SE2 106 EW76
SW9 101 DN82
Sutton SM2 158 DA107
Overton Rd E, SE2 106 EX76
Overtons Yd, Croy. CR0 142 DQ104
Overy St, Dart. DA1 128 FL86
Ovesdon Av, Har. HA2 60 BZ60
Ovett Cl, SE19 122 DS93
Ovex Cl, E14 204 E5
Ovington Ct, Wok. GU21
off Roundthorn Way 166 AT116
Ovington Gdns, SW3 198 C7
Ovington Ms, SW3 198 C7
Ovington Sq, SW3 198 C7
Ovington St, SW3 198 C7
Owen Cl, SE28 88 EW74
Croydon CR0 142 DR100
Hayes UB4 77 BV69
Northolt UB5 78 BY65
Romford RM5 51 FB51
Slough SL3 off Parsons Rd 93 AZ78
Owen Gdns, Wdf.Grn. IG8 48 EL51
Owenite St, SE2 106 EV77
Owen Pl, Lthd. KT22
off Church Rd 171 CH122
Owen Rd, N13 46 DQ50
Owen Rd, Hayes UB4 77 BV69
Owens Ms, E11 off Short Rd 68 EE61
Owen's Row, EC1 196 F2
Owen St, EC1 196 F1
Owens Way, SE23 123 DY87
Rickmansworth (Crox.Grn)
WD3 22 BN43
Owen Wk, SE20
off Sycamore Gro 122 DU94
Owen Waters Ho, Ilf. IG5 49 EM53
Owen Way, NW10 80 CQ65
Owgan Cl, SE5 off Benhill Rd 102 DR80
Owl Cl, S.Croy. CR2 161 DX110
Owlets Hall Cl, Horn. RM11
off Prospect Rd 72 FM55
Owl Pk, Loug. (High Beach)
IG10 32 EF40
Ownstead Gdns, S.Croy.
CR2 160 DT111
Ownsted Hill, Croy. (New Adgtn)
CR0 161 EC110
Oxberry Av, SW6 99 CY82
Oxdowne Cl, Cob. (Stoke D'Ab.)
KT11 154 CB114
Oxenden Wd Rd, Orp. BR6 164 EV107
Oxendon St, SW1 199 M1
Oxenford St, SE15 102 DT83
Oxenholme, NW1 195 L1
Oxenpark Av, Wem. HA9 62 CL59
Oxestalls Rd, SE8 203 L10
Oxford Av, N14 45 DJ46
SW20 139 CY96
Grays RM16 111 GG77
Hayes UB3 95 BT80
Hornchurch RM11 72 FN56
Hounslow TW5 96 CA78
★ Oxford Circ, W1 195 K8
⊖ Oxford Circus 195 K8
Oxford Circ Av, W1 195 K9
Oxford Cl, N9 46 DV47
Ashford TW15 115 BQ94
Gravesend DA12 131 GM89
Mitcham CR4 141 DJ97
Northwood HA6 39 BQ49
Romford RM2 71 FG57
Waltham Cross (Chsht) EN8 15 DX29
Oxford Ct, EC4 197 K10
W3 80 CN72
Brentwood (Warley) CM14 54 FX49
Feltham TW13
off Oxford Way 116 BX91
Oxford Cres, N.Mal. KT3 138 CR100
Oxford Dr, SE1 201 M3
Ruislip HA4 60 BW61
Oxford Gdns, N20 44 DD46
N21 46 DQ45
W4 98 CN78
W10 81 CY72
Uxbridge (Denh.) UB9 57 BF62
Oxford Gate, W6 99 CX77
Oxford Ms, Bex. DA5 126 FA88
Oxford Pl, NW10
off Neasden La N 62 CR62
Oxford Rd, E15 85 ED65
N4 65 DN60
N9 46 DV47
NW6 82 DA68
SE19 122 DR93
SW15 99 CY84
W5 79 CK73
Carshalton SM5 158 DE107
Enfield EN3 30 DV43
Gerrards Cross SL9 57 BA60
Harrow HA1 60 CC58
Harrow (Wealds.) HA3 61 CF55
Ilford IG1 69 EQ63
Redhill RH1 184 DE133
Romford RM3 52 FM51
Sidcup DA14 126 EV92
Teddington TW11 117 CD92
Uxbridge UB8, UB9 76 BJ65
Wallington SM6 159 DJ106
Woodford Green IG8 48 EJ50
Oxford Rd N, W4 98 CP78
Oxford Rd S, W4 98 CN78
Oxford Sq, W2 194 C9
Oxford St, W1 195 L8
Watford WD18 23 BV43
Oxford Wk, Sthl. UB1 78 BZ74
Oxford Way, Felt. TW13 116 BX91
Oxgate Cen Ind Est, NW2
off Oxgate La 63 CV61
Oxgate Gdns, NW2 63 CV62
Oxgate La, NW2 63 CV61
Oxhawth Cres, Brom. BR2 145 EN99
OXHEY, Wat. WD19 24 BW44
Oxhey Av, Wat. WD19 40 BX45
Oxhey Dr, Nthwd. HA6 39 BV50
Watford WD19 40 BW48
Oxhey Dr S, Nthwd. HA6 39 BV50
Oxhey La, Har. HA3 40 CA50
Pinner HA5 40 CA50
Watford WD19 40 BZ47
Oxhey Ridge Cl, Nthwd. HA6 39 BU50
Oxhey Rd, Wat. WD19 24 BW44
Ox La, Epsom KT17
off Church St 157 CU109
Oxleas, E6 87 EP72
Oxleas Cl, Well. DA16 105 ER82
Oxleay Ct, Har. HA2 60 CA60
Oxleay Rd, Har. HA2 60 CA60
Oxleigh Cl, N.Mal. KT3 138 CS99
Oxley Cl, SE1 202 A10
Romford RM2 52 FJ54
Oxleys Rd, NW2 63 CV62
Waltham Abbey EN9 16 EG32
Oxlip Cl, Croy. CR0
off Marigold Way 143 DX102
Oxlow La, Dag. RM9, RM10 70 FA63
Oxonian St, SE22 102 DT84
Oxo Twr Wf, SE1 200 E1
OXSHOTT, Lthd. KT22 155 CD113
⇌ Oxshott 154 CC113
Oxshott Ri, Cob. KT11 154 BX113
Oxshott Rd, Lthd. KT22 171 CE115
Oxshott Way, Cob. KT11 170 BY115
OXTED, RH8 187 ED129
⇌ Oxted 188 EE129
Oxted Cl, Mitch. CR4 140 DD97
Oxted Rd, Gdse. RH9 186 DW130
Oxtoby Way, SW16 141 DK96
Oyster Catchers Cl, E16
off Freemasons Rd 86 EH72
Oyster Catcher Ter, Ilf. IG5
off Tiptree Cres 69 EN55
Oystergate Wk, EC4
off Upper Thames St 84 DR73
Oyster La, W.Byf. (Byfleet)
KT14 152 BK110
Oyster Row, E1 off Lukin St 84 DW72
Oyster Wf, SW11 100 DD82
Ozolins Way, E16 86 EG72

P

Pablo Neruda Cl, SE24
off Shakespeare Rd 101 DP84
Paceheath Cl, Rom. RM5 51 FD51
Pace Pl, E1 off Bigland St 84 DV72
PACHESHAM PARK, Lthd.
KT22 171 CG116
Pachesham Pk, Lthd. KT22 171 CG117
Pacific Cl, Felt. TW14 115 BT88
Swanscombe DA10 130 FY85
Pacific Rd, E16 86 EG72
Pacific Wf, SE16
off Rotherhithe St 85 DX74
Packet Boat La, Uxb. UB8 76 BH72
Packham Cl, Orp. BR6
off Berrylands 146 EW104
Packham Ct, Wor.Pk. KT4
off Lavender Av 139 CW104
Packham Rd, Grav.
(Nthflt) DA11 131 GF90
Packhorse La, Borwd. WD6 26 CS37
Potters Bar (Ridge) EN6 10 CR31
Packhorse Rd, Ger.Cr. SL9 56 AY58
Sevenoaks TN13 190 FC123
Packington Rd, W3 98 CQ76
Packington Sq, N1 84 DQ67
Packington St, N1 83 DP67
Packmores Rd, SE9 125 ER85
Padbrook, Oxt. RH8 188 EG129
Padbrook Cl, Oxt. RH8 188 EH128
Padbury, SE17 102 DS78
Padbury Cl, Felt. TW14 115 BR88
Padbury Ct, E2 84 DT69
Padcroft Rd, West Dr. UB7 76 BK74
Paddenswick Rd, W6 99 CU76
PADDINGTON, W2 82 DB71
⇌ Paddington 82 DC72
⊖ Paddington 82 DC72
Paddington Cl, Hayes UB4 78 BX70
Paddington Grn, W2 194 A6
Paddington St, W1 194 F6
Paddock, The, Ger.Cr.
(Chal.St.P.) SL9 36 AY50
Slough (Datchet) SL3 92 AV81
Uxbridge (Ickhm) UB10 59 BP63
Westerham TN16 189 EQ126
Paddock Cl, SE3 104 EG82
SE26 123 DX91
Dartford (S.Darenth) DA4 148 FQ95
Northolt UB5 78 CA68
Orpington BR6
off State Fm Av 163 EP105
Oxted RH8 188 EF131
Watford WD19 24 BY44
Worcester Park KT4 138 CS102
Paddock Gdns, SE19
off Westow St 122 DS93
Paddock Rd, NW2 63 CU62
Bexleyheath DA6 106 EY84
Ruislip HA4 60 BX62
Paddocks, The, NW7 43 CY51
Addlestone (New Haw)
KT15 152 BH110
Barnet EN4 28 DF41
Rickmansworth (Chorl.)
WD3 21 BF42
Romford (Stap.Abb.) RM4 35 FF44
Sevenoaks TN13 191 FK124
Virginia Water GU25 132 AY100
Wembley HA9 62 CP61
Weybridge KT13 135 BS104
Paddocks Cl, Ashtd. KT21 172 CL118
Cobham KT11 154 BW114
Harrow HA2 60 CB63
Orpington BR5 146 EX103
Paddocks Mead, Wok. GU21 166 AS116
Paddocks Retail Pk, Wey.
KT13 152 BL111
Paddocks Way, Ashtd. KT21 172 CL118
Chertsey KT16 134 BH102
Paddock Wk, Warl. CR6 176 DV119
Paddock Way, SW15 119 CW87
Chislehurst BR7 125 ER94
Oxted RH8 188 EF131
Woking GU21 151 BB114
Padfield Ct, Wem. HA9
off Forty Av 62 CM62
Padfield Rd, SE5 102 DQ83
SW9 102 DQ83
Padgets, The, Wal.Abb. EN9 15 ED34
Padley Cl, Chess. KT9 156 CM106
Padnall Ct, Rom. RM6
off Padnall Rd 70 EX55
Padnall Rd, Rom. RM6 70 EX56
Padstow Cl, Orp. BR6 163 ET105
Slough SL3 92 AY76
Padstow Rd, Enf. EN2 29 DP40
Padstow Wk, Felt. TW14 115 BT88
Padua Rd, SE20 142 DW95
Pagden St, SW8 101 DH81
Pageant Av, NW9 42 CR53
Pageant Cl, Til. RM18 111 GJ81
Pageant Cres, SE16 203 L2
Pageantmaster Ct, EC4 196 F9
Pageant Wk, Croy. CR0 142 DS104
Page Av, Wem. HA9 62 CQ62
Page Cl, Dag. RM9 70 EY64
Dartford (Bean) DA2 129 FW90
Hampton TW12 116 BY93
Harrow HA3 62 CM58
Page Cres, Croy. CR0 159 DN106
Erith DA8 107 FF80
Page Grn Rd, N15 66 DU57
Page Grn Ter, N15 66 DT57
Page Heath La, Brom. BR1 144 EK97
Page Heath Vil, Brom. BR1 144 EK97
Pagehurst Rd, Croy. CR0 142 DV101
Page Meadow, NW7 43 CU52
Page Rd, Felt. TW14 115 BR86
Pages Hill, N10 44 DG54
Pages La, N10 44 DG54
Romford RM3 52 FP54
Uxbridge UB8 76 BJ65
Page St, NW7 43 CU53
SW1 199 N8
Pages Wk, SE1 201 M8
Pages Yd, W4 off Church St 98 CS79
Paget Av, Sutt. SM1 140 DD104
Paget Cl, Hmptn. TW12 117 CD91
Paget Gdns, Chis. BR7 145 EP95
Paget La, Islw. TW7 97 CD83
Paget Pl, Kings.T. KT2 118 CQ93
Thames Ditton KT7
off Brooklands Rd 137 CG102
Paget Ri, SE18 105 EN80
Paget Rd, N16 66 DR60
Ilford IG1 69 EP63
Slough SL3 93 AZ77
Uxbridge UB10 77 BQ70
Paget St, EC1 196 F2
Paget Ter, SE18 105 EN79
Pagette Way, Grays (Bad.Dene)
RM17 110 GA77
Pagitts Gro, Barn. EN4 28 DB39
Paglesfield, Brwd. (Hutt.)
CM13 55 GC44
Pagnell St, SE14 103 DZ80
Pagoda Av, Rich. TW9 98 CM83
Pagoda Gdns, SE3 103 ED82
Pagoda Gro, SE27
off Elmcourt Rd 121 DP89
Pagoda Vista, Rich. TW9 98 CM82
Paignton Rd, N15 66 DS58
Ruislip HA4 59 BU62
Paines Brook Rd, Rom. RM3
off Paines Brook Way 52 FM51
Paines Brook Way, Rom. RM3 52 FM51
Paines Cl, Pnr. HA5 60 BY55
Painesfield Dr, Cher. KT16 134 BG103
Paines La, Pnr. HA5 40 BY53
Pains Cl, Mitch. CR4 141 DH96
Painshill, Cob. KT11
off Portsmouth Rd 153 BT113
Pains Hill, Oxt. RH8 188 EJ132
★ Painshill Park, Cob. KT11 153 BS114
Painsthorpe Rd, N16
off Oldfield Rd 66 DS62
Painters Ash La, Grav.
(Nthflt) DA11 130 GD90
Painters La, Enf. EN3 31 DY35
Painters Ms, SE16
off Macks Rd 102 DU77
Painters Rd, Ilf. IG2 69 ET55
Paisley Rd, N22 45 DP53
Carshalton SM5 140 DD102
Paisley Ter, Cars. SM5 140 DD101
Pakeman St, N7 65 DM62
Pakenham Cl, SW12
off Balham Pk Rd 120 DG88
Pakenham St, WC1 196 C3
Pakes Way, Epp. (They.B.)
CM16 33 ES37
Palace Av, W8 82 DB74
Palace Cl, Kings L. WD4 6 BM30
Palace Ct, NW3 64 DB64
W2 82 DB73
Bromley BR1
off Palace Gro 144 EH95
Harrow HA3 62 CL58
Palace Ct Gdns, N10 65 DJ55
Palace Dr, Wey. KT13 135 BP104
Palace Gdns, Buck.H. IG9 48 EK46
Palace Gdns Ms, W8 82 DA74
Palace Gdns Prec, Enf. EN2 30 DR41
Palace Gdns Ter, W8 82 DA74
Palace Gate, W8 100 DC75
Palace Gates Rd, N22 45 DK53
Palace Grn, W8 100 DB75
Croydon CR0 161 DZ108
Palace Gro, SE19 122 DT94
Bromley BR1 144 EH95
Palace Ms, E17 67 DZ56
SW1 198 G9
SW6 off Hartismere Rd 99 CZ80
Palace of Industry, Wem. HA9 62 CN63
Palace Par, E17 67 EA56
Palace Pl, SW1 199 K6
Palace Rd, N8 65 DK57
N11 45 DL52
SE19 122 DT94
SW2 121 DM88
Bromley BR1 144 EH95
East Molesey KT8 137 CD97
Kingston upon Thames
KT1 137 CK98
Ruislip HA4 60 BY63
Westerham TN16 179 EN121
Palace Rd Est, SW2 121 DM88
Palace Sq, SE19 122 DT94
Palace St, SW1 199 K6
Palace Vw, SE12 124 EG89
Bromley BR1 144 EG97
Croydon CR0 161 DZ105
Palace Vw Rd, E4 47 EB50
Palace Way, Wey. KT13
off Palace Dr 135 BP104
Palamos Rd, E10 67 EA60
Palatine Av, N16
off Stoke Newington Rd 66 DT63
Palatine Rd, N16 66 DS63
Palemead Cl, SW6
off Eternit Wk 99 CX81
Palermo Rd, NW10 81 CU68
Palestine Gro, SW19 140 DD95
Palewell Cl, Orp. BR5 146 EV96
Palewell Common Dr, SW14 118 CR85
Palewell Pk, SW14 118 CR85
Paley Gdns, Loug. IG10 33 EP41
Palfrey Pl, SW8 101 DM80
Palgrave Av, Sthl. UB1 78 CA73
Palgrave Gdns, NW1 194 C4
Palgrave Ho, NW3
off Fleet Rd 64 DF64
Palgrave Rd, W12 99 CT76
Palissy St, E2 197 P3
Palladian Circ, Green. DA9 109 FW84
Palladino Ho, SW17
off Laurel Cl 120 DE92
Pallant Way, Orp. BR6 145 EN104
Pallet Way, SE18 104 EL81
Palliser Dr, Rain. RM13 89 FG71
Palliser Rd, W14 99 CY78

★ Place of interest ⇌ Railway station ⊖ London Underground station DLR Docklands Light Railway station Tra Tramlink station H Hospital Riv Pedestrian ferry landing stage

Palliser Rd, Ch.St.G. HP8 ....36 AU48
Pallister Ter, SW15
off Roehampton Vale 119 CT90
Pall Mall, SW1 ....199 L3
Pall Mall E, SW1 ....199 N2
Palmar Cres, Bexh. DA7 ....106 FA83
Palmar Rd, Bexh. DA7 ....106 FA82
Palmarsh Rd, Orp. BR5
off Wotton Grn 146 EX98
Palm Av, Sid. DA14 ....126 EX93
Palm Cl, E10 ....67 EB62
Palmeira Rd, Bexh. DA7 ....106 EX83
Palmer Av, Bushey WD23 ....24 CB43
Gravesend DA12 ....131 GK91
Sutton SM3 ....157 CW105
Palmer Cl, Houns. TW5 ....96 CA81
Northolt UB5 ....78 BY65
West Wickham BR4 ....143 ED104
Palmer Cres, Cher. (Ott.)
KT16 ....151 BD107
Kingston upon Thames
KT1 ....138 CL97
Palmer Gdns, Barn. EN5 ....27 CX43
Palmer Pl, N7 ....65 DN64
Palmer Rd, E13 ....86 EH70
Dagenham RM8 ....70 EX60
Palmers Av, Grays RM17 ....110 GC78
Palmers Dr, Grays RM17 ....110 GC77
Palmersfield Rd, Bans. SM7 .158 DA114
PALMERS GREEN, N13 ....45 DN48
⇌ **Palmers Green** 45 DM49
Palmers Gro, W.Mol. KT8 ..136 CA98
Palmers Hill, Epp. CM16 ....18 EU29
Palmers La, Enf. EN1, EN3 ...30 DV39
Palmers Moor La, Iver SL0 ..76 BG70
Palmers Orchard, Sev.
(Shore.) TN14 ....165 FF111
Palmers Pas, SW14
off Palmers Rd 98 CQ83
Palmers Rd, E2 ....85 DX68
N11 ....45 DJ50
SW14 ....98 CQ83
SW16 ....141 DM96
Borehamwood WD6 ....26 CP39
Palmerston Av, Slou. SL3 ...92 AV76
Palmerston Cl, Wok. GU21 ..151 AZ114
Palmerston Cres, N13 ....45 DM50
SE18 ....105 EQ79
Palmerstone Ct, Vir.W. GU25
off Sandhills La 132 AY99
Palmerston Gdns, Grays
RM20 ....109 FX78
Palmerston Gro, SW19 ....120 DA94
Palmerston Ho, SW11
off Strasburg Rd 100 DG81
Palmerston Rd, E7 ....68 EH64
E17 ....67 DZ56
N22 ....45 DM52
NW6 ....82 DA66
SW14 ....98 CQ84
SW19 ....120 DA94
W3 ....98 CQ76
Buckhurst Hill IG9 ....48 EH47
Carshalton SM5 ....158 DF105
Croydon CR0 ....142 DR99
Grays RM20 ....109 FX78
Harrow HA3 ....61 CF55
Hounslow TW3 ....96 CC81
Orpington BR6 ....163 EQ105
Rainham RM13 ....90 FJ68
Sutton SM1 *off Vernon Rd* ..158 DC106
Twickenham TW2 ....117 CF86
Palmerston Way, SW8
off Bradmead 101 DH80
Palmer St, SW1 ....199 M5
Palmers Way, Wal.Cr.
(Chsht) EN8 ....15 DY29
Palm Gro, W5 ....98 CL76
Palm Rd, Rom. RM7 ....71 FC57
Pamela Gdns, Pnr. HA5 ....59 BV57
Pamela Wk, E8
off Marlborough Av 84 DU67
Pampisford Rd, Pur. CR8 ....159 DN111
South Croydon CR2 ....159 DP108
Pams Way, Epsom KT19 ....156 CR106
Pancras La, EC4 ....197 J9
Pancras Rd, NW1 ....83 DK68
Pancroft, Rom. (Abridge) RM4 .34 EV41
Pandian Way, NW1
off Busby Pl 83 DK65
Pandora Rd, NW6 ....82 DA65
Panfield Ms, Ilf. IG2
off Cranbrook Rd 69 EN58
Panfield Rd, SE2 ....106 EU76
Pangbourne Av, W10 ....81 CW71
Pangbourne Dr, Stan. HA7 ...41 CK50
Pangbourne Ho, N7 ....65 DL64
Panhard Pl, Sthl. UB1 ....78 CB73
Pank Av, Barn. EN5 ....28 DC43
Pankhurst Av, E16
off Wesley Av 86 EH74
Pankhurst Cl, SE14
off Briant St 103 DX80
Isleworth TW7 ....97 CF83
Pankhurst Rd, Walt. KT12 ...136 BW101
Panmuir Rd, SW20 ....139 CV95
Panmure Cl, N5 ....65 DP63
Panmure Rd, SE26 ....122 DV90
Pannells Cl, Cher. KT16 ....133 BF102
Pansy Gdns, W12 ....81 CU73
Panters, Swan. BR8 ....127 FF94
Panther Dr, NW10 ....62 CR64
Pantile Rd, Wey. KT13 ....153 BR105
Pantile Row, Slou. SL3 ....93 BA77
Pantiles, The, NW11
off Willifield Way 63 CZ56
Bexleyheath DA7 ....106 EZ80
Bromley BR1 ....144 EL97
Bushey (Bushey Hth) WD23 .41 CD45
Pantiles Cl, N13 ....45 DP50
Woking GU21 ....166 AV118
Pantile Wk, Uxb. UB8
off The Pavilions 76 BJ66
Panton St, SW1 ....199 M1
Panyer All, EC4 ....197 H9
Papercourt La, Wok.
(Ripley) GU23 ....167 BF122
Papermill Cl, Cars. SM5 ....158 DG105
Papillons Wk, SE3 ....104 EG82
Papworth Gdns, N7
off Chillingworth Rd 65 DM64
Papworth Way, SW2 ....121 DN87
Parade, The, SW11 ....100 DF80
Parade, The, Brent. CM14
off Kings Rd 54 FW48
Dartford DA1
off Crayford Way 127 FF85
Epsom KT18 ....156 CR113
Epsom (Epsom Com.)
KT18 *off Spa Dr* 156 CN114
Esher (Clay.) KT10 ....155 CE107
Hampton TW12
off Hampton Rd 117 CD92
Romford RM3 ....52 FP51
South Ockendon (Aveley)
RM15 ....108 FQ75
Sunbury-on-Thames TW16 .115 BT94
Virginia Water GU25 ....132 AX100
Watford WD17 ....23 BV41
Watford (Carp.Pk) WD19 ...40 BY48
Watford (S.Oxhey) WD19
off Prestwick Rd 40 BX48
Parade Ms, SE27
off Norwood Rd 121 DP89
Paradise Cl, Wal.Cr.
(Chsht) EN7 ....14 DV28
Paradise Pas, N7 ....65 DN64
Paradise Path, SE28
off Birchdene Dr 88 EU74
Paradise Pl, SE18
off Godfrey Hill 104 EL77
Paradise Rd, SW4 ....101 DL82
Richmond TW9 ....117 CK85
Waltham Abbey EN9 ....15 EC34
Paradise Row, E2
off Bethnal Grn Rd 84 DV69
Paradise St, SE16 ....202 D5
Paradise Wk, SW3 ....100 DF79
Paragon, The, SE3 ....104 EF82
Paragon Cl, E16 ....86 EG72
Paragon Gro, Surb. KT5 ....138 CM100
Paragon Ms, SE1 ....201 L8
Paragon Pl, SE3 ....104 EF82
Surbiton KT5
off Berrylands Rd 138 CM100
Paragon Rd, E9 ....84 DW65
Parbury Ri, Chess. KT9 ....156 CL107
Parbury Rd, SE23 ....123 DY86
Parchment Cl, Amer. HP6 ....20 AS37
Parchmore Rd, Th.Hth. CR7 ..141 DP96
Parchmore Way, Th.Hth. CR7 .141 DP96
Pardoner St, SE1 ....201 L6
Pardon St, EC1 ....196 G4
Pares Cl, Wok. GU21 ....166 AX116
Parfett St, E1 ....84 DU71
Parfitt Cl, NW3
off North End 64 DC61
Parfour Dr, Ken. CR8 ....176 DQ116
Parfrey St, W6 ....99 CW79
Parham Dr, Ilf. IG2 ....69 EP58
Parham Way, N10 ....45 DJ54
Paris Gdn, SE1 ....200 F2
Parish Cl, Horn. RM11 ....71 FH61
Watford WD25 *off Crown Ri* .8 BX34
Parish Gate Dr, Sid. DA15 ...125 ES86
Parish La, SE20 ....123 DX93
Parish Ms, SE20 ....123 DX94
Parish Wf, SE18
off Woodhill 104 EL77
Park, The, N6 ....64 DG58
NW11 ....64 DB60
SE19 ....122 DS94
SE23 *off Park Hill* 122 DW88
W5 ....79 CK74
Carshalton SM5 ....158 DF106
Leatherhead (Bkhm) KT23 ..170 CA123
Sidcup DA14 ....125 ET92
Park App, Well. DA16 ....106 EV84
Park Av, E6 ....87 EN67
E15 ....86 EE65
N3 ....44 DB53
N13 ....45 DN48
N18 ....46 DU49
N22 ....45 DL54
NW2 ....81 CV65
NW10 ....80 CM69
NW11 ....64 DB60
SW14 ....98 CR84
Barking IG11 ....87 EQ65
Brentwood (Hutt.) CM13 ....55 GC46
Bromley BR1 ....124 EF93
Bushey WD23 ....24 BZ40
Carshalton SM5 ....158 DG107
Caterham CR3 ....176 DS124
Egham TW20 ....113 BC93
Enfield EN1 ....30 DS44
Gravesend DA12 ....131 GJ88
Gravesend (Perry St) DA11 .130 GE88
Grays RM20 ....109 FU79
Hounslow TW3 ....116 CB86
Ilford IG1 ....69 EN61
Mitcham CR4 ....121 DH94
Orpington BR6 ....146 EU103
Orpington (Farnboro.)
BR6 ....145 EM104
Potters Bar EN6 ....12 DC34
Radlett WD7 ....9 CH33
Rickmansworth (Chorl.)
WD3 ....22 BG43
Ruislip HA4 ....59 BR58
Southall UB1 ....78 CA74
Staines TW18 ....113 BF93
Staines (Wrays.) TW19 ....112 AX85
Upminster RM14 ....73 FS59
Watford WD18 ....23 BU42
West Wickham BR4 ....143 EC103
Woodford Green IG8 ....48 EH50
Park Av E, Epsom KT17 ....157 CU107
Park Av Ms, Mitch. CR4
off Park Av 121 DH94
Park Av N, N8 ....65 DK55
NW10 ....63 CV64
Park Av Rd, N17 ....46 DV52
Park Av S, N8 ....65 DK56
Park Av W, Epsom KT17 ....157 CU107
Park Boul, Rom. RM2 ....51 FF53
Park Cen Bldg, E3
off Fairfield Rd 85 EA68
Park Chase, Wem. HA9 ....62 CM63
Park Cliff Rd, Green. DA9 ...109 FW84
Park Cl, E9 ....84 DW67
NW2 ....63 CV62
NW10 ....80 CM69
SW1 ....198 D5
W4 ....98 CR78
W14 ....99 CZ76
Park Cl, Add. (New Haw)
KT15 ....152 BH110
Bushey WD23 ....24 BX41
Carshalton SM5 ....158 DF107
Epping (N.Wld Bas.) CM16 .18 FA27
Esher KT10 ....154 BZ107
Hampton TW12 ....136 CC95
Harrow HA3 ....41 CE53
Hatfield (Brook.Pk) AL9 ....11 CZ26
Hounslow TW3 ....116 CC85
Kingston upon Thames
KT2 ....138 CN95
Leatherhead (Fetch.) KT22 ..171 CD124
Oxted RH8 ....188 EF128
Rickmansworth WD3 ....39 BP49
Walton-on-Thames KT12 .135 BT103
Park Cor Rd, Grav.
(Sthflt) DA13 ....130 FZ91
Park Ct, SE26 ....122 DV93
SW11 *off Battersea Pk Rd* .101 DH81
Kingston upon Thames
(Hmptn W.) KT1 ....137 CJ95
New Malden KT3 ....138 CR98
Wembley HA9 ....62 CL64
West Byfleet KT14 ....152 BG113
Woking GU22
off Park Dr 167 AZ118
Park Cres, N3 ....44 DB52
W1 ....195 H5
Borehamwood (Els.) WD6 ..26 CM41
Enfield EN2 ....30 DR42
Erith DA8 ....107 FC79
Harrow HA3 ....41 CE53
Hornchurch RM11 ....71 FG59
Twickenham TW2 ....117 CD88
Park Cres Ms E, W1 ....195 J5
Park Cres Ms W, W1 ....195 H6
Park Cres Rd, Erith DA8 ....107 FD79
Park Cft, Edg. HA8 ....42 CQ53
Parkcroft Rd, SE12 ....124 EF87
Park Dale, N11 ....45 DK51
Parkdale Cres, Wor.Pk. KT4 ..138 CR104
Parkdale Rd, SE18 ....105 ES78
Park Dr, N21 ....30 DQ44
NW11 ....64 DB60
SE7 ....104 EL79
SW14 ....98 CR84
W3 ....98 CP75
Ashtead KT21 ....172 CN118
Dagenham RM10 ....71 FC62
Harrow (Har.Wld) HA3 ....41 CE51
Harrow (N.Har.) HA2 ....60 CA59
Potters Bar EN6 ....12 DA31
Romford RM1 ....71 FD56
Upminster RM14 ....72 FQ63
Weybridge KT13 ....153 BP106
Woking GU22 ....167 AZ118
Park Dr Cl, SE7 ....104 EL78
Park E Bldg, E3
off Fairfield Rd 85 EA68
Park End, NW3
off South Hill Pk 64 DE63
Bromley BR1 ....144 EF95
Park End Rd, Rom. RM1 ....71 FE56
Parker Av, Til. RM18 ....111 GJ81
Parker Cl, E16 ....86 EL74
Carshalton SM5 ....158 DF107
Parker Ms, WC2 ....196 A8
Parke Rd, SW13 ....99 CU81
Sunbury-on-Thames TW16 .135 BU98
Parker Rd, Croy. CR0 ....160 DQ105
Grays RM17 ....110 FZ78
Parkers Cl, Ashtd. KT21 ....172 CL119
Parkers Hill, Ashtd. KT21 ....172 CL119
Parkers La, Ashtd. KT21 ....172 CL119
Parkers Row, SE1 ....202 A5
Parker St, E16 ....86 EL74
WC2 ....196 A8
Watford WD24 ....23 BV39
Parkes Rd, Chig. IG7 ....49 ES50
Park Fm Cl, N2 ....64 DC55
Pinner HA5
off Field End Rd 59 BV57
Park Fm Rd, Brom. BR1 ....144 EK95
Kingston upon Thames
KT2 ....118 CL94
Upminster RM14 ....72 FM64
Parkfield, Rick. (Chorl.) WD3 ..21 BF42
Sevenoaks TN15 ....191 FM123
Parkfield Av, SW14 ....98 CS84
Feltham TW13 ....115 BU90
Harrow HA2 ....40 CC54
Northolt UB5 ....78 BX68
Uxbridge (Hlgdn) UB10 ....77 BP69
Parkfield Cl, Edg. HA8 ....42 CP51
Northolt UB5 ....78 BY68
Parkfield Cres, Felt. TW13 ...115 BU90
Harrow HA2 ....40 CC54
Ruislip HA4 ....60 BY62
Parkfield Dr, Nthlt. UB5 ....78 BX68
Parkfield Gdns, Har. HA2 ....60 CB55
Parkfield Rd, NW10 ....81 CU66
SE14 ....103 DZ81
Feltham TW13 ....115 BU90
Harrow HA2 ....60 CC62
Northolt UB5 ....78 BY68
Uxbridge (Ickhm) UB10 ....59 BP61
Parkfields, SW15 ....99 CW84
Croydon CR0 ....143 DZ102
Leatherhead (Oxshott)
KT22 ....155 CD111
Parkfields Av, NW9 ....62 CR60
SW20 ....139 CV95
Parkfields Cl, Cars. SM5
off Devonshire Rd 158 DG105
Parkfields Rd, Kings.T. KT2 ..118 CM92
Parkfield St, N1
off Berners Rd 83 DN68
Parkfield Vw, Pot.B. EN6 ....12 DB32
Parkfield Way, Brom. BR2 ...145 EM100
Park Gdns, NW9 ....62 CP55
Erith DA8 *off Valley Rd* 107 FD77
Kingston upon Thames
KT2 ....118 CM92
Park Gate, N2 ....64 DD55
N21 ....45 DM45
Parkgate, SE3 ....104 EF83
Park Gate, W5 ....79 CK71
Parkgate Av, Barn. EN4 ....28 DC39
Parkgate Cl, Kings.T. KT2
off Warboys App 118 CP93
Parkgate Cres, Barn. EN4 ....28 DC40
Parkgate Gdns, SW14 ....118 CR85
Parkgate Ms, N6
off Stanhope Rd 65 DJ59
Parkgate Rd, SW11 ....100 DE80
Orpington BR6 ....165 FB105
Wallington SM6 ....158 DG106
Watford WD24 ....24 BW37
Park Gates, Har. HA2 ....60 CA63
Park Gra Gdns, Sev. TN13
off Solefields Rd 191 FJ127
Park Grn, Lthd. (Bkhm) KT23 .170 CA124
Park Gro, E15 ....86 EG67
N11 ....45 DK52
Bexleyheath DA7 ....107 FC84
Bromley BR1 ....144 EH95
Chalfont St. Giles HP8 ....20 AX41
Edgware HA8 ....42 CM50
Park Gro Rd, E11 ....68 EE61
Park Hall Rd, N2 ....64 DE56
SE21 ....122 DQ90
Reigate RH2 ....184 DA132
Parkham Ct, Brom. BR2 ....144 EE96
Parkham St, SW11 ....100 DE81
Park Hill, SE23 ....122 DV89
SW4 ....121 DK85
W5 ....79 CK71
Bromley BR1 ....144 EL98
Carshalton SM5 ....158 DE107
Loughton IG10 ....32 EK43
Richmond TW10 ....118 CM86
Park Hill Cl, Cars. SM5 ....158 DE106
Parkhill Cl, Horn. RM12 ....72 FJ62
Park Hill Ct, SW17
off Beeches Rd 120 DF90
Park Hill Ri, Croy. CR0 ....142 DS103
Parkhill Rd, E4 ....47 EC46
NW3 ....64 DF64
Bexley DA5 ....126 EZ87
Park Hill Rd, Brom. BR2 ....144 EE96
Croydon CR0 ....142 DS103
Epsom KT17 ....157 CT111
Parkhill Rd, Sid. DA15 ....125 ER90
Park Hill Rd, Wall. SM6 ....159 DH108
Parkhill Wk, NW3 ....64 DF64
Parkholme Rd, E8 ....84 DT65
Park Ho, N21 ....45 DM45
Park Ho Gdns, Twick. TW1 ...117 CJ86
Parkhouse St, SE5 ....102 DR80
Parkhurst, Epsom KT19 ....156 CQ110
Parkhurst Gdns, Bex. DA5 ...126 FA87
Parkhurst Rd, E12 ....69 EN63
E17 ....67 DY56
N7 ....65 DL63
N11 ....44 DG49
N17 ....46 DU54
N22 ....45 DM52
Bexley DA5 ....126 FA87
Sutton SM1 ....158 DD105
Park Ind Est, St.Alb.
(Frog.) AL2 ....9 CE27
Parkinson Ho, SW1
off Tachbrook St 101 DK78
Parkland Av, Rom. RM1 ....71 FE55
Slough SL3 ....92 AX77
Upminster RM14 ....72 FP64
Parkland Cl, Chig. IG7 ....49 EQ48
Sevenoaks TN13 ....191 FJ129
Parkland Gdns, SW19 ....119 CX88
Parkland Gro, Ashf. TW15 ...114 BN91
Parkland Rd, N22 ....45 DM54
Ashford TW15 ....114 BN91
Woodford Green IG8 ....48 EG52
Parklands, N6 ....65 DH59
Addlestone KT15 ....152 BJ106
Chigwell IG7 ....49 EQ48
Epping (Cooper.) CM16 ....18 EX29
Leatherhead (Bkhm) KT23 ..170 CA123
Oxted RH8 ....188 EE131
Surbiton KT5 ....138 CM99
Waltham Abbey EN9 ....15 ED32
Parklands Cl, SW14 ....118 CQ85
Barnet EN4 ....28 DD38
Ilford IG2 ....69 EQ59
Parklands Ct, Houns. TW5 ...96 BX82
Parklands Dr, N3 ....63 CY55
Parklands Rd, SW16 ....121 DH92
Parklands Way, Wor.Pk. KT4 .138 CS104
Parkland Wk, N4 ....65 DM59
N6 ....65 DK59
N10 ....65 DH56
Park La, E15 *off High St* 85 ED67
N9 ....46 DT48
N17 ....46 DU52
W1 ....198 G3
Ashtead KT21 ....172 CM118
Banstead SM7 ....174 DD118
Carshalton SM5 ....158 DG105
Coulsdon CR5 ....175 DK121
Croydon CR0 ....142 DR104
Harrow HA2 ....60 CB62
Hayes UB4 ....77 BS71
Hornchurch RM11 ....71 FG58
Hornchurch (Elm Pk) RM12 .89 FH65
Hounslow TW5 ....95 BU80
Richmond TW9 ....97 CK84
Romford (Chad.Hth) RM6 ..70 EX58
Sevenoaks TN13 ....191 FJ124
Sevenoaks (Seal) TN15 ....191 FN121
Slough SL3 ....92 AV76
Slough (Horton) SL3 ....93 BA83
South Ockendon (Aveley)
RM15 ....91 FR74
Stanmore HA7 ....41 CG48
Sutton SM3 ....157 CY107
Swanley BR8 ....148 FJ96
Teddington TW11 ....117 CF93
Uxbridge (Hare.) UB9 ....38 BG53
Wallington SM6 ....158 DG105
Waltham Cross EN8 ....14 DW33
Waltham Cross (Chsht) EN7 .14 DU26
Wembley HA9 ....62 CL64
Park La Cl, N17 ....46 DU52
PARK LANGLEY, Beck. BR3 ..143 EC99
Parklawn Av, Epsom KT18 ...156 CP113
Park Lawn Rd, Wey. KT13 ...153 BQ105
Park Lawns, Wem. HA9 ....62 CM63
Parklea Cl, NW9 ....42 CS53
Parkleigh Rd, SW19 ....140 DB96
Park Ley Rd, Cat. (Wold.) CR3 .177 DX120
Parkleys, Rich. TW10 ....117 CK91
Parkmead, SW15 ....119 CV86
Park Mead, Har. HA2 ....60 CB62
Parkmead, Loug. IG10 ....33 EN43
Park Mead, Sid. DA15 ....126 EV85
Parkmead Gdns, NW7 ....43 CT51
Park Ms, SE10 *off Calvert Rd* ..104 EF78
SE24 *off Croxted Rd* 122 DQ86
Chislehurst BR7 ....125 EP93
East Molesey KT8 ....136 CC98
Hampton (Hmptn H.)
TW12 *off Park Rd* 116 CC92
Rainham RM13
off Sowrey Av 89 FG65
Parkmore Cl, Wdf.Grn. IG8 ..48 EG49
Park Nook Gdns, Enf. EN2 ...30 DR37
Park Par, NW10 ....81 CT68
Park Pl, E14 ....203 P2
N1 ....84 DR67
SW1 ....199 K3
W3 ....98 CN77
W5 ....79 CK74
Amersham HP6 ....20 AT38
Gravesend DA12 ....131 GJ86
Hampton (Hmptn H.) TW12 .116 CC93
St. Albans (Park St) AL2 ....9 CD27
Sevenoaks TN13 ....190 FD123
Wembley HA9 ....62 CM63
Woking GU22 *off Park Dr* .167 AZ118
Park Pl Vil, W2 ....82 DC71
Park Ridings, N8 ....65 DN55
Park Ri, SE23 ....123 DY88
Harrow HA3 ....41 CE53
Leatherhead KT22 ....171 CH121
Park Ri Cl, Lthd. KT22 ....171 CH121
Park Ri Rd, SE23 ....123 DY88
Park Rd, E6 ....86 EJ67
E10 ....67 EA60
E12 ....68 EH60
E15 ....86 EG67
E17 ....67 DZ57
N2 ....64 DD55
N8 ....65 DJ56
N11 ....45 DK52
N14 ....45 DK45
N15 ....65 DP56
N18 ....46 DT49
NW1 ....194 B2
NW4 ....63 CU59
NW8 ....194 B2
NW9 ....62 CR59
NW10 ....80 CS67
SE25 ....142 DS98
SW19 ....120 DD93
W4 ....98 CQ80
W7 ....79 CF73
Amersham HP6 ....20 AT37
Ashford TW15 ....115 BP92
Ashtead KT21 ....172 CL118
Banstead SM7 ....174 DB115
Barnet EN5 ....27 CZ42
Barnet (New Barn.) EN4 ....28 DE42
Beckenham BR3 ....123 DZ94
Brentwood CM14 ....54 FV46
Bromley BR1 ....144 EH95
Bushey WD23 ....24 CA44
Caterham CR3 ....176 DS123
Chislehurst BR7 ....125 EP93
Dartford DA1 ....128 FN87
East Molesey KT8 ....136 CC98
Egham TW20 ....113 BA91
Enfield EN3 ....31 DY36
Esher KT10 ....154 CB105
Feltham TW13 ....116 BX91
Gravesend DA11 ....131 GH88
Grays RM17 ....110 GB78
Hampton (Hmptn H.) TW12 .116 CB91
Hayes UB4 ....77 BS71
Hounslow TW3 ....96 CC84
Ilford IG1 ....69 ER62
Isleworth TW7 ....97 CH81
Kenley CR8 ....175 DP115
Kingston upon Thames
KT2 ....118 CM92
Kingston upon Thames
(Hmptn W.) KT1 ....137 CJ95
New Malden KT3 ....138 CR98
Orpington BR5 ....146 EW99
Oxted RH8 ....188 EF128
Potters Bar EN6 ....12 DG30
Radlett WD7 ....25 CG35
Redhill RH1 ....184 DF132
Richmond TW10 ....118 CM86
Rickmansworth WD3 ....38 BK45
Shepperton TW17 ....134 BN102
Staines (Stanw.) TW19 ....114 BH86
Sunbury-on-Thames TW16 .115 BV94
Surbiton KT5 ....138 CM99
Sutton SM3 ....157 CY107
Swanley BR8 ....147 FF97
Swanscombe DA10 ....130 FY86
Teddington TW11 ....117 CF93
Twickenham TW1 ....117 CJ86
Uxbridge UB8 ....76 BL66
Wallington SM6 ....159 DH106
Wallington (Hackbr.) SM6 .141 DH103
Waltham Cross EN8 ....15 DX33
Warlingham CR6 ....162 EE114
Watford WD17 ....23 BU39
Wembley HA0 ....80 CL65
Woking GU22 ....167 BA117
Park Rd E, W3 ....98 CP75
Uxbridge UB10
off Hillingdon Rd 76 BL68
Park Rd N, W3 ....98 CP75
W4 ....98 CR78
Park Row, SE10 ....103 ED79
PARK ROYAL, NW10 ....80 CN69
⊖ **Park Royal** 80 CN70
🄷 **Park Royal Cen for Mental Health**, NW10 ....80 CQ68
Park Royal Rd, NW10 ....80 CQ69
W3 ....80 CQ69
Parkshot, Rich. TW9 ....98 CL84
Parkside, N3 ....44 DB53
NW2 ....63 CU62
NW7 ....43 CU51
SE3 ....104 EF80
SW19 ....119 CX91
Addlestone (New Haw)
KT15 ....152 BH110
Buckhurst Hill IG9 ....48 EH47

★ Place of interest ⇌ Railway station ⊖ London Underground station DLR Docklands Light Railway station Tra Tramlink station H Hospital Riv Pedestrian ferry landing stage

Park Side, Epp. CM16 18 EV29
Parkside, Ger.Cr. (Chal.St.P.)
SL9 off Lower Rd 57 AZ56
Grays RM16 110 GE76
Hampton (Hmptn H.) TW12 117 CD92
Potters Bar EN6
off High St 12 DC32
Sevenoaks (Halst.) TN14 164 EZ113
Sidcup DA14 126 EV89
Sutton SM3 157 CY107
Waltham Cross EN8 15 DY34
Watford WD19 24 BW44
Parkside Av, SW19 119 CX92
Bexleyheath DA7 107 FD82
Bromley BR1 144 EL98
Romford RM1 71 FD55
Tilbury RM18 111 GH82
Parkside Business Est, SE8
off Rolt St 103 DY79
Parkside Cl, SE20 122 DW94
Parkside Ct, Wey. KT13 152 BN105
Parkside Cres, N7 65 DN62
Surbiton KT5 138 CQ100
Parkside Cross, Bexh. DA7 107 FE82
Parkside Dr, Edg. HA8 42 CN48
Watford WD17 23 BS40
Parkside Est, E9
off Rutland Rd 85 DX67
Parkside Gdns, SW19 119 CX91
Barnet EN4 44 DF46
Coulsdon CR5 175 DH117
H Parkside Hosp, SW19 119 CX90
Parkside Ho, Dag. RM10 71 FC62
Parkside Ms, Warl. CR6 177 EA116
H Parkside Oncology Clinic,
SW19 119 CX90
Parkside Pl, Stai. TW18 114 BG93
Parkside Rd, SW11 100 DG81
Belvedere DA17 107 FC77
Hounslow TW3 116 CB85
Northwood HA6 39 BT50
Parkside Ter, N18
off Great Cambridge Rd 46 DR49
Orpington BR6
off Willow Wk 145 EP104
Parkside Wk, SE10 205 H7
Slough SL1 92 AU76
Parkside Way, Har. HA2 60 CB56
Park St, SW11
off Austin Rd 100 DG81
Park Sq, Esher KT10
off Park Rd 154 CB105
Romford (Abridge) RM4 34 EY44
Park Sq E, NW1 195 H4
Park Sq Ms, NW1 195 H5
Park Sq W, NW1 195 H4
Parkstead Rd, SW15 119 CU85
Park Steps, W2
off St. Georges Flds 82 DE73
Parkstone Av, N18 46 DT50
Hornchurch RM11 72 FK58
Parkstone Rd, E17 67 EC55
SE15 off Rye La 102 DU82
PARK STREET, St.Alb. AL2 9 CD26
⇌ Park Street 9 CD26
Park St, SE1 201 H2
W1 194 F10
Croydon CR0 142 DQ103
St. Albans AL2 9 CD26
Slough SL1 92 AT76
Slough (Colnbr.) SL3 93 BD80
Teddington TW11 117 CE93
Park St La, St.Alb.
(Park St) AL2 8 CB30
Park Ter, Green. DA9 129 FV85
Sevenoaks (Sund.) TN14
off Main Rd 180 EX124
Worcester Park KT4 139 CU102
Parkthorne Cl, Har. HA2 60 CB58
Parkthorne Dr, Har. HA2 60 CA58
Parkthorne Rd, SW12 121 DK87
Park Twrs, W1 off Brick St 83 DH74
Park Vw, N21 45 DM45
W3 80 CQ71
New Malden KT3 139 CT97
Pinner HA5 40 BZ53
Potters Bar EN6 12 DC33
South Ockendon (Aveley)
RM15 91 FR74
Wembley HA9 62 CP64
Parkview Ct, SW18
off Broomhill Rd 120 DA86
Park Vw Ct, Ilf. IG2
off Brancaster Rd 69 ES58
Woking GU22 166 AY119
Park Vw Cres, N11 45 DH49
Parkview Dr, Mitch. CR4 140 DD96
Park Vw Est, E2 85 DX68
N5 66 DQ63
Park Vw Gdns, NW4 63 CW57
Grays RM17 110 GB78
Ilford IG4 69 EM56
Park Vw Ho, SE24
off Hurst St 121 DP86
Parkview Ho, Horn. RM12
off Sunrise Av 71 FH61
Park Vw Ms, SW9 101 DM82
Parkview Ms, Rain. RM13 89 FH71
Park Vw Rd, N3 44 DB53
N17 66 DU55
NW10 63 CT63
Parkview Rd, SE9 125 EP88
Park Vw Rd, W5 80 CL71
Caterham (Wold.) CR3 177 DY122
Parkview Rd, Croy. CR0 142 DU102
Park Vw Rd, Pnr. HA5 39 BV52
Southall UB1 78 CA74
Uxbridge UB8 76 BN72
Welling DA16 106 EW83
Park Vw Rd Est, N17 46 DV54
Park Village E, NW1 83 DH68
Park Village W, NW1 83 DH68
Park Vil, Rom. RM6 70 EX58
Parkville Rd, SW6 99 CZ80
Park Vista, SE10 103 ED79
Park Wk, N6 off North Rd 64 DG59
SE10 off Crooms Hill 103 ED80
SW10 100 DC79
Park Wk, Ashtd. KT21
off Rectory La 172 CM119
Parkway, N14 45 DL47
Park Way, N20 44 DF49
Parkway, NW1 83 DH67
Park Way, NW11 63 CY57
Parkway, SW20 139 CX98
Park Way, Bex. DA5 127 FE90
Brentwood (Shenf.) CM15 55 FZ46
Parkway, Croy. (New Adgtn)
CR0 161 EC109
Park Way, Edg. HA8 42 CP53
Enfield EN2 29 DN40
Parkway, Erith DA18 106 EY76
Park Way, Felt. TW14 115 BV87
Parkway, Ilf. IG3 69 ET62
Park Way, Lthd. (Bkhm) KT23 170 CA123
Parkway, Rain. RM13
off Upminster Rd S 89 FG70
Park Way, Rick. WD3 38 BJ46
Parkway, Rom. RM2 71 FF55
Park Way, Ruis. HA4 59 BU60
Parkway, Uxb. UB10 76 BN66
Park Way, W.Mol. KT8 136 CB97
Parkway, Wey. KT13 153 BR105
Woodford Green IG8 48 EJ50
Parkway, The, Hayes UB3,
UB4 78 BW72
Hounslow (Cran.) TW4, TW5 95 BV82
Iver SL0 75 BC68
Northolt UB5 78 BX69
Southall UB2 95 BU78
Parkway Trd Est, Houns. TW5 96 BW79
Park W, W2 194 C9
Park W Bldg, E3
off Fairfield Rd 85 EA68
Park W Pl, W2 194 C8
Parkwood, N20 44 DF48
Beckenham BR3 143 EA95
Parkwood Av, Esher KT10 136 CC102
Parkwood Cl, Bans. SM7 173 CX115
Parkwood Gro, Sun. TW16 135 BU97
Parkwood Ms, N6 65 DH58
Parkwood Rd, SW19 119 CZ92
Banstead SM7 173 CX115
Bexley DA5 126 EZ87
Isleworth TW7 97 CF81
Redhill (Nutfld) RH1 185 DL133
Westerham (Tats.) TN16 178 EL121
Parkwood Vw, Bans. SM7 173 CW116
Park Wks Rd, Red. RH1 185 DM133
Parlaunt Rd, Slou. SL3 93 BA77
Parley Dr, Wok. GU21 166 AW117
Parliament Ct, E1
off Sandy's Row 84 DS71
Parliament Hill, NW3 64 DE63
Parliament Ms, SW14
off Thames Bk 98 CQ82
Parliament Sq, SW1 199 P5
Parliament St, SW1 199 P5
Parliament Vw Apts, SE1 200 B8
Parma Cres, SW11 100 DF84
Parmiter St, E2 84 DV68
Parmoor Ct, EC1 197 H4
Parnell Cl, W12 99 CV76
Abbots Langley WD5 7 BT30
Edgware HA8 42 CP49
Grays (Chaff.Hun.) RM16 109 FW78
Parnell Gdns, Wey. KT13 152 BN111
Parnell Rd, E3 85 DZ67
Parnham St, E14
off Blount St 85 DY72
Parolles Rd, N19 65 DJ60
Paroma Rd, Belv. DA17 106 FA76
Parr Av, Epsom KT17 157 CV109
Parr Cl, N9 46 DV49
N18 46 DV49
Grays (Chaff.Hun.) RM16 109 FW77
Leatherhead KT22 171 CF120
Parr Ct, N1 off New N Rd 84 DR68
Feltham TW13 116 BW91
Parrock, The, Grav. DA12 131 GJ88
Parrock Av, Grav. DA12 131 GJ88
PARROCK FARM, Grav. DA12 131 GK91
Parrock Rd, Grav. DA12 131 GJ88
Parrock St, Grav. DA12 131 GH87
Parrotts Cl, Rick. (Crox.Grn)
WD3 22 BN42
Parr Pl, W4
off Chiswick High Rd 99 CT77
Parr Rd, E6 86 EK67
Stanmore HA7 41 CK53
Parrs Cl, S.Croy. CR2
off Florence Rd 160 DR109
Parrs Pl, Hmptn. TW12 116 CA94
Parr St, N1 84 DR68
Parry Av, E6 87 EM72
Parry Cl, Epsom KT17 157 CU108
Parry Dr, Wey. KT13 152 BN110
Parry Grn N, Slou. SL3 93 AZ77
Parry Grn S, Slou. SL3 93 AZ77
Parry Pl, SE18 105 EP77
Parry Rd, SE25 142 DS97
W10 81 CY69
Parry St, SW8 101 DL79
Parsifal Rd, NW6 64 DA64
Parsley Gdns, Croy. CR0
off Primrose La 143 DX102
Parsloes Av, Dag. RM9 70 EX63
Parsonage Bk, Dart. (Eyns.)
DA4 off Pollyhaugh 148 FL103
Parsonage Cl, Abb.L. WD5 7 BS30
Hayes UB3 77 BT72
Warlingham CR6 177 DY116
Parsonage Gdns, Enf. EN2 30 DQ40
Parsonage La, Dart.
(Sutt.H.) DA4 128 FP93
Enfield EN1, EN2 30 DR40
Sidcup DA14 126 EZ91
Parsonage Manorway,
Belv. DA17 106 FA79
Parsonage Rd, Ch.St.G. HP8 36 AW48
Egham (Eng.Grn) TW20 112 AX92
Grays RM20 109 FW79
Rainham RM13 90 FJ69
Rickmansworth WD3 38 BK45
Parsonage St, E14 204 E9
Parsons Cl, Sutt. SM1 140 DB104
Parsons Cres, Edg. HA8 42 CN48
Parsonsfield Cl, Bans. SM7 173 CX115
Parsonsfield Rd, Bans. SM7 173 CX116
PARSONS GREEN, SW6 100 DA81
⊖ Parsons Green 99 CZ81
Parsons Grn, SW6 100 DA81
Parsons Grn La, SW6 100 DA81
Parsons Gro, Edg. HA8 42 CN48
Parsons Ho, SW2
off New Pk Rd 121 DL87
Parson's Ho, W2 82 DD70
Parsons La, Dart. DA2 127 FH90
Parson's Mead, Croy. CR0 141 DP102
Parsons Mead, E.Mol. KT8 136 CC97
Parsons Pightle, Couls. CR5 175 DN120
Parsons Rd, E13 off Old St 86 EJ68
Slough SL3 93 AZ79
Parson St, NW4 63 CW56
Parthenia Rd, SW6 100 DA81
Parthia Cl, Tad. KT20 173 CV119
Partingdale La, NW7 43 CX50
Partington Cl, N19 65 DK60
Partridge Cl, E16
off Fulmer Rd 86 EK71
Barnet EN5 27 CW44
Bushey WD23 40 CB46
Chesham HP5 4 AS28
Stanmore HA7 42 CL49
Partridge Ct, EC1
off Percival St 83 DP70
Partridge Dr, Orp. BR6 145 EQ104
Partridge Grn, SE9 125 EN90
Partridge Knoll, Pur. CR8 159 DP112
Partridge Mead, Bans. SM7 173 CW116
Partridge Rd, Hmptn. TW12 116 BZ93
Sidcup DA14 125 ES90
Partridge Sq, E6
off Nightingale Way 86 EL71
Partridge Way, N22 45 DL53
Parvills, Wal.Abb. EN9 15 ED32
Parvin St, SW8 101 DK81
Parvis Rd, W.Byf. KT14 152 BG113
Pasadena Cl, Hayes UB3 95 BV75
Pasadena Cl Trd Est, Hayes
UB3 off Pasadena Cl 95 BV75
Pascal St, SW8 101 DK80
Pascoe Rd, SE13 123 ED85
Pasfield, Wal.Abb. EN9 15 ED33
Pasley Cl, SE17
off Penrose St 102 DQ78
Pasquier Rd, E17 67 DY55
Passey Pl, SE9 125 EM86
Passfield Dr, E14
off Uamvar St 85 EB71
Passfield Path, SE28
off Booth Cl 88 EV73
Passing All, EC1 196 G5
Passmore Gdns, N11 45 DK51
Passmore St, SW1 198 F9
★ Passport Office, SW1 199 J8
Pastens Rd, Oxt. RH8 188 EJ131
Pasteur Cl, NW9 42 CS54
Pasteur Dr, Rom. (Harold Wd)
RM3 52 FK54
Pasteur Gdns, N18 45 DP50
Paston Cl, E5
off Caldecott Way 67 DX62
Wallington SM6 141 DJ104
Paston Cres, SE12 124 EH87
Pastoral Way, Brwd. (Warley)
CM14 54 FV50
Pastor St, SE11 200 G8
Pasture Cl, Bushey WD23 40 CC45
Wembley HA0 61 CH62
Pasture Rd, SE6 124 EF88
Dagenham RM9 70 EZ63
Wembley HA0 61 CH61
Pastures, The, N20 43 CZ46
Watford WD19 40 BW45
Pastures Mead, Uxb. UB10 76 BN65
Patch, The, Sev. TN13 190 FE122
Patcham Ct, Sutt. SM2 158 DC109
Patcham Ter, SW8 101 DH81
Patch Cl, Uxb. UB10 76 BM67
PATCHETTS GREEN,
Wat. WD25 24 CC39
Patching Way, Hayes UB4 78 BY71
Paternoster Cl, Wal.Abb. EN9 16 EF33
Paternoster Hill, Wal.Abb. EN9 16 EF32
Paternoster La, EC4
off Warwick La 83 DP72
Paternoster Row, EC4 197 H9
Romford (Noak Hill) RM4 52 FJ47
Paternoster Sq, EC4 196 G9
Paterson Ct, EC1
off Peerless St 84 DR69
Paterson Rd, Ashf. TW15 114 BK92
Pater St, W8 100 DA76
Pates Manor Dr, Felt. TW14 115 BR87
Path, The, SW19 140 DB95
Pathfield Rd, SW16 121 DK93
Pathway, The, Rad. WD7 25 CF36
Watford WD19
off Anthony Cl 40 BX46
Patience Rd, SW11 100 DE82
Patio Cl, SW4 121 DK86
Patmore Est, SW8 101 DJ81
Patmore La, Walt. KT12 153 BT107
Patmore Rd, Wal.Abb. EN9 16 EE34
Patmore St, SW8 101 DJ81
Patmore Way, Rom. RM5 51 FB50
Patmos Rd, SW9 101 DP80
Paton Cl, E3 85 EA69
Paton St, EC1 197 H3
Patricia Ct, Chis. BR7
off Manor Pk Rd 145 ER95
Welling DA16 106 EV80
Patricia Dr, Horn. RM11 72 FL60
Patricia Gdns, Sutt. SM2
off The Crescent 158 DA111
Patrick Connolly Gdns, E3
off Talwin St 85 EB69
Patrick Gro, Wal.Abb. EN9
off Beaulieu Dr 15 EB33
Patrick Rd, E13 86 EJ69
Patrington Cl, Uxb. UB8
off Boulmer Rd 76 BJ69
Patriot Sq, E2 84 DV68
Patrol Pl, SE6 123 EB86
Patrons Dr, Uxb. (Denh.) UB9 57 BF58
Patshull Pl, NW5
off Patshull Rd 83 DJ65
Patshull Rd, NW5 83 DJ65
Patten All, Rich. TW10
off The Hermitage 117 CK85
Pattenden Rd, SE6 123 DZ88
Patten Rd, SW18 120 DE87
Patterdale Cl, Brom. BR1 124 EF93
Patterdale Rd, SE15 102 DW80
Dartford DA2 129 FR88
Patterson Ct, SE19 122 DT94
Dartford DA1 128 FN85
Patterson Rd, SE19 122 DT93
Pattina Wk, SE16 203 L3
Pattison Pt, E16 off Fife Rd 86 EG71
Pattison Rd, NW2 64 DA62
Pattison Wk, SE18 105 EQ78
Paul Cl, E15 86 EE66
Waltham Cross EN7
off Gladding Rd 14 DQ25
Paulet Rd, SE5 101 DP82
Paulet Way, NW10
off Church Rd 80 CS66
Paul Gdns, Croy. CR0 142 DT103
Paulhan Rd, Har. HA3 61 CK56
Paulin Dr, N21 45 DN45
Pauline Cres, Twick. TW2 116 CC88
Pauline Ho, E1
off Old Montague St 84 DU71
Paulinus Cl, Orp. BR5 146 EW96
Paul Julius Cl, E14 204 F1
Paul Robeson Cl, E6
off Eastbourne Rd 87 EN69
Pauls Grn, Wal.Cr. EN8
off Eleanor Rd 15 DY33
Paul's Pl, Ashtd. KT21 172 CP119
Paul St, E15 86 ED67
EC2 197 L5
Paul's Wk, EC4 196 G10
Paultons Sq, SW3 100 DD79
Paultons St, SW3 100 DD79
Pauntley St, N19 65 DJ60
Paved Ct, Rich. TW9 117 CK85
Paveley Dr, SW11 100 DE80
Paveley Ho, N1
off Priory Grn Est 83 DM68
Paveley St, NW8 194 C4
Pavement, The, SW4 101 DJ84
W5 off Popes La 98 CL76
Pavement Ms, Rom. RM6
off Clarissa Rd 70 EX59
Pavement Sq, Croy. CR0 142 DU102
Pavet Cl, Dag. RM10 89 FB65
Pavilion Gdns, Stai. TW18 114 BH94
Pavilion La, Beck. BR3 123 DZ93
Pavilion Ms, N3
off Windermere Av 44 DA54
Pavilion Rd, SW1 198 E7
Ilford IG1 69 EM59
Pavilions, The, Epp. (N.Wld Bas.)
CM16 19 FC25
Uxbridge UB8 76 BJ66
Pavilion Shop Cen, The,
Wal.Cr. EN8 15 DX34
Pavilion Sq, SW17 120 DE90
Pavilion St, SW1 198 E7
Pavilion Ter, E.Mol. KT8 137 CF98
Ilford IG2
off Southdown Cres 69 ES57
Pavilion Way, Amer. HP6 20 AW39
Edgware HA8 42 CP52
Ruislip HA4 60 BW61
Pawleyne Cl, SE20 122 DW94
Pawsey Cl, E13
off Plashet Rd 86 EG67
Pawson's Rd, Croy. CR0 142 DQ100
Paxford Rd, Wem. HA0 61 CH61
Paxton Cl, Rich. TW9 98 CM82
Walton-on-Thames KT12 136 BW101
Paxton Ct, Borwd. WD6
off Manor Way 26 CQ42
Paxton Gdns, Wok. GU21 151 BE112
Paxton Pl, SE27 122 DS91
Paxton Rd, N17 46 DT52
SE23 123 DY90
W4 98 CS79
Bromley BR1 124 EG94
Paxton Ter, SW1 101 DH79
Payne Cl, Bark. IG11 87 ES66
Paynell Ct, SE3 off Lawn Ter 104 EE83
Payne Rd, E3 85 EB68
Paynesfield Av, SW14 98 CR83
Paynesfield Rd, Bushey
(Bushey Hth) WD23 41 CF45
Westerham (Tats.) TN16 178 EK119
Payne St, SE8 103 DZ79
Paynes Wk, W6 99 CY79
Peabody Av, SW1 199 H10
Peabody Cl, SE10
off Devonshire Dr 103 EB81
SW1 off Lupus St 101 DH78
Croydon CR0
off Shirley Rd 142 DW102
Peabody Ct, Enf. EN3
off Martini Dr 31 EA37
Peabody Dws, WC1 195 P4
Peabody Est, EC1 197 J5
N1 (Islington)
off Greenman St 84 DQ67
N17 46 DS53
SE1 200 E3
SE24 122 DQ87
SW1 199 K8
SW3 off Margaretta Ter 100 DE79
SW6 off Lillie Rd 100 DA79
W6 off The Square 99 CW78
W10 81 CW71
Peabody Hill, SE21 121 DP88
Peabody Hill Est, SE21 121 DP87
Peabody Sq, SE1 200 F5
Peabody Twr, EC1
off Golden La 84 DQ70
Peabody Trust, SE1 201 H3
Peabody Yd, N1
off Greenman St 84 DQ67
Peace Cl, N14 29 DH43
SE25 142 DS98
Waltham Cross EN7
off Goffs La 14 DU29
Peace Dr, Wat. WD17 23 BU41
Peace Gro, Wem. HA9 62 CP62
Peace Prospect, Wat. WD17 23 BU41
Peace Rd, Iver SL0 75 AZ69
Slough SL3 75 BA68
Peace St, SE18
off Nightingale Vale 105 EP79
Peach Cft, Grav. (Nthflt) DA11 130 GE90
Peaches Cl, Sutt. SM2 157 CY108
Peachey Cl, Uxb. UB8 76 BK72
Peachey La, Uxb. UB8 76 BK71
Peach Gro, E11 67 ED62
Peach Rd, W10 81 CX69
Feltham TW13 115 BU88
Peach Tree Av, West Dr. UB7
off Pear Tree Av 76 BM72
Peachum Rd, SE3 104 EF79
Peachwalk Ms, E3
off Grove Rd 85 DX68
Peachy Cl, Edg. HA8
off Manor Pk Cres 42 CN51
Peacock Av, Felt. TW14 115 BR88
Peacock Cl, Dag. RM8 70 EW61
Hornchurch RM11 72 FL56
Peacock Gdns, S.Croy. CR2 161 DY110
Peacocks Cen, The, Wok.
GU21 166 AY117
Peacock St, SE17 200 G9
Gravesend DA12 131 GJ87
Peacock Wk, E16 86 EH72
Abbots Langley WD5 7 BU31
Peacock Yd, SE17 200 G9
Peak, The, SE26 122 DW90
Peakes La, Wal.Cr.
(Chsht) EN7 14 DT27
Peakes Way, Wal.Cr.
(Chsht) EN7 14 DT27
Peaketon Av, Ilf. IG4 68 EK56
Peak Hill, SE26 122 DW91
Peak Hill Av, SE26 122 DW91
Peak Hill Gdns, SE26 122 DW91
Peaks Hill, Pur. CR8 159 DK110
Peaks Hill Ri, Pur. CR8 159 DL110
Pea La, Upmin. RM14 91 FU66
Peal Gdns, W13
off Ruislip Rd E 79 CG70
Peall Rd, Croy. CR0 141 DM100
Pearce Cl, Mitch. CR4 140 DG96
Pearcefield Av, SE23 122 DW88
Pear Cl, NW9 62 CR56
SE14 off Southerngate Way 103 DY80
Pearcroft Rd, E11 67 ED61
Pearcy Cl, Rom. (Harold Hill)
RM3 52 FL52
Peardon St, SW8 101 DH82
Peareswood Gdns, Stan. HA7 41 CK53
Peareswood Rd, Erith DA8 107 FF81
Pearfield Rd, SE23 123 DY90
Pearl Cl, E6 87 EN72
NW2 63 CX59
Pearl Ct, Wok. GU21
off Langmans Way 166 AS116
Pearl Rd, E17 67 EA55
Pearl St, E1 202 E2
Pearmain Cl, Shep. TW17 135 BP99
Pearman St, SE1 200 E6
Pear Pl, SE1 200 D4
Pear Rd, E11 67 ED62
Pearscroft Ct, SW6 100 DB81
Pearscroft Rd, SW6 100 DB81
Pearse St, SE15
off Dragon Rd 102 DS79
Pearson Cl, SE5
off Medlar St 102 DQ81
Barnet EN5
off Woodville Rd 28 DB41
Purley CR8 159 DP111
Pearson Ms, SW4
off Edgeley Rd 101 DK83
Pearsons Av, SE14
off Tanners Hill 103 EA81
Pearson St, E2 84 DS68
Pearson Way, Dart. DA1 128 FM89
Mitcham CR4 140 DG95
Pears Rd, Houns. TW3 96 CC83
Peartree Av, SW17 120 DC90
Pear Tree Av, West Dr. UB7 76 BM72
Pear Tree Cl, E2 84 DT67
Addlestone KT15
off Pear Tree Rd 152 BG106
Amersham HP7
off Orchard End Av 20 AT39
Bromley BR2 144 EK99
Chessington KT9 156 CN106
Peartree Cl, Erith DA8 107 FD81
Pear Tree Cl, Mitch. CR4 140 DE96
Peartree Cl, S.Croy. CR2 160 DV114
South Ockendon RM15 91 FW68
Pear Tree Cl, Swan. BR8 147 FD96
Peartree Ct, E18
off Churchfields 48 EH53
Pear Tree Ct, EC1 196 E5
Peartree Gdns, Dag. RM8 70 EV63
Romford RM7 51 FB54
Peartree La, E1 202 G1
Pear Tree Rd, Add. KT15 152 BG106
Ashford TW15 115 BQ92
Peartree Rd, Enf. EN1 30 DS41
Pear Tree St, EC1 196 G4
Pear Tree Wk, Wal.Cr.
(Chsht) EN7 14 DR26
Peartree Way, SE10 205 M8
Peary Pl, E2 off Kirkwall Pl 84 DW69
Pease Cl, Horn. RM12
off Dowding Way 89 FH66
Peatfield Cl, Sid. DA15
off Woodside Rd 125 ES90
Peatmore Av, Wok. GU22 168 BG116
Peatmore Cl, Wok. GU22 168 BG116
Pebble Cl, Tad. KT20 182 CS128
PEBBLE COOMBE, Tad. KT20 182 CS128
Pebble Hill Rd, Bet. RH3 182 CS131
Tadworth KT20 182 CS131
Pebble La, Epsom KT18 172 CN121
Leatherhead KT22 182 CL125
Pebble Way, W3 80 CP74
Pebworth Rd, Har. HA1 61 CG61
Peckarmans Wd, SE26 122 DU90
Peckett Sq, N5
off Highbury Gra 65 DP63
Peckford Pl, SW9 101 DN82
PECKHAM, SE15 102 DU81
Peckham Gro, SE15 102 DS80
Peckham High St, SE15 102 DU81
Peckham Hill St, SE15 102 DU80
Peckham Pk Rd, SE15 102 DU80
Peckham Rd, SE5 102 DS81
SE15 102 DS81
⇌ Peckham Rye 102 DU82
Peckham Rye, SE15 102 DU83
SE22 102 DU84
Pecks Yd, E1 197 P6
Peckwater St, NW5 65 DJ64
Pedham Pl Ind Est, Swan.
BR8 147 FG99

Pedlars Wk, N7 83 DL65
Pedley Rd, Dag. RM8 70 EW60
Pedley St, E1 84 DT70
Pedro St, E5 67 DX62
Pedworth Gdns, SE16 202 F9
Peek Cres, SW19 119 CX92
Peel Cl, E4 47 EB47
N9 *off Plevna Rd* 46 DU48
Peel Dr, NW9 63 CT55
Ilford IG5 68 EL55
Peel Gro, E2 84 DW68
Peel Pas, W8 *off Peel St* 82 DA74
Peel Pl, Ilf. IG5 48 EL54
Peel Prec, NW6 82 DA68
Peel Rd, E18 48 EF53
NW6 81 CZ69
Harrow (Wealds.) HA3 61 CF55
Orpington BR6 163 EQ106
Wembley HA9 61 CK62
Peel St, W8 82 DA74
Peel Way, Rom. RM3 52 FM54
Uxbridge UB8 76 BL71
Peerage Way, Horn. RM11 72 FL59
Peerless Dr, Uxb. (Hare.) UB9 58 BJ57
Peerless St, EC1 197 K3
Pegamoid Rd, N18 46 DW48
Pegasus Cl, N16
off Green Las 66 DR63
Pegasus Ct, Abb.L. WD5
off Furtherfield 7 BT32
Gravesend DA12 131 GJ90
Pegasus Pl, SE11
off Clayton St 101 DN79
SW6 *off Ackmar Rd* 100 DA81
Pegasus Rd, Croy. CR0 159 DN107
Pegasus Way, N11 45 DH51
Pegelm Gdns, Horn. RM11 72 FM59
Peggotty Way, Uxb. UB8 77 BP72
Pegg Rd, Houns. TW5 96 BX80
Pegley Gdns, SE12 124 EG89
Pegmire La, Wat. (Ald.) WD25 24 CC39
Pegrum Dr, St.Alb. (Lon.Col.)
AL2 9 CH26
Pegwell St, SE18 105 ES80
Peket Cl, Stai. TW18 133 BE95
Pekin Cl, E14 *off Pekin St* 85 EA72
Pekin St, E14 85 EA72
Peldon Ct, Rich. TW9 98 CM84
Peldon Pas, Rich. TW10
off Worple Way 98 CM84
Peldon Wk, N1
off Britannia Row 83 DP67
Pelham Av, Bark. IG11 87 ET67
Pelham Cl, SE5 102 DS82
Pelham Cres, SW7 198 B9
Pelham Ho, W14
off Mornington Av 99 CZ77
Pelham Pl, SW7 198 B9
W13 *off Ruislip Rd E* 79 CF70
Pelham Rd, E18 68 EH55
N15 66 DT56
N22 45 DN54
SW19 120 DA94
Beckenham BR3 142 DW96
Bexleyheath DA7 106 FA83
Gravesend DA11 131 GF87
Ilford IG1 69 ER61
Pelham Rd S, Grav. DA11 131 GF88
Pelhams, The, Wat. WD25 24 BX35
Pelhams Cl, Esher KT10 154 CA105
Pelham St, SW7 198 A8
Pelhams Wk, Esher KT10 136 CA104
Pelham Ter, Grav. DA11
off Campbell Rd 131 GF87
Pelican Est, SE15 102 DT81
Pelican Ho, SE5
off Peckham Rd 102 DT81
Pelican Pas, E1
off Cambridge Heath Rd 84 DW70
Pelier St, SE17
off Langdale Cl 102 DQ79
Pelinore Rd, SE6 124 EE89
Pellant Rd, SW6 99 CY80
Pellatt Gro, N22 45 DN53
Pellatt Rd, SE22 122 DT85
Wembley HA9 62 CL61
Pellerin Rd, N16 66 DS64
Pelling Hill, Wind. (Old Wind.)
SL4 112 AV87
Pellings Cl, Brom. BR2 144 EE97
Pelling St, E14 85 EA72
Pellipar Cl, N13 45 DN48
Pellipar Gdns, SE18 105 EM78
Pelly Ct, Epp. CM16 17 ET31
Pelly Rd, E13 86 EG68
Pelman Way, Epsom KT19 156 CP110
Pelter St, E2 197 P2
Pelton Av, Sutt. SM2 158 DB110
Pelton Rd, SE10 205 H10
Pembar Av, E17 67 DY55
Pemberley Chase, Epsom
(W.Ewell) KT19 156 CP106
Pemberley Cl, Epsom
(W.Ewell) KT19 156 CP106
Pember Rd, NW10 81 CX69
Pemberton Av, Rom. RM2 71 FH55
Pemberton Gdns, N19 65 DJ62
Romford RM6 70 EY57
Swanley BR8 147 FE97
Pemberton Ho, SE26
off High Level Dr 122 DU91
Pemberton Pl, E8 *off Mare St* 84 DV66
Esher KT10
off Carrick Gate 136 CC104
Pemberton Rd, N4 65 DN57
East Molesey KT8 136 CC98
Pemberton Row, EC4 196 E8
Pemberton Ter, N19 65 DJ62
Pembrey Way, Horn. RM12 90 FJ65
Pembridge Av, Twick. TW2 116 BZ88
Pembridge Chase, Hem.H. (Bov.)
HP3 *off Pembridge Cl* 5 BA28
Pembridge Cl, Hem.H.
(Bov.) HP3 5 AZ28
Pembridge Cres, W11 82 DA73
Pembridge Gdns, W2 82 DA73
Pembridge Ms, W11 82 DA73
Pembridge Pl, SW15 120 DA85
W2 82 DA73
Pembridge Rd, W11 82 DA73
Hemel Hempstead
(Bov.) HP3 5 BA28
Pembridge Sq, W2 82 DA73
Pembridge Vil, W2 82 DA73
W11 82 DA73
Pembroke Av, N1 83 DL67
Enfield EN1 30 DV38
Harrow HA3 61 CG55
Pinner HA5 60 BX60
Surbiton KT5 138 CP99
Walton-on-Thames KT12 154 BX105
Pembroke Cl, SW1 198 G5
Banstead SM7 174 DB117
Erith DA8 *off Pembroke Rd* 107 FD77
Hornchurch RM11 72 FM56
Pembroke Cotts, W8
off Pembroke Sq 100 DA76
Pembroke Dr, S.Ock. RM15 108 FP75
Waltham Cross (Chsht) EN7 13 DP29
Pembroke Gdns, W8 99 CZ77
Dagenham RM10 71 FB62
Woking GU22 167 BA118
Pembroke Gdns Cl, W8 100 DA76
Pembroke Ms, E3
off Morgan St 85 DY69
N10 44 DG53
W8 *off Earls Wk* 100 DA76
Sevenoaks TN13
off Pembroke Rd 191 FH125
Pembroke Pl, W8 100 DA76
Dartford (Sutt.H.) DA4 148 FP95
Edgware HA8 42 CN52
Isleworth TW7
off Thornbury Rd 97 CE82
Pembroke Rd, E6 87 EM71
E17 67 EB57
N8 65 DL56
N10 44 DG53
N13 46 DQ48
N15 66 DT57
SE25 142 DS98
W8 100 DA77
Bromley BR1 144 EJ96
Erith DA8 107 FC78
Greenford UB6 78 CB70
Ilford IG3 69 ET60
Mitcham CR4 140 DG96
Northwood HA6 39 BQ48
Ruislip HA4 59 BS60
Sevenoaks TN13 191 FH125
Wembley HA9 61 CK62
Woking GU22 167 BA118
Pembroke Sq, W8 100 DA76
Pembroke St, N1 83 DL66
Pembroke Studios, W8 99 CZ76
Pembroke Vil, W8 100 DA77
Richmond TW9 97 CK84
Pembroke Wk, W8 100 DA77
Pembroke Way, Hayes UB3 95 BQ76
Pembry Cl, SW9 101 DN81
Pembury Av, Wor.Pk. KT4 139 CU101
Pembury Cl, Brom. BR2 144 EF101
Coulsdon CR5 158 DG114
Pembury Ct, Hayes UB3 95 BR79
Pembury Cres, Sid. DA14 126 EY89
Pembury Pl, E5 66 DV64
Pembury Rd, E5 66 DV64
N17 46 DT54
SE25 142 DU98
Bexleyheath DA7 106 EY80
Pemdevon Rd, Croy. CR0 141 DN101
Pemell Cl, E1
off Colebert Av 84 DW70
Pemerich Cl, Hayes UB3 95 BT78
Pempath Pl, Wem. HA9 61 CK61
Penally Pl, N1
off Shepperton Rd 84 DR67
Penang St, E1 202 E2
Penard Rd, Sthl. UB2 96 CA76
Penarth St, SE15 102 DW79
Penates, Esher KT10 155 CD105
Penberth Rd, SE6 123 EC89
Penbury Rd, Sthl. UB2 96 BZ77
Pencombe Ms, W11
off Denbigh Rd 81 CZ73
Pencraig Way, SE15 102 DV79
Pencroft Dr, Dart. DA1
off Shepherds La 128 FJ87
Pendall Cl, Barn. EN4 28 DE42
Penda Rd, Erith DA8 107 FB80
Pendarves Rd, SW20 139 CW95
Penda's Mead, E9
off Lindisfarne Way 67 DY63
Pendell Av, Hayes UB3 95 BT80
Pendell Ct, Red. (Bletch.)
RH1 185 DP131
Pendell Rd, Red. (Bletch.)
RH1 185 DP131
Pendennis Cl, W.Byf. KT14 152 BG114
Pendennis Rd, N17 66 DR55
SW16 121 DL91
Orpington BR6 146 EW103
Sevenoaks TN13 191 FH123
Penderel Rd, Houns. TW3 116 CA85
Penderry Ri, SE6 123 ED89
Penderyn Way, N7 65 DK63
Pendle Rd, SW16 121 DH93
Pendlestone Rd, E17 67 EA57
Pendolino Way, NW10 80 CN66
Pendragon Rd, Brom. BR1 124 EF90
Pendragon Wk, NW9 62 CS58
Pendrell Rd, SE4 103 DY82
Pendrell St, SE18 105 ER80
Pendula Dr, Hayes UB4 78 BX70
Pendulum Ms, E8
off Birkbeck Rd 66 DT64
Penerley Rd, SE6 123 EB88
Rainham RM13 89 FH71
Penfields Ho, N7
off York Way 83 DL65
Penfold Cl, Croy. CR0
off Epsom Rd 141 DN104
Penfold La, Bex. DA5 126 EX89
Penfold Pl, NW1 194 A6
Penfold Rd, N9 47 DX46
Penfold St, NW1 194 A5
NW8 194 A5
Penford Gdns, SE9 104 EK83
Penford St, SE5 101 DP82
Pengarth Rd, Bex. DA5 126 EX85
PENGE, SE20 122 DW94
⇌ **Penge East** 122 DW93
Penge Ho, SW11 *off Wye St* 100 DD83
Penge La, SE20 122 DW94
Pengelly Cl, Wal.Cr.
(Chsht) EN7 14 DV30
Penge Rd, E13 86 EJ66
SE20 142 DU97
SE25 142 DU97
⇌ **Penge West** 122 DV93
Penhale Cl, Orp. BR6 164 EU105
Penhall Rd, SE7 104 EK77
Penhill Rd, Bex. DA5 126 EW87
Penhurst, Wok. GU21 151 AZ114
Penhurst Pl, SE1 200 C7
Penhurst Rd, Ilf. IG6 49 EP52
Penifather La, Grnf. UB6 79 CD69
Peninsula Apts, W2
off Praed St 82 DE71
Peninsula Hts, SE1 200 A10
Peninsular Cl, Felt. TW14 115 BR86
Peninsular Pk Rd, SE7 205 N9
Penistone Rd, SW16 121 DL94
Penistone Wk, Rom. RM3
off Okehampton Rd 52 FJ51
Penketh Dr, Har. HA1 61 CD62
Penman Cl, St.Alb. AL2 8 CA27
Penman's Grn, Kings L. WD4 5 BF32
Penmans Hill, Kings L.
(Chipper.) WD4 5 BF33
Penmon Rd, SE2 106 EU76
Pennack Rd, SE15 102 DT79
Pennant Ms, W8 100 DB77
Pennant Ter, E17 47 DZ54
Pennard Rd, W12 99 CW75
Pennards, The, Sun. TW16 136 BW96
Penn Cl, Grnf. UB6 78 CB68
Harrow HA3 61 CJ56
Rickmansworth (Chorl.)
WD3 21 BD44
Uxbridge UB8 76 BK70
Penn Dr, Uxb. (Denh.) UB9 57 BF58
Penne Cl, Rad. WD7 9 CF34
Penner Cl, SW19 119 CY89
Penners Gdns, Surb. KT6 138 CL101
Pennethorne Cl, E9
off Victoria Pk Rd 84 DW67
Pennethorne Ho, SW11
off Wye St 100 DD83
Pennethorne Rd, SE15 102 DV80
Penney Cl, Dart. DA1 128 FK87
Penn Gdns, Chis. BR7 145 EP96
Romford RM5 50 FA52
Penn Gaskell La, Ger.Cr.
(Chal.St.P.) SL9 37 AZ50
Pennine Dr, NW2 63 CY61
Pennine Ho, N9 *off Plevna Rd* 46 DU48
Pennine La, NW2
off Pennine Dr 63 CY61
Pennine Way, Bexh. DA7 107 FE81
Gravesend (Nthflt) DA11 130 GE90
Hayes UB3 95 BR80
Pennington Cl, SE27
off Hamilton Rd 122 DR91
Romford RM5 50 FA50
Pennington Dr, N21 29 DL43
Weybridge KT13 135 BS104
Pennington Rd, Ger.Cr.
(Chal.St.P.) SL9 36 AX52
Penningtons, The, Amer. HP6 20 AS37
Pennington St, E1 202 C1
Pennington Way, SE12 124 EH89
Pennis La, Long. (Fawk.Grn)
DA3 149 FX100
Penniston Cl, N17 46 DQ54
Penn La, Bex. DA5 126 EX85
Penn Meadow, Slou.
(Stoke P.) SL2 74 AT67
Penn Pl, Rick. WD3
off Northway 38 BK45
Penn Rd, N7 65 DL64
Gerrards Cross (Chal.St.P.)
SL9 36 AX53
Rickmansworth (Mill End)
WD3 37 BF46
St. Albans (Park St) AL2 8 CC27
Slough (Datchet) SL3 92 AX81
Watford WD24 23 BV39
Penn St, N1 84 DR67
Penn Way, Rick. (Chorl.) WD3 21 BD44
Penny Cl, Rain. RM13 89 FH69
Pennycroft, Croy. CR0 161 DY109
Pennyfather La, Enf. EN2 30 DQ40
Pennyfield, Cob. KT11 153 BU113
Pennyfields, E14 85 EA73
Brentwood CM14 54 FW49
Penny La, Shep. TW17 135 BS101
Pennylets Grn, Slou.
(Stoke P.) SL2 74 AT66
Penny Ms, SW12
off Caistor Rd 121 DH87
Pennymoor Wk, W9
off Riverton Cl 81 CZ69
Penny Rd, NW10 80 CP69
Pennyroyal Av, E6 87 EN72
Penpoll Rd, E8 84 DV65
Penpool La, Well. DA16 106 EV83
Penrhyn Av, E17 47 DZ53
Penrhyn Cl, Cat. CR3 176 DR120
Penrhyn Cres, E17 47 EA53
SW14 98 CQ84
Penrhyn Gdns, Kings.T. KT1
off Surbiton Rd 137 CK98
Penrhyn Gro, E17 47 EA53
Penrhyn Rd, Kings.T. KT1 138 CL97
Penrith Cl, SW15 119 CY85
Beckenham BR3 143 EB95
Reigate RH2 184 DE133
Uxbridge UB8
off Chippendale Waye 76 BK66
Penrith Cres, Rain. RM13 71 FG64
Penrith Pl, SE27
off Harpenden Rd 121 DP89
Penrith Rd, N15 66 DR57
Ilford IG6 49 ET51
New Malden KT3 138 CR98
Romford RM3 52 FN51
Thornton Heath CR7 142 DQ96
Penrith St, SW16 121 DJ93
Penrose Av, Wat. WD19 40 BX47
Penrose Dr, Epsom KT19 156 CN111
Penrose Gro, SE17 102 DQ78
Penrose Ho, SE17 102 DQ78
Penrose Rd, Lthd. (Fetch.)
KT22 170 CC122
Penrose St, SE17 102 DQ78
Penryn St, NW1 83 DK68
Penry St, SE1 201 N9
Pensbury Pl, SW8 101 DJ82
Pensbury St, SW8 101 DJ82
Penscroft Gdns, Borwd. WD6 26 CR42
Pensford Av, Rich. TW9 98 CN82
Penshurst Av, Sid. DA15 126 EU86
Penshurst Cl, Ger.Cr.
(Chal.St.P.) SL9 36 AX54
Penshurst Gdns, Edg. HA8 42 CP50
Penshurst Grn, Brom. BR2 144 EF99
Penshurst Rd, E9 85 DX66
N17 46 DT52
Bexleyheath DA7 106 EZ81
Potters Bar EN6 12 DD31
Thornton Heath CR7 141 DP99
Penshurst Wk, Brom. BR2
off Hayesford Pk Dr 144 EF99
Penshurst Way, Orp. BR5
off Star La 146 EW98
Sutton SM2 158 DA108
Pensilver Cl, Barn. EN4 28 DE42
Pensons La, Ong. CM5 19 FG28
Penstemon Cl, N3 44 DA52
Penstemon Dr, Swans. DA10 130 FY85
Penstock Footpath, N22 65 DL55
Pentavia Retail Pk, NW7 43 CT52
Pentelow Gdns, Felt. TW14 115 BU86
Pentire Cl, Upmin. RM14 73 FS58
Pentire Rd, E17 47 ED53
Pentland Av, Edg. HA8 42 CP47
Shepperton TW17 134 BN99
Pentland Cl, N9 46 DW47
NW11 63 CY61
Pentland Gdns, SW18
off St. Ann's Hill 120 DC86
Pentland Pl, Nthlt. UB5 78 BY67
Pentland Rd, NW6 82 DA69
Bushey WD23 24 CC44
Pentlands Cl, Mitch. CR4 141 DH97
Pentland St, SW18 120 DC86
Pentland Way, Uxb. UB10 59 BQ62
Pentlow St, SW15 99 CW83
Pentlow Way, Buck.H. IG9 48 EL45
Pentney Rd, E4 47 ED46
SW12 121 DJ88
SW19 *off Midmoor Rd* 139 CY95
Penton Av, Stai. TW18 113 BF94
Penton Dr, Wal.Cr.
(Chsht) EN8 15 DX29
Penton Gro, N1 196 D1
Penton Hall Dr, Stai. TW18 134 BG95
Penton Hook Rd, Stai. TW18 114 BG94
Penton Ho, SE2
off Hartslock Dr 106 EX75
Penton Pk, Cher. KT16 134 BG97
Penton Pl, SE17 200 G10
Penton Ri, WC1 196 C2
Penton Rd, Stai. TW18 113 BF94
Penton St, N1 83 DN68
PENTONVILLE, N1 196 D1
Pentonville Rd, N1 196 B1
Pentrich Av, Enf. EN1 30 DU38
Pentridge St, SE15 102 DT80
Pentyre Av, N18 46 DR50
Penwerris Av, Islw. TW7 96 CC80
Penwith Rd, SW18 120 DB89
Penwith Wk, Wok. GU22 166 AX119
Penwood End, Wok. GU22 166 AV121
Penwood Ho, SW15
off Tunworth Cres 119 CT86
Penwortham Rd, SW16 121 DH93
South Croydon CR2 160 DQ110
Penylan Pl, Edg. HA8 42 CN52
Penywern Rd, SW5 100 DA78
Penzance Cl, Uxb. (Hare.) UB9 38 BK53
Penzance Gdns, Rom. RM3 52 FN51
Penzance Pl, W11 81 CY74
Penzance Rd, Rom. RM3 52 FN51
Penzance St, W11 81 CY74
Peony Cl, Brwd. (Pilg.Hat.)
CM15 54 FV44
Peony Ct, Wdf.Grn. IG8
off The Bridle Path 48 EE52
Peony Gdns, W12 81 CU73
Pepler Ms, SE5
off Cobourg Rd 102 DT79
Peplins Cl, Hat. AL9 11 CY26
Peplins Way, Hat. AL9 11 CY25
Peploe Rd, NW6 81 CX68
Peplow Cl, West Dr. UB7
off Tavistock Rd 76 BK74
Pepper All, Loug. (High Beach)
IG10 32 EG39
Pepper Cl, E6 87 EM71
Caterham CR3 186 DS125
Peppercorn Cl, Th.Hth. CR7 142 DR96
Pepper Hill, Grav. (Nthflt)
DA11 130 GC90
Pepperhill La, Grav. (Nthflt)
DA11 130 GC90
Peppermead Sq, SE13 123 EA85
Peppermint Cl, Croy. CR0 141 DL101
Peppermint Pl, E11
off Birch Gro 68 EE62
Pepper St, E14 204 B6
SE1 201 H4
Peppie Cl, N16
off Bouverie Rd 66 DS61
Pepys Cl, Ashtd. KT21 172 CN117
Dartford DA1 108 FN84
Gravesend (Nthflt) DA11 130 GD90
Slough SL3 93 BB79
Tilbury RM18 111 GJ81
Uxbridge UB10 59 BP63
Pepys Cres, E16 205 N2
Barnet EN5 27 CW43
Pepys Ri, Orp. BR6 145 ET102
Pepys Rd, SE14 103 DX81
SW20 139 CW95
Pepys St, EC3 197 N10
Perceval Av, NW3 64 DE64
Percheron Cl, Islw. TW7 97 CG83
Percheron Rd, Borwd. WD6 26 CR44
Perch St, E8 66 DT63
Percival Cl, Lthd. KT22 154 CB111
Percival Ct, N17 *off High Rd* 46 DT52
Northolt UB5 60 CA64
★ **Percival David Foundation
of Chinese Art**, WC1
off Gordon Sq 195 N5
Percival Gdns, Rom. RM6 70 EW58
Percival Rd, SW14 98 CQ84
Enfield EN1 30 DT42
Feltham TW13 115 BT89
Hornchurch RM11 72 FJ58
Percival Rd, Orp. BR6 145 EP103
Percival St, EC1 196 F4
Percival Way, Epsom KT19 156 CQ105
Percy Av, Ashf. TW15 114 BN92
Percy Bryant Rd, Sun. TW16 115 BS94
Percy Bush Rd, West Dr. UB7 94 BM76
Percy Circ, WC1 196 C2
Percy Gdns, Enf. EN3 31 DX43
Hayes UB4 77 BS69
Isleworth TW7 97 CG82
Worcester Park KT4 138 CR102
Percy Ms, W1 195 M7
Percy Pas, W1 195 L7
Percy Pl, Slou. (Datchet) SL3 92 AV81
Percy Rd, E11 68 EE59
E16 86 EE71
N12 44 DC50
N21 46 DQ45
SE20 143 DX95
SE25 142 DU99
W12 99 CU75
Bexleyheath DA7 106 EY82
Hampton TW12 116 CA94
Ilford IG3 70 EU59
Isleworth TW7 97 CG84
Mitcham CR4 140 DG101
Romford RM7 71 FB55
Twickenham TW2 116 CB88
Watford WD18 23 BV42
Percy St, W1 195 M7
Grays RM17 110 GC79
Percy Way, Twick. TW2 116 CC88
Percy Yd, WC1 196 C2
Peregrine Cl, NW10 62 CR64
Watford WD25 8 BY34
Peregrine Ct, SW16
off Leithcote Gdns 121 DM91
Welling DA16 105 ET81
Peregrine Gdns, Croy. CR0 143 DY103
Peregrine Ho, EC1 196 G2
Peregrine Rd, Ilf. IG6 50 EV50
Sunbury-on-Thames TW16 135 BT96
Waltham Abbey EN9 16 EG34
Peregrine Wk, Horn. RM12
off Heron Flight Av 89 FH65
Peregrine Way, SW19 119 CW94
Perham Rd, W14 99 CY78
Perham Way, St.Alb.
(Lon.Col.) AL2 9 CK26
Peridot St, E6 86 EL71
Perifield, SE21 122 DQ88
Perimeade Rd, Grnf. UB6 79 CJ68
Periton Rd, SE9 104 EK84
PERIVALE, Grnf. UB6 79 CJ67
⊖ **Perivale** 79 CG68
Perivale, Grnf. UB6 79 CF69
Perivale Gdns, W13
off Bellevue Rd 79 CH70
Watford WD25 7 BV34
Perivale Gra, Grnf. UB6 79 CG69
Perivale Ind Pk, Grnf. UB6 79 CG68
Perivale La, Grnf. UB6 79 CG69
Perivale New Business Cen,
Grnf. UB6 79 CH68
Perkin Cl, Houns. TW3 96 CB84
Wembley HA0 61 CH64
Perkins Cl, Green. DA9 129 FT85
Perkins Ct, Ashf. TW15 114 BM92
Perkin's Rents, SW1 199 M6
Perkins Rd, Ilf. IG2 69 ER57
Perkins Sq, SE1 201 J2
Perks Cl, SE3 *off Hurren Cl* 104 EE83
Perleybrooke La, Wok. GU21
off Bampton Way 166 AU117
Permain Cl, Rad. (Shenley)
WD7 9 CK33
Perpins Rd, SE9 125 ES86
Perram Cl, Brox. EN10 15 DY26
Perran Rd, SW2
off Christchurch Rd 121 DP89
Perran Wk, Brent. TW8 98 CL78
Perren St, NW5 *off Ryland Rd* 83 DH65
Perrers Rd, W6 99 CV77
Perrin Cl, Ashf. TW15
off Fordbridge Rd 114 BM92
Perrin Ct, Wok. GU21
off Blackmore Cres 167 BB115
Perrin Rd, Wem. HA0 61 CG63
Perrins Ct, NW3
off Hampstead High St 64 DC63
Perrins La, NW3 64 DC63
Perrin's Wk, NW3 64 DC63
Perriors Cl, Wal.Cr. (Chsht)
EN7 14 DU27
Perrott St, SE18 105 EQ77
Perry Av, W3 80 CR72
Perry Cl, Rain. RM13
off Lowen Rd 89 FD68
Uxbridge UB8 77 BP72
Perry Ct, E14 *off Napier Av* 103 EA78
N15 *off Albert Rd* 66 DS58
Perryfield Way, NW9 63 CT58
Richmond TW10 117 CH89
Perry Gdns, N9 *off Deansway* 46 DS48
Perry Garth, Nthlt. UB5 78 BW67
Perry Gro, Dart. DA1 108 FN84
Perry Hall Cl, Orp. BR6 146 EU101
Perry Hall Rd, Orp. BR6 145 ET100
Perry Hill, SE6 123 DZ90
Perry Ho, SW2
off Tierney Rd 121 DL87
Rainham RM13
off Lowen Rd 89 FD68
Perry How, Wor.Pk. KT4 139 CT102
Perryman Ho, Bark. IG11 87 EQ67
Perrymans Fm Rd, Ilf. IG2 69 ER58
Perry Mead, Bushey WD23 40 CB45
Enfield EN2 29 DP40
Perrymead St, SW6 100 DA81
Perryn Rd, SE16 202 D6
W3 80 CR73
Perry Ri, SE23 123 DY90
Perry Rd, Dag. RM9 88 EZ70
Perrysfield Rd, Wal.Cr.
(Chsht) EN8 15 DY27
Perrys La, Sev. (Knock.) TN14 164 EX113
Perrys Pl, W1 195 M8

★ Place of interest ⇌ Railway station ⊖ London Underground station DLR Docklands Light Railway station Tra Tramlink station H Hospital Riv Pedestrian ferry landing stage

PERRY STREET, Grav. DA11 .130 GE88
Perry St, Chis. BR7 .125 ER93
Dartford DA1 .107 FE84
Gravesend (Nthflt) DA11 .130 GE88
Perry St Gdns, Chis. BR7
off Old Perry St .125 ES93
Perry Vale, SE23 .122 DW89
Perry Way, S.Ock. (Aveley) RM15 .90 FQ73
Persant Rd, SE6 .124 EE89
Perseverance Cotts, Wok. (Ripley) GU23 .168 BJ121
Perseverance Pl, SW9 .101 DN80
Richmond TW9 *off Shaftesbury Rd* .98 CL83
Persfield Cl, Epsom KT17 .157 CU110
Pershore Cl, Ilf. IG2 .69 EP57
Pershore Gro, Cars. SM5 .140 DD100
Pert Cl, N10 .45 DH52
Perth Av, NW9 .62 CR59
Hayes UB4 .78 BW70
Perth Cl, SW20 *off Huntley Way* .139 CU96
Perth Rd, E10 .67 DY60
E13 .86 EH68
N4 .65 DN60
N22 .45 DP53
Barking IG11 .87 ER68
Beckenham BR3 .143 EC96
Ilford IG2 .69 EN58
Perth Ter, Ilf. IG2 .69 EQ59
Perwell Av, Har. HA2 .60 BZ60
Perwell Ct, Har. HA2 .60 BZ60
Peter Av, NW10 .81 CV66
Oxted RH8 .187 ED129
Peterboat Cl, SE10 .205 J8
Peterborough Av, Upmin. RM14 .73 FS60
Peterborough Gdns, Ilf. IG1 .68 EL59
Peterborough Ms, SW6 .100 DA82
Peterborough Rd, E10 .67 EC57
SW6 .100 DA82
Carshalton SM5 .140 DE100
Harrow HA1 .61 CE60
Peterborough Vil, SW6 .100 DB81
Peterchurch Ho, SE15 *off Commercial Way* .102 DV79
Petergate, SW11 .100 DC84
Peterhead Ms, Slou. SL3 .93 BA78
Peter Heathfield Ho, E15 *off High St* .85 ED67
Peterhill Cl, Ger.Cr. (Chal.St.P.) SL9 .36 AY50
Peterhouse Gdns, SW6 *off Bagley's La* .100 DB81
Peter James Business Cen, Hayes UB3 .95 BU75
Peterley Business Cen, E2 *off Hackney Rd* .84 DV68
★ Peter Pan Statue, W2 .82 DD74
Peters Av, St.Alb. (Lon.Col.) AL2 .9 CJ26
Peters Cl, Dag. RM8 .70 EX60
Stanmore HA7 .41 CK51
Welling DA16 .105 ES82
Petersfield Av, Rom. RM3 .52 FL51
Slough SL2 .74 AU74
Staines TW18 .114 BJ92
Petersfield Cl, N18 .46 DQ50
Romford RM3 .52 FN51
Petersfield Cres, Couls. CR5 .175 DL115
Petersfield Ri, SW15 .119 CV88
Petersfield Rd, W3 .98 CQ75
Staines TW18 .114 BJ92
PETERSHAM, Rich. TW10 .118 CL88
Petersham Av, W.Byf. (Byfleet) KT14 .152 BL112
Petersham Cl, Rich. TW10 .117 CK89
Sutton SM1 .158 DA106
West Byfleet (Byfleet) KT14 .152 BL112
Petersham Dr, Orp. BR5 .145 ET96
Petersham Gdns, Orp. BR5 .145 ET96
Petersham La, SW7 .100 DC76
Petersham Ms, SW7 .100 DC76
Petersham Pl, SW7 .100 DC76
Petersham Rd, Rich. TW10 .118 CL86
Peters Hill, EC4 .197 H10
Peter's La, EC1 .196 G6
Peterslea, Kings L. WD4 .7 BP29
Petersmead Cl, Tad. KT20 .173 CW123
Peters Path, SE26 .122 DV91
Peterstone Rd, SE2 .106 EV76
Peterstow Cl, SW19 .119 CY89
Peter St, W1 .195 L10
Gravesend DA12 .131 GH87
Peterwood Way, Croy. CR0 .141 DM103
Petherton Rd, N5 .66 DQ64
Petley Rd, W6 .99 CW79
Peto Pl, NW1 .195 J4
Peto St N, E16 *off Victoria Dock Rd* .86 EF73
Petrie Cl, NW2 .81 CY65
★ Petrie Mus of Egyptian Archaeology, WC1 *off Malet Pl* .195 M5
Petros Gdns, NW3 *off Lithos Rd* .64 DC64
Pettacre Cl, SE28 .105 EQ76
Pett Cl, Horn. RM11 .71 FH61
Petten Cl, Orp. BR5 .146 EX102
Petten Gro, Orp. BR5 .146 EW102
Petters Rd, Ashtd. KT21 .172 CM116
★ Petticoat La Mkt, E1 .197 N7
Petticoat Sq, E1 .197 P8
Petticoat Twr, E1 *off Petticoat Sq* .84 DT72
Pettits Boul, Rom. RM1 .51 FE53
Pettits Cl, Rom. RM1 .51 FE54
Pettits La, Rom. RM1 .51 FE54
Pettits La N, Rom. RM1 .51 FD53
Pettits Pl, Dag. RM10 .70 FA64
Pettits Rd, Dag. RM10 .70 FA64
Pettiward Cl, SW15 .99 CW84
Pettley Gdns, Rom. RM7 .71 FD57
Pettman Cres, SE28 .105 ER76
Pettsgrove Av, Wem. HA0 .61 CJ64
Petts Hill, Nthlt. UB5 .60 CB64
Petts La, Shep. TW17 .134 BN98
Pett St, SE18 .104 EL77
PETTS WOOD, Orp. BR5 .145 ER99
⇌ Petts Wood .145 EQ99
Petts Wd Rd, Orp. BR5 .145 EQ99
Petty France, SW1 .199 L6
Pettys Cl, Wal.Cr. (Chsht) EN8 .15 DX28
Petty Wales, EC3 .201 N1
Petworth Cl, Couls. CR5 .175 DJ119
Northolt UB5 .78 BZ66
Petworth Gdns, SW20 *off Hidcote Gdns* .139 CV97
Uxbridge UB10 .77 BQ67
Petworth Rd, N12 .44 DE50
Bexleyheath DA6 .126 FA85
Petworth St, SW11 .100 DE81
Petworth Way, Horn. RM12 .71 FF63
Petyt Pl, SW3 *off Old Ch St* .100 DE79
Petyward, SW3 .198 C9
Pevensey Av, N11 .45 DK50
Enfield EN1 .30 DR40
Pevensey Cl, Islw. TW7 .96 CC80
Pevensey Rd, E7 .68 EF63
SW17 .120 DD91
Feltham TW13 .116 BY88
Peverel, E6 *off Downings* .87 EN72
Peverel Ho, Dag. RM10 .70 FA61
Peveret Cl, N11 *off Woodland Rd* .45 DH50
Peveril Dr, Tedd. TW11 .117 CD92
Pewsey Cl, E4 .47 EA50
Peyton Pl, SE10 .103 EC80
Peyton's Cotts, Red. RH1 .185 DM132
Pharaoh Cl, Mitch. CR4 .140 DF101
Pharaoh's Island, Shep. TW17 .134 BM103
Pheasant Cl, E16 *off Maplin Rd* .86 EG72
Purley CR8 *off Partridge Knoll* .159 DP113
Pheasant Hill, Ch.St.G. HP8 .36 AW47
Pheasants Way, Rick. WD3 .38 BH45
Pheasant Wk, Ger.Cr. (Chal.St.P.) SL9 .36 AX49
Phelp St, SE17 .102 DR79
Phelps Way, Hayes UB3 .95 BT77
Phene St, SW3 .100 DE79
Philan Way, Rom. RM5 .51 FD51
Philbeach Gdns, SW5 .100 DA78
Phil Brown Pl, SW8 *off Daley Thompson Way* .101 DH82
Philchurch Pl, E1 *off Ellen St* .84 DU72
Philimore Cl, SE18 .105 ES78
Philip Av, Rom. RM7 .71 FD60
Swanley BR8 .147 FD98
Philip Cl, Brwd. CM15 .54 FV44
Romford RM7 *off Philip Av* .71 FD60
Philip Gdns, Croy. CR0 .143 DZ103
Philip La, N15 .66 DR56
Philipot Path, SE9 .125 EM86
Philippa Gdns, SE9 .124 EK85
Philippa Way, Grays RM16 .111 GH77
Philip Rd, Rain. RM13 .89 FE69
Staines TW18 .114 BK93
Philips Cl, Cars. SM5 .140 DG102
Philip St, E13 .86 EG70
Philip Sydney Rd, Grays RM16 .109 FX78
Philip Wk, SE15 .102 DU83
Phillida Rd, Rom. RM3 .52 FN54
Phillimore Gdns, NW10 .81 CW67
W8 .100 DA75
Phillimore Gdns Cl, W8 *off Phillimore Gdns* .100 DA76
Phillimore Pl, W8 .100 DA75
Radlett WD7 .25 CE36
Phillimore Wk, W8 .100 DA76
Phillipers, Wat. WD25 .24 BY35
Phillipp St, N1 .84 DS67
Phillips Cl, Dart. DA1 .127 FH86
Philpot La, EC3 .197 M10
Woking (Chobham) GU24 .150 AV113
Philpot Path, Ilf. IG1 *off Sunnyside Rd* .69 EQ62
Philpots Cl, West Dr. UB7 .76 BK73
Philpot Sq, SW6 *off Peterborough Rd* .100 DB83
Philpot St, E1 .84 DV72
Phineas Pett Rd, SE9 .104 EL83
[Tra] Phipps Bridge .140 DC97
Phipps Br Rd, SW19 .140 DC96
Mitcham CR4 .140 DC96
Phipps Hatch La, Enf. EN2 .30 DQ38
Phipp's Ms, SW1 .199 J7
Phipp St, EC2 .197 M4
Phoebeth Rd, SE4 .123 EA85
Phoenix Cl, E8 *off Stean St* .84 DT67
E17 .47 DZ54
Epsom KT19 .156 CN112
Northwood HA6 .39 BT49
West Wickham BR4 .144 EE103
Phoenix Ct, N.Mal. KT3 .139 CT97
Phoenix Dr, Kes. BR2 .144 EK104
Phoenix Pk, Brent. TW8 .97 CK78
Phoenix Pl, WC1 .196 C4
Dartford DA1 .128 FK87
Phoenix Rd, NW1 .195 M2
SE20 .122 DW93
Phoenix St, WC2 .195 N9
Phoenix Way, Houns. TW5 .96 BW79
Phoenix Wf, SE10 .205 K4
Phoenix Wf Rd, SE1 .202 A5
Phoenix Yd, WC1 .196 C3
★ Photographers' Gall, WC2 .195 N10
Phygtle, The, Ger.Cr. (Chal.St.P.) SL9 .36 AY51
Phyllis Av, N.Mal. KT3 .139 CV99
★ Physical Energy Statue, W2 .82 DC74
Physic Pl, SW3 *off Royal Hosp Rd* .100 DF79
Piazza, The, WC2 *off Covent Gdn* .83 DL73
Picardy Manorway, Belv. DA17 .107 FB76
Picardy Rd, Belv. DA17 .106 FA77
Picardy St, Belv. DA17 .106 FA76
Piccadilly, W1 .199 J3
Piccadilly Arc, SW1 .199 K2
⊖ Piccadilly Circus .199 L1
Piccadilly Circ, W1 .199 M1
Piccadilly Ct, N7 *off Caledonian Rd* .83 DM65
Piccadilly Pl, W1 .199 L1
Pickard Cl, N14 .45 DK46
Pickard St, EC1 .196 G2
Pickering Av, E6 .87 EN68
Pickering Cl, E9 *off Cassland Rd* .85 DX66
Pickering Gdns, N11 .44 DG51
Croydon CR0 .142 DT100
Pickering Ms, W2 *off Bishops Br Rd* .82 DB72
Pickering Pl, SW1 .199 L3
Pickering Rd, Bark. IG11 *off Church Rd* .87 EQ65
Pickering St, N1 *off Essex Rd* .83 DP67
Pickets Cl, Bushey (Bushey Hth) WD23 .41 CD46
Pickets St, SW12 .121 DH87
Pickett Cft, Stan. HA7 .41 CK53
Picketts Lock La, N9 .46 DW47
Pickford Cl, Bexh. DA7 .106 EY82
Pickford Dr, Slou. SL3 .75 AZ74
Pickford La, Bexh. DA7 .106 EY82
Pickford Rd, Bexh. DA7 .106 EY83
Pickfords Gdns, Slou. SL1 .74 AS74
Pickfords Wf, N1 .197 H1
Pick Hill, Wal.Abb. EN9 .16 EF32
Pickhurst Grn, Brom. BR2 .144 EF101
Pickhurst La, Brom. BR2 .144 EF102
West Wickham BR4 .144 EE100
Pickhurst Mead, Brom. BR2 .144 EF101
Pickhurst Pk, Brom. BR2 .144 EE99
Pickhurst Ri, W.Wick. BR4 .143 EC101
Pickins Piece, Slou. (Horton) SL3 .93 BA82
Pickle Herring St, SE1 *off Tooley St* .84 DS74
Pickmoss La, Sev. (Otford) TN14 .181 FH116
Pickwick Cl, Houns. TW4 *off Dorney Way* .116 BY85
Pickwick Ct, SE9 *off West Pk* .124 EL88
Pickwick Gdns, Grav. (Nthflt) DA11 .130 GD90
Pickwick Ms, N18 .46 DS50
Pickwick Pl, Har. HA1 .61 CE59
Pickwick Rd, SE21 .122 DR87
Pickwick St, SE1 .201 H5
Pickwick Ter, Slou. SL2 *off Maple Cres* .74 AV73
Pickwick Way, Chis. BR7 .125 EQ93
Pickworth Cl, SW8 *off Kenchester Cl* .101 DL80
Picquets Way, Bans. SM7 .173 CY116
Picton Pl, W1 .194 G9
Surbiton KT6 .138 CN102
Picton St, SE5 .102 DR80
Piedmont Rd, SE18 .105 ER78
Pield Heath Av, Uxb. UB8 .76 BN70
Pield Heath Rd, Uxb. UB8 .76 BM71
Piercing Hill, Epp. (They.B.) CM16 .33 ER35
Pier Head, E1 .202 D3
Piermont Grn, SE22 .122 DV85
Piermont Pl, Brom. BR1 .144 EL96
Piermont Rd, SE22 .122 DV85
Pier Par, E16 *off Pier Rd* .87 EN74
Pierrepoint Arc, N1 *off Islington High St* .83 DP68
Pierrepoint Rd, W3 .80 CP73
Pierrepoint Row, N1 *off Islington High St* .83 DP68
Pier Rd, E16 .105 EM75
Erith DA8 .107 FE79
Feltham TW14 .115 BV85
Gravesend (Nthflt) DA11 .131 GF86
Greenhithe DA9 .109 FV84
Pier St, E14 .204 E8
Pier Ter, SW18 *off Jew's Row* .100 DC84
Pier Wk, Grays RM17 .110 GA80
Pier Way, SE28 .105 ER76
Pigeonhouse La, Couls. CR5 .184 DC125
Pigeon La, Hmptn. TW12 .116 CA91
Piggs Cor, Grays RM17 .110 GC76
Piggy La, Rick. (Chorl.) WD3 .21 BB44
Pigott St, E14 .85 EA72
Pike Cl, Brom. BR1 .124 EH92
Uxbridge UB10 .76 BM67
Pike La, Upmin. RM14 .73 FT64
Pike Rd, NW7 *off Ellesmere Av* .42 CR49
Pikes End, Pnr. HA5 .59 BV56
Pikes Hill, Epsom KT17 .156 CS113
Pikestone Cl, Hayes UB4 *off Berrydale Rd* .78 BY70
Pike Way, Epp. (N.Wld Bas.) CM16 .18 FA27
Pilgrimage St, SE1 .201 K5
Pilgrim Cl, Mord. SM4 .140 DB101
St. Albans (Park St) AL2 .8 CC27
Pilgrim Hill, SE27 .122 DQ91
Orpington BR5 .146 EY96
Pilgrims Cl, N13 .45 DM49
Brentwood (Pilg.Hat.) CM15 .54 FT43
Northolt UB5 .60 CC64
Watford WD25 *off Kytes Dr* .8 BX33
Pilgrims Ct, SE3 .104 EG81
Dartford DA1 .128 FN85
PILGRIM'S HATCH, Brwd. CM15 .54 FU42
Pilgrim's La, NW3 .64 DD63
Pilgrims La, Cat. (Chaldon) CR3 .185 DM125
Grays (N.Stfd) RM16 .91 FW74
Oxted (Titsey) RH8 .188 EH125
Westerham TN16 .178 EL123
Pilgrims Ms, E14 *off Newport Av* .85 ED73
Pilgrims Pl, NW3 *off Hampstead High St* .64 DD63
Reigate RH2 .184 DA132
Pilgrims Ri, Barn. EN4 .28 DE43
Pilgrims Rd, Swans. DA10 .110 FY84
Pilgrim St, EC4 .196 F9
Pilgrims Vw, Green. DA9 .129 FW86
Pilgrims Way, E6 *off High St N* .86 EL67
N19 .65 DK60
Pilgrims' Way, Bet. RH3 .183 CY131
Caterham CR3 .185 DN126
Pilgrims Way, Dart. DA1 .128 FN88
Pilgrims' Way, Red. RH1 .185 DJ127
Pilgrims Way, Reig. RH2 .184 DA131
Sevenoaks (Chev.) TN14 .180 EV121
South Croydon CR2 .160 DT106
Pilgrim's Way, Wem. HA9 .62 CP60
Pilgrims Way, West. TN16 .179 EM123
Pilgrims Way W, Sev. (Otford) TN14 .181 FD116
Pilkington Rd, SE15 .102 DV82
Orpington BR6 .145 EQ103
Pillions La, Hayes UB4 .77 BR70
Pilot Cl, SE8 .103 DZ79
Pilots Pl, Grav. DA12 .131 GJ86
Pilsdon Cl, SW19 *off Inner Pk Rd* .119 CX88
Piltdown Rd, Wat. WD19 .40 BX49
Pilton Est, The, Croy. (Pitlake) CR0 *off Pitlake* .141 DP103
Pilton Pl, SE17 .201 J10
Pimento Ct, W5 *off Olive Rd* .97 CK76
PIMLICO, SW1 .199 K10
⊖ Pimlico .199 M10
Pimlico Rd, SW1 .198 F10
Pimlico Wk, N1 .197 M2
Pimpernel Way, Rom. RM3 .52 FK51
Pinchbeck Rd, Orp. BR6 .163 ET107
Pinchfield, Rick. (Map.Cr.) WD3 .37 BE50
Pinchin St, E1 .84 DU73
Pincott Pl, SE4 .103 DX84
Pincott Rd, SW19 .120 DC94
Bexleyheath DA6 .126 FA85
Pindar St, EC2 .197 M6
PINDEN, Dart. DA2 .149 FW96
Pindock Ms, W9 *off Warwick Av* .82 DB70
Pineapple Ct, SW1 .199 K6
Pineapple Rd, Amer. HP7 .20 AT39
Pine Av, E15 .67 ED64
Gravesend DA12 .131 GK88
West Wickham BR4 .143 EB102
Pine Cl, E10 *off Walnut Rd* .67 EB61
N14 .45 DJ45
N19 *off Hargrave Pk* .65 DJ61
SE20 .142 DW95
Addlestone (New Haw) KT15 .152 BH111
Kenley CR8 .176 DR117
Stanmore HA7 .41 CH49
Swanley BR8 .147 FF98
Waltham Cross (Chsht) EN8 .15 DX28
Woking GU21 .166 AW117
Pine Coombe, Croy. CR0 .161 DX105
Pine Ct, Upmin. RM14 .72 FN63
Pine Cres, Brwd. (Hutt.) CM13 .55 GD43
Carshalton SM5 .158 DD111
Pinecrest Gdns, Orp. BR6 .163 EP105
Pinecroft, Brwd. (Hutt.) CM13 .55 GB45
Romford (Gidea Pk) RM2 .72 FJ56
Pinecroft Cres, Barn. EN5 *off Hillside Gdns* .27 CY42
Pinedene, SE15 *off Meeting Ho La* .102 DV81
Pinefield Cl, E14 .85 EA73
Pine Gdns, Ruis. HA4 .59 BV60
Surbiton KT5 .138 CN100
Pine Glade, Orp. BR6 .163 EM105
Pine Gro, N4 .65 DL61
N20 .43 CZ46
SW19 .119 CZ92
Bushey WD23 .24 BZ40
Hatfield (Brook.Pk) AL9 .12 DB25
St. Albans (Brick.Wd) AL2 .8 BZ30
Weybridge KT13 .153 BP106
Pine Gro Ms, Wey. KT13 .153 BQ106
Pine Hill, Epsom KT18 .172 CR115
Pinehurst, Sev. TN14 .191 FL121
Pinehurst Cl, Abb.L. WD5 .7 BS32
Tadworth (Kgswd) KT20 .174 DA122
Pinehurst Wk, Orp. BR6 .145 ES102
Pinelands Cl, SE3 *off St. John's Pk* .104 EF80
Pinel Cl, Vir.W. GU25 .132 AY98
Pinemartin Cl, NW2 .63 CW62
Pine Ms, NW10 *off Clifford Gdns* .81 CX68
Pineneedle La, Sev. TN13 .191 FH123
Pine Pl, Bans. SM7 .157 CX114
Hayes UB4 .77 BT70
Pine Ridge, Cars. SM5 .158 DG109
Pine Rd, N11 .44 DG47
NW2 .63 CW63
Woking GU22 .166 AW120
Pines, The, N14 .29 DJ43
Borehamwood WD6 *off Anthony Rd* .26 CM40
Coulsdon CR5 .175 DH118
Purley CR8 .159 DP113
Sunbury-on-Thames TW16 .135 BU97
Woking GU21 .151 AZ114
Woodford Green IG8 .48 EG48
Pines Av, Enf. EN1 .30 DV36
Pines Cl, Nthwd. HA6 .39 BS51
Pines Rd, Brom. BR1 .144 EL96
Pine St, EC1 .196 D4
Pinetree Cl, Ger.Cr. (Chal.St.P.) SL9 .36 AW52
Pine Tree Cl, Houns. TW5 .95 BV81
Pine Tree Hill, Wok. GU22 .167 BD116
Pine Trees Dr, Uxb. UB10 .58 BL63
Pine Vw Manor, Epp. CM16 .18 EU30
Pine Wk, Bans. SM7 .174 DF117
Bromley BR1 .144 EJ95
Carshalton SM5 .158 DD110
Caterham CR3 .176 DS122
Cobham KT11 .154 BX114
Surbiton KT5 .138 CN100
Pine Way, Egh. (Eng.Grn) TW20 *off Ashwood Rd* .112 AV93
Pine Wd, Sun. TW16 .135 BU95
Pinewood Av, Add. (New Haw) KT15 .152 BJ109
Pinner HA5 .40 CB51
Rainham RM13 .89 FH70
Sevenoaks TN14 .191 FK121
Sidcup DA15 .125 ES88
Uxbridge UB8 .76 BM72
Pinewood Cl, Borwd. WD6 .26 CR39
Croydon CR0 .143 DY104
Gerrards Cross SL9 *off Oxford Rd* .56 AY59
Iver SL0 .75 BC66
Northwood HA6 .39 BV50
Pinewood Cl, Orp. BR6 .145 ER102
Pinner HA5 .40 CB51
Watford WD17 .23 BU39
Woking GU21 .151 BA114
Pinewood Dr, Orp. BR6 .163 ES106
Potters Bar EN6 .11 CZ31
Staines TW18 *off Cotswold Cl* .114 BG92
Pinewood Grn, Iver SL0 .75 BC66
Pinewood Gro, W5 .79 CJ72
Addlestone (New Haw) KT15 .152 BH110
Pinewood Ms, Stai. (Stanw.) TW19 .114 BK86
Pinewood Pk, Add. (New Haw) KT15 .152 BH111
Pinewood Pl, Dart. DA2 .127 FE89
Pinewood Ride, Iver SL0 .75 BA68
Slough SL3 .75 BA68
Pinewood Rd, SE2 .106 EX79
Bromley BR2 .144 EG98
Feltham TW13 .115 BV90
Iver SL0 .75 BB67
Romford (Hav.at.Bow.) RM4 .51 FC49
Virginia Water GU25 .132 AU98
Pinewood Way, Brwd. (Hutt.) CM13 .55 GD43
Pinfold Rd, SW16 .121 DL91
Bushey WD23 .24 BZ40
Pinglestone Cl, West Dr. UB7 .94 BL80
Pinkcoat Cl, Felt. TW13 *off Tanglewood Way* .115 BV90
Pinkerton Pl, SW16 .121 DK91
Pinkham Way, N11 .44 DG52
Pinks Hill, Swan. BR8 .147 FE99
Pinkwell Av, Hayes UB3 .95 BR77
Pinkwell La, Hayes UB3 .95 BQ77
Pinley Gdns, Dag. RM9 *off Stamford Rd* .88 EV67
Pinnacle Hill, Bexh. DA7 .107 FB84
Pinnacle Hill N, Bexh. DA7 .107 FB83
Pinnacles, Wal.Abb. EN9 .16 EE34
Pinn Cl, Uxb. UB8 *off High Rd* .76 BK72
Pinnell Rd, SE9 .104 EK84
PINNER, HA5 .60 BY56
⊖ Pinner .60 BY56
Pinner Ct, Pnr. HA5 .60 CA56
PINNER GREEN, Pnr. HA5 .40 BW53
Pinner Grn, Pnr. HA5 .40 BW54
Pinner Gro, Pnr. HA5 .60 BY56
Pinner Hill, Pnr. HA5 .40 BW53
Pinner Hill Rd, Pnr. HA5 .40 BW54
Pinner Pk, Pnr. HA5 .40 CA53
Pinner Pk Av, Har. HA2 .60 CB55
Pinner Pk Gdns, Har. HA2 .40 CC54
Pinner Rd, Har. HA1, HA2 .60 CB57
Northwood HA6 .39 BT53
Pinner HA5 .60 BZ56
Watford WD19 .24 BX44
Pinner Vw, Har. HA1, HA2 .60 CC58
PINNERWOOD PARK, Pnr. HA5 .40 BW52
Pinnocks Av, Grav. DA11 .131 GH88
Pinn Way, Ruis. HA4 .59 BS59
Pinstone Way, Ger.Cr. SL9 .57 BB61
Pintail Cl, E6 *off Swan App* .86 EL71
Pintail Rd, Wdf.Grn. IG8 .48 EH52
Pintail Way, Hayes UB4 .78 BX71
Pinter Ho, SW9 *off Grantham Rd* .101 DL82
Pinto Cl, Borwd. WD6 *off Percheron Rd* .26 CR44
Pinto Way, SE3 .104 EH84
Pioneer Cl, E14 *off Broomfield St* .85 EB71
Pioneer Pl, Croy. CR0 .161 EA109
Pioneers Ind Pk, Croy. CR0 .141 DL102
Pioneer St, SE15 .102 DU81
Pioneer Way, W12 *off Du Cane Rd* .81 CV72
Swanley BR8 .147 FE97
Watford WD18 .23 BT44
Piper Cl, N7 .83 DM65
Piper Rd, Kings.T. KT1 .138 CN97
Pipers Cl, Cob. KT11 .170 BX115
Pipers End, Vir.W. GU25 .132 AX97
Piper's Gdns, Croy. CR0 .143 DY101
Pipers Grn, NW9 .62 CQ57
Pipers Grn La, Edg. HA8 .42 CL48
Piper Way, Ilf. IG1 *off Vicarage La* .69 ER60
Pipewell Rd, Cars. SM5 .140 DE100
Pippin Cl, NW2 .63 CV62
Croydon CR0 .143 DZ102
Radlett (Shenley) WD7 .9 CK33
Pippins, The, Slou. SL3 *off Pickford Dr* .75 AZ74
Watford WD25 .8 BW34
Pippins Cl, West Dr. UB7 .94 BK76
Pippins Ct, Ashf. TW15 .115 BP93
Piquet Rd, SE20 .142 DW96
Pirbright Cres, Croy. (New Adgtn) CR0 .161 EC107
Pirbright Rd, SW18 .119 CZ88
Pirie Cl, SE5 *off Denmark Hill* .102 DR83
Pirie St, E16 .86 EH74
Pirrip Cl, Grav. DA12 .131 GM89
Pitcairn Cl, Rom. RM7 .70 FA56
Pitcairn Rd, Mitch. CR4 .120 DF94
Pitcairn's Path, Har. HA2 *off Eastcote Rd* .60 CC62
Pitchfont La, Oxt. RH8 .178 EF124
Pitchford St, E15 .85 ED66
Pitfield Cres, SE28 .88 EU74
Pitfield Est, N1 .197 L2
Pitfield St, N1 .197 M3
Pitfield Way, NW10 .80 CQ65
Enfield EN3 .30 DW39
Pitfold Cl, SE12 .124 EG86
Pitfold Rd, SE12 .124 EG86
Pitlake, Croy. CR0 .141 DP103
Pitman Ho, SE8 *off Tanners Hill* .103 EA81
Pitman St, SE5 .102 DQ80
Pitmaston Ho, SE13 *off Lewisham Rd* .103 EC82
Pitmaston Rd, SE13 *off Morden Hill* .103 EC82
Pitsea Pl, E1 *off Pitsea St* .85 DX72
Pitsea St, E1 .85 DX72
Pitshanger La, W5 .79 CH70

★ Pitshanger Manor & Gall, W5 ... 79 CJ74
Pitshanger Pk, W13 ... 79 CJ69
Pitson Cl, Add. KT15 ... 152 BK105
Pitt Cres, SW19 ... 120 DB91
Pitt Ho, SW11
off Maysoule Rd ... 100 DD84
Pittman Cl, Brwd. (Ingrave) CM13 ... 55 GC50
Pittman Gdns, Ilf. IG1 ... 69 EQ64
Pitt Pl, Epsom KT17 ... 156 CS114
Pitt Rd, Croy. CR0 ... 142 DQ99
Epsom KT17 ... 156 CS114
Orpington BR6 ... 163 EQ105
Thornton Heath CR7 ... 142 DQ99
Pitt's Head Ms, W1 ... 198 G3
Pittsmead Av, Brom. BR2 ... 144 EG101
Pitt St, W8 ... 100 DA75
Pittville Gdns, SE25 ... 142 DU97
Pittwood, Brwd. (Shenf.) CM15 ... 55 GA46
Pitwood Grn, Tad. KT20 ... 173 CW120
Pitwood Pk Ind Est, Tad. KT20 off Waterfield ... 173 CV120
Pixfield Ct, Brom. BR2
off Beckenham La ... 144 EF96
Pixley St, E14 ... 85 DZ72
Pixton Way, Croy. CR0 ... 161 DY109
Place Fm Av, Orp. BR6 ... 145 ER102
Place Fm Rd, Red. (Bletch.) RH1 ... 186 DR130
Placehouse La, Couls. CR5 ... 175 DM119
Plain, The, Epp. CM16 ... 18 EV29
PLAISTOW, E13 ... 86 EF69
PLAISTOW, Brom. BR1 ... 124 EF93
⊖ Plaistow ... 86 EF68
Plaistow Gro, E15 ... 86 EF67
Bromley BR1 ... 124 EH94
H Plaistow Hosp, E13 ... 86 EJ68
Plaistow La, Brom. BR1 ... 124 EH94
Plaistow Pk Rd, E13 ... 86 EH68
Plaistow Rd, E13 ... 86 EF67
E15 ... 86 EF67
Plaitford Cl, Rick. WD3 ... 38 BL47
Plane Av, Grav. (Nthflt) DA11 ... 130 GD87
Planes, The, Cher. KT16 ... 134 BJ101
Plane St, SE26 ... 122 DV90
Plane Tree Cres, Felt. TW13 ... 115 BV90
Plane Tree Wk, N2 ... 64 DD55
SE19 off Central Hill ... 122 DS93
Plantaganet Pl, Wal.Abb. EN9 ... 15 EB33
Plantagenet Cl, Wor.Pk. KT4 ... 156 CR105
Plantagenet Gdns, Rom. RM6 ... 70 EX59
Plantagenet Pl, Rom. RM6
off Broomfield Rd ... 70 EX59
Plantagenet Rd, Barn. EN5 ... 28 DC42
Plantain Gdns, E11
off Hollydown Way ... 67 ED62
Plantain Pl, SE1 ... 201 K4
Plantation, The, SE3 ... 104 EG82
Plantation Cl, SW4
off King's Av ... 121 DL85
Greenhithe DA9 ... 129 FT86
Plantation Dr, Orp. BR5 ... 146 EX102
Plantation La, EC3
off Rood La ... 84 DS73
Warlingham CR6 ... 177 DY119
Plantation Rd, Amer. HP6 ... 20 AS37
Erith DA8 ... 107 FG81
Swanley BR8 ... 127 FG94
Plantation Way, Amer. HP6 ... 20 AS37
Plantation Wf, SW11 ... 100 DC83
Plashet Gdns, Brwd. CM13 ... 55 GA49
Plashet Gro, E6 ... 86 EJ67
Plashet Rd, E13 ... 86 EG67
Plassy Rd, SE6 ... 123 EB87
Platford Grn, Horn. RM11 ... 72 FL56
Platina St, EC2 ... 197 L4
Platinum Ho, Har. HA1 ... 61 CF58
Plato Rd, SW2 ... 101 DL84
Platt, The, SW15 ... 99 CX83
Platts Av, Wat. WD17 ... 23 BV41
Platt's Eyot, Hmptn. TW12 ... 136 CA96
Platt's La, NW3 ... 64 DA63
Platts Rd, Enf. EN3 ... 30 DW39
Platt St, NW1 ... 83 DK68
Plawsfield Rd, Beck. BR3 ... 143 DX95
Plaxtol Cl, Brom. BR1 ... 144 EJ95
Plaxtol Rd, Erith DA8 ... 106 FA80
Plaxton Ct, E11
off Woodhouse Rd ... 68 EF62
Playfair St, W6
off Winslow Rd ... 99 CW78
Playfield Av, Rom. RM5 ... 51 FC53
Playfield Cres, SE22 ... 122 DT85
Playfield Rd, Edg. HA8 ... 42 CQ54
Playford Rd, N4 ... 65 DM61
Playgreen Way, SE6 ... 123 EA91
Playground Cl, Beck. BR3
off Churchfields Rd ... 143 DX96
Playhouse Ct, SE1
off Southwark Br Rd ... 102 DQ75
Playhouse Yd, EC4 ... 196 F9
Plaza Par, NW6
off Kilburn High Rd ... 82 DB68
Plaza Shop Cen, The, W1 ... 195 L8
Plaza W, Houns. TW3 ... 96 CB81
Pleasance, The, SW15 ... 99 CV84
Pleasance Rd, SW15 ... 119 CV85
Orpington BR5 ... 146 EV96
Pleasant Gro, Croy. CR0 ... 143 DZ104
Pleasant Pl, N1 ... 83 DP66
Rickmansworth (W.Hyde) WD3 ... 37 BE52
Walton-on-Thames KT12 ... 154 BW107
Pleasant Row, NW1 ... 83 DH67
Pleasant Vw, Erith DA8 ... 107 FE78
Pleasant Vw Pl, Orp. BR6
off High St ... 163 EP106
Pleasant Way, Wem. HA0 ... 79 CJ68
Pleasure Pit Rd, Ashtd. KT21 ... 172 CP118
Plender St, NW1 ... 83 DJ67
Pleshey Rd, N7 ... 65 DK63
Plesman Way, Wall. SM6 ... 159 DL109
Plevna Cres, N15 ... 66 DS58
Plevna Rd, N9 ... 46 DU48
Hampton TW12 ... 136 CB95
Plevna St, E14 ... 204 D6
Pleydell Av, SE19 ... 122 DT94
W6 ... 99 CT77
Pleydell Ct, EC4 ... 196 E9
Pleydell Est, EC1
off Radnor St ... 84 DQ69
Pleydell St, EC4 ... 196 E9
Plimley Pl, W12
off Sterne St ... 99 CX75
Plimsoll Cl, E14
off Grundy St ... 85 EB72
Plimsoll Rd, N4 ... 65 DN62
Plough Ct, EC3 ... 197 L10
Plough Fm Cl, Ruis. HA4 ... 59 BR58
Plough Hill, Pot.B. (Cuffley) EN6 ... 13 DL28
Plough Ind Est, Lthd. KT22 ... 171 CG120
Plough La, SE22 ... 122 DT86
SW17 ... 120 DB92
SW19 ... 120 DB92
Cobham (Down.) KT11 ... 169 BU116
Purley CR8 ... 159 DL109
Rickmansworth (Sarratt) WD3 ... 5 BF33
Slough (Stoke P.) SL2 ... 74 AV67
Teddington TW11 ... 117 CG92
Uxbridge (Hare.) UB9 ... 38 BJ51
Wallington SM6 ... 159 DL105
Plough La Cl, Wall. SM6 ... 159 DL106
Ploughlees La, Slou. SL1 ... 74 AS73
Ploughmans Cl, NW1
off Crofters Way ... 83 DK67
Ploughmans End, Islw. TW7 ... 117 CD85
Ploughmans Wk, N2
off Long La ... 44 DC54
Plough Ms, SW11
off Plough Ter ... 100 DD84
Plough Pl, EC4 ... 196 E8
Plough Ri, Upmin. RM14 ... 73 FS59
Plough Rd, SW11 ... 100 DD83
Epsom KT19 ... 156 CR109
Plough St, E1 off Leman St ... 84 DT72
Plough Ter, SW11 ... 100 DD84
Plough Way, SE16 ... 203 J8
Plough Yd, EC2 ... 197 N5
Plover Cl, Stai. TW18
off Waters Dr ... 113 BF90
Plover Gdns, Upmin. RM14 ... 73 FT60
Plover Way, SE16 ... 203 K6
Hayes UB4 ... 78 BX72
Plowden Bldgs, EC4
off Middle Temple La ... 83 DN72
Plowman Cl, N18 ... 46 DR50
Plowman Way, Dag. RM8 ... 70 EW60
Plumbers Row, E1 ... 84 DU71
Plumbridge St, SE10
off Blackheath Hill ... 103 EC81
Plum Cl, Felt. TW13 ... 115 BU88
Plum Garth, Brent. TW8 ... 97 CK77
Plum La, SE18 ... 105 EP80
Plummer La, Mitch. CR4 ... 140 DF96
Plummer Rd, SW4 ... 121 DK87
Plummers Cft, Sev. (Dunt.Grn) TN13 ... 190 FE121
Plumpton Av, Horn. RM12 ... 72 FL63
Plumpton Cl, Nthlt. UB5 ... 78 CA65
Plumpton Way, Cars. SM5 ... 140 DE104
PLUMSTEAD, SE18 ... 105 ES78
⇌ Plumstead ... 105 ER77
Plumstead Common Rd, SE18 ... 105 EP79
Plumstead High St, SE18 ... 105 ES77
Plumstead Rd, SE18 ... 105 EP77
Plumtree Cl, Dag. RM10 ... 89 FB65
Wallington SM6 ... 159 DK108
Plumtree Ct, EC4 ... 196 E8
Plumtree Mead, Loug. IG10 ... 33 EN41
Plymouth Dr, Sev. TN13 ... 191 FJ124
Plymouth Pk, Sev. TN13 ... 191 FJ124
Plymouth Rd, E16 ... 86 EG71
Bromley BR1 ... 144 EH95
Grays (Chaff.Hun.) RM16 ... 109 FW77
Plymouth Wf, E14 ... 204 F8
Plympton Av, NW6 ... 81 CZ66
Plympton Cl, Belv. DA17
off Halifield Dr ... 106 EY76
Plympton Pl, NW8 ... 194 B5
Plympton Rd, NW6 ... 81 CZ66
Plympton St, NW8 ... 194 B5
Plymstock Rd, Well. DA16 ... 106 EW80
Pocket Hill, Sev. TN13 ... 190 FG128
Pocketsdell La, Hem.H. (Bov.) HP3 ... 4 AX28
Pocklington Cl, NW9 ... 42 CS54
Pocock Av, West Dr. UB7 ... 94 BM76
Pococks La, Wind. (Eton) SL4 ... 92 AS78
Pocock St, SE1 ... 200 F4
Podium, The, E2
off Roman Rd ... 84 DW69
Podmore Rd, SW18 ... 100 DC84
Poets Gate, Wal.Cr. EN7 ... 14 DS28
Poets Rd, N5 ... 66 DR64
Poets Way, Har. HA1
off Blawith Rd ... 61 CE56
Point, The, E17 off Tower Ms ... 67 EA56
Ruislip HA4
off Bedford Rd ... 59 BU63
Pointalls Cl, N3 ... 44 DC54
Point Cl, SE10
off Point Hill ... 103 EC81
Pointer Cl, SE28 ... 88 EX72
Pointers, The, Ashtd. KT21 ... 172 CL120
Pointers Cl, E14 ... 204 B10
Pointers Rd, Cob. KT11 ... 169 BQ116
Point Hill, SE10 ... 103 EC80
Point of Thomas Path, E1 ... 202 G1
Point Pl, Wem. HA9 ... 80 CP66
Point Pleasant, SW18 ... 100 DA84
Point W, SW7
off Cromwell Rd ... 100 DB77
Point Wf La, Brent. TW8
off Town Meadow ... 98 CL80
Poland Ho, E15 ... 85 ED67
Poland St, W1 ... 195 L9
Polar Pk, West Dr. UB7 ... 94 BM80
Polebrook Rd, SE3 ... 104 EJ83
Pole Cat All, Brom. BR2 ... 144 EF103
Polecroft La, SE6 ... 123 DZ89
Polehamptons, The, Hmptn. TW12 off High St ... 116 CC94
Pole Hill Rd, E4 ... 47 EC45
Hayes UB4 ... 77 BQ69
Uxbridge UB10 ... 77 BQ69
Polesden Gdns, SW20 ... 139 CV96
Polesden La, Wok. (Ripley) GU23 ... 167 BF122
Poles Hill, Rick. (Sarratt) WD3 ... 5 BE33
Polesteeple Hill, West. (Bigg.H.) TN16 ... 178 EK117
Polesworth Ho, W2 ... 82 DA71
Polesworth Rd, Dag. RM9 ... 88 EX66
Polhill, Sev. (Halst.) TN14 ... 181 FC115
Police Sta La, Bushey WD23
off Sparrows Herne ... 40 CB45
Police Sta Rd, Walt. KT12 ... 154 BW107
★ Polish Inst & Sikorski Mus, SW7 off Princes Gate ... 198 A5
Polish War Mem, Ruis. HA4 ... 77 BV66
Pollard Av, Uxb. (Denh.) UB9 ... 57 BF58
Pollard Cl, E16 ... 86 EG73
N7 ... 65 DM64
Chigwell IG7 ... 50 EU50
Windsor (Old Wind.) SL4 ... 112 AV85
Pollard Rd, N20 ... 44 DE47
Morden SM4 ... 140 DD99
Woking GU22 ... 167 BB116
Pollard Row, E2 ... 84 DU69
Pollards, Rick. (Map.Cr.) WD3 ... 37 BD50
Pollards Cl, Loug. IG10 ... 32 EJ43
Waltham Cross (Chsht) EN7 ... 14 DQ29
Pollards Cres, SW16 ... 141 DL97
Pollards Hill E, SW16 ... 141 DM97
Pollards Hill N, SW16 ... 141 DL97
Pollards Hill S, SW16 ... 141 DL97
Pollards Hill W, SW16 ... 141 DL97
Pollards Oak Cres, Oxt. RH8 ... 188 EG132
Pollards Oak Rd, Oxt. RH8 ... 188 EG132
Pollard St, E2 ... 84 DU69
Pollards Wd Hill, Oxt. RH8 ... 188 EH130
Pollards Wd Rd, SW16 ... 141 DL96
Oxted RH8 ... 188 EH131
Pollard Wk, Sid. DA14 ... 126 EW93
Pollen St, W1 ... 195 J9
Pollitt Dr, NW8
off Cunningham Pl ... 82 DD70
★ Pollock's Toy Mus, W1 ... 195 L6
Pollyhaugh, Dart. (Eyns.) DA4 ... 148 FL104
Polperro Cl, Orp. BR6
off Cotswold Ri ... 145 ET100
Polperro Ms, SE11 ... 200 E8
Polsted Rd, SE6 ... 123 DZ87
Polsten Ms, Enf. EN3
off Martini Dr ... 31 EA37
Polthorne Est, SE18 ... 105 ER77
Polthorne Gro, SE18 ... 105 EQ77
Polworth Rd, SW16 ... 121 DL92
Polygon, The, SW4
off Old Town ... 101 DJ84
Polygon Rd, NW1 ... 195 M1
Polytechnic St, SE18 ... 105 EN77
Pomell Way, E1
off Commercial St ... 84 DT72
Pomeroy Cres, Wat. WD24 ... 23 BV36
Pomeroy St, SE14 ... 102 DW81
Pomfret Rd, SE5
off Flaxman Rd ... 101 DP83
Pomoja La, N19 ... 65 DK61
Pompadour Cl, Brwd. CM14
off Queen St ... 54 FW50
Pond Cl, N12 ... 44 DE51
SE3 ... 104 EF82
Ashtead KT21 ... 172 CL117
Uxbridge (Hare.) UB9 ... 38 BJ54
Walton-on-Thames KT12 ... 153 BU107
Pond Cottage La, W.Wick. BR4 ... 143 EA102
Pond Cotts, SE21 ... 122 DS88
PONDERS END, Enf. EN3 ... 30 DW43
⇌ Ponders End ... 31 DX43
Ponders End Ind Est, Enf. EN3 ... 31 DZ42
Pond Fm Cl, Tad. (Walt.Hill) KT20 ... 173 CU124
Pond Fld End, Loug. IG10 ... 48 EJ45
Pondfield La, Brwd. CM13 ... 55 GA49
Pondfield Rd, Brom. BR2 ... 144 EE102
Dagenham RM10 ... 71 FB64
Kenley CR8 ... 175 DP116
Orpington BR6 ... 145 EP104
Pond Grn, Ruis. HA4 ... 59 BS61
Pond Hill Gdns, Sutt. SM3 ... 157 CY107
Pond La, Ger.Cr. (Chal.St.P.) SL9 ... 36 AV53
Pond Lees Cl, Dag. RM10
off Leys Av ... 89 FD66
Pond Mead, SE21 ... 122 DR86
Pond Path, Chis. BR7
off Heathfield La ... 125 EQ93
Pond Piece, Lthd. (Oxshott) KT22 ... 154 CB114
Pond Pl, SW3 ... 198 B9
Pond Rd, E15 ... 86 EE68
SE3 ... 104 EF82
Egham TW20 ... 113 BC93
Hemel Hempstead HP3 ... 6 BN25
Woking GU22 ... 166 AU120
Ponds, The, Wey. KT13
off Ellesmere Rd ... 153 BS107
Pondside Cl, Hayes UB3
off Providence La ... 95 BR80
Pond Sq, N6 off South Gro ... 64 DG60
Pond St, NW3 ... 64 DE64
Pond Wk, Upmin. RM14 ... 73 FS61
Pond Way, Tedd. TW11
off Holmesdale Rd ... 117 CJ93
Pondwood Ri, Orp. BR6 ... 145 ES101
Ponler St, E1 ... 84 DV72
Ponsard Rd, NW10 ... 81 CV69
Ponsford St, E9 ... 84 DW65
Ponsonby Pl, SW1 ... 199 N10
Ponsonby Rd, SW15 ... 119 CV87
Ponsonby Ter, SW1 ... 199 N10
Pontefract Rd, Brom. BR1 ... 124 EF92
Pontoise Cl, Sev. TN13 ... 190 FF122
Ponton Rd, SW8 ... 101 DK79
DLR Pontoon Dock ... 86 EJ74
Pont St, SW1 ... 198 D7
Pont St Ms, SW1 ... 198 D7
Pontypool Pl, SE1 ... 200 F4
Pontypool Wk, Rom. RM3 ... 52 FJ51
Pony Chase, Cob. KT11 ... 154 BZ113
Pool Cl, Beck. BR3 ... 123 EA92
West Molesey KT8 ... 136 BZ99
Pool Ct, SE6 ... 123 EA89
Poole Cl, Ruis. HA4
off Chichester Av ... 59 BS61
Poole Ct Rd, Houns. TW4
off Vicarage Fm Rd ... 96 BY82
Poole Ho, SE11
off Lambeth Wk ... 101 DM76
Grays RM16 ... 111 GJ75
Pool End Cl, Shep. TW17 ... 134 BN99
Poole Rd, E9 ... 85 DX65
Epsom KT19 ... 156 CR107
Hornchurch RM11 ... 72 FM59
Woking GU21 ... 166 AY117
Pooles Bldgs, EC1 ... 196 D5
Pooles La, SW10 off Lots Rd ... 100 DC80
Dagenham RM9 ... 88 EY68
Pooles Pk, N4
off Seven Sisters Rd ... 65 DN61
Poole St, N1 ... 84 DR67
Poole Way, Hayes UB4 ... 77 BR69
Pooley Av, Egh. TW20 ... 113 BB92
POOLEY GREEN, Egh. TW20 ... 113 BC92
Pooley Grn Cl, Egh. TW20 ... 113 BB92
Pooley Grn Rd, Egh. TW20 ... 113 BB92
Pool Gro, Croy. CR0 ... 161 DY112
Pool La, Slou. SL1 ... 74 AS73
Poolmans St, SE16 ... 203 H4
Pool Rd, Har. HA1 ... 61 CD59
West Molesey KT8 ... 136 BZ100
Poolsford Rd, NW9 ... 62 CS56
Poonah St, E1
off Hardinge St ... 84 DW72
Pootings Rd, Eden. (Crock.H.) TN8 ... 189 ER134
Pope Cl, SW19 ... 120 DD93
Feltham TW14 ... 115 BT88
Pope Ho, SE16 ... 202 D9
Pope Rd, Brom. BR2 ... 144 EK99
Popes Av, Twick. TW2 ... 117 CE89
Popes Cl, Amer. HP6 ... 20 AT37
Slough (Colnbr.) SL3 ... 93 BB80
Popes Dr, N3 ... 44 DA53
Popes Gro, Croy. CR0 ... 143 DZ104
Twickenham TW1, TW2 ... 117 CF89
Pope's Head All, EC3
off Cornhill ... 84 DR72
Popes La, W5 ... 97 CK76
Oxted RH8 ... 188 EE134
Watford WD24 ... 23 BV37
Popes Rd, SW9 ... 101 DN83
Abbots Langley WD5 ... 7 BS31
Pope St, SE1 ... 201 N5
Popham Cl, Felt. TW13 ... 116 BZ90
Popham Gdns, Rich. TW9
off Lower Richmond Rd ... 98 CN83
Popham Rd, N1 ... 84 DQ67
Popham St, N1 ... 83 DP67
POPLAR, E14 ... 204 B2
DLR Poplar ... 204 B1
Poplar Av, Amer. HP7 ... 20 AT39
Gravesend DA12 ... 131 GJ91
Leatherhead KT22 ... 171 CH122
Mitcham CR4 ... 140 DF95
Orpington BR6 ... 145 EP103
Southall UB2 ... 96 CB76
West Drayton UB7 ... 76 BM73
Poplar Bath St, E14
off Lawless St ... 85 EB73
Poplar Business Pk, E14 ... 204 D1
Poplar Cl, E9
off Lee Conservancy Rd ... 67 DZ64
Pinner HA5 ... 40 BX53
Slough (Colnbr.) SL3 ... 93 BE81
South Ockendon RM15 ... 91 FX70
Poplar Ct, SW19 ... 120 DA92
Poplar Cres, Epsom KT19 ... 156 CQ107
Poplar Dr, Bans. SM7 ... 157 CX114
Brentwood (Hutt.) CM13 ... 55 GC44
Poplar Fm Cl, Epsom KT19 ... 156 CQ107
Poplar Gdns, N.Mal. KT3 ... 138 CR96
Poplar Gro, N11 ... 44 DG51
W6 ... 99 CW75
New Malden KT3 ... 138 CR97
Wembley HA9 ... 62 CQ62
Woking GU22 ... 166 AY119
Poplar High St, E14 ... 85 EA73
Poplar Mt, Belv. DA17 ... 107 FB77
Poplar Pl, SE28 ... 88 EW73
W2 ... 82 DB73
Hayes UB3 off Central Av ... 77 BU73
Poplar Rd, SE24 ... 102 DQ84
SW19 ... 140 DA96
Ashford TW15 ... 115 BQ92
Leatherhead KT22 ... 171 CH122
Sutton SM3 ... 139 CZ102
Uxbridge (Denh.) UB9 ... 58 BJ64
Poplar Rd S, SW19 ... 140 DA97
Poplar Row, Epp. (They.B.) CM16 ... 33 ES37
Poplars, The, N14 ... 29 DH43
Gravesend DA12 ... 131 GL87
Romford (Abridge) RM4
off Hoe La ... 34 EV41
Waltham Cross (Chsht) EN7 ... 14 DS26
Poplars Av, NW10 ... 81 CW65
Poplars Cl, Ruis. HA4 ... 59 BS60
Watford WD25 ... 7 BV32
Poplar Shaw, Wal.Abb. EN9 ... 16 EF33
Poplars Rd, E17 ... 67 EB58
Poplar St, Rom. RM7 ... 71 FC56
Poplar Vw, Wem. HA9
off Magnet Rd ... 61 CK61
Poplar Wk, SE24 ... 102 DQ84
Caterham CR3 ... 176 DS123
Croydon CR0 ... 142 DQ103
Poplar Way, Felt. TW13 ... 115 BU90
Ilford IG6 ... 69 EQ56
Poppins Ct, EC4 ... 196 F9
Poppleton Rd, E11 ... 68 EE58
Poppy Cl, Belv. DA17 ... 107 FB76
Brentwood (Pilg.Hat.) CM15 ... 54 FV43
Northolt UB5 ... 78 BZ65
Wallington SM6 ... 140 DG102
★ Poppy Factory Mus, The, Rich. TW10 ... 117 CK86
Poppy La, Croy. CR0 ... 142 DW101
Poppy Wk, Wal.Cr. EN7 ... 14 DR28
Porchester Cl, SE5 ... 102 DQ84
Hornchurch RM11 ... 72 FL58
Porchester Gdns, W2 ... 82 DB73
Porchester Gdns Ms, W2
off Porchester Gdns ... 82 DB72
Porchester Mead, Beck. BR3 ... 123 EB93
Porchester Ms, W2 ... 82 DB72
Porchester Pl, W2 ... 194 C9
Porchester Rd, W2 ... 82 DB71
Kingston upon Thames KT1 ... 138 CP96
Porchester Sq, W2 ... 82 DB72
Porchester Ter, W2 ... 82 DC73
Porchester Ter N, W2 ... 82 DB72
Porchfield Cl, Grav. DA12 ... 131 GJ89
Sutton SM2 ... 158 DB110
Porch Way, N20 ... 44 DF48
Porcupine Cl, SE9 ... 124 EL89
Porden Rd, SW2 ... 101 DM84
Porlock Av, Har. HA2 ... 60 CC60
Porlock Rd, Enf. EN1 ... 46 DT45
Porlock St, SE1 ... 201 K4
Porrington Cl, Chis. BR7 ... 145 EM95
Portal Cl, SE27 ... 121 DN90
Ruislip HA4 ... 59 BU63
Uxbridge UB10 ... 76 BL66
Portal Way, W3 ... 80 CR71
Port Av, Green. DA9 ... 129 FV86
Portbury Cl, SE15
off Clayton Rd ... 102 DU81
Port Cres, E13
off Jenkins Rd ... 86 EH70
★ Portcullis Ho, SW1
off Bridge St ... 199 P4
Portcullis Lo Rd, Enf. EN2 ... 30 DR41
Portelet Ct, N1
off De Beauvoir Est ... 84 DS67
Portelet Rd, E1 ... 85 DX69
Porten Rd, W14 ... 99 CY76
Porter Cl, Grays RM20 ... 109 FW79
Porter Rd, E6 ... 87 EM72
Porters Av, Dag. RM8, RM9 ... 88 EV65
Porters Cl, Brwd. CM14 ... 54 FU46
Portersfield Rd, Enf. EN1 ... 30 DS42
Porters Pk Dr, Rad. (Shenley) WD7 ... 9 CK33
Porter Sq, N19
off Hornsey Rd ... 65 DL60
Porter St, SE1 ... 201 J2
W1 ... 194 E6
Porters Wk, E1 ... 202 E1
Porters Way, N12 ... 44 DE52
West Drayton UB7 ... 94 BM76
Porteus Rd, W2 ... 82 DC71
Portgate Cl, W9 ... 81 CZ70
Porthallow Cl, Orp. BR6 ... 163 ET105
Porthcawe Rd, SE26 ... 123 DY91
Port Hill, Orp. BR6 ... 164 EV112
Porthkerry Av, Well. DA16 ... 106 EU84
Portia Way, E3 ... 85 DZ70
Portinscale Rd, SW15 ... 119 CY85
Portland Av, N16 ... 66 DT59
Gravesend DA12 ... 131 GH89
New Malden KT3 ... 139 CT101
Sidcup DA15 ... 126 EU86
Portland Cl, Rom. RM6 ... 70 EY57
Worcester Park KT4 ... 139 CV101
Portland Ct, SE1
off Falmouth Rd ... 102 DR76
Portland Cres, SE9 ... 124 EL89
Feltham TW13 ... 115 BR91
Greenford UB6 ... 78 CB70
Stanmore HA7 ... 41 CK54
Portland Dr, Enf. EN2 ... 30 DS38
Redhill (Merst.) RH1 ... 185 DK129
Waltham Cross (Chsht) EN7 ... 14 DU31
Portland Gdns, N4 ... 65 DP58
Romford RM6 ... 70 EX57
Portland Gro, SW8 ... 101 DM81
Portland Hts, Nthwd. HA6 ... 39 BT49
H Portland Hosp for Women & Children, The, W1 ... 195 J5
Portland Ho, Red. RH1 ... 185 DK129
Portland Ms, W1 ... 195 L9
Portland Pk, Ger.Cr. SL9 ... 56 AX58
Portland Pl, W1 ... 195 J7
Epsom KT17 ... 156 CS112
Portland Ri, N4 ... 65 DP60
Portland Ri Est, N4 ... 66 DQ60
Portland Rd, N15 ... 66 DT56
SE9 ... 124 EL89
SE25 ... 142 DU98
W11 ... 81 CY73
Ashford TW15 ... 114 BL90
Bromley BR1 ... 124 EJ91
Gravesend DA12 ... 131 GH88
Hayes UB4 ... 77 BS69
Kingston upon Thames KT1 ... 138 CL97
Mitcham CR4 ... 140 DE96
Southall UB2 ... 96 BZ76
Portland Sq, E1 ... 202 D2
Portland St, SE17 ... 201 K10
Portland Ter, Rich. TW9 ... 97 CK84
Portland Wk, SE17
off Portland St ... 102 DR79
Portley La, Cat. CR3 ... 176 DS121
Portley Wd Rd, Whyt. CR3 ... 176 DT120
Portman Av, SW14 ... 98 CR83
Portman Cl, W1 ... 194 E8
Bexley DA5 ... 127 FE88
Bexleyheath DA7
off Queen Anne's Gate ... 106 EX83
Portman Dr, Wdf.Grn. IG8 ... 48 EK54
Portman Gdns, NW9 ... 42 CR54
Uxbridge UB10 ... 76 BN66
Portman Gate, NW1 ... 194 C5
Portman Hall, Har. HA3 ... 41 CD50
Portman Ms S, W1 ... 194 F9
Portman Pl, E2 ... 84 DW69
Portman Rd, Kings.T. KT1 ... 138 CM96
Portman Sq, W1 ... 194 E8
Portman St, W1 ... 194 F9
Portmeadow Wk, SE2 ... 106 EX75
Portmeers Cl, E17
off Lennox Rd ... 67 DZ58
Portmore Gdns, Rom. RM5 ... 50 FA50
Portmore Pk Rd, Wey. KT13 ... 152 BN105
Portmore Quays, Wey. KT13
off Weybridge Rd ... 152 BM105
Portmore Way, Wey. KT13 ... 134 BN104
Portnall Dr, Vir.W. GU25 ... 132 AT99
Portnall Ri, Vir.W. GU25 ... 132 AT99
Portnall Rd, W9 ... 81 CZ68
Virginia Water GU25 ... 132 AT99
Portnalls Cl, Couls. CR5 ... 175 DH116
Portnalls Ri, Couls. CR5 ... 175 DH116
Portnalls Rd, Couls. CR5 ... 175 DH118
Portnoi Cl, Rom. RM1 ... 51 FD54
Portobello Ct, W11
off Westbourne Gro ... 81 CZ72

★ Place of interest ⇌ Railway station ⊖ London Underground station DLR Docklands Light Railway station Tra Tramlink station H Hospital Riv Pedestrian ferry landing stage

Portobello Ms, W11
off Portobello Rd 82 DA73
Portobello Rd, W10 81 CZ72
W11 81 CZ72
Port of Tilbury, Til. RM18 110 GE84
Porton Ct, Surb. KT6 137 CJ100
Portpool La, EC1 196 D6
Portree Cl, N22 45 DM52
Portree St, E14 85 ED72
Portsdown, Edg. HA8
off Rectory La 42 CN50
Portsdown Av, NW11 63 CZ58
Portsdown Ms, NW11 63 CZ58
Portsea Ms, W2 194 C9
Portsea Pl, W2 194 C9
Portsea Rd, Til. RM18 111 GJ81
Portslade Rd, SW8 101 DJ82
Portsmouth Av, T.Ditt. KT7 137 CG101
Portsmouth Ct, Slou. SL1 74 AS73
Portsmouth Ms, E16
off Wesley Av 86 EH74
Portsmouth Rd, SW15 119 CV87
Cobham KT11 153 BU114
Esher KT10 154 CC105
Kingston upon Thames
KT1 137 CJ99
Surbiton KT6 137 CJ99
Thames Ditton KT7 137 CE103
Woking GU23 168 BM119
Portsmouth St, WC2 196 B9
Portsoken St, E1 197 P10
Portugal Gdns, Twick. TW2
off Fulwell Pk Av 116 CC89
Portugal Rd, Wok. GU21 167 AZ116
Portugal St, WC2 196 B9
Portway, E15 86 EF67
Epsom KT17 157 CU110
Rainham RM13 89 FG67
Portway Cres, Epsom KT17 157 CU109
Portway Gdns, SE18
off Shooters Hill Rd 104 EK81
Postern Grn, Enf. EN2 29 DN40
Post La, Twick. TW2 117 CD88
Post Meadow, Iver SL0 75 BD69
Postmill Cl, Croy. CR0 143 DX104
Post Office App, E7 68 EH64
Post Office Ct, EC3 197 L9
Post Office La, Slou.
(Geo.Grn) SL3 74 AX72
Post Office Row, Oxt. RH8 188 EL131
Post Office Way, SW8 101 DK80
Post Rd, Sthl. UB2 96 CB76
Postway Ms, Ilf. IG1
off Clements Rd 69 EP62
Potier St, SE1 201 L7
Potter Cl, Mitch. CR4 141 DH96
Potterells, Hat. (N.Mymms)
AL9 11 CX25
Potteries, The, Cher. (Ott.)
KT16 151 BE107
Potterne Cl, SW19 119 CX87
POTTERS BAR, EN6 12 DA32
⇌ Potters Bar 12 DA32
H Potters Bar Comm Hosp,
Pot.B. EN6 12 DC34
★ Potters Bar Mus, The, Wyllyotts
Cen, Pot.B. EN6 11 CZ32
Potters Cl, SE15
off Chandler Way 102 DS80
Croydon CR0 143 DY102
Loughton IG10 32 EL40
Potters Ct, Pot.B. EN6 12 DA32
Potters Cross, Iver SL0 75 BE69
POTTERS CROUCH,
St.Alb. AL2 8 BX25
Potters Flds, SE1 201 N3
Potters Gro, N.Mal. KT3 138 CQ98
Potters Hts Cl, Pnr. HA5 39 BV52
Potters La, SW16 121 DK93
Barnet EN5 28 DA42
Borehamwood WD6 26 CQ39
Woking (Send) GU23 167 BB123
Potters Ms, Borwd. (Els.) WD6
off Elstree Hill N 25 CK44
Potters Rd, SW6 100 DC82
Barnet EN5 28 DB42
Potter St, Nthwd. HA6 39 BU53
Pinner HA5 39 BV53
Potter St Hill, Pnr. HA5 39 BV51
Pottery La, W11
off Portland Rd 81 CY73
Pottery Rd, Bex. DA5 127 FC89
Brentford TW8 98 CL79
Pottery St, SE16 202 D5
Pottiphere Pl, Brwd. (Warley)
CM14 54 FV49
Pott St, E2 84 DV69
Poulcott, Stai. (Wrays.) TW19 112 AY86
Poulett Gdns, Twick. TW1 117 CG88
Poulett Rd, E6 87 EM68
Poulters Wd, Kes. BR2 162 EK106
Poultney Cl, Rad. (Shenley)
WD7 10 CM32
Poulton Av, Sutt. SM1 140 DD104
Poulton Cl, E8 off Marcon Pl 66 DV64
Poultry, EC2 197 K9
Pound Cl, Orp. BR6 145 ER103
Surbiton KT6 137 CJ102
Pound Ct, Ashtd. KT21 172 CM118
Pound Ct Dr, Orp. BR6 145 ER103
Pound Cres, Lthd. (Fetch.)
KT22 171 CD121
Pound Fm Cl, Esher KT10 137 CD102
Poundfield, Wat. WD25
off Ashfields 23 BT35
Poundfield Ct, Wok. GU22
off High St 167 BC121
Poundfield Gdns, Wok. GU22 167 BC120
Poundfield Rd, Loug. IG10 33 EN43
Pound La, NW10 81 CU65
Epsom KT19 156 CR112
Radlett (Shenley) WD7 10 CM33
Sevenoaks TN13 191 FH124
Sevenoaks (Knock.P.) TN14 180 EX115
Pound Pk Rd, SE7 104 EK77
Pound Pl, SE9 125 EN86
Pound Rd, Bans. SM7 173 CZ117
Chertsey KT16 134 BH101
Pound St, Cars. SM5 158 DF106
Pound Way, Chis. BR7
off Royal Par 125 EQ94
Pounsley Rd, Sev. (Dunt.Grn)
TN13 190 FE121
Pountney Rd, SW11 100 DG83
POVEREST, Orp. BR5 145 ET99
Poverest Rd, Orp. BR5 145 ET99
Powder Mill La, Dart. DA1 128 FL89
Twickenham TW2 116 BZ88
Powdermill La, Wal.Abb. EN9 15 EB33
Powdermill Ms, Wal.Abb. EN9
off Powdermill La 15 EB33
Powdermill Way, Wal.Abb.
EN9 15 EB32
Powell Cl, Chess. KT9
off Coppard Gdns 155 CK106
Dartford DA2 129 FS89
Edgware HA8 42 CM51
Wallington SM6 159 DK108
Powell Gdns, Dag. RM10 70 FA63
Powell Rd, E5 66 DV62
Buckhurst Hill IG9 48 EJ45
Powell's Wk, W4 98 CS79
Powergate Business Pk,
NW10 80 CR69
Power Ind Est, Erith DA8 107 FG81
Power Rd, W4 98 CN77
Powers Ct, Twick. TW1 117 CK87
Powerscroft Rd, E5 66 DW63
Sidcup DA14 126 EW93
Powis Ct, Pot.B. EN6 12 DC34
Powis Gdns, NW11 63 CZ59
W11 81 CZ72
Powis Ms, W11
off Westbourne Pk Rd 81 CZ72
Powis Pl, WC1 196 A5
Powis Rd, E3 85 EB69
Powis Sq, W11 81 CZ72
Powis St, SE18 105 EN76
Powis Ter, W11 81 CZ72
Powle Ter, Ilf. IG1
off Oaktree Gro 69 EQ64
Powlett Pl, NW1
off Harmood St 83 DH65
Pownall Gdns, Houns. TW3 96 CB84
Pownall Rd, E8 84 DT67
Hounslow TW3 96 CB84
Pownsett Ter, Ilf. IG1
off Buttsbury Rd 69 EQ64
Powster Rd, Brom. BR1 124 EH92
Powys Cl, Bexh. DA7 106 EX79
Powys Ct, Borwd. WD6 26 CR41
Powys La, N13 45 DL50
N14 45 DL49
POYLE, Slou. SL3 93 BE81
Poyle Pk, Slou. (Colnbr.) SL3 93 BE83
Poyle Rd, Slou. (Colnbr.) SL3 93 BE83
Poyle Tech Cen, Slou. SL3 93 BE82
Poynder Rd, Til. RM18 111 GH81
Poynders Ct, SW4
off Poynders Rd 121 DJ86
Poynders Gdns, SW4 121 DJ87
Poynders Rd, SW4 121 DJ86
Poynings, The, Iver SL0 93 BF77
Poynings Cl, Orp. BR6 146 EW103
Poynings Rd, N19 65 DJ62
Poynings Way, N12 44 DA50
Romford RM3
off Arlington Gdns 52 FL53
Poyntell Cres, Chis. BR7 145 ER95
Poynter Ho, W11 81 CX74
Poynter Rd, Enf. EN1 30 DU43
Poynton Rd, N17 46 DU54
Poyntz Rd, SW11 100 DF82
Poyser St, E2 84 DV68
Prae, The, Wok. GU22 167 BF118
Praed Ms, W2 194 A8
Praed St, W2 194 B7
Pragel St, E13 86 EH68
Pragnell Rd, SE12 124 EH89
Prague Pl, SW2 121 DL85
Prah Rd, N4 65 DN61
Prairie Cl, Add. KT15 134 BH104
Prairie Rd, Add. KT15 134 BH104
Prairie St, SW8 100 DG82
Pratt Ms, NW1 off Pratt St 83 DJ67
PRATT'S BOTTOM,
Orp. BR6 164 EV110
Pratts La, Walt. KT12
off Molesey Rd 154 BX105
Pratts Pas, Kings.T. KT1
off Clarence St 138 CL96
Pratt St, NW1 83 DJ67
Pratt Wk, SE11 200 C8
Prayle Gro, NW2 63 CX60
Prebend Gdns, W4 99 CT76
W6 99 CT76
Prebend St, N1 84 DQ67
Precinct, The, Egh. TW20
off High St 113 BA92
West Molesey KT8
off Victoria Av 136 CB97
Precinct Rd, Hayes UB3 77 BU73
Precincts, The, Mord. SM4
off Green La 140 DA100
Premier Av, Grays RM16 110 GC75
Premier Cor, W9
off Kilburn La 81 CZ68
Premiere Pl, E14 203 P1
Premier Pk, NW10 80 CP67
Premier Pk Rd, NW10 80 CP68
Premier Pl, SW15
off Putney High St 99 CY84
Watford WD18 23 BT43
Prendergast Rd, SE3 104 EE83
Prentis Rd, SW16 121 DK91
Prentiss Ct, SE7 104 EK77
Presburg Rd, N.Mal. KT3 138 CS99
Presburg St, E5 off Glyn Rd 67 DX62
Prescelly Pl, Edg. HA8 42 CM53
Prescot St, E1 84 DT73
Prescott Av, Orp. BR5 145 EP100
Prescott Cl, SW16 121 DL94
Prescott Grn, Loug. IG10 33 EQ41
Prescott Ho, SE17
off Hillingdon St 101 DP79
Prescott Pl, SW4 101 DK83
Prescott Rd, Slou.
(Colnbr.) SL3 93 BE82
Waltham Cross (Chsht) EN8 15 DY27
Presentation Ms, SW2
off Palace Rd 121 DM88
President Dr, E1 202 D2
President St, EC1 197 H2
Prespa Cl, N9
off Hudson Way 46 DW47
Press Ct, SE1
off Marlborough Gro 102 DU78
Press Rd, NW10 62 CR62
Uxbridge UB8 76 BK65
Prestage Way, E14 85 EC73
Prestbury Ct, Wok. GU21
off Muirfield Rd 166 AU118
Prestbury Cres, Bans. SM7 174 DF116
Prestbury Rd, E7 86 EJ66
Prestbury Sq, SE9 125 EM91
Prested Rd, SW11
off St. John's Hill 100 DE84
Prestige Way, NW4
off Heriot Rd 63 CW57
PRESTON, Wem. HA9 61 CK59
Preston Av, E4 47 ED51
Preston Cl, SE1 201 M8
Twickenham TW2 117 CE90
Preston Ct, Walt. KT12
off St. Johns Dr 136 BW102
Preston Dr, E11 68 EJ57
Bexleyheath DA7 106 EX81
Epsom KT19 156 CS107
Preston Gdns, NW10
off Church Rd 80 CS65
Enfield EN3 31 DY37
Ilford IG1 68 EL58
Preston Gro, Ashtd. KT21 171 CJ117
Preston Hill, Har. HA3 62 CM58
Preston La, Tad. KT20 173 CV121
Preston Pl, NW2 81 CU65
Richmond TW10 118 CL85
⊖ Preston Road 62 CL60
Preston Rd, E11 68 EE58
SE19 121 DP93
SW20 119 CT94
Gravesend (Nthflt) DA11 130 GE88
Harrow HA3 62 CL59
Romford RM3 52 FK49
Shepperton TW17 134 BN99
Slough SL2 74 AW73
Wembley HA9 62 CL61
Prestons Rd, E14 204 E4
Bromley BR2 144 EG104
Preston Waye, Har. HA3 62 CL60
Prestwick Cl, Sthl. UB2
off Ringway 96 BY78
Prestwick Rd, Wat. WD19 40 BX50
Prestwood, Slou. SL2 74 AV72
Prestwood Av, Har. HA3 61 CH56
Prestwood Cl, SE18 106 EU80
Harrow HA3 61 CJ56
Prestwood Dr, Rom. RM5 51 FC50
Prestwood Gdns, Croy. CR0 142 DQ101
Prestwood St, N1 197 J1
Pretoria Av, E17 67 DY56
Pretoria Cl, N17
off Pretoria Rd 46 DT52
Pretoria Cres, E4 47 EC46
Pretoria Ho, Erith DA8
off Waterhead Cl 107 FE80
Pretoria Rd, E4 47 EC46
E11 67 ED60
E16 86 EF69
N17 46 DT52
SW16 121 DH93
Chertsey KT16 133 BF102
Ilford IG1 69 EP64
Romford RM7 71 FC56
Watford WD18 23 BU42
Pretoria Rd N, N18 46 DT51
Pretty La, Couls. CR5 175 DJ121
Prevost Rd, N11 44 DG47
Prey Heath, Wok. GU22 166 AV123
Prey Heath Cl, Wok. GU22 166 AW124
Prey Heath Rd, Wok. GU22 166 AV124
Price Cl, NW7 43 CY51
SW17 120 DF90
Price Rd, Croy. CR0 159 DP106
Price's Ct, SW11 100 DD83
Prices Ms, N1 83 DM67
Price's St, SE1 200 G3
Price Way, Hmptn. TW12
off Victors Dr 116 BY93
Pricklers Hill, Barn. EN5 28 DB44
Prickley Wd, Brom. BR2 144 EF102
Priddy's Yd, Croy. CR0
off Church St 142 DQ103
Prideaux Pl, W3 80 CR73
WC1 196 C2
Prideaux Rd, SW9 101 DL83
Pridham Rd, Th.Hth. CR7 142 DR98
Priest Ct, EC2 197 H8
Priestfield Rd, SE23 123 DY90
Priest Hill, Egh. TW20 112 AW90
Windsor (Old Wind.) SL4 112 AW90
Priestlands Pk Rd, Sid. DA15 125 ET90
Priestley Cl, N16
off Ravensdale Rd 66 DT59
Priestley Gdns, Rom. RM6 70 EV58
Priestley Rd, Mitch. CR4 140 DG96
Priestley Way, E17 67 DX55
NW2 63 CU60
Priestly Gdns, Wok. GU22 167 BA120
Priestman Pt, E3
off Rainhill Way 85 EB69
Priest Pk Av, Har. HA2 60 CA61
Priests Av, Rom. RM1 51 FD54
Priests Br, SW14 98 CS84
SW15 98 CS84
Priests Fld, Brwd. (Ingrave)
CM13 55 GC50
Priests La, Brwd. CM15 54 FY47
Prima Rd, SW9 101 DN80
Primrose Av, Enf. EN2 30 DR39
Romford RM6 70 EV59
Primrose Cl, E3 85 EA68
N3 44 DB54
SE6 123 EC92
Harrow HA2 60 BZ63
Wallington SM6 141 DH102
Primrose Dr, West Dr. UB7 94 BK77
Primrose Gdns, NW3 82 DE65
Bushey WD23 40 CB45
Ruislip HA4 60 BW64
Primrose Glen, Horn. RM11 72 FL56
PRIMROSE HILL, NW8 82 DF67
Primrose Hill, EC4 196 E9
Brentwood CM14 54 FW48
Primrose Hill, Kings L. WD4 7 BP28
Primrose Hill Ct, NW3 82 DF66
Primrose Hill Rd, NW3 82 DE66
Primrose Hill Studios, NW1
off Fitzroy Rd 82 DG67
Primrose La, Croy. CR0 143 DX102
Primrose Ms, NW1
off Sharpleshall St 82 DF66
SE3 104 EH80
W5 off St. Mary's Rd 97 CK75
Primrose Path, Wal.Cr.
(Chsht) EN7 14 DU31
Primrose Pl, Islw. TW7 97 CF82
Primrose Rd, E10 67 EB60
E18 48 EH54
Walton-on-Thames KT12 154 BW106
Primrose Sq, E9 84 DW66
Primrose St, EC2 197 M6
Primrose Wk, SE14
off Alexandra St 103 DY80
Epsom KT17 157 CT108
Primrose Way, Wem. HA0 79 CK68
Primula St, W12 81 CU72
Prince Albert Rd, NW1 194 C1
NW8 194 C1
Prince Alberts Wk, Wind. SL4 92 AU81
Prince Arthur Ms, NW3
off Perrins La 64 DC63
Prince Arthur Rd, NW3 64 DC64
Prince Charles Av, Dart.
(S.Darenth) DA4 149 FR96
Prince Charles Dr, NW4 63 CW59
Prince Charles Rd, SE3 104 EF81
Prince Charles Way, Wall.
SM6 141 DH104
Prince Consort Dr, Chis. BR7 145 ER95
Prince Consort Rd, SW7 100 DC76
Princedale Rd, W11 81 CY74
Prince Edwards Rd, E9 85 DZ65
Prince George Av, N14 29 DJ42
Prince George Duke of Kent Ct,
Chis. BR7
off Holbrook La 125 ER94
Prince George Rd, N16 66 DS63
Prince George's Av, SW20 139 CW96
Prince George's Rd, SW19 140 DD95
Prince Henry Rd, SE7 104 EK80
★ Prince Henry's Room,
EC4 196 D9
Prince Imperial Rd, SE18 105 EM81
Chislehurst BR7 125 EP94
Prince John Rd, SE9 124 EL85
Princelet St, E1 84 DT71
Prince of Orange La, SE10
off Greenwich High Rd 103 EC80
Prince of Wales Cl, NW4
off Church Ter 63 CV56
Prince of Wales Dr, SW8 101 DH80
SW11 100 DF81
Prince of Wales Footpath,
Enf. EN3 31 DY38
Prince of Wales Gate, SW7 198 B4
Prince of Wales Pas, NW1 195 K3
Prince of Wales Rd, NW5 82 DG65
SE3 104 EF81
Sutton SM1 140 DD103
Prince of Wales Ter, W4 98 CS78
W8 off Kensington Rd 100 DB75
DLR Prince Regent 86 EJ73
Prince Regent La, E13 86 EH69
E16 86 EJ71
Prince Regent Ms, NW1 195 K3
Prince Regent Rd, Houns.
TW3 96 CC83
Prince Rd, SE25 142 DS99
Prince Rupert Rd, SE9 105 EM84
Prince's Arc, SW1 199 L2
Princes Av, N3 44 DA53
N10 64 DG55
N13 45 DN50
N22 45 DK53
NW9 62 CP56
W3 98 CN76
Carshalton SM5 158 DF108
Dartford DA2 128 FP88
Enfield EN3 31 DY36
Greenford UB6 78 CB72
Orpington BR5 145 ES99
South Croydon CR2 176 DV115
Surbiton KT6 138 CN102
Watford WD18 23 BT43
Woodford Green IG8 48 EH49
Princes Cl, N4 65 DP60
NW9 62 CN56
SW4 off Old Town 101 DJ83
Edgware HA8 42 CN50
Epping (N.Wld Bas.) CM16 19 FC25
Sidcup DA14 126 EX90
South Croydon CR2 176 DV115
Teddington TW11 117 CD91
Princes Ct, SE16 203 M7
SW3 off Brompton Rd 100 DF75
Wembley HA9 62 CL64
Princes Ct Business Cen, E1 202 E1
Princes Dr, Har. HA1 61 CE55
Prince's Dr, Lthd. (Oxshott)
KT22 155 CE112
Princesfield Rd, Wal.Abb. EN9 16 EH33
Princes Gdns, SW7 198 A6
W3 80 CN71
W5 79 CJ70
Princes Gate, SW7 198 B5
Princes Gate Ct, SW7 198 A5
Princes Gate Ms, SW7 198 A6
Princes La, N10 65 DH55
Princes Ms, W2
off Hereford Rd 82 DA73
Princes Par, Pot.B. EN6
off High St 12 DC32
Princes Pk, Rain. RM13 89 FG66
Princes Pk Av, NW11 63 CY58
Hayes UB3 77 BR73
Princes Pk Circle, Hayes UB3 77 BR73
Princes Pk Cl, Hayes UB3 77 BR73
Princes Pk La, Hayes UB3 77 BR73
Princes Pk Par, Hayes UB3 77 BR73
Princes Pl, SW1 199 L2
W11 81 CY74
Princes Plain, Brom. BR2 144 EL101
Princes Ri, SE13 103 EC82
Princes Riverside Rd, SE16 203 H2
Princes Rd, N18 46 DW49
SE20 123 DX93
Princes Rd, SW14 98 CR83
SW19 120 DA93
W13 off Broomfield Rd 79 CH74
Ashford TW15 114 BM92
Buckhurst Hill IG9 48 EJ47
Dartford DA1, DA2 127 FG86
Egham TW20 113 AZ93
Feltham TW13 115 BT89
Gravesend DA12 131 GJ90
Ilford IG6 69 ER56
Kingston upon Thames
KT2 118 CN94
Richmond TW10 118 CM85
Richmond (Kew) TW9 98 CM80
Romford RM1 71 FG57
Swanley BR8 127 FG93
Teddington TW11 117 CD91
Weybridge KT13 153 BP106
Princess Alice Way, SE28 105 ER75
Princess Av, Wem. HA9 62 CL61
Princess Cl, SE28 88 EX72
Princess Cres, N4 65 DP61
Princesses Wk, Rich. TW9
off Kew Rd 98 CL80
Princess Gdns, Wok. GU22 167 BB116
H Princess Grace Hosp,
The, W1 194 F5
Princess La, Ruis. HA4 59 BS60
Princess Louise Cl, W2 194 A6
H Princess Louise Hosp,
W10 81 CX71
Princess Mary's Rd, Add.
KT15 152 BJ105
Princess May Rd, N16 66 DS63
Princess Ms, NW3
off Belsize Cres 82 DD65
Kingston upon Thames
KT1 138 CM97
Princess Par, Orp. BR6
off Crofton Rd 145 EN104
Princess Pk Manor, N11 44 DG50
Princes Sq, W2 82 DB73
Princess Rd, NW1 82 DG67
NW6 82 DA68
Croydon CR0 142 DQ100
Woking GU22 167 BB116
H Princess Royal Uni Hosp,
The, Orp. BR6 145 EN104
Princess St, SE1 200 G7
Princes St, EC2 197 K8
N17 off Queen St 46 DS51
W1 195 J9
Bexleyheath DA7 106 EZ84
Gravesend DA11 131 GH86
Richmond TW9
off Sheen Rd 118 CL85
Slough SL1 92 AV75
Sutton SM1 158 DD105
Princess Way, Red. RH1 184 DG133
Princes Ter, E13 86 EH67
Prince St, SE8 103 DZ79
Watford WD17 24 BW41
Princes Vw, Dart. DA1 128 FN88
Princes Way, SW19 119 CX87
Brentwood (Hutt.) CM13 55 GA46
Buckhurst Hill IG9 48 EJ47
Croydon CR0 159 DM106
Ruislip HA4 60 BY63
West Wickham BR4 162 EF105
Princes Yd, W11
off Princedale Rd 81 CY74
Princethorpe Ho, W2 82 DA71
Princethorpe Rd, SE26 123 DX91
Princeton Ct, SW15
off Felsham Rd 99 CX83
Princeton St, WC1 196 B6
Principal Sq, E9
off Chelmer Rd 67 DX64
Pringle Gdns, SW16 121 DJ91
Purley CR8 159 DM110
Printers Av, Wat. WD18 23 BS43
Printers Inn Ct, EC4 196 D8
Printers Ms, E3 85 DY67
Printer St, EC4 196 E8
Printing Ho La, Hayes UB3 95 BS75
Printing Ho Yd, E2 197 N2
Print Village, SE15
off Chadwick Rd 102 DT82
Priolo Rd, SE7 104 EJ78
Prior Av, Sutt. SM2 158 DE108
Prior Bolton St, N1 83 DP65
Prior Chase, Grays (Bad.Dene)
RM17 110 FZ77
Prioress Cres, Green. DA9 109 FW84
Prioress Ho, E3
off Bromley High St 85 EB69
Prioress Rd, SE27 121 DP90
Prioress St, SE1 201 L7
Prior Rd, Ilf. IG1 69 EN62
Priors, The, Ashtd. KT21 171 CK119
Priors Cl, Slou. SL1 92 AU76
Priors Ct, Wok. GU21 166 AU118
Priors Cft, E17 47 DY54
Woking GU22 167 BA120
Priors Fm La, Nthlt. UB5 78 BZ65
Priors Fld, Nthlt. UB5
off Arnold Rd 78 BY65
Priorsford Av, Orp. BR5 146 EU98
Priors Gdns, Ruis. HA4 60 BW64
Priors Mead, Enf. EN1 30 DS39
Priors Pk, Horn. RM12 72 FJ62
Prior St, SE10 103 EC80
Priory, The, SE3 104 EF84
Godstone RH9 186 DV131
Priory Av, E4 47 DZ48
E17 67 EA57
N8 65 DK56
W4 98 CS77
Orpington BR5 145 ER100
Sutton SM3 157 CX105
Uxbridge (Hare.) UB9 58 BJ56
Wembley HA0 61 CF63
Priory Cl, E4 47 DZ48
E18 48 EG53
N3 off Church Cres 43 CZ53
N14 29 DH43
N20 43 CZ45
SW19 off High Path 140 DB95
Beckenham BR3 143 DY97
Brentwood (Pilg.Hat.)
CM15 54 FU43
Chislehurst BR7 145 EM95
Dartford DA1 128 FJ85

Priory Cl, Haptn. TW12
off Priory Gdns **136** BZ95
Hayes UB3 . . . . **77** BV73
Ruislip HA4 . . . . **59** BT60
Stanmore HA7 . . . . **41** CF48
Sunbury-on-Thames TW16
off Staines Rd E **115** BU94
Uxbridge (Denh.) UB9 . . . . **58** BG62
Uxbridge (Hare.) UB9 . . . . **58** BH56
Walton-on-Thames KT12 . **135** BU104
Wembley (Sudbury) HA0 . . **61** CF63
Woking GU21 . . . . **151** BD113
Priory Ct, E17 . . . . **67** DZ55
EC4 off Carter La **83** DP72
SW8 . . . . **101** DK81
Bushey WD23
off Sparrows Herne **40** CC46
Epsom KT17
off Old Schs La **157** CT109
Priory Ct Est, E17
off Priory Ct **47** DZ54
Priory Cres, SE19 . . . . **122** DQ94
Sutton SM3 . . . . **157** CX105
Wembley HA0 . . . . **61** CG62
Priory Dr, SE2 . . . . **106** EX78
Stanmore HA7 . . . . **41** CF48
Priory Fld Dr, Edg. HA8 . . . . . **42** CP49
Priory Flds, Dart. (Fnghm)
DA4 . . . . **148** FM103
Priory Gdns, N6 . . . . **65** DH58
SE25 . . . . **142** DT98
SW13 . . . . **99** CT83
W4 . . . . **98** CS77
W5 off Hanger La **80** CM69
Ashford TW15 . . . . **115** BR92
Dartford DA1 . . . . **128** FK85
Hampton TW12 . . . . **116** BZ94
Uxbridge (Hare.) UB9 . . . . **58** BJ56
Wembley HA0 . . . . **61** CG63
Priory Gate, Wal.Cr. EN8 . . . . **15** DZ27
Priory Grn, Stai. TW18 . . . . . **114** BH92
Priory Grn Est, N1 . . . . **83** DM68
Priory Gro, SW8 . . . . **101** DL81
Barnet EN5 . . . . **28** DA43
Romford RM3 . . . . **52** FL48
Priory Hts, N1
off Wynford Rd **83** DM68
Priory Hill, Dart. DA1 . . . . **128** FK85
Wembley HA0 . . . . **61** CG63
H **Priory Hosp, The**, SW15 . . **99** CT84
H **Priory Hosp Hayes Gro,**
The, Brom. BR2 . . . . **144** EG103
H **Priory Hosp N London,**
N14 . . . . **45** DL46
Priory La, SW15 . . . . **118** CS86
Dartford (Fnghm) DA4 . . **148** FM102
Richmond TW9
off Forest Rd **98** CN80
West Molesey KT8 . . . . . . **136** CA98
Priory Ms, SW8 . . . . **101** DK81
Hornchurch RM11 . . . . **71** FH60
Staines TW18
off Chestnut Manor Cl . . . **114** BH92
Priory Pk, SE3 . . . . **104** EF83
Priory Pk Rd, NW6 . . . . **81** CZ67
Wembley HA0 . . . . **61** CG63
Priory Path, Rom. RM3 . . . . . . **52** FL48
Priory Pl, Dart. DA1 . . . . **128** FK86
Walton-on-Thames KT12 . **135** BU104
Priory Rd, E6 . . . . **86** EK67
N8 . . . . **65** DK56
NW6 . . . . **82** DB67
SW19 . . . . **120** DD94
W4 . . . . **98** CR76
Barking IG11 . . . . **87** ER66
Chessington KT9 . . . . **138** CL104
Croydon CR0 . . . . **141** DN101
Gerrards Cross (Chal.St.P.)
SL9 . . . . **56** AX55
Hampton TW12 . . . . **116** BZ94
Hounslow TW3 . . . . **116** CC85
Loughton IG10 . . . . **32** EL42
Richmond TW9 . . . . **98** CN79
Romford RM3 . . . . **52** FL48
Sutton SM3 . . . . **157** CX105
Priory Rd N, Dart. DA1 . . . . . **108** FK84
Priory Rd S, Dart. DA1 . . . . . **128** FK85
Priory Shop Cen, Dart. DA1 . **128** FL86
Priory St, E3 . . . . **85** EB69
Priory Ter, NW6 . . . . **82** DB67
Sunbury-on-Thames TW16
off Staines Rd E **115** BU94
Priory Vw, Bushey (Bushey Hth)
WD23 . . . . **41** CE45
Priory Wk, SW10 . . . . **100** DC78
Priory Way, Ger.Cr. (Chal.St.P.)
SL9 . . . . **56** AX55
Harrow HA2 . . . . **60** CB56
Slough (Datchet) SL3 . . . . **92** AV80
Southall UB2 . . . . **96** BX76
West Drayton UB7 . . . . **94** BL79
Priscilla Cl, N15
off Conway Rd **66** DQ57
Pritchard's Rd, E2 . . . . **84** DU67
Pritchett Cl, Enf. EN3 . . . . **31** EA37
Priter Rd, SE16 . . . . **202** C7
Priter Way, SE16
off Dockley Rd **102** DU76
Private Rd, Enf. EN1 . . . . **30** DS43
Probert Rd, SW2 . . . . **121** DN85
Probyn Ho, SW1 off Page St . **101** DK77
Probyn Rd, SW2 . . . . **121** DP89
Procter Ho, SE1 . . . . **202** B10
Procter St, WC1 . . . . **196** B7
Proctor Cl, Mitch. CR4 . . . . . **140** DG95
Proctors Cl, Felt. TW14 . . . . . **115** BU88
Profumo Rd, Walt. KT12 . . . **154** BX106
Progress Business Pk,
Croy. CR0 . . . . **141** DM103
Progress Way, N22 . . . . **45** DN53
Croydon CR0 . . . . **141** DM103
Enfield EN1 . . . . **30** DU43
Promenade, The, W4 . . . . **98** CS81
Promenade App Rd, W4 . . . . . **98** CS80
Promenade de Verdun,
Pur. CR8 . . . . **159** DK111
Promenade Mans, Edg.
HA8 off Hale La **42** CN50
Prospect Business Pk,
Loug. IG10 . . . . **33** EQ42
Prospect Cl, SE26 . . . . **122** DV91
Belvedere DA17 . . . . **106** FA77
Hounslow TW3 . . . . **96** BZ81
Prospect Cl, Ruis. HA4 . . . . . . **60** BX59
Prospect Cotts, SW18
off Point Pleasant **100** DA84
Prospect Cres, Twick. TW2 . . . **116** CC86
Prospect Gro, Grav. DA12 . . . **131** GK87
Prospect Hill, E17 . . . . **67** EB56
Prospect La, Egh. (Eng.Grn)
TW20 . . . . **112** AT92
Prospect Pl, E1 . . . . **202** F2
N2 . . . . **64** DD56
N7 off Parkhurst Rd **65** DL63
N17 . . . . **46** DS53
NW2 off Ridge Rd **63** CZ62
NW3 off Holly Wk **64** DC63
W4 off Chiswick High Rd . . **98** CR78
Bromley BR2 . . . . **144** EH97
Epsom KT17
off Clayton Rd **156** CS113
Gravesend DA12 . . . . **131** GK87
Grays RM17 . . . . **110** GB79
Romford RM5 . . . . **51** FC54
Staines TW18 . . . . **113** BF92
Prospect Pl Shop Pk, Dart.
DA1 . . . . **128** FK86
Prospect Quay, SW18 . . . . . . **100** DA84
Prospect Ring, N2 . . . . **64** DD55
Prospect Rd, NW2 . . . . **63** CZ62
Barnet EN5 . . . . **28** DA43
Hornchurch RM11 . . . . **72** FM55
Sevenoaks TN13 . . . . **191** FJ123
Surbiton KT6 . . . . **137** CJ100
Waltham Cross (Chsht) EN8 . **14** DW29
Woodford Green IG8 . . . . . . **48** EJ50
Prospect St, SE16 . . . . **202** E6
Prospect Vale, SE18 . . . . **104** EL77
Prospect Way, Brwd. (Hutt.)
CM13 . . . . **55** GE42
Prospero Rd, N19 . . . . **65** DJ60
Prossers, Tad. KT20 . . . . **173** CX121
Protea Cl, E16 off Hermit Rd . . **86** EF70
Prothero Gdns, NW4 . . . . **63** CV57
Prothero Ho, NW10 . . . . **80** CR66
Prothero Rd, SW6 . . . . **99** CY80
Prout Gro, NW10 . . . . **62** CS63
Prout Rd, E5 . . . . **66** DV62
Provence St, N1
off St. Peters St **84** DQ68
Providence Av, Har. HA2
off Goodwill Dr **60** CA60
Providence Cl, E9
off Wetherell Rd **85** DX67
Providence Ct, W1 . . . . **194** G10
Providence La, Hayes UB3 . . . **95** BR80
Providence Pl, N1
off Upper St **83** DP67
Epsom KT17 . . . . **156** CS112
Romford RM5 . . . . **50** EZ54
Woking GU22 . . . . **152** BG114
Providence Rd, West Dr. UB7 . **76** BL74
Providence Row, N1
off Pentonville Rd **83** DM68
Providence Row Cl, E2
off Ainsley St **84** DV69
Providence Sq, SE1
off Jacob St **102** DU75
Providence St, N1
off St. Peters St **84** DQ68
Greenhithe DA9 . . . . **129** FU85
Providence Yd, E2
off Ezra St **84** DU69
Provident Ind Est, Hayes UB3 . **95** BU75
Provost Est, N1 . . . . **197** K2
Provost Rd, NW3 . . . . **82** DF66
Provost St, N1 . . . . **197** K3
Prowse Av, Bushey (Bushey Hth)
WD23 . . . . **40** CC47
Prowse Pl, NW1 off Bonny St . **83** DH66
Pruden Cl, N14 . . . . **45** DJ47
Prudent Pas, EC2 . . . . **197** J8
Prune Hill, Egh. (Eng.Grn)
TW20 . . . . **112** AX94
Prusom St, E1 . . . . **202** E3
Pryor Cl, Abb.L. WD5 . . . . **7** BT32
Pryors, The, NW3 . . . . **64** DD62
★ **P.S. Tattershall Castle**,
SW1 . . . . **200** A3
H **Public Health Laboratory**
Service HQ, NW9 . . . . **62** CS55
★ **Public Record Office**, Rich.
TW9 . . . . **98** CP80
Puck La, Wal.Abb. EN9 . . . . . . **15** ED29
Pucknells Cl, Swan. BR8 . . . . **147** FC95
Puddenhole Cotts, Bet. RH3 . **182** CN133
Pudding La, EC3 . . . . **201** L1
Chigwell IG7 . . . . **49** ET46
Sevenoaks (Seal) TN15
off Church St **191** FN121
DLR **Pudding Mill Lane** **85** EB67
Pudding Mill La, E15 . . . . **85** EB67
Puddle Dock, EC4 . . . . **196** G10
Puddledock La, Dart. DA2 . . . **127** FE92
Westerham TN16 . . . . **189** ET133
Puers La, Beac. (Jordans)
HP9 . . . . **36** AS51
Puffin Cl, Bark. IG11 . . . . **88** EV69
Beckenham BR3 . . . . **143** DX99
Puffin Ter, Ilf. IG5
off Tiptree Cres **69** EN55
Pulborough Rd, SW18 . . . . . . **119** CZ87
Pulborough Way, Houns. TW4 . **96** BW84
Pulford Rd, N15 . . . . **66** DR58
Pulham Av, N2 . . . . **64** DC56
Pulham Ho, SW8
off Dorset Rd **101** DM80
Puller Rd, Barn. EN5 . . . . **27** CY40
Pulleyns Av, E6 . . . . **86** EL69
Pullman Ct, SW2 . . . . **121** DL88
Pullman Gdns, SW15 . . . . **119** CW86
Pullman Pl, SE9 . . . . **124** EL85
Pullmans Pl, Stai. TW18 . . . . . **114** BG92
Pulross Rd, SW9 . . . . **101** DM83
Pulse Apts, NW6
off Lymington Rd **64** DC64
Pulteney Cl, E3 . . . . **85** DZ67
Isleworth TW7
off Gumley Gdns **97** CG83
Pulteney Gdns, E18
off Pulteney Rd **68** EH55
Pulteney Rd, E18 . . . . **68** EH55
Pulteney Ter, N1 . . . . **83** DM67
Pulton Pl, SW6 . . . . **100** DA80
Puma Ct, E1 . . . . **197** P6
Pump All, Brent. TW8 . . . . **97** CK80
Pump Cl, Nthlt. UB5
off Union Rd **78** CA68
Pump Ct, EC4 . . . . **196** D9
Pumphandle Path, N2
off Tarling Rd **44** DC54
Pump Hill, Loug. IG10 . . . . **33** EM40
Pump Ho Cl, SE16 . . . . **202** G5
Bromley BR2 . . . . **144** EF96
Pump Ho Ms, E1
off Hooper St **84** DU73
Pumping Sta Rd, W4 . . . . **98** CS80
Pump La, SE14 . . . . **102** DW80
Chesham HP5 . . . . **4** AS32
Hayes UB3 . . . . **95** BV75
Orpington BR6 . . . . **165** FB106
Pump Pail N, Croy. CR0
off Old Town **142** DQ104
Pump Pail S, Croy. CR0
off Southbridge Rd **142** DQ104
Punchard Cres, Enf. EN3 . . . . . **31** EB38
Pundersons Gdns, E2 . . . . **84** DV69
Punjab La, Sthl. UB1
off Herbert Rd **78** BZ74
Purbeck Av, N.Mal. KT3 . . . . **139** CT100
Purbeck Cl, Red. (Merst.)
RH1 . . . . **185** DK128
Purbeck Dr, NW2 . . . . **63** CY61
Woking GU21 . . . . **151** AZ114
Purbeck Ho, SW8
off Bolney St **101** DM80
Purbeck Rd, Horn. RM11 . . . . . **71** FG60
Purberry Gro, Epsom KT17 . . **157** CT110
Purbrock Av, Wat. WD25 . . . . . **24** BW36
Purbrook Est, SE1 . . . . **201** N5
Purbrook St, SE1 . . . . **201** N6
Purcell Cl, Borwd. WD6 . . . . . . **25** CK39
Kenley CR8 . . . . **160** DR114
Purcell Cres, SW6 . . . . **99** CY80
Purcell Rd, Grnf. UB6 . . . . **78** CB71
Purcells Av, Edg. HA8 . . . . **42** CN50
Purcells Cl, Ashtd. KT21
off Albert Rd **172** CM118
Purcell St, N1 . . . . **84** DS68
Purchese St, NW1 . . . . **83** DK68
Purdy St, E3 . . . . **85** EB70
Purelake Ms, SE13 . . . . **103** ED83
PURFLEET, RM19 . . . . **108** FP77
⇌ **Purfleet** **108** FN78
Purfleet Bypass, Purf. RM19 . **108** FP77
Purfleet Ind Pk, S.Ock.
(Aveley) RM15 . . . . **108** FM75
Purfleet Rd, S.Ock. (Aveley)
RM15 . . . . **108** FN75
Purfleet Thames Terminal,
Purf. RM19 . . . . **108** FQ80
Purkis Cl, Uxb. UB8
off Dawley Rd **77** BQ72
Purland Cl, Dag. RM8 . . . . **70** EZ60
Purland Rd, SE28 . . . . **105** ET75
Purleigh Av, Wdf.Grn. IG8 . . . . **48** EL51
PURLEY, CR8 . . . . **159** DM111
⇌ **Purley** **159** DP112
Purley Av, NW2 . . . . **63** CY62
Purley Bury Av, Pur. CR8 . . . . **160** DQ110
Purley Bury Cl, Pur. CR8 . . . . **160** DQ111
Purley Cl, Ilf. IG5 . . . . **49** EN54
Purley Downs Rd, Pur. CR8 . . **160** DQ110
South Croydon CR2 . . . . . **160** DR111
Purley Hill, Pur. CR8 . . . . **159** DP112
Purley Knoll, Pur. CR8 . . . . . . **159** DM111
⇌ **Purley Oaks** **160** DQ109
Purley Oaks Rd, S.Croy. CR2 . **160** DR109
Purley Par, Pur. CR8
off High St **159** DN111
Purley Pk Rd, Pur. CR8 . . . . . **159** DP110
Purley Pl, N1
off Islington Pk St **83** DP66
Purley Ri, Pur. CR8 . . . . **159** DM112
Purley Rd, N9 . . . . **46** DR48
Purley CR8 . . . . **159** DN111
South Croydon CR2 . . . . . **160** DR108
Purley Vale, Pur. CR8 . . . . . . **159** DP113
H **Purley War Mem Hosp**,
Pur. CR8 . . . . **159** DN111
Purley Way, Croy. CR0 . . . . . . **141** DM101
Purley CR8 . . . . **159** DN108
Purley Way Cres, Croy. CR0
off Purley Way **141** DM101
Purlieu Way, Epp. (They.B.)
CM16 . . . . **33** ES35
Purlings Rd, Bushey WD23 . . . **24** CB43
Purneys Rd, SE9 . . . . **104** EK84
Purrett Rd, SE18 . . . . **105** ET78
Pursers Ct, Slou. SL2 . . . . **74** AS72
Purser's Cross Rd, SW6 . . . . . . **99** CZ81
Pursewardens Cl, W13 . . . . **79** CJ74
Pursley Gdns, Borwd. WD6 . . . **26** CN38
Pursley Rd, NW7 . . . . **43** CV52
Purves Rd, NW10 . . . . **81** CW68
Puteaux Ho, E2 . . . . **85** DX68
PUTNEY, SW15 . . . . **99** CY84
⇌ **Putney** **99** CY84
⊖ **Putney Bridge** **99** CY83
Putney Br, SW6 . . . . **99** CY83
SW15 . . . . **99** CY83
Putney Br App, SW6 . . . . **99** CY83
Putney Br Rd, SW15 . . . . **99** CY84
SW18 . . . . **99** CY84
Putney Common, SW15 . . . . . **99** CW83
Putney Ex Shop Cen, SW15 . . **99** CX84
Putney Gdns, Rom. (Chad.Hth)
RM6 off Heathfield Pk Dr . . . **70** EV58
PUTNEY HEATH, SW15 . . . . . **119** CW86
Putney Heath, SW15 . . . . **119** CW86
Putney Heath La, SW15 . . . . . **119** CX86
Putney High St, SW15 . . . . **99** CX84
Putney Hill, SW15 . . . . **119** CX86
Putney Pk Av, SW15 . . . . **99** CU84
Putney Pk La, SW15 . . . . **99** CV84
Putney Rd, Enf. EN3 . . . . **31** DX36
PUTNEY VALE, SW15 . . . . . . **119** CT90
Putney Wf Twr, SW15 . . . . **99** CY83
Puttenham Cl, Wat. WD19 . . . . **40** BW48
Pycroft Way, N9 . . . . **46** DU49
Pye Cl, Cat. CR3
off St. Lawrence Way . . . **176** DR123
Pyecombe Cor, N12 . . . . **43** CZ49
Pyghtle, The, Uxb. (Denh.)
UB9 . . . . **58** BG60
Pylbrook Rd, Sutt. SM1 . . . . . **140** DA104
Pyle Hill, Wok. GU22 . . . . **166** AX124
Pylon Way, Croy. CR0 . . . . . . **141** DL102
Pym Cl, Barn. EN4 . . . . **28** DD43
Pymers Mead, SE21 . . . . **122** DQ88
Pymmes Brook Dr, Barn. EN4 . **28** DE42
Pymmes Cl, N13 . . . . **45** DM50
N17 . . . . **46** DV53
Pymmes Gdns N, N9 . . . . **46** DT48
Pymmes Gdns S, N9 . . . . **46** DT48
Pymmes Grn Rd, N11 . . . . **45** DH49
Pymmes Rd, N13 . . . . **45** DL51
Pym Orchard, West.
(Brasted) TN16 . . . . **180** EW124
Pym Pl, Grays RM17 . . . . **110** GA77
Pynchester Cl, Uxb. UB10 . . . . **58** BN61
Pyne Rd, Surb. KT6 . . . . **138** CN102
Pynest Grn La, Wal.Abb. EN9 . **32** EG38
Pyne Ter, SW19
off Windlesham Gro **119** CX88
Pynfolds, SE16 . . . . **202** E5
Pynham Cl, SE2 . . . . **106** EU76
Pynnacles Cl, Stan. HA7 . . . . . **41** CH50
Pyrcroft La, Wey. KT13 . . . . . **153** BP106
Pyrcroft Rd, Cher. KT16 . . . . . **133** BF101
PYRFORD, Wok. GU22 . . . . . . **167** BE115
Pyrford Common Rd,
Wok. GU22 . . . . **167** BD116
★ **Pyrford Ct**, Wok. GU22 . . **167** BE117
PYRFORD GREEN, Wok.
GU22 . . . . **168** BH117
Pyrford Heath, Wok. GU22 . . **167** BF116
Pyrford Lock, Wok. (Wisley)
GU23 . . . . **168** BJ116
Pyrford Rd, W.Byf. KT14 . . . . **152** BG113
Woking GU22 . . . . **152** BG114
PYRFORD VILLAGE, Wok.
GU22 . . . . **168** BG118
Pyrford Wds Cl, Wok. GU22 . **167** BF115
Pyrford Wds Rd, Wok. GU22 . **167** BE115
Pyrland Rd, N5 . . . . **66** DR64
Richmond TW10 . . . . **118** CM86
Pyrles Grn, Loug. IG10 . . . . . . **33** EP39
Pyrles La, Loug. IG10 . . . . **33** EP40
Pyrmont Gro, SE27 . . . . **121** DP90
Pyrmont Rd, W4 . . . . **98** CN79
Ilford IG1 off High Rd **69** EQ61
Pytchley Cres, SE19 . . . . **122** DQ93
Pytchley Rd, SE22 . . . . **102** DS83

Q

Quadrangle, The, W2 . . . . **194** B8
Quadrangle Cl, SE1 . . . . **201** M8
Quadrangle Ho, E15
off Romford Rd **86** EE65
Quadrangle Ms, Stan. HA7 . . . **41** CJ52
Quadrant, The, SE24
off Herne Hill **122** DQ85
SW20 . . . . **139** CY95
Bexleyheath DA7 . . . . **106** EX80
Epsom KT17 . . . . **156** CS113
Purfleet RM19 . . . . **108** FQ77
Richmond TW9 . . . . **98** CL84
Sutton SM2 . . . . **158** DC107
Quadrant Arc, W1 . . . . **199** L1
Romford RM1 . . . . **71** FE57
Quadrant Cl, NW4
off The Burroughs **63** CV57
Quadrant Gro, NW5 . . . . **64** DF64
Quadrant Ho, Sutt. SM2 . . . . **158** DC107
Quadrant Rd, Rich. TW9 . . . . . . **97** CK84
Thornton Heath CR7 . . . . **141** DP98
Quadrant Way, Wey. KT13
off Weybridge Rd **152** BM105
Quad Rd, Wem. HA9
off Courtenay Rd **61** CK62
Quaggy Wk, SE3 . . . . **104** EG84
Quail Gdns, S.Croy. CR2 . . . . **161** DY110
Quainton St, NW10 . . . . **62** CR62
Quaker Cl, Sev. TN13 . . . . . . **191** FK123
Quaker Ct, E1 . . . . **197** P5
Quaker La, Sthl. UB2 . . . . **96** CA76
Waltham Abbey EN9 . . . . . . **15** EC34
Quakers Course, NW9 . . . . **43** CT53
Quakers Hall La, Sev. TN13 . . **191** FJ122
Quakers La, Islw. TW7 . . . . **97** CG81
Potters Bar EN6 . . . . **12** DB30
Quaker's Pl, E7 . . . . **68** EK64
Quaker St, E1 . . . . **197** P5
Quakers Wk, N21 . . . . **30** DR44
Quality Ct, WC2 . . . . **196** D8
Quality St, Red. (Merst.) RH1 . **185** DH128
Quantock Cl, Hayes UB3 . . . . **95** BR80
Slough SL3 . . . . **93** BA78
Quantock Dr, Wor.Pk. KT4 . . **139** CW103
Quantock Gdns, NW2 . . . . **63** CX61
Quantock Ms, SE15
off Choumert Gro **102** DU82
Quantock Rd, Bexh. DA7
off Cumbrian Av **107** FE82
Quarles Cl, Rom. RM5 . . . . **50** FA52
Quarles Pk Rd, Rom. RM6 . . . . **70** EV58
Quarrendon St, SW6 . . . . **100** DA82
Quarr Rd, Cars. SM5 . . . . **140** DD100
Quarry, The, Bet. RH3
off Station Rd **182** CS132
Quarry Cl, Lthd. KT22 . . . . . . **171** CK121
Oxted RH8 . . . . **188** EE130
Quarry Cotts, Sev. TN13 . . . . **190** FG123
Quarry Gdns, Lthd. KT22 . . . **171** CK121
Quarry Hill, Grays RM17 . . . . **110** GA78
Sevenoaks TN15 . . . . **191** FK123
Quarry Hill Pk, Reig. RH2 . . . **184** DC131
Quarry Ms, Purf. RM19 . . . . . **108** FN77
Quarry Pk Rd, Sutt. SM1 . . . . **157** CZ107
Quarry Ri, Sutt. SM1 . . . . **157** CZ107
Quarry Rd, SW18 . . . . **120** DC86
Godstone RH9 . . . . **186** DW128
Oxted RH8 . . . . **188** EE130
Quarryside Business Pk,
Red. RH1 . . . . **185** DH130
Quarterdeck, The, E14 . . . . . . **203** P5
Quartermaine Av, Wok.
GU22 . . . . **167** AZ122
Quarter Mile La, E10 . . . . **67** EB63
Quaves Rd, Slou. SL3 . . . . **92** AV76
Quay La, Green. DA9 . . . . **109** FV84
Quayside Wk, Kings.T. KT1
off Bishop's Hall **137** CK96
Quay W, Tedd. TW11 . . . . **117** CH92
Quebec Av, West. TN16 . . . . . **189** ER126
★ **Quebec Ho**, Wolfe's Ho,
West. TN16 . . . . **189** ER126
Quebec Ms, W1 . . . . **194** E9
Quebec Rd, Hayes UB4 . . . . . . **78** BW73
Ilford IG1, IG2 . . . . **69** EP59
Tilbury RM18 . . . . **111** GG82
Quebec Sq, West. TN16 . . . . . **189** ER126
Quebec Way, SE16 . . . . **203** J5
Queen Adelaide Rd, SE20 . . . **122** DW93
Queen Alexandra's Ct,
SW19 . . . . **119** CZ92
Queen Alexandra's Way,
Epsom KT19 . . . . **156** CN111
Queen Anne Av, N15
off Suffield Rd **66** DT57
Bromley BR2 . . . . **144** EF97
Queen Anne Dr, Esher
(Clay.) KT10 . . . . **155** CE108
Queen Anne Ms, W1 . . . . **195** J7
Queen Anne Rd, E9 . . . . **85** DX65
Queen Anne's Cl, Twick.
TW2 . . . . **117** CD90
Queen Anne's Gdns, W4 . . . . . **98** CS76
Queen Annes Gdns, W5 . . . . . **98** CL75
Enfield EN1 . . . . **30** DS44
Leatherhead KT22
off Linden Rd **171** CH121
Queen Anne's Gdns,
Mitch. CR4 . . . . **140** DF97
Queen Anne's Gate, SW1 . . . **199** M5
Bexleyheath DA7 . . . . **106** EX83
Queen Anne's Gro, W4 . . . . . . **98** CS76
Queen Annes Gro, W5 . . . . **98** CL75
Enfield EN1 . . . . **46** DR45
Queen Anne's Ms, Lthd.
KT22 off Fairfield Rd **171** CH121
Queen Annes Pl, Enf. EN1 . . . **30** DS44
Queen Annes Ter, Lthd. KT22
off Fairfield Rd **171** CH121
Queen Anne St, W1 . . . . **195** H8
Queen Anne's Wk, WC1
off Guilford St **83** DL70
Queen Anne Ter, E1
off Sovereign Cl **84** DV73
Queenborough Gdns, Chis.
BR7 . . . . **125** ER93
Ilford IG2 . . . . **69** EN56
Queen Caroline Est, W6 . . . . . **99** CW78
Queen Caroline St, W6 . . . . . . **99** CW77
H **Queen Charlotte's &**
Chelsea Hosp, W12 . . . . . **81** CU72
Queendale Ct, Wok. GU21
off Roundthorn Way **166** AT116
Queen Elizabeth Ct, Brox.
EN10 off Groom Rd **15** DZ26
Waltham Abbey EN9
off Greenwich Way **31** EC36
Queen Elizabeth Gdns,
Mord. SM4 . . . . **140** DA98
★ **Queen Elizabeth Hall &**
Purcell Room, SE1 . . . . . **200** B2
H **Queen Elizabeth Hosp**,
SE18 . . . . **104** EL80
Queen Elizabeth Rd, E17 . . . . **67** DY55
Kingston upon Thames
KT2 . . . . **138** CM95
Queen Elizabeths Cl, N16 . . . . **66** DR61
Queen Elizabeths Dr, N14 . . . **45** DL46
Queen Elizabeth's Dr, Croy.
(New Adgtn) CR0 . . . . . . **161** ED110
Queen Elizabeth II Br,
Dart. DA1 . . . . **109** FR82
Purfleet RM19 . . . . **109** FR82
★ **Queen Elizabeth II Conf**
Cen, SW1 . . . . **199** N5
Queen Elizabeth's Gdns, Croy.
(New Adgtn) CR0
off Queen Elizabeth's Dr . **161** ED110
★ **Queen Elizabeth's Hunting**
Lo, Epping Forest, E4 . . . . **48** EF45
Queen Elizabeth St, SE1 . . . . **201** N4
Queen Elizabeths Wk, N16 . . . **66** DR61
Queen Elizabeth's Wk, Wall.
SM6 . . . . **159** DK105
Queen Elizabeth Wk, SW13 . . **99** CV81
Windsor SL4 . . . . **92** AS82
Queen Elizabeth Way, Wok.
GU22 . . . . **167** AZ119
Queenhill Rd, S.Croy. CR2 . . . **160** DV110
Queenhithe, EC4 . . . . **197** J10
Queen Margaret's Gro, N1 . . . **66** DS64
Queen Mary Av, Mord. SM4 . **139** CX99
Queen Mary Cl, Rom. RM1 . . . **71** FF58
Surbiton KT6 . . . . **138** CN104
Woking GU22 . . . . **167** BC116
Queen Mary Ct, Stai. TW19
off Victory Cl **114** BL88
Queen Mary Rd, SE19 . . . . . . **121** DP93
Shepperton TW17 . . . . . . **135** BQ96
Queen Mary's Av, Cars. SM5 . **158** DF108
Queen Marys Av, Wat. WD18 . **23** BS42
Queen Marys Ct, Wal.Abb.
EN9 off Greenwich Way . . **31** EC35
Queen Marys Dr, Add.
(New Haw) KT15 . . . . **151** BF110
★ **Queen Mary's Gdns**,
NW1 . . . . **194** F3
H **Queen Mary's Hosp**,
NW3 . . . . **64** DC62
Sidcup DA14 . . . . **126** EU93
H **Queen Mary's Hosp for**
Children, Cars. SM5 . . . **140** DC102
H **Queen Mary's Hosp**
(Roehampton), SW15 . . . **119** CU86
Queen Mother's Dr, Uxb.
(Denh.) UB9 . . . . **57** BF58
Queen of Denmark Ct, SE16 . **203** M6
Queens Acre, Sutt. SM3 . . . . **157** CX108
Queens All, Epp. CM16 . . . . . . **17** ET31
Queens Av, N3 . . . . **44** DC52
N10 . . . . **64** DG55
N20 . . . . **44** DD47
Queen's Av, N21 . . . . **45** DP46
Queens Av, Felt. TW13 . . . . . . **116** BW91
Greenford UB6 . . . . **78** CB72
Stanmore HA7 . . . . **61** CJ55
Watford WD18 . . . . **23** BT42
West Byfleet (Byfleet) KT14 . **152** BK112
Woodford Green IG8 . . . . . . **48** EH50

★ Place of interest ⇌ Railway station ⊖ London Underground station DLR Docklands Light Railway station Tram Tramlink station H Hospital Riv Pedestrian ferry landing stage

Queensberry Ms W, SW7
off Queen's Gate ...100 DD77
Queensberry Pl, E12 ...68 EK64
SW7 ...100 DD77
Richmond TW9
off Friars La ...117 CK85
Queensberry Way, SW7
off Harrington Rd ...100 DD77
Queensborough Ms, W2
off Porchester Ter ...82 DC73
Queensborough Pas, W2
off Porchester Ter ...82 DC73
Queensborough Studios, W2
off Porchester Ter ...82 DC73
Queensborough Ter, W2 ...82 DB73
Queensbridge Pk, Islw. TW7 ...117 CE85
Queensbridge Rd, E2 ...84 DT67
E8 ...84 DT66
QUEENSBURY, Har. HA3 ...61 CK55
⊖ Queensbury ...62 CM55
Queensbury Circle Par, Har.
HA3 off Streatfield Rd ...62 CL55
Stanmore HA7
off Streatfield Rd ...62 CL55
Queensbury Rd, NW9 ...62 CR59
Wembley HA0 ...80 CM68
Queensbury Sta Par, Edg.
HA8 ...62 CM55
Queensbury St, N1 ...84 DQ66
Queen's Circ, SW8
off Queenstown Rd ...101 DH80
SW11 off Queenstown Rd ...101 DH80
Queens Cl, Edg. HA8 ...42 CN50
Tadworth (Walt.Hill) KT20 ...173 CU124
Wallington SM6
off Queens Rd ...159 DH106
Windsor (Old Wind.) SL4 ...112 AU85
★ Queens Club (Tennis Cen),
W14 ...99 CY78
Queens Club Gdns, W14 ...99 CY79
Queens Ct, SE23 ...122 DW88
Richmond TW10 ...118 CM86
Slough SL1 ...74 AT73
Queenscourt, Wem. HA9 ...62 CL63
Queens Ct, Wey. KT13 ...153 BR106
Woking GU22
off Hill Vw Rd ...167 AZ118
Queens Ct Ride, Cob. KT11 ...153 BU113
Queen's Cres, NW5 ...82 DG65
Queens Cres, Rich. TW10 ...118 CM85
Queenscroft Rd, SE9 ...124 EK85
Queensdale Cres, W11 ...81 CX74
Queensdale Pl, W11 ...81 CY74
Queensdale Rd, W11 ...81 CX74
Queensdale Wk, W11 ...81 CY74
Queensdown Rd, E5 ...66 DV63
Queens Dr, E10 ...67 EA59
N4 ...65 DP61
W3 ...80 CM72
W5 ...80 CM72
Abbots Langley WD5 ...7 BT32
Leatherhead (Oxshott)
KT22 ...154 CC111
Queen's Dr, Slou. SL3 ...75 AZ66
Queens Dr, Surb. KT5 ...138 CN101
Thames Ditton KT7 ...137 CG101
Waltham Cross EN8 ...15 EA34
Queens Dr, The, Rick.
(Mill End) WD3 ...37 BF45
Queens Elm Par, SW3
off Old Ch St ...100 DD78
Queen's Elm Sq, SW3
off Old Ch St ...100 DD78
Queensferry Wk, N17
off Jarrow Rd ...66 DV56
★ Queen's Gall, The, SW1 ...199 J5
Queens Gdns, NW4 ...63 CW57
W2 ...82 DC73
W5 ...79 CJ70
Dartford DA2 ...128 FP88
Queen's Gdns, Houns. TW5 ...96 BY81
Queens Gdns, Rain. RM13 ...89 FD68
Upminster RM14 ...73 FT58
Queen's Gate, SW7 ...100 DC75
Queensgate, Cob. KT11 ...154 BX112
Waltham Cross EN8 ...15 DZ34
Queen's Gate Gdns, SW7 ...100 DC76
Queens Gate Gdns, SW15
off Upper Richmond Rd ...99 CV84
Queensgate Gdns, Chis. BR7 ...145 ER95
Queen's Gate Ms, SW7 ...100 DC75
Queensgate Pl, NW6 ...82 DA66
Queen's Gate Pl, SW7 ...100 DC76
Queen's Gate Pl Ms, SW7 ...100 DC76
Queen's Gate Ter, SW7 ...100 DC76
Queen's Gro, NW8 ...82 DD67
Queen's Gro Ms, NW8 ...82 DD67
Queens Gro Rd, E4 ...47 ED46
Queen's Head Pas, EC4 ...197 H8
Queen's Head St, N1 ...83 DP67
Queens Head Yd, SE1 ...201 K3
Queens Ho, Tedd. TW11 ...117 CF93
★ Queen's Ice Rink, W2
off Queensway ...82 DB73
Queenside Ms, Horn. RM12 ...72 FL61
Queensland Av, N18 ...46 DQ51
SW19 ...140 DB95
Queensland Cl, E17 ...47 DZ54
Queensland Ho, E16
off Rymill St ...87 EN74
Queensland Rd, N7
off Benwell Rd ...65 DN63
Queens La, N10 ...65 DH55
Ashford TW15
off Clarendon Rd ...114 BM91
Queens Mkt, E13
off Green St ...86 EJ67
Queensmead, NW8 ...82 DD67
Queens Mead, Edg. HA8 ...42 CM51
Queensmead, Lthd. KT22 ...154 CC111
Slough (Datchet) SL3 ...92 AV80
Queensmead Av, Epsom
KT17 ...157 CV110
Queensmead Rd, Brom. BR2 ...144 EF96
Queensmere Cl, SW19 ...119 CX89
Queensmere Rd, SW19 ...119 CX89
Slough SL1
off Wellington St ...92 AU75
Queensmere Shop Cen,
Slou. SL1 ...92 AT75
Queens Ms, W2 ...82 DB73
Queensmill Rd, SW6 ...99 CX80
Queens Par, N11
off St. Johns Av ...44 DF50
W5 ...80 CM72
Queens Par Cl, N11
off Colney Hatch La ...44 DF50
⇌ Queen's Park ...81 CY68
⊖ Queen's Park ...81 CY68
Queens Pk Ct, W10 ...81 CX69
Queens Pk Gdns, Felt. TW13
off Vernon Rd ...115 BU90
★ Queens Park Rangers FC,
W12 ...81 CV74
Queens Pk Rd, Cat. CR3 ...176 DS123
Romford RM3 ...52 FM53
Queens Pas, Chis. BR7
off High St ...125 EP93
Queens Pl, Mord. SM4 ...140 DA98
Watford WD17 ...24 BW41
Queen's Prom, Kings.T. KT1
off Portsmouth Rd ...137 CK97
Queen Sq, WC1 ...196 A5
Queen Sq Pl, WC1 ...196 A5
Queens Reach, E.Mol. KT8 ...137 CE98
Queens Ride, SW13 ...99 CU83
SW15 ...99 CU83
Queen's Ride, Rich. TW10 ...118 CP88
Queens Ri, Rich. TW10 ...118 CM86
Queens Rd, E11 ...67 ED59
E13 ...86 EH67
Queen's Rd, E17 ...67 DZ58
Queens Rd, N3 ...44 DC53
N9 ...46 DV48
Queen's Rd, N11 ...45 DL52
Queens Rd, NW4 ...63 CW57
SE14 ...102 DV81
SE15 ...102 DV81
SW14 ...98 CR83
SW19 ...119 CZ93
W5 ...80 CL72
Barking IG11 ...87 EQ66
Barnet EN5 ...27 CX41
Beckenham BR3 ...143 DY96
Brentwood CM14 ...54 FW48
Bromley BR1 ...144 EG96
Buckhurst Hill IG9 ...48 EH47
Chislehurst BR7 ...125 EP93
Queen's Rd, Croy. CR0 ...141 DP100
Queens Rd, Egh. TW20 ...113 AZ93
Enfield EN1 ...30 DS42
Epping (N.Wld Bas.) CM16 ...19 FB26
Queen's Rd, Erith DA8 ...107 FE79
Queens Rd, Felt. TW13 ...115 BV88
Gravesend DA12 ...131 GJ90
Hampton (Hmptn H.) TW12 ...116 CB91
Hayes UB3 ...77 BS72
Queen's Rd, Houns. TW3 ...96 CB83
Queens Rd, Kings.T. KT2 ...118 CN94
Loughton IG10 ...32 EL41
Morden SM4 ...140 DA98
New Malden KT3 ...139 CT98
Richmond TW10 ...118 CM85
Queen's Rd, Slou. SL1 ...74 AT73
Queens Rd, Slou. (Datchet)
SL3 ...92 AU81
Southall UB2 ...96 BX75
Sutton SM2 ...158 DA110
Queen's Rd, Tedd. TW11 ...117 CE93
Thames Ditton KT7 ...137 CF99
Queens Rd, Twick. TW1 ...117 CF88
Queen's Rd, Uxb. UB8 ...76 BJ69
Queens Rd, Wall. SM6 ...159 DH106
Waltham Cross EN8 ...15 DY34
Walton-on-Thames KT12 ...153 BV106
Watford WD17 ...24 BW42
Queen's Rd, Well. DA16 ...106 EV82
Queens Rd, West Dr. UB7 ...94 BM75
Weybridge KT13 ...153 BQ105
⇌ Queens Road Peckham ...102 DW81
Queens Rd W, E13 ...86 EG68
Queen's Row, SE17 ...102 DR79
Queens Ter, E13 ...86 EH67
Queen's Ter, NW8 ...82 DD68
Queens Ter, Islw. TW7 ...97 CG84
Queens Ter Cotts, W7
off Boston Rd ...97 CE75
Queensthorpe Rd, SE26 ...123 DX91
★ Queen's Twr, SW7 ...100 DD76
Queenstown Gdns, Rain.
RM13 ...89 FF69
Queenstown Ms, SW8
off Queenstown Rd ...101 DH82
Queenstown Rd, SW8 ...101 DH79
⇌ Queenstown Road
(Battersea) ...101 DH81
Queen St, EC4 ...197 J10
N17 ...46 DS51
W1 ...199 H2
Bexleyheath DA7 ...106 EZ83
Brentwood (Warley) CM14 ...54 FW50
Chertsey KT16 ...134 BG102
Croydon CR0 ...160 DQ105
Erith DA8 ...107 FE79
Gravesend DA12 ...131 GH86
Kings Langley (Chipper.)
WD4 ...6 BG32
Romford RM7 ...71 FD58
Queen St Pl, EC4 ...201 J1
Queensville Rd, SW12 ...121 DK87
Queens Wk, E4
off The Green Wk ...47 ED46
NW9 ...62 CQ61
Queen's Wk, SE1 ...200 B3
SW1 ...199 K3
Queens Wk, W5 ...79 CJ70
Ashford TW15 ...114 BK91
Queen's Wk, Har. HA1 ...61 CE56
Queens Wk, Ruis. HA4 ...60 BX62
⊖ Queensway ...82 DB73
Queens Way, NW4 ...63 CW57
Queensway, W2 ...82 DB72
Queens Way, Croy. CR0 ...159 DM107
Queensway, Enf. EN3 ...30 DV42
Queens Way, Felt. TW13 ...116 BW91
Queensway, Orp. BR5 ...145 EQ99
Queens Way, Rad. (Shenley)
WD7 ...10 CL32
Queensway, Red. RH1 ...184 DF133
Sunbury-on-Thames TW16 ...135 BV96
Queens Way, Wal.Cr. EN8 ...15 DZ34
Queensway, W.Wick. BR4 ...144 EE104
Queensway, The, Ger.Cr.
(Chal.St.P.) SL9 ...56 AX55
Queensway N, Walt. KT12
off Robinsway ...154 BW105
Queensway S, Walt. KT12
off Trenchard Cl ...154 BW106
Queenswell Av, N20 ...44 DE48
Queenswood Av, E17 ...47 EC53
Brentwood (Hutt.) CM13 ...55 GD43
Hampton TW12 ...116 CB93
Hounslow TW3 ...96 BZ82
Thornton Heath CR7 ...141 DN99
Wallington SM6 ...159 DK105
Queenswood Cres, Wat. WD25 ...7 BU33
Queenswood Gdns, E11 ...68 EG60
Queenswood Pk, N3 ...43 CY54
Queen's Wd Rd, N10 ...65 DH58
Queenswood Rd, SE23 ...123 DX90
Sidcup DA15 ...125 ET85
Queens Yd, WC1 ...195 L5
Queen Victoria Av, Wem. HA0 ...79 CK66
★ Queen Victoria Mem,
SW1 ...199 K4
Queen Victoria St, EC4 ...196 G10
Queen Victoria's Wk, Wind.
SL4 ...92 AS81
Queen Victoria Ter, E1
off Sovereign Cl ...84 DV73
Quemerford Rd, N7 ...65 DM64
Quendon Dr, Wal.Abb. EN9 ...15 ED33
Quennell Cl, Ashtd. KT21
off Parkers La ...172 CM119
Quennel Way, Brwd. (Hutt.)
CM13 ...55 GC45
Quentin Pl, SE13 ...104 EE83
Quentin Rd, SE13 ...104 EE83
Quentins Dr, West. (Berry's Grn)
TN16 ...179 EP116
Quentins Wk, West. (Berry's Grn)
TN16 off St. Anns Way ...179 EP116
Quentin Way, Vir.W. GU25 ...132 AV98
Quernmore Cl, Brom. BR1 ...124 EG93
Quernmore Rd, N4 ...65 DN58
Bromley BR1 ...124 EG93
Querrin St, SW6 ...100 DC82
Quex Ms, NW6 off Quex Rd ...82 DA67
Quex Rd, NW6 ...82 DA67
Quickley La, Rick. (Chorl.)
WD3 ...21 BB44
Quickley Ri, Rick. (Chorl.)
WD3 ...21 BC44
Quickmoor La, Kings L. WD4 ...6 BH33
Quick Rd, W4 ...98 CS78
Quicks Rd, SW19 ...120 DB94
Quick St, N1 ...196 G1
Quick St Ms, N1 ...196 F1
Quickswood, NW3
off King Henry's Rd ...82 DE66
Quickwood Cl, Rick. WD3 ...22 BG44
Quiet Cl, Add. KT15 ...152 BG105
Quiet Nook, Brom. BR2
off Croydon Rd ...144 EK104
Quill Hall La, Amer. HP6 ...20 AT37
Quill La, SW15 ...99 CX84
Quillot, The, Walt. KT12 ...153 BT106
Quill St, N4 ...65 DN62
W5 ...80 CL69
Quilp St, SE1 ...201 H4
Quilter Gdns, Orp. BR5
off Tintagel Rd ...146 EW102
Quilter Rd, Orp. BR5 ...146 EW102
Quilter St, E2 ...84 DU69
SE18 ...105 ET78
Quilting Ct, SE16
off Poolmans St ...103 DX75
Quinbrookes, Slou. SL2 ...74 AW72
Quince Rd, SE13 ...103 EB82
Quince Tree Cl, S.Ock. RM15 ...91 FW70
Quincy Rd, Egh. TW20 ...113 BA92
Quinnell Cl, SE18
off Rippolson Rd ...105 ET78
Quinta Dr, Barn. EN5 ...27 CV43
Quintin Av, SW20 ...139 CZ95
Quintin Cl, Pnr. HA5
off High Rd ...59 BV57
Quinton Cl, Beck. BR3 ...143 EC97
Hounslow TW5 ...95 BV80
Wallington SM6 ...159 DH105
Quinton Rd, T.Ditt. KT7 ...137 CG102
Quinton St, SW18 ...120 DC89
Quintrell Cl, Wok. GU21 ...166 AV117
Quixley St, E14 ...85 ED73
Quorn Rd, SE22 ...102 DS84

R

Raans Rd, Amer. HP6 ...20 AT38
Rabbit La, Walt. KT12 ...153 BU108
Rabbit Row, W8
off Kensington Mall ...82 DA74
Rabbits Rd, E12 ...68 EL63
Dartford (S.Darenth) DA4 ...149 FR96
Rabbs Mill Ho, Uxb. UB8 ...76 BK68
Rabies Heath Rd, Gdse. RH9 ...186 DU134
Redhill (Bletch.) RH1 ...186 DS133
Rabournmead Dr, Nthlt. UB5 ...60 BY64
Raby Rd, N.Mal. KT3 ...138 CR98
Raby St, E14 off Salmon La ...85 DY72
Raccoon Way, Houns. TW4 ...96 BW82
Rachel Cl, Ilf. IG6 ...69 ER55
Rackham Cl, Well. DA16 ...106 EV82
Rackham Ms, SW16 ...121 DJ93
Racton Rd, SW6 ...100 DA79
Radbourne Av, W5 ...97 CJ77
Radbourne Cl, E5
off Overbury St ...67 DX63
Radbourne Cres, E17 ...47 ED54
Radbourne Rd, SW12 ...121 DJ87
Radcliffe Av, NW10 ...81 CU68
Enfield EN2 ...30 DQ39
Radcliffe Gdns, Cars. SM5 ...158 DE108
Radcliffe Ms, Hmptn. (Hmptn H.)
TW12 off Taylor Cl ...116 CC92
Radcliffe Path, SW8
off Robertson St ...101 DH82
Radcliffe Rd, N21 ...45 DP46
SE1 ...201 N6
Croydon CR0 ...142 DT103
Harrow HA3 ...41 CG54
Radcliffe Sq, SW15 ...119 CX86
Radcliffe Way, Nthlt. UB5 ...78 BX69
Radcot Av, Slou. SL3 ...93 BB76
Radcot Pt, SE23 ...123 DX90
Radcot St, SE11 ...101 DN78
Raddington Rd, W10 ...81 CY71
Radfield Way, Sid. DA15 ...125 ER87
Radford Rd, SE13 ...123 EC86
Radford Way, Bark. IG11 ...87 ET69
Radipole Rd, SW6 ...99 CZ81
Radius Pk, Felt. TW14 ...95 BT84
Radland Rd, E16 ...86 EF72
Radlet Av, SE26 ...122 DV90
RADLETT, WD7 ...25 CH35
⇌ Radlett ...25 CG35
Radlett Cl, E7 ...86 EF65
Radlett La, Rad. (Shenley)
WD7 ...25 CK35
Radlett Pk Rd, Rad. WD7 ...9 CG34
Radlett Pl, NW8 ...82 DE67
Radlett Rd, St.Alb. AL2 ...9 CE28
Watford WD17, WD24 ...24 BW41
Watford (Ald.) WD25 ...24 CB39
Radley Av, Ilf. IG3 ...69 ET63
Radley Cl, Felt. TW14 ...115 BT88
Radley Ct, SE16 ...203 J4
Radley Gdns, Har. HA3 ...62 CL56
Radley Ho, SE2
off Wolvercote Rd ...106 EX75
Radley Ms, W8 ...100 DA76
Radley Rd, N17 ...46 DS54
Radley's La, E18 ...48 EG54
Radleys Mead, Dag. RM10 ...89 FB65
Radley Sq, E5
off Dudlington Rd ...66 DW61
Radlix Rd, E10 ...67 EA60
Radnor Av, Har. HA1 ...61 CE57
Welling DA16 ...126 EV85
Radnor Cl, Chis. BR7
off Homewood Cres ...125 ES93
Mitcham CR4 ...141 DL98
Radnor Cres, SE18 ...106 EU79
Ilford IG4 ...69 EM57
Radnor Gdns, Enf. EN1 ...30 DS39
Twickenham TW1 ...117 CF89
Radnor Gro, Uxb. UB10
off Charnwood Rd ...76 BN68
Radnor Ms, W2 ...194 A9
Radnor Pl, W2 ...194 B9
Radnor Rd, NW6 ...81 CY67
SE15 ...102 DU80
Harrow HA1 ...61 CD57
Twickenham TW1 ...117 CF89
Weybridge KT13 ...134 BN104
Radnor St, EC1 ...197 J3
Radnor Ter, W14 ...99 CZ77
Radnor Wk, E14 ...204 A8
SW3 ...100 DE78
Croydon CR0 ...143 DZ100
Radnor Way, NW10 ...80 CP70
Slough SL3 ...92 AY77
Radolphs, Tad. KT20 ...173 CX122
Radstock Av, Har. HA3 ...61 CG55
Radstock Cl, N11 ...44 DG50
Radstock St, SW11 ...100 DE80
Radstock Way, Red.
(Merst.) RH1 ...185 DK128
Radstone Ct, Wok. GU22 ...167 AZ118
Radwell Path, Borwd. WD6
off Cromwell Rd ...26 CL39
Radzan Cl, Dart. DA2 ...127 FE89
Raebarn Gdns, Barn. EN5 ...27 CV43
Raeburn Av, Dart. DA1 ...127 FH85
Surbiton KT5 ...138 CP100
Raeburn Cl, NW11 ...64 DC58
Kingston upon Thames
KT1 ...117 CK94
Raeburn Ct, Wok. GU21
off Martin Way ...166 AU118
Raeburn Rd, Edg. HA8 ...42 CN54
Hayes UB4 ...77 BR68
Sidcup DA15 ...125 ES86
Raeburn St, SW2 ...101 DL84
Rafford Way, Brom. BR1 ...144 EH96
Raft Rd, SW18
off North Pas ...100 DA84
★ Ragged Sch Mus, E3 ...85 DY71
Raggleswood, Chis. BR7 ...145 EN95
Rag Hill Cl, West. (Tats.)
TN16 ...178 EL121
Rag Hill Rd, West. (Tats.)
TN16 ...178 EK121
Raglan Av, Wal.Cr. EN8 ...15 DX34
Raglan Cl, Houns. TW4 ...116 BZ85
Reigate RH2 ...184 DC132
Raglan Ct, SE12 ...124 EG85
South Croydon CR2 ...159 DP106
Wembley HA9 ...62 CM63
Raglan Gdns, Wat. WD19 ...39 BV46
Raglan Prec, Cat. CR3 ...176 DS122
Raglan Rd, E17 ...67 EC57
SE18 ...105 EQ78
Belvedere DA17 ...106 EZ77
Bromley BR2 ...144 EJ98
Enfield EN1 ...46 DS45
Reigate RH2 ...184 DB131
Woking (Knap.) GU21 ...166 AS118
Raglan St, NW5 ...83 DH65
Raglan Ter, Har. HA2 ...60 CB63
Raglan Way, Nthlt. UB5 ...78 CC65
Ragley Cl, W3 off Church Rd ...98 CQ75
Rags La, Wal.Cr. (Chsht) EN7 ...14 DS27
Ragwort Ct, SE26 ...122 DV92
Rahere Ho, EC1 ...197 H2
Rahn Rd, Epp. CM16 ...18 EU31
Raider Cl, Rom. RM7 ...50 FA53
Railey Ms, NW5 ...65 DJ64
Railpit La, Warl. CR6 ...177 EE115
Railshead Rd, Islw. TW7 ...97 CH84
Railstore, The, Rom.
(Gidea Pk) RM2 ...72 FJ55
Railton Rd, SE24 ...101 DN84
Railway App, N4
off Wightman Rd ...65 DN58
SE1 ...201 L2
Harrow HA3 ...61 CF56
Twickenham TW1 ...117 CG87
Wallington SM6 ...159 DH107
Railway Av, SE16 ...202 G4
Railway Children Wk, SE12
off Baring Rd ...124 EG89
Bromley BR1
off Reigate Rd ...124 EG89
Railway Cotts, Rad. WD7
off Shenley Hill ...25 CH35
Watford WD24 ...23 BV39
Railway Ms, E3
off Wellington Way ...85 EA69
W10 off Ladbroke Gro ...81 CY72
Railway Pas, Tedd. TW11
off Victoria Rd ...117 CG93
Railway Pl, SW19
off Hartfield Rd ...119 CZ93
Belvedere DA17 ...106 FA76
Gravesend DA12
off Stone St ...131 GH86
Railway Ri, SE22
off Grove Vale ...102 DS84
Railway Rd, Tedd. TW11 ...117 CF91
Waltham Cross EN8 ...15 DY33
Railway Side, SW13 ...98 CS83
Railway Sq, Brwd. CM14
off Fairfield Rd ...54 FW48
Railway St, N1 ...196 A1
Gravesend (Nthflt) DA11 ...130 GA85
Romford RM6 ...70 EW60
Railway Ter, SE13
off Ladywell Rd ...123 EB85
Kings Langley WD4 ...6 BN27
Slough SL2 ...74 AT74
Staines TW18 ...113 BD92
Westerham TN16 ...189 ER125
Rainborough Cl, NW10 ...80 CQ65
Rainbow Av, E14 ...204 B10
Rainbow Ct, Wat. WD19
off Oxhey Rd ...24 BW44
Woking GU21
off Langmans Way ...166 AS116
Rainbow Ind Est, West Dr.
UB7 ...76 BK73
Rainbow Quay, SE16 ...203 L7
Rainbow Rd, Grays (Chaff.Hun.)
RM16 ...109 FW77
Rainbow St, SE5 ...102 DS80
Rainer Cl, Wal.Cr. (Chsht) EN8 ...15 DX29
Raines Ct, N16
off Northwold Rd ...66 DT61
Raine St, E1 ...202 E2
RAINHAM, RM13 ...89 FG69
⇌ Rainham ...89 FF70
Rainham Cl, SE9 ...125 ER86
SW11 ...120 DE86
★ Rainham Hall, Rain. RM13 ...89 FG70
Rainham Rd, NW10 ...81 CW69
Rainham RM13 ...89 FE66
Rainham Rd N, Dag. RM10 ...71 FB61
Rainham Rd S, Dag. RM10 ...71 FB63
Rainhill Way, E3 ...85 EA69
Rainsborough Av, SE8 ...203 K9
Rainsford Cl, Stan. HA7
off Coverdale Cl ...41 CJ50
Rainsford Rd, NW10 ...80 CP69
Rainsford St, W2 ...194 B8
Rainsford Way, Horn. RM12 ...71 FG60
Rainton Rd, SE7 ...205 N10
Rainville Rd, W6 ...99 CW79
Raisins Hill, Pnr. HA5 ...60 BW55
Raith Av, N14 ...45 DK48
Raleana Rd, E14 ...204 E2
Raleigh Av, Hayes UB4 ...77 BV71
Wallington SM6 ...159 DK105
Raleigh Cl, NW4 ...63 CW57
Erith DA8 ...107 FF79
Pinner HA5 ...60 BX59
Ruislip HA4 ...59 BT61
Raleigh Ct, SE16
off Rotherhithe St ...85 DX74
SE19 off Lymer Av ...122 DT92
Beckenham BR3 ...143 EB95
Staines TW18 ...114 BG91
Wallington SM6 ...159 DH107
Raleigh Dr, N20 ...44 DE48
Esher (Clay.) KT10 ...155 CD106
Surbiton KT5 ...138 CQ102
Raleigh Gdns, SW2
off Brixton Hill ...121 DM86
Mitcham CR4 ...140 DF96
Raleigh Ms, N1
off Queen's Head St ...83 DP67
Orpington BR6
off Osgood Av ...163 ET106
Raleigh Rd, N8 ...65 DN56
SE20 ...123 DX94
Enfield EN2 ...30 DR42
Feltham TW13 ...115 BT90
Richmond TW9 ...98 CM83
Southall UB2 ...96 BY78
Raleigh St, N1 ...83 DP67
Raleigh Way, N14 ...45 DK46
Feltham TW13 ...116 BW92
Ralliwood Rd, Ashtd. KT21 ...172 CN119
Ralph Ct, W2 off Queensway ...82 DB72
Ralph Perring Ct, Beck. BR3 ...143 EA98
Ralston St, SW3
off Tedworth Sq ...100 DF78
Ralston Way, Wat. WD19 ...40 BX47
Rama Cl, SW16 ...121 DK94
Rama Ct, Har. HA1 ...61 CE61
Ramac Way, SE7 ...205 P9
Rama La, SE19 ...122 DT94
Rambler Cl, SW16 ...121 DJ91
Rambler La, Slou. SL3 ...92 AW76
Rame Cl, SW17 ...120 DG92
Ramilles Cl, SW2 ...121 DL86
Ramillies Pl, W1 ...195 K9
Ramillies Rd, NW7 ...42 CS47
W4 ...98 CR77
Sidcup DA15 ...126 EV86
Ramillies St, W1 ...195 K9
Ramney Dr, Enf. EN3 ...31 DY37
Ramornie Cl, Walt. KT12 ...154 BZ106
Rampart St, E1
off Commercial Rd ...84 DV72
Ram Pas, Kings.T. KT1
off High St ...137 CK96
Rampayne St, SW1 ...199 M10
Ram Pl, E9 off Chatham Pl ...84 DW65
Rampton Cl, E4 ...47 EA48
Ramsay Gdns, Rom. RM3 ...52 FJ53
Ramsay Ms, SW3
off King's Rd ...100 DE79
Ramsay Pl, Har. HA1 ...61 CE60
Ramsay Rd, E7 ...68 EE63
W3 ...98 CQ76
Ramscroft Cl, N9 ...46 DS45
Ramsdale Rd, SW17 ...120 DG92

★ Place of interest ⇌ Railway station ⊖ London Underground station DLR Docklands Light Railway station Tra Tramlink station H Hospital Riv Pedestrian ferry landing stage

RAMSDEN, Orp. BR5 146 EW102
Ramsden Cl, Orp. BR5 146 EW102
Ramsden Dr, Rom. RM5 50 FA52
Ramsden Rd, N11 44 DF50
SW12 120 DG86
Erith DA8 107 FD80
Orpington BR5, BR6 146 EV101
Ramsey Cl, NW9 63 CT58
Greenford UB6 60 CC64
Hatfield (Brook.Pk) AL9 12 DD27
Ramsey Ho, SW11
off Maysoule Rd 100 DD84
Wembley HA9 80 CL65
Ramsey Ms, N4
off Monsell Rd 65 DP62
Ramsey Rd, Th.Hth. CR7 141 DM100
Ramsey St, E2 84 DU70
Ramsey Wk, N1 84 DR65
Ramsey Way, N14 45 DJ45
Ramsfort Ho, SE16
off Manor Est 102 DV77
Ramsgate Cl, E16 205 P3
Ramsgate St, E8
off Dalston La 84 DT65
Ramsgill App, Ilf. IG2 69 ET56
Ramsgill Dr, Ilf. IG2 69 ET57
Rams Gro, Rom. RM6 70 EY56
Ram St, SW18 120 DB85
Ramulis Dr, Hayes UB4 78 BX70
Ramus Wd Av, Orp. BR6 163 ES106
Rancliffe Gdns, SE9 104 EL84
Rancliffe Rd, E6 86 EL68
Randall Av, NW2 63 CT62
Randall Cl, SW11 100 DE81
Erith DA8 107 FC79
Slough SL3 93 AZ78
Randall Ct, NW7 43 CU52
Randall Dr, Horn. RM12 72 FJ63
Randall Pl, SE10 103 EC80
Randall Rd, SE11 200 B10
Randall Row, SE11 200 B9
Randalls Cres, Lthd. KT22 171 CG120
Randalls Dr, Brwd. (Hutt.)
CM13 55 GE44
Randalls Pk Av, Lthd. KT22 171 CG120
Randalls Pk Dr, Lthd. KT22
off Randalls Rd 171 CG121
Randalls Rd, Lthd. KT22 171 CE119
Randall's Wk, St.Alb. AL2 8 BZ30
Randalls Way, Lthd. KT22 171 CG121
Randell's Rd, N1 83 DL67
Randle Rd, Rich. TW10 117 CJ91
Randlesdown Rd, SE6 123 EA91
Randles La, Sev. (Knock.)
TN14 180 EX115
Randolph App, E16 86 EK72
Randolph Av, W9 82 DC70
Randolph Cl, Bexh. DA7 107 FC83
Cobham (Stoke D'Ab.)
KT11 170 CA115
Kingston upon Thames
KT2 118 CQ92
Woking (Knap.) GU21
off Creston Av 166 AS117
Randolph Cres, W9 82 DC70
Randolph Gdns, NW6 82 DB68
Randolph Gro, Rom. RM6
off Donald Dr 70 EW57
Randolph Ho, Croy. CR0 142 DQ102
Randolph Ms, W9 82 DC70
Randolph Rd, E17 67 EB57
W9 82 DC70
Bromley BR2 145 EM102
Epsom KT17 157 CT114
Slough SL3 92 AY76
Southall UB1 96 BZ75
Randolph's La, West. TN16 189 EP126
Randolph St, NW1 83 DJ66
Randon Cl, Har. HA2 40 CB54
Ranelagh Av, SW6 99 CZ83
SW13 99 CU82
Ranelagh Br, W2
off Gloucester Ter 82 DB71
Ranelagh Cl, Edg. HA8 42 CN49
Ranelagh Dr, Edg. HA8 42 CN49
Twickenham TW1 117 CH85
★ **Ranelagh Gdns**, SW3 100 DG78
Ranelagh Gdns, E11 68 EJ57
SW6 99 CZ83
W4 off Grove Pk Gdns 98 CQ80
W6 99 CT76
Gravesend (Nthflt) DA11 131 GF87
Ilford IG1 69 EN60
Ranelagh Gdns Mans, SW6
off Ranelagh Gdns 99 CY83
Ranelagh Gro, SW1 198 G10
Ranelagh Ms, W5
off Ranelagh Rd 97 CK75
Ranelagh Pl, N.Mal. KT3 138 CS99
Ranelagh Rd, E6 87 EN67
E11 68 EE63
E15 86 EE67
N17 66 DS55
N22 45 DM53
NW10 81 CT68
SW1 off Lupus St 101 DJ78
W5 97 CK75
Redhill RH1 184 DE134
Southall UB1 78 BX74
Wembley HA0 61 CK64
Ranfurly Rd, Sutt. SM1 140 DA103
Rangefield Rd, Brom. BR1 124 EE92
Rangemoor Rd, N15 66 DT57
Range Rd, Grav. DA12 131 GL87
Rangers Rd, E4 48 EE45
Loughton IG10 48 EE45
Rangers Sq, SE10 103 ED81
Ranger Wk, Add. KT15
off Monks Cres 152 BH106
Range Way, Shep. TW17 134 BN101
Rangeworth Pl, Sid. DA15
off Priestlands Pk Rd 125 ET90
Rangoon St, EC3 197 P9
Rankin Cl, NW9 62 CS55
Ranleigh Gdns, Bexh. DA7 106 EZ80
Ranmere St, SW12
off Ormeley Rd 121 DH88
Ranmoor Cl, Har. HA1 61 CD56
Ranmoor Gdns, Har. HA1 61 CD56
Ranmore Av, Croy. CR0 142 DT104
Ranmore Cl, Red. RH1 184 DG131
Ranmore Path, Orp. BR5 146 EU98
Ranmore Rd, Sutt. SM2 157 CX109
Rannoch Cl, Edg. HA8 42 CP47
Rannoch Rd, W6 99 CW79
Rannock Av, NW9 62 CS59
Ranskill Rd, Borwd. WD6 26 CN39
Ransom Cl, Wat. WD19 40 BW45
Ransome's Dock Business Cen,
SW11 off Parkgate Rd 100 DE80
Ransom Rd, SE7
off Floyd Rd 104 EJ78
Ransom Wk, SE7
off Woolwich Rd 104 EJ77
Ranston Cl, Uxb. (Denh.) UB9
off Nightingale Way 57 BF58
Ranston St, NW1 194 B6
Ranulf Rd, NW2 63 CZ63
Ranwell Cl, E3 off Beale Rd 85 DZ67
Ranwell St, E3 85 DZ67
Ranworth Cl, Erith DA8 107 FE82
Ranworth Gdns, Pot.B. EN6 11 CX31
Ranworth Rd, N9 46 DW47
Ranyard Cl, Chess. KT9 138 CM104
Raphael Av, Rom. RM1 71 FF55
Tilbury RM18 111 GG80
Raphael Cl, Rad. (Shenley)
WD7 10 CL32
Raphael Dr, T.Ditt. KT7 137 CF101
Watford WD24 24 BX40
Raphael Rd, Grav. DA12 131 GK87
Raphael St, SW7 198 D5
Rapier Cl, Purf. RM19 108 FN77
Rasehill Cl, Rick. WD3 22 BJ43
Rashleigh St, SW8
off Peardon St 101 DH82
Rashleigh Way, Dart.
(Hort.Kir.) DA4 148 FQ98
Rasper Rd, N20 44 DC47
Rastell Av, SW2 121 DK89
Ratcliffe Cl, SE12 124 EG87
Uxbridge UB8 76 BK69
Ratcliffe Cross St, E1 85 DX72
Ratcliffe La, E14 85 DY72
Ratcliffe Orchard, E1 85 DX73
Ratcliff Rd, E7 68 EJ64
Rathbone Mkt, E16
off Barking Rd 86 EF71
Rathbone Pl, W1 195 M8
Rathbone St, E16 86 EF71
W1 195 L7
Rathcoole Av, N8 65 DM56
Rathcoole Gdns, N8 65 DM57
Rathfern Rd, SE6 123 DZ88
Rathgar Av, W13 79 CH74
Rathgar Cl, N3 43 CZ54
Rathgar Rd, SW9
off Coldharbour La 101 DP83
Rathmell Dr, SW4 121 DK86
Rathmore Rd, SE7 104 EH78
Gravesend DA11 131 GH87
Rathwell Path, Borwd. WD6 26 CL39
Rats La, Loug. (High Beach)
IG10 32 EH38
Rattray Rd, SW2 101 DN84
Raul Rd, SE15 102 DU81
Raveley St, NW5 65 DJ63
Ravel Gdns, S.Ock. (Aveley)
RM15 90 FQ72
Ravel Rd, S.Ock. (Aveley)
RM15 90 FQ72
Raven Cl, NW9 off Eagle Dr 42 CS54
Rickmansworth WD3 38 BJ45
Raven Ct, E5 off Stellman Cl 66 DU62
Ravencroft, Grays RM16
off Alexandra Cl 111 GH75
Ravendale Rd, Sun. TW16 135 BT96
Ravenet St, SW11
off Strasburg Rd 101 DH81
Ravenfield, Egh. (Eng.Grn)
TW20 112 AW93
Ravenfield Rd, SW17 120 DF90
Ravenhill Rd, E13 86 EJ68
Ravenna Rd, SW15 119 CX85
Ravenoak Way, Chig. IG7 49 ES50
Ravenor Pk Rd, Grnf. UB6 78 CB69
Raven Rd, E18 48 EJ54
Raven Row, E1 84 DV71
⇌ **Ravensbourne** 123 ED94
Ravensbourne Av, Beck. BR3 123 ED94
Bromley BR2 123 ED94
Staines TW19 114 BL88
Ravensbourne Cres, Rom.
RM3 72 FM55
Ravensbourne Gdns, W13 79 CH71
Ilford IG5 49 EN53
Ravensbourne Pk, SE6 123 EA87
Ravensbourne Pk Cres, SE6 123 DZ87
Ravensbourne Pl, SE13 103 EB82
Ravensbourne Rd, SE6 123 DZ87
Bromley BR1 144 EG97
Dartford DA1 107 FG83
Twickenham TW1 117 CJ86
Ravensbury Av, Mord. SM4 140 DC99
Ravensbury Ct, Mitch. CR4
off Ravensbury Gro 140 DD98
Ravensbury Gro, Mitch. CR4 140 DD98
Ravensbury La, Mitch. CR4 140 DD98
Ravensbury Path, Mitch. CR4 140 DD98
Ravensbury Rd, SW18 120 DA89
Orpington BR5 145 ET98
Ravensbury Ter, SW18 120 DB89
Ravenscar Rd, Brom. BR1 124 EE91
Surbiton KT6 138 CM103
Ravens Cl, Brom. BR2 144 EF96
Chessington KT9 137 CK100
Enfield EN1 30 DS40
Redhill RH1 184 DF132
Ravenscourt, Sun. TW16 135 BT95
Ravenscourt Av, W6 99 CU77
Ravenscourt Cl, Horn. RM12
off Ravenscourt Dr 72 FL62
Ruislip HA4 59 BQ59
Ravenscourt Dr, Horn. RM12 72 FL62
Ravenscourt Gdns, W6 99 CU77
Ravenscourt Gro, Horn. RM12 72 FL61
⊖ **Ravenscourt Park** 99 CU77
Ravenscourt Pk, W6 99 CU76
Ravenscourt Pl, W6 99 CV77
Ravenscourt Rd, W6 99 CV77
Orpington BR5 146 EU97
Ravenscourt Sq, W6 99 CU76
Ravenscraig Rd, N11 45 DH49
Ravenscroft, Wat. WD25 8 BY34
Ravenscroft Av, NW11 63 CZ59
Wembley HA9 62 CM60
Ravenscroft Cl, E16 86 EG71
Ravenscroft Cres, SE9 125 EM90
Ravenscroft Pk, Barn. EN5 27 CX42
Ravenscroft Pt, E9
off Kenton Rd 85 DX65
Ravenscroft Rd, E16 86 EG71
W4 98 CQ77
Beckenham BR3 142 DW96
Weybridge KT13 153 BQ111
Ravenscroft St, E2 84 DT68
Ravensdale Av, N12 44 DC49
Ravensdale Gdns, SE19 122 DR94
Hounslow TW4 96 BY83
Ravensdale Ms, Stai. TW18
off Worple Rd 114 BH93
Ravensdale Rd, N16 66 DT59
Hounslow TW4 96 BY83
Ravensdon St, SE11 101 DN78
Ravensfield, Slou. SL3 92 AX75
Ravensfield Cl, Dag. RM9 70 EX63
Ravensfield Gdns, Epsom
KT19 156 CS106
Ravenshaw St, NW6 63 CZ64
Ravenshead Cl, S.Croy. CR2 160 DW111
Ravenshill, Chis. BR7 145 EP95
Ravenshurst Av, NW4 63 CW56
Ravenside Cl, N18 47 DX51
Ravenside Retail Pk, N18 47 DX50
Ravenslea Rd, SW12 120 DF87
Ravensmead, Ger.Cr. (Chal.St.P.)
SL9 37 AZ50
Ravensmead Rd, Brom. BR2 123 ED94
Ravensmede Way, W4 99 CT77
Ravensmere, Epp. CM16 18 EU31
Ravens Ms, SE12
off Ravens Way 124 EG85
Ravenstone, SE17 102 DS78
Ravenstone Rd, N8 65 DM55
NW9 off West Hendon Bdy 63 CT58
Ravenstone St, SW12 120 DG88
Ravens Way, SE12 124 EG85
Ravenswold, Ken. CR8 176 DQ115
Ravenswood, Bex. DA5 126 EY88
Ravenswood Av, Surb. KT6 138 CM103
West Wickham BR4 143 EC102
Ravenswood Cl, Cob. KT11 170 BX115
Romford RM5 51 FB50
Ravenswood Ct, Kings.T. KT2 118 CP93
Woking GU22 167 AZ118
Ravenswood Cres, Har. HA2 60 BZ61
West Wickham BR4 143 EC102
Ravenswood Gdns, Islw. TW7 97 CE81
Ravenswood Pk, Nthwd. HA6 39 BU51
Ravenswood Rd, E17 67 EB56
SW12 121 DH87
Croydon CR0 141 DP104
Ravensworth Rd, NW10 81 CV69
SE9 125 EM91
Ravey St, EC2 197 M4
Ravine Gro, SE18 105 ES79
Rav Pinter Cl, N16 66 DS59
Rawlings Cl, Beck. BR3 143 EC99
Orpington BR6 163 ET106
Rawlings Cres, Wem. HA9 62 CP62
Rawlings St, SW3 198 D8
Rawlins Cl, N3 63 CY55
South Croydon CR2 161 DY108
Rawlinson Ho, SE13
off Mercator Rd 103 ED84
Rawlyn Cl, Grays (Chaff.Hun.)
RM16 109 FV78
Rawnsley Av, Mitch. CR4 140 DD99
Rawreth Wk, N1 off Basire St 84 DQ67
Rawson Ct, SW11
off Strasburg Rd 101 DH81
Rawson St, SW11
off Strasburg Rd 100 DG81
Rawsthorne Cl, E16
off Kennard St 87 EM74
Rawstone Wk, E13 86 EG68
Rawstorne Pl, EC1 196 F2
Rawstorne St, EC1 196 F2
Rayburn Rd, Horn. RM11 72 FN59
Ray Cl, Chess. KT9
off Merritt Gdns 155 CJ107
Raydean Rd, Barn. EN5 28 DB43
Raydon Rd, Wal.Cr. (Chsht)
EN8 15 DX32
Raydons Gdns, Dag. RM9 70 EY64
Raydons Rd, Dag. RM9 70 EY64
Raydon St, N19 65 DH61
Rayfield, Epp. CM16 18 EU30
Rayfield Cl, Brom. BR2 144 EL100
Rayford Av, SE12 124 EF87
Rayford Cl, Dart. DA1 128 FJ85
Ray Gdns, Bark. IG11 88 EU68
Stanmore HA7 41 CH50
Ray Lamb Way, Erith DA8 107 FH79
Raylands Mead, Ger.Cr. SL9
off Bull La 56 AW57
Rayleas Cl, SE18 105 EP81
Rayleigh Av, Tedd. TW11 117 CE93
Rayleigh Cl, N13
off Rayleigh Rd 46 DR48
Brentwood (Hutt.) CM13 55 GC44
Rayleigh Ct, Kings.T. KT1 138 CM96
Rayleigh Ri, S.Croy. CR2 160 DS107
Rayleigh Rd, E16 86 EH74
N13 46 DQ48
SW19 139 CZ95
Brentwood (Hutt.) CM13 55 GB44
Woodford Green IG8 48 EJ51
Ray Lo Rd, Wdf.Grn. IG8 48 EJ51
Ray Massey Way, E6
off Ron Leighton Way 86 EL67
Raymead, NW4
off Tenterden Gro 63 CW56
Raymead Av, Th.Hth. CR7 141 DN99
Raymead Cl, Lthd. (Fetch.)
KT22 171 CE122
Raymead Pas, Th.Hth. CR7
off Raymead Av 141 DN99
Raymead Way, Lthd. (Fetch.)
KT22 171 CE122
Raymere Gdns, SE18 105 ER80
Raymond Av, E18 68 EF55
W13 97 CG76
Raymond Bldgs, WC1 196 C6
Raymond Cl, SE26 122 DW92
Abbots Langley WD5 7 BR32
Slough (Colnbr.) SL3 93 BE81
Raymond Ct, N10
off Pembroke Rd 44 DG52
Raymond Ct, Pot. B. EN6
off St. Francis Cl 12 DC34
Raymond Gdns, Chig. IG7 50 EV48
Raymond Rd, E13 86 EJ66
SW19 119 CY93
Beckenham BR3 143 DY98
Ilford IG2 69 ER59
Slough SL3 93 BA76
Raymond Way, Esher (Clay.)
KT10 155 CG107
Raymouth Rd, SE16 202 E8
Rayne Ct, E18 68 EF56
Rayners Cl, Slou. (Colnbr.)
SL3 93 BC80
Wembley HA0 61 CK64
Rayners Ct, Grav. DA11 130 GB86
Harrow HA2 60 CA60
Rayners Cres, Nthlt. UB5 77 BV69
Rayners Gdns, Nthlt. UB5 77 BV68
RAYNERS LANE, Har. HA2 60 BZ60
⊖ **Rayners Lane** 60 BZ59
Rayners La, Har. HA2 60 CB61
Pinner HA5 60 BZ58
Rayners Rd, SW15 119 CY85
Rayner Twr, E10 67 EA59
Raynes Av, E11 68 EJ59
RAYNES PARK, SW20 139 CV97
⇌ **Raynes Park** 139 CW96
Raynham, W2
off Norfolk Cres 82 DE72
Raynham Av, N18 46 DU51
Raynham Rd, N18 46 DU50
W6 99 CV77
Raynham Ter, N18 46 DU50
Raynor Cl, Sthl. UB1 78 BZ74
Raynor Pl, N1
off Elizabeth Av 84 DQ67
Raynton Cl, Har. HA2 60 BY60
Hayes UB4 77 BT70
Raynton Dr, Hayes UB4 77 BT70
Raynton Rd, Enf. EN3 31 DX37
Ray Rd, Rom. RM5 51 FB50
West Molesey KT8 136 CB99
Rays Av, N18 46 DW49
Rays Hill, Dart. (Hort.Kir.)
DA4 148 FQ98
Rays Rd, N18 46 DW49
West Wickham BR4 143 EC101
Ray St, EC1 196 E5
Ray St Br, EC1 196 E5
Ray Wk, N7 off Andover Rd 65 DM61
Raywood Cl, Hayes UB3 95 BQ80
Reach, The, SE28 105 ES75
Reachview Cl, NW1
off Baynes St 83 DJ66
Read Cl, T.Ditt. KT7 137 CG101
Read Ct, Wal.Abb. EN9 16 EG33
Readens, The, Bans. SM7 174 DF116
Reade Wk, NW10
off Denbigh Cl 80 CS66
Reading Arch Rd, Red. RH1 184 DF134
Reading La, E8 84 DV65
Reading Rd, Nthlt. UB5 60 CB64
Sutton SM1 158 DC106
Readings, The, Rick. (Chorl.)
WD3 21 BF41
Reading Way, NW7 43 CX50
Read Rd, Ashtd. KT21 171 CK117
Reads Cl, Ilf. IG1
off Chapel Rd 69 EP62
Reads Rest La, Tad. KT20 173 CZ119
Read Way, Grav. DA12 131 GK92
Reapers Cl, NW1
off Crofters Way 83 DK67
Reapers Way, Islw. TW7
off Hall Rd 117 CD85
Reardon Ct, N21
off Cosgrove Cl 46 DQ47
Reardon Path, E1 202 E3
Reardon St, E1 202 D2
Reaston St, SE14 102 DW80
Reckitt Rd, W4 98 CS78
Record St, SE15 102 DW79
Recovery St, SW17 120 DE92
Recreation Av, Rom. RM7 71 FC57
Romford (Harold Wd) RM3 52 FM54
Recreation Rd, SE26 123 DX91
Bromley BR2 144 EF96
Sidcup DA15
off Woodside Rd 125 ES90
Southall UB2 96 BY77
Recreation Way, Mitch. CR4 141 DK97
Rector St, N1 84 DQ67
Rectory Chase, Brwd.
(Lt.Warley) CM13 73 FX56
Rectory Cl, E4 47 EA48
N3 43 CZ53
SW20 139 CW97
Ashtead KT21 172 CM119
Dartford DA1 107 FE84
Shepperton TW17 134 BN97
Sidcup DA14 126 EV91
Stanmore HA7 41 CH51
Surbiton KT6 137 CJ102
West Byfleet (Byfleet) KT14 152 BL113
Rectory Cres, E11 68 EJ58
Rectory Fm Rd, Enf. EN2 29 DM38
Rectory Fld Cres, SE7 104 EJ80
Rectory Gdns, N8 65 DL56
SW4 off Fitzwilliam Rd 101 DJ83
Chalfont St. Giles HP8 36 AV48
Northolt UB5 78 BZ67
Upminster RM14 73 FR61
Rectory Grn, Beck. BR3 143 DZ95
Rectory Gro, SW4 101 DJ83
Croydon CR0 141 DP103
Hampton TW12 116 BZ91
Rectory La, SW17 120 DG93
Ashtead KT21 172 CM118
Banstead SM7 158 DF114
Betchworth (Buckland) RH3 183 CT131
Edgware HA8 42 CN51
Kings Langley WD4 6 BN28
Loughton IG10 33 EN40
Radlett (Shenley) WD7 10 CN33
Rickmansworth WD3 38 BK46
Sevenoaks TN13 191 FJ126
Sidcup DA14 126 EV91
Stanmore HA7 41 CH50
Surbiton KT6 137 CH102
Wallington SM6 159 DJ105
West Byfleet (Byfleet) KT14 152 BL113
Westerham TN16 178 EL123
Rectory La, West. (Brasted)
TN16 180 EW123
Rectory Meadow, Grav.
(Sthflt) DA13 130 GA93
Rectory Orchard, SW19 119 CY91
Rectory Pk, S.Croy. CR2 160 DS113
Rectory Pk Av, Nthlt. UB5 78 BZ69
Rectory Pl, SE18 105 EN77
⇌ **Rectory Road** 66 DT62
Rectory Rd, E12 69 EM64
E17 67 EB55
N16 66 DT62
SW13 99 CU82
W3 80 CP74
Beckenham BR3 143 EA95
Coulsdon CR5 184 DD125
Dagenham RM10 88 FA66
Grays RM17 110 GD76
Hayes UB3 77 BU72
Hounslow TW4 95 BV81
Keston BR2 162 EK108
Rickmansworth WD3 38 BK46
Southall UB2 96 BZ76
Sutton SM1 140 DA104
Swanscombe DA10 130 FY87
Tilbury (W.Til.) RM18 111 GK79
Rectory Sq, E1 85 DX71
Rectory Way, Uxb. UB10 59 BP62
Reculver Ms, N18
off Lyndhurst Rd 46 DU49
Reculver Rd, SE16 203 H10
Red Anchor Cl, SW3
off Old Ch St 100 DE79
Redan Pl, W2 82 DB72
Redan St, W14 99 CX76
Redan Ter, SE5
off Flaxman Rd 102 DQ82
Redbarn Cl, Pur. CR8
off Whytecliffe Rd S 159 DP111
Red Barracks Rd, SE18 105 EM77
Redberry Gro, SE26 122 DW90
Redbourne Av, N3 44 DA53
Redbourne Dr, SE28 88 EX72
REDBRIDGE, Ilf. IG 69 EM58
⊖ **Redbridge** 68 EK58
Redbridge Enterprise Cen,
Ilf. IG1 69 EQ61
Redbridge Gdns, SE5 102 DS80
Redbridge La E, Ilf. IG4 68 EK58
Redbridge La W, E11 68 EH58
Redbridge Rbt, Ilf. IG4
off Eastern Av 68 EK58
Redburn St, SW3 100 DF79
Redbury Cl, Rain. RM13
off Deri Av 89 FH70
Redcar Cl, Nthlt. UB5 60 CB64
Redcar Rd, Rom. RM3 52 FM50
Redcar St, SE5 102 DQ80
Redcastle Cl, E1 84 DW73
Red Cedars Rd, Orp. BR6 145 ES101
Redchurch St, E2 197 P4
Redcliffe Cl, SW5
off Warwick Rd 100 DB78
Redcliffe Ct, E5
off Napoleon Rd 66 DV62
Redcliffe Gdns, SW5 100 DB78
SW10 100 DB78
W4 98 CP80
Ilford IG1 69 EN60
Redcliffe Ms, SW10 100 DB78
Redcliffe Pl, SW10 100 DC79
Redcliffe Rd, SW10 100 DC78
Redcliffe Sq, SW10 100 DB78
Redcliffe St, SW10 100 DB79
Redclose Av, Mord. SM4 140 DA99
Redclyffe Rd, E6 86 EJ67
Red Cottage Ms, Slou. SL3 92 AW76
Red Ct, Slou. SL1 74 AS74
Redcourt, Wok. GU22 167 BD115
Red Cow, Slou. SL1
off Mere Rd 92 AU76
Redcroft Rd, Sthl. UB1 78 CC73
Redcross Way, SE1 201 J4
Redden Ct Rd, Rom. RM3 72 FL55
Redding Cl, Dart. DA2 129 FS89
Reddings, The, NW7 43 CT48
Borehamwood WD6 26 CM41
Reddings Av, Bushey WD23 24 CB43
Reddings Cl, NW7 43 CT49
Reddington Cl, S.Croy. CR2 160 DR109
Reddington Dr, Slou. SL3 92 AY76
Reddington Ho, N1
off Priory Grn Est 83 DM68
Reddins Rd, SE15 102 DU79
Reddons Rd, Beck. BR3 123 DY94
Reddown Rd, Couls. CR5 175 DK118
Reddy Rd, Erith DA8 107 FF79
Rede Ct, Wey. KT13
off Old Palace Rd 135 BP104
Redenham Ho, SW15
off Tangley Gro 119 CT87
Rede Pl, W2 off Chepstow Pl 82 DA72
Redesdale Gdns, Islw. TW7 97 CG80
Redesdale St, SW3 100 DF79
Redfern Av, Houns. TW4 116 CA87
Redfern Cl, Uxb. UB8 76 BJ67
Redfern Gdns, Rom. RM2 52 FK54
Redfern Rd, NW10 80 CS66
SE6 123 EC87
Redfield La, SW5 100 DA77
Redfield Ms, SW5
off Redfield La 100 DA77
Redford Av, Couls. CR5 159 DH114
Thornton Heath CR7 141 DM98
Wallington SM6 159 DL107
Redford Cl, Felt. TW13 115 BT89
H **Redford Lo Psychiatric
Hosp**, N9 46 DU47
Redford Wk, N1
off Britannia Row 83 DP67
Redford Way, Uxb. UB8 76 BJ66
Redgate Dr, Brom. BR2 144 EH103
Redgate Ter, SW15 119 CY86
Redgrave Cl, Croy. CR0 142 DT100
Redgrave Rd, SW15 99 CX83
Redhall Ct, Cat. CR3 176 DR123
Redhall La, Rick. WD3 22 BL39

★ Place of interest ⇌ Railway station ⊖ London Underground station DLR Docklands Light Railway station Tra Tramlink station H Hospital Riv Pedestrian ferry landing stage

Redheath Cl, Wat. WD25 23 BT35
REDHILL, RH1 184 DG134
⇌ **Redhill** 184 DG133
Red Hill, Chis. BR7 125 EN92
Uxbridge (Denh.) UB9 57 BD61
Redhill Dr, Edg. HA8 42 CQ54
Redhill Rd, Cob. KT11 153 BP113
Redhill St, NW1 195 J2
★ **Red Ho**, William Morris Ho,
Bexh. DA6 106 EY84
Red Ho La, Bexh. DA6 106 EX84
Walton-on-Thames KT12 135 BU103
Redhouse Rd, Croy. CR0 141 DK100
Westerham (Tats.) TN16 178 EJ120
Red Ho Sq, N1 *off Ashby Gro* 84 DQ66
Redington Gdns, NW3 64 DB63
Redington Rd, NW3 64 DB63
Redland Gdns, W.Mol. KT8
off Dunstable Rd 136 BZ98
Redlands, Couls. CR5 175 DL116
Redlands Ct, Brom. BR1 124 EF94
Redlands Rd, Enf. EN3 31 DY39
Sevenoaks TN13 190 FF124
Redlands Way, SW2 121 DM87
Red La, Esher (Clay.) KT10 155 CG107
Oxted RH8 188 EH133
Redleaf Cl, Belv. DA17 106 FA79
Red Leaf Cl, Slou. SL3
off Pickford Dr 75 AZ74
Redleaves Av, Ashf. TW15 115 BP93
Redlees Cl, Islw. TW7 97 CG84
Red Leys, Uxb. UB8
off Park Rd 76 BL66
Red Lion Cl, SE17
off Red Lion Row 102 DQ79
Orpington BR5 146 EW100
Red Lion Ct, EC4 196 E8
Red Lion Hill, N2 44 DD54
Red Lion La, SE18 105 EN80
Hemel Hempstead HP3 6 BM26
Rickmansworth (Sarratt)
WD3 22 BG35
Woking (Chobham) GU24 150 AS109
Red Lion Pl, SE18
off Shooters Hill Rd 105 EN81
Red Lion Rd, Surb. KT6 138 CM103
Woking (Chobham) GU24 150 AS109
Red Lion Row, SE17 102 DQ79
Red Lion Sq, SW18
off Wandsworth High St 120 DA85
WC1 196 B7
Red Lion St, WC1 196 B6
Richmond TW9 117 CK85
Red Lion Yd, W1 198 G2
Watford WD17 *off High St* 24 BW42
Red Lo Cres, Bex. DA5 127 FD90
Red Lo Rd, Beck. BR3 143 ED100
Bexley DA5 127 FD90
West Wickham BR4 143 EC102
Redman Cl, Nthlt. UB5 78 BW68
Redmans La, Sev. (Shore.)
TN14 165 FE107
Redman's Rd, E1 84 DW71
Redmead La, E1 202 B3
Redmead Rd, Hayes UB3 95 BS77
Redmore Rd, W6 99 CV77
Red Oak Cl, Orp. BR6 145 EP104
Red Oaks Mead, Epp.
(They.B.) CM16 33 ER37
Red Path, E9 85 DZ65
Red Pl, W1 194 F10
Redpoll Way, Erith DA18 106 EX76
Red Post Hill, SE21 122 DR85
SE24 102 DR84
Redriffe Rd, E13 86 EF67
Redriff Est, SE16 203 M6
Redriff Rd, SE16 203 J7
Romford RM7 51 FB54
Red Rd, Borwd. WD6 26 CM41
Brentwood CM14 54 FV49
Redroofs Cl, Beck. BR3 143 EB95
Red Rover, SW15 99 CT83
Redruth Cl, N22 45 DM52
Redruth Gdns, Rom. RM3 52 FM50
Redruth Rd, E9 85 DX67
Romford RM3 52 FM50
Redruth Wk, Rom. RM3 52 FN50
Red Sq, N16 66 DR62
Redstart Cl, E6
off Columbine Av 86 EL71
SE14
off Southerngate Way 103 DY80
Croydon (New Adgtn) CR0 161 ED110
Redstart Mans, Ilf. IG1
off Mill Rd 69 EN62
Redstone Hill, Red. RH1 184 DG134
Redstone Manor, Red. RH1 184 DG134
Redstone Pk, Red. RH1 184 DG134
Redston Rd, N8 65 DK56
REDSTREET, Grav. DA13 130 GB93
Red St, Grav. (Sthflt) DA13 130 GA93
Redvers Rd, N22 45 DN54
Warlingham CR6 176 DW118
Redvers St, N1 197 N2
Redwald Rd, E5 67 DX63
Redway Dr, Twick. TW2 116 CC87
Redwing Cl, S.Croy. CR2 161 DX111
Redwing Gdns, W.Byf. KT14 152 BH112
Redwing Gro, Abb.L. WD5 7 BU31
Redwing Ms, SE5
off Vaughan Rd 102 DQ82
Redwing Path, SE28 105 ER75
Redwing Rd, Wall. SM6 159 DL108
Redwood, Egh. TW20 133 BE96
Redwood Chase, S.Ock. RM15 91 FW70
Redwood Cl, E3 85 EA68
N14 *off The Vale* 45 DK45
SE16 203 L3
Buckhurst Hill IG9
off Beech La 48 EH47
Kenley CR8 160 DQ114
Sidcup DA15 126 EU87
Uxbridge UB10
off The Larches 77 BP68
Watford WD19 40 BW49
Redwood Ct, NW6
off The Avenue 81 CY66
Redwood Est, Houns. TW5 95 BV79
Redwood Gdns, E4 31 EB44
Chigwell IG7 50 EU50
Redwood Ms, SW4
off Hannington Rd 101 DH83
Ashford TW15
off Napier Wk 115 BR94
Redwood Mt, Reig. RH2 184 DA131
Redwood Ri, Borwd. WD6 26 CN37
Redwoods, SW15 119 CU88
Addlestone KT15 152 BG107
Redwood Wk, Surb. KT6 137 CK102
Redwood Way, Barn. EN5 27 CX43
Reece Ms, SW7 100 DD77
Reed Av, Orp. BR6 145 ES104
Reed Cl, E16 86 EG71
SE12 124 EG85
Iver SL0 75 BE72
St. Albans (Lon.Col.) AL2 9 CK27
Reed Ct, Green. DA9 109 FW84
Reede Gdns, Dag. RM10 71 FB64
Reede Rd, Dag. RM10 88 FA65
Reede Way, Dag. RM10 89 FB65
⇌ **Reedham** 159 DM113
Reedham Cl, N17 66 DV56
St. Albans (Brick.Wd) AL2 8 CA29
Reedham Dr, Pur. CR8 159 DN113
Reedham Pk Av, Pur. CR8 175 DN116
Reedham St, SE15 102 DU82
Reedholm Vil, N16
off Winston Rd 66 DR63
Reed Pl, SW4 101 DK84
Shepperton TW17 134 BM102
West Byfleet KT14 151 BE113
Reed Pond Wk, Rom. RM2 51 FF54
Reed Rd, N17 46 DT54
Reeds Cres, Wat. WD24 24 BW40
Reedsfield Cl, Ashf. TW15
off Reedsfield Rd 115 BP91
Reedsfield Rd, Ashf. TW15 115 BP91
Reeds Pl, NW1
off Royal Coll St 83 DJ66
Reeds Wk, Wat. WD24 24 BW40
Reedworth St, SE11 200 E9
Ree La Cotts, Loug. IG10
off Englands La 33 EN39
Reenglass Rd, Stan. HA7 41 CK49
Rees Dr, Stan. HA7 42 CL49
Rees Gdns, Croy. CR0 142 DT100
Reesland Cl, E12 87 EN65
Rees St, N1 84 DQ67
Reets Fm Cl, NW9 62 CS58
Reeves Av, NW9 62 CR59
Tram **Reeves Corner** 141 DP103
Reeves Cor, Croy. CR0
off Roman Way 141 DP103
Reeves Cres, Swan. BR8 147 FD97
Reeves Ms, W1 198 F1
Reeves Rd, E3 85 EB70
SE18 105 EP79
Reflection, The, E16
off Woolwich Manor Way 105 EP75
Reform Row, N17 46 DT54
Reform St, SW11 100 DF82
Regal Cl, E1
off Old Montague St 84 DU71
W5 79 CK71
Regal Ct, N18 *off College Cl* 46 DT50
Regal Cres, Wall. SM6 141 DH104
Regal Dr, N11 45 DH50
Regal Ho, Ilf. IG2
off Eastern Av 69 ER58
Regal La, NW1
off Regents Pk Rd 82 DG67
Regal Pl, E3 *off Coborn St* 85 DZ69
SW6 *off Maxwell Rd* 100 DB80
Regal Row, SE15
off Astbury Rd 102 DW81
Regal Way, Har. HA3 62 CL58
Watford WD24 24 BW38
Regan Way, N1 197 M1
Regarder Rd, Chig. IG7 50 EU50
Regarth Av, Rom. RM1 71 FE58
Regatta Ho, Tedd. TW11
off Twickenham Rd 117 CG91
Regency Cl, W5 80 CL72
Chigwell IG7 49 EQ50
Hampton TW12 116 BZ92
Regency Ct, E18 48 EG54
Brentwood CM14 54 FW47
Sutton SM1
off Brunswick Rd 158 DB105
Regency Cres, NW4 43 CX54
Regency Dr, Ruis. HA4 59 BS60
West Byfleet KT14 151 BF113
Regency Gdns, Horn. RM11 72 FJ59
Walton-on-Thames KT12 136 BW102
Regency Ho, SW6
off The Boulevard 100 DC81
Regency Lo, Buck.H. IG9 48 EK47
Regency Ms, NW10
off High Rd 81 CU65
SW9 *off Lothian Rd* 101 DP80
Beckenham BR3 143 EC95
Isleworth TW7
off Queensbridge Pk 117 CE85
Regency Pl, SW1 199 N8
Regency St, NW10
off Victoria Rd 80 CS70
SW1 199 M8
Regency Ter, SW7
off Fulham Rd 100 DD78
Regency Wk, Croy. CR0 143 DY100
Richmond TW10
off Grosvenor Rd 118 CL85
Regency Way, Bexh. DA6 106 EX83
Woking GU22 167 BD115
Regeneration Rd, SE16 203 H9
Regent Av, Uxb. UB10 77 BP66
Regent Cl, N12 *off Nether St* 44 DC50
Addlestone (New Haw)
KT15 152 BK109
Grays RM16 110 GC75
Harrow HA3 62 CL58
Hounslow TW4 95 BV81
Redhill RH1 185 DJ129
Regent Ct, Slou. SL1 74 AS72
Regent Cres, Red. RH1 184 DF132
Regent Gdns, Ilf. IG3 70 EU58
Regent Gate, Wal.Cr. EN8 15 DY34
Regent Pk, Lthd. KT22 171 CG118
Regent Pl, SW19
off Haydons Rd 120 DB92
W1 195 L10
Regent Pl, Croy. CR0
off Grant Rd 142 DT102
Regent Rd, SE24 121 DP86
Epping CM16 17 ET30
Surbiton KT5 138 CM99
Regents Av, N13 45 DM50
Regents Br Gdns, SW8 101 DL80
Regents Cl, Hayes UB4
off Park Rd 77 BS71
Radlett WD7 9 CG34
South Croydon CR2 160 DS107
Whyteleafe CR3 176 DS118
Regents Dr, Kes. BR2 162 EK106
Woodford Green IG8 49 EN51
Regents Ms, NW8
off Langford Pl 82 DC68
REGENT'S PARK, NW1 194 G1
⊖ **Regent's Park** 194 H5
★ **Regent's Park, The**, NW1 194 E1
Regent's Pk Est, NW1 195 J3
Regents Pk Rd, N3 63 CZ55
NW1 82 DF67
Regents Pk Ter, NW1
off Oval Rd 83 DH67
Regent's Pl, SE3 104 EG82
Regents Pl, Loug. IG10 48 EK45
Regent Sq, E3 85 EB69
WC1 196 A3
Belvedere DA17 107 FB77
Regents Row, E8 84 DU67
Regent St, NW10
off Wellington Rd 81 CX69
SW1 199 M1
W1 195 J8
W4 98 CN78
Watford WD24 23 BV38
Regents Wf, N1
off All Saints St 83 DM68
Regina Cl, Barn. EN5 27 CX41
Reginald Rd, E7 86 EG66
SE8 103 EA80
Northwood HA6 39 BT53
Romford RM3 52 FN53
Reginald Sq, SE8 103 EA80
Regina Pt, SE16 202 G6
Regina Rd, N4 65 DM60
SE25 142 DU97
W13 79 CG74
Southall UB2 96 BY77
Regina Ter, W13 79 CG74
Regis Pl, SW2 101 DM84
Regis Rd, NW5 65 DH64
Regnart Bldgs, NW1 195 L4
Reid Av, Cat. CR3 176 DR121
Reid Cl, Couls. CR5 175 DH116
Hayes UB3 77 BS72
Pinner HA5 59 BU56
Reidhaven Rd, SE18 105 ES77
REIGATE, RH2 184 DA134
⇌ **Reigate** 184 DA133
Reigate Av, Sutt. SM1 140 DA102
Reigate Business Ms, Reig.
RH2 *off Albert Rd N* 183 CZ133
Reigate Hill, Reig. RH2 184 DB130
Reigate Hill Cl, Reig. RH2 184 DA131
Reigate Rd, Bet. RH3 182 CS132
Bromley BR1 124 EF90
Epsom KT17, KT18 157 CT110
Ilford IG3 69 ET61
Leatherhead KT22 171 CJ123
Redhill RH1 184 DB134
Reigate RH2 184 DB134
Tadworth KT20 173 CX117
Reigate Way, Wall. SM6 159 DL106
Reighton Rd, E5 66 DU62
Reinickendorf Av, SE9 125 EQ85
Reizel Cl, N16 66 DT60
Relay Rd, W12 81 CW73
Relf Rd, SE15 102 DU83
Reliance Sq, EC2 197 N4
Relko Ct, Epsom KT19 156 CR110
Relko Gdns, Sutt. SM1 158 DD106
Relton Ms, SW7 198 C6
Rembrandt Cl, E14 204 F7
SW1 198 F9
Rembrandt Ct, Epsom KT19 157 CT107
Rembrandt Dr, Grav. (Nthflt)
DA11 130 GD90
Rembrandt Rd, SE13 104 EE84
Edgware HA8 42 CN54
Rembrandt Way, Walt. KT12 135 BV104
Remington Rd, E6 86 EL72
N15 66 DR58
Remington St, N1 196 G1
Remnant St, WC2 196 B8
Remus Rd, E3 *off Monier Rd* 85 EA66
Renaissance Wk, SE10 205 L6
Rendle Cl, Croy. CR0 142 DT99
Rendlesham Av, Rad. WD7 25 CF37
Rendlesham Rd, E5 66 DU63
Enfield EN2 29 DP39
Rendlesham Way, Rick.
(Chorl.) WD3 21 BC44
Renforth St, SE16 202 G5
Renfree Way, Shep. TW17 134 BM101
Renfrew Cl, E6 87 EN73
Renfrew Ho, E17
off Priory Ct 47 DZ54
Renfrew Rd, SE11 200 F8
Hounslow TW4 96 BX82
Kingston upon Thames
KT2 118 CP94
Renmans, The, Ashtd. KT21 172 CM116
Renmuir St, SW17 120 DF93
Rennell St, SE13 103 EC83
Rennels Way, Islw. TW7 97 CE82
Renness Rd, E17 67 DY55
Rennets Cl, SE9 125 ES85
Rennets Wd Rd, SE9 125 ER85
Rennie Cl, Ashf. TW15 114 BK90
Rennie Ct, SE1 *off Upper Grd* 83 DP74
Rennie Est, SE16 202 E9
Rennie St, SE1 200 F2
Rennison Cl, Wal.Cr. EN7 14 DT27
Renovation, The, E16
off Woolwich Manor Way 105 EP75
Renown Cl, Croy. CR0 141 DP102
Romford RM7 50 FA53
Rensburg Rd, E17 67 DX57
Renshaw Cl, Belv. DA17
off Grove Rd 106 EZ79
Renters Av, NW4 63 CW58
Renton Dr, Orp. BR5 146 EX101
Renwick Ind Est, Bark. IG11 88 EV67
Renwick Rd, Bark. IG11 88 EV70
Repens Way, Hayes UB4
off Stipularis Dr 78 BX70
Rephidim St, SE1 201 M7
Replingham Rd, SW18 119 CZ88
Reporton Rd, SW6 99 CY81
Repository Rd, SE18 105 EM79
Repton Av, Hayes UB3 95 BR77
Romford RM2 71 FG55
Wembley HA0 61 CJ63
Repton Cl, Cars. SM5 158 DE106
Repton Ct, Beck. BR3 143 EB95
Ilford IG5 *off Repton Gro* 49 EM53
Repton Dr, Rom. RM2 71 FG56
Repton Gdns, Rom. RM2 71 FG55
Repton Gro, Ilf. IG5 49 EM53
Repton Pl, Amer. HP7 20 AU39
Repton Rd, Har. HA3 62 CM56
Orpington BR6 146 EU104
Repton St, E14 85 DY72
Repton Way, Rick. (Crox.Grn)
WD3 22 BN43
Repulse Cl, Rom. RM5 51 FB53
Reservoir Cl, Green. DA9 129 FW86
Thornton Heath CR7 142 DR98
Reservoir Rd, N14 29 DJ43
SE4 103 DY82
Ruislip HA4 59 BQ57
Resham Cl, Sthl. UB2 96 BW76
Resolution Wk, SE18 105 EM76
Resolution Way, SE8
off Deptford High St 103 EA80
Restavon Pk, West. (Berry's Grn)
TN16 179 EP116
Restell Cl, SE3 104 EE79
Restmor Way, Wall. SM6 140 DG103
Reston Cl, Borwd. WD6 26 CN38
Reston Path, Borwd. WD6 26 CN38
Reston Pl, SW7
off Hyde Pk Gate 100 DC75
Restons Cres, SE9 125 ER86
Restoration Sq, SW11
off Battersea High St 100 DD81
Restormel Cl, Houns. TW3 116 CA85
Retcar Cl, N19
off Dartmouth Pk Hill 65 DH61
Retcar Pl, N19 65 DH61
Retford Cl, Borwd. WD6
off The Campions 26 CN38
Romford RM3 52 FN51
Retford Path, Rom. RM3 52 FN51
Retford Rd, Rom. RM3 52 FM51
Retford St, N1 197 N1
Retingham Way, E4 47 EB47
Retreat, The, NW9 62 CR57
SW14 *off South Worple Way* 98 CS83
Addlestone KT15 152 BK106
Amersham HP6 20 AY39
Brentwood CM14 54 FV46
Brentwood (Hutt.) CM13 55 GB44
Egham (Eng.Grn) TW20 112 AX92
Grays RM17 110 GB79
Harrow HA2 60 CA59
Kings Langley WD4 7 BQ31
Orpington BR6 164 EV107
Surbiton KT5 138 CM100
Thornton Heath CR7 142 DR98
Worcester Park KT4 139 CV103
Retreat Cl, Har. HA3 61 CJ57
Retreat Pl, E9 84 DW65
Retreat Rd, Rich. TW9 117 CK85
Retreat Way, Chig. IG7 50 EV48
Reubens Rd, Brwd. (Hutt.)
CM13 55 GB44
Reunion Row, E1 202 E1
Reuters Plaza, E14
off South Colonnade 85 EB74
Reveley Sq, SE16 203 L5
Revell Cl, Lthd. (Fetch.) KT22 170 CB122
Revell Dr, Lthd. (Fetch.) KT22 170 CB122
Revell Ri, SE18 105 ET79
Revell Rd, Kings.T. KT1 138 CP95
Sutton SM1 157 CZ107
Revelon Rd, SE4 103 DY84
Revelstoke Rd, SW18 119 CZ89
Reventlow Rd, SE9 125 EQ88
Reverdy Rd, SE1 202 B9
Reverend Cl, Har. HA2 60 CB62
Revere Way, Epsom KT19 156 CS109
Revesby Rd, Cars. SM5 140 DD100
Review Rd, NW2 63 CT61
Dagenham RM10 89 FB67
Rewell St, SW6 *off King's Rd* 100 DC80
Rewley Rd, Cars. SM5 140 DD100
Rex Av, Ashf. TW15 114 BN93
Rex Cl, Rom. RM5 51 FB52
Rex Pl, W1 198 G1
Reydon Av, E11 68 EJ58
Reynard Cl, SE4
off Foxwell St 103 DY83
Bromley BR1 145 EM97
Reynard Dr, SE19 122 DT94
Reynard Pl, SE14
off Milton Ct Rd 103 DY79
Reynardson Rd, N17 46 DQ52
Reynards Way, St.Alb.
(Brick.Wd) AL2 8 BZ29
Reynolah Gdns, SE7
off Rathmore Rd 104 EH78
Reynolds Av, E12 69 EN64
Chessington KT9 156 CL108
Romford RM6 70 EW59
Reynolds Cl, NW11 64 DB59
SW19 140 DD95
Carshalton SM5 140 DF102
Reynolds Ct, E11
off Cobbold Rd 68 EF62
Romford RM6 70 EX55
Reynolds Dr, Edg. HA8 62 CM55
Reynolds Pl, SE3 104 EH80
Richmond TW10
off Cambrian Rd 118 CM86
Reynolds Rd, SE15 122 DW85
W4 98 CQ76
Hayes UB4 78 BW70
New Malden KT3 138 CR101
Reynolds Way, Croy. CR0 160 DS105
Rheidol Ms, N1
off Rheidol Ter 84 DQ68
Rheidol Ter, N1 83 DP68
Rheingold Way, Wall. SM6 159 DL109
Rheola Cl, N17 46 DT53
Rhoda St, E2 *off Brick La* 84 DT70
Rhodes Av, N22 45 DJ53
Rhodes Cl, Egh. TW20
off Mullens Rd 113 BC92
Rhodesia Rd, E11 67 ED61
SW9 101 DL82
Rhodes Moorhouse Ct,
Mord. SM4 140 DA100
Rhodes St, N7
off Mackenzie Rd 65 DM64
Rhodes Way, Wat. WD24 24 BX40
Rhodeswell Rd, E14 85 DY71
Rhododendron Ride, Egh.
TW20 112 AT94
Slough SL3 75 AZ69
Rhodrons Av, Chess. KT9 156 CL106
Rhondda Gro, E3 85 DY69
Rhyl Rd, Grnf. UB6 79 CF68
Rhyl St, NW5 82 DG65
Rhys Av, N11 45 DK52
Rialto Rd, Mitch. CR4 140 DG96
Ribble Cl, Wdf.Grn. IG8
off Prospect Rd 48 EJ51
Ribbledale, St.Alb. (Lon.Col.)
AL2 10 CM27
Ribblesdale Av, N11 44 DG51
Northolt UB5 78 CB65
Ribblesdale Rd, N8 65 DM56
SW16 121 DH93
Dartford DA2 128 FQ88
Ribbon Dance Ms, SE5
off Camberwell Gro 102 DR81
Ribchester Av, Grnf. UB6 79 CF69
Ribston Cl, Brom. BR2 145 EM102
Radlett (Shenley) WD7 9 CK33
Ricardo Path, SE28
off Byron Cl 88 EW74
Ricardo Rd, Wind. (Old Wind.)
SL4 112 AV86
Ricardo St, E14 85 EB72
Ricards Rd, SW19 119 CZ92
Richard Cl, SE18 104 EL77
Richard Fell Ho, E12
off Walton Rd 69 EN63
Richard Foster Cl, E17 67 DZ59
Richard Ho Dr, E16 86 EK72
Richard Robert Res, The, E15
off Broadway 85 ED65
Richards Av, Rom. RM7 71 FC57
Richards Cl, Bushey WD23 41 CD45
Harrow HA1 61 CG57
Hayes UB3 95 BR79
Uxbridge UB10 76 BN67
Richards Fld, Epsom KT19 156 CR109
Richardson Cl, E8
off Clarissa St 84 DT67
Greenhithe DA9
off Steele Av 129 FU85
St. Albans (Lon.Col.) AL2 10 CL27
Richardson Cres, Wal.Cr.
(Chsht) EN7 13 DP25
Richardson Rd, E15 86 EE68
Richardson's Ms, W1 195 K5
Richards Pl, E17 67 EA55
SW3 198 C8
Richards Rd, Cob. (Stoke D'Ab.)
KT11 154 CB114
Richard St, E1
off Commercial Rd 84 DV72
Richbell Cl, Ashtd. KT21 171 CK118
Richbell Pl, WC1 196 B6
Richborne Ter, SW8 101 DM80
Richborough Cl, Orp. BR5 146 EX98
Richborough Rd, NW2 63 CX63
Richbourne Ct, W1
off Harrowby St 82 DE72
Richens Cl, Houns. TW3 97 CD82
Riches Rd, Ilf. IG1 69 EQ61
Richfield Rd, Bushey WD23 40 CC45
Richford Rd, E15 86 EF67
Richford St, W6 99 CW75
Rich Ind Est, SE1 201 N7
RICHINGS PARK, Iver SL0 93 BE75
Richings Way, Iver SL0 93 BF76
Richland Av, Couls. CR5 158 DG114
Richlands Av, Epsom KT17 157 CU105
Rich La, SW5 *off Warwick Rd* 100 DB78
Richmer Rd, Erith DA8 107 FG80
RICHMOND, TW9 & TW10 118 CL86
⇌ **Richmond** 98 CL84
⊖ **Richmond** 98 CL84
Richmond Av, E4 47 ED50
N1 83 DM67
NW10 81 CW65
SW20 139 CY95
Feltham TW14 115 BS86
Uxbridge UB10 77 BP65
Richmond Br, Rich. TW9 117 CK86
Twickenham TW1 117 CK86
Richmond Bldgs, W1 195 M9
Richmond Circ, Rich. TW9
off Kew Rd 98 CL84
Richmond Cl, E17 67 DZ58
Amersham HP6 20 AT38
Borehamwood WD6 26 CR43
Epsom KT18 156 CS114
Leatherhead (Fetch.) KT22 170 CC124
Waltham Cross (Chsht) EN8 14 DW29
Westerham (Bigg.H.) TN16 178 EH119
Richmond Ct, Mitch. CR4
off Phipps Br Rd 140 DD97
Potters Bar EN6 12 DC31
Richmond Cres, E4 47 ED50
N1 83 DM67
N9 46 DU46
Slough SL1 74 AU74
Staines TW18 113 BF92
Richmond Dr, Grav. DA12 131 GL89
Shepperton TW17 135 BQ100
Watford WD17 23 BS39
Woodford Green IG8 49 EN52
Richmond Gdns, NW4 63 CU57
Harrow HA3 41 CF51
Richmond Grn, Croy. CR0 141 DL104
Richmond Gro, N1 83 DP66
Surbiton KT5 138 CM100
Richmond Hill, Rich. TW10 118 CL86
Richmond Hill Ct, Rich. TW10 118 CL86
Richmond Ho, NW1
off Park Village E 83 DH68
Richmond Ms, W1 195 M9
Teddington TW11
off Broad St 117 CF93

★ **Richmond Palace (remains)**, Rich. TW9 117 CJ85
★ **Richmond Park**, Rich. TW10 118 CN88
Richmond Pk, Kings.T. KT2 118 CN88
Loughton IG10
off Fallow Flds 48 EK45
Richmond TW10 118 CN88
Richmond Pk Rd, SW14 118 CQ85
Kingston upon Thames KT2 118 CL94
Richmond Pl, SE18 105 EQ77
Richmond Rd, E4 47 ED46
E7 68 EH64
E8 84 DT66
E11 67 ED61
N2 44 DC54
N11 45 DL51
N15 66 DS58
SW20 139 CV95
W5 98 CL75
Barnet EN5 28 DB43
Coulsdon CR5 175 DH115
Croydon CR0 141 DL104
Grays RM17 110 GC79
Ilford IG1 69 EQ62
Isleworth TW7 97 CG83
Kingston upon Thames KT2 117 CK92
Potters Bar EN6 12 DC31
Romford RM1 71 FF58
Staines TW18 113 BF92
Thornton Heath CR7 141 DP97
Twickenham TW1 117 CJ86
H **Richmond Royal Hosp**, Rich. TW9 98 CL83
Richmond St, E13 86 EG68
Richmond Ter, SW1 199 P4
Richmond Ter Ms, SW1
off Parliament St 101 DL75
Richmond Way, E11 68 EG61
W12 99 CX75
W14 99 CX76
Leatherhead (Fetch.) KT22 170 CB123
Rickmansworth (Crox.Grn) WD3 23 BQ42
Richmount Gdns, SE3 104 EG83
Rich St, E14 85 DZ73
Rickard Cl, NW4 63 CV56
SW2 121 DM88
West Drayton UB7 94 BK76
Rickards Cl, Surb. KT6 138 CL102
Ricketts Hill Rd, West. (Tats.) TN16 178 EK118
Rickett St, SW6 100 DA79
Rickman Cres, Add. KT15 134 BH104
Rickman Hill, Couls. CR5 175 DH118
Rickman Hill Rd, Couls. (Chipstead) CR5 175 DH118
Rickmans La, Slou. (Stoke P.) SL2 56 AS64
Rickman St, E1 *off Mantus Rd* 84 DW69
RICKMANSWORTH, WD3 38 BL45
⇌ **Rickmansworth** 38 BK45
⊖ **Rickmansworth** 38 BK45
Rickmansworth La, Ger.Cr. (Chal.St.P.) SL9 37 AZ50
Rickmansworth Pk, Rick. WD3 38 BK45
Rickmansworth Rd, Nthwd. HA6 39 BR52
Pinner HA5 39 BV54
Rickmansworth (Chorl.) WD3 21 BE41
Uxbridge (Hare.) UB9 38 BJ53
Watford WD17, WD18 23 BS42
Rick Roberts Way, E15 85 EC67
Rickthorne Rd, N19
off Landseer Rd 65 DL61
Rickyard Path, SE9 104 EL84
Ridding La, Grnf. UB6 61 CF64
Riddings, The, Cat. CR3 186 DT125
⇌ **Riddlesdown** 160 DR113
Riddlesdown Av, Pur. CR8 160 DQ112
Riddlesdown Rd, Pur. CR8 160 DQ111
Riddons Rd, SE12 124 EJ90
Ride, The, Brent. TW8 97 CH78
Enfield EN3 30 DW41
Rideout St, SE18 105 EM77
Rider Cl, Sid. DA15 125 ES86
Riders Way, Gdse. RH9 186 DW131
Ridgdale St, E3 85 EB68
RIDGE, Pot.B. EN6 10 CS34
Ridge, The, Bex. DA5 126 EZ87
Caterham (Wold.) CR3 187 EB126
Coulsdon CR5 159 DL114
Epsom KT18 172 CP117
Leatherhead (Fetch.) KT22 171 CD124
Orpington BR6 145 ER103
Purley CR8 159 DJ110
Surbiton KT5 138 CN99
Twickenham TW2 117 CD87
Woking GU22 167 BB117
Ridge Av, N21 46 DQ45
Dartford DA1 127 FF86
Ridgebrook Rd, SE3 104 EJ84
Ridge Cl, NW4 43 CX54
NW9 62 CR56
SE28 105 ER75
Woking GU22 166 AV121
Ridge Crest, Enf. EN2 29 DM39
Ridgecroft Cl, Bex. DA5 127 FC88
Ridgefield, Wat. WD17 23 BS37
Ridgegate Cl, Reig. RH2 184 DD132
RIDGEHILL, Rad. WD7 10 CQ30
Ridge Hill, NW11 63 CY60
Ridgehurst Av, Wat. WD25 7 BT34
Ridgelands, Lthd. (Fetch.) KT22 171 CD124
Ridge La, Wat. WD17 23 BS38
Ridge Langley, S.Croy. CR2 160 DU109
Ridgemead Cl, N14 45 DL47
Ridgemead Rd, Egh. (Eng.Grn) TW20 112 AU90
Ridgemont Gdns, Edg. HA8 42 CQ49
Ridgemount, Wey. KT13
off Oatlands Dr 135 BS103
Ridgemount Av, Couls. CR5 175 DH117
Croydon CR0 143 DX102
Ridgemount Cl, SE20 122 DV94
Ridgemount End, Ger.Cr. (Chal.St.P.) SL9 36 AY50
Ridgemount Gdns, Enf. EN2 29 DP40
Ridge Pk, Pur. CR8 159 DK110
Ridge Rd, N8 65 DM58
N21 46 DQ46
NW2 63 CZ62
Mitcham CR4 121 DH94
Sutton SM3 139 CY102
Ridge St, Wat. WD24 23 BV38
Ridgeview Cl, Barn. EN5 27 CX44
Ridgeview Lo, St.Alb. (Lon.Col.) AL2 10 CM28
Ridgeview Rd, N20 44 DB48
Ridge Way, SE19
off Central Hill 122 DS93
Ridgeway, SE28
off Pettman Cres 105 ER77
Brentwood (Hutt.) CM13 55 GB46
Bromley BR2 144 EG103
Ridge Way, Dart. (Cray.) DA1 127 FF86
Ridgeway, Dart. (Lane End) DA2 129 FS92
Epsom KT19 156 CQ112
Ridge Way, Felt. TW13 116 BY90
Ridgeway, Grays RM17 110 GE77
Ridge Way, Iver SL0 75 BE74
Ridgeway, Rick. WD3 38 BH45
Virginia Water GU25 132 AY99
Woking (Horsell) GU21 166 AX115
Woodford Green IG8 48 EJ49
Ridgeway, The, E4 47 EB47
N3 44 DB52
N11 44 DF49
N14 45 DL47
NW7 43 CU49
NW9 62 CS56
NW11 63 CZ60
W3 98 CN76
Croydon CR0 141 DM104
Enfield EN2 29 DN39
Gerrards Cross (Chal.St.P.) SL9 56 AY55
Harrow (Kenton) HA3 61 CJ58
Harrow (N.Har.) HA2 60 CA58
Leatherhead (Fetch.) KT22 171 CD123
Leatherhead (Oxshott) KT22 154 CC114
Potters Bar EN6 12 DD34
Potters Bar (Cuffley) EN6 12 DE28
Radlett WD7 25 CF37
Romford (Gidea Pk) RM2 71 FG56
Romford (Harold Wd) RM3 52 FL53
Ruislip HA4 59 BU59
South Croydon CR2 160 DS110
Stanmore HA7 41 CJ51
Walton-on-Thames KT12 135 BT102
Watford WD17 23 BS37
Ridgeway Av, Barn. EN4 28 DF44
Gravesend DA12 131 GH90
Ridgeway Cl, Lthd. (Oxshott) KT22 154 CC114
Woking GU21 166 AX116
Ridgeway Cres, Orp. BR6 145 ES104
Ridgeway Cres Gdns, Orp. BR6 145 ES103
Ridgeway Dr, Brom. BR1 124 EH91
Ridgeway E, Sid. DA15 125 ET85
Ridgeway Est, The, Iver SL0 75 BF74
Ridgeway Gdns, N6 65 DJ59
Ilford IG4 68 EL57
Woking GU21 166 AX115
Ridgeway Rd, SW9 101 DP83
Isleworth TW7 97 CE80
Redhill RH1 184 DE134
Ridgeway Rd N, Islw. TW7 97 CE79
Ridgeway Wk, Nthlt. UB5
off Fortunes Mead 78 BY65
Ridgeway W, Sid. DA15 125 ES85
Ridgewell Cl, N1
off Basire St 84 DQ67
SE26 123 DZ91
Dagenham RM10 89 FB67
Ridgewell Gro, Horn. RM12
off Airfield Way 89 FH65
Ridgmount Gdns, WC1 195 M5
Ridgmount Pl, WC1 195 M6
Ridgmount Rd, SW18 120 DB85
Ridgmount St, WC1 195 M6
Ridgway, SW19 119 CX93
Woking (Pyrford) GU22 167 BF115
Ridgway, The, Sutt. SM2 158 DD108
Ridgway Gdns, SW19 119 CX93
Ridgway Pl, SW19 119 CY93
Ridgway Rd, Wok. (Pyrford) GU22 167 BF115
Ridgwell Rd, E16 86 EJ71
Riding, The, NW11
off Golders Grn Rd 63 CZ59
Woking GU21 151 BB114
Riding Ct Rd, Slou. (Datchet) SL3 92 AW80
Riding Hill, S.Croy. CR2 160 DU113
Riding Ho St, W1 195 K7
Ridings, The, E11
off Malcolm Way 68 EG57
W5 80 CM70
Addlestone KT15 151 BF107
Ashtead KT21 171 CK117
Chesham (Latimer) HP5 20 AX36
Chigwell IG7
off Manford Way 50 EV49
Cobham KT11 154 CA112
Epsom KT18 172 CS115
Epsom (Ewell) KT17 157 CT109
Iver SL0 93 BF77
Reigate RH2 184 DD131
Sunbury-on-Thames TW16 135 BU95
Surbiton KT5 138 CN99
Tadworth KT20 173 CZ120
Westerham (Bigg.H.) TN16 178 EL117
Woking (Ripley) GU23 168 BG123
Ridings Av, N21 29 DP42
Ridings Cl, N6
off Hornsey La Gdns 65 DJ59
Ridings La, Wok. GU23 168 BN123
Ridlands Gro, Oxt. RH8 188 EL130
Ridlands La, Oxt. RH8 188 EK130
Ridlands Ri, Oxt. RH8 188 EL130
Ridler Rd, Enf. EN1 30 DS38
Ridley Av, W13 97 CH76
Ridley Cl, Bark. IG11 87 ET66
Romford RM3 51 FH53
Ridley Rd, E7 68 EJ63
E8 66 DT64
NW10 81 CU68
SW19 120 DB94
Ridley Rd, Brom. BR2 144 EF97
Warlingham CR6 176 DW118
Welling DA16 106 EV81
Ridsdale Rd, SE20 142 DV95
Woking GU21 166 AV117
Riefield Rd, SE9 105 EQ84
Riesco Dr, Croy. CR0 160 DW107
Riffel Rd, NW2 63 CW64
Riffhams, Brwd. CM13 55 GB48
Rifle Butts All, Epsom KT18 173 CT115
Rifle Ct, SE11 101 DN79
Rifle St, E14 85 EB71
Riga Ms, E1
off Commercial Rd 84 DU72
Rigault Rd, SW6 99 CY82
Rigby Cl, Croy. CR0 141 DN104
Rigby Gdns, Grays RM16 111 GH77
Rigby La, Hayes UB3 95 BR75
Rigby Ms, Ilf. IG1 69 EN61
Rigby Pl, Enf. EN3 31 EA37
Rigden St, E14 85 EB72
Rigeley Rd, NW10 81 CU69
Rigg App, E10 67 DX60
Rigge Pl, SW4 101 DK84
Riggindale Rd, SW16 121 DK92
Riley Cl, Epsom KT19 156 CP111
Riley Rd, SE1 201 N6
Enfield EN3 30 DW38
Riley St, SW10 100 DD79
Rinaldo Rd, SW12 121 DH87
Ring, The, W2 194 B10
Ring Cl, Brom. BR1
off Garden Rd 124 EH94
Ringcroft St, N7 65 DN64
Ringers Rd, Brom. BR1 144 EG97
Ringford Rd, SW18 119 CZ85
Ringlet Cl, E16 86 EH71
Ringlewell Cl, Enf. EN1
off Central Av 30 DV40
Ringley Pk Rd, Reig. RH2 184 DC134
Ringmer Av, SW6 99 CY81
Ringmer Gdns, N19
off Sussex Way 65 DL61
Ringmer Pl, N21 30 DR43
Ringmer Way, Brom. BR1 145 EM99
Ringmore Ri, SE23 122 DV87
Ringmore Rd, Walt. KT12 136 BW104
Ringmore Vw, SE23
off Ringmore Ri 122 DV87
Ring Rd, W12 81 CW73
Ringshall Rd, Orp. BR5 146 EU97
Ringslade Rd, N22 45 DM54
Ringstead Rd, SE6 123 EB87
Sutton SM1 158 DD105
Ringway, N11 45 DJ51
Southall UB2 96 BY78
Ringway Rd, St.Alb. (Park St) AL2 8 CB27
Ringwold Cl, Beck. BR3 123 DY94
Ringwood Av, N2 44 DF54
Croydon CR0 141 DL101
Hornchurch RM12 72 FK61
Orpington BR6 164 EW110
Redhill RH1 184 DF131
Ringwood Cl, Pnr. HA5 60 BW55
Ringwood Gdns, E14 204 A8
SW15 119 CU89
Ringwood Rd, E17 67 DZ58
Ringwood Way, N21 45 DP46
Hampton (Hmptn H.) TW12 116 CA91
RIPLEY, Wok. GU23 168 BJ122
Ripley Av, Egh. TW20 112 AY93
Ripley Bypass, Wok. GU23 168 BK122
Ripley Cl, Brom. BR1
off Ringmer Way 145 EM99
Croydon (New Adgtn) CR0 161 EC107
Slough SL3 92 AY77
Ripley Gdns, SW14 98 CR83
Sutton SM1 158 DC105
Ripley La, Wok. GU23 168 BL123
Ripley Ms, E11 68 EE58
Ripley Rd, E16 86 EJ72
Belvedere DA17 106 FA77
Enfield EN2 30 DQ39
Hampton TW12 116 CA94
Ilford IG3 69 ET61
RIPLEY SPRINGS, Egh. TW20 112 AY93
Ripley Vw, Loug. IG10 33 EP38
Ripley Vil, W5
off Castlebar Rd 79 CJ72
Ripley Way, Epsom KT19 156 CN111
Waltham Cross (Chsht) EN7 14 DV30
Riplington Ct, SW15
off Longwood Dr 119 CU87
Ripon Cl, Nthlt. UB5 60 CA64
Ripon Gdns, Chess. KT9 155 CK106
Ilford IG1 68 EL58
Ripon Rd, N9 46 DV45
N17 66 DR55
SE18 105 EP79
Ripon Way, Borwd. WD6 26 CQ43
Rippersley Rd, Well. DA16 106 EU81
Ripple Rd, Bark. IG11 87 EQ66
Dagenham RM9 88 EV67
Rippleside Commercial Est, Bark. IG11 88 EW68
Ripplevale Gro, N1 83 DM66
Rippolson Rd, SE18 105 ET78
Ripston Rd, Ashf. TW15 115 BR92
Risborough Dr, Wor.Pk. KT4 139 CU101
Risborough St, SE1 200 G4
Risdon St, SE16 202 G5
Rise, The, E11 68 EG57
N13 45 DN49
NW7 43 CT51
NW10 62 CR63
Bexley DA5 126 EW87
Borehamwood (Els.) WD6 26 CM43
Buckhurst Hill IG9 48 EK45
Dartford DA1 107 FF84
Edgware HA8 42 CP50
Epsom KT17 157 CT110
Gravesend DA12 131 GL91
Greenford UB6 61 CG64
St. Albans (Park St) AL2 9 CD25
Sevenoaks TN13 191 FJ129
South Croydon CR2 160 DW109
Tadworth KT20 173 CW121
Uxbridge UB10 76 BM68
Waltham Abbey EN9
off Breach Barn Mobile Home Pk 16 EH30
Risebridge Chase, Rom. RM1 51 FF52
Risebridge Rd, Rom. RM2 51 FF54
Risedale Rd, Bexh. DA7 107 FB83
Riseldine Rd, SE23 123 DY86
Rise Pk Boul, Rom. RM1 51 FF53
Rise Pk Par, Rom. RM1 51 FE54
Riseway, Brwd. CM15 54 FY48
Rising Hill Cl, Nthwd. HA6
off Ducks Hill Rd 39 BQ51
Risinghill St, N1 83 DM68
Risingholme Cl, Bushey WD23 40 CB45
Harrow HA3 41 CE53
Risingholme Rd, Har. HA3 41 CE54
Risings, The, E17 67 ED56
Rising Sun Ct, EC1 196 G7
Risley Av, N17 46 DQ53
Rita Rd, SW8 101 DM80
Ritches Rd, N15 66 DQ57
Ritchie Rd, Croy. CR0 142 DV100
Ritchie St, N1 83 DN68
Ritchings Av, E17 67 DY56
Ritherdon Rd, SW17 120 DG89
Ritson Rd, E8 84 DU65
Ritter St, SE18 105 EN79
Ritz Ct, Pot.B. EN6 12 DA31
Ritz Par, W5
off Connell Cres 80 CM70
Rivaz Pl, E9 84 DW65
Rivenhall Gdns, E18 68 EF56
River App, Edg. HA8 42 CQ53
River Ash Est, Shep. TW17 135 BT101
River Av, N13 45 DP48
Thames Ditton KT7 137 CG101
River Bk, N21 46 DQ45
East Molesey KT8 137 CE97
Riverbank, Stai. TW18 113 BF93
River Bk, T.Ditt. KT7 137 CF99
West Molesey KT8 136 BZ97
Riverbank Way, Brent. TW8 97 CJ79
River Barge Cl, E14 204 E5
River Brent Business Pk, W7 97 CE76
River Cl, E11 68 EJ58
Rainham RM13 89 FH71
Ruislip HA4 59 BT58
Southall UB2 96 CC75
Surbiton KT6
off Catherine Rd 137 CK99
Waltham Cross EN8 15 EA34
River Ct, SE1
off Upper Grd 83 DP73
Shepperton TW17 135 BQ101
Woking GU21 167 BC115
Rivercourt Rd, W6 99 CV77
River Crane Wk, Felt. TW13 116 BX88
Hounslow TW4 116 BX88
River Crane Way, Felt. TW13
off Watermill Way 116 BZ89
Riverdale, SE13
off Lewisham High St 103 EC83
Riverdale Cl, Bark. IG11 88 EV70
Riverdale Dr, SW18
off Knaresborough Dr 120 DB88
Woking GU22 167 AZ121
Riverdale Gdns, Twick. TW1 117 CJ86
Riverdale Rd, SE18 105 ET78
Bexley DA5 126 EZ87
Erith DA8 107 FB78
Feltham TW13 116 BY91
Twickenham TW1 117 CJ86
Riverdene, Edg. HA8 42 CQ48
Riverdene Rd, Ilf. IG1 69 EN62
River Dr, Upmin. RM14 72 FQ58
Riverfield Rd, Stai. TW18 113 BF93
River Front, Enf. EN1 30 DR41
River Gdns, Cars. SM5 140 DG103
Feltham TW14 115 BV85
River Gro Pk, Beck. BR3 143 DZ95
RIVERHEAD, Sev. TN13 190 FD122
Riverhead Cl, E17 47 DX54
Riverhead Dr, Sutt. SM2 158 DA110
River Hill, Cob. KT11 169 BV115
Riverhill, Sev. TN15 191 FL130
Riverhill Ms, Wor.Pk. KT4 138 CR104
Riverholme Dr, Epsom KT19 156 CR109
River Island Cl, Lthd. (Fetch.) KT22 171 CD121
River La, Lthd. KT22 171 CD120
Richmond TW10 117 CK88
Rivermead, E.Mol. KT8 136 CC97
West Byfleet (Byfleet) KT14 152 BM113
Rivermead Cl, Add. KT15 152 BJ108
Teddington TW11 117 CH92
Rivermead Ct, SW6 99 CZ83
Rivermead Ho, E9
off Kingsmead Way 67 DY64
Rivermead Rd, N18 47 DX51
Rivermeads Av, Twick. TW2 116 CA90
Rivermill, SW1
off Grosvenor Rd 101 DK78
Rivermount, Walt. KT12 135 BT101
Rivernook Cl, Walt. KT12 136 BW99
River Pk Av, Stai. TW18 113 BD91
River Pk Gdns, Brom. BR2 123 ED94
River Pk Rd, N22 45 DM54
River Pl, N1 84 DQ66
River Reach, Tedd. TW11 117 CJ92
River Rd, Bark. IG11 87 ES68
Brentwood CM14 54 FS49
Buckhurst Hill IG9 48 EL46
Staines TW18 133 BF95
River Rd Business Pk, Bark. IG11 87 ET69
Riversdale, Grav. (Nthflt) DA11 130 GE89
Riversdale Rd, N5 65 DP62
Romford RM5 51 FB52
Thames Ditton KT7 137 CG99
Riversdell Cl, Cher. KT16 133 BF101
Riversfield Rd, Enf. EN1 30 DS41
Riverside, NW4 63 CV59
SE7 205 P7
Chertsey KT16 134 BG97
Dartford (Eyns.) DA4 148 FK103
Egham (Runny.) TW20 113 BA90
Richmond TW9
off Water La 117 CK85
St. Albans (Lon.Col.) AL2 10 CL27
Shepperton TW17 135 BS101
Staines TW18 133 BF95
Staines (Wrays.) TW19 112 AW87
Twickenham TW1 117 CH88
Riverside, The, E.Mol. KT8 137 CD97
Riverside Av, E.Mol. KT8 137 CD99
Riverside Business Cen, SW18 120 DB88
Tilbury RM18 111 GH84
Riverside Cl, E5 66 DW60
W7 79 CE70
Kings Langley WD4 7 BP29
Kingston upon Thames KT1 137 CK98
Orpington BR5 146 EW96
Staines TW18 133 BF95
Wallington SM6 141 DH104
Riverside Ct, E4
off Chelwood Cl 31 EB44
SW8 101 DK79
Riverside Dr, NW11 63 CY58
W4 98 CS80
Esher KT10 154 CA105
Mitcham CR4 140 DE99
Richmond TW10 117 CH89
Rickmansworth WD3 38 BK46
Staines (Egh.H.) TW18 113 BE92
Riverside Gdns, N3 63 CY55
W6 99 CV78
Enfield EN2 30 DQ40
Wembley HA0 80 CL68
Woking (Old Wok.) GU22 167 BB121
Riverside Ind Est, Bark. IG11 88 EU69
Dartford DA1 128 FL85
Enfield EN3 31 DY44
Riverside Mans, E1 202 F1
Riverside Pk, Wey. KT13 152 BL106
Riverside Path, Wal.Cr. (Chsht) EN8 *off Dewhurst Rd* 15 DY29
Riverside Pl, Stai. (Stanw.) TW19 114 BK86
Riverside Retail Pk, Sev. TN14 181 FH119
Riverside Rd, E15 85 EC68
N15 66 DU58
SW17 120 DB91
Sidcup DA14 126 EY90
Staines TW18 113 BF94
Staines (Stanw.) TW19 114 BK85
Walton-on-Thames KT12 154 BX105
Watford WD19 23 BV44
Riverside Twr, SW6 100 DC82
Riverside Wk, E14
off Ferry St 103 EC78
Bexley DA5 126 EW87
Isleworth TW7 97 CE83
Kingston upon Thames KT1 *off High St* 137 CK97
Loughton IG10 33 EP44
West Wickham BR4
off The Alders 143 EB102
Riverside Way, Dart. DA1 128 FL85
St. Albans AL2 9 CD32
Uxbridge UB8 76 BH67
Riverside W, SW18
off Smugglers Way 100 DB84
Riverside Yd, SW17 120 DC91
Riverstone Cl, Har. HA2 61 CD60
River St, EC1 196 D2
River Ter, W6 *off Crisp Rd* 99 CW78
Riverton Cl, W9 81 CZ69
River Vw, Enf. EN2
off Chase Side 30 DQ41
Grays RM16 111 GG77
Riverview Gdns, SW13 99 CV79
Cobham KT11 153 BU113
Twickenham TW1 117 CF89
Riverview Gro, W4 98 CP79
River Vw Hts, SE16 202 B4
RIVERVIEW PARK, Grav. DA12 131 GK92
Riverview Pk, SE6 123 EA89
Riverview Rd, W4 98 CP79
Epsom KT19 156 CQ105
Greenhithe DA9 129 FU85
River Wk, Uxb. (Denh.) UB9 58 BJ64
Walton-on-Thames KT12 135 BU100
Riverway, N13 45 DN50
River Way, Epsom KT19 156 CR106
Loughton IG10 33 EN44
Riverway, Stai. TW18 134 BH95
River Way, Twick. TW2 116 CB89
River Wey Navigation, Wok. GU23 167 BB122
Riverwood La, Chis. BR7 145 ER95
Rivet Ho, SE1
off Rowcross St 102 DT77
Rivey Cl, W.Byf. KT14 151 BF114
Rivington Av, Wdf.Grn. IG8 48 EK54
Rivington Ct, NW10 81 CU67
Rivington Cres, NW7 43 CT52
Rivington Pl, EC2 197 N3
Rivington St, EC2 197 M3
Rivington Wk, E8
off Wilde Cl 84 DU67
Rivulet Rd, N17 46 DQ52
Rixon Cl, Slou. (Geo.Grn) SL3 74 AY72
Rixon Ho, SE18
off Barnfield Rd 105 EP79
Rixon St, N7 65 DN62
Rixsen Rd, E12 68 EL64
Roach Rd, E3 85 EA66
Roads Pl, N19 *off Hornsey Rd* 65 DL61
Roakes Av, Add. KT15 134 BH103
Roan St, SE10 103 EC79
Robarts Cl, Pnr. HA5
off Field End Rd 59 BV57
Robb Rd, Stan. HA7 41 CG51
Robert Adam St, W1 194 F8
Roberta St, E2 84 DU69
Robert Burns Ms, SE24
off Mayall Rd 121 DP85
Robert Cl, W9
off Randolph Av 82 DC70
Chigwell IG7 49 ET50
Potters Bar EN6 11 CY33
Walton-on-Thames KT12 153 BV106
Robert Dashwood Way, SE17 201 H9
Robert Keen Cl, SE15
off Cicely Rd 102 DU81
Robert Lowe Cl, SE14 103 DX80
Roberton Dr, Brom. BR1 144 EJ95

★ Place of interest ⇌ Railway station ⊖ London Underground station DLR Docklands Light Railway station Tra Tramlink station H Hospital Riv Pedestrian ferry landing stage

Robert Owen Ho, SW6 ...99 CX81
Robertsbridge Rd, Cars.
SM5 ...140 DC102
Roberts Cl, SE9 ...125 ER88
SE16 ...203 J5
Barking IG11
off Tanner St ...87 EQ65
Orpington BR5
off Sholden Gdns ...146 EW99
Romford RM3 ...51 FH53
Staines (Stanw.) TW19 ...114 BJ86
Sutton SM3 ...157 CX108
Thornton Heath CR7
off Kitchener Rd ...142 DR97
Waltham Cross (Chsht) EN8
off Norwood Rd ...15 DY30
West Drayton UB7 ...76 BL74
Roberts La, Ger.Cr. (Chal.St.P.)
SL9 ...37 BA50
Roberts Ms, SW1 ...198 F7
Orpington BR6 ...146 EU102
Robertson Cl, Brox. EN10 ...15 DY26
Robertson Ct, Wok. GU21 ...166 AS118
Robertson Rd, E15 ...85 EC67
Robertson St, SW8 ...101 DH83
Robert's Pl, EC1 ...196 E4
Roberts Pl, Dag. RM10 ...88 FA65
Robert Sq, SE13
off Bonfield Rd ...103 EC84
Roberts Rd, E17 ...47 EB53
NW7 ...43 CY51
Belvedere DA17 ...106 FA78
Watford WD18
off Tucker St ...24 BW43
Robert St, E16 ...87 EP74
NW1 ...195 J3
SE18 ...105 ER77
WC2 ...200 A1
Croydon CR0 off High St ...142 DQ104
Roberts Way, Egh. (Eng.Grn)
TW20 ...112 AW94
Roberts Wd Dr, Ger.Cr.
(Chal.St.P.) SL9 ...37 AZ50
Robeson St, E3
off Ackroyd Dr ...85 DZ71
Robeson Way, Borwd. WD6 ...26 CQ39
Robina Cl, Bexh. DA6 ...106 EX84
Northwood HA6 ...39 BT53
Robin Cl, NW7 ...42 CS48
Addlestone KT15 ...152 BK106
Hampton TW12 ...116 BY92
Romford RM5 ...51 FD52
Robin Ct, SE16 ...202 B8
Wallington SM6
off Carew Rd ...159 DJ107
Robin Cres, E6 ...86 EK71
Robin Gdns, Red. RH1 ...184 DG131
Robin Gro, N6 ...64 DG61
Brentford TW8 ...97 CJ79
Harrow HA3 ...62 CM58
Robin Hill Dr, Chis. BR7 ...124 EL93
Robin Hood, SW15
off Robin Hood Way ...118 CS90
Robinhood Cl, Mitch. CR4 ...141 DJ97
Robin Hood Cl, Wok. GU21 ...166 AT118
Robin Hood Cres, Wok.
(Knap.) GU21 ...166 AS117
Robin Hood Dr, Bushey WD23 .24 BZ39
Harrow HA3 ...41 CF52
Robin Hood Gdns, E14
off Woolmore St ...85 EC73
Robin Hood Grn, Orp. BR5 ...146 EU99
Robin Hood La, E14 ...85 EC73
SW15 ...118 CS91
Bexleyheath DA6 ...126 EY85
Guildford (Sutt.Grn) GU4 .167 AZ124
Robinhood La, Mitch. CR4 ...141 DJ97
Robin Hood La, Sutt. SM1 ...158 DA106
Robin Hood Rd, SW19 ...119 CV92
Brentwood CM15 ...54 FV45
Woking GU21 ...166 AT118
Robin Hood Way, SW15 ...118 CS91
SW20 ...118 CS91
Greenford UB6 ...79 CF65
Robin Ho, NW8
off Newcourt St ...82 DE68
Robinia Av, Grav. (Nthflt)
DA11 ...130 GD87
Robinia Cl, SE20
off Sycamore Gro ...142 DU95
Ilford IG6 ...49 ES51
Robinia Cres, E10 ...67 EB61
Robin La, NW4 ...63 CX55
Robins Cl, St.Alb. (Lon.Col.)
AL2 off High St ...10 CL27
Uxbridge UB8 off Newcourt .76 BJ71
Robins Ct, SE12 ...124 EJ90
Robinscroft Ms, SE10
off Sparta St ...103 EB81
Robins Gro, W.Wick. BR4 ...144 EG104
Robins La, Epp. (They.B.)
CM16 ...33 EQ36
Robinson Av, Wal.Cr.
(Chsht) EN7 ...13 DP28
Robinson Cl, E11 ...68 EE62
Enfield EN2 ...30 DQ41
Hornchurch RM12 ...89 FH66
Robinson Cres, Bushey
(Bushey Hth) WD23 ...40 CC46
Robinson Ho, W10
off Bramley Rd ...81 CX73
Robinson Rd, E2 ...84 DW68
SW17 ...120 DE93
Dagenham RM10 ...70 FA63
Robinsons Cl, W13 ...79 CG71
Robinson St, SW3
off Christchurch St ...100 DF79
Robins Orchard, Ger.Cr.
(Chal.St.P.) SL9 ...36 AY51
Robinsway, Wal.Abb. EN9
off Roundhills ...16 EE34
Walton-on-Thames KT12 .154 BW105
Robin Way, Orp. BR5 ...146 EV97
Potters Bar (Cuffley) EN6 ...13 DL28
Staines TW18 ...113 BF90
Robin Willis Way, Wind.
(Old Wind.) SL4 ...112 AU86
Robinwood Gro, Uxb. UB8 ...76 BM70
Robinwood Pl, SW15 ...118 CR91
Roborough Wk, Horn. RM12 ...90 FJ65
Robsart St, SW9 ...101 DM82
Robson Av, NW10 ...81 CU67
Robson Cl, E6
off Linton Gdns ...86 EL72
Enfield EN2 ...29 DP40
Gerrards Cross (Chal.St.P.)
SL9 ...36 AY50
Robson Rd, SE27 ...121 DP90
Robsons Cl, Wal.Cr. EN8 ...14 DW29
Robyns Cft, Grav. (Nthflt)
DA11 ...130 GE90
Robyns Way, Sev. TN13 ...190 FF122
Rocastle Rd, SE4 ...123 DY85
Roch Av, Edg. HA8 ...42 CM54
Rochdale Rd, E17 ...67 EA59
SE2 ...106 EV78
Rochdale Way, SE8
off Octavius St ...103 EA80
Rochelle Cl, SW11 ...100 DD84
Rochelle St, E2 ...197 P3
Rochemont Wk, E8
off Pownall Rd ...84 DT67
Roche Rd, SW16 ...141 DM95
Rochester Av, E13 ...86 EJ67
Bromley BR1 ...144 EH96
Feltham TW13 ...115 BT89
Rochester Cl, SW16 ...121 DL94
Enfield EN1 ...30 DS39
Sidcup DA15 ...126 EV86
Rochester Dr, Bex. DA5 ...126 EZ86
Pinner HA5 ...60 BX57
Watford WD25 ...8 BW34
Rochester Gdns, Cat. CR3 ...176 DS122
Croydon CR0 ...142 DS104
Ilford IG1 ...69 EM59
Rochester Ms, NW1 ...83 DJ66
Rochester Pl, NW1 ...83 DJ65
Rochester Rd, NW1 ...83 DJ65
Carshalton SM5 ...158 DF105
Dartford DA1 ...128 FN87
Gravesend DA12 ...131 GL87
Hornchurch RM12 ...89 FH66
Northwood HA6 ...59 BT55
Staines TW18 ...113 BD92
Rochester Row, SW1 ...199 L8
Rochester Sq, NW1 ...83 DJ66
Rochester St, SW1 ...199 M7
Rochester Ter, NW1 ...83 DJ65
Rochester Wk, SE1 ...201 K2
Rochester Way, SE3 ...104 EH81
SE9 ...105 EM83
Dartford DA1 ...127 FD87
Rickmansworth (Crox.Grn)
WD3 ...23 BP42
Rochester Way Relief Rd,
SE3 ...104 EH81
SE9 ...104 EL84
Roche Wk, Cars. SM5 ...140 DD100
Rochford Av, Brwd. (Shenf.)
CM15 ...55 GA43
Loughton IG10 ...33 EQ41
Romford RM6 ...70 EW57
Waltham Abbey EN9 ...15 ED33
Rochford Cl, E6
off Boleyn Rd ...86 EK68
Broxbourne EN10 ...15 DY26
Hornchurch RM12 ...89 FH65
Rochford Grn, Loug. IG10 ...33 EQ41
Rochfords Gdns, Slou. SL2 ...74 AW74
Rochford St, NW5 ...64 DF64
Rochford Wk, E8
off Wilman Gro ...84 DU66
Rochford Way, Croy. CR0 ...141 DL100
Rockall Ct, Slou. SL3 ...93 BB76
Rock Av, SW14
off South Worple Way ...98 CR83
Rockbourne Rd, SE23 ...123 DX88
Rockchase Gdns, Horn. RM11 .72 FL58
★ Rock Circ, W1 ...199 M1
Rock Cl, Mitch. CR4 ...140 DD96
Rockdale Rd, Sev. TN13 ...191 FH125
Rockells Pl, SE22 ...122 DV86
Rockfield Cl, Oxt. RH8 ...188 EF131
Rockfield Rd, Oxt. RH8 ...188 EF129
Rockford Av, Grnf. UB6 ...79 CG68
Rock Gdns, Dag. RM10 ...71 FB64
Rock Gro Way, SE16 ...202 C8
Rockhall Rd, NW2 ...63 CX63
Rockhall Way, NW2
off Midland Ter ...63 CX62
Rockhampton Cl, SE27 ...121 DN91
Rockhampton Rd, SE27 ...121 DN91
South Croydon CR2 ...160 DS107
Rock Hill, SE26 ...122 DT91
Orpington BR6 ...164 FA107
Rockingham Av, Horn. RM11 .71 FH58
Rockingham Cl, SW15 ...99 CT84
Uxbridge UB8 ...76 BJ67
Rockingham Est, SE1 ...201 H7
Rockingham Par, Uxb. UB8 ...76 BJ66
Rockingham Rd, Uxb. UB8 ...76 BH67
Rockingham St, SE1 ...201 H7
Rockland Rd, SW15 ...99 CY84
Rocklands Dr, Stan. HA7 ...41 CH54
Rockleigh Ct, Brwd. (Shenf.)
CM15 ...55 GA45
Rockley Rd, W14 ...99 CX75
Rockliffe Av, Kings L. WD4 ...6 BN30
Rockmount Rd, SE18 ...105 ET78
SE19 ...122 DR93
Rockshaw Rd, Red.
(Merst.) RH1 ...185 DM127
Rocks La, SW13 ...99 CU81
Rock St, N4 ...65 DN61
Rockware Av, Grnf. UB6 ...79 CD67
Rockways, Barn. EN5 ...27 CT44
Rockwell Gdns, SE19 ...122 DS92
Rockwell Rd, Dag. RM10 ...71 FB64
Rockwood Pl, W12 ...99 CW75
Rocky La, Reig. RH2 ...184 DF128
Rocliffe St, N1 ...196 G1
Rocombe Cres, SE23 ...122 DW87
Rocque La, SE3 ...104 EF83
Rodborough Rd, NW11 ...64 DA60
Roden Ct, N6 off Hornsey La .65 DK59
Roden Gdns, Croy. CR0 ...142 DS100
Rodenhurst Rd, SW4 ...121 DJ86
Roden St, N7 ...65 DM62
Ilford IG1 ...69 EN62
Rodeo Cl, Erith DA8 ...107 FH81
Roderick Rd, NW3 ...64 DF63
Rodgers Cl, Borwd. (Els.) WD6 .25 CK44
Roding Av, Wdf.Grn. IG8 ...48 EL51
Roding Gdns, Loug. IG10 ...32 EL44
Roding La, Buck.H. IG9 ...48 EL46
Chigwell IG7 ...49 EN46
Roding La N, Wdf.Grn. IG8 ...48 EK54
Roding La S, Ilf. IG4 ...68 EK56
Woodford Green IG8 ...68 EK56
Roding Ms, E1 ...202 C2
Roding Rd, E5 ...67 DX63
E6 ...87 EP71
Loughton IG10 ...32 EL43
Rodings, The, Upmin. RM14 ...73 FR58
Woodford Green IG8 ...48 EJ51
Rodings Row, Barn. EN5
off Leecroft Rd ...27 CY43
Roding Trd Est, Bark. IG11 ...87 EP66
⊖ Roding Valley ...48 EK49
Roding Vw, Buck.H. IG9 ...48 EK46
Roding Way, Rain. RM13 ...90 FK68
Rodmarton St, W1 ...194 E7
Rodmell Cl, Hayes UB4 ...78 BY70
Rodmell Slope, N12 ...43 CZ50
Rodmere St, SE10
off Trafalgar Rd ...104 EE78
Rodmill La, SW2 ...121 DL87
Rodney Cl, Croy. CR0 ...141 DP102
New Malden KT3 ...138 CS99
Pinner HA5 ...60 BY59
Walton-on-Thames KT12 .136 BW102
Rodney Ct, W9 off Maida Vale .82 DC70
Rodney Gdns, Pnr. HA5 ...59 BV57
West Wickham BR4 ...162 EG105
Rodney Grn, Walt. KT12 ...136 BW103
Rodney Pl, E17 ...47 DY54
SE17 ...201 J8
SW19 ...140 DC95
Rodney Rd, E11 ...68 EH56
SE17 ...201 J8
Mitcham CR4 ...140 DE96
New Malden KT3 ...138 CS99
Twickenham TW2 ...116 CA86
Walton-on-Thames KT12 .136 BW103
Rodney St, N1 ...83 DM68
Rodney Way, Rom. RM7 ...50 FA53
Slough (Colnbr.) SL3 ...93 BE81
Rodona Rd, Wey. KT13 ...153 BR111
Rodway Rd, SW15 ...119 CU87
Bromley BR1 ...144 EH95
Rodwell Cl, Ruis. HA4 ...60 BW60
Rodwell Ct, Add. KT15
off Garfield Rd ...152 BJ105
Rodwell Pl, Edg. HA8
off Whitchurch La ...42 CN51
Rodwell Rd, SE22 ...122 DT86
Roebourne Way, E16 ...105 EN75
Roebuck Cl, Ashtd. KT21 ...172 CL120
Feltham TW13 ...115 BV91
Reigate RH2 ...184 DB134
Roebuck La, N17 off High Rd .46 DT51
Buckhurst Hill IG9 ...48 EJ45
Roebuck Rd, Chess. KT9 ...156 CN106
Ilford IG6 ...50 EV50
Roedean Av, Enf. EN3 ...30 DW39
Roedean Cl, Enf. EN3 ...30 DW39
Orpington BR6 ...164 EV105
Roedean Cres, SW15 ...118 CS86
Roedean Dr, Rom. RM1 ...71 FE56
Roe End, NW9 ...62 CQ56
Roe Grn, NW9 ...62 CQ57
ROEHAMPTON, SW15 ...119 CU85
Roehampton Cl, SW15 ...99 CU84
Gravesend DA12 ...131 GL87
Roehampton Dr, Chis. BR7 ...125 EQ93
Roehampton Gate, SW15 ...118 CS86
Roehampton High St, SW15 .119 CV87
Roehampton La, SW15 ...99 CU84
Roehampton Vale, SW15 ...118 CS90
Roe La, NW9 ...62 CP56
Roe Way, Wall. SM6 ...159 DL107
Rofant Rd, Nthwd. HA6 ...39 BS51
Roffes La, Cat. (Chaldon)
CR3 ...176 DR124
Roffey Cl, Pur. CR8 ...175 DP116
Roffey St, E14 ...204 D5
Roffords, Wok. GU21 ...166 AV117
Rogate Ho, E5 off Muir Rd ...66 DU62
Roger Dowley Ct, E2 ...84 DW68
Rogers Cl, Cat. CR3
off Tillingdown Hill ...176 DV122
Coulsdon CR5 ...175 DP118
Waltham Cross (Chsht) EN7 .14 DR26
Rogers Ct, Swan. BR8 ...147 FG98
Rogers Est, E2 off Globe Rd ...84 DW69
Rogers Gdns, Dag. RM10 ...70 FA64
Rogers Ho, SW1 off Page St .101 DK77
Rogers La, Slou. (Stoke P.) SL2 .74 AT67
Warlingham CR6 ...177 DZ118
Rogers Mead, Gdse. RH9
off Ivy Mill La ...186 DV132
Rogers Rd, E16 ...86 EF72
SW17 ...120 DD91
Dagenham RM10 ...70 FA64
Grays RM17 ...110 GC77
Rogers Ruff, Nthwd. HA6 ...39 BQ53
Roger St, WC1 ...196 C5
Rogers Wk, N12
off Holden Rd ...44 DB48
Rojack Rd, SE23 ...123 DX88
Rokeby Ct, Wok. GU21 ...166 AT117
Rokeby Gdns, Wdf.Grn. IG8 ...48 EG53
Rokeby Pl, SW20 ...119 CV94
Rokeby Rd, SE4 ...103 DZ82
Rokeby St, E15 ...86 EE67
Roke Cl, Ken. CR8 ...160 DQ114
Roke Lo Rd, Ken. CR8 ...159 DP113
Roke Rd, Ken. CR8 ...176 DQ115
Roker Pk Av, Uxb. UB10 ...58 BL63
Rokesby Cl, Well. DA16 ...105 ER82
Rokesby Pl, Wem. HA0 ...61 CK64
Rokesly Av, N8 ...65 DL57
Roland Gdns, SW7 ...100 DC78
Feltham TW13 ...116 BY90
Roland Ms, E1
off Stepney Grn ...85 DX71
Roland Rd, E17 ...67 ED56
Roland Way, SE17 ...102 DR78
SW7 off Roland Gdns ...100 DC78
Worcester Park KT4 ...139 CT103
Roles Gro, Rom. RM6 ...70 EX56
Rolfe Cl, Barn. EN4 ...28 DE42
Rolinsden Way, Kes. BR2 ...162 EK105
Rollesby Rd, Chess. KT9 ...156 CN107
Rollesby Way, SE28 ...88 EW73
Rolleston Av, Orp. BR5 ...145 EP100
Rolleston Cl, Orp. BR5 ...145 EP101
Rolleston Rd, S.Croy. CR2 ...160 DR108
Roll Gdns, Ilf. IG2 ...69 EN57
Rollins St, SE15 ...102 DW79
Rollit Cres, Houns. TW3 ...116 CA85
Rollit St, N7 off Hornsey Rd ...65 DN64
Rollo Rd, Swan. BR8 ...127 FF94
Rolls Bldgs, EC4 ...196 D8
Rollscourt Av, SE24 ...122 DQ85
Rolls Pk Av, E4 ...47 EA51
Rolls Pk Rd, E4 ...47 EB50
Rolls Pas, EC4 ...196 D8
Rolls Rd, SE1 ...202 A10
Rolt St, SE8 ...103 DY79
Rolvenden Gdns, Brom. BR1 .124 EK94
Rolvenden Pl, N17 ...46 DU52
★ Roman Bath, WC2
off Strand La ...196 C10
Roman Cl, W3
off Avenue Gdns ...98 CP75
Feltham TW14 ...116 BW85
Rainham RM13 ...89 FD68
Uxbridge (Hare.) UB9 ...38 BH53
Romanfield Rd, SW2 ...121 DM87
Roman Gdns, Kings L. WD4 ...7 BP30
Roman Ho, Rain. RM13
off Roman Cl ...89 FD68
Romanhurst Av, Brom. BR2 .144 EE98
Romanhurst Gdns, Brom.
BR2 ...144 EE98
Roman Ind Est, Croy. CR0 ...142 DS101
Roman Ri, SE19 ...122 DR93
Roman Rd, E2 ...84 DW69
E3 ...85 DY68
E6 ...86 EL70
N10 ...45 DH52
NW2 ...63 CW62
W4 ...98 CS77
Brentwood CM15 ...55 GC41
Gravesend (Nthflt) DA11 ...130 GC90
Ilford IG1 ...87 EP65
Roman Sq, SE28 ...88 EU74
Romans Way, Wok. GU22 ...168 BG115
Roman Vil Rd, Dart. (S.Darenth)
DA2, DA4 ...128 FQ92
Roman Way, N7 ...83 DM65
SE15 off Clifton Way ...102 DW80
Carshalton SM5 ...158 DF109
Croydon CR0 ...141 DP103
Dartford DA1 ...127 FE85
Enfield EN1 ...30 DT43
Waltham Abbey EN9 ...31 EB35
Roman Way Ind Est, N1
off Offord St ...83 DM66
Romany Gdns, E17
off McEntee Av ...47 DY53
Sutton SM3 ...140 DA101
Romany Ri, Orp. BR5 ...145 EQ102
Roma Read Cl, SW15
off Bessborough Rd ...119 CV87
Roma Rd, E17 ...67 DY55
Romberg Rd, SW17 ...120 DG90
Romborough Gdns, SE13 ...123 EC85
Romborough Way, SE13 ...123 EC85
Rom Cres, Rom. RM7 ...71 FF59
Romeland, Borwd. (Els.) WD6 .25 CK44
Waltham Abbey EN9 ...15 EC33
Romero Cl, SW9
off Stockwell Rd ...101 DM83
Romero Sq, SE3 ...104 EJ84
Romeyn Rd, SW16 ...121 DM90
ROMFORD, RM1 - RM7 ...71 FF57
⇌ Romford ...71 FE58
Romford Rd, E7 ...68 EH64
E12 ...68 EL63
E15 ...86 EE66
Chigwell IG7 ...50 EU48
Romford RM5 ...50 EY52
South Ockendon (Aveley)
RM15 ...90 FQ73
Romford St, E1 ...84 DU71
Romilly Dr, Wat. WD19 ...40 BY49
Romilly Rd, N4 ...65 DP61
Romilly St, W1 ...195 M10
Rommany Rd, SE27 ...122 DR91
Romney Chase, Horn. RM11 ...72 FM58
Romney Cl, N17 ...46 DV53
NW11 ...64 DC60
SE14 off Kender St ...102 DW80
Ashford TW15 ...115 BQ92
Chessington KT9 ...156 CL105
Harrow HA2 ...60 CA59
Romney Dr, Brom. BR1 ...124 EK94
Harrow HA2 ...60 CA59
Romney Gdns, Bexh. DA7 ...106 EZ81
Romney Lock, Wind. SL4 ...92 AS79
Romney Ms, W1 ...194 F6
Romney Par, Hayes UB4
off Romney Rd ...77 BR68
Romney Rd, SE10 ...103 EC79
Gravesend (Nthflt) DA11 ...130 GE90
Hayes UB4 ...77 BR68
New Malden KT3 ...138 CR100
Romney Row, NW2
off Brent Ter ...63 CX61
Romney St, SW1 ...199 N7
Romola Rd, SE24 ...121 DP88
Romsey Cl, Orp. BR6 ...163 EP105
Slough SL3 ...93 AZ76
Romsey Gdns, Dag. RM9 ...88 EX67
Romsey Rd, W13 ...79 CG73
Dagenham RM9 ...88 EX67
Romside Pl, Rom. RM7
off Brooklands La ...71 FD56
Romulus Ct, Brent. TW8
off Justin Cl ...97 CK80
Rom Valley Way, Rom. RM7 ...71 FE59
Ronald Av, E15 ...86 EE69
Ronald Cl, Beck. BR3 ...143 DZ98
Ronald Ct, St.Alb. AL2 ...8 BY29
Ronald Ho, SE3
off Cambert Way ...104 EJ84
Ronald Rd, Rom. RM3 ...52 FN53
Ronaldsay Spur, Slou. SL1 ...74 AS71
Ronalds Rd, N5 ...65 DN64
Bromley BR1 ...144 EG95
Ronaldstone Rd, Sid.
DA15 ...125 ES86
Ronald St, E1
off Devonport St ...84 DW72
Rona Rd, NW3 ...64 DG63
Ronart St, Har. (Wealds.) HA3
off Stuart Rd ...61 CF55
Rona Wk, N1 off Ramsey Wk ...84 DR65
Rondu Rd, NW2 ...63 CY64
Ronelean Rd, Surb. KT6 ...138 CM104
Roneo Cor, Horn. RM12 ...71 FF60
Roneo Link, Horn. RM12 ...71 FF60
Ronfearn Av, Orp. BR5 ...146 EX99
Ron Grn Ct, Erith DA8 ...107 FD79
Ron Leighton Way, E6 ...86 EL67
Ronneby Cl, Wey. KT13 ...135 BS104
Ronnie La, E12 off Walton Rd .69 EN63
Ronson Way, Lthd. KT22 ...171 CG121
Ronver Rd, SE12 ...124 EF87
Rood La, EC3 ...197 M10
Roof of the World Caravan Pk,
Tad. (Box H.) KT20 ...182 CP132
Rookby Ct, N21 ...45 DP47
Rook Cl, Horn. RM12 ...89 FG66
Wembley HA9 ...62 CP62
Rookdean, Sev. (Chipstead)
TN13 ...190 FC122
Rookeries Cl, Felt. TW13 ...115 BV90
Rookery, The, Grays RM20 ...109 FU79
Rookery Cl, NW9 ...63 CT57
Leatherhead (Fetch.) KT22 ...171 CE124
Rookery Ct, Grays RM20 ...109 FU79
Rookery Cres, Dag. RM10 ...89 FB66
Rookery Dr, Chis. BR7 ...145 EN95
Rookery Gdns, Orp. BR5 ...146 EW99
Rookery Hill, Ashtd. KT21 ...172 CN118
Rookery La, Brom. BR2 ...144 EK100
Grays RM17 ...110 GD78
Rookery Mead, Couls. CR5 ...175 DK122
Rookery Rd, SW4 ...101 DJ84
Orpington BR6 ...163 EM110
Staines TW18 ...114 BH92
Rookery Vw, Grays RM17 ...110 GD78
Rookery Way, NW9 ...63 CT57
Tadworth (Lwr Kgswd)
KT20 ...183 CZ127
Rookesley Rd, Orp. BR5 ...146 EX101
Rooke Way, SE10 ...205 K10
Rookfield Av, N10 ...65 DJ56
Rookfield Cl, N10
off Cranmore Way ...65 DJ56
Rook La, Cat. (Chaldon) CR3 ...175 DM124
Rookley Cl, Sutt. SM2 ...158 DB110
Rooks Hill, Rick. (Loud.)
WD3 ...22 BK42
Rooksmead Rd, Sun. TW16 ...135 BT96
Rooks Nest, Gdse. RH9 ...187 DY130
Rookstone Rd, SW17 ...120 DF92
Rook Wk, E6
off Allhallows Rd ...86 EL72
Rookwood Av, Loug. IG10 ...33 EQ41
New Malden KT3 ...139 CU98
Wallington SM6 ...159 DK105
Rookwood Cl, Grays RM17 ...110 GB77
Redhill RH1 ...185 DH129
Rookwood Gdns, E4
off Whitehall Rd ...48 EF46
Loughton IG10 ...33 EQ41
Rookwood Ho, Bark. IG11
off St. Marys ...87 ER68
Rookwood Rd, N16 ...66 DT59
★ Roosevelt Mem, W1 ...194 G10
Roosevelt Way, Dag. RM10 ...89 FD65
Rootes Dr, W10 ...81 CX70
Ropemaker Rd, SE16 ...203 K5
Ropemakers Flds, E14 ...203 M1
Ropemaker St, EC2 ...197 K6
Roper La, SE1 ...201 N5
Ropers Av, E4 ...47 EC50
Ropers Orchard, SW3
off Danvers St ...100 DE79
Roper St, SE9 ...125 EM86
Ropers Wk, SW2
off Brockwell Pk Gdns ...121 DN87
Roper Way, Mitch. CR4 ...140 DG96
Ropery St, E3 ...85 DZ70
Rope St, SE16 ...203 L7
Rope Wk, Sun. TW16 ...136 BW97
Rope Wk Gdns, E1
off Commercial Rd ...84 DU72
Ropewalk Ms, E8
off Middleton Rd ...84 DT66
Rope Yd Rails, SE18 ...105 EP76
Ropley St, E2 ...84 DU68
Rosa Alba Ms, N5
off Kelross Rd ...66 DQ63
Rosa Av, Ashf. TW15 ...114 BN91
Rosaline Rd, SW6 ...99 CY80
Rosamond St, SE26 ...122 DV90
Rosamund Cl, S.Croy. CR2 ...160 DR105
Rosamun St, Sthl. UB2 ...96 BY77
Rosary, The, Egh. TW20 ...133 BD96
Rosary Cl, Houns. TW3 ...96 BY82
Rosary Ct, Pot.B. EN6 ...12 DB30
Rosary Gdns, SW7 ...100 DC77
Ashford TW15 ...115 BP91
Bushey WD23 ...41 CE45
Rosaville Rd, SW6 ...99 CZ80
Roscoe St, EC1 ...197 J5
Roscoff Cl, Edg. HA8 ...42 CQ53
Roseacre, Oxt. RH8 ...188 EG134
Roseacre Cl, W13
off Middlefielde ...79 CH71
Hornchurch RM11 ...72 FM60
Shepperton TW17 ...134 BN99
Roseacre Rd, Well. DA16 ...106 EV83
Rose All, EC2
off Bishopsgate ...84 DS71
SE1 ...201 J2
Rose & Crown Ct, EC2 ...197 H8
Rose & Crown Yd, SW1 ...199 L2
Roseary Cl, West Dr. UB7 ...94 BK77
Rose Av, E18 ...48 EH54
Gravesend DA12 ...131 GL88
Mitcham CR4 ...140 DF95
Morden SM4 ...140 DC99
Rosebank, SE20 ...122 DV94
Rose Bk, Brwd. CM14 ...54 FX48
Rosebank, Epsom KT18 ...156 CQ114
Waltham Abbey EN9 ...16 EE33
Rosebank Av, Horn. RM12 ...72 FJ64
Wembley HA0 ...61 CF63
Rosebank Cl, N12 ...44 DE50
Teddington TW11 ...117 CG93
Rose Bk Cotts, Wok. GU22 ...166 AY122
Rosebank Gdns, E3 ...85 DZ68
Gravesend (Nthflt) DA11 ...130 GE88
Rosebank Gro, E17 ...67 DZ55

★ Place of interest ⇌ Railway station ⊖ London Underground station DLR Docklands Light Railway station Tra Tramlink station H Hospital RIV Pedestrian ferry landing stage

Rosebank Rd, E17 .... 67 EB58
W7 .... 97 CE75
Rosebank Vil, E17 .... 67 EA56
Rosebank Wk, NW1
off Maiden La 83 DK66
SE18 *off Woodhill* 104 EL77
Rosebank Way, W3 .... 80 CR72
Rose Bates Dr, NW9 .... 62 CN56
Roseberry Cl, Upmin. RM14 .. 73 FT58
Roseberry Ct, Wat. WD17
off Grandfield Av 23 BU39
Roseberry Gdns, N4 .... 65 DP58
Dartford DA1 .... 128 FJ87
Orpington BR6 .... 145 ES104
Upminster RM14 .... 73 FT59
Roseberry Pl, E8 .... 84 DT65
Roseberry St, SE16 .... 202 D9
Rosebery Av, E12 .... 86 EL65
EC1 .... 196 D5
N17 .... 46 DU54
Epsom KT17 .... 156 CS114
Harrow HA2 .... 60 BZ63
New Malden KT3 .... 139 CT96
Sidcup DA15 .... 125 ES87
Thornton Heath CR7 .... 142 DQ96
Rosebery Cl, Mord. SM4 .... 139 CX100
Rosebery Ct, EC1
off Rosebery Av 83 DN70
Gravesend (Nthflt) DA11 .. 131 GF88
Rosebery Cres, Wok. GU22 .. 167 AZ121
Rosebery Gdns, N8 .... 65 DL57
W13 .... 79 CG72
Sutton SM1 .... 158 DB105
Rosebery Ms, N10 .... 45 DJ54
SW2 *off Rosebery Rd* 121 DL86
Rosebery Rd, N9 .... 46 DU48
N10 .... 45 DJ54
SW2 .... 121 DL86
Bushey WD23 .... 40 CB45
Epsom KT18 .... 172 CR119
Grays RM17 .... 110 FY79
Hounslow TW3 .... 116 CC85
Kingston upon Thames
KT1 .... 138 CP96
Sutton SM1 .... 157 CZ107
Rosebery Sq, EC1 .... 196 D5
Kingston upon Thames
KT1 .... 138 CN96
Rosebine Av, Twick. TW2 .... 117 CD87
Rosebriar Cl, Wok. GU22 .... 168 BG116
Rosebriars, Cat. CR3 .... 176 DS120
Esher KT10 .... 154 CC106
Rosebriar Wk, Wat. WD24 .... 23 BT36
Rosebury Rd, SW6 .... 100 DB82
Rosebury Sq, Wdf.Grn. IG8 .. 49 EN52
Rosebury Vale, Ruis. HA4 .... 59 BT60
Rose Bushes, Epsom KT17 .. 173 CV116
Rose Ct, E1 .... 197 P7
Pinner HA5
off Nursery Rd 60 BW55
Waltham Cross EN7 .... 14 DU27
Rosecourt Rd, Croy. CR0 .. 141 DM100
Rosecroft Av, NW3 .... 64 DA62
Rosecroft Cl, Orp. BR5 .... 146 EW100
Westerham (Bigg.H.) TN16
off Lotus Rd 179 EM118
Rosecroft Dr, Wat. WD17 .... 23 BS36
Rosecroft Gdns, NW2 .... 63 CU62
Twickenham TW2 .... 117 CD88
Rosecroft Rd, Sthl. UB1 .... 78 CA70
Rosecroft Wk, Pnr. HA5 .... 60 BX57
Wembley HA0 .... 61 CK64
Rosedale, Ashtd. KT21 .... 171 CJ118
Caterham CR3 .... 176 DS123
Rose Dale, Orp. BR6 .... 145 EP103
Rosedale Av, Hayes UB3 .... 77 BR71
Waltham Cross (Chsht) EN7 .14 DT29
Rosedale Cl, SE2
off Finchale Rd 106 EV76
W7 *off Boston Rd* 97 CF75
Dartford DA2 .... 128 FP87
St. Albans (Brick.Wd) AL2 .. 8 BY30
Stanmore HA7 .... 41 CH51
Rosedale Ct, N5 .... 65 DP63
Rosedale Dr, Dag. RM9 .... 88 EV67
Rosedale Gdns, Dag. RM9 .... 88 EV66
Rosedale Pl, Croy. CR0 .... 143 DX101
Rosedale Rd, E7 .... 68 EJ64
Dagenham RM9 .... 88 EV66
Epsom KT17 .... 157 CU106
Grays RM17 .... 110 GD78
Richmond TW9 .... 98 CL84
Romford RM1 .... 51 FC54
Rosedale Ter, W6
off Dalling Rd 99 CV76
Rosedale Way, Wal.Cr.
(Chsht) EN7 .... 14 DU29
Rosedene, NW6 .... 81 CX67
Rosedene Av, SW16 .... 121 DM90
Croydon CR0 .... 141 DM101
Greenford UB6 .... 78 CA69
Morden SM4 .... 140 DA99
Rosedene Ct, Dart. DA1
off Shepherds La 128 FJ87
Ruislip HA4 .... 59 BS60
Rosedene Gdns, Ilf. IG2 .... 69 EN56
Rosedene Ter, E10 .... 67 EB61
Rosedew Rd, W6 .... 99 CX79
Rose Dr, Chesh. HP5 .... 4 AS32
Rose End, Wor.Pk. KT4 .... 139 CX102
Rosefield, Sev. TN13 .... 190 FG124
Rosefield Cl, Cars. SM5 .... 158 DE106
Rosefield Gdns, E14 .... 85 EA73
Chertsey (Ott.) KT16 .... 151 BD107
Rosefield Rd, Stai. TW18 .... 114 BG91
Roseford Ct, W12 .... 99 CX75
Rose Gdn Cl, Edg. HA8 .... 42 CL51
Rose Gdns, W5 .... 97 CK76
Feltham TW13 .... 115 BU89
Southall UB1 .... 78 CA70
Staines (Stanw.) TW19
off Diamedes Av 114 BK87
Watford WD18 .... 23 BU43
Rose Glen, NW9 .... 62 CR56
Romford RM7 .... 71 FE60
Rosehart Ms, W11
off Westbourne Gro 82 DA72
Rosehatch Av, Rom. RM6 .... 70 EX55
Roseheath Rd, Houns. TW4 .. 116 BZ85
ROSEHILL, Sutt. SM1 .... 140 DB102
Rosehill, Esher (Clay.) KT10 .155 CG107
Hampton TW12 .... 136 CA95
Rose Hill, Sutt. SM1 .... 140 DB103
Rosehill Av, Sutt. SM1 .... 140 DC102
Woking GU21 .... 166 AW116
Rosehill Ct, Slou. SL1
off Yew Tree Rd 92 AU76
Rosehill Fm Meadow, Bans.
SM7 *off The Tracery* 174 DB115
Rosehill Gdns, Abb.L. WD5 .... 7 BQ32
Greenford UB6 .... 61 CF64
Sutton SM1 .... 140 DB103
Rosehill Pk W, Sutt. SM1 .... 140 DC102
Rosehill Rd, SW18 .... 120 DC86
Westerham (Bigg.H.) TN16 .. 178 EJ117
Roseland Cl, N17
off Cavell Rd 46 DR52
Rose La, Rom. RM6 .... 70 EX55
Woking (Ripley) GU23 .... 168 BJ121
Rose Lawn, Bushey (Bushey Hth)
WD23 .... 40 CC46
Roseleigh Av, N5 .... 65 DP63
Roseleigh Cl, Twick. TW1 .... 117 CK86
Rosemary Av, N3 .... 44 DB54
N9 .... 46 DV46
Enfield EN2 .... 30 DR39
Hounslow TW4 .... 96 BX82
Romford RM1 .... 71 FF55
West Molesey KT8 .... 136 CA97
Rosemary Cl, Croy. CR0 .... 141 DL100
Oxted RH8 .... 188 EG133
South Ockendon RM15 .... 91 FW69
Uxbridge UB8 .... 76 BN71
Rosemary Dr, E14 .... 85 ED72
Ilford IG4 .... 68 EK57
St. Albans (Lon.Col.) AL2 .. 9 CG26
Rosemary Gdns, SW14
off Rosemary La 98 CQ83
Chessington KT9 .... 156 CL105
Dagenham RM8 .... 70 EZ60
Rosemary La, SW14 .... 98 CQ83
Egham TW20 .... 133 BB97
Rosemary Rd, SE15 .... 102 DT80
SW17 .... 120 DC90
Welling DA16 .... 105 ET81
Rosemary St, N1
off Shepperton Rd 84 DR67
Rosemead, NW9 .... 63 CT59
Chertsey KT16 .... 134 BH101
Potters Bar EN6 .... 12 DC30
Rosemead Av, Felt. TW13 .. 115 BT89
Mitcham CR4 .... 141 DJ96
Wembley HA9 .... 62 CL64
Rosemead Gdns, Brwd.
(Hutt.) CM13 .... 55 GD42
Rosemont Av, N12 .... 44 DC51
Rosemont Rd, NW3 .... 82 DC65
W3 .... 80 CP73
New Malden KT3 .... 138 CQ97
Richmond TW10 .... 118 CL86
Wembley HA0 .... 80 CL67
Rosemoor St, SW3 .... 198 D9
Rosemount Av, W.Byf. KT14 .152 BG113
Rosemount Cl, Wdf.Grn. IG8
off Chapelmount Rd 49 EM51
Rosemount Dr, Brom. BR1 .. 145 EM98
Rosemount Pt, SE23
off Dacres Rd 123 DX90
Rosemount Rd, W13 .... 79 CG72
Rosenau Cres, SW11 .... 100 DE81
Rosenau Rd, SW11 .... 100 DE81
Rosendale Rd, SE21 .... 122 DQ87
SE24 .... 122 DQ87
Roseneath Av, N21 .... 45 DP46
Roseneath Cl, Orp. BR6 .... 164 EW108
Roseneath Pl, SW16
off Curtis Fld Rd 121 DM91
Roseneath Rd, SW11 .... 120 DG86
Roseneath Wk, Enf. EN1 .... 30 DS42
Rosens Wk, Edg. HA8 .... 42 CP48
Rosenthal Rd, SE6 .... 123 EB86
Rosenthorpe Rd, SE15 .... 123 DX85
Rose Pk, Add. KT15 .... 151 BE109
Rose Pk Cl, Hayes UB4 .... 78 BW70
Rosepark Ct, Ilf. IG5 .... 49 EM54
Roserton St, E14 .... 204 D5
Rosery, The, Croy. CR0 .... 143 DX100
Roses, The, Wdf.Grn. IG8 .... 48 EF52
Rose Sq, SW3 .... 198 A10
Rose St, EC4 .... 196 G8
WC2 .... 195 P10
Gravesend (Nthflt) DA11 .. 130 GB86
Rosethorn Cl, SW12 .... 121 DJ87
Rosetta Cl, SW8 .... 101 DL80
Rosetti Ter, Dag. RM8
off Marlborough Rd 70 EV63
Rose Valley, Brwd. CM14 .... 54 FW48
Roseveare Rd, SE12 .... 124 EJ91
Rose Vil, Dart. DA1 .... 128 FP87
Roseville Av, Houns. TW3 .... 116 CA85
Roseville Rd, Hayes UB3 .... 95 BU78
Rosevine Rd, SW20 .... 139 CW95
Rose Wk, Pur. CR8 .... 159 DK111
Surbiton KT5 .... 138 CP99
West Wickham BR4 .... 143 ED103
Rose Wk, The, Rad. WD7 .... 25 CH37
Rosewarne Cl, Wok. GU21
off Muirfield Rd 166 AU118
Rose Way, SE12 .... 124 EG85
Roseway, SE21 .... 122 DR86
Rose Way, Edg. HA8 .... 42 CQ49
Rosewell Cl, SE20 .... 122 DV94
Rosewood, Dart. DA2 .... 127 FE91
Esher KT10 .... 137 CG103
Sutton SM2 .... 158 DC110
Woking GU22 .... 167 BA119
Rosewood Av, Grnf. UB6 .... 61 CG64
Hornchurch RM12 .... 71 FG64
Rosewood Cl, Sid. DA14 .... 126 EW90
Rosewood Ct, Brom. BR1 .... 144 EJ95
Romford RM6 .... 70 EW57
Rosewood Dr, Enf. EN2 .... 29 DN35
Shepperton TW17 .... 134 BM99
Rosewood Gdns, SE13
off Morden Hill 103 EC82
Rosewood Gro, Sutt. SM1 .... 140 DC103
Rosewood Sq, W12
off Primula St 81 CU72
Rosewood Ter, SE20
off Laurel Gro 122 DW94
Rosher Cl, E15 .... 85 ED66
ROSHERVILLE, Grav. DA11 .. 131 GF85
Rosherville Way, Grav. DA11 .130 GE87
Rosina St, E9 .... 67 DX64
Roskell Rd, SW15 .... 99 CX83
Roslin Rd, W3 .... 98 CP76
Roslin Sq, W3 .... 98 CP76
Roslin Way, Brom. BR1 .... 124 EG92
Roslyn Cl, Mitch. CR4 .... 140 DD96
Roslyn Ct, Wok. GU21
off St. John's Rd 166 AU118
Roslyn Gdns, Rom. RM2 .... 51 FF54
Roslyn Rd, N15 .... 66 DR57
Rosmead Rd, W11 .... 81 CY73
Rosoman Pl, EC1 .... 196 E4
Rosoman St, EC1 .... 196 E3
Rossall Cl, Horn. RM11 .... 71 FG58
Rossall Cres, NW10 .... 80 CM69
Ross Av, NW7 .... 43 CY50
Dagenham RM8 .... 70 EZ61
Ross Cl, Har. HA3 .... 40 CC52
Hayes UB3 .... 95 BR77
Northolt UB5 .... 61 CD63
Ross Ct, E5 *off Napoleon Rd* .66 DV63
SW15 .... 119 CX87
Ross Cres, Wat. WD25 .... 23 BU35
Rossdale, Sutt. SM1 .... 158 DE106
Rossdale Dr, N9 .... 30 DW44
NW9 .... 62 CQ60
Rossdale Rd, SW15 .... 99 CW84
Rosse Ms, SE3 .... 104 EH81
Rossendale Cl, Enf. EN2 .... 29 DP37
Rossendale St, E5 .... 66 DV61
Rossendale Way, NW1 .... 83 DJ66
Rossetti Gdns, Couls. CR5 .. 175 DM118
Rossetti Ms, NW8
off Ordnance Hill 82 DD67
Rossetti Rd, SE16 .... 202 D10
Rossignol Gdns, Cars. SM5 .140 DG103
Rossindel Rd, Houns. TW3 .. 116 CA85
Rossington Av, Borwd. WD6 .26 CL38
Rossington Cl, Enf. EN1 .... 30 DV38
Rossington St, E5 .... 66 DU61
Rossiter Cl, Slou. SL3 .... 92 AY77
Rossiter Flds, Barn. EN5 .... 27 CY44
Rossiter Rd, SW12 .... 121 DH88
Rossland Cl, Bexh. DA6 .... 127 FB85
Rosslare Cl, West. TN16 .... 189 ER125
Rosslyn Av, E4 .... 48 EF47
SW13 .... 98 CS83
Barnet EN4 .... 28 DE44
Dagenham RM8 .... 70 EZ59
Feltham TW14 .... 115 BU86
Romford RM3 .... 52 FM54
Rosslyn Cl, Hayes UB3
off Morgans La 77 BR71
Sunbury-on-Thames TW16
off Cadbury Rd 115 BS93
West Wickham BR4 .... 144 EF104
Rosslyn Cres, Har. HA1 .... 61 CF57
Wembley HA9 .... 62 CL63
Rosslyn Gdns, Wem. HA9
off Rosslyn Cres 62 CL62
Rosslyn Hill, NW3 .... 64 DD63
Rosslyn Ms, NW3
off Rosslyn Hill 64 DD63
Rosslyn Pk, Wey. KT13 .... 153 BR105
Rosslyn Pk Ms, NW3
off Lyndhurst Rd 64 DD64
Rosslyn Rd, E17 .... 67 EC56
Barking IG11 .... 87 ER66
Twickenham TW1 .... 117 CJ86
Watford WD18 .... 23 BV41
Rossmore Ct, NW1 .... 194 D4
Rossmore Rd, NW1 .... 194 C5
Ross Par, Wall. SM6 .... 159 DH107
Ross Rd, SE25 .... 142 DR97
Cobham KT11 .... 154 BW113
Dartford DA1 .... 127 FG86
Twickenham TW2 .... 116 CB88
Wallington SM6 .... 159 DJ106
Ross Way, SE9 .... 104 EL83
Northwood HA6 .... 39 BT49
Rossway Dr, Bushey WD23 .. 24 CC43
Rosswood Gdns, Wall. SM6 .159 DJ107
Rostella Rd, SW17 .... 120 DD91
Rostrevor Av, N15 .... 66 DT58
Rostrevor Gdns, Hayes UB3 .. 77 BS74
Iver SL0 .... 75 BD68
Southall UB2 .... 96 BY78
Rostrevor Ms, SW6 .... 99 CZ81
Rostrevor Rd, SW6 .... 99 CZ81
SW19 .... 120 DA92
Roswell Cl, Wal.Cr.
(Chsht) EN8 .... 15 DY30
Rotary St, SE1 .... 200 F6
Rothbury Av, Rain. RM13 .... 89 FH71
Rothbury Gdns, Islw. TW7 .... 97 CG80
Rothbury Rd, E9 .... 85 DZ66
Rothbury Wk, N17 .... 46 DU52
Roth Dr, Brwd. (Hutt.) CM13 .. 55 GB47
Rother Cl, Wat. WD25 .... 8 BW34
Rotherfield Rd, Cars. SM5 .. 158 DG105
Enfield EN3 .... 31 DX37
Rotherfield St, N1 .... 84 DQ66
Rotherham Wk, SE1 .... 200 F3
Rotherhill Av, SW16 .... 121 DK93
ROTHERHITHE, SE16 .... 203 H6
⊖ **Rotherhithe** 202 G4
★ **Rotherhithe Heritage Mus**,
SE16 .... 203 L2
Rotherhithe New Rd, SE16 .. 102 DU78
Rotherhithe Old Rd, SE16 .. 203 H7
Rotherhithe St, SE16 .... 202 G4
Rotherhithe Tunnel, E1 .... 203 H2
Rotherhithe Tunnel App, E14 .85 DY73
SE16 .... 202 F5
Rothermere Rd, Croy. CR0 .. 159 DM106
Rotherwick Hill, W5 .... 80 CM70
Rotherwick Rd, NW11 .... 64 DA59
Rotherwood Cl, SW20 .... 139 CY95
Rotherwood Rd, SW15 .... 99 CX83
Rothery St, N1 *off Gaskin St* .83 DP67
Rothery Ter, SW9 .... 101 DP80
Rothesay Av, SW20 .... 139 CY96
Greenford UB6 .... 79 CD65
Richmond TW10 .... 98 CP84
Rothesay Rd, SE25 .... 142 DS98
Rothsay Rd, E7 .... 86 EJ66
Rothsay St, SE1 .... 201 M6
Rothsay Wk, E14 .... 204 A8
Rothschild Rd, W4 .... 98 CQ77
Rothschild St, SE27 .... 121 DP91
Roth Wk, N7 *off Durham Rd* .. 65 DM62
Rothwell Gdns, Dag. RM9 .... 88 EW66
Rothwell Rd, Dag. RM9 .... 88 EW67
Rothwell St, NW1 .... 82 DF67
Rotten Row, SW1 .... 198 F4
SW7 .... 198 B4
Rotterdam Dr, E14 .... 204 E7
Rouel Rd, SE16 .... 202 B7
Rouge La, Grav. DA12 .... 131 GH88
Rougemont Av, Mord. SM4 .140 DA100
Roughetts La, Gdse. RH9 .. 186 DS129
Redhill (Bletch.) RH1 .... 186 DS129
Roughlands, Wok. GU22 .... 167 BE115
Roughs, The, Nthwd. HA6 .... 39 BT48
Roughtallys, Epp. (N.Wld Bas.)
CM16 .... 18 EZ27
Roughwood Cl, Wat. WD17 .. 23 BS38
Roughwood La, Ch.St.G. HP8 .36 AY45
Roundacre, SW19
off Inner Pk Rd 119 CX89
Roundaway Rd, Ilf. IG5 .... 49 EM54
ROUND BUSH, Wat. WD25 .... 24 CC38
Roundcroft, Wal.Cr.
(Chsht) EN7 .... 14 DT26
Roundel Cl, SE4
off Adelaide Av 103 DZ84
Round Gro, Croy. CR0 .... 143 DX101
Roundhay Cl, SE23 .... 123 DX89
Roundhedge Way, Enf. EN2 .. 29 DM38
Round Hill, SE26 .... 122 DW89
Roundhill, Wok. GU22 .... 167 BB119
Roundhill Dr, Enf. EN2 .... 29 DM42
Woking GU22 .... 167 BB118
Roundhills, Wal.Abb. EN9 .... 16 EE34
Roundhill Way, Cob. KT11 .. 154 CB111
Roundlyn Gdns, Orp. (St.M.Cray)
BR5 *off Lynmouth Ri* 146 EV98
Roundmead Av, Loug. IG10 .. 33 EN41
Roundmead Cl, Loug. IG10 .. 33 EN41
Roundmoor Dr, Wal.Cr.
(Chsht) EN8 .... 15 DX29
Round Oak Rd, Wey. KT13 .. 152 BM105
Roundshaw Cen, Wall. SM6
off Meteor Way 159 DL108
Roundtable Rd, Brom. BR1 .. 124 EF90
Roundthorn Way, Wok.
GU21 .... 166 AT116
Roundtree Rd, Wem. HA0 .... 61 CH64
Roundway, Egh. TW20 .... 113 BC92
Westerham (Bigg.H.) TN16
off Norheads La 178 EK116
Roundway, The, N17 .... 46 DQ53
Esher (Clay.) KT10 .... 155 CF106
Watford WD18 .... 23 BT44
Roundways, Ruis. HA4 .... 59 BT62
Roundwood, Chis. BR7 .... 145 EP96
Kings Langley WD4 .... 6 BL26
Roundwood Av, Brwd.
(Hutt.) CM13 .... 55 GA46
Uxbridge UB11 .... 77 BQ74
Roundwood Cl, Ruis. HA4 .... 59 BR59
Roundwood Gro, Brwd.
(Hutt.) CM13 .... 55 GB45
Roundwood Lake, Brwd.
(Hutt.) CM13 .... 55 GB46
Roundwood Rd, NW10 .... 81 CT65
Amersham HP6 .... 20 AS38
Roundwood Vw, Bans. SM7 .173 CX115
Roundwood Way, Bans. SM7 .173 CX115
Rounton Rd, E3 .... 85 EA70
Waltham Abbey EN9 .... 16 EE33
Roupell Rd, SW2 .... 121 DM88
Roupell St, SE1 .... 200 E3
Rousden St, NW1 .... 83 DJ66
Rousebarn La, Rick. WD3 .... 23 BQ41
Rouse Gdns, SE21 .... 122 DS91
Rous Rd, Buck.H. IG9 .... 48 EL46
Routemaster Cl, E13 .... 86 EH69
Routh Ct, Felt. TW14 .... 115 BR88
Routh Rd, SW18 .... 120 DE87
Routh St, E6 .... 87 EM71
Routledge Cl, N19 .... 65 DK60
Rover Av, Ilf. IG6 .... 49 ET51
Rowallan Rd, SW6 .... 99 CY80
Rowan Av, E4 .... 47 DZ51
Egham TW20 .... 113 BC92
Rowan Cl, SW16 .... 141 DJ95
W5 .... 98 CL75
Ilford IG1 .... 69 ER64
New Malden KT3 .... 138 CS96
Radlett (Shenley) WD7
off Juniper Gdns 10 CL33
St. Albans (Brick.Wd) AL2 .. 8 CA31
Stanmore HA7
off Woodlands Dr 41 CF51
Wembley HA0 .... 61 CG62
Rowan Ct, Borwd. WD6
off Theobald St 26 CL39
Rowan Cres, SW16 .... 141 DJ95
Dartford DA1 .... 128 FJ88
Rowan Dr, NW9 .... 63 CU56
Broxbourne EN10 .... 15 DZ25
Rowan Gdns, Croy. CR0
off Radcliffe Rd 142 DT104
Iver SL0 .... 75 BC68
Rowan Grn, Wey. KT13 .... 153 BR105
Rowan Grn E, Brwd. CM13 .... 55 FZ48
Rowan Grn W, Brwd. CM13 .. 55 FZ49
Rowan Gro, Couls. CR5 .... 175 DH121
South Ockendon (Aveley)
RM15 .... 90 FQ73
Rowan Ho, NW3
off Maitland Pk Rd 82 DF65
Rowan Pl, Amer. HP6 .... 20 AT38
Hayes UB3 *off West Av* 77 BT73
Rowan Rd, SW16 .... 141 DJ96
W6 .... 99 CX77
Bexleyheath DA7 .... 106 EY83
Brentford TW8 .... 97 CH80
Swanley BR8 .... 147 FD97
West Drayton UB7 .... 94 BK77
Rowans, The, N13 .... 45 DP48
Gerrards Cross (Chal.St.P.)
SL9 .... 56 AX55
South Ockendon (Aveley)
RM15 *off Purfleet Rd* 90 FQ74
Sunbury-on-Thames TW16 .115 BT92
Woking GU22 .... 166 AY118
Rowans Cl, Long. DA3 .... 149 FX96
Rowans Way, Loug. IG10 .... 33 EM42
Rowan Ter, SE20
off Sycamore Gro 142 DU95
W6 *off Bute Gdns* 99 CX77
Rowantree Cl, N21 .... 46 DR46
Rowantree Rd, N21 .... 46 DR46
Enfield EN2 .... 29 DP40
Rowan Wk, N2 .... 64 DC58
N19 *off Bredgar Rd* 65 DJ61
W10 *off Droop St* 81 CY70
Rowan Wk, Barn. EN5 .... 28 DB43
Bromley BR2 .... 145 EM104
Hornchurch RM11 .... 72 FK56
Rowan Way, Rom. RM6 .... 70 EW55
South Ockendon RM15 .... 91 FX70
Rowanwood Av, Sid. DA15 .. 126 EU88
Rowanwood Ms, Enf. EN2 .... 29 DP40
Rowben Cl, N20 .... 44 DB46
Rowberry Cl, SW6 .... 99 CW80
Rowbourne Pl, Pot.B.
(Cuffley) EN6 .... 13 DK28
Rowcross St, SE1 .... 201 P10
Rowdell Rd, Nthlt. UB5 .... 78 CA67
Rowden Pk Gdns, E4
off Rowden Rd 47 EA51
Rowden Rd, E4 .... 47 EA51
Beckenham BR3 .... 143 DY95
Epsom KT19 .... 156 CP105
Rowditch La, SW11 .... 100 DG82
Rowdon Av, NW10 .... 81 CV66
Rowdown Cres, Croy.
(New Adgtn) CR0 .... 161 ED109
Rowdowns Rd, Dag. RM9 .... 88 EZ67
Rowe Gdns, Bark. IG11 .... 87 ET68
Rowe La, E9 .... 66 DW64
Rowena Cres, SW11 .... 100 DE82
Rowe Wk, Har. HA2 .... 60 CA62
Rowfant Rd, SW17 .... 120 DG88
Rowhedge, Brwd. CM13 .... 55 GA48
Row Hill, Add. KT15 .... 151 BF107
Rowhill Rd, E5 .... 66 DV63
Dartford DA2 .... 127 FF93
Swanley BR8 .... 127 FF93
Rowhurst Av, Add. KT15 .... 152 BH107
Leatherhead KT22 .... 171 CF117
Rowington Cl, W2 .... 82 DB71
Rowland Av, Har. HA3 .... 61 CJ56
Rowland Ct, E16 .... 86 EF70
Rowland Cres, Chig. IG7 .... 49 ES49
Rowland Gro, SE26
off Dallas Rd 122 DV90
Rowland Hill Av, N17 .... 46 DQ52
Rowland Hill St, NW3 .... 64 DE64
Rowlands Av, Pnr. HA5 .... 40 CA51
Rowlands Cl, N6
off North Hill 64 DG58
NW7 .... 43 CU52
Waltham Cross (Chsht)
EN8 .... 15 DX30
Rowlands Flds, Wal.Cr.
(Chsht) EN8 .... 15 DX29
Rowlands Rd, Dag. RM8 .... 70 EZ61
Rowland Wk, Rom. (Hav.at.Bow.)
RM4 .... 51 FE48
Rowland Way, SW19
off Hayward Cl 140 DB95
Ashford TW15
off Littleton Rd 115 BQ94
Rowlatt Cl, Dart. DA2 .... 128 FJ91
Rowlatt Rd, Dart. DA2
off Whitehead Cl 128 FJ91
Rowley Av, Sid. DA15 .... 126 EV87
Rowley Cl, Wat. WD19
off Lower Paddock Rd 24 BY44
Wembley HA0 .... 80 CM66
Woking (Pyrford) GU22 .. 168 BG116
Rowley Ct, Cat. CR3 .... 176 DQ122
Rowley Gdns, N4 .... 66 DQ59
Waltham Cross (Chsht)
EN8 *off Warwick Dr* 15 DX28
ROWLEY GREEN, Barn. EN5 .. 27 CT42
Rowley Grn Rd, Barn. EN5 .. 27 CT43
Rowley Ind Pk, W3 .... 98 CP76
Rowley La, Barn. EN5 .... 27 CT43
Borehamwood WD6 .... 26 CR39
Slough (Wexham) SL3 .... 74 AW67
Rowley Mead, Epp. (Thnwd)
CM16 .... 18 EW25
Rowley Rd, N15 .... 66 DQ57
Rowley Way, NW8 .... 82 DB67
Rowlheys Pl, West Dr. UB7 .. 94 BL76
Rowlls Rd, Kings.T. KT1 .... 138 CM97
Rowmarsh Cl, Grav. (Nthflt)
DA11 .... 130 GD91
Rowney Gdns, Dag. RM9 .... 88 EW65
Rowney Rd, Dag. RM9 .... 88 EV65
Rowntree Clifford Cl, E13
off Liddon Rd 86 EH69
Rowntree Cl, NW6
off Iverson Rd 82 DA65
Rowntree Path, SE28
off Booth Cl 88 EV73
Rowntree Rd, Twick. TW2 .... 117 CE88
Rowse Cl, E15 .... 85 EC67
Rowsley Av, NW4 .... 63 CW55
Rowstock Gdns, N7 .... 65 DK64
Rowton Rd, SE18 .... 105 EQ80
ROWTOWN, Add. KT15 .... 151 BF108
Rowtown, Add. KT15 .... 151 BF108
Rowzill Rd, Swan. BR8 .... 127 FF93
Roxborough Av, Har. HA1 .... 61 CD59
Isleworth TW7 .... 97 CF80
Roxborough Pk, Har. HA1 .... 61 CE59
Roxborough Rd, Har. HA1 .... 61 CD57
Roxbourne Cl, Nthlt. UB5 .... 78 BX65
Roxburgh Av, Upmin. RM14 .. 72 FQ62
Roxburgh Rd, SE27 .... 121 DP92
Roxburn Way, Ruis. HA4 .... 59 BT62
Roxby Pl, SW6 .... 100 DA79
ROXETH, Har. HA2 .... 61 CD61
Roxeth Ct, Ashf. TW15 .... 114 BN92
Roxeth Grn Av, Har. HA2 .... 60 CB62
Roxeth Gro, Har. HA2 .... 60 CB63
Roxeth Hill, Har. HA2 .... 61 CD61
Roxford Cl, Shep. TW17 .... 135 BS99
Roxley Rd, SE13 .... 123 EB86
Roxton Gdns, Croy. CR0 .... 161 EA106
Roxwell Gdns, Brwd.
(Hutt.) CM13 .... 55 GC43
Roxwell Rd, W12 .... 99 CU75
Barking IG11 .... 88 EU68
Roxwell Trd Pk, E10 .... 67 DX59
Roxwell Way, Wdf.Grn. IG8 .. 48 EJ52
Roxy Av, Rom. RM6 .... 70 EW59
★ **Royal Acad of Arts**, W1 .. 199 K1
★ **Royal Acad of Dramatic Art**
(R.A.D.A.), WC1 .... 195 M6

★ Place of interest ⇌ Railway station ⊖ London Underground station DLR Docklands Light Railway station Tra Tramlink station H Hospital Riv Pedestrian ferry landing stage

★ Royal Acad of Music, NW1 194 G5
H Royal Air Force, Headley Ct, Epsom KT18 172 CP123
★ Royal Air Force Museums, NW9 43 CU54
DLR Royal Albert 87 EL73
Royal Albert Dock, E16 87 EM73
★ Royal Albert Hall, SW7 100 DD75
Royal Albert Rbt, E16
off Royal Albert Way 86 EL73
Royal Albert Way, E16 86 EK73
Royal Arc, W1 199 K1
Royal Artillery Barracks, SE18
off Repository Rd 105 EN78
Royal Av, SW3 198 D10
Waltham Cross EN8 15 DY33
Worcester Park KT4 138 CS103
★ Royal Botanic Gdns, Kew, Rich. TW9 98 CL80
H Royal Brompton Hosp, SW3 198 B10
Annexe, SW3 198 A10
Royal Circ, SE27 121 DN90
Royal Cl, N16 off Manor Rd 66 DS60
SE8 103 DZ79
SW19 119 CX90
Ilford IG3 70 EU59
Orpington BR6 163 EP105
Uxbridge UB8 76 BM72
Worcester Park KT4 138 CS103
★ Royal Coll of Art, SW7 100 DC75
★ Royal Coll of Music, SW7 100 DD76
★ Royal Coll of Surgeons of England, WC2 196 C8
Royal Coll St, NW1 83 DJ66
Royal Ct, EC3 off Cornhill 84 DR72
SE16 203 M6
★ Royal Courts of Justice, WC2 196 C9
Royal Cres, W11 81 CX74
Ilford IG2 off Eastern Av 69 ER58
Ruislip HA4 60 BY63
Royal Cres Ms, W11
off Queensdale Rd 81 CX74
Royal Docks Rd, E6 87 EP72
Royal Dr, N11 44 DG50
Epsom KT18 173 CV118
Royal Duchess Ms, SW12
off Dinsmore Rd 121 DH87
Royale Leisure Pk, W3 80 CN70
★ Royal Exchange, EC3 197 L9
Royal Ex Av, EC3 197 L9
Royal Ex Bldgs, EC3 197 L9
Royal Ex Steps, EC3
off Cornhill 84 DR72
★ Royal Festival Hall, SE1 200 B2
H Royal Free Hosp, The, NW3 64 DE64
Royal Gdns, W7 97 CG76
★ Royal Geographical Society, SW7 100 DD75
Royal Herbert Pavilions, SE18 105 EM81
Royal Hill, SE10 103 EC80
Royal Horticultural Society Cotts, Wok. (Wisley) GU23
off Wisley La 168 BL116
★ Royal Horticultural Society (Lawrence Hall), SW1 199 M7
★ Royal Horticultural Society (Lindley Hall), SW1 199 M8
★ Royal Horticultural Society Wisley Gdn, Wok. GU22 168 BL118
★ Royal Hosp Chelsea & Mus, SW3 100 DG78
H Royal Hosp for Neuro-disability, SW15 119 CY86
Royal Hosp Rd, SW3 100 DF79
Royal La, Uxb. UB8 76 BM69
West Drayton UB7 76 BM72
Royal London Est, The, N17 46 DV51
H Royal London Homoeopathic Hosp, WC1 196 A6
H Royal London Hosp, The, St. Clements, E3 85 DZ69
Whitechapel, E1 84 DV71
H Royal London Hosp (Whitechapel) Dentistry Cen, E1 84 DV71
H Royal Marsden Hosp, The, SW3 198 A10
Sutton SM2 158 DC110
★ Royal Mews, The, SW1 199 J6
★ Royal Military Acad, SE18 105 EM80
Royal Mint Ct, EC3 202 A1
Royal Mint Pl, E1
off Blue Anchor Yd 84 DT73
Royal Mint St, E1 84 DT73
Royal Mt Ct, Twick. TW2 117 CE90
H Royal Nat Orthopaedic Hosp, W1 195 J5
Stanmore HA7 41 CJ47
★ Royal Nat Thea, SE1 200 C2
H Royal Nat Throat, Nose & Ear Hosp, WC1 196 B2
Royal Naval Pl, SE14 103 DZ80
⊖ Royal Oak 82 DB71
Royal Oak Ct, N1
off Pitfield St 84 DS69
Royal Oak Pl, SE22 122 DV86
Royal Oak Rd, E8 84 DV65
Bexleyheath DA6 126 EZ85
Woking GU21 166 AW118
Royal Oak Yd, SE1 201 M5
Royal Opera Arc, SW1 199 M2
★ Royal Opera Ho, WC2 196 A9
Royal Orchard Cl, SW18 119 CY87
Royal Par, SE3 104 EE82
SW6 off Dawes Rd 99 CY80
W5 off Western Av 80 CL69
Chislehurst BR7 125 EQ94
Richmond TW9
off Station App 98 CN81
Royal Par Ms, SE3
off Royal Par 104 EF82
Chislehurst BR7 125 EQ94
Royal Pier Ms, Grav. DA12
off Royal Pier Rd 131 GH86
Royal Pier Rd, Grav. DA12 131 GH86
Royal Pl, SE10 103 EC80
Royal Quarter, Kings.T. KT2 138 CL95
Royal Rd, E16 86 EK72
SE17 101 DP79
Dartford (Darenth) DA2 128 FN92
Sidcup DA14 126 EX90
Teddington TW11 117 CD92
Royal Route, Wem. HA9 62 CM63
Royal St, SE1 200 C6
Royalty Ms, W1 195 M9
DLR Royal Victoria 86 EG73
Royal Victoria Dock, E16 205 P1
Royal Victoria Patriotic Bldg, SW18 off Fitzhugh Gro 120 DD86
Royal Victoria Pl, E16
off Wesley Av 86 EH74
Royal Victoria Sq, E16 205 P1
Royal Victor Pl, E3 85 DX68
Royal Wk, Wall. SM6
off Prince Charles Way 141 DH104
Royce Gro, Wat. (Lvsdn) WD25 7 BT34
Roycraft Av, Bark. IG11 87 ET68
Roycraft Cl, Bark. IG11 87 ET68
Roycroft Cl, E18 48 EH53
SW2 121 DN88
Roydene Rd, SE18 105 ES79
Roydon Cl, SW11
off Reform St 100 DF82
Loughton IG10 48 EL45
Roydon Ct, Walt. KT12 153 BU105
Roydon St, SW11
off Southolm St 101 DH81
Roy Gdns, Ilf. IG2 69 ES56
Roy Gro, Hmptn. TW12 116 CB93
Royle Cl, Ger.Cr. (Chal.St.P.) SL9 37 AZ52
Romford RM2 71 FH57
Royle Cres, W13 79 CG70
Roy Rd, Nthwd. HA6 39 BT52
Roy Sq, E14 off Narrow St 85 DY73
Royston Av, E4 47 EA50
Sutton SM1 140 DD104
Wallington SM6 159 DK105
West Byfleet (Byfleet) KT14 152 BL112
Royston Cl, Houns. TW5 95 BV81
Walton-on-Thames KT12 135 BU102
Royston Ct, SE24
off Burbage Rd 122 DQ86
Richmond TW9 98 CM81
Surbiton KT6
off Hook Ri N 138 CN104
Royston Gdns, Ilf. IG1 68 EK58
Royston Gro, Pnr. HA5 40 BZ51
Royston Par, Ilf. IG1 68 EK58
Royston Pk Rd, Pnr. HA5 40 BZ51
Royston Rd, SE20 143 DX95
Dartford DA1 127 FF86
Richmond TW10 118 CL85
Romford RM3 52 FN52
West Byfleet (Byfleet) KT14 152 BL112
Roystons, The, Surb. KT5 138 CP99
Royston St, E2 84 DW68
Rozel Ct, N1 84 DS67
Rozel Rd, SW4 101 DJ82
Rubastic Rd, Sthl. UB2 96 BW76
Rubens Pl, SW4
off Dolman St 101 DM84
Rubens Rd, Nthlt. UB5 78 BW68
Rubens St, SE6 123 DZ89
Rubin Pl, Enf. EN3 31 EA37
Ruby Ms, E17 off Ruby Rd 67 EA55
Ruby Rd, E17 67 EA55
Ruby St, NW10
off Diamond St 80 CR66
SE15 102 DV79
Ruby Triangle, SE15
off Sandgate St 102 DV79
Ruckholt Cl, E10 67 EB62
Ruckholt Rd, E10 67 EA63
Rucklers La, Kings L. WD4 6 BK27
Rucklidge Av, NW10 81 CT68
Rudall Cres, NW3
off Willoughby Rd 64 DD63
Ruddington Cl, E5 67 DY63
Ruddock Cl, Edg. HA8 42 CQ52
Ruddstreet Cl, SE18 105 EP77
Ruden Way, Epsom KT17 173 CV116
Rudge Ri, Add. KT15 151 BF106
Rudgwick Ter, NW8
off Avenue Rd 82 DE67
Rudland Rd, Bexh. DA7 107 FB83
Rudloe Rd, SW12 121 DJ87
Rudolf Pl, SW8 off Miles St 101 DL79
Rudolph Rd, E13 86 EF68
NW6 82 DA68
Bushey WD23 24 CA44
Rudsworth Cl, Slou. (Colnbr.) SL3 93 BD80
Rudyard Gro, NW7 42 CQ51
Rue de St. Lawrence, Wal.Abb. EN9 off Quaker La 15 EC34
Ruffets Wd, Grav. DA12 131 GJ93
Ruffetts, The, S.Croy. CR2 160 DV108
Ruffetts Cl, S.Croy. CR2 160 DV108
Ruffetts Way, Tad. KT20 173 CY118
Ruffle Cl, West Dr. UB7 94 BL75
Rufford Cl, Har. HA3 61 CG58
Watford WD17 23 BT37
Rufford St, N1 83 DL67
Rufford Twr, W3 80 CP74
Rufus Cl, Ruis. HA4 60 BY62
Rufus St, N1 197 M3
Rugby Av, N9 46 DT46
Greenford UB6 79 CD65
Wembley HA0 61 CH64
Rugby Cl, Har. HA1 61 CE57
★ Rugby Football Union Twickenham, Twick. TW2 117 CE86
Rugby Gdns, Dag. RM9 88 EW65
Rugby La, Sutt. SM2
off Nonsuch Wk 157 CX109
Rugby Rd, NW9 62 CP56
W4 98 CS75
Dagenham RM9 88 EV66
Twickenham TW1 117 CE86
Rugby St, WC1 196 B5
Rugby Way, Rick. (Crox.Grn) WD3 23 BP43
Rugged La, Wal.Abb. EN9 16 EK33
Ruggles-Brise Rd, Ashf. TW15 114 BK92
Rugg St, E14 85 EA73
RUISLIP, HA4 59 BS59
⊖ Ruislip 59 BS60
Ruislip Cl, Grnf. UB6 78 CB70
RUISLIP COMMON, Ruis. HA4 59 BR57
Ruislip Ct, Ruis. HA4
off Courtfield Gdns 59 BT61
RUISLIP GARDENS, Ruis. HA4 59 BS63
⊖ Ruislip Gardens 59 BU63
RUISLIP MANOR, Ruis. HA4 59 BU61
⊖ Ruislip Manor 59 BU60
Ruislip Rd, Grnf. UB6 78 CA69
Northolt UB5 78 BX68
Southall UB1 78 CA69
Ruislip Rd E, W7 79 CD70
W13 79 CD70
Greenford UB6 79 CD70
Ruislip St, SW17 120 DF91
Rumania Wk, Grav. DA12 131 GM90
Rumbold Rd, SW6 100 DB80
Rum Cl, E1 202 F1
Rumsey Cl, Hmptn. TW12 116 BZ93
Rumsey Ms, N4
off Monsell Rd 65 DP62
Rumsey Rd, SW9 101 DM83
Rumsley, Wal.Cr. EN7 14 DU27
Runbury Circle, NW9 62 CR61
Runciman Cl, Orp. BR6 164 EW110
Runcorn Cl, N17 66 DV56
Runcorn Pl, W11 81 CY73
Rundell Cres, NW4 63 CV57
Rundell Twr, SW8
off Portland Gro 101 DM81
Runes Cl, Mitch. CR4 140 DD98
Runnel Fld, Har. HA1 61 CE62
Runnemede Rd, Egh. TW20 113 BA91
Running Horse Yd, Brent. TW8 off Pottery Rd 98 CL79
Running Waters, Brwd. CM13 55 GA49
Runnymede, SW19 140 DD95
Runnymede Cl, Twick. TW2 116 CB86
Runnymede Ct, Croy. CR0 142 DT103
Egham TW20 113 BA91
Runnymede Cres, SW16 141 DK95
Runnymede Gdns, Grnf. UB6 79 CD68
Twickenham TW2 116 CB86
H Runnymede Hosp, Cher. KT16 133 BD104
Runnymede Ho, E9
off Kingsmead Way 67 DY63
Runnymede Rd, Twick. TW2 116 CB86
Runrig Hill, Amer. HP6 20 AS35
Runway, The, Ruis. HA4 59 BV64
Rupack St, SE16 202 F5
Rupert Av, Wem. HA9 62 CL64
Rupert Ct, W1 195 M10
West Molesey KT8
off St. Peter's Rd 136 CA98
Rupert Gdns, SW9 101 DP82
Rupert Rd, N19
off Holloway Rd 65 DK62
NW6 81 CZ68
W4 98 CS76
Rupert St, W1 195 M10
Rural Cl, Horn. RM11 71 FH60
Rural Vale, Grav. (Nthflt) DA11 130 GE87
Rural Way, SW16 121 DH94
Redhill RH1 184 DG134
Rusbridge Cl, E8
off Amhurst Rd 66 DU64
Ruscoe Dr, Wok. GU22
off Pembroke Rd 167 BA117
Ruscoe Rd, E16 86 EF72
Ruscombe Dr, St.Alb. (Park St) AL2 8 CB26
Ruscombe Gdns, Slou. (Datchet) SL3 92 AU80
Ruscombe Way, Felt. TW14 115 BT87
Rush, The, SW19
off Kingston Rd 139 CZ95
Rusham Pk Av, Egh. TW20 113 AZ93
Rusham Rd, SW12 120 DF86
Egham TW20 113 AZ93
Rushbrook Cres, E17 47 DZ53
Rushbrook Rd, SE9 125 EQ89
Rush Common Ms, SW2 121 DM87
Rushcroft Rd, E4 47 EA52
SW2 101 DN84
Rushden Cl, SE19 122 DR94
Rushdene, SE2 106 EX76
Rushdene Av, Barn. EN4 44 DE45
Rushdene Cl, Nthlt. UB5 78 BW69
Rushdene Cres, Nthlt. UB5 78 BW68
Rushdene Rd, Brwd. CM15 54 FW45
Pinner HA5 60 BX58
Rushdene Wk, West. (Bigg.H.) TN16 178 EK117
Rushden Gdns, NW7 43 CW51
Ilford IG5 69 EN55
Rushdon Cl, Grays RM17 110 GA76
Romford RM1 71 FG57
Rush Dr, Wal.Abb. EN9 31 EC36
Rushen Wk, Cars. SM5
off Paisley Rd 140 DD102
Rushes Mead, Uxb. UB8
off Frays Waye 76 BJ67
Rushet Rd, Orp. BR5 146 EU96
Rushett Cl, T.Ditt. KT7 137 CH102
Rushett La, Epsom KT18 155 CJ111
Rushett Rd, T.Ditt. KT7 137 CH101
Rushey Cl, N.Mal. KT3 138 CR98
Rushey Grn, SE6 123 EB87
Rushey Hill, Enf. EN2 29 DM42
Rushey Mead, SE4 123 EA85
Rushfield, Pot.B. EN6 11 CX33
Rushford Rd, SE4 123 DZ86
RUSH GREEN, Rom. RM7 71 FC59
Rush Grn Gdns, Rom. RM7 71 FC60
Rush Grn Rd, Rom. RM7 71 FC60
Rushgrove Av, NW9 63 CT57
Rush Gro St, SE18 105 EM77
Rush Hill Ms, SW11
off Rush Hill Rd 100 DG83
Rush Hill Rd, SW11 100 DG83
Rushleigh Av, Wal.Cr. (Chsht) EN8 15 DX31
Rushley Cl, Kes. BR2 162 EK105
Rushmead, E2 off Florida St 84 DV69
Richmond TW10 117 CH90
Rushmead Cl, Croy. CR0 160 DT105
Rushmere Av, Upmin. RM14 72 FQ62
Rushmere Ct, Wor.Pk. KT4
off The Avenue 139 CU103
Rushmere Ho, SW15
off Fontley Way 119 CU88
Rushmere La, Chesh. (Orch.L.) HP5 4 AU28
Rushmere Pl, SW19 119 CX92
Egham (Eng.Grn) TW20 112 AY92
Rushmoor Cl, Pnr. HA5 59 BV56
Rickmansworth WD3 38 BK47
Rushmore Cl, Brom. BR1 144 EL97
Rushmore Cres, E5
off Rushmore Rd 67 DX63
Rushmore Hill, Orp. BR6 164 EW110
Sevenoaks (Knock.) TN14 164 EX112
Rushmore Rd, E5 66 DW63
Rusholme Av, Dag. RM10 70 FA62
Rusholme Gro, SE19 122 DS92
Rusholme Rd, SW15 119 CX86
Rushout Av, Har. HA3 61 CH58
Rushton Av, Wat. WD25 23 BU35
Rushton St, N1 84 DR68
Rushworth Rd, Reig. RH2 184 DA133
Rushworth St, SE1 200 G4
Rushy Meadow La, Cars. SM5 140 DE103
Ruskin Av, E12 86 EL65
Feltham TW14 115 BT86
Richmond TW9 98 CN80
Upminster RM14 72 FQ59
Waltham Abbey EN9 16 EE34
Welling DA16 106 EU83
Ruskin Cl, NW11 64 DB58
Waltham Cross (Chsht) EN7 14 DS26
Ruskin Dr, Orp. BR6 145 ES104
Welling DA16 106 EU83
Worcester Park KT4 139 CV103
Ruskin Gdns, W5 79 CK70
Harrow HA3 62 CM56
Romford RM3 51 FH52
Ruskin Gro, Dart. DA1 128 FN85
Welling DA16 106 EU82
Ruskin Pk Ho, SE5 102 DR83
Ruskin Rd, N17 46 DT53
Belvedere DA17 106 FA77
Carshalton SM5 158 DF106
Croydon CR0 141 DP103
Grays RM16 111 GG77
Isleworth TW7 97 CF83
Southall UB1 78 BY73
Staines TW18 113 BF94
Ruskin Wk, N9
off Durham Rd 46 DU47
SE24 122 DQ85
Bromley BR2 145 EM100
Ruskin Way, SW19 140 DD95
Rusland Av, Orp. BR6 145 ER104
Rusland Hts, Har. HA1
off Rusland Pk Rd 61 CE56
Rusland Pk Rd, Har. HA1 61 CE56
Rusper Cl, NW2 63 CW62
Stanmore HA7 41 CJ49
Rusper Rd, N22 46 DQ54
Dagenham RM9 88 EW65
Russell Av, N22 45 DP54
Russell Cl, NW10 80 CQ66
SE7 104 EJ80
W4 99 CT79
Amersham HP6 20 AX39
Beckenham BR3 143 EB97
Bexleyheath DA7 106 FA84
Brentwood CM15 54 FV45
Dartford DA1 107 FG83
Northwood HA6 39 BQ50
Ruislip HA4 60 BW61
Tadworth (Walt.Hill) KT20 183 CU125
Woking GU21 166 AW115
Russell Ct, SW1 199 L3
Leatherhead KT22 171 CH122
St. Albans (Brick.Wd) AL2 8 CA30
Russell Cres, Wat. WD25
off High Rd 23 BT35
Russell Dr, Stai. (Stanw.) TW19 114 BK86
Russell Gdns, N20 44 DE47
NW11 63 CY58
W14 99 CY76
Richmond TW10 117 CJ89
West Drayton UB7 94 BN78
Russell Gdns Ms, W14 99 CY76
Russell Grn Cl, Pur. CR8 159 DN110
Russell Gro, NW7 42 CS50
SW9 101 DN80
Russell Hill, Pur. CR8 159 DM110
Russell Hill Pl, Pur. CR8 159 DN111
Russell Hill Rd, Pur. CR8 159 DN110
Russell Kerr Cl, W4
off Burlington La 98 CQ80
Russell La, N20 44 DE47
Watford WD17 23 BR36
Russell Lo, SE1
off Spurgeon St 102 DR76
Russell Mead, Har. (Har.Wld) HA3 41 CF53
Russell Par, NW11
off Golders Grn Rd 63 CY58
Russell Pl, NW3
off Aspern Gro 64 DE64
SE16 203 K7
Dartford (Sutt.H.) DA4 148 FN95
Russell Rd, E4 47 DZ49
E10 67 EB58
E16 86 EG72
E17 67 DZ55
N8 65 DK58
N13 45 DM51
N15 66 DS57
N20 44 DE47
NW9 63 CT58
SW19 120 DA94
W14 99 CY76
Buckhurst Hill IG9 48 EH46
Enfield EN1 30 DT38
Gravesend DA12 131 GK86
Grays RM17 110 GA77
Mitcham CR4 140 DE97
Northolt UB5 60 CC64
Northwood HA6 39 BQ49
Shepperton TW17 135 BQ101
Tilbury RM18 110 GE81
Twickenham TW2 117 CF86
Walton-on-Thames KT12 135 BU100
Woking GU21 166 AW115
Russells, Tad. KT20 173 CX122
Russell's Footpath, SW16 121 DL92
⊖ Russell Square 195 P5
Russell Sq, WC1 195 P5
Longfield DA3
off Cavendish Sq 149 FX97
Russells Ride, Wal.Cr. (Chsht) EN8 15 DX31
Russell St, WC2 196 A10
Russell Wk, Rich. TW10
off Park Hill 118 CM86
Russell Way, Sutt. SM1 158 DA106
Watford WD19 39 BV45
Russell Wilson Ct, Rom. RM3 off Church Rd 52 FN53
Russet Cl, Stai. TW19 113 BF86
Uxbridge UB10
off Uxbridge Rd 77 BQ70
Walton-on-Thames KT12 136 BX104
Russet Cres, N7
off Stock Orchard Cres 65 DM64
Russet Dr, Croy. CR0 143 DY102
Radlett (Shenley) WD7 10 CL32
Russets, The, Ger.Cr. (Chal.St.P.) SL9 off Austenwood Cl 36 AX54
Russets Cl, E4
off Larkshall Rd 47 ED49
Russett Cl, Orp. BR6 164 EV106
Waltham Cross (Chsht) EN7 14 DS26
Russett Ct, Cat. CR3 186 DU125
Russett Hill, Ger.Cr. (Chal.St.P.) SL9 56 AY55
Russetts, Horn. RM11 72 FL56
Russetts Cl, Wok. GU21 167 AZ115
Russett Way, Swan. BR8 147 FD96
Russia Ct, EC2 197 J8
Russia Dock Rd, SE16 203 L3
Russia La, E2 84 DW68
Russia Row, EC2 197 J9
Russia Wk, SE16 203 K5
Russington Rd, Shep. TW17 135 BR100
Rusthall Av, W4 98 CR77
Rusthall Cl, Croy. CR0 142 DW100
Rustic Av, SW16 121 DH94
Rustic Cl, Upmin. RM14 73 FS60
Rustic Pl, Wem. HA0 61 CK63
Rustic Wk, E16
off Lambert Rd 86 EH72
Rustington Wk, Mord. SM4 139 CZ101
Ruston Av, Surb. KT5 138 CP101
Ruston Gdns, N14 off Bye Rd 28 DG44
Ruston Ms, W11
off St. Marks Rd 81 CY72
Ruston Rd, SE18 104 EL76
Ruston St, E3 85 DZ67
Rust Sq, SE5 102 DR80
Rutford Rd, SW16 121 DL92
Ruth Cl, Stan. HA7 62 CM56
Ruthen Cl, Epsom KT18 156 CP114
Rutherford Cl, Borwd. WD6 26 CQ40
Sutton SM2 158 DD107
Uxbridge UB8 76 BM70
Rutherford St, SW1 199 M8
Rutherford Twr, Sthl. UB1 78 CB72
Rutherford Way, Bushey (Bushey Hth) WD23 41 CD46
Wembley HA9 62 CN63
Rutherglen Rd, SE2 106 EU79
Rutherwick Ri, Couls. CR5 175 DL117
Rutherwyke Cl, Epsom KT17 157 CU107
Rutherwyk Rd, Cher. KT16 133 BE101
Ruthin Cl, NW9 62 CS58
Ruthin Rd, SE3 104 EG79
Ruthven Av, Wal.Cr. EN8 15 DX33
Ruthven St, E9
off Lauriston Rd 85 DX67
Rutland App, Horn. RM11 72 FN57
Rutland Av, Sid. DA15 126 EU87
Rutland Cl, SW14 98 CP83
SW19 off Rutland Rd 120 DE94
Ashtead KT21 172 CL117
Bexley DA5 126 EX88
Chessington KT9 156 CM107
Dartford DA1 128 FK87
Epsom KT19 156 CR110
Redhill RH1 184 DF133
Rutland Ct, SW7
off Knightsbridge 100 DE75
Enfield EN3 30 DW43
Rutland Dr, Horn. RM11 72 FN57
Morden SM4 139 CZ100
Richmond TW10 117 CK88
Rutland Gdns, N4 65 DP58
SW7 198 C5
W13 79 CG71
Croydon CR0 160 DS105
Dagenham RM8 70 EW64
Rutland Gdns Ms, SW7 198 C5
Rutland Gate, SW7 198 C5
Belvedere DA17 107 FB78
Bromley BR2 144 EF98
Rutland Gate Ms, SW7 198 B5
Rutland Gro, W6 99 CV78
Rutland Ms, NW8
off Boundary Rd 82 DB67
Rutland Ms E, SW7 198 B6
Rutland Ms S, SW7 198 B6
Rutland Ms W, SW7
off Ennismore St 100 DE76
Rutland Pk, NW2 81 CW65
SE6 123 DZ89
Rutland Pk Gdns, NW2
off Rutland Pk 81 CW65
Rutland Pk Mans, NW2
off Walm La 81 CW65
Rutland Pl, EC1 197 H5
Bushey (Bushey Hth) WD23
off The Rutts 41 CD46
Rutland Rd, E7 86 EK66
E9 84 DW67
E11 68 EH57
E17 67 EA58
SW19 120 DE94
Harrow HA1 60 CC58
Hayes UB3 95 BR77
Ilford IG1 69 EP63
Southall UB1 78 CA71
Twickenham TW2 117 CD89
Rutland St, SW7 198 C6
Rutland Wk, SE6 123 DZ89
Rutland Way, Orp. BR5 146 EW100
Rutley Cl, SE17 off Royal Rd 101 DP79

Rutley Cl, Rom. (Harold Wd) RM3 off Pasteur Dr 52 FK54
Rutlish Rd, SW19 .... 140 DA95
Rutson Rd, W.Byf. (Byfleet) KT14 .... 152 BM114
Rutter Gdns, Mitch. CR4 .... 140 DC98
Rutters Cl, West Dr. UB7 .... 94 BN75
Rutts, The, Bushey (Bushey Hth) WD23 .... 41 CD46
Rutts Ter, SE14 .... 103 DX81
Ruvigny Gdns, SW15 .... 99 CX83
Ruxbury Rd, Cher. KT16 .... 133 BC100
Ruxley Cl, Epsom KT19 .... 156 CP106
Sidcup DA14 .... 126 EX93
Ruxley Cor Ind Est, Sid. DA14 .... 126 EX93
Ruxley Cres, Esher (Clay.) KT10 .... 155 CH107
Ruxley Gdns, Shep. TW17 .... 135 BQ99
Ruxley La, Epsom KT19 .... 156 CR106
Ruxley Ms, Epsom KT19 .... 156 CP106
Ruxley Ridge, Esher (Clay.) KT10 .... 155 CG108
Ruxton Cl, Swan. BR8 .... 147 FE97
Ryall Cl, St.Alb. (Brick.Wd) AL2 .... 8 BY29
Ryalls Ct, N20 .... 44 DF48
Ryan Cl, SE3 .... 104 EJ84
Ruislip HA4 .... 59 BV60
Ryan Dr, Brent. TW8 .... 97 CG79
Ryan Way, Wat. WD24 .... 24 BW39
Ryarsh Cres, Orp. BR6 .... 163 ES105
Rybrook Dr, Walt. KT12 .... 136 BW103
Rycott Path, SE22 off Lordship La 122 DU87
Rycroft La, Sev. TN14 .... 190 FE130
Rycroft Way, N17 .... 66 DT55
Ryculff Sq, SE3 .... 104 EF82
Rydal Cl, NW4 .... 43 CY53
Purley CR8 .... 160 DR113
Rydal Ct, Wat. WD25 off Grasmere Cl 7 BV32
Rydal Cres, Grnf. UB6 .... 79 CH69
Rydal Dr, Bexh. DA7 .... 106 FA81
West Wickham BR4 .... 144 EE103
Rydal Gdns, NW9 .... 62 CS57
SW15 .... 118 CS92
Hounslow TW3 .... 116 CB86
Wembley HA9 .... 61 CJ60
Rydal Rd, SW16 .... 121 DK91
Rydal Way, Egh. TW20 .... 113 BB94
Enfield EN3 .... 30 DW44
Ruislip HA4 .... 60 BW63
Ryde, The, Stai. TW18 .... 134 BH95
Ryde Cl, Wok. (Ripley) GU23 .... 168 BJ121
Ryde Heron, Wok. (Knap.) GU21 .... 166 AS117
RYDENS, Walt. KT12 .... 136 BW103
Rydens Av, Walt. KT12 .... 135 BV103
Rydens Cl, Walt. KT12 .... 136 BW103
Rydens Gro, Walt. KT12 .... 154 BX105
Rydens Pk, Walt. KT12 off Rydens Rd 136 BX103
Rydens Rd, Walt. KT12 .... 136 BX103
Rydens Way, Wok. GU22 .... 167 BA120
Ryde Pl, Twick. TW1 .... 117 CJ86
Ryder Cl, Brom. BR1 .... 124 EH92
Bushey WD23 .... 24 CB44
Hemel Hempstead (Bov.) HP3 .... 5 BA28
Ryder Ct, SW1 .... 199 L2
Ryder Dr, SE16 .... 102 DV78
Ryder Gdns, Rain. RM13 .... 89 FF65
Ryder Ms, E9 off Homerton High St 66 DW64
Ryders Ter, NW8 off Blenheim Ter 82 DC68
Ryder St, SW1 .... 199 L2
Ryder Yd, SW1 .... 199 L2
Rydes Cl, Wok. GU22 .... 167 BC120
Ryde Vale Rd, SW12 .... 121 DH89
Rydon Business Cen, Lthd. KT22 .... 171 CH119
Rydons Cl, SE9 .... 104 EL83
Rydon's La, Couls. CR5 .... 176 DQ120
Rydon St, N1 off St. Paul St 84 DQ67
Rydon's Wd Cl, Couls. CR5 .... 176 DQ120
Rydston Cl, N7 off Sutterton St 83 DM66
Rye, The, N14 .... 45 DJ45
Ryebridge Cl, Lthd. KT22 .... 171 CG118
Ryebrook Rd, Lthd. KT22 .... 171 CG118
Rye Cl, Bex. DA5 .... 127 FB86
Hornchurch RM12 .... 72 FJ64
Ryecotes Mead, SE21 .... 122 DS88
Rye Ct, Slou. SL1 off Alpha St S 92 AU76
Rye Cres, Orp. BR5 .... 146 EX102
Ryecroft, Grav. DA12 .... 131 GL92
Ryecroft Av, Ilf. IG5 .... 49 EP54
Twickenham TW2 .... 116 CB87
Ryecroft Cres, Barn. EN5 .... 27 CV43
Ryecroft Rd, SE13 .... 123 EC85
SW16 .... 121 DN93
Orpington BR5 .... 145 ER100
Sevenoaks (Otford) TN14 .... 181 FG116
Ryecroft St, SW6 .... 100 DB81
Ryedale, SE22 .... 122 DV86
Ryedale Ct, Sev. TN13 off London Rd 190 FE121
Rye Fld, Ashtd. KT21 .... 171 CK117
Orpington BR5 .... 146 EX102
Ryefield Av, Uxb. UB10 .... 77 BP66
Ryefield Ct, Nthwd. HA6 off Ryefield Cres 39 BU54
Ryefield Cres, Nthwd. HA6 .... 39 BU54
Ryefield Par, Nthwd. HA6 off Ryefield Cres 39 BU54
Ryefield Path, SW15 .... 119 CU88
Ryefield Rd, SE19 .... 122 DQ93
Ryegates, SE15 off Caulfield Rd 102 DV82
Rye Hill Pk, SE15 .... 102 DW84
Ryeland Cl, West Dr. UB7 .... 76 BL72
Ryelands Cl, Cat. CR3 .... 176 DS121
Ryelands Ct, Lthd. KT22 .... 171 CG118
Ryelands Cres, SE12 .... 124 EJ86
Ryelands Pl, Wey. KT13 .... 135 BS104
Rye La, SE15 .... 102 DU81
Sevenoaks TN14 .... 181 FG117
Rye Pas, SE15 .... 102 DU83
Rye Rd, SE15 .... 103 DX84
Rye Wk, SW15 .... 119 CX85
Rye Way, Edg. HA8 off Canons Dr 42 CM51
Ryfold Rd, SW19 .... 120 DA90
Ryhope Rd, N11 .... 45 DH49
Rykhill, Grays RM16 .... 111 GH76
Ryland Cl, Felt. TW13 .... 115 BT91
Rylandes Rd, NW2 .... 63 CU62
South Croydon CR2 .... 160 DV109
Ryland Ho, Croy. CR0 .... 142 DQ104
Ryland Rd, NW5 .... 83 DH65
Rylett Cres, W12 .... 99 CT76
Rylett Rd, W12 .... 99 CT75
Rylston Rd, N13 .... 46 DR48
SW6 .... 99 CZ79
Rymer Rd, Croy. CR0 .... 142 DS101
Rymer St, SE24 .... 121 DP86
Rymill Cl, Hem.H. (Bov.) HP3 .... 5 BA28
Rymill St, E16 .... 87 EN74
Rysbrack St, SW3 .... 198 D6
Rysted La, West. TN16 .... 189 EQ126
Rythe Cl, Chess. KT9 off Nigel Fisher Way 155 CJ108
Rythe Ct, T.Ditt. KT7 .... 137 CG101
Rythe Rd, Esher (Clay.) KT10 .... 155 CD106
Ryvers Rd, Slou. SL3 .... 93 AZ76

S

Sabah Ct, Ashf. TW15 .... 114 BN91
Sabbarton St, E16 off Silvertown Way 86 EF72
Sabella Ct, E3 .... 85 DZ68
Sabina Rd, Grays RM16 .... 111 GJ77
Sabine Rd, SW11 .... 100 DF83
Sable Cl, Houns. TW4 .... 96 BW83
Sable St, N1 .... 83 DP66
Sach Rd, E5 .... 66 DV61
Sackville Av, Brom. BR2 .... 144 EG102
Sackville Cl, Har. HA2 .... 61 CD62
Sevenoaks TN13 .... 191 FH122
Sackville Ct, Rom. RM3 off Sackville Cres 52 FL53
Sackville Cres, Rom. RM3 .... 52 FL53
Sackville Est, SW16 .... 121 DL90
Sackville Gdns, Ilf. IG1 .... 69 EM60
Sackville Rd, Dart. DA2 .... 128 FK89
Sutton SM2 .... 158 DA108
Sackville St, W1 .... 199 L1
Saddington St, Grav. DA12 .... 131 GH87
Saddlebrook Pk, Sun. TW16 .... 115 BS94
Saddlers Cl, Barn. (Arkley) EN5 .... 27 CV43
Borehamwood WD6 off Farriers Way 26 CR44
Pinner HA5 .... 40 CA51
Saddlers Ms, SW8 off Portland Gro 101 DM81
Kingston upon Thames (Hmptn W.) KT1 .... 137 CJ95
Wembley HA0 off The Boltons 61 CF63
Saddler's Pk, Dart. (Eyns.) DA4 .... 148 FK104
Saddlers Path, Borwd. WD6 .... 26 CR43
Saddlers Way, Epsom KT18 .... 172 CR119
Saddlescombe Way, N12 .... 44 DA50
Saddleworth Rd, Rom. RM3 .... 52 FJ51
Saddleworth Sq, Rom. RM3 .... 52 FJ51
Saddle Yd, W1 .... 199 H2
Sadler Cl, Mitch. CR4 .... 140 DF96
Waltham Cross (Chsht) EN7 off Markham Rd 14 DQ25
Sadlers Ride, W.Mol. KT8 .... 136 CC96
★ Sadler's Wells Thea, EC1 .... 196 F2
Saffron Av, E14 .... 85 ED73
Saffron Cl, NW11 .... 63 CZ57
Croydon CR0 .... 141 DL100
Slough (Datchet) SL3 .... 92 AV81
Saffron Ct, Felt. TW14 off Staines Rd 115 BQ87
Saffron Hill, EC1 .... 196 E5
Saffron Rd, Grays (Chaff.Hun.) RM16 .... 109 FW77
Romford RM5 .... 51 FC54
Saffron St, EC1 .... 196 E6
Saffron Way, Surb. KT6 .... 137 CK102
Sage Cl, E6 off Bradley Stone Rd 87 EM71
Sage Ms, SE22 off Lordship La 122 DT85
Sage St, E1 off Cable St 84 DW73
Sage Way, WC1 .... 196 B3
Saigasso Cl, E16 off Royal Rd 86 EK72
Sailacre Ho, SE10 off Calvert Rd 104 EF78
Sail Ct, E14 off Newport Av 85 ED73
Sailmakers Ct, SW6 off William Morris Way 100 DC83
Sail St, SE11 .... 200 C8
Sainfoin Rd, SW17 .... 120 DG89
Sainsbury Cen, The, Cher. KT16 off Guildford St 134 BG101
Sainsbury Rd, SE19 .... 122 DS92
St. Agatha's Dr, Kings.T. KT2 .... 118 CM93
St. Agathas Gro, Cars. SM5 .... 140 DF102
St. Agnes Cl, E9 off Gore Rd 84 DW67
St. Agnes Pl, SE11 .... 101 DN79
St. Agnes Well, EC1 off Old St 84 DR70
St. Aidans Ct, W13 off St. Aidans Rd 97 CJ75
Barking IG11 off Choats Rd 88 EV69
St. Aidan's Rd, SE22 .... 122 DV86
St. Aidans Rd, W13 .... 97 CH75
St. Aidan's Way, Grav. DA12 .... 131 GL90
St. Albans Av, E6 .... 87 EM69
St. Alban's Av, W4 .... 98 CR77
St. Albans Av, Felt. TW13 .... 116 BX92
Upminster RM14 .... 73 FS60
Weybridge KT13 .... 134 BN104
St. Albans Cl, NW11 .... 64 DA60
Gravesend DA12 .... 131 GK90
St. Albans Ct, EC2 .... 197 J8
St. Albans Cres, N22 .... 45 DN53
St. Alban's Cres, Wdf.Grn. IG8 .... 48 EG52
St. Albans Gdns, Grav. DA12 .... 131 GK90
St. Alban's Gdns, Tedd. TW11 .... 117 CG92
St. Albans Gro, W8 .... 100 DB76
St. Alban's Gro, Cars. SM5 .... 140 DE101
St. Albans La, NW11 off West Heath Dr 64 DA60
Abbots Langley (Bedmond) WD5 .... 7 BT26
St. Alban's Pl, N1 .... 83 DP67
St. Albans Rd, NW5 .... 64 DG62
NW10 .... 80 CS67
Barnet EN5 .... 27 CX39
Dartford DA1 .... 128 FM87
Epping (Cooper.) CM16 .... 18 EX29
Ilford IG3 .... 69 ET60
St. Alban's Rd, Kings.T. KT2 .... 118 CL93
St. Albans Rd, Pot.B. (Dance.H.) EN6 .... 27 CV35
Potters Bar (S.Mimms) EN6 .... 11 CV34
Radlett (Shenley) WD7 .... 10 CQ30
Reigate RH2 .... 184 DA133
St. Albans (Lon.Col.) AL2 .... 10 CN28
St. Alban's Rd, Sutt. SM1 .... 157 CZ105
St. Albans Rd, Wat. WD17, WD24, WD25 .... 23 BV40
St. Alban's Rd, Wdf.Grn. IG8 .... 48 EG52
St. Albans St, SW1 .... 199 M1
St. Albans Ter, W6 off Margravine Rd 99 CY79
St. Alban's Vil, NW5 off Highgate Rd 64 DG62
St. Alfege Pas, SE10 .... 103 EC79
St. Alfege Rd, SE7 .... 104 EK79
St. Alphage Gdns, EC2 .... 197 J7
St. Alphage Highwalk, EC2 .... 197 K7
St. Alphage Wk, Edg. HA8 .... 42 CQ54
St. Alphege Rd, N9 .... 46 DW45
St. Alphonsus Rd, SW4 .... 101 DJ84
St. Amunds Cl, SE6 .... 123 EA91
H St. Andrew's at Harrow, Har. HA1 .... 61 CE61
St. Andrews Av, Horn. RM12 .... 71 FG64
Wembley HA0 .... 61 CG63
St. Andrew's Cl, N12 off Woodside Av 44 DC49
St. Andrews Cl, NW2 .... 63 CV62
SE16 off Ryder Dr 102 DV78
SE28 .... 88 EX72
St. Andrew's Cl, Islw. TW7 .... 97 CD81
St. Andrews Cl, Ruis. HA4 .... 60 BX61
St. Andrew's Cl, Shep. TW17 .... 135 BR98
Staines (Wrays.) TW19 .... 112 AY87
St. Andrews Cl, Stan. HA7 .... 41 CJ54
Thames Ditton KT7 .... 137 CH102
St. Andrew's Cl, Wind. (Old Wind.) SL4 .... 112 AU86
St. Andrews Cl, Wok. GU21 .... 166 AW117
St. Andrew's Ct, SW18 .... 120 DC89
St. Andrews Ct, Slou. (Colnbr.) SL3 off High St 93 BD80
Watford WD17 .... 23 BV39
St. Andrews Dr, Orp. BR5 .... 146 EV100
Stanmore HA7 .... 41 CJ53
St. Andrews Gdns, Cob. KT11 .... 154 BW113
St. Andrew's Gro, N16 .... 66 DR60
St. Andrew's Hill, EC4 .... 196 G10
St. Andrew's Ms, N16 .... 66 DS60
St. Andrews Ms, SE3 off Mycenae Rd 104 EG80
SW12 off Emmanuel Rd 121 DK88
St. Andrews Pl, NW1 .... 195 J4
Brentwood (Shenf.) CM15 .... 55 FZ47
St. Andrews Rd, E11 .... 68 EE58
E13 .... 86 EH69
E17 .... 47 DX54
N9 .... 46 DW45
NW9 .... 62 CR60
NW10 .... 81 CV65
NW11 .... 63 CZ58
W3 .... 80 CS73
W7 off Churchfield Rd 97 CE75
W14 .... 99 CY79
Carshalton SM5 .... 140 DE104
Coulsdon CR5 .... 174 DG116
Croydon CR0 off Lower Coombe St 160 DQ105
Enfield EN1 .... 30 DR41
St. Andrew's Rd, Grav. DA12 .... 131 GJ87
St. Andrews Rd, Ilf. IG1 .... 69 EM59
Romford RM7 .... 71 FD58
Sidcup DA14 .... 126 EX90
St. Andrew's Rd, Surb. KT6 .... 137 CK100
St. Andrews Rd, Til. RM18 .... 110 GE81
Uxbridge UB10 .... 76 BM66
Watford WD19 .... 40 BX48
St. Andrews Sq, W11 off Bartle Rd 81 CY72
St. Andrew's Sq, Surb. KT6 .... 137 CK100
St. Andrews Twr, Sthl. UB1 .... 78 CC73
St. Andrew St, EC4 .... 196 E7
St. Andrews Wk, Cob. KT11 .... 169 BV115
St. Andrews Way, E3 .... 85 EB70
Oxted RH8 .... 188 EL130
St. Anna Rd, Barn. EN5 off Sampson Av 27 CX43
St. Annes Av, Stai. (Stanw.) TW19 .... 114 BK87
St. Annes Boul, Red. RH1 .... 185 DH132
St. Anne's Cl, N6 off Highgate W Hill 64 DG62
St. Annes Cl, Wal.Cr. (Chsht) EN7 .... 14 DU28
St. Anne's Cl, Wat. WD19 .... 40 BW49
St. Anne's Ct, W1 .... 195 M9
St. Anne's Dr, Red. RH1 .... 184 DG133
St. Annes Dr N, Red. RH1 .... 184 DG132
St. Annes Gdns, NW10 .... 80 CM69
St. Anne's Mt, Red. RH1 .... 184 DG133
St. Annes Pas, E14 off Newell St 85 DZ72
St. Annes Ri, Red. RH1 .... 184 DG133
St. Annes Rd, E11 .... 67 ED61
St. Anne's Rd, St.Alb. (Lon.Col.) AL2 .... 9 CK27
Uxbridge (Hare.) UB9 .... 58 BJ55
Wembley HA0 .... 61 CK64
St. Anne's Row, E14 off Commercial Rd 85 DZ72
St. Anne St, E14 off Commercial Rd 85 DZ72
St. Anne's Way, Red. RH1 off St. Anne's Dr 184 DG133
St. Ann's, Bark. IG11 .... 87 EQ67
St. Anns Cl, Cher. KT16 .... 133 BF100
St. Ann's Cres, SW18 .... 120 DC86
St. Ann's Gdns, NW5 off Queen's Cres 82 DG65
St. Ann's Hill, SW18 .... 120 DB85
St. Anns Hill Rd, Cher. KT16 .... 133 BC100
H St. Ann's Hosp, N15 .... 66 DQ57
St. Ann's La, SW1 .... 199 N6
St. Ann's Pk Rd, SW18 .... 120 DC86
St. Ann's Pas, SW13 .... 98 CS83
St. Anns Rd, N9 .... 46 DT47
St. Ann's Rd, N15 .... 65 DP57
SW13 .... 99 CT82
St. Anns Rd, W11 .... 81 CX73
St. Ann's Rd, Bark. IG11 off Axe St 87 EQ67
St. Anns Rd, Cher. KT16 .... 133 BF100
St. Ann's Rd, Har. HA1 .... 61 CE58
St. Ann's Shop Cen, Har. HA1 .... 61 CE58
St. Ann's St, SW1 .... 199 N6
St. Ann's Ter, NW8 .... 82 DD68
St. Anns Vil, W11 .... 81 CX74
St. Anns Way, S.Croy. CR2 .... 159 DP107
Westerham (Berry's Grn) TN16 .... 179 EP116
St. Anselm's Pl, W1 .... 195 H9
St. Anselms Rd, Hayes UB3 .... 95 BT75
St. Anthonys Av, Wdf.Grn. IG8 .... 48 EJ51
St. Anthonys Cl, E1 .... 202 B2
SW17 off College Gdns 120 DE89
H St. Anthony's Hosp, Sutt. SM3 .... 139 CX102
St. Anthony's Way, Felt. TW14 .... 95 BT84
St. Antony's Rd, E7 .... 86 EH66
St. Arvans Cl, Croy. CR0 .... 142 DS104
St. Asaph Rd, SE4 .... 103 DX83
St. Aubins Ct, N1 off De Beauvoir Est 84 DR67
St. Aubyn's Av, SW19 .... 119 CZ92
St. Aubyns Av, Houns. TW3 .... 116 CA85
St. Aubyns Cl, Orp. BR6 .... 145 ET104
St. Aubyns Gdns, Orp. BR6 .... 145 ET103
St. Aubyn's Rd, SE19 .... 122 DT93
St. Audrey Av, Bexh. DA7 .... 106 FA82
St. Augustine Rd, Grays RM16 .... 111 GH77
St. Augustine's Av, W5 .... 80 CL68
St. Augustines Av, Brom. BR2 .... 144 EL99
St. Augustine's Av, S.Croy. CR2 .... 160 DQ107
St. Augustines Av, Wem. HA9 .... 62 CL62
St. Augustine's Path, N5 off Highbury New Pk 66 DQ63
St. Augustines Rd, NW1 .... 83 DK66
St. Augustine's Rd, Belv. DA17 .... 106 EZ77
St. Austell Cl, Edg. HA8 .... 42 CM54
St. Austell Rd, SE13 .... 103 EC82
St. Awdry's Rd, Bark. IG11 .... 87 ER66
St. Awdry's Wk, Bark. IG11 off Station Par 87 EQ66
St. Barnabas Cl, SE22 off East Dulwich Gro 122 DS85
Beckenham BR3 .... 143 EC96
St. Barnabas Ct, Har. HA3 .... 40 CC53
St. Barnabas Gdns, W.Mol. KT8 .... 136 CA99
St. Barnabas Rd, E17 .... 67 EA58
Mitcham CR4 .... 120 DG94
Sutton SM1 .... 158 DD106
Woodford Green IG8 .... 48 EH53
St. Barnabas St, SW1 .... 198 G10
St. Barnabas Ter, E9 .... 67 DX64
St. Barnabas Vil, SW8 .... 101 DL81
St. Bartholomews Cl, SE26 .... 122 DW91
H St. Bartholomew's Hosp, EC1 .... 196 G7
St. Bartholomew's Rd, E6 .... 86 EL67
★ St. Bartholomew-the-Great Ch, EC1 .... 196 G7
St. Benedict's Av, Grav. DA12 .... 131 GK89
St. Benedict's Cl, SW17 off Church La 120 DG92
St. Benet's Cl, SW17 off College Gdns 120 DE89
St. Benet's Gro, Cars. SM5 .... 140 DC101
St. Benet's Pl, EC3 .... 197 L10
St. Benjamins Dr, Orp. BR6 .... 164 EW109
St. Bernards, Croy. CR0 .... 142 DS104
St. Bernard's Cl, SE27 off St. Gothard Rd 122 DR91
H St. Bernard's Hosp, Sthl. UB1 .... 97 CD75
St. Bernard's Rd, E6 .... 86 EK67
St. Bernards Rd, Slou. SL3 .... 92 AW76
St. Blaise Av, Brom. BR1 .... 144 EH96
St. Botolph Rd, Grav. DA11 .... 130 GC90
St. Botolph Row, EC3 .... 197 P9
St. Botolph's Av, Sev. TN13 .... 190 FG124
St. Botolph's Rd, Sev. TN13 .... 190 FG124
St. Botolph St, EC3 .... 197 P9
St. Brides Av, EC4 .... 196 F9
Edgware HA8 .... 42 CM53
★ St. Bride's Ch & Crypt Mus, EC4 .... 196 F9
St. Brides Cl, Erith DA18 off St. Katherines Rd 106 EX75
St. Bride's Pas, EC4 .... 196 F9
St. Bride St, EC4 .... 196 F8
St. Catherines, Wok. GU22 .... 166 AW119
St. Catherines Cl, SW17 .... 120 DE89
St. Catherines Ct, Felt. TW13 .... 115 BU88
St. Catherines Cross, Red. (Bletch.) RH1 .... 186 DS134
St. Catherines Dr, SE14 off Kitto Rd 103 DX82
St. Catherines Fm Ct, Ruis. HA4 .... 59 BQ58
St. Catherine's Ms, SW3 .... 198 D8
St. Catherines Rd, E4 .... 47 EA47
Ruislip HA4 .... 59 BR57
St. Catherines Twr, E10 off Kings Cl 67 EB59
St. Cecelia's Pl, SE3 off Humber Rd 104 EG78
St. Cecilia Rd, Grays RM16 .... 111 GH77
St. Cecilia's Cl, Sutt. SM3 .... 139 CY102
St. Chads Cl, Surb. KT6 .... 137 CJ101
St. Chad's Dr, Grav. DA12 .... 131 GL90
St. Chad's Gdns, Rom. RM6 .... 70 EY59
St. Chad's Pl, WC1 .... 196 A2
St. Chad's Rd, Rom. RM6 .... 70 EY58
Tilbury RM18 .... 111 GG80
St. Chad's St, WC1 .... 196 A2
St. Charles Ct, Wey. KT13 .... 152 BN106
H St. Charles Hosp, W10 .... 81 CX71
St. Charles Pl, W10 off Chesterton Rd 81 CY71
Weybridge KT13 .... 152 BN106
St. Charles Rd, Brwd. CM14 .... 54 FV46
St. Charles Sq, W10 .... 81 CY71
St. Christopher Rd, Uxb. UB8 .... 76 BK71
St. Christopher's Cl, Islw. TW7 .... 97 CE81
St. Christopher's Dr, Hayes UB3 .... 77 BV73
St. Christophers Gdns, Th.Hth. CR7 .... 141 DN97
St. Christophers Ms, Wall. SM6 .... 159 DJ106
St. Christopher's Pl, W1 .... 194 G8
St. Clair Cl, Oxt. RH8 .... 187 EC130
Reigate RH2 .... 184 DC134
St. Clair Dr, Wor.Pk. KT4 .... 139 CV104
St. Clair Rd, E13 .... 86 EH68
St. Clair's Rd, Croy. CR0 .... 142 DS103
St. Clare Business Pk, Hmptn. TW12 .... 116 CC93
St. Clare Cl, Ilf. IG5 .... 49 EM54
St. Clare St, EC3 .... 197 P9
St. Clement Cl, Uxb. UB8 .... 76 BK72
★ St. Clement Danes Ch, WC2 .... 196 C9
St. Clements Av, Grays RM20 .... 109 FU79
St. Clement's Cl, Grav. (Nthflt) DA11 off Coldharbour Rd 131 GF90
St. Clements Ct, EC4 off Clements La 84 DR73
N7 off Arundel Sq 83 DM65
Purfleet RM19 .... 108 FN77
St. Clements Hts, SE26 .... 122 DU90
St. Clement's La, WC2 .... 196 C9
St. Clements Rd, Grays RM20 .... 109 FW80
St. Clements St, N7 .... 83 DN65
St. Clements Way, Grays RM20 .... 109 FT79
Greenhithe DA9 .... 129 FU85
St. Clements Yd, SE22 off Archdale Rd 122 DT85
St. Cloud Rd, SE27 .... 122 DQ91
St. Columba's Cl, Grav. DA12 .... 131 GL90
St. Crispins Cl, NW3 .... 64 DE63
Southall UB1 .... 78 BZ72
St. Crispins Way, Cher. (Ott.) KT16 .... 151 BC109
St. Cross St, EC1 .... 196 E6
St. Cuthberts Cl, Egh. (Eng.Grn) TW20 .... 112 AX92
St. Cuthberts Gdns, Pnr. HA5 off Westfield Pk 40 BZ52
St. Cuthberts Rd, N13 .... 45 DN51
NW2 .... 81 CZ65
St. Cyprian's St, SW17 .... 120 DF91
St. David Cl, Uxb. UB8 .... 76 BK71
St. Davids, Couls. CR5 .... 175 DM117
St. Davids Cl, SE16 off Masters Dr 102 DV78
Iver SL0 .... 75 BD67
St. David's Cl, Reig. RH2 .... 184 DC133
St. Davids Cl, Wem. HA9 .... 62 CQ62
St. David's Cl, W.Wick. BR4 .... 143 EB101
St. David's Ct, E17 .... 67 EC55
St. David's Cres, Grav. DA12 .... 131 GK91
St. Davids Dr, Edg. HA8 .... 42 CM53
St. David's Dr, Egh. (Eng.Grn) TW20 .... 112 AW94
St. Davids Ms, E3 off Morgan St 85 DY69
St. Davids Pl, NW4 .... 63 CV59
St. Davids Rd, Swan. BR8 .... 127 FF93
St. Davids Sq, E14 .... 204 C10
St. Denis Rd, SE27 .... 122 DR91
St. Denys Cl, Pur. CR8 .... 159 DP110
St. Dionis Rd, SW6 .... 99 CZ82
St. Donatts Rd, SE14 .... 103 DZ81
St. Dunstan's All, EC3 .... 197 M10
St. Dunstans Av, W3 .... 80 CR73
St. Dunstans Cl, Hayes UB3 .... 95 BT77
St. Dunstan's Ct, EC4 off Fleet St 83 DN72
St. Dunstan's Dr, Grav. DA12 .... 131 GL91
St. Dunstans Gdns, W3 off St. Dunstans Av 80 CR73
St. Dunstan's Hill, EC3 .... 201 M1
Sutton SM1 .... 157 CY106
St. Dunstan's La, EC3 .... 201 M1
Beckenham BR3 .... 143 EC100
St. Dunstan's Rd, E7 .... 86 EJ65
St. Dunstans Rd, SE25 .... 142 DT98
W6 .... 99 CX78
W7 .... 97 CE75
St. Dunstan's Rd, Felt. TW13 .... 115 BT90
St. Dunstans Rd, Houns. TW4 .... 96 BW82
H St. Ebba's Hosp, Epsom KT19 .... 156 CQ109
St. Edith Cl, Epsom KT18 off St. Elizabeth Dr 156 CQ114
St. Edmunds Av, Ruis. HA4 .... 59 BR58
St. Edmunds Cl, NW8 off St. Edmunds Ter 82 DF67
SW17 off College Gdns 120 DE89
Erith DA18 off St. Katherines Rd 106 EX75
St. Edmunds Dr, Stan. HA7 .... 41 CG53
St. Edmund's La, Twick. TW2 .... 116 CB87
St. Edmunds Rd, N9 .... 46 DU45
Dartford DA1 .... 108 FM84
Ilford IG1 .... 69 EM58
St. Edmunds Sq, SW13 .... 99 CW79
St. Edmunds Ter, NW8 .... 82 DE67
St. Edwards Cl, NW11 .... 64 DA58
Croydon (New Adgtn) CR0 .... 161 ED111
St. Edwards Way, Rom. RM1 .... 71 FD57
St. Egberts Way, E4 .... 47 EC46
St. Elizabeth Dr, Epsom KT18 .... 156 CQ114
St. Elmo Rd, W12 .... 81 CT74
St. Elmos Rd, SE16 .... 203 K4

★ Place of interest ⇌ Railway station ⊖ London Underground station DLR Docklands Light Railway station Tram Tramlink station H Hospital Riv Pedestrian ferry landing stage

St. Erkenwald Ms, Bark. IG11
off St. Erkenwald Rd 87 ER67
St. Erkenwald Rd, Bark. IG11 .87 ER67
St. Ermin's Hill, SW1 . . . . . . .199 M6
St. Ervans Rd, W10 . . . . .81 CY71
St. Faiths Cl, Enf. EN2 . . . . . . .30 DQ39
St. Faith's Rd, SE21 . . . . .121 DP88
St. Fidelis Rd, Erith DA8 . . . . .107 FD77
St. Fillans Rd, SE6 . . . . .123 EC88
St. Francis Av, Grav. DA12 . . .131 GL91
St. Francis Cl, Orp. BR5 . . . .145 ES100
Potters Bar EN6 . . . . .12 DC33
Watford WD19 . . . . .39 BV46
St. Francis Pl, SW12
off Malwood Rd 121 DH86
St. Francis Rd, SE22 . . . . . . .102 DS84
Erith DA8 *off West St* 107 FD77
Uxbridge (Denh.) UB9 . . . .57 BF58
St. Francis Way, Grays RM16 .111 GJ77
Ilford IG1 . . . . .69 ES63
St. Frideswides Ms, E14
off Lodore St 85 EC72
St. Gabriel's Cl, E11 . . . . .68 EH61
E14 *off Morris Rd* 85 EB71
St. Gabriels Rd, NW2 . . . . . . .63 CX64
St. Georges Av, E7 . . . . .86 EH66
N7 . . . . .65 DK63
NW9 . . . . .62 CQ56
St. George's Av, W5 . . . . .97 CK75
St. Georges Av, Grays RM17 .110 GC77
Hornchurch RM11 . . . . .72 FM59
Southall UB1 . . . . .78 BZ73
St. George's Av, Wey. KT13 . .153 BP107
St. George's Cen, Grav. DA11 .131 GH86
St. Georges Cen, Har. HA1 . . .61 CE58
St. Georges Circ, SE1 . . . . . . .200 F6
St. Georges Cl, NW11 . . . . . . .63 CZ58
SE28 *off Redbourne Dr* 88 EX72
St. George's Cl, SW8
off Patmore St 101 DJ81
St. Georges Cl, Wem. HA0 . . .61 CG62
St. George's Cl, Wey. KT13 . .153 BQ106
St. Georges Ct, E6 . . . . .87 EM70
EC4 . . . . .196 F8
SW7 *off Gloucester Rd* . . .100 DC76
St. Georges Cres, Grav.
DA12 . . . . .131 GK91
St. George's Dr, SW1 . . . . . .199 K10
St. Georges Dr, Uxb. UB10 . . .58 BM62
Watford WD19 . . . . .40 BY48
St. Georges Flds, W2 . . . . . .194 C9
St. Georges Gdns, Epsom
KT17 . . . . .157 CT114
St. George's Gdns, Surb.
KT6 . . . . .138 CP103
St. Georges Gro, SW17 . . . . .120 DD90
ST. GEORGE'S HILL,
Wey. KT13 . . . . .153 BQ110
H **St. George's Hosp**, SW17 .120 DD92
Hornchurch RM12 . . . . .72 FK63
St. Georges Ind Est,
Kings.T. KT2 . . . . .117 CK92
St. Georges La, EC3 . . . . . . .197 M10
St. George's Lo, Wey. KT13 . .153 BR106
St. Georges Ms, NW1
off Regents Pk Rd 82 DF66
SE1 . . . . .200 E6
SE8 *off Grove St* 103 DZ77
St. Georges Pl, Twick. TW1
off Church St 117 CG88
St. Georges Rd, E7 . . . . .86 EH65
E10 . . . . .67 EC62
N9 . . . . .46 DU48
N13 . . . . .45 DM48
NW11 . . . . .63 CZ58
SE1 . . . . .200 E6
St. George's Rd, SW19 . . . . .119 CZ93
St. Georges Rd, W4 . . . . .98 CS75
W7 . . . . .79 CF74
Addlestone KT15 . . . . .152 BJ105
St. George's Rd, Beck. BR3 . .143 EB95
St. Georges Rd, Brom. BR1 .145 EM96
Dagenham RM9 . . . . .70 EY64
Enfield EN1 . . . . .30 DT38
St. George's Rd, Felt. TW13 . .116 BX91
St. Georges Rd, Ilf. IG1 . . . . .69 EM59
St. George's Rd, Kings.T. KT2 .118 CN94
Mitcham CR4 . . . . .141 DH97
Orpington BR5 . . . . .145 ER100
St. Georges Rd, Rich. TW9 . . .98 CM83
St. George's Rd, Sev. TN13 . .191 FH122
Sidcup DA14 . . . . .126 EX93
St. Georges Rd, Swan. BR8 .147 FF98
Twickenham TW1 . . . . .117 CH85
Wallington SM6 . . . . .159 DH106
Watford WD24 . . . . .23 BV38
St. George's Rd, Wey. KT13 .153 BR107
St. Georges Rd W, Brom.
BR1 . . . . .144 EL95
St. Georges Sq, E7 . . . . .86 EH66
E14 *off Narrow St* 85 DY73
SE8 . . . . .203 M8
St. George's Sq, SW1 . . . . . .199 M10
New Malden KT3
off High St 138 CS97
St. George's Sq Ms, SW1 . . .101 DK78
St. Georges Ter, NW1
off Regents Pk Rd 82 DF66
St. George St, W1 . . . . .195 J9
St. Georges Wk, Croy. CR0 . .142 DQ104
St. Georges Way, SE15 . . . . .102 DS79
St. George Wf, SW8 . . . . . . .101 DL78
St. Gerards Cl, SW4 . . . . . . .121 DJ85
St. German's Pl, SE3 . . . . . . .104 EG81
St. Germans Rd, SE23 . . . . . .123 DY88
St. Giles Av, Dag. RM10 . . . . .89 FB66
Potters Bar EN6 . . . . .11 CV32
Uxbridge UB10 . . . . .59 BQ63
St. Giles Cl, Dag. RM10
off St. Giles Av 89 FB66
Hounslow TW5 . . . . .96 BY80
Orpington BR6 . . . . .163 ER106
St. Giles Ct, WC2
off St. Giles High St 83 DL72
St. Giles High St, WC2 . . . . .195 N8
St. Giles Pas, WC2 . . . . .195 N9
St. Giles Rd, SE5 . . . . .102 DS80
St. Gilles Ho, E2 . . . . .85 DX68
St. Gothard Rd, SE27 . . . . . .122 DR91
St. Gregory Cl, Ruis. HA4 . . . .60 BW63
St. Gregorys Cres, Grav.
DA12 . . . . .131 GL89
St. Helena Rd, SE16 . . . . . . .203 H9
St. Helena St, WC1 . . . . .196 D3
St. Helens Cl, Uxb. UB8 . . . . .76 BK72
St. Helens Ct, Epp. CM16
off Hemnall St 18 EU30
Rainham RM13 . . . . .89 FG70
St. Helens Cres, SW16
off St. Helens Rd 141 DM95
St. Helens Gdns, W10 . . . . . . .81 CX72
St. Helens Pl, EC3 . . . . .197 M8
St. Helens Rd, SW16 . . . . . . .141 DM95
St. Helen's Rd, W13
off Dane Rd 79 CJ74
St. Helens Rd, Erith DA18 . . .106 EX75
Ilford IG1 . . . . .69 EM58
ST. HELIER, Cars. SM5 . . . . .140 DD101
⇌ **St. Helier** 140 DA100
St. Helier Av, Mord. SM4 . . .140 DC101
H **St. Helier Hosp**,
Cars. SM5 . . . . .140 DC102
St. Heliers Av, Houns. TW3 . .116 CA85
St. Heliers Rd, E10 . . . . .67 EC58
St. Hildas Av, Ashf. TW15 . . .114 BL92
St. Hildas Cl, NW6 . . . . .81 CX66
SW17 . . . . .120 DE89
St. Hilda's Rd, SW13 . . . . .99 CV79
St. Hilda's Way, Grav. DA12 .131 GK91
St. Huberts Cl, Ger.Cr. SL9 . . .56 AY60
St. Huberts La, Ger.Cr. SL9 . . .57 AZ61
St. Hughe's Cl, SW17 . . . . . .120 DE89
St. Hughs Rd, SE20
off Ridsdale Rd 142 DV95
St. Ives Cl, Rom. RM3 . . . . . . .52 FM52
St. Ivians Dr, Rom. RM2 . . . . . .71 FG55
St. James Av, N20 . . . . .44 DE48
W13 . . . . .79 CG74
Epsom KT17 . . . . .157 CT111
Sutton SM1 . . . . .158 DA106
St. James Cl, N20 . . . . .44 DE48
NW8 *off Prince Albert Rd* . .82 DF67
SE18 *off Congleton Gro* . . .105 EQ78
Barnet EN4 . . . . .28 DD42
Epsom KT18 . . . . .156 CS114
New Malden KT3 . . . . .139 CT99
Ruislip HA4 . . . . .60 BW61
Woking GU21 . . . . .166 AU118
St. James Ct, Green. DA9 . . .129 FT86
St. James Gdns, Rom.
(Lt.Hth) RM6 . . . . .70 EV56
Wembley HA0 . . . . .79 CK66
St. James Gate, NW1
off St. Paul's Cres 83 DK66
St. James Gro, SW11
off Reform St 100 DF82
St. James La, Green. DA9 . . .129 FS88
St. James Ms, E14 . . . . .204 E7
E17 *off St. James's St* 67 DY57
Weybridge KT13 . . . . .153 BP105
St. James Oaks, Grav. DA11 .131 GG87
St. James Pl, Dart. DA1
off Spital St 128 FK86
St. James Rd, E15 . . . . .86 EF64
N9 *off Queens Rd* 46 DV47
Brentwood CM14 . . . . .54 FW48
Carshalton SM5 . . . . .140 DE104
Kingston upon Thames
KT1 . . . . .138 CL96
Mitcham CR4 . . . . .120 DG94
Purley CR8 . . . . .159 DP113
Sevenoaks TN13 . . . . .191 FH122
Surbiton KT6 . . . . .137 CK100
Sutton SM1 . . . . .158 DA106
Waltham Cross (Chsht) EN7 .14 DQ28
Watford WD18 . . . . .23 BV43
ST. JAMES'S, SW1 . . . . .199 L3
St. James's, SE14 . . . . .103 DY81
St. James's Av, E2 . . . . .84 DW68
Beckenham BR3 . . . . .143 DY97
Gravesend DA11 . . . . .131 GG87
Hampton (Hmptn H.) TW12 .116 CC92
St. James's Cl, SW17
off St. James's Dr 120 DF89
St. James's Cotts, Rich. TW9
off Paradise Rd 118 CL85
St. James's Ct, SW1 . . . . . . .199 L6
St. James's Cres, SW9 . . . . . .101 DN83
St. James's Dr, SW12 . . . . . .120 DF88
SW17 . . . . .120 DF88
St. James's Gdns, W11 . . . . . .81 CY74
St. James's La, N10 . . . . .65 DH56
St. James's Mkt, SW1 . . . . . .199 M1
★ **St. James's Palace**, SW1 .199 L4
★ **St. James's Park**, SW1 . .199 M4
⊖ **St. James's Park** 199 M6
St. James's Pk, Croy. CR0 . .142 DQ101
St. James's Pas, EC3 . . . . . . .197 N9
St. James's Pl, SW1 . . . . .199 K3
St. James's Rd, SE1 . . . . . . .202 C10
SE16 . . . . .202 C6
Croydon CR0 . . . . .141 DP101
Gravesend DA11 . . . . .131 GG86
Hampton (Hmptn H.) TW12 .116 CB92
St. James's Sq, SW1 . . . . . . .199 L2
St. James's St, E17 . . . . .67 DY57
SW1 . . . . .199 K2
Gravesend DA11 . . . . .131 GG86
St. James's Ter, NW8
off Prince Albert Rd 82 DF68
St. James's Ter Ms, NW8 . . . .82 DF67
⇌ **St. James Street** 67 DY57
St. James St, W6 . . . . .99 CW78
St. James's Wk, EC1 . . . . . . .196 F4
St. James Wk, Iver SL0 . . . . . .93 BE75
St. James Way, Sid. DA14 . . .126 EY92
St. Jeromes Gro, Hayes UB3 .77 BQ72
St. Joans Rd, N9 . . . . .46 DT46
St. John Fisher Rd, Erith
DA18 . . . . .106 EX76
ST. JOHN'S, SE8 . . . . .103 EA82
ST. JOHN'S, Wok. GU21 . . . .166 AV118
⇌ **St. John's** 103 EA82
St. Johns Av, N11 . . . . .44 DF50
St. John's Av, NW10 . . . . .81 CT67
SW15 . . . . .119 CX85
St. Johns Av, Brwd. CM14 . . . .54 FX49
St. John's Av, Epsom KT17 . .157 CT112
St. Johns Av, Lthd. KT22 . . . .171 CH121
St. John's Ch Rd, E9 . . . . .66 DW64
St. Johns Cl, N14 . . . . .29 DJ44
St. John's Cl, SW6
off Dawes Rd 100 DA80
St. Johns Cl, Lthd. KT22 . . . .171 CJ120
St. John's Cl, Pot.B. EN6 . . . . .12 DC33
St. Johns Cl, Rain. RM13 . . . . .89 FG66
St. John's Cl, Uxb. UB8 . . . . .76 BH67
Wembley HA9 . . . . .62 CL64
St. Johns Cl, West. (Berry's Grn)
TN16 *off St. Johns Ri* 179 EP116
St. John's Cotts, SE20
off Maple Rd 122 DW94
St. Johns Cotts, Rich. TW9
off Kew Foot Rd 98 CL84
St. Johns Ct, Buck.H. IG9 . . . .48 EH46
St. John's Ct, Egh. TW20 . . . .113 BA92
Isleworth TW7 . . . . .97 CF82
St. Johns Ct, Nthwd. HA6
off Murray Rd 39 BS53
St. John's Ct, Wok. GU21
off St. Johns Hill Rd 166 AU119
St. Johns Cres, SW9 . . . . . . .101 DN83
St. Johns Dr, SW18 . . . . .120 DB88
Walton-on-Thames KT12 .136 BW102
St. John's Est, N1 . . . . .197 L1
SE1 . . . . .201 P4
St. John's Gdns, W11 . . . . . . .81 CZ73
★ **St. John's Gate & Mus of the Order of St. John**, EC1 . .196 F5
St. Johns Gro, N19 . . . . .65 DJ61
SW13 *off Terrace Gdns* 99 CT82
Richmond TW9
off Kew Foot Rd 98 CL84
St. John's Hill, SW11 . . . . . . .100 DD84
Coulsdon CR5 . . . . .175 DN117
Purley CR8 . . . . .175 DN116
Sevenoaks TN13 . . . . .191 FJ123
St. John's Hill Gro, SW11 . . .100 DD84
St. Johns Hill Rd, Wok.
GU21 . . . . .166 AU119
★ **St. John's Jerusalem**,
Dart. DA4 . . . . .128 FP94
St. John's La, EC1 . . . . .196 F5
St. John's Lye, Wok. GU21 . .166 AT119
St. John's Ms, W11
off Ledbury Rd 82 DA72
Woking GU21 . . . . .166 AU119
St. Johns Par, Sid. DA14 . . . .126 EU91
St. John's Pk, SE3 . . . . .104 EF80
St. John's Pas, SW19
off Ridgway Pl 119 CY93
St. John's Path, EC1 . . . . . . .196 F5
St. Johns Pathway, SE23
off Devonshire Rd 122 DW88
St. John's Pl, EC1 . . . . .196 F5
St. Johns Ri, West. (Berry's Grn)
TN16 . . . . .179 EP116
Woking GU21 . . . . .166 AV119
St. John's Rd, E4 . . . . .47 EB48
E6 *off Ron Leighton Way* . . .86 EL67
St. Johns Rd, E16 . . . . .86 EG72
St. John's Rd, E17 . . . . .47 EB54
N15 . . . . .66 DS58
St. Johns Rd, NW11 . . . . .63 CZ58
St. John's Rd, SE20 . . . . .122 DW94
SW11 . . . . .100 DE84
SW19 . . . . .119 CY94
Barking IG11 . . . . .87 ES67
Carshalton SM5 . . . . .140 DE104
St. Johns Rd, Croy. CR0
off Sylverdale Rd 141 DP104
St. John's Rd, Dart. DA2 . . . .128 FQ87
St. Johns Rd, E.Mol. KT8 . . . .137 CD98
St. John's Rd, Epp. CM16 . . . .17 ET30
St. Johns Rd, Erith DA8 . . . . .107 FD78
St. John's Rd, Felt. TW13 . . . .116 BY91
St. Johns Rd, Grav. DA12 . . . .131 GK87
Grays RM16 . . . . .111 GH78
St. John's Rd, Har. HA1 . . . . .61 CF58
St. Johns Rd, Ilf. IG2 . . . . .69 ER59
St. John's Rd, Islw. TW7 . . . . .97 CE82
Kingston upon Thames
(Hmptn W.) KT1 . . . . .137 CJ96
St. Johns Rd, Lthd. KT22 . . . .171 CJ121
Loughton IG10 . . . . .33 EM40
New Malden KT3 . . . . .138 CQ97
St. John's Rd, Orp. BR5 . . . .145 ER100
Richmond TW9 . . . . .98 CL84
St. Johns Rd, Rom. RM5 . . . . .51 FC50
St. John's Rd, Sev. TN13 . . . .191 FH121
St. Johns Rd, Sid. DA14 . . . . .126 EV91
Slough SL2 . . . . .74 AU74
Southall UB2 . . . . .96 BY76
Sutton SM1 . . . . .140 DA103
Uxbridge UB8 . . . . .76 BH67
Watford WD17 . . . . .23 BV40
St. John's Rd, Well. DA16 . . .106 EV83
Wembley HA9 . . . . .61 CK63
Woking GU21 . . . . .166 AV118
St. John's Sq, EC1 . . . . .196 F5
St. Johns Ter, E7 . . . . .86 EH65
SE18 . . . . .105 EQ79
SW15 *off Kingston Vale* . . .118 CR91
W10 *off Harrow Rd* 81 CX70
St. John's Ter, Enf. EN2 . . . . . .30 DR37
St. John St, EC1 . . . . .196 G5
St. Johns Vale, SE8 . . . . .103 EA82
St. Johns Vil, N19 . . . . .65 DK61
St. John's Vil, W8
off St. Mary's Pl 100 DB76
St. John's Waterside, Wok.
GU21 *off Copse Rd* 166 AT118
St. Johns Way, N19 . . . . .65 DK60
St. John's Way, Cher. KT16 . .134 BG102
ST. JOHN'S WOOD, NW8 . . . . .82 DC69
⊖ **St. John's Wood** 82 DD68
St. Johns Wd Ct, NW8 . . . . . .194 A3
St. Johns Wd High St, NW8 .194 A1
St. John's Wd Pk, NW8 . . . . . .82 DD67
St. Johns Wd Rd, NW8 . . . . . .82 DD70
St. John's Wd Ter, NW8 . . . . . .82 DD68
St. Josephs Cl, W10
off Bevington Rd 81 CY71
St. Joseph's Cl, Orp. BR6 . . .163 ET105
St. Joseph's Ct, SE7 . . . . . . .104 EH79
St. Josephs Dr, Sthl. UB1 . . . .78 BY74
St. Joseph's Gro, NW4 . . . . . .63 CV56
St. Josephs Rd, N9 . . . . .46 DV45
St. Josephs Rd, Wal.Cr. EN8 .15 DY33
St. Josephs St, SW8
off Battersea Pk Rd 101 DH81
St. Joseph's Vale, SE3 . . . . .103 ED82
St. Judes Cl, Egh. (Eng.Grn)
TW20 . . . . .112 AW92
St. Jude's Rd, E2 . . . . .84 DV68
Egham (Eng.Grn) TW20 . . .112 AW90
St. Jude St, N16 . . . . .66 DS64
St. Julians, Sev. TN15 . . . . . .191 FN128
St. Julian's Cl, SW16 . . . . . . .121 DN91
St. Julian's Fm Rd, SE27 . . . .121 DN91
St. Julian's Rd, NW6 . . . . .82 DA66
St. Justin Cl, Orp. BR5 . . . . .146 EX97
★ **St. Katharine's Dock**, E1 .202 A1
RIV **St. Katharine's Pier** 201 P2
St. Katharines Prec, NW1
off Outer Circle 83 DH68
St. Katharine's Way, E1 . . . . .202 A2
St. Katherines Rd, Cat. CR3 .186 DU125
Erith DA18 . . . . .106 EX75
St. Katherine's Row, EC3 . . .197 N9
St. Katherine's Wk, W11
off Freston Rd 81 CX73
St. Keverne Rd, SE9 . . . . . . .124 EL91
St. Kilda Rd, W13 . . . . .79 CG74
Orpington BR6 . . . . .145 ET102
St. Kilda's Rd, N16 . . . . .66 DR60
Brentwood CM15 . . . . .54 FV45
Harrow HA1 . . . . .61 CE58
St. Kitts Ter, SE19 . . . . .122 DS92
St. Laurence Cl, NW6 . . . . . . .81 CX67
Orpington BR5 . . . . .146 EX97
Uxbridge UB8 . . . . .76 BJ71
St. Laurence Way, Slou. SL1 . .92 AU76
St. Lawrence Cl, Abb.L. WD5 . .7 BS30
Edgware HA8 . . . . .42 CM52
Hemel Hempstead (Bov.) HP3 .5 BA27
St. Lawrence Ct, Abb.L. WD5
off St. Lawrence Cl 7 BS30
St. Lawrence Dr, Pnr. HA5 . . .59 BV58
★ **St. Lawrence Jewry Ch**,
EC2 . . . . .197 J8
St. Lawrence Rd, Upmin.
RM14 . . . . .72 FQ61
St. Lawrence St, E14 . . . . . . .204 E2
St. Lawrence's Way, Reig.
RH2 *off Church St* 184 DA134
St. Lawrence Ter, W10 . . . . . . .81 CY71
St. Lawrence Way, SW9 . . . .101 DN81
Caterham CR3 . . . . .176 DQ123
St. Albans (Brick.Wd) AL2 . . .8 BZ30
St. Leonards Av, E4 . . . . .47 ED51
Harrow HA3 . . . . .61 CJ56
St. Leonards Cl, Bushey
WD23 . . . . .24 BY42
Grays RM17 . . . . .110 FZ79
St. Leonard's Cl, Well. DA16
off Hook La 106 EU83
St. Leonards Ct, N1 . . . . .197 J2
St. Leonard's Gdns,
Houns. TW5 . . . . .96 BY80
St. Leonards Gdns, Ilf. IG1 . . .69 EQ64
St. Leonards Ri, Orp. BR6 . . .163 ES105
St. Leonards Rd, E14 . . . . .85 EB71
NW10 . . . . .80 CR70
St. Leonard's Rd, SW14 . . . . .98 CP83
St. Leonards Rd, W13 . . . . . . .79 CJ73
Amersham HP6 . . . . .20 AS35
Croydon CR0 . . . . .141 DP104
Epsom KT18 . . . . .173 CW119
Esher (Clay.) KT10 . . . . . . .155 CF107
St. Leonard's Rd, Surb. KT6 .137 CK99
St. Leonards Rd, T.Ditt. KT7 .137 CG100
Waltham Abbey (Nazeing)
EN9 . . . . .16 EE25
St. Leonards Sq, NW5 . . . . . . .82 DG65
St. Leonard's Sq, Surb. KT6
off St. Leonard's Rd 137 CK99
St. Leonards St, E3 . . . . .85 EB69
St. Leonard's Ter, SW3 . . . . .100 DF78
St. Leonards Wk, SW16 . . . . .121 DM94
Iver SL0 . . . . .93 BF76
St. Leonards Way, Horn.
RM11 . . . . .71 FH61
St. Loo Av, SW3 . . . . .100 DE79
St. Louis Rd, SE27 . . . . .122 DQ91
St. Loy's Rd, N17 . . . . .46 DS54
St. Lucia Dr, E15 . . . . .86 EF67
St. Luke Cl, Uxb. UB8 . . . . . . .76 BK72
ST. LUKE'S, EC1 . . . . .197 J4
St. Luke's Av, SW4 . . . . .101 DK84
St. Lukes Av, Enf. EN2 . . . . . . .30 DR38
St. Luke's Av, Ilf. IG1 . . . . . . .69 EP64
St. Luke's Cl, EC1 . . . . .197 J4
SE25 . . . . .142 DV100
St. Lukes Cl, Dart. (Lane End)
DA2 . . . . .129 FS92
Swanley BR8 . . . . .147 FD96
St. Luke's Est, EC1 . . . . .197 K3
H **St. Luke's Hosp for the Clergy**,
W1 . . . . .195 K5
St. Lukes Ms, W11
off Basing St 81 CZ72
St. Lukes Rd, W11 . . . . .81 CZ71
Uxbridge UB10 . . . . .76 BL66
Whyteleafe CR3
off Whyteleafe Hill 176 DT118
Windsor (Old Wind.) SL4 . .112 AU86
St. Lukes Sq, E16 . . . . .86 EF72
St. Luke's St, SW3 . . . . .198 B10
H **St. Luke's Woodside Hosp**,
N10 . . . . .64 DG56
St. Luke's Yd, W9 . . . . .81 CZ68
St. Malo Av, N9 . . . . .46 DW48
St. Margaret Dr, Epsom
KT18 . . . . .156 CR114
ST. MARGARETS, Twick. TW1 .117 CG85
St. Margarets, Bark. IG11 . . . .87 ER67
St. Margarets Av, N15 . . . . . . .65 DP56
N20 . . . . .44 DC47
Ashford TW15 . . . . .115 BP92
Harrow HA2 . . . . .60 CC62
Sidcup DA15 . . . . .125 ER90
St. Margaret's Av, Sutt. SM3 .139 CY104
St. Margarets Av, Uxb. UB8 . .76 BN70
Westerham (Berry's Grn)
TN16 *off St. Anns Way* . .179 EP116
St. Margarets Cl, EC2
off Lothbury 84 DR72
Dartford DA2 . . . . .129 FR89
Iver SL0
off St. Margarets Gate . . .75 BD68
Orpington BR6 . . . . .164 EV105
St. Margaret's Ct, SE1 . . . . . .201 J3
St. Margaret's Cres, SW15 . .119 CV85
Gravesend DA12 . . . . .131 GL90
St. Margaret's Dr, Twick. TW1 .117 CH85
St. Margarets Gate, Iver SL0 .75 BD68
St. Margaret's Gro, E11 . . . . . .68 EF62
SE18 . . . . .105 EQ79
St. Margarets Gro, Twick.
TW1 . . . . .117 CG86
H **St. Margaret's Hosp**,
Epp. CM16 . . . . .18 EV29
St. Margarets La, W8 . . . . . .100 DB76
St. Margarets Pas, SE13
off Church Ter 104 EE83
St. Margarets Path, SE18 . . .105 EQ78
St. Margarets Rd, E12 . . . . . . .68 EJ61
St. Margaret's Rd, N17 . . . . . .66 DS55
NW10 . . . . .81 CW69
St. Margarets Rd, SE4 . . . . . .103 DZ84
W7 .97 CE75
Coulsdon CR5 . . . . .175 DH121
Dartford (S.Darenth)
DA2, DA4 . . . . .129 FS93
Edgware HA8 . . . . .42 CP50
St. Margaret's Rd, Grav.
(Nthflt) DA11 . . . . .130 GE89
St. Margarets Rd, Islw. TW7 . .97 CH84
St. Margarets Rd, Ruis. HA4 .59 BR58
St. Margarets Rd, Twick. TW1 .97 CH84
St. Margarets Sq, SE4
off Adelaide Av 103 DZ84
St. Margaret's St, SW1 . . . . . .199 P5
St. Margaret's Ter, SE18 . . . .105 EQ78
⇌ **St. Margarets (TW1)** 117 CH86
St. Marks Av, Grav.
(Nthflt) DA11 . . . . .131 GF87
St. Marks Cl, SE10
off Ashburnham Gro 103 EC80
SW6 *off Ackmar Rd* 100 DA81
W11 *off St. Marks Rd* 81 CY72
St. Mark's Cl, Barn. EN5 . . . . .28 DB41
St. Marks Cl, Har. HA1
off Nightingale Av 61 CH59
St. Marks Cres, NW1 . . . . . . .82 DG67
St. Mark's Gate, E9
off Cadogan Ter 85 DZ66
St. Mark's Gro, SW10 . . . . . .100 DB79
St. Mark's Hill, Surb. KT6 . . .138 CL100
St. Mark's Pl, SW19
off Wimbledon Hill Rd . . .119 CZ93
St. Marks Pl, W11 . . . . .81 CY72
St. Marks Ri, E8 . . . . .66 DT64
St. Marks Rd, SE25
off Coventry Rd 142 DU98
St. Mark's Rd, W5
off The Common 80 CL74
St. Marks Rd, W7 . . . . .97 CE75
W10 . . . . .81 CX72
W11 . . . . .81 CY72
Bromley BR2 . . . . .144 EH97
Enfield EN1 . . . . .30 DT44
St. Mark's Rd, Epsom KT18 .173 CW118
St. Marks Rd, Mitch. CR4 . . .140 DF96
St. Mark's Rd, Tedd. TW11 . . .117 CH94
St. Marks Sq, NW1 . . . . .82 DG67
St. Mark St, E1 . . . . .84 DT72
St. Martha's Av, Wok. GU22 .167 AZ121
St. Martin Cl, Uxb. UB8 . . . . .76 BK72
★ **St. Martin-in-the-Fields Ch**,
WC2 . . . . .199 P1
St. Martins, Nthwd. HA6 . . . .39 BR50
St. Martins App, Ruis. HA4 . . .59 BS59
St. Martins Av, E6 . . . . .86 EK68
Epsom KT18 . . . . .156 CS114
St. Martins Cl, NW1 . . . . .83 DJ67
Enfield EN1 . . . . .30 DV39
Epsom KT17
off Church Rd 156 CS113
Erith DA18
off St. Helens Rd 106 EX75
St. Martin's Cl, Wat. WD19
off Muirfield Rd 40 BW49
West Drayton UB7
off St. Martin's Rd 94 BK76
St. Martin's Ct, WC2
off St. Martin's La 83 DL73
Ashford TW15 . . . . .114 BJ92
St. Martins Dr, Walt. KT12 . .136 BW104
St. Martins Est, SW2 . . . . . .121 DN88
St. Martin's La, WC2 . . . . . . .195 P10
St. Martins La, Beck. BR3 . . .143 EB99
St. Martin's-le-Grand, EC1 . .197 H8
St. Martins Meadow, West.
(Brasted) TN16 . . . . .180 EW123
St. Martin's Ms, WC2 . . . . . .199 P1
St. Martins Ms, Wok.
(Pyrford) GU22 . . . . .168 BG116
St. Martin's Pl, WC2 . . . . . . .199 P1
St. Martins Rd, N9 . . . . .46 DV47
St. Martin's Rd, SW9 . . . . . . .101 DM82
St. Martins Rd, Dart. DA1 . . .128 FM86
St. Martin's Rd, West Dr. UB7 .94 BJ76
St. Martin's St, WC2 . . . . . . .199 N1
St. Martins Ter, N10
off Pages La 44 DG54
St. Martins Way, SW17 . . . . .120 DC90
St. Mary Abbots Pl, W8 . . . . . .99 CZ76
St. Mary Abbots Ter, W14
off Holland Pk Rd 99 CZ76
St. Mary at Hill, EC3 . . . . . . .201 M1
★ **St. Mary at Hill Ch**, EC3 .201 M1
St. Mary Av, Wall. SM6 . . . . .140 DG104
St. Mary Axe, EC3 . . . . .197 M9
St. Marychurch St, SE16 . . . .202 F5
ST. MARY CRAY, Orp. BR5 . .146 EW99
⇌ **St. Mary Cray** 146 EU98
St. Marylebone Cl, NW10
off Craven Pk Rd 80 CS67
★ **St. Mary-le-Bow Ch**, EC2 .197 J9
St. Mary Rd, E17 . . . . .67 EA56
St. Marys, Bark. IG11 . . . . .87 ER67
St. Marys App, E12 . . . . .69 EM64
St. Marys Av, E11 . . . . .68 EH58
St. Mary's Av, N3 . . . . .43 CY54
St. Marys Av, Brwd.
(Shenf.) CM15 . . . . .55 GA43
St. Mary's Av, Brom. BR2 . . . .144 EE97
Northwood HA6 . . . . .39 BS50
Staines (Stanw.) TW19 . . . .114 BK87
Teddington TW11 . . . . .117 CF93
St. Mary's Av Cen, Sthl. UB2 .96 CB77
St. Mary's Av N, Sthl. UB2 . . .96 CB77
St. Mary's Av S, Sthl. UB2 . . .96 CB77
St. Mary's Cl, N17
off Kemble Rd 46 DT53
St. Marys Cl, Chess. KT9 . . . .156 CM108
Epsom KT17 . . . . .157 CU108
St. Mary's Cl, Grav. DA12 . . .131 GJ89

★ Place of interest ⇌ Railway station ⊖ London Underground station DLR Docklands Light Railway station Tra Tramlink station H Hospital RIV Pedestrian ferry landing stage

St. Marys Cl, Grays RM17 off Dock Rd . 110 GD79
St. Mary's Cl, Lthd. (Fetch.) KT22 . 171 CD123
St. Marys Cl, Orp. BR5 . 146 EV96
St. Mary's Cl, Oxt. RH8 . 188 EE129
Staines (Stanw.) TW19 . 114 BK87
Sunbury-on-Thames TW16 off Green Way . 135 BU98
Uxbridge (Hare.) UB9 . 58 BH55
St. Marys Cl, Wat. WD18 off Church St . 24 BW42
St. Mary's Copse, Wor.Pk. KT4 . 138 CS103
St. Marys Ct, E6 . 87 EM70
St. Mary's Ct, SE7 . 104 EK80
W5 off St. Mary's Rd . 97 CK75
St. Mary's Cres, NW4 . 63 CV55
Hayes UB3 . 77 BT73
St. Marys Cres, Islw. TW7 . 97 CD80
St. Mary's Cres, Stai. (Stanw.) TW19 . 114 BK87
St. Marys Dr, Felt. TW14 . 115 BQ87
St. Mary's Dr, Sev. TN13 . 190 FE123
St. Mary's Gdns, SE11 . 200 E8
St. Mary's Gate, W8 . 100 DB76
St. Marys Grn, N2 off Thomas More Way . 64 DC55
Westerham (Bigg.H.) TN16 . 178 EJ118
St. Mary's Gro, N1 . 83 DP65
SW13 . 99 CV83
W4 . 98 CP79
Richmond TW9 . 98 CM84
St. Marys Gro, West. (Bigg.H.) TN16 . 178 EJ118
H St. Mary's Hosp, W2 . 194 A8
St. Mary's La, Upmin. RM14 . 72 FN61
St. Marys Mans, W2 . 82 DC71
St. Mary's Ms, NW6 off Priory Rd . 82 DB66
Richmond TW10 . 117 CJ89
St. Mary's Mt, Cat. CR3 . 176 DT124
St. Marys Path, N1 . 83 DP67
St. Mary's Pl, SE9 off Eltham High St . 125 EN86
W5 off St. Mary's Rd . 97 CK75
W8 . 100 DB76
St. Marys Rd, E10 . 67 EC62
E13 . 86 EH68
N8 off High St . 65 DL56
N9 . 46 DW46
St. Mary's Rd, NW10 . 80 CS67
St. Marys Rd, NW11 . 63 CY59
St. Mary's Rd, SE15 . 102 DW81
SE25 . 142 DS97
SW19 (Wimbledon) . 119 CY92
W5 . 97 CK75
Barnet EN4 . 44 DF45
Bexley DA5 . 127 FC88
St. Marys Rd, E.Mol. KT8 . 137 CD99
St. Mary's Rd, Grays RM16 . 111 GH77
Greenhithe DA9 . 129 FS85
Hayes UB3 . 77 BT73
St. Marys Rd, Ilf. IG1 . 69 EQ61
Leatherhead KT22 . 171 CH122
St. Mary's Rd, Slou. SL3 . 74 AY74
South Croydon CR2 . 160 DR110
St. Marys Rd, Surb. KT6 . 137 CK100
Surbiton (Long Dit.) KT6 . 137 CJ101
Swanley BR8 . 147 FD98
St. Mary's Rd, Uxb. (Denh.) UB9 . 57 BF58
Uxbridge (Hare.) UB9 . 58 BH56
Waltham Cross (Chsht) EN8 . 14 DW29
Watford WD18 . 23 BV42
St. Marys Rd, Wey. KT13 . 153 BR105
St. Mary's Rd, Wok. GU21 . 166 AW117
Worcester Park KT4 . 138 CS103
St. Marys Sq, W2 . 82 DD71
St. Mary's Sq, W5 off St. Mary's Rd . 97 CK75
St. Marys Ter, W2 . 82 DD71
St. Mary's Twr, EC1 off Fortune St . 84 DQ70
St. Mary St, SE18 . 105 EM77
St. Marys Vw, Har. HA3 . 61 CJ57
St. Mary's Vw, Wat. WD18 . 24 BW42
St. Mary's Wk, SE11 . 200 E8
Hayes UB3 off St. Mary's Rd . 77 BT73
Redhill (Bletch.) RH1 . 186 DR133
St. Mary's Way, Chig. IG7 . 49 EN50
Gerrards Cross (Chal.St.P.) SL9 . 36 AX54
St. Matthew Cl, Uxb. UB8 . 76 BK72
St. Matthew's Av, Surb. KT6 . 138 CL102
St. Matthews Cl, Rain. RM13 . 89 FG66
Watford WD19 . 24 BX44
St. Matthew's Dr, Brom. BR1 . 145 EM97
St. Matthew's Rd, SW2 . 101 DM84
St. Matthews Rd, W5 off The Common . 80 CL74
St. Matthew's Rd, Red. RH1 . 184 DF133
St. Matthew's Row, E2 . 84 DU69
St. Matthew St, SW1 . 199 M7
St. Matthias Cl, NW9 . 63 CT57
St. Maur Rd, SW6 . 99 CZ81
St. Mellion Cl, SE28 . 88 EX72
St. Merryn Cl, SE18 . 105 ER80
St. Michael's All, EC3 . 197 L9
St. Michaels Av, N9 . 46 DW45
St. Michael's Av, Wem. HA9 . 80 CN65
St. Michaels Cl, E16 off Fulmer Rd . 86 EK71
St. Michael's Cl, N3 . 43 CZ54
St. Michaels Cl, N12 . 44 DE50
Bromley BR1 . 144 EL97
Erith DA18 off St. Helens Rd . 106 EX75
South Ockendon (Aveley) RM15 . 90 FQ73
Walton-on-Thames KT12 . 136 BW103
Worcester Park KT4 . 139 CT103
St. Michaels Cres, Pnr. HA5 . 60 BY58
St. Michaels Dr, Wat. WD25 . 7 BV33
St. Michaels Gdns, W10 off St. Lawrence Ter . 81 CY71
St. Michael's Ms, SW1 off Graham Ter . 100 DG77
St. Michaels Rd, NW2 . 63 CW63
St. Michael's Rd, SW9 . 101 DM82
Ashford TW15 . 114 BN92
St. Michaels Rd, Cat. CR3 . 176 DR122
Croydon CR0 . 142 DQ102
Grays RM16 . 111 GH78
Wallington SM6 . 159 DJ107
Welling DA16 . 106 EV83
St. Michael's Rd, Wok. GU21 . 151 BD114
St. Michaels St, W2 . 194 A8
St. Michaels Ter, N22 . 45 DL54
St. Michaels Way, Pot.B. EN6 . 12 DB30
St. Mildred's Ct, EC2 off Poultry . 84 DR72
St. Mildreds Rd, SE12 . 124 EE87
St. Monica's Rd, Tad. (Kgswd) KT20 . 173 CZ121
St. Nazaire Cl, Egh. TW20 off Mullens Rd . 113 BC92
St. Neots Cl, Borwd. WD6 . 26 CN38
St. Neots Rd, Rom. RM3 . 52 FM52
St. Nicholas Av, Horn. RM12 . 71 FG62
St. Nicholas Cen, Sutt. SM1 off St. Nicholas Way . 158 DB106
St. Nicholas Cl, Amer. HP7 . 20 AV39
Borehamwood (Els.) WD6 . 25 CK44
Uxbridge UB8 . 76 BK72
St. Nicholas Cres, Wok. (Pyrford) GU22 . 168 BG116
St. Nicholas Dr, Sev. TN13 . 191 FH126
Shepperton TW17 . 134 BN101
St. Nicholas Glebe, SW17 . 120 DG93
St. Nicholas Gro, Brwd. (Ingrave) CM13 . 55 GC50
St. Nicholas Hill, Lthd. KT22 . 171 CH122
St. Nicholas Pl, Loug. IG10 . 33 EN42
St. Nicholas Rd, SE18 . 105 ET78
Sutton SM1 . 158 DB106
Thames Ditton KT7 . 137 CF100
St. Nicholas St, SE8 off Lucas St . 103 EA81
St. Nicholas Way, Sutt. SM1 . 158 DB105
St. Nicolas La, Chis. BR7 . 144 EL95
St. Ninian's Ct, N20 . 44 DF48
St. Norbert Grn, SE4 . 103 DY84
St. Norbert Rd, SE4 . 103 DY84
St. Normans Way, Epsom KT17 . 157 CU110
St. Olaf's Rd, SW6 . 99 CY80
St. Olaves Cl, Stai. TW18 . 113 BF94
St. Olaves Ct, EC2 . 197 K9
St. Olave's Est, SE1 . 201 N4
St. Olaves Gdns, SE11 . 200 D8
St. Olaves Rd, E6 . 87 EN67
St. Olave's Wk, SW16 . 141 DJ96
St. Olav's Sq, SE16 . 202 F6
St. Oswald's Pl, SE11 . 101 DM78
St. Oswald's Rd, SW16 . 141 DP95
St. Oswulf St, SW1 . 199 N9
ST. PANCRAS, WC1 . 195 P3
⇌ St. Pancras . 195 P2
H St. Pancras Hosp, NW1 . 83 DK67
St. Pancras Way, NW1 . 83 DJ66
St. Patrick's Ct, Wdf.Grn. IG8 . 48 EE52
St. Patrick's Gdns, Grav. DA12 . 131 GK90
St. Patricks Pl, Grays RM16 . 111 GJ77
St. Paul Cl, Uxb. UB8 . 76 BK71
⊖ St. Paul's . 197 H8
St. Paul's All, EC4 off St. Paul's Chyd . 83 DP72
St. Paul's Av, NW2 . 81 CV65
SE16 . 203 J2
St. Pauls Av, Har. HA3 . 62 CM57
Slough SL2 . 74 AT73
★ St. Paul's Cath, EC4 . 197 H9
St. Paul's Chyd, EC4 . 196 G9
St. Paul's Cl, SE7 . 104 EK78
W5 . 98 CM75
St. Pauls Cl, Add. KT15 . 152 BG106
St. Paul's Cl, Ashf. TW15 . 115 BQ92
Carshalton SM5 . 140 DE102
St. Pauls Cl, Chess. KT9 . 155 CK105
Hayes UB3 . 95 BR78
St. Paul's Cl, Houns. TW3 . 96 BY82
St. Pauls Cl, S.Ock. (Aveley) RM15 . 90 FQ73
Swanscombe DA10 . 130 FY87
St. Paul's Ct, W14 off Colet Gdns . 99 CX77
St. Pauls Ctyd, SE8 off Deptford High St . 103 EA79
ST. PAUL'S CRAY, Orp. BR5 . 146 EU96
St. Pauls Cray Rd, Chis. BR7 . 145 ER95
St. Paul's Cres, NW1 . 83 DK66
St. Pauls Dr, E15 . 67 ED64
St. Paul's Ms, NW1 . 83 DK66
St. Paul's Pl, N1 . 84 DR65
St. Pauls Pl, S.Ock. (Aveley) RM15 . 90 FQ73
St. Pauls Ri, N13 . 45 DP51
St. Paul's Rd, N1 . 83 DP65
N17 . 46 DU52
Barking IG11 . 87 EQ67
Brentford TW8 . 97 CK79
Erith DA8 . 107 FC80
Richmond TW9 . 98 CM83
Staines TW18 . 113 BD92
Thornton Heath CR7 . 142 DQ97
St. Pauls Rd, Wok. GU22 . 167 BA117
St. Paul's Shrubbery, N1 . 84 DR65
St. Pauls Sq, Brom. BR2 . 144 EG96
St. Paul's Ter, SE17 off Westcott Rd . 101 DP79
St. Pauls Twr, E10 . 67 EB59
St. Paul St, N1 . 84 DQ67
St. Pauls Wk, Kings.T. KT2 off Alexandra Rd . 118 CN94
St. Pauls Way, E3 . 85 DZ71
E14 . 85 DZ71
St. Paul's Way, N3 . 44 DB52
St. Pauls Way, Wal.Abb. EN9 off Rochford Av . 15 ED33
Watford WD24 . 24 BW40
St. Pauls Wd Hill, Orp. BR5 . 145 ES96
St. Peter's All, EC3 . 197 L9
St. Peter's Av, E2 off St. Peter's Cl . 84 DU68
E17 . 68 EE56
St. Peters Av, N18 . 46 DU49
Westerham (Berry's Grn) TN16 . 179 EP116
St. Petersburgh Ms, W2 . 82 DB73
St. Petersburgh Pl, W2 . 82 DB73
St. Peter's Cl, E2 . 84 DU68
St. Peters Cl, SW17 . 120 DE89
St. Peter's Cl, Barn. EN5 . 27 CV43
St. Peters Cl, Bushey (Bushey Hth) WD23 . 41 CD46
Chislehurst BR7 . 125 ER94
Gerrards Cross (Chal.St.P.) SL9 off Lewis La . 36 AY53
Ilford IG2 . 69 ES56
Rickmansworth (Mill End) WD3 . 38 BH46
St. Peter's Cl, Ruis. HA4 . 60 BX61
St. Peters Cl, Stai. TW18 . 113 BF93
Swanscombe DA10 . 130 FZ87
Windsor (Old Wind.) SL4 off Church Rd . 112 AU85
Woking GU22 . 167 BC120
St. Peter's Ct, NW4 . 63 CW57
St. Peters Ct, SE3 off Eltham Rd . 124 EF85
SE4 off Wickham Rd . 103 DZ82
Gerrards Cross (Chal.St.P.) SL9 off High St . 36 AY53
West Molesey KT8 . 136 CA98
St. Peter's Gdns, SE27 . 121 DN90
St. Peter's Gro, W6 . 99 CU77
H St. Peter's Hosp, Cher. KT16 . 133 BD104
St. Peters La, Orp. BR5 . 146 EU96
St. Peters Ms, N4 off Warham Rd . 65 DP57
St. Peter's Pl, W9 off Shirland Rd . 82 DB70
St. Peters Rd, N9 . 46 DW46
St. Peter's Rd, W6 . 99 CU78
St. Peters Rd, Brwd. CM14 off Crescent Rd . 54 FV49
St. Peter's Rd, Croy. CR0 . 160 DR105
Grays RM16 . 111 GH77
St. Peters Rd, Kings.T. KT1 . 138 CN96
Southall UB1 . 78 CA71
Twickenham TW1 . 117 CH85
Uxbridge UB8 . 76 BK71
St. Peter's Rd, W.Mol. KT8 . 136 CA98
St. Peters Rd, Wok. GU22 . 167 BB121
St. Peter's Sq, E2 off St. Peter's Cl . 84 DU68
W6 . 99 CU78
St. Peters St, N1 . 83 DP67
St. Peter's St, S.Croy. CR2 . 160 DR106
St. Peters Ter, SW6 . 99 CY80
St. Peter's Vil, W6 . 99 CU77
St. Peter's Way, N1 . 84 DS66
St. Peters Way, W5 . 79 CK71
St. Peter's Way, Add. KT15 . 134 BG104
Chertsey KT16 . 151 BD105
St. Peters Way, Hayes UB3 . 95 BR78
Rickmansworth (Chorl.) WD3 . 21 BB43
St. Philip's Av, Wor.Pk. KT4 . 139 CV103
St. Philips Gate, Wor.Pk. KT4 . 139 CV103
St. Philip Sq, SW8 . 101 DH82
St. Philip's Rd, E8 . 84 DU65
St. Philips Rd, Surb. KT6 . 137 CK100
St. Philip St, SW8 . 101 DH82
St. Philip's Way, N1 off Linton St . 84 DQ67
St. Pinnock Av, Stai. TW18 . 134 BG95
St. Quentin Ho, SW18 off Fitzhugh Gro . 120 DD86
St. Quentin Rd, Well. DA16 . 105 ET83
St. Quintin Av, W10 . 81 CW71
St. Quintin Gdns, W10 . 81 CW71
St. Quintin Rd, E13 . 86 EH68
St. Raphael's Way, NW10 . 62 CQ64
St. Regis Cl, N10 . 45 DH54
St. Ronan's Cl, Barn. EN4 . 28 DD38
St. Ronans Cres, Wdf.Grn. IG8 . 48 EG52
St. Rule St, SW8 . 101 DJ82
St. Saviour's Est, SE1 . 201 P6
St. Saviour's Rd, SW2 . 121 DM85
St. Saviours Rd, Croy. CR0 . 142 DQ100
Saints Cl, SE27 off Wolfington Rd . 121 DP91
Saints Dr, E7 . 68 EK64
St. Silas Pl, NW5 . 82 DG65
St. Silas St Est, NW5 . 82 DG65
St. Simon's Av, SW15 . 119 CW85
St. Stephens Av, E17 . 67 EC57
W12 . 99 CV75
W13 . 79 CH72
St. Stephen's Av, Ashtd. KT21 . 172 CL116
St. Stephens Cl, E17 . 67 EB57
NW8 off Avenue Cl . 82 DE67
Southall UB1 . 78 CA71
St. Stephens Cres, W2 . 82 DA72
Brentwood CM13 . 55 GA49
Thornton Heath CR7 . 141 DN97
St. Stephens Gdn Est, W2 off Shrewsbury Rd . 82 DA72
St. Stephens Gdns, SW15 off Manfred Rd . 119 CZ85
W2 . 82 DA72
Twickenham TW1 . 117 CJ86
St. Stephens Gro, SE13 . 103 EC83
St. Stephens Ms, W2 off Chepstow Rd . 82 DA71
St. Stephen's Par, E7 off Green St . 86 EJ66
St. Stephen's Pas, Twick. TW1 off Richmond Rd . 117 CJ86
St. Stephens Rd, E3 . 85 DZ68
St. Stephens Rd, E6 . 86 EJ66
St. Stephen's Rd, E17 off Grove Rd . 67 EB57
St. Stephens Rd, W13 . 79 CH72
St. Stephen's Rd, Barn. EN5 . 27 CX43
St. Stephens Rd, Enf. EN3 . 31 DX37
Hounslow TW3 . 116 CA86
St. Stephen's Rd, West Dr. UB7 . 76 BK74
St. Stephens Row, EC4 . 197 K9
St. Stephens Ter, SW8 . 101 DM80
St. Stephen's Wk, SW7 . 100 DC77
Saints Wk, Grays RM16 . 111 GJ77
St. Swithin's La, EC4 . 197 K10
St. Swithun's Rd, SE13 . 123 ED85
St. Teresa Wk, Grays RM16 . 111 GH76
St. Theresa Cl, Epsom KT18 . 156 CQ114
St. Theresa's Rd, Felt. TW14 . 95 BT84
St. Thomas' Cl, Surb. KT6 . 138 CM102
St. Thomas Cl, Wok. GU21 off St. Mary's Rd . 166 AW117
St. Thomas Ct, Bex. DA5 . 126 FA87
St. Thomas Dr, Orp. BR5 . 145 EQ102
St. Thomas' Dr, Pnr. HA5 . 40 BY53
St. Thomas Gdns, Ilf. IG1 . 87 EQ65
H St. Thomas' Hosp, SE1 . 200 B6
St. Thomas Rd, E16 . 86 EG72
N14 . 45 DK45
St. Thomas' Rd, W4 . 98 CQ79
St. Thomas Rd, Belv. DA17 . 107 FC75
Brentwood CM14 . 54 FX47
Gravesend (Nthflt) DA11 off St. Margaret's Rd . 130 GE89
St. Thomas's Av, Grav. DA11 . 131 GH88
St. Thomas's Cl, Wal.Abb. EN9 . 16 EH33
St. Thomas's Gdns, NW5 off Queen's Cres . 82 DG65
St. Thomas's Pl, E9 . 84 DW66
St. Thomas's Rd, N4 . 65 DN61
NW10 . 80 CS67
St. Thomas's Sq, E9 . 84 DV66
St. Thomas St, SE1 . 201 K3
St. Thomas's Way, SW6 . 99 CZ80
St. Thomas Wk, Slou. (Colnbr.) SL3 . 93 BD80
St. Timothy's Ms, Brom. BR1 off Wharton Rd . 144 EH95
St. Ursula Gro, Pnr. HA5 . 60 BX57
St. Ursula Rd, Sthl. UB1 . 78 CA72
St. Vincent Cl, SE27 . 121 DP92
St. Vincent Rd, Twick. TW2 . 116 CC86
Walton-on-Thames KT12 . 135 BV104
St. Vincents Av, Dart. DA1 . 128 FN85
ST. VINCENT'S HAMLET, Brwd. CM14 . 52 FP46
St. Vincents La, NW7 . 43 CW50
St. Vincents Rd, Dart. DA1 . 128 FN86
St. Vincent St, W1 . 194 G7
St. Vincents Way, Pot.B. EN6 . 12 DC33
St. Wilfrids Cl, Barn. EN4 . 28 DE43
St. Wilfrids Rd, Barn. EN4 . 28 DD43
St. Winefride's Av, E12 . 69 EM64
St. Winifreds, Ken. CR8 . 176 DQ115
St. Winifreds Cl, Chig. IG7 . 49 EQ50
St. Winifred's Rd, Tedd. TW11 . 117 CH93
Westerham (Bigg.H.) TN16 . 179 EM118
Saladin Dr, Purf. RM19 . 108 FN77
Sala Ho, SE3 off Pinto Way . 104 EH84
Salamanca Pl, SE1 . 200 B9
Salamanca St, SE1 . 200 A9
Salamander Cl, Kings.T. KT2 . 117 CJ92
Salamander Quay, Uxb. (Hare.) UB9 . 38 BG52
Salamons Way, Rain. RM13 . 89 FE72
Salcombe Dr, Mord. SM4 . 139 CX102
Romford RM6 . 70 EZ58
Salcombe Gdns, NW7 . 43 CW51
Salcombe Pk, Loug. IG10 . 32 EK43
Salcombe Rd, E17 . 67 DZ59
N16 . 66 DS64
Ashford TW15 . 114 BL91
Salcombe Vil, Rich. TW10 off The Vineyard . 118 CL85
Salcombe Way, Hayes UB4 off Portland Rd . 77 BS69
Ruislip HA4 . 59 BU61
Salcot Cres, Croy. (New Adgtn) CR0 . 161 EC110
Salcote Rd, Grav. DA12 . 131 GL92
Salcott Rd, SW11 . 120 DE85
Croydon CR0 . 141 DL104
Salehurst Cl, Har. HA3 . 62 CL57
Salehurst Rd, SE4 . 123 DZ86
Salem Pl, Croy. CR0 . 142 DQ104
Gravesend (Nthflt) DA11 . 130 GD87
Salem Rd, W2 . 82 DB73
Sale Pl, W2 . 194 B7
Salesian Gdns, Cher. KT16 . 134 BG102
Sale St, E2 off Hereford St . 84 DU70
Salford Rd, SW2 . 121 DK88
Salhouse Cl, SE28 off Rollesby Way . 88 EW72
Salisbury Av, N3 . 63 CZ55
Barking IG11 . 87 ES66
Sutton SM1 . 157 CZ107
Swanley BR8 . 147 FG98
Salisbury Cl, SE17 . 201 K8
Amersham HP7 . 20 AS39
Potters Bar EN6 . 12 DC32
Upminster RM14 off Canterbury Av . 73 FT61
Worcester Park KT4 . 139 CT104
Salisbury Ct, EC4 . 196 F9
Salisbury Cres, Wal.Cr. (Chsht) EN8 . 15 DX32
Salisbury Gdns, SW19 . 119 CY94
Buckhurst Hill IG9 . 48 EK47
Salisbury Hall Gdns, E4 . 47 EA51
Salisbury Ho, E14 off Hobday St . 85 EB72
Salisbury Ms, SW6 off Dawes Rd . 99 CZ80
Bromley BR2 off Salisbury Rd . 144 EL99
Salisbury Pl, SW9 . 101 DP80
W1 . 194 D6
West Byfleet KT14 . 152 BJ111
Salisbury Rd, E4 . 47 EA48
E7 . 86 EG65
E10 . 67 EC61
E12 . 68 EK64
E17 . 67 EC57
N4 . 65 DP57
N9 . 46 DU48
N22 . 45 DP53
SE25 . 142 DU100
SW19 . 119 CY94
W13 . 97 CG75
Banstead SM7 . 158 DB114
Barnet EN5 . 27 CY41
Bexley DA5 . 126 FA88
Bromley BR2 . 144 EL99
Carshalton SM5 . 158 DF107
Dagenham RM10 . 89 FB65
Dartford DA2 . 128 FQ88
Enfield EN3 . 31 DZ37
Feltham TW13 . 116 BW88
Godstone RH9 . 186 DW131
Gravesend DA11 . 131 GF88
Grays RM17 . 110 GC79
Harrow HA1 . 61 CD57
Hounslow TW4 . 96 BW83
Hounslow (Hthrw Air.) TW6 . 115 BQ85
Ilford IG3 . 69 ES61
New Malden KT3 . 138 CR97
Salisbury Rd, Pnr. HA5 . 59 BU56
Richmond TW9 . 98 CL84
Romford RM2 . 71 FH57
Southall UB2 . 96 BY77
Uxbridge UB8 . 76 BH68
Watford WD24 . 23 BV38
Woking GU22 . 166 AY119
Worcester Park KT4 . 139 CT104
Salisbury Sq, EC4 . 196 E9
Salisbury St, NW8 . 194 A5
W3 . 98 CQ75
Salisbury Ter, SE15 . 102 DW83
Salisbury Wk, N19 . 65 DJ61
Salix Cl, Lthd. (Fetch.) KT22 . 170 CB123
Sunbury-on-Thames TW16 off Oak Gro . 115 BV94
Salix Rd, Grays RM17 . 110 GD79
Salliesfield, Twick. TW2 . 117 CD86
Sally Murrey Cl, E12 off Grantham Rd . 69 EN63
Salmen Rd, E13 . 86 EF68
Salmond Cl, Stan. HA7 off Robb Rd . 41 CG51
Salmonds Gro, Brwd. (Ingrave) CM13 . 55 GC50
Salmon La, E14 . 85 DY72
Salmon Rd, Belv. DA17 . 106 FA78
Dartford DA1 . 108 FM83
Salmons La, Whyt. CR3 . 176 DU119
Salmons La W, Cat. CR3 . 176 DS120
Salmons Rd, N9 . 46 DU46
Chessington KT9 . 155 CK107
Salmon St, E14 off Salmon La . 85 DZ72
NW9 . 62 CP60
Salomons Rd, E13 off Chalk Rd . 86 EJ71
Salop Rd, E17 . 67 DX58
Saltash Cl, Sutt. SM1 . 157 CZ105
Saltash Rd, Ilf. IG6 . 49 ER52
Welling DA16 . 106 EW81
Salt Box Hill, West. TN16 . 162 EH113
Saltcoats Rd, W4 . 98 CS75
Saltcote Cl, Dart. DA1 . 127 FE86
Saltcroft Cl, Wem. HA9 . 62 CP60
Salter Cl, Har. HA2 . 60 BZ62
Salterford Rd, SW17 . 120 DG93
Salter Rd, SE16 . 203 H3
Salters Cl, Rick. WD3 . 38 BL46
Salters Gdns, Wat. WD17 . 23 BU39
Salters Hall Ct, EC4 . 197 K10
Salters Hill, SE19 . 122 DR92
Salters Rd, E17 . 67 ED56
W10 . 81 CX70
Salter St, E14 . 85 EA73
NW10 . 81 CU69
Salter St Allyway, NW10 off Hythe Rd . 81 CU69
Salterton Rd, N7 . 65 DL62
Saltford Cl, Erith DA8 . 107 FE78
Salthill Cl, Uxb. UB8 . 58 BL64
Saltley Cl, E6 off Dunnock Rd . 86 EL72
Saltoun Rd, SW2 . 101 DN84
Saltram Cl, N15 . 66 DT56
Saltram Cres, W9 . 81 CZ69
Saltwell St, E14 . 85 EA73
Saltwood Cl, Orp. BR6 . 164 EW105
Saltwood Gro, SE17 off Merrow St . 102 DR78
Salusbury Rd, NW6 . 81 CY67
Salutation Rd, SE10 . 205 J8
Salvia Gdns, Grnf. UB6 off Selborne Gdns . 79 CG68
Salvin Rd, SW15 . 99 CX83
Salway Cl, Wdf.Grn. IG8 . 48 EF52
Salway Pl, E15 off Broadway . 86 EE65
Salway Rd, E15 off Great Eastern Rd . 85 ED65
Samantha Cl, E17 . 67 DZ59
Samantha Ms, Rom. (Hav.at.Bow.) RM4 . 51 FE48
Sam Bartram Cl, SE7 . 104 EJ78
Sambruck Ms, SE6 . 123 EB88
Samels Ct, W6 off South Black Lion La . 99 CU78
Samford St, NW8 . 194 A5
Samira Cl, E17 off Colchester Rd . 67 EA58
Samos Rd, SE20 . 142 DV96
Samphire Ct, Grays RM17 off Salix Rd . 110 GE79
Sampson Av, Barn. EN5 . 27 CX43
Sampson Cl, Belv. DA17 off Carrill Way . 106 EX76
Sampsons Ct, Shep. TW17 off Linden Way . 135 BQ99
Sampson St, E1 . 202 C3
Samson St, E13 . 86 EJ68
Samuel Cl, E8 off Pownall Rd . 84 DT67
SE14 . 103 DX79
SE18 . 104 EL77
Samuel Gray Gdns, Kings.T. KT2 . 137 CK95
Samuel Johnson Cl, SW16 off Curtis Fld Rd . 121 DN91
Samuel Lewis Trust Dws, E8 off Amhurst Rd . 66 DU63
N1 off Liverpool Rd . 83 DN65
SW3 . 198 B9
SW6 . 100 DA80
Samuel Lewis Trust Est, SE5 off Warner Rd . 102 DQ81
Samuels Cl, W6 off South Black Lion La . 99 CU78
Samuel St, SE15 . 102 DT80
SE18 . 105 EM77
Sancroft Cl, NW2 . 63 CV62
Sancroft Rd, Har. HA3 . 41 CF54
Sancroft St, SE11 . 200 C10
Sanctuary, The, SW1 . 199 N5
Bexley DA5 . 126 EX86
Morden SM4 . 140 DA100
Sanctuary Cl, Dart. DA1 . 128 FJ86
Uxbridge (Hare.) UB9 . 38 BJ52
Sanctuary Ms, E8 off Queensbridge Rd . 84 DT65

★ Place of interest ⇌ Railway station ⊖ London Underground station DLR Docklands Light Railway station Tra Tramlink station H Hospital Riv Pedestrian ferry landing stage

Sanctuary Rd, Houns. (Hthrw Air.) TW6 .114 BN86
Sanctuary St, SE1 .201 J5
Sandale Cl, N16 off Stoke Newington Ch St .66 DR62
Sandall Cl, W5 .80 CL70
Sandall Ho, E3 off Daling Way .85 DY68
Sandall Rd, NW5 .83 DJ65
W5 .80 CL70
Sandal Rd, N18 .46 DU50
New Malden KT3 .138 CR99
Sandal St, E15 .86 EE67
Sandalwood Av, Cher. KT16 .133 BD104
Sandalwood Cl, E1 off Solebay St .85 DY70
Sandalwood Dr, Ruis. HA4 .59 BQ59
Sandalwood Rd, Felt. TW13 .115 BV90
Sandbach Pl, SE18 .105 EQ77
Sandbanks, Felt. TW14 .115 BS88
Sandbanks Hill, Dart. (Bean) DA2 .129 FV93
Sandbourne Av, SW19 .140 DB97
Sandbourne Rd, SE4 .103 DY82
Sandbrook Cl, NW7 .42 CR51
Sandbrook Rd, N16 .66 DS62
Sandby Grn, SE9 .104 EL83
Sandcliff Rd, Erith DA8 .107 FD77
Sandcroft Cl, N13 .45 DP51
Sandells Av, Ashf. TW15 .115 BQ91
Sandell St, SE1 .200 D4
Sanderling Way, Green. DA9 129 FU85
Sanders Cl, Hmptn. (Hmptn H.) TW12 .116 CC92
St. Albans (Lon.Col.) AL2 .9 CK27
Sandersfield Gdns, Bans. SM7 .174 DA115
Sandersfield Rd, Bans. SM7 .174 DB115
Sanders La, NW7 .43 CX52
Sanderson Av, Sev. (Bad.Mt) TN14 .164 FA110
Sanderson Cl, NW5 .65 DH63
Sanderson Rd, Uxb. UB8 .76 BJ65
SANDERSTEAD, S.Croy. CR2 .160 DT111
⇌ Sanderstead .160 DR109
Sanderstead Av, NW2 .63 CY61
Sanderstead Cl, SW12 off Atkins Rd .121 DJ87
Sanderstead Ct Av, S.Croy. CR2 .160 DU113
Sanderstead Hill, S.Croy. CR2 .160 DS111
Sanderstead Rd, E10 .67 DY60
Orpington BR5 .146 EV100
South Croydon CR2 .160 DR108
Sanders Way, N19 off Sussex Way .65 DK60
Sandes Pl, Lthd. KT22 .171 CG118
Sandfield Gdns, Th.Hth. CR7 .141 DP97
Sandfield Pas, Th.Hth. CR7 .142 DQ97
Sandfield Rd, Th.Hth. CR7 .141 DP97
Sandfields, Wok. (Send) GU23 .167 BD124
Sandford Av, N22 .46 DQ52
Loughton IG10 .33 EQ41
Sandford Cl, E6 .87 EM70
Sandford Ct, N16 .66 DS60
Sandford Rd, E6 .86 EL70
Bexleyheath DA7 .106 EY84
Bromley BR2 .144 EG98
Sandford St, SW6 off King's Rd .100 DB80
Sandgate Cl, Rom. RM7 .71 FD59
Sandgate La, SW18 .120 DE88
Sandgate Rd, Well. DA16 .106 EW80
Sandgates, Cher. KT16 .133 BE103
Sandgate St, SE15 .102 DV79
Sandham Pt, SE18 off Vincent Rd .105 EP77
Sandhills, Wall. SM6 .159 DK105
Sandhills La, Vir.W. GU25 .132 AY99
Sandhills Meadow, Shep. TW17 .135 BQ101
Sandhurst Av, Har. HA2 .60 CB58
Surbiton KT5 .138 CP101
Sandhurst Cl, NW9 .62 CN55
South Croydon CR2 .160 DS109
Sandhurst Dr, Ilf. IG3 .69 ET63
Sandhurst Rd, N9 .30 DW44
NW9 .62 CN55
SE6 .123 ED88
Bexley DA5 .126 EX85
Orpington BR6 .146 EU104
Sidcup DA15 .125 ET90
Tilbury RM18 .111 GJ82
Sandhurst Way, S.Croy. CR2 .160 DS108
Sandifer Dr, NW2 .63 CX62
Sandiford Rd, Sutt. SM3 .139 CZ103
Sandiland Cres, Brom. BR2 .144 EF103
Tram Sandilands .142 DT103
Sandilands, Croy. CR0 .142 DU103
Sevenoaks TN13 .190 FD122
Sandilands Rd, SW6 .100 DB81
Sandison St, SE15 .102 DT83
Sandlands Gro, Tad. (Walt.Hill) KT20 .173 CU123
Sandlands Rd, Tad. (Walt.Hill) KT20 .173 CU123
Sandland St, WC1 .196 C7
Sandling Ri, SE9 .125 EN90
Sandlings, The, N22 .45 DN54
Sandlings Cl, SE15 off Pilkington Rd .102 DV82
Sandmartin Way, Wall. SM6 .140 DG101
Sandmere Rd, SW4 .101 DL84
Sandon Cl, Esher KT10 .137 CD101
Sandon Rd, Wal.Cr. (Chsht) EN8 .14 DW30
Sandow Cres, Hayes UB3 .95 BT76
Sandown Av, Dag. RM10 .89 FC65
Esher KT10 .154 CC106
Hornchurch RM12 .72 FK61
Sandown Cl, Houns. TW5 .95 BU81
Sandown Ct, Sutt. SM2 off Grange Rd .158 DB108
Sandown Dr, Cars. SM5 .158 DG109
Sandown Gate, Esher KT10 .136 CC104
Sandown Ind Pk, Esher KT10 .136 CA103
★ Sandown Park Racecourse, Esher KT10 .136 CB104
Sandown Rd, SE25 .142 DV99
Coulsdon CR5 .174 DG116
Esher KT10 .154 CC105
Gravesend DA12 .131 GJ93
Watford WD24 .24 BW38
Sandown Way, Nthlt. UB5 .78 BY65
Sandpiper Cl, E17 .47 DX53
SE16 .203 M4
Greenhithe DA9 .129 FU86
Sandpiper Dr, Erith DA8 .107 FH80
Sandpiper Rd, S.Croy. CR2 .161 DX111
Sutton SM1 .157 CZ106
Sandpipers, The, Grav. DA12 .131 GK89
Sandpiper Way, Orp. BR5 .146 EX98
Sandpit Hall Rd, Wok. (Chobham) GU24 .150 AU112
Sandpit La, Brwd. (Pilg.Hat.) CM14, CM15 .54 FT46
Sandpit Pl, SE7 .104 EL78
Sandpit Rd, Brom. BR1 .124 EE92
Dartford DA1 .108 FJ84
Sandpits Rd, Croy. CR0 .161 DX105
Richmond TW10 .117 CK89
Sandra Cl, N22 off New Rd .46 DQ53
Hounslow TW3 .116 CB85
Sandridge Cl, Barn. EN4 .28 DE37
Harrow HA1 .61 CE56
Sandridge St, N19 .65 DJ61
Sandringham Av, SW20 .139 CY96
Sandringham Cl, SW19 .119 CX88
Enfield EN1 .30 DS40
Ilford IG6 .69 EQ55
Woking GU22 .168 BG116
Sandringham Ct, W9 off Maida Vale .82 DC69
Kingston upon Thames KT2 off Skerne Wk .138 CL95
Sandringham Cres, Har. HA2 .60 CA61
Sandringham Dr, Ashf. TW15 .114 BK91
Dartford DA2 .127 FE89
Welling DA16 .105 ES82
Sandringham Gdns, N8 .65 DL58
N12 .44 DC51
Hounslow TW5 .95 BU81
Ilford IG6 .69 EQ55
West Molesey KT8 off Rosemary Av .136 CA98
Sandringham Ms, W5 off High St .79 CK73
Hampton TW12 off Oldfield Rd .136 BZ95
Sandringham Pk, Cob. KT11 .154 BZ112
Sandringham Rd, E7 .68 EJ64
E8 .66 DT64
E10 .67 ED58
N22 .66 DQ55
NW2 .81 CV65
NW11 .63 CY59
Barking IG11 .87 ET65
Brentwood (Pilg.Hat.) CM15 .54 FV43
Bromley BR1 .124 EG92
Hounslow (Hthrw Air.) TW6 .114 BL85
Northolt UB5 .78 CA66
Potters Bar EN6 .12 DB30
Thornton Heath CR7 .142 DQ99
Watford WD24 .24 BW37
Worcester Park KT4 .139 CU104
Sandringham Way, Wal.Cr. EN8 .15 DX34
Sandrock Pl, Croy. CR0 .161 DX105
Sandrock Rd, SE13 .103 EA83
Sandroyd Way, Cob. KT11 .154 CA113
SANDS END, SW6 .100 DC81
Sand's End La, SW6 .100 DB81
Sandstone La, E16 .86 EH73
Sandstone Pl, N19 .65 DH61
Sandstone Rd, SE12 .124 EH89
Sands Way, Wdf.Grn. IG8 .48 EL51
Sandtoft Rd, SE7 .104 EH79
Sandway Path, Orp. BR5 off Okemore Gdns .146 EW98
Sandway Rd, Orp. BR5 .146 EW98
Sandwell Cres, NW6 .82 DA65
Sandwich St, WC1 .195 P3
Sandwick Cl, NW7 .43 CU52
Sandy Bk Rd, Grav. DA12 .131 GH88
Sandy Bury, Orp. BR6 .145 ER104
Sandy Cl, Wok. GU22 off Sandy La .167 BC117
Sandycombe Rd, Felt. TW14 .115 BU88
Richmond TW9 .98 CN83
Sandycoombe Rd, Twick. TW1 .117 CJ86
Sandycroft, SE2 .106 EU79
Epsom KT17 .157 CW110
Sandycroft Rd, Amer. HP6 .20 AV39
Sandy Dr, Cob. KT11 .154 CA111
Feltham TW14 .115 BS88
Sandy Hill Av, SE18 .105 EP78
Sandy Hill Rd, SE18 .105 EP78
Sandyhill Rd, Ilf. IG1 .69 EP63
Sandy Hill Rd, Wall. SM6 .159 DJ109
Sandy La, Bushey WD23 .24 CC41
Cobham KT11 .154 CA112
Dartford (Bean) DA2 .129 FW89
Grays (Chad.St.M.) RM16 .111 GH79
Grays (W.Thur.) RM20 off London Rd W Thurrock .109 FV79
Harrow HA3 .62 CM58
Kingston upon Thames KT1 .117 CG94
Leatherhead KT22 .154 CA112
Mitcham CR4 .140 DG95
Northwood HA6 .39 BU50
Orpington BR6 .146 EU101
Orpington (St.P.Cray) BR5 .146 EX95
Oxted RH8 .187 EC129
Oxted (Lmpfld) RH8 .188 EH127
Redhill (Bletch.) RH1 .185 DP132
Richmond TW10 .117 CJ89
Sevenoaks TN13 .191 FJ123
Sidcup DA14 .126 EX94
South Ockendon (Aveley) RM15 .90 FM73
Sutton SM2 .157 CY108
Tadworth (Kgswd) KT20 .173 CZ124
Teddington TW11 .117 CG94
Virginia Water GU25 .132 AY98
Walton-on-Thames KT12 .135 BV100
Sandy La, Wat. WD25 .24 CC41
Westerham TN16 .189 ER125
Woking GU22 .167 BC116
Woking (Chobham) GU24 .150 AS109
Woking (Pyrford) GU22 .167 BF117
Woking (Send) GU23 .167 BC123
Sandy La Est, Rich. TW10 .117 CK89
Sandy La N, Wall. SM6 .159 DK107
Sandy La S, Wall. SM6 .159 DK107
Sandy Lo La, Nthwd. HA6 .39 BR47
Sandy Lo Rd, Rick. WD3 .39 BP47
Sandy Lo Way, Nthwd. HA6 .39 BS50
Sandy Mead, Epsom KT19 .156 CN109
Sandymount Av, Stan. HA7 .41 CJ50
Sandy Ridge, Chis. BR7 .125 EN93
Sandy Ri, Ger.Cr. (Chal.St.P.) SL9 .36 AY53
Sandy Rd, NW3 .64 DB62
Addlestone KT15 .152 BG107
Sandy's Row, E1 .197 N7
Sandy Way, Cob. KT11 .154 CA112
Croydon CR0 .143 DZ104
Walton-on-Thames KT12 .135 BT102
Woking GU22 .167 BC117
Sanford La, N16 off Lawrence Bldgs .66 DT61
Sanford St, SE14 .103 DY79
Sanford Ter, N16 .66 DT62
Sanford Wk, N16 off Sanford Ter .66 DT61
SE14 off Cold Blow La .103 DY79
Sanger Av, Chess. KT9 .156 CL106
Sanger Dr, Wok. (Send) GU23 .167 BC123
Sangley Rd, SE6 .123 EB87
SE25 .142 DS98
Sangora Rd, SW11 .100 DD84
San Ho, E9 off Bradstock Rd .85 DX65
San Juan Dr, Grays (Chaff.Hun.) RM16 .109 FW77
San Luis Dr, Grays (Chaff.Hun.) RM16 .109 FW77
San Marcos Dr, Grays (Chaff.Hun.) RM16 .109 FW77
Sansom Rd, E11 .68 EE61
Sansom St, SE5 .102 DR80
Sans Wk, EC1 .196 E4
Santers La, Pot.B. EN6 .11 CY33
Santiago Way, Grays (Chaff.Hun.) RM16 .109 FX78
Santley St, SW4 .101 DM84
Santos Rd, SW18 .120 DA85
Santway, The, Stan. HA7 .41 CE50
Sanway Cl, W.Byf. (Byfleet) KT14 .152 BL114
Sanway Rd, W.Byf. (Byfleet) KT14 .152 BL114
Sapcote Trd Cen, NW10 .63 CT64
Saperton Wk, SE11 .200 C8
Sapho Pk, Grav. DA12 .131 GM91
Saphora Cl, Orp. BR6 .163 ER106
Sapperton Ct, EC1 .197 H4
Sapphire Cl, E6 .87 EN72
Dagenham RM8 .70 EW60
Sapphire Rd, NW10 off Hilltop Av .80 CR66
SE8 .203 L9
Sappho Ct, Wok. GU21 off Langmans Way .166 AS116
Saracen Cl, Croy. CR0 .142 DR100
Saracen's Head Yd, EC3 .197 N9
★ Saracens R.F.C., Wat. WD18 .23 BV43
Saracen St, E14 .85 EA72
Sara Ct, Beck. BR3 .143 EB95
Sara Cres, Green. DA9 .109 FU84
Sarah Ho, SW15 .99 CT84
Sara Ho, Erith DA8 off Larner Rd .107 FE80
Sara Pk, Grav. DA12 .131 GL91
Saratoga Rd, E5 .66 DW63
Sardinia St, WC2 .196 B9
Sargeant Cl, Uxb. UB8 off Ratcliffe Cl .76 BK69
Sarita Cl, Har. HA3 .41 CD54
Sarjant Path, SW19 off Queensmere Rd .119 CX89
Sark Cl, Houns. TW5 .96 CA80
Sark Ho, N1 off Clifton Rd .84 DQ65
Enfield EN3 off Eastfield Rd .31 DX38
Sark Wk, E16 .86 EH72
Sarnesfield Ho, SE15 off Pencraig Way .102 DV79
Sarnesfield Rd, Enf. EN2 off Church St .30 DR41
SARRATT, Rick. WD3 .22 BG35
Sarratt Bottom, Rick. (Sarratt) WD3 .21 BE36
Sarratt La, Rick. WD3 .22 BH40
Sarratt Rd, Rick. WD3 .22 BM41
Sarre Av, Horn. RM12 .90 FJ65
Sarre Rd, NW2 .63 CZ64
Orpington BR5 .146 EW99
Sarsby Dr, Stai. TW19 .113 BA89
Sarsen Av, Houns. TW3 .96 BZ82
Sarsfeld Rd, SW12 .120 DF88
Sarsfield Rd, Grnf. UB6 .79 CH68
Sartor Rd, SE15 .103 DX84
Sarum Complex, Uxb. UB8 .76 BH68
Sarum Grn, Wey. KT13 .135 BS104
Sarum Ter, E3 off Bow Common La .85 DZ70
Satanita Cl, E16 off High Meads Rd .86 EK72
Satchell Mead, NW9 .43 CT53
Satchwell Rd, E2 .84 DU69
Satis Ct, Epsom KT17 off Windmill Av .157 CT111
Sattar Ms, N16 off Clissold Rd .66 DR62
Sauls Grn, E11 off Napier Rd .68 EE62
Saunder Cl, Wal.Cr. EN8 off Welsummer Way .15 DX27
Saunders Cl, E14 .203 N1
Gravesend (Nthflt) DA11 .130 GE89
Ilford IG1 off Vicarage La .69 ER60
Saunders Copse, Wok. GU22 .166 AV122
Saunders La, Wok. GU22 .166 AS122
Saunders Ness Rd, E14 .204 E10
Saunders Rd, SE18 .105 ET78
Uxbridge UB10 .76 BM66
Saunders St, SE11 .200 D9
Saunders Way, SE28 off Oriole Way .88 EV73
Dartford DA1 .128 FM89
Saunderton Rd, Wem. HA0 .61 CH64
Saunton Av, Hayes UB3 .95 BT80
Saunton Rd, Horn. RM12 .71 FG61
Savage Gdns, E6 .87 EM72
EC3 .197 N10
Savannah Cl, SE15 off Chandler Way .102 DT80
Savay Cl, Uxb. (Denh.) UB9 .58 BG59
Savay La, Uxb. (Denh.) UB9 .58 BG58
Savernake Rd, N9 .30 DU44
NW3 .64 DF63
Savery Dr, Surb. KT6 .137 CJ101
Savile Cl, N.Mal. KT3 .138 CS99
Thames Ditton KT7 .137 CF102
Savile Gdns, Croy. CR0 .142 DT103
Savile Row, W1 .195 K10
Savill Cl, Wal.Cr. (Chsht) EN7 off Markham Rd .14 DQ25
Saville Cl, Epsom KT19 .156 CP111
Saville Cres, Ashf. TW15 .115 BR93
Saville Rd, E16 .86 EL74
W4 .98 CR76
Romford RM6 .70 EZ58
Twickenham TW1 .117 CF88
Saville Row, Brom. BR2 .144 EF102
Enfield EN3 .31 DX40
Savill Gdns, SW20 off Bodnant Gdns .139 CU97
Savill Ms, Egh. (Eng.Grn) TW20 .112 AX93
Savill Row, Wdf.Grn. IG8 .48 EF51
Savona Cl, SW19 .119 CY94
Savona Est, SW8 .101 DJ80
Savona St, SW8 .101 DJ80
Savoy Av, Hayes UB3 .95 BS78
Savoy Bldgs, WC2 .200 B1
Savoy Circ, W3 off Western Av .81 CT73
Savoy Cl, E15 off Arthingworth St .86 EE67
Edgware HA8 .42 CN50
Uxbridge (Hare.) UB9 .38 BK54
Savoy Ct, WC2 .200 A1
Savoy Hill, WC2 .200 B1
Savoy Ms, SW9 .101 DL83
RIV Savoy Pier .200 B1
Savoy Pl, WC2 .200 A1
Savoy Rd, Dart. DA1 .128 FK85
Savoy Row, WC2 .196 B10
Savoy Steps, WC2 off Savoy St .83 DM73
Savoy St, WC2 .196 B10
Savoy Way, WC2 .200 B1
Sawbill Cl, Hayes UB4 .78 BX71
Sawkins Cl, SW19 .119 CY89
Sawley Rd, W12 .81 CU74
Sawmill Yd, E3 .85 DY67
Sawtry Cl, Cars. SM5 .140 DE101
Sawtry Way, Borwd. WD6 .26 CN38
Sawyer Cl, N9 off Lion Rd .46 DU47
Sawyers Chase, Rom. (Abridge) RM4 .34 EV41
Sawyers Cl, Dag. RM10 .89 FC65
Sawyers Gro, Brwd. CM15 .54 FX46
Sawyers Hall La, Brwd. CM15 .54 FW45
Sawyer's Hill, Rich. TW10 .118 CP87
Sawyers La, Borwd. (Els.) WD6 .25 CH40
Potters Bar EN6 .11 CX34
Sawyers Lawn, W13 .79 CF72
Sawyer St, SE1 .201 H4
Saxby Rd, SW2 .121 DL87
Saxham Rd, Bark. IG11 .87 ES68
Saxlingham Rd, E4 .47 ED48
Saxon Av, Felt. TW13 .116 BZ89
Saxonbury Av, Sun. TW16 .135 BV97
Saxonbury Cl, Mitch. CR4 .140 DD97
Saxonbury Gdns, Surb. KT6 .137 CJ102
Saxon Cl, E17 .67 EA59
Amersham HP6 .20 AS38
Brentwood CM13 .55 GA48
Gravesend (Nthflt) DA11 .130 GC90
Romford RM3 .52 FM54
Sevenoaks (Otford) TN14 .181 FF117
Slough SL3 .93 AZ75
Surbiton KT6 .137 CK100
Uxbridge UB8 .76 BM71
Saxon Ct, Borwd. WD6 .26 CL40
Saxon Dr, W3 .80 CP72
Saxonfield Cl, SW2 .121 DM87
Saxon Gdns, Sthl. UB1 off Saxon Rd .78 BY73
Saxon Pl, Dart. (Hort.Kir.) DA4 .148 FQ99
Saxon Rd, E3 .85 DZ68
E6 .87 EM70
N22 .45 DP53
SE25 .142 DR99
Ashford TW15 .115 BR93
Bromley BR1 .124 EF94
Dartford (Hawley) DA2 .128 FL91
Ilford IG1 .87 EP65
Kingston upon Thames KT2 .138 CL95
Southall UB1 .78 BY74
Walton-on-Thames KT12 .136 BX104
Wembley HA9 .62 CQ62
Saxons, Tad. KT20 .173 CX121
Saxon Shore Way, Grav. DA12 .131 GM86
Saxon Ter, SE6 off Neuchatel Rd .123 DZ89
Saxon Wk, Sid. DA14 .126 EW93
Saxon Way, N14 .29 DK44
Reigate RH2 .183 CZ133
Waltham Abbey EN9 .15 EC33
West Drayton UB7 .94 BJ79
Windsor (Old Wind.) SL4 .112 AV86
Saxony Par, Hayes UB3 .77 BQ71
Saxton Cl, SE13 .103 ED83
Saxton Ms, Wat. WD17 .23 BU40
Saxville Rd, Orp. BR5 .146 EV97
Sayer Cl, Green. DA9 .129 FU85
Sayers Cl, Lthd. (Fetch.) KT22 .170 CC124
Sayers Wk, Rich. TW10 off Stafford Pl .118 CM87
Sayesbury La, N18 .46 DU50
Sayes Ct, SE8 off Sayes Ct St .103 DZ79
Sayes Ct, Add. KT15 .152 BJ106
Sayes Ct Fm Dr, Add. KT15 .152 BH106
Sayes Ct Rd, Orp. BR5 .146 EU98
Sayes Ct St, SE8 .103 DZ79
Scadbury Pk, Chis. BR7 .125 ET93
Scads Hill Cl, Orp. BR6 .145 ET100
Scala St, W1 .195 L6
Scales Rd, N17 .66 DT55
Scammel Way, Wat. WD18 .23 BT44
Scampston Ms, W10 .81 CX72
Scampton Rd, Houns. (Hthrw Air.) TW6 off Southampton Rd E .114 BM86
Scandrett St, E1 .202 D3
Scarba Wk, N1 off Marquess Rd .84 DR65
Scarborough Cl, Sutt. SM2 .157 CZ111
Westerham (Bigg.H.) TN16 .178 EJ118
Scarborough Rd, E11 .67 ED60
N4 .65 DN59
N9 .46 DW45
Hounslow (Hthrw Air.) TW6 off Southern Perimeter Rd .115 BQ86
Scarborough St, E1 off West Tenter St .84 DT72
Scarbrook Rd, Croy. CR0 .142 DQ104
Scarle Rd, Wem. HA0 .79 CK65
Scarlet Cl, Orp. BR5 .146 EV98
Scarlet Rd, SE6 .124 EE90
Scarlett Cl, Wok. GU21 .166 AT118
Scarlette Manor Way, SW2 off Papworth Way .121 DN87
Scarsbrook Rd, SE3 .104 EK83
Scarsdale Pl, W8 off Wrights La .100 DB76
Scarsdale Rd, Har. HA2 .60 CC62
Scarsdale Vil, W8 .100 DA76
Scarth Rd, SW13 .99 CT83
Scatterdells La, Kings L. (Chipper.) WD4 .5 BF30
Scawen Cl, Cars. SM5 .158 DG105
Scawen Rd, SE8 .103 DY78
Scawfell St, E2 .84 DT68
Scaynes Link, N12 .44 DA50
Sceaux Est, SE5 .102 DS81
Sceptre Rd, E2 .84 DW69
Schofield Wk, SE3 off Dornberg Cl .104 EH80
Scholars Cl, Barn. EN5 .27 CY42
Scholars Pl, N16 off Oldfield Rd .66 DS62
Scholars Rd, E4 .47 EC46
SW12 .121 DJ88
Scholars Wk, Ger.Cr. (Chal.St.P.) SL9 .36 AY51
Slough (Langley) SL3 .93 BA75
Scholars Way, Amer. HP6 .20 AT38
Romford RM2 .71 FG57
Scholefield Rd, N19 .65 DK60
Schomberg Ho, SW1 off Page St .101 DK77
Schonfeld Sq, N16 .66 DR61
Schoolbank Rd, SE10 .205 K8
Schoolbell Ms, E3 off Arbery Rd .85 DY68
School Cres, Dart. (Cray.) DA1 .107 FF84
Schoolfield Rd, Grays RM20 .109 FU79
School Grn La, Epp. (N.Wld Bas.) CM16 .19 FC25
School Hill, Red. (Merst.) RH1 .185 DJ128
Schoolhouse Gdns, Loug. IG10 .33 EP42
Schoolhouse La, E1 .85 DX73
School Ho La, Tedd. TW11 .117 CH94
Schoolhouse Yd, SE18 off Bloomfield Rd .105 EP78
School La, Add. KT15 .152 BG105
Bushey WD23 .40 CB45
Caterham CR3 .186 DT126
Chalfont St. Giles HP8 .36 AV47
Chigwell IG7 .49 ET49
Dartford (Bean) DA2 .129 FW90
Dartford (Hort.Kir.) DA4 .148 FQ98
Egham TW20 .113 BA92
Gerrards Cross (Chal.St.P.) SL9 .36 AX54
Kingston upon Thames KT1 off School Rd .137 CJ95
Leatherhead (Fetch.) KT22 .171 CD122
Longfield DA3 .149 FT100
Pinner HA5 .60 BY56
St. Albans (Brick.Wd) AL2 .8 CA31
Sevenoaks (Seal) TN15 .191 FM121
Shepperton TW17 .135 BP100
Slough SL2 .74 AT73
Slough (Stoke P.) SL2 .74 AV67
Surbiton KT6 .138 CN102
Swanley BR8 .147 FH95
Tadworth (Walt.Hill) KT20 off Chequers La .173 CU125
Welling DA16 .106 EV83
Woking (Ock.) GU23 .169 BP122
School Mead, Abb.L. WD5 .7 BS32
School Pas, Kings.T. KT1 .138 CM96
Southall UB1 .78 BZ74
School Rd, E12 off Sixth Av .69 EM63
NW10 .80 CR70
Ashford TW15 .115 BP93
Chislehurst BR7 .145 EQ95
Dagenham RM10 .88 FA67
East Molesey KT8 .137 CD98
Hampton (Hmptn H.) TW12 .116 CC93
Hounslow TW3 .96 CC83
Kingston upon Thames KT1 .137 CJ95
Ongar CM5 .19 FG32
Potters Bar EN6 .12 DC30
West Drayton UB7 .94 BK79
School Rd Av, Hmptn. (Hmptn H.) TW12 .116 CC93
School Sq, SE10 off Greenroof Way .104 EF76
School Wk, Slou. SL2 off Grasmere Av .74 AV73
Sunbury-on-Thames TW16 .135 BT98
School Way, N12 off High Rd .44 DC49
Schoolway, N12 (Woodhouse Rd) .44 DD51
School Way, Dag. RM8 .70 EW62
Schooner Cl, E14 .204 F7
SE16 .203 H4
Barking IG11 .88 EV69

★ Place of interest · ⇌ Railway station · London Underground station · DLR Docklands Light Railway station · Tram Tramlink station · H Hospital · RIV Pedestrian ferry landing stage

Schooner Ct, Dart. DA2 108 FQ84
Schroder Ct, Egh. (Eng.Grn) TW20 112 AV92
Schubert Rd, SW15 119 CZ85
Borehamwood (Els.) WD6 25 CK44
★ Science Mus, SW7 198 A7
Scilla Ct, Grays RM17 110 GD79
Sclater St, E1 197 P4
Scoble Pl, N16 *off Amhurst Rd* 66 DT63
Scoles Cres, SW2 121 DN88
Scope Way, Kings.T. KT1 138 CL98
Scoresby St, SE1 200 F3
Scorton Av, Grnf. UB6 79 CG68
Scotch Common, W13 79 CG71
Scoter Cl, Wdf.Grn. IG8 *off Mallards Rd* 48 EH52
Scot Gro, Pnr. HA5 40 BX52
Scotia Rd, SW2 121 DN87
Scotland Br Rd, Add. (New Haw) KT15 152 BG111
Scotland Grn, N17 46 DT54
Scotland Grn Rd, Enf. EN3 31 DX43
Scotland Grn Rd N, Enf. EN3 31 DX42
Scotland Pl, SW1 199 P2
Scotland Rd, Buck.H. IG9 48 EJ46
Scotney Cl, Orp. BR6 163 EN105
Scotney Wk, Horn. RM12 *off Bonington Rd* 72 FK64
Scotscraig, Rad. WD7 25 CF35
Scotsdale Cl, Orp. BR5 145 ES98
Sutton SM3 157 CY108
Scotsdale Rd, SE12 124 EH85
Scotshall La, Warl. CR6 161 EC114
Scots Hill, Rick. (Crox.Grn) WD3 22 BM44
Scots Hill Cl, Rick. (Crox.Grn) WD3 22 BM44
Scotsmill La, Rick. (Crox.Grn) WD3 22 BM44
Scotswood St, EC1 196 E4
Scotswood Wk, N17 46 DU52
Scott Cl, SW16 141 DM95
Epsom KT19 156 CQ106
West Drayton UB7 94 BM77
Scott Ct, SW8 *off Silverthorne Rd* 101 DH82
W3 *off Petersfield Rd* 98 CR75
Scott Cres, Erith DA8 *off Cloudesley Rd* 107 FF81
Harrow HA2 60 CB60
Scott Ellis Gdns, NW8 82 DD69
Scottes La, Dag. RM8 *off Valence Av* 70 EX60
Scott Fm Cl, T.Ditt. KT7 137 CH102
Scott Gdns, Houns. TW5 96 BX80
Scott Ho, E13 *off Queens Rd W* 86 EG68
N18 46 DU50
Scott Lidgett Cres, SE16 202 B5
Scott Rd, Grav. DA12 131 GK92
Grays RM16 111 GG77
Scott Russell Pl, E14 204 B10
Scotts Av, Brom. BR2 143 ED96
Sunbury-on-Thames TW16 115 BS94
Scotts Cl, Horn. RM12 *off Rye Cl* 72 FJ64
Staines TW19 114 BK88
Scotts Dr, Hmptn. TW12 116 CB94
Scotts Fm Rd, Epsom KT19 156 CQ107
Scotts La, Brom. BR2 143 ED97
Walton-on-Thames KT12 154 BX105
Scotts Pas, SE18 *off Spray St* 105 EP77
Scotts Rd, E10 67 EC60
W12 99 CV75
Bromley BR1 124 EG94
Southall UB2 96 BW76
Scott St, E1 84 DV70
Scotts Way, Sev. TN13 190 FE122
Sunbury-on-Thames TW16 115 BS93
Scottswood Cl, Bushey WD23 *off Scottswood Rd* 24 BY40
Scottswood Rd, Bushey WD23 24 BY40
Scott Trimmer Way, Houns. TW3 96 BY82
Scottwell Dr, NW9 63 CT57
Scoulding Rd, E16 86 EF72
Scouler St, E14 204 F1
Scout App, NW10 62 CS63
Scout La, SW4 *off Old Town* 101 DJ83
Scout Way, NW7 42 CR49
Scovell Cres, SE1 201 H5
Scovell Rd, SE1 201 H5
Scratchers La, Long. (Fawk.Grn) DA3 149 FR103
Scrattons Ter, Bark. IG11 88 EX68
Scriven St, E8 84 DT67
Scrooby St, SE6 123 EB86
Scrubbitts Pk Rd, Rad. WD7 25 CG35
Scrubbitts Sq, Rad. WD7 *off The Dell* 25 CG36
Scrubs La, NW10 81 CU69
W10 81 CU69
Scrutton Cl, SW12 121 DK87
Scrutton St, EC2 197 M5
Scudamore La, NW9 62 CQ55
Scudders Hill, Long. (Fawk.Grn) DA3 149 FV100
Scutari Rd, SE22 122 DW85
Scylla Cres, Houns. (Hthrw Air.) TW6 115 BP87
Scylla Pl, Wok. (St.John's) GU21 *off Church Rd* 166 AU119
Scylla Rd, SE15 102 DV83
Hounslow (Hthrw Air.) TW6 115 BP86
Seaborough Rd, Grays RM16 111 GJ76
Seabright St, E2 *off Bethnal Grn Rd* 84 DV69
Seabrook Ct, Pot.B. EN6 *off Station Cl* 12 DA32
Seabrook Dr, W.Wick. BR4 144 EE103
Seabrooke Ri, Grays RM17 110 GB79
Seabrook Gdns, Rom. RM7 70 FA59
Seabrook Rd, Dag. RM8 70 EX62
Kings Langley WD4 7 BR27
Seaburn Cl, Rain. RM13 89 FE68
Seacole Cl, W3 80 CR71
Seacon Twr, E14 203 N5
Seacourt Rd, SE2 106 EX75
Slough SL3 93 BB77
Seacroft Gdns, Wat. WD19 40 BX48
Seafield Rd, N11 45 DK49
Seaford Cl, Ruis. HA4 59 BR61
Seaford Rd, E17 67 EB55
N15 66 DR57
W13 79 CH74
Enfield EN1 30 DS42
Hounslow (Hthrw Air.) TW6 114 BK85
Seaford St, WC1 196 A3
Seaforth Av, N.Mal. KT3 139 CV99
Seaforth Cl, Rom. RM1 51 FE52
Seaforth Cres, N5 66 DQ64
Seaforth Dr, Wal.Cr. EN8 15 DX34
Seaforth Gdns, N21 45 DM45
Epsom KT19 157 CT105
Woodford Green IG8 48 EJ50
Seaforth Pl, SW1 *off Buckingham Gate* 101 DJ76
Seagrave Rd, SW6 100 DA79
Seagry Rd, E11 68 EG58
Seagull Cl, Bark. IG11 88 EU69
Seagull La, E16 86 EG73
SEAL, Sev. TN15 191 FN121
Sealand Rd, Houns. (Hthrw Air.) TW6 114 BN86
Sealand Wk, Nthlt. UB5 *off Wayfarer Rd* 78 BY69
Seal Dr, Sev. (Seal) TN15 191 FM121
Seal Hollow Rd, Sev. TN13, TN15 191 FJ124
Seally Rd, Grays RM17 110 GA78
Seal Rd, Sev. TN14, TN15 191 FJ121
Seal St, E8 66 DT63
Seaman Cl, St.Alb. (Park St) AL2 9 CD25
Searches La, Abb.L. (Bedmond) WD5 7 BV28
Searchwood Rd, Warl. CR6 176 DV118
Searle Pl, N4 *off Evershot Rd* 65 DM60
Searles Cl, SW11 100 DE80
Searles Dr, E6 87 EP71
Searles Rd, SE1 201 L8
Sears St, SE5 102 DR80
Seasprite Cl, Nthlt. UB5 78 BX69
Seaton Av, Ilf. IG3 69 ES64
Seaton Cl, E13 *off New Barn St* 86 EH70
SE11 200 E10
SW15 119 CV88
Twickenham TW2 117 CD86
Seaton Dr, Ashf. TW15 114 BL89
Seaton Gdns, Ruis. HA4 59 BU62
Seaton Pt, E5 66 DU63
Seaton Rd, Dart. DA1 127 FG87
Hayes UB3 95 BR77
Mitcham CR4 140 DE96
St. Albans (Lon.Col.) AL2 9 CK26
Twickenham TW2 116 CC86
Welling DA16 106 EW80
Wembley HA0 80 CL68
Seaton Sq, NW7 *off Tavistock Av* 43 CX52
Seaton St, N18 46 DU50
Sebastian Av, Brwd. (Shenf.) CM15 55 GA44
Sebastian Ct, Bark. IG11 *off Meadow Rd* 87 ET66
Sebastian St, EC1 196 G3
Sebastopol Rd, N9 46 DU49
Sebbon St, N1 83 DP66
Sebergham Gro, NW7 43 CU52
Sebert Rd, E7 68 EH64
Sebright Pas, E2 *off Hackney Rd* 84 DU68
Sebright Rd, Barn. EN5 27 CX40
Secker Cres, Har. HA3 40 CC53
Secker St, SE1 200 D3
Second Av, E12 68 EL63
E13 86 EG69
E17 67 EA57
N18 46 DW49
NW4 63 CX56
SW14 98 CS83
W3 81 CT74
W10 81 CY70
Dagenham RM10 89 FB67
Enfield EN1 30 DT43
Grays RM20 109 FU79
Hayes UB3 77 BT74
Romford RM6 70 EW57
Waltham Abbey EN9 *off Breach Barn Mobile Home Pk* 16 EH30
Walton-on-Thames KT12 135 BV100
Watford WD25 24 BX35
Wembley HA9 61 CK61
Second Cl, W.Mol. KT8 136 CC98
Second Cross Rd, Twick. TW2 117 CE89
Second Way, Wem. HA9 62 CP63
Sedan Way, SE17 201 M10
Sedcombe Cl, Sid. DA14 *off Knoll Rd* 126 EV91
Sedcote Rd, Enf. EN3 30 DW43
Sedding St, SW1 198 F8
Seddon Highwalk, EC2 *off Beech St* 84 DQ71
Seddon Ho, EC2 *off The Barbican* 84 DQ71
Seddon Rd, Mord. SM4 140 DD99
Seddon St, WC1 196 C3
Sedgebrook Rd, SE3 104 EK82
Sedgecombe Av, Har. HA3 61 CJ57
Sedge Ct, Grays RM17 110 GE80
Sedgefield Cl, Rom. RM3 52 FM49
Sedgefield Cres, Rom. RM3 52 FM49
Sedgeford Rd, W12 81 CT74
Sedgehill Rd, SE6 123 EA91
Sedgemere Av, N2 64 DC55
Sedgemere Rd, SE2 106 EW76
Sedgemoor Dr, Dag. RM10 70 FA63
Sedge Rd, N17 46 DW52
Sedgeway, SE6 124 EF88
Sedgewick Av, Uxb. UB10 77 BP66
Sedgewood Cl, Brom. BR2 144 EF101
Sedgmoor Pl, SE5 102 DS80
Sedgwick Rd, E10 67 EC61
Sedgwick St, E9 67 DX64
Sedleigh Rd, SW18 119 CZ86
Sedlescombe Rd, SW6 99 CZ79
Sedley, Grav. (Sthflt) DA13 130 GA93
Sedley Cl, Enf. EN1 30 DV38
Sedley Gro, Uxb. (Hare.) UB9 58 BJ56
Sedley Pl, W1 195 H9
Sedley Ri, Loug. IG10 33 EM40
Sedum Cl, NW9 62 CP57
Seeley Dr, SE21 122 DS91
Seelig Av, NW9 63 CU59
Seely Rd, SW17 120 DG93
Seer Grn La, Beac. (Jordans) HP9 36 AS52
Seething La, EC3 201 N1
Seething Wells La, Surb. KT6 137 CJ100
Sefton Av, NW7 42 CR50
Harrow HA3 41 CD53
Sefton Cl, Orp. BR5 145 ET98
Slough (Stoke P.) SL2 74 AT66
Sefton Paddock, Slou. (Stoke P.) SL2 74 AU66
Sefton Pk, Slou. (Stoke P.) SL2 74 AU66
Sefton Rd, Croy. CR0 142 DU102
Epsom KT19 156 CR110
Orpington BR5 145 ET98
Sefton St, SW15 99 CW82
Sefton Way, Uxb. UB8 76 BJ72
Segal Cl, SE23 123 DY87
Segrave Cl, Wey. KT13 152 BN108
Sekforde St, EC1 196 F5
Sekhon Ter, Felt. TW13 116 CA90
Selah Dr, Swan. BR8 147 FC95
Selan Gdns, Hayes UB4 77 BV71
Selbie Av, NW10 63 CT64
Selborne Av, E12 *off Walton Rd* 69 EN63
Bexley DA5 126 EY88
Selborne Gdns, NW4 63 CU56
Greenford UB6 79 CG67
Selborne Rd, E17 67 DZ57
N14 45 DL48
N22 45 DM53
SE5 *off Denmark Hill* 102 DR82
Croydon CR0 142 DS104
Ilford IG1 69 EN61
New Malden KT3 138 CS96
Sidcup DA14 126 EV91
Selbourne Av, E17 67 DZ56
Addlestone (New Haw) KT15 152 BH110
Surbiton KT6 138 CM103
Selbourne Cl, Add. (New Haw) KT15 152 BH109
Selbourne Sq, Gdse. RH9 186 DW130
Selbourne Wk, E17 *off Selbourne Wk Shop Cen* 67 DZ56
Selbourne Wk Shop Cen, E17 67 DZ56
Selby Chase, Ruis. HA4 59 BV61
Selby Cl, E6 *off Linton Gdns* 86 EL71
Chessington KT9 156 CL108
Chislehurst BR7 125 EN93
Selby Gdns, Sthl. UB1 78 CA70
Selby Grn, Cars. SM5 140 DE101
Selby Rd, E11 68 EE62
E13 86 EH71
N17 46 DS51
SE20 142 DU96
W5 79 CH70
Ashford TW15 115 BQ93
Carshalton SM5 140 DE101
Selby Sq, W10 81 CY69
Selby St, E1 84 DU70
Selby Wk, Wok. GU21 *off Wyndham Rd* 166 AV118
Selcroft Rd, Pur. CR8 159 DP112
Selden Rd, SE15 102 DW82
Selden Wk, N7 *off Durham Rd* 65 DM61
★ Selfridges, W1 194 G9
SELHURST, SE25 142 DS100
⇌ Selhurst 142 DS99
Selhurst Cl, SW19 119 CX88
Woking GU21 167 AZ115
Selhurst New Rd, SE25 142 DS100
Selhurst Pl, SE25 142 DS100
Selhurst Rd, N9 46 DR48
SE25 142 DS99
Selinas La, Dag. RM8 70 EY59
Selkirk Dr, Erith DA8 107 FE81
Selkirk Rd, SW17 120 DE91
Twickenham TW2 116 CC89
Sell Cl, Wal.Cr. (Chsht) EN7 *off Gladding Rd* 13 DP26
Sellers Cl, Borwd. WD6 26 CQ39
Sellers Hall Cl, N3 44 DA52
Sellincourt Rd, SW17 120 DE92
Sellindge Cl, Beck. BR3 123 DZ94
Sellons Av, NW10 81 CT67
Sellwood Dr, Barn. EN5 27 CX43
Sellwood St, SW2 *off Brockwell Pk Row* 121 DN87
SELSDON, S.Croy. CR2 160 DW110
Selsdon Av, S.Croy. CR2 160 DR107
Selsdon Cl, Rom. RM5 51 FC53
Surbiton KT6 138 CL99
Selsdon Cres, S.Croy. CR2 160 DW109
Selsdon Pk Rd, S.Croy. CR2 161 DX109
Selsdon Rd, E11 68 EG59
E13 86 EJ67
NW2 63 CT61
SE27 121 DP90
Addlestone (New Haw) KT15 152 BG111
South Croydon CR2 160 DR106
Selsdon Rd Ind Est, S.Croy. CR2 *off Selsdon Rd* 160 DR108
Selsdon Way, E14 204 C7
Selsea Pl, N16 *off Crossway* 66 DS64
Selsey Cres, Well. DA16 106 EX81
Selsey St, E14 85 EA71
Selvage La, NW7 42 CR50
Selway Cl, Pnr. HA5 59 BV56
Selwood Cl, Stai. (Stanw.) TW19 114 BJ86
Selwood Gdns, Stai. (Stanw.) TW19 114 BJ86
Selwood Pl, SW7 100 DD78
Selwood Rd, Brwd. CM14 54 FT48
Chessington KT9 155 CK105
Croydon CR0 142 DV103
Sutton SM3 139 CZ102
Woking GU22 167 BB120
Selwood Ter, SW7 *off Onslow Gdns* 100 DD78
Selworthy Cl, E11 68 EG57
Selworthy Ho, SW11 100 DD81
Selworthy Rd, SE6 123 DZ90
Selwyn Av, E4 47 EC51
Ilford IG3 69 ES58
Selwyn Av, Rich. TW9 98 CL83
Selwyn Cl, Houns. TW4 96 BY84
Selwyn Ct, SE3 104 EE83
Edgware HA8 *off Camrose Av* 42 CP52
Selwyn Cres, Well. DA16 106 EV84
Selwyn Pl, Orp. BR5 146 EV97
Selwyn Rd, E3 85 DZ68
E13 86 EH67
NW10 80 CR66
New Malden KT3 138 CR99
Tilbury RM18 *off Dock Rd* 111 GF82
Semley Pl, SW1 198 G9
Semley Rd, SW16 141 DL96
Semper Cl, Wok. (Knap.) GU21 166 AS117
Semper Rd, Grays RM16 111 GJ75
Senate St, SE15 102 DW82
Senator Wk, SE28 *off Broadwater Rd* 105 ER76
SEND, Wok. GU23 167 BC124
Sendall Ct, SW11 100 DD83
Send Barns La, Wok. (Send) GU23 167 BD124
Send Cl, Wok. (Send) GU23 167 BC123
SEND MARSH, Wok. GU23 167 BF124
Send Marsh Rd, Wok. GU23 167 BF123
Send Par Cl, Wok. (Send) GU23 *off Send Rd* 167 BC123
Send Rd, Wok. (Send) GU23 167 BB122
Seneca Rd, Th.Hth. CR7 142 DQ98
Senga Rd, Wall. SM6 140 DG102
Senhouse Rd, Sutt. SM3 139 CX104
Senior St, W2 82 DB71
Senlac Rd, SE12 124 EH88
Sennen Rd, Enf. EN1 46 DT45
Sennen Wk, SE9 124 EL90
Senrab St, E1 85 DX72
Sentamu Cl, SE24 *off Norwood Rd* 122 DQ87
Sentinel Cl, Nthlt. UB5 78 BY70
Sentinel Pt, SW8 *off St. George Wf* 101 DL79
Sentinel Sq, NW4 63 CW56
Sentis Ct, Nthwd. HA6 *off Carew Rd* 39 BS51
September Way, Stan. HA7 41 CH51
Sequoia Cl, Bushey (Bushey Hth) WD23 *off Giant Tree Hill* 41 CD46
Sequoia Gdns, Orp. BR6 145 ET101
Sequoia Pk, Pnr. HA5 40 CB51
Serbin Cl, E10 67 EC59
Serenaders Rd, SW9 101 DN82
Sergeants Grn La, Wal.Abb. EN9 16 EJ33
Sergeants Pl, Cat. CR3 *off Coulsdon Rd* 176 DQ122
Sergehill La, Abb.L. (Bedmond) WD5 7 BT27
Serjeants Inn, EC4 196 E9
Serle St, WC2 196 C8
Sermed Ct, Slou. SL2 74 AW74
Sermon Dr, Swan. BR8 147 FC97
Sermon La, EC4 197 H9
★ Serpentine, The, W2 198 B3
Serpentine Ct, Sev. TN13 191 FK122
★ Serpentine Gall, W2 198 A3
Serpentine Grn, Red. (Merst.) RH1 *off Malmstone Av* 185 DK129
Serpentine Rd, W2 198 D3
Sevenoaks TN13 191 FJ123
Service Rd, The, Pot.B. EN6 12 DA32
Serviden Dr, Brom. BR1 144 EK95
Setchell Rd, SE1 201 P8
Setchell Way, SE1 201 P8
Seth St, SE16 202 G5
Seton Gdns, Dag. RM9 88 EW66
Settle Pt, E13 *off London Rd* 86 EG68
Settle Rd, E13 *off London Rd* 86 EG68
Romford RM3 52 FN49
Settlers Ct, E14 *off Newport Av* 85 ED73
Settles St, E1 84 DU71
Settrington Rd, SW6 100 DB82
Seven Acres, Cars. SM5 140 DE103
Northwood HA6 39 BU51
Swanley BR8 147 FD100
Seven Arches App, Wey. KT13 152 BM108
Seven Arches Rd, Brwd. CM14 54 FX48
Seven Hills Cl, Walt. KT12 153 BS109
Seven Hills Rd, Cob. KT11 153 BS111
Iver SL0 75 BC65
Walton-on-Thames KT12 153 BS109
Seven Hills Rd S, Cob. KT11 153 BS113
SEVEN KINGS, Ilf. IG3 69 ES59
⇌ Seven Kings 69 ES60
Seven Kings Rd, Ilf. IG3 69 ET61
Seven Kings Way, Kings.T. KT2 138 CL95
SEVENOAKS, TN13 - TN15 191 FJ125
⇌ Sevenoaks 190 FG124
Sevenoaks Business Cen, Sev. TN14 191 FH121
Sevenoaks Bypass, Sev. TN14 190 FC123
Sevenoaks Cl, Bexh. DA7 107 FC84
Romford RM3 52 FJ49
Sutton SM2 158 DA110
SEVENOAKS COMMON, Sev. TN13 191 FH129
Sevenoaks Ct, Nthwd. HA6 39 BQ52
H Sevenoaks Hosp, Sev. TN13 191 FJ121
Sevenoaks Ho, SE25 142 DU97
★ Sevenoaks Mus, Sev. TN13 191 FJ125
Sevenoaks Rd, SE4 123 DY86
Orpington BR6 163 ET106
Orpington (Grn St Grn) BR6 163 ET108
Sevenoaks (Otford) TN14 181 FH116
Sevenoaks Way, Orp. BR5 126 EW94
Sidcup DA14 126 EW94
⇌ Seven Sisters 66 DS57
⊖ Seven Sisters 66 DS57
Seven Sisters Rd, N4 65 DM62
N7 65 DM62
N15 66 DQ59
Seven Stars Cor, W12 *off Goldhawk Rd* 99 CU76
Seven Stars Yd, E1 *off Brick La* 84 DT71
Seventh Av, E12 69 EM63
Hayes UB3 77 BU74
Severnake Cl, E14 204 A8
Severn Av, W10 *off Selby Sq* 81 CY69
Romford RM2 71 FH55
Severn Cres, Slou. SL3 93 BB78
Severn Dr, Enf. EN1 30 DU38
Esher KT10 137 CG103
Upminster RM14 73 FR58
Walton-on-Thames KT12 136 BX103
Severn Rd, S.Ock. (Aveley) RM15 90 FQ72
Severns Fld, Epp. CM16 18 EU29
Severnvale, St.Alb. (Lon.Col.) AL2 *off Thamesdale* 10 CM27
Severn Way, NW10 63 CT64
Watford WD25 8 BW34
Severus Rd, SW11 100 DE84
Seville Ms, N1 84 DS66
Seville St, SW1 198 E5
Sevington Rd, NW4 63 CV58
Sevington St, W9 82 DB70
Seward Rd, W7 97 CG75
Beckenham BR3 143 DX96
SEWARDSTONE, E4 32 EC39
SEWARDSTONEBURY, E4 32 EE42
Sewardstone Gdns, E4 31 EB43
Sewardstone Grn, E4 32 EE42
Sewardstone Rd, E2 84 DW68
E4 47 EB45
Waltham Abbey EN9 31 EC38
Sewardstone Rbt, Wal.Abb. EN9 31 EC35
Sewardstone St, Wal.Abb. EN9 15 EC34
Seward St, EC1 196 G4
Sewdley St, E5 67 DX62
Sewell Cl, Grays (Chaff.Hun.) RM16 109 FW78
Sewell Rd, SE2 106 EU76
Sewell St, E13 86 EG69
Sextant Av, E14 204 F8
Sexton Cl, Rain. RM13 *off Blake Cl* 89 FF67
Waltham Cross (Chsht) EN7 *off Shambrook Rd* 14 DQ25
Sexton Ct, E14 *off Newport Av* 85 ED73
Sexton Rd, Til. RM18 111 GF81
Seymer Rd, Rom. RM1 71 FD55
Seymour Av, N17 46 DU54
Caterham CR3 176 DQ123
Epsom KT17 157 CV109
Morden SM4 139 CX101
Seymour Cl, E.Mol. KT8 136 CC99
Loughton IG10 32 EL44
Pinner HA5 40 BZ53
Seymour Ct, E4 48 EF47
Seymour Dr, Brom. BR2 145 EM102
Seymour Gdns, SE4 103 DY83
Feltham TW13 116 BW91
Ilford IG1 69 EM60
Ruislip HA4 60 BX60
Surbiton KT5 138 CM99
Twickenham TW1 117 CH87
Seymour Ms, W1 194 F8
Seymour Pl, SE25 142 DV98
W1 194 D7
Hornchurch RM11 72 FK59
Seymour Rd, E4 47 EB46
E6 86 EK68
E10 67 DZ60
N3 44 DB52
N8 65 DN57
N9 46 DV47
SW18 119 CZ87
SW19 119 CX89
W4 98 CQ77
Carshalton SM5 158 DG106
Chalfont St. Giles HP8 36 AW49
East Molesey KT8 136 CC99
Gravesend (Nthflt) DA11 131 GF88
Hampton (Hmptn H.) TW12 116 CC92
Kingston upon Thames KT1 137 CK95
Mitcham CR4 140 DG101
Tilbury RM18 111 GF81
Seymours, The, Loug. IG10 33 EN39
Seymour St, SE18 105 EQ76
W1 194 D9
W2 194 D9
Seymour Ter, SE20 142 DV95
Seymour Vil, SE20 142 DV95
Seymour Wk, SW10 100 DC79
Swanscombe DA10 130 FY87
Seymour Way, Sun. TW16 115 BS93
Seyssel St, E14 204 E8
Shaa Rd, W3 80 CR73
Shacklands Rd, Sev. (Bad.Mt) TN14 165 FB111
Shackleford Rd, Wok. GU22 167 BA121
Shacklegate La, Tedd. TW11 117 CE91
Shackleton Cl, SE23 *off Featherstone Av* 122 DV89
Shackleton Ct, E14 *off Maritime Quay* 103 EA78
W12 99 CV75
Shackleton Rd, Slou. SL1 74 AT73
Southall UB1 78 BZ73
Shackleton Way, Abb.L. WD5 *off Lysander Way* 7 BU32
SHACKLEWELL, N16 66 DT63
Shacklewell Grn, E8 66 DT63
Shacklewell La, E8 66 DT64
Shacklewell Rd, N16 66 DT63
Shacklewell Row, E8 66 DT63
Shacklewell St, E2 84 DT70
Shadbolt Av, E4 47 DY50
Shadbolt Cl, Wor.Pk. KT4 139 CT103
Shad Thames, SE1 201 P3
SHADWELL, E1 202 F1
⊖ Shadwell 84 DW73
DLR Shadwell 84 DW73
Shadwell Ct, Nthlt. UB5 *off Shadwell Dr* 78 BZ68

★ Place of interest ⇌ Railway station ⊖ London Underground station DLR Docklands Light Railway station Tra Tramlink station H Hospital Riv Pedestrian ferry landing stage

Shadwell Dr, Nthlt. UB5 .....78 BZ69
Shadwell Gdns Est, E1
off Martha St 84 DW73
Shadwell Pierhead, E1 .....202 G1
Shadwell Pl, E1
off Sutton St 84 DW73
Shady Bush Cl, Bushey WD23 .40 CC45
Shady La, Wat. WD17 ....23 BV40
Shaef Way, Tedd. TW11 .....117 CG94
Shafter Rd, Dag. RM10 ....89 FC65
Shaftesbury, Loug. IG10 .....32 EK41
Shaftesbury Av, W1 ....195 M10
WC2 ....195 M10
Barnet EN5 ....28 DC42
Enfield EN3 ....31 DX40
Feltham TW14 ....115 BU86
Harrow HA2 ....60 CB60
Harrow (Kenton) HA3 .....61 CK58
Southall UB2 ....96 CA77
Shaftesbury Circle, Har. HA2
off Shaftesbury Av 60 CC60
Shaftesbury Ct, N1
off Shaftesbury St 84 DR68
SE1 off Alderney Ms 102 DR76
Shaftesbury Cres, Stai. TW18 .114 BK94
Shaftesbury Gdns, NW10 ....80 CS70
Shaftesbury La, Dart. DA1 ..108 FP84
Shaftesbury Ms, SW4
off Clapham Common
S Side 121 DJ85
W8 off Stratford Rd 100 DA76
Shaftesbury Pl, W14
off Warwick Rd 99 CZ77
Shaftesbury Pt, E13
off High St 86 EH68
Shaftesbury Rd, E4 ....47 ED46
E7 ....86 EJ66
E10 ....67 EA60
E17 ....67 EB58
N18 ....46 DS51
N19 ....65 DL60
Beckenham BR3 ....143 DZ96
Carshalton SM5 ....140 DD101
Epping CM16 ....17 ET29
Richmond TW9 ....98 CL83
Romford RM1 ....71 FF58
Watford WD17 ....24 BW41
Woking GU22 ....167 BA117
Shaftesburys, The, Bark. IG11 .87 EQ67
Shaftesbury St, N1 ....197 J1
Shaftesbury Way, Kings L.
WD4 ....7 BQ28
Twickenham TW2 ....117 CD90
Shaftesbury Waye, Hayes
UB4 ....77 BV71
Shafto Ms, SW1 ....198 D7
Shafton Rd, E9 ....85 DX67
Shaggy Calf La, Slou. SL2 ...74 AU73
Shakespeare Av, N11 ....45 DJ50
NW10 ....80 CR67
Feltham TW14 ....115 BU86
Hayes UB4 ....77 BV70
Tilbury RM18 ....111 GH82
Shakespeare Cres, E12 ......87 EM65
NW10 off Hillside 80 CR67
Shakespeare Dr, Har. HA3 ...62 CM58
Shakespeare Gdns, N2 ......64 DF56
Shakespeare Ho, N14
off High St 45 DK47
Shakespeare Rd, E17 ....47 DX54
N3 off Popes Dr 44 DA53
NW7 ....43 CT49
NW10 off Lawrence Av 80 CR67
SE24 ....121 DP85
W3 ....80 CQ74
W7 ....79 CF73
Addlestone KT15 ....152 BK105
Bexleyheath DA7 ....106 EY81
Dartford DA1 ....108 FN84
Romford RM1 ....71 FF58
★ Shakespeare's Globe Thea,
SE1 ....201 H1
Shakespeare Sq, Ilf. IG6 .....49 EQ51
Shakespeare St, Wat. WD24 ..23 BV38
Shakespeare Twr, EC2 ......197 J6
Shakespeare Way, Felt. TW13 .116 BW91
Shakspeare Ms, N16
off Shakspeare Wk 66 DS63
Shakspeare Wk, N16 ....66 DS63
Shalbourne Sq, E9 ....85 DZ65
Shalcomb St, SW10 ....100 DC79
Shalcross Dr, Wal.Cr.
(Chsht) EN8 ....15 DZ30
Shalden Ho, SW15
off Tunworth Cres 119 CT86
Shaldon Dr, Mord. SM4 ....139 CY99
Ruislip HA4 ....60 BW62
Shaldon Rd, Edg. HA8 ....42 CM53
Shaldon Way, Walt. KT12 ...136 BW104
Shale Grn, Red. (Merst.) RH1
off Bletchingley Rd 185 DK129
Shalfleet Dr, W10 ....81 CX73
Shalford Cl, Orp. BR6 ......163 EQ105
Shalimar Gdns, W3 ....80 CQ73
Shalimar Rd, W3
off Hereford Rd 80 CQ73
Shallons Rd, SE9 ....125 EP91
Shalstone Rd, SW14 ....98 CP83
Shalston Vil, Surb. KT6 ....138 CM100
Shambrook Rd, Wal.Cr.
(Chsht) EN7 ....13 DP25
Shamrock Cl, Lthd.
(Fetch.) KT22 ....171 CD121
Shamrock Ho, SE26
off Talisman Sq 122 DU91
Shamrock Rd, Croy. CR0 ...141 DM100
Gravesend DA12 ....131 GL87
Shamrock St, SW4 ....101 DK83
Shamrock Way, N14 ....45 DH46
Shandon Rd, SW4 ....121 DJ86
Shand St, SE1 ....201 M4
Shandy St, E1 ....85 DX71
Shanklin Cl, Wal.Cr. EN7 .....14 DT29
Shanklin Gdns, Wat. WD19 ...40 BW49
Shanklin Ho, E17
off Priory Ct 47 DZ54
Shanklin Rd, N8 ....65 DK57
N15 ....66 DU56
Shannon Cl, NW2 ....63 CX62
Southall UB2 ....96 BX78
Shannon Cor, SW20
off Beverley Way 139 CU97
Shannon Gro, SW9 ....101 DM84
Shannon Pl, NW8
off Allitsen Rd 82 DE68
Shannon Way, Beck. BR3 ...123 EB93
South Ockendon (Aveley)
RM15 ....90 FQ73
Shantock Hall La, Hem.H.
(Bov.) HP3 ....4 AY29
Shantock La, Hem.H.
(Bov.) HP3 ....4 AX30
Shap Cres, Cars. SM5 ......140 DF102
Shapland Way, N13 ....45 DM50
Shapwick Cl, N11 ....44 DF50
Shardcroft Av, SE24 ....121 DP85
Shardeloes Rd, SE4 ....103 DZ83
SE14 ....103 DZ83
Sharland Cl, Th.Hth. CR7
off Dunheved Rd N 141 DN100
Sharland Rd, Grav. DA12 ....131 GJ89
Sharman Ct, Sid. DA14 .....126 EU91
Sharman Row, Slou. SL3
off Ditton Rd 93 AZ78
Sharnbrooke Cl, Well. DA16 .106 EW83
Sharnbrook Ho, W14
off Marchbank Rd 100 DA79
Sharney Av, Slou. SL3 ......93 BB76
Sharon Cl, Epsom KT19 ....156 CQ113
Leatherhead (Bkhm) KT23 .170 CA124
Surbiton KT6 ....137 CJ102
Sharon Gdns, E9 ....84 DW67
Sharon Rd, W4 ....98 CR78
Enfield EN3 ....31 DY40
Sharpe Cl, W7
off Templeman Rd 79 CF71
Sharpleshall St, NW1 ....82 DF66
Sharpness Cl, Hayes UB4 ....78 BY71
Sharps La, Ruis. HA4 ....59 BR60
Sharp Way, Dart. DA1 ......108 FM83
Sharratt St, SE15 ....102 DW79
Sharsted St, SE17 ....101 DP78
Sharvel La, Nthlt. UB5 ....77 BU67
Shavers Pl, SW1 ....199 M1
Shaw Av, Bark. IG11 ....88 EY68
Shawbrooke Rd, SE9 ....124 EJ85
Shawbury Cl, NW9
off Kenley Av 42 CS54
Shawbury Rd, SE22 ....122 DT85
Shaw Cl, SE28 ....88 EV74
Bushey (Bushey Hth) WD23 .41 CE47
Chertsey (Ott.) KT16 .....151 BC107
Epsom KT17 ....157 CT111
Hornchurch RM11 ....71 FH60
South Croydon CR2 ......160 DT112
Waltham Cross (Chsht) EN8 .14 DW28
Shaw Ct, SW11 ....100 DD83
Morden SM4 ....140 DC101
Windsor SL4 ....112 AU85
Shaw Cres, E14 off Carr St ...85 DY72
Brentwood (Hutt.) CM13 ...55 GD43
South Croydon CR2 ......160 DT112
Tilbury RM18 ....111 GH81
Shaw Dr, Walt. KT12 ......136 BW101
Shawfield Ct, West Dr. UB7 ..94 BL76
Shawfield Pk, Brom. BR1 ...144 EK96
Shawfield St, SW3 ....100 DE78
Shawford Ct, SW15 ....119 CU87
Shawford Rd, Epsom KT19 ..156 CR107
Shaw Gdns, Bark. IG11 ......88 EY68
Slough SL3 ....93 AZ78
Shawley Cres, Epsom KT18 .173 CW118
Shawley Way, Epsom KT18 .173 CV118
Shaw Rd, SE22 ....102 DS84
Bromley BR1 ....124 EF90
Enfield EN3 ....31 DX39
Westerham (Tats.) TN16 ..178 EJ120
Shaws Cotts, SE23 ....123 DY90
Shaw Sq, E17 ....47 DY53
Shaw Way, Wall. SM6 ......159 DL108
Shaxton Cres, Croy. (New Adgtn)
CR0 ....161 EC109
Shearing Dr, Cars. SM5
off Stavordale Rd 140 DC101
Shearling Way, N7 ....83 DL65
Shearman Rd, SE3 ....104 EF84
Shears Ct, Sun. TW16
off Staines Rd W 115 BS94
Shearsmith Ho, E1
off Cable St 84 DU73
Shearwater Cl, Bark. IG11 ....88 EU69
Shearwater Rd, Sutt. SM1 ..157 CZ106
Shearwater Way, Hayes UB4 .78 BX72
Shearwood Cres, Dart. DA1 .107 FF83
Sheath's La, Lthd. KT22 ....154 CB113
Sheaveshill Av, NW9 ....62 CS56
Sheba Pl, E1 off Quaker St ...84 DT70
Sheehy Way, Slou. SL2 ......74 AV73
Sheen Common, SW14
off Fife Rd 118 CQ85
Sheen Common Dr, Rich.
TW10 ....98 CN84
Sheen Ct, Rich. TW10 ....98 CN84
Sheen Ct Rd, Rich. TW10 ....98 CN84
Sheendale Rd, Rich. TW9 ....98 CM84
Sheenewood, SE26 ....122 DV92
Sheen Gate Gdns, SW14 .....98 CQ84
Sheen Gate Mans Pas, SW14
off East Sheen Av 98 CR84
Sheen Gro, N1
off Richmond Av 83 DN67
Sheen La, SW14 ....98 CQ83
Sheen Pk, Rich. TW9 ....98 CM84
Sheen Rd, Orp. BR5 ....145 ET98
Richmond TW9, TW10 .....118 CL85
Sheen Way, Wall. SM6 .....159 DM106
Sheen Wd, SW14 ....118 CQ85
Sheepbarn La, Warl. CR6 ...162 EF112
Sheepcot Dr, Wat. WD25 .....8 BW34
Sheepcote Cl, Houns. TW5 ...95 BU80
Sheepcote Gdns, Uxb.
(Denh.) UB9 ....58 BG58
Sheepcote La, SW11 ....100 DF82
Orpington BR5 ....146 EZ99
Swanley BR8 ....146 EZ98
Sheepcote Rd, Har. HA1 .....61 CF58
Sheepcotes Rd, Rom. RM6 ...70 EX56
Sheepcot La, Wat. WD25 .....7 BV34
Sheephouse Way, N.Mal.
KT3 ....138 CS101
Sheep La, E8 ....84 DV67
Sheep Wk, Epsom KT18 ....172 CR122
Reigate RH2 ....183 CY131
Shepperton TW17 ....134 BM101
Sheep Wk, The, Wok. GU22 ..167 BE118
Sheep Wk Ms, SW19 ....119 CX93
Sheerness Ms, E16 ....105 EP75
SHEERWATER, Wok. GU21 ..151 BC113
Sheerwater Av, Add.
(Wdhm) KT15 ....151 BE112
Sheerwater Rd, E16 ....86 EK71
Addlestone (Wdhm) KT15 .151 BE112
West Byfleet KT14 ....151 BE112
Woking GU21 ....151 BE112
Sheffield Dr, Rom. RM3 ......52 FN50
Sheffield Gdns, Rom. RM3 ...52 FN50
Sheffield Rd, Houns.
(Hthrw Air.) TW6
off Southern Perimeter Rd .115 BR85
Sheffield Sq, E3
off Malmesbury Rd 85 DZ69
Sheffield St, WC2 ....196 B9
Sheffield Ter, W8 ....82 DA74
Shefton Ri, Nthwd. HA6 .....39 BU52
Sheila Cl, Rom. RM5 ....51 FB52
Sheila Rd, Rom. RM5 ....51 FB52
Sheilings, The, Horn. RM11 ...72 FM57
Shelbourne Cl, Pnr. HA5 .....60 BZ55
Shelbourne Pl, Beck. BR3 ...123 DZ94
Shelbourne Rd, N17 ....46 DV54
Shelburne Dr, Houns. TW4
off Hanworth Rd 116 CA86
Shelburne Rd, N7 ....65 DM63
Shelbury Cl, Sid. DA14 .....126 EU90
Shelbury Rd, SE22 ....122 DV85
Sheldon Av, N6 ....64 DE59
Ilford IG5 ....49 EP54
Sheldon Cl, SE12 ....124 EH85
SE20 ....142 DV95
Waltham Cross (Chsht) EN7 .14 DS26
Sheldon Ct, SW8
off Hartington Rd 101 DL80
Sheldon Pl, E2 ....84 DU68
Sheldon Rd, N18 ....46 DS49
NW2 ....63 CX63
Bexleyheath DA7 ....106 EZ81
Dagenham RM9 ....88 EY66
Sheldon Sq, W2 ....82 DC71
Sheldon St, Croy. CR0 .....142 DQ104
Sheldrake Cl, E16 ....87 EM74
Sheldrake Pl, W8 ....99 CZ75
Sheldrick Cl, SW19 ....140 DD96
Shelduck Cl, E15 ....68 EF64
Sheldwich Ter, Brom. BR2 ..144 EL100
Shelford Pl, N16
off Stoke Newington Ch St .66 DR62
Shelford Ri, SE19 ....122 DT94
Shelford Rd, Barn. EN5 ......27 CW44
Shelgate Rd, SW11 ....120 DE85
Shellbank La, Dart. (Bean)
DA2 ....129 FU93
★ Shell Cen, SE1 ....200 C3
Shell Cl, Brom. BR2 ....145 EM100
Shellduck Cl, NW9
off Swan Dr 42 CS54
Shelley Av, E12 ....86 EL65
Greenford UB6 ....79 CD69
Hornchurch RM12 ....71 FF61
Shelley Cl, SE15 ....102 DV82
Banstead SM7 ....173 CX115
Borehamwood WD6
off Melrose Av 26 CN42
Coulsdon CR5 ....175 DM117
Edgware HA8 ....42 CN49
Greenford UB6 ....79 CD69
Hayes UB4 ....77 BU71
Northwood HA6 ....39 BT50
Orpington BR6 ....145 ES104
Slough SL3 ....93 AZ78
Shelley Cres, Houns. TW5 ....96 BX82
Southall UB1 ....78 BZ72
Shelley Dr, Well. DA16 .....105 ES81
Shelley Gdns, Wem. HA0 ....61 CJ61
Shelley Gro, Loug. IG10 .....33 EM42
Shelley Ho, SW1
off Churchill Gdns 101 DJ78
Shelley La, Uxb. (Hare.) UB9 .38 BG53
Shelley Pl, Til. RM18
off Kipling Av 111 GH81
Shelley Rd, NW10 ....80 CR67
Brentwood (Hutt.) CM13 ...55 GD45
Shelleys La, Sev. (Knock.)
TN14 ....179 ET116
Shelley Way, SW19 ....120 DD93
Shellfield Cl, Stai. TW19 ....114 BG85
Shellgrove Est, N16 ....66 DS64
Shellness Rd, E5 ....66 DV64
Shell Rd, SE13 ....103 EB83
Shellwood Rd, SW11 ....100 DF82
Shelmerdine Cl, E3 ....85 EA71
Shelson Av, Felt. TW13 ....115 BT90
Shelton Av, Warl. CR6 .....176 DW117
Shelton Cl, Warl. CR6 ......176 DW117
Shelton Ct, Slou. SL3
off London Rd 92 AW76
Shelton Rd, SW19 ....140 DA95
Shelton St, WC2 ....195 P9
Shelvers Grn, Tad. KT20 ...173 CW121
Shelvers Hill, Tad. KT20
off Ashurst Rd 173 CV121
Shelvers Spur, Tad. KT20 ...173 CW121
Shelvers Way, Tad. KT20 ...173 CW121
Shenden Cl, Sev. TN13 .....191 FJ128
Shenden Way, Sev. TN13 ...191 FJ128
SHENFIELD, Brwd. CM15 .....55 GA45
⇌ Shenfield 55 GA45
Shenfield Cl, Couls. CR5
off Woodfield Cl 175 DJ119
Shenfield Common,
Brwd. CM15 ....54 FY48
Shenfield Cres, Brwd. CM15 ..54 FY47
Shenfield Gdns, Brwd.
(Hutt.) CM13 ....55 GB44
Shenfield Grn, Brwd. (Shenf.)
CM15 ....55 GA45
Shenfield Ho, SE18
off Shooters Hill Rd 104 EK80
Shenfield Pl, Brwd. (Shenf.)
CM15 ....54 FY45
Shenfield Rd, Brwd. CM15 ...54 FX46
Woodford Green IG8 ......48 EH52
Shenfield St, N1 ....197 N1
SHENLEY, Rad. WD7 ....10 CN33
Shenley Av, Ruis. HA4 ......59 BT61
Shenleybury, Rad. (Shenley)
WD7 ....10 CL30
Shenleybury Cotts, Rad.
(Shenley) WD7 ....10 CL31
Shenley Hill, Rad. WD7 ......25 CG35
Shenley La, St.Alb.
(Lon.Col.) AL2 ....9 CJ27
Shenley Rd, SE5 ....102 DS81
Borehamwood WD6 ......26 CN42
Dartford DA1 ....128 FN86
Hounslow TW5 ....96 BY81
Radlett WD7 ....9 CH34
Shenstone Cl, Dart. DA1 ....107 FD84
Shenstone Gdns, Rom. RM3 .52 FJ53
Shepcot Ho, N14 ....29 DJ44
Shepherd Cl, W1 off Lees Pl ..82 DG73
Abbots Langley WD5 ......7 BT30
Feltham (Han.) TW13 ....116 BY91
Shepherdess Pl, N1 ....197 J2
Shepherdess Wk, N1 ....84 DQ68
Shepherd Mkt, W1 ....199 H2
SHEPHERD'S BUSH, W12 ....81 CW74
⇌ Shepherd's Bush 99 CW75
⊖ Shepherd's Bush 99 CW75
Shepherds Bush Grn, W12 ...99 CW75
Shepherds Bush Mkt, W12 ...99 CW75
Shepherds Bush Pl, W12 .....99 CX75
Shepherds Bush Rd, W6 .....99 CW77
Shepherds Cl, N6 ....65 DH58
Leatherhead KT22 ....172 CL124
Orpington BR6
off Stapleton Rd 145 ET104
Romford RM6 ....70 EX57
Shepperton TW17 ....135 BP100
Stanmore HA7 ....41 CG50
Uxbridge (Cowley) UB8
off High St 76 BJ70
Shepherds Ct, W12
off Shepherds Bush Grn ...99 CX75
Shepherds Grn, Chis. BR7 ..125 ER94
Shepherds Hill, N6 ....65 DH58
Redhill (Merst.) RH1 .....185 DJ126
Romford RM3 ....52 FN54
Shepherds Ho, N7
off York Way 83 DL65
Shepherds La, E9 ....67 DX64
SE28 ....87 ES74
Shepherd's La, Brwd. CM14 ..54 FS45
Shepherds La, Dart. DA1 ...127 FG88
Rickmansworth WD3 ......37 BF45
Shepherds Path, Nthlt. UB5
off Fortunes Mead 78 BY65
Shepherd's Pl, W1 ....194 F10
Shepherds Rd, Wat. WD18 ...23 BT41
Shepherd St, W1 ....199 H3
Gravesend (Nthflt) DA11 ..130 GD87
Shepherds Wk, NW2 ....63 CU61
NW3 ....64 DD64
Bushey (Bushey Hth) WD23 .41 CD47
Shepherds' Wk, Epsom KT18 .172 CP121
Shepherds Way, Hat.
(Brook.Pk) AL9 ....12 DC27
Rickmansworth WD3 ......38 BH45
South Croydon CR2 ......161 DX108
Shepiston La, Hayes UB3 ....95 BR77
West Drayton UB7 ....95 BQ77
Shepley Cl, Cars. SM5 .....140 DG104
Shepley Ms, Enf. EN3 ....31 EA37
Sheppard Cl, Enf. EN1 ....30 DV38
Kingston upon Thames
KT1 off Beaufort Rd 138 CL98
Sheppard Dr, SE16 ....202 D10
Sheppard St, E16 ....86 EF70
SHEPPERTON, TW17 ....134 BN101
⇌ Shepperton 135 BQ99
Shepperton Business Pk,
Shep. TW17 ....135 BQ99
Shepperton Cl, Borwd. WD6 ..26 CR39
Shepperton Ct, Shep. TW17 .135 BP100
Shepperton Ct Dr, Shep.
TW17 ....135 BP99
Shepperton Rd, N1 ....84 DQ67
Orpington BR5 ....145 EQ100
Staines TW18 ....134 BJ97
Sheppey Cl, Erith DA8 .....107 FH80
Sheppey Gdns, Dag. RM9
off Sheppey Rd 88 EW66
Sheppey Rd, Dag. RM9 ......88 EV66
Sheppeys La, Abb.L. (Bedmond)
WD5 ....7 BS28
Sheppey Wk, N1
off Ashby Gro 84 DQ66
Sheppy Pl, Grav. DA12 .....131 GH87
Sherard Ct, N7
off Manor Gdns 65 DL62
Sherard Rd, SE9 ....124 EL85
Sheraton Business Cen,
Grnf. UB6 ....79 CH68
Sheraton Cl, Borwd. (Els.)
WD6 ....26 CM43
Sheraton Dr, Epsom KT19 ..156 CQ113
Sheraton Ms, Wat. WD18 ....23 BS42
Sheraton St, W1 ....195 M9
Sherborne Av, Enf. EN3 .....30 DW40
Southall UB2 ....96 CA77
Sherborne Cl, Epsom KT18 ..173 CW117
Hayes UB4 ....78 BW72
Slough (Colnbr.) SL3 .....93 BE81
Sherborne Cres, Cars. SM5 .140 DE101
Sherborne Gdns, NW9 ....62 CN55
W13 ....79 CH72
Romford RM5 ....50 FA50
Sherborne La, EC4 ....197 K10
Sherborne Pl, Nthwd. HA6 ...39 BR51
Sherborne Rd, Chess. KT9 ..156 CL106
Feltham TW14 ....115 BR87
Orpington BR5 ....145 ET98
Sutton SM3 ....140 DA103
Sherborne St, N1 ....84 DR67
Sherborne Wk, Lthd. KT22
off Windfield 171 CJ121
Sherborne Way, Rick.
(Crox.Grn) WD3 ....23 BP42
Sherboro Rd, N15
off Ermine Rd 66 DT58
Sherbourne Cotts, Wat. WD18
off Lammas Rd 24 BW43
Sherbourne Gdns, Shep.
TW17 ....135 BS101
Sherbourne Ho, SW8
off Bolney St 101 DM80
Sherbourne Pl, Stan. HA7 ....41 CG51
Sherbrooke Cl, Bexh. DA6 ..106 FA84
Sherbrooke Rd, SW6 ....99 CZ80
Sherbrooke Way, Wor.Pk.
KT4 ....139 CV101
Sherbrook Gdns, N21 ....45 DP45
Shere Av, Sutt. SM2 ....157 CW110
Shere Cl, Chess. KT9 ....155 CK106
Sheredan Rd, E4 ....47 ED50
Shere Rd, Ilf. IG2 ....69 EN57
Sherfield Av, Rick. WD3 .....38 BK47
Sherfield Cl, N.Mal. KT3 ....138 CP98
Sherfield Gdns, SW15 ......119 CT86
Sherfield Rd, Grays RM17 ...110 GB79
Sheridan Cl, Rom. RM3 .....51 FH52
Swanley BR8
off Willow Av 147 FF97
Uxbridge UB10
off Alpha Rd 77 BQ70
Sheridan Ct, Houns. TW4
off Vickers Way 116 BY85
Northolt UB5 ....60 CB64
Sheridan Cres, Chis. BR7 ...145 EP96
Sheridan Dr, Reig. RH2 .....184 DB132
Sheridan Gdns, Har. HA3 ....61 CK58
Sheridan Ms, E11
off Woodbine Pl 68 EG58
Sheridan Pl, SW13
off Brookwood Av 99 CT82
Hampton TW12 ....136 CB95
Sheridan Rd, E7 ....68 EF62
E12 ....68 EL64
SW19 ....139 CZ95
Belvedere DA17 ....106 FA77
Bexleyheath DA7 ....106 EY83
Richmond TW10 ....117 CJ90
Watford WD19 ....40 BX45
Sheridan St, E1
off Watney St 84 DV72
Sheridan Ter, Nthlt. UB5
off Whitton Av W 60 CB64
Sheridan Wk, NW11 ....64 DA58
Carshalton SM5
off Carshalton Pk Rd 158 DF106
Sheridan Way, Beck. BR3
off Turners Meadow Way .143 DZ95
Sheriff Way, Wat. WD25 ......7 BU33
Sheringham Av, E12 ....69 EM63
N14 ....29 DK43
Feltham TW13 ....115 BU90
Romford RM7 ....71 FC58
Twickenham TW2 ....116 BZ88
Sheringham Dr, Bark. IG11 ...69 ET64
Sheringham Rd, N7 ....83 DM65
SE20 ....142 DV97
Sheringham Twr, Sthl. UB1 ..78 CB73
Sherington Av, Pnr. HA5 .....40 CA52
Sherington Rd, SE7 ....104 EH79
Sherland Rd, Twick. TW1 ...117 CF88
Sherlies Av, Orp. BR6 ......145 ES103
★ Sherlock Holmes Mus,
NW1 ....194 E5
Sherlock Ms, W1 ....194 F6
Sherman Gdns, Rom. RM3 ...70 EW58
Sherman Rd, Brom. BR1 ....144 EG95
Slough SL1 ....74 AS71
Shernbroke Rd, Wal.Abb. EN9 .16 EF34
Shernhall St, E17 ....67 EC57
Sherrard Rd, E7 ....86 EJ65
E12 ....86 EK65
Sherrards Way, Barn. EN5 ....28 DA43
Sherrick Grn Rd, NW10 ......63 CV64
Sherriff Cl, Esher KT10 .....136 CB103
Sherriff Rd, NW6 ....82 DA65
Sherringham Av, N17 ....46 DU54
Sherrin Rd, E10 ....67 EA63
Sherrock Gdns, NW4 ....63 CU56
Sherry Ms, Bark. IG11
off Cecil Av 87 ER66
Sherwin Rd, SE14 ....103 DX81
Sherwood Av, E18 ....68 EH55
SW16 ....121 DK94
Greenford UB6 ....79 CE65
Hayes UB4 ....78 BV70
Potters Bar EN6 ....11 CY32
Ruislip HA4 ....59 BS58
Sherwood Cl, E17
off Priory Ct 47 DZ54
SW13 off Lower Common S .99 CV83
W13 ....79 CH74
Bexley DA5 ....126 EW86
Leatherhead (Fetch.) KT22 .170 CC122
Slough SL3 ....92 AY76
Sherwood Ct, Slou. (Colnbr.)
SL3 off High St 93 BD80
Watford WD25 off High Rd ..7 BU34
Sherwood Gdns, E14 ......204 A8
SE16 ....102 DU78
Barking IG11 ....87 ER66
Sherwood Pk Av, Sid. DA15 .126 EU87
Sherwood Pk Rd, Mitch. CR4 .141 DJ98
Sutton SM1 ....158 DA106
Sherwood Rd, NW4 ....63 CW55
SW19 ....119 CZ94
Coulsdon CR5 ....175 DJ116
Croydon CR0 ....142 DV101
Hampton (Hmptn H.) TW12 .116 CC92
Harrow HA2 ....60 CC61
Ilford IG6 ....69 ER56
Welling DA16 ....105 ES82
Woking (Knap.) GU21 ....166 AS117
Sherwoods Rd, Wat. WD19 ...40 BY45
Sherwood St, N20 ....44 DD48
W1 ....195 L10
Sherwood Ter, N20
off Green Rd 44 DD48
Sherwood Way, W.Wick. BR4 .143 EB103
Shetland Cl, Borwd. WD6 ....26 CR44
Shetland Rd, E3 ....85 DZ68
Shevon Way, Brwd. CM14 ....54 FT49
Shewens Rd, Wey. KT13 ....153 BR105
Shey Copse, Wok. GU22 ....167 BC117
Shield Dr, Brent. TW8 ....97 CG79
Shieldhall St, SE2 ....106 EW77
Shield Rd, Ashf. TW15 ......115 BQ91
Shifford Path, SE23 ....123 DX90
Shilburn Way, Wok. GU21 ...166 AU118
Shillibeer Pl, W1 ....194 C6
Shillibeer Wk, Chig. IG7 .....49 ET48
Shillingford Cl, NW7 ....43 CX52
Shillingford St, N1
off Cross St 83 DP66
Shillitoe Av, Pot.B. EN6 .....11 CX32
Shinfield St, W12 ....81 CW72
Shingle Ct, Wal.Abb. EN9 ....16 EG33

★ Place of interest ⇌ Railway station ⊖ London Underground station DLR Docklands Light Railway station Tra Tramlink station H Hospital Riv Pedestrian ferry landing stage

Shinglewell Rd, Erith DA8 .. 106 FA80
Shinners Cl, SE25 .. 142 DU99
Ship All, W4 off Thames Rd .. 98 CN79
Ship & Mermaid Row, SE1 .. 201 L4
Shipfield Cl, West. (Tats.) TN16 .. 178 EJ121
Ship Hill, West. (Tats.) TN16 .. 178 EJ121
Shipka Rd, SW12 .. 121 DH88
Ship La, SW14 .. 98 CQ82
Brentwood (Mtnsg) CM13 .. 55 GF41
Dartford (Sutt.H.) DA4 .. 148 FK95
Purfleet RM19 .. 109 FS76
South Ockendon (Aveley) RM15 .. 109 FR75
Swanley BR8 .. 148 FK95
Ship La Caravan Site, S.Ock. RM15 .. 109 FR76
Shipman Rd, E16 .. 86 EH72
SE23 .. 123 DX89
Ship St, SE8 .. 103 EA81
Ship Tavern Pas, EC3 .. 197 M10
Shipton Cl, Dag. RM8 .. 70 EX62
Shipton St, E2 .. 84 DT69
Shipwright Rd, SE16 .. 203 K5
Shipwright Yd, SE1 .. 201 M3
Ship Yd, E14 .. 204 B10
Weybridge KT13 off High St .. 153 BP105
Shirburn Cl, SE23 off Tyson Rd .. 122 DW87
Shirbutt St, E14 .. 85 EB73
Shirebrook Rd, SE3 .. 104 EK83
Shire Cl, Brox. EN10 off Groom Rd .. 15 DZ26
Shire Ct, Epsom KT17 .. 157 CT108
Erith DA18 off St. John Fisher Rd .. 106 EX76
Shirehall Cl, NW4 .. 63 CX58
Shirehall Gdns, NW4 .. 63 CX58
Shirehall La, NW4 .. 63 CX58
Shirehall Pk, NW4 .. 63 CX58
Shirehall Rd, Dart. DA2 .. 128 FK92
Shire Horse Way, Islw. TW7 .. 97 CF83
Shire La, Ger.Cr. (Chal.St.P.) SL9 .. 37 BD54
Keston BR2 .. 163 EM108
Orpington BR6 .. 163 ER107
Rickmansworth (Chorl.) WD3 .. 21 BB43
Uxbridge (Denh.) UB9 .. 57 BE55
Shiremeade, Borwd. (Els.) WD6 .. 26 CM43
Shire Pl, SW18 off Swaffield Rd .. 120 DB87
Shires, The, Rich. TW10 .. 118 CL91
Watford WD25 .. 7 BV31
Shires Cl, Ashtd. KT21 .. 171 CK118
Shires Ho, W.Byf. (Byfleet) KT14 off Eden Gro Rd .. 152 BL113
Shirland Ms, W9 .. 81 CZ69
Shirland Rd, W9 .. 82 DA69
SHIRLEY, Croy. CR0 .. 143 DX104
Shirley Av, Bex. DA5 .. 126 EX87
Coulsdon CR5 .. 175 DP119
Croydon CR0 .. 142 DW102
Sutton SM1 .. 158 DE105
Sutton (Cheam) SM2 .. 157 CZ109
Shirley Ch Rd, Croy. CR0 .. 143 DX104
Shirley Cl, E17 off Addison Rd .. 67 EB57
Dartford DA1 .. 108 FJ84
Hounslow TW3 .. 116 CC85
Waltham Cross (Chsht) EN8 .. 14 DW29
Shirley Ct, Croy. CR0 .. 143 DX104
Shirley Cres, Beck. BR3 .. 143 DY98
Shirley Dr, Houns. TW3 .. 116 CC85
Shirley Gdns, W7 .. 79 CF74
Barking IG11 .. 87 ES65
Hornchurch RM12 .. 72 FJ61
Shirley Gro, N9 .. 46 DW45
SW11 .. 100 DG83
Shirley Hts, Wall. SM6 .. 159 DJ109
Shirley Hills Rd, Croy. CR0 .. 161 DX106
Shirley Ho Dr, SE7 .. 104 EJ80
H Shirley Oaks Hosp, Croy. CR9 .. 142 DW101
Shirley Oaks Rd, Croy. CR0 .. 143 DX102
Shirley Pk Rd, Croy. CR0 .. 142 DV102
Shirley Rd, E15 .. 86 EE66
W4 .. 98 CR75
Abbots Langley WD5 .. 7 BT32
Croydon CR0 .. 142 DV101
Enfield EN2 .. 30 DQ41
Sidcup DA15 .. 125 ES90
Wallington SM6 .. 159 DJ109
Shirley St, E16 .. 86 EF72
Shirley Way, Croy. CR0 .. 143 DY104
Shirlock Rd, NW3 .. 64 DF63
Shirwell Cl, NW7 .. 43 CX52
Shobden Rd, N17 .. 46 DR53
Shobroke Cl, NW2 .. 63 CW62
Shoebury Rd, E6 .. 87 EM66
Shoe La, EC4 .. 196 E8
Sholden Gdns, Orp. BR5 .. 146 EW99
Sholto Rd, Houns. (Hthrw Air.) TW6 .. 114 BM85
Shona Ho, E13 off Prince Regent La .. 86 EJ71
Shonks Mill Rd, Rom. (Nave.) RM4 .. 35 FG37
Shooters Av, Har. HA3 .. 61 CJ56
SHOOTER'S HILL, SE18 .. 105 EQ81
Shooters Hill, SE18 .. 105 EN81
Welling DA16 .. 105 EN81
Shooters Hill Rd, SE3 .. 104 EF81
SE10 .. 103 ED81
SE18 .. 104 EH80
Shooters Rd, Enf. EN2 .. 29 DP39
Shoot Up Hill, NW2 .. 63 CY64
Shord Hill, Ken. CR8 .. 176 DR116
Shore, The, Grav. (Nthflt) DA11 .. 130 GD85
Gravesend (Rosh.) DA11 .. 131 GF86
Shore Cl, Felt. TW14 .. 115 BU87
Hampton TW12 off Stewart Cl .. 116 BY92
Shorediche Cl, Uxb. UB10 .. 58 BM62
SHOREDITCH, E1 .. 197 P5
Shoreditch High St, E1 .. 197 N5
Shoreditch Ho, N1 .. 197 L3
Shore Gro, Felt. TW13 .. 116 CA89
SHOREHAM, Sev. TN14 .. 165 FG111
⇌ Shoreham .. 165 FG111
Shoreham Cl, SW18 off Ram St .. 120 DB85
Bexley DA5 .. 126 EX88
Croydon CR0 .. 142 DW100
Shoreham La, Orp. BR6 .. 164 FA107
Sevenoaks TN13 .. 190 FF122
Sevenoaks (Halst.) TN14 .. 164 EZ112
Shoreham Pl, Sev. (Shore.) TN14 .. 165 FG112
Shoreham Rd, Orp. BR5 .. 146 EV95
Sevenoaks (Otford) TN14 .. 165 FH111
Shoreham Rd E, Houns. (Hthrw Air.) TW6 .. 114 BL85
Shoreham Rd W, Houns. (Hthrw Air.) TW6 .. 114 BL85
Shoreham Way, Brom. BR2 .. 144 EG100
Shore Pl, E9 .. 84 DW66
Shore Pt, Buck.H. IG9 off High Rd .. 48 EH47
Shore Rd, E9 .. 84 DW66
Shores Rd, Wok. GU21 .. 150 AY114
Shorncliffe Rd, SE1 .. 201 P10
Shorndean St, SE6 .. 123 EC88
Shorne Cl, Orp. BR5 .. 146 EX98
Sidcup DA15 .. 126 EV86
Shornefield Cl, Brom. BR1 .. 145 EN97
Shornells Way, SE2 off Willrose Cres .. 106 EW78
Shorrolds Rd, SW6 .. 99 CZ80
Shortacres, Red. RH1 .. 185 DM133
Shortcroft Rd, Epsom KT17 .. 157 CT108
Shortcrofts Rd, Dag. RM9 .. 88 EZ65
Shorter Av, Brwd. (Shenf.) CM15 .. 55 FZ44
Shorter St, E1 .. 197 P10
Shortfern, Slou. SL2 .. 74 AW72
Shortgate, N12 .. 43 CZ49
Short Hedges, Houns. TW3, TW5 .. 96 CB81
Short Hill, Har. HA1 off High St .. 61 CE60
SHORTLANDS, Brom. BR1 .. 144 EE97
⇌ Shortlands .. 144 EE96
Shortlands, W6 .. 99 CX77
Hayes UB3 .. 95 BR79
Shortlands Cl, N18 .. 46 DR48
Belvedere DA17 .. 106 EZ76
Shortlands Gdns, Brom. BR2 .. 144 EE96
Shortlands Gro, Brom. BR2 .. 143 ED97
Shortlands Rd, E10 .. 67 EB59
Bromley BR2 .. 143 ED97
Kingston upon Thames KT2 .. 118 CM94
Short La, Oxt. RH8 .. 188 EH132
St. Albans (Brick.Wd) AL2 .. 8 BZ30
Staines TW19 .. 114 BM88
Shortmead Dr, Wal.Cr. (Chsht) EN8 .. 15 DY31
Short Path, SE18 off Long Wk .. 105 EP79
Short Rd, E11 .. 68 EE61
W4 .. 98 CS79
Hounslow (Hthrw Air.) TW6 .. 114 BL86
Shorts Cft, NW9 .. 62 CP56
Shorts Gdns, WC2 .. 195 P9
Shorts Rd, Cars. SM5 .. 158 DE105
Short St, NW4 off New Brent St .. 63 CW56
SE1 .. 200 E4
Short Wall, E15 .. 85 EC69
Shortway, N12 .. 44 DE51
Short Way, SE9 .. 104 EL83
Twickenham TW2 .. 116 CC87
Shortwood Av, Stai. TW18 .. 114 BH90
Shortwood Common, Stai. TW18 .. 114 BH91
Shotfield, Wall. SM6 .. 159 DH107
Shothanger Way, Hem.H. (Bov.) HP3 .. 5 BC26
Shott Cl, Sutt. SM1 off Turnpike La .. 158 DC106
Shottendane Rd, SW6 .. 100 DA81
Shottery Cl, SE9 .. 124 EL90
Shottfield Av, SW14 .. 98 CS84
Shoulder of Mutton All, E14 off Narrow St .. 85 DY73
Shouldham St, W1 .. 194 C7
Showers Way, Hayes UB3 .. 77 BU74
Shrapnel Cl, SE18 .. 104 EL80
Shrapnel Rd, SE9 .. 105 EM83
SHREDING GREEN, Iver SL0 .. 75 BB72
Shrewsbury Av, SW14 .. 98 CQ84
Harrow HA3 .. 62 CL56
Shrewsbury Cl, Surb. KT6 .. 138 CL103
Shrewsbury Ct, EC1 off Whitecross St .. 84 DQ70
Shrewsbury Cres, NW10 .. 80 CR67
Shrewsbury La, SE18 .. 105 EP81
Shrewsbury Ms, W2 off Chepstow Rd .. 82 DA71
Shrewsbury Rd, E7 .. 68 EK64
N11 .. 45 DJ51
W2 .. 82 DA72
Beckenham BR3 .. 143 DY97
Carshalton SM5 .. 140 DE100
Hounslow (Hthrw Air.) TW6 .. 115 BQ86
Redhill RH1 .. 184 DE134
Shrewsbury St, W10 .. 81 CW70
Shrewsbury Wk, Islw. TW7 off South St .. 97 CG83
Shrewton Rd, SW17 .. 120 DF94
Shroffold Rd, Brom. BR1 .. 124 EE91
Shropshire Cl, Mitch. CR4 .. 141 DL98
Shropshire Ho, N18 .. 46 DV50
Shropshire Pl, WC1 .. 195 L5
Shropshire Rd, N22 .. 45 DM52
Shroton St, NW1 .. 194 B6
Shrubberies, The, E18 .. 48 EG54
Chigwell IG7 .. 49 EQ50
Shrubbery, The, E11 .. 68 EH57
Upminster RM14 .. 72 FQ62
Shrubbery Cl, N1 off St. Paul St .. 84 DQ67
Shrubbery Gdns, N21 .. 45 DP45
Shrubbery Rd, N9 .. 46 DU48
SW16 .. 121 DL91
Dartford (S.Darenth) DA4 .. 149 FR95
Gravesend DA12 .. 131 GH88
Southall UB1 .. 78 BZ74
Shrubland Cl, N20 .. 44 DD46
Shrubland Gro, Wor.Pk. KT4 .. 139 CW104
Shrubland Rd, E8 .. 84 DU67
E10 .. 67 EA59
E17 .. 67 EA57
Banstead SM7 .. 173 CZ116
Shrublands, Hat. AL9 .. 12 DB26
Shrublands, The, Pot.B. EN6 .. 11 CY33
Shrublands Av, Croy. CR0 .. 161 EA105
Shrublands Cl, SE26 .. 122 DW90
Chigwell IG7 .. 49 EQ51
Shrubsall Cl, SE9 .. 124 EL88
Shrubs Rd, Rick. WD3 .. 38 BM51
Shuna Wk, N1 off St. Paul's Rd .. 84 DR65
Shurland Av, Barn. EN4 .. 28 DD44
Shurland Gdns, SE15 off Rosemary Rd .. 102 DT80
Shurlock Av, Swan. BR8 .. 147 FD96
Shurlock Dr, Orp. BR6 .. 163 EQ105
Shuters Sq, W14 off Sun Rd .. 99 CZ78
Shuttle Cl, Sid. DA15 .. 125 ET87
Shuttlemead, Bex. DA5 .. 126 EZ87
Shuttle Rd, Dart. DA1 .. 107 FG83
Shuttle St, E1 off Buxton St .. 84 DU70
Shuttleworth Rd, SW11 .. 100 DE82
Siamese Ms, N3 off Station Rd .. 44 DA53
Siani Ms, N8 .. 65 DP56
Sibella Rd, SW4 .. 101 DK82
Sibley Cl, Bexh. DA6 .. 126 EY85
Bromley BR1 .. 144 EL99
Sibley Gro, E12 .. 86 EL66
Sibthorpe Rd, SE12 .. 124 EH86
Sibton Rd, Cars. SM5 .. 140 DE101
Sicilian Av, WC1 .. 196 A7
Sicklefield Cl, Wal.Cr. (Chsht) EN7 .. 14 DT26
Sidbury St, SW6 .. 99 CY81
SIDCUP, DA14 & DA15 .. 125 ET91
⇌ Sidcup .. 126 EU89
Sidcup Bypass, Chis. BR7 .. 125 ES91
Orpington BR5 .. 126 EX94
Sidcup DA14 .. 125 ES91
Sidcup High St, Sid. DA14 .. 126 EU91
Sidcup Hill, Sid. DA14 .. 126 EV91
Sidcup Hill Gdns, Sid. DA14 off Sidcup Hill .. 126 EW92
Sidcup Pl, Sid. DA14 .. 126 EU92
Sidcup Rd, SE9 .. 124 EK87
SE12 .. 124 EH85
Sidcup Tech Cen, Sid. DA14 .. 126 EX92
Siddeley Dr, Houns. TW4 .. 96 BY83
Siddons La, NW1 .. 194 E5
Siddons Rd, N17 .. 46 DU53
SE23 .. 123 DY89
Croydon CR0 .. 141 DN104
Side Rd, E17 .. 67 DZ57
Uxbridge (Denh.) UB9 .. 57 BD59
Sidewood Rd, SE9 .. 125 ER88
Sidford Ho, SE1 off Cosser St .. 101 DN76
Sidford Pl, SE1 .. 200 C7
Sidi Ct, N15 .. 65 DP55
Sidings, The, E11 .. 67 EC60
Loughton IG10 .. 32 EL44
Staines TW18 .. 114 BH91
Sidings Ms, N7 .. 65 DN62
Siding Way, St.Alb. (Lon.Col.) AL2 .. 9 CH26
Sidmouth Av, Islw. TW7 .. 97 CE82
Sidmouth Cl, Wat. WD19 .. 39 BV47
Sidmouth Dr, Ruis. HA4 .. 59 BU62
Sidmouth Par, NW2 off Sidmouth Rd .. 81 CW66
Sidmouth Rd, E10 .. 67 EC62
NW2 .. 81 CW66
Orpington BR5 .. 146 EV99
Welling DA16 .. 106 EW80
Sidmouth St, WC1 .. 196 A3
Sidney Av, N13 .. 45 DM50
Sidney Cl, Uxb. UB8 .. 76 BJ66
Sidney Elson Way, E6 off Edwin Av .. 87 EN68
Sidney Gdns, Brent. TW8 .. 97 CJ79
Sidney Gro, EC1 .. 196 F1
Sidney Rd, E7 .. 68 EG62
N22 .. 45 DM52
SE25 .. 142 DU99
SW9 .. 101 DM82
Beckenham BR3 .. 143 DY96
Epping (They.B.) CM16 .. 33 ER36
Harrow HA2 .. 60 CC55
Staines TW18 .. 114 BG91
Twickenham TW1 .. 117 CG86
Walton-on-Thames KT12 .. 135 BU101
Sidney Sq, E1 .. 84 DW72
Sidney St, E1 .. 84 DV71
Sidworth St, E8 .. 84 DV66
Siebert Rd, SE3 .. 104 EG79
Siemens Rd, SE18 .. 104 EK76
Sigdon Pas, E8 off Sigdon Rd .. 66 DU64
Sigdon Rd, E8 .. 66 DU64
Sigers, The, Pnr. HA5 .. 59 BV58
Signmakers Yd, NW1 off Delancey St .. 83 DH67
Sigrist Sq, Kings.T. KT2 .. 138 CL95
Silbury Av, Mitch. CR4 .. 140 DE95
Silbury Ho, SE26 off Sydenham Hill Est .. 122 DU90
Silbury St, N1 .. 197 K2
Silchester Rd, W10 .. 81 CX72
Silecroft Rd, Bexh. DA7 .. 106 FA81
Silesia Bldgs, E8 off London La .. 84 DV66
Silex St, SE1 .. 200 G5
Silk Cl, SE12 .. 124 EG85
Silkfield Rd, NW9 .. 62 CS57
Silkham Rd, Oxt. RH8 .. 187 ED127
Silkin Ho, Wat. WD19 .. 40 BW48
Silk Mill Ct, Wat. WD19 off Silk Mill Rd .. 39 BV45
Silk Mill Rd, Wat. WD19 .. 39 BV45
Silk Mills Cl, Sev. TN14 .. 191 FJ121
Silk Mills Pas, SE13 off Egeremont Rd .. 103 EB82
Silk Mills Path, SE13 off Lewisham Rd .. 103 EC83
Silk Mills Sq, E9 .. 85 DZ65
Silkstream Rd, Edg. HA8 .. 42 CQ53
Silk St, EC2 .. 197 J6
Silsden Cres, Ch.St.G. HP8 off London Rd .. 36 AX48
Silsoe Ho, NW1 off Park Village E .. 83 DH68
Silsoe Rd, N22 .. 45 DM54
Silver Birch Av, E4 .. 47 DZ51
Epping (N.Wld Bas.) CM16 .. 18 EY27
Silver Birch Cl, N11 .. 44 DG51
SE6 .. 123 DZ90
SE28 .. 88 EU74
Addlestone (Wdhm) KT15 .. 151 BE112
Dartford DA2 .. 127 FE91
Uxbridge UB10 .. 58 BL63
Silver Birch Ct, Wal.Cr. (Chsht) EN8 .. 15 DX31
Silver Birches, Brwd. (Hutt.) CM13 .. 55 GA46
Silver Birch Gdns, E6 .. 87 EM70
Silver Birch Ms, Ilf. IG6 off Fencepiece Rd .. 49 EQ51
Silverbirch Wk, NW3 off Queen's Cres .. 82 DG65
Silvercliffe Gdns, Barn. EN4 .. 28 DE42
Silver Cl, SE14 off Southerngate Way .. 103 DY80
Harrow HA3 .. 41 CD52
Tadworth (Kgswd) KT20 .. 173 CY124
Silver Cres, W4 .. 98 CP77
Silverdale, NW1 off Hampstead Rd .. 83 DJ69
SE26 .. 122 DW91
Enfield EN2 .. 29 DL42
Silverdale Av, Ilf. IG3 .. 69 ES57
Leatherhead (Oxshott) KT22 .. 154 CC114
Walton-on-Thames KT12 .. 135 BT104
Silverdale Cl, W7 .. 79 CE74
Northolt UB5 .. 60 BZ64
Sutton SM1 .. 157 CZ105
Silverdale Ct, Stai. TW18 off Leacroft .. 114 BH92
Silverdale Dr, SE9 .. 124 EL89
Hornchurch RM12 .. 71 FH64
Sunbury-on-Thames TW16 .. 135 BV96
Silverdale Gdns, Hayes UB3 .. 95 BU75
Silverdale Rd, E4 .. 47 ED51
Bexleyheath DA7 .. 107 FB82
Bushey WD23 .. 24 BY43
Hayes UB3 .. 95 BU75
Orpington (Petts Wd) BR5 .. 145 EQ98
Orpington (St.P.Cray) BR5 .. 146 EU97
Silver Dell, Wat. WD24 .. 23 BT35
Silvergate, Epsom KT19 .. 156 CQ106
Silverglade Business Pk, Chess. KT9 .. 155 CJ112
Silverhall St, Islw. TW7 .. 97 CG83
Silver Hill, Ch.St.G. HP8 .. 36 AV47
Silverholme Cl, Har. HA3 .. 61 CK59
Silver Jubilee Way, Houns. TW4 .. 95 BV82
Silverland St, E16 .. 87 EM74
Silver La, Pur. CR8 .. 159 DK112
West Wickham BR4 .. 143 ED103
Silverleigh Rd, Th.Hth. CR7 .. 141 DM98
Silverlocke Rd, Grays RM17 .. 110 GD79
Silvermead, E18 off Churchfields .. 48 EG53
Silvermere Av, Rom. RM5 .. 51 FB51
Silvermere Dr, N18 .. 47 DX51
Silvermere Rd, SE6 .. 123 EB86
Silver Pl, W1 .. 195 L10
Silver Rd, SE13 .. 103 EB83
W12 .. 81 CX73
Gravesend DA12 .. 131 GL89
Silversmiths Way, Wok. GU21 .. 166 AW118
Silver Spring Cl, Erith DA8 .. 107 FB79
Silverstead La, West. TN16 .. 179 ER121
Silverstone Cl, Red. RH1 off Goodwood Rd .. 184 DF132
Silverston Way, Stan. HA7 .. 41 CJ51
⇌ Silver Street .. 46 DT50
Silver St, N18 .. 46 DS49
Enfield EN1 .. 30 DR41
Romford (Abridge) RM4 .. 34 EV41
Waltham Abbey EN9 .. 15 EC34
Waltham Cross (Goffs Oak) EN7 .. 14 DR30
Silverthorne Rd, SW8 .. 101 DH82
Silverthorn Gdns, E4 .. 47 EA47
Silverton Rd, W6 .. 99 CX79
SILVERTOWN, E16 .. 104 EJ75
⇌ Silvertown & London City Airport .. 86 EK74
Silvertown Way, E16 .. 86 EF72
Silver Tree Cl, Walt. KT12 .. 135 BU104
Silvertree La, Grnf. UB6 off Cowgate Rd .. 79 CD69
Silver Trees, St.Alb. (Brick.Wd) AL2 .. 8 BZ30
Silver Wk, SE16 .. 203 M3
Silver Way, Rom. RM7 .. 71 FB55
Uxbridge UB10 off Oakdene Rd .. 77 BP68
Silverwood Cl, Beck. BR3 .. 123 EA94
Croydon CR0 .. 161 DZ109
Northwood HA6 .. 39 BQ53
Silvester Rd, SE22 .. 122 DT85
Silvester St, SE1 .. 201 J5
Silvocea Way, E14 .. 85 ED72
Silwood Est, SE16 off Reculver Rd .. 103 DX78
Silwood St, SE16 .. 202 G9
Simla Ho, SE1 .. 201 L5
Simmil Rd, Esher (Clay.) KT10 .. 155 CE106
Simmons Cl, N20 .. 44 DE46
Chessington KT9 .. 155 CJ107
Slough SL3 off Common Rd .. 93 BA77
Simmons Dr, Dag. RM8 .. 70 EY62
Simmons Gate, Esher KT10 .. 154 CC106
Simmons La, E4 .. 47 ED47
Simmons Pl, Stai. TW18 off Chertsey La .. 113 BE92
Simmons Rd, SE18 .. 105 EP78
Simmons Way, N20 .. 44 DE47
Simms Cl, Cars. SM5 .. 140 DE103
Simms Gdns, N2 .. 44 DC54
Simms Rd, SE1 .. 202 B9
Simnel Rd, SE12 .. 124 EH87
Simon Cl, W11 off Portobello Rd .. 81 CZ73
Simon Dean, Hem.H. (Bov.) HP3 .. 5 BA27
Simonds Rd, E10 .. 67 EA61
Simone Cl, Brom. BR1 .. 144 EK95
Simone Dr, Ken. CR8 .. 176 DQ116
Simons Cl, Cher. (Ott.) KT16 .. 151 BC107
Simons Wk, E15 off Waddington Rd .. 67 ED64
Egham (Eng.Grn) TW20 .. 112 AW94
Simplemarsh Ct, Add. KT15 off Simplemarsh Rd .. 152 BH105
Simplemarsh Rd, Add. KT15 .. 152 BG105
Simpson Cl, N21 off Macleod Rd .. 29 DL43
Simpson Dr, W3 .. 80 CR72
Simpson Rd, Houns. TW4 .. 116 BZ86
Rainham RM13 .. 89 FF65
Richmond TW10 .. 117 CJ91
Simpsons Rd, E14 .. 204 C1
Bromley BR2 .. 144 EG97
Simpson St, SW11 .. 100 DE82
Simpsons Way, Slou. SL1 .. 74 AS74
Simrose Ct, SW18 off Wandsworth High St .. 120 DA85
Sims Cl, Rom. RM1 .. 71 FF56
Sims Wk, SE3 .. 104 EF84
Sinclair Ct, Beck. BR3 .. 123 EA94
Sinclair Dr, Sutt. SM2 .. 158 DB109
Sinclair Gdns, W14 .. 99 CX75
Sinclair Gro, NW11 .. 63 CX58
Sinclair Pl, SE4 .. 123 EA86
Sinclair Rd, E4 .. 47 DZ50
W14 .. 99 CX75
Sinclair Way, Dart. (Lane End) DA2 .. 129 FR91
Sinclare Cl, Enf. EN1 .. 30 DT39
Sincots Rd, Red. RH1 off Lower Br Rd .. 184 DF134
Sinderby Cl, Borwd. WD6 .. 26 CL39
Singapore Rd, W13 .. 79 CG74
Singer St, EC2 .. 197 L3
Singles Cross La, Sev. (Knock.) TN14 .. 164 EW114
SINGLE STREET, West. TN16 .. 179 EN115
Single St, West. (Berry's Grn) TN16 .. 179 EP115
Singleton Cl, SW17 .. 120 DF94
Croydon CR0 off St. Saviours Rd .. 142 DQ101
Hornchurch RM12 off Carfax Rd .. 71 FF63
Singleton Rd, Dag. RM9 .. 70 EZ64
Singleton Scarp, N12 .. 44 DA50
SINGLEWELL, Grav. DA12 .. 131 GK93
Singlewell Rd, Grav. DA11 .. 131 GH89
Singret Pl, Uxb. (Cowley) UB8 off High St .. 76 BJ70
Sinnott Rd, E17 .. 47 DX53
Sion Rd, Twick. TW1 .. 117 CH88
SIPSON, West Dr. UB7 .. 94 BN79
Sipson Cl, West Dr. UB7 .. 94 BN79
Sipson La, Hayes UB3 .. 94 BN79
West Drayton UB7 .. 94 BN79
Sipson Rd, West Dr. UB7 .. 94 BN78
Sipson Way, West Dr. UB7 .. 94 BN80
Sir Alexander Cl, W3 .. 81 CT74
Sir Alexander Rd, W3 .. 81 CT74
Sir Cyril Black Way, SW19 .. 120 DA94
Sirdar Rd, N22 .. 65 DP55
W11 .. 81 CX73
Mitcham CR4 off Grenfell Rd .. 120 DG93
Sirdar Strand, Grav. DA12 .. 131 GM92
Sir Francis Way, Brwd. CM14 .. 54 FV47
Sirinham Pt, SW8 .. 101 DM79
Sirius Rd, Nthwd. HA6 .. 39 BU50
Sir James Black Ho, SE5 off Coldharbour La .. 102 DR82
Sir John Kirk Cl, SE5 off Bethwin Rd .. 102 DQ80
★ Sir John Soane's Mus, WC2 off Lincoln's Inn Flds .. 196 B8
Sir Robert Ms, Slou. SL3 off Cheviot Rd .. 93 BA78
Sir Thomas More Est, SW3 off Beaufort St .. 100 DD79
Sise La, EC4 .. 197 K9
Siskin Cl, Borwd. WD6 .. 26 CN42
Bushey WD23 .. 24 BY42
Sisley Rd, Bark. IG11 .. 87 ES67
Sispara Gdns, SW18 .. 119 CZ86
Sissinghurst Rd, Croy. CR0 .. 142 DU101
Sissulu Ct, E6 .. 86 EJ67
Sister Mabel's Way, SE15 off Radnor Rd .. 102 DU80
Sisters Av, SW11 .. 100 DF84
Sistova Rd, SW12 .. 121 DH88
Sisulu Pl, SW9 .. 101 DN83
Sittingbourne Av, Enf. EN1 .. 30 DR44
Sitwell Gro, Stan. HA7 .. 41 CF50
Siverst Cl, Nthlt. UB5 .. 78 CB65
Sivill Ho, E2 .. 84 DT69
Siviter Way, Dag. RM10 .. 89 FB66
Siward Rd, N17 .. 46 DR53
SW17 .. 120 DC90
Bromley BR2 .. 144 EH97
Six Acres Est, N4 .. 65 DN61
Six Bells La, Sev. TN13 .. 191 FJ126
Six Bridges Trd Est, SE1 .. 102 DU78
Sixth Av, E12 .. 69 EM63
W10 .. 81 CY69
Hayes UB3 .. 77 BT74
Watford WD25 .. 24 BX35
Sixth Cross Rd, Twick. TW2 .. 116 CC90
Skardu Rd, NW2 .. 63 CY64
Skarnings Ct, Wal.Abb. EN9 .. 16 EG33
Skeena Hill, SW18 .. 119 CY87
Skeet Hill La, Orp. BR5, BR6 .. 146 EY103
Skeffington Rd, E6 .. 86 EL67
Skeffington St, SE18 .. 105 EQ76
Skelbrook St, SW18 .. 120 DB89
Skelgill Rd, SW15 .. 99 CZ84
Skelley Rd, E15 .. 86 EF66
Skelton Cl, E8 off Buttermere Wk .. 84 DT65
Skelton Rd, E7 .. 86 EG65
Skeltons La, E10 .. 67 EB59
Skelwith Rd, W6 .. 99 CW79
Skenfrith Ho, SE15 off Commercial Way .. 102 DV79
Skerne Rd, Kings.T. KT2 .. 137 CK95
Skerne Wk, Kings.T. KT2 .. 137 CK95

★ Place of interest ⇌ Railway station ⊖ London Underground station DLR Docklands Light Railway station Tra Tramlink station H Hospital Riv Pedestrian ferry landing stage

Skerries Ct, Slou. (Langley) SL3 *off Blacksmith Row* 93 BA77
Sketchley Gdns, SE16 203 H10
Sketty Rd, Enf. EN1 30 DS41
Skibbs La, Orp. BR5, BR6 146 EZ103
Skid Hill La, Warl. CR6 162 EF113
Skidmore Way, Rick. WD3 38 BL46
Skiers St, E15 86 EE67
Skiffington Cl, SW2 121 DN88
Skillet Hill, Wal.Abb. EN9 32 EH35
Skinner Ct, E2 *off Parmiter St* 84 DV68
Skinner Pl, SW1 198 F9
★ **Skinners' Hall**, EC4 *off Dowgate Hill* 197 K10
Skinners La, EC4 197 J10
Ashtead KT21 171 CK118
Hounslow TW5 96 CB81
Skinner St, EC1 196 E3
Skinney La, Dart. (Hort.Kir.) DA4 148 FQ97
Skip La, Uxb. (Hare.) UB9 58 BL60
Skippers Cl, Green. DA9 129 FV85
Skips Cor, Epp. (N.Wld Bas.) CM16 19 FD25
Skipsea Ho, SW18 *off Fitzhugh Gro* 120 DD86
Skipsey Av, E6 87 EM69
Skipton Cl, N11 44 DG51
Skipton Dr, Hayes UB3 95 BQ76
Skipworth Rd, E9 84 DW67
Skomer Wk, N1 *off Ashby Gro* 84 DQ66
Skylark Rd, Uxb. (Denh.) UB9 57 BC60
Skylines Village, E14 204 D5
Sky Peals Rd, Wdf.Grn. IG8 47 ED53
Skyport Dr, West Dr. UB7 94 BK80
Slade,The, SE18 105 ES79
Sladebrook Rd, SE3 104 EK83
Slade Ct, Cher. (Ott.) KT16 151 BD107
Radlett WD7 25 CG35
Sladedale Rd, SE18 105 ES78
Slade End, Epp. (They.B.) CM16 33 ES36
Slade Gdns, Erith DA8 107 FF81
⇌ **Slade Green** 107 FG81
Slade Grn Rd, Erith DA8 107 FG80
Slade Ho, Houns. TW4 116 BZ86
Slade Oak La, Ger.Cr. SL9 57 BB55
Uxbridge (Denh.) UB9 57 BD59
Slade Rd, Cher. (Ott.) KT16 151 BD107
Slades Cl, Enf. EN2 29 DN41
Slades Dr, Chis. BR7 125 EQ90
Slades Gdns, Enf. EN2 29 DN40
Slades Hill, Enf. EN2 29 DN41
Slades Ri, Enf. EN2 29 DN41
Slade Twr, E10 67 EA61
Slade Wk, SE17 *off Heiron St* 101 DP79
Slagrove Pl, SE13 123 EA85
Slaidburn St, SW10 100 DC79
Slaithwaite Rd, SE13 103 EC84
Slaney Pl, N7 *off Hornsey Rd* 65 DN64
Slaney Rd, Rom. RM1 71 FE57
Slapleys, Wok. GU22 166 AX120
Slater Cl, SE18 *off Woolwich New Rd* 105 EN78
Slater Ms, SW4 *off Old Town* 101 DJ83
Slattery Rd, Felt. TW13 116 BW88
Sleaford Grn, Wat. WD19 40 BX48
Sleaford Ho, E3 85 EA70
Sleaford St, SW8 101 DJ80
Sledmere Ct, Felt. TW14 *off Kilross Rd* 115 BS88
Sleepers Fm Rd, Grays RM16 111 GH75
Slewins Cl, Horn. RM11 72 FJ57
Slewins La, Horn. RM11 72 FJ57
Slievemore Cl, SW4 *off Voltaire Rd* 101 DK83
Slines Oak Rd, Cat. (Wold.) CR3 177 EA123
Warlingham CR6 177 EA119
Slingsby Pl, WC2 195 P10
Slip,The, West. TN16 189 EQ126
Slippers Pl, SE16 202 E6
Slippers Pl Est, SE16 202 E7
Slipshoe St, Reig. RH2 *off West St* 184 DA134
Sloane Av, SW3 198 B8
Sloane Ct E, SW3 198 F10
Sloane Ct W, SW3 198 F10
Sloane Gdns, SW1 198 F9
Orpington BR6 145 EQ104
H **Sloane Hosp,The**, Beck. BR3 143 ED95
⊖ **Sloane Square** 198 F9
Sloane Sq, SW1 198 F9
Sloane St, SW1 198 E6
Sloane Ter, SW1 198 E8
Sloane Wk, Croy. CR0 143 DZ100
Slocock Hill, Wok. GU21 166 AW117
Slocum Cl, SE28 88 EW73
SLOUGH, SL1 - SL3 74 AS74
⇌ **Slough** 74 AT74
Slough La, NW9 62 CQ58
Betchworth (Buckland) RH3 183 CU133
Epsom (Headley) KT18 182 CQ125
★ **Slough Mus**, Slou. SL1 92 AU75
Slough Rd, Iver SL0 75 BE68
Slough (Datchet) SL3 92 AU78
Slowmans Cl, St.Alb. (Park St) AL2 8 CC28
Sly St, E1 *off Cannon St Rd* 84 DV72
Smaldon Cl, West Dr. UB7 *off Walnut Av* 94 BN76
Smallberry Av, Islw. TW7 97 CF82
Smallbrook Ms, W2 *off Craven Rd* 82 DD72
Smalley Cl, N16 66 DT62
Smalley Rd Est, N16 *off Smalley Cl* 66 DT62
Small Grains, Long. (Fawk.Grn) DA3 149 FV104
Smallholdings Rd, Epsom KT17 157 CW114
Smallwood Rd, SW17 120 DD91
Smardale Rd, SW18 *off Alma Rd* 120 DC85
Smarden Cl, Belv. DA17 *off Essenden Rd* 106 FA78
Smarden Gro, SE9 125 EM91
Smart Cl, Rom. RM3 51 FH53
Smarts Grn, Wal.Cr. (Chsht) EN7 14 DT27
Smarts Heath La, Wok. GU22 166 AU123
Smarts Heath Rd, Wok. GU22 166 AT123
Smarts La, Loug. IG10 32 EK42
Smarts Pl, N18 *off Fore St* 46 DU50
Smart's Pl, WC2 196 A8
Smarts Rd, Grav. DA12 131 GH89
Smart St, E2 85 DX69
Smeaton Cl, Chess. KT9 *off Merritt Gdns* 155 CK107
Waltham Abbey EN9 16 EE32
Smeaton Ct, SE1 201 H7
Smeaton Rd, SW18 120 DA87
Enfield EN3 31 EA37
Woodford Green IG8 49 EM50
Smeaton St, E1 202 D2
Smedley St, SW4 101 DK82
SW8 101 DK82
Smeed Rd, E3 85 EA66
Smiles Pl, SE13 103 EC82
⇌ **Smitham** 175 DL115
Smitham Bottom La, Pur. CR8 159 DJ111
Smitham Downs Rd, Pur. CR8 159 DK113
Smith Cl, SE16 203 H3
★ **Smithfield Cen Mkt**, EC1 196 G7
Smithfield St, EC1 196 F7
Smithies Ct, E15 67 EC64
Smithies Rd, SE2 106 EV77
Smiths Caravan Site, Iver SL0 75 BC74
Smith's Ct, W1 195 L10
Smiths Ct, Epp. (Thnwd) CM16 18 EW25
Smiths Fm Est, Nthlt. UB5 78 CA68
Smiths La, Eden. (Crock.H.) TN8 189 EQ133
Waltham Cross (Chsht) EN7 14 DR26
Smithson Rd, N17 46 DR53
Smiths Pt, E13 *off Brooks Rd* 86 EG67
Smith Sq, SW1 199 P7
Smith St, SW3 198 D10
Surbiton KT5 138 CM100
Watford WD18 24 BW42
Smiths Yd, SW18 *off Summerley St* 120 DC89
Smith's Yd, Croy. CR0 *off St. Georges Wk* 142 DQ104
Smith Ter, SW3 100 DF78
Smithwood Cl, SW19 119 CY88
Smithy Cl, Tad. (Lwr Kgswd) KT20 183 CZ126
Smithy La, Tad. (Lwr Kgswd) KT20 183 CZ127
Smithy St, E1 84 DW71
Smock Wk, Croy. CR0 142 DQ100
Smokehouse Yd, EC1 196 G6
Smugglers Wk, Green. DA9 129 FV85
Smugglers Way, SW18 100 DB84
Smug Oak Grn Business Cen, St.Alb. AL2 8 CB30
Smug Oak La, St.Alb. (Brick.Wd) AL2 8 CB30
Smyrks Rd, SE17 102 DS78
Smyrna Rd, NW6 82 DA66
Smythe Rd, Dart. (Sutt.H.) DA4 148 FN95
Smythe St, E14 85 EB73
Snag La, Sev. (Cudham) TN14 163 ES109
Snakes La, Barn. EN4 29 DH41
Snakes La E, Wdf.Grn. IG8 48 EJ51
Snakes La W, Wdf.Grn. IG8 48 EG51
Snakey La, Felt. TW13 115 BU91
Snape Spur, Slou. SL1 74 AS72
SNARESBROOK, E11 68 EE57
⊖ **Snaresbrook** 68 EG57
Snaresbrook Dr, Stan. HA7 41 CK49
Snaresbrook Rd, E11 68 EE56
Snarsgate St, W10 81 CW71
Snatts Hill, Oxt. RH8 188 EF129
Sneath Av, NW11 63 CZ59
Snelling Av, Grav. (Nthflt) DA11 130 GE89
Snellings Rd, Walt. KT12 154 BW106
Snells La, Amer. HP7 20 AV39
Snells Pk, N18 46 DT51
Snells Wd Ct, Amer. HP7 20 AW40
Sneyd Rd, NW2 63 CW63
Snipe Cl, Erith DA8 107 FH80
Snodland Cl, Orp. BR6 *off Mill La* 163 EN110
Snowberry Cl, E15 67 ED63
Snowbury Rd, SW6 100 DB82
Snowden Av, Uxb. UB10 77 BP68
Snowden St, EC2 197 M5
Snowdon Cres, Hayes UB3 95 BQ76
Snowdon Dr, NW9 62 CS58
Snowdon Rd, Houns. (Hthrw Air.) TW6 *off Southern Perimeter Rd* 115 BQ85
Snowdown Cl, SE20 143 DX95
Snowdrop Cl, Hmptn. TW12 *off Gresham Rd* 116 CA93
Snowdrop Path, Rom. RM3 52 FK52
Snow Hill, EC1 196 F7
Snow Hill Ct, EC1 196 G8
Snowman Ho, NW6 82 DB67
Snowsfields, SE1 201 L4
Snowshill Rd, E12 68 EL64
Snowy Fielder Waye, Islw. TW7 97 CH82
Soames St, SE15 102 DT83
Soames Wk, N.Mal. KT3 138 CS95
Soane Cl, W5 97 CK75
Socket La, Brom. BR2 144 EH100
SOCKETT'S HEATH, Grays RM16 110 GD76
Soham Rd, Enf. EN3 31 DZ37
SOHO, W1 195 M10
Soho Sq, W1 195 M8
Soho St, W1 195 M8
Sojourner Truth Cl, E8 *off Richmond Rd* 84 DV65
Solander Gdns, E1 *off Dellow St* 84 DV73
Solar Way, Enf. EN3 31 DZ36
Solebay St, E1 85 DY70
Sole Fm Cl, Lthd. (Bkhm) KT23 170 BZ124
Solefields Rd, Sev. TN13 191 FH128
Solent Ri, E13 86 EG69
Solent Rd, NW6 64 DA64
Soleoak Dr, Sev. TN13 191 FH127
Solesbridge Cl, Rick. (Chorl.) WD3 21 BF41
Solesbridge La, Rick. WD3 22 BG40
Soley Ms, WC1 196 D2
Solna Av, SW15 119 CW85
Solna Rd, N21 46 DR46
Solomon Av, N9 46 DU49
Solomons Hill, Rick. WD3 *off Northway* 38 BK45
Solomon's Pas, SE15 102 DV84
Solom's Ct Rd, Bans. SM7 174 DE117
Solon New Rd, SW4 101 DL84
Solon New Rd Est, SW4 *off Solon New Rd* 101 DL84
Solon Rd, SW2 101 DL84
Solway Cl, E8 *off Buttermere Wk* 84 DT65
Hounslow TW4 96 BY83
Solway Rd, N22 45 DP53
SE22 102 DU84
Somaford Gro, Barn. EN4 28 DD44
Somali Rd, NW2 63 CZ63
Somborne Ho, SW15 *off Fontley Way* 119 CU87
Somerby Rd, Bark. IG11 87 ER66
Somercoates Cl, Barn. EN4 28 DE41
Somerden Rd, Orp. BR5 146 EX101
Somerfield Cl, Tad. KT20 173 CY119
Somerfield Rd, N4 65 DP61
Somerfield St, SE16 203 H10
Somerford Cl, Pnr. HA5 59 BU56
Somerford Gro, N16 66 DT63
N17 46 DU52
Somerford Gro Est, N16 *off Somerford Gro* 66 DT63
Somerford St, E1 84 DV70
Somerford Way, SE16 203 K5
Somerhill Av, Sid. DA15 126 EV87
Somerhill Rd, Well. DA16 106 EV82
Somerleyton Pas, SW9 101 DP84
Somerleyton Rd, SW9 101 DN84
Somersby Gdns, Ilf. IG4 69 EM57
Somers Cl, NW1 *off Platt St* 83 DK68
Reigate RH2 184 DA133
Somers Cres, W2 194 B9
Somerset Av, SW20 139 CV96
Chessington KT9 155 CK105
Welling DA16 125 ET85
Somerset Cl, N17 46 DR54
Epsom KT19 156 CS109
New Malden KT3 138 CS100
Walton-on-Thames KT12 *off Queens Rd* 153 BV106
Woodford Green IG8 48 EG53
Somerset Est, SW11 100 DD81
Somerset Gdns, N6 64 DG59
N17 46 DS52
SE13 103 EB82
SW16 141 DM97
Hornchurch RM11 72 FN60
Teddington TW11 117 CE92
★ **Somerset Ho**, WC2 196 B10
Somerset Ho, SW19 119 CX90
Somerset Rd, E17 67 EA57
N17 66 DT55
N18 46 DT50
NW4 63 CW56
SW19 119 CY91
W4 98 CR76
W13 79 CH74
Barnet EN5 28 DB43
Brentford TW8 97 CJ79
Dartford DA1 127 FH86
Enfield EN3 31 EA38
Harrow HA1 60 CC57
Kingston upon Thames KT1 138 CM96
Orpington BR6 146 EU101
Southall UB1 78 BZ71
Teddington TW11 117 CE92
Somerset Sq, W14 99 CY75
Somerset Way, Iver SL0 93 BF75
Somerset Waye, Houns. TW5 96 BY79
Somersham Rd, Bexh. DA7 106 EY82
Somers Ms, W2 194 B9
Somers Pl, SW2 121 DM87
Reigate RH2 184 DA133
Somers Rd, E17 67 DZ56
SW2 121 DM86
Reigate RH2 183 CZ133
SOMERS TOWN, NW1 195 N2
Somers Way, Bushey WD23 40 CC45
Somerton Av, Rich. TW9 98 CP83
Somerton Cl, Pur. CR8 175 DN115
Somerton Rd, NW2 63 CY62
SE15 102 DV84
Somertrees Av, SE12 124 EH89
Somervell Rd, Har. HA2 60 BZ64
Somerville Av, SW13 99 CV79
Somerville Rd, SE20 123 DX94
Cobham KT11 154 CA114
Dartford DA1 128 FM86
Romford RM6 70 EW58
Sonderburg Rd, N7 65 DM61
Sondes St, SE17 102 DR79
Songhurst Cl, Croy. CR0 141 DM100
Sonia Cl, Wat. WD19 40 BW45
Sonia Ct, Har. HA1 61 CF58
Sonia Gdns, N12 *off Woodside Av* 44 DC49
NW10 63 CT63
Hounslow TW5 96 CA80
Sonnet Wk, West. (Bigg.H.) TN16 *off Kings Rd* 178 EH118
Sonning Gdns, Hmptn. TW12 116 BY93
Sonning Rd, SE25 142 DU100
Soper Cl, E4 47 DZ50
SE23 123 DX88
Soper Dr, Cat. CR3 *off Hambledon Rd* 176 DR123
Soper Ms, Enf. EN3 *off Harston Dr* 31 EA38
Sopers Rd, Pot.B. (Cuffley) EN6 13 DM29
Sophia Cl, N7 *off Mackenzie Rd* 83 DM65
Sophia Rd, E10 67 EB60
E16 86 EH72
Sophia Sq, SE16 203 K1
Sophie Gdns, Slou. SL3 92 AX75
Sopwith Av, Chess. KT9 156 CL106
Sopwith Cl, Kings.T. KT2 118 CM92
Westerham (Bigg.H.) TN16 178 EK116
Sopwith Dr, W.Byf. KT14 152 BL111
Weybridge KT13 152 BL111
Sopwith Rd, Houns. TW5 96 BW80
Sopwith Way, SW8 101 DH80
Kingston upon Thames KT2 138 CL95
Sorbie Cl, Wey. KT13 153 BR107
Sorrel Bk, Croy. CR0 161 DY110
Sorrel Cl, SE28 88 EU74
Sorrel Ct, Grays RM17 *off Salix Rd* 110 GD79
Sorrel Gdns, E6 86 EL71
Sorrel La, E14 85 ED72
Sorrell Cl, SE14 *off Southerngate Way* 103 DY80
Sorrel Wk, Rom. RM1 71 FF55
Sorrel Way, Grav. (Nthflt) DA11 130 GE91
Sorrento Rd, Sutt. SM1 140 DB104
Sotheby Rd, N5 65 DP62
Sotheran Cl, E8 84 DU67
Sotheron Rd, SW6 100 DB80
Watford WD17 24 BW40
Soudan Rd, SW11 100 DF81
Souldern Rd, W14 99 CX76
Souldern St, Wat. WD18 23 BU43
Sounds Lo, Swan. BR8 147 FC100
South Access Rd, E17 67 DY59
Southacre Way, Pnr. HA5 40 BW53
SOUTH ACTON, W3 98 CN76
⇌ **South Acton** 98 CQ76
South Acton Est, W3 98 CP75
South Africa Rd, W12 81 CV74
South Albert Rd, Reig. RH2 183 CZ133
SOUTHALL, UB1 & UB2 78 BX74
⇌ **Southall** 96 BZ75
Southall La, Houns. TW5 95 BV79
Southall UB2 95 BV79
Southall Pl, SE1 201 K5
Southall Way, Brwd. CM14 54 FT49
Southampton Bldgs, WC2 196 D8
Southampton Gdns, Mitch. CR4 141 DL99
Southampton Ms, E16 205 P2
Southampton Pl, WC1 196 A7
Southampton Rd, NW5 64 DF64
Southampton Rd E, Houns. (Hthrw Air.) TW6 114 BN86
Southampton Rd W, Houns. (Hthrw Air.) TW6 114 BL86
Southampton Row, WC1 196 A6
Southampton St, WC2 196 A10
Southampton Way, SE5 102 DR80
Southam St, W10 81 CY70
South App, Nthwd. HA6 39 BR48
South Audley St, W1 198 G1
South Av, E4 47 EB45
Carshalton SM5 158 DF108
Egham TW20 113 BC93
Richmond TW9 *off Sandycombe Rd* 98 CN82
Southall UB1 78 BZ73
Walton-on-Thames (Whiteley Vill.) KT12 153 BS110
South Av Gdns, Sthl. UB1 78 BZ73
South Bk, Chis. BR7 125 EQ91
Surbiton KT6 138 CL100
Southbank, T.Ditt. KT7 137 CH101
South Bk, West. TN16 189 ER126
Southbank Business Cen, SW8 101 DK79
South Bk Ter, Surb. KT6 138 CL100
SOUTH BEDDINGTON, Wall. SM6 159 DK107
⇌ **South Bermondsey** 202 F10
South Birkbeck Rd, E11 67 ED62
South Black Lion La, W6 99 CU78
South Bolton Gdns, SW5 100 DB78
South Border, The, Pur. CR8 159 DK111
SOUTHBOROUGH, Brom. BR2 145 EM100
Southborough Cl, Surb. KT6 137 CK102
Southborough La, Brom. BR2 144 EL99
Southborough Rd, E9 84 DW67
Bromley BR1 144 EL97
Surbiton KT6 138 CL102
Southbourne, Brom. BR2 144 EG101
Southbourne Av, NW9 42 CQ54
Southbourne Cl, Pnr. HA5 60 BY59
Southbourne Cres, NW4 63 CY56
Southbourne Gdns, SE12 124 EH85
Ilford IG1 69 EQ64
Ruislip HA4 59 BV60
Southbridge Pl, Croy. CR0 160 DQ105
Southbridge Rd, Croy. CR0 160 DQ105
Southbridge Way, Sthl. UB2 96 BY75
Southbrook Dr, Wal.Cr. (Chsht) EN8 15 DX28
Southbrook Ms, SE12 124 EF86
Southbrook Rd, SE12 124 EF86
SW16 141 DL95
⇌ **Southbury** 30 DV42
Southbury Av, Enf. EN1 30 DU43
Southbury Cl, Horn. RM12 72 FK64
Southbury Rd, Enf. EN1, EN3 30 DR41
South Carriage Dr, SW1 198 D4
SW7 198 A5
SOUTH CHINGFORD, E4 47 DZ50
Southchurch Rd, E6 87 EM68
South Circular Rd, SE6 (A205) 123 ED87
SE9 (A205) 105 EM83
SE12 (A205) 124 EH86
SE18 (A205) 105 EN79
SE21 (A205) 122 DS88
SE22 (A205) 122 DV88
SE23 (A205) 123 DZ88
SW2 (A205) 121 DN88
SW4 (A205) 120 DG85
SW11 (A3) 120 DE85
SW12 (A205) 121 DN88
SW14 (A205) 98 CS84
SW15 (A205) 99 CW84
SW18 (A3) 120 DE85
W4 (A205) 98 CN78
South Circular Rd, Brent. (A205) TW8 98 CN78
Richmond (A205) TW9 98 CP82
Southcliffe Dr, Ger.Cr. (Chal.St.P.) SL9 36 AY50
South Cl, N6 65 DH58
Barnet EN5 27 CZ41
Bexleyheath DA6 106 EX84
Dagenham RM10 88 FA67
Morden SM4 140 DA100
Pinner HA5 60 BZ59
St. Albans AL2 8 CB25
Twickenham TW2 116 CA90
West Drayton UB7 94 BM76
Woking GU21 166 AW116
South Cl Grn, Red. (Merst.) RH1 185 DH129
South Colonnade, E14 204 A2
Southcombe St, W14 99 CY77
South Common Rd, Uxb UB8. 76 BL65
Southcote, Wok. GU21 166 AX115
Southcote Av, Felt. TW13 115 BT89
Surbiton KT5 138 CP101
Southcote Ri, Ruis. HA4 59 BR59
Southcote Rd, E17 67 DX57
N19 65 DJ63
SE25 142 DV100
Redhill (S.Merst.) RH1 185 DJ129
South Croydon CR2 160 DS110
South Cottage Dr, Rick. (Chorl.) WD3 21 BF43
South Cottage Gdns, Rick. (Chorl.) WD3 21 BF43
Southcott Ms, NW8 194 B1
South Countess Rd, E17 67 DZ55
South Cres, E16 85 ED70
WC1 195 M7
South Cft, Egh. (Eng.Grn) TW20 112 AV92
Southcroft Av, Well. DA16 105 ES83
West Wickham BR4 143 EC103
Southcroft Rd, SW16 120 DG93
SW17 120 DG93
Orpington BR6 145 ES104
South Cross Rd, Ilf. IG6 69 EQ57
South Croxted Rd, SE21 122 DR90
SOUTH CROYDON, CR2 160 DQ107
⇌ **South Croydon** 160 DR106
Southdale, Chig. IG7 49 ER51
SOUTH DARENTH, Dart. DA4 149 FR95
Southdean Gdns, SW19 119 CZ89
South Dene, NW7 42 CR48
Southdene, Sev. (Halst.) TN14 164 EY113
Southdown Av, W7 97 CG76
Southdown Cres, Har. HA2 60 CB60
Ilford IG2 69 ES57
Southdown Dr, SW20 119 CX94
Southdown Rd, SW20 139 CX95
Carshalton SM5 158 DG109
Caterham (Wold.) CR3 177 DZ122
Hornchurch RM11 71 FH59
Walton-on-Thames KT12 154 BY105
Southdowns, Dart. (S.Darenth) DA4 149 FR96
South Dr, Bans. SM7 158 DE113
Brentwood CM14 54 FX49
Coulsdon CR5 175 DK115
Orpington BR6 163 ES106
Potters Bar (Cuffley) EN6 13 DL30
Romford RM2 72 FJ55
Ruislip HA4 59 BS60
Sutton SM2 157 CY110
Virginia Water GU25 132 AU102
⊖ **South Ealing** 97 CJ76
South Ealing Rd, W5 97 CK75
South Eastern Av, N9 46 DT48
South Eaton Pl, SW1 198 G8
South Eden Pk Rd, Beck. BR3 143 EB100
South Edwardes Sq, W8 99 CZ76
SOUTHEND, SE6 123 EB91
South End, W8 *off Ansdell St* 100 DB76
Croydon CR0 160 DQ105
Southend Arterial Rd, Brwd. CM13 73 FV57
Hornchurch RM11 52 FK54
Romford RM2, RM3 52 FK54
Upminster RM14 73 FR57
South End Cl, NW3 64 DE63
Southend Cl, SE9 125 EP86
Southend Cres, SE9 125 EN86
South End Grn, NW3 *off South End Rd* 64 DE63
Southend La, SE6 123 DZ91
SE26 123 DZ91
Waltham Abbey EN9 16 EH34
Southend Rd, E4 47 DY50
E6 87 EM66
E17 47 EB53
E18 48 EG53
South End Rd, NW3 64 DE63
Southend Rd, Beck. BR3 123 EA94
Grays RM17 110 GC77
South End Rd, Horn. RM12 89 FH65
Rainham RM13 89 FG67
Southend Rd, Wdf.Grn. IG8 48 EJ54
South End Row, W8 100 DB76
Southerland Cl, Wey. KT13 153 BQ105
Southern Av, SE25 142 DT97
Feltham TW14 115 BU88
Southern Dr, Loug. IG10 33 EM44
Southerngate Way, SE14 103 DY80
Southern Gro, E3 85 DZ69
Southernhay, Loug. IG10 32 EK43
Southern Perimeter Rd, Houns. (Hthrw Air.) TW6 115 BR85
Southern Pl, Har. HA1 61 CF63
Swanley BR8 147 FD98
Southern Rd, E13 86 EH68
N2 64 DF56
Southern Row, W10 81 CY70
Southerns La, Couls. CR5 184 DC125
Southern St, N1 83 DM68
Southern Way, SE10 205 L8
Romford RM7 70 FA58
Southerton Rd, W6 99 CW76
Southerton Way, Rad. (Shenley) WD7 10 CL33
South Esk Rd, E7 86 EJ65
Southey Ms, E16 205 N2
Southey Rd, N15 66 DS57

★ Place of interest ⇌ Railway station ⊖ London Underground station DLR Docklands Light Railway station Tra Tramlink station H Hospital Riv Pedestrian ferry landing stage

Southey Rd, SW9 . . . 101 DN81
SW19 . . . 120 DA94
Southey St, SE20 . . . 123 DX94
Southey Wk, Til. RM18 . . . 111 GH81
Southfield, Barn. EN5 . . . 27 CX44
Southfield Av, Wat. WD24 . . . 24 BW38
Southfield Cl, Uxb. UB8 . . . 76 BN69
Southfield Cotts, W7
off Oaklands Rd . . . 97 CF75
Southfield Gdns, Twick. TW1 . . 117 CF91
Southfield Pk, Har. HA2 . . . 60 CB56
Southfield Pl, Wey. KT13 . . . 153 BP108
Southfield Rd, N17
off The Avenue . . . 46 DS54
W4 . . . 98 CS76
Chislehurst BR7 . . . 145 ET97
Enfield EN3 . . . 30 DV44
Waltham Cross EN8 . . . 15 DY32
SOUTHFIELDS, SW18 . . . 120 DA88
⊖ Southfields . . . 119 CZ88
Southfields, NW4 . . . 63 CU55
East Molesey KT8 . . . 137 CE100
Swanley BR8 . . . 127 FE94
Southfields Av, Ashf. TW15 . . 115 BP93
Southfields Ct, SW19 . . . 119 CY88
Sutton SM1
off Sutton Common Rd . . 140 DA103
Southfields Ms, SW18
off Southfields Rd . . . 120 DA86
Southfields Pas, SW18 . . . 120 DA86
Southfields Rd, SW18 . . . 120 DA86
Caterham (Wold.) CR3 . . 177 EB123
SOUTHFLEET, Grav. DA13 . . 130 GB93
Southfleet Rd, Dart.
(Bean) DA2 . . . 129 FW91
Gravesend (Nthflt) DA11 . . 131 GF89
Orpington BR6 . . . 145 ES104
Swanscombe DA10 . . . 130 FZ87
South Gdns, SW19 . . . 120 DD94
SOUTHGATE, N14 . . . 45 DJ47
⊖ Southgate . . . 45 DJ46
Southgate, Purf. RM19 . . . 108 FQ77
Southgate Av, Felt. TW13 . . 115 BR91
Southgate Circ, N14
off The Bourne . . . 45 DK46
Southgate Gro, N1 . . . 84 DR66
Southgate Rd, N1 . . . 84 DR67
Potters Bar EN6 . . . 12 DC33
South Gipsy Rd, Well. DA16 . 106 EX83
South Glade, The, Bex. DA5 . 126 EZ88
South Grn, NW9
off Clayton Fld . . . 42 CS53
Slough SL1 . . . 74 AS73
⇌ South Greenford . . . 79 CE69
South Gro, E17 . . . 67 DZ57
N6 . . . 64 DG60
N15 . . . 66 DR57
Chertsey KT16 . . . 133 BF100
South Gro Ho, N6
off Highgate W Hill . . . 64 DG60
SOUTH HACKNEY, E9 . . . 84 DW66
South Hall Cl, Dart.
(Fnghm) DA4 . . . 148 FM101
South Hall Dr, Rain. RM13 . . 89 FH71
SOUTH HAMPSTEAD, NW6 . . 82 DB66
⇌ South Hampstead . . . 82 DC66
SOUTH HAREFIELD,
Uxb. UB9 . . . 58 BJ56
SOUTH HARROW, Har. HA2 . . 60 CB62
⊖ South Harrow . . . 60 CC62
South Hill, Chis. BR7 . . . 125 EM93
South Hill Av, Har. HA1, HA2 . 60 CC62
South Hill Gro, Har. HA1 . . . 61 CE63
South Hill Pk, NW3 . . . 64 DE63
South Hill Pk Gdns, NW3 . . . 64 DE63
South Hill Rd, Brom. BR2 . . . 144 EE97
Gravesend DA12 . . . 131 GH88
Southholme Cl, SE19 . . . 142 DS95
SOUTH HORNCHURCH,
Rain. RM13 . . . 89 FE67
South Huxley, N18 . . . 46 DR50
Southill La, Pnr. HA5 . . . 59 BU56
Southill Rd, Chis. BR7 . . . 124 EL94
Southill St, E14
off Chrisp St . . . 85 EB72
South Island Pl, SW9 . . . 101 DM80
SOUTH KENSINGTON, SW7 . 100 DB76
⊖ South Kensington . . . 198 A8
South Kensington Sta Arc,
SW7 off Pelham St . . . 100 DD77
South Kent Av, Grav.
(Nthflt) DA11 . . . 130 GC86
⇌ South Kenton . . . 61 CJ60
⊖ South Kenton . . . 61 CJ60
SOUTH LAMBETH, SW8 . . . 101 DL81
South Lambeth Pl, SW8 . . . 101 DL79
South Lambeth Rd, SW8 . . . 101 DL79
Southland Rd, SE18 . . . 105 ET80
Southlands Av, Orp. BR6 . . 163 ER105
Southlands Cl, Couls. CR5 . . 175 DM117
Southlands Dr, SW19 . . . 119 CX89
Southlands Gro, Brom. BR1 . 144 EL97
Southlands La, Oxt. RH8 . . 187 EB134
Southlands Rd, Brom.
BR1, BR2 . . . 144 EJ99
Iver SL0 . . . 57 BF64
Uxbridge (Denh.) UB9 . . . 57 BF63
Southland Way, Houns. TW3 . 117 CD85
South La, Kings.T. KT1 . . . 137 CK97
New Malden KT3 . . . 138 CR98
South La W, N.Mal. KT3 . . . 138 CR98
SOUTHLEA, Slou. SL3 . . . 92 AV82
Southlea Rd, Slou. (Datchet)
SL3 . . . 92 AV81
Windsor SL4 . . . 92 AU84
South Lo, SW7
off Knightsbridge . . . 100 DE75
South Lo Av, Mitch. CR4 . . . 141 DL98
South Lo Cres, Enf. EN2 . . . 29 DK42
South Lo Dr, N14 . . . 29 DL43
South Lo Rd, Walt. KT12 . . . 153 BU109
★ South London Art Gall,
SE5 . . . 102 DS81
Southly Cl, Sutt. SM1 . . . 140 DA104
South Mall, N9
off Edmonton Grn Shop Cen . 46 DU48
South Mead, NW9 . . . 43 CT53
Epsom KT19 . . . 156 CS108
Redhill RH1 . . . 184 DF131
Southmead Cres, Wal.Cr.
(Chsht) EN8 . . . 15 DY30
South Meadows, Wem. HA9 . 62 CM64
Southmead Rd, SW19 . . . 119 CY88
SOUTH MERSTHAM,
Red. RH1 . . . 185 DJ130
⇌ South Merton . . . 139 CZ97
SOUTH MIMMS, Pot.B. EN6 . . 11 CT32
South Molton La, W1 . . . 195 H9
South Molton Rd, E16 . . . 86 EG72
South Molton St, W1 . . . 195 H9
Southmont Rd, Esher KT10 . 137 CE103
Southmoor Way, E9 . . . 85 DZ65
SOUTH NORWOOD, SE25 . . 142 DT97
South Norwood Hill, SE25 . . 142 DS96
South Oak Rd, SW16 . . . 121 DM91
SOUTH OCKENDON, RM15 . . 91 FW70
Southold Ri, SE9 . . . 125 EM90
Southolm St, SW11 . . . 101 DH81
South Ordnance Rd, Enf. EN3 . 31 EA37
Southover, N12 . . . 44 DA49
Bromley BR1 . . . 124 EG92
SOUTH OXHEY, Wat. WD19 . . 40 BW48
South Par, SW3 . . . 198 A10
W4 . . . 98 CR77
Waltham Abbey EN9
off Sun St . . . 15 EC33
South Pk, SW6 . . . 100 DA82
Gerrards Cross SL9 . . . 57 AZ57
Sevenoaks TN13 . . . 191 FH125
South Pk Av, Rick.
(Chorl.) WD3 . . . 21 BF43
South Pk Cres, SE6 . . . 124 EF88
Gerrards Cross SL9 . . . 56 AY56
Ilford IG1 . . . 69 ER62
South Pk Dr, Bark. IG11 . . . 69 ES63
Gerrards Cross SL9 . . . 56 AY56
Ilford IG3 . . . 69 ES63
South Pk Gro, N.Mal. KT3 . . 138 CQ98
South Pk Hill Rd, S.Croy.
CR2 . . . 160 DR106
South Pk Ms, SW6 . . . 100 DB83
South Pk Rd, SW19 . . . 120 DA93
Ilford IG1 . . . 69 ER62
South Pk Ter, Ilf. IG1 . . . 69 ER62
South Pk Vw, Ger.Cr. SL9 . . . 57 AZ56
South Pk Way, Ruis. HA4 . . . 78 BW65
South Penge Pk Est, SE20 . . 142 DV96
South Perimeter Rd, Uxb.
UB8 off Kingston La . . . 76 BL69
South Pl, EC2 . . . 197 L6
Enfield EN3 . . . 30 DW43
Surbiton KT5 . . . 138 CM101
South Pl Ms, EC2 . . . 197 L7
South Pt, Sutt. SM1 . . . 158 DC107
Southport Rd, SE18 . . . 105 ER77
DLR South Quay . . . 204 B4
South Quay Plaza, E14 . . . 204 B4
South Ridge, Wey. KT13 . . . 153 BP110
Southridge Pl, SW20 . . . 119 CX94
South Riding, St.Alb.
(Brick.Wd) AL2 . . . 8 CA30
South Ri, Cars. SM5 . . . 158 DE109
South Ri Way, SE18 . . . 105 ER78
South Rd, N9 . . . 46 DU46
SE23 . . . 123 DX89
SW19 . . . 120 DC93
W5 . . . 97 CK77
Edgware HA8 . . . 42 CP53
Egham (Eng.Grn) TW20 . . 112 AW93
Erith DA8 . . . 107 FF79
Feltham TW13 . . . 116 BX92
Hampton TW12 . . . 116 BY93
Rickmansworth (Chorl.)
WD3 . . . 21 BC43
Romford (Chad.Hth) RM6 . . 70 EY58
Romford (Lt.Hth) RM6 . . . 70 EW57
South Ockendon RM15 . . . 91 FW72
Southall UB1 . . . 96 BZ75
Twickenham TW2 . . . 117 CD90
West Drayton UB7 . . . 94 BM76
Weybridge KT13 . . . 153 BQ106
Weybridge (St.Geo.H.)
KT13 . . . 153 BP109
Woking GU21 . . . 150 AX114
South Row, SE3 . . . 104 EF82
SOUTH RUISLIP, Ruis. HA4 . . 60 BW63
⇌ South Ruislip . . . 60 BW63
⊖ South Ruislip . . . 60 BW63
Southsea Av, Wat. WD18 . . . 23 BU42
Southsea Rd, Kings.T. KT1 . . 138 CL98
South Sea St, SE16 . . . 203 M6
South Side, W6 . . . 99 CT76
Southside, Ger.Cr. (Chal.St.P.)
SL9 . . . 56 AX55
Southside Common, SW19 . . 119 CW93
Southside Shop Cen, SW18 . 120 DB86
Southspring, Sid. DA15 . . . 125 ER87
South Sq, NW11 . . . 64 DB58
WC1 . . . 196 D7
SOUTH STIFFORD, Grays
RM20 . . . 109 FW78
SOUTH STREET, West. TN16 . 179 EM119
South St, W1 . . . 198 G2
Brentwood CM14 . . . 54 FW47
Bromley BR1 . . . 144 EG96
Enfield EN3 . . . 31 DX43
Epsom KT18 . . . 156 CR113
Gravesend DA12 . . . 131 GH87
Isleworth TW7 . . . 97 CG83
Rainham RM13 . . . 89 FC68
Romford RM1 . . . 71 FF58
Staines TW18 . . . 113 BF92
South Tenter St, E1 . . . 84 DT73
South Ter, SW7 . . . 198 B8
Surbiton KT6 . . . 138 CL100
SOUTH TOTTENHAM, N15 . . 66 DS57
⇌ South Tottenham . . . 66 DT57
South Vale, SE19 . . . 122 DS93
Harrow HA1 . . . 61 CE63
Southvale Rd, SE3 . . . 104 EE82
South Vw, Brom. BR1 . . . 144 EH96
Epsom KT19 . . . 156 CN110
Southview Av, NW10 . . . 63 CT64
South Vw Av, Til. RM18 . . . 111 GG81
Southview Cl, SW17 . . . 120 DG92
Bexley DA5 . . . 126 EZ86
Swanley BR8 . . . 147 FF98
Waltham Cross (Chsht) EN7 . 14 DS26
South Vw Ct, Wok. GU22
off Constitution Hill . . . 166 AY118
Southview Cres, Ilf. IG2 . . . 69 EP58
South Vw Dr, E18 . . . 68 EH55
Upminster RM14 . . . 72 FN62
Southview Gdns, Wall. SM6 . 159 DJ108
South Vw Rd, N8 . . . 65 DK55
Ashtead KT21 . . . 171 CK119
Southview Rd, Brom. BR1 . . 123 ED91
Caterham (Wold.) CR3 . . . 177 EB124
South Vw Rd, Dart. DA2 . . . 128 FK90
Gerrards Cross SL9 . . . 56 AX56
Grays RM20 . . . 109 FW79
Loughton IG10 . . . 33 EM44
Pinner HA5 . . . 39 BV51
Southview Rd, Warl. CR6 . . 176 DU119
Southviews, S.Croy. CR2 . . 161 DX109
South Vil, NW1 . . . 83 DK65
Southville, SW8 . . . 101 DK81
Southville Cl, Epsom KT19 . . 156 CR109
Feltham TW14 . . . 115 BS88
Southville Cres, Felt. TW14 . . 115 BS88
Southville Rd, Felt. TW14 . . 115 BS88
Thames Ditton KT7 . . . 137 CH101
South Wk, Hayes UB3
off Middleton Rd . . . 77 BR71
Reigate RH2 off Chartway . 184 DB134
West Wickham BR4 . . . 144 EE104
SOUTHWARK, SE1 . . . 200 G3
⊖ Southwark . . . 200 F3
Southwark Br, EC4 . . . 201 J2
SE1 . . . 201 J2
Southwark Br Rd, SE1 . . . 200 G6
★ Southwark Cath, SE1 . . . 201 K2
Southwark Pk, SE16 . . . 202 E7
Southwark Pk Est, SE16 . . . 202 E8
Southwark Pk Rd, SE16 . . . 202 A8
Southwark Pl, Brom. BR1 . . 145 EM97
Southwark St, SE1 . . . 200 G2
Southwater Cl, E14 . . . 85 DZ72
Beckenham BR3 . . . 123 EB94
South Way, N9 . . . 46 DW47
N11 off Ringway . . . 45 DJ51
Southway, N20 . . . 44 DA47
NW11 . . . 64 DB58
SW20 . . . 139 CW98
South Way, Abb.L. WD5 . . . 7 BT33
Bromley BR2 . . . 144 EG101
Southway, Cars. SM5 . . . 158 DD110
South Way, Croy. CR0 . . . 143 DY104
Harrow HA2 . . . 60 CA56
Purfleet RM19 . . . 109 FS76
Southway, Wall. SM6 . . . 159 DJ105
South Way, Wem. HA9 . . . 62 CN64
Southway Cl, W12
off Scotts Rd . . . 99 CV75
SOUTH WEALD, Brwd. CM14 . 54 FS47
South Weald Dr, Wal.Abb.
EN9 . . . 15 ED33
South Weald Rd, Brwd. CM14 . 54 FU48
Southwell Av, Nthlt. UB5 . . . 78 CA65
Southwell Cl, Grays (Chaff.Hun.)
RM16 . . . 109 FW78
Southwell Gdns, SW7 . . . 100 DC77
Southwell Gro Rd, E11 . . . 68 EE61
Southwell Rd, SE5 . . . 102 DQ83
Croydon CR0 . . . 141 DN100
Harrow HA3 . . . 61 CK58
South Western Rd, Twick.
TW1 . . . 117 CG86
Southwest Rd, E11 . . . 67 ED60
South Wf Rd, W2 . . . 82 DD72
Southwick Ms, W2 . . . 194 A8
Southwick Pl, W2 . . . 194 B9
Southwick St, W2 . . . 194 B8
SOUTH WIMBLEDON, SW19 . 120 DB94
⊖ South Wimbledon . . . 120 DB94
Southwold Dr, Bark. IG11 . . . 70 EU64
Southwold Rd, E5 . . . 66 DV61
Bexley DA5 . . . 127 FB86
Watford WD24 . . . 24 BW38
Southwold Spur, Slou. SL3 . . 93 BC75
Southwood Av, N6 . . . 65 DH59
Chertsey (Ott.) KT16 . . . 151 BC108
Coulsdon CR5 . . . 175 DJ115
Kingston upon Thames
KT2 . . . 138 CQ95
Southwood Cl, Brom. BR1 . . 145 EM98
Worcester Park KT4 . . . 139 CX102
Southwood Dr, Surb. KT5 . . 138 CQ101
SOUTH WOODFORD, E18 . . . 48 EF54
⊖ South Woodford . . . 48 EG54
South Woodford to Barking
Relief Rd, E11 . . . 68 EJ56
E12 . . . 69 EN62
E18 . . . 68 EJ56
Barking IG11 . . . 69 EN62
Ilford IG1, IG4 . . . 69 EN62
Southwood Gdns, Esher
KT10 . . . 137 CG104
Ilford IG2 . . . 69 EP56
H Southwood Hosp, N6 . . . 64 DG59
Southwood La, N6 . . . 64 DG59
Southwood Lawn Rd, N6 . . . 64 DG59
Southwood Rd, SE9 . . . 125 EP89
SE28 . . . 88 EV74
Southwood Smith St, N1
off Old Royal Free Sq . . . 83 DN67
South Worple Av, SW14 . . . 98 CS83
South Worple Way, SW14 . . . 98 CR83
Soval Ct, Nthwd. HA6
off Maxwell Rd . . . 39 BR52
Sovereign Cl, E1 . . . 202 E1
W5 . . . 79 CJ71
Purley CR8 . . . 159 DM110
Ruislip HA4 . . . 59 BS60
Sovereign Ct, W.Mol. KT8 . . 136 BZ98
Sovereign Cres, SE16 . . . 203 K1
Sovereign Gro, Wem. HA0 . . 61 CK62
Sovereign Hts, Slou. SL3 . . . 93 BA79
Sovereign Ms, E2
off Pearson St . . . 84 DT68
Barnet EN4 . . . 28 DF41
Sovereign Pk, NW10 . . . 80 CP70
Sovereign Pl, Har. HA1 . . . 61 CF57
Kings Langley WD4 . . . 6 BN29
Sovereign Rd, Bark. IG11 . . . 88 EW69
Sowerby Cl, SE9 . . . 124 EL85
Sowrey Av, Rain. RM13 . . . 89 FF65
Soyer Ct, Wok. GU21
off Raglan Rd . . . 166 AS118
Space Waye, Felt. TW14 . . . 115 BU85
Spa Cl, SE25 . . . 142 DS95
Spa Dr, Epsom KT18 . . . 156 CN114
Spafield St, EC1 . . . 196 D4
Spa Grn Est, EC1 . . . 196 E2
Spa Hill, SE19 . . . 142 DR95
Spalding Cl, Edg. HA8 . . . 42 CS52
Spalding Rd, NW4 . . . 63 CW58
SW17 . . . 121 DH92
Spalt Cl, Brwd. (Hutt.) CM13 . 55 GB47
Spanby Rd, E3 . . . 85 EA70
Spaniards Cl, NW11 . . . 64 DD60
Spaniards End, NW3 . . . 64 DC60
Spaniards Rd, NW3 . . . 64 DC61
Spanish Pl, W1 . . . 194 G8
Spanish Rd, SW18 . . . 120 DC85
Spareleaze Hill, Loug. IG10 . . 33 EM43
Sparepenny La, Dart.
(Eyns.) DA4 . . . 148 FL102
Sparkbridge Rd, Har. HA1 . . . 61 CE56
Sparkes Cl, Brom. BR2 . . . 144 EH98
Sparkford Gdns, N11 . . . 44 DG50
Sparkford Ho, SW11 . . . 100 DD81
Sparks Cl, W3 . . . 80 CR72
Dagenham RM8 . . . 70 EX61
Hampton TW12
off Victors Dr . . . 116 BY93
Spa Rd, SE16 . . . 201 P7
Sparrow Cl, Hmptn. TW12 . . 116 BY93
Sparrow Dr, Orp. BR5 . . . 145 EQ102
Sparrow Fm Dr, Felt. TW14 . 116 BX87
Sparrow Fm Rd, Epsom
KT17 . . . 157 CU105
Sparrow Grn, Dag. RM10 . . . 71 FB62
Sparrows Herne, Bushey
WD23 . . . 40 CB45
Sparrows La, SE9 . . . 125 EQ87
Sparrows Mead, Red. RH1 . . 184 DG131
Sparrows Way, Bushey WD23
off Sparrows Herne . . . 40 CC46
Sparrow Wk, Wat. WD25
off Gullet Wd Rd . . . 23 BU35
Sparsholt Rd, N19 . . . 65 DM60
Barking IG11 . . . 87 ES67
Sparta St, SE10 . . . 103 EB81
★ Speaker's Cor, W2 . . . 194 E10
Speaker's Ct, Croy. CR0
off St. James's Rd . . . 142 DR102
Spearman St, SE18 . . . 105 EN79
Spear Ms, SW5 . . . 100 DA77
Spearpoint Gdns, Ilf. IG2 . . . 69 ET56
Spears Rd, N19 . . . 65 DL60
Speart La, Houns. TW5 . . . 96 BY80
Spedan Cl, NW3 . . . 64 DB62
Speechly Ms, E8
off Alvington Cres . . . 66 DT64
Speedbird Way, West Dr. UB7 . 94 BH80
Speedgate Hill, Long.
(Fawk.Grn) DA3 . . . 149 FU103
Speed Highwalk, EC2
off Beech St . . . 84 DQ71
Speed Ho, EC2 . . . 197 K6
Speedwell Ct, Grays RM17 . . 110 GE80
Speedwell St, SE8
off Comet St . . . 103 EA80
Speedy Pl, WC1 . . . 195 P3
Speer Rd, T.Ditt. KT7 . . . 137 CF99
Speirs Cl, N.Mal. KT3 . . . 139 CT100
Spekehill, SE9 . . . 125 EM90
Speke Ho, SE5 . . . 102 DQ80
Speke Rd, Th.Hth. CR7 . . . 142 DR96
Speldhurst Cl, Brom. BR2 . . 144 EF99
Speldhurst Rd, E9 . . . 85 DX66
W4 . . . 98 CR76
Spellbrook Wk, N1
off Basire St . . . 84 DQ67
Spelman St, E1 . . . 84 DU71
Spelthorne Gro, Sun. TW16 . 115 BT94
Spelthorne La, Ashf. TW15 . . 135 BQ95
Spence Av, W.Byf. (Byfleet)
KT14 . . . 152 BL114
Spence Cl, SE16 . . . 203 M5
Spencer Av, N13 . . . 45 DM51
Hayes UB4 . . . 77 BU71
Waltham Cross (Chsht) EN7 . 14 DS26
Spencer Cl, N3 . . . 43 CZ54
NW10 . . . 80 CM69
Epsom KT18 . . . 172 CS119
Orpington BR6 . . . 145 ES103
Uxbridge UB8 . . . 76 BJ69
Woking GU21 . . . 151 BC113
Woodford Green IG8 . . . 48 EJ50
H Spencer Cl Mental Hosp,
Epp. CM16 . . . 18 EV29
Spencer Ctyd, N3
off Regents Pk Rd . . . 43 CZ54
Spencer Dr, N2 . . . 64 DC58
Spencer Gdns, SE9 . . . 125 EM85
SW14 . . . 118 CQ85
Egham (Eng.Grn) TW20 . . 112 AX92
Spencer Hill, SW19 . . . 119 CY93
Spencer Hill Rd, SW19 . . . 119 CY94
★ Spencer Ho, SW1 . . . 199 K3
Spencer Ms, SW8
off Lansdowne Way . . . 101 DM81
W6 off Greyhound Rd . . . 99 CY79
Spencer Pk, SW18 . . . 120 DD85
Spencer Pas, E2
off Pritchard's Rd . . . 84 DV68
Spencer Pl, N1
off Canonbury La . . . 83 DP66
Croydon CR0
off Gloucester Rd . . . 142 DS101
Spencer Ri, NW5 . . . 65 DH63
Spencer Rd, E6 . . . 86 EK67
E17 . . . 47 EC53
N8 . . . 65 DM57
N11 . . . 45 DH49
N17 . . . 46 DU53
SW18 . . . 100 DD84
SW20 . . . 139 CV95
W3 . . . 80 CQ74
W4 . . . 98 CQ80
Bromley BR1 . . . 124 EE94
Caterham CR3 . . . 176 DR121
Cobham KT11 . . . 169 BV115
East Molesey KT8 . . . 136 CC99
Harrow HA3 . . . 41 CE54
Ilford IG3 . . . 69 ET60
Isleworth TW7 . . . 97 CD81
Mitcham CR4 . . . 140 DG97
Mitcham (Bedd.Cor.) CR4 . 140 DG101
Rainham RM13 . . . 89 FD69
Slough SL3 . . . 93 AZ76
South Croydon CR2 . . . 160 DS106
Twickenham TW2 . . . 117 CE90
Wembley HA0 . . . 61 CJ61
Spencer St, EC1 . . . 196 F3
Gravesend DA11 . . . 131 GG87
Southall UB2 . . . 96 BX75
Spencer Wk, NW3 . . . 64 DD63
SW15 . . . 99 CX84
Rickmansworth WD3 . . . 22 BJ43
Spencer Wk, Til. RM18 . . . 111 GG82
Spencer Yd, SE3
off Blackheath Village . . 104 EF82
Spenser Av, Wey. KT13 . . . 152 BN108
Spenser Cres, Upmin. RM14 . 72 FQ59
Spenser Gro, N16 . . . 66 DS63
Spenser Ms, SE21
off Croxted Rd . . . 122 DR88
Spenser Rd, SE24 . . . 121 DN85
Spenser St, SW1 . . . 199 L6
Spensley Wk, N16
off Clissold Rd . . . 66 DR62
Speranza St, SE18 . . . 105 ET78
Sperling Rd, N17 . . . 46 DS54
Spert St, E14 . . . 85 DY73
Speyhawk Pl, Pot.B. EN6 . . . 12 DB30
Speyside, N14 . . . 29 DJ44
Spey St, E14 . . . 85 EC71
Spey Way, Rom. RM1 . . . 51 FE52
Spezia Rd, NW10 . . . 81 CU68
Sphere, The, E16
off Hallsville Rd . . . 86 EF72
Spice Quay Hts, SE1 . . . 202 A3
Spicer Cl, SW9 . . . 101 DP82
Walton-on-Thames KT12 . 136 BW100
Spicers Fld, Lthd. (Oxshott)
KT22 . . . 155 CD113
Spicersfield, Wal.Cr.
(Chsht) EN7 . . . 14 DU27
Spice's Yd, Croy. CR0 . . . 160 DQ105
Spielman Rd, Dart. DA1 . . . 108 FM84
Spigurnell Rd, N17 . . . 46 DR53
Spikes Br Moorings,
Hayes UB4 . . . 78 BY73
Spikes Br Rd, Sthl. UB1 . . . 78 BY72
Spilsby Rd, Rom. RM3 . . . 52 FK52
Spindle Cl, SE18 . . . 104 EL76
Spindles, Til. RM18 . . . 111 GG80
Spindlewood Gdns,
Croy. CR0 . . . 160 DS105
Spindlewoods, Tad. KT20 . . 173 CV122
Spindrift Av, E14 . . . 204 B8
Spinel Cl, SE18 . . . 105 ET78
Spingate Cl, Horn. RM12 . . . 72 FK64
Spinnaker Cl, Bark. IG11 . . . 88 EV69
Spinnells Rd, Har. HA2 . . . 60 BZ60
Spinney, The, N21 . . . 45 DN45
SW16 . . . 121 DK90
Barnet EN5 . . . 28 DB40
Brentwood (Hutt.) CM13 . . 55 GC44
Epsom KT18 . . . 173 CV119
Leatherhead (Bkhm) KT23 . 170 CB124
Leatherhead (Oxshott)
KT22 . . . 154 CC112
Potters Bar EN6 . . . 12 DD31
Purley CR8 . . . 159 DP111
Sidcup DA14 . . . 126 EY92
Stanmore HA7 . . . 42 CL49
Sunbury-on-Thames TW16 . 135 BU95
Sutton SM3 . . . 157 CW105
Swanley BR8 . . . 147 FE96
Watford WD17 . . . 23 BU39
Wembley HA0 . . . 61 CG62
Spinney Cl, Beck. BR3 . . . 143 EB98
Cobham KT11 . . . 154 CA111
New Malden KT3 . . . 138 CS99
Rainham RM13 . . . 89 FE68
West Drayton UB7
off Yew Av . . . 76 BL73
Worcester Park KT4 . . . 139 CT104
Spinneycroft, Lthd. KT22 . . 171 CD115
Spinney Dr, Felt. TW14 . . . 115 BQ87
Spinney Gdns, SE19 . . . 122 DT92
Dagenham RM9 . . . 70 EY64
Spinney Hill, Add. KT15 . . . 151 BE106
Spinney Oak, Brom. BR1 . . . 144 EL96
Chertsey (Ott.) KT16 . . . 151 BD107
Spinneys, The, Brom. BR1 . . 145 EM96
Spinney Way, Sev. (Cudham)
TN14 . . . 163 ER111
Spire Cl, Grav. DA12 . . . 131 GH88
Spire Ho, W2
off Lancaster Gate . . . 82 DC73
Spires, The, Dart. DA1 . . . 128 FK89
Spires Shop Cen, The,
Barn. EN5 . . . 27 CY41
Spirit Quay, E1 . . . 202 C2
★ Spitalfields City Fm, E1 . . 84 DU70
Spital La, Brwd. CM14 . . . 54 FT48
Spital Sq, E1 . . . 197 N6
Spital St, E1 . . . 84 DU70
Dartford DA1 . . . 128 FK86
Spital Yd, E1 . . . 197 N6
Spitfire Cl, Slou. SL3 . . . 93 BA77
Spitfire Est, Houns. TW5 . . . 96 BW78
Spitfire Rd, Wall. SM6 . . . 159 DL108
Spitfire Way, Houns. TW5 . . . 96 BW78
Spode Ho, SE11
off Lambeth Wk . . . 101 DN76
Spode Wk, NW6
off Dresden Cl . . . 64 DB64
Spondon Rd, N15 . . . 66 DU56
Spoonbill Way, Hayes UB4
off Cygnet Way . . . 78 BX71
Spooners Dr, St.Alb.
(Park St) AL2 . . . 8 CC27
Spooners Ms, W3
off Churchfield Rd . . . 80 CR74
Spooner Wk, Wall. SM6 . . . 159 DK106
Sporle Ct, SW11 . . . 100 DD83
Sportsbank St, SE6 . . . 123 EC87
Sportsman Ms, E2
off Whiston Rd . . . 84 DU67
Spotted Dog Path, E7
off Upton La . . . 86 EG65
Spottons Gro, N17
off Gospatrick Rd . . . 46 DQ53
Spout Hill, Croy. CR0 . . . 161 EA106
Spout La, Eden. (Crock.H.)
TN8 . . . 189 EQ134
Staines TW19 . . . 114 BG85
Spout La N, Stai. TW19 . . . 94 BH84
Spratt Hall Rd, E11 . . . 68 EG58
Spratts All, Cher. (Ott.) KT16 . 151 BE107
Spratts La, Cher. (Ott.) KT16 . 151 BE107
Spray La, Twick. TW2 . . . 117 CE86
Spray St, SE18 . . . 105 EP77

Spread Eagle Wk Shop Cen, Epsom KT19 *off High St* 156 CR113
Spreighton Rd, W.Mol. KT8 136 CB98
Spriggs Oak, Epp. CM16
off Palmers Hill 18 EU29
Sprimont Pl, SW3 198 D10
Springall St, SE15 102 DV80
Springate Fld, Slou. SL3 92 AY75
Spring Av, Egh. TW20 112 AY93
Springbank, N21 29 DM44
Springbank Av, Horn. RM12 72 FJ64
Springbank Rd, SE13 123 ED86
Springbank Wk, NW1
off St. Paul's Cres 83 DK66
Spring Bottom La, Red. (Bletch.) RH1 185 DN127
Springbourne Ct, Beck. BR3 143 EC95
Spring Br Ms, W5
off Spring Br Rd 79 CK73
Spring Br Rd, W5 79 CK73
Spring Cl, Barn. EN5 27 CX43
Borehamwood WD6 26 CN39
Chesham (Latimer) HP5 20 AX36
Dagenham RM8 70 EX60
Uxbridge (Hare.) UB9 38 BK53
Springclose La, Sutt. SM3 157 CY107
Spring Cotts, Surb. KT6
off St. Leonard's Rd 137 CK99
Spring Ct, Sid. DA15
off Station Rd 126 EU90
Spring Ct Rd, Enf. EN2 29 DN38
Springcroft Av, N2 64 DF56
Spring Cfts, Bushey WD23 24 CA43
Springdale Ms, N16
off Springdale Rd 66 DR63
Springdale Rd, N16 66 DR63
Spring Dr, Pnr. HA5
off Eastcote Rd 59 BU58
Spring Fm Cl, Rain. RM13 90 FK69
Springfield, E5 66 DV60
Bushey (Bushey Hth) WD23 41 CD46
Epping CM16 17 ET32
Oxted RH8 187 ED130
Springfield Av, N10 65 DJ55
SW20 139 CZ97
Brentwood (Hutt.) CM13 55 GE45
Hampton TW12 116 CB93
Swanley BR8 147 FF98
Springfield Cl, N12 44 DB50
Potters Bar EN6 12 DD31
Rickmansworth (Crox.Grn) WD3 23 BP43
Stanmore HA7 41 CG48
Woking (Knap.) GU21 166 AS118
Springfield Ct, Wall. SM6
off Springfield Rd 159 DH106
Springfield Dr, Ilf. IG2 69 EQ58
Leatherhead KT22 171 CE119
Springfield Gdns, E5 66 DV60
NW9 62 CR57
Bromley BR1 145 EM98
Ruislip HA4 59 BV60
Upminster RM14 72 FQ62
West Wickham BR4 143 EB103
Woodford Green IG8 48 EJ52
Springfield Gro, SE7 104 EJ79
Sunbury-on-Thames TW16 135 BT95
Springfield La, NW6 82 DB67
Weybridge KT13 153 BP105
Springfield Meadows, Wey. KT13 153 BP105
Springfield Mt, NW9 62 CS57
Springfield Pl, N.Mal. KT3 138 CQ98
Springfield Ri, SE26 122 DV90
Springfield Rd, E4 48 EE46
E6 86 EM66
E15 86 EE69
E17 67 DZ58
N11 45 DH50
N15 66 DU56
NW8 82 DC67
SE26 122 DV92
SW19 119 CZ92
W7 79 CE74
Ashford TW15 114 BM92
Bexleyheath DA7 107 FB83
Bromley BR1 145 EM98
Epsom KT17 157 CW110
Grays RM16 110 GD75
Harrow HA1 61 CE58
Hayes UB4 78 BW74
Kingston upon Thames KT1 138 CL97
Slough SL3 93 BB80
Teddington TW11 117 CG92
Thornton Heath CR7 142 DQ95
Twickenham TW2 116 CA88
Wallington SM6 159 DH106
Waltham Cross (Chsht) EN8 15 DY32
Watford WD25
off Haines Way 7 BV33
Welling DA16 106 EV83
Springfields, Wal.Abb. EN9 16 EE34
Springfields Cl, Cher. KT16 134 BH102
H **Springfield Uni Hosp**, SW17 120 DE89
Springfield Wk, NW6 82 DB67
Orpington BR6
off Place Fm Av 145 ER102
Spring Gdns, N5
off Grosvenor Av 66 DQ64
SW1 199 N2
Hornchurch RM12 71 FH63
Orpington BR6 164 EV107
Romford RM7 71 FC57
Wallington SM6 159 DJ106
Watford WD25 24 BW35
West Molesey KT8 136 CC99
Westerham (Bigg.H.) TN16 178 EJ118
Woodford Green IG8 48 EJ52
Spring Gdns Business Pk, Rom. RM7 71 FC57
SPRING GROVE, Islw. TW7 97 CF81
Spring Gro, SE19 *off Alma Pl* 122 DT94
W4 98 CN78
Gravesend DA12 131 GH88
Hampton TW12
off Plevna Rd 136 CB95
Spring Gro, Lthd. (Fetch.) KT22 170 CB123
Loughton IG10 32 EK44
Mitcham CR4 140 DG95
Spring Gro Cres, Houns. TW3 96 CC81
Spring Gro Rd, Houns. TW3 96 CB81
Isleworth TW7 96 CB81
Richmond TW10 118 CM85
Springhead Enterprise Pk, Grav. DA11 130 GC88
Springhead Rd, Erith DA8 107 FF79
Gravesend (Nthflt) DA11 130 GC87
Spring Hill, E5 66 DU59
SE26 122 DW91
Springhill Cl, SE5 102 DR83
Springholm Cl, West. (Bigg.H.) TN16 178 EJ118
Springhurst Cl, Croy. CR0 161 DZ105
Spring Lake, Stan. HA7 41 CH49
Spring La, E5 66 DV60
N10 64 DG55
SE25 142 DV100
Oxted RH8 187 ED131
Spring Ms, W1 194 E6
Epsom KT17
off Old Schs La 157 CT109
Richmond TW9
off Rosedale Rd 98 CL84
Spring Pk Av, Croy. CR0 143 DX103
Spring Pk Dr, N4 66 DQ60
Springpark Dr, Beck. BR3 143 EC97
Spring Pk Rd, Croy. CR0 143 DX103
Spring Pas, SW15
off Embankment 99 CX83
Spring Path, NW3 64 DD64
Spring Pl, N3
off Windermere Av 44 DA54
NW5 65 DH64
Springpond Rd, Dag. RM9 70 EY64
Springrice Rd, SE13 123 EC86
Spring Ri, Egh. TW20 112 AY93
Spring Rd, Felt. TW13 115 BT90
Springs, The, Brox. EN10 15 DY25
Springshaw Cl, Sev. TN13 190 FD123
Spring Shaw Rd, Orp. BR5 146 EU95
Spring St, W2 82 DD72
Epsom KT17 157 CT109
Spring Ter, Rich. TW9 118 CL85
Springtide Cl, SE15
off Staffordshire St 102 DU81
Spring Vale, Bexh. DA7 107 FB84
Greenhithe DA9 129 FW86
Springvale Av, Brent. TW8 97 CK78
Spring Vale Cl, Swan. BR8 147 FF95
Springvale Est, W14
off Blythe Rd 99 CY76
Spring Vale N, Dart. DA1 128 FK87
Springvale Retail Pk, Orp. BR5 146 EW97
Spring Vale S, Dart. DA1 128 FK87
Springvale Ter, W14 99 CX76
Springvale Way, Orp. BR5 146 EW97
Spring Vil Rd, Edg. HA8 42 CN52
Spring Wk, E1
off Old Montague St 84 DU71
Springwater Cl, SE18 105 EN81
Springway, Har. HA1 61 CD59
Springwell Av, NW10 81 CT67
Rickmansworth (Mill End) WD3 38 BG47
Springwell Cl, SW16
off Etherstone Rd 121 DN91
Springwell Ct, Houns. TW4 96 BX82
Springwell Hill, Uxb. (Hare.) UB9 38 BH51
Springwell La, Rick. WD3 38 BG49
Uxbridge (Hare.) UB9 38 BG49
Springwell Rd, SW16 121 DN91
Hounslow TW4, TW5 96 BX81
Springwood, Wal.Cr. (Chsht) EN7 14 DU26
Springwood Cl, E3 85 EA68
Uxbridge (Hare.) UB9 38 BK53
Springwood Cres, Edg. HA8 42 CP47
Springwood Pl, Wey. KT13 153 BP108
Spring Wds, Vir.W. GU25 132 AV98
Springwood Way, Rom. RM1 71 FG57
Sprowston Ms, E7 86 EG65
Sprowston Rd, E7 68 EG64
Spruce Cl, Red. RH1 184 DF133
Spruce Ct, W5
off Elderberry Rd 98 CL76
Sprucedale Cl, Swan. BR8 147 FE96
Sprucedale Gdns, Croy. CR0 161 DX105
Wallington SM6 159 DK109
Spruce Hills Rd, E17 47 EC54
Spruce Pk, Brom. BR2
off Cumberland Rd 144 EF98
Spruce Rd, West. (Bigg.H.) TN16 178 EK116
Spruce Way, St.Alb. (Park St) AL2 8 CB27
Sprules Rd, SE4 103 DY82
Spur, The, Wal.Cr. (Chsht) EN8
off Welsummer Way 15 DX28
Spur Cl, Abb.L. WD5 7 BR33
Romford (Abridge) RM4 34 EV41
Spurfield, W.Mol. KT8 136 CB97
Spurgate, Brwd. (Hutt.) CM13 55 GA47
Spurgeon Av, SE19 142 DR95
Spurgeon Rd, SE19 142 DR95
Spurgeon St, SE1 201 K7
Spurling Rd, SE22 102 DT84
Dagenham RM9 88 EZ65
Spurrell Av, Bex. DA5 127 FD91
Spur Rd, N15 *off Philip La* 66 DR56
SE1 200 D4
SW1 199 K5
Barking IG11 87 EQ68
Edgware HA8 42 CL49
Feltham TW14 115 BV85
Isleworth TW7 97 CH80
Orpington BR6 146 EU103
Spur Rd Est, Edg. HA8 42 CM49
Spurstowe Rd, E8
off Marcon Pl 66 DV64
Spurstowe Ter, E8 66 DV64
Squadrons App, Horn. RM12 90 FJ65
Square, The, E10 67 EC62
W6 99 CW78
Carshalton SM5 158 DG106
Hayes UB3 77 BR74
Ilford IG1 69 EN59
Square, The, Rich. TW9 117 CK85
Sevenoaks TN13
off Amherst Hill 190 FE122
Swanley BR8 147 FD97
Watford WD24
off The Harebreaks 23 BV37
West Drayton UB7 94 BH81
Westerham (Tats.) TN16 178 EJ120
Weybridge KT13 153 BQ105
Woking (Wisley) GU23 168 BL116
Woodford Green IG8 48 EG50
Square Rigger Row, SW11
off York Pl 100 DC83
Squarey St, SW17 120 DC90
Squerryes, The, Cat. CR3
off Portley La 176 DS121
★ **Squerryes Ct & Gdns**, West. TN16 189 EQ128
Squerryes Mede, West. TN16 189 EQ127
Squire Gdns, NW8
off St. John's Wd Rd 82 DD69
Squires, The, Rom. RM7 71 FC58
Squires Br Rd, Shep. TW17 134 BM98
Squires Ct, SW19 120 DA91
Chertsey KT16
off Springfields Cl 134 BH102
Squires Fld, Swan. BR8 147 FF95
Squires La, N3 44 DB54
Squires Mt, NW3
off East Heath Rd 64 DD62
Squires Rd, Shep. TW17 134 BM98
Squire's Wk, Ashf. TW15 115 BR94
Squires Way, Dart. DA2 127 FD91
Squires Wd Dr, Chis. BR7 124 EL94
Squirrel Cl, Houns. TW4 96 BW82
Squirrel Keep, W.Byf. KT14 152 BH112
Squirrel Ms, W13 79 CG73
Squirrels, The, SE13
off Belmont Hill 103 ED83
Bushey WD23 25 CD44
Pinner HA5 60 BZ55
Squirrels Chase, Grays (Orsett) RM16 *off Hornsby La* 111 GG75
Squirrels Cl, N12
off Woodside Av 44 DC49
Uxbridge UB10 76 BN66
Squirrels Grn, Lthd. (Bkhm) KT23 170 CA123
Worcester Park KT4 139 CT102
Squirrels Heath Av, Rom. RM2 71 FH55
Squirrels Heath La, Horn. RM11 72 FJ56
Romford RM2 72 FJ56
Squirrels Heath Rd, Rom. RM3 72 FL55
Squirrels La, Buck.H. IG9 48 EK48
Squirrels Trd Est, The, Hayes UB3 95 BU76
Squirrels Way, Epsom KT18 172 CR115
Squirrel Wd, W.Byf. KT14 152 BH112
Squirries St, E2 84 DU69
Stable Cl, Epsom KT18 172 CS119
Kingston upon Thames KT2 118 CM93
Northolt UB5 78 CA68
Stable Ms, Twick. TW1 117 CF88
Stables, The, Buck.H. IG9 48 EJ45
Cobham KT11 154 BZ114
Swanley BR8 147 FH95
Stables End, Orp. BR6 145 EQ104
Stables Ms, SE27 122 DQ92
Stables Way, SE11 200 D10
Stable Wk, N1
off Wharfdale Rd 83 DL68
N2 *off Old Fm Rd* 44 DD53
Stable Way, W10
off Latimer Rd 81 CW72
Stable Yd, SW1 199 K4
SW9 *off Broomgrove Rd* 101 DM82
SW15 *off Danemere St* 99 CW83
Stable Yd Rd, SW1 199 K3
Stacey Av, N18 46 DW49
Stacey Cl, E10
off Halford Rd 67 ED57
Gravesend DA12 131 GL92
Stacey St, N7 65 DN62
WC2 195 N9
Stackhouse St, SW3 198 D6
Stack Rd, Dart. (Hort.Kir.) DA4 149 FR97
Stacy Path, SE5
off Harris St 102 DS80
Staddon Cl, Beck. BR3 143 DY98
Stadium Business Cen, Wem. HA9 62 CP62
Stadium Retail Pk, Wem. HA9
off Wembley Pk Dr 62 CN62
Stadium Rd, NW2 63 CV59
SE18 104 EL80
Stadium Rd E, NW2 63 CW59
Stadium St, SW10 100 DC80
Stadium Way, Dart. DA1 127 FE85
Wembley HA9 62 CM63
Staffa Rd, E10 67 DY60
Stafford Av, Horn. RM11 72 FK55
Stafford Cl, E17 67 DZ58
N14 29 DJ43
NW6 82 DA69
Caterham CR3 176 DT123
Grays (Chaff.Hun.) RM16 109 FW77
Greenhithe DA9 129 FT85
Sutton SM3 157 CY107
Waltham Cross (Chsht) EN8 14 DV29
Stafford Ct, SW8
off Allen Edwards Dr 101 DL81
W8 100 DA76
Stafford Cripps Ho, E2
off Globe Rd 84 DW69
SW6 *off Clem Attlee Ct* 99 CZ79
Stafford Cross Business Pk, Croy. CR0 159 DM106
Stafford Gdns, Croy. CR0 159 DM106
Stafford Pl, SW1 199 K6
Richmond TW10 118 CM87
Stafford Rd, E3 85 DZ68
E7 86 EJ66
NW6 82 DA69
Caterham CR3 176 DT122
Croydon CR0 159 DN105
Harrow HA3 40 CC52
New Malden KT3 138 CQ97
Ruislip HA4 59 BT63
Stafford Rd, Sid. DA14 125 ES91
Wallington SM6 159 DJ107
Staffordshire St, SE15 102 DU81
Stafford Sq, Wey. KT13
off Rosslyn Pk 153 BR105
Stafford St, W1 199 K2
Stafford Ter, W8 100 DA76
Stafford Way, Sev. TN13 191 FJ127
Staff St, EC1 197 L3
Stagbury Av, Couls. (Chipstead) CR5 174 DE118
Stagbury Cl, Couls. (Chipstead) CR5 174 DE119
Stag Cl, Edg. HA8 42 CP54
Staggart Grn, Chig. IG7 49 ET51
Stagg Hill, Barn. EN4 28 DD35
Potters Bar EN6 28 DD35
Stag La, NW9 62 CQ55
SW15 119 CT89
Buckhurst Hill IG9 48 EH47
Edgware HA8 42 CP54
Rickmansworth (Chorl.) WD3 21 BC44
Stag Leys, Ashtd. KT21 172 CL120
Stag Leys Cl, Bans. SM7 174 DD115
Stag Pl, SW1 199 K6
Stag Ride, SW19 119 CT90
Stags Way, Islw. TW7 97 CF79
Stainash Cres, Stai. TW18 114 BH92
Stainash Par, Stai. TW18
off Kingston Rd 114 BH92
Stainbank Rd, Mitch. CR4 141 DH97
Stainby Cl, West Dr. UB7 94 BL76
Stainby Rd, N15 66 DT56
Stainer Ho, SE3 *off Ryan Cl* 104 EJ84
Stainer Rd, Borwd. WD6 25 CK39
Stainer St, SE1 201 L3
STAINES, TW18 & TW19 114 BG91
⇌ **Staines** 114 BG92
Staines Av, Sutt. SM3 139 CX103
Staines Br, Stai. TW18 113 BE92
Staines Bypass, Ashf. TW15 114 BH91
Staines TW18, TW19 114 BH91
Staines La, Cher. KT16 133 BF99
Staines La Cl, Cher. KT16 133 BF100
Staines Rd, Cher. KT16 133 BF97
Feltham TW14 115 BR87
Hounslow TW3, TW4 96 CB83
Ilford IG1 69 EQ63
Staines TW18 134 BH95
Staines (Wrays.) TW19 112 AY87
Twickenham TW2 116 CA90
Staines Rd E, Sun. TW16 115 BU94
Staines Rd W, Ashf. TW15 115 BP93
Sunbury-on-Thames TW16 115 BP93
Staines Wk, Sid. DA14
off Evry Rd 126 EW93
Stainford Cl, Ashf. TW15 115 BR92
Stainforth Rd, E17 67 EA56
Ilford IG2 69 ER59
Staining La, EC2 197 J8
Stainmore Cl, Chis. BR7 145 ER95
Stainsbury St, E2
off Royston St 84 DW68
Stainsby Rd, E14 85 EA72
Stains Cl, Wal.Cr. (Chsht) EN8 15 DY28
Stainton Rd, SE6 123 ED86
Enfield EN3 30 DW39
Stainton Wk, Wok. GU21
off Inglewood 166 AW118
Stairfoot La, Sev. (Chipstead) TN13 190 FC122
Staithes Way, Tad. KT20 173 CV120
Stalbridge St, NW1 194 C6
Stalham St, SE16 202 E7
Stalham Way, Ilf. IG6 49 EP53
Stalisfield Pl, Orp. BR6
off Mill La 163 EN110
Stambourne Way, SE19 122 DS94
West Wickham BR4 143 EC104
⊖ **Stamford Brook** 99 CT77
Stamford Brook Av, W6 99 CT76
Stamford Brook Gdns, W6
off Stamford Brook Rd 99 CT76
Stamford Brook Rd, W6 99 CT76
Stamford Cl, N15 66 DU56
Harrow HA3 41 CE52
Potters Bar EN6 12 DD32
Southall UB1 78 CA73
Stamford Cotts, SW10
off Billing St 100 DB80
Stamford Ct, W6
off Goldhawk Rd 99 CT77
Stamford Dr, Brom. BR2 144 EF98
Stamford Gdns, Dag. RM9 88 EW66
Stamford Grn Rd, Epsom KT18 156 CP113
Stamford Gro E, N16
off Oldhill St 66 DU60
Stamford Gro W, N16
off Oldhill St 66 DU60
STAMFORD HILL, N16 66 DS60
⇌ **Stamford Hill** 66 DS59
Stamford Hill, N16 66 DT61
Stamford Hill Est, N16 66 DT60
H **Stamford Hosp**, W6 99 CU77
Stamford Rd, E6 86 EL67
N1 84 DS66
N15 66 DU57
Dagenham RM9 88 EV67
Walton-on-Thames KT12
off Kenilworth Dr 136 BX104
Watford WD17 23 BV40
Stamford St, SE1 200 D3
Stamp Pl, E2 197 P2
Stanard Cl, N16 66 DS59
Stanborough Av, Borwd. WD6 26 CN37
Stanborough Cl, Borwd. WD6 26 CN38
Hampton TW12 116 BZ93
Stanborough Pk, Wat. WD25 23 BV35
Stanborough Pas, E8
off Kingsland Rd 84 DT65
Stanborough Rd, Houns. TW3 97 CD83
Stanbridge Pl, N21 45 DP47
Stanbridge Rd, SW15 99 CW83
Stanbrook Rd, SE2 106 EV75
Gravesend DA11 131 GF88
Stanbury Av, Wat. WD17 23 BS37
Stanbury Rd, SE15 102 DV81
Stancroft, NW9 62 CS56
Standale Gro, Ruis. HA4 59 BQ57
Standard Ind Est, E16 105 EM75
Standard Pl, EC2 197 N3
Standard Rd, NW10 80 CQ70
Belvedere DA17 106 FA78
Bexleyheath DA6 106 EY84
Enfield EN3 31 DY38
Hounslow TW4 96 BY83
Orpington BR6 163 EN110
Standen Av, Horn. RM12 72 FK62
Standen Rd, SW18 119 CZ87
Standfield, Abb.L. WD5 7 BS31
Standfield Gdns, Dag. RM10
off Standfield Rd 88 FA65
Standfield Rd, Dag. RM10 70 FA64
Standish Ho, SE3
off Elford Cl 104 EJ84
Standish Rd, W6 99 CU77
Standlake Pt, SE23 123 DX90
Stane Cl, SW19
off Hayward Cl 120 DB94
Stane Gro, SW9
off Clapham Rd 101 DL82
Stane St, Lthd. KT22 182 CL126
Stane Way, SE18 104 EK80
Epsom KT17 157 CU110
Stanfield Ho, NW8
off Frampton St 82 DD70
Stanfield Rd, E3 85 DY68
Stanford Cl, Hmptn. TW12 116 BZ93
Romford RM7 71 FB58
Ruislip HA4 59 BQ58
Woodford Green IG8 48 EL50
Stanford Ct, SW6
off Bagley's La 100 DB81
Waltham Abbey EN9 16 EG33
Stanford Gdns, S.Ock. (Aveley) RM15 91 FR74
Stanford Ho, Bark. IG11 88 EV68
Stanford Pl, SE17 201 M9
Stanford Rd, N11 44 DF50
SW16 141 DK96
W8 100 DB76
Grays RM16 110 GD76
Stanford St, SW1 199 M9
Stanford Way, SW16 141 DK96
Stangate, SE1 *off Royal St* 101 DM76
Stangate Cres, Borwd. WD6 26 CS43
Stangate Gdns, Stan. HA7 41 CH49
Stanger Rd, SE25 142 DU98
Stanham Pl, Dart. DA1
off Crayford Way 107 FG84
Stanham Rd, Dart. DA1 128 FJ85
Stanhope Av, N3 63 CZ55
Bromley BR2 144 EF102
Harrow HA3 41 CD53
Stanhope Cl, SE16 203 J4
Stanhope Gdns, N4 65 DP58
N6 65 DH58
NW7 43 CT50
SW7 100 DC77
Dagenham RM8 70 EZ62
Ilford IG1 69 EM60
Stanhope Gate, W1 198 G2
Stanhope Gro, Beck. BR3 143 DZ99
Stanhope Heath, Stai. (Stanw.) TW19 114 BJ86
Stanhope Ms E, SW7 100 DC77
Stanhope Ms S, SW7
off Gloucester Rd 100 DC77
Stanhope Ms W, SW7 100 DC77
Stanhope Par, NW1
off Stanhope St 83 DJ69
Stanhope Pk Rd, Grnf. UB6 78 CC70
Stanhope Pl, W2 194 D9
Stanhope Rd, E17 67 EB57
N6 65 DJ58
N12 44 DC50
Barnet EN5 27 CW44
Bexleyheath DA7 106 EY82
Carshalton SM5 158 DG108
Croydon CR0 142 DS104
Dagenham RM8 70 EZ61
Greenford UB6 78 CC71
Rainham RM13 89 FG68
Sidcup DA15 126 EU91
Swanscombe DA10 130 FZ85
Waltham Cross EN8 15 DY33
Stanhope Row, W1 199 H3
Stanhopes, Oxt. RH8 188 EH128
Stanhope St, NW1 195 K3
Stanhope Ter, W2 194 A10
Stanhope Way, Sev. TN13 190 FD122
Staines (Stanw.) TW19 114 BJ86
Stanier Cl, W14
off Aisgill Av 99 CZ78
Staniland Dr, Wey. KT13 152 BM110
Stanlake Ms, W12 81 CW74
Stanlake Rd, W12 81 CV74
Stanlake Vil, W12 81 CV74
Stanley Av, Bark. IG11 87 ET68
Beckenham BR3 143 EC96
Dagenham RM8 70 EZ60
Greenford UB6 78 CC67
New Malden KT3 139 CU99
Romford RM2 71 FG56
St. Albans AL2 8 CA25
Wembley HA0 80 CL66
Stanley Cl, SE9 125 EQ88
SW8 101 DM79
Coulsdon CR5 175 DM117
Greenhithe DA9 129 FS85
Hornchurch RM12
off Stanley Rd 72 FJ61
Romford RM2 71 FG56
Uxbridge UB8 76 BK67
Wembley HA0 80 CL66
Stanley Cotts, Slou. SL2 74 AT74
Stanley Ct, Cars. SM5
off Stanley Pk Rd 158 DG108
Stanley Cres, W11 81 CZ73
Gravesend DA12 131 GK92
Stanleycroft Cl, Islw. TW7 97 CE81
Stanley Gdns, NW2 63 CW64
W3 80 CS74
W11 81 CZ73
Borehamwood WD6 26 CL39
Mitcham CR4
off Ashbourne Rd 120 DG93
South Croydon CR2 160 DU112
Wallington SM6 159 DJ107
Walton-on-Thames KT12 154 BW107
Stanley Gdns Ms, W11
off Stanley Cres 81 CZ73
Stanley Gdns Rd, Tedd. TW11 117 CE92
Stanley Grn E, Slou. SL3 93 AZ77

★ Place of interest ⇌ Railway station ⊖ London Underground station DLR Docklands Light Railway station Tra Tramlink station H Hospital Riv Pedestrian ferry landing stage

Stanley Grn W, Slou. SL3 .... 93 AZ77
Stanley Gro, SW8 .... 100 DG82
Croydon CR0 .... 141 DN100
Stanley Pk Dr, Wem. HA0 .... 80 CM66
Stanley Pk Rd, Cars. SM5 .... 158 DF108
Wallington SM6 .... 159 DH107
Stanley Rd, E4 .... 47 ED46
E10 .... 67 EB58
E12 .... 68 EL64
E15 .... 85 ED67
E18 .... 48 EF53
N2 .... 64 DD55
N9 .... 46 DT46
N10 .... 45 DH52
N11 .... 45 DK51
N15 .... 65 DP56
NW9 *off West Hendon Bdy* .63 CU59
SW14 .... 98 CP84
SW19 .... 120 DA94
W3 .... 98 CQ76
Ashford TW15 .... 114 BL92
Bromley BR2 .... 144 EH98
Carshalton SM5 .... 158 DG108
Croydon CR0 .... 141 DN101
Enfield EN1 .... 30 DS41
Gravesend (Nthflt) DA11 .. 130 GE88
Grays RM17 .... 110 GB78
Harrow HA2 .... 60 CC61
Hornchurch RM12 .... 72 FJ61
Hounslow TW3 .... 96 CC84
Ilford IG1 .... 69 ER61
Mitcham CR4 .... 120 DG94
Morden SM4 .... 140 DA98
Northwood HA6 .... 39 BU53
Orpington BR6 .... 146 EU102
Sidcup DA14 .... 126 EU90
Southall UB1 .... 78 BY73
Sutton SM2 .... 158 DB107
Swanscombe DA10 .... 130 FZ86
Teddington TW11 .... 117 CE91
Twickenham TW2 .... 117 CD90
Watford WD17 .... 24 BW41
Wembley HA9 .... 80 CM65
Woking GU21 .... 167 AZ116
Stanley Rd N, Rain. RM13 .... 89 FE67
Stanley Rd S, Rain. RM13 .... 89 FF68
Stanley Sq, Cars. SM5 .... 158 DF109
Stanley St, SE8 .... 103 DZ80
Caterham CR3
off Coulsdon Rd 176 DQ122
Stanley Ter, N19 .... 65 DL61
Stanley Way, Orp. BR5 .... 146 EV99
Stanliff Ho, E14 .... 204 A6
Stanmer St, SW11 .... 100 DE81
STANMORE, HA7 .... 41 CG50
⊖ **Stanmore** 41 CK50
Stanmore Gdns, Rich. TW9 .. 98 CM83
Sutton SM1 .... 140 DC104
Stanmore Hall, Stan. HA7 .... 41 CH48
Stanmore Hill, Stan. HA7 .... 41 CG48
Stanmore Rd, E11 .... 68 EF60
N15 .... 65 DP56
Belvedere DA17 .... 107 FC77
Richmond TW9 .... 98 CM83
Watford WD24 .... 23 BV39
Stanmore St, N1
off Caledonian Rd 83 DM67
Stanmore Ter, Beck. BR3 .... 143 EA96
Stanmore Way, Loug. IG10 .... 33 EN39
Stanmount Rd, St.Alb. AL2 .... 8 CA25
Stannard Ms, E8 .... 84 DU65
Stannard Rd, E8 .... 84 DU65
Stannary Pl, SE11 .... 101 DN78
Stannary St, SE11 .... 101 DN79
Stannet Way, Wall. SM6 .... 159 DJ105
Stannington Path, Borwd.
WD6 .... 26 CN39
Stansbury Sq, W10
off Beethoven St 81 CY69
Stansfeld Rd, E6 .... 86 EK71
E16 .... 86 EK71
Stansfield Ho, SE1
off Longfield Est 102 DT77
Stansfield Rd, SW9 .... 101 DM83
Hounslow TW4 .... 95 BV82
Stansgate Rd, Dag. RM10 .... 70 FA61
Stanstead Cl, Brom. BR2 .... 144 EF99
Stanstead Gro, SE6
off Stanstead Rd 123 DZ88
Stanstead Manor, Sutt. SM1 .158 DA107
Stanstead Rd, E11 .... 68 EH57
SE6 .... 123 DX88
SE23 .... 123 DX88
Caterham CR3 .... 186 DR125
Hounslow (Hthrw Air.) TW6 .114 BM86
Stansted Cl, Horn. RM12 .... 89 FH65
Stansted Cres, Bex. DA5 .... 126 EX88
Stanswood Gdns, SE5 .... 102 DS80
Stanthorpe Cl, SW16 .... 121 DL92
Stanthorpe Rd, SW16 .... 121 DL92
Stanton Av, Tedd. TW11 .... 117 CE92
Stanton Cl, Epsom KT19 .... 156 CP106
Orpington BR5 .... 146 EW101
Worcester Park KT4 .... 139 CX102
Stanton Ho, SE16 .... 203 M4
Stanton Rd, SE26
off Stanton Way 123 DZ91
SW13 .... 99 CT82
SW20 .... 139 CX96
Croydon CR0 .... 142 DQ101
Stanton Sq, SE26
off Stanton Way 123 DZ91
Stanton Way, SE26 .... 123 DZ91
Slough SL3 .... 92 AY77
Stanway Cl, Chig. IG7 .... 49 ES50
Stanway Ct, N1 .... 197 N1
Stanway Gdns, W3 .... 80 CN74
Edgware HA8 .... 42 CQ50
Stanway Rd, Wal.Abb. EN9 .. 16 EG33
Stanway St, N1 .... 84 DS68
STANWELL, Stai. TW19 .... 114 BL87
Stanwell Cl, Stai. (Stanw.)
TW19 .... 114 BK86
Stanwell Gdns, Stai. (Stanw.)
TW19 .... 114 BK86
STANWELL MOOR, Stai.
TW19 .... 114 BG85
Stanwell Moor Rd, Stai.
TW19 .... 114 BH85
West Drayton UB7 .... 94 BH81
Stanwell New Rd, Stai.
TW18 .... 114 BH90
Stanwell Rd, Ashf. TW15 .... 114 BL89
Stanwell Rd, Felt. TW14 .... 115 BQ87
Slough (Horton) SL3 .... 93 BA83
Stanwick Rd, W14 .... 99 CZ77
Stanworth St, SE1 .... 201 P5
Stanwyck Dr, Chig. IG7 .... 49 EQ50
Stanwyck Gdns, Rom. RM3 .. 51 FH50
Stapenhill Rd, Wem. HA0 .... 61 CH62
Staple Cl, Bex. DA5 .... 127 FD90
Staplefield Cl, SW2 .... 121 DL88
Pinner HA5 .... 40 BY52
STAPLEFORD ABBOTTS,
Rom. RM4 .... 35 FC43
★ **Stapleford Airfield**,
Rom. RM4 .... 34 EZ40
Stapleford Av, Ilf. IG2 .... 69 ES57
Stapleford Cl, E4 .... 47 EC48
SW19 .... 119 CY87
Kingston upon Thames
KT1 .... 138 CN97
Stapleford Ct, Sev. TN13 .... 190 FF123
Stapleford Gdns, Rom. RM5 .. 50 FA51
Stapleford Rd, Rom. RM4 .... 35 FB42
Wembley HA0 .... 79 CK66
STAPLEFORD TAWNEY,
Rom. RM4 .... 35 FC37
Stapleford Way, Bark. IG11 .... 88 EV69
Staple Hill Rd, Wok. (Chob.Com.)
GU24 .... 150 AS105
Staplehurst Rd, SE13 .... 124 EE85
Carshalton SM5 .... 158 DE108
Staple Inn, WC1 .... 196 D7
Staple Inn Bldgs, WC1 .... 196 D7
Staples Cl, SE16 .... 203 K2
Staples Cor, NW2 .... 63 CV60
Staples Cor Business Pk,
NW2 .... 63 CV60
Staples Cor Retail Pk, NW2
off Geron Way 63 CV61
Staples Rd, Loug. IG10 .... 32 EL41
Staple St, SE1 .... 201 L5
Stapleton Cl, Pot.B. EN6 .... 12 DD31
Stapleton Cres, Rain. RM13 .. 89 FG65
Stapleton Gdns, Croy. CR0 .. 159 DN106
Stapleton Hall Rd, N4 .... 65 DM59
Stapleton Rd, SW17 .... 120 DG90
Bexleyheath DA7 .... 106 EZ80
Borehamwood WD6 .... 26 CN38
Orpington BR6 .... 145 ET104
Stapley Rd, Belv. DA17 .... 106 FA78
Stapylton Rd, Barn. EN5 .... 27 CY41
Star All, EC3 .... 197 N10
Star & Garter Hill, Rich.
TW10 .... 118 CL88
Starboard Av, Green. DA9 .. 129 FV86
Starboard Way, E14 .... 204 A6
Starbuck Cl, SE9 .... 125 EN87
Starch Ho La, Ilf. IG6 .... 49 ER54
Starcross St, NW1 .... 195 L3
Starfield Rd, W12 .... 99 CU75
Star Hill, Dart. DA1 .... 127 FE85
Woking GU22 .... 166 AW119
Star Hill Rd, Sev. (Dunt.Grn)
TN14 .... 180 EZ116
Starkey Cl, Wal.Cr. (Chsht)
EN7 *off Shambrook Rd* .. 14 DQ25
Star La, E16 .... 86 EE70
Coulsdon CR5 .... 174 DG122
Epping CM16 .... 18 EU30
Orpington BR5 .... 146 EW98
Starling Cl, Buck.H. IG9 .... 48 EG46
Croydon CR0 .... 143 DY100
Pinner HA5 .... 60 BW55
Starling La, Pot.B. (Cuffley)
EN6 .... 13 DM28
Starlings, The, Lthd. (Oxshott)
KT22 .... 154 CC113
Starling Wk, Hmptn. TW12
off Oak Av 116 BY92
Starmans Cl, Dag. RM9 .... 88 EY67
Star Path, Nthlt. UB5
off Brabazon Rd 78 CA68
Star Pl, E1 .... 202 A1
Star Rd, W14 .... 99 CZ79
Isleworth TW7 .... 97 CD82
Uxbridge UB10 .... 77 BQ70
Starrock La, Couls. (Chipstead)
CR5 .... 174 DF120
Starrock Rd, Couls. CR5 .... 175 DH119
Star St, E16 .... 86 EF71
W2 .... 194 A8
Starts Cl, Orp. BR6 .... 145 EN104
Starts Hill Av, Orp. BR6 .... 163 EP106
Starts Hill Rd, Orp. BR6 .... 145 EN104
Starveall Cl, West Dr. UB7 .... 94 BM76
Starwood Cl, W.Byf. KT14 .. 152 BJ111
Starwood Ct, Slou. SL3
off London Rd 92 AW76
Star Yd, WC2 .... 196 D8
State Fm Av, Orp. BR6 .... 163 EP105
Staten Bldg, E3
off Fairfield Rd 85 EA68
Staten Gdns, Twick. TW1 .... 117 CF88
Statham Gro, N16
off Green Las 66 DR63
N18 .... 46 DS50
Station App, E4 (Highams Pk)
off The Avenue 47 ED51
E7 *off Woodford Rd* 68 EH63
E11 (Snaresbrook)
off High St 68 EG57
N11 *off Friern Barnet Rd* .. 45 DH50
N12 (Woodside Pk) 44 DB49
N16 (Stoke Newington)
off Stamford Hill 66 DT61
NW10 *off Station Rd* 81 CT69
SE1 .... 200 C3
SE3 *off Kidbrooke Pk Rd* .104 EH83
SE9 (Mottingham) 125 EM88
SE26 (Lwr Sydenham)
off Worsley Br Rd 123 DZ92
SE26 (Sydenham)
off Sydenham Rd 122 DW91
SW6 .... 99 CY83
SW16 .... 121 DK92
W7 .... 79 CE74
Amersham (Lt.Chal.) HP7
off Chalfont Sta Rd 20 AX39
Ashford TW15 .... 114 BL91
Barnet (High Barn.) EN5
off Barnet Hill 28 DA42
Barnet (New Barn.) EN5 .. 28 DC42
Bexley DA5
off Bexley High St 126 FA87
Station App, Bexh. DA7
off Avenue Rd 106 EY82
Bexleyheath (Barne.) DA7 .107 FC82
Bromley (Hayes) BR2 .... 144 EG102
Buckhurst Hill IG9
off Cherry Tree Ri 48 EK49
Chislehurst BR7 .... 145 EN95
Chislehurst (Elm.Wds) BR7 .124 EL93
Coulsdon CR5 .... 175 DK116
Coulsdon (Chipstead) CR5 .. 174 DF118
Dartford DA1 .... 128 FL86
Dartford (Cray.) DA1 .... 127 FF86
Epping (They.B.) CM16
off Coppice Row 33 ES36
Epsom KT18 .... 156 CR113
Epsom (Ewell E.) KT17 .... 157 CV110
Epsom (Ewell W.) KT19
off Chessington Rd 157 CT109
Epsom (Stoneleigh) KT19 .157 CU106
Esher (Hinch.Wd) KT10 .... 137 CF104
Gerrards Cross SL9 .... 56 AY57
Grays RM17 .... 110 GA79
Greenford UB6 .... 79 CD66
Hampton TW12
off Milton Rd 136 CA95
Harrow HA1 .... 61 CE59
Hayes UB3 .... 95 BT75
Kenley CR8 *off Hayes La* .. 160 DQ114
Kingston upon Thames
KT1 .... 138 CN95
Leatherhead KT22 .... 171 CG121
Leatherhead (Oxshott)
KT22 .... 154 CC113
Loughton IG10 .... 32 EL43
Loughton (Debden) IG10 .. 33 EQ42
Northwood HA6 .... 39 BS52
Orpington BR6 .... 145 ET103
Orpington (Chels.) BR6 .. 164 EV106
Orpington (St.M.Cray) BR5 .146 EV98
Oxted RH8 .... 188 EE128
Pinner HA5 .... 60 BY55
Pinner (Hatch End) HA5
off Uxbridge Rd 40 CA52
Purley CR8
off Whytecliffe Rd S 159 DN111
Radlett WD7
off Shenley Hill 25 CG35
Richmond TW9 .... 98 CN81
Rickmansworth (Chorl.)
WD3 .... 21 BC42
Ruislip HA4 .... 59 BS60
Ruislip (S.Ruis.) HA4 .... 59 BV64
Shepperton TW17 .... 135 BQ100
South Croydon CR2
off Sanderstead Rd 160 DR109
Staines TW18 .... 114 BG92
Sunbury-on-Thames TW16 .135 BU95
Sutton (Belmont) SM2
off Brighton Rd 158 DB110
Sutton (Cheam) SM2 .... 157 CY108
Swanley BR8 .... 147 FE98
Tadworth KT20 .... 173 CW122
Upminster RM14 .... 72 FQ61
Uxbridge (Denh.) UB9
off Middle Rd 57 BD59
Virginia Water GU25 .... 132 AX98
Waltham Cross EN8 .... 15 DY34
Waltham Cross (Chsht) EN8 .15 DZ30
Watford WD18
off Cassiobury Pk Av 23 BT41
Watford (Carp.Pk) WD19
off Prestwick Rd 40 BX48
Welling DA16 .... 105 ET82
Wembley HA0 .... 79 CH65
West Byfleet KT14 .... 152 BG112
West Drayton UB7 .... 76 BL74
Weybridge KT13 .... 152 BN107
Whyteleafe CR3 .... 176 DU117
Woking GU22 .... 167 AZ117
Worcester Park KT4 .... 139 CU102
Station App N, Sid. DA15 .. 126 EU89
Station App Path, SE9
off Glenlea Rd 125 EM85
Station App Rd, W4 .... 98 CQ80
Coulsdon CR5 .... 175 DK115
Station Av, SW9
off Coldharbour La 101 DP83
Caterham CR3 .... 176 DU124
Epsom KT19 .... 156 CS109
New Malden KT3 .... 138 CS97
Richmond (Kew) TW9 .... 98 CN81
Walton-on-Thames KT12 .153 BU105
Station Cl, N3 .... 44 DA53
N12 (Woodside Pk) 44 DB49
Hampton TW12 .... 136 CB95
Hatfield AL9
off Station Rd 11 CY26
Potters Bar EN6 .... 11 CZ31
Station Ct, SW6 .... 100 DC81
Station Cres, N15 .... 66 DR56
SE3 .... 104 EG78
Ashford TW15 .... 114 BK90
Wembley HA0 .... 79 CH65
Stationers Hall Ct, EC4
off Ludgate Hill 83 DP72
Station Est, Beck. BR3
off Elmers End Rd 143 DX98
Station Est Rd, Felt. TW14 .. 115 BV88
Station Footpath, Kings L.
WD4 .... 7 BP31
Station Gar Ms, SW16
off Estreham Rd 121 DK93
Station Gdns, W4 .... 98 CQ80
Station Gro, Wem. HA0 .... 80 CL65
Station Hill, Brom. BR2 .... 144 EG103
Station Ho Ms, N9
off Fore St 46 DU49
Station La, Horn. RM12 .... 72 FK62
Station Ms Ter, SE3
off Halstow Rd 104 EG78
Station Par, E11 .... 68 EG57
N14 *off High St* 45 DK46
NW2 .... 81 CW65
SW12 *off Balham High Rd* .. 120 DG88
W3 .... 80 CN72
Ashford TW15
off Woodthorpe Rd 114 BM91
Barking IG11 .... 87 EQ66
Barnet EN4
off Cockfosters Rd 28 DG42
Feltham TW14 .... 115 BV87
Hornchurch RM12
off Rosewood Av 71 FH63
Station Par, Rich. TW9 .... 98 CN81
Sevenoaks TN13
off London Rd 190 FG124
Uxbridge (Denh.) UB9 .... 58 BG59
Virginia Water GU25 .... 132 AX98
Station Pas, E18
off Maybank Rd 48 EH54
SE15 .... 102 DW81
Station Path, E8
off Amhurst Rd 84 DV65
Staines TW18 .... 113 BF91
Station Pl, N4
off Seven Sisters Rd 65 DN61
Station Ri, SE27
off Norwood Rd 121 DP89
Station Rd, E4 (Chingford) .. 47 ED46
E7 .... 68 EG63
E12 .... 68 EK63
E17 .... 67 DY58
N3 .... 44 DA53
N11 .... 45 DH50
N17 .... 66 DU55
N19 .... 65 DJ62
N21 .... 45 DP46
N22 .... 45 DM54
NW4 .... 63 CU58
NW7 .... 42 CS50
NW10 .... 81 CT68
SE13 .... 103 EC83
SE20 .... 122 DW93
SE25 (Norwood Junct.) 142 DT98
SW13 .... 99 CU83
SW19 .... 140 DC95
W5 .... 80 CM72
W7 (Hanwell) 79 CE74
Addlestone KT15 .... 152 BJ105
Ashford TW15 .... 114 BM91
Barnet EN5 .... 28 DB43
Belvedere DA17 .... 106 FA76
Betchworth RH3 .... 182 CS131
Bexleyheath DA7 .... 106 EY83
Borehamwood WD6 .... 26 CN42
Brentford TW8 .... 97 CJ79
Bromley BR1 .... 144 EG95
Bromley (Short.) BR2 .... 144 EE96
Carshalton SM5 .... 158 DF105
Caterham (Wold.) CR3 .... 177 DZ123
Chertsey KT16 .... 133 BF102
Chessington KT9 .... 156 CL106
Chigwell IG7 .... 49 EP48
Cobham (Stoke D'Ab.)
KT11 .... 170 BY117
Croydon (E.Croy.) CR0 .. 142 DR103
Croydon (W.Croy.) CR0 .. 142 DQ102
Dartford (Cray.) DA1 .... 127 FF86
Dartford (Eyns.) DA4 .... 148 FK104
Dartford (S.Darenth) DA4 .148 FP96
Edgware HA8 .... 42 CN51
Egham TW20 .... 113 BA92
Epping CM16 .... 18 EU31
Epping (N.Wld Bas.) CM16 .19 FB27
Esher KT10 .... 137 CD103
Esher (Clay.) KT10 .... 155 CD106
Gerrards Cross SL9 .... 56 AY57
Gravesend (Betsham)
DA13 .... 130 GA91
Gravesend (Nthflt) DA11 .. 130 GB86
Greenhithe DA9 .... 109 FU84
Hampton TW12 .... 136 CA95
Harrow HA1 .... 61 CF59
Harrow (N.Har.) HA2 .... 60 CB57
Hatfield (Brook.Pk) AL9 .... 11 CX25
Hayes UB3 .... 95 BT76
Hounslow TW3 .... 96 CB84
Ilford IG1 .... 69 EP62
Ilford (Barkingside) IG6 .... 69 ER55
Kenley CR8 .... 160 DQ114
Kings Langley WD4 .... 7 BP29
Kingston upon Thames
KT2 .... 138 CN95
Kingston upon Thames
(Hmptn W.) KT1 .... 137 CJ95
Leatherhead KT22 .... 171 CG121
Loughton IG10 .... 32 EL42
New Malden (Mots.Pk)
KT3 .... 139 CV99
Orpington BR6 .... 145 ET103
Orpington (St.P.Cray) BR5 .146 EW98
Potters Bar (Cuffley) EN6 .. 13 DM29
Radlett WD7 .... 25 CG35
Redhill RH1 .... 184 DG133
Redhill (Merst.) RH1 .... 185 DJ128
Rickmansworth WD3 .... 38 BK45
Romford (Chad.Hth) RM6 .. 70 EX59
Romford (Gidea Pk) RM2 .. 71 FH56
Romford (Harold Wd) RM3 .52 FM53
St. Albans (Brick.Wd) AL2 .. 8 CA31
Sevenoaks (Dunt.Grn)
TN13 .... 181 FE120
Sevenoaks (Halst.) TN14 .. 164 EZ111
Sevenoaks (Otford) TN14 .181 FH116
Sevenoaks (Shore.) TN14 .165 FG111
Shepperton TW17 .... 135 BQ99
Sidcup DA15 .... 126 EU91
Slough (Langley) SL3 .... 93 BA76
Staines (Wrays.) TW19 .... 113 AZ86
Sunbury-on-Thames TW16 .115 BU94
Sutton (Belmont) SM2 .... 158 DA110
Swanley BR8 .... 147 FE98
Teddington TW11 .... 117 CF92
Thames Ditton KT7 .... 137 CF101
Twickenham TW1 .... 117 CF88
Upminster RM14 .... 72 FQ61
Uxbridge UB8 .... 76 BJ70
Waltham Cross EN8 .... 15 EA34
Watford WD17 .... 23 BV40
West Byfleet KT14 .... 152 BG112
West Drayton UB7 .... 76 BK74
West Wickham BR4 .... 143 EC102
Westerham (Brasted) TN16 .180 EV123
Whyteleafe CR3 .... 176 DT118
Woking (Chobham) GU24 .150 AT111
Station Rd E, Oxt. RH8 .... 188 EE128
Station Rd N, Belv. DA17 .... 107 FB76
Egham TW20 .... 113 BA92
Redhill (Merst.) RH1 .... 185 DJ128
Station Rd S, Red. (Merst.)
RH1 .... 185 DJ128
Station Rd W, Oxt. RH8 .... 188 EE129
Station Sq, Orp. (Petts Wd)
BR5 .... 145 EQ99
Romford RM2 .... 71 FH56
Station St, E15 .... 85 ED66
Station St, E16 .... 87 EP74
Station Ter, NW10 .... 81 CX68
SE5 .... 102 DQ81
St. Albans (Park St) AL2
off Park St 9 CD26
Station Vw, Grnf. UB6 .... 79 CD67
Station Way, Buck.H.
(Rod.Val.) IG9 .... 48 EJ49
Epsom KT19 .... 156 CR113
Esher (Clay.) KT10 .... 155 CE107
Sutton (Cheam) SM3 .... 157 CY107
Station Yd, Twick. TW1 .... 117 CG87
Staunton Rd, Kings.T. KT2 .. 118 CL93
Staunton St, SE8 .... 103 DZ79
★ **Stave Hill Ecological Pk**,
SE16 .... 203 K4
Staveley Cl, E9
off Churchill Wk 66 DW64
N7 .... 65 DL63
SE15 *off Asylum Rd* 102 DV81
Staveley Gdns, W4 .... 98 CR81
Staveley Rd, W4 .... 98 CR80
Ashford TW15 .... 115 BR93
Staveley Way, Wok. (Knap.)
GU21 .... 166 AS117
Staverton Rd, NW2 .... 81 CW66
Hornchurch RM11 .... 72 FK58
Stave Yd Rd, SE16 .... 203 K3
Stavordale Rd, N5 .... 65 DP63
Carshalton SM5 .... 140 DC101
Stayne End, Vir.W. GU25 .... 132 AU98
Stayner's Rd, E1 .... 85 DX70
Stayton Rd, Sutt. SM1 .... 140 DA104
Steadfast Rd, Kings.T. KT1 .. 137 CK95
Stead St, SE17 .... 201 K9
Steam Fm La, Felt. TW14 .... 95 BT84
Stean St, E8 .... 84 DT67
Stebbing Ho, W11 .... 81 CX74
Stebbing Way, Bark. IG11 .... 88 EU68
Stebondale St, E14 .... 204 E9
Stedham Pl, WC1 .... 195 P8
Stedman Cl, Bex. DA5 .... 127 FE90
Uxbridge UB10 .... 58 BN62
Steed Cl, Horn. RM11 .... 71 FH61
Steedman St, SE17 .... 201 H9
Steeds Rd, N10 .... 44 DF53
Steeds Way, Loug. IG10 .... 32 EL41
Steele Av, Green. DA9 .... 129 FT85
Steele Rd, E11 .... 68 EE63
N17 .... 66 DS55
NW10 .... 80 CQ68
W4 .... 98 CQ76
Isleworth TW7 .... 97 CG84
Steeles Ms N, NW3
off Steeles Rd 82 DF65
Steeles Ms S, NW3
off Steeles Rd 82 DF65
Steeles Rd, NW3 .... 82 DF65
Steele Wk, Erith DA8 .... 107 FB79
Steel's La, E1
off Devonport St 84 DW72
Steels La, Lthd. (Oxshott)
KT22 .... 154 CB114
Steelyard Pas, EC4
off Upper Thames St 84 DR73
Steen Way, SE22
off East Dulwich Gro 122 DS85
Steep Cl, Orp. BR6 .... 163 ET107
Steep Hill, SW16 .... 121 DK90
Croydon CR0 .... 160 DS105
Steeplands, Bushey WD23 .. 40 CB45
Steeple Cl, SW6 .... 99 CY82
SW19 .... 119 CY92
Steeple Ct, E1
off Coventry Rd 84 DV70
Steeple Gdns, Add. KT15
off Weatherall Cl 152 BH106
Steeple Hts Dr, West.
(Bigg.H.) TN16 .... 178 EK117
Steeplestone Cl, N18 .... 46 DQ50
Steeple Wk, N1 *off Basire St* .84 DQ67
Steerforth St, SW18 .... 120 DB89
Steers Mead, Mitch. CR4 .... 140 DF95
Steers Way, SE16 .... 203 L5
Stella Cl, Uxb. UB8 .... 77 BP71
Stellar Ho, N17 .... 46 DT51
Stella Rd, SW17 .... 120 DF93
Stelling Rd, Erith DA8 .... 107 FD80
Stellman Cl, E5 .... 66 DU62
Stembridge Rd, SE20 .... 142 DV96
Sten Cl, Enf. EN3 .... 31 EA37
Stents La, Cob. KT11 .... 170 BZ120
Stepbridge Path, Wok. GU21
off Goldsworth Rd 166 AX117
Stepgates, Cher. KT16 .... 134 BH101
Stepgates Cl, Cher. KT16 .. 134 BH101
Stephan Cl, E8 .... 84 DU67
Stephen Av, Rain. RM13 .... 89 FG65
Stephen Cl, Egh. TW20 .... 113 BC93
Orpington BR6 .... 145 ET104
Stephendale Rd, SW6 .... 100 DB82
Stephen Ms, W1 .... 195 M7
Stephen Pl, SW4
off Rectory Gro 101 DJ83
Stephen Rd, Bexh. DA7 .... 107 FC83
Stephens Cl, Rom. RM3 .... 52 FJ50
Stephenson Av, Til. RM18 .. 111 GG81
Stephenson Cl, Well. DA16
off Upper Wickham La .. 106 EU82
Stephenson Rd, E17 .... 67 DY57
W7 .... 79 CF72
Twickenham TW2 .... 116 CA87
Stephenson St, E16 .... 86 EE70
NW10 .... 80 CS69
Stephenson Way, NW1 .... 195 L4
Watford WD24 .... 24 BX41
Stephenson Wf, Hem.H. HP3 .. 6 BL25
Stephen's Rd, E15 .... 86 EE67
Stephen St, W1 .... 195 M7
STEPNEY, E1 .... 84 DW71
Stepney Causeway, E1 .... 85 DX72
Stepney Cl, Mitch. CR4 .... 140 DG95
⊖ **Stepney Green** 85 DX70
Stepney Grn, E1 .... 84 DW71
Stepney High St, E1 .... 85 DX71
Stepney Way, E1 .... 84 DV71
Sterling Av, Edg. HA8 .... 42 CM49

★ Place of interest ⇌ Railway station ⊖ London Underground station DLR Docklands Light Railway station Tra Tramlink station H Hospital Riv Pedestrian ferry landing stage

Sterling Av, Wal. Cr. EN8 15 DX34
Sterling Cl, N9 63 DW46
NW10 81 CU65
Sterling Gdns, SE14 103 DY79
Sterling Ho, SE3
off Cambert Way 104 EH84
Sterling Ind Est, Dag. RM10 71 FB63
Sterling Pl, W5 98 CL77
Weybridge KT13 153 BS105
Sterling Rd, Enf. EN2 30 DR39
Sterling St, SW7 198 C6
Sterling Way, N18 46 DR50
★ Sternberg Cen, N3 44 DB54
Stern Cl, Bark. IG11 88 EW68
Sterndale Rd, W14 99 CX76
Dartford DA1 128 FM87
Sterne St, W12 99 CX75
Sternhall La, SE15 102 DU83
Sternhold Av, SW2 121 DK89
Sterry Cres, Dag. RM10
off Alibon Rd 70 FA64
Sterry Dr, Epsom KT19 156 CS105
Thames Ditton KT7 137 CE100
Sterry Gdns, Dag. RM10 88 FA65
Sterry Rd, Bark. IG11 87 ET67
Dagenham RM10 70 FA63
Sterry St, SE1 201 K5
Steucers La, SE23 123 DY87
Steve Biko La, SE6 123 EA91
Steve Biko Rd, N7 65 DN62
Steve Biko Way, Houns. TW3 96 CA83
Stevedale Rd, Well. DA16 106 EW82
Stevedore St, E1 202 D2
Stevenage Cres, Borwd. WD6 26 CL39
Stevenage Rd, E6 87 EN65
SW6 99 CX80
Stevens Av, E9 84 DW65
Stevens Cl, Beck. BR3 123 EA93
Bexley DA5 127 FD91
Steven's Cl, Dart. (Lane End)
DA2 129 FS92
Stevens Cl, Epsom KT17
off Upper High St 156 CS113
Hampton TW12 116 BY93
Pinner HA5 off Bridle Rd 60 BW57
Stevens Grn, Bushey (Bushey Hth)
WD23 40 CC46
Stevens La, Esher (Clay.)
KT10 155 CG108
Stevenson Cl, Barn. EN5 28 DD44
Erith DA8 107 FH80
Stevenson Cres, SE16 202 C10
Stevens Pl, Pur. CR8 159 DP113
Stevens Rd, Dag. RM8 70 EV62
Stevens St, SE1 201 N6
Steven's Wk, Croy. CR0 161 DY111
Stevens Way, Chig. IG7 49 ES49
Steventon Rd, W12 81 CT73
Steward Cl, Wal.Cr.
(Chsht) EN8 15 DY30
Stewards Cl, Epp. CM16 18 EU33
Stewards Grn La, Epp. CM16 18 EV32
Stewards Grn Rd, Epp. CM16 18 EU33
Stewards Holte Wk, N11
off Coppies Gro 45 DH49
Steward St, E1 197 N7
Stewards Wk, Rom. RM1
off Western Rd 71 FE57
Stewart, Tad. KT20 173 CX121
Stewart Av, Shep. TW17 134 BN98
Slough SL1 74 AT71
Upminster RM14 72 FP62
Stewart Cl, NW9 62 CQ58
Abbots Langley WD5 7 BT32
Chislehurst BR7 125 EP92
Hampton TW12 116 BY92
Woking GU21 166 AT117
Stewart Rainbird Ho, E12 69 EN64
Stewart Rd, E15 67 EC63
Stewartsby Cl, N18 46 DQ50
Stewart's Gro, SW3 198 A10
Stewart's Rd, SW8 101 DJ80
Stewart St, E14 204 E5
Stew La, EC4 197 H10
Steyne Rd, W3 80 CQ74
Steyning Cl, Ken. CR8 175 DP116
Steyning Gro, SE9 125 EM91
Steynings Way, N12 44 DA50
Steyning Way, Houns. TW4 96 BW84
Steynton Av, Bex. DA5 126 EX89
Stickland Rd, Belv. DA17
off Picardy Rd 106 FA77
Stickleton Cl, Grnf. UB6 78 CB69
Stifford Hill, Grays (N.Stfd)
RM16 91 FX74
South Ockendon RM15 91 FW73
Stifford Rd, S.Ock. RM15 91 FR74
Stilecroft Gdns, Wem. HA0 61 CH62
Stile Hall Gdns, W4 98 CN78
Stile Hall Par, W4
off Chiswick High Rd 98 CN78
Stile Path, Sun. TW16 135 BU98
Stile Rd, Slou. SL3 92 AX76
Stiles Cl, Brom. BR2 145 EM100
Erith DA8
off Riverdale Rd 107 FB78
Stillingfleet Rd, SW13 99 CU79
Stillington St, SW1 199 L8
Stillness Rd, SE23 123 DY86
Stilton Path, Borwd. WD6 26 CN38
Stilwell Dr, Uxb. UB8 76 BM70
Stilwell Rbt, Uxb. UB8 77 BP72
Stipularis Dr, Hayes UB4 78 BX70
Stirling Av, Pnr. HA5 60 BY59
Wallington SM6 159 DL108
Stirling Cl, SW16 141 DJ95
Banstead SM7 173 CZ117
Rainham RM13 89 FH69
Sidcup DA14 125 ES91
Uxbridge UB8
off Ferndale Cres 76 BJ69
Stirling Cor, Barn. EN5 26 CR44
Borehamwood WD6 26 CR44
Stirling Dr, Orp. BR6 164 EV106
Stirling Gro, Houns. TW3 96 CC82
Stirling Ind Cen, Borwd. WD6 26 CR43
Stirling Rd, E13 86 EH68
E17 67 DY55
Stirling Rd, N17 46 DU53
N22 45 DP53
SW9 101 DL82
W3 98 CP76
Harrow HA3 61 CF55
Hayes UB3 77 BV73
Hounslow (Hthrw Air.) TW6 114 BM86
Twickenham TW2 116 CA87
Stirling Rd Path, E17 67 DY55
Stirling Wk, N.Mal. KT3 138 CQ99
Surbiton KT5 138 CP100
Stirling Way, Abb.L. WD5 7 BU32
Borehamwood WD6 26 CR44
Croydon CR0 141 DL101
Stites Hill Rd, Couls. CR5 175 DP120
Stiven Cres, Har. HA2 60 BZ62
Stoats Nest Rd, Couls. CR5 159 DL114
Stoats Nest Village, Couls.
CR5 175 DL115
Stockbury Rd, Croy. CR0 142 DW100
Stockdale Rd, Dag. RM8 70 EZ61
Stockdove Way, Grnf. UB6 79 CF69
Stocker Gdns, Dag. RM9 88 EW66
Stockers Fm Rd, Rick. WD3 38 BK48
Stockers La, Wok. GU22 167 AZ120
★ Stock Exchange, EC4 196 G8
Stockfield Rd, SW16 121 DM90
Esher (Clay.) KT10 155 CE106
Stockford Av, NW7 43 CX52
Stockham's Cl, S.Croy. CR2 160 DR111
Stock Hill, West. (Bigg.H.)
TN16 178 EK116
Stockholm Ho, E1 84 DU73
Stockholm Rd, SE16 102 DW78
Stockholm Way, E1 202 B2
Stockhurst Cl, SW15 99 CW82
Stockingswater La, Enf. EN3 31 DY41
Stockland Rd, Rom. RM7 71 FD58
Stock La, Dart. DA2 128 FJ91
Stockleigh Hall, NW8
off Prince Albert Rd 82 DF68
Stockley Cl, West Dr. UB7 95 BP75
Stockley Fm Rd, West Dr.
UB7 off Stockley Rd 95 BP76
Stockley Pk, Uxb. UB11 77 BP74
Stockley Pk Rbt, Uxb. UB11 77 BP74
Stockley Rd, Uxb. UB8 77 BP73
West Drayton UB7 95 BP77
Stock Orchard Cres, N7 65 DM64
Stock Orchard St, N7 65 DM64
Stockport Rd, SW16 141 DK95
Rickmansworth (Herons.)
WD3 37 BC45
Stocksfield Rd, E17 67 EC55
Stocks Pl, E14
off Grenade St 85 DZ73
Uxbridge UB10 76 BN67
Stock St, E13 86 EG68
Stockton Cl, Barn. EN5 28 DC42
Stockton Gdns, N17
off Stockton Rd 46 DQ52
NW7 42 CS48
Stockton Ho, E2
off Ellsworth St 84 DV69
Stockton Rd, N17 46 DQ52
N18 46 DU51
STOCKWELL, SW9 101 DM81
⊖ Stockwell 101 DL81
Stockwell Av, SW9 101 DM83
Stockwell Cl, Brom. BR1 144 EH96
Edgware HA8 42 CQ54
Waltham Cross (Chsht) EN7 14 DU28
Stockwell Gdns, SW9 101 DM82
Stockwell Gdns Est, SW9 101 DL82
Stockwell Grn, SW9 101 DM82
Stockwell La, SW9 101 DM82
Waltham Cross (Chsht) EN7 14 DU28
Stockwell Ms, SW9
off Stockwell Rd 101 DM82
Stockwell Pk Cres, SW9 101 DM82
Stockwell Pk Est, SW9 101 DN82
Stockwell Pk Rd, SW9 101 DM81
Stockwell Pk Wk, SW9 101 DM83
Stockwell Rd, SW9 101 DM82
Stockwell St, SE10 103 EC79
Stockwell Ter, SW9 101 DM81
Stodart Rd, SE20 142 DW95
Stofield Gdns, SE9
off Aldersgrove Av 124 EK90
Stoford Cl, SW19 119 CY87
Stoke Av, Ilf. IG6 50 EU51
Stoke Cl, Cob. (Stoke D'Ab.)
KT11 170 BZ116
Stoke Common Rd, Slou.
(Fulmer) SL3 56 AU63
Stoke Ct Dr, Slou.
(Stoke P.) SL2 74 AS67
STOKE D'ABERNON, Cob.
KT11 170 BZ116
Stoke Gdns, Slou. SL1 74 AS74
STOKE GREEN, Slou. SL2 74 AU70
Stoke Grn, Slou. (Stoke P.)
SL2 74 AU70
Stokenchurch St, SW6 100 DB81
STOKE NEWINGTON, N16 66 DS61
⇌ Stoke Newington 66 DT61
Stoke Newington Ch St, N16 66 DR62
Stoke Newington Common,
N16 66 DT62
Stoke Newington High St,
N16 66 DT62
Stoke Newington Rd, N16 66 DT64
Stoke Pl, NW10 81 CT69
STOKE POGES, Slou. SL2 74 AT66
Stoke Poges La, Slou.
SL1, SL2 74 AS72
Stoke Rd, Cob. KT11 170 BW115
Kingston upon Thames
KT2 118 CQ94
Rainham RM13 90 FK68
Slough SL2 74 AT71
Walton-on-Thames KT12 136 BW104
Stokesay, Slou. SL2 74 AT73
Stokesby Rd, Chess. KT9 156 CM107
Stokesheath Rd, Lthd.
(Oxshott) KT22 154 CC111
Stokesley St, W12 81 CT72
Stokes Ridings, Tad. KT20 173 CX123
Stokes Rd, E6 86 EL70
Croydon CR0 143 DX100
Stoke Wd, Slou. (Stoke P.)
SL2 56 AT63
Stoll Cl, NW2 63 CW62
Stompond La, Walt. KT12 135 BU103
Stonard Rd, N13 45 DN48
Dagenham RM8 70 EV64
Stonards Hill, Epp. CM16 18 EW31
Loughton IG10 33 EM44
Stondon Pk, SE23 123 DY87
Stondon Wk, E6 86 EK68
STONE, Green. DA9 129 FT85
Stonebanks, Walt. KT12 135 BU101
STONEBRIDGE, NW10 80 CP67
Stonebridge Common, E8
off Mayfield Rd 84 DT66
⇌ Stonebridge Park 80 CN66
⊖ Stonebridge Park 80 CN66
Stonebridge Pk, NW10 80 CR66
Stonebridge Rd, N15 66 DS57
Gravesend (Nthflt) DA11 130 GA85
Stonebridge Way, Wem. HA9 80 CP65
Stone Bldgs, WC2 196 C7
Stonechat Sq, E6
off Peridot St 86 EL71
Stone Cl, SW4
off Larkhall Ri 101 DJ82
Dagenham RM8 70 EZ61
West Drayton UB7 76 BM74
Stonecot Cl, Sutt. SM3 139 CY102
Stonecot Hill, Sutt. SM3 139 CY102
Stone Cres, Felt. TW14 115 BT87
Stonecroft Av, Iver SL0 75 BE72
Stonecroft Cl, Barn. EN5 27 CV42
Stonecroft Rd, Erith DA8 107 FC80
Stonecroft Way, Croy. CR0 141 DL101
Stonecrop Cl, NW9 62 CR55
⇌ Stone Crossing 129 FS85
Stonecutter Ct, EC4
off Stonecutter St 83 DP72
Stonecutter St, EC4 196 F8
Stonefield Cl, Bexh. DA7 106 FA83
Ruislip HA4 60 BY64
Stonefield St, N1 83 DN67
Stonefield Way, SE7
off Greenbay Rd 104 EK80
Ruislip HA4 60 BY63
Stonegate Cl, Orp. BR5
off Main Rd 146 EW97
Stonegrove, Edg. HA8 42 CL49
Stonegrove Est, Edg. HA8 42 CM49
Stonegrove Gdns, Edg. HA8 42 CM50
Stonehall Av, Ilf. IG1 68 EL58
Stone Hall Gdns, W8
off St. Mary's Gate 100 DB76
Stone Hall Pl, W8
off St. Mary's Gate 100 DB76
Stone Hall Rd, N21 45 DM45
Stoneham Rd, N11 45 DJ51
STONEHILL, Cher. KT16 150 AY107
Stonehill Cl, SW14 118 CR85
Stonehill Cres, Cher.
(Ott.) KT16 150 AY107
Stonehill Grn, Dart. DA2 127 FC94
Stonehill Rd, SW14 118 CQ85
W4 off Wellesley Rd 98 CN78
Chertsey (Ott.) KT16 151 BA105
Woking (Chobham) GU24 150 AW108
Stonehills Business Pk, N18
off Silvermere Dr 47 DX51
Stonehills Ct, SE21 122 DS90
Stonehill Wds Pk, Sid. DA14 127 FB93
Stonehorse Rd, Enf. EN3 30 DW43
Stone Ho Ct, EC3 197 M8
Stonehouse Gdns, Cat. CR3 186 DS125
H Stone Ho Hosp,
Dart. DA2 128 FQ86
Stonehouse La, Purf. RM19 109 FS79
Sevenoaks (Halst.) TN14 164 EX109
Stonehouse Rd, Sev.
(Halst.) TN14 164 EW110
Stoneings La, Sev. (Knock.)
TN14 179 ET118
Stone Lake Retail Pk, SE7 104 EH77
Stone Lake Rbt, SE7
off Woolwich Rd 104 EJ77
STONELEIGH, Epsom KT17 157 CU106
⇌ Stoneleigh 157 CU106
Stoneleigh Av, Enf. EN1 30 DV39
Worcester Park KT4 157 CU105
Stoneleigh Bdy, Epsom
KT17 157 CU106
Stoneleigh Cl, Wal.Cr. EN8 15 DX33
Stoneleigh Cres, Epsom
KT19 157 CT106
Stoneleigh Ms, E3
off Stanfield Rd 85 DY68
Stoneleigh Pk, Wey. KT13 153 BQ106
Stoneleigh Pk Av, Croy. CR0 143 DX100
Stoneleigh Pk Rd, Epsom
KT19 157 CT107
Stoneleigh Pl, W11 81 CX73
Stoneleigh Rd, N17 66 DT55
Carshalton SM5 140 DE101
Ilford IG5 68 EL55
Oxted RH8 188 EL130
Stoneleigh St, W11 81 CX73
Stoneleigh Ter, N19 65 DH61
Stonells Rd, SW11
off Chatham Rd 120 DF85
Stonemasons Cl, N15 66 DR56
Stoneness Rd, Grays RM20 109 FV79
Stonenest St, N4 65 DM60
Stone Pk Av, Beck. BR3 143 EA98
Stone Pl, Wor.Pk. KT4 139 CU103
Stone Pl Rd, Green. DA9 129 FS85
Stone Rd, Brom. BR2 144 EF99
Stones All, Wat. WD18 23 BV42
Stones Cross Rd, Swan. BR8 147 FC99
Stones End St, SE1 201 H5
Stones Rd, Epsom KT17 156 CS112
Stone St, Croy. CR0 159 DN106
Gravesend DA11 131 GH86
Stoneswood Rd, Oxt. RH8 188 EH130
Stonewall, E6 87 EN71
Stonewood, Dart. (Bean)
DA2 129 FW90
Stonewood Rd, Erith DA8 107 FE78
Stoney All, SE18 105 EN82
Stoneyard La, E14 204 B1
Stoney Br Rd, Wal.Abb. EN9 16 EG34
Stoney Cft, Couls. CR5 175 DJ122
Stoneycroft Cl, SE12 124 EF87
Stoneycroft Rd, Wdf.Grn. IG8 48 EL51
Stoneydeep, Tedd. TW11
off Twickenham Rd 117 CG91
Stoneydown, E17 67 DY56
Stoneydown Av, E17 67 DY56
Stoneyfield Rd, Couls. CR5 175 DM117
Stoneyfields Gdns, Edg. HA8 42 CQ49
Stoneyfields La, Edg. HA8 42 CQ50
Stoneylands Ct, Egh. TW20 113 AZ92
Stoneylands Rd, Egh. TW20 113 AZ92
Stoney La, E1 197 N8
SE19 off Church Rd 122 DT93
Hemel Hempstead (Bov.) HP3 5 BB27
Kings Langley (Chipper.)
WD4 5 BE30
Stoney St, SE1 201 K2
Stonhouse St, SW4 101 DK83
Stonny Cft, Ashtd. KT21 172 CM117
Stonor Rd, W14 99 CZ77
Stonycroft Cl, Enf. EN3
off Brimsdown Av 31 DY40
Stony La, Amer. HP6 20 AY38
Stony Path, Loug. IG10 33 EM40
Stonyshotts, Wal.Abb. EN9 16 EE34
Stoop Ct, W.Byf. KT14 152 BH112
Stopes St, SE15 102 DT80
Stopford Rd, E13 86 EG67
SE17 101 DP78
Store Rd, E16 105 EN75
Storers Quay, E14 204 F9
Store St, E15 67 ED64
WC1 195 M7
Storey Ct, NW8
off St. John's Wd Rd 82 DD69
Storey Rd, E17 67 DZ56
N6 64 DF58
Storey's Gate, SW1 199 N5
Storey St, E16 87 EN74
Stories Ms, SE5 102 DS82
Stories Rd, SE5 102 DS83
Stork Rd, E7 86 EF65
Storksmead Rd, Edg. HA8 42 CS52
Storks Rd, SE16 202 C7
Stormont Rd, N6 64 DF59
SW11 100 DG83
Stormont Way, Chess. KT9 155 CJ106
Stormount Dr, Hayes UB3 95 BQ75
Stornaway Rd, Slou. SL3 93 BC77
Stornaway Strand, Grav.
DA12 131 GM91
Storr Gdns, Brwd. (Hutt.)
CM13 55 GD43
Storrington Rd, Croy. CR0 142 DT102
Story St, N1
off Carnoustie Dr 83 DM66
Stothard Pl, E1
off Bishopsgate 84 DS71
Stothard St, E1
off Colebert Av 84 DW70
Stott Cl, SW18 120 DD86
Stoughton Av, Sutt. SM3 157 CX106
Stoughton Cl, SE11 200 C9
SW15 off Bessborough Rd 119 CU88
Stour Av, Sthl. UB2 96 CA76
Stourcliffe St, W1 194 D9
Stour Cl, Kes. BR2 162 EJ105
Stourhead Cl, SW19
off Castlecombe Dr 119 CX87
Stourhead Gdns, SW20 139 CU97
Stourhead Ho, SW1
off Tachbrook St 101 DK78
Stour Rd, E3 85 EA66
Dagenham RM10 70 FA61
Dartford DA1 107 FG83
Grays RM16 111 GG78
Stourton Av, Felt. TW13 116 BZ91
Stour Way, Upmin. RM14 73 FS58
Stowage, SE8 103 EA79
Stow Cres, E17 47 DY52
Stowe Ct, Dart. DA2 128 FQ87
Stowe Cres, Ruis. HA4 59 BP58
Stowe Gdns, N9 46 DT46
Stowell Av, Croy. (New Adgtn)
CR0 161 ED110
Stowe Pl, N15 66 DS55
Stowe Rd, W12 99 CV75
Orpington BR6 164 EV105
Stowting Rd, Orp. BR6 163 ES105
Stox Mead, Har. HA3 41 CD53
Stracey Rd, E7 68 EG63
NW10 80 CR67
Strachan Pl, SW19
off Woodhayes Rd 119 CW93
Stradbroke Dr, Chig. IG7 49 EN51
Stradbroke Gro, Buck.H. IG9 48 EK46
Ilford IG5 68 EL55
Stradbroke Pk, Chig. IG7 49 EP51
Stradbroke Rd, N5 66 DQ63
Stradbrook Cl, Har. HA2
off Stiven Cres 60 BZ62
Stradella Rd, SE24 122 DQ86
Strafford Av, Ilf. IG5 49 EN54
Strafford Cl, Pot.B. EN6
off Strafford Gate 12 DA32
Strafford Gate, Pot.B. EN6 12 DA32
Strafford Rd, W3 98 CQ75
Barnet EN5 27 CY41
Hounslow TW3 96 BZ83
Twickenham TW1 117 CG87
Strafford St, E14 203 P4
Strahan Rd, E3 85 DY69
Straight, The, Sthl. UB1 96 BX75
Straight Rd, Rom. RM3 52 FJ52
Windsor (Old Wind.) SL4 112 AU85
Straightsmouth, SE10 103 EC80
Strait Rd, E6 86 EL73
Straker's Rd, SE15 102 DV84
STRAND, WC2 195 P10
Strand, WC2 199 P1
Strand Cl, Epsom KT18 172 CR119
Strand Ct, SE18
off Strandfield Cl 105 ES78
Strand Dr, Rich. TW9 98 CP80
Strandfield Cl, SE18 105 ES78
Strand La, WC2 196 C10
Strand on the Grn, W4 98 CN79
Strand Pl, N18 46 DR49
Strand Sch App, W4
off Thames Rd 98 CN79
Strangeways, Wat. WD17 23 BS36
Strangways Ter, W14
off Melbury Rd 99 CZ76
Stranraer Gdns, Slou. SL1 74 AS74
Stranraer Rd, Houns.
(Hthrw Air.) TW6 114 BL86
Stranraer Way, N1 83 DL66
Strasburg Rd, SW11 101 DH81
Stratfield Pk Cl, N21 45 DP45
Stratfield Rd, Borwd. WD6 26 CN41
Slough SL1 92 AU75
STRATFORD, E15 85 EC65
⇌ Stratford 85 EC65
⊖ Stratford 85 EC66
DLR Stratford 85 EC66
Stratford Av, W8
off Stratford Rd 100 DA76
Uxbridge UB10 76 BM68
Stratford Cen, The, E15 85 ED66
Stratford Cl, Bark. IG11 88 EU66
Dagenham RM10 89 FC66
Stratford Ct, N.Mal. KT3
off Kingston Rd 138 CR98
Stratford Gro, SW15 99 CX84
Stratford Ho Av, Brom. BR1 144 EL97
⇌ Stratford International 85 EC65
Stratford Pl, W1 195 H9
Stratford Rd, E13 86 EF67
NW4 63 CX56
W8 100 DA76
Hayes UB4 77 BV70
Hounslow (Hthrw Air.) TW6 115 BP86
Southall UB2 96 BY77
Thornton Heath CR7 141 DN98
Watford WD17 23 BU40
Stratford Vil, NW1 83 DJ66
Stratford Way, St.Alb.
(Brick.Wd) AL2 8 BZ29
Watford WD17 23 BT40
Strathan Cl, SW18 119 CY86
Strathaven Rd, SE12 124 EH86
Strathblaine Rd, SW11 100 DD84
Strathbrook Rd, SW16 121 DM94
Strathcona Rd, Wem. HA9 61 CK61
Strathdale, SW16 121 DM92
Strathdon Dr, SW17 120 DD90
Strathearn Av, Hayes UB3 95 BT80
Twickenham TW2 116 CB88
Strathearn Pl, W2 194 A10
Strathearn Rd, SW19 120 DA92
Sutton SM1 158 DA106
Stratheden Par, SE3
off Stratheden Rd 104 EG80
Stratheden Rd, SE3 104 EG81
Strathfield Gdns, Bark. IG11 87 ER65
Strathleven Rd, SW2 121 DL85
Strathmore Cl, Cat. CR3 176 DS121
Strathmore Gdns, N3 44 DB53
W8 off Palace Gdns Ter 82 DA74
Edgware HA8 42 CP54
Hornchurch RM12 71 FF60
Strathmore Rd, SW19 120 DA90
Croydon CR0 142 DQ101
Teddington TW11 117 CE91
Strathnairn St, SE1 202 C9
Strathray Gdns, NW3 82 DE65
Strath Ter, SW11 100 DE84
Strathville Rd, SW18 120 DB89
Strathyre Av, SW16 141 DN97
Stratton Av, Enf. EN2 30 DR37
Wallington SM6 159 DK109
Stratton Chase Dr, Ch.St.G.
HP8 36 AU47
Stratton Cl, SW19 140 DA96
Bexleyheath DA7 106 EY83
Edgware HA8 42 CM52
Hounslow TW3 96 BZ81
Walton-on-Thames KT12
off St. Johns Dr 136 BW102
Strattondale St, E14 204 D6
Stratton Dr, Bark. IG11 69 ET64
Stratton Gdns, Sthl. UB1 78 BZ72
Stratton Rd, SW19 140 DA96
Bexleyheath DA7 106 EY83
Romford RM3 52 FN50
Sunbury-on-Thames TW16 135 BT96
Stratton St, W1 199 J2
Stratton Ter, West. TN16
off High St 189 EQ127
Stratton Wk, Rom. RM3 52 FN50
Strauss Rd, W4 98 CR75
Strawberry Cres, St.Alb. (Lon.Col.)
AL2 off Wistaria Dr 9 CH26
Strawberry Flds, Swan. BR8 147 FE95
STRAWBERRY HILL,
Twick. TW1 117 CE90
⇌ Strawberry Hill 117 CE90
Strawberry Hill, Twick. TW1 117 CF90
Strawberry Hill Cl, Twick.
TW1 117 CF90
Strawberry Hill Rd, Twick.
TW1 117 CF90
Strawberry La, Cars. SM5 140 DF104
Strawberry Vale, N2 44 DD53
Twickenham TW1 117 CG90
Straw Cl, Cat. CR3 176 DQ123
Strayfield Rd, Enf. EN2 29 DP37
Streakes Fld Rd, NW2 63 CU61
Stream Cl, W.Byf. (Byfleet)
KT14 152 BK112
Streamdale, SE2 106 EU79
Stream La, Edg. HA8 42 CP50
Streamline Ms, SE22 122 DU88
Streamside Cl, N9 46 DT46
Bromley BR2 144 EG98
Streamway, Belv. DA17 106 FA79
Streatfield Av, E6 87 EM67
Streatfield Rd, Har. HA3 61 CK55
STREATHAM, SW16 121 DL91
⇌ Streatham 121 DL92
Streatham Cl, SW16 121 DL89
⇌ Streatham Common 121 DK94
Streatham Common N,
SW16 121 DL92
Streatham Common S,
SW16 121 DL93
Streatham Ct, SW16 121 DL90
Streatham High Rd, SW16 121 DL92
STREATHAM HILL, SW2 121 DM87
⇌ Streatham Hill 121 DL89
Streatham Hill, SW2 121 DL89
STREATHAM PARK, SW16 121 DJ91
Streatham Pl, SW2 121 DL87
Streatham Rd, SW16 140 DG95
Mitcham CR4 140 DG95
Streatham St, WC1 195 N8
STREATHAM VALE, SW16 121 DK94
Streatham Vale, SW16 121 DJ94
Streathbourne Rd, SW17 120 DG89
Streatley Pl, NW3
off New End 64 DC63

★ Place of interest ⇌ Railway station ⊖ London Underground station DLR Docklands Light Railway station Tra Tramlink station H Hospital Riv Pedestrian ferry landing stage

Streatley Rd, NW6 . . . . .81 CZ66
Street, The, Ashtd. KT21 . . . .172 CL119
Dartford (Hort.Kir.) DA4 . .148 FP98
Kings Langley (Chipper.)
WD4 . . . . .6 BG31
Leatherhead (Fetch.) KT22 . .171 CD122
Streeters La, Wall. SM6 . . . .141 DK104
Streetfield Ms, SE3 . . . . . . .104 EG83
Streimer Rd, E15 . . . . .85 EC68
Strelley Way, W3 . . . . .80 CS73
Stretton Mans, SE8
off Glaisher St 103 EA79
Stretton Pl, Amer. HP6 . . . . .20 AT38
Stretton Rd, Croy. CR0 . . . . .142 DS101
Richmond TW10 . . . . .117 CJ89
Stretton Way, Borwd. WD6 . . .26 CL38
Strickland Av, Dart. DA1 . . . .108 FL83
Strickland Row, SW18 . . . . .120 DD87
Strickland St, SE8 . . . . .103 EA82
Strickland Way, Orp. BR6 . . .163 ET105
Stride Rd, E13 . . . . .86 EF68
Strides Ct, Cher. (Ott.) KT16
off Brox Rd 151 BC107
Strimon Cl, N9 . . . . .46 DW47
Stringhams Copse, Wok.
(Ripley) GU23 . . . . .167 BF124
Stripling Way, Wat. WD18 . . . .23 BU44
Strode Cl, N10 . . . . .44 DG52
Strode Rd, E7 . . . . .68 EG63
N17 . . . . .46 DS54
NW10 . . . . .81 CU65
SW6 . . . . .99 CX80
Strodes Coll La, Egh. TW20 . .113 AZ92
Strodes Cres, Stai. TW18 . . . .114 BJ92
Strode St, Egh. TW20 . . . . . .113 BA91
Strone Rd, E7 . . . . .86 EJ65
E12 . . . . .86 EK65
Strone Way, Hayes UB4 . . . . .78 BY70
Strongbow Cres, SE9 . . . . . .125 EM85
Strongbow Rd, SE9 . . . . . . .125 EM85
Strongbridge Cl, Har. HA2 . . .60 CA60
Stronsa Rd, W12 . . . . .99 CT75
Strood Av, Rom. RM7 . . . . . . .71 FD60
Stroud Cres, SW15 . . . . .119 CU90
STROUDE, Vir.W. GU25 . . . .133 AZ96
Stroude Rd, Egh. TW20 . . . .113 BA93
Virginia Water GU25 . . . . .132 AY98
Stroudes Cl, Wor.Pk. KT4 . . .138 CS101
Stroud Fld, Nthlt. UB5 . . . . . .78 BY65
Stroud Gate, Har. HA2 . . . . . .60 CB63
STROUD GREEN, N4 . . . . . . .65 DM58
Stroud Grn Gdns, Croy. CR0 .142 DW101
Stroud Grn Rd, N4 . . . . .65 DM60
Stroud Grn Way, Croy. CR0 . .142 DV101
Stroudley Wk, E3 . . . . .85 EB69
Stroud Rd, SE25 . . . . .142 DU100
SW19 . . . . .120 DA90
Strouds Cl, Rom. (Chad.Hth)
RM6 . . . . .70 EV57
Stroudwater Pk, Wey. KT13 .153 BP107
Stroud Way, Ashf. TW15
off Courtfield Rd 115 BP93
Strouts Pl, E2 . . . . .197 P2
Struan Gdns, Wok. GU21 . . .166 AY115
Strutton Grd, SW1 . . . . .199 M6
Struttons Av, Grav. (Nthflt)
DA11 . . . . .131 GF89
Strype St, E1 . . . . .197 P7
Stuart Av, NW9 . . . . .63 CU59
W5 .80 CM74
Bromley BR2 . . . . .144 EG102
Harrow HA2 . . . . .60 BZ62
Walton-on-Thames KT12 .135 BV102
Stuart Cl, Brwd. (Pilg.Hat.)
CM15 . . . . .54 FV43
Swanley BR8 . . . . .127 FF94
Uxbridge UB10 . . . . .76 BN65
Stuart Ct, Borwd. (Els.) WD6
off High St 25 CK44
Stuart Cres, N22 . . . . .45 DM53
Croydon CR0 . . . . .143 DZ104
Hayes UB3 . . . . .77 BQ72
Stuart Evans Cl, Well. DA16 .106 EW83
Stuart Gro, Tedd. TW11 . . . . .117 CE92
Stuart Mantle Way, Erith
DA8 . . . . .107 FD80
Stuart Pl, Mitch. CR4 . . . . . .140 DF95
Stuart Rd, NW6 . . . . .82 DA69
SE15 . . . . .102 DW84
SW19 . . . . .120 DA90
W3 .80 CQ74
Barking IG11 . . . . .87 ET66
Barnet EN4 . . . . .44 DE45
Gravesend DA11 . . . . .131 GG86
Grays RM17 . . . . .110 GB78
Harrow HA3 . . . . .41 CF54
Richmond TW10 . . . . .117 CH89
Thornton Heath CR7 . . . . .142 DQ98
Warlingham CR6 . . . . .176 DV120
Welling DA16 . . . . .106 EV81
Stuart Twr, W9 . . . . .82 DC70
Stuart Way, Stai. TW18 . . . . .114 BH93
Virginia Water GU25 . . . . .132 AU97
Waltham Cross (Chsht) EN7 .14 DV31
Stubbers La, Upmin. RM14 . .91 FR65
Stubbins Hall La, Wal.Abb.
EN9 . . . . .15 EB28
Stubbs Cl, NW9 . . . . .62 CQ57
Stubbs Dr, SE16 . . . . .202 D10
Stubbs End Cl, Amer. HP6 . . .20 AS37
Stubbs Hill, Sev. (Knock.)
TN14 . . . . .164 EW113
Stubbs La, Tad. (Lwr Kgswd)
KT20 . . . . .183 CZ128
Stubbs Ms, Dag. RM8
off Marlborough Rd 70 EV63
Stubbs Pt, E13 . . . . .86 EH70
Stubbs Way, SW19
off Ruskin Way 140 DD95
Stubbs Wd, Amer. HP6 . . . . . .20 AS36
Stucley Pl, NW1
off Hawley Cres 83 DH66
Stucley Rd, Houns. TW5 . . . . .96 CC80
Studdridge St, SW6 . . . . . . .100 DA82
Studd St, N1 . . . . .83 DP67
Stud Grn, Wat. WD25 . . . . .7 BV32
Studholme Ct, NW3 . . . . .64 DA63
Studholme St, SE15 . . . . . . .102 DV80
Studio Ms, NW4
off Glebe Cres 63 CW56
Studio Pl, SW1 . . . . .198 E5
Studios, The, Bushey WD23 . .24 CA44
Studios Rd, Shep. TW17 . . . .134 BM97
Studio Way, Borwd. WD6 . . . .26 CQ40
Studland, SE17 . . . . .201 K10
Studland Cl, Sid. DA15 . . . . .125 ET90
Studland Rd, SE26 . . . . .123 DX92
W7 .79 CD72
Kingston upon Thames
KT2 . . . . .118 CL93
West Byfleet (Byfleet)
KT14 . . . . .152 BM113
Studland St, W6 . . . . .99 CV77
Studley Av, E4 . . . . .47 ED52
Studley Cl, E5 . . . . .67 DY64
Studley Ct, E14
off Jamestown Way 85 ED73
Sidcup DA14 . . . . .126 EV92
Studley Dr, Ilf. IG4 . . . . .68 EK58
Studley Est, SW4 . . . . .101 DL81
Studley Gra Rd, W7 . . . . .97 CE75
Studley Rd, E7 . . . . .86 EH65
SW4 . . . . .101 DL81
Dagenham RM9 . . . . .88 EX66
Stukeley Rd, E7 . . . . .86 EH66
Stukeley St, WC1 . . . . .196 A8
WC2 . . . . .196 A8
Stump Rd, Epp. CM16 . . . . . .18 EW27
Stumps Hill La, Beck. BR3 . .123 EA93
Stumps La, Whyt. CR3 . . . . .176 DS117
Sturdy Rd, SE15 . . . . .102 DV82
Sturge Av, E17 . . . . .47 EB54
Sturgeon Rd, SE17 . . . . .102 DQ78
Sturges Fld, Chis. BR7 . . . . .125 ER93
Sturgess Av, NW4 . . . . .63 CV59
Sturge St, SE1 . . . . .201 H4
Sturlas Way, Wal.Cr. EN8 . . . .15 DX33
Sturmer Way, N7 . . . . .65 DM64
Sturminster Cl, Hayes UB4 . . .78 BW72
Sturrock Cl, N15 . . . . .66 DR56
Sturry St, E14 . . . . .85 EB72
Sturts La, Tad. (Walt.Hill)
KT20 . . . . .183 CT127
Sturt St, N1 . . . . .197 J1
Stutfield St, E1 . . . . .84 DU72
Stychens Cl, Red. (Bletch.)
RH1 . . . . .186 DQ133
Stychens La, Red. (Bletch.)
RH1 . . . . .186 DQ132
Stylecroft Rd, Ch.St.G. HP8 . .36 AX47
Styles Gdns, SW9 . . . . .101 DP83
Styles Way, Beck. BR3 . . . . .143 EC98
Styventon Pl, Cher. KT16 . . .133 BF101
Subrosa Dr, Red. (Merst.)
RH1 . . . . .185 DH130
Succombs Hill, Warl. CR6 . . .176 DV120
Whyteleafe CR3 . . . . .176 DV120
Succombs Pl, Warl. CR6 . . . .176 DV120
Sudbourne Rd, SW2 . . . . . . .121 DL85
Sudbrooke Rd, SW12 . . . . . .120 DF86
Sudbrook Gdns, Rich. TW10 .117 CK90
Sudbrook La, Rich. TW10 . . .118 CL88
SUDBURY, Wem. HA0 . . . . . .61 CG64
Sudbury, E6 off Newark Knok .87 EN72
⇌ Sudbury & Harrow Road .61 CH64
Sudbury Av, Wem. HA0 . . . . .61 CK62
Sudbury Ct, SW8
off Allen Edwards Dr 101 DL81
Sudbury Ct Dr, Har. HA1 . . . .61 CF62
Sudbury Ct Rd, Har. HA1 . . . .61 CF62
Sudbury Cres, Brom. BR1 . . .124 EG93
Wembley HA0 . . . . .61 CH64
Sudbury Cft, Wem. HA0 . . . . .61 CF63
Sudbury Gdns, Croy. CR0 . . .160 DS105
Sudbury Hts Av, Grnf. UB6 . . .61 CF64
⊖ Sudbury Hill 61 CE63
Sudbury Hill, Har. HA1 . . . . . .61 CE61
Sudbury Hill Cl, Wem. HA0 . . .61 CF63
⇌ Sudbury Hill Harrow 61 CE63
Sudbury Ho, SW18
off Wandsworth High St .120 DB85
Sudbury Rd, Bark. IG11 . . . . .69 ET64
⊖ Sudbury Town 79 CH65
Sudeley St, N1 . . . . .196 G1
Sudicamps Ct, Wal.Abb. EN9 .16 EG33
Sudlow Rd, SW18 . . . . .100 DA84
Sudrey St, SE1 . . . . .201 H5
Suez Av, Grnf. UB6 . . . . .79 CF68
Suez Rd, Enf. EN3 . . . . .31 DY42
Suffield Cl, S.Croy. CR2 . . . .161 DX112
Suffield Rd, E4 . . . . .47 EB48
N15 . . . . .66 DT57
SE20 . . . . .142 DW96
Suffolk Cl, Borwd. WD6 . . . . .26 CR43
St. Albans (Lon.Col.) AL2 . . .9 CJ25
Suffolk Ct, E10 . . . . .67 EA59
Ilford IG3 . . . . .69 ES58
Suffolk La, EC4 . . . . .197 K10
Suffolk Pk Rd, E17 . . . . .67 DY56
Suffolk Pl, SW1 . . . . .199 N2
Suffolk Rd, E13 . . . . .86 EF69
N15 . . . . .66 DR58
NW10 . . . . .80 CS66
SE25 . . . . .142 DT98
SW13 . . . . .99 CT80
Barking IG11 . . . . .87 ER66
Dagenham RM10 . . . . .71 FC64
Dartford DA1 . . . . .128 FL86
Enfield EN3 . . . . .30 DV43
Gravesend DA12 . . . . .131 GK86
Harrow HA2 . . . . .60 BZ58
Ilford IG3 . . . . .69 ES58
Potters Bar EN6 . . . . .11 CY32
Sidcup DA14 . . . . .126 EW93
Worcester Park KT4 . . . . .139 CT103
Suffolk St, E7 . . . . .68 EG64
SW1 . . . . .199 N2
Suffolk Way, Horn. RM11 . . . .72 FN56
Sevenoaks TN13 . . . . .191 FJ125
Sugar Bakers Ct, EC3
off Creechurch La 84 DS72
Sugar Ho La, E15 . . . . .85 EC68
Sugar Loaf Wk, E2
off Victoria Pk Sq 84 DW69
Sugar Quay Wk, EC3 . . . . . .201 N1
Sugden Rd, SW11 . . . . .100 DG83
Thames Ditton KT7 . . . . . . .137 CH102
Sugden Way, Bark. IG11 . . . . .87 ET68
Sulgrave Gdns, W6
off Sulgrave Rd 99 CW75
Sulgrave Rd, W6 . . . . .99 CW75
Sulina Rd, SW2 . . . . .121 DL87
Sulivan Ct, SW6 . . . . .100 DA83
Sulivan Rd, SW6 . . . . .100 DA83
Sulkin Ho, E2
off Knottisford St 84 DW69
Sullivan Av, E16 . . . . .86 EK71
Sullivan Cl, SW11 . . . . .100 DE83
Dartford DA1 . . . . .127 FH86
Hayes UB4 . . . . .78 BW71
West Molesey KT8
off Victoria Av 136 CA97
Sullivan Cres, Uxb. (Hare.)
UB9 . . . . .38 BK54
Sullivan Ho, SW1
off Churchill Gdns 101 DJ78
Sullivan Rd, SE11 . . . . .200 E8
Tilbury RM18 . . . . .111 GG81
Sullivans Reach, Walt. KT12 .135 BT101
Sullivan Way, Borwd. (Els.)
WD6 . . . . .25 CJ44
Sultan Rd, E11 . . . . .68 EH56
Sultan St, SE5 . . . . .102 DQ80
Beckenham BR3 . . . . .143 DX96
Sultan Ter, N22
off Vincent Rd 45 DN54
Sumatra Rd, NW6 . . . . .64 DA64
Sumburgh Rd, SW12 . . . . . .120 DG86
Sumburgh Way, Slou. SL1 . . .74 AS71
Summer Av, E.Mol. KT8 . . . .137 CE99
Summercourt Rd, E1 . . . . . . .84 DW72
Summer Crossing, T.Ditt.
KT7 . . . . .137 CE98
Summerene Cl, SW16 . . . . . .121 DJ94
Summerfield, Ashtd. KT21 . .171 CK119
Summerfield Av, NW6 . . . . . .81 CY68
Summerfield Cl, Add. KT15
off Spinney Hill 151 BF106
St. Albans (Lon.Col.) AL2 . . .9 CJ26
Summerfield La, Surb. KT6 .137 CK103
Summerfield Pl, Cher. (Ott.)
KT16 off Crawshaw Rd . .151 BD107
Summerfield Rd, W5 . . . . . . .79 CH70
Loughton IG10 . . . . .32 EK44
Watford WD25 . . . . .23 BU35
Summerfields Av, N12 . . . . . .44 DE51
Summerfield St, SE12 . . . . .124 EF87
Summer Gdns, E.Mol. KT8 . .137 CE99
Summer Gro, Borwd. (Els.)
WD6 . . . . .25 CK44
Summerhayes Cl, Wok.
GU21 . . . . .150 AY114
Summerhays, Cob. KT11 . . . .154 BX113
Summer Hill, Borwd. (Els.)
WD6 . . . . .26 CN43
Chislehurst BR7 . . . . .145 EN96
Summerhill Cl, Orp. BR6 . . .145 ES104
Summerhill Gro, Enf. EN1 . . .30 DS44
Summerhill Rd, N15 . . . . .66 DR56
Dartford DA1 . . . . .128 FK87
Summer Hill Vil, Chis. BR7 . .145 EN95
Summerhill Way, Mitch. CR4 .140 DG95
Summerhouse Av, Houns.
TW5 . . . . .96 BY81
Summerhouse Dr, Bex. DA5 .127 FD91
Dartford DA2 . . . . .127 FD91
Summerhouse La, Uxb.
(Hare.) UB9 . . . . .38 BG52
Watford (Ald.) WD25 . . . . . .24 CC40
West Drayton UB7 . . . . . . .94 BK79
Summerhouse Rd, N16 . . . . .66 DS61
Summerhouse Way, Abb.L.
WD5 . . . . .7 BT30
Summerland Gdns, N10 . . . . .65 DH55
Summerlands Av, W3 . . . . . . .80 CQ73
Summerlay Cl, Tad. KT20 . . .173 CY120
Summerlee Av, N2 . . . . .64 DF56
Summerlee Gdns, N2 . . . . . . .64 DF56
Summerley St, SW18 . . . . . .120 DB89
Summerly Av, Reig. RH2
off Burnham Dr 184 DA133
Summer Rd, E.Mol. KT8 . . . .137 CE99
Thames Ditton KT7 . . . . . .137 CF99
Summersby Rd, N6 . . . . .65 DH58
Summers Cl, Sutt. SM2
off Overton Rd 158 DA108
Wembley HA9 . . . . .62 CP60
Weybridge KT13 . . . . .152 BN111
Summerskill Cl, SE15
off Philip Wk 102 DV83
Summerskille Cl, N9
off Plevna Rd 46 DV47
Summers La, N12 . . . . .44 DD52
Summers Row, N12 . . . . .44 DE51
SUMMERSTOWN, SW17 . . . .120 DB90
Summerstown, SW17 . . . . . .120 DC90
Summer St, EC1 . . . . .196 D5
Summerswood Cl, Ken. CR8
off Longwood Rd 176 DR116
Summerswood La, Borwd.
WD6 . . . . .10 CS34
Summerton Way, SE28 . . . . . .88 EX72
Summer Trees, Sun. TW16
off The Avenue 135 BV95
Summerville Gdns, Sutt.
SM1 . . . . .157 CZ107
Summerwood Rd, Islw. TW7 .117 CF85
Summit, The, Loug. IG10 . . . .33 EM39
Summit Av, NW9 . . . . .62 CR57
Summit Cl, N14 . . . . .45 DJ47
NW9 . . . . .62 CR56
Edgware HA8 . . . . .42 CN52
Summit Ct, NW2 . . . . .63 CY64
Summit Dr, Wdf.Grn. IG8 . . . .48 EK54
Summit Est, N16 . . . . .66 DU59
Summit Pl, Wey. KT13
off Caenshill Rd 152 BN108
Summit Rd, E17 . . . . .67 EB56
Northolt UB5 . . . . .78 CA66
Potters Bar EN6 . . . . .11 CY30
Summit Way, N14 . . . . .45 DH47
SE19 . . . . .122 DS94
Sumner Av, SE15
off Peckham Rd 102 DT81
Sumner Cl, Lthd. (Fetch.)
KT22 . . . . .171 CD124
Orpington BR6 . . . . .163 EQ105
Sumner Ct, SW8
off Darsley Dr 101 DL81
Sumner Gdns, Croy. CR0 . . .141 DN102
Sumner Pl, SW7 . . . . .198 A9
Addlestone KT15 . . . . .152 BG106
Sumner Pl Ms, SW7 . . . . . . .198 A9
Sumner Rd, SE15 . . . . .102 DT80
Croydon CR0 . . . . .141 DN102
Harrow HA1 . . . . .60 CC59
Sumner Rd S, Croy. CR0 . . . .141 DN102
Sumner St, SE1 . . . . .200 G2
Sumpter Cl, NW3 . . . . .82 DC65
Sun All, Rich. TW9
off Kew Rd 98 CL84
Sunbeam Cres, W10 . . . . . . .81 CW70
Sunbeam Rd, NW10 . . . . .80 CQ70
SUNBURY, Sun. TW16 . . . . .153 BV107
⇌ Sunbury 135 BT95
Sunbury Av, NW7 . . . . .42 CR50
SW14 . . . . .98 CR84
Sunbury Cl, Walt. KT12 . . . . .135 BU100
Sunbury Ct, Sun. TW16 . . . . .136 BX96
Sunbury Ct Island, Sun.
TW16 . . . . .136 BX97
Sunbury Ct Ms, Sun. TW16
off Lower Hampton Rd . .136 BX96
Sunbury Ct Rd, Sun. TW16 . .136 BW96
Sunbury Cres, Felt. TW13
off Ryland Cl 115 BT91
Sunbury Cross Cen, Sun.
TW16 . . . . .115 BT94
Sunbury Gdns, NW7 . . . . . . .42 CR50
Sunbury La, SW11 . . . . .100 DD81
Walton-on-Thames KT12 .135 BU100
Sunbury Lock Ait, Walt.
KT12 . . . . .135 BV98
Sunbury Rd, Felt. TW13 . . . . .115 BT90
Sutton SM3 . . . . .139 CX104
Sunbury St, SE18 . . . . .105 EM76
Sunbury Way, Felt. TW13 . . . .116 BW92
Sun Ct, EC3 . . . . .197 L9
Erith DA8 . . . . .107 FF82
Suncroft Pl, SE26 . . . . .122 DW90
Sundale Av, S.Croy. CR2 . . . .160 DW110
Sunderland Ct, SE22 . . . . . . .122 DU87
Sunderland Gro, Wat.
(Lvsdn) WD25 . . . . .7 BT34
Sunderland Mt, SE23
off Sunderland Rd 123 DX89
Sunderland Rd, SE23 . . . . . .123 DX88
W5 .97 CK76
Sunderland Ter, W2 . . . . .82 DB72
Sunderland Way, E12 . . . . . . .68 EK61
Sundew Av, W12 . . . . .81 CU73
Sundew Cl, W12
off Sundew Av 81 CU73
Sundew Ct, Grays RM17
off Salix Rd 110 GD79
Sundial Av, SE25 . . . . .142 DT97
Sundon Cres, Vir.W. GU25 . . .132 AV99
Sundorne Rd, SE7 . . . . .104 EH78
Sundown Av, S.Croy. CR2 . . .160 DT111
Sundown Rd, Ashf. TW15 . . . .115 BQ92
Sundra Wk, E1
off Beaumont Gro 85 DX70
SUNDRIDGE, Brom. BR1 . . . .124 EJ93
SUNDRIDGE, Sev. TN14 . . . .180 EZ124
Sundridge Av, Brom. BR1 . . .144 EK95
Chislehurst BR7 . . . . .124 EK94
Welling DA16 . . . . .105 ER82
Sundridge Cl, Dart. DA1 . . . .128 FN86
Sundridge Ho, Brom. BR1
off Burnt Ash La 124 EH92
Sundridge La, Sev. TN14 . . . .180 EV117
⇌ Sundridge Park 124 EH94
Sundridge Pl, Croy. CR0
off Inglis Rd 142 DU102
Sundridge Rd, Croy. CR0 . . .142 DT101
Sevenoaks (Dunt.Grn)
TN14 . . . . .180 FA120
Woking GU22 . . . . .167 BA119
Sunfields Pl, SE3 . . . . .104 EH80
Sunflower Way, Rom. RM3 . . .52 FK53
Sun Hill, Long. (Fawk.Grn)
DA3 . . . . .149 FU104
Woking GU22 . . . . .166 AU121
Sun-In-The-Sands, SE3
off Shooters Hill Rd 104 EH80
Sunken Rd, Croy. CR0 . . . . . .160 DW106
Sunkist Way, Wall. SM6 . . . . .159 DL109
Sunland Av, Bexh. DA6 . . . . .106 EY84
Sun La, SE3 . . . . .104 EH80
Gravesend DA12 . . . . .131 GJ89
Sunleigh Rd, Wem. HA0 . . . . . .80 CL67
Sunley Gdns, Grnf. UB6 . . . . .79 CG67
Sunlight Cl, SW19 . . . . .120 DC93
Sunlight Sq, E2 . . . . .84 DV69
Sunmead Cl, Lthd. (Fetch.)
KT22 . . . . .171 CF122
Sunmead Rd, Sun. TW16 . . . .135 BU97
Sunna Gdns, Sun. TW16 . . . .135 BV96
Sunningdale, N14
off Wilmer Way 45 DK50
Sunningdale Av, W3 . . . . .80 CS73
Barking IG11 . . . . .87 ER67
Feltham TW13 . . . . .116 BY89
Rainham RM13 . . . . .89 FH70
Ruislip HA4 . . . . .60 BW60
Sunningdale Cl, E6 . . . . .87 EM69
SE16 off Ryder Dr 102 DV78
SE28 . . . . .88 EY72
Stanmore HA7 . . . . .41 CG52
Surbiton KT6
off Culsac Rd 138 CL103
Sunningdale Gdns, NW9 . . . .62 CQ57
W8 off Lexham Ms 100 DA76
Sunningdale Rd, Brom. BR1 .144 EL98
Rainham RM13 . . . . .89 FG66
Sutton SM1 . . . . .157 CZ105
Sunningfields Cres, NW4 . . . .43 CV54
Sunningfields Rd, NW4 . . . . .43 CV54
Sunning Hill, Grav. (Nthflt)
DA11 . . . . .130 GE89
Sunninghill Rd, SE13 . . . . . .103 EB82
Sunnings La, Upmin. RM14 . .90 FQ65
Sunningvale Av, West.
(Bigg.H.) TN16 . . . . .178 EJ115
Sunningvale Cl, West.
(Bigg.H.) TN16 . . . . .178 EK116
Sunny Bk, SE25 . . . . .142 DU97
Sunnybank, Epsom KT18 . . .172 CQ116
Sunny Bk, Warl. CR6 . . . . . .177 DY117
Sunnybank Rd, Pot.B. EN6 . . .12 DA33
Sunnybank Vil, Red. RH1 . . .186 DT132
Sunny Cres, NW10 . . . . .80 CQ66
Sunnycroft Gdns, Upmin.
RM14 . . . . .73 FT59
Sunnycroft Rd, SE25 . . . . . . .142 DU97
Hounslow TW3 . . . . .96 CB82
Southall UB1 . . . . .78 CA71
Sunnydale, Orp. BR6 . . . . . .145 EN103
Sunnydale Gdns, NW7 . . . . . .42 CR51
Sunnydale Rd, SE12 . . . . . . .124 EH85
Sunnydell, St.Alb. AL2 . . . . . . .8 CB26
Sunnydene Av, E4 . . . . .47 ED50
Sunnydene Av, Ruis. HA4 . . . .59 BU61
Sunnydene Cl, Rom. RM3 . . . .52 FM52
Sunnydene Gdns, Wem. HA0 .79 CJ65
Sunnydene Rd, Pur. CR8 . . . .159 DP113
Sunnydene St, SE26 . . . . . . .123 DY91
Sunnyfield, NW7 . . . . .43 CT49
Sunnyfield Rd, Chis. BR7 . . .146 EU97
Sunny Gdns Par, NW4
off Great N Way 43 CW54
Sunny Gdns Rd, NW4 . . . . . . .43 CV54
Sunny Hill, NW4 . . . . .63 CV55
Sunnyhill Cl, E5 . . . . .67 DY63
Sunnyhill Rd, SW16 . . . . . . .121 DL91
Rickmansworth (W.Hyde)
WD3 . . . . .37 BD51
Sunnyhurst Cl, Sutt. SM1 . . .140 DA104
Sunnymead Av, Mitch. CR4 .141 DJ97
Sunnymead Rd, NW9 . . . . . . .62 CR59
SW15 . . . . .119 CV85
SUNNYMEADS, Stai. TW19 . .92 AY84
⇌ Sunnymeads 92 AY83
Sunnymede, Chig. IG7 . . . . . .50 EV48
Sunnymede Av, Cars. SM5 . .158 DD111
Chesham HP5 . . . . .4 AS28
Epsom KT19 . . . . .156 CS109
Sunnymede Dr, Ilf. IG6 . . . . . .69 EP56
Sunny Ms, Rom. RM5 . . . . . . .51 FC52
Sunny Nook Gdns, S.Croy.
CR2 . . . . .160 DR107
Sunny Ri, Cat. (Chaldon) CR3 .176 DR124
Sunny Rd, The, Enf. EN3 . . . . .31 DX39
Sunnyside, NW2 . . . . .63 CZ62
SW19 . . . . .119 CY93
Walton-on-Thames KT12 .136 BW99
Sunnyside Cotts, Chesh. HP5 . .4 AU26
Sunnyside Dr, E4 . . . . .47 EC45
Sunnyside Gdns, Upmin.
RM14 . . . . .72 FQ61
Sunnyside Pas, SW19 . . . . . .119 CY93
Sunnyside Pl, SW19
off Sunnyside 119 CY93
Sunnyside Rd, E10 . . . . .67 EA60
N19 . . . . .65 DK59
W5 .79 CK74
Epping CM16 . . . . .17 ET32
Ilford IG1 . . . . .69 EQ62
Teddington TW11 . . . . .117 CD91
Sunnyside Rd E, N9 . . . . .46 DU48
Sunnyside Rd N, N9 . . . . .46 DT48
Sunnyside Rd S, N9 . . . . .46 DT48
Sunnyside Ter, NW9
off Edgware Rd 62 CR55
Sunny Vw, NW9 . . . . .62 CR57
Sunny Way, N12 . . . . .44 DE52
Sun Pas, SE16 . . . . .202 B6
Sunray Av, SE24 . . . . .102 DR84
Brentwood (Hutt.) CM13 . . .55 GE44
Bromley BR2 . . . . .144 EL100
Surbiton KT5 . . . . .138 CP103
West Drayton UB7 . . . . .94 BK75
Sunrise Av, Horn. RM12 . . . . .72 FJ62
Sunrise Cl, Felt. TW13
off Exeter Rd 116 BZ90
Sun Rd, W14 . . . . .99 CZ78
Swanscombe DA10 . . . . . . .130 FZ86
Sunset Av, E4 . . . . .47 EB46
Woodford Green IG8 . . . . . .48 EF49
Sunset Cl, Erith DA8 . . . . . . .107 FH81
Sunset Ct, Wdf.Grn. IG8
off Navestock Cres 48 EJ52
Sunset Dr, Rom. (Hav.at.Bow.)
RM4 . . . . .51 FH50
Sunset Gdns, SE25 . . . . .142 DT96
Sunset Ms, Rom. RM5 . . . . . .51 FC51
Sunset Rd, SE5 . . . . .102 DQ84
SE28 . . . . .106 EU75
Sunset Vw, Barn. EN5 . . . . . . .27 CY40
Sunshine Way, Mitch. CR4 . .140 DF96
Sunstone Gro, Red.
(Merst.) RH1 . . . . .185 DL129
Sun St, EC2 . . . . .197 M7
Waltham Abbey EN9 . . . . . . .15 EC33
Sun Wk, E1 . . . . .202 B1
Sunwell Cl, SE15
off Cossall Wk 102 DV82
Superior Dr, Orp. BR6 . . . . . .163 ET107
SURBITON, KT5 & KT6 . . . . .138 CM101
⇌ Surbiton 137 CK100
Surbiton Ct, Surb. KT6 . . . . .137 CJ100
Surbiton Cres, Kings.T. KT1 .138 CL98
Surbiton Hall Cl, Kings.T.
KT1 . . . . .138 CL98
Surbiton Hill Pk, Surb. KT5 .138 CN99
Surbiton Hill Rd, Surb. KT6 .138 CL98
H Surbiton Hosp,
Surb. KT6 . . . . .138 CL100
Surbiton Par, Surb. KT6
off St. Mark's Hill 138 CL100
Surbiton Rd, Kings.T. KT1 . . .138 CL98
Surlingham Cl, SE28 . . . . .88 EX73
Surma Cl, E1 . . . . .84 DV70
Surman Cres, Brwd. (Hutt.)
CM13 . . . . .55 GC45
Surmans Cl, Dag. RM9 . . . . . .88 EW67
Surrendale Pl, W9 . . . . .82 DA70
Surrey Canal Rd, SE14 . . . . .102 DW79
SE15 . . . . .102 DW79
Surrey Cl, N3 . . . . .63 CY55
Surrey Cres, W4 . . . . .98 CN78
★ Surrey Docks City Fm,
SE16 . . . . .203 M5
Surrey Dr, Horn. RM11 . . . . . .72 FN56
Surrey Gdns, N4
off Finsbury Pk Av 66 DQ58
Leatherhead (Eff.Junct.)
KT24 . . . . .169 BT123
Surrey Gro, SE17 off Alvey St .102 DS78
Sutton SM1 . . . . .140 DD104
Surrey Hills, Tad. (Box H.)
KT20 . . . . .182 CP130
Surrey Hills Av, Tad. (Box H.)
KT20 . . . . .182 CQ130
Surrey La, SW11 . . . . .100 DE81
Surrey La Est, SW11 . . . . . . .100 DE81
Surrey Lo, SE1 . . . . .200 D7
Surrey Ms, SE27
off Hamilton Rd 122 DS91

Surrey Mt, SE23 . . . . .122 DV88
⊖ Surrey Quays 203 H8
Surrey Quays Retail Cen,
SE16 . . . . .203 H7
Surrey Quays Rd, SE16 . . . . .202 G6
Surrey Rd, SE15 . . . . .123 DX85
Barking IG11 . . . . .87 ES67
Dagenham RM10 . . . . .71 FB64
Harrow HA1 . . . . .60 CC57
West Wickham BR4 . . . . . .143 EB102
Surrey Row, SE1 . . . . .200 F4
Surrey Sq, SE17 . . . . .201 M10
Surrey St, E13 . . . . .86 EH69
WC2 . . . . .196 C10
Croydon CR0 . . . . .142 DQ104
Surrey Ter, SE17 . . . . .201 N10
Surrey Twrs, Add. KT15
off Garfield Rd 152 BJ106
Surrey Water Rd, SE16 . . . . .203 J3
Surridge Cl, Rain. RM13 . . . . .90 FJ69
Surridge Gdns, SE19
off Hancock Rd 122 DR93
Surr St, N7 . . . . .65 DL64
Sury Basin, Kings.T. KT2 . . . .138 CL95
Susan Cl, Rom. RM7 . . . . .71 FC55
Susan Constant Ct, E14
off Newport Av 85 ED73
Susan Lawrence Ho, E12
off Walton Rd 69 EN63
Susannah St, E14 . . . . .85 EB72
Susan Rd, SE3 . . . . .104 EH82
Susan Wd, Chis. BR7 . . . . . .145 EN95
Sussex Av, Islw. TW7 . . . . . . .97 CE83
Romford RM3 . . . . .52 FM52
Sussex Cl, N19
off Cornwallis Rd 65 DL61
Chalfont St. Giles HP8 . . . .36 AV47
Ilford IG4 . . . . .69 EM58
New Malden KT3 . . . . .138 CS98
Slough SL1 . . . . .92 AV75
Twickenham TW1
off Westmorland Cl 117 CH86
Sussex Cres, Nthlt. UB5 . . . . .78 CA65
Sussex Gdns, N4 . . . . .66 DQ57
N6 .64 DF57
W2 .82 DD72
Chessington KT9 . . . . .155 CK107
Sussex Keep, Slou. SL1
off Sussex Cl 92 AV75
Sussex Ms, SE6
off Ravensbourne Pk 123 EA87
Sussex Ms E, W2 . . . . .194 A9
Sussex Ms W, W2 . . . . .194 A10
Sussex Pl, NW1 . . . . .194 D3
W2 . . . . .194 A9
W6 .99 CW78
Erith DA8 . . . . .107 FB80
New Malden KT3 . . . . .138 CS98
Slough SL1 . . . . .92 AV75
Sussex Ring, N12 . . . . .44 DA50
Sussex Rd, E6 . . . . .87 EN67
Brentwood CM14 . . . . .54 FV49
Carshalton SM5 . . . . .158 DF107
Dartford DA1 . . . . .128 FN87
Erith DA8 . . . . .107 FB80
Harrow HA1 . . . . .60 CC57
Mitcham CR4 off Lincoln Rd .141 DL99
New Malden KT3 . . . . .138 CS98
Orpington BR5 . . . . .146 EW100
Sidcup DA14 . . . . .126 EV92
South Croydon CR2 . . . . .160 DR107
Southall UB2 . . . . .96 BX76
Uxbridge UB10 . . . . .59 BQ63
Watford WD24 . . . . .23 BU38
West Wickham BR4 . . . . . .143 EB102
Sussex Sq, W2 . . . . .194 A10
Sussex St, E13 . . . . .86 EH69
SW1 . . . . .101 DH78
Sussex Way, N7 . . . . .65 DL61
N19 . . . . .65 DL60
Barnet EN4 . . . . .28 DG43
Uxbridge (Denh.) UB9 . . . .57 BF57
Sutcliffe Cl, NW11 . . . . .64 DB57
Bushey WD23 . . . . .24 CC42
Sutcliffe Ho, Hayes UB3 . . . . .77 BU72
Sutcliffe Rd, SE18 . . . . .105 ES79
Welling DA16 . . . . .106 EW82
Sutherland Av, W9 . . . . .82 DC69
W13 . . . . .79 CH72
Hayes UB3 . . . . .95 BU77
Orpington BR5 . . . . .145 ET100
Potters Bar (Cuffley) EN6 . .13 DK28
Sunbury-on-Thames TW16 .135 BT96
Welling DA16 . . . . .105 ES84
Westerham (Bigg.H.) TN16 . .178 EK117
Sutherland Cl, Barn. EN5 . . . .27 CY42
Greenhithe DA9 . . . . .129 FT85
Sutherland Ct, NW9 . . . . .62 CP57
Sutherland Dr, SW19 . . . . . .140 DD95
Sutherland Gdns, SW14 . . . . .98 CS83
Sunbury-on-Thames TW16
off Sutherland Av 135 BT96
Worcester Park KT4 . . . . . .139 CV102
Sutherland Gro, SW18 . . . . .119 CY86
Teddington TW11 . . . . .117 CE92
Sutherland Pl, W2 . . . . .82 DA72
Sutherland Rd, E17 . . . . .47 DX54
N9 .46 DU46
N17 . . . . .46 DU52
W4 .98 CS79
W13 . . . . .79 CG72
Belvedere DA17 . . . . .106 FA76
Croydon CR0 . . . . .141 DN101
Enfield EN3 . . . . .31 DX43
Southall UB1 . . . . .78 BZ72
Sutherland Rd Path, E17 . . . . .67 DX55
Sutherland Row, SW1 . . . . . .199 J10
Sutherland Sq, SE17 . . . . . .102 DQ78
Sutherland St, SW1 . . . . . . .199 H10
Sutherland Wk, SE17 . . . . . .102 DQ78
Sutherland Way, Pot.B.
(Cuffley) EN6 . . . . .13 DK28
Sutlej Rd, SE7 . . . . .104 EJ80
Sutterton St, N7 . . . . .83 DM65
SUTTON, SM1 - SM3 . . . . . .158 DB107
⇌ Sutton 158 DC107
SUTTON AT HONE,
Dart. DA4 . . . . .148 FN95
Sutton Av, Slou. SL3 . . . . .92 AW75
Woking GU21 . . . . .166 AS119
Sutton Cl, Beck. BR3 . . . . . . .143 EB95
Loughton IG10 . . . . .48 EL45
Pinner HA5 . . . . .59 BU57
⇌ Sutton Common 140 DB103
Sutton Common Rd, Sutt.
SM1, SM3 . . . . .139 CZ101
Sutton Ct, W4 . . . . .98 CQ79
Sutton SM2 . . . . .158 DC107
Sutton Ct Rd, E13 . . . . .86 EJ69
W4 .98 CQ80
Sutton SM1 . . . . .158 DC107
Uxbridge UB10 . . . . .77 BP67
Sutton Cres, Barn. EN5 . . . . . .27 CX43
Sutton Dene, Houns. TW3 . . . .96 CB81
Sutton Est, SW3 . . . . .198 C10
W10 . . . . .81 CW71
Sutton Est, The, N1 . . . . .83 DP66
Sutton Gdns, Bark. IG11
off Sutton Rd 87 ES67
Croydon CR0 . . . . .142 DT99
Redhill (Merst.) RH1 . . . . .185 DK129
Sutton Grn, Bark. IG11
off Sutton Rd 87 ES67
Sutton Gro, Sutt. SM1 . . . . .158 DD105
Sutton Hall Rd, Houns. TW5 . .96 CA80
★ Sutton Heritage Cen,
Cars. SM5 . . . . .158 DF105
H Sutton Hosp, Sutt. SM2 .158 DB110
★ Sutton Ho, E9 . . . . .66 DW64
Sutton La, EC1 . . . . .196 G5
Banstead SM7 . . . . .174 DB115
Hounslow TW3 . . . . .96 BZ83
Slough SL3 . . . . .93 BC78
Sutton SM2 . . . . .158 DB111
Sutton La N, W4 . . . . .98 CQ78
Sutton La S, W4 . . . . .98 CQ79
Sutton Par, NW4
off Church Rd 63 CW56
Sutton Pk Rd, Sutt. SM1 . . . .158 DB107
Sutton Path, Borwd. WD6
off Stratfield Rd 26 CN40
Sutton Pl, E9 . . . . .66 DW64
Dartford DA4 . . . . .128 FN92
Slough SL3 . . . . .93 BB79
Sutton Rd, E13 . . . . .86 EF70
E17 . . . . .47 DX53
N10 . . . . .44 DG54
Barking IG11 . . . . .87 ES68
Hounslow TW5 . . . . .96 CA81
Watford WD17 . . . . .24 BW41
Sutton Row, W1 . . . . .195 N8
Suttons Av, Horn. RM12 . . . . .72 FJ62
Suttons Gdns, Horn. RM12 . . .72 FK62
Suttons La, Horn. RM12 . . . . .72 FK64
Sutton Sq, E9 off Urswick Rd .66 DW64
Hounslow TW5 . . . . .96 BZ81
Sutton St, E1 . . . . .84 DW72
Sutton's Way, EC1 . . . . .197 J5
Sutton Wk, SE1 . . . . .200 C3
Sutton Way, W10 . . . . .81 CW71
Hounslow TW5 . . . . .96 BZ81
Swabey Rd, Slou. SL3 . . . . . . .93 BA77
Swaby Rd, SW18 . . . . .120 DC88
Swaffham Way, N22
off White Hart La 45 DP52
Swaffield Rd, SW18 . . . . . . .120 DB87
Sevenoaks TN13 . . . . .191 FJ122
Swain Cl, SW16 . . . . .121 DH93
Swain Rd, Th.Hth. CR7 . . . . .142 DQ99
Swains Cl, West Dr. UB7 . . . . .94 BL75
Swains La, N6 . . . . .64 DG62
Swainson Rd, W3 . . . . .99 CT75
Swains Rd, SW17 . . . . .120 DF94
Swain St, NW8 . . . . .194 B4
Swaisland Dr, Dart. (Cray.)
DA1 . . . . .127 FF85
Swaisland Rd, Dart. DA1 . . .127 FH85
Swakeleys Dr, Uxb. UB10 . . . .58 BM63
Swakeleys Rd, Uxb. (Ickhm)
UB10 . . . . .58 BM62
Swakeleys Rbt, Uxb. UB9 . . . .58 BL63
Swale Cl, S.Ock. (Aveley)
RM15 . . . . .90 FQ72
Swaledale Cl, N11
off Ribblesdale Av 44 DG51
Swaledale Rd, Dart. DA2 . . .128 FQ88
Swale Rd, Dart. DA1 . . . . . . .107 FG83
Swallands Rd, SE6 . . . . .123 EA90
Swallow Cl, SE14 . . . . .102 DW81
Bushey WD23 . . . . .40 CC46
Erith DA8 . . . . .107 FE81
Grays (Chaff.Hun.) RM16 . .109 FW77
Greenhithe DA9 . . . . .129 FT85
Rickmansworth WD3 . . . . . .38 BJ45
Staines TW18 . . . . .113 BF91
Swallowdale, Iver SL0 . . . . . .75 BD69
South Croydon CR2 . . . . . .161 DX109
Swallow Dr, NW10
off Kingfisher Way 80 CR65
Northolt UB5 . . . . .78 CA68
Swallowfield, NW1
off Munster Sq 83 DH69
Egham (Eng.Grn) TW20
off Heronfield 112 AV93
Swallowfield Rd, SE7 . . . . . .104 EH78
Swallowfields, Grav. (Nthflt)
DA11 off Hillary Av 130 GE90
Swallowfield Way, Hayes UB3 .95 BR75
Swallow Gdns, SW16 . . . . . .121 DK92
Swallow Ho, NW8
off Allitsen Rd 82 DE68
Swallow Oaks, Abb.L. WD5 . . . .7 BT31
Swallow Pas, W1
off Oxford St 83 DH72
Swallow Pl, W1 . . . . .195 J9
Swallow St, E6 . . . . .86 EL71
W1 . . . . .199 L1
Iver SL0 . . . . .75 BD69
Swallowtail Cl, Orp. BR5 . . . .146 EX98
Swallow Wk, Horn. RM12
off Heron Flight Av 89 FH65
Swanage Ho, SW8
off Dorset Rd 101 DM80
Swanage Rd, E4 . . . . .47 EC52
SW18 . . . . .120 DC86
Swanage Waye, Hayes UB4 . .78 BW72
Swan & Pike Rd, Enf. EN3 . . . .31 EA38
Swan App, E6 . . . . .86 EL71
Swan Av, Upmin. RM14 . . . . .73 FT60
Swanbourne Dr, Horn. RM12 .72 FJ64
Swanbridge Rd, Bexh. DA7 . .106 FA81
Swan Business Pk, Dart.
DA1 . . . . .108 FK84
Swan Cl, E17 . . . . .47 DY53
Croydon CR0 . . . . .142 DS101
Feltham TW13 . . . . .116 BY91
Orpington BR5 . . . . .146 EU97
Rickmansworth WD3
off Parsonage Rd 38 BK45
Swan Ct, SW3 off Flood St . .100 DE78
Swandon Way, SW18 . . . . . .100 DB84
Swan Dr, NW9 . . . . .42 CS54
Swanfield Rd, Wal.Cr. EN8 . . .15 DY33
Swanfield St, E2 . . . . .197 P3
Swanland Rd, Hat. (N.Mymms)
AL9 . . . . .11 CV28
Potters Bar (S.Mimms) EN6 . .11 CV33
Swan La, EC4 . . . . .201 K1
N20 . . . . .44 DC48
Dartford DA1 . . . . .127 FF87
Loughton IG10 . . . . .48 EJ45
SWANLEY, BR8 . . . . .147 FE98
⇌ Swanley 147 FD98
Swanley Bar La, Pot.B. EN6 . .12 DB28
Swanley Bypass, Sid. DA14 .147 FC97
Swanley BR8 . . . . .147 FC97
Swanley Cen, Swan. BR8 . . .147 FE97
Swanley Cres, Pot.B. EN6 . . . .12 DB29
Swanley La, Swan. BR8 . . . .147 FF97
Swanley Rd, Well. DA16 . . . .106 EW81
SWANLEY VILLAGE, Swan.
BR8 . . . . .148 FJ95
Swanley Village Rd, Swan.
BR8 . . . . .147 FH95
Swan Mead, SE1 . . . . .201 M7
Hemel Hempstead HP3 . . . . .6 BM25
Swan Ms, SW6
off Purser's Cross Rd 100 DA81
Romford RM7 . . . . .71 FB56
Swan Pas, E1
off Cartwright St 84 DT73
Swan Path, E10 off Jesse Rd .67 EC60
Swan Pl, SW13 . . . . .99 CT82
Swan Rd, SE16 . . . . .202 G4
SE18 . . . . .104 EK76
Feltham TW13 . . . . .116 BY92
Iver SL0 . . . . .75 BF72
Southall UB1 . . . . .78 CB72
West Drayton UB7 . . . . .94 BK75
SWANSCOMBE, DA10 . . . . . .130 FZ86
⇌ Swanscombe 130 FZ85
Swanscombe Ho, W11
off St. Anns Rd 81 CX74
Swanscombe Rd, W4 . . . . . . .98 CS78
W11 . . . . .81 CX74
Swanscombe St, Swans.
DA10 . . . . .130 FY87
Swansea Ct, E16
off Fishguard Way 87 EP74
Swansea Rd, Enf. EN3 . . . . . .30 DW42
Hounslow (Hthrw Air.) TW6
off Southern Perimeter Rd .115 BQ86
Swanshope, Loug. IG10 . . . . .33 EP40
Swansland Gdns, E17
off McEntee Av 47 DY53
Swanston Path, Wat. WD19 . .40 BW48
Swan St, SE1 . . . . .201 J6
Isleworth TW7 . . . . .97 CH83
Swanton Gdns, SW19 . . . . . .119 CX88
Swanton Rd, Erith DA8 . . . . .107 FB80
Swan Wk, SW3 . . . . .100 DF79
Shepperton TW17 . . . . . . .135 BS101
Swan Way, Enf. EN3 . . . . .31 DX40
Swanwick Cl, SW15 . . . . . . .119 CT87
Swan Yd, N1
off Highbury Sta Rd 83 DP65
Sward Rd, Orp. BR5 . . . . . . .146 EU100
Swaton Rd, E3 . . . . .85 EA70
Swaylands Rd, Belv. DA17 . . .106 FA79
Swaynesland Rd, Eden.
(Crock.H.) TN8 . . . . .189 EM134
Swaythling Cl, N18 . . . . .46 DV49
Swaythling Ho, SW15
off Tunworth Cres 119 CT86
Swedenborg Gdns, E1 . . . . . .84 DU73
Sweden Gate, SE16 . . . . . . .203 K7
Sweeney Cres, SE1 . . . . .202 A5
Sweeps Ditch Cl, Stai. TW18 .134 BG95
Sweeps La, Egh. TW20 . . . . .113 AZ92
Orpington BR5 . . . . .146 EX99
Sweet Briar Grn, N9 . . . . .46 DT48
Sweet Briar Gro, N9 . . . . .46 DT48
Sweet Briar La, Epsom KT18 .156 CR114
Sweet Briar Wk, N18 . . . . . . .46 DT49
Sweetcroft La, Uxb. UB10 . . . .76 BN66
Sweetmans Av, Pnr. HA5 . . . .60 BX55
Sweets Way, N20 . . . . .44 DD47
Swetenham Wk, SE18
off Sandbach Pl 105 EQ78
Swete St, E13 . . . . .86 EG68
Sweyne Rd, Swans. DA10 . . .130 FY86
Sweyn Pl, SE3 . . . . .104 EG82
Swievelands Rd, West.
(Bigg.H.) TN16 . . . . .178 EH119
Swift Cl, E17 . . . . .47 DY52
Harrow HA2 . . . . .60 CB61
Hayes UB3 off Church Rd . . .77 BT72
Upminster RM14 . . . . .73 FS60
Swift Rd, Felt. TW13 . . . . . . .116 BY90
Southall UB2 . . . . .96 BZ76
Swiftsden Way, Brom. BR1 . .124 EE93
Swift St, SW6 . . . . .99 CZ81
Swiftsure Rd, Grays (Chaff.Hun.)
RM16 . . . . .109 FW77
SWILLET, THE, Rick. WD3 . . . .21 BB44
Swinbrook Rd, W10 . . . . .81 CY71
Swinburne Ct, SE5
off Basingdon Way 102 DR84
Swinburne Cres, Croy. CR0 .142 DW100
Swinburne Gdns, Til. RM18 . .111 GH82
Swinburne Rd, SW15 . . . . . . .99 CU84
Swinderby Rd, Wem. HA0 . . . .80 CL65
Swindon Cl, Ilf. IG3
off Salisbury Rd 69 ES61
Romford RM3 . . . . .52 FM50
Swindon Gdns, Rom. RM3 . . . .52 FM50
Swindon La, Rom. RM3 . . . . .52 FM50
Swindon Rd, Houns. (Hthrw Air.)
TW6 . . . . .115 BQ85
Swindon St, W12 . . . . .81 CV74
Swinfield Cl, Felt. TW13 . . . . .116 BY91
Swinford Gdns, SW9 . . . . . . .101 DP83
Swingate La, SE18 . . . . .105 ES79
Swinnerton St, E9 . . . . .67 DY64
Swinton Cl, Wem. HA9 . . . . . .62 CP60
Swinton Pl, WC1 . . . . .196 B2
Swinton St, WC1 . . . . .196 B2
Swires Shaw, Kes. BR2 . . . . .162 EK105
Swiss Av, Wat. WD18 . . . . . . .23 BS42
Swiss Cl, Wat. WD18 . . . . . . .23 BS41
⊖ Swiss Cottage 82 DD66
Swiss Ct, W1 . . . . .199 N1
Swiss Ter, NW6 . . . . .82 DD66
Switch Ho, E14
off Blackwall Way 85 ED73
Swithland Gdns, SE9 . . . . . .125 EN91
Swyncombe Av, W5 . . . . .97 CH77
Swynford Gdns, NW4
off Handowe Cl 63 CU56
Sybil Ms, N4
off Lothair Rd N 65 DP58
Sybil Phoenix Cl, SE8 . . . . . .203 J10
Sybourn St, E17 . . . . .67 DZ59
Sycamore App, Rick. (Crox.Grn)
WD3 . . . . .23 BQ43
Sycamore Av, E3 . . . . .85 DZ67
W5 .97 CK76
Hayes UB3 . . . . .77 BS73
Sidcup DA15 . . . . .125 ET86
Upminster RM14 . . . . .72 FN62
Sycamore Cl, E16
off Clarence Rd 86 EE70
N9 off Pycroft Way 46 DU49
SE9 . . . . .124 EL89
W3 off Bromyard Av 80 CS74
Barnet EN4 . . . . .28 DD44
Bushey WD23 . . . . .24 BY40
Carshalton SM5 . . . . .158 DF105
Chalfont St. Giles HP8 . . . .36 AU48
Edgware HA8 off Ash Cl 42 CQ49
Feltham TW13 . . . . .115 BU90
Gravesend DA12 . . . . .131 GK87
Leatherhead (Fetch.) KT22 . .171 CE123
Loughton IG10 . . . . .33 EP40
Northolt UB5 . . . . .78 BY67
South Croydon CR2 . . . . .160 DS106
Waltham Cross EN7 . . . . . .14 DT27
Watford WD25 . . . . .23 BV35
West Drayton UB7
off Whitethorn Av 76 BM73
Sycamore Ct, Surb. KT6
off Penners Gdns 138 CL101
Sycamore Dr, Brwd. CM14
off Copperfield Gdns 54 FW46
St. Albans (Park St) AL2 . . . .9 CD27
Swanley BR8 . . . . .147 FE97
Sycamore Gdns, W6 . . . . .99 CV75
Mitcham CR4 . . . . .140 DD96
Sycamore Gro, NW9 . . . . .62 CQ59
SE6 . . . . .123 EC86
SE20 . . . . .122 DU94
New Malden KT3 . . . . .138 CR97
Romford RM2 . . . . .51 FG54
Sycamore Hill, N11 . . . . .44 DG51
Sycamore Ho, NW3
off Maitland Pk Vil 82 DF65
Warlingham CR6
off East Parkside 177 EB115
Sycamore Ms, SW4 . . . . .101 DJ83
Sycamore Ri, Bans. SM7 . . . .157 CX114
Chalfont St. Giles HP8 . . . .36 AU48
Sycamore Rd, SW19 . . . . . . .119 CW93
Chalfont St. Giles HP8 . . . .36 AU48
Dartford DA1 . . . . .128 FK88
Rickmansworth (Crox.Grn)
WD3 . . . . .23 BQ43
Sycamores, The, Lthd.
(Bkhm) KT23 . . . . .170 CC124
Radlett WD7 off The Avenue . .9 CH34
South Ockendon (Aveley)
RM15 off Dacre Av 91 FR74
Sycamore St, EC1 . . . . .197 H5
Sycamore Wk, W10
off Fifth Av 81 CY70
Egham (Eng.Grn) TW20 . . .112 AV93
Ilford IG6 off Civic Way 69 EQ56
Slough (Geo.Grn) SL3 . . . . .74 AY72
Sycamore Way, S.Ock. RM15 .91 FX70
Teddington TW11 . . . . .117 CJ93
Thornton Heath CR7 . . . . . .141 DN99
SYDENHAM, SE26 . . . . .122 DW92
⇌ Sydenham 122 DW91
Sydenham Av, N21
off Fleming Dr 29 DM43
SE26 . . . . .122 DV92
Sydenham Cl, Rom. RM1 . . . . .71 FF56
Sydenham Cotts, SE12 . . . . .124 EJ89
⇌ Sydenham Hill 122 DT90
Sydenham Hill, SE23 . . . . . .122 DV88
SE26 . . . . .122 DU90
Sydenham Hill Est, SE26 . . .122 DU90
Sydenham Pk, SE26 . . . . . . .122 DW90
Sydenham Pk Rd, SE26 . . . .122 DW90
Sydenham Ri, SE23 . . . . . . .122 DV89
Sydenham Rd, SE26 . . . . . . .122 DW92
Croydon CR0 . . . . .142 DR101
Sydmons Ct, SE23 . . . . .122 DW87
Sydner Ms, N16
off Sydner Rd 66 DT63
Sydner Rd, N16 . . . . .66 DT63
Sydney Av, Pur. CR8 . . . . . . .159 DM112
Sydney Chapman Way, Barn.
EN5 . . . . .27 CZ40
Sydney Cl, SW3 . . . . .198 A9
Sydney Cres, Ashf. TW15 . . . .115 BP93
Sydney Gro, NW4 . . . . .63 CW57
Sydney Ms, SW3 . . . . .198 A9
Sydney Pl, SW7 . . . . .198 A9
Sydney Rd, E11
off Mansfield Rd 68 EH58
N8 .65 DN56
N10 . . . . .44 DG53
SE2 . . . . .106 EW76
SW20 . . . . .139 CX96
W13 . . . . .79 CG74
Bexleyheath DA6 . . . . .106 EX84
Enfield EN2 . . . . .30 DR42
Feltham TW14 . . . . .115 BU88
Ilford IG6 . . . . .49 EQ54
Richmond TW9 . . . . .98 CL84
Sidcup DA14 . . . . .125 ES91
Sutton SM1 . . . . .158 DA105
Teddington TW11 . . . . .117 CF92
Tilbury RM18 . . . . .111 GG82
Watford WD18 . . . . .23 BS43
Woodford Green IG8 . . . . . .48 EG49
Sydney St, SW3 . . . . .198 B10
Syke Cluan, Iver SL0 . . . . .93 BE75
Syke Ings, Iver SL0 . . . . .93 BE76
Sykes Dr, Stai. TW18 . . . . . .114 BH92
Sylvana Cl, Uxb. UB10 . . . . . .76 BM67
Sylvan Av, N3 . . . . .44 DA54
N22 . . . . .45 DM52
NW7 . . . . .43 CT51
Hornchurch RM11 . . . . .72 FL58
Romford RM6 . . . . .70 EZ58
Sylvan Cl, Grays (Chaff.Hun.)
RM16 . . . . .110 FY77
Oxted RH8 . . . . .188 EH129
South Croydon CR2 . . . . .160 DV110
Woking GU22 . . . . .167 BB117
Sylvan Ct, N12 . . . . .44 DB49
Sylvan Est, SE19 . . . . .142 DT95
Sylvan Gdns, Surb. KT6 . . . .137 CK101
Sylvan Gro, NW2 . . . . .63 CX63
SE15 . . . . .102 DV80
Sylvan Hill, SE19 . . . . .142 DS95
Sylvan Ms, Green. DA9
off Watermans Way 109 FV84
Sylvan Rd, E7 . . . . .86 EG65
E11 . . . . .68 EG57
E17 . . . . .67 EA57
SE19 . . . . .142 DT95
Ilford IG1
off Hainault St 69 EQ61
Sylvan Wk, Brom. BR1 . . . . .145 EM97
Sylvan Way, Chig. IG7 . . . . . . .50 EV48
Dagenham RM8 . . . . .70 EV62
West Wickham BR4 . . . . . .162 EE105
Sylverdale Rd, Croy. CR0 . . .141 DP104
Purley CR8 . . . . .159 DP113
Sylvester Av, Chis. BR7 . . . . .125 EM93
Sylvester Gdns, Ilf. IG6 . . . . . .50 EV50
Sylvester Path, E8
off Sylvester Rd 84 DV65
Sylvester Rd, E8 . . . . .84 DV65
E17 . . . . .67 DZ59
N2 .44 DC54
Wembley HA0 . . . . .61 CJ64
Sylvestres, Sev. (Rvrhd) TN13 .190 FD121
Sylvestrus Cl, Kings.T. KT1 . .138 CN95
Sylvia Av, Brwd. (Hutt.) CM13 . .55 GC47
Pinner HA5 . . . . .40 BZ51
Sylvia Ct, Wem. HA9
off Harrow Rd 80 CP66
Sylvia Gdns, Wem. HA9 . . . . .80 CP66
Symes Ms, NW1
off Camden High St 83 DJ68
Symington Ho, SE1
off Deverell St 102 DR76
Symington Ms, E9
off Coopersale Rd 67 DX64
Symister Ms, N1 . . . . .197 M3
Symonds Ct, Wal.Cr. (Chsht)
EN8 off High St 15 DX28
Symons Cl, SE15
off Kimberley Av 102 DW82
Symons St, SW3 . . . . .198 E9
Symphony Cl, Edg. HA8 . . . . .42 CP52
Symphony Ms, W10
off Third Av 81 CY69
Syon Gate Way, Brent. TW8 . .97 CG80
★ Syon Ho & Pk, Brent. TW8 .97 CJ81
⇌ Syon Lane 97 CG80
Syon La, Islw. TW7 . . . . .97 CH80
Syon Pk Gdns, Islw. TW7 . . . .97 CF80
Syon Vista, Rich. TW9 . . . . . .97 CK81
Syracuse Av, Rain. RM13 . . . .90 FL69
Syringa Ct, Grays RM17 . . . .110 GD80
Sythwood, Wok. GU21 . . . . .166 AV117

T

Tabard Cen, SE1
off Prioress St 102 DR76
Tabard Gdn Est, SE1 . . . . . .201 L5
Tabard St, SE1 . . . . .201 K5
Tabarin Way, Epsom KT17 . . .173 CW116
Tabernacle Av, E13
off Barking Rd 86 EG70
Tabernacle St, EC2 . . . . .197 L5
Tableer Av, SW4 . . . . .121 DK85
Tabley Rd, N7 . . . . .65 DL63
Tabor Gdns, Sutt. SM3 . . . . .157 CZ107
Tabor Gro, SW19 . . . . .119 CY94
Tabor Rd, W6 . . . . .99 CV76
Tabors Ct, Brwd. (Shenf.) CM15
off Shenfield Rd 55 FZ45
Tabrums Way, Upmin. RM14 .73 FS59
Tachbrook Est, SW1 . . . . . . .101 DK78
Tachbrook Ms, SW1 . . . . . . .199 K8
Tachbrook Rd, Felt. TW14 . . .115 BT87
Southall UB2 . . . . .96 BX77
Uxbridge UB8 . . . . .76 BJ68
Tachbrook St, SW1 . . . . .199 L9
Tack Ms, SE4 . . . . .103 EA83
Tadema Ho, NW8 . . . . .194 A5
Tadema Rd, SW10 . . . . .100 DC80
Tadlows Cl, Upmin. RM14 . . . .72 FP64
Tadmor Cl, Sun. TW16 . . . . . .135 BT98
Tadmor St, W12 . . . . .81 CX74
Tadorne Rd, Tad. KT20 . . . . .173 CW121
TADWORTH, KT20 . . . . .173 CV121
⇌ Tadworth 173 CW122
Tadworth Av, N.Mal. KT3 . . . .139 CT99
Tadworth Cl, Tad. KT20 . . . . .173 CX122
Tadworth Par, Horn. RM12
off Maylands Av 71 FH63
Tadworth Rd, NW2 . . . . .63 CU61
Tadworth St, Tad. KT20 . . . . .173 CW123
Taeping St, E14 . . . . .204 B8
Taffy's How, Mitch. CR4 . . . .140 DE97
Taft Way, E3 off Franklin St . . .85 EB69
Tagalie Pl, Rad. (Shenley) WD7
off Porters Pk Dr 10 CL32
Tagg's Island, Hmptn. TW12 .137 CD96
Tailworth St, E1
off Chicksand St 84 DU71
Tait Ct, SW8
off Hartington Rd 101 DL81
Tait Rd, Croy. CR0 . . . . .142 DS101
Takeley Cl, Rom. RM5 . . . . . . .51 FD54
Waltham Abbey EN9 . . . . . . .15 ED33
Takhar Ms, SW11
off Cabul Rd 100 DE82
Talacre Rd, NW5 . . . . .82 DG65
Talbot Av, N2 . . . . .64 DD55

★ Place of interest   ⇌ Railway station   ⊖ London Underground station   DLR Docklands Light Railway station   Tra Tramlink station   H Hospital   Riv Pedestrian ferry landing stage

Talbot Av, Slough SL3 93 AZ76
Watford WD19 40 BY45
Talbot Cl, N15 66 DT56
Talbot Ct, EC3 197 L10
Talbot Cres, NW4 63 CU57
Talbot Gdns, Ilf. IG3 70 EU61
Talbot Ho, E14 off Giraud St 85 EB72
N7 off Harvist Est 65 DN62
Talbot Pl, SE3 104 EE82
Slough (Datchet) SL3 92 AW81
Talbot Rd, E6 87 EN68
E7 68 EG63
N6 64 DG58
N15 66 DT56
N22 45 DJ54
SE22 102 DS84
W2 82 DA72
W11 81 CZ72
W13 79 CG73
Ashford TW15 114 BK92
Bromley BR2
off Masons Hill 144 EH98
Carshalton SM5 158 DG106
Dagenham RM9 88 EZ65
Harrow HA3 41 CF54
Isleworth TW7 97 CG84
Rickmansworth WD3 38 BL46
Southall UB2 96 BY77
Thornton Heath CR7 142 DR98
Twickenham TW2 117 CE88
Wembley HA0 61 CK64
Talbot Sq, W2 194 A9
Talbot Wk, NW10
off Garnet Rd 80 CS65
W11 81 CY72
Talbot Yd, SE1 201 K3
Talbrook, Brwd. CM14 54 FT48
Taleworth Cl, Ashtd. KT21 171 CK120
Taleworth Pk, Ashtd. KT21 171 CK120
Taleworth Rd, Ashtd. KT21 171 CK119
Talfourd Pl, SE15 102 DT81
Talfourd Rd, SE15 102 DT81
Talgarth Rd, W6 99 CY78
W14 99 CY78
Talgarth Wk, NW9 62 CS57
Talisman Cl, Ilf. IG3 70 EV60
Talisman Sq, SE26 122 DU91
Talisman Way, Epsom KT17 173 CW116
Wembley HA9 62 CM62
Tallack Cl, Har. HA3
off College Hill Rd 41 CE52
Tallack Rd, E10 67 DZ60
Tall Elms Cl, Brom. BR2 144 EF99
Tallents Cl, Dart. (Sutt.H.)
DA4 128 FP94
Tallis Cl, E16 86 EH72
Tallis Ct, Rom. (Gidea Pk)
RM2 72 FJ55
Tallis Gro, SE7 104 EH79
Tallis St, EC4 196 E10
Tallis Vw, NW10 80 CR65
Tallis Way, Borwd. WD6 25 CK39
Brentwood (Warley) CM14 54 FV50
Tallon Rd, Brwd. (Hutt.) CM13 55 GE43
Tallow Rd, Brent. TW8 97 CJ79
Tall Trees, SW16 141 DM97
Slough (Colnbr.) SL3 93 BE81
Tall Trees Cl, Horn. RM11 72 FK58
Tally Ho Cor, N12 44 DC50
Tally Rd, Oxt. RH8 188 EL131
Talma Gdns, Twick. TW2 117 CE86
Talmage Cl, SE23
off Tyson Rd 122 DW87
Talman Gro, Stan. HA7 41 CK51
Talma Rd, SW2 101 DN84
Talus Cl, Purf. RM19
off Brimfield Rd 109 FR77
Talwin St, E3 85 EB69
Tamar Cl, E3 off Lefevre Wk 85 DZ67
Upminster RM14 73 FS58
Tamar Dr, S.Ock. (Aveley)
RM15 90 FQ72
Tamarind Yd, E1 202 C2
Tamarisk Cl, S.Ock. RM15 91 FW70
Tamarisk Rd, S.Ock. RM15 91 FW69
Tamarisk Sq, W12 81 CT73
Tamar Sq, Wdf.Grn. IG8 48 EH51
Tamar St, SE7
off Woolwich Rd 104 EL77
Tamar Way, N17 66 DU55
Slough SL3 93 BB78
Tamerton Sq, Wok. GU22 166 AY119
Tamesis Gdns, Wor.Pk. KT4 138 CS102
Tamesis Strand, Grav. DA12 131 GL92
Tamian Way, Houns. TW4 96 BW84
Tamworth Av, Wdf.Grn. IG8 48 EE51
Tamworth La, Mitch. CR4 141 DH96
Tamworth Pk, Mitch. CR4 141 DH98
Tamworth Pl, Croy. CR0 142 DQ103
Tamworth Rd, Croy. CR0 141 DP103
Tamworth St, SW6 100 DA79
Tancred Rd, N4 65 DP58
Tandem Cen, SW19 140 DD95
Tandem Way, SW19 140 DD95
TANDRIDGE, Oxt. RH8 187 EA133
Tandridge Ct, Cat. CR3 176 DU122
Tandridge Dr, Orp. BR6 145 ER102
Tandridge Gdns, S.Croy. CR2 160 DT113
Tandridge Hill La, Gdse. RH9 187 DZ128
Tandridge La, Oxt. (Tand.)
RH8 187 EA131
Tandridge Pl, Orp. BR6 145 ER102
Tandridge Rd, Warl. CR6 177 DX119
Tanfield Av, NW2 63 CT63
Tanfield Cl, Wal.Cr. EN7 14 DU27
Tanfield Rd, Croy. CR0 160 DQ105
Tangent Link, Rom. (Harold Hill)
RM3 52 FK53
Tangent Rd, Rom. RM3
off Ashton Rd 52 FK53
Tangier Rd, Rich. TW10 98 CP83
Tangier Way, Tad. KT20 173 CY117
Tangier Wd, Tad. KT20 173 CY118
Tanglebury Cl, Brom. BR1 145 EM98
Tangle Tree Cl, N3 44 DB54
Tanglewood Cl, Cher.
(Longcr.) KT16 132 AV104
Croydon CR0 142 DW104
Stanmore HA7 41 CE47
Uxbridge UB10 76 BN69
Woking GU22 167 BD116
Tanglewood Way, Felt. TW13 115 BV90
Tangley Gro, SW15 119 CT87
Tangley Pk Rd, Hmptn. TW12 116 BZ93
Tanglyn Av, Shep. TW17 135 BP99
Tangmere Cres, Horn. RM12 89 FH65
Tangmere Gdns, Nthlt. UB5 78 BW68
Tangmere Gro, Kings.T. KT2 117 CK92
Tangmere Way, NW9 42 CS54
Tanhouse Rd, Oxt. RH8 187 ED132
Tanhurst Wk, SE2
off Alsike Rd 106 EX76
Tankerton Rd, Surb. KT6 138 CM103
Tankerton St, WC1 196 A3
Tankerville Rd, SW16 121 DK93
Tank Hill Rd, Purf. RM19 108 FN78
Tank La, Purf. RM19 108 FN77
Tankridge Rd, NW2 63 CV61
Tanner Pt, E13 off Pelly Rd 86 EG67
Tanners Cl, Walt. KT12 135 BV100
Tanners Dean, Lthd. KT22 171 CJ122
Tanners End La, N18 46 DS49
Tanners Hill, SE8 103 DZ81
Abbots Langley WD5 7 BT31
Tanners La, Ilf. IG6 69 EQ55
Tanners Ms, SE8
off Tanners Hill 103 DZ81
Tanner St, SE1 201 N5
Barking IG11 87 EQ65
Tanners Wd Cl, Abb.L. WD5
off Tanners Wd La 7 BS32
Tanners Wd La, Abb.L. WD5 7 BS32
Tannery, The, Red. RH1
off Oakdene Rd 184 DE134
Tannery Cl, Beck. BR3 143 DX99
Dagenham RM10 71 FB62
Tannery La, Wok. (Send)
GU23 167 BF122
Tannington Ter, N5 65 DN62
Tannsfeld Rd, SE26 123 DX92
Tansley Cl, N7
off Hilldrop Rd 65 DK64
Tanswell Est, SE1 200 E5
Tanswell St, SE1 200 D5
Tansy Cl, E6 87 EN72
Romford RM3 52 FL51
Tantallon Rd, SW12 120 DG88
Tant Av, E16 86 EF72
Tantony Gro, Rom. RM6 70 EX55
Tanworth Cl, Nthwd. HA6 39 BQ51
Tanworth Gdns, Pnr. HA5 39 BV54
Tanyard La, Bex. DA5 126 FA88
Tanza Rd, NW3 64 DF63
Tapestry Cl, Sutt. SM2 158 DB108
Taplow, NW3 82 DD66
SE17 off Thurlow St 102 DS78
Taplow Rd, N13 46 DQ49
Taplow St, N1 197 J1
Tappesfield Rd, SE15 102 DW83
Tapp St, E1 84 DV70
Tapster St, Barn. EN5 27 CZ42
Tara Ms, N8 off Edison Rd 65 DK58
Taransay Wk, N1 off Essex Rd 84 DR65
Tarbert Ms, N15
off Roslyn Rd 66 DS57
Tarbert Rd, SE22 122 DS85
Tarbert Wk, E1
off Juniper St 84 DW73
Target Cl, Felt. TW14 115 BS86
Target Rbt, Nthlt. UB5
off Western Av 78 BZ67
Tariff Cres, SE8 203 M8
Tariff Rd, N17 46 DU51
Tarleton Gdns, SE23 122 DV88
Tarling Cl, Sid. DA14 126 EV90
Tarling Rd, E16 86 EF72
N2 44 DC54
Tarling St, E1 84 DV72
Tarling St Est, E1 84 DW72
Tarmac Way, West Dr. UB7 94 BH80
Tarnbank, Enf. EN2 29 DL43
Tarn St, SE1 201 H7
Tarnwood Pk, SE9 125 EM88
Tarnworth Rd, Rom. RM3 52 FN50
Tarpan Way, Brox. EN10 15 DZ26
Tarquin Ho, SE26 122 DU91
Tarragon Cl, SE14 103 DY80
Tarragon Gro, SE26 123 DX93
Tarrant Pl, W1 194 D7
Tarrington Cl, SW16 121 DK90
Tartar Rd, Cob. KT11 154 BW113
Tarver Rd, SE17 101 DP78
Tarves Way, SE10 103 EB80
Tash Pl, N11 off Woodland Rd 45 DH50
Tasker Cl, Hayes UB3 95 BQ80
Tasker Ho, Bark. IG11
off Dovehouse Mead 87 ER68
Tasker Rd, NW3 64 DF64
Grays RM16 111 GH76
Tasman Ct, E14
off Westferry Rd 103 EB77
Sunbury-on-Thames TW16 115 BS94
Tasmania Ho, Til. RM18
off Hobart Rd 111 GG81
Tasmania Ter, N18 46 DQ51
Tasman Rd, SW9 101 DL83
Tasman Wk, E16 off Royal Rd 86 EK72
Tasso Rd, W6 99 CY79
Tatam Rd, NW10 80 CQ66
Tatchbury Ho, SW15
off Tunworth Cres 119 CT86
Tate & Lyle Jetty, E16 104 EL75
★ Tate Britain, SW1 199 P9
Tate Cl, Lthd. KT22 171 CJ123
Tate Gdns, Bushey WD23 41 CE45
★ Tate Modern, SE1 200 G2
Tate Rd, E16 off Newland St 87 EM74
Gerrards Cross (Chal.St.P.)
SL9 37 AZ50
Sutton SM1 158 DA106
Tatham Pl, NW8 82 DD68
TATLING END, Ger.Cr. SL9 57 BB61
Tatnell Rd, SE23 123 DY86
TATSFIELD, West. TN16 178 EL120
Tatsfield App Rd, West.
(Tats.) TN16 178 EH123
Tatsfield La, West. (Tats.)
TN16 179 EM121
TATTENHAM CORNER,
Epsom KT18 173 CV118
⇌ Tattenham Corner 173 CV118
Tattenham Cor Rd,
Epsom KT18 173 CT117
Tattenham Cres, Epsom
KT18 173 CU118
Tattenham Gro, Epsom KT18 173 CV118
Tattenham Way, Tad. KT20 173 CX118
Tattersall Cl, SE9 124 EL85
Tatton Cres, N16
off Clapton Common 66 DT59
Tatum St, SE17 201 L9
Tauber Cl, Borwd. (Els.) WD6 26 CM42
Tauheed Cl, N4 66 DQ61
Taunton Av, SW20 139 CV96
Caterham CR3 176 DT123
Hounslow TW3 96 CC82
Taunton Cl, Bexh. DA7 107 FD82
Ilford IG6 49 ET51
Sutton SM3 140 DA102
Taunton Dr, N2 44 DC54
Enfield EN2 29 DN41
Taunton La, Couls. CR5 175 DN119
Taunton Ms, NW1 194 D5
Taunton Pl, NW1 194 D4
Taunton Rd, SE12 124 EE85
Gravesend (Nthflt) DA11 130 GA85
Greenford UB6 78 CB67
Romford RM3 52 FJ49
Taunton Vale, Grav. DA12 131 GK90
Taunton Way, Stan. HA7 62 CL55
Tavern Cl, Cars. SM5 140 DE101
Taverners Cl, W11
off Addison Av 81 CY74
Taverner Sq, N5
off Highbury Gra 66 DQ63
Taverners Way, E4
off Douglas Rd 48 EE46
Tavern La, SW9 101 DN82
Tavistock Av, E17 67 DY55
NW7 43 CX52
Greenford UB6 79 CG68
Tavistock Cl, N16
off Crossway 66 DS64
Potters Bar EN6 12 DD31
Romford RM3 52 FK53
Staines TW18 114 BK94
Tavistock Ct, WC2
off Tavistock St 83 DL73
Tavistock Cres, W11 81 CZ71
Mitcham CR4 141 DL98
Tavistock Gdns, Ilf. IG3 69 ES63
Tavistock Gate, Croy. CR0 142 DR102
Tavistock Gro, Croy. CR0 142 DR101
Tavistock Ms, E18
off Avon Way 68 EG56
Tavistock Pl, E18
off Avon Way 68 EG55
N14 29 DH44
WC1 195 N4
Tavistock Rd, E7 68 EF63
E15 86 EF65
E18 68 EG55
N4 66 DR58
NW10 81 CT68
W11 81 CZ72
Bromley BR2 144 EF98
Carshalton SM5 140 DD102
Croydon CR0 142 DR102
Edgware HA8 42 CN53
Uxbridge UB10 59 BQ64
Watford WD24 24 BX39
Welling DA16 106 EW81
West Drayton UB7 76 BK74
Tavistock Sq, WC1 195 N4
Tavistock St, WC2 196 A10
Tavistock Ter, N19 65 DK62
Tavistock Twr, SE16 203 K7
Tavistock Wk, Cars. SM5
off Tavistock Rd 140 DD102
Taviton St, WC1 195 M4
Tavy Cl, SE11 200 E10
Tawney Common, Epp.
(They.Mt) CM16 18 FA32
Tawney La, Ong. CM5 19 FC32
Romford (Stap.Taw.) RM4 35 FD35
Tawney Rd, SE28 88 EV73
Tawny Av, Upmin. RM14 72 FP64
Tawny Cl, W13 79 CH74
Feltham TW13
off Chervil Cl 115 BU90
Tawny Way, SE16 203 J8
Tayben Av, Twick. TW2 117 CE86
Taybridge Rd, SW11 100 DG83
Tayburn Cl, E14 85 EC72
Tayfield Cl, Uxb. UB10 59 BQ62
Tayler Cotts, Pot.B. EN6
off Crossoaks La 11 CT34
Tayles Hill, Epsom KT17
off Tayles Hill Dr 157 CT110
Tayles Hill Dr, Epsom KT17 157 CT110
Taylor Av, Rich. TW9 98 CP82
Taylor Cl, N17 46 DU52
SE8 103 DZ79
Epsom KT19 156 CN111
Hampton (Hmptn H.) TW12 116 CC92
Hounslow TW3 96 CC81
Orpington BR6 163 ET105
Romford RM5 50 FA52
Uxbridge (Hare.) UB9
off High St 38 BJ53
Taylor Ct, E15 off Clays La 67 EC64
Taylor Rd, Ashtd. KT21 171 CK117
Mitcham CR4 120 DE94
Wallington SM6 159 DH106
Taylor Row, Dart. DA2 128 FJ90
Romford (Noak Hill) RM3
off Cummings Hall La 52 FJ48
Taylors Bldgs, SE18
off Spray St 105 EP77
Taylors Cl, Sid. DA14 125 ET91
Taylors Ct, Felt. TW13 115 BU89
Taylors Grn, W3 80 CS72
Taylors La, NW10 80 CS66
SE26 122 DV91
Barnet EN5 27 CZ39
Taymount Ri, SE23 122 DW89
Taynton Dr, Red. (Merst.)
RH1 185 DK129
Tayport Cl, N1 83 DL66
Tayside Dr, Edg. HA8 42 CP48
Tay Way, Rom. RM1 51 FF53
Taywood Rd, Nthlt. UB5 78 BZ69
Teak Cl, SE16 203 L3
Teal Av, Orp. BR5 146 EX98
Teal Cl, E16 off Fulmer Rd 86 EK71
South Croydon CR2 161 DX111
Teal Ct, Wall. SM6
off Carew Rd 159 DJ107
Teal Dr, Nthwd. HA6 39 BQ52
Teale St, E2 84 DU68
Tealing Dr, Epsom KT19 156 CR105
Teal Pl, Sutt. SM1
off Sandpiper Rd 157 CZ106
Teal St, SE10 205 L6
Teal Way, Hem.H. HP3 6 BM25
Teardrop Ind Est, Swan. BR8 147 FH99
Teasel Cl, Croy. CR0 143 DX102
Teasel Cres, SE28 87 ES74
Teasel Way, E15 86 EE69
Teazle Meade, Epp. (Thnwd)
CM16 18 EV25
Teazle Wd Hill, Lthd. KT22 171 CE117
Teazlewood Pk, Lthd. KT22 171 CG117
Tebworth Rd, N17 46 DT52
Teck Cl, Islw. TW7 97 CG82
Tedder Cl, Chess. KT9 155 CJ107
Ruislip HA4
off West End Rd 59 BV64
Uxbridge UB10 76 BM66
Tedder Rd, S.Croy. CR2 160 DW108
TEDDINGTON, TW11 117 CG93
⇌ Teddington 117 CG93
Teddington Cl, Epsom KT19 156 CR110
Teddington Lock, Tedd. TW11 117 CH91
H Teddington Mem Hosp,
Tedd. TW11 117 CE93
Teddington Pk, Tedd. TW11 117 CF92
Teddington Pk Rd, Tedd.
TW11 117 CF91
Tedworth Gdns, SW3
off Tedworth Sq 100 DF78
Tedworth Sq, SW3 100 DF78
Tee, The, W3 80 CS72
Tees Av, Grnf. UB6 79 CE68
Tees Cl, Upmin. RM14 73 FR59
Teesdale Av, Islw. TW7 97 CG81
Teesdale Cl, E2 84 DV68
Teesdale Gdns, SE25 142 DS96
Isleworth TW7 97 CG81
Teesdale Rd, E11 68 EF58
Dartford DA2 128 FQ88
Teesdale St, E2 84 DV68
Teesdale Yd, E2
off Teesdale St 84 DV68
Tees Dr, Rom. RM3 52 FK48
Teeswater Ct, Erith DA18
off Middle Way 106 EX76
Teevan Cl, Croy. CR0 142 DU101
Teevan Rd, Croy. CR0 142 DU101
Teggs La, Wok. GU22 167 BF116
Teign Ms, SE9 124 EL89
Teignmouth Cl, SW4 101 DK84
Edgware HA8 42 CM54
Teignmouth Gdns, Grnf. UB6 79 CF68
Teignmouth Rd, NW2 63 CX64
Welling DA16 106 EW82
Telcote Way, Ruis. HA4
off Woodlands Av 60 BW59
★ Telecom Twr, W1 195 K6
Telegraph Hill, NW3 64 DB62
Telegraph La, Esher
(Clay.) KT10 155 CF107
Telegraph Ms, Ilf. IG3 70 EU60
Telegraph Path, Chis. BR7 125 EP92
Telegraph Pl, E14 204 B8
Telegraph Rd, SW15 119 CV87
Telegraph St, EC2 197 K8
Telegraph Track, Cars. SM5 158 DG110
Telemann Sq, SE3 104 EH83
Telephone Pl, SW6
off Lillie Rd 99 CZ79
Telfer Cl, W3 off Church Rd 98 CQ75
Telferscot Rd, SW12 121 DK88
Telford Av, SW2 121 DL88
Telford Cl, E17 67 DY59
SE19 off St. Aubyn's Rd 122 DT93
Watford WD25 24 BX35
Telford Dr, Walt. KT12 136 BW101
Telford Rd, N11 45 DJ51
NW9 off West Hendon Bdy 63 CU58
SE9 125 ER89
W10 81 CY71
St. Albans (Lon.Col.) AL2 9 CJ27
Southall UB1 78 CB73
Twickenham TW2 116 CA87
Telfords Yd, E1 202 C1
Telford Ter, SW1 101 DJ79
Telford Way, W3 80 CS71
Hayes UB4 78 BY71
Telham Rd, E6 87 EN68
Tell Gro, SE22 102 DT84
Tellisford, Esher KT10 154 CB105
Tellson Av, SE18 104 EL81
Telscombe Cl, Orp. BR6 145 ES103
Telston La, Sev. (Otford)
TN14 181 FF117
Temeraire Pl, Brent. TW8 98 CM78
Temeraire St, SE16 202 G5
Temperley Rd, SW12 120 DG87
Tempest Av, Pot.B. EN6 12 DC32
Tempest Mead, Epp. (N.Wld Bas.)
CM16 19 FB27
Tempest Rd, Egh. TW20 113 BC93
Tempest Way, Rain. RM13 89 FG65
Templar Ct, NW8
off St. John's Wd Rd 82 DD69
Templar Dr, SE28 88 EX72
Gravesend DA11 131 GG92
Templar Ho, NW2
off Shoot Up Hill 81 CZ65
Rainham RM13
off Chantry Way 89 FD68
Templar Pl, Hmptn. TW12 116 CA94
Templars Av, NW11 63 CZ58
Templars Cres, N3 44 DA54
Templars Dr, Har. HA3 41 CD51
Templars Ho, E15
off Clays La 67 EB64
Templar St, SE5 101 DP82
⊖ Temple 196 C10
★ Temple, The, EC4 196 D10
Temple Av, EC4 196 E10
N20 44 DD45
Croydon CR0 143 DZ103
Dagenham RM8 70 FA60
★ Temple Bar, EC4 196 D9
Temple Bar Rd, Wok. GU21 166 AT119
Temple Cl, E11 68 EE59
N3 off Cyprus Rd 43 CZ54
SE28 105 EQ76
Epsom KT19 156 CR112
Waltham Cross (Chsht) EN7 14 DU31
Temple Cl, Wat. WD17 23 BT40
Templecombe Ms, Wok. GU22
off Dorchester Ct 167 BA116
Templecombe Rd, E9 84 DW67
Templecombe Way, Mord.
SM4 139 CY99
Temple Ct, E1 off Rectory Sq 85 DX71
SW8 off Thorncroft St 101 DL80
Potters Bar EN6 11 CY31
Templecroft, Ashf. TW15 115 BR93
Templedene Av, Stai. TW18 114 BH94
Temple Dws, E2 off Temple St 84 DV68
Templefield Cl, Add. KT15 152 BH107
Temple Fortune Hill, NW11 64 DA57
Temple Fortune La, NW11 64 DA58
Temple Fortune Par, NW11
off Finchley Rd 63 CZ57
Temple Gdns, N21
off Barrowell Grn 45 DP47
NW11 63 CZ58
Dagenham RM8 70 EX62
Rickmansworth WD3 39 BP49
Staines TW18 133 BF95
Temple Gro, NW11 64 DA58
Enfield EN2 29 DP41
Temple Hill, Dart. DA1 128 FM86
Temple Hill Sq, Dart. DA1 128 FM85
Templehof Av, NW2 63 CW59
Temple La, EC4 196 E9
Templeman Cl, Pur. CR8
off Croftleigh Av 175 DP116
Templeman Rd, W7 79 CF71
Templemead Cl, W3 80 CS72
Temple Mead Cl, Stan. HA7 41 CH51
Templemead Ho, E9
off Kingsmead Way 67 DY63
Templemere, Wey. KT13 135 BR104
Temple Mill La, E15 67 EB63
★ Temple of Mithras, EC4
off Queen Victoria St 197 K9
Templepan La, Rick. WD3 22 BL37
Temple Pk, Uxb. UB8 76 BN69
Temple Pl, WC2 196 C10
Templer Av, Grays RM16 111 GG77
Temple Rd, E6 86 EL67
N8 65 DM56
NW2 63 CW63
W4 98 CQ76
W5 97 CK76
Croydon CR0 160 DR105
Epsom KT19 156 CR112
Hounslow TW3 96 CB84
Richmond TW9 98 CM83
Westerham (Bigg.H.) TN16 178 EK117
Temple Sheen, SW14 118 CQ85
Temple Sheen Rd, SW14 98 CP84
Temple St, E2 84 DV68
Templeton Av, E4 47 EA49
Templeton Cl, N16
off Boleyn Rd 66 DS64
SE19 142 DR95
Templeton Ct, NW7
off Kingsbridge Dr 43 CX52
Templeton Pl, SW5 100 DA77
Templeton Rd, N15 66 DR58
Temple Way, Sutt. SM1 140 DD104
Temple W Ms, SE11 200 F7
Templewood, W13 79 CH71
Templewood Av, NW3 64 DB62
Temple Wd Dr, Red. RH1 184 DF131
Templewood Gdns, NW3 64 DB62
Templewood La, Slou. SL2 56 AS63
Templewood Pk, Slou. SL2 56 AT63
Templewood Pt, NW2
off Granville Rd 63 CZ61
Temple Yd, E2 off Temple St 84 DV68
Tempsford Av, Borwd. WD6 26 CR42
Tempsford Cl, Enf. EN2
off Gladbeck Way 30 DQ41
Temsford Cl, Har. HA2 40 CC54
Ten Acre, Wok. GU21
off Chirton Wk 166 AU118
Ten Acre La, Egh. TW20 133 BC96
Ten Acres, Lthd. (Fetch.) KT22 171 CD124
Ten Acres Cl, Lthd. (Fetch.)
KT22 171 CD124
Tenbury Cl, E7
off Romford Rd 68 EK64
Tenbury Ct, SW2 121 DK88
Tenby Av, Har. HA3 41 CH54
Tenby Cl, N15 off Hanover Rd 66 DT56
Romford RM6 70 EY58
Tenby Gdns, Nthlt. UB5 78 CA65
Tenby Rd, E17 67 DY57
Edgware HA8 42 CM53
Enfield EN3 30 DW41
Romford RM6 70 EY58
Welling DA16 106 EX81
Tenchleys La, Oxt. RH8 188 EK131
Tench St, E1 202 D3
Tenda Rd, SE16 202 D9
Tendring Way, Rom. RM6 70 EW57
Tenham Av, SW2 121 DK88
Tenison Ct, W1 195 K10
Tenison Way, SE1 200 D3
Tennand Cl, Wal.Cr.
(Chsht) EN7 14 DT26
Tenniel Cl, W2
off Porchester Gdns 82 DC72
Tennis Ct La, E.Mol. KT8
off Hampton Ct Way 137 CF97
Tennison Av, Borwd. WD6 26 CP43
Tennison Cl, Couls. CR5 175 DP120
Tennison Rd, SE25 142 DT98
Tennis St, SE1 201 K4
Tenniswood Rd, Enf. EN1 30 DT39
Tennyson Av, E11 68 EG59
E12 86 EL66
NW9 62 CQ55
Grays RM17 110 GB76
New Malden KT3 139 CV99
Twickenham TW1 117 CF88
Waltham Abbey EN9 16 EE34
Tennyson Cl, Enf. EN3 31 DX43
Feltham TW14 115 BT86
Welling DA16 105 ES81
Tennyson Rd, E10 67 EB61

T

★ Place of interest ⇌ Railway station ⊖ London Underground station DLR Docklands Light Railway station Tra Tramlink station H Hospital Riv Pedestrian ferry landing stage

Tennyson Rd, E15 ..86 EE66
E17 ..67 DZ58
NW6 ..81 CZ67
NW7 ..43 CU50
SE20 ..123 DX94
SW19 ..120 DC93
W7 ..79 CF73
Addlestone KT15 ..152 BL105
Ashford TW15 ..114 BL92
Brentwood (Hutt.) CM13 ..55 GC45
Dartford DA1 ..128 FN85
Hounslow TW3 ..96 CC82
Romford RM3 ..52 FJ52
St. Albans AL2 ..8 CA26
Tennyson St, SW8 ..101 DH82
Tennyson Wk, Grav.
(Nthflt) DA11 ..130 GD90
Tilbury RM18 ..111 GH82
Tennyson Way, Horn. RM12 ..71 FF61
Tensing Av, Grav.
(Nthflt) DA11 ..130 GE90
Tensing Rd, Sthl. UB2 ..96 CA76
Tentelow La, Sthl. UB2 ..96 CA78
Tenterden Cl, NW4 ..63 CX55
SE9 ..125 EM91
Tenterden Dr, NW4 ..63 CX55
Tenterden Gdns, NW4 ..63 CX55
Croydon CR0 ..142 DU101
Tenterden Gro, NW4 ..63 CX56
Tenterden Rd, N17 ..46 DT52
Croydon CR0 ..142 DU101
Dagenham RM8 ..70 EZ61
Tenterden St, W1 ..195 J9
Tenter Grd, E1 ..197 P7
Tenter Pas, E1
off Mansell St ..84 DT72
Tent Peg La, Orp. BR5 ..145 EQ99
Tent St, E1 ..84 DV70
Terborch Way, SE22
off East Dulwich Gro ..122 DS85
Tercel Path, Chig. IG7 ..50 EV49
Teredo St, SE16 ..203 J7
Terence Cl, Grav. DA12 ..131 GM88
Terence Ct, Belv. DA17
off Nuxley Rd ..106 EZ79
Teresa Gdns, Wal.Cr. EN8 ..14 DW34
Teresa Ms, E17 ..67 EA56
Teresa Wk, N10
off Connaught Gdns ..65 DH57
Terling Cl, E11 ..68 EF62
Terling Rd, Dag. RM8 ..70 FA61
Terlings, The, Brwd. CM14 ..54 FU48
Terling Wk, N1
off Britannia Row ..84 DQ67
Terminus Pl, SW1 ..199 J7
Tern Gdns, Upmin. RM14 ..73 FS60
Tern Way, Brwd. CM14 ..54 FS49
Terrace, The, E4
off Chingdale Rd ..48 EE48
N3 *off Hendon La* ..43 CZ54
NW6 ..82 DA67
SW13 ..98 CS82
Addlestone KT15 ..152 BL106
Gravesend DA12 ..131 GH86
Sevenoaks TN13 ..190 FD122
Woodford Green IG8
off Broadmead Rd ..48 EG51
Terrace Gdns, SW13 ..99 CT82
Watford WD17 ..23 BV40
Terrace La, Rich. TW10 ..118 CL86
Terrace Rd, E9 ..84 DW66
E13 ..86 EG67
Walton-on-Thames KT12 ..135 BU101
Terraces, The, Dart. DA2 ..128 FQ87
Terrace St, Grav. DA12 ..131 GH86
Terrace Wk, Dag. RM9 ..70 EY64
Terrapin Rd, SW17 ..121 DH90
Terretts Pl, N1 *off Upper St* ..83 DP66
Terrick Rd, N22 ..45 DL53
Terrick St, W12 ..81 CV72
Terrilands, Pnr. HA5 ..60 BZ55
Terront Rd, N15 ..66 DQ57
Tersha St, Rich. TW9 ..98 CM84
Tessa Sanderson Pl, SW8 ..101 DH83
Tessa Sanderson Way, Grnf. UB6
off Lilian Board Way ..61 CD64
Testers Cl, Oxt. RH8 ..188 EH131
Testerton Wk, W11 ..81 CX73
Tetbury Pl, N1
off Upper St ..83 DP67
Tetcott Rd, SW10 ..100 DC80
Tetherdown, N10 ..64 DG55
Tetty Way, Brom. BR2 ..144 EG96
Teversham La, SW8 ..101 DL81
Teviot Av, S.Ock. (Aveley)
RM15 ..90 FQ72
Teviot Cl, Well. DA16 ..106 EV81
Teviot St, E14 ..85 EC71
Tewkesbury Av, SE23 ..122 DV88
Pinner HA5 ..60 BY57
Tewkesbury Cl, N15
off Tewkesbury Rd ..66 DR58
Barnet EN4
off Approach Rd ..28 DD42
Loughton IG10 ..32 EL44
West Byfleet (Byfleet)
KT14 ..152 BK111
Tewkesbury Gdns, NW9 ..62 CP55
Tewkesbury Rd, N15 ..66 DR58
W13 ..79 CG73
Carshalton SM5 ..140 DD102
Tewkesbury Ter, N11 ..45 DJ51
Tewson Rd, SE18 ..105 ES78
Teynham Av, Enf. EN1 ..30 DR44
Teynham Grn, Brom. BR2 ..144 EG99
Teynham Rd, Dart. DA2 ..128 FQ87
Teynton Ter, N17 ..46 DQ53
Thackeray Av, N17 ..46 DU54
Tilbury RM18 ..111 GH81
Thackeray Cl, SW19 ..119 CX94
Isleworth TW7 ..97 CG82
Uxbridge UB8 ..77 BP72
Thackeray Dr, Rom. RM6 ..70 EU59
Thackeray Rd, E6 ..86 EK68
SW8 ..101 DH82
Thackeray St, W8 ..100 DB75
Thakeham Cl, SE26 ..122 DV92
Thalia Cl, SE10 ..103 ED79
Thalmassing Cl, Brwd.
(Hutt.) CM13 ..55 GB47
Thame Rd, SE16 ..203 J4
Thames Av, SW10 ..100 DC81
Chertsey KT16 ..134 BG97
Dagenham RM9 ..89 FB70
Greenford UB6 ..79 CF68
Thames Bk, SW14 ..98 CQ82
Thamesbank Pl, SE28 ..88 EW72
Thames Circle, E14 ..204 A8
Thames Cl, Cher. KT16 ..134 BH101
Hampton TW12 ..136 CB96
Rainham RM13 ..89 FH72
Thames Ct, W.Mol. KT8 ..136 CB96
Thames Cres, W4
off Corney Rd ..98 CS80
Thamesdale, St.Alb. (Lon.Col.)
AL2 ..10 CM27
THAMES DITTON, KT7 ..137 CF100
⇌ **Thames Ditton** ..137 CF101
Thames Ditton Island, T.Ditt.
KT7 ..137 CG99
Thames Dr, Grays RM16 ..111 GG78
Ruislip HA4 ..59 BQ58
Thames Edge Ct, Stai. TW18
off Clarence St ..113 BE91
Thames Europort, Dart. DA2 ..109 FS84
Thamesfield Ct, Shep. TW17 ..135 BQ101
★ **Thames Flood Barrier &**
Visitors Cen, SE18 ..104 EK75
Thames Gate, Dart. DA1 ..128 FN85
Thamesgate Cen, Grav.
DA11 *off New Rd* ..131 GH86
Thamesgate Cl, Rich. TW10
off Locksmeade Rd ..117 CJ91
Thames Gateway, Dag. RM9 ..88 EZ68
Rainham RM13 ..89 FG72
South Ockendon RM15 ..108 FP75
Thames Gateway Pk, Dag.
RM9 ..88 EZ69
Thameshill Av, Rom. RM5 ..51 FC54
★ **Thames Ho**, SW1 ..199 P8
Thameside, Tedd. TW11 ..117 CK94
Thameside Ind Est, E16 ..104 EL75
Thameside Wk, SE28 ..87 ET72
THAMESMEAD, SE28 ..87 ET74
Thamesmead, Walt. KT12 ..135 BU101
THAMESMEAD NORTH,
SE28 ..88 EW72
Thames Meadow, Shep.
TW17 ..135 BR102
West Molesey KT8 ..136 CA96
Thamesmead Spine Rd, Belv.
DA17 ..107 FB75
THAMESMEAD WEST, SE18 ..105 EP76
Thamesmere Dr, SE28 ..88 EU73
Thames Pl, SW15 ..99 CX83
Thames Pt, SW6
off The Boulevard ..100 DC82
Thames Quay, SW10
off Harbour Av ..100 DC81
Thames Rd, E16 ..86 EK74
W4 ..98 CN79
Barking IG11 ..87 ET69
Dartford DA1 ..107 FF82
Grays RM17 ..110 GB80
Slough SL3 ..93 BA77
Thames Side, Cher. KT16 ..134 BJ100
Kingston upon Thames
KT1 ..137 CK95
Staines TW18 ..134 BH96
Thames Side Pl, Kings.T.
KT1 ..137 CK95
Thames St, SE10 ..103 EB79
Hampton TW12 ..136 CB95
Kingston upon Thames
KT1 ..137 CK96
Staines TW18 ..113 BE91
Sunbury-on-Thames TW16 ..135 BV98
Walton-on-Thames KT12 ..135 BT101
Weybridge KT13 ..135 BP103
Thames Tunnel Mills, SE16
off Rotherhithe St ..102 DW75
Thamesvale Cl, Houns. TW3 ..96 CA83
🄷 **Thames Valley Nuffield Hosp**,
Slou. SL2 ..74 AW67
Thames Vw, Grays RM16 ..111 GG78
Ilford IG1 *off High Rd* ..69 EQ61
Thames Village, W4 ..98 CQ81
Thames Way, Grav. DA11 ..130 GB86
Thames Wf, E16 ..205 K2
Thamley, Purf. RM19 ..108 FN77
Thanescroft Gdns, Croy. CR0 ..142 DS104
Thanet Dr, Kes. BR2
off Phoenix Dr ..144 EK104
Thanet Pl, Croy. CR0 ..160 DQ105
Thanet Rd, Bex. DA5 ..126 FA87
Erith DA8 ..107 FE80
Thanet St, WC1 ..195 P3
Thane Vil, N7 ..65 DM62
Thane Wks, N7 ..65 DM62
Thanington Ct, SE9 ..125 ES86
Thant Cl, E10 ..67 EB62
Tharp Rd, Wall. SM6 ..159 DK106
Thatcham Gdns, N20 ..44 DC45
Thatcher Cl, West Dr. UB7
off Classon Cl ..94 BL75
Thatcher Ct, Dart. DA1
off Heath St ..128 FK87
Thatchers Cl, Loug. IG10 ..33 EQ40
Thatchers Way, Islw. TW7 ..117 CD85
Thatches Gro, Rom. RM6 ..70 EY56
Thavies Inn, EC1 ..196 E8
Thaxted Ct, N1 ..197 K1
Thaxted Grn, Brwd.
(Hutt.) CM13 ..55 GC43
Thaxted Ho, Dag. RM10 ..89 FB66
Thaxted Pl, SW20 ..119 CX94
Thaxted Rd, SE9 ..125 EQ89
Buckhurst Hill IG9 ..48 EL45
Thaxted Wk, Rain. RM13
off Ongar Way ..89 FF67
Thaxted Way, Wal.Abb. EN9 ..15 ED33
Thaxton Rd, W14 ..99 CZ79
Thayers Fm Rd, Beck. BR3 ..143 DY95
Thayer St, W1 ..194 G7
Thaynesfield, Pot.B. EN6 ..12 DD31
★ **Theatre Mus**, WC2
off Russell St ..196 A10
★ **Theatre Royal**, WC2 ..196 A9
Theatre Sq, E15
off Great Eastern Rd ..85 ED65
Theatre St, SW11 ..100 DF83
Theberton St, N1 ..83 DN67
Theed St, SE1 ..200 D3
Thellusson Way, Rick. WD3 ..37 BF45
Thelma Cl, Grav. DA12 ..131 GM92
Thelma Gdns, SE3 ..104 EK81
Feltham TW13 ..116 BY90
Thelma Gro, Tedd. TW11 ..117 CG93
Theobald Cres, Har. HA3 ..40 CB53
Theobald Rd, E17 ..67 DZ59
Croydon CR0 ..141 DP103
Theobalds Av, N12 ..44 DC49
Grays RM17 ..110 GC78
Theobalds Cl, Pot.B.
(Cuffley) EN6 ..13 DM30
Theobalds Ct, N4
off Queens Dr ..66 DQ61
⇌ **Theobalds Grove** ..15 DX32
Theobalds La, Wal.Cr.
(Chsht) EN8 ..14 DV32
Theobalds Pk Rd, Enf. EN2 ..29 DP35
Theobald's Rd, WC1 ..196 B6
Theobalds Rd, Pot.B.
(Cuffley) EN6 ..13 DL30
Theobald St, SE1 ..201 K7
Borehamwood WD6 ..26 CM40
Radlett WD7 ..25 CH36
Theodora Way, Pnr. HA5 ..59 BT55
Theodore Rd, SE13 ..123 EC86
🅃 **Therapia Lane** ..141 DL101
Therapia La, Croy. CR0 ..141 DL100
Therapia Rd, SE22 ..122 DW86
Theresa Rd, W6 ..99 CU77
Theresas Wk, S.Croy. CR2
off Sanderstead Rd ..160 DR110
Therfield Ct, N4
off Brownswood Rd ..66 DQ61
Thermopylae Gate, E14 ..204 C9
Theseus Wk, N1 ..196 G1
Thesiger Rd, SE20 ..123 DX94
Thessaly Rd, SW8 ..101 DJ80
Thetford Cl, N13 ..45 DP51
Thetford Gdns, Dag. RM9 ..88 EX66
Thetford Rd, Ashf. TW15 ..114 BL91
Dagenham RM9 ..88 EX67
New Malden KT3 ..138 CR100
Thetis Ter, Rich. TW9
off Kew Grn ..98 CN79
THEYDON BOIS, Epp. CM16 ..33 ET37
⊖ **Theydon Bois** ..33 ET36
Theydon Bower, Epp. CM16 ..18 EU31
Theydon Ct, Wal.Abb. EN9 ..16 EG33
Theydon Gdns, Rain. RM13 ..89 FE66
THEYDON GARNON, Epp.
CM16 ..34 EW35
Theydon Gate, Epp. (They.B.)
CM16 *off Coppice Row* ..33 ES37
Theydon Gro, Epp. CM16 ..34 EU30
Woodford Green IG8 ..48 EJ51
THEYDON MOUNT, Epp.
CM16 ..18 FA34
Theydon Pk Rd, Epp.
(They.B.) CM16 ..33 ES39
Theydon Pl, Epp. CM16 ..17 ET31
Theydon Rd, E5 ..66 DW61
Epping CM16 ..17 ER34
Theydon St, E17 ..67 DZ59
Thicket, The, West Dr. UB7 ..76 BL72
Thicket Cres, Sutt. SM1 ..158 DC105
Thicket Gro, SE20
off Anerley Rd ..122 DU94
Dagenham RM9 ..88 EW65
Thicket Rd, SE20 ..122 DU94
Sutton SM1 ..158 DC105
Thicketts, Sev. TN13 ..191 FJ123
Thickthorne La, Stai. TW18 ..114 BJ94
Third Av, E12 ..68 EL63
E13 ..86 EG69
E17 ..67 EA57
W3 ..81 CT74
W10 ..81 CY69
Dagenham RM10 ..89 FB67
Enfield EN1 ..30 DT43
Grays RM20 ..109 FU79
Hayes UB3 ..77 BT74
Romford RM6 ..70 EW57
Waltham Abbey EN9
off Breach Barn Mobile
Home Pk ..16 EH30
Watford WD25 ..24 BX35
Wembley HA9 ..61 CK61
Third Cl, W.Mol. KT8 ..136 CB98
Third Cross Rd, Twick. TW2 ..117 CD89
Third Way, Wem. HA9 ..62 CP63
Thirleby Rd, SW1 ..199 L7
Edgware HA8 ..42 CR53
Thirlmere Av, Grnf. UB6 ..79 CJ69
Thirlmere Cl, Egh. TW20
off Keswick Rd ..113 BB94
Thirlmere Gdns, Nthwd. HA6 ..39 BQ51
Wembley HA9 ..61 CJ60
Thirlmere Ho, Islw. TW7
off Summerwood Rd ..117 CF85
Thirlmere Ri, Brom. BR1 ..124 EF93
Thirlmere Rd, N10 ..45 DH53
SW16 ..121 DK91
Bexleyheath DA7 ..107 FC82
Thirsk Cl, Nthlt. UB5 ..78 CA65
Thirsk Rd, SE25 ..142 DR98
SW11 ..100 DG83
Borehamwood WD6 ..26 CN37
Mitcham CR4 ..120 DG94
Thirston Path, Borwd. WD6 ..26 CN40
Thirza Rd, Dart. DA1 ..128 FM86
Thistlebrook, SE2 ..106 EW76
Thistlebrook Ind Est, SE2 ..106 EW75
Thistlecroft Gdns, Stan.
HA7 ..41 CK53
Thistlecroft Rd, Walt. KT12 ..154 BW105
Thistledene, T.Ditt. KT7 ..137 CE100
West Byfleet KT14 ..151 BF113
Thistledene Av, Har. HA2 ..60 BY62
Romford RM5 ..51 FB50
Thistledown, Grav. DA12 ..131 GK93
Thistlefield Cl, Bex. DA5 ..126 EX88
Thistle Gro, SW10 ..100 DC78
Thistlemead, Chis. BR7 ..145 EP96
Thistle Mead, Loug. IG10 ..33 EN41
Thistle Rd, Grav. DA12 ..131 GL87
Thistlewaite Rd, E5 ..66 DV62
Thistlewood Cl, N7 ..65 DM61
Thistlewood Cres, Croy.
(New Adgtn) CR0 ..161 ED112
Thistleworth Cl, Islw. TW7 ..97 CD80
Thistley Cl, N12
off Summerfields Av ..44 DE51
Thistley Ct, SE8
off Glaisher St ..103 EB79
Thomas a'Beckett Cl, Wem.
HA0 ..61 CF63
Thomas Av, Cat. CR3 ..176 DQ121
Thomas Baines Rd, SW11 ..100 DD83
Thomas Cl, Brwd. CM15 ..54 FY48
Thomas Cribb Ms, E6 ..87 EM72
Thomas Darby Ct, W11 ..81 CY72
Thomas Dean Rd, SE26
off Kangley Br Rd ..123 DZ91
Thomas Dinwiddy Rd, SE12 ..124 EH89
Thomas Doyle St, SE1 ..200 F6
Thomas Dr, Grav. DA12 ..131 GK89
Thomas Hardy Ho, N22 ..45 DM52
Thomas Hollywood Ho, E2
off Approach Rd ..84 DW68
Thomas La, SE6 ..123 EA87
Thomas More Ho, EC2
off The Barbican ..84 DQ71
Thomas More St, E1 ..202 B1
Thomas More Way, N2 ..64 DC55
Thomas Pl, W8
off St. Mary's Pl ..100 DB76
Thomas Rd, E14 ..85 DZ72
Thomas Rochford Way,
Wal.Cr. EN8 ..15 DZ27
Thomas Sims Ct, Horn. RM12 ..71 FH64
Thomas St, SE18 ..105 EN77
Thomas Wall Cl, Sutt. SM1
off Clarence Rd ..158 DB106
Thompson Av, Rich. TW9 ..98 CN83
Thompson Cl, Ilf. IG1
off High Rd ..69 EQ61
Slough SL3 ..93 BA77
Sutton SM3
off Barrington Rd ..140 DA102
Thompson Rd, SE22 ..122 DT86
Dagenham RM9 ..70 EZ62
Hounslow TW3 ..96 CB84
Uxbridge UB10 ..76 BL66
Thompson's Av, SE5 ..102 DQ80
Thompsons Cl, Wal.Cr.
(Chsht) EN7 ..14 DT29
Thompson's La, Loug.
(High Beach) IG10 ..32 EF39
Thompson Way, Rick. WD3 ..38 BG45
Thomson Cres, Croy. CR0 ..141 DN102
Thomson Rd, Har. HA3 ..61 CE55
Thong La, Grav. DA12 ..131 GM90
Thorburn Sq, SE1 ..202 B9
Thorburn Way, SW19 ..140 DC95
Thoresby St, N1 ..197 J2
Thorkhill Gdns, T.Ditt. KT7 ..137 CG102
Thorkhill Rd, T.Ditt. KT7 ..137 CH101
Thorley Cl, W.Byf. KT14 ..152 BG114
Thorley Gdns, Wok. GU22 ..152 BG114
Thornaby Gdns, N18 ..46 DU51
Thornash Cl, Wok. GU21 ..166 AW115
Thornash Rd, Wok. GU21 ..166 AW115
Thornash Way, Wok. GU21 ..166 AW115
Thorn Av, Bushey (Bushey Hth)
WD23 ..40 CC46
Thornbank Cl, Stai. TW19 ..114 BG85
Thornbridge Rd, Iver SL0 ..75 BC67
Thornbrook, Epp. (Thnwd)
CM16 ..18 EX25
Thornbury Av, Islw. TW7 ..97 CD80
Thornbury Cl, N16
off Boleyn Rd ..66 DS64
NW7 *off Kingsbridge Dr* ..43 CX52
Thornbury Gdns, Borwd. WD6 ..26 CQ42
Thornbury Rd, SW2 ..121 DL86
Isleworth TW7 ..97 CD81
Thornbury Sq, N6 ..65 DJ60
Thornby Rd, E5 ..66 DW62
Thorncliffe Rd, SW2 ..121 DL86
Southall UB2 ..96 BZ78
Thorn Cl, Brom. BR2 ..145 EN100
Northolt UB5 ..78 BZ69
Thorncombe Rd, SE22 ..122 DS85
Thorncroft, Egh. (Eng.Grn)
TW20 ..112 AW94
Hornchurch RM11 ..71 FH58
Thorncroft Cl, Couls. CR5
off Waddington Av ..175 DN119
Thorncroft Dr, Lthd. KT22 ..171 CH123
Thorncroft Rd, Sutt. SM1 ..158 DB105
Thorncroft St, SW8 ..101 DL80
Thorndales, Brwd. CM14 ..54 FX49
Thorndean St, SW18 ..120 DC89
Thorndene Av, N11 ..44 DG46
Thorndike Av, Nthlt. UB5 ..78 BX67
Thorndike Cl, SW10 ..100 DC80
Thorndike Ho, SW1
off Vauxhall Br Rd ..101 DK78
Thorndike Rd, N1 ..84 DQ65
Thorndike St, SW1 ..199 M9
Thorndon Cl, Orp. BR5 ..145 ET96
Thorndon Ct, Brwd. (Gt Warley)
CM13 ..53 FW51
Thorndon Gdns, Epsom
KT19 ..156 CS105
Thorndon Gate, Brwd.
(Ingrave) CM13 ..55 GC50
Thorndon Rd, Orp. BR5 ..145 ET96
Thorn Dr, Slou. (Geo.Grn) SL3 ..74 AY72
Thorndyke Ct, Pnr. HA5
off Westfield Pk ..40 BZ52
Thorne Cl, E11 ..68 EE63
E16 ..86 EG72
Ashford TW15 ..115 BQ94
Erith DA8 ..107 FC79
Esher KT10 ..155 CG108
Thorneloe Gdns, Croy. CR0 ..159 DN106
Thorne Pas, SW13 ..98 CS82
Thorne Rd, SW8 ..101 DL80
Thornes Cl, Beck. BR3 ..143 EC97
Thorne St, E16 ..86 EF72
SW13 ..98 CS83
Thornet Wd Rd, Brom. BR1 ..145 EN97
THORNEY, Iver SL0 ..94 BH76
Thorney Cres, SW11 ..100 DD80
Thorneycroft Cl, Walt. KT12 ..136 BW100
Thorneycroft Dr, Enf. EN3 ..31 EA38
Thorney Hedge Rd, W4 ..98 CP77
Thorney La N, Iver SL0 ..75 BF74
Thorney La S, Iver SL0 ..93 BF75
Thorney Mill Rd, Iver SL0 ..94 BG76
West Drayton UB7 ..94 BG76
Thorney St, SW1 ..199 P8
Thornfield Av, NW7 ..43 CY53
Thornfield Rd, W12 ..99 CV75
Banstead SM7 ..174 DA117
Thornford Rd, SE13 ..123 EC85
Thorngate Rd, W9 ..82 DA70
Thorngrove Rd, E13 ..86 EH67
Thornham Gro, E15 ..67 ED64
Thornham St, SE10 ..103 EB79
Thornhaugh Ms, WC1 ..195 N5
Thornhaugh St, WC1 ..195 N6
Thornhill, Epp. (N.Wld Bas.)
CM16 ..19 FC26
Thornhill Av, SE18 ..105 ES80
Surbiton KT6 ..138 CL103
Thornhill Br Wf, N1
off Caledonian Rd ..83 DM67
Thornhill Cres, N1 ..83 DM66
Thornhill Gdns, E10 ..67 EB61
Barking IG11 ..87 ES66
Thornhill Gro, N1
off Lofting Rd ..83 DM66
Thornhill Rd, E10 ..67 EB61
N1 ..83 DN66
Croydon CR0 ..142 DQ101
Northwood HA6 ..39 BQ49
Surbiton KT6 ..138 CL103
Uxbridge UB10 ..58 BM63
Thornhill Sq, N1 ..83 DM66
Thornhill Way, Shep. TW17 ..134 BN99
Thorn Ho, Beck. BR3 ..143 DY95
Thorn La, Rain. RM13 ..90 FK68
Thornlaw Rd, SE27 ..121 DN91
Thornley Cl, N17 ..46 DU52
Thornley Dr, Har. HA2 ..60 CB61
Thornley Pl, SE10
off Caradoc St ..104 EE78
Thornridge, Brwd. CM14 ..54 FV45
Thornsbeach Rd, SE6 ..123 EC88
Thornsett Pl, SE20 ..142 DV96
Thornsett Rd, SE20 ..142 DV96
SW18 ..120 DB89
Thornside, Edg. HA8
off High St ..42 CN51
Thorns Meadow, West.
(Brasted) TN16 ..180 EW123
Thorn Ter, SE15
off Nunhead Gro ..102 DW83
Thornton Av, SW2 ..121 DK88
W4 ..98 CS77
Croydon CR0 ..141 DM100
West Drayton UB7 ..94 BM76
Thornton Cl, West Dr. UB7 ..94 BM76
Thornton Ct, SW20 ..139 CX99
Thornton Cres, Couls. CR5 ..175 DN119
Thornton Dene, Beck. BR3 ..143 EA96
Thornton Gdns, SW12 ..121 DK88
Thornton Gro, Pnr. HA5 ..40 CA51
THORNTON HEATH, CR7 ..141 DP98
⇌ **Thornton Heath** ..142 DQ98
Thornton Hill, SW19 ..119 CY94
Thornton Ho, SE17
off Townsend St ..102 DS77
Thornton Pl, W1 ..194 E6
Thornton Rd, E11 ..67 ED61
N18 ..46 DW48
SW12 ..121 DK87
SW14 ..98 CR83
SW19 ..119 CX93
Barnet EN5 ..27 CY41
Belvedere DA17 ..107 FB77
Bromley BR1 ..124 EG92
Carshalton SM5 ..140 DD102
Croydon CR0 ..141 DM101
Ilford IG1 ..69 EP63
Potters Bar EN6 ..12 DC30
Thornton Heath CR7 ..141 DM101
Thornton Rd E, SW19
off Thornton Rd ..119 CX93
Thornton Rd Retail Pk,
Croy. CR0 ..141 DL100
Thornton Row, Th.Hth. CR7
off London Rd ..141 DN99
Thorntons Fm Av, Rom. RM7 ..71 FD60
Thornton St, SW9 ..101 DN82
Thornton Way, NW11 ..64 DB57
Thorntree Rd, SE7 ..104 EK78
Thornville Gro, Mitch. CR4 ..140 DC96
Thornville St, SE8 ..103 EA81
THORNWOOD, Epp. CM16 ..18 EW25
Thornwood Cl, E18 ..48 EH54
Thornwood Rd, SE13 ..124 EE85
Epping CM16 ..18 EV29
Thorogood Gdns, E15 ..68 EE64
Thorogood Way, Rain. RM13 ..89 FE67
Thorold Cl, S.Croy. CR2 ..161 DX110
Thorold Rd, N22 ..45 DL52
Ilford IG1 ..69 EP61
Thoroughfare, The, Tad.
(Walt.Hill) KT20 ..183 CU125
Thorparch Rd, SW8 ..101 DK81
THORPE, Egh. TW20 ..133 BC97
Thorpebank Rd, W12 ..81 CU74
Thorpe Bypass, Egh. TW20 ..133 BB96
Thorpe Cl, W10
off Cambridge Gdns ..81 CY72
Croydon (New Adgtn) CR0 ..161 EC111
Orpington BR6 ..145 ES103
🄷 **Thorpe Coombe Hosp**,
E17 ..67 EC55
Thorpe Cres, E17 ..47 DZ54
Watford WD19 ..40 BW45
Thorpedale Gdns, Ilf. IG2, IG6 ..69 EN56
Thorpedale Rd, N4 ..65 DL60
THORPE GREEN, Egh. TW20 ..133 BA98
Thorpe Hall Rd, E17 ..47 EC53
Thorpe Ind Est, Egh. TW20 ..133 BC96
THORPE LEA, Egh. TW20 ..113 BB93
Thorpe Lea Rd, Egh. TW20 ..113 BB93
Thorpe Lo, Horn. RM11 ..72 FL59
★ **Thorpe Park**, Cher. KT16 ..133 BE98
Thorpe Rd, E6 ..87 EM67
E7 ..68 EF63
E17 ..47 EC54
N15 ..66 DS58
Barking IG11 ..87 ER66
Chertsey KT16 ..133 BD99
Kingston upon Thames
KT2 ..118 CL94
Staines TW18 ..113 BD93
Thorpeside Cl, Stai. TW18 ..133 BE96
Thorpe Wk, Grnf. UB6 ..79 CE68
Thorpewood Av, SE26 ..122 DV89
Thorpland Av, Uxb. UB10 ..59 BQ62

★ Place of interest ⇌ Railway station ⊖ London Underground station DLR Docklands Light Railway station Tram Tramlink station 🄷 Hospital Riv Pedestrian ferry landing stage

Thorsden Cl, Wok. GU22 ....166 AY118
Thorsden Ct, Wok. GU22
off Guildford Rd 166 AY118
Thorsden Way, SE19
off Oaks Av 122 DS91
Thorverton Rd, NW2 ....63 CY62
Thoydon Rd, E3 ....85 DY68
Thrale Rd, SW16 ....121 DJ92
Thrale St, SE1 ....201 J3
Thrasher Cl, E8 off Stean St ..84 DT67
Thrawl St, E1 ....84 DT71
Threadneedle St, EC2 ......197 L9
Three Barrels Wk, EC4 ......197 J10
Three Colts Cor, E2
off Weaver St 84 DU70
Three Colts La, E2 ....84 DV70
Three Colt St, E14 ....85 DZ73
Three Cors, Bexh. DA7 .....107 FB82
Three Cranes Wk, EC4
off Bell Wf La 84 DQ73
Three Cups Yd, WC1 ....196 C7
Three Forests Way, Chig. IG7 .50 EW48
Loughton IG10
off The Clay Rd 32 EK38
Romford RM4 ....50 EW48
Waltham Abbey EN9 .....32 EK36
Three Gates Rd, Long.
(Fawk.Grn) DA3 ....149 FU102
Three Households, Ch.St.G.
HP8 ....36 AT49
Three Kings Rd, Mitch. CR4 .140 DG97
Three Kings Yd, W1 ....195 H10
Three Meadows Ms, Har. HA3 .41 CF53
Three Mill La, E3 ....85 EC69
Three Oak La, SE1 ....201 P4
Three Oaks Cl, Uxb. UB10 ...58 BM62
Three Quays Wk, EC3 ......201 N1
Three Valleys Way, Bushey
WD23 ....24 BX43
Threshers Pl, W11 ....81 CY73
Thriffwood, SE26 ....122 DW90
Thrift, The, Dart. (Bean) DA2 .129 FW90
Thrift Fm La, Borwd. WD6 ...26 CP40
Thrift Grn, Brwd. CM13
off Knight's Way 55 GA48
Thrift La, Sev. (Cudham)
TN14 ....179 ER117
Thrifts Hall Fm Ms, Epp.
(They.B.) CM16 ....33 ET37
Thrifts Mead, Epp. (They.B.)
CM16 ....33 ES37
Thrigby Rd, Chess. KT9 ....156 CM107
Throckmorten Rd, E16 ......86 EH72
Throgmorton Av, EC2 ......197 L8
Throgmorton St, EC2 ......197 L8
Throwley Cl, SE2 ....106 EW76
Throwley Rd, Sutt. SM1 ....158 DB106
Throwley Way, Sutt. SM1 ...158 DB105
Thrums, The, Wat. WD24 ....23 BV37
Thrupp Cl, Mitch. CR4 .....141 DH96
Thrupps Av, Walt. KT12 ....154 BX106
Thrupps La, Walt. KT12 ....154 BX106
Thrush Grn, Har. HA2 ....60 CA56
Rickmansworth WD3 ......38 BJ45
Thrush La, Pot.B. (Cuffley)
EN6 ....13 DL28
Thrush St, SE17 ....201 H10
Thunderer Rd, Dag. RM9 ....88 EY70
Thurbarn Rd, SE6 ....123 EB92
Thurland Ho, SE16
off Manor Est 102 DV77
Thurland Rd, SE16 ....202 B6
Thurlby Cl, Har. HA1
off Gayton Rd 61 CG58
Woodford Green IG8 ......49 EM50
Thurlby Rd, SE27 ....121 DN91
Wembley HA0 ....79 CK65
Thurleigh Av, SW12 ....120 DG86
Thurleigh Rd, SW12 ....120 DG86
Thurleston Av, Mord. SM4 ..139 CY99
Thurlestone Av, N12 ....44 DF51
Ilford IG3 ....69 ET63
Thurlestone Cl, Shep. TW17 .135 BQ100
Thurlestone Rd, SE27 ......121 DN90
Thurloe Cl, SW7 ....198 B8
Thurloe Gdns, Rom. RM1 ....71 FF58
Thurloe Pl, SW7 ....198 A8
Thurloe Pl Ms, SW7 ....198 A8
Thurloe Sq, SW7 ....198 B8
Thurloe St, SW7 ....198 A8
Thurloe Wk, Grays RM17 ...110 GA76
Thurlow Cl, E4
off Higham Sta Av 47 EB51
Thurlow Gdns, Ilf. IG6 ......49 ER51
Wembley HA0 ....61 CK64
Thurlow Hill, SE21 ....122 DQ88
Thurlow Pk Rd, SE21 ......121 DP88
Thurlow Rd, NW3 ....64 DD64
W7 ....97 CG75
Thurlow St, SE17 ....201 L10
Thurlow Ter, NW5 ....64 DG64
Thurlstone Rd, Ruis. HA4 ...59 BU62
Thurlton Ct, Wok. GU21
off Chobham Rd 166 AY116
Thurnby Ct, Twick. TW2 .....117 CE90
Thurnham Way, Tad. KT20 ..173 CW120
Thurrock Pk Way, Til. RM18 ..110 GD80
Thursby Rd, Wok. GU21 ....166 AU118
Thursland Rd, Sid. DA14 ....126 EY92
Thursley Cres, Croy. (New Adgtn)
CR0 ....161 ED108
Thursley Gdns, SW19 ......119 CX89
Thursley Rd, SE9 ....125 EM90
Thurso Cl, Rom. RM3 ....52 FP51
Thurso Ho, NW6
off Randolph Gdns 82 DB68
Thurso St, SW17 ....120 DD91
Thurstan Rd, SW20 ....119 CV94
Thurston Rd, SE13 ....103 EB82
Slough SL1 ....74 AS72
Southall UB1 ....78 BZ72
Thurston Rd Ind Est, SE13
off Jerrard St 103 EB83
Thurtle Rd, E2 ....84 DT67
Thwaite Cl, Erith DA8 ......107 FC79
Thyer Cl, Orp. BR6
off Isabella Dr 163 EQ105
Thyme Cl, SE3
off Nelson Mandela Rd ..104 EJ83
Thyra Gro, N12 ....44 DB51
Tibbatts Rd, E3 ....85 EB70
Tibbenham Pl, SE6 ....123 EA89
Tibbenham Wk, E13 ....86 EF68
Tibberton Sq, N1
off Popham Rd 84 DQ66
Tibbets Cl, SW19 ....119 CX88
Tibbet's Cor, SW15 ....119 CX87
Tibbet's Cor Underpass,
SW15 off West Hill 119 CX87
Tibbet's Ride, SW15 ....119 CX87
Tibbles Cl, Wat. WD25 ......24 BY35
Tibbs Hill Rd, Abb.L. WD5 ....7 BT30
Tiber Cl, E3 off Old Ford Rd ..85 EA67
Tiber Gdns, N1
off Copenhagen St 83 DM67
Ticehurst Cl, Orp. BR5
off Grovelands Rd 126 EU94
Ticehurst Rd, SE23 ....123 DY89
Tichborne, Rick. (Map.Cr.)
WD3 ....37 BD50
Tichmarsh, Epsom KT19 ....156 CQ110
Tickford Cl, SE2
off Ampleforth Rd 106 EW75
Tidal Basin Rd, E16 ....205 L1
Tidenham Gdns, Croy. CR0 .142 DS104
Tideslea Path, SE28
off Merbury Rd 87 ER74
Tideswell Rd, SW15 ....119 CW85
Croydon CR0 ....143 EA104
Tideway Cl, Rich. TW10
off Locksmeade Rd 117 CJ91
Tideway Ind Est, SW8 ......101 DJ79
Tideway Wk, SW8
off Cringle St 101 DJ80
Tidey St, E3 ....85 EA71
Tidford Rd, Well. DA16 .....105 ET82
Tidworth Rd, E3 ....85 EA70
Tidy's La, Epp. CM16 ....18 EV29
Tiepigs La, Brom. BR2 .....144 EE103
West Wickham BR4 ......144 EE103
Tierney Rd, SW2 ....121 DL88
Tiger Way, E5 ....66 DV63
Tigris Cl, N9 ....46 DW47
Tilbrook Rd, SE3 ....104 EJ83
Tilburstow Hill Rd, Gdse.
RH9 ....186 DW132
TILBURY, RM18 ....111 GG81
Tilbury Cl, SE15
off Sumner Rd 102 DT80
Orpington BR5 ....146 EV96
★ Tilbury Fort, Til. RM18 ...111 GJ84
Tilbury Rd, E6 ....87 EM68
E10 ....67 EC59
⇌ Tilbury Town 110 GE82
Tilbury Wk, Slou. SL3 ....93 BB76
Tildesley Rd, SW15 ....119 CW86
Tile Fm Rd, Orp. BR6 ......145 ER104
Tilehouse Cl, Borwd. WD6 ...26 CM41
Tilehouse La, Ger.Cr. SL9 ....37 BE53
Rickmansworth (W.Hyde)
WD3 ....37 BE53
Uxbridge (Denh.) UB9 ....57 BE58
Tilehouse Way, Uxb. (Denh.)
UB9 ....57 BF59
Tilehurst Pt, SE2
off Yarnton Way 106 EW75
Tilehurst Rd, SW18 ....120 DD88
Sutton SM3 ....157 CY106
Tilekiln Cl, Wal.Cr. (Chsht) EN7 .14 DS29
Tile Kiln La, N6 ....65 DJ60
N13 ....46 DQ50
Bexley DA5 ....127 FC89
Uxbridge (Hare.) UB9 .....59 BP59
Tilers Cl, Red. (S.Merst.) RH1 .185 DJ131
Tile Yd, E14
off Commercial Rd 85 DZ72
Tileyard Rd, N7 ....83 DL66
Tilford Av, Croy. (New Adgtn)
CR0 ....161 EC109
Tilford Gdns, SW19 ....119 CX89
Tilia Cl, Sutt. SM1 ....157 CZ106
Tilia Rd, E5 off Clarence Rd ..66 DV63
Tilia Wk, SW9
off Moorland Rd 101 DP84
Till Av, Dart. (Fnghm) DA4 ..148 FM102
Tiller Rd, E14 ....203 P6
Tillett Cl, NW10 ....80 CQ65
Tillett Sq, SE16 ....203 L5
Tillett Way, E2
off Gosset St 84 DU69
Tilley La, Epsom (Headley)
KT18 ....172 CQ123
Tilley Rd, Felt. TW13 ....115 BU88
Tillgate Common, Red.
(Bletch.) RH1 ....186 DQ133
Tillingbourne Gdns, N3 .....63 CZ55
Tillingbourne Grn, Orp. BR5 .146 EU98
Tillingbourne Way, N3
off Tillingbourne Gdns ...63 CZ55
Tillingdown Hill, Cat. CR3 ..176 DU122
Tillingdown La, Cat. CR3 ..176 DV124
Tillingham Ct, Wal.Abb. EN9 .16 EG33
Tillingham Way, N12 ....44 DA49
Tilling Rd, NW2 ....63 CW60
Tillings Cl, SE5
off Warner Rd 102 DQ81
Tilling Way, Wem. HA9 ......61 CK61
Tillman St, E1
off Bigland St 84 DV72
Tilloch St, N1
off Carnoustie Dr 83 DM66
Tillotson Ct, SW8
off Wandsworth Rd 101 DL81
Tillotson Rd, N9 ....46 DT47
Harrow HA3 ....40 CB52
Ilford IG1 ....69 EN59
Tilly's La, Stai. TW18 ....113 BF91
Tilmans Mead, Dart.
(Fnghm) DA4 ....148 FM101
Tilney Ct, EC1 ....197 J4
Tilney Dr, Buck.H. IG9 ....48 EG47
Tilney Gdns, N1 ....84 DR65
Tilney Rd, Dag. RM9 ....88 EZ65
Southall UB2 ....96 BW77
Tilney St, W1 ....198 G2
Tilson Cl, SE5
off Coleman Rd 102 DS80
Tilson Gdns, SW2 ....121 DL87
Tilson Ho, SW2
off Tilson Gdns 121 DL87
Tilson Rd, N17 ....46 DU53
Tilston Cl, E11
off Matcham Rd 68 EF62
Tilt Cl, Cob. KT11 ....170 BY116
Tilt Meadow, Cob. KT11 ....170 BY116
Tilton St, SW6 ....99 CY79
Tilt Rd, Cob. KT11 ....170 BW115
Tiltwood, The, W3
off Acacia Rd 80 CQ73
Tilt Yd App, SE9 ....125 EM86
Timber Cl, Chis. BR7 ....145 EN96
Woking GU22
off Hacketts La 151 BF114
Timber Ct, Grays RM17
off Columbia Wf Rd 110 GA79
Timbercroft, Epsom KT19 ...156 CS105
Timbercroft La, SE18 ......105 ES79
Timberdene, NW4 ....43 CX54
Timberdene Av, Ilf. IG6 .....49 EP53
Timberhill, Ashtd. KT21
off Ottways La 172 CL119
Timber Hill Cl, Cher.
(Ott.) KT16 ....151 BC108
Timber Hill Rd, Cat. CR3 ....176 DU124
Timberland Cl, SE15
off Peckham Hill St 102 DU80
Timberland Rd, E1 ....84 DV72
Timber La, Cat. CR3
off Timber Hill Rd 176 DU124
Timberling Gdns, S.Croy. CR2
off Sanderstead Rd 160 DR109
Timber Mill Way, SW4 ......101 DK83
Timber Pond Rd, SE16 .....203 J3
Timber Ridge, Rick. (Loud.)
WD3 ....22 BK42
Timberslip Dr, Wall. SM6 ...159 DK109
Timber St, EC1 ....197 H4
Timbertop Rd, West. (Bigg.H.)
TN16 ....178 EJ118
Timberwharf Rd, N16 ....66 DU58
Timbrell Pl, SE16 ....203 M3
Time Sq, E8 ....66 DT64
Times Sq, Sutt. SM1 ....158 DB106
Times Sq Shop Cen, Sutt.
SM1 off High St 158 DB106
Timms Cl, Brom. BR1 ......145 EM98
Timothy Cl, SW4 off Elms Rd .121 DJ85
Bexleyheath DA6 ....126 EY85
Timothy Ho, Erith DA18
off Kale Rd 106 EY75
Timothy Rd, E3 ....85 DZ71
Timperley Gdns, Red. RH1 ..184 DE132
Timsbury Wk, SW15 ....119 CU88
Timsway, Stai. TW18 ....113 BF92
Tindale Cl, S.Croy. CR2 ....160 DR111
Tindall Cl, Rom. RM3 ....52 FM54
Tindall Ms, Horn. RM12 .....72 FJ62
Tindal St, SW9 ....101 DP81
Tinderbox All, SW14 ....98 CR83
Tine Rd, Chig. IG7 ....49 ES50
Tingeys Top La, Enf. EN2 ....29 DN36
Tinniswood Cl, N5
off Drayton Pk 65 DN64
Tinsey Cl, Egh. TW20 ....113 BB92
Tinsley Cl, SE25
off Eldon Pk 142 DV98
Tinsley Rd, E1 ....84 DW71
Tintagel Cl, Epsom KT17 ...157 CT114
Tintagel Cres, SE22 ....102 DT84
Tintagel Dr, Stan. HA7 ......41 CK49
Tintagel Gdns, SE22
off Oxonian St 102 DT84
Tintagel Rd, Orp. BR5 ......146 EW103
Tintagel Way, Wok. GU22 ...167 BA116
Tintern Av, NW9 ....62 CP55
Tintern Cl, SW15 ....119 CY85
SW19 ....120 DC94
Tintern Ct, W13
off Green Man La 79 CG73
Tintern Gdns, N14 ....45 DL45
Tintern Path, NW9
off Ruthin Cl 62 CS58
Tintern Rd, N22 ....46 DQ53
Carshalton SM5 ....140 DD102
Tintern St, SW4 ....101 DL84
Tintern Way, Har. HA2 ......60 CB60
Tinto Rd, E16 ....86 EG70
Tinwell Ms, Borwd. WD6
off Cranes Way 26 CQ43
Tinworth St, SE11 ....200 A10
Tippendell La, St.Alb.
(Park St) AL2 ....8 CB26
Tippetts Cl, Enf. EN2 ....30 DQ39
Tipthorpe Rd, SW11 ....100 DG83
Tipton Cotts, Add. KT15
off Oliver Cl 152 BG105
Tipton Dr, Croy. CR0 ....160 DS105
Tiptree Cl, E4
off Mapleton Rd 47 EC48
Hornchurch RM11 ....72 FN60
Tiptree Cres, Ilf. IG5 ....69 EN55
Tiptree Dr, Enf. EN2 ....30 DR42
Tiptree Est, Ilf. IG5 ....69 EN55
Tiptree Rd, Ruis. HA4 ....59 BV63
Tirlemont Rd, S.Croy. CR2 ..160 DQ108
Tirrell Rd, Croy. CR0 ....142 DQ100
Tisbury Ct, W1 off Rupert St ..83 DK73
Tisbury Rd, SW16 ....141 DL96
Tisdall Pl, SE17 ....201 L9
Tissington Ct, SE16
off Rotherhithe New Rd .103 DX77
Titan Rd, Grays RM17 ......110 GA78
Titchborne Row, W2 ....194 C9
Titchfield Rd, NW8 ....82 DF67
Carshalton SM5 ....140 DD102
Enfield EN3 ....31 DY37
Titchfield Wk, Cars. SM5
off Titchfield Rd 140 DD101
Titchwell Rd, SW18 ....120 DD87
Tite Hill, Egh. TW20 ....112 AX92
Tite St, SW3 ....100 DF78
★ Tithe Barn Agricultural & Folk
Mus, The, Upmin. RM14 ..73 FR59
Tithe Barn Cl, Kings.T. KT2 ..138 CM95
Tithe Barn Ct, Abb.L. WD5
off Dairy Way 7 BT29
Tithe Barn Way, Nthlt. UB5 ..77 BV69
Tithe Cl, NW7 ....43 CU53
Hayes UB4
off Gledwood Dr 77 BT71
Virginia Water GU25 .....132 AX100
Walton-on-Thames KT12 .135 BV100
Tithe Ct, Slou. SL3 ....93 BA77
Tithe Fm Av, Har. HA2 ......60 CA62
Tithe Fm Cl, Har. HA2 ......60 CA62
Tithe La, Stai. (Wrays.) TW19 .113 BA86
Tithe Meadow, Wat. WD18 ...23 BR44
Tithe Meadows, Vir.W. GU25 .132 AW100
Tithepit Shaw La, Warl. CR6 .176 DV115
Tithe Wk, NW7 ....43 CU53
Titian Av, Bushey (Bushey Hth)
WD23 ....41 CE45
Titley Cl, E4 ....47 EA50
Titmus Cl, Uxb. UB8 ....77 BQ72
Titmuss Av, SE28 ....88 EV73
Titmuss St, W12
off Goldhawk Rd 99 CW75
TITSEY, Oxt. RH8 ....188 EH125
Titsey Hill, Oxt. (Titsey) RH8 .178 EF123
Titsey Rd, Oxt. RH8 ....188 EH125
Tiverton Av, Ilf. IG5 ....69 EN55
Tiverton Cl, Croy. CR0
off Exeter Rd 142 DT101
Tiverton Dr, SE9 ....125 EQ88
Tiverton Gro, Rom. RM3 .....52 FN50
Tiverton Ho, Enf. EN3 ....31 DX41
Tiverton Rd, N15 ....66 DR58
N18 ....46 DS50
NW10 ....81 CX67
Edgware HA8 ....42 CM54
Hounslow TW3 ....96 CC82
Potters Bar EN6 ....12 DD31
Ruislip HA4 ....59 BU62
Thornton Heath CR7
off Willett Rd 141 DN99
Wembley HA0 ....80 CL68
Tiverton St, SE1 ....201 H7
Tiverton Way, NW7 ....43 CX52
Chessington KT9 ....155 CJ106
Tivoli Ct, SE16 ....203 M4
Tivoli Gdns, SE18 ....104 EL77
Tivoli Rd, N8 ....65 DK57
SE27 ....122 DQ92
Hounslow TW4 ....96 BY84
Toad La, Houns. TW4 ....96 BZ84
Tobacco Dock, E1 ....202 D1
Tobacco Quay, E1 ....202 D1
Tobago St, E14 ....203 P4
Tobin Cl, NW3 ....82 DE66
Epsom KT19 ....156 CP111
Toby La, E1 ....85 DY70
Toby Way, Surb. KT5 ....138 CP103
Todd Cl, Rain. RM13 ....90 FK70
Todds Wk, N7 off Andover Rd .65 DM61
Toft Av, Grays RM17 ....110 GD77
Tokenhouse Yd, EC2 ....197 K8
Token Yd, SW15
off Montserrat Rd 99 CY84
TOKYNGTON, Wem. HA9 ....80 CP65
Tokyngton Av, Wem. HA9 ....80 CN65
Toland Sq, SW15 ....119 CU85
Tolcarne Dr, Pnr. HA5 ....59 BV55
Toldene Ct, Couls. CR5 .....175 DM120
Toley Av, Wem. HA9 ....62 CL59
Tolhurst Dr, W10
off Beethoven St 81 CY69
Toll Bar Ct, Sutt. SM2 ......158 DB109
Tollbridge Cl, W10
off Kensal Rd 81 CY70
Tolldene Cl, Wok. (Knap.) GU21
off Robin Hood Rd 166 AS117
Tollers La, Couls. CR5 ......175 DM119
Tollesbury Gdns, Ilf. IG6 ....69 ER55
Tollet St, E1 ....85 DX70
Tollgate Cl, Rick. (Chorl.) WD3 .21 BF41
Tollgate Dr, SE21 ....122 DS89
Hayes UB4 ....78 BX73
Tollgate Gdns, NW6 ....82 DB68
Tollgate Ho, NW6
off Tollgate Gdns 82 DB68
Tollgate Rd, E6 ....86 EK71
E16 ....86 EJ71
Dartford DA2 ....129 FR87
Waltham Cross EN8 ....31 DX35
Tollhouse La, Wall. SM6 ....159 DJ109
Tollhouse Way, N19 ....65 DJ61
Tollington Pk, N4 ....65 DM61
Tollington Pl, N4 ....65 DM61
Tollington Rd, N7 ....65 DM63
Tollington Way, N7 ....65 DL62
Tolmers Av, Pot.B. (Cuffley)
EN6 ....13 DL28
Tolmers Gdns, Pot.B. (Cuffley)
EN6 ....13 DL29
Tolmers Ms, Hert. (Newgate St)
SG13 ....13 DL25
Tolmers Pk, Hert. (Newgate St)
SG13 ....13 DL25
Tolmers Rd, Pot.B. (Cuffley)
EN6 ....13 DL27
Tolmers Sq, NW1 ....195 L4
Tolpits Cl, Wat. WD18 ....23 BT43
Tolpits La, Wat. WD18 ....23 BT44
Tolpuddle Av, E13
off Rochester Av 86 EJ67
Tolpuddle St, N1 ....83 DN68
Tolsford Rd, E5 ....66 DV64
Tolson Rd, Islw. TW7 ....97 CG83
Tolvaddon, Wok. GU21
off Cardingham 166 AU117
Tolverne Rd, SW20 ....139 CW95
TOLWORTH, Surb. KT6 .....138 CN103
⇌ Tolworth 138 CP103
Tolworth Bdy, Surb. KT6 ...138 CP102
Tolworth Cl, Surb. KT6 .....138 CP102
Tolworth Gdns, Rom. RM6 ...70 EX57
H Tolworth Hosp,
Surb. KT6 ....138 CN103
Tolworth Junct, Surb. KT5
off Kingston Bypass 138 CP103
Tolworth Pk Rd, Surb. KT6 ..138 CM103
Tolworth Ri N, Surb. KT5
off Elmbridge Av 138 CQ101
Tolworth Ri S, Surb. KT5
off Warren Dr S 138 CQ102
Tolworth Rd, Surb. KT6 ....138 CL103
Tolworth Twr, Surb. KT6 ....138 CP103
Tomahawk Gdns, Nthlt. UB5
off Javelin Way 78 BX69
Tom Coombs Cl, SE9
off Well Hall Rd 104 EL84
Tom Cribb Business Cen, SE28
off Tom Cribb Rd 105 ER76
Tom Cribb Rd, SE28 ....105 EQ76
Tom Gros Cl, E15
off Maryland St 67 ED64
Tom Hood Cl, E15
off Maryland St 67 ED64
Tom Jenkinson Rd, E16 .....205 N2
Tomkins Cl, Borwd. WD6
off Tallis Way 26 CL39
Tomkyns La, Upmin. RM14 ..73 FR56
Tomlin Cl, Epsom KT19 .....156 CR111
Tomlins Gro, E3 ....85 EA69
Tomlinson Cl, E2 ....84 DT69
W4 ....98 CP78
Tomlins Orchard, Bark. IG11 ..87 EQ67
Tomlins Ter, E14
off Rhodeswell Rd 85 DZ71
Tomlins Wk, N7
off Briset Way 65 DM61
Tomlyns Cl, Brwd. (Hutt.)
CM13 ....55 GE44
Tom Mann Cl, Bark. IG11 ....87 ES67
Tom Nolan Cl, E15 ....86 EE68
Tomo Ind Est, Uxb. UB8 .....76 BJ72
Tompion Ho, EC1
off Percival St 83 DP69
Tompion St, EC1 ....196 F3
Toms Hill, Kings L. WD4 .....22 BL36
Rickmansworth WD3 ......22 BL36
Toms La, Abb.L. (Bedmond)
WD5 ....7 BR28
Kings Langley WD4 ....7 BP29
Tom Smith Cl, SE10
off Maze Hill 104 EE79
Tomswood Ct, Ilf. IG6 ....49 EQ53
Tomswood Hill, Ilf. IG6 ......49 EP52
Tomswood Rd, Chig. IG7 .....49 EN51
Tom Thumbs Arch, E3
off Malmesbury Rd 85 EA68
Tom Williams Ho, SW6
off Clem Attlee Ct 99 CZ79
Tonbridge Cl, Bans. SM7 ...158 DF114
Tonbridge Cres, Har. HA3 ...62 CL56
Tonbridge Ho, SE25 ....142 DU97
Tonbridge Rd, Rom. RM3 ....52 FK52
Sevenoaks TN13 ....191 FJ127
West Molesey KT8 ......136 BY98
Tonbridge St, WC1 ....195 P2
Tonbridge Wk, WC1
off Tonbridge St 83 DL69
Tonfield Rd, Sutt. SM3 .....139 CZ102
Tonge Cl, Beck. BR3 ....143 EA99
Tonsley Hill, SW18 ....120 DB85
Tonsley Pl, SW18 ....120 DB85
Tonsley Rd, SW18 ....120 DB85
Tonsley St, SW18 ....120 DB85
Tonstall Rd, Epsom KT19 ...156 CR110
Mitcham CR4 ....140 DG96
Tony Cannell Ms, E3
off Maplin St 85 DZ69
Tooke Cl, Pnr. HA5 ....40 BY53
Tookey Cl, Har. HA3 ....62 CM59
Took's Ct, EC4 ....196 D8
Tooley St, SE1 ....201 L2
Gravesend (Nthflt) DA11 ..130 GD87
Toorack Rd, Har. HA3 ....41 CD54
TOOT HILL, Ong. CM5 ....19 FF30
Toot Hill Rd, Ong. CM5 ......19 FF29
⇌ Tooting 120 DG93
⊖ Tooting Bec 120 DF90
Tooting Bec, SW17 ....120 DF90
Tooting Bec Gdns, SW16 ....121 DK91
Tooting Bec Rd, SW16 .....120 DG90
SW17 ....120 DG90
⊖ Tooting Broadway 120 DE92
Tooting Bdy, SW17 ....120 DE91
TOOTING GRAVENEY,
SW17 ....120 DE93
Tooting Gro, SW17 ....120 DE92
Tooting High St, SW17 .....120 DE93
Tootswood Rd, Brom. BR2 ..144 EE99
Tooveys Mill Cl, Kings L. WD4 .6 BN28
Topaz Ho, E15 off Romford Rd .86 EF65
Topaz Wk, NW2 off Marble Dr .63 CX59
Topcliffe Dr, Orp. BR6 ......163 ER105
Top Dartford Rd, Dart. DA2 ..127 FF94
Swanley BR8 ....127 FF94
Topham Sq, N17 ....46 DQ53
Topham St, EC1 ....196 D4
Top Ho Ri, E4
off Parkhill Rd 47 EC45
Topiary, The, Ashtd. KT21 ...172 CL120
Topiary Sq, Rich. TW9 ....98 CM83
Topland Rd, Ger.Cr. (Chal.St.P.)
SL9 ....36 AX52
Toplands Av, S.Ock. (Aveley)
RM15 ....90 FP74
Topley St, SE9 ....104 EK84
Topmast Pt, E14 ....203 P5
Top Pk, Beck. BR3 ....144 EE99
Gerrards Cross SL9 ....56 AW58
Topping La, Uxb. UB8 ....76 BK69
Topp Wk, NW2 ....63 CW61
Topsfield Cl, N8
off Wolseley Rd 65 DK57
Topsfield Par, N8
off Tottenham La 65 DL57
Topsfield Rd, N8 ....65 DL57
Topsham Rd, SW17 ....120 DF90
Torbay Rd, NW6 ....81 CZ66
Harrow HA2 ....60 BY61
Torbay St, NW1
off Hawley Rd 83 DH66
Torbitt Way, Ilf. IG2 ....69 ET57
Torbridge Cl, Edg. HA8 ......42 CL52
Torbrook Cl, Bex. DA5 ......126 EY86
Torcross Dr, SE23 ....122 DW89
Torcross Rd, Ruis. HA4 ......59 BV62
Tor Gdns, W8 ....100 DA75
Tor Gro, SE28 ....87 ES74
Torin Ct, Egh. (Eng.Grn)
TW20 ....112 AW92
Torland Dr, Lthd. (Oxshott)
KT22 ....155 CD114
Tor La, Wey. KT13 ....153 BQ111
Tormead Cl, Sutt. SM1 .....158 DA107
Tormount Rd, SE18 ....105 ES79
Tornay Ho, N1
off Priory Grn Est 83 DM68
Toronto Av, E12 ....69 EM63
Toronto Rd, Ilf. IG1 ....69 EP60
Tilbury RM18 ....111 GG82
Torquay Gdns, Ilf. IG4 ....68 EK56
Torquay St, W2 off Harrow Rd .82 DB71
Torrance Cl, SE7 ....104 EK79
Hornchurch RM11 ....71 FH60
Torrens Rd, E15 ....86 EF65

Torrens Rd, SW2 121 DM85
Torrens Sq, E15 86 EE65
Torrens St, EC1 196 E1
Torrens Wk, Grav. DA12 131 GL92
Torres Sq, E14
off Maritime Quay 103 EA78
Torre Wk, Cars. SM5 140 DE102
Torrey Dr, SW9
off Overton Rd 101 DN82
Torriano Av, NW5 65 DK64
Torriano Cotts, NW5
off Torriano Av 65 DK64
Torriano Ms, NW5 65 DJ64
Torridge Gdns, SE15 102 DW84
Torridge Rd, Slou. SL3 93 BB79
Thornton Heath CR7 141 DP99
Torridon Cl, Wok. GU21 166 AV117
Torridon Ho, NW6
off Randolph Gdns 82 DB68
Torridon Rd, SE6 123 ED88
SE13 123 ED87
Torrington Av, N12 44 DD50
Torrington Cl, N12 44 DD49
Esher (Clay.) KT10 155 CE107
Torrington Dr, Har. HA2 60 CB63
Loughton IG10 33 EQ42
Potters Bar EN6 12 DD32
Torrington Gdns, N11 45 DJ51
Greenford UB6 79 CJ66
Loughton IG10 33 EQ42
Torrington Gro, N12 44 DE50
Torrington Pk, N12 44 DC50
Torrington Pl, E1 202 C2
WC1 195 L6
Torrington Rd, E18 68 EG55
Dagenham RM8 70 EZ60
Esher (Clay.) KT10 155 CE107
Greenford UB6 79 CJ67
Ruislip HA4 59 BT62
Torrington Sq, WC1 195 N5
Croydon CR0
off Tavistock Gro 142 DR101
Torrington Way, Mord. SM4 140 DA100
Tor Rd, Well. DA16 106 EW81
Torr Rd, SE20 123 DX94
Torver Rd, Har. HA1 61 CE56
Torver Way, Orp. BR6 145 ER104
Torwood La, Whyt. CR3 176 DT120
Torwood Rd, SW15 119 CU85
Torworth Rd, Borwd. WD6 26 CM39
Tothill Ho, SW1 *off Page St* 101 DK77
Tothill St, SW1 199 M5
Totnes Rd, Well. DA16 106 EV80
Totnes Wk, N2 64 DD56
Tottan Ter, E1 85 DX72
Tottenhall Rd, N13 45 DN51
TOTTENHAM, N17 46 DS53
⊖ **Tottenham Court Road** 195 M8
Tottenham Ct Rd, W1 195 L5
Tottenham Grn E, N15 66 DT56
TOTTENHAM HALE, N17 66 DV55
≠ **Tottenham Hale** 66 DV55
⊖ **Tottenham Hale** 66 DV55
Tottenham Hale, N15
off High Rd 66 DT55
Tottenham Hale Retail Pk,
N15 66 DU56
★ **Tottenham Hotspur FC**,
N17 46 DT52
Tottenham La, N8 65 DL57
Tottenham Ms, W1 195 L6
Tottenham Rd, N1 84 DS65
Tottenham St, W1 195 L7
Totterdown St, SW17 120 DF91
TOTTERIDGE, N20 43 CY46
⊖ **Totteridge & Whetstone** 44 DB47
Totteridge Common, N20 43 CU47
Totteridge Grn, N20 44 DA47
Totteridge Ho, SW11 100 DD82
Totteridge La, N20 44 DA47
Totteridge Rd, Enf. EN3 31 DX37
Totteridge Village, N20 43 CY46
Totternhoe Cl, Har. HA3 61 CJ57
Totton Rd, Th.Hth. CR7 141 DN97
Toucan Cl, NW10
off Abbeyfields Cl 80 CN69
Toulmin St, SE1 201 H5
Toulon St, SE5 102 DQ80
Tournay Rd, SW6 99 CZ80
Tours Pas, SW11 100 DD84
Toussaint Wk, SE16 202 C6
Tovey Cl, St.Alb. (Lon.Col.)
AL2 9 CK26
Tovil Cl, SE20 142 DU96
Tovy Ho, SE1
off Avondale Sq 102 DU78
Towcester Rd, E3 85 EB70
Tower, The, Couls. CR5 175 DK122
Tower 42, EC2 197 M8
Tower Br, E1 201 P3
SE1 201 P3
Tower Br App, E1 201 P2
★ **Tower Br Exhib**, SE1 201 P3
Tower Br Piazza, SE1 201 P3
Tower Br Rd, SE1 201 M7
Tower Br Wf, E1 202 B3
Tower Cl, NW3
off Lyndhurst Rd 64 DD64
SE20 122 DV94
Gravesend DA12 131 GL92
Ilford IG6 49 EP51
Orpington BR6 145 ET103
Woking GU21 166 AX117
Tower Ct, WC2 195 P9
Brentwood CM14 54 FV47
Tower Cft, Dart. (Eyns.) DA4
off High St 148 FL103
Tower Gdns, Esher (Clay.)
KT10 155 CG108
Tower Gdns Rd, N17 46 DQ53
Towergate Cl, Uxb. UB8 58 BL64
DLR **Tower Gateway** 84 DT73
Tower Gro, Wey. KT13 135 BS103
Tower Hamlets Rd, E7 68 EF63
E17 67 EA55
⊖ **Tower Hill** 197 P10
Tower Hill, EC3 201 P1
Brentwood CM14 54 FW47
Tower Hill, Kings L. (Chipper.)
WD4 5 BE29
Tower Hill Ter, EC3
off Byward St 84 DS73
Tower La, Wem. HA9
off Main Dr 61 CK62
Tower Ms, E17 67 EA56
★ **Tower Millennium Pier**,
EC3 201 N2
Tower Mill Rd, SE15 102 DS80
★ **Tower of London**, EC3 201 P1
Tower Pk Rd, Dart. DA1 127 FF85
Tower Pl, EC3 201 N1
Warlingham CR6 177 EA115
Tower Pl E, EC3
off Lower Thames St 84 DS73
Tower Pt, Enf. EN2 30 DR42
Tower Retail Pk, Dart. DA1 127 FF85
Tower Ri, Rich. TW9
off Jocelyn Rd 98 CL83
Tower Rd, NW10 81 CU66
Belvedere DA17 107 FC77
Bexleyheath DA7 107 FB84
Dartford DA1 128 FJ86
Epping CM16 17 ES30
Orpington BR6 145 ET103
Tadworth KT20 173 CW123
Twickenham TW1 117 CF90
Tower Royal, EC4 197 J10
Towers, The, Ken. CR8 176 DQ115
Towers Av, Uxb. (Hlgdn)
UB10 77 BQ69
Towers Pl, Rich. TW9
off Eton St 118 CL85
Towers Rd, Grays RM17 110 GC78
Pinner HA5 40 BY53
Southall UB1 78 CA70
Tower St, WC2 195 N9
Towers Wk, Wey. KT13 153 BP107
Towers Wd, Dart. (S.Darenth)
DA4 149 FR95
Tower Ter, N22 *off Mayes Rd* 45 DM54
SE4 *off Foxberry Rd* 103 DY84
Tower Vw, Croy. CR0 143 DX101
Towfield Rd, Felt. TW13 116 BZ89
Towing Path Wk, N1
off York Way 83 DL67
Town, The, Enf. EN2 30 DR41
Towncourt Cres, Orp. BR5 145 EQ99
Towncourt La, Orp. BR5 145 ER100
Town Ct Path, N4 66 DQ60
Town End, Cat. CR3 176 DS122
Town End Cl, Cat. CR3 176 DS122
Towney Mead, Nthlt. UB5 78 BZ68
Towney Mead Ct, Nthlt. UB5
off Towney Mead 78 BZ68
Town Fm Way, Stai. (Stanw.)
TW19 *off Town La* 114 BK87
Townfield, Rick. WD3 38 BJ45
Townfield Cor, Grav. DA12 131 GJ88
Town Fld La, Ch.St.G. HP8 36 AW48
Townfield Rd, Hayes UB3 77 BT74
Townfield Sq, Hayes UB3 77 BT74
Townfield Way, Islw. TW7 97 CG82
Towngate, Cob. KT11 170 BY115
Town Hall App, N16
off Milton Gro 66 DS63
Town Hall App Rd, N15 66 DT56
Town Hall Av, W4 98 CR78
Town Hall Rd, SW11 100 DF83
Townholm Cres, W7 97 CF76
Town La, Stai. (Stanw.) TW19 114 BK86
Townley Ct, E15 86 EF65
Townley Rd, SE22 122 DS85
Bexleyheath DA6 126 EZ85
Townley St, SE17 201 K10
Townmead, Red. (Bletch.)
RH1 186 DR133
Townmead Business Cen, SW6
off William Morris Way 100 DC83
Town Meadow, Brent. TW8 97 CK80
Townmead Rd, SW6 100 DC82
Richmond TW9 98 CP82
Waltham Abbey EN9 15 EC34
Town Path, Egh. TW20 113 BA92
Town Pier, Grav. DA11
off West St 131 GH86
Town Quay, Bark. IG11 87 EP67
Town Rd, N9 46 DV47
Townsend Av, N14 45 DK49
Townsend Ind Est, NW10 80 CR68
Townsend La, NW9 62 CR59
Woking GU22
off St. Peters Rd 167 BB121
Townsend Ms, SW18
off Waynflete St 120 DC89
Townsend Rd, N15 66 DT57
Ashford TW15 114 BL92
Southall UB1 78 BY74
Townsend St, SE17 201 L9
Townsend Way, Nthwd. HA6 39 BT52
Townsend Yd, N6 65 DH60
Townshend Cl, Sid. DA14 126 EV93
Townshend Est, NW8 82 DE68
Townshend Rd, NW8 82 DE67
Chislehurst BR7 125 EP92
Richmond TW9 98 CM84
Townshend Ter, Rich. TW9 98 CM84
Townslow La, Wok. (Wisley)
GU23 168 BJ116
Townson Av, Nthlt. UB5 77 BU69
Townson Way, Nthlt. UB5
off Townson Av 77 BU68
Town Sq, Erith DA8
off Pier Rd 107 FE79
Woking GU21
off Church St E 167 AZ117
Town Sq Cres, Green.
(Bluewater) DA9 129 FT87
Town Tree Rd, Ashf. TW15 114 BN92
Towpath, Shep. TW17 134 BM103
Towpath Rd, N18 47 DX51
Towpath Wk, E9 67 DZ64
Towpath Way, Croy. CR0 142 DT100
Towton Rd, SE27 122 DQ89
Toynbec Cl, Chis. BR7
off Beechwood Ri 125 EP91
★ **Toynbee Hall**, E1 84 DT71
Toynbee Rd, SW20 139 CY95
Toynbee St, E1 197 P7
Toyne Way, N6 *off Gaskell Rd* 64 DF58
Tracery, The, Bans. SM7 174 DB115
Tracey Av, NW2 63 CW64
Tracious Cl, Wok. GU21
off Sythwood 166 AV116
Tracious La, Wok. GU21 166 AV116
Tracy Av, Slou. SL3
off Ditton Rd 93 AZ79
Tracy Ct, Stan. HA7 41 CJ52
Trade Cl, N13 45 DN49
Trader Rd, E6 87 EP72
Tradescant Rd, SW8 101 DL80
Trading Est Rd, NW10 80 CQ70
Trafalgar Av, N17 46 DS51
SE15 102 DT78
Worcester Park KT4 139 CX102
Trafalgar Business Cen,
Bark. IG11 87 ET70
Trafalgar Cl, SE16 203 K8
Trafalgar Ct, E1 202 G1
Cobham KT11 153 BU113
Trafalgar Dr, Walt. KT12 135 BU104
Trafalgar Gdns, E1 85 DX71
W8 *off South End Row* 100 DB76
Trafalgar Gro, SE10 103 ED79
Trafalgar Ms, E9 85 DZ65
Trafalgar Pl, E11 68 EG56
N18 46 DU50
Trafalgar Rd, SE10 103 ED79
SW19 120 DB94
Dartford DA1 128 FL89
Gravesend DA11 131 GG87
Rainham RM13 89 FF68
Twickenham TW2 117 CD89
Trafalgar Sq, SW1 199 N2
WC2 199 N2
Trafalgar St, SE17 201 K10
Trafalgar Ter, Har. HA1
off Nelson Rd 61 CE60
Trafalgar Trd Est, Enf. EN3 31 DY42
Trafalgar Way, E14 204 D2
Croydon CR0 141 DM103
Trafford Cl, E15 67 EB64
Ilford IG6 49 ET51
Radlett (Shenley) WD7 10 CL32
Trafford Rd, Th.Hth. CR7 141 DM99
Trahorn Cl, E1 84 DU70
Tralee Ct, SE16 202 E10
Tramsheds Ind Est, Croy.
CR0 141 DK101
Tramway Av, E15 86 EE66
N9 46 DV45
Tramway Cl, SE20 142 DW95
Tramway Path, Mitch. CR4 140 DF99
Tranby Pl, E9
off Homerton High St 67 DX64
Tranley Ms, NW3 *off Fleet Rd* 64 DE64
Tranmere Rd, N9 46 DT45
SW18 120 DC89
Twickenham TW2 116 CB87
Tranquil Dale, Bet. (Buckland)
RH3 183 CT132
Tranquil Pas, SE3
off Tranquil Vale 104 EF82
Tranquil Ri, Erith DA8
off West St 107 FE78
Tranquil Vale, SE3 104 EE82
Transept St, NW1 194 B7
Transmere Cl, Orp. BR5 145 EQ100
Transmere Rd, Orp. BR5 145 EQ100
Transom Cl, SE16 203 L8
Transom Sq, E14 204 B9
Transport Av, Brent. TW8 97 CG78
Tranton Rd, SE16 202 C6
Trappes Ho, SE16
off Manor Est 102 DV77
Traps Hill, Loug. IG10 33 EM41
Traps La, N.Mal. KT3 138 CS95
Travellers Way, Houns. TW4 96 BW82
Travers Cl, E17 47 DX53
Travers Rd, N7 65 DN62
Treacy Cl, Bushey (Bushey Hth)
WD23 40 CC47
Treadgold St, W11 81 CX73
Treadway St, E2 84 DV68
Treadwell Rd, Epsom KT18 172 CS115
Treasury Cl, Wall. SM6 159 DK106
Treaty Cen, Houns. TW3 96 CB83
Treaty Rd, Houns. TW3
off Hanworth Rd 96 CB83
Treaty St, N1 83 DM67
Trebble Rd, Swans. DA10 130 FY86
Trebeck St, W1 199 H2
Trebovir Rd, SW5 100 DA78
Treby St, E3 85 DZ70
Trecastle Way, N7
off Carleton Rd 65 DK63
Tredegar Ms, E3
off Tredegar Ter 85 DZ69
Tredegar Rd, E3 85 DZ68
N11 45 DK52
Dartford DA2 127 FG89
Tredegar Sq, E3 85 DZ69
Tredegar Ter, E3 85 DZ69
Trederwen Rd, E8 84 DU67
Tredown Rd, SE26 122 DW92
Tredwell Cl, SW2
off Hillside Rd 121 DM89
Bromley BR2 144 EL98
Tredwell Rd, SE27 121 DP91
Treebourne Rd, West.
(Bigg.H.) TN16 178 EJ117
Tree Cl, Rich. TW10 117 CK88
Treemount Ct, Epsom KT17 156 CS113
Treen Av, SW13 99 CT83
Tree Rd, E16 86 EJ72
Treeside Cl, West Dr. UB7 94 BK77
Tree Tops, Brwd. CM15 54 FW46
Treetops, Grav. DA12 131 GH92
Whyteleafe CR3 176 DU118
Treetops Cl, SE2 106 EY78
Northwood HA6 39 BR50
Treetops Vw, Loug. IG10 48 EK45
Treeview Cl, SE19 142 DS95
Treewall Gdns, Brom. BR1 124 EH91
Tree Way, Reig. RH2 184 DB131
Trefgarne Rd, Dag. RM10 70 FA61
Trefil Wk, N7 65 DL63
Trefoil Ho, Erith DA18
off Kale Rd 106 EY75
Trefoil Rd, SW18 120 DC85
Trefusis Wk, Wat. WD17 23 BS39
Tregaron Av, N8 65 DL58
Tregaron Gdns, N.Mal. KT3
off Avenue Rd 138 CS98
Tregarthen Pl, Lthd. KT22 171 CJ121
Tregarth Pl, Wok. GU21 166 AT117
Tregarvon Rd, SW11 100 DG84
Tregenna Av, Har. HA2 60 BZ63
Tregenna Cl, N14 29 DJ43
Tregenna Ct, Har. HA2 60 CA63
Tregony Rd, Orp. BR6 163 ET105
Trego Rd, E9 85 EA66
Tregothnan Rd, SW9 101 DL83
Tregunter Rd, SW10 100 DC79
Trehearn Rd, Ilf. IG6 49 ER52
Treherne Ct, SW9
off Eythorne Rd 101 DN81
SW17 120 DG91
Trehern Rd, SW14 98 CR83
Trehurst St, E5 67 DY64
Trelawn Cl, Cher. (Ott.) KT16 151 BC108
Trelawney Av, Slou. SL3 92 AX76
Trelawney Cl, E17
off Orford Rd 67 EB56
Trelawney Est, E9 84 DW65
Trelawney Gro, Wey. KT13 152 BN107
Trelawney Rd, Ilf. IG6 49 ER52
Trelawn Rd, E10 67 EC62
SW2 121 DN85
Trellick Twr, W10 81 CZ70
Trellis Sq, E3
off Malmesbury Rd 85 DZ69
Treloar Gdns, SE19
off Hancock Rd 122 DR93
Tremadoc Rd, SW4 101 DK84
Tremaine Cl, SE4 103 EA82
Tremaine Rd, SE20 142 DV96
Trematon Pl, Tedd. TW11 117 CJ94
Tremlett Gro, N19 65 DJ62
Tremlett Ms, N19 65 DJ62
Trenance, Wok. GU21
off Cardingham 166 AU117
Trenance Gdns, Ilf. IG3 70 EU62
Trenchard Av, Ruis. HA4 59 BV63
Trenchard Cl, NW9
off Fulbeck Dr 42 CS53
Stanmore HA7 41 CG51
Walton-on-Thames KT12 154 BW106
Trenchard Ct, Mord. SM4
off Green La 140 DA100
Trenchard St, SE10 103 ED78
Trenches La, Slou. SL3 75 BA73
Trenchold St, SW8 101 DL79
Trenear Cl, Orp. BR6 164 EU105
Trenham Dr, Warl. CR6 176 DW116
Trenholme Cl, SE20 122 DV94
Trenholme Ct, Cat. CR3 176 DU122
Trenholme Rd, SE20 122 DV94
Trenholme Ter, SE20 122 DV94
Trenmar Gdns, NW10 81 CV69
Trent Av, W5 97 CJ76
Upminster RM14 73 FR58
Trentbridge Cl, Ilf. IG6 49 ET51
Trent Cl, Rad. (Shenley) WD7
off Edgbaston Dr 10 CL32
Trent Gdns, N14 29 DH44
Trentham Cres, Wok. GU22 167 BA121
Trentham Dr, Orp. BR5 146 EU98
Trentham St, SW18 120 DA88
★ **Trent Park Country Pk**,
Barn. EN4 29 DH40
Trent Rd, SW2 121 DM85
Buckhurst Hill IG9 48 EH46
Slough SL3 93 BB79
Trent Way, Hayes UB4 77 BS68
Worcester Park KT4 139 CW104
Trentwood Side, Enf. EN2 29 DM41
Treport St, SW18 120 DB87
Tresco Cl, Brom. BR1 124 EE93
Trescoe Gdns, Har. HA2 60 BY59
Romford RM5 51 FC50
Tresco Gdns, Ilf. IG3 70 EU61
Tresco Rd, SE15 102 DV84
Tresham Cres, NW8 194 B4
Tresham Rd, Bark. IG11 87 ET66
Tresham Wk, E9
off Churchill Wk 66 DW64
Tresilian Av, N21 29 DM43
Tresillian Way, Wok. GU21 166 AU116
Tressell Cl, N1
off Sebbon St 83 DP66
Tressillian Cres, SE4 103 EA83
Tressillian Rd, SE4 103 DZ84
Tresta Wk, Wok. GU21 166 AU115
Trestis Cl, Hayes UB4
off Jollys La 78 BY71
Treston Ct, Stai. TW18 113 BF92
Treswell Rd, Dag. RM9 88 EY67
Tretawn Gdns, NW7 42 CS49
Tretawn Pk, NW7 42 CS49
Trevanion Rd, W14 99 CY78
Treve Av, Har. HA1 60 CC59
Trevellance Way, Wat. WD25 8 BW33
Trevelyan Av, E12 69 EM63
Trevelyan Cl, Dart. DA1 108 FM84
Trevelyan Cres, Har. HA3 61 CK59
Trevelyan Gdns, NW10 81 CW67
Trevelyan Ho, E2
off Morpeth St 84 DW69
Trevelyan Rd, E15 68 EE63
SW17 120 DE92
Trevera Ct, Wal.Cr. EN8
off Eleanor Rd 15 DY33
Trevereux Hill, Oxt. RH8 189 EM131
Treveris St, SE1 200 F3
Treverton St, W10 81 CX70
Treves Cl, N21 29 DM43
Treville St, SW15 119 CV87
Treviso Rd, SE23
off Farren Rd 123 DX89
Trevithick Cl, Felt. TW14 115 BT88
Trevithick Dr, Dart. DA1 108 FM84
Trevithick Ho, SE16 202 E9
Trevithick St, SE8 103 EA78
Trevone Gdns, Pnr. HA5 60 BY58
Trevor Cl, Barn. EN4 28 DD43
Bromley BR2 144 EF101
Harrow HA3 *off Kenton La* 41 CF52
Isleworth TW7 117 CF85
Northolt UB5 78 BW68
Trevor Cres, Ruis. HA4 59 BT63
Trevor Gdns, Edg. HA8 42 CR53
Northolt UB5 78 BW68
Ruislip HA4
off Clyfford Rd 59 BU63
Trevor Pl, SW7 198 C5
Trevor Rd, SW19 119 CY94
Edgware HA8 42 CR53
Trevor Rd, Hayes UB3 95 BS75
Woodford Green IG8 48 EG52
Trevor Sq, SW7 198 D5
Trevor St, SW7 198 C5
Trevor Wk, SW7 *off Trevor Sq* 100 DF75
Trevose Av, W.Byf. KT14 151 BF114
Trevose Rd, E17 47 ED53
Trevose Way, Wat. WD19 40 BW48
Trewarden Av, Iver SL0 75 BD68
Trewenna Dr, Chess. KT9 155 CK106
Potters Bar EN6 12 DD32
Trewince Rd, SW20 139 CW95
Trewint St, SW18 120 DC89
Trewsbury Ho, SE2
off Hartslock Dr 106 EX75
Trewsbury Rd, SE26 123 DX92
Triandra Way, Hayes UB4 78 BX71
Triangle, The, EC1 196 G4
N13 *off Lodge Dr* 45 DN49
Barking IG11
off Tanner St 87 EQ65
Hampton TW12 *off High St* 136 CC95
Kingston upon Thames
KT1 *off Kenley Rd* 138 CQ96
Woking GU21 166 AW118
Triangle Business Cen, NW10
off Enterprise Way 81 CU69
Triangle Ct, E16
off Tollgate Rd 86 EK71
Triangle Est, SE11
off Kennington La 101 DN78
Triangle Pas, Barn. EN4
off Station App 28 DC42
Triangle Pl, SW4 101 DK84
Triangle Rd, E8 84 DV67
Trident Cen, Wat. WD24 24 BW39
Trident Gdns, Nthlt. UB5
off Jetstar Way 78 BX69
Trident Ind Est, Slou.
(Colnbr.) SL3 93 BE83
Trident Rd, Wat. WD25 7 BT34
Trident St, SE16 203 J8
Trident Way, Sthl. UB2 95 BV76
Trigg's Cl, Wok. GU22 166 AX119
Trigg's La, Wok. GU21, GU22 166 AW118
Trig La, EC4 197 H10
Trigo Ct, Epsom KT19
off Blakeney Cl 156 CR111
Trigon Rd, SW8 101 DM80
Trilby Rd, SE23 123 DX89
Trimmer Wk, Brent. TW8 98 CL79
Trim St, SE14 103 DZ79
Trinder Gdns, N19
off Trinder Rd 65 DL60
Trinder Ms, Tedd. TW11 117 CG92
Trinder Rd, N19 65 DL60
Barnet EN5 27 CW43
Tring Av, W5 80 CM74
Southall UB1 78 BZ72
Wembley HA9 80 CN65
Tring Cl, Ilf. IG2 69 EQ57
Romford RM3 52 FM49
Tring Gdns, Rom. RM3 52 FL49
Tring Grn, Rom. RM3 52 FM49
Tringham Cl, Cher. (Ott.)
KT16 151 BC107
Tring Wk, Rom. RM3 52 FL49
Trinidad Gdns, Dag. RM10 89 FD66
Trinidad St, E14 85 DZ73
Trinity Av, N2 64 DD55
Enfield EN1 30 DT44
Trinity Buoy Wf, E14 205 K1
Trinity Ch Pas, SW13 99 CV79
Trinity Ch Rd, SW13 99 CV79
Trinity Ch Sq, SE1 201 J6
Trinity Cl, E8 84 DT65
E11 68 EE61
NW3 *off Willoughby Rd* 64 DD63
SE13 103 ED84
SW4 *off The Pavement* 101 DJ84
Bromley BR2 144 EL102
Hounslow TW4 96 BY84
Northwood HA6 39 BS51
South Croydon CR2 160 DS109
Staines (Stanw.) TW19 114 BJ86
Trinity Cotts, Rich. TW9
off Trinity Rd 98 CM83
Trinity Ct, N1
off Downham Rd 84 DS66
NW2 *off Anson Rd* 63 CW64
SE7 *off Charlton La* 104 EK77
Trinity Cres, SW17 120 DF89
Trinity Dr, Uxb. UB8 77 BQ72
Trinity Gdns, E16
off Cliff Wk 86 EF71
SW9 101 DM84
Dartford DA1
off Summerhill Rd 128 FK86
Trinity Gro, SE10 103 EC81
Trinity Hall Cl, Wat. WD24 24 BW41
★ **Trinity Ho**, EC3 197 N10
Trinity La, Wal.Cr. EN8 15 DY32
Trinity Ms, SE20 142 DV95
W10 *off Cambridge Gdns* 81 CX72
Trinity Path, SE26 122 DW90
Trinity Pl, EC3 201 P1
Bexleyheath DA6 106 EZ84
Trinity Ri, SW2 121 DN88
Trinity Rd, N2 64 DD55
N22 45 DL53
SW17 120 DF89
SW18 120 DD85
SW19 120 DA93
Gravesend DA12 131 GJ87
Ilford IG6 69 EQ55
Richmond TW9 98 CM83
Southall UB1 78 BY74
Trinity Sq, EC3 201 N1
Trinity St, E16
off Vincent St 86 EG71
SE1 201 J5
Enfield EN2 30 DQ40
Trinity Wk, NW3 82 DC65
Trinity Way, E4 47 DZ51
W3 80 CS73
Trio Pl, SE1 201 J5
Tripps Hill, Ch.St.G. HP8 36 AU48
Tripps Hill Cl, Ch.St.G. HP8 36 AU48
Tristan Sq, SE3 104 EE83
Tristram Cl, E17 67 ED55
Tristram Dr, N9 46 DU48
Tristram Rd, Brom. BR1 124 EF91
Triton Sq, NW1 195 K4

Tritton Av, Croy. CR0 159 DL105
Tritton Rd, SE21 122 DR90
Trittons, Tad. KT20 173 CW121
Triumph Cl, Grays (Chaff.Hun.) RM16 109 FW77
Hayes UB3 95 BQ80
Triumph Ho, Bark. IG11 88 EV69
Triumph Rd, E6 87 EM72
Trivett Cl, Green. DA9 129 FU85
Trojan Way, Croy. CR0 141 DM104
Trolling Down Hill, Dart. DA2 128 FP89
Troon Cl, SE16 202 E10
SE28 off Fairway Dr 88 EX72
Troon St, E1 off White Horse Rd 85 DY72
Troopers Dr, Rom. RM3 52 FK49
Trosley Av, Grav. DA11 131 GH89
Trosley Rd, Belv. DA17 106 FA79
Trossachs Rd, SE22 122 DS85
Trothy Rd, SE1 202 C8
Trotsworth Av, Vir.W. GU25 132 AX98
Trotsworth Ct, Vir.W. GU25 132 AX98
Trotters Bottom, Barn. EN5 27 CU37
Trotters La, Wok. (Mimbr.) GU24 150 AV112
Trotter Way, Epsom KT19 156 CN112
Trott Rd, N10 44 DF52
Trotts La, West. TN16 189 EQ127
Trott St, SW11 100 DE81
Trotwood, Chig. IG7 49 ER51
Trotwood Cl, Brwd. (Shenf.) CM15 off Middleton Rd 54 FY46
Troughton Rd, SE7 205 P10
Troutbeck Cl, Slou. SL2 74 AU73
Troutbeck Rd, SE14 103 DY81
Trout La, West Dr. UB7 76 BJ73
Trout Ri, Rick. (Loud.) WD3 22 BH41
Trout Rd, West Dr. UB7 76 BK74
Troutstream Way, Rick. (Loud.) WD3 22 BH42
Trouville Rd, SW4 121 DJ86
Trowbridge Est, E9 off Osborne Rd 85 DZ65
Trowbridge Rd, E9 85 DZ65
Romford RM3 52 FK51
Trowers Way, Red. RH1 185 DH131
Trowley Ri, Abb.L. WD5 7 BS31
Trowlock Av, Tedd. TW11 117 CJ93
Trowlock Island, Tedd. TW11 117 CK92
Trowlock Way, Tedd. TW11 117 CK93
Troy Cl, Tad. KT20 173 CV120
Troy Ct, W8 off Kensington High St 100 DA76
Troy Rd, SE19 122 DR93
Troy Town, SE15 102 DU83
Trubshaw Rd, Sthl. UB2 off Havelock Rd 96 CB76
Truesdale Dr, Uxb. (Hare.) UB9 58 BJ57
Truesdale Rd, E6 87 EM72
Trulock Ct, N17 46 DU52
Trulock Rd, N17 46 DU52
Truman Cl, Edg. HA8 42 CQ52
Truman's Rd, N16 66 DS64
Trumpers Way, W7 97 CE76
Trumper Way, Uxb. UB8 76 BJ67
Trumpington Rd, E7 68 EF63
Trumps Grn Av, Vir.W. GU25 132 AX100
Trumps Grn Cl, Vir.W. GU25 off Trumpsgreen Rd 132 AY99
Trumpsgreen Rd, Vir.W. GU25 132 AX100
Trumps Mill La, Vir.W. GU25 133 AZ100
Trump St, EC2 197 J9
Trundlers Way, Bushey (Bushey Hth) WD23 41 CE46
Trundle St, SE1 201 H4
Trundleys Rd, SE8 203 J10
Trundleys Ter, SE8 203 J9
Trunks All, Swan. BR8 147 FB96
Truro Gdns, Ilf. IG1 68 EL59
Truro Rd, E17 67 DZ56
N22 45 DL52
Gravesend DA12 131 GK90
Truro St, NW5 82 DG65
Truro Wk, Rom. RM3 52 FJ51
Truro Way, Hayes UB4 off Portland Rd 77 BS69
Truslove Rd, SE27 121 DN92
Trussley Rd, W6 99 CW76
Trustees Way, Uxb. (Denh.) UB9 57 BF57
Trustons Gdns, Horn. RM11 71 FG59
Trust Rd, Wal.Cr. EN8 15 DY34
Trust Wk, SE21 off Peabody Hill 121 DP88
Tryfan Cl, Ilf. IG4 68 EK57
Tryon Cres, E9 84 DW67
Tryon St, SW3 198 D10
Trys Hill, Cher. (Lyne) KT16 133 AZ103
Trystings Cl, Esher (Clay.) KT10 155 CG107
Tuam Rd, SE18 105 ER79
Tubbenden Cl, Orp. BR6 145 ES103
Tubbenden Dr, Orp. BR6 163 ER105
Tubbenden La, Orp. BR6 145 ES104
Tubbenden La S, Orp. BR6 163 ER106
Tubbs Rd, NW10 81 CT68
Tubs Hill Par, Sev. TN13 190 FG124
Tubwell Rd, Slou. (Stoke P.) SL2 74 AV67
Tucker Rd, Cher. (Ott.) KT16 151 BD107
Tucker St, Wat. WD18 24 BW43
Tuckey Gro, Wok. (Ripley) GU23 167 BF124
Tuck Rd, Rain. RM13 89 FG65
Tudor Av, Hmptn. TW12 116 CA93
Romford RM2 71 FG55
Waltham Cross (Chsht) EN7 14 DU31
Watford WD24 24 BX38
Worcester Park KT4 139 CV104
Tudor Cl, N6 65 DJ59
NW3 64 DE64
NW7 43 CU51
NW9 62 CQ61
SW2 off Elm Pk 121 DM86
Ashford TW15 114 BL91
Banstead SM7 173 CY115
Brentwood (Shenf.) CM15 55 FZ44
Chessington KT9 156 CL106
Chigwell IG7 49 EN49
Chislehurst BR7 145 EM95
Cobham KT11 154 BZ113
Tudor Cl, Couls. CR5 175 DN118
Dartford DA1 127 FH86
Epsom KT17 157 CT110
Gravesend (Nthflt) DA11 130 GE88
Leatherhead (Bkhm) KT23 170 CA124
Pinner HA5 59 BU57
South Croydon CR2 176 DV115
Sutton SM3 157 CX106
Wallington SM6 159 DJ108
Waltham Cross (Chsht) EN7 14 DV31
Woking GU22 167 BA117
Woodford Green IG8 48 EH50
Tudor Ct, E17 67 DY59
Borehamwood WD6 26 CL40
Feltham TW13 116 BW91
Swanley BR8 147 FC101
Tudor Ct N, Wem. HA9 62 CN64
Tudor Ct S, Wem. HA9 62 CN64
Tudor Cres, Enf. EN2 29 DP39
Ilford IG6 49 EP51
Tudor Dr, Kings.T. KT2 118 CL92
Morden SM4 139 CX100
Romford RM2 71 FG56
Walton-on-Thames KT12 136 BX102
Watford WD24 24 BX38
Tudor Est, NW10 80 CP68
Tudor Gdns, NW9 62 CQ61
SW13 off Treen Av 98 CS83
W3 80 CN72
Harrow HA3 off Tudor Rd 41 CD54
Romford RM2 71 FG56
Twickenham TW1 117 CF88
Upminster RM14 72 FQ61
West Wickham BR4 143 EC104
Tudor Gro, E9 84 DW66
N20 off Church Cres 44 DE48
Tudor Ho, Surb. KT6 off Lenelby Rd 138 CN102
Tudor La, Wind. (Old Wind.) SL4 112 AW87
Tudor Manor Gdns, Wat. WD25 8 BX32
Tudor Ms, Rom. RM1 off Eastern Rd 71 FF57
Tudor Par, Rick. WD3 off Berry La 38 BG45
Tudor Pl, Mitch. CR4 120 DE94
Tudor Rd, E4 47 EB51
E6 86 EJ67
E9 84 DV67
N9 46 DV45
SE19 122 DT94
SE25 142 DV99
Ashford TW15 115 BR93
Barking IG11 87 ET67
Barnet EN5 28 DA41
Beckenham BR3 143 EB97
Hampton TW12 116 CA94
Harrow HA3 41 CD54
Hayes UB3 77 BR72
Hounslow TW3 97 CD84
Kingston upon Thames KT2 118 CN94
Pinner HA5 40 BW54
Southall UB1 78 BY73
Tudors, The, Reig. RH2 184 DC131
Tudor Sq, Hayes UB3 77 BR71
Tudor St, EC4 196 E10
Tudor Wk, Bex. DA5 126 EY86
Tudorwalk, Grays RM17 off Thurloe Wk 110 GA76
Tudor Wk, Lthd. KT22 171 CF120
Watford WD24 24 BX37
Weybridge KT13 off West Palace Gdns 135 BP104
Tudor Way, N14 45 DK46
W3 98 CN75
Orpington BR5 145 ER100
Rickmansworth (Mill End) WD3 38 BG46
Uxbridge UB10 76 BN65
Waltham Abbey EN9 15 ED33
Tudor Well Cl, Stan. HA7 41 CH50
Tudway Rd, SE3 104 EH83
Tufnail Rd, Dart. DA1 128 FM86
TUFNELL PARK, N7 65 DK63
⊖ Tufnell Park 65 DJ63
Tufnell Pk Rd, N7 65 DJ63
N19 65 DJ63
Tufter Rd, Chig. IG7 49 ET50
Tufton Gdns, W.Mol. KT8 136 CB96
Tufton Rd, E4 47 EA49
Tufton St, SW1 199 N6
Tugboat St, SE28 105 ES75
Tugela Rd, Croy. CR0 142 DR100
Tugela St, SE6 123 DZ89
Tugmutton Cl, Orp. BR6 163 EP105
Tugwood Cl, Couls. CR5 175 DK121
Tuilerie St, E2 84 DU68
Tulip Cl, E6 off Bradley Stone Rd 87 EM71
Brentwood (Pilg.Hat.) CM15 off Poppy Cl 54 FV43
Croydon CR0 143 DX102
Hampton TW12 off Partridge Rd 116 BZ93
Romford RM3 52 FJ51
Southall UB2 off Chevy Rd 96 CC75
Tulip Ct, Pnr. HA5 60 BW55
Tulip Gdns, Ilf. IG1 87 EP65
Tulip Tree Ct, Sutt. SM2 off The Crescent 158 DA111
Tulip Way, West Dr. UB7 94 BK77
Tull St, Mitch. CR4 140 DF101
Tulse Cl, Beck. BR3 143 EC97
TULSE HILL, SE21 122 DQ88
⇌ Tulse Hill 121 DP89
Tulse Hill, SW2 121 DN86
Tulse Hill Est, SW2 121 DN86
Tulsemere Rd, SE27 122 DQ89
Tulyar Cl, Tad. KT20 173 CV120
Tumber St, Epsom (Headley) KT18 182 CQ125
Tumblewood Rd, Bans. SM7 173 CY116
Tumbling Bay, Walt. KT12 135 BU100
Tummons Gdns, SE25 142 DS96
Tump Ho, SE28 off Miles Dr 87 ES74
Tuncombe Rd, N18 46 DS49
Tunis Rd, W12 81 CV74
Tunley Grn, E14 off Burdett Rd 85 DZ71
Tunley Rd, NW10 80 CS67
SW17 120 DG88
Tunmarsh La, E13 86 EJ69
Tunmers End, Ger.Cr. (Chal.St.P.) SL9 36 AW53
Tunnan Leys, E6 87 EN72
Tunnel Av, SE10 204 G4
Tunnel Est, Grays RM20 109 FT77
Tunnel Gdns, N11 45 DJ52
Tunnel Rd, SE16 202 F4
Reigate RH2 off Church St 184 DA134
Tunnel Wd Cl, Wat. WD17 23 BT37
Tunnel Wd Rd, Wat. WD17 23 BT37
Tunstall Av, Ilf. IG6 50 EU51
Tunstall Cl, Orp. BR5 163 ES105
Tunstall Rd, SW9 101 DM84
Croydon CR0 142 DS102
Tunstall Wk, Brent. TW8 98 CL79
Tunstock Way, Belv. DA17 106 EY76
Tunworth Cl, NW9 62 CQ58
Tunworth Cres, SW15 119 CT86
Tun Yd, SW8 off Peardon St 101 DH82
Tupelo Rd, E10 67 EB61
Tuppy St, SE28 105 EQ76
Tupwood Ct, Cat. CR3 186 DU125
Tupwood La, Cat. CR3 186 DU125
Tupwood Scrubbs Rd, Cat. CR3 186 DU128
Turenne Cl, SW18 100 DC84
Turfhouse La, Wok. (Chobham) GU24 150 AS109
Turin Rd, N9 46 DW45
Turin St, E2 84 DU69
Turkey Oak Cl, SE19 142 DS95
⇌ Turkey Street 30 DW37
Turkey St, Enf. EN1, EN3 30 DV37
Turks Cl, Uxb. UB8 off Harlington Rd 76 BN69
Turk's Head Yd, EC1 196 F6
Turks Row, SW3 198 E10
Turle Rd, N4 65 DM60
SW16 141 DL96
Turlewray Cl, N4 65 DM60
Turley Cl, E15 86 EE67
Turnagain La, EC4 196 F8
Dartford DA2 127 FG90
Turnage Rd, Dag. RM8 70 EY60
Turnberry Cl, NW4 43 CX54
SE16 off Ryder Dr 102 DV78
Turnberry Ct, Wat. WD19 40 BW48
Turnberry Dr, St.Alb. (Brick.Wd) AL2 8 BY30
Turnberry Quay, E14 204 C6
Turnberry Way, Orp. BR6 145 ER102
Turnbull Cl, Green. DA9 129 FS87
Turnbury Cl, SE28 88 EX72
Turnchapel Ms, SW4 off Cedars Rd 101 DH83
Turner Av, N15 66 DS56
Mitcham CR4 140 DF95
Twickenham TW2 116 CC90
Turner Cl, NW11 64 DB58
SW9 101 DP81
Hayes UB4 off Charville La 77 BQ68
Wembley HA0 61 CK64
Turner Ct, N15 off St. Ann's Rd 66 DR57
Dartford DA1 128 FJ85
Turner Dr, NW11 64 DB58
Turner Ho, E14 off Cassilis Rd 103 EA75
Turner Ms, Sutt. SM2 158 DB108
Turner Pl, SW11 off Cairns Rd 120 DE85
Turner Rd, E17 67 EC55
Bushey WD23 24 CC42
Dartford (Bean) DA2 129 FV90
Edgware HA8 62 CM55
Hornchurch RM12 71 FF61
New Malden KT3 138 CR101
Slough SL3 92 AW75
Westerham (Bigg.H.) TN16 162 EJ112
Turners Cl, N20 off Oakleigh Rd N 44 DF48
Staines TW18 114 BH92
Turners Ct, Rom. (Abridge) RM4 34 EV41
Turners Gdns, Sev. TN13 191 FJ128
Turners Hill, Wal.Cr. (Chsht) EN8 15 DX30
Turners La, Walt. KT12 153 BV107
Turners Meadow Way, Beck. BR3 143 DZ95
Turners Rd, E3 85 DZ71
Turner St, E1 84 DV71
E16 86 EF72
Turners Way, Croy. CR0 141 DN103
Turners Wd, NW11 64 DC59
Turners Wd Dr, Ch.St.G. HP8 36 AX48
Turneville Rd, W14 99 CZ79
Turney Grn, E14 off Wallwood St 85 DZ71
Turney Rd, SE21 122 DR87
Turneys Orchard, Rick. (Chorl.) WD3 21 BD43
TURNFORD, Brox. EN10 15 DZ26
⊖ Turnham Green 98 CS77
Turnham Grn Ter, W4 98 CS77
Turnham Grn Ter Ms, W4 off Turnham Grn Ter 98 CS77
Turnham Rd, SE4 123 DY85
Turnmill St, EC1 196 E5
Turnoak Av, Wok. GU22 166 AY120
Turnoak La, Wok. GU22 166 AY120
Turnpike Cl, SE8 off Amersham Vale 103 DZ80
Turnpike Dr, Orp. BR6 164 EW109
Turnpike Ho, EC1 196 G3
⊖ Turnpike Lane 65 DN55
Turnpike La, N8 65 DM56
Sutton SM1 158 DC106
Tilbury (W.Til.) RM18 111 GK78
Uxbridge UB10 76 BL69
Turnpike Link, Croy. CR0 142 DS103
Turnpike Ms, N8 off Turnpike La 65 DN55
Turnpike Way, Islw. TW7 97 CG81
Turnpin La, SE10 103 EC79
Turnstone Cl, E13 86 EG69
NW9 off Kestrel Cl 42 CS54
South Croydon CR2 161 DY110
Uxbridge (Ickhm) UB10 59 BP64
Turnstones, The, Grav. DA12 131 GK89
Watford WD25 24 BY36
Turp Av, Grays RM16 110 GC75
Turpentine La, SW1 199 J10
Turpin Av, Rom. RM5 50 FA52
Turpin Cl, Enf. EN3 off Burton Dr 31 EA37
Turpington Cl, Brom. BR2 144 EL100
Turpington La, Brom. BR2 144 EL101
Turpin Ho, SW11 off Strasburg Rd 101 DH81
Turpin La, Erith DA8 107 FG80
Turpin Rd, Felt. TW14 off Staines Rd 115 BT86
Turpins La, Wdf.Grn. IG8 49 EM50
Turpin Way, N19 65 DK61
Wallington SM6 159 DH108
Turquand St, SE17 201 J9
Turret Gro, SW4 101 DJ83
Turton Rd, Wem. HA0 62 CL64
Turville St, E2 197 P4
Tuscan Ho, E2 off Knottisford St 84 DW69
Tuscan Rd, SE18 105 ER78
Tuscany Ho, E17 off Priory Ct 47 DZ54
Tuskar St, SE10 104 EE78
Tussauds Cl, Rick. (Crox.Grn) WD3 22 BN43
Tustin Est, SE15 102 DW79
Tuttlebee La, Buck.H. IG9 48 EG47
Tuxford Cl, Borwd. WD6 26 CL38
Twankhams All, Epp. CM16 off Hemnall St 18 EU30
Tweedale Ct, E15 67 EC64
Tweeddale Gro, Uxb. UB10 59 BQ62
Tweeddale Rd, Cars. SM5 140 DD102
Tweed Glen, Rom. RM1 51 FD52
Tweed Grn, Rom. RM1 51 FE52
Tweedmouth Rd, E13 86 EH68
Tweed Rd, Slou. SL3 93 BA79
Tweed Way, Rom. RM1 51 FD52
Tweedy Cl, Enf. EN1 30 DT43
Tweedy Rd, Brom. BR1 144 EF95
Tweezer's All, WC2 196 D10
Twelve Acre Cl, Lthd. (Bkhm) KT23 170 BZ124
Twelve Acre Ho, E12 off Grantham Rd 69 EN62
Twelvetrees Business Pk, E3 off Twelvetrees Cres 85 ED69
Twelvetrees Cres, E3 85 EC70
Twentyman Cl, Wdf.Grn. IG8 48 EG50
TWICKENHAM, TW1 & TW2 117 CG89
⇌ Twickenham 117 CF87
Twickenham Br, Rich. TW9 117 CJ85
Twickenham TW1 117 CJ85
Twickenham Cl, Croy. CR0 141 DM104
Twickenham Gdns, Grnf. UB6 61 CG64
Harrow HA3 41 CE52
Twickenham Rd, E11 67 ED61
Feltham TW13 116 BZ90
Isleworth TW7 97 CG83
Richmond TW9 97 CJ84
Teddington TW11 117 CG92
Twickenham Trd Est, Twick. TW1 117 CF86
Twig Folly Cl, E2 off Roman Rd 85 DX68
Twigg Cl, Erith DA8 107 FE80
Twilley St, SW18 120 DB87
Twine Cl, Bark. IG11 off Thames Rd 88 EV69
Twine Ct, E1 84 DW73
Twineham Grn, N12 44 DA49
Twine Ter, E3 off Ropery St 85 DZ70
Twining Av, Twick. TW2 116 CC90
Twinn Rd, NW7 43 CY51
Twinoaks, Cob. KT11 154 CA113
Twin Tumps Way, SE28 88 EU73
Twisden Rd, NW5 65 DH63
Twisleton Ct, Dart. DA1 off Priory Hill 128 FK86
Twitchells La, Beac. (Jordans) HP9 36 AT51
TWITTON, Sev. TN14 181 FF116
Twitton La, Sev. (Otford) TN14 181 FD115
Twitton Meadows, Sev. (Otford) TN14 181 FE116
Two Rivers Retail Pk, Stai. TW18 off Mustard Mill Rd 113 BE91
Twybridge Way, NW10 80 CQ66
Twycross Ms, SE10 205 J9
Twyford Abbey Rd, NW10 80 CM69
Twyford Av, N2 64 DF55
W3 80 CN73
Twyford Cres, W3 80 CN74
Twyford Ho, N15 off Chisley Rd 66 DS58
Twyford Pl, WC2 196 B8
Twyford Rd, Cars. SM5 140 DD102
Harrow HA2 60 CB60
Ilford IG1 69 EQ64
Twyford St, N1 83 DM67
Twynersh Av, Cher. KT16 133 BF100
Tyas Rd, E16 86 EF70
Tybenham Rd, SW19 140 DA97
Tyberry Rd, Enf. EN3 30 DV41
Tyburn La, Har. HA1 61 CE59
Tyburns, The, Brwd. (Hutt.) CM13 55 GC47
Tyburn Way, W1 194 E10
Tycehurst Hill, Loug. IG10 33 EM42
Tydcombe Rd, Warl. CR6 176 DW119
Tye La, Epsom (Headley) KT18 182 CR127
Orpington BR6 163 EQ106
Tadworth KT20 off Dorking Rd 183 CT128
Tyers Est, SE1 201 M4
Tyers Gate, SE1 201 M4
Tyers St, SE11 200 B10
Tyers Ter, SE11 101 DM78
Tyeshurst Cl, SE2 106 EY78
Tyfield Cl, Wal.Cr. (Chsht) EN8 14 DW30
Tykeswater La, Borwd. (Els.) WD6 25 CJ39
Tylecroft Rd, SW16 141 DL96
Tyle Grn, Horn. RM11 72 FL56
Tylehurst Gdns, Ilf. IG1 69 EQ64
Tyle Pl, Wind. (Old Wind.) SL4 112 AU85
Tyler Cl, E2 84 DT68
Erith DA8 107 FB80
Tyler Gdns, Add. KT15 152 BJ105
Tyler Gro, Dart. DA1 off Spielman Rd 108 FM84
Tyler Rd, Sthl. UB2 off McNair Rd 96 CB76
Tylers Cl, Gdse. RH9 186 DV130
Kings Langley WD4 6 BL28
Loughton IG10 48 EL45
Tyler's Ct, W1 195 M9
Tylers Cres, Horn. RM12 72 FJ64
Tylersfield, Abb.L. WD5 7 BT31
Tylers Gate, Har. HA3 62 CL58
Tylers Grn Rd, Swan. BR8 147 FC100
Tylers Hill Rd, Chesh. HP5 4 AT30
Tylers Path, Cars. SM5 off Rochester Rd 158 DF105
Tyler St, SE10 104 EE78
Tylers Way, Wat. WD25 25 CD42
Tyler Wk, Slou. SL3 off Gilbert Way 93 AZ78
Tyler Way, Brwd. CM14 54 FV46
Tylney Av, SE19 122 DT92
Tylney Rd, E7 68 EJ63
Bromley BR1 144 EK96
Tymperley Ct, SW19 off Windlesham Gro 119 CY88
Tynan Cl, Felt. TW14 off Sandycombe Rd 115 BU88
Tyndale Ct, E14 204 B10
Tyndale La, N1 off Upper St 83 DP66
Tyndale Ter, N1 off Canonbury La 83 DP66
Tyndall Rd, E10 67 EC61
Welling DA16 105 ET83
Tyne Cl, Upmin. RM14 73 FR58
Tynedale, St.Alb. (Lon.Col.) AL2 off Thamesdale 10 CM27
Tynedale Cl, Dart. DA2 129 FR88
Tyne Gdns, S.Ock. (Aveley) RM15 90 FQ73
Tyneham Cl, SW11 off Shirley Gro 100 DG83
Tyneham Rd, SW11 100 DG82
Tynemouth Cl, E6 off Covelees Wall 87 EP72
Tynemouth Dr, Enf. EN1 30 DU38
Tynemouth Rd, N15 66 DT56
SE18 105 ET78
Mitcham CR4 120 DG94
Tynemouth St, SW6 100 DC82
Tyne St, E1 off Old Castle St 84 DT72
Tynsdale Rd, NW10 80 CS66
Tynwald Ho, SE26 off Sydenham Hill Est 122 DU90
Type St, E2 85 DX68
Tyrawley Rd, SW6 100 DB81
Tyre La, NW9 off Sheaveshill Av 62 CS56
Tyrell Cl, Har. HA1 61 CE63
Tyrell Ct, Cars. SM5 158 DF105
Tyrell Ri, Brwd. CM14 54 FW50
Tyrells Cl, Upmin. RM14 72 FN61
Tyrols Rd, SE23 off Wastdale Rd 123 DX88
Tyrone Rd, E6 87 EM68
Tyron Way, Sid. DA14 125 ES91
Tyrrell Av, Well. DA16 126 EU85
Tyrrell Rd, SE22 102 DU84
Tyrrells Hall Cl, Grays RM17 110 GD79
Tyrrell Sq, Mitch. CR4 140 DE95
TYRRELL'S WOOD, Lthd. KT22 172 CM123
Tyrrel Way, NW9 63 CT59
Tyrwhitt Rd, SE4 103 EA83
Tysea Hill, Rom. (Stap.Abb.) RM4 51 FF45
Tysoe Av, Enf. EN3 31 DZ36
Tysoe St, EC1 196 D3
Tyson Rd, SE23 122 DW87
Tyssen Pas, E8 84 DT65
Tyssen Pl, S.Ock. RM15 91 FW69
Tyssen Rd, N16 66 DT62
Tyssen St, E8 84 DT65
N1 off Hoxton St 84 DS68
Tytherton Rd, N19 65 DK62

U

Uamvar St, E14 85 EB71
Uckfield Gro, Mitch. CR4 140 DG95
Uckfield Rd, Enf. EN3 31 DX37
Udall Gdns, Rom. RM5 50 FA51
Udall St, SW1 199 L9
Udney Pk Rd, Tedd. TW11 117 CG92
Uffington Rd, NW10 81 CU67
SE27 121 DN91
Ufford Cl, Har. HA3 off Ufford Rd 40 CB52
Ufford Rd, Har. HA3 40 CB52
Ufford St, SE1 200 E4
Ufton Gro, N1 84 DR66
Ufton Rd, N1 84 DR66
Uhura Sq, N16 66 DS62
Ujima Ct, SW16 off Sunnyhill Rd 121 DL91
Ullathorne Rd, SW16 121 DJ91
Ulleswater Rd, N14 45 DL49
Ullin St, E14 off St. Leonards Rd 85 EC71
Ullswater Business Pk, Couls. CR5 175 DL116
Ullswater Cl, SW15 118 CR91
Bromley BR1 124 EE93
Hayes UB4 77 BS68
Ullswater Ct, Har. HA2 off Oakington Av 60 CA59
Ullswater Cres, SW15 118 CR91
Coulsdon CR5 175 DL116
Ullswater Rd, SE27 121 DP89
SW13 99 CU80
Ullswater Way, Horn. RM12 71 FG64

★ Place of interest ⇌ Railway station ⊖ London Underground station DLR Docklands Light Railway station Tra Tramlink station H Hospital Riv Pedestrian ferry landing stage

Ulstan Cl, Cat. (Wold.) CR3 .177 EA123
Ulster Gdns, N13 .46 DQ49
Ulster Pl, NW1 .195 H5
Ulster Ter, NW1 .195 H4
Ulundi Rd, SE3 .104 EE79
Ulva Rd, SW15
off Ravenna Rd .99 CX84
Ulverscroft Rd, SE22 .122 DT85
Ulverstone Rd, SE27 .121 DP89
Ulverston Rd, E17 .47 ED54
Ulwin Av, W.Byf. (Byfleet)
KT14 .152 BL113
Ulysses Rd, NW6 .63 CZ64
Umberstones, Vir.W. GU25 .132 AX100
Umberston St, E1
off Hessel St .84 DV72
Umbria St, SW15 .119 CU86
Umfreville Rd, N4 .65 DP58
Undercliff Rd, SE13 .103 EA83
UNDERHILL, Barn. EN5 .28 DA43
Underhill, Barn. EN5 .28 DA43
Underhill Pk Rd, Reig. RH2 .184 DA131
Underhill Pas, NW1
off Camden High St .83 DH67
Underhill Rd, SE22 .122 DV86
Underhill St, NW1
off Camden High St .83 DH67
Underne Av, N14 .45 DH47
UNDERRIVER, Sev. TN15 .191 FN130
Underriver Ho Rd, Sev.
(Undrvr) TN15 .191 FP130
Undershaft, EC3 .197 M9
Undershaw Rd, Brom. BR1 .124 EE90
Underwood, Croy. (New Adgtn)
CR0 .161 EC106
Underwood, The, SE9 .125 EM89
Underwood Rd, E1 .84 DU70
E4 .47 EB50
Caterham CR3 .186 DS126
Woodford Green IG8 .48 EK52
Underwood Row, N1 .197 J2
Underwood St, N1 .197 J2
Undine Rd, E14 .204 C8
Undine St, SW17 .120 DF92
Uneeda Dr, Grnf. UB6 .79 CD67
Unicorn Pas, SE1
off Tooley St .84 DS74
Unicorn Wk, Green. DA9 .129 FT85
Union Cl, E11 .67 ED63
Union Cotts, E15
off Welfare Rd .86 EE66
Union Ct, EC2 .197 M8
Richmond TW9 off Eton St .118 CL85
Union Dr, E1 off Canal Cl .85 DY70
Union Gro, SW8 .101 DK82
Union Jack Club, SE1 .200 D4
Union Pk, SE10
off Calvert Rd .104 EF78
Union Rd, N11 .45 DK51
SW4 .101 DK82
SW8 .101 DK82
Bromley BR2 .144 EK99
Croydon CR0 .142 DQ101
Northolt UB5 .78 CA68
Wembley HA0 .80 CL65
Union Sq, N1 .84 DQ67
Union St, E15 .85 EC67
SE1 .200 G3
Barnet EN5 .27 CY42
Kingston upon Thames
KT1 .137 CK96
Union Wk, E2 .197 N2
Union Wf, N1 .197 H1
West Drayton UB7
off Bentinck Rd .76 BK74
Unity Cl, NW10 .81 CU65
SE19 off Crown Dale .122 DQ92
Croydon (New Adgtn) CR0 .161 EB109
Unity Ct, SE1 off Mawbey Pl .102 DT78
Unity Rd, Enf. EN3 .30 DW37
Unity Ter, Har. HA2
off Scott Cres .60 CB60
Unity Trd Est, Wdf.Grn. IG8 .68 EK55
Unity Way, SE18 .104 EK76
Unity Wf, SE1 .202 A4
University Cl, NW7 .43 CT52
Bushey WD23 .24 CA42
H University Coll Hosp,
NW1 .195 L4
A&E & Out-Patients, WC1 .195 L4
Hosp for Tropical Diseases,
WC1 .195 L5
Maternity Wing, WC1 .195 L5
Private Wing, WC1 .195 L5
★ University Coll London,
WC1 .195 M4
University Gdns, Bex. DA5 .126 EZ87
H University Hosp Lewisham,
SE13 .123 EB85
★ University of London,
WC1 .195 N5
★ Royal Holloway Coll,
Egh. TW20 .112 AX93
University Pl, Erith DA8
off Belmont Rd .107 FC80
University Rd, SW19 .120 DD93
University St, WC1 .195 L5
University Way, E16 .87 EN73
Dartford DA1 .108 FP84
Unwin Av, Felt. TW14 .115 BS85
Unwin Cl, SE15 .102 DU79
Unwin Rd, SW7 .198 A6
Isleworth TW7 .97 CE83
Upbrook Ms, W2
off Chilworth St .82 DC72
Upcerne Rd, SW10 .100 DC80
Upchurch Cl, SE20 .122 DV94
Up Cor, Ch.St.G. HP8 .36 AW47
Up Cor Cl, Ch.St.G. HP8 .36 AV47
Upcroft Av, Edg. HA8 .42 CQ50
Updale Cl, Pot.B. EN6 .11 CY33
Updale Rd, Sid. DA14 .125 ET91
Upfield, Croy. CR0 .142 DV103
Upfield Rd, W7 .79 CF70
Upgrove Manor Way, SW2
off Trinity Ri .121 DN87
Uphall Rd, Ilf. IG1 .69 EP64
Upham Pk Rd, W4 .98 CS77
Uphavering Ho, Horn. RM12
off Parkhill Cl .72 FJ61
Uphill Dr, NW7 .42 CS50
NW9 .62 CQ57
Uphill Gro, NW7 .42 CS49
Uphill Rd, NW7 .42 CS49
Upland Ct Rd, Rom. RM3 .52 FM54
Upland Dr, Hat. AL9 .12 DB25
Upland Ms, SE22
off Upland Rd .122 DU85
Upland Rd, E13
off Sutton Rd .86 EF70
SE22 .122 DU85
Bexleyheath DA7 .106 EZ83
Caterham CR3 .177 EB120
Epping CM16 .17 ET25
South Croydon CR2 .160 DR106
Sutton SM2 .158 DD108
Uplands, Ashtd. KT21 .171 CK120
Beckenham BR3 .143 EA96
Rickmansworth (Crox.Grn)
WD3 .22 BM44
Uplands, The, Ger.Cr. SL9 .56 AY60
Loughton IG10 .33 EM41
Ruislip HA4 .59 BU60
St. Albans (Brick.Wd) AL2 .8 BY30
Uplands Av, E17
off Blackhorse La .47 DX54
Uplands Business Pk, E17 .47 DX54
Uplands Cl, SW14
off Monroe Dr .118 CP85
Gerrards Cross SL9 .56 AY60
Sevenoaks TN13 .190 FF123
Uplands Dr, Lthd. (Oxshott)
KT22 .155 CD113
Uplands End, Wdf.Grn. IG8 .48 EL52
Uplands Pk Rd, Enf. EN2 .29 DN41
Uplands Rd, N8 .65 DM57
Barnet EN4 .44 DG46
Brentwood (Warley) CM14 .54 FY50
Kenley CR8 .176 DQ116
Orpington BR6 .146 EV102
Romford RM6 .70 EX55
Woodford Green IG8 .48 EL52
Uplands Way, N21 .29 DN43
Sevenoaks TN13 .190 FF123
Upland Way, Epsom KT18 .173 CW118
UPMINSTER, RM14 .72 FQ62
⇌ Upminster .72 FQ61
⊖ Upminster .72 FQ61
⊖ Upminster Bridge .72 FN61
Upminster Rd, Horn. RM11,
RM12 .72 FM61
Upminster RM14 .72 FM61
Upminster Rd N, Rain. RM13 .90 FJ69
Upminster Rd S, Rain. RM13 .89 FG70
Upminster Trd Pk, Upmin.
RM14 .73 FX59
⊖ Upney .87 ET66
Upney Cl, Horn. RM12
off Tylers Cres .72 FJ64
Upney La, Bark. IG11 .87 ES65
Upnor Way, SE17 .201 N10
Uppark Dr, Ilf. IG2 .69 EQ58
Upper Abbey Rd, Belv. DA17 .106 EZ77
Upper Addison Gdns, W14 .99 CY75
Upper Bk St, E14 .204 B3
Upper Bardsey Wk, N1
off Clephane Rd .84 DQ65
Upper Belgrave St, SW1 .198 G6
Upper Berenger Wk, SW10
off World's End Est .100 DD80
Upper Berkeley St, W1 .194 D9
Upper Beulah Hill, SE19 .142 DS95
Upper Blantyre Wk, SW10
off World's End Est .100 DD80
Upper Bourne End La,
Hem.H. HP1 .5 BA25
Upper Brentwood Rd,
Rom. RM2 .72 FJ56
Upper Br Rd, Red. RH1 .184 DE134
Upper Brighton Rd,
Surb. KT6 .137 CK100
Upper Brockley Rd, SE4 .103 DZ82
Upper Brook St, W1 .198 F1
Upper Butts, Brent. TW8 .97 CJ79
Upper Caldy Wk, N1
off Clifton Rd .84 DQ65
Upper Camelford Wk, W11
off St. Marks Rd .81 CY72
Upper Cavendish Av, N3 .64 DA55
Upper Cheyne Row, SW3 .100 DE79
Upper Ch Hill, Green. DA9 .129 FS85
UPPER CLAPTON, E5 .66 DV60
Upper Clapton Rd, E5 .66 DV60
Upper Clarendon Wk, W11
off Clarendon Wk .81 CY72
Upper Cornsland, Brwd.
CM14 .54 FX48
Upper Ct Rd, Cat. (Wold.)
CR3 .177 EA123
Epsom KT19 .156 CQ111
Upper Dartrey Wk, SW10
off World's End Est .100 DD80
Upper Dengie Wk, N1
off Popham Rd .84 DQ67
Upper Dr, West. (Bigg.H.)
TN16 .178 EJ118
Upper Dunnymans, Bans.
SM7 off Basing Rd .157 CZ114
UPPER EDMONTON, N18 .46 DU51
UPPER ELMERS END,
Beck. BR3 .143 DZ100
Upper Elmers End Rd,
Beck. BR3 .143 DY98
Upper Fairfield Rd, Lthd.
KT22 .171 CH121
Upper Fm Rd, W.Mol. KT8 .136 BZ98
Upper Fosters, NW4
off New Brent St .63 CW57
Upper Grn E, Mitch. CR4 .140 DF97
Upper Grn W, Mitch. CR4
off London Rd .140 DF97
Upper Grenfell Wk, W11
off Whitchurch Rd .81 CX73
Upper Grosvenor St, W1 .198 F1
Upper Grotto Rd, Twick. TW1 .117 CF89
Upper Grd, SE1 .200 D2
Upper Gro, SE25 .142 DS98
Upper Gro Rd, Belv. DA17 .106 EZ79
Upper Guild Hall, Green.
(Bluewater) DA9
off Bluewater Parkway .129 FU88
Upper Gulland Wk, N1
off Nightingale Rd .84 DQ65
UPPER HALLIFORD, Shep.
TW17 .135 BS97
⇌ Upper Halliford .135 BS96
Upper Halliford Bypass,
Shep. TW17 .135 BS99
Upper Halliford Grn, Shep.
TW17 off Holmbank Dr .135 BS98
Upper Halliford Rd, Shep.
TW17 .135 BS96
Upper Hampstead Wk, NW3
off New End .64 DC63
Upper Ham Rd, Kings.T. KT2 .117 CK91
Richmond TW10 .117 CK91
Upper Handa Wk, N1
off Clephane Rd .84 DR65
Upper Hawkwell Wk, N1
off Popham Rd .84 DQ67
Upper High St, Epsom KT17 .156 CS113
Upper Highway, Abb.L. WD5 .7 BR33
Kings Langley WD4 .7 BQ32
Upper Hill Ri, Rick. WD3 .22 BH44
Upper Hitch, Wat. WD19 .40 BY46
UPPER HOLLOWAY, N19 .65 DJ62
⇌ Upper Holloway .65 DK61
Upper Holly Hill Rd, Belv.
DA17 .107 FB78
Upper James St, W1 .195 L10
Upper John St, W1 .195 L10
Upper Lismore Wk, N1
off Clephane Rd .84 DQ65
Upper Lo Way, Couls. CR5
off Netherne Dr .175 DK122
Upper Mall, W6 .99 CU78
Upper Marsh, SE1 .200 C6
Upper Montagu St, W1 .194 D6
Upper Mulgrave Rd, Sutt.
SM2 .157 CY108
Upper N St, E14 .85 EA71
UPPER NORWOOD, SE19 .122 DR94
Upper Paddock Rd, Wat.
WD19 .24 BY44
Upper Palace Rd, E.Mol. KT8 .136 CC97
Upper Pk, Loug. IG10 .32 EK42
Upper Pk Rd, N11 .45 DH50
NW3 .64 DF64
Belvedere DA17 .107 FB77
Bromley BR1 .144 EH95
Kingston upon Thames
KT2 .118 CN93
Upper Phillimore Gdns, W8 .100 DA75
Upper Pillory Down, Cars.
SM5 .158 DG113
Upper Pines, Bans. SM7 .174 DF117
Upper Rainham Rd, Horn.
RM12 .71 FF63
Upper Ramsey Wk, N1
off Clephane Rd .84 DR65
Upper Rawreth Wk, N1
off Popham Rd .84 DQ67
Upper Richmond Rd, SW15 .99 CY84
Upper Richmond Rd W,
SW14 .98 CP84
Richmond TW10 .98 CN84
Upper Rd, E13 .86 EG69
Uxbridge (Denh.) UB9 .57 BD59
Wallington SM6 .159 DK106
Upper Rose Gall, Green.
(Bluewater) DA9
off Bluewater Parkway .129 FU88
Upper Ryle, Brwd. CM14 .54 FV45
Upper St. Martin's La, WC2 .195 P10
Upper Sawley Wd, Bans.
SM7 .157 CZ114
Upper Selsdon Rd, S.Croy.
CR2 .160 DT108
Upper Sheppey Wk, N1
off Clephane Rd .84 DQ66
Upper Sheridan Rd, Belv.
DA17 off Coleman Rd .106 FA77
Upper Shirley Rd, Croy. CR0 .142 DW103
Upper Shott, Wal.Cr. (Chsht)
EN7 .14 DT26
Upper Sq, Islw. TW7 .97 CG83
Upper Sta Rd, Rad. WD7 .25 CG35
Upper St, N1 .83 DN68
Upper Sunbury Rd, Hmptn.
TW12 .136 BY95
Upper Sutton La, Houns. TW5 .96 CA80
Upper Swaines, Epp. CM16 .17 ET30
UPPER SYDENHAM, SE26 .122 DU91
Upper Tachbrook St, SW1 .199 K8
Upper Tail, Wat. WD19 .40 BY48
Upper Talbot Wk, W11
off Talbot Wk .81 CY72
Upper Teddington Rd,
Kings.T. KT1 .137 CJ95
Upper Ter, NW3 .64 DC62
Upper Thames St, EC4 .196 G10
Upper Thames Wk, Green.
(Bluewater) DA9
off Bluewater Parkway .129 FU88
Upper Tollington Pk, N4 .65 DN60
Upperton Rd, Sid. DA14 .125 ET92
Upperton Rd E, E13
off Inniskilling Rd .86 EJ69
Upperton Rd W, E13 .86 EJ69
UPPER TOOTING, SW17 .120 DE90
Upper Tooting Pk, SW17 .120 DF89
Upper Tooting Rd, SW17 .120 DF91
Upper Town Rd, Grnf. UB6 .78 CB70
Upper Tulse Hill, SW2 .121 DM87
Upper Vernon Rd, Sutt. SM1 .158 DD106
Upper Wk, Vir.W. GU25 .132 AY98
UPPER WALTHAMSTOW, E17 .67 EB56
Upper Walthamstow Rd, E17 .67 ED56
⇌ Upper Warlingham .176 DU118
Upper W St, Reig. RH2 .183 CZ134
Upper Whistler Wk, SW10
off World's End Est .100 DC80
Upper Wickham La, Well.
DA16 .106 EV80
Upper Wimpole St, W1 .195 H6
Upper Woburn Pl, WC1 .195 N3
Upper Woodcote Village,
Pur. CR8 .159 DK112
Uppingham Av, Stan. HA7 .41 CH53
Upsdell Av, N13 .45 DN51
UPSHIRE, Wal.Abb. EN9 .16 EJ32
Upshirebury Grn, Wal.Abb.
EN9 off Horseshoe Hill .16 EK33
Upshire Rd, Wal.Abb. EN9 .16 EF32
Upshott La, Wok. GU22 .167 BF117
Upstall St, SE5 .101 DP81
UPTON, E7 .86 EH66
UPTON, Slou. SL1 .92 AU76
Upton, Wok. GU21 .166 AV117
Upton Av, E7 .86 EG66
Upton Cl, NW2
off Somerton Rd .63 CY62
Bexley DA5 .126 EZ86
St. Albans (Park St) AL2 .9 CD25
Slough SL1 .92 AT76
Upton Ct, SE20
off Blean Gro .122 DW94
Upton Ct Rd, Slou. SL3 .92 AU76
Upton Dene, Sutt. SM2 .158 DB108
Upton Gdns, Har. HA3 .61 CH57
H Upton Hosp, Slou. SL1 .92 AT76
Upton La, E7 .86 EG66
Upton Lo Cl, Bushey WD23 .40 CC45
UPTON PARK, E6 .86 EJ67
UPTON PARK, Slou. SL1 .92 AT76
⊖ Upton Park .86 EH67
Upton Pk, Slou. SL1 .92 AT76
Upton Pk Rd, E7 .86 EH66
Upton Rd, N18 .46 DU50
SE18 .105 EQ79
Bexley DA5 .126 EZ86
Bexleyheath DA6 .106 EY84
Hounslow TW3 .96 CA83
Slough SL1 .92 AU76
Thornton Heath CR7 .142 DR96
Watford WD18 .23 BV42
Upton Rd S, Bex. DA5 .126 EZ86
Upway, N12 .44 DE52
Gerrards Cross (Chal.St.P.)
SL9 .37 AZ53
Upwood Rd, SE12 .124 EF86
SW16 .141 DL95
Urban Av, Horn. RM12 .72 FJ62
Urban Ms, N4 .65 DP59
Urlwin St, SE5 .102 DQ79
Urlwin Wk, SW9 .101 DN82
Urmston Dr, SW19 .119 CY88
Ursula Ms, N4
off Portland Ri .66 DQ60
Ursula St, SW11 .100 DE81
Urswick Gdns, Dag. RM9
off Urswick Rd .88 EY66
Urswick Rd, E9 .66 DW64
Dagenham RM9 .88 EX66
Usborne Ms, SW8 .101 DM80
Usher Rd, E3 .85 DZ68
Usherwood Cl, Tad. (Box H.)
KT20 .182 CP131
Usk Rd, SW11 .100 DC84
South Ockendon (Aveley)
RM15 .90 FQ72
Usk St, E2 .85 DX69
Utopia Village, NW1
off Chalcot Rd .82 DG67
Uvedale Cl, Croy. (New Adgtn)
CR0 off Uvedale Cres .161 ED111
Uvedale Cres, Croy. (New Adgtn)
CR0 .161 ED111
Uvedale Rd, Dag. RM10 .70 FA62
Enfield EN2 .30 DR43
Oxted RH8 .188 EF129
Uverdale Rd, SW10 .100 DC80
UXBRIDGE, UB8 - UB11 .76 BK66
⊖ Uxbridge .76 BK66
Uxbridge Gdns, Felt. TW13
off Marlborough Rd .116 BX89
UXBRIDGE MOOR, Iver SL0 .76 BG67
UXBRIDGE MOOR, Uxb. UB8 .76 BG67
Uxbridge Rd, W3 .80 CL73
W5 .79 CJ73
W5 (Ealing Com.) .80 CL73
W7 .79 CE74
W12 .81 CU74
W13 .79 CH74
Feltham TW13 .116 BW89
Hampton (Hmptn H.) TW12 .116 CA91
Harrow HA3 .40 CC52
Hayes UB4 .78 BW73
Iver SL0 .74 AY71
Kingston upon Thames
KT1 .137 CK98
Pinner HA5 .40 CB52
Rickmansworth WD3 .37 BF47
Slough SL1, SL2, SL3 .92 AU75
Southall UB1 .78 CA74
Stanmore HA7 .41 CF51
Uxbridge UB10 .76 BN69
Uxbridge St, W8 .82 DA74
Uxendon Cres, Wem. HA9 .62 CL60
Uxendon Hill, Wem. HA9 .62 CM60

V

Vache La, Ch.St.G. HP8 .36 AW47
Vache Ms, Ch.St.G. HP8 .36 AX46
Vaillant Rd, Wey. KT13 .153 BQ105
Valance Av, E4 .48 EF46
Valan Leas, Brom. BR2 .144 EE97
Vale, The, N10 .44 DG53
N14 .45 DK45
NW11 .63 CX62
SW3 .100 DD79
W3 .80 CR74
Brentwood CM14 .54 FW46
Coulsdon CR5 .159 DK114
Croydon CR0 .143 DX103
Feltham TW14 .115 BV86
Gerrards Cross (Chal.St.P.)
SL9 .36 AX53
Hounslow TW5 .96 BY79
Ruislip HA4 .60 BW63
Sunbury-on-Thames TW16
off Ashridge Way .115 BU93
Woodford Green IG8 .48 EG52
Vale Av, Borwd. WD6 .26 CP43
Vale Border, Croy. CR0 .161 DX111
Vale Cl, N2 off Church Vale .64 DF55
W9 off Maida Vale .82 DC69
Brentwood (Pilg.Hat.) CM15 .54 FT43
Gerrards Cross (Chal.St.P.)
SL9 .36 AX53
Orpington BR6 .163 EN105
Weybridge KT13 .135 BR104
Woking GU21 .166 AY116
Vale Cotts, SW15
off Kingston Vale .118 CR91
Vale Ct, W9 .82 DC69
Weybridge KT13 .135 BR104
Vale Cres, SW15 .118 CS90
Vale Cft, Esher (Clay.) KT10 .155 CE109
Pinner HA5 .60 BY57
Vale Dr, Barn. EN5 .27 CZ42
Vale End, SE22
off Grove Vale .102 DS84
Vale Fm Rd, Wok. GU21 .166 AX117
Vale Gro, N4 .66 DQ59
W3 off The Vale .80 CR74
Slough SL1 .92 AS76
Vale Ind Est, Wat. WD18 .39 BQ46
Vale La, W3 .80 CN71
Valence Av, Dag. RM8 .70 EX62
Valence Circ, Dag. RM8 .70 EX62
Valence Dr, Wal.Cr. (Chsht)
EN7 .14 DU28
★ Valence Ho Mus,
Dag. RM8 .70 EY61
Valence Rd, Erith DA8 .107 FD80
Valence Wd Rd, Dag. RM8 .70 EX62
Valencia Rd, Stan. HA7 .41 CJ49
Valency Cl, Nthwd. HA6 .39 BT49
Valentia Pl, SW9
off Brixton Sta Rd .101 DN84
Valentine Av, Bex. DA5 .126 EY89
Valentine Ct, SE23 .123 DX89
Valentine Pl, SE1 .200 F4
Valentine Rd, E9 .85 DX65
Harrow HA2 .60 CC62
Valentine Row, SE1 .200 F5
Valentines Rd, Ilf. IG1 .69 EP60
Valentines Way, Rom. RM7 .71 FE61
Valentine Way, Ch.St.G. HP8 .36 AX48
Valentyne Cl, Croy. (New Adgtn)
CR0 .162 EE111
Vale of Health, NW3
off East Heath Rd .64 DD62
Vale Par, SW15
off Kingston Vale .118 CR91
Valerian Way, E15 .86 EE69
Valerie Ct, Bushey WD23 .40 CC45
Sutton SM2 off Stanley Rd .158 DB108
Vale Ri, NW11 .63 CZ60
Vale Rd, E7 .86 EH65
N4 .66 DQ59
Bromley BR1 .145 EN96
Bushey WD23 .24 BY43
Dartford DA1 .127 FH88
Epsom KT19 .157 CT105
Esher (Clay.) KT10 .155 CE109
Gravesend (Nthflt) DA11 .130 GD87
Mitcham CR4 .141 DK97
Sutton SM1 .158 DB105
Weybridge KT13 .135 BR104
Worcester Park KT4 .157 CT105
Vale Rd N, Surb. KT6 .138 CL103
Vale Rd S, Surb. KT6 .138 CL103
Vale Row, N5
off Gillespie Rd .65 DP62
Vale Royal, N7 .83 DL66
Valery Pl, Hmptn. TW12 .116 CA94
Vale St, SE27 .122 DR90
Valeswood Rd, Brom. BR1 .124 EF92
Vale Ter, N4 .66 DQ58
Valetta Gro, E13 .86 EG68
Valetta Rd, W3 .98 CS75
Valette St, E9 .84 DV65
Valiant Cl, Nthlt. UB5
off Ruislip Rd .78 BX69
Romford RM7 .50 FA54
Valiant Ho, SE7 .104 EJ78
Valiant Path, NW9
off Blundell Rd .42 CS52
Valiant Way, E6 .87 EM71
Vallance Rd, E1 .84 DU70
E2 .84 DU69
N22 .45 DJ54
Vallentin Rd, E17 .67 EC56
Valley Av, N12 .44 DD49
Valley Cl, Dart. DA1 .127 FF86
Loughton IG10 .33 EM44
Pinner HA5
off Alandale Dr .39 BV54
Waltham Abbey EN9 .15 EC32
Valley Ct, Cat. CR3
off Beechwood Gdns .176 DU122
Kenley CR8
off Hayes La .160 DQ114
Valley Dr, NW9 .62 CN58
Gravesend DA12 .131 GK91
Sevenoaks TN13 .191 FH125
Valleyfield Rd, SW16 .121 DM92
Valley Flds Cres, Enf. EN2 .29 DN40
Valley Gdns, SW19 .120 DD94
Greenhithe DA9 .129 FV86
Wembley HA0 .80 CM66
★ Valley Gdns, The,
Egh. TW20 .132 AS96
Valley Gro, SE7 .104 EJ78
Valley Hill, Loug. IG10 .48 EL45
Valley Link Ind Est, Enf. EN3 .31 DY44
Valley Ms, Twick. TW1
off Cross Deep .117 CG89
Valley Ri, Wat. WD25 .7 BV33
Valley Rd, SW16 .121 DM91
Belvedere DA17 .107 FB77
Bromley BR2 .144 EE96
Dartford DA1 .127 FF86
Erith DA8 .107 FD77
Kenley CR8 .176 DR115
Longfield (Fawk.Grn) DA3 .149 FV102
Orpington BR5 .146 EV95
Rickmansworth WD3 .22 BG43
Uxbridge UB10 .76 BL68
Valley Side, E4 .47 EA47
Valley Side Par, E4
off Valley Side .47 EA47
Valley Vw, Barn. EN5 .27 CY44
Greenhithe DA9 .129 FV86
Waltham Cross (Chsht) EN7 .14 DQ28
Westerham (Bigg.H.) TN16 .178 EJ118
Valley Vw Gdns, Ken. CR8
off Godstone Rd .176 DS115
Valley Wk, Croy. CR0 .142 DW103
Rickmansworth (Crox.Grn)
WD3 .23 BQ43
Valley Way, Ger.Cr. SL9 .56 AW58
Valliere Rd, NW10 .81 CV69
Valliers Wd Rd, Sid. DA15 .125 ER88

Vallis Way, W13 79 CG71
Chessington KT9 155 CK105
Valmar Rd, SE5 102 DQ81
Val McKenzie Av, N7
off Parkside Cres 65 DN62
Valnay St, SW17 120 DF92
Valognes Av, E17 47 DY53
Valonia Gdns, SW18 119 CZ86
Vambery Rd, SE18 105 EQ79
Vanbrough Cres, Nthlt. UB5 78 BW67
Vanbrugh Cl, E16
off Fulmer Rd 86 EK71
Vanbrugh Dr, Walt. KT12 136 BW101
Vanbrugh Flds, SE3 104 EF80
Vanbrugh Hill, SE3 104 EF78
SE10 104 EF78
Vanbrugh Pk, SE3 104 EF80
Vanbrugh Pk Rd, SE3 104 EF80
Vanbrugh Pk Rd W, SE3 104 EF80
Vanbrugh Rd, W4 98 CR76
Vanbrugh Ter, SE3 104 EF81
Vanburgh Cl, Orp. BR6 145 ES102
Vancouver Cl, Epsom KT19 156 CQ111
Orpington BR6 164 EU105
Vancouver Rd, SE23 123 DY89
Broxbourne EN10 15 DY25
Edgware HA8 42 CP53
Hayes UB4 77 BV70
Richmond TW10 117 CJ91
Vanderbilt Rd, SW18 120 DC88
Vanderville Gdns, N2
off Tarling Rd 44 DD54
Vandome Cl, E16 86 EH72
Vandon Pas, SW1 199 L6
Vandon St, SW1 199 L6
Van Dyck Av, N.Mal. KT3 138 CR101
Vandyke Cl, SW15 119 CX87
Redhill RH1 184 DF131
Vandyke Cross, SE9 124 EL85
Vandy St, EC2 197 M5
Vane Cl, NW3 64 DD63
Harrow HA3 62 CM58
Vanessa Cl, Belv. DA17 106 FA78
Vanessa Wk, Grav. DA12 131 GM92
Vanessa Way, Bex. DA5 127 FD90
Vane St, SW1 199 L8
Van Gogh Cl, Islw. TW7
off Twickenham Rd 97 CG83
Vanguard Cl, E16 86 EG71
Croydon CR0 141 DP102
Romford RM7 51 FB54
Vanguard Ho, E8
off Martello St 84 DV66
Vanguard St, SE8 103 EA81
Vanguard Way, Cat. CR3 177 EB121
Wallington SM6 159 DL108
Warlingham CR6 177 EB121
Vanneck Sq, SW15 119 CU85
Vanner Pt, E9 *off Wick Rd* 85 DX65
Vanners Par, W.Byf. (Byfleet)
KT14 *off Brewery La* 152 BL113
Vanoc Gdns, Brom. BR1 124 EG90
Vanquisher Wk, Grav. DA12 131 GM90
Vansittart Rd, E7 68 EF63
Vansittart St, SE14 103 DY80
Vanston Pl, SW6 100 DA80
Vantage Ms, E14 204 E3
Vantage Pl, W8
off Abingdon Rd 100 DA76
Vant Rd, SW17 120 DF92
Varcoe Rd, SE16 102 DV78
Vardens Rd, SW11 100 DD84
Varden St, E1 84 DV72
Vardon Cl, W3 80 CR72
Varley Par, NW9 62 CS56
Varley Rd, E16 86 EH72
Varley Way, Mitch. CR4 140 DD96
Varna Rd, SW6 99 CY80
Hampton TW12 136 CB95
Varndell St, NW1 195 K2
Varney Cl, Wal.Cr. (Chsht) EN7 14 DU27
Varnishers Yd, N1
off Caledonian Rd 83 DL68
Varsity Dr, Twick. TW1 117 CE85
Varsity Row, SW14
off William's La 98 CQ82
Vartry Rd, N15 66 DR58
Vassall Rd, SW9 101 DN80
Vauban Est, SE16 202 A7
Vauban St, SE16 202 A7
Vaughan Av, NW4 63 CU57
W6 99 CT77
Hornchurch RM12 72 FK63
Vaughan Cl, Hmptn. TW12
off Oak Av 116 BY93
Vaughan Gdns, Ilf. IG1 69 EM59
Vaughan Rd, E15 86 EF65
SE5 102 DQ82
Harrow HA1 60 CC59
Thames Ditton KT7 137 CH101
Welling DA16 105 ET82
Vaughan St, SE16 203 M5
Vaughan Way, E1 202 B1
Vaughan Williams Cl, SE8
off Watson's St 103 EA80
Vaughan Williams Way,
Brwd. (Warley) CM14 53 FU51
Vaux Cres, Walt. KT12 153 BV107
VAUXHALL, SE11 101 DL78
⇌ **Vauxhall** 101 DL79
⊖ **Vauxhall** 101 DL79
Vauxhall Br, SE1 101 DL78
SW1 101 DL78
Vauxhall Br Rd, SW1 199 L8
Vauxhall Cl, Grav.
(Nthflt) DA11 131 GF87
Vauxhall Gdns, S.Croy. CR2 160 DQ107
Vauxhall Gdns Est, SE11 101 DM78
Vauxhall Gro, SW8 101 DL79
Vauxhall Pl, Dart. DA1 128 FL87
Vauxhall St, SE11 200 C10
Vauxhall Wk, SE11 200 B10
Vawdrey Cl, E1 84 DW70
Veals Mead, Mitch. CR4 140 DE95
Vectis Gdns, SW17
off Vectis Rd 121 DH93
Vectis Rd, SW17 121 DH93
Veda Rd, SE13 103 EA84
Vega Cres, Nthwd. HA6 39 BT50
Vegal Cres, Egh. (Eng.Grn)
TW20 112 AW92
Vega Rd, Bushey WD23 40 CC45
Veitch Cl, Felt. TW14 115 BT88
Veldene Way, Har. HA2 60 BZ62
Velde Way, SE22
off East Dulwich Gro 122 DS85
Velletri Ho, E2 85 DX68
Vellum Dr, Cars. SM5 140 DG104
Venables Cl, Dag. RM10 71 FB63
Venables St, NW8 194 A6
Vencourt Pl, W6 99 CU78
Venetian Rd, SE5 102 DQ82
Venetia Rd, N4 65 DP58
W5 97 CK75
Venette Cl, Rain. RM13 89 FH71
Venner Rd, SE26 122 DW93
Venners Cl, Bexh. DA7 107 FE82
Venn St, SW4 101 DJ84
Ventnor Av, Stan. HA7 41 CH53
Ventnor Dr, N20 44 DB48
Ventnor Gdns, Bark. IG11 87 ES65
Ventnor Rd, SE14 103 DX80
Sutton SM2 158 DB108
Venton Cl, Wok. GU21 166 AV117
Ventura Pk, St.Alb. AL2 9 CF29
Venture Cl, Bex. DA5 126 EY87
Venue St, E14 85 EC71
Venus Hill, Hem.H. (Bov.) HP3 5 BA31
Venus Ho, E14 *off Crews St* 103 EA77
Venus Ms, Mitch. CR4 140 DE97
Venus Rd, SE18 105 EM76
Veny Cres, Horn. RM12 72 FK64
Vera Av, N21 29 DN43
Vera Ct, Wat. WD19 40 BX45
Vera Lynn Cl, E7
off Dames Rd 68 EG63
Vera Rd, SW6 99 CY81
Verbena Cl, E16
off Pretoria Rd 86 EF70
South Ockendon RM15 91 FW72
West Drayton UB7
off Magnolia St 94 BK78
Verbena Gdns, W6 99 CU78
Verdant La, SE6 124 EE88
Verdayne Av, Croy. CR0 143 DX102
Verdayne Gdns, Warl. CR6 176 DW116
Verderers Rd, Chig. IG7 50 EU50
Verdi Cres, W10
off Herries St 81 CY68
Verdun Rd, SE18 106 EU79
SW13 99 CU79
Verdure Cl, Wat. WD25 8 BY32
Vereker Dr, Sun. TW16 135 BU97
Vereker Rd, W14 99 CY78
Vere Rd, Loug. IG10 33 EQ42
Vere St, W1 195 H9
Verity Cl, W11 81 CY72
Vermeer Gdns, SE15
off Elland Rd 102 DW84
Vermont Cl, Enf. EN2 29 DP42
Vermont Rd, SE19 122 DR93
SW18 120 DB86
Sutton SM1 140 DB104
Verney Gdns, Dag. RM9 70 EY63
Verney Rd, SE16 102 DU79
Dagenham RM9 70 EY64
Slough SL3 93 BA77
Verney St, NW10 62 CR62
Verney Way, SE16 102 DV78
Vernham Rd, SE18 105 EQ79
Vernon Av, E12 69 EM63
SW20 139 CX96
Enfield EN3 31 DY36
Woodford Green IG8 48 EH52
Vernon Cl, Cher. (Ott.) KT16 151 BD107
Epsom KT19 156 CQ107
Orpington BR5 146 EV97
Staines TW19 114 BL88
Vernon Ct, Stan. HA7
off Vernon Dr 41 CH53
Vernon Cres, Barn. EN4 28 DG44
Brentwood CM13 55 GA48
Vernon Dr, Cat. CR3 176 DQ122
Stanmore HA7 41 CG53
Uxbridge (Hare.) UB9 38 BJ53
Vernon Ms, E17 *off Vernon Rd* 67 DZ56
W14 *off Vernon St* 99 CY77
Vernon Pl, WC1 196 A7
Vernon Ri, WC1 196 C2
Greenford UB6 61 CD64
Vernon Rd, E3 85 DZ68
E11 68 EE60
E15 86 EE66
E17 67 DZ57
N8 65 DN55
SW14 98 CR83
Bushey WD23 24 BY43
Feltham TW13 115 BT89
Ilford IG3 69 ET60
Romford RM5 51 FC50
Sutton SM1 158 DC106
Swanscombe DA10 130 FZ86
Vernon Sq, WC1 196 C2
Vernon St, W14 99 CY77
Vernon Wk, Tad. KT20 173 CX120
Vernon Yd, W11
off Portobello Rd 81 CZ73
Veroan Rd, Bexh. DA7 106 EY82
Verona Cl, Uxb. UB8 76 BJ72
Verona Ct, W4
off Chiswick La 98 CS78
Verona Dr, Surb. KT6 138 CL103
Verona Gdns, Grav. DA12 131 GL91
Verona Ho, Erith DA8
off Waterhead Cl 107 FF80
Verona Rd, E7 *off Upton La* 86 EG66
Veronica Cl, Rom. RM3 52 FJ52
Veronica Gdns, SW16 141 DJ95
Veronica Rd, SW17 121 DH90
Veronique Gdns, Ilf. IG6 69 EP57
Verralls, Wok. GU22 167 BB117
Verran Rd, SW12
off Balham Gro 121 DH87
Versailles Rd, SE20 122 DU94
Verulam Av, E17 67 DZ58
Purley CR8 159 DJ112
Verulam Bldgs, WC1 196 C6
Verulam Ho, W6
off Hammersmith Gro 99 CW77
Verulam Pas, Wat. WD17 23 BV40
Verulam Rd, Grnf. UB6 78 CA70
Verulam St, WC1 196 D6
Verwood Dr, Barn. EN4 28 DF41
Verwood Rd, Har. HA2 40 CC54
Veryan, Wok. GU21 166 AU117
Veryan Cl, Orp. BR5 146 EW98
Vesage Ct, EC1
off Leather La 83 DN71
Vesey Path, E14
off East India Dock Rd 85 EB72
Vespan Rd, W12 99 CU75
Vesta Ct, SE1 *off Long La* 102 DS75
Vesta Rd, SE4 103 DY82
Vestris Rd, SE23 123 DX89
Vestry Ms, SE5 102 DS81
Vestry Rd, E17 67 EB56
SE5 102 DS81
Vestry St, N1 197 K2
Vevey St, SE6 123 DZ89
Vexil Cl, Purf. RM19 109 FR77
Veysey Gdns, Dag. RM10 70 FA62
Viaduct Pl, E2
off Viaduct St 84 DV69
Viaduct St, E2 84 DV69
Vian Av, Enf. EN3 31 DY35
Vian St, SE13 103 EB83
Vibart Gdns, SW2 121 DM87
Vibart Wk, N1 *off Outram Pl* 83 DL67
Vicarage Av, SE3 104 EG81
Egham TW20 113 BB93
Vicarage Cl, Brwd. CM14 54 FS49
Erith DA8 107 FC79
Northolt UB5 78 BZ66
Potters Bar EN6 11 CY32
Potters Bar (Northaw) EN6 12 DF30
Ruislip HA4 59 BR59
Tadworth KT20 173 CY124
Worcester Park KT4 138 CS102
Vicarage Ct, W8
off Vicarage Gate 100 DB75
Egham TW20 113 BB93
Feltham TW14 115 BQ87
Vicarage Cres, SW11 100 DD81
Egham TW20 113 BB92
Vicarage Dr, SW14 118 CR85
Barking IG11 87 EQ66
Beckenham BR3 143 EA95
Gravesend (Nthflt) DA11 130 GC86
Vicarage Fm Rd, Houns.
TW3, TW5 96 BY82
Vicarage Flds, Walt. KT12 136 BW100
Vicarage Fld Shop Cen,
Bark. IG11 87 EQ66
Vicarage Gdns, SW14
off Vicarage Rd 118 CQ85
W8 82 DA74
Mitcham CR4 140 DE97
Vicarage Gate, W8 100 DB75
Vicarage Gate Ms, Tad. KT20 173 CY124
Vicarage Gro, SE5 102 DR81
Vicarage Hill, West. TN16 189 ER126
Vicarage La, E6 87 EM69
E15 86 EE66
Chigwell IG7 49 EQ47
Epsom KT17 157 CU109
Hemel Hempstead
(Bov.) HP3 5 BB26
Ilford IG1 69 ER60
Kings Langley WD4 6 BM29
Leatherhead KT22 171 CH122
Sevenoaks (Dunt.Grn) TN13
off London Rd 181 FD119
Staines (Laleham) TW18 134 BH97
Staines (Wrays.) TW19 112 AY88
Vicarage Pk, SE18 105 EQ78
Vicarage Path, N8 65 DL59
Vicarage Pl, Slou. SL1 92 AU76
Vicarage Rd, E10 67 EB60
E15 86 EF66
N17 46 DU52
NW4 63 CU58
SE18 105 EQ78
SW14 118 CQ85
Bexley DA5 127 FB88
Croydon CR0 141 DN104
Dagenham RM10 89 FB65
Egham TW20 113 BB93
Epping (Cooper.) CM16 18 EW29
Hornchurch RM12 71 FG60
Kingston upon Thames
KT1 137 CK96
Kingston upon Thames
(Hmptn W.) KT1 137 CJ95
Staines TW18 113 BE91
Sunbury-on-Thames TW16 115 BT92
Sutton SM1 158 DB105
Teddington TW11 117 CG92
Twickenham TW2 117 CE89
Twickenham (Whitton) TW2 116 CC86
Watford WD18 23 BU44
Woking GU22 167 AZ121
Woodford Green IG8 48 EL52
Vicarage Sq, Grays RM17 110 GA79
Vicarage Wk, SW11
off Battersea Ch Rd 100 DD81
Reigate RH2 *off Chartway* 184 DB134
Vicarage Way, NW10 62 CR62
Gerrards Cross SL9 57 AZ58
Harrow HA2 60 CA59
Slough (Colnbr.) SL3 93 BC80
Vicars Br Cl, Wem. HA0 80 CL68
Vicars Cl, E9
off Northiam St 84 DW67
E15 86 EG67
Enfield EN1 30 DS40
Vicars Hill, SE13 103 EB84
Vicars Moor La, N21 45 DN45
Vicars Oak Rd, SE19 122 DS93
Vicars Rd, NW5 64 DG64
Vicars Wk, Dag. RM8 70 EV62
Viceroy Cl, N2 *off Market Pl* 64 DE56
Viceroy Ct, NW8
off Prince Albert Rd 82 DE68
Viceroy Par, N2 *off High Rd* 64 DE56
Viceroy Rd, SW8 101 DL81
Vickers Cl, Wall. SM6 159 DM108
Vickers Dr N, Wey. KT13 152 BL110
Vickers Dr S, Wey. KT13 152 BL111
Vickers Rd, Erith DA8 107 FD78
Vickers Way, Houns. TW4 116 BY85
Victor App, Horn. RM12
off Abbs Cross Gdns 72 FK60
Victor Cl, Horn. RM12 72 FK60
Victor Ct, Horn. RM12 72 FK60
Rainham RM13
off Askwith Rd 89 FD68
Victor Gdns, Horn. RM12 72 FK60
Victor Gro, Wem. HA0 80 CL66
⇌ **Victoria** 199 J8
⊖ **Victoria** 199 J8
★ **Victoria & Albert Mus**,
SW7 198 A7
Victoria Arc, SW1
off Terminus Pl 101 DH76
Victoria Av, E6 86 EK67
EC2 197 N7
N3 43 CZ53
Barnet EN4 28 DD42
Gravesend DA12
off Sheppy Pl 131 GH87
Grays RM16 110 GC75
Hounslow TW3 116 BZ85
Romford RM5 51 FB51
South Croydon CR2 160 DQ110
Surbiton KT6 137 CK101
Uxbridge UB10 77 BP66
Wallington SM6 140 DG104
Wembley HA9 80 CP65
West Molesey KT8 136 CA97
Victoria Cl, Barn. EN4 28 DD42
Grays RM16 110 GC75
Hayes UB3
off Commonwealth Av 77 BR72
Rickmansworth WD3
off Nightingale Rd 38 BK45
Waltham Cross EN8 15 DX30
West Molesey KT8
off Victoria Av 136 CA97
Weybridge KT13 135 BR104
★ **Victoria Coach Sta**, SW1 199 H9
Victoria Cotts, Rich. TW9 98 CM81
Victoria Ct, Wem. HA9 80 CN65
Victoria Cres, N15 66 DS57
SE19 122 DS93
SW19 119 CZ94
Iver SL0 76 BG73
Victoria Dock Rd, E16 86 EF72
Victoria Dr, SW19 119 CX87
Dartford (S.Darenth) DA4 149 FR96
Victoria Embk, EC4 200 B1
SW1 200 A4
WC2 200 B1
★ **Victoria Embankment Gdns**,
WC2 200 A1
Victoria Gdns, W11 82 DA74
Hounslow TW5 96 BY81
Westerham (Bigg.H.) TN16 178 EJ115
Victoria Gro, N12 44 DC50
W8 100 DC76
Victoria Gro Ms, W2
off Ossington St 82 DB73
Victoria Hill Rd, Swan. BR8 147 FF95
H **Victoria Hosp**, Rom. RM1 71 FF56
Victoria Ind Est, NW10 80 CS69
Victoria Ind Pk, Dart. DA1 128 FL85
Victoria La, Barn. EN5 27 CZ42
Hayes UB3 95 BQ78
Victoria Ms, E8
off Dalston La 66 DU64
NW6 82 DA67
SW4 *off Victoria Ri* 101 DH84
SW18 120 DC88
Victoria Mills Studios, E15
off Burford Rd 85 ED67
Victorian Gro, N16 66 DS62
Victorian Hts, SW8
off Thackeray Rd 101 DH82
Victorian Rd, N16 66 DS62
★ **Victoria Park**, E9 85 DY66
Victoria Pk Rd, E9 84 DW67
Victoria Pk Sq, E2 84 DW69
Victoria Pas, NW8
off Aberdeen Pl 82 DD70
Watford WD18 23 BV42
Victoria Pl, SE22
off Underhill Rd 122 DU85
SW1 199 J8
Epsom KT17 156 CS112
Richmond TW9 117 CK85
Victoria Pt, E13
off Victoria Rd 86 EG68
Victoria Retail Pk, Ruis. HA4 60 BX64
Victoria Ri, SW4 101 DH83
Victoria Rd, E4 48 EE46
E11 68 EE63
E13 86 EG68
E17 47 EC54
E18 48 EH54
N4 65 DM59
N9 46 DT49
N15 66 DU56
N18 46 DT49
N22 45 DJ53
NW4 63 CW56
NW6 81 CZ67
NW7 43 CT50
NW10 80 CR71
SW14 98 CR83
W3 80 CR71
W5 79 CH71
W8 100 DC76
Addlestone KT15 152 BK105
Barking IG11 87 EP65
Barnet EN4 28 DD42
Bexleyheath DA6 106 FA84
Brentwood (Warley) CM14 54 FW49
Bromley BR2 144 EK99
Buckhurst Hill IG9 48 EK47
Bushey WD23 40 CB46
Chislehurst BR7 125 EN92
Coulsdon CR5 175 DK115
Dagenham RM10 71 FB64
Dartford DA1 128 FK85
Erith DA8 107 FE79
Feltham TW13 115 BV88
Gravesend (Nthflt) DA11 131 GF88
Kingston upon Thames
KT1 138 CM96
Mitcham CR4 120 DE94
Romford RM1 71 FE58
Ruislip HA4 60 BW64
Sevenoaks TN13 191 FH125
Sidcup DA15 125 ET90
Slough SL2 74 AV74
Southall UB2 96 BZ76
Staines TW18 113 BE90
Surbiton KT6 137 CK100
Sutton SM1 158 DD106
Teddington TW11 117 CG93
Twickenham TW1 117 CG87
Uxbridge UB8
off New Windsor St 76 BJ67
Victoria Rd, Wal. Abb. EN9 15 EC34
Watford WD24 23 BV38
Weybridge KT13 135 BR104
Woking GU22 166 AY117
Victoria Scott Ct, Dart. DA1 107 FE83
Victoria Sq, SW1 199 J6
Victoria Steps, Brent. TW8
off Kew Br Rd 98 CM79
Victoria St, E15 86 EE66
SW1 199 K7
Belvedere DA17 106 EZ78
Egham (Eng.Grn) TW20 112 AW93
Slough SL1 92 AT75
Victoria Ter, N4 65 DN60
NW10 *off Old Oak La* 80 CS69
Harrow HA1 61 CE60
★ **Victoria Twr**, SW1 199 P6
Victoria Vil, Rich. TW9 98 CM83
Victoria Way, SE7 205 P10
Weybridge KT13 135 BR104
Woking GU21 166 AY117
Victoria Wf, E14 203 L1
Victoria Yd, E1
off Fairclough St 84 DU72
Victor Rd, NW10 81 CV69
SE20 123 DX94
Harrow HA2 60 CC55
Teddington TW11 117 CE91
Victors Cres, Brwd. (Hutt.)
CM13 55 GB47
Victors Dr, Hmptn. TW12 116 BY93
Victor Smith Ct, St.Alb.
(Brick.Wd) AL2 8 CA31
Victors Way, Barn. EN5 27 CZ41
Victor Vil, N9 46 DR48
Victor Wk, NW9 42 CS54
Hornchurch RM12
off Abbs Cross Gdns 72 FK60
Victory Av, Mord. SM4 140 DC99
Victory Business Cen,
Islw. TW7 97 CF83
Victory Cl, Grays (Chaff.Hun.)
RM16 109 FW77
Staines TW19 114 BL88
Victory Pk Rd, Add. KT15 152 BJ105
Victory Pl, E14
off Northey St 85 DY73
SE17 201 J8
SE19 *off Westow St* 122 DS93
Victory Rd, E11 68 EH56
SW19 120 DC94
Chertsey KT16 134 BG102
Rainham RM13 89 FG68
Victory Rd Ms, SW19
off Victory Rd 120 DC94
Victory Wk, SE8 *off Ship St* 103 EA81
Victory Way, SE16 203 L5
Dartford DA2 108 FQ84
Hounslow TW5 96 BW78
Romford RM7 51 FB54
Vidler Cl, Chess. KT9
off Merritt Gdns 155 CJ107
Vienna Cl, Ilf. IG5 68 EK55
View, The, SE2 106 EY78
View Cl, N6 64 DF59
Chigwell IG7 49 ER50
Harrow HA1 61 CD56
Westerham (Bigg.H.) TN16 178 EJ116
Viewfield Cl, Har. HA3 62 CL59
Viewfield Rd, SW18 119 CZ86
Bexley DA5 126 EW88
Viewland Rd, SE18 105 ET78
Viewlands Av, West. TN16 179 ES120
View Rd, N6 64 DF59
Potters Bar EN6 12 DC32
Viga Rd, N21 29 DN44
Vigerons Way, Grays RM16 111 GH77
Viggory La, Wok. GU21 166 AW115
Vigilant Cl, SE26 122 DU91
Vigilant Way, Grav. DA12 131 GL92
Vignoles Rd, Rom. RM7 70 FA59
Vigo St, W1 199 K1
Viking Cl, E3 *off Selwyn Rd* 85 DZ68
Viking Ct, SW6 100 DA79
Viking Gdns, E6
off Jack Dash Way 86 EL70
Viking Pl, E10 67 DZ60
Viking Rd, Grav. (Nthflt)
DA11 130 GC90
Southall UB1 78 BY73
Viking Way, Brwd. (Pilg.Hat.)
CM15 54 FV45
Erith DA8 107 FC76
Rainham RM13 89 FG70
Villa Ct, Dart. DA1
off Greenbanks 128 FL89
Villacourt Rd, SE18 106 EU80
Village, The, SE7 104 EJ79
Greenhithe (Bluewater)
DA9 129 FT87
Village Arc, E4
off Station Rd 47 ED46
Village Cl, E4 47 EC50
NW3 *off Belsize La* 64 DD64
Weybridge KT13 135 BR104
Village Ct, E17 *off Eden Rd* 67 EB57
Village Gdns, Epsom KT17 157 CT110
Village Grn Av, West. (Bigg.H.)
TN16 178 EL117
Village Grn Rd, Dart. DA1 107 FG84
Village Grn Way, West. (Bigg.H.)
TN16 *off Main Rd* 178 EL117
Village Hts, Wdf.Grn. IG8 48 EF50
Village Ms, NW9 62 CR61
Village Pk Cl, Enf. EN1 30 DS44
Village Rd, N3 43 CY53
Egham TW20 133 BC97
Enfield EN1 30 DS44
Uxbridge (Denh.) UB9 57 BF61
Village Row, Sutt. SM2 158 DA108
Village Sq, The, Couls. CR5
off Netherne Dr 175 DK122
Village Way, NW10 62 CR63
SE21 122 DR86
Amersham HP7 20 AX40
Ashford TW15 114 BM91
Beckenham BR3 143 EA96

Village Way, Ilf. IG6 69 EQ55
Pinner HA5 60 BY59
South Croydon CR2 160 DU113
Village Way E, Har. HA2 60 BZ59
Villa Rd, SW9 101 DN83
Villas Rd, SE18 105 EQ77
Villa St, SE17 102 DR78
Villiers, The, Wey. KT13 153 BR107
Villiers Av, Surb. KT5 138 CM99
Twickenham TW2 116 BZ88
Villiers Cl, E10 67 EA61
Surbiton KT5 138 CM98
Villiers Ct, N20
off Buckingham Av 44 DC45
Villiers Gro, Sutt. SM2 157 CX109
Villiers Path, Surb. KT5 138 CL99
Villiers Rd, NW2 81 CU65
Beckenham BR3 143 DX96
Isleworth TW7 97 CE82
Kingston upon Thames
KT1 138 CM97
Southall UB1 78 BZ74
Watford WD19 24 BY44
Villiers St, WC2 199 P1
Villier St, Uxb. UB8 76 BK68
Vincam Cl, Twick. TW2 116 CA87
Vincent Av, Cars. SM5 158 DD111
Croydon CR0 161 DY111
Surbiton KT5 138 CP102
Vincent Cl, SE16 203 K5
Barnet EN5 28 DA41
Bromley BR2 144 EH98
Chertsey KT16 133 BE101
Esher KT10 136 CB104
Ilford IG6 49 EQ51
Leatherhead (Fetch.) KT22 170 CB123
Sidcup DA15 125 ES88
Waltham Cross (Chsht) EN8 15 DY28
West Drayton UB7 94 BN79
Vincent Dr, Shep. TW17 135 BS97
Uxbridge UB10
off Birch Cres 76 BM67
Vincent Gdns, NW2 63 CT62
Vincent Grn, Couls. CR5 174 DF120
Vincent Ms, E3
off Fairfield Rd 85 EA68
Vincent Rd, E4 47 ED51
N15 66 DQ56
N22 45 DN54
SE18 105 EP77
W3 98 CQ76
Chertsey KT16 133 BE101
Cobham (Stoke D'Ab.)
KT11 170 BY116
Coulsdon CR5 175 DJ116
Croydon CR0 142 DS101
Dagenham RM9 88 EY66
Hounslow TW4 96 BX82
Isleworth TW7 97 CD81
Kingston upon Thames
KT1 138 CN97
Rainham RM13 90 FJ70
Wembley HA0 80 CM66
Vincent Row, Hmptn.
(Hmptn H.) TW12 116 CC93
Vincent's Cl, Couls. (Chipstead)
CR5 174 DF120
Vincents Path, Nthlt. UB5
off Arnold Rd 78 BY65
Vincent Sq, SW1 199 L8
Westerham (Bigg.H.) TN16 162 EJ113
Vincent St, E16 86 EF71
SW1 199 M8
Vincent Ter, N1 83 DP68
Vince St, EC1 197 L3
Vine, The, Sev. TN13 191 FH124
Vine Av, Sev. TN13 191 FH124
Vine Cl, Stai. TW19 114 BG85
Surbiton KT5 138 CM100
Sutton SM1 140 DC104
West Drayton UB7 94 BN77
Vine Ct, E1
off Whitechapel Rd 84 DU71
Harrow HA3 62 CL58
Vine Ct Rd, Sev. TN13 191 FJ124
Vinegar All, E17 67 EB56
Vine Gdns, Ilf. IG1 69 EQ64
Vinegar St, E1 202 D2
Vinegar Yd, SE1 201 M4
Vine Gro, Uxb. UB10 76 BN66
Vine Hill, EC1 196 D5
Vine La, SE1 201 N3
Uxbridge UB10 76 BM67
Vine Pl, W5 *off The Common* 80 CL74
Hounslow TW3 96 CB84
Viner Cl, Walt. KT12 136 BW100
Vineries, The, N14 29 DJ44
Enfield EN1 30 DS41
Vineries Bk, NW7 43 CV50
Vineries Cl, Dag. RM9
off Heathway 88 FA65
West Drayton UB7 94 BN79
Vine Rd, E15 86 EF66
SW13 99 CT83
East Molesey KT8 136 CC98
Orpington BR6 163 ET107
Slough (Stoke P.) SL2 74 AT65
Vines Av, N3 44 DB53
Vine Sq, W14 99 CZ78
Vine St, EC3 197 P10
W1 199 L1
Romford RM7 71 FC57
Uxbridge UB8 76 BK67
Vine St Br, EC1 196 E5
Vine Way, Brwd. CM14 54 FW46
Vine Yd, SE1 201 J4
Vineyard, The, Rich. TW10 118 CL85
Vineyard Av, NW7 43 CY52
Vineyard Cl, SE6 123 EA88
Kingston upon Thames
KT1 138 CM97
Vineyard Gro, N3 44 DB53
Vineyard Hill, Pot.B. (Northaw)
EN6 12 DG29
Vineyard Hill Rd, SW19 120 DA91
Vineyard Pas, Rich. TW9
off Paradise Rd 118 CL85
Vineyard Path, SW14 98 CR83
Vineyard Rd, Felt. TW13 115 BU90
Vineyard Row, Kings.T.
(Hmptn W.) KT1 137 CJ95
Vineyards Rd, Pot.B. EN6 12 DF30
Vineyard Wk, EC1 196 D4
Viney Bk, Croy. CR0 161 DZ109
Viney Rd, SE13 103 EB83
Vining St, SW9 101 DN84
Vinlake Av, Uxb. UB10 58 BM62
★ Vinopolis, SE1 201 J2
Vinson Cl, Orp. BR6 146 EU102
Vintners Ct, EC4 197 J10
Vintners Pl, EC4
off Upper Thames St 84 DQ73
Vintry Ms, E17
off Cleveland Pk Cres 67 EA56
Viola Av, SE2 106 EV77
Feltham TW14 116 BW86
Staines TW19 114 BK88
Viola Cl, S.Ock. RM15 91 FW69
Viola Sq, W12 81 CT73
Violet Av, Enf. EN2 30 DR38
Uxbridge UB8 76 BM71
Violet Cl, E16 86 EE70
SE8 *off Dorking Cl* 103 DZ79
Sutton SM3 139 CY102
Wallington SM6 140 DG102
Violet Gdns, Croy. CR0 159 DP106
Violet Hill, NW8 82 DC68
Violet La, Croy. CR0 159 DP106
Violet Rd, E3 85 EB70
E17 67 EA58
E18 48 EH54
Violet St, E2
off Three Colts La 84 DV70
Violet Way, Rick. (Loud.) WD3 22 BJ42
Virgil Pl, W1 194 D7
Virgil St, SE1 200 C6
Virginia Av, Vir.W. GU25 132 AW99
Virginia Beeches, Vir.W.
GU25 132 AW97
Virginia Cl, Ashtd. KT21
off Skinners La 171 CK118
New Malden KT3
off Willow Rd 138 CQ98
Romford RM5 51 FC52
Staines TW18
off Blacksmiths La 134 BJ97
Weybridge KT13 153 BQ107
Virginia Dr, Vir.W. GU25 132 AW99
Virginia Gdns, Ilf. IG6 49 EQ54
Virginia Pl, Cob. KT11 153 BU114
Virginia Rd, E2 197 P3
Thornton Heath CR7 141 DP95
Virginia St, E1 202 C1
Virginia Wk, SW2 121 DM86
Gravesend DA12 131 GK93
VIRGINIA WATER, GU25 132 AX99
⇌ Virginia Water 132 AY99
Visage Apts, NW3
off Winchester Rd 82 DD66
Viscount Cl, N11 45 DH50
Viscount Dr, E6 87 EM71
Viscount Gdns, W.Byf. KT14 152 BL112
Viscount Gro, Nthlt. UB5 78 BX69
Viscount Rd, Stai. (Stanw.)
TW19 114 BK88
Viscount St, EC1 197 H5
Viscount Way, Houns.
(Hthrw Air.) TW6 95 BS84
Vista, The, E4 47 ED45
SE9 124 EK86
Sidcup DA14
off Langdon Shaw 125 ET92
Vista Av, Enf. EN3 31 DX40
Vista Bldg, The, SE18
off Calderwood St 105 EN77
Vista Dr, Ilf. IG4 68 EK57
Vista Way, Har. HA3 62 CL58
Viveash Cl, Hayes UB3 95 BT76
Vivian Av, NW4 63 CV57
Wembley HA9 62 CN64
Vivian Cl, Wat. WD19 39 BU46
Vivian Comma Cl, N4
off Blackstock Rd 65 DP62
Vivian Ct, W9 *off Maida Vale* 82 DB68
Vivian Gdns, Wat. WD19 39 BU46
Wembley HA9 62 CN64
Vivian Rd, E3 85 DY68
Vivian Sq, SE15
off Scylla Rd 102 DV83
Vivian Way, N2 64 DD57
Vivien Cl, Chess. KT9 156 CL108
Vivienne Cl, Twick. TW1 117 CJ86
Voce Rd, SE18 105 ER80
Voewood Cl, N.Mal. KT3 139 CT100
Vogans Mill, SE1 *off Mill St* 102 DT75
Volta Cl, N9 *off Hudson Way* 46 DW48
Voltaire Rd, SW4 101 DK83
Voltaire Way, Hayes UB3
off Judge Heath La 77 BS73
Volt Av, NW10 80 CR69
Volta Way, Croy. CR0 141 DM102
Voluntary Pl, E11 68 EG58
Vorley Rd, N19 65 DJ61
Voss Ct, SW16 121 DL93
Voss St, E2 84 DU69
Voyagers Cl, SE28 88 EW72
Voysey Cl, N3 63 CY55
Vulcan Cl, E6 87 EN72
Vulcan Gate, Enf. EN2 29 DN40
Vulcan Rd, SE4 103 DZ82
Vulcan Sq, E14 204 A9
Vulcan Ter, SE4 103 DZ82
Vulcan Way, N7 83 DM65
Croydon (New Adgtn) CR0 162 EE110
Vyne, The, Bexh. DA7 107 FB83
Vyner Rd, W3 80 CR73
Vyner St, E2 84 DV67
Vyners Way, Uxb. UB10 58 BN64
Vyse Cl, Barn. EN5 27 CW42

W

Wacketts, Wal.Cr. (Chsht) EN7 14 DU27
Wadbrook St, Kings.T. KT1 137 CK96
Wadding St, SE17 201 K9
Waddington Av, Couls. CR5 175 DN120
Waddington Cl, Couls. CR5 175 DP119
Enfield EN1 30 DS42
Waddington Rd, E15 67 ED64
Waddington St, E15 85 ED65
Waddington Way, SE19 122 DQ94
WADDON, Croy. CR0 141 DN103
⇌ Waddon 159 DN105
Waddon Cl, Croy. CR0 141 DN104
Waddon Ct Rd, Croy. CR0 159 DN105
[Tram] Waddon Marsh 141 DM102
Waddon Marsh Way, Croy.
CR0 141 DM102
Waddon New Rd, Croy. CR0 141 DP104
Waddon Pk Av, Croy. CR0 159 DN105
Waddon Rd, Croy. CR0 141 DN104
Waddon Way, Croy. CR0 159 DP107
Wade Av, Orp. BR5 146 EX101
Wades Gro, N21 45 DN45
Wades Hill, N21 29 DN44
Wades La, Tedd. TW11
off High St 117 CG92
Wadeson St, E2 84 DV68
Wades Pl, E14 85 EB73
Wadeville Av, Rom. RM6 70 EZ59
Wadeville Cl, Belv. DA17 106 FA79
Wadham Av, E17 47 EB52
Wadham Cl, Shep. TW17 135 BQ101
Wadham Gdns, NW3 82 DE67
Greenford UB6 79 CD65
Wadham Rd, E17 47 EB53
SW15 99 CY84
Abbots Langley WD5 7 BT31
Wadhurst Cl, SE20 142 DV96
Wadhurst Rd, SW8 101 DJ81
W4 98 CR76
Wadley Rd, E11 68 EE59
Wadsworth Business Cen,
Grnf. UB6 79 CJ68
Wadsworth Cl, Enf. EN3 31 DX43
Greenford UB6 79 CJ68
Wadsworth Rd, Grnf. UB6 79 CH68
Wager St, E3 85 DZ70
Waggon Ms, N14
off Chase Side 45 DJ46
Waggon Rd, Barn. EN4 28 DC37
Waghorn Rd, E13 86 EJ67
Harrow HA3 61 CK55
Waghorn St, SE15 102 DU83
Wagner St, SE15 102 DW80
Wagon Rd, Barn. EN4 28 DB36
Wagon Way, Rick. (Loud.)
WD3 22 BJ41
Wagstaff Gdns, Dag. RM9 88 EW66
Wagtail Cl, NW9 *off Swan Dr* 42 CS54
Enfield EN1 30 DV39
Wagtail Gdns, S.Croy. CR2 161 DY110
Wagtail Wk, Beck. BR3 143 EC99
Wagtail Way, Orp. BR5 146 EX98
Waid Cl, Dart. DA1 128 FM86
Waights Ct, Kings.T. KT2 138 CL95
Wain Cl, Pot.B. EN6 12 DB29
Wainfleet Av, Rom. RM5 51 FC54
Wainford Cl, SW19
off Windlesham Gro 119 CX88
Wainwright Av, Brwd.
(Hutt.) CM13 55 GD44
Wainwright Gro, Islw. TW7 97 CD84
Waite Davies Rd, SE12 124 EF87
Waite St, SE15 102 DT79
Waithman St, EC4 196 F9
Wakefield Cl, W.Byf. (Byfleet)
KT14 152 BL112
Wakefield Cres, Slou.
(Stoke P.) SL2 74 AT66
Wakefield Gdns, SE19 122 DS94
Ilford IG1 68 EL58
Wakefield Ms, WC1 196 A3
Wakefield Rd, N11 45 DK50
N15 66 DT57
Greenhithe DA9 129 FW85
Richmond TW10 117 CK85
Wakefield St, E6 86 EK67
N18 46 DU50
WC1 196 A4
Wakefield Wk, Wal.Cr.
(Chsht) EN8 15 DY31
Wakeford Cl, SW4 121 DJ85
Wakehams Hill, Pnr. HA5 60 BZ55
Wakeham St, N1 84 DR65
Wakehurst Path, Wok. GU21 151 BC114
Wakehurst Rd, SW11 120 DE85
Wakeling La, Wem. HA0 61 CH62
Wakeling Rd, W7 79 CF71
Wakeling St, E14 85 DY72
Wakelin Rd, E15 86 EE68
Wakely Cl, West. (Bigg.H.)
TN16 178 EJ118
Wakeman Rd, NW10 81 CW69
Wakemans Hill Av, NW9 62 CR57
Wakerfield Cl, Horn. RM11 72 FM57
Wakering Rd, Bark. IG11 87 EQ65
Wakerley Cl, E6
off Truesdale Rd 87 EM72
Wake Rd, Loug. (High Beach)
IG10 32 EJ38
Wakley St, EC1 196 F2
Walberswick St, SW8 101 DL80
Walbrook, EC4 197 K10
Walbrook Ho, N9 46 DW46
Walbrook Wf, EC4
off Bell Wf La 84 DQ73
Walburgh St, E1
off Bigland St 84 DV72
Walburton Rd, Pur. CR8 159 DJ113
Walcorde Av, SE17 201 J9
Walcot Rd, Enf. EN3 31 DZ40
Walcot Sq, SE11 200 E8
Walcott St, SW1 199 L8
Waldair Ct, E16
off Barge Ho Rd 105 EP75
Waldair Wf, E16 105 EP75
Waldeck Gro, SE27 121 DP90
Waldeck Rd, N15 65 DP56
SW14
off Lower Richmond Rd 98 CQ83
W4 98 CN79
W13 79 CH72
Dartford DA1 128 FM86
Waldeck Ter, SW14
off Lower Richmond Rd 98 CQ83
Waldegrave Av, Tedd. TW11
off Waldegrave Rd 117 CF92
Waldegrave Ct, Upmin. RM14 72 FP60
Waldegrave Gdns, Twick.
TW1 117 CF89
Waldegrave Gdns, Upmin.
RM14 72 FP60
Waldegrave Pk, Twick. TW1 117 CF91
Waldegrave Rd, N8 65 DN55
SE19 122 DT94
W5 80 CM72
Bromley BR1 144 EL98
Dagenham RM8 70 EW61
Teddington TW11 117 CF91
Twickenham TW1 117 CF91
Waldegrove, Croy. CR0 142 DT104
Waldemar Av, SW6 99 CY81
W13 79 CJ74
Waldemar Rd, SW19 120 DA92
Walden Av, N13 46 DQ49
Chislehurst BR7 125 EM91
Rainham RM13 89 FD68
Walden Cl, Belv. DA17 106 EZ78
Walden Gdns, Th.Hth. CR7 141 DM97
Waldenhurst Rd, Orp. BR5 146 EX101
Walden Par, Chis. BR7
off Walden Rd 125 EM93
Walden Rd, N17 46 DR53
Chislehurst BR7 125 EM93
Hornchurch RM11 72 FK58
Waldens Cl, Orp. BR5 146 EX101
Waldenshaw Rd, SE23 122 DW88
Waldens Pk Rd, Wok. GU21 166 AW116
Waldens Rd, Orp. BR5 146 EY101
Woking GU21 166 AX117
Walden St, E1 84 DV72
Walden Way, NW7 43 CX51
Hornchurch RM11 72 FK58
Ilford IG6 49 ES52
Waldo Cl, SW4 121 DJ85
Waldon Ct, SW8
off Wandsworth Rd 101 DL81
Waldo Pl, Mitch. CR4 120 DE94
Waldorf Cl, S.Croy. CR2 159 DP109
Waldo Rd, NW10 81 CU69
Bromley BR1 144 EK97
Waldram Cres, SE23 122 DW88
Waldram Pk Rd, SE23 123 DX88
Waldram Pl, SE23
off Waldram Cres 122 DW88
Waldrist Way, Erith DA18 106 EZ75
Waldron Gdns, Brom. BR2 143 ED97
Waldronhyrst, S.Croy. CR2 159 DP105
Waldron Ms, SW3
off Old Ch St 100 DD79
Waldron Rd, SW18 120 DC90
Harrow HA1, HA2 61 CE60
Waldrons, The, Croy. CR0 159 DP105
Oxted RH8 188 EF131
Waldrons Path, S.Croy. CR2 160 DQ105
Waldstock Rd, SE28 88 EU73
Waleran Cl, Stan. HA7 41 CF51
Walerand Rd, SE13 103 EC82
Waleran Flats, SE1
off Old Kent Rd 102 DS77
Wales Av, Cars. SM5 158 DF106
Wales Cl, SE15 102 DV80
Wales Fm Rd, W3 80 CR71
Waleton Acres, Wall. SM6 159 DJ107
Waley St, E1 85 DX71
Walfield Av, N20 44 DB45
Walford Rd, N16 66 DS63
Uxbridge UB8 76 BJ68
Walfrey Gdns, Dag. RM9 88 EY66
WALHAM GREEN, SW6 100 DB80
Walham Grn Ct, SW6
off Waterford Rd 100 DB80
Walham Gro, SW6 100 DA80
Walham Ri, SW19 119 CY93
Walham Yd, SW6
off Estcourt Rd 100 DA80
Walk, The, Horn. RM11 72 FM61
Oxted (Tand.) RH8 187 EA133
Potters Bar EN6 12 DA32
Sunbury-on-Thames TW16 115 BT94
Walkden Rd, Chis. BR7 125 EN92
Walker Cl, N11 45 DJ49
SE18 105 EQ77
W7 79 CE74
Dartford DA1 107 FF83
Feltham TW14 115 BT87
Hampton TW12
off Fearnley Cres 116 BZ93
Walker Cres, Slou. SL3
off Ditton Rd 93 AZ78
Walker Ms, SW2 *off Effra Rd* 121 DN85
Walkers Ct, E8
off Wilton Way 84 DU65
W1 195 M10
Walkerscroft Mead, SE21 122 DQ88
Walkers Pl, SW15
off Felsham Rd 99 CY83
Walkfield Dr, Epsom KT18 173 CV117
Walkley Rd, Dart. DA1 127 FH85
Walks, The, N2 64 DD55
Walkynscroft, SE15
off Firbank Rd 102 DV82
Wallace Cl, SE28
off Haldane Rd 88 EX73
Shepperton TW17 135 BR98
Uxbridge UB10
off Grays Rd 76 BL68
★ Wallace Collection, W1 194 F8
Wallace Cres, Cars. SM5 158 DF106
Wallace Flds, Epsom KT17 157 CT112
Wallace Gdns, Swans. DA10 130 FY86
Wallace Rd, N1 84 DQ65
Grays RM17 110 GA76
Wallace Sq, Couls. CR5
off Cayton Rd 175 DK122
Wallace Wk, Add. KT15 152 BJ105
Wallace Way, N19
off Giesbach Rd 65 DK61
Romford RM1 51 FD53
Wallasey Cres, Uxb. UB10 58 BN61
Wallbutton Rd, SE4 103 DY82
Wallcote Av, NW2 63 CX60
Walled Gdn, The, Tad. KT20
off Heathcote 173 CX122
Walled Gdn Cl, Beck. BR3
off Coppice Cl 143 EB98
Wall End Rd, E6 87 EM66
Wallenger Av, Rom. RM2 71 FH55
Waller Dr, Nthwd. HA6 39 BU54
Waller La, Cat. CR3 176 DT123
Waller Rd, SE14 103 DX81
Wallers Cl, Dag. RM9 88 EY67
Woodford Green IG8 49 EM51
Wallers Hoppit, Loug. IG10 32 EL40
Waller Way, SE10
off Greenwich High Rd 103 EB80
Wallflower St, W12 81 CT73
Wallgrave Rd, SW5 100 DB77
Wallhouse Rd, Erith DA8 107 FH80
Wallingford Av, W10 81 CX71
Wallingford Rd, Uxb. UB8 76 BH68
WALLINGTON, SM6 159 DJ106
⇌ Wallington 159 DH107
Wallington Cl, Ruis. HA4 59 BQ58
Wallington Cor, Wall. SM6
off Manor Rd N 159 DH105
Wallington Rd, Ilf. IG3 69 ET59
Wallington Sq, Wall. SM6
off Woodcote Rd 159 DH107
Wallis All, SE1 201 J4
Wallis Cl, SW11 100 DD83
Dartford DA2 127 FF90
Hornchurch RM11 71 FH60
Wallis Ct, Slou. SL1
off Nixey Cl 92 AU76
Wallis Ms, N8 *off Courcy Rd* 65 DN55
Leatherhead (Fetch.) KT22 171 CG122
Wallis Pk, Grav. (Nthflt) DA11 130 GB85
Wallis Rd, E9 85 DZ65
Southall UB1 78 CB72
Wallis's Cotts, SW2 121 DL87
Wallman Pl, N22
off Bounds Grn Rd 45 DM53
Wallorton Gdns, SW14 98 CR84
Wallside, EC2 197 J7
Wall St, N1 84 DR65
Wallwood Rd, E11 67 ED60
Wallwood St, E14 85 DZ71
Walmar Cl, Barn. EN4 28 DD39
Walmer Cl, E4 47 EB47
Orpington BR6
off Tubbenden La S 163 ER105
Romford RM7 51 FB54
Walmer Gdns, W13 97 CG75
Walmer Ho, N9 46 DT45
Walmer Pl, W1 194 D6
Walmer Rd, W10
off Latimer Rd 81 CW72
W11 81 CY73
Walmer St, W1 194 D6
Walmer Ter, SE18 105 EQ77
Walmgate Rd, Grnf. UB6 79 CH67
Walmington Fold, N12 44 DA51
Walm La, NW2 63 CX64
Walmsley Ho, SW16
off Colson Way 121 DJ91
Walney Wk, N1
off St. Paul's Rd 84 DQ65
Walnut Av, West Dr. UB7 94 BN76
Walnut Cl, SE8 *off Clyde St* 103 DZ79
Carshalton SM5 158 DF106
Dartford (Eyns.) DA4 148 FK104
Epsom KT18 173 CT115
Hayes UB3 77 BS73
Ilford IG6 *off Civic Way* 69 EQ56
St. Albans (Park St) AL2 8 CB27
Walnut Ct, W5 98 CL75
Walnut Dr, Tad. (Kgswd) KT20
off Warren Lo Dr 173 CY124
Walnut Gdns, E15
off Burgess Rd 68 EE64
Walnut Grn, Bushey WD23 24 BZ40
Walnut Gro, Bans. SM7 157 CX114
Enfield EN1 30 DR43
Hornchurch RM12 72 FK60
Walnut Ms, Sutt. SM2 158 DC108
Walnut Rd, E10 67 EA61
Walnuts, The, Orp. BR6
off High St 146 EU102
Walnut Shop Cen, Orp. BR6 146 EU102
Walnuts Rd, Orp. BR6 146 EU102
Walnut Tree Av, Dart. DA1 128 FL89
Mitcham CR4
off De'Arn Gdns 140 DE97
Walnut Tree Cl, SW13 99 CT81
Banstead SM7 157 CY112
Chislehurst BR7 145 EQ95
Waltham Cross (Chsht) EN8 15 DX31
Walnut Tree Cotts, SW19
off Church Rd 119 CY91
Walnut Tree La, W.Byf.
(Byfleet) KT14 152 BK112
Walnut Tree Rd, SE10 104 EE78
Brentford TW8 98 CL79
Dagenham RM8 70 EX61
Erith DA8 107 FE78
Hounslow TW5 96 BZ79
Shepperton TW17 135 BQ96
Walnut Tree Wk, SE11 200 D8
Walnut Way, Buck.H. IG9 48 EK48
Ruislip HA4 78 BW65
Swanley BR8 147 FD96
Walpole Av, Couls. (Chipstead)
CR5 174 DF118
Richmond TW9 98 CM82
Walpole Cl, W13 97 CJ75
Grays RM17 *off Palmers Dr* 110 GC77
Pinner HA5 40 CA51
Walpole Cres, Tedd. TW11 117 CF92
Walpole Gdns, W4 98 CQ78
Twickenham TW2 117 CE89
Walpole Ms, NW8
off Queen's Gro 82 DD67
SW19 *off Walpole Rd* 120 DD93
Walpole Pk, W5 79 CJ74
Weybridge KT13 152 BN108
Walpole Pl, SE18
off Brookhill Rd 105 EP77
Teddington TW11 117 CF92
Walpole Rd, E6 86 EJ66
E17 67 DY56
E18 48 EF53
N17 (Downhills Way) 66 DQ55
N17 (Lordship La) 46 DQ54
SW19 120 DD93
Bromley BR2 144 EK99
Croydon CR0 142 DR103
Surbiton KT6 138 CL100
Teddington TW11 117 CF92
Twickenham TW2 117 CE89
Windsor (Old Wind.) SL4 112 AV87
Walpole St, SW3 198 D10
Walrond Av, Wem. HA9 62 CL64
Walsham Cl, N16
off Clarke Path 66 DU60
SE28 88 EX73

★ Place of interest ⇌ Railway station ⊖ London Underground station DLR Docklands Light Railway station Tra Tramlink station H Hospital Riv Pedestrian ferry landing stage

Walsham Rd, SE14 103 DX82
Feltham TW14 115 BV87
Walsh Cres, Croy. (New Adgtn)
CR0 162 EE112
Walshford Way, Borwd. WD6 26 CN38
Walsingham Gdns, Epsom
KT19 156 CS105
Walsingham Pk, Chis. BR7 145 ER96
Walsingham Pl, SW4
off Clapham Common W
Side 100 DF84
SW11 120 DG86
Walsingham Rd, E5 66 DU62
W13 79 CG74
Croydon (New Adgtn) CR0 161 EC110
Enfield EN2 30 DR42
Mitcham CR4 140 DF99
Orpington BR5 146 EV95
Walsingham Wk, Belv. DA17 106 FA79
Walsingham Way, St.Alb.
(Lon.Col.) AL2 9 CJ27
Walter Hurford Par, E12
off Walton Rd 69 EN63
Walter Rodney Cl, E6
off Stevenage Rd 87 EM65
Walters Cl, SE17 201 J9
Hayes UB3 95 BT75
Waltham Cross (Chsht)
EN7 13 DP25
Walters Ho, SE17
off Otto St 101 DP79
Walters Mead, Ashtd. KT21 172 CL117
Walters Rd, SE25 142 DS98
Enfield EN3 30 DW43
Walter St, E2 85 DX69
Kingston upon Thames
KT2 off Sopwith Way 138 CL95
Walters Way, SE23 123 DX86
Walters Yd, Brom. BR1 144 EG96
Walter Ter, E1 85 DX72
Walterton Rd, W9 81 CZ70
Walter Wk, Edg. HA8 42 CQ51
WALTHAM ABBEY, EN9 32 EF35
★ Waltham Abbey (ruins),
Wal.Abb. EN9 15 EC33
Waltham Av, NW9 62 CN58
Hayes UB3 95 BQ76
Waltham Cl, Brwd. (Hutt.)
CM13 off Bannister Dr 55 GC44
Dartford DA1 127 FG86
Orpington BR5 146 EX102
WALTHAM CROSS,
EN7 & EN8 15 DZ33
⇌ Waltham Cross 15 DY34
Waltham Dr, Edg. HA8 42 CN54
Waltham Gdns, Enf. EN3 30 DW36
Waltham Gate, Wal.Cr. EN8 15 DZ26
Waltham Pk Way, E17 47 EA53
Waltham Rd, Cars. SM5 140 DD101
Caterham CR3 176 DV122
Southall UB2 96 BY76
Waltham Abbey EN9 16 EF26
Woodford Green IG8 48 EL51
WALTHAMSTOW, E17 47 EB54
Walthamstow Av, E4 47 EA52
Walthamstow Business Cen,
E17 47 EC54
⇌ Walthamstow Central 67 EA56
⊖ Walthamstow Central 67 EA56
⇌ Walthamstow Queens
Road 67 DZ57
Waltham Way, E4 47 DZ49
Waltheof Av, N17 46 DR53
Waltheof Gdns, N17 46 DR53
Walton Av, Har. HA2 60 BZ64
New Malden KT3 139 CT98
Sutton SM3 139 CZ104
Wembley HA9 62 CP62
Walton Br, Shep. TW17 135 BS101
Walton-on-Thames KT12 135 BS101
Walton Br Rd, Shep. TW17 135 BS101
Walton Cl, E5 off Orient Way 67 DX62
NW2 63 CV61
SW8 101 DL80
Harrow HA1 61 CD56
H Walton Comm Hosp,
Walt. KT12 135 BV103
Walton Ct, Wok. GU21 167 BA116
Walton Cres, Har. HA2 60 BZ63
Walton Dr, NW10 80 CR65
Harrow HA1 61 CD56
Walton Gdns, W3 80 CP71
Brentwood (Hutt.) CM13 55 GC43
Feltham TW13 115 BT91
Waltham Abbey EN9 15 EB33
Wembley HA9 62 CL61
Walton Grn, Croy. (New Adgtn)
CR0 161 EC108
Walton La, Shep. TW17 135 BR101
Walton-on-Thames KT12 135 BQ102
Weybridge KT13 135 BP103
WALTON-ON-THAMES,
KT12 135 BT103
⇌ Walton-on-Thames 153 BU105
WALTON ON THE HILL,
Tad. KT20 183 CT125
Walton Pk, Walt. KT12 136 BX103
Walton Pk La, Walt. KT12 136 BX103
Walton Pl, SW3 198 D6
Walton Rd, E12 69 EN63
E13 86 EJ68
N15 66 DT57
Bushey WD23 24 BX42
East Molesey KT8 136 CA98
Epsom (Epsom Downs)
KT18 173 CT117
Epsom (Headley) KT18 172 CQ121
Harrow HA1 61 CD56
Romford RM5 50 EZ52
Sidcup DA14 126 EW89
Walton-on-Thames KT12 136 BW99
West Molesey KT8 136 BY99
Woking GU21 167 AZ116
Walton St, SW3 198 C8
Enfield EN2 30 DR39
Tadworth (Walt.Hill) KT20 173 CU124
Walton Ter, Wok. GU21 167 BB115
Walton Way, W3 80 CP71
Mitcham CR4 141 DJ98
Walt Whitman Cl, SE24
off Shakespeare Rd 101 DP84
Walverns Cl, Wat. WD19 24 BW44
WALWORTH, SE17 201 H10
★ Walworth Garden Fm -
Horticultural Training Cen,
SE17 101 DP78
Walworth Pl, SE17 102 DQ78
Walworth Rd, SE1 201 H8
SE17 201 H8
Walwyn Av, Brom. BR1 144 EK97
Wambrook Cl, Brwd.
(Hutt.) CM13 55 GC46
Wanborough Dr, SW15 119 CV88
Wanderer Dr, Bark. IG11 88 EV69
Wandle Bk, SW19 120 DD93
Croydon CR0 141 DL104
Wandle Ct, Epsom KT19 156 CQ105
Wandle Ct Gdns, Croy. CR0 159 DL105
Tra Wandle Park 141 DN103
Wandle Rd, SW17 120 DE89
Croydon CR0 142 DQ104
Croydon (Waddon) CR0 141 DL104
Morden SM4 140 DC98
Wallington SM6 141 DH103
Wandle Side, Croy. CR0 141 DM104
Wallington SM6 141 DH104
Wandle Tech Pk, Mitch. CR4
off Goat Rd 140 DF101
Wandle Trd Est, Mitch. CR4
off Budge La 140 DF101
Wandle Way, SW18 120 DB88
Mitcham CR4 140 DF99
Wandon Rd, SW6 100 DB80
WANDSWORTH, SW18 119 CZ85
Wandsworth Br, SW6 100 DB83
SW18 100 DB83
Wandsworth Br Rd, SW6 100 DB81
⇌ Wandsworth Common 120 DF88
Wandsworth Common,
SW12 120 DE86
Wandsworth Common W Side,
SW18 120 DC85
Wandsworth High St, SW18 120 DA85
★ Wandsworth Mus, SW18
off Garratt La 120 DB85
Wandsworth Plain, SW18 120 DB85
⇌ Wandsworth Road 101 DJ82
Wandsworth Rd, SW8 101 DK80
⇌ Wandsworth Town 100 DB84
Wandsworth Town, SW18 120 DA85
Wangey Rd, Rom. RM6 70 EX59
Wanless Rd, SE24 102 DQ83
Wanley Rd, SE5 102 DR84
Wanlip Rd, E13 86 EH70
Wanmer Ct, Reig. RH2
off Birkheads Rd 184 DA133
Wannions Cl, Chesh. HP5 4 AU30
Wannock Gdns, Ilf. IG6 49 EP52
Wansbeck Rd, E3 85 DZ66
E9 85 DZ66
Wansbury Way, Swan. BR8 147 FG99
Wansdown Pl, SW6
off Fulham Rd 100 DB80
Wansey St, SE17 201 J9
Wansford Cl, Brwd. CM14 54 FT48
Wansford Grn, Wok. GU21 166 AT117
Wansford Pk, Borwd. WD6 26 CS42
Wansford Rd, Wdf.Grn. IG8 48 EJ53
WANSTEAD, E11 68 EH59
⊖ Wanstead 68 EH58
Wanstead Cl, Brom. BR1 144 EJ96
Wanstead La, Ilf. IG1 68 EK58
⇌ Wanstead Park 68 EH63
Wanstead Pk, E11 68 EK59
Wanstead Pk Av, E12 68 EK61
Wanstead Pk Rd, Ilf. IG1 69 EM60
Wanstead Pl, E11 68 EG58
Wanstead Rd, Brom. BR1 144 EJ96
Wansunt Rd, Bex. DA5 127 FC88
Wantage Rd, SE12 124 EF85
Wantz La, Rain. RM13 89 FH70
Wantz Rd, Dag. RM10 71 FB63
Waplings, The, Tad. KT20 173 CV124
WAPPING, E1 202 C2
⊖ Wapping 202 F3
Wapping Dock St, E1 202 E3
Wapping High St, E1 202 B3
Wapping La, E1 202 E1
Wapping Wall, E1 202 F2
Wapseys La, Slou. (Hedg.)
SL2 56 AS58
Wapshott Rd, Stai. TW18 113 BE93
Warbank Cl, Croy. (New Adgtn)
CR0 162 EE111
Warbank Cres, Croy.
(New Adgtn) CR0 162 EE110
Warbank La, Kings.T. KT2 119 CT94
Warbeck Rd, W12 81 CV74
Warberry Rd, N22 45 DM54
Warblers Grn, Cob. KT11 154 BZ114
Warboys App, Kings.T. KT2 118 CP93
Warboys Cres, E4 47 EC50
Warboys Rd, Kings.T. KT2 118 CP93
Warburton Cl, N1
off Culford Rd 84 DS65
Harrow HA3 41 CD51
Warburton Rd, E8 84 DV66
Twickenham TW2 116 CB88
Warburton St, E8
off Warburton Rd 84 DV67
Warburton Ter, E17 47 EB54
War Coppice Rd, Cat. CR3 186 DR127
Wardalls Gro, SE14 102 DW80
Ward Av, Grays RM17 110 GA77
Ward Cl, Erith DA8 107 FD79
Iver SL0 75 BF72
South Croydon CR2 160 DS106
Waltham Cross (Chsht) EN7 14 DU27
Wardell Cl, NW7 42 CS52
Wardell Fld, NW9 42 CS53
Warden Av, Har. HA2 60 BZ60
Romford RM5 51 FC50
Warden Rd, NW5 82 DG65
Wardens Fld Cl, Orp. BR6 163 ES107
Wardens Gro, SE1 201 H3
Ward Gdns, Rom. (Harold Wd)
RM3 off Whitmore Av 52 FK54
Ward La, Warl. CR6 176 DW116
Wardle St, E9 67 DX64
Wardley St, SW18
off Garratt La 120 DB87
Wardo Av, SW6 99 CY81
Wardour Ms, W1 195 L9
Wardour St, W1 195 M10
Ward Pt, SE11 200 D9
Ward Rd, E15 85 ED67
Ward Rd, N19 65 DJ62
Wardrobe Pl, EC4
off Carter La 83 DP72
Wardrobe Ter, EC4 196 G9
Wards Dr, Rick. WD3 21 BF36
Wards La, Borwd. (Els.) WD6 25 CG40
Ward's Pl, Egh. TW20 113 BC93
Wards Rd, Ilf. IG2 69 ER59
Wards Wf App, E16 104 EK75
Wareham Cl, Houns. TW3 96 CB84
Waremead Rd, Ilf. IG2 69 EP57
Warenford Way, Borwd. WD6 26 CN39
Warenne Rd, Lthd.
(Fetch.) KT22 170 CC122
Ware Pt Dr, SE28 105 ER75
Warescot Cl, Brwd. CM15 54 FV45
Warescot Rd, Brwd. CM15 54 FV45
Warfield Rd, NW10 81 CX69
Feltham TW14 115 BS87
Hampton TW12 136 CB95
Warfield Yd, NW10
off Warfield Rd 81 CX69
Wargrave Av, N15 66 DT58
Wargrave Rd, Har. HA2 60 CC62
Warham Rd, N4 65 DN57
Harrow HA3 41 CF54
Sevenoaks (Otford) TN14 181 FH116
South Croydon CR2 160 DQ106
Warham St, SE5 101 DP80
Waring Cl, Orp. BR6 163 ET107
Waring Dr, Orp. BR6 163 ET107
Waring Rd, Sid. DA14 126 EW93
Waring St, SE27 122 DQ91
Warkworth Gdns, Islw. TW7 97 CG80
Warkworth Rd, N17 46 DR52
Warland Rd, SE18 105 ER80
WARLEY, Brwd. CM14 54 FV50
Warley Av, Dag. RM8 70 EZ59
Hayes UB4 77 BU71
Warley Cl, E10
off Millicent Rd 67 DZ60
Warley Gap, Brwd. (Lt.Warley)
CM13 53 FV52
Warley Hill, Brwd. CM13,
CM14 53 FV51
Warley Mt, Brwd. CM14 54 FW49
Warley Rd, N9 46 DW47
Brentwood CM13 53 FT54
Hayes UB4 77 BU72
Ilford IG5 49 EN53
Upminster RM14 52 FQ54
Woodford Green IG8 48 EH52
Warley St, E2 85 DX69
Brentwood (Gt Warley)
CM13 73 FW58
Upminster RM14 73 FW58
Warley St Flyover, Brwd.
CM13 73 FX57
Warley Wds Cres, Brwd.
CM14 54 FV49
WARLINGHAM, CR6 177 DX118
Warlingham Rd, Th.Hth. CR7 141 DP98
Warlock Rd, W9 82 DA70
Warlow Cl, Enf. EN3 31 EA37
Warlters Cl, N7
off Warlters Rd 65 DL63
Warlters Rd, N7 65 DL63
Warltersville Rd, N19 65 DL59
Warmington Cl, E5
off Orient Way 67 DX62
Warmington Rd, SE24 122 DQ86
Warmington St, E13
off Barking Rd 86 EG70
Warminster Gdns, SE25 142 DU96
Warminster Rd, SE25 142 DT96
Warminster Sq, SE25 142 DU96
Warminster Way, Mitch. CR4 141 DH95
Warmwell Av, NW9 42 CS53
Warndon St, SE16 202 G9
Warneford Pl, Wat. WD19 24 BY44
Warneford Rd, Har. HA3 61 CK55
Warneford St, E9 84 DV67
Warne Pl, Sid. DA15
off Westerham Dr 126 EV86
Warner Av, Sutt. SM3 139 CY103
Warner Cl, E15 68 EE64
NW9 63 CT59
Hampton TW12
off Tangley Pk Rd 116 BZ92
Hayes UB3 95 BR80
Warner Ho, SE13
off Conington Rd 103 EB82
Warner Par, Hayes UB3 95 BR80
Warner Pl, E2 84 DU68
Warner Rd, E17 67 DY56
N8 65 DK56
SE5 102 DQ81
Bromley BR1 124 EF94
Warners Cl, Wdf.Grn. IG8 48 EG50
Warners La, Kings.T. KT2 117 CK91
Warners Path, Wdf.Grn. IG8 48 EG50
Warner St, EC1 196 D5
Warner Ter, E14
off Broomfield St 85 EA71
Warner Yd, EC1 196 D5
Warnford Ho, SW15
off Tunworth Cres 119 CT86
Warnford Ind Est, Hayes UB3 95 BS75
Warnford Rd, Orp. BR6 163 ET106
Warnham Ct Rd, Cars. SM5 158 DF108
Warnham Rd, N12 44 DE50
Warple Ms, W3
off Warple Way 98 CS75
Warple Way, W3 80 CS74
Warren, The, E12 68 EL63
Ashtead KT21 172 CL119
Carshalton SM5 158 DD109
Gerrards Cross (Chal.St.P.)
SL9 37 AZ52
Gravesend DA12 131 GK91
Hayes UB4 77 BU72
Hounslow TW5 96 BZ80
Leatherhead (Oxshott)
KT22 154 CC112
Radlett WD7 9 CG33
St. Albans AL2
off How Wd 8 CC28
Tadworth (Kgswd) KT20 173 CY123
Worcester Park KT4 156 CR105
Warren Av, E10 67 EC62
Bromley BR1 124 EE94
Orpington BR6 163 ET106
Richmond TW10 98 CP84
Warren Av, S. Croy. CR2 161 DX108
Sutton SM2 157 CZ110
Warren Cl, N9 47 DX45
SE21 off Lairdale Cl 122 DQ87
Bexleyheath DA6 126 FA85
Esher KT10 154 CB105
Hayes UB4 78 BW71
Slough SL3 92 AY76
Wembley HA9 61 CK61
Warren Ct, SE7 104 EJ78
Chigwell IG7 49 ER49
Sevenoaks TN13 191 FJ125
Weybridge KT13 152 BN106
Warren Cres, N9 46 DT45
Warren Cutting, Kings.T. KT2 118 CR94
Warrender Rd, N19 65 DJ62
Chesham HP5 4 AS29
Warrender Way, Ruis. HA4 59 BU59
Warren Dr, Grnf. UB6 78 CB70
Hornchurch RM12 71 FG62
Orpington BR6 164 EV106
Ruislip HA4 60 BX59
Tadworth (Kgswd) KT20 173 CZ122
Warren Dr, The, E11 68 EJ59
Warren Dr N, Surb. KT5 138 CP102
Warren Dr S, Surb. KT5 138 CQ102
Warreners La, Wey. KT13 153 BR109
Warren Fld, Epp. CM16 18 EU32
Iver SL0 75 BC68
Warrenfield Cl, Wal.Cr.
(Chsht) EN7 14 DU31
Warren Flds, Stan. HA7
off Valencia Rd 41 CJ49
Warren Footpath, Twick. TW1 117 CK87
Warren Gdns, E15
off Ashton Rd 67 ED64
Orpington BR6 164 EU106
Warrengate La, Pot.B. EN6 11 CW31
Warrengate Rd, Hat. (N.Mymms)
AL9 11 CW28
Warren Gro, Borwd. WD6 26 CR42
Warren Hastings Ct, Grav.
DA11 off Pier Rd 131 GF86
Warren Hts, Grays (Chaff.Hun.)
RM16 110 FY77
Loughton IG10 32 EJ43
Warren Hill, Epsom KT18 172 CR116
Loughton IG10 32 EJ44
Warren Ho, E3
off Bromley High St 85 EB69
Warren La, SE18 105 EP76
Grays RM16 109 FW77
Leatherhead (Oxshott)
KT22 154 CC111
Oxted RH8 188 EF134
Stanmore HA7 41 CF48
Woking GU22 168 BH118
Warren La Gate, SE18 105 EP76
Warren Lo Dr, Tad. (Kgswd)
KT20 173 CY124
Warren Mead, Bans. SM7 173 CW115
Warren Ms, W1 195 K5
Warrenne Way, Reig. RH2 184 DA134
Warren Pk, Kings.T. KT2 118 CQ93
Tadworth (Box H.) KT20 182 CQ131
Warlingham CR6 177 DX118
Warren Pk Rd, Sutt. SM1 158 DD107
Warren Pond Rd, E4 48 EF46
Warren Ri, N.Mal. KT3 138 CR95
Warren Rd, E4 47 EC47
E10 67 EC62
E11 68 EJ60
NW2 63 CT61
SW19 120 DE93
Addlestone (New Haw)
KT15 152 BG110
Ashford TW15 115 BS94
Banstead SM7 157 CW114
Bexleyheath DA6 126 FA85
Bromley BR2 144 EG103
Bushey (Bushey Hth) WD23 40 CC46
Croydon CR0 142 DS102
Dartford DA1 128 FK90
Gravesend (Sthflt) DA13 130 GB92
Ilford IG6 69 ER57
Kingston upon Thames
KT2 118 CQ93
Orpington BR6 163 ET106
Purley CR8 159 DP111
Reigate RH2 184 DB133
Sidcup DA14 126 EW90
Twickenham TW2 116 CC86
Uxbridge UB10 58 BL63
Warrens Shawe La, Edg. HA8 42 CP46
⊖ Warren Street 195 L4
Warren St, W1 195 J5
Warren Ter, Grays RM16
off Arterial Rd W Thurrock 109 FX75
Romford RM6 70 EX56
Warren Wk, SE7 104 EJ79
Warren Way, NW7 43 CY51
Weybridge KT13 153 BQ106
Warren Wd Cl, Brom. BR2 144 EF103
Warriner Av, Horn. RM12 72 FK61
Warriner Dr, N9 46 DU48
Warriner Gdns, SW11 100 DF81
Warrington Cres, W9 82 DC70
Warrington Gdns, W9
off Warwick Av 82 DC70
Hornchurch RM11 72 FJ58
Warrington Rd, Croy. CR0 141 DP104
Dagenham RM8 70 EX61
Harrow HA1 61 CE57
Richmond TW10 117 CK85
Warrington Spur, Wind.
(Old Wind.) SL4 112 AV87
Warrington Sq, Dag. RM8 70 EX61
Warrior Av, Grav. DA12 131 GJ91
Warrior Cl, SE28 87 ER74
Warrior Sq, E12 69 EN63
Warsaw Cl, Ruis. HA4
off Glebe Av 77 BV65
Warsdale Dr, NW9
off Mardale Dr 62 CR57
Warspite Rd, SE18 104 EL76
Warton Rd, E15 85 EC66
Warwall, E6 87 EP72
⊖ Warwick Avenue 82 DC70
Warwick Av, W2 82 DC70
W9 82 DC70
Edgware HA8 42 CP48
Egham TW20 133 BC95
Harrow HA2 60 BZ63
Warwick Av, Pot.B. (Cuffley)
EN6 13 DK27
Staines TW18 114 BJ93
Warwick Bldg, SW8 101 DH79
Warwick Cl, Barn. EN4 28 DD43
Bexley DA5 126 EZ87
Bushey (Bushey Hth) WD23
off Magnaville Rd 41 CE45
Hampton TW12 116 CC94
Hornchurch RM11 72 FM56
Orpington BR6 146 EU104
Potters Bar (Cuffley) EN6 13 DK27
Warwick Ct, SE15 102 DU82
WC1 196 C7
Rickmansworth (Chorl.)
WD3 21 BF41
Surbiton KT6
off Hook Rd 138 CL103
Warwick Cres, W2 82 DC71
Hayes UB4 77 BT70
Warwick Deeping, Cher.
(Ott.) KT16 151 BC106
Warwick Dene, W5 80 CL74
Warwick Dr, SW15 99 CV83
Waltham Cross (Chsht) EN8 15 DX28
Warwick Est, W2 82 DB71
Warwick Gdns, N4 66 DQ57
W14 99 CZ76
Ashtead KT21 171 CJ117
Barnet EN5 off Great N Rd 27 CZ38
Ilford IG1 69 EP60
Romford RM2 72 FJ55
Thames Ditton KT7 137 CF99
Warwick Gro, E5 66 DV60
Surbiton KT5 138 CM101
Warwick Ho St, SW1 199 N2
Warwick La, EC4 196 G9
Rainham RM13 90 FM68
Upminster RM14 90 FP68
Woking GU21 166 AU119
Warwick Ms, Rick. (Crox.Grn)
WD3 22 BN44
Warwick Pas, EC4 196 G8
Warwick Pl, W5
off Warwick Rd 97 CK75
W9 82 DC71
Gravesend (Nthflt) DA11 130 GB85
Uxbridge UB8 76 BJ66
Warwick Pl N, SW1 199 K9
Warwick Quad Shop Mall, Red.
RH1 off London Rd 184 DG133
Warwick Rd, E4 47 EA50
E11 68 EH57
E12 68 EL64
E15 86 EF65
E17 47 DZ53
N11 45 DK51
N18 46 DS49
SE20 142 DV97
SW5 99 CZ77
W5 97 CK75
W14 99 CZ77
Ashford TW15 114 BL92
Barnet EN5 28 DB42
Borehamwood WD6 26 CR41
Coulsdon CR5 159 DJ114
Enfield EN3 31 DZ37
Hounslow TW4 95 BV83
Kingston upon Thames
KT1 137 CJ95
New Malden KT3 138 CQ97
Rainham RM13 90 FJ70
Redhill RH1 184 DF133
Sidcup DA14 126 EV92
Southall UB2 96 BZ76
Sutton SM1 158 DC105
Thames Ditton KT7 137 CF99
Thornton Heath CR7 141 DN97
Twickenham TW2 117 CE88
Welling DA16 106 EW83
West Drayton UB7 94 BL75
Warwick Row, SW1 199 J6
Warwickshire Path, SE8 103 DZ80
Warwick Sq, EC4 196 G8
SW1 199 K10
Warwick Sq Ms, SW1 199 K9
Warwick St, W1 195 L10
Warwick Ter, SE18 105 ER79
Warwick Way, SW1 199 K9
Dartford DA1 128 FL89
Rickmansworth (Crox.Grn)
WD3 23 BQ42
WARWICK WOLD, Red. RH1 185 DN129
Warwick Wold Rd, Red. RH1 185 DN128
Warwick Yd, EC1 197 J5
Washington Av, E12 68 EL63
Washington Cl, E3 85 EB69
Reigate RH2 184 DA131
Washington Rd, E6
off St. Stephens Rd 86 EJ66
E18 48 EF54
SW13 99 CU80
Kingston upon Thames
KT1 138 CN96
Worcester Park KT4 139 CV103
Wash La, Pot.B. EN6 11 CV33
Washneys Rd, Orp. BR6 164 EV113
Washpond La, Warl. CR6 177 EC118
Wash Rd, Brwd. (Hutt.) CM13 55 GD44
Wastdale Rd, SE23 123 DX88
Watchfield Ct, W4 98 CQ78
Watchgate, Dart. (Lane End)
DA2 129 FR91
Watcombe Cotts, Rich. TW9 98 CN79
Watcombe Pl, SE25
off Albert Rd 142 DV98
Watcombe Rd, SE25 142 DV99
Waterbank Rd, SE6 123 EB90
Waterbeach Rd, Dag. RM9 88 EW65
Waterbrook La, NW4 63 CW57
Water Circ, Green. (Bluewater)
DA9 129 FT88
Watercress Pl, N1
off Hertford Rd 84 DS66
Watercress Rd, Wal.Cr.
(Chsht) EN7 14 DR26
Watercress Way, Wok. GU21 166 AV117

★ Place of interest ⇌ Railway station ⊖ London Underground station DLR Docklands Light Railway station Tra Tramlink station H Hospital Riv Pedestrian ferry landing stage

Watercroft Rd, Sev. (Halst.)
TN14 . . . . . 164 EZ110
Waterdale Rd, SE2 . . . . . 106 EU79
Waterdales, Grav. (Nthflt)
DA11 . . . . . 130 GD88
Waterdell Pl, Rick. WD3
off Uxbridge Rd 38 BG47
Waterden Cres, E15
off Waterden Rd 67 EA64
Waterden Rd, E15 . . . . . 67 EA64
WATER END, Hat. AL9 . . . . . 11 CV26
Waterer Gdns, Tad. KT20 . . . 173 CX118
Waterer Ri, Wall. SM6 . . . . . 159 DK107
Waterfall Cl, N14 . . . . . 45 DJ48
Virginia Water GU25 . . . . . 132 AU97
Waterfall Cotts, SW19 . . . . . 120 DD93
Waterfall Rd, N11 . . . . . 45 DH49
N14 . . . . . 45 DJ48
SW19 . . . . . 120 DD93
Waterfall Ter, SW17 . . . . . 120 DE93
Waterfield, Rick. (Herons.)
WD3 . . . . . 37 BC45
Tadworth KT20 . . . . . 173 CV119
Waterfield Cl, SE28 . . . . . 88 EV74
Belvedere DA17 . . . . . 106 FA76
Waterfield Dr, Warl. CR6 . . . 176 DW119
Waterfield Gdns, SE25 . . . . . 142 DS99
Waterfield Grn, Tad. KT20 . . . 173 CW120
Waterfields, Lthd. KT22 . . . 171 CH119
Waterfields Shop Pk, Wat.
WD17 . . . . . 24 BX42
Waterfields Way, Wat. WD17 . 24 BX42
Waterford Cl, Cob. KT11 . . . 154 BY111
Waterford Rd, SW6 . . . . . 100 DB81
Waterford Way, NW10
off Cullingworth Rd 63 CV64
Waterfront Studios Business Cen,
E16 . . . . . 205 M2
Water Gdns, Stan. HA7 . . . . . 41 CH51
Water Gdns, The, W2 . . . . . 194 C8
Watergardens, The, Kings.T.
KT2 . . . . . 118 CQ93
Watergate, EC4 . . . . . 196 F10
Watergate, The, Wat. WD19 . . 40 BX47
Watergate St, SE8 . . . . . 103 EA79
Watergate Wk, WC2 . . . . . 200 A2
Waterglade Ind Pk, Grays
RM20 . . . . . 109 FT78
Waterhall Av, E4 . . . . . 48 EE49
Waterhall Cl, E17 . . . . . 47 DX53
Waterhead Cl, Erith DA8 . . . 107 FE80
Waterhouse Cl, E16 . . . . . 86 EK71
NW3 *off Lyndhurst Rd* 64 DD64
W6 *off Great Ch La* 99 CX78
Waterhouse La, Ken. CR8 . . 176 DQ119
Redhill (Bletch.) RH1 . . . . . 186 DT132
Tadworth (Kgswd) KT20 . . 173 CY121
Waterhouse Sq, EC1 . . . . . 196 D7
Wateridge Cl, E14 . . . . . 203 P7
Wateringbury Cl, Orp. BR5 . . 146 EV97
Water La, E15 . . . . . 86 EE65
EC3 . . . . . 201 M1
N9 . . . . . 46 DV46
NW1 *off Kentish Town Rd* . . 83 DH66
SE14 . . . . . 102 DW80
Cobham KT11 . . . . . 170 BY115
Hemel Hempstead (Bov.)
HP3 . . . . . 5 BA29
Ilford IG3 . . . . . 69 ES62
Kings Langley WD4 . . . . . 7 BP29
Kingston upon Thames
KT1 . . . . . 137 CK95
Oxted (Titsey) RH8 . . . . . 188 EG126
Purfleet RM19 . . . . . 108 FN77
Redhill RH1 . . . . . 185 DP130
Richmond TW9 . . . . . 117 CK85
Sevenoaks (Shore.) TN14 . 165 FF112
Sidcup DA14 . . . . . 126 EZ89
Twickenham TW1
off The Embankment 117 CG88
Watford WD17 . . . . . 24 BW42
Westerham TN16 . . . . . 189 ER127
Water Lily Cl, Sthl. UB2
off Navigator Dr 96 CC75
⇌ **Waterloo** 200 D4
⊖ **Waterloo** 200 D4
Waterloo Br, SE1 . . . . . 200 B1
WC2 . . . . . 200 B1
Waterloo Cl, E9
off Churchill Wk 66 DW64
Feltham TW14 . . . . . 115 BT88
⇌ **Waterloo East** 200 D3
Waterloo Est, E2 . . . . . 84 DW68
Waterloo Gdns, E2 . . . . . 84 DW68
N1 *off Barnsbury St* 83 DN66
Romford RM7 . . . . . 71 FD58
⇌ **Waterloo International** . . 200 C4
RIV **Waterloo Millennium Pier** 200 B4
Waterloo Pas, NW6 . . . . . 81 CZ66
Waterloo Pl, SW1 . . . . . 199 M2
Richmond TW9
off The Quadrant 98 CL84
Richmond (Kew) TW9 . . . . . 98 CN79
Waterloo Rd, E6 . . . . . 86 EJ66
E7 *off Wellington Rd* 68 EF64
E10 . . . . . 67 EA59
NW2 . . . . . 63 CU60
SE1 . . . . . 200 D4
Brentwood CM14 . . . . . 54 FW46
Epsom KT19 . . . . . 156 CR112
Ilford IG6 . . . . . 49 EQ54
Romford RM7 . . . . . 71 FE57
Sutton SM1 . . . . . 158 DD106
Uxbridge UB8 . . . . . 76 BJ67
Waterloo St, Grav. DA12 . . . 131 GJ87
Waterloo Ter, N1 . . . . . 83 DP66
Waterlow Ct, NW11
off Heath Cl 64 DB59
Waterlow Rd, N19 . . . . . 65 DJ60
Waterman Cl, Wat. WD19 . . . 23 BV44
★ **Watermans Art Cen**,
Brent. TW8 . . . . . 98 CL79
Waterman's Cl, Kings.T. KT2
off Woodside Rd 118 CL94
Waterman St, SW15 . . . . . 99 CX83
Waterman's Wk, EC4
off Upper Thames St 84 DR73
Watermans Wk, SE16 . . . . . 203 K6
Watermans Way, Epp.
(N.Wld Bas.) CM16 . . . . . 18 FA27
Greenhithe DA9 . . . . . 109 FV84
Waterman Way, E1 . . . . . 202 D2
Water Mead, Couls. (Chipstead)
CR5 . . . . . 174 DF117
Watermead, Felt. TW14 . . . . 115 BS88
Tadworth KT20 . . . . . 173 CV120
Woking GU21 . . . . . 166 AT116
Watermead Ho, E9
off Kingsmead Way 67 DY64
Watermead La, Cars. SM5
off Middleton Rd 140 DF101
Watermeadow Cl, Erith DA8 . 107 FH81
Watermeadow La, SW6 . . . . 100 DC82
Watermead Rd, SE6 . . . . . 123 EC91
Watermead Way, N17 . . . . . 66 DV55
Watermen's Sq, SE20 . . . . . 122 DW94
Water Ms, SE15 . . . . . 102 DW84
Watermill Cl, Rich. TW10 . . . 117 CJ90
Watermill La, N18 . . . . . 46 DS50
Watermill Way, SW19 . . . . . 140 DC95
Water Mill Way, Dart.
(S.Darenth) DA4 . . . . . 148 FP96
Watermill Way, Felt. TW13 . . 116 BZ89
Watermint Cl, Orp. BR5
off Wagtail Way 146 EX98
Watermint Quay, N16 . . . . . 66 DU59
Waterperry La, Wok. (Chobham)
GU24 . . . . . 150 AT110
Water Rd, Wem. HA0 . . . . . 80 CM67
Waters Dr, Rick. WD3 . . . . . 38 BL46
Staines TW18 . . . . . 113 BF90
Watersedge, Epsom KT19 . . 156 CQ105
Waters Edge Ct, Erith DA8
off Erith High St 107 FF78
Watersfield Way, Edg. HA8 . . 41 CK52
Waters Gdns, Dag. RM10 . . . 70 FA64
Waterside, Beck. BR3
off Rectory Rd 143 EA95
Dartford DA1 . . . . . 127 FE85
Gravesend DA11 . . . . . 130 GE86
Water Side, Kings L. WD4 . . . . 6 BN29
Waterside, Rad. WD7 . . . . . 9 CH34
St. Albans (Lon.Col.) AL2 . . 10 CL27
Uxbridge UB8 . . . . . 76 BJ71
Waterside Av, Beck. BR3
off Brockwell Av 143 EB99
Waterside Cl, E3 . . . . . 85 DZ67
SE16 . . . . . 202 C5
SE28 . . . . . 87 ET74
Barking IG11 . . . . . 70 EU63
Northolt UB5 . . . . . 78 BZ69
Romford (Harold Wd) RM3 . 52 FN52
Surbiton KT6
off Culsac Rd 138 CL103
Waterside Ct, SE13
off Weardale Rd 103 ED84
Kings Langley WD4
off Water Side 7 BP29
Waterside Dr, Slou. (Langley)
SL3 . . . . . 93 AZ75
Walton-on-Thames KT12 . 135 BU99
Waterside Ms, Uxb. (Hare.)
UB9 . . . . . 38 BG51
Waterside Path, SW18
off Smugglers Way 100 DB84
Waterside Pl, NW1
off Princess Rd 82 DG67
Waterside Pt, SW11 . . . . . 100 DE80
Waterside Rd, Sthl. UB2 . . . . 96 CA76
Waterside Twr, SW6 . . . . . 100 DC81
Waterside Trd Cen, W7 . . . . . 97 CE76
Waterside Way, SW17 . . . . . 120 DC91
Woking GU21
off Winnington Way 166 AV118
Watersmeet Way, SE28 . . . . . 88 EW72
Waterson Rd, Grays RM16 . . 111 GH77
Waterson St, E2 . . . . . 197 N2
Waters Pl, SW15
off Danemere St 99 CW82
Watersplash Cl, Kings.T. KT1 . 138 CL97
Watersplash La, Hayes UB3 . . 95 BU77
Hounslow TW5 . . . . . 95 BV78
Watersplash Rd, Shep. TW17 . 134 BN98
Waters Rd, SE6 . . . . . 124 EE90
Kingston upon Thames
KT1 . . . . . 138 CP96
Waters Sq, Kings.T. KT1 . . . . 138 CP97
Water St, WC2 . . . . . 196 C10
Waterton, Swan. BR8 . . . . . 147 FD98
Waterton Av, Grav. DA12 . . . 131 GL87
Water Twr Cl, Uxb. UB8 . . . . 58 BL64
Water Twr Hill, Croy. CR0 . . . 160 DR105
Water Twr Pl, N1
off Old Royal Free Sq 83 DN67
Water Twr Rd, Brwd. (Gt Warley)
CM14 . . . . . 54 FW50
Waterview Ho, E14 . . . . . 85 DY71
Waterway Rd, Lthd. KT22 . . . 171 CG122
Waterworks Cor, E18 . . . . . 48 EE54
Waterworks La, E5 . . . . . 67 DX61
Waterworks Rd, SW2 . . . . . 121 DL86
Waterworks Yd, Croy. CR0
off Surrey St 142 DQ104
Watery La, SW20 . . . . . 139 CZ96
Chertsey (Lyne) KT16 . . . . 133 BD101
Northolt UB5 . . . . . 78 BW68
St. Albans (Flam.) AL3 . . . . . 9 CK28
Sidcup DA14 . . . . . 126 EV93
Wates Way, Brwd. CM15 . . . . . 54 FX46
Mitcham CR4 . . . . . 140 DF100
Wateville Rd, N17 . . . . . 46 DQ53
WATFORD, WD17 - WD19;
WD24 & WD25 . . . . . 23 BT41
⊖ **Watford** 23 BT41
Watford Arches Trd Est, Wat.
WD17 . . . . . 24 BX43
Watford Business Pk, Wat.
WD18 . . . . . 23 BS44
Watford Bypass, Borwd. WD6 . 41 CG45
Watford Cl, SW11
off Petworth St 100 DE81
Watford Fld Rd, Wat. WD18 . . 24 BW43
★ **Watford FC**, Wat. WD18 . . . 23 BV43
H **Watford Gen Hosp**,
Wat. WD18 . . . . . 23 BV43
WATFORD HEATH, Wat. WD19 . 40 BY46
Watford Heath, Wat. WD19 . . 40 BX45
⇌ **Watford High Street** 24 BW42
⇌ **Watford Junction** 24 BW40
★ **Watford Mus**, Wat. WD17 . 24 BW43
⇌ **Watford North** 24 BW37
Watford Rd, E16 . . . . . 86 EG71
Borehamwood (Els.) WD6 . . 25 CJ44
Harrow HA1 . . . . . 61 CG61
Kings Langley WD4 . . . . . 7 BP32
Northwood HA6 . . . . . 39 BT52
Radlett WD7 . . . . . 25 CE36
Rickmansworth (Crox.Grn)
WD3 . . . . . 23 BQ43
St. Albans AL1, AL2 . . . . . 8 CA27
Wembley HA0 . . . . . 61 CG61
Watford Way, NW4 . . . . . 63 CU56
NW7 . . . . . 63 CU56
Watkin Rd, Wem. HA9 . . . . . 62 CP62
Watkins Cl, Nthwd. HA6
off Chestnut Av 39 BT53
Watkinson Rd, N7 . . . . . 83 DM65
Watkins Ri, Pot.B. EN6
off The Walk 12 DB32
Watling Av, Edg. HA8 . . . . . 42 CR52
Watling Ct, EC4 . . . . . 197 J9
Borehamwood WD6 . . . . . 25 CK44
Watling Fm Cl, Stan. HA7 . . . 41 CJ46
Watling Gdns, NW2 . . . . . 81 CY65
Watling Knoll, Rad. WD7 . . . . 9 CF33
Watlings Cl, Croy. CR0 . . . . 143 DY100
Watling St, EC4 . . . . . 197 H9
SE15 *off Dragon Rd* 102 DS79
Bexleyheath DA6 . . . . . 107 FB84
Borehamwood (Els.) WD6 . . 25 CJ40
Dartford DA1, DA2 . . . . . 128 FP87
Gravesend DA11, DA12,
DA13 . . . . . 130 GC90
Radlett WD7 . . . . . 9 CF32
St. Albans AL1, AL2 . . . . . 8 CC25
Watling St Caravan Site (Travellers),
St.Alb. (Park St) AL2 . . . . . 8 CC25
Watlington Gro, SE26 . . . . . 123 DY92
Watney Cotts, SW14
off Lower Richmond Rd . . . 98 CQ83
Watney Mkt, E1
off Commercial Rd 84 DV72
Watney Rd, SW14 . . . . . 98 CQ83
Watneys Rd, Mitch. CR4 . . . . 141 DK99
Watney St, E1 . . . . . 84 DV72
Watson Av, E6 . . . . . 87 EN66
Sutton SM3 . . . . . 139 CY103
Watson Cl, N16
off Matthias Rd 66 DR64
SW19 . . . . . 120 DE93
Grays RM20 . . . . . 109 FU81
Watson Gdns, Rom. (Harold Wd)
RM3 . . . . . 52 FK54
Watson's Ms, W1 . . . . . 194 C7
Watsons Rd, N22 . . . . . 45 DM53
Watson's St, SE8 . . . . . 103 EA80
Watson St, E13 . . . . . 86 EH68
Watsons Yd, NW2
off North Circular Rd 63 CT61
Wattendon Rd, Ken. CR8 . . . 175 DP116
Wattisfield Rd, E5 . . . . . 66 DW62
Watts Cl, N15 *off Seaford Rd* . 66 DS57
Tadworth KT20 . . . . . 173 CX122
Watts Cres, Purf. RM19 . . . . 108 FQ77
Watts Fm Par, Wok. (Chobham)
GU24 *off Barnmead* 150 AT110
Watts Gro, E3 . . . . . 85 EB71
Watts La, Chis. BR7 . . . . . 145 EP95
Tadworth KT20 . . . . . 173 CX122
Teddington TW11 . . . . . 117 CG92
Watts Mead, Tad. KT20 . . . . 173 CX122
Watts Rd, T.Ditt. KT7 . . . . . 137 CG101
Watts St, E1 . . . . . 202 E2
SE15 . . . . . 102 DT81
Watts Way, SW7 . . . . . 198 A6
Wat Tyler Rd, SE3 . . . . . 103 EC82
SE10 . . . . . 103 EC82
Wauthier Cl, N13 . . . . . 45 DP50
Wavell Cl, Wal.Cr. (Chsht) EN8 . 15 DY27
Wavell Dr, Sid. DA15 . . . . . 125 ES86
Wavel Ms, N8 . . . . . 65 DK56
NW6 *off Acol Rd* 82 DB66
Wavel Pl, SE26
off Sydenham Hill 122 DT91
Wavendene Av, Egh. TW20 . . 113 BB94
Wavendon Av, W4 . . . . . 98 CR78
Waveney Av, SE15 . . . . . 102 DV84
Waveney Cl, E1 . . . . . 202 C2
Waverley Av, E4 . . . . . 47 DZ49
E17 . . . . . 67 ED55
Kenley CR8 . . . . . 176 DS116
Surbiton KT5 . . . . . 138 CP100
Sutton SM1 . . . . . 140 DB103
Twickenham TW2 . . . . . 116 BZ88
Wembley HA9 . . . . . 62 CM64
Waverley Cl, E18 . . . . . 48 EJ53
Bromley BR2 . . . . . 144 EK99
Hayes UB3 . . . . . 95 BR77
West Molesey KT8 . . . . . 136 CA99
Waverley Ct, Wok. GU22 . . . 166 AY118
Waverley Cres, SE18 . . . . . 105 ER78
Romford RM3 . . . . . 52 FJ52
Waverley Dr, Cher. KT16 . . . 133 BD104
Virginia Water GU25 . . . . . 132 AU97
Waverley Gdns, E6
off Oliver Gdns 86 EL71
NW10 . . . . . 80 CM69
Barking IG11 . . . . . 87 ES68
Grays RM16 . . . . . 110 GA75
Ilford IG6 . . . . . 49 EQ54
Northwood HA6 . . . . . 39 BU53
Waverley Gro, N3 . . . . . 63 CY55
Waverley Ind Est, Har. HA1 . . . 61 CD55
Waverley Pl, N4
off Adolphus Rd 65 DP61
NW8 . . . . . 82 DD68
Leatherhead KT22
off Church Rd 171 CH122
Waverley Rd, E17 . . . . . 67 EC55
E18 . . . . . 48 EJ53
N8 . . . . . 65 DK58
N17 . . . . . 46 DV52
SE18 . . . . . 105 EQ78
SE25 . . . . . 142 DV98
Cobham (Stoke D'Ab.)
KT11 . . . . . 154 CB114
Enfield EN2 . . . . . 29 DP42
Epsom KT17 . . . . . 157 CV106
Harrow HA2 . . . . . 60 BZ60
Leatherhead (Oxshott)
KT22 . . . . . 154 CB114
Rainham RM13 . . . . . 89 FH69
Southall UB1 . . . . . 78 CA73
Waverley Rd, Wey. KT13 . . . . 152 BN106
Waverley Vil, N17 . . . . . 46 DT54
Waverley Wk, W2 . . . . . 82 DA71
Waverley Way, Cars. SM5 . . . 158 DE107
Waverton Ho, E3 . . . . . 85 DZ67
Waverton Rd, SW18 . . . . . 120 DC87
Waverton St, W1 . . . . . 198 G2
Wavertree Ct, SW2
off Streatham Hill 121 DL88
Wavertree Rd, E18 . . . . . 48 EG54
SW2 . . . . . 121 DL88
Waxlow Cres, Sthl. UB1 . . . . 78 CA72
Waxlow Rd, NW10 . . . . . 80 CQ68
Waxlow Way, Nthlt. UB5 . . . . 78 BZ70
Waxwell Cl, Pnr. HA5 . . . . . 40 BX54
Waxwell La, Pnr. HA5 . . . . . 40 BX54
Way, The, Reig. RH2 . . . . . 184 DD133
Wayborne Gro, Ruis. HA4 . . . . 59 BQ58
Waycross Rd, Upmin. RM14 . . 73 FS58
Waye Av, Houns. TW5 . . . . . 95 BU81
Wayfarer Rd, Nthlt. UB5 . . . . 78 BX70
Wayfaring Grn, Grays (Bad.Dene)
RM17 *off Curling La* 110 FZ78
Wayfield Link, SE9 . . . . . 125 ER86
Wayford St, SW11 . . . . . 100 DE82
Wayland Av, E8 . . . . . 66 DU64
Wayland Ho, SW9
off Robsart St 101 DN82
Waylands, Hayes UB3 . . . . . 77 BR71
Staines (Wrays.) TW19 . . . . 112 AY86
Swanley BR8 . . . . . 147 FF98
Waylands Cl, Sev. (Knock.)
TN14 . . . . . 180 EY115
Waylands Mead, Beck. BR3 . 143 EB95
Wayleave, The, SE28 . . . . . 88 EV73
Waylett Ho, SE11
off Loughborough St 101 DM78
Waylett Pl, SE27 . . . . . 121 DP90
Wembley HA0 . . . . . 61 CK63
Wayman Ct, E8 . . . . . 84 DV65
Waymouth Ho, SW8
off Bolney St 101 DM80
Wayne Cl, Orp. BR6 . . . . . 145 ET104
Wayneflete Twr Av, Esher
KT10 . . . . . 136 CA104
Waynflete Av, Croy. CR0 . . . 141 DP104
Waynflete Sq, W10 . . . . . 81 CX73
Waynflete St, SW18 . . . . . 120 DC89
Wayside, NW11 . . . . . 63 CY60
SW14 . . . . . 118 CQ85
Croydon CR0 *off Field Way* . 161 EB107
Kings Langley (Chipper.)
WD4 . . . . . 6 BH30
Potters Bar EN6 . . . . . 12 DD33
Radlett (Shenley) WD7 . . . . . 9 CK33
Wayside Av, Bushey WD23 . . . 25 CD44
Hornchurch RM12 . . . . . 72 FK61
Wayside Cl, N14 . . . . . 29 DJ44
Romford RM1 . . . . . 71 FF55
Wayside Commercial Est,
Bark. IG11 . . . . . 88 EU67
Wayside Ct, Twick. TW1 . . . . 117 CJ86
Wembley HA9
off Oakington Av 62 CN62
Woking GU21
off Langmans Way 166 AS116
Wayside Gdns, SE9
off Wayside Gro 125 EM91
Dagenham RM10 . . . . . 70 FA64
Gerrards Cross SL9 . . . . . 56 AX59
Wayside Gro, SE9 . . . . . 125 EM91
Wayside Ms, Ilf. IG2
off Gaysham Av 69 EN57
Wayville Rd, Dart. DA1 . . . . . 128 FP87
Way Volante, Grav. DA12 . . . 131 GL91
Weald, The, Chis. BR7 . . . . . 125 EM93
Weald Cl, SE16 . . . . . 202 D10
Brentwood CM14 . . . . . 54 FU48
Bromley BR2 . . . . . 144 EL103
Gravesend (Istead Rise)
DA13 . . . . . 130 GE94
★ **Weald Country Pk**, Brwd.
CM14 . . . . . 54 FS45
Weald Hall La, Epp. (Thnwd)
CM16 . . . . . 18 EW25
Weald La, Har. HA3 . . . . . 41 CD54
Weald Pk Way, Brwd. (S.Wld)
CM14 . . . . . 54 FS48
Weald Ri, Har. HA3 . . . . . 41 CF52
Weald Rd, Brwd. CM14 . . . . . 53 FR46
Sevenoaks TN13 . . . . . 191 FH129
Uxbridge UB10 . . . . . 76 BN68
Weald Sq, E5
off Rossington St 66 DV61
WEALDSTONE, Har. HA3 . . . . 61 CF55
Wealdstone Rd, Sutt. SM3 . . 139 CZ103
Weald Way, Cat. CR3 . . . . . 186 DS128
Wealdway, Grav. DA13 . . . . . 131 GH93
Weald Way, Hayes UB4 . . . . . 77 BS69
Romford RM7 . . . . . 71 FB58
Wealdwood Gdns, Pnr. HA5
off Highbanks Rd 40 CB51
Weale Rd, E4 . . . . . 47 ED48
Weall Cl, Pur. CR8 . . . . . 159 DM112
Weall Grn, Wat. WD25 . . . . . 7 BV32
Weardale Av, Dart. DA2 . . . . 128 FQ89
Weardale Gdns, Enf. EN2 . . . 30 DR39
Weardale Rd, SE13 . . . . . 103 ED84
Wear Pl, E2 . . . . . 84 DV69
Wearside Rd, SE13 . . . . . 103 EB84
Weasdale Ct, Wok. GU21
off Roundthorn Way 166 AT116
Weatherall Cl, Add. KT15 . . . 152 BH106
Weatherley Cl, E3 . . . . . 85 DZ71
Weaver Cl, E6 *off Trader Rd* . . 87 EP73
Croydon CR0 . . . . . 160 DT105
Weavers Cl, Grav. DA11 . . . . 131 GG88
Isleworth TW7 . . . . . 97 CE84
Weavers La, Sev. TN14 . . . . . 191 FJ121
Weavers Orchard, Grav.
(Sthflt) DA13 . . . . . 130 GA93
Weavers Ter, SW6 . . . . . 100 DA79
Weaver St, E1 . . . . . 84 DU70
Weavers Way, NW1 . . . . . 83 DK67
Weaver Wk, SE27 . . . . . 121 DP91
Webb Cl, W10 . . . . . 81 CW70
Slough SL3 . . . . . 92 AX77
Webber Cl, Borwd. (Els.)
WD6 *off Rodgers Cl* 25 CK44
Erith DA8 . . . . . 107 FH80
Webber Row, SE1 . . . . . 200 E6
Webber St, SE1 . . . . . 200 E4
Webb Est, E5 . . . . . 66 DU59
Webb Gdns, E13
off Kelland Rd 86 EG70
Webb Pl, NW10
off Old Oak La 81 CT69
Webb Rd, SE3 . . . . . 104 EF79
Webb's All, Sev. TN13, TN15 . 191 FJ125
Webbscroft Rd, Dag. RM10 . . . 71 FB63
Webbs Rd, SW11 . . . . . 120 DF85
Hayes UB4 . . . . . 77 BV69
Webb St, SE1 . . . . . 201 M7
Webheath Est, NW6 . . . . . 81 CZ66
Webley Ct, Enf. EN3
off Sten Cl 31 EA37
Webster Cl, Horn. RM12 . . . . 72 FK62
Leatherhead (Oxshott)
KT22 . . . . . 154 CB114
Waltham Abbey EN9 . . . . . 16 EG33
Webster Gdns, W5 . . . . . 79 CK74
Webster Rd, E11 . . . . . 67 EC62
SE16 . . . . . 202 C7
Websters Cl, Wok. GU22 . . . 166 AU120
Wedderburn Rd, NW3 . . . . . 64 DD64
Barking IG11 . . . . . 87 ER67
Wedgewood Cl, Epp. CM16
off Theydon Gro 18 EU30
Northwood HA6 . . . . . 39 BQ51
Wedgewoods, West. (Tats.)
TN16 *off Redhouse Rd* . . 178 EJ121
Wedgwood Ho, SE11
off Kennington Rd 101 DN76
Wedgwood Ms, W1 . . . . . 195 N9
Wedgwood Pl, Cob. KT11 . . . 153 BU114
Wedgwood Wk, NW6
off Dresden Cl 64 DB64
Wedgwood Way, SE19 . . . . . 122 DQ94
Wedlake Cl, Horn. RM11 . . . . 72 FL60
Wedlake St, W10
off Kensal Rd 81 CY70
Wedmore Av, Ilf. IG5 . . . . . 49 EN53
Wedmore Gdns, N19 . . . . . 65 DK61
Wedmore Ms, N19
off Wedmore St 65 DK62
Wedmore Rd, Grnf. UB6 . . . . 79 CD69
Wedmore St, N19 . . . . . 65 DK62
Wednesbury Gdns, Rom.
RM3 . . . . . 52 FM52
Wednesbury Grn, Rom. RM3
off Wednesbury Gdns 52 FM52
Wednesbury Rd, Rom. RM3 . . 52 FM52
Weech Rd, NW6 . . . . . 64 DA63
Weedington Rd, NW5 . . . . . 64 DG64
Weedon Cl, Ger.Cr. (Chal.St.P.)
SL9 . . . . . 36 AV53
Weekley Sq, SW11
off Thomas Baines Rd . . . 100 DD83
Weigall Rd, SE12 . . . . . 104 EG84
Weighhouse St, W1 . . . . . 194 G9
Weighton Rd, SE20 . . . . . 142 DV96
Harrow HA3 . . . . . 41 CD53
Weihurst Gdns, Sutt. SM1 . . 158 DD106
Weimar St, SW15 . . . . . 99 CY83
Weind, The, Epp. (They.B.)
CM16 . . . . . 33 ES36
Weirdale Av, N20 . . . . . 44 DF47
Weir Est, SW12 . . . . . 121 DJ87
Weir Hall Av, N18 . . . . . 46 DR51
Weir Hall Gdns, N18 . . . . . 46 DR50
Weir Hall Rd, N17 . . . . . 46 DR50
N18 . . . . . 46 DR50
Weir Pl, Stai. TW18 . . . . . 133 BE95
Weir Rd, SW12 . . . . . 121 DJ87
SW19 . . . . . 120 DB90
Bexley DA5 . . . . . 127 FB87
Chertsey KT16 . . . . . 134 BH101
Walton-on-Thames KT12 . 135 BU100
Weirside Gdns, West Dr. UB7 . 76 BK74
Weir's Pas, NW1 . . . . . 195 N2
Weiss Rd, SW15 . . . . . 99 CX83
Welbeck Av, Brom. BR1 . . . . 124 EG91
Hayes UB4 . . . . . 77 BV70
Sidcup DA15 . . . . . 126 EU88
Welbeck Cl, N12
off Torrington Pk 44 DD50
Borehamwood WD6 . . . . . 26 CN41
Epsom KT17 . . . . . 157 CU108
New Malden KT3 . . . . . 139 CT99
Welbeck Rd, E6 . . . . . 86 EK69
Barnet EN4 . . . . . 28 DD44
Carshalton SM5 . . . . . 140 DE102
Harrow HA2 . . . . . 60 CB60
Sutton SM1 . . . . . 140 DD103
Welbeck St, W1 . . . . . 195 H8
Welbeck Wk, Cars. SM5
off Welbeck Rd 140 DE102
Welbeck Way, W1 . . . . . 195 H8
Welby St, SE5 . . . . . 101 DP81
Welch Ho, Enf. EN3
off Beaconsfield Rd 31 DX37
Welch Pl, Pnr. HA5 . . . . . 40 BW53
Welcomes Rd, Ken. CR8 . . . . 176 DQ116
Welcote Dr, Nthwd. HA6 . . . . 39 BR51
Welden, Slou. SL2 . . . . . 74 AW72
Welders La, Beac. (Jordans)
HP9 . . . . . 36 AT52
Gerrards Cross (Chal.St.P.)
SL9 . . . . . 36 AT52
Weldon Cl, Ruis. HA4 . . . . . 77 BV65
Weldon Dr, W.Mol. KT8 . . . . . 136 BZ98
Weldon Way, Red. (Merst.)
RH1 . . . . . 185 DK129
Weld Pl, N11 . . . . . 45 DH50
Welfare Rd, E15 . . . . . 86 EE66
Welford Cl, E5
off Denton Way 67 DX62
Welford Pl, SW19 . . . . . 119 CY91
Welham Rd, SW16 . . . . . 120 DG92
SW17 . . . . . 120 DG92
Welhouse Rd, Cars. SM5 . . . 140 DE102
Wellacre Rd, Har. HA3 . . . . . 61 CH58
Wellan Cl, Sid. DA15 . . . . . 126 EV85
Welland Cl, Slou. SL3 . . . . . 93 BA79
Welland Gdns, Grnf. UB6 . . . 79 CF68
Welland Ms, E1 . . . . . 202 C2
Wellands Cl, Brom. BR1 . . . . 145 EM96
Welland St, SE10 . . . . . 103 EC79
Well App, Barn. EN5 . . . . . 27 CW43
Wellbrook Rd, Orp. BR6 . . . . 163 EN105
Well Cl, SW16 . . . . . 121 DM91
Ruislip HA4
off Parkfield Cres 60 BY62
Woking GU21 . . . . . 166 AW117
Wellclose Sq, E1 . . . . . 84 DU73
Wellclose St, E1 . . . . . 202 C1

★ Place of interest ⇌ Railway station ⊖ London Underground station DLR Docklands Light Railway station Tra Tramlink station H Hospital Riv Pedestrian ferry landing stage

Wellcome Av, Dart. DA1 108 FM84
★ Wellcome Trust, NW1 195 L4
Well Cottage Cl, E11 68 EJ59
Well Ct, EC4 197 J9
SW16 121 DM91
Welldon Cres, Har. HA1 61 CE58
WELL END, Borwd. WD6 26 CR38
Well End Rd, Borwd. WD6 26 CQ37
Weller Cl, Amer. HP6 20 AS37
Weller Pl, Orp. BR6 163 EN111
Weller Rd, Amer. HP6 20 AS37
Wellers Cl, West. TN16 189 EQ127
Wellers Gro, Wal.Cr. (Chsht) EN7 14 DU28
Weller St, SE1 201 H4
Wellesford Cl, Bans. SM7 173 CZ117
Wellesley Av, W6 99 CV76
Iver SL0 93 BF76
Northwood HA6 39 BT50
Wellesley Cl, SE7 off Wellington Gdns 104 EJ78
Wellesley Ct, W9 82 DC69
Wellesley Ct Rd, Croy. CR0 142 DR103
Wellesley Cres, Pot.B. EN6 11 CY33
Twickenham TW2 117 CE89
Wellesley Gro, Croy. CR0 142 DR103
Wellesley Pk Ms, Enf. EN2 29 DP40
Wellesley Pas, Croy. CR0 off Wellesley Rd 142 DQ103
Wellesley Path, Slou. SL1 off Wellesley Rd 92 AU75
Wellesley Pl, NW1 195 M3
Tram Wellesley Road 142 DQ103
Wellesley Rd, E11 68 EG57
E17 67 EA58
N22 45 DN54
NW5 64 DG64
W4 98 CN78
Brentwood CM14 54 FW46
Croydon CR0 142 DQ102
Harrow HA1 61 CE57
Ilford IG1 69 EP61
Slough SL1 92 AU75
Sutton SM2 158 DC107
Twickenham TW2 117 CD90
Wellesley St, E1 85 DX71
Wellesley Ter, N1 197 J2
Welley Av, Stai. (Wrays.) TW19 92 AY84
Welley Rd, Slou. (Horton) SL3 92 AY84
Staines (Wrays.) TW19 112 AX85
Well Fm Rd, Warl. CR6 176 DU119
Wellfield Av, N10 65 DH55
Wellfield Gdns, Cars. SM5 158 DE109
Wellfield Rd, SW16 121 DL91
Wellfields, Loug. IG10 33 EN41
Wellfield Wk, SW16 121 DM92
Wellfit St, SE24 off Hinton Rd 101 DP83
Wellgarth, Grnf. UB6 79 CH65
Wellgarth Rd, NW11 64 DB60
Well Gro, N20 44 DC45
Well Hall Par, SE9 off Well Hall Rd 105 EM84
Well Hall Rd, SE9 105 EM83
Well Hall Rbt, SE9 off Well Hall Rd 104 EL83
WELL HILL, Orp. BR6 165 FB107
Well Hill, Orp. BR6 165 FB107
Well Hill La, Orp. BR6 165 FB108
Well Hill Rd, Sev. TN14 165 FC107
Wellhouse La, Barn. EN5 27 CW42
Wellhouse Rd, Beck. BR3 143 DZ98
Wellhurst Cl, Orp. BR6 163 ET108
WELLING, DA16 106 EU83
⇌ Welling 106 EU82
Welling High St, Well. DA16 106 EV83
Wellings Ho, Hayes UB3 77 BV74
★ Wellington Arch, W1 198 G4
Wellington Av, E4 47 EA47
N9 46 DV48
N15 66 DT58
Hounslow TW3 116 CA85
Pinner HA5 40 BZ53
Sidcup DA15 126 EU86
Virginia Water GU25 132 AV99
Worcester Park KT4 157 CW105
Wellington Bldgs, SW1 off Ebury Br Rd 100 DG78
Wellington Cl, SE14 off Rutts Ter 103 DX81
W11 off Ledbury Rd 82 DA72
Dagenham RM10 89 FC66
Walton-on-Thames KT12 off Hepworth Way 135 BT102
Watford WD19 off Highfield 40 BZ48
Wellington Ct, NW8 off Wellington Rd 82 DD68
Ashford TW15 off Wellington Rd 114 BL92
Staines TW19 off Clare Rd 114 BL87
Wellington Cres, N.Mal. KT3 138 CQ97
Wellington Dr, Dag. RM10 89 FC66
Purley CR8 159 DM110
Wellington Gdns, SE7 104 EJ79
Twickenham TW2 117 CD91
Wellington Gro, SE10 off Crooms Hill 103 ED80
Wellington Hill, Loug. (High Beach) IG10 32 EG37
H Wellington Hosp, NW8 194 A1
Wellington Ho, Rom. (Gidea Pk) RM2 off Kidman Cl 72 FJ55
Wellingtonia Av, Rom. (Hav.at.Bow.) RM4 51 FE48
Wellington Ms, SE7 104 EJ79
SE22 off Peckham Rye 102 DU84
SW16 off Woodbourne Av 121 DK90
Wellington Pk Est, NW2 63 CU61
Wellington Pas, E11 off Wellington Rd 68 EG57
Wellington Pl, N2 off Great N Rd 64 DE57
NW8 194 A2
Brentwood CM14 54 FW50
Cobham KT11 154 BZ112
Wellington Rd, E6 87 EM68
E7 68 EF63
E10 67 DY60
E11 68 EG57
E17 67 DY55
NW8 82 DD68
NW10 81 CX69
Wellington Rd, SW19 120 DA89
W5 97 CJ76
Ashford TW15 114 BL92
Belvedere DA17 106 EZ78
Bexley DA5 126 EX86
Bromley BR2 144 EJ98
Caterham CR3 176 DQ122
Croydon CR0 141 DP101
Dartford DA1 128 FJ86
Enfield EN1 30 DS42
Epping (N.Wld Bas.) CM16 18 FA27
Feltham TW14 115 BS85
Hampton TW12 117 CD92
Harrow HA3 61 CE55
Orpington BR5 146 EV100
Pinner HA5 40 BZ53
St. Albans (Lon.Col.) AL2 9 CK26
Tilbury RM18 111 GG83
Twickenham TW2 117 CD92
Uxbridge UB8 76 BJ67
Watford WD17 23 BV40
Wellington Rd N, Houns. TW4 96 BZ83
Wellington Rd S, Houns. TW4 96 BZ84
Wellington Row, E2 84 DT69
Wellington Sq, SW3 198 D10
Wellington St, SE18 105 EN77
WC2 196 A10
Barking IG11 off Axe St 87 EQ67
Gravesend DA12 131 GJ87
Slough SL1 92 AT75
Wellington Ter, E1 202 D2
W2 off Notting Hill Gate 82 DB73
Harrow HA1 off West St 61 CD60
Woking (Knap.) GU21 off Victoria Rd 166 AS118
Wellington Way, E3 85 EA69
Weybridge KT13 152 BN110
Welling Way, SE9 105 ER83
Welling DA16 105 ER83
Well La, SW14 118 CQ85
Brentwood (Pilg.Hat.) CM15 54 FT41
Woking GU21 166 AW117
Wellmeade Dr, Sev. TN13 191 FH127
Wellmeadow Rd, SE6 124 EE87
SE13 124 EE86
W7 97 CG77
Wellow Wk, Cars. SM5 140 DD102
Well Pas, NW3 64 DD62
Well Path, Wok. GU21 off Well La 166 AW117
Well Rd, NW3 64 DD62
Barnet EN5 27 CW43
Potters Bar (Northaw) EN6 12 DE28
Wells, The, N14 45 DK45
Wells Cl, Lthd. KT23 170 CB124
Northolt UB5 off Yeading La 78 BW69
South Croydon CR2 160 DS106
Waltham Cross (Chsht) EN7 off Bloomfield Rd 14 DQ25
Wells Ct, Rom. RM1 off Regarth Av 71 FE58
Wells Dr, NW9 62 CR60
Wellsfield, Bushey WD23 24 BY43
Wells Gdns, Dag. RM10 71 FB64
Ilford IG1 68 EL59
Rainham RM13 89 FF65
Wells Ho Rd, NW10 80 CS71
Wellside Cl, Barn. EN5 27 CW42
Wellside Gdns, SW14 off Well La 118 CQ85
Wells Ms, W1 195 L7
Wellsmoor Gdns, Brom. BR1 145 EN97
Wells Pk Rd, SE26 122 DU90
Wells Path, Hayes UB4 77 BS69
Wells Pl, SW18 120 DC87
Redhill (Merst.) RH1 185 DH130
Westerham TN16 189 EQ127
Wellspring Cres, Wem. HA9 62 CP62
Wells Ri, NW8 82 DF67
Wells Rd, W12 99 CW75
Bromley BR1 145 EM96
Epsom KT18 156 CN114
Wells Sq, WC1 196 B3
Wells St, W1 195 K7
Wellstead Av, N9 46 DW45
Wellstead Rd, E6 87 EN68
Wells Ter, N4 65 DN61
Wellstones, Wat. WD17 23 BV41
Wellstones Yd, Wat. WD17 off Wellstones 23 BV41
Well St, E9 84 DV66
E15 86 EE65
Wells Way, SE5 102 DR79
SW7 100 DD76
Wells Yd S, N7 off George's Rd 65 DN64
Well Wk, NW3 64 DD63
Well Way, Epsom KT18 172 CN115
Wellwood Cl, Couls. CR5 off The Vale 159 DL114
Wellwood Rd, Ilf. IG3 70 EU60
Welmar Ms, SW4 101 DK84
Welsford St, SE1 202 B10
Welsh Cl, E13 86 EG69
Welshpool Ho, E8 off Benjamin Cl 84 DU67
Welshpool St, E8 off Broadway Mkt 84 DV67
Welshside Wk, NW9 off Fryent Gro 62 CS58
Welstead Way, W4 99 CT77
Welsummer Way, Wal.Cr. EN8 15 DX27
Weltje Rd, W6 99 CU78
Welton Rd, SE18 105 ES80
Welwyn Av, Felt. TW14 115 BT86
Welwyn St, E2 off Globe Rd 84 DW69
Welwyn Way, Hayes UB4 77 BS70
WEMBLEY, HA0 & HA9 62 CL64
⇌ Wembley Central 62 CL64
⊖ Wembley Central 62 CL64
Wembley Commercial Cen, Wem. HA9 61 CK61
★ Wembley Conf Cen, Wem. HA9 62 CM63
Wembley Hill Rd, Wem. HA9 62 CM64
WEMBLEY PARK, Wem. HA9 62 CM61
⊖ Wembley Park 62 CN62
Wembley Pk Business Cen, Wem. HA9 62 CP62
Wembley Pk Dr, Wem. HA9 62 CM62
Wembley Pt, Wem. HA9 80 CP66
Wembley Rd, Hmptn. TW12 116 CA94
★ Wembley Stadium, Wem. HA9 62 CN63
⇌ Wembley Stadium 62 CM64
Wembley Way, Wem. HA9 80 CP65
Wemborough Rd, Stan. HA7 41 CJ52
Wembury Ms, N6 off Wembury Rd 65 DH59
Wembury Rd, N6 65 DH59
Wemyss Rd, SE3 104 EF82
Wend, The, Couls. CR5 159 DK114
Croydon CR0 161 DZ111
Wendela Cl, Wok. GU22 167 AZ118
Wendela Ct, Har. HA1 61 CE62
Wendell Rd, W12 99 CT75
Wendle Ct, SW8 101 DL79
Wendle Sq, SW11 off Petworth St 100 DE81
Wendley Dr, Add. (New Haw) KT15 151 BF110
Wendling Rd, Sutt. SM1 140 DD102
Wendon St, E3 85 DZ67
Wendover, SE17 102 DS78
Wendover Cl, Hayes UB4 78 BX70
Wendover Dr, N.Mal. KT3 139 CT100
Wendover Gdns, Brwd. CM13 55 GB47
Wendover Pl, Stai. TW18 113 BD92
Wendover Rd, NW10 81 CT68
SE9 104 EK83
Bromley BR2 144 EH97
Staines TW18 113 BC92
Wendover Way, Bushey WD23 24 CC44
Hornchurch RM12 72 FJ64
Orpington BR6 off Glendower Cres 146 EU100
Welling DA16 126 EU85
Wendron Cl, Wok. GU21 166 AU118
Wendy Cl, Enf. EN1 30 DT44
Wendy Way, Wem. HA0 80 CL67
Wenham Gdns, Brwd. (Hutt.) CM13 off Bannister Dr 55 GC44
Wenlack Cl, Uxb. (Denh.) UB9 off Lindsey Rd 58 BG62
Wenlock Ct, N1 197 L1
Wenlock Gdns, NW4 off Rickard Cl 63 CU56
Wenlock Rd, N1 84 DQ68
Edgware HA8 42 CP52
Wenlock St, N1 197 J1
WENNINGTON, Rain. RM13 90 FK73
Wennington Rd, E3 85 DX68
Rainham RM13 89 FG70
Wensley Av, Wdf.Grn. IG8 48 EF52
Wensley Cl, N11 44 DG51
SE9 125 EM86
Romford RM5 50 FA50
Wensleydale Av, Ilf. IG5 48 EL54
Wensleydale Gdns, Hmptn. TW12 116 CB94
Wensleydale Pas, Hmptn. TW12 136 CA95
Wensleydale Rd, Hmptn. TW12 116 CA93
Wensley Rd, N18 46 DV51
Wensum Way, Rick. WD3 38 BK46
Wentbridge Path, Borwd. WD6 26 CN38
Wentland Cl, SE6 123 ED89
Wentland Rd, SE6 123 ED89
WENTWORTH, Vir.W. GU25 132 AS100
Wentworth Av, N3 44 DA52
Borehamwood (Els.) WD6 26 CM43
Wentworth Cl, N3 44 DB52
SE28 88 EX72
Ashford TW15 off Reedsfield Rd 115 BP91
Bromley BR2 off Hillside La 144 EG103
Gravesend DA11 131 GG92
Morden SM4 140 DA101
Orpington BR6 163 ES106
Potters Bar EN6 off Strafford Gate 12 DA31
Surbiton KT6 137 CK103
Watford WD17 23 BT38
Woking (Ripley) GU23 168 BH121
Wentworth Ct, Surb. KT6 off Culsac Rd 138 CL103
Wentworth Cres, SE15 102 DU80
Hayes UB3 95 BR76
Wentworth Dene, Wey. KT13 153 BP106
Wentworth Dr, Dart. DA1 127 FG86
Pinner HA5 59 BU57
Virginia Water GU25 132 AT98
Wentworth Gdns, N13 45 DP49
★ Wentworth Golf Course, Vir.W. GU25 132 AT100
Wentworth Hill, Wem. HA9 62 CM60
Wentworth Ms, E3 off Eric St 85 DZ70
W3 off Brassie Av 81 CT72
Wentworth Pk, N3 44 DA52
Wentworth Pl, Grays RM16 110 GD76
Stanmore HA7 off Greenacres Dr 41 CH51
Wentworth Rd, E12 68 EK63
NW11 63 CZ58
Barnet EN5 27 CX41
Croydon CR0 141 DN101
Southall UB2 96 BW77
Wentworth St, E1 197 P8
Wentworth Way, Pnr. HA5 60 BX56
Rainham RM13 89 FH69
South Croydon CR2 160 DU114
Wenvoe Av, Bexh. DA7 107 FB82
Wepham Cl, Hayes UB4 78 BX71
Wernbrook St, SE18 105 EQ79
Werndee Rd, SE25 142 DU98
Werneth Hall Rd, Ilf. IG5 69 EM55
Werrington St, NW1 195 L1
Werter Rd, SW15 99 CY84
Wescott Way, Uxb. UB8 76 BJ68
Wesleyan Pl, NW5 off Gordon Ho Rd 65 DH63
Wesley Av, E16 205 P2
NW10 80 CR69
Hounslow TW3 96 BY82
Wesley Cl, N7 65 DM61
SE17 200 G9
Harrow HA2 60 CC61
Orpington BR5 146 EW97
Waltham Cross (Chsht) EN7 14 DQ28
Wesley Dr, Egh. TW20 113 BA93
Wesley Rd, E10 67 EC59
Wesley Rd, NW10 80 CQ67
Hayes UB3 77 BU73
★ Wesley's Ho, EC1 197 L4
Wesley Sq, W11 off Bartle Rd 81 CY72
Wesley St, W1 194 G7
Wessels, Tad. KT20 173 CX121
Wessex Av, SW19 140 DA96
Wessex Cl, Ilf. IG3 69 ES58
Kingston upon Thames KT1 off Gloucester Rd 138 CP95
Thames Ditton KT7 137 CF103
Wessex Ct, Wem. HA9 62 CM61
Wessex Dr, Erith DA8 107 FE81
Pinner HA5 40 BY52
Wessex Gdns, NW11 63 CY60
Wessex Ho, SE1 off Old Kent Rd 102 DU78
Wessex La, Grnf. UB6 79 CD68
Wessex St, E2 84 DW69
Wessex Wk, Dart. DA2 off Sandringham Dr 127 FE89
Wessex Way, NW11 63 CY59
West 12 Shop Cen, W12 99 CX75
Westacott, Hayes UB4 77 BS71
Westacott Cl, N19 65 DK60
Westacres, Esher KT10 154 BZ108
WEST ACTON, W3 80 CN72
⊖ West Acton 80 CN72
Westall Rd, Loug. IG10 33 EP41
West App, Orp. BR5 145 EQ99
West Arbour St, E1 85 DX72
West Av, E17 67 EB56
N3 44 DA51
NW4 63 CX57
Hayes UB3 77 BT73
Pinner HA5 60 BZ58
St. Albans AL2 8 CB25
Southall UB1 78 BZ73
Wallington SM6 159 DL106
Walton-on-Thames (Whiteley Vill.) KT12 153 BS109
West Av Rd, E17 67 EA56
West Bk, N16 66 DS59
Barking IG11 off Highbridge Rd 87 EP67
Enfield EN2 30 DQ40
Westbank Rd, Hmptn. (Hmptn H.) TW12 116 CC93
WEST BARNES, N.Mal. KT3 139 CU99
West Barnes La, SW20 139 CV97
New Malden KT3 139 CV97
Westbeech Rd, N22 65 DN55
Westbere Dr, Stan. HA7 41 CK49
Westbere Rd, NW2 63 CY63
Westbourne Av, W3 80 CR72
Sutton SM3 139 CY103
Westbourne Br, W2 82 DC71
Westbourne Cl, Hayes UB4 77 BV70
Westbourne Cres, W2 82 DD73
Westbourne Cres Ms, W2 off Westbourne Cres 82 DD73
Westbourne Dr, SE23 123 DX89
Brentwood CM14 54 FT49
Westbourne Gdns, W2 82 DB72
WESTBOURNE GREEN, W2 82 DA71
Westbourne Gro, W2 82 DA72
W11 82 DA72
Westbourne Gro Ms, W11 off Westbourne Gro 82 DA72
Westbourne Gro Ter, W2 82 DB72
⊖ Westbourne Park 81 CZ71
Westbourne Pk Ms, W2 off Westbourne Gdns 82 DB72
Westbourne Pk Pas, W2 off Westbourne Pk Vil 82 DA71
Westbourne Pk Rd, W2 82 DA71
W11 81 CY72
Westbourne Pk Vil, W2 82 DA71
Westbourne Pl, N9 off Eastbournia Av 46 DV48
Westbourne Rd, N7 83 DN65
SE26 123 DX93
Bexleyheath DA7 106 EY80
Croydon CR0 142 DT100
Feltham TW13 115 BT90
Staines TW18 114 BH94
Uxbridge UB8 77 BP70
Westbourne St, W2 82 DD73
Westbourne Ter, SE23 off Westbourne Dr 123 DX89
W2 82 DD72
Westbourne Ter Ms, W2 82 DC72
Westbourne Ter Rd, W2 82 DC71
West Br Cl, W12 off Percy Rd 99 CU75
Westbridge Rd, SW11 100 DD81
WEST BROMPTON, SW10 100 DB79
⇌ West Brompton 100 DA78
⊖ West Brompton 100 DA78
Westbrook Av, Hmptn. TW12 116 BZ94
Westbrook Cl, Barn. EN4 28 DD41
Westbrook Cres, Barn. EN4 28 DD41
Westbrook Dr, Orp. BR5 146 EW102
Westbrooke Cres, Well. DA16 106 EW83
Westbrooke Rd, Sid. DA15 125 ER89
Welling DA16 106 EV83
Westbrook Rd, SE3 104 EH81
Hounslow TW5 96 BZ80
Staines TW18 off South St 113 BF92
Thornton Heath CR7 142 DR95
Westbrook Sq, Barn. EN4 off Westbrook Cres 28 DD41
Westbury Av, N22 65 DP55
Esher (Clay.) KT10 155 CF107
Southall UB1 78 CA70
Wembley HA0 80 CL66
Westbury Cl, Ruis. HA4 59 BU59
Shepperton TW17 off Burchetts Way 135 BP100
Whyteleafe CR3 off Station App 176 DU118
Westbury Dr, Brwd. CM14 54 FV47
Westbury Gro, N12 44 DA51
Westbury La, Buck.H. IG9 48 EJ47
Westbury Lo Cl, Pnr. HA5 60 BX55
Westbury Par, SW12 off Balham Hill 121 DH86
Westbury Pl, Brent. TW8 97 CK79
Westbury Rd, E7 68 EH64
E17 67 EA56
N11 45 DL51
N12 44 DA51
SE20 143 DX95
W5 80 CL72
Westbury Rd, Bark. IG11 87 ER67
Beckenham BR3 143 DY97
Brentwood CM14 54 FW47
Bromley BR1 144 EK95
Buckhurst Hill IG9 48 EJ47
Croydon CR0 142 DR100
Feltham TW13 116 BX88
Ilford IG1 69 EM61
New Malden KT3 138 CR98
Northwood HA6 39 BS49
Waltham Cross (Chsht) EN8 off Turners Hill 15 DX30
Watford WD18 23 BV43
Wembley HA0 80 CL66
Westbury St, SW8 101 DJ82
Westbury Ter, E7 86 EH65
Upminster RM14 73 FS61
Westerham TN16 189 EQ127
WEST BYFLEET, KT14 152 BH113
⇌ West Byfleet 152 BG112
Westcar La, Walt. KT12 153 BV107
West Carriage Dr, W2 198 A3
West Cen St, WC1 195 P8
West Cen Av, W10 off Harrow Rd 81 CV69
West Chantry, Har. HA3 off Chantry Rd 40 CB53
Westchester Dr, NW4 63 CX55
Westcliffe Apts, W2 off South Wf Rd 82 DD71
West Cl, N9 46 DT48
Ashford TW15 114 BL91
Barnet EN5 27 CV43
Barnet (Cockfos.) EN4 28 DG42
Greenford UB6 78 CC68
Hampton TW12 off Oak Av 116 BY93
Rainham RM13 89 FH70
Wembley HA9 62 CM60
Westcombe Av, Croy. CR0 141 DL100
Westcombe Ct, SE3 off Westcombe Pk Rd 104 EF80
Westcombe Dr, Barn. EN5 28 DA43
Westcombe Hill, SE3 104 EG78
SE10 104 EG78
Westcombe Lo Dr, Hayes UB4 77 BR71
⇌ Westcombe Park 104 EG78
Westcombe Pk Rd, SE3 104 EE79
West Common, Ger.Cr. SL9 56 AX57
West Common Cl, Ger.Cr. SL9 56 AY57
West Common Rd, Brom. BR2 144 EG103
Keston BR2 162 EH105
Uxbridge UB8 58 BK64
Westcoombe Av, SW20 139 CT95
Westcote Ri, Ruis. HA4 59 BQ59
Westcote Rd, SW16 121 DJ92
Epsom KT19 156 CP111
West Cotts, NW6 64 DA64
Westcott Av, Grav. (Nthflt) DA11 131 GG90
Westcott Cl, N15 off Ermine Rd 66 DT58
Bromley BR1 off Ringmer Way 144 EL99
Croydon (New Adgtn) CR0 off Castle Hill Av 161 EB109
Westcott Cres, W7 79 CE72
Westcott Rd, SE17 101 DP79
Westcott Way, Sutt. SM2 157 CW110
WESTCOURT, Grav. DA12 131 GL89
West Ct, SE18 off Prince Imperial Rd 105 EM81
Westcourt, Sun. TW16 135 BV96
West Ct, Wem. HA0 61 CJ61
West Cres Rd, Grav. DA12 131 GH86
Westcroft Cl, NW2 63 CY63
Enfield EN3 30 DW38
Westcroft Gdns, Mord. SM4 139 CZ97
Westcroft Rd, Cars. SM5 158 DG105
Wallington SM6 158 DG105
Westcroft Sq, W6 99 CU77
Westcroft Way, NW2 63 CY63
West Cromwell Rd, SW5 99 CZ77
W14 99 CZ77
West Cross Cen, Brent. TW8 97 CG79
West Cross Route, W10 81 CX73
W11 81 CX73
West Cross Way, Brent. TW8 97 CH79
⇌ West Croydon 142 DQ102
Tram West Croydon 142 DQ102
Westdale Pas, SE18 105 EP79
Westdale Rd, SE18 105 EP79
Westdean Av, SE12 124 EH88
Westdean Cl, SW18 120 DB86
West Dene, Sutt. SM3 off Park La 157 CY107
Westdene, Walt. KT12 153 BV105
West Dene Dr, Rom. RM3 52 FK50
Westdene Way, Wey. KT13 135 BS104
Westdown Rd, E15 67 EC63
SE6 123 EA87
WEST DRAYTON, UB7 94 BK76
⇌ West Drayton 76 BL74
West Drayton Pk Av, West Dr. UB7 94 BL76
West Drayton Rd, Uxb. UB8 76 BM72
Uxbridge (Hayes End) UB8 77 BP71
West Dr, SW16 121 DJ91
Carshalton SM5 158 DD110
Harrow HA3 41 CD51
Sutton (Cheam) SM2 157 CX109
Tadworth KT20 173 CX118
Virginia Water GU25 132 AT101
Watford WD25 23 BV36
West Dr Gdns, Har. HA3 41 CD51
WEST DULWICH, SE21 122 DR90
⇌ West Dulwich 122 DR88
⇌ West Ealing 79 CH73
West Eaton Pl, SW1 198 F8
West Eaton Pl Ms, SW1 198 F8
Wested La, Swan. BR8 147 FG101
West Ella Rd, NW10 80 CS66
WEST END, Esher KT10 154 BZ107
West End Av, E10 67 EC57
Pinner HA5 60 BX56

★ Place of interest ⇌ Railway station ⊖ London Underground station DLR Docklands Light Railway station Tram Tramlink station H Hospital Riv Pedestrian ferry landing stage

West End Cl, NW10 ... 80 CQ66
West End Ct, Pnr. HA5 ... 60 BX56
Slough (Stoke P.) SL2 ... 74 AT67
West End Gdns, Esher KT10 ... 154 BZ106
Northolt UB5
off Edward Cl ... 78 BW68
West End La, NW6 ... 82 DA66
Barnet EN5 ... 27 CX42
Esher KT10 ... 154 BZ107
Hayes UB3 ... 95 BQ80
Pinner HA5 ... 60 BX55
Slough (Stoke P.) SL2 ... 74 AS67
West End Rd, Nthlt. UB5 ... 78 BW66
Ruislip HA4 ... 59 BV64
Southall UB1 ... 78 BY74
Westerdale Rd, SE10 ... 104 EG78
Westerfield Rd, N15 ... 66 DT57
Westerfolds Cl, Wok. GU22 ... 167 BC116
Westergate Rd, SE2 ... 106 EY79
WESTERHAM, TN16 ... 189 EQ126
Westerham Av, N9 ... 46 DR48
Westerham Cl, Add. KT15 ... 152 BJ107
Sutton SM2 ... 158 DA110
Westerham Dr, Sid. DA15 ... 126 EV86
Westerham Hill, West. TN16 ... 179 EN121
Westerham Rd, E10 ... 67 EB58
Keston BR2 ... 162 EK107
Oxted RH8 ... 188 EF129
Sevenoaks TN13 ... 190 FC123
Westerham TN16 ... 189 EM128
Westerham (Brasted) TN16 ... 189 ET125
Westerley Cres, SE26 ... 123 DZ92
Westerley Ware, Rich. TW9
off Kew Grn ... 98 CN79
Westermain, Add. (New Haw)
KT15 ... 152 BJ110
Western Av, NW11 ... 63 CX58
W3 ... 80 CR71
W5 ... 80 CM69
Brentwood CM14 ... 54 FW46
Chertsey KT16 ... 134 BG97
Dagenham RM10 ... 89 FC65
Egham TW20 ... 133 BB97
Epping CM16 ... 17 ET32
Greenford UB6 ... 79 CF69
Northolt UB5 ... 78 BZ67
Romford RM2 ... 52 FJ54
Ruislip HA4 ... 77 BP65
Uxbridge (Denh.) UB9 ... 58 BJ63
Uxbridge (Ickhm) UB10 ... 77 BP65
Western Av Business Pk, W3
off Mansfield Rd ... 80 CP70
Western Av Underpass, W5
off Western Av ... 80 CM69
Western Beach Apts, E16 ... 205 M2
Western Cl, Cher. KT16
off Western Av ... 134 BG97
Western Ct, N3 off Huntley Dr ... 44 DA51
Western Cross Cl, Green.
DA9 off Johnsons Way ... 129 FW86
Western Dr, Shep. TW17 ... 135 BR100
[H] Western Eye Hosp, NW1 ... 194 D6
Western Gdns, W5 ... 80 CN73
Brentwood CM14 ... 54 FW47
Western Gateway, E16 ... 205 M1
Western La, SW12 ... 120 DG87
Western Ms, W9
off Great Western Rd ... 81 CZ70
Western Par, Barn. EN5
off Great N Rd ... 28 DA43
Western Pathway, Horn.
RM12 ... 90 FJ65
Western Perimeter Rd, Houns.
(Hthrw Air.) TW6 ... 94 BH83
Western Pl, SE16 ... 202 G4
Western Rd, E13 ... 86 EJ67
E17 ... 67 EC57
N2 ... 64 DF56
N22 ... 45 DM54
NW10 ... 80 CQ70
SW9 ... 101 DN83
SW19 ... 140 DD95
W5 ... 79 CK73
Brentwood CM14 ... 54 FW47
Epping CM16 ... 17 ET32
Mitcham CR4 ... 140 DD95
Romford RM1 ... 71 FE57
Southall UB2 ... 96 BX76
Sutton SM1 ... 158 DA106
Western Ter, W6
off Chiswick Mall ... 99 CU78
Western Trd Est, NW10 ... 80 CQ70
Western Vw, Hayes UB3 ... 95 BT75
Westernville Gdns, Ilf. IG2 ... 69 EQ59
Western Way, SE28 ... 105 ER76
Barnet EN5 ... 28 DA44
WEST EWELL, Epsom KT19 ... 156 CS108
West Fm Av, Ashtd. KT21 ... 171 CJ118
West Fm Cl, Ashtd. KT21 ... 171 CJ119
West Fm Dr, Ashtd. KT21 ... 171 CK119
[DLR] Westferry ... 85 EA73
Westferry Circ, E14 ... 203 P2
Westferry Rd, E14 ... 203 N2
WESTFIELD, Wok. GU22 ... 167 AZ122
Westfield, Ashtd. KT21 ... 172 CM118
Loughton IG10 ... 32 EJ43
Reigate RH2 ... 184 DB131
Sevenoaks TN13 ... 191 FJ122
Westfield Av, S.Croy. CR2 ... 160 DR113
Watford WD24 ... 24 BW37
Woking GU22 ... 166 AY121
Westfield Cl, NW9 ... 62 CQ55
SW10 ... 100 DC80
Enfield EN3 ... 31 DY41
Gravesend DA12 ... 131 GJ93
Sutton SM1 ... 157 CZ105
Waltham Cross EN8 ... 15 DZ31
Westfield Common, Wok.
GU22 ... 166 AY122
Westfield Dr, Har. HA3 ... 61 CK57
Leatherhead (Bkhm) KT23 ... 170 CA122
Westfield Gdns, Har. HA3 ... 61 CK56
Romford RM3 ... 70 EW58
Westfield Gro, Wok. GU22 ... 167 AZ120
Westfield La, Har. HA3 ... 61 CK56
Slough (Geo.Grn) SL3 ... 74 AX73
Westfield Par, Add. (New Haw)
KT15 ... 152 BK110
Westfield Pk, Pnr. HA5 ... 40 BZ52
Westfield Pk Dr, Wdf.Grn. IG8 ... 48 EL51
Westfield Rd, NW7 ... 42 CR48
W13 ... 79 CG74
Beckenham BR3 ... 143 DZ96
Bexleyheath DA7 ... 107 FC82
Croydon CR0 ... 141 DP103
Dagenham RM9 ... 70 EY63
Mitcham CR4 ... 140 DF96
Surbiton KT6 ... 137 CK99
Sutton SM1 ... 157 CZ105
Walton-on-Thames KT12 ... 136 BY101
Woking GU22 ... 166 AX122
Westfields, SW13 ... 99 CT83
Westfields Av, SW13 ... 98 CS83
Westfields Rd, W3 ... 80 CP71
Westfield St, SE18 ... 104 EK76
Westfield Wk, Wal.Cr. EN8
off Westfield Cl ... 15 DZ31
Westfield Way, E1 ... 85 DY69
Ruislip HA4 ... 59 BS62
Woking GU22 ... 166 AY122
⊖ West Finchley ... 44 DB51
West Gdn Pl, W2 ... 194 C9
West Gdns, E1 ... 202 E1
SW17 ... 120 DE93
Epsom KT17 ... 156 CS110
West Gate, W5 ... 80 CL69
Westgate Cl, Epsom KT18
off Chalk La ... 172 CR115
Westgate Ct, Wal.Cr. EN8
off Holmesdale ... 31 DX35
Westgate Est, Felt. TW14 ... 114 BN88
Westgate Ho, Brent. TW8 ... 97 CK78
Westgate Rd, SE25 ... 142 DV98
Beckenham BR3 ... 143 EB96
Dartford DA1 ... 128 FK86
Westgate St, E8 ... 84 DV67
Westgate Ter, SW10 ... 100 DB78
Westglade Ct, Har. HA3 ... 61 CK57
West Gorse, Croy. CR0 ... 161 DY112
WEST GREEN, N15 ... 66 DQ55
West Grn Pl, Grnf. UB6
off Uneeda Dr ... 79 CD67
West Grn Rd, N15 ... 65 DP56
West Gro, SE10 ... 103 EC81
Walton-on-Thames KT12 ... 153 BV105
Woodford Green IG8 ... 48 EJ51
Westgrove La, SE10 ... 103 EC81
West Halkin St, SW1 ... 198 F6
West Hallowes, SE9 ... 124 EK88
Westhall Pk, Warl. CR6 ... 176 DW119
West Hall Rd, Rich. TW9 ... 98 CP81
Westhall Rd, Warl. CR6 ... 176 DV119
WEST HAM, E15 ... 86 EF66
⇌ West Ham ... 86 EE69
⊖ West Ham ... 86 EE69
West Ham La, E15 ... 86 EE66
West Ham Pk, E7 ... 86 EG66
WEST HAMPSTEAD, NW6 ... 64 DB64
⇌ West Hampstead ... 82 DA65
⊖ West Hampstead ... 82 DA65
West Hampstead Ms, NW6 ... 82 DB65
⇌ West Hampstead
(Thameslink) ... 82 DA65
★ West Ham United FC, E13 ... 86 EJ68
West Harding St, EC4 ... 196 E8
West Harold, Swan. BR8 ... 147 FD97
WEST HARROW, Har. HA1 ... 60 CC59
⊖ West Harrow ... 60 CC58
West Hatch Manor, Ruis.
HA4 ... 59 BT60
Westhay Gdns, SW14 ... 118 CP85
WEST HEATH, SE2 ... 106 EX79
West Heath, Oxt. RH8 ... 188 EG130
West Heath Av, NW11 ... 64 DA60
West Heath Cl, NW3 ... 64 DA62
Dartford DA1
off West Heath Rd ... 127 FF86
West Heath Dr, NW11 ... 64 DA60
West Heath Gdns, NW3 ... 64 DA62
West Heath La, Sev. TN13 ... 191 FH128
West Heath Rd, NW3 ... 64 DA61
SE2 ... 106 EX79
Dartford DA1 ... 127 FF86
WEST HENDON, NW9 ... 62 CS59
West Hendon Bdy, NW9 ... 63 CT58
West Hill, SW15 ... 119 CX87
SW18 ... 120 DA85
Dartford DA1 ... 128 FK86
Epsom KT19 ... 156 CQ113
Harrow HA2 ... 61 CE61
Orpington BR6 ... 163 EM112
Oxted RH8 ... 187 ED130
South Croydon CR2 ... 160 DS110
Wembley HA9 ... 62 CM60
West Hill Av, Epsom KT19 ... 156 CQ112
West Hill Bk, Oxt. RH8 ... 187 ED130
Westhill Cl, Grav. DA12
off Leith Pk Rd ... 131 GH88
West Hill Ct, N6 ... 64 DG62
West Hill Dr, Dart. DA1 ... 128 FJ86
West Hill Pk, N6
off Merton La ... 64 DF61
West Hill Ri, Dart. DA1 ... 128 FK86
West Hill Rd, SW18 ... 120 DA86
Woking GU22 ... 166 AX119
West Hill Way, N20 ... 44 DB46
Westholm, NW11 ... 64 DB56
West Holme, Erith DA8 ... 107 FC81
Westholme, Orp. BR6 ... 145 ES101
Westholme Gdns, Ruis. HA4 ... 59 BU60
Westhorne Av, SE9 ... 124 EJ86
SE12 ... 124 EG87
Westhorpe Gdns, NW4 ... 63 CW55
Westhorpe Rd, SW15 ... 99 CW83
West Ho Cl, SW19 ... 119 CY88
Westhurst Dr, Chis. BR7 ... 125 EP92
West Hyde La, Ger.Cr.
(Chal.St.P.) SL9 ... 37 AZ52
West India Av, E14 ... 203 P2
West India Dock Rd, E14 ... 85 DZ72
[DLR] West India Quay ... 204 B1
⊖ West Kensington ... 99 CZ78
West Kensington Ct, W14
off Edith Vil ... 99 CZ78
West Kent Av, Grav. (Nthflt)
DA11 ... 130 GC86
West Kent Cold Storage, Sev.
(Dunt.Grn) TN14 ... 181 FF120
WEST KILBURN, W9 ... 81 CZ69
Westlake Cl, N13 ... 45 DN48
Hayes UB4 off Lochan Cl ... 78 BY70
Westlake Rd, Wem. HA9 ... 61 CK61
Westland Av, Horn. RM11 ... 72 FL60
Westland Cl, Stai. (Stanw.)
TW19 ... 114 BL86
Watford (Lvsdn) WD25 ... 7 BT34
Westland Dr, Brom. BR2 ... 144 EF103
Hatfield AL9 ... 11 CY27
Westland Ho, E16
off Rymill St ... 87 EN74
Westland Pl, N1 ... 197 K2
Westland Rd, Wat. WD17 ... 23 BV40
Westlands Cl, Hayes UB3
off Granville Rd ... 95 BU77
Westlands Ct, Epsom KT18 ... 172 CQ115
Westlands Ter, SW12
off Gaskarth Rd ... 121 DJ86
Westlands Way, Oxt. RH8 ... 187 ED127
West La, SE16 ... 202 D5
Westlea Av, Wat. WD25 ... 24 BY37
Westlea Rd, W7 ... 97 CG76
Westleigh Av, SW15 ... 119 CV85
Coulsdon CR5 ... 174 DG116
Westleigh Dr, Brom. BR1 ... 144 EL95
Westleigh Gdns, Edg. HA8 ... 42 CN53
Westlinks, Wem. HA0
off Alperton La ... 79 CK68
Westlinton Cl, NW7 ... 43 CY51
West Lo Av, W3 ... 80 CN74
Westlyn Cl, Rain. RM13 ... 90 FJ69
Westmacott Dr, Felt. TW14 ... 115 BT88
West Mall, W8
off Palace Gdns Ter ... 82 DA74
West Malling Way, Horn.
RM12 ... 72 FJ64
Westmark Pt, SW15
off Norley Vale ... 119 CV88
Westmead, SW15 ... 119 CV86
West Mead, Epsom KT19 ... 156 CS107
Ruislip HA4 ... 60 BW63
Westmead, Wok. GU21 ... 166 AV117
Westmead Cor, Cars. SM5
off Colston Av ... 158 DE105
Westmeade Cl, Wal.Cr.
(Chsht) EN7 ... 14 DV29
Westmead Rd, Sutt. SM1 ... 158 DD105
Westmede, Chig. IG7 ... 49 EQ51
Westmere Dr, NW7 ... 42 CR48
West Mersea Cl, E16 ... 205 P3
West Ms, N17 ... 46 DV51
SW1 ... 199 J9
[H] West Middlesex Uni Hosp,
Islw. TW7 ... 97 CG82
West Mill, Grav. DA11 ... 131 GF86
Westmill Ct, N4
off Brownswood Rd ... 66 DQ61
WESTMINSTER, SW1 ... 199 K6
⊖ Westminster ... 200 A5
★ Westminster Abbey,
SW1 ... 199 P6
★ Westminster Abbey Mus,
SW1 ... 199 P6
Westminster Av, Th.Hth. CR7 ... 141 DP96
Westminster Br, SE1 ... 200 A5
SW1 ... 200 A5
Westminster Br Rd, SE1 ... 200 C5
★ Westminster Cath, SW1 ... 199 K7
★ Westminster City Hall,
SW1 ... 199 L6
Westminster Cl, Felt. TW14 ... 115 BU88
Ilford IG6 ... 49 ER54
Teddington TW11 ... 117 CG92
Westminster Dr, N13 ... 45 DL50
Westminster Gdns, E4 ... 48 EE46
SW1 ... 199 P8
Barking IG11 ... 87 ES68
Ilford IG6 ... 49 EQ54
★ Westminster Millennium
Pier, SW1 ... 200 A4
[Riv] Westminster Millennium
Pier ... 200 A4
Westminster Rd, N9 ... 46 DV46
W7 ... 79 CE74
Sutton SM1 ... 140 DD103
Westmoat Cl, Beck. BR3 ... 123 EC94
WEST MOLESEY, KT8 ... 136 BZ99
Westmont Rd, Esher KT10 ... 137 CE103
Westmoor Gdns, Enf. EN3 ... 31 DX40
Westmoor Rd, Enf. EN3 ... 31 DX40
Westmoor St, SE7 ... 104 EJ76
Westmore Grn, West. (Tats.)
TN16 ... 178 EJ121
Westmoreland Av, Horn.
RM11 ... 72 FJ57
Welling DA16 ... 105 ES83
Westmoreland Bldgs, EC1
off Bartholomew Cl ... 84 DQ71
Westmoreland Dr, Sutt. SM2 ... 158 DB109
Westmoreland Pl, SW1 ... 101 DH78
W5 ... 79 CK71
Bromley BR1 ... 144 EG97
Westmoreland Rd, NW9 ... 62 CN56
SE17 ... 102 DQ79
SW13 ... 99 CT81
Bromley BR1, BR2 ... 144 EE99
Westmoreland St, W1 ... 194 G7
Westmoreland Ter, SW1 ... 101 DH78
Westmoreland Wk, SE17 ... 102 DR79
Westmore Rd, West. (Tats.)
TN16 ... 178 EJ121
Westmorland Cl, E12 ... 68 EK61
Epsom KT19 ... 156 CS110
Twickenham TW1 ... 117 CH86
Westmorland Rd, E17 ... 67 EA58
Harrow HA1 ... 60 CB57
Westmorland Sq, Mitch. CR4
off Westmorland Way ... 141 DL99
Westmorland Ter, SE20 ... 122 DV94
Westmorland Way, Mitch.
CR4 ... 141 DK98
Westmount Rd, SE9 ... 105 EM82
WEST NORWOOD, SE27 ... 122 DQ90
⇌ West Norwood ... 121 DP90
West Oak, Beck. BR3 ... 143 ED95
Westoe Rd, N9 ... 46 DV47
Weston Av, Add. KT15 ... 152 BG105
Grays RM20 ... 109 FT77
Thames Ditton KT7 ... 137 CE101
West Molesey KT8 ... 136 BY97
Weston Cl, Brwd. (Hutt.)
CM13 ... 55 GC45
Coulsdon CR5 ... 175 DM120
Potters Bar EN6 ... 11 CZ32
Weston Ct, N4 off Queens Dr ... 66 DQ62
Weston Ct, N20
off Farnham Cl ... 44 DC45
Weston Dr, Cat. CR3
off Coulsdon Rd ... 176 DQ122
Stanmore HA7 ... 41 CH53
West One Shop Cen, W1 ... 194 G9
Weston Gdns, Islw. TW7 ... 97 CD81
Woking GU22 ... 167 BE116
WESTON GREEN, T.Ditt. KT7 ... 137 CF102
Weston Grn, Dag. RM9 ... 70 EZ63
Thames Ditton KT7 ... 137 CE102
Weston Grn Rd, Esher KT10 ... 137 CD102
Thames Ditton KT7 ... 137 CE102
Weston Gro, Brom. BR1 ... 144 EF95
Weston Pk, N8 ... 65 DL58
Kingston upon Thames
KT1 off Clarence St ... 138 CL96
Thames Ditton KT7 ... 137 CE102
Weston Pk Cl, T.Ditt. KT7
off Weston Pk ... 137 CE102
Weston Ri, WC1 ... 196 C1
Weston Rd, W4 ... 98 CQ76
Bromley BR1 ... 124 EF94
Dagenham RM9 ... 70 EY63
Enfield EN2 ... 30 DR39
Epsom KT17 ... 156 CS111
Thames Ditton KT7 ... 137 CE102
Weston St, SE1 ... 201 L6
Weston Wk, E8 off Mare St ... 84 DV66
Weston Way, Wok. GU22 ... 167 BE116
Westover Cl, Sutt. SM2 ... 158 DB109
Westover Hill, NW3 ... 64 DA61
Westover Rd, SW18 ... 120 DC86
Westow Hill, SE19 ... 122 DS93
Westow St, SE19 ... 122 DS93
West Palace Gdns, Wey.
KT13 ... 135 BP104
West Pk, SE9 ... 124 EL89
West Pk Av, Rich. TW9 ... 98 CN81
West Pk Cl, Houns. TW5
off Heston Gra La ... 96 BZ79
Romford RM6 ... 70 EX57
West Pk Hill, Brwd. CM14 ... 54 FU48
[H] West Pk Hosp, Epsom
KT19 ... 156 CM112
West Pk Rd, Epsom KT19 ... 156 CM112
Richmond TW9 ... 98 CN81
Southall UB2 ... 78 CC74
West Parkside, SE10 ... 205 L7
Warlingham CR6 ... 177 EA115
West Pier, E1 ... 202 D3
West Pl, SW19 ... 119 CW92
West Pt, SE1 ... 202 B10
Westpoint Apts, N8
off Turnpike La ... 65 DM56
Westpoint Trd Est, W3 ... 80 CP71
Westpole Av, Barn. EN4 ... 28 DG42
Westport Rd, E13 ... 86 EH70
Westport St, E1 ... 85 DX72
West Poultry Av, EC1 ... 196 F7
West Quarters, W12 ... 81 CU72
West Quay Dr, Hayes UB4 ... 78 BY71
West Ramp, Houns. (Hthrw Air.)
TW6 ... 94 BN81
West Ridge Gdns, Grnf. UB6 ... 78 CC68
West Riding, St.Alb. (Brick.Wd)
AL2 ... 8 BZ30
West Rd, E15 ... 86 EF67
N17 ... 46 DV51
SW3 ... 100 DF79
SW4 ... 121 DK85
W5 ... 80 CL71
Barnet EN4 ... 44 DG46
Chessington KT9 ... 155 CJ112
Feltham TW14 ... 115 BR86
Kingston upon Thames
KT2 ... 138 CQ95
Romford (Chad.Hth) RM6 ... 70 EX58
Romford (Rush Grn) RM7 ... 71 FD59
South Ockendon RM15 ... 91 FV69
West Drayton UB7 ... 94 BM76
Weybridge KT13 ... 153 BP109
Westrow, SW15 ... 119 CW85
West Row, W10 ... 81 CY70
Westrow Dr, Bark. IG11 ... 87 ET65
Westrow Gdns, Ilf. IG3 ... 69 ET61
⇌ West Ruislip ... 59 BQ61
⊖ West Ruislip ... 59 BQ61
West Shaw, Long. DA3 ... 149 FX96
West Sheen Vale, Rich. TW9 ... 98 CM84
Westside, NW4 ... 43 CV54
West Side, Brox. EN10
off High Rd Turnford ... 15 DY25
West Side Common, SW19 ... 119 CW92
[DLR] West Silvertown ... 205 N3
West Smithfield, EC1 ... 196 F7
West Spur Rd, Uxb. UB8 ... 76 BK69
West Sq, SE11 ... 200 F7
Iver SL0 off High St ... 75 BF72
West St, E2 ... 84 DV68
E11 ... 68 EE62
E17 off Grove Rd ... 67 EB57
WC2 ... 195 N9
Bexleyheath DA7 ... 106 EZ84
Brentford TW8 ... 97 CJ79
Bromley BR1 ... 144 EG95
Carshalton SM5 ... 140 DF104
Croydon CR0 ... 160 DQ105
Epsom KT18 ... 156 CR113
Epsom (Ewell) KT17 ... 156 CS110
Erith DA8 ... 107 FD77
Gravesend DA11 ... 131 GG86
Grays RM17 ... 110 GA79
Harrow HA1 ... 61 CD60
Reigate RH2 ... 183 CY133
Sutton SM1 ... 158 DB106
Watford WD17 ... 23 BV40
Woking GU21
off Church St E ... 167 AZ117
West St La, Cars. SM5 ... 158 DF105
⇌ West Sutton ... 158 DA105
West Temple Sheen, SW14 ... 98 CP84
West Tenter St, E1 ... 84 DT72
West Thamesmead Business
Pk, SE28 ... 105 ET76
WEST THURROCK, Grays
RM20 ... 109 FU78
West Thurrock Way, Grays
RM20 ... 109 FT77
WEST TILBURY, Til. RM18 ... 111 GL79
West Twrs, Pnr. HA5 ... 60 BX58
Westvale Ms, W3 ... 80 CS74
West Valley Rd, Hem.H. HP3 ... 6 BJ25
West Vw, NW4 ... 63 CW56
Ashtead KT21
off West Fm Cl ... 171 CJ119
Feltham TW14 ... 115 BQ87
Loughton IG10 ... 33 EM41
West Vw Av, Whyt. CR3
off Station Rd ... 176 DU118
Westview Cl, NW10 ... 63 CT64
W7 ... 79 CE72
W10 ... 81 CW72
Rainham RM13 ... 90 FJ69
West Vw Ct, Borwd. (Els.)
WD6 off High St ... 25 CK44
Westview Cres, N9 ... 46 DS45
Westview Dr, Wdf.Grn. IG8 ... 48 EK54
West Vw Gdns, Borwd. (Els.)
WD6 off High St ... 25 CK44
West Vw Rd, Dart. DA1 ... 128 FM86
Swanley BR8 ... 147 FG98
Swanley (Crock.) BR8 ... 147 FD100
Westview Rd, Warl. CR6 ... 176 DV119
Westville Rd, W12 ... 99 CU75
Thames Ditton KT7 ... 137 CG102
West Wk, W5 ... 80 CL71
Barnet EN4 ... 44 DG45
Hayes UB3 ... 77 BU74
West Walkway, The, Sutt.
SM1 off Cheam Rd ... 158 DB106
Westward Rd, E4 ... 47 DZ50
Westward Way, Har. HA3 ... 62 CL58
West Warwick Pl, SW1 ... 199 K9
WEST WATFORD, Wat. WD18 ... 23 BU42
West Way, N18 ... 46 DR49
NW10 ... 62 CR62
Westway, SW20 ... 139 CV97
W2 ... 82 DA71
W9 ... 82 DA71
W10 ... 81 CY72
W12 ... 81 CU73
West Way, Brwd. CM14 ... 54 FU48
Carshalton SM5 ... 158 DD110
Westway, Cat. CR3 ... 176 DR122
West Way, Croy. CR0 ... 143 DY103
Edgware HA8 ... 42 CP51
Hounslow TW5 ... 96 BZ81
Westway, Orp. BR5 ... 145 ER99
West Way, Pnr. HA5 ... 60 BX56
Rickmansworth WD3 ... 38 BH46
Ruislip HA4 ... 59 BT60
Shepperton TW17 ... 135 BR100
West Wickham BR4 ... 143 ED100
Westway Cl, SW20 ... 139 CV97
Westway Cross Shop Pk,
Grnf. UB6 ... 79 CE67
West Way Gdns, Croy. CR0 ... 143 DX103
Westway Gdns, Red. RH1 ... 184 DG131
Westways, Epsom KT19 ... 157 CT105
Westerham TN16 ... 189 EQ126
Westwell Cl, Orp. BR5 ... 146 EX102
Westwell Rd, SW16 ... 121 DL93
Westwell Rd App, SW16
off Westwell Rd ... 121 DL93
Westwick Gdns, W14 ... 99 CX75
Hounslow TW4 ... 95 BV82
WEST WICKHAM, BR4 ... 143 EC103
⇌ West Wickham ... 143 EC101
Westwick Pl, Wat. WD25 ... 8 BW34
Westwood Av, SE19 ... 142 DQ95
Addlestone (Wdhm) KT15 ... 151 BF112
Brentwood CM14 ... 54 FU49
Harrow HA2 ... 60 CB63
Westwood Cl, Amer. HP6 ... 20 AX39
Bromley BR1 ... 144 EK97
Esher KT10 ... 136 CC104
Potters Bar EN6 ... 12 DA30
Ruislip HA4 ... 59 BP58
Westwood Dr, Amer. HP6 ... 20 AX39
Westwood Gdns, SW13 ... 99 CT83
Westwood Hill, SE26 ... 122 DU92
Westwood La, Sid. DA15 ... 126 EU85
Welling DA16 ... 105 ET83
Westwood Pk, SE23 ... 122 DV87
Westwood Pl, SE26 ... 122 DU91
Westwood Rd, E16 ... 205 P3
SW13 ... 99 CT83
Coulsdon CR5 ... 175 DK118
Gravesend (Sthflt) DA13 ... 130 FY93
Ilford IG3 ... 69 ET60
West Woodside, Bex. DA5 ... 126 EY87
Westwood Way, Sev. TN13 ... 190 FF122
West World, W5 ... 80 CL69
West Yoke, Sev. (Ash) TN15 ... 149 FX103
Wetheral Dr, Stan. HA7 ... 41 CH53
Wetherby Cl, Nthlt. UB5 ... 78 CB65
Wetherby Gdns, SW5 ... 100 DC77
Wetherby Ms, SW5
off Bolton Gdns ... 100 DB78
Wetherby Pl, SW7 ... 100 DC77
Wetherby Rd, Borwd. WD6 ... 26 CL39
Enfield EN2 ... 30 DQ39
Wetherby Way, Chess. KT9 ... 156 CL108
Wetherden St, E17 ... 67 DZ59
Wetherell Rd, E9 ... 85 DX67
Wetherill Rd, N10 ... 44 DG53
★ Wetland Cen, The, SW13 ... 99 CV80
Wettern Cl, S.Croy. CR2
off Purley Oaks Rd ... 160 DS110
Wetton Pl, Egh. TW20 ... 113 AZ92
Wexfenne Gdns, Wok. GU22 ... 168 BH116
Wexford Rd, SW12 ... 120 DF87
[H] Wexham Pk Hosp, Slou.
SL2 ... 74 AW70
Wexham Pk La, Slou.
(Wexham) SL3 ... 74 AW70
Wexham Pl, Slou. (Wexham)
SL2 ... 74 AX65
Wexham Rd, Slou. SL1, SL2 ... 74 AV71
Wexham Springs, Slou.
(Wexham) SL2 ... 74 AW66
WEXHAM STREET,
Slou. SL3 ... 74 AW67
Wexham St, Slou. SL2, SL3 ... 74 AW67
Wexham Wds, Slou. (Wexham)
SL3 ... 74 AW71
Wey Av, Cher. KT16 ... 134 BG97
Weybank, Wok. (Wisley)
GU23 ... 168 BL116
Wey Barton, W.Byf. (Byfleet)
KT14 ... 152 BM113
Weybourne Pl, S.Croy. CR2 ... 160 DR110
Weybourne St, SW18 ... 120 DC89
WEYBRIDGE, KT13 ... 152 BN105
⇌ Weybridge ... 152 BN107

Weybridge Business Pk, Add. KT15 .... **152** BL105
Weybridge Ct, SE16
off Argyle Way **102** DU78
🄷 **Weybridge Hosp**, Wey. KT13 .... **152** BN105
Weybridge Pk, Wey. KT13 .... **153** BP106
Weybridge Pt, SW11 .... **100** DG82
Weybridge Rd, Add. KT15 .... **134** BK104
Thornton Heath CR7 .... **141** DN98
Weybridge KT13 .... **134** BL104
Weybridge Trd Est, Add. KT15 .... **152** BL105
Wey Cl, W.Byf. KT14
off Broadoaks Cres **152** BH113
Wey Ct, Add. (New Haw) KT15 .... **152** BK109
Epsom KT19 .... **156** CQ105
Weydown Cl, SW19 .... **119** CY88
Weyhill Rd, E1
off Commercial Rd **84** DU72
Weylands Cl, Walt. KT12 .... **136** BZ102
Weylands Pk, Wey. KT13 .... **153** BR107
Weylond Rd, Dag. RM8 .... **70** EZ62
Wey Manor Rd, Add. (New Haw) KT15 .... **152** BK109
Weyman Rd, SE3 .... **104** EJ81
Weymead Cl, Cher. KT16 .... **134** BJ102
Wey Meadows, Wey. KT13 .... **152** BL106
Weymede, W.Byf. (Byfleet) KT14 .... **152** BM112
Weymouth Av, NW7 .... **42** CS50
W5 .... **97** CJ76
Weymouth Cl, E6
off Covelees Wall **87** EP72
Weymouth Ct, Sutt. SM2 .... **158** DA108
Weymouth Dr, Grays RM16 .... **109** FX78
Weymouth Ms, W1 .... **195** H6
Weymouth Rd, Hayes UB4 .... **77** BS69
Weymouth St, W1 .... **194** G7
Weymouth Ter, E2 .... **84** DT68
Weymouth Wk, Stan. HA7 .... **41** CG51
Wey Rd, Wey. KT13 .... **134** BM104
Weyside Cl, W.Byf. (Byfleet) KT14 .... **152** BM112
Weystone Rd, Add. KT15
off Weybridge Rd **152** BM105
Whadcote St, N4
off Seven Sisters Rd **65** DN61
Whalebone Av, Rom. RM6 .... **70** EZ58
Whalebone Ct, EC2 .... **197** L8
Whalebone Gro, Rom. RM6 .... **70** EZ58
Whalebone La, E15
off West Ham La **86** EE66
Whalebone La N, Rom. RM6 .... **70** EY57
Whalebone La S, Dag. RM8 .... **70** EZ59
Romford RM6 .... **70** EZ59
Whales Yd, E15
off West Ham La **86** EE66
Whaley Rd, Pot.B. EN6 .... **12** DC33
Wharfdale Cl, N11 .... **44** DG51
Wharfdale Ct, E5
off Rushmore Rd **67** DX63
Wharfdale Rd, N1 .... **83** DL68
Wharfedale Gdns, Th.Hth. CR7 .... **141** DM98
Wharfedale Rd, Dart. DA2 .... **128** FQ88
Wharfedale St, SW10 .... **100** DB78
Wharf La, Rick. WD3 .... **38** BL46
Twickenham TW1 .... **117** CG88
Woking (Ripley) GU23 .... **168** BJ118
Woking (Send) GU23 .... **167** BC123
Wharf Pl, E2 .... **84** DU67
Wharf Rd, N1 .... **84** DQ68
N1 (King's Cross) **83** DL68
Brentwood CM14 .... **54** FW48
Enfield EN3 .... **31** DY44
Gravesend DA12 .... **131** GL86
Grays RM17 .... **110** FZ79
Staines (Wrays.) TW19 .... **112** AW87
Wharf Rd S, Grays RM17 .... **110** FZ79
Wharfside Cl, Erith DA8 .... **107** FF78
Wharfside Rd, E16 .... **86** EE71
Wharf St, E16 .... **86** EE71
Wharncliffe Dr, Sthl. UB1 .... **79** CD74
Wharncliffe Gdns, SE25 .... **142** DS96
Wharncliffe Rd, SE25 .... **142** DS96
Wharton Cl, NW10 .... **80** CS65
Wharton Cotts, WC1
off Wharton St **83** DM69
Wharton Rd, Brom. BR1 .... **144** EH95
Wharton St, WC1 .... **196** C3
Whateley Rd, SE20 .... **123** DX94
SE22 .... **122** DT85
Whatley Av, SW20 .... **139** CY97
Whatman Rd, SE23 .... **123** DX87
Whatmore Cl, Stai. TW19 .... **114** BG86
Wheatash Rd, Add. KT15 .... **134** BH103
Wheatcroft, Wal.Cr. (Chsht) EN7 .... **14** DV28
Wheatfields, E6
off Oxleas **87** EP72
Enfield EN3 .... **31** DY40
Wheatfield Way, Kings.T. KT1 .... **138** CL96
Wheathill Rd, SE20 .... **142** DV97
Wheat Knoll, Ken. CR8 .... **176** DQ116
Wheatlands, Houns. TW5 .... **96** CA79
Wheatlands Rd, SW17
off Stapleton Rd **120** DG90
Slough SL3 .... **92** AV76
Wheatley Cl, NW4 .... **43** CU54
Greenhithe DA9
off Steele Av **129** FU85
Hornchurch RM11 .... **72** FK57
Wheatley Cres, Hayes UB3 .... **77** BU73
Wheatley Dr, Wat. WD25 .... **8** BW34
Wheatley Gdns, N9 .... **46** DS47
Wheatley Ho, SW15
off Tangley Gro **119** CU87
Wheatley Rd, Islw. TW7 .... **97** CF83
Wheatley's Ait, Sun. TW16 .... **135** BU99
Wheatley St, W1 .... **194** G7
Wheatley Ter Rd, Erith DA8 .... **107** FF79
Wheatley Way, Ger.Cr. (Chal.St.P.) SL9 .... **36** AY51
Wheat Sheaf Cl, E14 .... **204** B8
Wheatsheaf Cl, Cher. (Ott.) KT16 .... **151** BD107
Northolt UB5 .... **60** BY64
Woking GU21 .... **166** AY116
Wheatsheaf Hill, Sev. (Halst.) TN14 .... **164** EZ109
Wheatsheaf La, SW6 .... **99** CW80
SW8 .... **101** DL80
Staines TW18 .... **113** BF94
Wheatsheaf Rd, Rom. RM1 .... **71** FF58
Wheatsheaf Ter, SW6 .... **99** CZ80
Wheatstone Cl, Mitch. CR4 .... **140** DE95
Slough SL3 .... **92** AU76
Wheatstone Rd, W10 .... **81** CY71
Wheeler Av, Oxt. RH8 .... **187** ED129
Wheeler Cl, Wdf.Grn. IG8
off Chigwell Rd **49** EM50
Wheeler Gdns, N1
off Outram Pl **83** DL67
Wheeler Pl, Brom. BR2 .... **144** EH98
Wheelers, Epp. CM16 .... **17** ET29
Wheelers Cross, Bark. IG11 .... **87** ER68
Wheelers Dr, Ruis. HA4
off Wallington Cl **59** BQ58
Wheelers Fm Gdns, Epp. (N.Wld Bas.) CM16 .... **19** FB26
Wheelers La, Epsom KT18 .... **156** CP113
Wheelers Orchard, Ger.Cr. (Chal.St.P.) SL9 .... **36** AY51
Wheel Fm Dr, Dag. RM10 .... **71** FC62
Wheelock Cl, Erith DA8 .... **107** FB80
Wheelwright Cl, Bushey WD23 *off Ashfield Av* **24** CB44
Wheelwright St, N7 .... **83** DM66
Whelan Way, Wall. SM6 .... **141** DK104
Wheler St, E1 .... **197** P5
Whellock Rd, W4 .... **98** CS76
WHELPLEY HILL, Chesh. HP5 .... **4** AX26
Whelpley Hill Pk, Chesh. (Whel.Hill) HP5 .... **4** AX26
Whenman Av, Bex. DA5 .... **127** FC89
Whernside Cl, SE28 .... **88** EW73
WHETSTONE, N20 .... **44** DB47
Whetstone Cl, N20
off Oakleigh Rd N **44** DD47
Whetstone Pk, WC2 .... **196** B8
Whetstone Rd, SE3 .... **104** EJ82
Whewell Rd, N19 .... **65** DL61
Whichcote St, SE1 .... **200** D3
Whidborne Cl, SE8
off Cliff Ter **103** EA82
Whidborne St, WC1 .... **196** A3
Whiffins Orchard, Epp. (Cooper.) CM16 .... **18** EX29
Whimbrel Cl, SE28 .... **88** EW73
South Croydon CR2 .... **160** DR111
Whimbrel Way, Hayes UB4 .... **78** BX72
Whinchat Rd, SE28 .... **105** ER76
Whinfell Cl, SW16 .... **121** DK92
Whinfell Way, Grav. DA12 .... **131** GM91
Whinyates Rd, SE9 .... **104** EL83
Whippendell Cl, Orp. BR5 .... **146** EV95
Whippendell Hill, Kings L. WD4 .... **6** BJ30
Whippendell Rd, Wat. WD18 .... **23** BU43
Whippendell Way, Orp. BR5 .... **146** EV95
Whipps Cross Rd, E11 .... **67** ED57
🄷 **Whipps Cross Uni Hosp**, E11 .... **67** ED58
Whiskin St, EC1 .... **196** F3
Whisperwood, Rick. (Loud.) WD3 .... **22** BH41
Whisperwood Cl, Har. HA3 .... **41** CE52
Whistler Gdns, Edg. HA8 .... **42** CM54
Whistler Ms, SE15
off Kelly Av **102** DT80
Dagenham RM8
off Fitzstephen Rd **70** EV64
Whistlers Av, SW11 .... **100** DD80
Whistler St, N5 .... **65** DP63
Whistler Twr, SW10
off World's End Est **100** DC80
Whistler Wk, SW10
off World's End Est **100** DC80
Whiston Rd, E2 .... **84** DT68
Whitacre Ms, SE11
off Stannary St **101** DN78
Whitakers Way, Loug. IG10 .... **33** EM39
Whitbread Cl, N17 .... **46** DU53
Whitbread Rd, SE4 .... **103** DY84
Whitburn Rd, SE13 .... **103** EB84
Whitby Av, NW10 .... **80** CP69
Whitby Cl, Green. DA9 .... **129** FU85
Westerham (Bigg.H.) TN16 .... **178** EH119
Whitby Ct, N7 *off Camden Rd* **65** DL63
Whitby Gdns, NW9 .... **62** CN55
Sutton SM1 .... **140** DD103
Whitby Rd, SE18 .... **105** EM77
Harrow HA2 .... **60** CC62
Ruislip HA4 .... **59** BV62
Sutton SM1 .... **140** DD103
Whitby St, E1 .... **197** P4
Whitcher Cl, SE14 .... **103** DY79
Whitcher Pl, NW1
off Rochester Rd **83** DJ66
Whitchurch Av, Edg. HA8 .... **42** CM52
Whitchurch Cl, Edg. HA8 .... **42** CM51
Whitchurch Gdns, Edg. HA8 .... **42** CM51
Whitchurch La, Edg. HA8 .... **41** CK52
Whitchurch Rd, W11 .... **81** CX73
Romford RM3 .... **52** FK49
Whitcomb Ct, WC2
off Whitcomb St **83** DK73
Whitcomb St, WC2 .... **199** N1
Whitcome Ms, Rich. TW9 .... **98** CP81
Whiteadder Way, E14 .... **204** C8
Whitear Wk, E15 .... **85** ED65
White Av, Grav. (Nthflt) DA11 .... **131** GF90
Whitebarn La, Dag. RM10 .... **88** FA67
Whitebeam Av, Brom. BR2 .... **145** EN100
Whitebeam Cl, SW9
off Clapham Rd **101** DM80
Radlett (Shenley) WD7
off Mulberry Gdns **10** CM33
Waltham Cross EN7 .... **14** DS26
Whitebeam Dr, S.Ock. RM15 .... **91** FW69
Whitebeam Ho, NW3
off Maitland Pk Rd **82** DF65
White Beams, St.Alb. (Park St) AL2 .... **8** CC28
White Beam Way, Tad. KT20 .... **173** CU121
White Bear Pl, NW3
off New End Sq **64** DD63
White Br Av, Mitch. CR4 .... **140** DD98
Whitebridge Cl, Felt. TW14 .... **115** BT86
White Butts Rd, Ruis. HA4 .... **60** BX62
WHITECHAPEL, E1 .... **84** DU72
⊖ **Whitechapel** **84** DV71
★ **Whitechapel Art Gall**, E1 .... **84** DT72
Whitechapel High St, E1 .... **84** DT72
Whitechapel Rd, E1 .... **84** DU72
White Ch La, E1 .... **84** DU72
White Ch Pas, E1
off White Ch La **84** DU72
⊖ **White City** **81** CW73
White City Cl, W12 .... **81** CW73
White City Est, W12 .... **81** CV73
White City Rd, W12 .... **81** CV73
White Conduit St, N1
off Chapel Mkt **83** DN68
Whitecote Rd, Sthl. UB1 .... **78** CB72
White Craig Cl, Pnr. HA5 .... **40** CA50
Whitecroft, Swan. BR8 .... **147** FE96
Whitecroft Cl, Beck. BR3 .... **143** ED98
Whitecroft Way, Beck. BR3 .... **143** EC99
Whitecross Pl, EC2 .... **197** L6
Whitecross St, EC1 .... **197** J4
Whitefield Av, NW2 .... **63** CW59
Purley CR8 .... **175** DN116
Whitefield Cl, SW15 .... **119** CY86
Orpington BR5 .... **146** EW97
Whitefields Rd, Wal.Cr. (Chsht) EN8 .... **14** DW28
Whitefoot La, Brom. BR1 .... **123** EC91
Whitefoot Ter, Brom. BR1 .... **124** EE90
Whiteford Rd, Slou. SL2 .... **74** AS71
White Friars, Sev. TN13 .... **190** FG127
Whitefriars Av, Har. HA3 .... **41** CE54
Whitefriars Dr, Har. HA3 .... **41** CD54
Whitefriars St, EC4 .... **196** E9
White Gdns, Dag. RM10 .... **88** FA65
Whitegate Gdns, Har. HA3 .... **41** CF52
White Gates, Horn. RM12 .... **72** FJ61
Whitegates, Whyt. CR3
off Court Bushes Rd **176** DU119
Woking GU22 *off Loop Rd* **167** AZ120
Whitegates Cl, Rick. (Crox.Grn) WD3 .... **22** BN42
Whitegate Way, Tad. KT20 .... **173** CV120
Whitehall, SW1 .... **199** P2
White Hall, Rom. (Abridge) RM4 *off Market Pl* **34** EV41
Whitehall Cl, Chig. IG7 .... **50** EU48
Uxbridge UB8 .... **76** BJ67
Whitehall Ct, SW1 .... **199** P3
Whitehall Cres, Chess. KT9 .... **155** CK106
Whitehall Fm La, Vir.W. GU25 .... **132** AY96
Whitehall Gdns, E4 .... **48** EE46
SW1 .... **199** P3
W3 .... **80** CN74
W4 .... **98** CP79
Whitehall La, Buck.H. IG9 .... **48** EG47
Egham TW20 .... **113** AZ94
Erith DA8 .... **107** FF82
Grays RM17 .... **110** GC78
Staines (Wrays.) TW19 .... **113** BA86
Whitehall Pk, N19 .... **65** DJ60
Whitehall Pk Rd, W4 .... **98** CP79
Whitehall Pl, E7
off Brooking Rd **68** EG64
SW1 .... **199** P3
Wallington SM6
off Bernard Rd **159** DH105
Whitehall Rd, E4 .... **48** EE47
W7 .... **97** CG75
Bromley BR2 .... **144** EK99
Grays RM17 .... **110** GC77
Harrow HA1 .... **61** CE59
Thornton Heath CR7 .... **141** DN99
Uxbridge UB8 .... **76** BK67
Woodford Green IG8 .... **48** EE47
Whitehall St, N17 .... **46** DT52
White Hart Av, SE18 .... **105** ET76
SE28 .... **105** ET76
White Hart Cl, Ch.St.G. HP8 .... **36** AU48
Sevenoaks TN13 .... **191** FJ128
White Hart Ct, EC2
off Bishopsgate **84** DS72
Woking (Ripley) GU23 .... **168** BJ121
⇌ **White Hart Lane** **46** DT52
White Hart La, N17 .... **46** DR52
N22 .... **45** DN53
NW10 *off Church Rd* **81** CT65
SW13 .... **98** CS83
Romford RM7 .... **50** FA53
White Hart Meadows, Wok. (Ripley) GU23 .... **168** BJ121
White Hart Rd, SE18 .... **105** ES77
Orpington BR6 .... **146** EU101
White Hart Row, Cher. KT16
off Heriot Rd **134** BG101
White Hart Slip, Brom. BR1
off Market Sq **144** EG96
White Hart St, EC4 .... **196** G8
SE11 .... **200** E10
White Hart Wd, Sev. TN13 .... **191** FJ129
White Hart Yd, SE1 .... **201** K3
Whitehaven, Slou. SL1 .... **74** AT73
Whitehaven Cl, Brom. BR2 .... **144** EG98
Waltham Cross (Goffs Oak) EN7 .... **14** DS28
Whitehaven St, NW8 .... **194** B5
Whitehead Cl, N18 .... **46** DR50
SW18 .... **120** DC87
Dartford DA2 .... **128** FJ90
Whitehead's Gro, SW3 .... **198** C10
Whiteheart Av, Uxb. UB8 .... **77** BQ71
Whiteheath Av, Ruis. HA4 .... **59** BQ59
White Heron Ms, Tedd. TW11 .... **117** CF93
White Hill, Couls. (Chipstead) CR5 .... **174** DC124
Northwood HA6 .... **38** BN51
Rickmansworth WD3 .... **38** BN51
South Croydon CR2
off St. Mary's Rd **160** DR109
Whitehill La, Grav. DA12 .... **131** GK90
Redhill (Bletch.) RH1 .... **186** DR127
Woking (Ock.) GU23 .... **169** BQ123
Whitehill Par, Grav. DA12 .... **131** GJ90
Whitehill Pl, Vir.W. GU25 .... **132** AY99
White Hill Rd, Chesh. HP5 .... **4** AX26
Whitehill Rd, Dart. DA1 .... **127** FG85
Gravesend DA12 .... **131** GJ89
Gravesend (Hook Grn) DA13 .... **149** FX96
Longfield DA3 .... **149** FX96
Whitehills Rd, Loug. IG10 .... **33** EN41
White Horse All, EC1 .... **196** F6
White Horse Dr, Epsom KT18 .... **156** CQ114
Whitehorse Hill, Chis. BR7 .... **125** EN91
White Horse La, E1 .... **85** DX70
Whitehorse La, SE25 .... **142** DR98
White Horse La, St.Alb. (Lon.Col.) AL2 .... **10** CL25
Woking (Ripley) GU23 .... **168** BJ121
White Horse Ms, SE1 .... **200** E6
White Horse Rd, E1 .... **85** DY72
E6 .... **87** EM69
Whitehorse Rd, Croy. CR0 .... **142** DR100
Thornton Heath CR7 .... **142** DR100
White Horse St, W1 .... **199** H3
White Horse Yd, EC2 .... **197** K8
Whitehouse Apts, SE1
off Belvedere Rd **83** DM74
Whitehouse Av, Borwd. WD6 .... **26** CP41
White Ho Cl, Ger.Cr. (Chal.St.P.) SL9 .... **36** AY52
White Ho Dr, Stan. HA7 .... **41** CJ49
Whitehouse La, Abb.L. (Bedmond) WD5 .... **7** BV26
Enfield EN2
off Brigadier Hill **30** DQ39
White Ho La, Sev. TN14 .... **190** FF130
White Ho Rd, Sev. TN14 .... **190** FF130
Whitehouse Way, N14 .... **45** DH47
Iver SL0 .... **75** BD69
Slough SL3 .... **92** AW76
Whitehurst Dr, N18 .... **47** DX51
White Kennett St, E1 .... **197** N8
White Knights Rd, Wey. KT13 .... **153** BQ108
White Knobs Way, Cat. CR3 .... **186** DU125
Whitelands Av, Rick. (Chorl.) WD3 .... **21** BC42
Whitelands Cres, SW18 .... **119** CY87
Whitelands Way, Rom. RM3 .... **52** FK54
White La, Oxt. RH8 .... **178** EH123
Warlingham CR6 .... **178** EH123
Whiteledges, W13 .... **79** CJ72
Whitelegg Rd, E13 .... **86** EF68
Whiteley Rd, SE19 .... **122** DR92
Whiteleys Shop Cen, W2 .... **82** DB72
Whiteleys Way, Felt. TW13 .... **116** CA90
WHITELEY VILLAGE, Walt. KT12 .... **153** BS110
White Lion Cl, Amer. HP7 .... **20** AU39
White Lion Ct, EC3 .... **197** M9
White Lion Gate, Cob. KT11
off Virginia Pl **153** BU114
White Lion Hill, EC4 .... **196** G10
White Lion Rd, Amer. HP7 .... **20** AT38
White Lion St, N1 .... **196** D1
White Lo, SE19 .... **121** DP94
White Lo Cl, N2 .... **64** DD58
Isleworth TW7 .... **97** CG82
Sevenoaks TN13 .... **191** FH123
Sutton SM2 .... **158** DC108
White Lyon Ct, EC2
off Fann St **84** DQ70
White Lyons Rd, Brwd. CM14 .... **54** FW47
White Oak Business Pk, Swan. BR8 *off London Rd* **147** FE97
White Oak Dr, Beck. BR3 .... **143** EC96
White Oak Gdns, Sid. DA15 .... **125** ET87
White Oaks, Bans. SM7 .... **158** DB113
Whiteoaks La, Grnf. UB6 .... **79** CD68
White Orchards, N20 .... **43** CZ45
Stanmore HA7 .... **41** CG50
White Post Hill, Dart. (Fnghm) DA4 .... **148** FN101
Whitepost Hill, Red. RH1 .... **184** DE134
White Post La, E9 .... **85** DZ66
SE13 .... **103** EA83
White Post St, SE15 .... **102** DW80
White Rd, E15 .... **86** EE66
Betchworth RH3 .... **182** CN133
Tadworth (Box H.) KT20 .... **182** CN133
White Rose La, Wok. GU22 .... **167** AZ117
Whites Av, Ilf. IG2 .... **69** ES58
Whites Cl, Green. DA9 .... **129** FW86
Whites Grds, SE1 .... **201** N5
Whites Grds Est, SE1
off Whites Grds **102** DS75
White Shack La, Rick. WD3 .... **22** BM37
Whites La, Slou. (Datchet) SL3 .... **92** AV79
Whites Meadow, Brom. BR2
off Blackbrook La **145** EN98
White's Row, E1 .... **197** P7
White's Sq, SW4
off Nelson's Row **101** DK84
Whitestile Rd, Brent. TW8 .... **97** CJ78
Whitestone La, NW3
off Heath St **64** DC62
Whitestone Wk, NW3
off North End Way **64** DC62
White St, Sthl. UB1 .... **96** BX75
White Swan Ms, W4
off Bennett St **98** CS79
Whitethorn Av, Couls. CR5 .... **174** DG115
West Drayton UB7 .... **76** BL73
Whitethorn Gdns, Croy. CR0 .... **142** DV103
Enfield EN2 .... **30** DR43
Hornchurch RM11 .... **72** FJ58
Whitethorn Pl, West Dr. UB7
off Whitethorn Av **76** BM74
Whitethorn St, E3 .... **85** EA70
Whiteways Ct, Stai. TW18
off Pavilion Gdns **114** BH94
Whitewebbs La, Enf. EN2 .... **30** DS35
Whitewebbs Pk, Enf. EN2 .... **30** DQ35
Whitewebbs Rd, Enf. EN2 .... **29** DP35
Whitewebbs Way, Orp. BR5 .... **145** ET95
Whitewood Cotts, West. (Tats.) TN16 .... **178** EJ120
Whitfield Cres, Dart. DA2 .... **128** FQ87
Whitfield Pl, W1 .... **195** K5
Whitfield Rd, E6 .... **86** EJ66
SE3 .... **103** ED81
Bexleyheath DA7 .... **106** EZ80
Whitfield St, W1 .... **195** M7
Whitfield Way, Rick. (Mill End) WD3 .... **37** BF46
Whitford Gdns, Mitch. CR4 .... **140** DF97
Whitgift Av, S.Croy. CR2 .... **160** DQ106
Whitgift Cen, Croy. CR0 .... **142** DQ103
Whitgift Ho, SW11
off Westbridge Rd **100** DE81
Whitgift St, SE11 .... **200** B8
Croydon CR0 .... **142** DQ104
Whit Hern Ct, Wal.Cr. (Chsht) EN8 *off College Rd* **14** DW30
Whiting Av, Bark. IG11 .... **87** EP66
Whitings, Ilf. IG2 .... **69** ER57
Whitings Rd, Barn. EN5 .... **27** CW43
Whitings Way, E6 .... **87** EN71
Whitland Rd, Cars. SM5 .... **140** DD102
Whitlars Dr, Kings L. WD4 .... **6** BM28
Whitley Cl, Abb.L. WD5 .... **7** BU32
Staines (Stanw.) TW19 .... **114** BL86
Whitley Ho, SW1
off Churchill Gdns **101** DJ78
Whitley Rd, N17 .... **46** DS54
Whitlock Dr, SW19 .... **119** CY87
Whitman Rd, E3
off Mile End Rd **85** DY70
Whitmead Cl, S.Croy. CR2 .... **160** DS107
Whitmore Av, Rom. (Harold Wd) RM3 .... **52** FL54
Whitmore Cl, N11 .... **45** DH50
Whitmore Est, N1 .... **84** DS67
Whitmore Gdns, NW10 .... **81** CW68
Whitmore Rd, N1 .... **84** DS67
Beckenham BR3 .... **143** DZ97
Harrow HA1 .... **60** CC59
Whitmores Cl, Epsom KT18 .... **172** CQ115
Whitnell Way, SW15 .... **119** CX85
Whitney Av, Ilf. IG4 .... **68** EK56
Whitney Rd, E10 .... **67** EB59
Whitney Wk, Sid. DA14 .... **126** EY93
Whitstable Cl, Beck. BR3 .... **143** DZ95
Ruislip HA4
off Chichester Av **59** BS61
Whitstable Ho, W10 .... **81** CX72
Whitstable Pl, Croy. CR0 .... **160** DQ105
Whitstone La, Beck. BR3 .... **143** EB99
Whittaker Av, Rich. TW9
off Hill St **117** CK85
Whittaker Rd, E6 .... **86** EJ66
Sutton SM3 .... **139** CZ104
Whittaker St, SW1 .... **198** F9
Whittaker Way, SE1 .... **202** C9
Whitta Rd, E12 .... **68** EK63
Whittell Gdns, SE26 .... **122** DW90
Whittenham Cl, Slou. SL2 .... **74** AU74
Whittingstall Rd, SW6 .... **99** CZ81
Whittington Av, EC3 .... **197** M9
Hayes UB4 .... **77** BT71
Whittington Ct, N2 .... **64** DF57
🄷 **Whittington Hosp**, N19 .... **65** DJ61
Whittington Ms, N12 .... **44** DC49
Whittington Rd, N22 .... **45** DL52
Brentwood (Hutt.) CM13 .... **55** GC44
Whittington Way, Pnr. HA5 .... **60** BY57
Whittlebury Cl, Cars. SM5 .... **158** DF108
Whittle Cl, E17 .... **67** DY58
Southall UB1 .... **78** CB72
Watford (Lvsdn) WD25 .... **7** BT34
Whittle Rd, Houns. TW5 .... **96** BW80
Southall UB2 *off Post Rd* **96** CB75
Whittlesea Cl, Har. HA3 .... **40** CC52
Whittlesea Path, Har. HA3 .... **40** CC53
Whittlesea Rd, Har. HA3 .... **40** CC53
Whittlesey St, SE1 .... **200** D3
WHITTON, Twick. TW2 .... **116** CB87
⇌ **Whitton** **116** CC87
Whitton Av E, Grnf. UB6 .... **61** CE64
Whitton Av W, Grnf. UB6 .... **60** CC64
Northolt UB5 .... **60** CC64
Whitton Cl, Grnf. UB6 .... **79** CH65
Whitton Dene, Houns. TW3 .... **116** CB85
Isleworth TW7 .... **117** CD85
Whitton Dr, Grnf. UB6 .... **79** CG65
Whitton Manor Rd, Islw. TW7 .... **116** CC85
Whitton Rd, Houns. TW3 .... **96** CB84
Twickenham TW1, TW2 .... **117** CF86
Whitton Wk, E3 .... **85** EA68
Whitton Waye, Houns. TW3 .... **116** CA86
Whitwell Rd, E13 .... **86** EG69
Watford WD25 .... **24** BX35
Whitworth Cres, Enf. EN3
off Martini Dr **31** EA37
Whitworth Rd, SE18 .... **105** EN80
SE25 .... **142** DS97
Whitworth St, SE10 .... **205** J10
Whopshott Av, Wok. GU21 .... **166** AW116
Whopshott Cl, Wok. GU21 .... **166** AW116
Whopshott Dr, Wok. GU21 .... **166** AW116
Whorlton Rd, SE15 .... **102** DV83
Whybridge Cl, Rain. RM13 .... **89** FE67
Whychcote Pt, NW2
off Claremont Rd **63** CW59
Whymark Av, N22 .... **65** DN55
Whymark Cl, Rain. RM13 .... **89** FF68
Whytebeam Vw, Whyt. CR3 .... **176** DT118
Whytecliffe Rd N, Pur. CR8 .... **159** DP111
Whytecliffe Rd S, Pur. CR8 .... **159** DN111
Whytecroft, Houns. TW5 .... **96** BX80
WHYTELEAFE, Cat. CR3 .... **176** DS118
⇌ **Whyteleafe** **176** DT117
Whyteleafe Business Village, Whyt. CR3 *off Whyteleafe Hill* **176** DT117
Whyteleafe Hill, Whyt. CR3 .... **176** DT118
Whyteleafe Rd, Cat. CR3 .... **176** DS120
⇌ **Whyteleafe South** **176** DU119
Whyteville Rd, E7 .... **86** EH65
Wichling Cl, Orp. BR5 .... **146** EX102
Wickenden Rd, Sev. TN13 .... **191** FJ122
Wicken's Meadow, Sev. (Dunt.Grn) TN14 .... **181** FF119
Wickersley Rd, SW11 .... **100** DG82
Wickers Oake, SE19 .... **122** DT91
Wicker St, E1 *off Burslem St* **84** DV72
Wicket, The, Croy. CR0 .... **161** EA106
Wicket Rd, Grnf. UB6 .... **79** CG69
Wickets, The, Ashf. TW15 .... **114** BL91
Wickets End, Rad. (Shenley) WD7 .... **10** CL33
Wickets Way, Ilf. IG6 .... **49** ET51
Wickford Cl, Rom. RM3
off Wickford Dr **52** FM50
Wickford Dr, Rom. RM3 .... **52** FM50
Wickford St, E1 .... **84** DW70
Wickford Way, E17 .... **67** DX56
Wickham Av, Croy. CR0 .... **143** DY103
Sutton SM3 .... **157** CW106
Wickham Chase, W.Wick. BR4 .... **143** ED101
Wickham Cl, E1 .... **84** DW71
Enfield EN3 .... **30** DV41

★ Place of interest ⇌ Railway station ⊖ London Underground station DLR Docklands Light Railway station Tram Tramlink station 🄷 Hospital Riv Pedestrian ferry landing stage

Wickham Cl, N. Mal. KT3 . . .139 CT99
Uxbridge (Hare.) UB9 . . .38 BK53
Wickham Ct Rd, W.Wick. BR4 . . .143 EC103
Wickham Cres, W.Wick. BR4 .143 EC103
Wickham Fld, Sev. (Otford) TN14 . . .181 FF116
Wickham Gdns, SE4 . . .103 DZ83
Wickham La, SE2 . . .106 EU78
Egham TW20 . . .113 BA94
Welling DA16 . . .106 EU78
Wickham Ms, SE4 . . .103 DZ82
Wickham Rd, E4 . . .47 EC52
SE4 . . .103 DZ84
Beckenham BR3 . . .143 EB96
Croydon CR0 . . .143 DX103
Grays RM16 . . .111 GJ75
Harrow HA3 . . .41 CD54
Wickham St, SE11 . . .200 B10
Welling DA16 . . .105 ES82
Wickham Way, Beck. BR3 . . .143 EC98
Wick La, E3 . . .85 EA68
Egham (Eng.Grn) TW20 . . .112 AT92
Wickliffe Av, N3 . . .43 CY54
Wickliffe Gdns, Wem. HA9 . . .62 CP61
Wicklow St, WC1 . . .196 B2
Wick Rd, E9 . . .85 DX65
Egham (Eng.Grn) TW20 . . .112 AV94
Teddington TW11 . . .117 CH94
Wicks Cl, SE9 . . .124 EK91
Wicksteed Cl, Bex. DA5 . . .127 FD90
Wicksteed Ho, Brent. TW8 off Green Dragon La . . .98 CM78
Wickwood St, SE5 . . .101 DP82
Wid Cl, Brwd. (Hutt.) CM13 . . .55 GD43
Widdecombe Av, Har. HA2 . . .60 BY61
Widdenham Rd, N7 . . .65 DM63
Widdin St, E15 . . .85 ED66
Widecombe Cl, Rom. RM3 . . .52 FK53
Widecombe Gdns, Ilf. IG4 . . .68 EL56
Widecombe Rd, SE9 . . .124 EL90
Widecombe Way, N2 . . .64 DD57
Widecroft Rd, Iver SL0 . . .75 BE72
Widegate St, E1 . . .197 N7
Widenham Cl, Pnr. HA5 off Bridle Rd . . .60 BW57
Wide Way, Mitch. CR4 . . .141 DK97
Widewing Cl, Tedd. TW11 . . .117 CH94
Widgeon Cl, E16 off Maplin Rd . . .86 EH72
Widgeon Rd, Erith DA8 . . .107 FH80
Widgeon Way, Wat. WD25 . . .24 BY36
Widley Rd, W9 . . .82 DA69
WIDMORE, Brom. BR1 . . .144 EH97
WIDMORE GREEN, Brom. BR1 . . .144 EJ95
Widmore Lo Rd, Brom. BR1 .144 EK96
Widmore Rd, Brom. BR1 . . .144 EG96
Uxbridge UB8 . . .77 BP70
Widworthy Hayes, Brwd. (Hutt.) CM13 . . .55 GB46
Wieland Rd, Nthwd. HA6 . . .39 BU52
Wigan Ho, E5 off Warwick Gro . . .66 DV60
Wigeon Path, SE28 . . .105 ER76
Wigeon Way, Hayes UB4 . . .78 BX72
Wiggenhall Rd, Wat. WD18 . . .23 BV43
Wiggie La, Red. RH1 . . .184 DG132
Wiggins La, Rich. TW10 . . .117 CJ89
Wiggins Mead, NW9 . . .43 CT52
Wigginton Av, Wem. HA9 . . .80 CP65
Wigham Ho, Bark. IG11 . . .87 EQ66
Wightman Rd, N4 . . .65 DN57
N8 . . .65 DN56
Wigley Bush La, Brwd. (S.Wld) CM14 . . .54 FS47
Wigley Rd, Felt. TW13 . . .116 BX88
Wigmore Ct, W13 off Singapore Rd . . .79 CG74
Wigmore Pl, W1 . . .195 H8
Wigmore Rd, Cars. SM5 . . .140 DD103
Wigmore St, W1 . . .194 F9
Wigmore Wk, Cars. SM5 . . .140 DD103
Wigram Rd, E11 . . .68 EJ58
Wigram Sq, E17 . . .47 EC54
Wigston Cl, N18 . . .46 DS50
Wigston Rd, E13 . . .86 EH70
Wigton Gdns, Stan. HA7 . . .42 CL53
Wigton Pl, SE11 off Milverton St . . .101 DN78
Wigton Rd, E17 . . .47 DZ53
Romford RM3 . . .52 FL49
Wigton Way, Rom. RM3 . . .52 FL49
Wilberforce Ct, Kes. BR2 . . .162 EK107
Wilberforce Ms, SW4 off Stonhouse St . . .101 DK84
Wilberforce Rd, N4 . . .65 DP61
NW9 . . .63 CU58
Wilberforce Way, SW19 . . .119 CX93
Gravesend DA12 . . .131 GK92
Wilbraham Pl, SW1 . . .198 E8
Wilbury Av, Sutt. SM2 . . .157 CZ110
Wilbury Rd, Wok. GU21 . . .166 AX117
Wilbury Way, N18 . . .46 DR50
Wilby Ms, W11 . . .81 CZ74
Wilcon Way, Wat. WD25 . . .8 BX34
Wilcot Av, Wat. WD19 . . .40 BY45
Wilcot Cl, Wat. WD19 off Wilcot Av . . .40 BY45
Wilcox Cl, SW8 . . .101 DL80
Borehamwood WD6 . . .26 CQ39
Wilcox Gdns, Shep. TW17 . . .134 BM97
Wilcox Pl, SW1 . . .199 L7
Wilcox Rd, SW8 . . .101 DL80
Sutton SM1 . . .158 DB105
Teddington TW11 . . .117 CD91
Wildacres, Nthwd. HA6 . . .39 BT49
West Byfleet KT14 . . .152 BJ111
Wildbank Ct, Wok. GU22 off White Rose La . . .167 AZ118
Wild Ct, WC2 . . .196 B8
Wildcroft Gdns, Edg. HA8 . . .41 CK51
Wildcroft Rd, SW15 . . .119 CW87
Wilde Cl, E8 . . .84 DU67
Tilbury RM18 off Coleridge Rd . . .111 GJ82
Wilde Pl, N13 off Medesenge Way . . .45 DP51
Wilde Pl, SW18 off Heathfield Rd . . .120 DD87
Wilder Cl, Ruis. HA4 . . .59 BV60
Wilderness, The, E.Mol. KT8 .136 CC99
Hampton (Hmptn H.) TW12 off Park Rd . . .116 CB91
WILDERNESSE, Sev. TN15 . .191 FL122
Wildernesse Av, Sev. TN15 . .191 FL122
Wildernesse Mt, Sev. TN13 . .191 FK122
Wilderness Ms, SW4 off The Chase . . .101 DH84
Wilderness Rd, Chis. BR7 . . .125 EP94
Oxted RH8 . . .188 EE130
Wilde Rd, Erith DA8 . . .107 FB80
Wilders Cl, Wok. GU21 . . .166 AW118
Wilderton Rd, N16 . . .66 DS59
Wildfell Rd, SE6 . . .123 EB87
Wild Goose Dr, SE14 . . .102 DW81
Wild Grn N, Slou. SL3 off Verney Rd . . .93 BA77
Wild Grn S, Slou. SL3 . . .93 BA77
Wild Hatch, NW11 . . .64 DA58
Wild Oaks Cl, Nthwd. HA6 . . .39 BT51
Wild's Rents, SE1 . . .201 M6
Wild St, WC2 . . .196 A9
Wildwood, Nthwd. HA6 . . .39 BR51
Wildwood Av, St.Alb. (Brick.Wd) AL2 . . .8 BZ30
Wildwood Cl, SE12 . . .124 EF87
Woking GU22 . . .167 BF115
Wildwood Ct, Ken. CR8 . . .176 DR115
Wildwood Gro, NW3 off North End Way . . .64 DC60
Wildwood Ri, NW11 . . .64 DC60
Wildwood Rd, NW11 . . .64 DC59
Wildwood Ter, NW3 . . .64 DC60
Wilford Cl, Enf. EN2 . . .30 DR41
Northwood HA6 . . .39 BR52
Wilford Rd, Slou. SL3 . . .92 AY77
Wilfred Av, Rain. RM13 . . .89 FG71
Wilfred Owen Cl, SW19 off Tennyson Rd . . .120 DC93
Wilfred St, SW1 . . .199 K6
Gravesend DA12 . . .131 GH86
Woking GU21 . . .166 AX118
Wilfred Turney Est, W6 off Hammersmith Gro . . .99 CW75
Wilfrid Gdns, W3 . . .80 CQ71
Wilhelmina Av, Couls. CR5 . .175 DJ119
Wilkes Rd, Brent. TW8 . . .98 CL79
Brentwood (Hutt.) CM13 . . .55 GD43
Wilkes St, E1 . . .84 DT71
Wilkins Cl, Hayes UB3 . . .95 BT78
Mitcham CR4 . . .140 DE95
Wilkins Ho, SW1 off Churchill Gdns . . .101 DJ78
Wilkinson Cl, Dart. DA1 . . .108 FM84
Uxbridge UB10 . . .77 BP67
Waltham Cross (Chsht) EN7 . . .14 DQ26
Wilkinson Gdns, SE25 . . .142 DS95
Wilkinson Rd, E16 . . .86 EJ72
Wilkinson St, SW8 . . .101 DM80
Wilkinson Way, W4 . . .98 CR75
Wilkin St, NW5 . . .83 DH65
Wilkin St Ms, NW5 off Wilkin St . . .83 DH65
Wilkins Way, West. (Brasted) TN16 . . .180 EV124
Wilks Av, Dart. DA1 . . .128 FM89
Wilks Gdns, Croy. CR0 . . .143 DY102
Wilks Pl, N1 . . .197 N1
Willan Rd, N17 . . .46 DR54
Willan Wall, E16 off Victoria Dock Rd . . .86 EF73
Willard St, SW8 . . .101 DH83
Willats Cl, Cher. KT16 . . .133 BF100
Willcocks Cl, Chess. KT9 . . .138 CL104
Willcott Rd, W3 . . .80 CP74
Will Crooks Gdns, SE9 . . .104 EJ84
Willen Fld Rd, NW10 . . .80 CQ68
Willenhall Av, Barn. EN5 . . .28 DC44
Willenhall Dr, Hayes UB3 . . .77 BS73
Willenhall Rd, SE18 . . .105 EP78
Willersley Av, Orp. BR6 . . .145 ER104
Sidcup DA15 . . .125 ET88
Willersley Cl, Sid. DA15 . . .125 ET88
WILLESDEN, NW10 . . .81 CT65
WILLESDEN GREEN, NW10 . .81 CV66
⊖ Willesden Green . . .81 CW65
⇌ Willesden Junction . . .81 CT69
⊖ Willesden Junction . . .81 CT69
Willesden La, NW2 . . .81 CX65
NW6 . . .81 CX65
Willes Rd, NW5 . . .83 DH65
Willett Cl, Nthlt. UB5 off Broomcroft Av . . .78 BW69
Orpington BR5 . . .145 ES100
Willett Ho, E13 off Queens Rd W . . .86 EG68
Willett Pl, Th.Hth. CR7 off Willett Rd . . .141 DN99
Willett Rd, Th.Hth. CR7 . . .141 DN99
Willetts La, Uxb. (Denh.) UB9 .57 BF63
Willett Way, Orp. BR5 . . .145 ER99
Willey Broom La, Cat. (Chaldon) CR3 . . .185 DN125
Willey Fm La, Cat. (Chaldon) CR3 . . .186 DQ126
Willey La, Cat. (Chaldon) CR3 .186 DR125
William Barefoot Dr, SE9 . . .125 EN91
William Bonney Est, SW4 . . .101 DK84
William Booth Rd, SE20 . . .142 DU95
William Carey Way, Har. HA1 .61 CE59
William Cl, N2 off King St . . .64 DD55
SE13 . . .103 EC82
Romford RM5 . . .51 FC53
Southall UB2 off Windmill Av . . .96 CC75
William Cory Prom, Erith DA8 . . .107 FE78
William Covell Cl, Enf. EN2 . . .29 DM38
William Dr, Stan. HA7 . . .41 CG51
William Dunbar Ho, NW6 . . .81 CZ68
William Dyce Ms, SW16 off Babington Rd . . .121 DK91
William Ellis Cl, Wind. (Old Wind.) SL4 . . .112 AU85
William Ellis Way, SE16 . . .202 C7
William Evans Rd, Epsom KT19 . . .156 CN111
William IV St, WC2 . . .199 P1
William Gdns, SW15 . . .119 CV85
William Guy Gdns, E3 off Talwin St . . .85 EB69
William Harvey Ho, SW19 off Whitlock Dr . . .119 CY88
William Henry Wk, SW8 off Nine Elms La . . .101 DK79
William Hunter Way, Brwd. CM14 . . .54 FW47
William Margrie Cl, SE15 off Moncrieff St . . .102 DU82
William Ms, SW1 . . .198 E5
William Morley Cl, E6 . . .86 EK67
William Morris Cl, E17 . . .67 DZ55
★ William Morris Gall, E17 off Lloyd Pk . . .67 EA55
William Morris Way, SW6 . . .100 DC83
William Nash Ct, Orp. BR5 off Brantwood Way . . .146 EW97
William Perkin Ct, Grnf. UB6 off Greenford Rd . . .79 CE65
William Petty Way, Orp. BR5 .146 EW102
William Pl, E3 off Roman Rd . .85 DZ68
William Rd, NW1 . . .195 K3
SW19 . . .119 CY94
Caterham CR3 . . .176 DR122
Sutton SM1 . . .158 DC106
William Rushbrooke Ho, SE16 off Eveline Lowe Est . . .102 DU77
William Russell Ct, Wok. GU21 . . .166 AS118
Williams Av, E17 . . .47 DZ53
William Saville Ho, NW6 . . .81 CZ68
Williams Bldgs, E2 . . .84 DW70
Williams Cl, N8 off Coolhurst Rd . . .65 DK58
SW6 off Pellant Rd . . .99 CY80
Addlestone KT15 off Monks Cres . . .152 BH106
Williams Dr, Houns. TW3 . . .96 CA84
Williams Gro, N22 . . .45 DN53
Surbiton KT6 . . .137 CJ100
William's La, SW14 . . .98 CQ83
Williams La, Mord. SM4 . . .140 DC99
Williamson Cl, SE10 . . .205 K10
Williamson Rd, N4 . . .65 DP58
Williamson St, N7 . . .65 DL63
Williamson Way, NW7 . . .43 CY51
Rickmansworth WD3 . . .38 BG46
William Sq, SE16 . . .203 L1
Williams Rd, W13 . . .79 CG73
Southall UB2 . . .96 BY77
Williams Ter, Croy. CR0 . . .159 DN107
William St, E10 . . .67 EB58
N17 . . .46 DT52
SW1 . . .198 E5
Barking IG11 . . .87 EQ66
Bushey WD23 . . .24 BX41
Carshalton SM5 . . .140 DE104
Gravesend DA12 . . .131 GH87
Grays RM17 . . .110 GB79
Slough SL1 . . .74 AT74
Williams Way, Dart. DA2 . . .127 FD89
Radlett WD7 . . .25 CJ35
Willifield Way, NW11 . . .63 CZ56
Willingale Cl, Brwd. (Hutt.) CM13 off Fairview Av . . .55 GE44
Loughton IG10 off Willingale Rd . . .33 EQ40
Woodford Green IG8 . . .48 EK51
Willingale Rd, Loug. IG10 . . .33 EQ41
Willingdon Rd, N22 . . .45 DP54
Willinghall Cl, Wal.Abb. EN9 .15 ED32
Willingham Cl, NW5 . . .65 DJ64
Willingham Ter, NW5 . . .65 DJ64
Willingham Way, Kings.T. KT1 . . .138 CN97
Willington Ct, E5 off Mandeville St . . .67 DY62
Willington Rd, SW9 . . .101 DL83
Willis Av, Sutt. SM2 . . .158 DE107
Willis Cl, Epsom KT18 . . .156 CP113
Willis Ho, E12 off Grantham Rd . . .69 EN62
Willis Rd, E15 . . .86 EF67
Croydon CR0 . . .142 DQ101
Erith DA8 . . .107 FC77
Willis St, E14 . . .85 EB72
Willmore End, SW19 . . .140 DB95
Willoughby Av, Croy. CR0 . . .159 DM105
Willoughby Ct, St.Alb. (Lon.Col.) AL2 . . .9 CK26
Willoughby Dr, Rain. RM13 . .89 FE66
Willoughby Gro, N17 . . .46 DV52
Willoughby Ho, EC2 off The Barbican . . .84 DR71
Willoughby La, N17 . . .46 DV52
Willoughby Ms, SW4 off Wixs La . . .101 DH84
Willoughby Pk Rd, N17 . . .46 DV52
Willoughby Pas, E14 . . .203 P2
Willoughby Rd, N8 . . .65 DN55
NW3 . . .64 DD63
Kingston upon Thames KT2 . . .138 CM95
Slough SL3 . . .93 BA76
Twickenham TW1 . . .117 CK86
Willoughbys, The, SW14 off Upper Richmond Rd W .98 CS84
Willoughby St, WC1 . . .195 P7
Willoughby Way, SE7 . . .205 P8
Willow Av, SW13 . . .99 CT82
Sidcup DA15 . . .126 EU86
Swanley BR8 . . .147 FF97
Uxbridge (Denh.) UB9 . . .58 BJ64
West Drayton UB7 . . .76 BM73
Willow Bk, SW6 . . .99 CY83
Richmond TW10 . . .117 CH90
Woking GU22 . . .166 AY122
Willowbank Gdns, Tad. KT20 .173 CV122
Willowbank Pl, Pur. CR8 off Kingsdown Av . . .159 DP109
Willowbay Cl, Barn. EN5 . . .27 CX44
Willow Br Rd, N1 . . .84 DQ65
Willowbrook Est, SE15 off Sumner Rd . . .102 DT80
Willowbrook Rd, SE15 . . .102 DT79
Southall UB2 . . .96 CA76
Staines TW19 . . .114 BL89
Willow Business Cen, Mitch. CR4 off Willow La . . .140 DF99
Willow Cl, SE6 off Verdant La . . .124 EF88
Addlestone (Wdhm) KT15 . .151 BF111
Willow Cl, Bex. DA5 . . .126 EZ86
Brentford TW8 . . .97 CJ79
Brentwood (Hutt.) CM13 . . .55 GB44
Bromley BR2 . . .145 EM99
Buckhurst Hill IG9 . . .48 EK48
Erith DA8 off Willow Rd . .107 FG81
Hornchurch RM12 . . .71 FH62
Orpington BR5 . . .146 EV101
Slough (Colnbr.) SL3 . . .93 BC80
Thornton Heath CR7 . . .141 DP100
Waltham Cross (Chsht) EN7 .14 DS26
Willow Cotts, Mitch. CR4 . . .141 DJ97
Richmond TW9 off Kew Grn .98 CN79
Willow Ct, EC2 . . .197 M4
Edgware HA8 . . .42 CL49
Willowcourt Av, Har. HA3 . . .61 CH57
Willow Cres E, Uxb. (Denh.) UB9 . . .58 BJ64
Willow Cres W, Uxb. (Denh.) UB9 . . .58 BJ64
Willowdene, N6 off Denewood Rd . . .64 DF59
Brentwood (Pilg.Hat.) CM15 .54 FT43
Willow Dene, Bushey (Bushey Hth) WD23 . . .41 CE45
Pinner HA5 . . .40 BX54
Willowdene, Wal.Cr. EN8 . . .15 DY27
Willowdene Cl, Twick. TW2 . .116 CC87
Willowdene Ct, Brwd. CM14 .54 FW49
Willow Dr, Barn. EN5 . . .27 CY42
Woking (Ripley) GU23 . . .168 BG124
Willow Edge, Kings L. WD4 . . .6 BN29
Willow End, N20 . . .44 DA47
Northwood HA6 . . .39 BU51
Surbiton KT6 . . .138 CL102
Willow Fm La, SW15 off Queens Ride . . .99 CV83
Willowfield Cl, SE18 . . .105 ES78
Willow Gdns, Houns. TW3 . . .96 CA81
Ruislip HA4 . . .59 BT61
Willow Grn, NW9 off Clayton Fld . . .42 CS53
Borehamwood WD6 . . .26 CR43
Willow Gro, E13 off Libra Rd .86 EG68
Chislehurst BR7 . . .125 EN93
Ruislip HA4 . . .59 BT61
Willowhayne Dr, Walt. KT12 .135 BV101
Willowhayne Gdns, Wor.Pk. KT4 . . .139 CW104
Willowherb Wk, Rom. RM3 off Clematis Cl . . .52 FJ52
Willow Ho, NW3 off Maitland Pk Vil . . .82 DF65
Warlingham CR6 off East Parkside . . .177 EB115
Willow La, SE18 . . .105 EM77
Amersham HP7 . . .20 AT41
Mitcham CR4 . . .140 DF99
Watford WD18 . . .23 BU43
Willow Mead, Chig. IG7 . . .50 EU48
Willowmead, Stai. TW18 . . .134 BH95
Willowmead Cl, W5 . . .79 CK71
Woking GU21 . . .166 AU116
Willowmere, Esher KT10 . . .154 CC105
Willow Mt, Croy. CR0 off Langton Way . . .142 DS104
Willow Pk, Sev. (Otford) TN14 . . .181 FF117
Slough (Stoke P.) SL2 . . .74 AU66
Willow Path, Wal.Abb. EN9 . .16 EE34
Willow Pl, SW1 . . .199 L8
Willow Rd, NW3 . . .64 DD63
W5 . . .98 CL75
Dartford DA1 . . .128 FJ88
Enfield EN1 . . .30 DS41
Erith DA8 . . .107 FG81
New Malden KT3 . . .138 CQ98
Romford RM6 . . .70 EY58
Slough (Colnbr.) SL3 . . .93 BE82
Wallington SM6 . . .159 DH108
Willows, The, Buck.H. IG9 . . .48 EK48
Esher (Clay.) KT10 . . .155 CE107
Grays RM17 . . .110 GE79
Rickmansworth (Mill End) WD3 off Uxbridge Rd . . .38 BG47
Watford WD19 off Brookside Rd . . .39 BV45
West Byfleet (Byfleet) KT14 .152 BL113
Weybridge KT13 . . .134 BN104
Willows Av, Mord. SM4 . . .140 DB99
Willows Cl, Pnr. HA5 . . .40 BW54
Willowside, St.Alb. (Lon.Col.) AL2 . . .10 CL27
Willows Path, Epsom KT18 .156 CP114
Willow St, E4 . . .47 ED45
EC2 . . .197 M4
Romford RM7 . . .71 FC56
Willow Tree Cl, E3 off Birdsfield La . . .85 DZ67
SW18 off Cargill Rd . . .120 DB88
Hayes UB4 . . .78 BW70
Willowtree Cl, Nthlt. UB5 . . .78 BY65
Willow Tree Cl, Rom. (Abridge) RM4 . . .34 EV41
Uxbridge UB10 . . .59 BQ62
Willow Tree La, Hayes UB4 . .78 BW70
Willowtree Marina, Hayes UB4 . . .78 BY72
Willow Tree Wk, Brom. BR1 .144 EH95
Willowtree Way, Th.Hth. CR7 off Kensington Av . . .141 DN95
Willow Vale, W12 . . .81 CU74
Chislehurst BR7 . . .125 EP93
Leatherhead (Fetch.) KT22 . .170 CB123
Willow Vw, SW19 . . .140 DD95
Willow Wk, E17 . . .67 DZ57
N2 . . .44 DD54
N15 . . .65 DP56
N21 . . .29 DM44
SE1 . . .201 N8
Chertsey KT16 . . .134 BG101
Dartford DA1 . . .128 FJ85
Egham (Eng.Grn) TW20 . . .112 AW92
Orpington BR6 . . .145 EP104
Sutton SM3 . . .139 CZ104
Tadworth (Box H.) KT20 off Oak Dr . . .182 CQ130
Upminster RM14 . . .73 FS60
Willow Way, N3 . . .44 DB52
SE26 . . .122 DV90
W11 off Freston Rd . . .81 CX74
Epsom KT19 . . .156 CR107
Godstone RH9 . . .186 DV132
Willow Way, Pot. B. EN6 . . .12 DB33
Radlett WD7 . . .25 CE36
Romford RM3 . . .52 FP51
St. Albans AL2 . . .8 CA27
Sunbury-on-Thames TW16 .135 BU98
Tadworth (Box H.) KT20 off Oak Dr . . .182 CP130
Twickenham TW2 . . .116 CB89
Wembley HA0 . . .61 CG62
West Byfleet KT14 . . .152 BJ111
Woking GU22 . . .166 AX121
Willow Wd Cres, SE25 . . .142 DS100
Willrose Cres, SE2 . . .106 EW78
Wills Cres, Houns. TW3 . . .116 CB86
Wills Gro, NW7 . . .43 CU50
Willson Rd, Egh. (Eng.Grn) TW20 . . .112 AV92
Wilman Gro, E8 . . .84 DU66
Wilmar Cl, Hayes UB4 . . .77 BR70
Uxbridge UB8 . . .76 BK66
Wilmar Gdns, W.Wick. BR4 . .143 EB102
Wilmcote Ho, W2 . . .82 DA71
Wilmer Cl, Kings.T. KT2 . . .118 CM92
Wilmer Cres, Kings.T. KT2 . .118 CM92
Wilmer Gdns, N1 . . .84 DS67
Wilmerhatch La, Epsom KT18 . . .172 CP118
Wilmer Ho, E3 off Daling Way . . .85 DY68
Wilmer Lea Cl, E15 . . .85 EC66
Wilmer Pl, N16 off Stoke Newington Ch St .66 DT61
Wilmer Way, N14 . . .45 DK50
WILMINGTON, Dart. DA2 . . .128 FK91
Wilmington Av, W4 . . .98 CR80
Orpington BR6 . . .146 EW103
Wilmington Ct Rd, Dart. DA2 .127 FG90
Wilmington Gdns, Bark. IG11 .87 ER65
Wilmington Sq, WC1 . . .196 D3
Wilmington St, WC1 . . .196 D3
Wilmot Cl, N2 . . .44 DC54
SE15 . . .102 DU80
Wilmot Grn, Brwd. (Gt Warley) CM13 . . .53 FW51
Wilmot Pl, NW1 . . .83 DJ66
W7 off Boston Rd . . .79 CE74
Wilmot Rd, E10 . . .67 EB61
N17 . . .66 DR55
Carshalton SM5 . . .158 DF106
Dartford DA1 . . .127 FH85
Purley CR8 . . .159 DN112
Wilmots Cl, Reig. RH2 . . .184 DC133
Wilmot St, E2 . . .84 DV70
Wilmot Way, Bans. SM7 . . .158 DA114
Wilmount St, SE18 . . .105 EP77
Wilna Rd, SW18 . . .120 DC87
Wilsham St, W11 . . .81 CX74
Wilshaw Cl, NW4 . . .63 CU55
Wilshaw St, SE14 . . .103 EA81
Wilsman Rd, S.Ock. RM15 . . .91 FW68
Wilsmere Dr, Har. HA3 . . .41 CF52
Northolt UB5 . . .78 BY65
Wilson Av, Mitch. CR4 . . .120 DE94
Wilson Cl, S.Croy. CR2 off Bartlett St . . .160 DR106
Wembley HA9 . . .62 CM59
Wilson Dr, Cher. (Ott.) KT16 .151 BB106
Wembley HA9 . . .62 CM59
Wilson Gdns, Har. HA1 . . .60 CC59
Wilson Gro, SE16 . . .202 D5
Wilson La, Dart. DA4 . . .149 FT96
Wilson Rd, E6 . . .86 EK69
SE5 . . .102 DS81
Chessington KT9 . . .156 CM107
Ilford IG1 . . .69 EM59
Wilsons, Tad. KT20 . . .173 CX121
Wilsons Pl, E14 off Salmon La . . .85 DZ72
Wilsons Rd, W6 . . .99 CX78
Wilson St, E17 . . .67 EC57
EC2 . . .197 L6
N21 . . .45 DN45
Wilson Way, Wok. GU21 . . .166 AX116
Wilstone Cl, Hayes UB4 . . .78 BY70
Wilthorne Gdns, Dag. RM10 off Acre Rd . . .89 FB66
Wilton Av, W4 . . .98 CS78
Wilton Cl, West Dr. UB7 . . .94 BK79
Wilton Cres, SW1 . . .198 F5
SW19 . . .139 CZ95
Wilton Dr, Rom. RM5 . . .51 FC52
Wilton Gdns, Walt. KT12 . . .136 BX102
West Molesey KT8 . . .136 CA97
Wilton Gro, SW19 . . .139 CZ94
New Malden KT3 . . .139 CT100
Wilton Ms, SW1 . . .198 G6
Wilton Par, Felt. TW13 off Highfield Rd . . .115 BU89
Wilton Pk Ct, SE18 off Prince Imperial Rd . . .105 EN81
Wilton Pl, SW1 . . .198 F5
Addlestone (New Haw) KT15 . . .152 BK109
Wilton Rd, N10 . . .44 DG54
SE2 . . .106 EW76
SW1 . . .199 J7
SW19 . . .120 DE94
Barnet (Cockfos.) EN4 . . .28 DF42
Hounslow TW4 . . .96 BX83
Ilford IG1 off Ilford La . . .69 EP63
Wilton Row, SW1 . . .198 F5
Wilton Sq, N1 . . .84 DR67
Wilton St, SW1 . . .199 H6
Wilton Ter, SW1 . . .198 F6
Wilton Vil, N1 . . .84 DR67
Wilton Way, E8 . . .84 DU65
Wiltshire Av, Horn. RM11 . . .72 FM56
Wiltshire Cl, NW7 . . .43 CT50
SW3 . . .198 D8
Dartford DA2 . . .129 FR87
Wiltshire Gdns, N4 . . .66 DQ58
Twickenham TW2 . . .116 CC88
Wiltshire La, Pnr. HA5 . . .59 BT55
Wiltshire Rd, SW9 . . .101 DN83
Orpington BR6 . . .146 EU101
Thornton Heath CR7 . . .141 DN97
Wiltshire Row, N1 . . .84 DR67
Wilverley Cres, N.Mal. KT3 . .138 CS100
Wimbart Rd, SW2 . . .121 DM87
WIMBLEDON, SW19 . . .119 CY93
⇌ Wimbledon . . .119 CZ93
⊖ Wimbledon . . .119 CZ93
Tra Wimbledon . . .119 CZ93

★ Place of interest ⇌ Railway station ⊖ London Underground station DLR Docklands Light Railway station Tra Tramlink station H Hospital Riv Pedestrian ferry landing stage

★ Wimbledon (All England Tenn & Croquet Club), SW19 ..119 CY91
Wimbledon Br, SW19 ....119 CZ93
⇌ Wimbledon Chase 139 CY96
★ Wimbledon Common, SW19 ....119 CT91
Wimbledon Hill Rd, SW19 ..119 CY93
WIMBLEDON PARK, SW19 ..119 CZ90
⊖ Wimbledon Park 120 DA90
Wimbledon Pk, SW19 ....119 CZ89
Wimbledon Pk Est, SW19 ..119 CY88
Wimbledon Pk Rd, SW18 ..119 CZ87
SW19 ....119 CZ88
Wimbledon Pk Side, SW19 ..119 CX89
Wimbledon Rd, SW17 ....120 DC91
Wimbledon Stadium Business Cen, SW17 ....120 DB90
★ Wimbledon Windmill Mus, SW19 ....119 CV89
Wimbolt St, E2 ....84 DU69
Wimborne Av, Hayes UB4 ..77 BV72
Southall UB2 ....96 CA77
Wimborne Cl, SE12 ....124 EF85
Buckhurst Hill IG9 ....48 EH47
Epsom KT17 ....156 CS113
Worcester Park KT4 ..139 CW102
Wimborne Dr, NW9 ....62 CN55
Pinner HA5 ....60 BX59
Wimborne Gdns, W13 ....79 CH72
Wimborne Gro, Wat. WD17 ..23 BS37
Wimborne Rd, N9 ....46 DU47
N17 ....46 DS54
Wimborne Way, Beck. BR3 ..143 DX97
Wimbourne Av, Chis. BR7 ..145 ET98
Orpington BR5 ....145 ET98
Wimbourne Ct, N1 off Wimbourne St 84 DR68
Wimbourne Ho, SW8 off Dorset Rd 101 DM80
Wimbourne St, N1 ....84 DR68
Wimpole Cl, Brom. BR2 ....144 EJ98
Kingston upon Thames KT1 ....138 CM96
Wimpole Ms, W1 ....195 H6
Wimpole Rd, West Dr. UB7 ..76 BK74
Wimpole St, W1 ....195 H8
Wimshurst Cl, Croy. CR0 ..141 DL102
Winans Wk, SW9 ....101 DN82
Wincanton Cres, Nthlt. UB5 ..60 CA64
Wincanton Gdns, Ilf. IG6 ..69 EP55
Wincanton Rd, SW18 ....119 CZ87
Romford RM3 ....52 FK48
Winchcombe Rd, Cars. SM5 .140 DD101
Winchcomb Gdns, SE9 ....104 EK83
Winchelsea Av, Bexh. DA7 ..106 EZ80
Winchelsea Cl, SW15 ....119 CX85
Winchelsea Rd, E7 ....68 EG62
N17 ....66 DS55
NW10 ....80 CR67
Winchelsey Ri, S.Croy. CR2 .160 DT107
Winchendon Rd, SW6 ....99 CZ80
Teddington TW11 ....117 CD91
Winchester Av, NW6 ....81 CY67
NW9 ....62 CN55
Hounslow TW5 ....96 BZ79
Upminster RM14 ....73 FT60
Winchester Cl, E6 off Boultwood Rd 87 EM72
SE17 ....200 G9
Amersham HP7 ....20 AS39
Bromley BR2 ....144 EF97
Enfield EN1 ....30 DS43
Esher KT10 ....154 CA105
Kingston upon Thames KT2 ....118 CP94
Slough (Colnbr.) SL3 ....93 BE81
Waltham Abbey EN9 off Highbridge St 15 EB33
Winchester Ct, E17 off Billet Rd 47 DY53
Winchester Cres, Grav. DA12 .131 GK90
Winchester Dr, Pnr. HA5 ....60 BX57
Winchester Gro, Sev. TN13 ..191 FH123
Winchester Ho, SE18 off Shooters Hill Rd 104 EK80
Winchester Ms, NW3 off Winchester Rd 82 DD66
Worcester Park KT4 ....139 CX103
Winchester Pk, Brom. BR2 ..144 EF97
Winchester Pl, E8 off Kingsland High St 66 DT64
N6 ....65 DH60
W3 off Avenue Rd 98 CQ75
Winchester Rd, E4 ....47 EC52
N6 ....65 DH60
N9 ....46 DU46
NW3 ....82 DD66
Bexleyheath DA7 ....106 EX82
Bromley BR2 ....144 EF97
Feltham TW13 ....116 BZ90
Harrow HA3 ....62 CL56
Hayes UB3 ....95 BS80
Ilford IG1 ....69 ER62
Northwood HA6 ....59 BT55
Orpington BR6 ....164 EW105
Twickenham TW1 ....117 CH86
Walton-on-Thames KT12 .135 BU102
Winchester Sq, SE1 ....201 K2
Winchester St, SW1 ....199 J10
W3 ....80 CQ74
Winchester Wk, SE1 ....201 K2
Winchester Way, Rick. (Crox.Grn) WD3 ....23 BP43
Winchet Wk, Croy. CR0 ..142 DW100
Winchfield Cl, Har. HA3 ..61 CJ58
Winchfield Ho, SW15 off Highcliffe Dr 119 CT86
Winchfield Rd, SE26 ....123 DY92
Winchfield Way, Rick. WD3 ..38 BJ45
Winchilsea Cres, W.Mol. KT8 .136 CC96
WINCHMORE HILL, N21 ....45 DM45
⇌ Winchmore Hill 45 DN46
Winchmore Hill Rd, N14 ....45 DK46
N21 ....45 DK46
Winchstone Cl, Shep. TW17 .134 BM98
Winckley Cl, Har. HA3 ....62 CM57
Wincott St, SE11 ....200 E8
Wincrofts Dr, SE9 ....105 ER84
Windall Cl, SE19 ....124 DU95
Windborough Rd, Cars. SM5 .158 DG108
Windermere Av, N3 ....64 DA55
NW6 ....81 CY67
SW19 ....140 DB97
Windermere Av, Har. HA3 ....61 CJ59
Hornchurch RM12 ....71 FG64
Purfleet RM19 ....108 FQ78
Ruislip HA4 ....60 BW59
Wembley HA9 ....61 CJ59
Windermere Cl, Dart. DA1 ..127 FH88
Egham TW20 off Derwent Rd 113 BB94
Feltham TW14 ....115 BT88
Orpington BR6 ....145 EP104
Rickmansworth (Chorl.) WD3 ....21 BC43
Staines TW19 off Viola Av .114 BL88
Windermere Ct, SW13 ....99 CT79
Kenley CR8 ....175 DP115
Wembley HA9 off Windermere Av 61 CJ59
Windermere Gdns, Ilf. IG4 ..68 EL57
Windermere Gro, Wem. HA9 off Windermere Av 61 CJ60
Windermere Ho, Islw. TW7 off Summerwood Rd 117 CF85
Windermere Pt, SE15 off Ilderton Rd 102 DW80
Windermere Rd, N10 ....45 DH53
N19 off Holloway Rd 65 DJ61
SW15 ....118 CS91
SW16 ....141 DJ95
W5 ....97 CJ76
Bexleyheath DA7 ....107 FC82
Coulsdon CR5 ....175 DL115
Croydon CR0 ....142 DT102
Southall UB1 ....78 BZ71
West Wickham BR4 ....144 EE103
Windermere Way, Reig. RH2 .184 DD133
West Drayton UB7 off Providence Rd 76 BL74
Winders Rd, SW11 ....100 DE82
Windfield, Lthd. KT22 ....171 CH121
Windfield Cl, SE26 ....123 DX91
Windham Av, Croy. (New Adgtn) CR0 ....161 ED110
Windham Rd, Rich. TW9 ....98 CM83
Windhover Way, Grav. DA12 .131 GL91
Windings, The, S.Croy. CR2 .160 DT111
Winding Way, Dag. RM8 ....70 EW62
Harrow HA1 ....61 CE63
Windlass Pl, SE8 ....203 L9
Windlesham Gro, SW19 ....119 CX88
Windley Cl, SE23 ....122 DW89
Windmill All, W4 off Windmill Rd 98 CS77
Windmill Av, Epsom KT17 ..157 CT111
Southall UB2 ....96 CC75
Windmill Br Ho, Croy. CR0 ..142 DS102
Windmill Cl, SE1 ....202 C8
SE13 ....103 EC82
Caterham CR3 ....176 DQ121
Epsom KT17 ....157 CT112
Sunbury-on-Thames TW16 .115 BS94
Surbiton KT6 ....137 CH102
Upminster RM14 ....72 FN61
Waltham Abbey EN9 ....16 EE34
Windmill Ct, NW2 ....81 CY65
Windmill Dr, NW2 ....63 CY62
SW4 ....121 DJ85
Keston BR2 ....162 EJ105
Leatherhead KT22 ....171 CJ123
Reigate RH2 ....184 DD132
Rickmansworth (Crox.Grn) WD3 ....22 BM44
Windmill End, Epsom KT17 .157 CT112
Windmill Gdns, Enf. EN2 ....29 DN41
Windmill Grn, Shep. TW17 ..135 BS101
Windmill Gro, Croy. CR0 ..142 DQ101
WINDMILL HILL, Grav. DA11 .131 GG88
Windmill Hill, NW3 ....64 DC62
Enfield EN2 ....29 DP41
Kings Langley (Chipper.) WD4 ....5 BF32
Ruislip HA4 ....59 BT59
Windmill Ho, E14 ....203 P8
Windmill La, E15 ....85 ED65
Barnet EN5 ....27 CT44
Bushey (Bushey Hth) WD23 .41 CE46
Epsom KT17 ....157 CT112
Greenford UB6 ....78 CC71
Isleworth TW7 ....97 CE77
Southall UB2 ....96 CC76
Surbiton KT6 ....137 CH100
Waltham Cross (Chsht) EN8 .15 DX30
Windmill Ms, W4 off Windmill Rd 98 CS77
Windmill Pas, W4 ....98 CS77
Windmill Ri, Kings.T. KT2 ..118 CP94
Windmill Rd, N18 ....46 DR49
SW18 ....120 DD86
SW19 ....119 CV88
W4 ....98 CS77
W5 ....97 CJ77
Brentford TW8 ....97 CK78
Croydon CR0 ....142 DQ101
Gerrards Cross (Chal.St.P.) SL9 ....36 AX52
Hampton (Hmptn H.) TW12 .116 CB92
Mitcham CR4 ....141 DJ99
Sevenoaks TN13 ....191 FH130
Slough (Fulmer) SL3 ....56 AX64
Sunbury-on-Thames TW16 .135 BS95
Windmill Rd W, Sun. TW16 ..135 BS96
Windmill Row, SE11 ....101 DN78
Windmill Shott, Egh. TW20 off Rusham Rd 113 AZ93
Windmill St, W1 ....195 M7
Bushey (Bushey Hth) WD23 .41 CE46
Gravesend DA12 ....131 GH86
Windmill Trd Est, Mitch. CR4 .141 DJ98
Windmill Wk, SE1 ....200 E3
Windmill Way, Reig. RH2 ..184 DD132
Ruislip HA4 ....59 BT60
Windmore Av, Pot.B. EN6 ....11 CW31
Windmore Cl, Wem. HA0 ....61 CG64
Windover Av, NW9 ....62 CR56
Windrose Cl, SE16 ....203 H4
Windrush, N.Mal. KT3 ....138 CP98
Windrush Av, Slou. SL3 ....93 BB76
Windrush Cl, N17 off Linley Rd 46 DS54
SW11 off Maysoule Rd ..100 DD84
W4 ....98 CQ81
Uxbridge UB10 ....58 BM63
Windrush La, SE23 ....123 DX90
Windrush Rd, NW10 ....80 CR67
Windrush Sq, SW2 off Rushcroft Rd 101 DN84
Windsock Cl, SE16 ....203 M8
WINDSOR, SL4 ....92 AS82
Windsor Av, E17 ....47 DY54
SW19 ....140 DC95
Edgware HA8 ....42 CP49
Grays RM16 ....110 GB75
New Malden KT3 ....138 CQ99
Sutton SM3 ....139 CY104
Uxbridge UB10 ....77 BP67
West Molesey KT8 ....136 CA97
★ Windsor Castle, Wind. SL4 ....92 AS81
Windsor Cen, The, SE27 off Advance Rd 122 DQ91
Windsor Cl, N3 ....43 CY54
SE27 ....122 DQ91
Borehamwood WD6 ....26 CN39
Brentford TW8 ....97 CH79
Chislehurst BR7 ....125 EP92
Harrow HA2 ....60 CA62
Hemel Hempstead (Bov.) HP3 ....5 BA28
Northwood HA6 ....39 BU54
Waltham Cross (Chsht) EN7 .14 DU30
Windsor Ct, N14 ....45 DJ45
Sunbury-on-Thames TW16 off Windsor Rd 115 BU93
Windsor Ct Rd, Wok. (Chobham) GU24 ....150 AS109
Windsor Cres, Har. HA2 ....60 CA63
Wembley HA9 ....62 CP62
Windsor Dr, Ashf. TW15 ....114 BK91
Barnet EN4 ....28 DF44
Dartford DA1 ....127 FG86
Orpington BR6 ....164 EU107
Windsor Gdns, W9 ....82 DA71
Croydon CR0 off Richmond Rd 141 DL104
Hayes UB3 ....95 BR76
★ Windsor Great Pk, Ascot, Egh. & Wind. 112 AS93
Windsor Gt Pk, Ascot SL5 ..112 AS93
Egham TW20 ....112 AS93
Windsor Gro, SE27 ....122 DQ91
Windsor Ms, SE6 ....123 EC88
SE23 ....123 DY88
Windsor Pk Rd, Hayes UB3 ..95 BT80
Windsor Pl, SW1 ....199 L7
Chertsey KT16 off Windsor St 134 BG100
Windsor Rd, E4 off Chivers Rd 47 EB49
E7 ....68 EH64
E10 ....67 EB61
E11 ....68 EG60
N3 ....43 CY54
N7 ....65 DL62
N13 ....45 DN48
N17 ....46 DU54
NW2 ....81 CV65
W5 ....80 CL73
Barnet EN5 ....27 CX44
Bexleyheath DA6 ....106 EY84
Brentwood (Pilg.Hat.) CM15 .54 FV44
Dagenham RM8 ....70 EY62
Egham (Eng.Grn) TW20 ..113 AZ90
Enfield EN3 ....31 DX36
Gerrards Cross SL9 ....56 AW60
Gravesend DA12 ....131 GH90
Harrow HA3 ....41 CD53
Hornchurch RM11 ....72 FJ59
Hounslow TW4 ....95 BV82
Ilford IG1 ....69 EP63
Kingston upon Thames KT2 ....118 CL94
Richmond TW9 ....98 CM82
Slough SL1 ....92 AS76
Slough (Datchet) SL3 ....92 AT80
Slough (Stoke P.) SL2 ....56 AU63
Southall UB2 ....96 BZ76
Staines (Wrays.) TW19 ..112 AY86
Sunbury-on-Thames TW16 .115 BU93
Teddington TW11 ....117 CD92
Thornton Heath CR7 ....141 DP96
Watford WD24 ....24 BW38
Woking (Chobham) GU24 .150 AS109
Worcester Park KT4 ....139 CU103
Windsors, The, Buck.H. IG9 ..48 EL47
Windsor St, N1 ....83 DP67
Chertsey KT16 ....134 BG100
Uxbridge UB8 ....76 BJ66
Windsor Ter, N1 ....197 J2
Windsor Wk, SE5 ....102 DR82
Walton-on-Thames KT12 off King George Av 136 BX102
Weybridge KT13 ....153 BP106
Windsor Way, W14 ....99 CX77
Rickmansworth WD3 ....38 BG46
Woking GU22 ....167 BC116
Windsor Wf, E9 ....67 DZ64
Windsor Wd, Wal.Abb. EN9 off Monkswood Av 16 EE33
Windspoint Dr, SE15 off Ethnard Rd 102 DV79
Windus Rd, N16 ....66 DT60
Windus Wk, N16 ....66 DT60
Windward Cl, Enf. EN3 off Bullsmoor La 31 DX35
Windycroft Cl, Pur. CR8 ....159 DK113
Windy Hill, Brwd. (Hutt.) CM13 ....55 GC46
Windy Ridge, Brom. BR1 ....144 EL95
Windyridge Cl, SW19 ....119 CX92
Wine Cl, E1 ....202 F1
Wine Office Ct, EC4 ....196 E8
Winern Glebe, W.Byf. (Byfleet) KT14 ....152 BK113
Winery La, Kings.T. KT1 ....138 CM97
Winey Cl, Chess. KT9 off Nigel Fisher Way 155 CJ108
Winfield Mobile Home Pk, Wat. WD25 ....24 CB39
Winford Ho, E3 ....85 DZ66
Winford Par, Sthl. UB1 off Telford Rd 78 CB72
Winforton St, SE10 ....103 EC81
Winfrith Rd, SW18 ....120 DC87
Wingate Cres, Croy. CR0 ....141 DK100
Wingate Rd, W6 ....99 CV76
Ilford IG1 ....69 EP64
Sidcup DA14 ....126 EW92
Wingate Trd Est, N17 ....46 DU52
Wing Cl, Epp. (N.Wld Bas.) CM16 off Epping Rd 18 FA27
Wingfield, Grays (Bad.Dene) RM17 ....110 FZ78
Wingfield Bk, Grav. (Nthflt) DA11 ....130 GC89
Wingfield Cl, Add. (New Haw) KT15 ....152 BH110
Brentwood CM13 off Pondfield La 55 GA48
Wingfield Ct, E14 off Newport Av 85 ED73
Banstead SM7 ....174 DA115
Wingfield Gdns, Upmin. RM14 ....73 FT58
Wingfield Ho, NW6 off Tollgate Gdns 82 DB68
Wingfield Ms, SE15 off Wingfield St 102 DU83
Wingfield Rd, E15 ....68 EE64
E17 ....67 EB57
Gravesend DA12 ....131 GH87
Kingston upon Thames KT2 ....118 CN93
Wingfield St, SE15 ....102 DU83
Wingfield Way, Ruis. HA4 ....77 BV65
Wingford Rd, SW2 ....121 DL86
Wingletye La, Horn. RM11 ..72 FM60
Wingmore Rd, SE24 ....102 DQ83
Wingrave Cres, Brwd. CM14 ..54 FS49
Wingrave Rd, W6 ....99 CW79
Wingrove Dr, Purf. RM19 ..108 FP78
Wingrove Rd, SE6 ....124 EE89
Wings Cl, Sutt. SM1 ....158 DA105
Wing Way, Brwd. CM14 off Geary Dr 54 FW46
Winifred Av, Horn. RM12 ....72 FK63
Winifred Cl, Barn. EN5 ....27 CT44
Winifred Gro, SW11 ....100 DF84
Winifred Pl, N12 off High Rd .44 DC50
Winifred Rd, SW19 ....140 DA95
Coulsdon CR5 ....174 DG116
Dagenham RM8 ....70 EY61
Dartford DA1 ....127 FH85
Erith DA8 ....107 FE78
Hampton (Hmptn H.) TW12 .116 CA91
Winifred St, E16 ....87 EM74
Winifred Ter, E13 off Victoria Rd 86 EG68
Enfield EN1 off Great Cambridge Rd ..46 DT45
Winkers Cl, Ger.Cr. (Chal.St.P.) SL9 ....37 AZ53
Winkers La, Ger.Cr. (Chal.St.P.) SL9 ....37 AZ53
Winkfield Rd, E13 ....86 EH68
N22 ....45 DN53
Winkley St, E2 ....84 DV68
Winkworth Pl, Bans. SM7 off Bolters La 157 CZ114
Winkworth Rd, Bans. SM7 ..157 CZ114
Winlaton Rd, Brom. BR1 ....123 ED91
Winmill Rd, Dag. RM8 ....70 EZ62
Winnards, Wok. GU21 off Abercorn Way 166 AV118
Winn Common Rd, SE18 ..105 ES79
Winnett St, W1 ....195 M10
Winningales Ct, Ilf. IG5 off Vienna Cl 68 EL55
Winnings Wk, Nthlt. UB5 off Arnold Rd 78 BY65
Winnington Cl, N2 ....64 DD58
Winnington Rd, N2 ....64 DD59
Enfield EN3 ....30 DW38
Winnington Way, Wok. GU21 .166 AV118
Winnipeg Dr, Orp. BR6 ....163 ET107
Winnipeg Way, Brox. EN10 ..15 DY25
Winnock Rd, West Dr. UB7 ..76 BK74
Winn Rd, SE12 ....124 EG88
Winns Av, E17 ....67 DY55
Winns Ms, N15 off Grove Pk Rd 66 DS56
Winns Ter, E17 ....47 EA54
Winsbeach, E17 ....67 ED55
Winscombe Cres, W5 ....79 CK70
Winscombe St, N19 ....65 DH61
Winscombe Way, Stan. HA7 ..41 CG50
Winsford Rd, SE6 ....123 DZ90
Winsford Ter, N18 ....46 DR50
Winsham Gro, SW11 ....120 DG85
Winslade Rd, SW2 ....121 DL85
Winslade Way, SE6 off Rushey Grn 123 EB87
Winsland Ms, W2 off London St 82 DD72
Winsland St, W2 ....82 DD72
Winsley St, W1 ....195 K8
Winslow, SE17 ....102 DS78
Winslow Cl, NW10 off Neasden La N 62 CS62
Pinner HA5 ....59 BV58
Winslow Gro, E4 ....48 EE47
Winslow Rd, W6 ....99 CW79
Winslow Way, Felt. TW13 ..116 BX90
Walton-on-Thames KT12 .136 BW104
Winsor Ter, E6 ....87 EN71
Winstanley Cl, Cob. KT11 ..153 BV114
Winstanley Est, SW11 ....100 DD83
Winstanley Rd, SW11 ....100 DD83
Winstanley Wk, Cob. KT11 off Winstanley Cl 153 BV114
Winstead Gdns, Dag. RM10 ..71 FC64
Winston Av, NW9 ....62 CS59
Winston Churchill Way, Wal.Cr. (Chsht) EN8 ....14 DW33
Winston Cl, Green. DA9 ....129 FT85
Harrow HA3 ....41 CF51
Romford RM7 ....71 FB56
Winston Ct, Har. HA3 ....40 CB52
Winston Dr, Cob. (Stoke D'Ab.) KT11 ....170 BY116
Winston Rd, N16 ....66 DR63
Winston Wk, W4 off Beaconsfield Rd 98 CR77
Winston Way, Ilf. IG1 ....69 EP62
Potters Bar EN6 ....12 DA34
Woking (Old Wok.) GU22 .167 BB120
Winstre Rd, Borwd. WD6 ....26 CN39
Winter Av, E6 ....86 EL67
Winterborne Av, Orp. BR6 ..145 ER104
Winterbourne Gro, Wey. KT13 ....153 BQ107
Winterbourne Rd, SE6 ....123 DZ88
Dagenham RM8 ....70 EW61
Thornton Heath CR7 ....141 DN97
Winter Box Wk, Rich. TW10 ..98 CM84
Winterbrook Rd, SE24 ....122 DQ86
Winterburn Cl, N11 ....44 DG51
Winterdown Gdns, Esher KT10 ....154 BZ107
Winterdown Rd, Esher KT10 .154 BZ107
Winterfold Cl, SW19 ....119 CY89
Wintergarden, Green. (Bluewater) DA9 off Bluewater Parkway .129 FU87
Winter Gdn Cres, Green. (Bluewater) DA9 ....129 FU87
Winter Gdn Ho, WC2 off Macklin St 83 DL72
Wintergreen Cl, E6 off Yarrow Cres 86 EL71
Winters Cft, Grav. DA12 ....131 GK93
Wintersells Rd, W.Byf. (Byfleet) KT14 ....152 BK110
Winters Rd, T.Ditt. KT7 ....137 CH101
Winterstoke Gdns, NW7 ....43 CU50
Winterstoke Rd, SE6 ....123 DZ88
Winters Way, Wal.Abb. EN9 ..16 EG33
Winterton Ho, E1 ....84 DV72
Winterton Pl, SW10 off Park Wk 100 DC79
Winterwell Rd, SW2 ....121 DL85
Winthorpe Rd, SW15 ....99 CY84
Winthrop St, E1 ....84 DV71
Winthrop Wk, Wem. HA9 off Everard Way 62 CL62
Winton App, Rick. (Crox.Grn) WD3 ....23 BQ43
Winton Av, N11 ....45 DJ52
Winton Cl, N9 ....47 DX45
Winton Cres, Rick. (Crox.Grn) WD3 ....23 BP43
Winton Dr, Rick. (Crox.Grn) WD3 ....23 BP44
Waltham Cross (Chsht) EN8 .15 DY29
Winton Gdns, Edg. HA8 ....42 CM52
Winton Rd, Orp. BR6 ....163 EP105
Winton Way, SW16 ....121 DN92
Winvale, Slou. SL1 ....92 AS76
Winwood, Slou. SL2 ....74 AW72
Wireless Rd, West. (Bigg.H.) TN16 ....178 EK115
Wirrall Ho, SE26 off Sydenham Hill Est ..122 DU90
Wisbeach Rd, Croy. CR0 ....142 DR99
Wisborough Rd, S.Croy. CR2 .160 DT109
Wisdons Cl, Dag. RM10 ....71 FB60
Wise La, NW7 ....43 CV51
West Drayton UB7 ....94 BK77
Wiseman Ct, SE19 ....122 DS92
Wiseman Rd, E10 ....67 EA61
Wise Rd, E15 ....85 ED67
Wise's La, Hat. AL9 ....11 CW27
Wiseton Rd, SW17 ....120 DE88
Wishart Rd, SE3 ....104 EK81
Wishbone Way, Wok. GU21 .166 AT116
Wishford Ct, Ashtd. KT21 off The Marld 172 CM118
WISLEY, Wok. GU23 ....168 BL116
Wisley Common, Wok. GU23 .168 BN117
Wisley Ct, S.Croy. CR2 off Sanderstead Rd 160 DR110
Wisley Interchange, Cob. KT11 off Portsmouth Rd 169 BQ116
Wisley La, Wok. (Wisley) GU23 ....168 BL116
Wisley Rd, SW11 ....120 DG85
Orpington BR5 ....126 EU94
Wistaria Cl, Brwd. (Pilg.Hat.) CM15 ....54 FW43
Wistaria Dr, St.Alb. (Lon.Col.) AL2 ....9 CH26
Wisteria Cl, NW7 ....43 CT51
Ilford IG1 ....69 EP64
Orpington BR6 ....145 EP103
Wisteria Gdns, Swan. BR8 ..147 FD96
Wisteria Rd, SE13 ....103 ED84
Witanhurst La, N6 off Highgate W Hill 64 DG60
Witan St, E2 ....84 DV69
Witches La, Sev. TN13 ....190 FD122
Witcombe Pt, SE15 off Clayton Rd 102 DU81
Witham Cl, Loug. IG10 ....32 EL44
Witham Rd, SE20 ....142 DW97
W13 ....79 CG74
Dagenham RM10 ....70 FA64
Isleworth TW7 ....97 CD81
Romford RM2 ....71 FH57
Withens Cl, Orp. BR5 ....146 EW98
Witherby Cl, Croy. CR0 ....160 DS106
Witherings, The, Horn. RM11 .72 FL57
Witherington Rd, N5 ....65 DN64
Withers Cl, Chess. KT9 off Coppard Gdns 155 CJ107
Withers Mead, NW9 ....43 CT53
Witherston Way, SE9 ....125 EN89
Witheygate Av, Stai. TW18 ..114 BH93
Withies, The, Lthd. KT22 ..171 CH120
Woking (Knap.) GU21 ....166 AS117
Withybed Cor, Tad. (Walt.Hill) KT20 ....173 CV123
Withycombe Rd, SW19 ....119 CX87
Withycroft, Slou. (Geo.Grn) SL3 ....74 AY72
Withy La, Ruis. HA4 ....59 BQ57
Withy Mead, E4 ....47 ED48
Withy Pl, St.Alb. (Park St) AL2 .8 CC28
Witley Cres, Croy. (New Adgtn) CR0 ....161 EC107
Witley Gdns, Sthl. UB2 ....96 BZ77
Witley Pt, SW15 off Wanborough Dr 119 CV88
Witley Rd, N19 off Holloway Rd 65 DJ61
Witney Cl, Pnr. HA5 ....40 BZ51
Uxbridge UB10 ....58 BM63
Witney Path, SE23 ....123 DX90
Wittenham Way, E4 ....47 ED48
Wittering Cl, Kings.T. KT2 ..117 CK92

Wittering Wk, Horn. RM12 . . 90 FJ65
Wittersham Rd, Brom. BR1 . 124 EF92
Wivenhoe Cl, SE15 . . 102 DV83
Wivenhoe Ct, Houns. TW3 . . 96 BZ84
Wivenhoe Rd, Bark. IG11 . . 88 EU68
Wiverton Rd, SE26 . . 122 DW93
Wixom Ho, SE3
 off Romero Sq . . 104 EJ84
Wix Rd, Dag. RM9 . . 88 EX67
Wixs La, SW4 . . 101 DH84
Woburn Av, Epp. (They.B.)
 CM16 . . 33 ES37
 Hornchurch RM12 . . 71 FG63
 Purley CR8 off High St . . 159 DN111
Woburn Cl, SE28
 off Summerton Way . . 88 EX72
 SW19 . . 120 DC93
 Bushey WD23 . . 24 CC43
Woburn Ct, SE16
 off Masters Dr . . 102 DV78
Woburn Hill, Add. KT15 . . 134 BJ103
Woburn Pl, WC1 . . 195 N4
Woburn Rd, Cars. SM5 . . 140 DE102
 Croydon CR0 . . 142 DQ102
Woburn Sq, WC1 . . 195 N5
Woburn Wk, WC1 . . 195 N3
Wodeham Gdns, E1 . . 84 DU71
Wodehouse Av, SE5 . . 102 DT81
Wodehouse Rd, Dart. DA1 . . 108 FN84
Woffington Cl, Kings.T. KT1 . 137 CJ95
Wokindon Rd, Grays RM16 . . 111 GH76
WOKING, GU22 - GU24 . . 167 AZ117
≠ Woking . . 167 AZ117
Woking Business Pk,
 Wok. GU21 . . 167 BB115
Woking Cl, SW15 . . 99 CT84
H Woking Comm Hosp,
 Wok. GU22 . . 167 AZ118
H Woking Nuffield Hosp,
 The, Wok. GU21 . . 150 AY114
Wold, The, Cat. (Wold.) CR3 . 177 EA122
Woldham Pl, Brom. BR2 . . 144 EJ98
Woldham Rd, Brom. BR2 . . 144 EJ98
WOLDINGHAM, Cat. CR3 . . 177 EB122
≠ Woldingham . . 177 DX122
WOLDINGHAM GARDEN VILLAGE,
 Cat. CR3 . . 177 DY121
Woldingham Rd, Cat.
 (Wold.) CR3 . . 176 DV120
Wolds Dr, Orp. BR6 . . 163 EN105
Wolfe Cl, Brom. BR2 . . 144 EG100
 Hayes UB4 off Ayles Rd . . 77 BV69
Wolfe Cres, SE7 . . 104 EK78
 SE16 . . 203 H5
Wolferton Rd, E12 . . 69 EM63
Wolffe Gdns, E15 . . 86 EF65
Wolffram Cl, SE13 . . 124 EE85
Wolfington Rd, SE27 . . 121 DP91
Wolfs Hill, Oxt. RH8 . . 188 EG131
H Wolfson Med Rehab Cen,
 SW20 . . 119 CV94
Wolf's Row, Oxt. RH8 . . 188 EH130
Wolfs Wd, Oxt. RH8 . . 188 EG132
Wolftencroft Cl, SW11 . . 100 DD83
Wollaston Cl, SE1 . . 201 H8
Wolmer Cl, Edg. HA8 . . 42 CP49
Wolmer Gdns, Edg. HA8 . . 42 CN48
Wolseley Av, SW19 . . 120 DA89
Wolseley Gdns, W4 . . 98 CP79
Wolseley Rd, E7 . . 86 EH66
 N8 . . 65 DK58
 N22 . . 45 DM53
 W4 . . 98 CQ77
 Harrow HA3 . . 61 CE55
 Mitcham CR4 . . 140 DG101
 Romford RM7 . . 71 FD59
Wolseley St, SE1 . . 202 A5
Wolsey Av, E6 . . 87 EN69
 E17 . . 67 DZ55
 Thames Ditton KT7 . . 137 CF99
 Waltham Cross (Chsht) EN7 . 14 DT29
Wolsey Business Pk, Wat.
 WD18 . . 39 BR45
Wolsey Cl, SW20 . . 119 CV94
 Hounslow TW3 . . 96 CC84
 Kingston upon Thames
 KT2 . . 138 CP95
 Southall UB2 . . 96 CC76
 Worcester Park KT4 . . 157 CU105
Wolsey Cres, Croy. (New Adgtn)
 CR0 . . 161 EC109
 Morden SM4 . . 139 CY101
Wolsey Dr, Kings.T. KT2 . . 118 CL92
 Walton-on-Thames KT12 . 136 BX102
Wolsey Gdns, Ilf. IG6 . . 49 EQ51
Wolsey Gro, Edg. HA8 . . 42 CR52
 Esher KT10 . . 154 CB105
Wolsey Ms, NW5 . . 83 DJ65
 Orpington BR6 . . 163 ET106
Wolsey Pl Shop Cen, Wok. GU21
 off Commercial Way . . 167 AZ117
Wolsey Rd, N1 . . 66 DR64
 Ashford TW15 . . 114 BL91
 East Molesey KT8 . . 137 CD98
 Enfield EN1 . . 30 DV40
 Esher KT10 . . 154 CB105
 Hampton (Hmptn H.) TW12 . 116 CB93
 Northwood HA6 . . 39 BQ47
 Sunbury-on-Thames TW16 . 115 BT94
Wolsey St, E1
 off Sidney St . . 84 DW71
Wolsey Wk, Wok. GU21 . . 166 AY117
Wolsey Way, Chess. KT9 . . 156 CN106
Wolsley Cl, Dart. DA1 . . 127 FE85
Wolstan Cl, Uxb. (Denh.)
 UB9 off Lindsey Rd . . 58 BG62
Wolstonbury, N12 . . 44 DA50
Wolvercote Rd, SE2 . . 106 EX75
Wolverley St, E2
 off Bethnal Grn Rd . . 84 DV69
Wolverton, SE17 . . 201 L10
Wolverton Av, Kings.T. KT2 . 138 CN95
Wolverton Gdns, W5 . . 80 CM73
 W6 . . 99 CX77
Wolverton Rd, Stan. HA7 . . 41 CH51
Wolverton Way, N14 . . 29 DJ43
Wolves La, N13 . . 45 DN52
 N22 . . 45 DN52
Wombwell Gdns, Grav.
 (Nthflt) DA11 . . 130 GE89
WOMBWELL PARK, Grav.
 DA11 . . 130 GD89
Womersley Rd, N8 . . 65 DM58
Wonersh Way, Sutt. SM2 . . 157 CX109
Wonford Cl, Kings.T. KT2 . . 138 CS95
 Tadworth (Walt.Hill) KT20 . 183 CU126
Wontford Rd, Pur. CR8 . . 175 DN115
Wontner Cl, N1
 off Greenman St . . 84 DQ66
Wontner Rd, SW17 . . 120 DF89
Wooburn Cl, Uxb. UB8
 off Aldenham Dr . . 77 BP70
Woodall Cl, E14
 off Lawless St . . 85 EB73
 Chessington KT9 . . 155 CK108
Woodall Rd, Enf. EN3 . . 31 DX44
Wood Av, Purf. RM19 . . 108 FQ77
Woodbank, Rick. WD3 . . 22 BJ44
Woodbank Av, Ger.Cr. SL9 . . 56 AX58
Woodbank Dr, Ch.St.G. HP8 . . 36 AX48
Woodbank Rd, Brom. BR1 . . 124 EF90
Woodbastwick Rd, SE26 . . 123 DX92
Woodberry Av, N21 . . 45 DN47
 Harrow HA2 . . 60 CB56
Woodberry Cl, NW7 . . 43 CX52
 Sunbury-on-Thames TW16
 off Ashridge Way . . 115 BU93
Woodberry Cres, N10 . . 65 DH55
Woodberry Down, N4 . . 66 DQ59
 Epping CM16 . . 18 EU29
Woodberry Down Est, N4 . . 66 DQ59
Woodberry Gdns, N12 . . 44 DC51
Woodberry Gro, N4 . . 66 DQ59
 N12 . . 44 DC51
 Bexley DA5 . . 127 FD90
Woodberry Way, E4 . . 47 EC46
 N12 . . 44 DC51
Woodbine Cl, Twick. TW2 . . 117 CD89
 Waltham Abbey EN9 . . 32 EJ35
Woodbine Gro, SE20 . . 122 DV94
 Enfield EN2 . . 30 DR38
Woodbine La, Wor.Pk. KT4 . 139 CW104
Woodbine Pl, E11 . . 68 EG58
Woodbine Rd, Sid. DA15 . . 125 ES88
Woodbines Av, Kings.T. KT1 . 137 CK97
Woodbine Ter, E9
 off Morning La . . 84 DW65
Woodborough Rd, SW15 . . 99 CV84
Woodbourne Av, SW16 . . 121 DK90
Woodbourne Cl, SW16
 off Woodbourne Av . . 121 DL90
Woodbourne Dr, Esher
 (Clay.) KT10 . . 155 CF107
Woodbourne Gdns, Wall.
 SM6 . . 159 DH108
Woodbridge Av, Lthd. KT22 . 171 CG118
Woodbridge Cl, N7 . . 65 DM61
 NW2 . . 63 CU62
 Romford RM3 . . 52 FK49
Woodbridge Ct, Wdf.Grn. IG8 . 48 EL52
Woodbridge Gro, Lthd. KT22 . 171 CG118
Woodbridge La, Rom. RM3 . . 52 FK48
Woodbridge Rd, Bark. IG11 . . 69 ET64
Woodbridge St, EC1 . . 196 F4
Woodbrook Gdns, Wal.Abb.
 EN9 . . 16 EE33
Woodbrook Rd, SE2 . . 106 EU79
Woodburn Cl, NW4 . . 63 CX57
Woodbury Cl, E11 . . 68 EH56
 Croydon CR0 . . 142 DT103
 Westerham (Bigg.H.) TN16 . 179 EM118
Woodbury Dr, Sutt. SM2 . . 158 DC110
Woodbury Gdns, SE12 . . 124 EH90
Woodbury Hill, Loug. IG10 . . 32 EL41
Woodbury Hollow, Loug.
 IG10 . . 32 EL40
Woodbury Pk Rd, W13 . . 79 CH70
Woodbury Rd, E17 . . 67 EB56
 Westerham (Bigg.H.) TN16 . 179 EM118
Woodbury St, SW17 . . 120 DE92
Woodchester Sq, W2 . . 82 DB71
Woodchurch Cl, Sid. DA14 . . 125 ER90
Woodchurch Dr, Brom. BR1 . 124 EK94
Woodchurch Rd, NW6 . . 82 DA66
Wood Cl, E2 . . 84 DU70
 NW9 . . 62 CR59
 Bexley DA5 . . 127 FE90
 Harrow HA1 . . 61 CD59
Woodclyffe Dr, Chis. BR7 . . 145 EN96
Woodcock Ct, Har. HA3 . . 62 CL59
Woodcock Dell Av, Har. HA3 . 61 CK59
Woodcock Hill, Har. HA3 . . 61 CK59
 Rickmansworth WD3 . . 38 BL50
Woodcocks, E16 . . 86 EJ71
Woodcombe Cres, SE23 . . 122 DW88
WOODCOTE, Epsom KT18 . . 172 CQ116
WOODCOTE, Pur. CR8 . . 159 DK111
Woodcote Av, NW7 . . 43 CW51
 Hornchurch RM12 . . 71 FG63
 Thornton Heath CR7 . . 141 DP98
 Wallington SM6 . . 159 DH108
Woodcote Cl, Enf. EN3 . . 30 DW44
 Epsom KT18 . . 156 CR114
 Kingston upon Thames
 KT2 . . 118 CM92
 Waltham Cross (Chsht) EN8 . 14 DW30
Woodcote Dr, Orp. BR6 . . 145 ER102
 Purley CR8 . . 159 DK110
Woodcote End, Epsom KT18 . 172 CR115
Woodcote Grn, Wall. SM6 . . 159 DJ109
Woodcote Grn Rd, Epsom
 KT18 . . 172 CQ116
Woodcote Gro, Couls. CR5 . . 159 DH112
Woodcote Gro Rd, Couls.
 CR5 . . 175 DK115
Woodcote Hurst, Epsom
 KT18 . . 172 CQ116
Woodcote La, Pur. CR8 . . 159 DK111
Woodcote Ms, Loug. IG10 . . 48 EK45
 Wallington SM6 . . 159 DH107
Woodcote Pk, Epsom KT18 . 172 CQ117
Woodcote Pk Av, Pur. CR8 . . 159 DJ112
Woodcote Pk Rd, Epsom
 KT18 . . 172 CQ116
Woodcote Pl, SE27 . . 121 DP92
Woodcote Rd, E11 . . 68 EG59
 Epsom KT18 . . 156 CR114
 Purley CR8 . . 159 DJ109
 Wallington SM6 . . 159 DH107
Woodcote Side, Epsom
 KT18 . . 172 CP115
Woodcote Valley Rd, Pur.
 CR8 . . 159 DK113
Woodcott Ho, SW15
 off Ellisfield Dr . . 119 CU87
Wood Ct, W12
 off Heathstan Rd . . 81 CU72
Woodcrest Rd, Pur. CR8 . . 159 DL113
Woodcrest Wk, Reig. RH2 . . 184 DE132
Woodcroft, N21 . . 45 DM46
 SE9 . . 125 EM90
 Greenford UB6 . . 79 CG65
Woodcroft Av, NW7 . . 42 CS52
 Stanmore HA7 . . 41 CF53
Woodcroft Cres, Uxb. UB10 . . 77 BP67
Woodcroft Ms, SE8 . . 203 K9
Woodcroft Rd, Th.Hth. CR7 . 141 DP99
Woodcutters Av, Grays
 RM16 . . 110 GC75
Woodcutters Cl, Horn. RM11 . 72 FK56
Wood Dr, Chis. BR7 . . 124 EL93
 Sevenoaks TN13 . . 190 FF126
Woodedge Cl, E4 . . 48 EF46
Woodend, SE19 . . 122 DQ93
 Esher KT10 . . 136 CC103
Wood End, Hayes UB3 . . 77 BS72
 St. Albans (Park St) AL2 . . 8 CC28
Woodend, Sutt. SM1 . . 140 DC103
Wood End, Swan. BR8 . . 147 FC98
Woodend, The, Wall. SM6 . . 159 DH109
Wood End Av, Har. HA2 . . 60 CB63
Wood End Cl, Nthlt. UB5 . . 61 CD64
Woodend Cl, Wok. GU21 . . 166 AU119
Woodend Gdns, Enf. EN2 . . 29 DL42
Wood End Gdns, Nthlt. UB5 . . 60 CC64
Wood End Grn Rd, Hayes
 UB3 . . 77 BR71
Wood End La, Nthlt. UB5 . . 78 CB65
Woodend Pk, Cob. KT11 . . 170 BX115
Woodend Rd, E17 . . 47 EC54
Wood End Rd, Har. HA1 . . 61 CD63
Wood End Way, Nthlt. UB5 . . 60 CC64
Wooder Gdns, E7 . . 68 EF63
Wooderson Cl, SE25 . . 142 DS98
Woodfall Av, Barn. EN5 . . 27 CZ43
Woodfall Dr, Dart. DA1 . . 107 FE84
Woodfall Rd, N4 . . 65 DN60
Woodfall St, SW3 . . 100 DF78
Woodfarrs, SE5 . . 102 DR84
Woodfield, Ashtd. KT21 . . 171 CK117
Woodfield Av, NW9 . . 62 CS56
 SW16 . . 121 DK90
 W5 . . 79 CJ70
 Carshalton SM5 . . 158 DG107
 Gravesend DA11 . . 131 GH88
 Northwood HA6 . . 39 BS49
 Wembley HA0 . . 61 CJ62
Woodfield Cl, SE19 . . 122 DQ94
 Ashtead KT21 . . 171 CK117
 Coulsdon CR5 . . 175 DJ119
 Enfield EN1 . . 30 DS42
 Redhill RH1 . . 184 DE133
Woodfield Cres, W5 . . 79 CJ70
Woodfield Dr, Barn. EN4 . . 44 DG46
 Romford RM2 . . 71 FG56
Woodfield Gdns, W9
 off Woodfield Rd . . 81 CZ71
 New Malden KT3 . . 139 CT99
Woodfield Gro, SW16 . . 121 DK90
Woodfield Hill, Couls. CR5 . . 175 DH119
Woodfield La, SW16 . . 121 DK90
 Ashtead KT21 . . 172 CL116
Woodfield Pl, W9 . . 81 CZ70
Woodfield Ri, Bushey WD23 . . 41 CD45
Woodfield Rd, W5 . . 79 CJ70
 W9 . . 81 CZ71
 Ashtead KT21 . . 171 CK117
 Hounslow TW4 . . 95 BV82
 Radlett WD7 . . 25 CG36
 Thames Ditton KT7 . . 137 CF103
Woodfields, Sev. TN13 . . 190 FD122
Woodfields, The, S.Croy.
 CR2 . . 160 DT111
Woodfield Ter, Epp. (Thnwd)
 CM16 off High Rd . . 18 EW25
 Uxbridge (Hare.) UB9 . . 38 BH54
Woodfield Way, N11 . . 45 DK52
 Hornchurch RM12 . . 72 FK60
 Redhill RH1 . . 184 DE132
Woodfines, The, Horn. RM11 . 72 FK58
WOODFORD, Wdf.Grn. IG8 . . 48 EH51
⊖ Woodford . . 48 EH51
Woodford Av, Ilf. IG2, IG4 . . 69 EM57
 Woodford Green IG8 . . 68 EK55
WOODFORD BRIDGE,
 Wdf.Grn. IG8 . . 49 EM52
Woodford Br Rd, Ilf. IG4 . . 68 EK55
Woodford Ct, W12
 off Shepherds Bush Grn . . 99 CX75
 Waltham Abbey EN9 . . 16 EG33
Woodford Cres, Pnr. HA5 . . 39 BV54
WOODFORD GREEN, IG8 . . 48 EF49
Woodford New Rd, E17 . . 68 EE56
 E18 . . 48 EE53
 Woodford Green IG8 . . 48 EE53
Woodford Pl, Wem. HA9 . . 62 CL60
Woodford Rd, E7 . . 68 EH63
 E18 . . 68 EG56
 Watford WD17 . . 23 BV40
WOODFORD WELLS,
 Wdf.Grn. IG8 . . 48 EH49
Woodgate, Wat. WD25 . . 7 BV33
Woodgate Av, Chess. KT9 . . 155 CK106
 Potters Bar EN6 . . 13 DH33
Woodgate Cres, Nthwd. HA6 . . 39 BU51
Woodgate Dr, SW16 . . 121 DK94
Woodgavil, Bans. SM7 . . 173 CZ116
Woodger Rd, W12
 off Goldhawk Rd . . 99 CW75
Woodgers Gro, Swan. BR8 . . 147 FF96
Woodget Cl, E6
 off Remington Rd . . 86 EL72
Woodgrange Av, N12 . . 44 DD51
 W5 . . 80 CN74
 Enfield EN1 . . 30 DU44
 Harrow HA3 . . 61 CJ57
Woodgrange Cl, Har. HA3 . . 61 CK57
Woodgrange Gdns, Enf. EN1 . 30 DU44
≠ Woodgrange Park . . 68 EK64
Woodgrange Rd, E7 . . 68 EH63
Woodgrange Ter, Enf. EN1
 off Great Cambridge Rd . . 30 DU44
WOOD GREEN, N22 . . 45 DL53
⊖ Wood Green . . 45 DM54
Woodgreen Rd, Wal.Abb. EN9 . 32 EJ35
Wood Grn Shop City, N22 . . 45 DN54
Wood Grn Way, Wal.Cr.
 (Chsht) EN8 . . 15 DY31
Woodhall, NW1 off Robert St . 83 DJ69
Woodhall Av, SE21 . . 122 DT90
 Pinner HA5 . . 40 BY54
Woodhall Cl, Uxb. UB8 . . 58 BK64
Woodhall Cres, Horn. RM11 . . 72 FM59
Woodhall Dr, SE21 . . 122 DT90
 Pinner HA5 . . 40 BX53
Woodhall Gate, Pnr. HA5 . . 40 BX52
Woodhall Ho, SW18
 off Fitzhugh Gro . . 120 DD86
Woodhall La, Rad. (Shenley)
 WD7 . . 26 CL35
 Watford WD19 . . 40 BX49
Woodhall Rd, Pnr. HA5 . . 40 BX52
WOODHAM, Add. KT15 . . 151 BF111
Woodham Ct, E18 . . 68 EF56
Woodham La, Add. KT15 . . 152 BG110
 Woking GU21 . . 151 BB114
Woodham Pk Rd, Add.
 (Wdhm) KT15 . . 151 BF109
Woodham Pk Way, Add.
 (Wdhm) KT15 . . 151 BF111
Woodham Ri, Wok. GU21 . . 151 AZ114
Woodham Rd, SE6 . . 123 EC90
 Woking GU21 . . 166 AY115
Woodham Waye, Wok. GU21 . 151 BB113
Woodhatch Cl, E6
 off Remington Rd . . 86 EL72
Woodhatch Spinney,
 Couls. CR5 . . 175 DL116
Woodhaven Gdns, Ilf. IG6
 off Brandville Gdns . . 69 EQ56
Woodhaw, Egh. TW20 . . 113 BB91
Woodhayes Rd, SW19 . . 119 CW94
Woodhead Dr, Orp. BR6
 off Sherlies Av . . 145 ES103
Woodheyes Rd, NW10 . . 62 CR64
Woodhill, SE18 . . 104 EL77
Woodhill Av, Ger.Cr. SL9 . . 57 BA58
Woodhill Cres, Har. HA3 . . 61 CK58
Wood Ho, SW17
 off Laurel Cl . . 120 DE92
Woodhouse Av, Grnf. UB6 . . 79 CF68
Woodhouse Cl, SE22 . . 102 DU84
 Greenford UB6 . . 79 CF68
 Hayes UB3 . . 95 BS76
Woodhouse Eaves, Nthwd.
 HA6 . . 39 BU50
Woodhouse Gro, E12 . . 86 EL65
Woodhouse Rd, E11 . . 68 EF62
 N12 . . 44 DD51
Woodhurst Av, Orp. BR5 . . 145 EQ100
 Watford WD25 . . 24 BX35
Woodhurst Dr, Uxb.
 (Denh.) UB9 . . 57 BF57
Woodhurst La, Oxt. RH8 . . 188 EE130
Woodhurst Pk, Oxt. RH8 . . 188 EE130
Woodhurst Rd, SE2 . . 106 EU78
 W3 . . 80 CQ73
Woodhyrst Gdns, Ken. CR8 . . 175 DP115
Woodington Cl, SE9 . . 125 EN86
Woodknoll Dr, Chis. BR7 . . 145 EM95
Woodland App, Grnf. UB6 . . 79 CG65
Woodland Av, Brwd. (Hutt.)
 CM13 . . 55 GC43
Woodland Cl, NW9 . . 62 CQ58
 SE19 off Woodland Hill . . 122 DS93
 Brentwood (Hutt.) CM13 . . 55 GC43
 Epsom KT19 . . 156 CS107
 Uxbridge (Ickhm) UB10 . . 59 BP61
 Weybridge KT13
 off Woodland Gro . . 153 BR105
 Woodford Green IG8 . . 48 EH48
Woodland Ct, Oxt. RH8 . . 187 ED128
Woodland Cres, SE10 . . 104 EE79
 SE16 . . 203 H5
Woodland Dr, Wat. WD17 . . 23 BT39
Woodland Gdns, N10 . . 65 DH57
 Epsom KT18 . . 173 CW117
 Isleworth TW7 . . 97 CE82
 South Croydon CR2 . . 160 DW111
Woodland Gro, SE10 . . 104 EE78
 Epping CM16 . . 18 EU31
 Weybridge KT13 . . 153 BR105
Woodland Hts, SE3
 off Vanbrugh Hill . . 104 EF79
Woodland Hill, SE19 . . 122 DS93
Woodland La, Rick. (Chorl.)
 WD3 . . 21 BD41
Woodland Ms, SW16 . . 121 DL89
Woodland Pl, Rick. (Chorl.)
 WD3 . . 21 BF42
Woodland Ri, N10 . . 65 DH56
 Greenford UB6 . . 79 CG65
 Oxted RH8 . . 188 EE130
 Sevenoaks TN15 . . 191 FL123
Woodland Rd, E4 . . 47 EC46
 N11 . . 45 DH50
 SE19 . . 122 DS92
 Loughton IG10 . . 32 EL41
 Rickmansworth (Map.Cr.)
 WD3 . . 37 BD50
 Thornton Heath CR7 . . 141 DN98
WOODLANDS, Islw. TW7 . . 97 CE82
Woodlands, NW11 . . 63 CY58
 SW20 . . 139 CW98
 Gerrards Cross SL9 . . 57 AZ57
 Harrow HA2 . . 60 CA56
 Hatfield AL9 . . 12 DB26
 Radlett WD7 . . 9 CG34
 St. Albans (Park St) AL2 . . 8 CC27
 Woking GU22
 off Constitution Hill . . 166 AY118
Woodlands, The, N14 . . 45 DH46
 SE13 . . 123 ED87
 SE19 . . 122 DQ94
 Beckenham BR3 . . 143 EC95
 Esher KT10 . . 136 CC103
 Isleworth TW7 . . 97 CF82
 Orpington BR6 . . 164 EV107
 Wallington SM6 . . 159 DH109
Woodlands Av, E11 . . 68 EH60
 N3 . . 44 DC52
 W3 . . 80 CP74
 Hornchurch RM11 . . 72 FK57
 New Malden KT3 . . 138 CQ95
 Romford RM6 . . 70 EY58
 Ruislip HA4 . . 60 BW60
 Sidcup DA15 . . 125 ES88
Woodlands Av, W. Byf. KT14 . 151 BF113
 Worcester Park KT4 . . 139 CT103
Woodlands Cl, NW11 . . 63 CY57
 Borehamwood WD6 . . 26 CP42
 Bromley BR1 . . 145 EM96
 Chertsey (Ott.) KT16 . . 151 BB110
 Esher (Clay.) KT10 . . 155 CF108
 Gerrards Cross SL9 . . 57 BA58
 Grays RM16 . . 110 GE76
 Swanley BR8 . . 147 FF97
Woodlands Copse, Ashtd.
 KT21 . . 171 CK116
Woodlands Ct, Wok. GU22
 off Constitution Hill . . 166 AY119
Woodlands Dr, Kings L. WD4 . . 7 BQ28
 Stanmore HA7 . . 41 CF51
 Sunbury-on-Thames TW16 . 136 BW96
Woodlands Gro, Couls. CR5 . 174 DG117
 Isleworth TW7 . . 97 CE82
Woodlands La, Cob. (Stoke D'Ab.)
 KT11 . . 170 CA117
Woodlands Par, Ashf. TW15 . 115 BQ93
Woodlands Pk, Add. KT15 . . 151 BF106
 Bexley DA5 . . 127 FC91
 Tadworth (Box H.) KT20 . . 182 CP131
 Woking GU21
 off Blackmore Cres . . 151 BC114
Woodlands Pk Rd, N15 . . 65 DP57
 SE10 . . 104 EE79
Woodlands Ri, Swan. BR8 . . 147 FF96
Woodlands Rd, E11 . . 68 EE61
 E17 . . 67 EC55
 N9 . . 46 DW46
 SW13 . . 99 CT83
 Bexleyheath DA7 . . 106 EY83
 Bromley BR1 . . 144 EL96
 Bushey WD23 . . 24 BY43
 Enfield EN2 . . 30 DR39
 Epsom KT18 . . 172 CN115
 Harrow HA1 . . 61 CF57
 Hemel Hempstead HP3 . . 6 BN27
 Ilford IG1 . . 69 EQ62
 Isleworth TW7 . . 97 CE82
 Leatherhead KT22 . . 171 CD117
 Orpington BR6 . . 164 EU107
 Romford RM1 . . 71 FF55
 Romford (Harold Wd) RM3 . 52 FN53
 Southall UB1 . . 78 BX74
 Surbiton KT6 . . 137 CK101
 Virginia Water GU25 . . 132 AW98
 West Byfleet KT14 . . 151 BF114
Woodlands Rd E, Vir.W.
 GU25 . . 132 AW98
Woodlands Rd W, Vir.W.
 GU25 . . 132 AW97
Woodlands St, SE13 . . 123 ED87
Woodland St, E8
 off Dalston La . . 84 DT65
Woodlands Vw, Sev.
 (Bad.Mt) TN14 . . 164 FA110
Woodlands Way, SW15
 off Oakhill Rd . . 119 CZ85
 Ashtead KT21 . . 172 CN116
 Tadworth (Box H.) KT20 . 182 CQ130
Woodland Ter, SE7 . . 104 EL77
Woodland Wk, NW3 . . 64 DE64
 SE10 off Woodland Gro . . 104 EE78
 Bromley BR1 . . 124 EE91
 Epsom KT19 . . 156 CN107
Woodland Way, N21 . . 45 DN47
 NW7 . . 42 CS51
 SE2 . . 106 EX77
 Abbots Langley (Bedmond)
 WD5 . . 7 BT27
 Caterham CR3 . . 186 DS128
 Croydon CR0 . . 143 DY102
 Epping (They.B.) CM16 . . 33 ER35
 Greenhithe DA9 . . 109 FU84
 Mitcham CR4 . . 120 DG94
 Morden SM4 . . 139 CZ98
 Orpington BR5 . . 145 EQ98
 Purley CR8 . . 159 DN113
 Surbiton KT5 . . 138 CP103
 Tadworth (Kgswd) KT20 . . 173 CY122
 Waltham Cross (Chsht) EN7 . 13 DP28
 West Wickham BR4 . . 161 EB105
 Weybridge KT13 . . 153 BR106
 Woodford Green IG8 . . 48 EH48
Wood La, N6 . . 65 DH58
 NW9 . . 62 CS59
 W12 . . 81 CW72
 Caterham CR3 . . 176 DR124
 Dagenham RM8,
 RM9, RM10 . . 70 EW63
 Dartford (Lane End) DA2 . 129 FR91
 Hornchurch RM12 . . 71 FG64
 Isleworth TW7 . . 97 CF80
 Iver SL0 . . 75 BC71
 Ruislip HA4 . . 59 BR60
 Stanmore HA7 . . 41 CG48
 Tadworth KT20 . . 173 CZ116
 Weybridge KT13 . . 153 BQ109
 Woodford Green IG8 . . 48 EF50
Wood La Cl, Iver SL0 . . 75 BB69
Woodlawn Cl, SW15 . . 119 CZ85
Woodlawn Cres, Twick. TW2 . 116 CB89
Woodlawn Dr, Felt. TW13 . . 116 BX89
Woodlawn Gro, Wok. GU21 . 167 AZ115
Woodlawn Rd, SW6 . . 99 CX80
Woodlea Dr, Brom. BR2 . . 144 EE99
Woodlea Gro, Nthwd. HA6 . . 39 BQ51
Woodlea Rd, N16 . . 66 DS62
Woodlee Cl, Vir.W. GU25 . . 132 AW96
Woodleigh, E18
 off Churchfields . . 48 EG53
Woodleigh Av, N12 . . 44 DE51
Woodleigh Gdns, SW16 . . 121 DL90
Woodley Cl, SW17
 off Arnold Rd . . 120 DF94
Woodley La, Cars. SM5 . . 140 DD104
Woodley Rd, Orp. BR6 . . 146 EW103
Wood Lo Gdns, Brom. BR1 . . 124 EL94
Wood Lo La, W.Wick. BR4 . . 143 EC104
Woodmancote Gdns, W.Byf.
 KT14 . . 152 BG113
Woodman La, E4 . . 32 EE43
Woodman Ms, Rich. TW9
 off Melliss Av . . 98 CP81
Woodman Path, Ilf. IG6 . . 49 ES51
Woodman Rd, Brwd. (Warley)
 CM14 . . 54 FW50
 Coulsdon CR5 . . 175 DJ115
Woodmans Gro, NW10 . . 63 CT64

★ Place of interest ≠ Railway station ⊖ London Underground station DLR Docklands Light Railway station Tra Tramlink station H Hospital Riv Pedestrian ferry landing stage

Woodmans Ms, W12 ... 81 CV71
WOODMANSTERNE, Bans. SM7 ... 174 DD115
⇌ Woodmansterne ... 175 DH116
Woodmansterne La, Bans. SM7 ... 174 DB115
Carshalton SM5 ... 158 DF112
Wallington SM6 ... 159 DH111
Woodmansterne Rd, SW16 . 141 DK95
Carshalton SM5 ... 158 DE109
Coulsdon CR5 ... 175 DJ115
Woodmansterne St, Bans. SM7 ... 174 DE115
Woodman St, E16 ... 87 EN74
Wood Meads, Epp. CM16 ... 18 EU29
Woodmere, SE9 ... 125 EM88
Woodmere Av, Croy. CR0 ... 143 DX101
Watford WD24 ... 24 BX38
Woodmere Cl, SW11
off Lavender Hill ... 100 DG83
Croydon CR0 ... 143 DX101
Woodmere Gdns, Croy. CR0 . 143 DX101
Woodmere Way, Beck. BR3 . 143 ED99
Woodmount, Swan. BR8 ... 147 FC101
Woodnook Rd, SW16 ... 121 DH92
Woodpecker Cl, N9 ... 30 DV44
Bushey WD23 ... 40 CC46
Cobham KT11 ... 154 BY112
Harrow HA3 ... 41 CF53
Woodpecker Ms, SE13
off Mercator Rd ... 103 ED84
Woodpecker Mt, Croy. CR0 . 161 DY109
Woodpecker Rd, SE14 ... 103 DY79
SE28 ... 88 EW73
Woodpecker Way, Wok. GU22 ... 166 AX123
Woodplace Cl, Couls. CR5 . 175 DJ119
Woodplace La, Couls. CR5 . 175 DJ118
Wood Pt, E16 off Fife Rd ... 86 EG71
Woodquest Av, SE24 ... 122 DQ85
Woodredon Fm La, Wal.Abb. EN9 ... 32 EK35
Wood Retreat, SE18 ... 105 ER80
Woodridden Hill, Wal.Abb. EN9 ... 32 EK35
Wood Ride, Barn. EN4 ... 28 DD39
Orpington BR5 ... 145 ER98
Woodridge Cl, Enf. EN2 ... 29 DN39
Woodridge Way, Nthwd. HA6 . 39 BS51
Wood Riding, Wok. GU22
off Pyrford Wds Rd ... 167 BF115
Woodridings Av, Pnr. HA5 ... 40 BZ53
Woodridings Cl, Pnr. HA5 ... 40 BY52
Woodriffe Rd, E11 ... 67 ED59
Wood Ri, Pnr. HA5 ... 59 BU57
Wood Rd, NW10 ... 80 CQ66
Shepperton TW17 ... 134 BN98
Westerham (Bigg.H.) TN16 . 178 EJ118
Woodrow, SE18 ... 105 EM77
Woodrow Av, Hayes UB4 ... 77 BT71
Woodrow Cl, Grnf. UB6 ... 79 CH66
Woodrow Ct, N17
off Heybourne Rd ... 46 DV52
Woodrush Cl, SE14
off Southerngate Way ... 103 DY80
Woodrush Way, Rom. RM6 ... 70 EX56
Woods, The, Nthwd. HA6 ... 39 BU50
Radlett WD7 ... 9 CH34
Uxbridge UB10 ... 59 BP63
Wood's Bldgs, E1
off Whitechapel Rd ... 84 DV71
Woodseer St, E1 ... 84 DT71
Woodsford, SE17
off Portland St ... 102 DR78
Woodsford Sq, W14 ... 99 CY75
Woodshire Rd, Dag. RM10 ... 71 FB62
Woodshore Cl, Vir.W. GU25 . 132 AV100
Woodshots Meadow, Wat. WD18 ... 23 BR43
WOODSIDE, SE25 ... 142 DU100
WOODSIDE, Wat. WD25 ... 7 BU33
Tra Woodside ... 142 DV100
Woodside, NW11 ... 64 DA57
SW19 ... 119 CZ93
Borehamwood (Els.) WD6 . 26 CM42
Buckhurst Hill IG9 ... 48 EJ47
Epping (Thnwd) CM16 ... 18 EX27
Leatherhead (Fetch.) KT22 . 170 CB122
Orpington BR6 ... 164 EU106
Tadworth (Lwr Kgswd) KT20 ... 183 CZ128
Waltham Cross (Chsht) EN7 . 14 DU31
Walton-on-Thames KT12
off Ashley Rd ... 135 BU102
Watford WD24 ... 23 BU36
Woodside Av, N6 ... 64 DF57
N10 ... 64 DF57
N12 ... 44 DC49
SE25 ... 142 DV100
Chislehurst BR7 ... 125 EQ92
Esher KT10 ... 137 CE101
Walton-on-Thames KT12 . 153 BV105
Wembley HA0 ... 80 CL67
Woodside Cl, Bexh. DA7 ... 107 FD84
Brentwood (Hutt.) CM13 ... 55 GD43
Caterham CR3 ... 176 DS124
Gerrards Cross (Chal.St.P.) SL9 ... 36 AY54
Rainham RM13 ... 90 FJ70
Stanmore HA7 ... 41 CH50
Surbiton KT5 ... 138 CQ101
Wembley HA0 ... 80 CL67
Woodside Commercial Est, Epp. (Thnwd) CM16 ... 18 EX26
Woodside Ct, N12 ... 44 DB49
Woodside Ct Rd, Croy. CR0 . 142 DU101
Woodside Cres, Sid. DA15 . 125 ES90
Woodside Dr, Dart. DA2 ... 127 FE91
Woodside End, Wem. HA0 ... 80 CL67
Woodside Gdns, E4 ... 47 EB50
N17 ... 46 DS54
Woodside Gra Rd, N12 ... 44 DB49
Woodside Grn, SE25 ... 142 DV100
Woodside Gro, N12 ... 44 DC48
Woodside Hill, Ger.Cr. (Chal.St.P.) SL9 ... 36 AY54
Woodside La, N12 ... 44 DB48
Bexley DA5 ... 126 EX86
Woodside Ms, SE22
off Heber Rd ... 122 DT86
⊖ Woodside Park ... 44 DB49
Woodside Pk, SE25 ... 142 DU99
Woodside Pk Av, E17 ... 67 ED56
Woodside Pk Rd, N12 ... 44 DB49
Woodside Pl, Wem. HA0 ... 80 CL67
Woodside Rd, E13 ... 86 EJ70
N22 ... 45 DM52
SE25 ... 142 DV100
Abbots Langley WD5 ... 7 BV31
Bexleyheath DA7 ... 107 FD84
Bromley BR1 ... 144 EL99
Cobham KT11 ... 154 CA113
Kingston upon Thames KT2 ... 118 CL94
New Malden KT3 ... 138 CR96
Northwood HA6 ... 39 BT52
Purley CR8 ... 159 DK113
St. Albans (Brick.Wd) AL2 ... 8 BZ30
Sevenoaks TN13 ... 190 FG123
Sevenoaks (Sund.) TN14 . 180 EX124
Sidcup DA15 ... 125 ES90
Sutton SM1 ... 140 DC104
Watford WD25 ... 7 BV31
Woodford Green IG8 ... 48 EG49
Woodside Way, Croy. CR0 . 142 DV100
Mitcham CR4 ... 141 DH95
Virginia Water GU25 ... 132 AV97
Woods Ms, W1 ... 194 E10
Woodsome Lo, Wey. KT13 . 153 BQ107
Woodsome Rd, NW5 ... 64 DG62
Woods Pl, SE1 ... 201 N7
Woodspring Rd, SW19 ... 119 CY89
Woods Rd, SE15 ... 102 DV81
Woodstead Gro, Edg. HA8 ... 42 CL51
Woodstock, The, Sutt. SM3 . 139 CY101
Woodstock Av, NW11 ... 63 CY59
W13 ... 97 CG76
Isleworth TW7 ... 117 CG85
Romford RM3 ... 52 FP50
Slough SL3 ... 92 AX77
Southall UB1 ... 78 BZ69
Sutton SM3 ... 139 CZ101
Woodstock Cl, Bex. DA5 ... 126 EZ88
Stanmore HA7 ... 42 CL54
Woking GU21 ... 166 AY116
Woodstock Ct, SE12 ... 124 EG86
Woodstock Cres, N9 ... 30 DV44
Woodstock Dr, Uxb. UB10 ... 58 BL63
Woodstock Gdns, Beck. BR3 . 143 EB95
Hayes UB4 ... 77 BT71
Ilford IG3 ... 70 EU61
Woodstock Gro, W12 ... 99 CX75
Woodstock La N, Surb. KT6 . 137 CJ103
Woodstock La S, Chess. KT9 ... 155 CJ105
Esher (Clay.) KT10 ... 155 CH106
Woodstock Ms, W1 ... 194 G7
Woodstock Ri, Sutt. SM3 ... 139 CZ101
Woodstock Rd, E7 ... 86 EJ66
E17 ... 47 ED54
N4 ... 65 DN60
NW11 ... 63 CZ59
W4 ... 98 CS76
Bushey (Bushey Hth) WD23 . 41 CE45
Carshalton SM5 ... 158 DG106
Coulsdon CR5
off Chipstead Valley Rd . 175 DH116
Croydon CR0 ... 142 DR104
Wembley HA0 ... 80 CM66
Woodstock St, W1 ... 195 H9
Woodstock Ter, E14 ... 85 EB73
Woodstock Way, Mitch. CR4 . 141 DH96
Woodstone Av, Epsom KT17 . 157 CU106
⇌ Wood Street ... 67 EC56
Wood St, E17 ... 67 EC55
EC2 ... 197 J9
W4 ... 98 CS78
Barnet EN5 ... 27 CW42
Grays RM17 ... 110 GC79
Kingston upon Thames KT1 ... 137 CK95
Mitcham CR4 ... 140 DG101
Redhill (Merst.) RH1 ... 185 DJ129
Swanley BR8 ... 148 FJ96
Woodsway, Lthd. (Oxshott) KT22 ... 155 CE114
Woodsyre, SE26 ... 122 DT91
Woodthorpe Rd, SW15 ... 99 CV84
Ashford TW15 ... 114 BL91
Woodtree Cl, NW4
off Ashley La ... 43 CW54
Wood Vale, N10 ... 65 DJ57
SE23 ... 122 DV88
Woodvale Av, SE25 ... 142 DT97
Wood Vale Est, SE23 ... 122 DW86
Woodvale Wk, SE27
off Elder Rd ... 122 DQ92
Woodvale Way, NW11
off The Vale ... 63 CX62
Woodview, Chess. KT9 ... 155 CJ111
Grays RM16, RM17 ... 110 GE76
Wood Vw, Pot.B. (Cuffley) EN6 ... 13 DL27
Woodview Av, E4 ... 47 EC49
Woodview Cl, N4 ... 65 DP59
SW15 ... 118 CR91
Orpington BR6 ... 145 EQ103
South Croydon CR2 ... 160 DV114
Woodview Rd, Swan. BR8 . 147 FC96
Woodville, SE3 ... 104 EH81
Woodville Cl, SE12 ... 124 EG85
Teddington TW11 ... 117 CG91
Woodville Ct, Wat. WD17 ... 23 BU40
Woodville Gdns, NW11 ... 63 CX59
W5 ... 80 CL72
Ilford IG6 ... 69 EP55
Ruislip HA4 ... 59 BQ59
Woodville Gro, Well. DA16 . 106 EU83
Woodville Pl, Cat. CR3 ... 176 DQ121
Gravesend DA12 ... 131 GH87
Woodville Rd, E11 ... 68 EF60
E17 ... 67 DY56
E18 ... 48 EH54
N16 ... 66 DS64
NW6 ... 81 CZ68
NW11 ... 63 CX59
W5 ... 79 CK72
Barnet EN5 ... 28 DB41
Leatherhead KT22 ... 171 CH120
Morden SM4 ... 140 DA98
Richmond TW10 ... 117 CH90
Thornton Heath CR7 ... 142 DQ98
Woodville St, SE18
off Woodhill ... 104 EL77
Wood Wk, Rick. (Chorl.) WD3 . 21 BE40
Woodward Av, NW4 ... 63 CU57
Woodward Cl, Esher (Clay.) KT10 ... 155 CF107
Woodward Cl, Grays RM17 . 110 GB77
Woodwarde Rd, SE22 ... 122 DS86
Woodward Gdns, Dag. RM9
off Woodward Rd ... 88 EW66
Stanmore HA7 ... 41 CF52
Woodward Hts, Grays RM17 . 110 GB77
Woodward Rd, Dag. RM9 ... 88 EV66
Woodward Ter, Green. DA9 . 129 FS86
Woodway, Brwd. CM13, CM15 ... 55 GA46
Wood Way, Orp. BR6 ... 145 EN103
Woodway Cres, Har. HA1 ... 61 CG58
Woodwaye, Wat. WD19 ... 40 BW45
Woodwell St, SW18
off Huguenot Pl ... 120 DC85
Wood Wf, SE10 ... 103 EB79
Woodwicks, Rick. (Map.Cr.) WD3 ... 37 BD50
Woodyard, The, Epp. CM16 . 18 EW28
Woodyard Cl, NW5
off Gillies St ... 64 DG64
Woodyard La, SE21 ... 122 DS87
Woodyates Rd, SE12 ... 124 EG86
Woolacombe Rd, SE3 ... 104 EJ81
Woolacombe Way, Hayes UB3 ... 95 BS77
Woolbrook Rd, Dart. DA1 . 127 FE86
Wooler St, SE17 ... 102 DR78
Woolf Cl, SE28 ... 88 EV74
Woolf Ms, WC1 ... 195 N4
Woolf Wk, Til. RM18
off Coleridge Rd ... 111 GJ82
Woolhampton Way, Chig. IG7 . 50 EV48
Woolhams, Cat. CR3 ... 186 DT126
Woollard St, Wal.Abb. EN9 ... 15 EC34
Woollaston Rd, N4 ... 65 DP58
Woollett Cl, Dart. (Cray.) DA1 . 107 FG84
Woolmead Av, NW9 ... 63 CU59
Woolmer Cl, Borwd. WD6 ... 26 CN38
Woolmerdine Ct, Bushey WD23 ... 24 BX41
Woolmer Gdns, N18 ... 46 DU50
Woolmer Rd, N18 ... 46 DU50
Woolmore St, E14 ... 85 EC73
Woolneigh St, SW6 ... 100 DB83
Woolpack Ho, Enf. EN3 ... 31 DX37
Wool Rd, SW20 ... 119 CV93
Woolstaplers Way, SE16 ... 202 B7
Woolston Cl, E17
off Riverhead Cl ... 47 DX54
Woolstone Rd, SE23 ... 123 DY89
WOOLWICH, SE18 ... 105 EN78
⇌ Woolwich Arsenal ... 105 EP77
Woolwich Ch St, SE18 ... 104 EL76
★ Woolwich Common, SE18 ... 105 EM80
Woolwich Common, SE18 . 105 EM79
⇌ Woolwich Dockyard ... 105 EM77
Woolwich Ferry Pier, E16 . 105 EN75
Woolwich Foot Tunnel, E16 . 105 EN75
SE18 ... 105 EN75
Woolwich Garrison, SE18 ... 105 EM79
Woolwich High St, SE18 ... 105 EN76
Woolwich Ind Est, SE28
off Hadden Rd ... 105 ES76
Woolwich Manor Way, E6 ... 87 EM70
E16 ... 87 EP73
Woolwich Mkt, SE18 ... 105 EP77
Woolwich New Rd, SE18 ... 105 EN78
Woolwich Rd, SE2 ... 106 EX79
SE7 ... 104 EG78
SE10 ... 205 K10
Belvedere DA17 ... 106 EX79
Bexleyheath DA7 ... 106 FA84
Woolwich Trade Pk, SE28 ... 105 ER76
Wooster Gdns, E14 ... 85 ED72
Wooster Ms, Har. HA2
off Fairfield Dr ... 60 CC55
Wooster Pl, SE1 ... 201 L8
Wootton Cl, Epsom KT18 ... 173 CT115
Hornchurch RM11 ... 72 FK57
Wootton Gro, N3 ... 44 DA53
Wootton St, SE1 ... 200 E4
Worbeck Rd, SE20 ... 142 DV96
Worcester Av, N17 ... 46 DU52
Upminster RM14 ... 73 FT61
Worcester Cl, NW2
off Newfield Ri ... 63 CV62
Croydon CR0 ... 143 DZ103
Gravesend (Istead Rise) DA13 ... 131 GF94
Greenhithe DA9 ... 109 FV84
Mitcham CR4 ... 140 DG96
Worcester Ct, Walt. KT12
off Rodney Cl ... 136 BW102
Worcester Cres, NW7 ... 42 CS48
Woodford Green IG8 ... 48 EH50
Worcester Dr, W4 ... 98 CS75
Ashford TW15 ... 115 BP93
Worcester Gdns, SW11
off Grandison Rd ... 120 DF85
Greenford UB6 ... 78 CC65
Ilford IG1 ... 68 EL59
Worcester Park KT4 ... 138 CS104
Worcester Ho, SE11
off Kennington Rd ... 101 DN76
Worcester Ms, NW6
off Dresden Cl ... 82 DB65
WORCESTER PARK, KT4 ... 139 CT103
⇌ Worcester Park ... 139 CU102
Worcester Pk Rd, Wor.Pk. KT4 ... 138 CQ104
Worcester Rd, E12 ... 69 EM63
E17 ... 47 DX54
SW19 ... 119 CZ92
Reigate RH2 ... 183 CZ133
Sutton SM2 ... 158 DB107
Uxbridge UB8 ... 76 BJ71
Worcesters Av, Enf. EN1 ... 30 DU38
Wordsworth Av, E12 ... 86 EL66
E18 ... 68 EF55
Greenford UB6 ... 79 CD68
Kenley CR8 off Valley Rd . 176 DR115
Wordsworth Cl, Rom. RM3 ... 52 FJ53
Tilbury RM18 ... 111 GJ82
Wordsworth Dr, Sutt. SM3 . 157 CW105
Wordsworth Gdns, Borwd. WD6 ... 26 CN43
Wordsworth Mead, Red. RH1 ... 184 DG132
Wordsworth Pl, NW5
off Southampton Rd ... 64 DF64
Wordsworth Rd, N16 ... 66 DS63
SE1 ... 201 P9
Wordsworth Rd, SE20 ... 123 DX94
Addlestone KT15 ... 152 BK105
Hampton TW12 ... 116 BZ91
Wallington SM6 ... 159 DJ107
Welling DA16 ... 105 ES81
Wordsworth Wk, NW11 ... 63 CZ56
Wordsworth Way, Dart. DA1 . 108 FN84
West Drayton UB7 ... 94 BL77
Worfield St, SW11 ... 100 DE80
Worgan St, SE11 ... 200 B10
SE16 ... 203 J7
Worland Rd, E15 ... 86 EE66
WORLD'S END, Enf. EN2 ... 29 DN41
World's End, Cob. KT11 ... 153 BU114
World's End Est, SW10 ... 100 DC80
Worlds End La, N21 ... 29 DM43
Enfield EN2 ... 29 DM43
Orpington BR6 ... 163 ET107
World's End Pas, SW10
off Riley St ... 100 DD80
World's End Pl, SW10
off King's Rd ... 100 DC80
Worleys Dr, Orp. BR6 ... 163 ER105
Worlidge St, W6 ... 99 CW78
Worlingham Rd, SE22 ... 102 DT84
Wormholt Rd, W12 ... 81 CU73
Wormley Ct, Wal.Abb. EN9 ... 16 EG33
Wormwood St, EC2 ... 197 M8
Wormyngford Ct, Wal.Abb. EN9 off Ninefields ... 16 EG33
Wornington Rd, W10 ... 81 CY71
Woronzow Rd, NW8 ... 82 DD67
Worple, The, Stai. (Wrays.) TW19 ... 113 AZ86
Worple Av, SW19 ... 119 CX94
Isleworth TW7 ... 117 CG85
Staines TW18 ... 114 BH93
Worple Cl, Har. HA2 ... 60 BZ60
Worple Rd, SW19 ... 119 CY94
SW20 ... 139 CW96
Epsom KT18 ... 156 CS114
Isleworth TW7 ... 97 CG84
Leatherhead KT22 ... 171 CH123
Staines TW18 ... 114 BH94
Worple Rd Ms, SW19 ... 119 CZ93
⇌ Worplesdon ... 166 AV124
Worple St, SW14 ... 98 CR83
Worple Way, Har. HA2 ... 60 BZ60
Richmond TW10 ... 118 CL85
Worrin Cl, Brwd. (Shenf.) CM15 ... 55 FZ46
Worrin Rd, Brwd. (Shenf.) CM15 ... 55 FZ47
Worsfold Cl, Wok. (Send) GU23 ... 167 BB123
Worships Hill, Sev. TN13 ... 190 FE123
Worship St, EC2 ... 197 L5
Worslade Rd, SW17 ... 120 DD91
Worsley Br Rd, SE26 ... 123 DZ91
Beckenham BR3 ... 123 DZ92
Worsley Gra, Chis. BR7 ... 125 EQ93
Worsley Gro, E5 ... 66 DU63
Worsley Rd, E11 ... 68 EE63
Worsopp Dr, SW4 ... 121 DJ85
Worsted Grn, Red. (Merst.) RH1 ... 185 DJ129
Worth Cl, Orp. BR6 ... 163 ES105
Worthfield Cl, Epsom KT19 . 156 CR108
Worth Gro, SE17
off Merrow St ... 102 DR78
Worthing Cl, E15
off Mitre Rd ... 86 EE67
Grays RM20 ... 110 FY79
Worthing Rd, Houns. TW5 ... 96 BZ79
Worthington Cl, Mitch. CR4 . 141 DH97
Worthington Rd, Surb. KT6 . 138 CM102
Worthy Down Ct, SE18
off Prince Imperial Rd ... 105 EN81
Wortley Rd, E6 ... 86 EK66
Croydon CR0 ... 141 DN101
Worton Gdns, Islw. TW7 ... 97 CD82
Worton Hall Ind Est, Islw. TW7 ... 97 CE84
Worton Rd, Islw. TW7 ... 97 CE83
Worton Way, Houns. TW3 ... 97 CD82
Isleworth TW7 ... 96 CC81
Wotton Grn, Orp. BR5 ... 146 EX98
Wotton Rd, NW2 ... 63 CW63
SE8 ... 103 DZ79
Wotton Way, Sutt. SM2 ... 157 CW110
Wouldham Rd, E16 ... 86 EF72
Grays RM20 ... 110 FY79
Wrabness Way, Stai. TW18 . 134 BH95
Wragby Rd, E11 ... 68 EE62
Wrampling Pl, N9 ... 46 DU46
Wrangley Ct, Wal.Abb. EN9 ... 16 EG33
Wrangthorn Wk, Croy. CR0
off Epsom Rd ... 159 DN105
Wray Av, Ilf. IG5 ... 69 EN55
Wray Cl, Horn. RM11 ... 72 FJ59
Wray Common, Reig. RH2 . 184 DD132
Wray Common Rd, Reig. RH2 ... 184 DC133
Wray Cres, N4 ... 65 DL61
Wrayfield Av, Reig. RH2 ... 184 DC133
Wrayfield Rd, Sutt. SM3 ... 139 CX104
Wraylands Dr, Reig. RH2 ... 184 DD132
Wray La, Reig. RH2 ... 184 DC130
Wray Mill Pk, Reig. RH2 ... 184 DD132
Wray Pk Rd, Reig. RH2 ... 184 DB133
Wray Rd, Sutt. SM2 ... 157 CZ109
WRAYSBURY, Stai. TW19 ... 113 AZ86
⇌ Wraysbury ... 113 BA86
Wraysbury Cl, Houns. TW4 . 116 BY85
Wraysbury Gdns, Stai. TW18 . 113 BE91
Wraysbury Rd, Stai. TW18, TW19 ... 113 BC90
Wrays Way, Hayes UB4
off Balmoral Dr ... 77 BS70
Wrekin Rd, SE18 ... 105 EQ80
Wren Av, NW2 ... 63 CW64
Southall UB2 ... 96 BZ77
Wren Cl, E16 off Ibbotson Av . 86 EF72
N9 off Chaffinch Cl ... 47 DX46
Orpington BR5 ... 146 EX97
South Croydon CR2 ... 161 DX109
Wren Ct, Slou. SL3 ... 93 BA76
Wren Cres, Add. KT15 ... 152 BK106
Bushey WD23 ... 40 CC46
Wren Dr, Wal.Abb. EN9 ... 16 EG34
West Drayton UB7 ... 94 BK76
Wren Gdns, Dag. RM9 ... 70 EX64
Hornchurch RM12 ... 71 FF60
Wren Landing, E14 ... 204 A2
Wren Ms, SE13
off Lee High Rd ... 104 EE84
Wren Path, SE28 ... 105 ER76
Wren Pl, Brwd. CM14 ... 54 FX48
Wren Rd, SE5 ... 102 DR81
Dagenham RM9 ... 70 EX64
Sidcup DA14 ... 126 EW91
Wrens Av, Ashf. TW15 ... 115 BQ92
Wrens Cft, Grav. (Nthflt) DA11 ... 130 GE91
Wrens Hill, Lthd. (Oxshott) KT22 ... 170 CC115
Wren St, WC1 ... 196 C4
Wren Ter, Ilf. IG5
off Tiptree Cres ... 69 EN55
Wrentham Av, NW10 ... 81 CX68
Wrenthorpe Rd, Brom. BR1 . 124 EE91
Wren Wk, Til. RM18 ... 111 GH80
Wrenwood Way, Pnr. HA5 ... 59 BV56
Wrestlers Ct, EC3
off Camomile St ... 84 DS72
Wrexham Rd, E3 ... 85 EA68
Romford RM3 ... 52 FK48
Wricklemarsh Rd, SE3 ... 104 EH81
Wrigglesworth St, SE14 ... 103 DX80
Wright Cl, Swans. DA10 ... 129 FX86
Wright Gdns, Shep. TW17
off Laleham Rd ... 134 BN99
Wright Rd, N1 off Burder Cl . 84 DS65
Hounslow TW5 ... 96 BW80
Wrights All, SW19 ... 119 CW93
Wrightsbridge Rd, Brwd. CM14 ... 52 FN46
Wrights Cl, SE13 ... 103 ED84
Dagenham RM10 ... 71 FB62
Wrights Grn, SW4
off Nelson's Row ... 101 DK84
Wrights La, W8 ... 100 DB75
Wrights Pl, NW10
off Mitchell Way ... 80 CQ65
Wrights Rd, E3 ... 85 DZ68
SE25 ... 142 DS97
Wrights Row, Wall. SM6 ... 159 DH105
Wrights Wk, SW14 ... 98 CR83
Wrigley Cl, E4 ... 47 ED50
Wriotsley Way, Add. KT15
off Coombelands La ... 152 BG107
Writtle Wk, Rain. RM13 ... 89 FF67
Wrotham Business Pk, Barn. EN5 ... 27 CZ37
★ Wrotham Pk, Barn. EN5 . 27 CZ36
Wrotham Rd, NW1
off Agar Pl ... 83 DJ66
W13 off Mattock La ... 79 CJ74
Barnet EN5 ... 27 CY40
Gravesend DA11, DA13 ... 131 GG88
Welling DA16 ... 106 EW81
Wroths Path, Loug. IG10 ... 33 EM39
Wrottesley Rd, NW10 ... 81 CU68
SE18 ... 105 EQ79
Wroughton Rd, SW11 ... 120 DF86
Wroughton Ter, NW4 ... 63 CW56
Wroxall Rd, Dag. RM9 ... 88 EW65
Wroxham Gdns, N11 ... 45 DJ52
Enfield EN2 ... 29 DN35
Potters Bar EN6 ... 11 CX31
Wroxham Rd, SE28 ... 88 EX73
Wroxham Way, Ilf. IG6 ... 49 EP53
Wroxton Rd, SE15 ... 102 DV82
WRYTHE, THE, Cars. SM5 ... 140 DE103
Wrythe Grn, Cars. SM5
off Wrythe Grn Rd ... 140 DF104
Wrythe Grn Rd, Cars. SM5 . 140 DF104
Wrythe La, Cars. SM5 ... 140 DC102
Wulfstan St, W12 ... 81 CT72
Wulstan Pk, Pot.B. EN6
off Tempest Av ... 12 DD32
Wyatt Cl, SE16 ... 203 M5
Bushey (Bushey Hth) WD23 . 41 CE45
Feltham TW13 ... 116 BW88
Hayes UB4 ... 77 BU71
Wyatt Dr, SW13 ... 99 CW80
Wyatt Pk Rd, SW2 ... 121 DL89
Wyatt Rd, E7 ... 86 EG65
N5 ... 66 DQ62
Dartford DA1 ... 107 FF83
Staines TW18 ... 114 BG92
Wyatts Cl, Rick. (Chorl.) WD3 . 22 BG41
Wyatt's Covert Caravan Site, Uxb. (Denh.) UB9 ... 57 BE56
Wyatts La, E17 ... 67 EC55
Wyatts Rd, Rick. (Chorl.) WD3 . 21 BF42
Wybert St, NW1 ... 195 J4
Wyborne Way, NW10 ... 80 CQ66
Wyburn Av, Barn. EN5 ... 27 CZ41
Wyche Gro, S.Croy. CR2 ... 160 DQ108
Wych Elm Cl, Horn. RM11 ... 72 FN59
Wych Elm Dr, Brom. BR1
off London La ... 124 EF94
Wych Elm Pas, Kings.T. KT2 . 118 CM94
Wych Elm Rd, Horn. RM11 ... 72 FN58
Wych Elms, St.Alb. (Park St) AL2 ... 8 CB28
Wycherley Cl, SE3 ... 104 EF80
Wycherley Cres, Barn. EN5 . 28 DB44
Wych Hill, Wok. GU22 ... 166 AW119
Wych Hill La, Wok. GU22 ... 166 AY119
Wych Hill Pk, Wok. GU22 ... 166 AX119
Wych Hill Ri, Wok. GU22 ... 166 AW119
Wych Hill Way, Wok. GU22 . 166 AX120
Wychwood Av, Edg. HA8 ... 41 CK51
Thornton Heath CR7 ... 142 DQ97
Wychwood Cl, Edg. HA8 ... 41 CK51
Sunbury-on-Thames TW16 . 115 BU93
Wychwood End, N6 ... 65 DJ59
Wychwood Gdns, Ilf. IG5 ... 69 EM56
Wychwood Way, SE19
off Roman Ri ... 122 DR93
Northwood HA6 ... 39 BT52
Wyclif Ct, EC1
off St. John St ... 83 DP69
Wycliffe Cl, Wal.Cr. EN8 ... 15 DX28
Welling DA16 ... 105 ET81
Wycliffe Ct, Abb.L. WD5 ... 7 BS32
Wycliffe Rd, SW11 ... 100 DG82
SW19 ... 120 DB93
Wycliffe Row, Grav. (Nthflt) DA11 ... 131 GF88

★ Place of interest ⇌ Railway station ⊖ London Underground station DLR Docklands Light Railway station Tra Tramlink station H Hospital Riv Pedestrian ferry landing stage

Wyclif St, EC1 196 F3
Wycombe Gdns, NW11 64 DA61
Wycombe Pl, SW18 120 DC86
Wycombe Rd, N17 46 DU53
Ilford IG2 69 EM57
Wembley HA0 80 CN67
Wycombe Sq, W8 81 CZ74
Wydehurst Rd, Croy. CR0 142 DU101
Wydell Cl, Mord. SM4 139 CW100
Wydeville Manor Rd, SE12 124 EH91
Wyecliffe Gdns, Red. (S.Merst.) RH1 185 DJ130
Wye Cl, Ashf. TW15 115 BP91
Orpington BR6 145 ET101
Ruislip HA4 59 BQ58
Wyedale, St.Alb. (Lon.Col.) AL2 10 CM27
Wyemead Cres, E4 48 EE47
Wye Rd, Grav. DA12 131 GK89
Wye St, SW11 100 DD82
Wyeth's Ms, Epsom KT17 157 CT113
Wyeths Rd, Epsom KT17 157 CT113
Wyevale Cl, Pnr. HA5 59 BU55
Wyfields, Ilf. IG5 *off Ravensbourne Gdns* 49 EP53
Wyfold Ho, SE2 *off Wolvercote Rd* 106 EX75
Wyfold Rd, SW6 99 CY80
Wyhill Wk, Dag. RM10 89 FC65
Wyke Cl, Islw. TW7 97 CF79
Wyke Gdns, W7 97 CG76
Wykeham Av, Dag. RM9 88 EW65
Hornchurch RM11 72 FK58
Wykeham Cl, Grav. DA12 131 GL93
West Drayton UB7 94 BN78
Wykeham Grn, Dag. RM9 88 EW65
Wykeham Hill, Wem. HA9 62 CM60
Wykeham Ri, N20 43 CY46
Wykeham Rd, NW4 63 CW57
Harrow HA3 61 CH56
Wyke Rd, E3 85 EA66
SW20 139 CW96
Wylands Rd, Slou. SL3 93 BA77
Wylchin Cl, Pnr. HA5 59 BT56
Wyldes Cl, NW11 *off Wildwood Rd* 64 DC60
Wyldfield Gdns, N9 46 DT47
Wyld Way, Wem. HA9 80 CP65
Wyleu St, SE23 123 DY87
Wylie Rd, Sthl. UB2 96 CA76
Wyllen Cl, E1 84 DW70
Wyllyotts Cl, Pot.B. EN6 11 CZ32
Wyllyotts La, Pot.B. EN6 11 CZ32
Wyllyotts Pl, Pot.B. EN6 11 CZ32
Wylo Dr, Barn. EN5 27 CU44
Wymering Rd, W9 82 DA69
Wymond St, SW15 99 CW83
Wynan Rd, E14 204 B10
Wynash Gdns, Cars. SM5 158 DE106
Wynaud Ct, N22 *off Palmerston Rd* 45 DM51
Wyncham Av, Sid. DA15 125 ES88
Wynchgate, N14 45 DK46
N21 45 DL46
Harrow HA3 41 CE52
Wyncote Way, S.Croy. CR2 161 DX109
Wyncroft Cl, Brom. BR1 145 EM97
Wyndale Av, NW9 62 CN58
Wyndcliff Rd, SE7 104 EH79
Wyndcroft Cl, Enf. EN2 29 DP41
Wyndham Av, Cob. KT11 153 BU113
Wyndham Cl, Orp. BR6 145 EQ102
Sutton SM2 158 DA108
Wyndham Cres, N19 65 DJ62
Hounslow TW4 116 CA86
Wyndham Est, SE5 102 DQ80
Wyndham Ms, W1 194 D7
Wyndham Pl, W1 194 D7
Wyndham Rd, E6 86 EK66
SE5 101 DP80
W13 97 CH76
Barnet EN4 44 DF46
Kingston upon Thames KT2 118 CM94
Woking GU21 166 AV118
Wyndham St, W1 194 D6
Wyndham Yd, W1 194 D7
Wyndhurst Cl, S.Croy. CR2 159 DP108
Wyneham Rd, SE24 122 DR85
Wynell Rd, SE23 123 DX90
Wynford Gro, Orp. BR5 146 EV97
Wynford Pl, Belv. DA17 106 FA79
Wynford Rd, N1 83 DM68
Wynford Way, SE9 125 EM90
Wynlie Gdns, Pnr. HA5 39 BV54
Wynn Br Cl, Wdf.Grn. IG8 *off Chigwell Rd* 48 EJ53
Wynndale Rd, E18 48 EH53
Wynne Rd, SW9 101 DN82
Wynns Av, Sid. DA15 126 EU85
Wynnstay Gdns, W8 100 DA76
Wynnstow Pk, Oxt. RH8 188 EF131
Wynter St, SW11 100 DC84
Wynton Gdns, SE25 142 DT99
Wynton Gro, Walt. KT12 135 BU104
Wynton Pl, W3 80 CP72
Wynyard Cl, Rick. (Sarratt) WD3 22 BG36
Wynyard Ter, SE11 200 C10
Wynyatt St, EC1 196 F3
Wyre Gro, Edg. HA8 42 CP48
Hayes UB3 95 BU77
Wyresdale Cres, Grnf. UB6 79 CF69
Wyteleaf Cl, Ruis. HA4 59 BQ58
Wythburn Pl, W1 194 D9
Wythenshawe Rd, Dag. RM10 70 FA62
Wythens Wk, SE9 125 EP86
Wythes Cl, Brom. BR1 145 EM96
Wythes Rd, E16 86 EL74
Wythfield Rd, SE9 125 EM86
Wyvenhoe Rd, Har. HA2 60 CC62
Wyvern Cl, Dart. DA1 128 FJ87
Orpington BR6 146 EV104
Wyvern Est, N.Mal. KT3 139 CU98
Wyvern Gro, Hayes UB3 95 BP80
Wyvern Pl, Add. KT15 *off Green La* 152 BH105
Wyvern Rd, Pur. CR8 159 DP110
Wyvern Way, Uxb. UB8 76 BH66
Wyvil Est, SW8 *off Luscombe Way* 101 DL80
Wyvil Rd, SW8 101 DL79
Wyvis St, E14 85 EB71

Y

Yabsley St, E14 204 E2
Yaffle Rd, Wey. KT13 153 BQ110
Yalding Gro, Orp. BR5 146 EX98
Yalding Rd, SE16 202 B7
Yale Cl, Houns. TW4 116 BZ85
Yale Way, Horn. RM12 71 FG63
Yarborough Rd, SW19 140 DD95
Yarbridge Cl, Sutt. SM2 158 DB110
Yardley Cl, E4 31 EB43
Reigate RH2 184 DB132
Yardley Ct, Sutt. SM3 *off Hemingford Rd* 157 CW105
Yardley La, E4 31 EB43
Yardley St, WC1 196 D3
Yard Mead, Egh. TW20 113 BA90
Yarm Cl, Lthd. KT22 171 CJ123
Yarm Ct Rd, Lthd. KT22 171 CJ123
Yarmouth Cres, N17 66 DV57
Yarmouth Pl, W1 199 H3
Yarmouth Rd, Wat. WD24 24 BW38
Yarm Way, Lthd. KT22 171 CJ123
Yarnfield Sq, SE15 *off Clayton Rd* 102 DU81
Yarnton Way, SE2 106 EX75
Erith DA18 106 EZ76
Yarrow Cres, E6 86 EL71
Yarrowfield, Wok. GU22 166 AX123
Yarrowside, Amer. HP7 20 AV41
Yateley St, SE18 104 EK76
Yates Ct, NW2 81 CX65
Yates Ho, E2 *off Roberta St* 84 DU69
YEADING, Hayes UB4 77 BV69
Yeading Av, Har. HA2 60 BY61
Yeading Fork, Hayes UB4 78 BW71
Yeading Gdns, Hayes UB4 77 BV71
Yeading La, Hayes UB4 77 BV72
Northolt UB5 78 BW69
Yeames Cl, W13 79 CG72
Yeate St, N1 84 DR66
Yeatman Rd, N6 64 DF58
Yeats Cl, NW10 80 CS65
Yeats Ct, N15 *off Tynemouth Rd* 66 DT56
Ye Cor, Wat. WD19 24 BY44
Yeend Cl, W.Mol. KT8 136 CA98
Yeldham Rd, W6 99 CX78
Yellow Hammer Ct, NW9 *off Eagle Dr* 42 CS54
Yellowpine Way, Chig. IG7 50 EV49
Yelverton Cl, Rom. RM3 52 FK53
Yelverton Rd, SW11 100 DD82
Yenston Cl, Mord. SM4 140 DA100
Yeoman Cl, E6 *off Ferndale St* 87 EP73
SE27 121 DP90
Yeoman Dr, Stai. TW19 114 BL88
Yeoman Rd, Nthlt. UB5 78 BY66
Yeomanry Cl, Epsom KT17 *off Dirdene Gdns* 157 CT112
Yeomans Acre, Ruis. HA4 59 BU58
Yeomans Keep, Rick. (Chorl.) WD3 *off Rickmansworth Rd* 21 BF41
Yeomans Meadow, Sev. TN13 190 FG126
Yeoman's Ms, Islw. TW7 *off Queensbridge Pk* 117 CE85
Yeoman's Row, SW3 198 C7
Yeoman St, SE8 203 K8
Yeomans Way, Enf. EN3 30 DW40
Yeomans Yd, E1 *off Chamber St* 84 DT73
Yeomen Way, Ilf. IG6 49 EQ51
Yeo St, E3 85 EB71
Yeoveney Cl, Stai. TW19 113 BD89
Yeovil Cl, Orp. BR6 145 ES103
Yeovilton Pl, Kings.T. KT2 117 CJ92
Yerbury Rd, N19 65 DK62
Yester Dr, Chis. BR7 124 EL94
Yester Pk, Chis. BR7 125 EM94
Yester Rd, Chis. BR7 125 EM94
Yevele Way, Horn. RM11 72 FL59
Yew Av, West Dr. UB7 76 BL73
Yewbank Cl, Ken. CR8 176 DR115
Yew Cl, Buck.H. IG9 48 EK47
Waltham Cross EN7 14 DS27
Yewdale Cl, Brom. BR1 124 EE93
Yewdells Cl, Bet. (Buckland) RH3 183 CU133
Yewfield Rd, NW10 81 CT66
Yew Gro, NW2 63 CX63
Yewlands Cl, Bans. SM7 174 DC115
Yew Pl, Wey. KT13 135 BT104
Yews, The, Ashf. TW15 *off Reedsfield Rd* 115 BP91
Gravesend DA12 131 GK88
Yews Av, Enf. EN1 30 DV36
Yew Tree Bottom Rd, Epsom KT17, KT18 173 CV116
Yew Tree Cl, N21 45 DN45
Yewtree Cl, N22 45 DJ53
Yew Tree Cl, SE13 *off Bankside Av* 103 EC83
Brentwood (Hutt.) CM13 55 GB44
Chesham (Ley Hill) HP5 4 AU30
Coulsdon (Chipstead) CR5 174 DF119
Yewtree Cl, Har. HA2 60 CB56
Yew Tree Cl, Sev. TN13 190 FD123
Welling DA16 106 EU81
Worcester Park KT4 138 CS102
Yew Tree Ct, Borwd. (Els.) WD6 *off Barnet La* 25 CK44
Yew Tree Dr, Cat. CR3 186 DT125
Hemel Hempstead (Bov.) HP3 5 BB28
Yewtree End, St.Alb. (Park St) AL2 8 CB27
Yew Tree Gdns, Epsom KT18 172 CP115
Romford RM7 71 FD57
Romford (Chad.Hth) RM6 70 EY57
Yew Tree La, Reig. RH2 184 DB131
Yew Tree Rd, W12 81 CT73
Yewtree Rd, Beck. BR3 143 DZ97
Yew Tree Rd, Slou. SL1 92 AU76
Yew Tree Rd, Uxb. UB10 76 BM67
Yew Trees, Egh. TW20 133 BC97
Shepperton TW17 *off Laleham Rd* 134 BM98
Yew Tree Wk, Houns. TW4 116 BZ85
Purley CR8 160 DQ110
Yew Tree Way, Croy. CR0 161 DY110
Yew Wk, Har. HA1 61 CE60
YIEWSLEY, West Dr. UB7 76 BL74
Yoakley Rd, N16 66 DS61
Yoga Way, Wor.Pk. KT4 139 CU103
Yoke Cl, N7 *off Ewe Cl* 83 DL65
Yolande Gdns, SE9 124 EL85
Yonge Pk, N4 65 DN62
York Av, SW14 118 CQ85
W7 79 CE74
Hayes UB3 77 BQ71
Sidcup DA15 125 ES89
Stanmore HA7 41 CH53
York Br, NW1 194 F4
York Bldgs, WC2 200 A1
York Cl, E6 *off Boultwood Rd* 87 EM72
W7 *off York Av* 79 CE74
Amersham HP7 20 AT39
Brentwood (Shenf.) CM15 55 FZ45
Kings Langley WD4 6 BN29
Morden SM4 140 DB98
West Byfleet (Byfleet) KT14 152 BL112
York Cres, Borwd. WD6 26 CR40
Loughton IG10 32 EL41
Yorke Gdns, Reig. RH2 184 DA133
Yorke Gate Rd, Cat. CR3 176 DR122
Yorke Rd, Reig. RH2 183 CZ133
Rickmansworth (Crox.Grn) WD3 22 BN44
York Gdns, Walt. KT12 136 BX103
York Gate, N14 45 DL45
NW1 194 F5
York Gro, SE15 102 DW81
York Hill, SE27 121 DP90
Loughton IG10 32 EL41
York Hill Est, SE27 121 DP90
York Ho, Wem. HA9 62 CM63
York Ho Pl, W8 100 DB75
Yorkland Av, Well. DA16 105 ET83
York Ms, NW5 *off Kentish Town Rd* 65 DH64
Ilford IG1 69 EN62
York Par, Brent. TW8 97 CK78
York Pl, SW11 100 DD83
WC2 200 A1
Dagenham RM10 89 FC65
Ilford IG1 *off York Rd* 69 EN61
York Ri, NW5 65 DH62
Orpington BR6 145 ES102
York Rd, E4 47 EA50
E7 86 EG65
E10 67 EC62
E17 67 DX57
N11 45 DK51
N18 46 DV51
N21 46 DR45
SE1 200 C4
SW11 100 DC84
SW18 100 DC84
SW19 120 DC93
W3 80 CQ72
W5 97 CJ76
Barnet EN5 28 DD43
Brentford TW8 97 CK78
Brentwood (Shenf.) CM15 55 FZ45
Croydon CR0 141 DN101
Dartford DA1 128 FM87
Epping (N.Wld Bas.) CM16 18 FA27
Gravesend DA12 131 GJ90
Gravesend (Nthflt) DA11 130 GD87
Hounslow TW3 96 CB83
Ilford IG1 69 EN62
Kingston upon Thames KT2 118 CM94
Northwood HA6 39 BU54
Rainham RM13 89 FD66
Richmond TW10 *off Albert Rd* 118 CM85
South Croydon CR2 161 DX110
Sutton SM2 158 DA107
Teddington TW11 117 CE91
Uxbridge UB8 76 BK66
Waltham Cross EN8 15 DY34
Watford WD18 24 BW43
West Byfleet (Byfleet) KT14 152 BK112
Westerham (Bigg.H.) TN16 178 EH119
Weybridge KT13 153 BQ105
Woking GU22 166 AY118
Yorkshire Cl, N16 66 DS62
Yorkshire Gdns, N18 46 DV50
Yorkshire Grey, SE9 *off Westhorne Av* 124 EK85
Yorkshire Grey Pl, NW3 *off Heath St* 64 DC63
Yorkshire Grey Yd, WC1 196 B7
Yorkshire Rd, E14 85 DY72
Mitcham CR4 141 DL99
York Sq, E14 85 DY72
York St, W1 194 E6
Barking IG11 *off Abbey Rd* 87 EQ67
Mitcham CR4 140 DG101
Twickenham TW1 117 CG88
York Ter, Enf. EN2 30 DQ38
Erith DA8 107 FC81
York Ter E, NW1 194 G5
York Ter W, NW1 194 F5
Yorkton St, E2 84 DU68
York Way, N1 83 DL67
N7 83 DK65
N20 44 DF48
Borehamwood WD6 26 CR40
Chessington KT9 156 CL108
Feltham TW13 116 BZ90
Watford WD25 24 BX36
York Way Ct, N1 83 DL67
York Way Est, N7 *off York Way* 83 DL65
Youngmans Cl, Enf. EN2 30 DQ39
Young Rd, E16 86 EJ72
Young's Bldgs, EC1 197 J4
Youngs Ct, SW11 *off Charlotte Despard Av* 100 DG81
Youngs Rd, Ilf. IG2 69 ER57
Young St, W8 100 DB75
Youngstroat La, Wok. GU21, GU24 150 AY110
Yoxley App, Ilf. IG2 69 EQ58
Yoxley Dr, Ilf. IG2 69 EQ58
Yukon Rd, SW12 121 DH87
Broxbourne EN10 15 DY25
Yule Cl, St.Alb. (Brick.Wd) AL2 8 BZ30
Yunus Khan Cl, E17 67 EA57

Z

Zambezie Dr, N9 46 DW48
Zampa Rd, SE16 102 DW78
Zander Ct, E2 *off St. Peter's Cl* 84 DU68
Zangwill Rd, SE3 104 EK81
Zealand Av, West Dr. UB7 94 BK80
Zealand Rd, E3 85 DY68
Zelah Rd, Orp. BR5 146 EV101
Zeland Cl, NW2 63 CW60
Zennor Rd, SW12 121 DJ88
Zennor Rd Ind Est, SW12 *off Zennor Rd* 121 DJ88
Zenoria St, SE22 102 DT84
Zermatt Rd, Th.Hth. CR7 142 DQ98
Zetland St, E14 85 EB71
Zig Zag Rd, Ken. CR8 176 DQ116
Zion Ho, E1 *off Jubilee St* 84 DW72
Zion Pl, Grav. DA12 131 GH87
Thornton Heath CR7 142 DR98
Zion Rd, Th.Hth. CR7 142 DR98
Zion St, Sev. (Seal) TN15 *off Church Rd* 191 FM121
Zoar St, SE1 201 H2
Zodiac Business Pk, Uxb. (Cowley) UB8 76 BK72
Zoffany St, N19 65 DK61

★ Place of interest | Railway station | London Underground station | DLR Docklands Light Railway station | Tra Tramlink station | H Hospital | Riv Pedestrian ferry landing stage